J. W.]

C000211997

*Specialists in antiquarian and secondhand
cricket books, particularly
John Wisden's Cricketers' Almanack*

BOOKS AND COLLECTIONS BOUGHT

12 STONELEIGH PARK ROAD
EWELL, EPSOM, SURREY KT19 0QT
ENGLAND

CATALOGUES SENT ON REQUEST
01-393 7700

Sponsors of The McKenzie Thameside Cricket League

125th Year

WISDEN

CRICKETERS' ALMANACK

1988

EDITED BY GRAEME WRIGHT

PUBLISHED BY JOHN WISDEN & CO LTD

A COMPANY JOINTLY OWNED BY
GRAYS OF CAMBRIDGE (INTERNATIONAL) LIMITED
AND
NORTON OPAX PLC

SOFT COVER EDITION £14.50   CASED EDITION £16.50

PREFACE

The year past seems to have been one in which both the spirit and the letter of the Laws have been threatened by malevolence and near anarchy. Can this really be what happens when the Laws are omitted from *Wisden*? Neither the game nor the editor can chance another year's absence. The Laws of the Game return, with three new Laws – 2.1, 2.6 and 41.4 – replacing ones formerly experimental.

The dictates of size, nevertheless, mean that pages have had to be found from elsewhere, and to achieve this the scores of matches in South Africa, West Indies and New Zealand once more appear in the abbreviated form. When the decision was made to include full scorecards of first-class matches in those countries, as well as some in India and Pakistan, in the 1982 *Wisden*, the one-day international was not so rampant. In that edition, 29 were recorded; this year there are 61, excluding the World Cup, which is included even though it came after the usual *Wisden* terminus. Moreover, the number of Test and first-class matches has increased. *Wisden* will continue to give the full scorecards of matches in Australia, where no annual publication provides this information, as happens in most Test-playing countries.

With the help of Bill Frindall, Philip Bailey and Peter Wynne-Thomas, I have made a study of the career records which appear in *Wisden*. Where the research of statisticians has revealed errors in compilation, or shown a difference between scorebooks and published scores, the figures in *Wisden* have been amended. This is not to say that the scorebooks are always reliable; they are not. There are times when, with no evidence supporting either the scorebook or the published score, a decision has to be made. In such instances, I have taken the view that the scorebook, like the umpire, has the final say.

There are, in addition, some career records which may be affected by an interpretation of which matches, prior to 1947, were first-class. In such instances, the policy of previous *Wisden* editors has been adhered to. It has been said that history is a hard core of interpretation surrounded by a soft pulp of disputable facts, and that is certainly so here. I both respect and admire the immense and conscientious research that has been done. In a civilised society, it should be possible to differ without acrimony.

However, if cricket's history is not to be rewritten, those who compile it have a duty to ensure that it is written accurately initially – or corrected quickly. I am, therefore, grateful to the county scorers and statisticians who have checked *Wisden's* first-class scorecards throughout the 1987 season. That there were times when two scorers offered differing views merely highlights the difficulty of striving for accuracy.

It would help if the game's authorities saw the office of scorer as one of greater importance. Pakistan came to England last year without a scorer; as I understand, no country took its own scorer to the World Cup; and when England tour, the scorer has to pay his own travel and accommodation expenses. The number of versions of scores emanating from the World Cup, with sometimes little way of knowing which was right or wrong, is testament to the need for an official scorer with any touring team.

This edition is *Wisden's* 125th, and three of the articles in it assess the careers of players whose performances over the last 25 of those years have established their place in the Almanack's records. Derek Hodgson and Doug Ibbotson, who write of Geoffrey Boycott and Derek Underwood respectively, have watched those cricketers during that time and appreciate that it was more than statistical achievements alone which set them among the foremost batsmen and bowlers. To a new generation of cricket followers outside South Africa, Graeme Pollock is little more than a name: they have not been able to see him play. The MCC

Bicentenary match might have provided that opportunity; however, it was not thought politic to include him. Instead, rather like Banquo's ghost, he was at the revels but not seen by everyone. Charles Fortune, the South African broadcaster, has looked back over the career of this great left-handed batsman.

Each of these three cricketers built his game on technique and application, something I feel is often missing when I watch county cricket today. Don Wilson, head coach at Lord's, where he is concerned with the development of young cricketers, offers a coach's viewpoint of the contemporary scene. And finally, John Lawson, *Wisden's* Nottinghamshire correspondent, looks back at 150 years of cricket at Trent Bridge.

Technique and application were qualities in Salim Malik's batting which prompted his selection as a Cricketer of the Year. Leadership, an elusive quality, was manifest last year in David Hughes and Peter Roebuck, captains respectively of Lancashire and Somerset; in Roebuck's case, five first-class hundreds and an average of almost 50, in a season interrupted by injury, further advanced his claims. Jonathan Agnew accepted that life sometimes involves an uphill struggle and was rewarded with 101 first-class wickets, while Neil Foster, but for his well-merited inclusion in the England team throughout the summer, would surely have taken 100 wickets for the second season in succession. These, then, are *Wisden's* Five Cricketers of the Year.

My thanks go to those writers and statisticians without whose generous help *Wisden* would not be possible. I am also grateful, for their willing assistance, to the secretariats of MCC, TCCB, NCA and the Minor Counties, the county secretaries and their staffs, and the cricket masters at schools. For this year's edition, much of the proofreading has been undertaken by Gordon Burling, whose diligence and understanding will have saved the editor from additional readers' letters. To him, to Christine Forrest, who again has chevied and checked, to John Woodcock, whose advice as consultant editor was invaluable, and to our typesetters, SB Datagraphics, my special thanks.

GRAEME WRIGHT

Eastcote
Middlesex

ISBN

Cased edition 0 947766 09 X

Soft cover edition 0 947766 10 3

John Wisden & Co Ltd
Gray-Nicolls
Robertsbridge
East Sussex
TN32 5DH

Computer typeset by SB Datagraphics, Colchester

Printed in Great Britain by William Clowes Limited, Beccles

LIST OF CONTRIBUTORS

The editor acknowledges with gratitude the assistance afforded in the preparation of the Almanack by the following:

Jack Arlidge (Sussex)
John Arlott (Books)
R. L. Arrowsmith (Obituaries)
Chris Aspin (Lancashire Leagues)
Diane Back
Philip Bailey
Jack Bannister (Warwickshire)
Brian Bearshaw (Lancashire)
Michael Berry
Scyld Berry
John Billot (Glamorgan)
J. Watson Blair (Scotland)
Robert Brooke (Births and Deaths)
Kenneth R. Bullock (Canada)
Gordon Burling
C. R. Buttery (New Zealand)
John Callaghan (Yorkshire)
Terry Cooper (Middlesex)
Geoffrey Copinger
Tony Cozier (West Indies)
Patrick Eagar
Keith Edwards
Paton Fenton (Oxford University)
David Field (Surrey)
Charles Fortune
Bill Frindall (Records)
Nigel Fuller (Essex)
David Hallett (Cambridge University)
David Hardy (The Netherlands)
Peter Hargreaves (Denmark)
Lucy Hartley
Les Hatton
Eric Hill (Somerset)
Derek Hodgson
Grenville Holland (UAU)
Brian Hunt
James Hunt (Leicestershire)
Doug Ibbotson
Ken Ingman (ESCA)

Vic Isaacs (Hampshire)
Martin Johnson
Abid Ali Kazi (Pakistan)
Ken Kelly
C. J. Knott
Brian Langley
Stephanie Lawrence
John Lawson (Nottinghamshire)
Alan Lee
John Mackinnon (Australia)
John Minshull-Fogg
R. Mohan
Chris Moore (Worcestershire)
Dudley Moore (Kent)
Gerald Mortimer (Derbyshire)
David Munden
Adrian Murrell
Dr Vasant Naik
Don Neely
Graham Otway
A. L. A. Pichanick (Zimbabwe)
Qamar Ahmed
Andrew Radd (Northamptonshire)
Netta Rheinberg
Geoffrey Saulez
Derek Scott (Ireland)
Peter Sichel (South Africa)
Bill Smith
P. N. Sundaresan (India)
John Thicknesse
Bob Thomas
Gerry Vaidyasekera (Sri Lanka)
Mary Vaux
D. R. Walsh (HMC Schools)
Geoffrey Wheeler (Gloucestershire)
Don Wilson
A. S. R. Winlaw
Peter Wynne-Thomas

CONTENTS

INDEX

Note: For reasons of space, certain entries which appear in alphabetical order in sections of the Almanack are not included in this index. These include names that appear in Test Cricketers, Births and Deaths of Cricketers, Individual batting and bowling performances in the 1987 first-class season, and Oxford and Cambridge Blues.

c. = catches; d. = dismissals; p'ship = partnership; r. = runs; w. = wickets.

* Signifies not out or an unbroken partnership

Archer, R. G. (Aust.):- 1 Test hundred, *224;* Test p'ship records, *225.*

Arkwright, H. A.:- 18 w. v Gentlemen of Kent, *155.*

Arif Butt (Pak.):- Test p'ship record, *245.*

Arif-ud-Din (UBL):- 10 d. in match, *163;* 7 d. in innings, *162.*

Armstrong, N. F. (Leics.):- 36 hundreds, *137.*

Armstrong, W. W. (Aust.):- Test captain, *194;* All-round, *161;* 2,863 r. in Tests, *174;* 2,172 r. v England, *202;* 45 hundreds, *137;* 6 Test hundreds, *197, 221;* Hundred and double-hundred, *135;* 303* v Somerset, *132;* Carrying bat in Test, *176;* 428 for 6th wkt, *149;* Test p'ship record, *222.*

Arnold, E. G. (Eng.):- All-round, *161;* Wkt with 1st ball on Test début, *183;* 393 for 5th wkt, *149.*

Arnold, G. G. (Eng.):- 115 w. in Tests, *181.*

Arnold, J. (Eng.):- 37 hundreds, *137.*

Arshad Ali (Sukkur):- Obstructing the field, *152.*

Arshad Pervez (HBL):- 426 for 2nd wkt, *148.*

Arun Lal (Ind.):- Test p'ship record, *249.*

Arun, B. (Ind.):- Hat-trick, *156.*

Asda Challenge, *668-9.*

Ashdown, W. H. (Kent):- Highest for Kent, *133;* 332 v Essex, *131;* 307* in day, *143;* 305* v Derbyshire, *132;* 39 hundreds, *137.*

Ashes, The:- *193-202;* History of, *1283.*

Ashraf Ali (Pak.):- Test p'ship record, *251.*

Asif Din (Warwicks.):- Hundred before lunch, *286.*

Asif Iqbal (Pak.):- Test captain, *246;* 3,575 r. in Tests, *175;* 45 hundreds, *137;* 10 Test hundreds, *218, 231, 244, 247;* 350 for 4th wkt, *149;* 190 for 9th wkt, *150, 179, 218;* Test p'ship records, *218, 232, 241, 245.*

Asif Masood (Pak.):- Test p'ship record, *218.*

Aslam Ali (UBL):- 456 for 3rd wkt, *146, 149.*

Aslett, D. G. (Kent):- Hundred on début, *133.*

Astill, W. E. (Eng.):- All-round, *161, 162;* 2,431 w., *159;* 100 w. (9), *158.*

Athar Khan (Allied Bank):- Handled the ball, *151.*

Atherton, M. A. (CUCC & Lancs.):- Captain of Cambridge, *643;* Carrying bat in 1987, *287.*

Athey, C. W. J. (Eng.):- 4 successive hundreds, *135, 286;* 2 hundreds in match, *286;* 1 Test hundred, *217.*

Atkinson, D. St E. (WI):- Test hundred, *224;* All-round in Test, *185;* 347 for 7th wkt, *150, 225;* Test p'ship records, *225, 236.*

Atkinson, G. (Som.):- 1st wkt hundreds, *148.*

Attewell, W. (Eng.):- 1,950 w., *159;* 100 w. (10), *158.*

Australia:- Australia in Test cricket (*see p. 130*); B & H Challenge, *1008-13;* B & H World Series Cup, *1014-23;* Definition of first-class matches, *1248;* Domestic season 1986-87, *1034-66;* Highest individual Test innings, *169;* Highest Test innings,

188; Leading batsmen in Tests, *173-4;* Leading bowlers in Tests, *182;* Lowest Test innings, *190;* Most consecutive Test appearances, *192;* Most Test appearances, *126;* Most Test appearances as captain, *126;* Oldest Test player, *192;* Reliance World Cup, *263-85;* Representative body, *1191;* Sharjah Cup, *1024-8;* Summary of Tests, *193;* Test cricketers (1877-1987), *97-104;* Youngest and oldest on Test début, *191.*

Australia v England (Women), 1987, *1141-5.*

Australia v New Zealand, 1987-88, *1003.*

Australian team in South Africa, 1986-87, *1067, 1078-82.*

Azad, K. (Ind.):- Handled the ball, *151.*

Azhar Abbas (B'pur):- 10 d. in match, *163.*

Azharuddin, M. (Ind.):- 1,461 r. (avge 52.17) in Tests, *176;* 4 hundreds in succession, *135;* 6 Test hundreds, *171, 215, 247, 249;* Hundred on Test début, *171, 215;* 5 c. in innings, *265;* Test p'ship records, *216, 248, 249.*

Aziz Malik (Lahore Div.):- Hit the ball twice, *152.*

B

Bacchus, S. F. A. F. (WI):- 250 v India, *170, 237.*

Bacher, A. (SA):- Test captain, *220.*

Badcock, C. L. (Aust.):- 325 v Victoria, *131;* 1 Test hundred, *197.*

Badcock, F. T. (NZ):- Test p'ship record, *234.*

Baichan, L. (WI):- Hundred on Test début, *170, 240;* Hundred and double-hundred, *135;* 2 hundreds in match (2), *134.*

Baig, A. A. (Ind.):- Hundred on Test début, *170, 215;* Test p'ship record, *230.*

Bailey, T. E. (Eng.):- All-round, *161, 162;* *185;* 28,641 r., *141;* 2,290 r. in Tests, *173;* 1,000 r. (17), *138;* 1 Test hundred, *212;* Slow batting in Test, *178;* 2,082 w., *159;* 132 w. in Tests, *181;* 100 w. (9), *158;* 10 w. in innings, *153;* 10 w. or more in Test (1), *210;* Test p'ship record, *218.*

Bain Dawes Trophy, *840.*

Bairstow, D. L. (Eng.):- 1,024 d., *164;* 232 d. in Sunday League, *802;* 11 c. in match, *163;* 7 c. in innings, *162.*

Bakewell, A. H. (Eng.):- 1 Test hundred, *208;* 8 c. in match, *164.*

Balaskas, X. C. (SA):- 1 Test hundred, *234.*

Banerjee, S. N. (Ind.):- 249 for 10th wkt, *151.*

Banks, D. A. (Worcs.):- Hundred on début, *133.*

Bannerman, C. (Aust.):- Hundred on Test début, *170, 197.*

Bannister, J. D. (Warwicks.):- 10 w. in innings, *153.*

Baptiste, E. A. E. (WI):- 8 w. in innings, *287;* Test p'ship record, *210.*

E

MCC Schools Festival, 1987, *853-5*.

Masood Anwar (R'pindi):– 8 c. in match, *164*.

Masood Iqbal (HBL):– 7 d. in innings, *162*.

Massie, H. H. (Aust.):– Test captain, *195*.

Massie, R. A. L. (Aust.):– 16 w. in Test, *180, 201*; 10 w. or more in Test (1), *201*; 8 w. in Test innings (2), *180, 201*; Test p'ship record, *232*.

Matthews, F. C. L. (Notts.):– 17 w. in match, *154*.

Matthews, G. R. J. (Aust.):– 3 Test hundreds, *227, 229*; 10 w. or more in Test (1), *230*; Test p'ship records, *227, 232*.

Matthews, T. J. (Aust.):– Double hat-trick in Test, *156, 184*; 4 hat-tricks, *156*.

May, P. B. H. (Eng.):– Chairman of selectors, *1255*; Test captain, *126, 194, 203, 207, 211, 214*; 27,592 r. (avge 51.00), *141, 142*; 4,537 r. in Tests, *173*; 52 consecutive Tests, *192*; 85 hundreds, *136*; 13 Test hundreds, *196, 204, 209, 212, 215*; 4 successive hundreds, *136*; 2 hundreds in match (3), *134*; Hundred on Test début, *170, 204*; 285* v West Indies, *169, 209*; Test p'ship record, *179, 210*.

Maynard, M. P. (Glam.):– Hundred on début, *133*; Hundred before lunch, *286*; 50 in 14 min., *142, 286*; 30 r. in over, *145*.

Mayne, E. R. (Aust.):– 456 for 1st wkt, *146, 147, 148*.

Mead, C. P. (Eng.):– 55,061 r., *140*; 3,179 r. in season, *138*; 1,000 r. (27), *138*; 665 Championship appearances, *262*; 153 hundreds, *136*; 13 hundreds in season, *136*; 4 Test hundreds, *196, 204*; 2 hundreds in match (3), *134*; Hundred and double-hundred, *135*.

Mead, W. (Eng.):– 1,916 w., *159*; 100 w. (10), *158*; 17 w. in match, *154*.

Meckiff, I. (Aust.):– Test p'ship record, *222*.

Medlycott, K. T. (Surrey):– Hundred on début, *133*; 262 for 7th wkt, *287*.

Meetings in 1987:– ICC, *1255, 1256*; MCC, *334-5*; TCCB, *1255, 1256*.

Mehra, M. (Ind. Rlwys):– Obstructing the field, *152*.

Mehra, V. L. (Ind.):– Test cricket at 17, *191*.

Melville, A. (SA):– Test captain, *203*; 4 Test hundreds, *205*; 2 hundreds in same Test, *171, 205*; 299 for 7th wkt, *150*; Test p'ship record, *205*.

Mendis, G. D. (Lancs.):– 203* in 1987, *286*.

Mendis, L. R. D. (SL):– Test captain, *126, 219, 232, 245, 248, 250*; 23 Tests, *126, 192*; 4 Test hundreds, *219, 249*; 2 hundreds in same Test, *171, 249*; Test p'ship records, *219, 233, 249, 251*.

Mercer, J. (Sussex, Glam. and Northants):– 1,591 w., *159*; 100 w. (9), *158*; 10 w. in innings, *153*.

Merchant, U. M. (Bombay):– 360 for 5th wkt, *149*.

Merchant, V. M. (Ind.):– 13,248 r. (avge 71.22), *141*; 4 successive hundreds, *136*; 44 hundreds, *137*; 3 Test hundreds, *215*; 359* v Maharashtra, *131, 150*; 142 and hat-trick, *160*; 371 for 6th wkt, *150*.

Merrick, T. A. (Warwicks.):– 13 w. v Lancashire, *287*.

Metcalfe, A. A. (Yorks.):– Hundred on début, *133*.

Middlesex:– *349, 490-504*; Championship positions, *355-6*; Highest score, *165*; Highest individual score, *133*; Lowest score, *166*.

Middlesex II, *824, 825, 832-3*.

Milburn, C. (Eng.):– 2 Test hundreds, *208, 218*; Test p'ship record, *210*.

Miller, G. (Eng.):– Slow batting in Test, *178*.

Miller, K. R. (Aust.):– 2,958 r. in Tests, *174*; 41 hundreds, *137*; 7 Test hundreds, *198, 224*; 170 w. in Tests, *182*; 10 w. or more in Test (1), *201*; All-round in Tests, *184, 185*; Test p'ship records, *222, 225*.

Mills, J. E. (NZ):– Hundred on Test début, *170, 212*; 190* for 8th wkt, *150*; Test p'ship record, *213*.

Mills, P. T. (Glos.):– 5 w. for 0 r., *154*.

Milton, C. A. (Eng.):– 32,150 r., *140*; 1,000 r. (16), *138*; 56 hundreds, *137*; 2 hundreds in match (2), *134*; Hundred on Test début, *170, 212*; 758 c., *165*; 63 c. in season, *165*; 8 c. in match, *164*.

Milton, W. H. (SA):– Test captain, *203*.

Minor Counties:– *804-22*; B & H Cup, *694, 724*; Championship winners, *822*; Fixtures, 1988, *1292-1293*; Formation, *261-2*; Highest individual scores, *260*; NWB Trophy, *692*; Representative body, *1192*; Umpires, *1257*; v Pakistanis, *325*.

Miran Bux (Pak.):– Test début at 47, *191*; Oldest Pakistan Test player, *192*.

Mitchell, A. (Eng.):– 44 hundreds, *137*; 4 successive hundreds, *136*.

Mitchell, B. (SA):– 3,471 r. in Tests, *174*; 8 Test hundreds, *205, 234*; 2 hundreds in same Test, *171, 205*; 6 c. in Test, *188*; 299 for 7th wkt, *150*; Test p'ship records, *205-6, 234*.

Mitchell, F. (Eng. and SA):– Test captain, *203, 220*.

Mitchell, T. B. (Eng.):– 100 w. (10), *158*; 10 w. in innings, *153*.

Modi, R. S. (Ind.):– 1 Test hundred, *238*; 410 for 3rd wkt, *149*; 371 for 6th wkt, *150*.

Mohammad Farooq (Pak.):– Test p'ship record, *245*.

Mohammad Ilyas (Pak.):– 1 Test hundred, *244*; Test p'ship record, *245*.

Mohammad Iqbal (Muslim Model HS):– 475* v Islamia HS, *260*.

Mohol, S. N. (M'tra):– 4 w. with consecutive balls, *155*.

Mohsin Khan (Pak.):– 2,709 r. in Tests, *175*; 1,029 Test r. in year, *172*; 7 Test hundreds, *218, 231, 247, 250*; Handled the ball, *151*;

Nicholls, R. B. (Glos.):– 1,000 r. (15), *138*; 395 for 1st wkt, *147*.

Nichols, M. S. (Eng.):– All-round, *161*; 1,833 w., *159*; 100 w. (11), *158*.

Nicolson, J. F. W. (Natal):– 424 for 1st wkt, *147, 148*.

Nimbalkar, B. B. (M'tra):– 443* v Western Indian States, *131, 148*; 50 boundaries in innings, *146*; 455 for 2nd wkt, *146, 148*.

Nissan Shield (SA), *1076-7*.

Noble, M. A. (Aust.):– Test captain, *193*; 37 hundreds, *137*; 1 Test hundred, *198*; 121 w. in Tests, *182*; 10 w. or more in Test (2), *201*; All-round in Tests, *185*; 428 for 6th wkt, *149*.

Noreiga, J. M. (WI):– 9 w. in Test innings, *179*.

Norfolk, *806, 815-6*.

Northamptonshire:– *349, 505-20*; Championship positions, *355-6*; Highest score, *165*; Highest individual score, *133*; Lowest score, *166*.

Northamptonshire II, *824, 825, 833-4*.

Northumberland, *675, 806, 816-7*.

Nottinghamshire:– *349, 521-37*; Championship positions, *355-6*; Highest score, *165*; Highest individual score, *133*; Lowest score, *166*; NatWest Bank Trophy winners, *688-9*.

Nottinghamshire II, *824, 825, 834, 850*.

Nourse, A. D. (SA):– Test captain, *203, 220*; 12,472 r. (avge 51.53), *142*; 2,960 r. (avge 53.81) in Tests, *174, 176*; 621 r. in series, *206*; 41 hundreds, *137*; 9 Test hundreds, *205, 221*; Test p'ship record, *205*.

Nourse, A. W. (SA):– Handled the ball, *151*; Oldest South African Test player, *192*; 2,234 r. in Tests, *174*; 38 hundreds, *137*; 1 Test hundred, *221*; 304* v Transvaal, *132*; 53 boundaries in innings, *146*; Test p'ship records, *222*.

Nunes, R. K. (WI):– Test captain, *207*.

Nupen, E. P. (SA):– Test captain, *203*; 10 w. or more in Test (1), *206*; Test p'ship record, *206*.

Nurse, S. M. (WI):– 2,523 r. in Tests, *174*; 6 Test hundreds, *209, 225, 235*; 258 v New Zealand, *170, 235*; Test p'ship record, *210*.

O

Oates, T. W. (Notts.):– 10 d. in match, *163*.

O'Brien, Sir T. C. (Eng.):– Test captain, *203*.

Ochse, A. E. (SA):– Youngest South African Test player, *191*.

O'Connor, J. (Eng.):– 28,764 r., *141*; 1,000 r. (16), *138*; 72 hundreds, *136*.

O'Keeffe, K. J. (Aust.):– Test p'ship records, *227, 232*.

Old, C. M. (Eng.):– Fast scoring, *142*; 143 w. in Tests, *181*; 4 w. in 5 balls v Pakistan, *219*.

Oldest players on Test début, *191*.

Oldest Test players, *192*.

Oldfield, N. (Eng.):– 38 hundreds, *137*.

Oldfield, W. A. (Aust.):– 130 d. in Tests, *187*; 90 d. v England, *202*.

Oldroyd, E. (Yorks.):– 36 hundreds, *137*.

O'Neill, N. C. (Aust.):– 13,859 r. (avge 50.95), *142*; 2,779 r. in Tests, *174*; 45 hundreds, *137*; 6 Test hundreds, *198, 224, 229, 231*.

Ontong, R. C. (Glam.):– 5 c. in innings, *288*.

O'Reilly, W. J. (Aust.):– 144 w. in Tests, *182*; 102 w. v England, *202*; 10 w. or more in Test (3), *201*; Test p'ship record, *222*.

Ormiston, R. W. (Wgtn):– 226 for 6th wkt, *150*.

O'Shaughnessy, S. J. (Lancs.):– Hundred in 35 minutes, *142-3*.

Owen-Smith, H. G. (SA):– 1 Test hundred, *205*; Test p'ship record, *206*.

Oxford v Cambridge, *341-4*.

Oxford & Cambridge Universities:– v Pakistanis, *321-2*; in B & H Cup, *724*.

Oxford University 1987:– *635-43*; Blues, *653-6*.

Oxfordshire, *673-4, 805, 806, 817*.

P

PACO Cup (Pak.), *1107-8, 1122-3*.

Page, M. L. (NZ):– Test captain, *211, 233*; 1 Test hundred, *212*.

Pairaudeau, B. H. (WI):– Hundred on Test début, *170, 238*; Test p'ship record, *239*.

Pakistan:– B & H Challenge, *1008-13*; Champions Trophy, *1004-7*; Definition of first-class matches, *355*; Domestic season 1986-87, *1107-24*; Highest individual Test innings, *169*; Highest Test innings, *188*; Leading batsmen in Tests, *175*; Leading bowlers in Tests, *183*; Lowest Test innings, *190*; Most Test appearances, *126*; Most Test appearances as captain, *126*; Oldest Test player, *192*; Pakistan in Test cricket (*see p. 130*); Reliance World Cup, *263-83*; Representative body, *1192*; Sharjah Cup, *1024-8*; Summary of Tests, *193*; Test cricketers (1952-87), *122-5*; Youngest and oldest on Test début, *191*.

Pakistan v England, 1987-88, *1124*.

Pakistan B in Zimbabwe and Kenya, *1132-6, 1138*.

Palm, A. W. (SA):– 244* for 6th wkt, *150*.

Palmer, G. E. (Aust.):– 10 w. or more in Test (2), *201*.

Pandya, A. (Saurashtra):– Handled the ball, *151*.

Parfitt, P. H. (Eng.):– 26,924 r., *141*; 1,000 r. (15), *138*; 58 hundreds, *137*; 7 Test hundreds, *204, 212, 215, 218*; 2 hundreds in match (2) *134*; Test p'ship records, *213, 218*.

Parkar, G. A. (Ind.):– 421 for 1st wkt, *147*.

Parkar, Z. (Bombay):– 10 d. in match, *163*.

Parker, C. W. L. (Glos.):– 3,278 w., *158;* 200 w. (5), *157;* 100 w. (16), *158;* 100 w. by June 12, *158;* 17 w. in match, *154;* 10 w. in innings, *153;* 6 hat-tricks, *156;* Double hat-trick, *156.*

Parker, J. M. (NZ):– Test captain, *243;* 3 Test hundreds, *212, 227, 242;* Test p'ship records, *227.*

Parker, P. W. G. (Eng.):– Captain of Sussex, *570;* 32 r. in over, *144.*

Parkhouse, W. G. A. (Eng.):– Benefit match, *849;* 1,000 r. (15), *138.*

Parkin, C. H. (Eng.):– 200 w. (2), *157.*

Parks, H. W. (Sussex):– 42 hundreds, *137.*

Parks, J. H. (Eng.):– All-round, *161;* 3,003 r. in season, *138;* 41 hundreds, *137.*

Parks, J. M. (Eng.):– 36,673 r., *140;* 1,000 r. (20), *138;* 51 hundreds, *137;* 2 Test hundreds, *204, 208;* 1,181 d., *164;* 114 d. in Tests, *187;* 8 d. in Test, *186;* Test p'ship records, *205, 210.*

Parks, R. J. (Hants):– 10 d. in match, *163.*

Parsons, Rev. J. H. (Warwicks.):– 38 hundreds, *137.*

Partnerships:– First-wicket, *147;* Highest, *146;* Highest for each country, *148-51;* Highest in one-day ints, *255;* Highest in Tests, *179 (see individual series for records v countries);* In 1987, *287.*

Pascoe, L. S. (Aust.):– Test p'ship record, *227.*

Passailaigue, C. C. (WI):– 487* for 6th wkt, *146, 149.*

Pataudi (sen.), Nawab of (Eng. and Ind.):– Test captain, *214;* 4 successive hundreds, *136;* Hundred on Test début, *170, 196.*

Pataudi (jun.), Nawab of (Ind.):– Test captain, *126, 214, 228, 237, 241;* 2,793 r. in Tests, *175;* 6 Test hundreds, *215, 229, 242;* 2 hundreds in match (2), *134;* Slow batting in Test, *178.*

Patel, B. P. (Ind.):– 1 Test hundred, *238;* Test p'ship records, *239, 243.*

Patel, J. M. (Ind.):– 14 w. in Test, *180, 230;* 9 w. in Test innings, *179, 230.*

Patil, S. M. (Ind.):– 4 Test hundreds, *215, 229, 247;* Test p'ship record, *248, 249.*

Patron's Trophy (Pak.), *1107, 1110-1.*

Paynter, E. (Eng.):– 653 r. in series, *206;* 45 hundreds, *137;* 4 Test hundreds, *196, 204;* 2 hundreds in match (2), *134;* 2 hundreds in same Test, *171, 204;* 322 v Sussex, *131;* Test avge of 59.23, *176;* Test p'ship records, *200.*

Payton, W. R. D. (Notts.):– 39 hundreds, *137.*

Peach, H. A. (Surrey):– Fast scoring, *143;* 4 w. with consecutive balls, *155.*

Pearse, D. K. (Natal):– Handled the ball, *151.*

Pearson, A. J. G. (CUCC and Som.):– 10 w. in innings, *153.*

Peate, E. (Eng.):– 214 w. in season, *157;* 8 w. for 5 r., *154.*

Peel, R. (Eng.):– 1,753 w., *159;* 102 w. in Tests, *181;* 100 w. (8), *158;* 10 w. or more in Test (2), *201;* 292 for 8th wkt, *150.*

Pegler, S. J. (SA):– Test p'ship record, *222.*

Pellew, C. E. (Aust.):– 2 Test hundreds, *198.*

Perks, R. T. D. (Worcs.):– 2,233 w., *159;* 100 w. (16), *158.*

Perrin, P. A. (Essex):– Highest for Essex, *133;* 29,709 r., *141;* 1,000 r. (18), *138;* 66 hundreds, *136;* 2 hundreds in match (4), *134;* 343* v Derbyshire, *131, 133;* 68 boundaries in innings, *146.*

Pervez Akhtar (Pak. Rlwys):– 337* v Dera Ismail Khan, *131.*

Pervez Shah (Lahore):– Hat-trick, *156.*

Petherick, P. J. (NZ):– Hat-trick v Pakistan, *184.*

Phadkar, D. G. (Ind.):– 2 Test hundreds, *215, 229.*

Philip, I. L. (Scotland):– Hundred on début, *133.*

Phillips, H. (Sussex):– 10 d. in match, *163.*

Phillips, R. B. (Qld):– 7 d. in innings, *162.*

Phillips, W. B. (Aust.):– Hundred on Test début, *171, 231;* 2 Test hundreds, *224, 231;* 462* for 4th wkt, *146, 149, 1062;* Test p'ship records, *227, 232.*

Pickett, H. (Essex):– 10 w. in innings, *152.*

Pinch, C. (S. Aust.):– 2 hundreds in match (2), *134.*

Pithey, A. J. (SA):– 1 Test hundred, *205;* Test p'ship record, *206.*

Place, W. (Eng.):– 36 hundreds, *137;* 1 Test hundred, *208.*

Playle, W. R. (NZ):– Slow Test batting, *178.*

Pocock, P. I. (Eng.):– 1,607 w., *159;* 5 w. in 6 balls, *156;* 4 w. with consecutive balls, *155;* Test p'ship record, *210.*

Pollard, V. (NZ):– 2 Test hundreds, *212;* Test p'ship records, *213, 236, 242.*

Pollock, P. M. (SA):– 116 w. in Tests, *182;* 10 w. or more in Test (1), *206;* Test p'ship records, *222, 234.*

Pollock, R. G. (SA):– Handled the ball, *151;* 20,940 r. (avge 54.67), *142;* 2,256 r. (avge 60.97) in Tests, *174, 176;* 64 hundreds, *137;* 7 Test hundreds, *205, 221;* 2 hundreds in match (2), *134;* 274 v Australia, *169, 221;* 341 for 3rd wkt and 338 for 5th wkt, *149;* Test p'ship records, *222.*

Ponsford, W. H. (Aust.):– 13,819 r. (avge 65.18), *141;* 2,122 r. in Tests, *174;* 47 hundreds, *137;* 7 Test hundreds, *198-9, 224;* Hundred on Test début, *170;* 437 v Queensland, *131;* 429 v Tasmania, *131;* 352 v New South Wales, *131;* 336 v South Australia, *131;* 334 r. in day, *143;* 281* at Lord's, *259;* 266 v England, *169, 198;* 456 for 1st wkt, *146, 147;* 375 for 1st wkt, *147;* 451 for 2nd wkt, *146, 148, 179, 200;* Test p'ship records, *179, 200.*

Pooley, E. (Surrey):– 12 d. and 10 d. in matches, *163.*

Poore, M. B. (NZ):– Test p'ship record, *234.*

Vogler, A. E. E. (SA):– 36 w. in series, *181;* 16 w. in day, *155;* 10 w. in innings, *153;* 10 w. or more in Test (1), *206;* 6 c. in Test, *188.*

W

Wade, H. F. (SA):– Test captain, *203, 220.*
Wade, W. W. (SA):– 1 Test hundred, *205.*
Wadekar, A. L. (Ind.):– Test captain, *214, 237;* 2,113 r. in Tests, *175;* 36 hundreds, *137;* 1 Test hundred, *242;* 323 v Mysore, *131;* Test p'ship record, *216.*
Wadsworth, K. J. (NZ):– Test p'ship record, *236.*
Waheed Mirza (Sind):– 324 v Quetta, *131, 148;* 561 for 1st wkt, *146, 147, 148.*
Waite, J. H. B. (SA):– 2,405 r. in Tests, *174;* 50 Tests, *126, 192;* 4 Test hundreds, *205, 222, 234;* 141 d. in Tests, *187;* 26 d. in series, *187;* Test p'ship records, *206, 222.*
Walcott, C. L. (WI):– 11,820 r. (avge 56.55), *142;* 3,798 r. (avge 56.68) in Tests, *175, 176;* 827 r. in series, *172;* 40 hundreds, *137;* 15 Test hundreds, *209, 225, 235, 238, 240;* 2 hundreds in same Test, *171, 225;* 2 hundreds in match (2), *134;* 314* v Trinidad, *132, 149;* 574* for 4th wkt, *146, 149;* Test p'ship records, *236, 239, 240.*
Wales v Ireland, *664, 847.*
Walker, A. K. (Notts.):– 4 w. with consecutive balls.
Walker, M. H. N. (Aust.):– 138 w. in Tests, *182;* 8 w. in Test innings, *180;* Test p'ship record, *232.*
Walker, P. M. (Eng.):– 73 c., 69 c. and 65 c. in season, *165;* 8 c. in match, *164.*
Walker, V. E. (Middx):– 108 and 10 w., *160;* 10 w. in innings (2), *152.*
Walkley, E. (S. Aust.):– 232 for 9th wkt, *150.*
Wall, T. W. (Aust.):– 10 w. in innings, *153.*
Wallace, W. M. (NZ):– Test captain, *233;* 324 for 4th wkt, *149.*
Walters, C. F. (Eng.):– Test captain, *195;* 1 Test hundred, *215.*
Walters, K. D. (Aust.):– 5,357 r. in Tests, *173;* 45 hundreds, *137;* 15 Test hundreds, *199, 224, 227, 229, 231;* 2 hundreds in same Test, *171, 224;* Hundred and double-hundred, *135;* Hundred on Test début, *170, 199;* 250 v New Zealand, *170, 227;* Test p'ship records, *225, 227.*
Waqar Hassan (Pak.):– 1 Test hundred, *244;* 308 for 7th wkt v New Zealand, *150, 245.*
Ward, Alan (Eng.):– 4 w. in 4 balls in Sunday League, *802.*
Ward, Albert. (Eng.):– 1 Test hundred, *197.*
Ward, J. T. (NZ):– Test p'ship record, *242.*
Ward, W. (MCC):– 278 at Lord's, *259.*
Wardle, J. H. (Eng.):– 1,846 w., *159;* 102 w. in Tests, *181;* 100 w. (10), *158;* 10 w. or more in Test (1), *206.*
Warnapura, B. (SL):– Test captain, *219, 248, 250.*

Warner, Sir Pelham F. (Eng.):– Test captain, *194, 203;* 29,028 r., *141;* 60 hundreds, *137;* Hundred on Test début, *170, 204;* Carrying bat in Test, *176.*
Warr, J. J. (Eng.):– President of MCC, *333.*
Warren, A. (Eng.):– 283 for 9th wkt, *150.*
Warwick Under-25 Competition:– *840;* Fixtures, 1988, *1295.*
Warwickshire:– *349, 585-601;* Championship positions, *355-6;* Highest score, *165;* Highest individual score, *133;* Lowest score, *166.*
Warwickshire II, *824, 825, 837-8.*
Washbrook, C. (Eng.):– 34,101 r., *140;* 2,569 r. in Tests, *173;* 1,000 r. (20), *138;* 76 hundreds, *136;* 6 Test hundreds, *197, 204, 209, 212;* 1st wkt hundreds, *147;* Test p'ship record, *205.*
Wasim Akram (Pak.):– 10 w. or more in Test (1), *245;* Test p'ship record, *248.*
Wasim Bari (Pak.):– Test captain, *217;* 228 d. in Tests, *187;* 62 d. in one-day ints, *256;* 8 d. in Test, *186;* 7 d. in Test innings, *162, 186;* 7 d. in innings (2), *162;* Test p'ship records, *232, 241, 248.*
Wasim Raja (Pak.):– 2,821 r. in Tests, *175;* 4 Test hundreds, *218, 240, 247;* Test p'ship records, *241.*
Wass, T. G. (Notts.):– 1,666 w., *159;* 100 w. (10), *158;* 16 w. in day (2), *155.*
Wasu, H. (Vidarbha):– Obstructing the field, *152.*
Watkins, A. J. (Eng.):– 2 Test hundreds, *204, 215.*
Watkins, J. R. (Aust.):– Test p'ship record, *232.*
Watson, F. B. (Lancs.):– 50 hundreds, *137;* 300* v Surrey, *132;* 1st wkt hundreds, *148.*
Watson, W. (Eng.):– 25,670 r., *141;* 55 hundreds, *137;* 2 Test hundreds, *197, 209.*
Watson-Smith, R. (Border):– 183* and 125* in first two first-class innings, *134.*
Watts, E. A. (Surrey):– 10 w. in innings, *153.*
Wazir Mohammad (Pak.):– Test p'ship records, *241.*
Weekes, E. D. (WI):– 12,010 r. (avge 55.34), *142;* 4,455 r. (avge 58.61) in Tests, *174, 176;* 779 r. in series, *172;* 36 hundreds, *137;* 15 Test hundreds, *209-10, 225, 235, 238, 240;* 5 successive hundreds, *135;* 2 hundreds in same Test, *171, 238;* 304* v Cambridge Univ., *132;* Avge of 79.65 in English season, *139;* Test p'ship records, *210, 236, 239, 240.*
Weekes, K. H. (WI):– 1 Test hundred, *209.*
Weerasinghe, C. D. U. S. (SL):– Youngest Sri Lankan Test player, *191.*
Wellard, A. W. (Eng.):– All-round, *161;* 1,614 w., *159;* 66 sixes in season, *145;* 30 r. and 31 r. in over, *145;* 100 w. (8), *158.*
Wellham, D. M. (Aust.):– Hundred on début, *134;* Hundred on Test début, *134, 171, 199.*
Wells, C. M. (Sussex):– All-round, *288;* (with A. P. Wells) 303* for 4th wkt, *287, 577.*

INDEX OF FILLERS

NOTES BY THE EDITOR

There is a temptation, as I begin these Notes, to quote Voltaire, but it will be resisted, if for no better reason than that the quotation no longer applies. Certainly not in English cricket. There would appear to be no admirals. The game's leadership, if 1987 is any indication, comes from the quartermaster's store rather than the quarter-deck. As the society in which we live becomes more egalitarian, or so it is said, there are those who would argue that this is how it should be. But when those who lead are unable to rise above their former station, indeed do not consider it essential to do so, those they lead cannot be inspired to rise above their own routine levels of performance. English cricket, it seems to me, needs to be lifted beyond the routine performance.

That the game is capable still of freeing the spirit was evidenced during the MCC Bicentenary match at Lord's. Moreover, it offered a personal insight into one of the problems which sport faces today. Following any game made competitive by nationalism or commercialism can blind the spectator to those aspects of sport – enjoyment and entertainment – which are as important as winning. Sport was not meant to be a war substitute, and cricket must not find itself being forced into that role. Winning is not everything. This should be one of sport's primary lessons to society. Satisfaction can come from giving of one's best and even, in those few exquisite moments, from sur-passing personal expectations. Participants and spectators both need to be reminded of that from time to time, and at Lord's in August I was grateful for the reminder.

A truly sporting occasion

Although the rewards were generous, personal pride was the spur that drew from the players their best. Good manners prevailed, batsmen walked, bouncers were used sparingly and so were effective in surprising both the batsman and the spectator. In terms of technique, the game was a delight; from batsmen and bowlers there was variety. And throughout there was friendliness. Yet, honesty compels the admission, at first I was not en-chanted. Something seemed to be missing. It was the "edge", some would call it "needle", which after years of watching top-class sport I had come to accept as part of the occasion. Without it, that first day of the MCC Bicentenary match was like the first day without a cigarette after years of smoking. The next day, having realised why the fault was mine, I rejoiced in the occasion of cricket sportingly and well played. That morning I had sat on my station, with the sun on my back, reading a favourite book. I walked with the crowds to Lord's, all of us looking forward to a great day's cricket. We had not come to see anyone win or lose. We had come to see fine cricketers give of their best and it was a wonderful feeling.

An unhappy episode

Sadly, the year was not always so blessed, not even for the Marylebone Cricket Club in its bicentenary year. Concerned at what they felt was an encroachment by the Test and County Cricket Board on their rights at

Lord's, the club's premises, a group of members voted at the Annual General Meeting in May not to accept the club's Report and Accounts. There were also calls for the resignation of the President, M. C. Cowdrey. The dissatisfaction of those members had been prompted by the resignation of the Treasurer, D. G. Clark, the previous December, and the early retirement in January of the Secretary, J. A. Bailey. At a Special General Meeting at the end of July the Committee received, by a large majority, the support of the club's members, but they had been reminded of the importance of proper consultation and communication in today's world. In its way, this unhappy episode encapsulated a year in which censure and recrimination excited more attention than the cricket being played – or, as so often seemed the case, not being played.

Malevolence and mischief

The first two of the summer's Test matches between England and Pakistan were badly affected by the weather. At Old Trafford there were constant interruptions; at Lord's, there was no play on the second, fourth and fifth days. For players, managers and press, there was time to fill, and as an old saw has it, Satan finds some mischief still for idle hands to do. Certainly some mischief emanated from the enforced intervals of those two matches and the ramifications were to be bitter and widespread.

England and Pakistan had arrived at the Test series still tasting success from their winter series, Pakistan having drawn with West Indies at home and beaten India in India, England having retained the Ashes and won two international one-day tournaments in Australia. In terms of international prestige in the world of cricket, much was at stake in this series. With Imran Khan unable to bowl at Old Trafford, Pakistan were seriously handicapped, and as England set about building on the advantage secured by Robinson's century, Pakistan began to play for time. The weather was always going to be their ally, and the longer England batted, the better were Pakistan's chances of a draw. At one stage on the second day, they managed to bowl no more than eleven overs in an hour, and this without one bowler boasting a long run-up. Players came and substitutes went, and the rhythm of play was broken. Imran himself was off the field at the time, having required an X-ray of an injured thumb, and it was Javed Miandad who conducted the stalling operation. That it was deliberate time-wasting cannot be questioned. Unfortunately, all countries do it, and that England have been no exception is something England's newly appointed Team Manager, M. J. Stewart, should have considered when, at the evening's press conference, he criticised Pakistan's tactics. Commenting on the poor over-rate, and the need for a tightening-up on the use of substitutes, he said, "I feel there has to be a stricter control over what constitutes a genuine injury".

Some of the following morning's newspapers made a great play of Mr Stewart's comments. Later that day, a rain-interrupted Saturday, Imran and the Pakistan manager, Haseeb Ahsan, replied to the criticisms levelled at them. "We get slagged off and called cheats and I object to that", said Imran. "Maybe if I'd been in the field I'd have stepped things up. But both umpires said it was fine." Haseeb said, "The series has started off on the wrong foot. We've been labelled as cheats. I respect Stewart but he shouldn't have said what he did. If there's any problem we can sit down and talk it out. The umpires said there was no problem and yet talk of dirty tricks and all that nonsense has appeared in the press."

The battle lines had been drawn up: a fuse had been lit and it was to smoulder unchecked for another six months until, at Faisalabad in December, the charge exploded. Could not something have been done to defuse the situation before that? Or were the administrators at the TCCB aware even that there was a situation to defuse?

TCCB's support for umpire Constant

At Lord's, along with the rain, came a leak from the Pakistan management which was as subtle as any from a government department to Parliamentary correspondents. Its effect was to make public the TCCB's decision not to accede to Pakistan's request to remove two umpires, D. J. Constant and K. E. Palmer, from the Test match panel. Mr Constant had officiated in the Headingley Test match of the 1982 series between England and Pakistan, after which Imran had been critical of the umpiring, claiming that errors had cost his side the match and so the series. Pakistan's request in 1987 was not the first time that a visiting side had requested Mr Constant's omission from the Test match list. In 1982 the Indians, who came to England ahead of the Pakistanis, requested that he be replaced. This might have been a retaliatory move following complaints by England about umpiring standards in India during the previous winter: the 1981-82 tour on which the captain, K. W. R. Fletcher, expressed his dissent at an umpire's decision by hitting the stumps with his bat, an act which contributed to his being replaced as England's captain after the tour. It was also thought that the Indians had been unhappy with Mr Constant's umpiring during the final Test of the 1979 series. Whatever the reasons behind the Indians' request in 1982, the TCCB complied with it, although paying the umpire his match fee.

Last year, however, not only was the Pakistan request turned down on the grounds of prejudice, but A. C. Smith, the new Chief Executive of the TCCB, read a statement from the first-class umpires in support of their colleagues on the Test match panel. It was to be a year of supporting statements. All this time Mr Constant was the umpire officiating in the Test match at Lord's, and later both he and K. E. Palmer stood at The Oval in the final Test. At both venues, the Pakistan manager was publicly critical of Mr Constant and his umpiring, at one time describing him as "a disgraceful person". With or without justification, and I am not aware that there really was any, this was conduct unbecoming of a tour manager; but following some of Haseeb's other statements while in England, it surprised no-one. At Trent Bridge, during the touring team's match against Nottinghamshire, he attempted to interfere when the umpires officially warned a Pakistani bowler, Mohsin Kamal, for excessive use of the bouncer.

In view of Haseeb's conduct in England, it required the most optimistic of men to expect that England would not encounter some kind of retaliation when they stayed on in Pakistan after the World Cup. Without wishing to be pessimistic, or unduly cynical, little in the history of man's behaviour towards his fellow man, or nation's towards nation, could lead one to expect anything else, especially as Pakistan is a young, aggressive state fired by a fierce nationalism and a strict fundamentalist religion. Moreover, touring teams have repeatedly been critical of umpiring standards there, to the extent that the Pakistanis themselves had initiated a move towards neutral umpires for Test cricket.

At the end of the series in England, P. M. Lush, the England Tour Manager, said that he did not fear any reprisals. "If we want to have an umpire changed", he said, "there are procedures and I am sure that if we present the evidence on which our complaint is based, we will be given a fair hearing. It will be done without attracting publicity." His faith and his intentions were to be short-lived. By the end of the First Test in Pakistan, England's players and managers had become convinced that both the umpires and the conditions favoured the home side.

A dangerous state of mind

Yet even during the series in England last year, there were some players who felt that England were at a disadvantage because the umpires were giving Pakistan the benefit of the doubt following Haseeb's criticism of Mr Constant at Lord's. This is a dangerous state of mind for any team to be in, although for touring teams it is by no means unique. Before their game employed neutral referees for internationals, rugby union teams touring abroad invariably felt they were playing sixteen men. But even when cynicism about "local referees" might have been justified, there remained a code that the referee, however bad, had to be right. Even bad law is better than no law at all, for bad law in time can be changed. No law is anarchy. The way towards change, however, is not by dissent on the field of play. Nor is it by deliberate tit for tat; an eye for an eye.

An ugly aspect

Two touring teams in the closing months of last year felt that the odds were stacked against them: England in Pakistan and West Indies in India. In each country, the visiting captain expressed his anger, on the field of play, in the ugliest manner. There were complaints that pitches had been made to suit the local strength, which is spin bowling. Neither tour is covered by this edition of the Almanack but falls within the scope of the 1989 *Wisden*. None the less, what happened in Pakistan in November and December 1987 cannot stand in isolation from events in England in the preceding months, which is why a summary of the background has been provided in some detail. Other issues, too, require comment, for they are relevant to cricket and to the times in which we live.

An acceptable standard of behaviour

Britain has good reason to be proud of a tradition of civilised behaviour. But in recent years the tradition and indeed the civilisation have been endangered by the unacceptable increase in violent attitudes. I am not referring to criminal violence such as physical assault; rather the ill-tempered outbursts one encounters from otherwise law-abiding citizens. This behaviour is manifest on our roads, on public transport, in restaurants and at sports grounds. Consideration towards those about us is in decline; tolerance has given way to a short-fused temper.

There are some, among whom are our politicians, for whom such attitudes of verbal aggression are a device, a professional posturing. But politicians have a duty to society. When they are heard on the radio and television bickering, shrilly dissenting and by no means behaving in a civil manner, who can throw up his hands when the average citizen emulates those who are regarded as the country's leaders? It was not without significance that Mike Gatting, when called upon by the TCCB to apologise for his behaviour towards the Pakistani umpire, Shakoor Rana, was reported to have said, "Does Maggie [Mrs Thatcher, the Prime Minister] back down when she's given no choice?" The implication was that he could see no difference between his own outburst against an umpire he felt was behaving unjustly and that of the Prime Minister against her opponents.

No place for dissent

The refusal of Chris Broad, England's opening batsman, to leave the wicket when given out in the First Test in Pakistan cannot be condoned. He received a reprimand but was subject to no other disciplinary measure. On a rainy day at Nottingham, he would do well to read Sections One and Two of the Professional Golfers' Association code of ethics and thank his lucky stars he is a professional cricketer and not a golfer. Cited in mitigation were the frustrations of the England players which had been allowed to build up during the tour as a result of some bad umpiring. Sympathy was the prevailing sentiment. In the next Test match, at Faisalabad, Gatting lost his temper and indulged in an unedifying confrontation with Shakoor Rana. The nation was then held spellbound by the spectacle of two grown men standing on their dignity without a square inch of moral ground to support them. At the time of writing, no action had been taken against Gatting.

Whether or not it should have been, time will provide an answer. A glance at what has happened in two other sports, however, suggests it should have been. Rugby union and tennis have suffered at lower levels from the example of ill discipline at the highest level. When the British Lions rugby team toured South Africa in 1974, and won a series there for the first time, part and parcel of their game plan was the now infamous "99 call". In the event of provocation or aggression against a Lions forward, his fellow forwards would immediately pitch into the opposition. The purpose was two-fold. It showed the opposing side that the Lions could not be intimidated, and it made it impossible for the referee to send off any one player for retaliation. The consequences of this policy are still being felt today in club rugby, especially in Wales where a lack of discipline leads to outbursts of violence throughout the season. In tennis, the boorish behaviour of some leading players has permeated through to junior ranks so that coaches in England now complain that their young charges could win Wimbledon on the strength of their tantrums, but lack the tennis skills to match them.

I doubt if there is a cricketer anywhere who has not been upset by an umpire's decision, especially when – as can happen in club and village matches – that umpire has affiliations with "the other side". But without the unchallenged acceptance of the principle that the umpire's word is final, what chance does the game have? Professional sportsmen set the standards of behaviour for those who play the game at all levels, just as those in authority have a responsibility to ensure that they do. A cricket master, reporting on his school's season for *Wisden*, informed us that he had lost three senior players for disciplinary reasons. "All I can say after nineteen years with the XI", he wrote, "is that a schoolmaster must uphold behaviour standards, even at the cost of losing his best players."

The responsibility of captaincy

Like it or not, the England captain has a responsibility to English cricket. On the day that the national team left Heathrow for New Zealand, the Cricket Council announced its marketing strategy to introduce Kwik Cricket into primary schools, club colts sections and community groups. There is a significant sponsorship of £550,000 from the Milk Marketing Board. The launch was planned, in advance of the happenings in Pakistan, so that it would coincide with the England team's departure, partly to obtain maximum publicity, partly to show the Cricket Council's concern that cricket should be available to all. In the event, it was perhaps an unfortunate coincidence.

For Gatting, after the flush of success in Australia, 1987 was not the happiest of years. One would like to add the rider that as a batsman, his cricket was exemplary, for he stood alone as England's foremost batsman. Yet his dismissal resulting from a reverse sweep in the final of the World Cup is still fixed in the memory. At Edgbaston, there was an incident when the umpires stood in the middle, waiting to restart the Test match there after an interruption for bad light, only for the England team to remain closeted in their dressing-room, oblivious of the umpires' reappearance. Of the four Test series played fully under his captaincy to the end of 1987, three had been lost. And it might even be argued that, had he not been so concerned with standing up for his "rights" at Faisalabad, that series might have been drawn and not lost. England, by dint of some good cricket, had fought their way into a favourable position. At times, it was almost as if the prince had placed the crown on Falstaff's head and walked away.

A need for firm leadership

Never has cricket been more in need of firm leadership. The events in Pakistan showed that the management, in which I include the captain, instead of retaining a position from which they could provide leadership, allowed themselves to be drawn into the coterie of the players to the extent that sympathy for them was allowed to outweigh the most important issues.

Leadership is not simply issuing commands. As in business, it is a matter of understanding employees, conditions, resources and competition. History is something to be drawn upon; not put behind and forgotten. One wonders if in the offices of the TCCB there is a desk with a drawer filled with past managers' and captains' reports which have never been read again. This past tour was not the first to Pakistan by a cricket team, and nor will it be the last. Gatting had toured there twice before with England teams. He knew what the conditions were like and, as captain, should have helped his side rise above them. He could not; nor, it appears, could the Tour Manager or the Cricket Manager. Even the Chairman of the Cricket Council and TCCB, Raman Subba Row, was so moved by the players' pity for themselves that, without the sanction of the Board, he gave the players a bonus of £1,000 each. My first thought was to wonder how a soldier serving in Northern Ireland felt about that.

Gatting's outburst, of course, drew public support from those who suppose that Britain should stand up to the indignities perpetrated upon it by other countries, especially those of the third world. They ignore that what gives a nation its civilisation is its ability to accept these provocations without feeling a need to retaliate. It is an ability to judge when an issue is so morally wrong that action must be taken which makes a country great. A spat with an umpire in a cricket match is not one of those occasions.

The question of umpiring

It seems that, if nothing else, one outcome of the trouble in Pakistan will be a change in the way Test matches, and one-day internationals, are umpired. Of late, Pakistan and their captain, Imran Khan, have called for neutral umpires. In these Notes last year, an international panel was suggested. England would prefer the latter, given the experience of their first-class umpires, whose great advantage is that most have been first-class cricketers themselves. This is rarely the case in other countries. With one or two exceptions, they allow the game to move along, rather than trying to make their presence felt. If, however, the ICC decides in favour of neutral umpires, so that England no longer play international matches with English umpires officiating, English players will have no-one to blame but their countrymen. That was another initiative surrendered at Faisalabad.

Whichever alternative is employed, it will be expensive, and it will be cricketers who suffer. Assuming that Test cricketers will not contribute to the cost of independent umpires by a reduction in their match fees, the money will have to come from funds which would otherwise have been dispersed throughout the game. The same, incidentally, applies to Mr Subba Row's bonus of £15,000 to the England players.

Given that three, perhaps four, umpires would have to be allocated to each series, the opportunity to use one as a "third umpire" would present itself. He – or she, now that New Zealand has a female first-class umpire – would have reference to television playback facilities to give an opinion on appeals for certain dismissals. But which ones? Several times last year, it became apparent from television replays that Broad was unfortunate to be dismissed for "catches" at the wicket. Looking at his technique when playing fast bowlers, I can sympathise with the umpire standing 22 yards in front of him. It was often the replay from *behind* the wicket that made it apparent he had not touched the ball. Bat-pad catches, too, can assume a different aspect on a second or third viewing. I appreciate the arguments in favour of an umpire with a monitor, but I would be a most reluctant supporter. The flow of a match would be greatly interrupted, and it would be only a matter of time before batsmen and bowlers considered it an injustice unless every appeal was referred for appraisal. In all sporting games there have been and there always will be injustices. Life is full of them, and one of the virtues of sport is that it can set an example to society in how to accept setbacks with some dignity. Umpires, on the other hand, should remember that, while being both judge and jury, they are not above the Laws.

The World Cup

Although there was concern in some countries that the tournament would not eventuate, India and Pakistan staged cricket's fourth World Cup in a manner beyond expectation. In both countries, it caught the imagination of the population and there were large turn-outs for the matches, sometimes regardless of the countries playing. While India and Pakistan are to be congratulated on their successful organising of the World Cup, so too are Australia and England for reaching the final ahead of West Indies, the initial favourites, and the host countries. Australia's victory, on the eve of the country's bicentenary, was both deserved and welcome; it was not in the game's interest for one of its oldest participants to linger too long in the doldrums.

England's achievement confirmed the impression made since the start of the year that they are a strong competitor in limited-overs cricket. Their professionalism stood them in good stead in a form of cricket in which method is often preferable to basic technique. A sound technique, however, comes into its own in Test cricket, in which more than once England were found wanting. Able to ply their daily trade on pitches that do not punish a poor technique often enough, England's batsmen flounder on a pitch that does anything other than the ordinary. The bowlers, whose prime aim in the county game quickly becomes containment, struggle to take wickets on a good pitch and no longer have the same skills to exploit a poor one.

If Test cricket is to remain the indicator, England in the last five years have not been in good shape. Since the end of the 1982 season, they have played thirteen series and lost nine of them; of the 56 Test matches played, they have won eleven and lost 23. During that time they have had three captains, but the chairman of selectors has remained unchanged. His concern for the standards by which the game should be played is admirable and essential, but a policy, if there is a policy, which produces defeat more often than victory, is a matter of concern also.

Too much cricket . . .

One of the problems facing the selectors is that there is so little respite in the international calendar. They find themselves bound to a small group of regular players, and as the selection of the teams for England's two winter tours would suggest, the policy is towards a squad system. This can have tactical and psychological weaknesses. Taking into account the conditions which prevailed at Headingley in the past few years, it might, for example, have been advisable to play one or two Yorkshiremen in the Test matches there. But such "one-off" selections would not find favour under a squad system.

. . . of the wrong variety

The escalation of international cricket in the last ten years has been immense; but if the professional players are to be better paid, they have to perform for their rewards. The spectre of another Packer-style circus and rebel tours to South Africa still haunts the game's administrators. To alleviate what has correctly been described as a treadmill, one answer would be a reduction in the number of one-day internationals – but that is unlikely. Across the world the public prefers them to Test matches; and as economists tell us, the consumer dictates the market. Most children will eat hamburgers and chips in preference to a healthy well-balanced meal when given a choice.

Early in 1987, the Sri Lankan opening batsman, Sidath Wettimuny, who in his country's first Test in England, at Lord's in 1984, scored 190, announced his retirement from cricket at the age of 30. Not considered for the one-day internationals, he felt that with the number now being played by touring sides he was not getting sufficient match practice for Test cricket. He had, he said, stopped enjoying the game. Towards the end of the year, India dropped one of the Test matches scheduled against West Indies in favour of two extra one-day matches. If, as has been seen in India and Pakistan, attendances at Test matches fall away, will sponsorship be found to keep them going? England, having given birth to the one-day competition, could find itself the last bastion of the Test match. Let us hope that there are still cricketers able to play in them.

A struggle for the schools

While cricket continues to be popular among the young, the future of the game in Britain's schools has come under threat in the 1980s. For reasons either economic or political, sometimes both, cricket is no longer part of the sporting curriculum in many state schools. Fortunately, this gap has been filled by local clubs, often under the aegis of the county clubs, and coaching is available on a regional basis through the National Cricket Association. From 1988, however, the new GCSE examinations and the earlier sitting of A levels will result in a shortening of the summer term. I have seen one estimate that fewer than two months will be available for schools cricket. The changes being made to the education calendar could also have an effect on the MCC Schools Festival at Oxford, a most successful venture which for four days brings together four teams of the top schoolboy cricketers from the state and independent schools. As things will stand from this year, some schools will have broken up almost two weeks before the Festival is held in July. Already many of the independent schools are ensuring a full season by holding festivals in the first week of the holidays, and the cricket masters, who are therefore losing a week of their own holidays, deserve thanks for their efforts to keep the game healthy in these schools. So too do those many club cricketers who give their time to coach and transport young cricketers.

In the 1961 *Wisden*, H. S. Altham wrote, "However important may be the stimulus provided by the publicity and panache of 'big cricket' what matters, surely, is the healthy survival of the game as a whole as something integral to and reflecting the English way of life, a recreation in the truest and widest sense of the word for body, mind and spirit. That health is, I believe, to be assessed not so much in the attendance at a Test match, still less in the destiny of a rubber, but in the number of cricketers who will go on playing the game because they love it, on club grounds, on village greens, in the public parks, wherever, in fact, there is room to bowl and to hit a ball." That is a heritage which must be preserved.

A question of status

Two matches appear in this edition which have been designated first-class by the Pakistan Board of Control for Cricket: Zimbabwe B v Pakistan B, and Kenya v Pakistan B. There is no disputing Pakistan's right to decide the status of their matches in an Associate Member country. At a glance, in fact, Kenya's scores against a team containing seven Test players suggest they would give Oxford and Cambridge Universities a game. Nevertheless, tours are frequently being made by teams from Full or Foundation Members of the ICC to countries which are Associate Members. The ICC, in its classification of first-class matches, notes that "Governing bodies agree that the interest of first-class cricket will be served by ensuring first-class status is not accorded to any match in which one or other of the teams taking part cannot on a strict interpretation of the definition be adjudged first-class." The definition, *inter alia*, refers to a match "between two sides of eleven players officially judged first-class". When a team contains players without any first-class experience, I doubt that such a match complies with the definition.

I suspect it was for this reason that the New Zealand Cricket Council felt it was unable to confer first-class status on five matches played between its first-class provinces and the visiting Fiji side of 1947-48. No member of that side, as far as I am aware, had previously played in a first-class match, although it was strong enough to beat two first-class provinces and lost narrowly to two others. Last year, the ICC overturned the decision of the New Zealand Council and awarded first-class status to the five matches. Such retrospective action, especially taken after so many years, sets an unfortunate precedent. On the other hand, one cannot help but enjoy the pleasure felt by the team's captain, P. A. Snow, at entering the first-class lists at the age of 72.

To resolve the irresoluble

In 1988, more vexed matters than first-class status will concern the ICC. Umpires, short-pitched bowling and, perhaps, the preparation of pitches for Test matches may well be on the agenda. In addition, England will be re-shuffling some of their proposed future tours following the TCCB's decision to avoid "back-to-back" tours; not always easy when twin tours are being planned. But the issue with the farthest-reaching consequences is that of players having sporting contact with South Africa. Since last June, a working party has been considering a resolution that such players should cease to be eligible for international cricket; the full text may be found in "Meetings in 1987". It has been hinted that, rather than a blanket ban on these cricketers, members should respect the conditions of entry operated by a host country. Thus, if the government of country A is not prepared to accept players who have had sporting contact with South Africa, the cricketing authority of country B will not select them.

There is an irony here. In 1928, 1949 and 1960, Maori rugby players were not included in the All Black teams which toured South Africa. An argument given for the non-selection of Maori players was that, as guests, New Zealand should honour the conventions of their hosts.

In effect, England's cricketers will be most affected by any restriction on contact with South Africa, for it is one of the few countries where they can pursue their trade during the winter. Under English law, they have every right to go there. As recorded in the 1983 *Wisden*, the Prime Minister, speaking to the House of Commons, reaffirmed this right. The TCCB would be advised to seek the best counsel available if it is to be privy to any restriction of an Englishman's freedom. In his recently published book, *Sport and the Law*, Edward Grayson refers to the 1972 judgement in *Cooke v The Football Association*, in which the judge ruled FIFA's regulations to be in restraint of trade and told the Football Association to withdraw from the world governing body if FIFA would not alter its rules "to accord with the principles of English law" relating to restraint of trade.

The movement of cricketers

Already the TCCB has had to tread warily in respect of the legal rights of cricketers when trying to prevent an unofficial transfer market developing in cricket. It has done so by introducing Extraordinary Registration for any cricketer whose wish to move to another county is contested by his current county. The number of Extraordinary Registrations a county may have is restricted to one in any year and no more than two in five years. At the heart of the matter is the intention of preventing counties from "buying" a successful team at the expense of the other counties. The loyalty of players towards the county which nurtured them was much discussed, but it is common practice for an employee to move on to a new employer once he has gained training and experience. In reality, the answer lies with the counties themselves rather than with the players. If they honour the principle to which they subscribe as constituents of the TCCB, there is not a problem. Instead, during the last season, one still heard of approaches being made to contracted players.

Overseas players still dominate

One of the reasons why counties are now seeking players from other counties to improve their playing strength is the restriction on overseas players to one per match. Two are permitted if they were contracted before the 1979 season, but the passing years have reduced this category. In the coming season Nottinghamshire, the county champions and holders of the NatWest Bank Trophy, will be without Clive Rice and Richard Hadlee. Both made a major contribution to that county's success in the 1980s, and while the employment of overseas players ahead of English cricketers has its critics, those who watch and enjoy cricket cannot be anything but grateful that they have had the opportunity to watch Hadlee practise his craft throughout an English season. In eight full summers of county cricket, including 1986 when he played for New Zealand in the Test matches only, he was top of the first-class bowling averages five times and in second place twice. In 1984 he became the first player to do the double since the reduction in the number of Championship matches in 1969, and last season he was just three wickets from repeating the feat. His innings at Lord's to win last year's NatWest Bank Trophy final, when the match seemed lost, will rank high in the folklore of the great players of Trent Bridge. And as I write these Notes, he has equalled Ian Botham's record number of wickets in Test cricket.

An overseas player, Graeme Hick, was the season's leading run-scorer, while another, Martin Crowe, headed the batting averages. English batsmen were not overshadowed, more than twenty scoring 1,000 runs and averaging 40 or more in a wet summer, but only nine English bowlers took more than 50 wickets at an average of less than 25. Hemmings and Simmons were the only spinners to do so.

A wet summer but no "sticky dogs"

For a season, English cricket experimented with uncovered pitches during the hours of play in the hope that it would encourage spinners and make batsmen improve their techniques in difficult conditions. Neither hope was fulfilled, in part because, by allowing bowlers' run-ups to be covered, the seam bowlers were able to bowl in conditions made helpful by the rain. Secondly, the sun shone too infrequently to produce the kind of surface which might have been exploited by a spin bowler. In June and July, there were 7.05 inches of rain in England and Wales, compared with 6.57 inches in 1985, another poor summer. The figures for May and August, however, were not so bad: 4.72 inches last year compared with 7.16 in 1985. Given the way squares have been laid in modern times, I am not sure if such conditions would have eventuated anyway. Well grassed in beds of loam, today's pitches look capable of withstanding anything the elements could contrive. Not that it is relevant any more; at the Winter Meeting of the TCCB, the covering lobby won the day.

A new look to the season

This season sees the introduction of some four-day matches in the Britannic Assurance County Championship and a new limited-overs competition, the Refuge Assurance Cup. A knockout competition involving the top four teams in the Sunday League, the Cup will be contested at the end of the season. In order to accommodate it, the Sunday League commences a week earlier and finishes two Sundays earlier than it has in recent years. In one round of Championship matches, I notice, the fourth and final day falls on August Bank Holiday Monday. Perhaps it is not surprising that the reaction of counties, trying to sell sponsorship and hospitality facilities, has not always been favourably disposed towards the new-look fixture list. Although a majority of the counties seem to have made a profit last year, for some it was a struggle and at least five declared a loss. Other sports and other interests, such as education, hospitals and the arts, are in the business of raising funds, and if professional cricket is to maintain the lifestyle to which it has become accustomed in the past decade, it must project an image which appeals to the sponsor as well as the spectator. No matter how hard people work behind the scenes, ultimately the future rests with the players; and especially with those who captain them.

FIVE CRICKETERS OF THE YEAR

JONATHAN AGNEW

The Lancashire and former England opening batsman, David Lloyd, was halfway through a forward defensive push when his off stump was despatched halfway towards the Leicestershire wicket-keeper. It was August 1978, and with his fourth delivery in county cricket, a gangling eighteen year old just out of Uppingham School had discovered that he had enough pace to bother Test players as well as sixth formers. By the close of the season, that same bowler, Jonathan Agnew, had won a Whitbread Scholarship to Australia, and when invited to an England net in Melbourne, he struck the captain, Mike Brearley, a nasty blow in the face. It was, Agnew recalls, merely a gentle delivery off two paces that flew off a wet patch; but it did not deter the headline writers. Such early publicity did him no favours, but when a bowler arrives who is young, fast and English, a quiet settling-in period to one of the more difficult apprenticeships in sport is often denied him.

It was, therefore, only after some seasons of high promise but relatively modest delivery that JONATHAN PHILIP AGNEW realised his early potential and developed into a Test-match bowler. Born in Macclesfield on April 4, 1960, he was capped three times in 1984 and 1985, but it was not until last summer that he fully matured as a bowler. He took 101 wickets, the first Leicestershire player to take 100 since Jack Birkenshaw nineteen years earlier, and in doing so he helped his side recover from a disastrous start to third place in the County Championship. For reasons best known to themselves, the England selectors did not consider this good enough to earn Agnew a place on any of the three separate winter tours – to the World Cup, Pakistan or New Zealand.

Asked about Agnew's omission, the chairman of selectors, P. B. H. May, expressed concern about his fitness – rather a baffling statement to make about someone who bowled more overs than any other fast bowler in the Championship. There had been a time when the air at Grace Road would reverberate not just to the sound of leather upon willow, but also to the twanging of an Agnew hamstring; but the days had long since gone when the names of Agnew and another injury-prone Test player, Les Taylor, together on the same scorecard would startle collectors of memorabilia. ("Swap you an Agnew and a Taylor for a Ward and Shuttleworth?")

After four or five seasons of injury problems, probably the result of trying to bowl too fast, Agnew had by and large remained fit since 1983. But the injury-prone image had unfortunately stuck. He has never, for example, had back problems, although one annual cricket publication last year described that as the reason for long absences in his second season. He has had the occasional pulled muscle, which is a difficult achievement for someone with scarcely a muscle about his person. At almost 6ft 4in, he barely tips the scales at twelve stone, and this despite a gargantuan appetite which involves anything between three and six cooked meals a day. His pace comes from a whippy wrist action and co-ordination.

In the field, Agnew has at times appeared to be moving with his bootlaces tied together, but his long run-up was one of the more graceful in the game. However, it was the shortening of that run-up, and a cutting-down of pace, which led to last season's achievements – and, following James Whitaker, to his becoming the second Old Uppinghamian in consecutive years to be named one of *Wisden's* Cricketers of the Year.

Agnew had more often than not been given choice of ends with the new ball at Grace Road. This was invariably down the slope towards the pavilion, and with the prevailing wind. However, that became less automatic with the signing of the West Indian fast bowler, Winston Benjamin, and the advance of Phillip DeFreitas. An early-season game against Somerset saw Agnew running up the hill and into a gale. He cut down his run, strove for accuracy rather than pace, and took wickets. He has always been able to swing the ball, but he was often wayward off a full run. Now, by adhering to a fuller length, he became more dangerous, knowing that batsmen would remain reluctant to get forward with a full commitment because of his past reputation. And just to remind them of it, he could still produce the quick short delivery to force a sharp reappraisal of footwork. He also developed, and took many wickets with, an extremely effective slower ball.

Like DeFreitas at Middlesex, Agnew slipped through the coaching net at another county. He attended Alf Gover's school at Surrey at the age of sixteen, and played for two seasons during the summer holidays for Surrey's Second XI. Not a lot of interest was shown, he recalled, and it was probably only a coincidence that the coach at The Oval, Fred Titmus, was dismissed soon after Agnew's dramatic start with Leicestershire. He had been recommended to them by the senior coach at Uppingham, Les Berry, himself a former Leicestershire player, and secretary-manager Mike Turner arranged four times to see Agnew play. Because it rained or he did not bowl, he never did; so he signed him anyway on Berry's reputation as a judge of young cricketers.

Agnew was close to giving up the game in 1986, when he discovered that he was not enjoying it as he felt he ought to. He was also considering a career outside the game, preferably in the media, and that winter he joined the sports staff at BBC Radio Leicester, becoming in time a Sports Producer. He approached 1987 as his farewell season, but with the return of success and enjoyment, he has set his mind on attempting to regain an England place.

It will not, in all probability, be as an all-rounder, although he can certainly bat. After a bad injury, sustained in South Africa some years ago, fast bowlers have sometimes needed radar to locate him; but on his day he can destroy anything pitched up around off stump. He did so last season during his career-best 90 at Scarborough, while at the same time demonstrating that the Agnew of old, playing hard but always with a sense of fun, had resurfaced. When Leicestershire's captain, Peter Willey, came in to join his night-watchman, who was by then in the eighties, Agnew waited for him to take guard before walking down for a tactical discussion. "Now then, Will," he said, "just look for the ones and give me the strike. I'm in a bit of nick out here, you know." – Martin Johnson.

NEIL FOSTER

Although a good enough bowler to make his county début as an eighteen year old, still at school, and then picked for a full overseas England tour three years later, Neil Foster nevertheless took seven years to graduate from being considered a player with Test potential to holding down a regular place in the

England side in 1987. In the intervening years there was a brief flirtation with a career in soccer, a serious spinal injury, and sparse Test appearances which gave him too little time to establish himself.

In an age when state-controlled comprehensive schools were devoting more and more time to soccer, and less attention to cricket, NEIL ALAN FOSTER, born at Colchester on May 6, 1962, needed a keen cricketing father to maintain his interest in the summer game. At Philip Morant School in Colchester, Foster in his early teens was a tall, fast centre-forward, later turned central defender, who attracted the interest of the local Football League side. School cricket was, in the main, limited to twenty-over games after lessons, and Foster's development owed more to contacts at the nearby grammar school, who pushed him forward to the Essex Schools Under-14 side, and to his family.

Raised in the Essex village of Wivenhoe, Foster from a tender age was performing twelfth-man duties for the local club, where his father, Alan, was considered the "Geoff Boycott" of the side. Foster says, "He was a keen, if somewhat deliberate opening batsman, gentle in-swing bowler and immensely proud of his achievements at club level." Later they switched to another Essex side, Mistley, where Foster from the age of fourteen began to develop the high upright action that was to become the hallmark of his bowling in the years that followed. Impressive performances for Essex at the 1979 county youth festival at Cambridge, and a handful of Second XI games during the summer holidays, led to his being offered a two-year contract by Essex the following spring, and within weeks he made his first-class début.

It was on the night of his eighteenth birthday that Foster was summoned to Ilford to join an injury-hit side to play Kent the following day. With insufficient Second XI games under his belt to qualify for a cap or a sweater, he had to borrow equipment, and his career began inauspiciously when his first delivery produced four wides. "I'd only been used to the soft grounds of club cricket up until then, and on the harder Ilford surface I lost my footing in the delivery stride", he recalled. Fortunately his confidence did not suffer and he quickly claimed two impressive scalps. England Test batsmen Bob Woolmer and Chris Tavaré – the latter fresh from scoring 84 and 115 against Essex in the MCC match at Lord's – both fell to catches behind the wicket. In a later spell he also accounted for century-maker Alan Ealham, but even though he finished the innings with three for 51, it was to be his only Championship match until the start of the 1982 season.

Leaving school with six "O" levels and one "A", he was offered a two-week soccer trial the following winter with Ipswich, then managed by Bobby Robson, who was later to take charge of the England side. Eventually the trial lasted nearer three months while Robson tried to make up his mind whether Foster would make the grade as a professional footballer. With no decision forthcoming before Essex returned for pre-season training, he left Portman Road and played very little soccer thereafter. As a diversion from cricket, he later turned to golf with his wife, Romany, and at the end of last season was playing off a handy 16.

His only outing for Essex in 1981 was against the Sri Lankan tourists, but he made a big enough impression while playing for Young England against Young India to be awarded a Whitbread Scholarship, which sent him that winter to the Tasmanian club side, Glenorchy. There he began to suffer the occasional bout of back stiffness, which deteriorated on his return home. Specialists diagnosed stress fractures in two vertebrae near the base of his spine, and for three months he was forced to wear a corset of plaster as doctors hoped the injury would heal by itself. By September 1982, however, there was no improvement, and surgeons opted to insert two six-inch metal plates, secured by four screws, in his back.

Three months later, one of those screws had to be removed after it worked loose, but after supervised rehabilitation at a clinic in Clacton, he was passed fit to start the 1983 season with Essex. In August he was picked for his Test début against New Zealand at Lord's. By his own admission Foster did not bowl well in the match, claiming only the wicket of Jeremy Coney while conceding 75 runs in two innings. But there were extenuating circumstances. Shortly before the game, X-rays showed that another screw had loosened, and with a blood blister evident he was forced to have fluid drained from his spine twice a day during the Test. The match ended inside four days, and by the following Friday Foster was back in hospital having the plates and two abscesses removed. Fortunately it was to be almost six months before England began their winter tour to New Zealand and Pakistan, so giving Foster time to rebuild the strength in his back, despite the lack of a support.

For the next three years Foster was to be the yo-yo man of English cricket, popping up at home for the Lord's Tests of 1984 and 1985, but at least having the satisfaction of making each winter tour and producing match-winning figures of eleven for 163 against India at Madras on a pitch that had broken the hearts of many other pacemen.

Although with his late movement away from the bat Foster picked up 105 wickets for Essex in 1986, and was picked for England's tour of Australia, he failed to play in a Test and decided to reappraise his attitude towards playing for England. "I decided at the start of the 1987 series against Pakistan that if I got into the England team, I would simply try to produce my county form. In my early Tests I always felt on trial, and as a result tended to try to bowl defensively. Whereas with Essex I had always been regarded as an attacking bowler."

Bristling with an aggression which belies the soft burr of his East Anglian accent, Foster finally broke through at Leeds, where he took eight for 107 in 46.2 overs and emerged with credit from a match which England lost by an innings. Retained throughout the series, he finished the summer as England's leading wicket-taker with fifteen victims at an average of 22.60.

Although Essex's fortunes had fallen into sharp decline, Foster still took 86 first-class wickets in 1987, and with Ian Botham unavailable and Graham Dilley unfit, Foster, a mere onlooker in Australia less than twelve months earlier, departed with England for the World Cup in India and Pakistan as the side's leading strike bowler. His place in the side was strengthened by several useful late-order innings, in which he hit hard with a straight bat, and a growing reputation as an athletic outfielder with a strong, low return. – Graham Otway.

DAVID HUGHES

In the middle of the 1986 season David Hughes was considering retiring from first-class county cricket. He was 39, in the second team, and for two years he had felt he was no longer in Lancashire's first-team plans. He held back his letter of resignation as he led the second team to their championship, and within weeks he had been appointed captain of the county, one of the more surprising appointments in the club's 123-year history. It so shocked one former captain that he threatened to return his cap, blazer and sweaters. He described the decision as the worst he had ever known the club make.

It was a bold appointment. There had been no significant change in the team in 1986 under Clive Lloyd, the most successful Test captain of modern times, and Lancashire looked doomed to another season of desperation, another summer among the bottom teams in the County Championship. "I know I can't be around a long time", said Hughes at the time. "I can't go down in history as a great Lancashire captain. All I want is to see Lancashire moving up again, to restore the pride in the county. Too many people consider us a laughing stock."

As well as making Hughes captain, the committee appointed the second-team coach, Alan Ormrod, as coach/manager. Hughes and Ormrod's approach was positive and clear. Hughes made a point of speaking to each player before the season started and told them what was required. In essence, everybody was to give 100 per cent for Lancashire, and ill discipline would not be tolerated. Before the season started he promised, as many captains do, to play positive, attacking, entertaining cricket, always to be prepared to lose in order to force a win. Unlike most pre-season promises, his he managed to stick to from start to finish, and he led Lancashire in their attempt to become outright champions for the first time in 53 years, a challenge which failed by only four points.

Hughes's contribution as a batsman was disappointing, as a bowler non-existent, but as a captain inspirational and commanding. When he learnt he had been chosen as one of *Wisden's* Cricketers of the Year, he was staggered. "Perhaps I have underestimated my own contributions", he said.

DAVID PAUL HUGHES was born in Newton-le-Willows in South Lancashire on May 13, 1947, son of Lloyd Hughes, who had been a professional cricketer in the Bolton League. He was educated at Newton-le-Willows Grammar School, played for the town team in the Manchester Association and later joined Farnworth in the Bolton League. His introduction to the county was through the Club and Ground team in 1965 when he was eighteen, and two years later, when he was leading wicket-taker in the second team, he made his first-class début, against Oxford University at Old Trafford. Jack Bond started his successful five-year run as captain in 1968 – he was only 35 – and gave Hughes the opportunity to establish himself in the side. He took the chance and played in 23 of the 30 first-class matches, a promising left-arm spinner who took 31 wickets at 22.80 each but whose batting average of 14.48 hardly justified a position often as high as No. 7 in the order. The veteran off-spinner, John Savage, was his spinning partner that year. In 1969, the start of Lancashire's really successful period, it was Jack Simmons. The two of them quickly struck up a partnership which was to help take Lancashire to two John Player League championships and three Gillette Cup wins, all between 1969 and 1972.

Hughes's best years as a bowler were under Bond's care, his peak coming in 1970 and 1971 when he bowled more than 800 overs and took 82 first-class wickets each season. He took 296 wickets in the five years Bond was captain. Since then, under four other captains, he has only once exceeded 50 wickets in a season in first-class matches. He had taken 585 wickets for Lancashire by the end of the 1982 season, but in the next five claimed seven. As his bowling declined, so his batting blossomed, enabling him to reach 1,000 runs in a season for the first time in 1981. He followed this the next year with his best all-round season, averaging 48.25 with the bat and topping Lancashire's bowling averages with 31 wickets at 25.45 each. But he was unable to maintain that performance and gradually slipped into a more regular place in the second team than the first ... until his leadership qualities came through to persuade the committee to give him the daunting task of rejuvenating Lancashire.

Hughes once said he hoped he would not be for ever remembered only for his innings against Gloucestershire in the semi-final of the Gillette Cup in 1971, when he turned the match by hitting John Mortimore for 24 runs in one over. "I am mainly a bowler and that is how I would like to be remembered", he said. Perhaps, too, he will be recalled in years to come for his captaincy – Brian Bearshaw.

PETER ROEBUCK

For most of his 32 years, Peter Roebuck has nursed a burning ambition to be a highly successful member of a successful Somerset side. He played an important part in their emergence as a cricketing force when five limited-overs titles were won between 1979 and 1983, the first trophies in Somerset's long, diverting history. And he took a leading role in the rebuilding of the club after the divisive Richards-Garner-Botham controversy of 1986. His performance – as spokesman, batsman and captain – was vital to the 1987 improvement after that sad, vituperative episode.

His commitment stemmed from a fierce, competitive nature, based on a critical analysis of all the factors involved and the determination and talent to put his decisions to the test. His current vice-captain, Victor Marks, a friend of many years, said, "He seems to thrive on contest, competition and conflict. He rises to the occasion, is very much alive and always reacts in a positive way. He has improved dramatically over the past few years, with the security of his position and the captaincy. He puts a great deal more energy into his job than most people could." Somerset's coach, Peter Robinson, recalled many hours spent with the bowling machine, ironing out technical faults which he, Roebuck, had found.

Known for some time as a rather dour, studious, and bespectacled batsman, he revealed another side of his nature through his witty, pointed observations in his writings for a number of outlets. And in 1987, as he extended his range of strokes and even hit ten sixes, his batting has displayed a new dimension. "I now go in trying to take the initiative," he said, "instead of waiting for things to develop." The hundred he scored when his index finger was broken at Headingley in May was his fourth in all competitions in a thirteen-day period, and when he returned to the side after that injury, he took his tally of first-class hundreds to five. Only Hick, Athey, Crowe and Gatting hit more. He missed by a single run averaging 50 for the season.

Born in Oxford on March 6, 1956, PETER MICHAEL ROEBUCK, one of six children of schoolteachers, grew up initially in a third-floor flat in Bath. His father was a cricket enthusiast, his mother kept wicket for Oxford University ladies; one of his sisters later captained that team. Yet when it was apparent how badly bitten he was by the cricket bug – in the 1960s when professional cricket was at a very low ebb – it was felt he should be dissuaded from pursuing cricket as a living. Perhaps, it was thought, if he were hit and hurt by a cricket ball, he might share the view. Consequently, he was taken to

Peter Wight's indoor school at Bath, was hit, hurt and taken to hospital. "When I came back, I wanted to play just as much." That was the first hurdle overcome.

"I was completely wrapped up in Somerset cricket from about the age of ten, but one way of practising was soon stopped." Hitting a plastic ball against the wall of an adjoining flat, and giving a running commentary, was useful training. Unfortunately, the adjoining flat was used by a group holding séances ("trying to get in contact with Aunt Doris's poodle", suggested Roebuck), and having quite misinterpreted the tappings and the voice, they were very cross when the real source was discovered.

As his cricket came on in Bath junior circles, his parents decided to seek a scholarship at Millfield School, the nursery of many budding sportsmen. The first thing he saw when opening the study door of the founder, the highly individual R. J. O. Meyer, was an orange coming at him. He caught it. The intelligence test that followed he found totally incomprehensible, but the results were momentous for the family. Peter, his younger brother, and two of his sisters were given free scholarships, his parents were taken on the staff, and they were given a house in Street.

Quickly he appeared in the Somerset Second XI, "as a four foot two leg-spinner, with a good googly, who batted No. 11 with a sound technique but not enough strength to get runs against far bigger chaps". He was thirteen. In due course he went to Cambridge, worked hard for a degree (he ended with a First Class Honours in Law) and continued with the cricket he loved. He made 158 in the 1975 University Match, against Vic Marks, and both were in the Oxford and Cambridge side which beat Yorkshire in the Benson and Hedges Cup the next year.

However, 1976 brought another steep hurdle. The pace of the West Indian fast bowler, Andy Roberts, was outside Roebuck's experience at the time. Opening the innings for the Combined side at Fenner's, he ducked into a bouncer and, although feeling fairly well, was taken to hospital. A nurse, shown where he was hit, said, "Another quarter of an inch the other way and you'd have been a goner". Roebuck returned to the crease, and soon Roberts knocked his cap off. He went away, and in a dark room, playing a Joni Mitchell record, he realised that if he wanted to play first-class cricket, he had a lot to learn. He reckoned he had the talent, reflexes and ability to do it, so methodically he worked out what to do and how to do it. "Perhaps the most courageous thing I've done", he thinks. "You never know until you've been hit like that – the smell of leather, you know."

Life with Somerset was not always easy. So many remarkable characters surrounded him, making him even more withdrawn, but his first full season in 1978 was a success. Then came the triumphant Somerset period. He had never thought about captaining Somerset, but in 1983, when the World Cup required Botham, Marks, Richards and Garner, he found himself captaining a young side when Brian Rose was injured. The players reacted well, Roebuck enjoyed it, and subsequently he became involved in the broader issues of the club.

The rumblings of the 1986 row were present even then. "Too many people taking and not giving", and "Too many people putting their heads in too much sand for too long". He rationalised it, made his decision – "the most difficult and painful I've ever taken" – and helped to carry it through. Now Roebuck's ambitions are simple. "I want to see Somerset the best club in the land and winning the Championship. Oh, I'd also like to get in the top ten of Somerset run-scorers."

One of the best rewards of 1987, he said, was to note how great bowlers such as Marshall, Hadlee and Clarke seemed to bowl better at him than at others. "It can be uncomfortable, but I take it as a challenge – and as a compliment when I see how they look when they've got my wicket." – Eric Hill.

SALIM MALIK

In recent Test matches, Headingley has been a proving ground for the techniques of English and visiting batsmen. There the swinging and seaming ball sifts out the orthodox wheat. In 1986, when India defeated England at Headingley, the exposition of classical technique was given by Dilip Vengsarkar; last year, when Pakistan defeated England in the Test which settled the series, it was given by MUHAMMAD SALIM MALIK.

Brought up as they have been on pitches of unswerving rectitude, by no means all Pakistani batsmen have been models of orthodoxy. Zaheer Abbas gladly redirected the straight ball through cover-point, while Javed Miandad has been prone to whip it to leg with his dominant right hand. In the batting of Salim Malik, their heir-apparent as Pakistan's master batsman, there may be found a dedication to playing straight.

Salim gives thanks to his first coach for instilling in him this orthodoxy. Born in Lahore on April 16, 1963, the son of a Punjabi engaged in exporting linen-wear to Europe, he was taken when twelve by his elder brother to the Victorious Club in Iqbal Park. There he bowled leg-spin until the club coach, Rabb Nawaz, decided he could bat better than he could bowl. The coach then told him that the cut and the hook were the two riskiest strokes in cricket, and advised him to concentrate on hitting the ball in the "V" between mid-on and mid-off. It has been Salim's guiding principle ever since.

Developing at the precocious rate which seems almost to be the norm in that part of the cricket world, he was selected at sixteen for a Pakistan Under-19 tour of India and Sri Lanka. He made his first-class début for Lahore against Customs, and in his second match he scored a century against Muslim Commercial Bank. More significant, Salim thinks, was his performance for Pakistan Under-19s when they were hosts to the Australian Under-19s; with the matches being televised, he received wide exposure as Pakistan's leading run-scorer. As one for the future, he was taken on Pakistan's full tour to Australia in 1981-82. "I was very confused, there were so many senior players", he explains in improving English, his third language after Punjabi and Urdu. But on returning to Pakistan, those senior players revolted against the captaincy of Miandad and were dropped from the Test side. Salim was chosen as one of the replacements, made his Test début against Sri Lanka at Karachi, and hit a hundred, at 18 years and 328 days the youngest Pakistani to have done so on début.

Subsequently he did not score runs in a quantity befitting his technique or talent; yet Salim was still putting together a promising portfolio of Test centuries, with an average in the early forties, when a ball from Courtney Walsh reared from Faisalabad's re-laid pitch and hit him above the left wrist. It was the October 1986 Test match in which West Indies were dismissed for their lowest ever total of 53. Pakistan, having been 37 for five, were being rallied by Salim and Imran Khan when the fracture happened. In Pakistan's second innings, when runs were still vital, Salim batted left-handed at No. 11 for one ball and then right-handed in a stand of 32. He missed the rest of the series and, still bothered by stiffness in his left wrist, never got going in the following Test series in India.

However, on that tour of India, which preceded Pakistan's visit to England, he did play a one-day innings that was a wonder of its kind. In front of a capacity crowd in Calcutta, India were coasting to victory when Salim came in, for Pakistan had to score 78 in less than eight overs. He found it one of those magical days when the bowler pitched exactly where Salim wanted, and he proceeded to hit an unbeaten 72 from 35 balls, the best innings of its length in one-day internationals.

When he came to English pitches, he found he had to modify not his technique but his attitude. "I have a short temper but I learnt to be patient in England, to be more defensive and wait for the bad ball." He got out for 99 at Headingley in the last over of the day, he says, because he was nervous after not making a century for eighteen Tests. (He had hit five centuries in his first 21.) It eventually came two Tests later at The Oval, during a stand of 234 with Miandad.

A brilliant out-fielder with a pinpoint throw, Salim had to convert to first slip in England for want of anyone else. He did not like having to do the job with cold hands, but did well enough until the last morning of the series, when an edge from Gatting slipped out. As a slow in-swing bowler he has performed occasionally for Habib Bank, his present team, under the captaincy of Miandad, and he has not forgotten completely his leg-breaks.

An unmarried Muslim, Salim lives in Lahore and prays whenever cricket allows. During the World Cup, one of his prayers was answered by Imran, who let him bat at No. 3, the position he had wanted for a long time. But wherever he bats for Pakistan, Salim Malik has the class to score many runs for many years to come in model style. – Scyld Berry.

A COACH'S VIEWPOINT

By DON WILSON
(Head Coach, MCC)

To me, as a cricketer and a coach, the most enjoyable aspect of England's victories in Australia in 1986-87 was the way the players came together as a team under Micky Stewart. They practised properly, and when there was a function to attend, they were all there. The result of such team unity and team spirit was that it produced much success. It would be good, I thought, if that same attitude and commitment were to rub off on their fellow county players when the touring team returned home.

Last season, however, things started to go wrong again. It is easy to be critical, and often unrewarding. Instead, we need to understand why it is not always so easy for our modern first-class cricketers to achieve the success which the public, and the media, have come to expect, especially in Test matches. For a start, it is very difficult for the young players today. Immediately they come into the game, they are playing two or three different types of cricket – even the lads in the Second XIs.

As a coach, I want players to learn to bat all day. It is most important: one has only to look at the performances of Dilip Vengsarkar for India in 1986 and Salim Malik last year for Pakistan. By playing long innings, especially at Headingley where batting was far from easy, they won the matches for their countries. Batting from eleven in the morning until six o'clock has to be the hardest part of the game. It is a lot easier to slog or get on with it quickly. A coach's main contribution is to get into a batsman's head that if he bats all day, his side has a great chance of winning. One has only to think what happened when Bill Athey and Chris Broad played long innings in Australia.

It is always tempting to reach back into the past and consider the Huttons, the Comptons, the Mays and the Barringtons; to hold up as an example the way they used to play Test cricket. It seemed, in their day, that there was always one player, maybe two, who knew how to put together a big hundred. Or, if the wicket was doing something, stay there, not necessarily making runs, until the conditions improved for strokeplay. However, in cricketing terms, their level of concentration was higher; and it could afford to be. Peter May, for example, did not have to play one-day cricket. And, incidentally, imagine what we would have lost if he had. Those glorious drives we remember being despatched with precision to the boundary would have brought him only singles now that fields are set deep, with a "sweeper" deployed behind the inner fielders. Who stores singles in the memory, however beautifully the stroke is played?

Since May's day, the game has changed enormously. Geoff Boycott, who had the most amazing powers of concentration, could play one-day cricket well, but he did play it a little bit like a three-day game. His Test cricket was completely different. By being an opener, however, Boycott did have the advantage of being able to bat correctly in one-day cricket. This does not apply for a young man coming in at No. 4 or No. 5 with ten overs left. How on earth can he consider making a big score? And the answer is, we don't expect him to. But if he gets a quick 30, a big hand from the crowd and his name in the papers next morning, he thinks, "I've done marvellously. That's all I need; 30 or 40 and I'm magic."

I do think that the younger players today look at it that way. They get in, get their 30 or 40, and their concentration goes. I see it with the MCC Young Cricketers here at Lord's. There are some marvellous young batsmen, but when I look down the scoresheets, their ability is not always reflected in runs. When a batsman has 25 or 30, he should be on his way. He is seeing the ball, picking up the pace and the length of the bowlers; in other words, he's got his eye in; he's done all the graft. And yet here he is, throwing it away. I tell these lads, time and again, that once they get that far, they've cracked it. If you think about the great players, when they got to 25, they got 50, and when they got 50, they went on to a hundred.

The blame cannot be apportioned entirely to limited-overs cricket, although it is played a lot more in the schools these days. In my day, in Yorkshire, players knew little else but the leagues, and we didn't bat much more than 55 overs in an afternoon, even if it wasn't specifically limited-overs cricket. It seems to me, rather, that the attitude and temperament of people in general have changed. Many youngsters today would rather make big money doing something that requires little skill instead of taking up an apprenticeship. It's the same with travel. If we were going from Headingley to, say, Hove, we'd work out a nice, easy route, break the trip for a good meal at a pub along the A1, and not bother if we didn't get to our hotel until after midnight. Today, it seems to be A to B as fast as possible. Travel has come to mean movement. And I sometimes think that today's cricketer bats the way he drives. Life has become instant everything, and yet we are living in an age when there is supposed to be more leisure time.

Nor do the players talk about the game as much. If Yorkshire were playing Middlesex at Lord's in the 1950s, both teams would go together for a drink on the first night of the match. It was compulsory. And the talk would be cricket talk. As a youngster, I squeezed in between Denis Compton and Bill Edrich, and I probably did not open my mouth. I simply listened as Bill and Denis chatted about the game to Johnny Wardle, say, or Bob Appleyard. They were all nearing the end of their first-class careers, yet they were still intensely interested in techniques, and how other cricketers were playing the game. It was fascinating for us young players; it was part of our cricket education. Today, let's be quite honest about this, there are few people who want to listen.

One who does is Martin Crowe, but you've a different young man there. He has set out his stall to be the best batsman in the world. He's dedicated. I wonder sometimes what would have happened had David Gower been as dedicated as Martin Crowe, because David is a marvellous batsman, a great timer of the ball and wonderful to watch. On the other hand, it is possible, human nature being what it is, that he might have been only half the player he is.

Several times last year Martin, who was in tremendous form for Somerset, came to see me because he felt there were elements of his game that needed improvement. He felt I might see something that hadn't been seen down at Taunton. That is no reflection on the staff there. So often at counties the coach is with the youngsters; with the second team rather than the first. Therefore, the only time he sees the first-team players is in April – and then it is mostly gym work and fitness training. It's often too wet and cold for outdoor nets, and in addition the players, having in many instances spent the winter playing abroad, aren't always as keen as they used to be when April comes around.

April apart, the only time many of the coaches get a chance to see a first team player is if he's having a dreadful run and is given a week or so in the Seconds to sort himself out. However, I do think that there are times when the player has to go to the coach. A coach can't go on saying, "You should be doing this, you've got to do that"; not to a top player. He has to want help.

The situation in which Graham Gooch found himself last season provides a good example. He should never have been in the position he was, because one or two years ago some of the old players were getting worried about his stance and the way he was picking up the bat. Perhaps someone should have said to him then, "Come on, Graham, stop all this silliness. Play as you normally play." But it would have been difficult then, because he was getting a lot of runs. All of a sudden, when he was getting a run of noughts, the whole world started saying that something had gone wrong. It was too late then.

The players – some of them – say that they're happy with this stance with the bat held in mid-air. Personally, I don't like it. They also have these heavy bats which have virtually put spin bowlers out of the game, because a mis-hit now goes to the boundary whereas, with a lighter bat, it wouldn't have carried beyond the fielder threequarter-way back. What concerns me about the stance is that the batsman can easily pick the bat up incorrectly. It starts pointing towards slip, then towards second slip, and before the batsman knows it his feet are wrong. Once that happens, everything goes. I firmly believe – in all walks – that life revolves around a basic teaching. When golfers and tennis players have trouble with their game, they go back to basics with a coach. And I feel that this is what cricketers should do.

I am not advocating that everything must be straight from the text book. If anything, coaches have become a bit too text-bookish over the years. The most important thing about coaching is not to lose the natural ability of a player. The best players in the world have always had their own little idiosyncrasies, but they haven't ignored the basic tenets of the game.

What I see as a decline in technique does disturb me, and I'm equally disturbed because we are not doing enough as a game to halt it. I am a fortunate man, being based at Lord's, because I feel I'm at the centre of cricket. I see the players when they're here for Test matches and when they come for the county games. We have superb indoor and outdoor nets, plus modern aids such as video cameras so that players can actually see what they are doing. It has led me to think that perhaps cricket should have a place where first-class players can go to sort out their game – just as other sportsmen have. A change of environment. When you have a son or daughter growing up at home, you don't always notice how they're changing until, suddenly, it has happened. And I think cricketers have that problem at their counties. It needs someone not so close to home to look at their game with a critical eye. That's why I would like to see a cricketer, who was going through a bad patch, spend a few days at a "cricket farm", working with coaches who could help him through his problems.

I went through a bad spell myself when I came back from Australia in 1971; but we Yorkshire bowlers were lucky in those days in having Bill Bowes as our "travelling coach". Bill was writing for the Yorkshire evening papers and consequently was always with the team. After a day's play, we could go up to him in the bar or at the hotel and ask what we were doing wrong. Nearly always he'd be able to tell us. Bill also used to be there at pre-season training, along with Arthur Mitchell, the Yorkshire coach, and

Maurice Leyland, and I for one would always turn to him when I needed help. Today, I have a lot of respect for Ken Higgs as a coach for fast bowlers. He has a dry, hard sense of humour, which is a great asset for a fast bowler, and you have only to look at those on the staff at Leicestershire to see how good he is at his job. If I want help with slow bowlers, I'm always pleased when Fred Titmus is available.

But the whole concept of bowling has changed in recent years. The game today revolves around bowling twenty overs for, say, 40 or 50 runs. Once, not so long ago, if a bowler took four for 80 or 90 from fifteen overs, his team were in with a chance. Now, the aim is to stop the other side scoring runs. You have only to look at the fields that are set; at how quickly the fielders move into defensive positions, even in County Championship cricket. In schoolboy cricket I've seen a sweeper on the boundary. I think that's criminal, but television has shown them what the first-class players are doing, and they're the ones the young cricketers copy. Sadly, in English cricket we've lost the art of bowling sides out. The bowling is tighter than it has ever been, but the length bowled is also just that much shorter. That means bowlers no longer swing the ball, for if it isn't pitched up, it isn't going to swing.

I realise that one-day cricket is a big money-maker, but as things stand at the moment, without being a Test player, a young cricketer won't get to play in the big one-day internationals. So we come back to the five-day game, and the breeding ground for that in this country is the three-day game. I think as coaches we have to concentrate on this level and say that our aim is to produce good three-day county cricketers and Test cricketers. Then we might also have better cricket.

i

A SUMMER SCENE

[*David Munden*]
In 1987, England's weather again robbed spectators of hours of cricket. They bore their frustration stoically, their umbrellas providing a splash of colour under the grey skies.

ENGLAND'S VICTORIOUS TEAM IN AUSTRALIA

The England team which toured Australia in 1986-87, retained the Ashes and won the Benson and Hedges Challenge and World Series Cup. *Back row*: S. P. Austin (*scorer*), B. N. French, C. J. Richards, P. A. J. DeFreitas, G. R. Dilley, B. C. Broad, N. A. Foster, G. C. Small, J. J. Whitaker, W. N. Slack, C. W. J. Athey, L. G. Brown (*physiotherapist*). *Front row*: P. M. Lush (*manager*), P. H. Edmonds, D. I. Gower, M. W. Gatting (*captain*), J. E. Emburey, I. T. Botham, A. J. Lamb, M. J. Stewart (*assistant manager*).

[*TCCB*

AUSTRALIA WIN THE WORLD CUP

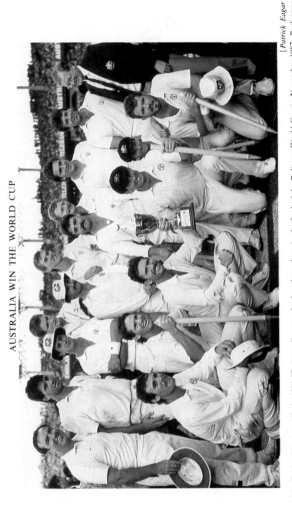

[*Patrick Eagar*

Outplayed by England in Australia in 1986-87, Australia came back to beat them in the final of the Reliance World Cup in November 1987. *Back row*: R. B. Simpson (*coach*), S. P. O'Donnell, T. B. A. May, T. M. Moody, G. C. Dyer, B. A. Reid, D. C. Boon, P. L. Taylor, A. K. Zesers, E. Alcott (*physiotherapist*), A. Crompton (*manager*). *Front row*: M. R. J. Veletta, D. M. Jones, A. R. Border (*captain*), G. R. Marsh, S. R. Waugh, C. J. McDermott.

THE NEW MOUND STAND AT LORD'S

[*Patrick Eagar*

Opened by HRH The Duke of Edinburgh on May 6, 1987, the new Mound Stand at Lord's quickly attracted much comment, especially on account of its "canopies". Not all of it was complimentary: "a pagoda in St John's Wood Road" and "an elongated spaceship" were just two descriptions. But on the big occasions at Lord's, when filled with spectators, it looked a splendid addition to the famous ground.

IMRAN ACHIEVES AN AMBITION

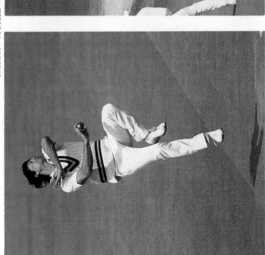

[*Patrick Eagar*

Imran Khan capped his Test match career by leading Pakistan to a 1-0 victory over England in the five-match series of 1987. His influence as captain was an essential ingredient of his young side's success. So too was his fast swing bowling. At Headingley, where David Gower ducks under an Imran bouncer, the 34-year-old Pakistan captain took ten wickets in the match, including seven for 40 in the second innings, to set up their victory.

THE MCC TEAM FOR THE MCC BICENTENARY MATCH

[*Patrick Eagar*

The MCC team which was selected for the Bicentenary match at Lord's against the Rest of the World. *Back row:* B. N. French, B. C. Broad, R. J. Shastri, P. H. Edmonds, J. E. Emburey, C. J. Richards. *Front row:* R. J. Hadlee, C. E. B. Rice, M. D. Marshall, M. W. Gatting (*captain*), M. J. Stewart (*manager*), D. I. Gower, G. A. Gooch, C. G. Greenidge.

THE REST OF THE WORLD TEAM FOR THE MCC BICENTENARY MATCH

[*Patrick Eagar*

The Rest of the World team which was selected for the Bicentenary match at Lord's against MCC. *Back row:* C. H. Lloyd (*manager*), Maninder Singh, J. R. Ratnayeke, R. A. Harper, C. A. Walsh, B. A. Reid, J. G. Bracewell, D. M. Jones, Imran Khan, Lt-Cdr P. J. W. Danks (*scorer*). *Front row:* P. J. L. Dujon, D. B. Vengsarkar, Abdul Qadir, S. M. Gavaskar, A. R. Border (*captain*), Kapil Dev, Javed Miandad, D. L. Haynes.

FIVE CRICKETERS OF THE YEAR

[*David Munden*

J. P. Agnew (Leicestershire)

FIVE CRICKETERS OF THE YEAR

[*Patrick Eagar*

N. A. Foster (England and Essex)

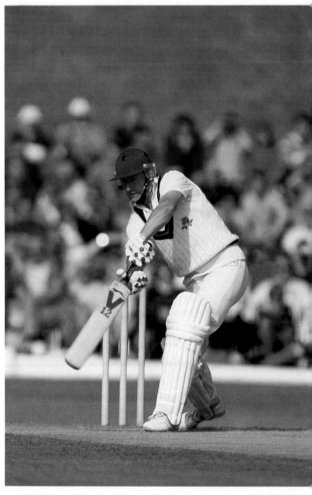

[*Bob Thomas*

D. P. Hughes (Lancashire)

FIVE CRICKETERS OF THE YEAR

[*David Munden*

P. M. Roebuck (Somerset)

[*Patrick Eagar*

Salim Malik (Pakistan)

THE MASTER CRAFTSMAN

A STUDY OF GEOFFREY BOYCOTT

By DEREK HODGSON

Geoffrey Boycott, an egocentric right-hand batsman of great defensive skills and an occasional in-swing bowler, will be remembered as much for his prodigious scoring record as for his impact, over 25 years, perhaps more, on the history of the Yorkshire county club. He has a facility for making enemies much faster than he made his runs, admits to very few friends, yet inspires a loyalty among his admirers that all politicians must envy.

As a cricketer, a batsman converted to opening in his early days with Yorkshire, he had no peers in England during his career. Abroad, only Sunil Gavaskar, the man who overtook Boycott's aggregate of Test match runs, could be compared in application, dedication, attention to detail, tactical acumen, patience and endurance. Even Boycott's critics would agree, too, that his runs were made often in far more difficult circumstances, in English conditions and on English pitches, than Gavaskar's. In batting on seaming or turning pitches, or when the ball cut or swung, Boycott for more than twenty years reigned supreme in the world.

This ability to score runs, albeit slowly, when all around him were grateful merely to survive, indicated that Boycott was far from limited in his strokeplay. All the shots were there, but only rarely was the full armoury uncovered; when he did settle upon an attacking innings, however, the ensuing firework display could be a brilliant memory. Three occasions come to mind, the first a brief burst at Bradford in 1977, when Yorkshire were chasing runs on the third afternoon against Northamptonshire and Boycott, astonishingly, was charging from his crease to lift the bowling straight. There was a humid Sunday afternoon at Worcester, where Boycott produced a dazzling 60 at a rate not even Milburn would have scorned.

But the outstanding recollection of Boycott in this mood must be of a World Series Cup match against Australia at Sydney during the 1979-80 tour under Mike Brearley. There had been speculation that Boycott might be dropped from the limited-overs side. Brearley, like every other captain, had his difficulties with Boycott, yet their relationship was only occasionally strained; and Brearley was able, as he was with most players, to inspire some remarkable performances. On December 11, Boycott walked out with Derek Randall and, against an attack featuring Lillee, Thomson and Walker, scored 105 off 124 balls, including seven fours. He reduced a rowdy Hill, primed to jeer him, to a respectful silence. Englishmen, by and large, are not disposed to embrace Geoffrey Boycott, but that was one time when he induced considerable emotion among the stiff upper lips.

The more customary Boycott, and the experience of batting with him, was summed up thus by a younger contemporary. "You were always conscious that you were on your own, in that he was one partner unlikely to surrender his wicket to save you and that you were his partner on his terms. That accepted, there was a lot to learn because his mind, computer-like, was always working.

[*Patrick Eagar*

Geoffrey Boycott – "A batting record that stretches, vast and almost unsurpassable, like a
distant view of the Himalayas."

"He would know who was to bowl and which end they would choose and why. He would anticipate bowling and fielding changes, calculating when and for what reason. He knew most bowlers backwards, most pitches, even the direction of the prevailing wind. You would always know when there was something he didn't like about one particular bowler when you found yourself with more of the strike than normal. Professionally he was a paragon, immaculate in his preparation and turn-out, and for all the jokes it was an education to stand at the other end and watch him play."

Bradman apart, it is hard to imagine a stronger-minded cricketer in the history of the game. He entered the Yorkshire dressing-room in 1962 and, with his short hair and rimless glasses, was regarded as a rather dull, painstaking young man from South Yorkshire who was unlikely to challenge the obvious rising stars, John Hampshire and Philip Sharpe among them. He was a mediocre fielder, and if anyone knew that he could bowl, his prowess remained a secret. Yet Boycott's will to succeed was so enormous that he swept into the Yorkshire and England teams with hardly a pause. He had achieved world class when political wranglings inside Yorkshire propelled him on to a larger stage.

By a process of mismanagement that would have brought courts-martial in another sphere, the Yorkshire committee allowed, from the sacking of Johnny Wardle in 1958 to the dismissal of Brian Close in 1970, almost a full Test match team to be dispersed. They preferred Boycott for the captaincy above two, possibly three, more experienced candidates; and then it was that the essential dichotomy in Boycott's character was fully revealed. How could a man so dedicated to personal accomplishment subordinate his own ambitions to the well-being of a team, and a young team at that, saddled with insecurities and the ever-present knowledge that they were forever being compared with their mighty predecessors? Other counties were opening their ranks to world-class players from overseas, making Yorkshire's task of competing doubly hard. Even the traditional reservoir of Yorkshire-born talent began to dry up as the leagues went over to limited-overs cricket. No Yorkshire captain, not Lord Hawke, nor Sellers nor Close, could have conjured up a Championship-winning team in those circumstances.

In a frustrating, difficult time, Boycott was the one link with a glorious past, the still unqualified success in an ever-gloomier world for the Yorkshire follower and member. Not surprisingly, he came to loom larger in the minds of the public, and of many Yorkshire members, than any officer of the club or any other player. Who were these little men who dared criticise the hero?

Boycott also found his international career in a cul-de-sac. What would have been a normal, acceptable and expected progress to the captaincy became complicated when he withdrew from consideration for selection in the mid-1970s mainly, it was alleged, because the England captaincy had not been offered when he expected it. When the crown became available, through Brearley's injury, in Pakistan and New Zealand in 1977-78, Boycott's leadership was not received well either by his hosts or his players.

His international career ended during the Calcutta Test of England's 1981-82 tour of India. He did not take the field on the final day of that match and returned home shortly afterwards on medical grounds. Memoirs published since, however, alleged that he was sent back as a disciplinary measure. He returned to domestic cricket, passing Yorkshire county records season by season until, in September 1986, the club brought his long career with them to an end by not offering a new contract. He remained, nevertheless, a member of the club's General Committee.

In 1987, Geoffrey Boycott published an autobiography, reviewers generally regarding it as a long, somewhat tedious attempt at self-justification. "A sad book" was an almost universal comment, a wry reflection on Boycott's own influence on the publication for his helper, Terry Brindle, is one of the most humorous of cricket writers. Nor is Boycott himself without humour, taking and giving the dressing-room horseplay with some relish. But he could also, in his time as Yorkshire's captain, make the dressing-room feared, almost hated, by young Yorkshire players.

So the paradox continues. Once asked to name his closest friend, he could not find one he was confident enough to nominate. Abominated by great Yorkshire contemporaries, he was found by many outside the game to be utterly charming.

Perhaps he was unfortunate to be born in an age when the public interest is served by a media intent upon prying and prising loose every single item, good but preferably bad. Had he lived in Victorian times he might have been regarded as one of the great eccentrics; "an intensely private man" is a phrase that might have been used. He would not have needed to appear continually before the cameras, the notebooks and the tape-recorders. Grace, MacLaren and Hawke never needed, nor were expected, to justify themselves. His resentment at the poking and probing into his manners, mores and style of life is understandable. A boy born into the South Yorkshire coalfield at any time in the last 50 years came into the world impressed with the need to retaliate first.

All over the world Boycott will be remembered for his batting: the ritual, almost fussy re-preparation before each ball, the tap of the bat, touch of the cap, reassurance that his pads were in place, and the relentless, straight-down-the-line forward push. Most of his runs came on the off side because that was where most bowlers bowled to him. The drive through cover, or extra, was minted silver. He was not less adept on the leg side, merely more circumspect, as if suspecting that the pull, hook or sweep all carried elements of risk. Such was his power and reputation at his peak that for him to be bowled was a major surprise. When an Oxford University bowler achieved that feat, the young man was a back-page sensation for a day.

Boycott's bowling was typical of the man, almost always of mean length and line with a huge in-swerve. He performed some notable little feats for Yorkshire on Sunday afternoons, but his captains knew they had to take him off the moment a batsman began to chance his arm. Boycott was deeply upset if he conceded many runs. He transformed himself from a poor fielder to an excellent boundary runner, with a strong, accurate arm, and from time to time he served his county well at slip. He might have been a great captain but for his notorious blind spots, for no-one disparages his knowledge and understanding of the game.

Yet when his career is fully assessed and settled into the record, early next century, will all his foibles and prejudices matter that much? A batting record that stretches, vast and almost unsurpassable, like a distant view of the Himalayas, must put much pettiness into perspective, leaving all the discord in his wake no more than the odd trickle down a great stone face.

G. BOYCOTT – FIRST-CLASS CAREER

	M	I	NO	R	HI	100s	50s	Avge
1962	5	9	2	150	47	0	0	21.42
1963	28	43	7	1,628	165*	3	11	45.22
1964	27	44	4	2,110	177	6	11	52.75
1964-65 (South Africa)	15	25	5	1,135	193*	4	6	56.75
1965	26	44	3	1,447	95	0	10	35.29
1965-66 (Australia/NZ)	13	21	2	784	156	1	7	41.26
1966	28	50	3	1,854	164	6	10	39.44
1967	24	40	4	1,910	246*	4	13	53.05
1967-68 (West Indies)	11	16	2	1,154	243	4	6	82.42
1968	20	30	7	1,487	180*	7	4	64.65
1969	23	39	6	1,283	128	3	6	38.87
1969-70 (Ceylon)	1	2	0	7	7	0	0	3.50
1970	25	42	5	2,051	260*	4	12	55.43
1970-71 (Australia)	12	22	6	1,535	173	6	7	95.93
1971	21	30	5	2,503	233	13	6	100.12
1971-72 (South Africa)	1	2	0	148	107	1	0	74.00
1972	13	22	5	1,230	204*	6	4	72.35
1973	18	30	6	1,527	141*	5	9	63.62
1973-74 (West Indies)	10	16	3	960	261*	3	4	73.84
1974	21	34	4	1,783	160*	6	8	59.43
1975	19	34	8	1,915	201*	6	8	73.65
1976	12	24	5	1,288	207*	5	2	67.78
1977	20	30	5	1,701	191	7	7	68.04
1977-78 (Pakistan/NZ)	13	20	3	867	123*	3	5	51.00
1978	16	25	1	1,233	131	6	3	51.37
1978-79 (Australia)	12	23	3	533	90*	0	4	26.65
1979	15	20	5	1,538	175*	6	7	102.53
1979-80 (Australia/India)	8	15	4	599	110	2	3	54.45
1980	17	28	4	1,264	154*	3	8	52.66
1980-81 (West Indies)	9	17	2	818	104*	1	7	54.53
1981	16	28	2	1,009	137	3	3	38.80
1981-82 (India)	8	14	5	701	105	2	6	77.88
(South Africa)	4	7	0	204	95	0	1	29.14
1982	21	37	6	1,913	159	6	10	61.70
1983	23	40	5	1,941	214*	7	4	55.45
1984	20	35	10	1,567	153*	4	9	62.68
1985	21	34	12	1,657	184	6	9	75.31
1986	13	20	1	992	135*	2	8	52.21
	609	1,014	162	48,426	261*	151	238	56.83

* *Signifies not out.*

Highest innings: 261*, MCC v West Indies Board of Control President's XI, at Bridgetown, 1973-74.

Bowling and Fielding: G. Boycott took 45 wickets during his career at a cost of 1,459 runs, average 32.42. His best bowling figures were 4-14, Yorkshire v Lancashire at Leeds, 1979. He held 264 catches.

G. BOYCOTT – TEST CAREER

	T	I	NO	R	HI	100s	50s	Avge
1964 v Australia	4	6	0	291	113	1	1	48.50
1964-65 v South Africa	5	8	2	298	117	1	2	49.66
1965 v New Zealand	2	4	1	157	76	0	1	52.33
v South Africa	2	4	0	75	31	0	0	18.75
1965-66 v Australia	5	9	2	300	84	0	3	42.85

	T	I	NO	R	HI	100s	50s	Avge
1965-66 v New Zealand	2	3	1	13	5	0	0	4.33
1966 v West Indies	4	7	0	186	71	0	2	26.57
1967 v India	2	3	1	277	246*	1	0	138.50
v Pakistan	1	2	1	16	15	0	0	16.00
1967-68 v India	5	8	1	463	116	1	4	66.14
1968 v Australia	3	5	0	162	49	0	0	32.40
1969 v West Indies	3	6	1	270	128	2	0	54.00
v New Zealand	3	5	0	101	47	0	0	20.20
1970-71 v Australia	5	10	3	657	142*	2	5	93.85
1971 v Pakistan	2	3	1	246	121*	2	0	123.00
v India	1	2	0	36	33	0	0	18.00
1972 v Australia	2	4	0	72	47	0	0	18.00
1973 v New Zealand	3	5	0	320	115	1	3	64.00
v West Indies	3	5	1	202	97	0	2	50.50
1973-74 v West Indies	5	9	0	421	112	1	3	46.77
1974 v India	1	2	0	16	10	0	0	8.00
1977 v Australia	3	5	2	442	191	2	1	147.33
1977-78 v Pakistan	3	5	1	329	100*	1	3	82.25
v New Zealand	3	5	0	166	77	0	2	33.20
1978 v New Zealand	2	3	0	159	131	1	0	53.00
1978-79 v Australia	6	12	0	263	77	0	1	21.91
1979 v India	4	5	0	378	155	2	0	75.60
1979-80 v Australia	3	6	1	176	99*	0	1	35.20
v India	1	2	1	65	43*	0	0	65.00
1980 v West Indies	5	10	1	368	86	0	3	40.88
1980 v Australia	1	2	1	190	128*	1	1	190.00
1980-81 v West Indies	4	8	1	295	104*	1	1	42.14
1981 v Australia	6	12	0	392	137	1	1	32.66
1981-82 v India	4	8	1	312	105	1	2	44.57
	108	193	23	8,114	246*	22	42	47.72

* *Signifies not out.*

Highest innings: 246* v India at Leeds, 1967.

Bowling and Fielding: G. Boycott bowled 148 overs (944 balls) in Test cricket, conceded 382 runs and took seven wickets, average 54.57. His best bowling figures were 3-47 v South Africa at Cape Town, 1964-65. He held 33 catches.

G. BOYCOTT – LIMITED-OVERS CAREER

	M	I	NO	R	HI	100s	50s	Avge
One-day Internationals	36	34	4	1,082	105	1	9	36.06
Gillette Cup/NatWest Bank Trophy	40	39	4	1,378	146	1	9	39.37
Benson and Hedges Cup	57	55	9	2,052	142	3	16	44.60
John Player League	163	157	24	5,051	108*	2	37	37.97

* *Signifies not out.*

Highest innings: 146, Yorkshire v Surrey at Lord's in the Gillette Cup final, 1965.

Bowling and Fielding: G. Boycott bowled 320.5 overs in limited-overs cricket, conceded 1,181 runs and took 29 wickets, average 40.72. His best bowling figures were 3-15, Yorkshire v Middlesex at Hull in the John Player League, 1983. He held 99 catches.

DEREK UNDERWOOD – AN APPRECIATION

By DOUG IBBOTSON

The full significance of Derek Underwood's retirement from first-class cricket will not properly be manifest until four o'clock, or thereabouts, on the last day of a moribund Championship match at Canterbury. Tardyshire, batting as only they can when challenged to score more than 4 runs an over, will be entrenched at 116 for three, many of the Faithful will be departing for Evensong, and seasoned correspondents will have advised their sports editors that the inevitable draw warrants no more than a brief litany.

Doubtless they will be right. Whereas, in the foregoing 25 years, the remarkable Derek Leslie Underwood frequently proved them wrong. For, in his capacity and determination to take, rather than buy, wickets on an unresponsive pitch, Underwood was a rare bird among spin bowlers. Whereas, against the average slow bowler, batsmen were principally alert to the prospect of punishing loose balls, when facing Underwood they steeled themselves against the unexpected – often to discover that, when it came, neither temperament nor technique was adequate. Not the least of their problems was that Underwood was not strictly a slow bowler in the traditional sense.

And so it would come to pass, shortly after the tea interval, with the match on its sick-bed and polite adjectives thin on the ground, that Underwood would peel off his sweater, trudge out his flat-footed run-up and wheel in to bowl. Alas, to elder statesmen deck-chair deep in disconsolation, it was not an edifying sight: the approach too long, the delivery too flat. Yet, even as they "hrrumphed" to the heavens in the name of Alfred Percy Freeman, Underwood's unique talents were at work. The obdurate batsman pushes forward and is caught off the handle. He takes his leave, a sadder – though little wiser – man, to be replaced by another who, already impregnated with doubt, dithers, dabbles and departs. The encircling vultures resettle and Underwood toils on until, at 6.15 in the final over, the last wicket falls and Kent win by 78 runs: Underwood six for 48.

In this typical scenario lay the real mark of a master bowler; a measure of the professionalism too often overlooked when, in league with a spiteful pitch, Underwood became virtually unplayable. Canterbury, 1984, and during the Championship match against Hampshire, overnight rain crept under the covers and lay brooding on a length. Those who had played and watched cricket only in recent years had never seen Underwood, or anyone else, bowl on a sticky patch. They were in for a salutary 90 minutes. So ruthlessly did Underwood exploit the conditions that, in 11.2 overs, he claimed seven wickets for 21 runs as Hampshire collapsed to summary defeat.

An easy haul? Comparatively speaking, yes. But, in the high summer and autumn of his professional career, such heaven-sent wickets had become a rare luxury. One would guess, in fact, that during a long and illustrious campaign, for each wicket plucked from a helpful pitch, Underwood quarried 50 from solid rock by the sweat of his brow and sheer tenacity of purpose.

[*Patrick Eagar*

Derek Underwood – "Individuality, honestly pursued, a generous sporting spirit and
professional skill, unstintingly applied."

Ironically, then, during the burgeoning maturity of his career the game's administrators, in their questionable wisdom, conspired to ensure that pitches should become as rock-like as possible; that, notwithstanding the odd, mischievous covers, they should remain dry and faithful to a new breed of batsmen who expected – nay demanded – that the ball maintain a line of such predictability that it may be cross-batted, almost with impunity, to all parts.

The declared object of the exercise was both mis-begotten and unsuccessful in that, far from providing maximum "entertainment" for the public (who were said to be interested only in positive results), it reduced the average Championship fixture to a two-and-a-half day bore between sides incapable of forcing a victory – followed by a limited-overs "accommodation" neither was prepared to lose. Under such circumstances Underwood's faculty for confounding the system was even more remarkable.

There was especial irony, therefore, when in his last season pitches were re-opened to the elements. Those among us who rejoiced scanned the sullen skies and smiled in anticipation of a rich Underwood harvest. Where, after all, were the batsmen with the technique to deal with the spinning ball on a steaming pitch? In the event it transpired that the turf technicians had done their work too well. Rain it certainly did, but pitches so rigorously tailored for batsmen produced not the anticipated "sticky dog" but rather the "Plasticine pup" on to which the bowler might as well lob a ball of wool. So Underwood was back to the hard graft: 611 overs and 45 wickets at 28.77 runs apiece. No mean performance, but neither an outstanding conclusion to a career during which, in his first season, he took 100 wickets – at eighteen, the youngest player to do so – and repeated the feat nine times.

Such are the bald statistics that all too often dominate the archives of achievement. Certainly they cannot be ignored. Underwood, D. L. – 86 Tests: First, West Indies 1966; Last, Sri Lanka 1981-82. Test wickets, 297; average 25.83. Best performance, against Pakistan at Lord's in 1974 – five for 20 in the first innings; eight for 51 in the second.

Most memorable, perhaps, was his match-winning seven for 50 at The Oval to square the 1968 series against Australia. Here was the young Underwood in his element. Torrential rain in the morning flooded the outfield, scores of volunteers joined the groundstaff in mopping up, and so began an agonising race against time that ended with five minutes to spare as the England spinner took his fourth wicket in 27 balls. A splendid statistic but, in perusing the Underwood curriculum vitae, it is equally pertinent to consider his analysis for the first innings of that same match – played on a pitch which yielded 494 runs for England and 324 for Australia. Underwood claimed only two wickets but, in so doing, conceded fewer than 1.7 runs for each of his 54 overs; a degree of economy, not to mention stamina, that seldom deserted him.

Facts and figures produce scope, for those so disposed, to speculate. What had he not forfeited two years of his Test career by defecting to World Series Cricket in 1977? Suppose he had not, in 1981, been banned from the international arena following an unauthorised tour of South Africa? Certainly he might have retired as the most prolific wicket-taker in Test history, which would have meant a great deal to archivists and doubtless something to Underwood himself. But if one respects individuality, honestly pursued, a generous sporting spirit and professional skill, unstintingly applied, then some may consider that many of Underwood's finest hours were spent in settings some way removed from the Ovals of Kennington or Adelaide.

He will be well remembered, albeit with somewhat grudging affection, at Bournemouth where, amid the sylvan charm of Dean Park, he invariably undid Hampshire. Likewise at Hastings where, in June 1964, he achieved a career-best bowling analysis of nine for 28 and, twenty years later, hit his maiden and only century.

Underwood's batting, like his bowling, though not a thing of beauty was rich in intent. Essentially fundamental in style, it relied on three basic strokes; the dogged forward thrust, the square, hunch-shouldered punch to the off, and the squat, short-arm pull between square leg and mid-wicket. It was a method which served Underwood well enough over the years, not least in scoring an unbeaten 45 against Lawry's Australians at Leeds in 1968. Even so, it was stretching credibility too far to imagine that, in his 40th year and at best a paid-up member of the night-watchmen's union, Underwood could coax, from such a limited repertoire, a first-class century.

Yet he did; nudge by nudge, stab by stab, scrambling between wickets in those Chaplinesque boots. And one suspects that, not until he stumbled into the 90s, was Underwood motivated by anything other than the responsibility of doing a job for his side to the utmost of his ability. Afterwards, of course, it was different. The unconfined delight as he acknowledged the congratulatory toasts of his peers was a joy to behold and to cherish – something that cannot be expressed in a mere statistic. So it was in everything Underwood approached; he took pleasure in his craft but placed craft above all.

Is he replaceable – if indeed there is to be encouragement in a changing game for bowlers of his ilk? Unless the TCCB decrees that, in future, all pitches are to be of rolled steel, the *fourth* day of a Championship match must offer rewards for even the most modest "flipper". Specialists such as Emburey, Hemmings, Marks and Gifford will undoubtedly enjoy a brisk trade. But what happens at the St Lawrence when Somerset sit on the splice? To whom do they turn at The Mote when Middlesex mount a rearguard action? No doubt the chaps in the deck-chairs will tell them.

D. L. UNDERWOOD – FIRST-CLASS CAREER

	M	O	M	R	W	BB	Avge
1963	27	941.4	376	2,134	101	6-88	21.12
1964	29	1,069.3	428	2,450	101	9-28	24.25
1965	31	982.4	423	2,259	89	6-26	25.38
1966	29	1,104.5	475	2,167	157	9-37	13.80
1966-67 (Pakistan)	6	245	102	406	13	4-21	31.23
1967	27	979.1	459	1,686	136	7-33	12.39
1967-68 (India/Ceylon)	2	77.4	43	96	24	8-10	4.00
1968	29	957.4	435	1,821	123	7-17	14.80
1968-69 (Ceylon/Pakistan)	6	189	71	380	20	6-40	19.00
1969	24	808.3	355	1,561	101	7-32	15.45
1969-70 (West Indies)	4	146	62	275	11	3-19	25.00
1970	21	851.2	307	2,043	89	7-103	22.95
1970-71 (Australia/NZ)	13	*422	110	1,123	43	6-12	26.11
1971	25	945.5	368	1,986	102	7-28	19.47
1972	18	652.4	227	1,485	71	8-70	20.91
1972-73 (India/Pakistan/SL)	10	442.5	164	934	26	4-56	35.92

	M	O	M	R	W	BB	Avge
1973	20	590.2	219	1,363	49	8-9	27.81
1973-74 (West Indies)	7	263.5	88	573	12	2-48	47.75
1974	16	563	229	1,181	65	8-51	18.16
1974-75 (Australia/NZ)	14	*412.3	102	1,214	48	7-113	25.29
1975	17	576.1	233	1,210	67	7-44	18.05
1975-76 (South Africa)	3	81	33	200	8	3-11	25.00
1976	20	859.2	317	2,139	78	7-56	27.42
1976-77 (India/SL/Aust.) {	8	329.5	130	640	36	5-84	17.77
	2	*48.6	15	101	8	3-16	12.62
1977	17	436.2	164	896	46	7-43	19.47
1978	22	815.1	359	1,594	110	9-32	14.49
1979	23	799.2	335	1,575	106	8-28	14.85
1979-80 (Australia/India)	6	260.1	81	609	25	7-66	24.36
1980	21	585.1	208	1,418	61	7-75	23.24
1981	23	774.3	282	1,788	78	7-93	22.92
1981-82 (India/Sri Lanka)	11	385.3	150	784	34	6-64	23.05
(South Africa)	2	45	10	128	2	1-36	64.00
1982	22	690.4	223	1,751	78	7-79	22.44
1983	25	936.3	358	2,044	106	7-55	19.28
1984	24	676.4	250	1,511	77	8-87	19.62
1985	25	807	290	1,802	67	6-56	26.89
1986	24	638.1	259	1,371	52	7-11	26.36
1987	23	611.3	211	1,295	45	5-43	28.77
	676	22,119.3 & 8,951 *883.1	49,993		2,465	9-28	20.28

* Eight-ball overs.

D. L. Underwood took 100 wickets in a season ten times, ten wickets in a match 47 times and five wickets in an innings 153 times.

Best bowling: 9-28, Kent v Sussex at Hastings, 1964.

Batting and Fielding: In 710 innings, 200 of them not out, D. L. Underwood scored 5,165 runs, average 10.12, with a highest innings of 111, Kent v Sussex at Hastings, 1984. This was his only hundred. He held 261 catches.

D. L. UNDERWOOD – TEST CAREER

		T	O	M	R	W	BB	Avge
1966	v West Indies	2	69	25	172	1	1-81	172.00
1967	v Pakistan	2	66	27	129	8	5-52	16.12
1968	v Australia	4	209.5	103	302	20	7-50	15.10
1968-69	v Pakistan	3	106	40	204	8	5-94	25.50
1969	v West Indies	2	53	29	101	6	4-55	16.83
	v New Zealand	3	150	70	220	24	7-32	9.16
1970-71	v Australia	5	*194.6	50	520	16	4-66	32.50
	v New Zealand	2	*84.1	28	205	17	6-12	12.05
1971	v Pakistan	1	41	13	102	0	0-102	—
	v India	1	63	20	121	4	3-72	30.25
1972	v Australia	2	125	49	266	16	6-45	16.62
1972-73	v India	4	214.4	82	457	15	4-56	30.46
	v Pakistan	2	96	35	215	3	3-48	71.66
1973	v New Zealand	1	18	6	41	0	0-14	—
	v West Indies	3	133	38	330	8	3-40	41.25
1973-74	v West Indies	4	137.5	45	314	5	2-48	62.80
1974	v India	3	67	25	146	4	1-18	36.50
	v Pakistan	3	113.5	48	218	17	8-51	12.82

	T	O	M	R	W	BB	Avge
1974-75 v Australia	5	*185	42	595	17	7-113	35.00
v New Zealand	2	*54.5	18	120	7	3-38	17.14
1975 v Australia	4	131	15	266	6	1-5	44.33
1976 v West Indies	5	224	59	631	17	5-39	37.11
1976-77 v India	5	252.5	95	509	29	5-84	17.55
v Australia	1	*23.6	4	54	4	3-16	13.50
1977 v Australia	5	169.1	61	362	13	6-66	27.84
1979-80 v Australia	3	160.2	48	405	13	3-71	31.15
v India	1	7	1	28	0	0-5	—
1980 v West Indies	1	29.2	7	108	1	1-108	108.00
1981-82 v India	6	228	99	438	10	3-45	43.80
v Sri Lanka	1	55.5	21	95	8	5-28	11.87
	86	2,920.4 & *542.2	1,239	7,674	297	8-51	25.83

* *Eight-ball overs.*

Best bowling: 8-51 v Pakistan at Lord's, 1974.

Batting and Fielding: In 116 innings, 35 of them not out, D. L. Underwood scored 937 runs, average 11.56, with a highest innings of 45 not out v Australia at Leeds, 1968. He held 44 catches.

D. L. UNDERWOOD – LIMITED-OVERS CAREER

	M	O	R	W	BB	Avge
One-day Internationals	26	213	734	32	4-44	22.93
Gillette Cup/NatWest Bank Trophy	57	582.4	1,711	77	8-31	22.22
Benson and Hedges Cup	86	832.4	2,435	107	5-35	22.75
John Player/Refuge Assurance League	229	1,574.3	5,846	346	6-12	16.89

Best bowling: 8-31, Kent v Scotland at Edinburgh in the NatWest Bank Trophy, 1987.

Batting and Fielding: In 192 innings, 79 of them not out, D. L. Underwood scored 790 runs, average 6.99, with a highest innings of 28, Kent v Sussex at Tunbridge Wells in the Gillette Cup, 1963. He held 108 catches.

150 YEARS AT TRENT BRIDGE

BY JOHN LAWSON

William Clarke would have been a satisfied man had he been at Trent Bridge last season to see Clive Rice and Richard Hadlee spearhead Nottinghamshire to the most glorious season in their marvellous history. Indeed, it could be said that he was there, at least in spirit. For Rice and Hadlee, like the other great names of Nottinghamshire cricket who went before them, would never have given so much pleasure and success to the county's cricketing public had it not been for the bricklayer-publican who founded that most welcoming of Test-match grounds.

Now Clarke's contribution to the game is to be highlighted in 1988 with the 150th anniversary of Trent Bridge. It is understandable that the occasion should not pass without celebration, and Nottinghamshire are rightly taking a leaf out of their founder's book by using the anniversary to fund-raising effect. "Trent Bridge 150" was fittingly launched in the middle of a week last September when Nottinghamshire not only captured the NatWest Bank Trophy – their first limited-overs success – but went on to win the County Championship for the second time in seven years. For good measure, they were also runners-up in the Refuge Assurance League.

The club, proud of their tradition as Test match hosts, are intent on raising sufficient money from the project to fund schemes that would be dear to Clarke's heart. Aiming for an initial target of £150,000, they hope to improve the Trent Bridge ground by redeveloping the Bridgford Road end and, it is hoped, creating a William Clarke Stand in the process. There are also plans to support financially the vital area of youth cricket to ensure that young, emerging talent in the county will be given every opportunity to perform on such a historic stage. Clarke would no doubt have approved of the bid to gain commercially from the anniversary. He saw such opportunities in cricket many years ago when sponsorship and advertising boards were much farther than a century away. It leads one to wonder what the commercial world has in store for the game 150 years hence.

William Clarke's ability to spot an opening and turn it to his advantage brought him rewards, and it also provided Nottinghamshire cricket with Trent Bridge. The landlord of the Bell Inn, a regular meeting-place for cricketers, in Nottingham's Market Place, he married Mary Chapman, the widowed landlady of the Trent Bridge Inn, in December 1837. He had played in a match near the Trent Bridge Inn that September, and there is some suggestion that the marriage was seen more as a business arrangement. Clarke had sensed the value of a piece of land adjacent to the Inn as a potential cricket ground and he did not let the grass grow under his feet.

Clarke, a useful batsman and successful exponent of the art of underarm bowling, had represented the North against the South at Lord's in 1836; and although he took no wickets, he did take a great deal of interest in the fact that the public paid an admission charge. On acquiring Trent Bridge, he was not unaware of the capacity for earning a penny or two from the game.

However, his plans did not produce the anticipated dividends. Until then, most of the cricket in the city had been played on the Forest, where spectators could gather to watch the game in pleasant surroundings at no cost. And while it was not difficult for Clarke to persuade the players to join him at Trent Bridge, because the gate money enabled him to pay them, Nottinghamshire suffered then – as it does today – from a fickle sporting public loathe to part with its hard-earned money. Clarke's decision to fence in the ground and charge a sixpence admission fee met with a poor response, with the result that the early matches at Trent Bridge did not attract the sizeable crowds for which he had hoped.

It was May 28, 1838, when the first ball was bowled at Trent Bridge, with Clarke's team, South of Nottingham, taking on the Forest Club. He later recruited leading players such as George Parr and John Wisden, but his ideas were bigger than he was able to put into operation in Nottingham. In 1846 he left for Lord's to join the staff as a professional bowler and gain the experience and contacts needed to form his All-England XI, whose tour around the counties proved to be both popular and profitable. The crowds flocked to see the leading players of the day, and Clarke, continuing with his underarm style, was a prominent figure in the side. He played almost until he died in 1856 at the age of 57.

For all his vision, Clarke was not the most popular man in the game. He had a reputation for playing practical – and at times not especially pleasant – jokes on his opponents, and his tendency to allow only his hands to untie the purse strings led to other problems. None the less, Nottinghamshire cricket owed him a considerable debt, for from those beginnings Trent Bridge was to blossom over many years, while always retaining its character and tradition.

When Clarke died, George Parr took over the captaincy and a committee was formed to supervise the club's affairs. The first Trent Bridge pavilion was built at the side of the old public house and stands were erected to accommodate spectators. On the field of play, Nottinghamshire became one of the most powerful sides of the day, winning the Championship ten times and sharing it on another five occasions in the 25 seasons between 1865 and 1889. And hand in hand with success in the middle came further development of the ground. During the 1880s the Ladies' Pavilion was built and the main pavilion was rebuilt at a cost of £5,000. More expenditure was made on improvements leading up to the first Test match at Trent Bridge in 1899.

Australia were the visitors, and with around 40,000 people watching the three days' play – the ground capacity in those days was between 20,000 and 25,000 – Test cricket was off to a satisfactory start. The match itself was drawn, with Ranjitsinhji saving England with a fine unbeaten innings of 93, and it saw the farewell Test appearance, at 50 years and 320 days, of W. G. Grace, who in 1871 had scored the first Championship hundred at Trent Bridge. Making his Test début in this same match was Wilfred Rhodes, who was to become the oldest Test cricketer.

Since the 1880s, Trent Bridge had also staged football. Nottingham Forest and Notts County, both of whose grounds are within immediate sight to this day, used the venue, but towards the end of the first decade of the new century, soccer was phased out. And Trent Bridge was put to another use during the First World War, when the pavilion was converted into a hospital where some 3,500 patients were treated.

Soon after the war, Nottinghamshire succeeded in securing the freehold of the ground without cost, and then capitalised by selling the Trent Bridge Inn to brewers – a piece of astute business which would have won the approval of William Clarke. In the post-war years the club was in the hands of Captain H. A. Brown, who stepped in as a temporary secretary in 1920 and, appointed to the post the following year, remained at Trent Bridge until 1958. Walter Marshall, whose many duties included that of groundsman, was another who made a notable contribution, not only to the ground but to its folklore. He kept chickens there, and behind the pavilion he cultivated a plot of land which would have done justice to a market gardener. Instrumental in improving facilities, he introduced mechanical power to replace Polly, the horse which had previously pulled along the rolling and cutting machinery.

The generosity of Sir Julien Cahn enabled the Radcliffe Road stand and Indoor Cricket School to be built, and these were in use by the time Nottinghamshire captured the County Championship title once more in 1929. That was to be their last major success until 1981, but in the intermediate period great players and great characters performed on the ground, beginning with the legendary fast-bowling partnership of Harold Larwood and Bill Voce. Both were at the centre of the bodyline controversy in Australia in 1932-33, and as if by way of settling a score, an Australian marked the centenary of the ground in spectacular style in 1938. Stan McCabe hammered the England bowling to the tune of 232 in just under four hours of the most punishing strokeplay ever seen.

During the Second World War, Trent Bridge had a fortunate escape when a 500lb bomb landed on nearby Swain Hall. When Championship cricket resumed afterwards, Nottinghamshire's displays suggested that a direct hit could not have done more damage as far as playing performances were concerned. In 1953, desperate to end the years of failure, Nottinghamshire registered the Australian leg-spinner, Bruce Dooland, who took 770 wickets and scored 4,782 runs in a five-year spell still fondly recalled by the county's supporters. Then, in 1968, Nottinghamshire surprised the cricketing world by attracting Garry Sobers, the greatest cricketer of his time, to Trent Bridge. He led Nottinghamshire to fourth place – their highest in post-war years – in his first full season, but he lacked support to make the transition from failure to success a permanent one. It was not until the Rice–Hadlee era that Nottinghamshire had a team to match the quality of their ground.

Under the management of Ken Taylor, whose contribution and influence should never be overlooked, Nottinghamshire were inspired by Rice and Hadlee to their first Championship title in 52 years. That, however, was just an appetiser for what was achieved last summer, when a "double" was won and a "treble" became a distinct possibility. It was a season that goes down in the 150-year history as the most memorable of all. William Clarke would indeed have been proud of those involved.

[All-Sport/Adrian Murrell

Official Test matches long since denied him, Graeme Pollock in his 40s could still take hundreds off the West Indian and Australian teams that visited South Africa in the 1980s.

GRAEME POLLOCK – A RETROSPECTIVE

By CHARLES FORTUNE

Graeme Pollock, the great South African batsman who too soon was denied occupation of cricket's more illustrious creases, retired from the first-class game at the end of the 1986-87 season. In January 1961, aged 16 years and 335 days, he scored his first Currie Cup century in Johannesburg, for Eastern Province against Transvaal B. Twenty-six summers later, with a score of 63 not out and now playing for Transvaal, he was there at the finish of the match which saw his team retain the Castle Currie Cup.

Heredity and environment each supposed that the Pollock brothers should go to the top in cricket. Their father, morning paper editor in the seaport where his family grew up, played for the Orange Free State. Their mother, an all-round games player of renown, came of a father who rose in cricket administration to a term of office as president of the South African Cricket Association. Frequently the family moved house, but always there was space for a practice wicket to be set down; for the brothers to bat and bowl through sun-drenched days. And should their contests become heated, always there to arbitrate was Mrs Pollock.

There is a similarity in the Pollock brothers' cricket background and that of W. G. Grace and his brothers. In both, the genes had given a touch of cricket to the blood. Environment lent itself to endless opportunity for practice, and there was a mother who saw only virtue in making her sons proficient. The analogy may be taken further. Right from their early schooldays, matches were played both with and against adult cricketers of some class.

Graeme, as did Peter, went as a day-boy to the Port Elizabeth high school, Grey College. "The Grey" has ever had a special care for its cricketers, and Graeme soon found himself at the nets where George Cox, a kindly, able and inspiring man from Sussex, was in charge. Just nine, Graeme was picked for the school's Under-eleven team. The venue was Graaff Reinet, a farming centre 150 miles distant. Bowling, he took all ten wickets; and then he scored the first century to come from his bat. Thus, while himself not yet into double figures, as a batsman he reached his first hundred. Peter, seventeen, beat his brother to a Nuffield South African Schools' cap, but junior came alongside a year later, aged but fifteen.

During the school summer vacation of 1960-61, and free from studies he did not relish, Graeme Pollock set out on his first-class cricket career with Eastern Province. His maiden century was entirely in keeping with the massive scores to follow; never once did this lanky, loose-limbed schoolboy deviate from the business of scoring runs. On Wanderers, the ground that was eventually to become his cricket home, the Transvaal B bowlers were irked that this "kid" should calmly and methodically press ever onwards. As he neared his hundred, the bowling became more physical and the batsman more mature. Pollock, in that maiden hundred, moved through the nineties with never a hesitation; as though, as indeed was so, to the manner born. He was not yet seventeen.

He was nineteen when chosen for the 1963-64 South African tour of Australia. On arrival in Western Australia, he was soon to learn that life with the Aussies is ever real. McKenzie bowled him first for 1 and then caught and bowled him for 0. Before the Springboks left Perth, however, Pollock showed his class, reaching a hundred in 88 minutes, with eighteen fours, against a Combined XI. His Test début came at Brisbane on December 6, 1963, but this was no happy match. Much interrupted by rain, it was the worse troubled by the abrupt end to a long-established Australian bowler's career. The South African innings had reached but the second ball of the second over on the second day when umpire Egar at square leg no-balled Ian Meckiff four times, and he did not bowl again. That rain poured down unceasingly on the third day somehow seemed appropriate to a wretched episode in what might have been a noble occasion.

Pollock came into his own in the Third Test on the Sydney Cricket Ground. His brother, Peter, having taken five first-innings Australian wickets for 83, Graeme made 122: his maiden Test century. Thus did the Sydney Cricket Ground set the pattern for the brotherly duets that became the hallmark of South Africa's Test matches. That match was drawn, and with the Australians one up from victory at Melbourne, the series moved on to Adelaide, where South Africa won by ten wickets.

All else in that Test gave place to the Barlow–Graeme Pollock third-wicket partnership. Coming together on the Saturday with three hours till close of play, they added 225. Adelaide, most genial of great cricket grounds, was on this Saturday packed to overflowing. No cloud in the sky, his partner well set, the younger Pollock moved through early assurance into total command. McKenzie, Hawke, Benaud could find nothing to halt or hinder his surging strokeplay. My broadcasting companion for the series was the renowned Australian captain, and grandsire of famous Australian cricketers, Victor Richardson. Came the moment when I glanced his way, indicating it was now his turn to talk, his response was a shaking of the head and a murmured – "No, no, you carry on". So captivated was this veteran stalwart that tiny tears of ecstasy shone in the corners of his eyes. He wanted only to sit back, the more fully to relish that day's batting. Never will one seasoned and long experienced in cricket confrontation pay a more sincere tribute to a young man than Victor Richardson spontaneously paid to Graeme Pollock that day.

Before 1964 had run its course, M. J. K. Smith and his MCC team had arrived in South Africa. Two good teams on slow wickets meandered through a dreary five-match series. England won at Durban, the first of the Tests, and Pollock was out twice to Titmus for 5 and 0. Of his eight dismissals in the five Tests, three went to Titmus and three to Allen: off-spinners both. There were times, bowling round the wicket and pushing the ball across him, when they seemed to be questioning the orthodoxy of his strict adherence to a sideways-on position. Against this, however, they, like all who bowled at him, were met by his marvellous judgement of length. Rarely was he brought forward unless the ball was there to play.

The power and the beauty of his batting came again in the last of the Tests on his home ground in Port Elizabeth. With one defeat and three drawn Tests, Port Elizabeth offered a last chance for South Africa, as in 1956-57, to square the series. Pollock made scores of 137 and 77 not out. Barlow and Bland, both in fine form throughout the rubber, could be kept in check by England's bowlers, but not Pollock. His driving into the covers had fieldsmen occasionally wringing their hands or, more often, groping in vain for the ball travelling hell-bent to the boundary. Several off-drives were self-retrieving. There is a low retaining wall, with a smooth cement surface, just beyond the boundary at long-off for the left-hander. Pollock's drives from it rebounded back towards the stumps at the bowler's end.

Rain put an early end to a scene set for a fighting finish to the series, but in July that year the contest was being resumed in England. Victory at Trent Bridge in the second of the three Tests gave South Africa the rubber; and that victory was a Pollock family affair. Graeme scored 125 and 59 while Peter took five wickets in each England innings: ten for 87 in all.

It is for his batting at Trent Bridge in 1965 that, in England, Graeme Pollock is best remembered; and this was the batting of a player only 21 years old. Of his hundred there, *Wisden* said that following the lunch break "... he reigned supreme for seventy more minutes while he lashed the bowling for 91 out of 102 ... he offered no chance." The power and the artistry of his strokeplay that day was awesome. Using his height (6ft 2½in) to full advantage, he drove the English bowling, off back foot and front, through the covers, regardless of length. The ball to which other batsmen would have offered a defensive bat was simply struck to the boundary. Ted Dexter later wrote of him: "... he could hit the good-length ball, given only a modicum of room outside the off stump, actually harder than he could hit the half-volley. Now that takes some doing."

Across the world cricket scene, that was pretty much the end for South Africa. Pollock was to play twice more against Australia in South Africa – Bobby Simpson's side in 1966-67 and Bill Lawry's in 1969-70 – and he was in England in 1970 for the series between England and the Rest of the World, which took the place of the cancelled tour by South Africa. A century in the fifth "Test", which incorporated with Garry Sobers a fifth-wicket partnership of 165, was his one big innings. His scores for eight innings averaged 31.25 and were below those of the other Springbok batsmen, Barlow, Procter and Richards.

At home, however, Pollock was consistently a heavy scorer, and in the two series with Australia he was often brilliant. Against Simpson's team came a double-century at Newlands. Four years later, when Lawry brought his team on from India, Pollock at Durban made 274 in the only South African innings and established a new record score by a South African in Test cricket. Thereafter, his and South Africa's international cricket were to be restricted to home series against "breakaway" visitors from England, Sri Lanka, the West Indies and Australia. The innings of 144 against an Australian XI with which he bowed out of international cricket in Port Elizabeth in 1986-87 was both convincing and memorable; it seemed hard to think of him as being 43 in three to four weeks' time.

If it is permissible to attach the word "genius" to the artistry of a batsman, then Graeme Pollock is such among cricketers. Like others so acknowledged he was ever the master craftsman. Perhaps the all-important factor was that from the start, the bowling he faced was more skilled and demanding than will have come the way of many others. Only Colin Cowdrey among the cricketers I have known has moved so easily up the rungs that take cricket toddlers to a Test match début. Pollock never underestimated the opposition, nor hesitated to meet a challenge. When thirteen, he became excited, even entranced, by the skill and application of the Australian, Neil Harvey, like himself a left-handed batsman. It was Harvey's dedication to the task of making runs, and still more runs, that determined Pollock never to yield his wicket while runs were there to be taken.

His move from Eastern Province to Transvaal in 1978-79 undoubtedly enriched and extended his playing days. So, too, did the SACU move that brought the "breakaway" touring teams to South Africa. Graeme Pollock, a supporter of full tours to South Africa by unofficial teams of international standard, is established in cricket administration: president of the South African Cricket Players' Association, board member and team selector with the Transvaal Cricket Council. We shall not see his like again at the crease, but he may yet become a prominent figure in cricket's council chambers.

R. G. POLLOCK – FIRST-CLASS CAREER

		M	I	NO	R	HI	100s	50s	Avge
1960-61		5	8	0	384	102	1	4	48.00
1961-62		5	10	1	346	79	0	4	38.44
1962-63		8	15	3	836	209*	3	3	69.66
1963-64	(Australia/NZ)	16	23	1	1,111	175	5	1	50.50
1964-65		9	16	2	734	137	2	5	52.42
1965	(England)	14	24	4	1,147	203*	3	5	57.35
1965-66		7	12	1	343	88	0	3	31.18
1966	(England)	1	2	0	51	29	0	0	25.50
1966-67		11	21	4	992	209	4	2	58.35
1967	(England)	2	2	1	111	59	0	2	111.00
1967-68		6	10	1	452	107*	1	3	50.22
1968	(England)	3	6	0	58	44	0	0	9.66
1968-69		8	14	2	1,043	196	3	5	86.92
1969	(England)	1	2	0	162	101	1	1	81.00
1969-70		9	16	0	1,005	274	4	4	62.81
1970	(England)	5	8	0	250	114	1	1	31.25
1970-71		8	13	0	548	146	1	3	42.15
1971-72		8	14	1	690	130*	2	3	53.07
1971-72	(Australia)	3	5	0	209	136	1	0	41.80
1972-73		2	4	1	118	47	0	0	39.33
1973-74		12	20	1	543	78	0	5	28.57
1974-75		11	21	5	1,126	167*	5	4	70.77
1975-76		10	19	4	1,013	194	3	5	67.53
1976-77		7	13	2	719	180*	2	3	65.36
1977-78		8	13	2	769	190*	2	2	69.90
1978-79		8	11	1	961	233	5	3	96.10
1979-80		9	13	2	739	168	2	2	67.18
1980-81		8	12	4	488	166*	1	3	61.00
1981-82		9	14	5	586	124	1	5	65.11
1982-83		13	19	2	818	197	2	3	48.11
1983-84		11	19	1	894	154	3	3	49.66
1984-85		10	15	0	567	114	1	4	37.80
1985-86		9	15	2	671	113	2	5	51.61
1986-87		6	8	1	456	144	2	3	65.14
		262	437	54	20,940	274	64	99	54.67

* *Signifies not out.*

R. G. POLLOCK – TEST CAREER

	T	I	NO	R	HI	100s	50s	Avge
1963-64 v Australia	5	7	0	399	175	2	0	57.00
1963-64 v New Zealand	1	2	0	53	30	0	0	26.50
1964-65 v England	5	10	2	459	137	1	4	57.37
1965 v England	3	6	0	291	125	1	2	48.50
1966-67 v Australia	5	9	2	537	209	2	2	76.71
1969-70 v Australia	4	7	0	517	274	1	3	73.85
	23	41	4	2,256	274	7	11	60.97

TEST CRICKETERS

FULL LIST FROM 1877 TO AUGUST 11, 1987

These lists have been compiled on a home and abroad basis, appearances abroad being printed in *italics*.

Abbreviations. E: England. A: Australia. SA: South Africa. WI: West Indies. NZ: New Zealand. In: India. P: Pakistan. SL: Sri Lanka.

All appearances are placed in this order of seniority. Hence, any England cricketer playing against Australia in England has that achievement recorded first and the remainder of his appearances at home (if any) set down before passing to matches abroad. Although the distinction between amateur and professional was abolished in 1963, initials of English professionals before that date are still given in brackets. The figures immediately following each name represent the total number of appearances in *all* Tests.

Where the season embraces two different years, the first year is given; i.e. 1876 indicates 1876-77.

When South Africa left the British Commonwealth in 1961 they ceased membership of the Imperial Cricket Conference, which in 1965 was renamed the International Cricket Conference. The rules of membership were changed then so that, although Pakistan have left the Commonwealth, they remain members of ICC.

ENGLAND

Number of Test cricketers: 526

Abel (R.) 13: v A 1888 (3) 1896 (3) 1902 (2); *v A 1891 (3); v SA 1888 (2)*
Absolom, C. A. 1: *v A 1878*
Agnew, J. P. 3: v A 1985 (1); v WI 1984 (1); v SL 1984 (1)
Allen (D. A.) 39: v A 1961 (4) 1964 (1); v SA 1960 (2); v WI 1963 (2) 1966 (1); v P 1962 (4); *v A 1962 (1) 1965 (4); v SA 1964 (4); v WI 1959 (5); v NZ 1965 (3); v In 1961 (5); v P 1961 (3)*
Allen, G. O. 25: v A 1930 (1) 1934 (2); v WI 1933 (1); v NZ 1931 (3); v In 1936 (3); *v A 1932 (5) 1936 (5); v WI 1947 (3); v NZ 1932 (2)*
Allom, M. J. C. 5: *v SA 1930 (1); v NZ 1929 (4)*
Allott, P. J. W. 13: v A 1981 (1) 1985 (4); v WI 1984 (3); v In 1982 (2); v SL 1984 (1); *v In 1981 (1); v SL 1981 (1)*
Ames, L. E. G.) 47: v A 1934 (5) 1938 (2); v SA 1929 (1) 1935 (4); v WI 1933 (3); v NZ 1931 (3) 1937 (3); v In 1932 (1); *v A 1932 (5) 1936 (5); v SA 1938 (5); v WI 1929 (4) 1934 (4); v NZ 1932 (2)*
Amiss, D. L. 50: v A 1968 (1) 1975 (2) 1977 (2); v WI 1966 (1) 1973 (3) 1976 (1); v NZ 1973 (3); v In 1967 (2) 1971 (1) 1974 (3); v P 1967 (1) 1971 (3) 1974 (3); *v A 1974 (5) 1976 (1); v WI 1973 (5) v NZ 1974 (2); v In 1972 (3) 1976 (5); v P 1972 (3)*
Andrew (K. V.) 2: v WI 1963 (1); *v A 1954 (1)*
Appleyard (R.) 9: v A 1956 (1); v SA 1955 (1); v P 1954 (1); *v A 1954 (4); v NZ 1954 (2)*
Archer, A. G. 1: *v SA 1898*
Armitage (T.) 2: *v A 1876 (2)*
Arnold (E. G.) 10: v A 1905 (4); v SA 1907 (2); *v A 1903 (4)*
Arnold, G. G. 34: v A 1972 (3) 1975 (1); v WI 1973 (3); v NZ 1969 (1) 1973 (3); v In 1974 (2); v P 1967 (2) 1974 (3); *v A 1974 (4); v WI 1973 (3); v NZ 1974 (2); v In 1972 (4); v P 1972 (3)*
Arnold (J.) 1: v NZ 1931
Astill (W. E.) 9: *v SA 1927 (5); v WI 1929 (4)*
Athey, C. W. J. 17: v A 1980 (1); v NZ 1986 (3); v In 1986 (2); v P 1987 (4); *v A 1986 (5); v WI 1980 (2)*
Attewell (W.) 10: v A 1890 (1); *v A 1884 (5) 1887 (1) 1891 (3)*

Bailey, T. E. 61: v A 1953 (5) 1956 (4); v SA 1951 (2) 1955 (5); v WI 1950 (2) 1957 (4); v NZ 1949 (4) 1958 (4); v P 1954 (3); *v A 1950 (4) 1954 (5) 1958 (5); v SA 1956 (5); v WI 1953 (5); v NZ 1950 (2) 1954 (2)*

Bairstow, D. L. 4: v A 1980 (1); v WI 1980 (1); v In 1979 (1); *v WI 1980 (1)*

Bakewell (A. H.) 6: v SA 1935 (2); v WI 1933 (1); v NZ 1931 (2); *v In 1933 (1)*

Balderstone J. C. 2: v WI 1976 (2)

Barber, R. W. 28: v A 1964 (1) 1968 (1); v SA 1960 (1) 1965 (3); v WI 1966 (2); v NZ 1965 (3); *v A 1965 (5); v SA 1964 (4); v In 1961 (5); v P 1961 (3)*

Barber (W.) 2: v SA 1935 (2)

Barlow, G. D. 3: v A 1977 (1); *v In 1976 (2)*

Barlow (R. G.) 17: v A 1882 (1) 1884 (3) 1886 (3); *v A 1881 (4) 1882 (4) 1886 (2)*

Barnes (S. F.) 27: v A 1902 (1) 1909 (3) 1912 (3); v SA 1912 (3); *v A 1901 (3) 1907 (5) 1911 (5); v SA 1913 (4)*

Barnes (W.) 21: v A 1880 (1) 1882 (1) 1884 (2) 1886 (2) 1888 (3) 1890 (2); *v A 1882 (4) 1884 (5) 1886 (2)*

Barnett (C. J.) 20: v A 1938 (3) 1948 (1); v SA 1947 (3); v WI 1933 (1); v NZ 1937 (3); v In 1936 (1); *v A 1936 (5); v In 1933 (3)*

Barratt (F.) 5: v SA 1929 (1); *v NZ 1929 (4)*

Barrington (K. F.) 82: v A 1961 (5) 1964 (5) 1968 (3); v SA 1955 (2) 1960 (4) 1965 (3); v WI 1963 (5) 1966 (2); v NZ 1965 (2); v In 1959 (5) 1967 (3); v P 1962 (4) 1967 (3); *v A 1962 (5) 1965 (5); v SA 1964 (5); v WI 1959 (5) 1967 (5); v NZ 1962 (3); v In 1961 (5) 1963 (1); v P 1961 (2)*

Barton (V. A.) 1: *v SA 1891*

Bates (W.) 15: *v A 1881 (4) 1882 (4) 1884 (5) 1886 (2)*

Bean (G.) 3: *v A 1891 (3)*

Bedser (A. V.) 51: v A 1948 (5) 1953 (5); v.SA 1947 (2) 1951 (5) 1955 (1); v WI 1950 (3); v NZ 1949 (2); v In 1946 (3) 1952 (4); v P 1954 (2); *v A 1946 (5) 1950 (5) 1954 (1); v SA 1948 (5); v NZ 1946 (1) 1950 (2)*

Benson, M. R. 1: v In 1986

Berry (R.) 2: v WI 1950 (2)

Binks, J. G. 2: *v In 1963 (2)*

Bird M. C. 10: *v SA 1909 (5) 1913 (5)*

Birkenshaw J. 5: *v WI 1973 (2); v In 1972 (2); v P 1972 (1)*

Bligh, Hon. I. F. W. 4: *v A 1882 (4)*

Blythe (C.) 19: v A 1905 (1) 1909 (2); v SA 1907 (3); *v A 1901 (5) 1907 (1); v SA 1905 (5) 1909 (2)*

Board (J. H.) 6: *v SA 1898 (2) 1905 (4)*

Bolus, J. B. 7: v WI 1963 (2); *v In 1963 (5)*

Booth (M. W.) 2: *v SA 1913 (2)*

Bosanquet, B. J. T. 7: v A 1905 (3); *v A 1903 (4)*

Botham, I. T. 94: v A 1977 (2) 1980 (1) 1981 (6) 1985 (6); v WI 1980 (5) 1984 (5); v NZ 1978 (3) 1983 (4) 1986 (1); v In 1979 (4) 1982 (3); v P 1978 (2) 1982 (3) 1987 (5); v SL 1984 (1); *v A 1978 (6) 1979 (3) 1982 (5) 1986 (4); v WI 1980 (4) 1985 (5); v NZ 1977 (3) 1983 (3); v In 1979 (1) 1981 (4); v P 1983 (1); v SL 1981 (1)*

Bowden, M. P. 2: *v SA 1888 (2)*

Bowes (W. E.) 15: v A 1934 (3) 1938 (2); v SA 1935 (4); v WI 1939 (2); v In 1932 (1) 1946 (1); *v A 1932 (1); v NZ 1932 (1)*

Bowley (E. H.) 5: v SA 1929 (2); *v NZ 1929 (3)*

Boycott, G. 108: v A 1964 (4) 1968 (3) 1972 (2) 1977 (3) 1980 (1) 1981 (6); v SA 1965 (2); v WI 1966 (4) 1969 (3) 1973 (3) 1980 (5); v NZ 1965 (2) 1969 (3) 1973 (3) 1978 (2); v In 1967 (2) 1971 (1) 1974 (1) 1979 (4); v P 1967 (1) 1971 (2); *v A 1965 (5) 1970 (5) 1978 (6) 1979 (3); v SA 1964 (5); v WI 1967 (5) 1973 (5) 1980 (4); v NZ 1965 (2) 1977 (3); v In 1979 (1) 1981 (4); v P 1977 (3)*

Bradley, W. M. 2: v A 1899 (2)

Braund (L. C.) 23: v A 1902 (5); v SA 1907 (3); *v A 1901 (5) 1903 (5) 1907 (5)*

Brearley, J. M. 39: v A 1977 (5) 1981 (4); v WI 1976 (2); v NZ 1978 (3); v In 1979 (4); v P 1978 (3); *v A 1976 (1) 1978 (6) 1979 (3); v In 1976 (5) 1979 (1); v P 1977 (2)*

Brearley, W. 4: v A 1905 (2) 1909 (1); v SA 1912 (1)

Brennan, D. V. 2: v SA 1951 (2)

Briggs (John) 33: v A 1886 (1) 1888 (3) 1893 (2) 1896 (1) 1899 (1); *v A 1884 (5) 1886 (2) 1887 (1) 1891 (3) 1894 (5) 1897 (5); v SA 1888 (2)*

Broad, B. C. 14: v WI 1984 (4); v P 1987 (4); v SL 1984 (1); *v A 1986 (5)*

Brockwell (W.) 7: v A 1893 (1) 1899 (1); *v A 1894 (5)*

Bromley-Davenport, H. R. 4: *v SA 1895 (3) 1898 (1)*

Brookes (D.) 1: *v WI 1947*

Brown (A.) 2: *v In 1961 (1)*; *v P 1961 (1)*
Brown, D. J. 26: v A 1968 (4); v SA 1965 (2); v WI 1966 (1) 1969 (3); v NZ 1969 (1); v In 1967 (2): *v A 1965 (4)*; *v WI 1967 (4)*; *v NZ 1965 (2)*; *v P 1968 (3)*
Brown, F. R. 22: v A 1953 (1); v SA 1951 (5); v WI 1950 (1); v NZ 1931 (2) 1937 (1) 1949 (2); v In 1932 (1); *v A 1950 (5)*; *v NZ 1932 (2) 1950 (2)*
Brown (G.) 7: v A 1921 (3); *v SA 1922 (4)*
Brown (J. T.) 8: v A 1896 (1) 1899 (1); *v A 1894 (5)*
Buckenham (C. P.) 4: *v SA 1909 (4)*
Butcher, A. R. 1: v In 1979
Butcher, R. O. 3: *v WI 1980 (3)*
Butler (H. J.) 2: v SA 1947 (1); *v WI 1947 (1)*
Butt (H. R.) 3: *v SA 1895 (3)*

Calthorpe, Hon. F. S. G. 4: *v WI 1929 (4)*
Capel, D. J. 1: v P 1987
Carr, A. W. 11: v A 1926 (4); v SA 1929 (2); *v SA 1922 (5)*
Carr, D. B. 2: *v In 1951 (2)*
Carr, D. W. 1: v A 1909
Cartwright, T. W. 5: v A 1964 (2); v SA 1965 (1); v NZ 1965 (1); *v SA 1964 (1)*
Chapman, A. P. F. 26: v A 1926 (4) 1930 (4); v SA 1924 (2); v WI 1928 (3); *v A 1924 (4) 1928 (4)*; *v SA 1930 (5)*
Charlwood (H. R. J.) 2: *v A 1876 (2)*
Chatterton (W.) 1: *v SA 1891*
Christopherson, S. 1: v A 1884
Clark (E. W.) 8: v A 1934 (2); v SA 1929 (1); v WI 1933 (2); *v In 1933 (3)*
Clay, J. C. 1: v SA 1935
Close (D. B.) 22: v A 1961 (1); v SA 1955 (1); v WI 1957 (2) 1963 (5) 1966 (1) 1976 (3); v NZ 1949 (1); v In 1959 (1) 1967 (3); *v P 1967 (3)*; *v A 1950 (1)*
Coldwell (L. J.) 7: v A 1964 (2); v P 1962 (2); *v A 1962 (2)*; *v NZ 1962 (1)*
Compton (D. C. S.) 78: v A 1938 (4) 1948 (5) 1953 (5) 1956 (1); v SA 1947 (5) 1951 (4) 1955 (5); v WI 1939 (3) 1950 (1); v NZ 1937 (1) 1949 (4); v In 1946 (3) 1952 (2); *v P 1954 (4)*; *v A 1946 (5) 1950 (4) 1954 (4)*; *v SA 1948 (5) 1956 (5)*; *v WI 1953 (5)*; *v NZ 1946 (1) 1950 (2)*
Cook (C.) 1: v SA 1947
Cook, G. 7: v In 1982 (3); *v A 1982 (3)*; *v SL 1981 (1)*
Cook, N. G. B. 9: v WI 1984 (2); v NZ 1983 (2); *v NZ 1983 (1)*; *v P 1983 (3)*
Cope, G. A. 3: *v P 1977 (3)*
Copson (W. H.) 3: v SA 1947 (1); v WI 1939 (2)
Cornford (W. L.) 4: *v NZ 1929 (4)*
Cottam, R. M. H. 4: *v In 1972 (2)*; *v P 1968 (2)*
Coventry, Hon. C. J. 2: *v SA 1888 (2)*
Cowans, N. G. 19: v A 1985 (1); v WI 1984 (1); v NZ 1983 (4); *v A 1982 (4)*; *v NZ 1983 (2)*; *v In 1984 (5)*; *v P 1983 (2)*
Cowdrey, C. S. 5: *v In 1984 (5)*
Cowdrey, M. C. 114: v A 1956 (5) 1961 (4) 1964 (3) 1968 (4); v SA 1955 (1) 1960 (5) 1965 (3); v WI 1957 (5) 1963 (2) 1966 (2); v NZ 1958 (4) 1965 (3); v In 1959 (5); v P 1962 (4) 1967 (2) 1971 (1); *v A 1954 (5) 1958 (5) 1962 (5) 1965 (4) 1970 (3) 1974 (5)*; *v SA 1956 (5)*; *v WI 1959 (5) 1967 (5)*; *v NZ 1954 (2) 1958 (2) 1962 (3) 1965 (3) 1970 (3)*; *v In 1963 (3)*; *v P 1968 (3)*
Coxon (A.) 1: v A 1948
Cranston, J. 1: v A 1890
Cranston, K. 8: v A 1948 (1); v SA 1947 (3); *v WI 1947 (4)*
Crapp (J. F.) 7: v A 1948 (3); *v SA 1948 (4)*
Crawford, J. N. 12: v SA 1907 (2); *v A 1907 (5)*; *v SA 1905 (5)*
Cuttell (W. R.) 2: *v SA 1898 (2)*

Dawson, E. W. 5: *v SA 1927 (1)*; *v NZ 1929 (4)*
Dean (H.) 3: v A 1912 (2); v SA 1912 (1)
DeFreitas, P. A. J. 5: v P 1987 (1); *v A 1986 (4)*
Denness, M. H. 28: v A 1975 (1); v NZ 1969 (1); v In 1974 (3); v P 1974 (3); *v A 1974 (5)*; *v WI 1973 (5)*; *v NZ 1974 (2)*; *v In 1972 (5)*; *v P 1972 (3)*
Denton (D.) 11: v A 1905 (1); *v SA 1905 (5) 1909 (5)*
Dewes, J. G. 5: v A 1948 (1); v WI 1950 (2); *v A 1950 (2)*

Dexter, E. R. 62: v A 1961 (5) 1964 (5) 1968 (2); v SA 1960 (5); v WI 1963 (5); v NZ 1958 (1) 1965 (2); v In 1959 (2); v P 1962 (5); *v A 1958 (2) 1962 (5); v SA 1964 (5); v WI 1959 (5); v NZ 1958 (2) 1962 (3); v In 1961 (5); v P 1961 (3)*

Dilley, G. R. 30: v A 1981 (3); v WI 1980 (3); v NZ 1983 (1) 1986 (2); v In 1986 (2); v P 1987 (4); *v A 1979 (2) 1986 (4); v WI 1980 (4); v In 1981 (4); v P 1983 (1)*

Dipper (A. E.) 1: v A 1921

Doggart, G. H. G. 2: v WI 1950 (2)

D'Oliveira, B. L. 44: v A 1968 (2) 1972 (5); v WI 1966 (4) 1969 (3); v NZ 1969 (3); v In 1967 (2) 1971 (3); v P 1967 (3) 1971 (3); *v A 1970 (6); v WI 1967 (5); v NZ 1970 (2); v P 1968 (3)*

Dollery (H. E.) 4: v A 1948 (1); v SA 1947 (1); v WI 1950 (1)

Dolphin (A.) 1: *v A 1920*

Douglas, J. W. H. T. 23: v A 1912 (1) 1921 (5); v SA 1924 (1); *v A 1911 (5) 1920 (5) 1924 (1); v SA 1913 (5)*

Downton, P. R. 27: v A 1981 (1) 1985 (6); v WI 1984 (5); v In 1986 (1); v SL 1984 (1); *v WI 1980 (3) 1985 (5); v In 1984 (5)*

Druce, N. F. 5: *v A 1897 (5)*

Ducat (A.) 1: v A 1921

Duckworth (G.) 24: v A 1930 (5); v SA 1924 (1) 1929 (4) 1935 (1); v WI 1928 (1); v In 1936 (3); *v A 1928 (5); v SA 1930 (3); v NZ 1932 (1)*

Duleepsinhji, K. S. 12: v A 1930 (4); v SA 1929 (1); v NZ 1931 (3); *v NZ 1929 (4)*

Durston (F. J.) 1: v A 1921

Edmonds, P. H. 51: v A 1975 (2) 1985 (5); v NZ 1978 (3) 1983 (2) 1986 (3); v In 1979 (4) 1982 (3) 1986 (2); v P 1978 (3) 1987 (5); *v A 1978 (1) 1986 (5); v WI 1985 (3); v NZ 1977 (3); v In 1984 (5); v P 1977 (2)*

Edrich, J. H. 77: v A 1964 (3) 1968 (5) 1972 (5) 1975 (4); v SA 1965 (1); v WI 1963 (3) 1966 (1) 1969 (3) 1976 (2); v NZ 1965 (1) 1969 (3); v In 1967 (2) 1971 (3) 1974 (3); v P 1971 (3) 1974 (3); *v A 1965 (5) 1970 (6) 1974 (4); v WI 1967 (5); v NZ 1965 (3) 1970 (2) 1974 (2); v In 1963 (2); v P 1968 (3)*

Edrich, W. J. 39: v A 1938 (4) 1948 (5) 1953 (3); v SA 1947 (4); v WI 1950 (2); v NZ 1949 (4); v In 1946 (1); v P 1954 (1); *v A 1946 (5) 1954 (4); v SA 1938 (5); v NZ 1946 (1)*

Elliott (H.) 4: v WI 1928 (1); *v SA 1927 (1); v In 1933 (2)*

Ellison, R. M. 11: v A 1985 (2); v WI 1984 (1); v In 1986 (1); v SL 1984 (1); *v WI 1985 (3); v In 1984 (3)*

Emburey, J. E. 46: v A 1980 (1) 1981 (4) 1985 (6); v WI 1980 (3); v NZ 1978 (1) 1986 (2); v In 1986 (3); v P 1987 (4); *v A 1978 (4) 1986 (5); v WI 1980 (4) 1985 (4); v In 1979 (1) 1981 (3); v SL 1981 (1)*

Emmett (G. M.) 1: v A 1948

Emmett (T.) 7: *v A 1876 (2) 1878 (1) 1881 (4)*

Evans, A. J. 1: v A 1921

Evans (T. G.) 91: v A 1948 (5) 1953 (5) 1956 (5); v SA 1947 (5) 1951 (3) 1955 (3); v WI 1950 (5) 1957 (5); v NZ 1949 (4) 1958 (5); v In 1946 (1) 1952 (4) 1959 (2); v P 1954 (4); *v A 1946 (4) 1950 (5) 1954 (4) 1958 (3); v SA 1948 (3) 1956 (5); v WI 1947 (4) 1953 (4); v NZ 1946 (1) 1950 (2) 1954 (2)*

Fagg (A. E.) 5: v WI 1939 (1); v In 1936 (2); *v A 1936 (2)*

Fairbrother, N. H. 1: v P 1987

Fane, F. L. 14: *v A 1907 (4); v SA 1905 (5) 1909 (5)*

Farnes, K. 15: v A 1934 (2) 1938 (4); *v A 1936 (2); v SA 1938 (5); v WI 1934 (2)*

Farrimond (W.) 4: v SA 1935 (1); *v SA 1930 (2); v WI 1934 (1)*

Fender, P. G. H. 13: v A 1921 (2); v SA 1924 (2) 1929 (1); *v A 1920 (3); v SA 1922 (5)*

Ferris, J. J. 1: *v SA 1891*

Fielder (A.) 6: *v A 1903 (2) 1907 (4)*

Fishlock (L. B.) 4: v In 1936 (2) 1946 (1); *v A 1946 (1)*

Flavell (J. A.) 4: v A 1961 (2) 1964 (2)

Fletcher, K. W. R. 59: v A 1968 (1) 1972 (1) 1975 (2); v WI 1973 (5); v NZ 1969 (2) 1973 (3); v In 1971 (2) 1974 (3); v P 1974 (3); *v A 1970 (5) 1974 (5) 1976 (1); v WI 1973 (4); v NZ 1970 (1) 1974 (2); v In 1972 (5) 1976 (3) 1981 (6); v P 1968 (3) 1972 (3); v SL 1981 (1)*

Flowers (W.) 8: v A 1893 (1); *v A 1884 (5) 1886 (2)*

Ford, F. G. J. 5: *v A 1894 (5)*

Foster, F. R. 11: v A 1912 (3); v SA 1912 (3); *v A 1911 (5)*

Foster, N. A. 19: v A 1985 (1); v WI 1984 (1); v In 1983 (1) 1986 (1); v In 1986 (1); v P 1987 (5); v WI 1985 (3); v NZ 1983 (2); v In 1984 (2); v P 1983 (2)

Foster, R. E. 8: v SA 1907 (3); v A 1903 (5)

Fothergill (A. J.) 2: v SA 1888 (2)

Fowler, G. 21: v WI 1984 (5); v NZ 1983 (2); v P 1982 (1); v SL 1984 (1); v A 1982 (3); v NZ 1983 (2); v In 1984 (5); v P 1983 (2)

Freeman (A. P.) 12: v SA 1929 (3); v WI 1928 (3); v A 1924 (2); v SA 1927 (4)

French, B. N. 9: v NZ 1986 (3); v In 1986 (2); v P 1987 (4)

Fry, C. B. 26: v A 1899 (5) 1902 (3) 1905 (4) 1909 (3) 1912 (3); v SA 1907 (3) 1912 (3); v SA 1895 (2)

Gatting, M. W. 58: v A 1980 (1) 1981 (6) 1985 (6); v WI 1980 (4) 1984 (1); v NZ 1983 (2) 1986 (3); v In 1986 (3); v P 1982 (3) 1987 (5); v A 1986 (5); v WI 1980 (1) 1985 (1); v NZ 1977 (1) 1983 (2); v In 1981 (5) 1984 (5); v P 1977 (1) 1983 (3)

Gay, L. H. 1: v A 1894

Geary (G.) 14: v A 1926 (2) 1930 (1) 1934 (2); v SA 1924 (1) 1929 (2); v A 1928 (4); v SA 1927 (2)

Gibb, P. A. 8: v In 1946 (2); v A 1946 (1); v SA 1938 (5)

Gifford, N. 15: v A 1964 (2) 1972 (3); v NZ 1973 (2); v In 1971 (2); v P 1971 (2); v In 1972 (2); v P 1972 (2)

Gilligan, A. E. R. 11: v SA 1924 (4); v A 1924 (5); v SA 1922 (2)

Gilligan, A. H. H. 4: v NZ 1929 (4)

Gimblett (H.) 3: v WI 1939 (1); v In 1936 (2)

Gladwin (C.) 8: v SA 1947 (2); v NZ 1949 (1); v SA 1948 (5)

Goddard (T. W.) 8: v A 1930 (1); v WI 1939 (2); v NZ 1937 (2); v SA 1938 (3)

Gooch, G. A. 59: v A 1975 (2) 1980 (1) 1981 (2) 1985 (6); v WI 1980 (5); v NZ 1978 (3) 1986 (3); v In 1979 (4) 1986 (3); v P 1978 (2); v A 1978 (6) 1979 (2); v WI 1980 (4) 1985 (5); v In 1979 (1) 1981 (6); v SL 1981 (1)

Gover (A. R.) 4: v NZ 1937 (2); v In 1936 (1) 1946 (1)

Gower, D. I. 96: v A 1980 (1) 1981 (5) 1985 (6); v WI 1980 (1) 1984 (1); v NZ 1978 (3) 1983 (2) 1986 (3); v In 1979 (4) 1982 (3) 1986 (2); v P 1978 (3) 1982 (3) 1987 (5); v SL 1984 (1); v A 1978 (6) 1979 (3) 1982 (5) 1986 (5); v WI 1980 (4) 1985 (5); v NZ 1983 (3); v In 1979 (1) 1981 (6) 1984 (5); v P 1983 (3); v SL 1981 (1)

Grace, E. M. 1: v A 1880

Grace, G. F. 1: v A 1880

Grace, W. G. 22: v A 1880 (1) 1882 (1) 1884 (3) 1886 (3) 1888 (3) 1890 (2) 1893 (2) 1896 (3) 1899 (1); v A 1891 (3)

Graveney, T. W. 79: v A 1953 (5) 1956 (2) 1968 (5); v SA 1951 (1) 1955 (5); v WI 1957 (4) 1966 (4) 1969 (1); v NZ 1958 (4); v In 1952 (4) 1967 (3); v P 1954 (3) 1962 (4) 1967 (3); v A 1954 (2) 1958 (5) 1962 (3); v WI 1953 (5) 1967 (5); v NZ 1954 (2) 1958 (2); v In 1951 (4); v P 1968 (3)

Greenhough (T.) 4: v SA 1960 (1); v In 1959 (3)

Greenwood (A.) 2: v A 1876 (2)

Greig, A. W. 58: v A 1972 (5) 1975 (4) 1977 (5); v WI 1973 (3) 1976 (5); v NZ 1973 (3); v In 1974 (3); v P 1974 (3); v A 1974 (6) 1976 (1); v WI 1973 (5); v NZ 1974 (2); v In 1972 (5) 1976 (5); v P 1972 (3)

Greig, I. A. 2: v P 1982 (2)

Grieve, B. A. F. 2: v SA 1888 (2)

Griffith, S. C. 3: v SA 1948 (2); v WI 1947 (1)

Gunn (G.) 15: v A 1909 (1); v A 1907 (5) 1911 (5); v WI 1929 (4)

Gunn (J.) 6: v A 1905 (1); v A 1901 (5)

Gunn (W.) 11: v A 1888 (2) 1890 (2) 1893 (2) 1896 (1) 1899 (1); v A 1886 (2)

Haig, N. E. 5: v A 1921 (1); v WI 1929 (4)

Haigh (S.) 11: v A 1905 (2) 1909 (1) 1912 (1); v SA 1898 (2) 1905 (5)

Hallows (C.) 2: v A 1921 (1); v WI 1928 (1)

Hammond, W. R. 85: v A 1930 (5) 1934 (5) 1938 (4); v SA 1929 (4) 1935 (5); v WI 1928 (3) 1933 (3) 1939 (3); v NZ 1931 (3) 1937 (3); v In 1932 (1) 1936 (2) 1946 (3); v A 1928 (5) 1932 (5) 1936 (5) 1946 (4); v SA 1927 (3) 1930 (5) 1938 (5); v WI 1934 (4); v NZ 1932 (2) 1946 (1)

Hampshire, J. H. 8: v A 1972 (1) 1975 (1); v WI 1969 (1); v A 1970 (2); v NZ 1970 (2)

Hardinge (H. T. W.) 1: v A 1921

Hardstaff (J.) 5: v A 1907 (5)

Hardstaff (J. jun.) 23: v A 1938 (3) 1948 (1); v SA 1935 (1); v WI 1939 (3); v NZ 1937 (3); v In 1936 (2) 1946 (2); v A 1936 (5) 1946 (1); v WI 1947 (3)

Harris, Lord 4: v A 1880 (1) 1884 (2); *v A 1878 (1)*
Hartley, J. C. 2: *v SA 1905 (2)*
Hawke, Lord 5: *v SA 1895 (3) 1898 (2)*
Hayes (E. G.) 5: v A 1909 (1); v SA 1912 (1); *v SA 1905 (3)*
Hayes, F. C. 9: v WI 1973 (3) 1976 (2); *v WI 1973 (4)*
Hayward (T. W.) 35: v A 1896 (2) 1899 (5) 1902 (1) 1905 (5) 1909 (1); v SA 1907 (3); *v A 1897 (5) 1901 (5) 1903 (5); v SA 1895 (3)*
Hearne (A.) 1: *v SA 1891*
Hearne (F.) 2: *v SA 1888 (2)*
Hearne (G. G.) 1: *v SA 1891*
Hearne (J. T.) 12: v A 1896 (3) 1899 (3); *v A 1897 (5); v SA 1891 (1)*
Hearne (J. W.) 24: v A 1912 (3) 1921 (1) 1926 (1); v SA 1912 (2) 1924 (3); *v A 1911 (5) 1920 (2) 1924 (4); v SA 1913 (3)*
Hemmings, E. E. 5: v P 1982 (2); *v A 1982 (3)*
Hendren (E. H.) 51: v A 1921 (2) 1926 (5) 1930 (2) 1934 (4); v SA 1924 (5) 1929 (4); v WI 1928 (1); *v A 1920 (5) 1924 (5) 1928 (5); v SA 1930 (5); v WI 1929 (4) 1934 (4)*
Hendrick, M. 30: v A 1977 (3) 1980 (1) 1981 (2); v WI 1976 (2) 1980 (2); v NZ 1978 (2); v In 1974 (3) 1979 (4); *v P 1974 (2); v A 1974 (2) 1978 (5); v NZ 1974 (1) 1977 (1)*
Heseltine, C. 2: v SA 1895 (2)
Higgs, K. 15: v A 1968 (1); v WI 1966 (5); v SA 1965 (1); v In 1967 (1); v P 1967 (3); *v A 1965 (1); v NZ 1965 (3)*
Hill (A.) 2: *v A 1876 (2)*
Hill, A. J. L. 3: *v SA 1895 (3)*
Hilton (M. J.) 4: v SA 1951 (1); v WI 1950 (1); *v In 1951 (2)*
Hirst (G. H.) 24: v A 1899 (1) 1902 (4) 1905 (3) 1909 (4); v SA 1907 (3); *v A 1897 (4) 1903 (5)*
Hitch (J. W.) 7: v A 1912 (1) 1921 (1); v SA 1912 (1); *v A 1911 (3) 1920 (1)*
Hobbs (J. B.) 61: v A 1909 (3) 1912 (3) 1921 (1) 1926 (5) 1930 (5); v SA 1912 (3) 1924 (4) 1929 (1); v WI 1928 (2); *v A 1907 (4) 1911 (5) 1920 (5) 1924 (5) 1928 (5); v SA 1909 (5) 1913 (5)*
Hobbs, R. N. S. 7: v In 1967 (3); v P 1967 (1) 1971 (1); *v WI 1967 (1); v P 1968 (1)*
Hollies (W. E.) 13: v A 1948 (1); v SA 1947 (3); v WI 1950 (2); v NZ 1949 (4); *v WI 1934 (3)*
Holmes, E. R. T. 5: v SA 1935 (1); *v WI 1934 (4)*
Holmes (P.) 7: v A 1921 (1); v In 1932 (1); *v SA 1927 (5)*
Hone, L. 1: *v A 1878*
Hopwood (J. L.) 2: v A 1934 (2)
Hornby, A. N. 3: v A 1882 (1) 1884 (1); *v A 1878 (1)*
Horton (M. J.) 2: v In 1959 (2)
Howard, N. D. 4: *v In 1951 (4)*
Howell (H.) 5: v A 1921 (1); v SA 1924 (1); *v A 1920 (3)*
Howorth (R.) 5: v SA 1947 (1); *v WI 1947 (4)*
Humphries (J.) 3: *v A 1907 (3)*
Hunter (J.) 5: *v A 1884 (5)*
Hutchings, K. L. 7: v A 1909 (2); *v A 1907 (5)*
Hutton (L.) 79: v A 1938 (3) 1948 (4) 1953 (5); v SA 1947 (5) 1951 (5); v WI 1939 (3) 1950 (3); v NZ 1937 (3) 1949 (4); v In 1946 (3) 1952 (4); v P 1954 (2); *v A 1946 (5) 1950 (5) 1954 (5); v SA 1938 (4) 1948 (5); v WI 1947 (2) 1953 (5); v NZ 1950 (2) 1954 (2)*
Hutton, R. A. 5: v In 1971 (3); v P 1971 (2)

Iddon (J.) 5: v SA 1935 (1); *v WI 1934 (4)*
Ikin (J. T.) 18: v SA 1951 (3) 1955 (1); v In 1946 (2) 1952 (2); *v A 1946 (5); v NZ 1946 (1); v WI 1947 (4)*
Illingworth (R.) 61: v A 1961 (2) 1968 (3) 1972 (5); v SA 1960 (4); v WI 1966 (2) 1969 (3) 1973 (3); v NZ 1958 (1) 1965 (1) 1969 (3) 1973 (3); v In 1959 (2) 1967 (3) 1971 (3); v P 1962 (1) 1967 (1) 1971 (3); *v A 1962 (3) 1970 (6); v WI 1959 (5); v NZ 1962 (3) 1970 (2)*
Insole, D. J. 9: v A 1956 (1); v SA 1955 (1); v WI 1950 (1) 1957 (1); *v SA 1956 (5)*

Jackman, R. D. 4: v P 1982 (2); *v WI 1980 (2)*
Jackson, F. S. 20: v A 1893 (2) 1896 (3) 1899 (5) 1902 (5) 1905 (5)
Jackson (H. L.) 2: v A 1961 (1); v NZ 1949 (1)
Jameson, J. A. 4: v In 1971 (2); *v WI 1973 (2)*
Jardine, D. R. 22: v WI 1928 (2) 1933 (2); v NZ 1931 (3); v In 1932 (1); *v A 1928 (5) 1932 (5); v NZ 1932 (1); v In 1933 (3)*
Jenkins (R. O.) 9: v WI 1950 (2); v In 1952 (2); *v SA 1948 (5)*

Jessop, G. L. 18: v A 1899 (1) 1902 (4) 1905 (1) 1909 (2); v SA 1907 (3) 1912 (2); *v A 1901* (5)

Jones, A. O. 12: v A 1899 (1) 1905 (2) 1909 (2); *v A 1901* (5) *1907* (2)

Jones, I. J. 15: v WI 1966 (2); *v A 1965* (4); *v WI 1967* (5); *v NZ 1965* (3); *v In 1963* (1)

Jupp (H.) 2: *v A 1876* (2)

Jupp, V. W. C. 8: v A 1921 (2); v WI 1928 (2); *v SA 1922* (4)

Keeton (W. W.) 2: v A 1934 (1); v WI 1939 (1)

Kennedy (A. S.) 5: *v SA 1922* (5)

Kenyon (D.) 8: v A 1953 (2); v SA 1955 (3); *v In 1951* (3)

Killick, E. T. 2: v SA 1929 (2)

Kilner (R.) 9: v A 1926 (4); v SA 1924 (2); *v A 1924* (3)

King (J. H.) 1: v A 1909

Kinneir (S. P.) 1: *v A 1911*

Knight (A. E.) 3: *v A 1903* (3)

Knight (B. R.) 29: v A 1968 (2); v WI 1966 (1) 1969 (3); v NZ 1969 (2); v P 1962 (2); *v A 1962* (1) *1965* (2); *v NZ 1962* (3) *1965* (2); *v In 1961* (4) *1963* (5); *v P 1961* (2)

Knight, D. J. 2: v A 1921 (2)

Knott, A. P. E. 95: v A 1968 (5) 1972 (5) 1975 (4) 1977 (5) 1981 (2); v WI 1969 (3) 1973 (3) 1976 (5) 1980 (4); v NZ 1969 (3) 1973 (3); v In 1971 (3) 1974 (3); v P 1967 (2) 1971 (3) 1974 (3); *v A 1970* (6) *1974* (6) *1976* (1); *v WI 1967* (2) *1973* (5); *v NZ 1970* (1) *1974* (2); *v In 1972* (5) *1976* (5); *v P 1968* (3) *1972* (3)

Knox, N. A. 2: v SA 1907 (2)

Laker (J. C.) 46: v A 1948 (3) 1953 (3) 1956 (5); v SA 1951 (2) 1955 (1); v WI 1950 (1) 1957 (4); v NZ 1949 (1) 1958 (4); v In 1952 (4); v P 1954 (1); *v A 1958* (4); *v SA 1956* (5); *v WI 1947* (4) *1953* (4)

Lamb, A. J. 51: v A 1985 (6); v WI 1984 (5); v NZ 1983 (4) 1986 (1); v In 1982 (3) 1986 (2); v P 1982 (3); v SL 1984 (1); *v A 1982* (5) *1986* (5); *v WI 1985* (5); *v NZ 1983* (3); *v In 1984* (5); *v P 1983* (3)

Langridge (James) 8: v SA 1935 (1); v WI 1933 (2); v In 1936 (1) 1946 (1); *v In 1933* (3)

Larkins, W. 6: v A 1981 (1); v WI 1980 (3); *v A 1979* (1); *v In 1979* (1)

Larter (J. D. F.) 10: v SA 1965 (2); v NZ 1965 (1); v P 1962 (1); *v NZ 1962* (3); *v In 1963* (3)

Larwood (H.) 21: v A 1926 (2) 1930 (3); v SA 1929 (3); v WI 1928 (2); v NZ 1931 (1); *v A 1928* (5) *1932* (5)

Leadbeater (E.) 2: *v In 1951* (2)

Lee (H. W.) 1: *v SA 1930*

Lees (W. S.) 5: *v SA 1905* (5)

Legge G. B. 5: *v SA 1927* (1); *v NZ 1929* (4)

Leslie, C. F. H. 4: *v A 1882* (4)

Lever, J. K. 21: v A 1977 (3); v WI 1980 (1); v In 1979 (1) 1986 (1); *v A 1976* (1) *1978* (1) *1979* (1); *v NZ 1977* (1); *v In 1976* (5) *1979* (1) *1981* (2); *v P 1977* (3)

Lever, P. 17: v A 1972 (1) 1975 (1); v In 1971 (1); v P 1971 (3); *v A 1970* (5) *1974* (2); *v NZ 1970* (2) *1974* (2)

Leveson Gower, H. D. G. 3: *v SA 1909* (3)

Levett, W. H. V. 1: *v In 1933*

Lewis, A. R. 9: v NZ 1973 (1); *v In 1972* (5); *v P 1972* (3)

Leyland (M.) 41: v A 1930 (3) 1934 (5) 1938 (1); v SA 1929 (5) 1935 (4); v WI 1928 (1) 1933 (1); v In 1936 (2); *v A 1928* (1) *1932* (5) *1936* (5); *v SA 1930* (5); *v WI 1934* (3)

Lilley (A. A.) 35: v A 1896 (3) 1899 (4) 1902 (5) 1905 (5) 1909 (5); v SA 1907 (3); *v A 1901* (5) *1903* (5)

Lillywhite (James jun.) 2: *v A 1876* (2)

Lloyd, D. 9: v In 1974 (2); v P 1974 (2); *v A 1974* (4)

Lloyd, T. A. 1: v WI 1984

Loader (P. J.) 13: v SA 1955 (1); v WI 1957 (2); v NZ 1958 (3); v P 1954 (1); *v A 1958* (2); *v SA 1956* (4)

Lock (G. A. R.) 49: v A 1953 (2) 1956 (4) 1961 (3); v SA 1955 (3); v WI 1957 (3) 1963 (3); v NZ 1958 (5); v In 1952 (2); v P 1962 (3); *v A 1958* (4); *v SA 1956* (1); *v WI 1953* (5) *1967* (2); *v NZ 1958* (2); *v In 1961* (5); *v P 1961* (2)

Lockwood (W. H.) 12: v A 1893 (2) 1899 (1) 1902 (4); *v A 1894* (5)

Lohmann (G. A.) 18: v A 1886 (3) 1888 (3) 1890 (2) 1896 (1); *v A 1886* (2) *1887* (1) *1891* (3); *v SA 1895* (3)

Lowson (F. A.) 7: v SA 1951 (2) 1955 (1); *v In 1951* (4)

Lucas, A. P. 5: v A 1880 (1) 1882 (1) 1884 (2); *v A 1887 (1)*
Luckhurst, B. W. 21: v A 1972 (4); v WI 1973 (2); v In 1971 (3); v P 1971 (3); *v A 1970 (5); 1974 (2); v NZ 1970 (2)*
Lyttelton, Hon. A. 4: v A 1880 (1) 1882 (1) 1884 (2)

Macaulay (G. G.) 8: v A 1926 (1); v SA 1924 (1); v WI 1933 (2); *v SA 1922 (4)*
MacBryan, J. C. W. 1: v SA 1924
McConnon (J. E.) 2: v P 1954 (2)
McGahey, C. P. 2: *v A 1901 (2)*
MacGregor, G. 8: v A 1890 (2) 1893 (3); *v A 1891 (3)*
McIntyre (A. J. W.) 3: v SA 1955 (1); v WI 1950 (1); *v A 1950 (10*
MacKinnon, F. A. 1: *v A 1878*
MacLaren, A. C. 35: v A 1896 (2) 1899 (4) 1902 (5) 1905 (4) 1909 (5); *v A 1894 (5) 1897 (5) 1901 (5)*
McMaster, J. E. P. 1: *v SA 1888*
Makepeace (H.) 4: *v A 1920 (4)*
Mann, F. G. 7: v NZ 1949 (2); *v SA 1948 (5)*
Mann, F. T. 5: *v SA 1922 (5)*
Marks, V. J. 6: v NZ 1983 (1); v P 1982 (1); *v NZ 1983 (1); v P 1983 (3)*
Marriott, C. S. 1: v WI 1933
Martin (F.) 2: v A 1890 (1); *v SA 1891 (1)*
Martin, J. W. 1: v SA 1947
Mason, J. R. 5: *v A 1897 (5)*
Matthews (A. D. G.) 1: v NZ 1937
May, P. B. H. 66: v A 1953 (2) 1956 (5) 1961 (4); v SA 1951 (2) 1955 (5); v WI 1957 (5); v NZ 1958 (5); v In 1952 (4) 1959 (3); v P 1954 (4); *v A 1954 (5) 1958 (5); v SA 1956 (5); v WI 1953 (5) 1959 (3); v NZ 1954 (2) 1958 (2)*
Mead (C. P.) 17: v A 1921 (2); *v A 1911 (4) 1928 (1); v SA 1913 (5) 1922 (5)*
Mead (W.) 1: v A 1899
Midwinter (W. E.) 4: *v A 1881 (4)*
Milburn, C. 9: v A 1968 (2); v WI 1966 (4); v In 1967 (1); v P 1967 (1); *v P 1968 (1)*
Miller, A. M. 1: *v SA 1895*
Miller, G. 34: v A 1977 (2); v WI 1976 (1) 1984 (2); v NZ 1978 (2); v In 1979 (3) 1982 (1); v P 1978 (3) 1982 (1); *v A 1978 (6) 1979 (1) 1982 (5); v WI 1980 (1); v NZ 1977 (3); v P 1977 (3)*
Milligan, F. W. 2: *v SA 1898 (2)*
Millman (G.) 6: v P 1962 (2); *v In 1961 (2); v P 1961 (2)*
Milton (C. A.) 6: v NZ 1958 (2); v In 1959 (2); *v A 1958 (2)*
Mitchell (A.) 6: v SA 1935 (2); v In 1936 (1); *v In 1933 (3)*
Mitchell, F. 2: *v SA 1898 (2)*
Mitchell (T. B.) 5: v A 1934 (2); v SA 1935 (1); *v A 1932 (1); v NZ 1932 (1)*
Mitchell-Innes, N. S. 1: v SA 1935
Mold (A. W.) 3: v A 1893 (3)
Moon, L. J. 4: *v SA 1905 (4)*
Morley (F.) 4: v A 1880 (1); *v A 1882 (3)*
Mortimore (J. B.) 9: v A 1964 (1); v In 1959 (2); *v A 1958 (1); v NZ 1958 (2); v In 1963 (3)*
Moss (A. E.) 9: v A 1956 (1); v SA 1960 (2); v In 1959 (3); *v WI 1953 (1) 1959 (2)*
Moxon, M. D. 3: v NZ 1986 (2); v P 1987 (1)
Murdoch, W. L. 1: *v SA 1891*
Murray, J. T. 21: v A 1961 (5); v WI 1966 (1); v In 1967 (3) 1962 1967; *v A 1962 (1); v SA 1964 (1); v NZ 1962 (1) 1965 (1); v In 1961 (3); v P 1961 (1)*

Newham (W.) 1: *v A 1887*
Nichols (M. S.) 14: v A 1930 (1); v SA 1935 (4); v WI 1933 (1) 1939 (1); *v NZ 1929 (4); v In 1933 (3)*

Oakman (A. S. M.) 2: v A 1956 (2)
O'Brien, T. C. 5: v A 1884 (1) 1888 (1); *v SA 1895 (3)*
O'Connor (J.) 4: v SA 1929 (1); *v WI 1929 (3)*
Old, C. M. 46: v A 1975 (3) 1977 (2) 1980 (1) 1981 (2); v WI 1973 (1) 1976 (2) 1980 (1); v NZ 1973 (2) 1978 (1); v P 1974 (3) 1978 (3); *v A 1974 (2) 1976 (1) 1978 (1); v WI 1973 (4) 1980 (1); v NZ 1974 (1) 1977 (2); v In 1972 (4) 1976 (4); v P 1972 (1) 1977 (1)*
Oldfield (N.) 1: v WI 1939

Padgett (D. E. V.) 2: v SA 1960 (2)
Paine (G. A. E.) 4: *v WI 1934 (4)*
Palairet, L. C. H. 2: v A 1902 (2)
Palmer, C. H. 1: *v WI 1953*
Palmer, K. E. 1: *v SA 1964*
Parfitt (P. H.) 37: v A 1964 (4) 1972 (3); v SA 1965 (4); v WI 1969 (1); v NZ 1965 (2); v P 1962 (5); *v A 1962 (2); v SA 1964 (5); v NZ 1962 (3) 1965 (3); v In 1961 (2) 1963 (3); v P 1961 (2)*
Parker (C. W. L.) 1: v A 1921
Parker, P. W. G. 1: v A 1981
Parkhouse (W. G. A.) 7: v WI 1950 (2); v In 1959 (2); *v A 1950 (2); v NZ 1950 (1)*
Parkin (C. H.) 10: v A 1921 (4); v SA 1924 (1); *v A 1920 (5)*
Parks (J. H.) 1: v NZ 1937
Parks (J. M.) 46: v A 1964 (5); v SA 1960 (5) 1965 (3); v WI 1963 (4) 1966 (4); v NZ 1965 (3); v P 1954 (1); *v A 1965 (5); v SA 1964 (5); v WI 1959 (1) 1967 (3); v NZ 1965 (2); v In 1963 (5)*
Pataudi, Nawab of, 3: v A 1934 (1); *v A 1932 (2)*
Paynter (E.) 20: v A 1938 (4); v WI 1939 (2); v NZ 1931 (1) 1937 (2); v In 1932 (1); *v A 1932 (3); v SA 1938 (5); v NZ 1932 (2)*
Peate (E.) 9: v A 1882 (1) 1884 (3) 1886 (1); *v A 1881 (4)*
Peebles, I. A. R. 13: v A 1930 (2); v NZ 1931 (3); *v A 1927 (4) 1930 (2)*
Peel (R.) 20: v A 1888 (3) 1890 (1) 1893 (1) 1896 (1); *v A 1884 (5) 1887 (1) 1891 (3) 1894 (5)*
Penn, F. 1: v A 1880
Perks (R. T. D.) 2: v WI 1939 (1); *v SA 1938 (1)*
Philipson, (H.) 5: *v A 1891 (1) 1894 (4)*
Pigott, A. C. S. 1: *v NZ 1983*
Pilling (R.) 8: v A 1884 (1) 1886 (1) 1888 (1); *v A 1881 (4) 1887 (1)*
Place (W.) 3: *v WI 1947 (3)*
Pocock, P. I. 25: v A 1968 (1); v WI 1976 (2) 1984 (2); v SL 1984 (1); *v WI 1967 (2) 1973 (4); v In 1972 (4) 1984 (5); v P 1968 (1) 1972 (3)*
Pollard (R.) 4: v A 1948 (2); v In 1946 (1); *v NZ 1946 (1)*
Poole (C. J.) 3: *v In 1951 (3)*
Pope (G. H.) 1: v SA 1947
Pougher (A. D.) 1: *v SA 1891*
Price, J. S. E. 15: v A 1964 (2) 1972 (1); v In 1971 (3); v P 1971 (1); *v SA 1964 (4); v In 1963 (4)*
Price (W. F. F.) 1: v A 1938
Prideaux, R. M. 3: v A 1968 (1); *v P 1968 (2)*
Pringle, D. R. 14: v WI 1984 (2); v NZ 1986 (1); v In 1982 (3) 1986 (3); v P 1982 (1); *v A 1982 (3)*
Pullar (G.) 28: v A 1961 (5); v SA 1960 (3); v In 1959 (3); v P 1962 (2); *v A 1962 (4); v WI 1959 (5); v In 1961 (3); v P 1961 (3)*

Quaife (W. G.) 7: v A 1899 (2); *v A 1901 (5)*

Radford, N. V. 2: v NZ 1986 (1); v In 1986 (1)
Radley, C. T. 8: v NZ 1978 (3); v P 1978 (3); *v NZ 1977 (2)*
Randall, D. W. 47: v A 1977 (5); v WI 1984 (1); v NZ 1983 (3); v In 1979 (3) 1982 (3); v P 1982 (3); *v A 1976 (1) 1978 (6) 1979 (2) 1982 (4); v NZ 1977 (3) 1983 (3); v In 1976 (4); v P 1977 (3) 1983 (3)*
Ranjitsinhji, K. S. 15: v A 1896 (2) 1899 (5) 1902 (3); *v A 1897 (5)*
Read, H. D. 1: v SA 1935
Read (J. M.) 17: v A 1882 (1) 1890 (2) 1893 (1); *v A 1884 (5) 1886 (2) 1887 (1) 1891 (3); v SA 1888 (2)*
Read, W. W. 18: v A 1884 (2) 1886 (3) 1888 (3) 1890 (2) 1893 (2); *v A 1882 (3) 1887 (1); v SA 1891 (1)*
Relf (A. E.) 13: v A 1909 (1); *v A 1903 (2); v SA 1905 (5) 1913 (5)*
Rhodes (H. J.) 2: v In 1959 (2)
Rhodes (W.) 58: v A 1899 (3) 1902 (5) 1905 (4) 1909 (4) 1912 (3) 1921 (1) 1926 (1); v SA 1912 (3); *v A 1903 (5) 1907 (5) 1911 (5) 1920 (5); v SA 1909 (5) 1913 (5); v WI 1929 (4)*
Richards, C. J. 6: v P 1987 (1); *v A 1986 (5)*
Richardson (D. W.) 1: v WI 1957
Richardson (P. E.) 34: v A 1956 (5); v WI 1957 (5) 1963 (1); v NZ 1958 (4); *v A 1958 (4); v SA 1956 (5); v NZ 1958 (2); v In 1961 (5); v P 1961 (3)*
Richardson (T.) 14: v A 1893 (1) 1896 (3); *v A 1894 (5) 1897 (5)*
Richmond (T. L.) 1: v A 1921

Ridgway (F.) 5: *v In 1951* (5)

Robertson (J. D.) 11: v SA 1947 (1); v NZ 1949 (1); *v WI 1947* (4); *v In 1951* (5)

Robins, R. W. V. 19: v A 1930 (2); v SA 1929 (1) 1935 (3); v WI 1933 (2); v NZ 1931 (1) 1937 (3); v In 1932 (1) 1936 (2); *v A 1936* (4)

Robinson, R. T. 21: v A 1985 (6); v In 1986 (1); v P 1987 (5); *v WI 1985* (4); *v In 1984* (5)

Roope, G. R. J. 21: v A 1975 (1) 1977 (2); v WI 1973 (1); v NZ 1973 (3) 1978 (1); v P 1978 (3); *v NZ 1977* (3); *v In 1972* (2); *v P 1972* (2) *1977* (3)

Root (C. F.) 3: v A 1926 (3)

Rose, B. C. 9: v WI 1980 (3); *v WI 1980* (1); *v NZ 1977* (2); *v P 1977* (3)

Royle, V. P. F. A. 1: *v A 1878*

Rumsey, F. E. 5: v A 1964 (1); v SA 1965 (1); v NZ 1965 (3)

Russell (A. C.) 10: v A 1921 (2); *v A 1920* (4); *v SA 1922* (4)

Russell, W. E. 10: SA 1965 (1); v WI 1966 (2); v P 1967 (1); *v A 1965* (1); *v NZ 1965* (3); *v In 1961* (1); *v P 1961* (1)

Sandham (A.) 14: v A 1921 (1); v SA 1924 (2); *v A 1924* (2); *v SA 1922* (5); *v WI 1929* (4)

Schultz, S. S. 1: *v A 1878*

Scotton (W. H.) 15: v A 1884 (1) 1886 (3); *v A 1881* (4) *1884* (5) *1886* (2)

Selby (J.) 6: *v A 1876* (2) *1881* (4)

Selvey, M. W. W. 3: v WI 1976 (2); *v In 1976* (1)

Shackleton (D.) 7: v SA 1951 (1); v WI 1950 (1) 1963 (4); *v In 1951* (1)

Sharp (J.) 3: v A 1909 (3)

Sharpe (J. W.) 3: v A 1890 (1); *v A 1891* (2)

Sharpe, P. J. 12: v A 1964 (2); v WI 1963 (3) 1969 (3); v NZ 1969 (3); *v In 1963* (1)

Shaw (A.) 7: v A 1880 (1); *v A 1876* (2) *1881* (4)

Sheppard, Rev. D. S. 22: v A 1956 (2); v WI 1950 (1) 1957 (2); v In 1952 (2); v P 1954 (2) 1962 (2); *v A 1950* (2) *1962* (5); *v NZ 1950* (1) *1963* (3)

Sherwin (M.) 3: v A 1888 (1); *v A 1886* (2)

Shrewsbury (A.) 23: v A 1884 (2) 1886 (3) 1890 (2) 1893 (3); *v A 1881* (4) *1884* (5) *1886* (2) *1887* (1)

Shuter, J. 1: v A 1888

Shuttleworth, K. 5: v P 1971 (1); *v A 1970* (2); *v NZ 1970* (2)

Sidebottom, A. 1: v A 1985

Simpson, R. T. 27: v A 1953 (3); v SA 1951 (3); v WI 1950 (3); v NZ 1949 (2); v In 1952 (2); v P 1954 (3); *v A 1950* (5) *1954* (1); *v SA 1948* (1); *v NZ 1950* (2) *1954* (2)

Simpson-Hayward, G. H. 5: *v SA 1909* (5)

Sims (J. M.) 4: v SA 1935 (1); v In 1936 (1); *v A 1936* (2)

Sinfield (R. A.) 1: v A 1938

Slack, W. N. 3: v In 1986 (1); *v WI 1985* (2)

Smailes (T. F.) 1: v In 1946

Small, G. C. 4: v NZ 1986 (2); *v A 1986* (2)

Smith, A. C. 6: *v A 1962* (4); *v NZ 1962* (2)

Smith, C. A. 1: *v SA 1888*

Smith (C. I. J.) 5: v NZ 1937 (1); *v WI 1934* (4)

Smith, C. L. 8: v NZ 1983 (2); v In 1986 (1); *v NZ 1983* (2); *v P 1983* (3)

Smith (D.) 2: v SA 1935 (2)

Smith D. M. 2: *v WI 1985* (2)

Smith (D. R.) 5: *v In 1961* (5)

Smith (D. V.) 3: v WI 1957 (3)

Smith (E. J.) 11: v A 1912 (3); v SA 1912 (3); *v A 1911* (4); *v SA 1913* (1)

Smith (H.) 1: v WI 1928

Smith, M. J. K. 50: v A 1961 (1) 1972 (3); v SA 1960 (4) 1965 (3); v WI 1966 (1); v NZ 1958 (3) 1965 (3); v In 1959 (2); *v A 1965* (5); *v SA 1964* (5); *v WI 1959* (5); *v NZ 1965* (3); *v In 1961* (4) *1963* (5); *v P 1961* (3)

Smith (T. P. B.) 4: v In 1946 (1); *v A 1946* (2); *v NZ 1946* (1)

Smithson (G. A.) 2: *v WI 1947* (2)

Snow, J. A. 49: v A 1968 (5) 1972 (5) 1975 (4); v SA 1965 (1); v WI 1966 (3) 1969 (3) 1973 (3) 1976 (3); v NZ 1965 (1) 1969 (2) 1973 (3); v In 1967 (3) 1971 (2); v P 1967 (1); *v A 1970* (6); *v WI 1967* (4); *v P 1968* (2)

Southerton (J.) 2: *v A 1876* (2)

Spooner, R. H. 10: v A 1905 (2) 1909 (2) 1912 (3); v SA 1912 (3)

Spooner (R. T.) 7: v SA 1955 (1); *v In 1951* (5); *v WI 1953* (1)

Stanyforth, R. T. 4: *v SA 1927* (4)

Staples (S. J.) 3: *v SA 1927 (3)*

Statham (J. B.) 70: v A 1953 (1) 1956 (3) 1961 (4); v SA 1951 (2) 1955 (4) 1960 (5) 1965 (1); v WI 1957 (3) 1963 (2); v NZ 1958 (2); v In 1959 (3); v P 1954 (4) 1962 (3); *v A 1954 (5) 1958 (4) 1962 (5); v SA 1956 (4); v WI 1953 (4) 1959 (3); v NZ 1950 (1) 1954 (2); v In 1951 (5)*

Steel, A. G. 13: v A 1880 (1) 1882 (1) 1884 (3) 1886 (3) 1888 (1); *v A 1882 (4)*

Steele, D. S. 8: v A 1975 (3); v WI 1976 (5)

Stevens, G. T. S. 10: v A 1926 (2); *v SA 1922 (1) 1927 (5); v WI 1929 (2)*

Stevenson, G. B. 2: *v WI 1980 (1); v In 1979 (1)*

Stewart (M. J.) 8: v WI 1963 (4); v P 1962 (2); *v In 1963 (2)*

Stoddart, A. E. 16: v A 1893 (3) 1896 (2); *v A 1887 (1) 1891 (3) 1894 (5) 1897 (2)*

Storer (W.) 6: v A 1899 (1); *v A 1897 (5)*

Street (G. B.) 1: *v SA 1922*

Strudwick (H.) 28: v A 1921 (2) 1926 (5); v SA 1924 (1); *v A 1911 (1) 1920 (4) 1924 (5); v SA 1909 (5) 1913 (5)*

Studd, C. T. 5: v A 1882 (1); *v A 1882 (4)*

Studd, G. B. 4: *v A 1882 (4)*

Subba Row, R. 13: v A 1961 (5); v SA 1960 (4); v NZ 1958 (1); v In 1959 (1); *v WI 1959 (2)*

Sugg (F. H.) 2: v A 1888 (2)

Sutcliffe (H.) 54: v A 1926 (5) 1930 (4) 1934 (4); v SA 1924 (5) 1929 (5) 1935 (2); v WI 1928 (3) 1933 (2); v NZ 1931 (2); v In 1932 (1); *v A 1924 (5) 1928 (4) 1932 (5); v SA 1927 (5); v NZ 1932 (2)*

Swetman (R.) 11: v In 1959 (3); *v A 1958 (2); v WI 1959 (4); v NZ 1958 (2)*

Tate (F. W.) 1: v A 1902

Tate (M. W.) 39: v A 1926 (5) 1930 (5); v SA 1924 (5) 1929 (3) 1935 (1); v WI 1928 (3); v NZ 1931 (1); *v A 1924 (5) 1928 (5); v SA 1930 (5); v NZ 1932 (1)*

Tattersall (R.) 16: v A 1953 (1); v SA 1951 (5); v P 1954 (1); *v A 1950 (2); v NZ 1950 (2); v In 1951 (5)*

Tavaré, C. J. 30: v A 1981 (2); v WI 1980 (2) 1984 (1); v NZ 1983 (4); v In 1982 (3); v P 1982 (3); v SL 1984 (3); *v A 1982 (5); v NZ 1983 (2); v In 1981 (6); v SL 1981 (1)*

Taylor (K.) 3: v A 1964 (1); v In 1959 (2)

Taylor, L. B. 2: v A 1985 (2)

Taylor, R. W. 57: v A 1981 (3); v NZ 1978 (3) 1983 (4); v In 1979 (3) 1982 (3); v P 1978 (3) 1982 (3); *v A 1978 (6) 1979 (3) 1982 (5); v NZ 1970 (1) 1977 (3) 1983 (3); v In 1979 (1) 1981 (6); v P 1977 (3) 1983 (3); v SL 1981 (1)*

Tennyson, Hon. L. H. 9: v A 1921 (4); *v SA 1913 (5)*

Terry, V. P. 2: v WI 1984 (2)

Thomas, J. G. 5: v NZ 1986 (1); *v WI 1985 (4)*

Thompson (G. J.) 6: v A 1909 (1); *v SA 1909 (5)*

Thomson, N. I. 5: *v SA 1964 (5)*

Titmus (F. J.) 53: v A 1964 (5); v SA 1955 (2) 1965 (3); v WI 1963 (4) 1966 (3); v NZ 1965 (3); v P 1962 (2) 1967 (2); *v A 1962 (5) 1965 (5) 1974 (4); v SA 1964 (5); v WI 1967 (2); v NZ 1962 (3); v In 1963 (5)*

Tolchard, R. W. 4: *v In 1976 (4)*

Townsend, C. L. 2: v A 1899 (2)

Townsend, D. C. H. 3: *v WI 1934 (3)*

Townsend (L. F.) 4: *v WI 1929 (1); v In 1933 (3)*

Tremlett (M. F.) 3: *v WI 1947 (3)*

Trott (A. E.) 2: *v SA 1898 (2)*

Trueman (F. S.) 67: v A 1953 (1) 1956 (2) 1961 (4) 1964 (4); v SA 1955 (1) 1960 (5); v WI 1957 (5) 1963 (5); v NZ 1958 (5) 1965 (2); v In 1952 (4) 1959 (5); v P 1962 (4); *v A 1958 (3) 1962 (5); v WI 1953 (3) 1959 (5); v NZ 1958 (2) 1962 (2)*

Tufnell, N. C. 1: *v SA 1909*

Turnbull, M. J. 9: v WI 1933 (2); v In 1936 (1); *v SA 1930 (5); v NZ 1929 (1)*

Tyldesley (E.) 14: v A 1921 (3) 1926 (1); v SA 1924 (1); v WI 1928 (3); *v A 1928 (1); v SA 1927 (5)*

Tyldesley (J. T.) 31: v A 1899 (2) 1902 (5) 1905 (5) 1909 (4); v SA 1907 (3); *v A 1901 (5) 1903 (5); v SA 1898 (2)*

Tyldesley (R. K.) 7: v A 1930 (2); v SA 1924 (4); *v A 1924 (1)*

Tylecote, E. F. S. 6: v A 1886 (2); *v A 1882 (4)*

Tyler (E. J.) 1: *v SA 1895*

Tyson (F. H.) 17: v A 1956 (1); v SA 1955 (2); v P 1954 (1); *v A 1954 (5) 1958 (2); v SA 1956 (2); v NZ 1954 (2) 1958 (2)*

Ulyett (G.) 25: v A 1882 (1) 1884 (3) 1886 (3) 1888 (2) 1890 (1); *v A 1876 (2) 1878 (1) 1881 (4) 1884 (5) 1887 (1); v SA 1888 (2)*

Underwood, D. L. 86: v A 1968 (4) 1972 (2) 1975 (4) 1977 (5); v WI 1966 (2) 1969 (2) 1973 (3) 1976 (5) 1980 (1); v NZ 1969 (3) 1973 (1); v In 1971 (1) 1974 (3); v P 1967 (2) 1971 (1) 1974 (3); *v A 1970 (5) 1974 (5) 1976 (1) 1979 (3); v WI 1973 (4); v NZ 1970 (2) 1974 (2); v In 1972 (4) 1976 (5) 1979 (1) 1981 (6); v P 1968 (3) 1972 (2); v SL 1981 (1)*

Valentine, B. H. 7: *v SA 1938 (5); v In 1933 (2)*

Verity (H.) 40: v A 1934 (5) 1938 (4); v SA 1935 (4); v WI 1933 (2) 1939 (1); v NZ 1931 (2) 1937 (1); v In 1936 (3); *v A 1932 (4) 1936 (5); v SA 1938 (5); v NZ 1932 (1); v In 1933 (3)*

Vernon, G. F. 1: *v A 1882*

Vine (J.) 2: *v A 1911 (2)*

Voce (W.) 27: v NZ 1931 (1) 1937 (1); v In 1932 (1) 1936 (1) 1946 (1); *v A 1932 (4) 1936 (5) 1946 (2); v SA 1930 (5); v WI 1929 (4); v NZ 1932 (2)*

Waddington (A.) 2: *v A 1920 (2)*

Wainwright (E.) 5: v A 1893 (1); *v A 1897 (4)*

Walker (P. M.) 3: v SA 1960 (3)

Walters, C. F. 11: v A 1934 (5); v WI 1933 (3); *v In 1933 (5)*

Ward, A. 5: v WI 1976 (1); v NZ 1969 (3); v P 1971 (1)

Ward (A.) 7: v A 1893 (2); *v A 1894 (5)*

Wardle (J. H.) 28: v A 1953 (3) 1956 (1); v SA 1951 (2) 1955 (3); v WI 1950 (1) 1957 (1); v P 1954 (4); *v A 1954 (4); v SA 1956 (4); v WI 1947 (1) 1953 (2); v NZ 1954 (2)*

Warner, P. F. 15: v A 1909 (1) 1912 (1); v SA 1912 (1); *v A 1903 (5); v SA 1898 (2) 1905 (5)*

Warr, J. J. 2: *v A 1950 (2)*

Warren (A. R.) 1: v A 1905

Washbrook (C.) 37: v A 1948 (4) 1956 (3); v SA 1947 (5); v WI 1950 (2); v NZ 1937 (1) 1949 (2); v In 1946 (3); *v A 1946 (5) 1950 (5); v SA 1948 (5); v NZ 1946 (1) 1950 (1)*

Watkins (A. J.) 15: v A 1948 (1); v NZ 1949 (1); v In 1952 (3); *v SA 1948 (5); v In 1951 (5)*

Watson (W.) 23: v A 1953 (3) 1956 (2); v SA 1951 (1) 1955 (1); v NZ 1958 (2); v In 1952 (1); *v A 1958 (2); v WI 1953 (5); v NZ 1958 (2)*

Webbe, A. J. 1: *v A 1878*

Wellard (A. W.) 2: v A 1938 (1); v NZ 1937 (1)

Wharton (A.) 1: v NZ 1949

Whitaker, J. J. 1: *v A 1986*

White (D. W.) 2: *v P 1961 (2)*

White, J. C. 15: v A 1921 (1) 1930 (1); v SA 1929 (3); v WI 1928 (1); *v A 1928 (5); v SA 1930 (4)*

Whysall (W. W.) 4: v A 1930 (1); *v A 1924 (3)*

Wilkinson (L. L.) 3: *v SA 1938 (3)*

Willey, P. 26: v A 1980 (1) 1981 (4) 1985 (1); v WI 1976 (2) 1980 (5); v NZ 1986 (1); v In 1979 (1); *v A 1979 (3); v WI 1980 (4) 1985 (4)*

Willis, R. G. D. 90: v A 1977 (5) 1981 (6); v WI 1973 (1) 1976 (2) 1980 (4) 1984 (3); v NZ 1978 (3) 1983 (3); v In 1974 (1) 1979 (3) 1982 (3); v P 1974 (1) 1978 (3) 1982 (2); *v A 1970 (4) 1974 (5) 1976 (1) 1978 (6) 1979 (3) 1982 (5); v WI 1973 (3); v NZ 1970 (1) 1977 (3) 1983 (3); v In 1976 (5) 1981 (5); v P 1977 (3) 1983 (1); v SL 1981 (1)*

Wilson, C. E. M. 2: *v SA 1898 (2)*

Wilson, D. 6: *v NZ 1970 (1); v In 1963 (5)*

Wilson, E. R. 1: *v A 1920*

Wood (A.) 4: v A 1938 (1); v WI 1939 (3)

Wood, B. 12: v A 1972 (1) 1975 (3); v WI 1976 (1); v P 1978 (1); *v NZ 1974 (2); v In 1972 (3); v P 1972 (1)*

Wood, G. E. C. 3: v SA 1924 (3)

Wood (H.) 4: v A 1888 (1); *v SA 1888 (2) 1891 (1)*

Wood (R.) 1: *v A 1886*

Woods S. M. J. 3: *v SA 1895 (3)*

Woolley (F. E.) 64: v A 1909 (1) 1912 (3) 1921 (5) 1926 (5) 1930 (2) 1934 (1); v SA 1912 (3) 1924 (5) 1929 (3); v NZ 1931 (1); v In 1932 (1); *v A 1911 (5) 1920 (5) 1924 (5); v SA 1909 (5) 1913 (5) 1922 (5); v NZ 1929 (4)*

Woolmer, R. A. 19: v A 1975 (2) 1977 (5) 1981 (2); v WI 1976 (5) 1980 (2); *v A 1976 (1); v In 1976 (2)*

Worthington (T. S.) 9: v In 1936 (2); *v A 1936 (3); v NZ 1929 (4)*

Wright, C. W. 3: *v SA 1895 (3)*

Wright (D. V. P.) 34: v A 1938 (3) 1948 (1); v SA 1947 (4); v WI 1939 (3) 1950 (1); v NZ 1949 (1); v In 1946 (2); *v A 1946 (5) 1950 (5); v SA 1938 (3) 1948 (3); v NZ 1946 (1)*

Wyatt, R. E. S. 40: v A 1930 (1) 1934 (4); v SA 1929 (2) 1935 (5); v WI 1933 (2); v In 1936 (1); *v A 1932 (5) 1936 (2); v SA 1927 (5) 1930 (5); v WI 1929 (2) 1934 (4); v NZ 1932 (2)*

Wynyard, E. G. 3: v A 1896 (1); *v SA 1905 (2)*

Yardley, N. W. D. 20: v A 1948 (5); v SA 1947 (5); v WI 1950 (3); *v A 1946 (5); v SA 1938 (1); v NZ 1946 (1)*

Young (H. I.) 2: v A 1899 (2)

Young (J. A.) 8: v A 1948 (3); v SA 1947 (1); v NZ 1949 (2); *v SA 1948 (2)*

Young, R. A. 2: *v A 1907 (2)*

AUSTRALIA

Number of Test cricketers: 340

A'Beckett, E. L. 4: v E 1928 (2); v SA 1931 (1); *v E 1930 (1)*

Alderman, T. M. 22: v E 1982 (1); v WI 1981 (2) 1984 (3); v P 1981 (3); *v E 1981 (6); v WI 1983 (3); v NZ 1981 (3); v P 1982 (1)*

Alexander, G. 2: v E 1884 (1); *v E 1880 (1)*

Alexander, H. H. 1: v E 1932

Allan, F. E. 1: v E 1878

Allan, P. J. 1: v E 1965

Allen, R. C. 1: v E 1886

Andrews, T. J. E. 16: v E 1924 (3); *v E 1921 (5) 1926 (5); v SA 1921 (3)*

Archer, K. A. 5: v E 1950 (3); v WI 1951 (2)

Archer, R. G. 19: v E 1954 (4); v SA 1952 (1); *v E 1953 (3) 1956 (5); v WI 1954 (5); v P 1956 (1)*

Armstrong, W. W. 50: v E 1901 (4) 1903 (3) 1907 (5) 1911 (5) 1920 (5); v SA 1910 (5); *v E 1902 (5) 1905 (5) 1909 (5) 1921 (5); v SA 1902 (3)*

Badcock, C. L. 7: v E 1936 (3); *v E 1938 (4)*

Bannerman, A. C. 28: v E 1878 (1) 1881 (3) 1882 (4) 1884 (4) 1886 (1) 1887 (1) 1891 (3); *v E 1880 (1) 1882 (1) 1884 (3) 1888 (3) 1893 (3)*

Bannerman, C. 3: v E 1876 (2) 1878 (1)

Bardsley, W. 41: v E 1911 (4) 1920 (5) 1924 (3); v SA 1910 (5); *v E 1909 (5) 1912 (3) 1921 (5) 1926 (5); v SA 1912 (3) 1921 (3)*

Barnes, S. G. 13: v E 1946 (4); v In 1947 (5); *v E 1938 (1) 1948 (4); v NZ 1945 (1)*

Barnett, B. A. 4: *v E 1938 (4)*

Barrett, J. E. 2: *v E 1890 (2)*

Beard, G. R. 3: v P 1979 (3)

Benaud, J. 3: v P 1972 (2); *v WI 1972 (1)*

Benaud, R. 63: v E 1954 (5) 1958 (5) 1962 (5); v SA 1952 (4) 1963 (4); v WI 1951 (1) 1960 (5); *v E 1953 (3) 1956 (5) 1961 (4); v SA 1957 (5); v WI 1954 (5); v In 1956 (3) 1959 (5); v P 1956 (1) 1959 (3)*

Bennett, M. J. 3: v WI 1984 (2); *v E 1985 (1)*

Blackham, J. McC. 35: v E 1876 (2) 1878 (1) 1881 (4) 1882 (4) 1884 (2) 1886 (1) 1887 (1) 1891 (3) 1894 (1); *v E 1880 (1) 1882 (1) 1884 (3) 1886 (3) 1888 (3) 1890 (3) 1893 (3)*

Blackie, D. D. 3: v E 1928 (3)

Bonnor, G. J. 17: v E 1882 (4) 1884 (3); *v E 1880 (1) 1882 (1) 1884 (3) 1886 (2) 1888 (3)*

Boon, D. C. 23: v E 1986 (4); v WI 1984 (3); v NZ 1985 (3); v In 1985 (3); *v E 1985 (4); v NZ 1985 (3); v In 1986 (3)*

Booth, B. C. 29: v E 1962 (5) 1965 (3); v SA 1963 (4); v P 1964 (1); *v E 1961 (2) 1964 (5); v WI 1964 (5); v In 1964 (3); v P 1964 (1)*

Border, A. R. 89: v E 1978 (3) 1979 (3) 1982 (5) 1986 (5); v WI 1979 (3) 1981 (3) 1984 (5); v NZ 1980 (3) 1985 (3); v In 1980 (3) 1985 (3); v P 1978 (2) 1981 (3) 1983 (5); *v E 1980 (1) 1981 (6) 1985 (6); v WI 1983 (5); v NZ 1981 (3) 1985 (3); v In 1979 (6) 1986 (3); v P 1979 (3) 1982 (3); v SL 1982 (1)*

Boyle, H. F. 12: v E 1878 (1) 1881 (4) 1882 (1) 1884 (1); *v E 1880 (1) 1882 (1) 1884 (3)*

Bradman, D. G. 52: v E 1928 (4) 1932 (4) 1936 (5) 1946 (5); v SA 1931 (5); v WI 1930 (5); v In 1947 (5); *v E 1930 (5) 1934 (5) 1938 (4) 1948 (5)*

Bright, R. J. 25: v E 1979 (1); v WI 1979 (1); v NZ 1985 (1); v In 1985 (1); *v E 1977 (3) 1980 (1) 1981 (5); v NZ 1985 (2); v In 1986 (3); v P 1979 (3) 1982 (2)*

Bromley, E. H. 2: v E 1932 (1); *v E 1934 (1)*
Brown, W. A. 22: v E 1936 (2); v In 1947 (3); *v E 1934 (5) 1938 (4) 1948 (2); v SA 1935 (5); v NZ 1945 (1)*
Bruce, W. 14: v E 1884 (2) 1891 (3) 1894 (4); *v E 1886 (2) 1893 (3)*
Burge, P. J. 42: v E 1954 (1) 1958 (1) 1962 (3) 1965 (4); v SA 1963 (5); v WI 1960 (2); *v E 1956 (3) 1961 (5) 1964 (5); v SA 1957 (1); v WI 1954 (1); v In 1956 (3) 1959 (2) 1964 (3); v P 1959 (2) 1964 (1)*
Burke, J. W. 24: v E 1950 (2) 1954 (2) 1958 (5); v WI 1951 (1); *v E 1956 (5); v SA 1957 (5); v In 1956 (3); v P 1956 (1)*
Burn, K. E. 2: *v E 1890 (2)*
Burton, F. J. 2: v E 1886 (1) 1887 (1)

Callaway, S. T. 3: v E 1891 (2) 1894 (1)
Callen, I. W. 1: v In 1977
Carkeek, W. 6: *v E 1912 (3); v SA 1912 (3)*
Carlson, P. H. 2: v E 1978 (2)
Carter, H. 28: v E 1907 (5) 1911 (5) 1920 (2); v SA 1910 (5); *v E 1909 (5) 1921 (4); v SA 1921 (2)*
Chappell, G. S. 87: v E 1970 (5) 1974 (6) 1976 (1) 1979 (3) 1982 (5); v WI 1975 (6) 1979 (3) 1981 (3); v NZ 1973 (3) 1980 (3); v In 1980 (3); v P 1972 (3) 1976 (3) 1981 (3) 1983 (5); *v E 1972 (5) 1975 (4) 1977 (5) 1980 (1); v WI 1972 (5); v NZ 1973 (3) 1976 (2) 1981 (3); v P 1979 (3); v SL 1982 (1)*
Chappell, I. M. 75: v E 1965 (2) 1970 (6) 1974 (6) 1979 (2); v WI 1968 (5) 1975 (6) 1979 (1); v NZ 1973 (3); v In 1967 (4); *v P 1964 (1) 1972 (5) 1975 (4); v SA 1966 (5) 1969 (4); v WI 1972 (5); v NZ 1973 (3); v In 1969 (5)*
Chappell, T. M. 3: *v E 1981 (3)*
Charlton, P. C. 2: *v E 1890 (2)*
Chipperfield, A. G. 14: v E 1936 (3); *v E 1934 (5) 1938 (1); v SA 1935 (5)*
Clark, W. M. 10: v In 1977 (5); v P 1978 (1); *v WI 1977 (4)*
Colley, D. J. 3: *v E 1972 (3)*
Collins, H. L. 19: v E 1920 (5) 1924 (5); *v E 1921 (3) 1926 (3); v SA 1921 (3)*
Coningham, A. 1: v E 1894
Connolly, A. N. 29: v E 1965 (1) 1970 (1); v SA 1963 (3); v WI 1968 (5); v In 1967 (3); *v E 1968 (5); v SA 1969 (4); v In 1964 (2); 1969 (5)*
Cooper, B. B. 1: v E 1876
Cooper, W. H. 2: v E 1881 (1) 1884 (1)
Corling, G. E. 5: *v E 1964 (5)*
Cosier, G. J. 18: v E 1976 (1) 1978 (2); v WI 1975 (3); v In 1977 (4); v P 1976 (3); *v WI 1977 (3); v NZ 1976 (2)*
Cottam, W. J. 1: v E 1886
Cotter, A. 21: v E 1903 (2) 1907 (2) 1911 (4); v SA 1910 (5); *v E 1905 (3) 1909 (5)*
Coulthard, G. 1: v E 1881
Cowper, R. M. 27: v E 1965 (4); v In 1967 (4); v P 1964 (1); *v E 1964 (1) 1968 (4); v SA 1966 (5); v WI 1964 (5); v In 1964 (2); v P 1964 (1)*
Craig, I. D. 11: v SA 1952 (1); *v E 1956 (2); v SA 1957 (5); v In 1956 (2); v P 1956 (1)*
Crawford, W. P. A. 4: *v E 1956 (1); v In 1956 (3)*

Darling, J. 34: v E 1894 (5) 1897 (5) 1901 (5); *v E 1896 (3) 1899 (5) 1902 (5) 1905 (5); v SA 1902 (3)*
Darling, L. S. 12: v E 1932 (2) 1936 (1); *v E 1934 (4); v SA 1935 (5)*
Darling, W. M. 14: v E 1978 (4); v In 1977 (1); v P 1978 (1); *v WI 1977 (3); v In 1979 (5)*
Davidson, A. K. 44: v E 1954 (3) 1958 (5) 1962 (5); v WI 1960 (4); *v E 1953 (5) 1956 (2) 1961 (5); v SA 1957 (5); v In 1956 (1) 1959 (2); v P 1956 (1) 1959 (3)*
Davis, I. C. 15: v E 1976 (1); v NZ 1973 (3); v P 1976 (2); *v E 1977 (3); v NZ 1973 (3) 1976 (2)*
Davis, S. P. 1: *v NZ 1985*
De Courcy, J. H. 3: *v E 1953 (3)*
Dell, A. R. 2: v E 1970 (1); v NZ 1973 (1)
Donnan, H. 5: v E 1891 (2); *v E 1896 (3)*
Dooland, B. 3: v E 1946 (2); v In 1947 (1)
Duff, R. A. 22: v E 1901 (4) 1903 (5); *v E 1902 (5) 1905 (5); v SA 1902 (3)*
Duncan, J. R. F. 1: v E 1970
Dyer, G. C. 1: v E 1986
Dymock, G. 21: v E 1974 (1) 1978 (3) 1979 (3); v WI 1979 (2); v NZ 1973 (1); v P 1978 (1); *v In 1973 (2); v In 1979 (5); v P 1979 (3)*

Dyson, J. 30: v WI 1982 (5); v WI 1981 (2) 1984 (3); v NZ 1980 (3); v In 1977 (3) 1980 (3); *v E 1981 (5); v NZ 1981 (3); v P 1982 (3)*

Eady, C. J. 2: v E 1901 (1); *v E 1896 (1)*
Eastwood, K. H. 1: v E 1970
Ebeling, H. I. 1: *v E 1934*
Edwards, J. D. 3: *v E 1888 (3)*
Edwards, R. 20: v E 1974 (5); v P 1972 (2); *v E 1972 (4) 1975 (4); v WI 1972 (5)*
Edwards, W. J. 3: v E 1974 (3)
Emery, S. H. 4: *v E 1912 (2); v SA 1912 (2)*
Evans, E. 6: v E 1881 (2) 1882 (1) 1884 (1); *v E 1886 (2)*

Fairfax, A. G. 10: v E 1928 (1); v WI 1930 (5); *v E 1930 (4)*
Favell, L. E. 19: v E 1954 (4) 1958 (2); v WI 1960 (4); *v WI 1954 (2); v In 1959 (4); v P 1959 (3)*
Ferris, J. J. 8: v E 1886 (2) 1887 (1); *v E 1888 (3) 1890 (2)*
Fingleton, J. H. 18: v E 1932 (3) 1936 (5); v SA 1931 (1); *v E 1938 (4); v SA 1935 (5)*
Fleetwood-Smith, L. O'B. 10: v E 1936 (3); *v E 1938 (4); v SA 1935 (3)*
Francis, B. C. 3: *v E 1972 (3)*
Freeman, E. W. 11: v WI 1968 (4); v In 1967 (2); *v E 1968 (2); v SA 1969 (2); v In 1969 (1)*
Freer, F. W. 1: v E 1946

Gannon, J. B. 3: v In 1977 (3)
Garrett, T. W. 19: v E 1876 (2) 1878 (1) 1881 (3) 1882 (3) 1884 (3) 1886 (2) 1887 (1); *v E 1882 (1) 1886 (3)*
Gaunt, R. A. 3: v SA 1963 (1); *v E 1961 (1); v SA 1957 (1)*
Gehrs, D. R. A. 6: v E 1903 (1); v SA 1910 (4); *v E 1905 (1)*
Giffen, G. 31: v E 1881 (3) 1882 (4) 1884 (3) 1891 (3) 1894 (5); *v E 1882 (1) 1884 (3) 1886 (3) 1893 (3) 1896 (3)*
Giffen, W. F. 3: v E 1886 (1) 1891 (2)
Gilbert, D. R. 9: v NZ 1985 (3); v In 1985 (2); *v E 1985 (1); v NZ 1985 (1); v In 1986 (2)*
Gilmour, G. J. 15: v E 1976 (1); v WI 1975 (5); v NZ 1973 (2); v P 1976 (3); *v E 1975 (1); v NZ 1973 (1) 1976 (2)*
Gleeson, J. W. 29: v E 1970 (5); v WI 1968 (5); v In 1967 (4); *v E 1968 (5) 1972 (3); v SA 1969 (4); v In 1969 (3)*
Graham, H. 6: v E 1894 (2); *v E 1893 (3) 1896 (1)*
Gregory, D. W. 3: v E 1876 (2) 1878 (1)
Gregory, E. J. 1: v E 1876
Gregory, J. M. 24: v E 1920 (5) 1924 (5) 1928 (1); *v E 1921 (5) 1926 (5); v SA 1921 (3)*
Gregory, R. G. 2: v E 1936 (2)
Gregory, S. E. 58: v E 1891 (1) 1894 (5) 1897 (5) 1901 (5) 1903 (4) 1907 (2) 1911 (1); *v E 1890 (2) 1893 (3) 1896 (3) 1899 (5) 1902 (5) 1905 (3) 1909 (5) 1912 (3); v SA 1902 (3) 1912 (3)*
Grimmett, C. V. 37: v E 1924 (1) 1928 (5) 1932 (5); v SA 1931 (5); v WI 1930 (5); *v E 1926 (3) 1930 (5) 1934 (5); v SA 1935 (5)*
Groube, T. U. 1: *v E 1880*
Grout, A. T. W. 51: v E 1958 (5) 1962 (2) 1965 (5); v SA 1963 (5); v WI 1960 (5); *v E 1961 (5) 1964 (5); v SA 1957 (5); v WI 1964 (5); v In 1959 (4) 1964 (1); v P 1959 (3) 1964 (1)*
Guest, C. E. J. 1: v E 1962

Hamence, R. A. 3: v E 1946 (1); v In 1947 (2)
Hammond, J. R. 5: *v WI 1972 (5)*
Harry, J. 1: v E 1894
Hartigan, R. J. 2: v E 1907 (2)
Hartkopf, A. E. V. 1: v E 1924
Harvey, M. R. 1: v E 1946
Harvey, R. N. 79: v E 1950 (5) 1954 (5) 1958 (5) 1962 (5); v SA 1952 (5); v WI 1951 (5) 1960 (4); v In 1947 (2); *v E 1948 (2) 1953 (5) 1956 (5) 1961 (5); v SA 1949 (5) 1957 (4); v WI 1954 (5); v In 1956 (3) 1959 (5); v P 1956 (1) 1959 (3)*
Hassett, A. L. 43: v E 1946 (5) 1950 (5); v SA 1952 (5); v WI 1951 (4); v In 1947 (4); *v E 1938 (4) 1948 (5) 1953 (5); v SA 1949 (5); v NZ 1945 (1)*
Hawke, N. J. N. 27: v E 1962 (1) 1965 (4); v SA 1963 (4); v In 1967 (1); v P 1964 (1); *v E 1964 (5) 1968 (2); v SA 1966 (2); v WI 1964 (5); v In 1964 (1); v P 1964 (1)*
Hazlitt, G. R. 9: v E 1907 (2) 1911 (1); *v E 1912 (3); v SA 1912 (3)*

Hendry, H. L. 11: v E 1924 (1) 1928 (4); *v E 1921 (4)*; *v SA 1921 (2)*

Hibbert, P. A. 1: v In 1977

Higgs, J. D. 22: v E 1978 (5) 1979 (1); v WI 1979 (1); v NZ 1980 (3); v In 1980 (2); *v WI 1977 (4)*; *v In 1979 (6)*

Hilditch, A. M. J. 18: v E 1978 (1); v WI 1984 (2); v NZ 1985 (1); v P 1978 (2); *v E 1985 (6)*; *v In 1979 (6)*

Hill, C. 49: v E 1897 (5) 1901 (5) 1903 (5) 1907 (5) 1911 (5); v SA 1910 (5); *v E 1896 (3) 1899 (3) 1902 (5) 1905 (5); v SA 1902 (3)*

Hill, J. C. 3: *v E 1953 (2)*; *v WI 1954 (1)*

Hoare, D. E. 1: v WI 1960

Hodges, J. H. 2: v E 1876 (2)

Hogan, T. G. 7: v P 1983 (1); *v WI 1983 (5)*; *v SL 1982 (1)*

Hogg, R. M. 38: v E 1978 (6) 1982 (3); v WI 1979 (2) 1984 (4); v NZ 1980 (2); v In 1980 (2); v P 1978 (2) 1983 (4); *v E 1981 (2); v WI 1983 (4); v In 1979 (6); v SL 1982 (1)*

Hole, G. B. 18: v E 1950 (1) 1954 (3); v SA 1952 (4); v WI 1951 (5); *v E 1953 (5)*

Holland, R. G. 11: v WI 1984 (3); v NZ 1985 (3); v In 1985 (1); *v E 1985 (4)*

Hookes, D. W. 23: v E 1976 (1) 1982 (5); v WI 1979 (1); v NZ 1985 (2); v In 1985 (2); *v E 1977 (5); v WI 1983 (5); v P 1979 (1); v SL 1982 (1)*

Hopkins, A. J. Y. 20: v E 1901 (2) 1903 (5); *v E 1902 (5) 1905 (3) 1909 (2); v SA 1902 (3)*

Horan, T. P. 15: v E 1876 (1) 1878 (1) 1881 (4) 1882 (4) 1884 (4); *v E 1882 (1)*

Hordern, H. V. 7: v E 1911 (5); v SA 1910 (2)

Hornibrook, P. M. 6: v E 1928 (1); *v E 1930 (5)*

Howell, W. P. 18: v E 1897 (3) 1901 (4) 1903 (3); *v E 1899 (5) 1902 (1); v SA 1902 (2)*

Hughes, K. J. 70: v E 1978 (6) 1979 (3) 1982 (5); v WI 1979 (3) 1981 (3) 1984 (4); v NZ 1980 (3); v In 1977 (2) 1980 (3); v P 1978 (2) 1981 (3) 1983 (5); *v E 1977 (1) 1980 (1) 1981 (6); v WI 1983 (5); v NZ 1981 (3); v In 1979 (6); v P 1979 (3) 1982 (3)*

Hughes, M. G. 5: v E 1986 (4); v In 1985 (1)

Hunt, W. A. 1: v SA 1931

Hurst, A. G. 12: v E 1978 (6); v NZ 1973 (1); v In 1977 (1); v P 1978 (2); *v In 1979 (2)*

Hurwood, A. 2: v WI 1930 (2)

Inverarity, R. J. 6: v WI 1968 (1); *v E 1968 (2) 1972 (3)*

Iredale, F. A. 14: v E 1894 (5) 1897 (4); *v E 1896 (2) 1899 (3)*

Ironmonger, H. 14: v E 1928 (2) 1932 (4); v SA 1931 (4); v WI 1930 (4)

Iverson, J. B. 5: v E 1950 (5)

Jackson, A. 8: v E 1928 (2); v WI 1930 (4); *v E 1930 (2)*

Jarman, B. N. 19: v E 1962 (3); v WI 1968 (4); v In 1967 (4); v P 1964 (1); *v E 1968 (4); v In 1959 (1); 1964 (2)*

Jarvis, A. H. 11: v E 1884 (3) 1894 (4); *v E 1886 (2) 1888 (2)*

Jenner, T. J. 9: v E 1970 (2) 1974 (2); v WI 1975 (1); *v WI 1972 (4)*

Jennings, C. B. 6: *v E 1912 (3); v SA 1912 (3)*

Johnson I. W. 45: v E 1946 (4) 1950 (4) 1954 (4); v SA 1952 (1); v WI 1951 (5); v In 1947 (4); *v E 1948 (4) 1956 (5); v SA 1949 (5); v WI 1954 (5); v NZ 1945 (1); v In 1956 (2); v P 1956 (1)*

Johnson, L. J. 1: v In 1947

Johnston W. A. 40: v E 1950 (5) 1954 (4); v SA 1952 (5); v WI 1951 (5); v In 1947 (4); *v E 1948 (5) 1953 (3); v SA 1949 (5); v WI 1954 (4)*

Jones, D. M. 10: v E 1986 (5); *v WI 1983 (2); v In 1986 (3)*

Jones, E. 19: v E 1894 (1) 1897 (5) 1901 (2); *v E 1896 (3) 1899 (5) 1902 (2); v SA 1902 (1)*

Jones, S. P. 12: v E 1881 (2) 1884 (2) 1886 (1) 1887 (1); *v E 1882 (1) 1886 (3)*

Joslin, L. R. 1: v In 1967

Kelleway, C. 26: v E 1911 (4) 1920 (5) 1924 (5) 1928 (1); v SA 1910 (5); *v E 1912 (3); v SA 1912 (3)*

Kelly, J. J. 36: v E 1897 (5) 1901 (5) 1903 (5); *v E 1896 (3) 1899 (5) 1902 (5) 1905 (5); v SA 1902 (3)*

Kelly, T. J. D. 2: v E 1876 (1) 1878 (1)

Kendall, T. 2: v E 1876 (2)

Kent, M. F. 3: *v E 1981 (3)*

Kerr, R. B. 2: v NZ 1985 (2)

Kippax, A. F. 22: v E 1924 (1) 1928 (5) 1932 (1); v SA 1931 (4); v WI 1930 (1); *v E 1930 (5) 1934 (1)*

Kline L. F. 13: v E 1958 (2); v WI 1960 (2); v SA 1957 (5); *v In 1959 (3); v P 1959 (1)*

Laird, B. M. 21: v E 1979 (2); v WI 1979 (3) 1981 (3); v P 1981 (3); *v E 1980 (1); v NZ 1981 (3); v P 1979 (3) 1982 (3)*

Langley, G. R. A. 26: v E 1954 (2); v SA 1952 (5); v WI 1951 (5); *v E 1953 (4) 1956 (3); v WI 1954 (4); v In 1956 (2); v P 1956 (1)*

Laughlin, T. J. 3: v E 1978 (1); *v WI 1977 (2)*

Laver, F. 15: v E 1901 (1) 1903 (1); *v E 1899 (4) 1905 (5) 1909 (4)*

Lawry, W. M. 67: v E 1962 (5) 1965 (5) 1970 (5); v SA 1963 (5); v WI 1968 (5); v In 1967 (4); v P 1964 (1); *v E 1961 (5) 1964 (5) 1968 (4); v SA 1966 (5) 1969 (4); v WI 1964 (5); v In 1964 (3) 1969 (5); v P 1964 (3)*

Lawson, G. F. 37: v E 1982 (5) 1986 (1); v WI 1981 (1) 1984 (5); v NZ 1980 (1) 1985 (2); v P 1983 (5); *v E 1981 (3) 1985 (6); v WI 1983 (5); v P 1982 (3)*

Lee, P. K. 2: v E 1932 (1); v SA 1931 (1)

Lillee, D. K. 70: v E 1970 (2) 1974 (6) 1976 (1) 1979 (3) 1982 (1); v WI 1975 (5) 1979 (3) 1981 (3); v NZ 1980 (3); v In 1980 (3); v P 1972 (3) 1976 (3) 1981 (3) 1983 (5); *v E 1972 (5) 1975 (4) 1980 (1) 1981 (6); v WI 1972 (1); v NZ 1976 (2) 1981 (3); v P 1979 (3); v SL 1982 (1)*

Lindwall, R. R. 61: v E 1946 (4) 1950 (5) 1954 (4) 1958 (2); v SA 1952 (4); v WI 1951 (5); v In 1947 (5); *v E 1948 (5) 1953 (5) 1956 (4); v SA 1949 (4); v WI 1954 (5); v NZ 1945 (1); v In 1956 (3) 1959 (2); v P 1956 (1) 1959 (3)*

Love, H. S. B. 1: v E 1932

Loxton, S. J. E. 12: v In 1947 (1); *v E 1948 (3); v SA 1949 (5)*

Lyons, J. J. 14: v E 1886 (1) 1891 (3) 1894 (3) 1897 (1); *v E 1888 (3) 1890 (3) 1893 (3)*

McAlister, P. A. 8: v E 1903 (2) 1907 (4); *v E 1909 (2)*

Macartney, C. G. 35: v E 1907 (5) 1911 (1) 1920 (2); v SA 1910 (4); *v E 1909 (5) 1912 (3) 1921 (5) 1926 (5); v SA 1912 (3) 1921 (2)*

McCabe, S. J. 39: v E 1932 (1) 1936 (5); v SA 1931 (5); v WI 1930 (5); *v E 1930 (5) 1934 (5) 1938 (4); v SA 1935 (5)*

McCool, C. L. 14: v E 1946 (5); v In 1947 (3); *v SA 1949 (5) v NZ 1945 (1)*

McCormick, E. L. 12: v E 1936 (4); *v E 1938 (3); v SA 1935 (5)*

McCosker, R. B. 25: v E 1974 (3) 1976 (1) 1979 (2); v WI 1975 (4) 1979 (1); v P 1976 (3); *v E 1975 (4) 1977 (5); v NZ 1976 (2)*

McDermott, C. J. 17: v E 1986 (1); v WI 1984 (2); v NZ 1985 (2); v In 1985 (2); *v E 1985 (6); v NZ 1985 (2); v In 1986 (2)*

McDonald, C. C. 47: v E 1954 (2) 1958 (5); v SA 1952 (5); v WI 1951 (1) 1960 (5); *v E 1956 (5) 1961 (3); v SA 1957 (5); v WI 1954 (5); v In 1956 (2) 1959 (5); v P 1956 (1) 1959 (3)*

McDonald, E. A. 11: v E 1920 (3); *v E 1921 (5); v SA 1921 (3)*

McDonnell, P. S. 19: v E 1881 (4) 1882 (3) 1884 (2) 1886 (2) 1887 (1); *v E 1880 (1) 1884 (3) 1888 (3)*

McIlwraith, J. 1: *v E 1886*

Mackay K. D. 37: v E 1958 (5) 1962 (3); v WI 1960 (5); *v E 1956 (3) 1961 (5); v SA 1957 (5); v In 1956 (3) 1959 (5); v P 1959 (3)*

McKenzie, G. D. 60: v E 1962 (5) 1965 (4) 1970 (3); v SA 1963 (5); v WI 1968 (5); v In 1967 (2); v P 1964 (1); *v E 1961 (3) 1964 (5) 1968 (5); v SA 1966 (5) 1969 (3); v WI 1964 (5); v In 1964 (3) 1969 (5); v P 1964 (1)*

McKibbin, T. R. 5: v E 1894 (1) 1897 (2); *v E 1896 (2)*

McLaren, J. W. 1: v E 1911

Maclean, J. A. 4: v E 1978 (4)

McLeod, C. E. 17: v E 1894 (1) 1897 (5) 1901 (2) 1903 (3); *v E 1899 (1) 1905 (5)*

McLeod, R. W. 6: v E 1891 (3); *v E 1893 (3)*

McShane, P. G. 3: v E 1884 (1) 1886 (1) 1887 (1)

Maddocks, L. V. 7: v E 1954 (3); *v E 1956 (2); v WI 1954 (1); v In 1956 (1)*

Maguire, J. N. 3: v P 1983 (1); *v WI 1983 (2)*

Mailey, A. A. 21: v E 1920 (2) 1924 (5); *v E 1921 (3) 1926 (5); v SA 1921 (3)*

Mallett, A. A. 38: v E 1970 (2) 1974 (5) 1979 (1); v WI 1968 (1) 1975 (6) 1979 (1); v NZ 1973 (3); v P 1972 (2); *v E 1968 (1) 1972 (2) 1975 (4) 1980 (1); v SA 1969 (1); v NZ 1973 (3); v In 1969 (5)*

Malone, M. F. 1: *v E 1977*

Mann, A. L. 4: v In 1977 (4)

Marr, A. P. 1: v E 1884

Marsh, G. R. 14: v E 1986 (5); v In 1985 (3); *v NZ 1985 (3); v In 1986 (3)*

Marsh, R. W. 96: v E 1970 (6) 1974 (6) 1976 (1) 1979 (3) 1982 (5); v WI 1975 (6) 1979 (3) 1981 (3); v NZ 1973 (3) 1980 (3); v In 1980 (3); v P 1972 (3) 1976 (3) 1981 (3) 1983 (5); *v E 1972 (5) 1975 (4) 1977 (5) 1980 (1) 1981 (6); v WI 1972 (5); v NZ 1973 (3) 1976 (2) 1981 (3); v P 1979 (3) 1982 (3)*

Martin, J. W. 8: v SA 1963 (1); v WI 1960 (3); *v SA 1966 (1); v In 1964 (2); v P 1964 (1)*

Massie, H. H. 9: v E 1881 (4) 1882 (3) 1884 (1); *v E 1882 (1)*

Massie, R. A. L. 6: v P 1972 (2); *v E 1972 (4)*

Matthews, C. D. 2: v E 1986 (2)

Matthews, G. R. J. 21: v E 1986 (4); v WI 1984 (1); v NZ 1985 (3); v P 1983 (2); *v E 1985 (1); v WI 1983 (1); v NZ 1985 (3); v In 1986 (3)*

Matthews, T. J. 8: v E 1911 (2); *v E 1912 (3); v SA 1912 (3)*

Mayne, E. R. 4: *v E 1912 (1); v SA 1912 (1) 1921 (2)*

Mayne, L. C. 6: *v SA 1969 (2); v WI 1964 (3); v In 1969 (1)*

Meckiff, I. 18: v E 1958 (4); v SA 1963 (1); v WI 1960 (2); *v SA 1957 (4); v In 1959 (5); v P 1959 (2)*

Meuleman, K. D. 1: *v NZ 1945*

Midwinter, W. E. 8: v E 1876 (2) 1882 (1) 1886 (2); *v E 1884 (3)*

Miller, K. R. 55: v E 1946 (5) 1950 (5) 1954 (4); v SA 1952 (4); v WI 1951 (5); v In 1947 (5); *v E 1948 (5) 1953 (5) 1956 (5); v SA 1949 (5); v WI 1954 (5); v NZ 1945 (1); v P 1956 (1)*

Minnett, R. B. 9: v E 1911 (5); *v E 1912 (1); v SA 1912 (3)*

Misson, F. M. 5: v WI 1960 (3); *v E 1961 (2)*

Moroney, J. R. 7: v E 1950 (1); v WI 1951 (1); *v SA 1949 (5)*

Morris, A. R. 46: v E 1946 (5) 1950 (5) 1954 (4); v SA 1952 (5); v WI 1951 (4); v In 1947 (4); *v E 1948 (5) 1953 (5); v SA 1949 (5); v WI 1954 (4)*

Morris, S. 1: v E 1884

Moses, H. 6: v E 1886 (2) 1887 (1) 1891 (2) 1894 (1)

Moss, J. K. 1: v P 1978

Moule, W. H. 1: *v E 1880*

Murdoch, W. L. 18: v E 1876 (1) 1878 (1) 1881 (4) 1882 (4) 1884 (1); *v E 1880 (1) 1882 (1) 1884 (3) 1890 (2)*

Musgrove, H. 1: v E 1884

Nagel, L. E. 1: v E 1932

Nash, L. J. 2: v E 1936 (1); v SA 1931 (1)

Nitschke, H. C. 2: v SA 1931 (2)

Noble, M. A. 42: v E 1897 (4) 1901 (5) 1903 (5) 1907 (5); *v E 1899 (5) 1902 (5) 1905 (5) 1909 (5); v SA 1902 (3)*

Noblet, G. 3: v SA 1952 (1); v WI 1951 (1); *v SA 1949 (1)*

Nothling, O. E. 1: v E 1928

O'Brien, L. P. J. 5: v E 1932 (2) 1936 (1); *v SA 1935 (2)*

O'Connor, J. D. A. 4: v E 1907 (3); *v E 1909 (1)*

O'Donnell, S. P. 6: v NZ 1985 (1); *v E 1985 (5)*

Ogilvie, A. D. 5: v In 1977 (3); *v WI 1977 (2)*

O'Keeffe, K. J. 24: v E 1970 (2) 1976 (1); v NZ 1973 (3); v P 1972 (2) 1976 (3); *v E 1977 (3); v WI 1972 (5); v NZ 1973 (3) 1976 (2)*

Oldfield, W. A. 54: v E 1920 (3) 1924 (5) 1928 (5) 1932 (4) 1936 (5); v SA 1931 (5); v WI 1930 (5); *v E 1921 (1) 1926 (5) 1930 (5) 1934 (5); v SA 1921 (1) 1935 (5)*

O'Neill, N. C. 42: v E 1958 (5) 1962 (5); v SA 1963 (4); v WI 1960 (5); *v E 1961 (5) 1964 (4); v WI 1964 (4); v In 1959 (5) 1964 (2); v P 1959 (3)*

O'Reilly, W. J. 27: v E 1932 (5) 1936 (5); v SA 1931 (2); *v E 1934 (5) 1938 (4); v SA 1935 (5); v NZ 1945 (1)*

Oxenham, R. K. 7: v E 1928 (3); v SA 1931 (1); v WI 1930 (3)

Palmer, G. E. 17: v E 1881 (4) 1882 (4) 1884 (2); *v E 1880 (1) 1884 (3) 1886 (3)*

Park, R. L. 1: v E 1920

Pascoe, L. S. 14: v E 1979 (2); v WI 1979 (1) 1981 (1); v NZ 1980 (3); v In 1980 (3); *v E 1977 (3) 1980 (1)*

Pellew, C. E. 10: v E 1920 (4); *v E 1921 (5); v SA 1921 (1)*

Phillips, W. B. 27: v WI 1984 (2); v NZ 1985 (3); v In 1985 (3); v P 1983 (3); *v E 1985 (6); v WI 1983 (5); v NZ 1985 (3)*

Philpott, P. I. 8: v E 1965 (3); *v WI 1964 (5)*

Ponsford, W. H. 29: v E 1924 (5) 1928 (2) 1932 (3); v SA 1931 (4); v WI 1930 (5); *v E 1926 (2) 1930 (4) 1934 (4)*

Pope, R. J. 1: v E 1884

Rackemann, C. G. 5: v E 1982 (1); v WI 1984 (1); v P 1983 (2); *v WI 1983 (1)*

Ransford, V. S. 20: v E 1907 (5) 1911 (5); v SA 1910 (5); *v E 1909 (5)*

Redpath, I. R. 66: v E 1965 (1) 1970 (6) 1974 (6); v WI 1968 (5) 1975 (6); v In 1967 (3); v P 1972 (3); *v E 1964 (5) 1968 (5); v SA 1966 (5) 1969 (4); v WI 1972 (5); v NZ 1973 (3); v In 1964 (2) 1969 (5); v P 1964 (1)*

Reedman, J. C. 1: v E 1894

Reid, B. A. 13: v E 1986 (5); v In 1985 (3); *v NZ 1985 (3); v In 1986 (2)*

Renneberg, D. A. 8: v In 1967 (3); *v SA 1966 (5)*

Richardson, A. J. 9: v E 1924 (4); *v E 1926 (5)*

Richardson, V. Y. 19: v E 1924 (3) 1928 (2) 1932 (5); *v E 1930 (4); v SA 1935 (5)*

Rigg, K. E. 8: v E 1936 (3); v SA 1931 (4); v WI 1930 (1)

Ring, D. T. 13: v SA 1952 (5); v WI 1951 (5); v In 1947 (1); *v E 1948 (1) 1953 (1)*

Ritchie, G. M. 30: v E 1986 (4); v WI 1984 (1); v NZ 1985 (3); v In 1985 (2); *v E 1985 (6); v WI 1983 (5); v NZ 1985 (3); v In 1986 (3); v P 1982 (5)*

Rixon, S. J. 13: v WI 1984 (3); v In 1977 (5); *v WI 1977 (5)*

Robertson, W. R. 1: v E 1884

Robinson, R. D. 3: *v E 1977 (3)*

Robinson, R. H. 1: v E 1936

Rorke, G. F. 4: v E 1958 (2); *v In 1959 (2)*

Rutherford, J. W. 1: *v In 1956*

Ryder, J. 20: v E 1920 (5) 1924 (3) 1928 (5); *v E 1926 (4); v SA 1921 (3)*

Saggers, R. A. 6: *v E 1948 (1); v SA 1949 (5)*

Saunders, J. V. 14: v E 1901 (1) 1903 (2) 1907 (5); *v E 1902 (4); v SA 1902 (2)*

Scott, H. J. H. 8: v E 1884 (2); *v E 1884 (3) 1886 (3)*

Sellers, R. H. D. 1: *v In 1964*

Serjeant, C. S. 12: v In 1977 (4); *v E 1977 (3); v WI 1977 (5)*

Sheahan, A. P. 31: v E 1970 (2); v WI 1968 (5); v NZ 1973 (2); v In 1967 (4); v P 1972 (2); *v E 1968 (5) 1972 (2); v SA 1969 (4); v In 1969 (5)*

Shepherd, B. K. 9: v E 1962 (2); v SA 1963 (4); v P 1964 (1); *v WI 1964 (2)*

Sievers, M. W. 3: v E 1936 (3)

Simpson, R. B. 62: v E 1958 (1) 1962 (5) 1965 (3); v SA 1963 (5); v WI 1960 (5); v In 1967 (3) 1977 (5); v P 1964 (1); *v E 1961 (5) 1964 (5); v SA 1957 (5) 1966 (5); v WI 1964 (5) 1977 (5); v In 1964 (3); v P 1964 (1)*

Sincock, D. J. 3: v E 1965 (1); v P 1964 (1); *v WI 1964 (1)*

Slater, K. N. 1: v E 1958

Sleep, P. R. 7: v E 1986 (3); v P 1978 (1); *v In 1979 (2); v P 1982 (1)*

Slight, J. 1: *v E 1880*

Smith, D. B. M. 2: *v E 1912 (2)*

Smith, S. B. 3: *v WI 1983 (3)*

Spofforth, F. R. 18: v E 1876 (1) 1878 (1) 1881 (1) 1882 (4) 1884 (3) 1886 (1); *v E 1882 (1) 1884 (3) 1886 (3)*

Stackpole, K. R. 43: v E 1965 (2) 1970 (6); v WI 1968 (5); v NZ 1973 (3); v P 1972 (1); *v E 1972 (5); v SA 1966 (5) 1969 (4); v WI 1972 (5); v NZ 1973 (3); v In 1969 (5)*

Stevens, G. B. 4: *v In 1959 (2); v P 1959 (2)*

Taber, H. B. 16: v WI 1968 (1); *v E 1968 (1); v SA 1966 (5); 1969 (4); v In 1969 (5)*

Tallon, D. 21: v E 1946 (5) 1950 (5); v In 1947 (5); *v E 1948 (4) 1953 (1); v NZ 1945 (1)*

Taylor, J. M. 20: v E 1920 (5) 1924 (5); *v E 1921 (5) 1926 (3); v SA 1921 (2)*

Taylor, P. L. 1: v E 1986

Thomas, G. 8: v E 1965 (3); *v WI 1964 (5)*

Thompson, N. 2: v E 1876 (2)

Thoms, G. R. 1: v WI 1951

Thomson, A. L. 4: v E 1970 (4)

Thomson, J. R. 51: v E 1974 (5) 1979 (1) 1982 (4); v WI 1975 (6) 1979 (1) 1981 (2); v In 1977 (5); v P 1972 (1) 1976 (1) 1981 (3); *v E 1975 (4) 1977 (5) 1985 (2); v WI 1977 (5); v NZ 1981 (3); v P 1982 (3)*

Thurlow, H. M. 1: v SA 1931

Toohey, P. M. 15: v E 1978 (5) 1979 (1); v WI 1979 (1); v In 1977 (5); *v WI 1977 (3)*

Toshack, E. R. H. 12: v E 1946 (5); v In 1947 (2); *v E 1948 (4); v NZ 1945 (1)*

Travers, J. P. F. 1: v E 1901

Tribe, G. E. 3: v E 1946 (3)

Trott, A. E. 3: v E 1894 (3)
Trott, G. H. S. 24: v E 1891 (3) 1894 (5) 1897 (5); *v E 1888 (3) 1890 (2) 1893 (3) 1896 (3)*
Trumble, H. 32: v E 1894 (1) 1897 (5) 1901 (5) 1903 (4); *v E 1890 (2) 1893 (3) 1896 (3) 1899 (5) 1902 (3); v SA 1902 (1)*
Trumble, J. W. 7: v E 1884 (4); *v E 1886 (3)*
Trumper, V. T. 48: v E 1901 (5) 1903 (5) 1907 (5) 1911 (5); v SA 1910 (5); *v E 1899 (5) 1902 (5) 1905 (5) 1909 (5); v SA 1902 (3)*
Turner, A. 14: v WI 1975 (6); v P 1976 (3); *v E 1975 (3); v NZ 1976 (2)*
Turner, C. T. B. 17: v E 1886 (2) 1887 (1) 1891 (3) 1894 (3); *v E 1888 (3) 1890 (2) 1893 (3)*

Veivers, T. R. 21: v E 1965 (4); v SA 1963 (3); v P 1964 (1); *v E 1964 (5); v SA 1966 (4); v In 1964 (3); v P 1964 (1)*

Waite, M. G. 2: *v E 1938 (2)*
Walker, M. H. N. 34: v E 1974 (6); 1976 (1); v WI 1975 (3); v NZ 1973 (1); v P 1972 (2) 1976 (2); *v E 1975 (4); 1977 (5); v WI 1972 (5); v NZ 1973 (3) 1976 (2)*
Wall, T. W. 18: v E 1928 (1) 1932 (4); v SA 1931 (3); v WI 1930 (1); *v E 1930 (5) 1934 (4)*
Walters, F. H. 1: v E 1884
Walters, K. D. 74: v E 1965 (5) 1970 (6) 1974 (6) 1976 (1); v WI 1968 (4); v NZ 1973 (3) 1980 (3); v In 1967 (2) 1980 (3); v P 1972 (1) 1976 (3); *v E 1968 (5) 1972 (4) 1975 (4) 1977 (5); v SA 1969 (4); v WI 1972 (5); v NZ 1973 (3) 1976 (2); v In 1969 (5)*
Ward, F. A. 4: v E 1936 (3); *v E 1938 (1)*
Watkins, J. R. 1: v P 1972
Watson, G. D. 5: *v E 1972 (2); v SA 1966 (3)*
Watson, W. 4: v E 1954 (1); *v WI 1954 (3)*
Waugh, S. R. 13: v E 1986 (5); v In 1985 (2); *v NZ 1985 (3); v In 1986 (3)*
Wellham, D. M. 6: v E 1986 (1); v WI 1981 (1); v P 1981 (2); *v E 1981 (1) 1985 (1)*
Wessels, K. C. 24: v E 1982 (4); v WI 1984 (5); v NZ 1985 (1); v P 1983 (5); *v E 1985 (6); v WI 1983 (2); v SL 1982 (1)*
Whatmore, D. F. 7: v P 1978 (2); *v In 1979 (5)*
Whitney, M. R. 2: *v E 1981 (2)*
Whitty, W. J. 14: v E 1911 (2); v SA 1910 (5); *v E 1909 (1) 1912 (3); v SA 1912 (3)*
Wiener, J. M. 6: v E 1979 (2); v WI 1979 (2); *v P 1979 (2)*
Wilson, J. W. 1: *v In 1956*
Wood, G. M. 53: v E 1978 (6) 1982 (1); v WI 1981 (3) 1984 (5); v NZ 1980 (3); v In 1977 (1) 1980 (3); v P 1978 (1) 1981 (3); *v E 1980 (1) 1981 (6) 1985 (5); v WI 1977 (5) 1983 (1); v NZ 1981 (3); v In 1979 (2); v P 1982 (3); v SL 1982 (1)*
Woodcock, A. J. 1: v NZ 1973
Woodfull, W. M. 35: v E 1928 (5) 1932 (5); v SA 1931 (5); v WI 1930 (5); *v E 1926 (5) 1930 (5) 1934 (5)*
Woods, S. M. J. 3: *v E 1888 (3)*
Woolley, R. D. 2: *v WI 1983 (1); v SL 1982 (1)*
Worrall, J. 11: v E 1884 (1) 1887 (1) 1894 (1) 1897 (1); *v E 1888 (3) 1899 (2)*
Wright, K. J. 10: v E 1978 (2); v P 1978 (2); *v In 1979 (6)*

Yallop, G. N. 39: v E 1978 (6); v WI 1975 (3) 1984 (1); v In 1977 (1); v P 1978 (1) 1981 (1) 1983 (5); *v E 1980 (1) 1981 (6); v WI 1977 (4); v In 1979 (6); v P 1979 (3); v SL 1982 (1)*
Yardley, B. 33: v E 1978 (4) 1982 (5); v WI 1981 (3); v In 1977 (1) 1980 (2); v P 1978 (1) 1981 (3); *v WI 1977 (5); v NZ 1981 (3); v In 1979 (3); v P 1982 (2); v SL 1982 (1)*

Zoehrer, T. J. 10: v E 1986 (4); *v NZ 1985 (3); v In 1986 (3)*

SOUTH AFRICA

Number of Test cricketers: 235

Adcock, N. A. T. 26: v E 1956 (5); v A 1957 (5); v NZ 1953 (5) 1961 (2); *v E 1955 (4) 1960 (5)*
Anderson, J. H. 1: v A 1902
Ashley, W. H. 1: v E 1888

Bacher, A. 12: v A 1966 (5) 1969 (4); *v E 1965 (3)*
Balaskas, X. C. 9: v E 1930 (2) 1938 (1); v A 1935 (3); *v E 1935 (1); v NZ 1931 (2)*

Barlow, E. J. 30: v E 1964 (5); v A 1966 (5) 1969 (4); v NZ 1961 (5); *v E 1965 (3)*; *v A 1963 (5)*; *v NZ 1963 (3)*

Baumgartner, H. V. 1: v E 1913

Beaumont, R. 5: v E 1913 (2); *v E 1912 (1)*; *v A 1912 (2)*

Begbie, D. W. 5: v E 1948 (3); v A 1949 (2)

Bell, A. J. 16: v E 1930 (3); *v E 1929 (3) 1935 (3)*; *v A 1931 (5)*; *v NZ 1931 (2)*

Bisset, M. 3: v E 1898 (2) 1909 (1)

Bissett, G. F. 4: v E 1927 (4)

Blanckenberg, J. M. 18: v E 1913 (5) 1922 (5); v A 1921 (3); *v E 1924 (5)*

Bland, K. C. 21: v E 1964 (5); v A 1966 (1); v NZ 1961 (5); *v E 1965 (3)*; *v A 1963 (4)*; *v NZ 1963 (3)*

Bock, E. G. 1: v A 1935

Bond, G. E. 1: v E 1938

Botten, J. T. 3: *v E 1965 (3)*

Brann, W. H. 3: v E 1922 (3)

Briscoe, A. W. 2: v E 1938 (1); v A 1935 (1)

Bromfield, H. D. 9: v E 1964 (3); v NZ 1961 (5); *v E 1965 (1)*

Brown, L. S. 2: *v A 1931 (1)*; *v NZ 1931 (1)*

Burger, C. G. de V. 2: v A 1957 (2)

Burke, S. F. 2: v E 1964 (1); v NZ 1961 (1)

Buys, I. D. 1: v E 1922

Cameron, H. B. 26: v E 1927 (5) 1930 (5); *v E 1929 (4) 1935 (5)*; *v A 1931 (5)*; *v NZ 1931 (2)*

Campbell, T. 5: v E 1909 (4); *v E 1912 (1)*

Carlstein, P. R. 8: v A 1957 (1); *v E 1960 (5)*; *v A 1963 (2)*

Carter, C. P. 10: v E 1913 (2); v A 1921 (3); *v E 1912 (2) 1924 (3)*

Catterall, R. H. 24: v E 1922 (5) 1927 (5) 1930 (4); *v E 1924 (5) 1929 (5)*

Chapman, H. W. 2: v E 1913 (1); v A 1921 (1)

Cheetham, J. E. 24: v E 1948 (1); v A 1949 (3); v NZ 1953 (5); *v E 1951 (5) 1955 (3)*; *v A 1952 (5)*; *v NZ 1952 (2)*

Chevalier, G. A. 1: v A 1969

Christy, J. A. J. 10: v E 1930 (1); *v E 1929 (2)*; *v A 1931 (5)*; *v NZ 1931 (2)*

Chubb, G. W. A. 5: *v E 1951 (5)*

Cochran, J. A. K. 1: v E 1930

Coen, S. K. 2: v E 1927 (2)

Commaille, J. M. M. 12: v E 1909 (5) 1927 (2); *v E 1924 (5)*

Conyngham, D. P. 1: v E 1922

Cook, F. J. 1: v E 1895

Cooper, A. H. C. 1: v E 1913

Cox, J. L. 3: v E 1913 (3)

Cripps, G. 1: v E 1891

Crisp, R. J. 9: v A 1935 (4); *v E 1935 (5)*

Curnow, S. H. 7: v E 1930 (3); *v A 1931 (4)*

Dalton, E. L. 15: v E 1930 (1) 1938 (4); v A 1935 (1); *v E 1929 (1) 1935 (4)*; *v A 1931 (2)*; *v NZ 1931 (2)*

Davies, E. Q. 5: v E 1938 (3); v A 1935 (2)

Dawson, O. C. 9: v E 1948 (4); *v E 1947 (5)*

Deane, H. G. 17: v E 1927 (5) 1930 (2); *v E 1924 (5) 1929 (5)*

Dixon, C. D. 1: v E 1913

Dower, R. R. 1: v E 1898

Draper, R. G. 2: v A 1949 (2)

Duckworth, C. A. R. 2: v E 1956 (2)

Dumbrill, R. 5: v A 1966 (2); *v E 1965 (3)*

Duminy, J. P. 3: v E 1927 (2); *v E 1929 (1)*

Dunell, O. R. 2: v E 1888 (2)

Du Preez, J. H. 2: v A 1966 (2)

Du Toit, J. F. 1: v E 1891

Dyer, D. V. 3: *v E 1947 (3)*

Elgie, M. K. 3: v NZ 1961 (3)

Endean, W. R. 28: v E 1956 (5); v A 1957 (5); v NZ 1953 (5); *v E 1951 (1) 1955 (5)*; *v A 1952 (5)*; *v NZ 1952 (2)*

Farrer, W. S. 6: v NZ 1961 (3); *v NZ 1963 (3)*
Faulkner, G. A. 25: v E 1905 (5) 1909 (5); *v E 1907 (3) 1912 (3) 1924 (1)*; *v A 1910 (5) 1912 (3)*
Fellows-Smith, J. P. 4: *v E 1960 (4)*
Fichardt, C. G. 2: v E 1891 (1) 1895 (1)
Finlason, C. E. 1: v E 1888
Floquet, C. E. 1: v E 1909
Francis, H. H. 2: v E 1898 (2)
Francois, C. M. 5: v E 1922 (5)
Frank, C. N. 3: v A 1921 (3)
Frank, W. H. B. 1: v E 1895
Fuller, E. R. H. 7: v A 1957 (1); *v E 1955 (2)*; *v A 1952 (2)*; *v NZ 1952 (2)*
Fullerton, G. M. 7: v A 1949 (2); *v E 1947 (2) 1951 (3)*
Funston, K. J. 18: v E 1956 (3); v A 1957 (5); v NZ 1953 (3); *v A 1952 (5)*; *v NZ 1952 (2)*

Gamsy, D. 2: v A 1969 (2)
Gleeson, R. A. 1: v E 1895
Glover, G. K. 1: v E 1895
Goddard, T. L. 41: v E 1956 (5) 1964 (5); v A 1957 (5) 1966 (5) 1969 (3); *v E 1955 (5) 1960 (5)*; *v A 1963 (5)*; *v NZ 1963 (3)*
Gordon, N. 5: v E 1938 (5)
Graham, R. 2: v E 1898 (2)
Grieveson, R. E. 2: v E 1938 (2)
Griffin, G. M. 2: *v E 1960 (2)*

Hall, A. E. 7: v E 1922 (4) 1927 (2) 1930 (1)
Hall, G. G. 1: v E 1964
Halliwell, E. A. 8: v E 1891 (1) 1895 (3) 1898 (1); v A 1902 (3)
Halse, C. G. 3: *v A 1963 (3)*
Hands, P. A. M. 7: v E 1913 (5); v A 1921 (1); *v E 1924 (1)*
Hands, R. H. M. 1: v E 1913
Hanley, M. A. 1: v E 1948
Harris, T. A. 3: v E 1948 (1); *v E 1947 (2)*
Hartigan, G. P. D. 5: v E 1913 (3); *v E 1912 (1)*; *v A 1912 (1)*
Harvey, R. L. 2: v A 1935 (2)
Hathorn, C. M. H. 12: v E 1905 (5); v A 1902 (3); *v E 1907 (3)*; *v A 1910 (1)*
Hearne, F. 4: v E 1891 (1) 1895 (3)
Hearne, G. A. L. 3: v E 1922 (2); *v E 1924 (1)*
Heine, P. S. 14: v E 1956 (5); v A 1957 (4); v NZ 1961 (1); *v E 1955 (4)*
Hime, C. F. W. 1: v E 1895
Hutchinson, P. 2: v E 1888 (2)

Ironside, D. E. J. 3: v NZ 1953 (3)
Irvine, B. L. 4: v A 1969 (4)

Johnson, C. L. 1: v E 1895

Keith, H. J. 8: v E 1956 (3); *v E 1955 (4)*; *v A 1952 (1)*
Kempis, G. A. 1: v E 1888
Kotze, J. J. 3: v A 1902 (2); *v E 1907 (1)*
Kuys, F. 1: v E 1898

Lance, H. R. 13: v A 1966 (5) 1969 (3); v NZ 1961 (2); *v E 1965 (3)*
Langton, A. B. C. 15: v E 1938 (5); v A 1935 (5); *v E 1935 (5)*
Lawrence, G. B. 5: v NZ 1961 (5)
Le Roux, F. le S. 1: v E 1913
Lewis, P. T. 1: v E 1913
Lindsay, D. T. 19: v E 1964 (3); v A 1966 (5) 1969 (2); *v E 1965 (3)*; *v A 1963 (3)*; *v NZ 1963 (3)*
Lindsay, J. D. 3: *v E 1947 (3)*
Lindsay, N. V. 1: v A 1921
Ling, W. V. S. 6: v E 1922 (3); v A 1921 (3)
Llewellyn, C. B. 15: v E 1895 (1) 1898 (1); v A 1902 (3); *v E 1912 (3)*; *v A 1910 (5) 1912 (2)*
Lundie, E. B. 1: v E 1913

Macaulay, M. J. 1: v E 1964
McCarthy, C. N. 15: v E 1948 (5); v A 1949 (5); *v E 1951* (5)
McGlew, D. J. 34: v E 1956 (1); v A 1957 (5); v NZ 1953 (5) 1961 (5); *v E 1951* (2) *1955* (5) *1960* (5); *v A 1952* (4); *v NZ 1952* (2)
McKinnon, A. H. 8: v E 1964 (2); v A 1966 (2); v NZ 1961 (1); *v E 1960* (1) *1965* (2)
McLean, R. A. 40: v E 1956 (5) 1964 (2); v A 1957 (4); v NZ 1953 (4) 1961 (5); *v E 1951* (3) *1955* (5) *1960* (5); *v A 1952* (5); *v NZ 1952* (2)
McMillan, Q. 13: v E 1930 (5); *v E 1929* (2); *v A 1931* (4); *v NZ 1931* (2)
Mann, N. B. F. 19: v E 1948 (5); v A 1949 (5); *v E 1947* (5) *1951* (4)
Mansell, P. N. F. 13: *v E 1951* (2) *1955* (4); *v A 1952* (5); *v NZ 1952* (2)
Markham, L. A. 1: v E 1948
Marx, W. F. E. 3: v A 1921 (3)
Meintjes, D. J. 2: v E 1922 (2)
Melle, M. G. 7: v A 1949 (2); *v E 1951* (1); *v A 1952* (4)
Melville, A. 11: v E 1938 (5) 1948 (1); *v E 1947* (5)
Middleton, J. 6: v E 1895 (2) 1898 (2); v A 1902 (2)
Mills, C. 1: v E 1891
Milton, W. H. 3: v E 1888 (2) 1891 (1)
Mitchell, B. 42: v E 1930 (5) 1938 (5) 1948 (5); v A 1935 (5); *v E 1929* (5) *1935* (5) *1947* (5); *v A 1931* (5); *v NZ 1931* (2)
Mitchell, F. 3: *v E 1912* (1); *v A 1912* (2)
Morkel, D. P. B. 16: v E 1927 (5); *v E 1929* (5); *v A 1931* (5); *v NZ 1931* (1)
Murray, A. R. A. 10: v NZ 1953 (4); *v A 1952* (4); *v NZ 1952* (2)

Nel, J. D. 6: v A 1949 (5) 1957 (1)
Newberry, C. 4: v E 1913 (4)
Newson, E. S. 3: v E 1930 (1) 1938 (2)
Nicholson, F. 4: v A 1935 (4)
Nicolson, J. F. W. 3: v E 1927 (3)
Norton, N. O. 1: v E 1909
Nourse, A. D. 34: v E 1938 (5) 1948 (5); v A 1935 (5) 1949 (5); *v E 1935* (4) *1947* (5) *1951* (5)
Nourse, A. W. 45: v E 1905 (5) 1909 (5) 1913 (5) 1922 (5); v A 1902 (3) 1921 (3); *v E 1907* (3) *1912* (3) *1924* (5); *v A 1910* (5) *1912* (3)
Nupen, E. P. 17: v E 1922 (4) 1927 (5) 1930 (3); v A 1921 (2) 1935 (1); *v E 1924* (2)

Ochse, A. E. 2: v E 1888 (2)
Ochse, A. L. 3: v E 1927 (1); *v E 1929* (2)
O'Linn, S. 7: v NZ 1961 (2); *v E 1960* (5)
Owen-Smith, H. G. 5: *v E 1929* (5)

Palm, A. W. 1: v E 1927
Parker, G. M. 2: *v E 1924* (2)
Parkin, D. C. 1: v E 1891
Partridge, J. T. 11: v E 1964 (3); *v A 1963* (5); *v NZ 1963* (3)
Pearse, O. C. 3: *v A 1910* (3)
Pegler, S. J. 16: v E 1909 (1); *v E 1912* (3) *1924* (5); *v A 1910* (4) *1912* (3)
Pithey, A. J. 17: v E 1956 (1) 1964 (5); *v E 1960* (2); *v A 1963* (4); *v NZ 1963* (3)
Pithey, D. B. 8: v A 1966 (2); *v A 1963* (3); *v NZ 1963* (3)
Plimsoll, J. B. 1: *v E 1947*
Pollock, P. M. 28: v E 1964 (5); v A 1966 (5) 1969 (4); v NZ 1961 (3); *v E 1965* (3); *v A 1963* (5); *v NZ 1963* (3)
Pollock, R. G. 23: v E 1964 (5); v A 1966 (5) 1969 (4); *v E 1965* (3); *v A 1963* (5); *v NZ 1963* (1)
Poore, R. M. 3: v E 1895 (3)
Pothecary, J. E. 3: *v E 1960* (3)
Powell, A. W. 1: v E 1898
Prince, C. F. H. 1: v E 1898
Procter, M. J. 7: v A 1966 (3) 1969 (4)
Promnitz, H. L. E. 2: v E 1927 (2)

Quinn, N. A. 12: v E 1930 (1); *v E 1929* (4); *v A 1931* (5); *v NZ 1931* (2)

Reid, N. 1: v A 1921
Richards, A. R. 1: v E 1895
Richards, B. A. 4: v A 1969 (4)
Richards, W. H. 1: v E 1888
Robertson, J. B. 3: v A 1935 (3)
Rose-Innes, A. 2: v E 1888 (2)
Routledge, T. W. 4: v E 1891 (1) 1895 (3)
Rowan, A. M. B. 15: v E 1948 (5); *v E 1947 (5) 1951 (5)*
Rowan, E. A. B. 26: v E 1938 (4) 1948 (4); v A 1935 (3); 1949 (5); *v E 1935 (5) 1951 (5)*
Rowe, G. A. 5: v E 1895 (2) 1898 (2); v A 1902 (1)

Samuelson, S. V. 1: v E 1909
Schwarz, R. O. 20: v E 1905 (5) 1909 (4); *v E 1907 (3) 1912 (1); v A 1910 (5) 1912 (2)*
Seccull, A. W. 1: v E 1895
Seymour, M. A. 7: v E 1964 (2); v A 1969 (1); *v A 1963 (4)*
Shalders, W. A. 12: v E 1898 (1) 1905 (5); v A 1902 (3); *v E 1907 (3)*
Shepstone, G. H. 2: v E 1895 (1) 1898 (1)
Sherwell, P. W. 13: v E 1905 (5); *v E 1907 (3); v A 1910 (5)*
Siedle, I. J. 18: v E 1927 (1) 1930 (5); v A 1935 (5); *v E 1929 (3) 1935 (4)*
Sinclair, J. H. 25: v E 1895 (3) 1898 (2) 1905 (5) 1909 (4); v A 1902 (3); *v E 1907 (3); v A 1910 (5)*
Smith, C. J. E. 3: v A 1902 (3)
Smith, F. W. 3: v E 1888 (2) 1895 (1)
Smith, V. I. 9: v A 1949 (3) 1957 (1); *v E 1947 (4) 1955 (1)*
Snooke, S. D. 1: *v E 1907*
Snooke, S. J. 26: v E 1905 (5) 1909 (5) 1922 (3); *v E 1907 (3) 1912 (3); v A 1910 (5) 1912 (2)*
Solomon, W. R. 1: v E 1898
Stewart, R. B. 1: v E 1888
Stricker, L. A. 13: v E 1909 (4); *v E 1912 (2); v A 1910 (5) 1912 (2)*
Susskind, M. J. 5: *v E 1924 (5)*

Taberer, H. M. 1: v A 1902
Tancred, A. B. 2: v E 1888 (2)
Tancred, L. J. 14: v E 1905 (5) 1913 (1); v A 1902 (3); *v E 1907 (1) 1912 (2); v A 1912 (2)*
Tancred, V. M. 1: v E 1898
Tapscott, G. L. 1: v E 1913
Tapscott, L. E. 2: v E 1922 (2)
Tayfield, H. J. 37: v E 1956 (5); v A 1949 (5) 1957 (5); v NZ 1953 (5); *v E 1955 (5) 1960 (5); v A 1952 (5); v NZ 1952 (2)*
Taylor, A. I. 1: v E 1956
Taylor, D. 2: v E 1913 (2)
Taylor, H. W. 42: v E 1913 (5) 1922 (5) 1927 (5) 1930 (4); v A 1921 (3); *v E 1912 (3) 1924 (5) 1929 (3); v A 1912 (3) 1931 (5); v NZ 1931 (1)*
Theunissen, N. H. G. de J. 1: v E 1888
Thornton, P. G. 1: v A 1902
Tomlinson, D. S. 1: *v E 1935*
Traicos, A. J. 3: v A 1969 (3)
Trimborn, P. H. J. 4: v A 1966 (3) 1969 (1)
Tuckett, L. 9: v E 1948 (4); *v E 1947 (5)*
Tuckett, L. R. 1: v E 1913
Twentyman-Jones, P. S. 1: v A 1902

van der Bijl, P. G. V. 5: v E 1938 (5)
Van der Merwe, E. A. 2: v A 1935 (1); *v E 1929 (1)*
Van der Merwe, P. L. 15: v E 1964 (2); v A 1966 (5); *v E 1965 (3); v A 1963 (3); v NZ 1963 (2)*
Van Ryneveld, C. B. 19: v E 1956 (5); v A 1957 (4); v NZ 1953 (5); *v E 1951 (5)*
Varnals, G. D. 3: v E 1964 (3)
Viljoen, K. G. 27: v E 1930 (3) 1938 (4) 1948 (2); v A 1935 (4); *v E 1935 (4) 1947 (5); v A 1931 (4); v NZ 1931 (1)*
Vincent, C. L. 25: v E 1927 (5) 1930 (5); *v E 1929 (4) 1935 (4); v A 1931 (5); v NZ 1931 (2)*
Vintcent, C. H. 3: v E 1888 (2) 1891 (1)
Vogler, A. E. E. 15: v E 1905 (5) 1909 (5); *v E 1907 (3); v A 1910 (2)*

Wade, H. F. 10: v A 1935 (5); *v E 1935 (5)*
Wade, W. W. 11: v E 1938 (3) 1948 (5); v A 1949 (3)
Waite, J. H. B. 50: v E 1956 (5); 1964 (2); v A 1957 (5); v NZ 1953 (5) 1961 (5); *v E 1951 (4) 1955 (5) 1960 (5); v A 1952 (5) 1963 (4); v NZ 1952 (2) 1963 (3)*
Walter, K. A. 2: v NZ 1961 (2)
Ward, T. A. 23: v E 1913 (5) 1922 (5); v A 1921 (3); *v E 1912 (2) 1924 (5); v A 1912 (3)*
Watkins, J. C. 15: v E 1956 (2); v A 1949 (3); v NZ 1953 (3); *v A 1952 (5); v NZ 1952 (2)*
Wesley, C. 3: *v E 1960 (3)*
Westcott, R. J. 5: v A 1957 (2); v NZ 1953 (3)
White, G. C. 17: v E 1905 (5) 1909 (4); *v E 1907 (3) 1912 (2); v A 1912 (3)*
Willoughby, J. T. I. 2: v E 1895 (2)
Wimble, C. S. 1: v E 1891
Winslow, P. L. 5: v A 1949 (2); *v E 1955 (3)*
Wynne, O. E. 6: v E 1948 (3); v A 1949 (3)

Zulch, J. W. 16: v E 1909 (5) 1913 (3); v A 1921 (3); *v A 1910 (5)*

WEST INDIES

Number of Test cricketers: 188

Achong, E. 6: v E 1929 (1) 1934 (2); *v E 1933 (3)*
Alexander, F. C. M. 25: v E 1959 (5); v P 1957 (5); *v E 1957 (2); v A 1960 (5); v In 1958 (5); v P 1958 (3)*
Ali, Imtiaz 1: v In 1975
Ali, Inshan 12: v E 1973 (2); v A 1972 (3); v In 1970 (1); v P 1976 (1); v NZ 1971 (3); *v E 1973 (1); v A 1975 (1)*
Allan, D. W. 5: v A 1964 (1); v In 1961 (3); *v E 1966 (2)*
Asgarali, N. 2: *v E 1957 (2)*
Atkinson, D. St E. 22: v E 1953 (4); v A 1954 (4); v P 1957 (1); *v E 1957 (2); v A 1951 (2); v NZ 1951 (1) 1955 (4); v In 1948 (4)*
Atkinson, E. St E. 8: v P 1957 (3); *v In 1958 (3); v P 1958 (2)*
Austin, R. A. 2: v A 1977 (2)

Bacchus, S. F. A. F. 19: v A 1977 (2); *v E 1980 (5); v A 1981 (2); v In 1978 (6); v P 1980 (4)*
Baichan, L. 3: *v A 1975 (1); v P 1974 (2)*
Baptiste, E. A. E. 9: v A 1983 (3); *v E 1984 (5); v In 1983 (1)*
Barrow, I. 11: v E 1929 (1) 1934 (1); *v E 1933 (3) 1939 (1); v A 1930 (5)*
Barrett, A. G. 6: v E 1973 (2); v In 1970 (2); *v In 1974 (2)*
Bartlett, E. L. 5: *v E 1928 (1); v A 1930 (4)*
Best, C. A. 3: v E 1985 (3)
Betancourt, N. 1: v E 1929
Binns, A. P. 5: v A 1954 (1); v In 1952 (1); *v NZ 1955 (3)*
Birkett, L. S. 4 *v A 1930 (4)*
Boyce, K. D. 21: v E 1973 (4); v A 1972 (4); v In 1970 (1); *v E 1973 (3); v A 1975 (4); v In 1974 (3); v P 1974 (2)*
Browne, C. R. 4: v E 1929 (2); *v E 1928 (2)*
Butcher, B. F. 44: v E 1959 (2) 1967 (5); v A 1964 (5); *v E 1963 (5) 1966 (5) 1969 (3); v A 1968 (5); v NZ 1968 (3); v In 1958 (5) 1966 (3); v P 1958 (3)*
Butler, L. 1: v A 1954
Butts, C. G. 4: v NZ 1984 (1); *v NZ 1986 (1); v P 1986 (2)*
Bynoe, M. R. 4: *v In 1966 (3); v P 1958 (1)*

Camacho, G. S. 11: v E 1967 (5); v In 1970 (2); *v E 1969 (2); v A 1968 (2)*
Cameron, F. J. 5: *v In 1948 (5)*
Cameron, J. H. 2: *v E 1939 (2)*
Carew, G. M. 4: v E 1934 (1) 1947 (2); *v In 1948 (1)*
Carew, M. C. 19: v E 1967 (1); v NZ 1971 (3); v In 1970 (3); *v E 1963 (2) 1966 (1) 1969 (1); v A 1968 (5); v NZ 1968 (3)*
Challenor, G. 3: *v E 1928 (3)*

Chang, H. S. 1: *v In 1978*

Christiani, C. M. 4: v E 1934 (4)

Christiani, R. J. 22: v E 1947 (4) 1953 (1); v In 1952 (2); *v E 1950 (4); v A 1951 (5); v NZ 1951 (1); v In 1948 (5)*

Clarke, C. B. 3: *v E 1939 (3)*

Clarke, S. T. 11: v A 1977 (1); *v A 1981 (1); v In 1978 (5); v P 1980 (4)*

Constantine, L. N. 18: v E 1929 (3) 1934 (3); *v E 1928 (3) 1933 (1) 1939 (3); v A 1930 (5)*

Croft, C. E. H. 27: v E 1980 (4); v A 1977 (2); v P 1976 (5); *v E 1980 (3); v A 1979 (3) 1981 (3); v NZ 1979 (3); v P 1980 (4)*

Da Costa, O. C. 5: v E 1929 (1) 1934 (1); *v E 1933 (3)*

Daniel, W. W. 10: v A 1983 (2); v In 1975 (1); *v E 1976 (4) v In 1983 (3)*

Davis, B. A. 4: v A 1964 (4)

Davis, C. A. 15: v A 1972 (2); v NZ 1971 (5); v In 1970 (4); *v E 1969 (3); v A 1968 (1)*

Davis, W. W. 11: v A 1983 (1); v NZ 1984 (2); v In 1982 (1); *v E 1984 (1); v In 1983 (6)*

De Caires, F. I. 3: v E 1929 (3)

Depeiza, C. C. 5: v A 1954 (3); *v NZ 1955 (2)*

Dewdney, T. 9: v A 1954 (2); v P 1957 (3); *v E 1957 (1); v NZ 1955 (3)*

Dowe, U. G. 4: v A 1972 (1); v NZ 1971 (1); v In 1970 (2)

Dujon, P. J. L. 43: v E 1985 (4); v A 1983 (5); v NZ 1984 (4); v In 1982 (5); *v E 1984 (5); v A 1981 (3) 1984 (5); v NZ 1986 (3); v In 1983 (6); v P 1986 (3)*

Edwards, R. M. 5: *v A 1968 (2); v NZ 1968 (3)*

Ferguson, W. 8: v E 1947 (4) 1953 (1); *v In 1948 (3)*

Fernandes, M. P. 2: v E 1929 (1); *v E 1928 (1)*

Findlay, T. M. 10: v A 1972 (1); v NZ 1971 (5); v In 1970 (2); *v E 1969 (2)*

Foster, M. L. C. 14: v E 1973 (1); v A 1972 (4) 1977 (1); v NZ 1971 (3); v In 1970 (2); v P 1976 (1); *v E 1969 (1) 1973 (1)*

Francis, G. N. 10: v E 1929 (1); *v E 1928 (3) 1933 (1); v A 1930 (5)*

Frederick, M. C. 1: v E 1953

Fredericks, R. C. 59: v E 1973 (5); v A 1972 (5); v NZ 1971 (5); v In 1970 (4) 1975 (4); v P 1976 (5); *v E 1969 (3) 1973 (3) 1976 (5); v A 1968 (4) 1975 (6); v NZ 1968 (3); v In 1974 (5); v P 1974 (2)*

Fuller, R. L. 1: v E 1934

Furlonge, H. A. 3: v A 1954 (1); *v NZ 1955 (2)*

Ganteaume, A. G. 1: v E 1947

Garner, J. 58: v E 1980 (4) 1985 (5); v A 1977 (2) 1983 (5); v NZ 1984 (4); v In 1982 (4); v P 1976 (5); *v E 1980 (5) 1984 (5); v A 1979 (3) 1981 (3) 1984 (5); v NZ 1979 (3) 1986 (2); v P 1980 (3)*

Gaskin, B. B. M. 2: v E 1947 (2)

Gibbs, G. L. R. 1: v A 1954

Gibbs, L. R. 79: v E 1967 (5) 1973 (5); v A 1964 (5) 1972 (5); v NZ 1971 (2); v In 1961 (5) 1970 (1); v P 1957 (4); *v E 1963 (5) 1966 (5) 1969 (3) 1973 (3); v A 1960 (3) 1968 (5) 1975 (6); v NZ 1968 (3); v In 1958 (1) 1966 (3) 1974 (5); v P 1958 (3) 1974 (2)*

Gilchrist, R. 13: v P 1957 (5); *v E 1957 (4); v In 1958 (4)*

Gladstone, G. 1: v E 1929

Goddard, J. D. C. 27: v E 1947 (4); *v E 1950 (4) 1957 (5); v A 1951 (4); v NZ 1951 (2) 1955 (3); v In 1948 (5)*

Gomes, H. A. 60: v E 1980 (4) 1985 (5); v A 1977 (3) 1983 (2); v NZ 1984 (4); v In 1982 (5); *v E 1976 (2) 1984 (5); v A 1981 (3) 1984 (5); v NZ 1986 (3); v In 1978 (6) 1983 (6); v P 1980 (4) 1986 (3)*

Gomez, G. E. 29: v E 1947 (4) 1953 (4); v In 1952 (4); *v E 1939 (2) 1950 (4); v A 1951 (5); v NZ 1951 (1); v In 1948 (5)*

Grant, G. C. 12: v E 1934 (4); *v E 1933 (3); v A 1930 (5)*

Grant, R. S. 7: v E 1934 (4); *v E 1939 (3)*

Gray, A. H. 5: *v NZ 1986 (2); v P 1986 (3)*

Greenidge, A. E. 6: v A 1977 (2); *v In 1978 (4)*

Greenidge, C. G. 77: v E 1980 (4) 1985 (5); v A 1977 (2) 1983 (5); v NZ 1984 (4); v In 1982 (5); v P 1976 (5); *v E 1976 (5) 1980 (5) 1984 (5); v A 1975 (2) 1979 (3) 1981 (2) 1984 (5); v NZ 1979 (3); v In 1974 (5) 1983 (6); v P 1986 (3)*

Greenidge, G. A. 5: v A 1972 (3); v NZ 1971 (2)

Grell, M. G. 1: v E 1929

Griffith, C. C. 28: v E 1959 (1) 1967 (4); v A 1964 (5); *v E 1963 (5) 1966 (5); v A 1968 (3); v NZ 1968 (2); v In 1966 (3)*

Griffith, H. C. 13: v E 1929 (3); *v E 1928 (3) 1933 (2); v A 1930 (5)*

Guillen, S. C. 5: *v A 1951 (3); v NZ 1951 (2)*

Hall, W. W. 48: v E 1959 (5) 1967 (4); v A 1964 (5); v In 1961 (5); *v E 1963 (5) 1966 (5); v A 1960 (5) 1968 (2); v NZ 1968 (1); v In 1958 (5) 1966 (3); v P 1958 (3)*

Harper, R. A. 19: v E 1985 (2); v A 1983 (4); v NZ 1984 (1); *v E 1984 (5); v A 1984 (2); v In 1983 (2); v P 1986 (3)*

Haynes, D. L. 65: v E 1980 (4) 1985 (5); v A 1977 (2) 1983 (5); v NZ 1984 (4); v In 1982 (5); *v E 1980 (5) 1984 (5); v A 1979 (3) 1981 (3) 1984 (5); v NZ 1979 (3) 1986 (3); v In 1983 (6); v P 1980 (4) 1986 (3)*

Headley, G. A. 22: v E 1929 (4) 1934 (4) 1947 (1) 1953 (1); *v E 1933 (3) 1939 (3); v A 1930 (5); v In 1948 (1)*

Headley, R. G. A. 2: *v E 1973 (2)*

Hendriks, J. L. 20: v A 1964 (4); v In 1961 (1); *v E 1966 (3) 1969 (1); v A 1968 (5); v NZ 1968 (3); v In 1966 (3)*

Hoad, E. L. G. 4: v E 1929 (1); *v E 1928 (1) 1933 (2)*

Holder, V. A. 40: v E 1973 (1); v A 1972 (3) 1977 (3); v NZ 1971 (4); v In 1970 (3) 1975 (1); v P 1976 (1); *v E 1969 (3) 1973 (2) 1976 (2); v A 1975 (3); v In 1974 (4) 1978 (6); v P 1974 (2)*

Holding, M. A. 60: v E 1980 (4) 1985 (4); v A 1983 (3); v NZ 1984 (3); v In 1975 (4) 1982 (5); *v E 1976 (4) 1980 (5) 1984 (4); v A 1975 (5) 1979 (3) 1981 (3) 1984 (3); v NZ 1979 (3) 1986 (1); v In 1983 (6)*

Holford, D. A. J. 24: v E 1967 (4); v NZ 1971 (5); v In 1970 (1) 1975 (2); v P 1976 (1); *v E 1966 (5); v A 1968 (2); v NZ 1968 (3); v In 1966 (1)*

Holt, J. K. 17: v E 1953 (5); v A 1954 (5); *v In 1958 (5); v P 1958 (2)*

Howard, A. B. 1: v NZ 1971

Hunte, C. C. 44: v E 1959 (5); v A 1964 (5); v In 1961 (5); v P 1957 (5); *v E 1963 (5) 1966 (5); v A 1960 (5); v In 1958 (5) 1966 (3); v P 1958 (1)*

Hunte, E. A. C. 3: v E 1929 (3)

Hylton, L. G. 6: v E 1934 (4); *v E 1939 (2)*

Johnson, H. H. H. 3: v E 1947 (1); *v E 1950 (2)*

Johnson, T. F. 1: *v E 1939*

Jones, C. M. 4: v E 1929 (1) 1934 (3)

Jones, P. E. 9: v E 1947 (1); *v E 1950 (2); v A 1951 (1); v In 1948 (5)*

Julien, B. D. 24: v E 1973 (5); v In 1975 (4); v P 1976 (1); *v E 1973 (3) 1976 (2); v A 1975 (3); v In 1974 (4); v P 1974 (2)*

Jumadeen, R. R. 12: v A 1972 (1) 1977 (2); v NZ 1971 (1); v In 1975 (4); v P 1976 (1); *v E 1976 (1); v In 1978 (2)*

Kallicharran, A. I. 66: v E 1973 (5); v A 1972 (5) 1977 (5); v NZ 1971 (2); v In 1975 (4); v P 1976 (5); *v E 1973 (3) 1976 (3) 1980 (5); v A 1975 (6) 1979 (3); v NZ 1979 (3); v In 1974 (5) 1978 (6); v P 1974 (2) 1980 (4)*

Kanhai, R. B. 79: v E 1959 (5) 1967 (5) 1973 (5); v A 1964 (5) 1972 (5); v In 1961 (5) 1970 (5); v P 1957 (5); *v E 1957 (5) 1963 (5) 1966 (5) 1973 (3); v A 1960 (5) 1968 (5); v In 1958 (5) 1966 (3); v P 1958 (3)*

Kentish, E. S. M. 2: v E 1947 (1) 1953 (1)

King, C. L. 9: v P 1976 (1); *v E 1976 (3) 1980 (1); v A 1979 (1); v NZ 1979 (3)*

King, F. M. 14: v E 1953 (3); v A 1954 (4); v In 1952 (5); *v NZ 1955 (2)*

King, L. A. 2: v E 1967 (1); v In 1961 (1)

Lashley, P. D. 4: *v E 1966 (2); v A 1960 (2)*

Legall, R. 4: v In 1952 (4)

Lewis, D. M. 3: v In 1970 (3)

Lloyd, C. H. 110: v E 1967 (5) 1973 (5) 1980 (4); v A 1972 (3) 1977 (2) 1983 (4); v NZ 1971 (2); v In 1970 (5) 1975 (4) 1982 (5); v P 1976 (5); *v E 1969 (3) 1973 (3) 1976 (5) 1980 (4) 1984 (5); v A 1968 (4) 1975 (6) 1979 (2) 1981 (3) 1984 (5); v NZ 1968 (3) 1979 (3); v In 1966 (3) 1974 (5) 1983 (6); v P 1974 (2) 1980 (4)*

Logie, A. L. 16: v A 1983 (1); v NZ 1984 (4); v In 1982 (5); *v NZ 1986 (3); v In 1983 (3)*

McMorris, E. D. A. 13: v E 1959 (4); v In 1961 (4); v P 1957 (1); *v E 1963 (2) 1966 (2)*
McWatt, C. A. 6: v E 1953 (5); v A 1954 (1)
Madray, I. S. 2: v P 1957 (2)
Marshall, M. D. 51: v E 1980(1) 1985 (5); v A 1983 (4); v NZ 1984 (4); v In 1982 (5); *v E 1980 (4) 1984 (4); v A 1984 (5); v NZ 1986 (3); v In 1978 (3) 1983 (6); v P 1980 (4) 1986 (3)*
Marshall, N. E. 1: v A 1954
Marshall, R. E. 4: *v A 1951 (2); v NZ 1951 (2)*
Martin, F. R. 9: v E 1929 (1); *v E 1928 (3); v A 1930 (5)*
Martindale, E. A. 10: v E 1934 (4); *v E 1933 (3) 1939 (3)*
Mattis, E. H. 4: v E 1980 (4)
Mendonca, I. L. 2: v In 1961 (2)
Merry, C. A. 2: *v E 1933 (2)*
Miller, R. 1: v In 1952
Moodie, G. H. 1: v E 1934
Murray, D. A. 19: v E 1980 (4); v A 1977 (3); *v A 1981 (2); v In 1978 (6); v P 1980 (4)*
Murray, D. L. 62: v E 1967 (5) 1973 (5); v A 1972 (4) 1977 (2); v In 1975 (4); v P 1976 (5); *v E 1963 (5) 1973 (3) 1976 (5) 1980 (5); v A 1975 (6) 1979 (3); v NZ 1979 (3); v In 1974 (5); v P 1974 (2)*

Nanan, R. 1: *v P 1980*
Neblett, J. M. 1: v E 1934
Noreiga, J. M. 4: v In 1970 (4)
Nunes, R. K. 4: v E 1929 (1); *v E 1928 (3)*
Nurse, S. M. 29: v E 1959 (1) 1967 (5); v A 1964 (4); v In 1961 (1); *v E 1966 (5); v A 1960 (3) 1968 (5); v NZ 1968 (3); v In 1966 (2)*

Padmore, A. L. 2: v In 1975 (1); *v E 1976 (1)*
Pairaudeau, B. H. 13: v E 1953 (2); v In 1952 (5): *v E 1957 (2); v NZ 1955 (4)*
Parry, D. R. 12: v A 1977 (5); *v NZ 1979 (1); v In 1978 (6)*
Passailaigue, C. C. 1: v E 1929
Patterson, B. P. 6: v E 1985 (5); *v P 1986 (1)*
Payne, T. R. O. 1: v E 1985
Phillip, N. 9: v A 1977 (3); *v In 1978 (6)*
Pierre, L. R. 1: v E 1947

Rae, A. F. 15: v In 1952 (2); *v E 1950 (4); v A 1951 (3); v NZ 1951 (1); v In 1948 (5)*
Ramadhin, S. 43: v E 1953 (5) 1959 (4); v A 1954 (4); v In 1952 (4); *v E 1950 (4) 1957 (5); v A 1951 (5) 1960 (2); v NZ 1951 (2) 1955 (4); v In 1958 (2); v P 1958 (2)*
Richards, I. V. A. 88: v E 1980 (4) 1985 (5); v A 1977 (2) 1983 (5); v NZ 1984 (4); v In 1975 (4) 1982 (5); v P 1976 (5); *v E 1976 (4) 1980 (5) 1984 (5); v A 1975 (6) 1979 (3) 1981 (3) 1984 (5); v NZ 1986 (3); v In 1974 (5) 1983 (6); v P 1974 (2) 1980 (4) 1986 (3)*
Richardson, R. B. 26: v E 1985 (5); v A 1983 (5); v NZ 1984 (4); *v A 1984 (5); v NZ 1986 (3); v In 1983 (1); v P 1986 (3)*
Rickards, K. R. 2: v E 1947 (1); *v A 1951 (1)*
Roach, C. A. 16: v E 1929 (4) 1934 (1); *v E 1928 (3) 1933 (3); v A 1930 (5)*
Roberts, A. M. E. 47: v E 1973 (1) 1980 (3); v A 1977 (2); v In 1975 (2) 1982 (5); v P 1976 (5); *v E 1976 (5) 1980 (3); v A 1975 (5) 1979 (3) 1981 (3); v NZ 1979 (2); v In 1974 (5) 1983 (2); v P 1974 (2)*
Roberts, A. T. 1: *v NZ 1955*
Rodriguez, W. V. 5: v E 1967 (1); v A 1964 (1); v In 1961 (2); *v E 1963 (1)*
Rowe, L. G. 30: v E 1973 (5); v A 1972 (3); v NZ 1971 (4); v In 1975 (4); *v E 1976 (2); v A 1975 (6) 1979 (3); v NZ 1979 (3)*

St Hill, E. L. 2: v E 1929 (2)
St Hill, W. H. 3: v E 1929 (1); *v E 1928 (2)*
Scarlett, R. O. 3: v E 1959 (3)
Scott, A. P. H. 1: v In 1952
Scott, O. C. 8: v E 1929 (1); *v E 1928 (2); v A 1930 (5)*
Sealey, B. J. 1: *v E 1933*
Sealy, J. E. D. 11: v E 1929 (2) 1934 (4); *v E 1939 (3); v A 1930 (2)*
Shepherd, J. N. 5: v In 1970 (2); *v E 1969 (3)*
Shillingford, G. C. 7: v NZ 1971 (2); v In 1970 (3); *v E 1969 (2)*

Shillingford, I. T. 4: v A 1977 (1); v P 1976 (3)
Shivnarine, S. 8: v A 1977 (3); *v In 1978 (5)*
Singh, C. K. 2: v E 1959 (2)
Small, J. A. 3: v E 1929 (1); *v E 1928 (2)*
Small, M. A. 2: v A 1983 (1); *v E 1984 (1)*
Smith, C. W. 5: v In 1961 (1); *v A 1960 (4)*
Smith, O. G. 26: v A 1954 (4); v P 1957 (5); *v E 1957 (5); v NZ 1955 (4); v In 1958 (5); v P 1958 (3)*
Sobers, G. S. 93: v E 1953 (1) 1959 (5) 1967 (5) 1973 (4); v A 1954 (4) 1964 (5); v NZ 1971 (5); v In 1961 (5); 1970 (5); v P 1957 (5); *v E 1957 (5) 1963 (5) 1966 (5) 1969 (3) 1973 (3); v A 1960 (5) 1968 (5); v NZ 1955 (4) 1968 (3); v In 1958 (5) 1966 (3); v P 1958 (3)*
Solomon, J. S. 27: v E 1959 (2); v A 1964 (4); v In 1961 (4); *v E 1963 (5); v A 1960 (5); v In 1958 (4); v P 1958 (3)*
Stayers, S. C. 4: v In 1961 (4)
Stollmeyer, J. B. 32: v E 1947 (2) 1953 (5); v A 1954 (2); v In 1952 (5); *v E 1939 (1) 1950 (4); v A 1951 (5); v NZ 1951 (2); v In 1948 (4)*
Stollmeyer, V. H. 1: *v E 1939*

Taylor, J. 3: v P 1957 (1); *v In 1958 (1); v P 1958 (1)*
Trim, J. 4: v E 1947 (1); *v A 1951 (1); v In 1948 (2)*

Valentine, A. L. 36: v E 1953 (3); v A 1954 (3); v In 1952 (5) 1961 (2); v P 1957 (1); *v E 1950 (4) 1957 (2); v A 1951 (5) 1960 (5); v NZ 1951 (2) 1955 (4)*
Valentine, V. A. 2: *v E 1933 (2)*

Walcott, C. L. 44: v E 1947 (4) 1953 (5) 1959 (2); v A 1954 (5); v In 1952 (5); v P 1957 (4); *v E 1950 (4) 1957 (5); v A 1951 (3); v NZ 1951 (2); v In 1948 (5)*
Walcott, L. A. 1: v E 1929
Walsh, C. A. 13: v E 1985 (1); v NZ 1984 (1); *v A 1984 (5); v NZ 1986 (3); v P 1986 (3)*
Watson, C. 7: v E 1959 (5); v In 1961 (1); *v A 1960 (1)*
Weekes, E. D. 48: v E 1947 (4) 1953 (4); v A 1954 (5) v In 1952 (5); v P 1957 (5); *v E 1950 (4) 1957 (5); v A 1951 (5); v NZ 1951 (2) 1955 (4); v In 1948 (5)*
Weekes, K. H. 2: *v E 1939 (2)*
White, W. A. 2: v E 1964 (2)
Wight, C. V. 2: v E 1929 (1); *v E 1928 (1)*
Wight, G. L. 1: v In 1952
Wiles, C. A. 1: *v E 1933*
Willett, E. T. 5: v A 1972 (3); *v In 1974 (2)*
Williams, A. B. 7: v A 1977 (3); *v In 1978 (4)*
Williams, E. A. V. 4: v E 1947 (3); *v E 1939 (1)*
Wishart, K. L. 1: v E 1934
Worrell, F. M. M. 51: v E 1947 (3) 1953 (4) 1959 (4); v A 1954 (4); v In 1952 (5) 1961 (5); *v E 1950 (4) 1957 (5) 1963 (5); v A 1951 (5) 1960 (5); v NZ 1951 (2)*

NEW ZEALAND

Number of Test cricketers: 163

Alabaster, J. C. 21: v E 1962 (2); v WI 1955 (1); v In 1967 (4); *v E 1958 (2); v SA 1961 (5); v WI 1971 (2); v In 1955 (4); v P 1955 (1)*
Allcott, C. F. W. 6: v E 1929 (2); v SA 1931 (1); *v E 1931 (3)*
Anderson, R. W. 9: v E 1977 (3); *v E 1978 (3); v P 1976 (3)*
Anderson, W. M. 1: v A 1945
Andrews, B. 2: *v A 1973 (2)*

Badcock, F. T. 7: v E 1929 (3) 1932 (2); v SA 1931 (2)
Barber, R. T. 1: v WI 1955
Bartlett, G. A. 10: v E 1965 (2); v In 1967 (2); v P 1964 (1); *v SA 1961 (5)*
Barton, P. T. 7: v E 1962 (3); *v SA 1961 (4)*
Beard, D. D. 4: v WI 1951 (2) 1955 (2)
Beck, J. E. F. 8: v WI 1955 (4); *v SA 1953 (4)*

Bell, W. 2: *v SA 1953* (2)

Bilby, G. P. 2: v E 1965 (2)

Blain, T. E. 1: *v E 1986*

Blair, R. W. 19: v E 1954 (1) 1958 (2) 1962 (2); v SA 1952 (2) 1963 (3); v WI 1955 (2) *v E 1958* (3); *v SA 1953* (4)

Blunt, R. C. 9: v E 1929 (4); v SA 1931 (2); *v E 1931* (3)

Bolton, B. A. 2: v E 1958 (2)

Boock, S. L. 28: v E 1977 (3) 1983 (2); v WI 1979 (3) 1986 (2); v P 1978 (3) 1984 (2); *v E 1978* (3); *v A 1985* (1); *v WI 1984* (3); *v P 1984* (3); *v SL 1983* (3)

Bracewell, B. P. 6: v P 1978 (1) 1984 (1); *v E 1978* (3); *v A 1980* (1)

Bracewell, J. G. 24: v A 1985 (2); v WI 1986 (3); v In 1980 (1); *v E 1983* (4) *1986* (3); *v A 1980* (3) *1985* (2); *v WI 1984* (1); *v P 1984* (2); *v SL 1983* (2) *1986* (1)

Bradburn, W. P. 2: v SA 1963 (2)

Brown, V. R. 2: *v A 1985* (2)

Burgess, M. G. 50: v E 1970 (1) 1977 (3); v A 1973 (1) 1976 (2); v WI 1968 (2); v In 1967 (4) 1975 (3); v P 1972 (3) 1978 (3); *v E 1969* (2) *1973* (3) *1978* (3); *v A 1980* (3); *v WI 1971* (5); *v In 1969* (3) *1976* (3); *v P 1969* (3) *1976* (3)

Burke, C. 1: v A 1945

Burtt, T. B. 10: v E 1946 (1) 1950 (2); v SA 1952 (1); v WI 1951 (2); *v E 1949* (4)

Butterfield, L. A. 1: v A 1945

Cairns, B. L. 43: v E 1974 (1) 1977 (1) 1983 (3); v A 1976 (1) 1981 (3); v WI 1979 (3); v In 1975 (1) 1980 (3); v P 1978 (3) 1984 (3); *v E 1978* (2) *1983* (4); *v A 1973* (1) *1980* (3) *1985* (1); *v WI 1984* (2); *v In 1976* (2); *v P 1976* (2); *v SL 1983* (2)

Cameron, F. J. 19: v E 1962 (3); v SA 1963 (3); v P 1964 (3); *v E 1965* (2); *v SA 1961* (5); *v In 1964* (1); *v P 1964* (3)

Cave, H. B. 19: v E 1954 (2); v WI 1955 (3); *v E 1949* (4) *1958* (2); *v In 1955* (5); *v P 1955* (3)

Chapple, M. E. 14: v E 1954 (1) 1965 (1); v SA 1952 (1) 1963 (3); v WI 1955 (1); *v SA 1953* (5) *1961* (2)

Chatfield, E. J. 33: v E 1974 (1) 1977 (1) 1983 (3); v A 1976 (2) 1981 (1) 1985 (3); v WI 1986 (3); v P 1984 (3); v SL 1982 (2); *v E 1983* (4) *1986* (1); *v A 1985* (2); *v WI 1984* (4); *v P 1984* (1); *v SL 1983* (2) *1986* (1)

Cleverley, D. C. 2: v SA 1931 (1); v A 1945 (1)

Collinge, R. O. 35: v E 1970 (2) 1974 (2) 1977 (3); v A 1973 (3); v In 1967 (2) 1975 (3); v P 1964 (3) 1972 (2); *v E 1965* (3) *1969* (1) *1973* (3) *1978* (1); *v In 1964* (2) *1976* (1); *v P 1964* (2) *1976* (2)

Colquhoun, I. A. 2: v E 1954 (2)

Coney, J. V. 52: v E 1983 (3); v A 1973 (2) 1981 (3) 1985 (3); v WI 1979 (3) 1986 (3); v In 1980 (3); v P 1978 (3) 1984 (3); v SL 1982 (2); *v E 1983* (4) *1986* (3); *v A 1973* (2) *1980* (2) *1985* (3); *v WI 1984* (4); *v P 1984* (3); *v SL 1983* (3)

Congdon, B. E. 61: v E 1965 (3) 1970 (2) 1974 (2) 1977 (3); v A 1973 (3) 1976 (2); v WI 1968 (3); v In 1967 (4) 1975 (3); v P 1964 (3) 1972 (3); *v E 1965* (3) *1969* (3) *1973* (3) *1978* (3); *v A 1973* (3); *v WI 1971* (5); *v In 1964* (3) *1969* (3); *v P 1964* (1) *1969* (3)

Cowie, J. 9: v E 1946 (1); v A 1945 (1); *v E 1937* (3) *1949* (4)

Cresswell G. F. 3: v E 1950 (2); *v E 1949* (1)

Cromb, I. B. 5: v SA 1931 (2); *v E 1931* (3)

Crowe, J. J. 30: v E 1983 (3); v WI 1986 (3); v P 1984 (3); v SL 1982 (2); *v E 1983* (3) *1986* (3); *v A 1985* (3); *v WI 1984* (4); *v P 1984* (3); *v SL 1983* (3) *1986* (1)

Crowe, M. D. 36: v E 1983 (3); v A 1981 (3) 1985 (3); v WI 1986 (3); v P 1984 (3); *v E 1983* (4) *1986* (3); *v A 1985* (3); *v WI 1984* (4); *v P 1984* (3); *v SL 1983* (3) *1986* (1)

Cunis, R. S. 20: v E 1965 (3) 1970 (2); v SA 1963 (1); v WI 1968 (3); *v E 1969* (1); *v WI 1971* (5); *v In 1969* (3); *v P 1969* (2)

D'Arcy, J. W. 5: *v E 1958* (5)

Dempster, C. S. 10: v E 1929 (4) 1932 (2); v SA 1931 (2); *v E 1931* (2)

Dempster, E. W. 5: v SA 1952 (1); *v SA 1953* (4)

Dick, A. E. 17: v E 1962 (3); v SA 1963 (2); v P 1964 (3); *v E 1965* (2); *v SA 1961* (5); *v P 1964* (3)

Dickinson, G. R. 3: v E 1929 (2); v SA 1931 (1)

Donnelly, M. P. 7: *v E 1937* (3) *1949* (4)

Dowling, G. T. 39: v E 1962 (3) 1970 (2); v In 1967 (4); v SA 1963 (1); v WI 1968 (3); v P 1964 (2); *v E 1965* (3) *1969* (3); *v SA 1961* (4); *v WI 1971* (2); *v In 1964* (4) *1969* (3); *v P 1964* (2) *1969* (3)

Dunning, J. A. 4: v E 1932 (1); *v E 1937* (3)

Edgar, B. A. 39: v E 1983 (3); v A 1981 (3) 1985 (3); v WI 1979 (3); v In 1980 (3); v P 1978 (3); v SL 1982 (2); *v E 1978 (3) 1983 (4) 1986 (3); v A 1980 (3) 1985 (3); v P 1984 (3)*
Edwards, G. N. 8: v E 1977 (1); v A 1976 (2); v In 1980 (3); *v E 1978 (2)*
Emery, R. W. G. 2: v WI 1951 (2)

Fisher, F. E. 1: v SA 1952
Foley, H. 1: v E 1929
Franklin, T. J. 2: v A 1985 (1); *v E 1983 (1)*
Freeman, D. L. 2: v E 1932 (2)

Gallichan, N. 1: *v E 1937*
Gedye, S. G. 4: v SA 1963 (3); v P 1964 (1)
Gillespie, S. R. 1: v A 1985
Gray, E. J. 8: *v E 1983 (2) 1986 (3); v P 1984 (2); v SL 1986 (1)*
Guillen, S. C. 3: v WI 1955 (3)
Guy, J. W. 12: v E 1958 (2); v WI 1955 (2); *v SA 1961 (2); v In 1955 (5); v P 1955 (1)*

Hadlee, D. R. 26: v E 1974 (2) 1977 (1); v A 1973 (3) 1976 (1); v In 1975 (3); v P 1972 (2); *v E 1969 (2) 1973 (3); v A 1973 (3); v In 1969 (3); v P 1969 (3)*
Hadlee, R. J. 70: v E 1977 (3) 1983 (3); v A 1973 (2) 1976 (2) 1981 (3) 1985 (3); v WI 1979 (3) 1986 (3); v In 1975 (2) 1980 (3); v P 1972 (1) 1978 (3) 1984 (3); v SL 1982 (2); *v E 1973 (1) 1978 (3) 1983 (4) 1986 (3); v A 1973 (3) 1980 (3) 1985 (3); v WI 1984 (4); v In 1976 (3); v P 1976 (3); v SL 1983 (3) 1986 (1)*
Hadlee, W. A. 11: v E 1946 (1) 1950 (2); v A 1945 (1); *v E 1937 (3) 1949 (4)*
Harford, N. S. 8: *v E 1958 (4); v In 1955 (2); v P 1955 (2)*
Harford, R. I. 3: v In 1967 (3)
Harris, P. G. Z. 9: v P 1964 (1); *v SA 1961 (5); v In 1955 (1); v P 1955 (2)*
Harris, R. M. 2: v E 1958 (2)
Hastings, B. F. 31: v E 1974 (2); v A 1973 (3); v WI 1968 (3); v In 1975 (1); v P 1972 (2); *v E 1969 (3) 1973 (3); v A 1973 (3); v WI 1971 (5); v In 1969 (3); v P 1969 (3)*
Hayes, J. A. 15: v E 1950 (2) 1954 (1); v WI 1951 (2); *v E 1958 (4); v In 1955 (5); v P 1955 (1)*
Henderson, M. 1: v E 1929
Horne, P. A. 2: v WI 1986 (1); *v SL 1986 (1)*
Hough, K. W. 2: v E 1958 (2)
Howarth, G. P. 47: v E 1974 (2) 1977 (3) 1983 (3); v A 1976 (2) 1981 (3); v WI 1979 (3); v In 1980 (3); v P 1978 (3) 1984 (3); v SL 1982 (2); *v E 1978 (3) 1983 (4); v A 1980 (2); v WI 1984 (4); v In 1976 (2); v P 1976 (2); v SL 1983 (3)*
Howarth, H. J. 30: v E 1970 (2) 1974 (2); v A 1973 (3) 1976 (2); v In 1975 (3); v P 1972 (3); *v E 1969 (3) 1973 (2); v WI 1971 (5); v In 1969 (3); v P 1969 (3)*

James, K. C. 11: v E 1929 (4) 1932 (2); v SA 1931 (2); *v E 1931 (3)*
Jarvis, T. W. 13: v E 1965 (1); v P 1972 (3); *v WI 1971 (4); v In 1964 (2); v P 1964 (3)*
Jones, A. H. 1: *v SL 1986*

Kerr, J. L. 7: v E 1932 (2); v SA 1931 (1); *v E 1931 (2) 1937 (2)*

Lees, W. K. 21: v E 1977 (2); v A 1976 (1); v WI 1979 (3); v P 1978 (3); v SL 1982 (2); *v E 1983 (2); v A 1980 (2); v In 1976 (3); v P 1976 (3)*
Leggat, I. B. 1: *v SA 1953*
Leggat, J. G. 9: v E 1954 (1); v SA 1952 (1); v WI 1951 (1) 1955 (1); *v In 1955 (3); v P 1955 (2)*
Lissette, A. F. 2: v WI 1955 (2)
Lowry, T. C. 7: v E 1929 (4); *v E 1931 (3)*

MacGibbon, A. R. 26: v E 1950 (2) 1954 (2); v SA 1952 (1); v WI 1955 (3); *v E 1958 (5); v SA 1953 (5); v In 1955 (5); v P 1955 (3)*
McEwan, P. E. 4: v WI 1979 (1); *v A 1980 (2); v P 1984 (1)*
McGirr, H. M. 2: v E 1929 (2)
McGregor, S. N. 25: v E 1954 (2) 1958 (2); v SA 1963 (3); v WI 1955 (4); v P 1964 (2); *v SA 1961 (5); v In 1955 (4); v P 1955 (3)*
McLeod E. G. 1: v E 1929
McMahon T. G. 5: v WI 1955 (1); *v In 1955 (3); v P 1955 (1)*
McRae, D. A. N. 1: v A 1945

Matheson, A. M. 2: v E 1929 (1); *v E 1931 (1)*
Meale, T. 2: *v E 1958 (2)*
Merritt, W. E. 6: v E 1929 (4); *v E 1931 (2)*
Meuli, E. M. 1: v SA 1952
Milburn, B. D. 3: v WI 1968 (3)
Miller, L. S. M. 13: v SA 1952 (2); v WI 1955 (3); *v E 1958 (4); v SA 1953 (4)*
Mills, J. E. 7: v E 1929 (3) 1932 (1); *v E 1931 (3)*
Moir, A. M. 17: v E 1950 (2) 1954 (2) 1958 (2); v SA 1952 (1); v WI 1951 (2) 1955 (1); *v E 1958 (2); v In 1955 (2); v P 1955 (3)*
Moloney D. A. R. 3: *v E 1937 (3)*
Mooney, F. L. H. 14: v E 1950 (2); v SA 1952 (2); v WI 1951 (2); *v E 1949 (3); v SA 1953 (5)*
Morgan, R. W. 20: v E 1965 (2) 1970 (2); v WI 1968 (1); v P 1964 (2); *v E 1965 (3); v WI 1971 (3); v In 1964 (4); v P 1964 (3)*
Morrison, B. D. 1: v E 1962
Morrison, J. F. M. 17: v E 1974 (2); v A 1973 (3) 1981 (3); v In 1975 (3); *v A 1973 (3); v In 1976 (1); v P 1976 (2)*
Motz, R. C. 32: v E 1962 (2) 1965 (3); v SA 1963 (3); v WI 1968 (3); v In 1967 (4); v P 1964 (3); *v E 1965 (3) 1969 (3); v SA 1961 (5); v In 1964 (4); v P 1964 (1)*
Murray, B. A. G. 13: v E 1970 (1); v In 1967 (4); *v E 1969 (2); v In 1969 (3); v P 1969 (3)*

Newman J. 3: v E 1932 (2); v SA 1931 (1)

O'Sullivan, D. R. 11: v In 1975 (1); v P 1972 (3); *v A 1973 (3); v In 1976 (3); v P 1976 (3)*
Overton, G. W. F. 3: *v SA 1953 (3)*

Page, M. L. 14: v E 1929 (4) 1932 (2); v SA 1931 (2); *v E 1931 (3) 1937 (3)*
Parker, J. M. 36: v E 1974 (2) 1977 (3); v A 1973 (3) 1976 (2); v WI 1979 (3); v In 1975 (3); v P 1972 (1) 1978 (2); *v E 1973 (3) 1978 (2); v A 1973 (3) 1980 (3); v In 1976 (3); v P 1976 (3)*
Parker, N. M. 3: *v In 1976 (2); v P 1976 (1)*
Patel, D. N. 3: v WI 1986 (3)
Petherick, P. J. 6: v A 1976 (1); *v In 1976 (3); v P 1976 (2)*
Petrie, E. C. 14: v E 1958 (2) 1965 (3); *v E 1958 (5); v In 1955 (3); v P 1955 (3)*
Playle, W. R. 8: v E 1962 (3); *v E 1958 (5)*
Pollard, V. 32: v E 1965 (3) 1970 (1); v WI 1968 (3); v In 1967 (4); v P 1972 (1); *v E 1965 (3) 1969 (3) 1973 (3); v In 1964 (4) 1969 (1); v P 1964 (3) 1969 (3)*
Poore, M. B. 14: v E 1954 (1); v SA 1952 (1); *v SA 1953 (5); v In 1955 (4); v P 1955 (3)*
Puna, N. 3: v E 1965 (3)

Rabone, G. O. 12: v E 1954 (2); v SA 1952 (1); v WI 1951 (2); *v E 1949 (4); v SA 1953 (3)*
Redmond, R. E. 1: v P 1972
Reid, J. F. 19: v A 1985 (3); v In 1980 (3); v P 1978 (1) 1984 (3); *v A 1985 (3); v P 1984 (3); v SL 1983 (3)*
Reid, J. R. 58: v E 1950 (2) 1954 (2) 1958 (2) 1962 (3); v SA 1952 (3) 1963 (3); v WI 1951 (2) 1955 (4); v P 1964 (3); *v E 1949 (2) 1958 (5) 1965 (3); v SA 1953 (5) 1961 (5); v In 1955 (5) 1964 (4); v P 1955 (3) 1964 (3)*
Roberts, A. D. G. 7: v In 1975 (2); *v In 1976 (3); v P 1976 (2)*
Roberts, A. W. 5: v E 1929 (1); v SA 1931 (2); *v E 1937 (2)*
Robertson, G. K. 1: v A 1985
Rowe, C. G. 1: v A 1945
Rutherford, K. R. 11: v A 1985 (3); v WI 1986 (2); *v E 1986 (1); v WI 1984 (4); v SL 1986 (1)*

Scott, R. H. 1: v E 1946
Scott, V. J. 10: v E 1946 (1) 1950 (2); v A 1945 (1); v WI 1951 (2); *v E 1949 (4)*
Shrimpton, M. J. F. 10: v E 1962 (2) 1965 (3) 1970 (2); v SA 1963 (1); *v A 1973 (2) In 1964 (2); v P 1964 (3)*
Sinclair, B. W. 21: v E 1962 (3) 1965 (3); v SA 1963 (3); v In 1967 (3); v P 1964 (2); *v E 1965 (3); v In 1964 (2); v P 1964 (3)*
Sinclair, I. M. 2: v WI 1955 (2)
Smith, F. B. 4: v E 1946 (1); v WI 1951 (1); *v E 1949 (2)*
Smith, H. D. 1: v E 1932
Smith, I. D. S. 37: v E 1983 (3); v A 1981 (3) 1985 (3); v WI 1986 (3); v In 1980 (3); v P 1984 (3); *v E 1983 (2) 1986 (2); v A 1980 (1) 1985 (3); v WI 1984 (4); v P 1984 (3); v SL 1983 (3) 1986 (1)*
Snedden, C. A. 1: v E 1946

Snedden, M. C. 13: v E 1983 (1); v A 1981 (3); v WI 1986 (1); v In 1980 (3); v SL 1982 (2); *v E 1983 (1); v A 1985 (1); v SL 1986 (1)*
Sparling, J. T. 11: v E 1958 (2) 1962 (1); v SA 1963 (2); *v E 1958 (3); v SA 1961 (3)*
Stirling, D. A. 6: *v E 1986 (2); v WI 1984 (1); v P 1984 (3)*
Sutcliffe, B. 42: v E 1946 (1) 1950 (2) 1954 (2) 1958 (2); v SA 1952 (2); v WI 1951 (2) 1955 (2); *v E 1949 (4) 1958 (4) 1965 (1); v SA 1953 (5); v In 1955 (5) 1964 (4); v P 1955 (3) 1964 (3)*

Taylor, B. R. 30: v E 1965 (1); v WI 1968 (3); v In 1967 (3); v P 1972 (3); *v E 1965 (2) 1969 (2) 1973 (3); v WI 1971 (4); v In 1964 (3) 1969 (2); v P 1964 (3) 1969 (1)*
Taylor, D. D. 3: v E 1946 (1); v WI 1955 (2)
Thomson, K. 2: v In 1967 (2)
Tindill, E. W. T. 5: v E 1946 (1); v A 1945 (1); *v E 1937 (3)*
Troup, G. B. 15: v A 1981 (2) 1985 (2); v WI 1979 (3); v In 1980 (3); v P 1978 (2); *v A 1980 (2); v WI 1984 (1); v In 1976 (1)*
Truscott, P. B. 1: v P 1964
Turner, G. M. 41: v E 1970 (2) 1974 (2); v A 1973 (3) 1976 (2); v WI 1968 (3); v In 1975 (3); v P 1972 (3); v SL 1982 (2); *v E 1969 (2) 1973 (3); v A 1973 (2); v WI 1971 (5); v In 1969 (3) 1976 (3); v P 1969 (1) 1976 (2)*

Vivian, G. E. 5: *v WI 1971 (4); v In 1964 (1)*
Vivian, H. G. 7: v E 1932 (1); v SA 1931 (1); *v E 1931 (2) 1937 (3)*

Wadsworth, K. J. 33: v E 1970 (2) 1974 (2); v A 1973 (3); v In 1975 (3); v P 1972 (3); *v E 1969 (3) 1973 (3); v A 1973 (3); v WI 1971 (5); v In 1969 (3); v P 1969 (3)*
Wallace, W. M. 13: v E 1946 (1) 1950 (2); v A 1945 (1); v SA 1952 (2); *v E 1937 (3) 1949 (4)*
Ward, J. T. 8: v SA 1963 (1); v In 1967 (1); v P 1964 (1); *v E 1965 (1); v In 1964 (4)*
Watson, W. 2: *v E 1986 (2)*
Watt, L. 1: v E 1954
Webb, M. G. 3: v E 1970 (1); v A 1973 (1); *v WI 1971 (1)*
Webb, P. N. 2: v WI 1979 (2)
Weir, G. L. 11: v E 1929 (3) 1932 (2); v SA 1931 (1); *v E 1931 (3) 1937 (1)*
Whitelaw, P. E. 2: v E 1932 (2)
Wright, J. G. 52: v E 1977 (3) 1983 (3); v A 1981 (3) 1985 (2); v WI 1979 (3) 1986 (3); v In 1980 (3); v P 1978 (3) 1984 (3); v SL 1982 (2); *v E 1978 (2) 1983 (3) 1986 (3); v A 1980 (3) 1985 (3); v WI 1984 (4); v P 1984 (3); v SL 1983 (3)*

Yuile, B. W. 17: v E 1962 (2); v WI 1968 (3); v In 1967 (1); v P 1964 (3); *v E 1965 (1); v In 1964 (3) 1969 (1); v P 1964 (1) 1969 (2)*

INDIA

Number of Test cricketers: 177

Abid Ali, S. 29: v E 1972 (4); v A 1969 (1); v WI 1974 (2); v NZ 1969 (3); *v E 1971 (3) 1974 (3); v A 1967 (4); v WI 1970 (2); v NZ 1967 (4)*
Adhikari, H. R. 21: v E 1951 (3); v A 1956 (2); v WI 1948 (5) 1958 (1); v P 1952 (2); *v E 1952 (3); v A 1947 (5)*
Amarnath, L. 24: v E 1933 (3) 1951 (3); v WI 1948 (5); v P 1952 (5); *v E 1946 (3); v A 1947 (5)*
Amarnath, M. 66: v E 1976 (2) 1984 (5); v A 1969 (1) 1979 (1) 1986 (3); v WI 1978 (2) 1983 (3); v NZ 1976 (3); v P 1983 (2) 1986 (5); v SL 1986 (2); *v E 1979 (2) 1986 (2); v A 1977 (5) 1985 (3); v WI 1975 (4) 1982 (5); v NZ 1975 (3); v P 1978 (3) 1982 (6) 1984 (2); v SL 1985 (2)*
Amarnath, S. 10: v E 1976 (2); *v WI 1975 (2); v NZ 1975 (3); v P 1978 (3)*
Amar Singh 7: v E 1933 (3); *v E 1932 (1) 1936 (3)*
Amir Elahi 1: *v A 1947*
Apte, A. L. 1: *v E 1959*
Apte, M. L. 7: v P 1952 (2); *v WI 1952 (5)*
Arun, B. 2: v SL 1986 (2)
Arun Lal 5: v P 1986 (1); v SL 1982 (1); *v P 1982 (3)*
Azad, K. 7: v E 1981 (3); v WI 1983 (2); v P 1983 (1); *v NZ 1980 (1)*

Azharuddin, M. 21 : v E 1984 (3); v A 1986 (3); v P 1986 (5); v SL 1986 (1); *v E 1986 (3); v A 1985 (3); v SL 1985 (3)*

Baig, A. A. 10 : v A 1959 (3); v WI 1966 (2); v P 1960 (3); *v E 1959 (2)*
Banerjee, S. A. 1 : v WI 1948
Banerjee, S. N. 1 : v WI 1948
Baqa Jilani, M. 1 : *v E 1936*
Bedi, B. S. 67 : v E 1972 (5) 1976 (5); v A 1969 (5); v WI 1966 (2) 1974 (4) 1978 (3); v NZ 1969 (3) 1976 (3); *v E 1967 (3) 1971 (3) 1974 (3) 1979 (3); v A 1967 (2) 1977 (5); v WI 1970 (5) 1975 (4); v NZ 1967 (4) 1975 (2); v P 1978 (3)*
Bhandari, P. 3 : v A 1956 (1); v NZ 1955 (1); *v P 1954 (1)*
Bhat, A. R. 2 : v WI 1983 (1); v P 1983 (1)
Binny, R. M. H. 27 : v E 1979 (1); v WI 1983 (6); v P 1979 (6) 1983 (2) 1986 (3); *v E 1986 (3); v A 1980 (1) 1985 (2); v NZ 1980 (1); v P 1984 (1); v SL 1985 (1)*
Borde, C. G. 55 : v E 1961 (5) 1963 (5); v A 1959 (5) 1964 (3) 1969 (1); v WI 1958 (4) 1966 (3); v NZ 1964 (4); v P 1960 (5); *v E 1959 (4) 1967 (3); v A 1967 (4); v WI 1961 (5); v NZ 1967 (4)*

Chandrasekhar, B. S. 58 : v E 1963 (4) 1972 (5) 1976 (5); v A 1964 (2); v WI 1966 (3) 1974 (4) 1978 (4); v NZ 1964 (2) 1976 (3); *v E 1967 (3) 1971 (3) 1974 (2) 1979 (1); v A 1967 (2) 1977 (5); v WI 1975 (4); v NZ 1975 (3); v P 1978 (3)*
Chauhan, C. P. S. 40 : v E 1972 (2); v A 1969 (1) 1979 (6); v WI 1978 (6); v NZ 1969 (2); v P 1979 (6); *v E 1979 (4); v A 1977 (4) 1980 (3); v NZ 1980 (3); v P 1978 (3)*
Chowdhury, N. R. 2 : v E 1951 (1); v WI 1948 (1)
Colah, S. H. M. 2 : v E 1933 (1); *v E 1932 (1)*
Contractor, N. J. 31 : v E 1961 (5); v A 1956 (1) 1959 (5); v WI 1958 (5); v NZ 1955 (4); v P 1960 (5); *v E 1959 (4); v WI 1961 (2)*

Dani, H. T. 1 : v P 1952
Desai, R. B. 28 : v E 1961 (4) 1963 (2); v A 1959 (3); v WI 1958 (3); v NZ 1964 (3); v P 1960 (5); *v E 1959 (5); v A 1967 (1); v WI 1961 (3); v NZ 1967 (1)*
Dilawar Hussain 3 : v E 1933 (2); *v E 1936 (1)*
Divecha, R. V. 5 : v E 1951 (2); v P 1952 (1); *v E 1952 (2)*
Doshi, D. R. 33 : v E 1979 (1) 1981 (6); v A 1979 (6); v P 1979 (6) 1983 (1); v SL 1982 (1); *v E 1982 (3); v A 1980 (3); v NZ 1980 (2); v P 1982 (4)*
Durani, S. A. 29 : v E 1961 (5) 1963 (5) 1972 (3); v A 1959 (1) 1964 (3); v WI 1966 (1); v NZ 1964 (3); *v WI 1961 (5) 1970 (3)*

Engineer, F. M. 46 : v E 1961 (4) 1972 (5); v A 1969 (5); v WI 1966 (1) 1974 (5); v NZ 1964 (4) 1969 (2); *v E 1967 (3) 1971 (3) 1974 (3); v A 1967 (4); v WI 1961 (3); v NZ 1967 (4)*

Gadkari, C. V. 6 : *v WI 1952 (3); v P 1954 (3)*
Gaekwad, A. D. 40 : v E 1976 (4) 1984 (3); v WI 1974 (3) 1978 (5) 1983 (6); v NZ 1976 (3); v P 1983 (3); *v E 1979 (2); v A 1977 (1); v WI 1975 (3) 1982 (5); v P 1984 (2)*
Gaekwad, D. K. 11 : v WI 1958 (1); v P 1952 (2) 1960 (1); *v E 1952 (1) 1959 (4); v WI 1952 (2)*
Gaekwad, H. G. 1 : v P 1952
Gandotra, A. 2 : v A 1969 (1); v NZ 1969 (1)
Gavaskar, S. M. 125 : v E 1972 (5) 1976 (5) 1979 (1) 1981 (6) 1984 (5); v A 1979 (6) 1986 (3); v WI 1974 (2) 1978 (6) 1983 (6); v NZ 1976 (3); v P 1979 (6) 1983 (6) 1986 (4); v SL 1982 (1) 1986 (3); *v E 1971 (3) 1974 (3) 1979 (4) 1982 (3) 1986 (3); v A 1977 (5) 1980 (3) 1985 (3); v WI 1970 (4) 1975 (4) 1982 (5); v NZ 1975 (3) 1980 (3); v P 1978 (3) 1982 (6) 1984 (2); v SL 1985 (3)*
Ghavri, K. D. 39 : v E 1976 (3) 1979 (1); v A 1979 (6); v WI 1974 (3) 1978 (6); v NZ 1976 (2); v P 1979 (6); *v E 1979 (4); v A 1977 (3) 1980 (3); v NZ 1980 (1); v P 1978 (3)*
Ghorpade, J. M. 8 : v A 1956 (1); v WI 1958 (1); v NZ 1955 (1); *v E 1959 (3); v WI 1952 (2)*
Ghulam Ahmed 22 : v E 1951 (2); v A 1956 (2); v WI 1948 (3) 1958 (2); v NZ 1955 (1); v P 1952 (4); *v E 1952 (4); v P 1954 (4)*
Gopalan, M. J. 1 : v E 1933
Gopinath, C. D. 8 : v E 1951 (3); v A 1959 (1); v WI 1958 (1); *v E 1952 (1); v P 1954 (2)*
Guard, G. M. 2 : v A 1959 (1); v WI 1958 (1)
Guha, S. 4 : v A 1969 (3); *v E 1967 (1)*
Gul Mahomed 8 : v P 1952 (2); *v E 1946 (1); v A 1947 (5)*
Gupte, B. P. 3 : v E 1963 (1); v NZ 1964 (1); v P 1960 (1)
Gupte, S. P. 36 : v E 1951 (1) 1961 (2); v A 1956 (3); v WI 1958 (5); v NZ 1955 (5); v P 1952 (2) 1960 (3); *v E 1959 (5); v WI 1952 (5); v P 1954 (5)*

Milkha Singh, A. G. 4: v E 1961 (1); v A 1959 (1); v P 1960 (2)
Modi, R. S. 10: v E 1951 (1); v WI 1948 (5); v P 1952 (1); *v E 1946 (3)*
More, K. S. 13: v A 1986 (2); v P 1986 (5); v SL 1986 (3); *v E 1986 (3)*
Muddiah, V. M. 2: v A 1959 (1); v P 1960 (1)
Mushtaq Ali, S. 11: v E 1933 (2) 1951 (1); v WI 1948 (3); *v E 1936 (3) 1946 (2)*

Nadkarni, R. G. 41: v E 1961 (1) 1963 (5); v A 1959 (5) 1964 (3); v WI 1958 (1) 1966 (1); v NZ 1955 (1) 1964 (4); v P 1960 (4); *v E 1959 (4); v A 1967 (3); v WI 1961 (5); v NZ 1967 (4)*
Naik, S. S. 3: v WI 1974 (2); *v E 1974 (1)*
Naoomal Jeoomal 3: v E 1933 (2); *v E 1932 (1)*
Narasimha Rao, M. V. 4: v A 1979 (2); v WI 1978 (2)
Navle, J. G. 2: v E 1933 (1); *v E 1932 (1)*
Nayak, S. V. 2: *v E 1982 (2)*
Nayudu, C. K. 7: v E 1933 (3); *v E 1932 (1) 1936 (3)*
Nayudu, C. S. 11: v E 1933 (2) 1951 (1); *v E 1936 (2) 1946 (2); v A 1947 (4)*
Nazir Ali, S. 2: v E 1933 (1); *v E 1932 (1)*
Nissar, Mahomed 6: v E 1933 (2); *v E 1932 (1) 1936 (3)*
Nyalchand, S. 1: v P 1952

Pai, A. M. 1: v NZ 1969
Palia, P. E. 2: *v E 1932 (1) 1936 (1)*
Pandit, C. S. 3: v A 1986 (2); *v E 1986 (1)*
Parkar, G. A. 1: *v E 1982*
Parkar, R. D. 2: v E 1972 (2)
Parsana, D. D. 2: v WI 1978 (2)
Patankar, C. T. 1: v NZ 1955
Pataudi sen., Nawab of, 3: *v E 1946 (3)*
Pataudi jun., Nawab of (now Mansur Ali Khan) 46: v E 1961 (3) 1963 (5) 1972 (3); v A 1964 (3) 1969 (5); v WI 1966 (3) 1974 (4); v NZ 1964 (4) 1969 (3); *v E 1967 (3); v A 1967 (3); v WI 1961 (3); v NZ 1967 (4)*
Patel, B. P. 21: v E 1976 (5); v WI 1974 (3); v NZ 1976 (3); *v E 1974 (2); v A 1977 (2); v WI 1975 (3); v NZ 1975 (3)*
Patel, J. M. 7: v A 1956 (2) 1959 (3); v NZ 1955 (1); *v P 1954 (1)*
Patiala, Yuvraj of, 1: v E 1933
Patil, S. M. 29: v E 1979 (1) 1981 (4) 1984 (2); v WI 1983 (2); v P 1979 (2) 1983 (3); v SL 1982 (1); *v E 1982 (2); v A 1980 (3); v NZ 1980 (3); v P 1982 (4) 1984 (2)*
Patil, S. R. 1: v NZ 1955
Phadkar, D. G. 31: v E 1951 (4); v A 1956 (1); v WI 1948 (4) 1958 (1); v NZ 1955 (4); v P 1952 (2); *v E 1952 (4); v A 1947 (4); v WI 1952 (4); v P 1954 (3)*
Prabhakar, M. 2: v E 1984 (2)
Prasanna, E. A. S. 49: v E 1961 (1) 1972 (3) 1976 (4); v A 1969 (5); v WI 1966 (1) 1974 (5); v NZ 1969 (3); *v E 1967 (3) 1974 (2); v A 1967 (4) 1977 (4); v WI 1961 (1) 1970 (3) 1975 (3); v NZ 1967 (4) 1975 (3); v P 1978 (2)*
Punjabi, P. H. 5: *v P 1954 (5)*

Rai Singh, K. 1: *v A 1947*
Rajinder Pal 1: v E 1963
Rajindernath, V. 1: v P 1952
Rajput, L. S. 2: *v SL 1985 (2)*
Ramaswami, C. 2: *v E 1936 (2)*
Ramchand, G. S. 33: v A 1956 (3) 1959 (5); v WI 1958 (3); v NZ 1955 (5); v P 1952 (3); *v E 1952 (4); v WI 1952 (5); v P 1954 (5)*
Ramji, L. 1: v E 1933
Rangachary, C. R. 4: v WI 1948 (2); *v A 1947 (2)*
Rangnekar, K. M. 3: *v A 1947 (3)*
Ranjane, V. B. 7: v E 1961 (3) 1963 (1); v A 1964 (1); v WI 1958 (1); *v WI 1961 (1)*
Reddy, B. 4: *v E 1979 (4)*
Rege, M. R. 1: v WI 1948
Roy, A. 4: v A 1969 (2); v NZ 1969 (2)
Roy, Pankaj 43: v E 1951 (5); v A 1956 (3) 1959 (5); v WI 1958 (5); v NZ 1955 (3); v P 1952 (3) 1960 (1); *v E 1952 (4) 1959 (5); v WI 1952 (4); v P 1954 (5)*
Roy, Pranab 2: v E 1981 (2)

Sandhu, B. S. 8: v WI 1983 (1); *v WI 1982 (4); v P 1982 (3)*

Sardesai, D. N. 30: v E 1961 (1) 1963 (5) 1972 (1); v A 1964 (3) 1969 (1); v WI 1966 (2); v NZ 1964 (3); *v E 1967 (1) 1971 (3); v A 1967 (2); v WI 1961 (3) 1970 (5)*

Sarwate, C. T. 9: v E 1951 (1); v WI 1948 (2); *v E 1946 (1); v A 1947 (5)*

Saxena, R. C. 1: *v E 1967*

Sekar, T. A. P. 2: *v P 1982 (2)*

Sen, P. 14: v E 1951 (2); v WI 1948 (5); v P 1952 (2); *v E 1952 (2); v A 1947 (3)*

Sengupta, A. K. 1: v WI 1958

Sharma, Chetan 16: v E 1984 (3); v A 1986 (2); v SL 1986 (2); *v E 1986 (2); v A 1985 (2); v P 1984 (2); v SL 1985 (3)*

Sharma, Gopal 4: v E 1984 (1); v P 1986 (2); *v SL 1985 (1)*

Sharma, P. 5: v E 1976 (2); v WI 1974 (2); *v WI 1975 (1)*

Shastri, R. J. 54: v E 1981 (6) 1984 (5); v A 1986 (3); v WI 1983 (6); v P 1983 (2) 1986 (5); v SL 1986 (3); *v E 1982 (3) 1986 (3); v A 1985 (3); v WI 1982 (5); v NZ 1980 (3); v P 1982 (2) 1984 (2); v SL 1985 (3)*

Shinde, S. G. 7: v E 1951 (3); v WI 1948 (1); *v E 1946 (1) 1952 (2)*

Shodhan, R. H. 3: v P 1952 (1); *v WI 1952 (2)*

Shukla, R. C. 1: v SL 1982

Sidhu, N. S. 2: v WI 1983 (2)

Sivaramakrishnan, L. 9: v E 1984 (5); *v A 1985 (2); v WI 1982 (1); v SL 1985 (1)*

Sohoni, S. W. 4: v E 1951 (1); *v E 1946 (2); v A 1947 (1)*

Solkar, E. D. 27: v E 1972 (5) 1976 (1); v A 1969 (4); v WI 1974 (4); v NZ 1969 (1); *v E 1971 (3) 1974 (3); v WI 1970 (5) 1975 (1)*

Sood, M. M. 1: v A 1959

Srikkanth, K. 28: v E 1981 (4) 1984 (2); v A 1986 (3); v P 1986 (5); v SL 1986 (3); *v E 1986 (3); v A 1985 (3); v P 1982 (2); v SL 1985 (3)*

Srinivasan, T. E. 1: *v NZ 1980*

Subramanya, V. 9: v WI 1966 (2); v NZ 1964 (1); *v E 1967 (2); v A 1967 (2); v NZ 1967 (2)*

Sunderram, G. 2: v NZ 1955 (2)

Surendranath, R. 11: v A 1959 (2); v WI 1958 (2); v P 1960 (2); *v E 1959 (5)*

Surti, R. F. 26: v E 1963 (1); v A 1964 (2) 1969 (1); v WI 1966 (2); v NZ 1964 (1) 1969 (2); v P 1960 (2); *v E 1967 (2); v A 1967 (4); v WI 1961 (5); v NZ 1967 (4)*

Swamy, V. N. 1: v NZ 1955

Tamhane, N. S. 21: v A 1956 (3) 1959 (1); v WI 1958 (4); v NZ 1955 (4); v P 1960 (2); *v E 1959 (2); v P 1954 (5)*

Tarapore, K. K. 1: v WI 1948

Umrigar, P. R. 59: v E 1951 (5) 1961 (4); v A 1956 (3) 1959 (3); v WI 1948 (1) 1958 (5); v NZ 1955 (5); v P 1952 (5) 1960 (5); *v E 1952 (4) 1959 (4); v WI 1952 (5) 1961 (5); v P 1954 (5)*

Vengsarkar, D. B. 95: v E 1976 (1) 1979 (1) 1981 (6) 1984 (5); v A 1979 (6) 1986 (2); v WI 1978 (6) 1983 (5); v P 1979 (5) 1983 (1) 1986 (5); v SL 1982 (1) 1986 (3); *v E 1979 (4) 1982 (3) 1986 (3); v A 1977 (5) 1980 (3) 1985 (3); v WI 1975 (2) 1982 (5); v NZ 1975 (3) 1980 (3); v P 1978 (3) 1982 (6) 1984 (2); v SL 1985 (3)*

Venkataraghavan, S. 57: v E 1972 (2) 1976 (1); v A 1969 (5) 1979 (3); v WI 1966 (2) 1974 (2) 1978 (6); v NZ 1964 (4) 1969 (2) 1976 (3); v P 1983 (2); *v E 1967 (1) 1971 (3) 1974 (2) 1979 (4); v A 1977 (1); v WI 1970 (5) 1975 (3) 1982 (5); v NZ 1975 (1)*

Viswanath, G. R. 91: v E 1972 (5) 1976 (5) 1979 (1) 1981 (6); v A 1969 (4) 1979 (6); v WI 1974 (5) 1978 (6); v NZ 1976 (3); v SL 1982 (1); v P 1979 (6); *v E 1971 (3) 1974 (3) 1979 (4) 1982 (3); v A 1977 (5) 1980 (3); v WI 1970 (3) 1975 (4); v NZ 1975 (3) 1980 (3); v P 1978 (3) 1982 (6)*

Viswanath, S. 3: *v SL 1985 (3)*

Vizianagram, Maharaj Sir Vijaya 3: *v E 1936 (3)*

Wadekar, A. L. 37: v E 1972 (5); v A 1969 (5); v WI 1966 (2); v NZ 1969 (3); *v E 1967 (2) 1971 (3) 1974 (3); v A 1967 (4); v WI 1970 (5); v NZ 1967 (4)*

Wazir Ali, S. 7: v E 1933 (3); *v E 1932 (1) 1936 (3)*

Yadav, N. S. 35: v E 1979 (1) 1981 (1) 1984 (4); v A 1979 (5) 1986 (3); v WI 1983 (3); v P 1979 (5) 1986 (4); v SL 1986 (2); *v A 1980 (2) 1985 (3); v NZ 1980 (1); v P 1984 (1)*

Yajurvindra Singh 4: v E 1976 (2); v A 1979 (1); *v E 1979 (1)*

Yashpal Sharma 37: v E 1979 (1) 1981 (2); v A 1979 (6); v WI 1983 (1); v P 1979 (6) 1983 (3); v SL 1982 (1); *v E 1979 (3) 1982 (3); v A 1980 (3); v WI 1982 (5); v NZ 1980 (1); v P 1982 (2)*

Yograj Singh 1: *v NZ 1980*

Note: Hafeez, on going later to Oxford University, took his correct name, Kardar.

PAKISTAN

Number of Test cricketers: 107

Abdul Kadir 4: v A 1964 (1); *v A 1964 (1); v NZ 1964* (2)
Abdul Qadir 48: v E 1977 (3) 1983 (3); v A 1982 (3); v WI 1980 (2) 1986 (3); v NZ 1984 (3); v In 1982 (5) 1984 (1); v SL 1985 (3); *v E 1982 (3) 1987 (4); v A 1983 (5); v NZ 1984 (2); v In 1979 (3) 1986 (3); v SL 1985* (2)
Afaq Hussain 2: v E 1961 (1); *v A 1964 (1)*
Aftab Baloch 2: v WI 1974 (1); v NZ 1969 (1)
Aftab Gul 6: v E 1968 (2); v NZ 1969 (1); *v E 1971 (3)*
Agha Saadat Ali 1: v NZ 1955
Agha Zahid 1: v WI 1974
Alim-ud-Din 25: v E 1961 (2); v A 1956 (1) 1959 (1); v WI 1958 (1); v NZ 1955 (3); v In 1954 (5); *v E 1954 (3) 1962 (3); v WI 1957 (5); v In 1960 (1)*
Amir Elahi 5: *v In 1952 (5)*
Anil Dalpat 9: v E 1983 (3); v NZ 1984 (3); *v NZ 1984 (3)*
Anwar Hussain 4: *v In 1952 (4)*
Anwar Khan 1: *v NZ 1978*
Arif Butt 3: *v A 1964 (1); v NZ 1964* (2)
Ashraf Ali 5: v In 1984 (2); v SL 1981 (2) 1985 (1)
Asif Iqbal 58: v E 1968 (3) 1972 (3); v A 1964 (1); v WI 1974 (2); v NZ 1964 (3) 1969 (3) 1976 (3); v In 1978 (3); *v E 1967 (3) 1971 (3) 1974 (3); v A 1964 (1) 1972 (3) 1976 (3) 1978 (2); v WI 1976 (5); v NZ 1964 (3) 1972 (3) 1978 (2); v In 1979* (6)
Asif Masood 16: v E 1968 (2) 1972 (1); v WI 1974 (2); v NZ 1969 (1); *v E 1971 (3) 1974 (3); v A 1972 (3) 1976 (1)*
Asif Mujtaba 2: v WI 1986 (2)
Azeem Hafeez 18: v E 1983 (2); v NZ 1984 (3); v In 1984 (2); *v A 1983 (5); v NZ 1984 (3); v In 1983 (3)*
Azhar Khan 1: v A 1979
Azmat Rana 1: v A 1979

Burki, J. 25: v E 1961 (3); v A 1964 (1); v NZ 1964 (3) 1969 (1); *v E 1962 (5) 1967 (3); v A 1964 (1); v NZ 1964 (3); v In 1960 (5)*

D'Souza, A. 6: v E 1961 (2); v WI 1958 (1); *v E 1962 (3)*

Ehtesham-ud-Din 5: v A 1979 (1); *v E 1982 (1); v In 1979 (3)*

Farooq Hamid 1: *v A 1964*
Farrukh Zaman 1: v NZ 1976
Fazal Mahmood 34: v E 1961 (1); v A 1956 (1) 1959 (2); v WI 1958 (3); v NZ 1955 (2); v In 1954 (4); *v E 1954 (4) 1962 (2); v WI 1957 (5); v In 1952 (5) 1960 (5)*

Ghazali, M. E. Z. 2: *v E 1954 (2)*
Ghulam Abbas 1: *v E 1967*
Gul Mahomed 1: v A 1956

Hanif Mohammad 55: v E 1961 (3) 1968 (3); v A 1956 (1) 1959 (3) 1964 (1); v WI 1958 (1); v NZ 1955 (3) 1964 (3) 1969 (1); v In 1954 (5); *v E 1954 (4) 1962 (5) 1967 (3); v A 1964 (1); v WI 1957 (5); v NZ 1964 (3); v In 1952 (5) 1960 (5)*
Haroon Rashid 23: v E 1977 (3); v A 1979 (2) 1982 (3); v In 1982 (1); v SL 1981 (2); *v E 1978 (3) 1982 (1); v A 1976 (1) 1978 (1); v WI 1976 (5); v NZ 1978 (1)*
Haseeb Ahsan 12: v E 1961 (2); v A 1959 (1); v WI 1958 (1); *v WI 1957 (3); v In 1960 (5)*

Ibadulla, K. 4: v A 1964 (1); *v E 1967 (2); v NZ 1964 (1)*
Ijaz Ahmed 5: *v E 1987 (4); v In 1986 (1)*
Ijaz Butt 8: v A 1959 (2); v WI 1958 (3); *v E 1962 (3)*
Ijaz Faqih 3: v WI 1980 (1); *v A 1981 (1); v In 1986 (1)*

Imran Khan 70: v A 1979 (2) 1982 (3); v WI 1980 (4) 1986 (3); v NZ 1976 (3); v In 1978 (3) 1982 (6); v SL 1981 (1) 1985 (3); *v E 1971 (1) 1974 (3) 1982 (3) 1987 (5); v A 1976 (3) 1982 (3) 1981 (3) 1983 (2); v WI 1976 (5); v NZ 1978 (2); v In 1979 (5) 1986 (5); v SL 1985 (3)*

Imtiaz Ahmed 41: v E 1961 (3); v A 1956 (1) 1959 (3); v WI 1958 (3); v NZ 1955 (3); v In 1954 (5); *v E 1954 (4) 1962 (4); v WI 1957 (5); v In 1952 (5) 1960 (5)*

Intikhab Alam 47: v E 1961 (2) 1968 (3) 1972 (3); v A 1959 (1) 1964 (1); v WI 1974 (2); v NZ 1964 (3) 1969 (3) 1976 (3); *v E 1962 (3) 1967 (3) 1971 (3) 1974 (3); v A 1964 (1) 1972 (3); v WI 1976 (1); v NZ 1964 (3) 1972 (3); v In 1960 (3)*

Iqbal Qasim 44: v E 1977 (3); v A 1979 (3) 1982 (2); v WI 1980 (4); v NZ 1984 (3); v In 1978 (3) 1982 (2); v SL 1981 (3); *v E 1978 (3); v A 1976 (3) 1981 (2); v WI 1976 (2); v NZ 1984 (1); v In 1979 (6) 1983 (1) 1986 (3)*

Israr Ali 4: v A 1959 (2); *v In 1952 (2)*

Jalal-ud-Din 6: v A 1982 (1); v In 1982 (2) 1984 (2); v SL 1985 (1)

Javed Akhtar 1: *v E 1962*

Javed Miandad 86: v E 1977 (3); v A 1979 (3) 1982 (3); v WI 1980 (4) 1986 (3); v NZ 1976 (3) 1984 (3); v In 1978 (3) 1982 (6) 1984 (2); v SL 1981 (3) 1985 (3); *v E 1978 (3) 1982 (3) 1987 (5); v A 1976 (3) 1978 (3) 1981 (3) 1983 (5); v WI 1976 (1); v NZ 1978 (3) 1984 (3); v In 1979 (6) 1983 (3) 1986 (4); v SL 1985 (3)*

Kardar, A. H. 23: v A 1956 (1); v NZ 1955 (3); v In 1954 (5); *v E 1954 (4); v WI 1957 (5); v In 1952 (5)*

Khalid Hassan 1: *v E 1954*

Khalid Wazir 2: *v E 1954 (2)*

Khan Mohammad 13: v A 1956 (1); v NZ 1955 (3); v In 1954 (4); *v E 1954 (2); v WI 1957 (2); v In 1952 (1)*

Liaqat Ali 5: v E 1977 (2); v WI 1974 (1); *v E 1978 (2)*

Mahmood Hussain 27: v E 1961 (1); v WI 1958 (1); v NZ 1955 (1); v In 1954 (5); *v E 1954 (2) 1962 (3); v WI 1957 (3); v In 1952 (4) 1960 (5)*

Majid Khan 63: v E 1968 (3) 1972 (3); v A 1964 (1) 1979 (3); v WI 1974 (2) 1980 (4); v NZ 1964 (3) 1976 (3); v In 1978 (3) 1982 (1); v SL 1981 (1); *v E 1967 (3) 1971 (2) 1974 (3) 1982 (1); v A 1972 (3) 1976 (3) 1978 (2) 1981 (3); v WI 1976 (5); v NZ 1972 (3) 1978 (2); v In 1979 (6)*

Mansoor Akhtar 18: v A 1982 (3); v WI 1980 (2); v In 1982 (3); v SL 1981 (1); *v E 1982 (3) 1987 (5); v A 1981 (1)*

Manzoor Elahi 4: v NZ 1984 (1); v In 1984 (1); *v In 1986 (2)*

Maqsood Ahmed 16: v NZ 1955 (2); v In 1954 (5); *v E 1954 (4); v In 1952 (5)*

Mathias, Wallis 21: v E 1961 (1); v A 1956 (1) 1959 (2); v WI 1958 (3); v NZ 1955 (1); *v E 1962 (3); v WI 1957 (5); v In 1960 (5)*

Miran Bux 2: v In 1954 (2)

Mohammad Aslam 1: *v E 1954*

Mohammad Farooq 7: v NZ 1964 (3); *v E 1962 (2); v In 1960 (2)*

Mohammad Ilyas 10: v E 1968 (2); v NZ 1964 (3); *v E 1967 (1); v A 1964 (1); v NZ 1964 (3)*

Mohammad Munaf 4: v E 1961 (2); v A 1959 (2)

Mohammad Nazir 14: v E 1972 (1); v WI 1980 (4); v NZ 1969 (3); *v A 1983 (3); v In 1983 (3)*

Mohsin Kamal 7: v E 1983 (1); v SL 1985 (1); *v E 1987 (4); v SL 1985 (1)*

Mohsin Khan 48: v E 1977 (1) 1983 (3); v A 1982 (3); v WI 1986 (3); v NZ 1984 (2); v In 1982 (6) 1984 (2); v SL 1981 (2) 1985 (2); *v E 1978 (3) 1982 (3); v A 1978 (1) 1981 (2) 1983 (5); v NZ 1978 (1) 1984 (3); v In 1983 (3); v SL 1985 (3)*

Mudassar Nazar 65: v E 1977 (3) 1983 (1); v A 1979 (3) 1982 (3); v WI 1986 (3); v NZ 1984 (3); v In 1978 (3) 1982 (6) 1984 (2); v SL 1981 (1) 1985 (3); *v E 1978 (3) 1982 (3) 1987 (5); v A 1976 (1) 1978 (3) 1981 (3) 1983 (5); v NZ 1978 (1) 1984 (3); v In 1979 (5) 1983 (3); v SL 1985 (3)*

Mufasir-ul-Haq 1: *v NZ 1964*

Munir Malik 3: v A 1959 (1); *v E 1962 (2)*

Mushtaq Mohammad 57: v E 1961 (3) 1968 (3) 1972 (3); v WI 1958 (1) 1974 (2); v NZ 1969 (2) 1976 (3); v In 1978 (3); *v E 1962 (5) 1967 (3) 1971 (3) 1974 (3); v A 1972 (3) 1976 (3) 1978 (2); v WI 1976 (5); v NZ 1972 (2) 1978 (3); v In 1960 (5)*

Nasim-ul-Ghani 29: v E 1961 (2); v A 1959 (2) 1964 (1); v WI 1958 (3); *v E 1962 (5) 1967 (2); v A 1964 (1) 1972 (1); v WI 1957 (5); v NZ 1964 (3); v In 1960 (4)*

Naushad Ali 6: v NZ 1964 (3); *v NZ 1964 (3)*

Nazar Mohammad 5: *v In 1952 (5)*
Nazir Junior (*see* Mohammad Nazir)
Niaz Ahmed 2: v E 1968 (1); *v E 1967 (1)*

Pervez Sajjad 19: v E 1968 (1) 1972 (2); v A 1964 (1); v NZ 1964 (3) 1969 (3); *v E 1971 (3); v NZ 1964 (3) 1972 (3)*

Qasim Omar 26: v E 1983 (3); v WI 1986 (3); v NZ 1984 (3); v In 1984 (2); v SL 1985 (3); *v A 1983 (5); v NZ 1984 (3); v In 1983 (1); v SL 1985 (3)*

Ramiz Raja 16: v E 1983 (2); v WI 1986 (3); v SL 1985 (1); *v E 1987 (2); v In 1986 (5); v SL 1985 (3)*
Rashid Khan 4: v SL 1981 (2); *v A 1983 (1); v NZ 1984 (1)*
Rehman, S. F. 1: *v WI 1957*
Rizwan-uz-Zaman 9: v WI 1986 (1); v SL 1981 (2); *v A 1981 (1); v In 1986 (5)*

Sadiq Mohammad 41: v E 1972 (3) 1977 (2); v WI 1974 (1) 1980 (3); v NZ 1969 (3) 1976 (3); v In 1978 (1); *v E 1971 (3) 1974 (3) 1978 (3); v A 1972 (3) 1976 (2); v WI 1976 (5); v NZ 1972 (3); v In 1979 (3)*
Saeed Ahmed 41: v E 1961 (3) 1968 (3); v A 1959 (3) 1964 (1); v WI 1958 (3); v NZ 1964 (3); *v E 1962 (5) 1967 (3) 1971 (1); v A 1964 (1) 1972 (2); v WI 1957 (5); v NZ 1964 (3); v In 1960 (3)*
Salah-ud-Din 5: v E 1968 (1); v NZ 1964 (3) 1969 (1)
Saleem Jaffer 3: v WI 1986 (1); *v In 1986 (2)*
Salim Altaf 21: v E 1972 (3); v NZ 1969 (2); v In 1978 (1); *v E 1967 (2) 1971 (2); v A 1972 (3) 1976 (2); v WI 1976 (3); v NZ 1972 (3)*
Salim Malik 41: v E 1983 (3); v WI 1986 (1); v NZ 1984 (3); v In 1982 (6) 1984 (2); v SL 1981 (2) 1985 (3); *v E 1987 (5); v A 1983 (3); v NZ 1984 (3); v In 1983 (2) 1986 (5); v SL 1985 (3)*
Salim Yousuf 16: v WI 1986 (1); v SL 1981 (1) 1985 (2); *v E 1987 (5); v In 1986 (5)*
Sarfraz Nawaz 55: v E 1968 (1) 1972 (2) 1977 (2) 1983 (3); v WI 1974 (2) 1980 (2); v NZ 1976 (3); v In 1978 (3) 1982 (6); *v E 1974 (3) 1978 (2) 1982 (1); v A 1972 (2) 1976 (2) 1978 (2) 1981 (3) 1983 (3); v WI 1976 (4); v NZ 1972 (3) 1978 (3)*
Shafiq Ahmad 6: v E 1977 (3); v WI 1980 (2); *v E 1974 (1)*
Shafqat Rana 5: v E 1968 (2); v A 1964 (1); v NZ 1969 (2)
Shahid Israr 1: v NZ 1974
Shahid Mahmood 1: *v E 1962*
Sharpe, D. 3: v A 1959 (3)
Shoaib Mohammad 13: v E 1983 (1); v NZ 1984 (1); v SL 1985 (1); *v E 1987 (4); v NZ 1984 (1); v In 1983 (2) 1986 (3)*
Shuja-ud-Din 19: v E 1961 (2); v A 1959 (3); v WI 1958 (3); v NZ 1955 (3); v In 1954 (5); *v E 1954 (3)*
Sikander Bakht 26: v E 1977 (2); v WI 1980 (1); v NZ 1976 (1); v In 1978 (2) 1982 (1); *v E 1978 (3) 1982 (2); v A 1978 (2) 1981 (3); v WI 1976 (1); v NZ 1978 (3); v In 1979 (5)*

Tahir Naqqash 15: v A 1982 (3); v In 1982 (2); v SL 1981 (3); *v E 1982 (2); v A 1983 (1); v NZ 1984 (1); v In 1983 (3)*
Talat Ali 10: v E 1972 (3); *v E 1978 (2); v A 1972 (1); v NZ 1972 (1) 1978 (3)*
Taslim Arif 6: v A 1979 (3); v WI 1980 (2); *v In 1979 (1)*
Tauseef Ahmed 22: v E 1983 (2); v A 1979 (3); v WI 1986 (3); v NZ 1984 (1); v In 1984 (1); v SL 1981 (3) 1985 (1); *v E 1987 (2); v In 1986 (4); v SL 1985 (2)*

Waqar Hassan 21: v A 1956 (1) 1959 (1); v WI 1958 (1); v NZ 1955 (3); v In 1954 (5); *v E 1954 (4); v WI 1957 (1); v In 1952 (5)*
Wasim Akram 20: v WI 1986 (2); v SL 1985 (1); *v E 1987 (5); v NZ 1984 (2); v In 1986 (5); v SL 1985 (3)*
Wasim Bari 81: v E 1968 (3) 1972 (3) 1977 (3); v A 1982 (3); v WI 1974 (2) 1980 (2); v NZ 1969 (3) 1976 (2); v In 1978 (3) 1982 (6); *v E 1967 (3) 1971 (3) 1974 (3) 1978 (3) 1982 (3); v A 1972 (3) 1976 (3) 1978 (2) 1981 (3) 1983 (5); v WI 1976 (5); v NZ 1972 (3) 1978 (3); v In 1979 (6); 1983 (3)*
Wasim Raja 57: v E 1972 (1) 1977 (3) 1983 (3); v A 1979 (3); v WI 1974 (2) 1980 (4); v NZ 1976 (1) 1984 (1); v In 1982 (1) 1984 (1); v SL 1981 (3); *v E 1974 (2) 1978 (3) 1982 (1); v A 1978 (1) 1981 (3) 1983 (2); v WI 1976 (5); v NZ 1972 (3) 1978 (3) 1984 (2); v In 1979 (6) 1983 (3)*

Wazir Mohammad 20: v A 1956 (1) 1959 (1); v WI 1958 (3); v NZ 1955 (2); v In 1954 (5); *v E 1954 (2); v WI 1957 (5); v In 1952 (1)*

Younis Ahmed 4: v NZ 1969 (2); *v In 1986 (2)*

Zaheer Abbas 78: v E 1972 (2) 1983 (2); v A 1979 (2) 1982 (3); v WI 1974 (2) 1980 (3); v NZ 1969 (1) 1976 (3) 1984 (3); v In 1978 (3) 1982 (6) 1984 (2); v SL 1981 (1) 1985 (2); *v E 1971 (3) 1974 (3) 1982 (3); v A 1972 (3) 1976 (3) 1978 (2) 1981 (2) 1983 (5); v WI 1976 (3); v NZ 1972 (3) 1978 (2) 1984 (2); v In 1979 (5) 1983 (3)*
Zakir Khan 1: *v SL 1985*
Zulfiqar Ahmed 9: v A 1956 (1); v NZ 1955 (3); *v E 1954 (2); v In 1952 (1)*
Zulqarnain 3: *v SL 1985 (3)*

SRI LANKA

Number of Test cricketers: 39

Ahangama, F. S. 3: v In 1985 (3)
Amalean, K. N. 1: v P 1985
Amerasinghe, A. M. J. G. 2: v NZ 1983 (2)
Anurasiri, S. D. 4: v NZ 1986 (1); v P 1985 (2); *v In 1986 (1)*
de Alwis, R. G. 10: v A 1982 (1); v NZ 1983 (3); v P 1985 (2); *v NZ 1982 (1); v In 1986 (3)*
de Mel, A. L. F. 17: v E 1981 (1); v A 1982 (1); v In 1985 (3); v P 1985 (3); *v E 1984 (1); v In 1982 (1) 1986 (1); v P 1981 (3) 1985 (3)*
de Silva, D. S. 12: v E 1981 (1); v A 1982 (1); v NZ 1983 (3); *v E 1984 (1); v NZ 1982 (2); v In 1982 (1); v P 1981 (3)*
de Silva, E. A. R. 5: v In 1985 (1); v P 1985 (1); *v In 1986 (3)*
de Silva, G. R. A. 4: v E 1981 (1); *v In 1982 (1); v P 1981 (2)*
de Silva, P. A. 13: v In 1985 (3); v P 1985 (3); *v E 1984 (1); v In 1986 (3); v P 1985 (3)*
Dias, R. L. 20: v E 1981 (1); v A 1982 (1); v NZ 1983 (2) 1986 (1); v In 1985 (3); v P 1985 (1); *v E 1984 (1); v In 1982 (1) 1986 (3); v P 1981 (3) 1985 (3)*

Fernando, E. R. N. S. 5: v A 1982 (1); v NZ 1983 (2); *v NZ 1982 (2)*

Goonatillake, H. M. 5: v E 1981 (1); *v In 1982 (1); v P 1981 (3)*
Gunasekera, Y. 2: *v NZ 1982 (2)*
Guneratne, R. P. W. 1: v A 1982
Gurusinha, A. P. 7: v NZ 1986 (1); v P 1985 (2); *v In 1986 (3); v P 1985 (1)*

Jayasekera, R. S. A. 1: *v P 1981*
Jeganathan, S. 2: *v NZ 1982 (2)*
John, V. B. 6: v NZ 1983 (3); *v E 1984 (1); v NZ 1982 (2)*
Jurangpathy, B. R. 2: v In 1985 (1); *v In 1986 (1)*

Kaluperuma, L. W. 2: v E 1981 (1); *v P 1981 (1)*
Kaluperuma, S. M. S. 3: v NZ 1983 (3)
Kuruppu, D. S. B. P. 1: v NZ 1986
Kuruppuarachchi, A. K. 2: v NZ 1986 (1); v P 1985 (1)

Labrooy, G. F. 1: *v In 1986*

Madugalle, R. S. 19: v E 1981 (1); v A 1982 (1); v NZ 1983 (3) 1986 (1); v In 1985 (3); *v E 1984 (1); v NZ 1982 (2); v In 1982 (1); v P 1981 (3) 1985 (3)*
Mahanama, R. S. 3: v NZ 1986 (1); v P 1985 (2)
Mendis, L. R. D. 23: v E 1981 (1); v A 1982 (1); v NZ 1983 (3) 1986 (1); v In 1985 (3); v P 1985 (3); *v E 1984 (1); v In 1982 (1) 1986 (3); v P 1981 (3) 1985 (3)*

Ranasinghe, A. N. 2: *v In 1982 (1); v P 1981 (1)*
Ranatunga, A. 22: v E 1981 (1); v A 1982 (1); v NZ 1983 (3) 1986 (1); v In 1985 (3); v P 1985 (3); *v E 1984 (1); v In 1982 (1) 1986 (3); v P 1981 (2) 1985 (3)*

Ratnayake, R. J. 14: v A 1982 (1); v NZ 1983 (1) 1986 (1); v In 1985 (3); v P 1985 (1); *v NZ 1982 (2); v In 1986 (2); v P 1985 (3)*

Ratnayake, J. R. 18: v NZ 1983 (2) 1986 (1); v P 1985 (3); *v E 1984 (1); v NZ 1982 (2); v In 1982 (1) 1986 (3); v P 1981 (2) 1985 (3)*

Silva, S. A. R. 8: v In 1985 (3); v P 1985 (1); *v E 1984 (1); v NZ 1982 (1); v P 1985 (2)*

Warnapura, B. 4: v E 1981 (1); *v In 1982 (1); v P 1981 (2)*
Warnaweera, K. P. J. 1: v P 1985
Weerasinghe, C. D. U. S. 1: v In 1985
Wettimuny, M. D. 2: *v NZ 1982 (2)*
Wettimuny, S. 23: v E 1981 (1); v A 1982 (1); v NZ 1983 (3); v In 1985 (3); v P 1985 (3); *v E 1984 (1); v NZ 1982 (2); v In 1986 (3); v P 1981 (3) 1985 (3)*
Wijesuriya, R. G. C. E. 4: *v P 1981 (1) 1985 (3)*

TWO COUNTRIES

Twelve cricketers have appeared for two countries in Test matches, namely:

Amir Elahi, *India and Pakistan*.
J. J. Ferris, *Australia and England*.
S. C. Guillen, *West Indies and NZ*.
Gul Mahomed, *India and Pakistan*.
F. Hearne, *England and South Africa*.
A. H. Kardar, *India and Pakistan*.

W. E. Midwinter, *England and Australia*.
F. Mitchell, *England and South Africa*.
W. L. Murdoch, *Australia and England*.
Nawab of Pataudi, sen., *England and India*.
A. E. Trott, *Australia and England*.
S. M. J. Woods, *Australia and England*.

MOST TEST APPEARANCES FOR EACH COUNTRY

England: M. C. Cowdrey 114.
Australia: R. W. Marsh 96.
South Africa: J. H. B. Waite 50.
West Indies: C. H. Lloyd 110.
New Zealand: R. J. Hadlee 70.

India: S. M. Gavaskar 125.
Pakistan: Javed Miandad 86.
Sri Lanka: L. R. D. Mendis and
S. Wettimuny 23.

MOST TEST APPEARANCES AS CAPTAIN FOR EACH COUNTRY

England: P. B. H. May 41.
Australia: G. S. Chappell 48.
South Africa: H. W. Taylor 18.
West Indies: C. H. Lloyd 74.

New Zealand: J. R. Reid 34.
India: S. M. Gavaskar 47.
Pakistan: Imran Khan 30.
Sri Lanka: L. R. D. Mendis 19.

ENGLAND v REST OF THE WORLD

The following were awarded England caps for playing against the Rest of the World in England in 1970, although the five matches played are now generally considered not to have rated as full Tests: D. L. Amiss (1), G. Boycott (2), D. J. Brown (2), M. C. Cowdrey (4), M. H. Denness (1), B. L. D'Oliveira (4), J. H. Edrich (2), K. W. R. Fletcher (4), A. W. Greig (3), R. Illingworth (5), A. Jones (1), A. P. E. Knott (5), P. Lever (1), B. W. Luckhurst (5), C. M. Old (2), P. J. Sharpe (1), K. Shuttleworth (1), J. A. Snow (5), D. L. Underwood (3), A. Ward (1), D. Wilson (2).

CRICKET RECORDS

Amended by BILL FRINDALL to end of the 1987 season in England

Unless stated to be of a minor character, all records apply only to first-class cricket including some performances in the distant past which have always been recognised as of exceptional merit.

* Denotes not out or an unbroken partnership.

(A), (SA), (WI), (NZ), (I), (P) or (SL) indicates either the nationality of the player, or the country in which the record was made.

FIRST-CLASS RECORDS

BATTING RECORDS

BOWLING RECORDS

ALL-ROUND RECORDS

WICKET-KEEPING RECORDS

FIELDING RECORDS

TEAM RECORDS

TEST MATCH RECORDS

BATTING RECORDS

BOWLING RECORDS

ALL-ROUND RECORDS

WICKET-KEEPING RECORDS

FIELDING RECORDS

TEAM RECORDS

TEST SERIES

LIMITED-OVERS INTERNATIONAL RECORDS

MISCELLANEOUS

FIRST-CLASS RECORDS

BATTING RECORDS

HIGHEST INDIVIDUAL SCORES

499	Hanif Mohammad	Karachi v Bahawalpur at Karachi	1958-59
452*	D. G. Bradman	NSW v Queensland at Sydney	1929-30
443*	B. B. Nimbalkar	Maharashtra v Kathiawar at Poona	1948-49
437	W. H. Ponsford	Victoria v Queensland at Melbourne	1927-28
429	W. H. Ponsford	Victoria v Tasmania at Melbourne	1922-23
428	Aftab Baloch	Sind v Baluchistan at Karachi	1973-74
424	A. C. MacLaren	Lancashire v Somerset at Taunton	1895
385	B. Sutcliffe	Otago v Canterbury at Christchurch	1952-53
383	C. W. Gregory	NSW v Queensland at Brisbane	1906-07
369	D. G. Bradman	South Australia v Tasmania at Adelaide	1935-36
365*	C. Hill	South Australia v NSW at Adelaide	1900-01
365*	G. S. Sobers	West Indies v Pakistan at Kingston	1957-58
364	L. Hutton	England v Australia at The Oval	1938
359*	V. M. Merchant	Bombay v Maharashtra at Bombay	1943-44
359	R. B. Simpson	NSW v Queensland at Brisbane	1963-64
357*	R. Abel	Surrey v Somerset at The Oval	1899
357	D. G. Bradman	South Australia v Victoria at Melbourne	1935-36
356	B. A. Richards	South Australia v W. Australia at Perth	1970-71
355	B. Sutcliffe	Otago v Auckland at Dunedin	1949-50
352	W. H. Ponsford	Victoria v NSW at Melbourne	1926-27
350	Rashid Israr	Habib Bank v National Bank at Lahore	1976-77
345	C. G. Macartney	Australians v Nottinghamshire at Nottingham	1921
344*	G. A. Headley	Jamaica v Lord Tennyson's XI at Kingston	1931-32
344	W. G. Grace	MCC v Kent at Canterbury	1876
343*	P. A. Perrin	Essex v Derbyshire at Chesterfield	1904
341	G. H. Hirst	Yorkshire v Leicestershire at Leicester	1905
340*	D. G. Bradman	NSW v Victoria at Sydney	1928-29
340	S. M. Gavaskar	Bombay v Bengal at Bombay	1981-82
338*	R. C. Blunt	Otago v Canterbury at Christchurch	1931-32
338	W. W. Read	Surrey v Oxford University at The Oval	1888
337*	Pervez Akhtar	Railways v Dera Ismail Khan at Lahore	1964-65
337†	Hanif Mohammad	Pakistan v West Indies at Bridgetown	1957-58
336*	W. R. Hammond	England v New Zealand at Auckland	1932-33
336	W. H. Ponsford	Victoria v South Australia at Melbourne	1927-28
334	D. G. Bradman	Australia v England at Leeds	1930
333	K. S. Duleepsinhji	Sussex v Northamptonshire at Hove	1930
332	W. H. Ashdown	Kent v Essex at Brentwood	1934
331*	J. D. Robertson	Middlesex v Worcestershire at Worcester	1949
325*	H. L. Hendry	Victoria v New Zealanders at Melbourne	1925-26
325	A. Sandham	England v West Indies at Kingston	1929-30
325	C. L. Badcock	South Australia v Victoria at Adelaide	1935-36
324	J. B. Stollmeyer	Trinidad v British Guiana at Port-of-Spain	1946-47
324	Waheed Mirza	Karachi Whites v Quetta at Karachi	1976-77
323	A. L. Wadekar	Bombay v Mysore at Bombay	1966-67
322	E. Paynter	Lancashire v Sussex at Hove	1937
322	I. V. A. Richards	Somerset v Warwickshire at Taunton	1985
321	W. L. Murdoch	NSW v Victoria at Sydney	1881-82
319	Gul Mahomed	Baroda v Holkar at Baroda	1946-47
318*	W. G. Grace	Gloucestershire v Yorkshire at Cheltenham	1876
317	W. R. Hammond	Gloucestershire v Nottinghamshire at Gloucester . . .	1936
317	K. R. Rutherford	New Zealanders v D. B. Close's XI at Scarborough .	1986
316*	J. B. Hobbs	Surrey v Middlesex at Lord's	1926
316*	V. S. Hazare	Maharashtra v Baroda at Poona	1939-40
316	R. H. Moore	Hampshire v Warwickshire at Bournemouth	1937

First-Class Records – Batting

315*	T. W. Hayward	Surrey v Lancashire at The Oval	1898
315*	P. Holmes	Yorkshire v Middlesex at Lord's	1925
315*	A. F. Kippax	NSW v Queensland at Sydney	1927-28
314*	C. L. Walcott	Barbados v Trinidad at Port-of-Spain	1945-46
313	H. Sutcliffe	Yorkshire v Essex at Leyton	1932
312*	W. W. Keeton	Nottinghamshire v Middlesex at The Oval‡	1939
312*	J. M. Brearley	MCC Under 25 v North Zone at Peshawar ...	1966-67
311*	G. M. Turner	Worcestershire v Warwickshire at Worcester ..	1982
311	J. T. Brown	Yorkshire v Sussex at Sheffield	1897
311	R. B. Simpson	Australia v England at Manchester	1964
311	Javed Miandad	Karachi Whites v National Bank at Karachi ...	1974-75
310*	J. H. Edrich	England v New Zealand at Leeds	1965
310	H. Gimblett	Somerset v Sussex at Eastbourne	1948
309	V. S. Hazare	The Rest v Hindus at Bombay	1943-44
308*	F. M. M. Worrell	Barbados v Trinidad at Bridgetown	1943-44
307	M. C. Cowdrey	MCC v South Australia at Adelaide	1962-63
307	R. M. Cowper	Australia v England at Melbourne	1965-66
306*	A. Ducat	Surrey v Oxford University at The Oval	1919
306*	E. A. B. Rowan	Transvaal v Natal at Johannesburg	1939-40
306*	D. W. Hookes	South Australia v Tasmania at Adelaide	1986-87
305*	F. E. Woolley	MCC v Tasmania at Hobart	1911-12
305*	F. R. Foster	Warwickshire v Worcestershire at Dudley	1914
305*	W. H. Ashdown	Kent v Derbyshire at Dover	1935
304*	A. W. Nourse	Natal v Transvaal at Johannesburg	1919-20
304*	P. H. Tarilton	Barbados v Trinidad at Bridgetown	1919-20
304*	E. D. Weekes	West Indians v Cambridge University at Cambridge	1950
304	R. M. Poore	Hampshire v Somerset at Taunton	1899
304	D. G. Bradman	Australia v England at Leeds	1934
303*	W. W. Armstrong	Australians v Somerset at Bath	1905
303*	Mushtaq Mohammad	Karachi Blues v Karachi University at Karachi	1967-68
303*	Abdul Azeem	Hyderabad v Tamil Nadu at Hyderabad	1986-87
302*	P. Holmes	Yorkshire v Hampshire at Portsmouth	1920
302*	W. R. Hammond	Gloucestershire v Glamorgan at Bristol	1934
302	W. R. Hammond	Gloucestershire v Glamorgan at Newport	1939
302	L. G. Rowe	West Indies v England at Bridgetown	1973-74
301*	E. H. Hendren	Middlesex v Worcestershire at Dudley	1933
301	W. G. Grace	Gloucestershire v Sussex at Bristol	1896
300*	V. T. Trumper	Australians v Sussex at Hove	1899
300*	F. B. Watson	Lancashire v Surrey at Manchester	1928
300*	Imtiaz Ahmed	PM's XI v Commonwealth XI at Bombay	1950-51
300	J. T. Brown	Yorkshire v Derbyshire at Chesterfield	1898
300	D. C. S. Compton	MCC v N. E. Transvaal at Benoni	1948-49
300	Raman Subba Row	Northamptonshire v Surrey at The Oval	1958

† *Hanif Mohammad batted for 16 hours 10 minutes – the longest innings in first-class cricket.*
‡ *Played at The Oval because Lord's was required for Eton v Harrow.*

HIGHEST FOR TEAMS

For English Teams in Australia

307	M. C. Cowdrey	MCC v South Australia at Adelaide	1962-63
287	R. E. Foster	England v Australia at Sydney	1903-04

Against Australians in England

364	L. Hutton	England v Australia at The Oval	1938
219	A. Sandham	Surrey at The Oval (record for any county) ..	1934

For Australian Teams in England

345	C. G. Macartney	v Nottinghamshire at Nottingham	1921
334	D. G. Bradman	Australia v England at Leeds	1930

Against English Teams in Australia

307	R. M. Cowper	Australia v England at Melbourne	1965-66
280	A. J. Richardson	South Australia v MCC at Adelaide	1922-23

For Each First-Class County

Derbyshire	274	G. Davidson v Lancashire at Manchester		1896
Essex	343*	P. A. Perrin v Derbyshire at Chesterfield		1904
Glamorgan	287*	D. E. Davies v Gloucestershire at Newport		1939
Gloucestershire	318*	W. G. Grace v Yorkshire at Cheltenham		1876
Hampshire	316	R. H. Moore v Warwickshire at Bournemouth		1937
Kent	332	W. H. Ashdown v Essex at Brentwood		1934
Lancashire	424	A. C. MacLaren v Somerset at Taunton		1895
Leicestershire	252*	S. Coe v Northamptonshire at Leicester		1914
Middlesex	331*	J. D. Robertson v Worcestershire at Worcester		1949
Northamptonshire	300	R. Subba Row v Surrey at The Oval		1958
Nottinghamshire	312*	W. W. Keeton v Middlesex at The Oval†		1939
Somerset	322	I. V. A. Richards v Warwickshire at Taunton		1985
Surrey	357*	R. Abel v Somerset at The Oval		1899
Sussex	333	K. S. Duleepsinhji v Northamptonshire at Hove		1930
Warwickshire	305*	F. R. Foster v Worcestershire at Dudley		1914
Worcestershire	311*	G. M. Turner v Warwickshire at Worcester		1982
Yorkshire	341	G. H. Hirst v Leicestershire at Leicester		1905

† *Played at The Oval because Lord's was required for Eton v Harrow.*

HUNDRED ON DEBUT IN BRITISH ISLES

(The following list does not include instances of players who have previously appeared in first-class cricket outside the British Isles or who performed the feat before 1946. Particulars of the latter are in *Wisdens* prior to 1984.)

114	F. W. Stocks	Nottinghamshire v Kent at Nottingham	1946
108	A. Fairbairn	Middlesex v Somerset at Taunton	†‡1947
124	P. Hearn	Kent v Warwickshire at Gillingham	1947
215*	G. H. G. Doggart	Cambridge University v Lancashire at Cambridge	1948
106	J. R. Gill	Ireland v MCC at Dublin	1948
107*	G. Barker	Essex v Canadians at Clacton	†1954
135	J. K. E. Slack	Cambridge University v Middlesex at Cambridge	1954
100*	E. A. Clark	Middlesex v Cambridge University at Cambridge	1959
113	G. J. Chidgey	Free Foresters v Cambridge U. at Cambridge	1962
108	D. R. Shepherd	Gloucestershire v Oxford University at Oxford	1965
110*	A. J. Harvey-Walker	Derbyshire v Oxford University at Burton upon Trent	†1971
173	J. Whitehouse	Warwickshire v Oxford University at Oxford	1971
106	J. B. Turner	Minor Counties v Pakistanis at Jesmond	1974
112	J. A. Claughton	Oxford University v Gloucestershire at Oxford	†1976
100*	A. W. Lilley	Essex v Nottinghamshire at Nottingham	1978
146*	J. S. Johnson	Minor Counties v Indians at Wellington	1979
110	N. R. Taylor	Kent v Sri Lankans at Canterbury	1979
146*	D. G. Aslett	Kent v Hampshire at Bournemouth	1981
116	M. D. Moxon	Yorkshire v Essex at Leeds	†1981
100	D. A. Banks	Worcestershire v Oxford University at Oxford	1983
122	A. A. Metcalfe	Yorkshire v Nottinghamshire at Bradford	1983
117*	K. T. Medlycott } 101*	N. J. Falkner } Surrey v Cambridge University at Banstead	§1984
106	A. C. Storie	Northamptonshire v Hampshire at Northampton	†1985
102	M. P. Maynard	Glamorgan v Yorkshire at Swansea	1985
117*	R. J. Bartlett	Somerset v Oxford University at Oxford	1986
100*	P. D. Bowler	Leicestershire v Hampshire at Leicester	1986
145	I. L. Philip	Scotland v Ireland at Glasgow	1986

† *In his second innings.*

‡ *A. Fairbairn (Middlesex) in 1947 scored hundreds in the second innings of his first two matches in first-class cricket: 108 as above, 110* Middlesex v Nottinghamshire at Nottingham.*

§ *The only instance in England of two players performing the feat in the same match.*

Notes: A number of players abroad have also made a hundred on a first appearance.

The highest innings on début was hit by W. F. E. Marx when he made 240 for Transvaal against Griqualand West at Johannesburg in 1920-21.

There are three instances of a cricketer making two separate hundreds on début: A. R. Morris, New South Wales, 148 and 111 against Queensland in 1940-41, N. J. Contractor, Gujarat, 152 and 102* against Baroda in 1952-53, and Aamer Malik, Lahore "A", 132* and 110* against Railways in 1979-80.

J. S. Solomon, British Guiana, scored a hundred in each of his first three innings in first-class cricket: 114* v Jamaica; 108 v Barbados in 1956-57; 121 v Pakistanis in 1957-58.

R. Watson-Smith, Border, scored 310 runs before he was dismissed in first-class cricket, including not-out centuries in his first two innings: 183* v Orange Free State and 125* v Griqualand West in 1969-70.

G. R. Viswanath and D. M. Wellham alone have scored a hundred on both their début in first-class cricket and in Test cricket. Viswanath scored 230 for Mysore v Andhra in 1967-68 and 137 for India v Australia in 1969-70. Wellham scored 100 for New South Wales v Victoria in 1980-81 and 103 for Australia v England in 1981.

TWO SEPARATE HUNDREDS IN A MATCH

Eight times: Zaheer Abbas.

Seven times: W. R. Hammond.

Six times: J. B. Hobbs, G. M. Turner.

Five times: C. B. Fry.

Four times: D. G. Bradman, G. S. Chappell, J. H. Edrich, L. B. Fishlock, T. W. Graveney, C. G. Greenidge, H. T. W. Hardinge, E. H. Hendren, Javed Miandad, G. L. Jessop, P. A. Perrin, B. Sutcliffe, H. Sutcliffe.

Three times: L. E. G. Ames, G. Boycott, I. M. Chappell, D. C. S. Compton, M. C. Cowdrey, D. Denton, K. S. Duleepsinhji, R. E. Foster, R. C. Fredericks, S. M. Gavaskar, W. G. Grace, G. Gunn, M. R. Hallam, Hanif Mohammad, M. J. Harris, T. W. Hayward, V. S. Hazare, D. W. Hookes, L. Hutton, A. Jones, P. N. Kirsten, R. B. McCosker, P. B. H. May, C. P. Mead, A. C. Russell, Sadiq Mohammad, J. T. Tyldesley.

Twice: Agha Zahid, D. L. Amiss, L. Baichan, A. R. Border, B. J. T. Bosanquet, R. J. Boyd-Moss, C. C. Dacre, G. M. Emmett, A. E. Fagg, L. E. Favell, H. Gimblett, C. Hallows, R. A. Hamence, A. L. Hassett, G. A. Headley, A. I. Kallicharran, J. H. King, A. F. Kippax, J. G. Langridge, H. W. Lee, E. Lester, C. B. Llewellyn, C. G. Macartney, C. A. Milton, A. R. Morris, P. H. Parfitt, Nawab of Pataudi jun., E. Paynter, C. Pinch, R. G. Pollock, R. M. Prideaux, Qasim Omar, W. Rhodes, B. A. Richards, Rizwan-uz-Zaman, Pankaj Roy, James Seymour, Shafiq Ahmed, R. B. Simpson, G. S. Sobers, E. Tyldesley, C. L. Walcott, W. W. Whysall, G. N. Yallop.

Notes: W. Lambert scored 107 and 157 for Sussex v Epsom at Lord's in 1817 and it was not until W. G. Grace made 130 and 102* for South of the Thames v North of the Thames at Canterbury in 1868 that the feat was repeated.

T. W. Hayward (Surrey) set up a unique record in 1906 when in one week – six days – he hit four successive hundreds, 144 and 100 v Nottinghamshire at Nottingham and 143 and 125 v Leicestershire at Leicester.

D. W. Hookes (South Australia) scored four successive hundreds in eleven days at Adelaide in 1976-77: 185 and 105 v Queensland (tied match) and 135 and 156 v New South Wales.

A. E. Fagg is alone in scoring two double-hundreds in the same match: 244 and 202* for Kent v Essex at Colchester, 1938.

L. G. Rowe is alone in scoring hundreds in each innings on his first appearance in Test cricket: 214 and 100* for West Indies v New Zealand at Kingston in 1971-72.

Zaheer Abbas (Gloucestershire) set a unique record in 1976 by twice scoring a double hundred and a hundred in the same match without being dismissed: 216* and 156* v Surrey at The Oval and 230* and 104* v Kent at Canterbury. In 1977 he achieved this feat for a third time, scoring 205* and 108* v Sussex at Cheltenham, and in 1981 for a fourth time, scoring 215* and 150* v Somerset at Bath.

M. R. Hallam (Leicestershire), opening the batting each time, achieved the following treble: 210* and 157 v Glamorgan at Leicester, 1959; 203* and 143* v Sussex at Worthing, 1961; 107* and 149* v Worcestershire at Leicester, 1965. In the last two matches he was on the field the whole time.

C. J. B. Wood, 107* and 117* for Leicestershire against Yorkshire at Bradford, 1911, is alone in carrying his bat and scoring hundreds in each innings.

W. L. Foster, 140 and 172*, and R. E. Foster, 134 and 101*, for Worcestershire v Hampshire at Worcester in July 1899, were the first brothers each to score two separate hundreds in the same first-class match.

The brothers I. M. Chappell, 145 and 121, and G. S. Chappell, 247* and 133, for Australia v New Zealand at Wellington in 1973-74, became the first players on the same side each to score a hundred in each innings of a Test match.

G. Gunn, 183, and G. V. Gunn, 100*, for Nottinghamshire v Warwickshire at Birmingham in 1931, provide the only instance of father and son each hitting a century in the same innings of a first-class match.

Most recent instances

In 1986-87

B. G. Cooper	105	100	Northern Districts v Canterbury at Gisborne.
M. D. Crowe	144	151	Central Districts v Canterbury at New Plymouth.
A. du Toit	118	135	Boland v Eastern Province at Stellenbosch.
P. N. Kirsten	173	105*	South Africa v Australian XI at Cape Town.
D. P. le Roux	127	109	Orange Free State v Border at Bloemfontein.
L. S. Rajput	105	109	West Zone v South Zone at Bombay.
Shafiq Ahmed	124	103*	United Bank v Lahore at Lahore.
K. C. Wessels	135	105*	South Africa v Australian XI at Port Elizabeth.

In 1987: See Features of 1987.

HUNDRED AND DOUBLE-HUNDRED IN A MATCH

C. B. Fry	125	229	Sussex v Surrey at Hove	1900
W. W. Armstrong	157*	245	Victoria v South Australia at Melbourne.	1920-21
H. T. W. Hardinge	207	102*	Kent v Surrey at Blackheath	1921
C. P. Mead	113	224	Hampshire v Sussex at Horsham	1921
K. S. Duleepsinhji	115	246	Sussex v Kent at Hastings	1929
D. G. Bradman	124	225	Woodfull's XI v Ryder's XI at Sydney	1929-30
B. Sutcliffe	243	100*	New Zealanders v Essex at Southend	1949
M. R. Hallam	210*	157	Leicestershire v Glamorgan at Leicester	1959
M. R. Hallam	203*	143*	Leicestershire v Sussex at Worthing	1961
Hanumant Singh	109	213*	Rajasthan v Bombay at Bombay	1966-67
Salah-ud-Din	256	102*	Karachi v East Pakistan at Karachi	1968-69
K. D. Walters	242	103	Australia v West Indies at Sydney	1968-69
S. M. Gavaskar	124	220	India v West Indies at Port-of-Spain	1970-71
L. G. Rowe	214	100*	West Indies v New Zealand at Kingston	1971-72
G. S. Chappell	247*	133	Australia v New Zealand at Wellington	1973-74
L. Baichan	216*	102	Berbice v Demerara at Georgetown	1973-74
Zaheer Abbas	216*	156*	Gloucestershire v Surrey at The Oval	1976
Zaheer Abbas	230*	104*	Gloucestershire v Kent at Canterbury	1976
Zaheer Abbas	205*	108*	Gloucestershire v Sussex at Cheltenham	1977
Saadat Ali	141	222	Income Tax v Multan at Multan	1977-78
Talat Ali	214*	104	PIA v Punjab at Lahore	1978-79
Shafiq Ahmed	129	217*	National Bank v MCB at Karachi	1978-79
D. W. Randall	209	146	Nottinghamshire v Middlesex at Nottingham	1979
Zaheer Abbas	215*	150*	Gloucestershire v Somerset at Bath	1981
Qasim Omar	210*	110	MCB v Lahore at Lahore	1982-83
A. I. Kallicharran	200*	117*	Warwickshire v Northamptonshire at Birmingham	1984

FOUR HUNDREDS OR MORE IN SUCCESSION

Six in succession: C. B. Fry 1901; D. G. Bradman 1938-39; M. J. Procter 1970-71.

Five in succession: E. D. Weekes 1955-56.

Four in succession: C. W. J. Athey 1987; M. Azharuddin 1984-85; A. R. Border 1985; D. G. Bradman 1931-32, 1948-49; D. C. S. Compton 1946-47; N. J. Contractor 1957-58; K. S.

Duleepsinhji 1931; C. B. Fry 1911; C. G. Greenidge 1986; W. R. Hammond 1936-37, 1945-46; H. T. W. Hardinge 1913; T. W. Hayward 1906; J. B. Hobbs 1920, 1925; D. W. Hookes 1976-77; P. N. Kirsten 1976-77; J. G. Langridge 1949; C. G. Macartney 1921; K. S. McEwan 1977; P. B. H. May 1956-57; V. M. Merchant 1941-42; A. Mitchell 1933; Nawab of Pataudi sen. 1931; L. G. Rowe 1971-72; Pankaj Roy 1962-63; Sadiq Mohammad 1976; Saeed Ahmed 1961-62; H. Sutcliffe 1931, 1939; E. Tyldesley 1926; W. W. Whysall 1930; F. E. Woolley 1929; Zaheer Abbas 1970-71, 1982-83.

Note: The most fifties in consecutive innings is ten – by E. Tyldesley in 1926 and by D. G. Bradman in the 1947-48 and 1948 seasons.

MOST HUNDREDS IN A SEASON

Eighteen: D. C. S. Compton in 1947. These included six hundreds against the South Africans in which matches his average was 84.78. His aggregate for the season was 3,816, also a record.

Sixteen: J. B. Hobbs in 1925, when aged 42, played 16 three-figure innings in first-class matches. It was during this season that he exceeded the number of hundreds obtained in first-class cricket by W. G. Grace.

Fifteen: W. R. Hammond in 1938.

Fourteen: H. Sutcliffe in 1932.

Thirteen: G. Boycott in 1971, D. G. Bradman in 1938, C. B. Fry in 1901, W. R. Hammond in 1933 and 1937, T. W. Hayward in 1906, E. H. Hendren in 1923, 1927 and 1928, C. P. Mead in 1928, H. Sutcliffe in 1928 and 1931.

MOST HUNDREDS IN A CAREER

(35 or More)

	Hundreds Total	Abroad	100th 100		Hundreds Total	Abroad	100th 100
J. B. Hobbs	197	22	1923	D. G. Bradman	117	41†	1947-48
E. H. Hendren	170	19	1928-29	Zaheer Abbas	108	70†	1982-83
W. R. Hammond	167	33	1935	M. C. Cowdrey	107	27	1973
C. P. Mead	153	8	1927	A. Sandham	107	20	1935
G. Boycott	151	27	1977	T. W. Hayward	104	4	1913
H. Sutcliffe	149	14	1932	J. H. Edrich	103	13	1977
F. E. Woolley	145	10	1929	G. M. Turner	103	85†	1982
L. Hutton	129	24	1951	L. E. G. Ames	102	13	1950
W. G. Grace	126	1	1895	D. L. Amiss	102	15	1986
D. C. S. Compton	123	31	1952	E. Tyldesley	102	8	1934
T. W. Graveney	122	31	1964				

† *"Abroad" for D. G. Bradman is outside Australia; for Zaheer Abbas, outside Pakistan; for G. M. Turner, outside New Zealand.*

E. H. Hendren and D. G. Bradman scored their 100th hundreds in Australia, Zaheer Abbas scored his in Pakistan. Zaheer Abbas and G. Boycott did so in Test matches.

J. W. Hearne	96	B. A. Richards	80	W. G. Quaife	72
C. B. Fry	94	C. H. Lloyd	79	K. S. Ranjitsinhji	72
I. V. A. Richards	93	C. G. Greenidge	78	D. Brookes	71
W. J. Edrich	86	K. F. Barrington	76	A. C. Russell	71
G. S. Sobers	86	J. G. Langridge	76	D. Denton	69
J. T. Tyldesley	86	C. Washbrook	76	M. J. K. Smith	69
P. B. H. May	85	H. T. W. Hardinge	75	Javed Miandad	68
R. E. S. Wyatt	85	R. Abel	74	K. S. McEwan	68
A. I. Kallicharran	84	G. S. Chappell	74	R. E. Marshall	68
J. Hardstaff, jun.	83	D. Kenyon	74	R. N. Harvey	67
R. B. Kanhai	83	Majid Khan	73	P. Holmes	67
S. M. Gavaskar	81	Mushtaq Mohammad	72	J. D. Robertson	67
M. Leyland	80	J. O'Connor	72	P. A. Perrin	66

R. G. Pollock ... 64	W. Gunn ... 48	W. E. Russell ... 41
R. T. Simpson ... 64	E. G. Hayes ... 48	K. C. Wessels ... 41
K. W. R. Fletcher ... 63	B. W. Luckhurst ... 48	R. C. Fredericks ... 40
G. Gunn ... 62	M. J. Procter ... 48	J. Gunn ... 40
G. A. Gooch ... 60	Shafiq Ahmed ... 48	W. Larkins ... 40
V. S. Hazare ... 60	M. W. Gatting ... 47	Mudassar Nazar ... 40
G. H. Hirst ... 60	A. J. Lamb ... 47	M. J. Smith ... 40
R. B. Simpson ... 60	A. C. MacLaren ... 47	C. L. Walcott ... 40
P. F. Warner ... 60	W. H. Ponsford ... 47	P. Willey ... 40
I. M. Chappell ... 59	J. Iddon ... 46	D. M. Young ... 40
A. L. Hassett ... 59	A. R. Morris ... 46	W. H. Ashdown ... 39
A. Shrewsbury ... 59	C. T. Radley ... 46	J. B. Bolus ... 39
A. E. Fagg ... 58	Younis Ahmed ... 46	W. A. Brown ... 39
P. H. Parfitt ... 58	W. W. Armstrong ... 45	M. D. Crowe ... 39
W. Rhodes ... 58	Asif Iqbal ... 45	R. J. Gregory ... 39
L. B. Fishlock ... 56	L. G. Berry ... 45	W. R. D. Payton ... 39
A. Jones ... 56	J. M. Brearley ... 45	D. W. Randall ... 39
C. A. Milton ... 56	A. W. Carr ... 45	J. R. Reid ... 39
C. Hallows ... 56	C. Hill ... 45	F. M. M. Worrell ... 39
Hanif Mohammad ... 55	N. C. O'Neill ... 45	F. L. Bowley ... 38
W. Watson ... 55	E. Paynter ... 45	P. J. Burge ... 38
D. J. Insole ... 54	C. E. B. Rice ... 45	J. F. Crapp ... 38
W. W. Keeton ... 54	Rev. D. S. Sheppard ... 45	D. I. Gower ... 38
W. Bardsley ... 53	K. D. Walters ... 45	D. Lloyd ... 38
B. F. Davison ... 53	J. G. Wright ... 45	V. L. Manjrekar ... 38
A. E. Dipper ... 53	H. H. I. Gibbons ... 44	A. W. Nourse ... 38
G. L. Jessop ... 53	P. N. Kirsten ... 44	N. Oldfield ... 38
James Seymour ... 53	V. M. Merchant ... 44	Rev. J. H. Parsons ... 38
E. H. Bowley ... 52	A. Mitchell ... 44	W. W. Read ... 38
D. B. Close ... 52	P. E. Richardson ... 44	J. Sharp ... 38
A. Ducat ... 52	B. Sutcliffe ... 44	L. J. Todd ... 38
E. R. Dexter ... 51	G. R. Viswanath ... 44	J. Arnold ... 37
J. M. Parks ... 51	E. J. Barlow ... 43	G. Brown ... 37
W. W. Whysall ... 51	B. L. D'Oliveira ... 43	G. M. Emmett ... 37
G. Cox jun. ... 50	J. H. Hampshire ... 43	H. W. Lee ... 37
H. E. Dollery ... 50	A. F. Kippax ... 43	M. A. Noble ... 37
K. S. Duleepsinhji ... 50	H. Makepeace ... 43	H. S. Squires ... 37
H. Gimblett ... 50	D. B. Vengsarkar ... 43	R. T. Virgin ... 37
W. M. Lawry ... 50	James Langridge ... 42	C. J. B. Wood ... 37
Sadiq Mohammad ... 50	H. W. Parks ... 42	N. F. Armstrong ... 36
F. B. Watson ... 50	T. F. Shepherd ... 42	E. Oldroyd ... 36
C. G. Macartney ... 49	V. T. Trumper ... 42	W. Place ... 36
M. J. Stewart ... 49	M. J. Harris ... 41	A. L. Wadekar ... 36
K. G. Suttle ... 49	K. R. Miller ... 41	E. D. Weekes ... 36
P. M. Umrigar ... 49	A. D. Nourse ... 41	C. S. Dempster ... 35
W. M. Woodfull ... 49	J. H. Parks ... 41	D. R. Jardine ... 35
C. J. Barnett ... 48	R. M. Prideaux ... 41	B. H. Valentine ... 35
A. R. Border ... 48	G. Pullar ... 41	

3,000 RUNS IN A SEASON

	Season	I	NO	R	HI	100s	Avge
D. C. S. Compton ...	1947	50	8	3,816	246	18	90.85
W. J. Edrich ...	1947	52	8	3,539	267*	12	80.43
T. W. Hayward ...	1906	61	8	3,518	219	13	66.37
L. Hutton ...	1949	56	6	3,429	269*	12	68.58
F. E. Woolley ...	1928	59	4	3,352	198	12	60.94
H. Sutcliffe ...	1932	52	7	3,336	313	14	74.13
W. R. Hammond ...	1933	54	5	3,323	264	13	67.81
E. H. Hendren ...	1928	54	7	3,311	209*	13	70.44
R. Abel ...	1901	68	8	3,309	247	7	55.15

	Season	I	NO	R	HI	100s	Avge
W. R. Hammond	1937	55	5	3,252	217	13	65.04
M. J. K. Smith	1959	67	11	3,245	200*	8	57.94
E. H. Hendren	1933	65	9	3,186	301*	11	56.89
C. P. Mead	1921	52	6	3,179	280*	10	69.10
T. W. Hayward	1904	63	5	3,170	203	11	54.65
K. S. Ranjitsinhji	1899	58	8	3,159	197	8	63.18
C. B. Fry	1901	43	3	3,147	244	13	78.67
K. S. Ranjitsinhji	1900	40	5	3,065	275	11	87.57
L. E. G. Ames	1933	57	5	3,058	295	9	58.80
J. T. Tyldesley	1901	60	5	3,041	221	9	55.29
C. P. Mead	1928	50	10	3,027	180	13	75.67
J. B. Hobbs	1925	48	5	3,024	266*	16	70.32
E. Tyldesley	1928	48	10	3,024	242	10	79.57
W. E. Alley	1961	64	11	3,019	221*	11	56.96
W. R. Hammond	1938	42	2	3,011	271	15	75.27
E. H. Hendren	1923	51	12	3,010	200*	13	77.17
H. Sutcliffe	1931	42	11	3,006	230	13	96.96
J. H. Parks	1937	63	4	3,003	168	11	50.89
H. Sutcliffe	1928	44	5	3,002	228	13	76.97

Notes: W. G. Grace scored 2,739 runs in 1871 – the first batsman to reach 2,000 runs in a season. He made ten hundreds and twice exceeded 200, with an average of 78.25 in all first-class matches. At the time, the over consisted of four balls.

The highest aggregate in a season since the reduction of County Championship matches in 1969 is 2,559 by G. A. Gooch (45 innings) in 1984.

1,000 RUNS IN A SEASON MOST TIMES

(Includes Overseas Tours and Seasons)

28 times: W. G. Grace 2,000 (6); F. E. Woolley 3,000 (1), 2,000 (12).

27 times: M. C. Cowdrey 2,000 (2); C. P. Mead 3,000 (1), 2,000 (9).

26 times: G. Boycott 2,000 (3); J. B. Hobbs 3,000 (1), 2,000 (16).

25 times: E. H. Hendren 3,000 (3), 2,000 (12).

24 times: D. L. Amiss 2,000 (3); W. G. Quaife 2,000 (1); H. Sutcliffe 3,000 (3), 2,000 (12).

23 times: A. Jones.

22 times: T. W. Graveney 2,000 (7); W. R. Hammond 3,000 (3), 2,000 (9).

21 times: D. Denton 2,000 (5); J. H. Edrich 2,000 (6); W. Rhodes 2,000 (2).

20 times: D. B. Close; K. W. R. Fletcher; G. Gunn; T. W. Hayward 3,000 (2), 2,000 (8); James Langridge 2,000 (1); J. M. Parks 2,000 (3); A. Sandham 2,000 (8); M. J. K. Smith 3,000 (1), 2,000 (5); C. Washbrook 2,000 (2).

19 times: J. W. Hearne 2,000 (4); G. H. Hirst 2,000 (1); D. Kenyon 2,000 (7); E. Tyldesley 3,000 (1), 2,000 (5); J. T. Tyldesley 3,000 (1), 2,000 (4).

18 times: L. G. Berry 2,000 (1); H. T. W. Hardinge 2,000 (5); R. E. Marshall 2,000 (6); P. A. Perrin; G. M. Turner 2,000 (5); R. E. S. Wyatt 2,000 (5).

17 times: L. E. G. Ames 3,000 (1), 2,000 (5); T. E. Bailey 2,000 (1); D. Brookes 2,000 (6); D. C. S. Compton 3,000 (1), 2,000 (5); L. Hutton 3,000 (1), 2,000 (8); J. G. Langridge 2,000 (11); M. Leyland 2,000 (3); K. G. Suttle 2,000 (1); Zaheer Abbas 2,000 (2).

16 times: D. G. Bradman 2,000 (4); D. E. Davies 2,000 (1); C. G. Greenidge 2,000 (1); E. G. Hayes 2,000 (2); C. A. Milton 2,000 (1); J. O'Connor 2,000 (4); C. T. Radley; James Seymour 2,000 (1).

15 times: G. Barker; K. F. Barrington 2,000 (3); E. H. Bowley 2,000 (4); M. H. Denness; A. E. Dipper 2,000 (5); H. E. Dollery 2,000 (2); W. J. Edrich 3,000 (1), 2,000 (8); J. H. Hampshire; P. Holmes 2,000 (7); Mushtaq Mohammad; R. B. Nicholls 2,000 (1); P. H. Parfitt 2,000 (3); W. G. A. Parkhouse 2,000 (1); B. A. Richards 2,000 (1); I. V. A. Richards 2,000 (1); J. D. Robertson 2,000 (9); G. S. Sobers; M. J. Stewart 2,000 (1).

Notes: F. E. Woolley reached 1,000 runs in 28 consecutive seasons (1907-1938). C. P. Mead did so 27 seasons in succession (1906-1936).

Outside England, 1,000 runs in a season has been reached most times by D. G. Bradman (in 12 seasons in Australia).

Three batsmen have scored 1,000 runs in a season in each of four different countries: G. S. Sobers in West Indies, England, India and Australia; M. C. Cowdrey and G. Boycott in England, South Africa, West Indies and Australia.

HIGHEST AGGREGATES OUTSIDE ENGLAND

	Season	I	NO	R	HI	100s	Avge
In Australia							
D. G. Bradman	1928-29	24	6	1,690	340*	7	93.88
In South Africa							
J. R. Reid	1961-62	30	2	1,915	203	7	68.39
In West Indies							
E. H. Hendren	1929-30	18	5	1,765	254*	6	135.76
In New Zealand							
M. D. Crowe	1986-87	21	3	1,676	175*	8	93.11
In India							
C. G. Borde	1964-65	28	3	1,604	168	6	64.16
In Pakistan							
Saadat Ali	1983-84	27	1	1,649	208	4	63.42
In Sri Lanka							
A. Ranatunga	1985-86	16	2	739	135*	3	52.78

Note: In more than one country, the following aggregates of over 2,000 runs have been recorded.

	Season	I	NO	R	HI	100s	Avge
M. Amarnath (P/I/WI)	1982-83	34	6	2,234	207	9	79.78
J. R. Reid (SA/A/NZ) .	1961-62	40	2	2,188	203	7	57.57
S. M. Gavaskar (I/P) .	1978-79	30	6	2,121	205	10	88.37
R. B. Simpson (I/P/A/WI)	1964-65	34	4	2,063	201	8	68.76

HIGHEST AVERAGES IN AN ENGLISH SEASON

(Qualification: 12 innings)

	Season	I	NO	R	HI	100s	Avge
D. G. Bradman	1938	26	5	2,429	278	13	115.66
G. Boycott	1979	20	5	1,538	175*	6	102.53
W. A. Johnston	1953	17	16	102	28*	0	102.00
G. Boycott	1971	30	5	2,503	233	13	100.12
D. G. Bradman	1930	36	6	2,960	334	10	98.66
H. Sutcliffe	1931	42	11	3,006	230	13	96.96
R. M. Poore	1899	21	4	1,551	304	7	91.23
D. R. Jardine	1927	14	3	1,002	147	5	91.09
D. C. S. Compton	1947	50	8	3,816	246	18	90.85
G. M. Turner	1982	16	3	1,171	311*	5	90.07
D. G. Bradman	1948	31	4	2,428	187	11	89.92
Zaheer Abbas	1981	36	10	2,306	215*	10	88.69
K. S. Ranjitsinhji	1900	40	5	3,065	275	11	87.57
D. R. Jardine	1928	17	4	1,133	193	3	87.15
W. R. Hammond	1946	26	5	1,783	214	7	84.90
D. G. Bradman	1934	27	3	2,020	304	7	84.16
R. B. Kanhai	1975	22	9	1,073	178*	3	82.53
Mudassar Nazar	1982	16	6	825	211*	4	82.50
C. G. Greenidge	1984	16	3	1,069	223	4	82.23
J. B. Hobbs	1928	38	7	2,542	200*	12	82.00
C. B. Fry	1903	40	7	2,683	234	9	81.30
W. J. Edrich	1947	52	8	3,539	267*	12	80.43

25,000 RUNS IN A CAREER

Dates in italics denote the first half of an overseas season; i.e. *1945* denotes the 1945-46 season.

	Career	R	I	NO	HI	100s	Avge
J. B. Hobbs	1905-34	61,237	1,315	106	316*	197	50.65
F. E. Woolley	1906-38	58,969	1,532	85	305*	145	40.75
E. H. Hendren	1907-38	57,611	1,300	166	301*	170	50.80
C. P. Mead	1905-36	55,061	1,340	185	280*	153	47.67
†W. G. Grace	1865-1908	54,896	1,493	105	344	126	39.55
W. R. Hammond	1920-51	50,551	1,005	104	336*	167	56.10
H. Sutcliffe	1919-45	50,138	1,088	123	313	149	51.95
G. Boycott	1962-86	48,426	1,014	162	261*	151	56.83
T. W. Graveney	1948-71	47,793	1,223	159	258	122	44.91
T. W. Hayward	1893-1914	43,551	1,138	96	315*	104	41.79
D. L. Amiss	1960-87	43,423	1,139	126	262*	102	42.86
M. C. Cowdrey	1950-76	42,719	1,130	134	307	107	42.89
A. Sandham	1911-37	41,284	1,000	79	325	107	44.82
L. Hutton	1934-60	40,140	814	91	364	129	55.51
M. J. K. Smith	1951-75	39,832	1,091	139	204	69	41.84
W. Rhodes	1898-1930	39,802	1,528	237	267*	58	30.83
J. H. Edrich	1956-78	39,790	979	104	310*	103	45.47
R. E. S. Wyatt	1923-57	39,405	1,141	157	232	85	40.04
D. C. S. Compton	1936-64	38,942	839	88	300	123	51.85
E. Tyldesley	1909-36	38,874	961	106	256*	102	45.46
J. T. Tyldesley	1895-1923	37,897	994	62	295*	86	40.66
K. W. R. Fletcher	1962-87	37,362	1,153	167	228*	63	37.89
J. W. Hearne	1909-36	37,252	1,025	116	285*	96	40.98
L. E. G. Ames	1926-51	37,248	951	95	295	102	43.51
D. Kenyon	1946-67	37,002	1,159	59	259	74	33.63
W. J. Edrich	1934-58	36,965	964	92	267*	86	42.39
J. M. Parks	1949-76	36,673	1,227	172	205*	51	34.76
D. Denton	1894-1920	36,479	1,163	70	221	69	33.37
G. H. Hirst	1891-1929	36,323	1,215	151	341	60	34.13
A. Jones	1957-83	36,049	1,168	72	204*	56	32.89
W. G. Quaife	1894-1928	36,012	1,203	185	255*	72	35.37
R. E. Marshall	1945-72	35,725	1,053	59	228*	68	35.94
G. Gunn	1902-32	35,208	1,061	82	220	62	35.96
D. B. Close	1949-86	34,994	1,225	173	198	52	33.26
Zaheer Abbas	1965-86	34,843	768	92	274	108	51.54
J. G. Langridge	1928-55	34,380	984	66	250*	76	37.45
G. M. Turner	1964-82	34,346	792	101	311*	103	49.70
C. Washbrook	1933-64	34,101	906	107	251*	76	42.67
M. Leyland	1920-48	33,660	932	101	263	80	40.50
H. T. W. Hardinge	1902-33	33,519	1,021	103	263*	75	36.51
R. Abel	1881-1904	33,124	1,007	73	357*	74	35.46
C. G. Greenidge	1970-87	32,799	780	67	273*	78	46.00
C. A. Milton	1948-74	32,150	1,078	125	170	56	33.73
J. D. Robertson	1937-59	31,914	897	46	331*	67	37.50
J. Hardstaff, jun.	1930-55	31,847	812	94	266	83	44.35
James Langridge	1924-53	31,716	1,058	157	167	42	35.20
K. F. Barrington	1953-68	31,714	831	136	256	76	45.63
A. I. Kallicharran	1966-86	31,331	775	82	243*	84	45.21
C. H. Lloyd	1963-86	31,232	730	96	242*	79	49.26
Mushtaq Mohammad	1956-85	31,091	843	104	303*	72	42.07
C. B. Fry	1892-1921	30,886	658	43	258*	94	50.22
D. Brookes	1934-59	30,874	925	70	257	71	36.10
P. Holmes	1913-35	30,573	810	84	315*	67	42.11
R. T. Simpson	1944-63	30,546	852	55	259	64	38.32
L. G. Berry	1924-51	30,225	1,056	57	232	45	30.25
K. G. Suttle	1949-71	30,225	1,064	92	204*	49	31.09

	Career	R	I	NO	HI	100s	Avge
P. A. Perrin	1896-1928	29,709	918	91	343*	66	35.92
I. V. A. Richards	1971-86	29,061	626	41	322	93	49.67
P. F. Warner	1894-1929	29,028	875	75	244	60	36.28
R. B. Kanhai	1954-81	28,774	669	82	256	83	49.01
J. O'Connor	1921-39	28,764	903	79	248	72	34.90
T. E. Bailey	1945-67	28,641	1,072	215	205	28	33.42
E. H. Bowley	1912-34	28,378	859	47	283	52	34.94
B. A. Richards	1964-82	28,358	576	58	356	80	54.74
G. S. Sobers	1952-74	28,315	609	93	365*	86	54.87
A. E. Dipper	1908-32	28,075	865	69	252*	53	35.27
D. G. Bradman	1927-48	28,067	338	43	452*	117	95.14
J. H. Hampshire	1961-84	28,059	924	112	183*	43	34.55
P. B. H. May	1948-63	27,592	618	77	285*	85	51.00
Majid Khan	1961-84	27,444	700	62	241	73	43.01
A. C. Russell	1908-30	27,358	717	59	273	71	41.57
E. G. Hayes	1896-1926	27,318	896	48	276	48	32.21
A. E. Fagg	1932-57	27,291	803	46	269*	58	36.05
James Seymour	1900-26	27,237	911	62	218*	53	32.08
P. H. Parfitt	1956-73	26,924	845	104	200*	58	36.33
B. F. Davison	1967-85	26,923	745	78	189	53	40.36
G. L. Jessop	1894-1914	26,698	855	37	286	53	32.63
D. E. Davies	1924-54	26,564	1,032	80	287*	32	27.90
A. Shrewsbury	1875-1902	26,505	813	90	267	59	36.65
M. J. Stewart	1954-72	26,492	898	93	227*	49	32.90
C. T. Radley	1964-87	26,441	880	134	200	46	35.44
Younis Ahmed	1961-86	26,063	762	118	221*	46	40.47
P. E. Richardson	1949-65	26,055	794	41	185	44	34.60
M. H. Denness	1959-80	25,886	838	65	195	33	33.48
S. M. Gavaskar	1966-87	25,834	563	61	340	81	51.46
H. Makepeace	1906-30	25,799	778	66	203	43	36.23
W. Gunn	1880-1904	25,691	850	72	273	48	33.02
W. Watson	1939-64	25,670	753	109	257	55	39.86
G. Brown	1908-33	25,649	1,012	52	232*	37	26.71
G. M. Emmett	1936-59	25,602	865	50	188	37	31.41
J. B. Bolus	1956-75	25,598	833	81	202*	39	34.03
W. E. Russell	1956-72	25,525	796	64	193	41	34.87
C. J. Barnett	1927-53	25,389	821	45	259	48	32.71
L. B. Fishlock	1931-52	25,376	699	54	253	56	39.34
D. J. Insole	1947-63	25,241	743	72	219*	54	37.61
J. M. Brearley	1961-83	25,185	768	102	312*	45	37.81
J. Vine	1896-1922	25,171	920	79	202	34	29.92
R. M. Prideaux	1958-74	25,136	808	75	202*	41	34.29
J. H. King	1895-1926	25,122	988	69	227*	34	27.33

† *In recent years some statisticians have removed from W. G. Grace's record a number of matches which they consider not to have been first-class. The above figures are those which became universally accepted upon appearance in W. G. Grace's obituary in the* Wisden *of 1916. Some works of reference give his career record as being 54,211–1,478–104–344–124–39.45. These figures also appeared in the 1981 edition of* Wisden.

CAREER AVERAGE OVER 50

(Qualification: 10,000 runs)

Avge		Career	I	NO	R	HI	100s
95.14	D. G. Bradman	1927-48	338	43	28,067	452*	117
71.22	V. M. Merchant	1929-51	229	43	13,248	359*	44
65.18	W. H. Ponsford	1920-34	235	23	13,819	437	47
64.99	W. M. Woodfull	1921-34	245	39	13,388	284	49
58.24	A. L. Hassett	1932-53	322	32	16,890	232	59

Avge		Career	I	NO	R	HI	100s
58.19	V. S. Hazare	1934-66	365	45	18,621	316*	60
57.22	A. F. Kippax	1918-35	256	33	12,762	315*	43
56.83	G. Boycott	1962-86	1,014	162	48,426	261*	151
56.55	C. L. Walcott	1941-63	238	29	11,820	314*	40
56.37	K. S. Ranjitsinhji	1893-1920	500	62	24,692	285*	72
56.22	R. B. Simpson	1952-77	436	62	21,029	359	60
56.10	W. R. Hammond	1920-51	1,005	104	50,551	336*	167
55.51	L. Hutton	1934-60	814	91	40,140	364	129
55.34	E. D. Weekes	1944-64	241	24	12,010	304*	36
55.23	M. D. Crowe	1979-87	249	39	11,600	242*	39
54.87	G. S. Sobers	1952-74	609	93	28,315	365*	86
54.74	B. A. Richards	1964-82	576	58	28,358	356	80
54.67	R. G. Pollock	1960-86	437	54	20,940	274	64
54.24	F. M. M. Worrell	1941-64	326	49	15,025	308*	39
53.78	R. M. Cowper	1959-69	228	31	10,595	307	26
53.67	A. R. Morris	1940-63	250	15	12,614	290	46
53.46	A. R. Border	1976-87	355	51	16,253	200	48
53.33	Javed Miandad	1973-87	547	86	24,586	311	68
52.32	Hanif Mohammad	1951-75	371	45	17,059	499	55
52.27	P. R. Umrigar	1944-67	350	41	16,154	252*	49
52.20	G. S. Chappell	1966-83	542	72	24,535	247*	74
51.95	H. Sutcliffe	1919-45	1,088	123	50,138	313	149
51.85	D. C. S. Compton	1936-64	839	88	38,942	300	123
51.54	Zaheer Abbas	1965-86	768	92	34,843	274	108
51.53	A. D. Nourse	1931-52	269	27	12,472	260*	41
51.46	S. M. Gavaskar	1966-87	563	61	25,834	340	81
51.44	W. A. Brown	1932-49	284	15	13,838	265*	39
51.34	D. B. Vengsarkar	1975-87	312	40	13,965	210	43
51.00	P. B. H. May	1948-63	618	77	27,592	285*	85
50.95	N. C. O'Neill	1955-67	306	34	13,859	284	45
50.93	R. N. Harvey	1946-62	461	35	21,699	231*	67
50.90	W. M. Lawry	1955-71	417	49	18,734	266	50
50.90	A. V. Mankad	1963-82	326	71	12,980	265	31
50.80	E. H. Hendren	1907-38	1,300	166	57,611	301*	170
50.65	J. B. Hobbs	1905-34	1,315	106	61,237	316*	197
50.47	Shafiq Ahmed	1967-86	383	47	16,959	217*	48
50.23	K. C. Wessels	1973-86	331	26	15,323	254	41
50.22	C. B. Fry	1892-1921	658	43	30,886	258*	94

FAST FIFTIES

Minutes

8†	C. C. Inman (57)	Leicestershire v Nottinghamshire at Nottingham ...	1965
11	C. I. J. Smith (66)	Middlesex v Gloucestershire at Bristol	1938
14	S. J. Pegler (50)	South Africans v Tasmania at Launceston	1910-11
14	F. T. Mann (53)	Middlesex v Nottinghamshire at Lord's	1921
14	H. B. Cameron (56)	Transvaal v Orange Free State at Johannesburg ...	1934-35
14	C. I. J. Smith (52)	Middlesex v Kent at Maidstone	1935
14	M. P. Maynard (61*)	Glamorgan v Yorkshire at Cardiff	1987

† *Full tosses were bowled to expedite a declaration.*

FASTEST HUNDREDS

Minutes

35	P. G. H. Fender (113*)	Surrey v Northamptonshire at Northampton ..	1920
35	S. J. O'Shaughnessy (105)	Lancashire v Leicestershire at Manchester	1983
37	C. M. Old (107)	Yorkshire v Warwickshire at Birmingham	1977
40	G. L. Jessop (101)	Gloucestershire v Yorkshire at Harrogate	1897
41	N. F. M. Popplewell (143)	Somerset v Gloucestershire at Bath	1983

Minutes

42	G. L. Jessop (191)	Gentlemen of South v Players of South at Hastings	1907
43	A. H. Hornby (106)	Lancashire v Somerset at Manchester	1905
43	D. W. Hookes (107)	South Australia v Victoria at Adelaide	1982-83
44	R. N. S. Hobbs (100)	Essex v Australians at Chelmsford	1975

Notes: The fastest recorded hundred in terms of balls received was scored off 34 balls by D. W. Hookes (above).

Research of the scorebook has shown that P. G. H. Fender scored his hundred from between 40 and 46 balls. He contributed 113 to an unfinished sixth-wicket partnership of 171 in 42 minutes with H. A. Peach.

S. J. O'Shaughnessy scored his hundred on the final afternoon of the season and against a succession of long-hops and full-tosses offered by occasional bowlers to expedite a declaration.

E. B. Alletson (Nottinghamshire) scored 189 out of 227 runs in 90 minutes against Sussex at Hove in 1911. It has been estimated that his last 139 runs took 37 minutes.

FASTEST DOUBLE-HUNDREDS

Minutes

113	R. J. Shastri (200*)	Bombay v Baroda at Bombay	1984-85
120	G. L. Jessop (286)	Gloucestershire v Sussex at Hove	1903
120	C. H. Lloyd (201*)	West Indians v Glamorgan at Swansea	1976
130	G. L. Jessop (234)	Gloucestershire v Somerset at Bristol	1905
131	V. T. Trumper (293)	Australians v Canterbury at Christchurch	1913-14

FASTEST TRIPLE-HUNDREDS

Minutes

181	D. C. S. Compton (300)	MCC v N. E. Transvaal at Benoni	1948-49
205	F. E. Woolley (305*)	MCC v Tasmania at Hobart	1911-12
205	C. G. Macartney (345)	Australians v Nottinghamshire at Nottingham	1921
213	D. G. Bradman (369)	South Australia v Tasmania at Adelaide	1935-36

300 RUNS IN ONE DAY

345	C. G. Macartney	Australians v Nottinghamshire at Nottingham	1921
334	W. H. Ponsford	Victoria v New South Wales at Melbourne	1926-27
333	K. S. Duleepsinhji	Sussex v Northamptonshire at Hove	1930
331*	J. D. Robertson	Middlesex v Worcestershire at Worcester	1949
325*	B. A. Richards	S. Australia v W. Australia at Perth	1970-71
322†	E. Paynter	Lancashire v Sussex at Hove	1937
322	I. V. A. Richards	Somerset v Warwickshire at Taunton	1985
318	C. W. Gregory	New South Wales v Queensland at Brisbane	1906-07
317	K. R. Rutherford	New Zealanders v D. B. Close's XI at Scarborough	1986
316†	R. H. Moore	Hampshire v Warwickshire at Bournemouth	1937
315*	R. C. Blunt	Otago v Canterbury at Christchurch	1931-32
312*	J. M. Brearley	MCC Under 25 v North Zone at Peshawar	1966-67
311*	G. M. Turner	Worcestershire v Warwickshire at Worcester	1982
309*	D. G. Bradman	Australia v England at Leeds	1930
307*	W. H. Ashdown	Kent v Essex at Brentwood	1934
306*	A. Ducat	Surrey v Oxford University at The Oval	1919
305*	F. R. Foster	Warwickshire v Worcestershire at Dudley	1914

† E. Paynter's 322 and R. H. Moore's 316 were scored on the same day: *July 28, 1937.*

1,000 RUNS IN MAY

		Runs	Avge
W. G. Grace, May 9 to May 30, 1895 (22 days):			
13, 103, 18, 25, 288, 52, 257, 73*, 18, 169		1,016	112.88
"W.G." was within two months of completing his 47th year.			
W. R. Hammond, May 7 to May 31, 1927 (25 days):			
27, 135, 108, 128, 17, 11, 99, 187, 4, 30, 83, 7, 192, 14		1,042	74.42
Hammond scored his 1,000th run on May 28, thus equalling			
"W.G.'s" record of 22 days.			
C. Hallows, May 5 to May 31, 1928 (27 days):			
100, 101, 51*, 123, 101*, 22, 74, 104, 58, 34*, 232		1,000	125.00

1,000 RUNS IN APRIL AND MAY

	Runs	Avge
T. W. Hayward, April 16 to May 31, 1900:		
120*, 55, 108, 131*, 55, 193, 120, 5, 6, 3, 40, 146, 92	1,074	97.63
D. G. Bradman, April 30 to May 31, 1930:		
236, 185*, 78, 9, 48*, 66, 4, 44, 252*, 32, 47*	1,001	143.00
On April 30 Bradman scored 75 not out.		
D. G. Bradman, April 30 to May 31, 1938:		
258, 58, 137, 278, 2, 143, 145*, 5, 30*	1,056	150.85
Bradman scored 258 on April 30, and his 1,000th run on May 27.		
W. J. Edrich, April 30 to May 31, 1938:		
104, 37, 115, 63, 20*, 182, 71, 31, 53*, 45, 15, 245, 0, 9, 20*	1,010	84.16
Edrich scored 21 not out on April 30. All his runs were scored at		
Lord's.		
G. M. Turner, April 24 to May 31, 1973:		
41, 151*, 143, 85, 7, 8, 17*, 81, 13, 53, 44, 153*, 3, 2, 66*, 30, 10*,		
111	1,018	78.30

1,000 RUNS IN TWO SEPARATE MONTHS

Only four batsmen, C. B. Fry, K. S. Ranjitsinhji, H. Sutcliffe and L. Hutton, have scored over 1,000 runs in each of two months in the same season. L. Hutton, by scoring 1,294 in June 1949, made more runs in a single month than anyone else. He also made 1,050 in August 1949.

MOST RUNS SCORED OFF ONE OVER

(All instances refer to six-ball overs)

36	G. S. Sobers	off M. A. Nash, Nottinghamshire v Glamorgan at Swansea (six 6s)	1968
36	R. J. Shastri	off Tilak Raj, Bombay v Baroda at Bombay (six 6s)	1984-85
34	E. B. Alletson	off E. H. Killick, Nottinghamshire v Sussex at Hove (46604446; including two no-balls)	1911
34	F. C. Hayes	off M. A. Nash, Lancashire v Glamorgan at Swansea (646666)	1977
32	I. T. Botham	off I. R. Snook, England XI v Central Districts at Palmerston North (466464)	1983-84
32	C. C. Inman	off N. W. Hill, Leicestershire v Nottinghamshire at Nottingham (466664; full tosses were provided for him to hit)	1965
32	T. E. Jesty	off R. J. Boyd-Moss, Hampshire v Northamptonshire at Southampton (466662)	1984
32	P. W. G. Parker	off A. I. Kallicharran, Sussex v Warwickshire at Birmingham (466664)	1982

32	I. R. Redpath	off N. Rosendorff, Australians v Orange Free State at Bloemfontein (666644)	1969-70
32	C. C. Smart	off G. Hill, Glamorgan v Hampshire at Cardiff (664664)	1935
31	M. H. Bowditch (1) and M. J. Procter (30)	off A. A. Mallett, Western Province v Australians at Cape Town (Procter hit five 6s)	1969-70
31	A. W. Wellard	off F. E. Woolley, Somerset v Kent at Wells (666661)	1938
30	I. T. Botham	off P. A. Smith, Somerset v Warwickshire at Taunton (4466460 including one no-ball)	1982
30	D. G. Bradman	off A. P. Freeman, Australians v England XI at Folkestone (466464)	1934
30	H. B. Cameron	off H. Verity, South Africans v Yorkshire at Sheffield (444666)	1935
30	G. A. Gooch	off S. R. Gorman, Essex v Cambridge U. at Cambridge (662664)	1985
30	A. J. Lamb	off A. I. Kallicharran, Northamptonshire v Warwickshire at Birmingham (644664)	1982
30	D. T. Lindsay	off W. T. Greensmith, South African Fezela XI v Essex at Chelmsford (066666 to win the match)	1961
30	Majid Khan	off R. C. Davis, Pakistanis v Glamorgan at Swansea (606666)	1967
30	M. P. Maynard	off K. Sharp, Glamorgan v Yorkshire at Cardiff (464466)	1987
30	A. W. Wellard	off T. R. Armstrong, Somerset v Derbyshire at Wells (066666)	1936
30	D. Wilson	off R. N. S. Hobbs, Yorkshire v MCC at Scarborough (466266)	1966
30	P. L. Winslow	off J. T. Ikin, South Africans v Lancashire at Manchester (446646)	1955
30	Zaheer Abbas	off D. Breakwell, Gloucestershire v Somerset at Taunton (466626)	1979

Note: The greatest number of runs scored off an eight-ball over is 34 (40446664) by R. M. Edwards off M. C. Carew, Governor-General's XI v West Indians at Auckland, 1968-69.

MOST SIXES IN AN INNINGS

15	J. R. Reid (296)	Wellington v N. Districts at Wellington	1962-63
13	Majid Khan (147*)	Pakistanis v Glamorgan at Swansea	1967
13	C. G. Greenidge (273*)	D. H. Robins' XI v Pakistanis at Eastbourne	1974
13	C. G. Greenidge (259)	Hampshire v Sussex at Southampton	1975
13	G. W. Humpage (254)	Warwickshire v Lancashire at Southport	1982
13	R. J. Shastri (200*)	Bombay v Baroda at Bombay	1984-85
12	Gulfraz Khan (207)	Railways v Universities at Lahore	1976-77
12	I. T. Botham (138*)	Somerset v Warwickshire at Birmingham	1985
12	R. A. Harper (234)	Northamptonshire v Gloucestershire at Northampton	1986
11	C. K. Nayudu (153)	Hindus v MCC at Bombay	1926-27
11	C. J. Barnett (194)	Gloucestershire v Somerset at Bath	1934
11	R. Benaud (135)	Australians v T. N. Pearce's XI at Scarborough	1953

Note: W. J. Stewart (Warwickshire) hit seventeen 6s in the match v Lancashire, at Blackpool, 1959; ten in his first innings of 155 and seven in his second innings of 125.

MOST SIXES IN A SEASON

| 80 | I. T. Botham | 1985 | 66 | A. W. Wellard | 1935 |

Note: A. W. Wellard hit 50 or more sixes in a season four times. His number of 6s in 1935 has in the past been given as 72, but recent research has caused this to be adjusted.

MOST BOUNDARIES IN AN INNINGS

68	P. A. Perrin (343*)	Essex v Derbyshire at Chesterfield	1904
65	A. C. MacLaren (424)	Lancashire v Somerset at Taunton	1895
64	Hanif Mohammad (499)	Karachi v Bahawalpur at Karachi	1958-59
57	J. H. Edrich (310*)	England v New Zealand at Leeds	1965
55	C. W. Gregory (383)	NSW v Queensland at Brisbane	1906-07
54	G. H. Hirst (341)	Yorkshire v Leicestershire at Leicester	1905
53	A. W. Nourse (304*)	Natal v Transvaal at Johannesburg	1919-20
53	K. R. Rutherford (317)	New Zealanders v D. B. Close's XI at Scarborough.	1986
51	C. G. Macartney (345)	Australians v Nottinghamshire at Nottingham	1921
50	D. G. Bradman (369)	South Australia v Tasmania at Adelaide	1935-36
50	A. Ducat (306*)	Surrey v Oxford University at The Oval	1919
50	B. B. Nimbalkar (443*)	Maharashtra v Kathiawar at Poona	1948-49
50	J. R. Reid (296)	Wellington v N. Districts at Wellington	1962-63
50	I. V. A. Richards (322)	Somerset v Warwickshire at Taunton	1985

Note: Boundaries include sixes.

HIGHEST PARTNERSHIPS

577	V. S. Hazare (288) and Gul Mahomed (319), fourth wicket, Baroda v Holkar at Baroda	1946-47
574*	F. M. M. Worrell (255*) and C. L. Walcott (314*), fourth wicket, Barbados v Trinidad at Port-of-Spain	1945-46
561	Waheed Mirza (324) and Mansoor Akhtar (224*), first wicket, Karachi Whites v Quetta at Karachi	1976-77
555	P. Holmes (224*) and H. Sutcliffe (313), first wicket, Yorkshire v Essex at Leyton	1932
554	J. T. Brown (300) and J. Tunnicliffe (243), first wicket, Yorkshire v Derbyshire at Chesterfield	1898
502*	F. M. M. Worrell (308*) and J. D. C. Goddard (218*), fourth wicket, Barbados v Trinidad at Bridgetown	1943-44
490	E. H. Bowley (283) and J. G. Langridge (195), first wicket, Sussex v Middlesex at Hove	1933
487*	G. A. Headley (344*) and C. C. Passailaigue (261*), sixth wicket, Jamaica v Lord Tennyson's XI at Kingston	1931-32
470	A. I. Kallicharran (230*) and G. W. Humpage (254), fourth wicket, Warwickshire v Lancashire at Southport	1982
465*	J. A. Jameson (240*) and R. B. Kanhai (213*), second wicket, Warwickshire v Gloucestershire at Birmingham	1974
462*	D. W. Hookes (306*) and W. B. Phillips (213*), fourth wicket, South Australia v Tasmania at Adelaide	1986-87
456	W. H. Ponsford (248) and E. R. Mayne (209), first wicket, Victoria v Queensland at Melbourne	1923-24
456	Khalid Irtiza (290) and Aslam Ali (236), third wicket, United Bank v Multan at Karachi	1975-76
455	K. V. Bhandarkar (205) and B. B. Nimbalkar (443*), second wicket, Maharashtra v Kathiawar at Poona	1948-49
451	D. G. Bradman (244) and W. H. Ponsford (266), second wicket, Australia v England, Fifth Test, at The Oval	1934
451*	S. Desai (218*) and R. M. H. Binny (211*), first wicket, Karnataka v Kerala at Chikmagalur	1977-78
451	Mudassar Nazar (231) and Javed Miandad (280*), third wicket, Pakistan v India, Fourth Test, at Hyderabad	1982-83

PARTNERSHIPS FOR FIRST WICKET

561	Waheed Mirza and Mansoor Akhtar, Karachi Whites v Quetta at Karachi	1976-77
555	P. Holmes and H. Sutcliffe, Yorkshire v Essex at Leyton	1932
554	J. T. Brown and J. Tunnicliffe, Yorkshire v Derbyshire at Chesterfield	1898
490	E. H. Bowley and J. G. Langridge, Sussex v Middlesex at Hove	1933
456	E. R. Mayne and W. H. Ponsford, Victoria v Queensland at Melbourne ..	1923-24
451*	S. Desai and R. M. H. Binny, Karnataka v Kerala at Chikmagalur	1977-78
428	J. B Hobbs and A. Sandham, Surrey v Oxford University at The Oval	1926
424	J. F. W. Nicholson and I. J. Siedle, Natal v Orange Free State at Bloemfontein	1926-27
421	S. M. Gavaskar and G. A. Parkar, Bombay v Bengal at Bombay	1981-82
417	Kamal Najamuddin and Khalid Alvi, Karachi v Railways at Karachi	1980-81
413	V. Mankad and Pankaj Roy, India v New Zealand at Madras (world Test record)	1955-56
405	C. P. S. Chauhan and M. S. Gupte, Maharashtra v Vidarbha at Poona ...	1972-73
395	D. M. Young and R. B. Nicholls, Gloucestershire v Oxford University at Oxford	1962
391	A. O. Jones and A. Shrewsbury, Nottinghamshire v Gloucestershire at Bristol	1899
390	G. L. Wight and G. L. R. Gibbs, B. Guiana v Barbados at Georgetown ..	1951-52
390	B. Dudleston and J. F. Steele, Leicestershire v Derbyshire at Leicester	1979
389	Majid Khan and Shafiq Ahmed, Punjab A v Sind A at Karachi	1974-75
389	Mudassar Nazar and Mansoor Akhtar, United Bank v Rawalpindi at Lahore	1981-82
388	K. C. Wessels and R. B. Kerr, Queensland v Victoria at St Kilda, Melbourne	1982-83
387	G. M. Turner and T. W. Jarvis, New Zealand v West Indies at Georgetown	1971-72
382	R. B. Simpson and W. M. Lawry, Australia v West Indies at Bridgetown .	1964-65
380	H. Whitehead and C. J. B. Wood, Leicestershire v Worcestershire at Worcester	1906
379	R. Abel and W. Brockwell, Surrey v Hampshire at The Oval	1897
378	J. T. Brown and J. Tunnicliffe, Yorkshire v Sussex at Sheffield	1897
377*	N. F. Horner and Khalid Ibadulla, Warwickshire v Surrey at The Oval ...	1960
375	W. H. Ponsford and W. M. Woodfull, Victoria v New South Wales at Melbourne	1926-27

FIRST-WICKET HUNDREDS IN BOTH INNINGS

B. Sutcliffe and D. D. Taylor, for Auckland v Canterbury in 1948-49, scored for the first wicket 220 in the first innings and 286 in the second innings. This is the only instance of two double-century opening stands in the same match.

T. W. Hayward and J. B. Hobbs in 1907 accomplished a performance without parallel by scoring over 100 together for Surrey's first wicket four times in one week: 106 and 125 v Cambridge University at The Oval, and 147 and 105 v Middlesex at Lord's.

L. Hutton and C. Washbrook, in three consecutive Test match innings which they opened together for England v Australia in 1946-47, made 138 in the second innings at Melbourne, and 137 and 100 at Adelaide. They also opened with 168 and 129 at Leeds in 1948.

J. B. Hobbs and H. Sutcliffe, in three consecutive Test match innings which they opened together for England v Australia in 1924-25, made 157 and 110 at Sydney and 283 at Melbourne. On 26 occasions – 15 times in Test matches – Hobbs and Sutcliffe took part in a three-figure first-wicket partnership. Seven of these stands exceeded 200.

G. Boycott and J. H. Edrich, in three consecutive Test match innings which they opened together for England v Australia in 1970-71, made 161* in the second innings at Melbourne, and 107 and 103 at Adelaide.

In 1971 R. G. A. Headley and P. J. Stimpson of Worcestershire shared in first-wicket hundred partnerships on each of the first four occasions they opened the innings together: 125 and 147 v Northamptonshire at Worcester, 102 and 128* v Warwickshire at Birmingham.

J. B. Hobbs during his career, which extended from 1905 to 1934, helped to make 100 or more for the first wicket in first-class cricket 166 times – 15 of them in 1926, when in consecutive innings he helped to make 428, 182, 106 and 123 before a wicket fell. As many as 117 of the 166 stands were made for Surrey. In all first-class matches Hobbs and A. Sandham shared 66 first-wicket partnerships of 100 or more runs.

P. Holmes and H. Sutcliffe made 100 or more runs for the first wicket of Yorkshire on 69 occasions; J. B. Hobbs and A. Sandham for Surrey on 63 occasions; W. W. Keeton and C. B. Harris of Nottinghamshire on 46; T. W. Hayward and J. B. Hobbs of Surrey on 40; G. Gunn and W. W. Whysall of Nottinghamshire on 40; J. D. Robertson and S. M. Brown of Middlesex on 34; C. B. Fry and J. Vine of Sussex on 33; R. E. Marshall and J. R. Gray of Hampshire on 33; D. E. Davies and A. H. Dyson of Glamorgan on 32; and G. Boycott and R. G. Lumb of Yorkshire on 27.

J. Douglas and A. E. Stoddart in 1896 scored over 150 runs for the Middlesex first wicket three times within a fortnight. In 1901, J. Iremonger and A. O. Jones obtained over 100 for the Nottinghamshire first wicket four times within eight days, scoring 134 and 144* v Surrey at The Oval, 238 v Essex at Leyton, and 119 v Derbyshire at Welbeck.

J. W. Lee and F. S. Lee, brothers, for Somerset in 1934, scored over 100 runs thrice in succession in the County Championship.

W. G. Grace and A. E. Stoddart, in three consecutive innings against the Australians in 1893, made over 100 runs for each opening partnership.

C. Hallows and F. B. Watson, in consecutive innings for Lancashire in 1928, opened with 200, 202, 107, 118; reached three figures twelve times, 200 four times.

H. Sutcliffe, in the period 1919-1939 inclusive, shared in 145 first-wicket partnerships of 100 runs or more.

There were four first-wicket hundred partnerships in the match between Somerset and Cambridge University at Taunton in 1960. G. Atkinson and R. T. Virgin scored 172 and 112 for Somerset and R. M. Prideaux and A. R. Lewis 198 and 137 for Cambridge University.

PARTNERSHIP RECORDS FOR ALL COUNTRIES

Best First-Wicket Stands

Pakistan	561	Waheed Mirza (324) and Mansoor Akhtar (224*), Karachi Whites v Quetta at Karachi	1976-77
English	555	P. Holmes (224*) and H. Sutcliffe (313), Yorkshire v Essex at Leyton	1932
Australian	456	W. H. Ponsford (248) and E. R. Mayne (209), Victoria v Queensland at Melbourne	1923-24
Indian	451*	S. Desai (218*) and R. M. H. Binny (211*), Karnataka v Kerala at Chikmagalur	1977-78
South African	424	J. F. W. Nicolson (252*) and I. J. Siedle (174), Natal v Orange Free State at Bloemfontein	1926-27
West Indian	390	G. L. Wight (262*) and G. L. R. Gibbs (216), British Guiana v Barbados at Georgetown	1951-52
New Zealand	387	G. M. Turner (259) and T. W. Jarvis (182), New Zealand v West Indies at Georgetown	1971-72

Best Second-Wicket Stands

English	465*	J. A. Jameson (240*) and R. B. Kanhai (213*), Warwickshire v Gloucestershire at Birmingham	1974
Indian	455	K. V. Bhandarkar (205) and B. B. Nimbalkar (443*), Maharashtra v Kathiawar at Poona	1948-49
Australian	451	W. H. Ponsford (266) and D. G. Bradman (244), Australia v England at The Oval	1934
West Indian	446	C. C. Hunte (260) and G. S. Sobers (365*), West Indies v Pakistan at Kingston	1957-58
Pakistan	426	Arshad Pervez (220) and Mohsin Khan (220), Habib Bank v Income Tax Dept at Lahore	1977-78
New Zealand	317	R. T. Hart (167*) and P. S. Briasco (157), Central Districts v Canterbury at New Plymouth	1983-84
South African	305	S. K. Coen (165) and J. M. M Commaille (186), Orange Free State v Natal at Bloemfontein	1926-27

Best Third-Wicket Stands

Pakistan	456	Khalid Irtiza (290) and Aslam Ali (236), United Bank v Multan at Karachi	1975-76
New Zealand	445	P. E. Whitelaw (195) and W. N. Carson (290), Auckland v Otago at Dunedin (in 268 minutes)	1936-37
West Indian	434	J. B. Stollmeyer (324) and G. E. Gomez (190), Trinidad v British Guiana at Port-of-Spain	1946-47
English	424*	W. J. Edrich (168*) and D. C. S. Compton (252*), Middlesex v Somerset at Lord's	1948
Indian	410	L. Amarnath (262) and R. S. Modi (156), India in England v The Rest at Calcutta	1946-47
Australian	390*	J. M. Wiener (221*) and J. K. Moss (200*), Victoria v Western Australia at St Kilda, Melbourne	1981-82
South African	341	E. J. Barlow (201) and R. G. Pollock (175), South Africa v Australia at Adelaide	1963-64

Best Fourth-Wicket Stands

Indian	577	V. S. Hazare (288) and Gul Mahomed (319), Baroda v Holkar at Baroda	1946-47
West Indian	574*	C. L. Walcott (314*) and F. M. M. Worrell (255*), Barbados v Trinidad at Port-of-Spain	1945-46
English	470	A. I. Kallicharran (230*) and G. W. Humpage (254), Warwickshire v Lancashire at Southport	1982
Australian	462*	D. W. Hookes (306*) and W. B. Phillips (213*), South Australia v Tasmania at Adelaide	1986-87
Pakistan	350	Mushtaq Mohammad (201) and Asif Iqbal (175), Pakistan v New Zealand at Dunedin	1972-73
South African	342	E. A. B. Rowan (196) and P. J. M. Gibb (203), Transvaal v N. E. Transvaal at Johannesburg	1952-53
New Zealand	324	J. R. Reid (188*) and W. M. Wallace (197), New Zealanders v Cambridge University at Cambridge	1949

Best Fifth-Wicket Stands

Australian	405	S. G. Barnes (234) and D. G. Bradman (234), Australia v England at Sydney	1946-47
English	393	E. G. Arnold (200*) and W. B. Burns (196), Worcestershire v Warwickshire at Birmingham	1909
Indian	360	U. M. Merchant (217) and M. N. Raiji (170), Bombay v Hyderabad at Bombay	1947-48
Pakistan	355	Altaf Shah (276) and Tariq Bashir (196), House Building Finance Corporation v Multan at Multan	1976-77
South African	338	R. G. Pollock (194) and A. L. Wilmot (152), Eastern Province v Natal at Port Elizabeth	1975-76
West Indian	335	B. F. Butcher (151) and C. H. Lloyd (201*), West Indians v Glamorgan at Swansea	1969
New Zealand	319	K. R. Rutherford (317) and E. J. Gray (88), New Zealanders v D. B. Close's XI at Scarborough	1986

Best Sixth-Wicket Stands

West Indian	487*	G. A. Headley (344*) and C. C. Passailaigue (261*), Jamaica v Lord Tennyson's XI at Kingston	1931-32
Australian	428	M. A. Noble (284) and W. W. Armstrong (172*), Australians v Sussex at Hove	1902

English	411	R. M. Poore (304) and E. G. Wynyard (225), Hampshire v Somerset at Taunton	1899
Indian	371	V. M. Merchant (359*) and R. S. Modi (168), Bombay v Maharashtra at Bombay	1943-44
Pakistan	353	Salah-ud-Din (256) and Zaheer Abbas (197), Karachi v East Pakistan at Karachi	1968-69
South African	244*	J. M. M. Commaille (132*) and A. W. Palm (106*), Western Province v Griqualand West at Johannesburg	1923-24
New Zealand	226	E. J. Gray (126) and R. W. Ormiston (93), Wellington v Central Districts at Wellington	1981-82

Best Seventh-Wicket Stands

West Indian	347	D. St E. Atkinson (219) and C. C. Depeiza (122), West Indies v Australia at Bridgetown	1954-55
English	344	K. S. Ranjitsinhji (230) and W. Newham (153), Sussex v Essex at Leyton	1902
Australian	335	C. W. Andrews (253) and E. C. Bensted (155), Queensland v New South Wales at Sydney	1934-35
Pakistan	308	Waqar Hassan (189) and Imtiaz Ahmed (209), Pakistan v New Zealand at Lahore	1955-56
South African	299	B. Mitchell (159) and A. Melville (153), Transvaal v Griqualand West at Kimberley	1946-47
Indian	274	K. C. Ibrahim (250) and K. M. Rangnekar (138), Bijapur XI v Bengal XI at Bombay	1942-43
New Zealand	265	J. L. Powell (164) and N. Dorreen (105*), Canterbury v Otago at Christchurch	1929-30

Best Eighth-Wicket Stands

Australian	433	A. Sims (184*) and V. T. Trumper (293), An Australian XI v Canterbury at Christchurch	1913-14
English	292	R. Peel (210*) and Lord Hawke (166), Yorkshire v Warwickshire at Birmingham	1896
West Indian	255	E. A. V. Williams (131*) and E. A. Martindale (134), Barbados v Trinidad at Bridgetown	1935-36
Pakistan	240	Gulfraz Khan (207) and Raja Sarfraz (102), Railways v Universities at Lahore	1976-77
Indian	236	C. T. Sarwate (235) and R. P. Singh (88), Holkar v Delhi and District at Delhi	1949-50
South African	222	D. P. B. Morkel (114) and S. S. L. Steyn (261*), Western Province v Border at Cape Town	1929-30
New Zealand	190*	J. E. Mills (104*) and C. F. W. Allcott (102*), New Zealanders v Civil Service at Chiswick	1927

Best Ninth-Wicket Stands

English	283	J. Chapman (165) and A. Warren (123), Derbyshire v Warwickshire at Blackwell	1910
Indian	245	V. S. Hazare (316*) and N. D. Nagarwalla (98), Maharashtra v Baroda at Poona	1939-40
New Zealand	239	H. B. Cave (118) and I. B. Leggat (142*), Central Districts v Otago at Dunedin	1952-53
Australian	232	C. Hill (365*) and E. Walkley (53), South Australia v New South Wales at Adelaide	1900-01
South African	221	N. V. Lindsay (160*) and G. R. McCubbin (97), Transvaal v Rhodesia at Bulawayo	1922-23
Pakistan	190	Asif Iqbal (146) and Intikhab Alam (51), Pakistan v England at The Oval	1967
West Indian	161	C. H. Lloyd (161*) and A. M. E. Roberts (68), West Indies v India at Calcutta	1983-84

Best Tenth-Wicket Stands

Australian	307	A. F. Kippax (260*), and J. E. H. Hooker (62), New South Wales v Victoria at Melbourne	1928-29
Indian	249	C. T. Sarwate (124*) and S. N. Banerjee (121), Indians v Surrey at The Oval	1946
English	235	F. E. Woolley (185) and A. Fielder (112*), Kent v Worcestershire at Stourbridge	1909
Pakistan	196*	Nadim Yousuf (202*) and Maqsood Kundi (109*) Muslim Commercial Bank v National Bank at Lahore	1981-82
New Zealand	184	R. C. Blunt (338*) and W. Hawkesworth (21), Otago v Canterbury at Christchurch	1931-32
South African	174	H. R. Lance (168) and D. Mackay-Coghill (57*), Transvaal v Natal at Johannesburg	1965-66
West Indian	138	E. L. G. Hoad (149*) and H. C. Griffith (84), West Indians v Sussex at Hove	1933

Note: All the English record wicket partnerships were made in the County Championship.

OUT HANDLED THE BALL

J. Grundy	MCC v Kent at Lord's	1857
G. Bennett	Kent v Sussex at Hove	1872
W. H. Scotton	Smokers v Non-Smokers at East Melbourne	1886-87
C. W. Wright	Nottinghamshire v Gloucestershire at Bristol	1893
E. Jones	South Australia v Victoria at Melbourne	1894-95
A. W. Nourse	South Africans v Sussex at Hove	1907
E. T. Benson	MCC v Auckland at Auckland	1929-30
A. W. Gilbertson	Otago v Auckland at Auckland	1952-53
W. R. Endean	South Africa v England at Cape Town	1956-57
P. J. Burge	Queensland v New South Wales at Sydney	1958-59
Dildar Awan	Services v Lahore at Lahore	1959-60
Mahmood-ul-Hasan	Karachi University v Railways-Quetta at Karachi	1960-61
Ali Raza	Karachi Greens v Hyderabad at Karachi	1961-62
Mohammad Yusuf	Rawalpindi v Peshawar at Peshawar	1962-63
A. Rees	Glamorgan v Middlesex at Lord's	1965
Pervez Akhtar	Multan v Karachi Greens at Sahiwal	1971-72
Javed Mirza	Railways v Punjab at Lahore	1972-73
R. G. Pollock	Eastern Province v Western Province at Cape Town	1973-74
C. I. Dey	Northern Transvaal v Orange Free State at Bloemfontein	1973-74
Nasir Valika	Karachi Whites v National Bank at Karachi	1974-75
Haji Yousuf	National Bank v Railways at Lahore	1974-75
Masood-ul-Hasan	PIA v National Bank B at Lyallpur	1975-76
D. K. Pearse	Natal v Western Province at Cape Town	1978-79
A. M. J. Hilditch	Australia v Pakistan at Perth	1978-79
Musleh-ud-Din	Railways v Lahore at Lahore	1979-80
Jalal-ud-Din	IDBP v Habib Bank at Bahawalpur	1981-82
Mohsin Khan	Pakistan v Australia at Karachi	1982-83
D. L. Haynes	West Indies v India at Bombay	1983-84
K. Azad	Delhi v Punjab at Amritsar	1983-84
Athar A. Khan	Allied Bank v HBFC at Sialkot	1983-84
A. Pandya	Saurashtra v Baroda at Baroda	1984-85
G. N. Linton	Barbados v Windward Islands at Bridgetown	1985-86
R. B. Gartrell	Tasmania v Victoria at Melbourne	1986-87

OUT OBSTRUCTING THE FIELD

C. A. Absolom	Cambridge University v Surrey at The Oval	1868
T. Straw	Worcestershire v Warwickshire at Worcester	1899
T. Straw	Worcestershire v Warwickshire at Birmingham	1901
J. P. Whiteside	Leicestershire v Lancashire at Leicester	1901

L. Hutton	England v South Africa at The Oval	1951
J. A. Hayes	Canterbury v Central Districts at Christchurch	1954-55
D. D. Deshpande	Madhya Pradesh v Uttar Pradesh at Benares	1956-57
M. Mehra	Railways v Delhi at Delhi	1959-60
K. Ibadulla	Warwickshire v Hampshire at Coventry	1963
Qaiser Khan	Dera Ismail Khan v Railways at Lahore	1964-65
Ijaz Ahmed	Lahore Greens v Lahore Blues at Lahore	1973-74
Qasim Feroze	Bahawalpur v Universities at Lahore	1974-75
T. Quirk	Northern Transvaal v Border at East London	1978-79
Mahmood Rashid	United Bank v Muslim Commercial Bank at Bahawalpur	1981-82
Arshad Ali	Sukkur v Quetta at Quetta	1983-84
H. Wasu	Vidarbha v Rajasthan at Akola	1984-85
Khalid Javed	Railways v Lahore at Lahore	1985-86

OUT HIT THE BALL TWICE

H. E. Bull	MCC v Oxford University at Lord's	1864
H. R. J. Charlwood	Sussex v Surrey at Hove	1872
R. G. Barlow	North v South at Lord's	1878
P. S. Wimble	Transvaal v Griqualand West at Kimberley	1892-93
G. B. Nicholls	Somerset v Gloucestershire at Bristol	1896
A. A. Lilley	Warwickshire v Yorkshire at Birmingham	1897
J. H. King	Leicestershire v Surrey at The Oval	1906
A. P. Binns	Jamaica v British Guiana at Georgetown	1956-57
K. Bavanna	Andhra v Mysore at Guntur	1963-64
Zaheer Abbas	PIA A v Karachi Blues at Karachi	1969-70
Anwar Miandad	IDBP v United Bank at Lahore	1979-80
Anwar Iqbal	Hyderabad v Sukkur at Hyderabad	1983-84
Iqtidar Ali	Allied Bank v Muslim Commercial Bank at Lahore	1983-84
Aziz Malik	Lahore Division v Faisalabad at Sialkot	1984-85
Javed Mohammad	Multan v Karachi Whites at Sahiwal	1986-87

BOWLING RECORDS

TEN WICKETS IN ONE INNINGS

	O	M	R		
E. Hinkly (Kent)				v England at Lord's	1848
*J. Wisden (North)				v South at Lord's	1850
V. E. Walker (England)	43	17	74	v Surrey at The Oval	1859
V. E. Walker (Middlesex)	44.2	5	104	v Lancashire at Manchester	1865
G. Wootton (All England)	31.3	9	54	v Yorkshire at Sheffield	1865
W. Hickton (Lancashire)	36.2	19	46	v Hampshire at Manchester	1870
S. E. Butler (Oxford)	24.1	11	38	v Cambridge at Lord's	1871
James Lillywhite (South)	60.2	22	129	v North at Canterbury	1872
A. Shaw (MCC)	36.2	8	73	v North at Lord's	1874
E. Barratt (Players)	29	11	43	v Australians at The Oval	1878
G. Giffen (Australian XI)	26	10	66	v The Rest at Sydney	1883-84
W. G. Grace (MCC)	36.2	17	49	v Oxford University at Oxford	1886
G. Burton (Middlesex)	52.3	25	59	v Surrey at The Oval	1888
†A. E. Moss (Canterbury)	21.3	10	28	v Wellington at Christchurch	1889-90
S. M. J. Woods (Cambridge U.)	31	6	69	v Thornton's XI at Cambridge	1890
T. Richardson (Surrey)	15.3	3	45	v Essex at The Oval	1894
H. Pickett (Essex)	27	11	32	v Leicestershire at Leyton	1895
E. J. Tyler (Somerset)	34.3	15	49	v Surrey at Taunton	1895
W. P. Howell (Australians)	23.2	14	28	v Surrey at The Oval	1899
C. H. G. Bland (Sussex)	25.2	10	48	v Kent at Tonbridge	1899
J. Briggs (Lancashire)	28.5	7	55	v Worcestershire at Manchester	1900
A. E. Trott (Middlesex)	14.2	5	42	v Somerset at Taunton	1900
F. Hinds (A. B. St Hill's XI)	19.1	6	36	v Trinidad at Port-of-Spain	1900-01

	O	M	R		
A. Fielder (Players)	24.5	1	90	v Gentlemen at Lord's	1906
E. G. Dennett (Gloucestershire)	19.4	7	40	v Essex at Bristol	1906
A. E. E. Vogler (E. Province)	12	2	26	v Griqualand West at Johannesburg	1906-07
C. Blythe (Kent)	16	7	30	v Northamptonshire at Northampton	1907
A. Drake (Yorkshire)	8.5	0	35	v Somerset at Weston-super-Mare	1914
W. Bestwick (Derbyshire)	19	2	40	v Glamorgan at Cardiff	1921
A. A. Mailey (Australians)	28.4	5	66	v Gloucestershire at Cheltenham	1921
C. W. L. Parker (Glos.)	40.3	13	79	v Somerset at Bristol	1921
T. Rushby (Surrey)	17.5	4	43	v Somerset at Taunton	1921
J. C. White (Somerset)	42.2	11	76	v Worcestershire at Worcester	1921
G. C. Collins (Kent)	19.3	4	65	v Nottinghamshire at Dover	1922
H. Howell (Warwickshire)	25.1	5	51	v Yorkshire at Birmingham	1923
A. S. Kennedy (Players)	22.4	10	37	v Gentlemen at The Oval	1927
G. O. Allen (Middlesex)	25.3	10	40	v Lancashire at Lord's	1929
A. P. Freeman (Kent)	42	9	131	v Lancashire at Maidstone	1929
G. Geary (Leicestershire)	16.2	8	18	v Glamorgan at Pontypridd	1929
C. V. Grimmett (Australians)	22.3	8	37	v Yorkshire at Sheffield	1930
A. P. Freeman (Kent)	30.4	8	53	v Essex at Southend	1930
H. Verity (Yorkshire)	18.4	6	36	v Warwickshire at Leeds	1931
A. P. Freeman (Kent)	36.1	9	79	v Lancashire at Manchester	1931
V. W. C. Jupp (Northants)	39	6	127	v Kent at Tunbridge Wells	1932
H. Verity (Yorkshire)	19.4	16	10	v Nottinghamshire at Leeds	1932
T. W. Wall (South Australia)	12.4	2	36	v New South Wales at Sydney	1932-33
T. B. Mitchell (Derbyshire)	19.1	4	64	v Leicestershire at Leicester	1935
J. Mercer (Glamorgan)	26	10	51	v Worcestershire at Worcester	1936
T. W. Goddard (Glos.)	28.4	4	113	v Worcestershire at Cheltenham	1937
T. F. Smailes (Yorkshire)	17.1	5	47	v Derbyshire at Sheffield	1939
E. A. Watts (Surrey)	24.1	8	67	v Warwickshire at Birmingham	1939
*W. E. Hollies (Warwickshire)	20.4	4	49	v Nottinghamshire at Birmingham	1946
J. M. Sims (East)	18.4	2	90	v West at Kingston	1948
T. E. Bailey (Essex)	39.4	9	90	v Lancashire at Clacton	1949
J. K. Graveney (Glos.)	18.4	2	66	v Derbyshire at Chesterfield	1949
R. Berry (Lancashire)	36.2	9	102	v Worcestershire at Blackpool	1953
S. P. Gupte (President's XI)	24.2	7	78	v Combined XI at Bombay	1954-55
J. C. Laker (Surrey)	46	18	88	v Australians at The Oval	1956
J. C. Laker (England)	51.2	23	53	v Australia at Manchester	1956
G. A. R. Lock (Surrey)	29.1	18	54	v Kent at Blackheath	1956
K. Smales (Nottinghamshire)	41.3	20	66	v Gloucestershire at Stroud	1956
P. Chatterjee (Bengal)	19	11	20	v Assam at Jorhat	1956-57
J. D. Bannister (Warwickshire)	23.3	11	41	v Comb. Services at Birmingham	1959
A. J. G. Pearson (Cambridge University)	30.3	8	78	v Leicestershire at Loughborough	1961
N. I. Thomson (Sussex)	34.2	19	49	v Warwickshire at Worthing	1964
P. J. Allan (Queensland)	15.6	3	61	v Victoria at Melbourne	1965-66
I. J. Brayshaw (W. Australia)	17.6	4	44	v Victoria at Perth	1967-68
Shahid Mahmood (Karachi Whites)	25	5	58	v Khairpur at Karachi	1969-70
E. E. Hemmings (International XI)	49.3	14	175	v West Indies XI at Kingston	1982-83
P. Sunderam (Rajasthan)	22	5	78	v Vidarbha at Jodhpur	1985-86

*J. Wisden and W. E. Hollies achieved the feat without the direct assistance of a fielder. Wisden's ten were all bowled; Hollies bowled seven and had three leg-before-wicket.

† On debut in first-class cricket.

Note: The following instances were achieved in 12-a-side matches:

	O	M	R		
E. M. Grace (MCC)	32.2	7	69	v Gents of Kent at Canterbury	1862
W. G. Grace (MCC)	46.1	15	92	v Kent at Canterbury	1873

OUTSTANDING ANALYSES

	O	M	R	W		
H. Verity (Yorkshire)	19.4	16	10	10	v Nottinghamshire at Leeds	1932
G. Elliott (Victoria)	19	17	2	9	v Tasmania at Launceston	1857-58
Ahad Khan (Railways)	6.3	4	7	9	v Dera Ismail Khan at Lahore	1964-65
J. C. Laker (England)	14	12	2	8	v The Rest at Bradford	1950
D. Shackleton (Hampshire)	11.1	7	4	8	v Somerset at Weston-super-Mare	1955
E. Peate (Yorkshire)	16	11	5	8	v Surrey at Holbeck	1883
F. R. Spofforth (Australians)	8.3	6	3	7	v England XI at Birmingham	1884
W. A. Henderson (N.E. Transvaal)	9.3	7	4	7	v Orange Free State at Bloemfontein	1937-38
Rajinder Goel (Haryana)	7	4	4	7	v Jammu and Kashmir at Chandigarh	1977-78
V. I. Smith (South Africans)	4.5	3	1	6	v Derbyshire at Derby	1947
S. Cosstick (Victoria)	21.1	20	1	6	v Tasmania at Melbourne	1868-69
Israr Ali (Bahawalpur)	11	10	1	6	v Dacca U. at Bahawalpur	1957-58
A. D. Pougher (MCC)	3	3	0	5	v Australians at Lord's	1896
G. R. Cox (Sussex)	6	6	0	5	v Somerset at Weston-super-Mare	1921
R. K. Tyldesley (Lancashire)	5	5	0	5	v Leicestershire at Manchester	1924
P. T. Mills (Gloucestershire)	6.4	6	0	5	v Somerset at Bristol	1928

MOST WICKETS IN A MATCH

19-90	J. C. Laker	England v Australia at Manchester	1956
17-48	C. Blythe	Kent v Northamptonshire at Northampton	1907
17-50	C. T. B. Turner	Australians v England XI at Hastings	1888
17-54	W. P. Howell	Australians v Western Province at Cape Town	1902-03
17-56	C. W. L. Parker	Gloucestershire v Essex at Gloucester	1925
17-67	A. P. Freeman	Kent v Sussex at Hove	1922
17-89	W. G. Grace	Gloucestershire v Nottinghamshire at Cheltenham	1877
17-89	F. C. L. Matthews	Nottinghamshire v Northants at Nottingham	1923
17-91	H. Dean	Lancashire v Yorkshire at Liverpool	1913
17-91	H. Verity	Yorkshire v Essex at Leyton	1933
17-92	A. P. Freeman	Kent v Warwickshire at Folkestone	1932
17-103	W. Mycroft	Derbyshire v Hampshire at Southampton	1876
17-106	G. R. Cox	Sussex v Warwickshire at Horsham	1926
17-106	T. W. Goddard	Gloucestershire v Kent at Bristol	1939
17-119	W. Mead	Essex v Hampshire at Southampton	1895
17-137	W. Brearley	Lancashire v Somerset at Manchester	1905
17-159	S. F. Barnes	England v South Africa at Johannesburg	1913-14
17-201	G. Giffen	South Australia v Victoria at Adelaide	1885-86
17-212	J. C. Clay	Glamorgan v Worcestershire at Swansea	1937

Notes: H. A. Arkwright took eighteen wickets for 96 runs in a 12-a-side match for Gentlemen of MCC v Gentlemen of Kent at Canterbury in 1861.

W. Mead took seventeen wickets for 205 runs for Essex v Australians at Leyton in 1893, the year before Essex were raised to first-class status.

F. P. Fenner took seventeen wickets for Cambridge Town Club v University of Cambridge at Cambridge in 1844.

SIXTEEN OR MORE WICKETS IN A DAY

17-48	C. Blythe	Kent v Northamptonshire at Northampton	1907
17-91	H. Verity	Yorkshire v Essex at Leyton	1933
17-106	T. W. Goddard	Gloucestershire v Kent at Bristol	1939
16-38	T. Emmett	Yorkshire v Cambridgeshire at Hunslet	1869
16-52	J. Southerton	South v North at Lord's	1875
16-69	T. G. Wass	Nottinghamshire v Lancashire at Liverpool	1906
16-38	A. E. E. Vogler	E. Province v Griqualand West at Johannesburg .	1906-07
16-103	T. G. Wass	Nottinghamshire v Essex at Nottingham	1908
16-83	J. C. White	Somerset v Worcestershire at Bath	1919

FOUR WICKETS WITH CONSECUTIVE BALLS

J. Wells	Kent v Sussex at Brighton	1862
G. Ulyett	Lord Harris's XI v New South Wales at Sydney	1878-79
G. Nash	Lancashire v Somerset at Manchester	1882
J. B. Hide	Sussex v MCC and Ground at Lord's	1890
F. J. Shacklock	Nottinghamshire v Somerset at Nottingham	1893
A. D. Downes	Otago v Auckland at Dunedin	1893-94
F. Martin	MCC and Ground v Derbyshire at Lord's	1895
A. W. Mold	Lancashire v Nottinghamshire at Nottingham	1895
W. Brearley†	Lancashire v Somerset at Manchester	1905
S. Haigh	MCC v Army XI at Pretoria	1905-06
A. E. Trott‡	Middlesex v Somerset at Lord's	1907
F. A. Tarrant	Middlesex v Gloucestershire at Bristol	1907
A. Drake	Yorkshire v Derbyshire at Chesterfield	1914
S. G. Smith	Northamptonshire v Warwickshire at Birmingham ...	1914
H. A. Peach	Surrey v Sussex at The Oval	1924
A. F. Borland	Natal v Griqualand West at Kimberley	1926-27
J. E. H. Hooker†	New South Wales v Victoria at Sydney	1928-29
R. K. Tyldesley†	Lancashire v Derbyshire at Derby	1929
R. J. Crisp	Western Province v Griqualand West at Johannesburg .	1931-32
R. J. Crisp	Western Province v Natal at Durban	1933-34
A. R. Gover	Surrey v Worcestershire at Worcester	1935
W. H. Copson	Derbyshire v Warwickshire at Derby	1937
W. A. Henderson	N.E. Transvaal v Orange Free State at Bloemfontein ...	1937-38
F. Ridgway	Kent v Derbyshire at Folkestone	1951
A. K. Walker§	Nottinghamshire v Leicestershire at Leicester	1956
S. N. Mohol	Board of Control President's XI v Minister for Small	
	Savings' XI at Poona	1965-66
P. I. Pocock	Surrey v Sussex at Eastbourne	1972

† *Not all in the same innings.*

‡ *Trott achieved another hat-trick in the same innings of this, his benefit match.*

§ *Walker dismissed Firth with the last ball of the first innings and Lester, Tompkin and Smithson
with the first three balls of the second innings, a feat without parallel.*

Notes: In their match with England at The Oval in 1863, Surrey lost four wickets in the course of
a four-ball over from G. Bennett.

Sussex lost five wickets in the course of the final (six-ball) over of their match with Surrey at
Eastbourne in 1972. P. I. Pocock, who had taken three wickets in his previous over, captured
four more, taking in all seven wickets with eleven balls, a feat unique in first-class matches. (The
eighth wicket fell to a run-out.)

P. G. H. Fender (Surrey) took six Middlesex wickets with eleven balls (including five with
seven) at Lord's in 1927.

HAT-TRICKS

Double Hat-Trick

Besides Trott's performance, which is given in the preceding section, the following instances are recorded of players having performed the hat-trick twice in the same match, Rao doing so in the same innings.

A. Shaw	Nottinghamshire v Gloucestershire at Nottingham	1884
T. J. Matthews	Australia v South Africa at Manchester	1912
C. W. L. Parker	Gloucestershire v Middlesex at Bristol	1924
R. O. Jenkins	Worcestershire v Surrey at Worcester	1949
J. S. Rao	Services v Northern Punjab at Amritsar	1963-64
Amin Lakhani	Combined XI v Indians at Multan	1978-79

Five Wickets with Six Consecutive Balls

W. H. Copson	Derbyshire v Warwickshire at Derby	1937
W. A. Henderson	NE Transvaal v Orange Free State at Bloemfontein	1937-38
P. I. Pocock	Surrey v Sussex at Eastbourne	1972

Most Hat-Tricks

Seven times: D. V. P. Wright.
Six times: T. W. Goddard, C. W. L. Parker.
Five times: S. Haigh, V. W. C. Jupp, A. E. G. Rhodes, F. A. Tarrant.
Four times: R. G. Barlow, J. T. Hearne, J. C. Laker, G. A. R. Lock, G. G. Macaulay, T. J. Matthews, M. J. Procter, T. Richardson, F. R. Spofforth, F. S. Trueman.
Three times: W. M. Bradley, H. J. Butler, S. T. Clarke, W. H. Copson, R. J. Crisp, J. W. H. T. Douglas, J. A. Flavell, A. P. Freeman, G. Giffen, K. Higgs, A. Hill, W. A. Humphries, R. D. Jackman, R. O. Jenkins, A. S. Kennedy, W. H. Lockwood, E. A. McDonald, T. L. Pritchard, J. S. Rao, A. Shaw, J. B. Statham, M. W. Tate, H. Trumble, D. Wilson, G. A. Wilson.

Unusual Hat-Tricks

All "Stumped":	by W. H. Brain off C. L. Townsend, Gloucestershire v Somerset at Cheltenham	1893
All "Caught":	by G. J. Thompson off S. G. Smith, Northamptonshire v Warwickshire at Birmingham	1914
	by Cyril White off R. Beesly, Border v Griqualand West at Queenstown	1946-47
	by G. O. Dawkes (wicket-keeper) off H. L. Jackson, Derbyshire v Worcestershire at Kidderminster	1958
All "LBW":	H. Fisher, Yorkshire v Somerset at Sheffield	1932
	J. A. Flavell, Worcestershire v Lancashire at Manchester	1963
	M. J. Procter, Gloucestershire v Essex at Westcliff	1972
	B. J. Ikin, Griqualand West v OFS at Kimberley	1973-74
	M. J. Procter, Gloucestershire v Yorkshire at Cheltenham	1979
	Aamer Wasim, Zone C v Lahore at Lahore	1985-86

Most recent instances

In 1986-87

B. Arun	Tamil Nadu v Goa at Panjim.
B. Burman	Bengal v Tripura at Calcutta.
Farrukh Zaman	MCB v PIA at Lahore.
M. G. Holmes	Natal B v Eastern Province B at Uitenhage.
Kazim Mehdi	HBFC v PIA at Karachi.
J. N. Maguire	Australian XI v Eastern Province at Port Elizabeth.
Pervez Shah	Lahore v Rawalpindi at Rawalpindi.

In 1987: See Features of 1987.

200 WICKETS IN A SEASON

	Season	O	M	R	W	Avge
A. P. Freeman	1928	1,976.1	423	5,489	304	18.05
A. P. Freeman	1933	2,039	651	4,549	298	15.26
T. Richardson	1895‡	1,690.1	463	4,170	290	14.37
C. T. B. Turner**	1888†	2,427.2	1,127	3,307	283	11.68
A. P. Freeman	1931	1,618	360	4,307	276	15.60
A. P. Freeman	1930	1,914.3	472	4,632	275	16.84
T. Richardson	1897‡	1,603.4	495	3,945	273	14.45
A. P. Freeman	1929	1,670.5	381	4,879	267	18.27
W. Rhodes	1900	1,553	455	3,606	261	13.81
J. T. Hearne	1896	2,003.1	818	3,670	257	14.28
A. P. Freeman	1932	1,565.5	404	4,149	253	16.39
W. Rhodes	1901	1,565	505	3,797	251	15.12
T. W. Goddard	1937	1,478.1	359	4,158	248	16.76
W. C. Smith	1910	1,423.3	420	3,225	247	13.05
T. Richardson	1896‡	1,656.2	526	4,015	246	16.32
A. E. Trott	1899‡	1,772.4	587	4,086	239	17.09
T. W. Goddard	1947	1,451.2	344	4,119	238	17.30
M. W. Tate	1925	1,694.3	472	3,415	228	14.97
J. T. Hearne	1898‡	1,802.2	781	3,120	222	14.05
C. W. L. Parker	1925	1,512.3	478	3,311	222	14.91
G. A. Lohmann	1890‡	1,759.1	737	2,998	220	13.62
M. W. Tate	1923	1,608.5	331	3,061	219	13.97
C. F. Root	1925	1,493.2	416	3,770	219	17.21
C. W. L. Parker	1931	1,320.4	386	3,125	219	14.26
H. Verity	1936	1,289.3	463	2,847	216	13.18
G. A. R. Lock	1955	1,408.4	497	3,109	216	14.39
C. Blythe	1909	1,273.5	343	3,128	215	14.54
E. Peate	1882†	1,853.1	868	2,466	214	11.52
A. W. Mold	1895‡	1,629	598	3,400	213	15.96
W. Rhodes	1902	1,306.3	405	2,801	213	13.15
C. W. L. Parker	1926	1,739.5	556	3,920	213	18.40
J. T. Hearne	1893‡	1,741.4	667	3,492	212	16.47
A. P. Freeman	1935	1,503.2	320	4,562	212	21.51
G. A. R. Lock	1957	1,194.1	449	2,550	212	12.02
A. E. Trott	1900	1,547.1	363	4,923	211	23.33
G. G. Macaulay	1925	1,338.2	307	3,268	211	15.48
H. Verity	1935	1,279.2	453	3,032	211	14.36
J. Southerton	1870†	1,876.5	709	3,074	210	14.63
G. A. Lohmann	1888†	1,649.1	783	2,280	209	10.90
C. H. Parkin	1923	1,356.2	356	3,543	209	16.94
G. H. Hirst	1906	1,306.1	271	3,434	208	16.50
F. R. Spofforth	1884†	1,577	653	2,654	207	12.82
A. W. Mold	1894‡	1,288.3	456	2,548	207	12.30
C. W. L. Parker	1922	1,294.5	445	2,712	206	13.16
A. S. Kennedy	1922	1,346.4	366	3,444	205	16.80
M. W. Tate	1924	1,469.5	465	2,818	205	13.74
E. A. McDonald	1925	1,249.4	282	3,828	205	18.67
A. P. Freeman	1934	1,744.4	440	4,753	205	23.18
C. W. L. Parker	1924	1,303.5	411	2,913	204	14.27
G. A. Lohmann	1889‡	1,614.1	646	2,714	202	13.43
H. Verity	1937	1,386.2	487	3,168	202	15.68
A. Shaw	1878†	2,630	1,586	2,201	201	10.89
E. G. Dennett	1907	1,216.2	305	3,227	201	16.05
A. R. Gover	1937	1,219.4	191	3,816	201	18.98
C. H. Parkin	1924	1,162.5	357	2,735	200	13.67
T. W. Goddard	1935	1,553	384	4,073	200	20.36
A. R. Gover	1936	1,159.2	185	3,547	200	17.73
T. W. Goddard	1939§	819	139	2,973	200	14.86
R. Appleyard	1951	1,313.2	391	2,829	200	14.14

† *Indicates 4-ball overs;* ‡ *5-ball overs. All others were 6-ball overs except* § *8-ball overs.*
** *Exclusive of matches not reckoned as first-class.*

Notes: In four consecutive seasons (1928-31), A. P. Freeman took 1,122 wickets, and in eight consecutive seasons (1928-35), 2,090 wickets. In each of these eight seasons he took over 200 wickets.

T. Richardson took 1,005 wickets in four consecutive seasons (1894-97).

In 1896, J. T. Hearne took his 100th wicket as early as June 12. In 1931, C. W. L. Parker did the same and A. P. Freeman obtained his 100th wicket a day later.

The most wickets in a season since the reduction of Championship matches in 1969 is 134 by M. D. Marshall (822 overs) in 1982.

100 WICKETS IN A SEASON MOST TIMES

(Includes Overseas Tours and Seasons)

23 times: W. Rhodes 200 wkts (3).

20 times: D. Shackleton (In successive seasons – 1949 to 1968 inclusive).

17 times: A. P. Freeman 300 wkts (1), 200 wkts (7).

16 times: T. W. Goddard 200 wkts (4), C. W. L. Parker 200 wkts (5), R. T. D. Perks, F. J. Titmus.

15 times: J. T. Hearne 200 wkts (3), G. H. Hirst 200 wkts (1), A. S. Kennedy 200 wkts (1).

14 times: C. Blythe 200 wkts (1), W. E. Hollies, G. A. R. Lock 200 wkts (2), M. W. Tate 200 wkts (3), J. C White.

13 times: J. B. Statham.

12 times: J. Briggs, E. G. Dennett 200 wkts (1), C. Gladwin, D. J. Shepherd, N. I. Thomson, F. S. Trueman.

11 times: A. V. Bedser, G. Geary, S. Haigh, J. C. Laker, M. S. Nichols, A. E. Relf.

10 times: W. Attewell, W. G. Grace, R. Illingworth, H. L. Jackson, V. W. C. Jupp, G. G. Macaulay 200 wkts (1), W. Mead, T. B. Mitchell, T. Richardson 200 wkts (3), J. Southerton 200 wkts (1), R. K. Tyldesley, D. L. Underwood, J. H. Wardle, T. G. Wass, D. V. P. Wright.

9 times: W. E. Astill, T. E. Bailey, W. E. Bowes, C. Cook, R. Howorth, J. Mercer, A. W. Mold 200 wkts (2), J. Newman, C. F. Root 200 wkts (1), A. Shaw 200 wkts (1), H. Verity 200 wkts (3).

8 times: T. W. Cartwright, H. Dean, J. A. Flavell, A. R. Gover 200 wkts (2), H. Larwood, G. A. Lohmann 200 wkts (3), R. Peel, J. M. Sims, F. A. Tarrant, R. Tattersall, G. J. Thompson, G. E. Tribe, A. W. Wellard, F. E. Woolley, J. A. Young.

100 WICKETS IN A SEASON OUTSIDE ENGLAND

W		Season	Country	R	Avge
116	M. W. Tate	1926-27	India/Ceylon	1,599	13.78
107	Ijaz Faqih	1985-86	Pakistan	1,719	16.06
106	C. T. B. Turner ...	1887-88	Australia	1,441	13.59
106	R. Benaud	1957-58	South Africa	2,056	19.39
104	S. F. Barnes	1913-14	South Africa	1,117	10.74
103	Abdul Qadir	1982-83	Pakistan	2,367	22.98

1,500 WICKETS IN A CAREER

Dates in italics denote the first half of an overseas season; i.e. *1970* denotes the 1970-71 season.

	Career	W	R	Avge
W. Rhodes	1898-1930	4,187	69,993	16.71
A. P. Freeman	1914-36	3,776	69,577	18.42
C. W. L. Parker	1903-35	3,278	63,817	19.46
J. T. Hearne	1888-1923	3,061	54,352	17.75
T. W. Goddard	1922-52	2,979	59,116	19.84
†W. G. Grace	1865-1908	2,876	51,545	17.92
A. S. Kennedy	1907-36	2,874	61,034	21.23
D. Shackleton	1948-69	2,857	53,303	18.65

	Career	W	R	Avge
G. A. R. Lock	1946-70	2,844	54,709	19.23
F. J. Titmus	1949-82	2,830	63,313	22.37
M. W. Tate	1912-37	2,784	50,571	18.16
G. H. Hirst	1891-1929	2,739	51,282	18.72
C. Blythe	1899-1914	2,506	42,136	16.81
D. L. Underwood	1963-87	2,465	49,993	20.28
W. E. Astill	1906-39	2,431	57,783	23.76
J. C. White	1909-37	2,356	43,759	18.57
W. E. Hollies	1932-57	2,323	48,656	20.94
F. S. Trueman	1949-69	2,304	42,154	18.29
J. B. Statham	1950-68	2,260	36,995	16.36
R. T. D. Perks	1930-55	2,233	53,770	24.07
J. Briggs	1879-1900	2,221	35,430	15.95
D. J. Shepherd	1950-72	2,218	47,302	21.32
E. G. Dennett	1903-26	2,147	42,571	19.82
T. Richardson	1892-1905	2,104	38,794	18.43
T. E. Bailey	1945-67	2,082	48,170	23.13
R. Illingworth	1951-83	2,072	42,023	20.28
F. E. Woolley	1906-38	2,068	41,066	19.85
G. Geary	1912-38	2,063	41,339	20.03
D. V. P. Wright	1932-57	2,056	49,307	23.98
N. Gifford	1960-87	2,037	47,755	23.44
J. Newman	1906-30	2,032	51,111	25.15
‡A. Shaw	1864-97	2,027	24,579	12.12
S. Haigh	1895-1913	2,012	32,091	15.94
H. Verity	1930-39	1,956	29,146	14.90
W. Attewell	1881-1900	1,950	29,896	15.33
J. C. Laker	1946-64	1,944	35,791	18.41
A. V. Bedser	1939-60	1,924	39,279	20.41
W. Mead	1892-1913	1,916	36,388	18.99
A. E. Relf	1900-21	1,897	39,724	20.94
P. G. H. Fender	1910-36	1,894	47,458	25.05
J. W. H. T. Douglas ...	1901-30	1,893	44,159	23.32
J. H. Wardle	1946-67	1,846	35,027	18.97
G. R. Cox	1895-1928	1,843	42,136	22.86
G. A. Lohmann	1884-97	1,841	25,295	13.73
J. W. Hearne	1909-36	1,839	44,926	24.42
G. G. Macaulay	1920-35	1,837	32,440	17.65
M. S. Nichols	1924-39	1,833	39,666	21.63
J. B. Mortimore	1950-75	1,807	41,904	23.18
C. Cook	1946-64	1,782	36,578	20.52
R. Peel	1882-99	1,753	28,442	16.22
H. L. Jackson	1947-63	1,733	30,101	17.36
T. P. B. Smith	1929-52	1,697	45,059	26.55
J. Southerton	1854-79	1,681	24,290	14.44
A. E. Trott	*1892*-1911	1,674	35,317	21.09
A. W. Mold	1889-1901	1,673	26,010	15.54
T. G. Wass	1896-1920	1,666	34,092	20.46
V. W. C. Jupp	1909-38	1,658	38,166	23.01
C. Gladwin	1939-58	1,653	30,265	18.30
J. K. Lever	1967-87	1,653	39,896	24.13
W. E. Bowes	1928-47	1,639	27,470	16.76
A. W. Wellard	1927-50	1,614	39,302	24.35
P. I. Pocock	1964-86	1,607	42,648	26.53
N. I. Thomson	1952-72	1,597	32,867	20.58
J. Mercer	1919-47	1,591	37,210	23.38
G. J. Thompson	1897-1922	1,591	30,058	18.89
J. M. Sims	1929-53	1,581	39,401	24.92
T. Emmett	1866-88	1,571	21,314	13.56
Intikhab Alam	*1957*-82	1,571	43,474	27.67
B. S. Bedi	*1961*-80	1,560	33,843	21.69

	Career	W	R	Avge
W. Voce	1927-52	1,558	35,961	23.08
A. R. Gover	1928-48	1,555	36,753	23.63
T. W. Cartwright	1952-77	1,536	29,357	19.11
K. Higgs	1958-86	1,536	36,267	23.61
James Langridge	1924-53	1,530	34,524	22.56
J. A. Flavell	1949-67	1,529	32,847	21.48
C. F. Root	1910-33	1,512	31,933	21.11
R. K. Tyldesley	1919-35	1,509	25,980	17.21

† *In recent years some statisticians have removed from W. G. Grace's record a number of matches which they consider not to have been first-class. The above figures are those which became universally accepted upon appearance in W. G. Grace's obituary in the* Wisden *of 1916. Some works of reference gave his career record as being 2,809–50,999–18.15 (these figures also appeared in the 1981 edition of* Wisden*), and subsequently it has been amended to 2,808–50,982–18.15.*

‡ *The figures for A. Shaw exclude one wicket for which no analysis is available.*

ALL-ROUND RECORDS

HUNDRED AND TEN WICKETS IN ONE INNINGS

V. E. Walker, England v Surrey at The Oval; ten for 74, four for 17, 20* and 108.	1859
W. G. Grace, MCC v Oxford University at Oxford; two for 60, ten for 49, and 104.	1886

Note: E. M. Grace, for MCC v Gentlemen of Kent in a 12-a-side match at Canterbury in 1862, scored 192* and took five for 77 and ten for 69.

HUNDRED IN EACH INNINGS AND FIVE WICKETS TWICE

G. H. Hirst, Yorkshire v Somerset at Bath; six for 70, five for 45, 111 and 117*. 1906

HUNDRED AND HAT-TRICK

G. Giffen, Australians v Lancashire at Manchester; 13, 113, and six for 55 including hat-trick	1884
W. E. Roller, Surrey v Sussex at The Oval; 204, four for 28 including hat-trick, and two for 16. (Unique instance of 200 and hat-trick.)	1885
W. B. Burns, Worcestershire v Gloucestershire at Worcester; 102*, three for 56, including hat-trick, and two for 21	1913
V. W. C. Jupp, Sussex v Essex at Colchester; 102, six for 61, including hat-trick, and six for 78	1921
R. E. S. Wyatt, MCC v Ceylon at Colombo; 124 and five for 39 including hat-trick.	1926-27
L. N. Constantine, West Indians v Northamptonshire at Northampton; seven for 45, including hat-trick, 107 (five 6s), and six for 67	1928
D. E. Davies, Glamorgan v Leicestershire at Leicester; 139, four for 27, and three for 31 including hat-trick	1937
V. M. Merchant, Dr C. R. Pereira's XI v Sir Homi Mehta's XI at Bombay; 1, 142, three for 31 including hat-trick, and no wicket for 17	1946-47
M. J. Procter, Gloucestershire v Essex at Westcliff-on-Sea; 51, 102, three for 43, and five for 30 including hat-trick (all lbw)	1972
M. J. Procter, Gloucestershire v Leicestershire at Bristol; 122, no wkt for 32, and seven for 26 including hat-trick	1979

Note: W. G. Grace, for MCC v Kent in a 12-a-side match at Canterbury in 1874, scored 123 and took five for 82 and six for 47 including a hat-trick.

SEASON DOUBLES

2,000 RUNS AND 200 WICKETS

1906   G. H. Hirst   2,385 runs and 208 wickets

3,000 RUNS AND 100 WICKETS

1937   J. H. Parks   3,003 runs and 101 wickets

2,000 RUNS AND 100 WICKETS

	Season	R	W		Season	R	W
W. G. Grace	1873	2,139	106	F. E. Woolley	1914	2,272	125
W. G. Grace	1876	2,622	129	J. W. Hearne	1920	2,148	142
C. L. Townsend	1899	2,440	101	V. W. C. Jupp	1921	2,169	121
G. L. Jessop	1900	2,210	104	F. E. Woolley	1921	2,101	167
G. H. Hirst	1904	2,501	132	F. E. Woolley	1922	2,022	163
G. H. Hirst	1905	2,266	110	F. E. Woolley	1923	2,091	101
W. Rhodes	1909	2,094	141	L. F. Townsend	1933	2,268	100
W. Rhodes	1911	2,261	117	D. E. Davies	1937	2,012	103
F. A. Tarrant	1911	2,030	111	James Langridge	1937	2,082	101
J. W. Hearne	1913	2,036	124	T. E Bailey	1959	2,011	100
J. W. Hearne	1914	2,116	123				

1,000 RUNS AND 200 WICKETS

	Season	R	W		Season	R	W
A. E. Trott	1899	1,175	239	M. W. Tate	1923	1,168	219
A. E. Trott	1900	1,337	211	M. W. Tate	1924	1,419	205
A. S. Kennedy	1922	1,129	205	M. W. Tate	1925	1,290	228

1,000 RUNS AND 100 WICKETS

Sixteen times: W. Rhodes.   **Fourteen times:** G. H. Hirst.

Ten times: V. W. C. Jupp.   **Nine times:** W. E. Astill.

Eight times: T. E. Bailey, W. G. Grace, M. S. Nichols, A. E. Relf, F. A. Tarrant, M. W. Tate†, F. J. Titmus, F. E. Woolley.

Seven times: G. E. Tribe.

Six times: P. G. H. Fender, R. Illingworth, James Langridge.

Five times: J. W. H. T. Douglas, J. W. Hearne, A. S. Kennedy, J. Newman.

Four times: E. G. Arnold, J. Gunn, R. Kilner, B. R. Knight.

Three times: W. W. Armstrong (Australians), L. C. Braund, G. Giffen (Australians), N. E. Haig, R. Howorth, C. B. Llewellyn, J. B. Mortimore, Ray Smith, S. G. Smith, L. F. Townsend, A. W. Wellard.

† *M. W. Tate also scored 1,193 runs and took 116 wickets for MCC in first-class matches on the 1926-27 MCC tour of India and Ceylon.*

Note : R. J. Hadlee in 1984 was the first player to perform the feat since the reduction of County Championship matches. A complete list of those performing the feat before then will be found on p. 202 of the 1982 *Wisden.*

WICKET-KEEPERS' DOUBLE

	Season	R	D
L. E. G. Ames	1928	1,919	122
L. E. G. Ames	1929	1,795	128
L. E. G. Ames	1932	2,482	104
J. T. Murray	1957	1,025	104

20,000 RUNS AND 2,000 WICKETS IN A CAREER

	Career	R	Avge	W	Avge	'Doubles'
W. E. Astill	1906-39	22,731	22.55	2,431	23.76	9
T. E. Bailey	1945-67	28,642	33.42	2,082	23.13	8
W. G. Grace	1865-1908	54,896	39.55	2,876	17.92	8
G. H. Hirst	1891-1929	36,323	34.13	2,739	18.72	14
R. Illingworth	1951-83	24,134	28.06	2,072	20.28	6
W. Rhodes	1898-1930	39,802	30.83	4,187	16.71	16
M. W. Tate	1912-37	21,717	25.01	2,784	18.16	8
F. J. Titmus	1949-82	21,588	23.11	2,830	22.37	8
F. E. Woolley	1906-38	58,969	40.75	2,068	19.85	8

WICKET-KEEPING RECORDS

MOST DISMISSALS IN AN INNINGS

8 (all ct)	A. T. W. Grout	Queensland v Western Australia at Brisbane	1959-60
8 (all ct)	D. E. East	Essex v Somerset at Taunton	†1985
7 (4ct, 3st)	E. J. Smith	Warwickshire v Derbyshire at Birmingham	1926
7 (6ct, 1st)	W. Farrimond	Lancashire v Kent at Manchester	1930
7 (all ct)	W. F. F. Price	Middlesex v Yorkshire at Lord's	1937
7 (3ct, 4st)	D. Tallon	Queensland v Victoria at Brisbane	1938-39
7 (all ct)	R. A. Saggers	New South Wales v Combined XI at Brisbane ...	1940-41
7 (1ct, 6st)	H. Yarnold	Worcestershire v Scotland at Dundee	1951
7 (4ct, 3st)	J. Brown	Scotland v Ireland at Dublin	1957
7 (6ct, 1st)	N. Kirsten	Border v Rhodesia at East London	1959-60
7 (all ct)	M. S. Smith	Natal v Border at East London	1959-60
7 (all ct)	K. V. Andrew	Northamptonshire v Lancashire at Manchester ..	1962
7 (all ct)	A. Long	Surrey v Sussex at Hove	1964
7 (all ct)	R. M. Schofield	Central Districts v Wellington at Wellington	1964-65
7 (all ct)	R. W. Taylor	Derbyshire v Glamorgan at Derby	1966
7 (6ct, 1st)	H. B. Taber	New South Wales v South Australia at Adelaide ..	1968-69
7 (6ct, 1st)	E. W. Jones	Glamorgan v Cambridge University at Cambridge.	1970
7 (6ct, 1st)	S. Benjamin	Central Zone v North Zone at Bombay	1973-74
7 (all ct)	R. W. Taylor	Derbyshire v Yorkshire at Chesterfield	1975
7 (6ct, 1st)	Shahid Israr	Karachi Whites v Quetta at Karachi	1976-77
7 (4ct, 3st)	Wasim Bari	PIA v Sind at Lahore	1977-78
7 (all ct)	J. A. Maclean	Queensland v Victoria at Melbourne	1977-78
7 (5ct, 2st)	Taslim Arif	National Bank v Punjab at Lahore	1978-79
7 (all ct)	Wasim Bari	Pakistan v New Zealand at Auckland	1978-79
7 (all ct)	R. W. Taylor	England v India at Bombay	1979-80
7 (all ct)	D. L. Bairstow	Yorkshire v Derbyshire at Scarborough	1982
7 (6ct, 1st)	R. B. Phillips	Queensland v New Zealanders at Bundaberg	1982-83
7 (3ct, 4st)	Masood Iqbal	Habib Bank v Lahore at Lahore	1982-83
7 (3ct, 4st)	Arif-ud-Din	United Bank v PACO at Sahiwal	1983-84
7 (6ct, 1st)	R. J. East	OFS v Western Province B at Cape Town	1984-85
7 (all ct)	B. A. Young	Northern Districts v Canterbury at Christchurch ..	1986-87

† *The first eight wickets to fall.*

WICKET-KEEPERS' HAT-TRICKS

W. H. Brain, Gloucestershire v Somerset at Cheltenham, 1893 – three stumpings off successive balls from C. L. Townsend.

G. O. Dawkes, Derbyshire v Worcestershire at Kidderminster, 1958 – three catches off successive balls from H. L. Jackson.

R. C. Russell, Gloucestershire v Surrey at The Oval, 1986 – three catches off successive balls from C. A. Walsh and D. V. Lawrence (2).

MOST DISMISSALS IN A MATCH

12 (8ct, 4st)	E. Pooley	Surrey v Sussex at The Oval	1868
12 (9ct, 3st)	D. Tallon	Queensland v New South Wales at Sydney	1938-39
12 (9ct, 3st)	H. B. Taber	New South Wales v South Australia at Adelaide .	1968-69
11 (all ct)	A. Long	Surrey v Sussex at Hove	1964
11 (all ct)	R. W. Marsh	Western Australia v Victoria at Perth	1975-76
11 (all ct)	D. L. Bairstow	Yorkshire v Derbyshire at Scarborough	1982
10 (5ct, 5st)	H. Phillips	Sussex v Surrey at The Oval	1872
10 (2ct, 8st)	E. Pooley	Surrey v Kent at The Oval	1878
10 (9ct, 1st)	T. W. Oates	Nottinghamshire v Middlesex at Nottingham ...	1906
10 (1ct, 9st)	F. H. Huish	Kent v Surrey at The Oval	1911
10 (9ct, 1st)	J. C. Hubble	Kent v Gloucestershire at Cheltenham	1923
10 (8ct, 2st)	H. Elliott	Derbyshire v Lancashire at Manchester	1935
10 (7ct, 3st)	P. Corrall	Leicestershire v Sussex at Hove	1936
10 (9ct, 1st)	R. A. Saggers	New South Wales v Combined XI at Brisbane ...	1940-41
10 (all ct)	A. E. Wilson	Gloucestershire v Hampshire at Portsmouth	1953
10 (7ct, 3st)	B. N. Jarman	South Australia v New South Wales at Adelaide .	1961-62
10 (all ct)	L. A. Johnson	Northamptonshire v Sussex at Worthing	1963
10 (all ct)	R. W. Taylor	Derbyshire v Hampshire at Chesterfield	1963
10 (8ct, 2st)	L. A. Johnson	Northamptonshire v Warwickshire at Birmingham	1965
10 (9ct, 1st)	R. C. Jordon	Victoria v South Australia at Melbourne	1970-71
10 (all ct)	R. W. Marsh†	Western Australia v South Australia at Perth ...	1976-77
10 (6ct, 4st)	Taslim Arif	National Bank v Punjab at Lahore	1978-79
10 (9ct, 1st)	Arif-ud-Din	United Bank v Karachi B at Karachi	1978-79
10 (all ct)	R. W. Taylor	England v India at Bombay	1979-80
10 (all ct)	R. J. Parks	Hampshire v Derbyshire at Portsmouth	1981
10 (9ct, 1st)	A. Ghosh	Bihar v Assam at Bhagalpur	1981-82
10 (8ct, 2st)	Z. Parkar	Bombay v Maharashtra at Bombay	1981-82
10 (all ct)	R. V. Jennings	Transvaal v Arosa Sri Lankans at Johannesburg .	1982-83
10 (9ct, 1st)	Kamal Najamuddin	Karachi v Lahore at Multan	1982-83
10 (all ct)	D. A. Murray	West Indies XI v South Africa at Port Elizabeth .	1983-84
10 (7ct, 3st)	Azhar Abbas	Bahawalpur v Lahore City Greens at Bahawalpur	1983-84
10 (7ct, 3st)	B. N. French	Nottinghamshire v Oxford University at Oxford .	1984
10 (8ct, 2st)	R. J. Ryall	Western Province v Transvaal at Cape Town ...	1984-85
10 (all ct)	S. J. Rixon	Australian XI v South Africa at Johannesburg .	1985-86
10 (8ct, 2st)	Anil Dalpat	Karachi v United Bank at Lahore	1985-86
10 (all ct)	R. V. Jennings	Transvaal v Northern Transvaal at Verwoerdburg	1986-87
10 (all ct)	S. J. Rixon	Australian XI v South Africa at Johannesburg .	1986-87
10 (all ct)	R. V. Jennings	Transvaal v Orange Free State at Johannesburg .	1986-87
10 (9ct, 1st)	C. J. Richards	Surrey v Sussex at Guildford	1987

† *Marsh also scored a hundred (104), a unique "double".*

MOST DISMISSALS IN A SEASON

128 (79ct, 49st)	L. E. G. Ames	Kent	1929
122 (70ct, 52st)	L. E. G. Ames	Kent	1928
110 (63ct, 47st)	H. Yarnold	Worcestershire	1949
107 (77ct, 30st)	G. Duckworth	Lancashire	1928
107 (96ct, 11st)	J. G. Binks	Yorkshire	1960
104 (40ct, 64st)	L. E. G. Ames	Kent	1932
104 (82ct, 22st)	J. T. Murray	Middlesex	1957
102 (69ct, 33st)	F. H. Huish	Kent	1913
102 (95ct, 7st)	J. T. Murray	Middlesex	1960
101 (62ct, 39st)	F. H. Huish	Kent	1911
101 (85ct, 16st)	R. Booth	Worcestershire	1960
100 (91ct, 9st)	R. Booth	Worcestershire	1964

MOST DISMISSALS IN A CAREER

Dates in italics denote the first half of an overseas season; i.e. *1914* denotes the 1914-15 season.

	Career	M	Ct	St	Total
R. W. Taylor	1960-86	638	1,473	175	1,648
J. T. Murray	1952-75	635	1,270	257	1,527
H. Strudwick	1902-27	675	1,242	255	1,497
A. P. E. Knott	1964-85	511	1,211	133	1,344
F. H. Huish	1895-1914	497	933	377	1,310
B. Taylor	1949-73	572	1,083	211	1,294
D. Hunter	1889-1909	548	906	347	1,253
H. R. Butt	1890-1912	550	953	275	1,228
J. H. Board	1891-*1914*	525	852	355	1,207
H. Elliott	1920-47	532	904	302	1,206
J. M. Parks	1949-76	739	1,088	93	1,181
R. Booth	1951-70	468	948	178	1,126
L. E. G. Ames	1926-51	593	703	418	1,121
G. Duckworth	1923-47	504	753	342	1,095
H. W. Stephenson	1948-64	462	748	334	1,082
J. G. Binks	1955-75	502	895	176	1,071
T. G. Evans	1939-69	465	816	250	1,066
A. Long	1960-80	452	922	124	1,046
G. O. Dawkes	1937-61	482	895	148	1,043
R. W. Tolchard	1965-83	483	912	125	1,037
D. L. Bairstow	1970-87	428	888	136	1,024
W. L. Cornford	1921-47	496	675	342	1,017

FIELDING RECORDS

(Excluding wicket-keepers)

Most Catches in an Innings

7	M. J. Stewart	Surrey v Northamptonshire at Northampton	1957
7	A. S. Brown	Gloucestershire v Nottinghamshire at Nottingham	1966

Most Catches in a Match

10	W. R. Hammond	Gloucestershire v Surrey at Cheltenham	†1928
8	W. B. Burns	Worcestershire v Yorkshire at Bradford	1907
8	A. H. Bakewell	Northamptonshire v Essex at Leyton	1928
8	W. R. Hammond	Gloucestershire v Worcestershire at Cheltenham	1932
8	K. J. Grieves	Lancashire v Sussex at Manchester	1951
8	C. A. Milton	Gloucestershire v Sussex at Hove	1952
8	G. A. R. Lock	Surrey v Warwickshire at The Oval	1957
8	J. M. Prodger	Kent v Gloucestershire at Cheltenham	1961
8	P. M. Walker	Glamorgan v Derbyshire at Swansea	1970
8	Javed Miandad	Habib Bank v Universities at Lahore	1977-78
8	Masood Anwar	Rawalpindi v Lahore Division at Rawalpindi	1983-84

† *Hammond also scored a hundred in each innings.*

Most Catches in a Season

78	W. R. Hammond	1928	65	D. W. Richardson	1961
77	M. J. Stewart	1957	64	K. F. Barrington	1957
73	P. M. Walker	1961	64	G. A. R. Lock	1957
71	P. J. Sharpe	1962	63	J. Tunnicliffe	1896
70	J. Tunnicliffe	1901	63	J. Tunnicliffe	1904
69	J. G. Langridge	1955	63	K. J. Grieves	1950
69	P. M. Walker	1960	63	C. A. Milton	1956
66	J. Tunnicliffe	1895	61	J. V. Wilson	1955
65	W. R. Hammond	1925	61	M. J. Stewart	1958
65	P. M. Walker	1959			

Note: The most catches by a fielder since the reduction of County Championship matches in 1969 is 49 by C. J. Tavaré in 1979.

Most Catches in a Career

Dates in italics denote the first half of an overseas season; i.e. *1970* denotes the 1970-71 season.

1,018	F. E. Woolley (1906-38)	784	J. G. Langridge (1928-55)
887	W. G. Grace (1865-1908)	764	W. Rhodes (1898-1930)
831	G. A. R. Lock (1946-*70*)	758	C. A. Milton (1948-74)
819	W. R. Hammond (1920-51)	754	E. H. Hendren (1907-38)
813	D. B. Close (1949-86)		

TEAM RECORDS

HIGHEST TOTALS

1,107	Victoria v New South Wales at Melbourne	1926-27
1,059	Victoria v Tasmania at Melbourne	1922-23
951-7 dec.	Sind v Baluchistan at Karachi	1973-74
918	New South Wales v South Australia at Sydney	1900-01
912-8 dec.	Holkar v Mysore at Indore	1945-46
910-6 dec.	Railways v Dera Ismail Khan at Lahore	1964-65
903-7 dec.	England v Australia at The Oval	1938
887	Yorkshire v Warwickshire at Birmingham	1896
849	England v West Indies at Kingston	1929-30
843	Australians v Oxford and Cambridge Universities Past and Present at Portsmouth	1893

HIGHEST FOR EACH FIRST-CLASS COUNTY

Derbyshire	645	v Hampshire at Derby	1898
Essex	692	v Somerset at Taunton	1895
Glamorgan	587-8	v Derbyshire at Cardiff	1951
Gloucestershire	653-6	v Glamorgan at Bristol	1928
Hampshire	672-7	v Somerset at Taunton	1899
Kent	803-4	v Essex at Brentwood	1934
Lancashire	801	v Somerset at Taunton	1895
Leicestershire	701-4	v Worcestershire at Worcester	1906
Middlesex	642-3	v Hampshire at Southampton	1923
Northamptonshire	557-6	v Sussex at Hove	1914
Nottinghamshire	739-7	v Leicestershire at Nottingham	1903
Somerset	675-9	v Hampshire at Bath	1924
Surrey	811	v Somerset at The Oval	1899
Sussex	705-8	v Surrey at Hastings	1902
Warwickshire	657-6	v Hampshire at Birmingham	1899
Worcestershire	633	v Warwickshire at Worcester	1906
Yorkshire	887	v Warwickshire at Birmingham	1896

LOWEST TOTALS

12	Oxford University v MCC and Ground at Oxford	†1877
12	Northamptonshire v Gloucestershire at Gloucester	1907
13	Auckland v Canterbury at Auckland	1877-78
13	Nottinghamshire v Yorkshire at Nottingham	1901
14	Surrey v Essex at Chelmsford	1983
15	MCC v Surrey at Lord's	1839
15	Victoria v MCC at Melbourne	†1903-04
15	Northamptonshire v Yorkshire at Northampton	†1908
15	Hampshire v Warwickshire at Birmingham	1922
	(Following on, Hampshire scored 521 and won by 155 runs.)	
16	MCC and Ground v Surrey at Lord's	1872
16	Derbyshire v Nottinghamshire at Nottingham	1879
16	Surrey v Nottinghamshire at The Oval	1880
16	Warwickshire v Kent at Tonbridge	1913
16	Trinidad v Barbados at Bridgetown	1942-43
16	Border v Natal at East London (first innings)	1959-60
17	Gentlemen of Kent v Gentlemen of England at Lord's	1850
17	Gloucestershire v Australians at Cheltenham	1896
18	The Bs v England at Lord's	1831
18	Kent v Sussex at Gravesend	†1867
18	Tasmania v Victoria at Melbourne	1868-69
18	Australians v MCC and Ground at Lord's	†1896
18	Border v Natal at East London (second innings)	1959-60
19	Sussex v Surrey at Godalming	1830
19	Sussex v Nottinghamshire at Hove	†1873
19	MCC and Ground v Australians at Lord's	1878
19	Wellington v Nelson at Nelson	1885-86

† *Signifies that one man was absent.*

Note: At Lord's in 1810, The Bs, with one man absent, were dismissed by England for 6.

LOWEST TOTAL IN A MATCH

34	(16 and 18) Border v Natal at East London	1959-60
42	(27 and 15) Northamptonshire v Yorkshire at Northampton	1908

Note: Northamptonshire batted one man short in each innings.

LOWEST FOR EACH FIRST-CLASS COUNTY

Derbyshire	16	v Nottinghamshire at Nottingham	1879
Essex	30	v Yorkshire at Leyton	1901
Glamorgan	22	v Lancashire at Liverpool	1924
Gloucestershire	17	v Australians at Cheltenham	1896
Hampshire	15	v Warwickshire at Birmingham	1922
Kent	18	v Sussex at Gravesend	1867
Lancashire	25	v Derbyshire at Manchester	1871
Leicestershire	25	v Kent at Leicester	1912
Middlesex	20	v MCC at Lord's	1864
Northamptonshire	12	v Gloucestershire at Gloucester	1907
Nottinghamshire	13	v Yorkshire at Nottingham	1901
Somerset	25	v Gloucestershire at Bristol	1947
Surrey	14	v Essex at Chelmsford	1983
Sussex	19	v Nottinghamshire at Hove	1873
Warwickshire	16	v Kent at Tonbridge	1913
Worcestershire	24	v Yorkshire at Huddersfield	1903
Yorkshire	23	v Hampshire at Middlesbrough	1965

HIGHEST MATCH AGGREGATES

2,376 for 38 wickets	Maharashtra v Bombay at Poona	1948-49
2,078 for 40 wickets	Bombay v Holkar at Bombay	1944-45
1,981 for 35 wickets	England v South Africa at Durban	1938-39
1,929 for 39 wickets	New South Wales v South Australia at Sydney	1925-26
1,911 for 34 wickets	New South Wales v Victoria at Sydney	1908-09
1,905 for 40 wickets	Otago v Wellington at Dunedin	1923-24

In England

1,723 for 31 wickets	England v Australia at Leeds	1948
1,601 for 29 wickets	England v Australia at Lord's	1930
1,507 for 28 wickets	England v West Indies at The Oval	1976
1,502 for 28 wickets	MCC v New Zealanders at Lord's	1927
1,499 for 31 wickets	T. N. Pearce's XI v Australians at Scarborough	1961
1,496 for 24 wickets	England v Australia at Nottingham	1938
1,494 for 37 wickets	England v Australia at The Oval	1934

LOWEST MATCH AGGREGATE

105 for 31 wickets	MCC v Australians at Lord's	1878

Note: The lowest aggregate since 1900 is 158 for 22 wickets, Surrey v Worcestershire at The Oval, 1954.

HIGHEST FOURTH INNINGS TOTALS

(Unless otherwise stated, the side making the runs won the match.)

654-5 England v South Africa at Durban 1938-39
 (After being set 696 to win. The match was left drawn on the tenth day.)
604 Maharashtra v Bombay at Poona 1948-49
 (After being set 959 to win.)
576-8 Trinidad v Barbados at Port-of-Spain 1945-46
 (After being set 672 to win. Match drawn on fifth day.)
572 New South Wales v South Australia at Sydney 1907-08
 (After being set 593 to win.)
529-9 Combined XI v South Africans at Perth 1963-64
 (After being set 579 to win. Match drawn on fourth day.)
518 Victoria v Queensland at Brisbane 1926-27
 (After being set 753 to win.)
507-7 Cambridge University v MCC and Ground at Lord's 1896
502-6 Middlesex v Nottinghamshire at Nottingham 1925
 (Game won by an unfinished stand of 271; a county record.)
502-8 Players v Gentlemen at Lord's 1900
500-7 South African Universities v Western Province at Stellenbosch 1978-79

LARGEST VICTORIES

Largest Innings Victories

Inns and 851 runs:	Railways (910-6 dec.) v Dera Ismail Khan (Lahore)	1964-65
Inns and 666 runs:	Victoria (1,059) v Tasmania (Melbourne)	1922-23
Inns and 656 runs:	Victoria (1,107) v New South Wales (Melbourne)	1926-27
Inns and 605 runs:	New South Wales (918) v South Australia (Sydney)	1900-01
Inns and 579 runs:	England (903-7 dec.) v Australia (The Oval)	1938
Inns and 575 runs:	Sind (951-7 dec.) v Baluchistan (Karachi)	1973-74
Inns and 527 runs:	New South Wales (713) v South Australia (Adelaide)	1908-09
Inns and 517 runs:	Australians (675) v Nottinghamshire (Nottingham)	1921

Largest Victories by Runs Margin

685 runs:	New South Wales (235 and 761-8 dec.) v Queensland (Sydney)	1929-30
675 runs:	England (521 and 342-8 dec.) v Australia (Brisbane)	1928-29
638 runs:	New South Wales (304 and 770) v South Australia (Adelaide)	1920-21
625 runs:	Sargodha (376 and 416) v Lahore Municipal Corporation (Faisalabad)	1978-79
609 runs:	Muslim Commercial Bank (575 and 282-0 dec.) v WAPDA (Lahore).	1977-78
571 runs:	Victoria (304 and 649) v South Australia (Adelaide)	1926-27
562 runs:	Australia (701 and 327) v England (The Oval)	1934

Victory Without Losing a Wicket

Lancashire (166-0 dec. and 66-0) beat Leicestershire by ten wickets (Manchester)	1956
Karachi A (277-0 dec.) beat Sind A by an innings and 77 runs (Karachi)	1957-58
Railways (236-0 dec. and 16-0) beat Jammu and Kashmir by ten wickets (Srinagar)	1960-61
Karnataka (451-0 dec.) beat Kerala by an innings and 186 runs (Chikmagalur) .	1977-78

TIED MATCHES IN FIRST-CLASS CRICKET

There have been 35 tied matches since the First World War.

Somerset v Sussex at Taunton	1919
(The last Sussex batsman not allowed to bat under Law 45 [subsequently Law 17 and now Law 31])	
Orange Free State v Eastern Province at Bloemfontein	1925-26
(Eastern Province had two wickets to fall.)	
Essex v Somerset at Chelmsford	1926
(Although Essex had one man to go in, MCC ruled that the game should rank as a tie. The ninth wicket fell half a minute before time.)	
Gloucestershire v Australians at Bristol	1930
Victoria v MCC at Melbourne	1932-33
(Victoria's third wicket fell to the last ball of the match when one run was needed to win.)	
Worcestershire v Somerset at Kidderminster	1939
Southern Punjab v Baroda at Patiala	1945-46
Essex v Northamptonshire at Ilford	1947
Hampshire v Lancashire at Bournemouth	1947
D. G. Bradman's XI v A. L. Hassett's XI at Melbourne	1948-49
Hampshire v Kent at Southampton	1950
Sussex v Warwickshire at Hove	1952
Essex v Lancashire at Brentwood	1952
Northamptonshire v Middlesex at Peterborough	1953
Yorkshire v Leicestershire at Huddersfield	1954
Sussex v Hampshire at Eastbourne	1955
Victoria v New South Wales at Melbourne	1956-57
T. N. Pearce's XI v New Zealanders at Scarborough	1958
Essex v Gloucestershire at Leyton	1959
Australia v West Indies (First Test) at Brisbane	1960-61
Bahawalpur v Lahore B at Bahawalpur	1961-62
Hampshire v Middlesex at Portsmouth	1967
England XI v England Under-25 XI at Scarborough	1968
Yorkshire v Middlesex at Bradford	1973
Sussex v Essex at Hove	1974
South Australia v Queensland at Adelaide	1976-77
Central Districts v England XI at New Plymouth	1977-78
Victoria v New Zealanders at Melbourne	1982-83
Muslim Commercial Bank v Railways at Sialkot	1983-84
Sussex v Kent at Hastings	1984
Northamptonshire v Kent at Northampton	1984
Eastern Province B v Boland at Albany SC, Port Elizabeth	1985-86
Natal B v Eastern Province B at Pietermaritzburg	1985-86
India v Australia (First Test) at Madras	1986-87
Gloucestershire v Derbyshire at Bristol	1987

Note: Since 1948 a tie has been recognised only when the scores are level with all the wickets down in the fourth innings. This ruling applies to all grades of cricket, and in the case of a one-day match to the second innings, provided that the match has not been brought to a further conclusion.

MATCHES BEGUN AND FINISHED ON FIRST DAY

Since 1900. A fuller list may be found in the Wisden of 1981 and preceding editions.

Yorkshire v Worcestershire at Bradford, May 7	1900
MCC and Ground v London County at Lord's, May 20	1903
Transvaal v Orange Free State at Johannesburg, December 30	1906
Middlesex v Gentlemen of Philadelphia at Lord's, July 20	1908
Gloucestershire v Middlesex at Bristol, August 26	1909
Eastern Province v Orange Free State at Port Elizabeth, December 26	1912
Kent v Sussex at Tonbridge, June 21	1919
Lancashire v Somerset at Manchester, May 21	1925
Madras v Mysore at Madras, November 4	1934
Ireland v New Zealanders at Dublin, September 11	1937
Derbyshire v Somerset at Chesterfield, June 11	1947
Lancashire v Sussex at Manchester, July 12	1950
Surrey v Warwickshire at The Oval, May 16	1953
Somerset v Lancashire at Bath, June 6 (H. T. F. Buse's benefit)	1953
Kent v Worcestershire at Tunbridge Wells, June 15	1960

TEST MATCH RECORDS

BATTING RECORDS

HIGHEST INDIVIDUAL INNINGS

365*	G. S. Sobers, West Indies v Pakistan at Kingston	1957-58
364	L. Hutton, England v Australia at The Oval	1938
337	Hanif Mohammad, Pakistan v West Indies at Bridgetown	1957-58
336*	W. R. Hammond, England v New Zealand at Auckland	1932-33
334	D. G. Bradman, Australia v England at Leeds	1930
325	A. Sandham, England v West Indies at Kingston	1929-30
311	R. B. Simpson, Australia v England at Manchester	1964
310*	J. H. Edrich, England v New Zealand at Leeds	1965
307	R. M. Cowper, Australia v England at Melbourne	1965-66
304	D. G. Bradman, Australia v England at Leeds	1934
302	L. G. Rowe, West Indies v England at Bridgetown	1973-74
299*	D. G. Bradman, Australia v South Africa at Adelaide	1931-32
291	I. V. A. Richards, West Indies v England at The Oval	1976
287	R. E. Foster, England v Australia at Sydney	1903-04
285*	P. B. H. May, England v West Indies at Birmingham	1957
280*	Javed Miandad, Pakistan v India at Hyderabad	1982-83
278	D. C. S. Compton, England v Pakistan at Nottingham	1954
274	R. G. Pollock, South Africa v Australia at Durban	1969-70
274	Zaheer Abbas, Pakistan v England at Birmingham	1971
270*	G. A. Headley, West Indies v England at Kingston	1934-35
270	D. G. Bradman, Australia v England at Melbourne	1936-37
268	G. N. Yallop, Australia v Pakistan at Melbourne	1983-84
266	W. H. Ponsford, Australia v England at The Oval	1934
262*	D. L. Amiss, England v West Indies at Kingston	1973-74
261	F. M. M. Worrell, West Indies v England at Nottingham	1950
260	C. C. Hunte, West Indies v Pakistan at Kingston	1957-58
260	Javed Miandad, Pakistan v England at The Oval	1987

259	G. M. Turner, New Zealand v West Indies at Georgetown	1971-72
258	T. W. Graveney, England v West Indies at Nottingham	1957
258	S. M. Nurse, West Indies v New Zealand at Christchurch	1968-69
256	R. B. Kanhai, West Indies v India at Calcutta	1958-59
256	K. F. Barrington, England v Australia at Manchester	1964
255*	D. J. McGlew, South Africa v New Zealand at Wellington	1952-53
254	D. G. Bradman, Australia v England at Lord's	1930
251	W. R. Hammond, England v Australia at Sydney	1928-29
250	K. D. Walters, Australia v New Zealand at Christchurch	1976-77
250	S. F. A. F. Bacchus, West Indies v India at Kanpur	1978-79

The highest individual innings for other countries are:

236*	S. M. Gavaskar, India v West Indies at Madras	1983-84
201*	D. S. B. P. Kuruppu, Sri Lanka v New Zealand at Colombo (CCC)	1986-87

HUNDRED ON TEST DEBUT

C. Bannerman (165*)	Australia v England at Melbourne	1876-77
W. G. Grace (152)	England v Australia at The Oval	1880
H. Graham (107)	Australia v England at Lord's	1893
†K. S. Ranjitsinhji (154*)	England v Australia at Manchester	1896
†P. F. Warner (132*)	England v South Africa at Johannesburg	1898-99
†R. A. Duff (104)	Australia v England at Melbourne	1901-02
R. E. Foster (287)	England v Australia at Sydney	1903-04
G. Gunn (119)	England v Australia at Sydney	1907-08
†R. J. Hartigan (116)	Australia v England at Adelaide	1907-08
†H. L. Collins (104)	Australia v England at Sydney	1920-21
W. H. Ponsford (110)	Australia v England at Sydney	1924-25
A. A. Jackson (164)	Australia v England at Adelaide	1928-29
†G. A. Headley (176)	West Indies v England at Bridgetown	1929-30
J. E. Mills (117)	New Zealand v England at Wellington	1929-30
Nawab of Pataudi (102)	England v Australia at Sydney	1932-33
B. H. Valentine (136)	England v India at Bombay	1933-34
†L. Amarnath (118)	India v England at Bombay	1933-34
†P. A. Gibb (106)	England v South Africa at Johannesburg	1938-39
S. C. Griffith (140)	England v West Indies at Port-of-Spain	1947-48
A. G. Ganteaume (112)	West Indies v England at Port-of-Spain	1947-48
†J. W. Burke (101*)	Australia v England at Adelaide	1950-51
P. B. H. May (138)	England v South Africa at Leeds	1951
R. H. Shodhan (110)	India v Pakistan at Calcutta	1952-53
B. H. Pairaudeau (115)	West Indies v India at Port-of-Spain	1952-53
†O. G. Smith (104)	West Indies v Australia at Kingston	1954-55
A. G. Kripal Singh (100*)	India v New Zealand at Hyderabad	1955-56
C. C. Hunte (142)	West Indies v Pakistan at Bridgetown	1957-58
C. A. Milton (104*)	England v New Zealand at Leeds	1958
†A. A. Baig (112)	India v England at Manchester	1959
Hanumant Singh (105)	India v England at Delhi	1963-64
Khalid Ibadulla (166)	Pakistan v Australia at Karachi	1964-65
B. R. Taylor (105)	New Zealand v India at Calcutta	1964-65
K. D. Walters (155)	Australia v England at Brisbane	1965-66
J. H. Hampshire (107)	England v West Indies at Lord's	1969
†G. R. Viswanath (137)	India v Australia at Kanpur	1969-70
G. S. Chappell (108)	Australia v England at Perth	1970-71
‡L. G. Rowe (214, 100*)	West Indies v New Zealand at Kingston	1971-72
A. I. Kallicharran (100*)	West Indies v New Zealand at Georgetown	1971-72
R. E. Redmond (107)	New Zealand v Pakistan at Auckland	1972-73
†F. C. Hayes (106*)	England v West Indies at The Oval	1973
†C. G. Greenidge (107)	West Indies v India at Bangalore	1974-75
†L. Baichan (105*)	West Indies v Pakistan at Lahore	1974-75
G. J. Cosier (109)	Australia v West Indies at Melbourne	1975-76

S. Amarnath (124)	India v New Zealand at Auckland	1975-76
Javed Miandad (163)	Pakistan v New Zealand at Lahore	1976-77
†A. B. Williams (100)	West Indies v Australia at Georgetown	1977-78
†D. M. Wellham (103)	Australia v England at The Oval	1981
†Salim Malik (100*)......	Pakistan v Sri Lanka at Karachi	1981-82
K. C. Wessels (162)	Australia v England at Brisbane	1982-83
W. B. Phillips (159)	Australia v Pakistan at Perth	1983-84
§M. Azharuddin (110)	India v England at Calcutta	1984-85
D. S. B. P. Kuruppu (201*)	Sri Lanka v New Zealand at Colombo (CCC) .	1986-87

† *In his second innings of the match.*
‡ *L. G. Rowe is the only batsman to score a hundred in each innings on début.*
§ *M. Azharuddin is the only batsman to score hundreds in each of his first three Tests.*

300 RUNS IN FIRST TEST

314	L. G. Rowe (214, 100*)	West Indies v New Zealand at Kingston	1971-72
306	R. E. Foster (287, 19)	England v Australia at Sydney	1903-04

TWO SEPARATE HUNDREDS IN A TEST

Three times: S. M. Gavaskar v West Indies (1970-71), v Pakistan (1978-79), v West Indies (1978-79).

Twice in one series: C. L. Walcott v Australia (1954-55).

Twice: H. Sutcliffe v Australia (1924-25), v South Africa (1929); G. A. Headley v England (1929-30 and 1939); G. S. Chappell v New Zealand (1973-74), v West Indies (1975-76); ‡A. R. Border v Pakistan (1979-80), v New Zealand (1985-86).

Once: W. Bardsley v England (1909); A. C. Russell v South Africa (1922-23); W. R. Hammond v Australia (1928-29); E. Paynter v South Africa (1938-39); D. C. S. Compton v Australia (1946-47); A. R. Morris v England (1946-47); A. Melville v England (1947); B. Mitchell v England (1947); D. G. Bradman v India (1947-48); V. S. Hazare v Australia (1947-48); E. D. Weekes v India (1948-49); J. Moroney v South Africa (1949-50); G. S. Sobers v Pakistan (1957-58); R. B. Kanhai v Australia (1960-61); Hanif Mohammad v England (1961-62); R. B. Simpson v Pakistan (1964-65); K. D. Walters v West Indies (1968-69); †L. G. Rowe v New Zealand (1971-72); I. M. Chappell v New Zealand (1973-74); G. M. Turner v Australia (1973-74); C. G. Greenidge v England (1976); G. P. Howarth v England (1977-78); L. R. D. Mendis v India (1982-83); Javed Miandad v New Zealand (1984-85).

† *L. G. Rowe's two hundreds were on his Test début.*
‡ *A. R. Border scored 150* and 153 against Pakistan to become the first batsman to score 150 in each innings of a Test match.*

HUNDRED AND DOUBLE-HUNDRED IN SAME TEST

K. D. Walters (Australia)	242 and 103 v West Indies at Sydney	1968-69
S. M. Gavaskar (India)	124 and 220 v West Indies at Port-of-Spain	1970-71
†L. G. Rowe (West Indies)	214 and 100* v New Zealand at Kingston	1971-72
G. S. Chappell (Australia)	247* and 133 v New Zealand at Wellington	1973-74

† *On Test début.*

MOST RUNS IN A SERIES

	T	I	NO	R	HI	100s	Avge		
D. G. Bradman ...	5	7	0	974	334	4	139.14	A v E	1930
W. R. Hammond .	5	9	1	905	251	4	113.12	E v A	1928-29
R. N. Harvey	5	9	0	834	205	4	92.66	A v SA	1952-53
I. V. A. Richards .	4	7	0	829	291	3	118.42	WI v E	1976
C. L. Walcott	5	10	0	827	155	5	82.70	WI v A	1954-55
G. S. Sobers	5	8	2	824	365*	3	137.33	WI v P	1957-58
D. G. Bradman ...	5	9	0	810	270	3	90.00	A v E	1936-37
D. G. Bradman ...	5	5	1	806	299*	4	201.50	A v SA	1931-32
E. D. Weekes	5	7	0	779	194	4	111.28	WI v I	1948-49
†S. M. Gavaskar ..	4	8	3	774	220	4	154.80	I v WI	1970-71
Mudassar Nazar ..	6	8	2	761	231	4	126.83	P v I	1982-83
D. G. Bradman ...	5	8	0	758	304	2	94.75	A v E	1934
D. C. S. Compton	5	8	0	753	208	4	94.12	E v SA	1947

† Gavaskar's aggregate was achieved in his first Test series.

1,000 TEST RUNS IN A CALENDAR YEAR

	T	I	NO	R	HI	100s	Avge	Year
I. V. A. Richards (*West Indies*) .	11	19	0	1,710	291	7	90.00	1976
S. M. Gavaskar (*India*)	18	27	1	1,555	221	5	59.80	1979
G. R. Viswanath (*India*)	17	26	3	1,388	179	5	60.34	1979
R. B. Simpson (*Australia*)	14	26	3	1,381	311	3	60.04	1964
D. L. Amiss (*England*)	13	22	2	1,379	262*	5	68.95	1974
S. M. Gavaskar (*India*)	18	32	4	1,310	236*	5	46.78	1983
G. S. Sobers (*West Indies*)	7	12	3	1,193	365*	5	132.55	1958
D. B. Vengsarkar (*India*)	18	27	4	1,174	146*	5	51.04	1979
K. J. Hughes (*Australia*)	15	28	4	1,163	130*	2	48.45	1979
D. C. S. Compton (*England*) ...	9	15	1	1,159	208	6	82.78	1947
C. G. Greenidge (*West Indies*) ..	14	22	4	1,149	223	4	63.83	1984
I. T. Botham (*England*)	14	22	0	1,095	208	3	49.77	1982
K. W. R. Fletcher (*England*) ...	13	22	4	1,090	178	2	60.55	1973
M. Amarnath (*India*)	14	24	1	1,077	120	4	46.82	1983
A. R. Border (*Australia*)	14	27	3	1,073	162	3	44.70	1979
C. Hill (*Australia*)	12	21	2	1,061	142	2	55.78	1902
D. I. Gower (*England*)	14	25	2	1,061	114	1	46.13	1982
W. M. Lawry (*Australia*)	14	27	2	1,056	157	2	42.24	1964
S. M. Gavaskar (*India*)	9	15	2	1,044	205	4	80.30	1978
K. F. Barrington (*England*)	12	22	2	1,039	132*	3	51.95	1963
E. R. Dexter (*England*)	11	15	1	1,038	205	2	74.14	1962
K. F. Barrington (*England*)	10	17	4	1,032	172	4	79.38	1961
Mohsin Khan (*Pakistan*)	10	17	3	1,029	200	4	73.50	1982
D. G. Bradman (*Australia*)	8	13	4	1,025	201	5	113.88	1948
S. M. Gavaskar (*India*)	11	20	1	1,024	156	4	53.89	1976
A. R. Border (*Australia*)	11	19	3	1,000	140	5	62.50	1986

Note: The earliest date for completing 1,000 runs is May 3 by M. Amarnath in 1983.

MOST RUNS IN A CAREER

(Qualification: 2,000 runs)

ENGLAND

	T	I	NO	R	HI	100s	Avge
G. Boycott	108	193	23	8,114	246*	22	47.72
M. C. Cowdrey	114	188	15	7,624	182	22	44.06
W. R. Hammond	85	140	16	7,249	336*	22	58.45
L. Hutton	79	138	15	6,971	364	19	56.67
K. F. Barrington	82	131	15	6,806	256	20	58.67
D. I. Gower	96	164	12	6,789	215	14	44.66
D. C. S. Compton	78	131	15	5,807	278	17	50.06
J. B. Hobbs	61	102	7	5,410	211	15	56.94
J. H. Edrich	77	127	9	5,138	310*	12	43.54
I. T. Botham	94	150	5	5,057	208	14	34.87
T. W. Graveney	79	123	13	4,882	258	11	44.38
H. Sutcliffe	54	84	9	4,555	194	16	60.73
P. B. H. May	66	106	9	4,537	285*	13	46.77
E. R. Dexter	62	102	8	4,502	205	9	47.89
A. P. E. Knott	95	149	15	4,389	135	5	32.75
G. A. Gooch	59	105	4	3,746	196	7	37.08
D. L. Amiss	50	88	10	3,612	262*	11	46.30
A. W. Greig	58	93	4	3,599	148	8	40.43
M. W. Gatting	58	100	13	3,563	207	9	40.95
E. H. Hendren	51	83	9	3,525	205*	7	47.63
F. E. Woolley	64	98	7	3,283	154	5	36.07
K. W. R. Fletcher	59	96	14	3,272	216	7	39.90
M. Leyland	41	65	5	2,764	187	9	46.06
A. J. Lamb	51	88	7	2,644	137*	7	32.64
C. Washbrook	37	66	6	2,569	195	6	42.81
B. L. D'Oliveira	44	70	8	2,484	158	5	40.06
D. W. Randall	47	79	5	2,470	174	7	33.37
W. J. Edrich	39	63	2	2,440	219	6	40.00
T. G. Evans	91	133	14	2,439	104	2	20.49
L. E. G. Ames	47	72	12	2,434	149	8	40.56
W. Rhodes	58	98	21	2,325	179	2	30.19
T. E. Bailey	61	91	14	2,290	134*	1	29.74
M. J. K. Smith	50	78	6	2,278	121	3	31.63
P. E. Richardson	34	56	1	2,061	126	5	37.47

AUSTRALIA

	T	I	NO	R	HI	100s	Avge
G. S. Chappell	87	151	19	7,110	247*	24	53.86
D. G. Bradman	52	80	10	6,996	334	29	99.94
A. R. Border	89	157	26	6,917	196	21	52.80
R. N. Harvey	79	137	10	6,149	205	21	48.41
K. D. Walters	74	125	14	5,357	250	15	48.26
I. M. Chappell	75	136	10	5,345	196	14	42.42
W. M. Lawry	67	123	12	5,234	210	13	47.15
R. B. Simpson	62	111	7	4,869	311	10	46.81
I. R. Redpath	66	120	11	4,737	171	8	43.45
K. J. Hughes	70	124	6	4,415	213	9	37.41
R. W. Marsh	96	150	13	3,633	132	3	26.51
A. R. Morris	46	79	3	3,533	206	12	46.48
C. Hill	49	89	2	3,412	191	7	39.21
V. T. Trumper	48	89	8	3,163	214*	8	39.04

	T	I	NO	R	HI	100s	Avge
G. M. Wood	53	101	5	3,109	172	8	32.38
C. C. McDonald	47	83	4	3,107	170	5	39.32
A. L. Hassett	43	69	3	3,073	198*	10	46.56
K. R. Miller	55	87	7	2,958	147	7	36.97
W. W. Armstrong	50	84	10	2,863	159*	6	38.68
K. R. Stackpole	43	80	5	2,807	207	7	37.42
N. C. O'Neill	42	69	8	2,779	181	6	45.55
G. N. Yallop	39	70	3	2,756	268	8	41.13
S. J. McCabe	39	62	5	2,748	232	6	48.21
W. Bardsley	41	66	5	2,469	193*	6	40.47
W. M. Woodfull	35	54	4	2,300	161	7	46.00
P. J. Burge	42	68	8	2,290	181	4	38.16
S. E. Gregory	58	100	7	2,282	201	4	24.53
R. Benaud	63	97	7	2,201	122	3	24.45
C. G. Macartney	35	55	4	2,131	170	7	41.78
W. H. Ponsford	29	48	4	2,122	266	7	48.22
R. M. Cowper	27	46	2	2,061	307	5	46.84

SOUTH AFRICA

	T	I	NO	R	HI	100s	Avge
B. Mitchell	42	80	9	3,471	189*	8	48.88
A. D. Nourse	34	62	7	2,960	231	9	53.81
H. W. Taylor	42	76	4	2,936	176	7	40.77
E. J. Barlow	30	57	2	2,516	201	6	45.74
T. L. Goddard	41	78	5	2,516	112	1	34.46
D. J. McGlew	34	64	6	2,440	255*	7	42.06
J. H. B. Waite	50	86	7	2,405	134	4	30.44
R. G. Pollock	23	41	4	2,256	274	7	60.97
A. W. Nourse	45	83	8	2,234	111	1	29.78
R. A. McLean	40	73	3	2,120	142	5	30.28

WEST INDIES

	T	I	NO	R	HI	100s	Avge
G. S. Sobers	93	160	21	8,032	365*	26	57.78
C. H. Lloyd	110	175	14	7,515	242*	19	46.67
I. V. A. Richards	88	131	8	6,472	291	20	52.61
R. B. Kanhai	79	137	6	6,227	256	15	47.53
C. G. Greenidge	77	128	14	5,509	223	13	48.32
E. D. Weekes	48	81	5	4,455	207	15	58.61
A. I. Kallicharran	66	109	10	4,399	187	12	44.43
R. C. Fredericks	59	109	7	4,334	169	8	42.49
D. L. Haynes	65	108	12	4,012	184	6	41.79
F. M. M. Worrell	51	87	9	3,860	261	9	49.48
C. L. Walcott	44	74	7	3,798	220	15	56.68
C. C. Hunte	44	78	6	3,245	260	8	45.06
H. A. Gomes	60	91	11	3,171	143	9	39.63
B. F. Butcher	44	78	6	3,104	209*	7	43.11
S. M. Nurse	29	54	1	2,523	258	6	47.60
G. A. Headley	22	40	4	2,190	270*	10	60.83
J. B. Stollmeyer	32	56	5	2,159	160	4	42.33
L. G. Rowe	30	49	2	2,047	302	7	43.55
P. J. L. Dujon	43	57	4	2,020	139	4	38.11

NEW ZEALAND

	T	I	NO	R	HI	100s	Avge
B. E. Congdon	61	114	7	3,448	176	7	32.22
J. R. Reid	58	108	5	3,428	142	6	33.28
G. M. Turner	41	73	6	2,991	259	7	44.64
J. G. Wright	52	92	4	2,874	141	6	32.65
B. Sutcliffe	42	76	8	2,727	230*	5	40.10
M. G. Burgess	50	92	6	2,684	119*	5	31.20
J. V. Coney	52	85	14	2,668	174*	3	37.57
R. J. Hadlee	70	111	16	2,622	151*	2	27.60
G. P. Howarth	47	83	5	2,531	147	6	32.44
G. T. Dowling	39	77	3	2,306	239	3	31.16
M. D. Crowe	36	59	6	2,162	188	7	40.79

INDIA

	T	I	NO	R	HI	100s	Avge
S. M. Gavaskar	125	214	16	10,122	236*	34	51.12
G. R. Viswanath	91	155	10	6,080	222	14	41.93
D. B. Vengsarkar	95	153	20	5,951	166	15	44.74
M. Amarnath	66	108	10	4,322	138	11	44.10
Kapil Dev	88	126	12	3,668	163	5	32.17
P. R. Umrigar	59	94	8	3,631	223	12	42.22
V. L. Manjrekar	55	92	10	3,208	189*	7	39.12
C. G. Borde	55	97	11	3,061	177*	5	35.59
Nawab of Pataudi jun.	46	83	3	2,793	203*	6	34.91
S. M. H. Kirmani	88	124	22	2,759	102	2	27.04
F. M. Engineer	46	87	3	2,611	121	2	31.08
R. J. Shastri	54	79	11	2,463	142	7	36.22
Pankaj Roy	43	79	4	2,442	173	5	32.56
V. S. Hazare	30	52	6	2,192	164*	7	47.65
A. L. Wadekar	37	71	3	2,113	143	1	31.07
V. Mankad	44	72	5	2,109	231	5	31.47
C. P. S. Chauhan	40	68	2	2,084	97	0	31.57
M. L. Jaisimha	39	71	4	2,056	129	3	30.68
D. N. Sardesai	30	55	4	2,001	212	5	39.23

PAKISTAN

	T	I	NO	R	HI	100s	Avge
Javed Miandad	86	133	18	6,251	280*	15	54.35
Zaheer Abbas	78	124	11	5,062	274	12	44.79
Majid Khan	63	106	5	3,931	167	8	38.92
Hanif Mohammad	55	97	8	3,915	337	12	43.98
Mudassar Nazar	65	99	8	3,745	231	9	41.15
Mushtaq Mohammad .	57	100	7	3,643	201	10	39.17
Asif Iqbal	58	99	7	3,575	175	11	38.85
Saeed Ahmed	41	78	4	2,991	172	5	40.41
Wasim Raja	57	92	14	2,821	125	4	36.16
Imran Khan	70	101	17	2,770	135*	4	32.97
Mohsin Khan	48	79	6	2,709	200	7	37.10
Sadiq Mohammad	41	74	2	2,579	166	5	35.81
Imtiaz Ahmed	41	72	1	2,079	209	3	29.28

SRI LANKA: The highest aggregate is 1,354, average 36.59, by A. Ranatunga.

HIGHEST AVERAGES

(Qualification: 20 innings)

Avge		T	I	NO	R	HI	100s
99.94	D. G. Bradman (A)	52	80	10	6,996	334	29
60.97	R. G. Pollock (SA)	23	41	4	2,256	274	7
60.83	G. A. Headley (WI)	22	40	4	2,190	270*	10
60.73	H. Sutcliffe (E)	54	84	9	4,555	194	16
59.23	E. Paynter (E)	20	31	5	1,540	243	4
58.67	K. F. Barrington (E)	82	131	15	6,806	256	20
58.61	E. D. Weekes (WI)	48	81	5	4,455	207	15
58.45	W. R. Hammond (E)	85	140	16	7,249	336*	22
57.78	G. S. Sobers (WI)	93	160	21	8,032	365*	26
56.94	J. B. Hobbs (E)	61	102	7	5,410	211	15
56.68	C. L. Walcott (WI)	44	74	7	3,798	220	15
56.67	L. Hutton (E)	79	138	15	6,971	364	19
55.00	E. Tyldesley (E)	14	20	2	990	122	3
54.35	Javed Miandad (P)	86	133	18	6,251	280*	15
54.20	C. A. Davis (WI)	15	29	5	1,301	183	4
53.86	G. S. Chappell (A)	87	151	19	7,110	247*	24
53.81	A. D. Nourse (SA)	34	62	7	2,960	231	9
52.80	A. R. Border (A)	89	157	26	6,917	196	21
52.61	I. V. A. Richards (WI)	88	131	8	6,472	291	20
52.17	M. Azharuddin (I)	21	31	3	1,461	199	6
51.62	J. Ryder (A)	20	32	5	1,394	201*	3
51.12	S. M. Gavaskar (I)	125	214	16	10,122	236*	34
50.06	D. C. S. Compton (E)	78	131	15	5,807	278	17

MOST HUNDREDS

Total		E	A	SA	WI	NZ	I	P	SL
34	S. M. Gavaskar (India)	4	8	—	13	2	—	5	2
29	D. G. Bradman (Australia)	19	—	4	2	0	4	—	—
26	G. S. Sobers (West Indies)	10	4	0	—	1	8	3	—
24	G. S. Chappell (Australia)	9	—	0	5	3	1	6	0
22	W. R. Hammond (England)	—	9	6	1	4	2	—	—
22	M. C. Cowdrey (England)	—	5	3	6	2	3	3	—
22	G. Boycott (England)	—	7	1	5	2	4	3	0
21	R. N. Harvey (Australia)	6	—	8	3	0	4	—	—
21	A. R. Border (Australia)	7	—	—	3	4	5	—	—
20	K. F. Barrington (England)	—	5	2	3	3	3	4	—
20	I. V. A. Richards (West Indies)	8	4	—	—	1	6	1	—

CARRYING BAT THROUGH TEST INNINGS

(Figures in brackets show side's total)

A. B. Tancred	26*	(47)	South Africa v England at Cape Town	1888-89
J. E. Barrett	67*	(176)	Australia v England at Lord's	1890
R. Abel	132*	(307)	England v Australia at Sydney	1891-92
P. F. Warner	132*	(237)	England v South Africa at Johannesburg	1898-99
W. W. Armstrong	159*	(309)	Australia v South Africa at Johannesburg	1902-03
J. W. Zulch	43*	(103)	South Africa v England at Cape Town	1909-10
W. Bardsley	193*	(383)	Australia v England at Lord's	1926
W. M. Woodfull	30*	(66)‡	Australia v England at Brisbane	1928-29
W. M. Woodfull	73*	(193)†	Australia v England at Adelaide	1932-33
W. A. Brown	206*	(422)	Australia v England at Lord's	1938
L. Hutton	202*	(344)	England v West Indies at The Oval	1950

L. Hutton	156* (272)	England v Australia at Adelaide	1950-51
Nazar Mohammad ..	124* (331)	Pakistan v India at Lucknow	1952-53
F. M. M. Worrell ..	191* (372)	West Indies v England at Nottingham ..	1957
T. L. Goddard	56* (99)	South Africa v Australia at Cape Town ..	1957-58
D. J. McGlew	127* (292)	South Africa v New Zealand at Durban ..	1961-62
C. C. Hunte	60* (131)	West Indies v Australia at Port-of-Spain .	1964-65
G. M. Turner	43* (131)	New Zealand v England at Lord's	1969
W. M. Lawry	49* (107)	Australia v India at Delhi	1969-70
W. M. Lawry	60* (116)†	Australia v England at Sydney	1970-71
G. M. Turner	223* (386)	New Zealand v West Indies at Kingston .	1971-72
I. R. Redpath	159* (346)	Australia v New Zealand at Auckland ..	1973-74
G. Boycott	99* (215)	England v Australia at Perth	1979-80
S. M. Gavaskar	127* (286)	India v Pakistan at Faisalabad	1982-83
Mudassar Nazar ...	152* (323)	Pakistan v India at Lahore	1982-83
S. Wettimuny	63* (144)	Sri Lanka v New Zealand at Christchurch	1982-83
D. C. Boon	58* (103)	Australia v New Zealand at Auckland ..	1985-86
D. L. Haynes	88* (211)	West Indies v Pakistan at Karachi	1986-87

      † *One man absent.*   ‡ *Two men absent.*

Notes: G. M. Turner (223*) holds the record for the highest score by a player carrying his bat through a Test innings. He is also the youngest player to do so, being 22 years 63 days old when he first achieved the feat (1969).

     Nazar Mohammad and Mudassar Nazar are the only instance of father and son carrying their bat through a Test innings.

     D. L. Haynes (55 and 105) opened the batting and was last man out in each innings for West Indies v New Zealand at Dunedin, 1979-80.

FASTEST FIFTIES

Minutes

28	J. T. Brown	England v Australia at Melbourne	1894-95
29	S. A. Durani	India v England at Kanpur	1963-64
30	E. A. V. Williams .	West Indies v England at Bridgetown ...	1947-48
30	B. R. Taylor	New Zealand v West Indies at Auckland ...	1968-69
33	C. A. Roach	West Indies v England at The Oval	1933
34	C. R. R. Browne ..	West Indies v England at Georgetown ...	1929-30

The fastest fifties in terms of balls received (where recorded) are:

Balls

32	I. T. Botham	England v New Zealand at The Oval	1986
33	R. C. Fredericks ...	West Indies v Australia at Perth	1975-76
33	Kapil Dev	India v England at Manchester	1982
33	I. V. A. Richards ..	West Indies v England at St John's	1985-86

FASTEST HUNDREDS

Minutes

70	J. M. Gregory	Australia v South Africa at Johannesburg	1921-22
75	G. L. Jessop	England v Australia at The Oval	1902
78	R. Benaud	Australia v West Indies at Kingston	1954-55
80	J. H. Sinclair	South Africa v Australia at Cape Town	1902-03
81	I. V. A. Richards ..	West Indies v England at St John's	1985-86
86	B. R. Taylor	New Zealand v West Indies at Auckland ...	1968-69

The fastest hundreds in terms of balls received (where recorded) are:

Balls

56	I. V. A. Richards ..	West Indies v England at St John's	1985-86
67	J. M. Gregory	Australia v South Africa at Johannesburg	1921-22
71	R. C. Fredericks ...	West Indies v Australia at Perth	1975-76
74	Majid Khan	Pakistan v New Zealand at Karachi	1976-77
75	G. L. Jessop	England v Australia at The Oval	1902

FASTEST DOUBLE-HUNDREDS

Minutes

214	D. G. Bradman ...	Australia v England at Leeds		1930
223	S. J. McCabe	Australia v England at Nottingham		1938
226	V. T. Trumper	Australia v South Africa at Adelaide		1910-11
234	D. G. Bradman ...	Australia v England at Lord's		1930
240	W. R. Hammond ..	England v New Zealand at Auckland		1932-33
241	S. E. Gregory	Australia v England at Sydney		1894-95
245	D. C. S. Compton .	England v Pakistan at Nottingham		1954

FASTEST TRIPLE-HUNDREDS

Minutes

288	W. R. Hammond ..	England v New Zealand at Auckland	1932-33
336	D. G. Bradman ..	Australia v England at Leeds	1930

MOST RUNS IN A DAY BY A BATSMAN

309	D. G. Bradman	Australia v England at Leeds	1930
295	W. R. Hammond	England v New Zealand at Auckland	1932-33
273	D. C. S. Compton	England v Pakistan at Nottingham	1954
271	D. G. Bradman	Australia v England at Leeds	1934

SLOWEST INDIVIDUAL BATTING

2* in 80 minutes	C. E. H. Croft, West Indies v Australia at Brisbane	1979-80
3* in 100 minutes	J. T. Murray, England v Australia at Sydney	1962-63
5 in 102 minutes	Nawab of Pataudi jun, India v England at Bombay ...	1972-73
7 in 123 minutes	G. Miller, England v Australia at Melbourne	1978-79
9 in 125 minutes	T. W. Jarvis, New Zealand v India at Madras	1964-65
10* in 133 minutes	T. G. Evans, England v Australia at Adelaide	1946-47
16 in 188 minutes	G. M. Ritchie, Australia v New Zealand at Sydney	1985-86
18 in 194 minutes	W. R. Playle, New Zealand v England at Leeds	1958
19 in 217 minutes	M. D. Crowe, New Zealand v Sri Lanka at Colombo (SSC)	1983-84
28* in 250 minutes	J. W. Burke, Australia v England at Brisbane	1958-59
31 in 264 minutes	K. D. Mackay, Australia v England at Lord's	1956
34* in 271 minutes	Younis Ahmed, Pakistan v India at Ahmedabad	1986-87
35 in 332 minutes	C. J. Tavaré, England v India at Madras	1981-82
55 in 336 minutes	B. A. Edgar, New Zealand v Australia at Wellington ...	1981-82
57 in 346 minutes	G. S. Camacho, West Indies v England at Bridgetown ..	1967-68
58 in 367 minutes	Ijaz Butt, Pakistan v Australia at Karachi	1959-60
60 in 390 minutes	D. N. Sardesai, India v West Indies at Bridgetown	1961-62
62 in 408 minutes	Ramiz Raja, Pakistan v West Indies at Karachi	1986-87
68 in 458 minutes	T. E. Bailey, England v New Zealand at Brisbane	1958-59
99 in 505 minutes	M. L. Jaisimha, India v Pakistan at Kanpur	1960-61
105 in 575 minutes	D. J. McGlew, South Africa v Australia at Durban	1957-58
114 in 591 minutes	Mudassar Nazar, Pakistan v England at Lahore	1977-78
120* in 609 minutes	J. J. Crowe, New Zealand v Sri Lanka, Colombo (CCC) .	1986-87
158 in 648 minutes	C. T. Radley, England v New Zealand at Auckland	1977-78
172 in 708 minutes	S. M. Gavaskar, India v England at Bangalore	1981-82
337 in 970 minutes	Hanif Mohammad, Pakistan v West Indies at Bridgetown	1957-58

SLOWEST HUNDREDS

557 minutes	Mudassar Nazar, Pakistan v England at Lahore	1977-78
545 minutes	D. J. McGlew, South Africa v Australia at Durban	1957-58
515 minutes	J. J. Crowe, New Zealand v Sri Lanka, Colombo (CCC)	1986-87
488 minutes	P. E. Richardson, England v South Africa at Johannesburg	1956-57

Notes: The slowest hundred for any Test in England is 458 minutes (329 balls) by K. W. R. Fletcher, England v Pakistan, The Oval, 1974.

The slowest double-hundred in a Test was scored in 776 minutes (517 balls) by D. S. B. P. Kuruppu for Sri Lanka v New Zealand at Colombo (CCC), 1986-87, on his début. It is also the slowest-ever first-class double-hundred.

HIGHEST WICKET PARTNERSHIPS

413 for 1st	V. Mankad (231) and Pankaj Roy (173) for India v New Zealand at Madras	1955-56
451 for 2nd	W. H. Ponsford (266) and D. G. Bradman (244) for Australia v England at The Oval	1934
451 for 3rd	Mudassar Nazar (231) and Javed Miandad (280*) for Pakistan v India at Hyderabad	1982-83
411 for 4th	P. B. H. May (285*) and M. C. Cowdrey (154) for England v West Indies at Birmingham	1957
405 for 5th	S. G. Barnes (234) and D. G. Bradman (234) for Australia v England at Sydney	1946-47
346 for 6th	J. H. W. Fingleton (136) and D. G. Bradman (270) for Australia v England at Melbourne	1936-37
347 for 7th	D. St E. Atkinson (219) and C. C. Depeiza (122) for West Indies v Australia at Bridgetown	1954-55
246 for 8th	L. E. G. Ames (137) and G. O. Allen (122) for England v New Zealand at Lord's	1931
190 for 9th	Asif Iqbal (146) and Intikhab Alam (51) for Pakistan v England at The Oval	1967
151 for 10th	B. F. Hastings (110) and R. O. Collinge (68*) for New Zealand v Pakistan at Auckland	1972-73

BOWLING RECORDS

MOST WICKETS IN AN INNINGS

10-53	J. C. Laker	England v Australia at Manchester	1956
9-28	G. A. Lohmann	England v South Africa at Johannesburg	1895-96
9-37	J. C. Laker	England v Australia at Manchester	1956
9-52	R. J. Hadlee	New Zealand v Australia at Brisbane	1985-86
9-69	J. M. Patel	India v Australia at Kanpur	1959-60
9-83	Kapil Dev	India v West Indies at Ahmedabad	1983-84
9-86	Sarfraz Nawaz	Pakistan v Australia at Melbourne	1978-79
9-95	J. M. Noreiga	West Indies v India at Port-of-Spain	1970-71
9-102	S. P. Gupte	India v West Indies at Kanpur	1958-59
9-103	S. F. Barnes	England v South Africa at Johannesburg	1913-14
9-113	H. J. Tayfield	South Africa v England at Johannesburg	1956-57
9-121	A. A. Mailey	Australia v England at Melbourne	1920-21
8-7	G. A. Lohmann	England v South Africa at Port Elizabeth	1895-96
8-11	J. Briggs	England v South Africa at Cape Town	1888-89
8-29	S. F. Barnes	England v South Africa at The Oval	1912
8-29	C. E. H. Croft	West Indies v Pakistan at Port-of-Spain	1976-77
8-31	F. Laver	Australia v England at Manchester	1909
8-31	F. S. Trueman	England v India at Manchester	1952
8-34	I. T. Botham	England v Pakistan at Lord's	1978
8-35	G. A. Lohmann	England v Australia at Sydney	1886-87
8-38	L. R. Gibbs	West Indies v India at Bridgetown	1961-62
8-43†	A. E. Trott	Australia v England at Adelaide	1894-95
8-43	H. Verity	England v Australia at Lord's	1934
8-43	R. G. D. Willis	England v Australia at Leeds	1981
8-51	D. L. Underwood	England v Pakistan at Lord's	1974

8-52	V. Mankad	India v Pakistan at Delhi	1952-53
8-53	G. B. Lawrence	South Africa v New Zealand at Johannesburg	1961-62
8-53†	R. A. L. Massie	Australia v England at Lord's	1972
8-55	V. Mankad	India v England at Madras	1951-52
8-56	S. F. Barnes	England v South Africa at Johannesburg	1913-14
8-58	G. A. Lohmann	England v Australia at Sydney	1891-92
8-58	Imran Khan	Pakistan v Sri Lanka at Lahore	1981-82
8-59	C. Blythe	England v South Africa at Leeds	1907
8-59	A. A. Mallett	Australia v Pakistan at Adelaide	1972-73
8-60	Imran Khan	Pakistan v India at Karachi	1982-83
8-65	H. Trumble	Australia v England at The Oval	1902
8-68	W. Rhodes	England v Australia at Melbourne	1903-04
8-69	H. J. Tayfield	South Africa v England at Durban	1956-57
8-69	Sikander Bakht	Pakistan v India at Delhi	1979-80
8-70	S. J. Snooke	South Africa v England at Johannesburg	1905-06
8-71	G. D. McKenzie	Australia v West Indies at Melbourne	1968-69
8-72	S. Venkataraghavan	India v New Zealand at Delhi	1964-65
8-76	E. A. S. Prasanna	India v New Zealand at Auckland	1975-76
8-79	B. S. Chandrasekhar	India v England at Delhi	1972-73
8-81	L. C. Braund	England v Australia at Melbourne	1903-04
8-83	J. R. Ratnayeke	Sri Lanka v Pakistan at Sialkot	1985-86
8-84†	R. A. L. Massie	Australia v England at Lord's	1972
8-85	Kapil Dev	India v Pakistan at Lahore	1982-83
8-86	A. W. Greig	England v West Indies at Port-of-Spain	1973-74
8-92	M. A. Holding	West Indies v England at The Oval	1976
8-94	T. Richardson	England v Australia at Sydney	1897-98
8-103	I. T. Botham	England v West Indies at Lord's	1984
8-104†	A. L. Valentine	West Indies v England at Manchester	1950
8-106	Kapil Dev	India v Australia at Adelaide	1985-86
8-107	B. J. T. Bosanquet	England v Australia at Nottingham	1905
8-107	N. A. Foster	England v Pakistan at Leeds	1987
8-112	G. F. Lawson	Australia v West Indies at Adelaide	1984-85
8-126	J. C. White	England v Australia at Adelaide	1928-29
8-141	C. J. McDermott	Australia v England at Manchester	1985
8-143	M. H. N. Walker	Australia v England at Melbourne	1974-75

† *On Test début.*

MOST WICKETS IN A MATCH

19-90	J. C. Laker	England v Australia at Manchester	1956
17-159	S. F. Barnes	England v South Africa at Johannesburg	1913-14
16-137†	R. A. L. Massie	Australia v England at Lord's	1972
15-28	J. Briggs	England v South Africa at Cape Town	1888-89
15-45	G. A. Lohmann	England v South Africa at Port Elizabeth	1895-96
15-99	C. Blythe	England v South Africa at Leeds	1907
15-104	H. Verity	England v Australia at Lord's	1934
15-123	R. J. Hadlee	New Zealand v Australia at Brisbane	1985-86
15-124	W. Rhodes	England v Australia at Melbourne	1903-04
14-90	F. R. Spofforth	Australia v England at The Oval	1882
14-99	A. V. Bedser	England v Australia at Nottingham	1953
14-102	W. Bates	England v Australia at Melbourne	1882-83
14-116	Imran Khan	Pakistan v Sri Lanka at Lahore	1981-82
14-124	J. M. Patel	India v Australia at Kanpur	1959-60
14-144	S. F. Barnes	England v South Africa at Durban	1913-14
14-149	M. A. Holding	West Indies v England at The Oval	1976
14-199	C. V. Grimmett	Australia v South Africa at Adelaide	1931-32

† *On Test début.*

Notes: The best for South Africa is 13-165 by H. J. Tayfield against Australia at Melbourne, 1952-53.

The best for Sri Lanka is 9-125 by R. J. Ratnayake against India at Colombo (PSO), 1985-86.

MOST WICKETS IN A SERIES

	T	R	W	*Avge*		
S. F. Barnes	4	536	49	10.93	England v South Africa.	1913-14
J. C. Laker	5	442	46	9.60	England v Australia ...	1956
C. V. Grimmett	5	642	44	14.59	Australia v South Africa	1935-36
T. M. Alderman	6	893	42	21.26	Australia v England ...	1981
R. M. Hogg	6	527	41	12.85	Australia v England ...	1978-79
Imran Khan	6	558	40	13.95	Pakistan v India	1982-83
A. V. Bedser	5	682	39	17.48	England v Australia ...	1953
D. K. Lillee	6	870	39	22.30	Australia v England ...	1981
M. W. Tate	5	881	38	23.18	England v Australia ...	1924-25
W. J. Whitty	5	632	37	17.08	Australia v South Africa	1910-11
H. J. Tayfield	5	636	37	17.18	South Africa v England.	1956-57
A. E. E. Vogler	5	783	36	21.75	South Africa v England.	1909-10
A. A. Mailey	5	946	36	26.27	Australia v England ...	1920-21
G. A. Lohmann	3	203	35	5.80	England v South Africa.	1895-96
B. S. Chandrasekhar	5	662	35	18.91	India v England	1972-73

MOST WICKETS IN A CAREER

(Qualification: 100 wickets)

ENGLAND

	T	Balls	R	W	*Avge*	5 W/i	10 W/m
I. T. Botham	94	20,801	10,392	373	27.86	27	4
R. G. D. Willis	90	17,357	8,190	325	25.20	16	—
F. S. Trueman	67	15,178	6,625	307	21.57	17	3
D. L. Underwood	86	21,862	7,674	297	25.83	17	6
J. B. Statham	70	16,056	6,261	252	24.84	9	1
A. V. Bedser	51	15,918	5,876	236	24.89	15	5
J. A. Snow	49	12,021	5,387	202	26.66	8	1
J. C. Laker	46	12,027	4,101	193	21.24	9	3
S. F. Barnes	27	7,873	3,106	189	16.43	24	7
G. A. R. Lock	49	13,147	4,451	174	25.58	9	3
M. W. Tate	39	12,523	4,055	155	26.16	7	1
F. J. Titmus	53	15,118	4,931	153	32.22	7	—
H. Verity	40	11,173	3,510	144	24.37	5	2
C. M. Old	46	8,858	4,020	143	28.11	4	—
A. W. Greig	58	9,802	4,541	141	32.20	6	2
T. E. Bailey	61	9,712	3,856	132	29.21	5	1
W. Rhodes	58	8,231	3,425	127	26.96	6	1
P. H. Edmonds	51	12,028	4,273	125	34.18	2	—
D. A. Allen	39	11,297	3,779	122	30.97	4	—
R. Illingworth	61	11,934	3,807	122	31.20	3	—
J. Briggs	33	5,332	2,094	118	17.74	9	4
G. G. Arnold	34	7,650	3,254	115	28.29	6	—
J. E. Emburey	46	10,868	3,855	115	33.52	6	—
G. A. Lohmann	18	3,821	1,205	112	10.75	9	5
D. V. P. Wright	34	8,135	4,224	108	39.11	6	1
R. Peel	20	5,216	1,715	102	16.81	6	2
J. H. Wardle	28	6,597	2,080	102	20.39	5	1
C. Blythe	19	4,546	1,863	100	18.63	9	4

AUSTRALIA

	T	Balls	R	W	Avge	5 W/i	10 W/m
D. K. Lillee	70	18,467	8,493	355	23.92	23	7
R. Benaud	63	19,108	6,704	248	27.03	16	1
G. D. McKenzie	60	17,681	7,328	246	29.78	16	3
R. R. Lindwall	61	13,650	5,251	228	23.03	12	—
C. V. Grimmett	37	14,513	5,231	216	24.21	21	7
J. R. Thomson	51	10,535	5,601	200	28.00	8	—
A. K. Davidson	44	11,587	3,819	186	20.53	14	2
K. R. Miller	55	10,461	3,906	170	22.97	7	1
W. A. Johnston	40	11,048	3,826	160	23.91	7	—
G. F. Lawson	37	8,705	4,420	145	30.48	10	2
W. J. O'Reilly	27	10,024	3,254	144	22.59	11	3
H. Trumble	32	8,099	3,072	141	21.78	9	3
M. H. N. Walker ...	34	10,094	3,792	138	27.47	6	—
A. A. Mallett	38	9,990	3,940	132	29.84	6	1
B. Yardley	33	8,909	3,986	126	31.63	6	1
R. M. Hogg	38	7,633	3,503	123	28.47	6	2
M. A. Noble	42	7,159	3,025	121	25.00	9	2
I. W. Johnson	45	8,780	3,182	109	29.19	3	—
G. Giffen	31	6,391	2,791	103	27.09	7	1
A. N. Connolly	29	7,818	2,981	102	29.22	4	—
C. T. B. Turner	17	5,179	1,670	101	16.53	11	2

SOUTH AFRICA

	T	Balls	R	W	Avge	5 W/i	10 W/m
H. J. Tayfield	37	13,568	4,405	170	25.91	14	2
T. L. Goddard	41	11,736	3,226	123	26.22	5	—
P. M. Pollock	28	6,522	2,806	116	24.18	9	1
N. A. T. Adcock	26	6,391	2,195	104	21.10	5	—

WEST INDIES

	T	Balls	R	W	Avge	5 W/i	10 W/m
L. R. Gibbs	79	27,115	8,989	309	29.09	18	2
J. Garner	58	13,169	5,433	259	20.97	7	—
M. A. Holding	60	12,680	5,898	249	23.68	13	2
M. D. Marshall	51	11,278	5,194	240	21.64	14	2
G. S. Sobers	93	21,599	7,999	235	34.03	6	—
A. M. E. Roberts	47	11,136	5,174	202	25.61	11	2
W. W. Hall	48	10,421	5,066	192	26.38	9	1
S. Ramadhin	43	13,939	4,579	158	28.98	10	1
A. L. Valentine	36	12,953	4,215	139	30.32	8	2
C. E. H. Croft	27	6,165	2,913	125	23.30	3	—
V. A. Holder	40	9,095	3,627	109	33.27	3	—

NEW ZEALAND

	T	Balls	R	W	Avge	5 W/i	10 W/m
R. J. Hadlee	70	18,091	7,976	355	22.46	29	7
B. L. Cairns	43	10,628	4,280	130	32.92	6	1
R. O. Collinge	35	7,689	3,392	116	29.24	3	—
B. R. Taylor	30	6,334	2,953	111	26.60	4	—
R. C. Motz	32	7,034	3,148	100	31.48	5	—
E. J. Chatfield	33	7,749	3,102	100	31.02	3	1

INDIA

	T	Balls	R	W	Avge	5 W/i	10 W/m
Kapil Dev	88	18,547	9,145	311	29.40	19	2
B. S. Bedi	67	21,364	7,637	266	28.71	14	1
B. S. Chandrasekhar ..	58	15,963	7,199	242	29.74	16	2
E. A. S. Prasanna	49	14,353	5,742	189	30.38	10	2
V. Mankad	44	14,686	5,236	162	32.32	8	2
S. Venkataraghavan ..	57	14,877	5,634	156	36.11	3	1
S. P. Gupte	36	11,284	4,403	149	29.55	12	1
R. J. Shastri	54	12,526	4,683	119	39.35	2	—
D. R. Doshi	33	9,322	3,502	114	30.71	6	—
K. D. Ghavri	39	7,042	3,656	109	33.54	4	—
N. S. Yadav	35	8,349	3,580	102	35.09	3	—

PAKISTAN

	T	Balls	R	W	Avge	5 W/i	10 W/m
Imran Khan	70	16,358	6,903	311	22.19	21	5
Sarfraz Nawaz	55	13,927	5,798	177	32.75	4	1
Abdul Qadir	48	12,041	5,508	161	34.21	11	2
Iqbal Qasim	44	11,710	4,361	149	29.26	6	2
Fazal Mahmood	34	9,834	3,434	139	24.70	13	4
Intikhab Alam	47	10,474	4,494	125	35.95	5	2

SRI LANKA: The highest aggregate is 59 wickets, average 36.94, by A. L. F. de Mel.

WICKET WITH FIRST BALL IN TEST CRICKET

	Batsman dismissed			
A. Coningham	A. C. MacLaren	A v E	Melbourne	1894-95
W. M. Bradley	F. Laver	E v A	Manchester	1899
E. G. Arnold	V. T. Trumper	E v A	Sydney	1903-04
G. G. Macaulay	G. A. L. Hearne	E v SA	Cape Town	1922-23
M. W. Tate	M. J. Susskind	E v SA	Birmingham	1924
M. Henderson	E. W. Dawson	NZ v E	Christchurch	1929-30
H. D. Smith	E. Paynter	NZ v E	Christchurch	1932-33
T. F. Johnson	W. W. Keeton	WI v E	The Oval	1939
R. Howorth	D. V. Dyer	E v SA	The Oval	1947
Intikhab Alam	C. C. McDonald	P v A	Karachi	1959-60

HAT-TRICKS

F. R. Spofforth	Australia v England at Melbourne	1878-79
W. Bates	England v Australia at Melbourne	1882-83
J. Briggs	England v Australia at Sydney	1891-92
G. A. Lohmann ...	England v South Africa at Port Elizabeth	1895-96
J. T. Hearne	England v Australia at Leeds	1899
H. Trumble	Australia v England at Melbourne	1901-02
H. Trumble	Australia v England at Melbourne	1903-04
T. J. Matthews† ... ⎱ Australia v South Africa at Manchester		1912
T. J. Matthews .... ⎰		
M. J. C. Allom‡ ...	England v New Zealand at Christchurch	1929-30
T. W. Goddard	England v South Africa at Johannesburg	1938-39
P. J. Loader	England v West Indies at Leeds	1957
L. F. Kline	Australia v South Africa at Cape Town	1957-58
W. W. Hall	West Indies v Pakistan at Lahore	1958-59
G. M. Griffin	South Africa v England at Lord's	1960
L. R. Gibbs	West Indies v Australia at Adelaide	1960-61
P. J. Petherick‡ ...	New Zealand v Pakistan at Lahore	1976-77

† *T. J. Matthews did the hat-trick in each innings of the same match.*
‡ *On Test début.*

MOST BALLS BOWLED IN A TEST

S. Ramadhin (West Indies) sent down 774 balls in 129 overs against England at Birmingham, 1957. It was the most delivered by any bowler in a Test, beating H. Verity's 766 for England against South Africa at Durban, 1938-39. In this match Ramadhin also bowled the most balls (588) in any single first-class innings, including Tests.

It should be noted that six balls were bowled to the over in the Australia v England Test series of 1928-29 and 1932-33, when the eight-ball over was otherwise in force in Australia.

ALL-ROUND RECORDS

100 RUNS AND FIVE WICKETS IN AN INNINGS

England

A. W. Greig	148	6-164	v West Indies	Bridgetown	1973-74
I. T. Botham	103	5-73	v New Zealand	Christchurch	1977-78
I. T. Botham	108	8-34	v Pakistan	Lord's	1978
I. T. Botham	. 114	6-58 7-48	v India	Bombay	1979-80
I. T. Botham	149*	6-95	v Australia	Leeds	1981
I. T. Botham	138	5-59	v New Zealand	Wellington	1983-84

Australia

C. Kelleway	114	5-33	v South Africa	Manchester	1912
J. M. Gregory	100	7-69	v England	Melbourne	1920-21
K. R. Miller	109	6-107	v West Indies	Kingston	1954-55
R. Benaud	100	5-84	v South Africa	Johannesburg	1957-58

South Africa

J. H. Sinclair	106	6-26	v England	Cape Town	1898-99
G. A. Faulkner	123	5-120	v England	Johannesburg	1909-10

West Indies

D. St E. Atkinson	219	5-56	v Australia	Bridgetown	1954-55
O. G. Smith	100	5-90	v India	Delhi	1958-59
G. S. Sobers	104	5-63	v India	Kingston	1961-62
G. S. Sobers	174	5-41	v England	Leeds	1966

New Zealand

B. R. Taylor†	105	5-86	v India	Calcutta	1964-65

India

V. Mankad	184	5-196	v England	Lord's	1952
P. R. Umrigar	172*	5-107	v West Indies	Port-of-Spain	1961-62

Pakistan

Mushtaq Mohammad	201	5-49	v New Zealand	Dunedin	1972-73
Mushtaq Mohammad	121	5-28	v West Indies	Port-of-Spain	1976-77
Imran Khan	117	6-98 5-82 }	v India	Faisalabad	1982-83

† *On début.*

100 RUNS AND FIVE DISMISSALS IN AN INNINGS

D. T. Lindsay	182	6ct	SA v A	Johannesburg	1966-67
I. D. S. Smith	113*	4ct, 1st	NZ v E	Auckland	1983-84
S. A. R. Silva	111	5ct	SL v I	Colombo (PSO)	1985-86

100 RUNS AND TEN WICKETS IN A TEST

A. K. Davidson	44 80	5-135 6-87 }	A v WI	Brisbane	1960-61
I. T. Botham	114	6-58 7-48 }	E v I	Bombay	1979-80
Imran Khan	117	6-98 5-82 }	P v I	Faisalabad	1982-83

1,000 RUNS AND 100 WICKETS IN A CAREER

	Tests	Runs	Wkts	Tests for Double
England				
T. E. Bailey	61	2,290	132	47
I. T. Botham	94	5,057	373	21
J. E. Emburey	46	1,027	115	46
A. W. Greig	58	3,599	141	37
R. Illingworth	61	1,836	122	47
W. Rhodes	58	2,325	127	44
M. W. Tate	39	1,198	155	33
F. J. Titmus	53	1,449	153	40
Australia				
R. Benaud	63	2,201	248	32
A. K. Davidson	44	1,328	186	34
G. Giffen	31	1,238	103	30
I. W. Johnson	45	1,000	109	45
R. R. Lindwall	61	1,502	228	38
K. R. Miller	55	2,958	170	33
M. A. Noble	42	1,997	121	27

	Tests	Runs	Wkts	Tests for Double
South Africa				
T. L. Goddard	41	2,516	123	36
West Indies				
M. D. Marshall	51	1,068	240	49
G. S. Sobers	93	8,032	235	48
New Zealand				
R. J. Hadlee	70	2,622	355	28
India				
Kapil Dev	88	3,668	311	25
V. Mankad	44	2,109	162	23
R. J. Shastri	54	2,463	119	44
Pakistan				
Imran Khan	70	2,770	311	30
Intikhab Alam	47	1,493	125	41
Sarfraz Nawaz	55	1,045	177	55

1,000 RUNS, 100 WICKETS AND 100 CATCHES

	Tests	Runs	Wkts	Ct
I. T. Botham	94	5,057	373	109
G. S. Sobers	93	8,032	235	109

WICKET-KEEPING RECORDS

Most Dismissals in an Innings

7 (all ct)	Wasim Bari	Pakistan v New Zealand at Auckland ...	1978-79
7 (all ct)	R. W. Taylor	England v India at Bombay	1979-80
6 (all ct)	A. T. W. Grout ...	Australia v South Africa at Johannesburg	1957-58
6 (5ct, 1st)	S. M. H. Kirmani .	India v New Zealand at Christchurch ..	1975-76
6 (all ct)	D. T. Lindsay	South Africa v Australia at Johannesburg	1966-67
6 (all ct)	R. W. Marsh	Australia v England at Brisbane	1982-83
6 (all ct)	J. T. Murray	England v India at Lord's	1967
6 (all ct)	S. A. R. Silva	Sri Lanka v India at Colombo (SSC)	1985-86

Most Dismissals in One Test

10 (all ct)	R. W. Taylor	England v India at Bombay	1979-80
9 (8ct, 1st)	G. R. A. Langley ..	Australia v England at Lord's	1956
9 (all ct)	R. W. Marsh	Australia v England at Brisbane	1982-83
9 (all ct)	D. A. Murray	West Indies v Australia at Melbourne ...	1981-82
9 (all ct)	S. A. R. Silva	Sri Lanka v India at Colombo (SSC)	1985-86
9 (8ct, 1st)	S. A. R. Silva	Sri Lanka v India at Colombo (PSO)	1985-86
8 (6ct, 2st)	L. E. G. Ames	England v West Indies at The Oval	1933
8 (6ct, 2st)	A. T. W. Grout ...	Australia v Pakistan at Lahore	1959-60
8 (all ct)	A. T. W. Grout ...	Australia v England at Lord's	1961
8 (all ct)	J. J. Kelly	Australia v England at Sydney	1901-02
8 (all ct)	G. R. A. Langley ..	Australia v West Indies at Kingston	1954-55
8 (all ct)	W. K. Lees	New Zealand v Sri Lanka at Wellington .	1982-83
8 (all ct)	D. T. Lindsay	South Africa v Australia at Johannesburg	1966-67
8 (all ct)	R. W. Marsh	Australia v West Indies at Melbourne ...	1975-76
8 (all ct)	R. W. Marsh	Australia v New Zealand at Christchurch	1976-77
8 (7ct, 1st)	R. W. Marsh	Australia v India at Sydney	1980-81
8 (all ct)	R. W. Marsh	Australia v England at Adelaide	1982-83
8 (all ct)	J. M. Parks	England v New Zealand at Christchurch .	1965-66
8 (7ct, 1st)	H. B. Taber	Australia v South Africa at Johannesburg	1966-67
8 (all ct)	Wasim Bari	Pakistan v England at Leeds	1971

Note: S. A. R. Silva made 18 dismissals in two successive Tests.

Most Dismissals in a Series

(Played in 5 Tests unless otherwise stated)

28 (all ct)	R. W. Marsh	Australia v England	1982-83
26 (all ct)	R. W. Marsh	Australia v West Indies (6 Tests)	1975-76
26 (23ct, 3st)	J. H. B. Waite	South Africa v New Zealand	1961-62
24 (21ct, 3st)	A. P. E. Knott	England v Australia (6 Tests)	1970-71
24 (all ct)	D. T. Lindsay	South Africa v Australia	1966-67
24 (22ct, 2st)	D. L. Murray	West Indies v England	1963
23 (22ct, 1st)	F. C. M. Alexander.	West Indies v England	1959-60
23 (21ct, 2st)	A. E. Dick	New Zealand v South Africa	1961-62
23 (20ct, 3st)	A. T. W. Grout	Australia v West Indies	1960-61
23 (22ct, 1st)	A. P. E. Knott	England v Australia (6 Tests)	1974-75
23 (21ct, 2st)	R. W. Marsh	Australia v England	1972
23 (all ct)	R. W. Marsh	Australia v England (6 Tests)	1981
23 (16ct, 7st)	J. H. B. Waite	South Africa v New Zealand	1953-54
22 (all ct)	S. J. Rixon	Australia v India	1977-78
22 (21ct, 1st)	S. A. R. Silva	Sri Lanka v India (3 Tests)	1985-86
21 (20ct, 1st)	A. T. W. Grout	Australia v England	1961
21 (16ct, 5st)	G. R. A. Langley ..	Australia v West Indies	1951-52
21 (all ct)	R. W. Marsh	Australia v Pakistan	1983-84
21 (13ct, 8st)	R. A. Saggers	Australia v South Africa	1949-50
21 (15ct, 6st)	H. Strudwick	England v South Africa	1913-14
20 (19ct, 1st)	P. R. Downton	England v Australia (6 Tests)	1985
20 (19ct, 1st)	P. J. L. Dujon	West Indies v Australia	1983-84
20 (18ct, 2st)	T. G. Evans	England v South Africa	1956-57
20 (17ct, 3st)	A. T. W. Grout	Australia v England	1958-59
20 (16ct, 4st)	G. R. A. Langley ..	Australia v West Indies (4 Tests)	1954-55
20 (19ct, 1st)	H. B. Taber	Australia v South Africa	1966-67
20 (16ct, 4st)	D. Tallon	Australia v England	1946-47
20 (18ct, 2st)	R. W. Taylor	England v Australia (6 Tests)	1978-79

Most Dismissals in a Career

	T	*Ct*	*St*	*Total*
R. W. Marsh (Australia)	96	343	12	355
A. P. E. Knott (England)	95	250	19	269
Wasim Bari (Pakistan)	81	201	27	228
T. G. Evans (England)	91	173	46	219
S. M. H. Kirmani (India)	88	160	38	198
D. L. Murray (West Indies)	62	181	8	189
A. T. W. Grout (Australia)	51	163	24	187
R. W. Taylor (England)	57	167	7	174
P. J. L. Dujon (West Indies)	43	139	3	142
J. H. B. Waite (South Africa)	50	124	17	141
W. A. Oldfield (Australia)	54	78	52	130
J. M. Parks (England)	46	103	11	114
I. D. S. Smith (New Zealand)	37	103	6	109

Notes: The records for P. J. L. Dujon and J. M. Parks each include two catches taken when not keeping wicket in two and three Tests respectively.

S. A. R. Silva (30ct, 1st) made most dismissals for Sri Lanka.

FIELDING RECORDS

(Excluding wicket-keepers)

Most Catches in an Innings

5	V. Y. Richardson	Australia v South Africa at Durban	1935-36
5	Yajurvindra Singh	India v England at Bangalore	1976-77

Most Catches in One Test

7	G. S. Chappell	Australia v England at Perth	1974-75
7	Yajurvindra Singh	India v England at Bangalore	1976-77
6	A. Shrewsbury	England v Australia at Sydney	1887-88
6	A. E. E. Vogler	South Africa v England at Durban	1909-10
6	F. E. Woolley	England v Australia at Sydney	1911-12
6	J. M. Gregory	Australia v England at Sydney	1920-21
6	B. Mitchell	South Africa v Australia at Melbourne	1931-32
6	V. Y. Richardson	Australia v South Africa at Durban	1935-36
6	R. N. Harvey	Australia v England at Sydney	1962-63
6	M. C. Cowdrey	England v West Indies at Lord's	1963
6	E. D. Solkar	India v West Indies at Port-of-Spain	1970-71
6	G. S. Sobers	West Indies v England at Lord's	1973
6	I. M. Chappell	Australia v New Zealand at Adelaide	1973-74
6	A. W. Greig	England v Pakistan at Leeds	1974
6	D. F. Whatmore	Australia v India at Kanpur	1979-80
6	A. J. Lamb	England v New Zealand at Lord's	1983

Most Catches in a Series

15	J. M. Gregory	Australia v England	1920-21
14	G. S. Chappell	Australia v England (6 Tests)	1974-75
13	R. B. Simpson	Australia v South Africa	1957-58
13	R. B. Simpson	Australia v West Indies	1960-61

Most Catches in a Career

G. S. Chappell (Australia)	122 in 87 matches
M. C. Cowdrey (England)	120 in 114 matches
R. B. Simpson (Australia)	110 in 62 matches
W. R. Hammond (England)	110 in 85 matches
G. S. Sobers (West Indies)	109 in 93 matches
I. T. Botham (England)	109 in 94 matches
S. M. Gavaskar (India)	108 in 125 matches
I. M. Chappell (Australia)	105 in 75 matches

TEAM RECORDS

HIGHEST INNINGS TOTALS

903-7 dec.	England v Australia at The Oval	1938
849	England v West Indies at Kingston	1929-30
790-3 dec.	West Indies v Pakistan at Kingston	1957-58
758-8 dec.	Australia v West Indies at Kingston	1954-55
729-6 dec.	Australia v England at Lord's	1930
708	Pakistan v England at The Oval	1987
701	Australia v England at The Oval	1934
695	Australia v England at The Oval	1930
687-8 dec.	West Indies v England at The Oval	1976
681-8 dec.	West Indies v England at Port-of-Spain	1953-54
676-7	India v Sri Lanka at Kanpur	1986-87
674-6	Pakistan v India at Faisalabad	1984-85
674	Australia v India at Adelaide	1947-48
668	Australia v West Indies at Bridgetown	1954-55
659-8 dec.	Australia v England at Sydney	1946-47
658-8 dec.	England v Australia at Nottingham	1938
657-8 dec.	Pakistan v West Indies at Bridgetown	1957-58
656-8 dec.	Australia v England at Manchester	1964
654-5	England v South Africa at Durban	1938-39
652-7 dec.	England v India at Madras	1984-85
652-8 dec.	West Indies v England at Lord's	1973
652	Pakistan v India at Faisalabad	1982-83
650-6 dec.	Australia v West Indies at Bridgetown	1964-65

The highest innings for the countries not mentioned on previous page are:

622-9 dec.	South Africa v Australia at Durban	1969-70
553-7 dec.	New Zealand v Australia at Brisbane	1985-86
491-7 dec.	Sri Lanka v England at Lord's	1984

HIGHEST FOURTH INNINGS TOTALS

To win

406-4	India v West Indies at Port-of-Spain	1975-76
404-3	Australia v England at Leeds	1948
362-7	Australia v West Indies at Georgetown	1977-78
348-5	West Indies v New Zealand at Auckland	1968-69
344-1	West Indies v England at Lord's	1984

To tie

347	India v Australia at Madras	1986-87

To draw

654-5	England (needing 696 to win) v South Africa at Durban	1938-39
429-8	India (needing 438 to win) v England at The Oval	1979
423-7	South Africa (needing 451 to win) v England at The Oval	1947
408-5	West Indies (needing 836 to win) v England at Kingston	1929-30

To lose

445	India (lost by 47 runs) v Australia at Adelaide	1977-78
440	New Zealand (lost by 38 runs) v England at Nottingham	1973
417	England (lost by 45 runs) v Australia at Melbourne	1976-77
411	England (lost by 193 runs) v Australia at Sydney	1924-25

MOST RUNS IN A DAY (BOTH SIDES)

588	England (398-6), India (190-0) at Manchester (2nd day)	1936
522	England (503-2), South Africa (19-0) at Lord's (2nd day)	1924
508	England (221-2), South Africa (287-6) at The Oval (3rd day)	1935

MOST RUNS IN A DAY (ONE SIDE)

503	England (503-2) v South Africa at Lord's (2nd day)	1924
494	Australia (494-6) v South Africa at Sydney (1st day)	1910-11
475	Australia (475-2) v England at The Oval (1st day)	1934
471	England (471-8) v India at The Oval (1st day)	1936
458	Australia (458-3) v England at Leeds (1st day)	1930
455	Australia (455-1) v England at Leeds (2nd day)	1934

MOST WICKETS IN ONE DAY

27	England (18-3 to 53 out and 62) v Australia (60) at Lord's (2nd day)	1888
25	Australia (112 and 48-5) v England (61) at Melbourne (1st day)	1901-02

HIGHEST MATCH AGGREGATES

Runs	Wkts			Days played
1,981	35	South Africa v England at Durban	1938-39	10†
1,815	34	West Indies v England at Kingston	1929-30	9‡
1,764	39	Australia v West Indies at Adelaide	1968-69	5
1,753	40	Australia v England at Adelaide	1920-21	6
1,723	31	England v Australia at Leeds	1948	5
1,661	36	West Indies v Australia at Bridgetown	1954-55	6

† *No play on one day.*   ‡ *No play on two days.*

LOWEST INNINGS TOTALS

26	New Zealand v England at Auckland	1954-55
30	South Africa v England at Port Elizabeth	1895-96
30	South Africa v England at Birmingham	1924
35	South Africa v England at Cape Town	1898-99
36	Australia v England at Birmingham	1902
36	South Africa v Australia at Melbourne	1931-32
42	Australia v England at Sydney	1887-88
42	New Zealand v Australia at Wellington	1945-46
42†	India v England at Lord's	1974
43	South Africa v England at Cape Town	1888-89
44	Australia v England at The Oval	1896
45	England v Australia at Sydney	1886-87
45	South Africa v Australia at Melbourne	1931-32
47	South Africa v England at Cape Town	1888-89
47	New Zealand v England at Lord's	1958

The lowest innings for the countries not mentioned above are:

53	West Indies v Pakistan at Faisalabad	1986-87
62	Pakistan v Australia at Perth	1981-82
93	Sri Lanka v New Zealand at Wellington	1982-83

† *Batted one man short.*

FEWEST RUNS IN A FULL DAY'S PLAY

95 At Karachi, October 11, 1956. Australia 80 all out; Pakistan 15 for two (first day, 5½ hours).

104 At Karachi, December 8, 1959. Pakistan 0 for no wicket to 104 for five v Australia (fourth day, 5½ hours).

106 At Brisbane, December 9, 1958. England 92 for two to 198 all out v Australia (fourth day, 5 hours). *England were dismissed five minutes before the close of play, leaving no time for Australia to start their second innings.*

112 At Karachi, October 15, 1956. Australia 138 for six to 187 all out; Pakistan 63 for one (fourth day, 5½ hours).

117 At Madras, October 19, 1956. India 117 for five v Australia (first day, 5½ hours).

117 At Colombo (SSC), March 21, 1984. New Zealand 6 for no wicket to 123 for four (fifth day, 5 hours, 47 minutes).

In England

151 At Lord's, August 26, 1978. England 175 for two to 289 all out; New Zealand 37 for seven (third day, 6 hours).

159 At Leeds, July 10, 1971. Pakistan 208 for four to 350 all out; England 17 for one (third day, 6 hours).

LOWEST MATCH AGGREGATES

(For a completed match)

Runs	Wkts			Days played
234	29	Australia v South Africa at Melbourne	1931-32	3†
291	40	England v Australia at Lord's	1888	2
295	28	New Zealand v Australia at Wellington	1945-46	2
309	29	West Indies v England at Bridgetown	1934-35	3
323	30	England v Australia at Manchester	1888	2

† *No play on one day.*

YOUNGEST TEST PLAYERS

Years	Days			
15	124	Mushtaq Mohammad ...	Pakistan v West Indies at Lahore ...	1958-59
16	191	Aftab Baloch	Pakistan v New Zealand at Dacca ..	1969-70
16	248	Nasim-ul-Ghani	Pakistan v West Indies at Bridgetown	1957-58
16	352	Khalid Hassan	Pakistan v England at Nottingham ..	1954
17	118	L. Sivaramakrishnan ...	India v West Indies at St John's	1982-83
17	122	J. E. D. Sealy	West Indies v England at Bridgetown	1929-30
17	189	C. D. U. S. Weerasinghe	Sri Lanka v India at Colombo (PSO)	1985-86
17	193	Maninder Singh	India v Pakistan at Karachi	1982-83
17	239	I. D. Craig	Australia v South Africa at Melbourne	1952-53
17	245	G. S. Sobers	West Indies v England at Kingston ..	1953-54
17	265	V. L. Mehra	India v New Zealand at Bombay	1955-56
17	300	Hanif Mohammad	Pakistan v India at Delhi	1952-53
17	341	Intikhab Alam	Pakistan v Australia at Karachi	1959-60

Note: The youngest Test players for countries not mentioned above are: England – D. B. Close, 18 years 149 days, v New Zealand at Manchester, 1949; New Zealand – D. L. Freeman, 18 years 197 days, v England at Christchurch, 1932-33; South Africa – A. E. Ochse, 19 years 1 day, v England at Port Elizabeth, 1888-89.

OLDEST PLAYERS ON TEST DEBUT

Years	Days			
49	119	J. Southerton	England v Australia at Melbourne ...	1876-77
47	284	Miran Bux	Pakistan v India at Lahore	1954-55
46	253	D. D. Blackie	Australia v England at Sydney	1928-29
46	237	H. Ironmonger	Australia v England at Brisbane	1928-29
42	242	N. Betancourt	West Indies v England at Port-of-Spain	1929-30
41	337	E. R. Wilson	England v Australia at Sydney	1920-21
41	27	R. J. D. Jamshedji	India v England at Bombay	1933-34
40	345	C. A. Wiles	West Indies v England at Manchester	1933
40	216	S. P. Kinneir	England v Australia at Sydney	1911-12
40	110	H. W. Lee	England v South Africa at Johannesburg	1930-31
40	56	G. W. A. Chubb	South Africa v England at Nottingham.	1951
40	37	C. Ramaswami	India v England at Manchester	1936

Note: The oldest Test player on début for New Zealand was H. M. McGirr, 38 years 101 days, v England at Auckland, 1929-30; for Sri Lanka, D. S. de Silva, 39 years 251 days, v England at Colombo (PSO), 1981-82.

OLDEST TEST PLAYERS

(Age on final day of their last Test match)

Years	Days			
52	165	W. Rhodes	England v West Indies at Kingston ...	1929-30
50	327	H. Ironmonger	Australia v England at Sydney	1932-33
50	320	W. G. Grace	England v Australia at Nottingham ...	1899
50	303	G. Gunn	England v West Indies at Kingston ...	1929-30
49	139	J. Southerton	England v Australia at Melbourne ...	1876-77
47	302	Miran Bux	Pakistan v India at Peshawar	1954-55
47	249	J. B. Hobbs	England v Australia at The Oval	1930
47	87	F. E. Woolley	England v Australia at The Oval	1934
46	309	D. D. Blackie	Australia v England at Adelaide	1928-29
46	206	A. W. Nourse	South Africa v England at The Oval ..	1924
46	202	H. Strudwick	England v Australia at The Oval	1926
46	41	E. H. Hendren	England v West Indies at Kingston ...	1934-35
45	245	G. O. Allen	England v West Indies at Kingston ...	1947-48
45	215	P. Holmes	England v India at Lord's	1932
45	140	D. B. Close	England v West Indies at Manchester .	1976

MOST TEST MATCH APPEARANCES

For	Total		E	A	SA	WI	NZ	I	P	SL
England	114	M. C. Cowdrey	—	43	14	21	18	8	10	—
Australia	96	R. W. Marsh	42	—	—	17	14	3	20	—
South Africa	50	J. H. B. Waite	21	14	—	—	15	—	—	—
West Indies	110	C. H. Lloyd	34	29	—	—	8	28	11	—
New Zealand	70	R. J. Hadlee	17	19	—	10	—	8	10	6
India	125	S. M. Gavaskar	38	20	—	27	9	—	24	7
Pakistan	86	Javed Miandad	14	19	—	8	12	24	—	9
Sri Lanka	23	L. R. D. Mendis	2	1	—	—	4	7	9	—
	23	S. Wettimuny	2	1	—	—	5	6	9	—

MOST CONSECUTIVE TEST APPEARANCES

106	S. M. Gavaskar, India	Bombay 1974-75 to Madras 1986-87
87	G. R. Viswanath, India	Georgetown 1970-71 to Karachi 1982-83
86	A. R. Border, Australia	Melbourne 1978-79 to Sydney 1986-87
85	G. S. Sobers, West Indies ...	Port-of-Spain 1954-55 to Port-of-Spain 1971-72
71	I. M. Chappell, Australia ...	Adelaide 1965-66 to Melbourne 1975-76
66	Kapil Dev, India	Faisalabad 1978-79 to Delhi 1984-85
65	I. T. Botham, England	Wellington 1977-78 to Karachi 1983-84
65	A. P. E. Knott, England	Auckland 1970-71 to The Oval 1977
63	D. L. Haynes, West Indies ..	Brisbane 1979-80 to Christchurch 1986-87
61	R. B. Kanhai, West Indies ..	Birmingham 1957 to Sydney 1968-69
58†	A. W. Greig, England	Manchester 1972 to The Oval 1977
58†	J. R. Reid, New Zealand ...	Manchester 1949 to Leeds 1965
57	I. V. A. Richards, West Indies	Nottingham 1980 to Christchurch 1986-87
56	S. M. H. Kirmani, India	Madras 1979-80 to Kanpur 1984-85
53	K. J. Hughes, Australia	Brisbane 1978-79 to Sydney 1982-83
53	Javed Miandad, Pakistan	Lahore 1977-78 to Sydney 1983-84
52	R. W. Marsh, Australia	Brisbane 1970-71 to The Oval 1977
52	P. B. H. May, England	The Oval 1953 to Leeds 1959
52	F. E. Woolley, England	The Oval 1909 to The Oval 1926
51	G. S. Chappell, Australia ...	Perth 1970-71 to The Oval 1977
51	D. I. Gower, England	Bombay 1981-82 to Lord's 1986

† *Indicates complete Test career.*

SUMMARY OF ALL TEST MATCHES

To end of 1987 season in England

		Tests	Won by								Tied	Drawn
			E	A	SA	WI	NZ	I	P	SL		
England	v Australia	262	88	97	–	–	–	–	–	–	–	77
	v South Africa	102	46	–	18	–	–	–	–	–	–	38
	v West Indies	90	21	–	–	35	–	–	–	–	–	34
	v New Zealand	63	30	–	–	–	4	–	–	–	–	29
	v India	75	30	–	–	–	–	11	–	–	–	34
	v Pakistan	44	13	–	–	–	–	–	4	–	–	27
	v Sri Lanka	2	1	–	–	–	–	–	–	0	–	1
Australia	v South Africa	53	–	29	11	–	–	–	–	–	–	13
	v West Indies	62	–	27	–	19	–	–	–	–	1	15
	v New Zealand	21	–	9	–	–	5	–	–	–	–	7
	v India	45	–	20	–	–	–	8	–	–	1	16
	v Pakistan	28	–	11	–	–	–	–	8	–	–	9
	v Sri Lanka	1	–	1	–	–	–	–	–	0	–	0
South Africa	v New Zealand	17	–	–	9	–	2	–	–	–	–	6
West Indies	v New Zealand	24	–	–	–	8	4	–	–	–	–	12
	v India	54	–	–	–	22	–	5	–	–	–	27
	v Pakistan	22	–	–	–	8	–	–	5	–	–	9
New Zealand	v India	25	–	–	–	–	4	10	–	–	–	11
	v Pakistan	27	–	–	–	–	3	–	10	–	–	14
	v Sri Lanka	6	–	–	–	–	4	–	–	0	–	2
India	v Pakistan	40	–	–	–	–	–	4	7	–	–	29
	v Sri Lanka	7	–	–	–	–	–	2	–	1	–	4
Pakistan	v Sri Lanka	9	–	–	–	–	–	–	5	1	–	3
		1,079	229	194	38	92	26	40	39	2	2	417

	Tests	Won	Lost	Drawn	Tied	Toss Won
England	638	229	169	240	–	314
Australia	472	194	139	137	2	237
South Africa	172	38	77	57	–	80
West Indies	252	92	62	97	1	135
New Zealand	183	26	76	81	–	90
India	246	40	84	121	1	121
Pakistan	170	39	40	91	–	89
Sri Lanka	25	2	13	10	–	13

ENGLAND v AUSTRALIA

		Captains				
Season	England	Australia	T	E	A	D
1876-77	James Lillywhite	D. W. Gregory	2	1	1	0
1878-79	Lord Harris	D. W. Gregory	1	0	1	0
1880	Lord Harris	W. L. Murdoch	1	1	0	0
1881-82	A. Shaw	W. L. Murdoch	4	0	2	2
1882	A. N. Hornby	W. L. Murdoch	1	0	1	0

THE ASHES

		Captains					
Season	England	Australia	T	E	A	D	Held by
1882-83	Hon. Ivo Bligh	W. L. Murdoch	4*	2	2	0	E
1884	Lord Harris[1]	W. L. Murdoch	3	1	0	2	E
1884-85	A. Shrewsbury	T. Horan[2]	5	3	2	0	E
1886	A. G. Steel	H. J. H. Scott	3	3	0	0	E

Captains

Season	England	Australia	T	E	A	D	Held by
1886-87	A. Shrewsbury	P. S. McDonnell	2	2	0	0	E
1887-88	W. W. Read	P. S. McDonnell	1	1	0	0	E
1888	W. G. Grace[3]	P. S. McDonnell	3	2	1	0	E
1890†	W. G. Grace	W. L. Murdoch	2	2	0	0	E
1891-92	W. G. Grace	J. McC. Blackham	3	1	2	0	A
1893	W. G. Grace[4]	J. McC. Blackham	3	1	0	2	E
1894-95	A. E. Stoddart	G. Giffen[5]	5	3	2	0	E
1896	W. G. Grace	G. H. S. Trott	3	2	1	0	E
1897-98	A. E. Stoddart[6]	G. H. S. Trott	5	1	4	0	A
1899	A. C. MacLaren[7]	J. Darling	5	0	1	4	A
1901-02	A. C. MacLaren	J. Darling[8]	5	1	4	0	A
1902	A. C. MacLaren	J. Darling	5	1	2	2	A
1903-04	P. F. Warner	M. A. Noble	5	3	2	0	E
1905	Hon. F. S. Jackson	J. Darling	5	2	0	3	E
1907-08	A. O. Jones[9]	M. A. Noble	5	1	4	0	A
1909	A. C. MacLaren	M. A. Noble	5	1	2	2	A
1911-12	J. W. H. T. Douglas	C. Hill	5	4	1	0	E
1912	C. B. Fry	S. E. Gregory	3	1	0	2	E
1920-21	J. W. H. T. Douglas	W. W. Armstrong	5	0	5	0	A
1921	Hon. L. H. Tennyson[10]	W. W. Armstrong	5	0	3	2	A
1924-25	A. E. R. Gilligan	H. L. Collins	5	1	4	0	A
1926	A. W. Carr[11]	H. L. Collins[12]	5	1	0	4	E
1928-29	A. P. F. Chapman[13]	J. Ryder	5	4	1	0	E
1930	A. P. F. Chapman[14]	W. M. Woodfull	5	1	2	2	A
1932-33	D. R. Jardine	W. M. Woodfull	5	4	1	0	E
1934	R. E. S. Wyatt[15]	W. M. Woodfull	5	1	2	2	A
1936-37	G. O. Allen	D. G. Bradman	5	2	3	0	A
1938†	W. R. Hammond	D. G. Bradman	4	1	1	2	A
1946-47	W. R. Hammond[16]	D. G. Bradman	5	0	3	2	A
1948	N. W. D. Yardley	D. G. Bradman	5	0	4	1	A
1950-51	F. R. Brown	A. L. Hassett	5	1	4	0	A
1953	L. Hutton	A. L. Hassett	5	1	0	4	E
1954-55	L. Hutton	I. W. Johnson[17]	5	3	1	1	E
1956	P. B. H. May	I. W. Johnson	5	2	1	2	E
1958-59	P. B. H. May	R. Benaud	5	0	4	1	A
1961	P. B. H. May[18]	R. Benaud[19]	5	1	2	2	A
1962-63	E. R. Dexter	R. Benaud	5	1	1	3	A
1964	E. R. Dexter	R. B. Simpson	5	0	1	4	A
1965-66	M. J. K. Smith	R. B. Simpson[20]	5	1	1	3	A
1968	M. C. Cowdrey[21]	W. M. Lawry[22]	5	1	1	3	A
1970-71†	R. Illingworth	W. M. Lawry[23]	6	2	0	4	E
1972	R. Illingworth	I. M. Chappell	5	2	2	1	E
1974-75	M. H. Denness[24]	I. M. Chappell	6	1	4	1	A
1975	A. W. Greig[25]	I. M. Chappell	4	0	1	3	A
1976-77‡	A. W. Greig	G. S. Chappell	1	0	1	0	—
1977	J. M. Brearley	G. S. Chappell	5	3	0	2	E
1978-79	J. M. Brearley	G. N. Yallop	6	5	1	0	E
1979-80‡	J. M. Brearley	G. S. Chappell	3	0	3	0	—
1980‡	I. T. Botham	G. S. Chappell	1	0	0	1	—
1981	J. M. Brearley[26]	K. J. Hughes	6	3	1	2	E
1982-83	R. G. D. Willis	G. S. Chappell	5	1	2	2	A
1985	D. I. Gower	A. R. Border	6	3	1	2	E
1986-87	M. W. Gatting	A. R. Border	5	2	1	2	E

			T	E	A	D
In Australia			139	51	67	21
In England			123	37	30	56
Totals			262	88	97	77

* *The Ashes were awarded in 1882-83 after a series of three matches which England won 2-1. A fourth unofficial match was played, each innings being played on a different pitch, and this was won by Australia.*

† *The matches at Manchester in 1890 and 1938 and at Melbourne (Third Test) in 1970-71 were abandoned without a ball being bowled and are excluded.*

‡ *The Ashes were not at stake in these series.*

Notes: The following deputised for the official touring captain or were appointed by the home authority for only a minor proportion of the series:

[1]A. N. Hornby (First). [2]W. L. Murdoch (First), H. H. Massie (Third), J. McC. Blackham (Fourth). [3]A. G. Steel (First). [4]A. E. Stoddart (First). [5]J. McC. Blackham (First). [6]A. C. MacLaren (First, Second and Fifth). [7]W. G. Grace (First). [8]H. Trumble (Fourth and Fifth). [9]F. L. Fane (First, Second and Third). [10]J. W. H. T. Douglas (First and Second). [11]A. P. F. Chapman (Fifth). [12]W. Bardsley (Third and Fourth). [13]J. C. White (Fifth). [14]R. E. S. Wyatt (Fifth). [15]C. F. Walters (First). [16]N. W. D. Yardley (Fifth). [17]A. R. Morris (Second). [18]M. C. Cowdrey (First and Second). [19]R. N. Harvey (Second). [20]B. C. Booth (First and Third). [21]T. W. Graveney (Fourth). [22]B. N. Jarman (Fourth). [23]I. M. Chappell (Seventh). [24]J. H. Edrich (Fourth). [25]M. H. Denness (First). [26]I. T. Botham (First and Second).

HIGHEST INNINGS TOTALS

For England in England: 903-7 dec. at The Oval	1938
in Australia: 636 at Sydney	1928-29
For Australia in England: 729-6 dec. at Lord's	1930
in Australia: 659-8 dec. at Sydney	1946-47

LOWEST INNINGS TOTALS

For England in England: 52 at The Oval	1948
in Australia: 45 at Sydney	1886-87
For Australia in England: 36 at Birmingham	1902
in Australia: 42 at Sydney	1887-88

INDIVIDUAL HUNDREDS

For England (186)

132*‡	R. Abel, Sydney 1891-92	128*	G. Boycott, Lord's 1980
120	L. E. G. Ames, Lord's 1934	137	G. Boycott, The Oval 1981
185	R. W. Barber, Sydney ... 1965-66	103*	L. C. Braund, Adelaide ... 1901-02
134	W. Barnes, Adelaide 1884-85	102	L. C. Braund, Sydney 1903-04
129	C. J. Barnett, Adelaide .. 1936-37	121	J. Briggs, Melbourne 1884-85
126	C. J. Barnett, Nottingham . 1938	162	B. C. Broad, Perth 1986-87
132*	K. F. Barrington, Adelaide . 1962-63	116	B. C. Broad, Adelaide ... 1986-87
101	K. F. Barrington, Sydney .. 1962-63	112	B. C. Broad, Melbourne ... 1986-87
256	K. F. Barrington, Manchester 1964	140	J. T. Brown, Melbourne ... 1894-95
		121	A. P. F. Chapman, Lord's . 1930
102	K. F. Barrington, Adelaide 1965-66	102†	D. C. S. Compton, Nottingham 1938
115	K. F. Barrington, Melbourne 1965-66		
		147 ⎱	D. C. S. Compton, Adelaide 1946-47
119*	I. T. Botham, Melbourne . 1979-80	103* ⎰	
149*	I. T. Botham, Leeds 1981	184	D. C. S. Compton, Nottingham 1948
118	I. T. Botham, Manchester . 1981		
138	I. T. Botham, Brisbane .. 1986-87	145*	D. C. S. Compton, Manchester 1948
113	G. Boycott, The Oval 1964		
142*	G. Boycott, Sydney 1970-71	102	M. C. Cowdrey, Melbourne 1954-55
119*	G. Boycott, Adelaide 1970-71	100*	M. C. Cowdrey, Sydney ... 1958-59
107	G. Boycott, Nottingham ... 1977	113	M. C. Cowdrey, Melbourne 1962-63
191	G. Boycott, Leeds 1977		

104	M. C. Cowdrey, Melbourne	1965-66
104	M. C. Cowdrey, Birmingham	1968
188	M. H. Denness, Melbourne	1974-75
180	E. R. Dexter, Birmingham	1961
174	E. R. Dexter, Manchester	1964
158	B. L. D'Oliveira, The Oval	1968
117	B. L. D'Oliveira, Melbourne	1970-71
173†	K. S. Duleepsinhji, Lord's	1930
120†	J. H. Edrich, Lord's	1964
109	J. H. Edrich, Melbourne	1965-66
103	J. H. Edrich, Sydney	1965-66
164	J. H. Edrich, The Oval	1968
115*	J. H. Edrich, Perth	1970-71
130	J. H. Edrich, Adelaide	1970-71
175	J. H. Edrich, Lord's	1975
119	W. J. Edrich, Sydney	1946-47
111	W. J. Edrich, Leeds	1948
146	K. W. R. Fletcher, Melbourne	1974-75
287†	R. E. Foster, Sydney	1903-04
144	C. B. Fry, The Oval	1905
160	M. W. Gatting, Manchester	1985
100*	M. W. Gatting, Birmingham	1985
100	M. W. Gatting, Adelaide	1986-87
196	G. A. Gooch, The Oval	1985
102	D. I. Gower, Perth	1978-79
114	D. I. Gower, Adelaide	1982-83
166	D. I. Gower, Nottingham	1985
215	D. I. Gower, Birmingham	1985
157	D. I. Gower, The Oval	1985
136	D. I. Gower, Perth	1986-87
152†	W. G. Grace, The Oval	1880
170	W. G. Grace, The Oval	1886
111	T. W. Graveney, Sydney	1954-55
110	A. W. Greig, Brisbane	1974-75
119†	G. Gunn, Sydney	1907-08
122*	G. Gunn, Sydney	1907-08
102*	W. Gunn, Manchester	1893
251	W. R. Hammond, Sydney	1928-29
200	W. R. Hammond, Melbourne	1928-29
119* 177	W. R. Hammond, Adelaide	1928-29
113	W. R. Hammond, Leeds	1930
112	W. R. Hammond, Sydney	1932-33
101	W. R. Hammond, Sydney	1932-33
231*	W. R. Hammond, Sydney	1936-37
240	W. R. Hammond, Lord's	1938
169*	J. Hardstaff jun., The Oval	1938
130	T. W. Hayward, Manchester	1899
137	T. W. Hayward, The Oval	1899
114	J. W. Hearne, Melbourne	1911-12
127*	E. H. Hendren, Lord's	1926
169	E. H. Hendren, Brisbane	1928-29
132	E. H. Hendren, Manchester	1934
126*	J. B. Hobbs, Melbourne	1911-12
187	J. B. Hobbs, Adelaide	1911-12
178	J. B. Hobbs, Melbourne	1911-12

107	J. B. Hobbs, Lord's	1912
122	J. B. Hobbs, Melbourne	1920-21
123	J. B. Hobbs, Adelaide	1920-21
115	J. B. Hobbs, Sydney	1924-25
154	J. B. Hobbs, Melbourne	1924-25
119	J. B. Hobbs, Adelaide	1924-25
119	J. B. Hobbs, Lord's	1926
100	J. B. Hobbs, The Oval	1926
142	J. B. Hobbs, Melbourne	1928-29
126	K. L. Hutchings, Melbourne	1907-08
100†	L. Hutton, Nottingham	1938
364	L. Hutton, The Oval	1938
122*	L. Hutton, Sydney	1946-47
156*‡	L. Hutton, Adelaide	1950-51
145	L. Hutton, Lord's	1953
103	Hon. F. S. Jackson, The Oval	1893
118	Hon. F. S. Jackson, The Oval	1899
128	Hon. F. S. Jackson, Manchester	1902
144*	Hon. F. S. Jackson, Leeds	1905
113	Hon. F. S. Jackson, Manchester	1905
104	G. L. Jessop, The Oval	1902
106*	A. P. E. Knott, Adelaide	1974-75
135	A. P. E. Knott, Nottingham	1977
137†	M. Leyland, Melbourne	1928-29
109	M. Leyland, Lord's	1934
153	M. Leyland, Manchester	1934
110	M. Leyland, The Oval	1934
126	M. Leyland, Brisbane	1936-37
111*	M. Leyland, Melbourne	1936-37
187	M. Leyland, The Oval	1938
131	B. W. Luckhurst, Perth	1970-71
109	B. W. Luckhurst, Melbourne	1970-71
120	A. C. MacLaren, Melbourne	1894-95
109	A. C. MacLaren, Sydney	1897-98
124	A. C. MacLaren, Adelaide	1897-98
116	A. C. MacLaren, Sydney	1901-02
140	A. C. MacLaren, Nottingham	1905
117	H. Makepeace, Melbourne	1920-21
104	P. B. H. May, Sydney	1954-55
101	P. B. H. May, Leeds	1956
113	P. B. H. May, Melbourne	1958-59
182*	C. P. Mead, The Oval	1921
102†	Nawab of Pataudi, Sydney	1932-33
216*	E. Paynter, Nottingham	1938
174†	D. W. Randall, Melbourne	1976-77
150	D. W. Randall, Sydney	1978-79
115	D. W. Randall, Perth	1982-83
154*†	K. S. Ranjitsinhji, Manchester	1896
175	K. S. Ranjitsinhji, Sydney	1897-98
117	W. W. Read, The Oval	1884
179	W. Rhodes, Melbourne	1911-12

133	C. J. Richards, Perth	1986-87	115†	H. Sutcliffe, Sydney	1924-25
104	P. E. Richardson, Manchester	1956	176 127	} H. Sutcliffe, Melbourne	1924-25
175†	R. T. Robinson, Leeds	1985	143	H. Sutcliffe, Melbourne	1924-25
148	R. T. Robinson, Birmingham	1985	161	H. Sutcliffe, The Oval	1926
135*	A. C. Russell, Adelaide	1920-21	135	H. Sutcliffe, Melbourne	1928-29
101	A. C. Russell, Manchester	1921	161	H. Sutcliffe, The Oval	1930
102*	A. C. Russell, The Oval	1921	194	H. Sutcliffe, Sydney	1932-33
105	J. Sharp, The Oval	1909	138	J. T. Tyldesley, Birmingham	1902
113	Rev. D. S. Sheppard, Manchester	1956	100	J. T. Tyldesley, Leeds	1905
113	Rev. D. S. Sheppard, Melbourne	1962-63	112*	J. T. Tyldesley, The Oval	1905
105*	A. Shrewsbury, Melbourne	1884-85	149	G. Ulyett, Melbourne	1881-82
164	A. Shrewsbury, Lord's	1886	117	A. Ward, Sydney	1894-95
106	A. Shrewsbury, Lord's	1893	112	C. Washbrook, Melbourne	1946-47
156*	R. T. Simpson, Melbourne	1950-51	143	C. Washbrook, Leeds	1948
135*	A. G. Steel, Sydney	1882-83	109†	W. Watson, Lord's	1953
148	A. G. Steel, Lord's	1884	133*	F. E. Woolley, Sydney	1911-12
134	A. E. Stoddart, Adelaide	1891-92	123	F. E. Woolley, Sydney	1924-25
173	A. E. Stoddart, Melbourne	1894-95	149	R. A. Woolmer, The Oval	1975
112†	R. Subba Row, Birmingham	1961	120	R. A. Woolmer, Lord's	1977
137	R. Subba Row, The Oval	1961	137	R. A. Woolmer, Manchester	1977

† *Signifies hundred on first appearance in England–Australia Tests.*
‡ *Carried his bat.*

Note: In consecutive innings in 1928-29, W. R. Hammond scored 251 at Sydney, 200 and 32 at Melbourne, and 119* and 177 at Adelaide.

For Australia (203)

133*	W. W. Armstrong, Melbourne	1907-08	131	D. G. Bradman, Nottingham	1930
158	W. W. Armstrong, Sydney	1920-21	254	D. G. Bradman, Lord's	1930
121	W. W. Armstrong, Adelaide	1920-21	334	D. G. Bradman, Leeds	1930
			232	D. G. Bradman, The Oval	1930
123*	W. W. Armstrong, Melbourne	1920-21	103*	D. G. Bradman, Melbourne	1932-33
118	C. L. Badcock, Melbourne	1936-37	304	D. G. Bradman, Leeds	1934
165*†	C. Bannerman, Melbourne	1876-77	244	D. G. Bradman, The Oval	1934
136 130	} W. Bardsley, The Oval	1909	270	D. G. Bradman, Melbourne	1936-37
193*‡	W. Bardsley, Lord's	1926	212	D. G. Bradman, Adelaide	1936-37
234	S. G. Barnes, Sydney	1946-47	169	D. G. Bradman, Melbourne	1936-37
141	S. G. Barnes, Lord's	1948			
128	G. J. Bonnor, Sydney	1884-85	144*	D. G. Bradman, Nottingham	1938
103	D. C. Boon, Adelaide	1986-87	102*	D. G. Bradman, Lord's	1938
112	B. C. Booth, Brisbane	1962-63	103	D. G. Bradman, Leeds	1938
103	B. C. Booth, Melbourne	1962-63	187	D. G. Bradman, Brisbane	1946-47
115	A. R. Border, Perth	1979-80	234	D. G. Bradman, Sydney	1946-47
123*	A. R. Border, Manchester	1981	138	D. G. Bradman, Nottingham	1948
106*	A. R. Border, The Oval	1981			
196	A. R. Border, Lord's	1985	173*	D. G. Bradman, Leeds	1948
146*	A. R. Border, Manchester	1985	105	W. A. Brown, Lord's	1934
125	A. R. Border, Perth	1986-87	133	W. A. Brown, Nottingham	1938
100*	A. R. Border, Adelaide	1986-87			
112	D. G. Bradman, Melbourne	1928-29	206*‡	W. A. Brown, Lord's	1938
			181	P. J. Burge, The Oval	1961
123	D. G. Bradman, Melbourne	1928-29	103	P. J. Burge, Sydney	1962-63

160	P. J. Burge, Leeds	1964	117	K. J. Hughes, Lord's	1980
120	P. J. Burge, Melbourne	1965-66	137	K. J. Hughes, Sydney	1982-83
101*†	J. W. Burke, Adelaide	1950-51	140	F. A. Iredale, Adelaide	1894-95
108†	G. S. Chappell, Perth	1970-71	108	F. A. Iredale, Manchester	1896
131	G. S. Chappell, Lord's	1972	164†	A. A. Jackson, Adelaide	1928-29
113	G. S. Chappell, The Oval	1972	184*	D. M. Jones, Sydney	1986-87
144	G. S. Chappell, Sydney	1974-75	147	C. Kelleway, Adelaide	1920-21
102	G. S. Chappell, Melbourne	1974-75	100	A. F. Kippax, Melbourne	1928-29
			130	W. M. Lawry, Lord's	1961
112	G. S. Chappell, Manchester	1977	102	W. M. Lawry, Manchester	1961
			106	W. M. Lawry, Manchester	1964
114	G. S. Chappell, Melbourne	1979-80	166	W. M. Lawry, Brisbane	1965-66
			119	W. M. Lawry, Adelaide	1965-66
117	G. S. Chappell, Perth	1982-83	108	W. M. Lawry, Melbourne	1965-66
115	G. S. Chappell, Adelaide	1982-83	135	W. M. Lawry, The Oval	1968
111	I. M. Chappell, Melbourne	1970-71	100	R. R. Lindwall, Melbourne	1946-47
104	I. M. Chappell, Adelaide	1970-71	134	J. J. Lyons, Sydney	1891-92
118	I. M. Chappell, The Oval	1972	170	C. G. Macartney, Sydney	1920-21
192	I. M. Chappell, The Oval	1975	115	C. G. Macartney, Leeds	1921
104†	H. L. Collins, Sydney	1920-21	133*	C. G. Macartney, Lord's	1926
162	H. L. Collins, Adelaide	1920-21	151	C. G. Macartney, Leeds	1926
114	H. L. Collins, Sydney	1924-25	109	C. G. Macartney, Manchester	1926
307	R. M. Cowper, Melbourne	1965-66			
101	J. Darling, Sydney	1897-98	187*	S. J. McCabe, Sydney	1932-33
178	J. Darling, Adelaide	1897-98	137	S. J. McCabe, Manchester	1934
160	J. Darling, Sydney	1897-98	112	S. J. McCabe, Melbourne	1936-37
104†	R. A. Duff, Melbourne	1901-02	232	S. J. McCabe, Nottingham	1938
146	R. A. Duff, The Oval	1905	104*	C. L. McCool, Melbourne	1946-47
102	J. Dyson, Leeds	1981	127	R. B. McCosker, The Oval	1975
170*	R. Edwards, Nottingham	1972	107	R. B. McCosker, Nottingham	1977
115	R. Edwards, Perth	1974-75	170	C. C. McDonald, Adelaide	1958-59
100	J. H. Fingleton, Brisbane	1936-37			
136	J. H. Fingleton, Melbourne	1936-37	133	C. C. McDonald, Melbourne	1958-59
161	G. Giffen, Sydney	1894-95	147	P. S. McDonnell, Sydney	1881-82
107†	H. Graham, Lord's	1893	103	P. S. McDonnell, The Oval	1884
105	H. Graham, Sydney	1894-95	124	P. S. McDonnell, Adelaide	1884-85
100	J. M. Gregory, Melbourne	1920-21			
201	S. E. Gregory, Sydney	1894-95	112	C. E. McLeod, Melbourne	1897-98
103	S. E. Gregory, Lord's	1896	110†	G. R. Marsh, Brisbane	1986-87
117	S. E. Gregory, The Oval	1899	110*	R. W. Marsh, Melbourne	1976-77
112	S. E. Gregory, Adelaide	1903-04	141*	K. R. Miller, Adelaide	1946-47
116†	R. J. Hartigan, Adelaide	1907-08	145*	K. R. Miller, Sydney	1950-51
112†	R. N. Harvey, Leeds	1948	109	K. R. Miller, Lord's	1953
122	R. N. Harvey, Manchester	1953	155	A. R. Morris, Melbourne	1946-47
162	R. N. Harvey, Brisbane	1954-55	122 ⎫	A. R. Morris, Adelaide	1946-47
167	R. N. Harvey, Melbourne	1958-59	124* ⎭		
114	R. N. Harvey, Birmingham	1961	105	A. R. Morris, Lord's	1948
154	R. N. Harvey, Adelaide	1962-63	182	A. R. Morris, Leeds	1948
128	A. L. Hassett, Brisbane	1946-47	196	A. R. Morris, The Oval	1948
137	A. L. Hassett, Nottingham	1948	206	A. R. Morris, Adelaide	1950-51
115	A. L. Hassett, Nottingham	1953	153	A. R. Morris, Brisbane	1954-55
104	A. L. Hassett, Lord's	1953	153*	W. L. Murdoch, Sydney	1880
112	H. L. Hendry, Sydney	1928-29	211	W. L. Murdoch, The Oval	1884
119	A. M. J. Hilditch, Leeds	1985	133	M. A. Noble, Sydney	1903-04
188	C. Hill, Melbourne	1897-98	117	N. C. O'Neill, The Oval	1961
135	C. Hill, Lord's	1899	100	N. C. O'Neill, Adelaide	1962-63
119	C. Hill, Sheffield	1902	116	C. E. Pellew, Melbourne	1920-21
160	C. Hill, Adelaide	1907-08	104	C. E. Pellew, Adelaide	1920-21
124	T. P. Horan, Melbourne	1881-82			
129	K. J. Hughes, Brisbane	1978-79	110†	W. H. Ponsford, Sydney	1924-25

128	W. H. Ponsford, Melbourne	1924-25	185*	V. T. Trumper, Sydney	1903-04
110	W. H. Ponsford, The Oval	1930	113	V. T. Trumper, Adelaide	1903-04
181	W. H. Ponsford, Leeds	1934	166	V. T. Trumper, Sydney	1907-08
266	W. H. Ponsford, The Oval	1934	113	V. T. Trumper, Sydney	1911-12
143*	V. S. Ransford, Lord's	1909	155†	K. D. Walters, Brisbane	1965-66
171	I. R. Redpath, Perth	1970-71	115	K. D. Walters, Melbourne	1965-66
105	I. R. Redpath, Sydney	1974-75	112	K. D. Walters, Brisbane	1970-71
100	A. J. Richardson, Leeds	1926	103	K. D. Walters, Perth	1974-75
138	V. Y. Richardson, Melbourne	1924-25	103†	D. M. Wellham, The Oval	1981
146	G. M. Ritchie, Nottingham	1985	162†	K. C. Wessels, Brisbane	1982-83
201*	J. Ryder, Adelaide	1924-25	100	G. M. Wood, Melbourne	1978-79
112	J. Ryder, Melbourne	1928-29	112	G. M. Wood, Lord's	1980
102	H. J. H. Scott, The Oval	1884	172	G. M. Wood, Nottingham	1985
311	R. B. Simpson, Manchester	1964	141	W. M. Woodfull, Leeds	1926
225	R. B. Simpson, Adelaide	1965-66	117	W. M. Woodfull, Manchester	1926
207	K. R. Stackpole, Brisbane	1970-71	111	W. M. Woodfull, Sydney	1928-29
136	K. R. Stackpole, Adelaide	1970-71	107	W. M. Woodfull, Melbourne	1928-29
114	K. R. Stackpole, Nottingham	1972	102	W. M. Woodfull, Melbourne	1928-29
108	J. M. Taylor, Sydney	1924-25	155	W. M. Woodfull, Lord's	1930
143	G. H. S. Trott, Lord's	1896	102†	G. N. Yallop, Brisbane	1978-79
135*	V. T. Trumper, Lord's	1899	121	G. N. Yallop, Sydney	1978-79
104	V. T. Trumper, Manchester	1902	114	G. N. Yallop, Manchester	1981

† *Signifies hundred on first appearance in England–Australia Tests.*

‡ *Carried his bat.*

Notes: D. G. Bradman's scores in 1930 were 8 and 131 at Nottingham, 254 and 1 at Lord's, 334 at Leeds, 14 at Manchester, and 232 at The Oval.

D. G. Bradman scored a hundred in eight successive Tests against England in which he batted – three in 1936-37, three in 1938 and two in 1946-47. He was injured and unable to bat at The Oval in 1938.

W. H. Ponsford and K. D. Walters each hit hundreds in their first two Tests.

C. Bannerman and H. Graham each scored their maiden hundred in first-class cricket in their first Test.

No right-handed batsman has obtained two hundreds for Australia in a Test match against England, and no left-handed batsman for England against Australia.

H. Sutcliffe, in his first two games for England, scored 59 and 115 at Sydney and 176 and 127 at Melbourne in 1924-25. In the latter match, which lasted into the seventh day, he was on the field throughout except for 86 minutes, namely 27 hours and 52 minutes.

C. Hill made 98 and 97 at Adelaide in 1901-02, and F. E. Woolley 95 and 93 at Lord's in 1921.

H. Sutcliffe in 1924-25, C. G. Macartney in 1926 and A. R. Morris in 1946-47 made three hundreds in consecutive innings.

J. B. Hobbs and H. Sutcliffe shared eleven first-wicket three-figure partnerships.

L. Hutton and C. Washbrook twice made three-figure stands in each innings, at Adelaide in 1946-47 and at Leeds in 1948.

H. Sutcliffe, during his highest score of 194, v Australia in 1932-33, took part in three stands each exceeding 100, viz. 112 with R. E. S. Wyatt for the first wicket, 188 with W. R. Hammond for the second wicket, and 123 with the Nawab of Pataudi for the third wicket. In 1903-04 R. E. Foster, in his historic innings of 287, added 192 for the fifth wicket with L. C. Braund, 115 for the ninth with A. E. Relf, and 130 for the tenth with W. Rhodes.

When L. Hutton scored 364 at The Oval in 1938 he added 382 for the second wicket with M. Leyland, 135 for the third wicket with W. R. Hammond and 215 for the sixth wicket with J. Hardstaff jun.

D. C. S. Compton and A. R. Morris at Adelaide in 1946-47 provide the only instance of a player on each side hitting two separate hundreds in a Test match.

G. S. and I. M. Chappell at The Oval in 1972 provide the first instance in Test matches of brothers each scoring hundreds in the same innings.

RECORD PARTNERSHIPS FOR EACH WICKET

For England

323 for 1st	J. B. Hobbs and W. Rhodes at Melbourne	....	1911-12
382 for 2nd†	L. Hutton and M. Leyland at The Oval	....	1938
262 for 3rd	W. R. Hammond and D. R. Jardine at Adelaide	.....	1928-29
222 for 4th	W. R. Hammond and E. Paynter at Lord's	....	1938
206 for 5th	E. Paynter and D. C. S. Compton at Nottingham	...	1938
215 for 6th	{ L. Hutton and J. Hardstaff jun. at The Oval	.....	1938
	{ G. Boycott and A. P. E. Knott at Nottingham	.....	1977
143 for 7th	F. E. Woolley and J. Vine at Sydney	....	1911-12
124 for 8th	E. H. Hendren and H. Larwood at Brisbane	....	1928-29
151 for 9th	W. H. Scotton and W. W. Read at The Oval	......	1884
130 for 10th†	R. E. Foster and W. Rhodes at Sydney	....	1903-04

For Australia

244 for 1st	R. B. Simpson and W. M. Lawry at Adelaide	......	1965-66
451 for 2nd†	W. H. Ponsford and D. G. Bradman at The Oval	....	1934
276 for 3rd	D. G. Bradman and A. L. Hassett at Brisbane	.....	1946-47
388 for 4th†	W. H. Ponsford and D. G. Bradman at Leeds	......	1934
405 for 5th†‡	S. G. Barnes and D. G. Bradman at Sydney	....	1946-47
346 for 6th†	J. H. Fingleton and D. G. Bradman at Melbourne	..	1936-37
165 for 7th	C. Hill and H. Trumble at Melbourne	....	1897-98
243 for 8th	R. J. Hartigan and C. Hill at Adelaide	....	1907-08
154 for 9th†	S. E. Gregory and J. McC. Blackham at Sydney	....	1894-95
127 for 10th†	J. M. Taylor and A. A. Mailey at Sydney	....	1924-25

  † *Denotes record partnership against all countries.*
  ‡ *Record fifth-wicket partnership in first-class cricket.*

MOST RUNS IN A SERIES

England in England	....	732 (average 81.33)	D. I. Gower	1985
England in Australia	....	905 (average 113.12)	W. R. Hammond	1928-29
Australia in England	....	974 (average 139.14)	D. G. Bradman	1930
Australia in Australia	....	810 (average 90.00)	D. G. Bradman	1936-37

TEN WICKETS OR MORE IN A MATCH

For England (37)

13-163 (6-42, 7-121)	S. F. Barnes, Melbourne	1901-02
14-102 (7-28, 7-74)	W. Bates, Melbourne	1882-83
10-105 (5-46, 5-59)	A. V. Bedser, Melbourne	1950-51
14-99 (7-55, 7-44)	A. V. Bedser, Nottingham	1953
11-102 (6-44, 5-58)	C. Blythe, Birmingham	1909
11-176 (6-78, 5-98)	I. T. Botham, Perth	1979-80
10-253 (6-125, 4-128)	I. T. Botham, The Oval	1981
11-74 (5-29, 6-45)	J. Briggs, Lord's	1886
12-136 (6-49, 6-87)	J. Briggs, Adelaide	1891-92
10-148 (5-34, 5-114)	J. Briggs, The Oval	1893
10-104 (6-77, 4-27)†	R. M. Ellison, Birmingham	1985
10-179 (5-102, 5-77)†	K. Farnes, Nottingham	1934
10-60 (6-41, 4-19)	J. T. Hearne, The Oval	1896
11-113 (5-58, 6-55)	J. C. Laker, Leeds	1956
19-90 (9-37, 10-53)	J. C. Laker, Manchester	1956
10-124 (5-96, 5-28)	H. Larwood, Sydney	1932-33
11-76 (6-48, 5-28)	W. H. Lockwood, Manchester	1902
12-104 (7-36, 5-68)	G. A. Lohmann, The Oval	1886
10-87 (8-35, 2-52)	G. A. Lohmann, Sydney	1886-87

10-142 (8-58, 2-84)	G. A. Lohmann, Sydney	1891-92
12-102 (6-50, 6-52)†	F. Martin, The Oval	1890
10-58 (5-18, 5-40)	R. Peel, Sydney	1887-88
11-68 (7-31, 4-37)	R. Peel, Manchester	1888
15-124 (7-56, 8-68)	W. Rhodes, Melbourne	1903-04
10-156 (5-49, 5-107)†	T. Richardson, Manchester	1893
11-173 (6-39, 5-134)	T. Richardson, Lord's	1896
13-244 (7-168, 6-76)	T. Richardson, Manchester	1896
10-204 (8-94, 2-110)	T. Richardson, Sydney	1897-98
11-228 (6-130, 5-98)†	M. W. Tate, Sydney	1924-25
11-88 (5-58, 6-30)	F. S. Trueman, Leeds	1961
10-130 (4-45, 6-85)	F. H. Tyson, Sydney	1954-55
10-82 (4-37, 6-45)	D. L. Underwood, Leeds	1972
11-215 (7-113, 4-102)	D. L. Underwood, Adelaide	1974-75
15-104 (7-61, 8-43)	H. Verity, Lord's	1934
10-57 (6-41, 4-16)	W. Voce, Brisbane	1936-37
13-256 (5-130, 8-126)	J. C. White, Adelaide	1928-29
10-49 (5-29, 5-20)	F. E. Woolley, The Oval	1912

For Australia (35)

10-239 (4-129, 6-110)	L. O'B. Fleetwood-Smith, Adelaide	1936-37
10-160 (4-88, 6-72)	G. Giffen, Sydney	1891-92
11-82 (5-45, 6-37)†	C. V. Grimmett, Sydney	1924-25
10-201 (5-107, 5-94)	C. V. Grimmett, Nottingham	1930
10-122 (5-65, 5-57)	R. M. Hogg, Perth	1978-79
10-66 (5-30, 5-36)	R. M. Hogg, Melbourne	1978-79
12-175 (5-85, 7-90)†	H. V. Hordern, Sydney	1911-12
10-161 (5-95, 5-66)	H. V. Hordern, Sydney	1911-12
10-164 (7-88, 3-76)	E. Jones, Lord's	1899
11-134 (6-47, 5-87)	G. F. Lawson, Brisbane	1982-83
10-181 (5-58, 5-123)	D. K. Lillee, The Oval	1972
11-165 (6-26, 5-139)	D. K. Lillee, Melbourne	1976-77
11-138 (6-60, 5-78)	D. K. Lillee, Melbourne	1979-80
11-159 (7-89, 4-70)	D. K. Lillee, The Oval	1981
11-85 (7-58, 4-27)	C. G. Macartney, Leeds	1909
10-302 (5-160, 5-142)	A. A. Mailey, Adelaide	1920-21
13-236 (4-115, 9-121)	A. A. Mailey, Melbourne	1920-21
16-137 (8-84, 8-53)†	R. A. L. Massie, Lord's	1972
10-152 (5-72, 5-80)	K. R. Miller, Lord's	1956
13-77 (7-17, 6-60)	M. A. Noble, Melbourne	1901-02
11-103 (5-51, 6-52)	M. A. Noble, Sheffield	1902
10-129 (5-63, 5-66)	W. J. O'Reilly, Melbourne	1932-33
11-129 (4-75, 7-54)	W. J. O'Reilly, Nottingham	1934
10-122 (5-66, 5-56)	W. J. O'Reilly, Leeds	1938
11-165 (7-68, 4-97)	G. E. Palmer, Sydney	1881-82
10-126 (7-65, 3-61)	G. E. Palmer, Melbourne	1882-83
13-110 (6-48, 7-62)	F. R. Spofforth, Melbourne	1878-79
14-90 (7-46, 7-44)	F. R. Spofforth, The Oval	1882
11-117 (4-73, 7-44)	F. R. Spofforth, Sydney	1882-83
10-144 (4-54, 6-90)	F. R. Spofforth, Sydney	1884-85
12-89 (6-59, 6-30)	H. Trumble, The Oval	1896
10-128 (4-75, 6-53)	H. Trumble, Manchester	1902
12-173 (8-65, 4-108)	H. Trumble, The Oval	1902
12-87 (5-44, 7-43)	C. T. B. Turner, Sydney	1887-88
10-63 (5-27, 5-36)	C. T. B. Turner, Lord's	1888

† *Signifies ten wickets or more on first appearance in England–Australia Tests.*

Note: J. Briggs, J. C. Laker, T. Richardson in 1896, R. M. Hogg, A. A. Mailey, H. Trumble and C. T. B. Turner took ten wickets or more in successive Tests. J. Briggs was omitted, however, from the England team for the first Test match in 1893.

MOST WICKETS IN A SERIES

England in England	46 (average 9.60)	J. C. Laker	1956
England in Australia	38 (average 23.18)	M. W. Tate	1924-25
Australia in England	42 (average 21.26)	T. M. Alderman (6 Tests)	1981
Australia in Australia	41 (average 12.85)	R. M. Hogg (6 Tests)	1978-79

WICKET-KEEPING – MOST DISMISSALS

	M	Ct	St	Total
†R. W. Marsh (Australia)	42	141	7	148
A. P. E. Knott (England)	34	97	8	105
†W. A. Oldfield (Australia)	38	59	31	90
A. A. Lilley (England)	32	65	19	84
A. T. W. Grout (Australia)	22	69	7	76
T. G. Evans (England)	31	63	12	75

† *The number of catches by R. W. Marsh (141) and stumpings by W. A. Oldfield (31) are respective records in England–Australia Tests.*

SCORERS OF OVER 2,000 RUNS

	T	I	NO	R	HI	Avge
D. G. Bradman	37	63	7	5,028	334	89.78
J. B. Hobbs	41	71	4	3,636	187	54.26
G. Boycott	38	71	9	2,945	191	47.50
W. R. Hammond	31	58	3	2,852	251	51.85
H. Sutcliffe	27	46	5	2,741	194	66.85
C. Hill	41	76	1	2,660	188	35.46
J. H. Edrich	32	57	3	2,644	175	48.96
G. S. Chappell	35	65	8	2,619	144	45.94
D. I. Gower	31	56	3	2,479	215	46.77
M. C. Cowdrey	43	75	4	2,433	113	34.26
L. Hutton	27	49	6	2,428	364	56.46
R. N. Harvey	37	68	5	2,416	167	38.34
A. R. Border	29	55	13	2,342	196	55.76
V. T. Trumper	40	74	5	2,263	185*	32.79
W. M. Lawry	29	51	5	2,233	166	48.54
S. E. Gregory	52	92	7	2,193	201	25.80
W. W. Armstrong	42	71	9	2,172	158	35.03
I. M. Chappell	30	56	4	2,138	192	41.11
K. F. Barrington	23	39	6	2,111	256	63.96
A. R. Morris	24	43	2	2,080	206	50.73

BOWLERS WITH 100 WICKETS

	T	Balls	R	W	5 W/i	Avge
D. K. Lillee	29	8,516	3,507	167	11	21.00
I. T. Botham	33	7,999	3,852	145	9	26.56
H. Trumble	31	7,895	2,945	141	9	20.88
R. G. D. Willis	35	7,294	3,346	128	7	26.14
M. A. Noble	39	6,845	2,860	115	9	24.86
R. R. Lindwall	29	6,728	2,559	114	6	22.44
W. Rhodes	41	5,791	2,616	109	6	24.00
S. F. Barnes	20	5,749	2,288	106	12	21.58
C. V. Grimmett	22	9,224	3,439	106	11	32.44
D. L. Underwood	29	8,000	2,770	105	4	26.38
A. V. Bedser	21	7,065	2,859	104	7	27.49
G. Giffen	31	6,325	2,791	103	7	27.09
W. J. O'Reilly	19	7,864	2,587	102	8	25.36
R. Peel	20	5,216	1,715	102	6	16.81
C. T. B. Turner	17	5,195	1,670	101	11	16.53
J. R. Thomson	21	4,951	2,418	100	5	24.18

ENGLAND v SOUTH AFRICA

Captains

Season	England	South Africa	T	E	SA	D
1888-89	C. A. Smith[1]	O. R. Dunell[2]	2	2	0	0
1891-92	W. W. Read	W. H. Milton	1	1	0	0
1895-96	Lord Hawke[3]	E. A. Halliwell[4]	3	3	0	0
1898-99	Lord Hawke	M. Bisset	2	2	0	0
1905-06	P. F. Warner	P. W. Sherwell	5	1	4	0
1907	R. E. Foster	P. W. Sherwell	3	1	0	2
1909-10	H. D. G. Leveson Gower[5]	S. J. Snooke	5	2	3	0
1912	C. B. Fry	F. Mitchell[6]	3	3	0	0
1913-14	J. W. H. T. Douglas	H. W. Taylor	5	4	0	1
1922-23	F. T. Mann	H. W. Taylor	5	2	1	2
1924	A. E. R. Gilligan[7]	H. W. Taylor	5	3	0	2
1927-28	R. T. Stanyforth[8]	H. G. Deane	5	2	2	1
1929	J. C. White[9]	H. G. Deane	5	2	0	3
1930-31	A. P. F. Chapman	H. G. Deane[10]	5	0	1	4
1935	R. E. S. Wyatt	H. F. Wade	5	0	1	4
1938-39	W. R. Hammond	A. Melville	5	1	0	4
1947	N. W. D. Yardley	A. Melville	5	3	0	2
1948-49	F. G. Mann	A. D. Nourse	5	2	0	3
1951	F. R. Brown	A. D. Nourse	5	3	1	1
1955	P. B. H. May	J. E. Cheetham[11]	5	3	2	0
1956-57	P. B. H. May	C. B. van Ryneveld[12]	5	2	2	1
1960	M. C. Cowdrey	D. J. McGlew	5	3	0	2
1964-65	M. J. K. Smith	T. L. Goddard	5	1	0	4
1965	M. J. K. Smith	P. L. van der Merwe	3	0	1	2

			T	E	SA	D
In South Africa			58	25	13	20
In England			44	21	5	18
Totals			102	46	18	38

Notes: The following deputised for the official touring captain or were appointed by the home authority for only a minor proportion of the series:

[1]M. P. Bowden (Second). [2]W. H. Milton (Second). [3]Sir T. C. O'Brien (First). [4]A. R. Richards (Third). [5]F. L. Fane (Fourth and Fifth). [6]L. J. Tancred (Second and Third). [7]J. W. H. T. Douglas (Fourth). [8]G. T. S. Stevens (Fifth). [9]A. W. Carr (Fourth and Fifth). [10]E. P. Nupen (First), H. B. Cameron (Fourth and Fifth). [11]D. J. McGlew (Third and Fourth). [12]D. J. McGlew (Second).

HIGHEST INNINGS TOTALS

For England in England: 554-8 dec. at Lord's	1947
in South Africa: 654-5 at Durban	1938-39
For South Africa in England: 538 at Leeds	1951
in South Africa: 530 at Durban	1938-39

LOWEST INNINGS TOTALS

For England in England: 76 at Leeds	1907
in South Africa: 92 at Cape Town	1898-99
For South Africa in England: 30 at Birmingham	1924
in South Africa: 30 at Port Elizabeth	1895-96

INDIVIDUAL HUNDREDS

For England (87)

120	R. Abel, Cape Town	1888-89
148*	L. E. G. Ames, The Oval	1935
115	L. E. G. Ames, Cape Town	1938-39
148*	K. F. Barrington, Durban	1964-65
121	K. F. Barrington, Johannesburg	1964-65
117	G. Boycott, Port Elizabeth	1964-65
104†	L. C. Braund, Lord's	1907
208	D. C. S. Compton, Lord's	1947
163‡	D. C. S. Compton, Nottingham	1947
115	D. C. S. Compton, Manchester	1947
113	D. C. S. Compton, The Oval	1947
114	D. C. S. Compton, Johannesburg	1948-49
112	D. C. S. Compton, Nottingham	1951
158	D. C. S. Compton, Manchester	1955
101	M. C. Cowdrey, Cape Town	1956-57
155	M. C. Cowdrey, The Oval	1960
105	M. C. Cowdrey, Nottingham	1965
104	D. Denton, Johannesburg	1909-10
172	E. R. Dexter, Johannesburg	1964-65
119†	J. W. H. T. Douglas, Durban	1913-14
219	W. J. Edrich, Durban	1938-39
191	W. J. Edrich, Manchester	1947
189	W. J. Edrich, Lord's	1947
143	F. L. Fane, Johannesburg	1905-06
129	C. B. Fry, The Oval	1907
106†	P. A. Gibb, Johannesburg	1938-39
120	P. A. Gibb, Durban	1938-39
138*	W. R. Hammond, Birmingham	1929
101*	W. R. Hammond, The Oval	1929
136*	W. R. Hammond, Durban	1930-31
181	W. R. Hammond, Cape Town	1938-39
120	W. R. Hammond, Durban	1938-39
140	W. R. Hammond, Durban	1938-39
122	T. W. Hayward, Johannesburg	1895-96
132	E. H. Hendren, Leeds	1924
142	E. H. Hendren, The Oval	1924
124	A. J. L. Hill, Cape Town	1895-96
187	J. B. Hobbs, Cape Town	1909-10
211	J. B. Hobbs, Lord's	1924
100	L. Hutton, Leeds	1947
158	L. Hutton, Johannesburg	1948-49
123	L. Hutton, Johannesburg	1948-49

100	L. Hutton, Leeds	1951
110*	D. J. Insole, Durban	1956-57
102	M. Leyland, Lord's	1929
161	M. Leyland, The Oval	1935
136*	F. G. Mann, Port Elizabeth	1948-49
138†	P. B. H. May, Leeds	1951
112	P. B. H. May, Lord's	1955
117	P. B. H. May, Manchester	1955
102	C. P. Mead, Johannesburg	1913-14
117	C. P. Mead, Port Elizabeth	1913-14
181	C. P. Mead, Durban	1922-23
122*	P. H. Parfitt, Johannesburg	1964-65
108*	J. M. Parks, Durban	1964-65
117† ⎫	E. Paynter, Johannesburg	1938-39
100 ⎭		
243	E. Paynter, Durban	1938-39
175	G. Pullar, The Oval	1960
152	W. Rhodes, Johannesburg	1913-14
117†	P. E. Richardson, Johannesburg	1956-57
108	R. W. V. Robins, Manchester	1935
140 ⎫	A. C. Russell, Durban	1922-23
111 ⎭		
137	R. T. Simpson, Nottingham	1951
121	M. J. K. Smith, Cape Town	1964-65
119†	R. H. Spooner, Lord's	1912
122	H. Sutcliffe, Lord's	1924
102	H. Sutcliffe, Johannesburg	1927-28
114	H. Sutcliffe, Birmingham	1929
100	H. Sutcliffe, Lord's	1929
104 ⎫	H. Sutcliffe, The Oval	1929
109* ⎭		
100*	M. W. Tate, Lord's	1929
122†	E. Tyldesley, Johannesburg	1927-28
100	E. Tyldesley, Durban	1927-28
112	J. T. Tyldesley, Cape Town	1898-99
112	B. H. Valentine, Cape Town	1938-39
132*†‡	P. F. Warner, Johannesburg	1898-99
195	C. Washbrook, Johannesburg	1948-49
111	A. J. Watkins, Johannesburg	1948-49
134*	H. Wood, Cape Town	1891-92
115*	F. E. Woolley, Johannesburg	1922-23
134*	F. E. Woolley, Lord's	1924
154	F. E. Woolley, Manchester	1929
113	R. E. S. Wyatt, Manchester	1929
149	R. E. S. Wyatt, Nottingham	1935

For South Africa (58)

138	E. J. Barlow, Cape Town	1964-65
144*	K. C. Bland, Johannesburg	1964-65

127	K. C. Bland, The Oval	1965
120	R. H. Catterall, Birmingham	1924

120	R. H. Catterall, Lord's	1924		112	A. D. Nourse, Cape Town	1948-49
119	R. H. Catterall, Durban	1927-28		208	A. D. Nourse, Nottingham	1951
117	E. L. Dalton, The Oval	1935		129	H. G. Owen-Smith, Leeds	1929
102	E. L. Dalton, Johannesburg	1938-39		154	A. J. Pithey, Cape Town	1964-65
116*	W. R. Endean, Leeds	1955		137	R. G. Pollock, Port Elizabeth	1964-65
123	G. A. Faulkner, Johannesburg	1909-10		125	R. G. Pollock, Nottingham	1965
112	T. L. Goddard, Johannesburg	1964-65		156*	E. A. B. Rowan, Johannesburg	1948-49
102	C. M. H. Hathorn, Johannesburg	1905-06		236	E. A. B. Rowan, Leeds	1951
				115	P. W. Sherwell, Lord's	1907
104*	D. J. McGlew, Manchester	1955		141	I. J. Siedle, Cape Town	1930-31
133	D. J. McGlew, Leeds	1955		106	J. H. Sinclair, Cape Town	1898-99
142	R. A. McLean, Lord's	1955		109	H. W. Taylor, Durban	1913-14
100	R. A. McLean, Durban	1956-57		176	H. W. Taylor, Johannesburg	1922-23
109	R. A. McLean, Manchester	1960				
103	A. Melville, Durban	1938-39		101	H. W. Taylor, Johannesburg	1922-23
189	A. Melville, Nottingham	1947		102	H. W. Taylor, Durban	1922-23
104*				101	H. W. Taylor, Johannesburg	1927-28
117	A. Melville, Lord's	1947		121	H. W. Taylor, The Oval	1929
123	B. Mitchell, Cape Town	1930-31		117	H. W. Taylor, Cape Town	1930-31
164*	B. Mitchell, Lord's	1935		125	P. G. V. van der Bijl, Durban	1938-39
128	B. Mitchell, The Oval	1935				
109	B. Mitchell, Durban	1938-39		124	K. G. Viljoen, Manchester	1935
120	B. Mitchell, The Oval	1947		125	W. W. Wade, Port Elizabeth	1948-49
189*						
120	B. Mitchell, Cape Town	1948-49		113	J. H. B. Waite, Manchester	1955
120	A. D. Nourse, Cape Town	1938-39		147	G. C. White, Johannesburg	1905-06
103	A. D. Nourse, Durban	1938-39		118	G. C. White, Durban	1909-10
149	A. D. Nourse, Nottingham	1947		108	P. L. Winslow, Manchester	1955
115	A. D. Nourse, Manchester	1947				
129*	A. D. Nourse, Johannesburg	1948-49				

† *Signifies hundred on first appearance in England–South Africa Tests.*

‡ *P. F. Warner carried his bat through the second innings.*

Notes: The highest score by a South African batsman on début is 93* by A. W. Nourse at Johannesburg in 1905-06.

P. N. F. Mansell made 90 at Leeds in 1951, the best on début in England.

A. Melville's four hundreds were made in successive Test innings.

H. Wood scored the only hundred of his career in a Test match.

RECORD PARTNERSHIP FOR EACH WICKET

For England

359 for 1st†	L. Hutton and C. Washbrook at Johannesburg	1948-49
280 for 2nd	P. A. Gibb and W. J. Edrich at Durban	1938-39
370 for 3rd†	W. J. Edrich and D. C. S. Compton at Lord's	1947
197 for 4th	W. R. Hammond and L. E. G. Ames at Cape Town	1938-39
237 for 5th	D. C. S. Compton and N. W. D. Yardley at Nottingham	1947
206* for 6th	K. F. Barrington and J. M. Parks at Durban	1964-65
115 for 7th	M. C. Bird and J. W. H. T. Douglas at Durban	1913-14
154 for 8th	C. W. Wright and H. R. Bromley-Davenport at Johannesburg	1895-96
71 for 9th	H. Wood and J. T. Hearne at Cape Town	1891-92
92 for 10th	A. C. Russell and A. E. R. Gilligan at Durban	1922-23

For South Africa

260 for 1st†	I. J. Siedle and B. Mitchell at Cape Town	1930-31
198 for 2nd†	E. A. B. Rowan and C. B. van Ryneveld at Leeds	1951
319 for 3rd	A. Melville and A. D. Nourse at Nottingham	1947

214 for 4th†	H. W. Taylor and H. G. Deane at The Oval	1929
157 for 5th†	A. J. Pithey and J. H. B. Waite at Johannesburg	1964-65
171 for 6th	J. H. B. Waite and P. L. Winslow at Manchester	1955
123 for 7th	H. G. Deane and E. P. Nupen at Durban	1927-28
109* for 8th	B. Mitchell and L. Tuckett at The Oval	1947
137 for 9th†	E. L. Dalton and A. B. C. Langton at The Oval	1935
103 for 10th†	H. G. Owen-Smith and A. J. Bell at Leeds	1929

    † *Denotes record partnership against all countries.*

MOST RUNS IN A SERIES

England in England	753 (average 94.12)	D. C. S. Compton .	1947
England in South Africa	653 (average 81.62)	E. Paynter	1938-39
South Africa in England	621 (average 69.00)	A. D. Nourse	1947
South Africa in South Africa .	582 (average 64.66)	H. W. Taylor	1922-23

TEN WICKETS OR MORE IN A MATCH

For England (23)

11-110 (5-25, 6-85)†	S. F. Barnes, Lord's	1912
10-115 (6-52, 4-63)	S. F. Barnes, Leeds	1912
13-57 (5-28, 8-29)	S. F. Barnes, The Oval	1912
10-105 (5-57, 5-48)	S. F. Barnes, Durban	1913-14
17-159 (8-56, 9-103)	S. F. Barnes, Johannesburg	1913-14
14-144 (7-56, 7-88)	S. F. Barnes, Durban	1913-14
12-112 (7-58, 5-54)	A. V. Bedser, Manchester	1951
11-118 (6-68, 5-50)	C. Blythe, Cape Town	1905-06
15-99 (8-59, 7-40)	C. Blythe, Leeds	1907
10-104 (7-46, 3-58)	C. Blythe, Cape Town	1909-10
15-28 (7-17, 8-11)	J. Briggs, Cape Town	1888-89
13-91 (6-54, 7-37)†	J. J. Ferris, Cape Town	1891-92
10-207 (7-115, 3-92)	A. P. Freeman, Leeds	1929
12-171 (7-71, 5-100)	A. P. Freeman, Manchester	1929
12-130 (7-70, 5-60)	G. Geary, Johannesburg	1927-28
11-90 (6-7, 5-83)	A. E. R. Gilligan, Birmingham	1924
10-119 (4-64, 6-55)	J. C. Laker, The Oval	1951
15-45 (7-38, 8-7)†	G. A. Lohmann, Port Elizabeth	1895-96
12-71 (9-28, 3-43)	G. A. Lohmann, Johannesburg	1895-96
11-97 (6-63, 5-34)	J. B. Statham, Lord's	1960
12-101 (7-52, 5-49)	R. Tattersall, Lord's	1951
12-89 (5-53, 7-36)	J. H. Wardle, Cape Town	1956-57
10-175 (5-95, 5-80)	D. V. P. Wright, Lord's	1947

For South Africa (6)

11-112 (4-49, 7-63)†	A. E. Hall, Cape Town	1922-23
11-150 (5-63, 6-87)	E. P. Nupen, Johannesburg	1930-31
10-87 (5-53, 5-34)	P. M. Pollock, Nottingham	1965
12-127 (4-57, 8-70)	S. J. Snooke, Johannesburg	1905-06
13-192 (4-79, 9-113)	H. J. Tayfield, Johannesburg	1956-57
12-181 (5-87, 7-94)	A. E. E. Vogler, Johannesburg	1909-10

    † *Signifies ten wickets or more on first appearance in England–South Africa Tests.*

Note: S. F. Barnes took ten wickets or more in his first five Tests v South Africa and in six of his seven Tests v South Africa. A. P. Freeman and G. A. Lohmann took ten wickets or more in successive matches.

MOST WICKETS IN A SERIES

England in England	34 (average 8.29)	S. F. Barnes	1912
England in South Africa	49 (average 10.93)	S. F. Barnes	1913-14
South Africa in England	26 (average 21.84)	H. J. Tayfield	1955
South Africa in England	26 (average 22.57)	N. A. T. Adcock ..	1960
South Africa in South Africa .	37 (average 17.18)	H. J. Tayfield	1956-57

ENGLAND v WEST INDIES

	Captains					
Season	*England*	*West Indies*	*T*	*E*	*WI*	*D*
1928	A. P. F. Chapman	R. K. Nunes	3	3	0	0
1929-30	Hon. F. S. G.					
	Calthorpe	E. L. G. Hoad[1]	4	1	1	2
1933	D. R. Jardine[2]	G. C. Grant	3	2	0	1
1934-35	R. E. S. Wyatt	G. C. Grant	4	1	2	1
1939	W. R. Hammond	R. S. Grant	3	1	0	2
1947-48	G. O. Allen[3]	J. D. C. Goddard[4]	4	0	2	2
1950	N. W. D. Yardley[5]	J. D. C. Goddard	4	1	3	0
1953-54	L. Hutton	J. B. Stollmeyer	5	2	2	1
1957	P. B. H. May	J. D. C. Goddard	5	3	0	2
1959-60	P. B. H. May[6]	F. C. M. Alexander	5	1	0	4

THE WISDEN TROPHY

	Captains						
Season	*England*	*West Indies*	*T*	*E*	*WI*	*D*	*Held by*
1963	E. R. Dexter	F. M. M. Worrell	5	1	3	1	WI
1966	M. C. Cowdrey[7]	G. S. Sobers	5	1	3	1	WI
1967-68	M. C. Cowdrey	G. S. Sobers	5	1	0	4	E
1969	R. Illingworth	G. S. Sobers	3	2	0	1	E
1973	R. Illingworth	R. B. Kanhai	3	0	2	1	WI
1973-74	M. H. Denness	R. B. Kanhai	5	1	1	3	WI
1976	A. W. Greig	C. H. Lloyd	5	0	3	2	WI
1980	I. T. Botham	C. H. Lloyd[8]	5	0	1	4	WI
1980-81†	I. T. Botham	C. H. Lloyd	4	0	2	2	WI
1984	D. I. Gower	C. H. Lloyd	5	0	5	0	WI
1985-86	D. I. Gower	I. V. A. Richards	5	0	5	0	WI
	In England		49	14	20	15	
	In West Indies		41	7	15	19	
	Totals		90	21	35	34	

† *The Test match at Georgetown, scheduled as the second of the series, was cancelled owing to political pressure.*

Notes: The following deputised for the official touring captain or were appointed by the home authority for only a minor proportion of the series:
[1]N. Betancourt (Second), M. P. Fernandes (Third), R. K. Nunes (Fourth). [2]R. E. S. Wyatt (Third). [3]K. Cranston (First). [4]G. A. Headley (First), G. E. Gomez (Second). [5]F. R. Brown (Fourth). [6]M. C. Cowdrey (Fourth and Fifth). [7]M. J. K. Smith (First), D. B. Close (Fifth). [8]I. V. A. Richards (Fifth).

HIGHEST INNINGS TOTALS

For England in England: 619-6 dec. at Nottingham   1957
　　　　　　in West Indies: 849 at Kingston   1929-30
For West Indies in England: 687-8 dec. at The Oval   1976
　　　　　　in West Indies: 681-8 dec. at Port-of-Spain   1953-54

LOWEST INNINGS TOTALS

For England in England: 71 at Manchester   1976
　　　　　　in West Indies: 103 at Kingston   1934-35
For West Indies in England: 86 at The Oval   1957
　　　　　　in West Indies: 102 at Bridgetown   1934-35

INDIVIDUAL HUNDREDS

For England (81)

105	L. E. G. Ames, Port-of-Spain	1929-30
149	L. E. G. Ames, Kingston . .	1929-30
126	L. E. G. Ames, Kingston . .	1934-35
174	D. L. Amiss, Port-of-Spain .	1973-74
262*	D. L. Amiss, Kingston	1973-74
118	D. L. Amiss, Georgetown .	1973-74
203	D. L. Amiss, The Oval . . .	1976
107†	A. H. Bakewell, The Oval . .	1933
128†	K. F. Barrington, Bridgetown	1959-60
121	K. F. Barrington, Port-of-Spain	1959-60
143	K. F. Barrington, Port-of-Spain	1967-68
116	G. Boycott, Georgetown . .	1967-68
128	G. Boycott, Manchester . . .	1969
106	G. Boycott, Lord's	1969
112	G. Boycott, Port-of-Spain . .	1973-74
104*	G. Boycott, St John's	1980-81
120†	D. C. S. Compton, Lord's . .	1939
133	D. C. S. Compton, Port-of-Spain	1953-54
154†	M. C. Cowdrey, Birmingham	1957
152	M. C. Cowdrey, Lord's . . .	1957
114	M. C. Cowdrey, Kingston .	1959-60
119	M. C. Cowdrey, Port-of-Spain	1959-60
101	M. C. Cowdrey, Kingston .	1967-68
148	M. C. Cowdrey, Port-of-Spain	1967-68
136*†	E. R. Dexter, Bridgetown .	1959-60
110	E. R. Dexter, Georgetown .	1959-60
146	J. H. Edrich, Bridgetown . .	1967-68
104	T. G. Evans, Manchester . .	1950
129*	K. W. R. Fletcher, Bridgetown	1973-74
106	G. Fowler, Lord's	1984
123	G. A. Gooch, Lord's	1980

116	G. A. Gooch, Bridgetown .	1980-81
153	G. A. Gooch, Kingston . . .	1980-81
154*	D. I. Gower, Kingston	1980-81
258	T. W. Graveney, Nottingham	1957
164	T. W. Graveney, The Oval	1957
109	T. W. Graveney, Nottingham	1966
165	T. W. Graveney, The Oval	1966
118	T. W. Graveney, Port-of-Spain	1967-68
148	A. W. Greig, Bridgetown . .	1973-74
121	A. W. Greig, Georgetown .	1973-74
116	A. W. Greig, Leeds	1976
140†	S. C. Griffith, Port-of-Spain	1947-48
138	W. R. Hammond, The Oval	1939
107†	J. H. Hampshire, Lord's . . .	1969
106*†	F. C. Hayes, The Oval	1973
205*	E. H. Hendren, Port-of-Spain	1929-30
123	E. H. Hendren, Georgetown	1929-30
159	J. B. Hobbs, The Oval	1928
196†	L. Hutton, Lord's	1939
165*	L. Hutton, The Oval	1939
202*‡	L. Hutton, The Oval	1950
169	L. Hutton, Georgetown . . .	1953-54
205	L. Hutton, Kingston	1953-54
113	R. Illingworth, Lord's	1969
127	D. R. Jardine, Manchester .	1933
116	A. P. E. Knott, Leeds	1976
110	A. J. Lamb, Lord's	1984
100	A. J. Lamb, Leeds	1984
100*	A. J. Lamb, Manchester . .	1984
135	P. B. H. May, Port-of-Spain	1953-54
285*	P. B. H. May, Birmingham	1957
104	P. B. H. May, Nottingham	1957
126*	C. Milburn, Lord's	1966
112†	J. T. Murray, The Oval . . .	1966
101*†	J. M. Parks, Port-of-Spain .	1959-60
107	W. Place, Kingston	1947-48

126	P. E. Richardson, Nottingham	1957	100†	R. Subba Row, Georgetown	1959-60
107	P. E. Richardson, The Oval	1957	122†	E. Tyldesley, Lord's	1928
133	J. D. Robertson, Port-of-Spain	1947-48	114†	C. Washbrook, Lord's	1950
152†	A. Sandham, Bridgetown	1929-30	102	C. Washbrook, Nottingham	1950
325	A. Sandham, Kingston	1929-30	116†	W. Watson, Kingston	1953-54
108	M. J. K. Smith, Port-of-Spain	1959-60	100*	P. Willey, The Oval	1980
106†	D. S. Steele, Nottingham	1976	102*	P. Willey, St John's	1980-81

For West Indies (91)

105	I. Barrow, Manchester	1933	101	C. H. Lloyd, Manchester	1980
133	B. F. Butcher, Lord's	1963	100	C. H. Lloyd, Bridgetown	1980-81
209*	B. F. Butcher, Nottingham	1966	137	S. M. Nurse, Leeds	1966
107	G. M. Carew, Port-of-Spain	1947-48	136	S. M. Nurse, Port-of-Spain	1967-68
103	C. A. Davis, Lord's	1969	106	A. F. Rae, Lord's	1950
101	P. J. Dujon, Manchester	1984	109	A. F. Rae, The Oval	1950
150	R. C. Fredericks, Birmingham	1973	232†	I. V. A. Richards, Nottingham	1976
138	R. C. Fredericks, Lord's	1976	135	I. V. A. Richards, Manchester	1976
109	R. C. Fredericks, Leeds	1976	291	I. V. A. Richards, The Oval	1976
112†	A. G. Ganteaume, Port-of-Spain	1947-48	145	I. V. A. Richards, Lord's	1980
143	H. A. Gomes, Birmingham	1984	182*	I. V. A. Richards, Bridgetown	1980-81
104*	H. A. Gomes, Lord's	1984	114	I. V. A. Richards, St John's	1980-81
134 } C. G. Greenidge, Manchester	1976	117	I. V. A. Richards, Birmingham	1984
101 }				
115	C. G. Greenidge, Leeds	1976	110*	I. V. A. Richards, St John's	1985-86
214*	C. G. Greenidge, Lord's	1984	102	R. B. Richardson, Port-of-Spain	1985-86
223	C. G. Greenidge, Manchester	1984	160	R. B. Richardson, Bridgetown	1985-86
184	D. L. Haynes, Lord's	1980	122	C. A. Roach, Bridgetown	1929-30
125	D. L. Haynes, The Oval	1984	209	C. A. Roach, Georgetown	1929-30
131	D. L. Haynes, St John's	1985-86	120	L. G. Rowe, Kingston	1973-74
176†	G. A. Headley, Bridgetown	1929-30	302	L. G. Rowe, Bridgetown	1973-74
114 } G. A. Headley, Georgetown	1929-30	123	L. G. Rowe, Port-of-Spain	1973-74
112 }			161†	O. G. Smith, Birmingham	1957
223	G. A. Headley, Kingston	1929-30	168	O. G. Smith, Nottingham	1957
169*	G. A. Headley, Manchester	1933	226	G. S. Sobers, Bridgetown	1959-60
270*	G. A. Headley, Kingston	1934-35	147	G. S. Sobers, Kingston	1959-60
106 } G. A. Headley, Lord's	1939	145	G. S. Sobers, Georgetown	1959-60
107 }			102	G. S. Sobers, Leeds	1963
105*	D. A. J. Holford, Lord's	1966	161	G. S. Sobers, Manchester	1966
166	J. K. Holt, Bridgetown	1953-54	163*	G. S. Sobers, Lord's	1966
182	C. C. Hunte, Manchester	1963	174	G. S. Sobers, Leeds	1966
108*	C. C. Hunte, The Oval	1963	113*	G. S. Sobers, Kingston	1967-68
135	C. C. Hunte, Manchester	1966	152	G. S. Sobers, Georgetown	1967-68
121	B. D. Julien, Lord's	1973	150*	G. S. Sobers, Lord's	1973
158	A. I. Kallicharran, Port-of-Spain	1973-74	168*	C. L. Walcott, Lord's	1950
119	A. I. Kallicharran, Bridgetown	1973-74	220	C. L. Walcott, Bridgetown	1953-54
110	R. B. Kanhai, Port-of-Spain	1959-60	124	C. L. Walcott, Port-of-Spain	1953-54
104	R. B. Kanhai, The Oval	1966	116	C. L. Walcott, Kingston	1953-54
153	R. B. Kanhai, Port-of-Spain	1967-68	141	E. D. Weekes, Kingston	1947-48
150	R. B. Kanhai, Georgetown	1967-68	129	E. D. Weekes, Nottingham	1950
157	R. B. Kanhai, Lord's	1973	206	E. D. Weekes, Port-of-Spain	1953-54
118†	C. H. Lloyd, Port-of-Spain	1967-68			
113*	C. H. Lloyd, Bridgetown	1967-68			
132	C. H. Lloyd, The Oval	1973			

137	K. H. Weekes, The Oval .. 1939	167	F. M. M. Worrell, Port-of-Spain 1953-54
131*	F. M. M. Worrell, Georgetown 1947-48	191*‡	F. M. M. Worrell, Nottingham 1957
261	F. M. M. Worrell, Nottingham 1950	197*	F. M. M. Worrell, Bridgetown 1959-60
138	F. M. M. Worrell, The Oval 1950		

† *Signifies hundred on first appearance in England–West Indies Tests. S. C. Griffith provides the only instance for England of a player hitting his maiden century in first-class cricket in his first Test.*
‡ *Carried his bat.*

RECORD PARTNERSHIPS FOR EACH WICKET

For England

212 for 1st	C. Washbrook and R. T. Simpson at Nottingham	1950
266 for 2nd	P. E. Richardson and T. W. Graveney at Nottingham	1957
264 for 3rd	L. Hutton and W. R. Hammond at The Oval	1939
411 for 4th†	P. B. H. May and M. C. Cowdrey at Birmingham	1957
130* for 5th	C. Milburn and T. W. Graveney at Lord's	1966
163 for 6th	A. W. Greig and A. P. E. Knott at Bridgetown	1973-74
197 for 7th	M. J. K. Smith and J. M. Parks at Port-of-Spain	1959-60
217 for 8th	T. W. Graveney and J. T. Murray at The Oval	1966
109 for 9th	G. A. R. Lock and P. I. Pocock at Georgetown	1967-68
128 for 10th	K. Higgs and J. A. Snow at The Oval	1966

For West Indies

206 for 1st	R. C. Fredericks and L. G. Rowe at Kingston	1973-74
287* for 2nd	C. G. Greenidge and H. A. Gomes at Lord's	1984
338 for 3rd†	E. D. Weekes and F. M. M. Worrell at Port-of-Spain	1953-54
399 for 4th†	G. S. Sobers and F. M. M. Worrell at Bridgetown	1959-60
265 for 5th†	S. M. Nurse and G. S. Sobers at Leeds	1966
274* for 6th†	G. S. Sobers and D. A. J. Holford at Lord's	1966
155* for 7th‡	G. S. Sobers and B. D. Julien at Lord's	1973
99 for 8th	C. A. McWatt and J. K. Holt at Georgetown	1953-54
150 for 9th	E. A. E. Baptiste and M. A. Holding at Birmingham	1984
67* for 10th	M. A. Holding and C. E. H. Croft at St John's	1980-81

† *Denotes record partnership against all countries.*
‡ *231 runs were added for this wicket in two separate partnerships: G. S. Sobers retired ill and was replaced by K. D. Boyce when 155 had been added.*

TEN WICKETS OR MORE IN A MATCH

For England (10)

11-98 (7-44, 4-54)	T. E. Bailey, Lord's	1957
10-93 (5-54, 5-39)	A. P. Freeman, Manchester	1928
13-156 (8-86, 5-70)	A. W. Greig, Port-of-Spain	1973-74
11-48 (5-28, 6-20)	G. A. R. Lock, The Oval	1957
11-96 (5-37, 6-59)†	C. S. Marriott, The Oval	1933
10-142 (4-82, 6-60)	J. A. Snow, Georgetown	1967-68
10-195 (5-105, 5-90)†	G. T. S. Stevens, Bridgetown	1929-30
11-152 (6-100, 5-52)	F. S. Trueman, Lord's	1963
12-119 (5-75, 7-44)	F. S. Trueman, Birmingham	1963
11-149 (4-79, 7-70)	W. Voce, Port-of-Spain	1929-30

For West Indies (10)

11-147 (5-70, 6-77)†	K. D. Boyce, The Oval	1973
11-229 (5-137, 6-92)	W. Ferguson, Port-of-Spain	1947-48
11-157 (5-59, 6-98)†	L. R. Gibbs, Manchester	1963

10-106 (5-37, 5-69)	L. R. Gibbs, Manchester	1966
14-149 (8-92, 6-57)	M. A. Holding, The Oval	1976
10-96 (5-41, 5-55)†	H. H. H. Johnson, Kingston	1947-48
11-152 (5-66, 6-86)	S. Ramadhin, Lord's	1950
10-123 (5-60, 5-63)	A. M. E. Roberts, Lord's	1976
11-204 (8-104, 3-100)†	A. L. Valentine, Manchester	1950
10-160 (4-121, 6-39)	A. L. Valentine, The Oval	1950

† *Signifies ten wickets or more on first appearance in England–West Indies Tests.*

Note: F. S. Trueman took ten wickets or more in successive matches.

ENGLAND v NEW ZEALAND

Captains

Season	England	New Zealand	T	E	NZ	D
1929-30	A. H. H. Gilligan	T. C. Lowry	4	1	0	3
1931	D. R. Jardine	T. C. Lowry	3	1	0	2
1932-33	D. R. Jardine[1]	M. L. Page	2	0	0	2
1937	R. W. V. Robins	M. L. Page	3	1	0	2
1946-47	W. R. Hammond	W. A. Hadlee	1	0	0	1
1949	F. G. Mann[2]	W. A. Hadlee	4	0	0	4
1950-51	F. R. Brown	W. A. Hadlee	2	1	0	1
1954-55	L. Hutton	G. O. Rabone	2	2	0	0
1958	P. B. H. May	J. R. Reid	5	4	0	1
1958-59	P. B. H. May	J. R. Reid	2	1	0	1
1962-63	E. R. Dexter	J. R. Reid	3	3	0	0
1965	M. J. K. Smith	J. R. Reid	3	3	0	0
1965-66	M. J. K. Smith	B. W. Sinclair[3]	3	0	0	3
1969	R. Illingworth	G. T. Dowling	3	2	0	1
1970-71	R. Illingworth	G. T. Dowling	2	1	0	1
1973	R. Illingworth	B. E. Congdon	3	2	0	1
1974-75	M. H. Denness	B. E. Congdon	2	1	0	1
1977-78	G. Boycott	M. G. Burgess	3	1	1	1
1978	J. M. Brearley	M. G. Burgess	3	3	0	0
1983	R. G. D. Willis	G. P. Howarth	4	3	1	0
1983-84	R. G. D. Willis	G. P. Howarth	3	0	1	2
1986	M. W. Gatting	J. V. Coney	3	0	1	2
	In New Zealand		29	11	2	16
	In England		34	19	2	13
	Totals		63	30	4	29

Notes: The following deputised for the official touring captain or were appointed by the home authority for only a minor proportion of the series:
[1]R. E. S. Wyatt (Second). [2]F. R. Brown (Third and Fourth). [3]M. E. Chapple (First).

HIGHEST INNINGS TOTALS

For England in England: 546-4 dec. at Leeds	1965
in New Zealand: 593-6 dec. at Auckland	1974-75
For New Zealand in England: 551-9 dec. at Lord's	1973
in New Zealand: 537 at Wellington	1983-84

LOWEST INNINGS TOTALS

For England in England: 187 at Manchester	1937
in New Zealand: 64 at Wellington	1977-78
For New Zealand in England: 47 at Lord's	1958
in New Zealand: 26 at Auckland	1954-55

INDIVIDUAL HUNDREDS

For England (68)

122†	G. O. Allen, Lord's	1931	111†	D. I. Gower, The Oval	1978
137†	L. E. G. Ames, Lord's	1931	112*	D. I. Gower, Leeds	1983
103	L. E. G. Ames, Christchurch	1932-33	108	D. I. Gower, Lord's	1983
			131	D. I. Gower, The Oval	1986
138*†	D. L. Amiss, Nottingham	1973	139†	A. W. Greig, Nottingham	1973
164*	D. L. Amiss, Christchurch	1974-75	100*	W. R. Hammond, The Oval	1931
134*	T. E. Bailey, Christchurch	1950-51	227	W. R. Hammond, Christchurch	1932-33
126†	K. F. Barrington, Auckland	1962-63			
163	K. F. Barrington, Leeds	1965	336*	W. R. Hammond, Auckland	1932-33
137	K. F. Barrington, Birmingham	1965	140	W. R. Hammond, Lord's	1937
103	I. T. Botham, Christchurch	1977-78	114†	J. Hardstaff jun., Lord's	1937
103	I. T. Botham, Nottingham	1983	103	J. Hardstaff jun., The Oval	1937
138	I. T. Botham, Wellington	1983-84			
109	E. H. Bowley, Auckland	1929-30	100	L. Hutton, Manchester	1937
115	G. Boycott, Leeds	1973	101	L. Hutton, Leeds	1949
131	G. Boycott, Nottingham	1978	206	L. Hutton, The Oval	1949
114	D. C. S. Compton, Leeds	1949	125†	B. R. Knight, Auckland	1962-63
116	D. C. S. Compton, Lord's	1949	101	A. P. E. Knott, Auckland	1970-71
128*	M. C. Cowdrey, Wellington	1962-63	102*†	A. J. Lamb, The Oval	1983
119	M. C. Cowdrey, Lord's	1965	137*	A. J. Lamb, Nottingham	1983
181	M. H. Denness, Auckland	1974-75	196	G. B. Legge, Auckland	1929-30
141	E. R. Dexter, Christchurch	1958-59	113*	P. B. H. May, Leeds	1958
100	B. L. D'Oliveira, Christchurch	1970-71	101	P. B. H. May, Manchester	1958
			124*	P. B. H. May, Auckland	1958-59
117	K. S. Duleepsinhji, Auckland	1929-30	104*†	C. A. Milton, Leeds	1958
109	K. S. Duleepsinhji, The Oval	1931	131*†	P. H. Parfitt, Auckland	1962-63
			158	C. T. Radley, Auckland	1977-78
310*†	J. H. Edrich, Leeds	1965	164	D. W. Randall, Wellington	1983-84
155	J. H. Edrich, Lord's	1969	104	D. W. Randall, Auckland	1983-84
115	J. H. Edrich, Nottingham	1969	100†	P. E. Richardson, Birmingham	1958
100	W. J. Edrich, The Oval	1949			
178	K. W. R. Fletcher, Lord's	1973	121†	J. D. Robertson, Lord's	1949
216	K. W. R. Fletcher, Auckland	1974-75	111	P. J. Sharpe, Nottingham	1969
			103†	R. T. Simpson, Manchester	1949
105†	G. Fowler, The Oval	1983	117†	H. Sutcliffe, The Oval	1931
121	M. W. Gatting, The Oval	1986	109*	H. Sutcliffe, Manchester	1931
183	G. A. Gooch, Lord's	1986	109†	C. J. Tavaré, The Oval	1983
			103*	C. Washbrook, Leeds	1949

For New Zealand (29)

110	J. G. Bracewell, Nottingham	1986	206	M. P. Donnelly, Lord's	1949
104	M. G. Burgess, Auckland	1970-71	116	W. A. Hadlee, Christchurch	1946-47
105	M. G. Burgess, Lord's	1973			
174*	J. V. Coney, Wellington	1983-84	122	} G. P. Howarth, Auckland	1977-78
104	B. E. Congdon, Christchurch	1965-66	102		
			123	G. P. Howarth, Lord's	1978
176	B. E. Congdon, Nottingham	1973	117†	J. E. Mills, Wellington	1929-30
175	B. E. Congdon, Lord's	1973	104	M. L. Page, Lord's	1931
128	J. J. Crowe, Auckland	1983-84	121	J. M. Parker, Auckland	1974-75
100	M. D. Crowe, Wellington	1983-84	116	V. Pollard, Nottingham	1973
106	M. D. Crowe, Lord's	1986	105*	V. Pollard, Lord's	1973
136	C. S. Dempster, Wellington	1929-30	100	J. R. Reid, Christchurch	1962-63
120	C. S. Dempster, Lord's	1931	114	B. W. Sinclair, Auckland	1965-66

113*	I. D. S. Smith, Auckland	1983-84	130	J. G. Wright, Auckland	1983-84
101	B. Sutcliffe, Manchester	1949	119	J. G. Wright, The Oval	1986
116	B. Sutcliffe, Christchurch	1950-51			

† *Signifies hundred on first appearance in England–New Zealand Tests.*

RECORD PARTNERSHIPS FOR EACH WICKET

For England

223 for 1st	G. Fowler and C. J. Tavaré at The Oval	1983
369 for 2nd	J. H. Edrich and K. F. Barrington at Leeds	1965
245 for 3rd	W. R. Hammond and J. Hardstaff jun. at Lord's	1937
266 for 4th	M. H. Denness and K. W. R. Fletcher at Auckland	1974-75
242 for 5th	W. R. Hammond and L. E. G. Ames at Christchurch	1932-33
240 for 6th†	P. H. Parfitt and B. R. Knight at Auckland	1962-63
149 for 7th	A. P. E. Knott and P. Lever at Auckland	1970-71
246 for 8th†	L. E. G. Ames and G. O. Allen at Lord's	1931
163* for 9th†	M. C. Cowdrey and A. C. Smith at Wellington	1962-63
59 for 10th	A. P. E. Knott and N. Gifford at Nottingham	1973

For New Zealand

276 for 1st	C. S. Dempster and J. E. Mills at Wellington	1929-30
131 for 2nd	B. Sutcliffe and J. R. Reid at Christchurch	1950-51
210 for 3rd	B. A. Edgar and M. D. Crowe at Lord's	1986
154 for 4th	J. G. Wright and J. J. Crowe at Auckland	1983-84
177 for 5th	B. E. Congdon and V. Pollard at Nottingham	1973
117 for 6th	M. G. Burgess and V. Pollard at Lord's	1973
104 for 7th	B. Sutcliffe and V. Pollard at Birmingham	1965
104 for 8th	A. W. Roberts and D. A. R. Moloney at Lord's	1937
118 for 9th†	J. V. Coney and B. L. Cairns at Wellington	1983-84
57 for 10th	F. L. H. Mooney and J. Cowie at Leeds	1949

† *Denotes record partnership against all countries.*

TEN WICKETS OR MORE IN A MATCH

For England (7)

11-140 (6-101, 5-39)	I. T. Botham, Lord's	1978
10-149 (5-98, 5-51)	A. W. Greig, Auckland	1974-75
11-65 (4-14, 7-51)	G. A. R. Lock, Leeds	1958
11-84 (5-31, 6-53)	G. A. R. Lock, Christchurch	1958-59
11-70 (4-38, 7-32)†	D. L. Underwood, Lord's	1969
12-101 (6-41, 6-60)	D. L. Underwood, The Oval	1969
12-97 (6-12, 6-85)	D. L. Underwood, Christchurch	1970-71

For New Zealand (4)

10-144 (7-74, 3-70)	B. L. Cairns, Leeds	1983
10-140 (4-73, 6-67)	J. Cowie, Manchester	1937
10-100 (4-74, 6-26)	R. J. Hadlee, Wellington	1977-78
10-140 (6-80, 4-60)	R. J. Hadlee, Nottingham	1986

† *Signifies ten wickets or more on first appearance in England–New Zealand Tests.*

Note: D. L. Underwood took twelve wickets in successive matches against New Zealand in 1969 and 1970-71.

HAT-TRICK AND FOUR WICKETS IN FIVE BALLS

M. J. C. Allom, in his first Test match, v New Zealand at Christchurch in 1929-30, dismissed C. S. Dempster, T. C. Lowry, K. C. James, and F. T. Badcock to take four wickets in five balls (w-www).

ENGLAND v INDIA

Captains

Season	England	India	T	E	I	D
1932	D. R. Jardine	C. K. Nayudu	1	1	0	0
1933-34	D. R. Jardine	C. K. Nayudu	3	2	0	1
1936	G. O. Allen	Maharaj of Vizianagram	3	2	0	1
1946	W. R. Hammond	Nawab of Pataudi sen.	3	1	0	2
1951-52	N. D. Howard[1]	V. S. Hazare	5	1	1	3
1952	L. Hutton	V. S. Hazare	4	3	0	1
1959	P. B. H. May[2]	D. K. Gaekwad[3]	5	5	0	0
1961-62	E. R. Dexter	N. J. Contractor	5	0	2	3
1963-64	M. J. K. Smith	Nawab of Pataudi jun.	5	0	0	5
1967	D. B. Close	Nawab of Pataudi jun.	3	3	0	0
1971	R. Illingworth	A. L. Wadekar	3	0	1	2
1972-73	A. R. Lewis	A. L. Wadekar	5	1	2	2
1974	M. H. Denness	A. L. Wadekar	3	3	0	0
1976-77	A. W. Greig	B. S. Bedi	5	3	1	1
1979	J. M. Brearley	S. Venkataraghavan	4	1	0	3
1979-80	J. M. Brearley	G. R. Viswanath	1	1	0	0
1981-82	K. W. R. Fletcher	S. M. Gavaskar	6	0	1	5
1982	R. G. D. Willis	S. M. Gavaskar	3	1	0	2
1984-85	D. I. Gower	S. M. Gavaskar	5	2	1	2
1986	M. W. Gatting[4]	Kapil Dev	3	0	2	1
	In England		35	20	3	12
	In India		40	10	8	22
	Totals		75	30	11	34

Notes: The 1932 Indian touring team was captained by the Maharaj of Porbandar but he did not play in the Test match.

The following deputised for the official touring captain or were appointed by the home authority for only a minor proportion of the series:

[1]D. B. Carr (Fifth). [2]M. C. Cowdrey (Fourth and Fifth). [3]Pankaj Roy (Second). [4]D. I. Gower (First).

HIGHEST INNINGS TOTALS

For England in England: 633-5 dec. at Birmingham	1979
in India: 652-7 dec. at Madras	1984-85
For India in England: 510 at Leeds	1967
in India: 553-8 dec. at Kanpur	1984-85

LOWEST INNINGS TOTALS

For England in England: 101 at The Oval	1971
in India: 102 at Bombay	1981-82
For India in England: 42 at Lord's	1974
in India: 83 at Madras	1976-77

INDIVIDUAL HUNDREDS

For England (61)

188	D. L. Amiss, Lord's	1974	200*†	D. I. Gower, Birmingham	1979
179	D. L. Amiss, Delhi	1976-77	175†	T. W. Graveney, Bombay	1951-52
151*	K. F. Barrington, Bombay	1961-62	151	T. W. Graveney, Lord's	1967
172	K. F. Barrington, Kanpur	1961-62	148	A. W. Greig, Bombay	1972-73
113*	K. F. Barrington, Delhi	1961-62	106	A. W. Greig, Lord's	1974
137	I. T. Botham, Leeds	1979	103	A. W. Greig, Calcutta	1976-77
114	I. T. Botham, Bombay	1979-80	167	W. R. Hammond, Manchester	1936
142	I. T. Botham, Kanpur	1981-82	217	W. R. Hammond, The Oval	1936
128	I. T. Botham, Manchester	1982	205*	J. Hardstaff jun., Lord's	1946
208	I. T. Botham, The Oval	1982	150	L. Hutton, Lord's	1952
246*†	G. Boycott, Leeds	1967	104	L. Hutton, Manchester	1952
155	G. Boycott, Birmingham	1979	107	R. Illingworth, Manchester	1971
125	G. Boycott, The Oval	1979	127	B. R. Knight, Kanpur	1963-64
105	G. Boycott, Delhi	1981-82	107	A. J. Lamb, The Oval	1982
160	M. C. Cowdrey, Leeds	1959	125	A. R. Lewis, Kanpur	1972-73
107	M. C. Cowdrey, Calcutta	1963-64	214*	D. Lloyd, Birmingham	1974
151	M. C. Cowdrey, Delhi	1963-64	101	B. W. Luckhurst, Manchester	1971
118	M. H. Denness, Lord's	1974	106	P. B. H. May, Nottingham	1959
100	M. H. Denness, Birmingham	1974	121	P. H. Parfitt, Kanpur	1963-64
126*	E. R. Dexter, Kanpur	1961-62	131	G. Pullar, Manchester	1959
109†	B. L. D'Oliveira, Leeds	1967	119	G. Pullar, Kanpur	1961-62
100*	J. H. Edrich, Manchester	1974	126	D. W. Randall, Lord's	1982
113	T. G. Evans, Lord's	1952	160	R. T. Robinson, Delhi	1984-85
113	K. W. R. Fletcher, Bombay	1972-73	119	D. S. Sheppard, The Oval	1952
123*	K. W. R. Fletcher, Manchester	1974	100†	M. J. K. Smith, Manchester	1959
201	G. Fowler, Madras	1984-85	149	C. J. Tavaré, Delhi	1981-82
136	M. W. Gatting, Bombay	1984-85	136†	B. H. Valentine, Bombay	1933-34
207	M. W. Gatting, Madras	1984-85	102	C. F. Walters, Madras	1933-34
183*	M. W. Gatting, Birmingham	1986	137*†	A. J. Watkins, Delhi	1951-52
129	G. A. Gooch, Madras	1981-82	128	T. S. Worthington, The Oval	1936
114	G. A. Gooch, Lord's	1986			

For India (50)

118†	L. Amarnath, Bombay	1933-34	108	V. L. Manjrekar, Madras	1963-64
110†	M. Azharuddin, Calcutta	1984-85	184	V. Mankad, Lord's	1952
105	M. Azharuddin, Madras	1984-85	114	V. M. Merchant, Manchester	1936
122	M. Azharuddin, Kanpur	1984-85	128	V. M. Merchant, The Oval	1946
112†	A. A. Baig, Manchester	1959	154	V. M. Merchant, Delhi	1951-52
121	F. M. Engineer, Bombay	1972-73	112	Mushtaq Ali, Manchester	1936
101	S. M. Gavaskar, Manchester	1974	122*	R. G. Nadkarni, Kanpur	1963-64
108	S. M. Gavaskar, Bombay	1976-77	103	Nawab of Pataudi jun., Madras	1961-62
221	S. M. Gavaskar, The Oval	1979	203*	Nawab of Pataudi jun., Delhi	1963-64
172	S. M. Gavaskar, Bangalore	1981-82	148	Nawab of Pataudi jun., Leeds	1967
105†	Hanumant Singh, Delhi	1963-64	129*	S. M. Patil, Manchester	1982
164*	V. S. Hazare, Delhi	1951-52	115	D. G. Phadkar, Calcutta	1951-52
155	V. S. Hazare, Bombay	1951-52	140	Pankaj Roy, Bombay	1951-52
127	M. L. Jaisimha, Delhi	1961-62	111	Pankaj Roy, Madras	1951-52
129	M. L. Jaisimha, Calcutta	1963-64	142	R. J. Shastri, Bombay	1984-85
116	Kapil Dev, Kanpur	1981-82	111	R. J. Shastri, Calcutta	1984-85
192	S. M. H. Kirmani, Bombay	1984-85	130*	P. R. Umrigar, Madras	1951-52
192	B. K. Kunderan, Madras	1963-64	118	P. R. Umrigar, Manchester	1959
100	B. K. Kunderan, Delhi	1963-64			
133	V. L. Manjrekar, Leeds	1952			
189*	V. L. Manjrekar, Delhi	1961-62			

147*	P. R. Umrigar, Kanpur	... 1961-62	113	G. R. Viswanath, Bombay	.	1972-73
103	D. B. Vengsarkar, Lord's	1979	113	G. R. Viswanath, Lord's	..	1979
157	D. B. Vengsarkar, Lord's	.. 1982	107	G. R. Viswanath, Delhi	...	1981-82
137	D. B. Vengsarkar, Kanpur	1984-85	222	G. R. Viswanath, Madras	.	1981-82
126*	D. B. Vengsarkar, Lord's	.. 1986	140	Yashpal Sharma, Madras		1981-82
102*	D. B. Vengsarkar, Leeds	.. 1986				

† *Signifies hundred on first appearance in England–India Tests.*

Note: M. Azharuddin scored hundreds in each of his first three Tests.

RECORD PARTNERSHIPS FOR EACH WICKET

For England

178 for 1st	G. Fowler and R. T. Robinson at Madras	1984-85
241 for 2nd	G. Fowler and M. W. Gatting at Madras	1984-85
169 for 3rd	R. Subba Row and M. J. K. Smith at The Oval	1959
266 for 4th	W. R. Hammond and T. S. Worthington at The Oval	1936
254 for 5th†	K. W. R. Fletcher and A. W. Greig at Bombay	1972-73
171 for 6th	I. T. Botham and R. W. Taylor at Bombay	1979-80
125 for 7th	D. W. Randall and P. H. Edmonds at Lord's	1982
168 for 8th	R. Illingworth and P. Lever at Manchester	1971
83 for 9th	K. W. R. Fletcher and N. Gifford at Madras	1972-73
70 for 10th	P. J. W. Allott and R. G. D. Willis at Lord's	1982

For India

213 for 1st	S. M. Gavaskar and C. P. S. Chauhan at The Oval	1979
192 for 2nd	F. M. Engineer and A. L. Wadekar at Bombay	1972-73
316 for 3rd†‡	G. R. Viswanath and Yashpal Sharma at Madras	1981-82
222 for 4th†	V. S. Hazare and V. L. Manjrekar at Leeds	1952
214 for 5th†	M. Azharuddin and R. J. Shastri at Calcutta	1984-85
130 for 6th	S. M. H. Kirmani and Kapil Dev at The Oval	1982
235 for 7th†	R. J. Shastri and S. M. H. Kirmani at Bombay	1984-85
128 for 8th	R. J. Shastri and S. M. H. Kirmani at Delhi	1981-82
104 for 9th	R. J. Shastri and Madan Lal at Delhi	1981-82
51 for 10th	{ R. G. Nadkarni and B. S. Chandrasekhar at Calcutta	1963-64
	{ S. M. H. Kirmani and C. Sharma at Madras	1984-85

† *Denotes record partnership against all countries.*

‡ *415 runs were added between the fall of the 2nd and 3rd wickets: D. B. Vengsarkar retired hurt when he and Viswanath had added 99 runs.*

TEN WICKETS OR MORE IN A MATCH

For England (7)

10-78 (5-35, 5-43)†	G. O. Allen, Lord's	1936
11-145 (7-49, 4-96)†	A. V. Bedser, Lord's	1946
11-93 (4-41, 7-52)	A. V. Bedser, Manchester	1946
13-106 (6-58, 7-48)	I. T. Botham, Bombay	1979-80
11-163 (6-104, 5-59)†	N. A. Foster, Madras	1984-85
10-70 (7-46, 3-24)†	J. K. Lever, Delhi	1976-77
11-153 (7-49, 4-104)	H. Verity, Madras	1933-34

For India (4)

10-177 (6-105, 4-72)	S. A. Durani, Madras	1961-62
12-108 (8-55, 4-53)	V. Mankad, Madras	1951-52
10-188 (4-130, 6-58)	Chetan Sharma, Birmingham	1986
12-181 (6-64, 6-117)†	L. Sivaramakrishnan, Bombay	1984-85

† *Signifies ten wickets or more on first appearance in England–India Tests.*

Note: A. V. Bedser took eleven wickets in a match in the first two Tests of his career.

ENGLAND v PAKISTAN

Captains

Season	England	Pakistan	T	E	P	D
1954	L. Hutton[1]	A. H. Kardar	4	1	1	2
1961-62	E. R. Dexter	Imtiaz Ahmed	3	1	0	2
1962	E. R. Dexter[2]	Javed Burki	5	4	0	1
1967	D. B. Close	Hanif Mohammad	3	2	0	1
1968-69	M. C. Cowdrey	Saeed Ahmed	3	0	0	3
1971	R. Illingworth	Intikhab Alam	3	1	0	2
1972-73	A. R. Lewis	Majid Khan	3	0	0	3
1974	M. H. Denness	Intikhab Alam	3	0	0	3
1977-78	J. M. Brearley[3]	Wasim Bari	3	0	0	3
1978	J. M. Brearley	Wasim Bari	3	2	0	1
1982	R. G. D. Willis[4]	Imran Khan	3	2	1	0
1983-84	R. G. D. Willis[5]	Zaheer Abbas	3	0	1	2
1987	M. W. Gatting	Imran Khan	5	0	1	4
	In England		29	12	3	14
	In Pakistan		15	1	1	13
	Totals		44	13	4	27

Notes: [1]D. S. Sheppard captained in Second and Third Tests. [2]M. C. Cowdrey captained in Third Test. [3]G. Boycott captained in Third Test. [4]D. I. Gower captained in Second Test. [5]D. I. Gower captained in Second and Third Tests.

HIGHEST INNINGS TOTALS

For England in England: 558-6 dec. at Nottingham	1954
in Pakistan: 546-8 dec. at Faisalabad	1983-84
For Pakistan in England: 708 at The Oval	1987
in Pakistan: 569-9 dec. at Hyderabad	1972-73

LOWEST INNINGS TOTALS

For England in England: 130 at The Oval	1954
in Pakistan: 159 at Karachi	1983-84
For Pakistan in England: 87 at Lord's	1954
in Pakistan: 199 at Karachi	1972-73

INDIVIDUAL HUNDREDS

For England (40)

112	D. L. Amiss, Lahore	1972-73	100*	G. Boycott, Hyderabad	1977-78
158	D. L. Amiss, Hyderabad	1972-73	278	D. C. S. Compton, Nottingham	1954
183	D. L. Amiss, The Oval	1974			
123	C. W. J. Athey, Lord's	1987	159†	M. C. Cowdrey, Birmingham	1962
139†	K. F. Barrington, Lahore	1961-62	182	M. C. Cowdrey, The Oval	1962
148	K. F. Barrington, Lord's	1967	100	M. C. Cowdrey, Lahore	1968-69
109*	K. F. Barrington, Nottingham	1967	205	E. R. Dexter, Karachi	1961-62
142	K. F. Barrington, The Oval	1967	172	E. R. Dexter, The Oval	1962
100†	I. T. Botham, Birmingham	1978	114*	B. L. D'Oliveira, Dacca	1968-69
108	I. T. Botham, Lord's	1978	122	K. W. R. Fletcher, The Oval	1974
121*	G. Boycott, Lord's	1971			
112	G. Boycott, Leeds	1971	124	M. W. Gatting, Birmingham	1987

150*	M. W. Gatting, The Oval	1987	139	C. Milburn, Karachi	1968-69
152	D. I. Gower, Faisalabad	1983-84	111	P. H. Parfitt, Karachi	1961-62
173*	D. I. Gower, Lahore	1983-84	101*	P. H. Parfitt, Birmingham	1962
153	T. W. Graveney, Lord's	1962	119	P. H. Parfitt, Leeds	1962
114	T. W. Graveney, Notting-		101*	P. H. Parfitt, Nottingham	1962
	ham	1962	165	G. Pullar, Dacca	1961-62
105	T. W. Graveney, Karachi	1968-69	106†	C. T. Radley, Birmingham	1978
116	A. P. E. Knott, Birmingham	1971	105	D. W. Randall, Birmingham	1982
108*†	B. W. Luckhurst, Bir-		166†	R. T. Robinson, Manchester	1987
	mingham	1971	101	R. T. Simpson, Nottingham	1954

For Pakistan (29)

109	Alim-ud-Din, Karachi	1961-62	114†	Mudassar Nazar, Lahore	1977-78
146	Asif Iqbal, The Oval	1967	124	Mudassar Nazar, Birming-	
104*	Asif Iqbal, Birmingham	1971		ham	1987
102	Asif Iqbal, Lahore	1972-73	100*	Mushtaq Mohammad, Not-	
111	} Hanif Mohammad, Dacca	1961-62		tingham	1962
104			100	Mushtaq Mohammad, Bir-	
187*	Hanif Mohammad, Lord's	1967		mingham	1971
122†	Haroon Rashid, Lahore	1977-78	157	Mushtaq Mohammad, Hy-	
108	Haroon Rashid, Hydera-			derabad	1972-73
	bad	1977-78	101	Nasim-ul-Ghani, Lord's	1962
118	Imran Khan, The Oval	1987	119	Sadiq Mohammad, Lahore	1972-73
138	Intikhab Alam, Hyderabad	1972-73	116	Salim Malik, Faisalabad	1983-84
138†	Javed Burki, Lahore	1961-62	102	Salim Malik, The Oval	1987
140	Javed Burki, Dacca	1961-62	112	Wasim Raja, Faisalabad	1983-84
101	Javed Burki, Lord's	1962	274†	Zaheer Abbas, Birming-	
260	Javed Miandad, The Oval	1987		ham	1971
200	Mohsin Khan, Lord's	1982	240	Zaheer Abbas, The Oval	1974
104	Mohsin Khan, Lahore	1983-84			

† *Signifies hundred on first appearance in England–Pakistan Tests.*

Note: Three batsmen – Majid Khan, Mushtaq Mohammad and D. L. Amiss – were dismissed for 99 at Karachi, 1972-73: the only instance in Test matches.

RECORD PARTNERSHIPS FOR EACH WICKET

For England

198 for 1st	G. Pullar and R. W. Barber at Dacca	1961-62
248 for 2nd	M. C. Cowdrey and E. R. Dexter at The Oval	1962
201 for 3rd	K. F. Barrington and T. W. Graveney at Lord's	1967
188 for 4th	E. R. Dexter and P. H. Parfitt at Karachi	1961-62
192 for 5th	D. C. S. Compton and T. E. Bailey at Nottingham	1954
153* for 6th	P. H. Parfitt and D. A. Allen at Birmingham	1962
167 for 7th	D. I. Gower and V. J. Marks at Faisalabad	1983-84
99 for 8th	P. H. Parfitt and D. A. Allen at Leeds	1962
76 for 9th	T. W. Graveney and F. S. Trueman at Lord's	1962
79 for 10th	R. W. Taylor and R. G. D. Willis at Birmingham	1982

For Pakistan

173 for 1st	Mohsin Khan and Shoaib Mohammad at Lahore	1983-84
291 for 2nd†	Zaheer Abbas and Mushtaq Mohammad at Birmingham	1971
180 for 3rd	Mudassar Nazar and Haroon Rashid at Lahore	1977-78
234 for 4th	Javed Miandad and Salim Malik at The Oval	1987
197 for 5th	Javed Burki and Nasim-ul-Ghani at Lord's	1962
145 for 6th	Mushtaq Mohammad and Intikhab Alam at Hyderabad	1972-73
89 for 7th	Ijaz Ahmed and Salim Yousuf at The Oval	1987
130 for 8th†	Hanif Mohammad and Asif Iqbal at Lord's	1967
190 for 9th†	Asif Iqbal and Intikhab Alam at The Oval	1967
62 for 10th	Sarfraz Nawaz and Asif Masood at Leeds	1974

† *Denotes record partnership against all countries.*

TEN WICKETS OR MORE IN A MATCH

For England (2)

11-83 (6-65, 5-18)†	N. G. B. Cook, Karachi	1983-84
13-71 (5-20, 8-51)	D. L. Underwood, Lord's	1974

For Pakistan (3)

10-194 (5-84, 5-110)	Abdul Qadir, Lahore	1983-84
12-99 (6-53, 6-46)	Fazal Mahmood, The Oval	1954
10-77 (3-37, 7-40)	Imran Khan, Leeds	1987

† *Signifies ten wickets or more on first appearance in England–Pakistan Tests.*

FOUR WICKETS IN FIVE BALLS

C. M. Old, v Pakistan at Birmingham in 1978, dismissed Wasim Raja, Wasim Bari, Iqbal Qasim and Sikander Bakht to take four wickets in five balls (ww-ww).

ENGLAND v SRI LANKA

			Captains				
Season	England		Sri Lanka	T	E	SL	D
1981-82	K. W. R. Fletcher		B. Warnapura	1	1	0	0
1984	D. I. Gower		L. R. D. Mendis	1	0	0	1
	Totals			2	1	0	1

Highest innings total for England: 370 at Lord's		1984
for Sri Lanka: 491-7 dec. at Lord's		1984
Lowest innings total for England: 223 at Colombo (PSO)		1981-82
for Sri Lanka: 175 at Colombo (PSO)		1981-82

INDIVIDUAL HUNDREDS

For England (1)		For Sri Lanka (3)	
107† A. J. Lamb, Lord's 1984		111 L. R. D. Mendis, Lord's	1984
		102*† S. A. R. Silva, Lord's	1984
		190 S. Wettimuny, Lord's	1984

† *Signifies hundred on first appearance in England–Sri Lanka Tests.*

Best bowling in an innings for England: 6-33 by J. E. Emburey at Colombo (PSO) 1981-82
for Sri Lanka: 4-70 by A. L. F. de Mel at Colombo (PSO) 1981-82

Best wicket partnerships for England: 87 for 6th by A. J. Lamb and R. M. Ellison at
Lord's 1984
for Sri Lanka: 150 for 5th by S. Wettimuny and
L. R. D. Mendis at Lord's 1984

ENGLAND v REST OF THE WORLD

In 1970, owing to the cancellation of the South African tour to England, a series of matches was arranged, with the trappings of a full Test series, between England and the Rest of the World. It was played for the Guinness Trophy.

The following players represented the Rest of the World: E. J. Barlow (5), F. M. Engineer (2), L. R. Gibbs (4), Intikhab Alam (5), R. B. Kanhai (5), C. H. Lloyd (5), G. D. McKenzie (3), D. L. Murray (3), Mushtaq Mohammad (2), P. M. Pollock (1), R. G. Pollock (5), M. J. Procter (5), B. A. Richards (5), G. S. Sobers (5).

A list of players who appeared for England in these matches may be found on page 126.

AUSTRALIA v SOUTH AFRICA

		Captains				
Season	Australia	South Africa	T	A	SA	D
1902-03S	J. Darling	H. M. Taberer[1]	3	2	0	1
1910-11A	C. Hill	P. W. Sherwell	5	4	1	0
1912E	S. E. Gregory	F. Mitchell[2]	3	2	0	1
1921-22S	H. L. Collins	H. W. Taylor	3	1	0	2
1931-32A	W. M. Woodfull	H. B. Cameron	5	5	0	0
1935-36S	V. Y. Richardson	H. F. Wade	5	4	0	1
1949-50S	A. L. Hassett	A. D. Nourse	5	4	0	1
1952-53A	A. L. Hassett	J. E. Cheetham	5	2	2	1
1957-58S	I. D. Craig	C. B. van Ryneveld[3]	5	3	0	2
1963-64A	R. B. Simpson[4]	T. L. Goddard	5	1	1	3
1966-67S	R. B. Simpson	P. L. van der Merwe	5	1	3	1
1969-70S	W. M. Lawry	A. Bacher	4	0	4	0
	In South Africa		30	15	7	8
	In Australia		20	12	4	4
	In England		3	2	0	1
	Totals		53	29	11	13

S Played in South Africa.   A Played in Australia.   E Played in England.

Notes: The following deputised for the official touring captain or were appointed by the home authority for only a minor proportion of the series:
[1]J. H. Anderson (Second), E. A. Halliwell (Third). [2]L. J. Tancred (Third). [3]D. J. McGlew (First). [4]R. Benaud (First).

HIGHEST INNINGS TOTALS

For Australia in Australia: 578 at Melbourne	1910-11
in South Africa: 549-7 dec. at Port Elizabeth	1949-50
For South Africa in Australia: 595 at Adelaide	1963-64
in South Africa: 622-9 dec. at Durban	1969-70

LOWEST INNINGS TOTALS

For Australia in Australia: 153 at Melbourne	1931-32
in South Africa: 75 at Durban	1949-50
For South Africa in Australia: 36† at Melbourne	1931-32
in South Africa: 85 at Johannesburg	1902-03

† *Scored 45 in the second innings giving the smallest aggregate of 81 (12 extras) in Test cricket.*

INDIVIDUAL HUNDREDS

For Australia (55)

159*‡	W. W. Armstrong, Johannesburg	1902-03
132	W. W. Armstrong, Melbourne	1910-11
132†	W. Bardsley, Sydney	1910-11
121	W. Bardsley, Manchester	1912
164	W. Bardsley, Lord's	1912
122	R. Benaud, Johannesburg	1957-58
100	R. Benaud, Johannesburg	1957-58
169†	B. C. Booth, Brisbane	1963-64
102*	B. C. Booth, Sydney	1963-64
226†	D. G. Bradman, Brisbane	1931-32
112	D. G. Bradman, Sydney	1931-32
167	D. G. Bradman, Melbourne	1931-32
299*	D. G. Bradman, Adelaide	1931-32
121	W. A. Brown, Johannesburg	1935-36
189	J. W. Burke, Cape Town	1957-58
109†	A. G. Chipperfield, Durban	1935-36
203	H. L. Collins, Johannesburg	1921-22
112	J. H. Fingleton, Cape Town	1935-36
108	J. H. Fingleton, Johannesburg	1935-36
118	J. H. Fingleton, Durban	1935-36
119	J. M. Gregory, Johannesburg	1921-22
178	R. N. Harvey, Cape Town	1949-50
151*	R. N. Harvey, Durban	1949-50
116	R. N. Harvey, Port Elizabeth	1949-50
100	R. N. Harvey, Johannesburg	1949-50
109	R. N. Harvey, Brisbane	1952-53
190	R. N. Harvey, Sydney	1952-53
116	R. N. Harvey, Adelaide	1952-53
205	R. N. Harvey, Melbourne	1952-53
112†	A. L. Hassett, Johannesburg	1949-50
167	A. L. Hassett, Port Elizabeth	1949-50
163	A. L. Hassett, Adelaide	1952-53
142†	C. Hill, Johannesburg	1902-03
191	C. Hill, Sydney	1910-11
100	C. Hill, Melbourne	1910-11
114	C. Kelleway, Manchester	1912
102	C. Kelleway, Lord's	1912
157	W. M. Lawry, Melbourne	1963-64
101†	S. J. E. Loxton, Johannesburg	1949-50
137	C. G. Macartney, Sydney	1910-11
116	C. G. Macartney, Durban	1921-22
149	S. J. McCabe, Durban	1935-36
189*	S. J. McCabe, Johannesburg	1935-36
154	C. C. McDonald, Adelaide	1952-53
118 101* }	J. Moroney, Johannesburg	1949-50
111	A. R. Morris, Johannesburg	1949-50
157	A. R. Morris, Port Elizabeth	1949-50
127†	K. E. Rigg, Sydney	1931-32
142	J. Ryder, Cape Town	1921-22
153	R. B. Simpson, Cape Town	1966-67
134	K. R. Stackpole, Cape Town	1966-67
159	V. T. Trumper, Melbourne	1910-11
214*	V. T. Trumper, Adelaide	1910-11
161	W. M. Woodfull, Melbourne	1931-32

For South Africa (36)

114†	E. J. Barlow, Brisbane	1963-64
109	E. J. Barlow, Melbourne	1963-64
201	E. J. Barlow, Adelaide	1963-64
127	E. J. Barlow, Cape Town	1969-70
110	E. J. Barlow, Johannesburg	1969-70
126	K. C. Bland, Sydney	1963-64
162*	W. R. Endean, Melbourne	1952-53
204	G. A. Faulkner, Melbourne	1910-11
115	G. A. Faulkner, Adelaide	1910-11
122*	G. A. Faulkner, Manchester	1912
152	C. N. Frank, Johannesburg	1921-22
102	B. L. Irvine, Port Elizabeth	1969-70
182	D. T. Lindsay, Johannesburg	1966-67
137	D. T. Lindsay, Durban	1966-67
131	D. T. Lindsay, Johannesburg	1966-67
108	D. J. McGlew, Johannesburg	1957-58
105	D. J. McGlew, Durban	1957-58
231	A. D. Nourse, Johannesburg	1935-36
114	A. D. Nourse, Cape Town	1949-50
111	A. W. Nourse, Johannesburg	1921-22
122	R. G. Pollock, Sydney	1963-64
175	R. G. Pollock, Adelaide	1963-64
209	R. G. Pollock, Cape Town	1966-67
105	R. G. Pollock, Port Elizabeth	1966-67
274	R. G. Pollock, Durban	1969-70
140	B. A. Richards, Durban	1969-70
126	B. A. Richards, Port Elizabeth	1969-70
143	E. A. B. Rowan, Durban	1949-50

101	J. H. Sinclair, Johannesburg	1902-03	115	J. H. B. Waite, Johannesburg	1957-58
104	J. H. Sinclair, Cape Town	1902-03	134	J. H. B. Waite, Durban	1957-58
103	S. J. Snooke, Adelaide	1910-11	105	J. W. Zulch, Adelaide	1910-11
111	K. G. Viljoen, Melbourne	1931-32	150	J. W. Zulch, Sydney	1910-11

† *Signifies hundred on first appearance in Australia–South Africa Tests.*
‡ *Carried his bat.*

RECORD PARTNERSHIPS FOR EACH WICKET

For Australia

233 for 1st	J. H. Fingleton and W. A. Brown at Cape Town	1935-36
275 for 2nd	C. C. McDonald and A. L. Hassett at Adelaide	1952-53
242 for 3rd	C. Kelleway and W. Bardsley at Lord's	1912
168 for 4th	R. N. Harvey and K. R. Miller at Sydney	1952-53
143 for 5th	W. W. Armstrong and V. T. Trumper at Melbourne	1910-11
107 for 6th	C. Kelleway and V. S. Ransford at Melbourne	1910-11
160 for 7th	R. Benaud and G. D. McKenzie at Sydney	1963-64
83 for 8th	A. G. Chipperfield and C. V. Grimmett at Durban	1935-36
78 for 9th	{ D. G. Bradman and W. J. O'Reilly at Adelaide	1931-32
	{ K. D. Mackay and I. Meckiff at Johannesburg	1957-58
82 for 10th	V. S. Ransford and W. J. Whitty at Melbourne	1910-11

For South Africa

176 for 1st	D. J. McGlew and T. L. Goddard at Johannesburg	1957-58
173 for 2nd	L. J. Tancred and C. B. Llewellyn at Johannesburg	1902-03
341 for 3rd†	E. J. Barlow and R. G. Pollock at Adelaide	1963-64
206 for 4th	C. N. Frank and A. W. Nourse at Johannesburg	1921-22
129 for 5th	J. H. B. Waite and W. R. Endean at Johannesburg	1957-58
200 for 6th†	R. G. Pollock and H. R. Lance at Durban	1969-70
221 for 7th	D. T. Lindsay and P. L. van der Merwe at Johannesburg	1966-67
124 for 8th†	A. W. Nourse and E. A. Halliwell at Johannesburg	1902-03
85 for 9th	R. G. Pollock and P. M. Pollock at Cape Town	1966-67
53 for 10th	L. A. Stricker and S. J. Pegler at Adelaide	1910-11

† *Denotes record partnership against all countries.*

TEN WICKETS OR MORE IN A MATCH

For Australia (5)

14-199 (7-116, 7-83)	C. V. Grimmett, Adelaide	1931-32
10-88 (5-32, 5-56)	C. V. Grimmett, Cape Town	1935-36
10-110 (3-70, 7-40)	C. V. Grimmett, Johannesburg	1935-36
13-173 (7-100, 6-73)	C. V. Grimmett, Durban	1935-36
11-24 (5-6, 6-18)	H. Ironmonger, Melbourne	1931-32

For South Africa (2)

| 10-116 (5-43, 5-73) | C. B. Llewellyn, Johannesburg | 1902-03 |
| 13-165 (6-84, 7-81) | H. J. Tayfield, Melbourne | 1952-53 |

Note: C. V. Grimmett took ten wickets or more in three consecutive matches in 1935-36.

AUSTRALIA v WEST INDIES

			Captains					
Season	*Australia*		*West Indies*	*T*	*A*	*WI*	*T*	*D*
1930-31*A*	W. M. Woodfull		G. C. Grant	5	4	1	0	0
1951-52*A*	A. L. Hassett[1]		J. D. C. Goddard[2]	5	4	1	0	0
1954-55*W*	I. W. Johnson		D. S. Atkinson[3]	5	3	0	0	2
1960-61*A*	R. Benaud		F. M. M. Worrell	5†	2	1	1	1

THE FRANK WORRELL TROPHY

			Captains						
Season	*Australia*		*West Indies*	*T*	*A*	*WI*	*T*	*D*	*Held by*
1964-65*W*	R. B. Simpson		G. S. Sobers	5	1	2	0	2	WI
1968-69*A*	W. M. Lawry		G. S. Sobers	5	3	1	0	1	A
1972-73*W*	I. M. Chappell		R. B. Kanhai	5	2	0	0	3	A
1975-76*A*	G. S. Chappell		C. H. Lloyd	6	5	1	0	0	A
1977-78*W*	R. B. Simpson	A. I. Kallicharran[4]		5	1	3	0	1	WI
1979-80*A*	G. S. Chappell		C. H. Lloyd[5]	3	0	2	0	1	WI
1981-82*A*	G. S. Chappell		C. H. Lloyd	3	1	1	0	1	WI
1983-84*W*	K. J. Hughes		C. H. Lloyd[6]	5	0	3	0	2	WI
1984-85*A*	A. R. Border[7]		C. H. Lloyd	5	1	3	0	1	WI
	In Australia			37	20	11	1	5	
	In West Indies			25	7	8	0	10	
	Totals			62	27	19	1	15	

† *The First Test at Brisbane resulted in a tie. This is the only instance of a Test match resulting in a tie.*

A Played in Australia.   W Played in West Indies.

Notes: The following deputised for the official touring captain or were appointed by the home authority for only a minor proportion of the series:
[1]A. R. Morris (Third). [2]J. B. Stollmeyer (Fifth). [3]J. B. Stollmeyer (Second and Third). [4]C. H. Lloyd (First and Second). [5]D. L. Murray (First). [6]I. V. A. Richards (Second). [7]K. J. Hughes (First and Second).

HIGHEST INNINGS TOTALS

For Australia in Australia: 619 at Sydney	1968-69
in West Indies: 758-8 dec. at Kingston	1954-55
For West Indies in Australia: 616 at Adelaide	1968-69
in West Indies: 573 at Bridgetown	1964-65

LOWEST INNINGS TOTALS

For Australia in Australia: 76 at Perth	1984-85
in West Indies: 90 at Port-of-Spain	1977-78
For West Indies in Australia: 78 at Sydney	1951-52
in West Indies: 109 at Georgetown	1972-73

INDIVIDUAL HUNDREDS

For Australia (64)

128	R. G. Archer, Kingston ...	1954-55
121	R. Benaud, Kingston	1954-55
117	B. C. Booth, Port-of-Spain	1964-65
126	A. R. Border, Adelaide ...	1981-82
100*	A. R. Border, Port-of-Spain	1983-84
223	D. G. Bradman, Brisbane .	1930-31
152	D. G. Bradman, Melbourne	1930-31
106	G. S. Chappell, Bridgetown	1972-73
123 ⎫ 109* ⎭	‡G. S. Chappell, Brisbane .	1975-76
182*	G. S. Chappell, Sydney ...	1975-76
124	G. S. Chappell, Brisbane .	1979-80
117†	I. M. Chappell, Brisbane .	1968-69
165	I. M. Chappell, Melbourne .	1968-69
106*	I. M. Chappell, Bridgetown	1972-73
109	I. M. Chappell, Georgetown	1972-73
156	I. M. Chappell, Perth	1975-76
109†	G. J. Cosier, Melbourne ...	1975-76
143	R. M. Cowper, Port-of-Spain	1964-65
102	R. M. Cowper, Bridgetown	1964-65
127*†	J. Dyson, Sydney	1981-82
133	R. N. Harvey, Kingston ...	1954-55
133	R. N. Harvey, Port-of-Spain	1954-55
204	R. N. Harvey, Kingston ...	1954-55
132	A. L. Hassett, Sydney	1951-52
102	A. L. Hassett, Melbourne .	1951-52
113†	A. M. J. Hilditch, Melbourne	1984-85
130*†	K. J. Hughes, Brisbane ...	1979-80
100*	K. J. Hughes, Adelaide ...	1981-82
146†	A. F. Kippax, Adelaide ...	1930-31
210	W. M. Lawry, Bridgetown .	1964-65
105	W. M. Lawry, Brisbane ...	1968-69
205	W. M. Lawry, Melbourne .	1968-69
151	W. M. Lawry, Sydney	1968-69
118	R. R. Lindwall, Bridgetown	1954-55
109*	R. B. McCosker, Melbourne	1975-76
110	C. C. McDonald, Port-of-Spain	1954-55
127	C. C. McDonald, Kingston	1954-55
129	K. R. Miller, Sydney	1951-52
147	K. R. Miller, Kingston	1954-55
137	K. R. Miller, Bridgetown .	1954-55
109	K. R. Miller, Kingston	1954-55
111	A. R. Morris, Port-of-Spain	1954-55
181†	N. C. O'Neill, Brisbane ...	1960-61
120	W. B. Phillips, Bridgetown .	1983-84
183	W. H. Ponsford, Sydney ...	1930-31
109	W. H. Ponsford, Brisbane .	1930-31
132	I. R. Redpath, Sydney	1968-69
102	I. R. Redpath, Melbourne .	1975-76
103	I. R. Redpath, Adelaide ...	1975-76
101	I. R. Redpath, Melbourne .	1975-76
124	C. S. Serjeant, Georgetown	1977-78
201	R. B. Simpson, Bridgetown	1964-65
142	K. R. Stackpole, Kingston .	1972-73
122	P. M. Toohey, Kingston ...	1977-78
136	A. Turner, Adelaide	1975-76
118	K. D. Walters, Sydney	1968-69
110	K. D. Walters, Adelaide ...	1968-69
242 ⎫ 103 ⎭	K. D. Walters, Sydney	1968-69
102*	K. D. Walters, Bridgetown .	1972-73
112	K. D. Walters, Port-of-Spain	1972-73
173	K. C. Wessels, Sydney	1984-85
126	G. M. Wood, Georgetown .	1977-78

‡ *G. S. Chappell is the only player to score hundreds in both innings of his first Test as captain.*

For West Indies (63)

108	F. C. M. Alexander, Sydney	1960-61
219	D. St E. Atkinson, Bridgetown	1954-55
117	B. F. Butcher, Port-of-Spain	1964-65
101	B. F. Butcher, Sydney	1968-69
118	B. F. Butcher, Adelaide	1968-69
122	C. C. Depeiza, Bridgetown .	1954-55
130	P. J. L. Dujon, Port-of-Spain	1983-84
139	P. J. L. Dujon, Perth	1984-85
125†	M. L. C. Foster, Kingston .	1972-73
169	R. C. Fredericks, Perth	1975-76
101†	H. A. Gomes, Georgetown .	1977-78
115	H. A. Gomes, Kingston ...	1977-78
126	H. A. Gomes, Sydney	1981-82
124*	H. A. Gomes, Adelaide ...	1981-82
127	H. A. Gomes, Perth	1984-85
120*	H. A. Gomes, Adelaide ...	1984-85
120*	C. G. Greenidge, Georgetown	1983-84
127	C. G. Greenidge, Kingston .	1983-84
103*	D. L. Haynes, Georgetown .	1983-84
145	D. L. Haynes, Bridgetown ..	1983-84
102*	G. A. Headley, Brisbane ...	1930-31
105	G. A. Headley, Sydney	1930-31
110	C. C. Hunte, Melbourne ...	1960-61
101	A. I. Kallicharran, Brisbane	1975-76
127	A. I. Kallicharran, Port-of-Spain	1977-78
126	A. I. Kallicharran, Kingston	1977-78
106	A. I. Kallicharran, Adelaide	1979-80
117 ⎫ 115 ⎭	R. B. Kanhai, Adelaide	1960-61

129	R. B. Kanhai, Bridgetown .	1964-65	154	R. B. Richardson, St John's	1983-84
121	R. B. Kanhai, Port-of-Spain	1964-65	138	R. B. Richardson, Brisbane.	1984-85
105	R. B. Kanhai, Bridgetown .	1972-73	107	L. G. Rowe, Brisbane	1975-76
129†	C. H. Lloyd, Brisbane	1968-69	104†	O. G. Smith, Kingston	1954-55
178	C. H. Lloyd, Georgetown .	1972-73	132	G. S. Sobers, Brisbane ...	1960-61
149	C. H. Lloyd, Perth	1975-76	168	G. S. Sobers, Sydney	1960-61
102	C. H. Lloyd, Melbourne ..	1975-76	110	G. S. Sobers, Adelaide ...	1968-69
121	C. H. Lloyd, Adelaide	1979-80	113	G. S. Sobers, Sydney	1968-69
114	C. H. Lloyd, Brisbane	1984-85	104	J. B. Stollmeyer, Sydney ...	1951-52
123*	F. R. Martin, Sydney	1930-31	108	C. L. Walcott, Kingston ...	1954-55

Note: F. C. M. Alexander and C. C. Depeiza scored the only hundreds of their careers in a Test match.

TEN WICKETS OR MORE IN A MATCH

For Australia (9)

11-222 (5-135, 6-87)†	A. K. Davidson, Brisbane		1960-61
11-183 (7-87, 4-96)†	C. V. Grimmett, Adelaide		1930-31
10-115 (6-72, 4-43)	N. J. N. Hawke, Georgetown		1964-65
10-144 (6-54, 4-90)	R. G. Holland, Sydney		1984-85
11-79 (7-23, 4-56)	H. Ironmonger, Melbourne		1930-31
11-181 (8-112, 3-69)	G. F. Lawson, Adelaide		1984-85
10-127 (7-83, 3-44)	D. K. Lillee, Melbourne		1981-82
10-159 (8-71, 2-88)	G. D. McKenzie, Melbourne		1968-69
10-185 (3-87, 7-98)	B. Yardley, Sydney		1981-82

For West Indies (3)

10-113 (7-55, 3-58)	G. E. Gomez, Sydney		1951-52
11-107 (5-45, 6-62)	M. A. Holding, Melbourne		1981-82
10-107 (5-69, 5-38)	M. D. Marshall, Adelaide		1984-85

† *Signifies ten wickets or more on first appearance in Australia–West Indies Tests.*

AUSTRALIA v NEW ZEALAND

	Captains					
Season	Australia	New Zealand	T	A	NZ	D
1945-46N	W. A. Brown	W. A. Hadlee	1	1	0	0
1973-74A	I. M. Chappell	B. E. Congdon	3	2	0	1
1973-74N	I. M. Chappell	B. E. Congdon	3	1	1	1
1976-77N	G. S. Chappell	G. M. Turner	2	1	0	1
1980-81A	G. S. Chappell	G. P. Howarth[1]	3	2	0	1
1981-82N	G. S. Chappell	G. P. Howarth	3	1	1	1

TRANS-TASMAN TROPHY

	Captains						
Season	Australia	New Zealand	T	A	NZ	D	Held by
1985-86A	A. R. Border	J. V. Coney	3	1	2	0	NZ
1985-86N	A. R. Border	J. V. Coney	3	0	1	2	NZ

In Australia		9	5	2	2
In New Zealand		12	4	3	5
Totals		21	9	5	7

A Played in Australia. N Played in New Zealand.

Note: The following deputised for the official touring captain: [1]M. G. Burgess (Second).

HIGHEST INNINGS TOTALS

For Australia in Australia: 477 at Adelaide		1973-74
in New Zealand: 552 at Christchurch		1976-77
For New Zealand in Australia: 553-7 dec. at Brisbane		1985-86
in New Zealand: 484 at Wellington		1973-74

LOWEST INNINGS TOTALS

For Australia in Australia: 162 at Sydney		1973-74
in New Zealand: 103 at Auckland		1985-86
For New Zealand in Australia: 121 at Perth		1980-81
in New Zealand: 42 at Wellington		1945-46

INDIVIDUAL HUNDREDS

For Australia (20)

152*	A. R. Border, Brisbane 1985-86	115†	G. R. J. Matthews, Brisbane 1985-86
140	A. R. Border, Christchurch 1985-86	130	G. R. J. Matthews, Wellington 1985-86
114*			
247*	G. S. Chappell, Wellington . 1973-74	159*‡	I. R. Redpath, Auckland .. 1973-74
133		122†	K. R. Stackpole, Melbourne 1973-74
176	G. S. Chappell, Christchurch 1981-82	104*	K. D. Walters, Auckland .. 1973-74
145	I. M. Chappell, Wellington 1973-74	250	K. D. Walters, Christchurch 1976-77
121			
101	G. J. Gilmour, Christchurch 1976-77	107	K. D. Walters, Melbourne . 1980-81
118	G. R. Marsh, Auckland .. 1985-86	111†	G. M. Wood, Brisbane 1980-81
132	R. W. Marsh, Adelaide ... 1973-74	100	G. M. Wood, Auckland ... 1981-82

For New Zealand (13)

101*	J. V. Coney, Wellington ... 1985-86	101	B. F. Hastings, Wellington . 1973-74
132	B. E. Congdon, Wellington . 1973-74	117	J. F. M. Morrison, Sydney . 1973-74
107*	B. E. Congdon, Christchurch 1976-77	108	J. M. Parker, Sydney 1973-74
		108†	J. F. Reid, Brisbane 1985-86
188	M. D. Crowe, Brisbane ... 1985-86	101	G. M. Turner, Christchurch 1973-74
137	M. D. Crowe, Christchurch 1985-86	110*	
161	B. A. Edgar, Auckland 1981-82	141	J. G. Wright, Christchurch . 1981-82

† *Signifies hundred on first appearance in Australia–New Zealand Tests.*
‡ *Carried his bat.*

Notes: G. S. and I. M. Chappell at Wellington in 1973-74 provide the only instance in Test matches of brothers both scoring a hundred in each innings and in the same Test.

G. S. Chappell's match aggregate of 380 (247* and 133) for Australia at Wellington in 1973-74 is the record in Test matches.

RECORD PARTNERSHIPS FOR EACH WICKET

For Australia

106 for 1st	B. M. Laird and G. M. Wood at Auckland	1981-82
168 for 2nd	G. R. Marsh and W. B. Phillips at Auckland	1985-86
264 for 3rd	I. M. Chappell and G. S. Chappell at Wellington	1973-74
106 for 4th	I. R. Redpath and I. C. Davis at Christchurch	1973-74
213 for 5th	G. M. Ritchie and G. R. J. Matthews at Wellington	1985-86
197 for 6th	A. R. Border and G. R. J. Matthews at Brisbane	1985-86
217 for 7th†	K. D. Walters and G. J. Gilmour at Christchurch	1976-77
93 for 8th	G. J. Gilmour and K. J. O'Keeffe at Auckland	1976-77
57 for 9th	R. W. Marsh and L. S. Pascoe at Perth	1980-81
60 for 10th	K. D. Walters and J. D. Higgs at Melbourne	1980-81

For New Zealand

107 for 1st	G. M. Turner and J. M. Parker at Auckland	1973-74
108 for 2nd	G. M. Turner and J. F. M. Morrison at Wellington	1973-74
224 for 3rd	J. F. Reid and M. D. Crowe at Brisbane	1985-86
229 for 4th†	B. E. Congdon and B. F. Hastings at Wellington	1973-74
88 for 5th	J. V. Coney and G. Burgess at Perth	1980-81
109 for 6th	K. R. Rutherford and J. V. Coney at Wellington	1985-86
132* for 7th	J. V. Coney and R. J. Hadlee at Wellington	1985-86
53 for 8th	B. A. Edgar and R. J. Hadlee at Brisbane	1980-81
73 for 9th	H. J. Howarth and D. R. Hadlee at Christchurch	1976-77
124 for 10th	J. G. Bracewell and S. L. Boock at Sydney	1985-86

† *Denotes record partnership against all countries.*

TEN WICKETS OR MORE IN A MATCH

For Australia (2)

10-174 (6-106, 4-68)	R. G. Holland, Sydney	1985-86
11-123 (5-51, 6-72)	D. K. Lillee, Auckland	1976-77

For New Zealand (3)

10-106 (4-74, 6-32)	J. G. Bracewell, Auckland	1985-86
15-123 (9-52, 6-71)	R. J. Hadlee, Brisbane	1985-86
11-155 (5-65, 6-90)	R. J. Hadlee, Perth	1985-86

AUSTRALIA v INDIA

Season	Australia	*Captains* India	T	A	I	T	D
1947-48*A*	D. G. Bradman	L. Amarnath	5	4	0	0	1
1956-57*I*	I. W. Johnson[1]	P. R. Umrigar	3	2	0	0	1
1959-60*I*	R. Benaud	G. S. Ramchand	5	2	1	0	2
1964-65*I*	R. B. Simpson	Nawab of Pataudi jun.	3	1	1	0	1
1967-68*A*	R. B. Simpson[2]	Nawab of Pataudi jun.[3]	4	4	0	0	0
1969-70*I*	W. M. Lawry	Nawab of Pataudi jun.	5	3	1	0	1
1977-78*A*	R. B. Simpson	B. S. Bedi	5	3	2	0	0
1979-80*I*	K. J. Hughes	S. M. Gavaskar	6	0	2	0	4
1980-81*A*	G. S. Chappell	S. M. Gavaskar	3	1	1	0	1
1985-86*A*	A. R. Border	Kapil Dev	3	0	0	0	3
1986-87*I*	A. R. Border	Kapil Dev	3	0	0	1	2
	In Australia		20	12	3	0	5
	In India		25	8	5	1	11
	Totals		45	20	8	1	16

A Played in Australia.   I Played in India.

Notes: The following deputised for the official touring captain or were appointed by the home authority for only a minor proportion of the series:
[1] R. R. Lindwall (Second).   [2] W. M. Lawry (Third and Fourth).   [3] C. G. Borde (First).

HIGHEST INNINGS TOTALS

For Australia in Australia: 674 at Adelaide	1947-48
in India: 574-7 dec. at Madras	1986-87
For India in Australia: 600-4 dec. at Sydney	1985-86
in India: 517-5 dec. at Bombay	1986-87

LOWEST INNINGS TOTALS

For Australia in Australia: 83 at Melbourne	1980-81
in India: 105 at Kanpur	1959-60
For India in Australia: 58 at Brisbane	1947-48
in India: 135 at Delhi	1959-60

INDIVIDUAL HUNDREDS

For Australia (45)

112	S. G. Barnes, Adelaide	1947-48
123†	D. C. Boon, Adelaide	1985-86
131	D. C. Boon, Sydney	1985-86
122	D. C. Boon, Madras	1986-87
162†	A. R. Border, Madras	1979-80
124	A. R. Border, Melbourne	1980-81
163	A. R. Border, Melbourne	1985-86
106	A. R. Border, Madras	1986-87
185†	D. G. Bradman, Brisbane	1947-48
132	D. G. Bradman, Melbourne	1947-48
127*		
201	D. G. Bradman, Adelaide	1947-48
161	J. W. Burke, Bombay	1956-57
204†	G. S. Chappell, Sydney	1980-81
151	I. M. Chappell, Melbourne	1967-68
138	I. M. Chappell, Delhi	1969-70
108	R. M. Cowper, Adelaide	1967-68
165	R. M. Cowper, Sydney	1967-68
101	L. E. Favell, Madras	1959-60
153	R. N. Harvey, Melbourne	1947-48
140	R. N. Harvey, Bombay	1956-57
114	R. N. Harvey, Delhi	1959-60
102	R. N. Harvey, Bombay	1959-60

198*	A. L. Hassett, Adelaide	1947-48
100	K. J. Hughes, Madras	1979-80
213	K. J. Hughes, Adelaide	1980-81
210†	D. M. Jones, Madras	1986-87
100	W. M. Lawry, Melbourne	1967-68
105	A. L. Mann, Perth	1977-78
101	G. R. Marsh, Bombay	1986-87
100*	G. R. J. Matthews, Melbourne	1985-86
100*	A. R. Morris, Melbourne	1947-48
163	N. C. O'Neill, Bombay	1959-60
113	N. C. O'Neill, Calcutta	1959-60
128†	G. M. Ritchie, Adelaide	1985-86
114	A. P. Sheahan, Kanpur	1969-70
103	R. B. Simpson, Adelaide	1967-68
109	R. B. Simpson, Melbourne	1967-68
176	R. B. Simpson, Perth	1977-78
100	R. B. Simpson, Adelaide	1977-78
103†	K. R. Stackpole, Bombay	1969-70
102	K. D. Walters, Madras	1969-70
125	G. M. Wood, Adelaide	1980-81
121†	G. N. Yallop, Adelaide	1977-78
167	G. N. Yallop, Calcutta	1979-80

For India (31)

100	M. Amarnath, Perth	1977-78
138	M. Amarnath, Sydney	1985-86
108	N. J. Contractor, Bombay	1959-60
113†	S. M. Gavaskar, Brisbane	1977-78
127	S. M. Gavaskar, Perth	1977-78
118	S. M. Gavaskar, Melbourne	1977-78
115	S. M. Gavaskar, Delhi	1979-80
123	S. M. Gavaskar, Bombay	1979-80
166*	S. M. Gavaskar, Adelaide	1985-86
172	S. M. Gavaskar, Sydney	1985-86
103	S. M. Gavaskar, Bombay	1986-87
116	V. S. Hazare, Adelaide	1947-48
145		
101	M. L. Jaisimha, Brisbane	1967-68
119	Kapil Dev, Madras	1986-87
101*	S. M. H. Kirmani, Bombay	1979-80
116	V. Mankad, Melbourne	1947-48

111	V. Mankad, Melbourne	1947-48
128*†	Nawab of Pataudi, Madras	1964-65
174	S. M. Patil, Adelaide	1980-81
123	D. G. Phadkar, Adelaide	1947-48
109	G. S. Ramchand, Bombay	1956-57
121*	R. J. Shastri, Bombay	1986-87
116	K. Srikkanth, Sydney	1985-86
112	D. B. Vengsarkar, Bangalore	1979-80
164*	D. B. Vengsarkar, Bombay	1986-87
137†	G. R. Viswanath, Kanpur	1969-70
161*	G. R. Viswanath, Bangalore	1979-80
131	G. R. Viswanath, Delhi	1979-80
114	G. R. Viswanath, Melbourne	1980-81
100*	Yashpal Sharma, Delhi	1979-80

† *Signifies hundred on first appearance in Australia–India Tests.*

RECORD PARTNERSHIPS FOR EACH WICKET

For Australia

217 for 1st	D. C. Boon and G. R. Marsh at Sydney	1985-86
236 for 2nd	S. G. Barnes and D. G. Bradman at Adelaide	1947-48
222 for 3rd	A. R. Border and K. J. Hughes at Madras	1979-80
178 for 4th	D. M. Jones and A. R. Border at Madras	1986-87
223* for 5th	A. R. Morris and D. G. Bradman at Melbourne	1947-48
151 for 6th	T. R. Veivers and B. N. Jarman at Bombay	1964-65
64 for 7th	T. R. Veivers and J. W. Martin at Madras	1964-65
73 for 8th	T. R. Veivers and G. D. McKenzie at Madras	1964-65
87 for 9th	I. W. Johnson and W. P. A. Crawford at Madras	1956-57
77 for 10th	A. R. Border and D. R. Gilbert at Melbourne	1985-86

For India

192 for 1st	S. M. Gavaskar and C. P. S. Chauhan at Bombay	1979-80
224 for 2nd	S. M. Gavaskar and M. Amarnath at Sydney	1985-86
159 for 3rd	S. M. Gavaskar and G. R. Viswanath at Delhi	1979-80
159 for 4th	D. B. Vengsarkar and G. R. Viswanath at Bangalore	1979-80
109 for 5th	A. A. Baig and R. B. Kenny at Bombay	1959-60
298* for 6th†	D. B. Vengsarkar and R. J. Shastri at Bombay	1986-87
132 for 7th	V. S. Hazare and H. R. Adhikari at Adelaide	1947-48
127 for 8th	S. M. H. Kirmani and K. D. Ghavri at Bombay	1979-80
57 for 9th	S. M. H. Kirmani and K. D. Ghavri at Sydney	1980-81
94 for 10th	S. M. Gavaskar and N. S. Yadav at Adelaide	1985-86

† *Denotes record partnership against all countries.*

TEN WICKETS OR MORE IN A MATCH

For Australia (8)

11-105 (6-52, 5-53)	R. Benaud, Calcutta	1956-57
12-124 (5-31, 7-93)	A. K. Davidson, Kanpur	1959-60
12-166 (5-99, 7-67)	G. Dymock, Kanpur	1979-80
10-91 (6-58, 4-33)†	G. D. McKenzie, Madras	1964-65
10-151 (7-66, 3-85)	G. D. McKenzie, Melbourne	1967-68
10-144 (5-91, 5-53)	A. A. Mallett, Madras	1969-70
10-249 (5-103, 5-146)	G. R. J. Matthews, Madras	1986-87
11-31 (5-2, 6-29)†	E. R. H. Toshack, Brisbane	1947-48

For India (6)

10-194 (5-89, 5-105)	B. S. Bedi, Perth	1977-78
12-104 (6-52, 6-52)	B. S. Chandrasekhar, Melbourne	1977-78
10-130 (7-49, 3-81)	Ghulam Ahmed, Calcutta	1956-57
11-122 (5-31, 6-91)	R. G. Nadkarni, Madras	1964-65
14-124 (9-69, 5-55)	J. M. Patel, Kanpur	1959-60
10-174 (4-100, 6-74)	E. A. S. Prasanna, Madras	1969-70

† *Signifies ten wickets or more on first appearance in Australia–India Tests.*

AUSTRALIA v PAKISTAN

Season	Australia	Captains Pakistan	T	A	P	D
1956-57 *P*	I. W. Johnson	A. H. Kardar	1	0	1	0
1959-60 *P*	R. Benaud	Fazal Mahmood[1]	3	2	0	1
1964-65 *P*	R. B. Simpson	Hanif Mohammad	1	0	0	1
1964-65 *A*	R. B. Simpson	Hanif Mohammad	1	0	0	1
1972-73 *A*	I. M. Chappell	Intikhab Alam	3	3	0	0
1976-77 *A*	G. S. Chappell	Mushtaq Mohammad	3	1	1	1
1978-79 *A*	G. N. Yallop[2]	Mushtaq Mohammad	2	1	1	0
1979-80 *P*	G. S. Chappell	Javed Miandad	3	0	1	2
1981-82 *A*	G. S. Chappell	Javed Miandad	3	2	1	0
1982-83 *P*	K. J. Hughes	Imran Khan	3	0	3	0
1983-84 *A*	K. J. Hughes	Imran Khan[3]	5	2	0	3
	In Pakistan		11	2	5	4
	In Australia		17	9	3	5
	Totals		28	11	8	9

A Played in Australia.   P Played in Pakistan.

Notes: [1] Imtiaz Ahmed captained in Second Test. [2] K. J. Hughes captained in Second Test. [3] Zaheer Abbas captained in First, Second and Third Tests.

HIGHEST INNINGS TOTALS

For Australia in Australia: 585 at Adelaide 1972-73
          in Pakistan: 617 at Faisalabad 1979-80
For Pakistan in Australia: 624 at Adelaide 1983-84
          in Pakistan: 501-6 dec. at Faisalabad 1982-83

LOWEST INNINGS TOTALS

For Australia in Australia: 125 at Melbourne 1981-82
          in Pakistan: 80 at Karachi 1956-57
For Pakistan in Australia: 62 at Perth 1981-82
          in Pakistan: 134 at Dacca 1959-60

INDIVIDUAL HUNDREDS

For Australia (32)

142	J. Benaud, Melbourne	1972-73	105	R. B. McCosker, Melbourne		1976-77
105†	A. R. Border, Melbourne	1978-79	118†	R. W. Marsh, Adelaide		1972-73
150*	A. R. Border, Lahore	1979-80	134	N. C. O'Neill, Lahore		1959-60
153			159†	W. B. Phillips, Perth		1983-84
118	A. R. Border, Brisbane	1983-84	135	I. R. Redpath, Melbourne		1972-73
117*	A. R. Border, Adelaide	1983-84	106*	G. M. Ritchie, Faisalabad		1982-83
116*	G. S. Chappell, Melbourne	1972-73	127	A. P. Sheahan, Melbourne		1972-73
121	G. S. Chappell, Melbourne	1976-77	153†	R. B. Simpson, Karachi		1964-65
235	G. S. Chappell, Faisalabad	1979-80	115			
201	G. S. Chappell, Brisbane	1981-82	107	K. D. Walters, Adelaide		1976-77
150*	G. S. Chappell, Brisbane	1983-84	179	K. C. Wessels, Adelaide		1983-84
182	G. S. Chappell, Sydney	1983-84	100	G. M. Wood, Melbourne		1981-82
196	I. M. Chappell, Adelaide	1972-73	172	G. N. Yallop, Faisalabad		1979-80
168	G. J. Cosier, Melbourne	1976-77	141	G. N. Yallop, Perth		1983-84
105†	I. C. Davis, Adelaide	1976-77	268	G. N. Yallop, Melbourne		1983-84
106	K. J. Hughes, Perth	1981-82				
106	K. J. Hughes, Adelaide	1983-84				

For Pakistan (25)

152*	Asif Iqbal, Adelaide	1976-77	135	Mohsin Khan, Lahore	1982-83
120	Asif Iqbal, Sydney	1976-77	149	Mohsin Khan, Adelaide	1983-84
134*	Asif Iqbal, Perth	1978-79	152	Mohsin Khan, Melbourne	1983-84
101*	Hanif Mohammad, Karachi	1959-60	121	Mushtaq Mohammad, Sydney	1972-73
104	Hanif Mohammad, Melbourne	1964-65	113	Qasim Omar, Adelaide	1983-84
129*	Javed Miandad, Perth	1976-77	137	Sadiq Mohammad, Melbourne	1972-73
106*	Javed Miandad, Faisalabad	1979-80	105	Sadiq Mohammad, Melbourne	1976-77
138	Javed Miandad, Lahore	1982-83	166	Saeed Ahmed, Lahore	1959-60
131	Javed Miandad, Adelaide	1983-84	210*	Taslim Arif, Faisalabad	1979-80
166†	Khalid Ibadulla, Karachi	1964-65	101	Zaheer Abbas, Adelaide	1976-77
158	Majid Khan, Melbourne	1972-73	126	Zaheer Abbas, Faisalabad	1982-83
108	Majid Khan, Melbourne	1978-79			
110*	Majid Khan, Lahore	1979-80			
111	Mansoor Akhtar, Faisalabad	1982-83			

† *Signifies hundred on first appearance in Australia–Pakistan Tests.*

RECORD PARTNERSHIPS FOR EACH WICKET

For Australia

134 for 1st	I. C. Davis and A. Turner at Melbourne	....	1976-77
259 for 2nd	W. B. Phillips and G. N. Yallop at Perth	....	1983-84
203 for 3rd	G. N. Yallop and K. J. Hughes at Melbourne	....	1983-84
217 for 4th	G. S. Chappell and G. N. Yallop at Faisalabad	....	1979-80
171 for 5th	{ G. S. Chappell and G. J. Cosier at Melbourne	....	1976-77
	A. R. Border and G. S. Chappell at Brisbane	....	1983-84
139 for 6th	R. M. Cowper and T. R. Veivers at Melbourne	....	1964-65
185 for 7th	G. N. Yallop and G. R. J. Matthews at Melbourne	....	1983-84
117 for 8th	G. J. Cosier and K. J. O'Keeffe at Melbourne	....	1976-77
83 for 9th	J. R. Watkins and R. A. L. Massie at Sydney	....	1972-73
52 for 10th	{ D. K. Lillee and M. H. N. Walker at Sydney	....	1976-77
	G. F. Lawson and T. M. Alderman at Lahore	....	1982-83

For Pakistan

249 for 1st†	Khalid Ibadulla and Abdul Kadir at Karachi	....	1964-65
233 for 2nd	Mohsin Khan and Qasim Omar at Adelaide	....	1983-84
223* for 3rd	Taslim Arif and Javed Miandad at Faisalabad	....	1979-80
155 for 4th	Mansoor Akhtar and Zaheer Abbas at Faisalabad	....	1982-83
186 for 5th	Javed Miandad and Salim Malik at Adelaide	....	1983-84
115 for 6th	Asif Iqbal and Javed Miandad at Sydney	....	1976-77
104 for 7th	Intikhab Alam and Wasim Bari at Adelaide	....	1972-73
111 for 8th	Majid Khan and Imran Khan at Lahore	....	1979-80
56 for 9th	Intikhab Alam and Afaq Hussain at Melbourne	....	1964-65
87 for 10th	Asif Iqbal and Iqbal Qasim at Adelaide	....	1976-77

† *Denotes record partnership against all countries.*

TEN WICKETS OR MORE IN A MATCH

For Australia (2)

10-111 (7-87, 3-24)†	R. J. Bright, Karachi	....	1979-80
10-135 (6-82, 4-53)	D. K. Lillee, Melbourne	....	1976-77
11-118 (5-32, 6-86)†	C. G. Rackemann, Perth	....	1983-84

For Pakistan (5)

11-218 (4-76, 7-142)	Abdul Qadir, Faisalabad	....	1982-83
13-114 (6-34, 7-80)†	Fazal Mahmood, Karachi	....	1956-57
12-165 (6-102, 6-63)	Imran Khan, Sydney	....	1976-77
11-118 (4-69, 7-49)	Iqbal Qasim, Karachi	....	1979-80
11-125 (2-39, 9-86)	Sarfraz Nawaz, Melbourne	....	1978-79

† *Signifies ten wickets or more on first appearance in Australia–Pakistan Tests.*

AUSTRALIA v SRI LANKA

		Captains					
Season	*Australia*		*Sri Lanka*	*T*	*A*	*SL*	*D*
1982-83*SL*	G. S. Chappell		L. R. D. Mendis	1	1	0	0

SL Played in Sri Lanka.

The only match played was at Kandy.

INDIVIDUAL HUNDREDS

For Australia (2)

143*† D. W. Hookes, Kandy ... 1982-83 | 141† K. C. Wessels, Kandy ... 1982-83

† *Signifies hundred on first appearance in Australia–Sri Lanka Tests.*

Highest score for Sri Lanka: 96 by S. Wettimuny.

Best bowling in an innings for Australia: 5-66 by T. G. Hogan.
for Sri Lanka: 2-113 by A. L. F. de Mel.

Best wicket partnerships for Australia:170 for the 2nd by K. C. Wessels and G. N. Yallop.
155* for the 5th by D. W. Hookes and A. R. Border.
for Sri Lanka: 96 for the 5th by L. R. D. Mendis and
A. Ranatunga.

Highest innings total for Australia: 514-4 dec.
for Sri Lanka: 271.

SOUTH AFRICA v NEW ZEALAND

		Captains				
Season	*South Africa*	*New Zealand*	*T*	*SA*	*NZ*	*D*
1931-32*N*	H. B. Cameron	M. L. Page	2	2	0	0
1952-53*N*	J. E. Cheetham	W. M. Wallace	2	1	0	1
1953-54*S*	J. E. Cheetham	G. O. Rabone[1]	5	4	0	1
1961-62*S*	D. J. McGlew	J. R. Reid	5	2	2	1
1963-64*N*	T. L. Goddard	J. R. Reid	3	0	0	3
	In New Zealand		7	3	0	4
	In South Africa		10	6	2	2
	Totals		17	9	2	6

N Played in New Zealand. S Played in South Africa.
Note: [1]B. Sutcliffe captained in Fourth and Fifth Tests.

HIGHEST INNINGS TOTALS

For South Africa in South Africa: 464 at Johannesburg 1961-62
in New Zealand: 524-8 at Wellington 1952-53
For New Zealand in South Africa: 505 at Cape Town 1953-54
in New Zealand: 364 at Wellington 1931-32

LOWEST INNINGS TOTALS

For South Africa in South Africa: 148 at Johannesburg 1953-54
in New Zealand: 223 at Dunedin 1963-64
For New Zealand in South Africa: 79 at Johannesburg 1953-54
in New Zealand: 138 at Dunedin 1963-64

INDIVIDUAL HUNDREDS

For South Africa (11)

122*	X. C. Balaskas, Wellington	1931-32	101	R. A. McLean, Durban ...	1953-54
103†	J. A. J. Christy, Christchurch	1931-32	113	R. A. McLean, Cape Town	1961-62
116	W. R. Endean, Auckland ..	1952-53	113†	B. Mitchell, Christchurch ..	1931-32
255*†	D. J. McGlew, Wellington ..	1952-53	109†	A. R. A. Murray, Wellington	1952-53
127*‡	D. J. McGlew, Durban ...	1961-62			
120	D. J. McGlew, Johannesburg	1961-62	101	J. H. B. Waite, Johannesburg	1961-62

For New Zealand (7)

109	P. T. Barton, Port Elizabeth	1961-62	135	J. R. Reid, Cape Town ...	1953-54
101	P. G. Z. Harris, Cape Town	1961-62	142	J. R. Reid, Johannesburg	1961-62
107	G. O. Rabone, Durban	1953-54	138	B. W. Sinclair, Auckland ..	1963-64
			100†	H. G. Vivian, Wellington .	1931-32

† *Signifies hundred on first appearance in South Africa–New Zealand Tests.*
‡ *Carried his bat.*

RECORD PARTNERSHIPS FOR EACH WICKET

For South Africa

196 for 1st	J. A. J. Christy and B. Mitchell at Christchurch	1931-32
76 for 2nd	J. A. J. Christy and H. B. Cameron at Wellington	1931-32
112 for 3rd	D. J. McGlew and R. A. McLean at Johannesburg	1961-62
135 for 4th	K. J. Funston and R. A. McLean at Durban	1953-54
130 for 5th	W. R. Endean and J. E. Cheetham at Auckland	1952-53
83 for 6th	K. C. Bland and D. T. Lindsay at Auckland	1963-64
246 for 7th†	D. J. McGlew and A. R. A. Murray at Wellington	1952-53
95 for 8th	J. E. Cheetham and H. J. Tayfield at Cape Town	1953-54
60 for 9th	P. M. Pollock and N. A. T. Adcock at Port Elizabeth	1961-62
47 for 10th	D. J. McGlew and H. D. Bromfield at Port Elizabeth	1961-62

For New Zealand

126 for 1st	G. O. Rabone and M. E. Chapple at Cape Town	1953-54
51 for 2nd	W. P. Bradburn and B. W. Sinclair at Dunedin	1963-64
94 for 3rd	M. B. Poore and B. Sutcliffe at Cape Town	1953-54
171 for 4th	B. W. Sinclair and S. N. McGregor at Auckland	1963-64
174 for 5th	J. R. Reid and J. E. F. Beck at Cape Town	1953-54
100 for 6th	H. G. Vivian and F. T. Badcock at Wellington	1931-32
84 for 7th	J. R. Reid and G. A. Bartlett at Johannesburg	1961-62
73 for 8th	P. G. Z. Harris and G. A. Bartlett at Durban	1961-62
69 for 9th	C. F. W. Allcott and I. B. Cromb at Wellington	1931-32
49* for 10th	A. E. Dick and F. J. Cameron at Cape Town	1961-62

† *Denotes record partnership against all countries.*

TEN WICKETS OR MORE IN A MATCH

For South Africa (1)

11-196 (6-128, 5-68)†	S. F. Burke, Cape Town	1961-62

† *Signifies ten wickets or more on first appearance in South Africa–New Zealand Tests.*

Note: The best match figures by a New Zealand bowler are 8-180 (4-61, 4-119), J. C. Alabaster at Cape Town, 1961-62.

WEST INDIES v NEW ZEALAND

	Captains					
Season	*West Indies*	*New Zealand*	*T*	*WI*	*NZ*	*D*
1951-52N	J. D. C. Goddard	B. Sutcliffe	2	1	0	1
1955-56N	D. St E. Atkinson	J. R. Reid[1]	4	3	1	0
1968-69N	G. S. Sobers	G. T. Dowling	3	1	1	1
1971-72W	G. S. Sobers	G. T. Dowling[2]	5	0	0	5
1979-80N	C. H. Lloyd	G. P. Howarth	3	0	1	2
1984-85W	I. V. A. Richards	G. P. Howarth	4	2	0	2
1986-87N	I. V. A. Richards	J. V. Coney	3	1	1	1
	In New Zealand		15	6	4	5
	In West Indies		9	2	0	7
	Totals		24	8	4	12

N Played in New Zealand. W Played in West Indies.

Notes: The following deputised for the official touring captain or were appointed by the home authority for only a minor proportion of the series:
[1]H. B. Cave (First). [2]B. E. Congdon (Third, Fourth and Fifth).

HIGHEST INNINGS TOTALS

For West Indies in West Indies: 564-8 at Bridgetown		1971-72
in New Zealand: 546-6 dec. at Auckland		1951-52
For New Zealand in West Indies: 543-3 dec. at Georgetown		1971-72
in New Zealand: 460 at Christchurch		1979-80

LOWEST INNINGS TOTALS

For West Indies in West Indies: 133 at Bridgetown		1971-72
in New Zealand: 77 at Auckland		1955-56
For New Zealand in West Indies: 94 at Bridgetown		1984-85
in New Zealand: 74 at Dunedin		1955-56

INDIVIDUAL HUNDREDS

By West Indies (25)

109†	M. C. Carew, Auckland	1968-69
183	C. A. Davis, Bridgetown	1971-72
163	R. C. Fredericks, Kingston	1971-72
100	C. G. Greenidge, Port-of-Spain	1984-85
213	C. G. Greenidge, Auckland	1986-87
105†	D. L. Haynes, Dunedin	1979-80
122	D. L. Haynes, Christchurch	1979-80
121	D. L. Haynes, Wellington	1986-87
100*†	A. I. Kallicharran, Georgetown	1971-72
101	A. I. Kallicharran, Port-of-Spain	1971-72
100*	C. L. King, Christchurch	1979-80
168†	S. M. Nurse, Auckland	1968-69
258	S. M. Nurse, Christchurch	1968-69
105	I. V. A. Richards, Bridgetown	1984-85
185	R. B. Richardson, Georgetown	1984-85
214† } 100* }	L. G. Rowe, Kingston	1971-72
100	L. G. Rowe, Christchurch	1979-80
142	G. S. Sobers, Bridgetown	1971-72
152	J. B. Stollmeyer, Auckland	1951-52
115	C. L. Walcott, Auckland	1951-52
123	E. D. Weekes, Dunedin	1955-56
103	E. D. Weekes, Christchurch	1955-56
156	E. D. Weekes, Wellington	1955-56
100	F. M. M. Worrell, Auckland	1951-52

By New Zealand (17)

101	M. G. Burgess, Kingston ..	1971-72	117* B. F. Hastings, Christ-church 1968-69
166*	B. E. Congdon, Port-of-Spain	1971-72	105 B. F. Hastings, Bridge-town 1971-72
126	B. E. Congdon, Bridge-town	1971-72	147 G. P. Howarth, Christ-church 1979-80
112	J. J. Crowe, Kingston	1984-85	182 T. W. Jarvis, Georgetown . 1971-72
188	M. D. Crowe, Georgetown .	1984-85	124† B. R. Taylor, Auckland . 1968-69
119	M. D. Crowe, Wellington .	1986-87	223*‡ G. M. Turner, Kingston . 1971-72
104	M. D. Crowe, Auckland ...	1986-87	259 G. M. Turner, Georgetown . 1971-72
127	B. A. Edgar, Auckland	1979-80	138 J. G. Wright, Wellington . 1986-87
103	R. J. Hadlee, Christchurch .	1979-80	

† *Signifies hundred on first appearance in West Indies–New Zealand Tests.*
‡ *Carried his bat.*

Notes: E. D. Weekes in 1955-56 made three hundreds in consecutive innings.

L. G. Rowe and A. I. Kallicharran each scored hundreds in their first two innings in Test cricket, Rowe being the only batsman to do so in his first match.

RECORD PARTNERSHIPS FOR EACH WICKET

For West Indies

225 for 1st	C. G. Greenidge and D. L. Haynes at Christchurch	1979-80
269 for 2nd	R. C. Fredericks and L. G. Rowe at Kingston	1971-72
185 for 3rd	C. G. Greenidge and R. B. Richardson at Port-of-Spain	1984-85
162 for 4th {	E. D. Weekes and O. G. Smith at Dunedin	1955-56
	C. G. Greenidge and A. I. Kallicharran at Christchurch	1979-80
189 for 5th	F. M. M. Worrell and C. L. Walcott at Auckland	1951-52
254 for 6th	C. A. Davis and G. S. Sobers at Bridgetown	1971-72
143 for 7th	D. St E. Atkinson and J. D. C. Goddard at Christchurch	1955-56
83 for 8th	I. V. A. Richards and M. D. Marshall at Bridgetown	1984-85
70 for 9th	M. D. Marshall and J. Garner at Bridgetown	1984-85
31 for 10th	T. M. Findlay and G. C. Shillingford at Bridgetown	1971-72

For New Zealand

387 for 1st†	G. M. Turner and T. W. Jarvis at Georgetown	1971-72
210 for 2nd†	G. P. Howarth and J. J. Crowe at Kingston	1984-85
241 for 3rd†	J. G. Wright and M. D. Crowe at Wellington	1986-87
175 for 4th	B. E. Congdon and B. F. Hastings at Bridgetown	1971-72
142 for 5th	M. D. Crowe and J. V. Coney at Georgetown	1984-85
220 for 6th	G. M. Turner and K. J. Wadsworth at Kingston	1971-72
143 for 7th	M. D. Crowe and I. D. S. Smith at Georgetown	1984-85
136 for 8th†	B. E. Congdon and R. S. Cunis at Port-of-Spain	1971-72
62* for 9th	V. Pollard and R. S. Cunis at Auckland	1968-69
41 for 10th	B. E. Congdon and J. C. Alabaster at Port-of-Spain	1971-72

† *Denotes record partnership against all countries.*

TEN WICKETS OR MORE IN A MATCH

For West Indies (1)

11-120 (4-40, 7-80)	M. D. Marshall, Bridgetown	1984-85

For New Zealand (3)

10-124 (4-51, 6-73)†	E. J. Chatfield, Port-of-Spain	1984-85
11-102 (5-34, 6-68)†	R. J. Hadlee, Dunedin	1979-80
10-166 (4-71, 6-95)	G. B. Troup, Auckland	1979-80

† *Signifies ten wickets or more on first appearance in West Indies–New Zealand Tests.*

WEST INDIES v INDIA

Captains

Season	West Indies	India	T	WI	I	D
1948-49*I*	J. D. C. Goddard	L. Amarnath	5	1	0	4
1952-53*W*	J. B. Stollmeyer	V. S. Hazare	5	1	0	4
1958-59*I*	F. C. M. Alexander	Ghulam Ahmed[1]	5	3	0	2
1961-62*W*	F. M. M. Worrell	N. J. Contractor[2]	5	5	0	0
1966-67*I*	G. S. Sobers	Nawab of Pataudi jun.	3	2	0	1
1970-71*W*	G. S. Sobers	A. L. Wadekar	5	0	1	4
1974-75*I*	C. H. Lloyd	Nawab of Pataudi jun.[3]	5	3	2	0
1975-76*I*	C. H. Lloyd	B. S. Bedi	4	2	1	1
1978-79*I*	A. I. Kallicharran	S. M. Gavaskar	6	0	1	5
1982-83*W*	C. H. Lloyd	Kapil Dev	5	2	0	3
1983-84*I*	C. H. Lloyd	Kapil Dev	6	3	0	3
	In India		30	12	3	15
	In West Indies		24	10	2	12
	Totals		54	22	5	27

I Played in India. W Played in West Indies.

Notes: The following deputised for the official touring captain or were appointed by the home authority for only a minor proportion of the series:
[1]P. R. Umrigar (First), V. Mankad (Fourth), H. R. Adhikari (Fifth). [2]Nawab of Pataudi jun. (Third, Fourth and Fifth). [3]S. Venkataraghavan (Second).

HIGHEST INNINGS TOTALS

For West Indies in West Indies: 631-8 dec. at Kingston	1961-62
in India: 644-8 dec. at Delhi	1958-59
For India in West Indies: 469-7 at Port-of-Spain	1982-83
in India: 644-7 dec. at Kanpur	1978-79

LOWEST INNINGS TOTALS

For West Indies in West Indies: 214 at Port-of-Spain	1970-71
in India: 151 at Madras	1978-79
For India in West Indies: 97† at Kingston	1975-76
in India: 90 at Calcutta	1983-84

† *Five men absent hurt.*

INDIVIDUAL HUNDREDS

For West Indies (67)

250	S. F. A. F. Bacchus, Kanpur	1978-79	107†	C. G. Greenidge, Bangalore	1974-75
103	B. F. Butcher, Calcutta	1958-59	154*	C. G. Greenidge, St John's	1982-83
142	B. F. Butcher, Madras	1958-59	194	C. G. Greenidge, Kanpur	1983-84
107†	R. J. Christiani, Delhi	1948-49	136	D. L. Haynes, St John's	1982-83
125*	C. A. Davis, Georgetown	1970-71	123	J. K. Holt, Delhi	1958-59
105	C. A. Davis, Port-of-Spain	1970-71	101	C. C. Hunte, Bombay	1966-67
110	P. J. L. Dujon, St John's	1982-83	124†	A. I. Kallicharran, Bangalore	1974-75
100	R. C. Fredericks, Calcutta	1974-75	103*	A. I. Kallicharran, Port-of-Spain	1975-76
104	R. C. Fredericks, Bombay	1974-75	187	A. I. Kallicharran, Bombay	1978-79
123	H. A. Gomes, Port-of-Spain	1982-83	256	R. B. Kanhai, Calcutta	1958-59
101†	G. E. Gomez, Delhi	1948-49			

138	R. B. Kanhai, Kingston ...	1961-62
139	R. B. Kanhai, Port-of-Spain	1961-62
158*	R. B. Kanhai, Kingston ...	1970-71
163	C. H. Lloyd, Bangalore ...	1974-75
242*	C. H. Lloyd, Kingston ...	1974-75
102	C. H. Lloyd, Bombay ...	1975-76
143	C. H. Lloyd, Port-of-Spain .	1982-83
106	C. H. Lloyd, St John's ..	1982-83
103	C. H. Lloyd, Delhi ...	1983-84
161*	C. H. Lloyd, Calcutta ...	1983-84
130	A. L. Logie, Bridgetown ..	1982-83
125†	E. D. A. McMorris, Kingston	1961-62
115†	B. H. Pairaudeau, Port-of-Spain ...	1952-53
104	A. F. Rae, Bombay ...	1948-49
109	A. F. Rae, Madras ...	1948-49
192*	I. V. A. Richards, Delhi .	1974-75
142	I. V. A. Richards, Bridgetown ...	1975-76
130	I. V. A. Richards, Port-of-Spain	1975-76
177	I. V. A. Richards, Port-of-Spain	1975-76
109	I. V. A. Richards, Georgetown ...	1982-83
120	I. V. A. Richards, Bombay	1983-84
100	O. G. Smith, Delhi ...	1958-59
142*†	G. S. Sobers, Bombay ...	1958-59
198	G. S. Sobers, Kanpur ...	1958-59
106*	G. S. Sobers, Calcutta ...	1958-59
153	G. S. Sobers, Kingston ...	1961-62
104	G. S. Sobers, Kingston ...	1961-62
108*	G. S. Sobers, Georgetown .	1970-71
178*	G. S. Sobers, Bridgetown ..	1970-71
132	G. S. Sobers, Port-of-Spain	1970-71
100*	J. S. Solomon, Delhi ...	1958-59
160	J. B. Stollmeyer, Madras .	1948-49
104*	J. B. Stollmeyer, Port-of-Spain ...	1952-53
152†	C. L. Walcott, Delhi ...	1948-49
108	C. L. Walcott, Calcutta ..	1948-49
125	C. L. Walcott, Georgetown	1952-53
118	C. L. Walcott, Kingston ..	1952-53
128†	E. D. Weekes, Delhi ...	1948-49
194	E. D. Weekes, Bombay ...	1948-49
162 } 101	E. D. Weekes, Calcutta ..	1948-49
207	E. D. Weekes, Port-of-Spain ...	1952-53
161	E. D. Weekes, Port-of-Spain ...	1952-53
109	E. D. Weekes, Kingston ..	1952-53
111	A. B. Williams, Calcutta ..	1978-79
237	F. M. M. Worrell, Kingston	1952-53

For India (49)

114*†	H. R. Adhikari, Delhi	1948-49
101*	M. Amarnath, Kanpur	1978-79
117	M. Amarnath, Port-of-Spain ...	1982-83
116	M. Amarnath, St John's ..	1982-83
163*	M. L. Apte, Port-of-Spain .	1952-53
109	C. G. Borde, Delhi ...	1958-59
121	C. G. Borde, Bombay ...	1966-67
125	C. G. Borde, Madras	1966-67
104	S. A. Durani, Port-of-Spain	1961-62
109	F. M. Engineer, Madras ..	1966-67
102	A. D. Gaekwad, Kanpur ..	1978-79
116	S. M. Gavaskar, Georgetown ...	1970-71
117*	S. M. Gavaskar, Bridgetown ...	1970-71
124 } 220	S. M. Gavaskar, Port-of-Spain ...	1970-71
156	S. M. Gavaskar, Port-of-Spain ...	1975-76
102	S. M. Gavaskar, Port-of-Spain ...	1975-76
205	S. M. Gavaskar, Bombay ..	1978-79
107 } 182*	S. M. Gavaskar, Calcutta .	1978-79
120	S. M. Gavaskar, Delhi	1978-79
147*	S. M. Gavaskar, Georgetown ...	1982-83
121	S. M. Gavaskar, Delhi ...	1983-84
236*	S. M. Gavaskar, Madras ..	1983-84
134*	V. S. Hazare, Bombay	1948-49
122	V. S. Hazare, Bombay	1948-49
126*	Kapil Dev, Delhi ...	1978-79
100*	Kapil Dev, Port-of-Spain ..	1982-83
118	V. L. Manjrekar, Kingston	1952-53
112	R. S. Modi, Bombay ...	1948-49
106†	Mushtaq Ali, Calcutta	1948-49
115*	B. P. Patel, Port-of-Spain ..	1975-76
150	P. Roy, Kingston ...	1952-53
212	D. N. Sardesai, Kingston ..	1970-71
112	D. N. Sardesai, Port-of-Spain ...	1970-71
150	D. N. Sardesai, Bridgetown	1970-71
102	R. J. Shastri, St John's	1982-83
102	E. D. Solkar, Bombay	1974-75
130	P. R. Umrigar, Port-of-Spain ...	1952-53
117	P. R. Umrigar, Kingston ..	1952-53
172*	P. R. Umrigar, Port-of-Spain ...	1961-62
157*	D. B. Vengsarkar, Calcutta	1978-79
109	D. B. Vengsarkar, Delhi ...	1978-79
159	D. B. Vengsarkar, Delhi ...	1983-84
100	D. B. Vengsarkar, Bombay .	1983-84
139	G. R. Viswanath, Calcutta .	1974-75
112	G. R. Viswanath, Port-of-Spain ...	1975-76
124	G. R. Viswanath, Madras ..	1978-79
179	G. R. Viswanath, Kanpur .	1978-79

† *Signifies hundred on first appearance in West Indies–India Tests.*

RECORD PARTNERSHIPS FOR EACH WICKET

For West Indies

296 for 1st†	C. G. Greenidge and D. L. Haynes at St John's	1982-83
255 for 2nd	E. D. A. McMorris and R. B. Kanhai at Kingston	1961-62
220 for 3rd	I. V. A. Richards and A. I. Kallicharran at Bridgetown	1975-76
267 for 4th	C. L. Walcott and G. E. Gomez at Delhi	1948-49
219 for 5th	E. D. Weekes and B. H. Pairaudeau at Port-of-Spain	1952-53
250 for 6th	C. H. Lloyd and D. L. Murray at Bombay	1974-75
130 for 7th	C. G. Greenidge and M. D. Marshall at Kanpur	1983-84
124 for 8th†	I. V. A. Richards and K. D. Boyce at Delhi	1974-75
161 for 9th†	C. H. Lloyd and A. M. E. Roberts at Calcutta	1983-84
98* for 10th†	F. M. M. Worrell and W. W. Hall at Port-of-Spain	1961-62

For India

153 for 1st	S. M. Gavaskar and C. P. S. Chauhan at Bombay	1978-79
344* for 2nd†	S. M. Gavaskar and D. B. Vengsarkar at Calcutta	1978-79
159 for 3rd	M. Amarnath and G. R. Viswanath at Port-of-Spain	1975-76
172 for 4th	G. R. Viswanath and A. D. Gaekwad at Kanpur	1978-79
204 for 5th	S. M. Gavaskar and B. P. Patel at Port-of-Spain	1975-76
170 for 6th	S. M. Gavaskar and R. J. Shastri at Madras	1983-84
186 for 7th	D. N. Sardesai and E. D. Solkar at Bridgetown	1970-71
107 for 8th	Yashpal Sharma and B. S. Sandhu at Kingston	1982-83
143* for 9th	S. M. Gavaskar and S. M. H. Kirmani at Madras	1983-84
62 for 10th	D. N. Sardesai and B. S. Bedi at Bridgetown	1970-71

† *Denotes record partnership against all countries.*

TEN WICKETS OR MORE IN A MATCH

For West Indies (2)

11-126 (6-50, 5-76)	W. W. Hall, Kanpur	1958-59
12-121 (7-64, 5-57)	A. M. E. Roberts, Madras	1974-75

For India (3)

11-235 (7-157, 4-78)†	B. S. Chandrasekhar, Bombay	1966-67
10-223 (9-102, 1-121)	S. P. Gupte, Kanpur	1958-59
10-135 (1-52, 9-83)	Kapil Dev, Ahmedabad	1983-84

† *Signifies ten wickets or more on first appearance in West Indies–India Tests.*

WEST INDIES v PAKISTAN

	Captains					
Season	West Indies	Pakistan	T	WI	P	D
1957-58*W*	F. C. M. Alexander	A. H. Kardar	5	3	1	1
1958-59*P*	F. C. M. Alexander	Fazal Mahmood	3	1	2	0
1974-75*P*	C. H. Lloyd	Intikhab Alam	2	0	0	2
1976-77*W*	C. H. Lloyd	Mushtaq Mohammad	5	2	1	2
1980-81*P*	C. H. Lloyd	Javed Miandad	4	1	0	3
1986-87*P*	I. V. A. Richards	Imran Khan	3	1	1	1
In West Indies			10	5	2	3
In Pakistan			12	3	3	6
Totals			22	8	5	9

P Played in Pakistan.   W Played in West Indies.

HIGHEST INNINGS TOTALS

For West Indies in West Indies: 790-3 dec. at Kingston 1957-58
              in Pakistan: 493 at Karachi 1974-75
For Pakistan in West Indies: 657-8 dec. at Bridgetown 1957-58
            in Pakistan: 406-8 dec. at Karachi 1974-75

LOWEST INNINGS TOTALS

For West Indies in West Indies: 154 at Port-of-Spain 1976-77
             in Pakistan: 53 at Faisalabad 1986-87
For Pakistan in West Indies: 106 at Bridgetown 1957-58
           in Pakistan: 77 at Lahore 1986-87

INDIVIDUAL HUNDREDS

For West Indies (17)

105*† L. Baichan, Lahore 1974-75	157	C. H. Lloyd, Bridgetown .. 1976-77
120 R. C. Fredericks, Port-of-Spain 1976-77	120*	I. V. A. Richards, Multan . 1980-81
100 C. G. Greenidge, Kingston 1976-77	120	I. T. Shillingford, Georgetown 1976-77
142† C. C. Hunte, Bridgetown .. 1957-58	365*	G. S. Sobers, Kingston 1957-58
260 C. C. Hunte, Kingston 1957-58	125	G. S. Sobers, Georgetown . 1957-58
114 C. C. Hunte, Georgetown .. 1957-58	109*	
101 B. D. Julien, Karachi 1974-75	145	C. L. Walcott, Georgetown 1957-58
115 A. I. Kallicharran, Karachi 1974-75	197†	E. D. Weekes, Bridgetown . 1957-58
217 R. B. Kanhai, Lahore 1958-59		

Pakistan (14)

135 Asif Iqbal, Kingston 1976-77	121	Mushtaq Mohammad, Port-of-Spain 1976-77
337† Hanif Mohammad, Bridgetown 1957-58	150	Saeed Ahmed, Georgetown 1957-58
103 Hanif Mohammad, Karachi 1958-59	107*	Wasim Raja, Karachi 1974-75
122 Imtiaz Ahmed, Kingston .. 1957-58	117*	Wasim Raja, Bridgetown .. 1976-77
123 Imran Khan, Lahore 1980-81	106	Wazir Mohammad, Kingston 1957-58
100 Majid Khan, Karachi 1974-75	189	Wazir Mohammad, Port-of-Spain 1957-58
167 Majid Khan, Georgetown . 1976-77		
123 Mushtaq Mohammad, Lahore 1974-75		

† *Signifies hundred on first appearance in West Indies–Pakistan Tests.*

RECORD PARTNERSHIPS FOR EACH WICKET

For West Indies

182 for 1st	R. C. Fredericks and C. G. Greenidge at Kingston	1976-77
446 for 2nd†	C. C. Hunte and G. S. Sobers at Kingston	1957-58
162 for 3rd	R. B. Kanhai and G. S. Sobers at Lahore	1958-59
188* for 4th	G. S. Sobers and C. L. Walcott at Bridgetown	1957-58
185 for 5th	E. D. Weekes and O. G. Smith at Bridgetown	1957-58
151 for 6th	C. H. Lloyd and D. L. Murray at Bridgetown	1976-77
70 for 7th	C. H. Lloyd and J. Garner at Bridgetown	1976-77
50 for 8th	B. D. Julien and V. A. Holder at Karachi	1974-75
46 for 9th	J. Garner and C. E. H. Croft at Port-of-Spain	1976-77
44 for 10th	R. Nanan and S. T. Clarke at Faisalabad	1980-81

For Pakistan

159 for 1st‡	Majid Khan and Zaheer Abbas at Georgetown	1976-77
178 for 2nd	Hanif Mohammad and Saeed Ahmed at Karachi	1958-59
169 for 3rd	Saeed Ahmed and Wazir Mohammad at Port-of-Spain	1957-58
154 for 4th	Wazir Mohammad and Hanif Mohammad at Port-of-Spain	1957-58
87 for 5th	Mushtaq Mohammad and Asif Iqbal at Kingston	1976-77
166 for 6th	Wazir Mohammad and A. H. Kardar at Kingston	1957-58
128 for 7th	Wasim Raja and Wasim Bari at Karachi	1974-75
73 for 8th	Imran Khan and Sarfraz Nawaz at Port-of-Spain	1976-77
73 for 9th	Wasim Raja and Sarfraz Nawaz at Bridgetown	1976-77
133 for 10th†	Wasim Raja and Wasim Bari at Bridgetown	1976-77

† *Denotes record partnership against all countries.*

‡ *219 runs were added for this wicket in two separate partnerships: Sadiq Mohammad retired hurt and was replaced by Zaheer Abbas when 60 had been added. The highest partnership by two opening batsmen is 152 by Hanif Mohammad and Imtiaz Ahmed at Bridgetown, 1957-58.*

TEN WICKETS OR MORE IN A MATCH

For Pakistan (1)

12-100 (6-34, 6-66)	Fazal Mahmood, Dacca	1958-59

Note: The best match figures by a West Indian bowler are 9-187 (5-66, 4-121), A. M. E. Roberts at Lahore, 1974-75, and 9-95 (8-29, 1-66), C. E. H. Croft at Port-of-Spain, 1976-77.

NEW ZEALAND v INDIA

Season	New Zealand	Captains India	T	NZ	I	D
1955-56*I*	H. B. Cave	P. R. Umrigar[1]	5	0	2	3
1964-65*I*	J. R. Reid	Nawab of Pataudi jun.	4	0	1	3
1967-68*N*	G. T. Dowling[2]	Nawab of Pataudi jun.	4	1	3	0
1969-70*I*	G. T. Dowling	Nawab of Pataudi jun.	3	1	1	1
1975-76*N*	G. M. Turner	B. S. Bedi[3]	3	1	1	1
1976-77*I*	G. M. Turner	B. S. Bedi	3	0	2	1
1980-81*N*	G. P. Howarth	S. M. Gavaskar	3	1	0	2
	In India		15	1	6	8
	In New Zealand		10	3	4	3
	Totals		25	4	10	11

I Played in India. N Played in New Zealand.

Notes: [1]Ghulam Ahmed captained in First Test. [2]B. W. Sinclair captained in First Test. [3]S. M. Gavaskar captained in First Test.

HIGHEST INNINGS TOTALS

For New Zealand in New Zealand: 502 at Christchurch		1967-68
in India: 462-9 dec. at Calcutta		1964-65
450-2 dec. at Delhi		1955-56
For India in New Zealand: 414 at Auckland		1975-76
in India: 537-3 dec. at Madras		1955-56

LOWEST INNINGS TOTALS

For New Zealand in New Zealand: 100 at Wellington 1980-81
in India: 127 at Bombay 1969-70

For India in New Zealand: 81 at Wellington 1975-76
in India: 88 at Bombay 1964-65

INDIVIDUAL HUNDREDS

For New Zealand (16)

120	G. T. Dowling, Bombay ...	1964-65
143	G. T. Dowling, Dunedin ..	1967-68
239	G. T. Dowling, Christchurch	1967-68
102†	J. W. Guy, Hyderabad	1955-56
137*	G. P. Howarth, Wellington	1980-81
104	J. M. Parker, Bombay	1976-77
123*	J. F. Reid, Christchurch	1980-81
119*	J. R. Reid, Delhi	1955-56

120	J. R. Reid, Calcutta	1955-56
137*†	B. Sutcliffe, Hyderabad ...	1955-56
230*	B. Sutcliffe, Delhi	1955-56
151*	B. Sutcliffe, Calcutta	1964-65
105†	B. R. Taylor, Calcutta	1964-65
117	G. M. Turner, Christchurch	1975-76
113	G. M. Turner, Kanpur	1976-77
110	J. G. Wright, Auckland ...	1980-81

For India (20)

124†	S. Amarnath, Auckland ...	1975-76
109	C. G. Borde, Bombay	1964-65
116†	S. M. Gavaskar, Auckland	1975-76
119	S. M. Gavaskar, Bombay ..	1976-77
100*†	A. G. Kripal Singh, Hyderabad	1955-56
118†	V. L. Manjrekar, Hyderabad	1955-56
177	V. L. Manjrekar, Delhi ...	1955-56
102*	V. L. Manjrekar, Madras ..	1964-65
223	V. Mankad, Bombay	1955-56
231	V. Mankad, Madras	1955-56

153	Nawab of Pataudi jun., Calcutta	1964-65
113	Nawab of Pataudi jun., Delhi	1964-65
106*	G. S. Ramchand, Calcutta .	1955-56
100	Pankaj Roy, Calcutta	1955-56
173	Pankaj Roy, Madras	1955-56
200*	D. N. Sardesai, Bombay ..	1964-65
106	D. N. Sardesai, Delhi	1964-65
223†	P. R. Umrigar, Hyderabad	1955-56
103*	G. R. Viswanath, Kanpur .	1976-77
143	A. L. Wadekar, Wellington	1967-68

† *Signifies hundred on first appearance in New Zealand-India Tests. B. R. Taylor provides the only instance for New Zealand of a player scoring his maiden hundred in first-class cricket in his first Test.*

RECORD PARTNERSHIPS FOR EACH WICKET

For New Zealand

126 for 1st	B. A. G. Murray and G. T. Dowling at Christchurch	1967-68
155 for 2nd	G. T. Dowling and B. E. Congdon at Dunedin	1967-68
222* for 3rd	B. Sutcliffe and J. R. Reid at Delhi	1955-56
103 for 4th	G. T. Dowling and M. G. Burgess at Christchurch	1967-68
119 for 5th	G. T. Dowling and K. Thomson at Christchurch	1967-68
87 for 6th	J. W. Guy and A. R. MacGibbon at Hyderabad	1955-56
163 for 7th	B. Sutcliffe and B. R. Taylor at Calcutta	1964-65
81 for 8th	V. Pollard and G. E. Vivian at Calcutta	1964-65
69 for 9th	M. G. Burgess and J. C. Alabaster at Dunedin	1967-68
61 for 10th	J. T. Ward and R. O. Collinge at Madras	1964-65

For India

413 for 1st†	V. Mankad and Pankaj Roy at Madras	1955-56
204 for 2nd	S. M. Gavaskar and S. Amarnath at Auckland	1975-76
238 for 3rd	P. R. Umrigar and V. L. Manjrekar at Hyderabad	1955-56
171 for 4th	P. R. Umrigar and A. G. Kripal Singh at Hyderabad	1955-56
127 for 5th	V. L. Manjrekar and G. S. Ramchand at Delhi	1955-56
193* for 6th	D. N. Sardesai and Hanumant Singh at Bombay	1964-65
116 for 7th	B. P. Patel and S. M. H. Kirmani at Wellington	1975-76
143 for 8th†	R. G. Nadkarni and F. M. Engineer at Madras	1964-65
105 for 9th	{ S. M. H. Kirmani and B. S. Bedi at Bombay	1976-77
	{ S. M. H. Kirmani and N. S. Yadav at Auckland	1980-81
57 for 10th	R. B. Desai and B. S. Bedi at Dunedin	1967-68

† *Denotes record partnership against all countries.*

TEN WICKETS OR MORE IN A MATCH

For New Zealand (1)

11-58 (4-35, 7-23)	R. J. Hadlee, Wellington	1975-76

For India (2)

11-140 (3-64, 8-76)	E. A. S. Prasanna, Auckland	1975-76
12-152 (8-72, 4-80)	S. Venkataraghavan, Delhi	1964-65

NEW ZEALAND v PAKISTAN

	Captains					
Season	New Zealand	Pakistan	T	NZ	P	D
1955-56P	H. B. Cave	A. H. Kardar	3	0	2	1
1964-65N	J. R. Reid	Hanif Mohammad	3	0	0	3
1964-65P	J. R. Reid	Hanif Mohammad	3	0	2	1
1969-70P	G. T. Dowling	Intikhab Alam	3	1	0	2
1972-73N	B. E. Congdon	Intikhab Alam	3	0	1	2
1976-77P	G. M. Turner[1]	Mushtaq Mohammad	3	0	2	1
1978-79N	M. G. Burgess	Mushtaq Mohammad	3	0	1	2
1984-85P	J. V. Coney	Zaheer Abbas	3	0	2	1
1984-85N	G. P. Howarth	Javed Miandad	3	2	0	1
	In Pakistan		15	1	8	6
	In New Zealand		12	2	2	8
	Totals		27	3	10	14

N Played in New Zealand. P Played in Pakistan.
Note: [1]J. M. Parker captained in Third Test.

HIGHEST INNINGS TOTALS

For New Zealand in New Zealand 492 at Wellington	1984-85
in Pakistan: 482-6 dec. at Lahore	1964-65
For Pakistan in New Zealand: 507-6 dec. at Dunedin	1972-73
in Pakistan: 565-9 dec. at Karachi	1976-77
561 at Lahore	1955-56

LOWEST INNINGS TOTALS

For New Zealand in New Zealand: 156 at Dunedin	1972-73
in Pakistan: 70 at Dacca	1955-56
For Pakistan in New Zealand: 169 at Auckland	1984-85
in Pakistan: 114 at Lahore	1969-70

INDIVIDUAL HUNDREDS

For New Zealand (16)

119*	M. G. Burgess, Dacca	1969-70	107†	R. E. Redmond, Auckland	1972-73
111	M. G. Burgess, Lahore	1976-77	106	J. F. Reid, Hyderabad	1984-85
111*	J. V. Coney, Dunedin	1984-85	148	J. F. Reid, Wellington	1984-85
129†	B. A. Edgar, Christchurch	1978-79	158*	J. F. Reid, Auckland	1984-85
110	B. F. Hastings, Auckland	1972-73	128	J. R. Reid, Karachi	1964-65
114	G. P. Howarth, Napier	1978-79	130	B. W. Sinclair, Lahore	1964-65
152	W. K. Lees, Karachi	1976-77	110†	G. M. Turner, Dacca	1969-70
111	S. N. McGregor, Lahore	1955-56	107	J. G. Wright, Karachi	1984-85

For Pakistan (26)

175	Asif Iqbal, Dunedin	1972-73	126	Mohammad Ilyas, Karachi	1964-65
166	Asif Iqbal, Lahore	1976-77	106	Mudassar Nazar, Hyderabad	1984-85
104	Asif Iqbal, Napier	1978-79	201	Mushtaq Mohammad, Dunedin	1972-73
103	Hanif Mohammad, Dacca	1955-56			
100*	Hanif Mohammad, Christchurch	1964-65	101	Mushtaq Mohammad, Hyderabad	1976-77
203*	Hanif Mohammad, Lahore	1964-65	107	Mushtaq Mohammad, Karachi	1976-77
209	Imtiaz Ahmed, Lahore	1955-56			
163†	Javed Miandad, Lahore	1976-77	166	Sadiq Mohammad, Wellington	1972-73
206	Javed Miandad, Karachi	1976-77			
160*	Javed Miandad, Christchurch	1978-79	103*	Sadiq Mohammad, Hyderabad	1976-77
104	Javed Miandad, Hyderabad	1984-85	172	Saeed Ahmed, Karachi	1964-65
103*	Javed Miandad, Hyderabad	1984-85	119*	Salim Malik, Karachi	1984-85
110	Majid Khan, Auckland	1972-73	189	Waqar Hassan, Lahore	1955-56
112	Majid Khan, Karachi	1976-77	135	Zaheer Abbas, Auckland	1978-79
119*	Majid Khan, Napier	1978-79			

† *Signifies hundred on first appearance in New Zealand–Pakistan Tests.*

Note: Mushtaq and Sadiq Mohammad, at Hyderabad in 1976-77, provide the fourth instance in Test matches, after the Chappells (thrice), of brothers each scoring hundreds in the same innings.

RECORD PARTNERSHIPS FOR EACH WICKET

For New Zealand

159 for 1st	R. E. Redmond and G. M. Turner at Auckland	1972-73
195 for 2nd	J. G. Wright and G. P. Howarth at Napier	1978-79
178 for 3rd	B. W. Sinclair and J. R. Reid at Lahore	1964-65
128 for 4th	B. F. Hastings and M. G. Burgess at Wellington	1972-73
183 for 5th†	M. G. Burgess and R. W. Anderson at Lahore	1976-77
145 for 6th	J. F. Reid and R. J. Hadlee at Wellington	1984-85
186 for 7th†	W. K. Lees and R. J. Hadlee at Karachi	1976-77
100 for 8th	B. W. Yuile and D. R. Hadlee at Karachi	1969-70
96 for 9th	M. G. Burgess and R. S. Cunis at Dacca	1969-70
151 for 10th†	B. F. Hastings and R. O. Collinge at Auckland	1972-73

For Pakistan

147 for 1st‡	Sadiq Mohammad and Majid Khan at Karachi	1976-77
114 for 2nd	Mohammad Ilyas and Saeed Ahmed at Rawalpindi	1964-65
212 for 3rd	Mudassar Nazar and Javed Miandad at Hyderabad	1984-85
350 for 4th†	Mushtaq Mohammad and Asif Iqbal at Dunedin	1972-73
281 for 5th†	Javed Miandad and Asif Iqbal at Lahore	1976-77
217 for 6th†	Hanif Mohammad and Majid Khan at Lahore	1964-65
308 for 7th†	Waqar Hassan and Imtiaz Ahmed at Lahore	1955-56
89 for 8th	Anil Dalpat and Iqbal Qasim at Karachi	1984-85
52 for 9th	Intikhab Alam and Arif Butt at Auckland	1964-65
65 for 10th	Salah-ud-Din and Mohammad Farooq at Rawalpindi	1964-65

† *Denotes record partnership against all countries.*
‡ *In the preceding Test of this series, at Hyderabad, 164 runs were added for this wicket by Sadiq Mohammad, Majid Khan and Zaheer Abbas. Sadiq Mohammad retired hurt after 136 had been scored.*

TEN WICKETS OR MORE IN A MATCH

For Pakistan (4)

10-182 (5-91, 5-91)	Intikhab Alam, Dacca	1969-70
11-130 (7-52, 4-78)	Intikhab Alam, Dunedin	1972-73
10-128 (5-56, 5-72)	Wasim Akram, Dunedin	1984-85
11-79 (5-37, 6-42)†	Zulfiqar Ahmed, Karachi	1955-56

† *Signifies ten wickets or more on first appearance in New Zealand–Pakistan Tests.*
Note: The best match figures by a New Zealand bowler are 9-70 (4-36, 5-34), F. J. Cameron at Auckland, 1964-65.

NEW ZEALAND v SRI LANKA

	Captains					
Season	*New Zealand*	*Sri Lanka*	*T*	*NZ*	*SL*	*D*
1982-83*N*	G. P. Howarth	D. S. de Silva	2	2	0	0
1983-84*S*	G. P. Howarth	L. R. D. Mendis	3	2	0	1
1986-87*S*†	J. J. Crowe	L. R. D. Mendis	1	0	0	1
	In New Zealand		2	2	0	0
	In Sri Lanka		4	2	0	2
	Totals		6	4	0	2

N Played in New Zealand. S Played in Sri Lanka.

† *The Second and Third Tests were cancelled owing to civil disturbances.*

HIGHEST INNINGS TOTALS

For New Zealand in New Zealand: 344 at Christchurch		1982-83
in Sri Lanka: 459 at Colombo (CCC)		1983-84
For Sri Lanka in New Zealand: 240 at Wellington		1982-83
in Sri Lanka: 397-9 dec. at Colombo (CCC)		1986-87

LOWEST INNINGS TOTALS

For New Zealand in New Zealand: 201 at Wellington		1982-83
in Sri Lanka: 198 at Colombo (SSC)		1983-84
For Sri Lanka in New Zealand: 93 at Wellington		1982-83
in Sri Lanka: 97 at Kandy		1983-84

INDIVIDUAL HUNDREDS

For New Zealand (3)	**For Sri Lanka (2)**
120* J. J. Crowe, Colombo (CCC) 1986-87	108† R. L. Dias, Colombo (SSC) 1983-84
151* R. J. Hadlee, Colombo (CCC) 1986-87	201*† D. S. B. P. Kuruppu, Colombo (CCC) 1986-87
180 J. F. Reid, Colombo (CCC) 1983-84	

† *Signifies hundred on first appearance in New Zealand–Sri Lanka Tests.*

Best wicket partnership for New Zealand: 246* for the 6th† by J. J. Crowe and
R. J. Hadlee at Colombo (CCC) 1986-87
for Sri Lanka: ‡159* for the 3rd by S. Wettimuny and
R. L. Dias at Colombo (SSC) 1983-84

† *Denotes record partnership against all countries.*

‡ *163 runs were added for this wicket in two separate partnerships: S. Wettimuny retired hurt and was replaced by L. R. D. Mendis when 159 had been added.*

TEN WICKETS OR MORE IN A MATCH

For New Zealand (1)

10-102 (5-73, 5-29)   R. J. Hadlee, Colombo (CCC) 1983-84
Note: The best match figures by a Sri Lankan bowler are 8-159 (5-86, 3-73), V. B. John at Kandy, 1983-84.

INDIA v PAKISTAN

	Captains					
Season	India	Pakistan	T	I	P	D
1952-53*I*	L. Amarnath	A. H. Kardar	5	2	1	2
1954-55*P*	V. Mankad	A. H. Kardar	5	0	0	5
1960-61*I*	N. J. Contractor	Fazal Mahmood	5	0	0	5
1978-79*P*	B. S. Bedi	Mushtaq Mohammad	3	0	2	1
1979-80*I*	S. M. Gavaskar[1]	Asif Iqbal	6	2	0	4
1982-83*P*	S. M. Gavaskar	Imran Khan	6	0	3	3
1983-84*I*	Kapil Dev	Zaheer Abbas	3	0	0	3
1984-85*P*	S. M. Gavaskar	Zaheer Abbas	2	0	0	2
1986-87*I*	Kapil Dev	Imran Khan	5	0	1	4
	In India		24	4	2	18
	In Pakistan		16	0	5	11
	Totals		40	4	7	29

I Played in India.   P Played in Pakistan.
Note: [1]G. R. Viswanath captained in Sixth Test.

HIGHEST INNINGS TOTALS

For India in India: 539-9 dec. at Madras	1960-61
in Pakistan: 500 at Faisalabad	1984-85
For Pakistan in India: 487-9 dec. at Madras	1986-87
in Pakistan: 674-6 at Faisalabad	1984-85

LOWEST INNINGS TOTALS

For India in India: 106 at Lucknow	1952-53
in Pakistan: 145 at Karachi	1954-55
For Pakistan in India: 116 at Bangalore	1986-87
in Pakistan: 158 at Dacca	1954-55

INDIVIDUAL HUNDREDS

For India (28)

109*	M. Amarnath, Lahore	1982-83	128	R. J. Shastri, Karachi	1982-83
120	M. Amarnath, Lahore	1982-83	139	R. J. Shastri, Faisalabad	1984-85
103*	M. Amarnath, Karachi	1982-83	125	R. J. Shastri, Jaipur	1986-87
101*	M. Amarnath, Lahore	1984-85	110†	R. H. Shodhan, Calcutta	1952-53
141	M. Azharuddin, Calcutta	1986-87	123	K. Srikkanth, Madras	1986-87
110	M. Azharuddin, Jaipur	1986-87	102	P. R. Umrigar, Bombay	1952-53
177*	C. G. Borde, Madras	1960-61	108	P. R. Umrigar, Peshawar	1954-55
201	A. D. Gaekwad, Jullundur	1983-84	115	P. R. Umrigar, Kanpur	1960-61
111	} S. M. Gavaskar, Karachi	1978-79	117	P. R. Umrigar, Madras	1960-61
137			112	P. R. Umrigar, Delhi	1960-61
166	S. M. Gavaskar, Madras	1979-80	146*	D. B. Vengsarkar, Delhi	1979-80
127*‡	S. M. Gavaskar, Faisalabad	1982-83	109	D. B. Vengsarkar, Ahmeda-	
103*	S. M. Gavaskar, Bangalore	1983-84		bad	1986-87
146*	V. S. Hazare, Bombay	1952-53	145†	G. R. Viswanath, Faisala-	
127	S. M. Patil, Faisalabad	1984-85		bad	1978-79

For Pakistan (35)

103*	Alim-ud-Din, Karachi	1954-55	152*†	Mudassar Nazar, Lahore	1982-83
104†	Asif Iqbal, Faisalabad	1978-79	152	Mudassar Nazar, Karachi	1982-83
142	Hanif Mohammad, Baha-		199	Mudassar Nazar, Faisalabad	1984-85
	walpur	1954-55	101	Mushtaq Mohammad,	
160	Hanif Mohammad, Bom-			Delhi	1960-61
	bay	1960-61	124*‡	Nazar Mohammad, Luck-	
105†	Ijaz Faqih, Ahmedabad	1986-87		now	1952-53
135	Imtiaz Ahmed, Madras	1960-61	210	Qasim Omar, Faisalabad	1984-85
117	Imran Khan, Faisalabad	1982-83	114	Ramiz Raja, Jaipur	1986-87
135*	Imran Khan, Madras	1986-87	121†	Saeed Ahmed, Bombay	1960-61
154*†	Javed Miandad, Faisalabad	1978-79	103	Saeed Ahmed, Madras	1960-61
100	Javed Miandad, Karachi	1978-79	107	Salim Malik, Faisalabad	1982-83
126	Javed Miandad, Faisala-		102*	Salim Malik, Faisalabad	1984-85
	bad	1982-83	101	Shoaib Mohammad, Madras	1986-87
280*	Javed Miandad, Hydera-		125	Wasim Raja, Jullundur	1983-84
	bad	1982-83	176†	Zaheer Abbas, Faisalabad	1978-79
101*†	Mohsin Khan, Lahore	1982-83	235*	Zaheer Abbas, Lahore	1978-79
126	Mudassar Nazar, Bangalore	1979-80	215	Zaheer Abbas, Lahore	1982-83
119	Mudassar Nazar, Karachi	1982-83	186	Zaheer Abbas, Karachi	1982-83
231	Mudassar Nazar, Hydera-		168	Zaheer Abbas, Faisalabad	1982-83
	bad	1982-83	168*	Zaheer Abbas, Lahore	1984-85

† *Signifies hundred on first appearance in India–Pakistan Tests.*
‡ *Carried his bat.*

RECORD PARTNERSHIPS FOR EACH WICKET

For India

200 for 1st	S. M. Gavaskar and K. Srikkanth at Madras	1986-87
125 for 2nd	S. M. Gavaskar and M. Amarnath at Hyderabad	1982-83
190 for 3rd	M. Amarnath and Yashpal Sharma at Lahore	1982-83
183 for 4th	V. S. Hazare and P. R. Umrigar at Bombay	1952-53

200 for 5th	S. M. Patil and R. J. Shastri at Faisalabad	1984-85
143 for 6th	M. Azharuddin and Kapil Dev at Calcutta	1986-87
155 for 7th	R. M. H. Binny and Madan Lal at Bangalore	1983-84
122 for 8th	S. M. H. Kirmani and Madan Lal at Faisalabad	1982-83
149 for 9th†	P. G. Joshi and R. B. Desai at Bombay	1960-61
109 for 10th†	H. R. Adhikari and Ghulam Ahmed at Delhi	1952-53

For Pakistan

162 for 1st	Hanif Mohammad and Imtiaz Ahmed at Madras	1960-61
250 for 2nd	Mudassar Nazar and Qasim Omar at Faisalabad	1984-85
451 for 3rd†	Mudassar Nazar and Javed Miandad at Hyderabad	1982-83
287 for 4th	Javed Miandad and Zaheer Abbas at Faisalabad	1982-83
213 for 5th	Zaheer Abbas and Mudassar Nazar at Karachi	1982-83
207 for 6th	Salim Malik and Imran Khan at Faisalabad	1982-83
154 for 7th	Imran Khan and Ijaz Faqih at Ahmedabad	1986-87
112 for 8th	Imran Khan and Wasim Akram at Madras	1986-87
60 for 9th	Wasim Bari and Iqbal Qasim at Bangalore	1979-80
104 for 10th	Zulfiqar Ahmed and Amir Elahi at Madras	1952-53

† *Denotes record partnership against all countries.*

TEN WICKETS OR MORE IN A MATCH

For India (3)

11-146 (4-90, 7-56)	Kapil Dev, Madras	1979-80
10-126 (7-27, 3-99)	Maninder Singh, Bangalore	1986-87
13-131 (8-52, 5-79)†	V. Mankad, Delhi	1952-53

For Pakistan (5)

12-94 (5-52, 7-42)	Fazal Mahmood, Lucknow	1952-53
11-79 (3-19, 8-60)	Imran Khan, Karachi	1982-83
11-180 (6-98, 5-82)	Imran Khan, Faisalabad	1982-83
10-175 (4-135, 6-40)	Iqbal Qasim, Bombay	1979-80
11-190 (8-69, 3-121)	Sikander Bakht, Delhi	1979-80

† *Signifies ten wickets or more on first appearance in India–Pakistan Tests.*

INDIA v SRI LANKA

Season	India	*Captains* Sri Lanka	T	I	SL	D
1982-83*I*	S. M. Gavaskar	B. Warnapura	1	0	0	1
1985-86*S*	Kapil Dev	L. R. D. Mendis	3	0	1	2
1986-87*I*	Kapil Dev	L. R. D. Mendis	3	2	0	1
	In India		4	2	0	2
	In Sri Lanka		3	0	1	2
	Totals		7	2	1	4

I Played in India. S Played in Sri Lanka.

HIGHEST INNINGS TOTALS

For India in India: 676-7 at Kanpur	1986-87
in Sri Lanka: 325-5 dec. at Kandy	1985-86
For Sri Lanka in India: 420 at Kanpur	1986-87
in Sri Lanka: 385 at Colombo (PSO)	1985-86

LOWEST INNINGS TOTALS

For India in India: 400 at Cuttack 1986-87
        in Sri Lanka: 198 at Colombo (PSO) 1985-86
For Sri Lanka in India: 141 at Nagpur 1986-87
        in Sri Lanka: 198 at Kandy 1985-86

INDIVIDUAL HUNDREDS

For India (9)

116*	M. Amarnath, Kandy	1985-86	163	Kapil Dev, Kanpur	1986-87
131	M. Amarnath, Nagpur	1986-87	114*†	S. M. Patil, Madras	1982-83
199	M. Azharuddin, Kanpur ..	1986-87	153	D. B. Vengsarkar, Nagpur .	1986-87
155†	S. M. Gavaskar, Madras ..	1982-83	166	D. B. Vengsarkar, Cuttack .	1986-87
176	S. M. Gavaskar, Kanpur ..	1986-87			

For Sri Lanka (7)

106	R. L. Dias, Kandy	1985-86	124	L. R. D. Mendis, Kandy ..	1985-86
103	R. S. Madugalle, Colombo (SSC)	1985-86	111	A. Ranatunga, Colombo (SSC)	1985-86
105 105 }	†L. R. D. Mendis, Madras .	1982-83	111	S. A. R. Silva, Colombo (PSO)	1985-86

† *Signifies hundred on first appearance in India–Sri Lanka Tests.*

RECORD PARTNERSHIPS FOR EACH WICKET

For India

156 for 1st	S. M. Gavaskar and Arun Lal at Madras	1982-83
173 for 2nd	S. M. Gavaskar and D. B. Vengsarkar at Madras	1982-83
173 for 3rd	M. Amarnath and D. B. Vengsarkar at Nagpur	1986-87
163 for 4th	S. M. Gavaskar and M. Azharuddin at Kanpur	1986-87
78 for 5th	M. Amarnath and M. Azharuddin at Kandy	1985-86
272 for 6th	M. Azharuddin and Kapil Dev at Kanpur	1986-87
78* for 7th	S. M. Patil and Madan Lal at Madras	1982-83
70 for 8th	Kapil Dev and L. Sivaramakrishnan at Colombo (PSO)	1985-86
16 for 9th	S. M. Gavaskar and Gopal Sharma at Colombo (SSC)	1985-86
29 for 10th	Kapil Dev and Chetan Sharma at Colombo (PSO)	1985-86

For Sri Lanka

159 for 1st†	S. Wettimuny and J. R. Ratnayeke at Kanpur	1986-87
95 for 2nd	S. A. R. Silva and R. S. Madugalle at Colombo (PSO)	1985-86
153 for 3rd	R. L. Dias and L. R. D. Mendis at Madras	1982-83
216 for 4th	R. L. Dias and L. R. D. Mendis at Kandy	1985-86
144 for 5th	R. S. Madugalle and A. Ranatunga at Colombo (SSC)	1985-86
89 for 6th	L. R. D. Mendis and A. N. Ranasinghe at Madras	1982-83
77 for 7th†	R. S. Madugalle and D. S. de Silva at Madras	1982-83
40* for 8th	P. A. de Silva and A. L. F. de Mel at Kandy	1985-86
42 for 9th	J. R. Ratnayeke and A. L. F. de Mel at Madras	1982-83
44 for 10th	R. J. Ratnayake and E. A. R. de Silva at Nagpur	1986-87

† *Denotes record partnership against all countries.*

TEN WICKETS OR MORE IN A MATCH

For India (1)

10-107 (3-56, 7-51)　　Maninder Singh, Nagpur 1986-87

Note: The best match figures by a Sri Lankan bowler are 9-125 (4-76, 5-49) by R. J. Ratnayake against India at Colombo (PSO), 1985-86.

PAKISTAN v SRI LANKA

		Captains					
Season	Pakistan		Sri Lanka	T	P	SL	D
1981-82P	Javed Miandad		B. Warnapura[1]	3	2	0	1
1985-86P	Javed Miandad		L. R. D. Mendis	3	2	0	1
1985-86S	Imran Khan		L. R. D. Mendis	3	1	1	1
	In Pakistan			6	4	0	2
	In Sri Lanka			3	1	1	1
	Totals			9	5	1	3

P Played in Pakistan. S Played in Sri Lanka.

Note: [1]L. R. D. Mendis captained in the Second Test.

HIGHEST INNINGS TOTALS

For Pakistan in Pakistan: 555-3 at Faisalabad 1985-86
　　　　　　　　in Sri Lanka: 318 at Colombo (PSO) 1985-86
For Sri Lanka in Pakistan: 479 at Faisalabad 1985-86
　　　　　　　　in Sri Lanka: 323-3 at Colombo (PSO) 1985-86

LOWEST INNINGS TOTALS

For Pakistan in Pakistan: 259 at Sialkot 1985-86
　　　　　　　　in Sri Lanka: 132 at Colombo (CCC) 1985-86
For Sri Lanka in Pakistan: 149 at Karachi 1981-82
　　　　　　　　in Sri Lanka: 101 at Kandy 1985-86

INDIVIDUAL HUNDREDS

For Pakistan (7)

153† Haroon Rashid, Karachi . 1981-82	122 Ramiz Raja, Colombo	
203* Javed Miandad, Faisalabad 1985-86	(PSO) 1985-86	
129 Mohsin Khan, Lahore ... 1981-82	100*† Salim Malik, Karachi 1981-82	
206† Qasim Omar, Faisalabad . 1985-86	134† Zaheer Abbas, Lahore ... 1981-82	

For Sri Lanka (6)

122† P. A. de Silva, Faisalabad 1985-86	135* A. Ranatunga, Colombo	
105 P. A. de Silva, Karachi . 1985-86	(PSO) 1985-86	
109 R. L. Dias, Lahore 1981-82	157 S. Wettimuny, Faisalabad 1981-82	
116* A. P. Gurusinha, Colombo		
(PSO) 1985-86		

† *Signifies hundred on first appearance in Pakistan–Sri Lanka Tests.*

RECORD PARTNERSHIPS FOR EACH WICKET

For Pakistan

98* for 1st	Mudassar Nazar and Mohsin Khan at Karachi	1985-86
151 for 2nd	Mohsin Khan and Majid Khan at Lahore	1981-82
397 for 3rd	Qasim Omar and Javed Miandad at Faisalabad	1985-86
162 for 4th	Salim Malik and Javed Miandad at Karachi	1981-82
102 for 5th	Mudassar Nazar and Salim Malik at Kandy	1985-86
100 for 6th	Zaheer Abbas and Imran Khan at Lahore	1981-82
104 for 7th	Haroon Rashid and Tahir Naqqash at Karachi	1981-82
29 for 8th	⎰ Ashraf Ali and Iqbal Qasim at Faisalabad	1981-82
	⎱ Salim Yousuf and Abdul Qadir at Sialkot	1985-86
	⎱ Salim Yousuf and Abdul Qadir at Karachi	1985-86
127 for 9th	Haroon Rashid and Rashid Khan at Karachi	1981-82
48 for 10th	Rashid Khan and Tauseef Ahmed at Faisalabad	1981-82

For Sri Lanka

77 for 1st	S. Wettimuny and H. M. Goonatillake at Faisalabad	1981-82
217 for 2nd†	S. Wettimuny and R. L. Dias at Faisalabad	1981-82
85 for 3rd	S. Wettimuny and R. L. Dias at Faisalabad	1985-86
240* for 4th†	A. P. Gurusinha and A. Ranatunga at Colombo (PSO)	1985-86
58 for 5th	R. L. Dias and L. R. D. Mendis at Lahore	1981-82
121 for 6th	A. Ranatunga and P. A. de Silva at Faisalabad	1985-86
57 for 7th	P. A. de Silva and J. R. Ratnayake at Faisalabad	1985-86
61 for 8th†	R. S. Madugalle and D. S. de Silva at Faisalabad	1981-82
52 for 9th†	P. A. de Silva and R. J. Ratnayake at Faisalabad	1985-86
36 for 10th	R. J. Ratnayake and R. G. C. E. Wijesuriya at Faisalabad	1985-86

† *Denotes record partnership against all countries.*

TEN WICKETS OR MORE IN A MATCH

For Pakistan (1)

14-116 (8-58, 6-58)	Imran Khan, Lahore	1981-82

Note: The best match figures by a Sri Lankan bowler are 9-162 (4-103, 5-59), D. S. de Silva at Faisalabad, 1981-82.

TEST MATCH GROUNDS

In Chronological Sequence

	City and Ground	Date of First Test	Match
1.	Melbourne, Melbourne Cricket Ground	March 15, 1877	Australia v England
2.	London, Kennington Oval	September 6, 1880	England v Australia
3.	Sydney, Sydney Cricket Ground (No. 1)	February 17, 1882	Australia v England
4.	Manchester, Old Trafford	July 11, 1884	Australia v England

This match was due to have started on July 10, but rain prevented any play.

5.	London, Lord's	July 21, 1884	England v Australia
6.	Adelaide, Adelaide Oval	December 12, 1884	Australia v England
7.	Port Elizabeth, St George's Park	March 12, 1889	South Africa v England
8.	Cape Town, Newlands	March 25, 1889	South Africa v England
9.	Johannesburg, Old Wanderers*	March 2, 1896	South Africa v England
10.	Nottingham, Trent Bridge	June 1, 1899	England v Australia

	City and Ground	Date of First Test	Match
11.	Leeds, Headingley	June 29, 1899	England v Australia
12.	Birmingham, Edgbaston	May 29, 1902	England v Australia
13.	Sheffield, Bramall Lane*	July 3, 1902	England v Australia
14.	Durban, Lord's*	January 21, 1910	South Africa v England
15.	Durban, Kingsmead	January 18, 1923	South Africa v England
16.	Brisbane, Exhibition Ground*	November 30, 1928	Australia v England
17.	Christchurch, Lancaster Park	January 10, 1930	New Zealand v England
18.	Bridgetown, Kensington Oval	January 11, 1930	West Indies v England
19.	Wellington, Basin Reserve	January 24, 1930	New Zealand v England
20.	Port-of-Spain, Queen's Park Oval	February 1, 1930	West Indies v England
21.	Auckland, Eden Park	February 17, 1930	New Zealand v England

This match was due to have started on February 14, but rain prevented any play on the first two days. February 16 was a Sunday.

22.	Georgetown, Bourda	February 21, 1930	West Indies v England
23.	Kingston, Sabina Park	April 3, 1930	West Indies v England
24.	Brisbane, Woolloongabba	November 27, 1931	Australia v South Africa
25.	Bombay, Gymkhana Ground*	December 15, 1933	India v England
26.	Calcutta, Eden Gardens	January 5, 1934	India v England
27.	Madras, Chepauk (Chidambaram Stadium)	February 10, 1934	India v England
28.	Delhi, Feroz Shah Kotla	November 10, 1948	India v West Indies
29.	Bombay, Brabourne Stadium*	December 9, 1948	India v West Indies
30.	Johannesburg, Ellis Park*	December 27, 1948	South Africa v England
31.	Kanpur, Green Park (Modi Stadium)	January 12, 1952	India v England
32.	Lucknow, University Ground*	October 25, 1952	India v Pakistan
33.	Dacca, Dacca Stadium*	January 1, 1955	Pakistan v India
34.	Bahawalpur, Dring Stadium	January 15, 1955	Pakistan v India
35.	Lahore, Lawrence Gardens (Bagh-i-Jinnah)*	January 29, 1955	Pakistan v India
36.	Peshawar, Peshawar Club Ground	February 13, 1955	Pakistan v India
37.	Karachi, National Stadium	February 26, 1955	Pakistan v India
38.	Dunedin, Carisbrook	March 11, 1955	New Zealand v England
39.	Hyderabad, Fateh Maidan (Lal Bahadur Stadium)	November 19, 1955	India v New Zealand
40.	Madras, Corporation Stadium*	January 6, 1956	India v New Zealand
41.	Johannesburg, New Wanderers	December 24, 1956	South Africa v England
42.	Lahore, Gaddafi Stadium	November 21, 1959	Pakistan v Australia
43.	Rawalpindi, Rawalpindi Club Ground	March 27, 1965	Pakistan v New Zealand
44.	Nagpur, Vidarbha Cricket Association Ground	October 3, 1969	India v New Zealand
45.	Perth, Western Australian Cricket Association Ground	December 11, 1970	Australia v England
46.	Hyderabad, Niaz Stadium	March 16, 1973	Pakistan v England
47.	Bangalore, Karnataka State Cricket Association Ground	November 22, 1974	India v West Indies
48.	Bombay, Wankhede Stadium	January 23, 1975	India v West Indies
49.	Faisalabad, Iqbal Park	October 16, 1978	Pakistan v India
50.	Napier, McLean Park	February 16, 1979	New Zealand v Pakistan
51.	Multan, Ibn-e-Qasim Bagh Stadium	December 30, 1980	Pakistan v West Indies
52.	St John's (Antigua), Recreation Ground	March 27, 1981	West Indies v England
53.	Colombo, P. Saravanamuttu Oval	February 17, 1982	Sri Lanka v England
54.	Kandy, Asgiriya Stadium	April 22, 1983	Sri Lanka v Australia
55.	Jullundur, Burlton Park	September 24, 1983	India v Pakistan
56.	Ahmedabad, Gujarat Stadium	November 12, 1983	India v West Indies
57.	Colombo, Singhalese Sports Club Ground	March 16, 1984	Sri Lanka v New Zealand
58.	Colombo, Colombo Cricket Club Ground	March 24, 1984	Sri Lanka v New Zealand
59.	Sialkot, Jinnah Park	October 27, 1985	Pakistan v Sri Lanka
60.	Cuttack, Barabati Stadium	January 4, 1987	India v Sri Lanka
61.	Jaipur, Sawai Mansingh Stadium	February 21, 1987	India v Pakistan

* *Denotes no longer used for Test matches. In some instances the ground is no longer in existence.*

FAMILIES IN TEST CRICKET

FATHERS AND SONS

England

M. C. Cowdrey (114 Tests, 1954-55–1974-75) and C. S. Cowdrey (5 Tests, 1984-85).

J. Hardstaff (5 Tests, 1907-08) and J. Hardstaff jun. (23 Tests, 1935–1948).

L. Hutton (79 Tests, 1937–1954-55) and R. A. Hutton (5 Tests, 1971).

F. T. Mann (5 Tests, 1922-23) and F. G. Mann (7 Tests, 1948-49–1949).

J. H. Parks (1 Test, 1937) and J. M. Parks (46 Tests, 1954–1967-68).

F. W. Tate (1 Test, 1902) and M. W. Tate (39 Tests, 1924–1935).

C. L. Townsend (2 Tests, 1899) and D. C. H. Townsend (3 Tests, 1934-35).

Australia

E. J. Gregory (1 Test, 1876-77) and S. E. Gregory (58 Tests, 1890–1912).

South Africa

F. Hearne (4 Tests, 1891-92–1895-96) and G. A. L. Hearne (3 Tests, 1922-23–1924).
  F. Hearne also played 2 Tests for England in 1888-89.

J. D. Lindsay (3 Tests, 1947) and D. T. Lindsay (19 Tests, 1963-64–1969-70).

A. W. Nourse (45 Tests, 1902-03–1924) and A. D. Nourse (34 Tests, 1935–1951).

L. R. Tuckett (1 Test, 1913-14) and L. Tuckett (9 Tests, 1947–1948-49).

West Indies

G. A. Headley (22 Tests, 1929-30–1953-54) and R. G. A. Headley (2 Tests, 1973).

O. C. Scott (8 Tests, 1928–1930-31) and A. P. H. Scott (1 Test, 1952-53).

New Zealand

W. M. Anderson (1 Test, 1945-46) and R. W. Anderson (9 Tests, 1976-77–1978).

W. A. Hadlee (11 Tests, 1937–1950-51) and D. R. Hadlee (26 Tests, 1969–1977-78); R. J. Hadlee (70 Tests, 1972-73–1986-87).

H. G. Vivian (7 Tests, 1931–1937) and G. E. Vivian (5 Tests, 1964-65–1971-72).

India

L. Amarnath (24 Tests, 1933-34–1952-53) and M. Amarnath (66 Tests, 1969-70–1986-87); S. Amarnath (10 Tests, 1975-76–1978-79).

D. K. Gaekwad (11 Tests, 1952–1960-61) and A. D. Gaekwad (40 Tests, 1974-75–1984-85).

Nawab of Pataudi (Iftikhar Ali Khan) (3 Tests, 1946) and Nawab of Pataudi (Mansur Ali Khan) (46 Tests, 1961-62–1974-75).
  Nawab of Pataudi sen. also played 3 Tests for England, 1932-33–1934.

V. Mankad (44 Tests, 1946–1958-59) and A. V. Mankad (22 Tests, 1969-70–1977-78).

Pankaj Roy (43 Tests, 1951-52–1960-61) and Pranab Roy (2 Tests, 1981-82).

India and Pakistan

M. Jahangir Khan (4 Tests, 1932–1936) and Majid Khan (63 Tests, 1964-65–1982-83).

S. Wazir Ali (7 Tests, 1932–1936) and Khalid Wazir (2 Tests, 1954).

Pakistan

Hanif Mohammad (55 Tests, 1954–1969-70) and Shoaib Mohammad (13 Tests, 1983-84–1987).

Nazar Mohammad (5 Tests, 1952-53) and Mudassar Nazar (65 Tests, 1976-77–1987).

GRANDFATHERS AND GRANDSONS

Australia

V. Y. Richardson (19 Tests, 1924-25–1935-36) and G. S. Chappell (87 Tests, 1970-71–1983-84); I. M. Chappell (75 Tests, 1964-65–1979-80); T. M. Chappell (3 Tests, 1981).

GREAT-GRANDFATHER AND GREAT-GRANDSON

Australia

W. H. Cooper (2 Tests, 1881-82 and 1884-85) and A. P. Sheahan (31 Tests, 1967-68–1973-74).

BROTHERS IN SAME TEST TEAM

England

E. M., G. F. and W. G. Grace: 1 Test, 1880.
C. T. and G. B. Studd: 4 Tests, 1882-83.
A. and G. G. Hearne: 1 Test, 1891-92.
  F. Hearne, their brother, played in this match for South Africa.
D. W. and P. E. Richardson: 1 Test, 1957.

Australia

E. J. and D. W. Gregory: 1 Test, 1876-77.
C. and A. C. Bannerman: 1 Test, 1878-79.
G. and W. F. Giffen: 2 Tests, 1891-92.
G. H. S. and A. E. Trott: 3 Tests, 1894-95.
I. M. and G. S. Chappell: 43 Tests, 1970-71–1979-80.

South Africa

S. J. and S. D. Snooke: 1 Test, 1907.
D. and H. W. Taylor: 2 Tests, 1913-14.
R. H. M. and P. A. M. Hands: 1 Test, 1913-14.
E. A. B. and A. M. B. Rowan: 9 Tests, 1948-49–1951.
P. M. and R. G. Pollock: 23 Tests, 1963-64–1969-70.
A. J. and D. B. Pithey: 5 Tests, 1963-64.

West Indies

G. C. and R. S. Grant: 4 Tests, 1934-35.
J. B. and V. H. Stollmeyer: 1 Test, 1939.
D. St E. and E. St E. Atkinson: 1 Test, 1957-58.

New Zealand

J. J. and M. D. Crowe: 28 Tests, 1983–1986-87.
D. R. and R. J. Hadlee: 10 Tests, 1973–1977-78.
H. J. and G. P. Howarth: 4 Tests, 1974-75–1976-77.
J. M. and N. M. Parker: 3 Tests, 1976-77.
B. P. and J. G. Bracewell: 1 Test, 1980-81.

India

S. Wazir Ali and S. Nazir Ali: 2 Tests, 1932–1933-34.
L. Ramji and Amar Singh: 1 Test, 1933-34.
C. K. and C. S. Nayudu: 4 Tests, 1933-34–1936.
A. G. Kripal Singh and A. G. Milkha Singh: 1 Test, 1961-62.
S. and M. Amarnath: 8 Tests, 1975-76–1978-79.

Pakistan

Wazir and Hanif Mohammad: 18 Tests, 1952-53–1959-60.
Wazir and Mushtaq Mohammad: 1 Test, 1958-59.
Hanif and Mushtaq Mohammad: 19 Tests, 1960-61–1969-70.
Hanif, Mushtaq and Sadiq Mohammad: 1 Test, 1969-70.
Mushtaq and Sadiq Mohammad: 26 Tests, 1969-70–1978-79.
Wasim and Ramiz Raja: 2 Tests, 1983-84.

Sri Lanka

M. D. and S. Wettimuny: 2 Tests, 1982-83.

LIMITED-OVERS INTERNATIONAL RECORDS

Notes: Limited-overs international matches do not have first-class status.
The following records take into account the 1987-88 World Cup in India and Pakistan.

3,000 OR MORE RUNS

	M	I	NO	R	HI	100s	Avge
I. V. A. Richards (*West Indies*)	137	124	20	5,587	189*	10	53.72
D. L. Haynes (*West Indies*)	128	127	16	4,549	148	9	40.98
Javed Miandad (*Pakistan*)	126	121	28	4,235	119*	5	45.53
A. R. Border (*Australia*)	159	150	20	4,135	127*	3	31.80
C. G. Greenidge (*West Indies*)	87	87	8	3,652	115	9	46.22
S. M. Gavaskar (*India*)	107	102	14	3,092	103*	1	35.13

HIGHEST INDIVIDUAL SCORE FOR EACH COUNTRY

189*	I. V. A. Richards	**West Indies** v England at Manchester	1984
175*	Kapil Dev	**India** v Zimbabwe at Tunbridge Wells	1983
171*	G. M. Turner	**New Zealand** v East Africa at Birmingham	1975
158	D. I. Gower	**England** v New Zealand at Brisbane	1982-83
138*	G. S. Chappell	**Australia** v New Zealand at Sydney	1980-81
123	Zaheer Abbas	**Pakistan** v Sri Lanka at Lahore	1981-82
121	R. L. Dias	**Sri Lanka** v India at Bangalore	1982-83

FIVE OR MORE HUNDREDS

Total		E	A	WI	NZ	I	P	SL	Others
10	I. V. A. Richards (*West Indies*) ..	3	3	–	1	2	0	1	0
9	C. G. Greenidge (*West Indies*)	0	1	–	3	2	1	1	1
9	D. L. Haynes (*West Indies*)	0	6	–	2	0	0	1	0
7	D. I. Gower (*England*)	–	2	0	3	0	1	1	0
7	Zaheer Abbas (*Pakistan*)	0	2	0	1	3	–	1	0
5	Javed Miandad (*Pakistan*)	1	0	0	0	3	–	1	0

HIGHEST PARTNERSHIP FOR EACH WICKET

212 for 1st	G. R. Marsh (104) and D. C. Boon (111), Australia v India at Jaipur	1986-87
221 for 2nd	C. G. Greenidge (115) and I. V. A. Richards (149), West Indies v India at Jamshedpur	1983-84
224* for 3rd	D. M. Jones (99*) and A. R. Border (118*), Australia v Sri Lanka at Adelaide	1984-85
173 for 4th	D. M. Jones (121) and S. R. Waugh (82), Australia v Pakistan at Perth	1986-87
152 for 5th	I. V. A. Richards (98) and C. H. Lloyd (89*), West Indies v Sri Lanka at Brisbane	1984-85
144 for 6th	Imran Khan (102*) and Shahid Mahboob (77), Pakistan v Sri Lanka at Leeds	1983
115 for 7th	P. J. L. Dujon (57*) and M. D. Marshall (66), West Indies v Pakistan at Gujranwala	1986-87
117 for 8th	D. L. Houghton (141) and I. P. Butchart (54), Zimbabwe v New Zealand at Hyderabad (Pakistan)	1987-88
126* for 9th	Kapil Dev (175*) and S. M. H. Kirmani (24*), India v Zimbabwe at Tunbridge Wells	1983
106* for 10th	I. V. A. Richards (189*) and M. A. Holding (12*), West Indies v England at Manchester	1984

100 OR MORE WICKETS

	M	Balls	R	W	BB	4W/i	Avge
J. Garner (*West Indies*)	98	5,330	2,752	146	5-31	5	18.84
M. A. Holding (*West Indies*)	102	5,473	3,034	142	5-26	6	21.36
Kapil Dev (*India*)	112	5,821	3,654	135	5-43	2	27.06
R. J. Hadlee (*New Zealand*)	94	4,994	2,702	128	5-25	5	21.10
I. T. Botham (*England*)	95	5,076	3,398	116	4-56	1	29.29
Imran Khan (*Pakistan*)	101	4,196	2,531	115	6-14	4	22.00
M. D. Marshall (*West Indies*)	86	4,553	2,530	111	4-23	3	22.79
E. J. Chatfield (*New Zealand*)	90	4,792	2,816	110	5-34	2	25.60
D. K. Lillee (*Australia*)	63	3,593	2,145	103	5-34	6	20.82
Mudassar Nazar (*Pakistan*)	107	4,225	2,993	102	5-28	2	29.34

BEST BOWLING FOR EACH COUNTRY

7-51	W. W. Davis	**West Indies** v Australia at Leeds	1983
6-14	G. J. Gilmour	**Australia** v England at Leeds	1975
6-14	Imran Khan	**Pakistan** v India at Sharjah	1984-85
5-20	V. J. Marks	**England** v New Zealand at Wellington	1983-84
5-23	R. O. Collinge	**New Zealand** v India at Christchurch	1975-76
5-26	U. S. H. Karnain	**Sri Lanka** v New Zealand at Moratuwa	1983-84
5-43	Kapil Dev	**India** v Australia at Nottingham	1983

HAT-TRICKS

Jalal-ud-Din	Pakistan v Australia at Hyderabad	1982-83
B. A. Reid	Australia v New Zealand at Sydney	1985-86
Chetan Sharma	India v New Zealand at Nagpur	1987-88

MOST DISMISSALS IN A MATCH

5 (all ct)	R. W. Marsh	Australia v England at Leeds	1981
5 (all ct)	R. G. de Alwis	Sri Lanka v Australia at Colombo (PSO)	1982-83
5 (all ct)	S. M. H. Kirmani	India v Zimbabwe at Leicester	1983
5 (3 ct, 2 st)	S. Viswanath	India v England at Sydney	1984-85

50 OR MORE DISMISSALS

	M	Ct	St	Total
P. J. L. Dujon (*West Indies*)	106	122	12	134
R. W. Marsh (*Australia*)	91	119	4	123
Wasim Bari (*Pakistan*)	51	52	10	62

MOST CATCHES IN A MATCH

(Excluding wicket-keepers)

4	Salim Malik	Pakistan v New Zealand at Sialkot	1984-85
4	S. M. Gavaskar	India v Pakistan at Sharjah	1984-85

50 OR MORE CATCHES

	M	Ct		M	Ct
V. A. Richards (*West Indies*)	137	64	A. R. Border (*Australia*)	159	54

ALL-ROUND

1,000 Runs and 50 Wickets

	M	R	W
I. T. Botham (*England*)	95	1,693	116
J. V. Coney (*New Zealand*)	87	1,847	54
G. S. Chappell (*Australia*)	73	2,329	71
R. J. Hadlee (*New Zealand*)	94	1,310	128
Imran Khan (*Pakistan*)	101	1,785	115
Kapil Dev (*India*)	112	2,262	135
Mudassar Nazar (*Pakistan*)	107	2,314	102
I. V. A. Richards (*West Indies*)	137	5,587	78
R. J. Shastri (*India*)	90	1,753	89

1,000 Runs and 100 Dismissals

	M	R	D
P. J. L. Dujon (*West Indies*)	106	1,166	134
R. W. Marsh (*Australia*)	91	1,220	123

HIGHEST INNINGS TOTALS

360-4	(50 overs)	**West Indies** v Sri Lanka at Karachi	1987-88
338-5	(60 overs)	**Pakistan** v Sri Lanka at Swansea	1983
334-4	(60 overs)	**England** v India at Lord's	1975
333-8	(45 overs)	West Indies v India at Jamshedpur	1983-84
333-9	(60 overs)	England v Sri Lanka at Taunton	1983
330-6	(60 overs)	Pakistan v Sri Lanka at Nottingham	1975
328-5	(60 overs)	**Australia** v Sri Lanka at The Oval	1975
323-2	(50 overs)	Australia v Sri Lanka at Adelaide	1984-85
322-6	(60 overs)	England v New Zealand at The Oval	1983
320-8	(55 overs)	England v Australia at Birmingham	1980
320-9	(60 overs)	Australia v India at Nottingham	1983
313-9	(50 overs)	West Indies v Australia at St John's	1977-78
309-6	(50 overs)	West Indies v Sri Lanka at Perth	1984-85
309-5	(60 overs)	**New Zealand** v East Africa at Birmingham	1975
304-5	(50 overs)	New Zealand v Sri Lanka at Auckland	1982-83
302-8	(50 overs)	Australia v New Zealand at Melbourne	1982-83

Note: The highest score by **India** is 289-6 (50 overs) v Australia at New Delhi, 1987-88, and the highest by **Sri Lanka** is 288-9 (60 overs) v Pakistan at Swansea, 1983.

HIGHEST TOTALS BATTING SECOND

Winning

297-6	(48.5 overs)	New Zealand v England at Adelaide	1982-83

Losing

289-7	(40 overs)	Sri Lanka v India at Bombay	1986-87
288-9	(60 overs)	Sri Lanka v Pakistan at Swansea	1983

HIGHEST MATCH AGGREGATES

626-14	(120 overs)	Pakistan v Sri Lanka at Swansea	198.
619-19	(118 overs)	England v Sri Lanka at Taunton	198.
604-9	(120 overs)	Australia v Sri Lanka at The Oval	197.

LOWEST INNINGS TOTALS

45	(40.3 overs)	Canada v England at Manchester	1979
55	(28.3 overs)	**Sri Lanka** v West Indies at Sharjah	1986-87
63	(25.5 overs)	**India** v Australia at Sydney	1980-81
64	(35.5 overs)	New Zealand v Pakistan at Sharjah	1985-86
70	(25.2 overs)	**Australia** v England at Birmingham	1977
70	(26.3 overs)	Australia v New Zealand at Adelaide	1985-86
74	(29 overs)	New Zealand v Australia at Wellington	1981-82
78	(24.1 overs)	India v Sri Lanka at Kanpur	1986-87
79	(34.2 overs)	India v Pakistan at Sialkot	1978-79
85	(47 overs)	**Pakistan** v England at Manchester	1978
86	(37.2 overs)	Sri Lanka v West Indies at Manchester	1975
87	(32.5 overs)	Pakistan v India at Sharjah	1984-85
91	(35.5 overs)	Sri Lanka v Australia at Adelaide	1984-85
91	(35.4 overs)	Australia v West Indies at Perth	1986-87
93	(36.2 overs)	**England** v Australia at Leeds	1975
94	(31.7 overs)	England v Australia at Melbourne	1978-79
94	(52.3 overs)	East Africa v England at Birmingham	1975
96	(41 overs)	Sri Lanka v India at Sharjah	1983-84

Note: This section does not take into account those matches in which the number of overs wa reduced.

The lowest innings total by **West Indies** is 111 (41.4 overs) v Pakistan at Melbourne, 1983-84.

LARGEST VICTORIES

232 runs	Australia (323-2 in 50 overs) v Sri Lanka (91 in 35.5 overs) at Adelaide 1984-85
206 runs	New Zealand (276-7 in 50 overs) v Australia (70 in 26.3 overs) at Adelaide 1985-86
202 runs	England (334-4 in 60 overs) v India (132-3 in 60 overs) at Lord's 1975

By ten wickets: There have been seven instances of victory by ten wickets.

TIED MATCH

West Indies 222-5 (50 overs), Australia 222-9 (50 overs) at Melbourne 1983-84

WORLD CUP FINALS

1975 (60 overs)   West Indies (291-8) beat Australia (274) by 17 runs at Lord's.
1979 (60 overs)   West Indies (286-9) beat England (194) by 92 runs at Lord's.
1983 (60 overs)   India (183) beat West Indies (140) by 43 runs at Lord's.
1987 (50 overs)   Australia (253-5) beat England (246-8) by 7 runs at Calcutta.

MISCELLANEOUS

LARGE ATTENDANCES

Test Series

943,000	Australia v England (5 Tests)	1936-37
In England		
549,650	England v Australia (5 Tests)	1953

Test Match

†350,534	Australia v England, Melbourne (Third Test)	1936-37
325,000+	India v England, Calcutta (Second Test)	1972-73
In England		
158,000+	England v Australia, Leeds (Fourth Test)	1948
137,915	England v Australia, Lord's (Second Test)	1953

Test Match Day

90,800	Australia v West Indies, Melbourne (Fifth Test, 2nd day)	1960-61

Other First-Class Matches in England

80,000+	Surrey v Yorkshire, The Oval (3 days)	1906
78,792	Yorkshire v Lancashire, Leeds (3 days)	1904
76,617	Lancashire v Yorkshire, Manchester (3 days)	1926

One-day International

86,133‡	Australia v West Indies, Melbourne	1983-84

† *Although no official figures are available, the attendance at the Fourth Test between India and England at Calcutta, 1981-82, was thought to have exceeded this figure.*
‡ *It is estimated that a crowd of more than 90,000 attended the one-day international between India and Pakistan at Calcutta, 1986-87. However, this figure has not been confirmed.*

LORD'S CRICKET GROUND

Lord's and the MCC were founded in 1787. The Club has enjoyed an uninterrupted career since that date, but there have been three grounds known as Lord's. The first (1787-1810) was situated where Dorset Square now is; the second (1809-13), at North Bank, had to be abandoned owing to the cutting of the Regent's Canal; and the third, opened in 1814, is the present one at St John's Wood. It was not until 1866 that the freehold of Lord's was secured by the MCC. The present pavilion was erected in 1890 at a cost of £21,000.

HIGHEST INDIVIDUAL SCORES MADE AT LORD'S

316*	J. B. Hobbs	Surrey v Middlesex	1926
315*	P. Holmes	Yorkshire v Middlesex	1925
281*	W. H. Ponsford	Australians v MCC	1934
278	W. Ward	MCC v Norfolk (with E. H. Budd, T. Vigne and	
		F. Ladbroke)	1820
278	D. G. Bradman	Australians v MCC	1938
277*	E. H. Hendren	Middlesex v Kent	1922

Note: The longest innings in a Test match at Lord's was played by S. Wettimuny (642 minutes, 190 runs) for Sri Lanka v England, 1984.

HIGHEST TOTALS OBTAINED AT LORD'S

First-Class Matches

729-6	Australia v England	1930
665	West Indians v Middlesex	1939
652-8	West Indies v England	1973
629	England v India	1974
612-8	Middlesex v Nottinghamshire	1921
610-5	Australians v Gentlemen	1948
609-8	Cambridge University v MCC and Ground	1913
608-7	Middlesex v Hampshire	1919
607	MCC and Ground v Cambridge University	1902

Minor Match

735-9	MCC and Ground v Wiltshire	1888

BIGGEST HIT AT LORD'S

The only known instance of a batsman hitting a ball over the present pavilion at Lord's occurred when A. E. Trott, appearing for MCC against Australians on July 31, August 1, 2, 1899, drove M. A. Noble so far and high that the ball struck a chimney pot and fell behind the building.

HIGHEST IN A MINOR COUNTY MATCH

323*	F. E. Lacey	Hampshire v Norfolk at Southampton	1887

HIGHEST IN MINOR COUNTIES CHAMPIONSHIP

282	E. Garnett	Berkshire v Wiltshire at Reading	1908
254	H. E. Morgan	Glamorgan v Monmouthshire at Cardiff	1901
253*	G. J. Whittaker	Surrey II v Gloucestershire II at The Oval	1950
253	A. Booth	Lancashire II v Lincolnshire at Grimsby	1950
252	J. A. Deed	Kent II v Surrey II at The Oval (on début)	1924

HIGHEST FOR ENGLISH PUBLIC SCHOOL

278	J. L. Guise	Winchester v Eton at Eton	1921

HIGHEST IN OTHER MATCHES

628*	A. E. J. Collins, Clark's House v North Town at Clifton College. (A Junior House match. His innings of 6 hours 50 minutes was spread over four afternoons.)	1899
566	C. J. Eady, Break-o'-Day v Wellington at Hobart	1901-02
515	D. R. Havewalla, B.B. and C.I. Rly v St Xavier's at Bombay	1933-34
506*	J. C. Sharp, Melbourne GS v Geelong College at Melbourne	1914-15
502*	Chaman Lal, Mehandra Coll., Patiala v Government Coll., Rupar at Patiala	1956-57
485	A. E. Stoddart, Hampstead v Stoics at Hampstead	1886
475*	Mohammad Iqbal, Muslim Model HS v Islamia HS, Sialkot at Lahore	1958-59
466*	G. T. S. Stevens, Beta v Lambda (University College School House match) at Neasden	1919
459	J. A. Prout, Wesley College v Geelong College at Geelong	1908-09

RECORD HIT

The Rev. W. Fellows, while at practice on the Christ Church ground at Oxford in 1856, drove a ball bowled by Charles Rogers 175 yards from hit to pitch.

THROWING THE CRICKET BALL

140 yards 2 feet, Robert Percival, on the Durham Sands, Co. Durham Racecourse		c 1882
140 yards 9 inches, Ross Mackenzie, at Toronto	....	1872

Notes: W. F. Forbes, on March 16, 1876, threw 132 yards at the Eton College sports. He was then eighteen years of age.

Onochie Onuorah, on June 5, 1987, threw a $4\frac{3}{4}$oz ball 100 yards 1 foot $8\frac{1}{4}$ inches (91.94 metres) at The Abbey School, Westgate, sports. He was then thirteen years of age.

William Yardley, while a boy at Rugby, threw 100 yards with his right hand and 78 yards with his left .

Charles Arnold, of Cambridge, once threw 112 yards with the wind and 108 against.

W. H. Game, at The Oval in 1875, threw the ball 111 yards and then back the same distance. W. G. Grace threw 109 yards one way and back 105, and George Millyard 108 with the wind and 103 against. At The Oval in 1868, W. G. Grace made three successive throws of 116, 117 and 118 yards, and then threw back over 100 yards. D. G. Foster (Warwickshire) threw 133 yards, and in 1930 he made a Danish record with 120.1 metres – about 130 yards.

DATES OF FORMATION OF COUNTY CLUBS NOW FIRST-CLASS

County	First known county organisation	Original date	Present Club Reorganisation, if substantial
Derbyshire	November 4, 1870	November 4, 1870	—
Essex	By May, 1790	January 14, 1876	—
Glamorgan	1863	July 6, 1888	—
Gloucestershire	November 3, 1863	1871	—
Hampshire	April 3, 1849	August 12, 1863	July, 1879
Kent	August 6, 1842	March 1, 1859	December 6, 1870
Lancashire	January 12, 1864	January 12, 1864	—
Leicestershire	By August, 1820	March 25, 1879	—
Middlesex	December 15, 1863	February 2, 1864	—
Northamptonshire	1820	1820	July 31, 1878
Nottinghamshire	March/April, 1841	March/April, 1841	December 11, 1866
Somerset	October 15, 1864	August 18, 1875	—
Surrey	August 22, 1845	August 22, 1845	—
Sussex	June 16, 1836	March 1, 1839	August, 1857
Warwickshire	May, 1826	1882	—
Worcestershire	1844	March 5, 1865	—
Yorkshire	March 7, 1861	January 8, 1863	December 10, 1891

DATES OF FORMATION OF CLUBS IN THE CURRENT MINOR COUNTIES CHAMPIONSHIP

County	First known county organisation	Present Club
Bedfordshire	May, 1847	November 3, 1899
Berkshire	By May, 1841	March 17, 1895
Buckinghamshire	November, 1864	January 15, 1891
Cambridgeshire	March 13, 1844	June 6, 1891
Cheshire	1819	September 29, 1908

	First known	
County	*county organisation*	*Present Club*
Cornwall	1813	November 12, 1894
Cumberland	January 2, 1884	April 10, 1948
Devon	1824	November 26, 1899
Dorset	1862 *or* 1871	February 5, 1896
Durham	January 24, 1874	May 10, 1882
Hertfordshire	1838	March 8, 1876
Lincolnshire	1853	September 28, 1906
Norfolk	January 11, 1827	October 14, 1876
Northumberland	1834	December, 1895
Oxfordshire	1787	December 14, 1921
Shropshire	1819 *or* 1829	June 28, 1956
Staffordshire	November 24, 1871	November 24, 1871
Suffolk	July 27, 1864	August, 1932
Wiltshire	February 24, 1881	January, 1893

CONSTITUTION OF COUNTY CHAMPIONSHIP

There are references in the sporting press to a champion county as early as 1825, but the list is not continuous and in some years only two counties contested the title. The earliest reference in any cricket publication is from 1864, and at this time there were eight leading counties who have come to be regarded as first-class from that date – Cambridgeshire, Hampshire, Kent, Middlesex, Nottinghamshire, Surrey, Sussex and Yorkshire. The newly formed Lancashire club began playing inter-county matches in 1865, Gloucestershire in 1870 and Derbyshire in 1871, and they are therefore regarded as first-class from these respective dates. Cambridgeshire dropped out after 1871, Hampshire, who had not played inter-county matches in certain seasons, after 1885, and Derbyshire after 1887. Somerset, who had played matches against the first-class counties since 1879, were regarded as first-class from 1882 to 1885, and were admitted formally to the Championship in 1891. In 1894, Derbyshire, Essex, Leicestershire and Warwickshire were granted first-class status, but did not compete in the Championship until 1895 when Hampshire returned. Worcestershire, Northamptonshire and Glamorgan were admitted to the Championship in 1899, 1905 and 1921 respectively and are regarded as first-class from these dates. An invitation in 1921 to Buckinghamshire to enter the Championship was declined, owing to the lack of necessary playing facilities, and an application by Devon in 1948 was unsuccessful.

MOST COUNTY CHAMPIONSHIP APPEARANCES

763	W. Rhodes	Yorkshire	1898-1930
707	F. E. Woolley	Kent	1906-38
665	C. P. Mead	Hampshire	1906-36

MOST CONSECUTIVE COUNTY CHAMPIONSHIP APPEARANCES

423	K. G. Suttle	Sussex	1954-69
412	J. G. Binks ,,,,,,,,	Yorkshire	1955-69
399	J. Vine	Sussex	1899-1914
344	E. H. Killick	Sussex	1898-1912
326	C. N. Woolley	Northamptonshire	1913-31
305	A. H. Dyson	Glamorgan	1930-47
301	B. Taylor	Essex	1961-72

Notes: J. Vine made 417 consecutive appearances for Sussex in all first-class matches between July 1900 and September 1914.

J. G. Binks did not miss a Championship match for Yorkshire between making his début in June 1955 and retiring at the end of the 1969 season.

THE RELIANCE WORLD CUP, 1987-88

The fourth World Cup was more widely watched, more closely fought, and more colourful than any of its three predecessors held in England. Any doubts about it were dispelled by the opening matches when Pakistan, the favourites, were run close by Sri Lanka; when India, the holders, were beaten by Australia by 1 run; when England succeeded in scoring 35 off their last three overs to beat West Indies; and when the gallant amateurs of Zimbabwe lost by only 3 runs to New Zealand.

If the rest of the Reliance Cup, as it was officially known and seldom called, could not quite live up to such a start, the experiment of an oriental World Cup was still acknowledged to have been a great success. The semi-finals in Lahore and Bombay held the sub-continent by the ears and eyes, even if they did not produce the results desired by the tens of millions who were following the matches on radio and television. The arrangements for the final, at Eden Gardens in Calcutta, were praised to the full by the winning Australian captain, and rightly.

Any drawbacks resulted from the geographical enormity of the two host countries and the determination of the Indo-Pakistan Joint Management Committee to spread the games around as many as 21 venues. It was the equivalent of staging a tournament in Europe, barring only the Soviet Union, without quite the same facility of transport and telecommunications. Fewer centres would have meant less travelling, a shorter and more compact competition – it took six weeks against less than a month for the 1983 World Cup – and increased enjoyment all round. For successive matches, the Sri Lankans were shunted from Peshawar, in the North-West Frontier Province of Pakistan, to Kanpur in central India, back to Faisalabad, then across the border again to Pune: two-day journeys every time, with hours spent in transit lounges at airports waiting for flights.

Nevertheless, in circumstances which were perhaps more arduous than they need have been, the organisers did excellently. In return, the weather was kind to them. To all intents, only one match was affected by rain, when Australia and New Zealand were reduced to 30 overs each in Indore. (Happily, the rule that a match could not be carried over to its second day was never exposed in its absurdity.) Otherwise the matches were of 50 overs per side, and on good pitches totals similar to those in previous 60-over World Cups were raised. Viv Richards, and West Indies as a team, set up new records against Sri Lanka for World Cup innings.

If the umpiring was not of the very highest standard, its "neutrality" served to minimise grievances. Poor neutral umpiring, however, can never be a substitute for good umpiring, whether by home or neutral officials. The standard of scoring, it has to be recorded, was inadequate in many centres, done as it was by local scorers unfamiliar with visiting players, while the telegraph boards were not always kept up to date.

One especial virtue in staging the World Cup in India and Pakistan was that spin had a full part to play, whereas previous competitions in England had been dominated by repetitive seamers. Not one over of spin was risked in the 1975 final. Australia were untypical in that they usually allotted only ten overs to spin; the majority of teams fielded two spinners and benefited on the slow batting pitches that prevailed. In the qualifying rounds, seven of the nine most economical bowlers were spinners. That said, the leading wicket-takers were both fast bowlers, Craig McDermott equalling the World Cup record of eighteen and Imran Khan capturing seventeen in one match less.

Batsmen were not troubled by dew when batting first, as some had feared, but by the strain of batting second. Out of 27 matches, nineteen were won by the side batting first. The received wisdom had been to bowl first in one-day internationals and to determine the target. Now every side wanted to bat first, then watch the opposition – fatigued by three and a half hours' fielding in the heat – make mistakes and panic as the run-rate climbed to 7 and 8 an over. The side batting first played the ball according to its merits; the side batting second seemed to play it according to the run-rate required.

In this context, Australia were fortunate to bat first in five of their six qualifying games, and to be able to do so again in their semi-final and final, on pitches which lost what bounce they had. This luck aside, they were still the team most deserving of victory: they appeared to put the most into the tournament – the sweat was dripping from the peaks of the batsmen's caps when they "warmed up" in Madras – and they gained their first success of note since 1984. England, the runners-up, arrived with a specialist in tropical diseases and a microwave oven but with only three batsmen capable of scoring at a run a ball. They won whenever their bowlers were able to make up for the deficiencies in their batting.

Co-hosts India and Pakistan, as holders and favourites, had been expected to meet in the final but never met at all, not even in a hastily conceived third-place play-off match which fell through owing to the exorbitant demands of some players. Indeed, it was perhaps as well that their paths never crossed, for there were reports of communal conflict in India after the semi-final results. Pakistan blew hot too soon, winning their first five qualifying games, largely on the basis of some overwhelming bowling from Imran Khan and Abdul Qadir, only for their luck to turn in the semi-final.

In a sense, India handicapped themselves by playing in the weaker qualifying group, much as England had in 1979. In both cases the hosts qualified without having the weak links in their bowling exposed. India's batting was collectively the most brilliant in the tournament but not always the most effective. The demands of their crowds for spectacular hitting, and enticing awards from a sponsor for every four and six they hit, cannot have been beneficial influences; likewise a never settled dispute which the senior Indian players had with their Board over insignia.

West Indies, in transition, missed their fast bowlers of experience. It is not inconceivable that Malcolm Marshall could have won the World Cup for them had he played. New Zealand, too, were in transition in the absence of Richard Hadlee. Sri Lanka, in the field, were utterly defensive, and confronted by mountainous totals their talented batsmen were crushed.

Like the Sri Lankans, the Zimbabweans returned home without a victory, but they gained many friends by their fielding – giving themselves as professionals never quite could – and many sympathisers by their naïve mistakes and run-outs. For sheer heroism, the innings of the World Cup was David Houghton's 141 against New Zealand.

The Australians had the same keen, uncynical spirit as the Zimbabweans. They worked and worked as a team; and every follower of the game had to be pleased in some measure when, at the end of the Australians' victory lap around Eden Gardens, Allan Border was raised on the shoulders of his team-mates and the gold Reliance Cup placed in his hands. – Scyld Berry.

GROUP A

†AUSTRALIA v INDIA

At Madras, October 9. Australia won by 1 run. Toss: India. Kapil Dev's sportsmanship proved the deciding factor in a close-run match. One of Jones's two sixes, in his 39 from 35 balls, had been signalled as four; but between innings Kapil concurred with the Australians' insistence that the ball cleared the boundary. That India's target was increased by 2 seemed insignificant when Gavaskar (32 balls, one six, six fours), Srikkanth (83 balls, seven fours) and Sidhu (79 balls, five sixes, four fours) sent them racing past 200 for the loss of only two wickets. McDermott's first four overs went for 31 runs, but he came back strongly to whip out the middle order. Even so, India, with four wickets in hand, needed just 15 from the last four overs; when the last over began, the requirement was 6, with the last man, Maninder Singh, taking strike. He managed two 2s, but along with his sang-froid went his off stump. Australia's innings, like India's, had been built around the top-order batsmen. On a pitch of little pace or bounce, Marsh and Boon put on 100 at almost 5 an over. Jones played quite beautifully, but the middle order lost the initiative. Marsh, in 95-degree heat and high humidity, batted more than three hours and hit a six and seven fours in 141 balls.

Man of the Match: G. R. Marsh.

Australia

D. C. Boon lbw b Shastri	49	S. R. Waugh not out	19
G. R. Marsh c Azharuddin		S. P. O'Donnell run out	7
b Prabhakar	.110	L-b 18, w 2, n-b 2	22
D. M. Jones c Sidhu b Maninder	39		
*A. R. Border b Binny	16	1/110 2/174 3/228 (6 wkts, 50 overs)	270
T. M. Moody c Kapil Dev b Prabhakar	8	4/237 5/251 6/270	

†G. C. Dyer, P. L. Taylor, C. J. McDermott and B. A. Reid did not bat.

Bowling: Kapil Dev 10-0-41-0; Prabhakar 10-0-47-2; Binny 7-0-46-1; Maninder 10-0-48-1; Shastri 10-0-50-1; Azharuddin 3-0-20-0.

India

S. M. Gavaskar c Reid b Taylor	37	R. M. H. Binny run out	0
K. Srikkanth lbw b Waugh	70	M. Prabhakar run out	5
N. S. Sidhu b McDermott	73	Maninder Singh b Waugh	4
D. B. Vengsarkar c Jones b McDermott	29	B 2, l-b 7, w 2	11
M. Azharuddin b McDermott	10		
*Kapil Dev c Boon b O'Donnell	6	1/69 2/131 3/207 (49.5 overs)	269
R. J. Shastri c and b McDermott	12	4/229 5/232 6/246	
†K. S. More not out	12	7/256 8/256 9/265	

Bowling: McDermott 10-0-56-4; Reid 10-2-35-0; O'Donnell 9-1-32-1; Taylor 5-0-46-1; Waugh 9.5-0-52-2; Border 6-0-39-0.

Umpires: D. M. Archer and H. D. Bird.

†NEW ZEALAND v ZIMBABWE

At Hyderabad, India, October 10. New Zealand won by 3 runs. Toss: Zimbabwe. An innings of great character, 141 from 138 balls, by Houghton, Zimbabwe's wicket-keeper-batsman, gave New Zealand a scare in their opening match of the tournament. Adding 117 with Butchart – a record for the eighth wicket in one-day internationals – Houghton had taken his side to within 22 of their target when he was out in the 47th over, having hit three sixes and thirteen fours. Zimbabwe wanted 6 from the final over, but Butchart was run out off the fourth ball. New Zealand had surprisingly ended their batting with Snedden, their seam bowler, who hit 64 off 97 balls, while Martin Crowe batted elegantly as they put on 84. Everything, however, paled when set alongside Houghton's heroic attempt to lift Zimbabwe from 104 for seven to within a gasp of history.

Man of the Match: D. L. Houghton.

New Zealand

M. C. Snedden c Waller b Rawson 64	†I. D. S. Smith c Brown b Curran 29
J. G. Wright c Houghton b Traicos ... 17	S. L. Boock not out 0
M. D. Crowe c and b Rawson 72	B 4, l-b 5, w 4, n-b 3 16
A. H. Jones c Brandes b Shah 0	
*J. J. Crowe c Brown b Curran 31	1/59 2/143 3/145 (7 wkts, 50 overs) 242
D. N. Patel lbw b Shah 0	4/166 5/169
J. G. Bracewell not out 13	6/205 7/240

E. J. Chatfield and W. Watson did not bat.

Bowling: Curran 10-0-51-2; Rawson 10-0-62-2; Brandes 7-2-23-0; Traicos 10-2-28-1; Butchart 4-0-27-0; Shah 9-0-42-2.

Zimbabwe

R. D. Brown c J. J. Crowe b Chatfield . 1	I. P. Butchart run out 54
A. H. Shah lbw b Snedden 5	E. A. Brandes run out 0
†D. L. Houghton c M. D. Crowe	*A. J. Traicos not out 4
b Snedden .141	
A. J. Pycroft run out 12	L-b 8, w 1, n-b 1 10
K. M. Curran c Boock b Watson 4	
A. C. Waller c Smith b Watson 5	1/8 2/10 3/61 (49.4 overs) 239
G. A. Paterson c Smith b Boock 2	4/67 5/86 6/94
P. W. E. Rawson lbw b Boock 1	7/104 8/221 9/221

Bowling: Chatfield 10-2-26-1; Snedden 9-0-53-2; Watson 10-2-36-2; Bracewell 7-0-47-0; Patel 5-0-27-0; Boock 8.4-0-42-2.

Umpires: Mahboob Shah and P. W. Vidanagamage.

†AUSTRALIA v ZIMBABWE

At Madras, October 13. Australia won by 96 runs. Toss: Zimbabwe. Border, dropped by Jarvis off a straightforward return catch when he had scored 1, put on 113 with Marsh after Australia had shown signs of nerves at 20 for two. Working the ball solidly off his legs, he faced 88 balls in an innings of 67 which took him past 4,000 runs in one-day matches for Australia. Zimbabwe broke back, dismissing both batsmen in quick succession, only for Waugh to step up the rate with 45 from 40 balls. And when Zimbabwe batted, he gave away just 7 runs in his six overs. McDermott looked sharp and accurate, while the inclusion of May, an off-spinner, hinted at a better balance.
Man of the Match: S. R. Waugh.

Australia

G. R. Marsh c Curran b Shah 62	C. J. McDermott c Brown b Curran ... 1
D. C. Boon c Houghton b Curran 2	T. B. A. May run out 1
D. M. Jones run out 2	
*A. R. Border c Shah b Butchart 67	W 8 8
S. R. Waugh 45	
S. P. O'Donnell run out 3	1/10 2/20 3/133 (9 wkts, 50 overs) 235
†G. C. Dyer c Paterson b Butchart 27	4/143 5/155 6/202
P. L. Taylor not out 17	7/228 8/230 9/235

B. A. Reid did not bat.

Bowling: Curran 8-0-29-2; Jarvis 10-0-40-0; Rawson 6-0-39-0; Butchart 10-1-59-2; Traicos 10-0-36-0; Shah 6-0-32-1.

Zimbabwe

R. D. Brown b O'Donnell	3	I. P. Butchart c Jones b O'Donnell	18
G. A. Paterson run out	16	*A. J. Traicos c and b O'Donnell	6
†D. L. Houghton c O'Donnell b May	11	M. P. Jarvis not out	1
A. J. Pycroft run out	9	B 2, l-b 3, w 3, n-b 1	9
K. M. Curran b O'Donnell	30		
A. C. Waller c and b May	19	1/13 2/27 3/41	(42.4 overs) 139
A. H. Shah b McDermott	2	4/44 5/79 6/97	
P. W. E. Rawson b Reid	15	7/97 8/124 9/137	

Bowling: McDermott 7-1-13-1; Reid 7-1-21-1; O'Donnell 9.4-1-39-4; Waugh 6-3-7-0; May 8-0-29-2; Taylor 5-0-25-0.

Umpires: Khizar Hayat and D. R. Shepherd.

†INDIA v NEW ZEALAND

At Bangalore, October 14. India won by 16 runs. Toss: New Zealand. Asked to bat first when the conditions were not easy – the pace of the pitch was variable and the outfield slow – India were not helped by an eccentric whim which took hold of Srikkanth and led to both openers being run out. Srikkanth actually appeared oblivious of the danger when Rutherford dismissed him. Sidhu (71 balls, four sixes, four fours) got the innings going from a position of 21 for three in the tenth over, but when he was fifth out, at 114, something special was required if India were to set any sort of target. Kapil Dev (58 balls, one six, four fours) and More provided it, adding 82 runs in dashing fashion off the last 51 balls. New Zealand, without Wright, who was ill with a virus, batted soundly but never quickly enough. Martin Crowe, the one batsman capable of developing the run-rate, was classically beaten by the slow left-armer, Maninder Singh, one of three spin bowlers employed by India.

Man of the Match: Kapil Dev.

India

K. Srikkanth run out	9	M. Prabhakar c and b Chatfield	3
S. M. Gavaskar run out	2	†K. S. More not out	42
N. S. Sidhu c Jones b Patel	75	L-b 4, w 2	6
D. B. Vengsarkar c and b Watson	0		
M. Azharuddin c Boock b Patel	21	1/11 2/16 3/21	(7 wkts, 50 overs) 252
R. J. Shastri c and b Patel	22	4/86 5/114	
*Kapil Dev not out	72	6/165 7/170	

Maninder Singh and L. Sivaramakrishnan did not bat.

Bowling: Chatfield 10-1-39-1; Snedden 10-1-56-0; Watson 9-0-59-1; Boock 4-0-26-0; Bracewell 7-0-32-0; Patel 10-0-36-3.

New Zealand

M. C. Snedden c Shastri b Azharuddin	33	S. L. Boock not out	7
K. R. Rutherford c Srikkanth b Shastri	75	W. Watson not out	2
M. D. Crowe st More b Maninder	9		
A. H. Jones run out	64	B 5, l-b 9, w 5, n-b 1	20
*J. J. Crowe c Vengsarkar b Maninder	7		
D. N. Patel run out	1	1/67 2/86 3/146	(8 wkts, 50 overs) 236
J. G. Bracewell c Maninder b Shastri	8	4/168 5/170 6/189	
†I. D. S. Smith b Prabhakar	10	7/206 8/225	

E. J. Chatfield did not bat.

Bowling: Kapil Dev 10-1-54-0; Prabhakar 8-0-38-1; Azharuddin 4-0-11-1; Sivaramakrishnan 8-0-34-0; Maninder 10-0-40-2; Shastri 10-0-45-2.

Umpires: D. M. Archer and H. D. Bird.

†INDIA v ZIMBABWE

At Bombay, October 17. India won by eight wickets. Toss: Zimbabwe. India, having bowled out Zimbabwe for 135 well within the allocation of overs, wasted no time in achieving victory, conscious of the importance of a good run-rate should it be the deciding factor at the end of the group matches. Gavaskar (51 balls) scored his first 36 runs from his nine boundaries; Vengsarkar picked off the runs with a deadly intent. Zimbabwe's decision to bat first on a dewy morning rebounded as Prabhakar, swinging the ball disconcertingly, took four wickets in seventeen balls. Pycroft, with 61 from 102 balls, saw that Zimbabwe at least reached three figures.

Man of the Match: M. Prabhakar.

Zimbabwe

G. A. Paterson b Prabhakar	6	M. A. Meman run out	19
K. J. Arnott lbw b Prabhakar	1	*A. J. Traicos c Gavaskar	
†D. L. Houghton b Prabhakar	0	b Sivaramakrishnan	0
A. J. Pycroft st More b Shastri	61	M. P. Jarvis not out	8
K. M. Curran c More b Prabhakar	0	B 2, l-b 6, w 6	14
A. C. Waller st More b Maninder	16		
I. P. Butchart c Sivaramakrishnan		1/3 2/12 3/13	(44.2 overs) 135
b Maninder	10	4/13 5/47 6/67	
A. H. Shah c More b Maninder	0	7/67 8/98 9/99	

Bowling: Kapil Dev 8-1-17-0; Prabhakar 8-1-19-4; Maninder 10-0-21-3; Azharuddin 1-0-6-0; Sivaramakrishnan 9-0-36-1; Shastri 8.2-0-28-1.

India

K. Srikkanth c Paterson b Traicos	31
S. M. Gavaskar st Houghton b Traicos	43
M. Prabhakar not out	11
D. B. Vengsarkar not out	46
L-b 1, w 4	5

1/76 2/80　　　(2 wkts, 27.5 overs) 136

N. S. Sidhu, M. Azharuddin, *Kapil Dev, R. J. Shastri, †K. S. More, L. Sivaramakrishnan and Maninder Singh did not bat.

Bowling: Curran 6-0-32-0; Jarvis 4-0-22-0; Butchart 3-0-20-0; Traicos 8-0-27-2; Meman 6.5-0-34-0.

Umpires: Mahboob Shah and D. R. Shepherd.

†AUSTRALIA v NEW ZEALAND

At Indore, October 18, 19. Australia won by 3 runs. Toss: New Zealand. This was a match New Zealand needed to win to leave themselves in a position to challenge for a semi-final place; and they should not have lost it. Postponed for a day because of heavy rain, it was curtailed to 30 overs a side after the captains expressed their preference for a game rather than sharing the points for a "no result". Boon's 87 from 87 balls laid the foundation for an Australian total that was to set New Zealand a target of 6.66 an over. He and Jones (49 balls) added 117 from 98 balls against some indifferent slow bowling, and Border improvised to score 34 off 26 balls. Wright and Rutherford sparked New Zealand's reply, putting on 83 in twelve overs, and with Martin Crowe on 58 from 46 balls, they began the final over requiring 7 runs with four wickets in hand. Crowe departed to Waugh's first ball, misjudging the length and lofting it to deep cover; the next ball, a yorker, sent back Smith. For New Zealand, it was all over. Waugh, the last-over hero against India, allowed only 3 singles and ran out Snedden.

Man of the Match: D. C. Boon.

Australia

D. C. Boon c Wright b Snedden	 87	T. M. Moody not out	 0
G. R. Marsh c J. J. Crowe b Snedden	. 5	B 1, l-b 5, w 2	 8
D. M. Jones c Rutherford b Patel	 52		
*A. R. Border c M. D. Crowe b Chatfield	34	1/17 2/134 3/171 (4 wkts, 30 overs) 199	
S. R. Waugh not out	 13	4/196	

S. P. O'Donnell, †G. C. Dyer, T. B. A. May, C. J. McDermott and B. A. Reid did not bat.

Bowling: Snedden 6-0-35-2; Chatfield 6-0-28-1; Watson 6-0-34-0; Patel 6-0-45-1; Bracewell 6-0-51-0.

New Zealand

K. R. Rutherford b O'Donnell	 37	M. C. Snedden run out	 1
J. G. Wright c Dyer b O'Donnell	 47	E. J. Chatfield not out	 0
M. D. Crowe c Marsh b Waugh	 58	W. Watson not out	 2
A. H. Jones c Marsh b McDermott	... 15	B 4, l-b 5, w 4	 13
*J. J. Crowe c and b Reid	 3		
D. N. Patel run out	 13	1/83 2/94 3/133 (9 wkts, 30 overs) 196	
J. G. Bracewell c and b Reid	 6	4/140 5/165 6/183	
†I. D. S. Smith b Waugh	 1	7/193 8/193 9/195	

Bowling: McDermott 6-0-30-1; Reid 6-0-38-2; May 6-0-39-0; O'Donnell 6-0-44-2; Waugh 6-0-36-2.

Umpires: D. M. Archer and Khizar Hayat.

†AUSTRALIA v INDIA

At New Delhi, October 22. India won by 56 runs. Toss: Australia. The prospect of India's finishing second in this group, and so having to play Pakistan in a semi-final in Pakistan, lessened after their convincing victory. The pitch was ideal for strokeplaying batsmen; the outfield was fast and the boundaries were not too distant. Containment, therefore, was going to be the key, and with the ball coming on to the bat, the Australians' all-seam attack proved to be more vulnerable. Gavaskar and Srikkanth got India off to a flying start with 50 in ten overs, Sidhu hit his third successive fifty, and Vengsarkar (59 balls) and Azharuddin (47 balls), batting with authority and *élan*, added 65 in ten overs. Marsh and Boon (55 balls, seven fours) responded with 88 in eighteen overs, but the introduction of the left-arm spinners, Maninder and Shastri, after seventeen overs changed the complexion of the match. Turn, flight and a modicum of frustration brought about Australia's undoing. Waugh (53 balls) displayed technique and temperament, but while the spinners dictated the terms, Australia slipped further and further behind.

Man of the Match: M. Azharuddin.

India

K. Srikkanth c Dyer b McDermott	... 26	R. J. Shastri c and b Waugh	 8
S. M. Gavaskar b O'Donnell	 61	†K. S. More not out	 5
N. S. Sidhu c Moody b McDermott	... 51	B 1, l-b 6, w 11	 18
D. B. Vengsarkar c O'Donnell b Reid	. 63		
*Kapil Dev c Dyer b McDermott	 3	1/50 2/125 3/167 (6 wkts, 50 overs) 289	
M. Azharuddin not out	 54	4/178 5/243 6/274	

M. Prabhakar, Chetan Sharma and Maninder Singh did not bat.

Bowling: O'Donnell 9-1-45-1; Reid 10-0-65-1; Waugh 10-0-59-1; McDermott 10-0-61-3; Moody 2-0-15-0; Zesers 9-1-37-0.

Australia

G. R. Marsh st More b Maninder	33		C. J. McDermott c and b Azharuddin	4
D. C. Boon c More b Shastri	62		A. K. Zesers not out	2
D. M. Jones c Kapil Dev b Maninder	36		B. A. Reid c Sidhu b Azharuddin	1
*A. R. Border c Prabhakar b Maninder	12		L-b 11, w 8	19
S. R. Waugh c Sidhu b Kapil Dev	42			
T. M. Moody run out	2		1/88 2/104 3/135	(49 overs) 233
S. P. O'Donnell b Azharuddin	5		4/164 5/167 6/182	
†G. C. Dyer c Kapil Dev b Prabhakar	15		7/214 8/227 9/231	

Bowling: Kapil Dev 8-1-41-1; Prabhakar 10-0-56-1; Chetan 7.1-0-37-0; Maninder 10-0-34-3; Shastri 10-0-35-1; Azharuddin 3.5-0-19-3.

Umpires: Khalid Aziz and D. R. Shepherd.

†NEW ZEALAND v ZIMBABWE

At Calcutta, October 23. New Zealand won by four wickets. Toss: New Zealand. When Martin Crowe, having hit eight fours in 58 from 58 balls, was fourth out at 125, New Zealand looked in some difficulty. However, they were seen to their second win of the tournament by his older brother, Jeff, the captain, whose sterling 88 not out, from 105 balls, included eight fours also. Zimbabwe again owed much to Houghton and Pycroft. Arnott and Shah were sound, but slow, and when Pycroft replaced Shah at 121 for three, only fifteen overs remained. He played the supporting role as Houghton carved 50 from 58 balls, then expanded his own repertoire of hitting to reach his half-century before the innings closed.

Man of the Match: J. J. Crowe.

Zimbabwe

G. A. Paterson run out	0		A. C. Waller not out	8
A. H. Shah c M. D. Crowe b Watson	41			
K. J. Arnott run out	51		L-b 7, w 6	13
†D. L. Houghton c M. D. Crowe b Boock	50			
A. J. Pycroft not out	52		1/1 2/82 3/121	(5 wkts, 50 overs) 227
K. M. Curran b Boock	12		4/180 5/216	

I. P. Butchart, E. A. Brandes, *A. J. Traicos and M. P. Jarvis did not bat.

Bowling: Snedden 10-2-32-0; Chatfield 10-2-47-0; Patel 10-1-52-0; Watson 10-1-45-1; Boock 10-1-44-2.

New Zealand

K. R. Rutherford b Brandes	22		M. C. Snedden b Jarvis	4
J. G. Wright b Shah	12		†I. D. S. Smith not out	17
M. D. Crowe c Butchart b Shah	58		B 1, l-b 5, w 4, n-b 1	11
D. N. Patel c Arnott b Brandes	1			
*J. J. Crowe not out	88		1/37 2/53 3/56	(6 wkts, 47.4 overs) 228
A. H. Jones c Jarvis b Traicos	15		4/125 5/158 6/182	

S. L. Boock, W. Watson and E. J. Chatfield did not bat.

Bowling: Curran 2-0-12-0; Jarvis 7.4-0-39-1; Brandes 10-1-44-2; Shah 10-0-34-2; Butchart 8-0-50-0; Traicos 10-0-43-1.

Umpires: Khizar Hayat and P. W. Vidanagamage.

†INDIA v ZIMBABWE

At Ahmedabad, October 26. India won by seven wickets. Toss: India. With run-rate becoming such an essential factor in this group, India's top-order batting was decidedly dilatory, even taking into account the slow pitch and the distraction of unruly, stone-throwing spectators. Gavaskar took 114 balls over his 50, and although Kapil Dev, promoting himself to No. 5 and hitting three sixes, scored 41 in 25 balls to win the match in the 42nd over, he did not salvage the situation entirely. India's run-rate was now 5.18 to Australia's 5.20. For Zimbabwe, Arnott, coming in when Shah was run out in the second over, batted 43 overs for his 60.

Man of the Match: Kapil Dev.

Zimbabwe

R. D. Brown c More b Chetan	13	P. W. E. Rawson not out		16
A. H. Shah run out	0	E. A. Brandes not out		3
K. J. Arnott b Kapil Dev	60	B 1, l-b 12, w 9, n-b 1		23
A. J. Pycroft c More b Chetan	2			
†D. L. Houghton c Kapil Dev b Shastri	22	1/4 2/36 3/40	(7 wkts, 50 overs)	191
A. C. Waller c Shastri b Maninder	39	4/83 5/150		
I. P. Butchart b Kapil Dev	13	6/155 7/184		

M. P. Jarvis and *A. J. Traicos did not bat.

Bowling: Kapil Dev 10-2-44-2; Prabhakar 7-2-12-0; Chetan 10-0-41-2; Maninder 10-1-32-1; Shastri 10-0-35-1; Azharuddin 3-0-14-0.

India

K. Srikkanth lbw b Jarvis	6	*Kapil Dev not out		41
S. M. Gavaskar c Butchart b Rawson	50	L-b 6, w 3		9
N. S. Sidhu c Brandes b Rawson	55			
D. B. Vengsarkar not out	33	1/11 2/105 3/132	(3 wkts, 42 overs)	194

M. Azharuddin, R. J. Shastri, †K. S. More, M. Prabhakar, Chetan Sharma and Maninder Singh did not bat.

Bowling: Brandes 6-0-28-0; Jarvis 8-1-21-1; Shah 8-0-40-0; Traicos 10-0-39-0; Rawson 8-0-46-2; Butchart 2-0-14-0.

Umpires: D. M. Archer and H. D. Bird.

†AUSTRALIA v NEW ZEALAND

At Chandigarh, October 27. Australia won by 17 runs. Toss: Australia. The Australians, looking for a total of 260 or more to improve their run-rate in the hope of avoiding a semi-final with Pakistan, had to thank an uncharacteristically loose final over by Chatfield for scoring as many as 251. The New Zealand seamer, usually so accurate, was hit for 19 runs, including two leg-side sixes by Marsh. It had taken Australia 45 overs to reach 200, with only Marsh, the third player after S. M. Gavaskar and G. M. Turner to bat throughout a World Cup innings, showing any application once Jones (80 balls) was caught in the 36th over. Marsh's 126, his fourth one-day hundred for Australia and second of this World Cup, contained three sixes and twelve fours. New Zealand suffered an unlucky setback when Martin Crowe, the non-striker, was run out by Waugh's deflection of a straight drive from Wright. Rutherford batted neatly, Wright solidly, but Border never let the Australians relax their grip. He also bowled seven tidy overs of left-arm slows and took two wickets to expose New Zealand's limited lower-order batting.

Man of the Match: G. R. Marsh.

Australia

G. R. Marsh not out	126	T. B. A. May run out		15
D. C. Boon run out	14	A. K. Zesers not out		8
D. M. Jones c Smith b Watson	56			
*A. R. Border b Snedden	1	L-b 10, w 7		17
M. R. J. Veletta run out	0			
S. R. Waugh b Watson	1	1/25 2/151 3/158	(8 wkts, 50 overs)	251
†G. C. Dyer b Chatfield	8	4/158 5/175 6/193		
C. J. McDermott lbw b Chatfield	5	7/201 8/228		

B. A. Reid did not bat.

Bowling: Snedden 10-0-48-1; Chatfield 10-2-52-2; Boock 10-1-45-0; Bracewell 4-0-24-0; Patel 8-0-26-0; Watson 8-0-46-2.

New Zealand

M. C. Snedden b Waugh	32	S. L. Boock run out	12
J. G. Wright c and b Zesers	61	W. Watson run out	8
M. D. Crowe run out	4	E. J. Chatfield not out	5
K. R. Rutherford c Jones b McDermott	44	B 1, l-b 7, w 4, n-b 2	14
*J. J. Crowe c and b Border	27		
D. N. Patel st Dyer b Border	3	1/72 2/82 3/127	(48.4 overs) 234
J. G. Bracewell run out	12	4/173 5/179 6/186	
†I. D. S. Smith c Boon b Waugh	12	7/206 8/208 9/221	

Bowling: McDermott 10-1-43-1; Reid 6-0-30-0; Waugh 9.4-0-37-2; Zesers 6-0-37-1; May 10-0-52-0; Border 7-0-27-2.

Umpires: Khizar Hayat and D. R. Shepherd.

†AUSTRALIA v ZIMBABWE

At Cuttack, October 30. Australia won by 70 runs. Toss: Zimbabwe. Australia did well to reach 266 on a pitch viewed with some suspicion; rightly so as it proved. When Zimbabwe batted, a ball from Reid rose sharply to strike Waller a nasty blow on the bridge of his nose. Boon, hitting a six and nine fours, had the measure of the conditions, putting on 90 in 23 overs with Marsh and 58 in ten with Jones; but the Victorian's not out 58 included only a six and a four in boundaries. Traicos, extracting turn, took two wickets before Veletta strengthened his claims for a batting place in the middle order. Zimbabwe were again slow to start. Waller's injury made them tentative, and when May, the Australian off-spinner, dismissed Curran in the 27th over, followed by Houghton in the 29th, that effectively snuffed out Zimbabwe's challenge. Waller came back bravely to resume his innings, but an asking-rate of almost 9 an over from the final twenty overs was too demanding a task for the ICC Trophy holders.

Man of the Match: D. C. Boon.

Australia

D. C. Boon c Houghton b Butchart	93	S. R. Waugh not out	10
G. R. Marsh run out	37		
D. M. Jones not out	58	B 3, l-b 3, w 6	12
C. J. McDermott c Rawson b Traicos	9		
*A. R. Border st Houghton b Traicos	4	1/90 2/148 3/159	(5 wkts, 50 overs) 266
M. R. J. Veletta run out	43	4/170 5/248	

S. P. O'Donnell, †G. C. Dyer, T. B. A. May and B. A. Reid did not bat.

Bowling: Rawson 9-0-41-0; Jarvis 6-0-33-0; Shah 7-0-31-0; Brandes 10-1-58-0; Traicos 10-0-45-2; Butchart 8-0-52-1.

Zimbabwe

A. H. Shah b Waugh	32	P. W. E. Rawson not out	24
A. C. Waller c Waugh b McDermott	38	E. A. Brandes not out	18
K. M. Curran c Waugh b May	29	L-b 5, w 6, n-b 2	13
A. J. Pycroft c Dyer b McDermott	38		
†D. L. Houghton lbw b May	1	1/55 2/89 3/92	(6 wkts, 50 overs) 196
I. P. Butchart st Dyer b Border	3	4/97 5/139 6/156	

M. P. Jarvis, K. J. Arnott and *A. J. Traicos did not bat.

Bowling: McDermott 10-0-43-2; Reid 9-2-30-0; Waugh 4-0-9-1; O'Donnell 7-1-21-0; May 10-1-30-2; Border 8-0-36-1; Jones 1-0-5-0; Boon 1-0-17-0.

Umpires: Mahboob Shah and P. W. Vidanagamage.

†INDIA v NEW ZEALAND

At Nagpur, October 31. India won by nine wickets. Toss: New Zealand. India won this group through batting of breathtaking brilliance. To edge ahead of Australia, they had to score at a rate of 5.25 an over; with New Zealand having chosen to bat first, and been restricted to 221, this meant scoring the runs in 42.2 overs. In Srikkanth they had the ideal opener; the surprise was Gavaskar, who had been said to be unwell prior to the match. He matched Srikkanth stroke for stroke in the bravura of his batting. They took 18 off the first two overs, 21 came off Chatfield's third over as Gavaskar hit the first four balls for successive sixes and then successive fours, and the 50 was posted in the eighth over. The next 50 took just six overs. Srikkanth had three sixes and nine fours in his 75 (58 balls); Gavaskar, finishing with three sixes and ten fours, went on to record his first century, off 85 balls, in 106 one-day internationals. India met their target ten overs ahead of schedule. Earlier, Chetan Sharma had provided the excitement by bowling Rutherford, Smith and Chatfield with the last three balls of the 42nd over – the first hat-trick in a World Cup match. Only a partnership of 39 between Snedden and Watson at the end retrieved another unconvincing display by New Zealand.

Man of the Match: S. M. Gavaskar and Chetan Sharma (shared).

New Zealand

J. G. Wright run out	35	E. J. Chatfield b Chetan 0
P. A. Horne b Prabhakar	18	W. Watson not out 12
M. D. Crowe c Pandit b Azharuddin	21	
*J. J. Crowe b Maninder	24	L-b 14, w 7, n-b 1 22
D. N. Patel c Kapil Dev b Shastri	40	
K. R. Rutherford b Chetan	26	1/46 2/84 3/90 (9 wkts, 50 overs) 221
M. C. Snedden run out	23	4/122 5/181 6/182
†I. D. S. Smith b Chetan	0	7/182 8/182 9/221

D. K. Morrison did not bat.

Bowling: Kapil Dev 6-0-24-0; Prabhakar 7-0-23-1; Chetan 10-2-51-3; Azharuddin 7-0-26-1; Maninder 10-0-51-1; Shastri 10-1-32-1.

India

K. Srikkanth c Rutherford b Watson .. 75
S. M. Gavaskar not out 103
M. Azharuddin not out 41
    L-b 1, w 2, n-b 2 5

1/136   (1 wkt, 32.1 overs) 224

N. S. Sidhu, D. B. Vengsarkar, *Kapil Dev, R. J. Shastri, †C. S. Pandit, M. Prabhakar, Chetan Sharma and Maninder Singh did not bat.

Bowling: Morrison 10-0-69-0; Chatfield 4.1-1-39-0; Snedden 4-0-29-0; Watson 10-0-50-1; Patel 4-0-36-0.

Umpires: H. D. Bird and D. R. Shepherd.

GROUP A FINAL TABLE

	P	W	L	Pts	Run-rate
India	6	5	1	20	5.39
Australia	6	5	1	20	5.19
New Zealand	6	2	4	8	4.88
Zimbabwe	6	0	6	0	3.76

GROUP B

†PAKISTAN v SRI LANKA

At Hyderabad, Pakistan, October 8. Pakistan won by 15 runs. Toss: Pakistan. Sri Lanka, with their exciting young opener, Mahanama, in the vanguard, made a courageous attempt at a target that required more than 5 runs an over. As he began to accelerate in a partnership of 79 with Gurusinha, it began to look as if Mahanama (one six, seven fours) might orchestrate an upset. With his dismissal, however, Sri Lanka again fell behind the run-rate. Pakistan's total was built on Javed Miandad's fifth one-day international hundred (96 balls, six fours). He passed 50 for the ninth consecutive match and reached 4,000 runs in his 120th one-day match for Pakistan. Ramiz, with whom he added 113, was the anchorman, taking 30 overs to reach 50. Imran took his 100th wicket in this cricket when he snuffed out Sri Lanka's challenge by bowling the belligerent de Silva, but the bowling honours went to Abdul Qadir, economical and at times unreadable.

Man of the Match: Javed Miandad.

Pakistan

Ramiz Raja c Ratnayake b Anurasiri	..	76	*Imran Khan b Ratnayake	2
Ijaz Ahmed c Kuruppu b Ratnayake	..	16	†Salim Yousuf not out	1
Mansoor Akhtar c Ratnayake				
b Ratnayeke		12	L-b 15, w 9, n-b 1	25
Javed Miandad b Ratnayeke		103		
Wasim Akram run out		14	1/48 2/67 3/180 (6 wkts, 50 overs) 267	
Salim Malik not out		18	4/226 5/259 6/266	

Mudassar Nazar, Abdul Qadir and Tauseef Ahmed did not bat.

Bowling: John 10–2–37–0; Ratnayake 10–0–64–2; Ratnayeke 9–0–47–2; de Silva 10–0–44–0; Anurasiri 10–0–52–1; Gurusinha 1–0–8–0.

Sri Lanka

†D. S. B. P. Kuruppu c Yousuf b Imran	9	R. J. Ratnayake c Mudassar b Wasim	8
R. S. Mahanama c Miandad b Mansoor	89	V. B. John not out	1
R. L. Dias b Qadir	5	S. D. Anurasiri run out	0
A. Ranatunga b Tauseef	24	B 7, l-b 14, w 7, n-b 1	29
*L. R. D. Mendis run out	1		
A. P. Gurusinha b Qadir	37	1/29 2/57 3/100 (49.2 overs) 252	
P. A. de Silva b Imran	42	4/103 5/182 6/190	
J. R. Ratnayeke c Yousuf b Wasim	7	7/209 8/223 9/251	

Bowling: Imran 10–2–42–2; Wasim 9.2–1–41–2; Mudassar 9–0–63–0; Qadir 10–1–30–2; Tauseef 10–0–48–1; Mansoor 1–0–7–1.

Umpires: V. K. Ramaswamy and S. J. Woodward.

†ENGLAND v WEST INDIES

At Gujranwala, October 9. England won by two wickets. Toss: England. Lamb (68 balls, one six, five fours), with a reprise of his heroic innings against Australia in Sydney in January, and Walsh, conceding 31 runs in his last two overs, allowed England to win a match that looked beyond their grasp when they needed 91 from the last ten overs with four wickets remaining. Earlier, West Indies had themselves conjured 92 from their last ten, having been restricted by tight bowling and good fielding to 151 for four in 40 overs. Logie, Dujon and Harper (22 off Pringle's last over, the 49th) cut loose as England's control slackened. England's innings began slowly, and when Gatting and Gooch, who put on 58 in nine overs, were out to Hooper's slow-medium in the 27th over, they were in trouble. But Lamb, slow to start, found allies in

Embury (fifteen balls) and DeFreitas (21 balls). The target from three overs was 35, but Walsh went for 16, Lamb scoring 15 of them. Patterson's last over realised just 6, leaving 13 till required. At Sydney, Lamb had hit Reid's last over for 18; now he hit 2 and 4 from the first two balls. Then Walsh gave away 4 leg-side wides and followed this immediately with a no-ball, from which Lamb took a single. The hapless bowler's third attempt at his third ball, a full toss, was carved to the boundary by Foster.

Man of the Match: A. J. Lamb.

West Indies

D. L. Haynes run out	19	C. L. Hooper not out	1
C. A. Best b DeFreitas	5	W. K. M. Benjamin not out	7
R. B. Richardson b Foster	53	L-b 9, n-b 3	12
*I. V. A. Richards b Foster	27		
†P. J. L. Dujon run out	46	1/8 2/53 3/105 (7 wkts, 50 overs) 243
A. L. Logie b Foster	49	4/122 5/205
R. A. Harper b Small	24	6/235 7/235

C. A. Walsh and B. P. Patterson did not bat.

Bowling: DeFreitas 10-2-31-1; Foster 10-0-53-3; Emburey 10-1-22-0; Small 10-0-45-1; Pringle 10-0-83-0.

England

G. A. Gooch c Dujon b Hooper	47	P. A. J. DeFreitas b Patterson	23
B. C. Broad c Dujon b Walsh	3	N. A. Foster not out	9
R. T. Robinson run out	12		
*M. W. Gatting b Hooper	25	L-b 14, w 6, n-b 3	23
A. J. Lamb not out	67		
D. R. Pringle c Best b Hooper	12	1/14 2/40 3/98 (8 wkts, 49.3 overs) 246
†P. R. Downton run out	3	4/99 5/123 6/131
J. E. Emburey b Patterson	22	7/162 8/209

G. C. Small did not bat.

Bowling: Patterson 10-0-49-2; Walsh 9.3-0-65-1; Harper 10-0-44-0; Benjamin 10-2-32-0; Hooper 10-0-42-3.

Umpires: A. R. Crafter and R. B. Gupta.

†ENGLAND v PAKISTAN

At Rawalpindi, October 12, 13. Pakistan won by 18 runs. Toss: England. England's defeat was of their own making: with six wickets in hand, and 34 required from the last four overs, they contrived by an excess of panic and insufficient intelligent batting to lose all six for 15 runs in sixteen balls. The decisive over was the 47th, the last of Qadir's quota: Lamb, Emburey and Downton made their exits during it. Yet in the field, England had done well, containing Pakistan to under 4 an over for the first 30 overs. A marvellous throw from Broad sent back Ramiz, while wickets in successive overs by DeFreitas removed Miandad (not without a tantrum) and Malik (80 balls, eight fours) just when they were looking to accelerate. However, Imran, despite suffering from food poisoning, helped Ijaz (60 balls, one six, four fours) add 79. Even though the Pakistan captain did not bowl or field, England were unable to capitalise on his absence. Gooch and Broad put on 52 in fourteen overs, but Robinson's 33 from 62 balls in 21 overs left England needing 99 from fifteen overs. It was not the kind of pressure their later batsmen needed. Heavy rain, which turned the outfield into a mud-field, although the pitch remained undamaged, precluded the possibility of play on the first day.

Man of the Match: Abdul Qadir.

Pakistan

Mansoor Akhtar c Downton b Foster	6	†Salim Yousuf not out	1
Ramiz Raja run out	15	Abdul Qadir not out	1
Salim Malik c Downton b DeFreitas	65	L-b 10, w 3, n-b 3	1
Javed Miandad lbw b DeFreitas	23		
Ijaz Ahmed c Robinson b Small	59	1/13 2/51 3/112 (7 wkts, 50 overs) 23	
*Imran Khan b Small	22	4/123 5/202	
Wasim Akram b DeFreitas	5	6/210 7/210	

Tauseef Ahmed and Saleem Jaffer did not bat.

Bowling: DeFreitas 10-1-42-3; Foster 10-1-35-1; Small 10-1-47-2; Pringle 10-0-54-0; Emburey 10-0-51-0.

England

G. A. Gooch b Qadir	21	P. A. J. DeFreitas not out	3
B. C. Broad b Tauseef	36	N. A. Foster run out	6
R. T. Robinson b Qadir	33	G. C. Small lbw b Jaffer	0
*M. W. Gatting b Jaffer	43	B 6, l-b 26, w 8	40
A. J. Lamb lbw b Qadir	30		
D. R. Pringle run out	8	1/52 2/92 3/141 (48.4 overs) 221	
J. E. Emburey run out	1	4/186 5/206 6/207	
†P. R. Downton c Yousuf b Qadir	0	7/207 8/213 9/221	

Bowling: Wasim 9-0-32-0; Jaffer 9.4-0-42-2; Tauseef 10-0-39-1; Qadir 10-0-31-4; Malik 7-0-29-0; Mansoor 3-0-16-0.

Umpires: A. R. Crafter and R. B. Gupta.

†SRI LANKA v WEST INDIES

At Karachi, October 13. West Indies won by 191 runs. Toss: Sri Lanka. Richards, coming in with Ratnayeke on a hat-trick, set about the Sri Lankan bowling with such savagery that his own record highest score in a one-day international (189 not out off 170 balls against England) looked certain to be eclipsed. Instead, caught when aiming for another six, he had to settle for the highest individual score in a World Cup innings: 181 from 125 balls, with six sixes and sixteen fours. It was Richards's tenth hundred in one-day matches for West Indies, while Haynes's 105 (109 balls, one six, nine fours) was his ninth. West Indies' total was the highest in a one-day international, the previous being Pakistan's 338 for five off 60 overs in the 1983 World Cup. Then, as now, Sri Lanka's bowlers were on the receiving end. In reply, Mahanama and Kuruppu set off at a rate of 12 an over; but this spectacular flourish did not survive the third over.

Man of the Match: I. V. A. Richards.

West Indies

D. L. Haynes b Gurusinha	105	A. L. Logie not out	31
C. A. Best b Ratnayeke	18	R. A. Harper not out	5
R. B. Richardson c Kuruppu b Ratnayeke	0	B 4, l-b 8, w 4, n-b 4	20
*I. V. A. Richards c Mahanama b de Mel	181	1/45 2/45 3/227 (4 wkts, 50 overs) 360	
		4/343	

C. L. Hooper, †P. J. L. Dujon, W. K. M. Benjamin, C. A. Walsh and B. P. Patterson did not bat.

Bowling: John 10-1-48-0; Ratnayeke 8-0-68-2; Anurasiri 10-0-39-0; de Mel 10-0-97-1; de Silva 6-0-35-0; Ranatunga 2-0-18-0; Gurusinha 4-0-43-1.

Sri Lanka

R. S. Mahanama c Dujon b Walsh	 12	*L. R. D. Mendis not out	....	37
*D. S. B. P. Kuruppu lbw b Patterson	. 14	B 1, l-b 2, w 6	....	9
A. P. Gurusinha b Hooper	 36			
P. A. de Silva c Dujon b Hooper	 9	1/24 2/31 3/57	(4 wkts, 50 overs)	169
A. Ranatunga not out	 52	4/112		

R. S. Madugalle, J. R. Ratnayeke, A. L. F. de Mel, V. B. John and S. D. Anurasiri did not bat.

Bowling: Patterson 7-0-32-1; Walsh 7-2-23-1; Harper 10-2-15-0; Benjamin 4-0-11-0; Hooper 10-0-39-2; Richards 8-0-22-0; Richardson 4-0-24-0.

Umpires: V. K. Ramaswamy and S. J. Woodward.

---

†PAKISTAN v WEST INDIES

At Lahore, October 16. Pakistan won by one wicket. Toss: West Indies. Another of the nail-biting finishes for which this World Cup was becoming renowned saw Pakistan finish their first round of group matches with an unbeaten record. Yet it could not have been closer. With their last pair at the wicket they wanted 14 from the last over, to be bowled – as in West Indies' match against England – by Walsh. He went for 112622, all but the second single scored by Qadir, whose straight-hit six raised a crowd of more than 50,000 to new heights of ecstacy. When 110 for five in the 35th over, Pakistan looked out of it. However, Imran and Yousuf (49 balls, seven fours) added 73 in eleven overs, and with three overs remaining the target was 21 with four wickets in hand. Yousuf, who had enjoyed at least three lives, was finally caught in Walsh's penultimate over; Patterson's final over brought two wickets while only 2 runs were added. So came the finale. Walsh, off the very last ball, could have run out Jaffer for backing up too soon, but good sportsmanship prevailed. In West Indies' innings, Simmons made an impressive début, hitting 50 from 51 balls with eight fours, but only Richards after him played a commanding innings. Imran came back to dismiss Richards and Harper with successive balls and swept away the tail. Qadir, without a wicket, was saving his magic for later.

Man of the Match: Salim Yousuf.

West Indies

D. L. Haynes b Jaffer	 37	E. A. E. Baptiste b Imran	....	14
P. V. Simmons c and b Tauseef	 50	C. A. Walsh lbw b Imran	....	7
R. B. Richardson c Ijaz b Jaffer	 11	B. P. Patterson not out	....	0
*I. V. A. Richards c Malik b Imran	.. 51	B 1, l-b 14, w 2	....	17
A. L. Logie c Mansoor b Jaffer	 2			
C. L. Hooper lbw b Wasim	 22	1/91 2/97 3/118	(49.3 overs)	216
†P. J. L. Dujon lbw b Wasim	 5	4/121 5/169 6/184		
R. A. Harper c Mansoor b Imran	 0	7/184 8/196 9/207		

Bowling: Imran 8.3-2-37-4; Wasim 10-0-45-2; Qadir 8-0-42-0; Tauseef 10-2-35-1; Jaffer 10-0-30-3; Malik 3-0-12-0.

Pakistan

Ramiz Raja c Richards b Harper	 42	Abdul Qadir not out	....	16
Mansoor Akhtar b Patterson	 10	Tauseef Ahmed run out	....	0
Salim Malik c Baptiste b Walsh	 4	Saleem Jaffer not out	....	1
Javed Miandad c and b Hooper	 33	B 5, l-b 12, w 7	....	24
Ijaz Ahmed b Walsh	 6			
*Imran Khan c Logie b Walsh	 18	1/23 2/28 3/92	(9 wkts, 50 overs)	217
†Salim Yousuf c Hooper b Walsh	 56	4/104 5/110 6/183		
Wasim Akram c Richardson b Patterson	7	7/200 8/202 9/203		

Bowling: Patterson 10-1-51-2; Walsh 10-1-40-4; Baptiste 8-1-33-0; Harper 10-0-28-1; Hooper 10-0-38-1; Richards 2-0-10-0.

Umpires: A. R. Crafter and S. J. Woodward.

†ENGLAND v SRI LANKA

At Peshawar, October 17. England won by 109 runs, Sri Lanka failing to achieve a revised target of 267 off 45 overs. Toss: England. By bringing in Hemmings and Athey, England looked a more balanced attacking side, although against such weak opposition the true value of the changes was difficult to assess. Most obviously effective was the revised batting order which gave the quick run-getters time to build a big total. Broad (60 balls) never got going, but Gooch (100 balls, eight fours) and Gatting (63 balls) were in their element against commonplace bowling on a good batting strip of sun-baked mud. With Lamb (58 balls, two sixes, three fours) and Emburey (nineteen balls, one six, three fours) also partaking of the run feast, the last ten overs realised 101 runs. England's greatest concern was with the dark clouds that had been rolling down from the Khyber all morning. The covers were out during lunch but by getting in their 25 overs, they made sure that the result would be decided – in their favour – on run-rate should a storm break. Subsequently, only five overs were lost to rain, and Sri Lanka's revised target was still well beyond their reach.

Man of the Match: A. J. Lamb.

England

G. A. Gooch c and b Anurasiri	84		C. W. J. Athey not out	2
B. C. Broad c de Silva b Ratnayeke	28		L-b 13, w 5	18
*M. W. Gatting b Ratnayake	58			
A. J. Lamb c de Silva b Ratnayake	76		1/89 2/142 3/218 (4 wkts, 50 overs)	296
J. E. Emburey not out	30		4/287	

†P. R. Downton, P. A. J. DeFreitas, D. R. Pringle, E. E. Hemmings and G. C. Small did not bat.

Bowling: Ratnayeke 9–0–62–2; John 10–0–44–0; de Silva 7–0–33–0; Ratnayake 10–0–60–1; Anurasiri 8–0–44–1; Ranatunga 6–0–40–0.

Sri Lanka

R. S. Mahanama c Gooch b Pringle	11		J. R. Ratnayeke c Broad b Emburey	1
†D. S. B. P. Kuruppu c Hemmings b Emburey	13		R. J. Ratnayake not out	14
A. P. Gurusinha run out	1		V. B. John not out	8
R. S. Madugalle b Hemmings	30		B 2, l-b 9, w 6, n-b 3	20
A. Ranatunga lbw b DeFreitas	40			
*L. R. D. Mendis run out	14		1/31 2/32 3/37 (8 wkts, 45 overs)	158
P. A. de Silva c Emburey b Hemmings	6		4/99 5/105 6/113	
			7/119 8/137	

S. D. Anurasiri did not bat.

Bowling: DeFreitas 9–2–24–1; Small 7–0–27–0; Pringle 4–1–11–1; Emburey 10–1–26–2; Hemmings 10–1–31–2; Gooch 2–0–9–0; Athey 1–0–10–0; Broad 1–0–6–0; Lamb 1–0–3–0.

Umpires: R. B. Gupta and V. K. Ramaswamy.

†ENGLAND v PAKISTAN

At Karachi, October 20. Pakistan won by seven wickets to be assured of a place in the semi-finals. Toss: Pakistan. The loss of Athey and Gatting within the space of three balls, after they had added 135 in 24 overs, arrested England's progress. The next three wickets produced only 19 runs as Imran brought himself back to take advantage of the breach. Athey (104 balls, two sixes, six fours) and Gatting (65 balls) were both out sweeping, Athey attempting the controversial reverse variety in the 37th over. On a true batting pitch 244 did not seem enough runs, and so it proved. Certainly, England could not afford the luxury of giving Ramiz two lives: an easy chance to Gatting at square leg when he was 6 and another to Athey at mid-on when he was 62. That they felt Ramiz had been stumped off Emburey later in his innings was of less significance. With Malik (92 balls, seven fours), Ramiz put on 167 in a partnership built on good placement and quick running. There were 62 singles, as well as five fours, in Ramiz's 113 from 148 balls. During the afternoon, play was suspended for a time after stones were thrown on to the outfield.

Man of the Match: Imran Khan.

England

G. A. Gooch c Wasim b Imran	16	N. A. Foster not out	20
R. T. Robinson b Qadir	16	G. C. Small run out	0
C. W. J. Athey b Tauseef	86	E. E. Hemmings not out	4
M. W. Gatting c Yousuf b Qadir	60	L-b 7, w 4	11
A. J. Lamb b Imran	9		
J. E. Emburey lbw b Qadir	3	1/26 2/52 3/187 (9 wkts, 50 overs) 244	
†P. R. Downton c Yousuf b Imran	6	4/187 5/192 6/203	
P. A. J. DeFreitas c Yousuf b Imran	13	7/206 8/230 9/230	

Bowling: Imran 9-0-37-4; Wasim 8-0-44-0; Tauseef 10-0-46-1; Qadir 10-0-31-3; Jaffer 8-0-44-0; Malik 5-0-35-0.

Pakistan

Ramiz Raja c Gooch b DeFreitas	113	Ijaz Ahmed not out	4
Mansoor Akhtar run out	29	L-b 6, w 1	7
Salim Malik c Athey b Emburey	88		
Javed Miandad not out	6	1/61 2/228 3/243 (3 wkts, 49 overs) 247	

*Imran Khan, †Salim Yousuf, Wasim Akram, Abdul Qadir, Tauseef Ahmed and Saleem Jaffer did not bat.

Bowling: DeFreitas 8-2-41-1; Foster 10-0-51-0; Hemmings 10-1-40-0; Emburey 10-0-34-1; Small 9-0-63-0; Gooch 2-0-12-0.

Umpires: A. R. Crafter and V. K. Ramaswamy.

†SRI LANKA v WEST INDIES

At Kanpur, October 21. West Indies won by 25 runs. Toss: Sri Lanka. That West Indies would not run riot a second time against the Sri Lankans became apparent as Simmons, an accomplished strokeplayer, took 37 overs over his 89 (eleven fours) on a tardy pitch. Logie, with his ability to improvise, was the only other West Indian batsman to overcome the conditions. When Sri Lanka batted, however, Ranatunga outshone them both, hitting 86 from 92 balls to accelerate an innings that began with all the haste of a dowager. While a requirement of 9 an over was being met, Sri Lanka looked capable of avenging their massive defeat in Karachi; but with 37 needed from the last four overs, Patterson returned to bowl a mean spell which left an almost impossible 28 to be scored from the final over. Benjamin never looked like conceding that many.

Man of the Match: P. V. Simmons.

West Indies

D. L. Haynes b Anurasiri	24	R. A. Harper b Ratnayeke	3
P. V. Simmons c Madugalle b Ratnayeke	89	W. K. M. Benjamin b Ratnayeke	0
R. B. Richardson c Mahanama b Jeganathan	4	C. A. Walsh not out	9
*I. V. A. Richards c Ratnayeke b de Silva	14	B 2, l-b 7, w 7	16
A. L. Logie not out	65	1/62 2/80 3/115 (8 wkts, 50 overs) 236	
C. L. Hooper st Kuruppu b de Silva	6	4/155 5/168 6/199	
†P. J. L. Dujon c Kuruppu b Ratnayeke	6	7/213 8/214	

B. P. Patterson did not bat.

Bowling: Ratnayeke 10-1-41-3; John 5-1-25-0; Ratnayeke 5-0-39-1; Jeganathan 10-1-33-1; Anurasiri 10-1-46-1; de Silva 10-0-43-2.

Sri Lanka

R. S. Mahanama b Patterson	0	S. Jeganathan run out	
†D. S. B. P. Kuruppu c and b Hooper	33	V. B. John not out	
J. R. Ratnayeke lbw b Benjamin	15		
R. S. Madugalle c Haynes b Harper	18	B 2, l-b 11, n-b 10	2
A. Ranatunga not out	86		
*L. R. D. Mendis b Walsh	19	(8 wkts, 50 overs) 21	
P. A. de Silva b Patterson	8	1/2 2/28 3/66	
R. J. Ratnayake c Walsh b Patterson	5	4/86 5/156 6/184	
		7/200 8/209	

S. D. Anurasiri did not bat.

Bowling: Patterson 10–0–31–3; Walsh 9–2–43–1; Benjamin 10–0–43–1; Harper 10–1–29–1 Hooper 8–0–35–1; Richards 3–0–17–0.

Umpires: Amanullah Khan and Mahboob Shah.

†PAKISTAN v SRI LANKA

At Faisalabad, October 25. Pakistan won by 113 runs. Toss: Pakistan. Salim Malik's first one day international century, from 85 balls with ten fours, ensured Pakistan of a total which Sri Lanka showed no interest in challenging. With Wasim Akram twice swinging the ball away for six, Ijaz hitting 30 from eighteen balls and Imran scoring 39 off 37 balls, 154 runs came from the last fifteen overs. Sri Lanka's innings, on the other hand, was a pedestrian affair although there was momentary concern for Pakistan's supporters when Imran pulled up feeling his ankle, and did not complete his fourth over. Saleem Jaffer was already being rested because of an ankle injury, but Imran's discomfort resulted from nothing more serious than bruising.

Man of the Match: Salim Malik.

Pakistan

Ramiz Raja c and b Anurasiri	32	Manzoor Elahi not out	4
Mansoor Akhtar b Jeganathan	33	†Salim Yousuf not out	11
Salim Malik b Ratnayeke	100	L-b 6, w 2	8
Javed Miandad run out	1		
Wasim Akram c Ranatunga b de Silva	39	1/64 2/72 3/77	(7 wkts, 50 overs) 297
Ijaz Ahmed c and b John	30	4/137 5/197	
*Imran Khan run out	39	6/264 7/285	

Abdul Qadir and Tauseef Ahmed did not bat.

Bowling: Ratnayeke 10–0–58–1; John 8–1–53–1; de Mel 10–0–53–0; Jeganathan 9–1–45–1; Anurasiri 7–0–45–1; de Silva 6–0–37–1.

Sri Lanka

R. S. Mahanama run out	8	S. Jeganathan c Yousuf b Miandad	1
†D. S. B. P. Kuruppu c Yousuf b Imran	0	V. B. John not out	1
J. R. Ratnayeke run out	22		
R. S. Madugalle c Yousuf b Manzoor	15	B 4, l-b 4, w 6, n-b 2	16
A. Ranatunga c and b Qadir	50		
*L. R. D. Mendis b Qadir	58	(8 wkts, 50 overs) 184	
P. A. de Silva not out	13	1/4 2/11 3/41	
A. L. F. de Mel b Qadir	0	4/70 5/150 6/173	
		7/173 8/179	

S. D. Anurasiri did not bat.

Bowling: Imran 3.2–1–13–1; Wasim 7–0–34–0; Manzoor 9.4–0–32–1; Tauseef 10–1–23–0; Qadir 10–0–40–3; Malik 7–1–29–0; Miandad 3–0–5–1.

Umpires: R. B. Gupta and S. J. Woodward.

†ENGLAND v WEST INDIES

At Jaipur, October 26. England won by 34 runs. Toss: West Indies. A marvellously disciplined innings by Gooch (137 balls, seven fours) and some indisciplined bowling by West Indies, who gave away 22 runs – and extra balls – in wides, brought England the victory they needed to have a realistic chance of qualifying for the semi-finals. So profligate was West Indies' early bowling that, after 30 overs, England were 151 for two. A controlled spell by Richards, however, pegged them back to 35 from the next ten, and when Patterson returned to dismiss Lamb and Gooch, it took some inventive batting from Emburey (sixteen balls, four fours) and DeFreitas (nine balls) to realise 83 from the final fifth. While Richards (51 in 51 balls) was adding 82 in almost eighteen overs with Richardson, hitting Emburey once and Hemmings twice for six, the match was swinging West Indies' way. Then Hemmings bowled him, off stump, to reward England's decision to play both their spinners on a pitch sufficiently green to provide some movement off the seam for much of the day. Next, Hemmings caught Logie to end another promising partnership, and when, from backward point, he hit the stumps at the far end to run out Harper, his cup was overflowing. There were two good catches, well to his right, by Downton to dismiss Hooper and Richardson (130 balls, one six, eight fours) as, under pressure, West Indies cracked. They had begun the 41st over needing 65 with six wickets in hand; in eight overs they lost them for 30 runs.

Man of the Match: G. A. Gooch.

England

G. A. Gooch c Harper b Patterson	....	92	P. A. J. DeFreitas not out	 16
R. T. Robinson b Patterson	....	13		
C. W. J. Athey c Patterson b Harper	..	21	B 5, l-b 10, w 22, n-b 1	 38
*M. W. Gatting lbw b Richards	......	25		
A. J. Lamb c Richardson b Patterson	..	40	1/35 2/90 3/154 (5 wkts, 50 overs) 269	
J. E. Emburey not out	....	24	4/209 5/250	

†P. R. Downton, N. A. Foster, E. E. Hemmings and G. C. Small did not bat.

Bowling: Patterson 9–0–56–3; Walsh 10–0–24–0; Benjamin 10–0–63–0; Harper 10–1–52–1; Hooper 3–0–27–0; Richards 8–0–32–1.

West Indies

D. L. Haynes c Athey b DeFreitas	...	9	W. K. M. Benjamin c Foster b DeFreitas	8
P. V. Simmons b Emburey	....	25	C. A. Walsh b Hemmings	 2
R. B. Richardson c Downton b Small	..	93	B. P. Patterson not out	 4
*I. V. A. Richards b Hemmings	......	51	L-b 7, w 1, n-b 1	 9
A. L. Logie c Hemmings b Emburey	..	22		
C. L. Hooper c Downton b DeFreitas ..		8	1/18 2/65 3/147 (48.1 overs) 235	
†P. J. L. Dujon c Downton b Foster	...	1	4/182 5/208 6/211	
R. A. Harper run out	....	3	7/219 8/221 9/224	

Bowling: DeFreitas 9.1–2–28–3; Foster 10–0–52–1; Emburey 9–0–41–2; Small 10–0–61–1; Hemmings 10–0–46–2.

Umpires: Mahboob Shah and P. W. Vidanagamage.

†ENGLAND v SRI LANKA

At Pune, October 30. England won by eight wickets. Toss: Sri Lanka. England had to win to be sure of a place in the semi-finals and they did so convincingly, though not having things entirely their own way. Dias, playing only for the second time in this World Cup and benefiting from being dropped by Downton when 1, batted with considerable charm on an easy-paced pitch. His 80, from 105 balls, included three sixes and six fours, and with Sri Lanka snatching 75 runs from the last ten overs, England received a timely reminder that lapses can be costly in this kind of game. They dropped four catches, the first of them in the opening over by Gooch, who in doing so dislocated a finger on his right hand and was allowed to sit out the rest of the innings. Any discomfort was well concealed as he and Robinson built a perfect platform with 123 in 23.3 overs against the friendliest of attacks. Gooch faced 79 balls, Robinson 75, each hit seven fours, and when they were out, Athey (55 balls) and Gatting (40 balls) quickly finished off the job.

Man of the Match: G. A. Gooch.

Sri Lanka

R. S. Mahanama c Emburey b DeFreitas	14	A. L. F. de Mel c Lamb b Hemmings	.	(
J. R. Ratnayeke lbw b Small	7	S. Jeganathan not out		2(
†A. P. Gurusinha run out	34			
R. L. Dias st Downton b Hemmings	80	L-b 3, w 3, n-b 5		11
*L. R. D. Mendis b DeFreitas	7			
R. S. Madugalle c sub (P. W. Jarvis)		1/23 2/25 3/113 (7 wkts, 50 overs)	218	
b Hemmings	22	4/125 5/170		
P. A. de Silva not out	23	6/177 7/180		

V. B. John and S. D. Anurasiri did not bat.

Bowling: DeFreitas 10-2-46-2; Small 10-1-33-1; Foster 10-0-37-0; Emburey 10-1-42-0; Hemmings 10-0-57-3.

England

G. A. Gooch c and b Jeganathan	61
R. T. Robinson b Jeganathan	55
C. W. J. Athey not out	40
*M. W. Gatting not out	46
B 1, l-b 13, w 3	17

1/123 2/132 (2 wkts, 41.2 overs) 219

A. J. Lamb, †P. R. Downton, J. E. Emburey, P. A. J. DeFreitas, N. A. Foster, G. C. Small and E. E. Hemmings did not bat.

Bowling: Ratnayeke 8-1-37-0; John 6-2-19-0; de Mel 4.2-0-34-0; Jeganathan 10-0-45-2; Anurasiri 10-0-45-0; de Silva 3-0-25-0.

Umpires: D. M. Archer and Khizar Hayat.

†PAKISTAN v WEST INDIES

At Karachi, October 30. West Indies won by 28 runs. Toss: West Indies. This was like old times: aggravating students, running battles with the police, teargas drifting across the enclosures and West Indies rolling over the opposition. True, Pakistan's performance was decidedly off song, especially in the field where catches were put down and they needed a hurry-up from Imran to avoid the imposition of fines for a slow over-rate. Richards's was a convincing presence throughout, initially with the bat and then marshalling his resources in the field. Taking 74 balls for his 67, he added 137 in 23 overs with Richardson, whose highest one-day score for West Indies, from 136 balls, included a straight-driven six off Imran and another 38 in boundaries. Pakistan began tardily, only 26 coming from the first ten overs. The rate had improved to 4 an over by the time Mudassar was bowled, but when the innings required a quicker tempo, Richards and his bowlers dictated the beat. Imran had good reason for expressing his dissatisfaction after the match.

Man of the Match: R. B. Richardson.

West Indies

D. L. Haynes c Imran b Mudassar	25	W. K. M. Benjamin c Mudassar b Imran	0	
P. V. Simmons b Wasim	6	†P. J. L. Dujon not out	1	
R. B. Richardson c Qadir b Imran	110	B 3, l-b 10, w 16, n-b 1	30	
*I. V. A. Richards b Wasim	67			
A. L. Logie c Mudassar b Imran	12	1/19 2/84 3/221 (7 wkts, 50 overs)	258	
R. A. Harper b Wasim	2	4/242 5/248		
C. L. Hooper not out	5	6/255 7/255		

C. A. Walsh and B. P. Patterson did not bat.

Bowling: Imran 9-0-57-3; Wasim 10-0-45-3; Qadir 10-1-29-0; Mudassar 10-0-47-1; Jaffer 6-0-37-0; Malik 5-0-30-0.

Pakistan

Mudassar Nazar b Harper	40	Abdul Qadir not out	8
Ramiz Raja c Hooper b Patterson	70	Shoaib Mohammad b Benjamin	0
Salim Malik c Richards b Walsh	23	Saleem Jaffer not out	8
Javed Miandad b Benjamin	38	B 4, l-b 6, w 10, n-b 2	22
Ijaz Ahmed b Benjamin	6		
*Imran Khan c Harper b Walsh	8	1/78 2/128 3/147 (9 wkts, 50 overs) 230	
†Salim Yousuf b Patterson	7	4/167 5/186 6/202	
Wasim Akram lbw b Patterson	8	7/202 8/208 9/208	

Bowling: Patterson 10-1-34-3; Walsh 10-1-34-2; Harper 10-0-38-1; Benjamin 10-0-69-3; Richards 10-0-45-0.

Umpires: R. B. Gupta and V. K. Ramaswamy.

GROUP B FINAL TABLE

	P	W	L	Pts	Run-rate
Pakistan	6	5	1	20	5.01
England	6	4	2	16	5.12
West Indies	6	3	3	12	5.16
Sri Lanka	6	0	6	0	4.04

SEMI-FINALS

†AUSTRALIA v PAKISTAN

At Lahore, November 4. Australia won by 18 runs. Toss: Australia. Pakistan, losing semi-finalists in 1979 and 1983, again failed to reach the World Cup final. They were beaten by a superior all-round performance as Border's Australian side, scarcely rated at the start of the tournament, came of age. Until Imran returned to take three for 17 in five overs, their batsmen had contributed solidly; and at the very end, Waugh, previously the provider of heroic last overs with the ball, struck a vital 18 runs off Saleem Jaffer, beginning with a six over long-on. Jaffer had earlier conceded 39 from his first five overs (the 50th over was only his sixth) as Marsh and Boon put on 73 in eighteen overs. Malik's direct hit from square leg ran out Marsh, but Boon (91 balls, four fours) and Jones (45 balls) added 82 before Pakistan broke through in the 31st and 32nd overs. Miandad, who stumped Boon, had taken the gloves when Yousuf was struck on the mouth by a deflection off Jones's pad in the nineteenth over. Another wicket now would have put Pakistan on top, but Border and Veletta (55 balls) kept the momentum going with a stand worth 60 runs. Pakistan made a disastrous start, losing three wickets in 10.1 overs. Ramiz, sent back, was run out in the first over, Mansoor always struggled, and Malik, playing across the line, spooned the first ball of Waugh's spell to extra-cover. Miandad (104 balls, four fours) and Imran (83 balls, four fours) rebuilt the innings with 112 in 26 overs, reducing the target to 118 from fifteen overs. While Miandad remained it was always possible, but his dismissal, swinging at Reid in the 44th over, left the last three wickets to muster 56 runs. Instead, McDermott, bowling fast and accurately, took all three to finish with the first five-wicket return of the tournament and dash the dreams of a nation.

Man of the Match: C. J. McDermott.

Australia

G. R. Marsh run out	31	C. J. McDermott b Imran	1
D. C. Boon st Miandad b Malik	65	T. B. A. May not out	0
D. M. Jones b Tauseef	38		
*A. R. Border run out	18	B 1, l-b 19, w 13, n-b 1	34
M. R. J. Veletta b Imran	48		
S. R. Waugh not out	32	1/73 2/155 3/155 (8 wkts, 50 overs) 267	
S. P. O'Donnell run out	0	4/215 5/236 6/236	
†G. C. Dyer b Imran	0	7/241 8/249	

B. A. Reid did not bat.

Bowling: Imran 10-1-36-3; Jaffer 6-0-57-0; Wasim 10-0-54-0; Qadir 10-0-39-0; Tauseef 10-1-39-1; Malik 4-0-22-1.

Pakistan

Mansoor Akhtar b McDermott	9	Abdul Qadir not out	2⬚
Ramiz Raja run out	1	Saleem Jaffer c Dyer b McDermott	⬚
Salim Malik c McDermott b Waugh	25	Tauseef Ahmed c Dyer b McDermott	⬚
Javed Miandad b Reid	70	L-b 6, w 10	16
*Imran Khan c Dyer b Border	58		
Wasim Akram b McDermott	20	1/2 2/37 3/38	(49 overs) 24⬚
Ijaz Ahmed c Jones b Reid	8	4/150 5/177 6/192	
†Salim Yousuf c Dyer b McDermott	21	7/212 8/236 9/247	

Bowling: McDermott 10-0-44-5; Reid 10-2-41-2; Waugh 9-1-51-1; O'Donnell⬚ 10-1-45-0; May 6-0-36-0; Border 4-0-26-1.

Umpires: H. D. Bird and D. R. Shepherd.

†ENGLAND v INDIA

At Bombay, November 5. England won by 35 runs. Toss: India. Kapil Dev put England in, believing that the ball would swing early in the day. In the event it did not. The pitch, slow and providing turn, was more suited to spin bowling, thought to be India's strength but countered masterfully by Gooch (136 balls, eleven fours) and Gatting (62 balls, five fours). Adopting a policy of sweeping and pulling the two slow left-arm bowlers, they put on 117 in nineteen overs. And when Gooch, who survived a difficult running chance to Srikkanth when 82, was fourth out, caught on the mid-wicket boundary in the 43rd over – Gatting was out in the 41st – Lamb (29 balls) saw that another 51 runs were added. India, with Vengsarkar unable to play because of a stomach upset, suffered an early setback when DeFreitas knocked over Gavaskar's off stump. It was the break England wanted, and they never let India take the initiative. Srikkanth (55 balls) and Sidhu (40 balls), both strokeplayers, did not manage a single boundary. When Azharuddin and Pandit took 27 from Hemmings's first three overs, Gooch bowled three tidy overs and Foster struck again to remove Pandit. Kapil Dev fell victim to his own impetuosity, caught on the mid-wicket boundary immediately after Gatting had stationed himself there. For Hemmings, it was the start of a 34-ball spell in which he took four for 21, his next wicket being the important one of Azharuddin (74 balls, seven fours). With five wickets and ten overs in hand, India were looking for 5 runs an over, but with Azharuddin gone, panic and recklessness set in. Shastri remained a potential threat until the last, but Lamb's marvellous running catch, to put paid to Chetan Sharma's first-ball fling, was testimony to England's all-round commitment.

Man of the Match: G. A. Gooch.

England

G. A. Gooch c Srikkanth b Maninder	115	P. A. J. DeFreitas b Kapil Dev	7
R. T. Robinson st More b Maninder	13	†P. R. Downton not out	1
C. W. J. Athey c More b Chetan	4	B 1, l-b 18, w 1	20
*M. W. Gatting b Maninder	56		
A. J. Lamb not out	32	1/40 2/79 3/196	(6 wkts, 50 overs) 254
J. E. Emburey lbw b Kapil Dev	6	4/203 5/219 6/231	

N. A. Foster, G. C. Small and E. E. Hemmings did not bat.

Bowling: Kapil Dev 10-1-38-2; Prabhakar 9-1-40-0; Maninder 10-0-54-3; Chetan 9-0-41-1; Shastri 10-0-49-0; Azharuddin 2-0-13-0.

India

K. Srikkanth b Foster	31	M. Prabhakar c Downton b Small	4
S. M. Gavaskar b DeFreitas	4	Chetan Sharma c Lamb b Hemmings	0
N. S. Sidhu c Athey b Foster	22	Maninder Singh not out	0
M. Azharuddin lbw b Hemmings	64	B 1, l-b 9, w 6, n-b 3	19
C. S. Pandit lbw b Foster	24		
*Kapil Dev c Gatting b Hemmings	30	1/7 2/58 3/73	(45.3 overs) 219
R. J. Shastri c Downton b Hemmings	21	4/121 5/168 6/204	
†K. S. More c and b Emburey	0	7/205 8/218 9/219	

Bowling: DeFreitas 7–0–37–1; Small 6–0–22–1; Emburey 10–1–35–1; Foster 10–0–47–3; Hemmings 9.3–1–52–4; Gooch 3–0–16–0.

Umpires: A. R. Crafter and S. J. Woodward.

FINAL

†AUSTRALIA v ENGLAND

At Calcutta, November 8. Australia won by 7 runs. Toss: Australia. Batting first suited Australia; and when they took the field to defend a total of 253, it was in the knowledge that no side batting second had scored 254 to win in this World Cup. England, 135 for two at 31 overs, and with Australia beginning to show signs of disarray in the field, were then almost on target. But in a moment too crass to contemplate, Gatting handed back the initiative. To Border's first ball, bowled on the line of his leg stump, the England captain attempted to play a reverse sweep. Having in the semi-final swept the ball on to his leg stump, he now contrived to hit it on to his shoulder, whence it looped into Dyer's gloves. The Australians' joy was unconcealed.

England had conceded points from the start, an erratic opening spell from DeFreitas and Small helping Marsh and Boon post 52 in ten overs. Foster and the two spinners repaired the damage, with Foster's eight overs costing just 16 runs and bringing the wicket of Marsh in the eighteenth over. Gooch, too, was economical until coming under fire as Border and Veletta (31 balls, six fours) added 73 in the ten overs following Boon's dismissal. Boon's 75 (125 balls, seven fours) was his fifth score of 50 or more in six innings. DeFreitas, brought back to bowl the last over, went for 11 to bring to 65 the runs scored from England's last six overs.

Robinson, undone by pace to no-one's great surprise, was out first ball to McDermott's fourth. Gooch (57 balls) and Athey put on 65 in seventeen overs, Athey and Gatting (45 balls) 69 in thirteen, Athey (104 balls) and Lamb 35 in just over eight. It was Waugh whose throw ran out Athey as he went for a third run; and with England slipping farther behind the run-rate (75 from ten overs had drifted to 46 from five), he bowled Lamb (55 balls) in the 47th over. DeFreitas gave England renewed hope with 14 (464) in McDermott's penultimate over, but Waugh conceded just 2 runs, as well as having DeFreitas caught, in the 49th. That left 17 runs needed from the final over, and there was no way McDermott was going to allow that.

Man of the Match: D. C. Boon.   *Attendance:* 70,000 approx.

Australia

D. C. Boon c Downton b Hemmings	75	S. R. Waugh not out		5
G. R. Marsh b Foster	24	B 1, l-b 13, w 5, n-b 7		26
D. M. Jones c Athey b Hemmings	33			
C. J. McDermott b Gooch	14	1/75 (2) 2/151 (3)	(5 wkts, 50 overs)	253
*A. R. Border run out	31	3/166 (4) 4/168 (1)		
M. R. J. Veletta not out	45	5/241 (5)		

S. P. O'Donnell, †G. C. Dyer, T. B. A. May and B. A. Reid did not bat.

Bowling: DeFreitas 6–1–34–0; Small 6–0–33–0; Foster 10–0–38–1; Hemmings 10–1–48–2; Emburey 10–0–44–0; Gooch 8–1–42–1.

England

G. A. Gooch lbw b O'Donnell	35	N. A. Foster not out		7
R. T. Robinson lbw b McDermott	0	G. C. Small not out		3
C. W. J. Athey run out	58	B 1, l-b 14, w 2, n-b 4		21
*M. W. Gatting c Dyer b Border	41			
A. J. Lamb b Waugh	45	1/1 (2) 2/66 (1)	(8 wkts, 50 overs)	246
†P. R. Downton c O'Donnell b Border	9	3/135 (4) 4/170 (3)		
J. E. Emburey run out	10	5/188 (6) 6/218 (5)		
P. A. J. DeFreitas c Reid b Waugh	17	7/220 (7) 8/235 (8)		

E. E. Hemmings did not bat.

Bowling: McDermott 10–1–51–1; Reid 10–0–43–0; Waugh 9–0–37–2; O'Donnell 10–1–35–1; May 4–0–27–0; Border 7–0–38–2.

Umpires: R. B. Gupta and Mahboob Shah.

FEATURES OF 1987

Double-Hundreds

R. J. Blakey	204*	Yorkshire v Gloucestershire at Leeds.
M. D. Crowe	206*	Somerset v Warwickshire at Birmingham.
Javed Miandad (2) ..	211*	Pakistanis v Sussex at Hove.
	260	Pakistan v England (Fifth Test) at The Oval.
G. D. Mendis	203*	Lancashire v Middlesex at Manchester.
M. Newell	203*	Nottinghamshire v Derbyshire at Derby.
C. L. Smith	217	Hampshire v Warwickshire at Birmingham.
R. A. Smith	209*	Hampshire v Essex at Southend.

Four Hundreds in Successive Innings

C. W. J. Athey (Gloucestershire) – 115, 114*, 160 and 101*.

Three Hundreds in Successive Innings

G. A. Hick (Worcestershire) – 126, 156 and 140*.

Hundred in Each Innings of a Match

| C. W. J. Athey ..... | 115 | 114* | Gloucestershire v Warwickshire at Birmingham. |
| H. Morris .... | 115 | 105 | Glamorgan v Warwickshire at Birmingham. |

Fastest Hundred

(For the Walter Lawrence Trophy)

R. O. Butcher ...... 73 balls Middlesex v Sussex at Hove.
In 96 minutes and including four sixes and nine fours.

Fast Fifty

M. P. Maynard .... 19 balls Glamorgan v Yorkshire at Cardiff.
In fourteen minutes from fourteen scoring strokes including five sixes, and with 30 runs (464466) off one over from K. Sharp.

Hundred Before Lunch

Asif Din	104*	Warwickshire v Gloucestershire at Birmingham (3rd day).
J. D. Carr	111*	Middlesex v Surrey at Lord's (1st day).
M. D. Crowe	105	Somerset v Worcestershire at Worcester (3rd day).
M. A. Lynch	100*	Surrey v Gloucestershire at Cheltenham (2nd day).
M. P. Maynard	101*	Glamorgan v Somerset at Weston-super-Mare (1st day).

Carr and Maynard both achieved the feat on August 1.

First to 1,000 Runs

M. D. Crowe (Somerset) on July 1.

For the first season since 1980, no batsman scored 2,000 runs. The highest aggregate was 1,879 by G. A. Hick (Worcestershire).

Carrying Bat Through Completed Innings

M. A. Atherton .... 109* (185) Cambridge University v Derbyshire at Cambridge.
A. R. Butcher ...... 135* (275) Glamorgan v Worcestershire at Neath.
P. M. Roebuck ..... 165* (300) Somerset v Hampshire at Weston-super-Mare.
N. R. Taylor .... 123* (219) Kent v Nottinghamshire at Canterbury.

Innings totals shown in brackets.

Notable Partnerships

First Wicket
347† V. P. Terry/C. L. Smith, Hampshire v Warwickshire at Birmingham.

Second Wicket
303* Shoaib Mohammad/Mansoor Akhtar, Pakistanis v Worcestershire at Worcester.
258 T. S. Curtis/G. A. Hick, Worcestershire v Middlesex at Lord's.

Third Wicket
311 C. G. Greenidge/D. R. Turner, Hampshire v Gloucestershire at Gloucester.
285 M. R. Benson/C. J. Tavaré, Kent v Worcestershire at Worcester.

Fourth Wicket
303* A. P. Wells/C. M. Wells, Sussex v Kent at Hove.

Seventh Wicket
262† C. J. Richards/K. T. Medlycott, Surrey v Kent at The Oval.

Ninth Wicket
151 R. Sharma/O. H. Mortensen, Derbyshire v Yorkshire at Chesterfield.

† County record.

Thirteen Wickets in a Match

T. A. Merrick ...... 13-115 Warwickshire v Lancashire at Birmingham.

Eight Wickets in an Innings

E. A. E. Baptiste ... 8-76 Kent v Warwickshire at Birmingham (before lunch).
S. T. Clarke .... 8-62 Surrey v Northamptonshire at The Oval.
N. A. Foster .... 8-107 England v Pakistan (Third Test) at Leeds.
N. A. Radford ..... 8-55 Worcestershire v Nottinghamshire at Kidderminster.

Four Wickets in Five Balls

S. T. Clarke .... Surrey v Essex at Colchester.

Hat-tricks

S. T. Clarke .... Surrey v Essex at Colchester.
R. J. Hadlee .... Nottinghamshire v Kent at Canterbury.
K. B. S. Jarvis ..... Kent v Middlesex at Lord's.
O. H. Mortensen ... Derbyshire v Leicestershire at Derby.

Outstanding Analyses

K. W. McLeod ...... 7-2-8-5 Lancashire v Leicestershire at Leicester.

First to 100 Wickets

N. V. Radford (Worcestershire) on September 4.

1,000 Runs and 50 Wickets

R. J. Hadlee (Nottinghamshire)   1,111 runs and 97 wickets.
C. M. Wells (Sussex)   1,456 runs and 52 wickets.

Match Double (100 runs and 10 wickets)

R. J. Hadlee   101   23*   6-42   6-41   Nottinghamshire v Somerset at Nottingham.

Ten Wicket-Keeping Dismissals in a Match

10   C. J. Richards (9ct, 1st) . . . .   Surrey v Sussex at Guildford.

Five Catches in the Field

5   R. C. Ontong . . . .   Glamorgan v Yorkshire at Cardiff.
5   D. W. Randall . . . .   Nottinghamshire v Yorkshire at Nottingham.

Highest Innings Totals

708 . . . .   Pakistan v England (Fifth Test) at The Oval.
521 . . . .   England v Pakistan (Fourth Test) at Edgbaston.

Lowest Innings Totals

52
66 } . . . .   Oxford University v Nottinghamshire at Oxford.
71 . . . .   Cambridge University v Essex at Cambridge.
71 . . . .   Leicestershire v Lancashire at Leicester.
71 . . . .   Derbyshire v Leicestershire at Derby.
72 . . . .   Warwickshire v Derbyshire at Derby.

Most Extras in an Innings

60 (B 15, l-b 25, w 8, n-b 12) . . . .   Worcestershire v Warwickshire at Birmingham.
52 (B 1, l-b 24, w 11, n-b 16) . . . .   England v Pakistan (Fourth Test) at Birmingham.

Tied Match

Gloucestershire (288 and 278) v Derbyshire (340 and 226-5 dec.) at Bristol.

Career Aggregate Milestones†

20,000 runs . . . .   G. Cook, P. Willey.
10,000 runs . . . .   J. Abrahams, K. J. Barnett, M. D. Crowe, G. Fowler, R. J. Hadlee,
                            M. A. Lynch, V. J. Marks.
1,000 wickets . . . . . .   J. E. Emburey.
1,000 dismissals . . . .   D. L. Bairstow.

† *Achieved since September 1986.*

FIRST-CLASS AVERAGES, 1987

BATTING AND FIELDING

(Qualification: 8 innings, average 10.00)

* Signifies not out. † Denotes a left-handed batsman.

	M	I	NO	R	HI	100s	Avge	Ct/St
M. D. Crowe (*Somerset*) ...	18	29	5	1,627	206*	6	67.79	15
Javed Miandad (*Pak. & R of W*)	12	14	1	822	260	2	63.23	5
†K. D. James (*Hants*)	17	16	6	620	142*	2	62.00	5
M. W. Gatting (*Middx*)	19	29	2	1,646	196	6	60.96	13
R. K. Illingworth (*Worcs.*) ..	20	19	11	448	120*	1	56.00	8
†R. J. Hadlee (*Notts.*)	21	28	7	1,111	133*	2	52.90	16
G. A. Hick (*Worcs.*)	25	38	2	1,879	173	8	52.19	13
P. M. Roebuck (*Somerset*) ..	16	29	5	1,199	165*	5	49.95	15
C. G. Greenidge (*Hants*) ...	12	18	0	899	163	3	49.94	21
†D. R. Turner (*Hants*)	25	35	8	1,328	184*	2	49.18	8
R. A. Smith (*Hants*)	18	25	7	869	209*	1	48.27	18
R. A. Harper (*Northants & R of W*)	7	9	5	193	127*	1	48.25	7
†G. Fowler (*Lancs.*)	24	43	5	1,800	169*	3	47.36	12
T. S. Curtis (*Worcs.*)	25	40	6	1,601	138*	4	47.08	10
C. L. Smith (*Hants*)	26	42	9	1,519	217	4	46.03	26
C. E. B. Rice (*Notts.*)	22	32	8	1,103	138	3	45.95	26
C. M. Wells (*Sussex*)	24	39	7	1,456	148*	5	45.50	15
R. G. Williams (*Northants*) .	22	27	7	898	104	1	44.90	5
N. E. Briers (*Leics.*)	21	32	4	1,257	104	2	44.89	11
C. W. J. Athey (*Glos.*)	21	34	5	1,295	160	2	44.65	14
†D. I. Gower (*Leics.*)	20	31	4	1,197	125	2	44.33	5
†M. R. Benson (*Kent*)	24	39	0	1,725	131	5	44.23	17
†J. W. Lloyds (*Glos.*)	23	32	4	1,213	130	2	43.32	17
B. Roberts (*Derbys.*)	25	41	3	1,643	184	4	43.23	22
V. P. Terry (*Hants*)	23	37	5	1,382	122	2	43.18	29
K. M. Curran (*Glos.*)	21	33	6	1,142	119	3	42.29	11
†N. H. Fairbrother (*Lancs.*) .	21	30	6	1,014	109*	3	42.25	18
T. J. Boon (*Leics.*)	20	26	2	1,009	94	0	42.04	15
J. D. Carr (*Middx*)	24	41	4	1,541	156	3	41.64	10
R. J. Blakey (*Yorks.*)	24	38	5	1,361	204*	4	41.24	28
G. W. Humpage (*Warwicks.*)	24	41	9	1,318	99*	0	41.18	31/3
P. J. Newport (*Worcs.*)	25	25	12	534	64*	0	41.07	8
R. F. Pienaar (*Kent*)	7	8	0	327	153	1	40.87	2
M. C. J. Nicholas (*Hants*) ...	25	38	9	1,183	147	4	40.79	12
M. P. Maynard (*Glam.*)	26	45	5	1,626	160	2	40.65	30
D. A. Reeve (*Sussex*)	17	23	8	606	87*	0	40.40	14
†A. R. Butcher (*Glam.*)	15	27	2	1,009	135	3	40.36	6
R. J. Shastri (*Glam.*)	13	22	3	765	103	1	40.26	8
M. D. Moxon (*Yorks.*)	22	37	4	1,321	130	2	40.03	26
Imran Khan (*Pak. & R of W*)	13	14	3	431	118	1	39.18	6
R. T. Robinson (*Notts.*)	21	36	4	1,250	166	3	39.06	14
M. Newell (*Notts.*)	20	34	7	1,054	203*	3	39.03	15
†W. N. Slack (*Middx*)	25	42	0	1,636	173	3	38.95	14
G. A. Gooch (*Essex*)	24	41	6	1,361	171	3	38.88	20
G. D. Mendis (*Lancs.*)	24	42	6	1,390	203*	3	38.61	6
M. A. Atherton (*CUCC & Lancs.*)	21	35	4	1,193	110	2	38.48	7
P. E. Robinson (*Yorks.*)	7	13	2	421	95	0	38.27	8

	M	I	NO	R	HI	100s	Avge	Ct/St
A. J. Stewart (*Surrey*)	22	34	2	1,219	132	3	38.09	20
†D. M. Smith (*Surrey*)	17	27	4	873	121*	1	37.95	10
†J. Abrahams (*Lancs.*)	9	15	1	525	140*	1	37.50	5
G. S. le Roux (*Sussex*)	13	15	5	375	73	0	37.50	3
R. J. Bailey (*Northants*)	26	42	8	1,274	158	3	37.47	18
P. R. Downton (*Middx*)	26	39	9	1,120	103*	1	37.33	57/8
C. T. Radley (*Middx*)	9	13	3	373	72	0	37.30	4
†J. G. Wright (*Derbys.*)	10	17	2	558	118	1	37.20	6
N. R. Taylor (*Kent*)	24	38	3	1,300	142*	3	37.14	14
C. J. Richards (*Surrey*)	20	26	6	738	172*	1	36.90	68/6
P. A. Neale (*Worcs.*)	25	34	7	994	103*	2	36.81	10
K. J. Barnett (*Derbys.*)	25	40	1	1,429	130	3	36.64	12
J. J. Whitaker (*Leics.*)	27	39	5	1,245	126	2	36.61	17
P. Johnson (*Notts.*)	25	39	4	1,257	125	3	35.91	20
M. D. Marshall (*Hants*)	22	22	5	610	99	0	35.88	7
I. G. Swallow (*Yorks.*)	5	9	2	249	114	1	35.57	4
†D. J. Bicknell (*Surrey*)	12	20	3	600	105	1	35.29	5
P. Bainbridge (*Glos.*)	17	25	6	668	151	2	35.15	9
B. R. Hardie (*Essex*)	27	43	4	1,370	143	3	35.12	22
D. W. Randall (*Notts.*)	13	20	1	665	133	1	35.00	18
W. Larkins (*Northants*)	25	43	4	1,364	120	3	34.97	17
†T. A. Lloyd (*Warwicks.*)	25	46	3	1,503	162	3	34.95	11
T. E. Jesty (*Surrey*)	24	36	5	1,074	124*	1	34.64	8
J. E. Morris (*Derbys.*)	26	40	1	1,343	162	3	34.43	13
P. Willey (*Leics.*)	26	40	3	1,256	122	2	33.94	10
I. P. Butcher (*Leics.*)	8	12	0	407	88	0	33.91	5
M. Watkinson (*Lancs.*)	19	27	4	776	91	0	33.73	17
R. J. Parks (*Hants*)	25	19	8	370	62*	0	33.63	56/5
D. B. D'Oliveira (*Worcs.*)	25	37	4	1,106	131*	2	33.51	25
D. L. Bairstow (*Yorks.*)	20	23	1	736	128	2	33.45	32/4
P. J. Prichard (*Essex*)	11	16	3	434	72	0	33.38	3
A. J. Moles (*Warwicks.*)	25	46	3	1,431	151	4	33.27	24
M. A. Lynch (*Surrey*)	26	39	5	1,127	128*	2	33.14	24
C. J. Tavaré (*Kent*)	26	42	7	1,157	152	1	33.05	29
†I. J. Gould (*Sussex*)	21	29	5	792	111	1	33.00	23
Asif Din (*Warwicks.*)	23	36	4	1,056	115*	2	33.00	12
A. J. Lamb (*Northants*)	23	34	4	982	101*	1	32.73	19
J. E. Emburey (*Middx*)	18	26	4	710	74	0	32.27	9
†B. C. Broad (*Notts.*)	15	26	4	708	80	0	32.18	15
A. P. Wells (*Sussex*)	23	37	4	1,058	161*	3	32.06	11
†S. G. Hinks (*Kent*)	21	33	2	992	112	2	32.00	18
P. B. Clift (*Leics.*)	17	22	3	608	88	0	32.00	8
R. C. Ontong (*Glam.*)	16	27	8	600	100	1	31.57	13
J. D. Birch (*Notts.*)	23	32	3	914	82	0	31.51	10
A. W. Lilley (*Essex*)	20	29	4	783	102	1	31.32	11
G. R. Cowdrey (*Kent*)	5	8	1	219	68	0	31.28	4
A. A. Metcalfe (*Yorks.*)	24	42	4	1,178	152	2	31.00	8
C. S. Cowdrey (*Kent*)	25	37	6	958	135	3	30.90	21
I. A. Greig (*Surrey*)	26	35	6	887	104*	1	30.58	17
D. G. Aslett (*Kent*)	25	40	8	969	101*	1	30.28	13
G. Cook (*Northants*)	25	41	9	969	111*	1	30.28	15
†G. S. Clinton (*Surrey*)	19	30	2	848	93	0	30.28	6
D. L. Amiss (*Warwicks.*)	25	46	3	1,300	123	2	30.23	8
I. T. Botham (*Worcs.*)	16	22	2	598	126*	1	29.90	10
†A. J. T. Miller (*Middx*)	10	15	2	387	97	0	29.76	1
†D. J. Wild (*Northants*)	22	23	6	501	102*	1	29.47	15
M. J. Kilborn (*OUCC*)	8	12	2	294	59	0	29.40	8
D. R. Pringle (*Essex*)	22	33	9	705	84*	0	29.37	15
K. T. Medlycott (*Surrey*)	25	30	5	734	153	1	29.36	13
M. A. Crawley (*OUCC*)	7	10	1	263	140	1	29.22	2
M. R. Ramprakash (*Middx*)	8	14	3	321	71	0	29.18	6

	M	I	NO	R	HI	100s	Avge	Ct/St
R. A. Cobb (*Leics.*)	17	26	5	612	88	0	29.14	9
K. W. R. Fletcher (*Essex*)	24	35	3	925	121	1	28.90	12
†J. J. E. Hardy (*Somerset*)	24	40	2	1,089	119	1	28.65	8
P. W. Romaines (*Glos.*)	25	42	2	1,144	119	2	28.60	8
A. J. Wright (*Glos.*)	23	38	2	1,022	161	1	28.38	17
†H. Morris (*Glam.*)	26	48	2	1,304	143	3	28.34	15
P. J. W. Allott (*Lancs.*)	22	27	4	641	88	0	27.86	24
J. D. Love (*Yorks.*)	21	30	7	639	79*	0	27.78	7
R. D. Sardesai (*OUCC*)	7	9	1	222	63*	0	27.75	2
R. O. Butcher (*Middx*)	17	22	1	580	118	1	27.61	15
K. R. Brown (*Middx*)	15	24	3	579	70	0	27.57	15
†R. C. Russell (*Glos.*)	26	38	9	798	57*	0	27.51	54/10
M. W. Alleyne (*Glos.*)	20	30	7	628	82	0	27.30	7
J. P. Stephenson (*Essex*)	13	22	3	515	67*	0	27.10	10
S. J. S. Kimber (*Sussex*)	8	9	3	161	54	0	26.83	2
†K. Sharp (*Yorks.*)	20	32	4	751	81*	0	26.82	6
R. J. Boyd-Moss (*Northants*)	8	13	1	321	77	0	26.75	3
†N. A. Felton (*Somerset*)	24	41	0	1,094	110	1	26.68	18
V. S. Greene (*Glos.*)	8	11	4	186	62*	0	26.57	4
†N. D. Burns (*Somerset*)	24	35	7	729	100*	0	26.03	44/6
R. Sharma (*Derbys.*)	17	27	4	596	111	1	25.91	19
C. K. Bullen (*Surrey*)	11	13	3	259	65	0	25.90	14
K. P. Tomlins (*Glos.*)	7	9	1	207	100	1	25.87	1
E. A. E. Baptiste (*Kent*)	16	23	3	517	95	0	25.85	6
V. J. Marks (*Somerset*)	22	31	6	635	63*	0	25.40	9
D. G. Price (*CUCC*)	8	12	1	279	57	0	25.36	0
L. Potter (*Leics.*)	14	20	4	401	68	0	25.06	22
D. Ripley (*Northants*)	25	24	5	474	125*	0	24.94	40/9
G. C. Holmes (*Glam.*)	25	43	6	922	95	0	24.91	9
†G. J. Parsons (*Warwicks.*)	16	19	2	422	67*	0	24.82	6
G. D. Rose (*Somerset*)	18	23	4	470	95	0	24.73	10
M. A. Roseberry (*Middx*)	10	14	3	270	52	0	24.54	7
R. J. Finney (*Derbys.*)	23	36	5	760	77	0	24.51	11
D. W. Varey (*Lancs.*)	7	10	1	220	59	0	24.44	1
A. M. Green (*Sussex*)	20	36	2	821	115	1	24.14	9
A. W. Stovold (*Glos.*)	26	43	2	988	88	0	24.09	3
D. J. Capel (*Northants*)	22	30	3	639	91*	0	23.66	10
R. J. Harden (*Somerset*)	19	30	6	568	59	0	23.66	9
S. J. O'Shaughnessy (*Lancs.*)	9	16	4	275	61*	0	22.91	15
A. C. Storie (*Warwicks.*)	16	26	8	410	66*	0	22.77	16
J. G. Wyatt (*Somerset*)	8	13	2	250	58*	0	22.72	2
S. J. Rhodes (*Worcs.*)	25	31	7	544	80	0	22.66	51/6
†C. Gladwin (*Essex*)	10	17	2	339	77	0	22.60	5
M. J. Weston (*Worcs.*)	14	21	2	426	54	0	22.42	6
W. K. Hegg (*Lancs.*)	13	20	4	350	130	1	21.87	24/11
R. I. Alikhan (*Sussex*)	19	34	3	666	78	0	21.48	9
I. S. Anderson (*Derbys.*)	15	21	2	407	87*	0	21.42	6
B. J. M. Maher (*Derbys.*)	25	41	2	834	105	1	21.38	72/4
S. D. Weale (*OUCC*)	8	9	0	192	76	0	21.33	0
C. D. M. Tooley (*OUCC*)	8	10	1	189	61*	0	21.00	4
T. D. Topley (*Essex*)	12	15	4	231	66	0	21.00	2
†G. J. Lord (*Worcs.*)	12	19	2	353	66	0	20.76	3
K. B. K. Ibadulla (*Glos.*)	5	8	1	145	46*	0	20.71	2
S. P. James (*Glam.*)	8	13	1	246	106	1	20.50	4
E. E. Hemmings (*Notts.*)	25	27	8	389	75	0	20.47	5
N. J. Pringle (*Somerset*)	11	18	1	347	79	0	20.41	1
B. N. French (*Notts.*)	18	20	2	365	70	0	20.27	45/4
P. W. G. Parker (*Sussex*)	19	32	4	565	85	0	20.17	16
N. A. Foster (*Essex*)	21	23	2	419	49*	0	19.95	6
J. Derrick (*Glam.*)	18	27	7	398	57	0	19.90	7
A. C. S. Pigott (*Sussex*)	19	27	4	456	62	0	19.82	12

	M	I	NO	R	HI	100s	Avge	Ct/St
N. G. Cowley (*Hants*)	10	12	2	197	96	0	19.70	5
P. A. J. DeFreitas (*Leics.*) ..	18	23	2	412	74	0	19.61	9
P. A. Todd (*Glam.*)	14	24	0	470	135	1	19.58	13
D. J. Fell (*CUCC*)	9	14	1	254	67*	0	19.53	5
G. V. Palmer (*Somerset*) ...	14	16	4	234	68	0	19.50	4
P. A. Smith (*Warwicks.*) ...	17	31	5	506	89	0	19.46	1
†D. J. Thomas (*Surrey*)	17	17	4	243	49	0	18.69	5
S. A. Marsh (*Kent*)	21	27	5	411	72*	0	18.68	39/2
S. N. Hartley (*Yorks.*)	10	18	2	298	63	0	18.62	5
A. E. Warner (*Derbys.*)	18	28	4	444	72	0	18.50	4
P. A. C. Bail (*CUCC*)	9	14	0	257	90	0	18.35	1
P. J. Hartley (*Yorks.*)	22	26	7	347	49	0	18.26	7
A. Needham (*Middx*)	10	12	3	164	33	0	18.22	3
P. G. Newman (*Derbys.*) ...	17	24	5	341	42	0	17.94	5
P. A. Cottey (*Glam.*)	7	10	1	161	42*	0	17.88	2
C. W. Scott (*Notts.*)	12	15	1	250	45	0	17.85	27/2
D. M. Ward (*Surrey*)	6	10	0	178	44	0	17.80	7
P. Moores (*Sussex*)	18	24	2	385	55	0	17.50	19
D. J. R. Martindale (*Notts.*)	9	13	2	192	103	1	17.45	3
P. Carrick (*Yorks.*)	24	29	2	471	61	0	17.44	8
M. A. Holding (*Derbys.*) ...	13	18	2	278	63*	0	17.37	10
D. P. Hughes (*Lancs.*)	25	35	6	503	81	0	17.34	20
P. H. Edmonds (*Middx*)	16	18	6	208	32	0	17.33	6
D. K. Standing (*Sussex*)	17	29	3	443	56	0	17.03	5
J. P. Agnew (*Leics.*)	25	27	4	387	90	0	16.82	1
†H. A. Page (*Essex*)	15	20	4	266	60	0	16.62	5
N. G. B. Cook (*Northants*) .	26	25	7	299	64	0	16.61	13
C. P. Metson (*Glam.*)	25	37	7	493	81	0	16.43	47/6
N. A. Mallender (*Somerset*) .	15	17	9	131	20*	0	16.37	6
A. Sidebottom (*Yorks.*)	18	22	6	261	33	0	16.31	5
P. W. Jarvis (*Yorks.*)	24	24	11	212	32	0	16.30	6
G. C. Small (*Warwicks.*) ...	12	20	4	257	42	0	16.06	4
I. Smith (*Glam.*)	18	23	5	288	45	0	16.00	6
A. A. Donald (*Warwicks.*) ..	11	10	3	111	37*	0	15.85	1
T. A. Merrick (*Warwicks.*) ..	14	19	5	220	74*	0	15.71	6
M. D. Harman (*Somerset*) ..	6	8	2	94	41	0	15.66	7
†A. Walker (*Northants*)	18	10	5	78	41*	0	15.60	6
D. E. East (*Essex*)	27	32	3	449	73	0	15.48	57/4
J. A. Hopkins (*Glam.*)	15	26	2	371	39*	0	15.45	13
M. P. Bicknell (*Surrey*)	14	14	7	108	18	0	15.42	5
†R. A. Pick (*Notts.*)	17	15	5	154	42*	0	15.40	2
J. G. Thomas (*Glam.*)	10	15	2	200	48	0	15.38	3
D. L. Underwood (*Kent*) ...	23	20	9	168	29*	0	15.27	3
G. Miller (*Essex*)	23	30	5	371	33*	0	14.84	29
†C. Penn (*Kent*)	17	18	2	237	53	0	14.81	7
I. Folley (*Lancs.*)	25	31	7	355	38	0	14.79	18
M. A. Feltham (*Surrey*)	11	12	3	129	39	0	14.33	6
W. W. Davis (*Northants*) ...	19	18	5	186	25*	0	14.30	7
P. Whitticase (*Leics.*)	26	31	6	351	59	0	14.04	67/2
S. P. Hughes (*Middx*)	18	20	7	182	26*	0	14.00	6
R. E. Morris (*OUCC*)	6	9	2	98	34	0	14.00	1
G. A. Tedstone (*Warwicks.*).	10	14	1	180	51	0	13.84	13/2
T. M. Tremlett (*Hants*)	24	17	5	161	42	0	13.41	7
A. H. Gray (*Surrey*)	10	8	3	67	35	0	13.40	4
J. Simmons (*Lancs.*)	22	24	5	252	64	0	13.26	16
G. A. Pointer (*CUCC*)	8	11	3	104	33	0	13.00	1
N. F. Williams (*Middx*)	10	9	4	64	18*	0	12.80	1
S. J. Base (*Glam.*)	8	14	4	127	38	0	12.70	1
†J. H. Childs (*Essex*)	22	22	13	113	26	0	12.55	6
O. H. Mortensen (*Derbys.*) .	19	24	10	168	74*	0	12.00	6
M. Jean-Jacques (*Derbys.*) ..	16	20	4	192	47	0	12.00	6

	M	I	NO	R	HI	100s	Avge	Ct/St
A. R. C. Fraser (*Middx*) ...	22	22	5	202	38	0	11.88	4
S. R. Gorman (*CUCC*)	7	11	1	117	39	0	11.70	4
I. Redpath (*Essex*)	7	12	1	128	46	0	11.63	2
N. V. Radford (*Worcs.*)	23	21	4	197	31	0	11.58	14
P. A. W. Heseltine (*Sussex*) .	18	18	0	172	26	0	11.46	3
K. B. S. Jarvis (*Kent*)	11	8	7	11	4*	0	11.00	0
L. B. Taylor (*Leics.*)	9	9	3	66	16	0	11.00	0
T. A. Munton (*Warwicks.*)..	16	16	5	116	38	0	10.54	3
G. J. F. Ferris (*Leics.*)	13	13	4	93	25	0	10.33	0
S. D. Fletcher (*Yorks.*)	15	12	6	61	15	0	10.16	3
S. R. Lampitt (*Worcs.*)	13	14	3	111	24	0	10.09	6
†N. Gifford (*Warwicks.*)	25	25	12	131	36	0	10.07	1
†G. R. Dilley (*Worcs.*)	11	9	3	60	29	0	10.00	2

BOWLING

(Qualification: 10 wickets in 10 innings)

† *Denotes left-arm bowler.*

	O	M	R	W	BB	5 W/i	Avge
R. J. Hadlee (*Notts.*)	591	189	1,227	97	6-20	9	12.64
A. H. Gray (*Surrey*)	291.1	59	748	48	5-46	2	15.58
K. J. Barnett (*Derbys*)	88.2	27	225	13	4-31	0	17.30
S. T. Clarke (*Surrey*)	456.4	124	1,160	67	8-62	6	17.31
N. G. Cowans (*Middx*)	341.3	78	958	51	5-43	2	18.78
T. M. Tremlett (*Hants*)	547	153	1,407	72	6-53	3	19.54
O. H. Mortensen (*Derbys.*) ..	432.5	111	1,084	55	5-57	2	19.70
M. D. Marshall (*Hants*)	594.1	152	1,508	76	5-49	1	19.84
P. J. W. Allott (*Lancs.*)	535.2	166	1,222	59	7-42	1	20.71
N. V. Radford (*Worcs.*)	741.5	126	2,269	109	8-55	8	20.81
A. Walker (*Northants*)	390.2	104	1,011	48	4-22	0	21.06
T. E. Jesty (*Surrey*)	72.4	11	212	10	6-81	1	21.20
J. Simmons (*Lancs.*)	640.3	196	1,425	67	6-20	4	21.26
S. J. W. Andrew (*Hants*)	316.1	61	1,022	48	7-92	2	21.29
G. J. F. Ferris (*Leics.*)	359.1	69	1,143	52	6-42	4	21.98
N. A. Foster (*Essex*)	674.5	147	1,892	86	8-107	5	22.00
G. R. Dilley (*Worcs.*)	265.3	52	817	35	6-43	2	23.34
M. Watkinson (*Lancs.*)	318	66	986	42	7-25	4	23.47
S. J. Base (*Glam.*)	203.1	38	660	28	5-67	2	23.57
Imran Khan (*Pak. & R of W*)	338.4	77	898	38	7-40	3	23.63
M. P. Bicknell (*Surrey*)	363.2	94	997	42	6-63	2	23.73
G. S. le Roux (*Sussex*)	266.5	54	768	32	5-64	1	24.00
†K. W. McLeod (*Lancs.*)	126.4	24	409	17	5-8	2	24.05
E. E. Hemmings (*Notts.*)	872.4	295	2,119	88	6-62	7	24.07
J. P. Agnew (*Leics.*)	777	144	2,451	101	7-46	9	24.26
P. G. Newman (*Derbys.*)	364	75	1,093	45	5-46	1	24.28
P. B. Clift (*Leics.*)	405.1	114	900	37	6-64	2	24.32
M. A. Holding (*Derbys.*)	391.2	72	1,194	49	5-41	2	24.36
N. A. Mallender (*Somerset*) .	351	61	1,129	46	7-61	1	24.54
P. W. Jarvis (*Yorks.*)	644.1	149	1,991	81	7-82	2	24.58
†I. Folley (*Lancs.*)	753.1	240	1,865	74	7-15	5	25.20
T. A. Merrick (*Warwicks.*) ..	433.3	71	1,439	57	7-45	4	25.24
T. A. Munton (*Warwicks.*) ..	341.1	72	992	39	6-69	2	25.43
C. A. Walsh (*Glos. & R of W*)	524.4	108	1,609	63	5-38	3	25.53
R. G. Williams (*Northants*) ..	241.4	61	667	26	5-81	1	25.65
G. D. Rose (*Somerset*)	314.4	56	976	38	5-24	1	25.68
K. E. Cooper (*Notts.*)	158.3	50	387	15	3-38	0	25.80

	O	M	R	W	BB	5 W/i	Avge
D. J. M. Kelleher (*Kent*)	301	72	878	34	6-109	2	25.82
P. A. J. DeFreitas (*Leics.*) ..	487.2	107	1,450	56	7-85	3	25.89
†P. Carrick (*Yorks.*)	575.4	198	1,323	51	5-42	1	25.94
A. A. Donald (*Warwicks.*) ...	301.4	36	1,012	39	6-74	2	25.94
L. B. Taylor (*Leics.*)	154.4	20	545	21	6-47	2	25.95
A. P. Igglesden (*Kent*)	382.3	54	1,351	52	5-45	3	25.98
B. P. Patterson (*Lancs.*)	419.1	61	1,359	52	6-40	4	26.13
D. J. Capel (*Northants*)	464.5	87	1,396	53	7-46	4	26.33
D. R. Pringle (*Essex*)	599.4	155	1,457	55	5-70	1	26.49
E. A. E. Baptiste (*Kent*)	519.3	117	1,495	56	8-76	2	26.69
C. K. Bullen (*Surrey*)	225.4	71	564	21	6-119	1	26.85
K. Saxelby (*Notts.*)	452.1	121	1,278	47	6-49	1	27.19
W. W. Davis (*Northants*)	591.1	100	1,906	70	6-57	5	27.22
T. D. Topley (*Essex*)	300.2	66	840	30	4-75	0	28.00
†J. A. Afford (*Notts.*)	276.4	89	729	26	5-79	1	28.03
P. Bainbridge (*Glos.*)	288.4	62	927	33	5-70	1	28.09
S. D. Fletcher (*Yorks.*)	276.3	54	903	32	4-22	0	28.21
V. S. Greene (*Glos.*)	234.5	32	819	29	7-96	1	28.24
C. E. B. Rice (*Notts.*)	308.3	90	800	28	4-42	0	28.57
A. N. Jones (*Somerset*)	517.1	85	1,800	63	7-85	3	28.57
†D. L. Underwood (*Kent*)	611.3	211	1,295	45	5-43	1	28.77
†R. J. Maru (*Hants*)	802.4	229	2,061	71	5-45	3	29.02
†N. G. B. Cook (*Northants*) ..	705.2	227	1,574	54	6-77	1	29.14
J. G. Thomas (*Glam.*)	245.3	48	875	30	6-109	2	29.16
A. E. Warner (*Derbys.*)	328.5	67	1,026	35	4-12	0	29.31
A. Sidebottom (*Yorks.*)	446.5	83	1,261	43	4-46	0	29.32
C. M. Wells (*Sussex*)	546.1	98	1,531	52	6-34	2	29.44
D. A. Reeve (*Sussex*)	450	108	1,240	42	7-37	1	29.52
†P. C. R. Tufnell (*Middx*)	335.2	75	984	33	6-60	1	29.81
M. A. Feltham (*Surrey*)	412.1	101	1,202	40	5-66	1	30.05
†D. A. Graveney (*Glos.*)	356.1	112	848	28	5-37	1	30.28
C. Penn (*Kent*)	439.1	78	1,469	48	5-52	2	30.60
P. M. Such (*Leics.*)	490.1	142	1,256	41	6-123	1	30.63
V. J. Marks (*Somerset*)	778.5	203	2,155	70	5-35	3	30.78
R. A. Pick (*Notts.*)	361.4	74	1,206	39	4-75	0	30.92
†R. J. Finney (*Derbys.*)	275.2	57	839	27	3-39	0	31.07
G. Miller (*Essex*)	379.3	84	995	32	7-59	1	31.09
†N. Gifford (*Warwicks.*)	453	136	1,121	36	5-71	2	31.13
J. Derrick (*Glam.*)	321.3	70	1,064	34	5-50	1	31.29
G. C. Small (*Warwicks.*)	350	71	1,067	34	4-80	0	31.38
R. A. Harper (*Northants & R of W*)	256	56	662	21	5-28	2	31.52
K. B. S. Jarvis (*Kent*)	251.2	41	884	28	5-48	1	31.57
†J. K. Lever (*Essex*)	396	99	1,079	34	5-59	2	31.73
†R. J. Shastri (*Glam.*)	461.1	100	1,181	37	5-100	1	31.91
A. C. S. Pigott (*Sussex*)	455.2	86	1,443	45	5-32	3	32.06
G. A. Gooch (*Essex*)	250.3	64	687	21	4-42	0	32.71
A. P. Pridgeon (*Worcs.*)	344	80	920	28	7-44	1	32.85
C. A. Connor (*Hants*)	397	87	1,061	32	4-26	0	33.15
†J. H. Childs (*Essex*)	479.3	143	1,228	37	5-40	2	33.18
H. A. Page (*Essex*)	340.2	52	1,172	35	5-26	1	33.48
P. Willey (*Leics.*)	219.2	46	614	18	4-32	0	34.11
†P. H. Edmonds (*Middx*)	481.5	160	1,094	32	4-34	0	34.18
A. R. C. Fraser (*Middx*)	568.1	143	1,506	44	4-50	0	34.22
R. C. Ontong (*Glam.*)	469.4	89	1,410	41	6-91	2	34.39
N. G. Cowley (*Hants*)	250.1	57	689	20	4-35	0	34.45
D. E. Malcolm (*Derbys.*)	255	45	898	26	3-47	0	34.53
W. K. M. Benjamin (*Leics.*) .	207.2	54	525	15	5-50	1	35.00
I. L. Pont (*Essex*)	183	19	671	19	5-73	1	35.31
†P. G. Edwards (*OUCC*)	172.4	42	500	14	4-93	0	35.71
I. A. Greig (*Surrey*)	413.4	86	1,257	35	4-47	0	35.91

	O	M	R	W	BB	5 W/i	Avge
G. J. Parsons (*Warwicks.*) ...	418.5	82	1,229	34	5-80	1	36.14
P. J. Hartley (*Yorks.*)	501	89	1,726	47	4-52	0	36.72
D. V. Lawrence (*Glos.*)	350.5	44	1,411	38	6-63	1	37.13
†D. J. Thomas (*Surrey*)	357	61	1,230	33	5-73	1	37.27
J. E. Emburey (*Middx*)	570.3	153	1,311	35	5-60	1	37.45
D. J. Foster (*Somerset*)	111.5	10	490	13	4-56	0	37.69
S. R. Barwick (*Glam.*)	603.1	122	1,799	47	4-60	0	38.27
M. A. Robinson (*Northants*) .	150	25	501	13	3-45	0	38.53
†K. T. Medlycott (*Surrey*) ...	546.4	148	1,640	42	5-103	1	39.04
M. Jean-Jacques (*Derbys.*) ...	325	59	1,068	27	4-39	0	39.55
†K. D. James (*Hants*)	206.1	36	757	19	5-62	1	39.84
W. W. Daniel (*Middx*)	348.1	47	1,275	32	4-69	0	39.84
I. Smith (*Glam.*)	211.3	40	757	19	3-65	0	39.84
G. V. Palmer (*Somerset*)	316	54	1,162	29	4-63	0	40.06
S. P. Hughes (*Middx*)	358	55	1,167	29	3-74	0	40.24
J. W. Lloyds (*Glos.*)	403.2	62	1,466	36	6-57	2	40.72
†A. M. G. Scott (*CUCC*)	250.3	50	744	18	5-97	1	41.33
G. A. Hick (*Worcs.*)	310.2	59	1,042	25	4-31	0	41.68
I. T. Botham (*Worcs.*)	260	47	883	21	3-51	0	42.04
†R. K. Illingworth (*Worcs.*) ..	478.2	117	1,391	33	4-28	0	42.15
R. Sharma (*Derbys.*)	206	46	640	15	6-80	1	42.66
A. J. Moles (*Warwicks.*)	182.3	47	513	12	3-21	0	42.75
A. M. Babington (*Sussex*) ...	248.1	44	898	21	3-44	0	42.76
P. J. Newport (*Worcs.*)	504.3	79	1,839	42	4-28	0	43.78
N. F. Williams (*Middx*)	189.4	32	575	13	3-55	0	44.23
Abdul Qadir (*Pak. & R of W*)	352.1	82	987	22	7-96	1	44.86
A. Needham (*Middx*)	179	34	545	12	4-96	0	45.41
C. S. Cowdrey (*Kent*)	278.1	64	871	19	2-30	0	45.84
P. A. W. Heseltine (*Sussex*) .	316.2	75	963	21	3-33	0	45.85
†M. R. Davis (*Somerset*)	153.5	25	505	11	3-43	0	45.90
P. A. Smith (*Warwicks.*)	177.5	21	783	17	3-31	0	46.05
†R. P. Davis (*Kent*)	153	35	473	10	3-68	0	47.30
M. Beardshall (*Derbys.*)	158.2	21	572	12	4-68	0	47.66
D. J. Wild (*Northants*)	214.4	68	531	11	2-11	0	48.27
†G. E. Sainsbury (*Glos.*)	344.2	79	922	19	3-48	0	48.52
T. Firth (*OUCC*)	209.3	29	682	14	4-129	0	48.71
S. J. S. Kimber (*Surrey*)	152	21	639	12	2-13	0	53.25
†G. A. Pointer (*CUCC*)	176	25	568	10	3-52	0	56.80
M. W. Alleyne (*Glos.*)	172.4	35	709	11	4-128	0	64.45

The following bowlers took ten wickets but bowled in fewer than ten innings:

	O	M	R	W	BB	5 W/i	Avge
P. J. Bakker (*Hants*)	92.5	23	249	12	7-31	1	20.75
†G. Smith (*Northants*)	81	10	308	13	6-72	1	23.69
†M. K. Bore (*Notts.*)	148.2	58	344	13	4-52	0	26.46
R. F. Pienaar (*Kent*)	135.4	27	427	15	4-66	0	28.46
†S. Monkhouse (*Glam.*)	82	7	326	11	2-21	0	29.63
S. R. Waugh (*Somerset*)	112	22	348	11	3-48	0	31.63
I. G. Swallow (*Yorks.*)	111	25	349	11	7-95	1	31.72
C. J. P. G. van Zyl (*Glam.*) .	172	37	511	14	3-35	0	36.50

INDIVIDUAL SCORES OF 100 AND OVER

There were 244 three-figure innings in first-class cricket in 1987, eleven fewer than in 1986. The following list includes 197 hit in the County Championship, and 34 in other first-class games, but not the thirteen hit by the Pakistani touring team, which can be found in that section.

* *Signifies not out.*

G. A. Hick (8)
173 Worcs. v Middx, Lord's
156 Worcs. v Essex, Colchester
140* Worcs. v Northants, Worcester
138 Worcs. v Glos., Gloucester
132 Worcs. v Somerset, Worcester
126 Worcs. v Warwicks., Birmingham
107 Worcs. v Sussex, Worcester
107 Worcs. v Northants, Northampton

C. W. J. Athey (6)
160 Glos. v Notts., Nottingham
123 England v Pakistan, Lord's
115
114* } Glos. v Warwicks., Birmingham
101* Glos. v Yorks., Leeds
101* Glos. v Glam., Bristol

M. D. Crowe (6)
206 Somerset v Warwicks., Birmingham
148 Somerset v Surrey, Taunton
148 Somerset v Glam., Weston-super-Mare
105 Somerset v Worcs., Worcester
102* Somerset v Middx, Bath
100 Somerset v Essex, Chelmsford

M. W. Gatting (6)
196 Middx v Somerset, Bath
179 MCC v Rest of the World, Lord's
150* England v Pakistan, The Oval
132 Middx v Essex, Chelmsford
124 England v Pakistan, Birmingham
111 MCC v Essex, Lord's

M. R. Benson (5)
131 Kent v Surrey, The Oval
122 Kent v Worcs., Worcester
114 Kent v Sussex, Hove
113 Kent v Northants, Northampton
106 Kent v Oxford U., Oxford

P. M. Roebuck (5)
165* Somerset v Hants, Weston-super-Mare
135* Somerset v Worcs., Worcester
122 Somerset v Glam., Weston-super-Mare
112 Somerset v Yorks., Leeds
103* Somerset v Surrey, Taunton

C. M. Wells (5)
148* Sussex v Essex, Eastbourne
140* Sussex v Kent, Hove
118 Sussex v Warwicks., Hove
106 Sussex v Derbys., Chesterfield
105* Sussex v Somerset, Hove

R. J. Blakey (4)
204* Yorks. v Glos., Leeds
124* Yorks. v Lancs., Manchester
108 Yorks. v Northants, Northampton
101* Yorks. v Glam., Cardiff

T. S. Curtis (4)
138* Worcs. v Notts., Nottingham
129 Worcs. v Middx, Lord's
110 Worcs. v Notts., Kidderminster
106* Worcs. v Sussex, Worcester

A. J. Moles (4)
151 Warwicks. v Kent, Birmingham
145* Warwicks. v Somerset, Birmingham
137 Warwicks. v Worcs., Birmingham
101 Warwicks. v Yorks., Scarborough

M. C. J. Nicholas (4)
147 Hants v Sussex, Horsham
133 Hants v Kent, Bournemouth
110* Hants v Worcs., Worcester
103* Hants v Derbys., Heanor

B. Roberts (4)
184 Derbys. v Sussex, Chesterfield
137* Derbys. v Leics., Leicester
128 Derbys. v Kent, Canterbury
106 Derbys. v Hants, Heanor

C. L. Smith (4)
217 Hants v Warwicks., Birmingham
132* Hants v Middx, Southampton
118* Hants v Worcs., Worcester
102* Hants v Surrey, The Oval

R. J. Bailey (3)
158 Northants v Lancs., Northampton
152* Northants v Yorks., Northampton
137* Northants v Sussex, Hove

K. J. Barnett (3)
130 Derbys. v Notts., Nottingham
125 Derbys. v Warwicks., Derby
110 Derbys. v Glos., Bristol

A. R. Butcher (3)
135* Glam. v Worcs., Neath
135 Glam. v Leics., Abergavenny
113* Glam. v Derbys., Cardiff

J. D. Carr (3)
156 Middx v Essex, Lord's
133 Middx v Surrey, Lord's
123* Middx v Surrey, The Oval

C. S. Cowdrey (3)
135 Kent v Hants, Bournemouth
100 Kent v Oxford U., Oxford
100* Kent v Glam., Canterbury

K. M. Curran (3)
119 Glos. v Kent, Cheltenham
114* Glos. v Essex, Bristol
102* Glos. v Glam., Swansea

N. H. Fairbrother (3)
109* Lancs. v Notts., Manchester
101 Lancs. v Leics., Leicester
100 Lancs. v Somerset, Taunton

G. Fowler (3)
169* Lancs. v Kent, Liverpool
121 Lancs. v Essex, Manchester
100 Lancs. v Kent, Maidstone

G. A. Gooch (3)
171 Essex v Glos., Bristol
159 Essex v Northants, Ilford
117 MCC v Rest of the World, Lord's

C. G. Greenidge (3)
163 Hants v Glos., Gloucester
122 MCC v Rest of the World, Lord's
106 Hants v Glos., Southampton

B. R. Hardie (3)
143 Essex v Cambridge U., Cambridge
111 Essex v Leics., Leicester
111 Essex v Sussex, Eastbourne

P. Johnson (3)
125 Notts. v Leics., Nottingham
108 Notts. v Kent, Canterbury
106 Notts. v Derbys., Nottingham

W. Larkins (3)
120 Northants v Hants, Southampton
115 Northants v Worcs., Northampton
101* Northants v Yorks., Northampton

T. A. Lloyd (3)
162 Warwicks. v Sussex, Hove
151* Warwicks. v Glam., Birmingham
150* Warwicks. v Oxford U., Oxford

G. D. Mendis (3)
203* Lancs. v Middx, Manchester
155 Lancs. v Yorks., Manchester
100* Lancs. v Yorks., Leeds

H. Morris (3)
143 Glam. v Oxford U., Oxford
115
105 } Glam. v Warwicks., Birmingham

J. E. Morris (3)
162 Derbys. v Notts., Derby
113* Derbys. v Somerset, Taunton
106 Derbys. v Notts., Nottingham

M. Newell (3)
203* Notts. v Derbys., Derby
133* Notts. v Essex, Chelmsford
116 Notts. v Lancs., Manchester

C. E. B. Rice (3)
138 Notts. v Leics., Leicester
115 Notts. v Yorks., Nottingham
104* Notts. v Glam., Nottingham

R. T. Robinson (3)
166 England v Pakistan, Manchester
137 Notts. v Essex, Chelmsford
102 Notts. v Northants, Nottingham

W. N. Slack (3)
173 Middx v Glam., Lord's
149 Middx v Cambridge U., Cambridge
116 Middx v Lancs., Manchester

A. J. Stewart (3)
132 Surrey v Yorks., The Oval
127 Surrey v Middx, The Oval
105 Surrey v Somerset, The Oval

N. R. Taylor (3)
142* Kent v Essex, Ilford
123* Kent v Notts., Canterbury
113 Kent v Glam., Canterbury

A. P. Wells (3)
161* Sussex v Kent, Hove
119 Sussex v Middx, Hove
119 Sussex v Warwicks., Nuneaton

D. L. Amiss (2)
123 Warwicks. v Worcs., Worcester
120 Warwicks. v Leics., Hinckley

Asif Din (2)
115* Warwicks. v Glos., Birmingham
110 Warwicks. v Sussex, Hove

M. A. Atherton (2)
110 MCC v Yorks., Scarborough
109* Cambridge U. v Derbys., Cambridge

P. Bainbridge (2)
151 Glos. v Surrey, Cheltenham
134* Glos. v Sussex, Hove

D. L. Bairstow (2)
128 Yorks. v Leics., Scarborough
104 Yorks. v Derbys., Harrogate

N. E. Briers (2)
104 Leics. v Yorks., Scarborough
102* Leics. v Glos., Leicester

D. B. D'Oliveira (2)
131* Worcs. v Pakistanis, Worcester
121* Worcs. v Derbys., Worcester

D. I. Gower (2)
125 Leics. v Derbys., Derby
105* Leics. v Glos., Cheltenham

R. J. Hadlee (2)
133* Notts. v Somerset, Taunton
101 Notts. v Somerset, Nottingham

S. G. Hinks (2)
112 Kent v Middx, Lord's
104* Kent v Oxford U., Oxford

K. D. James (2)
142* Hants v Notts., Bournemouth
103* Hants v Oxford U., Oxford

J. W. Lloyds (2)
130 Glos. v Glam., Swansea
105 Glos. v Leics., Leicester

M. A. Lynch (2)
128* Surrey v Somerset, Taunton
114 Surrey v Glos., Cheltenham

B. J. M. Maher (2)
105 Derbys. v Surrey, Chesterfield
100* Derbys. v Cambridge U., Cambridge

M. P. Maynard (2)
160 Glam. v Somerset, Weston-super-Mare
119 Glam. v Derbys., Cardiff

A. A. Metcalfe (2)
152 Yorks. v MCC, Scarborough
113 Yorks. v Sussex, Sheffield

M. D. Moxon (2)
130 Yorks. v Derbys., Harrogate
104 Yorks. v Essex, Leeds

P. A. Neale (2)
103* Worcs. v Somerset, Worcester
100* Worcs. v Essex, Colchester

P. W. Romaines (2)
119 Glos. v Oxford U., Oxford
115 Glos. v Somerset, Bristol

V. P. Terry (2)
122 Hants v Warwicks., Birmingham
119* Hants v Pakistanis, Southampton

D. R. Turner (2)
184* Hants v Glos., Gloucester
104* Hants v Derbys., Heanor

S. R. Waugh (2)
137* Somerset v Glos., Bristol
111* Somerset v Surrey, The Oval

J. J. Whitaker (2)
126 Leics. v Cambridge U., Cambridge
105 Leics. v Yorks., Scarborough

P. Willey (2)
122 Leics. v Derbys., Leicester
113 Leics. v Somerset, Leicester

The following each played one three-figure innings:

J. Abrahams, 140*, Lancs. v Surrey, Manchester; D. G. Aslett, 101*, Kent v Derbys., Derby. D. J. Bicknell, 105, Surrey v Hants, The Oval; I. T. Botham, 126*, Worcs. v Somerset, Taunton; N. D. Burns, 100*, Somerset v Essex, Chelmsford; R. O. Butcher, 118, Middx v Sussex, Hove.

G. Cook, 111*, Northants v Worcs., Northampton; M. A. Crawley, 140, Oxford U. v Cambridge U., Lord's.

P. R. Downton, 103*, Middx v Surrey, The Oval.

N. A. Felton, 110, Somerset v Worcs., Worcester; K. W. R. Fletcher, 121, Essex v Middx, Lord's.

S. M. Gavaskar, 188, Rest of the World v MCC, Lord's; I. J. Gould, 111, Sussex v Northants, Hove; I. A. Greig, 104*, Surrey v Cambridge U., Cambridge; A. M. Green, 115, Sussex v Worcs., Worcester.

J. J. E. Hardy, 119, Somerset v Glos., Taunton; R. A. Harper, 127*, Northants v Worcs., Worcester; D. L. Haynes, 130, Rest of the World XI v Glos., Bristol; W. K. Hegg, 130, Lancs. v Northants, Northampton.

R. K. Illingworth, 120*, Worcs. v Warwicks., Worcester.

S. P. James, 106, Glam. v Oxford U., Oxford; T. E. Jesty, 124*, Surrey v Lancs., Manchester.

A. J. Lamb, 101*, Northants v Kent, Northampton; N. J. Lenham, 104*, Sussex v Pakistanis, Hove; A. W. Lilley, 102, Essex v Middx, Chelmsford.

A. McBrine, 102, Ireland v Scotland, Coleraine; D. J. R. Martindale, 103, Notts. v Warwicks., Worksop; K. T. Medlycott, 153, Surrey v Kent, The Oval.

R. C. Ontong, 100, Glam. v Lancs., Swansea.

R. F. Pienaar, 153, Kent v Derbys., Derby.

D. W. Randall, 133, Notts. v Warwicks., Birmingham; C. J. Richards, 172*, Surrey v Kent, The Oval; D. Ripley, 125*, Northants v Derbys., Derby.

R. Sharma, 111, Derbys. v Yorks., Chesterfield; R. J. Shastri, 103, Glam. v Northants, Swansea; D. M. Smith, 121*, Surrey v Worcs., The Oval; R. A. Smith, 209*, Hants v Essex, Southend; I. D. Swallow, 114, Yorks. v MCC, Scarborough.

C. J. Tavaré, 152, Kent v Worcs., Worcester; P. A. Todd, 135, Glam. v Worcs., Worcester; K. P. Tomlins, 100, Glos. v Oxford U., Oxford.

D. B. Vengsarkar, 173*, Rest of the World XI v Glos., Bristol.

D. J. Wild, 102*, Northants v Worcs., Worcester; R. G. Williams, 104, Northants v Notts., Nottingham; A. J. Wright, 161, Glos. v Glam., Bristol; J. G. Wright, 118, Derbys. v Somerset, Taunton.

TEN WICKETS IN A MATCH

There were twenty instances of bowlers taking ten or more wickets in a match in first-class cricket in 1987, fourteen fewer than in 1986. The list includes eighteen in the County Championship, and two by the Pakistani touring team.

J. P. Agnew (2)
11-126 Leics. v Derbys., Derby
10-106 Leics. v Northants, Leicester

S. T. Clarke (2)
12-105 Surrey v Northants, The Oval
10-127 Surrey v Derbys., The Oval

W. W. Davis (2)
10-115 Northants v Somerset, Northampton
10-149 Northants v Middx, Lord's

R. J. Hadlee (2)
12-83 Notts. v Somerset, Nottingham
10-46 Notts. v Sussex, Nottingham

The following each took ten wickets in a match on one occasion:

Abdul Qadir, 10-211, Pakistan v England, The Oval.
E. A. E. Baptiste, 10-146, Kent v Warwicks., Birmingham.
J. H. Childs, 10-160, Essex v Middx, Chelmsford.
I. Folley, 12-57, Lancs. v Warwicks., Southport; N. A. Foster, 10-170, Essex v Glos., Bristol.
E. E. Hemmings, 10-79, Notts. v Warwicks., Worksop.
Imran Khan, 10-77, Pakistan v England, Leeds.
A. N. Jones, 10-146, Somerset v Notts., Nottingham.
T. A. Merrick, 13-115, Warwicks. v Lancs., Birmingham; G. Miller, 11-133, Essex v Lancs., Manchester.
N. V. Radford, 10-118, Worcs. v Notts., Kidderminster.
J. Simmons, 12-123, Lancs. v Worcs., Manchester.

THE CRICKET COUNCIL

The Cricket Council, which was set up in 1968 and reconstituted in 1974 and 1983, acts as the governing body for cricket in the British Isles. It comprises the following, the officers listed being those for 1986-87.

Chairman: R. Subba Row.
Vice-Chairman: J. D. Robson.
8 Representatives of the Test and County Cricket Board: R. Subba Row, C. R. M. Atkinson, D. J. Insole, F. G. Mann, D. N. Perry, H. J. Pocock, A. D. Steven, F. M. Turner.
5 Representatives of the National Cricket Association: J. D. Robson, F. R. Brown, F. H. Elliott, E. K. Ingman, J. G. Overy.
3 Representatives of the Marylebone Cricket Club: D. G. Clark (until Dec. 1986), E. A. Clark (from Jan. 1987), G. H. G. Doggart, J. J. Warr.
1 Representative (non-voting) of the Minor Counties Cricket Association: G. L. B. August.
1 Representative (non-voting) of the Irish Cricket Union: D. Scott.
1 Representative (non-voting) of the Scottish Cricket Union: R. W. Barclay.

Secretary: A. C. Smith.

THE TEST AND COUNTY CRICKET BOARD

The TCCB was set up in 1968 to be responsible for Test matches, official tours, and first-class and minor county competitions. It is composed of representatives of the seventeen first-class counties; Marylebone Cricket Club; Minor Counties Cricket Association; Oxford University Cricket Club, Cambridge University Cricket Club, the Irish Cricket Union and the Scottish Cricket Union.

Officers 1986-87

Chairman: R. Subba Row.

Chairmen of Committees: R. Subba Row (Executive); F. G. Mann (Adjudication); M. C. Cowdrey (County Pitches); O. S. Wheatley (Cricket); D. J. Insole (Overseas Tours); P. R. Bromage (Discipline); A. D. Steven (Finance); C. R. M. Atkinson (PR and Marketing); D. R. W. Silk (Registration); P. B. H. May (Selection); A. C. Smith (Umpires); M. D. Vockins (Under-25 and Second XI Competitions).

Chief Executive: A. C. Smith. *Assistant Secretary (Administration):* B. Langley. *Assistant Secretary (Cricket):* M. E. Gear. *Accountant:* C. A. Barker. *PR and Marketing Manager:* P. M. Lush. *Sales and Promotion Manager:* K. Deshayes.

THE NATIONAL CRICKET ASSOCIATION

With the setting up of the Cricket Council in 1968 it was necessary to form a separate organisation to represent the interests of all cricket below the first-class game, and it is the National Cricket Association that carries out this function. It comprises representatives from 51 county cricket associations and seventeen national cricketing organisations.

Officers 1986-87

President: F. R. Brown.
Chairman: J. D. Robson.
Vice-Chairman: F. H. Elliott.

Chief Executive: K. V. Andrew.
General Secretary: B. J. Aspital.
Hon. Treasurer: D. W. Carter.

THE PAKISTANIS IN ENGLAND, 1987

Having, earlier in the year, fulfilled one ambition by leading Pakistan to their first series victory in India, Imran Khan achieved another when, under his captaincy, Pakistan won their first series in England. For the 34-year-old all-rounder, in his benefit year and nearing the end of his international career, it was a memorable double. It would not be doing an injustice to his team-mates to say that, without Imran's leadership, or his ability as a player, such triumphs would not have been celebrated.

Victory over England, by an innings at Headingley with the other four Tests drawn, provided compensation for defeat by two Tests to one in 1982, Pakistan's previous tour to England. At the time Imran, rankled, had expressed his dissatisfaction with some of the umpiring; five years older, he was more circumspect. His team's manager, Haseeb Ahsan, who had come to England with the 1962 Pakistan team, was less so. He had, in 1962, suffered foot trouble in the first match and had returned home early. By way of coincidence, if somewhat surprisingly, this was Pakistan's first full tour of England since then.

The wet, often cold weather which blighted so much of the tour was ironically Pakistan's ally in the first two Test matches. Principally, it allowed Imran to recover from a stomach muscle strained while he was lifting weights two days before the Old Trafford Test. He did not bowl there, and never slipped himself at Lord's. When he did so at Headingley, feeling the ground firm under his feet, he was at once a formidable strike bowler, swinging the ball prodigiously and taking ten wickets as England were beaten in three days and 24 minutes. One of those ten was his 300th Test wicket. At Edgbaston, when Pakistan's batting showed signs of the vulnerability once associated with it, Imran kept out England's bowlers for more than two hours and then, with England needing 124 from eighteen overs, he and Wasim Akram, his young charge, bowled through to deny them. Finally, at The Oval, where England had to win to square the series, he hit his fourth Test hundred as Pakistan amassed 708, their highest total in Tests.

At the outset of the tour, when Imran was often absent from the party of players, the young team looked uncertain of purpose. Kent beat them by an innings, but with Imran in charge they humbled Essex, the county champions, by 210 runs. The arrival of Javed Miandad, the vice-captain, produced a further transformation. Miandad had stayed in Pakistan until the birth of his son: within three days of arriving in England, he celebrated with an unbeaten double-hundred against Sussex and followed it with 113, 71 not out and 68 in the Texaco Trophy series. With his ability to pick up the line quickly, his sure footwork and his placement of the ball, he looked then as if he would cause England's bowlers all kinds of problems. But it was not until the last Test, when he batted more than ten hours for 260, that England again suffered from his genius.

Instead, when it mattered, it was Salim Malik who thwarted them, reaching maturity – if not his sixth Test hundred – with an innings of 99 at Headingley that was full of authority and Test-match temperament. As much as Imran's bowling, it was essential to Pakistan's victory. Settled into the No. 5 spot, he brought to the middle order a much needed solidity. After him came batting that could produce runs freely and attractively, especially

302

THE PAKISTANIS IN ENGLAND, 1987

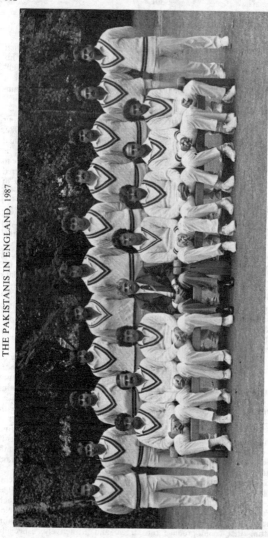

[*Patrick Eagar*

Back row: Shoaib Mohammad, Asif Mujtaba, Ramiz Raja, Salim Yousuf, Mohsin Kamal, Wasim Akram, Saleem Jaffer, Zakir Ahmed, Ijaz Ahmed, Mansoor Akhtar, Manzoor Elahi. **Front row:** Salim Malik, Iqbal Qasim (*assistant manager*), Abdul Qadir, Haseeb Ahsan (*manager*), Imran Khan (*captain*), Javed Miandad, Mudassar Nazar, Tauseef Ahmed.

against a weary attack: the gifted eighteen-year-old, Ijaz Ahmed, an exciting strokeplayer and a fascinating prospect; Salim Yousuf, at times an untidy wicket-keeper but a stylish batsman; Wasim Akram, a ferocious left-handed belter of the ball either straight or over mid-wicket; and of course Imran.

At the top of the order, however, Pakistan were less sure. Injury to Ramiz Raja, who dislocated his shoulder while fielding against Northamptonshire, forced the return of Mudassar Nazar to a role as opener: initially the intention was to play him in the middle order, but his calm temperament stood Pakistan in equally good stead at the start. He averaged 57.75 in the Tests, with an invaluable hundred at Edgbaston. His partners, Shoaib Mohammad and Ramiz, who began the series as the opening pair, could not match his resolve. Shoaib, son of Hanif, betrayed in the Tests the patience that was his father's hallmark but made a good impression with hundreds in the county matches. Ramiz looked the better batsman, technically sound and with time to play his strokes or adjust to defence.

At No. 3 Mansoor Akhtar, apart from a disciplined 75 at Old Trafford, disappointed in the Test matches but delighted around the counties with his wristy cover drives, quickness to pull anything short and his neat, almost classical leg-glance. He hit four hundreds and was the only tourist to exceed 1,000 runs. The little left-hander, Asif Mujtaba, who had been capped within days of his nineteenth birthday against West Indies the previous November, never came to terms with the varying pace and movement of the ball off English pitches. But his fielding, in a team of athletic fielders, was quite outstanding. In the one-day series, with no restriction on the tactical substitution of a bowler once he finished his spell, Mujtaba's was a frequent appearance.

There were times when Pakistan's bowling looked ordinary: at others it looked of the highest class. Wasim Akram, left-arm fast-medium, finished the tour with most wickets and justified all one had heard of him. From an easy, economical run-up and a whippy action, he could let slip a genuinely fast ball, especially if it was a bouncer, and at 21 he possessed impressive control of pace and movement. Mohsin Kamal, lively medium-fast, had trouble with his line at times, but when on target his late movement into or away from the bat troubled anyone not going fully forward. He developed well on tour and took the chance offered him by the injury to Saleem Jaffer. Hailed as the find of the 1986-87 season by his captain, Jaffer, a fast-medium left-armer, was troubled by a groin injury sustained during Pakistan's tour of India and played only twice on this tour. His record in one-day cricket suggested that his absence was especially felt in the Texaco Trophy series, which England won 2-1 by coming back spectacularly in the final stages of the third match.

Few opportunities were afforded to Zakir Khan, a tall, medium-pace bowler who kept a useful line and length, or to Manzoor Elahi, a stockily built all-rounder. The effort Manzoor put into his bowling did not compensate for his inability to use the ball in English conditions; with the bat, his plane was as often horizontal as vertical but he struck the ball hard. Six sixes in an over off Kirti Azad in a charity match at West Bromwich bore testimony to that. Azeem Hafeez, a left-arm medium-fast bowler, capped eighteen times, who happened to be in England on holiday, was drafted into the side midway through the tour, as was Zulqarnain, a wicket-keeper with three Test appearances. Yousuf was the only wicket-keeper in the tour party and he played in all but two of the team's 25 scheduled fixtures.

For spin, Pakistan depended on Abdul Qadir and Tauseef Ahmed, although it had been thought that the assistant manager, Iqbal Qasim, a left-arm spinner with 44 Tests' experience, might strengthen this arm of the attack. This became even more of a possibility when, for the first 50 days of the tour, the whereabouts of Abdul Qadir remained something of a mystery. Having stayed at home to look after his wife, who was ill, he eventually arrived in time for the Second Test and, with Tauseef out with a broken finger, was immediately called into action. However, it was not until the Oval Test, when he at last gave the ball time in the air, that his leg-spin and googly bowling was seen at its best. He took ten of his eleven wickets in the series there; seven in the first innings. Tauseef, the off-spinner, gave the ball quite a tweak but bowled too flat and fast for the English pitches of 1987.

The tour was not without its less salutary moments. Accusations of cheating were levelled against some of the Pakistan players following incidents in the one-day international at The Oval and the Test match at Headingley. At Old Trafford, time-wasting was the charge when, with Imran off the field for an X-ray of his thumb, only eleven overs were bowled in an hour after tea on the second day. This is a practice by no means unique to Pakistan, but the situation was exacerbated by statements to the press from both the England and Pakistan managements. In addition, Pakistan's grievance over the selection of D. J. Constant and K. E. Palmer to the Test match umpires' panel, and the TCCB's subsequent refusal to replace them, was allowed into the public domain. A less loquacious manager might have stilled some of the off-the-field controversies. Unfortunately, Haseeb, albeit a charming man, served only to fuel them. – G.W.

PAKISTANI TOUR RESULTS

Test matches – Played 5: Won 1, Drawn 4.
First-class matches – Played 17: Won 2, Lost 1, Drawn 14.
Wins – England, Essex.
Loss – Kent.
Draws – England (4), Glamorgan, Hampshire, Leicestershire, Middlesex, Northamptonshire, Nottinghamshire, Oxford & Cambridge Universities, Surrey, Sussex, Worcestershire.
Non first-class matches – Played 8: Won 4, Lost 3, Drawn 1. Abandoned 2. *Wins* – England, Ireland (2), Scotland. *Losses* – England (2), Somerset. *Draw* – Minor Counties. *Abandoned* – Lavinia, Duchess of Norfolk's XI, Derbyshire.

TEST MATCH AVERAGES

ENGLAND – BATTING

	T	I	NO	R	HI	100s	Avge
M. W. Gatting	5	8	1	445	150*	2	63.57
R. T. Robinson ...	5	8	0	299	166	1	37.37
C. W. J. Athey	4	6	1	186	123	1	37.20
I. T. Botham	5	8	1	232	51*	0	33.14
J. E. Emburey	4	5	0	162	58	0	32.40
D. I. Gower	5	8	0	236	61	0	29.50
B. C. Broad	4	7	0	193	55	0	27.57
B. N. French	4	5	1	103	59	0	25.75
P. H. Edmonds ...	5	7	4	66	24*	0	22.00
N. A. Foster	5	6	0	93	29	0	15.50
G. R. Dilley	4	5	2	20	17	0	6.66

Played in one Test: D. J. Capel 53, 28; P. A. J. DeFreitas 11; N. H. Fairbrother 0; M. D. Moxon 8, 15; C. J. Richards 6, 2.

* Signifies not out.

BOWLING

	O	M	R	W	BB	Avge
N. A. Foster	137.2	36	339	15	8-107	22.60
G. R. Dilley	133.3	26	388	14	6-154	27.71
P. H. Edmonds	92.3	36	219	4	1-2	54.75
I. T. Botham	134.3	30	433	7	3-217	61.85

Also bowled: D. J. Capel 18–1–64–0; P. A. J. DeFreitas 12–4–36–1; J. E. Emburey 07–21–222–0; M. W. Gatting 22–5–40–0; M. D. Moxon 6–2–27–0.

PAKISTAN – BATTING

	T	I	NO	R	HI	100s	Avge
Javed Miandad	5	5	0	360	260	1	72.00
Salim Yousuf	5	4	1	187	91*	0	62.33
Mudassar Nazar	5	5	1	231	124	1	57.75
Salim Malik	5	5	0	248	102	1	49.60
Imran Khan	5	5	1	191	118	1	47.75
Ijaz Ahmed	4	4	0	150	69	0	37.50
Mansoor Akhtar	5	5	0	152	75	0	30.40
Shoaib Mohammad ...	4	4	0	84	50	0	21.00
Wasim Akram	5	4	0	80	43	0	20.00
Ramiz Raja	2	2	0	29	15	0	14.50
Mohsin Kamal	4	3	2	13	10	0	13.00
Abdul Qadir	4	4	0	28	20	0	7.00

Played in two Tests: Tauseef Ahmed 0*.

* *Signifies not out.*

BOWLING

	O	M	R	W	BB	Avge
Imran Khan	168.2	33	455	21	7-40	21.66
Wasim Akram	180.4	38	464	16	4-111	29.00
Mohsin Kamal	94.4	14	332	9	4-127	36.88
Tauseef Ahmed	91.1	28	203	5	2-52	40.60
Abdul Qadir	175.4	46	450	11	7-96	40.90

Also bowled: Javed Miandad 4–2–10–0; Mudassar Nazar 110–26–303–3.

PAKISTANI TOUR AVERAGES – FIRST-CLASS MATCHES

BATTING

	M	I	NO	R	HI	100s	Avge
Javed Miandad	11	14	1	822	260	2	63.23
Mansoor Akhtar	16	24	3	1,156	169*	4	55.04
Salim Malik	17	22	4	901	102	1	50.05
Mudassar Nazar	13	16	2	588	124	2	42.00
Shoaib Mohammad	16	23	5	727	121*	2	40.38
Imran Khan	12	13	3	349	118	1	34.90
Salim Yousuf	16	14	4	347	91*	0	34.70
Ramiz Raja	11	15	0	501	150	1	33.40
Ijaz Ahmed	11	13	1	382	69	0	31.83
Manzoor Elahi	4	6	0	182	74	0	30.33
Wasim Akram	14	11	2	245	59*	0	27.22
Tauseef Ahmed	8	6	4	54	16*	0	27.00
Zakir Khan	8	4	2	48	22*	0	24.00
Mohsin Kamal	12	11	6	69	28	0	13.80
Abdul Qadir	10	7	0	70	24	0	10.00
Asif Mujtaba	4	5	0	11	5	0	2.20

Played in one match: Zulqarnain 0*; Azeem Hafeez, Iqbal Qasim and Saleem Jaffer did not bat.

* Signifies not out.

BOWLING

	O	M	R	W	BB	5W/i	Avge
Imran Khan	300.4	67	768	36	7-40	3	21.33
Wasim Akram	394	82	1,095	39	6-34	2	28.07
Mohsin Kamal	288.4	47	1,046	36	6-100	1	29.05
Mudassar Nazar	212	51	545	15	5-28	1	36.33
Tauseef Ahmed	212.2	66	477	13	4-51	0	36.69
Zakir Khan	165	32	554	14	4-27	0	39.57
Abdul Qadir	299.5	66	845	19	7-96	1	44.47

Also bowled: Asif Mujtaba 1-0-2-0; Azeem Hafeez 15-2-84-2; Ijaz Ahmed 4-0-21-0; Iqbal Qasim 18-6-41-1; Javed Miandad 5-2-11-0; Mansoor Akhtar 5-0-10-2; Manzoor Elahi 31.3-5-106-2; Saleem Jaffer 18-10-17-3; Salim Malik 29-6-71-2; Shoaib Mohammad 18.3-3-69-2.

FIELDING

39 – Salim Yousuf (37 ct, 2 st); 9 – Ijaz Ahmed; 8 – Salim Malik; 7 – Asif Mujtaba, Wasim Akram; 5 – Imran Khan, Javed Miandad, Mansoor Akhtar, Mohsin Kamal, Mudassar Nazar; 4 – Manzoor Elahi, Shoaib Mohammad, substitutes, Tauseef Ahmed, Zakir Khan; 2 – Abdul Qadir; 1 – Azeem Hafeez, Ramiz Raja.

HUNDREDS FOR PAKISTANIS

The following seventeen three-figure innings were played for the Pakistanis, thirteen in first-class matches and four in non first-class matches.

Mansoor Akhtar (4)
169* v Worcs., Worcester
137 v Notts., Nottingham
135 v Middx, Lord's
127 v Hants, Southampton

Javed Miandad (3)
260 v England, The Oval (Fifth Test)
211* v Sussex, Hove
†113 v England, The Oval (First Texaco Trophy)

Shoaib Mohammad (3)
121* v Worcs., Worcester
†101* v Ireland, Dublin
100 v Leics., Leicester

Mudassar Nazar (2)
124 v England, Birmingham (Fourth Test)
100 v Notts., Nottingham

Ijaz Ahmed (1)
†104 v Minor Counties, Burton upon Trent

Imran Khan (1)
118 v England, The Oval (Fifth Test)

Manzoor Elahi (1)
†109 v Ireland, Dublin

Ramiz Raja (1)
150 v Hants, Southampton

Salim Malik (1)
102 v England, The Oval (Fifth Test)

* Signifies not out.   † Not first-class.

Note: Those matches which follow which were not first-class are signified by the use of a dagger.

†LAVINIA, DUCHESS OF NORFOLK'S XI v PAKISTANIS

At Arundel, April 30. Abandoned.

SURREY v PAKISTANIS

At The Oval, May 2, 3, 4. Drawn. Toss: Surrey. The touring team, unacclimatised to, and joints stiffened by, the unforgiving chill of an early English summer day, were dismissed for their lowest total in seven encounters with Surrey. Their first innings had promised more when Ramiz and Mansoor were playing themselves in, but Feltham capitalised on a welter of loose shots with five wickets. The Pakistanis rallied by having Surrey 117 for seven on a second day of seven stoppages as bad light, rain, hail and a biting north-easterly wind made the cricket an uncomfortable experience for the players and the sparse gathering of spectators. However, Bullen made light of the conditions and went on to a maiden half-century. Mudassar and Mansoor, too, struck fluent fifties as the Pakistanis gained batting practice on the final afternoon.

Close of play: First day, Surrey 54-3 (D. M. Smith 11*, K. T. Medlycott 2*); Second day, Surrey 192-7 (C. K. Bullen 35*, M. A. Feltham 37*).

Pakistanis

*Mudassar Nazar c Lynch b Feltham		8	– b Medlycott	52
Shoaib Mohammad c Falkner b Feltham		32	– b Gray	43
Ramiz Raja b Medlycott		41	– c and b Bullen	9
Mansoor Akhtar c Falkner b Feltham		41	– not out	52
Salim Malik lbw b Feltham		11	– not out	10
Ijaz Ahmed run out		2		
Manzoor Elahi c Brown b Gray		13		
†Salim Yousuf c Feltham b Gray		2		
Wasim Akram c Bullen b Gray		29		
Tauseef Ahmed not out		7		
Mohsin Kamal b Feltham		0		
B 2, l-b 6, n-b 1		9	L-b 4, n-b 1	5

1/15 2/76 3/94 4/111 5/125   195   1/82 2/93 3/126   (3 wkts) 171
6/153 7/155 8/157 9/190

Bowling: *First Innings*—Gray 17-2-49-3; Feltham 23.2-8-66-5; Greig 13-3-32-0; Medlycott 12-2-40-1. *Second Innings*—Gray 13-1-32-1; Feltham 11-2-28-0; Medlyco 22-2-76-1; Bullen 15-5-31-1.

Surrey

N. J. Falkner b Wasim	19	M. A. Feltham st Yousuf b Tauseef ... 3
G. S. Clinton c Yousuf b Mohsin	12	A. H. Gray c Tauseef b Mohsin	1
D. M. Smith c Manzoor b Mudassar	26	†G. E. Brown not out	1
M. A. Lynch c Manzoor b Wasim	7	
K. T. Medlycott lbw b Mohsin	2	B 1, l-b 10, w 4, n-b 4	1
D. M. Ward c Yousuf b Manzoor	37	
*I. A. Greig c and b Mudassar	5	1/32 2/32 3/43 4/54 5/97	25
C. K. Bullen c Yousuf b Manzoor	65	6/110 7/117 8/198 9/221	

Bowling: Wasim 35-6-79-2; Mohsin 27-5-89-3; Mudassar 13-3-23-2; Tausee 15-5-34-1; Manzoor 9.3-2-21-2.

Umpires: D. J. Constant and K. J. Lyons.

KENT v PAKISTANIS

At Canterbury, May 6, 7, 8. Kent won by an innings and 57 runs. Toss: Pakistanis. The touring team recovered from a poor start through a third-wicket stand of 113 off 39 overs between Shoaib and Mansoor, but then collapsed against the pace and seam movement of Penn and Baptiste, losing five wickets for 9 runs in five overs. Hinks and Tavaré laid the foundations for Kent and, despite some encouraging medium-fast bowling by Mohsin, Chris Cowdrey and Penn increased the tempo. Pakistan, 228 behind, again got off to a bad start and Igglesden and Baptiste always worried them. Ramiz made a sparkling half-century out of 61 off 30 balls, hitting one six and seven fours, but it was not in keeping with the situation, and when Salim Malik's later resistance was ended, Kent hurried to an easy victory.

Close of play: First day, Kent 111-2 (S. G. Hinks 60*, C. J. Tavaré 10*); Second day, Pakistanis 25-1 (Shoaib Mohammad 10*, Tauseef Ahmed 3*).

Pakistanis

*Mudassar Nazar c Taylor b Igglesden	0	- c Taylor b Igglesden	11
Shoaib Mohammad c C. S. Cowdrey b Baptiste	50	- c Hinks b Baptiste	11
Ramiz Raja c Taylor b Igglesden	2	- (4) b Baptiste	50
Mansoor Akhtar c Farbrace b Baptiste	74	- (5) c Tavaré b Igglesden	5
Salim Malik lbw b Penn	1	- (7) c Aslett b Igglesden	41
Asif Mujtaba c Farbrace b Penn	0	- c Farbrace b Baptiste	1
Manzoor Elahi b C. S. Cowdrey	21	- (8) c Baptiste b Underwood	15
†Salim Yousuf c G. R. Cowdrey b Penn	0	- (9) c Tavaré b Underwood	13
Tauseef Ahmed c Aslett b Igglesden	15	- (3) c Farbrace b Igglesden	7
Zakir Khan lbw b C. S. Cowdrey	0	- (11) not out	9
Mohsin Kamal not out	4	- (10) b Igglesden	5
B 1, l-b 4, w 1, n-b 2	8	L-b 2, n-b 1	3

1/4 2/12 3/125 4/133 5/133   175   1/18 2/30 3/48 4/78 5/79   171
6/133 7/134 8/171 9/171   6/96 7/124 8/153 9/157

Bowling: *First Innings*—Igglesden 13.1-3-38-3; Baptiste 15.4-4-34-2; C. S. Cowdrey 14-3-41-2; Penn 19-5-51-3; Underwood 2-0-6-0. *Second Innings*—Baptiste 14-3-52-3; Igglesden 15.2-1-60-5; Underwood 11-5-28-2; Penn 9-3-23-0; Aslett 1-0-6-0.

Kent

. G. Hinks c Mansoor b Mohsin	70	†P. Farbrace not out	13
J. R. Taylor lbw b Mohsin	18	A. P. Igglesden not out	20
D. G. Aslett c Yousuf b Mohsin	12		
. J. Tavaré c Manzoor b Mohsin	87	B 4, l-b 13, w 1, n-b 9	27
G. R. Cowdrey lbw b Malik	21		
. A. E. Baptiste c sub b Zakir	7	1/37 2/66 3/135 (8 wkts dec.) 403	
C. S. Cowdrey c Shoaib b Mohsin	75	4/187 5/194 6/272	
. Penn c Tauseef b Mohsin	53	7/342 8/382	

D. L. Underwood did not bat.

Bowling: Mohsin 31–7–100–6; Zakir 26–4–103–1; Manzoor 4–0–25–0; Tauseef 2–11–53–0; Mudassar 21–3–69–0; Malik 13–2–36–1.

Umpires: N. T. Plews and D. R. Shepherd.

ESSEX v PAKISTANIS

At Chelmsford, May 9, 10, 11. Pakistanis won by 210 runs. Toss: Pakistanis. Wasim Akram hurried the tourists to their first victory, following his unbeaten 59, which included four sixes, with five wickets. Among his victims were Gooch, who picked up his second "pair" in consecutive matches at Chelmsford, and Hardie, one of the few Essex batsmen to impart authority. Page hit the ball cleanly to reach the boundary eleven times during the Essex first innings before Imran, who marked his first appearance on tour by bowling Gooch first ball, removed him. Salim Malik also hit eleven fours in his 99 from 212 balls, producing many stylish strokes, but the Pakistanis were throwing away their advantage in the second innings before Manzoor and Wasim came to their rescue. These two hard hitters joined forces when Imran had to go to hospital to receive seven stitches after playing a delivery from Page on to his cheekbone.

Close of play: First day, Pakistanis 331-7 (Salim Yousuf 19*, Wasim Akram 26*); Second day, Pakistanis 150-6 (Manzoor Elahi 45*, Wasim Akram 27*).

Pakistanis

Ramiz Raja c and b Lever	28	– c Page b Lever	1
Shoaib Mohammad c East b Topley	41	– c Miller b Page	7
Mansoor Akhtar c East b Topley	8	– lbw b Topley	18
Asif Mujtaba b Lever	3	– c East b Page	2
Salim Malik c Gladwin b Page	99	– (6) c East b Topley	8
*Imran Khan c East b Childs	24	– (8) retired hurt	11
Manzoor Elahi c Gladwin b Lever	44	– c sub b Miller	74
†Salim Yousuf not out	19	– (5) lbw b Gooch	20
Wasim Akram not out	26	– not out	59
B 1, l-b 16, w 3, n-b 19	39	B 1, l-b 9, w 3, n-b 4	17

1/61 2/82 3/96 4/123 5/178   (7 wkts dec.) 331   1/5 2/22 3/24   (7 wkts dec.) 217
6/272 7/299   4/32 5/61 6/70 7/217

Tauseef Ahmed and Zakir Khan did not bat.

Bowling: *First Innings*—Lever 29–6–91–3; Page 23–5–87–1; Topley 29–5–78–2; Gooch 6–2–21–0; Childs 12–3–26–1; Miller 2–0–11–0. *Second Innings*—Lever 12–1–38–1; Page 20–2–74–2; Childs 3–0–15–0; Gooch 12–3–24–1; Topley 15–6–49–2; Miller 1.5–0–7–1.

Essex

*G. A. Gooch b Imran	0	– c and b Wasim	
C. Gladwin c Zakir b Imran	12	– c Manzoor b Wasim	
B. R. Hardie b Zakir	47	– lbw b Wasim	8
A. W. Lilley c Asif b Zakir	8	– c sub b Wasim	1
G. Miller b Wasim	3	– c Imran b Tauseef	30
M. G. Field-Buss c Asif b Tauseef	2	– c Yousuf b Zakir	14
H. A. Page c Tauseef b Imran	60	– c Yousuf b Tauseef	
†D. E. East lbw b Wasim	0	– c Ramiz b Tauseef	
T. D. Topley b Tauseef	1	– c Asif b Tauseef	29
J. H. Childs not out	4	– not out	0
J. K. Lever b Imran	0	– b Wasim	0
L-b 5, w 1, n-b 7	13	L-b 6, w 3, n-b 7	16

1/0 2/26 3/63 4/83 5/83   150   1/0 2/1 3/52 4/103 5/134   188
6/106 7/115 8/130 9/150   6/139 7/139 8/188 9/188

Bowling: *First Innings*—Imran 15.2–5–51–4; Wasim 13–3–44–2; Zakir 9–2–26–2; Tauseef 11–4–24–2. *Second Innings*—Wasim 11.3–2–40–5; Imran 13–3–34–0; Zakir 13–2–40–1; Manzoor 6–1–15–0; Tauseef 19–4–51–4; Asif 1–0–2–0.

Umpires: B. J. Meyer and K. E. Palmer.

†DERBYSHIRE v PAKISTANIS

At Derby, May 12. Abandoned.

†SOMERSET v PAKISTANIS

At Taunton, May 14. Somerset won by 79 runs. Toss: Pakistanis. In cold, windy weather, Hardy and Felton put on 54 in fifteen overs before Crowe, 75 in 63 balls, led a stand of 86 in fifteen overs with Waugh, who was making his first appearance for the county. Although four Pakistani batsmen reached 20, application was lacking. Somerset fielded excellently and only Salim Malik, 32 in 36 balls, made much progress.

Somerset

N. A. Felton c Malik b Mudassar	26	G. D. Rose run out	7
*P. M. Roebuck b Wasim	0	G. V. Palmer not out	1
J. J. E. Hardy b Manzoor	34	B 8, l-b 6, w 2, n-b 6	22
S. R. Waugh c Yousuf b Mohsin	34		
M. D. Crowe lbw b Wasim	75	1/9 2/63 3/71 (8 wkts, 50 overs) 217	
R. J. Harden c Malik b Tauseef	1	4/157 5/168 6/193	
†N. D. Burns c Mudassar b Tauseef	17	7/211 8/217	

M. R. Davis and A. N. Jones did not bat.

Bowling: Wasim 10–2–33–2; Mohsin 9.1–2–33–1; Manzoor 11–1–53–1; Mudassar 11–0–34–1; Tauseef 7.5–0–46–2; Malik 1–0–4–0.

Pakistanis

Mudassar Nazar c Roebuck b Jones	4	†Salim Yousuf c Burns b Jones	6
Ijaz Ahmed b Davis	20	Tauseef Ahmed not out	13
Ramiz Raja c Crowe b Rose	1	Mohsin Kamal absent injured	
Mansoor Akhtar run out	21		
*Javed Miandad b Palmer	23	L-b 3	3
Salim Malik run out	32		
Wasim Akram c Harden b Jones	13	1/10 2/26 3/26 4/60 5/89 (39.1 overs) 138	
Manzoor Elahi c Waugh b Palmer	2	6/115 7/119 8/120 9/138	

Bowling: Jones 9.1–1–32–3; Davis 9–3–23–1; Rose 5–2–14–1; Waugh 6–0–29–0; Palmer 10–1–37–2.

Umpires: J. H. Harris and A. A. Jones.

SUSSEX v PAKISTANIS

At Hove, May 16, 17, 18. Drawn. Toss: Pakistanis. A brilliant double-hundred by Javed Miandad and a maiden century off 210 balls by Lenham were the batting highlights of a match spoiled in the end by rain and bad light. Miandad, where once he had been a player, reigned as king on the opening day, hitting a six and 27 fours as he achieved hundreds in each of the afternoon sessions: 199 runs were added between lunch and tea. On a cold Sunday, Imran took centre stage before rescue acts from the brothers Wells and Lenham and Reeve warmed the Sussex supporters. Rain caused a 2.30 p.m. start and brought two stoppages on the last day, but Lenham continued with commendable coolness to his hundred, playing neat, carefully placed strokes and hitting sixteen fours.

Close of play: First day, Pakistanis 444-4 (Javed Miandad 211*, Salim Malik 86*); Second day, Sussex 209-5 (N. J. Lenham 44*, D. A. Reeve 27*).

Pakistanis

Mudassar Nazar run out	25	Salim Malik not out		86
Shoaib Mohammad lbw b Pringle	39	W 1, n-b 21		22
Ramiz Raja c Parker b Pringle	4			—
Javed Miandad not out	211	1/63 2/72 3/109	(4 wkts dec.)	444
Mansoor Akhtar c Kimber b Reeve	57	4/232		

Imran Khan, Wasim Akram, †Salim Yousuf, Tauseef Ahmed and Zakir Khan did not bat.

Bowling: Pringle 16-4-45-2; Kimber 16-2-89-0; Reeve 23-5-95-1; C. M. Wells 9-2-48-0; Heseltine 21-4-94-0; A. P. Wells 9-0-63-0; Standing 1-0-10-0.

Sussex

R. I. Alikhan c Yousuf b Imran	3	M. W. Pringle c and b Zakir		12
D. K. Standing c Yousuf b Imran	5	S. J. S. Kimber not out		6
P. W. G. Parker c Yousuf b Imran	17			
A. P. Wells c Malik b Imran	55	B 3, l-b 5, w 4, n-b 5		17
C. M. Wells c Yousuf b Mudassar	45			—
N. J. Lenham not out	104	1/4 2/12 3/31	(8 wkts dec.)	299
D. A. Reeve b Imran	30	4/107 5/138 6/232		
P. Moores c Mansoor b Zakir	5	7/243 8/275		

*A. W. Heseltine did not bat.

Bowling: Imran 23-4-61-5; Wasim 23-3-69-0; Zakir 26-7-73-2; Mudassar 15-2-29-1; Tauseef 19.3-7-45-0; Shoaib 1-1-0-0; Malik 3-1-14-0.

Umpires: A. G. T. Whitehead and P. B. Wight.

†ENGLAND v PAKISTAN

First Texaco Trophy Match

At The Oval, May 21. England won by seven wickets. Toss: England. Played on a pitch of gentle pace, and on a cold day, the match revolved around major innings from Miandad and Broad. The difference lay in Broad's support from Athey (61 balls) and Lamb for 23 overs each. When Gatting, with a toe infection, did not resume after tea (England 83 for one), Lamb (71 balls, one six, three fours) picked up the pace. The light was deteriorating, and 50 from 61 balls by Broad and Lamb, in a partnership of 116, was just what England needed. Put in, Pakistan made the worst possible start. Ramiz, without facing a ball, was beaten by Foster's underarm throw to Richards in the first over. But from the seventh over, Miandad took charge, at first streakily and then with invention and audacity. With Mudassar (132 balls) he put on 110 in 36 overs, hit his fourth one-day international hundred off 130 balls, and when Lamb, running some twenty yards at third man, caught a top-edged flail, he had faced 142 balls and hit ten fours. Broad (168 balls, four fours) was more orthodox and unlucky to miss his hundred: the square-cut 2 which brought his 50 should have been 4 runs as Ramiz had his boot over the boundary rope when picking up the ball. That said, Broad was desperately close to being run out when 77. Salim Malik, diving to his right at cover, and Mujtaba, sprinting back to long-off to dismiss Lamb, held catches that matched the excellence of Lamb's.

Man of the Match: B. C. Broad.   *Attendance:* 14,578; *receipts* £170,952.

Pakistan

Mudassar Nazar c DeFreitas b Foster	.	45
Ramiz Raja run out		0
Manzoor Akhtar c Gatting b Dilley	...	12
Javed Miandad c Lamb b Dilley		113
*Imran Khan c Broad b Foster		7
Wasim Akram b Emburey		12
Manzoor Elahi not out		18

Salim Malik not out ....

B 1, l-b 8, w 4, n-b 4 1

1/0 (2) 2/18 (3)   (6 wkts, 55 overs) 23
3/128 (1) 4/169 (5)
5/206 (6) 6/208 (4)

Ijaz Ahmed, †Salim Yousuf and Tauseef Ahmed did not bat.

Bowling: Dilley 11–1–63–2; DeFreitas 11–3–50–0; Botham 11–2–38–0; Foster 11–0–36–2;
Emburey 11–1–36–1.

England

B. C. Broad c sub (Asif Mujtaba)		
	b Wasim	99
C. W. J. Athey c Malik b Mudassar	...	33
*M. W. Gatting retired hurt	....	2
A. J. Lamb c sub (Asif Mujtaba)		
	b Tauseef	61

D. I. Gower not out ....
I. T. Botham not out ....

L-b 9, w 2, n-b 6 ....

1/76 (2) 2/199 (4)   (3 wkts, 53.1 overs) 23
3/218 (1)

†C. J. Richards, J. E. Emburey, P. A. J. DeFreitas, N. A. Foster and G. R. Dilley did not bat.

Bowling: Imran 8–0–30–0; Manzoor 11–1–31–0; Wasim 11–0–60–1; Mudassar 11–1–41–1;
Tauseef 10.1–0–47–1; Mansoor 2–0–15–0.

Umpires: D. R. Shepherd and A. G. T. Whitehead.

†ENGLAND v PAKISTAN

Second Texaco Trophy Match

At Nottingham, May 23. Pakistan won by six wickets. Toss: Pakistan. Winning the toss was a
decisive factor in conditions which favoured the seam bowlers until mid-afternoon. Athey was
never comfortable against Imran's swing, Gooch, in for the injured Gatting, drove one
imperious four off Mohsin before twice being struck on the pads in the tenth over, and only
Broad had the measure of the bowlers. He was out immediately after reaching his fifty in 81
balls with his third four. Gower, surviving an early chance, and Lamb put on 42 in thirteen
overs before a smart leg-side catch off the bottom edge by the wicket-keeper began a fatal
slide. Next over, the 39th, Gower drove too soon at Mudassar, and in the 40th Botham hoisted
a high catch to long leg. Thereafter it was left to the acting-captain, Emburey, to fashion 25 in
his unique way. With Miandad (128 balls, three fours) in such scintillating form, and Botham
in a profligate mood, a target of 158 was always on. When Foster, the pick of England's
bowlers, ran out Malik with a direct throw from backward square leg to the bowler's end,
Imran hastened the end with a straight six off Emburey. Broad's misfield, turning 1 into 4 to
level the scores, summed up England's day.

Man of the Match: Javed Miandad.   *Attendance: 12,080; receipts £130,380.*

England

B. C. Broad c Yousuf b Wasim	......	52
C. W. J. Athey lbw b Imran	....	1
G. A. Gooch lbw b Mohsin	...	9
A. J. Lamb c Yousuf b Tauseef	......	26
D. I. Gower b Mudassar	....	24
I. T. Botham c Mohsin b Tauseef	.....	0
†C. J. Richards c Manzoor b Mohsin	...	0
*J. E. Emburey b Wasim	....	25
P. A. J. DeFreitas c Manzoor b Imran	.	3

N. A. Foster run out ....
G. R. Dilley not out ....

L-b 8, w 4 ....

1/15 (2) 2/45 (3)   (51.1 overs) 157
3/75 (1) 4/117 (4) 5/117 (5)
6/117 (6) 7/121 (7) 8/144 (9)
9/157 (10) 10/157 (8)

Bowling: Imran 9–1–31–2; Mohsin 11–1–31–2; Wasim 9.1–1–18–2; Mudassar 11–1–36–1;
Tauseef 11–1–33–2.

Pakistan

Mudassar Nazar lbw b Foster	12	*Imran Khan not out	2
Ramiz Raja c Gooch b DeFreitas	13	L-b 8, w 2, n-b 1	1
Mansoor Akhtar b Foster	21		
Javed Miandad not out	71	1/23 (2) 2/29 (1) (4 wkts, 52 overs) 15	
Salim Malik run out	9	3/64 (3) 4/81 (5)	

Manzoor Elahi, Wasim Akram, †Salim Yousuf, Tauseef Ahmed and Mohsin Kamal di
not bat.

Bowling: Dilley 9–4–16–0; DeFreitas 11–2–30–1; Foster 11–1–25–2; Botham 7–0–34–0
Emburey 11–2–33–0; Gooch 3–0–12–0.

Umpires: D. J. Constant and B. J. Meyer.

†ENGLAND v PAKISTAN

Third Texaco Trophy Match

At Birmingham, May 25. England won by one wicket to take the Texaco series 2–1. Toss
England. There was high drama from the first over to the last, but sadly a match of such
marvellous cricket was marred by ugly scenes, beyond the boundary, provoked by racial pride
racial prejudice and alcohol. Put in, with the conditions again overcast, Pakistan found
themselves 0 for two after three balls from Thomas, who replaced the unfit Dilley. But
Miandad was at his most brilliant, putting on 73 in 24 overs with Ramiz (72 balls, six fours) and
95 in twenty with Malik (61 balls). He had faced 128 balls for his 68 when, lashing out, he
was spectacularly caught by Gower, diving far to his right; and without him, Pakistan
disintegrated. Emburey took two wickets in the 45th over, two more fell in the next, and
Pakistan had lost five wickets for 2 runs in eighteen deliveries. Only Imran, clubbing Thomas
over the pavilion and out of the ground, and Emburey high over deep mid-wicket, prevented
England's target being less than 200.
England had fielded wonderfully well and so did Pakistan. Miandad took two brilliant
catches at point, the second dismissing Gatting (56 balls, six fours) in the 35th over; Malik
accounted for Richards with a hard, flat throw from the square-leg boundary and came in fast
from third man to run out Emburey. England had needed 63 from the last ten overs; now the
target was 47 from 40 balls as DeFreitas came in. He cast caution to the wind, swinging Imran
over mid-wicket for six, added three fours, and had taken 33 from 22 balls when he chopped
on. Foster and Thomas had eleven balls in which to score 5, and although Foster could
should, have been run out, scampering a leg-bye to level the scores, they made it with a four
through slips.
Man of the Match: P. A. J. DeFreitas. *Attendance*: 17,000; *receipts* £147,844.
Men of the Series: England – B. C. Broad; Pakistan – Javed Miandad.

Pakistan

Mudassar Nazar lbw b Thomas	0	Tauseef Ahmed b Foster	0
Ramiz Raja run out	46	Mohsin Kamal not out	1
Mansoor Akhtar c Richards b Thomas	0	B 2, l-b 13, w 1, n-b 3	19
Javed Miandad c Gower b Foster	68		
Salim Malik b Emburey	45	1/0 (1) 2/0 (3) (9 wkts, 55 overs) 213	
*Imran Khan not out	24	3/73 (2) 4/168 (4)	
Manzoor Elahi b Emburey	0	5/170 (5) 6/170 (7)	
†Salim Yousuf run out	0	7/170 (8) 8/170 (9)	
Wasim Akram c Richards b Foster	0	9/178 (10)	

Bowling: Thomas 11–0–59–2; DeFreitas 11–1–30–0; Botham 11–1–31–0; Foster
11–1–29–3; Emburey 11–1–49–2.

·ngland

. C. Broad c Miandad b Mohsin	....	15
. W. J. Athey c Yousuf b Imran	....	5
·. I. Gower b Mudassar	....	11
. J. Lamb c Mansoor b Mudassar	....	14
M. W. Gatting c Miandad b Mohsin	.	41
T. Botham c sub (Asif Mujtaba)		
	b Tauseef	. 24
C. J. Richards run out	....	16
E. Emburey run out	....	16
·. A. Foster not out	....	14

P. A. J. DeFreitas b Imran	....	33
J. G. Thomas not out	....	1
L-b 14, w 12, n-b 1	....	27

1/18 (2) 2/31 (1) (9 wkts, 54.3 overs) 217
3/34 (3) 4/75 (4)
5/105 (5) 6/140 (6)
7/155 (7) 8/167 (8)
9/209 (10)

Bowling: Imran 11–0–43–2; Mohsin 11–0–47–2; Wasim 10.3–2–34–0; Mudassar ·4–2–17–2; Tauseef 11–0–62–1.

Umpires: H. D. Bird and K. E. Palmer.

†IRELAND v PAKISTANIS

·t Dublin, May 27. Pakistanis won by 114 runs. Toss: Pakistanis. Shoaib's unbeaten 101, ·om 157 balls, included three sixes and seven fours, while there were three sixes and nine ·urs in Mansoor's 78-ball 87. Mansoor, when 2, was forced to retire after being struck on the ·and and resumed at the fall of the second wicket.

·akistanis

·amiz Raja c and b Corlett	....	4
·hoaib Mohammad not out	101
·ansoor Akhtar c Warke b Garth	....	87
·alim Malik c Milling b McBrine	....	42
·anzoor Elahi c Garth b Milling	.....	8
·alim Yousuf c Jackson b Milling	....	11

Asif Mujtaba not out	....	16
L-b 3, w 1, n-b 3	....	7

1/5 2/85 3/206 (5 wkts, 60 overs) 276
4/222 5/245

·auseef Ahmed, Mohsin Kamal, Zakir Khan and Saleem Jaffer did not bat.

Bowling: Corlett 12–2–52–1; Milling 12–3–39–2; Garth 10–1–43–1; Masood 7–1–45–0; ·cBrine 11–1–48–1; Halliday 8–0–46–0.

·reland

·. J. S. Warke c and b Mohsin	....	13
·. F. Cohen st Yousuf b Asif	....	53
·. A. Masood c Malik b Zakir	......	16
·. G. Dennison c Yousuf b Asif	......	11
·. D. Garth c Asif b Tauseef	....	4
·. D. Harrison b Malik	....	25
·. C. Corlett c Mohsin b Asif	......	17
·. McBrine c Manzoor b Asif	.....	3

*†P. B. Jackson b Malik	....	4
M. Halliday not out	....	1
H. Milling not out	....	4
L-b 8, w 2, n-b 1	....	11

1/22 2/67 3/90 (9 wkts, 60 overs) 162
4/105 5/105 6/134
7/143 8/152 9/158

Bowling: Mohsin 7–2–21–1; Jaffer 7–0–14–0; Zakir 8–2–16–1; Manzoor 10–1–33–0; ·auseef 12–5–25–1; Asif 11–3–25–4; Ramiz 3–0–14–0; Malik 2–0–6–2.

Umpires: M. Henderson and L. Hogan.

†IRELAND v PAKISTANIS

·At Dublin, May 28. Pakistanis won on faster scoring-rate after rain ended play. Toss: ·akistanis. Manzoor Elahi scored 109 in 79 minutes after lunch, hitting six sixes and eleven ·ours. Salim Malik hit two sixes and eleven fours.

Pakistanis

*Mudassar Nazar c Cohen b Milling	34	Mohsin Kamal c Cohen b Garth	......
Shoaib Mohammad c Jackson b Milling	10	Tauseef Ahmed not out	....
Ijaz Ahmed c Cohen b Harrison	59	B 4, l-b 12, w 5, n-b 1	2?
Salim Malik run out	82		
Manzoor Elahi c Masood b Corlett	109	1/45 2/60 3/192	(7 wkts, 60 overs) 37?
Asif Mujtaba c Harrison b Corlett	47	4/212 5/343	
†Salim Yousuf not out	8	6/363 7/371	

Mansoor Akhtar and Zakir Khan did not bat.

Bowling: Corlett 12-1-71-2; Milling 12-0-57-2; Garth 9-3-58-1; Halliday 10-1-62-(; McBrine 7-1-36-0; Harrison 8-0-55-1; Masood 2-0-21-0.

Ireland

S. J. S. Warke c Asif b Mohsin	1
M. F. Cohen not out	39
M. A. Masood c Manzoor b Tauseef	89
D. G. Dennison not out	2
B 1, l-b 2, w 9, n-b 1	13

1/5 2/139   (2 wkts, 31.1 overs) 144

J. D. Garth, G. D. Harrison, A. McBrine, S. C. Corlett, M. Halliday, *†P. B. Jackson an? H. Milling did not bat.

Bowling: Ijaz 8-1-34-0; Mohsin 7-1-36-1; Zakir 7-0-40-0; Malik 8-0-27-0; Tause? 1.1-0-4-1.

Umpires: B. Carpenter and M. Moore.

MIDDLESEX v PAKISTANIS

At Lord's, May 30, 31, June 1. Drawn. Toss: Pakistanis. Mansoor Akhtar's stylish centur? gave the Pakistanis command from the start, but with the First Test approaching, and in nee? of batting practice, they declined to push for victory. There was enough movement off th? pitch for the seam bowlers to bring Downton five catches and Salim Yousuf four in the firs? innings. Wasim Akram ended the Middlesex innings after lunch on the second day by takin? the last six wickets for 10 runs in 34 balls. When Imran chose not to enforce the follow-o? Mansoor, coming in when Shoaib injured his right hand, once more mastered the attack, h? and Ramiz averaging 4 an over as the Pakistanis' first wicket realised 176 runs. Malik was th? main contributor as the tourists added 138 on the final morning before declaring at lunch? Middlesex displayed much improved batting, with Carr reaching 50 off 68 balls before th? match tailed off.

Close of play: First day, Middlesex 18-1 (W. N. Slack 16*, J. D. Carr 1*); Second day? Pakistanis 204-2 (Javed Miandad 10*, Salim Malik 4*).

Pakistanis

Ramiz Raja c Downton b Cowans	17	– run out	8?
Shoaib Mohammad c Gatting b Hughes	14	– retired hurt	?
Mansoor Akhtar c Butcher b Edmonds	135	– c Downton b Emburey	8?
Javed Miandad c Downton b Slack	9	– c Butcher b Hughes	4?
Salim Malik c Downton b Hughes	34	– sub b Edmonds	9?
*Imran Khan c Downton b Hughes	10	– not out	1?
Manzoor Elahi c Downton b Williams	15		
†Salim Yousuf b Slack b Emburey	13		
Wasim Akram lbw b Cowans	16		
Tauseef Ahmed not out	9		
Mohsin Kamal not out	9		
L-b 9, w 1, n-b 6	16	L-b 9, n-b 8	1?

1/21 2/60 3/77 4/148 5/164   (9 wkts dec.) 297   1/176 2/198 3/283 (4 wkts dec.) 34?
6/213 7/254 8/268 9/281   4/342

Bowling: *First Innings*—Williams 13–2–53–1; Cowans 15–4–41–2; Hughes 20.5–3–77–3; Slack 6–2–17–1; Edmonds 24–6–60–1; Emburey 20–4–40–1. *Second Innings*—Hughes 5–2–62–1; Cowans 12–1–55–0; Williams 12–0–63–0; Gatting 10–0–32–0; Edmonds 8.1–0–53–1; Emburey 17–4–48–1; Slack 2–0–7–0; Carr 3–0–13–0.

Middlesex

P. H. Edmonds c Yousuf b Imran	0			
W. N. Slack b Mohsin	36	– (1) c Yousuf b Malik	32
J. D. Carr c Yousuf b Imran	18	– (2) not out	81
M. W. Gatting c Yousuf b Wasim	19			
C. O. Butcher c Yousuf b Wasim	41			
†P. R. Downton lbw b Wasim	8	– (3) not out	45
J. E. Emburey b Wasim	0			
N. F. Williams c Mohsin b Wasim	0			
S. P. Hughes not out	8			
N. G. Cowans b Wasim	2			
A. J. T. Miller absent injured				
L-b 6, w 2, n-b 4	12	B 7, l-b 2, n-b 3	12

1/0 2/57 3/57 4/116 5/122   144   1/89   (1 wkt) 170
6/122 7/122 8/134 9/144

Bowling: *First Innings*—Imran 14–4–35–2; Wasim 14.5–2–34–6; Mohsin 13–2–48–1; Manzoor 7–0–21–0. *Second Innings*—Imran 7–1–17–0; Wasim 13–4–41–0; Manzoor 9–2–24–0; Mohsin 9–2–30–0; Tauseef 17–5–40–0; Malik 4–1–9–1.

Umpires: K. J. Lyons and R. Palmer.

ENGLAND v PAKISTAN

First Cornhill Test

At Manchester, June 4, 5, 6, 8, 9. Drawn. Toss: Pakistan. Just over half the match was lost to the weather, only fourteen hours eighteen minutes' play being possible. England held a promising position by the end of the third day when Pakistan were 93 for three, needing 248 to avoid following on, but only 26 overs were possible on the fourth day and none on the last. England's original choice of thirteen players included two who had not been to Australia in the winter, Robinson and Capel. This became three when Broad broke his thumb and Fairbrother was brought in for his début on his home ground. Dilley was declared unfit on the morning of the match, Capel was left out, and England's team showed five changes from the one which lost the Fifth Test in Sydney. Broad, Small and Dilley were injured, Lamb and Richards were dropped, and in came Robinson, Fairbrother, DeFreitas, Foster and French. Pakistan were still without Qadir and showed four changes from the team which won the final Test against India in Bangalore in March. Shoaib Mohammad, Mudassar Nazar, Mansoor Akhtar and Mohsin Kamal replaced Rizwan-uz-Zaman, Manzoor Elahi, Iqbal Qasim and Saleem Jaffer.

Play was able to start at 2.45 p.m. on the first day, but only after matting had been laid over a sodden, muddy-looking nearby pitch. Imran won the toss and, although not fit to bowl, he put England in and could have been moderately satisfied with holding them to 145 for three at the end of the day. Wasim Akram, 21 the previous day, took the first wicket in the 30th over and Mohsin gave Pakistan encouragement with two wickets in an over in the closing half-hour. Gatting was bowled and Fairbrother, sent in with 25 minutes to go, let a bouncer go by, was beaten outside off stump and let the third delivery pass. He made no shot to the fourth, which came in to him, and was sadly lbw. French went in as night-watchman and the following day, in which only 37 minutes were lost, went on to his first Test fifty in a stand of 113 with his Nottinghamshire colleague, Robinson.

Gower top-edged a catch to the wicket-keeper, but Robinson, whose fourth Test century occupied 366 minutes and 264 balls, went on for a total of 528 minutes and 365 balls and hit sixteen fours until, hooking tiredly, he was caught behind. Botham hit five fours and a six before he was caught in the outfield and play ended 37 minutes early because of rain with

England 402 for seven. A bright innings from Edmonds dominated a last-wicket stand of 3 on the third day, and before play again ended early, England had claimed three wickets Shoaib edged his seventh ball to the wicket-keeper, Ramiz was well caught by the divin Emburey at square leg, and Miandad was caught by French, standing up to Botham.

By the end of the third day, 308 minutes' play had been lost – 121 on the first day, 37 on th second, and 150 on the third. The rain made sure there would be little more, just 86 minutes on the fourth day which was highlighted by a superb piece of fielding by DeFreitas, supported by alert wicket-keeping, to run out Malik. Another feature of the match was the use of the standby umpire, J. Birkenshaw, who deputised briefly when H. D. Bird was hit on the leg by fielder's throw on the second day. – Brian Bearshaw.

Man of the Match: R. T. Robinson.   *Attendance*: 31,823; *receipts* £229,276.

Close of play: First day, England 145-3 (R. T. Robinson 62*, B. N. French 6*); Second day England 402-7 (J. E. Emburey 14*, P. A. J. DeFreitas 5*); Third day, Pakistan 93-3 (Mansoo Akhtar 42*, Salim Malik 3*); Fourth day, Pakistan 140-5 (Imran Khan 10*, Mudassa Nazar 0*).

England

C. W. J. Athey b Wasim	19	P. A. J. DeFreitas b Wasim 1
R. T. Robinson c Yousuf b Mohsin	166	N. A. Foster b Tauseef ....
*M. W. Gatting b Mohsin	42	P. H. Edmonds not out 2
N. H. Fairbrother lbw b Mohsin	0	B 9, l-b 15, w 1, n-b 5 .... 3*
†B. N. French c Imran b Wasim	59	
D. I. Gower c Yousuf b Wasim	22	1/50 (1) 2/133 (3) 3/133 (4) 4/246 (5) 44
I. T. Botham c Wasim b Tauseef	48	5/284 (6) 6/373 (2) 7/397 (7)
J. E. Emburey c Shoaib b Mohsin	19	8/413 (9) 9/413 (8) 10/447 (10)

Bowling: Wasim 46–11–111–4; Mohsin 39–4–127–4; Tauseef 21.4–4–52–2; Mudassa 37–8–133–0.

Pakistan

Ramiz Raja c Emburey b DeFreitas	15	*Imran Khan not out .... 1(
Shoaib Mohammad c French b Foster	0	Mudassar Nazar not out .... (
Mansoor Akhtar c Fairbrother		B 9, l-b 2, w 1, n-b 1 .... 1:
b Edmonds	75	
Javed Miandad c French b Botham	21	1/9 (2) 2/21 (1) 3/74 (4) (5 wkts) 14*
Salim Malik run out	6	4/100 (5) 5/139 (3)

†Salim Yousuf, Wasim Akram, Tauseef Ahmed and Mohsin Kamal did not bat.

Bowling: Foster 15–3–34–1; DeFreitas 12–4–36–1; Botham 14–7–29–1; Emburey 16–3–28–0; Edmonds 7–5–2–1.

Umpires: H. D. Bird and B. J. Meyer.

†SCOTLAND v PAKISTANIS

At Glasgow, June 11. Pakistanis won by 56 runs. Toss: Scotland. Rain, which delayed the start by 45 minutes, later caused the Pakistanis' innings to be closed after 42 overs. When play resumed, Scotland's target was adjusted to 184 from 38 overs.

Pakistanis

Ijaz Ahmed lbw b McIntyre	27	Ramiz Raja c Ker b Burnett .... (
Shoaib Mohammad retired ill	36	Iqbal Qasim not out 4
Salim Malik c Brown b Ker	47	
Wasim Akram c Rajput b Ker	40	B 3, l-b 1, w 1 5
†Salim Yousuf st Brown b Burnett	28	
Asif Mujtaba b Burnett	3	1/38 2/111 3/178 (6 wkts, 42 overs) 20:
*Javed Miandad not out	7	4/186 5/187 6/193

Zakir Khan and Barkatullah did not bat.

Bowling: Duthie 7-1-30-0; Ker 9-1-49-2; Rajput 9-0-30-0; McIntyre 9-0-35-1; Burnett -0-55-3.

Scotland

L. Philip c Yousuf b Iqbal	28	P. G. Duthie c Shoaib b Miandad	9
S. Rajput c Yousuf b Zakir	13	E. J. McIntyre not out	1
C. Scott b Wasim	0		
R. G. Swan c Ramiz b Iqbal	14	B 2, l-b 4, w 2, n-b 6	14
A. B. Russell c sub b Shoaib	12		
D. L. Snodgrass c Barkatullah b Iqbal	14	1/38 2/38 3/55 (8 wkts, 38 overs)	128
N. W. Burnett c Miandad b Shoaib	10	4/70 5/91 6/93	
A. Brown not out	13	7/107 8/123	

E. Ker did not bat.

Bowling: Barkatullah 7-1-19-0; Zakir 7-1-20-1; Wasim 7-1-21-1; Iqbal 8-1-28-3; Asif -1-14-0; Shoaib 3-0-11-2; Miandad 1-0-9-1.

Umpires: J. B. Connell and A. Wood.

NORTHAMPTONSHIRE v PAKISTANIS

At Bletchley, June 13, 14, 15. Drawn. Toss: Pakistanis. Local sponsorship took a touring team to Manor Fields again after visits by the West Indians in 1980 and 1984. But the decision did not please Imran, who described the conditions on the first day as "a disgrace" after a fortnight's heavy rain; and although the Pakistanis went close to victory, it was not a happy match for them. Injuries in the field to Ramiz (dislocated shoulder) and Tauseef, who broke a finger catching Capel, precluded both from selection for the Lord's Test, and this after Ramiz had gained some useful first-innings practice. The county side crumbled against Mudassar's medium-pace, and having at one time lost six wickets in as many overs, they conceded a lead of 88. Miandad (one six, eight fours) and Shoaib built attractively on that advantage and, having to bat for at least 45 overs or score an improbable 287 to win, Northamptonshire were saved only be determined batting from Wild and Ripley.

Close of play: First day, Pakistanis 178-6 (Mudassar Nazar 37*, Salim Yousuf 34*); Second day, Pakistanis 45-1 (Shoaib Mohammad 16*, Mansoor Akhtar 6*).

Pakistanis

Ramiz Raja c Larkins b Harper	60		
Shoaib Mohammad b Brown	1	– (1) not out	61
Mansoor Akhtar b Capel	17	3 – st Ripley b Harper	17
Javed Miandad c Boyd-Moss b Brown	5	– c and b Wild	86
Salim Malik c Ripley b Stevenson	17		
*Imran Khan b Cook	12	– (2) c Bailey b Capel	18
Mudassar Nazar c Cook b Harper	72		
†Salim Yousuf c Capel b Brown	41		
Wasim Akram c Ripley b Wild	3		
Tauseef Ahmed not out	16		
Mohsin Kamal lbw b Stevenson	1		
L-b 10, w 3	13	B 10, l-b 6	16
1/8 2/13 3/32 4/62 5/101	244	1/39 2/62 3/198 (3 wkts dec.)	198
6/111 7/195 8/198 9/243			

Bowling: *First Innings*—Capel 7-0-18-1; Brown 20-4-67-3; Cook 17-2-41-1; Stevenson 11-1-34-2; Harper 19-3-43-2; Williams 8-1-24-0; Wild 10-5-7-1. *Second Innings*—Capel 12-1-35-1; Brown 7-3-18-0; Stevenson 10-2-33-0; Harper 11-0-44-1; Williams 8-1-31-0; Cook 7-2-18-0; Wild 3.1-1-3-1.

Northamptonshire

R. J. Bailey c Wasim b Mudassar	56	– lbw b Imran	
*W. Larkins b Wasim	0	– c Yousuf b Imran	
R. J. Boyd-Moss b Mohsin	17	– c Shoaib b Mohsin	2
D. J. Capel c Mohsin b Mudassar	15	– c Tauseef b Mudassar	1
R. G. Williams c Yousuf b Mudassar	35	– c sub b Mohsin	1
D. J. Wild b Wasim	0	– c Wasim b Mansoor	2
R. A. Harper lbw b Mudassar	0	– lbw b Mohsin	
†D. Ripley run out	0	– not out	2
G. B. Stevenson b Mudassar	2	– c and b Mansoor	
N. G. B. Cook not out	19	– not out	
S. J. Brown b Tauseef	1		
L-b 6, w 1, n-b 4	11	B 6, l-b 1, w 1, n-b 2	1

1/1 2/31 3/75 4/116 5/126   156   1/5 2/10 3/33 4/69 5/69 (8 wkts) 13
6/131 7/134 8/136 9/138   6/71 7/121 8/121

Bowling: *First Innings*—Wasim 12–3–28–2; Imran 9–2–19–0; Tauseef 6.4–2–23–1; Mohsin 10–1–52–1; Mudassar 11–4–28–5. *Second Innings*—Imran 9–4–14–2; Wasim 12–6–17–0 Mudassar 14–6–23–1; Mohsin 9–1–50–3; Tauseef 1–0–4–0; Shoaib 5–1–11–0; Mansoor 3–0–7–2.

Umpires: J. Birkenshaw and B. Hassan.

ENGLAND v PAKISTAN

Second Cornhill Test

At Lord's, June 18, 19, 20, 22, 23. Drawn. Toss: England. The playing area was flooded or the eve of the match; it was flooded again on the final morning. Between times, there was opportunity for only seven hours ten minutes of cricket, and even this would have been greatly diminished but for the heroic work, at all hours of day and night, of the groundsman, Mic Hunt, and his staff. It was one of the most frustrating Test matches of recent times and following similar events at Old Trafford, it effectively reduced the series to a three-match rubber.

For the first time since its inception three seasons earlier, a payout was applicable on the TCCB's pluvius insurance policy, which guarantees ticket-holders a refund if a full day's pla is lost. As no cricket was possible on the second and fourth days (when tickets had been sol in advance), as well as the fifth (when no tickets were issued and no-one paid for entry), the potential claims amounted to some £230,000. Receipts for the match were an impressive £610,963 from the sale of 63,651 tickets.

That the first scheduled day contained 73 overs and was cut short only by poor light was a baffling achievement to those who had witnessed the ground on Wednesday afternoon, when it resembled nothing so much as a boating lake. Both teams were able to start at something near full strength, England reinstating Broad and Dilley at the expense of Fairbrother and DeFreitas. Pakistan could not consider either Ramiz Raja or Tauseef Ahmed because o injuries; Ijaz Ahmed, a prodigious talent at eighteen, was introduced to the middle order and Abdul Qadir, having at last joined the tour, was thrust directly into Test action.

The other important adjustment to Pakistan's strength concerned the captain, Imran Khan who was satisfied that he was now fit to bowl again and confirmed the point when England elected to bat on a dry pitch of little pace or bounce. Broad and Robinson, the Nottingham shire pair, opening together for the first time at Test level, were both severely examined by Imran's early-morning swing. It was, however, the first-change bowler, Mohsin Kamal, wh divided them, Robinson being adjudged caught behind down the leg side.

The one substantial contribution to a match otherwise devoid of memories now began Athey, who had managed only four half-centuries in 25 previous innings for his country, came in at No. 3, knowing that his place was once more under severe threat. By close of play he wa 107 not out, having acted on the advice of the team manager, M. J. Stewart, and adopted positive attitude. This transmitted itself immediately, for when Qadir was brought on for the velfth over of the innings, Athey refused to let him settle, sweeping him three times in that pening over and thereafter punishing anything which strayed from a good length. With Qadir understandably rusty, this amounted to a good deal.

Broad picked up the threads of his consistency in Australia with another half-century, ntirely commanding, before the niggling accuracy of Mudassar undid him and, soon fterwards, the impatient Gower. Gatting, arriving at 128 for three, survived a confident lbw ppeal from Wasim; umpire Constant gave him not out and was later berated by the Pakistan nanager, Haseeb Ahsan, who had tried unsuccessfully to have Constant removed from the anel for the series.

This sticky period in mid-afternoon was quickly left behind as Athey and Gatting added 02. Athey reached his maiden Test century, from 167 deliveries after 256 minutes, and Gatting seemed on the brink of something worthwhile when he set off for an injudicious econd run to Salim Malik at long leg.

There was no more play until 2.45 p.m. on Saturday, by which time a further 3,000 gallons f water had been removed from the outfield. Athey, after an innings of five and a quarter ours, during which he hit fourteen fours, was bowled by a very quick delivery from Imran, vith the new ball, and another perky night-watchman's contribution from French was ended y Wasim, who then disappointed the capacity crowd by disposing of Botham. England's last hree wickets added 63 runs, but there was no time for Pakistan to commence their reply on he Saturday; little did anyone imagine that they would not be granted a chance on the emaining days, either. – Alan Lee.

Man of the Match: C. W. J. Athey.

Close of play: First day, England 231-4 (C. W. J. Athey 107*, B. N. French 1*); Second day, No play; Third day, England 368; Fourth day, No play.

England

B. C. Broad b Mudassar	55	N. A. Foster b Qadir	21	
R. T. Robinson c Yousuf b Mohsin	7	P. H. Edmonds not out	17	
C. W. J. Athey b Imran	123	G. R. Dilley c Yousuf b Imran	17	
D. I. Gower c Yousuf b Mudassar	8	L-b 12, w 1, n-b 4	17	
M. W. Gatting run out	43			
B. N. French b Wasim	42	1/29 (2) 2/118 (1) 3/128 (4) 4/230 (5)	368	
I. T. Botham c Miandad b Wasim	6	5/272 (3) 6/294 (6) 7/305 (7)		
J. E. Emburey run out	12	8/329 (9) 9/340 (8) 10/368 (11)		

Bowling: Imran 34.5–7–90–2; Wasim 28–1–98–2; Mohsin 9–2–42–1; Qadir 25–1–100–1; Mudassar 16–6–26–2.

Pakistan

Mudassar Nazar, Shoaib Mohammad, Mansoor Akhtar, Javed Miandad, Salim Malik, Ijaz Ahmed, *Imran Khan, †Salim Yousuf, Wasim Akram, Abdul Qadir and Mohsin Kamal.

Umpires: D. J. Constant and A. G. T. Whitehead.

OXFORD & CAMBRIDGE UNIVERSITIES v PAKISTANIS

At Oxford, June 24, 25, 26. Drawn. Toss: Pakistanis. Rain once more denied the touring eam, robbing them of any play on the second and third days. On a slow, damp pitch, Atherton and Kilborn overcame the early loss of Bail, taking the score to 74 at lunch. Atherton, the Cambridge freshman, batted with considerable style and authority, and when he combined side lost five wickets for 26, Price, whose batting had been out of sorts all term, put on 50 with Weale and 33 with Perry before reaching his half-century. Saleem Jaffer, in nis second match of the tour, extracted lift but again aggravated the groin injury that had roubled him since the team's arrival in England.

Oxford & Cambridge Universities

P. A. C. Bail c Yousuf b Zakir	0	G. A. Pointer run out	
M. A. Atherton c Asif b Jaffer	43	J. N. Perry b Iqbal	2
M. J. Kilborn c Yousuf b Jaffer	28	T. Firth c Asif b Qadir	
*C. D. M. Tooley b Qadir	11		
R. D. Sardesai b Qadir	2	B 6, l-b 3, w 1, n-b 2	1
†D. J. Fell c Asif b Jaffer	2		
D. G. Price not out	51	1/2 2/74 3/82 4/85 5/90	20
S. D. Weale c and b Qadir	27	6/100 7/150 8/157 9/190	

Bowling: Zakir 17–6–32–1; Jaffer 18–10–17–3; Qadir 34.4–6–98–4; Iqbal 18–6–41–1; Mali 3–1–2–0; Mansoor 1–0–2–0.

Pakistanis

Ijaz Ahmed c Sardesai b Firth	6
Shoaib Mohammad not out	32
*Mansoor Akhtar not out	8
N-b 2	2

1/17   (1 wkt) 48

Salim Malik, Zakir Khan, Asif Mujtaba, †Salim Yousuf, Iqbal Qasim, Abdul Qadir, Mudassar Nazar and Saleem Jaffer did not bat.

Bowling: Firth 6–0–19–1; Pointer 5–0–25–0; Weale 1–0–4–0.

Umpires: P. J. Eele and D. S. Thompsett.

LEICESTERSHIRE v PAKISTANIS

At Leicester, June 27, 28, 29. Drawn. Toss: Leicestershire. The touring team availed themselves of batting practice on a good wicket, occupying a day and one session before declaring. Shoaib, getting slower the longer he batted, took 6 hours 22 minutes over his century and hit nine fours; Ijaz, Malik and Miandad all helped themselves to rather pedestrian half-centuries. The match lost significance as a contest when Leicestershire batted on until 4.15 p.m. on the final day. Boon took 251 minutes over his 81, hitting ten fours and two sixes, Willey an hour and 40 minutes over 76 (thirteen fours) and Cobb, ever cautious, used up 295 minutes in making 72. Leicestershire's 392 was their highest total against a touring side from Pakistan.

Close of play: First day, Pakistanis 237–3 (Shoaib Mohammad 84*, Salim Malik 26*). Second day, Leicestershire 146–3 (R. A. Cobb 62*, T. J. Boon 16*).

Pakistanis

Ijaz Ahmed c Briers b Such	60	– not out	6
Shoaib Mohammad c Benjamin b Willey	111		
Mansoor Akhtar b Such	8	– (2) c Cobb b DeFreitas	5
Javed Miandad c Gower b DeFreitas	52		
Salim Malik lbw b Clift	55	– (3) not out	50
*Imran Khan b Willey	25		
†Salim Yousuf not out	22		
Wasim Akram c Briers b Such	0		
Mohsin Kamal not out	8		
L-b 8, w 2, n-b 6	16	L-b 1	1

1/109 2/123 3/199 4/288   (7 wkts dec.) 346   1/21   (1 wkt) 11
5/294 6/329 7/330

Zakir Khan and Abdul Qadir did not bat.

Bowling: *First Innings*—DeFreitas 28–7–75–1; Benjamin 20–8–55–0; Clift 26–6–62–1; Such 26–3–85–3; Briers 4–0–10–0; Willey 21–3–51–2. *Second Innings*—DeFreitas 7–0–22–1; Clift 3–2–9–0; Such 8–0–16–0; Willey 3–0–7–0; Whitaker 5–0–33–0; Gower 1–0–9–0; Boon 3–0–22–0.

Leicestershire

R. A. Cobb lbw b Wasim	72		P. A. J. DeFreitas b Shoaib	29
N. E. Briers c Malik b Mohsin	13		W. K. M. Benjamin st Yousuf b Shoaib	12
D. I. Gower c Mansoor b Mohsin	26		P. M. Such not out	0
J. J. Whitaker c Imran b Zakir	22			
T. J. Boon b Wasim	81		B 1, l-b 9, w 8, n-b 8	26
*P. Willey b Imran	76			
P. B. Clift b Wasim	32		1/34 2/78 3/113 4/167 5/288	392
†P. Whitticase c Ijaz b Zakir	3		6/331 7/336 8/360 9/391	

Bowling: Imran 27–6–53–1; Mohsin 28–9–102–2; Wasim 23–4–82–3; Zakir 29–5–105–2; Shoaib 7.3–1–25–2; Mansoor 1–0–1–0; Ijaz 2–0–14–0.

Umpires: J. W. Holder and H. J. Rhodes.

ENGLAND v PAKISTAN

Third Cornhill Test

At Leeds, July 2, 3, 4, 6. Pakistan won by an innings and 18 runs, needing only five overs and one ball for victory on the fourth morning. For England, it was a dismal reminder of their defeat by India on the same ground a year earlier. Because it contained cracks and its bounce was irregular, the pitch was criticised, but more culpable were England's batsmen. Of their bowlers, only Foster used the conditions properly, moving the ball into and away from the bat and forcing the batsmen to play. He took the first six wickets to fall and finished with eight, a display of fast-medium bowling that matched Imran's. Dilley's away-swing rarely threatened, Capel's line and length did not pass muster, and Edmonds vacillated between attack and containment. England had omitted Emburey in favour of a fourth seamer, Capel, while Richards stood in for French, who had not recovered from chicken-pox. Pakistan were unchanged.

England chose to bat first on a sunny morning of high cloud and little breeze. It seemed ideal for batting, and yet after 63 minutes they were 31 for five, undone in the main by pace and swing. Robinson, to the third ball, was not fully forward; Athey, in the seventh over, played late; Broad, in the eighth, was neither forward nor back; Gatting played no stroke; and Gower played on, trying to take his bat away from a ball that lifted and was leaving him. Imran's figures were 7–1–16–3; Wasim Akram's, when he gave way to Mudassar, were 10–4–20–2.

Botham's watchful approach saw him through almost two hours before Mudassar, having already bruised Botham's instep so that he would not take the field when Pakistan batted, tempted him to drive at a gentle out-swinger. Richards played no stroke to an in-swinger from Wasim, and when the young left-armer tired, Mohsin Kamal wound up the innings with three wickets in nine balls. Capel, 47 not out at tea, had no sooner reached a début fifty with his sixth boundary than he drove a ball of full length and Mohsin took the return catch above his head. He had batted well for three hours thirteen minutes, proving the wisdom of a full forward defence.

Pakistan had 27 overs to stumps and in that time England put down three catches off Foster's bowling. Mansoor, first ball and then in the 26th over, survived hard chances to Edmonds and Emburey in the slips, and Emburey also dropped Yousuf, second ball, a straightforward catch and a costly miss as the night-watchman batted throughout the Friday morning session.

Until he drove a full toss to cover in the final over, needing 1 for his hundred, Salim Malik quietly imposed himself on the second day's play. His innings, a lesson in application and technique, occupied five and a half hours and his 99 came from 238 balls with eight fours. Adding 72 runs to the side having been taking the game away from England, and on the third morning Ijaz and Wasim Akram took it beyond reach. Ijaz captivated the Saturday crowd with his dashing strokes: four off the back foot behind point and then, with two dancing steps, a straight boundary off successive balls from Edmonds; a turn of the wrists brought a ninth four and his fifty. Wasim Akram's 43 from 41 balls was a swashbuckler's innings containing four sixes and two fours. Edmonds put an end to the second stage of England's misery by running in from fine leg to dismiss him with a lovely tumbling catch.

But stage three began immediately, Broad and Robinson going in Imran's first and second overs. Athey and Gower then put on 35 in the 38 minutes to lunch, batting as if there were no tomorrow. Broad had been unlucky, adjudged caught behind off Imran's second ball, which brushed his left hand after he had removed it from the bat and was snatched up in front of him by the wicket-keeper. The TV replay, after several viewings, suggested Broad was luckless on two counts. Yousuf was less successful in the afternoon when, having dropped the ball and then retrieved it, he appealed to have Botham caught behind. The umpire was not impressed. Nor was Botham, who reacted angrily, and umpire Palmer had to be quick to separate them. Imran also acted smartly, dressing down Yousuf in no uncertain manner.

While Qadir kept one end tight through 23 successive overs, the quick bowlers operated from the Football Stand end to exploit the uncertain bounce. Imran bowled immaculately, and with his fifth wicket, that of Richards, well taken at forward short leg, he became the eighth bowler to capture 300 Test wickets. On the fourth morning, he took his tally for the innings to seven and for the match to ten. Capel had again batted soundly for three hours, but England's fate had been sealed since Thursday morning's gambit. That Imran would have made the same opening move was little consolation to Gatting. – G.W.

Man of the Match: Imran Khan.   *Attendance:* 44,500; *receipts* £303,057.

Close of play: First day, Pakistan 76-2 (Mansoor Akhtar 24*, Salim Yousuf 4*); Second day, Pakistan 280-7 (Ijaz Ahmed 33*, Wasim Akram 0*); Third day, England 186-7 (D. J. Capel 26*, N. A. Foster 13*).

England

B. C. Broad c Yousuf b Wasim	8	– c Yousuf b Imran	4
R. T. Robinson lbw b Imran	0	– c Malik b Imran	2
C. W. J. Athey c Yousuf b Imran	4	– lbw b Imran	26
D. I. Gower b Imran	10	– b Imran	55
*M. W. Gatting lbw b Wasim	8	– c Miandad b Wasim	9
I. T. Botham c Yousuf b Mudassar	26	– (8) c Mudassar b Mohsin	24
D. J. Capel c and b Mohsin	53	– (6) c Ijaz b Imran	28
†C. J. Richards lbw b Wasim	6	– (7) c Ijaz b Imran	2
N. A. Foster c Malik b Mohsin	9	– b Wasim	22
P. H. Edmonds c Yousuf b Mohsin	0	– not out	0
G. R. Dilley not out	1	– b Imran	0
B 1, l-b 8, w 1, n-b 1	11	B 5, l-b 12, w 7, n-b 3	27
	136		**199**

1/1 (2) 2/13 (3) 3/13 (1) 4/31 (5)   1/4 (1) 2/9 (2) 3/60 (3) 4/94 (5)
5/31 (4) 6/85 (6) 7/113 (8)   5/120 (4) 6/122 (7) 7/160 (8)
8/133 (7) 9/133 (10) 10/136 (9)   8/197 (6) 9/197 (9) 10/199 (11)

Bowling: *First Innings*—Imran 19-3-37-3; Wasim 14-4-36-3; Qadir 5-0-14-0; Mudassar 14-5-18-1; Mohsin 8.4-2-22-3. *Second Innings*—Imran 19.1-5-40-7; Wasim 21-5-55-2; Qadir 27-5-60-0; Mudassar 2-0-8-0; Mohsin 9-4-19-1.

Pakistan

Mudassar Nazar lbw b Foster	24	
Shoaib Mohammad c Richards b Foster	16	
Mansoor Akhtar lbw b Foster	29	
†Salim Yousuf c Athey b Foster	37	
Javed Miandad c Gatting b Foster	0	
Salim Malik c Gower b Edmonds	99	
*Imran Khan c Richards b Foster	26	
Ijaz Ahmed c Athey b Foster	50	
Wasim Akram c Edmonds b Foster	43	
Abdul Qadir b Dilley	2	
Mohsin Kamal not out	3	
B 5, l-b 13, w 1, n-b 5	24	
	353	

1/22 (2) 2/60 (1) 3/86 (3) 4/86 (5)   353
5/152 (4) 6/208 (7) 7/280 (6)
8/318 (8) 9/328 (10) 10/353 (9)

Bowling: Dilley 33-7-89-1; Foster 46.2-15-107-8; Capel 18-1-64-0; Edmonds 25-10-59-1; Gatting 9-3-16-0.

Umpires: K. E. Palmer and D. R. Shepherd.

†MINOR COUNTIES v PAKISTANIS

At Burton upon Trent, July 9, 10. Drawn. Toss: Pakistanis. Two days of glorious strokeplay and exciting hitting came to an end with Minor Counties 36 runs short of a target of 245 in 158 minutes. For the visitors, Shoaib was in excellent touch, setting the tone for the match with 90 in 142 minutes, including 60 in boundaries, although Greensword, the 43-year-old Durham medium-pace bowler, gave nothing away. Thanks to the left-handed Henderson, with two sixes and eleven fours in two and a half hours, and Plumb, Minor Counties were in a position to declare at their overnight score, whereupon Ijaz, hitting fifteen fours, exhibited some breathtaking strokes in reaching a hundred by lunch. Atkinson and Herbert made it clear that the chase was on, the former taking 26 off one over from Iqbal Qasim, including two off-drives on to the pavilion roof. However, with the Pakistanis bowling only fourteen overs in an hour before the last twenty overs, the target was kept out of reach.

Pakistanis

*Mudassar Nazar c Atkinson b Bunting	11		
Shoaib Mohammad c Garnham b Bunting	90	– (1) not out	75
Mansoor Akhtar lbw b Greensword	27		
Ijaz Ahmed lbw b Greensword	0	– (2) b Herbert	104
Asif Mujtaba c Henderson b Green	62	– not out	41
Manzoor Elahi c Herbert b Green	5	– (3) lbw b Herbert	4
Iqbal Qasim c Roope b Greensword	0		
Zakir Khan b Greensword	2		
Mohsin Kamal not out	0	– (4) c Bunting b Herbert	0
L-b 6, w 1	7	B 4, l-b 4, w 1	9

1/28 2/78 3/79 4/173 5/188   (8 wkts dec.) 204   1/154 2/164   (3 wkts dec.) 233
6/190 7/204 8/204   3/164

Azeem Hafeez and †Zulqarnain did not bat.

Bowling: *First Innings*—Merry 9–1–34–0; Bunting 10–2–62–2; Green 13.1–1–49–2; Greensword 11–3–25–4; Herbert 3–0–20–0; Plumb 2–1–8–0. *Second Innings*—Green 9–2–22–0; Bunting 8–2–34–0; Merry 7–0–40–0; Greensword 7–0–35–0; Roope 11–2–33–0; Herbert 11.5–0–61–3.

Minor Counties

S. R. Atkinson c Iqbal b Zakir	17	– c Zulqarnain b Azeem	60
*S. G. Plumb c Azeem b Manzoor	57	– (6) b Mohsin	1
S. P. Henderson c Mudassar b Mohsin	82	– c Asif b Zakir	21
D. A. Banks not out	16	– lbw b Zakir	13
†M. A. Garnham not out	9	– not out	38
R. Herbert (did not bat)		– (2) c Ijaz b Zakir	60
G. R. J. Roope (did not bat)		– not out	3
L-b 10, w 2	12	B 1, l-b 4, w 8	13

1/28 2/137 3/173   (3 wkts dec.) 193   1/112 2/149 3/149   (5 wkts) 209
    4/181 5/200

S. Greensword, R. C. Green, W. G. Merry and R. A. Bunting did not bat.

Bowling: *First Innings*—Mohsin 17–4–52–1; Zakir 8–2–13–1; Azeem 12–0–66–0; Iqbal 6–1–34–0; Asif 1–0–5–0; Manzoor 6–2–13–1. *Second Innings*—Mohsin 14–1–60–1; Zakir 8–1–38–3; Iqbal 4–0–34–0; Azeem 11–0–46–1; Manzoor 5–1–26–0.

Umpires: D. B. Harrison and C. T. Spencer.

NOTTINGHAMSHIRE v PAKISTANIS

At Nottingham, July 11, 13, 14. Drawn. Toss: Pakistanis. The tourists were content to use this game as batting practice for the Fourth Test, but when Nottinghamshire provided little resistance on the second day they had an opportunity to press for victory. Rain, however, ended play during the afternoon session on the final day. Without Hadlee and Rice in the home team's attack, the Pakistanis scored heavily on the first day, Mansoor hitting 102 of his 137 (186 minutes) in boundaries and Mudassar batting for 249 minutes while playing a supporting role. By the end of the second day, Miandad not having enforced the follow-on, they had extended their lead to 410, despite being kept in check by a fine spell from Saxelby. Nottinghamshire had to bat throughout the last day to save the game, and, helped by Robinson, Birch played with sufficient authority to thwart the Pakistani bowlers until the rain came. Earlier, there were acrimonious scenes when Miandad, prompted by a note from the team's manager, disputed the right of umpire Dudleston to no-ball and officially warn for a second time Mohsin Kamal, who had bowled five short-pitched balls in an over to Birch. Mohsin had already had an unofficial warning from umpire Hampshire. Miandad argued that there had been no decision to limit the number of bouncers per over on the tour, but the umpires insisted they were correct in applying Law 42.8. This was upheld by the TCCB.

Close of play: First day, Pakistanis 412-9 (Zulqarnain 0*); Second day, Pakistanis 186-6 (Mudassar Nazar 61*, Zakir Khan 22*).

Pakistanis

Mudassar Nazar c K. P. Evans b Birch	100	– (6) not out	61
Shoaib Mohammad c Saxelby b Fraser-Darling	14	– (1) c R. J. Evans b Saxelby	0
Mansoor Akhtar c Saxelby b Birch	137	– (5) lbw b K. P. Evans	33
*Javed Miandad b K. P. Evans	7	– (2) c Robinson b K. P. Evans	46
Salim Malik c Fraser-Darling b Birch	39	– (4) c French b Saxelby	0
Ijaz Ahmed b Hemmings	34	– (3) c Birch b Saxelby	19
Abdul Qadir c Robinson b Fraser-Darling	24	– b Saxelby	4
Zakir Khan c Hemmings b K. P. Evans	17	– not out	22
Mohsin Kamal b K. P. Evans	28		
†Zulqarnain not out	0		
B 7, l-b 1, w 3, n-b 1	12	N-b 1	1

1/27 2/251 3/259 4/265 5/335   (9 wkts dec.) 412   1/0 2/52 3/52   (6 wkts dec.) 186
6/344 7/362 8/412 9/412   4/82 5/104 6/109

Azeem Hafeez did not bat.

Bowling: *First Innings*—Saxelby 19-1-66-0; Fraser-Darling 18-2-97-2; K. P. Evans 17.3-0-65-3; Birch 15-4-58-3; Hemmings 23-8-81-1; Afford 9-0-37-0. *Second Innings*—Saxelby 14.5-5-36-4; Fraser-Darling 11-0-76-0; K. P. Evans 12-2-37-2; Birch 7-1-27-0; R. J. Evans 2-0-10-0.

Nottinghamshire

D. W. Randall b Qadir	38	– c Mohsin b Azeem	5
*R. T. Robinson c and b Zakir	11	– c Shoaib b Mohsin	49
P. Johnson c Mudassar b Mohsin	7	– (5) c Ijaz b Zakir	13
J. D. Birch c Ijaz b Zakir	26	– (3) not out	71
R. J. Evans c Ijaz b Zakir	4	– (4) c Malik b Mohsin	0
†B. N. French c Qadir b Azeem	17	– c sub b Qadir	14
C. D. Fraser-Darling b Qadir	33	– not out	0
K. P. Evans lbw b Qadir	21		
K. Saxelby c Azeem b Mohsin	9		
E. E. Hemmings not out	2		
J. A. Afford c Ijaz b Zakir	0		
B 2, l-b 3, w 4, n-b 1	10	L-b 12, w 7, n-b 3	22

1/37 2/60 3/67 4/80 5/95   188   1/13 2/106 3/106   (5 wkts) 174
6/134 7/150 8/173 9/187   4/147 5/174

Bowling: *First Innings*—Mohsin 13-1-44-2; Azeem 9-1-58-1; Zakir 13-4-27-4; Qadir 17-2-54-3. *Second Innings*—Mohsin 13-0-55-2; Azeem 6-1-26-1; Mudassar 8-1-30-0; Zakir 13-1-45-1; Qadir 1.3-0-6-1.

Umpires: B. Dudleston and J. H. Hampshire.

GLAMORGAN v PAKISTANIS

At Cardiff, July 15, 16, 17. Drawn. Toss: Glamorgan. Rain prevented any play on the first day and delayed the start on the final day until three o'clock. The county resumed in a desperate plight at 19 for four, Wasim Akram having found steep bounce the previous evening on a pitch that gave assistance throughout; but Maynard and Todd rallied them with a spectacular partnership of 139. Todd, signed by Glamorgan after making a Benson and Hedges century for Minor Counties against them in May, scored 90 in 97 minutes with two sixes and fifteen fours. Often it was more swashbuckling than scientific, but it was always splendid entertainment and quite in contrast to Shoaib Mohammad's batting the previous day, when he took just over three hours to score 63. Maynard contributed to the barrage of big hits, with one six and ten fours providing the major part of his 66 not out.

Close of play: First day, No play; Second day, Glamorgan 19-4 (M. P. Maynard 4*, M. L. Roberts 2*).

Pakistanis

Ramiz Raja c Derrick b Smith	1	†Salim Yousuf not out		6
Shoaib Mohammad c Todd b Derrick	63			
Ijaz Ahmed c Maynard b Derrick	20	L-b 1, w 8, n-b 11		20
*Javed Miandad c Roberts b van Zyl	1			
Salim Malik not out	50	1/3 2/53 3/73	(5 wkts dec.)	166
Asif Mujtaba c Roberts b Derrick	5	4/130 5/135		

Zakir Khan, Abdul Qadir, Wasim Akram and Mohsin Kamal did not bat.

Bowling: van Zyl 20.2-4-60-1; Smith 10-0-46-1; Derrick 24-7-42-3; Ontong 3-1-2-0; Holmes 5-2-15-0.

Glamorgan

S. P. James b Wasim	3	P. A. Todd c Asif b Mohsin		90
*H. Morris c Miandad b Wasim	0	R. C. Ontong not out		4
A. R. Butcher c Miandad b Wasim	2	L-b 2, w 2, n-b 8		12
G. C. Holmes c Yousuf b Mohsin	4			
M. P. Maynard not out	66	1/3 2/7 3/8 4/13	(6 wkts)	187
†M. L. Roberts c Zakir b Mohsin	6	5/37 6/176		

J. Derrick, I. Smith and C. J. P. G. van Zyl did not bat.

Bowling: Wasim 14-3-58-3; Mohsin 11-1-41-3; Zakir 7-0-52-0; Qadir 8-0-33-0; Miandad 1-0-1-0.

Umpires: J. Birkenshaw and D. O. Oslear.

WORCESTERSHIRE v PAKISTANIS

At Worcester, July 18, 19, 20. Drawn. Toss: Pakistanis. Spectacular batting by Shoaib and Mansoor compensated for a day of stoppages and an early finish because of rain: after the departure of Mudassar in the second over, they put on 303 in 218 minutes, a second-wicket record for the Pakistanis in England. The previous one was 291 by Zaheer Abbas and Mushtaq Mohammad in the First Test at Birmingham in 1971. Only 39 balls were bowled on the second day, and on the third Worcestershire laboured to 100 for three before the game came alive again during an unbeaten partnership between D'Oliveira and Neale, who added 214 in 56 overs. D'Oliveira, who reached his hundred in 164 minutes, hit four sixes and thirteen fours in all, while Neale, who faced 134 balls for his second half-century of the season, hit eleven fours.

Close of play: First day, Pakistanis 304-1 (Shoaib Mohammad 121*, Mansoor Akhtar 169*); Second day, Worcestershire 17-0 (T. S. Curtis 9*, G. J. Lord 3*).

Pakistanis

Mudassar Nazar c D'Oliveira b Ellcock 0
Shoaib Mohammad not out 121
Mansoor Akhtar not out 169
    L-b 6, w 4, n-b 4 14

1/1   (1 wkt dec.) 304

Salim Malik, *Imran Khan, Ijaz Ahmed, Ramiz Raja, †Salim Yousuf, Abdul Qadir, Wasim Akram and Zakir Khan did not bat.

Bowling: Dilley 8–1–42–0; Ellcock 10–0–69–1; Newport 8–0–36–0; Pridgeon 10–3–29–0; Illingworth 12–2–60–0; Hick 9–0–62–0.

Worcestershire

T. S. Curtis lbw b Mudassar 35	*P. A. Neale not out 69	
G. J. Lord c Malik b Imran 6	B 5, l-b 7, w 6, n-b 5 23	
G. A. Hick b Mudassar 11		
D. B. D'Oliveira not out 131	1/23 2/54 3/61 (3 wkts) 275	

†S. J. Rhodes, P. J. Newport, R. K. Illingworth, R. M. Ellcock, G. R. Dilley and A. P. Pridgeon did not bat.

Bowling: Imran 15–5–29–1; Wasim 15–4–47–0; Mudassar 13–5–21–2; Qadir 28–7–75–0; Zakir 12–1–51–0; Shoaib 5–0–33–0; Ijaz 2–0–7–0.

Umpires: M. J. Kitchen and D. S. Thompsett.

ENGLAND v PAKISTAN

Fourth Cornhill Test

At Birmingham, July 23, 24, 25, 27, 28. Drawn. A placid Edgbaston pitch looked certain to produce a draw from the time Pakistan dealt comfortably with Gatting's decision to bowl first after winning the toss. The match, however, suddenly sprang to life after lunch on the final day, with England going close to achieving a remarkable victory.

An incisive spell of fast bowling from Foster, supported well by Botham, brought a swift and unexpected end to Pakistan's second innings and left England with the difficult, but not impossible, target of 124 from the last eighteen overs. Given a brisk start by Broad, who made 30 of an opening stand of 37 in five overs, England should have levelled the series. But Pakistan were able to harness the talents of Imran Khan and Wasim Akram throughout the run-chase, and without the one-day restrictions on short-pitched bowling and wides, or of fielding circles, England were kept in check as wickets fell. In the end they were just 15 runs short of their goal.

Both captains later agreed that England, with their vast experience of one-day cricket, should have achieved victory; but it was Gatting himself who had to field a great deal of criticism, some of it particularly unsavoury in the tabloid press, on the first two days. He had assumed that, with Birmingham suffering as badly as elsewhere during the prolonged spell of wet weather, a greener than normal pitch might respond to his bowlers early in the match.

It was surprising, therefore, that England chose to omit Radford from their twelve, at a time when he was the leading wicket-taker in the County Championship, and opted instead to play two spinners. This left England a pace bowler short, and Pakistan cashed in by reaching 250 for three by stumps on the first day. It was occupied throughout by Mudassar Nazar, who scored his ninth Test century, mainly in the company of Javed Miandad. Miandad made the most of being dropped at slip by Botham when 15 and scored 75 in a third-wicket partnership of 135.

Rain and bad light delayed the start of the second day until 1.25 p.m. and there were several stoppages during the afternoon, one of which attracted particular attention. Umpires Whitehead and Meyer emerged from the pavilion, only to be left standing alone on the square, waiting to restart the game, while the England team remained in their dressing-room. It later emerged that no player was keeping a lookout, and while blame was later apportioned in several directions, England's absence was not well received. As it turned out, the light again deteriorated and the umpires, to the bemusement of the crowd, returned to their own quarters with England still nowhere in sight.

In between the interruptions, Dilley slowed down the Pakistan advance by taking the wickets of Mudassar, after almost seven hours, Malik and Imran in the space of four overs on the way to only his second five-wicket return in Test cricket. But the tourists were then allowed to reach 439. Botham dropped Salim Yousuf when he was 4 and the wicket-keeper went on to score 91, his highest in fifteen Tests.

England's response on the third day was dominated by an opening stand of 119 between Broad and Robinson. The innings faltered in the middle as Imran, extracting more from the pitch than any bowler previously, worked his way towards his 21st Test haul of five wickets or more; but Gatting, either side of the rest day, silenced some of his critics with a fighting 124. He batted for 6 hours 39 minutes, hit sixteen fours, and with help from Emburey and Foster, earned his side an 82-run advantage.

Just under an hour was left of the fourth day when Pakistan began their second innings. There had been nothing to suggest that anything other than a draw would be achieved, and by lunch on the fifth day (74 for one) they had all but erased the arrears. Foster, however, sent a shiver of panic through the Pakistan dressing-room as Shoaib, Mansoor and Miandad were dismissed in quick succession. Botham lifted England's hopes further with an acrobatic return catch to account for Malik and followed up by bowling Ijaz. But a crucial break of thirteen minutes for bad light and a stubborn innings of 37 from Imran kept England in the field until the start of the final hour.

England's pursuit of their target after the departure of Broad was hampered by three run-outs. Athey was involved, though not wholly to blame, in all of them, and in the later stages of the innings he could manage only 14 runs in seven overs – a disappointing performance that was to cost him his place in the Fifth Test.

With poor weather dominating the first four days, the attendance was just 42,500 with receipts totalling £287,080. Thankfully, there was no repetition of the crowd trouble which had marred the one-day international between the two sides at Edgbaston in May. The match profits, however, were considerably reduced by the necessity of having a large police and stewarding presence on the ground throughout the five days. – Graham Otway.

Man of the Match: M. W. Gatting.

Close of play: First day, Pakistan 250-3 (Mudassar Nazar 102*, Salim Malik 13*); Second day, England 18-0 (B. C. Broad 14*, R. T. Robinson 2*); Third day, England 273-5 (M. W. Gatting 35*, I. T. Botham 16*); Fourth day, Pakistan 38-0 (Mudassar Nazar 6*, Shoaib Mohammad 32*).

Pakistan

Mudassar Nazar lbw b Dilley	124	– b Dilley	10
Shoaib Mohammad c Foster b Edmonds	18	– lbw b Foster	50
Mansoor Akhtar b Foster	26	– lbw b Foster	17
Javed Miandad lbw b Dilley	75	– c Emburey b Foster	4
Salim Malik c French b Dilley	24	– c and b Botham	17
Ijaz Ahmed lbw b Botham	20	– b Botham	11
*Imran Khan c Emburey b Dilley	0	– lbw b Foster	37
†Salim Yousuf not out	91	– c Gatting b Edmonds	17
Wasim Akram c Botham b Foster	26	– c Edmonds b Dilley	6
Abdul Qadir c Edmonds b Dilley	6	– run out	20
Mohsin Kamal run out	10	– not out	0
B 4, l-b 11, w 1, n-b 3	19	L-b 13, w 1, n-b 2	16

1/44(2) 2/83 (3) 3/218 (4) 4/284 (1)   439   1/47 (1) 2/80 (3) 3/85 (4)   205
5/289 (5) 6/289 (7) 7/317 (6)   4/104 (5) 5/104 (2) 6/116 (6)
8/360 (9) 9/384 (10) 10/439 (11)   7/156 (8) 8/165 (9) 9/204 (7)
                                  10/205 (10)

Bowling: *First Innings*—Dilley 35-6-92-5; Foster 37-8-107-2; Emburey 26-7-48-0; Edmonds 24.3-12-50-1; Botham 48-13-121-1; Gatting 3-0-6-0. *Second Innings*—Foster 27-7-59-4; Dilley 18-3-53-2; Emburey 4-1-3-0; Botham 20.3-3-66-2; Edmonds 4-1-11-1.

England

B. C. Broad c Yousuf b Imran	54	– c Mudassar b Imran	30
R. T. Robinson c Yousuf b Wasim	80	– c Imran b Wasim	4
C. W. J. Athey b Imran	0	– (6) not out	14
D. I. Gower c Yousuf b Imran	61	– (3) b Imran	18
*M. W. Gatting c Wasim b Imran	124	– run out	8
†B. N. French b Imran	0	– (9) not out	1
I. T. Botham c and b Wasim	37	– (4) c Mohsin b Wasim	6
J. E. Emburey lbw b Wasim	58	– (7) run out	20
N. A. Foster run out	29		
P. H. Edmonds not out	24	– (8) run out	0
G. R. Dilley b Imran	2		
B 1, l-b 24, w 11, n-b 16	52	L-b 7, w 1	8

1/119 (1) 2/132 (3) 3/157 (2) 4/251 (4)   521   1/37 (1) 2/39 (2)   (7 wkts) 109
5/251 (6) 6/300 (7) 7/443 (8)   3/53 (4) 4/72 (3)
8/484 (5) 9/512 (9) 10/521 (11)   5/73 (5) 6/108 (7)
    7/108 (8)

Bowling: *First Innings*—Imran 41.5-8-129-6; Wasim 43-12-83-3; Qadir 21-4-65-0; Mudassar 35-7-97-0; Mohsin 29-2-122-0. *Second Innings*—Imran 9-0-61-2; Wasim 8.4-0-41-2.

Umpires: B. J. Meyer and A. G. T. Whitehead.

HAMPSHIRE v PAKISTANIS

At Southampton, August 1, 2, 3. Drawn. Toss: Pakistanis. The match was destined to end in a draw once Imran Khan, who did not take an active part on the second and third days, had opted to give his side batting practice rather than set Hampshire a sporting target. The first day was dominated by Ramiz Raja, back after a shoulder injury, who pulled and cut sixteen fours in an innings lasting four and a half hours. Terry (seventeen fours) and Turner, between several interruptions for rain, mastered the guile of Qadir and the left-arm pace of Wasim Akram to enable Hampshire, 107 behind, to declare before the start of the third morning in the hope of a run-chase in the afternoon. A scintillating innings of 127 by Mansoor in just 105 minutes, which included eight sixes and twelve fours, entertained the spectators: of a fifth-wicket stand of 59 with Shoaib, he scored 58. The late declaration enabled Chris Smith enough time to hit his 1,000th run of the season.

Close of play: First day, Hampshire 17-0 (V. P. Terry 12*, C. L. Smith 4*); Second day, Hampshire 256-4 (V. P. Terry 119*, N. G. Cowley 12*).

Pakistanis

Ramiz Raja b Connor	150	– (2) lbw b Tremlett	25
Shoaib Mohammad c Cowley b Connor	9	– (6) not out	1
Ijaz Ahmed c Nicholas b Tremlett	8	– c Parks b Bakker	20
Mansoor Akhtar c R. A. Smith b Maru	20	– c Terry b Tremlett	127
Salim Malik lbw b Maru	40	– c Connor b Tremlett	17
Mudassar Nazar b Maru	15	– (1) c R. A. Smith b Tremlett	13
*Imran Khan c Parks b Bakker	48		
†Salim Yousuf st Parks b Maru	24		
Wasim Akram c Connor b Cowley	32		
Abdul Qadir c C. L. Smith b Cowley	14		
Mohsin Kamal not out	1		
L-b 2	2	L-b 6, n-b 1	7

1/31 2/46 3/112 4/185 5/214   363   1/26 2/46 3/74   (5 wkts dec.) 210
6/283 7/293 8/343 9/361   4/151 5/210

Bowling: *First Innings*—Connor 25-4-75-2; Bakker 20-2-58-1; Tremlett 15-2-52-1; Cowley 23-0-88-2; Maru 32-5-88-4. *Second Innings*—Connor 9-2-24-0; Bakker 16-3-45-1; Tremlett 17.2-2-84-4; Maru 2-0-6-0; Cowley 4-0-45-0.

Hampshire

V. P. Terry not out	119	– lbw b Mudassar	20
C. L. Smith c Mansoor b Mohsin	22	– not out	58
*M. C. J. Nicholas c Yousuf b Mohsin	3	– not out	28
D. R. Turner c Yousuf b Mohsin	71		
R. A. Smith b Mohsin	17		
N. G. Cowley not out	12		
B 4, l-b 5, w 1, n-b 2	12	L-b 3	3

1/50 2/62 3/216 4/242   (4 wkts dec.) 256   1/51   (1 wkt) 109

†R. J. Parks, T. M. Tremlett, R. J. Maru, C. A. Connor and P. J. Bakker did not bat.

Bowling: *First Innings*—Qadir 28–2–111–0; Wasim 17–2–68–0; Mohsin 21–4–62–4; Malik 2–1–6–0. *Second Innings*—Wasim 10–2–24–0; Mohsin 9–0–41–0; Malik 4–0–4–0; Qadir 7–3–18–0; Mudassar 7–1–19–1.

Umpires: K. Taylor and R. A. White.

ENGLAND v PAKISTAN

Fifth Cornhill Test

At The Oval, August 6, 7, 8, 10, 11. Drawn. Toss: Pakistan. Gatting and Botham stoically withstood Pakistan's push for victory on the final day to bring England belated solace in a summer of diminishing returns. Their four and a quarter hours' diligence pegged Pakistan to a 1-0 win in the series, their first series victory in England.

To overturn such a proficient side, England needed to bat first on a sound, somewhat slowish pitch. But Imran called correctly for the first time in four Tests, and by lunch on the second day his batsmen had ensured England's third successive defeat in a home series. By tea on the third, England were engaged in a formidable rearguard action; by the close of play on the fourth, and already following on, they were still 381 runs behind with seven wickets in hand.

England replaced Athey, after a run of fourteen Tests, with Moxon and again omitted Radford to accommodate both spinners. Pakistan recalled Ramiz Raja and Tauseef Ahmed after injury and left out Shoaib Mohammad and Mohsin Kamal for the first time in the series. When Botham and Dilley removed Ramiz and Mansoor in the first 50 minutes, there seemed no possible scenario for Pakistan to compile a record score. However, Miandad undermined England's bid to square the series by first completing an overdue maiden Test century against them and then progressing to his fourth double-hundred in Tests, the seventh batsman to achieve this distinction. Having survived the most difficult of chances to Foster at long leg when 9, Miandad passed 6,000 runs in Tests on the first day, when the measured Mudassar and the more flamboyant Malik accompanied him to his fifteenth Test hundred, made from 197 balls. England were hampered by injuries to Dilley (ankle) and Foster (strained side) and had to forego Foster's services for the remainder of the innings.

Imaginative strokeplay sent Malik darting from 64 to the 90s early on the second day as he moved impressively to his sixth Test hundred – the first outside his homeland. Out soon afterwards, in almost four and a half hours he had faced 237 balls, hit only six fours and added 234 with Miandad, a record for Pakistan's fourth wicket against England. Next Imran, who insisted this was to be his last Test, registered his first hundred against England, racing from 57 to three figures while Miandad remained runless. Miandad, by now, had tired, despite his intention of attacking Sobers's Test record of 365 not out, and after ten hours seventeen minutes, during which he faced 521 balls and hit a six and 28 fours, he tapped back a return catch to Dilley. Good work by Radford and Botham ended Imran's innings as he went for a fourth run on the stroke from Ijaz which brought up the 600. He had batted for four and a quarter hours, hitting one six and eleven fours.

On the third morning, Ijaz and Yousuf continued their partnership to 89, a record for Pakistan's seventh wicket against England, and Dilley picked up late wickets to return six for 154, his best bowling analysis in Test cricket. Because of the worsening light, Imran had had to abandon any notion of declaring and so the innings ran its mammoth course. Pakistan's 708, in 13 hours 40 minutes, was their highest total, surpassing their 674 for six against India in Faisalabad in 1984-85; it was also the sixth largest in any Test match and the second highest conceded by England. The 217 runs conceded by Botham, from 52 overs, were the most by an England bowler, passing the 204 by I. A. R. Peebles, from 71 overs, against Australia, also at The Oval, in 1930.

England's position worsened when Broad was caught behind off Imran's fourth ball, and the miserable canvas soon portrayed 78 for four before Gatting, with a sturdy half-century, and Botham saw them to Saturday's close without further loss. For England to survive, either of these two had to bat throughout the fourth day. But soon Qadir's bouncy leg-spin began to have its effect. Only Emburey withstood to any extent, hitting a six and six fours as Qadir brought England to their knees with his best Test figures of seven for 96, including a spell of three for 13 in 37 balls.

Following on, 476 runs behind, England contemplated the humiliation of losing by a bigger margin than any previous England defeat. And that ignominy took on a realistic look when they lost Moxon, Robinson and Gower. On the final day, however, when Pakistan were without Wasim Akram, in hospital for an appendix operation, the wicket of Broad was their only setback. Gatting reached his ninth Test hundred, the fifth in his last fourteen matches, and although giving chances of varying degrees of difficulty at 5, 23, 58, 60 and 107 he batted for five and threequarter hours in all, hitting 21 fours in his unbeaten 150. Botham, batting with immense responsibility, denied the attacking principles on which his game had been founded for ten years by refusing to commit the slightest indiscretion. He joined the fight 45 minutes before lunch and stayed with his captain until the grim, necessary job was completed at 5.25 p.m. – David Field.

Man of the Match: Javed Miandad.   *Attendance:* 52,104; *receipts* £500,399.

Men of the Series: England – M. W. Gatting; Pakistan – Imran Khan.

Close of play: First day, Pakistan 297-3 (Javed Miandad 131*, Salim Malik 64*); Second day, Pakistan 616-6 (Ijaz Ahmed 22*, Salim Yousuf 6*); Third day, England 144-4 (M. W. Gatting 50*, I. T. Botham 23*); Fourth day, England 95-3 (B. C. Broad 26*, M. W. Gatting 5*).

Pakistan

Mudassar Nazar c Moxon b Botham	..	73
Ramiz Raja b Botham		14
Mansoor Akhtar c French b Dilley		5
Javed Miandad c and b Dilley		260
Salim Malik c Gower b Botham		102
*Imran Khan run out		118
Ijaz Ahmed c Moxon b Dilley		69
†Salim Yousuf c and b Dilley		42
Wasim Akram c Botham b Dilley		5
Abdul Qadir c Moxon b Dilley		0
Tauseef Ahmed not out		0
B 2, l-b 18		20
		708

1/40 (2) 2/45 (3) 3/148 (1) 4/382 (5) 5/573 (4) 6/601 (6) 7/690 (8) 8/707 (7) 9/707 (10) 10/708 (9)

Bowling: Dilley 47.3-10-154-6; Foster 12-3-32-0; Botham 52-7-217-3; Emburey 61-10-143-0; Edmonds 32-8-97-0; Gatting 10-2-18-0; Moxon 6-2-27-0.

England

B. C. Broad c Yousuf b Imran	0	– c Ijaz b Qadir		42
M. D. Moxon c Miandad b Qadir	8	– c Yousuf b Tauseef		15
R. T. Robinson b Qadir	30	– c Wasim b Qadir		10
D. I. Gower b Tauseef	28	– c Mudassar b Qadir		34
*M. W. Gatting c Imran b Qadir	61	– not out		150
I. T. Botham b Qadir	34	– not out		51
J. E. Emburey c Malik b Qadir	53			
†B. N. French c Malik b Qadir	1			
N. A. Foster c Ijaz b Tauseef	4			
P. H. Edmonds lbw b Qadir	2			
G. R. Dilley not out	0			
B 4, l-b 3, w 1, n-b 3	11	B 4, l-b 5, w 1, n-b 3		13
	232		**(4 wkts)**	**315**

1/0 (1) 2/32 (2) 3/54 (3) 4/78 (4) 5/165 (6) 6/166 (5) 7/184 (8) 8/198 (9) 9/223 (10) 10/232 (7)

1/22 (2) 2/40 (3) 3/89 (4) 4/139 (1)

Bowling: First Innings—Imran 18-2-39-1; Wasim 14-2-37-0; Qadir 44.4-15-96-7; Tauseef 23-9-53-2. *Second Innings*—Imran 26.3-8-59-0; Wasim 6-3-3-0; Qadir 53-21-115-3; Tauseef 46.3-15-98-1; Mudassar 6-0-21-0; Miandad 4-2-10-0.

Umpires: D. J. Constant and K. E. Palmer.

THE MARYLEBONE CRICKET CLUB, 1987

In the year of MCC's Bicentenary, a group of members used the occasion of the 200th Annual General Meeting, held at Lord's on May 6, 1987, to express their disquiet about certain aspects of the club's affairs, notably MCC's relationship with the Test and County Cricket Board, following the resignation in December 1986 of D. G. Clark, the Treasurer and a Trustee of the club, and the retirement of J. A. Bailey, Secretary from 1974 until January 1987. The President, who was in the chair, had written to members in February to explain the circumstances of the departure of two of the club's senior officers and to outline the relationship between MCC and the TCCB. However, not all of those among the 500 present were satisfied that the Committee was insisting on the necessary safeguards to members' rights, and amid some confusion, the Annual Report for 1987 and the Accounts for 1986 were not adopted.

(At the beginning of June, the Committee announced that it would re-present the Report and Accounts at a Special General Meeting on July 30, and because the matter was sufficiently important for the whole membership to be informed and consulted, a postal vote was held.)

J. J. Warr was nominated by M. C. Cowdrey to succeed him as President of MCC on October 1, 1987. Captain of Middlesex from 1958 to 1960, as a right-arm fast-medium bowler he played twice for England in Australia in 1950-51, and in a first-class career of 344 matches took 956 wickets. Australia's representative on the ICC, of which by custom he became Chairman, he had been a member of the organising committee of the World Cup since its inception and was a member in 1979 of the ICC delegation to South Africa. He had been a member of MCC's Committee since 1984 and was due to retire by rotation on September 30, 1987, as were E. A. Clark, N. J. Cosh and T. M. B. Sissons. As a result of a postal ballot, held among members because there were more nominations than vacancies, C. A. Fry, D. L. Hudd, N. E. J. Pocock and D. R. W. Silk were nominated to join the Committee from October 1, 1987.

The Committee nominated D. J. Insole as a Trustee, to serve until September 30, 1988, and G. H. G. Doggart as Treasurer following the resignation of D. G. Clark. Lt-Colonel J. R. Stephenson, OBE, had become Acting Secretary on the retirement of J. A. Bailey and on April 20, 1987, he was appointed to be MCC's twelfth Secretary.

At a Special General Meeting immediately following the Annual Meeting, three changes were approved to the 1980 Code of the Laws of Cricket. These had received the approval of the ICC and related to Law 2.1 – Substitutes, Law 2.6 – Runner's Equipment, and Law 41.4 – Fieldsman's Protective Helmets.

At the Special General Meeting on July 30, 1987, held at Westminster Central Hall, London and attended by 799 members, the Treasurer took the chair in the absence of M. C. Cowdrey, who had undergone open-heart surgery earlier in the month. The members were asked to consider the resolution "That the club's Annual Report 1987, as supplemented by the Memorandum dated 8th July, 1987 from the Committee to the members, and the Accounts for 1986 be and are adopted".

The Memorandum dealt primarily with MCC's relationship with the TCCB, which had been influenced by two conflicting views as to the interests of MCC and its members. The first view recognised that the TCCB had, since 1968, been responsible for running first-class cricket in the United Kingdom and that MCC should seek to foster good working relationships with its officers and be flexible in dealings with the TCCB as long as the rights of MCC members were protected. The contrary view saw the TCCB as seeking to encroach upon MCC's authority at Lord's, thereby justifying MCC's adopting a defensive attitude.

The relationship between MCC and the TCCB had been deteriorating: there was a "real risk" that at least one major match might be taken away from Lord's. The Committee believed that one of its major duties to members was to ensure the preservation of a full programme at Lord's and was confident that, with improved understanding and trust between the Secretariat of MCC and the TCCB, recognition of the Board's overall responsibility would not cause serious difficulties. Members were assured that if the Board's responsibilities were exercised in a way that affected the rights of members, MCC had a legal obligation to put the matter to its members before any action was taken.

The discussion was opened on behalf of the Committee by T. M. B. Sissons, after which members contributed from the floor. The President Designate, J. J. Warr, concluded on behalf of the Committee. With the postal votes taken into account, the resolution was passed by 7,138 to 981, comfortably exceeding the two-thirds majority required in the instance of a postal vote.

The Accounts for 1986 reflected the continuing programme of improvements and general maintenance at Lord's, with major items including the extension and refurbishing of the Secretariat offices and the rewiring and refurbishment of the Pavilion. To meet the requirements of the Safety at Sports Grounds Act, the benches had been anchored to the ground and the arrangement of the turnstiles at the Nursery End had been altered. Work would also have to be undertaken to strengthen or replace many of the balustrades. The cost of rebuilding the Mound Stand (officially opened by HRH The Duke of Edinburgh on May 6, 1987) was now expected to be £4·335 million, and when professional fees, furniture and equipment were taken into account, the cost was approximately £5·5 million. Extra expenditure had been incurred to meet the requirement of the caterers, and the estimate of costs had been affected by the strengthening during the year of the German mark against the pound, so increasing the price paid for steel. However, the club's income had increased, with the result that the final surplus after tax had risen to £10,168 from £2,140 the previous year.

The membership of the club on December 31, 1986 was 19,925, made up of 17,936 full members and 1,989 associate members. These comprised the following: 10,849 full and 1,522 associate town members, 2,298 full and 271 associate country members, 3,268 at the over-65 rate, 214 full and 175 associate members at the under-25 rate, 279 full and 21 associate members at the special schoolmasters' rate, 711 on the abroad list, 64 life members, 20 60-year life members, 39 honorary cricket members and 194 honorary life members. In addition, there were 30 out-match members, and the number of candidates on the waiting list was 12,215. In 1986, 462 vacancies occurred, owing to 236 deaths, 103 resignations and 123 lapsed memberships.

MCC v ESSEX

At Lord's, April 22, 23, 24. Drawn. Toss: Essex. Just as DeFreitas, with nine wickets, and Richards, with eight catches, were to do later in the match, Foster, Morris and Whitaker caught the eye on the opening morning. A cover drive from Morris, played off the back foot, was as heartening as the sunshine that warmed a useful-sized crowd. Gatting gave them good entertainment in the afternoon. He went from 87 to three figures in one over from Childs, hit seventeen fours in all, and with Ontong (160 minutes) put on 150 in 41 overs. The pitch, easy paced on the first day, provided lively movement and even some lift, especially for DeFreitas, on the second as Essex lost their last eight wickets in 21 overs. At times Gatting set four slips, and there was plenty to occupy them, as there was Richards. Gladwin batted almost till lunch and Hardie, resolute as ever, stayed just under three hours. Foster's line and pace again impressed when MCC batted a second time, but they made steady progress towards a declaration that set Essex to score 303 in four hours. A tardy over-rate, as well as DeFreitas, made this a stiff proposition. And when Gooch was out in the first over after tea, followed soon by Fletcher and Miller, Essex at 130 for six were in danger of defeat. Pringle and East, however, with sensible application, saw them past it. A strain kept Gatting in the Pavilion on the final day – Edmonds was in charge – and when Jarvis, Metcalfe and Ontong were also there, MCC had four substitute fielders employed.

Close of play: First day, Essex 23-1 (C. Gladwin 3*, D. E. East 11*); Second day, MCC 89-3 (J. E. Morris 10*, R. C. Ontong 1*).

MCC

A. A. Metcalfe c Hardie b Foster	10	– lbw b Foster	6
R. T. Robinson lbw b Foster	17	– c Pringle b Gooch	45
J. J. Whitaker b Foster	52	– c Fletcher b Foster	25
J. E. Morris c East b Gooch	18	– lbw b Pringle	20
*M. W. Gatting run out	111		
R. C. Ontong not out	63	– (5) not out	46
†C. J. Richards not out	9	– not out	38
P. A. J. DeFreitas (did not bat)	–	– (6) c Gooch b Page	3
B 1, l-b 11, w 1, n-b 4	17	L-b 4, n-b 1	5

1/27 2/40 3/87 4/124 5/274   (5 wkts dec.) 297   1/8 2/71 3/87   (5 wkts dec.) 188
                                               4/114 5/117

P. H. Edmonds, J. G. Thomas and P. W. Jarvis did not bat.

Bowling: *First Innings*—Foster 20-4-71-3; Page 17-2-76-0; Pringle 19-3-45-0; Gooch 5-1-11-1; Childs 15-5-48-0; Miller 7-0-34-0. *Second Innings*—Foster 20-7-32-2; Page 19-5-57-1; Pringle 18-3-47-1; Gooch 9-1-32-1; Miller 1-1-0-0; Childs 2.4-0-16-0.

Essex

*G. A. Gooch c Richards b DeFreitas	6	– lbw b DeFreitas	55
C. Gladwin c Richards b DeFreitas	29	– c Richards b Thomas	19
†D. E. East c Robinson b Thomas	12	– (8) not out	36
B. R. Hardie c Richards b Jarvis	79	– (3) c Richards b DeFreitas	10
P. J. Prichard c Ontong b DeFreitas	0	– (4) b DeFreitas	2
K. W. R. Fletcher c Robinson b Thomas	2	– (6) lbw b Jarvis	15
D. R. Pringle c Richards b Jarvis	20	– (5) not out	30
G. Miller lbw b DeFreitas	9	– (7) c Richards b DeFreitas	9
N. A. Foster c Ontong b Jarvis	6		
H. A. Page c Richards b DeFreitas	5		
J. H. Childs not out	0		
L-b 4, w 2, n-b 9	15	B 4, l-b 2, w 1, n-b 16	23

1/9 2/29 3/101 4/101 5/104   183   1/41 2/61 3/73   (6 wkts) 199
6/152 7/171 8/177 9/179   4/116 5/116 6/130

Bowling: *First Innings*—Thomas 17-5-57-2; Jarvis 17-3-62-5; Ontong 5-1-13-0; Edmonds 2-0-4-0. *Second Innings*—Thomas 13-3-62-1; DeFreitas 15-1-68-4; Jarvis 10-2-31-1; Edmonds 10-4-25-0; Robinson 2-0-7-0.

Umpires: J. Birkenshaw and R. Julian.

†At Lord's, May 21. MCC Young Cricketers won by four wickets. MCC 219 for five dec. (A. M. de Silva 49, R. J. Lanchbury 32, S. C. Wundke 70 not out, S. M. N. Zaidi 32); MCC Young Cricketers 223 for six (I. A. Kidd 45, R. G. Twose 79, R. J. Robinson 36).

At Oxford, June 10, 11, 12. MCC drew with Oxford University (See Oxford University section).

At Cambridge, June 13, 14, 15. MCC drew with Cambridge University (See Cambridge University section).

At Lord's, July 22. MCC v MCC Schools. Abandoned.

At Lord's, August 5, 6. Ireland won by four wickets. MCC 250 for seven dec. (P. R. Oliver 54, N. E. J. Pocock 46, C. R. Trembath 45) and 199 for three dec. (R. J. Lanchbury 73, C. J. C. Rowe 63, P. R. Oliver 48); Ireland 193 for seven (S. J. S. Warke 30, S. C. Corlett 35, A. McBrine 43; P. J. Kippax four for 56) and 260 for six (M. F. Cohen 91, M. A. Masood 91).

At Aberdeen, August 12, 13, 14. MCC drew with Scotland (See Other Matches, 1987).

MCC v REST OF THE WORLD

MCC Bicentenary Match

At Lord's, August 20, 21, 22, 24, 25. Drawn. Rain washed out the last day's play with the Rest of the World, 13 for one overnight, needing another 340 to win. It was a sad finish to a match which provided many marvellous moments while, off the field, friendships were renewed and nostalgia was indulged in as cricketers, young and old, came together to celebrate the 200th anniversary of MCC. In memory there will be cameos rather than a broad sweep of canvas, or in the modern sporting context this was a game rather than a contest. It may even have been appropriate that neither side won. In their performances and their sportsmanship, the finest players in the world had recognised that cricket should be the winner. Because of the spirit in which the match was played, MCC increased from £25,000 to £30,000 the prizemoney to be shared by the two teams in the event of a draw. The winners would have received 25,000 and the losers £12,000.

If it is futile to speculate who might have won, it is none the less fascinating to ponder. The pitch was perfect for batting, as it had been from the start. On the fourth day MCC had scored their 318 in 88 overs, indeed having to keep a tight rein on the innings at the end to stop it from bolting. And although the Rest had lost Gavaskar, bowled off stump in Marshall's first over that evening before bad light stopped play, they possessed batsmen of the calibre to challenge such a target. Moreover, Javed Miandad, troubled by a back strain, had been unable to express his unique talent in the first innings. The second would have provided an opportunity.

From the teams originally chosen, there were three changes. For MCC, M. D. Crowe and I. T. Botham were unfit and replaced by Gooch and Rice. The latter's inclusion gave the celebrations a South African presence, for no-one from that country had been invited. With so many players coming from countries hostile to the South African government, MCC had avoided possible embarrassment by restricting selection to players currently engaged in county cricket (MCC) or, not being current county cricketers, from the Test-playing countries (Rest of the World). I. V. A. Richards withdrew from the Rest XI in order to play a match for Rishton in the Lancashire League and was replaced by Vengsarkar.

The sun shone in a blue sky when Gatting won the toss with a Spade Guinea, minted in 1787, the year of the first game at Thomas Lord's original ground. And when Greenidge clipped Imran's first ball for four, it signalled the batting feast to follow. Broad, playing no stroke, missed out, but this brought in Gooch. He had had an unhappy summer. Now, although beaten early on by Imran and Walsh, he was to rediscover his form and his confidence. By lunch Greenidge had reached fifty, off 91 balls with nine fours, but in the second over of the afternoon, stepping out, he lifted Qadir over – so he must have thought – mid-on; only for Harper, 6ft 5in tall, to intercept the ball as it passed overhead.

Impressive in its casualness, the catch was nothing to his dismissal of Gooch in the evening. Gower, out of tune, had come and gone, walking without waiting, and Gooch and Gatting had added 103 when Gooch went down the wicket and drove Harper straight. In an instant Harper fielded the ball, and while Gooch was still moving forward with the momentum of his stroke, threw down the stumps, the action of taking and throwing being as one. Even Gooch was drawn to smile in admiration, and well he could afford to. His 117, from 210 balls in hours 50 minutes, had taken him from a shadow into sunlight. In recent seasons he has swayed at the crease like an oak in the wind: here, he was upright and still, waiting for the ball and punching it with the authority of his best years. He hit eighteen fours and had, in addition, removed Qadir from the attack, bruising the bowler's fingers with a straight drive. It was in finishing this over that Miandad strained his back.

Gatting, in a sunhat, and Rice, helmeted, put on 201 in a partnership of contrasts. Gatting hitting his fourth hundred in a month – two of them in Tests – was in wonderful form, especially powerful off the back foot and deft with orthodox and unorthodox sweeps. He scored 90 of the 136 runs that came on the second morning and there were 26 fours in his 179 made from 273 balls in five and a quarter hours. Rice, who was not timing the ball so well, batted with determination rather than dash, his unbeaten 59 taking 202 minutes (156 balls).

The Rest's innings began at 2.15 with a no-ball from Marshall. His first legitimate delivery fast and low, struck Gavaskar on the pad and he was fortunate to get away with a leg-bye instead of a leg-before. Next ball, Haynes was dropped by Gatting at third slip. Almost an hour later, Rice showed how such catches can be taken, moving low to his right at first slip and grasping the ball two-handed. He took another splendid catch to dismiss Border late in the day, diving wide and low to his left at cover.

When Shastri was bowling his slow left-arm spin to Gavaskar and Vengsarkar, with the canopies of the new Mound Stand behind them, the setting could have been the sub-continent; but not when Hadlee or Marshall was bowling from the Pavilion End after tea (69 for one). For the first time in the match, a competitive edge could be felt. Hadlee to Gavaskar was a duel between two masters, the bowler probing with all his skills for an opening, the batsman correct and studious in defence, awaiting the chance to counter-attack. Gavaskar won the bout. But if Hadlee's weapon was the épée, Marshall's was the sabre. From round the wicket, on so placid a pitch, he removed Vengsarkar with a ball that kicked, took the shoulder of the bat and flew to Gooch, the finer of two gullies. Border, gritty, rode the storm, and when Gavaskar reached his fifty (121 balls) with a flowing cover drive off Marshall, they had entered calmer waters. The evening was made charming by the artistry of these two small men against the spinners: driving or deflecting, the execution of their strokes was classical.

Gavaskar, when 75, had a lucky escape when the ball rolled from his pads to rest against the stumps; and next day, contemplating a suicidal second run to bring him his first hundred at Lord's, he was firmly sent back by Imran Khan. Here was a moment to savour. Earlier in the year, Imran had dismissed Gavaskar with the first ball in the Test match at Jaipur. Now he was rescuing him. The smiles on their faces were large. Next over, when Gavaskar turned Shastri backward of square, the hug of congratulation from the bowler was spontaneous. His hundred had taken Gavaskar 215 balls, and when he clipped Hadlee through mid-wicket, then rocked back and hooked him for another boundary, a second hundred looked possible. The sky was clearing after an overcast start; play began at 11.30 on Saturday after excellent work by the groundstaff had removed the effects of heavy overnight rain.

Imran was an ideal foil for the "Little Master." Once he had seen him to his hundred, he hit Emburey straight for six, reached fifty with two lovely off-side fours in an over from Hadlee, and carted Emburey high into the President's box above the Tavern concourse. When he was bowled, making room to cut, he and Gavaskar had put on 180 in 2 hours 40 minutes. Kapil Dev kept up the entertainment for twenty minutes until he was caught in front of the Pavilion.

Gavaskar now was 177, making steady and stylish progress towards a Bicentenary double-hundred. So it came as some surprise when Shastri, with a little flight and a little turn, beguiled him into a return catch. Gavaskar had batted for six and threequarter hours, faced 351 balls and hit 22 fours. He was accorded an outstanding reception – he had announced his retirement from Test cricket the previous evening – and as if the gods too were mourning his leaving, it rained during the tea interval. Play did not resume until 5.46, when Harper and Walsh, almost indistinguishable in the dark, added 30 before rain returned at six o'clock. Walsh hit a mighty six, they ran, with their giant strides, 4 to third man: and all the while lightning and thunder raged above them.

Border's declaration that evening put the onus on Gatting to set a target. It also gave Greenidge the opportunity to score the hundred he had desired on the first day. He was careful over it, batting for five hours and needing 223 balls, but Gooch (118 balls), Gower (73 balls) and Hadlee (39 balls) kept the score moving nicely. Qadir ran through his repertoire all afternoon, unchanged except to change ends; but he bowled as much to contain as to attack: a pity. By late afternoon, however, the sky was threatening rain, and soon all that had passed would be merely memories. But what memories.

Awards of £2,000 each were made to the Batsman of the Match, S. M. Gavaskar, the Bowler of the Match, M. D. Marshall, and the Fielder of the Match, C. E. B. Rice. D. C. S. Compton chose the batsman, Sir George Allen the bowler, and they consulted on the fielder. – G.W.

Attendance: 80,555; *receipts:* £691,233.50.

Close of play: First day, MCC 291-4 (M. W. Gatting 68*, C. E. B. Rice 14*); Second day, Rest of the World 169-3 (S. M. Gavaskar 80*, P. J. L. Dujon 8*); Third day, Rest of the World 421-7 dec.; Fourth day, Rest of the World 13-1 (D. L. Haynes 3*, R. A. Harper 9*).

MCC

C. G. Greenidge c Harper b Qadir	52	– b Qadir	122
B. C. Broad lbw b Imran	10	– c Dujon b Kapil Dev	2
G. A. Gooch run out	117	– b Harper	70
D. I. Gower c Dujon b Harper	8	– c Border b Imran	40
*M. W. Gatting b Walsh	179		
C. E. B. Rice not out	59	– (8) not out	4
R. J. Hadlee (did not bat)		– (5) c Imran b Walsh	36
R. J. Shastri (did not bat)		– (6) not out	10
J. E. Emburey (did not bat)		– (7) c Haynes b Qadir	7
B 11, l-b 15, w 1, n-b 3	30	B 15, l-b 11, n-b 1	27

1/21 2/96 3/151 4/254 5/455   (5 wkts dec.) 455   1/11 2/146 3/231   (6 wkts dec.) 318
4/289 5/293 6/308

M. D. Marshall and †B. N. French did not bat.

Bowling: *First Innings*—Imran 25-6-97-1, Walsh 28.1-6-102-1; Kapil Dev 24-8-54-0; Qadir 16.2-7-30-1; Harper 34-5-125-1; Miandad 5.4-0-21-0. *Second Innings*—Imran 13-4-33-1; Kapil Dev 7-0-21-1; Walsh 12-3-54-1; Qadir 36-9-112-2; Harper 20-2-72-1.

Rest of the World

S. M. Gavaskar c and b Shastri	188	– b Marshall	0
D. L. Haynes c Rice b Marshall	23	– not out	3
D. B. Vengsarkar c Gooch b Marshall	22		
*A. R. Border c Rice b Shastri	26		
†P. J. L. Dujon c Gooch b Marshall	9		
Imran Khan b Shastri	82		
Kapil Dev c Marshall b Emburey	13		
R. A. Harper not out	17	– (3) not out	9
C. A. Walsh not out	21		
B 3, l-b 8, w 4, n-b 5	20	L-b 1	1

1/46 2/93 3/148 4/173   (7 wkts dec.) 421   1/2   (1 wkt) 13
5/353 6/372 7/389

Javed Miandad and Abdul Qadir did not bat.

Bowling: *First Innings*—Marshall 20-3-53-3; Hadlee 21-2-71-0; Rice 12-1-63-0; Shastri 42-4-130-3; Emburey 29-7-93-1. *Second Innings*—Marshall 2.3-0-10-1; Hadlee 2-1-2-0.

Umpires: H. D. Bird and D. R. Shepherd.

In addition to the above players, the following reserves were selected: MCC – P. H. Edmonds, M. A. Holding and C. J. Richards; Rest of the World – J. G. Bracewell, J. Garner, D. M. Jones, Maninder Singh, J. R. Ratnayeke and B. A. Reid.

The selectors of the two squads were M. C. Cowdrey, P. B. H. May and M. W. Gatting for MCC and G. H. G. Doggart, C. H. Lloyd and A. R. Border for the Rest of the World.

At Scarborough, September 2, 3, 4. MCC beat Yorkshire by six wickets (See Other Matches, 1987).

MCC ENGLAND HONORARY CRICKET MEMBERS

C. J. Barnett	J. Hardstaff	D. B. Close, CBE
H. Larwood	J. B. Statham, CBE	B. L. D'Oliveira, OBE
L. E. G. Ames, CBE	F. S. Trueman	R. Illingworth, CBE
Sir Leonard Hutton	T. W. Graveney, OBE	G. Pullar
D. C. S. Compton, CBE	G. A. R. Lock	F. J. Titmus, MBE
D. V. P. Wright	C. Milburn	D. J. Brown
T. G. Evans, CBE	D. A. Allen	M. H. Denness
C. Washbrook	R. W. Barber	J. M. Brearley, OBE
A. V. Bedser, CBE	E. R. Dexter	R. W. Taylor, MBE
P. B. H. May, CBE	P. H. Parfitt	R. G. D. Willis, MBE
W. Watson	F. H. Tyson	J. H. Edrich, MBE
P. E. Richardson	M. C. Cowdrey, CBE	A. P. E. Knott
T. E. Bailey	J. T. Murray, MBE	C. M. Old
M. J. K. Smith, OBE	J. M. Parks	J. A. Snow

COUNTY CAPS AWARDED IN 1987

Derbyshire	B. J. M. Maher, A. E. Warner.
Glamorgan	S. R. Barwick, A. R. Butcher, M. P. Maynard, C. P. Metson.
Gloucestershire	G. E. Sainsbury, A. J. Wright.
Kent	C. Penn.
Lancashire	I. Folley, B. P. Patterson, M. Watkinson.
Leicestershire	P. Whitticase.
Middlesex	J. D. Carr.
Northamptonshire	N. G. B. Cook, W. W. Davis, D. Ripley, A. Walker.
Nottinghamshire	M. Newell, R. A. Pick.
Somerset	N. D. Burns, J. J. E. Hardy, A. N. Jones, N. A. Mallender.
Surrey	I. A. Greig.
Warwickshire	Asif Din, A. J. Moles, G. J. Parsons.
Worcestershire	I. T. Botham, G. R. Dilley.
Yorkshire	R. J. Blakey, P. J. Hartley.

No caps were awarded by Essex, Hampshire or Sussex.

COUNTY BENEFITS AWARDED FOR 1988

Gloucestershire	A. J. Brassington.	Somerset	V. J. Marks.
Hampshire	N. G. Cowley.	Surrey	C. J. Richards.
Kent	C. J. Tavaré.	Sussex	P. W. G. Parker.
Lancashire	J. Abrahams.	Worcestershire	P. A. Neale.
Middlesex	M. W. Gatting.	Yorkshire	A. Sidebottom.
Northamptonshire	A. J. Lamb.		

No benefits have been awarded by Derbyshire, Essex, Glamorgan, Leicestershire, Nottinghamshire or Warwickshire.

OTHER MATCHES AT LORD'S, 1987

June 18, 19, 20, 22, 23. Second Cornhill Test. ENGLAND drew with PAKISTAN (See Pakistani tour section).

OXFORD UNIVERSITY v CAMBRIDGE UNIVERSITY

July 1, 2, 3. Drawn. Toss: Cambridge University. Oxford, having been in command for much of the first two days, never threatened to bowl Cambridge out a second time. In the first innings, their opening bowlers, Firth and Henderson, had set an effective attack in the dismissal of Cambridge for 207. On the second day, Crawley completed a maiden hundred in just under three and threequarter hours as Oxford gained a lead of 140, thus following M. J. K. Smith (1954) and the Nawab of Pataudi (1960) in becoming the third Oxford freshman since World War Two to score a hundred in the University Match. Crawley, who entered at 91 for four, patiently built his innings, hitting thirteen fours, and he had a determined partner in Weale, who likewise completed a career-best score. They added 191 runs for the sixth wicket. When Crawley was out, bowled by the left-arm medium-fast Scott, who took five for 97, Oxford declared, and their hopes of a victory were further enhanced when Firth had Atherton lbw for the second time in the match. But thereon the Cambridge batsmen, led by Hooper and Bail, confidently frustrated Oxford – and their eight bowlers – for most of the final day.

Close of play: First day, Oxford University 63-3 (M. J. Kilborn 20*, R. D. Sardesai 29*); Second day, Cambridge University 41-1 (A. M. Hooper 14*, J. M. Tremellen 21*).

Cambridge University

P. A. C. Bail (*Millfield and Downing*) lbw b Henderson	5	– (4) c Kilborn b Weale	90
M. A. Atherton (*Manchester GS and Downing*) lbw b Firth	7	– lbw b Firth	0
A. M. Hooper (*Latymer Upper and St John's*) b Edwards	15	– (1) c Tooley b Edwards	89
†D. J. Fell (*John Lyon and Trinity*) c Kilborn b Henderson	0	– (5) not out	67
*D. G. Price (*Haberdashers' Aske's and Homerton*) b Firth	46	– (6) c Kilborn b Tooley	57
S. R. Gorman (*St Peter's, York and Emmanuel*) c Cope b Crawley	26		
J. M. Tremellen (*Bradfield and St Catharine's*) b Edwards	28	– (3) b Edwards	39
G. A. Pointer (*St Dunstan's and St John's*) lbw b Firth	33		
J. N. Perry (*Ampleforth and Trinity*) b Weale	10		
A. M. G. Scott (*Seaford Head and Queens'*) not out	11		
M. R. Middleton (*Harrow and Caius*) b Crawley	6		
B 1, l-b 6, w 3, n-b 10	20	B 2, l-b 8, w 2, n-b 13	25
	207	(5 wkts dec.)	**367**

1/16 2/16 3/18 4/54 5/104 6/122 7/158 8/177 9/190

1/1 2/123 3/183 4/261 5/367

Bowling: *First Innings*—Firth 21-4-64-3; Henderson 9-0-29-2; Edwards 22-7-50-2; Weale 13-4-27-1; Crawley 7.1-1-30-2. *Second Innings*—Firth 26-6-101-1; Henderson 12-1-75-0; Edwards 22.9-9-63-2; Crawley 17-6-38-0; Weale 11-2-25-1; Kilborn 3-0-23-0; Tooley 5.3-1-21-1; Morris 2-0-11-0.

Oxford University

R. E. Morris (*Dyffryn Conwy, Llanrwst and Oriel*)
lbw b Scott .... 0 – (2) not out 13
A. R. Beech (*John XXIII Coll., Perth, Univ. of
Western Australia and Magdalen*) c Fell b Perry 1 – (1) c Fell b Pointer 6
M. J. Kilborn (*Farrer Agric. HS, Univ. of NSW
and St John's*) c and b Scott .... 59 – not out 6
*C. D. M. Tooley (*St Dunstan's and Magdalen*)
lbw b Scott 5
R. D. Sardesai (*St Xavier's Coll., Bombay, Univ. of
Bombay and University*) lbw b Atherton 40
M. A. Crawley (*Manchester GS and Oriel*)
b Scott 140
S. D. Weale (*Westminster City and Keble*) b Scott 76
I. M. Henderson (*Laxton and Pembroke*) not out 4
    B 7, l-b 7, w 2, n-b 6 22   L-b 2, n-b 2 4
                   ——   ——

1/0 2/5 3/11 4/91 5/135   (7 wkts dec.) 347   1/13   (1 wkt) 29
6/326 7/347

†J. E. B. Cope (*St John's, Leatherhead and Keble*), P. G. Edwards (*Canford and Christ Church*)
and T. Firth (*Stockport GS and Oriel*) did not bat.

Bowling: *First Innings*—Scott 33.3–7–97–5; Perry 19–3–50–1; Pointer 23–2–61–0;
Middleton 15–1–47–0; Atherton 22–0–66–1; Tremellen 2–0–12–0. *Second Innings*—Pointer
5–1–9–1; Perry 3–0–14–0; Atherton 1–0–4–0.

Umpires: J. H. Harris and J. A. Jameson.

OXFORD v CAMBRIDGE, RESULTS AND HUNDREDS

The University match dates back to 1827. Altogether there have been 143 official matches,
Cambridge winning 54 and Oxford 46, with 43 drawn. Results since 1950:

1950	Drawn	
1951	Oxford won by 21 runs	
1952	Drawn	
1953	Cambridge won by two wickets	
1954	Drawn	
1955	Drawn	
1956	Drawn	
1957	Cambridge won by an innings and 186 runs	
1958	Cambridge won by 99 runs	
1959	Oxford won by 85 runs	
1960	Drawn	
1961	Drawn	
1962	Drawn	
1963	Drawn	
1964	Drawn	
1965	Drawn	
1966	Oxford won by an innings and 9 runs	
1967	Drawn	
1968	Drawn	
1969	Drawn	
1970	Drawn	
1971	Drawn	
1972	Cambridge won by an innings and 25 runs	
1973	Drawn	
1974	Drawn	
1975	Drawn	
1976	Oxford won by ten wickets	
1977	Drawn	
1978	Drawn	
1979	Cambridge won by an innings and 52 runs	
1980	Drawn	
1981	Drawn	
1982	Cambridge won by seven wickets	
1983	Drawn	
1984	Oxford won by five wickets	
1985	Drawn	
1986	Cambridge won by five wickets	
1987	Drawn	

Ninety-three three-figure innings have been played in the University matches. For those scored before 1919 see 1940 *Wisden*. Those subsequent to 1919 include the seven highest:

238*	Nawab of Pataudi	1931 Oxford		121	J. N. Grover	1937 Oxford
211	G. Goonesena	1957 Cam.		119	J. M. Brearley	1964 Cam.
201*	M. J. K. Smith	1954 Oxford		118	H. Ashton	1921 Cam.
201	A. Ratcliffe	1931 Cam.		118	D. R. W. Silk	1954 Oxford
200	Majid Khan	1970 Cam.		117	M. J. K. Smith	1956 Oxford
193	D. C. H. Townsend	1934 Oxford		116*	D. R. W. Silk	1953 Cam.
174	P. A. C. Bail	1986 Cam.		116	M. C. Cowdrey	1953 Oxford
170	M. Howell	1919 Oxford		115	A. W. Allen	1934 Cam.
167	B. W. Hone	1932 Oxford		114*	D. R. Owen-Thomas	1972 Cam.
158	P. M. Roebuck	1975 Cam.		114	J. F. Pretlove	1955 Cam.
157	D. R. Wilcox	1932 Cam.		113*	J. M. Brearley	1962 Cam.
155	F. S. Goldstein	1968 Oxford		113	E. R. T. Holmes	1927 Oxford
149	J. T. Morgan	1929 Cam.		112*	E. D. Fursdon	1975 Oxford
149	G. J. Toogood	1985 Oxford		111*	G. W. Cook	1957 Cam.
146	R. O'Brien	1956 Cam.		109	C. H. Taylor	1923 Oxford
146	D. R. Owen-Thomas	1971 Cam.		109	G. J. Toogood	1984 Oxford
145*	H. E. Webb	1948 Oxford		108	F. G. H. Chalk	1934 Oxford
142	D. P. Toft	1967 Oxford		106	Nawab of Pataudi	1929 Oxford
142	M. P. Donnelly	1946 Oxford		105	E. J. Craig	1961 Cam.
140	M. A. Crawley	1987 Oxford		104*	D. A. Thorne	1986 Oxford
139	R. J. Boyd-Moss	1983 Cam.		104	H. J. Enthoven	1924 Cam.
136	E. T. Killick	1930 Cam.		104	M. J. K. Smith	1955 Oxford
135	H. A. Pawson	1947 Oxford		103*	A. R. Lewis	1962 Cam.
131	Nawab of Pataudi	1960 Oxford		103	D. R. Pringle	1979 Cam.
129	H. J. Enthoven	1925 Cam.		102*	A. P. F. Chapman	1922 Cam.
128*	A. J. T. Miller	1984 Oxford		101*	R. W. V. Robins	1928 Cam.
127	D. S. Sheppard	1952 Cam.		101	N. W. D. Yardley	1937 Cam.
124	A. K. Judd	1927 Cam.		100*	M. Manasseh	1964 Oxford
124	A. Ratcliffe	1932 Cam.		100	P. J. Dickinson	1939 Cam.
124	R. J. Boyd-Moss	1983 Cam.		100	N. J. Cosh	1967 Cam.
122	P. A. Gibb	1938 Cam.		100	R. J. Boyd-Moss	1982 Cam.

* *Signifies not out.*

Highest Totals

503	Oxford	1900	432-9	Cambridge	1936
457	Oxford	1947	431	Cambridge	1932
453-8	Oxford	1931	425	Cambridge	1938

Lowest Totals

32	Oxford	1878	42	Oxford	1890
39	Cambridge	1858	47	Cambridge	1838

Notes: A. P. F. Chapman and M. P. Donnelly enjoy the following distinction: Chapman scored a century at Lord's in the University match (102*, 1922); for Gentlemen v Players (160, 1922), (108, 1926); and for England v Australia (121, 1930). M. P. Donnelly scored a century at Lord's in the University match (142, 1946); for Gentlemen v Players (162*, 1947); and for New Zealand v England (206, 1949).

A. Ratcliffe's 201 for Cambridge remained a record for the match for only one day, being beaten by the Nawab of Pataudi's 238* for Oxford next day.

M. J. K. Smith (Oxford) and R. J. Boyd-Moss (Cambridge) are the only players who have scored three hundreds. Smith scored 201* in 1954, 104 in 1955, and 117 in 1956; Boyd-Moss scored 100 in 1982 and 139 and 124 in 1983. His aggregate of 489 surpassed Smith's previous record of 477.

The following players have scored two hundreds: W. Yardley (Cambridge) 100 in 1870 an 130 in 1872; H. J. Enthoven (Cambridge) 104 in 1924 and 129 in 1925; Nawab of Patau (Oxford) 106 in 1929 and 238* in 1931; A. Ratcliffe (Cambridge) 201 in 1931 and 12 in 1932; D. R. W. Silk (Cambridge) 116* in 1953 and 118 in 1954; J. M. Brearley (Cam bridge) 113* in 1962 and 119 in 1964; D. R. Owen-Thomas (Cambridge) 146 in 1971 an 114* in 1972; G. J. Toogood (Oxford) 109 in 1984 and 149 in 1985.

F. C. Cobden, in the Oxford v Cambridge match in 1870, performed the hat-trick by takin the last three wickets and won an extraordinary game for Cambridge by 2 runs. The feat i without parallel in first-class cricket. Other hat-tricks, all for Cambridge, have been credite to A. G. Steel (1879), P. H. Morton (1880), J. F. Ireland (1911), and R. G. H. Lowe (1926)

S. E. Butler, in the 1871 match, took all the wickets in the Cambridge first innings. The fea is unique in University matches. He bowled 24.1 overs. In the follow-on he took five wicket for 57, giving him match figures of fifteen for 95 runs.

The best all-round performances in the history of the match have come from P. R Le Couteur, who scored 160 and took eleven Cambridge wickets for 66 runs in 1910, an G. J. Toogood, who in 1985 scored 149 and took ten Cambridge wickets for 93.

D. W. Jarrett (Oxford 1975, Cambridge 1976), S. M. Wookey (Cambridge 1975-76), Oxfor 1978) and G. Pathmanathan (Oxford 1975-78, Cambridge 1983) are alone in gaining cricke Blues for both Universities.

ETON v HARROW

July 4. Drawn. Toss: Harrow. Harrow set Eton 197 to win in 140 minutes but, although th captain, MacLeay, played a resolute innings of 70 not out, a draw was soon the likelihoo Eton received only 44 overs compared with Harrow's 74. A record Harrovian first-wicke stand in the 152 matches against Eton was set when Boralessa and de Souza Girao put on 116 runs. But Erith broke this partnership soon after lunch, and when Boralessa was run out fo 68, there was a Harrow collapse of five wickets for 6 runs. The accuracy of Eton's left-arr spinner, Fleming, was well conveyed by figures of two for 33 off 27 overs, but les commendable was the provision to Harrow's total of 20 runs from wides and no-balls, th opening bowlers being the principal offenders.

Harrow

M. B. T. de C. de Souza Girao b Erith	38	R. D. Nelson not out		
H. Boralessa run out	68	J. A. R. Hill not out		
*D. C. Manasseh c Trusted b Erith	17			
C. Keey c Shirazi b Fleming	3	B 3, l-b 10, w 8, n-b 12		3
R. C. Hamilton c Trusted b Erith	0			
J. K. Bourne c MacLeay b Erith	0	1/116 2/142 3/143	(8 wkts dec.)	19
A. C. W. Snow c and b Fleming	17	4/147 5/147 6/148		
†A. K. C. Green c Jenkins b Fairbairn	14	7/178 8/186		

D. W. F. Berry-Green did not bat.

Bowling: Erith 24-6-70-4; Fairbairn 11-1-48-1; Shirazi 5-0-25-0; Winter 7-4-7-0 Fleming 27-12-33-2.

Eton

*R. D. O. MacLeay not out	70	S. H. Shirazi not out		
J. B. Bowman-Shaw b Hill	18			
C. A. C. Winter run out	16	B 7, l-b 17, w 9, n-b 5		3
J. B. A. Jenkins b Snow	3			
A. R. G. Lunt c Manasseh b Berry-Green	21	1/75 2/107 3/116	(5 wkts)	16
G. P. F. Selmon b Snow	0	4/158 5/161		

†J. T. Trusted, J. K. Erith, T. P. M. Fleming and J. H. M. Fairbairn did not bat.

Bowling: Snow 13-1-38-2; Berry-Green 6-0-28-1; Hill 16-2-42-1; Manasseh 6-0-20-0 Nelson 3-0-17-0.

Umpires: P. Adams and D. J. Dennis.

ETON v HARROW, RESULTS AND HUNDREDS

Of the 152 matches played Eton have won 50, Harrow 44 and 58 have been drawn. This is the generally published record, but Harrow men object strongly to the first game in 1805 being treated as a regular contest between the two schools, contending that it is no more correct to count that one than the fixture of 1857 which has been rejected.

The matches played during the war years 1915-18 and 1940-45 are not reckoned as belonging to the regular series.

Results since 1950:

1950 Drawn	1969 Drawn
1951 Drawn	1970 Eton won by 97 runs
1952 Harrow won by seven wickets	1971 Drawn
1953 Eton won by ten wickets	1972 Drawn
1954 Harrow won by nine wickets	1973 Drawn
1955 Eton won by 38 runs	1974 Harrow won by eight wickets
1956 Drawn	1975 Harrow won by an innings and 151
1957 Drawn	runs
1958 Drawn	1976 Drawn
1959 Drawn	1977 Eton won by six wickets
1960 Harrow won by 124 runs	1978 Drawn
1961 Harrow won by an innings and 12	1979 Drawn
runs	1980 Drawn
1962 Drawn	1981 Drawn
1963 Drawn	1982 Drawn
1964 Eton won by eight wickets	1983 Drawn
1965 Harrow won by 48 runs	1984 Drawn
1966 Drawn	1985 Eton won by 3 runs
1967 Drawn	1986 Drawn
1968 Harrow won by seven wickets	1987 Drawn

Forty-five three-figure innings have been played in matches between these two schools. Those since 1918:

161*	M. K. Fosh	1975 Harrow	106	D. M. Smith	1966 Eton
159	E. W. Dawson	1923 Eton	104	R. Pulbrook	1932 Harrow
158	I. S. Akers-Douglas	1928 Eton	103	L. G. Crawley	1921 Harrow
153	N. S. Hotchkin	1931 Eton	103	T. Hare	1947 Eton
151	R. M. Tindall	1976 Harrow	102*	P. H. Stewart-Brown	1923 Harrow
135	J. C. Atkinson-Clark	1930 Eton	102	R. V. C. Robins	1953 Eton
115	E. Crutchley	1939 Harrow	100	R. H. Cobbold	1923 Eton
112	A. W. Allen	1931 Eton	100*	P. V. F. Cazalet	1926 Eton
112*	T. M. H. James	1978 Harrow	100	A. N. A. Boyd	1934 Eton
111	R. A. A. Holt	1937 Harrow	100*	P. M. Studd	1935 Harrow
109	K. F. H. Hale	1929 Eton	100	S. D. D. Sainsbury	1947 Eton
109	N. S. Hotchkin	1932 Eton	100	M. J. J. Faber	1968 Eton
107	W. N. Coles	1946 Eton			

* Signifies not out.

In 1904, D. C. Boles of Eton, making 183, set a record for the match, beating the 152 obtained for Eton in 1841 by Emilius Bayley, afterwards the Rev. Sir John Robert Laurie Emilius Bayley Laurie. M. C. Bird, Harrow, in 1907, scored 100 not out and 131, the only batsman who has made two 100s in the match. N. S. Hotchkin, Eton, played the following innings: 1931, 153; 1932, 109 and 96; 1933, 88 and 12.

July 11. Benson and Hedges Cup final. YORKSHIRE beat NORTHAMPTONSHIRE, having taken more wickets with the scores tied (See Benson and Hedges Cup section).

MCC SCHOOLS v NATIONAL ASSOCIATION OF YOUNG CRICKETERS

July 23. Abandoned.

MCC Schools

C. J. Adams (*Repton*), A. L. Penberthy (*Camborne*), D. A. Graham (*Chipping Camden*), G. P. Thorpe (*Farnham College*), M. R. Newton (*Peter Symonds, Winchester*), P. J. Rendall (*Broadoak, Weston-super-Mare*), N. A. Derbyshire (*Ampleforth*), *H. R. J. Trump (*Millfield*), †W. M. I. Bailey (*Clifton*), P. J. Martin (*Danum, Doncaster*) and I. J. Houseman (*Harrogate GS*).

National Association of Young Cricketers

*†M. P. Speight (*Sussex*), T. Orrell (*Lancashire*), M. Pooley (*Gloucestershire*), O. C. K. Smith (*Gloucestershire*), S. J. Green (*Warwickshire*), G. Yates (*Lancashire*), N. Shahid (*Suffolk*), M. J. Doidge (*Yorkshire*), A. M. Smith (*Yorkshire*), T. Kirk (*Derbyshire*) and M. Saxelby (*Nottinghamshire*).

Umpires: D. F. Dean and F. S. Tillson.

The National Cricket Association selected the following to play for NCA Young Cricketers against Combined Services: *†M. P. Speight (*Sussex*), T. Orrell (*Lancashire*), M. Pooley (*Gloucestershire*), O. C. K. Smith (*Gloucestershire*), D. A. Graham (*Gloucestershire*), M. R. Newton (*Hampshire*), H. R. J. Trump (*Somerset*), N. Shahid (*Suffolk*), A. M. Smith (*Yorkshire*), I. J. Houseman (*Yorkshire*) and N. A. Derbyshire (*Yorkshire*).

July 24. Drawn. Combined Services 163 for four (44 overs) (A. Ward 41 not out, M. V. Fleming 46) v NCA Young Cricketers.

OLD HILL v TEDDINGTON

Cockspur Cup Final

August 28. Old Hill won by five wickets. Toss: Teddington. A commanding half-century by Morgan, a Minor Counties cricketer for Suffolk, was the feature of the morning's play. But having reached it in the over before lunch by driving Mushtaq for the second of his two sixes, he was bowled around his legs next ball. Headley, seventeen-year-old son of R. G. A. and grandson of G. A., had made the initial breakthrough, bowling at a brisk pace, and it was his direct hit from near the third man boundary to run out Holliday which further checked Teddington's progress. A partnership of 109 between Mushtaq and Hemsley put Old Hill well on the way to victory, and although Harris came back to take three wickets, Wilkinson saw his side become national club champions for the third time in four years. Morgan of Teddington won the Man of the Match award, by tradition given to a member of the losing side.

Teddington

G. Morgan b Mushtaq	52	†R. S. Luddington not out		6
S. Munday c Green b Headley	21	P. H. D. Eastland not out		5
K. MacKintosh b Headley	4	L-b 6, w 5, n-b 2		13
W. A. Donald b Derham	10			
D. C. Holliday run out	30	1/57 2/67 3/90	(7 wkts, 45 overs)	185
D. J. Malan c Derham b Webster	27	4/94 5/143		
*J. P. C. Mills b Webster	17	6/173 7/179		

G. Harris and S. Reed did not bat.

Bowling: Webster 9-0-38-2; Frost 9-1-40-0; Derham 9-1-40-1; Headley 9-0-32-2; Mushtaq 9-0-29-1.

Old Hill

C. Hemsley b MacKintosh	57	A. E. Brookes lbw b Harris	0
P. R. Oliver c MacKintosh b Harris	7	†M. Green not out	4
Mushtaq Mohammad c Holliday		L-b 8, w 6, n-b 1	15
b Harris	64		
R. J. Lanchbury b Harris	31	1/19 2/128 3/160 (5 wkts, 44.3 overs) 188
*K. W. Wilkinson not out	10	4/180 5/180	

D. W. Headley, A. Webster, S. Derham and M. Frost did not bat.

Bowling: Harris 9-1-21-4; Malan 9-1-33-0; Donald 9-1-23-0; Reed 7-0-43-0; MacKintosh 8.3-1-51-1; Eastland 2-0-9-0.

Umpires: F. Garrett and K. Rayner.

NATIONAL CLUB CHAMPIONSHIP WINNERS 1969-87

1969 HAMPSTEAD beat Pocklington Pixies by 14 runs.
1970 CHELTENHAM beat Stockport by three wickets.
1971 BLACKHEATH beat Ealing by eight wickets.
1972 SCARBOROUGH beat Brentham by six wickets.
1973 WOLVERHAMPTON beat The Mote by five wickets.
1974 SUNBURY beat Tunbridge Wells by seven wickets.
1975 YORK beat Blackpool by six wickets.
1976 SCARBOROUGH beat Dulwich by five wickets.
1977 SOUTHGATE beat Bowdon by six wickets.
1978 CHELTENHAM beat Bishop's Stortford by 15 runs.
1979 SCARBOROUGH beat Reading by two wickets.
1980 MOSELEY beat Gosport Borough by nine wickets.
1981 SCARBOROUGH beat Blackheath by 57 runs.
1982 SCARBOROUGH beat Finchley by 4 runs.
1983 SHREWSBURY beat Hastings and St Leonards Priory by 2 runs.
1984 OLD HILL beat Bishop's Stortford by five wickets.
1985 OLD HILL beat Reading by nine wickets.
1986 STOURBRIDGE beat Weston-super-Mare by four wickets.
1987 OLD HILL beat Teddington by five wickets.

From 1969 to 1975, the Championship was contested for the D. H. Robins Trophy, from 1976 to 1982 for the John Haig Trophy, from 1983 to 1986 for the William Younger Cup, and in 1987 for the Cockspur Cup.

LONGPARISH v TREETON WELFARE

Norsk Hydro Village Championship Final

August 31. Longparish won by 76 runs. Toss: Longparish. A Bank Holiday crowd of some 3,000 saw Longparish of Hampshire take the Village Championship title to the south of England for the first time since 1978, when Linton Park of Kent held it. Heagren, under-keeper to his gamekeeper father and his successor as captain of Longparish, held his team's innings together with batting of considerable style, especially his cover driving. The Yorkshiremen – from a mining village near Rotherham – gave nothing away in the field and accurate returns resulted in four run-outs. But when they batted, Treeton were in trouble from the start. Only Jacobs offered any real resistance and they were dismissed in 37.1 overs for 90, a meagre total but one which still left Longparish's 82 for nine in 1980 the lowest in a village final at Lord's. Heagren senior was the Longparish captain that day.

Longparish

*J. D. Heagren st Meadows b Thorpe	63	†S. Mundy b Thorpe	0
K. Sutcliffe c Meadows b Hinchliffe	6	R. H. Jones not out	5
R. D. Smith lbw b Harris	0	B. J. Smith run out	0
K. C. Finch c Meadows b Allsopp	2	B 3, l-b 14, w 9, n-b 2	28
S. N. Paine b Thorpe	14		
R. D. Sturt run out	22	1/28 2/30 3/35	(39.5 overs) 166
J. W. Hibberd run out	17	4/77 5/111 6/143	
R. J. Copping run out	9	7/150 8/150 9/166	

Bowling: Hinchliffe 8-1-29-1; Harris 8.5-0-30-1; Allsopp 5-0-22-1; Foster 9-0-32-0; Thorpe 9-0-36-3.

Treeton Welfare

S. A. Rogers b Sturt	2	*D. M. Allsopp c Heagren b Copping	18
J. C. Blagden c Mundy b Sturt	8	M. Thorpe b B. J. Smith	3
A. Jarvis c Mundy b Sturt	0	L. Harris not out	3
J. Foster lbw b Sutcliffe	2	B 1, l-b 6, w 5, n-b 2	14
J. N. Jacobs b B. J. Smith	21		
G. Ellis b Sutcliffe	3	1/10 2/13 3/16	(37.1 overs) 90
†F. B. Meadows c Copping b Heagren	9	4/17 5/21 6/44	
S. Hinchliffe b B. J. Smith	7	7/57 8/64 9/74	

Bowling: Sturt 8-2-14-3; Sutcliffe 9-1-20-2; Heagren 9-2-15-1; B. J. Smith 9-1-26-3; Finch 2-0-8-0; Copping 0.1-0-0-1.

Umpires: R. E. A. Frost and K. Naylor.

VILLAGE CHAMPIONSHIP WINNERS 1972-87

1972 TROON (Cornwall) beat Astwood Bank (Worcestershire) by seven wickets.
1973 TROON (Cornwall) beat Gowerton (Glamorgan) by 12 runs.
1974 BOMARSUND (Northumberland) beat Collingham (Nottinghamshire) by three wickets.
      (Played at Edgbaston after being rained off at Lord's).
1975 GOWERTON (Glamorgan) beat Isleham (Cambridgeshire) by six wickets.
1976 TROON (Cornwall) beat Sessay (Yorkshire) by 18 runs.
1977 COOKLEY (Worcestershire) beat Lindal Moor (Cumbria) by 28 runs.
1978 LINTON PARK (Kent) beat Toft (Cheshire) by four wickets.
1979 EAST BIERLEY (Yorkshire) beat Ynysygerwn (Glamorgan) by 92 runs.
1980 MARCHWIEL (Clwyd) beat Longparish (Hampshire) by 79 runs.
1981 ST FAGANS (Glamorgan) beat Broad Oak (Yorkshire) by 22 runs.
1982 ST FAGANS (Glamorgan) beat Collingham (Nottinghamshire) by six wickets.
1983 QUARNDON (Derbyshire) beat Troon (Cornwall) by eight wickets.
1984 MARCHWIEL (Clwyd) beat Hursley Park (Hampshire) by 8 runs.
1985 FREUCHIE (Fifeshire) beat Rowledge (Surrey) by virtue of fewer wickets lost with the scores level.
1986 FORGE VALLEY (Yorkshire) beat Ynysygerwn (Glamorgan) by 5 runs.
1987 LONGPARISH (Hampshire) beat Treeton Welfare (Yorkshire) by 76 runs.

From 1972 to 1977, the Village Championship was sponsored by John Haig Ltd, in 1978 by The Cricketer, from 1979 to 1984 by Samuel Whitbread and Co. Ltd, and since 1986 by Norsk Hydro Fertilizers. There was no sponsor in 1985.

September 5, 7. NatWest Bank Trophy final. NOTTINGHAMSHIRE beat NORTHAMPTONSHIRE by three wickets (See NatWest Bank Trophy section).

BRITANNIC ASSURANCE
COUNTY CHAMPIONSHIP, 1987

Nottinghamshire won the County Championship for the second time in seven years. And just as in 1981, when they beat Sussex by two points, the title was not decided until the final round. In 1987, however, Nottinghamshire, having finished their fixtures with a 24-point win over Glamorgan, had to wait to see if Lancashire would nudge them off the top of the table by picking up 24 points at Chelmsford. When they were unable to gain more than two batting points, Nottinghamshire were champions, while Lancashire, who went on to beat Essex, finished four points adrift in second place. They had won one more match than Nottinghamshire – ten against nine – and of those ten, half had been won away from home. All but two of Nottinghamshire's wins were at home.

Top of the table from May 22 until June 23, Lancashire had slipped as low as eighth within a month, but they came storming back to win their last six games and pick up 125 points. Nottinghamshire in the same period collected only 67 points, and as their lead was being whittled away, Rice again took over the captaincy. He had stepped down at the end of May so that Robinson would gain experience.

Nottinghamshire, at that early stage of the season, were seventeenth, a position owing more to their programme than anything else. They had played only two Championship matches; Lancashire by then had played five and won three. Not until their eighth match, at the end of June, did Nottinghamshire record their first win, but they had steadily been banking bonus

Continued over

BRITANNIC ASSURANCE CHAMPIONSHIP

						Bonus points		
Win = 16 points	*Played*	*Won*	*Lost*	*Tied*	*Drawn*	*Batting*	*Bowling*	*Points*
1 – Nottinghamshire (4) ..	23	9	1	0	13	68	80	292
2 – Lancashire (15)	24	10	4	0	10	55	73	288
3 – Leicestershire (7)	24	8	3	0	13	57	75	260
4 – Surrey (3)	24	7	4	0	13	65	73	250
5 – Hampshire (6)	24	7	3	0	14	59	73	244
6 – Derbyshire (11)	24	6	5	1	12	51	70	225
7 – Northamptonshire (9) .	24	7	4	0	13	48	68	224
8 – Yorkshire (10)	23	7	3	0	13	52	58	222
9 – Worcestershire (5) ...	24	5	4	0	15	58	68	206
10 – Gloucestershire (2) ..	24	5	8	1	10	62	50	200
11 – Somerset (16)	24	2	3	0	19	61	70	163
12 – Essex (1)	24	2	4	0	18	45	77	162
13 – Glamorgan (17)	24	3	9	0	12	40	70	158
14 – Kent (8)	24	2	7	0	15	53	66	151
15 – Warwickshire (12) ...	24	2	7	0	15	48	67	147
16 – Middlesex (12)	23	2	8	0	13	47	60	139
17 – Sussex (14)	23	1	8	0	14	47	56	119

1986 positions are shown in brackets.

The total for Northamptonshire includes 12 points for a win in a one-innings match and that for Essex includes 8 points for levelling the scores in a drawn match.

The following two matches were abandoned and are not included in the above table: July 18, 20, 21 – Middlesex v Nottinghamshire at Lord's and Sussex v Yorkshire at Hastings.

points: 52 from eight games against Lancashire's 63 from eleven. This first win coincided with the first of three consecutive defeats for Lancashire in an eleven-day period which saw them add just 11 points. When the two counties met at Old Trafford at the end of July, the draw left them equal third with 148 points.

Above them were Yorkshire and Northamptonshire. Yorkshire had moved easily into the lead as Lancashire began to slip, had been overtaken by Northamptonshire for a week in July and then, with an innings victory over Leicestershire, had gone back on top. Northamptonshire, however, who had won their first two games (as had Yorkshire) and then four in succession in late June and early July, had four games in hand over Yorkshire, two over Lancashire and one over Nottinghamshire. They went back on top in the first week of August, but Nottinghamshire's convincing home wins over Warwickshire and Somerset made them Championship leaders on August 11. From then on, they were never headed. Northamptonshire and Yorkshire began to fade, although Yorkshire remained in the top three until the end of the month.

Leicestershire, like their neighbours, Nottinghamshire, spent May and June in the lower reaches: their second win, at the beginning of July, took them from sixteenth to eleventh, and their rise from then came evenly as another six matches were won. Surrey, third in mid-July but seventh a month later, fought their way back to finish fourth with three consecutive wins, pushing Hampshire, third on September 1 after four successive wins, back into fifth place. Hampshire's other three wins, in mid-season, were also in a sequence. Derbyshire, one place away from the prizemoney, had jumped from ninth to second in May and never been lower than eighth after that.

The defending champions, Essex, were without a win from April until July, and although for a time in June they were third, they never looked like serious contenders. That same month, Glamorgan, who had beaten Lancashire and Yorkshire in Wales in May, climbed to fourth. Meanwhile Gloucestershire, runners-up in 1986, had been lingering at the bottom of the table and were to remain there until mid-July, when Sussex and Middlesex dropped to seventeenth and sixteenth respectively. They remained there, occasionally split by Warwickshire, until the end of the season.

REGULATIONS FOR BRITANNIC ASSURANCE CHAMPIONSHIP

(As applied in 1987)

1. Prizemoney

First (Nottinghamshire)	£25,000
Second (Lancashire)	£12,500
Third (Leicestershire)	£6,500
Fourth (Surrey)	£3,500
Fifth (Hampshire)	£2,000
Winner of each match	£210
Championship Player of the Year (R. J. Hadlee)	£500
County of the Month	£750
Player of the Month	£250

2. Scoring of Points

(a) For a win, sixteen points, plus any points scored in the first innings.

(b) In a tie, each side to score eight points, plus any points scored in the first innings.

(c) If the scores are equal in a drawn match, the side batting in the fourth innings to score eight points, plus any points scored in the first innings.

(d) **First Innings Points** (awarded only for performances **in the first 100 overs** of each first innings and retained whatever the result of the match).

    (i) A maximum of four batting points to be available as under:

        150 to 199 runs – 1 point; 200 to 249 runs – 2 points; 250 to 299 runs – 3 points; 300 runs or over – 4 points.

    (ii) A maximum of four bowling points to be taken as under:

        3 to 4 wickets taken – 1 point; 5 to 6 wickets taken – 2 points; 7 to 8 wickets taken – 3 points; 9 to 10 wickets taken – 4 points.

(e) If play starts when fewer than eight hours' playing time remains and a one innings match is played, no first innings points shall be scored. The side winning on the one innings to score twelve points.

(f) The side which has the highest aggregate of points gained at the end of the season shall be the Champion County. Should any sides in the Championship table be equal on points the side with most wins will have priority.

3. Hours of Play

1st and 2nd days . . . . .   11.00 a.m. to 6.30 p.m. or after 110 overs, whichever is the later. (For Sunday play, the home county may decide to play from 12 noon to 7.30 p.m.)

3rd day . . . .   11.00 a.m. to 6.00 p.m. or after 102 overs, whichever is the later.

(a) If play is suspended (including any interval between innings) the minimum number of overs to be bowled in a day to be reduced by one over for each $3\frac{1}{2}$ minutes or part thereof of such suspension or suspensions in aggregate.

(b) If at 5.00 p.m. on the third day, nineteen overs or fewer remain to be bowled, the umpires shall indicate that play shall continue until a minimum of a further twenty overs has been bowled, or until 6.00 p.m., whichever is the later. Play may cease on the third day at any time between 5.30 p.m. and 6.00 p.m. by mutual agreement of the captains.

(c) The captain's may agree or, in the event of disagreement, the umpires may decide to play 30 minutes (or minimum ten overs) extra time at the end of the first and/or second day's play if, in their opinion, it would bring about a definite result on that day. In the event of the possibility of a finish disappearing before the full period has expired, the whole period must be played out. Any time so claimed does not effect the timing for cessation of play on the third day.

(d) If an innings ends during the course of an over, that part shall count as a full over so far as the minimum number of overs per day is concerned.

Intervals

Lunch: 1.15 p.m. to 1.55 p.m. (1st and 2nd days), 2.15 p.m. to 2.55 p.m. on Sundays when play commences at 12 noon
       1.00 p.m. to 1.40 p.m. (3rd day)

Tea: 4.10 p.m. to 4.30 p.m. (1st and 2nd days), 5.10 p.m. to 5.30 p.m. on Sundays when play commences at 12 noon, or when 40 overs remain to be bowled, whichever is the later. 3.40 p.m. to 4.00 p.m. (3rd day), or when 40 overs remain to be bowled, whichever is the later.

4. Substitutes

A substitute shall be allowed as of right in the event of a cricketer currently playing in a Championship match being required to join the England team for a Test match (or one-day international). Such substitutes may be permitted to bat or bowl in that match, subject to the approval of the TCCB. The player who is substituted may not take further part in the match, even though he might not be required by England. If batting at the time, the player substituted shall be retired "not out" and his substitute may be permitted to bat subject to the approval of the TCCB.

The opposing captain shall have no right of objection to any player acting as substitute in the field, nor as to where he shall field. However, no substitute may act as wicket-keeper.

5. New ball

The captain of the fielding side shall have the choice of taking the new ball after 100 overs have been bowled with the old one.

Covering of Pitches and Bowling Ends

The whole pitch shall be covered:

(a) The night before a match and, if necessary, until the first ball is bowled.

(b) On each night of a match and, if necessary, throughout Sunday. In the event of rain falling during the specified hours of play, as soon as play has been abandoned for the day.

The bowling ends shall be covered to a distance of four feet in front of the popping creases if, during the hours of play, the match is suspended.

Declarations

Law 14 will apply, but, in addition, a captain may also forfeit his first innings, subject to the provisions set out in Law 14.2. If, owing to weather conditions, the match has not started when fewer than eight hours of playing time remain, the first innings of each side shall automatically be forfeited and a one-innings match played.

CHAMPION COUNTY SINCE 1864

Note: The earliest county champions were decided usually by the fewest matches lost, but in 1888 an unofficial points system was introduced. In 1890, the Championship was constituted officially. From 1977 to 1983 it was sponsored by Schweppes, and since 1984 by Britannic Assurance.

1864	Surrey	1900	Yorkshire	1950 { Lancashire / Surrey
1865	Nottinghamshire	1901	Yorkshire
1866	Middlesex	1902	Yorkshire	1951 Warwickshire
1867	Yorkshire	1903	Middlesex	1952 Surrey
1868	Nottinghamshire	1904	Lancashire	1953 Surrey
1869 { Nottinghamshire / Yorkshire	1905	Yorkshire	1954 Surrey
		1906	Kent	1955 Surrey
1870	Yorkshire	1907	Nottinghamshire	1956 Surrey
1871	Nottinghamshire	1908	Yorkshire	1957 Surrey
1872	Nottinghamshire	1909	Kent	1958 Surrey
1873 { Gloucestershire / Nottinghamshire	1910	Kent	1959 Yorkshire
		1911	Warwickshire	1960 Yorkshire
1874	Gloucestershire	1912	Yorkshire	1961 Hampshire
1875	Nottinghamshire	1913	Kent	1962 Yorkshire
1876	Gloucestershire	1914	Surrey	1963 Yorkshire
1877	Gloucestershire	1919	Yorkshire	1964 Worcestershire
1878	Undecided	1920	Middlesex	1965 Worcestershire
1879 { Nottinghamshire / Lancashire	1921	Middlesex	1966 Yorkshire
		1922	Yorkshire	1967 Yorkshire
1880	Nottinghamshire	1923	Yorkshire	1968 Yorkshire
1881	Lancashire	1924	Yorkshire	1969 Glamorgan
1882 { Nottinghamshire / Lancashire	1925	Yorkshire	1970 Kent
		1926	Lancashire	1971 Surrey
1883	Nottinghamshire	1927	Lancashire	1972 Warwickshire
1884	Nottinghamshire	1928	Lancashire	1973 Hampshire
1885	Nottinghamshire	1929	Nottinghamshire	1974 Worcestershire
1886	Nottinghamshire	1930	Lancashire	1975 Leicestershire
1887	Surrey	1931	Yorkshire	1976 Middlesex
1888	Surrey	1932	Yorkshire	1977 { Middlesex / Kent
1889 { Surrey / Lancashire / Nottinghamshire	1933	Yorkshire	
		1934	Lancashire	1978 Kent
		1935	Yorkshire	1979 Essex
1890	Surrey	1936	Derbyshire	1980 Middlesex
1891	Surrey	1937	Yorkshire	1981 Nottinghamshire
1892	Surrey	1938	Yorkshire	1982 Middlesex
1893	Yorkshire	1939	Yorkshire	1983 Essex
1894	Surrey	1946	Yorkshire	1984 Essex
1895	Surrey	1947	Middlesex	1985 Middlesex
1896	Yorkshire	1948	Glamorgan	1986 Essex
1897	Lancashire	1949 { Middlesex / Yorkshire	1987 Nottinghamshire
1898	Yorkshire		
1899	Surrey		

Notes: The title has been won outright as follows: Yorkshire 31 times, Surrey 1
Nottinghamshire 14, Middlesex 9, Lancashire 8, Kent 6, Essex 4, Gloucestershire
Warwickshire 3, Worcestershire 3, Glamorgan 2, Hampshire 2, Derbyshire 1, Leicestershire

Eight times the title has been shared as follows: Nottinghamshire 5, Lancashire
Middlesex 2, Surrey 2, Yorkshire 2, Gloucestershire 1, Kent 1.

The earliest date the Championship has been won in any season since it was expanded
1895 was August 12, 1910, by Kent.

BRITANNIC ASSURANCE CHAMPIONSHIP
STATISTICS FOR 1987

County	For			Against		
	Runs	Wickets	Avge	Runs	Wickets	Avg
Derbyshire	9,201	343	26.82	9,220	305	30.2
Essex	7,928	289	27.43	9,074	299	30.3
Glamorgan	9,340	371	25.17	9,311	268	34.7
Gloucestershire	9,495	321	29.57	8,718	247	35.2
Hampshire	9,021	224	40.27	8,612	330	26.0
Kent	9,107	311	29.28	9,409	285	33.0
Lancashire	9,224	301	30.64	8,637	340	25.4
Leicestershire	8,865	293	30.25	8,832	324	27.2
Middlesex	8,798	284	30.97	8,683	275	31.5
Northamptonshire ..	8,120	255	31.84	8,777	310	28.3
Nottinghamshire	8,984	270	33.27	8,235	337	29.4
Somerset	9,670	308	31.39	9,901	300	33.0
Surrey	9,423	296	31.83	9,392	328	28.6
Sussex	8,562	308	27.79	8,268	246	33.6
Warwickshire	9,672	345	28.03	9,294	284	32.7
Worcestershire	9,022	264	34.17	9,681	304	31.8
Yorkshire	8,322	278	29.93	8,710	279	31.2
	152,754	5,061	30.18	152,754	5,061	30.

COUNTY CHAMPIONSHIP – MATCH RESULTS, 1864-1987

County	Years of Play	Played	Won	Lost	Tied	Draw
Derbyshire	1871-87; 1895-1987	2,046	501	753	1	79
Essex	1895-1987	2,009	555	587	3	86
Glamorgan	1921-1987	1,544	337	534	0	67
Gloucestershire ..	1870-1987	2,285	678	842	2	76
Hampshire	1864-85; 1895-1987	2,118	554	734	4	82
Kent	1864-1987	2,406	879	732	4	79
Lancashire	1865-1987	2,484	931	502	3	1,04
Leicestershire ...	1895-1987	1,976	425	743	1	80
Middlesex	1864-1987	2,186	816	564	5	80
Northamptonshire	1905-1987	1,743	413	619	3	70
Nottinghamshire .	1864-1987	2,315	705	602	0	1,00
Somerset	1882-85; 1891-1987	2,016	473	835	3	70
Surrey	1864-1987	2,563	1,027	559	4	97
Sussex	1864-1987	2,455	692	846	5	91
Warwickshire ...	1895-1987	1,990	517	584	1	88
Worcestershire ...	1899-1987	1,931	464	696	1	77
Yorkshire	1864-1987	2,584	1,182	417	2	98
Cambridgeshire ..	1864-69; 1871	19	8	8	0	
		18,335	11,157	11,157	22	7,15

Notes: Matches abandoned without a ball bowled are wholly excluded.

Counties participated in the years shown, except that there were no matches in the yea
1915-18 and 1940-45; Hampshire did not play inter-county matches in 1868-69, 1871-74 an
1879; Worcestershire did not take part in the Championship in 1919.

COUNTY CHAMPIONSHIP – FINAL POSITIONS, 1890-1987

Year	Derbyshire	Essex	Glamorgan	Gloucestershire	Hampshire	Kent	Lancashire	Leicestershire	Middlesex	Northamptonshire	Nottinghamshire	Somerset	Surrey	Sussex	Warwickshire	Worcestershire	Yorkshire
1890	—	—	—	6	—	3	2	—	7	—	5	—	1	8	—	—	3
1891	—	—	—	9	—	5	2	—	3	—	4	5	1	7	—	—	8
1892	—	—	—	7	—	7	4	—	5	—	2	3	1	9	—	—	6
1893	—	—	—	9	—	4	2	—	3	—	6	8	5	7	—	—	1
1894	—	—	—	9	—	4	4	—	3	—	7	6	1	8	—	—	2
1895	—	9	—	4	10	14	2	12	6	—	12	8	1	11	6	—	3
1896	7	5	—	10	8	9	2	13	3	—	6	11	4	14	12	—	1
1897	14	3	—	5	9	12	1	13	8	—	10	11	2	6	7	—	4
1898	9	5	—	3	12	7	6	13	2	—	8	13	4	9	9	—	1
1899	15	6	—	9	10	8	4	13	2	—	10	13	1	5	7	12	3
1900	13	10	—	7	15	3	2	14	7	—	5	11	7	3	6	12	1
1901	15	10	—	14	7	7	3	12	2	—	9	12	6	4	5	11	1
1902	10	13	—	14	15	7	5	11	12	—	3	7	4	2	6	9	1
1903	12	8	—	13	14	8	4	14	1	—	5	10	11	2	7	6	3
1904	10	14	—	9	15	3	1	7	4	—	5	12	11	6	7	13	2
1905	14	12	—	8	16	6	2	5	11	13	10	15	4	3	7	8	1
1906	16	7	—	9	8	1	4	15	11	11	5	11	3	10	6	14	2
1907	16	7	—	10	12	8	6	11	5	15	1	14	4	13	9	2	2
1908	14	11	—	10	9	2	7	13	4	15	8	16	3	5	12	6	1
1909	15	14	—	16	8	1	2	13	6	7	10	11	5	4	12	8	3
1910	15	11	—	12	6	1	4	10	3	9	5	16	2	7	14	13	8
1911	14	6	—	12	11	2	4	15	3	10	8	16	5	13	1	9	7
1912	12	15	—	11	6	3	4	13	5	2	8	14	7	10	9	16	1
1913	13	15	—	9	10	1	8	14	6	4	5	16	3	7	11	12	2
1914	12	8	—	16	5	3	11	13	2	9	10	15	1	6	7	14	4
1919	9	14	—	8	7	2	5	9	13	12	3	5	4	11	15	—	1
1920	16	9	—	8	11	5	2	13	1	14	7	10	3	6	12	15	4
1921	12	15	17	7	6	4	5	11	1	13	8	10	2	9	16	14	3
1922	11	8	16	13	6	4	5	14	7	15	2	10	3	9	12	17	1
1923	10	13	16	11	7	5	3	14	8	17	2	9	4	6	12	15	1
1924	17	15	13	6	12	5	4	11	2	16	6	8	3	10	9	14	1
1925	14	7	17	10	9	5	3	12	6	11	4	15	2	13	8	16	1
1926	11	9	8	15	7	3	1	13	6	16	4	14	5	10	12	17	2
1927	5	8	15	12	13	4	1	7	9	16	2	14	6	10	11	17	3
1928	10	16	15	5	12	2	1	9	8	13	3	14	6	7	11	17	4
1929	7	12	17	4	11	8	2	9	6	13	1	15	10	4	14	16	2
1930	9	6	11	2	13	5	1	12	16	17	4	13	8	7	15	10	3
1931	7	10	15	2	12	3	6	16	11	17	5	13	8	4	9	14	1
1932	10	14	15	13	8	3	6	12	10	16	4	7	5	2	9	17	1
1933	6	4	16	10	14	3	5	17	12	13	8	11	9	2	7	15	1
1934	3	8	13	7	14	5	1	12	10	17	9	15	11	2	4	16	5
1935	2	9	13	15	16	10	4	6	3	17	5	14	11	7	8	12	1
1936	1	9	16	4	10	8	11	15	2	17	5	7	6	14	13	12	3
1937	8	7	11	4	14	12	9	16	2	17	10	13	8	5	11	15	1
1938	5	6	16	7	14	9	4	12	11	17	12	7	3	8	13	11	1
1939	4	8	13	3	15	5	6	17	2	16	12	14	8	10	11	7	1
1946	15	8	6	5	10	6	3	11	2	16	13	4	11	17	14	8	1
1947	5	11	9	2	16	4	3	14	1	17	11	11	6	9	15	7	7
1948	6	13	1	8	9	15	5	11	3	17	14	12	2	16	7	10	4
1949	15	9	8	7	16	13	11	17	1	6	11	9	5	13	4	3	1

	Derbyshire	Essex	Glamorgan	Gloucestershire	Hampshire	Kent	Lancashire	Leicestershire	Middlesex	Northamptonshire	Nottinghamshire	Somerset	Surrey	Sussex	Warwickshire	Worcestershire	Yorkshire
1950	5	17	11	7	12	9	1	16	14	10	15	7	1	13	4	6	3
1951	11	8	5	12	9	16	3	15	7	13	17	14	6	10	1	4	2
1952	4	10	7	9	12	15	3	6	5	8	16	17	1	13	10	14	2
1953	6	12	10	6	14	16	3	3	5	11	8	17	1	2	9	15	12
1954	3	15	4	13	14	11	10	16	7	7	5	17	1	9	6	11	2
1955	8	14	16	12	3	13	9	6	5	7	11	17	1	4	9	15	2
1956	12	11	13	3	6	16	2	17	5	4	8	15	1	9	14	9	7
1957	4	5	9	12	13	14	6	17	7	2	15	8	1	9	11	16	3
1958	5	6	15	14	2	8	7	12	10	4	17	3	1	13	16	9	11
1959	7	9	6	2	8	13	5	16	10	11	17	12	3	15	4	14	1
1960	5	6	11	8	12	10	2	17	3	9	16	14	7	4	15	13	1
1961	7	6	14	5	1	11	13	9	3	16	17	10	15	8	12	4	2
1962	7	9	14	4	10	11	16	17	13	8	15	6	5	12	3	2	1
1963	17	12	2	8	10	13	15	16	6	7	9	3	11	4	4	14	1
1964	12	10	11	17	12	7	14	16	6	3	15	8	4	9	2	1	5
1965	9	15	3	10	12	5	13	14	6	2	17	7	8	16	11	1	4
1966	9	16	14	15	11	4	12	8	12	5	17	3	7	10	6	2	1
1967	6	15	14	17	12	2	11	2	7	9	15	8	4	13	10	5	1
1968	8	14	3	16	5	2	6	9	10	13	4	12	15	17	11	7	1
1969	16	6	1	2	5	10	15	14	11	9	8	17	3	7	4	12	13
1970	7	12	2	17	10	1	3	15	16	14	11	13	5	9	7	6	4
1971	17	10	16	8	9	4	3	5	6	14	12	7	1	11	2	15	13
1972	17	5	13	3	9	2	15	6	8	4	14	11	12	16	1	7	10
1973	16	8	11	5	1	4	12	9	13	3	17	10	2	15	7	6	14
1974	17	12	16	14	2	10	8	4	6	3	15	5	7	13	9	1	11
1975	15	7	9	16	3	5	4	1	11	8	13	12	6	17	14	10	2
1976	15	6	17	3	12	14	16	4	1	2	13	7	9	10	5	11	8
1977	7	6	14	3	11	1	16	5	1	9	17	4	14	8	10	13	12
1978	14	2	13	10	8	1	12	6	3	17	7	5	16	9	11	15	4
1979	16	1	17	10	12	5	13	6	14	11	9	8	3	4	15	2	7
1980	9	8	13	7	17	16	15	10	1	12	3	5	2	4	14	11	6
1981	12	5	14	13	7	9	16	8	4	15	1	3	6	2	17	11	10
1982	11	7	16	15	3	13	2	1	9	4	6	5	8	17	14	14	10
1983	9	1	15	12	3	7	12	4	2	6	11	10	8	11	5	16	17
1984	12	1	13	17	15	5	16	4	3	11	2	7	8	6	9	10	14
1985	13	4	12	3	2	9	14	16	1	10	8	17	6	7	15	5	11
1986	11	1	17	2	6	8	15	7	12	9	4	16	3	14	12	5	10
1987	6	12	13	10	5	14	2	3	16	7	1	11	4	14	15	9	8

Note: From 1969 onwards, positions have been given in accordance with the Championship regulations which state that "Should *any* sides in the table be equal on points the side with most wins will have priority".

DERBYSHIRE

President: The Duke of Devonshire
Chairman: C. N. Middleton
Chairman, Cricket Committee: G. L. Willatt
Secretary: I. Edwards
    County Ground, Nottingham Road, Derby
    DE2 6DA (Telephone: 0332-383211)
Captain: K. J. Barnett
Coach: P. E. Russell

Derbyshire finished sixth in the Britannic Assurance Championship, their highest final placing since 1967, and were in contention for the Refuge Assurance Sunday League title up to the final match of the season. Their Second XI, led by Alan Hill, won the Bain Dawes Trophy, although it was ironic that three of the most successful players in the final against Hampshire, Iain Anderson, Andrew Brown and Paul Taylor, were among the four released. Off-spinner Chris Rudd was the other one to go.

The success owed much to Kim Barnett's leadership, and was especially pleasing as Derbyshire knew when the 1986 season ended that they were short of a spin bowler and at least one batsman. Winter endeavours to sign experienced players, including Ian Botham and Geoffrey Boycott, came to nothing, and only the registration of the Jamaican-born fast bowler, Devon Malcolm, as English for county purposes improved their potential.

Lack of depth in the batting was, to a large extent, overcome by the advance of Bruce Roberts, who more than doubled his modest 1986 aggregate. Roberts opened the season with a masterly 184 in the victory over Sussex, hit four Championship centuries, and was out in the nineties three times in first-class games. He scored hundreds in two of the one-day competitions, and his powerful driving made him one of the most attractive batsmen in the country. Barnett and John Morris also passed 1,000 runs without matching the consistency they can achieve. Barnett's century against Nottinghamshire was widely praised as one of the best innings seen from a visiting player at Trent Bridge for years. He frequently gave Derbyshire a flying start, although his attacking instincts inevitably made him appear rash when he failed. Morris, who signed a five-year contract after returning from a coaching post in Australia, tended to be out when apparently set, then came through strongly in the last month.

With John Wright, who shared the overseas place with Michael Holding, not finding his touch until late in his benefit season, Derbyshire relied on useful, rather than major, contributions from other sources. Rajeshwar Sharma advanced sufficiently to score a maiden century against Yorkshire, and Philip Russell, the coach, has tried to create a situation in which runs can come from almost anywhere in the order. Bernard Maher showed some of the required adaptability. He is short of the necessary class to open the innings but determination carries him part of the way. In his specialist role, he dismissed more batsmen (76) than any wicket-keeper in the country.

Maher's 72 catches showed that the Derbyshire bowlers were finding regular edges. Holding and Ole Mortensen formed the spearhead, Mortensen bowling exceptionally well in all competitions despite frequent knee trouble. For all that he is Danish, he is in the true Derbyshire tradition of grudging seam bowlers. The pace attack was balanced when Paul Newman and Allan Warner were in support, and both were greatly missed when they were injured in mid-season. However, Warner did enough to be capped, as was Maher. Malcolm, out for some time through injury, did not make the expected improvement, although he is capable of bowling as fast as anybody in the country.

The spin department gained an unexpected recruit through force of circumstances. Roger Finney, never the most naturally supple of cricketers, completely lost his ability to bowl the nippy in-swing which had made him such an important component of the team. With great determination, he maintained his batting form and switched to a combination of left-arm spin and cut, finding a measure of success. He and Sharma, whose off-spin remains of the occasional variety, were instrumental in Derbyshire's gaining a tie with Gloucestershire, their first in their 2,219th first-class match. Barnett's leg-spin was vital in two victories, over Lancashire and Glamorgan, and many consider he should bowl more often.

Derbyshire were occasionally prone to spectacular collapses and four of their five defeats were by an innings. To set against those, they registered six victories, one more than in 1986, and were close to winning three other games. They threw away a good position in their final Benson and Hedges Cup group match and, after an exciting victory over Kent, were outplayed by Nottinghamshire in the NatWest Bank Trophy. For much of the summer, they led the Refuge Assurance League but lost their advantage when, in July and August, they were twice beaten between two abandoned games.

Few Derbyshire seasons are complete without some kind of upheaval and, in April, Roger Pearman left after five and a half years as chief executive. The parting was said to be by mutual consent, but Pearman also spoke of a breakdown in his relations with the committee. Ian Edwards, previously the club's accountant, was promoted to secretary and the wider concept of a chief executive was scrapped. – Gerald Mortimer.

DERBYSHIRE 1987

[Bill Smith

Back row: B. J. M. Maher, B. Roberts, M. Jean-Jacques, R. Sharma, P. G. Newman, O. H. Mortensen, D. E. Malcolm, M. Beardshall. Front row: R. J. Finney, M. A. Holding, K. J. Barnett (captain), J. E. Morris, I. S. Anderson.

DERBYSHIRE RESULTS

All first-class matches – Played 25: Won 7, Lost 5, Tied 1, Drawn 12.

County Championship matches – Played 24: Won 6, Lost 5, Tied 1, Drawn 12.

Bonus points – Batting 51, Bowling 70.

Competition placings – Britannic Assurance County Championship, 6th; NatWest Bank Trophy, q-f; Benson and Hedges Cup, 3rd in Group A; Refuge Assurance League, 5th.

BRITANNIC ASSURANCE CHAMPIONSHIP AVERAGES

BATTING

	Birthplace	M	I	NO	R	HI	Avge
‡B. Roberts	*Lusaka, N. Rhodesia*	24	40	3	1,544	184	41.72
§J. G. Wright	*Darfield, NZ*	10	17	2	558	118	37.20
‡K. J. Barnett	*Stoke-on-Trent*	24	39	1	1,370	130	36.05
‡J. E. Morris	*Crewe*	24	37	1	1,294	162	35.94
R. Sharma	*Nairobi, Kenya*	17	27	4	596	111	25.91
‡R. J. Finney	*Darley Dale*	22	34	4	683	77	22.76
‡I. S. Anderson	*Derby*	14	20	2	363	87*	20.16
‡P. G. Newman	*Leicester*	16	22	5	332	42	19.52
‡A. E. Warner	*Birmingham*	17	27	4	444	72	19.30
‡B. J. M. Maher	*Hillingdon*	24	39	1	716	105	18.84
§‡M. A. Holding	*Kingston, Jamaica*	13	18	2	278	63*	17.37
§‡O. H. Mortensen	*Vejle, Denmark*	19	24	10	168	74*	12.00
M. Jean-Jacques	*Soufrière, Dominica*	15	18	2	183	47	11.43
M. Beardshall	*Barnsley*	8	8	3	47	25	9.40
T. J. G. O'Gorman . . .	*Woking*	2	4	1	19	11*	6.33
D. E. Malcolm	*Kingston, Jamaica*	13	16	4	43	9*	3.58

Also batted: C. F. B. P. Rudd (*Sutton Coldfield*) (2 matches) 9, 3*, 0.

* Signifies not out.   ‡ Denotes county cap.   § Not qualified for England.

The following played a total of thirteen three-figure innings for Derbyshire in County Championship matches: B. Roberts 4, K. J. Barnett 3, J. E. Morris 3, B. J. M. Maher 1, R. Sharma 1, J. G. Wright 1.

BOWLING

	O	M	R	W	BB	Avge
O. H. Mortensen	432.5	111	1,084	55	5-57	19.70
M. A. Holding	391.2	72	1,194	49	5-41	24.36
P. G. Newman	341	69	1,059	42	5-46	25.21
R. J. Finney	254.2	55	779	26	3-39	29.96
A. E. Warner	304.5	59	986	32	4-12	30.81
D. E. Malcolm	255	45	898	26	3-47	34.53
R. Sharma	206	46	640	15	6-80	42.66
M. Jean-Jacques	312	52	1,051	24	4-39	43.79
M. Beardshall	158.2	21	572	12	4-68	47.66

Also bowled: I. S. Anderson 10–0–42–1; K. J. Barnett 68.2–19–194–9; J. E. Morris 5.3–0–61–1; B. Roberts 64.2–14–189–8; C. F. B. P. Rudd 29–6–126–1.

Wicket-keeper: B. J. M. Maher 70 ct, 4 st.

Leading Fielders: B. Roberts 22, R. Sharma 19.

DERBYSHIRE v SUSSEX

At Chesterfield, April 25, 26, 27. Derbyshire won by nine wickets. Derbyshire 24 pts, Sussex 6 pts. Toss: Derbyshire. Roberts opened the season with a magnificent, career-best 184, said by his captain to be one of the finest innings he had seen from a Derbyshire player. In glorious weather, Roberts hit the ball with immense strength on a good, but not fast, pitch and reached 100 in 141 minutes. In all, he faced 188 balls, batted for 205 minutes and hit two sixes and 25 fours. With Morris he added 176 in 41 overs. On the second day Sussex were held together only by Colin Wells, who reached 100 in 202 minutes with fourteen fours. Warner, Mortensen and Newman bowled well throughout the match and Sussex, forced to follow on, were saved from an innings defeat by le Roux (79 balls) and Colin Wells, who put on 97 for the ninth wicket. Maher held eight catches in the match, a figure bettered only three times in Derbyshire's history.

Close of play: First day, Sussex 23-0 (R. I. Alikhan 8*, A. M. Green 14*); Second day, Sussex 56-2 (A. P. Wells 12*, A. C. S. Pigott 7*).

Derbyshire

*K. J. Barnett c Green b le Roux	6	– not out	30
J. G. Wright c C. M. Wells b le Roux	6		
B. Roberts c Waring b C. M. Wells	184	– not out	33
J. E. Morris c le Roux b Reeve	76		
†B. J. M. Maher lbw b le Roux	37	– (2) c Gould b le Roux	0
I. S. Anderson c C. M. Wells b Reeve	4		
R. J. Finney b Reeve	4		
P. G. Newman b le Roux	42		
A. E. Warner c Reeve b le Roux	4		
M. Jean-Jacques not out	11		
O. H. Mortensen b Standing	2		
L-b 4, w 1, n-b 3	8	N-b 1	1

1/9 2/18 3/194 4/290 5/297   384   1/5   (1 wkt) 64
6/312 7/355 8/369 9/369

Bonus points – Derbyshire 4, Sussex 4.

Bowling: *First Innings*—le Roux 18-3-64-5; Pigott 17-1-55-0; Reeve 20-2-82-3; Waring 17-1-70-0; C. M. Wells 18-4-84-1; Standing 2.2-0-11-1; Myles 2-0-14-0. *Second Innings*—le Roux 6-0-14-1; Pigott 4-0-29-0; Reeve 3-0-21-0.

Sussex

R. I. Alikhan c Warner b Mortensen	22	– lbw b Finney	6
A. M. Green b Warner	44	– (5) b Mortensen	0
D. K. Standing c Maher b Warner	25	– (2) c Maher b Roberts	27
A. P. Wells c Roberts b Mortensen	4	– (3) c Mortensen b Newman	16
C. M. Wells c Morris b Warner	106	– (7) lbw b Warner	55
S. D. Myles c Roberts b Warner	0	– c Maher b Mortensen	1
D. A. Reeve c Maher b Newman	8	– (6) lbw b Warner	10
*†I. J. Gould c Maher b Newman	0	– (9) c Maher b Warner	10
A. C. S. Pigott c Roberts b Newman	0	– (4) c Morris b Mortensen	18
G. S. le Roux c Maher b Newman	2	– c Maher b Roberts	73
I. C. Waring not out	0	– not out	0
L-b 5, n-b 13	18	L-b 3, n-b 3	6

1/42 2/50 3/107 4/109 5/140   233   1/22 2/41 3/61 4/61 5/71   212
6/140 7/156 8/219 9/233   6/74 7/96 8/113 9/210

Bonus points – Sussex 2, Derbyshire 4.

Bowling: *First Innings*—Newman 22.2-7-44-4; Mortensen 18-6-39-2; Jean-Jacques 16-4-43-0; Finney 6-1-28-0; Warner 16-2-44-4; Roberts 10-2-30-0. *Second Innings*—Newman 16-4-29-1; Jean-Jacques 15-2-51-0; Finney 12-4-21-1; Warner 16-3-52-3; Mortensen 18-7-42-3; Roberts 9.2-2-14-2.

Umpires: H. D. Bird and N. T. Plews.

At The Oval, April 29, 30, May 1. DERBYSHIRE lost to SURREY by an innings and 3 runs.

At Cambridge, May 6, 7, 8. DERBYSHIRE beat CAMBRIDGE UNIVERSITY by 164 runs.

At Derby, May 12. DERBYSHIRE v PAKISTANIS. Abandoned.

At Worcester, May 20, 21, 22. DERBYSHIRE drew with WORCESTERSHIRE.

DERBYSHIRE v WARWICKSHIRE

At Derby, May 23, 25, 26. Derbyshire won by an innings and 107 runs. Derbyshire 23 pts, Warwickshire 2 pts. Toss: Warwickshire. High-class bowling by Holding and Mortensen routed Warwickshire on the first day. While the pitch and the atmosphere helped the bowlers, the batting was poor. Barnett and Maher passed Warwickshire's total without being parted, Barnett scoring 52 of the first 54 runs and hitting eleven fours as he reached his hundred in 163 minutes. Derbyshire failed to collect a fourth batting point, Morris and Anderson both being run out when the score was 299 in the 100th over, but with Holding hitting 50 from 50 balls they established a lead of 297. Warwickshire were soon in trouble again, losing six wickets in 29 overs, although Humpage provided some belated resolution. Derbyshire claimed an extra half-hour without success but needed only five balls to finish the match on the third morning.

Close of play: First day, Derbyshire 213-2 (B. Roberts 35*, R. J. Finney 2*); Second day, Warwickshire 188-9 (G. W. Humpage 87*, N. Gifford 0*).

Warwickshire

T. A. Lloyd b Holding	2	– (2) c Maher b Holding	1
A. J. Moles lbw b Mortensen	8	– (1) lbw b Mortensen	11
A. C. Storie b Mortensen	13	– c Maher b Mortensen	23
D. L. Amiss c Newman b Holding	2	– c Holding b Newman	2
†G. W. Humpage c Morris b Holding	0	– not out	87
P. A. Smith c Maher b Mortensen	14	– c Holding b Mortensen	0
Asif Din c Jean-Jacques b Newman	11	– b Newman	1
G. J. Parsons b Newman	7	– b Warner	23
T. A. Merrick b Mortensen	1	– c Jean-Jacques b Warner	19
T. A. Munton c Maher b Newman	3	– c and b Roberts	2
*N. Gifford not out	5	– b Holding	2
B 4, l-b 2	6	B 5, l-b 5, w 1, n-b 8	19

1/6 2/22 3/29 4/29 5/31   72   1/3 2/26 3/29 4/55 5/57   190
6/50 7/59 8/61 9/65   6/58 7/120 8/156 9/184

Bonus points – Derbyshire 4.

Bowling: *First Innings*—Holding 9-2-19-3; Mortensen 14-3-38-4; Newman 5.3-2-9-3. *Second Innings*—Holding 15.5-2-36-2; Mortensen 16-7-13-3; Newman 11-0-50-2; Warner 13-3-51-2; Jean-Jacques 10-0-22-0; Roberts 3-1-8-1.

Derbyshire

*K. J. Barnett b Munton	125	A. E. Warner c Humpage b Parsons ... 1
†B. J. M. Maher b Merrick	42	M. Jean-Jacques c Moles b Parsons ... 1
B. Roberts c Humpage b Munton	52	O. H. Mortensen lbw b Parsons	1
R. J. Finney c Merrick b Parsons	30	
J. E. Morris run out	25	B 9, l-b 6, n-b 3 18
I. S. Anderson run out	10	
P. G. Newman b Merrick	1	1/124 2/205 3/241 4/271 5/299 369
M. A. Holding not out	63	6/299 7/311 8/312 9/355

Bonus points – Derbyshire 3, Warwickshire 2 (Score at 100 overs: 299-6).

Bowling: Merrick 29–8–100–2; Smith 15–1–61–0; Munton 21–5–51–2; Parsons 25–4–81–4; Moles 8–3–25–0; Gifford 19–6–36–0; Asif Din 1–1–0–0.

Umpires: D. G. L. Evans and B. Leadbeater.

DERBYSHIRE v GLAMORGAN

At Chesterfield, May 30, June 1, 2. Drawn. Derbyshire 7 pts, Glamorgan 6 pts. Toss: Derbyshire. Holding, who bowled superbly, reduced Glamorgan to 4 for three but Morris, their captain, began a recovery which was carried on by a career-highest innings from Cottey. Forced to retire when hit on the left knee by a full toss from Jean-Jacques, he returned to help the last two wickets add 71. Rain took 43 overs from the first day and shortened the second, when van Zyl bowled an impressive opening spell, by a further 35. Although both captains were prepared to attack to achieve a result, they could do nothing when the third day was washed out.

Close of play: First day, Glamorgan 206; Second day, Glamorgan 21-1 (J. A. Hopkins 15*, C. P. Metson 0*).

Glamorgan

J. A. Hopkins c Anderson b Holding	0	– not out	15
*H. Morris c Holding b Jean-Jacques	24	– c Morris b Holding	5
P. A. Todd c Roberts b Holding	3		
G. C. Holmes c Maher b Holding	0		
M. P. Maynard hit wkt b Holding	19		
P. A. Cottey not out	42		
J. G. Thomas c Morris b Mortensen	22		
†C. P. Metson lbw b Mortensen	17	– (3) not out	0
I. Smith c Maher b Holding	13		
C. J. P. G. van Zyl c Roberts b Warner	35		
S. R. Barwick c Maher b Newman	14		
L-b 7, w 4, n-b 6	17	L-b 1	1
1/0 2/4 3/4 4/36 5/89	206	1/21	(1 wkt) 21
6/105 7/133 8/135 9/177			

Bonus points – Glamorgan 2, Derbyshire 4.

Bowling: *First Innings*—Holding 14–2–42–5; Mortensen 13–5–21–2; Newman 9.4–2–28–1; Warner 14–1–60–1; Jean-Jacques 8–2–21–1; Finney 7–1–27–0. *Second Innings*—Holding 6–3–6–1; Mortensen 3–0–13–0; Newman 2–1–1–0.

Derbyshire

*K. J. Barnett c Metson b Thomas	10	M. A. Holding c Todd b Thomas	14
†B. J. M. Maher c Morris b Barwick	5	M. Jean-Jacques c Morris b Thomas ... 12
B. Roberts c Metson b Barwick	37	O. H. Mortensen b Thomas	0
J. E. Morris c sub b van Zyl	56	
I. S. Anderson lbw b van Zyl	17	L-b 9, w 3, n-b 14 26
R. J. Finney c Maynard b van Zyl	40	
P. G. Newman not out	24	1/11 2/45 3/86 4/138 5/146 251
A. E. Warner c Todd b Barwick	10	6/190 7/204 8/225 9/243

Bonus points – Derbyshire 3, Glamorgan 4.

Bowling: Thomas 16–3–66–4; van Zyl 20–4–77–2; Barwick 23–5–95–4; Holmes 2–1–4–0.

Umpires: B. Dudleston and D. O. Oslear.

At Harrogate, June 6, 8, 9. DERBYSHIRE lost to YORKSHIRE by an innings and 169 runs.

DERBYSHIRE v LANCASHIRE

At Derby, June 17, 18, 19. Drawn. Derbyshire 5 pts, Lancashire 7 pts. Toss: Lancashire. With Mortensen maintaining his good form, Lancashire were several times on the verge of collapse, but they always found somebody to give the innings a fresh impetus, suggesting that their position at the top of the table came through a team effort. Rain prevented Derbyshire from batting until the second morning, when Patterson was hostile despite a slow pitch. Morris batted well in an uneven Derbyshire innings. Lancashire scored freely in the final session to extend their lead to 178, only for rain to wash out the third day.

Close of play: First day, Lancashire 258; Second day, Lancashire 118-2 (G. D. Mendis 53*, N. H. Fairbrother 23*).

Lancashire

G. D. Mendis c Maher b Mortensen	4	– not out	53
G. Fowler c Roberts b Mortensen	42	– lbw b Holding	10
D. W. Varey c Maher b Holding	3	– lbw b Barnett	27
N. H. Fairbrother c Anderson b Newman	38	– not out	23
*D. P. Hughes lbw b Holding	39		
M. Watkinson c Jean-Jacques b Warner	33		
I. D. Austin lbw b Mortensen	37		
P. J. W. Allott c Maher b Warner	3		
I. Folley c Maher b Mortensen	28		
†J. Stanworth lbw b Finney	1		
B. P. Patterson not out	0		
B 5, l-b 12, w 7, n-b 6	30	B 1, l-b 1, w 1, n-b 2	5

1/9 2/12 3/70 4/135 5/135   258   1/27 2/78   (2 wkts) 118
6/194 7/201 8/254 9/258

Bonus points – Lancashire 3, Derbyshire 4.

Bowling: *First Innings*—Holding 19–7–44–2; Mortensen 17–4–40–4; Warner 14–1–45–2; Newman 15–3–46–1; Jean-Jacques 8–0–45–0; Roberts 3–0–13–0; Finney 2.1–0–8–1. *Second Innings*—Holding 7–1–39–1; Mortensen 8–1–20–0; Warner 2–0–10–0; Newman 8–0–26–0; Barnett 8–2–21–1.

Derbyshire

*K. J. Barnett b Patterson	3		M. A. Holding run out	1
†B. J. M. Maher lbw b Folley	25		M. Jean-Jacques c Allott b Patterson	14
B. Roberts c Stanworth b Patterson	2		O. H. Mortensen not out	2
J. E. Morris c Stanworth b Folley	60			
I. S. Anderson run out	21		B 4, l-b 9, n-b 6	19
R. J. Finney b Patterson	18			
P. G. Newman b Folley	7		1/15 2/20 3/62 4/129 5/129	198
A. E. Warner b Patterson	26		6/140 7/180 8/181 9/191	

Bonus points – Derbyshire 1, Lancashire 4.

Bowling: Patterson 15.1–1–44–5; Allott 7–2–16–0; Watkinson 11–3–29–0; Folley 32–13–79–3; Austin 13–3–17–0.

Umpires: B. Leadbeater and K. E. Palmer.

At Manchester, June 27, 29, 30. DERBYSHIRE beat LANCASHIRE by 3 runs.

At Leicester, July 1, 2, 3. DERBYSHIRE lost to LEICESTERSHIRE by 47 runs.

DERBYSHIRE v HAMPSHIRE

At Heanor, July 4, 5, 6. Derbyshire won by four wickets. Derbyshire 19 pts, Hampshire 7 pts. Toss: Hampshire. Although they lost only eight wickets in the match, Hampshire were beaten with two balls to spare in the first Championship fixture on this ground. The pitch was excellent for batting but the playing area was far smaller than is desirable for three-day cricket. Nicholas reached a century from 221 balls (a six and fifteen fours) and Turner his in 153 balls (a six and fourteen fours) as they shared an unbroken partnership of 194. During Derbyshire's solid reply, Marshall was warned for intimidatory bowling by umpire Kitchen and taken off at the end of the over by Nicholas. Barnett, who hit sixteen fours in his 91, had already been struck on the helmet when Marshall subjected him to five bouncers in nine balls. A third declaration set Derbyshire 297 in what turned out to be 59 overs. Roberts hit his third Championship century of the season from 117 balls (four sixes, twelve fours) to set Derbyshire on the way, and Finney's excellent half-century steered them to a thrilling victory.

Close of play: First day, Derbyshire 45-0 (K. J. Barnett 27*, J. G. Wright 13*); Second day, Hampshire 86-1 (C. G. Greenidge 52*, M. C. J. Nicholas 4*).

Hampshire

C. G. Greenidge c Roberts b Jean-Jacques	67	– c and b Newman	73
C. L. Smith c Roberts b Newman	58	– lbw b Beardshall	26
*M. C. J. Nicholas not out	103	– c Wright b Newman	18
D. R. Turner not out	104	– c Barnett b Jean-Jacques	0
V. P. Terry (did not bat)		– not out	54
M. D. Marshall (did not bat)		– c Finney b Newman	26
N. G. Cowley (did not bat)		– b Warner	12
†R. J. Parks (did not bat)		– not out	43
L-b 4, w 1, n-b 12	17	L-b 4, w 1, n-b 4	9

1/114 2/155   (2 wkts dec.) 349   1/71 2/122 3/123   (6 wkts dec.) 261
                                                      4/123 5/153 6/169

T. M. Tremlett, R. J. Maru and S. J. W. Andrew did not bat.

Bonus points – Hampshire 4 (Score at 100 overs: 340-2).

Bowling: *First Innings*—Newman 26-7-79-1; Warner 28-9-89-0; Jean-Jacques 22-4-77-1; Finney 2-0-20-0; Beardshall 18.3-2-63-0; Sharma 6-0-17-0. *Second Innings*—Newman 22-2-92-3; Jean-Jacques 25-7-64-1; Beardshall 13.4-1-59-1; Warner 4-1-18-1; Sharma 6-1-24-0.

Derbyshire

*K. J. Barnett b Maru	91	– c Parks b Maru	22
J. G. Wright lbw b Andrew	15	– c Greenidge b Maru	39
B. Roberts c Terry b Marshall	16	– c Terry b Maru	106
J. E. Morris c Turner b Maru	42	– lbw b Cowley	24
†B. J. M. Maher run out	13	– lbw b Marshall	24
R. J. Finney c Greenidge b Cowley	37	– not out	53
R. Sharma not out	48	– c Greenidge b Maru	2
P. G. Newman b Maru	1	– not out	17
A. E. Warner not out	33		
B 4, l-b 6, w 3, n-b 5	18	B 2, l-b 4, n-b 5	11

1/50 2/75 3/152 4/183   (7 wkts dec.) 314   1/45 2/91 3/140   (6 wkts) 298
5/189 6/249 7/250   4/216 5/248 6/266

M. Jean-Jacques and M. Beardshall did not bat.

Bonus points – Derbyshire 3, Hampshire 3 (Score at 100 overs: 268-7).

Bowling: *First Innings*—Andrew 8–2–34–1; Marshall 18–4–38–1; Maru 33–11–90–3; Tremlett 14–3–53–0; Cowley 34–7–89–1. *Second Innings*—Andrew 2–0–13–0; Marshall 14–2–52–1; Maru 23.4–3–123–4; Tremlett 7–0–41–0; Cowley 12–1–63–1.

Umpires: J. A. Jameson and M. J. Kitchen.

DERBYSHIRE v KENT

At Derby, July 15, 16, 17. Drawn. Derbyshire 5 pts, Kent 7 pts. Toss: Derbyshire. Poor catching, especially by Derbyshire, helped to prevent a positive conclusion to a dull match. On a first day reduced by 28 overs because of rain, Derbyshire missed seven clear chances and, with the exception of Mortensen, bowled indifferently. Sharma, who spent two seasons in Kent's second team, held Derbyshire together with the highest score of his career, and when they batted into the third morning, Kent settled for playing out the day. Graham Cowdrey failed to avoid the first ball he received, from Holding, and retired with a broken jaw. Pienaar, on his 26th birthday, reached 100 from 162 balls, hitting two sixes and eleven fours and passing his previous best, made in South Africa, while Aslett squeezed in an unbeaten 101 (168 balls, ten fours) before the game drifted to its end.

Close of play: First day, Kent 216–5 (G. R. Cowdrey 55*, R. F. Pienaar 10*); Second day, Derbyshire 262–7 (M. Jean-Jacques 36*, M. Beardshall 1*).

Kent

M. R. Benson c Sharma b Beardshall	42	– b Holding	19
N. R. Taylor c Maher b Newman	34	– (7) not out	0
G. R. Cowdrey c Maher b Mortensen	68	– retired hurt	0
C. J. Tavaré c Sharma b Mortensen	32	– b Beardshall	22
D. G. Aslett c Roberts b Newman	2	– not out	101
*C. S. Cowdrey c Maher b Beardshall	25	– c Maher b Finney	0
R. F. Pienaar b Mortensen	41	– (2) c Holding b Finney	153
†S. A. Marsh c Maher b Mortensen	7		
A. P. Igglesden b Mortensen	2		
D. L. Underwood b Beardshall	8		
K. B. S. Jarvis not out	3		
B 4, l-b 14, w 5	23	B 5, l-b 5, w 1, n-b 3	14
	287	(4 wkts dec.)	309

1/67 2/89 3/132 4/141 5/187 6/250 7/268 9/283

1/32 2/81 3/287 4/298

Bonus points – Kent 3, Derbyshire 2 (Score at 100 overs: 259-6).

Bowling: *First Innings*—Holding 22–5–41–0; Mortensen 27–8–57–5; Jean-Jacques 27–5–85–0; Newman 8–0–20–2; Beardshall 23.2–4–66–3. *Second Innings*—Holding 13–1–40–1; Jean-Jacques 11–1–42–0; Mortensen 10–2–30–0; Beardshall 6–0–42–1; Sharma 18–2–65–0; Finney 20.3–2–80–2.

Derbyshire

*K. J. Barnett c G. R. Cowdrey b Jarvis	33	M. Beardshall not out	10
†B. J. M. Maher b C. S. Cowdrey	30	M. A. Holding b Igglesden	3
B. Roberts c G. R. Cowdrey b Jarvis	2	O. H. Mortensen c Benson b Pienaar	1
J. E. Morris c Tavaré b Jarvis	49		
R. J. Finney c Marsh b Pienaar	7	B 1, l-b 7, w 1, n-b 2	11
R. Sharma c Marsh b Jarvis	74		
P. G. Newman c Taylor b Pienaar	20		287
M. Jean-Jacques c Marsh b Pienaar	47		

1/46 2/50 3/93 4/123 5/136 6/190 7/261 8/275 9/284

Bonus points – Derbyshire 3, Kent 4.

Bowling: Igglesden 20–0–77–1; Jarvis 19–3–65–4; Underwood 15–9–28–0; Pienaar 22.1–3–66–4; C. S. Cowdrey 15–4–43–1.

Umpires: B. Leadbeater and B. J. Meyer.

At Southend, July 18, 20, 21. DERBYSHIRE drew with ESSEX.

DERBYSHIRE v NOTTINGHAMSHIRE

At Derby, July 22, 23, 24. Nottinghamshire won by an innings and 33 runs. Nottinghamshire 24 pts, Derbyshire 1 pt. Toss: Derbyshire. At the age of 22, Newell became the youngest player in Nottinghamshire's history to score a double-century, taking that distinction away from Tim Robinson. Newell, whose only previous century was against Oxford University in 1986, displayed sound technique, exemplary concentration and, as his confidence increased, a developing range of strokes to bat for 464 minutes, face 402 balls and hit a six and twenty fours. Hemmings took full advantage of some feeble batting to make Derbyshire follow on 285 runs behind, but on the final day Morris delayed Nottinghamshire with a fine 162, facing 217 balls and hitting 26 runs. Although Hadlee did not bowl in the second innings because of knee trouble, the visitors won in comfort as Rice finished the match with three wickets in eleven balls.

Close of play: First day, Nottinghamshire 310-4 (M. Newell 126*, R. J. Hadlee 41*); Second day, Derbyshire 48-2 (B. Roberts 20*, J. E. Morris 21*).

Nottinghamshire

M. Newell not out	203	†C. W. Scott c Holding b Jean-Jacques	4
P. Pollard c Morris b Jean-Jacques	31	E. E. Hemmings not out	8
P. Johnson b Holding	26		
*C. E. B. Rice lbw b Holding	0		
J. D. Birch b Malcolm	69	B 1, l-b 12, w 5, n-b 2	20
R. J. Hadlee c Roberts b Mortensen	70		
D. J. R. Martindale c Maher		1/72 2/107 3/109 4/224 (7 wkts dec.) 433	
b Jean-Jacques	2	5/350 6/389 7/403	

R. A. Pick and K. Saxelby did not bat.

Bonus points – Nottinghamshire 4, Derbyshire 1 (Score at 100 overs: 307-4).

Bowling: Holding 33-6-92-2; Malcolm 22.2-2-100-1; Mortensen 30-2-107-1; Jean-Jacques 26-5-74-3; Sharma 8-2-18-0; Finney 12-2-29-0.

Derbyshire

*K. J. Barnett c Johnson b Pick	19	– c Scott b Saxelby	5
†B. J. M. Maher b Saxelby	18	– c Pollard b Rice	0
B. Roberts b Pick	0	– b Saxelby	30
J. E. Morris c Martindale b Hemmings	62	– b Hemmings	162
R. J. Finney c Martindale b Saxelby	0	– b Saxelby	27
R. Sharma c Saxelby b Hemmings	11	– b Pick	17
I. S. Anderson b Hemmings	27	– b Hemmings	2
M. A. Holding c Martindale b Hemmings	0	– b Rice	3
M. Jean-Jacques c Pollard b Hemmings	4	– b Rice	0
O. H. Mortensen c Johnson b Rice	4	– not out	1
D. E. Malcolm not out	0	– b Rice	0
L-b 1, n-b 2	3	L-b 2, n-b 3	5

1/28 2/28 3/70 4/78 5/104   148   1/4 2/6 3/87 4/173 5/218   252
6/125 7/138 8/143 9/148   6/231 7/251 8/251 9/252

Bonus points – Nottinghamshire 4.

Bowling: *First Innings*—Hadlee 14-7-26-0; Pick 16-5-38-2; Rice 8.1-1-19-1; Saxelby 7-2-26-2; Hemmings 19-7-38-5; Birch 1-1-0-0. *Second Innings*—Saxelby 17-4-48-3; Rice 13.5-0-42-4; Pick 14-1-80-1; Hemmings 29-9-80-2.

Umpires: J. W. Holder and A. A. Jones.

At Bristol, July 25, 27, 28. DERBYSHIRE tied with GLOUCESTERSHIRE.

At Canterbury, August 1, 3, 4. DERBYSHIRE drew with KENT.

DERBYSHIRE v YORKSHIRE

At Chesterfield, August 5, 6, 7. Drawn. Derbyshire 7 pts, Yorkshire 5 pts. Toss: Yorkshire. Derbyshire, without a Championship win over Yorkshire since 1957, were frustrated by poor light after a good match. In his first Championship appearance of the season, Robinson scored an aggressive 95, hitting twelve fours, and was well supported by Neil Hartley. Roberts also reached 95 in Derbyshire's reply, hitting fourteen fours, but it was the ninth-wicket partnership of 151 between Sharma and Mortensen that gave them their decisive lead. Sharma, stuck on 99 overnight, reached his maiden hundred from 221 balls, with eleven fours, and Mortensen passed 50 for the first time. Yorkshire lost six wickets before they cleared the deficit, but Barnett had to wait for a break in the clouds before he could bring back Holding. The Derbyshire captain was then told by the umpires that they would go off if Holding bowled: Holding had expected to send down at least one ball before such a ruling could be made.

Close of play: First day, Derbyshire 121-3 (B. Roberts 65*, I. S. Anderson 7*); Second day, Derbyshire 351-8 (R. Sharma 99*, O. H. Mortensen 49*).

Yorkshire

†R. J. Blakey c Finney b Holding	4	– c Finney b Malcolm	1
A. A. Metcalfe c Maher b Mortensen	8	– c Sharma b Jean-Jacques	56
K. Sharp c Finney b Holding	9	– lbw b Holding	11
J. D. Love c Jean-Jacques b Holding	12	– c Maher b Malcolm	2
P. E. Robinson c Roberts b Jean-Jacques	95	– c Maher b Jean-Jacques	26
S. N. Hartley c Maher b Mortensen	63	– not out	17
*P. Carrick c Mortensen b Holding	3	– c Sharma b Jean-Jacques	3
A. Sidebottom c Jean-Jacques b Roberts	25	– c Maher b Jean-Jacques	33
P. J. Hartley not out	13	– not out	3
P. W. Jarvis c Maher b Roberts	2		
C. Shaw c Maher b Mortensen	0		
L-b 5, w 2, n-b 7	14	L-b 8, n-b 8	16

1/10 2/21 3/24 4/38 5/176   248   1/1 2/36 3/40 4/96   (7 wkts) 168
6/183 7/227 8/235 9/242   5/104 6/113 7/157

Bonus points – Yorkshire 2, Derbyshire 4.

Bowling: *First Innings*—Holding 22-3-85-4; Mortensen 20.1-4-46-3; Malcolm 11-1-50-0; Jean-Jacques 10-0-48-1; Roberts 6-1-14-2. *Second Innings*—Holding 11-3-20-1; Malcolm 9-1-31-2; Jean-Jacques 20-3-61-4; Sharma 3-0-21-0; Roberts 15-6-27-0.

Derbyshire

*K. J. Barnett b Jarvis	22	M. A. Holding b P. J. Hartley	9
†B. J. M. Maher lbw b Jarvis	0	M. Jean-Jacques c Jarvis b Carrick	7
B. Roberts b Carrick	95	O. H. Mortensen not out	74
J. E. Morris c Metcalfe b P. J. Hartley	19	D. E. Malcolm b Sidebottom	6
I. S. Anderson lbw b Jarvis	17	B 3, l-b 13, w 1, n-b 7	24
R. J. Finney b Sidebottom	15		
R. Sharma c P. J. Hartley		1/4 2/34 3/101 4/135 5/171	399
b Sidebottom	111	6/195 7/212 8/222 9/373	

Bonus points – Derbyshire 3, Yorkshire 3 (Score at 100 overs: 263-8).

Bowling: Jarvis 35-8-99-3; Sidebottom 26-3-81-3; P. J. Hartley 30-5-82-2; Shaw 12-3-44-0; Carrick 42-13-77-2.

Umpires: A. A. Jones and B. J. Meyer.

DERBYSHIRE v SURREY

At Chesterfield, August 8, 10, 11. Drawn. Derbyshire 7 pts, Surrey 6 pts. Toss: Derbyshire. Barnett and Maher gave Derbyshire a fine start with a partnership of 140 in 42 overs. Maher held the innings together with his maiden Championship hundred, which he reached in 195 minutes, from 253 balls, with ten fours. It looked as if Derbyshire would miss a fourth batting

)int until Holding carried them past 300 with a remarkable display of power, hitting five xes and two fours in the first 37 balls he faced. Surrey scored freely and Greig, after irviving an appeal for a catch at the wicket, added 116 in 21 overs with Richards before eclaring with the scores level. Maher and Roberts (sixteen fours) put on 169 for Derbyshire's econd wicket but, on the last afternoon, the match drifted into a testy stalemate. Rain, which ad spoiled Chesterfield week, came as a relief at tea.

Close of play: First day, Derbyshire 305-6 (R. Sharma 9*, M. A. Holding 49*); Second day,)erbyshire 72-1 (B. J. M. Maher 34*, B. Roberts 20*).

Derbyshire

K. J. Barnett c Richards b Feltham	86	– c Bullen b Gray	15
B. J. M. Maher c and b Medlycott	105	– c Bullen b Jesty	75
. Roberts c Gray b Medlycott	33	– c Richards b Jesty	93
E. Morris c Richards b Medlycott	1	– b Medlycott	36
S. Anderson c Stewart b Bullen	1	– st Richards b Medlycott	1
.. J. Finney b Medlycott	11	– not out	20
.. Sharma c Richards b Gray	9	– lbw b Bullen	16
1. A. Holding c Bullen b Gray	49		
1. Jean-Jacques lbw b Gray	7	– (8) c Gray b Medlycott	3
1. Beardshall c Clinton b Gray	1	– (9) not out	4
). E. Malcolm not out	9		
B 2, l-b 4, w 1, n-b 4	11	B 4, l-b 2, w 2, n-b 5	13
	323	(7 wkts)	276

/140 2/193 3/207 4/212 5/241   1/20 2/189 3/198 4/203
/248 7/305 8/311 9/314   5/241 6/259 7/264

Bonus points – Derbyshire 4, Surrey 2 (Score at 100 overs: 302-6).

Bowling: *First Innings*—Gray 13.4-3-59-4; Thomas 6-2-26-0; Feltham 34-9-87-1; Greig 2-2-33-0; Medlycott 29-13-86-4; Bullen 14.5-5-26-1. *Second Innings*—Gray 12-2-36-1; 'eltham 23-8-66-0; Medlycott 34-15-74-3; Greig 8-1-38-0; Jesty 16-2-38-2; Bullen -3-18-1.

Surrey

i. S. Clinton c Morris b Holding	58	K. T. Medlycott c Sharma	
.. K. Bullen c Anderson b Malcolm	20	b Jean-Jacques	8
A. J. Stewart c Maher b Jean-Jacques	23	M. A. Feltham not out	4
1. A. Lynch c Beardshall b Malcolm	25	B 5, l-b 8, w 2, n-b 14	29
'. E. Jesty c Sharma b Holding	28		
C. J. Richards not out	68	1/23 2/68 3/126 4/163 (7 wkts dec.)	323
I. A. Greig c Morris b Jean-Jacques	60	5/179 6/295 7/307	

A. H. Gray and D. J. Thomas did not bat.

Bonus points – Surrey 4, Derbyshire 3.

Bowling: Holding 20-3-90-2; Malcolm 17-7-43-2; Jean-Jacques 17-0-107-3; Beardshall 4.5-1-64-0; Sharma 1-0-6-0.

Umpires: A. A. Jones and B. J. Meyer.

DERBYSHIRE v LEICESTERSHIRE

At Derby, August 15, 17. Leicestershire won by an innings and 25 runs. Leicestershire 24 pts,)erbyshire 4 pts. Toss: Derbyshire. The match was effectively decided on the first morning, vhen Derbyshire were swept aside by Agnew's superb bowling. The pitch was green, the tmosphere helpful, and Agnew, bowling the right line and length, was in a vein of excellent orm. Even so, Derbyshire's capitulation in fewer than 25 overs was a pathetic effort; they lost heir last five wickets for 4 runs. Leicestershire were ahead in the twentieth over of their nnings and led by 234 at the close of the first day. Gower reached his second century of the season, including thirteen fours, from 175 balls, but on the second morning Mortense brought Leicestershire's innings to an end with his first hat-trick, dismissing Agnew, Ferr and, after an over from the other end, Such. An unbeaten 87 in 246 minutes by Anders restored some dignity to Derbyshire but they were beaten in two days, Agnew returning matc figures of eleven for 126 to boost Leicestershire's late challenge for the Championship.

Close of play: First day, Leicestershire 305-6 (D. I. Gower 119*, P. Whitticase 12*).

Derbyshire

*K. J. Barnett c Whitticase b Agnew	31	– (7) c Whitticase b Ferris 1
†B. J. M. Maher c Whitticase b Ferris	6	– c Whitticase b Agnew ....
B. Roberts lbw b Agnew	0	– b Ferris 1
J. E. Morris c Whitticase b DeFreitas	5	– (1) lbw b Agnew 1
I. S. Anderson lbw b Agnew	0	– (4) not out 8
R. J. Finney b Agnew	11	– (5) c Whitticase b Clift ....
R. Sharma c Whitticase b DeFreitas	5	– (6) lbw b Ferris 3
A. E. Warner b Agnew	0	– c DeFreitas b Agnew ....
M. A. Holding c Whitticase b Agnew	3	– lbw b Clift 16
M. Beardshall not out	1	– lbw b Agnew ....
O. H. Mortensen lbw b Agnew	0	– b DeFreitas 21
L-b 3, n-b 6	9	B 1, l-b 12, w 1, n-b 4 18

1/34 2/42 3/43 4/47 5/49   **71**   1/3 2/34 3/34 4/68 5/131   **239**
6/67 7/67 8/67 9/71   6/153 7/166 8/189 9/190

Bonus points – Leicestershire 4.

Bowling: *First Innings*—Agnew 12.4-1-46-7; Ferris 7-3-14-1; DeFreitas 5-1-8-2. *Second Innings*—Agnew 26-6-80-4; Ferris 16-2-70-3; DeFreitas 18.2-6-33-1; Clift 16-8-28-2; Such 4-1-15-0.

Leicestershire

I. P. Butcher lbw b Mortensen	40		J. P. Agnew b Mortensen	3
N. E. Briers lbw b Holding	2		G. J. F. Ferris c Maher b Mortensen ..	0
*P. Willey c Anderson b Warner	62		P. M. Such lbw b Mortensen	0
D. I. Gower c Maher b Mortensen 125			B 4, l-b 8, w 1, n-b 9	22
J. J. Whitaker b Holding	12			
P. B. Clift c Anderson b Holding	8			
P. A. J. DeFreitas c Roberts b Finney .	32		1/7 2/81 3/126 4/164 5/180	**335**
†P. Whitticase not out	29		6/257 7/319 8/335 9/335	

Bonus points – Leicestershire 4, Derbyshire 4.

Bowling: Holding 26-5-67-3; Mortensen 25.1-7-71-5; Beardshall 13-0-69-0; Warner 16-0-62-1; Finney 15-3-44-1; Sharma 2-0-10-0.

Umpires: J. H. Harris and D. O. Oslear.

DERBYSHIRE v ESSEX

At Derby, August 22, 24, 25. Drawn. Derbyshire 5 pts, Essex 5 pts. Toss: Essex. Play was possible only on the second day, during which twenty wickets fell. In conditions which favoured the seam bowlers, only Roberts batted with any sustained authority for Derbyshire. Essex appeared to be building a strong position until Newman and Mortensen rattled through their innings, nine wickets falling for 80 runs. Newman took three for 10 in 26 balls to start the slide and Mortensen capped this with three for 2 in fifteen balls. However, a promising situation came to nothing because of rain on the third day.

Derbyshire

K. J. Barnett b Lever	19	M. A. Holding lbw b Pont	1
B. J. M. Maher lbw b Pringle	18	O. H. Mortensen lbw b Foster	5
. Roberts c Lilley b Pont	62	D. E. Malcolm not out	1
. E. Morris c Stephenson b Pringle	8		
S. Anderson c East b Foster	18	L-b 3, w 1, n-b 4	8
R. Sharma c Miller b Foster	6		—
A. E. Warner c Fletcher b Foster	25	1/27 2/55 3/68 4/114 5/129	171
P. G. Newman c Pringle b Pont	0	6/139 7/139 8/147 9/170	

Bonus points – Derbyshire 1, Essex 4.

Bowling: Lever 11–4–19–1; Foster 18.3–4–60–4; Pont 14–1–55–3; Pringle 10–1–34–2.

Essex

D. E. East c Mortensen b Holding	11	N. A. Foster c and b Malcolm	27
P. Stephenson c Maher b Newman	30	I. L. Pont c Mortensen b Holding	15
R. Hardie c Maher b Newman	42	J. K. Lever not out	4
A. W. Lilley c Sharma b Newman	8		
K. W. R. Fletcher c Maher b Mortensen	2	L-b 5, n-b 2	7
A. J. Prichard c and b Mortensen	0		—
D. R. Pringle lbw b Mortensen	3	1/19 2/77 3/91 4/98 5/98	157
G. Miller c Barnett b Malcolm	8	6/99 7/107 8/134 9/138	

Bonus points – Essex 1, Derbyshire 4.

Bowling: Holding 15.2–3–53–2; Mortensen 18–3–47–3; Malcolm 8–3–22–2; Newman 1–0–30–3.

Umpires: J. H. Harris and P. B. Wight.

At Northampton, August 26, 27, 28. DERBYSHIRE drew with NORTHAMPTONSHIRE.

At Nottingham, August 29, 31, September 1. DERBYSHIRE drew with NOTTINGHAM-SHIRE.

At Cardiff, September 2, 3, 4. DERBYSHIRE beat GLAMORGAN by three wickets.

At Taunton, September 9, 10, 11. DERBYSHIRE drew with SOMERSET.

DERBYSHIRE v MIDDLESEX

At Derby, September 12, 14, 15. Derbyshire won by five wickets. Derbyshire 22 pts, Middlesex 4 pts. Toss: Derbyshire. Warner, who was awarded his county cap, gave Derbyshire an early grip by taking four for 12 in ten overs, and Holding made sure there was no escape for Middlesex. By the close of the first day, however, Derbyshire had lost five wickets to Cowans and Fraser, but Finney's excellent 77, his highest of the season, helped the last five wickets to add 174. Barnett was unable to field because of damaged ankle ligaments, so Holding led the side and bowled superbly on the second afternoon. Newman took four for 9 in 52 balls and Maher collected the two catches he needed to head the wicket-keepers' table. Derbyshire had two sessions in which to score 105, and although they slumped to 65 for five, Middlesex applied no pressure. Sharma and Warner made sure of victory in the final match for the fourth season in succession.

Close of play: First day, Derbyshire 102-5 (R. Sharma 20*, R. J. Finney 20*); Second day, Middlesex 143-5 (M. W. Gatting 30*, P. R. Downton 5*).

Middlesex

J. D. Carr c Roberts b Holding	8	– c Sharma b Newman	3
W. N. Slack lbw b Warner	37	– lbw b Holding	7
*M. W. Gatting b Warner	8	– (6) b Newman	43
K. R. Brown c Maher b Warner	2	– (3) lbw b Warner	1
M. R. Ramprakash c Maher b Warner	0	– lbw b Holding	48
M. A. Roseberry c Sharma b Mortensen	33	– (4) b Holding	14
†P. R. Downton c Holding b Mortensen	13	– c Maher b Newman	32
J. E. Emburey b Holding	2	– c Maher b Mortensen	0
S. P. Hughes not out	6	– not out	10
A. R. C. Fraser c Barnett b Holding	17	– c Morris b Newman	5
N. G. Cowans b Holding	0	– b Newman	7
L-b 3	3	B 3, l-b 11, n-b 2	16
	129		**214**

1/24 2/47 3/54 4/54 5/65   1/21 2/30 3/40 4/87 5/118   214
6/89 7/96 8/110 9/129   6/177 7/184 8/196 9/204

Bonus points – Derbyshire 4.

Bowling: *First Innings*—Holding 18.3-1-48-4; Newman 9-2-23-0; Warner 10-3-12-4; Mortensen 17-5-43-2. *Second Innings*—Holding 27-8-69-3; Newman 23.2-9-46-5; Warner 14-4-36-1; Sharma 13-5-24-0; Mortensen 15-6-25-1.

Derbyshire

*K. J. Barnett c Downton b Cowans	13		
†B. J. M. Maher c Carr b Cowans	20	– c Ramprakash b Fraser	24
B. Roberts c Slack b Fraser	17	– lbw b Cowans	2
J. E. Morris c Brown b Cowans	5	– (1) c Slack b Cowans	5
T. J. G. O'Gorman b Fraser	2	– (4) c and b Hughes	4
R. Sharma c Downton b Fraser	27	– (5) not out	28
R. J. Finney b Hughes	77	– (6) c Brown b Emburey	9
A. E. Warner c and b Hughes	17	– (7) not out	27
M. A. Holding c Emburey b Cowans	35		
P. G. Newman not out	13		
O. H. Mortensen b Cowans	1		
B 2, l-b 4, w 1, n-b 9	16	B 1, l-b 2, n-b 3	6
	239	(5 wkts)	**105**

1/23 2/42 3/49 4/54 5/65   1/19 2/21 3/26   (5 wkts) 105
6/131 7/151 8/214 9/237   4/49 5/65

Bonus points – Derbyshire 2, Middlesex 4.

Bowling: *First Innings*—Cowans 22.2-6-58-5; Fraser 32-4-94-3; Hughes 16-1-65-2; Gatting 4-1-16-0. *Second Innings*—Cowans 8-1-14-2; Fraser 14-6-25-1; Hughes 5-0-17-1; Emburey 7-2-37-1; Brown 2-1-8-0; Ramprakash 1-0-1-0.

Umpires: J. Birkenshaw and J. A. Jameson.

ESSEX

President: T. N. Pearce
Chairman: D. J. Insole
Chairman, Cricket Committee: D. J. Insole
Secretary/General Manager: P. J. Edwards
County Ground, New Writtle Street,
Chelmsford CM2 0PG
(Telephone: 0245-354533)
Captain: 1987 – G. A. Gooch
1988 – K. W. R. Fletcher

After scaling the heights in recent years, Essex found the 1987 season was one of disappointments. They finished twelfth in the Britannic Assurance Championship, equal fourteenth in the Refuge Assurance Sunday League, failed to reach the quarter-finals of the Benson and Hedges Cup, and were knocked out in the quarter-finals of the NatWest Bank Trophy. It can be argued that their cause was not helped by a long list of injuries, the most severe of which deprived them of Paul Prichard. His finger was shattered by Warwickshire's Allan Donald in April and this kept him out of action until the last month of the season. However, to put forward injuries as the major excuse for the county's decline would be to ignore the fundamental reason. In short, too many players failed to display consistency of form or application.

There were fears before the start of the summer that there would be too much reliance on Graham Gooch to provide the launching pad for big totals. And they proved well founded. He started well enough with 171 against Gloucestershire at Bristol, but in his first four innings at Chelmsford he recorded "pairs" against Warwickshire and the Pakistanis. That was the prelude to several miserable weeks for him and for Essex, who, following their victory at Bristol, had to wait until the beginning of July for their only other Championship victory – at Old Trafford. Gooch did rediscover some of his form during the latter half of the season, and scored a hundred for MCC in the Bicentenary match at Lord's, but he seldom looked the dominant batsman of old. At the end of the season, he announced he was giving up the captaincy to concentrate on his batting.

That Essex should entrust Keith Fletcher with the leadership once again came as little surprise. No-one doubted his powers of motivation or his shrewd tactical brain, yet the decision to turn to him again must have been taken with some reluctance. He would be 44 in the opening weeks of the 1988 season, and with an eye to the long-term future, a younger player would have been preferable. That was why Fletcher gave way to Gooch in 1986, but no such heir was around this time. Last season, Fletcher was again one of the county's leading batsmen, and his century against Middlesex at Lord's confirmed that he still possessed the skill and concentration to go with his wealth of experience. When it came to gathering runs, however, Brian Hardie was the most consistent for Essex. While Gooch lived through his nightmare in May and the greater part of June, it was the determined Scot who held the batting together, and although some of his strokes are not in coaching manuals, their effectiveness helped bring him some 2,000 runs in all competitions.

The player who had most reason for satisfaction was Neil Foster. He began the season looking set to take 100 wickets again, and that he finished with 86 first-class wickets, rather than 100, was because he emerged during the summer as England's main strike bowler. Career best figures of eight for 107 against Pakistan in the Third Test at Headingley emphasised this point, and his selection as one of *Wisden's* Five Cricketers of the Year complements his achievements of the past two seasons. Unfortunately, Hugh Page failed to live up to expectations as Foster's new-ball partner. Signed as the overseas replacement for Allan Border, the South African fast bowler was constantly called for no-balling during the opening weeks, and he also found that bowling a consistent line and length was a demanding task in English conditions. A knee injury eventually put paid to his hopes of ending the summer on a promising note, but long before then he had been forced to make room for John Lever.

Geoff Miller, having moved from Derbyshire, had almost as much difficulty as Page in making an impact. He did prove a match-winner with eleven wickets in the win over Lancashire, but that accounted for more than a third of his Championship wickets. He also struggled with the bat and failed to register one half-century. David East, despite his competence behind the stumps, was another to gain little satisfaction from his season's run-making which fell a long way short of his 1986 aggregate. Derek Pringle, without ever rising to great heights, showed his value as an all-rounder with 54 wickets and 655 runs in the Championship. He also attracted the attentions once more of England's selectors, who included him in their team for the World Cup. Alan Lilley, whose 783 first-class runs included his first Championship century for nine years, had his rewarding moments, but one was left reflecting at the season's end that Essex may have to wait some time before re-emerging as a powerful force. Border made one appearance, in the NatWest quarter-final against Northamptonshire, and the county were hoping that he would be available to rejoin them in 1988. Essex desperately needed someone of his stature to provide stability.

Two who will be missing from the county's ranks in 1988 are Chris Gladwin and David Acfield. Gladwin, an aggressive left-handed batsman who came to prominence in 1984 with 1,396 runs and the award of his county cap, was released after three barren years, while Acfield announced his retirement following more than twenty years with the county. Acfield's deadpan expression and his dry sense of humour will be missed as much as his bowling. As the off-spinner bowed out with 950 first-class wickets at an average of 28.21 runs each, that can be regarded as a compliment. – Nigel Fuller.

[Bill Smith]

Back row: C. Grinyer, A. D. Brown, A. K. Golding, J. P. Stephenson, N. Hussain, I. Redpath, M. G. Field-Buss. *Middle row:* R. Cole (*physiotherapist*), P. J. Prichard, T. D. Topley, C. Gladwin, I. L. Pont, H. A. Page, N. A. Foster, A. W. Lilley, G. Miller. *Front row:* D. E. East, B. R. Hardie, K. W. R. Fletcher, G. A. Gooch (*captain*), J. K. Lever, D. L. Acfield, D. R. Pringle.

ESSEX RESULTS

All first-class matches – Played 27: Won 3, Lost 5, Drawn 19.

County Championship matches – Played 24: Won 2, Lost 4, Drawn 18.

Bonus points – Batting 45, Bowling 77.

Competition placings – Britannic Assurance County Championship, 12th; NatWest Bank Trophy q-f; Benson and Hedges Cup, 3rd in Group C; Refuge Assurance League, 14th equal.

BRITANNIC ASSURANCE CHAMPIONSHIP AVERAGES

BATTING

	Birthplace	M	I	NO	R	HI	Avge
‡G. A. Gooch	Leytonstone	20	34	6	1,100	171	39.2
‡P. J. Prichard	Billericay	9	12	2	335	72	33.5
‡A. W. Lilley	Ilford	19	27	4	759	102	33.0
‡K. W. R. Fletcher	Worcester	22	31	3	865	121	30.8
‡B. R. Hardie	Stenhousemuir	24	38	4	1,008	111	29.6
‡D. R. Pringle	Nairobi, Kenya	21	31	8	655	84*	28.4
J. P. Stephenson	Stebbing	13	22	3	515	67*	27.1
‡N. A. Foster	Colchester	14	15	2	305	49*	23.4
T. D. Topley	Canterbury	11	13	4	201	66	22.3
‡C. Gladwin	East Ham	7	12	2	202	76	20.20
I. L.Pont	Brentwood	6	7	2	86	39	17.20
§H. A. Page	Salisbury, S. Rhodesia	12	16	4	201	42*	16.75
‡D. E. East	Clapton	24	26	1	394	73	15.76
G. Miller	Chesterfield	20	25	4	290	33*	13.80
‡J. H. Childs	Plymouth	19	19	10	109	26	12.11
‡J. K. Lever	Stepney	13	7	2	60	18	12.00
I. Redpath	Basildon	7	12	1	128	46	11.63

Also batted: M. G. Field-Buss (*Mtarfa, Malta*) (1 match) 6, 34*; N. Hussain (*Madras, India*) (2 matches) 12, 18, 2.

* *Signifies not out.* ‡ *Denotes county cap.* § *Not qualified for England.*

The following played a total of six three-figure innings for Essex in County Championship matches – G. A. Gooch 2, B. R. Hardie 2, K. W. R. Fletcher 1, A. W. Lilley 1.

BOWLING

	O	M	R	W	BB	Avge
N. A. Foster	472.3	93	1,397	61	7-33	22.90
D. R. Pringle	562.4	149	1,365	54	5-70	25.27
T. D. Topley	256.2	55	713	26	4-75	27.42
G. Miller	349.3	74	923	29	7-59	31.82
G. A. Gooch	212.3	55	584	18	4-42	32.44
J. H. Childs	424	126	1,100	33	5-40	33.33
H. A. Page	240.2	34	839	25	4-36	33.56
J. K. Lever	324	77	906	26	5-59	34.84
I. L. Pont	183	19	671	19	5-73	35.31

Also bowled: D. E. East 1-0-5-0; K. W. R. Fletcher 2-0-9-0; B. R. Hardie 13-1-65-0; A. W. Lilley 12-1-77-0; J. P. Stephenson 25.1-3-94-1.

Wicket-keeper: D. E. East 49 ct, 4 st.

Leading Fielders: G. Miller 27, B. R. Hardie 20, G. A. Gooch 16.

At Cambridge, April 18, 20, 21. ESSEX beat CAMBRIDGE UNIVERSITY by 249 runs.

At Lord's, April 22, 23, 24. ESSEX drew with MCC.

At Bristol, April 25, 26, 27. ESSEX beat GLOUCESTERSHIRE by ten wickets.

ESSEX v WARWICKSHIRE

At Chelmsford, April 29, 30, May 1. Drawn. Essex 8 pts, Warwickshire 6 pts. Toss: Essex. Foster, on course for all ten wickets in Warwickshire's second innings until bad light forced his withdrawal from the attack, emerged with the consolation of a career-best seven for 33 when the weather saved the visitors. Fletcher displayed all his experience and skill in compiling two half-centuries but Gooch suffered the ignominy of a "pair". Warwickshire's new fast bowler, Donald, showed promise until injuring his back, but like his fellow South African, Page, Essex's newcomer, he was frequently no-balled.

Close of play: First day, Warwickshire 6-0 (T. A. Lloyd 2*, A. J. Moles 3*); Second day, Essex 45-3 (K. W. R. Fletcher 3*, H. A. Page 2*).

Essex

*G. A. Gooch c Asif Din b Small	0	– b Donald	0
C. Gladwin c Lloyd b Moles	33	– c Lloyd b Donald	24
B. R. Hardie c Thorne b Donald	4	– b Donald	1
P. J. Prichard c Asif Din b Moles	61	– retired hurt	8
K. W. R. Fletcher b Moles	86	– not out	54
D. R. Pringle c Thorne b Parsons	7	– (7) lbw b Donald	3
G. Miller c Humpage b Parsons	1	– (8) b Donald	1
†D. E. East c Humpage b Small	12	– (9) b Donald	11
N. A. Foster c Humpage b Parsons	20	– (10) c Gifford b Moles	40
H. A. Page not out	35	– (6) run out	10
J. H. Childs c Lloyd b Donald	11	– b Moles	0
B 9, l-b 11, w 7, n-b 11	38	B 7, l-b 2, w 4, n-b 4	17

1/0 2/15 3/83 4/141 5/150   308   1/2 2/13 3/36 4/64 5/67   169
6/154 7/173 8/218 9/277   6/70 7/93 8/169 9/169

Bonus points – Essex 4, Warwickshire 4 (Score at 100 overs: 304-9).

Bowling: *First Innings*—Small 15-6-35-2; Donald 19.3-1-84-2; Parsons 38-5-114-3; Gifford 1-0-5-0; Moles 27-9-50-3. *Second Innings*—Donald 20.1-2-74-6; Parsons 24-6-48-0; Moles 4.4-0-38-2.

Warwickshire

T. A. Lloyd b Pringle	12	– c Hardie b Foster	39
A. J. Moles c Gooch b Pringle	28	– c Pringle b Foster	10
P. A. Smith c Miller b Foster	4	– (7) c East b Foster	8
D. L. Amiss c Miller b Pringle	43	– (4) c East b Foster	0
†G. W. Humpage c sub b Page	15	– c and b Foster	12
Asif Din c Miller b Page	1	– c East b Foster	0
D. A. Thorne b Page	20	– (3) c East b Foster	0
G. J. Parsons c Prichard b Gooch	6	– lbw b Miller	13
G. C. Small b Pringle	42	– not out	0
A. A. Donald c and b Page	15	– not out	2
*N. Gifford not out	10		
B 1, l-b 1, w 3, n-b 16	27	L-b 3, w 2, n-b 3	8

1/52 2/53 3/120 4/120 5/127   223   1/50 2/52 3/52 4/65   (8 wkts) 92
6/135 7/138 8/164 9/197   5/65 6/70 7/79 8/90

Bonus points – Warwickshire 2, Essex 4.

Bowling: *First Innings*—Foster 25.4–7–60–1; Page 24.2–5–89–4; Pringle 24.5–8–48–4; Gooch 9–2–18–1. *Second Innings*—Foster 17–4–33–7; Page 6–1–25–0; Pringle 11–4–20–0; Childs 9–6–8–0; Miller 7–5–3–1.

Umpires: H. D. Bird and D. O. Oslear.

At Leicester, May 6, 7, 8. ESSEX drew with LEICESTERSHIRE.

At Chelmsford, May 9, 10, 11. ESSEX lost to PAKISTANIS by 210 runs (See Pakistani tour section).

ESSEX v GLAMORGAN

At Chelmsford, May 20, 21, 22. Drawn. Essex 6 pts, Glamorgan 4 pts. Toss: Glamorgan. The visitors soon rued their decision to bat first on a lively pitch, and Essex were also finding run-gathering difficult until Lilley, with eight fours in a robust innings, enlisted the support of the tailenders to set Glamorgan a challenging task for the final day. However, Holmes batted resolutely and repeated interference from the weather condemned the match to a draw.

Close of play: First day, Essex 75–4 (G. Miller 10*, D. R. Pringle 5*); Second day, Glamorgan 69–0 (J. A. Hopkins 31*, H. Morris 33*).

Glamorgan

J. A. Hopkins lbw b Pringle	21	– c East b Lever	31
*H. Morris lbw b Page	3	– lbw b Lever	33
A. R. Butcher run out	10	– c Lilley b Topley	25
G. C. Holmes lbw b Page	12	– c Fletcher b Page	74
M. P. Maynard lbw b Topley	0	– not out	39
J. Derrick lbw b Pringle	1	– not out	1
†C. P. Metson c Hardie b Pringle	24		
I. Smith c Pringle b Lever	10		
C. J. P. G. van Zyl c East b Topley	23		
P. D. North c Fletcher b Pringle	6		
S. R. Barwick not out	2		
L-b 2, w 1, n-b 4	7	B 2, l-b 7, w 1, n-b 3	13

1/7 2/31 3/45 4/45 5/50   119   1/69 2/72   (4 wkts dec.) 216
6/57 7/72 8/110 9/112   3/142 4/213

Bonus points – Essex 4.

Bowling: *First Innings*—Lever 22–7–35–1; Page 14–7–23–2; Pringle 16.5–4–34–4; Topley 9–1–25–2. *Second Innings*—Lever 27–5–69–2; Page 13–3–35–1; Pringle 17–5–33–0; Topley 25–9–43–1; Miller 5–1–27–0.

Essex

C. Gladwin c North b Smith	1	†D. E. East lbw b van Zyl	10
I. Redpath c Metson b van Zyl	0	T. D. Topley c Metson b Barwick	31
B. R. Hardie b Smith	0	J. K. Lever c Butcher b Derrick	12
*K. W. R. Fletcher c Metson b Derrick	20		
G. Miller run out	20	L-b 7, w 6, n-b 7	20
D. R. Pringle c Morris b Barwick	18		
A. W. Lilley not out	80	1/1 2/1 3/51 4/61 5/100	253
H. A. Page c Smith b Derrick	10	6/115 7/133 8/158 9/220	

Bonus points – Essex 2, Glamorgan 4 (Score at 100 overs: 224–9).

Bowling: van Zyl 34–7–79–2; Smith 27–7–62–2; Barwick 34–9–64–2; Derrick 10.1–0–32–3; Holmes 4–1–9–0.

Umpires: B. Dudleston and D. G. L. Evans.

At The Oval, May 23, 25, 26. ESSEX drew with SURREY.

At Worcester, May 30, June 1, 2. ESSEX drew with WORCESTERSHIRE.

At Lord's, June 3, 4, 5. ESSEX drew with MIDDLESEX.

At Tunbridge Wells, June 6, 8, 9. ESSEX drew with KENT.

ESSEX v KENT

At Ilford, June 13, 15, 16. Drawn. Essex 14 pts, Kent 5 pts. Toss: Kent. Both captains entered into the right spirit to set up a thrilling finish. Foster, who had joined Pringle with 62 required from the final eight overs, was run out off the last ball by Cowdrey as he went for the second run that would have signalled an Essex victory. However, Essex had the consolation of receiving an additional 8 points as the side batting second with the scores finishing level. In a match frequently interrupted by rain, Pienaar, an all-rounder from Northern Transvaal, marked his début for Kent by top-scoring in the first innings and twice removing Gooch. East, with 73 from 95 deliveries, saved Essex's first innings, and on the last day Taylor, who hit seventeen fours, and Tavaré, whose 88 came from 92 balls, sent Kent racing to a declaration with 153 in 90 minutes as Hardie and Lilley tossed the ball up.

Close of play: First day, Essex 54-4 (K. W. R. Fletcher 14*, D. R. Pringle 2*); Second day, Kent 78-0 (M. R. Benson 35*, N. R. Taylor 38*).

Kent

M. R. Benson c East b Pringle	31	– lbw b Page	43
N. R. Taylor lbw b Page	0	– not out	142
S. G. Hinks c Hardie b Page	4	– b Pringle	14
C. J. Tavaré b Foster	23	– not out	88
D. G. Aslett c Miller b Pringle	5		
*C. S. Cowdrey c East b Pringle	13		
R. F. Pienaar c Childs b Foster	41		
†S. A. Marsh b Foster	0		
C. Penn c and b Page	17		
A. P. Igglesden b Page	6		
D. L. Underwood not out	2		
B 1, l-b 1, w 1, n-b 7	10	B 1, l-b 7, w 3, n-b 4	15

1/2 2/6 3/56 4/64 5/68   152   1/103 2/149   (2 wkts dec.) 302
6/83 7/85 8/126 9/139

Bonus points – Kent 1, Essex 4.

Bowling: *First Innings*—Foster 24.3–4–56–3; Page 12–2–36–4; Miller 7–3–16–0; Childs 4–1–7–0; Pringle 15–6–25–3; Gooch 7–3–10–0. *Second Innings*—Foster 20–7–45–0; Page 16–4–32–1; Gooch 10–3–33–0; Pringle 15–4–33–1; Childs 3–2–1–0; Miller 3–0–8–0; Hardie 13–1–65–0; Lilley 12–1–77–0.

Essex

*G. A. Gooch c Marsh b Pienaar	12	– c Marsh b Pienaar	11
C. Gladwin b Igglesden	7	– lbw b Igglesden	0
B. R. Hardie c Hinks b Igglesden	6	– c Hinks b Pienaar	40
K. W. R. Fletcher c Marsh b Penn	29		
G. Miller c Aslett b Penn	7		
D. R. Pringle lbw b Penn	37	– (4) not out	84
A. W. Lilley c Marsh b Pienaar	2	– (5) run out	23
H. A. Page run out	15	– (7) b Penn	0
†D. E. East lbw b Underwood	73	– (6) c Pienaar b Penn	7
N. A. Foster c Marsh b Pienaar	10	– (8) run out	37
J. H. Childs not out	6		
L-b 11, w 7, n-b 1	19	B 12, l-b 15, w 2	29

1/11 2/19 3/28 4/43 5/85	223	1/4 2/32 3/89 4/150 (7 wkts) 231
6/98 7/125 8/146 9/179		5/170 6/171 7/231

Bonus points – Essex 2, Kent 4.

Bowling: *First Innings*—Igglesden 29–8–50–2; Pienaar 34–11–84–3; Penn 20–3–52–3; Underwood 13.2–7–26–1. *Second Innings*—Pienaar 12–0–50–2; Igglesden 10–0–38–1; Penn 15–0–71–2; Underwood 9–2–45–0.

Umpires: M. J. Kitchen and D. R. Shepherd.

ESSEX v NORTHAMPTONSHIRE

At Ilford, June 17, 18, 19. Drawn. Essex 7 pts, Northamptonshire 3 pts. Toss: Essex. Gooch, after a lean season, returned to form with an innings that contained 23 boundaries and lasted 280 minutes. It was only the second time in twelve completed innings that the Essex captain had topped 50. Northamptonshire, 85 runs behind at the end of the second day, declared in the hope of being set a target, but once again the weather was the victor. Well under an hour's play was all that was possible on the third day – there was no play elsewhere in the Championship – and during that time Essex were fed runs by Northamptonshire's occasional bowlers. Ripley, their wicket-keeper, claimed the first Championship wickets of his career.

Close of play: First day, Essex 159-2 (G. A. Gooch 93*, K. W. R. Fletcher 14*); Second day, Northamptonshire 216-8 (D. J. Wild 20*, W. W. Davis 18*).

Essex

*G. A. Gooch lbw b Walker	159		
I. Redpath c Lamb b Capel	28	– c N. G. B. Cook b Lamb	46
B. R. Hardie c Ripley b Davis	13	– not out	45
K. W. R. Fletcher c Ripley b Davis	24		
G. Miller not out	33		
D. R. Pringle not out	21		
A. W. Lilley (did not bat)		– (1) c Walker b Ripley	7
†D. E. East (did not bat)		– (4) c Capel b Ripley	13
H. A. Page (did not bat)		– (5) not out	42
L-b 13, w 1, n-b 9	23	L-b 2	2

1/64 2/105 3/185 4/276	(4 wkts dec.) 301	1/7 2/81 3/96 (3 wkts) 155

J. K. Lever and J. H. Childs did not bat.

Bonus points – Essex 4, Northamptonshire 1.

Bowling: *First Innings*—Davis 21–2–83–2; Capel 21–2–84–1; N. G. B. Cook 23.1–8–53–0; Williams 2–0–9–0; Walker 24–5–59–1. *Second Innings*—G. Cook 3–0–29–0; Ripley 9–0–89–2; Lamb 2–0–18–1; Larkins 4.2–0–17–0.

Northamptonshire

*G. Cook c Hardie b Lever	0	N. G. B. Cook c Gooch b Pringle	0
W. Larkins c Miller b Pringle	42	W. W. Davis not out	18
R. J. Bailey lbw b Page	29		
A. J. Lamb b Gooch	33	L-b 1, n-b 4	5
D. J. Capel c Lilley b Page	24		
R. G. Williams c Fletcher b Page	37	1/0 2/49 3/100	(8 wkts dec.) 216
D. J. Wild not out	20	4/120 5/160 6/175	
†D. Ripley b Pringle	8	7/192 8/192	

A. Walker did not bat.

Bonus points – Northamptonshire 2, Essex 3.

Bowling: Lever 14–3–41–1; Page 16–3–53–3; Gooch 7–2–36–1; Pringle 13–5–30–3; Miller 7–3–20–0; Childs 8–2–35–0.

Umpires: M. J. Kitchen and D. R. Shepherd.

At Leeds, June 20, 22, 23. ESSEX lost to YORKSHIRE by nine wickets.

ESSEX v SOMERSET

At Chelmsford, June 27, 29, 30. Drawn. Essex 5 pts, Somerset 7 pts. Toss: Essex. A masterful display by Crowe, who batted for 260 minutes, highlighted Somerset's first innings and Burns, playing against his former county, dominated their second with his maiden century. Coming in after four wickets had fallen for 41, Burns attacked the bowling from the start and hit fourteen fours to reach three figures from 161 deliveries. Gooch and Fletcher were the only Essex batsmen to look at ease in the Essex first innings, with the Essex captain again confirming his return to form when the match was condemned to a tame draw by Somerset's unrealistic declaration.

Close of play: First day, Essex 26-0 (G. A. Gooch 8*, J. P. Stephenson 14*); Second day, Somerset 41-3 (N. A. Felton 25*, N. J. Pringle 5*).

Somerset

N. A. Felton lbw b Gooch	51	– (2) c Hardie b Miller	49
*V. J. Marks lbw b Foster	0	– (1) c Fletcher b Foster	8
J. J. E. Hardy lbw b Topley	50	– c Miller b Pringle	0
M. D. Crowe c Miller b Childs	100	– c Gooch b Pringle	0
N. J. Pringle c East b Topley	21	– lbw b Pringle	5
†N. D. Burns b Pringle	3	– not out	100
G. D. Rose c East b Topley	3	– c Hardie b Topley	24
G. V. Palmer c and b Foster	10	– c Pringle b Foster	4
M. D. Harman c East b Foster	4	– c Lilley b Topley	11
N. A. Mallender not out	8	– not out	0
A. N. Jones c Gooch b Childs	0		
L-b 11, w 4, n-b 11	26	B 1, l-b 10, w 1, n-b 7	19

1/1 2/72 3/136 4/172 5/176	276	1/25 2/28 3/28	(8 wkts dec.) 220
6/201 7/232 8/256 9/276		4/41 5/130 6/190	
		7/197 8/216	

Bonus points – Somerset 3, Essex 3 (Score at 100 overs: 276-8).

Bowling: *First Innings*—Foster 26–3–109–3; Pringle 18–4–35–1; Miller 9–1–15–0; Topley 26–4–56–3; Gooch 13–2–28–1; Childs 8.3–3–22–2. *Second Innings*—Foster 27–5–80–2; Pringle 15–5–27–3; Miller 16–4–33–1; Topley 9–0–37–2; Gooch 2–0–3–0; Childs 9–0–29–0.

Essex

*G. A. Gooch c Harman b Jones	46	– not out	56
J. P. Stephenson c Felton b Rose	24	– c Mallender b Rose	41
B. R. Hardie lbw b Palmer	6		
K. W. R. Fletcher c Rose b Palmer	61		
G. Miller c Harman b Marks	18		
D. R. Pringle c Burns b Rose	6	– (3) c Burns b Rose	9
A. W. Lilley b Marks	6	– (4) not out	8
N. A. Foster c Harman b Palmer	5		
†D. E. East b Marks	21		
T. D. Topley not out	7		
J. H. Childs c Hardy b Marks	0		
B 4, l-b 11, w 10, n-b 6	31	L-b 2, w 2	4

1/47 2/61 3/110 4/145 5/156   231   1/95 2/106   (2 wkts) 118
6/178 7/199 8/224 9/225

Bonus points – Essex 2, Somerset 4.

Bowling: *First Innings*—Jones 14–3–27–1; Mallender 10–1–36–0; Rose 17–5–30–2; Palmer 19–4–52–3; Pringle 4–1–13–0; Marks 24.4–6–48–4; Harman 8–1–10–0. *Second Innings*—Rose 11–1–35–2; Palmer 8–1–34–0; Marks 12–2–47–0.

Umpires: B. Leadbeater and D. Lloyd.

At Manchester, July 1, 2, 3. ESSEX beat LANCASHIRE by 73 runs.

ESSEX v HAMPSHIRE

At Southend, July 15, 16, 17. Drawn. Essex 2 pts, Hampshire 8 pts. Toss: Hampshire. Rain denied Hampshire the chance of victory, robbing them of seventeen overs in the final hour after washing out that morning's session. Robin Smith, arriving at the crease after three wickets had fallen in fewer than five overs, batted magnificently on a good batting wicket to record a career-best 209 not out off 269 balls. Among his 30 fours were commanding drives on either side of the wicket, while anything short was hooked or cut with conviction. The memory does not recall his giving a chance, and having put the Essex attack in its place, he received fine support in century stands from Turner and Parks. Poor strokes, lack of application and a burst of three wickets in five balls by Connor were the reasons for Essex's being asked to follow on 282 behind.

Close of play: First day, Essex 24–2 (G. A. Gooch 7*, B. R. Hardie 3*); Second day, Essex 47–1 (G. A. Gooch 33*, T. D. Topley 8*).

Hampshire

C. G. Greenidge c East b Topley	0	†R. J. Parks c Stephenson b Miller	58
C. L. Smith run out	1	T. M. Tremlett not out	17
*M. C. J. Nicholas c Pringle b Foster	3	L-b 11, n-b 9	20
D. R. Turner b Foster	61		
R. A. Smith not out	209	1/1 2/4 3/5 (6 wkts dec.) 373	
N. G. Cowley b Page	4	4/170 5/186 6/319	

R. J. Maru, C. A. Connor and S. J. W. Andrew did not bat.

Bonus points – Hampshire 4, Essex 2.

Bowling: Foster 23–6–66–2; Topley 18–3–70–1; Page 15–0–71–1; Childs 11–2–48–0; Miller 25–1–82–1; Gooch 8–2–25–0.

Essex

*G. A. Gooch c Parks b Connor	18	– c Nicholas b Maru	48
J. P. Stephenson c Greenidge b Connor	8	– b Connor	3
T. D. Topley c R. A. Smith b Andrew	6	– c Parks b Maru	10
B. R. Hardie c Parks b Connor	5	– not out	44
K. W. R. Fletcher b Connor	0	– lbw b Tremlett	26
G. Miller c R. A. Smith b Tremlett	10	– lbw b Tremlett	6
D. R. Pringle b Maru	26	– b Maru	8
H. A. Page b Tremlett	1	– not out	0
N. A. Foster c Parks b Andrew	9		
†D. E. East c R. A. Smith b Maru	1		
J. H. Childs not out	0		
B 4, l-b 2, w 1	7	B 3, l-b 3, w 1, n-b 3	10
	91		**(6 wkts) 155**

1/8 2/21 3/37 4/37 5/38   1/27 2/66 3/71   (6 wkts) 155
6/75 7/77 8/87 9/89   4/130 5/140 6/151

Bonus points – Hampshire 4.

Bowling: *First Innings*—Andrew 14–5–38–2; Connor 14–5–26–4; Tremlett 15–8–10–2; Maru 12.4–4–11–2. *Second Innings*—Andrew 13–2–49–0; Connor 14–4–27–1; Maru 22–9–31–3; Tremlett 17–8–23–2; Cowley 9.3–5–19–0; C. L. Smith 1–1–0–0.

Umpires: D. J. Constant and J. W. Holder.

ESSEX v DERBYSHIRE

At Southend, July 18, 20, 21. Drawn. Toss: Essex. The final two days were completely washed out after just eight overs had been possible on the opening day.

Derbyshire

*K. J. Barnett b Foster	0
J. G. Wright not out	4
B. Roberts not out	5
L-b 1	1
	10

1/0   (1 wkt) 10

J. E. Morris, †B. J. M. Maher, R. J. Finney, R. Sharma, M. Beardshall, M. Jean-Jacques, O. H. Mortensen and D. E. Malcolm did not bat.

Bowling: Foster 4–4–0–1; Lever 4–1–9–0.

Essex

*G. A. Gooch, J. P. Stephenson, B. R. Hardie, K. W. R. Fletcher, G. Miller, A. W. Lilley, N. A. Foster, †D. E. East, T. D. Topley, J. H. Childs and J. K. Lever.

Umpires: D. J. Constant and J. W. Holder.

At Portsmouth, July 25, 27, 28. ESSEX drew with HAMPSHIRE.

At Eastbourne, August 5, 6, 7. ESSEX drew with SUSSEX.

At Northampton, August 8, 10, 11. ESSEX drew with NORTHAMPTONSHIRE.

ESSEX v MIDDLESEX

At Chelmsford, August 15, 17, 18. Drawn. Essex 6 pts, Middlesex 3 pts. Toss: Middlesex. Having been set a target of 230 in 47 overs, Essex were a considerable way short when stumps were drawn midway through the final hour. Ramprakash, with his highest score, held the Middlesex innings together on the first day, and in the second innings Gatting thrashed five sixes and fifteen fours while racing to 132 from 150 deliveries. Three of his sixes came from successive balls by Childs, but on a pitch always giving a little encouragement, the Essex left-arm spinner bowled well to end with ten wickets in the match. Lilley, with his first century since marking his début with 100 not out against Nottinghamshire nine years earlier, batted for almost four and threequarter hours to put Essex in a sound position on the second day.

Close of play: First day, Essex 104-3 (A. W. Lilley 36*, P. J. Prichard 11*); Second day, Middlesex 123-1 (J. D. Carr 68*, M. W. Gatting 38*).

Middlesex

W. N. Slack st East b Childs	20	– lbw b Foster	11
J. D. Carr lbw b Foster	7	– c East b Foster	78
*M. W. Gatting b Pringle	7	– c Foster b Childs	132
K. R. Brown c Childs b Pringle	4	– c Childs b Miller	42
M. R. Ramprakash b Miller	71	– lbw b Childs	0
†P. R. Downton b Childs	12	– c Lilley b Childs	3
J. E. Emburey c Miller b Childs	11	– st East b Childs	25
A. R. C. Fraser lbw b Miller	17	– c Foster b Childs	14
N. G. Cowans c East b Childs	3	– c Stephenson b Miller	4
P. C. R. Tufnell c Pringle b Childs	2	– not out	1
W. W. Daniel not out	0	– not out	9
L-b 10, n-b 2	12	B 4, l-b 8, n-b 2	14

1/11 2/23 3/34 4/53 5/89   166   1/25 2/163 3/264   (9 wkts dec.) 333
6/101 7/159 8/164 9/164   4/265 5/271 6/278
                             7/311 8/320 9/323

Bonus points – Middlesex 1, Essex 4.

Bowling: *First Innings*—Foster 21-2-59-1; Pringle 18-8-29-2; Childs 24.5-11-40-5; Gooch 4-1-13-0; Miller 9-3-15-2. *Second Innings*—Foster 20-3-86-2; Childs 31-4-120-5; Pringle 13-3-42-0; Gooch 2-0-5-0; Miller 21-2-68-2.

Essex

*G. A. Gooch c Gatting b Cowans	1	– c Emburey b Daniel	6
J. P. Stephenson c Brown b Tufnell	46	– c Ramprakash b Daniel	29
B. R. Hardie b Daniel	1	– not out	55
A. W. Lilley b Tufnell	102	– c Slack b Daniel	9
P. J. Prichard c Brown b Emburey	37		
K. W. R. Fletcher lbw b Emburey	0	– (5) not out	23
D. R. Pringle c Carr b Fraser	1		
G. Miller c Brown b Emburey	28		
N. A. Foster st Downton b Emburey	11		
†D. E. East c Ramprakash b Tufnell	13		
J. H. Childs not out	10		
B 1, l-b 11, w 1, n-b 7	20	B 6, l-b 7, n-b 7	20

1/1 2/4 3/70 4/150 5/152   270   1/36 2/52 3/69   (3 wkts) 142
6/156 7/235 8/235 9/249

Bonus points – Essex 2, Middlesex 2 (Score at 100 overs: 225-6).

Bowling: *First Innings*—Daniel 11-2-32-1; Cowans 9-2-30-1; Emburey 48.1-11-95-4; Tufnell 30-3-82-3; Fraser 17-7-19-1. *Second Innings*—Cowans 2-0-9-0; Daniel 8-0-33-3; Emburey 14-2-30-0; Tufnell 15-1-57-0.

Umpires: A. A. Jones and B. Leadbeater.

ESSEX v NOTTINGHAMSHIRE

At Chelmsford, August 19, 20, 21. Drawn. Essex 4 pts, Nottinghamshire 5 pts. Toss: Nottinghamshire. Coming to the last twenty overs needing 95 to win and with six wickets in hand, Essex were favourably placed to beat the Championship leaders, who were without four key players because of the MCC Bicentenary match at Lord's. However, they lost four wickets in five overs and Foster and Pont had to bat through nine overs to secure the draw. Robinson, dropped three times before he reached 50, and Newell put on 216 as Nottinghamshire scored freely on the opening day, Robinson hitting fourteen fours in his 137 and Newell a six and seven fours in his 133. They also shared a century opening stand in the second innings. Hardie and Stephenson batted attractively in putting on 135 at the start of Essex's first innings, while Prichard looked to be in excellent form as he consolidated their bid to score 292 in 69 overs' minimum. For Nottinghamshire, Hemmings, on a pitch almost devoid of grass, sent down 37 overs and claimed five victims during a spell interrupted only by tea.

Close of play: First day, Essex 11-0 (B. R. Hardie 6*, J. P. Stephenson 4*); Second day, Nottinghamshire 90-0 (R. T. Robinson 50*, M. Newell 38*).

Nottinghamshire

*R. T. Robinson c Miller	137	– c Stephenson b Miller	76
P. Pollard lbw b Foster	9		
M. Newell not out	133	– (2) c Pringle b Miller	55
P. Johnson c Childs b Miller	52	– (3) c East b Pont	8
J. D. Birch not out	9	– (4) lbw b Miller	5
D. J. R. Martindale (did not bat)		– (5) not out	19
†C. W. Scott (did not bat)		– (6) c Pont b Miller	0
E. E. Hemmings (did not bat)		– (7) not out	6
B 1, l-b 10, n-b 9	20	B 4, l-b 8	12

1/22 2/238 3/316   (3 wkts dec.) 360   1/120 2/133 3/142   (5 wkts dec.) 181
                                                  4/155 5/155

R. A. Pick, K. Saxelby and M. K. Bore did not bat.

Bonus points – Nottinghamshire 4, Essex 1 (Score at 100 overs: 324-3).

Bowling: *First Innings*—Foster 14-5-30-1; Pont 17-1-86-0; Pringle 15-3-52-0; Miller 39-12-125-2; Childs 21-5-56-0. *Second Innings*—Foster 6-0-29-0; Pont 23-2-65-1; Pringle 2-2-0-0; Childs 6-1-16-0; Miller 21-4-59-4.

Essex

B. R. Hardie lbw b Hemmings	71	– lbw b Hemmings	15
J. P. Stephenson b Pick	67	– b Saxelby	4
A. W. Lilley b Bore	4	– lbw b Hemmings	36
*K. W. R. Fletcher b Bore	11	– (6) lbw b Hemmings	30
P. J. Prichard not out	35	– (4) st Scott b Bore	72
D. R. Pringle not out	35	– (5) c Birch b Hemmings	41
†D. E. East (did not bat)		– lbw b Hemmings	5
N. A. Foster (did not bat)		– not out	4
G. Miller (did not bat)		– lbw b Bore	1
I. L. Pont (did not bat)		– not out	4
B 4, l-b 14, w 1, n-b 8	27	B 6, l-b 10, n-b 4	20

1/135 2/145 3/171 4/171   (4 wkts dec.) 250   1/7 2/61 3/62 4/137   (8 wkts) 234
                                                   5/212 6/222 7/222 8/228

J. H. Childs did not bat.

Bonus points – Essex 3, Nottinghamshire 1.

Bowling: *First Innings*—Saxelby 12-4-31-0; Pick 18-2-58-1; Hemmings 28-6-74-1; Bore 33.2-13-66-2; Newell 2-0-3-0. *Second Innings*—Saxelby 11-0-25-1; Pick 14-3-23-0; Hemmings 37-11-112-5; Bore 16-4-58-2.

Umpires: A. A. Jones and B. Leadbeater.

At Derby, August 22, 24, 25. ESSEX drew with DERBYSHIRE.

ESSEX v SURREY

At Colchester, August 29, 31, September 1. Surrey won by three wickets. Surrey 22 pts, Essex 4 pts. Toss: Surrey. Clarke's hat-trick to remove Lilley, Gooch and Fletcher with the first three balls of his seventh over, and the dismissal of Prichard with his fifth, rocked Essex on a pitch that had been affected by rain. Although Surrey then built a useful first-innings lead, Essex batted with greater application second time around to leave the visitors requiring 147 to win in a minimum of 57 overs. When they were 90 for six, it seemed that Essex might pull off an unexpected triumph, but Lynch, with eight fours in an unbeaten 69, saw Surrey to victory halfway through the final twenty overs.

Close of play: First day, Surrey 110-4 (T. E. Jesty 1*, D. M. Ward 1*); Second day, Essex 199-5 (K. W. R. Fletcher 25*, G. Miller 12*).

Essex

B. R. Hardie c Richards b Feltham	14	– c Richards b Clarke	54
J. P. Stephenson c Richards b Clarke	28	– c Ward b Mays	32
A. W. Lilley c Richards b Clarke	6	– c Richards b Feltham	42
*G. A. Gooch lbw b Clarke	0	– c Lynch b Feltham	5
K. W. R. Fletcher c Medlycott b Clarke	0	– lbw b Feltham	25
P. J. Prichard c Mays b Clarke	0	– run out	12
G. Miller b Feltham	13	– c Greig b Clarke	26
N. A. Foster lbw b Feltham	12	– c and b Clarke	48
†D. E. East c Stewart b Feltham	9	– c Bicknell b Clarke	19
I. L. Pont lbw b Medlycott	0	– c Richards b Feltham	6
J. H. Childs not out	3	– not out	0
B 1	1	B 11, l-b 8, w 3, n-b 2	24
	86		293

1/25 2/32 3/32 4/32 5/32   86   1/81 2/143 3/143 4/151 5/173   293
6/53 7/73 8/78 9/79   6/199 7/221 8/277 9/291

Bonus points – Surrey 4.

Bowling: *First Innings*—Clarke 13–5–41–5; Feltham 12.1–6–24–4; Medlycott 10–2–20–1. *Second Innings*—Clarke 37.4–10–86–4; Feltham 35–8–82–4; Mays 11–0–39–1; Medlycott 22–7–55–0; Greig 8–1–12–0.

Surrey

D. J. Bicknell c Gooch b Foster	8	– lbw b Gooch	25
†C. J. Richards b Foster	42	– c Miller b Pont	5
A. J. Stewart c Prichard b Childs	23	– lbw b Gooch	6
M. A. Lynch c Hardie b Miller	31	– not out	69
T. E. Jesty lbw b Foster	39	– c Lilley b Foster	13
D. M. Ward c East b Foster	19	– b Foster	0
*I. A. Greig b Pont	0	– lbw b Gooch	11
K. T. Medlycott c East b Foster	28	– c Stephenson b Gooch	8
M. A. Feltham b Childs	18	– not out	8
C. S. Mays not out	5		
S. T. Clarke c Miller b Childs	3		
B 4, l-b 8, w 2, n-b 3	17	L-b 2, n-b 2	4
	233	(7 wkts)	149

1/22 2/57 3/108 4/108 5/159   233   1/13 2/35 3/48 4/63   (7 wkts) 149
6/160 7/169 8/220 9/224   5/69 6/90 7/123

Bonus points – Surrey 2, Essex 4.

Bowling: *First Innings*—Foster 25–3–72–4; Pont 11–0–48–2; Childs 23.1–6–63–3; Gooch 8–3–13–0; Miller 6–0–25–1. *Second Innings*—Foster 16–4–67–2; Pont 7–1–25–1; Gooch 21–5–42–4; Childs 6.2–2–13–0.

Umpires: P. J. Eele and B. J. Meyer.

ESSEX v WORCESTERSHIRE

At Colchester, September 2, 3, 4. Worcestershire won by 119 runs. Worcestershire 20 pts, Essex 2 pts. Toss: Essex. A masterful century from Hick, his seventh of the season and one containing a six and nineteen fours, kept the match alive after the opening day had been washed out. Neale was also at his best, hitting seventeen fours in an unbeaten hundred. A declaration at their overnight score by Worcestershire, followed by Worcestershire's forfeiting their second innings, left the home side to score 340 on the final day. Despite the efforts of Gooch and Pringle, they never threatened to reach their objective once Radford had plunged them into early difficulty. When he bowled Lilley, the Worcestershire fast bowler became the first of the season to take 100 wickets.

Close of play: First day, No play; Second day, Essex 11-0 (B. R. Hardie 4*, J. P. Stephenson 4*).

Worcestershire

T. S. Curtis b Foster	44	S. R. Lampitt not out	11
G. J. Lord c East b Foster	1		
G. A. Hick c and b Stephenson	156	B 1, l-b 16, w 1, n-b 1	19
D. B. D'Oliveira lbw b Foster	1		
*P. A. Neale not out	100	1/1 2/135 3/145 (5 wkts dec.) 350	
M. J. Weston lbw b Pringle	18	4/247 5/331	

†S. J. Rhodes, N. V. Radford, P. J. Newport and S. M. McEwan did not bat.

Bonus points – Worcestershire 4, Essex 2.

Bowling: Foster 24-3-71-3; Lever 13-2-50-0; Pringle 19-4-67-1; Gooch 7-0-32-0; Childs 28.2-9-93-0; Stephenson 8-2-20-1.

Worcestershire forfeited their second innings.

Essex

B. R. Hardie not out	4	– lbw b Radford	16	
J. P. Stephenson not out	4	– b Radford	0	
A. W. Lilley (did not bat)		– b Radford	46	
P. J. Prichard (did not bat)		– b Newport	2	
*G. A. Gooch (did not bat)		– c Weston b Newport	63	
K. W. R. Fletcher (did not bat)		– b Radford	0	
D. R. Pringle (did not bat)		– not out	63	
N. A. Foster (did not bat)		– lbw b Weston	1	
†D. E. East (did not bat)		– b Newport	13	
J. K. Lever (did not bat)		– c Lampitt b Radford	1	
J. H. Childs (did not bat)		– b Newport	4	
L-b 2, w 1	3	B 1, l-b 9, w 1	11	
(no wkt dec.)	11	1/3 2/33 3/38 4/94 5/98	220	
		6/162 7/163 8/202 9/205		

Bowling: *First Innings*—Newport 3-1-3-0; McEwan 3-1-5-0; Hick 1-0-1-0. *Second Innings*—Radford 19-2-77-5; Newport 23.1-4-84-4; McEwan 6-1-22-0; Weston 9-4-27-1.

Umpires: P. J. Eele and B. J. Meyer.

ESSEX v LANCASHIRE

At Chelmsford, September 12, 14, 15. Lancashire won by 89 runs. Lancashire 20 pts, Essex 6 pts. Toss: Essex. Lancashire won with 7.1 overs to spare to make certain of finishing runners-up to Nottinghamshire in the Championship. Their sixth successive victory, it was never really in doubt from the moment that their spinners, Folley and Simmons, captured four wickets in six overs immediately after tea on the third day. If they were to go ahead of

Nottinghamshire, Lancashire had to take maximum points from this match, but losing the toss meant batting first on a pitch of inconsistent bounce in conditions favouring the Essex seam bowlers. Abrahams stayed almost four hours for his 64, but their fate was settled when the last five wickets fell in ten overs. Pont, who took three of them in eight balls, finished with career-best figures. Lilley sustained Essex's reply, and when Lancashire went in a second time, Fowler, with 76 from 98 balls, and Atherton answered the call for quick runs. Hughes's declaration gave his bowlers at least 52 overs in which to break down Essex's final-innings resistance.

Close of play: First day, Lancashire 155-5 (J. Abrahams 43*, W. K. Hegg 7*); Second day, Lancashire 53-1 (G. Fowler 24*, I. Folley 3*).

Lancashire

G. D. Mendis c Gooch b Pringle	22	– c Lilley b Pont	23
G. Fowler lbw b Pont	2	– c Hardie b Pringle	76
M. A. Atherton lbw b Pont	28	– (4) c and b Gooch	60
J. Abrahams c Pringle b Pont	64	– (5) b Gooch	22
M. Watkinson b Pringle	26	– (6) not out	7
*D. P. Hughes c Hardie b Foster	15		
†W. K. Hegg lbw b Childs	31	– (7) not out	7
P. J. W. Allott b Childs	1		
J. Simmons not out	8		
I. Folley b Pont	0	– (3) c East b Gooch	19
B. P. Patterson b Pont	0		
B 1, l-b 10, w 1, n-b 11	23	B 2, l-b 1, n-b 3	6

1/7 2/43 3/65 4/106 5/140   220   1/50 2/120 3/122   (5 wkts dec.) 220
6/193 7/197 8/213 9/213   4/188 5/213

Bonus points – Lancashire 2, Essex 4.

Bowling: *First Innings*—Foster 23-4-59-1; Pont 18-1-73-5; Pringle 28-9-60-2; Childs 12-6-17-2. *Second Innings*—Pont 14-2-50-1; Pringle 8-1-31-1; Childs 17-0-45-0; Gooch 10-4-32-3; Stephenson 11.1-0-59-0.

Essex

B. R. Hardie c Watkinson b Allott	1	– b Watkinson	24
J. P. Stephenson c Hegg b Folley	23	– c Hegg b Allott	0
A. W. Lilley c Folley b Abrahams	88	– c and b Folley	29
N. Hussain c Watkinson b Fowler	18	– (5) c Mendis b Simmons	2
I. L. Pont c Allott b Fowler	39	– (9) c and b Folley	4
*G. A. Gooch not out	6	– (4) c Allott b Simmons	16
D. R. Pringle not out	6	– (6) c Hegg b Folley	9
P. J. Prichard (did not bat)		– (7) c Allott b Abrahams	22
†D. E. East (did not bat)		– (8) b Watkinson	27
N. A. Foster (did not bat)		– b Watkinson	13
J. H. Childs (did not bat)		– not out	0
B 8, l-b 6, n-b 6	20	B 1, l-b 1, n-b 2	4

1/1 2/116 3/141 4/188 5/191   (5 wkts dec.) 201   1/2 2/44 3/67 4/72 5/83   150
                                         6/83 7/116 8/121 9/144

Bonus points – Essex 2, Lancashire 2.

Bowling: *First Innings*—Patterson 8-1-22-0; Allott 6-3-8-1; Folley 14-5-19-1; Watkinson 7-1-24-0; Simmons 8-0-18-0; Atherton 4-0-16-0; Abrahams 11-2-37-1; Fowler 10.3-0-43-2. *Second Innings*—Patterson 3-0-14-0; Allott 5-2-16-1; Watkinson 8.5-0-33-3; Folley 21-4-43-3; Simmons 10-2-25-2; Abrahams 7-3-17-1.

Umpires: B. Dudleston and R. Palmer.

GLAMORGAN

Patron: HRH The Prince of Wales
President: His Honour Rowe Harding
Chairman: G. Craven
Chairman, Cricket Committee: A. R. Lewis
Secretary: P. G. Carling
Sophia Gardens, Cardiff CF1 9XR
(Telephone: 0222-343478)
Assistant Secretary (Cricket): J. F. Steele
Captain: H. Morris
Coach: A. Jones

Although an improved playing record enabled Glamorgan to scramble from the bottom of the Britannic Assurance Championship table and leave four teams below them, there remained much unfulfilled promise in the team. For Hugh Morris, the youngest county captain to have served two consecutive summers in command since World War Two, it was a particularly frustrating season. He saw the balanced attack at his disposal in April being torn apart by injuries until his resources became inadequate; and the demands of leadership, especially with key players injured, inevitably took their toll. Nevertheless, the left-hander continued to carry the stamp of a possible Test player. His defiance in carrying his bat on an unpredictable Headingley pitch, as his team were dismissed for 83 in the NatWest Bank Trophy, typified his indomitable spirit, and his innings finds a niche in Glamorgan's cricket history. It was perhaps the most memorable 16 runs – with as many bruises – of its kind by a Glamorgan player.

It contrasted vividly with the numerous colourful performances by Matthew Maynard, at 21 one of the most exciting attacking batsmen in the county game. While Morris so often played the anchorman role to protect his strokemakers against the new ball, Maynard wasted little time. He hit the fastest half-century in his county's history, off nineteen deliveries against Yorkshire at Cardiff in May, and was awarded his county cap in the match against Somerset at Weston-super-Mare after scoring 160 on the Saturday and then the fastest televised Refuge Assurance League 50, off 34 deliveries, on the Sunday. Rising from No. 7 in the order at the start of the summer to his rightful place at No. 4, Maynard emerged as Glamorgan's leading batsman with 1,626 first-class runs at 40.65 per innings. He hit two centuries and twelve half-centuries, ten of them in the Championship, and he was top of the national catching list with 30, many of them brilliantly taken in the outfield. There were those who suggested he was too impetuous early in an innings; but his game developed at an amazing pace and Glamorgan were confident that he would make all the adjustments necessary without suffering any inhibitions.

Another success was Colin Metson, the wicket-keeper signed from Middlesex. He too was awarded his cap, as were Alan Butcher and Stephen Barwick, and he fitted into the team smoothly and unostentatiously. A bonus was his confident batting, often as night-watchman. Although the experienced Butcher, who joined from Surrey, was out for a long spell with a torn calf muscle, he finished the summer impressively with three hundreds in the course of six matches and completed 1,000 runs along with Morris and Maynard. Butcher took over the duties of opening the innings with Morris when John Hopkins lost form, and a reassuring confidence emanated from the pair of left-handers.

Another newcomer of considerable reputation was Ravi Shastri, the Indian Test all-rounder. He played on the slow turners in South Wales and where conditions suited in away matches, while Corrie van Zyl, the new fast bowler from South Africa, operated almost exclusively on the faster pitches. Unfortunately, a recurrence of a foot problem meant that van Zyl did not play after the end of July. His eleven Championship wickets cost 39.90 runs each. Shastri took 34 wickets with his left-arm spin, but at just under 31 runs per wicket, and it was his cultured batting that most marked his contribution. He enjoyed hitting straight sixes, and while Maynard finished as the most prolific striker of sixes in first-class cricket in 1987 with 30, Shastri was next in line with 22.

Rodney Ontong was another dogged by injuries and did not reach 500 runs in the Championship. However, his off-spin was invaluable in what became a threadbare and limited attack, and his six for 91 helped bring victory over Yorkshire at Cardiff. Ontong's 41 wickets were bettered only by Barwick, who returned from a winter of cricket in South Africa fitter than he had ever been and more mature. However, his wickets came at a high cost of more than 38 runs each for often he had to be a stock as well as a strike bowler.

Simon Base had taken only six wickets until late in August in a few appearances and then, with Gregory Thomas injured, he made the most of his opportunities. The seamer had a match analysis of nine wickets in successive matches against Worcestershire and Surrey, including a career-best five for 67 at The Oval. Such instant success saw him top the county's Championship averages with 28 wickets at 23.57 apiece. Steve Monkhouse, signed from Warwickshire, had few opportunities as a medium-paced left-armer and the same applied to Philip North, the left-arm spinner, who took six wickets in the victory over Worcestershire at Neath.

Hopkins lost his place for a long time in the Championship team, though the opening batsman continued to prove a reliable performer in limited-overs matches. Geoff Holmes just failed to complete 1,000 runs; Paul Todd, the former Nottinghamshire batsman, who scored a century to help Minor Counties defeat Glamorgan in the Benson and Hedges competition, was recruited when Butcher was injured and hit a hundred at Worcester; and there were useful performances by Anthony Cottey, Steve James, Ian Smith and John Derrick.

However, Gregory Thomas was dogged by injuries, missed half the Championship programme as a result, and requested to be released from his final year's contract in order to join a county where he could bowl on faster wickets. The club, having suspended Thomas late in the season for going ahead with an ankle operation without permission, were not prepared to agree to his going, and it is to be hoped that the committee and the player can settle their differences as Glamorgan celebrate their centenary season. – John Billot.

391

GLAMORGAN 1987

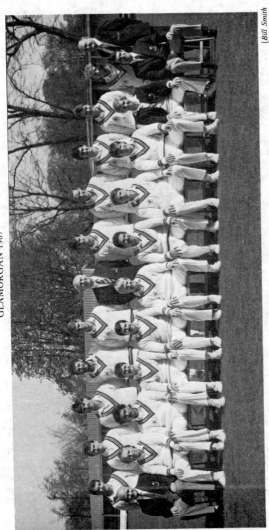

[*Bill Smith*

Back row: P. D. North, C. P. Metson, J. Derrick, S. R. Barwick, S. Monkhouse, T. Jones (*physiotherapist*), I. Smith, S. J. Base, M. L. Roberts, M. P. Maynard, P. A. Cottey, G. Lewis (*scorer*). *Front row*: P. G. Carling (*secretary*), A. R. Butcher, R. J. Shastri, G. C. Holmes, J. A. Hopkins, H. Morris (*captain*), R. C. Ontong, J. G. Thomas, C. J. P. G. van Zyl, A. Jones (*coach*), J. F. Steele (*assistant secretary, cricket*).

GLAMORGAN RESULTS

All first-class matches – Played 26: Won 3, Lost 9, Drawn 14.

County Championship matches – Played 24: Won 3, Lost 9, Drawn 12.

Bonus points – Batting 40, Bowling 70.

Competition placings – Britannic Assurance County Championship, 13th; NatWest Bank Trophy, 2nd round; Benson and Hedges Cup, 3rd in Group D; Refuge Assurance League, 14th equal.

BRITANNIC ASSURANCE CHAMPIONSHIP AVERAGES

BATTING

	Birthplace	M	I	NO	R	HI	Avge
‡A. R. Butcher	Croydon	14	26	2	1,007	135*	41.95
§R. J. Shastri	Bombay, India	12	21	2	755	103	39.73
‡M. P. Maynard	Oldham	24	43	4	1,508	160	38.66
‡H. Morris	Cardiff	24	46	2	1,161	115	26.38
‡G. C. Holmes	Newcastle-upon-Tyne	23	41	6	912	95	26.05
‡R. C. Ontong	Johannesburg, SA	14	24	5	487	100	25.63
J. Derrick	Cwmaman	16	26	6	380	57	19.00
§C. J. P. G. van Zyl ..	Bloemfontein, SA	6	5	0	85	35	17.00
P. A. Todd	Morton	13	23	0	380	135	16.52
‡C. P. Metson	Goffs Oak	24	37	7	493	81	16.43
P. A. Cottey	Swansea	6	9	1	130	42*	16.25
‡J. A. Hopkins	Maesteg	14	25	2	369	39*	16.04
I. Smith	Chopwell	16	23	5	288	45	16.00
‡J. G. Thomas	Trebanos	9	15	2	200	48	15.38
S. P. James	Lydney	6	11	1	137	43*	13.70
S. J. Base	Maidstone	8	14	4	127	38	12.70
‡S. R. Barwick	Neath	23	30	10	150	27*	7.50
P. D. North	Newport	5	7	1	39	15	6.50
S. Monkhouse	Bury	5	8	3	23	15	4.60

Also batted: M. J. Cann (*Cardiff*) (2 matches) 16*, 8*.

* *Signifies not out.*   ‡ *Denotes county cap.*   § *Not qualified for England.*

The following played a total of ten three-figure innings for Glamorgan in County Championship matches – A. R. Butcher 3, M. P. Maynard 2, H. Morris 2, R. C. Ontong 1, R. J. Shastri 1, P. A. Todd 1.

BOWLING

	O	M	R	W	BB	Avge
S. J. Base	203.1	38	660	28	5-67	23.57
J. G. Thomas	215.3	40	756	27	6-109	28.00
R. J. Shastri	419.1	96	1,051	34	5-100	30.91
J. Derrick	291.3	61	1,015	31	5-50	32.74
R. C. Ontong	461.4	87	1,395	41	6-91	34.02
S. R. Barwick	603.1	122	1,799	47	4-60	38.27
C. J. P. G. van Zyl ..	138	25	439	11	3-35	39.90
I. Smith	195.3	38	692	17	3-65	40.70

Also bowled: A. R. Butcher 21-1-52-3; M. J. Cann 23.5-3-110-1; G. C. Holmes 94.4-15-340-2; M. P. Maynard 20-3-68-1; S. Monkhouse 70-4-305-9; H. Morris 5-1-20-0; P. D. North 103.3-27-242-7.

Wicket-keeper: C. P. Metson 45 ct, 6 st.

Leading Fielders: M. P. Maynard 29, H. Morris 15.

At Birmingham, April 25, 26, 27. GLAMORGAN drew with WARWICKSHIRE.

At Canterbury, April, 29, 30, May 1. GLAMORGAN lost to KENT by an innings and 116 runs.

GLAMORGAN v LANCASHIRE

At Swansea, May 6, 7, 8. Glamorgan won by an innings and 132 runs. Glamorgan 23 pts, Lancashire 2 pts. Toss: Glamorgan. Ontong's seventeenth century for Glamorgan, scored in four hours with a six and eleven fours, together with an admirable 98 by Butcher, helped rebuild the innings after the loss of two early wickets. With the pitch showing signs of favouring spin on the first day, Glamorgan extended their innings into the morning of the second day, and then Ontong, with off-spin, and Shastri, with flighted left-arm spin, made it an early finish on the third day. This was Glamorgan's first Championship success at Swansea for almost three years and their first victory by an innings on a home ground since they defeated Warwickshire at Cardiff in 1981.

Close of play: First day, Glamorgan 348-5 (G. C. Holmes 68*, M. P. Maynard 18*); Second day, Lancashire 47-4 (J. Abrahams 13*, D. P. Hughes 4*).

Glamorgan

J. A. Hopkins c Stanworth b Hayhurst	15	J. G. Thomas c Hughes b McLeod		10
*H. Morris c Abrahams b McLeod	5	I. Smith not out		14
A. R. Butcher c Fairbrother b Folley	98	†C. P. Metson not out		7
R. J. Shastri b Simmons	32	L-b 8, w 2, n-b 7		17
R. C. Ontong c Folley b McLeod	100			
G. C. Holmes lbw b McLeod	95	1/21 2/32 3/97 4/230 (8 wkts. dec.)		416
M. P. Maynard c Hughes b McLeod	23	5/292 6/359 7/391 8/399		

S. R. Barwick did not bat.

Bonus points – Glamorgan 3, Lancashire 1 (Score at 100 overs: 283-4).

Bowling: McLeod 26-1-94-5; Hayhurst 15-2-76-1; O'Shaughnessy 21-4-77-0; Simmons 38-7-101-1; Folley 27-11-60-1.

Lancashire

G. D. Mendis b Thomas	33	c Metson b Barwick		7
G. Fowler c Hopkins b Ontong	27	c Thomas b Barwick		6
J. Abrahams c Ontong b Thomas	10	c Hopkins b Ontong		30
N. H. Fairbrother b Shastri	33	b Barwick		0
S. J. O'Shaughnessy c Ontong b Shastri	9	c Hopkins b Shastri		14
*D. P. Hughes c Maynard b Ontong	4	c Morris b Thomas		4
A. N. Hayhurst c and b Shastri	2	c Metson b Thomas		0
I. Folley not out	15	b Shastri		38
J. Simmons c Shastri b Ontong	2	(11) not out		2
†J. Stanworth c Maynard b Ontong	5	(9) c Maynard b Shastri		0
K. W. McLeod c Holmes b Shastri	1	(10) c Maynard b Ontong		27
B 8, l-b 1, n-b 3	12	L-b 2, n-b 1		3

1/39 2/52 3/91 4/117 5/124 ... 153   1/9 2/22 3/22 4/39 5/47 ... 131
6/130 7/130 8/132 9/144   6/51 7/77 8/82 9/129

Bonus points – Lancashire 1, Glamorgan 4.

Bowling: *First Innings*—Thomas 16-2-69-2; Barwick 5-1-12-0; Ontong 26-5-47-4; Shastri 15.4-5-16-4. *Second Innings*—Thomas 16-6-33-2; Barwick 13-8-15-3; Ontong 18.2-5-46-2; Shastri 16-5-35-3.

Umpires: D. J. Constant and M. J. Kitchen.

At Chelmsford, May 20, 21, 22. GLAMORGAN drew with ESSEX.

GLAMORGAN v YORKSHIRE

At Cardiff, May 23, 25, 26. Glamorgan won by 73 runs. Glamorgan 19 pts, Yorkshire 6 pts. Toss: Yorkshire. An absorbing contest built up to a fascinating final day on which the home side registered their eleventh victory in 65 years against Yorkshire. Play did not begin until 4.00 p.m. on Saturday and Glamorgan, put in, were never comfortable, though Shastri batted securely. When Blakey had completed his maiden century, an unbeaten 101 in just over three hours with eleven fours, Carrick declared 54 runs behind, which set up the excitement of the last day on a turning pitch. First, Glamorgan promoted Metson to open because Hopkins had been concussed while batting in the Sunday League match, and the new wicket-keeper contributed 81 in just over two hours. But everyone else was overshadowed by Maynard, who hit the fastest half-century in Glamorgan's history, his fourteen minutes (nineteen balls) improving on the fifteen minutes by D. J. Shepherd against the Australians in 1961. However, it should be added that Yorkshire were bowling for a declaration. Sharp gave away 52 runs in two overs, one of which Maynard hammered for 30 runs (464466) – the most by a Glamorgan batsman since J. Mercer's 31 off an eight-ball over by Worcestershire's R. Howorth at the Arms Park in 1939. Maynard hit six sixes and four fours in his unbeaten 61 from 22 deliveries in seventeen minutes. Yorkshire, set 281 in 66 overs, were then spun out by Ontong, who held four return catches, and Shastri, despite a fearless 55 from Bairstow, who was batting with a fractured index finger on his left hand.

Close of play: First day, Glamorgan 127-3 (R. J. Shastri 53*, R. C. Ontong 27*); Second day, Yorkshire 216-2 dec.

Glamorgan

J. A. Hopkins lbw b Jarvis	11			
*H. Morris c Moxon b Sidebottom	5	– (1) c sub b Love	33
A. R. Butcher lbw b Hartley	10			
R. J. Shastri c Bairstow b Sidebottom	58			
R. C. Ontong b Fletcher	43	– (4) c Metcalfe b Carrick	15
G. C. Holmes c Sidebottom b Hartley	15	– (3) c and b Love	27
M. P. Maynard b Hartley	5	– (5) not out	61
†C. P. Metson b Jarvis	47	– (2) c and b Metcalfe	81
I. Smith b Sidebottom	13	– (6) not out	4
S. J. Base b Hartley	11			
S. R. Barwick not out	21			
B 7, l-b 11, w 5, n-b 8	31	L-b 4, n-b 1	5

1/18 2/18 3/52 4/138 5/159   270   1/66 2/133   (4 wkts. dec.) 226
6/168 7/172 8/200 9/237   3/156 4/195

Bonus points – Glamorgan 3, Yorkshire 4.

Bowling: *First Innings*—Jarvis 22.1–4–76–2; Sidebottom 21–5–45–3; Fletcher 16–1–55–1; P. J. Hartley 17–3–61–4; Carrick 2–0–12–0; Moxon 2–1–3–0. *Second Innings*—Jarvis 2–2–0–0; Sidebottom 2–1–6–0; Carrick 7–2–14–1; Sharp 13–0–102–0; Love 19–1–72–2; Metcalfe 4.2–0–28–1.

Yorkshire

M. D. Moxon lbw b Base	16	– c Hopkins b Barwick	3
A. A. Metcalfe c Maynard b Ontong	37	– b Shastri	51
R. J. Blakey not out	101	– c and b Ontong	16
K. Sharp not out	46	– c and b Ontong	13
J. D. Love (did not bat)		– c and b Ontong	37
†D. L. Bairstow (did not bat)		– c Base b Ontong	55
*P. Carrick (did not bat)		– c Maynard b Ontong	8
A. Sidebottom (did not bat)		– st Metson b Shastri	2
P. J. Hartley (did not bat)		– c Ontong b Shastri	0
P. W. Jarvis (did not bat)		– c and b Ontong	0
S. D. Fletcher (did not bat)		– not out	13
L-b 8, w 1, n-b 7	16	L-b 2, w 3, n-b 4	9

1/33 2/77   (2 wkts. dec.) 216   1/8 2/71 3/75 4/105 5/133   207
                                   6/161 7/164 8/166 9/167

Bonus points – Yorkshire 2.

Bowling: *First Innings*—Barwick 9–1–34–0; Smith 4–1–16–0; Base 8–1–31–1; Ontong 18–3–57–1; Shastri 25·5–5–59–0; Holmes 8–3–11–0. *Second Innings*—Barwick 4–1–26–1; Shastri 25–6–64–3; Ontong 23.4–2–91–6; Smith 4–0–24–0.

Umpires: A. G. T. Whitehead and P. B. Wight.

At Chesterfield, May 30, June 1, 2. GLAMORGAN drew with DERBYSHIRE.

GLAMORGAN v HAMPSHIRE

At Swansea, June 3, 4, 5. Drawn. Glamorgan 3 pts, Hampshire 6 pts. Toss: Glamorgan. Only two hours' play was possible late on the first day, during which time Andrew's lively pace caused a collapse, and next day Glamorgan were subjected to the demoralising speed of Marshall. Hampshire overtook the home total before they lost their fourth wicket, Greenidge leading the way with a typically dynamic innings. On the day that a World War II German bomb was dredged up in Swansea Bay, just off-shore from the cricket ground, Greenidge produced another of his batting explosions: he struck four sixes and nine fours including a blow off Shastri that went out of the ground through the members' gate and into the garden of a guest house on the opposite side of Bryn Road. It was considered one of the biggest hits witnessed at St Helen's. Glamorgan, comprehensively outplayed, were grateful when a downpour ended play at midday on the final day.

Close of play: First day, Glamorgan 67-4 (H. Morris 22*); Second day, Hampshire 237-8 (R. J. Maru 14*, I. J. Chivers 20*).

Glamorgan

J. A. Hopkins c Smith b Andrew	3	– c Marshall b Maru		18
*H. Morris c Maru b Marshall	25	– c Parks b Andrew		0
P. A. Todd c Marshall b Andrew	12	– c Greenidge b Andrew		18
R. J. Shastri lbw b Andrew	12			
G. C. Holmes st Parks b Chivers	14	– (4) not out		5
R. C. Ontong lbw b Marshall	1			
M. P. Maynard c Terry b Marshall	18	– (5) c Parks b Andrew		6
J. Derrick not out	26	– (6) not out		0
J. G. Thomas c Turner b Maru	11			
†C. P. Metson b Maru	0			
S. R. Barwick c Marshall b Maru	0			
W 4, n-b 1	5	B 4		4

1/12 2/26 3/39 4/67 5/71   127   1/1 2/23 3/44 4/51   (4 wkts) 51
6/74 7/91 8/112 9/121

Bonus points – Hampshire 4.

Bowling: *First Innings*—Andrew 19–6–48–3; Marshall 19–6–42–3; Maru 17–9–13–3; James 7–2–20–0; Chivers 3–1–4–1. *Second Innings*—Andrew 10–3–20–3; Marshall 5–1–22–0; Maru 5–3–5–1.

Hampshire

C. G. Greenidge c Metson b Barwick	76	R. J. Maru not out	14
V. P. Terry c Hopkins b Thomas	14	I. J. Chivers not out	20
*M. C. J. Nicholas c Metson b Thomas	8		
D. R. Turner c Maynard b Derrick	51	B 2, l-b 2, n-b 5	9
C. L. Smith c Thomas b Derrick	21		
K. D. James c Hopkins b Derrick	6	1/59 2/85 3/106 (8 wkts dec.) 237
M. D. Marshall c Hopkins b Derrick	16	4/172 5/180 6/188
†R. J. Parks c Maynard b Derrick	2	7/192 8/206

S. J. W. Andrew did not bat.

Bonus points – Hampshire 2, Glamorgan 3.

Bowling: Thomas 26–7–76–2; Barwick 18–9–39–1; Shastri 9–1–35–0; Ontong 9–2–33–0; Derrick 13–3–50–5.

Umpires: D. J. Constant and D. R. Shepherd.

GLAMORGAN v SOMERSET

At Swansea, June 6, 7, 8. Drawn. Glamorgan 4 pts, Somerset 6 pts. Toss: Somerset. Water-logged surrounds prevented a start on the first day. Barwick, a much improved seam bowler after a winter in South Africa, and Derrick provided too many problems for Somerset on a slow-paced pitch and their last six wickets went down for an addition of 42 runs. Even so, Felton and Crowe had made a sound enough start before a stunt-pilot caused a distraction with aerobatics overhead, and amid the confusion Crowe found himself at the same end as Harden. The umpires decided that Crowe was run out, just 2 runs short of his half-century. Glamorgan's batting was dismal and they followed on 117 runs behind, only to save the match by a grim rearguard operation. Morris, the captain, batted 22 overs for 4 runs and Holmes stayed more than two hours for his unbeaten 25.

Close of play: First day, No play; Second day, Glamorgan 53-5 (C. P. Metson 2*, R. J. Shastri 0*).

Somerset

J. G. Wyatt c Metson b Derrick	22	M. R. Davis c Hopkins b Barwick 4
N. A. Felton b Derrick	53	N. A. Mallender c Metson b Derrick .. 3
J. J. E. Hardy run out	30	A. N. Jones not out 1
M. D. Crowe run out	48	
R. J. Harden c Morris b Barwick	26	B 1, l-b 15, w 2, n-b 3 21
*V. J. Marks c Thomas b Barwick	0	
†N. D. Burns b Derrick	9	1/58 2/117 3/123 4/194 5/194 236
G. D. Rose lbw b Barwick	19	6/205 7/209 8/222 9/231

Bonus points – Somerset 2, Glamorgan 4.

Bowling: Thomas 12–0–43–0; Barwick 25.2–4–60–4; Shastri 8–1–25–0; Derrick 26–9–69–4; Holmes 6–1–23–0.

Glamorgan

J. A. Hopkins c Harden b Mallender	1 – c Jones b Rose	11
*H. Morris c Mallender b Rose	21 – st Burns b Marks	4
P. A. Todd c Davis b Jones	16 – c Burns b Rose	25
G. C. Holmes c Burns b Marks	6 – not out	25
M. P. Maynard c and b Marks	0 – c Marks b Rose	1
†C. P. Metson b Rose	2 – (9) c Wyatt b Rose	9
R. J. Shastri c Rose b Marks	22 – (6) b Rose	5
J. Derrick st Burns b Marks	12 – (7) lbw b Marks	3
J. G. Thomas not out	11 – (8) c Crowe b Marks	4
P. D. North c Wyatt b Marks	2 – not out	2
S. R. Barwick b Mallender	14	
B 6, l-b 5, w 1	12	L-b 4, w 2, n-b 1 7
1/2 2/29 3/47 4/47 5/53	119	1/18 2/22 3/51 4/55 (8 wkts) 96
6/54 7/84 8/88 9/94		5/60 6/65 7/69 8/92

Bonus points – Somerset 4.

Bowling: *First Innings*—Jones 12–6–20–1; Mallender 13.2–2–29–2; Davis 7–2–10–0; Rose 9–3–14–2; Marks 17–8–35–5. *Second Innings*—Jones 7–2–5–0; Mallender 8–4–20–0; Davis 6–4–3–0; Rose 15.5–7–24–5; Marks 26–11–40–3.

Umpires: D. J. Constant and D. R. Shepherd.

GLAMORGAN v WARWICKSHIRE

At Cardiff, June 13, 15, 16. Drawn. Glamorgan 4 pts, Warwickshire 6 pts. Toss: Warwickshire. Glamorgan's young captain, Morris, and the vastly experienced Gifford, leading Warwickshire, engineered a fascinating finish to a rain-ravaged fixture with their declarations on the final day. Glamorgan had only ten batsmen because Cann went down with chickenpox, but they took up the challenge to try to make 211 in 40 overs. Morris recaptured missing form to inspire his team and there was adventure from Maynard, whose first two strokes went for six, and Shastri, who was dropped when he had made 8. Had Lloyd held the steepling catch at mid-off, Gifford would have claimed a sixth wicket and probably won the match. As it was, Barwick had to block out a fiery last over from Donald.

Close of play: First day, Warwickshire 308-6 (A. C. Storie 41*, G. J. Parsons 59*); Second day, Glamorgan 153-3 (G. C. Holmes 46*, R. J. Shastri 20*).

Warwickshire

T. A. Lloyd lbw b Thomas	17	– c Derrick b Shastri	25
A. J. Moles c Metson b Thomas	20	– not out	34
D. A. Thorne c Metson b Thomas	0	– (4) c Metson b Thomas	1
D. L. Amiss c Maynard b Shastri	64	– (3) c Shastri b Thomas	0
†G. W. Humpage c Metson b Barwick	55		
P. A. Smith c Shastri b Barwick	14	– (5) not out	6
A. C. Storie not out	66		
G. J. Parsons b Thomas	65		
A. R. K. Pierson b Thomas	0		
A. A. Donald st Metson b Shastri	9		
*N. Gifford b Thomas	3		
B 10, l-b 11, w 6, n-b 13	40	B 10, l-b 6, w 2, n-b 1 ...	19

1/46 2/46 3/51 4/171 5/193   353   1/61 2/63 3/77   (3 wkts dec.) 85
6/194 7/322 8/326 9/349

Bonus points – Warwickshire 3, Glamorgan 2 (Score at 100 overs: 295-6).

Bowling: *First Innings*—Thomas 35.3–6–109–6; Barwick 21–3–50–2; Derrick 10–1–33–0; Shastri 49–13–104–2; Cann 10–2–36–0. *Second Innings*—Thomas 10–1–26–2; Derrick 6–2–24–0; Shastri 4–0–19–1.

Glamorgan

J. A. Hopkins c and b Parsons	22	– c Parsons b Gifford	5
*H. Morris c Moles b Donald	2	– st Humpage b Gifford	67
G. C. Holmes c and b Donald	49	– st Humpage b Pierson	8
M. P. Maynard c Storie b Moles	32	– c Thorne b Pierson	20
R. J. Shastri c Humpage b Gifford	46	– c Pierson b Gifford	51
P. A. Cottey c Storie b Gifford	8	– b Gifford	2
J. G. Thomas c Amiss b Gifford	0	– c Pierson b Donald	21
J. Derrick not out	17	– b Gifford	0
†C. P. Metson c Amiss b Pierson	14	– not out	6
S. R. Barwick not out	0	– not out	0
B 20, l-b 5, w 1, n-b 12	38	B 3, l-b 2, w 3, n-b 2 ...	10

1/12 2/58 3/110 4/164 5/182   (8 wkts dec.) 228   1/26 2/49 3/88   (8 wkts) 190
6/182 7/193 8/227   4/116 5/130 6/173
7/173 8/190

M. J. Cann did not bat.

Bonus points – Glamorgan 2, Warwickshire 3.

Bowling: *First Innings*—Donald 20–4–45–2; Smith 11–4–27–0; Gifford 32–13–60–3; Parsons 18–4–36–1; Moles 4–1–15–1; Pierson 13–6–20–1. *Second Innings*—Donald 5–2–11–1; Smith 5–0–21–0; Gifford 17–3–71–5; Pierson 13–1–82–2.

Umpires: H. D. Bird and R. Palmer.

At Hove, June 17, 18, 19. GLAMORGAN drew with SUSSEX.

At Oxford, June 20, 22, 23. GLAMORGAN drew with OXFORD UNIVERSITY.

At Lord's, June 27, 29, 30. GLAMORGAN drew with MIDDLESEX.

GLAMORGAN v NORTHAMPTONSHIRE

At Swansea, July 1, 2, 3. Northamptonshire won by eight wickets. Northamptonshire 19 pts, Glamorgan 6 pts. Toss: Glamorgan. After taking a first-innings lead of 96, Glamorgan collapsed for 77, their lowest total in a home match for seven years. Yet on the first day, as Shastri was making his first century for the county, with two sixes and ten fours in just over three hours, it appeared as if Glamorgan were shaping a well-organised victory. However, they were held up by Williams, who survived an emphatic appeal second ball for a catch at the wicket off Shastri and proceeded to assault the bowling spectacularly. He struck one six and fifteen fours in making 79. After Glamorgan had batted so abysmally against the steep bounce obtained by Harper, Larkins (one six, eight fours), Lamb (two sixes, six fours) and Geoff Cook took full advantage of the swing of fortunes.

Close of play: First day, Glamorgan 282-5 (P. A. Cottey 38*, J. G. Thomas 11*); Second day, Glamorgan 50-7 (C. P. Metson 4*, M. J. Cann 0*).

Glamorgan

J. A. Hopkins run out	12	– b Brown	0
S. P. James lbw b Walker	2	– c Larkins b Harper	2
*H. Morris b Harper	57	– c G. Cook b Brown	13
M. P. Maynard c G. Cook b Harper	57	– b Harper	0
R. J. Shastri b Wild	103	– (6) c sub b Harper	1
P. A. Cottey c G. Cook b Brown	42	– (5) lbw b N. G. B. Cook	9
J. G. Thomas c G. Cook b Brown	11	– c Harper b Williams	18
†C. P. Metson c Brown b N. G. B. Cook	2	– c G. Cook b Harper	4
M. J. Cann not out	16	– not out	8
S. R. Barwick c Harper b N. G. B. Cook	0	– c and b Harper	0
S. Monkhouse b N. G. B. Cook	0	– b Williams	15
L-b 3	3	B 4, l-b 3	7

1/3 2/23 3/111 4/156 5/269   305   1/0 2/8 3/12 4/20 5/21   77
6/286 7/287 8/293 9/294   6/37 7/50 8/50 9/52

Bonus points – Glamorgan 2, Northamptonshire 1 (Score at 100 overs: 221-4).

Bowling: *First Innings*—Walker 10–6–14–1; Brown 24–5–69–2; Larkins 4–1–11–0; Wild 13–3–28–1; Harper 32–7–84–2; N. G. B. Cook 33–10–69–3; Williams 17–5–27–0. *Second Innings*—Brown 10–4–11–2; Wild 2–0–7–0; Harper 25–15–28–5; N. G. B. Cook 10–5–10–1; Williams 8–4–14–2.

Northamptonshire

*G. Cook c Maynard b Thomas	0	– not out	67
W. Larkins c Metson b Thomas	16	– c Hopkins b Cann	55
R. J. Bailey c Metson b Barwick	4	– c and b Shastri	2
A. J. Lamb lbw b Barwick	2	– not out	46
R. G. Williams c Metson b Monkhouse	79		
R. A. Harper c Maynard b Shastri	23		
D. J. Wild c Barwick b Shastri	31		
†D. Ripley c Hopkins b Shastri	28		
N. G. B. Cook c Hopkins b Shastri	7		
A. Walker c Metson b Monkhouse	3		
S. J. Brown not out	0		
B 4, l-b 7, n-b 5	16	B 2, n-b 3	5

1/0 2/5 3/23 4/27 5/106   209   1/69 2/72   (2 wkts) 175
6/160 7/166 8/191 9/197

Bonus points – Northamptonshire 2, Glamorgan 4.

Bowling: *First Innings*—Thomas 8-1-28-2; Barwick 19-6-50-2; Shastri 25.2-8-60-4; Cann 4-0-26-0; Monkhouse 10-1-34-2. *Second Innings*—Thomas 3-1-18-0; Barwick 8-2-22-0; Monkhouse 4-0-16-0; Shastri 17-2-69-1; Cann 9.5-1-48-1.

Umpires: R. Julian and D. Lloyd.

GLAMORGAN v GLOUCESTERSHIRE

At Swansea, July 4, 5, 7. Gloucestershire won by 105 runs. Gloucestershire 24 pts, Glamorgan 6 pts. Toss: Gloucestershire. Glamorgan, having battled almost throughout the final day, took the match into the last twenty overs but could not prevent their opponents from winning their first Championship match of the season. The game was unusual in that the first two days were played on Saturday and Sunday and the third on Tuesday. Monday featured a match between the counties under Sunday League regulations, watched by the Prince of Wales (patron of Glamorgan) and Princess (patron of Gloucestershire) to launch Glamorgan's centenary celebrations. Lawrence dismissed six Glamorgan batsmen for 63 in their first innings of the Championship match to follow up a career-best 65 not out (two sixes, six fours). Lloyds had batted attractively for his 130 in just over three hours in 56, and he moved the scoring along briskly in the second innings, hitting eleven fours in 56. After Curran had completed his century, an unbeaten 102 in 174 minutes (one six, fourteen fours), Graveney set Glamorgan to score 359 in 84 overs. It was a question of trying to hold out. Metson was 52 minutes before scoring, while Base provided a career-best 38 after Shastri had hit three sixes in a defiant 62; but Walsh, fast and whippy, kept Gloucestershire in the hunt.

Close of play: First day, Glamorgan 26-0 (S. P. James 13*, H. Morris 10*); Second day, Gloucestershire 158-4 (K. M. Curran 59*, M. W. Alleyne 11*).

Gloucestershire

A. W. Stovold c Metson b Shastri	46	– c Maynard b Barwick	4
A. J. Wright c Maynard b Monkhouse	32	– b Base	8
P. W. Romaines b Shastri	9	– c Metson b Barwick	6
K. M. Curran c Metson b Smith	21	– not out	102
J. W. Lloyds c Metson b Shastri	130	– c Smith b Maynard	56
K. P. Tomlins lbw b Smith	0	– (7) not out	5
M. W. Alleyne c and b Smith	4	– (6) c Monkhouse b Barwick	34
†R. C. Russell c Metson b Shastri	21		
C. A. Walsh b Shastri	3		
D. V. Lawrence not out	65		
*D. A. Graveney c Maynard b Barwick	7	B 8, l-b 12, w 1, n-b 2	23
B 4, l-b 11, n-b 5	20		

1/47 2/62 3/103 4/144 5/148   358   1/12 2/14 3/36   (5 wkts dec.) 238
6/152 7/208 8/230 9/320   4/132 5/221

Bonus points – Gloucestershire 4, Glamorgan 4 (Score at 100 overs: 334-9).

Bowling: *First Innings*—Barwick 17.1–3–69–1; Base 18–2–63–0; Shastri 44–7–100–5; Monkhouse 10–1–46–1; Smith 15–3–65–3. *Second Innings*—Barwick 27–5–82–3; Base 17.1–4–67–1; Smith 6–2–22–0; Monkhouse 6–0–22–0; Maynard 9–2–25–1.

Glamorgan

S. P. James lbw b Lawrence	30	– c Russell b Walsh 10
*H. Morris b Curran b Walsh	14	– c Curran b Lawrence 0
G. C. Holmes c Russell b Lawrence	50	– c Graveney b Walsh 20
M. P. Maynard c Stovold b Graveney	51	– b Walsh 20
P. A. Cottey c Lloyds b Lawrence	1	– (6) b Lloyds 21
†C. P. Metson b Lawrence	0	– (7) c Graveney b Walsh 41
R. J. Shastri lbw b Lawrence	57	– (5) st Russell b Graveney 62
I. Smith b Walsh	6	– c Russell b Graveney 4
S. J. Base not out	6	– lbw b Lloyds 38
S. R. Barwick c Russell b Walsh	7	– not out 13
S. Monkhouse b Lawrence	1	– b Walsh 2
L-b 7, n-b 8	15	B 8, l-b 6, w 8 22

1/30 2/75 3/105 4/109 5/111   238   1/0 2/19 3/51 4/54 5/105   253
6/187 7/216 8/222 9/237   6/143 7/151 8/212 9/224

Bonus points – Glamorgan 2, Gloucestershire 4.

Bowling: *First Innings*—Walsh 20–4–78–3; Lawrence 16.1–0–63–6; Graveney 16–8–39–1; Lloyds 8–0–29–0; Curran 4–0–22–0. *Second Innings*—Walsh 17.4–3–38–5; Lawrence 16–2–60–1; Graveney 25–9–75–2; Lloyds 22–6–66–2.

Umpires: R. Julian and D. Lloyd.

At Cardiff, July 6. GLAMORGAN lost to GLOUCESTERSHIRE by seven wickets (See Other Matches, 1987).

At Cardiff, July 15, 16, 17. GLAMORGAN drew with PAKISTANIS (See Pakistani tour section).

GLAMORGAN v SURREY

At Cardiff, July 18, 20, 21. Surrey won by 65 runs. Surrey 23 pts, Glamorgan 5 pts. Toss: Surrey. On a pitch providing turn and bounce this was an interesting contest. On the second day Glamorgan's first innings fell apart until Smith, with a six and seven fours in a career-best 44, injected some much needed determination against the short-pitched bowling of Gray. On the final day Medlycott made a further decisive contribution to Surrey's cause with 65 and then took four wickets in 31 overs with his flat left-arm spin. Glamorgan, set to score 261 off 76 overs, held out until the final over. Barwick, the last man in, had faced 25 balls and survived; but Surrey could not use their quick bowlers because of the poor light. Lynch was called on to bowl the last over, and with the third ball he had the prodding Derrick caught ankle-high at silly mid-off. Richards, Surrey's wicket-keeper, claimed nine dismissals in the match to pass the record eight against Glamorgan by J. T. Murray, of Middlesex, at Lord's 27 years earlier.

Close of play: First day, Surrey 226-7 (D. J. Thomas 24*, K. T. Medlycott 16*); Second day, Surrey 44-2 (G. S. Clinton 21*, K. T. Medlycott 5*).

Surrey

G. S. Clinton c Todd b Barwick	5	– c Todd b Ontong	53
D. M. Smith lbw b Shastri	56	– b Smith	6
A. J. Stewart lbw b Smith	1	– run out	10
M. A. Lynch c Todd b Smith	0	– (6) b Barwick	0
T. E. Jesty c Morris b Ontong	84	– (7) not out	4
†C. J. Richards c Todd b Shastri	14		
*I. A. Greig b Ontong	15	– (5) not out	4
D. J. Thomas b Shastri	49		
K. T. Medlycott c James b Ontong	32	– (4) c Metson b Barwick	65
C. K. Bullen c Morris b Shastri	5		
A. H. Gray not out	1		
B 2, l-b 1, w 2, n-b 6	11	B 1, l-b 3, w 1	5

1/12 2/17 3/17 4/107 5/149   273   1/8 2/38 3/139   (5 wkts dec.) 147
6/181 7/186 8/251 9/266   4/139 5/139

Bonus points – Surrey 3, Glamorgan 4.

Bowling: *First Innings*—Barwick 19–5–43–1; Derrick 4–0–25–0; Ontong 28–6–75–3; Shastri 32.1–7–77–4; Holmes 5–1–15–0. *Second Innings*—Barwick 8–2–22–2; Smith 3–0–12–1; Ontong 17–2–70–1; Shastri 11–2–39–0.

Glamorgan

S. P. James c Richards b Gray	6	– c Richards b Thomas	2
*H. Morris b Thomas	14	– c Stewart b Gray	0
G. C. Holmes lbw b Medlycott	11	– c Richards b Gray	28
M. P. Maynard c Greig b Gray	10	– st Richards b Medlycott	53
R. J. Shastri c Richards b Gray	13	– c Thomas b Medlycott	47
P. A. Todd c Greig b Gray	2	– st Richards b Medlycott	6
R. C. Ontong c Lynch b Gray	0	– c Jesty b Gray	13
J. Derrick lbw b Bullen	15	– c Smith b Lynch	18
†C. P. Metson not out	31	– b Bullen	4
I. Smith st Richards b Medlycott	44	– c Richards b Medlycott	5
S. R. Barwick c Richards b Bullen	1	– not out	1
B 1, l-b 1, n-b 11	13	B 8, l-b 4, n-b 6	18

1/6 2/31 3/35 4/57 5/58   160   1/3 2/3 3/74 4/119 5/128   195
6/60 7/96 8/98 9/151   6/152 7/163 8/179 9/186

Bonus points – Glamorgan 1, Surrey 4.

Bowling: *First Innings*—Gray 16–1–46–5; Thomas 18–4–48–1; Medlycott 15–5–47–2; Bullen 8.1–3–17–2. *Second Innings*—Gray 15–3–39–3; Thomas 6–1–17–1; Medlycott 31–11–70–4; Bullen 23–10–57–1; Lynch 0.3–0–0–1.

Umpires: J. Birkenshaw and D. O. Oslear.

At Leeds, July 22, 23, 24. GLAMORGAN drew with YORKSHIRE.

At Weston-super-Mare, August 1, 3, 4. GLAMORGAN lost to SOMERSET by seven wickets.

GLAMORGAN v LEICESTERSHIRE

At Abergavenny, August 5, 6, 7. Drawn. Glamorgan 5 pts, Leicestershire 4 pts. Toss: Glamorgan. After two mainly tedious days of slow batting on an easy-paced pitch, there was a much needed urgency on the third day. Shastri played with an enchanting mixture of grace and high-velocity hitting, striking four sixes before Glamorgan set Leicestershire to chase 330 off 62 overs; and though they were steadily on course for an assault, when Briers was fifth out for 84 they thought better of it. Earlier in the match Alan Butcher hit his first century for Glamorgan. Made in just over four and a half hours, with eighteen fours, his 135 was the highest innings on the ground by a Glamorgan player and equalled the record score there by P. A. Neale, of Worcestershire, in 1983. Ian Butcher, his younger brother, batted excellently in both innings for the visitors.

Close of play: First day, Glamorgan 322-6 (R. J. Shastri 56*, C. P. Metson 1*); Second day, Leicestershire 277-5 (L. Potter 47*, J. P. Agnew 0*).

Glamorgan

A. R. Butcher c Potter b Such	135	– c Such b Potter	64
*H. Morris c Butcher b Willey	56	– b Willey	3
M. P. Maynard b Whitaker b Potter	35	– (4) c DeFreitas b Potter	38
G. C. Holmes c Whitticase b Agnew	26	– (5) not out	44
P. A. Todd c and b Potter	4	– (3) c Whitaker b Willey	17
R. J. Shastri lbw b Clift	56	– not out	49
J. Derrick lbw b Agnew	0		
†C. P. Metson c Potter b Agnew	31		
I. Smith b Clift	14		
S. R. Barwick b Clift	12		
R. C. Ontong not out	6		
L-b 2, n-b 9	11	B 5	5

1/156 2/233 3/233 4/237 5/320   386   1/21 2/53 3/122   (4 wkts dec.) 220
6/320 7/322 8/343 9/362   4/137

Bonus points – Glamorgan 3, Leicestershire 1 (Score at 100 overs: 277-4).

Bowling: *First Innings*—Agnew 36.2-6-129-3; DeFreitas 13-3-31-0; Clift 28-6-71-3; Such 23-7-60-1; Willey 18-3-54-1; Potter 10-3-39-2. *Second Innings*—Agnew 5-0-25-0; Clift 3-1-5-0; Willey 8-1-48-2; Such 19-1-71-0; Potter 14-2-66-2.

Leicestershire

I. P. Butcher c and b Shastri	88	– c Todd b Shastri	67
N. E. Briers c Metson b Barwick	18	– c Holmes b Ontong	84
R. A. Cobb b sub b Derrick	78		
J. J. Whitaker c and b Shastri	2	– c Ontong b Shastri	9
*P. Willey c Ontong b Derrick	30	– (3) c Maynard b Ontong	26
L. Potter not out	47	– not out	7
J. P. Agnew not out	0		
P. A. J. DeFreitas (did not bat)		– (5) b Shastri	18
P. B. Clift (did not bat)		– (7) not out	4
B 10, l-b 4	14	B 4, l-b 3, n-b 2	9

1/45 2/188 3/194 4/194 5/268   (5 wkts dec.) 277   1/130 2/175 3/187   (5 wkts) 224
                                             4/210 5/220

†P. Whitticase and P. M. Such did not bat.

Bonus points – Leicestershire 3, Glamorgan 2.

Bowling: *First Innings*—Barwick 15-2-46-1; Smith 4-1-20-0; Ontong 17-4-53-0; Shastri 33-8-72-2; Derrick 27-5-71-2; Holmes 1-0-1-0. *Second Innings*—Barwick 2-1-1-0; Derrick 7-1-33-0; Ontong 22-5-103-2; Shastri 25-7-80-3.

Umpires: B. Leadbeater and R. A. White.

At Worcester, August 15, 17, 18. GLAMORGAN drew with WORCESTERSHIRE.

GLAMORGAN v MIDDLESEX

At Cardiff, August 19, 20, 21. Drawn. Glamorgan 7 pts, Middlesex 5 pts. Toss: Middlesex. Glamorgan were reported to the TCCB for allegedly "doctoring" the pitch, which was closely shaved at one end to assist Ontong's off-spin. In the event, Middlesex, without their leading spin bowlers, Emburey and Edmonds, who were at Lord's for the MCC Bicentenary match, almost won. Glamorgan collapsed on the final day and their last pair, Base and Barwick, had to endure three overs to save the match. Slack and Brown batted splendidly in both innings, while Carr played a purposeful innings before Middlesex declared to set a target of 230 from what turned out to be 48 overs. Sykes, emulating the first-innings success of Ontong, took four wickets with his off-breaks in an exciting climax.

Close of play: First day, Middlesex 237; Second day, Middlesex 40-0 (W. N. Slack 11*, J. D. Carr 26*).

Middlesex

W. N. Slack c Derrick b Ontong	70	– lbw b Butcher	90
J. D. Carr lbw b Base	16	– c Smith b Ontong	43
K. R. Brown c Maynard b Ontong	65	– c Maynard b Butcher	58
M. R. Ramprakash c Holmes b Ontong	1	– st Metson b Butcher	0
M. A. Roseberry c Metson b Base	11	– (6) not out	7
*†P. R. Downton c Metson b Ontong	13	– (5) not out	34
J. F. Sykes c Maynard b Ontong	8		
S. P. Hughes b Barwick	19		
A. R. C. Fraser lbw b Barwick	0		
N. G. Cowans b Barwick	17		
P. C. R. Tufnell not out	0		
B 2, l-b 7, w 5, n-b 3	17	B 10, l-b 10, w 2, n-b 2 . .	24
	237	(4 wkts dec.)	**256**

1/33 2/143 3/149 4/172 5/190   1/79 2/210 3/214
6/192 7/211 8/212 9/232   4/219

Bonus points – Middlesex 2, Glamorgan 4.

Bowling: *First Innings*—Barwick 25.4–1–75–3; Base 17–5–42–2; Smith 8–2–26–0; Derrick 9–1–27–0; Ontong 22–2–58–5. *Second Innings*—Barwick 15–1–52–0; Base 10–1–28–0; Ontong 28–2–79–1; Holmes 6–2–22–0; Butcher 14–1–35–3; Morris 5–1–20–0.

Glamorgan

A. R. Butcher lbw b Fraser	37	– run out	35
*H. Morris lbw b Fraser	15	– (5) c Slack b Tufnell	18
P. A. Todd b Tufnell	54	– (2) b Cowans	8
M. P. Maynard b Sykes	18	– c Roseberry b Sykes	33
R. C. Ontong c Downton b Tufnell	23	– (6) c Fraser b Sykes	8
G. C. Holmes lbw b Fraser	1	– (3) c Downton b Cowans	0
J. Derrick b Hughes	44	– (8) b Sykes b Tufnell	22
†C. P. Metson c Sykes b Fraser	10	– (9) b Sykes	0
I. Smith b Tufnell	32	– (7) b Sykes	20
S. J. Base not out	2	– not out	1
S. R. Barwick b Hughes	0	– not out	0
B 6, l-b 7, w 1, n-b 14	28	B 5, l-b 4, n-b 2	11
	264	(9 wkts)	**156**

1/60 2/71 3/93 4/163 5/172   1/15 2/15 3/59   (9 wkts) 156
6/172 7/204 8/254 9/264   4/82 5/104 6/112
                            7/155 8/155 9/155

Bonus points – Glamorgan 3, Middlesex 3 (Score at 100 overs: 263-8).

Bowling: *First Innings*—Cowans 9–2–28–0; Hughes 24.4–5–57–2; Sykes 21–8–42–1; Fraser 20–8–50–4; Tufnell 26–6–74–3. *Second Innings*—Cowans 4–1–19–2; Hughes 4–1–15–0; Sykes 20–6–49–4; Fraser 5–0–16–0; Tufnell 15–5–48–2.

Umpires: J. W. Holder and A. G. T. Whitehead.

GLAMORGAN v WORCESTERSHIRE

At Neath, August 22, 24, 25. Glamorgan won by seven wickets. Glamorgan 23 pts, Worcestershire 5 pts. Toss: Worcestershire. Maynard's natural aggression was given full rein on the last day with his team needing only 158 runs from a minimum of 50 overs. He struck three sixes and twelve fours in making an unbeaten 80 off 57 deliveries and Glamorgan won with more than an hour to spare. Butcher was awarded his county cap at the end of the match, having carried his bat for 135 in just under four and a half hours on a slow, low pitch. He hit eighteen fours, and there were ten fours in his second-innings 59. Base, who had taken only six wickets during the season, finished with a match analysis of nine for 145, including a then career-best five for 108, from his medium-pace seamers. North, a left-arm spinner, bowling for the first time in the Championship in 1987, also made a notable contribution, dismissing Hick and Botham in both innings without either noted hitter being able to launch an assault. Radford's six for 67 in Glamorgan's first innings was a highly commendable performance on an unresponsive pitch.

Close of play: First day, Glamorgan 28-1 (A. R. Butcher 13*, G. C. Holmes 5*); Second day, Worcestershire 77-2 (T. S. Curtis 39*, R. K. Illingworth 2*).

Worcestershire

T. S. Curtis c Metson b Derrick	25	– c Morris b Base		49
G. J. Lord b Barwick	11	– c Maynard b Ontong		25
G. A. Hick c Holmes b North	32	– st Metson b North		9
D. B. D'Oliveira c Maynard b North	43	– (5) lbw b Base		56
*P. A. Neale b Base	37	– (6) c sub b Base		26
I. T. Botham b North	6	– (7) c Metson b North		2
†S. J. Rhodes b North	11	– (8) not out		17
P. J. Newport c Metson b Base	9	– (9) c Metson b Base		0
R. K. Illingworth lbw b Base	2	– (4) c Maynard b Base		30
N. V. Radford not out		– b Ontong		13
A. P. Pridgeon c Morris b Base	0	– b Ontong		1
B 1, l-b 9, w 2, n-b 1	13	L-b 10, w 1		11
	193			**239**

1/32 2/68 3/75 4/153 5/163   1/53 2/72 3/101 4/174 5/181
6/175 7/187 8/187 9/193   6/188 7/212 8/212 9/237

Bonus points – Worcestershire 1, Glamorgan 4.

Bowling: First Innings—Barwick 19-5-39-1; Base 15.2-1-37-4; North 29-10-43-4; Ontong 17-2-47-0; Derrick 6-1-17-1. *Second Innings*—Barwick 4-1-8-0; Base 29-8-108-5; Ontong 33-13-52-3; North 27-10-45-2; Derrick 1-0-2-0; Butcher 6-0-14-0.

Glamorgan

A. R. Butcher not out	135	– c Rhodes b Newport		59
*H. Morris c Illingworth b Pridgeon	9	– c Botham b Radford		0
G. C. Holmes c Radford b Illingworth	10	– c Hick b Radford		12
M. P. Maynard b Hick	42	– not out		80
R. C. Ontong c Botham b Radford	25	– not out		7
P. A. Todd c D'Oliveira b Radford	0			
J. Derrick c and b D'Oliveira	19			
†C. P. Metson c Rhodes b Radford	2			
P. D. North b Radford	15			
S. J. Base b Radford	3			
S. R. Barwick b Radford	0			
B 9, l-b 5, n-b 1	15	L-b 1, w 1		2
	275	(3 wkts)		**160**

1/16 2/39 3/102 4/162 5/162   1/5 2/43 3/131
6/219 7/238 8/269 9/275

Bonus points – Glamorgan 3, Worcestershire 4.

Bowling: *First Innings*—Radford 24–5–67–6; Pridgeon 4–0–12–1; Illingworth 22–4–63–1; Hick 26–9–85–1; D'Oliveira 8–3–30–1; Botham 1–0–4–0. *Second Innings*—Radford 11–1–55–2; Pridgeon 3–1–5–0; Hick 9–2–33–0; Lord 2–0–24–0; D'Oliveira 2–0–25–0; Newport 2–0–7–1; Botham 1–0–6–0; Neale 0.1–0–4–0.

Umpires: J. W. Holder and A. G. T. Whitehead.

At The Oval, August 26, 27, 28. GLAMORGAN lost to SURREY by five wickets.

GLAMORGAN v DERBYSHIRE

At Cardiff, September 2, 3, 4. Derbyshire won by three wickets. Derbyshire 23 pts, Glamorgan 6 pts. Toss: Derbyshire. Not many matches are won in such manner as this eventful and thrilling contest. With 6 runs required from the final ball, Maher struck a tremendous blow, high over mid-wicket, when Holmes sent down a short delivery. Maynard saved Glamorgan on the opening day with a brilliant hundred on a greenish pitch on which Holding returned his best figures of the season – five for 41. He hit a six and eighteen fours in just over three hours, scoring 119 out of 171 runs before he was seventh out. Solid contributions, and a swift, spirited onslaught by Warner and Holding, put Derbyshire 47 runs ahead. Butcher, after recovering from a knock on the arm, received while batting in the first innings, hit his third Glamorgan century in a month, his unbeaten 113 in three and a half hours containing eleven fours. Barnett and Morris gave Derbyshire a secure start to their attempt to score 216 in 70 minutes plus twenty overs. Roberts and Holding increased the momentum, but the chase was to provide tingling tension right to that last ball.

Close of play: First day, Derbyshire 106–2 (B. Roberts 11*, J. E. Morris 0*); Second day, Glamorgan 55–0 (J. E. Morris 19*, G. C. Holmes 9*).

Glamorgan

A. R. Butcher c Maher b Holding	6	– not out	113
*H. Morris c Maher b Sharma	30	– c O'Gorman b Finney	25
G. C. Holmes c Maher b Holding	0	– st Maher b Barnett	36
M. P. Maynard c Maher b Mortensen	119	– c Maher b Finney	0
R. C. Ontong c Sharma b Holding	6	– c Morris b Barnett	9
P. A. Todd c Finney b Holding	0	– b Finney	5
J. Derrick c Morris b Holding	0	– lbw b Barnett	0
†C. P. Metson not out	23	– lbw b Barnett	0
I. Smith c Maher b Mortensen	1	– c O'Gorman b Holding	45
S. J. Base c Warner b Malcolm	18	– c Barnett b Malcolm	9
S. R. Barwick b Mortensen	5	– b Holding	3
B 5, l-b 16, w 1, n-b 5	27	L-b 8, w 4, n-b 5	17
	239		**262**

1/10 2/10 3/94 4/138 5/138   1/73 2/73 3/98 4/98 5/104
6/169 7/181 8/184 9/213   6/105 7/105 8/183 9/237

Bonus points – Glamorgan 2, Derbyshire 4.

In the second innings A. R. Butcher, when 20, retired hurt at 35 and resumed at 98.

Bowling: *First Innings*—Holding 17–7–41–5; Malcolm 15–2–43–1; Warner 13–2–53–0; Mortensen 20.3–4–60–3; Sharma 4–1–21–1. *Second Innings*—Holding 21.4–3–72–2; Warner 5–1–13–0; Mortensen 5–1–12–0; Malcolm 9–1–40–1; Finney 28–11–47–3; Barnett 31–11–70–4.

Derbyshire

*K. J. Barnett c Todd b Ontong	48	– st Metson b Ontong	45
†B. J. M. Maher c Todd b Smith	39	– (8) not out	12
B. Roberts c Metson b Smith	20	– c Derrick b Ontong	47
J. E. Morris c Morris b Derrick	38	– (2) c Butcher b Smith	39
T. J. G. O'Gorman c Todd b Base	2	– (9) not out	11
R. Sharma c Maynard b Base	17	– st Metson b Ontong	4
R. J. Finney c Todd b Ontong	29	– run out	13
A. E. Warner c Metson b Base	43	– (4) c sub b Holmes	4
M. A. Holding c Maynard b Ontong	26	– (5) b Ontong	32
O. H. Mortensen not out	5		
D. E. Malcolm b Base	3		
B 1, l-b 10, n-b 5	16	B 4, l-b 5	9

1/75 2/103 3/122 4/139 5/172   286   1/71 2/109 3/116   (7 wkts) 216
6/194 7/238 8/270 9/282   4/153 5/166 6/190 7/192

Bonus points – Derbyshire 3, Glamorgan 4.

Bowling: *First Innings*—Barwick 11–1–37–0; Base 18.3–2–67–4; Derrick 14–4–47–1; Ontong 20–8–46–3; Smith 18–3–69–2; Holmes 2–1–9–0. *Second Innings*—Base 5–0–33–0; Smith 6–0–34–1; Ontong 16–1–85–4; Holmes 12–1–55–1.

Umpires: B. Dudleston and R. A. White.

At Nottingham, September 9, 10, 11. GLAMORGAN lost to NOTTINGHAMSHIRE by nine wickets.

At Bristol, September 12, 14, 15. GLAMORGAN lost to GLOUCESTERSHIRE by 114 runs.

GLOUCESTERSHIRE

Patron: HRH The Princess of Wales
President: G. W. Parker
Chairman: D. N. Perry
Chairman, Cricket Committee: D. G. Stone
Secretary: P. G. M. August
    Phoenix County Ground, Nevil Road, Bristol
    BS7 9EJ (Telephone: 0272-45216)
Captain: D. A. Graveney
Senior Coach: J. N. Shepherd
Youth Coach: G. G. Wiltshire

A much improved performance in the limited-overs competitions provided some compensation for Gloucestershire's decline in the Britannic Assurance Championship, in which they fell to tenth place after finishing third in 1985 and second in 1986. After nine matches they had 31 points, so a final total of 200 was something of an achievement, the last fifteen games having produced five wins and a tie. Like most counties, Gloucestershire suffered from the appalling weather, and in five matches they were unable to bowl for bonus points. This accounts, to a degree, for their having fewer bowling points than any other team; but it has also to be said that the bowling was not as demanding as in the two previous years.

Courtney Walsh, the leading wicket-taker in the country in 1986, began to show the effects of three years' almost continuous cricket and had to be used more sparingly. Even though he missed three matches while away with the Rest of the World XI, his total of overs in the Championship was down from 790 to 471 and his return of wickets was halved to 59. Only twice did he claim five wickets in an innings, compared with twelve times in 1986. Nevertheless he was again the county's leading bowler. David Lawrence, after some good days, broke down at Cheltenham early in August and did not play again. Hopes that Kevin Curran might have regained full fitness were not realised, and although he put in some useful spells in the NatWest Bank Trophy, he was rarely risked in the three-day games. Indeed, there were times when Gloucestershire had enough injured players to keep a sports injuries clinic working full time. Only Jack Russell and Andy Stovold appeared in all 24 Championship games. Phil Bainbridge, who took two nasty knocks, missed a third of the programme, and David Graveney, having overcome a back problem, gashed both hands and towards the end was kept going by painkillers.

Runs were not usually in short supply, indifferent starts often being repaired in attractive style by Curran, Jeremy Lloyds and Russell. Only Nottinghamshire and Surrey gained more batting points. Lloyds played many sparkling innings, with a high proportion of boundaries, leaving bowlers to curse their luck at finding such an accomplished player at No. 7. Bill Athey had a strange season. He scored consistently in the Benson and Hedges Cup and made his maiden Test century at Lord's, but he lost his England place two games later. At that point his highest Championship score was 29, yet he came back to form so well that he hit five hundreds – four in succession – and a 98 in the last six weeks of the season. He also did well as captain when Graveney and Bainbridge were absent.

Gloucestershire's player of the year, however, was Russell, whose wicket-keeping touched new heights and whose batting continued to improve. Two brilliant displays in televised games brought him a host of new admirers, and he was chosen for England's tour of Pakistan, surely the first of many representative honours.

"Vibert" Greene, a Barbadian, signed as deputy for Walsh, proved an interesting newcomer – a flamboyant batsman and a hard-working fast bowler. He will be one of the county's two overseas players in 1988, the other being the Australian fast bowler, Craig McDermott, who was recruited on the recommendation of Allan Border. No sooner had Gary Sainsbury announced his retirement than, with Lawrence unfit, he became a regular member of the attack again. The decision to award him his cap, just before the end of the season, was a popular one. Tony Wright, on the staff since 1980, was also given his cap and celebrated with a career-best 161 against Glamorgan.

Paul Romaines had his best season for some time, while Stovold, in his benefit year, played few long innings but was usually good value. For nineteen-year-old Mark Alleyne, his second season was one of learning. He played many useful innings, was outstanding in the field, and showed some promise as a bowler of medium pace. Kassim Ibadulla, son of the former Pakistan and Warwickshire player, was taken on to the staff and on his few appearances revealed potential as a batsman and off-spin bowler.

Gloucestershire won the toughest of the Benson and Hedges Cup qualifying groups, only to lose their quarter-final to Kent off the final ball. Having overcome their bogey team, Lancashire, in the first round of the NatWest Bank Trophy, they saw off Sussex and Warwickshire with little trouble, Stovold and Wright contributing century partnerships in both games. But by the semi-final with Nottinghamshire, the injury position was at its most critical. A patched-up team did well in the field, only to collapse when chasing a reasonable target. Third in the Refuge Assurance League was three places higher than previously achieved in the Sunday competition and it could have been even better. Gloucestershire should have won at Old Trafford, when Lancashire rested some leading players, and the game with Derbyshire could easily have gone in their favour. By the end of the season, therefore, it was clear that, at full strength, they were still a side to be reckoned with. Nevertheless, the sequence of near misses in the challenge for trophies was becoming frustrating for players and supporters alike. – Geoffrey Wheeler.

GLOUCESTERSHIRE 1987

[Bill Smith

Back row: V. S. Greene, M. W. Alleyne, J. W. Lloyds, K. M. Curran, D. V. Lawrence, A. J. Wright, R. C. Russell, K. P. Tomlins. Front row: C. A. Walsh, P. Bainbridge, D. A. Graveney (captain), A. W. Stovold, P. W. Romaines. Inset: C. W. J. Athey.

GLOUCESTERSHIRE RESULTS

All first-class matches – Played 26: Won 5, Lost 8, Tied 1, Drawn 12.

County Championship matches – Played 24: Won 5, Lost 8, Tied 1, Drawn 10.

Bonus points – Batting 62, Bowling 50.

Competition placings – Britannic Assurance County Championship, 10th; NatWest Bank Trophy, s-f; Benson and Hedges Cup, q-f; Refuge Assurance League, 3rd.

BRITANNIC ASSURANCE CHAMPIONSHIP AVERAGES

BATTING

	Birthplace	M	I	NO	R	HI	Avge
‡C. W. J. Athey	Middlesbrough	16	26	4	1,069	160	48.59
‡J. W. Lloyds	Penang, Malaya	22	30	4	1,159	130	44.57
§‡K. M. Curran	Rusape, S. Rhodesia	20	31	6	1,067	119	42.68
‡P. Bainbridge	Stoke-on-Trent	16	23	6	628	151	36.94
‡R. C. Russell	Stroud	24	34	7	779	57*	28.85
‡A. J. Wright	Stevenage	22	36	2	975	161	28.67
‡P. W. Romaines	Bishop Auckland	23	39	1	1,004	115	26.42
M. W. Alleyne	Tottenham	18	26	7	499	82	26.26
‡A. W. Stovold	Bristol	24	40	2	897	88	23.60
§V. S. Greene	Barbados	6	8	2	141	62*	23.50
K. B. K. Ibadulla	Birmingham	4	6	1	113	46*	22.60
K. P. Tomlins	Kingston-upon-Thames	6	8	1	107	34	15.28
‡D. A. Graveney	Bristol	17	16	3	121	30	9.30
‡D. V. Lawrence	Gloucester	17	19	4	138	65*	9.20
§‡C. A. Walsh	Kingston, Jamaica	17	21	1	166	27	8.30
‡G. E. Sainsbury	Wanstead	11	14	7	15	5	2.14

Also batted: ‡J. N. Shepherd (*Belleplaine, Barbados*) (1 match) 5, 1.

* *Signifies not out.*   ‡ *Denotes county cap.*   § *Not qualified for England.*

The following played a total of fourteen three-figure innings for Gloucestershire in County Championship matches – C. W. J. Athey 5, K. M. Curran 3, P. Bainbridge 2, J. W. Lloyds 2, P. W. Romaines 1, A. J. Wright 1.

BOWLING

	O	M	R	W	BB	Avge
C. A. Walsh	471.3	95	1,433	59	5-38	24.28
P. Bainbridge	271.4	59	885	30	5-70	29.50
V. S. Greene	167.5	18	625	20	7-96	31.25
D. A. Graveney	324.2	97	812	25	5-37	32.48
D. V. Lawrence	350.5	44	1,411	38	6-63	37.13
J. W. Lloyds	364.4	57	1,315	32	6-57	41.09
G. E. Sainsbury	298.2	71	798	17	3-48	46.94

Also bowled: M. W. Alleyne 149.4–32–577–9; C. W. J. Athey 37.4–3–136–2; K. M. Curran 48–5–203–2; K. B. K. Ibadulla 43–8–112–4; R. C. Russell 0.1–0–0–0; J. N. Shepherd 28–9–92–2.

Wicket-keeper: R. C. Russell 50 ct, 8 st.

Leading Fielders: A. J. Wright 17, J. W. Lloyds 16.

GLOUCESTERSHIRE v ESSEX

At Bristol, April 25, 26, 27. Essex won by ten wickets. Essex 24 pts, Gloucestershire 4 pts.
Toss: Essex. This early-season match between the two leading teams of 1986 was won with
authority by the reigning champions, for whom Foster and Gooch were outstanding. Curran's
century in 149 balls saw to it that Gloucestershire's first innings achieved respectability, but
with their attack missing Walsh and Graveney, and with Gooch at his imperious best,
needing only 206 balls for his 171, the home side were given a fearful drubbing on the second
day. The Essex captain batted for almost four and a quarter hours and hit 28 fours.
Gloucestershire entertained hopes of saving the game while Stovold was in full flow, his 88
coming off 93 balls, but his dismissal opened the way for Foster and Pringle to hurry Essex
to victory.

Close of play: First day, Essex 85-0 (G. A. Gooch 41*, C. Gladwin 43*); Second day,
Gloucestershire 50-1 (A. W. Stovold 38*, R. C. Russell 0*).

Gloucestershire

A. W. Stovold	c East b Foster	10	– c Page b Lever	88
P. W. Romaines	c Gooch b Foster	45	– c East b Pringle	10
C. W. J. Athey	c Miller b Foster	13	– (4) lbw b Pringle	19
*P. Bainbridge	c Hardie b Foster	0	– (5) b Pringle	0
A. J. Wright	c East b Lever	13	– (6) not out	9
M. W. Alleyne	c and b Foster	6	– (7) c Gladwin b Gooch	9
K. M. Curran	not out	114	– (8) c Pringle b Foster	22
J. W. Lloyds	c East b Foster	32	– (9) c Miller b Gooch	7
†R. C. Russell	c East b Page	21	– (3) c Miller b Gooch	23
G. E. Sainsbury	c East b Gooch	0	– b Foster	1
D. V. Lawrence	c Prichard b Page	2	– c Gladwin b Pringle	0
	L-b 8, w 3, n-b 1	12	L-b 2, w 1, n-b 4	7

1/23 2/45 3/45 4/78 5/88   **268**   1/50 2/112 3/145 4/145 5/145   **222**
6/110 7/178 8/249 9/264   6/165 7/198 8/207 9/209

Bonus points – Gloucestershire 3, Essex 4.

Bowling: *First Innings*—Lever 22-5-68-1; Foster 25-4-75-6; Pringle 18-4-42-0; Page
17-2-54-2; Gooch 7-1-21-1. *Second Innings*—Lever 13-3-30-1; Foster 26-4-95-4; Pringle
17-3-38-3; Page 5-0-30-0; Gooch 12-7-24-2; Miller 8-5-3-0.

Essex

*G. A. Gooch	c Sainsbury b Lloyds	171	– not out	18
C. Gladwin	c Lloyds b Bainbridge	76	– not out	7
B. R. Hardie	b Curran	61		
P. J. Prichard	run out	70		
K. W. R. Fletcher	b Lloyds	36		
D. R. Pringle	not out	27		
	B 9, l-b 13, w 1, n-b 2	25		

1/172 2/313 3/338   (5 wkts dec.) **466**   (no wkt) **25**
4/411 5/466

G. Miller, †D. E. East, N. A. Foster, H. A. Page and J. K. Lever did not bat.

Bonus points – Essex 4, Gloucestershire 1 (Score at 100 overs: 416-4).

Bowling: *First Innings*—Lawrence 21-1-122-0; Sainsbury 27-6-70-0; Curran 21-4-93-1;
Bainbridge 18-3-66-1; Lloyds 11-1-54-0; Alleyne 10-1-39-0. *Second Innings*—Lawrence
3-0-20-0; Sainsbury 2-0-5-0.

Umpires: D. G. L. Evans and P. B. Wight.

At Hove, April 29, 30, May 1. GLOUCESTERSHIRE drew with SUSSEX.

At Oxford, May 20, 21, 22. GLOUCESTERSHIRE drew with OXFORD UNIVERSITY.

At Taunton, May 23, 25, 26. GLOUCESTERSHIRE lost to SOMERSET by an innings and 83 runs.

At Southampton, May 30, June 1, 2. GLOUCESTERSHIRE drew with HAMPSHIRE.

GLOUCESTERSHIRE v LANCASHIRE

At Bristol, June 3, 4, 5. Drawn. Gloucestershire 6 pts, Lancashire 4 pts. Toss: Gloucestershire. The home side called the tune for much of the match and were still in a winning position against the Championship leaders when rain washed out play after 29 overs on the third day. Lancashire were 91 runs ahead with four second-innings wickets in hand. Lawrence and Walsh soon had Lancashire on the rack on the opening day and only Allott, with nine boundaries in a spirited 67, played with any confidence. Although Patterson proved equally devastating for Lancashire, Wright and Romaines had already put on 93 for the second wicket, and Lloyds hit effectively to gain a lead of 85. That Lancashire lost only four wickets in clearing this deficit was due mainly to a stubborn innings by Fowler, and Allott was again going well when the weather intervened.

Close of play: First day, Gloucestershire 78-1 (A. J. Wright 51*, P. W. Romaines 18*); Second day, Lancashire 80-4 (G. Fowler 34*, I. Folley 0*).

Lancashire

G. D. Mendis c Wright b Walsh	4	– c Russell b Lawrence	3
M. R. Chadwick c and b Walsh	11	– c Alleyne b Lawrence	4
D. W. Varey b Lawrence	9	– c Russell b Lawrence	21
G. Fowler c Wright b Lawrence	0	– c and b Bainbridge	62
*D. P. Hughes c Russell b Walsh	11	– lbw b Walsh	9
M. Watkinson c Russell b Lawrence	0	– (7) not out	12
J. Simmons b Lawrence	0		
P. J. W. Allott b Walsh	67	– not out	36
I. Folley lbw b Bainbridge	17	– (6) c Russell b Bainbridge	12
†J. Stanworth b Bainbridge	1		
B. P. Patterson not out	0		
L-b 3, n-b 3	6	B 7, l-b 2, n-b 8	17

1/4 2/25 3/25 4/32 5/35   126   1/4 2/19 3/42 4/76   (6 wkts) 176
6/35 7/69 8/110 9/126   5/122 6/129

Bonus points – Gloucestershire 4.

Bowling: *First Innings*—Walsh 22-9-47-4; Lawrence 14-5-42-4; Bainbridge 9.3-1-25-2; Graveney 2-1-9-0. *Second Innings*—Walsh 25-7-62-1; Lawrence 23-5-87-3; Lloyds 1-1-0-0; Bainbridge 9-3-18-2.

Gloucestershire

A. W. Stovold c Chadwick b Allott	6	C. A. Walsh c Stanworth b Patterson	0
A. J. Wright b Patterson	67	*D. A. Graveney c Folley b Watkinson	2
P. W. Romaines c Stanworth b Patterson	34	D. V. Lawrence c Hughes b Watkinson	0
P. Bainbridge c Folley b Patterson	4		
K. M. Curran c Stanworth b Watkinson	1	B 1, l-b 4, n-b 13	18
J. W. Lloyds not out	57		
M. W. Alleyne c Stanworth b Allott	6	1/10 2/103 3/114 4/117 5/117	211
†R. C. Russell b Patterson	16	6/143 7/190 8/191 9/211	

Bonus points – Gloucestershire 2, Lancashire 4.

Bowling: Patterson 23-4-87-5; Allott 17-3-50-2; Watkinson 23-10-55-3; Simmons 7-3-11-0; Folley 4-2-3-0.

Umpires: B. Dudleston and K. E. Palmer.

At Lord's, June 6, 8, 9. GLOUCESTERSHIRE drew with MIDDLESEX.

At Worcester, June 17, 18, 19. GLOUCESTERSHIRE drew with WORCESTERSHIRE.

GLOUCESTERSHIRE v WORCESTERSHIRE

At Gloucester, June 27, 29, 30. Worcestershire won by 160 runs. Worcestershire 24 pts, Gloucestershire 4 pts. Toss: Worcestershire. A second-wicket partnership of 231 between the fluent Hick and the dogged Curtis, after Botham had been caught first ball, effectively decided this match in Worcestershire's favour, for it was the only period when batsmen were in control. Once Hick's commanding innings had ended, Walsh and Lloyds swept through the rest of the batting; but with Dilley bowling a penetrating opening spell Gloucestershire were soon facing the prospect of following on. Curran and Lloyds later removed this threat. Worcestershire, however, happily traded wickets for quick runs before setting a target of 329 in 88 overs. With Stovold and Bainbridge handicapped by injuries, Gloucestershire had little to offer except more bold hitting from Curran (two sixes, eight fours) before the last five wickets fell for 17 runs.

Close of play: First day, Gloucestershire 17-2 (A. J. Wright 7*, P. Bainbridge 4*); Second day, Worcestershire 140-5 (P. J. Newport 23*, R. K. Illingworth 0*).

Worcestershire

T. S. Curtis c Russell b Lloyds	91	– c Lloyds b Graveney	36
I. T. Botham c Athey b Lawrence	0	– (8) run out	6
G. A. Hick c Russell b Lloyds	138	– lbw b Walsh	24
D. B. D'Oliveira b Lloyds	14	– c and b Walsh	5
*P. A. Neale c Graveney b Lloyds	8	– (2) c Wright b Lawrence	0
†S. J. Rhodes c Russell b Walsh	2	– (5) c Wright b Lawrence	48
P. J. Newport c and b Walsh	0	– (6) c Walsh b Graveney	44
R. K. Illingworth not out	19	– (7) run out	16
N. V. Radford c sub b Walsh	31	– c Curran b Lawrence	8
G. R. Dilley c Wright b Lloyds	0	– c Wright b Graveney	3
A. P. Pridgeon b Walsh	1	– not out	2
L-b 1, w 1, n-b 4	12	L-b 2, w 1, n-b 2	5
	316		197

1/4 2/235 3/249 4/260 5/263 6/264 7/266 8/305 9/314

1/6 2/52 3/61 4/82 5/134 6/176 7/184 8/184 9/188

Bonus points – Worcestershire 4, Gloucestershire 3 (Score at 100 overs: 306-8).

Bowling: First Innings—Walsh 24.3-2-70-4; Lawrence 17-2-55-1; Bainbridge 17-2-77-0; Graveney 22-9-34-0; Lloyds 24-5-73-5. *Second Innings*—Walsh 16-3-48-2; Lawrence 13.2-1-63-3; Bainbridge 10-5-12-0; Graveney 16-5-45-3; Lloyds 8-2-27-0.

Gloucestershire

A. J. Wright c Rhodes b Dilley	22	– c Illingworth b Dilley	1
P. W. Romaines lbw b Dilley	4	– b Dilley	1
†R. C. Russell c D'Oliveira b Dilley	0	– (6) c Botham b Illingworth	16
P. Bainbridge b Dilley	4	– (11) not out	2
A. W. Stovold run out	37	– b Botham	21
C. W. J. Athey lbw b Radford	3	– (3) b Botham	29
K. M. Curran c Neale b Newport	40	– (4) b Illingworth	61
J. W. Lloyds c Botham b Newport	40	– (7) c D'Oliveira b Illingworth	12
*D. A. Graveney c Hick b Newport	15	– (8) c Rhodes b Botham	0
C. A. Walsh b Dilley	4	– (9) c Rhodes b Illingworth	14
D. V. Lawrence not out	1	– (10) run out	1
B 2, l-b 7, n-b 6	15	L-b 8, w 1, n-b 1	10
	185		168

1/6 2/6 3/23 4/46 5/75 6/76 7/147 8/170 9/181

1/6 2/7 3/71 4/111 5/125 6/151 7/151 8/151 9/152

Bonus points – Gloucestershire 1, Worcestershire 4.

Bowling: *First Innings*—Dilley 20–2–67–5; Radford 14–4–39–1; Newport 14–3–28–3; Botham 5–1–21–0; Illingworth 1–0–2–0; Pridgeon 5–0–19–0. *Second Innings*—Dilley 6–3–6–2; Radford 7–1–28–0; Newport 4–0–18–0; Pridgeon 5–1–27–0; Botham 15–3–53–3; Illingworth 10.1–5–28–4.

Umpires: J. Birkenshaw and D. G. L. Evans (B. Dudleston on 2nd and 3rd days).

GLOUCESTERSHIRE v HAMPSHIRE

At Gloucester, July 1, 2, 3. Hampshire won by an innings and 107 runs. Hampshire 24 pts, Gloucestershire 1 pt. Toss: Gloucestershire. This was a painfully one-sided affair, Gloucestershire being buried under a mountain of runs as Hampshire made a mockery of the home county's miserable first-innings total. Their batting varied between the careless and the overcautious. Although Gloucestershire hit back quickly by dismissing Smith and Nicholas, the third-wicket pair of Greenidge and Turner soon showed that there were no demons in the pitch. On the second day they took their partnership to 311, a Hampshire record against Gloucestershire, before Greenidge gave himself up after hitting four sixes and seventeen fours. The declaration was delayed so that Turner, who hit 25 fours in six hours at the crease, could better his previous best of 181 not out, made against Surrey eighteen years previously. Gloucestershire made more of a fight of it in their second innings, but when Russell and Curran threatened to drop anchor, Nicholas called up Marshall, who took four wickets in eighteen balls.

Close of play: First day, Hampshire 136-2 (C. G. Greenidge 69*, D. R. Turner 38*); Second day, Gloucestershire 101-2 (K. P. Tomlins 25*, R. C. Russell 4*).

Gloucestershire

A. J. Wright b Maru	15	– c Cowley b Tremlett	16
P. W. Romaines c Greenidge b Marshall	19	– lbw b Tremlett	45
K. P. Tomlins b Maru	2	– b Tremlett	25
K. M. Curran lbw b Tremlett	2	– (5) b Marshall	46
A. W. Stovold b Maru	21	– (6) b Cowley	5
M. W. Alleyne c Maru b Andrew	15	– (7) c Smith b Marshall	3
J. W. Lloyds c Terry b Andrew	13	– (8) not out	29
†R. C. Russell c Parks b Maru	14	– (4) b Marshall	23
C. A. Walsh c Parks b Maru	10	– b Marshall	0
*D. A. Graveney c Greenidge b Marshall	4	– lbw b Marshall	0
D. V. Lawrence not out	0	– st Parks b Maru	9
B 3, l-b 12, n-b 6	21	B 2, l-b 8, w 1, n-b 7	18
	136		**219**

1/26 2/36 3/39 4/50 5/86 6/105 7/107 8/117 9/136

1/34 2/90 3/101 4/163 5/175 6/176 7/181 8/182 9/182

Bonus points – Hampshire 4.

Bowling: *First Innings*—Marshall 11–1–35–2; Andrew 14–3–26–2; Maru 23.2–8–48–5; Tremlett 10–5–8–1; Cowley 6–3–4–0. *Second Innings*—Marshall 15–3–49–5; Andrew 10–3–39–0; Maru 22.3–6–50–1; Tremlett 15–2–36–3; Cowley 16–6–35–1.

Hampshire

C. G. Greenidge st Russell b Lloyds	163	M. D. Marshall not out	61
C. L. Smith c Russell b Walsh	18	B 5, l-b 21, w 1, n-b 7	34
*M. C. J. Nicholas c Lloyds b Lawrence	2		
D. R. Turner not out	184	1/35 2/38 3/349 (4 wkts dec.) 462	
V. P. Terry c Wright b Walsh	0	4/354	

†R. J. Parks, N. G. Cowley, T. M. Tremlett, R. J. Maru and S. J. W. Andrew did not bat.

Bonus points – Hampshire 4, Gloucestershire 1 (Score at 100 overs: 394-4).

Bowling: Walsh 27–6–81–2; Lawrence 24–2–98–1; Curran 13–1–49–0; Graveney 17–2–56–0; Lloyds 27–3–120–1; Alleyne 5–0–32–0.

Umpires: J. Birkenshaw and P. J. Eele.

At Swansea, July 4, 5, 7. GLOUCESTERSHIRE beat GLAMORGAN by 105 runs.

At Cardiff, July 6. GLOUCESTERSHIRE beat GLAMORGAN by seven wickets (See Other Matches, 1987).

GLOUCESTERSHIRE v MIDDLESEX

At Bristol, July 15, 16, 17. Gloucestershire won by 118 runs. Gloucestershire 19 pts, Middlesex 4 pts. Toss: Middlesex. Gloucestershire moved off the bottom of the Championship table by winning a game which was seriously affected by the weather on the first two days. After negotiations and two declarations on the third morning, Middlesex were set 306 in 90 overs. Lawrence quickly upset them, taking the first three wickets in sixteen balls, but Gatting banged the ball about as if he believed the target was readily attainable. However, Lloyds, finding substantial turn to achieve his best figures since leaving Somerset, was too much for most of the other batsmen and he also ended Gatting's resistance by having him caught in the deep, ninth out after hitting fourteen fours.

Close of play: First day, Gloucestershire 84-1 (A. W. Stovold 51*, C. W. J. Athey 10*); Second day, Middlesex 5-1 (J. D. Carr 4*, M. W. Gatting 0*).

Gloucestershire

A. W. Stovold c Brown b Emburey	68	– c Emburey b Hughes 0
A. J. Wright c Downton b Williams	15	– c Williams b Carr 5
*C. W. J. Athey c Emburey b Edmonds	26	– (6) not out 1
P. W. Romaines c Gatting b Emburey	10	– (5) c Butcher b Brown 0
K. M. Curran b Edmonds	26	
J. W. Lloyds c Gatting b Edmonds	8	
M. W. Alleyne st Downton b Edmonds	59	– (3) b Brown 12
†R. C. Russell c Hughes b Williams	40	– (4) not out 12
D. V. Lawrence b Emburey	6	
C. A. Walsh lbw b Emburey	1	
G. E. Sainsbury not out	3	
B 1, l-b 7, w 1, n-b 8	17	L-b 1 1

1/63 2/109 3/121 4/151 5/163   279   1/0 2/8 3/26   (4 wkts dec.) 31
6/164 7/248 8/261 9/265   4/26

Bonus points – Gloucestershire 3, Middlesex 4.

Bowling: *First Innings*—Daniel 6-0-36-0; Hughes 7-1-20-0; Williams 10-1-38-2; Edmonds 41.1-13-104-4; Emburey 34-9-69-4; Gatting 1-0-4-0. *Second Innings*—Hughes 2-0-12-1; Carr 4-0-11-1; Brown 3-0-7-2.

Middlesex

W. N. Slack c Russell b Lawrence	1	– c Walsh b Lawrence 17
J. D. Carr not out	4	– c Russell b Lawrence 7
*M. W. Gatting not out	0	– c Wright b Lloyds 78
K. R. Brown (did not bat)		– c Russell b Lawrence 4
R. O. Butcher (did not bat)		– c Sainsbury b Lloyds 16
†P. R. Downton (did not bat)		– c Wright b Lloyds 0
J. E. Emburey (did not bat)		– b Walsh 23
P. H. Edmonds (did not bat)		– c Walsh b Lloyds 24
N. F. Williams (did not bat)		– b Lloyds 0
S. P. Hughes (did not bat)		– c Romaines b Lloyds 2
W. W. Daniel (did not bat)		– not out 5
		B 2, l-b 1, w 2, n-b 6 11

1/5   (1 wkt dec.) 5   1/27 2/29 3/33 4/66 5/66   187
                                            6/129 7/178 8/178 9/182

Bowling: *First Innings*—Walsh 1–0–4–0; Lawrence 0.3–0–1–1. *Second Innings*—Walsh 12–3–54–1; Lawrence 10–1–48–3; Lloyds 15.5–3–57–6; Sainsbury 8–2–25–0.

Umpires: H. D. Bird and A. A. Jones.

GLOUCESTERSHIRE v NORTHAMPTONSHIRE

At Bristol, July 18, 20, 21. Drawn. Gloucestershire 4 pts, Northamptonshire 4 pts. Toss: Gloucestershire. Northamptonshire's bonus points took them to the head of the Championship table for the first time since 1976, but they finished the game requiring the weather's intervention to maintain their unbeaten record. Davis, with some hostile fast bowling, was the key figure on the opening day, although he was checked by Wright and Romaines. And, with Capel off line, Lloyds hit a six and eight fours in his 62 to ensure a reasonable total. Russell and Graveney gathered in the fourth batting point during Monday's brief spell of play. Given a stiff target of 346 in a minimum of 90 overs, Northamptonshire were launched by a flurry of boundaries from Larkins and were up with the clock until Alleyne's spell of three for 14 in six overs – his first Championship wickets – set them back. Williams, missed twice, took up the chase but Graveney had reduced the visitors to eight wickets down before the rain came. The players re-emerged with eight of the final twenty overs remaining but only one was bowled before the final storm.

Close of play: First day, Gloucestershire 251-7 (R. C. Russell 13*); Second day, Gloucestershire 307-9 (R. C. Russell 36*, D. A. Graveney 16*).

Gloucestershire

A. W. Stovold c Ripley b Davis	4	
A. J. Wright c Bailey b Davis	65	
C. W. J. Athey c Bailey b Davis	2	
P. W. Romaines c N. G. B. Cook b Davis	69	– (3) lbw b Walker ... 6
K. M. Curran c Larkins b Davis	4	
J. W. Lloyds c Lamb b N. G. B. Cook	62	– (5) not out ... 16
M. W. Alleyne b N. G. B. Cook	9	– (2) lbw b Walker ... 1
†R. C. Russell not out	36	– (1) c Ripley b Walker ... 0
V. S. Greene c Wild b N. G. B. Cook	1	– (4) not out ... 13
D. V. Lawrence b Davis	9	
*D. A. Graveney not out	16	
L-b 15, w 4, n-b 11	30	B 2 ... 2

1/8 2/23 3/138 4/148 5/194 (9 wkts dec.) 307   1/0 2/3 3/14 (3 wkts dec.) 38
6/229 7/251 8/253 9/264

Bonus points – Gloucestershire 4, Northamptonshire 4.

Bowling: *First Innings*—Davis 28–4–94–6; Capel 18–2–77–0; Walker 6–3–18–0; N. G. B. Cook 22–6–45–3; Wild 14–4–52–0; Williams 3.1–0–6–0. *Second Innings*—Walker 5–1–19–3; N. G. B. Cook 4–0–17–0.

Northamptonshire

Northamptonshire forfeited their first innings.

*G. Cook lbw b Lawrence	13	†D. Ripley c Lloyds b Graveney ... 22
W. Larkins c Lawrence b Alleyne	45	N. G. B. Cook not out ... 5
R. J. Bailey b Greene	11	W. W. Davis not out ... 23
A. J. Lamb b Alleyne	21	B 5, l-b 5, w 5, n-b 8 ... 23
D. J. Capel c Russell b Alleyne	8	
R. G. Williams b Graveney	63	1/42 2/62 3/104 4/108 (8 wkts) 252
D. J. Wild b Graveney	18	5/132 6/168 7/220 8/225

A. Walker did not bat.

Bowling: Lawrence 17–1–55–1; Greene 20–3–58–1; Alleyne 18–6–66–3; Graveney 13–3–33–3; Lloyds 9–1–30–0.

Umpires: H. D. Bird and A. A. Jones.

At Folkestone, July 22, 23, 24. GLOUCESTERSHIRE drew with KENT.

GLOUCESTERSHIRE v DERBYSHIRE

At Bristol, July 25, 27, 28. Tied. Gloucestershire 14 pts, Derbyshire 15 pts. Toss: Derbyshire. Barnett's generous declaration, which set Gloucestershire to score 279 in four hours, looked like going unrewarded when the home side recovered so effectively from 125 for five that they had two wickets in hand with the scores level and three balls of the final over remaining. A powerful hit from Lawrence looked to have won the match, only for Barnett to bring off a fine stop. Sharma then bowled Lawrence through a wild heave and yorked Walsh with the last ball to provide Derbyshire with the first tied match in their first-class history. On an increasingly dusty pitch, Sharma, with off-spin, and Finney had almost put Gloucestershire out of contention, but Lloyds and Alleyne revived the innings as they had the previous day. Although there were thirteen half-centuries in the match, only the admirable Barnett went on to three figures. He completed his hundred in the morning session of the third day when, with Graveney and Walsh absent from the attack, Derbyshire scored 167 runs.

Close of play: First day, Derbyshire 329-8 (I. S. Anderson 54*, M. Beardshall 24*); Second day, Derbyshire 59-1 (K. J. Barnett 25*, B. Roberts 24*).

Derbyshire

*K. J. Barnett c Bainbridge b Lawrence	80	– lbw b Bainbridge	110
†B. J. M. Maher c Russell b Lawrence	5	– b Lawrence	1
B. Roberts c Russell b Walsh	53	– c Russell b Lloyds	69
J. E. Morris b Walsh	6	– c Bainbridge b Lloyds	0
R. J. Finney c Romaines b Walsh	0	– st Russell b Bainbridge	28
R. Sharma st Russell b Lloyds	55		
I. S. Anderson c Russell b Lawrence	59		
M. A. Holding b Walsh	9	– (6) not out	2
M. Jean-Jacques b Lloyds	15		
M. Beardshall c Russell b Lawrence	25		
O. H. Mortensen not out	5		
B 7, l-b 18, w 1, n-b 2	28	B 4, l-b 8, n-b 4	16

1/27 2/134 3/140 4/142 5/165   340   1/7 2/174 3/174   (5 wkts dec.) 226
6/242 7/255 8/290 9/331   4/211 5/226

Bonus points – Derbyshire 3, Gloucestershire 3 (Score at 100 overs: 295-8).

Bowling: *First Innings*—Walsh 27-6-77-4; Lawrence 14.3-1-61-4; Sharma 24-4-63-3; Bainbridge 12-2-34-0; Graveney 30-7-57-0. *Second Innings*—Lawrence 15-1-47-1; Bainbridge 14.1-1-56-2; Lloyds 22-1-95-2; Alleyne 2-0-16-0.

Gloucestershire

A. W. Stovold c Morris b Mortensen	11	– b Finney	51
A. J. Wright c Barnett b Holding	14	– lbw b Sharma	2
P. W. Romaines lbw b Holding	8	– lbw b Sharma	16
P. Bainbridge c Barnett b Sharma	53	– b Sharma	20
K. M. Curran c Beardshall b Holding	0	– c Sharma b Finney	24
J. W. Lloyds c Holding b Finney	66	– b Holding	64
M. W. Alleyne b Sharma	51	– c Maher b Finney	53
†R. C. Russell c Holding b Finney	54	– not out	19
D. V. Lawrence b Sharma	0	– (10) b Sharma	14
C. A. Walsh b Finney	14	– (11) b Sharma	0
*D. A. Graveney not out	1	– (9) c Barnett b Sharma	1
B 6, l-b 4, w 1, n-b 5	16	L-b 10, n-b 4	14

1/17 2/32 3/38 4/42 5/132   288   1/18 2/71 3/73 4/119 5/125   278
6/198 7/256 8/256 9/281   6/221 7/249 8/258 9/278

Bonus points – Gloucestershire 3, Derbyshire 4.

Bowling: *First Innings*—Holding 17-2-74-3; Mortensen 8-3-11-1; Sharma 24-4-63-3; Jean-Jacques 4-0-27-0; Barnett 8-0-48-0; Beardshall 5-0-16-0; Finney 16-6-39-3. *Second Innings*—Holding 20-1-76-1; Jean-Jacques 5-0-29-0; Sharma 32-12-80-6; Finney 19-1-83-3.

Umpires: K. E. Palmer and P. B. Wight.

GLOUCESTERSHIRE v LEICESTERSHIRE

At Cheltenham, August 1, 3, 4. Leicestershire won by 63 runs. Leicestershire 24 pts, Gloucestershire 7 pts. Toss: Leicestershire. Leicestershire's fifth win in eight Championship games came with 35 balls to spare after they had set Gloucestershire 315 in at least 63 overs. Splendid fast bowling by DeFreitas, despite his problems with overstepping, had reduced Gloucestershire to 107 for six, only for their last four wickets to add 144 in 80 minutes. Greene, with a six and thirteen fours, and Russell struck about them with great relish. Earlier in the day, batting of a more classical style had been seen from Gower, who, with seventeen fours from 177 balls, stroked his first Championship hundred for Leicestershire since 1985, albeit against a rather toothless attack. Another batsman back among the runs was Romaines, whose battling first-innings 99, with seventeen fours, was his highest in the Championship for three seasons.

Close of play: First day, Gloucestershire 47-2 (C. W. J. Athey 10*, R. C. Russell 1*); Second day, Leicestershire 86-2 (N. E. Briers 46*, D. I. Gower 27*).

Leicestershire

R. A. Cobb b Lawrence	1	– c Alleyne b Greene	4
N. E. Briers c Lloyds b Greene	91	– c Alleyne b Bainbridge	46
*P. Willey b Lawrence	12	– c Russell b Lawrence	2
D. I. Gower c Russell b Sainsbury	56	– not out	105
J. J. Whitaker b Greene	62	– not out	66
P. B. Clift c Bainbridge b Lloyds	1		
P. A. J. DeFreitas b Greene	16		
†P. Whitticase c and b Bainbridge	59		
J. P. Agnew run out	31		
G. J. F. Ferris c Athey b Bainbridge	12		
P. M. Such not out	7		
B 4, l-b 10, n-b 5	19	L-b 6, w 1, n-b 5	12

1/6 2/32 3/108 4/237 5/238   367   1/21 2/30 3/86   (3 wkts dec.) 235
6/238 7/262 8/323 9/356

Bonus points – Leicestershire 4, Gloucestershire 4.

Bowling: *First Innings*—Lawrence 18-3-84-2; Greene 22-3-87-3; Sainsbury 20-5-50-1; Bainbridge 7-0-40-2; Alleyne 14-6-37-0; Lloyds 18-1-55-1. *Second Innings*—Lawrence 7-1-22-1; Greene 17-3-72-1; Sainsbury 21-4-57-0; Bainbridge 13-4-49-1; Alleyne 7-2-29-0.

Gloucestershire

A. W. Stovold run out	14	– c Clift b Agnew	14
A. J. Wright c Willey b DeFreitas	21	– c Whitaker b Such	42
C. W. J. Athey c and b Clift	48	– c sub b DeFreitas	21
†R. C. Russell c Whitticase b Clift	20	– (8) c Whitticase b DeFreitas	50
*P. Bainbridge c Gower b Agnew	4	– (4) c Whitticase b DeFreitas	8
J. W. Lloyds c Clift b Such	27	– (5) c sub b DeFreitas	27
P. W. Romaines c Cobb b DeFreitas	99	– (6) lbw b DeFreitas	0
M. W. Alleyne c Whitticase b Agnew	5	– (7) lbw b Clift	1
V. S. Greene c and b Such	30	– not out	62
D. V. Lawrence b Agnew	1	– b DeFreitas	6
G. E. Sainsbury not out	0	– c Whitaker b Such	1
L-b 8, w 1, n-b 10	19	L-b 12, w 1, n-b 6	19

1/22 2/44 3/104 4/115 5/115   288   1/21 2/83 3/91 4/104 5/104   251
6/178 7/195 8/254 9/284   6/107 7/141 8/218 9/238

Bonus points – Gloucestershire 3, Leicestershire 4.

Bowling: *First Innings*—Agnew 29-4-86-3; Ferris 12-3-41-0; DeFreitas 19.5-2-88-2; Clift 21-7-39-2; Such 10-3-26-2. *Second Innings*—Agnew 14-0-74-1; DeFreitas 24-5-94-6; Clift 11-2-39-1; Such 10.1-1-32-2.

Umpires: J. A. Jameson and D. R. Shepherd.

GLOUCESTERSHIRE v SURREY

At Cheltenham, August 5, 6, 7. Gloucestershire won by 52 runs. Gloucestershire 24 pts, Surrey 8 pts. Toss: Gloucestershire. Another splendid batting pitch helped produce a match never lacking in interest. Gloucestershire recovered from the loss of two wickets to Clarke without a run on the board to set the trend, although it might have been a different story had Bainbridge not been missed in the slips in Clarke's second over. He went on to dominate century stands with Wright and Curran, hitting 21 fours in his 151. Surrey's response was a hundred before lunch on the second day from Lynch, who needed just 99 balls and hit two sixes and seventeen fours: in all, 189 runs were scored in that session. However, Walsh and Bainbridge struck back in the afternoon, and with Clarke unfit to bowl, Gloucestershire scored freely before asking Surrey to make 316 in 66 overs. They passed 100 with only one wicket down and with Bullen, a stand-in opener, and Stewart going well. The turning-point was a brilliant caught-and-bowled by Graveney to remove Lynch – at the cost of ten stitches in his right hand – and it set the standard for some fine catches that were held as Surrey chased their target all the way down the order.

Close of play: First day, Surrey 60-1 (D. M. Smith 31*, A. J. Stewart 18*); Second day, Gloucestershire 144-3 (K. M. Curran 57*, J. W. Lloyds 32*).

Gloucestershire

A. W. Stovold c Feltham b Clarke	0	– c Bullen b Clarke	35
A. J. Wright run out	53	– (6) c Jesty b Greig	56
C. W. J. Athey lbw b Clarke	0	– (2) c Bullen b Clarke	12
P. Bainbridge c Lynch b Thomas	151	– (7) c Thomas b Bullen	41
K. M. Curran b Smith b Thomas	34	– (4) c Stewart b Greig	67
P. W. Romaines b Feltham	17	– (3) c and b Thomas	2
J. W. Lloyds c Bullen b Greig	1	– (5) c Richards b Thomas	63
†R. C. Russell not out	50	– not out	8
C. A. Walsh c Feltham b Greig	20	– c Bullen b Greig	1
D. V. Lawrence c Smith b Greig	0		
*D. A. Graveney not out	0		
B 5, l-b 8, w 1, n-b 13	27	N-b 7	7

1/0 2/0 3/120 4/226 5/265   (9 wkts dec.) 353   1/27 2/53 3/55   (8 wkts dec.) 292
6/266 7/308 8/345 9/349   4/163 5/199 6/270
                                                    7/290 8/292

Bonus points – Gloucestershire 4, Surrey 4.

Bowling: *First Innings*—Clarke 21–3–56–2; Thomas 16–1–98–2; Feltham 28–2–95–1; Greig 18.3–2–66–3; Bullen 9–3–25–0. *Second Innings*—Clarke 14–4–48–2; Thomas 18–1–84–2; Greig 14.1–1–78–3; Feltham 16–5–39–0; Jesty 3–0–28–0; Bullen 5–1–15–1.

Surrey

G. S. Clinton c Russell b Lawrence	3	– c Russell b Lawrence	14
D. M. Smith c Lloyds b Bainbridge	66	– (8) c Russell b Walsh	6
A. J. Stewart lbw b Walsh	21	– c Russell b Walsh	65
M. A. Lynch c Curran b Bainbridge	114	– c and b Graveney	6
T. E. Jesty c Lloyds b Graveney	42	– c Russell b Walsh	47
†C. J. Richards c Russell b Bainbridge	9	– c Athey b Bainbridge	0
*I. A. Greig c Athey b Walsh	16	– run out	17
D. J. Thomas lbw b Walsh	21	– (9) not out	20
M. A. Feltham c and b Bainbridge	7	– (10) c Curran b Lloyds	9
C. K. Bullen not out	9	– (2) c Romaines b Lawrence	57
S. T. Clarke b Bainbridge	3	– c Lawrence b Lloyds	5
B 1, l-b 6, n-b 12	19	L-b 5, n-b 12	17

1/10 2/68 3/157 4/249 5/266   330   1/31 2/109 3/116 4/190 5/191   263
6/275 7/295 8/312 9/322   6/201 7/219 8/224 9/246

Bonus points – Surrey 4, Gloucestershire 4.

Bowling: _First Innings_—Walsh 26–2–99–3; Lawrence 16–0–92–1; Bainbridge 25.1–8–70–5; Graveney 8–1–34–1; Lloyds 2–0–28–0. _Second Innings_—Walsh 19.4–1–86–3; Lawrence 16–0–80–2; Bainbridge 9–0–42–1; Graveney 2.2–1–10–1; Lloyds 6.5–0–40–2.

Umpires: N. T. Plews and D. R. Shepherd.

GLOUCESTERSHIRE v KENT

At Cheltenham, August 8, 10, 11. Drawn. Gloucestershire 7 pts, Kent 5 pts. Toss: Kent. Rain set in just before lunch on the third day, at which point Gloucestershire were 243 ahead with their last fit batsmen at the crease. Moreover, as Lawrence was unable to bowl, and Walsh and Bainbridge were also handicapped by injury, they would have had problems had Kent been given a chance to go for victory. With Curran hitting two sixes and fifteen fours in his third hundred of the season, and Athey (seventeen fours) returning to form, Gloucestershire delighted their supporters by dashing to 436 for seven on the opening day. On the Monday, the consistent Benson gave Kent a good start, but there was a mid-innings hiccup before Aslett and Underwood saw them past the follow-on figure. Gloucestershire seemed to be cruising towards a declaration on the third day until Igglesden, who took nine wickets in the match, and Underwood dismissed five batsmen for 23 runs, setting up the prospect of an interesting finish.

Close of play: First day, Gloucestershire 436-7 (R. C. Russell 57*, D. V. Lawrence 5*); Second day, Gloucestershire 64-2 (C. W. J. Athey 27*, K. M. Curran 24*).

Gloucestershire

A. W. Stovold b Igglesden	1	– c Benson b Igglesden	7
P. W. Romaines c Hinks b Jarvis	36	– c Marsh b Igglesden	0
C. W. J. Athey b Baptiste	86	– c Aslett b Underwood	45
*P. Bainbridge retired hurt	3		
K. M. Curran c Underwood b Igglesden	119	– (4) b Igglesden	46
J. W. Lloyds b Igglesden	19	– (5) lbw b Igglesden	5
M. W. Alleyne c Tavaré b Penn	82	– (6) not out	10
†R. C. Russell not out	57	– (7) b Underwood	0
C. A. Walsh c Tavaré b Igglesden	6	– (8) lbw b Igglesden	0
D. V. Lawrence not out	5		
G. E. Sainsbury (did not bat)		– (9) not out	1
L-b 13, n-b 9	22	L-b 4, w 1, n-b 11	16

1/111 2/145 3/168 4/330   (7 wkts dec.) 436   1/2 2/19 3/100 4/108   (7 wkts) 130
5/385 6/399 7/424   5/117 6/118 7/123

Bonus points – Gloucestershire 4, Kent 1 (Score at 100 overs: 355-4).

In the first innings A. W. Stovold, when 0, retired hurt at 0 and resumed at 385; P. Bainbridge retired hurt at 129.

Bowling: _First Innings_—Igglesden 23.1–1–100–4; Jarvis 22–2–115–1; Penn 18–3–74–1; Baptiste 23–3–63–1; Underwood 24–5–71–0. _Second Innings_—Igglesden 18–1–53–5; Baptiste 6–3–8–0; Penn 4–1–15–0; Jarvis 8–1–22–0; Underwood 12–2–28–2.

Kent

M. R. Benson c Alleyne b Walsh	98	A. P. Igglesden lbw b Sainsbury	1
N. R. Taylor lbw b Walsh	8	D. L. Underwood not out	21
S. G. Hinks c Alleyne b Lloyds	29		
*C. J. Tavaré c Russell b Walsh	24	B 1, l-b 6, n-b 10	17
D. G. Aslett not out	71		
E. A. E. Baptiste c Curran b Alleyne	37	1/11 2/90 3/164 (8 wkts dec.) 323
†S. A. Marsh lbw b Sainsbury	1	4/179 5/244 6/250
C. Penn c Romaines b Alleyne	16	7/271 8/277

K. B. S. Jarvis did not bat.

Bonus points – Kent 4, Gloucestershire 3.

Bowling: Walsh 20–1–81–3; Lawrence 9.2–1–31–0; Sainsbury 23–4–72–2; Alleyne 16.4–4–50–2; Lloyds 15–2–75–1; Athey 3–0–7–0.

Umpires: J. H. Harris and N. T. Plews.

At Bristol, August 15, 16, 17. GLOUCESTERSHIRE drew with REST OF THE WORLD XI (See Other Matches, 1987).

At Birmingham, August 19, 20, 21. GLOUCESTERSHIRE beat WARWICKSHIRE by four wickets.

At Nottingham, August 22, 24, 25. GLOUCESTERSHIRE drew with NOTTINGHAMSHIRE.

At Leeds, August 26, 27, 28. GLOUCESTERSHIRE lost to YORKSHIRE by 44 runs.

At Manchester, August 29, 31, September 1. GLOUCESTERSHIRE lost to LANCASHIRE by three wickets.

GLOUCESTERSHIRE v SOMERSET

At Bristol, September 2, 3, 4. Drawn. Gloucestershire 6 pts, Somerset 7 pts. Toss: Somerset. A marvellous hundred by the Australian, Waugh, was the highlight of a match which finished quietly after both sides had had the advantage wrested from them. Somerset's seam bowlers wasted the helpful conditions on the opening day, when Romaines (fifteen fours) progressed doggedly towards his first Championship hundred since 1984. Walsh and Bainbridge quickly reduced Somerset to 138 for eight, but by now Waugh was beginning to dominate. Mallender played the supporting role in a stand of 113 as Waugh set about the bowling with strokes of power and quality. He had batted for three hours and hit nineteen fours when Roebuck declared, a strategy rewarded by the capture of three cheap wickets before the close. Athey, hitting thirteen boundaries, rebuilt the innings next day, but with more than three hours remaining, Gloucestershire led by only 196 with two wickets in hand. One of those, however, was that of Stovold, who had a back strain, and he and Alleyne removed any prospect of defeat. Somerset, set 251 in 38 overs, settled for a draw.

Close of play: First day, Somerset 6-1 (N. A. Felton 2*, J. J. E. Hardy 4*); Second day, Gloucestershire 18-3 (G. E. Sainsbury 5*, C. W. J. Athey 2*).

Gloucestershire

A. W. Stovold c Rose b Mallender	12	– (10) not out	37
A. J. Wright c and b Jones	13	– (1) lbw b Jones	2
P. W. Romaines c Hardy b Marks	115	– (2) c sub b Mallender	2
C. W. J. Athey lbw b Pringle	18	– (5) lbw b Mallender	98
K. M. Curran lbw b Waugh	41	– (6) c Hardy b Jones	22
*P. Bainbridge c Waugh b Marks	8	– (7) c Burns b Jones	9
M. W. Alleyne lbw b Mallender	11	– (8) not out	26
K. B. K. Ibadulla c Burns b Marks	19	– (9) lbw b Mallender	0
†R. C. Russell c sub b Mallender	15	– (3) c Felton b Jones	6
C. A. Walsh c Roebuck b Marks	4		
G. E. Sainsbury not out	1	– (4) b Jones	5
B 8, l-b 8, w 3, n-b 6	25	L-b 6, n-b 6	12
	282	(8 wkts dec.)	**219**

1/17 2/52 3/98 4/198 5/217 6/226 7/250 8/275 9/278

1/2 2/10 3/12 4/24 5/102 6/116 7/165 8/165

Bonus points – Gloucestershire 3, Somerset 4.

Bowling: *First Innings*—Jones 17-4-63-1; Mallender 21-7-44-3; Rose 3-1-9-0; Waugh 26-7-72-1; Pringle 8-0-33-1; Marks 18.3-7-45-4. *Second Innings*—Jones 20-2-66-5; Mallender 24-8-52-3; Marks 16-3-48-0; Waugh 14-1-47-0.

Somerset

N. A. Felton c Curran b Walsh	8	– c Athey b Sainsbury	5
*P. M. Roebuck c Romaines b Walsh	0	– not out	23
J. J. E. Hardy c and b Bainbridge	47		
J. G. Wyatt c Athey b Bainbridge	22	– not out	28
S. R. Waugh not out	137	– (3) lbw b Bainbridge	12
N. J. Pringle c Romaines b Bainbridge	4		
†N. D. Burns c Ibadulla b Sainsbury	2		
V. J. Marks c Alleyne b Walsh	1		
G. D. Rose c Russell b Walsh	0		
N. A. Mallender not out	14		
B 4, l-b 8, n-b 4	16	N-b 2	2

1/1 2/21 3/80 4/92   (8 wkts dec.) 251   1/10 2/33   (2 wkts) 70
5/107 6/112 7/138 8/138

A. N. Jones did not bat.

Bonus points – Somerset 3, Gloucestershire 3.

Bowling: *First Innings*—Walsh 29–5–81–4; Sainsbury 17–2–57–1; Bainbridge 20.2–6–60–3; Alleyne 6–0–17–0; Ibadulla 7–0–24–0. *Second Innings*—Walsh 10–0–40–0; Sainsbury 4–3–1–1; Ibadulla 11–6–9–0; Bainbridge 5–0–20–1.

Umpires: J. A. Jameson and D. O. Oslear.

At Leicester, September 9, 10, 11. GLOUCESTERSHIRE lost to LEICESTERSHIRE by eight wickets.

GLOUCESTERSHIRE v GLAMORGAN

At Bristol, September 12, 14, 15. Gloucestershire won by 114 runs. Gloucestershire 20 pts, Glamorgan 1 pt. Toss: Glamorgan. With nearly all of the first day lost to rain, three declarations were needed to produce a positive result. Wright, capped before the match, hit a career-best 161, including 29 fours, against a below-strength attack; he and Athey (eighteen fours) dealing mainly in boundaries as they added 190 for the third wicket. Glamorgan declared at their overnight score, 213 behind, Gloucestershire batted to the dictates of target-setting, and eventually Glamorgan set off in pursuit of 316 in 78 overs. Maynard underlined his potential with some splendid hitting, especially of Lloyds's off-breaks, but Graveney bowled cleverly to dispose of the middle order. Walsh, held back for the purpose, made short work of the tail.

Close of play: First day, Gloucestershire 27-1 (A. J. Wright 9*, P. W. Romaines 3*); Second day, Glamorgan 121-1 (J. A. Hopkins 39*, H. Morris 26*).

Gloucestershire

A. W. Stovold c Holmes b Monkhouse	13	– c Metson b Barwick	40
A. J. Wright c Holmes b Monkhouse	161	– lbw b Monkhouse	0
P. W. Romaines b Derrick	31	– c Butcher b Derrick	22
C. W. J. Athey not out	101		
P. Bainbridge not out	17		
†R. C. Russell (did not bat)		– (4) c Butcher b Barwick	2
M. W. Alleyne (did not bat)		– (5) not out	19
C. A. Walsh (did not bat)		– (6) not out	12
L-b 3, n-b 8	11	B 1, l-b 3, n-b 3	7

1/18 2/107 3/297   (3 wkts dec.) 334   1/3 2/54 3/56   (4 wkts dec.) 102
4/88

J. W. Lloyds, *D. A. Graveney and G. E. Sainsbury did not bat.

Bonus points – Gloucestershire 4, Glamorgan 1.

Bowling: *First Innings*—Barwick 19–6–47–0; Monkhouse 16–2–73–2; Derrick 20.1–4–86–1; North 14–0–61–0; Butcher 1–0–3–0; Holmes 9–1–35–0; Maynard 6–1–26–0. *Second Innings*—Barwick 14–3–37–2; Monkhouse 5–0–30–1; Derrick 9–1–31–1.

Glamorgan

A. R. Butcher c Wright b Bainbridge	48	– c Graveney b Sainsbury 0
J. A. Hopkins not out	39	– c Walsh b Bainbridge 13
*H. Morris not out	26	– c Lloyds b Bainbridge 38
M. P. Maynard (did not bat)		– c Lloyds b Graveney 81
G. C. Holmes (did not bat)		– c Wright b Graveney 30
P. A. Todd (did not bat)		– c Stovold b Graveney 4
J. Derrick (did not bat)		– c Russell b Walsh 25
†C. P. Metson (did not bat)		– c Sainsbury b Walsh 0
P. D. North (did not bat)		– c Athey b Walsh 0
S. R. Barwick (did not bat)		– c Wright b Graveney 3
S. Monkhouse (did not bat)		– not out 0
B 4, l-b 1, w 1, n-b 2	8	L-b 3, n-b 4 7

1/66   (1 wkt dec.) 121   1/0 2/23 3/136 4/136 5/140   201
                                           6/183 7/192 8/198 9/201

Bowling: *First Innings*—Sainsbury 12–0–36–0; Walsh 8–0–42–0; Bainbridge 9–3–26–1; Graveney 3–1–3–0; Lloyds 3–1–9–0. *Second Innings*—Sainsbury 7–1–30–1; Walsh 14–5–30–3; Bainbridge 12–5–29–2; Graveney 17.4–3–54–4; Lloyds 8–1–55–0.

Umpires: J. W. Holder and R. A. White.

FIELDING IN 1987

(Qualification: 20 dismissals)

76	B. J. M. Maher (72 ct, 4 st)	28	R. J. Blakey
74	C. J. Richards (68 ct, 6 st)	26	M. D. Moxon
69	P. Whitticase (67 ct, 2 st)	26	C. E. B. Rice
65	P. R. Downton (57 ct, 8 st)	26	C. L. Smith
64	R. C. Russell (54 ct, 10 st)	25	D. B. D'Oliveira
61	D. E. East (57 ct, 4 st)	25	J. Stanworth (21 ct, 4 st)
61	R. J. Parks (56 ct, 5 st)	24	P. J. W. Allott
57	S. J. Rhodes (51 ct, 6 st)	24	M. A. Lynch
53	C. P. Metson (47 ct, 6 st)	24	R. J. Maru
50	N. D. Burns (44 ct, 6 st)	24	A. J. Moles
49	B. N. French (45 ct, 4 st)	23	I. J. Gould
49	D. Ripley (40 ct, 9 st)	22	B. R. Hardie
41	S. A. Marsh (39 ct, 2 st)	22	L. Potter
36	D. L. Bairstow (32 ct, 4 st)	22	B. Roberts
35	W. K. Hegg (24 ct, 11 st)	21	C. S. Cowdrey
34	G. W. Humpage (31 ct, 3 st)	21	C. G. Greenidge
30	M. P. Maynard	20	G. A. Gooch
29	G. Miller	20	D. P. Hughes
29	C. W. Scott (27 ct, 2 st)	20	P. Johnson
29	C. J. Tavaré	20	A. J. Stewart
29	V. P. Terry		

HAMPSHIRE

President: C. G. A. Paris
Chairman: D. Rich
Chairman, Cricket Committee: C. J. Knott
Chief Executive: A. F. Baker
  Northlands Road, Southampton SO9 2TY
  (Telephone: 0703-333788)
Captain: M. C. J. Nicholas
Coach: P. J. Sainsbury

A combination of injuries, bad weather and inconsistent performances conspired to make Hampshire's 1987 season one in which potential and expectations were not fully matched by achievement. On the credit side was the late run they made in the Britannic Assurance Championship. After a disappointing start – they lost their opening two games – Hampshire came back well with three consecutive wins between June 20 and July 3. But it was not until the second half of August that they made their real challenge with a run of four victories. Lying third in the table after that spurt, Hampshire eventually finished fifth to take a share of the prizemoney.

Few counties were harder hit by the weather than Hampshire in one of England's soggiest summers. They lost just over 100 hours' play in the Championship and it would be fair to say that rain robbed them of four victories. In the end, they won seven Championship matches, the same number as in 1986, but they lost one fewer.

Despite what was once again an embarrassment of riches on paper, Hampshire's batting lacked consistency at times, but it did show a marked improvement on the previous season. Whereas in 1986 their batsmen hit just eight first-class centuries – six of them by Gordon Greenidge – there were seventeen in 1987 with seven players making three-figure scores compared with three the previous year.

The injuries which were to bedevil Hampshire – Greenidge played in fewer than half the first-class games – began in the first week of the campaign when Robin Smith broke a thumb. But for that injury, however, David Turner might well have spent most of the summer out of the side. Instead, the veteran left-hander, who made his Hampshire début 21 years earlier, was one of the successes of the season. He hit a career-best 184 not out at Gloucester and his aggregate was just 37 runs short of his previous best for a season.

Mark Nicholas and Paul Terry, both of whom had poor seasons in 1986, weathered uncertain starts to finish with more than 1,000 first-class runs. Terry, whose total of 1,382 was his best, had the added satisfaction of participating in a record Hampshire first-wicket stand of 347 with Chris Smith against Warwickshire at Edgbaston. Smith, with a career-best 217, dominated the partnership, which bettered by 97 runs the previous record set by Greenidge and Terry in 1986. Robin Smith has still to find the consistency to match his abundant talent, but he too achieved a career-best with an unbeaten 209 against Essex on his return after injury.

Kevan James, a left-handed all-rounder, had his best season with the bat and not only topped the Hampshire batting averages but was also the highest-placed England-qualified cricketer in the national list. James, once of Middlesex, will become an even bigger asset when he achieves more accuracy as a bowler, especially in one-day cricket.

Tim Tremlett, helped by the 34 wickets he took in August, usually a lean month for him, was Hampshire's leading bowler in the national averages. He took 72 first-class wickets, the same number as Malcolm Marshall took for Hampshire, and he would have topped the county's Championship averages but for Paul Jan Bakker's amazing performance against Kent at Bournemouth. The Dutch seam bowler took seven wickets in the second innings to bowl Hampshire to a 75-run win. Rajesh Maru, the slow left-arm bowler who also joined Hampshire from Middlesex, in 1984, had another fine season and his tally of 71 wickets fell just two short of his season's best in 1985. A major bonus for Hampshire was the advance made by the young fast bowler, Stephen Andrew. He is tall, works up a lively pace, and he was beginning to be talked about as an England prospect when a foot injury put him out for seven weeks.

Hampshire, for the most part, caught and fielded well, with Terry outstanding in any position and Maru relishing his new role as slip. Nicholas's captaincy was again positive, challenging and imaginative.

Although strongly fancied by the bookmakers, Hampshire again showed their tendency to "freeze" in the two knockout competitions. After fighting back from a losing position against Essex to qualify for the last eight in the Benson and Hedges Cup, they failed their supporters by going down tamely to Yorkshire in the quarter-finals. The NatWest Bank Trophy, the other avenue to Lord's, brought even earlier disappointment, with Hampshire bowing out to Leicestershire in the second round – this despite making the most runs scored by a side batting second in a one-day match anywhere in the world. Defending their Sunday League title, they made a good start and then faded.

As cover for Marshall, who along with Greenidge seemed certain to be touring England with the West Indians in 1988, Hampshire signed a one-year contract with the Australian left-arm swing bowler, Bruce Reid, only to learn during the winter that an injury suffered during the Australian season might rule him out. Moreover, although they had offered Greenidge a contract for the 1989 season, the question remained as to whether he would play for the county again. His departure would be a big disappointment to cricket enthusiasts in and outside Hampshire, for no batsman has provided better entertainment over so long a period as this belligerent opening batsman. – Victor Isaacs.

426

HAMPSHIRE 1987

[*Bill Smith*]

Back row: V. H. Isaacs (*scorer*), C. L. Smith, K. D. James, T. M. Tremlett, S. J. W. Andrew, R. A. Smith, C. A. Connor, R. J. Parks, R. J. Maru. *Front row*: M. D. Marshall, N. G. Cowley, M. C. J. Nicholas (*captain*), V. P. Terry, D. R. Turner. *Inset*: C. G. Greenidge.

HAMPSHIRE RESULTS

All first-class matches – Played 26: Won 7, Lost 3, Drawn 16.

County Championship matches – Played 24: Won 7, Lost 3, Drawn 14.

Bonus points – Batting 59, Bowling 73.

Competition placings – Britannic Assurance County Championship, 5th; NatWest Bank Trophy,
2nd round; Benson and Hedges Cup, q-f; Refuge Assurance League, 7th equal.

BRITANNIC ASSURANCE CHAMPIONSHIP AVERAGES

BATTING

	Birthplace	M	I	NO	R	HI	Avge
K. D. James	Lambeth	16	15	5	517	142*	51.70
‡R. A. Smith	Durban, SA	17	24	7	852	209*	50.11
‡D. R. Turner	Chippenham	23	33	8	1,240	184*	49.60
§‡C. G. Greenidge	St Peter, Barbados	11	16	0	725	163	45.31
‡C. L. Smith	Durban, SA	24	38	7	1,382	217	44.58
‡M. C. J. Nicholas	London	23	34	7	1,115	147	41.29
‡V. P. Terry	Osnabruck, WG	21	34	4	1,172	122	39.06
§‡M. D. Marshall	St Michael, Barbados	21	22	5	610	99	35.88
‡R. J. Parks	Cuckfield	23	19	8	370	62*	33.63
‡T. M. Tremlett	Wellington, Somerset	22	16	4	157	42	13.08
‡N. G. Cowley	Shaftesbury	8	10	1	89	30	9.88
‡R. J. Maru	Nairobi, Kenya	24	14	3	92	15	8.36
C. A. Connor	The Valley, Anguilla	13	9	5	31	11*	7.75

Also batted: S. J. W. Andrew (*London*) (13 matches) 3, 4*; A. N. Aymes (*Southampton*)
(1 match) 58; P. J. Bakker (*Vlaardingen, The Netherlands*) (2 matches) 0; I. J. Chivers
(*Southampton*) (1 match) 20*; T. C. Middleton (*Winchester*) (1 match) 7.

* *Signifies not out.*   ‡ *Denotes county cap.*   § *Not qualified for England.*

The following played a total of fifteen three-figure innings for Hampshire in County
Championship matches – M. C. J. Nicholas 4, C. L. Smith 4, C. G. Greenidge 2, D. R.
Turner 2, K. D. James 1, R. A. Smith 1, V. P. Terry 1.

BOWLING

	O	M	R	W	BB	Avge
P. J. Bakker	56.5	18	146	10	7-31	14.60
T. M. Tremlett	503.4	146	1,251	66	6-53	18.95
M. D. Marshall	571.4	149	1,445	72	5-49	20.06
S. J. W. Andrew	302.1	56	996	46	7-92	21.65
R. J. Maru	751.4	218	1,937	66	5-45	29.34
C. A. Connor	350	74	943	28	4-26	33.67
N. G. Cowley	205.1	51	521	14	4-77	37.21
K. D. James	192.1	33	728	19	5-62	38.31

Also bowled: I. J. Chivers 3-1-4-1; M. C. J. Nicholas 6.5-0-31-0; R. J. Parks 8-0-56-0;
C. L. Smith 25-5-75-1; R. A. Smith 12-0-88-2.

Wicket-keepers: R. J. Parks 53 ct, 4 st; A. N. Aymes 1 ct.

Leading Fielders: V. P. Terry 28, R. J. Maru 24, C. G. Greenidge 21, C. L. Smith 21,
R. A. Smith 16.

HAMPSHIRE v NORTHAMPTONSHIRE

At Southampton, April 25, 26, 27. Northamptonshire won by five wickets. Northamptonshire 22 pts, Hampshire 8 pts. Toss: Northamptonshire. Robin Smith and Terry began a recovery after the home side had been put in on a green pitch, Davis, despite trouble with no-balls, having troubled the early batsmen on his début for Northamptonshire. Turner moved into the Hampshire list of top ten run-scorers, overtaking N. T. McCorkell when he reached 48. On the second day, Northamptonshire also had to stage a comeback with Capel and Williams saving their side after Tremlett and James had reduced them to 92 for five. Geoff Cook passed 20,000 first-class runs. A belligerent 90 from Robin Smith (one six, nine fours) and a hard-hitting innings from James (three sixes, eight fours) allowed Nicholas to set Northamptonshire a sporting target of 269 in 59 overs. With Larkins sparkling, hitting two sixes and thirteen fours in 120 off 149 balls, they achieved their task with one over remaining.

Close of play: First day, Hampshire 303-7 (M. D. Marshall 90*, R. J. Parks 6*); Second day, Hampshire 81-3 (R. A. Smith 22*, D. R. Turner 5*).

Hampshire

V. P. Terry b Walker	30	– lbw b Capel 12
C. L. Smith c Ripley b Capel	5	– c Bailey b Walker 5
*M. C. J. Nicholas c Ripley b Davis	3	– c G. Cook b Walker 25
R. A. Smith c Bailey b Walker	24	– st Ripley b N. G. B. Cook 90
D. R. Turner c Larkins b Williams	81	– b N. G. B. Cook 11
K. D. James c Ripley b Davis	25	– st Ripley b N. G. B. Cook 67
M. D. Marshall not out	90	– b N. G. B. Cook 2
T. M. Tremlett c Ripley b Capel	9	– not out 7
†R. J. Parks not out	6	
L-b 6, w 4, n-b 20	30	L-b 9, w 2, n-b 10 21

1/10 2/13 3/67 4/78   (7 wkts dec.) 303   1/15 2/33 3/62   (7 wkts dec.) 240
5/131 6/245 7/272   4/100 5/203
                                        6/219 7/240

R. J. Maru and C. A. Connor did not bat.

Bonus points – Hampshire 4, Northamptonshire 3.

Bowling: *First Innings*—Davis 24–3–84–2; Capel 25–2–85–2; Walker 23–7–57–2; N. G. B. Cook 15–5–48–0; Williams 5–1–23–1. *Second Innings*—Davis 16–1–41–0; Capel 14–2–52–1; Walker 20–5–46–2; N. G. B. Cook 14.5–3–49–4; Williams 10–2–43–0.

Northamptonshire

*G. Cook b Connor	6	– run out 20
W. Larkins c Parks b Tremlett	33	– c Parks b Marshall 120
R. J. Boyd-Moss lbw b Tremlett	17	– c Parks b Connor 18
A. J. Lamb c Terry b James	12	– c James b Maru 45
R. J. Bailey c Terry b James	6	– c R. A. Smith b Maru 13
D. J. Capel not out	91	– not out 16
R. G. Williams lbw b Maru	42	– not out 19
†D. Ripley c Parks b James	25	
N. G. B. Cook c Terry b James	0	
W. W. Davis lbw b James	0	
A. Walker c Parks b Marshall	12	
L-b 22, w 1, n-b 8	31	L-b 9, w 4, n-b 5 18

1/8 2/59 3/70 4/81 5/92   275   1/80 2/145 3/204   (5 wkts) 269
6/169 7/221 8/233 9/233   4/229 5/236

Bonus points – Northamptonshire 3, Hampshire 4.

Bowling: *First Innings*—Marshall 14.3–3–46–1; Connor 18–0–78–1; Tremlett 13–4–44–2; James 18–3–62–5; Maru 15–3–23–1. *Second Innings*—Marshall 18–1–66–1; Connor 9–1–39–1; James 7–0–38–0; Maru 20–2–87–2; Tremlett 4–0–30–0.

Umpires: K. E. Palmer and R. Palmer.

At Oxford, April 29, 30, May 1. HAMPSHIRE drew with OXFORD UNIVERSITY.

At Leeds, May 6, 7, 8. HAMPSHIRE lost to YORKSHIRE by 15 runs.

HAMPSHIRE v NOTTINGHAMSHIRE

At Bournemouth, May 20, 21, 22. Drawn. Hampshire 7 pts, Nottinghamshire 4 pts. Toss: Nottinghamshire. Dropped catches and finally a thunderstorm deprived Hampshire of their first Championship victory of the season. A spell of four for 8 in fourteen balls by Tremlett took the back out of the Nottinghamshire first innings with only Johnson resisting. The home side themselves were struggling at 60 for four, but James, with a dogged, career-best 142 not out (three sixes, twenty fours), his third first-class century, and a sprightly 62 not out from Parks, gave Hampshire a lead of 133. At 92 for five, with Marshall and Andrew causing problems, Nottinghamshire were heading for defeat, but fine rearguard batting from Birch and Hadlee, assisted by some fielding lapses, left Hampshire requiring 117 to win in eighteen overs. Before they could start, the skies opened and play was abandoned shortly afterwards.

Close of play: First day, Hampshire 45-2 (M. C. J. Nicholas 0*, D. R. Turner 4*); Second day, Nottinghamshire 23-1 (R. T. Robinson 5*, D. W. Randall 17*).

Nottinghamshire

M. Newell c Smith b Maru	26	– c Parks b Marshall		0
R. T. Robinson c Terry b James	27	– c Tremlett b Marshall		26
D. W. Randall lbw b Marshall	13	– c Nicholas b Andrew		32
*C. E. B. Rice b Andrew	19	– c Greenidge b Andrew		2
P. Johnson not out	60	– c Maru b Marshall		18
J. D. Birch c Terry b Tremlett	7	– c Greenidge b Maru		82
R. J. Hadlee c Terry b Tremlett	7	– c Nicholas b Maru		44
E. E. Hemmings c Smith b Tremlett	0	– (9) c Turner b Marshall		13
†B. N. French c Greenidge b Tremlett	0	– (8) c Nicholas b James		9
R. A. Pick c Greenidge b James	22	– c Tremlett b Andrew		6
J. A. Afford lbw b James	0	– not out		0
L-b 16, w 1	17	L-b 16, w 1		17
	198			**249**

1/53 2/77 3/77 4/116 5/129   1/0 2/53 3/55 4/79 5/92
6/141 7/141 8/141 9/198   6/191 7/220 8/235 9/249

Bonus points – Nottinghamshire 1, Hampshire 4.

Bowling: *First Innings*—Marshall 13-3-42-1; Andrew 16-1-63-1; Tremlett 18-6-49-4; James 4.3-1-11-3; Maru 6-2-17-1. *Second Innings*—Marshall 26-4-71-4; Andrew 20-6-39-3; Maru 15.2-6-36-2; Tremlett 16-4-50-0; James 10-1-37-1.

Hampshire

C. G. Greenidge b Hadlee	36	T. M. Tremlett run out		1
V. P. Terry c Randall b Hadlee	0	†R. J. Parks not out		62
*M. C. J. Nicholas c Afford b Pick	8			
D. R. Turner c Randall b Hemmings	45	B 4, l-b 8, n-b 3		15
C. L. Smith lbw b Pick	6			
K. D. James not out	142	1/4 2/41 3/54 4/60	(7 wkts dec.)	**331**
M. D. Marshall c Johnson b Hadlee	16	5/138 6/174 7/179		

R. J. Maru and S. J. W. Andrew did not bat.

Bonus points – Hampshire 3, Nottinghamshire 3 (Score at 100 overs: 268-7).

Bowling: Hadlee 27-12-44-3; Pick 27-4-79-2; Rice 19-5-60-0; Hemmings 26-7-74-1; Afford 16-4-62-0.

Umpires: J. H. Harris and K. J. Lyons.

HAMPSHIRE v GLOUCESTERSHIRE

At Southampton, May 30, June 1, 2. Drawn. Hampshire 8 pts, Gloucestershire 5 pts. Toss: Hampshire. Greenidge, Terry and Turner were the mainstays of Hampshire's first innings, with Greenidge scoring his 106, out of 134, in 148 minutes. Although batting with a damaged right knee, which required surgery the following week, he hooked and drove with his customary force, despatching the ball for two sixes and seventeen fours. Bainbridge and some aggressive strokeplay by Lloyds (65 in 60 balls) revived Gloucestershire after they were 52 for three, while Andrew, with a career-best seven for 92, showed the form he had promised for some time, his height allowing him to find extra bounce. Despite losing Greenidge to the fourth ball of the second innings, Hampshire had increased their lead to 92 by the close on the second day, but heavy rain throughout the final morning led to the match being called off at 2.30 p.m.

Close of play: First day, Gloucestershire 14-0 (A. W. Stovold 9*, K. P. Tomlins 4*); Second day, Hampshire 62-1 (V. P. Terry 24*, M. C. J. Nicholas 35*).

Hampshire

C. G. Greenidge c Walsh b Graveney	106	– lbw b Walsh		0
V. P. Terry c Graveney b Lawrence	67	– not out		24
*M. C. J. Nicholas c Tomlins b Walsh	0	– not out		35
D. R. Turner c Russell b Walsh	63			
C. L. Smith not out	38			
K. D. James c Athey b Lloyds	26			
M. D. Marshall run out	1			
†R. J. Parks not out	2			
L-b 6, w 3, n-b 2	11	L-b 1, n-b 2		3

1/134 2/142 3/229 4/258   (6 wkts dec.) 314   1/0   (1 wkt) 62
5/297 6/304

T. M. Tremlett, R. J. Maru and S. J. W. Andrew did not bat.

Bonus points – Hampshire 4, Gloucestershire 2 (Score at 100 overs: 313-6).

Bowling: *First Innings*—Walsh 25–9–58–2; Lawrence 23–4–76–1; Bainbridge 8–1–45–0; Graveney 24–8–56–1; Lloyds 21–4–73–1. *Second Innings*—Walsh 8–3–11–1; Lawrence 6–2–29–0; Bainbridge 4–1–16–0; Graveney 4–3–1–0; Lloyds 2–0–4–0.

Gloucestershire

A. W. Stovold c Parks b Andrew	22	C. A. Walsh c Marshall b James		5
K. P. Tomlins c Terry b Marshall	11	*D. A. Graveney b Marshall		19
C. W. J. Athey c Parks b Andrew	11	D. V. Lawrence c Terry b Andrew		5
P. Bainbridge c Maru b Andrew	55			
P. W. Romaines b Andrew	25	B 4, l-b 9, n-b 1		14
K. M. Curran b Andrew	12			
J. W. Lloyds lbw b Andrew	65	1/27 2/41 3/52 4/126 5/131		284
†R. C. Russell not out	40	6/196 7/211 8/224 9/258		

Bonus points – Gloucestershire 3, Hampshire 4.

Bowling: Andrew 26.2–4–92–7; Marshall 22–9–50–2; James 11–3–36–1; Tremlett 20–3–63–0; Maru 9–2–30–0.

Umpires: K. E. Palmer and A. G. T. Whitehead.

At Swansea, June 3, 4, 5. HAMPSHIRE drew with GLAMORGAN.

At Horsham, June 6, 8, 9. HAMPSHIRE drew with SUSSEX.

At The Oval, June 13, 15, 16. HAMPSHIRE drew with SURREY.

HAMPSHIRE v YORKSHIRE

At Basingstoke, June 17, 18, 19. Drawn. Toss: Hampshire. Despite the excellent efforts of the groundstaff, 1,000 minutes of a scheduled 1,140 were lost to the elements. When play was possible on the second day, Chris Smith's style was suited to the soft conditions, and Terry drove one ball from Carrick out of the ground, on to the slates of the houses across the road.

Close of play: First day, No play; Second day, Hampshire 139-0 (V. P. Terry 59*, C. L. Smith 69*).

Hampshire

V. P. Terry not out	. . . .	59
C. L. Smith not out	. . . .	69
	B 9, l-b 2	11

(no wkt) 139

*M. C. J. Nicholas, D. R. Turner, R. A. Smith, K. D. James, M. D. Marshall, †R. J. Parks, R. J. Maru, T. M. Tremlett and S. J. W. Andrew did not bat.

Bowling: Jarvis 11-3-20-0; Sidebottom 10-3-24-0; Hartley 9-2-36-0; Carrick 9-2-26-0; Berry 6-1-22-0.

Yorkshire

M. D. Moxon, A. A. Metcalfe, R. J. Blakey, J. D. Love, K. Sharp, †D. L. Bairstow, *P. Carrick, A. Sidebottom, P. J. Hartley, P. W. Jarvis and P. J. Berry.

Umpires: K. J. Lyons and R. Palmer.

HAMPSHIRE v MIDDLESEX

At Southampton, June 20, 22, 23. Hampshire won by eight wickets. Hampshire 20 pts, Middlesex 3 pts. Toss: Middlesex. Middlesex, weakened by Test calls and injuries, were grateful to their former England batsman, Butcher, who alone stood firm against the hostility of Marshall and Andrew, unleashing a series of pulls and cuts to bring an air of respectability to their first innings. Hampshire were themselves in trouble at the close with four wickets down for 50, but heavy overnight rain, and more the following morning, changed the nature of the game. The friendly bowling of Parks – James kept wicket – and Robin Smith allowed the visitors to set Hampshire 270 to win in four hours, whereupon Terry and Chris Smith, back to his best form, put Hampshire in the driving seat with a century opening stand. A flamboyant innings by the captain, Nicholas, took them closer to their first Championship victory of the season, which was achieved with Smith 132 not out (one six, sixteen fours) after an innings of early caution and developing aggression.

Close of play: First day, Hampshire 50-4 (D. R. Turner 18*, R. A. Smith 1*); Second day, No play.

Middlesex

W. N. Slack c Nicholas b Tremlett	37	– c Turner b R. A. Smith 28
J. D. Carr c Turner b Andrew	9	– c Parks b R. A. Smith 24
A. J. T. Miller lbw b Maru	9	– not out 23
C. T. Radley c Parks b Andrew	30	– not out 25
R. O. Butcher c R. A. Smith b Andrew	73	
M. A. Roseberry c Turner b James	0	
*†P. R. Downton c Parks b Marshall	17	
A. Needham c Marshall b Andrew	27	
N. F. Williams lbw b Marshall	4	
S. P. Hughes b Marshall	0	
A. R. C. Fraser not out	3	
B 1, l-b 3, n-b 6	10	

1/20 2/51 3/61 4/160 5/167　　　　　　219　　1/49 2/53　　　(2 wkts dec.) 100
6/167 7/197 8/201 9/201

Bonus points – Middlesex 2, Hampshire 4.

Bowling: *First Innings*—Marshall 18-3-44-3; Andrew 17.1-3-61-4; Maru 10-3-22-1; Tremlett 20-2-56-1; James 14-7-32-1. *Second Innings*—Parks 8-0-56-0; R. A. Smith 7-0-44-2.

Hampshire

V. P. Terry c Downton b Hughes	5	– c Butcher b Needham 59
C. L. Smith c Needham b Hughes	5	– not out 132
*M. C. J. Nicholas c Radley b Fraser	15	– lbw b Fraser 49
D. R. Turner not out	18	– not out 16
R. J. Maru c Downton b Fraser	0	
R. A. Smith not out	1	
N-b 6	6	B 1, l-b 6, n-b 7 14

1/8 2/15 3/42 4/47　　　　　(4 wkts dec.) 50　　1/126 2/226　　　(2 wkts) 270

K. D. James, M. D. Marshall, †R. J. Parks, T. M. Tremlett and S. J. W. Andrew did not bat.

Bonus point – Middlesex 1.

Bowling: *First Innings*—Williams 9-2-18-0; Hughes 5-1-12-2; Fraser 8-0-13-2; Needham 4-1-7-0. *Second Innings*—Williams 7-2-27-0; Hughes 9-3-18-0; Fraser 17-1-70-1; Slack 10-0-41-0; Needham 21-1-86-1; Carr 3-0-21-0.

Umpires: H. D. Bird and J. H. Harris.

At Birmingham, June 27, 29, 30. HAMPSHIRE beat WARWICKSHIRE by nine wickets.

At Gloucester, July 1, 2, 3. HAMPSHIRE beat GLOUCESTERSHIRE by an innings and 107 runs.

At Heanor, July 4, 5, 6. HAMPSHIRE lost to DERBYSHIRE by four wickets.

At Southend, July 15, 16, 17. HAMPSHIRE drew with ESSEX.

HAMPSHIRE v WARWICKSHIRE

At Bournemouth, July 18, 19, 20. Drawn. Hampshire 4 pts, Warwickshire 4 pts. Toss: Hampshire. A brave attempt by Nicholas to force a result from another rain-spoilt match came to nothing when Warwickshire failed to accept the challenge to score 115 in 33 overs. Greenidge, Chris Smith and Nicholas gave the home team a good start on the opening day before the rain-affected wicket lent Parsons and Merrick greater assistance. Torrential rain at four o'clock on the second afternoon turned the ground into a lake, casting memories back to similar scenes on the same ground in 1974, when Hampshire failed to gain the three points they needed to win the Championship. Humpage, batting with a runner after aggravating a back injury, mixed aggressive pulls with some good fortune on what had become a tricky wicket to allow Gifford to declare, and Hampshire forfeited their second innings to set up the final act. However, when Marshall removed both openers, Asif Din and Amiss put their minds to achieving a draw.

Close of play: First day, Hampshire 178-8 (K. D. James 14*, R. J. Maru 2*); Second day, Warwickshire 6-1 (A. J. Moles 3*, P. A. Smith 1*).

Hampshire

C. G. Greenidge c Tedstone b Merrick	35	T. M. Tremlett c Tedstone b Parsons	5
C. L. Smith c Moles b Parsons	22	R. J. Maru c and b Merrick	10
*M. C. J. Nicholas lbw b Parsons	45	C. A. Connor not out	11
D. R. Turner c Thorne b Merrick	20	B 4, l-b 2, w 1, n-b 1	8
R. A. Smith c Tedstone b Merrick	13		
K. D. James not out	35	1/50 2/85 3/125 (9 wkts dec.)	224
M. D. Marshall c Thorne b Parsons	12	4/133 5/143 6/156	
†R. J. Parks c Thorne b Parsons	1	7/158 8/170 9/198	

Bonus points – Hampshire 2, Warwickshire 4.

Bowling: Merrick 33-5-100-4; Smith 5-1-22-0; Parsons 35-7-80-5; Moles 6-2-13-0; Thorne 2-0-3-0.

Hampshire forfeited their second innings.

Warwickshire

A. J. Moles c Parks b Connor	7	– (2) c C. L. Smith b Marshall	10
T. A. Lloyd c Parks b Marshall	1	– (1) c Nicholas b Marshall	0
P. A. Smith c Greenidge b Marshall	6	– c James b Connor	10
D. L. Amiss c Parks b Tremlett	19	– not out	18
G. W. Humpage c Greenidge b Marshall	51		
Asif Din not out	23	– (5) not out	18
†G. A. Tedstone c C. L. Smith b Marshall	0		
D. A. Thorne not out	0		
L-b 3	3	L-b 1, n-b 1	2
1/3 2/15 3/15 4/65 (6 wkts dec.)	110	1/0 2/11 3/26 (3 wkts)	58
5/98 6/100			

G. J. Parsons, T. A. Merrick and *N. Gifford did not bat.

Bonus points – Hampshire 2.

Bowling: *First Innings*—Marshall 17-7-32-4; Connor 11-3-29-1; Maru 13-5-29-0; Tremlett 8-2-17-1. *Second Innings*—Marshall 8-5-9-2; Connor 5-2-11-1; Maru 9-1-33-0; Tremlett 4-2-2-0; James 3-2-2-0.

Umpires: B. Dudleston and R. Julian.

HAMPSHIRE v SUSSEX

At Portsmouth, July 22, 23, 24. Drawn. Hampshire 4 pts, Sussex 2 pts. Toss: Sussex. Yet another match was badly affected by the weather, with no play until after tea on the first day or from 2.30 p.m. on the third. Sussex, batting first on a slow, green and damp wicket, found Maru a problem as it began to dry and the left-arm spin bowler returned his best figures of the season. Hampshire lost both openers early on, but Nicholas and Turner, after slow starts, allowed the captain to declare 37 runs behind on the second evening. Sussex, hoping to set a target, had in Parker and Colin Wells two batsmen able to master the conditions; but the return of the rain confounded all their enterprise.

Close of play: First day, Sussex 51-3 (A. P. Wells 11*, A. C. S. Pigott 4*); Second day, Sussex 1-1 (R. I. Alikhan 1*, A. C. S. Pigott 0*).

Sussex

R. I. Alikhan c C. L. Smith b Marshall	2	– c Parks b Maru	13
A. M. Green c Parks b Connor	8	– lbw b Tremlett	0
P. W. G. Parker c Terry b Connor	25	– (4) c Maru b James	45
A. P. Wells c Maru b Marshall	16	– (5) b Maru	10
A. C. S. Pigott c Parks b Maru	14	– (3) b Connor	0
C. M. Wells c Nicholas b Maru	35	– not out	34
D. K. Standing c Parks b Tremlett	2	– not out	25
*†I. J. Gould b Maru	3		
G. S. le Roux not out	35		
P. A. W. Heseltine c James b Maru	12		
A. M. Babington c Tremlett b Maru	8		
B 1, l-b 2, n-b 2	5	B 2, l-b 5, w 2, n-b 11	20

1/4 2/12 3/47 4/58 5/90   165   1/0 2/1 3/51   (5 wkts dec.) 147
6/93 7/105 8/116 9/148   4/74 5/89

Bonus points – Sussex 1, Hampshire 4.

Bowling: *First Innings*—Marshall 18-6-37-2; Connor 23-7-27-2; Maru 28.5-6-59-5; Tremlett 11-2-36-1; James 1-0-1-0; C. L. Smith 1-0-2-0. *Second Innings*—Connor 10-5-10-1; Maru 20-10-28-2; Tremlett 5-2-20-1; Marshall 5-2-10-0; James 13.1-0-48-1; Nicholas 5.5-0-24-0.

Hampshire

V. P. Terry lbw b le Roux	1	R. A. Smith not out	7
C. L. Smith c Gould b C. M. Wells	7	L-b 6, n-b 2	8
*M. C. J. Nicholas b C. M. Wells	56		
D. R. Turner not out	49	1/4 2/16 3/114	(3 wkts dec.) 128

K. D. James, M. D. Marshall, T. M. Tremlett, †R. J. Parks, R. J. Maru and C. A. Connor did not bat.

Bonus point – Sussex 1.

Bowling: le Roux 9-5-6-1; Pigott 8-2-24-0; C. M. Wells 17-6-44-2; Heseltine 9-2-22-0; Babington 6-0-26-0.

Umpires: J. A. Jameson and D. Lloyd.

HAMPSHIRE v ESSEX

At Portsmouth, July 25, 27, 28. Drawn. Hampshire 6 pts, Essex 5 pts. Toss: Hampshire. A three-hour stay by Chris Smith held Hampshire's first innings together as Pringle's bowling caused a variety of problems on a low, slow wicket. Essex in turn found Marshall difficult, but they gained the advantage on the third day by reducing Hampshire to 128 for six, Lever bowling his left-arm seam to good effect. Marshall and Tremlett fought back, however, and Hampshire were able to set Essex to score 222 to win in a minimum of 58 overs. Stephenson, hitting ten fours and cutting and pulling with some style, was the mainstay of the Essex innings, but with Maru making the ball turn they abandoned the chase. The match was called off with seven overs of the last twenty remaining.

Close of play: First day, Essex 28-1 (J. P. Stephenson 8*, B. R. Hardie 14*); Second day, Hampshire 92-2 (M. C. J. Nicholas 8*, D. R. Turner 4*).

Hampshire

C. G. Greenidge c East b Pringle	4	– c Pringle b Childs	51
C. L. Smith c Miller b Childs	82	– c Fletcher b Childs	28
*M. C. J. Nicholas lbw b Pringle	0	– lbw b Lever	10
D. R. Turner b Miller	39	– b Lever	20
R. A. Smith c East b Lever	0	– c East b Lever	9
M. D. Marshall b Lever	24	– not out	45
N. G. Cowley st East b Childs	9	– c Miller b Lever	3
†R. J. Parks c East b Pringle	17	– c Lilley b Lever	3
T. M. Tremlett lbw b Pringle	1	– c Hardie b Childs	24
R. J. Maru b Childs	15		
C. A. Connor not out	2		
B 2, l-b 1, n-b 3	12	L-b 7	7

1/5 2/17 3/122 4/123 5/159	205	1/75 2/84 3/94 (8 wkts dec.) 200
6/165 7/186 8/186 9/189		4/117 5/124 6/128
		7/148 8/200

Bonus points – Hampshire 2, Essex 4.

Bowling: *First Innings*—Lever 20-6-33-2; Pringle 24-6-47-4; Topley 6-1-15-0; Miller 21-5-62-1; Childs 20.4-8-39-3. *Second Innings*—Lever 24-8-59-5; Pringle 16-6-36-0; Childs 20.4-6-56-3; Miller 1-1-0-0; Topley 7-1-25-0; Gooch 6-2-17-0.

Essex

*G. A. Gooch c Parks b Connor	3	– c Parks b Maru	9
J. P. Stephenson c Parks b Maru	27	– not out	67
B. R. Hardie c C. L. Smith b Tremlett	38	– c Parks b Tremlett	11
K. W. R. Fletcher b Cowley	30	– (5) c R. A. Smith b Maru	5
A. W. Lilley c Parks b Marshall	14	– (6) not out	10
D. R. Pringle c Maru b Marshall	11	– (4) b Maru	6
G. Miller c Maru b Tremlett	19		
†D. E. East c Greenidge b Marshall	1		
T. D. Topley c C. L. Smith b Cowley	17		
J. K. Lever c R. A. Smith b Marshall	18		
J. H. Childs not out	2		
L-b 1, w 2, n-b 1	4	B 9, l-b 6	15

1/4 2/68 3/76 4/108 5/124	184	1/19 2/46 3/65 (4 wkts) 123
6/126 7/128 8/151 9/179		4/90

Bonus points – Essex 1, Hampshire 4.

Bowling: *First Innings*—Marshall 25-6-51-4; Connor 14-2-39-1; Maru 20-7-39-1; Tremlett 11-1-27-2; Cowley 16-5-27-2. *Second Innings*—Marshall 10-4-7-0; Connor 5-0-14-0; Maru 20-4-53-3; Cowley 9-4-20-0; Tremlett 8-5-9-1; C. L. Smith 2-1-5-0.

Umpires: J. A. Jameson and D. Lloyd.

At Southampton, August 1, 2, 3. HAMPSHIRE drew with PAKISTANIS (See Pakistani tour section).

At Weston-super-Mare, August 5, 6, 7. HAMPSHIRE drew with SOMERSET.

HAMPSHIRE v LANCASHIRE

At Southampton, August 8, 10, 11. Drawn. Hampshire 6 pts, Lancashire 6 pts. Toss: Lancashire. No play was possible after lunch on the third day. On a pitch helping spin rather than seam, Lancashire made heavy weather of their first innings until Hegg, Allott, Folley and Patterson added 155 for the last three wickets. Allott, with three sixes and eleven fours, mainly from straight drives and some brave hooking, particularly off Marshall, initiated the revival and hit a career-best 88. Patterson, finding some lift from the slow wicket, dismissed both openers, but troubled by some 24 no-balls, including six in his twelve-minute first over, he did not have the happiest of times. Hampshire declared after their third batting point, rather than bat into the third morning; but before the declaration bowlers could assist Lancashire's batsmen to set up a target, the rain fell.

Close of play: First day, Lancashire 273-8 (W. K. Hegg 30*, I. Folley 0*); Second day, Hampshire 256-7 (R. J. Parks 12*, T. M. Tremlett 22*).

Lancashire

G. D. Mendis c Cowley b Connor	53	– c Greenidge b Tremlett	34
G. Fowler lbw b Marshall	14	– b Connor	5
M. A. Atherton c Greenidge b Cowley	43	– c Parks b Cowley	15
N. H. Fairbrother b Tremlett	12	– not out	36
M. Watkinson lbw b Cowley	13	– not out	41
*D. P. Hughes c Greenidge b Maru	8		
†W. K. Hegg lbw b Cowley	40		
J. D. Fitton c Maru b Cowley	3		
P. J. W. Allott c Maru b Marshall	88		
I. Folley c Cowley b Maru	27		
B. P. Patterson not out	4		
L-b 7, n-b 3	10	L-b 16	16
	315	(3 wkts)	**147**

1/34 2/96 3/114 4/140 5/147   1/8 2/61 3/74
6/151 7/160 8/267 9/299

Bonus points – Lancashire 3, Hampshire 3 (Score at 100 overs: 265-7).

Bowling: *First Innings*—Marshall 23.5-56-2; Connor 30-7-77-1; Maru 29.5-8-70-2; Tremlett 13-4-28-1; Cowley 26-6-77-4. *Second Innings*—Marshall 5-2-6-0; Connor 7-1-25-1; Maru 12-6-14-0; Tremlett 5-1-13-1; Cowley 3-0-8-1; R. A. Smith 5-0-44-0; Nicholas 1-0-7-0; C. L. Smith 3-0-14-0.

Hampshire

C. G. Greenidge c Watkinson b Patterson	19	N. G. Cowley c and b Folley	12
C. L. Smith c Hegg b Patterson	0	†R. J. Parks not out	12
V. P. Terry lbw b Allott	24	T. M. Tremlett not out	22
*M. C. J. Nicholas b Allott	60	L-b 2, n-b 23	25
R. A. Smith b Fitton	61	1/13 2/50 3/52 4/151 (7 wkts dec.) 256
M. D. Marshall c Watkinson b Patterson	21	5/187 6/221 7/221

R. J. Maru and C. A. Connor did not bat.

Bonus points – Hampshire 3, Lancashire 3.

Bowling: Patterson 23-4-90-3; Allott 20-7-35-2; Folley 29-9-74-1; Watkinson 11-2-32-0; Fitton 7-0-23-1.

Umpires: R. Julian and D. O. Oslear.

HAMPSHIRE v KENT

At Bournemouth, August 19, 20, 21. Hampshire won by 75 runs. Hampshire 22 pts, Kent 6 pts. Toss: Hampshire. Bakker, a Dutchman playing his first Championship game of the season, returned remarkable figures of seven for 31 to assist Hampshire to their first Championship victory since early July. Batting first on a slow wicket, they had toiled, especially against Underwood who was playing his last match on a ground where he had reaped a good harvest in the past. Kent were soon in trouble, losing four cheap wickets, but Cowdrey, playing a captain's role, gained in confidence to hit his highest score of the season, his 135 from 232 balls containing twenty fours and a six. Nicholas, assisted by some friendly bowling, replied in kind for Hampshire with his third three-figure innings of the season (24 fours), and his declaration set Kent to chase 252 in a minimum of 42 overs. To their credit they pursued it almost to the end, but Bakker's accurate seam bowling, helped by some faulty strokes, kept the advantage with Hampshire.

Close of play: First day, Hampshire 222-7 (K. D. James 62*, T. M. Tremlett 1*); Second day, Hampshire 44-1 (C. L. Smith 28*, M. C. J. Nicholas 16*).

Hampshire

V. P. Terry c Cowdrey b Underwood	47	– c Hinks b Baptiste 0
C. L. Smith c Marsh b Penn	31	– c Marsh b Penn 46
*M. C. J. Nicholas c Taylor b Underwood	27	– c Cowdrey b Aslett 133
D. R. Turner c Marsh b Baptiste	15	– c Marsh b Tavaré 71
R. A. Smith b Underwood	5	– not out 47
K. D. James lbw b Baptiste	64	– not out 6
†R. J. Parks b Underwood	18	
R. J. Maru b Baptiste	0	
T. M. Tremlett b Penn	8	
C. A. Connor not out	1	
P. J. Bakker c Benson b Penn	0	
B 2, l-b 7, w 5, n-b 4	18	L-b 2, n-b 2 4

1/64 2/103 3/121 4/128 5/130   234   1/0 2/112 3/216   (4 wkts dec.) 307
6/209 7/219 8/228 9/232   4/280

Bonus points – Hampshire 2, Kent 3 (Score at 100 overs: 222-7).

Bowling: *First Innings*—Igglesden 10–4–30–0; Baptiste 28–7–66–3; Underwood 29–16–27–4; Penn 25-6-67-3; Cowdrey 15-5-35-0. *Second Innings*—Baptiste 12-4-34-1; Penn 10-1-51-0; Underwood 16-6-48-0; Aslett 18.1-0-128-1; Tavaré 8-0-44-1.

Kent

M. R. Benson c Maru b Bakker	13	– c Terry b Bakker 4
N. R. Taylor c Parks b Connor	6	– c and b Maru 42
S. G. Hinks c Connor b James	13	– c James b Maru 30
C. J. Tavaré c Maru b Connor	0	– c Turner b Maru 42
D. G. Aslett run out	52	– c Connor b Bakker 14
*C. S. Cowdrey b Tremlett	135	– c Tremlett b Bakker 24
E. A. E. Baptiste c R. A. Smith b Tremlett	14	– c Connor b Bakker 4
†S. A. Marsh b Tremlett	37	– lbw b Bakker 2
C. Penn c Maru b Tremlett	0	– not out 2
D. L. Underwood b Tremlett	4	– b Bakker 0
A. P. Igglesden not out	1	– c Connor b Bakker 0
L-b 8, n-b 7	15	B 4, l-b 8 12

1/19 2/19 3/19 4/37 5/127   290   1/13 2/78 3/109 4/140 5/145   176
6/170 7/284 8/284 9/289   6/170 7/173 8/174 9/174

Bonus points – Kent 3, Hampshire 4.

Bowling: *First Innings*—Connor 22-4-50-2; Bakker 20-8-63-1; James 8-1-28-1; Tremlett 17.5-5-57-5; Maru 22-2-84-0. *Second Innings*—Connor 9-0-28-0; Bakker 13.5-2-31-7; Maru 22-5-84-3; Tremlett 7-0-21-0.

Umpires: D. J. Constant and D. S. Thompsett.

HAMPSHIRE v SOMERSET

At Bournemouth, August 22, 24, 25. Hampshire won by 129 runs. Hampshire 20 pts, Somerset 3 pts. Toss: Hampshire. The home side, with some good all-round batting, quickly made up for a rain-delayed start. Roebuck, the Somerset captain, declared overnight after Hardy, formerly of Hampshire, had struck a fine half-century in an unbroken partnership of 129 with

Wyatt. Terry and Chris Smith again batted enterprisingly and Somerset were set 263 to win in some 60 overs, only to find the left-arm spin of Maru impeding their progress. Hampshire's win was their second of the Bournemouth festival week, both coming while they were without Greenidge or Marshall, who were at Lord's for the MCC Bicentenary match.

Close of play: First day, Hampshire 178-2 (M. C. J. Nicholas 50*, R. J. Maru 0*); Second day, Somerset 215-2 (J. J. E. Hardy 75*, J. G. Wyatt 58*).

Hampshire

V. P. Terry lbw b Rose	80	– lbw b Rose	88
C. L. Smith lbw b Palmer	41	– not out	83
*M. C. J. Nicholas c Burns b Jones	53		
R. J. Maru c Marks b Jones	6		
D. R. Turner not out	61		
R. A. Smith not out	43		
L-b 11, w 5, n-b 1	17	L-b 5	5

1/85 2/178 3/189 4/197   (4 wkts dec.) 301   1/176   (1 wkt dec.) 176

K. D. James, †R. J. Parks, T. M. Tremlett, C. A. Connor and P. J. Bakker did not bat.

Bonus points – Hampshire 4, Somerset 1.

Bowling: *First Innings*—Jones 20-5-54-2; Mallender 19-4-54-0; Palmer 28-6-85-1; Rose 20.1-4-59-1; Marks 10-1-38-0. *Second Innings*—Jones 4-0-11-0; Mallender 8-1-23-0; Palmer 11-0-52-0; Marks 18-3-63-0; Rose 5.5-0-22-1.

Somerset

N. A. Felton c Parks b Tremlett	27	– (2) c Tremlett b Maru	16
*P. M. Roebuck lbw b Bakker	45	– (1) c Terry b Maru	17
J. J. E. Hardy not out	75	– c Tremlett b Connor	8
J. G. Wyatt not out	58	– c C. L. Smith b Tremlett	23
R. J. Harden (did not bat)		– lbw b Maru	6
V. J. Marks (did not bat)		– c Parks b Maru	1
†N. D. Burns (did not bat)		– c C. L. Smith b Maru	18
G. D. Rose (did not bat)		– c Terry b Tremlett	10
G. V. Palmer (did not bat)		– not out	19
N. A. Mallender (did not bat)		– lbw b Bakker	11
A. N. Jones (did not bat)		– c Terry b Connor	0
B 4, l-b 3, n-b 3	10	B 4	4

1/53 2/86   (2 wkts dec.) 215   1/32 2/35 3/47 4/56 5/66   133
                                        6/84 7/100 8/106 9/133

Bonus points – Somerset 2.

Bowling: *First Innings*—Connor 14-2-37-0; Bakker 11-4-21-1; Tremlett 14-8-16-1; Maru 23-3-64-0; James 11-0-37-0; C. L. Smith 6-0-33-0. *Second Innings*—Connor 9.2-1-29-2; Bakker 12-4-31-1; Maru 23-7-45-5; Tremlett 9-4-24-2.

Umpires: D. J. Constant and D. S. Thompsett.

At Worcester, August 26, 27, 28. HAMPSHIRE beat WORCESTERSHIRE by 31 runs.

At Maidstone, August 29, 31, September 1. HAMPSHIRE beat KENT by seven wickets.

HAMPSHIRE v LEICESTERSHIRE

At Southampton, September 2, 3, 4. Drawn. Hampshire 8 pts, Leicestershire 6 pts. Toss: Leicestershire. The umpires requested a visit from the TCCB's Inspector of Pitches after Marshall and Andrew had made the ball lift dangerously on the first morning, when the visitors were reduced to 82 for five. Clift, with sound defence, and DeFreitas, hitting five sixes and being particularly severe on Maru, led the recovery with 101 in 70 minutes. Rain and bad light, however, took Hampshire past 100 hours lost in first-class matches in 1987, frustrating the ambitions of both teams. Each still had an outside chance of winning the Championship. Hampshire, with Robin Smith particularly punishing, pushed hard to establish an advantage but, held up by Boon's defiant 94, they were left to score 229 in the final session. When both openers went in quick succession, the captains agreed to an early finish.

Close of play: First day, Leicestershire 257-7 (P. B. Clift 70*, J. P. Agnew 0*); Second day, Hampshire 278-5 (R. A. Smith 85*, M. D. Marshall 1*).

Leicestershire

T. J. Boon c Parks b Andrew	3	– c C. L. Smith b Maru	94
N. E. Briers c Tremlett b Andrew	4	– c Terry b Marshall	1
*P. Willey c Terry b Marshall	15	– c Terry b Tremlett	44
D. I. Gower c Terry b Andrew	41	– c Nicholas b James	46
J. J. Whitaker b Andrew	5	– not out	36
P. B. Clift c Maru b Marshall	79	– c Parks b Andrew	1
P. A. J. DeFreitas c R. A. Smith b Andrew	74	– st Parks b Maru	2
†P. Whitticase b Tremlett	21	– not out	4
J. P. Agnew not out	14		
G. J. F. Ferris b Marshall	2		
P. M. Such c Parks b Marshall	2		
B 1, l-b 8, n-b 17	26	L-b 10, w 1, n-b 7	18

1/9 2/13 3/49 4/54 5/82   286   1/7 2/64 3/165   (6 wkts dec.) 246
6/183 7/256 8/271 9/278   4/211 5/226 6/239

Bonus points – Leicestershire 3, Hampshire 4.

Bowling: *First Innings*—Marshall 21.1-6-57-4; Andrew 24-0-119-5; Tremlett 13-0-48-1; Maru 10-2-53-0. *Second Innings*—Marshall 8-2-33-1; Andrew 13-1-56-1; Maru 24-4-83-2; Tremlett 6-0-16-1; C. L. Smith 1-0-2-0; James 7-1-46-1.

Hampshire

V. P. Terry c Boon b Such	44	– c Whitticase b Agnew	40
C. L. Smith run out	28	– b DeFreitas	43
*M. C. J. Nicholas c Clift b Agnew	36	– (4) not out	0
D. R. Turner c Whitaker b Such	19		
R. A. Smith lbw b Agnew	94	– (3) not out	2
K. D. James c Clift b Willey	34		
M. D. Marshall c Whitticase b Agnew	5		
†R. J. Parks not out	8		
T. M. Tremlett c Briers b DeFreitas	3		
B 5, l-b 6, w 4, n-b 18	33	L-b 4, n-b 3	7

1/56 2/120 3/142 4/169 5/274   (8 wkts dec.) 304   1/87 2/91   (2 wkts) 92
6/289 7/298 8/304

R. J. Maru and S. J. W. Andrew did not bat.

Bonus points – Hampshire 4, Leicestershire 3.

Bowling: *First Innings*—Ferris 11-3-45-0; Agnew 15-1-50-3; Clift 13-2-23-0; DeFreitas 19.2-0-82-1; Such 18-6-65-2; Willey 8-1-28-1. *Second Innings*—Agnew 12-1-48-1; Ferris 7-0-19-0; DeFreitas 4-1-21-1.

Umpires: A. A. Jones and N. T. Plews.

At Lord's, September 9, 10, 11. HAMPSHIRE drew with MIDDLESEX.

KENT

Patron: HRH The Duke of Kent
President: 1987 – T. G. Denne
1988 – H. J. Pocock
Chairman: 1987 – M. A. O'B. ffrench Blake
Secretary: D. B. Dalby
St Lawrence Ground, Old Dover Road,
Canterbury CT1 3NZ
(Telephone: 0227-456886)
Captain: C. S. Cowdrey
Director of Coaching: J. C. T. Page
Cricket Administrator: B. W. Luckhurst

Kent knew a hard season lay ahead when it was learnt that their international opening bowlers, Graham Dilley and Terry Alderman, would not be playing for the county in 1987. The previous season Dilley, in between Tests, had taken 44 Championship wickets and Alderman 98, and the enormity of their loss was amplified by the inability of Richard Ellison, because of back and leg injuries, to play one first-class match in 1987. Nor was that the end of Kent's difficulties. On the slow pitches of their home grounds, Kent's batsmen found it hard to score runs, and as injuries manifested themselves regularly, the side was subject to almost continuous change. The result was that in the Britannic Assurance Championship, the county slid from eighth to fourteenth, and their two wins were the least since 1980, which in turn was the first time since 1897 that only two wins had been recorded.

Yet the season had started well with Glamorgan beaten by an innings in the first home Championship game. Alan Igglesden, the promising young fast bowler, took 23 wickets in his first four matches, and Chris Penn, becoming a more regular member of the attack in the absence of Ellison, was also in good form. Eldine Baptiste, now the county's only overseas player, responded to his chance with 23 wickets in his first five three-day matches, and Kent qualified for the quarter-finals of the Benson and Hedges Cup. Injury laid low Igglesden, but Danny Kelleher, promoted from the Second XI, was an instant success with his medium-fast pace. Then, in the Benson and Hedges Cup semi-final against Northamptonshire at Canterbury, came the cruellest blow. Baptiste, having bowled an opening spell of six overs for 8 runs, sustained side and groin muscle injuries while fielding. He limped off and the match was lost in a thrilling finish. Immediately Roy Pienaar, a South African who was spending the season with Worcestershire, was registered and played as a medium-pace bowler, even though his more obvious talent lay in his batting.

Form in the Refuge Assurance Sunday League, in which three of the first four games were won, became patchy, and when the last two games were washed out, Kent finished fifth in the table and out of the prizemoney. Derek Underwood, in his farewell season, found a rare wicket to suit him in Scotland to bowl Kent into the second round of the NatWest Bank Trophy, but another last-over finish at Canterbury went against them as Derbyshire won a place in the quarter-finals.

In the Championship, a losing run of four games was halted by a tame draw against Leicestershire at Canterbury, where the spotlight was almost exclusively on Underwood. In an emotional three days, he signed off after a distinguished career of 25 years by bowling 59 overs in the match, taking four for 89 in the first innings and none for 40 in 27 overs in the second. Richard Davis, his successor as Kent's slow left-arm spinner, played more regularly once Underwood's intended retirement had been confirmed, and he showed promise.

For the third year in succession Mark Benson led the batting, this time with his highest aggregate of 1,725 first-class runs. Showing a high standard of consistency, he passed 50 fifteen times and went on to score five hundreds. Not one of those hundreds, however, came on a Kent ground, lending credence to the point made earlier about Kent wickets. Apart from Benson, only Neil Taylor and Chris Tavaré scored 1,000 runs, although Simon Hinks, who lost his place for a spell, Derek Aslett and the captain, Christopher Cowdrey, finished with more than 900. The captain's first-class season, after a tremendous start, fell away to such an extent that from May 24 he had to wait until mid-August before reaching the half-century mark again. In the limited-overs game it was a different story. Eight times he passed 50, and in addition to scoring 812 runs, he took 31 wickets.

Graham Cowdrey, playing principally in one-day cricket – he twice took four wickets in a Sunday game – had just been given his chance to bat at No. 3 in the Championship side when he sustained a broken jaw while batting at Derby in mid-July and was sidelined for the rest of the summer. And when Trevor Ward, a young opening batsman, was given the opportunity of an extended run in the last few games of the season, he broke a thumb and did not play again. Even the wicket-keeper, Steven Marsh, struck a nasty blow in the eye, did not escape injury. However, his absence did provide a chance for Paul Farbrace to show his promise behind the stumps, as well as with the bat.

Long before the season ended, speculation about their future gave several players cause for concern. With no guarantee of Ellison's fitness, there was talk of acquiring a new overseas fast bowler, and it must have been reassuring for Penn when he received his county cap. But for Aslett, Baptiste, Steven Goldsmith and Kevin Jarvis, whose benefit season was blighted by injury, there was no further future with Kent. Instead, the county offered terms to Mark Harman, an off-spinner who was released by Somerset.

With Underwood's departure, it was the end of an era. Whether a new era will dawn in 1988 remains to be seen. So much could depend on the fitness of Ellison and the acquisition of a new fast bowler. Should neither be forthcoming, 1988 could provide another long, hard struggle to prevent the "empty eighties" succeeding those fast-receding glory years of the seventies. – Dudley Moore.

KENT 1987

[*Bill Smith*]

Back row: P. Farbrace, S. C. Goldsmith, R. P. Davis, C. Penn, T. R. Ward, D. J. Sabine. *Middle row:* G. Popplewell (*physiotherapist*), G. R. Cowdrey, A. P. Igglesden, D. J. M. Kelleher, S. G. Hinks, C. Lewis (*scorer*). *Front row:* M. R. Benson, N. R. Taylor, S. A. Marsh, C. J. Tavaré, C. S. Cowdrey (*captain*), K. B. S. Jarvis, R. M. Ellison, D. G. Aslett, R. A. Woolmer (*coach*). *Inset:* R. F. Pienaar.

KENT RESULTS

All first-class matches – Played 26: Won 3, Lost 7, Drawn 16.

County Championship matches – Played 24: Won 2, Lost 7, Drawn 15.

Bonus points – Batting 53, Bowling 66.

Competition placings – Britannic Assurance County Championship, 14th; NatWest Bank Trophy, 2nd round; Benson and Hedges Cup, s-f; Refuge Assurance League, 6th.

BRITANNIC ASSURANCE CHAMPIONSHIP AVERAGES

BATTING

	Birthplace	M	I	NO	R	HI	Avge
‡M. R. Benson	Shoreham	23	38	0	1,619	131	42.60
§R. F. Pienaar	Johannesburg, SA	7	8	0	327	153	40.87
‡N. R. Taylor	Orpington	22	36	3	1,224	142*	37.09
G. R. Cowdrey	Farnborough, Kent	4	7	1	198	68	33.00
‡C. J. Tavaré	Orpington	24	40	7	1,035	152	31.36
P. Farbrace	Ash	4	6	2	121	75*	30.25
‡D. G. Aslett	Dover	23	37	7	895	101*	29.83
‡S. G. Hinks	Northfleet	19	31	1	818	112	27.26
§‡E. A. E. Baptiste ...	Liberta, Antigua	15	22	3	510	95	26.84
‡C. S. Cowdrey	Farnborough, Kent	23	35	5	783	135	26.10
‡S. A. Marsh	Westminster	20	26	5	387	72*	18.42
‡D. L. Underwood	Bromley	21	20	9	168	29*	15.27
S. C. Goldsmith	Ashford	2	4	0	49	25	12.25
‡C. Penn	Dover	15	16	1	175	37	11.66
‡K. B. S. Jarvis	Dartford	10	8	7	11	4*	11.00
R. P. Davis	Margate	7	9	4	43	21*	8.60
D. J. M. Kelleher ...	Southwark	12	12	1	81	30	7.36
A. P. Igglesden	Farnborough, Kent	12	14	3	69	30	6.27

Also batted: T. R. Ward (*Farningham*) (1 match) 6, 13*.

* Signifies not out. ‡ Denotes county cap. § Not qualified for England.

The following played a total of thirteen three-figure innings for Kent in County Championship matches – M. R. Benson 4, N. R. Taylor 3, C. S. Cowdrey 2, D. G. Aslett 1, S. G. Hinks 1, R. F. Pienaar 1, C. J. Tavaré 1.

BOWLING

	O	M	R	W	BB	Avge
D. J. M. Kelleher ...	301	72	878	34	6-109	25.82
E. A. E. Baptiste ...	490.3	110	1,409	51	8-76	27.62
R. F. Pienaar	135.4	27	427	15	4-66	28.46
A. P. Igglesden	332	48	1,189	39	5-45	30.48
C. Penn	387.1	66	1,313	43	5-52	30.53
D. L. Underwood	562.3	192	1,201	38	5-43	31.60
K. B. S. Jarvis	224.2	32	827	26	5-48	31.80
R. P. Davis	153	35	473	10	3-68	47.30
C. S. Cowdrey	259.1	58	817	17	2-30	48.05

Also bowled: D. G. Aslett 63.1-6-288-2; M. R. Benson 2-0-8-0; G. R. Cowdrey 8-2-43-0; S. C. Goldsmith 6-0-37-1; S. G. Hinks 9-0-51-0; C. J. Tavaré 29.1-5-124-1; N. R. Taylor 2-0-15-0.

Wicket-keepers: S. A. Marsh 38 ct, 1 st; P. Farbrace 7 ct.

Leading Fielders: C. J. Tavaré 22, C. S. Cowdrey 18, M. R. Benson 17, S. G. Hinks 16.

At Oxford, April 22, 23, 24. KENT drew with OXFORD UNIVERSITY.

At Worcester, April 25, 26, 27. KENT lost to WORCESTERSHIRE by two wickets.

KENT v GLAMORGAN

At Canterbury, April 29, 30, May 1. Kent won by an innings and 116 runs. Kent 23 pts, Glamorgan 2 pts. Toss: Kent. Benson and Taylor launched Kent towards a big total with an opening stand of 168 off 60 overs, Taylor going on to 113 off 247 balls and hitting thirteen fours. The innings faltered for a time, but Cowdrey and Marsh effected a telling recovery with an unbroken stand of 162 from 34 overs. Cowdrey reached his century in 139 minutes with ten fours. Glamorgan made a bad start and never recovered. When they followed on, the pace of Igglesden was soon hurrying Kent to an early victory, for after Hopkins the only real resistance came from Maynard, who hit nine fours in a spirited 70-minute innings.

Close of play: First day, Kent 351-5 (C. S. Cowdrey 83*, S. A. Marsh 33*); Second day, Glamorgan 51-2 (J. A. Hopkins 29*, R. J. Shastri 3*).

Kent

M. R. Benson lbw b Barwick	78	†S. A. Marsh not out 72
N. R. Taylor c Metson b Thomas	113	
S. G. Hinks c Hopkins b Ontong	1	B 4, l-b 10, w 1, n-b 3 18
C. J. Tavaré c Metson b Smith	10	
D. G. Aslett lbw b Barwick	15	1/168 2/181 3/208 (5 wkts dec.) 407
*C. S. Cowdrey not out	100	4/223 5/245

C. Penn, D. L. Underwood, A. P. Igglesden and K. B. S. Jarvis did not bat.

Bonus points – Kent 3, Glamorgan 2 (Score at 100 overs: 282-5).

Bowling: Thomas 17-3-63-1; Smith 13-2-58-1; Barwick 28-5-74-2; Ontong 28-7-69-1; Shastri 29-6-80-0; Holmes 9-0-49-0.

Glamorgan

J. A. Hopkins c Hinks b Igglesden	5	– c Penn b Igglesden	35
*H. Morris c Tavaré b Jarvis	24	– c Aslett b Igglesden	4
A. R. Butcher lbw b Jarvis	12	– c Marsh b Igglesden	10
R. J. Shastri lbw b Jarvis	15	– c Penn b Jarvis	3
R. C. Ontong c Benson b Penn	3	– c Marsh b Igglesden	1
G. C. Holmes c Benson b Penn	4	– lbw b Cowdrey	7
M. P. Maynard c Hinks b Igglesden	29	– c Marsh b Underwood	46
J. G. Thomas c Aslett b Penn	5	– c Hinks b Cowdrey	2
†C. P. Metson b Underwood	14	– lbw b Penn	9
I. Smith c Benson b Underwood	16	– not out	6
S. R. Barwick not out	0	– b Igglesden	18
L-b 3, w 2, n-b 6	11	L-b 4, w 3, n-b 5	12

1/14 2/38 3/48 4/58 5/67   138   1/12 2/35 3/52 4/59 5/62   153
6/71 7/77 8/119 9/138   6/92 7/96 8/128 9/128

Bonus points – Kent 4.

Bowling: *First Innings*—Igglesden 14-3-35-2; Jarvis 15-3-49-3; Penn 10-1-36-3; Cowdrey 5-2-12-0; Underwood 2-1-3-2. *Second Innings*—Jarvis 9.5-0-30-1; Igglesden 16-4-45-5; Cowdrey 12.1-5-33-2; Penn 9-1-35-1; Underwood 3-1-6-1.

Umpires: B. J. Meyer and P. B. Wight.

At Canterbury, May 6, 7, 8. KENT beat PAKISTANIS by an innings and 57 runs (See Pakistani tour section).

KENT v SUSSEX

At Dartford, May 20, 21, 22. Drawn. Kent 6 pts, Sussex 6 pts. Toss: Kent. With Jarvis pulling a calf muscle while batting and unable to bowl, Baptiste's all-round form stood Kent in good stead on the first two days. Sussex, in turn, had reason to appreciate the batting skills of their opening bowler, Reeve, who with Moores and Heseltine saw them to safety from troubled waters. Kent struggled early in their second innings, but on the final day there were frequent stoppages because of bad weather. Eventually Sussex were set 184 to win in 35 minutes plus the last twenty overs – a task with which, understandably, they did not concern themselves.

Close of play: First day, Sussex 10-0 (R. I. Alikhan 2*, A. M. Green 8*); Second day, Kent 51-3 (N. R. Taylor 34*, D. G. Aslett 9*).

Kent

M. R. Benson c Reeve b Heseltine	39	– lbw b Babington	8
N. R. Taylor c Parker b C. M. Wells	26	– c and b Heseltine	48
S. G. Hinks lbw b le Roux	33	– c Moores b C. M. Wells	5
C. J. Tavaré c Moores b C. M. Wells	11	– b Babington	3
D. G. Aslett run out	1	– c Reeve b Babington	9
*C. S. Cowdrey c Moores b Reeve	11	– c Lenham b le Roux	29
E. A. E. Baptiste c Reeve b C. M. Wells	64	– b le Roux	0
†S. A. Marsh c C. M. Wells b Reeve	8	– b le Roux	41
C. Penn c le Roux b Heseltine	12	– c Parker b Heseltine	24
D. L. Underwood c Green b Heseltine	4	– not out	13
K. B. S. Jarvis not out	3	– not out	4
B 5, l-b 10, n-b 6	21	B 1, l-b 3, n-b 1	5
	233	(9 wkts dec.)	189

1/68 2/70 3/86 4/88 5/107 6/177 7/198 8/224 9/224

1/19 2/34 3/43 4/64 5/105 6/105 7/105 8/166 9/176

Bonus points – Kent 2, Sussex 4 (Score at 100 overs: 233-9).

Bowling: *First Innings*—le Roux 13-2-36-1; Reeve 25-9-55-2; Babington 13-3-39-0; C. M. Wells 26-8-26-3; Heseltine 24.3-9-62-3. *Second Innings*—le Roux 18-6-40-3; Reeve 10-6-15-0; Babington 18-7-49-3; C. M. Wells 18.1-3-39-1; Heseltine 16-4-42-2.

Sussex

R. I. Alikhan c sub b Baptiste	10	– retired hurt	6
A. M. Green b Penn	17	– lbw b Baptiste	11
*P. W. G. Parker c Taylor b Baptiste	8	– not out	34
A. P. Wells b Baptiste	20	– b Underwood	10
C. M. Wells b Baptiste	19	– b Underwood	0
N. J. Lenham lbw b Underwood	6	– not out	1
D. A. Reeve not out	87		
G. S. le Roux c Marsh b Underwood	3		
†P. Moores lbw b Baptiste	35		
P. A. W. Heseltine run out	26		
A. M. Babington c Marsh b Baptiste	0		
L-b 5, w 1, n-b 2	8	N-b 2	2
	239	(3 wkts)	64

1/24 2/35 3/36 4/65 5/76 6/88 7/98 8/155 9/229

1/17 2/40 3/42

Bonus points – Sussex 2, Kent 4.

Bowling: *First Innings*—Baptiste 30-5-69-6; Penn 24-5-60-1; Underwood 27-7-66-2; Cowdrey 12-1-39-0. *Second Innings*—Baptiste 5-1-16-1; Penn 2-0-4-0; Underwood 11-6-13-2; Tavaré 8-4-31-0.

Umpires: A. A. Jones and R. Julian.

At Northampton, May 30, June 1, 2. KENT drew with NORTHAMPTONSHIRE.

KENT v SURREY

At Tunbridge Wells, June 3, 4, 5. Drawn. Kent 6 pts, Surrey 6 pts. Toss: Surrey. Clinton continued his habit of getting runs against his former county, reaching 53 out of 76 in 75 minutes with ten fours, but after that, apart from Lynch, Surrey faded as Kelleher, in only his second Championship match, gave the Kent attack fresh impetus. On the second day only 6.3 overs were possible, and on the final day Kent's night-watchman, Marsh, checked Surrey's progress. In their second innings Surrey ran into early trouble, but Lynch, hitting 41 out of 45 with six fours in 35 minutes, retrieved the situation, only for rain to wash out any prospects of a finish.

Close of play: First day, Kent 85-2 (N. R. Taylor 34*, S. A. Marsh 3*); Second day, Kent 91-3 (S. A. Marsh 5*, C. J. Tavaré 0*).

Surrey

G. S. Clinton c Marsh b Kelleher	72	– (2) c Benson b Baptiste	0
D. M. Smith c Taylor b Penn	1		
A. J. Stewart lbw b Kelleher	8	– b Kelleher	10
M. A. Lynch c Aslett b Baptiste	68	– c Marsh b Baptiste	41
T. E. Jesty c Taylor b Kelleher	0	– not out	9
†C. J. Richards b Penn	11	– not out	0
*I. A. Greig c Tavaré b Penn	7		
D. J. Thomas c Benson b Kelleher	15		
K. T. Medlycott not out	12	– (1) c Hinks b Baptiste	11
C. K. Bullen c Cowdrey b Baptiste	4		
S. T. Clarke c Tavaré b Kelleher	0		
B 1, l-b 4, w 1, n-b 4	10	B 7, n-b 1	8

1/5 2/56 3/102 4/104 5/131   208   1/3 2/16 3/61 4/79   (4 wkts) 79
6/141 7/188 8/192 9/203

Bonus points – Surrey 2, Kent 4.

Bowling: *First Innings*—Baptiste 22-3-62-2; Penn 15-3-46-3; Kelleher 21.4-3-76-5; Underwood 5-0-19-0. *Second Innings*—Baptiste 13-2-52-3; Underwood 13-6-20-0; Kelleher 1-1-0-1.

Kent

M. R. Benson c Lynch b Thomas	35	D. G. Aslett b Thomas	19
N. R. Taylor lbw b Thomas	34	D. J. M. Kelleher c and b Bullen	20
S. G. Hinks b Thomas	9	D. L. Underwood not out	0
†S. A. Marsh c Richards b Thomas	67		
C. J. Tavaré st Richards b Bullen	14	B 2, l-b 8	10
*C. S. Cowdrey c Bullen b Medlycott	7		
E. A. E. Baptiste c Smith b Bullen	0	1/56 2/74 3/87 4/123 5/142	220
C. Penn c sub b Medlycott	5	6/143 7/160 8/181 9/220	

Bonus points – Kent 2, Surrey 4.

Bowling: Clarke 5-1-12-0; Thomas 22-6-73-5; Greig 15-5-35-0; Jesty 3-1-8-0; Medlycott 15-4-36-2; Bullen 13.1-3-46-3.

Umpires: J. H. Harris and A. G. T. Whitehead.

KENT v ESSEX

At Tunbridge Wells, June 6, 8, 9. Drawn. Kent 4 pts, Essex 2 pts. Toss: Kent. Taylor and Tavaré put Kent on the right course, and after Graham Cowdrey had been involved in a mis-understanding which saw his brother and captain run out, he responded with a half-century in his first Championship match of the season. His first 10 runs took him nineteen overs, and he batted for more than two and a half hours. The rain returned on the second day, when Gooch and Hardie added 85 off 22 overs, and on the third every effort was made to achieve a result. Gooch declared, Kent forfeited their second innings, and Essex embarked on the task of scoring 186 to win on a day which everyone knew the rain would curtail. It did, after Baptiste had shocked Essex by taking three wickets in seven balls without conceding a run.

Close of play: First day, Kent 304-6 (E. A. E. Baptiste 28*, S. A. Marsh 0*); Second day, Essex 119-3 (K. W. R. Fletcher 4*, G. Miller 1*).

Kent

M. R. Benson c Redpath b Page	20	E. A. E. Baptiste not out	28
N. R. Taylor c Pringle b Childs	81	†S. A. Marsh not out	0
S. G. Hinks c Miller b Pringle	31	L-b 10, w 2, n-b 6	18
C. J. Tavaré c East b Pringle	63		
G. R. Cowdrey c Miller b Page	62	1/32 2/110 3/168 (6 wkts dec.)	304
*C. S. Cowdrey run out	1	4/225 5/226 6/302	

C. Penn, D. J. M. Kelleher and D. L. Underwood did not bat.

Bonus points – Kent 3, Essex 2 (Score at 100 overs: 265-5).

Bowling: Lever 22–3–60–0; Page 18–0–54–2; Pringle 27–4–56–2; Gooch 14–0–44–0; Childs 24–9–62–1; Miller 6–0–18–0.

Kent forfeited their second innings.

Essex

*G. A. Gooch c G. R. Cowdrey b Penn	41	– not out	19
I. Redpath c Hinks b Baptiste	10	– c Hinks b Baptiste	1
B. R. Hardie c Hinks b Kelleher	55	– c Benson b Baptiste	1
K. W. R. Fletcher not out	4	– c Marsh b Baptiste	0
G. Miller not out	1	– not out	1
L-b 7, w 1	8		

1/17 2/102 3/117 (3 wkts dec.) 119   1/19 2/21 3/21 (3 wkts) 22

D. R. Pringle, A. W. Lilley, H. A. Page, †D. E. East, J. K. Lever and J. H. Childs did not bat.

Bonus point – Kent 1.

Bowling: *First Innings*—Baptiste 10–1–42–1; Kelleher 11–2–30–1; Penn 11–3–40–1; Underwood 1–1–0–0. *Second Innings*—Baptiste 5–2–15–3; Kelleher 2–2–0–0; Underwood 2.1–0–7–0.

Umpires: J. H. Harris and A. G. T. Whitehead.

At Ilford, June 13, 15, 16. KENT drew with ESSEX.

At Bath, June 17, 18, 19. KENT drew with SOMERSET.

At Liverpool, June 20, 22, 23. KENT drew with LANCASHIRE.

KENT v NOTTINGHAMSHIRE

At Canterbury, June 27, 29, 30. Nottinghamshire won by ten wickets. Nottinghamshire 24 pts, Kent 6 pts. Toss: Kent. A dominating century by Johnson was the main feature of the first day, when he and Hadlee pulled Nottinghamshire round after three wickets had fallen for 9 runs in three overs. They put on 107 off 21 overs, Johnson reaching 100 in 158 minutes with eighteen fours. Taylor, hitting fifteen fours as he became the 22nd Kent player to carry his bat, resisted for 352 minutes and then became the first victim in the second hat-trick of Hadlee's career as Kent followed on. By the close on the second day Hadlee had taken five for 24 in 7.5 overs, and although Graham Cowdrey and Pienaar added 99 off 41 overs, Nottinghamshire's easy victory was inevitable.

Close of play: First day, Kent 20-0 (M. R. Benson 15*, N. R. Taylor 5*); Second day, Kent 50-5 (C. S. Cowdrey 20*).

Nottinghamshire

B. C. Broad lbw b Pienaar	30	– not out	16
*R. T. Robinson c Tavaré b Pienaar	18	– not out	5
D. W. Randall c Aslett b Kelleher	45		
P. Johnson c Taylor b Underwood	108		
C. E. B. Rice c Farbrace b Kelleher	0		
J. D. Birch c Underwood b Pienaar	4		
R. J. Hadlee c Tavaré b Kelleher	67		
†C. W. Scott b Igglesden	39		
E. E. Hemmings b Igglesden	40		
K. Saxelby not out	9		
K. E. Cooper lbw b Igglesden	0		
L-b 13, w 2, n-b 6	21	W 1	1

1/53 2/66 3/163 4/163 5/172   381   (no wkt) 22
6/279 7/290 8/368 9/381

Bonus points – Nottinghamshire 4, Kent 4.

Bowling: *First Innings*—Igglesden 18–1–87–3; Kelleher 32–8–93–3; Pienaar 20–1–87–3; Underwood 18–0–48–1; G. R. Cowdrey 8–2–43–0; C. S. Cowdrey 1–0–10–0. *Second Innings*—C. S. Cowdrey 1–0–6–0; Pienaar 2–1–4–0; Aslett 1–0–6–0; Benson 1–0–4–0; Tavaré 0.4–0–2–0.

Kent

M. R. Benson lbw b Cooper	15	– c and b Hadlee	20
N. R. Taylor not out	123	– b Hadlee	4
D. G. Aslett c Johnson b Hemmings	15	– b Hadlee	0
C. J. Tavaré c Robinson b Hemmings	9	– c Rice b Hadlee	0
*C. S. Cowdrey b Saxelby	3	– c Scott b Hadlee	22
G. R. Cowdrey b Scott b Cooper	9	– (7) c Scott b Cooper	57
R. F. Pienaar b Hemmings	1	– (8) b Saxelby	50
D. J. M. Kelleher c Scott b Hadlee	7	– (5) st Scott b Hemmings	3
†P. Farbrace c sub b Hemmings	20	– (6) c Robinson b Hadlee	0
A. P. Igglesden b Hemmings	1	– c Robinson b Hemmings	4
D. L. Underwood c Scott b Cooper	4	– not out	5
B 9, n-b 3	12	B 7, l-b 9, w 1, n-b 1	18

1/20 2/44 3/68 4/78 5/104   219   1/9 2/9 3/9 4/44 5/50   183
6/115 7/156 8/199 9/210   6/53 7/152 8/167 9/171

Bonus points – Kent 2, Nottinghamshire 4 (Score at 100 overs: 210-9).

Bowling: *First Innings*—Hadlee 20–5–53–1; Saxelby 22–8–49–1; Hemmings 37–16–70–5; Cooper 23.3–11–38–3. *Second Innings*—Hadlee 22–7–44–6; Saxelby 16–3–36–1; Hemmings 26–7–62–2; Cooper 10–3–21–1; Birch 1–0–4–0.

Umpires: D. J. Constant and A. A. Jones.

KENT v YORKSHIRE

At Canterbury, July 1, 2, 3. Yorkshire won by two wickets. Yorkshire 22 pts, Kent 5 pts. Toss: Kent. The pace of Jarvis had Kent struggling as he took three for 27 in his first 56 balls and Kent lost three wickets for 3 runs in five overs before lunch. Farbrace rescued them with a career-best 75 not out, hitting thirteen fours in his 119-minute innings. Yorkshire declared behind soon after Neil Hartley and Carrick had added 61 off twenty overs, and this initiative was rewarded when Kent collapsed on the final day. Jarvis again caused problems, and after some middle-order resistance, Kent lost their last six wickets for 29 in eleven overs. Yorkshire's target looked a comfortable one as Metcalfe and Blakey added 69 off sixteen overs. But four wickets fell for 24 in fourteen overs, and it needed some enterprising hitting by Carrick and Sidebottom before Yorkshire reached their target with thirteen balls to spare in an exciting finish.

Close of play: First day, Yorkshire 11-0 (M. D. Moxon 7*, A. A. Metcalfe 4*); Second day, Kent 31-2 (N. R. Taylor 10*, P. Farbrace 0*).

Kent

M. R. Benson c Moxon b Jarvis	50	– c Love b Jarvis		14
N. R. Taylor lbw b Jarvis	6	– c Moxon b Jarvis		11
D. G. Aslett b Jarvis	20	– b P. J. Hartley		3
C. J. Tavaré b Berry	1	– (5) c Blakey b Carrick		42
*C. S. Cowdrey lbw b S. N. Hartley	36	– (6) lbw b Sidebottom		33
G. R. Cowdrey b P. J. Hartley	1	– (7) b Jarvis		1
E. A. E. Baptiste b S. N. Hartley	35	– (8) c Sharp b Carrick		6
C. Penn c Blakey b Jarvis	37	– (9) c P. J. Hartley b Carrick		0
D. J. M. Kelleher c Blakey b P. J. Hartley	7	– (10) c Blakey b P. J. Hartley		0
†P. Farbrace not out	75	– (4) c Blakey b Jarvis		7
D. L. Underwood b Jarvis	18	– not out		4
B 2, l-b 7, n-b 6	15	L-b 11, n-b 4		15
	301			**136**

1/15 2/82 3/83 4/85 5/94 6/157 7/162 8/200 9/224

1/23 2/31 3/38 4/50 5/107 6/108 7/119 8/125 9/132

Bonus points – Kent 3, Yorkshire 4 (Score at 100 overs: 293-9).

Bowling: *First Innings*—Jarvis 28.3–8–65–5; Sidebottom 20–6–40–0; P. J. Hartley 24–4–80–2; Carrick 15–4–49–0; Berry 6–2–23–1; S. N. Hartley 8–1–35–2. *Second Innings*—Jarvis 15–3–37–4; Sidebottom 10–1–30–1; P. J. Hartley 9.2–4–21–2; Carrick 14–5–37–3.

Yorkshire

M. D. Moxon b Kelleher	35	– b Baptiste		11
A. A. Metcalfe lbw b Kelleher	11	– b Underwood		38
†R. J. Blakey c C. S. Cowdrey b Penn	54	– b Baptiste		45
K. Sharp b C. S. Cowdrey	14	– c sub b Underwood		11
J. D. Love c Tavaré b C. S. Cowdrey	28	– c Farbrace b Penn		11
S. N. Hartley c Tavaré b Penn	58	– lbw b Baptiste		0
*P. Carrick b Penn	44	– c Tavaré b Underwood		20
A. Sidebottom not out	1	– (9) b Penn		12
P. J. Hartley (did not bat)		– (8) not out		14
P. W. Jarvis (did not bat)		– not out		10
B 2, l-b 10, n-b 2	14	L-b 6, n-b 4		10
	(7 wkts dec.) 259			**(8 wkts) 182**

1/18 2/95 3/114 4/136 5/181 6/242 7/259

1/21 2/90 3/109 4/111 5/114 6/145 7/147 8/163

P. J. Berry did not bat.

Bonus points – Yorkshire 2, Kent 2 (Score at 100 overs: 223-5).

Bowling: *First Innings*—Baptiste 2–0–5–0; Kelleher 28–6–69–2; Underwood 30–14–44–0; Penn 25.3–6–72–3; C. S. Cowdrey 23–7–57–2. *Second Innings*—Kelleher 11–3–26–0; Baptiste 14–7–17–3; Penn 13.5–2–59–2; Underwood 24–9–51–3; C. S. Cowdrey 3–0–23–0.

Umpires: D. J. Constant and A. A. Jones.

At Hove, July 4, 6, 7. KENT drew with SUSSEX.

At Derby, July 15, 16, 17. KENT drew with DERBYSHIRE.

KENT v GLOUCESTERSHIRE

At Folkestone, July 22, 23, 24. Drawn. Toss: Gloucestershire. Folkestone's only county match of the season was ruined by the weather. No play was possible on the first two days, and when a one-innings match began on the third day Kent were indebted to a solid innings by Taylor, who reached his half-century in 143 minutes with four fours. Lloyds then took three for 2 in nine balls, but Aslett and Pienaar retrieved the position, adding 83 off 23 overs. Gloucestershire, left 75 minutes plus the last twenty overs, were progressing at 4 an over when rain had the last word.

Kent

M. R. Benson c Lloyds b Greene	7	R. F. Pienaar lbw b Lloyds	37
N. R. Taylor c Russell b Lloyds	52	†S. A. Marsh not out	11
S. G. Hinks b Bainbridge	25	B 2, l-b 2, n-b 2	6
C. J. Tavaré c Russell b Lloyds	25		
D. G. Aslett not out	49	1/11 2/52 3/112 (6 wkts dec.) 212
*C. S. Cowdrey c Bainbridge b Lloyds	0	4/113 5/115 6/198

D. J. M. Kelleher, D. L. Underwood and K. B. S. Jarvis did not bat.

Bowling: Lawrence 7–4–13–0; Greene 7–1–17–1; Alleyne 4–0–20–0; Bainbridge 6.3–2–13–1; Graveney 25.3–7–52–0; Lloyds 25–2–93–4.

Gloucestershire

A. W. Stovold c Pienaar b Jarvis	1
A. J. Wright not out	36
K. M. Curran not out	14
N-b 1	1
1/14 (1 wkt) 52	

P. W. Romaines, M. W. Alleyne, P. Bainbridge, J. W. Lloyds, †R. C. Russell, V. S. Greene, D. V. Lawrence and *D. A. Graveney did not bat.

Bowling: Jarvis 6.3–1–32–1; Kelleher 6–1–20–0.

Umpires: K. E. Palmer and P. B. Wight.

At Lord's, July 25, 27, 28. KENT beat MIDDLESEX by one wicket.

KENT v DERBYSHIRE

At Canterbury, August 1, 3, 4. Drawn. Kent 4 pts, Derbyshire 6 pts. Toss: Kent. A fine opening spell by Jean-Jacques on a slow wicket – three for 37 in 16.1 overs – made Kent struggle, and Beardshall ensured that they continued to do so with a career-best performance. Derbyshire, Roberts excepted, found run-scoring equally difficult. Roberts batted 233 minutes and hit nineteen fours in a superb innings, but Derbyshire's hopes of a big lead went when they lost their last five wickets for 47 runs in 50 minutes. Rain, Benson's seventh fifty of the season and a third-wicket stand of 86 in 31 overs between Hinks and Tavaré ensured Kent's safety.

Close of play: First day, Derbyshire 31-0 (K. J. Barnett 15*, J. G. Wright 15*); Second day, Derbyshire 271-5 (B. Roberts 128*, R. Sharma 8*).

Kent

M. R. Benson b Jean-Jacques	30	– lbw b Malcolm	58
N. R. Taylor c Maher b Jean-Jacques	13	– c Finney b Sharma	15
S. G. Hinks c Roberts b Jean-Jacques	13	– c Barnett b Finney	72
C. J. Tavaré b Beardshall	13	– not out	35
D. G. Aslett lbw b Beardshall	36	– not out	10
*C. S. Cowdrey c Wright b Beardshall	5		
E. A. E. Baptiste c Maher b Malcolm	42		
†S. A. Marsh b Beardshall	3		
R. P. Davis c Maher b Malcolm	10		
D. L. Underwood not out	29		
K. B. S. Jarvis b Malcolm	0		
B 4, l-b 6, w 3, n-b 5	18	L-b 2	2

1/32 2/54 3/61 4/100 5/119   212   1/44 2/83 3/169   (3 wkts) 192
6/122 7/134 8/178 9/179

Bonus points – Kent 2, Derbyshire 4.

Bowling: *First Innings*—Malcolm 19.5–4–47–3; Jean-Jacques 32–10–69–3; Beardshall 38–10–68–4; Sharma 4–1–18–0. *Second Innings*—Malcolm 12–2–36–1; Jean-Jacques 2–0–10–0; Sharma 26–7–61–1; Beardshall 6–1–33–0; Finney 25–11–50–1.

Derbyshire

*K. J. Barnett c Marsh b Davis	51	M. Jean-Jacques c Tavaré b Baptiste	6
J. G. Wright c and b Baptiste	36	M. Beardshall c Benson b Underwood	4
B. Roberts c Tavaré b Jarvis	128	D. E. Malcolm b Baptiste	1
J. E. Morris c Benson b Davis	0		
†B. J. M. Maher lbw b Jarvis	24	L-b 4, w 1, n-b 3	8
R. J. Finney c Underwood b Cowdrey	18		
R. Sharma c Cowdrey b Jarvis	8	1/77 2/111 3/111 4/185 5/243	318
I. S. Anderson not out	34	6/271 7/276 8/297 9/308	

Bonus points – Derbyshire 2, Kent 2 (Score at 100 overs: 243-5).

Bowling: Baptiste 37.5–8–85–3; Jarvis 25–6–50–3; Underwood 30–9–79–1; Davis 34–10–75–2; Cowdrey 8–1–25–1.

Umpires: R. Julian and R. Palmer.

KENT v MIDDLESEX

At Canterbury, August 5, 6, 7. Drawn. Kent 3 pts, Middlesex 6 pts. Toss: Middlesex. Another slow Canterbury wicket and some typically economical bowling by Underwood saw Middlesex in trouble until Downton, hitting nine fours, organised a fightback in a stay of 187 minutes. Kent fared even worse against the pace of Cowans and Fraser and the left-arm spin of Tufnell; and when Middlesex wanted runs to set a target, they came up against Underwood's best return of the season. To win, Kent required 219 in 64 overs, and Benson and Tavaré, with a stand of 60 off seventeen overs, put them in a challenging position. However, when Tavaré was caught, having hit 50 off 78 balls, Middlesex got on top. Five wickets fell for 28 in six overs as Tufnell enjoyed career-best figures, but Jarvis, going in with 22 balls remaining, helped Baptiste stave off defeat.

Close of play: First day, Middlesex 291-9 (A. R. C. Fraser 38*, P. C. R. Tufnell 0*); Second day, Middlesex 9-1 (J. D. Carr 6*).

Middlesex

J. D. Carr c Cowdrey b Davis	58	– (2) c Taylor b Underwood	22
W. N. Slack c Davis b Underwood	20	– (1) b Underwood	3
A. J. T. Miller c Aslett b Underwood	7	– lbw b Underwood	16
K. R. Brown lbw b Jarvis	7	– not out	23
R. O. Butcher c Tavaré b Baptiste	3	– c Davis b Jarvis	6
*†P. R. Downton b Davis	74	– c Marsh b Underwood	2
A. Needham c Cowdrey b Aslett	33	– b Underwood	5
S. P. Hughes b Baptiste	22	– not out	22
A. R. C. Fraser b Baptiste	38		
N. G. Cowans b Baptiste	13		
P. C. R. Tufnell not out	0		
B 2, l-b 10, n-b 4	16	B 1, l-b 3	4

1/45 2/58 3/72 4/84 5/116   291   1/9 2/42 3/43   (6 wkts dec.) 103
6/199 7/223 8/252 9/280   4/54 5/57 6/63

Bonus points – Middlesex 2, Kent 2 (Score at 100 overs: 221-6).

Bowling: *First Innings*—Jarvis 22–4–69–1; Baptiste 26.3–6–63–4; Underwood 30–10–54–2; Davis 21–7–55–2; Cowdrey 10–3–19–0; Aslett 8–2–19–1. *Second Innings*—Baptiste 11–2–25–0; Underwood 19–5–43–5; Jarvis 5–1–13–1; Davis 4–0–18–0.

Kent

M. R. Benson c Butcher b Cowans	0	– c Needham b Tufnell	55
N. R. Taylor run out	16	– c Downton b Fraser	9
S. G. Hinks c Downton b Cowans	25	– c Fraser b Tufnell	18
C. J. Tavaré c and b Tufnell	2	– c Cowans b Tufnell	56
D. G. Aslett lbw b Fraser	47	– c Butcher b Tufnell	0
*C. S. Cowdrey c Butcher b Cowans	35	– c Butcher b Tufnell	6
E. A. E. Baptiste c Downton b Fraser	7	– not out	29
†S. A. Marsh st Downton b Tufnell	11	– b Fraser	2
R. P. Davis c Brown b Tufnell	1	– run out	0
D. L. Underwood b Cowans	21	– c Brown b Tufnell	1
K. B. S. Jarvis not out	1	– not out	0
B 4, l-b 3, n-b 3	10	B 1, l-b 8	9

1/0 2/32 3/44 4/45 5/111   176   1/29 2/62 3/122   (9 wkts) 185
6/123 7/146 8/149 9/154   4/136 5/151 6/151
                                 7/174 8/177 9/179

Bonus points – Kent 1, Middlesex 4 (Score at 100 overs: 169-9).

Bowling: *First Innings*—Cowans 25.5–10–42–4; Hughes 11–2–25–0; Tufnell 37–13–68–3; Fraser 23–11–16–2; Needham 7–2–18–0. *Second Innings*—Cowans 8–0–25–0; Hughes 5–1–7–0; Fraser 15–5–41–2; Needham 13–3–43–0; Tufnell 23–4–60–6.

Umpires: R. Julian and R. Palmer.

At Cheltenham, August 8, 10, 11. KENT drew with GLOUCESTERSHIRE.

At The Oval, August 15, 17, 18. KENT drew with SURREY.

At Bournemouth, August 19, 20, 21. KENT lost to HAMPSHIRE by 75 runs.

KENT v LANCASHIRE

At Maidstone, August 26, 27, 28. Lancashire won by six wickets. Lancashire 21 pts, Kent 3 pts. Toss: Lancashire. A marvellous hundred from 126 balls by Fowler crowned a convincing performance by Lancashire. Allott's superb fast bowling had begun it, helping reduce Kent to 48 for five in the 23rd over. It needed Baptiste's 95 out of 122 in 149 minutes to save the home side from complete humiliation, but they fought back through the medium pace of Penn, who had a spell of four for 28 in eleven overs in his career-best return. It was the spin of Folley and Simmons that undermined Kent's second innings, their last seven wickets falling for 25 runs in 56 minutes. With Fairbrother nursing an ankle injury, Lancashire needed a sound start and Fowler, hitting fourteen fours and two sixes, did not let them down. Victory was achieved with eight balls to spare.

Close of play: First day, Kent 172-9 (D. J. M. Kelleher 14*, R. P. Davis 2*); Second day, Kent 25-0 (N. R. Taylor 8*, T. R. Ward 13*).

Kent

N. R. Taylor lbw b Allott	3	– c sub b Patterson	20
T. R. Ward c Allott b Patterson	6	– not out	13
S. G. Hinks lbw b Allott	11	– c Watkinson b Folley	29
C. J. Tavaré c Hegg b Allott	1	– c Fowler b Simmons	35
D. G. Aslett c Fowler b Allott	14	– st Hegg b Folley	23
*C. S. Cowdrey c Fowler b Simmons	7	– c Hegg b Folley	19
E. A. E. Baptiste lbw b Allott	95	– b Simmons	2
†S. A. Marsh b Watkinson b Allott	1	– c Hegg b Simmons	7
C. Penn c Allott b Patterson	4	– b Folley	10
D. J. M. Kelleher c Hegg b Allott	17	– lbw b Folley	1
R. P. Davis not out	10	– c Hughes b Simmons	0
B 6, l-b 3, n-b 5	14	L-b 1, n-b 6	7
	183		166

1/14 2/14 3/21 4/26 5/48 6/68 7/76 8/93 9/170

1/50 2/95 3/127 4/141 5/146 6/148 7/165 8/165 9/166

Bonus points – Kent 1, Lancashire 4.

In the second innings T. R. Ward, when 13, retired hurt at 25 and resumed at 166.

Bowling: *First Innings*—Patterson 15-2-51-2; Allott 26.5-8-42-7; Watkinson 15-4-42-0; Simmons 9-0-31-1; Folley 6-2-8-0. *Second Innings*—Patterson 10-0-44-1; Allott 9-4-19-0; Watkinson 8-4-25-0; Folley 22-8-54-5; Simmons 14.5-6-23-4.

Lancashire

G. D. Mendis c Cowdrey b Penn	38	– c Taylor b Penn	30
G. Fowler c Aslett b Penn	35	– c Kelleher b Baptiste	100
M. A. Atherton not out	37	– lbw b Cowdrey	37
M. Watkinson b Penn	2	– b Baptiste	1
†W. K. Hegg c Marsh b Penn	4		
P. J. W. Allott b Davis	5	– (6) not out	11
I. Folley c Davis b Penn	14		
*D. P. Hughes not out	9	– (5) not out	13
L-b 4, n-b 2	6	B 5, l-b 6, n-b 1	12
	(6 wkts dec.) 150		(4 wkts) 204

1/62 2/95 3/97 4/101 5/106 6/127

1/77 2/168 3/171 4/187

N. H. Fairbrother, J. Simmons and B. P. Patterson did not bat.

Bonus points – Lancashire 1, Kent 2.

Bowling: *First Innings*—Baptiste 10.5-2-38-0; Kelleher 8-2-17-0; Cowdrey 11-5-21-0; Penn 20-4-52-5; Davis 11-2-18-1. *Second Innings*—Baptiste 15.4-3-56-2; Kelleher 4-0-19-0; Davis 16-0-67-0; Penn 9-1-29-1; Cowdrey 4-0-22-1.

Umpires: K. J. Lyons and N. T. Plews.

KENT v HAMPSHIRE

At Maidstone, August 29, 31, September 1. Hampshire won by seven wickets. Hampshire 21 pts, Kent 5 pts. Toss: Kent. A spell of four for 1 in twenty balls by Tremlett accounted for half the Kent side being dismissed for 83 in the 33rd over. Taylor, missed early on, batted resolutely despite a blow on the hand from Marshall. Hampshire, after a recovery from Terry and Turner, lost their last five wickets for 4 runs in seven overs, but Tremlett bowled them back into the game with a spell of three for 1 in nine balls. Tavaré and Baptiste pulled Kent round until an explosive spell by Marshall (four for 19 in thirteen overs) left Hampshire requiring 221 in a minimum of 66 overs. Robin Smith set them on the way with 47 (two sixes, six fours) off 67 balls, and although they faltered slightly, Terry and Nicholas won the game with an unbroken stand of 133 off 33 overs.

Close of play: First day, Hampshire 36-2 (V. P. Terry 18*, D. R. Turner 0*); Second day, Kent 130-4 (C. J. Tavaré 49*, E. A. E. Baptiste 26*).

Kent

M. R. Benson c Maru b Tremlett	25	– b Tremlett	13
N. R. Taylor c Turner b Cowley	85	– (11) c Connor b Maru	1
S. G. Hinks lbw b Tremlett	0	– (2) lbw b Tremlett	25
C. J. Tavaré lbw b Tremlett	0	– (3) c C. L. Smith b Marshall	54
D. G. Aslett c R. A. Smith b Tremlett	0	– (4) lbw b Tremlett	0
*C. S. Cowdrey c Maru b Connor	19	– (5) c C. L. Smith b Tremlett	0
E. A. E. Baptiste b Tremlett	23	– (6) c Terry b Marshall	31
†S. A. Marsh lbw b Marshall	4	– (7) c R. A. Smith b Marshall	8
C. Penn c R. A. Smith b Marshall	0	– (8) lbw b Marshall	19
D. J. M. Kelleher not out	2	– (9) c Cowley b Maru	5
D. L. Underwood b Marshall	15	– (10) not out	1
L-b 9, l-b 2, w 1, n-b 4	16	B 4, l-b 4, w 1, n-b 24	33
	189		**190**

1/36 2/36 3/42 4/42 5/83   **189**   1/45 2/54 3/54 4/58 5/136   **190**
6/149 7/164 8/164 9/172   6/158 7/159 8/187 9/189

Bonus points – Kent 1, Hampshire 4.

Bowling: *First Innings*—Marshall 19.1-6-50-3; Connor 10-2-33-1; Maru 18-8-42-0; Tremlett 15-5-28-5; Cowley 7-2-25-1. *Second Innings*—Marshall 28-3-58-4; Connor 15-3-35-0; Tremlett 23-6-52-4; Cowley 11-6-13-0; Maru 11.1-4-24-2.

Hampshire

V. P. Terry st Marsh b Underwood	74	– not out	83
C. L. Smith c Benson b Kelleher	14	– (3) lbw b Underwood	1
*M. C. J. Nicholas c Marsh b Baptiste	0	– (5) not out	65
D. R. Turner c Marsh b Penn	36	– c Baptiste b Penn	18
R. A. Smith c Hinks b Underwood	1	– (2) lbw b Penn	47
M. D. Marshall c Marsh b Penn	5		
N. G. Cowley c Tavaré b Kelleher	14		
†R. J. Parks lbw b Kelleher	0		
T. M. Tremlett c Hinks b Underwood	0		
R. J. Maru b Kelleher	0		
C. A. Connor not out	0		
L-b 10, n-b 5	15	B 1, l-b 3, n-b 6	10
	159	(3 wkts)	**224**

1/28 2/33 3/111 4/120 5/133   **159**   1/65 2/67 3/91   (3 wkts) **224**
6/155 7/156 8/159 9/159

Bonus points – Hampshire 1, Kent 4.

Bowling: *First Innings*—Penn 15-2-45-2; Baptiste 17-5-37-1; Kelleher 16.2-4-35-4; Cowdrey 5-2-18-0; Underwood 18-12-14-3. *Second Innings*—Baptiste 16-5-64-0; Kelleher 5-0-32-0; Underwood 22-1-59-1; Penn 14-3-44-2; Cowdrey 5-0-21-0.

Umpires: K. J. Lyons and N. T. Plews.

At Birmingham, September 2, 3, 4. KENT lost to WARWICKSHIRE by 133 runs.

KENT v LEICESTERSHIRE

At Canterbury, September 12, 14, 15. Drawn. Kent 6 pts, Leicestershire 7 pts. Toss: Leicestershire. Briers and Willey shared in a stand of 163 for the second wicket on a rain-affected first day. On the Monday, Underwood, in his farewell game, took three wickets for 13 in nine overs before Potter steered his side to their fourth batting point. Kent declared behind to open up the game, Agnew having captured his 100th wicket of the season when he dismissed Benson, who passed 50 for the fifteenth time. Next day, after Kelleher had a spell of three for 19 in nineteen balls, Briers and Gower added 72 off 24 overs. Briers batted in all for 196 minutes and hit eight fours. Kent, with a minimum of 40 overs in which to score 250, never really got into their stride.

Close of play: First day, Leicestershire 222-2 (N. E. Briers 81*, D. I. Gower 11*); Second day, Leicestershire 10-0 (T. J. Boon 9*, N. E. Briers 0*).

Leicestershire

T. J. Boon b Cowdrey	19	– c Farbrace b Kelleher	35
N. E. Briers b Baptiste	82	– not out	82
*P. Willey c Hinks b Underwood	83	– (6) not out	16
D. I. Gower c Cowdrey b Underwood	21	– (5) c Tavaré b Goldsmith	41
J. J. Whitaker c Farbrace b Underwood	5	– (3) c Goldsmith b Kelleher	16
L. Potter not out	34	– (4) c Farbrace b Kelleher	0
†P. Whitticase b Underwood	2		
W. K. M. Benjamin lbw b Baptiste	9		
J. P. Agnew not out	15		
B 13, l-b 9, w 1, n-b 10	33	L-b 5, n-b 1	6

1/40 2/203 3/234 4/235 (7 wkts dec.) 303   1/65 2/87 3/92 (4 wkts dec.) 196
5/241 6/247 7/262   4/164

P. M. Such and L. B. Taylor did not bat.

Bonus points – Leicestershire 4, Kent 3.

Bowling: *First Innings*—Baptiste 31.4–10–69–2; Kelleher 7–1–28–0; Cowdrey 14–3–40–1; Penn 12–2–53–0; Underwood 32–8–89–4; Aslett 2–0–2–0. *Second Innings*—Baptiste 14–4–37–0; Underwood 27–6–40–0; Kelleher 12–0–62–3; Aslett 2–0–5–0; Cowdrey 1–0–6–0; Goldsmith 6–0–37–1; Benson 1–0–4–0.

Kent

M. R. Benson c Benjamin b Agnew	55	– c Whitticase b Agnew	16
S. G. Hinks b Such	41	– run out	43
S. C. Goldsmith b Such	4	– c Whitaker b Such	25
D. G. Aslett b Willey	38	– (5) not out	16
*C. S. Cowdrey not out	56	– (6) not out	8
E. A. E. Baptiste c Whitaker b Willey	10		
†P. Farbrace c Whitticase b Benjamin	5		
D. J. M. Kelleher lbw b Benjamin	12		
C. J. Tavaré not out	22	– (4) b Benjamin	19
L-b 3, n-b 4	7	L-b 3, w 1, n-b 3	7

1/72 2/76 3/142 4/154 (7 wkts dec.) 250   1/44 2/83 3/107 (4 wkts) 134
5/188 6/207 7/223   4/120

C. Penn and D. L. Underwood did not bat.

Bonus points – Kent 3, Leicestershire 3.

Bowling: *First Innings*—Agnew 21–2–64–1; Taylor 9–3–37–0; Such 21.5–6–66–2; Benjamin 16–7–44–2; Willey 8–1–36–2. *Second Innings*—Agnew 7–0–35–1; Benjamin 10–2–24–1; Such 13–4–39–1; Taylor 6–0–25–0; Potter 1–0–8–0.

Umpires: J. H. Hampshire and M. J. Kitchen.

LANCASHIRE

Patron: HM The Queen
President: B. J. Howard
Chairman: R. Bennett
Secretary: C. D. Hassell
County Cricket Ground, Old Trafford,
Manchester M16 0PX
(Telephone: 061-848 7021)
Captain: D. P. Hughes
Coach: J. A. Ormrod

Lancashire had a marvellous season, one that will be remembered for many years despite their not winning anything. For the first time in twelve years they did not finish in the bottom six of the County Championship, rising from fifteenth place in 1986 to the giddy heights of second, only four points behind the winners and their best position since 1960. Their transformation was remarkable, particularly after much of the close season had been a shambles. The first-team coach, Peter Lever, manager Jack Bond, and the captain, Clive Lloyd, had all been relieved of their positions soon after the 1986 NatWest Bank Trophy final. Lloyd later decided to retire, and at the beginning of February Cedric Rhoades, chairman since 1969, was forced to resign by intense pressure from an action group who were intending to call a special meeting of members. This might well have overthrown the committee.

Lancashire, therefore, approached the season with a new captain, David Hughes, a new coach/manager, Alan Ormrod, and a new chairman in Bob Bennett, a former player who accepted the invitation to return to the committee he had left two years earlier. All three can take a huge amount of credit for a season which restored interest, pride and enthusiasm in a great club which had been in decline for too long. Hughes's contribution in runs and wickets – he averaged 15.07 batting and bowled 22 overs in 24 Britannic Assurance Championship matches – was hardly noticed as he led the team with care, vigour, imagination and a positive approach at all times.

The Championship season fell into three distinct parts. By the end of May Lancashire had won three of their first five matches and were top of the table. They won only one of the next thirteen and entered the last six games in the middle of August 62 points behind Nottinghamshire, the leaders, having played the same number of games. They won those six matches, collected 125 points, and kept Nottinghamshire waiting until the penultimate day of the season before they could claim the Championship. Lancashire were left to rue two matches at Old Trafford in June when Yorkshire's last pair held out for 17.5 overs to secure a draw, and when they lost to Derbyshire by 3 runs after needing 5 to win with three wickets standing.

Lancashire's performances in limited-overs games were not so good. They were affected by an unusually high number of injuries at the start of the season, particularly among their seam bowlers, and failed to qualify for the quarter-finals of the Benson and Hedges Cup. They lost to

Gloucestershire in the first round of the NatWest Bank Trophy, but won three of their last five Refuge Assurance Sunday League matches to finish ninth, three places higher than in 1986.

Ian Folley and Mike Watkinson came of age in the summer, and they and the West Indian Test fast bowler, Patrick Patterson, were capped in the closing stages of the season. Folley played in 24 of the 25 first-class matches, bowled 711.3 overs, and took 70 wickets, twelve of them in the ten-wicket win over Warwickshire at Southport. Watkinson did not get into the Championship team until the beginning of June but soon established his position; in the remaining nineteen games he scored 776 runs and took 42 wickets. Graeme Fowler also had his best season in ten years with Lancashire, his total of 1,800 runs in first-class matches being the highest by any batsman for the county for 22 years. Only Worcestershire's Graeme Hick scored more, yet Fowler was not chosen for any England team or for a winter tour.

Gehan Mendis, Neil Fairbrother and Michael Atherton, who was in his début season, also scored more than 1,000 runs in the season. Atherton, who was nineteen, spent the first half of the summer with Cambridge University and the second half with Lancashire, where he soon established himself at No. 3, scoring 602 runs for an average of over 35 and playing several significant innings in the challenge for the Championship. Another important run-scorer was Paul Allott who, in addition to taking 56 Championship wickets and heading the bowling averages, scored 612 runs in a fine all-round season. John Abrahams, who has been awarded a benefit in 1988, was dropped after the first five games but returned at the end of the season, when Fairbrother was injured, to play several crucial innings, notably in the victory over Surrey when he scored 140 not out and 92.

Lancashire's successful season was also reflected in four bowlers – Patterson, Simmons, Folley and Allott – topping 50 wickets. Simmons's batting deteriorated, but at the age of 46 he bowled 640 overs in the first-class game and was as economical and cunning as ever. He was also responsible for an uncharacteristic outburst after the first Yorkshire match when he publicly accused Stuart Fletcher of cheating. He was suspended by the club for a week and reprimanded by the TCCB. Injuries to Chris Maynard, who was unable to play all season, and John Stanworth enabled nineteen-year-old Warren Hegg, Young England's wicket-keeper in Sri Lanka, to have a long run in the first team. He impressed not only with his enthusiastic wicket-keeping but with his batting, which produced a maiden century at Northampton.

Lancashire released several players, all with first-team experience, at the end of the season, the only capped player being Steve O'Shaughnessy. He had another disappointing season and had been unable to ally undoubted talent with temperament. The others to leave were Kevin Hayes, the former Oxford University captain, Søren Henriksen, Ian Davidson, Mark Chadwick and David Varey. – Brian Bearshaw.

458

LANCASHIRE 1987

[Bob Thomas

Back row: I. D. Austin, G. D. Lloyd, J. D. Fitton, N. J. Speak, A. N. Hayhurst, A. J. Murphy, W. K. Hegg, K. A. Hayes. *Middle row*: I. C. Davidson, I. Folley, M. R. Chadwick, M. Watkinson, S. P. Titchard, D. W. Varey, S. Henriksen, J. Stanworth, C. Maynard. *Front row*: J. A. Ormrod (*coach*), G. D. Mendis, P. J. W. Allott, J. Simmons, D. P. Hughes (*captain*), G. Fowler, J. Abrahams, N. H. Fairbrother, S. J. O'Shaughnessy. *Insets*: M. A. Atherton, B. P. Patterson.

LANCASHIRE RESULTS

All first-class matches – Played 25: Won 10, Lost 4, Drawn 11.

County Championship matches – Played 24: Won 10, Lost 4, Drawn 10.

Bonus points – Batting 55, Bowling 73.

Competition placings – Britannic Assurance County Championship, 2nd; NatWest Bank Trophy, 1st round; Benson and Hedges Cup, 4th in Group B; Refuge Assurance League, 9th.

BRITANNIC ASSURANCE CHAMPIONSHIP AVERAGES

BATTING

	Birthplace	M	I	NO	R	HI	Avge
‡G. Fowler	Accrington	23	41	5	1,689	169*	46.91
‡N. H. Fairbrother . . .	Warrington	19	27	5	963	109*	43.77
‡G. D. Mendis	Colombo, Ceylon	23	40	6	1,384	203*	40.70
‡J. Abrahams	Cape Town, SA	8	14	1	515	140*	39.61
M. A. Atherton	Manchester	11	19	2	602	76*	35.41
‡M. Watkinson	Westhoughton	19	27	4	776	91	33.73
‡P. J. W. Allott	Altrincham	21	26	4	612	88	27.81
D. W. Varey	Darlington	7	10	1	220	59	24.44
‡S. J. O'Shaughnessy . .	Bury	8	14	3	243	61*	22.09
W. K. Hegg	Whitefield	13	20	4	350	130	21.87
§K. W. McLeod	St Elizabeth, Jamaica	6	6	0	92	31	15.33
‡D. P. Hughes	Newton-le-Willows	24	34	6	422	43*	15.07
‡I. Folley	Burnley	23	29	6	341	38	14.82
A. N. Hayhurst	Manchester	4	4	1	37	30*	12.33
‡J. Simmons	Clayton-le-Moors	21	23	5	188	43*	10.44
§‡B. P. Patterson	Portland, Jamaica	17	16	8	65	29	8.12
J. Stanworth	Oldham	11	9	3	39	14*	6.50

Also batted: I. D. Austin (*Haslingden*) (2 matches) 37; M. R. Chadwick (*Rochdale*) (2 matches) 11, 4, 38; J. D. Fitton (*Littleborough*) (1 match) 3; A. J. Murphy (*Manchester*) (1 match) 5.

* Signifies not out.   ‡ Denotes county cap.   § Not qualified for England.

The following played a total of eleven three-figure innings for Lancashire in County Championship matches – N. H. Fairbrother 3, G. Fowler 3, G. D. Mendis 3, J. Abrahams 1, W. K. Hegg 1.

BOWLING

	O	M	R	W	BB	Avge
P. J. W. Allott	504.3	151	1,188	56	7-42	21.21
J. Simmons	613.3	178	1,397	63	6-20	22.17
M. Watkinson	318	66	986	42	7-25	23.47
K. W. McLeod	126.4	24	409	17	5-8	24.05
I. Folley	678.3	212	1,668	68	7-15	24.52
B. P. Patterson	419.1	61	1,359	52	6-40	26.13

Also bowled: J. Abrahams 23–6–65–2; M. A. Atherton 51–6–187–4; I. D. Austin 33.5–7–64–3; N. H. Fairbrother 22–2–111–2; J. D. Fitton 7–0–23–1; G. Fowler 13.3–3–43–3; A. N. Hayhurst 92.4–20–299–8; D. P. Hughes 24–4–87–2; G. D. Mendis 10–1–33–0; A. J. Murphy 36–5–133–4; S. J. O'Shaughnessy 96–18–289–4.

Wicket-keepers: W. K. Hegg 24 ct, 11 st; J. Stanworth 19 ct, 3 st.

Leading Fielders: P. J. W. Allott 22, D. P. Hughes 20, I. Folley 18, N. H. Fairbrother 17, M. Watkinson 17, J. Simmons 16.

At Cambridge, April 22, 23, 24. LANCASHIRE drew with CAMBRIDGE UNIVERSITY.

At Taunton, April 25, 26, 27. LANCASHIRE beat SOMERSET by six wickets.

LANCASHIRE v MIDDLESEX

At Manchester, April 29, 30, May 1. Drawn. Lancashire 7 pts, Middlesex 3 pts. Toss: Middlesex. Gatting's decision to field first backfired as three of the first four Lancashire wickets produced century partnerships and Mendis, with 24 fours in seven and threequarter hours, scored the first-ever double-hundred for Lancashire against Middlesex. The previous highest had been Washbrook's 182 at Old Trafford in 1946. Lancashire batted for another 75 minutes on the second day and then bowled out Middlesex by the close. Middlesex followed on 209 behind the following morning, but Slack batted for 4 hours 40 minutes to ensure a draw on a placid pitch. McLeod, a Jamaican left-arm medium-pace bowler, made his début for Lancashire.

Close of play: First day, Lancashire 379-3 (G. D. Mendis 162*, S. J. O'Shaughnessy 42*); Second day, Middlesex 244.

Lancashire

G. D. Mendis not out	203	I. Folley b Daniel		8
G. Fowler c and b Emburey	68	K. W. McLeod run out		3
J. Abrahams c Downton b Edmonds	0	†J. Stanworth not out		0
N. H. Fairbrother c Fraser b Edmonds	89	B 4, l-b 14, n-b 8		26
S. J. O'Shaughnessy b Daniel	47			
*D. P. Hughes c Downton b Daniel	2	1/127 2/128 3/290	(9 wkts dec.)	453
A. N. Hayhurst c Gatting b Daniel	5	4/395 5/399 6/407		
J. Simmons c Slack b Fraser	2	7/414 8/437 9/449		

Bonus points – Lancashire 3, Middlesex 1 (Score at 100 overs: 298-3).

Bowling: Daniel 22.2-4-69-4; Hughes 14-1-58-0; Fraser 27-4-106-1; Edmonds 34-9-85-2; Emburey 32-9-80-1; Gatting 7-0-32-0; Roseberry 1-0-4-0; Carr 1-0-1-0.

Middlesex

W. N. Slack run out	26	– b Hayhurst	116
A. J. T. Miller c Mendis b McLeod	97	– c Simmons b Folley	29
*M. W. Gatting c Stanworth b Hayhurst	7	– c Hughes b Folley	43
J. D. Carr c Stanworth b Hayhurst	0	– b Folley	24
M. A. Roseberry c Folley b Simmons	28	– not out	23
†P. R. Downton c Simmons b Folley	21	– run out	9
J. E. Emburey not out	45	– not out	18
P. H. Edmonds c O'Shaughnessy b McLeod	5		
S. P. Hughes b McLeod	0		
W. W. Daniel c Stanworth b Hayhurst	0		
A. R. C. Fraser c Fairbrother b Hayhurst	2		
L-b 3, w 2, n-b 8	13	B 1, n-b 2	3

1/68 2/79 3/83 4/146 5/190	244	1/79 2/156 3/196	(5 wkts) 265
6/192 7/202 8/212 9/242		4/220 5/245	

Bonus points – Middlesex 2, Lancashire 4.

Bowling: *First Innings*—McLeod 19–3–67–3; Hayhurst 14.4–6–27–4; O'Shaughnessy 12–2–31–0; Simmons 20–7–44–1; Folley 19–1–72–1. *Second Innings*—McLeod 13–3–33–0; Hayhurst 19–5–40–1; O'Shaughnessy 12–0–45–0; Simmons 19–9–45–0; Folley 25–5–78–3; Abrahams 5–1–11–0; Hughes 5–3–12–0.

Umpires: J. W. Holder and B. Leadbeater.

At Swansea, May 6, 7, 8. LANCASHIRE lost to GLAMORGAN by an innings and 132 runs.

At Leicester, May 20, 21, 22. LANCASHIRE beat LEICESTERSHIRE by an innings and 116 runs.

LANCASHIRE v WORCESTERSHIRE

At Manchester, May 23, 25, 26. Lancashire won by 117 runs. Lancashire 23 pts, Worcestershire 5 pts. Toss: Lancashire. Simmons's best match return of his career, twelve wickets for 123 runs, enabled Lancashire to strengthen their place at the head of the Championship table. Winning the toss was important, but Lancashire still needed an eighth-wicket century partnership between Allott and Folley to help them pass 300. Worcestershire's last-wicket pair averted the follow-on, and when Lancashire batted again Mendis and Fowler, their openers, had to retire hurt after being hit on the head by balls from Radford. They came together again to share an unbroken eighth-wicket partnership of 84, which enabled Lancashire to declare and leave Worcestershire two sessions in which to score 278 for victory. Once Weston and D'Oliveira were separated, Simmons ran through the opposition on a pitch taking spin quite sharply.

Close of play: First day, Lancashire 290-9 (J. Stanworth 8*, K. W. McLeod 3*); Second day, Lancashire 42-2 (G. D. Mendis 19*, S. J. O'Shaughnessy 11*).

Lancashire

G. D. Mendis lbw b Pridgeon	12	– not out	52
G. Fowler c Rhodes b Weston	28	– not out	45
J. Abrahams b Radford	29	– lbw b Radford	1
N. H. Fairbrother c D'Oliveira b Weston	38	– b Radford	2
S. J. O'Shaughnessy c Rhodes b Radford	0	– lbw b Hick	14
*D. P. Hughes b Newport	36	– b Hick	10
J. Simmons c Neale b Illingworth	4	– b Hick	4
P. J. W. Allott c Rhodes b Illingworth	74	– c Pridgeon b Illingworth	3
I. Folley lbw b Illingworth	33	– c Weston b Hick	2
†J. Stanworth not out	14		
K. W. McLeod c Lampitt b Illingworth	31		
B 1, l-b 16, n-b 9	26	B 8, l-b 2, n-b 9	19

1/13 2/65 3/99 4/99 5/137   325   1/11 2/14 3/58   (7 wkts dec.) 152
6/145 7/160 8/265 9/287   4/62 5/65
                                       6/67 7/68

Bonus points – Lancashire 3, Worcestershire 3 (Score at 100 overs: 251-7).

Bowling: *First Innings*—Radford 24–7–46–2; Pridgeon 21–6–40–1; Weston 19–4–37–2; Newport 19–5–59–1; Illingworth 30.1–2–87–4; Lampitt 1–0–7–0; D'Oliveira 8–1–30–0; Hick 2–0–2–0. *Second Innings*—Radford 12–1–43–2; Pridgeon 7–2–11–0; Illingworth 20–5–57–1; Hick 15–5–31–4.

Worcestershire

T. S. Curtis lbw b Allott	5	– c Abrahams b Allott	7
M. J. Weston c Fairbrother b Simmons	54	– lbw b Allott	51
G. A. Hick c Stanworth b Allott	0	– st Stanworth b Folley	11
D. B. D'Oliveira c O'Shaughnessy b Folley	14	– b Simmons	42
*P. A. Neale c Fairbrother b Simmons	33	– c Fairbrother b Simmons	0
†S. J. Rhodes c O'Shaughnessy b Simmons	1	– b Simmons	1
S. R. Lampitt c Allott b Folley	5	– (8) c sub b Folley	1
P. J. Newport not out	58	– (7) not out	25
N. V. Radford c Fairbrother b Simmons	7	– c Folley b Simmons	19
R. K. Illingworth c Fairbrother b Simmons	0	– lbw b Simmons	1
A. P. Pridgeon c Allott b Simmons	17	– c Stanworth b Simmons	0
B 2, l-b 3, n-b 1	6	B 1, l-b 1	2

1/7 2/7 3/34 4/102 5/106   200   1/40 2/51 3/104 4/104 5/108   160
6/117 7/119 8/138 9/146   6/125 7/128 8/151 9/152

Bonus points – Worcestershire 2, Lancashire 4.

Bowling: *First Innings*—Allott 13–2–27–2; McLeod 9–1–34–0; Folley 27–8–72–2; Simmons 32.4–11–62–6. *Second Innings*—Allott 14–6–22–2; McLeod 2–0–16–0; Simmons 22.4–8–61–6; Folley 22–7–59–2.

Umpires: J. A. Jameson and R. A. White.

At Bristol, June 3, 4, 5. LANCASHIRE drew with GLOUCESTERSHIRE.

At Nottingham, June 6, 8, 9. LANCASHIRE drew with NOTTINGHAMSHIRE.

LANCASHIRE v YORKSHIRE

At Manchester, June 13, 14, 15. Drawn. Lancashire 4 pts, Yorkshire 1 pt. Toss: Lancashire. A superb batting wicket had produced 677 runs for the loss of four wickets by the time the third declaration set up an exciting finish to a rain-affected game. Both teams had opening century partnerships in the first innings – Mendis batted 312 minutes and hit sixteen fours – and after the second day had been shortened by 150 minutes, Yorkshire declared 223 behind on the third morning. Lancashire batted for twenty overs before setting Yorkshire a target of 320 in 79 overs, generous enough in view of the easy-paced pitch, but after Patterson had taken out the heart of the innings with three wickets – all lbw – in fourteen balls, only Blakey stood between Lancashire and victory. Blakey, who batted all but the opening over, hit fourteen fours, and the last man, Fletcher, stayed with him for 17.5 overs to make it the eleventh successive Roses draw. Lancashire claimed that Fletcher had given a bat-pad catch off Simmons's bowling, an appeal turned down by umpire Evans, and Simmons later accused Fletcher of cheating. His public outburst led to a week's suspension imposed by the Lancashire committee.

Close of play: First day, Yorkshire 21–0 (M. D. Moxon 10*, A. A. Metcalfe 7*); Second day, Yorkshire 179–1 (M. D. Moxon 88*, R. J. Blakey 4*).

Lancashire

G. D. Mendis b Jarvis	155	– not out	42
G. Fowler c Sidebottom b Carrick	77	– not out	51
D. W. Varey c Bairstow b Jarvis	59		
N. H. Fairbrother not out	47		
*D. P. Hughes not out	43		
B 5, l-b 14, w 2	21	L-b 3	3

1/153 2/289 3/318   (3 wkts dec.) 402   (no wkt dec.) 96

M. Watkinson, I. Folley, J. Simmons, P. J. W. Allott, †J. Stanworth and B. P. Patterson did not bat.

Bonus points – Lancashire 4 (Score at 100 overs: 310-2).

Bowling: *First Innings*—Jarvis 20–4–73–2; Sidebottom 17–4–63–0; Hartley 18–1–68–0; Fletcher 16–1–75–0; Carrick 36–10–80–1; Love 6–1–24–0. *Second Innings*—Jarvis 5–2–11–0; Sidebottom 5–0–29–0; Hartley 5–1–13–0; Fletcher 5–0–40–0.

Yorkshire

M. D. Moxon not out	88	– c Watkinson b Allott	36
A. A. Metcalfe st Stanworth b Folley	78	– c Fairbrother b Allott	0
R. J. Blakey not out	4	– not out	124
K. Sharp (did not bat)		– c and b Simmons	11
J. D. Love (did not bat)		– lbw b Patterson	7
†D. L. Bairstow (did not bat)		– lbw b Patterson	3
*P. Carrick (did not bat)		– lbw b Patterson	0
A. Sidebottom (did not bat)		– lbw b Simmons	6
P. J. Hartley (did not bat)		– c Simmons b Watkinson	2
P. W. Jarvis (did not bat)		– c Fairbrother b Simmons	1
S. D. Fletcher (did not bat)		– not out	9
L-b 1, n-b 8	9	B 1, l-b 16, w 1, n-b 6	24

1/165   (1 wkt dec.) 179   1/4 2/84 3/114 4/138   (9 wkts) 223
                                        5/147 6/147 7/165
                                        8/176 9/185

Bonus point – Yorkshire 1.

Bowling: *First Innings*—Patterson 12–1–43–0; Allott 13–3–40–0; Simmons 13–1–42–0; Watkinson 5–0–13–0; Folley 18–6–40–1. *Second Innings*—Patterson 16–2–50–3; Allott 16–3–28–2; Folley 14–4–45–0; Simmons 25–8–40–3; Watkinson 8–0–43–1.

Umpires: D. G. L. Evans and K. E. Palmer.

At Derby, June 17, 18, 19. LANCASHIRE drew with DERBYSHIRE.

LANCASHIRE v KENT

At Liverpool, June 20, 22, 23. Drawn. Lancashire 8 pts. Toss: Kent. By the end of the opening day Lancashire were in the strongest of positions with an unbroken opening partnership of 116 after bowling out Kent for 130. But 78 overs were lost on the second day, 36 on the third, and Lancashire were unable to press for their first victory over Kent in fourteen years. Kent looked to be establishing their innings with an opening stand of 82 on the first morning, but four wickets in nine balls by Patterson after lunch wrecked it. Mendis and Fowler shared their fourth opening century partnership of the season and Fowler went on to his first century, a magnificent innings spread over three days and including sixteen fours and six sixes. Varey was totally overshadowed by him in their stand of 163 and on the final morning scored only three singles out of 56 added. Kent, needing 170 to avoid an innings defeat, showed more determination in the second innings.

Close of play: First day, Lancashire 116-0 (G. D. Mendis 63*, G. Fowler 49*); Second day, Lancashire 244-1 (G. Fowler 122*, D. W. Varey 34*).

Kent

M. R. Benson c and b Folley	26	– c Fairbrother b Patterson	0
N. R. Taylor b Austin	49	– c Stanworth b Watkinson	19
D. G. Aslett st Stanworth b Folley	27	– not out	74
C. J. Tavaré b Patterson	2	– c and b Hayhurst	40
*C. S. Cowdrey lbw b Patterson	0	– not out	4
R. F. Pienaar b Patterson	0		
†S. A. Marsh b Patterson	0		
D. J. M. Kelleher lbw b Folley	3		
R. P. Davis not out	1		
A. P. Igglesden lbw b Austin	3		
D. L. Underwood b Austin	3		
B 4, l-b 9, n-b 3	16	B 1, l-b 4, w 1, n-b 4	10

1/82 2/84 3/93 4/97 5/97   130   1/0 2/50 3/136   (3 wkts) 147
6/97 7/118 8/121 9/124

Bonus points – Lancashire 4.

Bowling: *First Innings*—Patterson 15-5-19-4; Watkinson 11-4-26-0; Hayhurst 5-0-24-0; Folley 19-9-20-3; Austin 15.5-4-28-3. *Second Innings*—Patterson 11-2-38-1; Watkinson 12-2-32-1; Folley 9-3-19-0; Austin 5-0-19-0; Hayhurst 5-0-22-1; Fairbrother 2-0-12-0.

Lancashire

G. D. Mendis c Tavaré b Kelleher	77
G. Fowler not out	169
D. W. Varey not out	37
B 2, l-b 14, w 1	17

1/137   (1 wkt dec.) 300

N. H. Fairbrother, *D. P. Hughes, M. Watkinson, I. D. Austin, A. N. Hayhurst, I. Folley, B. P. Patterson and †J. Stanworth did not bat.

Bonus points – Lancashire 4.

Bowling: Igglesden 22-4-93-0; Pienaar 8-1-27-0; Kelleher 19-4-59-1; Underwood 22-5-54-0; Davis 18-3-51-0.

Umpires: J. Birkenshaw and B. Leadbeater.

LANCASHIRE v DERBYSHIRE

At Manchester, June 27, 29, 30. Derbyshire won by 3 runs. Derbyshire 18 pts, Lancashire 4 pts. Toss: Derbyshire. Only 33.2 overs were possible on the opening day and by the end of the second Lancashire were 174 behind with eight wickets standing. They declared at the start of the third day, Derbyshire declared at lunch, and Lancashire had 73 overs in which to score 276 to win. After a faltering start they were rallied by a fifth-wicket stand of 154 in 37 overs by Fairbrother and Watkinson and looked to be on course for victory when Barnett came on with his leg-breaks and dismissed them both. Lancashire went into the last over wanting 4 runs with two wickets standing, but Allott's spirited innings ended when he was stumped off Barnett's third ball. Patterson, failing to beat Barnett's throw, was run out off the next. Folley's five-wicket return in the first innings was his third in Championship cricket. Stanworth badly bruised his hand when a door shut on it on the morning of the second day, so Fowler kept wicket for the remainder of the first innings and Hughes took over in the second.

Close of play: First day, Derbyshire 107-3 (J. E. Morris 20*, B. J. M. Maher 0*); Second day, Lancashire 52-2 (S. J. O'Shaughnessy 30*, N. H. Fairbrother 14*).

Derbyshire

*K. J. Barnett lbw b Watkinson	39	– b Watkinson	36
J. G. Wright c O'Shaughnessy b Folley	26	– not out	39
B. Roberts c Watkinson b Patterson	17	– b Watkinson	4
J. E. Morris c and b Folley	64	– c and b Watkinson	7
†B. J. M. Maher c O'Shaughnessy b Simmons	14	– c Simmons b O'Shaughnessy	0
R. J. Finney c Fairbrother b Folley	23	– not out	7
P. G. Newman not out	23		
A. E. Warner c O'Shaughnessy b Folley	0		
C. F. B. P. Rudd c O'Shaughnessy b Simmons	0		
O. H. Mortensen b Simmons	5		
D. E. Malcolm c Hughes b Folley	7		
B 1, l-b 1, n-b 6	8	B 4, n-b 4	8

1/49 2/67 3/105 4/165 5/173   226   1/53 2/57 3/67   (4 wkts dec.) 101
6/192 7/192 8/193 9/211   4/83

Bonus points – Derbyshire 2, Lancashire 4.

Bowling: *First Innings*—Patterson 13–1–53–1; Allott 17–2–44–0; Watkinson 3–0–17–1; Simmons 29–12–43–3; Folley 23.4–5–67–5. *Second Innings*—Patterson 5–0–19–0; Allott 8–0–30–0; Watkinson 5–0–22–3; O'Shaughnessy 3–0–9–1; Simmons 4–2–3–0; Folley 3–0–6–0; Fairbrother 1–0–8–0.

Lancashire

G. D. Mendis c Barnett b Malcolm	0	– c Newman b Malcolm	19
G. Fowler c Finney b Malcolm	1	– c Wright b Mortensen	11
S. J. O'Shaughnessy not out	30	– c Maher b Mortensen	1
N. H. Fairbrother not out	14	– b Barnett	82
*D. P. Hughes (did not bat)		– b Mortensen	10
M. Watkinson (did not bat)		– c Mortensen b Barnett	91
P. J. W. Allott (did not bat)		– st Maher b Barnett	32
J. Simmons (did not bat)		– run out	4
I. Folley (did not bat)		– c Finney b Barnett	7
B. P. Patterson (did not bat)		– run out	0
†J. Stanworth (did not bat)		– not out	0
B 1, l-b 1, w 1, n-b 4	7	B 1, l-b 8, w 5, n-b 1	15

1/0 2/11   (2 wkts dec.) 52   1/31 2/37 3/39 4/64 5/218   272
                              6/236 7/243 8/271 9/272

Bowling: *First Innings*—Malcolm 7–0–22–2; Mortensen 8–1–17–0; Newman 3–0–9–0; Warner 1–0–2–0. *Second Innings*—Malcolm 11–2–47–1; Mortensen 23–6–65–3; Newman 12–0–33–0; Rudd 10–2–37–0; Warner 6–1–38–0; Barnett 10.4–0–43–4.

Umpires: N. T. Plews and A. G. T. Whitehead.

LANCASHIRE v ESSEX

At Manchester, July 1, 2, 3. Essex won by 73 runs. Essex 23 pts, Lancashire 3 pts. Toss: Essex. Eighteen wickets fell to the spinners on the final day when Folley had a career-best Championship return and Miller his best for Essex. The toss proved vital and, having elected to bat, Essex were well served by Fletcher, in his 26th season, who stayed for 61 overs with good support from the middle order. Fowler's second Championship century of the season dominated Lancashire's reply – he hit a six and twelve fours – but by the end of the second day

Essex were in a commanding position, 137 in front with nine wickets standing. The spinners controlled the final day, Folley taking his six wickets in the morning session when Essex lost their last seven wickets for 35 runs. Lancashire had to get 257 in 76 overs and started well with a half-century stand before Miller and Childs ran through them. Mendis had a virus infection, was not well enough to bat in the first innings and went in No. 7 in the second.

Close of play: First day, Essex 322-8 (J. P. Stephenson 13*); Second day, Essex 29-1 (G. A. Gooch 20*, D. E. East 0*).

Essex

*G. A. Gooch c O'Shaughnessy b Allott	26	– c Watkinson b Folley	60
J. P. Stephenson c Hegg b Patterson	17	– c O'Shaughnessy b Allott	7
B. R. Hardie c O'Shaughnessy b Allott	3	– (4) c Hughes b Folley	15
K. W. R. Fletcher c Hughes b Simmons	82	– (6) b Simmons	12
G. Miller c Fairbrother b Simmons	30	– (8) st Hegg b Folley	0
D. R. Pringle c Folley b Patterson	70	– (5) st Hegg b Folley	0
A. W. Lilley b Allott	50	– c Fowler b Folley	15
H. A. Page c Allott b Patterson	3	– (10) c Fairbrother b Folley	0
†D. E. East c Watkinson b Allott	20	– (3) b Simmons	25
T. D. Topley not out	5	– (9) not out	6
J. H. Childs c Hegg b Patterson	13	– run out	0
B 9, l-b 16, n-b 5	30	B 2, l-b 4, n-b 2	8

1/35 2/67 3/144 4/193 5/280		349
6/287 7/311 8/322 9/327		

1/19 2/71 3/113 4/113 5/114		148
6/138 7/142 8/142 9/142		

Bonus points – Essex 3, Lancashire 1 (Score at 100 overs: 269-4).

In the first innings J. P. Stephenson, when 12, retired hurt at 32 and resumed at 311.

Bowling: *First Innings*—Patterson 22-1-82-4; Allott 19-5-50-4; Watkinson 12-0-42-0; Simmons 35-8-71-2; Folley 29-9-79-0. *Second Innings*—Patterson 6-0-30-0; Allott 9-2-27-1; Simmons 14-2-50-2; Folley 10.1-1-35-6.

Lancashire

G. Fowler lbw b Topley	121	– c Lilley b Miller	41
I. Folley c East b Miller	20	– st East b Childs	12
S. J. O'Shaughnessy c Fletcher b Childs	1	– c Fletcher b Miller	5
N. H. Fairbrother c East b Miller	20	– c and b Childs	4
M. Watkinson c Stephenson b Miller	24	– c Pringle b Miller	40
*D. P. Hughes c and b Topley	17	– c Hardie b Miller	0
P. J. W. Allott c Miller b Childs	8	– (8) c Stephenson b Miller	5
J. Simmons lbw b Topley	5	– (9) not out	43
†W. K. Hegg c Hardie b Miller	1	– (10) c Hardie b Miller	2
B. P. Patterson not out	8	– (11) b Childs	6
G. D. Mendis absent ill		– (7) c and b Miller	11
B 1, l-b 10, w 1, n-b 4	16	B 2, l-b 8, w 2, n-b 2	14

1/56 2/67 3/117 4/171 5/213		241
6/216 7/231 8/232 9/241		

1/51 2/62 3/67 4/67 5/67		183
6/94 7/106 8/145 9/152		

Bonus points – Lancashire 2, Essex 4.

Bowling: *First Innings*—Pringle 19-6-46-0; Page 5-1-19-0; Miller 29.3-6-74-4; Childs 30-12-53-2; Topley 12-1-38-3. *Second Innings*—Pringle 9-4-17-0; Topley 2-0-14-0; Childs 32-6-83-3; Miller 27-8-59-7.

Umpires: N. T. Plews and A. G. T. Whitehead.

At Northampton, July 4, 6, 7. LANCASHIRE lost to NORTHAMPTONSHIRE by nine wickets.

LANCASHIRE v WARWICKSHIRE

At Southport, July 22, 23. Lancashire won by ten wickets. Lancashire 22 pts, Warwickshire 4 pts. Toss: Lancashire. Warwickshire, put in to bat on a soft, drying pitch, lost all their wickets for 64 runs after an opening stand of 52, and by the end of the first day Lancashire were in a winning position, 2 runs ahead with eight wickets standing. Atherton, the Cambridge University batsman making his first appearance in the Championship, shared in a stand of 108 with Fairbrother to help Lancashire to a first-innings lead of 114. Folley, whose first-innings return was the best of his career and the best by a Lancashire spinner for 23 years, took five more wickets when Warwickshire again collapsed, leaving Lancashire with four overs in which to get the 20 runs needed for a two-day win. Folley's match analysis of 45.3–25–57–12 was the finest by any Lancashire bowler since J. B. Statham's fifteen for 108 against Leicestershire in 1964 and the best by a Lancashire spinner since M. J. Hilton's fourteen for 88 against Somerset in 1956. Thorne, the Warwickshire batsman, was taken from the team's Southport hotel to hospital with appendicitis the night before the game and N. M. K. Smith, son of M. J. K. Smith, the former Warwickshire and England captain, made his début.

Close of play: First day, Lancashire 118-2 (M. A. Atherton 42*, N. H. Fairbrother 53*).

Warwickshire

A. J. Moles b Simmons	25	– (2) b Allott	4
T. A. Lloyd c Hegg b Patterson	26	– (1) c Hughes b Patterson	4
P. A. Smith c Fairbrother b Folley	2	– b Patterson	0
D. L. Amiss c Fairbrother b Folley	6	– c Allott b Folley	23
Asif Din c Simmons b Folley	0	– c Fowler b Simmons	11
†G. A. Tedstone b Folley	15	– c Hegg b Folley	6
A. C. Storie c Fairbrother b Simmons	14	– lbw b Simmons	26
G. J. Parsons lbw b Folley	21	– lbw b Folley	19
N. M. K. Smith not out	1	– c Hughes b Folley	23
T. A. Merrick st Hegg b Folley	0	– not out	5
*N. Gifford b Folley	0	– b Folley	1
L-b 6	6	B 5, l-b 3, n-b 3	11
	116		**133**

1/52 2/54 3/58 4/60 5/63   1/8 2/8 3/8 4/45 5/50
6/82 7/94 8/116 9/116   6/53 7/83 8/109 9/131

Bonus points – Lancashire 4.

Bowling: *First Innings*—Patterson 13–5–24–1; Allott 9–4–15–0; Watkinson 6–2–13–0; Simmons 22–8–43–2; Folley 21.1–13–15–7. *Second Innings*—Patterson 14–3–33–2; Allott 12–6–18–1; Simmons 22–8–32–2; Folley 24.2–12–42–5.

Lancashire

G. D. Mendis lbw b Gifford	19	– not out	2
G. Fowler c N. M. K. Smith b Parsons	0	– not out	10
M. A. Atherton lbw b Merrick	53		
N. H. Fairbrother c Storie b Gifford	73		
*D. P. Hughes lbw b Merrick	1		
M. Watkinson b Gifford	27		
†W. K. Hegg b Gifford	1		
P. J. W. Allott c Merrick b N. M. K. Smith	22		
I. Folley c Storie b N. M. K. Smith	4		
J. Simmons lbw b Gifford	13		
B. P. Patterson not out	1		
B 6, l-b 10	16	L-b 8	8
	230	(no wkt)	**20**

1/8 2/36 3/144 4/146 5/156
6/160 7/199 8/204 9/225

Bonus points – Lancashire 2, Warwickshire 4.

Bowling: *First Innings*—Merrick 25–4–54–2; Parsons 6–0–11–1; Gifford 42.4–19–76–5; N. M. K. Smith 23–3–73–2. *Second Innings*—Merrick 2–0–7–0; Parsons 1.3–1–5–0.

Umpires: R. Julian and H. J. Rhodes.

LANCASHIRE v NOTTINGHAMSHIRE

At Manchester, July 25, 27, 28. Drawn. Lancashire 8 pts, Nottinghamshire 4 pts. Toss: Nottinghamshire. Repeated interruptions by rain on the final day condemned the match to a draw. Newell again opened the batting in the absence of Broad and Robinson, who were at the Test, and again seized his opportunity, following a double-century in the previous match with a determined hundred after Nottinghamshire had been 97 for six. He and Hemmings put on 144 for the seventh wicket. Fairbrother scored his third hundred of the season, batting 239 minutes, hitting two sixes and eleven fours, and sharing in a century stand with Watkinson, and the teams ended the second day with Nottinghamshire 7 runs behind with all wickets standing. They batted right through the shortened final day, starting with a century stand before both openers were stumped in the space of three balls. Rice was bowled at 99 to become the sixth first-class victim of Fairbrother, one of ten bowlers used by Lancashire.

Close of play: First day, Nottinghamshire 248. Second day, Nottinghamshire 45-0 (M. Newell 15*, P. Pollard 27*).

Nottinghamshire

M. Newell c Hegg b Watkinson	116	– st Hegg b Hughes 41
P. Pollard b Patterson	7	– st Hegg b Atherton 59
P. Johnson b Patterson	0	– b Atherton 22
*C. E. B. Rice c Allott b Watkinson	3	– b Fairbrother 99
J. D. Birch b Folley	14	– lbw b Fowler 0
R. J. Hadlee c Hughes b Patterson	16	– c Allott b Fairbrother 22
†C. W. Scott lbw b Watkinson	7	– c sub b Atherton 9
E. E. Hemmings b Watkinson	66	– not out 21
R. A. Pick b Simmons	3	– not out 26
K. Saxelby lbw b Watkinson	0	
M. K. Bore not out	2	
B 3, l-b 5, n-b 6	14	B 8, l-b 6, w 1, n-b 4 19

1/12 2/13 3/29 4/57 5/75	248	1/103 2/103 3/155 (7 wkts) 318
6/97 7/241 8/244 9/244		4/159 5/226
		6/260 7/260

Bonus points – Nottinghamshire 2, Lancashire 4.

Bowling: *First Innings*—Patterson 19-2-52-3; Allott 13-4-26-0; Watkinson 20-5-42-5; Simmons 29.3-6-72-1; Folley 18-6-48-1. *Second Innings*—Patterson 4-0-27-0; Allott 6-4-10-0; Simmons 8-3-21-0; Folley 5-3-12-0; Hughes 6-0-30-1; Atherton 17-2-72-3; Fairbrother 19-2-91-2; Fowler 3-3-0-1; Mendis 10-1-33-0; Watkinson 4-0-8-0.

Lancashire

G. D. Mendis b Pick	10	†W. K. Hegg not out 3
G. Fowler c Rice b Saxelby	80	
M. A. Atherton c Scott b Bore	11	B 4, l-b 13, w 2, n-b 1 20
N. H. Fairbrother not out	109	
M. Watkinson c Birch b Rice	53	1/21 2/54 3/132 (5 wkts dec.) 300
*D. P. Hughes c Birch b Hemmings	14	4/237 5/283

J. Simmons, P. J. W. Allott, I. Folley and B. P. Patterson did not bat.

Bonus points – Lancashire 4, Nottinghamshire 2.

Bowling: Saxelby 26-5-60-1; Pick 12-0-40-1; Rice 12-2-47-1; Bore 15-2-58-1; Hemmings 30-11-78-1.

Umpires: B. Dudleston and J. W. Holder.

At Leeds, August 1, 3, 4. LANCASHIRE drew with YORKSHIRE.

LANCASHIRE v NORTHAMPTONSHIRE

At Manchester, August 5, 6, 7. Drawn. Lancashire 5 pts, Northamptonshire 8 pts. Toss: Lancashire. Northamptonshire came to Manchester as Championship leaders and left it frustrated by the rain that wiped out the final day and a promising position. Only two Lancashire batsmen failed to reach double figures on an opening day on which the Northamptonshire spinners bowled all but fourteen of the overs, took nine wickets, and were helped by Wild's four excellent catches at short leg. Cook, who took six of the wickets, followed with his best innings for Northamptonshire when they were stumbling at 154 for seven, while Ripley (seventeen fours) scored the second century of his career. Between them, the pair put on 164, beating the county's eighth-wicket record of 155 by A. E. Nutter and F. R. Brown, established in 1952. Lancashire, with Mendis already out and still 117 behind at the end of the second day, were happy to see the rain come to their assistance.

Close of play: First day, Northamptonshire 40-0 (R. J. Bailey 16*, W. Larkins 21*); Second day, Lancashire 23-1 (G. Fowler 14*, I. Folley 3*).

Lancashire

G. D. Mendis c Lamb b Smith	9	– c Wild b N. G. B. Cook	4
G. Fowler c and b N. G. B. Cook	32	– not out	14
M. A. Atherton b N. G. B. Cook	47		
N. H. Fairbrother b Harper	39		
M. Watkinson c Larkins b N. G. B. Cook	18		
*D. P. Hughes c Wild b Harper	18		
†W. K. Hegg c Wild b Harper	14		
P. J. W. Allott c Wild b N. G. B. Cook	15		
J. Simmons c Wild b N. G. B. Cook	6		
I. Folley not out	13	– (3) not out	3
K. W. McLeod b N. G. B. Cook	21		
L-b 7	7	L-b 2	2

1/25 2/71 3/113 4/139 5/159   239   1/18   (1 wkt) 23
6/173 7/194 8/198 9/219

Bonus points – Lancashire 2, Northamptonshire 4.

Bowling: *First Innings*—Capel 8–0–31–0; Smith 6–0–36–1; Harper 44–11–87–3; N. G. B. Cook 38.5–17–77–6; Williams 1–0–1–0. *Second Innings*—Capel 2–0–14–0; Harper 4–1–4–0; N. G. B. Cook 3–1–3–1.

Northamptonshire

R. J. Bailey c Simmons b Folley	61	N. G. B. Cook c Fowler b McLeod	64
W. Larkins c Folley b McLeod	38	G. Smith not out	29
A. J. Lamb st Hegg b Folley	0		
D. J. Capel run out	0	B 3, l-b 9, n-b 8	20
R. G. Williams b Folley	10		
R. A. Harper b Allott	5	1/70 2/71 3/71 (8 wkts dec.) 379
D. J. Wild c and b Simmons	27	4/103 5/112 6/130
†D. Ripley not out	125	7/154 8/318

*G. Cook did not bat.

Bonus points – Northamptonshire 4, Lancashire 3 (Score at 100 overs: 310-7).

Bowling: Allott 20–5–66–1; McLeod 21–5–88–2; Simmons 17–4–49–1; Folley 33–12–77–3; Atherton 7–1–24–0; Hughes 7–0–23–0; Watkinson 7–0–40–0.

Umpires: H. D. Bird and P. B. Wight.

At Southampton, August 8, 10, 11. LANCASHIRE drew with HAMPSHIRE.

At Manchester, August 12, 13, 14. LANCASHIRE v REST OF THE WORLD XI. Abandoned.

At Manchester, August 14. LANCASHIRE lost to REST OF THE WORLD XI by four wickets (See Other Matches, 1987).

LANCASHIRE v SUSSEX

At Lytham, August 19, 20, 21. Lancashire won by 54 runs. Lancashire 20 pts, Sussex 5 pts. Toss: Lancashire. There were three career-best bowling performances, starting with Reeve, who followed his seven for 37 with the highest score of the match to give Sussex a first-innings lead of 27 on a pitch and in conditions which helped seam bowling throughout. Colin Wells took the honours in Lancashire's second innings with six for 34, but Fowler followed his admirable 61 of the first innings with 44 to help Lancashire set Sussex a target of 151 in 76 overs. Watkinson surpassed everybody else by taking seven for 25, the first four coming at a cost of 2 runs in a spell of nineteen balls as Sussex fell from an encouraging 63 for two to 73 for seven. When the last three wickets fell at 96, Lancashire gained the first of the six successive wins that were to take them so close to the Championship.

Close of play: First day, Sussex 101-6 (D. A. Reeve 49*, P. A. W. Heseltine 0*); Second day, Lancashire 133-6 (D. P. Hughes 23*, P. J. W. Allott 8*).

Lancashire

G. D. Mendis b Reeve	4	– lbw b Wells	24	
G. Fowler c Heseltine b Reeve	61	– c Kimber b Pigott	44	
M. A. Atherton lbw b Reeve	0	– lbw b Wells	0	
N. H. Fairbrother c Green b Heseltine	3	– lbw b Pigott	23	
M. Watkinson b Heseltine	8	– c Moores b Heseltine	0	
*D. P. Hughes not out	25	– lbw b Wells	35	
†W. K. Hegg c Pigott b Reeve	7	– lbw b Wells	6	
P. J. W. Allott lbw b Reeve	9	– c Standing b Pigott	22	
J. Simmons c Parker b Reeve	2	– c Greenfield b Wells	8	
I. Folley c Greenfield b Reeve	1	– not out	7	
B. P. Patterson b Wells	1	– c Gould b Wells	0	
B 1, l-b 3, w 1, n-b 5	10	L-b 4, w 3, n-b 1	8	

1/5 2/6 3/35 4/57 5/104   **131**   1/40 2/42 3/95 4/96 5/96   **177**
6/112 7/122 8/128 9/130   6/120 7/149 8/170 9/171

Bonus points – Sussex 4.

Bowling: *First Innings*—Pigott 17–3–47–0; Reeve 21–6–37–7; Heseltine 8–2–20–2; Wells 10.1–5–12–1; Kimber 4–0–11–0. *Second Innings*—Pigott 21–6–53–3; Reeve 30–9–59–0; Wells 21.4–10–34–6; Heseltine 14–7–23–1; Green 1–0–4–0.

Sussex

D. K. Standing c Simmons b Patterson	0	– c Watkinson b Allott	1	
A. M. Green c Hegg b Patterson	5	– lbw b Watkinson	40	
P. W. G. Parker c Mendis b Allott	10	– c Simmons b Allott	2	
P. Moores c Watkinson b Patterson	6	– (6) c Allott b Watkinson	1	
C. M. Wells lbw b Allott	2	– c Folley b Simmons	0	
K. Greenfield c Watkinson b Patterson	18	– (4) c Mendis b Watkinson	11	
D. A. Reeve c Simmons b Patterson	64	– c sub b Watkinson	1	
P. A. W. Heseltine lbw b Allott	25	– (11) lbw b Watkinson	0	
*†I. J. Gould c Hegg b Allott	2	– (8) not out	10	
A. C. S. Pigott c Fowler b Patterson	8	– (9) c Hegg b Watkinson	14	
S. J. S. Kimber not out	1	– (10) c Allott b Watkinson	0	
L-b 2, w 1, n-b 14	17	B 5, l-b 2, n-b 9	16	

1/0 2/14 3/24 4/26 5/32   **158**   1/1 2/18 3/63 4/64 5/64   **96**
6/100 7/125 8/129 9/156   6/70 7/73 8/96 9/96

Bonus points – Sussex 1, Lancashire 4.

Bowling: *First Innings*—Patterson 24–5–70–6; Allott 25.5–8–42–4; Watkinson 9–1–21–0; Simmons 4–2–9–0; Folley 3–1–14–0. *Second Innings*—Patterson 9–1–21–0; Allott 8–3–22–2; Watkinson 10.4–3–25–7; Simmons 10–2–21–1.

Umpires: N. T. Plews and P. B. Wight.

At Birmingham, August 22, 24, 25. LANCASHIRE beat WARWICKSHIRE by 25 runs.

At Maidstone, August 26, 27, 28. LANCASHIRE beat KENT by six wickets.

LANCASHIRE v GLOUCESTERSHIRE

At Manchester, August 29, 31, September 1. Lancashire won by three wickets. Lancashire 21 pts, Gloucestershire 5 pts. Toss: Gloucestershire. A fine all-round performance in the first innings by Watkinson, who took five wickets and scored 47 runs, gave Lancashire a handy lead of 24. Gloucestershire started the final day only 107 ahead with six wickets down, but Ibadulla defied Lancashire as he shared in partnerships of 37 with Russell and 40, for the last wicket, with Graveney. This left Lancashire needing 208 in 46 overs. Mendis and Fowler gave them a wonderful start, Atherton and Abrahams maintained the brisk scoring-rate, and Lancashire went into the last ten overs needing 52 with eight wickets standing. They then ran into trouble, losing four wickets, and reached the final over wanting 7 runs. Hegg was out to the third ball, and when Folley faced his first delivery, 3 runs were needed from two balls. He prodded forward at Greene and a thick edge produced the required runs to the accompaniment of prolonged cheering from the members.

Close of play: First day, Lancashire 77-4 (M. A. Atherton 3*, W. K. Hegg 1*); Second day, Gloucestershire 131-6 (P. W. Romaines 28*, R. C. Russell 1*).

Gloucestershire

A. W. Stovold b Watkinson	22	– lbw b Folley	12
A. J. Wright c Allott b Watkinson	20	– c Allott b Folley	31
P. W. Romaines st Hegg b Simmons	23	– c Hughes b Simmons	30
C. W. J. Athey lbw b Watkinson	0	– b Folley	7
K. M. Curran c Allott b Watkinson	10	– b Simmons	22
J. W. Lloyds c Atherton b Folley	8	– c Allott b Atherton	21
K. B. K. Ibadulla lbw b Watkinson	7	– (9) not out	46
†R. C. Russell c Fowler b Simmons	49	– (8) c Folley b Simmons	23
V. S. Greene st Hegg b Folley	22	– (10) lbw b Simmons	5
*D. A. Graveney b Simmons	2	– (11) c Hughes b Allott	23
G. E. Sainsbury not out	3	– (7) b Patterson	0
B 2, l-b 1	3	B 4, l-b 4, n-b 3	11

1/40 2/45 3/45 4/57 5/66   169   1/45 2/46 3/54 4/85 5/122   231
6/93 7/93 8/141 9/148   6/124 7/142 8/179 9/191

Bonus points – Gloucestershire 1, Lancashire 4.

Bowling: *First Innings*—Patterson 10–4–17–0; Allott 7–1–18–0; Watkinson 18–4–57–5; Folley 23–9–38–2; Simmons 15.5–2–36–3. *Second Innings*—Patterson 16–2–53–1; Allott 7.4–3–10–1; Simmons 44–15–80–4; Folley 35–10–68–3; Atherton 7–2–12–1.

Lancashire

G. D. Mendis b Graveney	22	– b Sainsbury	55
G. Fowler b Graveney	49	– lbw b Sainsbury	38
M. A. Atherton b Ibadulla	26	– lbw b Graveney	40
J. Abrahams lbw b Graveney	0	– c Athey b Graveney	32
I. Folley lbw b Lloyds	0	– (9) not out	3
†W. K. Hegg b Lloyds	27	– (8) c Curran b Greene	5
M. Watkinson c Wright b Graveney	47	– (5) b Graveney	10
*D. P. Hughes b Ibadulla	1	– (6) c sub b Greene	8
P. J. W. Allott st Russell b Graveney	15	– (7) not out	6
J. Simmons not out	3		
B. P. Patterson st Russell b Ibadulla	0		
L-b 2, n-b 1	3	B 1, l-b 7, n-b 3	11

193   (7 wkts) 208

1/71 2/72 3/72 4/75 5/116   1/85 2/118 3/172 4/181
6/157 7/169 8/189 9/190   5/194 6/194 7/204

Bonus points – Lancashire 1, Gloucestershire 4.

Bowling: *First Innings*—Greene 7–0–23–0; Sainsbury 7–0–23–0; Lloyds 27–5–71–2; Graveney 34–17–37–5; Ibadulla 14–1–37–3. *Second Innings*—Greene 16.5–0–77–2; Sainsbury 13–2–43–2; Lloyds 4–0–19–0; Graveney 11–0–52–3; Ibadulla 1–0–9–0.

Umpires: D. J. Constant and J. A. Jameson.

LANCASHIRE v SURREY

At Manchester, September 9, 10, 11. Lancashire won by four wickets. Lancashire 22 pts, Surrey 7 pts. Toss: Surrey. Another run-chase, this time in appalling light, enabled Lancashire to go into their final game at Chelmsford needing 24 points to snatch the Championship from Nottinghamshire. Jesty, in his last match for Surrey, stopped a middle-order collapse with his first century of the season and Surrey, who started the game with a chance of finishing Championship runners-up, ended their first innings in a powerful position. However, Abrahams, recalled for the previous match because of injury to Fairbrother, played his best innings of the season, hitting a six and nineteen fours as he saw Lancashire from 23 for two to a declaration at 334 for eight. Surrey, led by Bicknell, scored quickly on the final day to set Lancashire a target of 276 in 60 overs, achieved with fourteen balls to spare after another magnificent innings from Abrahams. He shared in stands of 93 with Atherton and 97 in fourteen overs with Watkinson, whose 57 came from 50 balls and who had the satisfaction of celebrating the recent award of his cap by hitting the winning runs.

Close of play: First day, Surrey 365-8 (T. E. Jesty 119*, C. S. Mays 0*); Second day, Surrey 5-1 (D. J. Bicknell 3*, K. T. Medlycott 0*).

Surrey

D. J. Bicknell st Hegg b Simmons	61	– not out	85
D. M. Smith b Folley	19	– lbw b Allott	1
A. J. Stewart c Mendis b Folley	60	– (4) run out	66
M. A. Lynch b Simmons	5	– (5) st Hegg b Folley	37
T. E. Jesty not out	124	– (6) b Simmons	4
†C. J. Richards lbw b Simmons	53		
*I. A. Greig c Folley b Hughes	21		
K. T. Medlycott c Hegg b Patterson	0	– (3) c Hughes b Patterson	23
M. A. Feltham c Hughes b Patterson	0		
C. S. Mays b Allott	2		
S. T. Clarke b Allott	6		
B 1, l-b 9, w 1, n-b 17	28	B 4, l-b 4, n-b 6	14

379   (5 wkts dec.) 230

1/51 2/147 3/164 4/165 5/305   1/3 2/45 3/153
6/364 7/365 8/365 9/369   4/225 5/230

Bonus points – Surrey 4, Lancashire 2 (Score at 100 overs: 365-6).

Bowling: *First Innings*—Patterson 16–2–49–2; Allott 11–3–21–2; Watkinson 11–4–17–0; Folley 33–4–136–2; Simmons 23–3–78–3; Atherton 10–0–46–0; Hughes 4–1–22–1. *Second Innings*—Patterson 8–1–29–1; Allott 8–1–45–1; Watkinson 4–0–30–0; Folley 14–1–68–1; Simmons 10.5–1–50–1.

Lancashire

G. D. Mendis c Richards b Medlycott	62	– c Smith b Clarke	32
G. Fowler c Richards b Feltham	0	– lbw b Clarke	18
M. A. Atherton b Clarke	9	– run out	45
J. Abrahams not out	140	– c Richards b Clarke	92
M. Watkinson lbw b Medlycott	35	– not out	57
*D. P. Hughes b Feltham b Medlycott	18	– c Greig b Feltham	2
†W. K. Hegg lbw b Mays	6	– (8) not out	4
P. J. W. Allott c Richards b Feltham	33	– (7) c Stewart b Clarke	9
J. Simmons b Feltham	15		
I. Folley not out	3		
B 4, l-b 9	13	B 8, l-b 8, w 1	17

1/4 2/23 3/96 4/162 5/204 (8 wkts dec.) 334 1/46 2/55 3/148 (6 wkts) 276
6/229 7/290 8/318 4/245 5/248 6/257

B. P. Patterson did not bat.

Bonus points – Lancashire 4, Surrey 3 (Score at 100 overs: 323-8).

Bowling: *First Innings*—Clarke 17–6–41–1; Feltham 14–3–46–3; Medlycott 34–8–115–3; Mays 30–5–94–1; Lynch 7–2–25–0. *Second Innings*—Clarke 18.4–1–79–4; Feltham 10–1–54–1; Medlycott 12–1–49–0; Mays 15–2–68–0; Lynch 2–0–10–0.

Umpires: R. Julian and D. O. Oslear.

At Chelmsford, September 12, 14, 15. LANCASHIRE beat ESSEX by 89 runs.

KWIK CRICKET

In what is regarded as an essential development for the future of cricket at all levels, the Test and County Cricket Board, National Cricket Association and English Schools Cricket Association have combined resources to promote cricket in the United Kingdom through a specially devised concept called Kwik Cricket.

While intended to benefit cricket in general, it is specifically aimed at children from the ages of five to eleven, boys and girls both, as an introduction to the conventional form of cricket. It may be played indoors or outdoors, and the rules, which aim at maximum activity and maximum involvement, may be adapted to suit any length of time and any number of players. Primary schools, club colts and community groups are the areas into which the governing bodies hope to distribute Kwik Cricket sets.

The equipment, made of high technology plastic, has been developed to give the "feel" and appearance of conventional equipment. Each set consists of two bats, two balls and two sets of stumps. The bats are light enough for young children to use, are hard wearing, and when picked up have the genuine feel of a cricket bat. The ball is soft enough so that protective equipment is not required, but it bounces like a conventional cricket ball, thereby encouraging the natural development of the usual range of strokes. Because it is difficult to hit the ball great distances, games of Kwik Cricket can be contained within a small area and be played without damage to property in the immediate vicinity.

LEICESTERSHIRE

Chairman: C. H. Palmer
Chairman, Cricket Committee: J. J. Palmer
Secretary/Cricket Manager: F. M. Turner
   County Cricket Ground, Grace Road,
   Leicester LE2 8AD
   (Telephone: 0533-831880/832128)
Captain: 1987 – P. Willey
            1988 – D. I. Gower
Coach: K. Higgs

Leicestershire's 1987 season was one of such contrasting fortunes that, for many at the club, September could not come quickly enough. Others, however, would gladly have played on into winter. There can hardly have been a time when the county experienced so much media attention and speculation. Unhappily, much of it had little to do with playing performances, which at times were considerable, but with personal and personnel problems. Rumours frequently overshadowed the side's actual achievements, and this marred what would otherwise have been recognised as a highly successful season. By finishing in the top three in the Britannic Assurance Championship, they achieved something only four previous Leicestershire teams had managed, and by reaching the semi-final of the NatWest Bank Trophy they equalled the club's best progress in the 60-overs competition.

Both these achievements were peppered with some fine individual performances, the most notable of which were the bowling of Jonathan Agnew and the batting of Nigel Briers. Agnew, bowling off a shorter run and with a wicked slower ball added to his armoury, became the first Leicestershire player since J. Birkenshaw in 1968 to take 100 first-class wickets in a season; Briers, after a poor start in the middle order, moved up to open the innings and scored 806 runs in the final month and a half, totalling 1,257 first-class runs in all.

Leicestershire began the season with an optimism born of having their strongest and largest squad for many years. However, keeping such a talented gathering happy and playing was bound to be a problem, and so it proved. Before the season was a month old, all-rounder Paddy Clift, in his last term at the club, threatened to resign after being omitted from a limited-overs match. After talks with the management, the threat was never carried out, and Clift went on to enjoy one of his best years at Leicestershire. Ian Butcher, also dissatisfied at failing to command a regular first-team place, asked the committee not to renew his contract and he later joined Gloucestershire.

But it was the county's England all-rounder, Phillip DeFreitas, who posed the greatest problem, following his emergence as a player of daunting potential on England's successful tour of Australia the previous winter. Indeed, it may have been his disappointment at failing to live up to the exacting standards set on that tour which led to the many rumours concerning his involvement in dressing-room rifts and conflict with the new captain, Peter Willey. However, the rumours would have remained no more than that but for a notorious incident in which DeFreitas poured a pot of salt over Agnew's lunch on the final day of the Championship match against Sussex late in June. Agnew responded by throwing DeFreitas's kit over the dressing-room balcony, and the all-rounder left the ground for two hours before returning and, in dramatic fashion, helping Leicestershire to their first Championship victory. For DeFreitas, the troubles did not end there. He lost his England place and was then dropped from the county's first team for disciplinary reasons. It was a sorry state of affairs, and in the end it was to prove too much for Willey. During the close season he resigned the captaincy, though saying he hoped to continue as a member of the side.

For Leicestershire, the victory over Sussex marked the beginning of a resolute transformation, and they went on to win five of their next ten matches, laying the foundation of their challenge for the Championship. George Ferris, the Antiguan fast bowler, emerged from the doldrums of the previous two years to produce genuine hostility and prove an ideal foil for Agnew. In reserve, the county's seam attack had another West Indian, Winston Benjamin, and the promising Chris Lewis, Guyana born but eligible for England. At the end of the season, with DeFreitas more settled, Leicestershire's fast bowling looked as strong as any in the country, and was young enough to develop its menace.

The batting, however, did not fulfil expectations. Leicestershire struggled to find a reliable opening pair, with Butcher, Cobb and Potter all failing to fit the bill, and the committee eventually settled on Briers and Boon. Both seemed to relish the challenge and passed 1,000 runs for the county, as did Willey and James Whitaker. Of the four, Whitaker would have been disappointed not to have consolidated his promise and remain in contention for an England place.

In the limited-overs competitions, Leicestershire's season, the NatWest apart, was not so rewarding. They failed to qualify for the quarter-finals of the Benson and Hedges Cup, while in the Refuge Assurance Sunday League they suffered more than any other county from the weather. Seven of their games either did not start or failed to produce a result. Consequently they did not figure significantly.

Although 1987 should best be considered a season of qualified success, it should also be remembered for some vintage innings by David Gower, enjoying his benefit year and free from the pressures of international cricket. He scored nearly 1,000 first-class runs for Leicestershire, and in the last six weeks of the season he produced batting of the highest quality which was almost worth a decade of internal squabbles and tribulations. – James Hunt.

476

LEICESTERSHIRE 1987

[*Bill Smith*]

Back row: C. Mortimer (*physiotherapist*), P. Whitticase, J. J. Whitaker, G. J. F. Ferris, J. P. Agnew, C. C. Lewis, P. A. J. DeFreitas, L. Potter, R. A. Cobb, I. P. Butcher. *Front row:* N. E. Briers, D. I. Gower, P. Willey (*captain*), L. B. Taylor, P. B. Clift. *Inset:* T. J. Boon.

LEICESTERSHIRE RESULTS

All first-class matches – Played 26: Won 9, Lost 3, Drawn 14.

County Championship matches – Played 24: Won 8, Lost 3, Drawn 13.

Bonus points – Batting 57, Bowling 75.

Competition placings – Britannic Assurance County Championship, 3rd; NatWest Bank Trophy, s-f; Benson and Hedges Cup, 5th in Group A; Refuge Assurance League, 12th equal.

BRITANNIC ASSURANCE CHAMPIONSHIP AVERAGES

BATTING

	Birthplace	M	I	NO	R	HI	Avge
‡D. I. Gower	Tunbridge Wells	12	19	4	840	125	56.00
‡N. E. Briers	Leicester	20	31	4	1,244	104	46.07
‡T. J. Boon	Doncaster	18	24	2	858	94	39.00
J. J. Whitaker	Skipton	24	35	5	1,020	105	34.00
‡P. Willey	Sedgefield	24	38	4	1,153	122	32.02
‡P. B. Clift	Salisbury, S. Rhodesia	16	21	3	576	88	32.00
I. P. Butcher	Farnborough, Kent	7	11	0	320	88	29.09
‡R. A. Cobb	Leicester	16	25	5	540	88	27.00
L. Potter	Bexleyheath	13	19	4	333	47*	22.20
‡P. A. J. DeFreitas	Scotts Head, Dominica	15	20	2	369	74	20.50
‡J. P. Agnew	Macclesfield	24	27	4	387	90	16.82
‡P. Whitticase	Solihull	24	29	5	336	59	14.00
C. C. Lewis	Georgetown, Guyana	4	4	0	53	42	13.25
‡L. B. Taylor	Earl Shilton	8	9	3	66	16	11.00
§G. J. F. Ferris	Urlings Village, Antigua	13	13	4	93	25	10.33
§W. K. M. Benjamin	St John's, Antigua	7	8	1	57	30	8.14
P. M. Such	Helensburgh	19	16	8	28	12	3.50

* *Signifies not out.*   ‡ *Denotes county cap.*   § *Not qualified for England.*

The following played a total of seven three-figure innings for Leicestershire in County Championship matches – N. E. Briers 2, D. I. Gower 2, P. Willey 2, J. J. Whitaker 1.

BOWLING

	O	M	R	W	BB	Avge
G. J. F. Ferris	359.1	69	1,143	52	6-42	21.98
P. B. Clift	376.1	106	829	36	6-64	23.02
J. P. Agnew	750	132	2,409	99	7-46	24.33
P. A. J. DeFreitas	408.2	92	1,187	44	7-85	26.97
L. B. Taylor	143.4	19	524	18	6-47	29.11
W. K. M. Benjamin	187.2	46	470	15	5-50	31.33
P. M. Such	420.3	117	1,099	31	3-50	35.45
P. Willey	173.2	33	524	12	2-36	43.66

Also bowled: N. E. Briers 3-1-8-0; I. P. Butcher 2-0-4-0; C. C. Lewis 63-9-167-5; L. Potter 40-6-163-4.

Wicket-keeper: P. Whitticase 65 ct, 1 st.

Leading Fielders: L. Potter 21, J. J. Whitaker 16.

At Cambridge, April 25, 27, 28. LEICESTERSHIRE beat CAMBRIDGE UNIVERSITY by an innings and 220 runs.

LEICESTERSHIRE v ESSEX

At Leicester, May 6, 7, 8. Drawn. Leicestershire 6 pts, Essex 7 pts. Toss: Leicestershire. Soon after a cloud of sulphur dioxide, reportedly from a nearby power station, had passed over the ground, Foster, on a slow pitch of variable bounce, brought Leicestershire's first innings to an end with a spell of six wickets for 19 off 39 deliveries. In Essex's reply, Hardie compiled a solid if unattractive 111 in five hours off 263 balls, hitting thirteen boundaries, and the game seemed destined for a draw as Whitaker recorded his second half-century. However, when three wickets fell midway through the last afternoon, Leicestershire were only 111 in front with the tail remaining and Essex having time aplenty for a run-chase. Improbably long innings by Taylor and Such, who both batted for nearly an hour, kept the champions at bay as Boon reached his half-century and Essex were left needing 232 to win with only sixteen overs remaining.

Close of play: First day, Essex 78-2 (B. R. Hardie 29*, K. W. R. Fletcher 12*); Second day, Leicestershire 86-2 (J. P. Agnew 2*).

Leicestershire

L. Potter lbw b Childs	41	– c East b Pringle	23
I. P. Butcher c Hardie b Pringle	11	– c East b Pringle	50
*P. Willey run out	45	– (4) c Gooch b Miller	18
J. J. Whitaker c Page b Foster	62	– (5) c East b Foster	51
D. I. Gower c and b Miller	9	– (6) c East b Pringle	34
T. J. Boon c Miller b Foster	35	– (7) not out	64
P. A. J. DeFreitas c Gladwin b Foster	3	– (8) lbw b Pringle	0
†P. Whitticase lbw b Foster	12	– (9) c Lilley b Page	20
J. P. Agnew not out	15	– (3) b Pringle	3
L. B. Taylor b Foster	6	– c Gooch b Foster	15
P. M. Such lbw b Foster	0	– b Childs	12
B 4, l-b 3, w 5, n-b 12	24	B 3, l-b 23, w 3, n-b 7	36

1/35 2/108 3/137 4/172 5/210   263   1/73 2/86 3/87 4/141 5/204   326
6/214 7/241 8/242 9/263   6/206 7/206 8/255 9/289

Bonus points – Leicestershire 3, Essex 4.

Bowling: *First Innings*—Foster 23.5-2-86-6; Page 12-0-47-0; Pringle 16-5-43-1; Gooch 2-1-2-0; Childs 8-2-39-1; Miller 15-4-39-1. *Second Innings*—Foster 24-4-58-2; Page 13-2-41-1; Childs 24.3-9-55-1; Pringle 25-6-70-5; Miller 33-9-54-1; Gooch 3-1-8-0; Fletcher 2-0-9-0; East 1-0-5-0.

Essex

*G. A. Gooch c Potter b Agnew	27	– not out	2
C. Gladwin c Whitticase b Agnew	2	– not out	3
B. R. Hardie c Whitaker b Taylor	111		
K. W. R. Fletcher c Potter b Agnew	14		
A. W. Lilley b Such	37		
D. R. Pringle lbw b Taylor	29		
G. Miller c DeFreitas b Willey	7		
H. A. Page run out	21		
†D. E. East c Whitaker b Agnew	21		
N. A. Foster not out	49		
J. H. Childs b Such	26		
L-b 5, n-b 9	14	N-b 1	1

1/4 2/52 3/82 4/165 5/228   358   (no wkt) 6
6/239 7/240 8/277 9/282

Bonus points – Essex 3, Leicestershire 3 (Score at 100 overs: 268-7).

Bowling: *First Innings*—DeFreitas 22–5–81–0; Agnew 28–4–107–4; Taylor 27–5–71–2; Such 28.3–8–54–2; Willey 13–2–40–1. *Second Innings*—DeFreitas 3–2–2–0; Butcher 2–0–4–0.

Umpires: H. D. Bird and A. A. Jones.

LEICESTERSHIRE v LANCASHIRE

At Leicester, May 20, 21, 22. Lancashire won by an innings and 116 runs. Lancashire 24 pts. Toss: Lancashire. For the first time since the introduction of the current points system, a team gained the maximum allocation while their opponents failed to gain a single point. Such was the ease of Lancashire's victory, achieved by dint of injudicious batting from Leicestershire, who were bowled out twice in only 117.4 overs, and splendid seam bowling by McLeod and Allott. On the first day, Fairbrother had continued his early-season promise with a fine hundred off 162 balls on what was developing into a difficult two-paced wicket. He batted for three hours fifteen minutes and hit three sixes and ten fours. Leicestershire were quickly in trouble when they lost Butcher and Willey to successive deliveries from McLeod in the second over, and at 12 for five after nine overs they were heading for their lowest total. Clift and Whitticase averted this embarrassment by adding 48 for the sixth wicket. Asked to follow on 273 behind, Leicestershire fared little better second time around and were bowled out for 157 as storm clouds gathered round the ground.

Close of play: First day, Lancashire 344-4 (S. J. O'Shaughnessy 6*, D. P. Hughes 14*); Second day, Leicestershire 100-4 (P. Willey 27*, P. Whitticase 8*).

Lancashire

G. D. Mendis c Boon b Such	68	*D. P. Hughes not out		14
D. W. Varey b Such	57			
J. Abrahams b Benjamin	80	B 1, l-b 10, w 1, n-b 6		18
N. H. Fairbrother c Whitticase				
b Agnew	101	1/115 2/143 3/320	(4 wkts dec.)	344
S. J. O'Shaughnessy not out	6	4/324		

I. Folley, J. Simmons, †J. Stanworth, P. J. W. Allott and K. W. McLeod did not bat.

Bonus points – Lancashire 4 (Score at 100 overs: 314-2).

Bowling: Agnew 25–2–83–1; Benjamin 25–6–70–1; Clift 20–5–43–0; Taylor 14–1–69–0; Such 23–9–53–2; Willey 3–0–15–0.

Leicestershire

L. Potter c Abrahams b Allott	7	– c and b Folley	41
I. P. Butcher c Stanworth b McLeod	0	– c Stanworth b O'Shaughnessy	6
*P. Willey c O'Shaughnessy b McLeod	0	– c Abrahams b Allott	29
J. J. Whitaker c Stanworth b Allott	3	– c Allott b Folley	5
T. J. Boon c Hughes b McLeod	0	– lbw b Allott	10
†P. Whitticase c and b McLeod	15	– c Mendis b Folley	11
P. B. Clift b Folley	35	– c Varey b McLeod	18
W. K. M. Benjamin lbw b Allott	0	– lbw b Allott	0
J. P. Agnew b Folley	6	– b Allott	17
L. B. Taylor c Stanworth b McLeod	0	– c Hughes b McLeod	16
P. M. Such not out	1	– not out	0
L-b 2, n-b 2	4	L-b 1, w 1, n-b 2	4

1/4 2/4 3/10 4/12 5/12	71	1/22 2/63 3/69 4/92 5/103	157
6/60 7/61 8/70 9/70		6/109 7/114 8/136 9/153	

Bonus points – Lancashire 4.

Bowling: *First Innings*—Allott 14–5–35–3; McLeod 7–2–8–5; O'Shaughnessy 4–1–12–0; Simmons 2–0–4–0; Folley 6–3–10–2. *Second Innings*—Allott 28–11–46–4; McLeod 11.4–4–35–2; O'Shaughnessy 15–7–31–1; Simmons 3–1–3–0; Folley 27–17–41–3.

Umpires: B. J. Meyer and R. Palmer.

At Northampton, May 23, 24, 25. LEICESTERSHIRE drew with NORTHAMPTON-SHIRE.

LEICESTERSHIRE v SOMERSET

At Leicester, May 30, June 1, 2. Drawn. Leicestershire 8 pts, Somerset 7 pts. Toss: Somerset. Torrential rain washed out the final day's play of a match enlivened by some noteworthy performances. Agnew, bowling off a shortened run to make the most of the cloudy conditions, took four for 39 in a seventeen-over spell and finished with six for 85 after useful contributions by Hardy, Felton and Crowe had given Somerset a solid start. Leicestershire's reply centred largely on their captain, Willey, who reached his hundred with the third of three sixes, having batted for 86 minutes and faced 86 balls, eighteen of which were despatched to the boundary. Willey's innings followed rumours of dressing-room discontent, but such matters were set aside as he put on 147 in 27 overs for the second wicket with Cobb.

Close of play: First day, Somerset 173-2 (J. J. E. Hardy 71*, M. D. Crowe 14*); Second day, Leicestershire 326-9 (D. I. Gower 48*, P. M. Such 0*).

Somerset

B. C. Rose c Willey b Agnew	......	28
N. A. Felton c Potter b Agnew	......	52
J. J. E. Hardy c Whitticase b DeFreitas		82
M. D. Crowe c Whitaker b Agnew	......	44
R. J. Harden lbw b Agnew	......	0
*V. J. Marks c Willey b Agnew	......	18
†N. D. Burns c Potter b Such	....	21
G. D. Rose c Boon b DeFreitas	.....	10
G. V. Palmer c Boon b Agnew	......	6
N. A. Mallender not out	......	11
A. N. Jones c Whitticase b DeFreitas	.	0
L-b 5, n-b 8	....	13

1/52 2/127 3/218 4/219 5/219   285
6/258 7/258 8/267 9/285

Bonus points – Somerset 3, Leicestershire 4.

Bowling: Agnew 37–5–85–6; Benjamin 20–2–80–0; DeFreitas 16–3–54–3; Such 21–5–52–1; Willey 2–0–9–0.

Leicestershire

L. Potter c Burns b Marks	....	23
R. A. Cobb lbw b Marks	....	88
*P. Willey c and b Mallender	....	113
J. J. Whitaker b Mallender	....	0
D. I. Gower not out	....	48
T. J. Boon lbw b Palmer	....	6
†P. Whitticase c Felton b Marks	......	0
P. A. J. DeFreitas lbw b G. D. Rose	...	21
W. K. M. Benjamin c Crowe b G. D. Rose	3
J. P. Agnew c and b G. D. Rose	...	15
P. M. Such not out	......	0
B 1, l-b 4, w 1, n-b 3	....	9

1/77 2/224 3/230 4/234   (9 wkts) 326
5/255 6/256 7/279 8/297 9/323

Bonus points – Leicestershire 4, Somerset 4.

Bowling: Jones 10–1–55–0; Mallender 16–1–73–2; G. D. Rose 14–1–67–3; Palmer 8–1–40–1; Marks 23–6–74–3; Crowe 3–1–12–0.

Umpires: J. H. Hampshire and M. J. Kitchen.

At Birmingham, June 3, 4, 5. LEICESTERSHIRE drew with WARWICKSHIRE.

LEICESTERSHIRE v WORCESTERSHIRE

At Leicester, June 6, 8, 9. Drawn. Leicestershire 3 pts, Worcestershire 4 pts. Toss: Leicestershire. The match was abandoned early on the final day after the last two sessions of the previous day had been lost through incessant rain. Worcestershire's batsmen, Weston apart, had looked far more comfortable on the two-paced wicket than their Leicestershire counterparts, with Curtis and Illingworth scoring half-centuries as they added 116 for the first wicket in 30 overs.

Close of play: First day, Worcestershire 4-0 (R. K. Illingworth 4*, T. S. Curtis 0*); Second day, Worcestershire 143-2 (R. K. Illingworth 59*, G. A. Hick 16*).

Leicestershire

L. Potter lbw b Radford	16	J. P. Agnew b Pridgeon	20
R. A. Cobb c and b Radford	6	L. B. Taylor c Illingworth b Pridgeon	8
*P. Willey b Radford	71	P. M. Such not out	2
J. J. Whitaker c Hick b Pridgeon	8		
T. J. Boon c Hick b Pridgeon	87	B 1, l-b 3, w 2, n-b 8	14
N. E. Briers c Hick b Pridgeon	31		
†P. Whitticase b Pridgeon	0	1/15 2/35 3/64 4/154 5/229	263
C. C. Lewis c D'Oliveira b Pridgeon	0	6/230 7/232 8/239 9/258	

Bonus points – Leicestershire 3, Worcestershire 4.

Bowling: Radford 23–4–63–3; Pridgeon 24.3–10–44–7; Newport 14–2–56–0; Illingworth 12–3–30–0; Hick 4–0–12–0; Weston 11–2–39–0; Lampitt 6–0–15–0.

Worcestershire

R. K. Illingworth not out	59
T. S. Curtis c Briers b Lewis	54
M. J. Weston b Lewis	0
G. A. Hick not out	16
L-b 12, w 1, n-b 1	14

1/116 2/116   (2 wkts) 143

D. B. D'Oliveira, S. R. Lampitt, *P. A. Neale, †S. J. Rhodes, P. J. Newport, N. V. Radford and A. P. Pridgeon did not bat.

Bowling: Agnew 9–2–35–0; Taylor 5–0–35–0; Lewis 15–2–40–2; Such 11–4–21–0.

Umpires: D. Lloyd and K. E. Palmer.

At Worcester, June 13, 15, 16. LEICESTERSHIRE drew with WORCESTERSHIRE.

LEICESTERSHIRE v SUSSEX

At Leicester, June 20, 22, 23. Leicestershire won by four wickets. Leicestershire 20 pts, Sussex 3 pts. Toss: Sussex. Leicestershire's first victory in the Championship came at a time when rumours of dressing-room unrest were at their highest and speculation about Willey's captaincy was at its most intense. Furthermore, an off-the-field incident involving Agnew and DeFreitas overshadowed what was a splendid finish after both sides had contrived a run-chase following the loss of six hours twenty minutes' play on the last two days. Sussex's first innings looked like being a modest affair until a robust, undefeated 72 off 120 balls by le Roux, coming in at No. 8, saw them to a third bonus point. When Willey declared, Sussex reciprocated, and Leicestershire were set 284 to win in 72 overs. Boon, Briers and Whitaker scored half-centuries and DeFreitas, with some bold hitting, struck the winning runs.

Close of play: First day, Sussex 124-6 (R. I. Alikhan 45*, G. S. le Roux 10*); Second day, Leicestershire 32-0 (R. A. Cobb 13*, N. E. Briers 17*).

Sussex

R. I. Alikhan c Cobb b Clift	45	– c Whitticase b Benjamin	9
A. M. Green c Boon b DeFreitas	1	– b Benjamin	7
D. K. Standing b Agnew	1	– st Whitticase b Such	4
A. P. Wells c Whitticase b Clift	9	– c DeFreitas b Such	7
C. M. Wells b Clift	0	– not out	0
*I. J. Gould c Cobb b Agnew	43	– not out	13
D. A. Reeve c Whitticase b Clift	8		
G. S. le Roux not out	72		
†P. Moores c sub b DeFreitas	31		
A. C. S. Pigott c Boon b Clift	23		
A. M. Babington c Whitticase b Clift	0		
B 4, l-b 1, n-b 13	18	L-b 2	2

1/3 2/13 3/27 4/27 5/95   251   1/16 2/19   (4 wkts dec.) 64
6/111 7/124 8/199 9/238   3/22 4/33

Bonus points – Sussex 3, Leicestershire 4.

Bowling: *First Innings*—DeFreitas 30–10–82–2; Agnew 18–6–43–2; Benjamin 20–4–57–0; Clift 24.5–6–64–6. *Second Innings*—DeFreitas 5–1–8–0; Benjamin 6–1–10–2; Clift 3–1–2–0; Such 8–4–21–2; Willey 6–1–21–0.

Leicestershire

R. A. Cobb not out	13	– c Moores b Babington	46
N. E. Briers not out	17	– c Alikhan b Reeve	54
*P. Willey (did not bat)		– b Reeve	13
J. J. Whitaker (did not bat)		– b Pigott	55
T. J. Boon (did not bat)		– b Babington	61
P. B. Clift (did not bat)		– c Moores b le Roux	20
P. A. J. DeFreitas (did not bat)		– not out	26
W. K. M. Benjamin (did not bat)		– not out	9
L-b 1, n-b 1	2	L-b 3, n-b 1	4

(no wkt dec.) 32   1/100 2/112 3/114   (6 wkts) 288
                      4/194 5/251 6/259

†P. Whitticase, J. P. Agnew and P. M. Such did not bat.

Bowling: *First Innings*—le Roux 5–1–11–0; Babington 4–1–6–0; C. M. Wells 3–1–6–0; Pigott 4–1–4–0; Reeve 2–1–4–0. *Second Innings*—le Roux 15.2–2–73–1; Babington 18–2–77–2; Pigott 13–1–53–1; Reeve 10–1–42–2; C. M. Wells 12–1–40–0.

Umpires: B. Dudleston and D. R. Shepherd.

At Leicester, June 27, 28, 29. LEICESTERSHIRE drew with PAKISTANIS (See Pakistani tour section).

LEICESTERSHIRE v DERBYSHIRE

At Leicester, July 1, 2, 3. Leicestershire won by 47 runs. Leicestershire 24 pts, Derbyshire 7 pts. Toss: Leicestershire. The wicket having eased by the third day, Leicestershire built on their first-innings superiority with considerable authority. Willey, typically aggressive, fashioned his 122 in just 126 minutes, hitting a six and sixteen fours, whereas Briers, in marked contrast, had but four boundaries in his 179-minute 76 not out. Derbyshire, needing 309 to win in just over two sessions, were in desperate trouble at 5 for two before Roberts rallied their cause. He batted for 221 minutes, hitting 21 fours, until he lost all his partners, the last of whom, Mortensen, was dismissed in unusual circumstances. Batting with a runner, he set off for a single, forgetting that he should not leave his crease. Willey, alert to Law 2.7, instructed the wicket-keeper to remove the bails and Mortensen, by now at the bowler's end with his runner, was run out.

Close of play: First day, Derbyshire 41-3 (J. E. Morris 13*, R. J. Finney 5*); Second day, Leicestershire 83-1 (N. E. Briers 34*, P. Willey 31*).

Leicestershire

R. A. Cobb c Maher b Malcolm	1	– c Holding b Warner	9
N. E. Briers c Maher b Finney	45	– not out	76
*P. Willey c Maher b Mortensen	30	– c Sharma b Holding	122
J. J. Whitaker b Holding	51	– not out	26
T. J. Boon c Holding b Sharma	51		
P. B. Clift b Warner	56		
†P. Whitticase c Maher b Newman	31		
P. A. J. DeFreitas b Newman	18		
J. P. Agnew b Warner	5		
G. J. F. Ferris lbw b Newman	3		
P. M. Such not out	0		
B 2, l-b 12, w 2, n-b 10	26	L-b 10, w 1, n-b 2	13

1/4 2/46 3/99 4/193 5/201   317   1/20 2/209   (2 wkts dec.) 246
6/289 7/289 8/298 9/314

Bonus points – Leicestershire 4, Derbyshire 4.

Bowling: *First Innings*—Holding 19-2-71-1; Malcolm 9-1-49-1; Mortensen 8-3-17-1; Finney 7-0-39-1; Newman 21.5-5-59-3; Sharma 26-8-53-1; Warner 4-0-15-2. *Second Innings*—Holding 18-2-69-1; Warner 14-2-46-1; Malcolm 9-1-39-0; Sharma 16-1-82-0; Barnett 2-2-0-0.

Derbyshire

*K. J. Barnett b Agnew	1	– b DeFreitas	4
†B. J. M. Maher lbw b Agnew	1	– c Whitticase b DeFreitas	10
B. Roberts c Clift b Agnew	15	– (4) not out	137
J. E. Morris b Willey	53	– (5) c and b Such	20
R. J. Finney c Whitaker b Clift	8	– (6) c Boon b Ferris	24
R. Sharma not out	62	– (7) c Whitticase b DeFreitas	23
P. G. Newman c Whitticase b Ferris	35	– (8) b Ferris	5
A. E. Warner c Whitticase b Ferris	1	– (9) c Whitticase b DeFreitas	15
M. A. Holding c Boon b Ferris	4	– (10) c Whitticase b Ferris	8
O. H. Mortensen c Whitaker b Such	8	– (11) run out	0
D. E. Malcolm b Clift	2	– (3) b Agnew	0
B 1, l-b 5, w 1, n-b 18	25	B 4, l-b 4, w 1, n-b 6	15

1/6 2/21 3/28 4/130 5/134   255   1/4 2/5 3/23 4/64 5/164   261
6/209 7/212 8/216 9/252   6/203 7/229 8/248 9/261

Bonus points – Derbyshire 3, Leicestershire 4.

Bowling: *First Innings*—DeFreitas 19-2-66-0; Agnew 24-7-61-3; Ferris 22-2-71-3; Such 13-1-27-1; Clift 8-2-16-2; Willey 6-3-8-1. *Second Innings*—DeFreitas 13-0-73-4; Agnew 8-1-52-1; Such 11-2-35-1; Ferris 11.4-0-38-3; Willey 13-3-33-0; Clift 7-0-22-0.

Umpires: M. J. Kitchen and R. Palmer.

At The Oval, July 4, 6, 7. LEICESTERSHIRE beat SURREY by an innings and 24 runs.

At Nottingham, July 15, 16, 17. LEICESTERSHIRE lost to NOTTINGHAMSHIRE by an innings and 32 runs.

At Taunton, July 18, 20, 21. LEICESTERSHIRE drew with SOMERSET.

LEICESTERSHIRE v MIDDLESEX

At Leicester, July 22, 23, 24. Leicestershire won by an innings and 30 runs. Leicestershire 22 pts, Middlesex 4 pts. Toss: Leicestershire. No play was possible before lunch on the first day. With the pitch offering help to the seamers, Middlesex struggled to a paltry 119 in 70.2 overs. Clift gave an object lesson in line and length in taking five wickets, while Ferris's five were the product of a more hostile approach. The gloomy weather, which was threatening to end the match prematurely, persuaded Leicestershire to go for their runs quickly, and Boon and Whitaker added 84 in 95 minutes for the fourth wicket. Play was delayed until 1.25 p.m. on the final day, when Middlesex resumed needing 124 to make Leicestershire bat again. However, with Agnew making amends for going without a wicket in the first innings, and Ferris improving his match figures to eight for 63, they never looked like achieving this.

Close of play: First day, Middlesex 99-8 (S. P. Hughes 3*, A. R. C. Fraser 11*); Second day, Middlesex 2-1 (W. N. Slack 0*, S. P. Hughes 0*).

Middlesex

J. D. Carr c Cobb b Ferris	7	– lbw b Lewis	1
W. N. Slack c Whitticase b Ferris	21	– b Agnew	35
K. R. Brown lbw b Clift	7	– (4) c Cobb b Ferris	2
C. T. Radley c Potter b Clift	9	– (5) lbw b Agnew	0
R. O. Butcher c Whitticase b Clift	0	– (6) b Ferris	0
*†P. R. Downton lbw b Ferris	22	– (7) c Whitticase b Lewis	15
A. Needham c Lewis b Clift	0	– (8) lbw b Agnew	15
N. F. Williams c Willey b Ferris	0	– (9) c Whitticase b Agnew	17
S. P. Hughes b Clift	3	– (3) b Agnew	0
A. R. C. Fraser c Cobb b Ferris	27	– not out	2
N. G. Cowans not out	2	– c Briers b Agnew	2
L-b 2, n-b 2	4	L-b 1, w 3, n-b 3	7
	119		**96**

1/22 2/33 3/37 4/37 5/48   1/1 2/9 3/20 4/23 5/24
6/55 7/84 8/85 9/111   6/52 7/64 8/87 9/93

Bonus points – Leicestershire 4.

Bowling: *First Innings*—Ferris 23.2–9–38–5; Agnew 14–5–30–0; Clift 21–9–33–5; Lewis 12–4–16–0. *Second Innings*—Ferris 12–4–25–3; Lewis 7–1–26–2; Agnew 16.3–6–44–5.

Leicestershire

R. A. Cobb c Downton b Williams	22	C. C. Lewis c Downton b Cowans	6
N. E. Briers c Downton b Fraser	18	G. J. F. Ferris b Cowans	0
*P. Willey lbw b Fraser	2		
J. J. Whitaker b Needham	77	B 2, l-b 8, n-b 6	16
T. J. Boon c Carr b Cowans	71		
L. Potter c Butcher b Williams	0	1/35 2/37 3/80	(9 wkts dec.) 245
P. B. Clift not out	33	4/164 5/187 6/237	
†P. Whitticase c Carr b Needham	0	7/238 8/245 9/245	

J. P. Agnew did not bat.

Bonus points – Leicestershire 2, Middlesex 4.

Bowling: Williams 21–4–49–2; Cowans 19–6–53–3; Fraser 16–5–45–2; Hughes 19–5–51–0; Needham 15–6–30–2; Slack 3–0–7–0.

Umpires: D. J. Constant and R. Palmer.

LEICESTERSHIRE v YORKSHIRE

At Leicester, July 25, 27, 28. Yorkshire won by an innings and 86 runs. Yorkshire 23 pts, Leicestershire 1 pt. Toss: Yorkshire. Leicestershire's indifferent batting on a pitch helping the seam bowlers early on – it had been used previously in the Middlesex match – was put firmly into perspective by Moxon and Blakey, who added 155 in 61 overs for Yorkshire's second wicket. Moxon, taking 176 balls to reach 50, went on to face 253 deliveries in all. Second time round, Leicestershire's batsmen ignored their opponents' good sense in playing forward on a pitch of variable bounce, and they again suffered the consequences. Fletcher, who had impressed with his economy on the first day, took a wicket with the first ball of his second spell and three in four overs without conceding a run. For Leicestershire, matters off the field were equally disturbing, with F. M. Turner, their secretary/manager, accusing Worcestershire's chairman, C. D. Fearnley, of making an illegal approach to the much troubled all-rounder, DeFreitas. It was also confirmed that Boon, whose hand was struck by Jarvis in the first innings, had suffered a fracture and would be out for several weeks.

Close of play: First day, Yorkshire 77-1 (M. D. Moxon 33*, R. J. Blakey 18*); Second day, Leicestershire 41-0 (N. E. Briers 24*, R. A. Cobb 12*).

Leicestershire

R. A. Cobb c Bairstow b Shaw	20	– lbw b Hartley	20
N. E. Briers c Moxon b Hartley	0	– lbw b Jarvis	24
*P. Willey b Jarvis	28	– c Hartley b Jarvis	9
J. J. Whitaker b Shaw	0	– c Blakey b Hartley	5
T. J. Boon retired hurt	32	– absent injured	
L. Potter b Fletcher	7	– (5) not out	18
P. B. Clift c Blakey b Fletcher	2	– (6) b Fletcher	6
P. A. J. DeFreitas b Fletcher	7	– (7) c Blakey b Fletcher	0
†P. Whitticase c Bairstow b Hartley	0	– (8) b Fletcher	3
J. P. Agnew b Jarvis	19	– (9) c Sharp b Fletcher	7
G. J. F. Ferris not out	11	– (10) c Blakey b Jarvis	20
B 2, l-b 3	5	B 5, l-b 6, n-b 1	12

1/2 2/45 3/47 4/70 5/83   131   1/41 2/63 3/63 4/70 5/76   124
6/85 7/101 8/101 9/131   6/76 7/84 8/92 9/124

Bonus points – Yorkshire 4.

Bowling: *First Innings*—Jarvis 13.5-4-46-2; Hartley 14-4-26-2; Shaw 8-1-18-2; Fletcher 13-3-36-3. *Second Innings*—Jarvis 19-5-52-3; Hartley 13-4-30-2; Fletcher 11-6-22-4; Shaw 6-3-9-0.

Yorkshire

M. D. Moxon c Whitticase b DeFreitas	84	P. W. Jarvis b Agnew	32
A. A. Metcalfe c Whitticase b DeFreitas	6	S. D. Fletcher b Clift	2
R. J. Blakey lbw b Ferris	76	C. Shaw not out	2
K. Sharp b Agnew	34		
J. D. Love b Ferris	16	B 7, l-b 10, w 1, n-b 19	37
†D. L. Bairstow b Clift	35		
*P. Carrick lbw b Ferris	0	1/37 2/192 3/198 4/252 5/252	341
P. J. Hartley b Clift	17	6/256 7/295 8/318 9/338	

Bonus points – Yorkshire 3, Leicestershire 1 (Score at 100 overs: 252-3).

Bowling: Agnew 33.4-6-94-2; Ferris 24-5-80-3; DeFreitas 33-8-69-2; Clift 32-9-61-3; Willey 6-0-20-0.

Umpires: D. J. Constant and R. Palmer.

At Cheltenham, August 1, 3, 4. LEICESTERSHIRE beat GLOUCESTERSHIRE by 63 runs.

At Abergavenny, August 5, 6, 7. LEICESTERSHIRE drew with GLAMORGAN.

LEICESTERSHIRE v WARWICKSHIRE

At Hinckley, August 8, 10, 11. Drawn. Leicestershire 6 pts, Warwickshire 4 pts. Toss: Leicestershire. The early signs were favourable for the home county, on their annual visit to Hinckley, when their West Indian fast bowler, Ferris, claimed Warwickshire's first three wickets without conceding a run in a devastating spell of nineteen deliveries. Only Humpage, with some resolute hitting in his 61, averted a complete disaster. In reply, Leicestershire managed a 99-run lead, and had the visitors 76 for three before Moles, Amiss and Humpage set about saving the match on the third day. A fifth-wicket partnership of 154 in 35 overs saw Amiss score his 102nd century (fifteen fours, 200 balls), and when rain washed out play at tea, Humpage, having hit a six and nine fours, was unbeaten on 99.

Close of play: First day, Leicestershire 32-0 (I. P. Butcher 7*, N. E. Briers 21*); Second day, Warwickshire 76-3 (A. J. Moles 24*, D. L. Amiss 1*).

Warwickshire

T. A. Lloyd c Potter b Ferris	12	– (2) b Clift	7
A. J. Moles c Potter b Ferris	0	– (1) c Potter b Ferris	51
Asif Din lbw b Clift	13	– b Ferris	35
D. L. Amiss c Whitticase b Ferris	0	– (5) c Whitaker b Willey	120
G. W. Humpage c Potter b Ferris	61	– (6) not out	99
P. A. Smith b Ferris	13	– (7) not out	5
†G. A. Tedstone lbw b Clift	8		
G. C. Small c Whitticase b Ferris	8	– (4) c Potter b Ferris	3
T. A. Merrick c Butcher b Clift	4		
T. A. Munton b Clift	4		
*N. Gifford not out	6		
B 2, l-b 12, n-b 5	19	L-b 12, n-b 10	22

1/10 2/20 3/21 4/90 5/103   148   1/10 2/70 3/74   (5 wkts) 342
6/119 7/123 8/135 9/136   4/155 5/309

Bonus points – Leicestershire 4.

Bowling: *First Innings*—Agnew 14-4-42-0; Ferris 20-5-42-6; Clift 16.2-8-26-4; Lewis 6-0-24-0. *Second Innings*—Ferris 28-6-86-3; Agnew 4-0-14-0; Clift 27-6-81-1; Lewis 10-0-22-0; Potter 13-1-48-0; Willey 28-5-79-1.

Leicestershire

I. P. Butcher lbw b Merrick	22	C. C. Lewis b Merrick	5
N. E. Briers c Humpage b Small	65	J. P. Agnew b Munton	43
R. A. Cobb b Merrick	3	G. J. F. Ferris not out	8
J. J. Whitaker lbw b Small	25		
*P. Willey c Moles b Munton	7	L-b 8, n-b 15	23
L. Potter c Humpage b Merrick	7		
P. B. Clift b Merrick	37	1/65 2/78 3/125 4/131 5/139	247
†P. Whitticase c Moles b Munton	2	6/150 7/155 8/169 9/205	

Bonus points – Leicestershire 2, Warwickshire 4.

Bowling: Small 24-0-89-2; Merrick 27-4-84-5; Munton 29-7-65-3; Gifford 2-1-1-0.

Umpires: J. Birkenshaw and D. Lloyd.

At Derby, August 15, 17. LEICESTERSHIRE beat DERBYSHIRE by an innings and 25 runs.

At Scarborough, August 19, 20, 21. LEICESTERSHIRE drew with YORKSHIRE.

LEICESTERSHIRE v NOTTINGHAMSHIRE

At Leicester, August 26, 27, 28. Drawn. Leicestershire 7 pts, Nottinghamshire 7 pts. Toss: Leicestershire. Leicestershire, in a bid to throw open the Championship race, took a leaf from the book of their opponents and local rivals. They prepared a lush pitch, won the toss, and in 8.4 overs had three Nottinghamshire wickets down for 11 runs. Unfortunately for their bowlers, they then encountered Rice at his most determined. His superb innings of 138 was a combination of cautious, sound defence and an ability to adapt quickly to the unpredictability of the wicket. With Birch, he added 114 in 127 minutes, and in all he batted for 244 minutes, hitting twenty boundaries. Inclement weather – there was no play after lunch on the first day – further dampened Leicestershire's hopes of a result, and settling for maximum batting points, they continued their innings well into the third day.

Close of play: First day, Nottinghamshire 105-4 (C. E. B. Rice 58*, J. D. Birch 16*); Second day, Leicestershire 156-4 (D. I. Gower 68*, J. J. Whitaker 4*).

Nottinghamshire

B. C. Broad b Agnew	6	– c Butcher b Lewis	19
*R. T. Robinson lbw b Ferris	0	– not out	41
M. Newell b Ferris	2		
P. Johnson c Whitticase b Ferris	12	– (3) not out	36
C. E. B. Rice lbw b Agnew	138		
J. D. Birch b Ferris	55		
R. J. Hadlee c Briers b Agnew	44		
†B. N. French not out	19		
E. E. Hemmings c Briers b Ferris	0		
K. Saxelby not out	10		
L-b 4, w 5, n-b 5	14	B 1, l-b 1, w 2, n-b 1	5

1/2 2/9 3/11 4/67 5/181   (8 wkts dec.) 300   1/36   (1 wkt dec.) 101
6/256 7/275 8/276

K. E. Cooper did not bat.

Bonus points – Nottinghamshire 4, Leicestershire 3.

Bowling: *First Innings*—Agnew 25-6-85-3; Ferris 27.1-2-115-5; Clift 15-2-49-0; Lewis 5-2-14-0; Such 13-5-33-0. *Second Innings*—Agnew 6-2-17-0; Ferris 3-0-6-0; Lewis 8-0-25-1; Such 14-3-33-0; Willey 8-1-18-0.

Leicestershire

I. P. Butcher c French b Cooper	16	C. C. Lewis c Hemmings b Cooper	42
N. E. Briers c French b Saxelby	37	G. J. F. Ferris c French b Hadlee	7
*P. Willey lbw b Hadlee	27	P. M. Such not out	0
D. I. Gower c Birch b Rice	74		
J. P. Agnew c Johnson b Saxelby	0	B 1, l-b 7	8
J. J. Whitaker c Rice b Hadlee	14		
P. B. Clift b Hadlee	88	1/30 2/64 3/148 4/148 5/172	324
†P. Whitticase c Johnson b Cooper	11	6/176 7/203 8/307 9/321	

Bonus points – Leicestershire 4, Nottinghamshire 3 (Score at 100 overs: 307-8).

Bowling: Hadlee 28.3-8-76-4; Saxelby 20-4-53-2; Rice 19-4-61-1; Cooper 21-7-56-3; Hemmings 17-3-70-0.

Umpires: D. Lloyd and R. A. White.

LEICESTERSHIRE v NORTHAMPTONSHIRE

At Leicester, August 29, 31, September 1. Leicestershire won by an innings and 125 runs. Leicestershire 24 pts, Northamptonshire 3 pts. Toss: Northamptonshire. In a match vital to the Championship aspirations of both teams, Northamptonshire were punished for their positive approach. Taking first use of a green pitch after winning the toss, they were in disarray at 83 for seven by lunch on the first day. Agnew, off an economical run, kept the batsmen under pressure with a 22-over spell which was interrupted only by lunch and two brief stoppages for light rain. However, Nick Cook held up his former county's progress with an unbeaten 55, his half-century coming in 133 minutes. Leicestershire's innings could not have been more of a contrast. Their experimental opening pair of Briers and Boon put on 154, with Boon's 94 in 222 minutes including twelve fours; Gower was at his fluid best, stroking eleven fours and two sixes during a stay of 146 minutes; and Whitaker, batting for 204 minutes, hit ten fours in his unbeaten 82. Northamptonshire's second innings was all over by five past twelve on the final day. Agnew again claimed five wickets, and DeFreitas at one point had figures of three for 3 in six deliveries. DeFreitas, included in England's winter tour parties over the weekend, had originally been dropped by Leicestershire for "disciplinary reasons", and he was included for this match only because his replacement, C. C. Lewis, was ill.

Close of play: First day, Leicestershire 140-0 (T. J. Boon 58*, N. E. Briers 64*); Second day, Northamptonshire 56-3 (G. Cook 31*, N. G. B. Cook 10*).

Northamptonshire

*G. Cook b Agnew	5	– c Whitticase b Agnew	37
W. Larkins lbw b Agnew	17	– b Agnew	2
R. J. Bailey b DeFreitas	6	– b Agnew	5
A. J. Lamb c Whitticase b Ferris	46	– b DeFreitas	4
D. J. Capel c Whitticase b DeFreitas	4	– (7) lbw b DeFreitas	4
R. J. Boyd-Moss c Whitticase b Agnew	0	– lbw b DeFreitas	0
D. J. Wild c Boon b DeFreitas	1	– absent injured	
†D. Ripley c Clift b Agnew	1	– lbw b DeFreitas	0
N. G. B. Cook not out	55	– (5) b Agnew	32
W. W. Davis b Agnew	1	– (9) c Whitticase b Agnew	8
S. J. Brown lbw b Willey	20	– (10) not out	0
B 6, l-b 8, w 1, n-b 3	18	L-b 4, w 1, n-b 8	13

1/17 2/26 3/41 4/47 5/52   174   1/9 2/24 3/37 4/65 5/66   105
6/57 7/58 8/104 9/105   6/73 7/73 8/102 9/105

Bonus points – Northamptonshire 1, Leicestershire 4.

Bowling: *First Innings*—Ferris 11–2–45–1; Agnew 22–5–59–5; DeFreitas 17–3–44–3; Clift 8–3–8–0; Willey 2.2–1–4–1. *Second Innings*—Ferris 6–2–12–0; Agnew 17.1–4–47–5; DeFreitas 12–1–42–4.

Leicestershire

T. J. Boon c G. Cook b N. G. B. Cook	94	J. P. Agnew b Boyd-Moss	12
N. E. Briers lbw b Davis	69	G. J. F. Ferris b Capel	0
*P. Willey lbw b Capel	7	P. M. Such c Capel b N. G. B. Cook	0
D. I. Gower c sub b Davis	79		
J. J. Whitaker not out	82	B 8, l-b 15, n-b 16	39
P. B. Clift c Boyd-Moss b Capel	9		
†P. Whitticase lbw b Capel	0	1/154 2/169 3/229 4/317 5/333	404
P. A. J. DeFreitas c sub b N. G. B. Cook	13	6/335 7/372 8/393 9/403	

Bonus points – Leicestershire 4, Northamptonshire 2 (Score at 100 overs: 336-6).

Bowling: Davis 31–5–107–2; Capel 28–4–92–4; Brown 15–0–22–0; N. G. B. Cook 34–9–68–3; Bailey 4–0–18–0; Larkins 8–3–23–0; Boyd-Moss 15–4–51–1.

Umpires: B. Leadbeater and R. A. White.

At Southampton, September 2, 3, 4. LEICESTERSHIRE drew with HAMPSHIRE.

LEICESTERSHIRE v GLOUCESTERSHIRE

At Leicester, September 9, 10, 11. Leicestershire won by eight wickets. Leicestershire 22 pts, Gloucestershire 8 pts. Toss: Leicestershire. DeFreitas, finding movement where Agnew and Ferris had failed, took seven for 85, his best return of the season, and Gloucestershire had good reason to be grateful for Lloyds's 105 in 178 minutes, a superb innings which included a six and fifteen fours. Lloyds played with admirable correctness, and deserved his good fortune when, on 97, he chopped the ball on to his stumps but did not dislodge a bail. Leicestershire's reply fell way short of expectations, but Taylor, playing his first Championship match since breaking a toe in mid-June, put them in a winning position with six wickets in a sustained spell of seam bowling after DeFreitas and Ferris had left the field with injuries. Agnew bowled unchanged for 21 overs and took his total of first-class wickets for the season to 99. Needing 230 to win, Leicestershire scored them with a fair amount of dash as adverse weather threatened on the horizon. Gower provided the impetus with an unbeaten 62 off 70 balls, hitting nine fours and one six and adding 122 in 81 minutes with Briers, whose 102 not out came in 210 minutes and included thirteen fours. Briers's second fifty, however, off 52 balls, took just 51 minutes.

Close of play: First day, Leicestershire 52-3 (P. Willey 4*, P. Whitticase 4*); Second day, Gloucestershire 153.

Gloucestershire

A. W. Stovold c and b DeFreitas	53	– b Ferris		35
A. J. Wright c Whitticase b DeFreitas	7	– b Taylor		23
P. W. Romaines b DeFreitas	5	– lbw b Agnew		2
*C. W. J. Athey lbw b DeFreitas	24	– c Boon b Taylor		4
P. Bainbridge run out	0	– b Taylor		1
K. M. Curran b Ferris	49	– not out		20
J. W. Lloyds c Whitticase b DeFreitas	105	– c and b Agnew		11
†R. C. Russell c Potter b DeFreitas	27	– c Whitticase b Taylor		19
J. N. Shepherd c Briers b DeFreitas	5	– b Taylor		1
C. A. Walsh c Potter b Taylor	2	– c Potter b Agnew		26
G. E. Sainsbury not out	0	– b Taylor		0
B 1, l-b 4, w 2, n-b 18	25	L-b 3, n-b 8		11

1/32 2/60 3/91 4/96 5/118   302   1/37 2/42 3/58 4/60 5/82   153
6/187 7/277 8/291 9/301   6/109 7/110 8/143 9/145

Bonus points – Gloucestershire 4, Leicestershire 4.

In the second innings K. M. Curran, when 16, retired hurt at 89 and resumed at 145.

Bowling: *First Innings*—Agnew 21-2-70-0; Ferris 11-1-41-1; DeFreitas 30.2-5-85-7; Taylor 16-1-85-1; Willey 9-2-16-0. *Second Innings*—Agnew 20.2-0-76-3; Ferris 8-1-27-1; Taylor 12-1-47-6.

Leicestershire

T. J. Boon c Athey b Walsh	18	– b Sainsbury		50
N. E. Briers c Curran b Walsh	14	– not out		102
*P. Willey c Shepherd b Sainsbury	8	– c Russell b Walsh		9
D. I. Gower c Shepherd b Sainsbury	7	– not out		62
†P. Whitticase run out	33			
J. J. Whitaker b Walsh	61			
L. Potter c Curran b Shepherd	4			
P. A. J. DeFreitas c Lloyds b Shepherd	18			
J. P. Agnew b Walsh	10			
G. J. F. Ferris c and b Walsh	25			
L. B. Taylor not out	12			
B 4, l-b 7, n-b 5	16	B 2, l-b 5		7

1/36 2/37 3/45 4/56 5/125   226   1/85 2/108   (2 wkts) 230
6/142 7/168 8/181 9/207

Bonus points – Leicestershire 2, Gloucestershire 4.

Bowling: *First Innings*—Walsh 28.4-3-112-5; Sainsbury 19-5-48-2; Bainbridge 6-3-13-0; Shepherd 15-5-42-2. *Second Innings*—Walsh 15-4-35-1; Sainsbury 18-2-61-1; Bainbridge 11-0-49-0; Shepherd 13-4-50-0; Lloyds 6-0-28-0.

Umpires: J. H. Harris and A. A. Jones.

At Canterbury, September 12, 14, 15. LEICESTERSHIRE drew with KENT.

MIDDLESEX

Patron: HRH The Duke of Edinburgh
President: F. G. Mann
Chairman: M. P. Murray
Chairman, Cricket Committee:
  1987 – R. V. C. Robins
  1988 – M. O. C. Sturt
Secretary: T. M. Lamb
  Lord's Cricket Ground, St John's Wood,
  London NW8 8QN (Telephone: 01-289 1300)
Captain: M. W. Gatting
Coach: D. Bennett

While believing that sixteenth place in the Britannic Assurance Championship was cruelly low, Middlesex conceded that the good days might be over and that the rest of the 1980s could be occupied with rehabilitation. It would be a strong contrast to J. M. Brearley's era of six titles which was extended as four more were won in Mike Gatting's first four years as captain. In 1986, however, even though a Lord's final was won, the signs of decline were there with the fall from champions to twelfth.

Last year there was too much poor batting, and neither pace nor spin bowling functioned to expectation. Only once before had Middlesex won just two Championship games, in 1919, the season of two-day matches, and only twice (1930 and 1970) had they finished sixteenth. The failures in limited-overs cricket were also significant, for Middlesex had been as successful at winning finals as Championships. In 1987, they failed to qualify for the quarter-finals of the Benson and Hedges Cup; Nottinghamshire eliminated them in the second round of the NatWest Bank Trophy; and there was the routine lack of challenge in the Refuge Assurance Sunday League, in which Middlesex finished tenth.

All counties had ill luck with the weather and all suffered from injuries. For Middlesex, it was clear early in 1987 that their fortune would be worse than average when five players missed the first fixture. Gatting endured four separate injuries before June – strained thigh, broken and dislocated fingers, and a poisoned toe – but when he was fit his form was prolific. Middlesex have seldom been let down by the captain, whose Championship average between 1980 and 1987 was 58.77.

When Gatting went to lead England, Middlesex had already lost to Yorkshire and Northamptonshire and followed on against Lancashire. The first of two wins over Sussex, who finished seventeenth, preceded five more defeats in mid-season, and the losing run ended with a succession of draws as the batting became relatively secure and the bowlers' penetration increased.

Their lowly ranking did not generate complete despair because among the disappointments there were encouraging signs. The promotion of John Carr to opener, when Andy Miller was hurt, was instantly successful as he hit 81 not out and 156 against the Pakistani tourists and Essex respectively. His strokeplay was clean and audacious, he scored and ran quickly, and he formed a dovetailing alliance with Wilf Slack. Their highlights were stands of 173 and 221 in Middlesex's two matches against Surrey. Further investment in young batsmen, at the expense of Clive Radley and Roland Butcher, was also worthwhile. Nobody with the county's future at heart wanted to overpraise Mark Ramprakash, who made his début at seventeen in the first match, but he entranced watchers with his exquisite, powerful strokes. Next day he was back at college. After term, however, there were some more glowing innings, plus the inevitable ducks. "Do not burden him by expecting too much," Gatting asked, but it must be recorded that Ramprakash displayed the strokes and authority of Gatting at a similar age. Mike Roseberry could not achieve a large score, but Keith Brown, with five half-centuries in the Championship, suggested that technical work could make him the grafting successor to Radley.

Radley was left out after the midway point of his second benefit season, but happily he will extend his time at Lord's beyond a quarter of a century by helping to organise the hoped-for revival as captain of the Second XI. Butcher aired his trademark – the match-winning innings – but only once, and his form became so poor that he was dropped. Paul Downton and John Emburey sometimes disguised cracks in the batting by their widely contrasting methods, but even so Middlesex could not average two batting points per match. Downton, who relished the demands of vice-captaincy and was in charge twelve times to Gatting's eleven, improved his already valuable contribution of runs and was selected for the World Cup as wicket-keeper-batsman.

It had been, reluctantly, accepted in 1986 that Phil Edmonds and Emburey were not the match-winners of old. Unhelpful, flat pitches were advanced as the reason why this pair lost their potency, and their transformation into toilers epitomised the way that Middlesex were no longer feared. As the season ended, Edmonds – a lovely, watchable cricketer, but a man who exasperated those in authority – made one unusual demand too many. His wish to play periodically as an amateur could not be granted and so his distinguished seventeen years at Lord's concluded with the committee paying due tribute to his part in the triumphs between 1975 and 1986. His successor, Philip Tufnell, was alone in giving the merest hint that the post-war tradition of high-class spin bowling at Lord's would be maintained.

The unexpected weakness was the pace bowling. Norman Cowans needed a pre-season hernia operation and was not available until late July. By then, his efforts were urgently needed, for Wayne Daniel was experiencing by far his worst year, lacking the capacity to blast out top batsmen. With Neil Williams struggling for fitness and Simon Hughes also having an unproductive summer, 21-year-old Angus Fraser found himself undertaking an unscheduled heavy workload. He responded with accuracy and fortitude, despite having recently recovered from a stress fracture of the back, and became a dependable first change in the attack. – Terry Cooper.

MIDDLESEX 1987

[Bill Smith

Back row: S. P. Hughes, A. J. T. Miller, K. R. Brown, G. K. Brown, J. D. Carr, M. A. Roseberry, A. Needham, M. R. Ramprakash. Middle row:
D. Bennett (coach), A. Jones (Second XI scorer), N. R. C. MacLaurin, P. C. R. Tufnell, J. F. Sykes, A. R. C. Fraser, A. G. J. Fraser, I. J. F. Hutchinson,
N. F. Williams, N. G. Cowans, H. P. Sharp (scorer). Front row: W. N. Slack, P. R. Downton, C. T. Radley, M. W. Gatting (captain), J. E. Emburey,
W. W. Daniel, P. H. Edmonds, R. O. Butcher.

MIDDLESEX RESULTS

All first-class matches – Played 25: Won 2, Lost 8, Drawn 15. Abandoned 1.

County Championship matches – Played 23: Won 2, Lost 8, Drawn 13. Abandoned 1.

Bonus points – Batting 47, Bowling 60.

Competition placings – Britannic Assurance County Championship, 16th; NatWest Bank Trophy, 2nd round; Benson and Hedges Cup, 4th in Group C; Refuge Assurance League, 10th equal.

BRITANNIC ASSURANCE CHAMPIONSHIP AVERAGES

BATTING

	Birthplace	M	I	NO	R	HI	Avge
‡M. W. Gatting	Kingsbury	11	18	1	892	196	52.47
‡J. D. Carr	St John's Wood	22	37	3	1,385	156	40.73
‡W. N. Slack	Troumaca, St Vincent	23	39	0	1,419	173	36.38
‡J. E. Emburey	Peckham	12	19	4	541	74	36.06
‡P. R. Downton	Farnborough, Kent	23	34	6	995	103*	35.53
A. J. T. Miller	Chesham	8	13	1	354	97	29.50
M. R. Ramprakash	Bushey	8	14	3	321	71	29.18
K. R. Brown	Edmonton	15	24	3	579	70	27.57
‡R. O. Butcher	East Point, Barbados	14	18	1	466	71	27.41
‡C. T. Radley	Hertford	7	10	2	182	45*	22.75
M. A. Roseberry	Houghton-le-Spring	9	13	2	248	52	22.54
A. Needham	Calow	9	11	2	161	33	17.88
‡P. H. Edmonds	Lusaka, N. Rhodesia	9	10	2	142	32	17.75
‡N. F. Williams	Hope Well, St Vincent	8	8	4	64	18*	16.00
‡S. P. Hughes	Kingston-upon-Thames	16	19	6	174	26*	13.38
A. R. C. Fraser	Billinge	21	21	5	173	38	10.81
§‡W. W. Daniel	St Philip, Barbados	15	12	8	31	9*	7.75
‡N. G. Cowans	Enfield St Mary, Jamaica	12	14	3	77	24	7.00
P. C. R. Tufnell	Barnet	8	8	4	21	12*	5.25

Also batted: J. F. Sykes (*Shoreditch*) (3 matches) 8, 10, 3*.

* Signifies not out.   ‡ Denotes county cap.   § Not qualified for England.

The following played a total of nine three-figure innings for Middlesex in County Championship matches – J. D. Carr 3, M. W. Gatting 2, W. N. Slack 2, R. O. Butcher 1, P. R. Downton 1.

BOWLING

	O	M	R	W	BB	Avge
N. G. Cowans	281.3	65	781	44	5-43	17.75
P. H. Edmonds	335.1	114	733	26	4-34	28.19
J. E. Emburey	397.3	117	908	32	5-60	28.37
P. C. R. Tufnell	316.2	66	939	31	6-60	30.29
A. R. C. Fraser	532.1	128	1,420	44	4-5	32.27
N. F. Williams	148.4	28	420	11	3-55	38.18
S. P. Hughes	303.1	48	955	24	3-74	39.79
W. W. Daniel	333	43	1,246	29	4-69	42.96

Also bowled: K. R. Brown 13-1-54-3; R. O. Butcher 2.3-1-9-0; J. D. Carr 15-3-54-2; M. W. Gatting 41-10-137-5; A. J. T. Miller 1-0-4-0; A. Needham 155-24-508-9; M. R. Ramprakash 1-0-1-0; M. A. Roseberry 5-0-25-0; W. N. Slack 25-7-69-1; J. F. Sykes 50-16-115-6.

Wicket-keeper: P. R. Downton 47 ct, 5 st.

Leading Fielder: K. R. Brown 15.

MIDDLESEX v YORKSHIRE

At Lord's, April 25, 26, 27. Yorkshire won by two wickets. Yorkshire 21 pts, Middlesex 7 pts. Toss: Middlesex. Slack and Miller fulfilled their responsibilities as Middlesex's only experienced specialist batsmen with a large stand; and after a collapse induced by Carrick and Jarvis, the home side regained control, first through Downton's batting and then through Embury's four for 31 in thirteen overs from the less familiar Nursery End. Middlesex, 45 for two at the second-day close, were taken out of trouble by Roseberry and Ramprakash, whose hundred partnership was laced with boundaries. Ramprakash hit one six and seven fours off 99 balls and made a glowing impression on his first-class début. Then it was back to school the following day for the seventeen-year-old, who had come in because of injuries to Gatting, Radley and Butcher. Yorkshire were set 264 in 60 overs, and after Moxon and Blakey had prepared the way, Sharp, whose first-innings 56 had needed 46 overs, struck 75 from 75 balls. The target became 131 off the last twenty overs and 61 off ten; at 154 for five Middlesex had looked favourites, but Carrick, Hartley and Sidebottom benefited as Middlesex tried to buy wickets and Yorkshire won, off a no-ball from Daniel, with eight balls in hand.

Close of play: First day, Yorkshire 17-0 (M. D. Moxon 8*, R. J. Blakey 7*); Second day, Middlesex 45-2 (W. N. Slack 26*, M. R. Ramprakash 0*).

Middlesex

W. N. Slack c Moxon b Carrick	84	– c Bairstow b Sidebottom	28
A. J. T. Miller c Moxon b Carrick	69	– c Blakey b Sidebottom	2
J. D. Carr lbw b Jarvis	0	– c Blakey b Sidebottom	12
M. R. Ramprakash c Blakey b Jarvis	17	– not out	63
M. A. Roseberry b Carrick	45	– run out	52
†P. R. Downton not out	59	– b Sidebottom	11
*J. E. Emburey b Jarvis	1	– not out	12
P. H. Edmonds c Moxon b Dennis	23		
S. P. Hughes not out	7		
B 4, l-b 11, n-b 9	24	B 4, l-b 6, n-b 8	18

1/159 2/159 3/173 4/190   (7 wkts. dec.) 292   1/7 2/45 3/50   (5 wkts. dec.) 198
5/202 6/208 7/263   4/166 5/184

A. R. C. Fraser and W. W. Daniel did not bat.

Bonus points – Middlesex 3, Yorkshire 3 (Score at 100 overs: 276-7).

Bowling: *First Innings*—Jarvis 19-6-44-3; P. J. Hartley 17-1-71-0; Carrick 25-10-41-3; Sidebottom 19-3-55-0; Dennis 21-3-66-1. *Second Innings*—Jarvis 11-4-36-0; Sidebottom 13.2-0-54-4; Dennis 8-0-53-0; Carrick 8-3-15-0; P. J. Hartley 9-1-30-0.

Yorkshire

M. D. Moxon c Downton b Fraser	24	– c Ramprakash b Edmonds	30
R. J. Blakey c Miller b Edmonds	21	– c Daniel b Edmonds	44
K. Sharp c Roseberry b Emburey	56	– c and b Edmonds	75
J. D. Love c Carr b Edmonds	17	– lbw b Fraser	18
S. N. Hartley c Downton b Emburey	13	– c Downton b Fraser	5
†D. L. Bairstow c Downton b Hughes	34	– c Downton b Fraser	5
*P. Carrick lbw b Hughes	17	– lbw b Emburey	16
A. Sidebottom b Emburey	9	– (9) not out	32
P. J. Hartley c Roseberry b Emburey	4	– (8) b Daniel	22
P. W. Jarvis not out	11	– not out	17
S. J. Dennis c Downton b Fraser	4		
L-b 5, n-b 12	17	L-b 5, n-b 2	7

1/49 2/51 3/85 4/124 5/155   227   1/56 2/95 3/128 4/130   (8 wkts) 267
6/191 7/196 8/209 9/210   5/154 6/194 7/202 8/243

Bonus points – Yorkshire 2, Middlesex 4.

Bowling: *First Innings*—Daniel 19–1–54–0; Hughes 16–2–49–2; Emburey 17–6–38–4; Edmonds 24–8–49–2; Fraser 16.2–4–32–2. *Second Innings*—Daniel 9.4–2–40–1; Hughes 6–2–16–0; Edmonds 19–1–85–3; Fraser 12–4–55–3; Emburey 12–0–66–1.

Umpires: J. Birkenshaw and J. H. Harris.

At Manchester, April 29, 30, May 1. MIDDLESEX drew with LANCASHIRE.

MIDDLESEX v NORTHAMPTONSHIRE

At Lord's, May 6, 7, 8. Northamptonshire won by ten wickets. Northamptonshire 24 pts, Middlesex 5 pts. Toss: Northamptonshire. Middlesex batted without conviction on the first morning but in the afternoon Downton and Embury, in contrasting styles, engineered a revival. Their entertaining stand of 137 lasted 44 overs. For Northamptonshire, Larkins was at his hard-hitting best, and until he was run out two balls after Lamb's dismissal, no bowler had suggested he could be removed in any other way. Williams and Wild then added 143 in 37 overs, and such was the supremacy of bat over ball that 190 of Northamptonshire's 302 came in boundaries. Demoralised, Middlesex were in no state to combat Davis, and Gatting was forced to risk further injury to the finger he had broken while fielding to take the game into the third day. Northamptonshire knocked off the winning runs shortly after lunch, whereupon Middlesex staged a unique practice in the middle in an effort to reverse their poor form.

Close of play: First day, Northamptonshire 58-1 (W. Larkins 41*, N. G. B. Cook 3*); Second day, Middlesex 121-8 (M. W. Gatting 20*, A. R. C. Fraser 2*).

Middlesex

W. N. Slack b Capel	2	– b Davis		14
A. J. T. Miller c G. Cook b Davis	11	– b Davis		21
*M. W. Gatting b Walker	18	– (8) c Williams b Davis		24
R. O. Butcher c Ripley b Walker	14	– c Bailey b Capel		9
C. T. Radley c Ripley b Walker	11	– b Davis		15
†P. R. Downton c Bailey b Davis	81	– (3) c Lamb b Davis		8
J. E. Emburey c sub b Davis	73	– (6) b Davis		1
P. H. Edmonds b Walker	11	– (7) c Bailey b Capel		4
A. R. C. Fraser run out	4	– (10) c Bailey b Capel		8
S. P. Hughes lbw b Davis	13	– (9) c N. G. B. Cook b Walker		13
W. W. Daniel not out	0	– not out		4
L-b 1, n-b 8	18	L-b 3, w 3, n-b 11		17

1/7 2/24 3/44 4/49 5/78   256   1/22 2/44 3/57 4/57 5/62   138
6/215 7/228 8/248 9/250   6/68 7/86 8/112 9/133

Bonus points – Middlesex 3, Northamptonshire 4.

Bowling: *First Innings*—Davis 27–2–92–4; Capel 20–2–57–1; Walker 20.2–5–42–4; Wild 19–7–40–0; N. G. B. Cook 7–2–15–0. *Second Innings*—Davis 22–5–57–6; Capel 21–4–58–3; Walker 7–1–12–1; Wild 2–1–2–0; N. G. B. Cook 5–3–6–0.

Northamptonshire

*G. Cook c Edmonds b Daniel	12	– not out		24
W. Larkins run out	87	– not out		66
N. G. B. Cook b Hughes	13			
R. J. Bailey b Daniel	0			
A. J. Lamb c Butcher b Hughes	37			
D. J. Capel c Downton b Hughes	3			
R. G. Williams not out	74			
D. J. Wild not out	59			
B 1, l-b 6, w 10	17	L-b 1, n-b 3		4

1/47 2/85 3/86 4/156   (6 wkts. dec.) 302   (no wkt) 94
5/159 6/159

†D. Ripley, A. Walker and W. W. Davis did not bat.

Bonus points – Northamptonshire 4, Middlesex 2.

Bowling: *First Innings*—Daniel 23–6–95–2; Fraser 19–4–65–0; Hughes 23–2–100–3; Emburey 5–1–24–0; Edmonds 2–0–11–0. *Second Innings*—Daniel 4–0–30–0; Hughes 3–0–27–0; Emburey 8–3–11–0; Edmonds 7–1–17–0; Butcher 1.3–1–4–0; Miller 1–0–4–0.

Umpires: B. Dudleston and D. G. L. Evans.

At Cambridge, May 20, 21, 22. MIDDLESEX drew with CAMBRIDGE UNIVERSITY.

At Hove, May 23, 25, 26. MIDDLESEX beat SUSSEX by three wickets.

At Lord's, May 30, 31, June 1. MIDDLESEX drew with PAKISTANIS (See Pakistani tour section).

MIDDLESEX v ESSEX

At Lord's, June 3, 4, 5. Drawn. Middlesex 7 pts, Essex 5 pts. Toss: Middlesex. Gooch put his poor form behind him and his morning's effort was consolidated by Fletcher and Pringle in unpleasant conditions. Pringle retired hurt when 41 after being hit on the helmet by a ball from Williams; Fletcher took many knocks – especially on the hand – from the lifting ball but battled for four hours to his hundred in one of the braver innings of his distinguished career. For Middlesex, Slack was forceful but Carr was inspired, producing the county's best innings of the season to date and easily improving on his previous Championship highest. At 168 for one, a storm during the tea interval ruined a promising contest and influenced Downton to bat on for full batting points. Carr, 90 when the rain stopped play, batted even more powerfully on the third day and had faced 203 balls and struck 23 fours when caught behind. Downton's decision not to engage in declarations was vindicated when rain, as forecast, returned in the last hour.

Close of play: First day, Essex 268-6 (K. W. R. Fletcher 102*, T. D. Topley 2*); Second day, Middlesex 168-1 (J. D. Carr 90*).

Essex

*G. A. Gooch lbw b Daniel	53	– c Butcher b Slack	36
I. Redpath b Daniel	1	– retired hurt	4
B. R. Hardie c Downton b Hughes	18	– lbw b Fraser	15
K. W. R. Fletcher c Downton b Fraser	121		
D. R. Pringle not out	69	– (4) c Downton b Carr	18
M. G. Field-Buss lbw b Daniel	6	– (5) not out	34
H. A. Page c Needham b Williams	9	– (6) not out	1
†D. E. East lbw b Hughes	7		
T. D. Topley b Daniel	7		
J. K. Lever b Hughes	10		
J. H. Childs run out	8		
L-b 6, w 5, n-b 21	32	B 4, w 1, n-b 3	8

1/10 2/53 3/104 4/226 5/250   341   1/57 2/57 3/115   (3 wkts) 116
6/264 7/274 8/304 9/323

Bonus points – Essex 4, Middlesex 3 (Score at 100 overs: 317-8).

In the first innings D. R. Pringle, when 41, retired hurt; he resumed at 274.

Bowling: *First Innings*—Daniel 27–2–109–4; Williams 25–5–76–1; Hughes 28.3–6–74–3; Fraser 22–3–64–1; Needham 3–0–12–0. *Second Innings*—Daniel 6–0–26–0; Williams 3–0–14–0; Hughes 3–0–12–0; Slack 9–7–5–1; Fraser 6–2–11–1; Needham 9–2–23–0; Carr 7–3–21–1.

Middlesex

W. N. Slack b Childs	77	R. O. Butcher not out		18
J. D. Carr c East b Gooch	156	L-b 1, n-b 1		2
C. T. Radley not out	45			
M. A. Roseberry lbw b Gooch	2	1/168 2/264 3/266	(3 wkts dec.)	300

*†P. R. Downton, A. Needham, N. F. Williams, S. P. Hughes, A. R. C. Fraser and
W. W. Daniel did not bat.

Bonus points – Middlesex 4, Essex 1.

Bowling: Lever 17–2–66–0; Page 14–1–62–0; Pringle 21–4–61–0; Childs 12–3–45–1; Topley
13–5–42–0; Gooch 7.3–2–23–2.

Umpires: K. J. Lyons and D. O. Oslear.

MIDDLESEX v GLOUCESTERSHIRE

At Lord's, June 6, 8, 9. Drawn. Middlesex 1 pt. Toss: Middlesex. Play did not start until four
o'clock on the Saturday, the captains deciding to offer some entertainment even though the
umpires considered the ground unfit. The second and third days were washed out.

Gloucestershire

A. W. Stovold c Downton b Hughes	24	K. M. Curran not out		4
A. J. Wright b Williams	9	L-b 5, n-b 4		9
K. P. Tomlins c Downton b Williams	34			
P. Bainbridge not out	35	1/24 2/48 3/93	(3 wkts)	115

J. W. Lloyds, M. W. Alleyne, †R. C. Russell, C. A. Walsh, *D. A. Graveney and
D. V. Lawrence did not bat.

Bonus point – Middlesex 1.

Bowling: Daniel 6–1–34–0; Williams 11–2–19–2; Fraser 12.1–5–17–0; Hughes 10–2–24–1;
Slack 3–0–16–0.

Middlesex

W. N. Slack, J. D. Carr, A. J. T. Miller, R. O. Butcher, C. T. Radley, *†P. R. Downton,
A. Needham, N. F. Williams, S. P. Hughes, A. R. C. Fraser and W. W. Daniel.

Umpires: K. J. Lyons and D. O. Oslear.

At Bath, June 13, 15, 16. MIDDLESEX drew with SOMERSET.

At Southampton, June 20, 22, 23. MIDDLESEX lost to HAMPSHIRE by eight wickets.

MIDDLESEX v GLAMORGAN

At Lord's, June 27, 29, 30. Drawn. Middlesex 8 pts, Glamorgan 4 pts. Toss: Glamorgan. The
game emulated the pattern of many recent contests between these counties at Lord's, with
Middlesex compiling a large total and making Glamorgan follow on. While those at the other
end all played brisk, brief innings, Slack anchored Middlesex for 97 overs, hitting the ball
sweetly on the on-side. The Middlesex bowlers took twelve wickets on the second day, but
only six on the third, Glamorgan's batsmen having already hinted at resistance by taking the
first innings into the final hour of the second evening. The game was swung by two second-
innings stands, each of which lasted two hours. Morris and Maynard's effort was ended when

Emburey removed both, but then Holmes and Thomas blocked on. Three wickets around the start of the last hour looked to let Middlesex in, but Holmes, who batted for three hours, and Derrick, both of whom had been injured earlier in the match, held them off for the final seventeen overs.

Close of play : First day, Middlesex 483-9 (N. F. Williams 9*, A. R. C. Fraser 3*); Second day, Glamorgan 21-2 (C. P. Metson 0*, H. Morris 0*).

Middlesex

W. N. Slack c Metson b Thomas	173	W. W. Daniel c James b van Zyl 4
J. D. Carr b Monkhouse	 36	N. F. Williams not out 9
*M. W. Gatting c Maynard b van Zyl .	52	A. R. C. Fraser not out 3
K. R. Brown lbw b Thomas	 13	B 16, l-b 6, w 10, n-b 8 40
R. O. Butcher lbw b Thomas	 20	
†P. R. Downton lbw b Barwick	 59	1/70 2/148 3/186 (9 wkts dec.) 483
J. E. Emburey b Thomas	 64	4/216 5/366 6/397
P. H. Edmonds c Morris b Thomas	 10	7/409 8/453 9/473

Bonus points – Middlesex 4, Glamorgan 3 (Score at 100 overs: 416-7).

Bowling: Thomas 30-4-132-5; van Zyl 29-5-116-2; Barwick 25-2-110-1; Monkhouse 11-0-50-1; Derrick 15-4-53-0.

Glamorgan

J. A. Hopkins c Carr b Gatting	 29	– c Butcher b Fraser 4
S. P. James c Brown b Daniel	 0	– c Downton b Fraser 14
*H. Morris b Edmonds	 46	– (4) b Emburey 45
M. P. Maynard c Slack b Edmonds	 16	– (5) b Emburey 54
J. Derrick b Fraser	 4	– (10) not out 11
†C. P. Metson lbw b Emburey	 8	– (3) lbw b Daniel 14
J. G. Thomas c Downton b Edmonds	... 9	– (6) c Gatting b Edmonds 48
G. C. Holmes not out	 24	– (7) not out 29
C. J. P. G. van Zyl lbw b Daniel	... 25	– (8) b Daniel 2
S. R. Barwick c Daniel b Edmonds	... 10	– (9) lbw b Edmonds 5
S. Monkhouse b Daniel	 1	
L-b 1, n-b 8	 9	B 1, l-b 4, w 1, n-b 11 17

1/1 2/79 3/79 4/103 5/111	181	1/18 2/20 3/43 4/139 (8 wkts) 243
6/119 7/158 8/171 9/176		5/144 6/209 7/212 8/223

Bonus points – Glamorgan 1, Middlesex 4.

Bowling: *First Innings*—Daniel 20-3-56-3; Williams 12-4-20-0; Fraser 7.5-2-16-1; Edmonds 33-19-34-4; Emburey 25-7-43-1; Gatting 4-2-11-1. *Second Innings*—Williams 16-2-36-0; Fraser 14.5-1-46-2; Daniel 19-4-76-2; Edmonds 43-20-51-2; Emburey 38-27-29-2.

Umpires: J. H. Harris and J. A. Jameson.

At The Oval, July 1, 2, 3. MIDDLESEX lost to SURREY by two wickets.

At Bristol, July 15, 16, 17. MIDDLESEX lost to GLOUCESTERSHIRE by 118 runs.

MIDDLESEX v NOTTINGHAMSHIRE

At Lord's, July 18, 20, 21. Abandoned.

At Leicester, July 22, 23, 24. MIDDLESEX lost to LEICESTERSHIRE by an innings and 30 runs.

MIDDLESEX v KENT

At Lord's, July 25, 27, 28. Kent won by one wicket. Kent 21 pts, Middlesex 5 pts. Toss: Middlesex. Middlesex batted consistently, without anyone going on to a big score, and the fourth bonus point was acquired in the 99th over. After the second morning was lost to rain, Cowans, in his first Championship match of the season, bowled the night-watchman, only for Benson and Hinks to add 179 in 40 overs. Hinks reached his century with a six which Slack caught as he stepped over the rope; Benson, seeking his hundred with a similar shot to square leg, was less fortunate. Kent declared overnight and Jarvis began a personally memorable day with the first wicket. Carr mustered resistance as Middlesex crumbled, but Jarvis turned the game in one over. Without help from a fielder, he dismissed Carr, Fraser, and Cowans with successive balls, and the last ball of the over induced a mis-hook which flew from Williams's gloves into his face to end the innings abruptly. Kent, with at least 66 overs in which to score 173, stuttered in mid-innings. Aslett hooked Cowans and Daniel for six, but at 121 for eight Middlesex seemed likely winners. However, Marsh kept his head, Underwood stayed while 38 came from the ninth wicket, and finally Jarvis survived ten balls while the last 14 runs were gathered amid great tension.

Close of play: First day, Kent 26-1 (M. R. Benson 11*, S. A. Marsh 7*); Second day, Kent 262-4 (C. J. Tavaré 14*, D. G. Aslett 3*).

Middlesex

J. D. Carr c Cowdrey b Pienaar	41	– (2) b Jarvis		77
W. N. Slack c Marsh b Cowdrey	49	– (1) b Jarvis		1
K. R. Brown c Marsh b Cowdrey	39	– c Benson b Igglesden		0
C. T. Radley c Cowdrey b Igglesden	17	– lbw b Jarvis		4
R. O. Butcher c Benson b Underwood	44	– c Marsh b Igglesden		2
*†P. R. Downton c Tavaré b Pienaar	49	– lbw b Pienaar		3
A. Needham not out	32	– c Marsh b Cowdrey		20
N. F. Williams not out	7	– retired hurt		18
A. R. C. Fraser (did not bat)		– lbw b Jarvis		0
N. G. Cowans (did not bat)		– b Jarvis		0
W. W. Daniel (did not bat)		– not out		1
B 4, l-b 4, w 7, n-b 10	25	L-b 2, n-b 3		5

1/86 2/94 3/127 4/182   (6 wkts dec.) 303   1/3 2/14 3/33 4/44 5/51   131
5/210 6/286   6/87 7/125 8/125 9/125

Bonus points – Middlesex 4, Kent 2.

Bowling: *First Innings*—Igglesden 16-4-65-1; Jarvis 21-2-66-0; Cowdrey 30-7-87-2; Pienaar 17.3-6-44-2; Underwood 14-7-33-1. *Second Innings*—Igglesden 13-1-43-2; Jarvis 10-1-48-5; Pienaar 5-0-25-1; Cowdrey 2-0-13-1.

Kent

M. R. Benson c Slack b Brown	97	– lbw b Cowans		10
N. R. Taylor c Downton b Cowans	6	– b Daniel		42
†S. A. Marsh b Cowans	12	– (8) not out		38
S. G. Hinks c Fraser b Needham	112	– (3) lbw b Fraser		10
C. J. Tavaré not out	14	– (4) c Downton b Fraser		0
D. G. Aslett not out	3	– (5) lbw b Cowans		28
*C. S. Cowdrey (did not bat)		– (6) lbw b Cowans		9
R. F. Pienaar (did not bat)		– (7) c Downton b Fraser		4
A. P. Igglesden (did not bat)		– c Radley b Daniel		2
D. L. Underwood (did not bat)		– b Cowans		13
K. B. S. Jarvis (did not bat)		– not out		0
W 1, n-b 17	18	L-b 8, n-b 9		17

1/13 2/35 3/214 4/259   (4 wkts dec.) 262   1/32 2/64 3/67   (9 wkts) 173
                                                   4/80 5/92 6/101
                                                   7/119 8/121 9/159

Bonus points – Kent 3, Middlesex 1.

Bowling: *First Innings*—Daniel 12-2-52-0; Cowans 15-5-43-2; Fraser 6-0-26-0; Williams 12-2-56-0; Brown 7-0-33-1; Butcher 1-0-5-0; Needham 16-0-47-1. *Second Innings*—Daniel 17-0-74-2; Cowans 17-4-47-4; Fraser 21-6-44-3.

Umpires: H. D. Bird and R. A. White.

MIDDLESEX v SURREY

At Lord's, August 1, 3, 4. Drawn. Middlesex 4 pts, Surrey 2 pts. Toss: Middlesex. A month earlier, Carr and Slack had put on 173 at The Oval. Now they transferred their liking for Surrey's bowling across the river. Again Carr was significantly more assertive, and his century by one o'clock was the first hundred before lunch for Middlesex at Lord's since J. D. Robertson's against Sussex in 1957. Taking on the spinners from down the pitch and driving to long-on and extra cover, he hit nineteen fours. Slack was out six overs after lunch and Carr nine overs into the afternoon. Rain throughout Monday meant last-day manoeuvrings, which ended with Surrey being set 358 in 82 overs. The return of the rain, however, was decisive.

Close of play: First day, Surrey 9-0 (G. S. Clinton 1*, D. M. Smith 7*); Second day, No play.

Middlesex

J. D. Carr c Smith b Bullen 133	W. W. Daniel c Clinton b Bullen 0
W. N. Slack c Richards b Gray 89	A. R. C. Fraser lbw b Thomas 0
*M. W. Gatting c Medlycott b Greig .. 27	N. G. Cowans not out 0
K. R. Brown c Greig b Bullen 0	
R. O. Butcher c Richards b Gray 2	B 10, l-b 9, n-b 7 26
†P. R. Downton c Richards b Bullen .. 56	
J. E. Emburey c Lynch b Bullen 74	1/221 2/231 3/231 4/234 5/273 411
P. H. Edmonds b Bullen 4	6/398 7/404 8/404 9/407

Bonus points — Middlesex 4, Surrey 2 (Score at 100 overs: 403-6).

Bowling: Gray 19-6-56-2; Thomas 17-3-58-1; Greig 15-5-55-1; Medlycott 10-2-64-0; Bullen 33.2-3-119-6; Lynch 8-0-40-0.

Middlesex forfeited their second innings.

Surrey

G. S. Clinton b Cowans	3	– c Gatting b Cowans	6
D. M. Smith lbw b Fraser	19	– not out	38
A. J. Stewart not out	7	– c Gatting b Emburey	13
M. A. Lynch not out	14	– not out	8
B 4, l-b 6, n-b 1	11	B 6, l-b 2	8

1/20 2/29	(2 wkts dec.) 54	1/12 2/56	(2 wkts) 73

T. E. Jesty, †C. J. Richards, *I. A. Greig, D. J. Thomas, K. T. Medlycott, C. K. Bullen and A. H. Gray did not bat.

Bowling: *First Innings*—Daniel 2-0-4-0; Cowans 5-1-13-1; Fraser 6-1-8-1; Emburey 6-1-13-0; Edmonds 2-0-6-0. *Second Innings*—Cowans 4-0-12-1; Daniel 3-0-4-0; Emburey 9-4-17-1; Edmonds 7-1-28-0; Fraser 3-1-4-0.

Umpires: D. Lloyd and N. T. Plews.

At Canterbury, August 5, 6, 7. MIDDLESEX drew with KENT.

MIDDLESEX v WORCESTERSHIRE

At Lord's, August 8, 10, 11. Drawn. Middlesex 3 pts, Worcestershire 8 pts. Hick was the senior partner in a double-hundred stand with Curtis as Worcestershire dominated the opening exchanges. His 173 featured nineteen powerfully hit fours, needed 245 balls, and lasted 305 minutes. Curtis hit sixteen fours and batted for 374 minutes. Middlesex responded stubbornly. The openers began warily, Miller took three hours to reach 50, and the follow-on was avoided on the last morning with three wickets in hand. A crisp knock by D'Oliveira enabled Worcestershire to set a target of 268 in 58 overs. After positive batting from the openers, Downton and Brown added 100 in 21 overs and were promising to score the necessary 62 from the final ten overs when rain ended play.

Close of play: First day, Worcestershire 341-2 (G. A. Hick 158*, D. B. D'Oliveira 6*); Second day, Middlesex 241-6 (A. Needham 15*, A. R. C. Fraser 5*).

Worcestershire

T. S. Curtis b Fraser	129	– c Downton b Daniel	18
G. J. Lord c Brown b Cowans	25	– b Cowans	12
G. A. Hick b Daniel	173	– lbw b Cowans	4
D. B. D'Oliveira b Daniel	14	– not out	54
*P. A. Neale lbw b Cowans	2	– c Butcher b Tufnell	15
S. R. Lampitt not out	17		
†S. J. Rhodes not out	18	– (6) not out	10
B 4, l-b 18, n-b 1	23	L-b 8, w 1, n-b 2	11

1/68 2/326 3/359 (5 wkts dec.) 401 1/34 2/38 3/38 (4 wkts dec.) 124
4/366 5/368 4/107

P. J. Newport, R. K. Illingworth, N. V. Radford and A. P. Pridgeon did not bat.

Bonus points – Worcestershire 4 (Score at 100 overs: 312-1).

Bowling: *First Innings*—Daniel 29-6-81-2; Cowans 25-4-100-2; Fraser 31-7-86-1; Tufnell 30-12-69-0; Needham 8-0-37-0; Brown 1-0-6-0. *Second Innings*—Daniel 10-1-38-1; Cowans 10-4-19-2; Fraser 7-1-30-0; Tufnell 6-0-29-1.

Middlesex

J. D. Carr c Newport b Pridgeon	15	– (2) c Curtis b Radford	48
W. N. Slack c Rhodes b Newport	29	– (1) lbw b Radford	33
A. J. T. Miller c Rhodes b Lampitt	64		
K. R. Brown b Lampitt	70	– not out	58
R. O. Butcher c Newport b Radford	4		
*†P. R. Downton b Radford	17	– (3) not out	61
A. Needham retired hurt	15		
A. R. C. Fraser not out	14		
N. G. Cowans lbw b Pridgeon	2		
W. W. Daniel c Rhodes b Newport	1		
P. C. R. Tufnell c and b Pridgeon	4		
B 1, l-b 3, w 1, n-b 8	13	L-b 6	6

1/24 2/71 3/184 4/189 5/207 258 1/51 2/93 (2 wkts) 206
6/226 7/248 8/253 9/258

Bonus points – Middlesex 3, Worcestershire 4.

Bowling: *First Innings*—Radford 29-5-68-2; Pridgeon 19.3-3-50-3; Newport 16-2-39-2; Hick 8-0-23-0; Illingworth 15-2-37-0; Lampitt 10-1-37-2. *Second Innings*—Radford 14-0-64-2; Pridgeon 10-1-32-0; Newport 6-1-21-0; Hick 1-0-2-0; Illingworth 14-3-57-0; Lampitt 3-0-24-0.

Umpires: J. H. Hampshire and H. J. Rhodes.

At Chelmsford, August 15, 17, 18. MIDDLESEX drew with ESSEX.

At Cardiff, August 19, 20, 21. MIDDLESEX drew with GLAMORGAN.

At Wellingborough School, August 22, 24, 25. MIDDLESEX drew with NORTHAMPTON-SHIRE.

MIDDLESEX v WARWICKSHIRE

At Uxbridge, August 26, 27, 28. Drawn. Middlesex 2 pts, Warwickshire 3 pts. Toss: Warwickshire. Gifford won the toss on Wednesday morning but play did not begin until four o'clock on the second day. Asif Din drove effectively across the damp outfield, and Warwickshire batted for 100 overs before their declaration and two forfeitures left 51 overs. With Carr, capped at the start of the game, being run out without facing a ball, all depended on Gatting. He hammered one six and eleven fours, but when he was stumped, Middlesex had no-one to maintain the rate. Nor had Warwickshire any bowlers to extend the breach.

Close of play: First day, No play; Second day, Warwickshire 115-2 (Asif Din 56*, D. L. Amiss 25*).

Warwickshire

A. J. Moles c Downton b Emburey	 18	A. C. Storie not out	 14
T. A. Lloyd lbw b Cowans	 9	G. C. Small not out	 14
Asif Din c Downton b Emburey	 92	B 5, l-b 12, w 3	 20
D. L. Amiss c Downton b Hughes	 44		
G. W. Humpage c Hughes b Tufnell	.. 28	1/17 2/35 3/155	(6 wkts dec.) 274
†G. A. Tedstone lbw b Cowans	 35	4/184 5/214 6/253	

T. A. Merrick, T. A. Munton and *N. Gifford did not bat.

Bonus points – Warwickshire 3, Middlesex 2.

Bowling: Cowans 19-3-48-2; Hughes 14-3-38-1; Fraser 24-9-41-0; Emburey 19-4-51-2; Tufnell 24-3-79-1.

Warwickshire forfeited their second innings.

Middlesex

Middlesex forfeited their first innings.

W. N. Slack c Humpage b Munton	 37	M. R. Ramprakash not out	 16
J. D. Carr run out	 0		
*M. W. Gatting st Tedstone b Gifford	. 63	B 5, l-b 5, n-b 1	 11
J. E. Emburey not out	 32		
K. R. Brown lbw b Small	 8	1/0 2/102 3/106 4/126	(4 wkts) 167

†P. R. Downton, S. P. Hughes, A. R. C. Fraser, N. G. Cowans and P. C. R. Tufnell did not bat.

Bowling: Small 10-2-36-1; Merrick 11-3-35-0; Gifford 12-2-60-1; Munton 3-1-10-1; Asif Din 5-1-16-0.

Umpires: B. Dudleston and J. H. Hampshire.

MIDDLESEX v SUSSEX

At Uxbridge, August 29, 31, September 1. Middlesex won by 86 runs. Middlesex 23 pts, Sussex 6 pts. Toss: Middlesex. Pigott bowled with great hostility in taking Middlesex's first two wickets, and when he returned to remove Carr and the in-form Gatting, they urgently needed Emburey's vigorous batting. His 70 included 50 in boundaries (three sixes, eight fours) and was supplemented by Cowans's 24 in an over from Heseltine which featured three sixes.

Green and Alikhan gave Sussex a bright start, only for the innings to stumble as Fraser gained response from the pitch. Reeve's fighting fifty pulled the innings together on the second day. When Middlesex batted again, Carr played beautifully and, with Gatting holding himself back, Brown and Ramprakash lent useful support. To win, Sussex needed 306 from a minimum of 87 overs and they made the worst possible start when Hughes claimed two wickets in consecutive balls. Undaunted, Colin Wells hit 55 out of 77 in the hour before lunch, Parker drove six sixes after the interval, and for a moment Middlesex supporters might have entertained thoughts of being pushed into last place in the Championship. However, Cowans removed three of Parker's partners, Tufnell had him stumped, and Middlesex ran out comfortable winners.

Close of play: First day, Sussex 134-6 (D. A. Reeve 7*, I. J. Gould 8*); Second day, Middlesex 263-6 (M. W. Gatting 52*, S. P. Hughes 3*).

Middlesex

W. N. Slack c Alikhan b Pigott	1	– lbw b Reeve	9
J. D. Carr c and b Pigott	38	– c Pigott b Green	92
K. R. Brown c Gould b Pigott	2	– b Green	26
M. R. Ramprakash lbw b Reeve	24	– c sub b Green	38
*M. W. Gatting b Pigott	49	– (6) b Babington	60
†P. R. Downton b Babington	1	– (5) lbw b Reeve	2
J. E. Emburey b Babington	70	– lbw b C. M. Wells	10
S. P. Hughes lbw b Reeve	11	– c Gould b Reeve	3
A. R. C. Fraser c Pigott b Heseltine	5	– not out	6
N. G. Cowans b Pigott	24	– b Babington	1
P. C. R. Tufnell not out	12	– c Gould b Babington	2
B 4, l-b 15, n-b 3	22	B 4, l-b 17, w 2, n-b 11	34

1/12 2/22 3/61 4/100 5/101   259   1/13 2/92 3/189 4/193 5/193   283
6/139 7/168 8/223 9/223   6/229 7/268 8/272 9/278

Bonus points – Middlesex 3, Sussex 4.

Bowling: *First Innings*—Pigott 20.1–3–83–5; Reeve 20–9–26–2; C. M. Wells 14–3–52–0; Babington 12–1–54–2; Heseltine 3–1–25–1. *Second Innings*—Pigott 12–1–39–0; Reeve 21–3–64–3; Heseltine 4–0–17–0; Babington 13.5–0–44–3; Green 21–4–68–3; C. M. Wells 10–0–31–1.

Sussex

R. I. Alikhan c Tufnell b Fraser	28	– b Cowans	4
A. M. Green lbw b Fraser	44	– c Downton b Hughes	6
P. W. G. Parker c Tufnell b Emburey	14	– st Downton b Tufnell	85
A. P. Wells c Hughes b Fraser	11	– c and b Hughes	0
C. M. Wells b Slack b Emburey	10	– c Cowans b Tufnell	67
P. Moores b Fraser	4	– c Brown b Cowans	3
D. A. Reeve not out	57	– lbw b Cowans	0
*†I. J. Gould lbw b Emburey	18	– c Ramprakash b Cowans	5
A. C. S. Pigott b Tufnell	23	– c Cowans b Tufnell	38
P. A. W. Heseltine c Ramprakash b Tufnell	0	– c Slack b Tufnell	1
A. M. Babington c Gatting b Tufnell	16	– not out	4
B 4, l-b 5, n-b 3	12	L-b 3, n-b 3	6

1/42 2/66 3/89 4/110 5/114   237   1/4 2/10 3/10 4/128 5/162   219
6/119 7/154 8/197 9/207   6/162 7/173 8/180 9/192

Bonus points – Sussex 2, Middlesex 4.

Bowling: *First Innings*—Cowans 15–4–57–0; Hughes 6–0–28–0; Fraser 19–2–58–4; Emburey 28–5–63–3; Tufnell 13.2–5–22–3. *Second Innings*—Cowans 14–3–44–4; Hughes 5–0–26–2; Fraser 4–1–24–0; Emburey 11–2–50–0; Tufnell 18–2–72–4.

Umpires: B. Dudleston and A. A. Jones.

MIDDLESEX v HAMPSHIRE

At Lord's, September 9, 10, 11. Drawn. Middlesex 4 pts, Hampshire 7 pts. Toss: Hampshire. Although Gatting and his opening bowlers reduced Hampshire to 93 for six, Marshall and Parks revived the innings by adding 123 in 41 overs. Having swept to 99, Marshall cut Fraser into his stumps. Middlesex also lost six wickets cheaply on the opening day, Andrew claiming three for 1 run and Marshall two in an over. Hampshire toiled through most of the second afternoon, building towards a declaration which set Middlesex to score 337 in the final day plus seven overs that evening. Rain caused four interruptions on Friday and play continued in virtual twilight after tea, when Marshall ended Carr's admirable attempt at the target with a flier off the dampened pitch. With Embury and Downton together, 75 were needed over the last twenty overs, but the weather allowed only seven of them to be bowled.

Close of play: First day, Middlesex 76-6 (M. W. Gatting 9*, A. R. C. Fraser 0*); Second day, Middlesex 17-0 (W. N. Slack 9*, J. D. Carr 2*).

Hampshire

V. P. Terry c Downton b Fraser	19	– c Brown b Cowans 4
C. L. Smith c Slack b Cowans	0	– lbw b Gatting 14
*M. C. J. Nicholas lbw b Gatting	17	– c Downton b Cowans 33
D. R. Turner c Downton b Fraser	0	– c Carr b Embury 52
R. A. Smith b Gatting	30	– c Brown b Tufnell 24
M. D. Marshall b Fraser	99	– c Gatting b Tufnell 12
N. G. Cowley lbw b Gatting	0	– b Embury 30
†R. J. Parks c Slack b Embury	43	– not out 30
R. J. Maru b Fraser	15	– not out 9
C. A. Connor b Cowans	10	
S. J. W. Andrew not out	4	
B 5, l-b 2, w 2, n-b 4	13	B 5, l-b 1 6

1/9 2/33 3/33 4/48 5/93	250	1/9 2/46 3/60 (7 wkts dec.) 214
6/93 7/216 8/220 9/246		4/123 5/140
		6/144 7/200

Bonus points – Hampshire 3, Middlesex 4.

Bowling: *First Innings*—Cowans 14.4-1-39-2; Fraser 24-4-67-4; Gatting 9-2-40-3; Embury 19-4-49-1; Tufnell 12-1-36-0; Sykes 2-0-12-0. *Second Innings*—Fraser 14-5-34-0; Cowans 13.4-3-38-2; Gatting 11-5-16-1; Embury 18.2-3-35-2; Tufnell 19-2-85-2.

Middlesex

J. D. Carr c Parks b Andrew	18	– c Parks b Marshall 88
W. N. Slack b Andrew	26	– c Andrew b Connor 21
K. R. Brown c C. L. Smith b Andrew	6	– (4) c C. L. Smith b Maru 40
M. R. Ramprakash lbw b Marshall	0	– (5) b Maru 12
*M. W. Gatting b Maru	42	– (3) lbw b Cowley 43
†P. R. Downton c R. A. Smith b Marshall	0	– not out 17
J. E. Embury lbw b Connor	10	– b Marshall 53
A. R. C. Fraser b Connor	5	
J. F. Sykes c R. A. Smith b Andrew	10	– (8) not out 3
N. G. Cowans not out	0	
P. C. R. Tufnell b Maru	0	
B 3, l-b 6, w 1, n-b 1	11	B 12, l-b 5, n-b 2 19

1/48 2/54 3/55 4/55 5/55	128	1/33 2/109 3/195 (6 wkts) 296
6/76 7/102 8/128 9/128		4/213 5/225 6/291

Bonus points – Hampshire 4.

Bowling: *First Innings*—Andrew 19-4-48-4; Connor 11-3-21-2; Marshall 15-4-49-2; Maru 1.2-0-1-2. *Second Innings*—Marshall 23-6-60-2; Connor 15-2-48-1; Andrew 14-1-42-0; Maru 24-5-84-2; Cowley 16-0-45-1.

Umpires: B. Leadbeater and R. Palmer.

At Derby, September 12, 14, 15. MIDDLESEX lost to DERBYSHIRE by five wickets.

NORTHAMPTONSHIRE

Patron: The Earl of Dalkeith
President: D. C. Lucas
Chairman: W. R. F. Chamberlain
Chairman, Cricket Committee: A. P. Arnold
Secretary/Manager: S. P. Coverdale
   County Ground, Wantage Road,
   Northampton NN1 4TJ
   (Telephone: 0604-32917)
Captain: G. Cook
Coach: R. M. Carter
Cricket Development Officer: B. L. Reynolds

When the Northamptonshire side arrived at Lord's on the second Saturday in July for the Benson and Hedges Cup final against Yorkshire, a historic hat-trick of titles looked within the realms of possibility. Yet, by the time the same players began the return journey to Northampton after losing to Nottinghamshire in the NatWest Bank Trophy final eight weeks later, the dream had been shattered. Richard Hadlee's heroic innings on that momentous Monday afternoon ensured that Northamptonshire shared Middlesex's unhappy experience of 1975, reaching both major one-day finals, only to lose them both. And seventh place in the Britannic Assurance Championship, although an improvement of two places on 1986, was a disappointing outcome after their being among the pace-setters for a good part of the season.

Unkind weather and inconsistent cricket put paid to Northamptonshire's chances of a first three-day title. The last of their seven Championship victories came as early as July 28, after which rain intervened to nullify strong positions against Warwickshire and Lancashire. The challenge fell away with crushing defeats at the hands of Nottinghamshire, the eventual champions, and Leicestershire.

The aftermath of the defeat in the NatWest final, without doubt the nadir of the season, was a depressing and emotional time for Northamptonshire's captain, Geoff Cook, who was forced to reflect on his seventh season as the county's leader without one trophy to show for his efforts. "I know we fell at the last fence again," he commented, "but we've all learnt lessons from this year. I think it's taken us another step nearer to becoming a really formidable outfit."

Certainly, the signing of the West Indian fast bowler, Winston Davis, proved a successful move, and Northamptonshire's belief in him was rewarded with 70 Championship wickets, the county's best individual return for ten years. Despite Davis's tendency to overstep – 211 no-balls in nineteen three-day matches – his penetrative, hostile bowling brought a new edge to the seam attack. Only three bowling bonus points were missed out of a possible 40 on Northamptonshire's County Ground pitches. The presence of Davis had an effect on other players, too. With genuine fast bowling at the other end, Alan Walker looked a much more formidable proposition, and it was sad that the back injury which disrupted his season also cast a shadow over his long-term prospects.

With Davis occupying the overseas player's place for much of the season, Roger Harper's appearances were limited to a handful of Championship games and a regular place in the side on Sundays. However, not even his vivid and exciting talents could lift the county above equal tenth in the Refuge Assurance League, in which only Leicestershire had more games washed out than Northamptonshire. At other times, Harper enjoyed the title of the best – and most expensive – substitute fielder in the country. His absence placed the responsibility of spin bowling on Nick Cook, who, although rarely threatening to run through a side, bowled steadily enough to earn himself 54 first-class wickets and a place on England's tour to Pakistan.

Allan Lamb and David Capel were also chosen for various stages of England's winter travels, and at Headingley in July last year, Capel became the first Northampton-born player for nearly 80 years to win an England cap. As with Walker and Simon Brown, a promising eighteen-year-old left-arm seamer, injury prevented Capel from enjoying a more productive season with the ball, and both he and Lamb had most of their best batting moments in the one-day competitions. This was particularly true in the Benson and Hedges Cup, with Lamb's memorable 126 not out at Canterbury getting Northamptonshire to Lord's, where Capel delighted the full house with a mature 97.

Otherwise, the batting tended to fluctuate between exhilarating and alarmingly brittle. With pressures increasing as the season developed, it was not surprising that Geoff Cook was less prolific than usual, and only Wayne Larkins and Robert Bailey completed 1,000 first-class runs. Larkins scored 1,363 in the Championship and rounded off the season with 87 in the NatWest final to exorcise the unhappy memories of 1986. Bailey, after a patchy start, hit his first Championship hundred of the season against Yorkshire at the end of June, featuring in a match-winning stand of 208 with Capel which was possibly the county's batting highlight of the season. He followed his unbeaten 152 with 158 against Lancashire a week later, but then had to wait until the penultimate game, against Sussex, to complete his third hundred.

For many, the return to form of Richard Williams was the most pleasing aspect of the season. He fought his way back with great character after spending most of the previous year in the Second XI, batted consistently in all competitions, bowled tidily and was a deserving recipient of the club's Player of the Year award. However, it was another largely frustrating season for the talented Duncan Wild, although he did manage one Championship hundred. So, too, did David Ripley, whose wicket-keeping, in line with the close catching generally, showed improved consistency.

The lessons talked about by Geoff Cook must indeed be put into practice in the future. And everyone connected with the county will hope that the experience of the 1987 season, with all its drama and its anticlimax, will bring Northamptonshire closer to the long-awaited breakthrough. – Andrew Radd.

507

NORTHAMPTONSHIRE 1987

[Bill Smith]

Back row: B. Clarke (*scorer*), M. A. Robinson, A. Walker, D. J. Capel, W. W. Davis, R. J. Bailey, D. Ripley, N. G. B. Cook, D. J. Wild, R. Norman (*physiotherapist*). *Front row*: R. A. Harper, W. Larkins, G. Cook (*captain*), A. J. Lamb, R. G. Williams. *Insets*: R. J. Boyd-Moss, S. N. V. Waterton.

NORTHAMPTONSHIRE RESULTS

All first-class matches – Played 26: Won 7, Lost 4, Drawn 15.

County Championship matches – Played 24: Won 7, Lost 4, Drawn 13.

Bonus points – Batting 48, Bowling 68.

Competition placings – Britannic Assurance County Championship, 7th; NatWest Bank Trophy,
finalists; Benson and Hedges Cup, finalists; Refuge Assurance League, 10th equal.

BRITANNIC ASSURANCE CHAMPIONSHIP AVERAGES

BATTING

	Birthplace	M	I	NO	R	HI	Avge
§‡R. A. Harper	Georgetown, BG	5	5	3	165	127*	82.50
‡R. G. Williams	Bangor	20	24	6	775	104	43.05
‡W. Larkins	Roxton	24	41	4	1,363	120	36.83
‡R. J. Bailey	Biddulph	24	38	7	1,099	158	35.45
‡A. J. Lamb	Langebaanweg, SA	23	34	4	982	101*	32.73
‡G. Cook	Middlesbrough	24	40	9	957	111*	30.87
‡D. J. Wild	Northampton	20	19	5	406	102*	29.00
‡D. Ripley	Leeds	23	21	4	439	125*	25.82
S. J. Brown	Cleadon	3	4	3	24	20	24.00
‡D. J. Capel	Northampton	19	25	3	503	91*	22.86
‡R. J. Boyd-Moss	Hatton, Ceylon	6	10	1	203	60	22.55
‡A. Walker	Emley	17	9	5	78	41*	19.50
‡N. G. B. Cook	Leicester	24	22	5	268	64	15.76
§‡W. W. Davis	Sion Hill, St Vincent	19	18	5	186	25*	14.30
G. Smith	Jarrow	5	5	1	47	29*	11.75
M. A. Robinson	Hull	7	6	2	4	2	1.00

Also batted: S. N. V. Waterton (*Dartford*) (1 match) 4, 50*.

* Signifies not out.   ‡ Denotes county cap.   § Not qualified for England.

The following played a total of twelve three-figure innings for Northamptonshire in County
Championship matches – R. J. Bailey 3, W. Larkins 3, G. Cook 1, R. A. Harper 1, A. J.
Lamb 1, D. Ripley 1, D. J. Wild 1, R. G. Williams 1.

BOWLING

	O	M	R	W	BB	Avge
A. Walker	373.5	97	989	44	4-39	22.47
R. G. Williams	225.4	59	612	26	5-81	23.53
R. A. Harper	172	46	378	16	5-28	23.62
G. Smith	81	10	308	13	6-72	23.69
D. J. Capel	416.5	78	1,266	50	7-46	25.32
W. W. Davis	591.1	100	1,906	70	6-57	27.22
N. G. B. Cook	659.2	216	1,478	52	6-77	28.42
M. A. Robinson	150	25	501	13	3-45	38.53

Also bowled: R. J. Bailey 14-5-33-1; R. J. Boyd-Moss 25-6-79-1; S. J. Brown
42-11-106-4; G. Cook 10.1-2-71-0; A. J. Lamb 2-0-18-1; W. Larkins 16.2-4-51-0;
D. Ripley 9-0-89-2; D. J. Wild 186.3-53-510-7.

Wicket-keeper: D. Ripley 38 ct, 8 st.

Leading Fielders: A. J. Lamb 19, R. J. Bailey 17, W. Larkins 16.

At Southampton, April 25, 26, 27. NORTHAMPTONSHIRE beat HAMPSHIRE by five wickets.

At Cambridge, April 29, 30, May 1. NORTHAMPTONSHIRE drew with CAMBRIDGE UNIVERSITY.

At Lord's, May 6, 7, 8. NORTHAMPTONSHIRE beat MIDDLESEX by ten wickets.

NORTHAMPTONSHIRE v LEICESTERSHIRE

At Northampton, May 23, 24, 25. Drawn. Northamptonshire 6 pts, Leicestershire 5 pts. Toss: Northamptonshire. A blank first day and some dour cricket brought about the seventeenth Championship draw between these neighbouring counties since 1976. Northamptonshire were 110 for seven as skilful pace bowling from Benjamin, Agnew and Taylor undid them on a pitch offering some movement off the seam, but then Ripley and Nick Cook put on 100 for the eighth wicket. Cook relished the struggle against his former county, and Ripley went on to an unbeaten 69 in 172 minutes. Leicestershire's reply occupied 84.3 overs, 46 of which Potter spent in scoring 37, and Capel's three for 8 in 21 balls was a welcome highlight as yet another Bank Holiday match at Northampton drifted to an aimless conclusion.

Close of play: First day, No play; Second day, Leicestershire 29-0 (L. Potter 7*, R. A. Cobb 15*).

Northamptonshire

*G. Cook lbw b Benjamin	5	– c Benjamin b Such	13
W. Larkins c Cobb b Agnew	24	– lbw b Benjamin	7
R. J. Bailey c Whitaker b Agnew	8	– not out	28
R. J. Boyd-Moss b Taylor	37	– not out	13
D. J. Capel b Taylor	11		
R. G. Williams b Benjamin	17		
D. J. Wild b Benjamin	0		
†D. Ripley not out	69		
N. G. B. Cook c Potter b Agnew	35		
W. W. Davis c Briers b Benjamin	1		
A. Walker b Benjamin	1		
L-b 5, w 3, n-b 7	15	B 2, l-b 2, n-b 1	5

1/9 2/37 3/37 4/58 5/108   223   1/14 2/43   (2 wkts dec.) 66
6/108 7/110 8/210 9/211

Bonus points – Northamptonshire 2, Leicestershire 4.

Bowling: *First Innings*—Agnew 25-3-73-3; Benjamin 26.2-6-50-5; Taylor 15-0-45-2; Such 16-6-32-0; Potter 1-0-1-0; Willey 5-2-9-0; Briers 3-1-8-0. *Second Innings*—Agnew 6-0-24-0; Benjamin 5-1-10-1; Such 6-1-10-1; Taylor 5-1-17-0; Potter 1-0-1-0.

Leicestershire

L. Potter c Walker b N. G. B. Cook	37	J. P. Agnew b Capel	1
R. A. Cobb c N. G. B. Cook b Davis	20	L. B. Taylor not out	9
*P. Willey c G. Cook b N. G. B. Cook	10	P. M. Such b Capel	0
J. J. Whitaker c Ripley b Walker	15		
T. J. Boon b Davis	6	B 5, l-b 5, n-b 14	24
N. E. Briers b Williams	31		
†P. Whitticase b Williams	9	1/42 2/65 3/85 4/98 5/130	165
W. K. M. Benjamin b Capel	3	6/146 7/151 8/152 9/165	

Bonus points – Leicestershire 1, Northamptonshire 4.

Bowling: Davis 21-7-57-2; Capel 16.3-5-28-3; N. G. B. Cook 21-11-23-2; Walker 17-4-38-1; Williams 9-5-9-2.

Umpires: D. O. Oslear and N. T. Plews.

NORTHAMPTONSHIRE v KENT

At Northampton, May 30, June 1, 2. Drawn. Northamptonshire 6 pts, Kent 3 pts. Toss: Northamptonshire. Rain spoiled the match, cutting short the first day and preventing any play on the third. On a slow pitch, Cook and Larkins led off with an opening stand of 133, many of Larkins's fourteen boundaries coming from fine drives, and then Lamb took over. He reacted to the news over the weekend of his omission from the England side for the First Test by completing his 30th century for the county early on Monday, having faced 171 balls and hit a six and fourteen fours. His partnership of 72 in nineteen overs with Williams made sure that Northamptonshire got their fourth batting point. Benson and Taylor hit back strongly for Kent with 166 for the first wicket, but despite the former's workmanlike century, a result looked unlikely long before the final downpour.

Close of play: First day, Northamptonshire 230-3 (A. J. Lamb 68*, D. J. Capel 17*); Second day, Kent 248-5 (C. J. Tavaré 8*).

Northamptonshire

*G. Cook lbw b Kelleher	57	R. G. Williams not out		37
W. Larkins b Kelleher	75	B 8, n-b 2		10
R. J. Bailey b Baptiste	5			
A. J. Lamb not out	101	1/133 2/144 3/148	(4 wkts dec.)	302
D. J. Capel c Benson b Baptiste	17	4/230		

D. J. Wild, †D. Ripley, N. G. B. Cook, W. W. Davis and A. Walker did not bat.

Bonus points – Northamptonshire 4, Kent 1.

Bowling: Baptiste 31–7–97–2; Penn 17–2–60–0; Kelleher 28–6–82–2; Underwood 18–5–44–0; Aslett 1–1–0–0; Tavaré 3.3–0–11–0.

Kent

M. R. Benson c G. Cook b Walker	113	*C. S. Cowdrey c Larkins b Williams		7
N. R. Taylor c Bailey b Davis	81	B 2, l-b 3, n-b 10		15
S. G. Hinks c Bailey b Walker	24			
C. J. Tavaré not out	8	1/166 2/232 3/233	(5 wkts)	248
D. G. Aslett b Walker	0	4/235 5/248		

E. A. E. Baptiste, †S. A. Marsh, C. Penn, D. J. M. Kelleher and D. L. Underwood did not bat.

Bonus points – Kent 2, Northamptonshire 2.

Bowling: Davis 14–0–53–1; Capel 9–2–32–0; N. G. B. Cook 25–8–49–0; Williams 25.4–5–63–1; Walker 17–4–34–3; Wild 6–1–7–0; Bailey 2–1–5–0.

Umpires: J. Birkenshaw and A. A. Jones.

NORTHAMPTONSHIRE v SURREY

At Northampton, June 6, 8, 9. Drawn. Northamptonshire 4 pts, Surrey 2 pts. Toss: Northamptonshire. The wretched late-spring weather ruined another game at Northampton, washing out the last two days after an absorbing Saturday's play finished with Northamptonshire 18 for the loss of Geoff Cook. Surrey, put in to bat, were indebted to Stewart's diligence for 191 minutes, which prevented a complete collapse, and when a four-wicket burst after tea from Capel had the visitors in trouble again, Medlycott found a determined last-wicket partner in Bicknell. Together they added 80 in less than an hour. Medlycott hit twelve fours, including five in one over from Nick Cook.

Surrey

G. S. Clinton b Davis	4	K. T. Medlycott not out		63
D. M. Smith c G. Cook b Walker	8	A. H. Gray c Bailey b Capel		1
A. J. Stewart c Ripley b N. G. B. Cook	66	M. P. Bicknell b N. G. B. Cook		16
M. A. Lynch lbw b Capel	17	B 2, l-b 6, n-b 4		12
†C. J. Richards c Ripley b Davis	10			
T. E. Jesty c sub b Capel	27	1/12 2/20 3/65 4/85 5/134		231
*I. A. Greig c Larkins b Capel	5	6/146 7/150 8/150 9/151		
D. J. Thomas c Bailey b Capel	2			

Bonus points – Surrey 2, Northamptonshire 4.

Bowling: Davis 22–7–59–2; Walker 17–7–44–1; N. G. B. Cook 19–7–54–2; Capel 18–4–66–5.

Northamptonshire

*G. Cook lbw b Gray	0
W. Larkins not out	13
R. J. Bailey not out	3
N-b 2	2
1/0 (1 wkt)	18

A. J. Lamb, D. J. Capel, R. G. Williams, D. J. Wild, †D. Ripley, N. G. B. Cook, W. W. Davis and A. Walker did not bat.

Bowling: Gray 4–1–10–1; Thomas 4–3–8–0.

Umpires: J. W. Holder and B. Leadbeater.

At Bletchley, June 13, 14, 15. NORTHAMPTONSHIRE drew with PAKISTANIS (See Pakistani tour section).

At Ilford, June 17, 18, 19. NORTHAMPTONSHIRE drew with ESSEX.

NORTHAMPTONSHIRE v WARWICKSHIRE

At Luton, June 20, 22, 23. Northamptonshire won by eight wickets. Northamptonshire 12 pts. Toss: Warwickshire. Despite the efforts of a helicopter, called in to help drying operations, Wardown Park was unplayable on the first day and more rain ruled out any play on the second. Consequently a single-innings match was played for 12 points. Warwickshire struggled against Walker, Harper and Nick Cook on a damp pitch, which eased as the day progressed, and Harper returned his best figures for the county. Only a restrained Humpage stood firm, frustrating the home side's bowlers for two and a half hours. Needing 173 in the final session, Northamptonshire paced their innings perfectly and won with eight balls to spare. Larkins, in outstanding form, included a six and twelve fours in his 72 off 86 balls.

Warwickshire

A. J. Moles lbw b Walker	10	*N. Gifford c and b Harper		0
T. A. Lloyd c Lamb b Walker	17	T. A. Munton not out		14
P. A. Smith b Harper	1	A. A. Donald b Williams		0
D. L. Amiss c Lamb b N. G. B. Cook	21			
†G. W. Humpage c Lamb b Harper	66	B 5, l-b 3		8
A. C. Storie c Harper b N. G. B. Cook	22			
Asif Din c Lamb b Harper	5	1/28 2/29 3/29 4/52 5/123		174
G. J. Parsons c Wild b Harper	10	6/140 7/151 8/160 9/166		

Bowling: Capel 3–1–12–0; Walker 15–6–40–2; Harper 25–7–46–5; N. G. B. Cook 22–7–47–2; Williams 6.3–0–21–1.

Northamptonshire

*G. Cook c Moles b Parsons	....	15
W. Larkins lbw b Munton	....	70
R. J. Bailey not out	....	27
A. J. Lamb not out	....	47
L-b 9, w 5, n-b 3	....	17

1/69 2/96   (2 wkts) 178

D. J. Capel, R. G. Williams, D. J. Wild, R. A. Harper, †D. Ripley, N. G. B. Cook and A. Walker did not bat.

Bowling: Donald 8–0–43–0; Smith 3–1–16–0; Parsons 8–2–34–1; Gifford 13.4–3–41–0; Munton 6–0–35–1.

Umpires: B. J. Meyer and R. Palmer.

NORTHAMPTONSHIRE v YORKSHIRE

At Northampton, June 27, 29, 30. Northamptonshire won by seven wickets. Northamptonshire 20 pts, Yorkshire 1 pt. Toss: Northamptonshire. Capel produced an outstanding all-round performance to decide a match which, following the loss of the first day, featured some cricket of the highest quality. The 24-year-old all-rounder celebrated his England call-up for the Third Test with a career-best seven for 46 to bowl out the Championship leaders on a green pitch. But in conditions helpful to the bowlers, Blakey's century was a gem. There were fifteen fours in his three and threequarter hours at the crease. Larkins was more spectacular, 88 of his 101 runs coming in boundaries, but Blakey was again outstanding as Yorkshire pushed on towards a declaration on the last afternoon. They set Northamptonshire a formidable 283 in 100 minutes plus the last twenty overs, and, after the early loss of the openers, 158 were still needed in the last hour. However, Bailey (128 balls, four sixes, eighteen fours) and Capel (85 balls, eleven fours) drove the home side to a thrilling victory with nine balls to spare, adding 208 in 27.3 overs of brilliant strokeplay.

Close of play: First day, No play; Second day, Yorkshire 22-0 (M. D. Moxon 5*, A. A. Metcalfe 9*).

Yorkshire

M. D. Moxon c Lamb b Capel	....	1	– c Ripley b Capel	12
A. A. Metcalfe c Ripley b Capel	....	0	– c Davis b N. G. B. Cook	26
R. J. Blakey c Ripley b Capel	....	108	– b N. G. B. Cook	60
K. Sharp c Wild b Davis	....	0	– st Ripley b Williams	49
J. D. Love c Larkins b Davis	....	7	– not out	48
†D. L. Bairstow c Walker b Capel	....	15		
*P. Carrick c Ripley b Capel	....	2	– (7) not out	22
A. Sidebottom lbw b Walker	....	1	– (6) c Larkins b Williams	3
P. J. Hartley c Davis b Capel	....	23		
P. W. Jarvis c Ripley b Capel	....	3		
S. D. Fletcher not out	....	1		
B 3, l-b 4, w 10, n-b 9	....	26	B 1, l-b 10, w 1, n-b 1	13

1/0 2/1 3/6 4/30 5/90   187   1/37 2/67 3/154   (5 wkts dec.) 233
6/97 7/98 8/178 9/186   4/169 5/185

Bonus points – Yorkshire 1, Northamptonshire 4.

Bowling: *First Innings*—Capel 18.2–3–46–7; Davis 21–4–73–2; Walker 15–5–51–1; N. G. B. Cook 9–6–10–0. *Second Innings*—Davis 10–2–24–0; Capel 10–7–10–1; N. G. B. Cook 21–3–48–2; Wild 7–1–35–0; Walker 11–1–35–0; Williams 11–3–29–2; G. Cook 7–2–41–0.

Northamptonshire

*G. Cook not out	31	– b Sidebottom	7
W. Larkins not out	101	– lbw b Jarvis	2
R. J. Bailey (did not bat)		– not out	152
A. J. Lamb (did not bat)		– c and b Fletcher	14
D. J. Capel (did not bat)		– not out	91
B 4, l-b 1, n-b 1	6	B 1, l-b 16	17

(no wkt dec.) 138   1/9 2/9 3/75   (3 wkts) 283

R. G. Williams, D. J. Wild, †D. Ripley, N. G. B. Cook, W. W. Davis and A. Walker did not bat.

Bowling: *First Innings*—Jarvis 8–1–53–0; Sidebottom 10–4–25–0; Hartley 6–1–32–0; Fletcher 6–2–22–0; Carrick 1–0–1–0. *Second Innings*—Jarvis 14–2–85–1; Sidebottom 11.3–0–66–1; Hartley 8–0–57–0; Fletcher 8–1–42–1; Carrick 2–0–16–0.

Umpires: R. Julian and K. J. Lyons.

At Swansea, July 1, 2, 3. NORTHAMPTONSHIRE beat GLAMORGAN by eight wickets.

NORTHAMPTONSHIRE v LANCASHIRE

At Northampton, July 4, 6, 7. Northamptonshire won by nine wickets. Northamptonshire 24 pts, Lancashire 4 pts. Toss: Lancashire. Northamptonshire completed a "double" over the Roses counties at Northampton, despite an outstanding maiden hundred from Hegg in his fourth Championship match. Coming in as night-watchman, with his side 184 behind on the second evening, the nineteen-year-old wicket-keeper batted for nearly four and a quarter hours, hitting eighteen fours and sharing a stand of 106 with Fairbrother. His dismissal, however, triggered a collapse, with Davis taking four for 26 in 38 balls after tea, and Northamptonshire's batsmen were left with a straightforward task. The home side had earlier built up an imposing lead of 216, chiefly through a fine display from Bailey (275 minutes, two sixes, 23 fours). He and Cook (ten fours) put on 157 for the second wicket, and then Lamb (one six, nine fours) helped him add 119 in 39 overs to press home the advantage.

Close of play: First day, Northamptonshire 119-1 (G. Cook 35*, R. J. Bailey 75*); Second day, Lancashire 58-2 (G. Fowler 30*, W. K. Hegg 10*).

Lancashire

G. Fowler lbw b Davis	20	– b N. G. B. Cook	63
I. Folley c Ripley b Davis	31	– lbw b Robinson	3
D. W. Varey c G. Cook b Davis	0	– c N. G. B. Cook b Davis	1
N. H. Fairbrother c Davis	2	– (5) c Larkins b Robinson	45
S. J. O'Shaughnessy c sub b Robinson	8	– (6) b Davis	9
M. Watkinson lbw b Robinson	0	– (7) c G. Cook b Wild	0
*D. P. Hughes c sub b Wild	37	– (8) lbw b Davis	0
P. J. W. Allott c sub b Wild	27	– (9) c Boyd-Moss b Davis	30
J. Simmons run out	4	– (10) lbw b Davis	0
†W. K. Hegg not out	26	– (4) b Wild	130
B. P. Patterson c Ripley b N. G. B. Cook	29	– not out	1
B 6, l-b 15, n-b 9	30	B 1, l-b 5, n-b 22	28

1/30 2/30 3/43 4/66 5/66	214	1/18 2/32 3/105 4/211 5/272	310
6/73 7/134 8/142 9/168		6/272 7/273 8/288 9/288	

Bonus points – Lancashire 2, Northamptonshire 4.

Bowling: *First Innings*—Davis 26–4–90–4; Brown 3–2–4–0; Robinson 19–6–36–2; N. G. B. Cook 17.2–7–24–1; Wild 13–2–39–2. *Second Innings*—Davis 25.2–0–116–5; Robinson 22–2–72–2; N. G. B. Cook 31–13–62–1; Boyd-Moss 10–2–28–0; Wild 11–6–26–2.

Northamptonshire

*G. Cook c Folley b Simmons	55	– not out 36
W. Larkins lbw b Patterson	6	– c Hegg b Allott 2
R. J. Bailey lbw b O'Shaughnessy	158	– not out 45
A. J. Lamb c O'Shaughnessy b Simmons	89	
R. J. Boyd-Moss c Patterson b Watkinson	60	
D. J. Wild run out	2	
†D. Ripley b Allott	4	
N. G. B. Cook b Allott	5	
W. W. Davis not out	25	
S. J. Brown retired hurt	4	
M. A. Robinson c Hegg b Watkinson	1	
B 7, l-b 4, n-b 10	21	L-b 8, w 1, n-b 3 ... 12

1/13 2/170 3/289 4/340 5/343   430   1/12   (1 wkt) 95
6/383 7/391 8/413 9/430

Bonus points – Northamptonshire 4, Lancashire 2 (Score at 100 overs: 349-5).

Bowling: *First Innings*—Patterson 23–2–101–1; Allott 22–5–83–2; Watkinson 16.3–3–0–73–2; O'Shaughnessy 12–0–50–1; Simmons 24–13–45–2; Folley 25–3–67–0. *Second Innings*—Patterson 7–0–35–0; Allott 8–2–36–1; Simmons 1.5–0–16–0.

Umpires: D. J. Constant and J. H. Harris.

At Bristol, July 18, 20, 21. NORTHAMPTONSHIRE drew with GLOUCESTERSHIRE.

NORTHAMPTONSHIRE v SOMERSET

At Northampton, July 22, 23, 24. Drawn. Northamptonshire 4 pts, Somerset 5 pts. Toss: Somerset. A well-grassed pitch, freshened by occasional rain, ensured that the bowlers held sway throughout a match which produced an exciting climax, Somerset finishing eight wickets down and 4 runs short of victory. Chasing 174 in 49 overs, they were put on course by Crowe, only for the innings to lose momentum until Burns and Marks joined forces with enterprising strokeplay and running. However, 9 runs off the last over, from Davis, proved beyond the visitors' reach. On the first day, in gloomy conditions which brought four stoppages, Mallender took four of the first five wickets against his former colleagues; but Williams averted complete disarray with 49 off 64 balls. Davis and Walker struck back for Northamptonshire to restrict Somerset's lead to 19. And as batting conditions eased, Geoff Cook, batting carefully for two and a half hours, steered his side into a position to set a run-chase. His calculations were not made easier by rain either side of lunch which took 33 overs from the day's allotment.

Close of play: First day, Northamptonshire 132; Second day, Northamptonshire 108-2 (G. Cook 47*, A. J. Lamb 15*).

Northamptonshire

*G. Cook c Burns b Foster	3	– not out 67
W. Larkins c Burns b Mallender	0	– c Mallender b Palmer ... 2
R. J. Bailey c Crowe b Mallender	3	– c Roebuck b Mallender .. 39
A. J. Lamb c Felton b Mallender	11	– c Foster b Palmer ... 39
D. J. Capel c Burns b Mallender	3	– b Marks 33
R. G. Williams c Harden b Palmer	49	– not out 3
D. J. Wild c Roebuck b Palmer	2	
†D. Ripley c Felton b Foster	15	
N. G. B. Cook c Burns b Foster	0	
W. W. Davis c Crowe b Palmer	14	
A. Walker not out	2	
B 2, l-b 7, w 4, n-b 17	30	B 1, n-b 8 9

1/3 2/17 3/19 4/39 5/40   132   1/25 2/83 3/135   (4 wkts dec.) 192
6/47 7/83 8/103 9/122   4/188

Bonus points – Somerset 4.

Bowling: *First Innings*—Mallender 14–2–37–4; Foster 11–1–53–3; Palmer 12.3–3–33–3. *Second Innings*—Mallender 19–5–42–1; Foster 6–0–51–0; Palmer 22–4–84–2; Marks 6–1–14–1; Pringle 2–2–0–0.

Somerset

N. A. Felton lbw b Davis	41	– c Bailey b Walker	1
*P. M. Roebuck hit wkt b Davis	0	– c Williams b Walker	6
J. J. E. Hardy c Bailey b Walker	18	– run out	43
M. D. Crowe c Lamb b Davis	0	– lbw b Davis	44
N. J. Pringle lbw b Davis	31	– c Ripley b Davis	6
R. J. Harden b Walker	13	– c Capel b Walker	17
†N. D. Burns c Ripley b Walker	8	– c Davis	21
V. J. Marks c Lamb b Davis	11	– c Capel b Davis	17
G. V. Palmer c and b Davis	3	– not out	6
N. A. Mallender c Ripley b Walker	10	– not out	2
D. J. Foster not out	0		
B 9, l-b 3, n-b 4	16	B 1, l-b 5, n-b 1	7

1/1 2/26 3/27 4/97 5/104　　　　　　　151　　1/7 2/8 3/68 4/78　　　　(8 wkts) 170
6/124 7/128 8/133 9/151　　　　　　　　　　5/113 6/142 7/144 8/165

Bonus points – Somerset 1, Northamptonshire 4.

Bowling: *First Innings*—Davis 21.1–3–58–6; Capel 12–1–33–0; Walker 20–6–43–4; Wild 2–1–4–0; N. G. B. Cook 1–0–1–0. *Second Innings*—Davis 17–1–57–4; Walker 17–1–70–3; N. G. B. Cook 7–1–27–0; Capel 8–3–10–0.

Umpires: J. Birkenshaw and D. R. Shepherd.

NORTHAMPTONSHIRE v SUSSEX

At Northampton, July 25, 27, 28. Northamptonshire won by five wickets. Northamptonshire 22 pts, Sussex 5 pts. Toss: Sussex. Northamptonshire's victory was not achieved without a few anxious moments when, needing 125 to win after lunch on the last day, they lost five wickets for 71. However, Geoff Cook, although handicapped by a badly bruised heel, came in to join Bailey and prevent any further alarms. Bailey's responsible 81, the highest individual score of a match dominated by seam bowling, included a six and eleven fours and, despite the delicate situation, came off just 109 balls. The decisive phase of the match was in the last hour of the second day when Sussex, beginning their second innings 7 runs ahead, lost four wickets for 16 to Capel and Davis. Capel recaptured his best bowling form with match figures of nine for 79, but in such favourable conditions Sussex were unlucky to lose le Roux early in Northamptonshire's first innings. A stomach strain prevented him from bowling again in the match.

Close of play: First day, Northamptonshire 26–2 (R. J. Bailey 8*, A. J. Lamb 9*); Second day, Sussex 26–4 (C. M. Wells 2*, D. K. Standing 7*).

Sussex

R. I. Alikhan c Ripley b Davis	0	– lbw b Davis	7
A. M. Green c Larkins b Davis	15	– b Capel	0
P. W. G. Parker c N. G. B. Cook b Capel	31	– c Bailey b Davis	3
A. P. Wells c Ripley b Capel	28	– c Walker b Capel	2
C. M. Wells c and b Capel	4	– c Robinson b Capel	2
D. K. Standing c Ripley b Capel	56	– c N. G. B. Cook b Davis	22
*H. J. Gould run out	46	– b Capel	0
G. S. le Roux b Williams	0	– not out	44
A. C. S. Pigott c Ripley b Capel	7	– c Ripley b Davis	4
P. A. W. Heseltine c Ripley b Walker	6	– b Walker	19
A. M. Babington not out	0	– run out	1
B 2, l-b 6, n-b 7	15	W 1, n-b 12	13

1/1 2/27 3/78 4/79 5/88　　　　　　　208　　1/7 2/10 3/16 4/16 5/29　　　　117
6/165 7/166 8/191 9/208　　　　　　　　　　6/29 7/56 8/69 9/103

Bonus points – Sussex 2, Northamptonshire 4.

Bowling: *First Innings*—Davis 14–1–50–2; Capel 24.2–6–57–5; Walker 13–4–25–1; Robinson 6–2–20–0; N. G. B. Cook 13–5–22–0; Williams 14–3–26–1. *Second Innings*—Davis 21–7–51–4; Capel 11–4–22–4; N. G. B. Cook 5–3–6–0; Walker 10–1–38–1.

Northamptonshire

*G. Cook lbw b le Roux	2	– (7) not out	18
W. Larkins lbw b le Roux	6	– c sub b Babington	9
R. J. Bailey c A. P. Wells b Babington	43	– (1) not out	81
A. J. Lamb c and b C. M. Wells	25	– (3) c Standing b Pigott	11
D. J. Capel c Gould b Heseltine	44	– (4) c and b C. M. Wells	4
R. G. Williams not out	42	– (5) c Gould b Pigott	0
†D. Ripley c C. M. Wells b Pigott	1	– (6) c A. P. Wells b Pigott	0
N. G. B. Cook c Gould b Pigott	1		
W. W. Davis c Parker b C. M. Wells	13		
A. Walker not out	11		
B 1, l-b 4, w 1, n-b 7	13	L-b 3, n-b 1	4

1/4 2/9 3/62 4/103 5/157   (8 wkts dec.) 201   1/19 2/51 3/62   (5 wkts) 127
6/160 7/162 8/179   4/65 5/71

M. A. Robinson did not bat.

Bonus points – Northamptonshire 2, Sussex 3.

Bowling: *First Innings*—le Roux 9.2–3–20–2; Pigott 26.4–5–64–2; Babington 13–3–30–1; C. M. Wells 19.4–1–43–2; Heseltine 16–5–39–1. *Second Innings*—Pigott 16–2–50–3; Babington 9–3–37–1; C. M. Wells 11–2–26–1; Heseltine 1–0–7–0; Alikhan 0.1–0–4–0.

Umpires: J. H. Hampshire and D. R. Shepherd.

At Birmingham, August 1, 3, 4. NORTHAMPTONSHIRE drew with WARWICKSHIRE.

At Manchester, August 5, 6, 7. NORTHAMPTONSHIRE drew with LANCASHIRE.

NORTHAMPTONSHIRE v ESSEX

At Northampton, August 8, 10, 11. Drawn. Northamptonshire 6 pts, Essex 7 pts. Toss: Northamptonshire. Rain ended the prospect of a potentially interesting finish after Essex had been set 213 to win in a minimum of 39 overs. The weather had also intervened on the first day, cutting 39 overs from the day's quota, and in gloomy conditions only Cook, Williams and Lamb came to terms with some testing bowling from Lever and Topley. Lamb, who was at a local hospital where his wife was about to give birth to their first child, was recalled to the County Ground as wickets fell and hit 40 quick runs before resuming bedside duties. Gooch was restrained but solid when Essex replied, batting three and threequarter hours for his 75, and on the last morning he saw his bowlers reduce Northamptonshire to 84 for five before Waterton, in his first Championship match of the season, helped Wild steady the innings with an unbroken partnership of 105.

Close of play: First day, Northamptonshire 223-7 (R. G. Williams 60*, N. G. B. Cook 3*); Second day, Essex 249-8 (T. D. Topley 25*, I. L. Pont 18*).

Northamptonshire

*G. Cook c Stephenson b Gooch	53	– c Gooch b Pont	12
W. Larkins c and b Lever	26	– c Hussain b Topley	27
R. J. Bailey lbw b Topley	6	– c East b Lever	11
†S. N. V. Waterton c East b Topley	4	– (7) not out	50
D. J. Capel lbw b Topley	17		
R. G. Williams c Lilley b Lever	66	– (5) c Miller b Topley	15
D. J. Wild b Lever	3	– (6) not out	59
A. J. Lamb c Topley b Pont	40	– (4) c Hussain b Lever	7
N. G. B. Cook c East b Lever	11		
W. W. Davis not out	20		
G. Smith c Stephenson b Lever	11		
L-b 10, w 1, n-b 5	16	L-b 8	8

1/55 2/64 3/83 4/103 5/119   273   1/13 2/36 3/44   (5 wkts dec.) 189
6/147 7/208 8/237 9/239   4/63 5/84

Bonus points – Northamptonshire 3, Essex 4.

Bowling: *First Innings*—Lever 26–6–71–5; Pont 27–6–86–1; Topley 25–6–62–3; Gooch 11–4–44–1. *Second Innings*—Lever 6–1–29–2; Pont 13–1–48–1; Topley 18–6–45–2; Miller 14–3–49–0; Gooch 5–1–10–0.

Essex

*G. A. Gooch b Wild	75	– not out	7
J. P. Stephenson b Capel	9	– not out	6
B. R. Hardie c Lamb b Capel	8		
A. W. Lilley lbw b Smith	33		
N. Hussain b N. G. B. Cook	12		
P. J. Prichard c Davis b Capel	16		
G. Miller c Lamb b Davis	12		
†D. E. East b Davis	17		
T. D. Topley not out	25		
I. L. Pont not out	18		
B 5, l-b 9, w 1, n-b 10	25	L-b 4, n-b 1	5

1/33 2/51 3/108 4/133   (8 wkts dec.) 250   (no wkt) 18
5/168 6/168 7/199 8/204

J. K. Lever did not bat.

Bonus points – Essex 3, Northamptonshire 3.

Bowling: *First Innings*—Davis 27–3–75–2; Capel 19–4–60–3; Smith 7–1–30–1; N. G. B. Cook 13–7–29–1; Wild 23–10–42–1. *Second Innings*—Davis 2–0–9–0; Smith 2–0–5–0.

Umpires: R. A. White and A. G. T. Whitehead.

At Nottingham, August 15, 17, 18. NORTHAMPTONSHIRE lost to NOTTINGHAM-SHIRE by an innings and 132 runs.

NORTHAMPTONSHIRE v WORCESTERSHIRE

At Northampton, August 19, 20, 21. Drawn. Northamptonshire 8 pts, Worcestershire 5 pts. Toss: Northamptonshire. Much good, positive cricket was played in a match which produced more than 1,000 runs and three centuries and reached a climax on the final afternoon. Hick, in outstanding form, followed his first-innings 87 (two sixes, thirteen fours) with a masterly 107 off 150 balls, which included sixteen fours and took Worcestershire within sight of their target of 281. They were favourites to win during a stand of 111 in 29 overs between Hick and D'Oliveira, but the challenge faltered when three wickets fell in four balls with 18 still required. Worcestershire began the last over 12 short, and Newport failed to make contact with the final ball, from Williams, which he needed to hit for six. Larkins (sixteen fours) dominated the first day with 115 in just under four hours, adding 125 in 42 overs with Lamb, and Cook held Northamptonshire's second innings together with his first Championship hundred of the season.

Close of play: First day, Worcestershire 17-0 (T. S. Curtis 8*, G. J. Lord 7*); Second day, Northamptonshire 73-2 (G. Cook 30*).

Northamptonshire

*G. Cook b Radford	16	– not out	111
W. Larkins lbw b Pridgeon	115	– lbw b Radford	10
R. J. Bailey c D'Oliveira b Pridgeon	17	– c Rhodes b Newport	22
A. J. Lamb c Newport b Hick	56	– lbw b Radford	3
D. J. Capel c Radford b Illingworth	24	– c Rhodes b Radford	22
R. G. Williams not out	45	– c Radford b Newport	6
D. J. Wild st Rhodes b Illingworth	48	– not out	23
L-b 8, n-b 4	12	B 6, l-b 6, w 1, n-b 9	22

1/28 2/82 3/207 4/215   (6 wkts. dec.) 333   1/21 2/73 3/78   (5 wkts. dec.) 219
5/254 6/333   4/116 5/135

†D. Ripley, N. G. B. Cook, W. W. Davis and A. Walker did not bat.

Bonus points – Northamptonshire 4, Worcestershire 2 (Score at 100 overs: 309-5).

Bowling: *First Innings*—Radford 23-3-67-1; Pridgeon 20-8-39-2; Newport 14-0-76-0; Illingworth 23.5-5-65-2; Hick 16-2-59-1; Lampitt 7-1-19-0. *Second Innings*—Radford 21-1-75-3; Pridgeon 11-1-41-0; Newport 14-1-56-2; Lampitt 5-1-16-0; Illingworth 7-1-19-0.

Worcestershire

T. S. Curtis c Lamb b Williams	35	– lbw b Walker	19
G. J. Lord lbw b Capel	19	– c Walker b Williams	10
G. A. Hick c Bailey b Walker	87	– lbw b Williams	107
D. B. D'Oliveira b Williams	15	– st Ripley b Williams	42
*P. A. Neale c Ripley b Walker	46	– c Larkins b Williams	29
S. R. Lampitt lbw b Walker	2	– (8) run out	0
†S. J. Rhodes c Wild b Williams	3	– b N. G. B. Cook	9
P. J. Newport c Ripley b Walker	22	– (9) not out	2
R. K. Illingworth b Williams	16	– (10) not out	9
N. V. Radford c Williams b N. G. B. Cook	8	– (6) c Capel b Williams	29
A. P. Pridgeon not out	0		
B 5, l-b 6, n-b 8	19	B 10, l-b 9, n-b 3	22

1/61 2/64 3/87 4/208 5/218   272   1/19 2/59 3/170 4/202   (8 wkts) 275
6/223 7/225 8/261 9/272   5/243 6/263 7/263 8/263

Bonus points – Worcestershire 3, Northamptonshire 4.

Bowling: *First Innings*—Davis 20-3-71-0; Capel 14-2-46-1; Walker 17-4-39-4; Williams 21-11-44-4; Wild 4-1-13-0; N. G. B. Cook 17.2-6-48-1. *Second Innings*—Davis 14-2-63-0; Walker 6-1-22-1; Wild 4-1-21-0; Williams 26-7-81-5; N. G. B. Cook 16-0-69-1.

Umpires: J. A. Jameson and K. E. Palmer.

NORTHAMPTONSHIRE v MIDDLESEX

At Wellingborough School, August 22, 24, 25. Drawn. Middlesex 4 pts. Toss: Middlesex. Northamptonshire's annual visit to Wellingborough School was ruined by rain, which allowed only 95 minutes' play on the first day and washed out the third. In between, batting was far from easy on a slow pitch devoid of bounce. Bailey, for example, was restricted to 36 in 55 overs. However, Carr and Ramprakash managed to provide a splash of colour with some attractive strokeplay in the last hour of the second day. Williams, suffering from bruised ribs and lungs, was unable to bat for Northamptonshire, and Daniel returned to Barbados during the match following the death of his mother.

Close of play: First day, Northamptonshire 51-1 (G. Cook 22*, R. J. Bailey 13*); Second day, Middlesex 88-2 (J. D. Carr 47*, M. R. Ramprakash 31*).

Northamptonshire

*G. Cook b Edmonds	27	A. Walker not out		8
W. Larkins c Daniel b Edmonds	12	M. A. Robinson lbw b Cowans		2
R. J. Bailey c Brown b Edmonds	36	R. G. Williams absent ill		
A. J. Lamb lbw b Cowans	2			
D. J. Wild lbw b Cowans	0	L-b 4, n-b 3		7
†D. Ripley lbw b Cowans	28			
N. G. B. Cook c Carr b Cowans	4	1/29 2/56 3/63 4/63 5/102		127
W. W. Davis b Sykes	1	6/108 7/109 8/117 9/127		

Bonus points – Middlesex 4.

Bowling: Daniel 4-0-14-0; Cowans 22-5-43-5; Edmonds 29-15-23-3; Fraser 14-3-31-0; Sykes 7-2-12-1.

Middlesex

W. N. Slack c sub b Davis	4
J. D. Carr not out	47
*†P. R. Downton lbw b Walker	5
M. R. Ramprakash not out	31
N-b 1	1
1/7 2/12 (2 wkts)	88

M. A. Roseberry, K. R. Brown, J. F. Sykes, P. H. Edmonds, A. R. C. Fraser, N. G. Cowans and W. W. Daniel did not bat.

Bowling: Davis 9-5-13-1; Walker 14-3-29-1; N. G. B. Cook 11-4-32-0; Robinson 5-2-8-0; Bailey 2-0-6-0.

Umpires: J. A. Jameson and K. E. Palmer.

NORTHAMPTONSHIRE v DERBYSHIRE

At Northampton, August 26, 27, 28. Drawn. Northamptonshire 4 pts. Toss: Northamptonshire. Outplayed for all but the last two hours of the match, Derbyshire none the less came closer to winning as the home side lost their way chasing 250 in 42 overs. Rain prevented play after lunch on the first day and before lunch on the second, interrupting Derbyshire's troubled progress against Davis, who exploited the advantageous seam-bowling conditions with the help of fine close-catching. Larkins's 46 off 35 balls paved the way for Cook to declare 55 behind, but his hopes of a second Derbyshire collapse on the second evening were not realised as Wright dug in. However, when Derbyshire's remaining eight wickets went for 72 on the last day, the task facing Northamptonshire appeared well within their capabilities. Cook and Larkins led off with 47 before the innings ran into trouble, and with Mortensen in a hostile mood – he had been struck on the foot and helmet in Derbyshire's first innings – it was left to Davis and Nick Cook to play out the final four overs for a draw.

Close of play: First day, Derbyshire 92-4 (B. J. M. Maher 8*, R. Sharma 0*); Second day, Derbyshire 122-2 (J. G. Wright 52*, J. E. Morris 8*).

Derbyshire

*K. J. Barnett c Capel b Davis	9	– c Davis b N. G. B. Cook	40
J. G. Wright c Larkins b N. G. B. Cook	19	– run out	65
B. Roberts c Wild b Davis	21	– b Davis	18
J. E. Morris c Wild b Capel	31	– b Davis	9
†B. J. M. Maher c Lamb b Walker	22	– c Ripley b Walker	5
R. Sharma c Lamb b Walker	4	– c Ripley b Walker	1
R. J. Finney c Capel b Davis	4	– c Larkins b N. G. B. Cook	19
A. E. Warner run out	14	– b N. G. B. Cook	21
P. G. Newman c Capel b Davis	2	– b Bailey	3
O. H. Mortensen not out	4	– not out	1
D. E. Malcolm b Davis	4	– c Wild b Davis	1
L-b 6, w 1, n-b 6	13	L-b 4, n-b 7	11

1/12 2/48 3/57 4/89 5/106   147   1/64 2/94 3/130 4/144 5/145   194
6/115 7/119 8/122 9/141   6/146 7/183 8/192 9/192

Bonus points – Northamptonshire 4.

Bowling: *First Innings*—Davis 21.3–6–64–5; Walker 16–5–47–2; N. G. B. Cook 8–1–14–1; Capel 5–2–13–1; Wild 2–1–3–0. *Second Innings*—Davis 18.1–3–59–3; Walker 12.3–2–47–2; Capel 18–4–43–0; N. G. B. Cook 30–17–32–3; Bailey 6–4–4–1; Wild 9.3–6–5–0.

Northamptonshire

*G. Cook not out	24	– c Warner b Newman	22
W. Larkins c sub b Malcolm	46	– run out	48
R. J. Bailey c Roberts b Malcolm	16	– b Mortensen	1
A. J. Lamb not out	1	– c Maher b Newman	7
D. J. Capel (did not bat)		– st Maher b Finney	12
R. J. Boyd-Moss (did not bat)		– b Mortensen	7
D. J. Wild (did not bat)		– b Malcolm	1
†D. Ripley (did not bat)		– b Mortensen	10
N. G. B. Cook (did not bat)		– not out	0
W. W. Davis (did not bat)		– not out	0
L-b 1, n-b 4	5	L-b 8	8

1/67 2/89   (2 wkts dec.) 92   1/47 2/58 3/80 4/86   (8 wkts) 116
                                     5/101 6/101 7/116 8/116

A. Walker did not bat.

Bowling: *First Innings*—Newman 5–0–26–0; Malcolm 8–0–36–2; Warner 4–0–26–0; Finney 2–0–3–0. *Second Innings*—Malcolm 8.5–4–15–1; Newman 10–0–48–2; Mortensen 16–5–34–3; Finney 6–2–11–1; Barnett 1–1–0–0.

Umpires: J. H. Harris and R. Palmer.

At Leicester, August 29, 31, September 1. NORTHAMPTONSHIRE lost to LEICESTERSHIRE by an innings and 125 runs.

At The Oval, September 2, 3, 4. NORTHAMPTONSHIRE lost to SURREY by ten wickets.

At Hove, September 9, 10, 11. NORTHAMPTONSHIRE drew with SUSSEX.

At Worcester, September 12, 14, 15. NORTHAMPTONSHIRE lost to WORCESTERSHIRE by four wickets.

NOTTINGHAMSHIRE

President: J. W. Baddiley
Chairman: C. W. Gillott
Chairman, Cricket Committee: R. T. Simpson
Secretary: B. Robson
County Cricket Ground, Trent Bridge,
Nottingham NG2 6AG
(Telephone: 0602-821525)
Cricket Manager: K. A. Taylor
Captain: 1987 – C. E. B. Rice
1988 – R. T. Robinson

A scriptwriter could not have devised anything better for the swan-song of Clive Rice and Richard Hadlee, the South African and New Zealander who had done so much to transform Nottinghamshire into one of the most successful county sides. At one time, with the Britannic Assurance Championship, NatWest Bank Trophy and Refuge Assurance League in their sights, it looked as if Nottinghamshire would capture a remarkable treble. Then, for an agonising fortnight at the end of August, all the old doubts and uncertainties returned. However, determination had always been as significant a quality of Rice and Hadlee as their natural talent, and they were determined to capture honours as proof of the best season in the club's history. So it was. First came the NatWest Trophy, then the Championship, and they were denied the treble by Worcestershire's winning the Sunday League, having to settle for the runners-up prizemoney.

Although the winning of the NatWest final in a wonderful fightback against Northamptonshire at Lord's ended Nottinghamshire's quest for a one-day trophy, there was perhaps more inner – and more lasting – satisfaction in taking the County Championship title for the second time in seven seasons. Yet it had seemed such an unlikely event in the early weeks of the season. They had seven successive draws, and in some of them experienced the frustration of getting into winning positions, only to be denied, largely, by the weather. It was not until the last day of June, when they defeated Kent at Canterbury, that their Championship challenge began, but by the end of July they had put themselves in a position from which they could press home their advantage.

An unbalanced fixture list left Nottinghamshire with seven of their last nine matches at home, and it was then that the surge came. Five of those games ended in victories – and convincing ones at that. This led to a repeat of the 1981 rumblings over the Trent Bridge pitch being prepared to suit the bowling of Hadlee. No doubt the pitches did favour the brilliant New Zealander, whose match-winning talents were exploited to the limit, but he had been a formidable proposition on any pitch. Hadlee apart, was it not the same for both sides?

Over the years – not just in 1981 and 1987 – Ron Allsopp, the Nottinghamshire groundsman, has attempted to change Trent Bridge's feather-bed pitches in pursuit of those which encouraged positive cricket, greater entertainment, and more results. As with such efforts anywhere, there have been times when the odds favoured the bowlers; but there have also been times when the pendulum has swung the other way. This was seen last season on that farcical occasion when Derbyshire were offered "gift" bowlers in the hope of a result being manufactured. If that is the alternative to wickets which provide a result, then it has to be asked what is better for the future of the game.

Of special significance in the closing stages of the Championship campaign was the decision to reinstate Rice as captain for Championship games. Tim Robinson had been given the opportunity to gain experience in the role; but with Rice once more in control, Nottinghamshire rounded off their programme with emphatic home wins over Sussex and Glamorgan to take a clear lead. The champagne, however, had to stay on ice, for Lancashire, who had been winning repeatedly to come back into contention, could pip Nottinghamshire by taking maximum points from their last game. Their failure at Chelmsford to get the necessary batting points meant the return of the Championship pennant to Trent Bridge.

Once more, as far as Nottinghamshire were concerned, Hadlee was the man of the season, failing by three wickets to achieve the double for the second time in four years and heading both their batting and bowling averages. Just how they will fare without him and Rice is open to question. Hadlee, without question, proved himself the most effective, and most consistent, cricketer in the county game and is virtually irreplaceable. None the less, he and Rice, whose positive ideas and actions contributed as much to the county over the years, left Nottinghamshire in much better shape than when they arrived.

Robinson, Chris Broad, Bruce French and Eddie Hemmings were involved with England over the winter. Derek Randall, before a broken thumb restricted his contribution, had rediscovered his appetite for the game with batting that showed there was still much to come from one of cricket's most colourful characters. Moreover, there is rich promise in the new breed of Nottinghamshire cricketers. Paul Johnson can be one of the most destructive of attacking batsmen, while Mick Newell's 1,054 runs in twenty first-class games last season showed that he can hold his own in the best of company.

With the loss of Hadlee as a strike bowler, heavy responsibility lies with the emerging Andy Pick and Kevin Saxelby, who could play a key role if he adds consistency to his game. In spin, Nottinghamshire are as well off as most counties. Hemmings took 88 first-class wickets in his benefit season to win an England recall, and much will be expected of the young left-armer, Andy Afford, provided he steers clear of the back injury that forced him to miss much of 1987. Fortunately for him, and for every other spectator at Trent Bridge, it was a memorable season to watch. – John Lawson.

523

NOTTINGHAMSHIRE 1987

[*Bill Smith*

Back row: P. Pollard, R. J. Evans, C. D. Fraser-Darling, K. P. Evans, J. A. Afford, M. Newell. *Middle row*: D. J. R. Martindale, C. W. Scott, R. A. Pick, K. Saxelby, D. J. Millns, K. E. Cooper, P. Johnson. *Front row*: B. N. French, E. E. Hemmings, D. W. Randall, R. T. Robinson, K. A. Taylor (*manager*), C. E. B. Rice (*captain*), B. C. Broad, J. D. Birch, M. K. Bore. *Inset*: R. J. Hadlee.

NOTTINGHAMSHIRE RESULTS

All first-class matches – Played 25: Won 10, Lost 1, Drawn 14. Abandoned 1.

County Championship matches – Played 23: Won 9, Lost 1, Drawn 13. Abandoned 1.

Bonus points – Batting 68, Bowling 80.

Competition placings – Britannic Assurance County Championship, winners; NatWest Bank Trophy, winners; Benson and Hedges Cup, 4th in Group A; Refuge Assurance League, 2nd.

BRITANNIC ASSURANCE CHAMPIONSHIP AVERAGES

BATTING

	Birthplace	M	I	NO	R	HI	Avge
§‡R. J. Hadlee	Christchurch, NZ	20	27	7	1,075	133*	53.75
§‡C. E. B. Rice	Johannesburg, SA	21	30	6	1,040	138	43.33
‡R. T. Robinson	Sutton-in-Ashfield	13	23	4	808	137	42.52
‡B. C. Broad	Bristol	10	17	4	503	80	38.69
‡P. Johnson	Newark	23	36	4	1,232	125	38.50
‡M. Newell	Blackburn	19	33	7	1,001	203*	38.50
‡D. W. Randall	Retford	11	17	1	601	133	37.56
‡J. D. Birch	Nottingham	21	29	2	774	82	28.66
‡E. E. Hemmings	Leamington Spa	23	25	6	377	75	19.84
P. Pollard	Nottingham	5	7	0	132	59	18.85
C. W. Scott	Thorpe-on-the-Hill	12	15	1	250	45	17.85
D. J. R. Martindale	Harrogate	9	13	2	192	103	17.45
‡R. A. Pick	Nottingham	16	15	5	154	42*	15.40
‡B. N. French	Warsop	11	12	1	161	29	14.63
J. A. Afford	Crowland	9	9	6	23	16	7.66
‡K. Saxelby	Worksop	17	14	6	60	14	7.50
‡K. E. Cooper	Hucknall	6	6	1	22	17	4.40
‡M. K. Bore	Hull	6	5	1	13	7	3.25

Also batted: C. D. Fraser-Darling (*Sheffield*) (1 match) 16.

* *Signifies not out.*   ‡ *Denotes county cap.*   § *Not qualified for England.*

The following played a total of fifteen three-figure innings for Nottinghamshire in County Championship matches – P. Johnson 3, M. Newell 3, C. E. B. Rice 3, R. J. Hadlee 2, R. T. Robinson 2, D. J. R. Martindale 1, D. W. Randall 1.

BOWLING

	O	M	R	W	BB	Avge
R. J. Hadlee	568	186	1,154	97	6-20	11.89
E. E. Hemmings	816.4	267	2,004	82	6-62	24.43
K. E. Cooper	158.3	50	387	15	3-38	25.80
C. E. B. Rice	296.3	89	737	28	4-42	26.32
M. K. Bore	148.2	58	344	13	4-52	26.46
K. Saxelby	393.1	101	1,140	38	6-49	30.00
J. A. Afford	251.4	79	675	21	5-79	32.14
R. A. Pick	344.4	67	1,185	36	4-75	32.91

Also bowled: J. D. Birch 16.2–3–55–1; C. D. Fraser-Darling 17–4–69–0; P. Johnson 6–0–64–0; M. Newell 8.3–0–45–2.

Wicket-keepers: B. N. French 37 ct, 3 st; C. W. Scott 27 ct, 2 st.

Leading Fielders: C. E. B. Rice 24, P. Johnson 18, D. W. Randall 17, R. J. Hadlee 16, B. C. Broad 15.

NOTTINGHAMSHIRE v SURREY

At Nottingham, April 25, 26, 27. Drawn. Nottinghamshire 7 pts, Surrey 6 pts. Toss: Surrey. Greig marked his début as Surrey captain with an unbeaten half-century in 83 minutes on the final day before setting Nottinghamshire a difficult target of 233 in 85 minutes plus twenty overs. They never looked capable of reaching it, and when four wickets went down quickly, Broad and Rice batted out time. On the first day Greig had linked with Richards in a valuable stand of 118 to prevent Hemmings, who took six for 99, from dismissing Surrey cheaply. Hemmings – in addition to Broad – also made a useful contribution with the bat to give Nottinghamshire a first-innings lead, but time was always against their forcing a positive result.

Close of play: First day, Nottinghamshire 55-1 (B. C. Broad 32*, M. Newell 7*); Second day, Surrey 47-0 (G. S. Clinton 23*, D. M. Smith 23*).

Surrey

G. S. Clinton run out	46	– lbw b Afford	23
D. M. Smith b Hemmings	17	– lbw b Hemmings	23
A. J. Stewart c Johnson b Hemmings	0	– c Rice b Hemmings	61
M. A. Lynch c Rice b Hemmings	7	– c Rice b Pick	40
T. E. Jesty c Newell b Hemmings	3	– run out	3
†C. J. Richards st French b Hemmings	84	– c Broad b Saxelby	39
*I. A. Greig c French b Afford	46	– not out	50
C. K. Bullen c French b Hemmings	24	– c Randall b Saxelby	1
K. T. Medlycott b Afford	3	– c French b Saxelby	3
M. P. Bicknell not out	14	– not out	1
S. T. Clarke b Pick	9		
L-b 12, w 1	13	B 8, l-b 13, n-b 1	22
	266	(8 wkts dec.)	266

1/50 2/50 3/72 4/80 5/81 6/199 7/218 8/221 9/247

1/47 2/47 3/134 4/158 5/166 6/239 7/250 8/264

Bonus points – Surrey 3, Nottinghamshire 4.

Bowling: *First Innings*—Pick 12.3-4-41-1; Saxelby 4-0-22-0; Rice 10-3-29-0; Hemmings 31-5-99-6; Afford 32-11-63-2. *Second Innings*—Pick 8-3-26-1; Rice 4-0-10-0; Hemmings 32-11-83-2; Afford 29-3-100-1; Saxelby 6-0-26-3.

Nottinghamshire

B. C. Broad c and b Bullen	80	– not out	32
R. T. Robinson c Smith b Bicknell	8	– b Clarke	0
M. Newell b Bicknell	17	– c Smith b Greig	14
*C. E. B. Rice c Lynch b Clarke	10	– (6) not out	25
P. Johnson c Lynch b Clarke	18	– (4) b Medlycott	6
D. W. Randall lbw b Greig	0	– (5) b Medlycott	0
†B. N. French c Lynch b Medlycott	25		
E. E. Hemmings b Bullen	54		
R. A. Pick not out	42		
K. Saxelby b Bicknell	3		
J. A. Afford lbw b Greig	16		
B 8, l-b 15, w 2, n-b 2	27	B 5, w 2	7
	300	(4 wkts)	84

1/10 2/76 3/108 4/138 5/139 6/147 7/196 8/249 9/270

1/0 2/34 3/43 4/43

Bonus points – Nottinghamshire 3, Surrey 3 (Score at 100 overs: 252-8).

Bowling: *First Innings*—Clarke 30-10-62-2; Bicknell 25-5-70-3; Greig 13.4-2-45-2; Medlycott 27-6-62-1; Bullen 18-3-38-2. *Second Innings*—Bicknell 4-3-2-0; Clarke 10-2-27-1; Medlycott 11-1-31-2; Greig 3-0-19-1; Bullen 2-2-0-0.

Umpires: J. H. Hampshire and R. A. White.

At Bournemouth, May 20, 21, 22. NOTTINGHAMSHIRE drew with HAMPSHIRE.

At Oxford, May 23, 25, 26. NOTTINGHAMSHIRE beat OXFORD UNIVERSITY by an innings and 140 runs.

At Middlesbrough, May 30, June 1, 2. NOTTINGHAMSHIRE drew with YORKSHIRE.

At Taunton, June 3, 4, 5. NOTTINGHAMSHIRE drew with SOMERSET.

NOTTINGHAMSHIRE v LANCASHIRE

At Nottingham, June 6, 8, 9. Drawn. Nottinghamshire 4 pts, Lancashire 7 pts. Toss: Nottinghamshire. Lancashire had the better of the encounter before rain cut short play on the second day and wiped out the third. Nottinghamshire always struggled after winning the toss and only a typically aggressive 57 by Hadlee – to 50 in 52 minutes – gave the innings respectability against the wiles of Simmons. Lancashire themselves were in trouble at 95 for five, but Watkinson and Simmons put on 100 for the eighth wicket in 33 overs to give them a 73-run lead, Watkinson batting for just over three hours in only his second appearance of the season. Before the rain came, Nottinghamshire's young pair of Newell and Martindale withstood an uncomfortable spell from Patterson and Allott.

Close of play: First day, Lancashire 95-3 (M. R. Chadwick 28*, I. Folley 1*); Second day, Nottinghamshire 26-0 (M. Newell 9*, D. J. R. Martindale 15*).

Nottinghamshire

M. Newell lbw b Watkinson	8	– not out	9
D. J. R. Martindale c Stanworth b Watkinson	11	– not out	15
D. W. Randall c Simmons b Allott	28		
P. Johnson c Watkinson b Simmons	25		
*C. E. B. Rice c Watkinson b Simmons	23		
J. D. Birch c Stanworth b Allott	7		
R. J. Hadlee b Simmons	57		
†C. W. Scott c Allott b Folley	14		
E. E. Hemmings c Hughes b Simmons	6		
R. A. Pick c Hughes b Simmons	0		
K. Saxelby not out	0		
L-b 1, w 2, n-b 4	7	L-b 1, w 1	2

1/18 2/21 3/74 4/79 5/93   186   (no wkt) 26
6/129 7/174 8/184 9/184

Bonus points – Nottinghamshire 1, Lancashire 4.

Bowling: *First Innings*—Patterson 15-2-51-0; Allott 19-7-44-2; Watkinson 8-1-34-2; Simmons 19-4-55-5; Folley 1.1-0-1-1. *Second Innings*—Patterson 5-1-13-0; Allott 6-2-9-0; Watkinson 2-0-2-0; Simmons 1.1-1-0-0; Folley 1-0-1-0.

Lancashire

G. D. Mendis c Scott b Rice	24	J. Simmons c Scott b Pick	37
M. R. Chadwick c Newell b Hemmings	38	†J. Stanworth c Scott b Hadlee	10
D. W. Varey c Scott b Hadlee	6	B. P. Patterson not out	0
G. Fowler c Randall b Hemmings	28		
I. Folley c Scott b Saxelby	1	B 2, l-b 16	18
*D. P. Hughes c Hadlee b Saxelby	0		
M. Watkinson c Hadlee b Hemmings	78	1/33 2/44 3/87 4/95 5/95	259
P. J. W. Allott c Rice b Pick	19	6/127 7/149 8/249 9/259	

Bonus points – Lancashire 3, Nottinghamshire 3 (Score at 100 overs: 250-8).

Bowling: Hadlee 26-8-44-2; Pick 16.1-2-56-2; Rice 15-6-47-1; Saxelby 22-7-47-2; Hemmings 23-8-47-3.

Umpires: J. A. Jameson and A. A. Jones.

At Birmingham, June 17, 18, 19. NOTTINGHAMSHIRE drew with WARWICKSHIRE.

NOTTINGHAMSHIRE v WORCESTERSHIRE

At Nottingham, June 20, 22, 23. Drawn. Nottinghamshire 6 pts, Worcestershire 4 pts. Toss: Nottinghamshire. Curtis batted throughout the first day on a green pitch to make 129 and was unbeaten on 138 when the visitors declared on Monday, having batted for 422 minutes and hit eighteen fours. Nottinghamshire were more sprightly in reply, with Randall making 83 off 118 balls and Johnson 75 off 107 balls with thirteen fours before they declared 52 runs behind. Another half-century by Curtis, who had a productive season against Nottinghamshire, and an elegant 69 by Hick enabled Worcestershire to set a target of 247 in 125 minutes and twenty overs. While Hadlee and Birch were together, Nottinghamshire were on course for their first Championship win of the season, but as the light deteriorated, wickets tumbled. Worcestershire were pushing for victory at the close, but Hemmings denied them by playing out a fiery last over from Radford.

Close of play: First day, Worcestershire 271-7 (T. S. Curtis 129*, R. K. Illingworth 23*); Second day, Nottinghamshire 257-6 (C. E. B. Rice 4*, R. J. Hadlee 5*).

Worcestershire

T. S. Curtis not out	138	– c Cooper b Pick		62
M. J. Weston lbw b Hadlee	9	– c Randall b Hemmings		37
G. A. Hick c Scott b Hadlee	2	– c Randall b Newell		69
D. B. D'Oliveira b Cooper	67	– b Pick		4
*P. A. Neale b Cooper	0			
S. R. Lampitt lbw b Pick	23			
†S. J. Rhodes lbw b Pick	1	– (5) not out		13
P. J. Newport b Hemmings	1			
R. K. Illingworth lbw b Pick	46			
N. V. Radford b Pick	0			
B 2, l-b 16, w 1, n-b 3	22	B 4, l-b 4, n-b 1		9

1/27 2/29 3/151 4/151 5/195   (9 wkts dec.) 309   1/67 2/149   (4 wkts dec.) 194
6/205 7/206 8/309 9/309   3/160 4/194

A. P. Pridgeon did not bat.

Bonus points – Worcestershire 2, Nottinghamshire 3 (Score at 100 overs: 231-7).

Bowling: *First Innings*—Hadlee 26–7–63–2; Pick 28.5–8–75–4; Cooper 22–12–37–2; Rice 10–3–25–0; Hemmings 38–16–91–1. *Second Innings*—Hadlee 10–4–20–0; Pick 10.2–49–2; Hemmings 21–3–83–1; Cooper 8–2–26–0; Birch 1–0–8–0; Newell 0.3–0–0–1.

Nottinghamshire

D. W. Randall c Weston b Radford	83	– c Curtis b Radford		4
M. Newell c Rhodes b Pridgeon	28	– c Lampitt b Radford		1
P. Johnson b Radford	75	– c Radford b Illingworth		34
J. D. Birch lbw b Illingworth	19	– (5) c Newport b Hick		53
D. J. R. Martindale c Rhodes b Illingworth	0	– (7) lbw b Illingworth		8
†C. W. Scott c Neale b Hick	35	– (8) c D'Oliveira b Radford		2
*C. E. B. Rice not out	4	– (6) c Radford b Illingworth		29
R. J. Hadlee not out	5	– (6) c and b Radford		47
R. A. Pick (did not bat)		– c and b Illingworth		7
E. E. Hemmings (did not bat)		– not out		0
K. E. Cooper (did not bat)		– not out		0
L-b 2, n-b 6	8	B 6, l-b 13, n-b 2		21

1/85 2/133 3/160 4/160   (6 wkts dec.) 257   1/3 2/25 3/55 4/96   (9 wkts) 206
5/241 6/251   5/172 6/190 7/195
                                           8/201 9/206

Bonus points – Nottinghamshire 3, Worcestershire 2.

Bowling: *First Innings*—Radford 19–5–68–2; Pridgeon 16–1–53–1; Newport 14–2–46–0; Illingworth 19–4–70–2; Hick 7–1–18–1. *Second Innings*—Radford 14–2–42–4; Pridgeon 9–0–48–0; Illingworth 21–5–62–4; Newport 6–0–32–0; Hick 4–2–3–1.

Umpires: R. Julian and K. E. Palmer.

At Canterbury, June 27, 29, 30. NOTTINGHAMSHIRE beat KENT by ten wickets.

At Kidderminster, July 1, 2, 3. NOTTINGHAMSHIRE lost to WORCESTERSHIRE by ten wickets.

NOTTINGHAMSHIRE v YORKSHIRE

At Nottingham, July 4, 6. Nottinghamshire won by eight wickets. Nottinghamshire 24 pts, Yorkshire 5 pts. Toss: Yorkshire. Of the 32 wickets to fall in the match, 28 fell to spin bowlers. Yorkshire always struggled on the opening day against Afford and Hemmings, but the Yorkshire spinners, Carrick and Swallow, did not exploit the conditions when Nottinghamshire replied, even though Swallow enjoyed a spell of four wickets in eight balls in his career-best figures. Rice and Johnson, who went on to share a partnership of 169, gave Nottinghamshire the lead with only two wickets down, and Rice duly completed his first century of the season on the second day, his 115 coming off 163 deliveries and including twenty boundaries. Although there were useful partnerships between Moxon and Metcalfe and Neil Hartley and Bairstow, Yorkshire perished a second time to the spinners, leaving Nottinghamshire to achieve a comfortable win inside two days.

Close of play: First day, Nottinghamshire 211-2 (P. Johnson 85*, C. E. B. Rice 76*).

Yorkshire

M. D. Moxon c French b Afford	50	– lbw b Hemmings	22
A. A. Metcalfe b Pick	2	– c Randall b Afford	38
R. J. Blakey b Hemmings	18	– c Randall b Afford	6
K. Sharp b Afford	32	– c French b Hemmings	11
J. D. Love c French b Afford	4	– c Randall b Hemmings	0
S. N. Hartley c Randall b Hemmings	17	– lbw b Hadlee	38
†D. L. Bairstow c Johnson b Hemmings	16	– lbw b Afford	35
*P. Carrick c Hadlee b Afford	14	– c Randall b Hadlee	0
I. G. Swallow run out	5	– not out	4
P. J. Hartley not out	13	– c Hadlee b Afford	5
P. W. Jarvis c French b Afford	0	– c Randall b Hemmings	11
B 3, l-b 6	9	B 3, l-b 12, w 1, n-b 1	17
	180		**187**

1/6 2/41 3/87 4/93 5/130 6/138 7/161 8/161 9/179

1/60 2/72 3/91 4/91 5/92 6/161 7/161 8/165 9/171

Bonus points – Yorkshire 1, Nottinghamshire 4.

Bowling: *First Innings*—Hadlee 5–1–11–0; Pick 6–0–18–1; Hemmings 29–13–50–3; Saxelby 5–0–13–0; Afford 23–7–79–5. *Second Innings*—Hadlee 9–3–6–2; Pick 2–0–6–0; Afford 33–12–80–4; Hemmings 25.3–3–80–4.

Nottinghamshire

D. W. Randall c Blakey b Swallow	30	– c Moxon b Carrick	4
M. Newell c Moxon b Swallow	7	– not out	6
P. Johnson b Carrick	96	– st Bairstow b Carrick	23
*C. E. B. Rice c Blakey b Swallow	115	– not out	7
J. D. Birch c and b Swallow	34		
R. J. Hadlee b Swallow	0		
†B. N. French lbw b Swallow	0		
E. E. Hemmings lbw b Swallow	0		
R. A. Pick c Carrick	15		
K. Saxelby c Moxon b Carrick	4		
J. A. Afford not out	0		
B 16, l-b 6, n-b 2	24	L-b 3	3

1/36 2/61 3/230 4/294 5/294   325   1/4 2/32   (2 wkts) 43
6/294 7/294 8/317 9/323

Bonus points – Nottinghamshire 4, Yorkshire 4.

Bowling: *First Innings*—Jarvis 10–2–45–0; P. J. Hartley 2–0–8–0; Swallow 20–2–95–7; Carrick 30.2–4–116–3; Love 13–1–39–0. *Second Innings*—Carrick 6–2–16–2; Swallow 4–0–23–0; Sharp 1–0–1–0.

Umpires: B. Dudleston and A. G. T. Whitehead.

At Nottingham, July 11, 13, 14. NOTTINGHAMSHIRE drew with PAKISTANIS (See Pakistani tour section).

NOTTINGHAMSHIRE v LEICESTERSHIRE

At Nottingham, July 15, 16, 17. Nottinghamshire won by an innings and 32 runs. Nottinghamshire 24 pts, Leicestershire 3 pts. Toss: Leicestershire. Nottinghamshire outplayed their East Midlands rivals from start to finish and, despite hold-ups for rain and bad light, won comfortably. Leicestershire, electing to bat first, were always in trouble against a Nottinghamshire attack which, because of injury, included the veteran left-armer, Bore. Nottinghamshire's batsmen quickly capitalised on their bowlers' performance, despite losing Randall with a broken finger when he was hit by a ball from DeFreitas. Johnson's 125, which included sixteen fours and came off 209 balls, was the cornerstone of their reply, and Hadlee, hitting 77 off 83 balls, made sure that the lead was a demoralising one. Briers and Willey gave the visitors some hope of saving the match with a second-wicket stand of 113, but Hadlee, in a spell of 83 balls, took the wickets of Briers, Boon and Clift in the space of five deliveries and he went on to finish with match figures of nine for 83.

Close of play: First day, Nottinghamshire 58-2 (R. T. Robinson 32*, D. W. Randall 0*); Second day, Leicestershire 43-1 (N. E. Briers 14*, P. Willey 7*).

Leicestershire

R. A. Cobb c Broad b Hadlee	10	– c Johnson b Bore	22
N. E. Briers c Birch b Saxelby	6	– b Hadlee	71
*P. Willey b Rice	5	– c French b Saxelby	57
D. I. Gower lbw b Bore	18	– c Saxelby b Hemmings	1
J. J. Whitaker c Rice b Bore	11	– c Johnson b Hemmings	2
T. J. Boon c Hemmings b Saxelby	50	– lbw b Hadlee	0
P. B. Clift c Broad b Hadlee	39	– b Hadlee	0
P. A. J. DeFreitas c and b Hadlee	16	– c Rice b Hadlee	8
†P. Whitticase c French b Hadlee	1	– not out	9
J. P. Agnew c French b Hemmings	7	– b Hadlee	0
P. M. Such not out	0	– lbw b Hemmings	3
B 4, l-b 7	11	B 4, l-b 8	12

1/16 2/22 3/22 4/38 5/57   174   1/26 2/139 3/154 4/160 5/160   185
6/113 7/157 8/163 9/172   6/160 7/160 8/178 9/182

Bonus points – Leicestershire 1, Nottinghamshire 4.

Bowling: *First Innings*—Hadlee 23–7–54–4; Saxelby 17.1–4–40–2; Rice 13–2–32–1; Bore 13–7–14–2; Hemmings 7–2–23–1. *Second Innings*—Hadlee 17–6–29–5; Saxelby 12–4–35–1; Hemmings 27.3–6–70–3; Bore 12–5–26–1; Rice 8–4–13–0.

Nottinghamshire

B. C. Broad b Such 19	†B. N. French b Agnew 16
*R. T. Robinson c Whitaker b Willey . 47	E. E. Hemmings not out 0
K. Saxelby c Whitticase b Agnew 0	M. K. Bore b Agnew 0
D. W. Randall retired hurt 26	
P. Johnson c Such b DeFreitas 125	B 4, l-b 13, n-b 8 25
C. E. B. Rice c Clift b Agnew 39	—
J. D. Birch c Briers b Agnew 17	1/57 2/58 3/119 4/178 5/208 391
R. J. Hadlee c Such b Clift 77	6/365 7/388 8/391 9/391

Bonus points – Nottinghamshire 4, Leicestershire 2 (Score at 100 overs: 357-5).

Bowling: Agnew 29.5–6–132–5; DeFreitas 26–7–78–1; Clift 23–5–70–1; Such 22–3–70–1; Willey 6–0–24–1.

Umpires: J. H. Hampshire and R. Julian.

At Lord's, July 18, 20, 21. MIDDLESEX v NOTTINGHAMSHIRE. Abandoned.

At Derby, July 22, 23, 24. NOTTINGHAMSHIRE beat DERBYSHIRE by an innings and 33 runs.

At Manchester, July 25, 27, 28. NOTTINGHAMSHIRE drew with LANCASHIRE.

At Eastbourne, August 1, 3, 4. NOTTINGHAMSHIRE drew with SUSSEX.

NOTTINGHAMSHIRE v WARWICKSHIRE

At Worksop, August 5, 6, 7. Nottinghamshire won by an innings and 34 runs. Nottinghamshire 23 pts, Warwickshire 3 pts. Toss: Nottinghamshire. After a somewhat hesitant start, Nottinghamshire dominated the game and, despite the loss of more than two hours to the weather, registered another emphatic victory. Martindale returned to form in splendid fashion, his century coming in 177 minutes and including one six and thirteen fours; and with Hemmings and Scott adding 107 for the eighth wicket, Nottinghamshire were able to declare and attempt to enforce the follow-on. This they achieved, despite Warwickshire's obsession with survival; their total of 123 was scored in 82.3 overs. Hemmings, whose 34 overs in the first innings included 28 maidens, did much of the damage when Warwickshire batted again, and despite a defiant 69 by Humpage, with 50 coming from boundaries, Nottinghamshire romped home.

Close of play: First day, Nottinghamshire 332-7 (C. W. Scott 23*, E. E. Hemmings 46*); Second day, Warwickshire 90-6 (G. A. Tedstone 7*, N. M. K. Smith 1*).

Nottinghamshire

M. Newell b Small	24	R. J. Hadlee c Amiss b P. A. Smith	24
P. Pollard c Asif Din b Gifford	15	†C. W. Scott not out	33
P. Johnson c Moles b Merrick	39	E. E. Hemmings lbw b Gifford	75
*C. E. B. Rice c Humpage b Gifford	2	B 5, l-b 24, n-b 3	32
J. D. Birch c Tedstone b N. M. K. Smith	28		
D. J. R. Martindale c Small		1/33 2/71 3/78 4/93 (8 wkts dec.) 375	
b N. M. K. Smith	103	5/154 6/204 7/268 8/375	

R. A. Pick and J. A. Afford did not bat.

Bonus points – Nottinghamshire 3, Warwickshire 3 (Score at 100 overs: 276-7).

Bowling: Small 29-12-62-1; Merrick 29-6-66-1; Gifford 36-8-92-3; Moles 8-2-24-0; N. M. K. Smith 19-3-79-2; P. A. Smith 5-1-23-1.

Warwickshire

T. A. Lloyd c Scott b Hemmings	39	– (2) c Johnson b Hemmings	32
A. J. Moles c Newell b Hadlee	0	– (1) c Johnson b Pick	4
Asif Din c Hadlee b Rice	9	– c Newell b Hemmings	17
D. L. Amiss c Birch b Hadlee	13	– c Newell b Rice	41
G. W. Humpage c Scott b Hemmings	0	– b Afford	69
P. A. Smith c Birch b Hadlee	11	– lbw b Hemmings	1
†G. A. Tedstone c Rice b Hadlee	7	– lbw b Hemmings	0
N. M. K. Smith c Newell b Hemmings	9	– lbw b Afford	23
G. C. Small not out	17	– b Hemmings	9
T. A. Merrick c Pollard b Hemmings	0	– c Pollard b Hemmings	6
*N. Gifford c Newell b Hadlee	0	– not out	0
B 13, l-b 4, w 1	18	B 9, l-b 7	16

1/1 2/32 3/52 4/52 5/80	123	1/4 2/48 3/68 4/114 5/127	218
6/84 7/90 8/114 9/114		6/127 7/201 8/212 9/212	

Bonus points – Nottinghamshire 4.

Bowling: *First Innings*—Hadlee 22.3-5-39-5; Pick 6-2-18-0; Hemmings 34-28-17-4; Rice 8-3-11-1; Afford 12-6-21-0. *Second Innings*—Pick 8-1-28-1; Rice 10-2-31-1; Hemmings 38-16-62-6; Afford 25-15-48-2; Hadlee 8-1-33-0.

Umpires: J. W. Holder and K. J. Lyons.

NOTTINGHAMSHIRE v SOMERSET

At Nottingham, August 8, 10, 11. Nottinghamshire won by five wickets. Nottinghamshire 23 pts, Somerset 7 pts. Toss: Somerset. Victory took Nottinghamshire to the top of the Championship table for the first time in 1987. The match was dominated by Hadlee, who became the first Nottinghamshire player since 1921 to score a hundred and take ten wickets in a match at Trent Bridge. Somerset chose to bat, and although there was an excellent 93 by Crowe, with fourteen boundaries, Hadlee's six for 42 curbed the other batsmen. Nottinghamshire lost three quick wickets in reply, but Rice and Birch added 117 and then Hadlee took over. His 101 included two sixes and twelve fours. With Crowe nursing a broken thumb, the legacy of a blow by Rice when he made 49 in the first innings, Somerset perished much quicker against Hadlee in their second innings, leaving Nottinghamshire to chase 110 with time no object. As Jones increased his match tally to ten, they lost five wickets for 64 to raise an element of doubt, but Rice and Hadlee soon removed any threat of defeat.

Close of play: First day, Nottinghamshire 2-0 (M. Newell 2*, P. Pollard 0*); Second day, Somerset 43-3 (J. J. E. Hardy 7*, V. J. Marks 22*).

Somerset

N. A. Felton c Scott b Rice	9	– b Cooper	7
*P. M. Roebuck c Scott b Cooper	48	– c Rice b Hadlee	3
J. J. E. Hardy lbw b Cooper	20	– b Hadlee	11
M. D. Crowe lbw b Cooper	93	– absent injured	
R. J. Harden c Scott b Hadlee	0	– (4) lbw b Hadlee	1
V. J. Marks b Hadlee	9	– (5) c Scott b Hadlee	30
†N. D. Burns b Hadlee	49	– (6) b Afford	15
G. V. Palmer c Newell b Hadlee	13	– (7) c Scott b Hadlee	24
G. D. Rose lbw b Hadlee	0	– (8) b Hadlee	37
M. D. Harman not out	2	– (9) lbw b Hemmings	4
A. N. Jones b Hadlee	15	– (10) not out	0
B 2, l-b 6, n-b 1	9	B 4, l-b 1, w 2	7

1/19 2/56 3/101 4/106 5/126   267   1/9 2/13 3/14 4/47 5/68   139
6/212 7/250 8/250 9/251   6/94 7/108 8/139 9/139

Bonus points – Somerset 3, Nottinghamshire 4.

Bowling: *First Innings*—Hadlee 25.1-9-42-6; Rice 15-9-26-1; Cooper 26-5-87-3; Hemmings 16-0-82-0; Afford 4-0-22-0. *Second Innings*—Hadlee 16-5-41-6; Cooper 13-4-30-1; Hemmings 15-8-34-1; Afford 12-5-29-1.

Nottinghamshire

M. Newell c Felton b Jones	4	– b Jones	6
P. Pollard lbw b Palmer	2	– c Roebuck b Marks	9
P. Johnson c Roebuck b Jones	6	– c Burns b Jones	37
*C. E. B. Rice b Harman	48	– (6) not out	20
J. D. Birch c Burns b Jones	77	– (4) c Roebuck b Jones	1
D. J. R. Martindale b Jones	1	– (5) b Marks	8
R. J. Hadlee c Harman b Jones	101	– not out	23
†C. W. Scott c sub b Harman	30		
E. E. Hemmings c Burns b Jones	13		
K. E. Cooper c Rose b Jones	4		
J. A. Afford not out	2		
L-b 7, n-b 2	9	L-b 5, n-b 1	6

1/6 2/6 3/21 4/138 5/140   297   1/18 2/18 3/29   (5 wkts) 110
6/140 7/242 8/276 9/294   4/64 5/64

Bonus points – Nottinghamshire 3, Somerset 4.

Bowling: *First Innings*—Jones 22.2-5-85-7; Palmer 15-1-67-1; Marks 22-6-57-0; Rose 3-0-13-0; Harman 19-4-68-2. *Second Innings*—Jones 12-1-61-3; Palmer 3.1-0-7-0; Marks 13-4-37-2.

Umpires: B. Leadbeater and K. J. Lyons.

NOTTINGHAMSHIRE v NORTHAMPTONSHIRE

At Nottingham, August 15, 17, 18. Nottinghamshire won by an innings and 132 runs. Nottinghamshire 24 pts, Northamptonshire 2 pts. Toss: Nottinghamshire. The match was billed as a potential Championship decider, but Nottinghamshire soon took a grip and never relaxed. After Robinson had won the toss, he and Broad put on 162 for the first wicket against an ineffective attack and Robinson went on to reach his hundred off 195 balls. On the second day, Nottinghamshire batted on for an hour and a half to put the game beyond Northamptonshire's reach, and then gave them a testing time before lunch as Hadlee accounted for Cook, Larkins and Bailey in 21 deliveries. Lamb became his fourth victim in his first over after lunch. Despite a splendid innings by Williams, who batted 186 minutes and hit seventeen boundaries in his 104, Northamptonshire were a long way short of avoiding the follow-on. Cook and Larkins gave them a stronger platform when they batted again; but from 46 without loss, Northamptonshire were hurried out for 97, Saxelby taking three for 0 in ten balls before Hemmings took up the attack to finish with five for 19.

Close of play: First day, Nottinghamshire 352-4 (P. Johnson 20*, J. D. Birch 4*); Second day, Northamptonshire 16-0 (G. Cook 9*, W. Larkins 5*).

Nottinghamshire

B. C. Broad b Williams	67	†B. N. French c Davis b N. G. B. Cook	21
*R. T. Robinson c Wild		E. E. Hemmings not out	9
b N. G. B. Cook	102	K. Saxelby not out	8
M. Newell st Ripley b Williams	72	L-b 22, n-b 11	33
C. E. B. Rice st Ripley b Williams	65		
P. Johnson c Lamb b Davis	31	1/162 2/194 3/310 (8 wkts dec.)	452
J. D. Birch b Capel	8	4/343 5/359 6/380	
R. J. Hadlee b Walker	36	7/423 8/435	

J. A. Afford did not bat.

Bonus points – Nottinghamshire 4 (Score at 100 overs: 300-2).

Bowling: Davis 24–6–78–1; Capel 20–2–75–1; Walker 18–3–61–1; Williams 32–6–87–3; N. G. B. Cook 38–8–106–2; Wild 9–2–23–0.

Northamptonshire

*G. Cook c Johnson b Hadlee	0	– c Broad b Hadlee	29
W. Larkins lbw b Hadlee	25	– c sub b Saxelby	20
R. J. Bailey c French b Hadlee	6	– c Newell b Hemmings	3
A. J. Lamb c Rice b Hadlee	7	– b Saxelby	0
D. J. Capel c Rice b Hemmings	32	– c French b Saxelby	0
R. G. Williams st French b Hemmings	104	– b Hemmings	4
D. J. Wild c French b Hemmings	0	– c French b Hemmings	0
†D. Ripley b Hadlee	21	– not out	12
N. G. B. Cook lbw b Hadlee	0	– c Newell b Hadlee	7
W. W. Davis b Rice	20	– c Broad b Hemmings	8
A. Walker not out	0	– c Hadlee b Hemmings	0
L-b 5, n-b 3	8	B 7, l-b 4, n-b 3	14
1/0 2/32 3/33 4/43 5/107	223	1/46 2/58 3/58 4/60 5/60	97
6/109 7/175 8/175 9/217		6/60 7/67 8/80 9/93	

Bonus points – Northamptonshire 2, Nottinghamshire 4.

Bowling: *First Innings*—Hadlee 17–2–60–6; Saxelby 12–3–53–0; Hemmings 21.4–5–49–3; Rice 11–2–41–1; Afford 8–3–15–0. *Second Innings*—Hadlee 15–8–25–2; Saxelby 13–2–42–3; Hemmings 15.4–6–19–5.

Umpires: N. T. Plews and R. A. White.

At Chelmsford, August 19, 20, 21. NOTTINGHAMSHIRE drew with ESSEX.

NOTTINGHAMSHIRE v GLOUCESTERSHIRE

At Nottingham, August 22, 24, 25. Drawn. Nottinghamshire 4 pts, Gloucestershire 8 pts. Toss: Nottinghamshire. In a match badly affected by the weather, Nottinghamshire missed Hadlee, Rice, Broad and French, who were playing in the MCC Bicentenary match at Lord's. After a long delay at the start, Gloucestershire, put in to bat, lost three wickets for 37 before Athey took charge. He batted for 246 minutes and hit 28 fours in his 160 from 199 balls as Gloucestershire flourished against a second-string attack. Nottinghamshire, in reply, reached 90 for one before the hostile Greene, taking the place of Walsh, who was also on duty at Lord's, began to make inroads. He looked like denying Nottinghamshire any batting points, but the last man, Bore, managed to take them to 150 before they were forced to follow on. However, only 23 overs remained, and Robinson and Newell comfortably batted out time.

Close of play: First day, Gloucestershire 37-1 (A. J. Wright 21*, P. W. Romaines 13*); Second day, Nottinghamshire 66-1 (R. T. Robinson 30*, P. Johnson 32*).

Gloucestershire

A. W. Stovold c Birch b Saxelby	2	V. S. Greene c Johnson b Bore	0
A. J. Wright c Robinson b Pick	21	*D. A. Graveney c Scott b Saxelby	30
P. W. Romaines c Newell b Saxelby	13	G. E. Sainsbury not out	0
C. W. J. Athey c Scott b Bore	160		
K. M. Curran c Scott b Bore	38	B 1, l-b 4, w 2, n-b 5	12
M. W. Alleyne c Newell b Bore	0		
K. B. K. Ibadulla lbw b Hemmings	36	1/2 2/37 3/37 4/123 5/123	360
†R. C. Russell b Pick	48	6/259 7/299 8/299 9/360	

Bonus points – Gloucestershire 4, Nottinghamshire 3 (Score at 100 overs: 357-8).

Bowling: Saxelby 21–6–86–3; Pick 17.2–1–84–2; Fraser-Darling 17–4–69–0; Hemmings 23–5–64–1; Bore 25–11–52–4.

Nottinghamshire

*R. T. Robinson c Russell b Greene	43	– not out	30
M. Newell c Russell b Greene	3	– not out	15
P. Johnson c Graveney b Greene	43		
J. D. Birch c Graveney b Sainsbury	14		
D. J. R. Martindale c Wright b Greene	5		
†C. W. Scott c Athey b Greene	2		
C. D. Fraser-Darling c Sainsbury b Greene	16		
E. E. Hemmings c and b Greene	0		
R. A. Pick not out	13		
K. Saxelby b Sainsbury	0		
M. K. Bore b Sainsbury	3		
L-b 1, w 2, n-b 6	9	L-b 1	1

1/9 2/90 3/92 4/108 5/111	151	(no wkt)	46
6/113 7/114 8/134 9/135			

Bonus points – Nottinghamshire 1, Gloucestershire 4.

Bowling: *First Innings*—Greene 25–2–96–7; Sainsbury 22.2–11–48–3; Graveney 2–0–5–0; Alleyne 1–0–1–0. *Second Innings*—Greene 5–0–22–0; Sainsbury 5–1–6–0; Alleyne 3–2–1–0; Athey 4–0–16–0.

Umpires: D. Lloyd and D. O. Oslear.

At Leicester, August 26, 27, 28. NOTTINGHAMSHIRE drew with LEICESTERSHIRE.

NOTTINGHAMSHIRE v DERBYSHIRE

At Nottingham, August 29, 31, September 1. Drawn. Nottinghamshire 7 pts, Derbyshire 7 pts. Toss: Derbyshire. Question marks about Nottinghamshire's Championship prospects appeared with this fourth successive draw. On a "soft" pitch, Barnett led from the front to score 130, including nineteen fours, in 211 minutes as Derbyshire reached a healthy 339. Johnson responded for Nottinghamshire, scoring 106 off 140 deliveries with seventeen fours, and with Hadlee and Birch adding 130, Nottinghamshire took a first-innings lead of 50. Although the pitch continued to favour the batsmen, only 20 runs came in the first hour of Derbyshire's second innings and quick runs were offered in the hope of a declaration. Consequently, Morris, hitting his second 50 off 21 balls, raced to what should remain one of the least satisfying of his first-class hundreds. Barnett set Nottinghamshire a challenging target of 210 at around 6 runs an over, and when Malcolm and Mortensen produced the best bowling of the match, a Derbyshire victory looked more probable. However, Birch and Hadlee steadied the innings, and Hadlee plundered 22 off an over from Morris before a halt was called with eight overs remaining.

Close of play: First day, Derbyshire 313-7 (R. J. Finney 39*, P. G. Newman 8*); Second day, Derbyshire 2-0 (B. J. M. Maher 0*, J. G. Wright 0*).

Derbyshire

*K. J. Barnett c Robinson b Hemmings	130	– (5) c Rice b Birch	36
J. G. Wright c Johnson b Hemmings	11	– (2) c French b Hemmings	15
B. Roberts c French b Pick	44	– c Robinson b Pick	35
J. E. Morris c Broad b Rice	44	– c French b Newell	106
†B. J. M. Maher b Bore	7	– (1) c Rice b Hemmings	12
R. Sharma c French b Hadlee	54		
R. J. Finney b Hadlee	54		
A. E. Warner b Rice	6	– (6) not out	37
P. G. Newman c French b Hadlee	12		
O. H. Mortensen not out	2		
D. E. Malcolm b Hadlee	0		
B 3, l-b 13, n-b 7	23	B 5, l-b 8, n-b 3	16
	339	(5 wkts dec.)	**259**

1/76 2/178 3/208 4/215 5/241   339   1/26 2/37 3/91   (5 wkts dec.) 259
6/256 7/272 8/334 9/339   4/208 5/252

Bonus points – Derbyshire 3, Nottinghamshire 3 (Score at 100 overs: 276-7).

Bowling: *First Innings*—Hadlee 27–7–71–4; Pick 21–2–97–1; Hemmings 39–12–91–2; Bore 23–13–32–1; Rice 12–2–32–2. *Second Innings*—Hadlee 13–8–13–0; Hemmings 33–16–38–2; Bore 11–3–38–0; Rice 9–4–8–0; Pick 4–1–32–1; Johnson 4–0–53–0; Newell 6–0–42–1; Birch 5–0–22–1.

Nottinghamshire

B. C. Broad c Roberts b Newman	0	– c Sharma b Malcolm	13
*R. T. Robinson c Maher b Malcolm	28	– c Sharma b Mortensen	11
M. Newell c sub b Newman	9	– c Finney b Malcolm	10
P. Johnson c Sharma b Malcolm	106	– c Maher b Mortensen	8
C. E. B. Rice c Malcolm b Sharma	58	– b Mortensen	6
J. D. Birch c Sharma b Finney	63	– not out	12
R. J. Hadlee c Warner b Sharma	77	– not out	44
†B. N. French c Newman b Finney	19		
E. E. Hemmings c Sharma b Finney	2		
M. K. Bore c Malcolm b Sharma	7		
R. A. Pick not out	1		
B 1, l-b 14, n-b 4	19	L-b 1	1
	389	(5 wkts)	**105**

1/0 2/22 3/67 4/190 5/225   389   1/18 2/29 3/42   (5 wkts) 105
6/355 7/355 8/367 9/378   4/48 5/50

Bonus points – Nottinghamshire 4, Derbyshire 4.

Bowling: *First Innings*—Newman 12–3–42–2; Malcolm 17–3–71–2; Mortensen 14–1–58–0; Warner 15–3–61–0; Finney 18.4–1–82–3; Sharma 14–2–60–3. *Second Innings*—Malcolm 8–1–30–2; Mortensen 8–3–19–3; Sharma 1–0–2–0; Finney 5–2–5–0; Barnett 1–1–0–0; Morris 3–0–48–0.

Umpires: H. D. Bird and R. Palmer.

NOTTINGHAMSHIRE v SUSSEX

At Nottingham, September 2, 3, 4. Nottinghamshire won by eight wickets. Nottinghamshire 20 pts, Sussex 4 pts. Toss: Sussex. With Nottinghamshire badly needing a victory, Rice took over the captaincy and saw Sussex slump to 73 for seven by lunch on the opening day. A spirited 42 by Gould held up Nottinghamshire but Hadlee, finishing with six for 20, polished off the tail. Nottinghamshire faced a similar struggle when they batted against Pigott and Reeve in conditions tailor-made for seam bowling, and they owed much to Broad's 73. With the ball continuing to move about, Sussex had nothing to offer in their second innings. Saxelby upstaged Hadlee to take six for 49 while the New Zealander had figures of four for 26 to finish with ten wickets in the match. Nottinghamshire were left with the task of scoring just 71, and although Broad and the promoted French went cheaply, Robinson and Johnson took Nottinghamshire to victory.

Close of play: First day, Nottinghamshire 77-4 (B. C. Broad 44*, E. E. Hemmings 0*); Second day, Nottinghamshire 6-0 (B. C. Broad 6*, R. T. Robinson 0*).

Sussex

R. I. Alikhan b Pick	12	– lbw b Hadlee	8
A. M. Green c Hadlee b Pick	31	– c Hadlee b Saxelby	14
P. W. G. Parker c French b Hadlee	6	– lbw b Hadlee	6
A. P. Wells c Broad b Hadlee	1	– c Bore b Saxelby	8
C. M. Wells c Broad b Hadlee	6	– c French b Saxelby	8
K. Greenfield c Rice b Saxelby	3	– (8) c French b Saxelby	2
D. A. Reeve c Rice b Hadlee	0	– c Hemmings b Saxelby	11
*I. J. Gould c Rice b Pick	42	– (6) b Hadlee	10
†P. Moores lbw b Hadlee	7	– b Saxelby	11
A. C. S. Pigott c Robinson b Hadlee	4	– lbw b Hadlee	1
A. M. Babington not out	2	– not out	0
B 1, l-b 7, n-b 5	13	B 1, l-b 2	3

1/37 2/42 3/52 4/55 5/62   123   1/20 2/30 3/30 4/42 5/47   80
6/62 7/68 8/86 9/93   6/57 7/64 8/71 9/80

Bonus points – Nottinghamshire 4.

Bowling: *First Innings*—Hadlee 18–4–20–6; Saxelby 11–3–32–1; Pick 12.5–2–58–3; Hemmings 1–0–5–0. *Second Innings*—Hadlee 19.1–6–26–4; Saxelby 20–7–49–6; Hemmings 1–0–2–0.

Nottinghamshire

B. C. Broad c Reeve b Pigott	73	– c Moores b Reeve	10
R. T. Robinson lbw b Reeve	14	– not out	27
*C. E. B. Rice c Reeve b Pigott	5		
P. Johnson c Moores b Pigott	2	– not out	31
J. D. Birch c Alikhan b C. M. Wells	9		
E. E. Hemmings c C. M. Wells b Reeve	3		
R. J. Hadlee run out	0		
†B. N. French c A. P. Wells b Pigott	15	– (3) b Reeve	2
R. A. Pick not out	5		
K. Saxelby c Moores b Pigott	0		
M. K. Bore c Moores b Reeve	1		
L-b 4, n-b 2	6	N-b 1	1

1/35 2/48 3/50 4/76 5/85   133   1/16 2/20   (2 wkts) 71
6/90 7/124 8/127 9/128

Bonus points – Sussex 4.

Bowling: *First Innings*—Pigott 17–5–35–5; Babington 4–0–22–0; Reeve 20.1–6–42–3; Green 2–0–12–0; C. M. Wells 7–1–18–1. *Second Innings*—Pigott 13–3–33–0; Reeve 9–2–20–2; C. M. Wells 4–1–12–0; Gould 1–0–1–0; Parker 0.2–0–5–0.

Umpires: H. D. Bird and J. W. Holder.

NOTTINGHAMSHIRE v GLAMORGAN

At Nottingham, September 9, 10, 11. Nottinghamshire won by nine wickets. Nottinghamshire 24 pts, Glamorgan 2 pts. Toss: Glamorgan. Nottinghamshire made no mistake in taking maximum points from their final match to put pressure on Lancashire, the only side capable of catching them. Glamorgan, electing to bat, started promisingly, but only the openers, Butcher and Hopkins, who batted 166 minutes for his 37, offered lengthy resistance. Once the wickets began to tumble, Hemmings mopped up the tail and Glamorgan were all out for 111. Nottinghamshire then set about chasing maximum batting points as quickly as possible, with Rice accepting the responsibility. His unbeaten 104 came in 189 minutes and contained two sixes and eleven fours. Maynard, with a polished 93, and Derrick, with a hard-hitting 57, denied Nottinghamshire a two-day victory, but Hadlee whipped out the tail on the final morning to leave only 38 runs required for victory.

Close of play: First day, Nottinghamshire 139-3 (P. Johnson 53*, C. E. B. Rice 28*); Second day, Glamorgan 221-8 (J. Derrick 54*, P. D. North 0*).

Glamorgan

A. R. Butcher c Broad b Rice	29	– b Hadlee	0
J. A. Hopkins c Pick b Hemmings	37	– lbw b Hadlee	8
*H. Morris lbw b Rice	0	– c French b Pick	20
M. P. Maynard c Broad b Saxelby	13	– c Robinson b Hemmings	93
G. C. Holmes c Hadlee b Hemmings	8	– c French b Hemmings	10
P. A. Todd c Rice b Hadlee	1	– b Hadlee	7
J. Derrick c Newell b Hemmings	2	– c French b Hadlee	57
I. Smith c Rice b Hadlee	0	– c Broad b Hadlee	0
†C. P. Metson not out	4	– b Pick	12
P. D. North st French b Hemmings	12	– c French b Hadlee	2
S. J. Base c French b Hemmings	4	– not out	0
N-b 1	1	B 1, l-b 5, n-b 11	17

1/36 2/36 3/61 4/77 5/83   111   1/0 2/14 3/64 4/107 5/126   226
6/89 7/89 8/91 9/105   6/158 7/158 8/220 9/223

Bonus points – Nottinghamshire 4.

Bowling: *First Innings*—Hadlee 23–9–38–2; Saxelby 11–2–39–1; Pick 7–3–10–0; Rice 8–4–12–2; Hemmings 12.4–7–12–5. *Second Innings*—Hadlee 18.4–6–38–6; Saxelby 11–3–34–0; Hemmings 29–8–97–2; Pick 15–5–39–2; Rice 5–2–12–0.

Nottinghamshire

B. C. Broad c and b Derrick	28	– not out	21
R. T. Robinson lbw b Smith	14	– c Metson b Derrick	9
M. Newell c Metson b Derrick	12	– not out	5
P. Johnson c Derrick b Smith	55		
*C. E. B. Rice not out	104		
J. D. Birch c and b North	65		
R. J. Hadlee not out	15		
L-b 4, w 1, n-b 2	7	L-b 3, n-b 1	4

1/18 2/54 3/65 4/146 5/264   (5 wkts dec.) 300   1/20   (1 wkt) 39

†B. N. French, E. E. Hemmings, R. A. Pick and K. Saxelby did not bat.

Bonus points – Nottinghamshire 4, Glamorgan 2.

Bowling: *First Innings*—Smith 17.3–4–61–2; Base 5.3–2–11–0; Derrick 29–9–92–2; North 33.3–7–93–1; Holmes 10–2–39–0. *Second Innings*—Smith 3–1–5–0; Derrick 4.4–1–20–1; Maynard 2–0–11–0.

Umpires: J. H. Hampshire and D. Lloyd.

HONOURS' LIST

In 1987, the following were decorated for their services to cricket:

New Year's Honours: G. T. Dowling (New Zealand) OBE, F. J. Cameron (New Zealand) MBE.
Queen's Birthday Honours: M. W. Gatting (England) OBE.

SOMERSET

President: C. R. M. Atkinson
Chairman: 1987 – M. F. Hill
1988 – J. Gardner
Chairman, Cricket Committee: R. E. Marshall
Secretary: A. S. Brown
The County Ground, St James's Street,
Taunton TA1 1JT
(Telephone: 0823-272946/253666)
Captain: P. M. Roebuck
Coach: P. J. Robinson

Following the bitterness of the winter the remodelled Somerset side of 1987 had an encouraging season. To lose three of the world's best players, to suffer from injuries to leading players, and yet to improve the playing record, as well as the membership and sponsorship, was a major achievement – a tribute to all involved with the club and notably to the captain, Peter Roebuck.

Somerset improved by five places in the Britannic Assurance Championship, and although only two matches were won, they went close to seven more victories. Only rain at Swansea saved Glamorgan in a match already reduced to two days. Tight finishes against Surrey (twice), Yorkshire (away), Leicestershire (home), Northamptonshire (away) and Warwickshire (away) could have brought wins. It was a splendid performance, after losing the toss, to beat Gloucestershire by an innings on a pitch with a large wet patch at one end.

For the first time since 1984, Somerset reached the Benson and Hedges Cup quarter-finals, winning their group, and in the Refuge Assurance League, fourth was their best Sunday position since 1983. Only in the NatWest Bank Trophy was there a serious slip, an embarrassing defeat by Buckinghamshire in the first round. This provided a severe test of character, but it was triumphantly passed and the excellent team spirit was immediately recaptured.

The reasons for renewed optimism at Taunton were easy to find. A vital factor was the batting and captaincy of Roebuck, whose example underlined why he had been a leading spokesman in the controversies of 1986. Showing a wider range of strokes, he started superbly in all competitions, suffered a hand injury which put him out for seven weeks, but returned with another flow of runs. Martin Crowe, before losing four of the last five weeks with a broken thumb, was first in the country to 1,000 Championship runs and to 2,000 in all competitions; yet the importance of his return cannot be measured only by his output of classically made runs.

A scouting tour by Brian Rose, the former captain and now Cricket Development Officer, produced essential recruits: opening bowlers Adrian Jones (from Sussex) and Neil Mallender (from Northamptonshire), a largely untried all-rounder, Graham Rose (from Middlesex), and wicket-keeper-batsman Neil Burns (from Essex). All exceeded expectations. For the first time in some years, the bowling tended to be more reliable than the batting.

The spate of injuries was a setback. After Nick Taylor had resigned in April, it soon became clear that Colin Dredge would play little in his benefit year, because of recurring shoulder troubles; and in the event he did not play at all. At one time in mid-season, four seamers were out of action. Mark Davis, after a useful start, was again injured and he left the club in September; Mallender, Gary Palmer and Graham Rose had bad backs, the last-mentioned breaking down early in three matches, which upset the balance of the attack. Palmer had some good days, especially in the Sunday League.

As ever, Victor Marks, who took over as vice-captain, was a tower of strength in all departments. A magnificent club man, he richly deserves his benefit in 1988. Some spin help was forthcoming for him last season, but while Mark Harman's off-breaks were steady, they were insufficiently penetrative. As he could not replace Marks, he was released at the end of the year. In the final match, Robert Woolston, a nineteen-year-old slow left-armer signed hurriedly in June, suggested a useful future.

The batting relied heavily on Roebuck and Crowe. Although Jonathan Hardy and Nigel Felton both passed 1,000 runs, rather more would have been acceptable. Richard Harden's final figures look unconvincing, but he frequently met a challenge with an important contribution. Few present at Taunton will forget the gritty half-centuries with which he and Burns rescued Somerset from 18 for five against Leicestershire. Nick Pringle, occasionally pressed into service as an emergency seamer, batted well at times, while at the end of the season Julian Wyatt produced some useful scores. Ricky Bartlett had wretched luck, breaking the same rib twice following fighting innings. One youngster to show much improvement was the 21-year-old seam bowler, Darren Foster.

When Crowe was required by New Zealand for their suddenly arranged – but soon to be abandoned – tour of Sri Lanka, Somerset hastily signed the young Australian all-rounder, Stephen Waugh, as cover. He played in only four Championship matches, but two superb match-saving centuries indicated his class, and his bowling was also of fine quality. In fact, the abandonment of that Sri Lanka tour produced an interesting insight into the new and refreshing spirit in the team. Crowe caught the first available flight from Colombo to England and, having embarked on his journey at midnight on Thursday, found himself going in to bat at midday on Saturday, in the first match of the season, with Somerset 24 for two. He made 65 runs. That example of enthusiasm, loyalty and dedication, and the way all the team seemed prepared to give 100 per cent, whatever the situation, typified the improvement seen at Taunton last summer and provided hope for the future. Many felt that it justified the dreadful happenings of the previous winter. – Eric Hill.

SOMERSET 1987

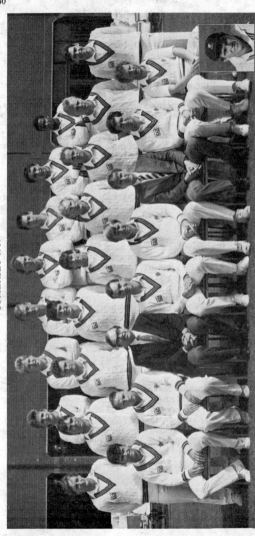

[*Bill Smith*]

Back row: R. J. Bartlett, M. Cleal, J. C. M. Atkinson, J. J. E. Hardy, A. R. Phillips, H. R. J. Trump, D. J. Foster. *Middle row*: J. G. Wyatt, R. J. Harden, A. N. Jones, G. D. Rose, G. V. Palmer, N. A. Mallender, M. R. Davis, N. J. Pringle, N. D. Burns. *Front row*: N. A. Felton, V. J. Marks, M. F. Hill (*chairman*), P. M. Roebuck (*captain*), B. C. Rose, A. S. Brown (*secretary*), C. H. Dredge, T. Gard. *Inset*: M. D. Crowe.

SOMERSET RESULTS

All first-class matches – Played 24: Won 2, Lost 3, Drawn 19.

County Championship matches – Played 24: Won 2, Lost 3, Drawn 19.

Bonus points – Batting 61, Bowling 70.

Competition placings – Britannic Assurance County Championship, 11th; NatWest Bank Trophy, 1st round; Benson and Hedges Cup, q-f; Refuge Assurance League, 4th.

BRITANNIC ASSURANCE CHAMPIONSHIP AVERAGES

BATTING

	Birthplace	M	I	NO	R	HI	Avge
§S. R. Waugh	Sydney, Australia	4	6	3	340	137*	113.33
§‡M. D. Crowe	Auckland, NZ	18	29	5	1,627	206*	67.79
‡P. M. Roebuck	Oxford	16	29	5	1,199	165*	49.95
‡J. J. E. Hardy	Nakaru, Kenya	24	40	2	1,089	119	28.65
‡N. A. Felton	Guildford	24	41	0	1,094	110	26.68
‡N. D. Burns	Chelmsford	24	35	7	729	100*	26.03
‡V. J. Marks	Middle Chinnock	22	31	6	635	63*	25.40
G. D. Rose	Tottenham	18	23	4	470	95	24.73
R. J. Harden	Bridgwater	19	30	6	568	59	23.66
J. G. Wyatt	Paulton	8	13	2	250	58*	22.72
N. J. Pringle	Weymouth	11	18	1	347	79	20.41
G. V. Palmer	Taunton	14	16	4	234	68	19.50
‡N. A. Mallender	Kirk Sandall	15	17	9	131	20*	16.37
M. D. Harman	Aylesbury	6	8	2	94	41	15.66
‡B. C. Rose	Dartford	3	4	0	60	31	15.00
‡A. N. Jones	Woking	21	21	8	114	15	8.76
M. R. Davis	Kilve	8	8	1	57	23*	8.14

Also batted: R. J. Bartlett (*Ash Priors*) (1 match) 0; D. J. Foster (*Tottenham*) (5 matches) 9, 0*, 16; R. G. Woolston (*Enfield*) (1 match) 0.

* *Signifies not out.*   ‡ *Denotes county cap.*   § *Not qualified for England.*

The following played a total of sixteen three-figure innings for Somerset in County Championship matches – M. D. Crowe 6, P. M. Roebuck 5, S. R. Waugh 2, N. D. Burns 1, N. A. Felton 1, J. J. E. Hardy 1.

BOWLING

	O	M	R	W	BB	Avge
N. A. Mallender	351	61	1,129	46	7-61	24.54
G. D. Rose	314.4	56	976	38	5-24	25.68
A. N. Jones	517.1	85	1,800	63	7-85	28.57
V. J. Marks	778.5	203	2,155	70	5-35	30.78
S. R. Waugh	112	22	348	11	3-48	31.63
D. J. Foster	111.5	10	490	13	4-56	37.69
G. V. Palmer	316	54	1,162	29	4-63	40.06
M. R. Davis	153.5	25	505	11	3-43	45.90

Also bowled: M. D. Crowe 33-8-100-0; R. J. Harden 2-0-8-0; M. D. Harman 131-35-369-7; N. J. Pringle 93-14-341-4; P. M. Roebuck 13-1-54-0; R. G. Woolston 43-10-107-2.

Wicket-keeper: N. D. Burns 44 ct, 6 st.

Leading Fielders: N. A. Felton 18, M. D. Crowe 15, P. M. Roebuck 15.

SOMERSET v LANCASHIRE

At Taunton, April 25, 26, 27. Lancashire won by six wickets. Lancashire 21 pts, Somerset 7 pts. Toss: Lancashire. Crowe, who had left Sri Lanka only 36 hours before, having been touring there with the New Zealand team, made 65 from 145 balls to rescue Somerset after they had been put in on a lively pitch. Graham Rose and Burns, each in his first innings for Somerset, hit maiden half-centuries and added 102 for the seventh wicket. Fowler (156 balls), O'Shaughnessy and Hayhurst (112 balls) just saved Lancashire from the follow-on and so set the scene for a remarkable last day. First Simmons profited from some untidy batting. Then, after Lancashire had faltered to 69 for three in pursuit of 240 in 63 overs, Fairbrother, with a brilliant century from 125 balls which included two sixes and thirteen fours, put on 151 in 37 overs with O'Shaughnessy, who steered Lancashire home with three overs to spare.

Close of play: First day, Somerset 300-7 (G. D. Rose 72*, M. R. Davis 11*); Second day, Lancashire 203-8 (A. N. Hayhurst 23*, A. J. Murphy 4*).

Somerset

N. A. Felton c Simmons b Allott	7	– b Hayhurst	8
*P. M. Roebuck c Simmons b Murphy	16	– c Murphy b Simmons	17
J. J. E. Hardy lbw b Allott	25	– c O'Shaughnessy b Simmons	0
M. D. Crowe lbw b Murphy	65	– retired hurt	15
B. C. Rose c O'Shaughnessy b Allott	1	– lbw b Simmons	0
V. J. Marks c Allott b O'Shaughnessy	43	– c Fowler b Simmons	24
†N. D. Burns c Fowler b Simmons	52	– (8) not out	4
G. D. Rose c Abrahams b Murphy	95	– (7) lbw b Simmons	18
M. R. Davis lbw b Murphy	12	– b Simmons	0
N. A. Mallender not out	17		
A. N. Jones not out	12		
L-b 8, w 2	10	B 4, l-b 5	9

1/24 2/24 3/81 4/87 5/146   (9 wkts dec.) 355   1/17 2/25 3/34   (7 wkts dec.) 95
6/173 7/275 8/303 9/336   4/46 5/85
                                                 6/95 7/95

Bonus points – Somerset 3, Lancashire 3 (Score at 100 overs: 275-7).

Bowling: *First Innings*—Allott 26.1-5-66-3; Murphy 32-5-115-4; O'Shaughnessy 17-4-34-1; Hayhurst 20-5-62-0; Simmons 31.5-11-70-1. *Second Innings*—Murphy 4-0-18-0; Hayhurst 14-2-48-1; Simmons 10.4-3-20-6.

Lancashire

G. D. Mendis c Hardy b Mallender	20	– c Felton b Mallender	20
G. Fowler c Burns b Marks	72	– c Burns b G. D. Rose	37
J. Abrahams lbw b G. D. Rose	7	– b Marks	8
N. H. Fairbrother b Davis	9	– st Burns b Marks	100
S. J. O'Shaughnessy c Roebuck b G. D. Rose	38	– not out	61
*D. P. Hughes c Burns b Marks	0	– not out	3
A. N. Hayhurst not out	30		
J. Simmons c Burns b Davis	9		
†J. Stanworth c Crowe b Marks	8		
A. J. Murphy b Marks	5		
P. J. W. Allott absent injured			
B 2, l-b 1, w 4, n-b 6	13	B 1, l-b 7, w 1, n-b 2	11

1/42 2/57 3/67 4/156 5/156   211   1/43 2/67 3/69   (4 wkts) 240
6/160 7/178 8/191 9/211   4/220

Bonus points – Lancashire 2, Somerset 4.

Bowling: *First Innings*—Jones 12-0-56-0; Mallender 11-5-31-1; Marks 27.4-10-46-4; G. D. Rose 17-5-23-2; Davis 15-3-36-2; Crowe 9-2-16-0. *Second Innings*—Jones 9-0-41-0; Mallender 13-1-46-1; Davis 7-1-42-0; G. D. Rose 8-0-36-1; Marks 20-7-54-2; Crowe 3-1-13-0.

Umpires: B. Dudleston and D. R. Shepherd.

SOMERSET v SURREY

At Taunton, May 6, 7, 8. Drawn. Somerset 8 pts, Surrey 6 pts. Toss: Somerset. Crowe, who batted beautifully through 201 deliveries, hitting three sixes and sixteen fours, put on 114 in 34 overs with Felton against several hostile spells from Clarke to rectify Somerset's uncertain start. Then he and Harden added 125 in 27 overs to ensure a full hand of batting points. Surrey failed to capitalise after Smith and Clinton – the latter was missed twice – had opened with a brisk 104. Only Jesty, Bullen and Clarke made progress thereafter. Somerset's second innings revolved around Roebuck's hundred in 161 balls, and with Crowe helping him put on 104 in 21 overs, he eventually set Surrey a target of 305 in 58 overs. Lynch led the way with three sixes and fourteen fours from 155 balls, and while he and Smith were putting on 122 in 26 overs Surrey looked likely winners. However, a fine catch by Jones abruptly changed the pattern, although it was only when 71 were needed in seven overs from the last three wickets that Surrey settled for a draw.

Close of play: First day, Somerset 380-6 (N. D. Burns 31*); Second day, Somerset 45-0 (N. A. Felton 21*, P. M. Roebuck 23*).

Somerset

N. A. Felton c Ward b Feltham	66	– lbw b Greig	22
*P. M. Roebuck c Brown b Clarke	0	– not out	103
J. J. E. Hardy c Clarke b Feltham	27	– c Lynch b Clarke	10
M. D. Crowe b Clarke	148	– c Clarke b Feltham	52
R. J. Harden c Clarke b Feltham	44	– not out	23
V. J. Marks c Ward b Greig	45		
†N. D. Burns not out	31		
B 3, l-b 8, n-b 8	19	B 1, l-b 11, n-b 2	14

1/9 2/46 3/160 4/285   (6 wkts dec.) 380   1/51 2/72 3/176   (3 wkts dec.) 224
5/308 6/380

G. V. Palmer, M. R. Davis, N. A. Mallender and A. N. Jones did not bat.

Bonus points – Somerset 4, Surrey 2 (Score at 100 overs: 346-5).

Bowling: *First Innings*—Clarke 22–5–58–2; Feltham 32–6–109–3; Greig 31–6–81–1; Medlycott 11–2–59–0; Bullen 14–3–62–0. *Second Innings*—Clarke 22–5–69–1; Feltham 19.4–1–83–1; Greig 17–3–60–1.

Surrey

G. S. Clinton c Burns b Palmer	38	– c Hardy b Davis	11
D. M. Smith c Crowe b Palmer	65	– c Jones b Marks	56
M. A. Lynch c Roebuck b Jones	23	– not out	128
T. E. Jesty c Marks b Palmer	47	– c Burns b Jones	6
D. M. Ward run out	5	– c Burns b Marks	6
C. K. Bullen c Davis b Mallender	36	– (9) not out	4
M. A. Feltham run out	12	– (8) c Burns b Davis	5
K. T. Medlycott lbw b Davis	0		
S. T. Clarke b Jones	31	– (7) b Marks	3
*I. A. Greig not out	15	– (6) run out	11
†G. E. Brown not out	5		
L-b 10, n-b 13	23	L-b 8, w 2, n-b 5	15

1/104 2/121 3/168 4/190 5/203   (9 wkts dec.) 300   1/35 2/157 3/170 4/192 (7 wkts) 245
6/230 7/230 8/275 9/287   5/219 6/227 7/234

Bonus points – Surrey 4, Somerset 4.

Bowling: *First Innings*—Jones 14–2–61–2; Mallender 14.2–1–51–1; Davis 13–1–51–1; Marks 31–9–68–0; Crowe 5–2–18–0; Palmer 11–3–41–3. *Second Innings*—Jones 11–1–43–1; Davis 9–0–36–2; Marks 23–4–90–3; Palmer 10–0–51–0; Crowe 4–0–17–0.

Umpires: R. A. White and A. G. T. Whitehead.

At Taunton, May 14. SOMERSET beat PAKISTANIS by 79 runs (See Pakistani tour section).

At Leeds, May 20, 21, 22. SOMERSET drew with YORKSHIRE.

SOMERSET v GLOUCESTERSHIRE

At Taunton, May 23, 25, 26. Somerset won by an innings and 83 runs. Somerset 24 pts, Gloucestershire 3 pts. Toss: Gloucestershire. Despite a large wet patch on an otherwise dry pitch after a cover had leaked, Somerset, put in, batted splendidly. Felton and Brian Rose did the early vital work in difficult conditions, and then Hardy, profiting from two fielding errors, made his first century for Somerset in 241 balls. Crowe helped him put on 135 in 38 overs and Burns added useful runs. With the wet patch still drying on the second day, only Lloyds made any progress in Gloucestershire's first innings. Romaines, Bainbridge and Tomlins resisted with much more application in the second, and Alleyne confirmed the excellent impression he had made in the first, but no large stand was allowed to develop. Marks, Somerset's acting-captain, and Mallender again bowled admirably and less than an hour was needed on the final day to seal Gloucestershire's fate.

Close of play: First day, Somerset 341-7 (N. D. Burns 42*, M. R. Davis 9*); Second day, Gloucestershire 122-5 (K. P. Tomlins 22*, R. C. Russell 1*).

Somerset

B. C. Rose c Wright b Bainbridge	 31	M. R. Davis not out	....	23
N. A. Felton c Russell b Walsh	 28	N. A. Mallender lbw b Lawrence	.....	0
J. J. E. Hardy c Lloyds b Walsh	119	A. N. Jones not out	....	4
M. D. Crowe lbw b Walsh	 61	B 5, l-b 23, w 6, n-b 7	....	41
R. J. Harden c Russell b Bainbridge	... 12			
*V. J. Marks b Lloyds	 7	1/60 2/66 3/201	(9 wkts dec.)	376
†N. D. Burns b Bainbridge	 50	4/230 5/249 6/323		
G. D. Rose c Russell b Walsh	 0	7/323 8/354 9/361		

Bonus points – Somerset 4, Gloucestershire 3 (Score at 100 overs: 341-7).

Bowling: Lawrence 22-2-92-1; Walsh 28-10-57-4; Bainbridge 32-8-78-3; Alleyne 10-4-25-0; Graveney 16-1-59-0; Lloyds 8-0-37-1.

Gloucestershire

A. W. Stovold c Marks b Mallender	 11	– c G. D. Rose b Marks	....	8
P. W. Romaines b Jones	 2	– b Mallender	....	32
A. J. Wright c B. C. Rose b Mallender	 8	– c Harden b Marks	....	8
P. Bainbridge c Burns b Mallender	 6	– c Crowe b Marks	....	17
K. P. Tomlins b Marks	 8	– b Marks	....	22
J. W. Lloyds c Burns b Mallender	 28	– lbw b G. D. Rose	....	25
M. W. Alleyne not out	 11	– (8) not out	....	25
†R. C. Russell c Burns b G. D. Rose	 12	– (7) lbw b Marks	....	5
*D. A. Graveney c Harden b Marks	 1	– (11) c Hardy b Jones	....	0
C. A. Walsh c sub b Marks	 5	– (9) c Jones b Mallender	....	27
D. V. Lawrence run out	 13	– (10) b Mallender	....	1
L-b 1, w 1, n-b 4	 6	L-b 8, n-b 4	....	12
1/16 2/16 3/28 4/35 5/65	111	1/23 2/39 3/69 4/77 5/117		182
6/69 7/87 8/88 9/94		6/123 7/127 8/160 9/161		

Bonus points – Somerset 4.

Bowling: *First Innings*—Jones 5-1-11-1; Mallender 14-2-37-4; G. D. Rose 7.5-1-25-1; Marks 10-5-13-3; Davis 2-0-24-0. *Second Innings*—Mallender 15-4-50-3; Davis 4-1-8-0; Marks 28-11-70-5; G. D. Rose 10-3-24-1; Crowe 6-2-15-0; Jones 1.3-0-7-1.

Umpires: J. H. Harris and D. Lloyd.

At Leicester, May 30, June 1, 2. SOMERSET drew with LEICESTERSHIRE.

SOMERSET v NOTTINGHAMSHIRE

At Taunton, June 3, 4, 5. Drawn. Somerset 5 pts, Nottinghamshire 8 pts. Toss: Somerset. On a grassy pitch, Hardy and Crowe added 98 in 31 overs to redress a poor start, but after several rainstorms Hadlee, with four for 3 in 29 balls, Rice and Hemmings captured the last eight wickets for 44 in 24 overs. Nottinghamshire were themselves in difficulty until Hadlee, dropped when 6, and Randall, missed at 40, took control, putting on 127 in eighteen overs. Randall faced 111 balls for his 97 and Hadlee's powerful strokeplay brought him four sixes and twelve fours in 133 from 132 balls. On the final morning Pick and Hadlee tested Somerset severely, but Crowe held firm through 26 overs. Rain prevented any play after lunch.

Close of play: First day, Somerset 174; Second day, Nottinghamshire 336-9 (R. J. Hadlee 133*, K. Saxelby 1*).

Somerset

J. G. Wyatt lbw b Saxelby	10	– c Scott b Pick	2
N. A. Felton c Randall b Saxelby	19	– lbw b Hadlee	23
J. J. E. Hardy lbw b Rice	51	– lbw b Pick	3
M. D. Crowe c Hadlee b Rice	44	– not out	42
R. J. Harden c Rice b Hemmings	9	– not out	1
*V. J. Marks c Scott b Hadlee	19		
†N. D. Burns c Rice b Hadlee	4		
G. D. Rose lbw b Hadlee	0		
M. R. Davis lbw b Hemmings	0		
N. A. Mallender not out	5		
A. N. Jones c Hemmings b Hadlee	3		
L-b 9, n-b 1	10	B 4, l-b 1	5
	174		**(3 wkts) 76**

1/29 2/32 3/130 4/137 5/155 6/165 7/165 8/166 9/166

1/5 2/11 3/63

Bonus points – Somerset 1, Nottinghamshire 4.

Bowling: *First Innings*—Hadlee 18.5-5-35-4; Pick 8-2-35-0; Saxelby 21-7-51-2; Rice 17-6-33-2; Hemmings 6-2-11-2. *Second Innings*—Hadlee 11-4-26-1; Pick 7-2-9-2; Saxelby 6-1-19-0; Rice 7-2-15-0; Hemmings 3-1-2-0.

Nottinghamshire

M. Newell lbw b Rose	12	E. E. Hemmings lbw b Marks	12
D. J. R. Martindale b Mallender	10	R. A. Pick c Felton b Jones	0
D. W. Randall b Mallender	97	K. Saxelby not out	1
P. Johnson c Felton b Mallender	39	B 7, l-b 5, w 2, n-b 1	15
*C. E. B. Rice lbw b Davis	0		
J. D. Birch lbw b Davis	4	1/24 2/30 3/106	**(9 wkts dec.) 336**
R. J. Hadlee not out	133	4/109 5/114 6/241	
†C. W. Scott c Mallender b Marks	13	7/290 8/332 9/333	

Bonus points – Nottinghamshire 4, Somerset 4.

Bowling: Jones 14-2-74-1; Mallender 15-3-58-3; Rose 12-1-68-1; Marks 21-1-69-2; Davis 12-0-55-2.

Umpires: J. A. Jameson and R. Julian.

At Swansea, June 6, 7, 8. SOMERSET drew with GLAMORGAN.

SOMERSET v MIDDLESEX

At Bath, June 13, 15, 16. Drawn. Somerset 6 pts, Middlesex 7 pts. Toss: Middlesex. Gatting's innings dominated the first day, his runs coming in 297 minutes from 269 balls with a six and 31 fours. On the Monday, Crowe (135 balls) and Marks (79 balls) launched a Somerset recovery from 101 for four and Burns superintended the saving of the follow-on with a valuable 45 from 114 balls. The final day was bedevilled by rain, but Middlesex made a positive result virtually impossible by setting Somerset 256 in 123 minutes on a drying pitch. However, while Hardy went steadily against the spinners, Crowe, having escaped a sharp chance when 8, batted gloriously for 90 minutes. He needed 109 balls for his unbeaten 102 and hit two sixes and thirteen fours.

Close of play: First day, Somerset 27-0 (N. A. Felton 12*, J. G. Wyatt 13*); Second day, Middlesex 71-2 (P. R. Downton 24*, S. P. Hughes 0*).

Middlesex

W. N. Slack c Rose b Marks	54	– b Mallender 8
J. D. Carr b Jones	18	– lbw b Rose 34
*M. W. Gatting c and b Mallender	196	
M. A. Roseberry c Felton b Mallender	43	
R. O. Butcher c Burns b Jones	17	
†P. R. Downton b Mallender	13	– (3) not out 40
J. E. Emburey c Burns b Marks	17	
P. H. Edmonds not out	17	
N. F. Williams not out	0	
S. P. Hughes (did not bat)		– (4) not out 26
B 1, l-b 10, n-b 17	28	B 5, l-b 1, w 4 10

1/44 2/128 3/249 4/270 5/350   (7 wkts dec.) 403   1/13 2/69   (2 wkts dec.) 118
6/371 7/395

W. W. Daniel did not bat.

Bonus points – Middlesex 4, Somerset 3.

Bowling: *First Innings*—Jones 15-0-65-2; Mallender 19-0-86-3; Rose 20-2-66-0; Davis 23-3-79-0; Marks 23-4-96-2. *Second Innings*—Jones 6-0-39-0; Mallender 10-2-47-1; Rose 8-4-21-1; Marks 2-0-5-0.

Somerset

N. A. Felton b Daniel	20	
J. G. Wyatt c Gatting b Williams	25	– lbw b Williams 0
J. J. E. Hardy lbw b Emburey	26	– (1) not out 39
M. D. Crowe c Downton b Emburey	64	– (3) not out 102
R. J. Harden lbw b Emburey	2	
*V. J. Marks st Downton b Emburey	29	
†N. D. Burns c Emburey b Williams	45	
G. D. Rose b Edmonds	18	
N. A. Mallender c Roseberry b Emburey	6	
M. R. Davis lbw b Williams	2	
A. N. Jones not out	1	
L-b 13, n-b 15	28	N-b 1 1

1/39 2/73 3/89 4/101 5/185   266   1/1   (1 wkt) 142
6/194 7/229 8/237 9/263

Bonus points – Somerset 3, Middlesex 3 (Score at 100 overs: 257-8).

Bowling: *First Innings*—Williams 19.4-4-55-3; Daniel 16-1-58-1; Emburey 35-16-60-5; Edmonds 23-7-45-1; Hughes 7-0-29-0; Gatting 3-0-6-0. *Second Innings*—Williams 3-0-12-1; Hughes 1-0-4-0; Edmonds 15-3-66-0; Emburey 12-1-48-0; Gatting 2-0-12-0.

Umpires: J. W. Holder and R. A. White.

SOMERSET v KENT

At Bath, June 17, 18, 19. Drawn. Somerset 4 pts, Kent 4 pts. Toss: Somerset. Rain cut into the first two days and washed out the third. Kelleher, who returned his best figures to date, had Somerset struggling at 125 for six, but Marks, Rose and Harman, the last-mentioned making his highest first-class score, brought about a recovery. Kent's slow reply, on a pitch now bland and lacking pace, was led by Benson, who faced 157 balls for his half-century.

Close of play: First day, Somerset 207-8 (G. D. Rose 30*, M. D. Harman 21*); Second day, Kent 139-3 (C. J. Tavaré 15*, C. S. Cowdrey 15*).

Somerset

J. G. Wyatt c Tavaré b Kelleher	6		N. A. Mallender c Marsh b Kelleher	0
N. A. Felton b Davis	47		M. D. Harman run out	41
J. J. E. Hardy lbw b Penn	29		A. N. Jones c Taylor b Kelleher	5
M. D. Crowe lbw b Kelleher	5			
R. J. Harden c Benson b Kelleher	10		B 1, l-b 8, w 1, n-b 5	15
*V. J. Marks b Kelleher	45			
†N. D. Burns run out	2		1/9 2/52 3/59 4/93 5/122	250
G. D. Rose not out	45		6/125 7/178 8/178 9/238	

Bonus points – Somerset 3, Kent 4.

Bowling: Pienaar 15-4-40-0; Kelleher 35-7-109-6; Penn 20-2-55-1; Underwood 15-5-24-0; Davis 11-6-13-1.

Kent

M. R. Benson c Harman b Rose	55		*C. S. Cowdrey not out	15
N. R. Taylor lbw b Rose	19		L-b 2, w 1, n-b 1	4
D. G. Aslett lbw b Mallender	31			
C. J. Tavaré not out	15		1/37 2/98 3/114	(3 wkts) 139

R. F. Pienaar, †S. A. Marsh, D. J. M. Kelleher, R. P. Davis, D. L. Underwood and C. Penn did not bat.

Bonus point – Somerset 1.

Bowling: Jones 6-0-20-0; Mallender 11-3-24-1; Rose 13.4-0-34-2; Harman 15-7-19-0; Marks 17-2-40-0.

Umpires: J. W. Holder and R. A. White.

At Chelmsford, June 27, 29, 30. SOMERSET drew with ESSEX.

At Birmingham, July 1, 2, 3. SOMERSET drew with WARWICKSHIRE.

SOMERSET v WORCESTERSHIRE

At Taunton, July 15, 16, 17. Drawn. Somerset 1 pt, Worcestershire 3 pts. Toss: Somerset. The much-heralded return to Taunton of Botham brought an unusually high gate of £4,500, although the weather destroyed the match. It did not, however, stop the nominal hero from fulfilling one ambition. The first day consisted of eleven overs, wherein Rose and Palmer broke down, and next day, on an awkward pitch, Curtis, Lord and D'Oliveira went slowly to 140 for four in 69 overs. Botham, after a sober start, opened up to reach 53 in 60 balls at the close of a day which had seen Marks bowling throughout. Only one hour was possible on the final day, but that was time enough for Botham to race characteristically to 100 from 102 balls and go on to 126 not out from 111 balls with three sixes and sixteen fours. Neale, who had batted steadily the previous day, also struck out as they took their stand to 197 runs from 36 overs, 125 of which came in the sixteen overs before rain ended matters.

Close of play: First day, Worcestershire 29-0 (T. S. Curtis 12*, G. J. Lord 16*); Second day, Worcestershire 212-4 (P. A. Neale 51*, I. T. Botham 53*).

Worcestershire

T. S. Curtis lbw b Marks	42	I. T. Botham not out	126
G. J. Lord run out	29		
G. A. Hick b Marks	0	B 1, l-b 10, w 4, n-b 2	17
D. B. D'Oliveira c Felton b Jones	26		
*P. A. Neale not out	97	1/60 2/61 3/85 4/140 (4 wkts) 337	

†S. J. Rhodes, P. J. Newport, R. K. Illingworth, N. V. Radford and G. R. Dilley did not bat.

Bonus points – Worcestershire 3, Somerset 1 (Score at 100 overs: 278-4).

Bowling: Jones 27–8–79–1; Rose 1.2–0–8–0; Palmer 10.4–0–62–0; Marks 40.1–15–74–2; Pringle 24–6–95–0; Harden 2–0–8–0.

Somerset

*P. M. Roebuck, N. A. Felton, J. J. E. Hardy, M. D. Crowe, N. J. Pringle, R. J. Harden, V. J. Marks, †N. D. Burns, G. D. Rose, G. V. Palmer and A. N. Jones.

Umpires: K. J. Lyons and P. B. Wight.

SOMERSET v LEICESTERSHIRE

At Taunton, July 18, 20, 21. Drawn. Somerset 3 pts, Leicestershire 4 pts. Toss: Somerset. Despite 68 overs being lost on the first two days, this was made into an interesting match. On a damp pitch Ferris soon had Somerset 18 for five, but courageous batting by Harden (229 balls), who was missed twice, and Burns (117 balls) saved them. Palmer's lively 68 contained one six and ten fours. Leicestershire responded briskly and, declaring 146 behind, soon had Somerset in trouble again. The victory target was 295 in 250 minutes, or a minimum of 70 overs, and was attacked enthusiastically after the early depredations of Foster. Willey and Clift, each hitting nine fours, led the first and last half of the chase respectively, but when 39 were needed from five overs with three wickets in hand, the shutters were closed.

Close of play: First day, Somerset 163-7 (V. J. Marks 25*, G. V. Palmer 5*); Second day, Somerset 57-3 (P. M. Roebuck 29*, N. J. Pringle 10*).

Somerset

N. A. Felton lbw b Agnew	0	– lbw b Ferris	6
*P. M. Roebuck b Ferris	5	– c Whitticase b Ferris	41
J. J. E. Hardy b Ferris	0	– run out	5
M. D. Crowe b Ferris	0	– c Whitticase b Agnew	1
N. J. Pringle run out	1	– c Whitticase b Ferris	15
R. J. Harden b Agnew	59	– not out	42
†N. D. Burns c Whitticase b Clift	59	– b Such	4
V. J. Marks c Whitticase b Clift	38	– b Such	8
G. V. Palmer c Cobb b Agnew	68	– b Agnew	18
A. N. Jones not out	6	– not out	0
D. J. Foster c Willey b Agnew	9		
B 2, l-b 4, w 1, n-b 5	12	L-b 4, w 1, n-b 3	8

1/0 2/3 3/5 4/7 5/18   257   1/15 2/23 3/28 (8 wkts dec.) 148
6/119 7/148 8/242 9/242   4/69 5/74 6/82
                                 7/90 8/143

Bonus points – Somerset 3, Leicestershire 4 (Score at 100 overs: 253-9).

Bowling: *First Innings*—Agnew 31.4–8–92–4; Ferris 23–5–76–3; Clift 29–11–39–2; Such 17–6–44–0. *Second Innings*—Agnew 9–2–22–2; Ferris 17–3–57–3; Such 7–1–23–2; Clift 4–2–6–0; Willey 11–4–36–0.

Leicestershire

R. A. Cobb not out	27	– c Burns b Foster	19
N. E. Briers b Pringle	30	– c Crowe b Foster	4
*P. Willey c Crowe b Foster	17	– b Jones	61
D. I. Gower not out	19	– c Palmer b Marks	21
J. J. Whitaker (did not bat)		– b Jones	21
T. J. Boon (did not bat)		– c Harden b Marks	20
P. B. Clift (did not bat)		– not out	74
†P. Whitticase (did not bat)		– c Harden b Foster	14
J. P. Agnew (did not bat)		– b Jones	23
G. J. F. Ferris (did not bat)		– not out	4
L-b 7, w 6, n-b 5	18	B 2, l-b 4, n-b 1	7

1/55 2/75   (2 wkts dec.) 111   1/10 2/35 3/82 4/128   (8 wkts) 268
                                                 5/133 6/175 7/214 8/256

P. M. Such did not bat.

Bowling: *First Innings*—Jones 5-0-17-0; Foster 8-0-42-1; Palmer 8-2-26-0; Pringle 4-0-13-1; Marks 1-0-6-0. *Second Innings*—Jones 20-4-56-3; Foster 16.5-0-77-3; Marks 28-4-87-2; Palmer 7-1-27-0; Pringle 2-0-15-0.

Umpires: K. J. Lyons and P. B. Wight.

At Northampton, July 22, 23, 24. SOMERSET drew with NORTHAMPTONSHIRE.

At Worcester, July 25, 27, 28. SOMERSET drew with WORCESTERSHIRE.

SOMERSET v GLAMORGAN

At Weston-super-Mare, August 1, 3, 4. Somerset won by seven wickets. Somerset 23 pts, Glamorgan 6 pts. Toss: Glamorgan. Glamorgan were lifted from 5 for two by a superb 160 in 177 balls from Maynard, who hit three sixes and 25 fours and set the tone for a free-scoring match with a century before lunch off 98 balls. With Morris, Glamorgan's anchorman, he put on 239 for the third wicket. Crowe, with a beautifully fashioned innings that also included 25 fours, dominated Somerset's reply, and after a declaration 79 behind, Maynard and Holmes gave Morris the opportunity to set a target of 321 in four hours. Roebuck, 122 from 178 balls, masterminded the attempt in a partnership of 178 in 41 overs with Hardy, whose fine innings of 136 balls contained three sixes and eight fours. Harden, with a breezy 39, saw it to completion with fourteen balls to spare.

Close of play: First day, Somerset 13-0 (N. A. Felton 9*, P. M. Roebuck 4*); Second day, Glamorgan 74-0 (A. R. Butcher 29*, H. Morris 35*).

Glamorgan

A. R. Butcher c Crowe b Jones	0	– c and b Jones	35
*H. Morris c Crowe b Jones	92	– st Burns b Marks	46
G. C. Holmes b Foster	5	– not out	70
M. P. Maynard c Jones b Foster	160	– lbw b Pringle	52
R. J. Shastri c Jones b Palmer	20	– (6) not out	4
P. A. Todd c Felton b Jones	10	– (5) c Roebuck b Pringle	16
J. Derrick b Foster	6		
†C. P. Metson c Felton b Marks	5		
I. Smith c and b Foster	19		
R. C. Ontong not out	3		
S. R. Barwick not out	8		
B 4, l-b 4, w 2, n-b 13	23	B 4, l-b 6, w 1, n-b 7	18

1/0 2/5 3/244 4/289 5/302   (9 wkts dec.) 351   1/87 2/109   (4 wkts dec.) 241
6/303 7/317 8/317 9/342   3/196 4/228

Bonus points – Glamorgan 4, Somerset 4 (Score at 100 overs: 350-9).

Bowling: *First Innings*—Jones 21–2–77–3; Foster 17–4–56–4; Palmer 19–4–70–1; Marks 32–13–91–1; Pringle 12–0–49–0. *Second Innings*—Jones 11–4–24–1; Foster 9–0–49–0; Marks 20–3–74–1; Palmer 13–3–49–0; Pringle 8–0–35–2.

Somerset

N. A. Felton lbw b Derrick	35	– c Butcher b Ontong	37
*P. M. Roebuck c Smith b Derrick	22	– b Shastri	122
J. J. E. Hardy c Todd b Smith	4	– run out	93
M. D. Crowe run out	148	– not out	19
N. J. Pringle b Barwick	22		
R. J. Harden not out	26	– (5) not out	39
†N. D. Burns not out	3		
L-b 10, w 1, n-b 1	12	B 7, l-b 4	11

1/48 2/53 3/73 4/167 5/268   (5 wkts dec.) 272   1/74 2/252 3/270   (3 wkts) 321

V. J. Marks, G. V. Palmer, A. N. Jones and D. J. Foster did not bat.

Bonus points – Somerset 3, Glamorgan 2.

Bowling: *First Innings*—Barwick 17–5–37–1; Smith 14–4–47–1; Shastri 24–8–42–0; Holmes 2–0–3–0; Derrick 17–4–72–2; Ontong 16–1–55–0; Maynard 3–0–6–0. *Second Innings*—Barwick 17–1–80–0; Smith 3–1–13–0; Shastri 19–3–63–1; Derrick 5–0–19–0; Ontong 26.4–2–135–1.

Umpires: J. Birkenshaw and J. H. Hampshire.

SOMERSET v HAMPSHIRE

At Weston-super-Mare, August 5, 6, 7. Drawn. Somerset 6 pts, Hampshire 4 pts. Toss: Somerset. Rocked by Tremlett's early burst of three for 2, Somerset were indebted to their captain's patience and skill as he carried his bat. It was Roebuck's fifth Championship hundred of the season and, coming off 342 balls, contained a six and seventeen fours. Jones, Waugh – making his first Championship appearance – and Harman worked through the Hampshire order gradually, and there was a spectacular gully catch from Palmer to dismiss Chris Smith. When Somerset slipped to 128 for six, they were only 235 ahead with five hours left, but Waugh and Palmer added 97 in 24 overs to make the final calculation 333 in 210 minutes. On a slow pitch with the ball tending to keep low, this seemed of little interest to Hampshire after they lost Greenidge first ball. However, a partnership of 151 between Terry and Robin Smith encouraged Hampshire into the extra half-hour, but Palmer removed both of them in one over.

Close of play: First day, Somerset 300; Second day, Somerset 74-3 (J. J. E. Hardy 20*, S. R. Waugh 1*).

Somerset

N. A. Felton c Greenidge b Tremlett	16	– b Tremlett	25
*P. M. Roebuck not out	165	– c R. A. Smith b Marshall	19
J. J. E. Hardy lbw b Tremlett	0	– c Terry b Cowley	26
N. J. Pringle b Tremlett	1	– st Parks b Maru	9
S. R. Waugh lbw b Maru	1	– not out	71
R. J. Harden lbw b Cowley	26	– c Parks b Tremlett	10
†N. D. Burns c and b Marshall	20	– run out	9
G. V. Palmer c Parks b Tremlett	15	– not out	43
M. D. Harman run out	16		
A. N. Jones c Parks b Tremlett	7		
D. J. Foster b Tremlett	16		
B 2, l-b 11, w 3, n-b 1	17	B 6, l-b 7	13

1/36 2/50 3/52 4/53 5/103   300   1/29 2/52 3/70   (6 wkts dec.) 225
6/134 7/170 8/247 9/259   4/84 5/113 6/128

Bonus points – Somerset 2, Hampshire 3 (Score at 100 overs: 246-7).

Bowling: *First Innings*—Marshall 18–4–46–1; Connor 21–4–82–0; Tremlett 27.5–7–53–6; Maru 32–11–65–1; Cowley 16–3–41–1. *Second Innings*—Marshall 15–2–44–1; Connor 12–3–22–0; Tremlett 14–7–33–2; Cowley 23.4–4–55–1; Maru 20–4–58–1.

Hampshire

C. G. Greenidge b Jones	12	– lbw b Jones	0
C. L. Smith c Palmer b Waugh	3	– c Burns b Waugh	34
*V. P. Terry c and b Jones	32	– b Palmer	98
D. R. Turner lbw b Waugh	35	– c Palmer b Harman	0
R. A. Smith b Foster	12	– lbw b Palmer	68
M. D. Marshall lbw b Jones	38	– not out	1
N. G. Cowley c Burns b Waugh	5	– not out	0
†R. J. Parks lbw b Harman	27		
T. M. Tremlett not out	10		
R. J. Maru lbw b Palmer	2		
C. A. Connor c Waugh b Harman	2		
L-b 8, n-b 9	17	B 5, l-b 13, w 1, n-b 5	24

1/14 2/41 3/55 4/77 5/121   193   1/0 2/67 3/68   (5 wkts) 225
6/127 7/179 8/183 9/186   4/219 5/220

Bonus points – Hampshire 1, Somerset 4.

Bowling: *First Innings*—Jones 13–1–41–3; Foster 12–2–39–1; Waugh 20–3–63–3; Harman 19.5–5–38–2; Palmer 3–1–4–1. *Second Innings*—Jones 9–3–23–1; Foster 5–0–28–0; Harman 20.4–6–57–1; Waugh 14–3–33–1; Roebuck 6–1–24–0; Palmer 6–1–25–2; Pringle 2–1–17–0.

Umpires: J. Birkenshaw and J. H. Hampshire.

At Nottingham, August 8, 10, 11. SOMERSET lost to NOTTINGHAMSHIRE by five wickets.

SOMERSET v YORKSHIRE

At Taunton, August 15, 17, 18. Drawn. Somerset 5 pts, Yorkshire 4 pts. Toss: Yorkshire. In hot weather, Moxon and Metcalfe gave Yorkshire a sound start and later on Bairstow, with 88 from 140 balls, completed a useful first day for the visitors. Although Marks bowled 45 consecutive overs, the pitch had hinted at help for the seamers, and so it proved on the second day. However, Felton (195 balls) and Hardy (212 balls) batted with great application and some luck. When Somerset enterprisingly declared 59 behind, blows around the hands forced the retirement of Metcalfe and Sharp on the second evening to join the fielding casualties, Bartlett and Moxon. Next day, Yorkshire slipped from 71 for one to 125 for eight against Marks and Jones, but late aggression brought 61 runs from the last ten overs and made Somerset's target a stiff one – 246 in 54 overs. Harden hit a brave 35 after getting a painful blow on the foot, but at 166 for six, with twelve overs left, Somerset turned their thoughts to a draw.

Close of play: First day, Yorkshire 343; Second day, Yorkshire 37-0 (R. J. Blakey 19*, P. Carrick 3*).

Yorkshire

M. D. Moxon lbw b Marks	60	– (5) c Roebuck b Harman	4
A. A. Metcalfe c Harman b Jones	30	– (1) b Marks	6
R. J. Blakey c and b Marks	51	– (2) b Rose	26
K. Sharp c Felton b Marks	8	– (3) b Jones	8
P. E. Robinson c Burns b Foster	24	– (6) b Jones	7
†D. L. Bairstow c Burns b Rose	88	– (7) c Roebuck b Marks	2
*P. Carrick lbw b Marks	28	– (4) c sub b Marks	61
P. J. Hartley c Felton b Rose	12	– b Jones	5
P. W. Jarvis c Foster b Rose	16	– not out	30
S. D. Fletcher c Harden b Marks	6	– c Roebuck b Marks	7
C. Shaw not out	0	– not out	22
B 2, l-b 7, w 1, n-b 18	28	B 2, l-b 4, n-b 2	8

1/96 2/103 3/103 4/169 5/195   343   1/71 2/80 3/93   (9 wkts dec.) 186
6/267 7/320 8/321 9/338   4/113 5/115 6/115
                                   7/124 8/125 9/153

Bonus points – Yorkshire 3, Somerset 2 (Score at 100 overs: 294-6).

In the second innings A. A. Metcalfe, when 6, retired hurt at 11 and resumed at 115-5; K. Sharp, when 8, retired hurt at 34 and resumed at 80.

Bowling: *First Innings*—Jones 17-3-41-1; Foster 18-2-60-1; Rose 16-3-48-3; Marks 45.2-11-117-5; Harman 13-2-68-0. *Second Innings*—Jones 14-4-51-3; Foster 9-1-35-0; Marks 15-3-50-0; Rose 6.4-2-20-1; Harman 8-1-24-1.

Somerset

N. A. Felton b Fletcher	96	– c and b Carrick	42
*P. M. Roebuck c Bairstow b Jarvis	7	– b Carrick	25
J. J. E. Hardy lbw b Carrick	77	– c Robinson b Carrick	0
R. J. Harden not out	58	– st Bairstow b Carrick	35
†N. D. Burns lbw b Carrick	7	– (6) c Bairstow b Jarvis	20
V. J. Marks not out	15	– (5) c Sharp b Carrick	17
G. D. Rose (did not bat)		– not out	22
M. D. Harman (did not bat)		– b Jarvis	12
R. J. Bartlett (did not bat)		– lbw b Jarvis	0
A. N. Jones (did not bat)		– not out	1
L-b 11, w 3, n-b 10	24	B 4, l-b 1, n-b 6	11

1/21 2/174 3/227 4/235   (4 wkts dec.) 284   1/46 2/52 3/93 4/116   (8 wkts) 185
                                   5/134 6/166 7/180 8/180

D. J. Foster did not bat.

Bonus points – Somerset 3, Yorkshire 1.

Bowling: *First Innings*—Jarvis 15.2-2-50-1; Hartley 15-0-58-0; Shaw 16-4-38-0; Fletcher 12-2-23-1; Carrick 29-9-67-2; Sharp 6-0-37-0. *Second Innings*—Jarvis 13.5-2-45-3; Hartley 11-1-51-0; Carrick 22-11-42-5; Fletcher 3-0-14-0; Shaw 4-0-28-0.

Umpires: B. Dudleston and R. Julian.

At The Oval, August 19, 20, 21. SOMERSET drew with SURREY.

At Bournemouth, August 22, 24, 25. SOMERSET lost to HAMPSHIRE by 129 runs.

At Hove, August 26, 27, 28. SOMERSET drew with SUSSEX.

At Bristol, September 2, 3, 4. SOMERSET drew with GLOUCESTERSHIRE.

SOMERSET v DERBYSHIRE

At Taunton, September 9, 10, 11. Drawn. Somerset 7 pts, Derbyshire 7 pts. Toss: Derbyshire. On a bare pitch, which did not wear as expected, Derbyshire were well placed at 221 for three; but they were all out 33 runs later as Mallender, with a remarkable spell of six for 8 in 25 balls, achieved his best return for Somerset. Morris, having escaped three difficult chances, remained unbeaten on 113 from 215 balls, his innings containing fifteen fours. Roebuck and Felton overcame a hostile opening attack to put together Somerset's best start in 1987, and Crowe's polished 72 in 92 balls, plus a tail-end flourish led by Rose, saw the home side draw ahead. Wright (215 balls, two sixes, fifteen fours) and Barnett then registered Derbyshire's best opening stand of the year, Woolston took his first Championship wickets, and eventually Somerset were set to score 264 in 165 minutes. Only when Crowe (56 balls) and Rose (35 balls) were adding 66 in ten overs did the task seem feasible. When wickets fell, Roberts taking an unbelievable catch to get rid of Rose, Marks and Mallender had to block out the final twelve overs.

Close of play: First day, Somerset 22-0 (N. A. Felton 6*, P. M. Roebuck 13*); Second day, Derbyshire 78-0 (K. J. Barnett 46*, J. G. Wright 29*).

Derbyshire

*K. J. Barnett lbw b Mallender	4	– c Hardy b Marks	82
J. G. Wright run out	78	– st Burns b Woolston	118
B. Roberts c Felton b Rose	16	– c Crowe b Marks	2
J. E. Morris not out	113		
†B. J. M. Maher c Marks b Jones	15	– (4) lbw b Mallender	4
R. Sharma lbw b Mallender	0	– (5) b Woolston	14
R. J. Finney c Crowe b Mallender	0	– (6) not out	20
A. E. Warner b Mallender	2	– (7) not out	25
P. G. Newman b Mallender	0		
M. Beardshall b Mallender	2		
D. E. Malcolm b Mallender	0		
B 4, l-b 12, w 3, n-b 5	24	L-b 6, n-b 4	10

1/11 2/59 3/149 4/221 5/226   254   1/163 2/173 3/180   (5 wkts dec.) 275
6/230 7/232 8/232 9/244   4/219 5/228

Bonus points – Derbyshire 3, Somerset 4.

Bowling: *First Innings*—Jones 14–2–30–1; Mallender 17.4–0–61–7; Rose 17–1–54–1; Marks 24–6–56–0; Woolston 16–3–37–0. *Second Innings*—Jones 3.2–0–28–0; Mallender 15–1–53–1; Marks 38–9–92–2; Rose 8–1–26–0; Woolston 27–7–70–2.

Somerset

N. A. Felton c Maher b Newman	29	– c Maher b Warner	9
*P. M. Roebuck c Maher b Beardshall	67	– c Sharma b Newman	27
J. J. E. Hardy c Maher b Newman	0	– c Maher b Newman	16
M. D. Crowe b Finney	72	– c Roberts b Beardshall	46
J. G. Wyatt b Finney	12	– (6) st Maher b Finney	11
V. J. Marks c Maher b Beardshall	5	– (7) not out	14
†N. D. Burns b Newman	7	– (8) b Finney	0
G. D. Rose not out	27	– (5) c Roberts b Finney	39
N. A. Mallender c Sharma b Warner	14	– not out	10
R. G. Woolston lbw b Warner	0		
A. N. Jones b Warner	13		
L-b 9, w 5, n-b 6	20	L-b 2, w 1, n-b 1	4

1/81 2/85 3/142 4/158 5/185   266   1/28 2/38 3/73 4/139   (7 wkts) 176
6/197 7/205 8/246 9/246   5/145 6/156 7/156

Bonus points – Somerset 3, Derbyshire 4.

Bowling: *First Innings*—Malcolm 23–6–61–0; Newman 20–8–47–3; Warner 25.5–8–55–3; Beardshall 15–2–70–2; Finney 13–4–24–2. *Second Innings*—Malcolm 11–3–29–0; Warner 10–2–23–1; Newman 8–3–31–2; Finney 10–0–47–3; Beardshall 5–0–22–1; Sharma 2–0–15–0; Barnett 3.4–1–7–0.

Umpires: J. W. Holder and J. A. Jameson.

SURREY

Patron: HM The Queen
President: A. V. Bedser
Chairman: D. H. Newton
Chairman, Cricket Committee: J. A. F. Fulford
Secretary: 1987 – I. F. B. Scott-Browne
         1988 – D. Seward
  Kennington Oval, London SE11 5SS
  (Telephone: 01-582 6660)
Captain: I. A. Greig
Coaches: G. G. Arnold and C. E. Waller

The name of Ian Greig was never mentioned outside the committee room at The Oval when speculation was mounting over the new man to inherit the Surrey captaincy. Greig himself was 13,000 miles away, running an indoor school in Brisbane, when he received the call that was to bring him back to county cricket after a year's absence, enforced by Sussex's decision in 1985 to release him. Consequently, he arrived amid some mild astonishment to succeed Pat Pocock. But when he packed his bats away in mid-September, he had exceeded most expectations, having guided Surrey to fourth place in the Britannic Assurance Championship and into the semi-finals of the Benson and Hedges Cup.

Those achievements would, for many counties, reflect a summer of achievement. To the denizens of The Oval, however, it was another season of unfulfilment from a side possessing an envied strike force in Sylvester Clarke and Tony Gray, and a powerful batting line-up. Lack of an experienced spinner, allied to a curious shortage of confidence, diluted their potency. This was no reflection on Greig, whose dressing-room presence was a major bonus. He proved to be a tough, decision-making cricketer who won the respect of his men and eliminated the thread of disharmony which lingered in 1986.

Surrey's failure to mount a serious bid for the Championship could be traced to an unproductive week in the second half of August. First, Kent's last-wicket pair held out for the final hour, and then Somerset denied them 11 runs off the last over. Those setbacks took on a greater significance when, after rain washed them out at Hove, the next three matches were won and Surrey moved into third place with one game to play. Gambling for a fourth victory, Greig set Lancashire a challenging, some felt too challenging, target, but he was let down by his bowlers in the middle of a drizzle-dampened run-chase. Surrey, however, accumulated 73 bowling points and 65 for batting, figures second only to Nottinghamshire, the champions. Both totals were better than the previous year, when Surrey held on to third place in the final hour of the season.

Clarke (66 Championship wickets) and Gray (44) both bowled impressively, but because of the registration regulations, they could never operate in tandem. Even taking into account the developing promise of Martin Bicknell, Surrey were a trifle short of fire-power at one end. In the batting, there was, it seemed, a hint of complacency. Alec Stewart,

Monte Lynch and Trevor Jesty all passed 1,000 runs but should really have recorded higher aggregates. With such depth in batting, enhanced by the return of David Smith to The Oval, Surrey automatically geared their strategy to fast scoring, each batsman knowing that there was run-power in reserve if he failed.

Jack Richards had a fine season, finishing second in the national wicket-keeping list. He effected a career-best ten dismissals in the home match against Sussex at the end of June and was the central figure in a piece of Surrey history, putting on 262 against Kent with Keith Medlycott at more than 5 an over to set a record for the county's seventh wicket. It was also Surrey's first record wicket partnership since 1936, in itself a quite extraordinary statistic.

Medlycott, while emerging as an extremely useful lower-order batsman, took only 38 wickets in the Championship with his left-arm spin. More was expected of him as the successor to Pocock as Surrey's major spinner. Because of this shortfall, Surrey often found themselves playing on turning pitches with the opposition content that there would be no serious retaliation. Chris Bullen, with off-breaks, collected nineteen wickets in addition to producing useful all-round performances in the limited-overs games. As were all the bowlers, he was supported by outstanding close catching.

There was continued improvement in the Refuge Assurance League, equal seventh being attained after an unsatisfactory twelfth in 1986 and last in 1985. There were two remarkable Sunday finishes. Lynch, the most occasional of bowlers, conjured two wickets in the final over to beat Northamptonshire at Guildford. But when Surrey needed 4 runs off the last over to beat Gloucestershire, fate conspired against them. Walsh took four wickets in the September twilight.

During the year, Micky Stewart, Surrey's Director of Cricket, left to take up his appointment as England's team manager, but the youth policy he had nurtured was showing handsome dividends before the sun set on the 1987 season. Surprisingly not retained for the county, Jesty, at 39, became a victim of it. Surrey calculated that to retain a middle-order batsman in his advancing cricketing years might retard the development, and so damage the ambition, of younger claimants. – David Field.

556

SURREY 1987

[Bill Smith

Back row: J. Deary (*physiotherapist*), N. M. Kendrick, P. D. Atkins, D. J. Bicknell, J. D. Robinson, G. E. Brown, T. Billson (*scorer*). *Middle row*: G. G. Arnold (*coach*), N. J. Falkner, A. J. Stewart, C. K. Bullen, M. A. Feltham, K. T. Medlycott, D. M. Ward, Zahid Sadiq, C. E. Waller (*coach*). *Front row*: D. M. Smith, T. E. Jesty, C. J. Richards, I. A. Greig (*captain*), G. S. Clinton, S. T. Clarke, M. A. Lynch, D. J. Thomas. *Insets*: M. P. Bicknell, A. H. Gray.

SURREY RESULTS

All first-class matches – Played 26: Won 7, Lost 4, Drawn 15.

County Championship matches – Played 24: Won 7, Lost 4, Drawn 13.

Bonus points – Batting 65, Bowling 73.

*Competition placings – Britannic Assurance County Championship, 4th; NatWest Bank Trophy,
2nd round; Benson and Hedges Cup, s-f; Refuge Assurance League, 7th equal.*

BRITANNIC ASSURANCE CHAMPIONSHIP AVERAGES

BATTING

	Birthplace	M	I	NO	R	HI	Avge
‡A. J. Stewart	Merton	21	33	2	1,217	132	39.25
‡D. M. Smith	Balham	16	26	4	847	121*	38.50
‡C. J. Richards	Penzance	18	22	4	683	172*	37.94
D. J. Bicknell	Guildford	11	19	3	599	105	37.43
‡T. E. Jesty	Gosport	23	35	5	1,074	124*	35.80
‡M. A. Lynch	Georgetown, BG	24	37	5	1,057	128*	33.03
‡G. S. Clinton	Sidcup	17	28	2	825	93	31.73
K. T. Medlycott	Whitechapel	23	28	5	719	153	31.26
‡I. A. Greig	Queenstown, SA	24	33	5	778	88	27.78
G. E. Brown	Balham	4	5	4	26	8*	26.00
C. K. Bullen	Clapham	9	11	3	172	57	21.50
‡D. J. Thomas	Solihull	16	16	4	220	49	18.33
D. M. Ward	Croydon	5	9	0	141	44	15.66
M. P. Bicknell	Guildford	14	14	7	108	18	15.42
§‡A. H. Gray	Port-of-Spain, Trinidad	9	7	3	54	35	13.50
N. J. Falkner	Redhill	3	4	0	47	29	11.75
M. A. Feltham	St John's Wood	10	11	3	90	18	11.25
§§S. T. Clarke	Christ Church, Barbados	14	15	1	131	44	9.35

Also batted: C. S. Mays (*Brighton*) (2 matches) 5*, 2; R. J. Doughty (*Bridlington*) (1 match)
0, 5.

* Signifies not out. ‡ Denotes county cap. § Not qualified for England.

The following played a total of ten three-figure innings for Surrey in County Championship
matches – A. J. Stewart 3, M. A. Lynch 2, D. J. Bicknell 1, T. E. Jesty 1, K. T. Medlycott 1,
C. J. Richards 1, D. M. Smith 1.

BOWLING

	O	M	R	W	BB	Avge
A. H. Gray	261.1	56	667	44	5-46	15.15
S. T. Clarke	440.4	121	1,123	66	8-62	17.01
T. E. Jesty	72.4	11	212	10	6-81	21.20
M. P. Bicknell	363.2	94	997	42	6-63	23.73
C. K. Bullen	190.4	57	504	19	6-119	26.52
M. A. Feltham	377.5	91	1,108	35	4-24	31.65
I. A. Greig	397.4	82	1,220	35	4-47	34.85
K. T. Medlycott	485.4	134	1,469	38	5-103	38.65
D. J. Thomas	348	58	1,205	31	5-73	38.87

Also bowled: R. J. Doughty 26-3-76-0; M. A. Lynch 51.3-8-184-2; C. S. Mays
56-7-201-2.

Wicket-keepers: C. J. Richards 58 ct, 6 st; G. E. Brown 6 ct; A. J. Stewart 8 ct; D. M. Ward
3 ct.

Leading Fielders: M. A. Lynch 23, I. A. Greig 16.

At Nottingham, April 25, 26, 27. SURREY drew with NOTTINGHAMSHIRE.

SURREY v DERBYSHIRE

At The Oval, April 29, 30, May 1. Surrey won by an innings and 3 runs. Surrey 24 pts, Derbyshire 5 pts. Toss: Derbyshire. Derbyshire scarcely had a moment to settle before Clarke's biting pace undid them on a pitch assisting the quicker bowlers. However, helped by a rousing 72 in 58 balls by Warner, with 54 coming in boundaries, they made a partial recovery to 217. This was largely offset by a 74-run start by Clinton and Smith, which they improved to 137 next day, and Greig, who had been awarded his county cap the previous evening by Surrey's president, Alec Bedser, lifted his side to 361 with an invigorating 88 in 106 deliveries. Only Morris and later Newman displayed any real appetite for the fight that was needed for Derbyshire to avoid an innings defeat, and on the final morning Surrey required only 80 minutes to provide Greig with a victory in his first home match as captain.

Close of play: First day, Surrey 74-0 (G. S. Clinton 38*, D. M. Smith 31*); Second day, Derbyshire 84-5 (J. E. Morris 37*, P. G. Newman 17*).

Derbyshire

*K. J. Barnett b Clarke	8	– c Richards b Thomas	12
†B. J. M. Maher c Richards b Feltham	6	– c Stewart b Clarke	0
B. Roberts c Richards b Clarke	0	– c sub b Clarke	13
J. E. Morris c Smith b Clarke	11	– c Richards b Thomas	37
I. S. Anderson c Stewart b Feltham	51	– c Richards b Greig	1
R. Sharma c Richards b Clarke	11	– b Greig	0
P. G. Newman c Lynch b Thomas	16	– c Falkner b Feltham	32
A. E. Warner c Richards b Feltham	72	– c Richards b Clarke	14
M. Jean-Jacques c Lynch b Clarke	16	– b Clarke	25
O. H. Mortensen not out	11	– hit wkt b Clarke	2
D. E. Malcolm b Feltham	9	– not out	0
B 2, l-b 2, n-b 2	6	B 1, l-b 1, n-b 3	5

1/10 2/10 3/22 4/37 5/55   217   1/7 2/13 3/49 4/53 5/53   141
6/87 7/177 8/178 9/198   6/86 7/103 8/133 9/141

Bonus points – Derbyshire 2, Surrey 4.

Bowling: *First Innings*—Clarke 22-6-63-5; Feltham 22-10-63-4; Thomas 16-5-43-1; Greig 12-5-38-0; Medlycott 3-0-6-0. *Second Innings*—Clarke 21-6-64-5; Thomas 14-1-36-2; Feltham 13.4-4-31-1; Greig 3-1-8-2.

Surrey

G. S. Clinton c Roberts b Jean-Jacques	72	M. A. Feltham lbw b Mortensen	10
D. M. Smith lbw b Jean-Jacques	74	K. T. Medlycott not out	2
A. J. Stewart b Warner	9	S. T. Clarke c Morris b Jean-Jacques	8
N. J. Falkner c and b Jean-Jacques	14		
†C. J. Richards c Maher b Anderson	26	B 8, l-b 8, w 1, n-b 4	21
*I. A. Greig b Mortensen	88		
D. J. Thomas c Maher b Malcolm	31	1/137 2/154 3/179 4/183 5/263	361
M. A. Lynch c and b Malcolm	6	6/333 7/335 8/342 9/352	

Bonus points – Surrey 4, Derbyshire 3 (Score at 100 overs: 342-8).

Bowling: Warner 14-4-47-1; Jean-Jacques 16-3-39-4; Malcolm 20-1-87-2; Newman 16-0-64-0; Mortensen 26-8-47-2; Anderson 10-0-42-1; Roberts 4-0-19-0.

Umpires: D. J. Constant and K. J. Lyons.

At The Oval, May 2, 3, 4. SURREY drew with PAKISTANIS (See Pakistani tour section).

At Taunton, May 6, 7, 8. SURREY drew with SOMERSET.

At Birmingham, May 20, 21, 22. SURREY lost to WARWICKSHIRE by seven wickets.

SURREY v ESSEX

At The Oval, May 23, 25, 26. Drawn. Surrey 7 pts, Essex 4 pts. Toss: Essex. After the first day was lost to rain, Surrey had trouble coping with the Essex seam bowlers on a pitch of erratic bounce which was to take on a nastier character. However, from 149 for seven they were revitalised by adventurous batting from Thomas and Medlycott, who added 50 for the eighth wicket. Clarke struck immediately, and next day he ravaged the Essex first innings to finish with a career-best analysis of seven for 31. Facing him was an ordeal from which the batsmen were happy to emerge with their bones in one piece. Many deliveries reared to head height, others sped through unpredictably low. Obliged to follow on, Essex must have harboured thoughts of a further battering, but unaccountably Clarke's penetration deserted him and, with the stoical Hardie sustaining the effort, they survived in relative comfort.

Close of play: First day, No play; Second day, Essex 16-1 (I. Redpath 9*, T. D. Topley 2*).

Surrey

N. J. Falkner c Fletcher b Lever	0	K. T. Medlycott not out	74
D. J. Bicknell lbw b Pringle	39	S. T. Clarke c Pringle b Topley	5
M. A. Lynch c Redpath b Lever	19	M. P. Bicknell not out	9
T. E. Jesty lbw b Topley	29	B 1, l-b 8	9
†D. M. Ward c Hardie b Pringle	7		
*I. A. Greig c East b Pringle	29	1/0 2/28 3/79	(9 wkts dec.) 260
D. J. Thomas c East b Childs	40	4/97 5/112 6/147	
C. K. Bullen b Pringle	0	7/149 8/199 9/214	

Bonus points – Surrey 3, Essex 4.

Bowling: Lever 19-3-63-2; Pringle 33-12-79-4; Topley 24-3-84-2; Miller 8-2-12-0; Childs 16-9-13-1.

Essex

C. Gladwin lbw b Clarke	0	– c Lynch b Greig	30
I. Redpath c Clarke b M. P. Bicknell	16	– c Ward b M. P. Bicknell	13
T. D. Topley c Jesty b Clarke	12		
B. R. Hardie b Clarke	2	– (3) b Clarke	53
*K. W. R. Fletcher b Clarke	15	– (4) c Lynch b Thomas	30
G. Miller c Medlycott b Greig	7	– (5) c Ward b Thomas	4
D. R. Pringle c Lynch b Jesty	21	– (6) not out	7
A. W. Lilley c D. J. Bicknell b Clarke	28	– (7) not out	8
†D. E. East c Bullen b Clarke	6		
J. K. Lever not out	11		
J. H. Childs c Medlycott b Clarke	0		
B 3, l-b 2, w 1	6	B 13, l-b 13, w 1, n-b 1	28

1/2 2/24 3/27 4/40 5/58	124	1/25 2/51 3/128	(5 wkts) 173
6/58 7/96 8/107 9/124		4/132 5/155	

Bonus points – Surrey 4.

Bowling: *First Innings*—Clarke 17-6-31-7; M. P. Bicknell 11-4-26-1; Greig 4-0-23-1; Thomas 9-2-30-0; Jesty 4-0-9-1. *Second Innings*—M. P. Bicknell 8-2-23-1; Clarke 12-4-41-1; Thomas 15-2-54-2; Greig 4-0-18-1; Medlycott 8-4-11-0; Bullen 4-4-0-0.

Umpires: R. Julian and K. J. Lyons.

At Tunbridge Wells, June 3, 4, 5. SURREY drew with KENT.

At Northampton, June 6, 8, 9. SURREY drew with NORTHAMPTONSHIRE.

SURREY v HAMPSHIRE

At The Oval, June 13, 15, 16. Drawn. Surrey 8 pts, Hampshire 4 pts. Toss: Hampshire. Surrey's hostile bowling had Hampshire in dreadful difficulty at 49 for six, but the parlous position was improved by Marshall's violent hitting, which was soon to be dampened by the storm that shortened the first day. Aymes, making his first-class début, celebrated his call-up by moving on to a half-century on Monday. The day, however, belonged to the young Surrey left-hander, Darren Bicknell. While his brother was in hospital with suspected appendicitis, he moved to within touching distance of a maiden century, which he duly completed on the third morning. Jesty hit a handsome 79 against his former county, putting on 140 in a spectacular hour with Greig, whose 79 came from only 44 balls and featured six sixes and five fours. However, what hopes Greig entertained of bowling out Hampshire again were countered by the pitch. It remained slow and reliable, and Chris Smith moulded an unbeaten hundred as the match moved serenely to its conclusion.

Close of play: First day, Hampshire 130-7 (A. N. Aymes 27*, T. M. Tremlett 9*); Second day, 188-1 (D. J. Bicknell 95*, A. J. Stewart 44*).

Hampshire

V. P. Terry c Clinton b Gray	0	– lbw b Thomas	7
C. L. Smith c M. P. Bicknell b Gray	6	– not out	102
*M. C. J. Nicholas c Gray b M. P. Bicknell	12	– lbw b Gray	21
D. R. Turner c Stewart b Thomas	1	– not out	20
R. A. Smith c Richards b Thomas	10		
K. D. James c Stewart b M. P. Bicknell	3		
M. D. Marshall c Richards b M. P. Bicknell	46		
†A. N. Aymes c Gray b Jesty	58		
T. M. Tremlett lbw b Gray	42		
R. J. Maru not out	1		
S. J. W. Andrew c Richards b Gray	3		
L-b 6, w 4, n-b 9	19	B 5, l-b 4, w 1, n-b 11	21
1/0 2/13 3/14 4/30 5/41	201	1/16 2/79 (2 wkts)	171
6/49 7/104 8/196 9/196			

Bonus points – Hampshire 2, Surrey 4.

Bowling: *First Innings*—Gray 22.3–7–40–4; Thomas 21–6–50–2; M. P. Bicknell 15–3–45–3; Greig 11–3–28–0; Medlycott 11–4–21–0; Lynch 3–2–7–0; Jesty 2–0–4–1. *Second Innings*—Gray 14–5–19–1; Thomas 13–0–57–1; Jesty 7–2–15–0; Medlycott 16–4–44–0; Greig 2–0–6–0; Lynch 6–0–21–0.

Surrey

D. J. Bicknell c Aymes b Andrew	105	*I. A. Greig c Nicholas b James	79
G. S. Clinton b C. L. Smith	37		
A. J. Stewart c Maru b Andrew	45	L-b 11, w 1, n-b 9	21
M. A. Lynch c Maru b Andrew	11		
T. E. Jesty not out	79	1/94 2/194 3/204 (6 wkts dec.)	383
†C. J. Richards c Maru b Andrew	6	4/229 5/243 6/383	

D. J. Thomas, K. T. Medlycott, A. H. Gray and M. P. Bicknell did not bat.

Bonus points – Surrey 4, Hampshire 2.

Bowling: Andrew 22–1–91–4; Maru 30–6–119–0; Marshall 14–3–51–0; Tremlett 9–0–38–0; James 13.3–1–61–1; C. L. Smith 6–1–12–1.

Umpires: B. J. Meyer and D. O. Oslear.

At Cambridge, June 17, 18, 19. SURREY drew with CAMBRIDGE UNIVERSITY.

SURREY v SUSSEX

At Guildford, June 27, 29, 30. Surrey won by 109 runs. Surrey 22 pts, Sussex 6 pts. Toss: Sussex. A pitch of pedestrian pace committed Surrey to a struggle for runs on the first day as the Sussex seam bowlers pecked away at the innings. Pigott, finishing with a spell of four for 4 in 28 balls, took five wickets in his second Championship match since completing a four-week suspension. Sussex were themselves soon perplexed at 40 for four, but Colin Wells and Gould retrieved the position and Surrey's eventual advantage was only 5. Enterprising batting by Clinton and Stewart was augmented by innings of more aggressive tenor from Richards and Greig, who fired off four sixes and five fours to score 56 in twenty minutes. The declaration left Sussex a challenging target of 308 in four and a half hours, and when 119 for eight at tea, they were obliged to plot a survival course. Pigott almost saw them through it safely, but with sixteen balls remaining, Richards stumped Heseltine to collect his tenth victim of the match, a career-best performance.

Close of play: First day, Sussex 95-4 (C. M. Wells 35*, I. J. Gould 23*); Second day, Surrey 174-4 (T. E. Jesty 23*, C. J. Richards 8*).

Surrey

D. J. Bicknell lbw b C. M. Wells	19	– lbw b Pigott	8
G. S. Clinton lbw b Pigott	32	– lbw b Pigott	61
A. J. Stewart c Green b Reeve	11	– c Gould b Pigott	58
M. A. Lynch c Moores b Reeve	8	– c Moores b Pigott	4
T. E. Jesty c Moores b C. M. Wells	73	– c A. P. Wells b Heseltine	43
†C. J. Richards c Standing b Heseltine	23	– b Heseltine	57
*I. A. Greig b Pigott	28	– c A. P. Wells b Standing	56
D. J. Thomas lbw b Pigott	2	– not out	0
K. T. Medlycott c Reeve b Pigott	4		
A. H. Gray not out	1		
M. P. Bicknell c A. P. Wells b Pigott	1		
B 1, l-b 3, w 2, n-b 3	9	B 1, l-b 11, w 1, n-b 2	15

1/38 2/57 3/74 4/79 5/127 211   1/27 2/138 3/139 (7 wkts dec.) 302
6/193 7/199 8/205 9/210   4/156 5/242
                                      6/277 7/302

Bonus points – Surrey 2, Sussex 4.

Bowling: *First Innings*—le Roux 12-2-43-0; Pigott 14-4-32-5; C. M. Wells 19-3-40-2; Reeve 19-4-51-2; Heseltine 15-4-41-1. *Second Innings*—le Roux 6-0-23-0; Pigott 24-3-93-4; Reeve 16-3-30-0; Heseltine 21-10-56-2; C. M. Wells 7-1-32-0; Standing 14-4-56-1.

Sussex

R. I. Alikhan lbw b Thomas	2	– lbw b Gray	38
A. M. Green c and b Thomas	1	– (7) c Richards b M. P. Bicknell	8
D. K. Standing c Richards b Gray	14	– (2) c Richards b Gray	7
A. P. Wells c Richards b Thomas	7	– c Medlycott b Gray	6
C. M. Wells c Richards b Gray	50	– c Richards b Greig	7
*I. J. Gould c Clinton b M. P. Bicknell	54	– c Richards b Gray	44
D. A. Reeve c Richards b Greig	21	– (3) lbw b M. P. Bicknell	10
G. S. le Roux not out	20	– b M. P. Bicknell	0
†P. Moores c Richards b M. P. Bicknell	7	– b Greig	0
A. C. S. Pigott c D. J. Bicknell b Gray	6	– not out	42
P. A. W. Heseltine c Greig b Gray	1	– st Richards b Medlycott	13
B 4, l-b 3, w 6, n-b 10	23	B 8, l-b 2, w 4, n-b 9	23

1/7 2/8 3/26 4/40 5/124 206   1/54 2/59 3/65 4/80 5/92 198
6/165 7/167 8/190 9/198   6/106 7/106 8/119 9/148

Bonus points – Sussex 2, Surrey 4.

Bowling: *First Innings*—Gray 21.4-4-56-4; Thomas 19-1-77-3; M. P. Bicknell 21-5-49-2; Greig 11-4-17-1. *Second Innings*—Gray 26-7-71-4; Thomas 7-3-17-0; M. P. Bicknell 15-2-43-3; Greig 16-3-42-2; Medlycott 9.2-5-15-1.

Umpires: R. A. White and P. B. Wight.

SURREY v MIDDLESEX

At The Oval, July 1, 2, 3. Surrey won by two wickets. Surrey 21 pts, Middlesex 5 pts. Toss: Middlesex. After the loss of Slack without a run on the board, the Middlesex innings was gradually consolidated by consistent middle-order batting. Downton's sturdy perseverance was rewarded with an unbeaten hundred while Butcher, having begun watchfully, made 74 off 90 balls. Middlesex declared immediately on the second morning, whereupon Darren Bicknell, Clinton and Stewart built profitably on a benign pitch. Progress was arrested by the Middlesex second-string spinners, Needham and Tufnell, but Greig opened up the game by declaring, 61 behind, 70 minutes before the close. Carr and Slack's opening stand of 173 prompted Downton to set Surrey 334 in 205 minutes, a stern requirement at first inspection, but the pitch had quickened along with Surrey's ambitions. An exhilarating partnership of 208 in 42 overs between Stewart and Lynch set up the chase, which ended thrillingly when Martin Bicknell hit a six and then took a single from the last two balls of the match, bowled by Needham.

Close of play: First day, Middlesex 337-8 (P. R. Downton 103*, W. W. Daniel 3*); Second day, Middlesex 54-0 (J. D. Carr 12*, W. N. Slack 40*).

Middlesex

W. N. Slack b Gray	0	– (2) c Greig b Medlycott	96
J. D. Carr c Greig b Gray	20	– (1) not out	123
K. R. Brown c Brown b Thomas	60	– not out	42
C. T. Radley lbw b Thomas	26		
R. O. Butcher c Stewart b Greig	74		
*†P. R. Downton not out	103		
A. Needham lbw b Thomas	0		
S. P. Hughes c Greig b M. P. Bicknell	15		
A. R. C. Fraser lbw b M. P. Bicknell	0		
W. W. Daniel not out	3		
B 11, l-b 7, w 1, n-b 17	36	B 3, l-b 4, w 1, n-b 3	11

1/0 2/35 3/110 4/133 5/229   (8 wkts. dec.) 337   1/173   (1 wkt dec.) 272
6/236 7/321 8/321

P. C. R. Tufnell did not bat.

Bonus points – Middlesex 3, Surrey 2 (Score at 100 overs: 288-6).

Bowling: *First Innings*—Gray 16–2–61–2; Thomas 23–4–54–3; M. P. Bicknell 24–6–63–2; Greig 12–4–20–1; Medlycott 35–4–121–0. *Second Innings*—Gray 4–0–12–0; Thomas 13–2–63–0; M. P. Bicknell 12–2–44–0; Medlycott 18.4–0–84–1; Greig 9–2–29–0; Lynch 8–0–33–0.

Surrey

D. J. Bicknell c Slack b Tufnell	61	– c Downton b Daniel	5
G. S. Clinton c Tufnell b Hughes	93	– b Hughes	0
A. J. Stewart not out	67	– b Needham	127
M. A. Lynch c Downton b Tufnell	15	– c Downton b Fraser	95
T. E. Jesty c Downton b Tufnell	15	– c Brown b Needham	29
*I. A. Greig c Tufnell b Needham	4	– c Butcher b Needham	17
D. J. Thomas not out	8	– c Butcher b Needham	6
K. T. Medlycott (did not bat)		– run out	9
A. H. Gray (did not bat)		– not out	9
M. P. Bicknell (did not bat)		– not out	5
B 3, l-b 3, w 2, n-b 5	13	B 9, l-b 12, w 2, n-b 2	25

1/120 2/195 3/229 4/247 5/254   (5 wkts. dec.) 276   1/4 2/15 3/223 4/261   (8 wkts) 334
5/286 6/290 7/306 8/319

†G. E. Brown did not bat.

Bonus points – Surrey 3, Middlesex 2 (Score at 100 overs: 262-5).

Bowling: *First Innings*—Daniel 6–0–20–0; Hughes 15–3–51–1; Fraser 16–4–46–0; Needham 34–9–68–1; Tufnell 33–7–85–3. *Second Innings*—Daniel 17–3–71–1; Hughes 7–0–36–1; Tufnell 15–2–73–0; Needham 18–0–96–4; Fraser 5–0–37–1.

Umpires: R. A. White and P. B. Wight.

SURREY v LEICESTERSHIRE

At The Oval, July 4, 6, 7. Leicestershire won by an innings and 24 runs. Leicestershire 24 pts, Surrey 3 pts. Toss: Surrey. Put in, Leicestershire on Saturday had the best of the pitch and conditions, but Monday morning provided a steamy haze which helped Agnew capture five wickets in 22 deliveries as the ball swung freely. Surrey followed on 211 behind – the deficit would have been greater but for the stoical Stewart and Clarke – and Leicestershire continued to flourish through a combination of spin, seam and pace. The rout was complete 70 minutes into the third day.

Close of play: First day, Surrey 26-0 (G. S. Clinton 14*, D. J. Bicknell 7*); Second day, Surrey 154-5 (I. A. Greig 22*, D. J. Thomas 10*).

Leicestershire

R. A. Cobb c Stewart b Clarke	47	†P. Whitticase not out 24
N. E. Briers lbw b Thomas	10	J. P. Agnew c Medlycott b M. P. Bicknell 8
*P. Willey c Greig b Clarke	82	
J. J. Whitaker c Clarke b M. P. Bicknell	46	B 8, l-b 9, w 1, n-b 3 21
T. J. Boon c Clinton b Medlycott	36	
P. B. Clift c Brown b M. P. Bicknell	47	1/24 2/144 3/155 (8 wkts dec.) 339
P. A. J. DeFreitas c M. P. Bicknell		4/226 5/246 6/274
b Medlycott	18	7/327 8/339

G. J. F. Ferris and P. M. Such did not bat.

Bonus points – Leicestershire 4, Surrey 3.

Bowling: Clarke 24–9–46–2; Thomas 25–3–88–1; Greig 4–1–24–0; M. P. Bicknell 15.4–1–47–3; Medlycott 31–7–117–2.

Surrey

D. J. Bicknell lbw b Agnew	7	– lbw b Ferris	3
G. S. Clinton c Willey b DeFreitas	15	– b Such	37
A. J. Stewart c Whitticase b Clift	39	– c Willey b Such	9
M. A. Lynch c Whitticase b Agnew	0	– c Boon b Clift	48
T. E. Jesty b Agnew	2	– b Ferris	4
*I. A. Greig c Briers b Agnew	2	– c sub b Ferris	25
D. J. Thomas c Whitticase b DeFreitas	1	– c Whitticase b Ferris	10
K. T. Medlycott b Agnew	0	– c Whitticase b Ferris	0
S. T. Clarke c Whitticase b Ferris	44	– c Whitaker b DeFreitas	2
M. P. Bicknell c Willey b Ferris	0	– not out	16
†G. E. Brown not out	4	– lbw b Clift	8
L-b 6, w 3, n-b 5	14	B 1, l-b 11, w 9, n-b 4	25

1/27 2/27 3/27 4/29 5/34   128   1/5 2/45 3/92 4/99 5/133   187
6/36 7/37 8/102 9/116   6/154 7/154 8/159 9/166

Bonus points – Leicestershire 4.

Bowling: *First Innings*—DeFreitas 15–5–27–2; Agnew 12–3–37–5; Ferris 12–1–53–2; Such 1–0–1–0; Clift 2–1–4–1. *Second Innings*—DeFreitas 22–8–44–1; Ferris 17–5–37–5; Clift 20–4–47–2; Such 24–11–39–2; Willey 6–2–8–0.

Umpires: J. H. Hampshire and B. Leadbeater.

SURREY v YORKSHIRE

At The Oval, July 15, 16, 17. Drawn. Surrey 8 pts, Yorkshire 1 pt. Toss: Surrey. Yorkshire, Championship leaders and winners of the Benson and Hedges Cup the previous Saturday, were brought down from such dizzy heights by the fine seam bowling of Greig. The Surrey captain's four wickets, after he had put the visitors in, sustained an all-round team effort which had Yorkshire out for their lowest total in two years. Stewart drove home Surrey's advantage against an ineffectual attack weakened by the absence, until late in the day, of Sidebottom. He had been concussed, as well as dismissed, after deflecting a ball from Clarke on to his helmet. Stewart, having shared a stand of 114 with Smith, reached his hundred off 141 balls and figured in another century partnership with Lynch as he extended his stay at the crease to four hours three minutes. Surrey, in a position to press for an innings victory, were thwarted by the weather, which allowed only five overs' play on the final day.

Close of play: First day, Surrey 223-2 (A. J. Stewart 123*, M. A. Lynch 50*); Second day, Yorkshire 4-0 (M. D. Moxon 0*, A. A. Metcalfe 2*).

Yorkshire

M. D. Moxon c Richards b Clarke	2	– not out	14
A. A. Metcalfe c Thomas b Bicknell	15	– not out	4
R. J. Blakey b Thomas	16		
K. Sharp c Richards b Greig	8		
J. D. Love c Lynch b Greig	6		
†D. L. Bairstow c Greig b Thomas	1		
*P. Carrick b Greig	20		
A. Sidebottom c Greig b Clarke	16		
P. J. Hartley c Richards b Greig	27		
P. W. Jarvis run out	2		
S. D. Fletcher not out	4		
B 1, l-b 3	4	B 1, n-b 3	4

1/15 2/19 3/44 4/50 5/51   121   (no wkt) 22
6/51 7/81 8/87 9/92

Bonus points – Surrey 4.

Bowling: *First Innings*—Clarke 13-6-30-2; Thomas 10-2-19-2; Bicknell 6-2-21-1; Greig 11.2-3-47-4. *Second Innings*—Thomas 4-1-9-0; Bicknell 1-0-2-0; Clarke 2-0-10-0.

Surrey

G. S. Clinton b Hartley	6	†C. J. Richards not out	25
D. M. Smith b Jarvis	39	L-b 6, n-b 1	7
A. J. Stewart c Bairstow b Sidebottom	132		
M. A. Lynch not out	87	1/7 2/121 3/234	(4 wkts dec.) 303
T. E. Jesty c Metcalfe b Sidebottom	7	4/248	

*I. A. Greig, D. J. Thomas, K. T. Medlycott, S. T. Clarke and M. P. Bicknell did not bat.

Bonus points – Surrey 4, Yorkshire 1.

Bowling: Jarvis 19-4-77-1; Hartley 16-2-66-1; Fletcher 16-1-68-0; Carrick 7-3-15-0; Moxon 7-0-23-0; Sidebottom 17-3-47-2; Love 1-0-1-0.

Umpires: D. R. Shepherd and A. G. T. Whitehead.

At Cardiff, July 18, 20, 21. SURREY beat GLAMORGAN by 65 runs.

SURREY v WORCESTERSHIRE

At The Oval, July 22, 23, 24. Drawn. Surrey 3 pts, Worcestershire 1 pt. Toss: Worcestershire. Both sides tried in vain to wring a positive result from a match which did not begin until 4.20 on the second afternoon, only for rain at tea on the final day to end Worcestershire's attempt to make 261 in a minimum of 67 overs. With Dilley, Radford and Botham all required by England for the Birmingham Test, Clinton and Smith were largely untroubled as they put on 80 from twenty overs, but against the spin of Illingworth and Hick, they could manage only 19 from the day's last nineteen overs. Smith progressed to an unbeaten hundred on the third day, while a crisp 76 in 66 balls from Jesty formed the basis of their partnership of 120 in 65 minutes.

Close of play: First day, No play; Second day, Surrey 99-0 (G. S. Clinton 32* D. M. Smith 57*).

Surrey

G. S. Clinton retired hurt	32	D. J. Thomas not out	1
D. M. Smith not out	121		
A. J. Stewart c D'Oliveira b Pridgeon	0	L-b 9, w 1, n-b 3	13
M. A. Lynch c Hick b Pridgeon	3		
T. E. Jesty c D'Oliveira b Hick	76	1/99 2/111 3/231	(4 wkts dec.) 260
*I. A. Greig c Curtis b Hick	14	4/257	

†C. J. Richards, K. T. Medlycott, M. A. Feltham and S. T. Clarke did not bat.

Bonus points – Surrey 3, Worcestershire 1.

Bowling: Pridgeon 16–2–41–2; Newport 9–0–53–0; McEwan 6–0–25–0; Hick 27–6–87–2; Illingworth 16.1–4–45–0.

Surrey forfeited their second innings.

Worcestershire

Worcestershire forfeited their first innings.

T. S. Curtis b Clarke	13	M. J. Weston not out	0
G. J. Lord lbw b Feltham	21		
G. A. Hick lbw b Greig	30	L-b 8	8
D. B. D'Oliveira b Lynch	12		
*P. A. Neale not out	17	1/30 2/66 3/74 4/97	(4 wkts) 101

†S. J. Rhodes, P. J. Newport, R. K. Illingworth, S. M. McEwan and A. P. Pridgeon did not bat.

Bowling: Clarke 11–2–25–1; Thomas 8–2–13–0; Feltham 5–2–10–1; Greig 4–1–20–1; Medlycott 6–2–17–0; Lynch 5–2–8–1.

Umpires: H. D. Bird and J. H. Harris.

At Lord's, August 1, 3, 4. SURREY drew with MIDDLESEX.

At Cheltenham, August 5, 6, 7. SURREY lost to GLOUCESTERSHIRE by 52 runs.

At Chesterfield, August 8, 10, 11. SURREY drew with DERBYSHIRE.

SURREY v KENT

At The Oval, August 15, 17, 18. Drawn. Surrey 5 pts, Kent 7 pts. Toss: Surrey. The match began on a historical note for Surrey but ended on a frustrating one when Kent's last pair held out for a draw. Surrey, having lost half their first-innings batting for 110, were taken towards a formidable 473 for seven in 97 overs by the daring and determined efforts of Richards and

Medlycott, whose stand of 262 at more than 5 an over was a record for Surrey's seventh wicket, surpassing the 200 of T. F. Shepherd and J. W. Hitch, also against Kent, in 1921. It was Surrey's first record wicket partnership since 1936, and both batsmen posted career-best scores, Richards hitting 23 fours in his 172 not out and Medlycott seventeen fours in his 153. On a rain-interrupted second day, Surrey were met by a more sombre innings from Benson (thirteen fours), who needed 86 balls to move from 80 to his fifth hundred of the season. Hinks (fourteen fours) just missed three figures as they added 180 for the second wicket. When Kent declared, 132 behind, Smith bludgeoned a 92-ball 79 not out so that Kent were set 317 in 70 overs. Sustained for a long time by Tavaré and Cowdrey, they belatedly lost three wickets in nine balls and required Igglesden and Jarvis to survive from the eighth over of the final hour.

Close of play: First day, Kent 36-0 (M. R. Benson 22*, N. R. Taylor 11*); Second day, Kent 341-6 (E. A. E. Baptiste 7*, S. A. Marsh 17*).

Surrey

G. S. Clinton c Marsh b Baptiste	24	– c Cowdrey b Igglesden	14
D. M. Smith b Igglesden	2	– not out	79
A. J. Stewart b Igglesden	0	– b Jarvis	12
M. A. Lynch c Marsh b Jarvis	10		
T. E. Jesty c Cowdrey b Igglesden	34	– (4) c Marsh b Davis	29
†C. J. Richards not out	172	– c Taylor b Davis	0
*I. A. Greig c Marsh b Baptiste	47	– not out	18
K. T. Medlycott c Baptiste b Cowdrey	153	– (5) c Aslett b Davis	29
C. K. Bullen not out	12		
B 9, l-b 1, w 4, n-b 5	19	L-b 3	3

1/25 2/25 3/40 4/56 5/110   (7 wkts dec.) 473   1/20 2/47 3/105   (5 wkts dec.) 184
6/191 7/453   4/157 5/158

M. A. Feltham and M. P. Bicknell did not bat.

Bonus points – Surrey 4, Kent 3.

Bowling: *First Innings*—Igglesden 16-1-77-3; Baptiste 21-1-99-2; Jarvis 17-1-83-1; Davis 19-2-97-0; Cowdrey 12-1-61-1; Aslett 12-2-46-0. *Second Innings*—Igglesden 5-0-24-1; Jarvis 7-0-34-1; Baptiste 11-1-55-0; Davis 9-0-68-3.

Kent

M. R. Benson c Richards b Feltham	131	– b Feltham	17
N. R. Taylor b Greig	38	– c Richards b Bicknell	4
S. G. Hinks c Richards b Feltham	97	– c and b Medlycott	22
C. J. Tavaré c Richards b Bicknell	10	– b Bullen	84
D. G. Aslett c and b Medlycott	15	– c Richards b Medlycott	21
*C. S. Cowdrey c Bullen b Feltham	12	– b Medlycott	64
E. A. E. Baptiste not out	7	– c Bicknell b Medlycott	1
†S. A. Marsh not out	17	– c Greig b Bullen	3
A. P. Igglesden (did not bat)		– not out	0
R. P. Davis (did not bat)		– b Medlycott	0
K. B. S. Jarvis (did not bat)		– not out	0
B 9, l-b 2, w 1, n-b 2	14	B 1, w 1, n-b 2	4

1/92 2/272 3/281 4/296   (6 wkts dec.) 341   1/19 2/23 3/56   (9 wkts) 220
5/317 6/317   4/120 5/186 6/187
                                                                                 7/219 8/219 9/219

Bonus points – Kent 4, Surrey 1 (Score at 100 overs: 311-4).

Bowling: *First Innings*—Feltham 27-6-79-3; Bicknell 17-5-61-1; Medlycott 19-2-55-1; Bullen 21-8-44-0; Greig 13-1-47-1; Jesty 3-1-14-0; Lynch 12-2-40-0. *Second Innings*—Feltham 12-2-59-1; Bicknell 9-3-20-1; Medlycott 29-9-103-5; Bullen 17-6-37-2.

Umpires: J. H. Hampshire and D. Lloyd.

SURREY v SOMERSET

At The Oval, August 19, 20, 21. Drawn. Surrey 7 pts, Somerset 6 pts. Toss: Somerset. For the second time in a week, Surrey had victory snatched from their grasp. Chasing a target of 217 in 36 overs, they needed 11 from the last one but lost three wickets for 5 runs and held on because Clinton, despite a fractured finger, came in last. Stewart's third Championship hundred of the summer, from 174 balls with thirteen fours, earned Surrey a useful if not imposing first-innings lead of 75. Somerset had been sustained by Hardy and Roebuck as Bicknell returned career-best figures. Roebuck's second fifty was overshadowed by a stylish first Championship hundred from the Australian all-rounder, Waugh. As Somerset attempted to defend the wide open spaces of The Oval by setting far-flung fields, Stewart aggressively added 93 to his hundred, but in the end it was Clinton's stoicism for which Surrey were most grateful.

Close of play: First day, Surrey 28-0 (G. S. Clinton 14*, D. M. Smith 7*); Second day, Somerset 96-1 (P. M. Roebuck 54*, J. J. E. Hardy 13*).

Somerset

N. A. Felton c Stewart b Clarke	4	– c Jesty b Greig ... 22
*P. M. Roebuck b Greig	54	– lbw b Clarke ... 59
J. J. E. Hardy c Stewart b Bicknell	59	– c Doughty b Clarke ... 16
R. J. Harden c Stewart b Greig	0	– c Stewart b Clarke ... 0
S. R. Waugh b Bicknell	8	– not out ... 111
N. J. Pringle c Stewart b Bicknell	30	– c Stewart b Clarke ... 0
†N. D. Burns c Lynch b Clarke	9	– c sub b Clarke ... 0
V. J. Marks not out	27	– b Medlycott ... 35
G. D. Rose c Stewart b Bicknell	6	– c Jesty b Greig ... 7
G. V. Palmer c Greig b Bicknell	0	– c Greig b Medlycott ... 0
A. N. Jones b Bicknell	9	– c Doughty b Bicknell ... 15
B 1, l-b 8, w 1, n-b 6	16	B 13, l-b 10, w 3 ... 26

1/5 2/98 3/100 4/121 5/146   222   1/53 2/99 3/99 4/110 5/110   291
6/163 7/192 8/204 9/204   6/114 7/215 8/234 9/239

Bonus points – Somerset 2, Surrey 4.

Bowling: *First Innings*—Clarke 22-6-49-2; Bicknell 24.2-6-63-6; Doughty 13-3-38-0; Greig 28-9-57-2; Medlycott 5-2-6-0. *Second Innings*—Clarke 32-11-74-5; Bicknell 27-7-76-1; Doughty 13-0-38-0; Greig 23-2-64-2; Medlycott 13-9-16-2.

Surrey

G. S. Clinton c Burns b Marks	66	– (11) not out ... 0
D. M. Smith c Waugh b Rose	7	– c Marks b Rose ... 4
†A. J. Stewart st Burns b Marks	105	– c Harden b Jones ... 93
M. A. Lynch c Roebuck b Rose	1	– (1) lbw b Rose ... 9
D. M. Ward b Waugh	17	– b Waugh ... 43
K. T. Medlycott b Palmer	13	– (7) b Waugh ... 14
*I. A. Greig c Pringle b Marks	15	– (6) c Hardy b Waugh ... 7
T. E. Jesty c Rose b Palmer	21	– (4) c Harden b Marks ... 17
R. J. Doughty c and b Palmer	6	– (8) c Burns b Jones ... 5
S. T. Clarke not out	6	– (9) c Burns b Jones ... 1
M. P. Bicknell b Palmer	18	– (10) not out ... 0
B 10, l-b 6, w 6, n-b 6	28	B 7, l-b 10, w 1 ... 18

1/28 2/148 3/156 4/173 5/196   297   1/15 2/20 3/50   (9 wkts) 211
6/241 7/273 8/273 9/273   4/137 5/153 6/205
    7/210 8/211 9/211

Bonus points – Surrey 3, Somerset 4.

Bowling: *First Innings*—Jones 17-2-51-0; Rose 15-3-48-2; Waugh 18-5-63-1; Palmer 16-3-63-4; Marks 16-4-56-3. *Second Innings*—Jones 7-0-55-3; Rose 8-0-29-2; Waugh 11-0-48-3; Marks 7-0-42-1; Palmer 3-0-20-0.

Umpires: D. Lloyd and R. Palmer.

At Hove, August 22, 24, 25. SURREY drew with SUSSEX.

SURREY v GLAMORGAN

At The Oval, August 26, 27, 28. Surrey won by five wickets. Surrey 23 pts, Glamorgan 5 pts. Toss: Surrey. Although making heavy weather of scoring 43 to win, Surrey enhanced their prospects of being among the Championship prizemoney winners. Gray's pace was the key to their victory, although Glamorgan's Base made his presence felt by claiming four late wickets to increase his return to nine for the match and to eighteen for a successful week of medium-fast bowling. Glamorgan lost six wickets on a cheerless first day and were dismissed for 152 on an even bleaker second. Half-centuries from Smith and Medlycott helped Surrey to a lead of 136, but on the final day Holmes played grimly in the cause of the Welsh county, using up 59 overs and almost four and a half hours over his 45. When he departed, lbw to Feltham soon after tea on the final afternoon, Surrey were home.

Close of play: First day, Glamorgan 122-6 (J. Derrick 17*, C. P. Metson 19*); Second day, Glamorgan 1-0 (A. R. Butcher 1*, H. Morris 0*).

Glamorgan

A. R. Butcher c Feltham b Gray	7	– c Richards b Gray	10
*H. Morris b Gray	6	– c Richards b Greig	8
G. C. Holmes lbw b Feltham	4	– lbw b Feltham	45
M. P. Maynard lbw b Greig	20	– c Feltham b Gray	41
R. C. Ontong b Greig	14	– c M. P. Bicknell b Gray	14
P. A. Cottey lbw b Greig	1	– b Jesty b M. P. Bicknell	4
J. Derrick b Greig	20	– b Feltham	16
†C. P. Metson c Lynch b M. P. Bicknell	20	– b Gray	8
S. J. Base b Feltham	16	– c Richards b Gray	4
S. R. Barwick c M. P. Bicknell b Feltham	5	– b Feltham	1
S. Monkhouse not out	2	– not out	2
B 6, l-b 6, w 4, n-b 21	37	B 1, l-b 4, w 1, n-b 19	25
	152		178

1/18 2/22 3/34 4/62 5/68   152   1/18 2/35 3/100 4/117 5/127   178
6/87 7/126 8/126 9/149   6/151 7/164 8/164 9/167

Bonus points – Glamorgan 1, Surrey 4.

Bowling: *First Innings*—Gray 18-3–38–3; Feltham 20.2-3–58–3; M. P. Bicknell 10-4-15–1; Greig 13-1-29–3. *Second Innings*—Gray 24.2-2–57–5; Feltham 21-8-40–3; Greig 10-0-42–1; M. P. Bicknell 17-6-30–1; Jesty 2-1-4-0.

Surrey

D. J. Bicknell lbw b Base	5	– b Derrick	15
D. M. Smith c Maynard b Base	69	– b Base	5
A. J. Stewart c Metson b Derrick	44	– lbw b Base	0
M. A. Lynch lbw b Derrick	1	– c Cottey b Base	2
T. E. Jesty c Derrick b Monkhouse	5	– not out	15
†C. J. Richards lbw b Base	38	– b Base	1
*I. A. Greig c Cottey b Base	12	– not out	4
K. T. Medlycott c Butcher b Derrick	54		
M. A. Feltham c Maynard b Base	1		
A. H. Gray lbw b Monkhouse	35		
M. P. Bicknell not out	9		
B 5, l-b 2, w 3, n-b 5	15	L-b 3, n-b 1	4
	288	(5 wkts)	46

1/21 2/106 3/108 4/121 5/151   288   1/12 2/12 3/22   (5 wkts) 46
6/181 7/186 8/204 9/274   4/41 5/42

Bonus points – Surrey 3, Glamorgan 4.

Bowling: *First Innings*—Barwick 15-0-72–0; Base 23-3-67–5; Derrick 23-4-79–3; Monkhouse 8-0-34–2; Ontong 9-0-29-0. *Second Innings*—Barwick 4-1-12-0; Base 6.4-1-17–4; Derrick 3-0-14-1.

Umpires: K. E. Palmer and P. B. Wight.

At Colchester, August 29, 31, September 1. SURREY beat ESSEX by three wickets.

SURREY v NORTHAMPTONSHIRE

At The Oval, September 2, 3, 4. Surrey won by ten wickets. Surrey 24 pts, Northamptonshire 4 pts. Toss: Northamptonshire. Clarke's pace and penetration claimed six wickets on the last day, taking his total for the match to twelve and Surrey into third place on the Championship table with their third successive victory. Surrey were put on a sound footing when Lynch and Jesty stylishly stabilised the middle of their first innings with 136 in 26 overs. And a solid score of 304 took on an imposing air as Clarke and Martin Bicknell worked their way through the Northamptonshire order on the second day. Only Geoff Cook, and for a while Lamb, remained for any length of time. The last six wickets went for 7 runs in five overs, and when Northamptonshire followed on, the same bowlers had three more wickets in the bag by the close. Next day, only Lamb stood firm as Clarke moved unrelentingly towards career-best innings and match figures, leaving Darren Bicknell and Smith to complete the formalities for a maximum-points win.

Close of play: First day, Surrey 304; Second day, Northamptonshire 70-3 (A. J. Lamb 7*, R. J. Boyd-Moss 2*).

Surrey

D. J. Bicknell b Davis	7	– not out	24
D. M. Smith lbw b Davis	0	– not out	34
A. J. Stewart b Robinson	26		
M. A. Lynch b N. G. B. Cook	69		
T. E. Jesty b Smith	72		
†C. J. Richards c Ripley b N. G. B. Cook	0		
*I. A. Greig st Ripley b N. G. B. Cook	33		
K. T. Medlycott b Robinson	20		
M. A. Feltham not out	16		
S. T. Clarke lbw b Robinson	5		
M. P. Bicknell c Lamb b N. G. B. Cook	8		
B 5, l-b 20, w 1, n-b 22	48	B 2, l-b 3, n-b 1	6

1/3 2/24 3/42 4/178 5/179   **304**   (no wkt) **64**
6/217 7/261 8/268 9/275

Bonus points – Surrey 4, Northamptonshire 4.

Bowling: *First Innings*—Davis 22-2-83-2; Capel 9-3-26-0; Robinson 26-4-85-3; Smith 13-1-52-1; N. G. B. Cook 17.4-7-33-4. *Second Innings*—Davis 6-1-15-0; Robinson 3-0-18-0; N. G. B. Cook 5-0-19-0; Smith 3-1-6-0; G. Cook 0.1-0-1-0.

Northamptonshire

*G. Cook c Greig b M. P. Bicknell	51	– b Clarke	20
W. Larkins b Clarke	4	– c and b Clarke	30
R. J. Bailey c Lynch b M. P. Bicknell	12	– lbw b M. P. Bicknell	0
A. J. Lamb c D. J. Bicknell b Feltham	29	– b M. P. Bicknell	70
R. J. Boyd-Moss lbw b Clarke	16	– c Smith b Clarke	35
D. J. Capel c Richards b M. P. Bicknell	8	– b Clarke	28
†D. Ripley b Clarke	1	– c Lynch b Clarke	3
N. G. B. Cook not out	1	– c Stewart b Clarke	8
W. W. Davis c Medlycott b Clarke	0	– c Richards b Clarke	17
G. Smith c Clarke b M. P. Bicknell	1	– b Clarke	0
M. A. Robinson b M. P. Bicknell	0	– not out	0
B 3, l-b 4, w 6, n-b 1	14	B 4, l-b 13, n-b 2	19

1/8 2/34 3/91 4/110 5/130   **137**   1/57 2/58 3/64 4/164 5/172   **230**
6/135 7/136 8/136 9/137   6/183 7/204 8/229 9/229

Bonus points – Surrey 4.

Bowling: *First Innings*—Clarke 17-3-43-4; Feltham 12-3-36-1; M. P. Bicknell 21-10-28-5; Greig 8-1-23-0. *Second Innings*—Clarke 32.2-8-62-8; Feltham 18-4-47-0; M. P. Bicknell 22-7-72-2; Greig 4-0-11-0; Medlycott 8-2-21-0.

Umpires: M. J. Kitchen and K. J. Lyons.

At Manchester, September 9, 10, 11. SURREY lost to LANCASHIRE by four wickets.

SUSSEX

President: A. M. Caffyn
Chairman: R. M. Leadley
Chairman, Cricket & Ground Sub-Committee:
    A. N. C. Wadey
Secretary: 1987 – R. H. Renold
         1988 – N. Bett
    County Ground, Eaton Road,
    Hove BN3 3AN
    (Telephone: 0273-732161)
Captain: 1987 – I. J. Gould
       1988 – P. W. G. Parker
Coach: 1988 – J. A. Jameson

With only seven matches won in all the major competitions, this was a most disappointing season for Sussex. They were last in the Britannic Assurance Championship, last but one in the Refuge Assurance Sunday League, and were soon out of the Benson and Hedges Cup and the NatWest Bank Trophy, which they had won the previous year. Only one match was won in the Championship, and that away from home, at Worcester, at the beginning of May.

The summer ended on a definite down, with Sussex winning only one of their final 26 matches and Ian Gould, who had led them to victory at Lord's twelve months earlier, resigning after only one full season in charge. It had been a demanding season for a small staff, weakened by the loss of Imran Khan – with the Pakistani touring team – and by injuries to several key players. The absence of a full-time coach to replace Stewart Storey, who was dismissed during the close season, was also felt. It was among the reasons Gould gave for his resignation. He also felt that the pressure of captaincy and the handicap of a stubborn knee injury were preventing him from producing his best form.

However, he rounded off the season in a belligerent batting mood. His 111 against Northamptonshire was his highest score for Sussex, and he went from his fifty to his hundred off 25 balls. Other big scores that day, in a total of 408 for six declared, were 96 and 79 respectively from the Wells brothers, Colin and Alan. Colin Wells was considered by many shrewd judges to be unfortunate to miss selection for one of the winter tours. He scored more than 1,000 first-class runs for the fifth time in eight full seasons and took 52 wickets, a better record than some of the all-rounders chosen. During the "winter of discontent", he had initially refused a three-year contract, but in spite of receiving offers from five other counties, the stalwart all-rounder allowed his heart to rule his head, as he put it, and stayed.

Sussex had every reason to be grateful, for the contribution of the two brothers would have been sorely missed: 2,514 runs, 55 wickets and 26 catches in first-class matches alone. Among those runs was an unbroken fourth-wicket partnership of 303 off 75 overs against Kent at Hove, which bettered the previous Sussex record for brothers of 297, by J. H. and H. W. Parks for the fifth wicket against Hampshire at Portsmouth in

1937. The family connection between the Parks family and Sussex was revived when Jim Parks, son of J. H. and father of the current Hampshire wicket-keeper, took over as the club's marketing manager, having also helped to coach at Hove during the season. Other former Sussex players who turned out to help, cheerfully sharing the duties, were Ian Thomson and John Snow. At the end of the season, the club announced that John Jameson, the former Warwickshire batsman and a first-class umpire, would become the county's full-time coach.

The club's other pressing vacancy, that of captain, was quickly filled by the appointment of Paul Parker, who in addition to this new responsibility takes a benefit in 1988. He will be hoping to produce more consistent form than in last season's Championship matches, when he received a setback with his left arm being broken by a sharply rising ball from Daniel in the match against Middlesex at Hove.

Another to suffer from Daniel's hostility at Hove was Neil Lenham, who sustained a broken finger, having already missed the early matches following a knee operation. And when he returned to the side in August, at Sheffield, his season was immediately terminated by a broken bone in his left foot, the legacy of a yorker from Dennis. His injury was a cruel blow, for he had given a sample of his ability with a maiden hundred against the Pakistani tourists.

Garth le Roux, in his farewell season with Sussex, was another whose season was curtailed by injury. He did, however, leave Sussex supporters something to remember him by with a match-winning 83 not out from 54 balls in the Sunday League against Hampshire at Horsham. When Sussex needed 5 runs off the last ball, he hit it for the sixth of his sixes in the match. The big-hitting South African scored 354 runs in this competition at an average of 70.80.

On top of sadness at le Roux's departure came the announcement from Dermot Reeve that he felt he should seek another club because the Hove wicket did not suit his swing bowling. His best performances, he informed the committee, had been made away from the County Ground. There was, however, the good news that Imran Khan would be playing in the one-day matches in 1988. It is hoped that his experience will greatly assist other members of the attack, such as Andy Babington, Peter Heseltine and Simon Kimber.

At the end of the season, Sussex released Ian Waring, a fast bowler, left-arm spinner Courtney Ricketts, and Simon Myles, a batsman. Gould said that rebuilding was crucial if the county's position was to improve, with the immediate need being two or three seam bowlers, a class spin bowler and a top-quality batsman. Towards this end, Sussex signed the 25-year-old Surrey opener, Nick Falkner. Of those already with the county, Peter Moores had impressed as Gould's deputy behind the stumps, and Keith Greenfield, an eighteen-year-old Brighton-born batsman, who joined the staff on a youth training scheme, had earned his first-class début following a run of good scores in the Second XI. – Jack Arlidge.

SUSSEX 1987

[Bill Smith]

Back row: A. J. Pugh, S. J. S. Kimber, A. M. Babington, P. V. Boarer. Middle row: C. P. Cale (assistant coach), D. K. Standing, C. I. O. Ricketts, N. J. Lenham, I. C. Waring, S. D. Myles. Front row: D. A. Reeve, A. M. Green, A. C. S. Pigott, I. J. Gould (captain), A. P. Wells, P. W. G. Parker, C. M. Wells. Insets: P. A. W. Heseltine, R. I. Alikhan.

SUSSEX RESULTS

All first-class matches – Played 24: Won 1, Lost 8, Drawn 15. Abandoned 1.

County Championship matches – Played 23: Won 1, Lost 8, Drawn 14. Abandoned 1.

Bonus points – Batting 47, Bowling 56.

Competition placings – Britannic Assurance County Championship, 17th; NatWest Bank Trophy, 2nd round; Benson and Hedges Cup, 4th in Group D; Refuge Assurance League, 14th equal.

BRITANNIC ASSURANCE CHAMPIONSHIP AVERAGES

BATTING

	Birthplace	M	I	NO	R	HI	Avge
‡C. M. Wells	Newhaven	23	38	7	1,411	148*	45.51
‡D. A. Reeve	Kowloon, Hong Kong	16	22	8	576	87*	41.14
§‡G. S. le Roux	Cape Town, SA	13	15	5	375	73	37.50
‡I. J. Gould	Slough	21	29	5	792	111	33.00
‡A. P. Wells	Newhaven	22	36	4	1,003	161*	31.34
S. J. S. Kimber	Ormskirk	7	8	2	155	54	25.83
‡A. M. Green	Pulborough	20	36	2	821	115	24.14
R. I. Alikhan	London	18	33	3	663	78	22.10
N. J. Lenham	Worthing	3	4	3	22	12*	22.00
‡P. W. G. Parker	Bulawayo, S. Rhodesia	18	31	4	548	85	20.29
‡A. C. S. Pigott	London	19	27	4	456	62	19.82
P. Moores	Macclesfield	17	23	2	380	55	18.09
D. K. Standing	Brighton	16	28	3	438	56	17.52
P. A. W. Heseltine	Barnsley	17	18	3	172	26	11.46
K. Greenfield	Brighton	2	4	0	34	18	8.50
A. M. Babington	London	14	15	8	58	16	8.28

Also batted: S. D. Myles (*Mansfield*) (2 matches) 0, 1, 18*; C. I. O. Ricketts (*Kennington*) (3 matches) 29; I. C. Waring (*Chesterfield*) (2 matches) 0*, 0*, 0.

* *Signifies not out.* ‡ *Denotes county cap.* § *Not qualified for England.*

The following played a total of ten three-figure innings for Sussex in County Championship matches – C. M. Wells 5, A. P. Wells 3, I. J. Gould 1, A. M. Green 1.

BOWLING

	O	M	R	W	BB	Avge
G. S. le Roux	266.5	54	768	32	5-64	24.00
D. A. Reeve	427	103	1,145	41	7-37	27.92
C. M. Wells	527.1	96	1,483	52	6-34	28.51
A. C. S. Pigott	455.2	86	1,443	45	5-32	32.06
P. A. W. Heseltine	295.2	71	869	21	3-33	41.38
A. M. Babington	248.1	44	898	21	3-44	42.76
S. J. S. Kimber	136	19	550	12	2-13	45.83

Also bowled: R. I. Alikhan 0.1-0-4-0; I. J. Gould 1-0-1-0; A. M. Green 38-7-130-4; S. D. Myles 4-0-28-0; P. W. G. Parker 2.2-0-15-0; C. I. O. Ricketts 71.4-8-253-5; D. K. Standing 30.2-6-147-2; I. C. Waring 50-9-172-2; A. P. Wells 22-1-119-3.

Wicket-keepers: I. J. Gould 21 ct; P. Moores 10 ct.

Leading Fielders: P. W. G. Parker 15, C. M. Wells 15.

At Chesterfield, April 25, 26, 27. SUSSEX lost to DERBYSHIRE by nine wickets.

SUSSEX v GLOUCESTERSHIRE

At Hove, April 29, 30, May 1. Drawn. Sussex 3 pts, Gloucestershire 4 pts. Toss: Gloucestershire. With the loss of the second day to rain, the captains agreed on a formula which saw Sussex set a target of 281 in 59 overs. After eleven overs they were 42 for three, and they were in deeper trouble at 77 for five. However, Standing's 73-minute 45, a stubborn unbeaten innings by Reeve and determined batting from the tailenders defied the visiting bowlers. Bainbridge took three wickets to complement his first-day 134 which, coming off 208 balls, contained seventeen fours.

Close of play: First day, Sussex 14-0 (R. I. Alikhan 4*, A. M. Green 6*); Second day, No play.

Gloucestershire

A. W. Stovold c A. P. Wells b C. M. Wells	21	– not out	5
P. W. Romaines c Gould b C. M. Wells	81	– not out	9
C. W. J. Athey c Pigott b Reeve	11		
P. Bainbridge not out	134		
A. J. Wright lbw b C. M. Wells	0		
K. M. Curran c and b Ricketts	1		
J. W. Lloyds b Ricketts	51		
†R. C. Russell c A. P. Wells b le Roux	20		
L-b 5, n-b 5	10	W 4, n-b 1	5

1/35 2/52 3/192 4/192 5/196   (7 wkts dec.) 329   (no wkt dec.) 19
6/274 7/329

*D. A. Graveney, C. A. Walsh and D. V. Lawrence did not bat.

Bonus points – Gloucestershire 4, Sussex 3.

Bowling: *First Innings*—le Roux 11.3-0-39-1; Pigott 20-4-72-0; C. M. Wells 20-2-62-3; Reeve 13-2-44-1; Ricketts 24-3-82-2; Standing 5-1-25-0. *Second Innings*—Parker 2-0-10-0; A. P. Wells 2-0-9-0.

Sussex

R. I. Alikhan not out	33	– c Russell b Walsh	6
A. M. Green not out	27	– c Lloyds b Lawrence	0
P. W. G. Parker (did not bat)		– b Walsh	24
A. P. Wells (did not bat)		– c Lloyds b Curran	25
C. M. Wells (did not bat)		– c and b Bainbridge	13
D. K. Standing (did not bat)		– st Russell b Graveney	45
D. A. Reeve (did not bat)		– not out	32
A. C. S. Pigott (did not bat)		– c Russell b Bainbridge	19
*†H. J. Gould (did not bat)		– c Wright b Bainbridge	16
G. S. le Roux (did not bat)		– not out	0
B 4, l-b 1, n-b 3	8	B 4, l-b 2, n-b 6	12

(no wkt dec.) 68   1/1 2/25 3/41 4/67   (8 wkts) 192
5/77 6/141 7/170 8/188

C. I. O. Ricketts did not bat.

Bowling: *First Innings*—Lawrence 10-3-26-0; Walsh 9-4-19-0; Bainbridge 2-0-7-0; Curran 4-0-9-0; Lloyds 2-1-2-0; Russell 0.1-0-0-0. *Second Innings*—Lawrence 11-0-44-1; Walsh 16-3-59-2; Curran 6-0-30-1; Bainbridge 12-1-40-3; Graveney 12.5-7-13-1; Lloyds 1-1-0-0.

Umpires: R. Palmer and D. R. Shepherd.

At Worcester, May 6, 7, 8. SUSSEX beat WORCESTERSHIRE by three wickets.

At Hove, May 16, 17, 18. SUSSEX drew with PAKISTANIS (See Pakistani tour section).

At Dartford, May 20, 21, 22. SUSSEX drew with KENT.

SUSSEX v MIDDLESEX

At Hove, May 23, 25, 26. Middlesex won by three wickets. Middlesex 22 pts, Sussex 7 pts. Toss: Middlesex. Sussex, on a cold Saturday, met hostile bowling by Daniel which left Parker with a broken left arm and Lenham with a broken index finger on his right hand. Standing, for 3 hours 42 minutes, and Alan Wells, with two sixes and fourteen fours in his 119, were their heroes, putting on 180 for the second wicket. Downton, batting for 194 minutes, provided the substance of the Middlesex reply, and on the last day, with the outfield fast, Alan Wells and Reeve put on 128 in 33 overs as Sussex sought to make a challenging yet sporting declaration. Middlesex's target was 256 from a minimum of 43 overs and they achieved it with two balls to spare, thanks to Butcher's 96-minute hundred off 73 balls. His 118, off 98 balls, contained four sixes and ten fours, and with Downton he put on 143 in twenty overs.

Close of play: First day, Middlesex 7-0 (W. N. Slack 5*, A. J. T. Miller 2*); Second day, Sussex 41-0 (D. K. Standing 17*, A. M. Green 19*).

Sussex

D. K. Standing b Hughes	53	– run out		27
A. M. Green c Downton b Daniel	4	– c Carr b Daniel		22
*P. W. G. Parker retired hurt	0			
A. P. Wells b Edmonds	119	– (3) not out		78
C. M. Wells c Daniel b Hughes	5	– (4) c Carr b Edmonds		18
N. J. Lenham retired hurt	3			
D. A. Reeve c Daniel b Edmonds	30	– (5) not out		54
G. S. le Roux c Downton b Fraser	26			
†P. Moores b Edmonds	0			
P. A. W. Heseltine c and b Edmonds	13			
A. M. Babington not out	0			
L-b 5, w 3, n-b 13	21	L-b 3, w 1, n-b 17		21

1/11 2/191 3/197 4/199 5/256   286   1/60 2/61 3/92   (3 wkts dec.) 220
6/260 7/260 8/286

Bonus points – Sussex 3, Middlesex 3 (Score at 100 overs: 278-7).

Bowling: *First Innings*—Daniel 21–4-83-1; Hughes 22-2-49-2; Fraser 25-7-62-1; Edmonds 34-9-87-4. *Second Innings*—Hughes 15-5-35-0; Daniel 15-1-57-1; Edmonds 22-8-42-1; Fraser 9-1-21-0; Needham 7-0-41-0; Roseberry 4-0-21-0.

Middlesex

W. N. Slack lbw b Babington	5	– lbw b C. M. Wells		40
A. J. T. Miller c Green b le Roux	6	– c C. M. Wells b le Roux		0
J. D. Carr c Reeve b C. M. Wells	33	– lbw b Reeve		17
M. A. Roseberry lbw b le Roux	19	– lbw b C. M. Wells		8
R. O. Butcher c C. M. Wells b Reeve	36	– c A. P. Wells b le Roux		118
*†P. R. Downton c Green b C. M. Wells	93	– run out		50
A. Needham c Wells b sub b Reeve	8	– lbw b le Roux		0
P. H. Edmonds lbw b Reeve	32	– not out		12
S. P. Hughes c sub b Reeve	2	– not out		0
A. R. C. Fraser c Reeve b le Roux	3			
W. W. Daniel not out	4			
L-b 1, w 2, n-b 7	10	L-b 3, w 1, n-b 7		11

1/7 2/23 3/59 4/68 5/159   251   1/1 2/36 3/64 4/90   (7 wkts) 256
6/175 7/219 8/226 9/245   5/233 6/234 7/251

Bonus points – Middlesex 3, Sussex 4.

Bowling: *First Innings*—le Roux 21–2–51–4; Reeve 27–9–48–3; Babington 16–4–57–1; C. M. Wells 19.3–1–52–2; Heseltine 9–3–17–0; A. P. Wells 3–0–25–0. *Second Innings*—le Roux 10.4–0–56–3; Babington 8–0–53–0; C. M. Wells 10–1–31–2; Reeve 16–0–79–1; Heseltine 4–0–34–0.

Umpires: B. Dudleston and A. A. Jones.

SUSSEX v HAMPSHIRE

At Horsham, June 6, 8, 9. Drawn. Sussex 2 pts, Hampshire 5 pts. Toss: Hampshire. For the third year in succession, rain spoilt Sussex's visit to the pretty Horsham ground, allowing only 42 overs on the second day and no play on the third. Nicholas, dropped at second slip off Colin Wells when 10, drove and pulled in an innings of refound assurance, reaching with his fifteenth four his first Championship hundred since August 1985.

Close of play: First day, Sussex 6–1 (A. M. Green 4*, P. Moores 1*); Second day, Sussex 79–4 (S. D. Myles 18*, C. M. Wells 12*).

Hampshire

V. P. Terry c Reeve b C. M. Wells	6	M. D. Marshall not out		0
T. C. Middleton lbw b Reeve	7			
*M. C. J. Nicholas c Myles b Reeve	147	B 3, l-b 3, w 2, n-b 9		17
D. R. Turner b Ricketts	64			
C. L. Smith c Moores b C. M. Wells	23	1/8 2/19 3/148	(5 wkts dec.)	307
K. D. James not out	43	4/223 5/307		

T. M. Tremlett, †R. J. Parks, R. J. Maru and S. J. W. Andrew did not bat.

Bonus points – Hampshire 4, Sussex 2.

Bowling: le Roux 18–4–51–0; Reeve 20.3–6–48–2; C. M. Wells 22–4–73–2; Heseltine 13–2–47–0; A. P. Wells 3–0–18–0; Ricketts 17–2–50–1; Myles 2–0–14–0.

Sussex

D. K. Standing c Middleton b Andrew	0	C. M. Wells not out		12
A. M. Green b Marshall	35			
†P. Moores lbw b Tremlett	7	L-b 3, w 2, n-b 2		7
S. D. Myles not out	18			
A. P. Wells b Maru	0	1/4 2/32 3/58 4/59	(4 wkts)	79

*I. J. Gould, D. A. Reeve, G. S. le Roux, P. A. W. Heseltine and C. I. O. Ricketts did not bat.

Bonus point – Hampshire 1.

Bowling: Andrew 7–1–23–1; Marshall 10–6–9–1; Tremlett 11–7–11–1; Maru 12–5–23–1; James 5–1–10–0.

Umpires: R. Palmer and P. B. Wight.

SUSSEX v GLAMORGAN

At Hove, June 17, 18, 19. Drawn. Sussex 2 pts, Glamorgan 1 pt. Toss: Glamorgan. Play was possible only on the second day, when Alikhan batted soundly for a career-best 78. There was a best score, too, for the nineteen-year-old Glamorgan opener, James, whose début had been against these same opponents at Cardiff in 1985. On that occasion rain allowed only one hour's play and, down to bat at No. 3, he did not leave the pavilion.

Sussex

R. I. Alikhan b van Zyl	78	C. M. Wells not out	24
A. M. Green c Metson b Barwick	39	B 2, l-b 4, w 1, n-b 2	9
D. K. Standing b Derrick	34		
A. P. Wells not out	16	1/83 2/159 3/159 (3 wkts dec.)	200

*I. J. Gould, D. A. Reeve, G. S. le Roux, †P. Moores, P. A. W. Heseltine and A. M. Babington did not bat.

Bonus points – Sussex 2, Glamorgan 1.

Bowling: van Zyl 19–5–46–1; Smith 12–1–34–0; Barwick 18–3–57–1; Derrick 11.3–1–38–1; Holmes 5–0–19–0.

Glamorgan

J. A. Hopkins c Gould b C. M. Wells	20
S. P. James not out	43
*H. Morris not out	32
L-b 2, n-b 2	4
1/34 (1 wkt)	99

G. C. Holmes, M. P. Maynard, P. A. Cottey, J. Derrick, †C. P. Metson, I. Smith, C. J. P. G. van Zyl and S. R. Barwick did not bat.

Bowling: le Roux 6–2–15–0; Babington 10–3–25–0; C. M. Wells 11–3–20–1; Reeve 9–3–14–0; Heseltine 8–1–23–0.

Umpires: H. D. Bird and B. J. Meyer.

At Leicester, June 20, 22, 23. SUSSEX lost to LEICESTERSHIRE by four wickets.

At Guildford, June 27, 29, 30. SUSSEX lost to SURREY by 109 runs.

SUSSEX v KENT

At Hove, July 4, 6, 7. Drawn. Sussex 3 pts, Kent 8 pts. Toss: Kent. Sussex-born batsmen held sway, and Shoreham, in the form of Benson, who batted solidly for four hours on Saturday, finally had to concede to Newhaven's brothers Wells after Kent forced the home county to follow on. With Sussex needing to bat long into the final day to save the match, Alan and Colin Wells put together an unbroken stand of 303 to surpass the 50-year-old record for a partnership by brothers for Sussex: 297 for the fifth wicket by J. H. and H. W. Parks against Hampshire at Portsmouth. There were three sixes and nineteen fours in Alan's career-best 161 (279 balls) and two sixes and seventeen fours in Colin's 140 (211 balls), although Kent's use of nine bowlers fairly reflects their interest in the later stages.

Close of play: First day, Kent 367-9 (P. Farbrace 14*, D. L. Underwood 2*); Second day, Sussex 82-0 (R. I. Alikhan 29*, A. M. Green 45*).

Kent

M. R. Benson c Pigott b le Roux	114	†P. Farbrace not out	14
N. R. Taylor lbw b le Roux	6	A. P. Igglesden c Reeve b C. M. Wells	30
S. G. Hinks c Moores b Pigott	8	D. L. Underwood not out	2
C. J. Tavaré b Pigott	30	B 9, l-b 4, w 1, n-b 8	22
D. G. Aslett c and b Reeve	80		
*C. S. Cowdrey lbw b Reeve	42	1/19 2/51 3/132 (9 wkts dec.)	367
E. A. E. Baptiste b C. M. Wells	15	4/202 5/292 6/313	
D. J. M. Kelleher run out	4	7/317 8/323 9/358	

Bonus points – Kent 4, Sussex 2 (Score at 100 overs: 313-6).

Bowling: le Roux 20–7–40–2; Pigott 23–2–89–2; Reeve 26–3–80–2; C. M. Wells 24–2–97–2; Heseltine 16–2–48–0; A. P. Wells 1–1–0–0.

Sussex

R. I. Alikhan c Tavaré b Igglesden	20	– b Kelleher	70
A. M. Green c Hinks b Baptiste	4	– b Kelleher	57
P. W. G. Parker b Cowdrey	19	– b Cowdrey	15
A. P. Wells c Cowdrey b Kelleher	11	– not out	161
C. M. Wells lbw b Kelleher	36	– not out	140
*I. J. Gould c Farbrace b Kelleher	1		
D. A. Reeve c Farbrace b Igglesden	8		
G. S. le Roux c Cowdrey b Kelleher	41		
A. C. S. Pigott run out	9		
†P. Moores not out	32		
P. A. W. Heseltine c and b Cowdrey	0		
B 2, l-b 5, w 6, n-b 1	14	B 2, l-b 6, w 8, n-b 1	17

1/20 2/28 3/57 4/70 5/71   195   1/106 2/140 3/157   (3 wkts dec.) 460
6/83 7/126 8/147 9/192

Bonus points – Sussex 1, Kent 4.

Bowling: *First Innings*—Igglesden 19–5–62–2; Baptiste 15–3–53–1; Kelleher 23–11–35–4; Cowdrey 18–3–30–2; Underwood 6–2–8–0. *Second Innings*—Igglesden 15–4–38–0; Baptiste 16–6–36–0; Kelleher 31–11–86–2; Cowdrey 21–5–74–1; Underwood 21–11–34–0; Aslett 19–1–82–0; Tavaré 9–1–36–0; Hinks 9–0–51–0; Taylor 2–0–15–0.

Umpires: J. Birkenshaw and K. J. Lyons.

At Nuneaton, July 15, 16, 17. SUSSEX drew with WARWICKSHIRE.

SUSSEX v YORKSHIRE

At Hastings, July 18, 20, 21. Abandoned.

At Portsmouth, July 22, 23, 24. SUSSEX drew with HAMPSHIRE.

At Northampton, July 25, 27, 28. SUSSEX lost to NORTHAMPTONSHIRE by five wickets.

SUSSEX v NOTTINGHAMSHIRE

At Eastbourne, August 1, 3, 4. Drawn. Sussex 5 pts, Nottinghamshire 7 pts. Toss: Sussex. The presence of Hadlee, who had taken six wickets in their first innings, made a target of 252 in 49 overs unlikely for Sussex; a thunderstorm at tea on the third day ruled out the possibility of a Nottinghamshire victory. A greenish pitch that encouraged movement made batting a trial, but Newell and Rice, with 117 for the fourth wicket, established the visitors on the opening day. Sussex were soon in trouble when play began 90 minutes late on Monday, Hadlee beating the bat repeatedly and taking four for 41 in sixteen overs. However, Moores and Gould saved them from the follow-on, and as the pitch eased Kimber revealed a range of attacking strokes. Broad's fifty in an hour, containing eight fours, and a hurry-along from Rice set up Nottinghamshire's declaration – but it was all to no avail.

Close of play: First day, Sussex 2-0 (R. I. Alikhan 0*, D. K. Standing 1*); Second day, Sussex 221-8 (S. J. S. Kimber 54*, P. A. W. Heseltine 9*).

Nottinghamshire

B. C. Broad c Gould b Kimber	11	– c Standing b Kimber	51
*R. T. Robinson c Pigott b C. M. Wells	42	– c Parker b Heseltine	65
M. Newell c Pigott b Kimber	65	– c Gould b Babington	15
P. Johnson c Gould b C. M. Wells	19	– c and b Heseltine	13
C. E. B. Rice b Pigott	54	– not out	32
J. D. Birch b Pigott	29	– c Alikhan b Heseltine	2
R. J. Hadlee c Babington b Pigott	6	– not out	1
†B. N. French c Gould b C. M. Wells	29		
E. E. Hemmings lbw b C. M. Wells	6		
R. A. Pick b Pigott	1		
K. Saxelby not out	7		
L-b 13, w 1, n-b 7	21	B 1, l-b 5, n-b 8	14

1/39 2/61 3/93 4/210 5/210   **290**   1/79 2/128 3/146   (5 wkts dec.) **193**
6/217 7/263 8/281 9/283   4/165 5/177

Bonus points – Nottinghamshire 3, Sussex 3 (Score at 100 overs: 270-7).

Bowling: *First Innings*—Pigott 26.3–7–67–4; Babington 17–1–43–0; Kimber 22–10–46–2; C. M. Wells 26–3–80–4; Heseltine 15–4–41–0. *Second Innings*—Pigott 6–0–17–0; Babington 12–1–69–1; Kimber 8–0–47–1; C. M. Wells 3–0–21–0; Heseltine 9–0–33–3.

Sussex

R. I. Alikhan c Newell b Hadlee	8	– not out	20
D. K. Standing c French b Hadlee	14	– lbw b Pick	20
P. W. G. Parker c Hadlee b Pick	14	– not out	0
A. P. Wells c Broad b Hadlee	6		
C. M. Wells c Broad b Hadlee	12		
P. Moores b Rice	55		
*†I. J. Gould c Newell b Hadlee	34		
A. C. S. Pigott c French b Pick	1		
S. J. S. Kimber c and b Hadlee	54		
P. A. W. Heseltine b Pick	15		
A. M. Babington not out	3		
B 1, l-b 5, w 6, n-b 4	16	N-b 2	2

1/19 2/38 3/40 4/58 5/63   **232**   1/39   (1 wkt) **42**
6/134 7/142 8/182 9/227

Bonus points – Sussex 2, Nottinghamshire 4.

Bowling: *First Innings*—Pick 23–7–54–3; Saxelby 15–6–55–0; Hadlee 27.1–10–53–6; Hemmings 13–2–32–0; Rice 16–6–32–1. *Second Innings*—Hadlee 5–2–8–0; Saxelby 5–1–18–0; Pick 2–0–9–1; Hemmings 2–0–7–0.

Umpires: M. J. Kitchen and D. O. Oslear.

SUSSEX v ESSEX

At Eastbourne, August 5, 6, 7. Drawn. Sussex 3 pts, Essex 8 pts. Toss: Essex. Colin Wells, batting for five hours and hitting three sixes and nineteen fours, rescued Sussex after Lever and Pont had reduced them to 54 for four by the eighth over of the final morning. With his brother, Alan, he added 80, with Moores 76, and finally, to make the game safe, 148 with Gould. Conditions at the Saffrons continued to favour seam bowling, and when Essex put them in, Sussex desperately needed the eighth-wicket pair, Pigott (107 balls) and Kimber, to lift them with 85 in 29 overs. Gooch looked in good touch in the evening, but it was Hardie, with thirteen fours in his hundred, and Fletcher (216 balls) who put Essex in a commanding position, adding 214 in 70 overs on the second day. Both were out in successive overs immediately after tea.

Close of play: First day, Essex 83-1 (J. P. Stephenson 28*, H. A. Page 7*); Second day, Sussex 21-1 (R. I. Alikhan 5*, P. A. W. Heseltine 5*).

Sussex

R. I. Alikhan b Page	14	– c Gooch b Pont	14
D. K. Standing c Miller b Pont	15	– b Pringle	8
P. W. G. Parker c East b Pringle	18	– (4) c Hardie b Lever	10
A. P. Wells run out	20	– (5) lbw b Page	50
C. M. Wells lbw b Pringle	4	– (6) not out	148
P. Moores c Gooch b Pringle	21	– (7) c Miller b Pont	30
*†I. J. Gould c East b Pont	20	– (8) not out	64
A. C. S. Pigott not out	57		
S. J. S. Kimber b Miller	43		
P. A. W. Heseltine run out	0	– (3) c Hardie b Lever	14
A. M. Babington c Miller b Pringle	1		
L-b 4, w 3, n-b 8	15	B 4, 1-b 10, w 2, n-b 4 ...	20

1/21 2/38 3/61 4/73 5/78   228   1/14 2/39 3/45   (6 wkts dec.) 358
6/109 7/134 8/219 9/221   4/54 5/134 6/210

Bonus points – Sussex 2, Essex 4.

Bowling: *First Innings*—Lever 13-5-22-0; Pont 20-1-67-2; Pringle 21-2-55-4; Page 11-1-34-1; Gooch 13-5-29-0; Miller 4-1-17-1. *Second Innings*—Lever 26-7-97-2; Pringle 16-3-44-1; Pont 19-3-68-2; Page 12-0-45-1; Gooch 12-2-35-0; Miller 8-1-40-0; Stephenson 6-1-15-0.

Essex

*G. A. Gooch lbw b Babington	39	D. R. Pringle c Pigott b Kimber	5
J. P. Stephenson c Alikhan b Pigott	43	G. Miller not out	21
H. A. Page b C. M. Wells	19	†D. E. East not out	11
B. R. Hardie c Alikhan b Pigott	111	L-b 15, n-b 10	25
K. W. R. Fletcher c C. M. Wells b Kimber	92	1/65 2/108 3/110 4/324 (7 wkts dec.) 397
A. W. Lilley c Moores b Pigott	31	5/326 6/342 7/375

J. K. Lever and I. L. Pont did not bat.

Bonus points – Essex 4, Sussex 1 (Score at 100 overs: 303-3).

Bowling: Pigott 30-5-103-3; Babington 24-5-81-1; C. M. Wells 31-6-68-1; Heseltine 17-3-33-0; Kimber 22-2-97-2.

Umpires: M. J. Kitchen and D. O. Oslear.

At Sheffield, August 8, 10, 11. SUSSEX drew with YORKSHIRE.

SUSSEX v WARWICKSHIRE

At Hove, August 15, 17, 18. Drawn. Sussex 6 pts, Warwickshire 7 pts. Toss: Warwickshire. With Sussex hanging on grimly to avoid defeat, Alan Wells was required to come in with a cracked left thumb and face the last two balls from Merrick. That more than 1,100 runs and three hundreds were scored in three days owed a lot to the splendid batting pitch but as much to the lack of penetration in the bowling of the two counties propping up the Championship: Sussex and Warwickshire began and ended the match seventeenth and fifteenth respectively. Even though 100 minutes were lost to poor light on the second evening, Sussex still managed to collect full batting points that day. On the last day, as Warwickshire pressed towards a declaration, Amiss reached 1,000 runs for the 24th season, and after Merrick had hit Heseltine for three sixes, Gifford set a target of 293 in a minimum of 49 overs. Encouraged by the spin of Gifford and Asif Din, Sussex went for the runs until the tenth over of the final twenty, when Kimber and Pigott turned their thoughts to saving the game and Small and Merrick were brought back to set up the nail-biting finale.

Close of play: First day, Sussex 13-1 (A. M. Green 9*, A. C. S. Pigott 2*); Second day, Sussex 301-7 dec.

Warwickshire

T. A. Lloyd c Reeve b C. M. Wells	162	– c and b Pigott	5
A. J. Moles c Gould b Pigott	21	– lbw b Reeve	31
Asif Din c Gould b C. M. Wells	110	– b Kimber	52
D. L. Amiss c Parker b Kimber	14	– c Moores b Heseltine	81
G. W. Humpage c Parker b C. M. Wells	12	– b Heseltine	18
†G. A. Tedstone not out	6	– b Reeve	20
A. C. Storie not out	4	– not out	11
G. C. Small (did not bat)		– b Reeve	4
T. A. Merrick (did not bat)		– not out	20
L-b 1, n-b 16	17	L-b 1, w 1, n-b 3	5

1/56 2/277 3/296 4/317	(5 wkts dec.) 346	1/6 2/50 3/134 (7 wkts dec.) 247
5/338		4/187 5/194
		6/218 7/222

T. A. Munton and *N. Gifford did not bat.

Bonus points – Warwickshire 4, Sussex 2 (Score at 100 overs: 338-5).

Bowling: *First Innings*—Pigott 20–2–78–1; Kimber 18–0–76–1; Reeve 26–6–78–0; C. M. Wells 27.4–6–71–3; Heseltine 12–1–42–0. *Second Innings*—Pigott 8–2–34–1; Reeve 12–3–59–3; C. M. Wells 4–0–24–0; Heseltine 14.5–0–75–2; Kimber 11–0–54–1.

Sussex

D. K. Standing b Small	2	– c Storie b Gifford	19
A. M. Green b Merrick	82	– b Gifford	15
A. C. S. Pigott lbw b Merrick	9	– (8) b Small	25
P. W. G. Parker b Merrick	0	– (3) c Merrick b Asif Din	17
A. P. Wells lbw b Small	1	– (11) not out	0
C. M. Wells st Tedstone b Gifford	118	– (4) c Small b Asif Din	33
P. Moores c Tedstone b Asif Din	52	– (5) c Lloyd b Asif Din	15
D. A. Reeve not out	20	– (7) b Gifford	10
*†I. J. Gould not out	5	– (6) c Asif Din b Gifford	60
S. J. S. Kimber (did not bat)		– (9) c Storie b Merrick	6
P. A. W. Heseltine (did not bat)		– (10) not out	2
B 2, l-b 7, n-b 3	12	B 13, l-b 5	18

1/2 2/27 3/27 4/36	(7 wkts dec.) 301	1/31 2/56 3/56 4/96 (9 wkts) 220
5/173 6/253 7/293		5/145 6/177 7/187
		8/216 9/220

Bonus points – Sussex 4, Warwickshire 3.

Bowling: *First Innings*—Small 21–3–74–2; Merrick 19–2–67–3; Munton 21–4–74–0; Moles 3–1–12–0; Gifford 21–4–48–1; Humpage 2–0–8–0; Asif Din 2–0–9–1. *Second Innings*—Small 6–0–24–1; Merrick 10–3–26–1; Gifford 21–5–66–4; Asif Din 17–2–86–3.

Umpires: K. J. Lyons and A. G. T. Whitehead.

At Lytham, August 19, 20, 21. SUSSEX lost to LANCASHIRE by 54 runs.

SUSSEX v SURREY

At Hove, August 22, 24, 25. Drawn. Sussex 4 pts, Surrey 4 pts. Toss: Surrey. Rain ruined this match between neighbours and old rivals, with only eighteen overs possible on the first day and the third washed out. On a sunny second day, Alikhan and Green took their opening partnership to 119, and on another good Hove pitch Sussex looked set for a full hand of batting points. However, with Jesty's medium pace bringing him his best figures for Surrey, Sussex needed Reeve and Pigott to see them to 300 as they put on 104 in eighteen overs.

Close of play: First day, Sussex 78-0 (R. I. Alikhan 28*, A. M. Green 39*); Second day, Surrey 79-1 (D. J. Bicknell 38*, K. T. Medlycott 6*).

Sussex

R. I. Alikhan c Stewart b M. P. Bicknell	43	A. C. S. Pigott c D. J. Bicknell
A. M. Green c Lynch b M. P. Bicknell	59	b Medlycott 62
P. W. G. Parker b Jesty	29	P. A. W. Heseltine not out 1
A. P. Wells lbw b Jesty	13	A. M. Babington lbw b Jesty 0
C. M. Wells c Lynch b Jesty	6	B 12, l-b 7, n-b 16 35
P. Moores c Lynch b Jesty	25	
D. A. Reeve lbw b Jesty	54	1/119 2/120 3/154 4/165 5/174 349
*†I. J. Gould c Lynch b Thomas	22	6/208 7/241 8/345 9/349

Bonus points – Sussex 4, Surrey 4.

Bowling: Clarke 5–2–6–0; Thomas 18–1–99–1; M. P. Bicknell 23–0–71–2; Greig 19–6–49–0; Jesty 28.4–4–81–6; Medlycott 5–2–24–1.

Surrey

D. J. Bicknell not out	38
D. M. Smith lbw b C. M. Wells	32
K. T. Medlycott not out	6
L-b 1, n-b 2	3

1/71   (1 wkt) 79

A. J. Stewart, M. A. Lynch, T. E. Jesty, †C. J. Richards, *I. A. Greig, D. J. Thomas, S. T. Clarke and M. P. Bicknell did not bat.

Bowling: Pigott 6–0–33–0; Reeve 6–3–6–0; Babington 5–2–13–0; Heseltine 7–1–18–0; C. M. Wells 2–0–8–1.

Umpires: B. Leadbeater and B. J. Meyer.

SUSSEX v SOMERSET

At Hove, August 26, 27, 28. Drawn. Toss: Somerset. Play was not possible until midway through the second day and there were two early declarations before the match got going in earnest. Colin Wells kept Sussex on the move with his fifth hundred of the season, his unbeaten 105 taking just over three hours and including thirteen fours. Somerset's target was 274 in 57 overs but, 60 for one at tea, they never seriously looked like attacking it. When Colin Wells sent back Pringle, it was his 50th wicket of the season. Earlier in the month, against Warwickshire, he had completed 1,000 runs for the fifth time in his nine seasons with Sussex.

Close of play: First day, No play; Second day, Sussex 105-3 (A. P. Wells 31*, C. M. Wells 14*).

Sussex

R. I. Alikhan c Waugh b Mallender	8	– b Mallender	5
A. M. Green not out	18	– b Waugh	44
P. W. G. Parker not out	12	– c Burns b Waugh	7
A. P. Wells (did not bat)		– c Burns b Mallender	46
C. M. Wells (did not bat)		– not out	105
P. Moores (did not bat)		– b Jones	21
D. A. Reeve (did not bat)		– not out	23
N-b 7	7	B 6, l-b 3, w 1, n-b 13	23

1/14   (1 wkt dec.) 45   1/19 2/53 3/70   (5 wkts dec.) 274
                                           4/143 5/195

*†I. J. Gould, A. C. S. Pigott, A. M. Babington and P. A. W. Heseltine did not bat.

Bowling: *First Innings*—Mallender 6–0–28–1; Palmer 5–1–17–0. *Second Innings*—Jones 19–4–55–1; Mallender 14–1–57–2; Waugh 9–3–22–2; Rose 16.2–0–54–0; Palmer 9–2–35–0; Pringle 9–1–22–0; Roebuck 5–0–20–0.

Somerset

N. A. Felton c Gould b Babington	12	– c Moores b Reeve	19
N. J. Pringle not out	21	– (3) c Parker b C. M. Wells	13
†N. D. Burns not out	12	– (7) not out	31
*P. M. Roebuck (did not bat)		– (2) c Green b Reeve	55
J. G. Wyatt (did not bat)		– (4) c C. M. Wells b Heseltine	31
J. J. E. Hardy (did not bat)		– (5) c Parker b Heseltine	13
G. D. Rose (did not bat)		– (6) not out	41
L-b 1	1	L-b 9, w 2, n-b 4	15

1/31   (1 wkt dec.) 46   1/46 2/74 3/125   (5 wkts) 218
                                              4/127 5/151

S. R. Waugh, N. A. Mallender, A. N. Jones and G. V. Palmer did not bat.

Bowling: *First Innings*—Reeve 5.3–0–20–0; Babington 5–1–25–1. *Second Innings*—Pigott 10–4–52–0; Reeve 16–1–56–2; C. M. Wells 10–0–40–1; Heseltine 13–3–43–2; Green 3–0–8–0; Babington 4–0–10–0.

Umpires: M. J. Kitchen and B. Leadbeater.

At Uxbridge, August 29, 31, September 1. SUSSEX lost to MIDDLESEX by 86 runs.

At Nottingham, September 2, 3, 4. SUSSEX lost to NOTTINGHAMSHIRE by eight wickets.

SUSSEX v NORTHAMPTONSHIRE

At Hove, September 9, 10, 11. Drawn. Sussex 5 pts, Northamptonshire 6 pts. Toss: Sussex. Gould, resigned to Sussex finishing last in the Championship, vented his season's frustrations on Northamptonshire's bowlers, hammering five sixes and ten fours in 111 from 95 balls. His second fifty took just 25 balls. With Davis, Capel and Walker injured or ill, there were runs aplenty for Sussex, and Colin Wells fell just 4 short of his sixth hundred of the season. On the second day, after an hour's delay because of overnight rain, Bailey continued the feast of hitting with a six and 21 fours in a welcome return to form after scoring only 40 runs in his previous six innings. But in the last hour a bowler took centre stage, Smith, a quick left-armer, rocking Sussex with four for 17 in 25 balls. However, Reeve's unbeaten half-century held up Northamptonshire next day, and no sooner had they begun their chase for 260 than the weather closed in to thwart them. So ended the season at Hove, where only one visiting side, Middlesex, had managed a victory.

Close of play: First day, Sussex 408-6 dec.; Second day, Sussex 39-6 (I. J. Gould 4*, D. A. Reeve 0*).

Sussex

R. I. Alikhan lbw b Robinson	13	– c Ripley b Smith	2
A. M. Green c N. G. B. Cook b Smith	22	– b Smith	1
P. W. G. Parker st Ripley b Harper	40	– b Robinson	6
A. P. Wells b Wild	79	– lbw b Robinson	4
C. M. Wells c Larkins b N. G. B. Cook	96	– (6) b Smith	10
*†I. J. Gould c and b Williams	111	– (7) b Smith	9
D. A. Reeve not out	22	– (8) not out	56
P. Moores (did not bat)		– (5) c Larkins b Smith	8
A. C. S. Pigott (did not bat)		– c Harper b Smith	13
S. J. S. Kimber (did not bat)		– c Ripley b Robinson	13
A. M. Babington (did not bat)		– not out	11
B 4, l-b 9, w 1, n-b 11	25	B 1, l-b 6, w 13	20

1/41 2/53 3/116 4/248   (6 wkts dec.) 408   1/2 2/11 3/11   (9 wkts dec.) 153
5/309 6/408   4/20 5/34 6/38
                                            7/68 8/88 9/122

Bonus points – Sussex 4, Northamptonshire 2.

Bowling: *First Innings*—Robinson 15–2–83–1; Smith 12–0–43–1; Harper 27–1–102–1; Wild 22–5–65–1; N. G. B. Cook 15–1–64–1; Williams 5.2–0–38–1. *Second Innings*—Robinson 16–2–45–3; Smith 23–5–72–6; Harper 11–3–18–0; Wild 5–1–11–0.

Northamptonshire

*G. Cook b Babington	35	– not out	2
W. Larkins c Reeve b Pigott	32	– not out	2
R. J. Bailey not out	137		
A. J. Lamb lbw b Reeve	52		
R. G. Williams c Babington b Green	24		
R. A. Harper not out	2		
B 1, l-b 6, n-b 13	20	L-b 1	1

1/56 2/75 3/221 4/292　　　(4 wkts dec.) 302　　　(no wkt) 5

G. Smith, D. J. Wild, †D. Ripley, N. G. B. Cook and M. A. Robinson did not bat.

Bonus points – Northamptonshire 4, Sussex 1.

Bowling: *First Innings*—Pigott 8–0–34–1; Reeve 23–6–63–2; Babington 9.2–0–57–1; Kimber 18–1–86–0; C. M. Wells 10–4–22–0; Green 8–1–33–1. *Second Innings*—Pigott 1–0–2–0; Reeve 0.5–0–2–0.

Umpires: M. J. Kitchen and K. J. Lyons.

THE CRICKETER CUP WINNERS, 1967-1987

Sponsored by The Cricketer

1967	REPTON PILGRIMS	beat Radley Rangers by 96 runs.

Final Sponsored by Champagne Mercier

1968	OLD MALVERNIANS	beat Harrow Wanderers by five wickets.
1969	OLD BRIGHTONIANS	beat Stowe Templars by 156 runs.
1970	OLD WYKEHAMISTS	beat Old Tonbridgians by 94 runs.

Final Sponsored by Moët & Chandon

1971	OLD TONBRIDGIANS	beat Charterhouse Friars on faster scoring-rate.
1972	OLD TONBRIDGIANS	beat Old Malvernians by 114 runs.
1973	RUGBY METEORS	beat Old Tonbridgians by five wickets.
1974	OLD WYKEHAMISTS	beat Old Alleynians on faster scoring-rate.
1975	OLD MALVERNIANS	beat Harrow Wanderers by 97 runs.
1976	OLD TONBRIDGIANS	beat Old Blundellians by 170 runs.
1977	SHREWSBURY SARACENS	beat Oundle Rovers by nine wickets.
1978	CHARTERHOUSE FRIARS	beat Oundle Rovers by nine wickets.
1979	OLD TONBRIDGIANS	beat Uppingham Rovers by 5 runs.
1980	MARLBOROUGH BLUES	beat Old Wellingtonians by 31 runs.
1981	CHARTERHOUSE FRIARS	beat Old Wykehamists by nine wickets.
1982	OLD WYKEHAMISTS	beat Old Malvernians on faster scoring-rate.
1983	REPTON PILGRIMS	beat Haileybury Hermits by seven wickets.
1984	OLD TONBRIDGIANS	beat Old Malvernians by seven wickets.
1985	OUNDLE ROVERS	beat Repton Pilgrims by three wickets.
1986	OLD MALVERNIANS	beat Downside Wanderers by six wickets.
1987	SHREWSBURY SARACENS	beat Old Cliftonians by 58 runs.

From 1967 to 1983 the final was played at Burton Court, Chelsea. Since then, it has been played at Vincent Square, Westminster.

WARWICKSHIRE

President: The Earl of Aylesford
Chairman: 1987 – A. D. Steven
          1988 – R. J. Evans
Chairman, Cricket Committee: M. J. K. Smith
Secretary: D. M. W. Heath
  County Ground, Edgbaston,
  Birmingham B5 7QU
  (Telephone: 021-440 4292)
Cricket Manager: 1987 – D. J. Brown
Captain: 1987 – N. Gifford
      1988 – T. A. Lloyd
Coach: 1987 – A. S. M. Oakman

Warwickshire's most shapeless season of the 1980s produced just five wins against first-class county opposition from 44 attempts. It ended with a members' petition calling for a Special General Meeting to debate a vote of no confidence in the chairman and the committee, following the resignation of Bob Willis as chairman of cricket.

Given the atmosphere of administrative disunity, it was not surprising that the club finished fifteenth in the Britannic Assurance Championship and bottom of the Refuge Assurance League, having also failed to qualify for the knockout stages of the Benson and Hedges Cup. In the NatWest Bank Trophy, they went out in the quarter-finals after beating Minor Counties teams in the first two rounds. Warwickshire's wooden spoon in the Sunday League was their fourth since 1979 and the third since they won the title in 1980.

The decision not to register Alvin Kallicharran instead of one of their two overseas fast bowlers, Tony Merrick and Allan Donald, further exacerbated a batting problem caused by the erratic form of the specialist batsmen early on. And even though Merrick and Donald took 94 wickets between them – the registration rules prevented their playing in the same match – they did not bring in an adequate tally of bowling points. Injuries deprived Norman Gifford of Gladstone Small's bowling for all but two of the first fifteen Championship matches and of Gordon Parsons's for the last nine. But just two wins – notwithstanding winning 17 of the 24 tosses – underlined the purposeless and erratic cricket which, all too often, was played by a side lacking tenacity and confidence.

The bowling problems of recent years surfaced too many times to suggest that a permanent solution was near. Gifford's output understandably declined (36 Championship wickets from 447 overs compared with 58 from 542.3 in 1986), off-spinner Adrian Pierson bowled only 26 overs, and Paul Smith's contribution (seventeen wickets at 46.05 each) was again infuriatingly short of his potential. Tim Munton had a satisfactory second season, although a mid-season injury, coupled with a slow start, limited him to 38 wickets.

The batting failed too frequently in the first half of the season for Warwickshire to mount a serious challenge in any of the four competitions. Only four counties obtained fewer batting points, in spite of a second-half revival by the newly capped Asif Din and Andy Moles, plus more solid support from Geoff Humpage, Andy Lloyd and Dennis Amiss. Such was the dearth of young batting talent on the staff that the reserve wicket-keeper, Geoff Tedstone, was brought in for eight matches.

Lloyd was the heaviest scorer with 1,503 runs in first-class matches, and three hundreds from Moles in the last three matches took him to 1,431 runs in his first full season. In particular, his 151 out of 236 for six against Kent, on a far from straightforward pitch, was an impressive innings. His power off the back foot, on both sides of the wicket, is rare among English batsmen, and his all-round technique is solid enough to suggest that he has the ability to play the game at the highest level. Asif Din passed 1,000 runs for the first time, in his seventh season, but his batting did not flourish until he was promoted to No. 3. He then scored 778 runs from eighteen completed innings, including two hundreds and a 92. His career must have been in doubt, and it was pleasing to see him take so ably his first opportunity to bat regularly at the top of the order.

For the first time since 1979, Humpage failed to get a hundred, although rain robbed him at Hinckley, where he ended unbeaten with 99. His position in the national averages, 31st, reflects that he never managed a decisive innings, and his wicket-keeping fell slightly below his standards of previous years. Amiss scored two hundreds in his 1,300 – the 23rd time he reached 1,000 runs in 28 seasons of county cricket. His final position of eleventh in the all-time list of run-makers is a true indication of an approach to batting that has never been short of dedication and skill. He broke every Warwickshire batting record and more than an era ended with his retirement.

An approach was made to Amiss to stay with the club as commercial manager, Jim Cumbes having moved on to Old Trafford, and it was the circumstances of the breakdown of negotiations which led indirectly to the Special General Meeting of members. Part of the trouble seemed to stem from the reluctance of the secretary, David Heath, to relinquish the chairmanship of the cricket committee once he had joined the paid staff on October 1, 1986. A close vote in the general committee on July 13 last year forced him to step down, whereupon he was replaced by Willis. However, the club's former captain stayed in office for only seven weeks before resigning in the belief that he could better serve the interests of the membership outside the confidentiality of the General Purpose and Finance committee, on which he sat as cricket chairman. At the end of the season, Tony Steven resigned as chairman of the club to enable his successor, Bob Evans, to address the special meeting on November 11; and it was the new chairman's clear analysis of the problems within the club which led to the members backing the committee by 507 votes to 450. A week later, it was announced that David Brown, after eight seasons as cricket manager, was relinquishing the post and that Alan Oakman, the county's coach for seventeen years, would become assistant secretary (cricket). So ended one of the saddest years at Edgbaston for a long time. – Jack Bannister.

WARWICKSHIRE 1987

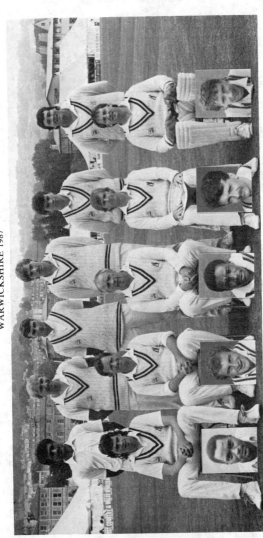

[*Bill Smith*]

Back row: Asif Din, A. A. Donald, A. R. K. Pierson, T. A. Munton, D. A. Thorne, A. J. Moles. *Front row*: P. A. Smith, D. L. Amiss, N. Gifford (*captain*), T. A. Lloyd, G. W. Humpage. *Insets*: T. A. Merrick, G. J. Parsons, G. C. Small, G. A. Tedstone, A. C. Storie.

WARWICKSHIRE RESULTS

All first-class matches – Played 25: Won 2, Lost 7, Drawn 16.

County Championship matches – Played 24: Won 2, Lost 7, Drawn 15.

Bonus points – Batting 48, Bowling 67.

Competition placings – Britannic Assurance County Championship, 15th; NatWest Bank Trophy, q-f; Benson and Hedges Cup, 3rd in Group B; Refuge Assurance League, 17th.

BRITANNIC ASSURANCE CHAMPIONSHIP AVERAGES

BATTING

	Birthplace	M	I	NO	R	HI	Avge
‡G. W. Humpage	Birmingham	23	40	8	1,315	99*	41.09
‡Asif Din	Kampala, Uganda	22	36	4	1,056	115*	33.00
‡A. J. Moles	Solihull	24	45	3	1,355	151	32.26
‡T. A. Lloyd	Oswestry	24	45	2	1,353	162	31.46
‡D. L. Amiss	Birmingham	24	44	1	1,276	123	29.67
‡G. J. Parsons	Slough	15	19	2	422	67*	24.82
A. C. Storie	Bishopbriggs, Glasgow	15	25	8	391	66*	23.00
‡P. A. Smith	Jesmond	17	31	5	506	89	19.46
N. M. K. Smith	Birmingham	2	4	1	56	23	18.66
E. T. Milburn	Nuneaton	3	4	2	37	24	18.50
‡G. C. Small	St George, Barbados	12	20	4	257	42	16.06
§A. A. Donald	Bloemfontein, SA	10	10	3	111	37*	15.85
§T. A. Merrick	St John's, Antigua	14	19	5	220	74*	15.71
G. A. Tedstone	Southport	10	14	1	180	51	13.84
T. A. Munton	Melton Mowbray	15	16	5	116	38	10.54
‡N. Gifford	Ulverston	24	25	12	131	36	10.07
D. A. Thorne	Coventry	9	14	1	116	43	8.92

Also batted: A. R. K. Pierson (*Enfield*) (1 match) 0.

* Signifies not out.   *‡ Denotes county cap.*   *§ Not qualified for England.*

The following played a total of ten three-figure innings for Warwickshire in County Championship matches – A. J. Moles 4, D. L. Amiss 2, Asif Din 2, T. A. Lloyd 2.

BOWLING

	O	M	R	W	BB	Avge
T. A. Merrick	433.3	71	1,439	57	7-45	25.24
T. A. Munton	336.1	70	982	38	6-69	25.84
A. A. Donald	281.4	35	968	37	6-74	26.16
N. Gifford	447	134	1,116	36	5-71	31.00
G. C. Small	350	71	1,067	34	4-80	31.38
G. J. Parsons	391.5	74	1,178	33	5-80	35.69
P. A. Smith	177.5	21	783	17	3-31	46.05

Also bowled: Asif Din 52–9–233–5; G. W. Humpage 2–0–8–0; T. A. Lloyd 1–0–1–0; E. T. Milburn 36–6–128–2; A. J. Moles 173.4–47–492–9; A. R. K. Pierson 26–7–102–3; N. M. K. Smith 42–6–152–4; D. A. Thorne 13–2–45–0.

Wicket-keepers: G. W. Humpage 23 ct, 2 st; G. A. Tedstone 13 ct, 2 st.

Leading Fielder: A. J. Moles 24.

WARWICKSHIRE v GLAMORGAN

At Birmingham, April 25, 26, 27. Drawn. Warwickshire 6 pts, Glamorgan 5 pts. Toss: Warwickshire. A high-scoring match on a good batting pitch looked likely to provide a positive result when Glamorgan were struggling on the second evening. Next day, however, Morris went on to complete a century in each innings for the first time. His 220 runs in the match, in an aggregate stay of eight hours twenty minutes, during which he hit 32 fours, held his side together in a match they might otherwise have lost. In the first innings he shared a second-wicket stand of 189 with Butcher; a stand of 192 with Holmes for the fourth wicket in the second innings prevented Warwickshire from capitalising on an early breakthrough by their new fast bowler, Donald. Lloyd marked his return to the first-class game with an unbeaten 151, which included 24 fours in an innings of five and threequarter hours.

Close of play: First day, Glamorgan 350-7 (C. P. Metson 11*, I. Smith 0*); Second day, Glamorgan 38-3 (H. Morris 10*, G. C. Holmes 5*).

Glamorgan

J. A. Hopkins c Humpage b Donald	7	– lbw b Parsons	7
*H. Morris c Amiss b Munton	115	– c and b Moles	105
A. R. Butcher lbw b Parsons	87	– c Thorne b Donald	6
R. C. Ontong lbw b Donald	25	– lbw b Donald	2
G. C. Holmes lbw b Munton	0	– c and b Moles	80
M. P. Maynard c Asif Din b Parsons	52	– not out	20
J. G. Thomas c Moles b Parsons	13	– not out	15
†C. P. Metson not out	11		
I. Smith not out	0		
B 15, l-b 11, w 4, n-b 10	40	B 11, l-b 9, w 1, n-b 3	24

1/37 2/226 3/254 4/254 (7 wkts dec.) 350 1/13 2/20 3/24 (5 wkts dec.) 259
5/285 6/324 7/350   4/216 5/239

C. J. P. G. van Zyl and S. R. Barwick did not bat.

Bonus points – Glamorgan 4, Warwickshire 2 (Score at 100 overs: 324-5).

Bowling: *First Innings*—Donald 19-2-62-2; Smith 9-1-45-0; Parsons 28-4-81-3; Munton 21-5-68-2; Moles 11-3-22-0; Gifford 21-8-44-0; Asif Din 1-0-2-0. *Second Innings*—Donald 12-2-35-2; Parsons 14-6-20-1; Munton 6-3-19-0; Gifford 1-1-0-0; Smith 2-0-10-0; Asif Din 18-4-88-0; Thorne 11-2-42-0; Moles 7-1-25-2.

Warwickshire

T. A. Lloyd not out	151	– (2) run out	68
A. J. Moles b Thomas	32	– (1) c and b Ontong	26
P. A. Smith lbw b Barwick	33	– lbw b Ontong	9
D. L. Amiss c Morris b van Zyl	38	– c Morris b Holmes	26
†G. W. Humpage not out	10	– not out	11
B 5, l-b 11, w 1, n-b 19	36	L-b 14, n-b 5	19

1/117 2/225 3/280 (3 wkts dec.) 300 1/96 2/108 3/139 4/159 (4 wkts) 159

Asif Din, D. A. Thorne, G. J. Parsons, T. A. Munton, A. A. Donald and *N. Gifford did not bat.

Bonus points – Warwickshire 4, Glamorgan 1.

Bowling: *First Innings*—Thomas 19-4-72-1; van Zyl 18-2-56-1; Barwick 17-1-73-1; Smith 15-2-34-0; Ontong 22-7-49-0. *Second Innings*—Thomas 7-2-21-0; van Zyl 5-0-30-0; Ontong 12-1-38-2; Barwick 10-1-43-0; Holmes 1.4-0-12-1; Smith 1-0-1-0.

Umpires: D. Lloyd and B. J. Meyer.

At Chelmsford, April 29, 30, May 1. WARWICKSHIRE drew with ESSEX.

WARWICKSHIRE v SURREY

At Birmingham, May 20, 21, 22. Warwickshire won by seven wickets. Warwickshire 24 pts, Surrey 3 pts. Toss: Warwickshire. Warwickshire's decisive win was marked by a match-winning aggregate of eight wickets for 89 by Munton, and crucial batting contributions from Lloyd (sixteen fours) and Humpage. In Surrey's first innings, Munton received good seam-bowling support from Smith and Parsons, and the injury-stricken visitors never looked like avoiding the follow-on. In their second innings, Darren Bicknell, a promising left-hander making his first-class début, held up Warwickshire with a stylish 63, but Munton's best Championship performance ensured the win.

Close of play: First day, Surrey 7-1 (D. J. Bicknell 3*, K. T. Medlycott 0*); Second day, Surrey 144-2 (D. J. Bicknell 63*, T. E. Jesty 9*).

Warwickshire

T. A. Lloyd c Brown b Thomas	92	– (2) c Medlycott b Gray		9
A. J. Moles lbw b Greig	16	– (1) lbw b M. P. Bicknell		18
D. A. Thorne lbw b Gray	1			
D. L. Amiss c Medlycott b M. P. Bicknell	13	– c Ward b Gray		8
†G. W. Humpage c Brown b Gray	79	– not out		19
P. A. Smith b M. P. Bicknell	48			
A. C. Storie c Brown b Gray	21	– (3) not out		27
G. J. Parsons c and b Medlycott	4			
T. A. Merrick c Ward b Medlycott	24			
T. A. Munton not out	1			
*N. Gifford c Jesty b Medlycott	0			
B 8, l-b 7, w 2, n-b 6	23	B 13, l-b 2, w 5, n-b 1		21

1/62 2/75 3/124 4/128 5/212   322   1/29 2/29 3/54   (3 wkts) 102
6/285 7/289 8/303 9/322

Bonus points – Warwickshire 4, Surrey 3 (Score at 100 overs: 316-8).

Bowling: *First Innings*—Gray 23-7-48-3; Thomas 22-2-58-1; Greig 21-7-56-1; M. P. Bicknell 24-9-84-2; Jesty 4-0-21-0; Medlycott 7.4-1-40-3. *Second Innings*—Gray 12-3-19-2; Thomas 4-0-26-0; M. P. Bicknell 11.2-2-42-1.

Surrey

D. J. Bicknell c Moles b Smith	21	– (2) c Moles b Merrick		63
N. J. Falkner c Lloyd b Smith	4	– (1) c Storie b Gifford		29
K. T. Medlycott c Humpage b Munton	51	– b Munton		34
M. A. Lynch c and b Smith	4	– (3) sub b Munton		32
T. E. Jesty b Munton	14	– (4) b Munton		30
D. M. Ward lbw b Munton	0	– (5) lbw b Merrick		44
*I. A. Greig run out	22	– (6) b Parsons		0
D. J. Thomas lbw b Parsons	0	– (7) b Merrick		14
A. H. Gray lbw b Parsons	0	– c Storie b Munton		7
M. P. Bicknell c Humpage b Parsons	0	– lbw b Munton		4
†G. E. Brown not out	1	– not out		8
L-b 5, n-b 2	7	B 14, l-b 18, n-b 2		34

1/6 2/49 3/57 4/84 5/88   124   1/70 2/131 3/148 4/182 5/183   299
6/116 7/117 8/117 9/119   6/223 7/256 8/271 9/277

Bonus points – Warwickshire 4.

Bowling: *First Innings*—Merrick 15-4-49-0; Smith 9-2-31-3; Gifford 1-0-1-0; Munton 9.1-2-18-3; Parsons 5-0-20-3. *Second Innings*—Merrick 31-4-90-3; Smith 6-1-20-0; Munton 28-3-71-5; Parsons 18-5-49-1; Gifford 14-4-26-1; Moles 5-2-11-0.

Umpires: D. J. Constant and J. A. Jameson.

At Derby, May 23, 25, 26. WARWICKSHIRE lost to DERBYSHIRE by an innings and 107 runs.

At Oxford, May 30, June 1, 2. WARWICKSHIRE drew with OXFORD UNIVERSITY.

WARWICKSHIRE v LEICESTERSHIRE

At Birmingham, June 3, 4, 5. Drawn. Warwickshire 6 pts, Leicestershire 4 pts. Toss: Warwickshire. Bowlers dominated a match in which 4 hours 39 minutes were lost to bad weather. Only Lloyd, with an unbeaten 88, topped 50. For Leicestershire, Taylor's seven wickets in the match rewarded his control and hostility, while for the home side Donald underlined his potential as a fast bowler with his first five-wicket return in a Championship innings. When Leicestershire set out to meet a target of 220 in 41 overs, he quickly captured another wicket before the rain returned to end the match.

Close of play: First day, Warwickshire 147-6 (Asif Din 9*, G. J. Parsons 4*); Second day, Leicestershire 141-9 (P. Whitticase 2*, P. M. Such 0*).

Warwickshire

T. A. Lloyd c Whitticase b Agnew	13	– (2) not out	88
A. J. Moles c Boon b Taylor	33	– (1) c Potter b Benjamin	15
D. A. Thorne c and b Such	12	– c Benjamin b Agnew	9
D. L. Amiss c Potter b Agnew	29	– b Taylor	23
†G. W. Humpage lbw b Benjamin	17	– c Whitticase b Taylor	1
A. C. Storie c Whitticase b Taylor	8	– not out	8
Asif Din c Whitticase b Taylor	36		
G. J. Parsons lbw b Agnew	12		
A. A. Donald c Boon b Taylor	3		
T. A. Munton not out	5		
*N. Gifford c Benjamin b Taylor	8		
B 5, l-b 11, w 4, n-b 11	31	L-b 9, w 3, n-b 3	15

1/21 2/40 3/90 4/116 5/126   207   1/57 2/97 3/140   (4 wkts dec.) 159
6/138 7/173 8/176 9/197   4/144

Bonus points – Warwickshire 2, Leicestershire 4.

Bowling: *First Innings*—Agnew 28–5–78–3; Benjamin 26–8–45–1; Such 20–7–21–1; Taylor 22.4–5–47–5. *Second Innings*—Agnew 17.1–1–59–1; Taylor 12–2–46–2; Such 7–1–27–0; Benjamin 3–1–6–1; Willey 4–0–12–0.

Leicestershire

L. Potter c Storie b Gifford	15		
R. A. Cobb c and b Parsons	2	– (1) not out	4
*P. Willey c Moles b Donald	6	– not out	0
J. J. Whitaker c Moles b Gifford	44		
T. J. Boon c Humpage b Gifford	10		
N. E. Briers c Amiss b Donald	21		
W. K. M. Benjamin c Munton b Gifford	30		
J. P. Agnew b Donald	1		
†P. Whitticase not out	3	– (2) c Thorne b Donald	1
L. B. Taylor c Storie b Donald	0		
P. M. Such b Donald	1		
B 5, l-b 2, w 1, n-b 6	14		

1/9 2/19 3/52 4/85 5/90   147   1/5   (1 wkt) 5
6/136 7/138 8/141 9/141

Bonus points – Warwickshire 4.

Bowling: *First Innings*—Donald 13–1–42–5; Parsons 13–2–49–1; Gifford 20–9–27–4; Munton 5–0–22–0. *Second Innings*—Donald 2–1–4–1; Parsons 2–1–1–0.

Umpires: J. H. Hampshire and A. A. Jones.

At Cardiff, June 13, 15, 16. WARWICKSHIRE drew with GLAMORGAN.

WARWICKSHIRE v NOTTINGHAMSHIRE

At Birmingham, June 17, 18, 19. Drawn. Warwickshire 6 pts, Nottinghamshire 7 pts. Toss: Warwickshire. The loss of the third day, because of rain, thwarted both sides after Randall's first hundred since 1985 had given the visitors an early advantage. The former England batsman dominated a second-wicket stand of 172 with Newell, and although the other Nottinghamshire batsmen found the accurate seam bowling of Munton a problem, he had seventeen fours in his bright 133 from 199 deliveries. Munton's figures of six for 69 were his best in first-class cricket. For Warwickshire, Parsons hit his highest score since joining the county, a defiant 67 which rescued them when they were 114 for six.

Close of play: First day, Nottinghamshire 276-8 (K. Saxelby 13*, K. E. Cooper 17*); Second day, Nottinghamshire 52-2 (M. Newell 25*, P. Johnson 10*).

Nottinghamshire

M. Newell b Smith	43	– (2) not out	25
D. J. R. Martindale c Moles b Donald	0	– (3) c Moles b Parsons	10
D. W. Randall c Lloyd b Parsons	133	– (1) c Humpage b Smith	3
P. Johnson run out	1	– not out	10
*C. E. B. Rice c Amiss b Munton	14		
R. J. Hadlee c Moles b Munton	26		
†C. W. Scott b Munton	4		
E. E. Hemmings lbw b Munton	1		
K. Saxelby c Storie b Munton	14		
K. E. Cooper lbw b Munton	17		
J. A. Afford not out	0		
B 4, l-b 16, w 4, n-b 2	26	L-b 2, w 2	4

1/3 2/175 3/187 4/204 5/208   279   1/5 2/33   (2 wkts) 52
6/237 7/241 8/246 9/278

Bonus points – Nottinghamshire 3, Warwickshire 4.

Bowling: *First Innings*—Donald 20-5-56-1; Smith 11-0-40-1; Munton 28.3-9-69-6; Parsons 20-4-66-1; Gifford 5-1-13-0; Moles 2-0-15-0. *Second Innings*—Donald 5-2-17-0; Smith 5-1-8-1; Munton 6-0-17-0; Parsons 7-4-8-1; Gifford 1-1-0-0.

Warwickshire

A. J. Moles c Scott b Hadlee	14	A. A. Donald b Rice	6
T. A. Lloyd c Randall b Hadlee	22	T. A. Munton c Rice b Afford	0
P. A. Smith b Cooper	6	*N. Gifford lbw b Rice	1
D. L. Amiss c Rice b Cooper	20		
†G. W. Humpage lbw b Hemmings	43	L-b 5, n-b 1	6
A. C. Storie b Hadlee	4		
Asif Din c Randall b Afford	25	1/29 2/38 3/46 4/92 5/112	214
G. J. Parsons not out	67	6/114 7/206 8/212 9/213	

Bonus points – Warwickshire 4, Nottinghamshire 4.

Bowling: Hadlee 15-6-23-3; Saxelby 15-2-71-0; Cooper 14-2-37-2; Rice 11.3-4-23-2; Hemmings 15-6-37-1; Afford 10-1-18-2.

Umpires: J. Birkenshaw and P. B. Wight.

At Luton, June 20, 22, 23. WARWICKSHIRE lost to NORTHAMPTONSHIRE by eight wickets.

WARWICKSHIRE v HAMPSHIRE

At Birmingham, June 27, 29, 30. Hampshire won by nine wickets. Hampshire 24 pts, Warwickshire 1 pt. Toss: Hampshire. A magnificent opening partnership of 347 between Terry and Chris Smith eclipsed the Hampshire record for the first wicket which Terry had established with Greenidge the previous season and set up a win which, on the final day, was delayed by Warwickshire's determined rearguard action. Smith led the way with his maiden double-hundred – his 32nd first-class hundred – hitting a six and 31 fours and facing 342 deliveries. Terry was more subdued, taking six minutes longer to reach his hundred than it took Smith to reach 200 (309 minutes). The overall run-rate of 3½ an over gave the Hampshire bowlers valuable extra time to force victory, and this proved its worth when determined innings from Moles, Humpage and Asif Din threatened to save the game. Tremlett returned the best figures, with a match haul of eight for 105, but it was the menace of Marshall which had the final say.

Close of play: First day, Hampshire 39-0 (V. P. Terry 9*, C. L. Smith 23*); Second day, Warwickshire 33-1 (A. J. Moles 14*, P. A. Smith 14*).

Warwickshire

A. J. Moles c Parks b Andrew	9	– b Maru	41
T. A. Lloyd c Terry b Andrew	0	– lbw b Andrew	1
P. A. Smith c Nicholas b Tremlett	17	– lbw b Tremlett	14
D. L. Amiss c C. L. Smith b Tremlett	13	– lbw b Marshall	17
†G. W. Humpage lbw b Andrew	9	– c Parks b Tremlett	64
A. C. Storie c Nicholas b Maru	28	– b Marshall	1
Asif Din c C. L. Smith b Marshall	29	– c Parks b Tremlett	49
G. J. Parsons c Parks b Tremlett	13	– lbw b Tremlett	28
E. T. Milburn c Terry b Andrew	24	– retired hurt	2
A. A. Donald c James b Tremlett	0	– c Maru b Marshall	27
*N. Gifford not out	0	– not out	7
B 1, l-b 12, w 10, n-b 3	26	B 2, l-b 10, w 5, n-b 3	20

1/4 2/17 3/41 4/48 5/72   168   1/3 2/42 3/80 4/92 5/93   271
6/128 7/128 8/151 9/151   6/187 7/223 8/234 9/271

Bonus points – Warwickshire 1, Hampshire 4.

Bowling: First Innings—Marshall 19-12-22-1; Andrew 12.4-3-35-4; Tremlett 17-5-38-4; Maru 17-7-27-1; James 8-1-33-0. *Second Innings*—Andrew 21-7-60-1; Marshall 22.5-5-66-3; Maru 20-13-23-1; Tremlett 23-7-67-4; James 8-0-43-0; C. L. Smith 2-2-0-0.

Hampshire

V. P. Terry b Donald	122	– lbw b Smith	11
C. L. Smith b Milburn	217	– not out	15
D. R. Turner not out	17		
R. A. Smith not out	11		
*M. C. J. Nicholas (did not bat)		– (3) not out	13
L-b 19, w 5, n-b 5	29	W 4, n-b 1	5

1/347 2/380   (2 wkts dec.) 396   1/13   (1 wkt) 44

K. D. James, M. D. Marshall, †R. J. Parks, T. M. Tremlett, R. J. Maru and S. J. W. Andrew did not bat.

Bonus points – Hampshire 4 (Score at 100 overs: 347-1).

Bowling: First Innings—Donald 21-2-91-1; Smith 14-2-52-0; Parsons 20-1-83-0; Moles 18-7-48-0; Milburn 18-4-52-1; Gifford 19-4-51-0. *Second Innings*—Donald 5-0-22-0; Smith 4.5-0-22-1.

Umpires: J. H. Hampshire and D. O. Oslear.

WARWICKSHIRE v SOMERSET

At Birmingham, July 1, 2, 3. Drawn. Warwickshire 5 pts, Somerset 5 pts. Toss: Warwickshire. Crowe became the first of the season to 1,000 runs with a superb double-hundred, the second in successive matches at Edgbaston. The New Zealander's unbeaten 206 from 322 balls, containing a six and 22 fours, brought about a recovery from 42 for three; but from Warwickshire's viewpoint it meant that, in three innings, their bowlers had conceded 847 runs for seven wickets off 219.5 overs. Nothing more effectively underlined the problem of the continued absence of Small from the attack. Moles replied with 145 not out, his career highest and his first hundred of the season. He, too, hit 22 fours and shared in two century partnerships. A target of 306 from at least 60 overs was too demanding for the home team, but Smith followed his best score of the season with a second unbeaten innings to secure the draw.

Close of play: First day, Warwickshire 22-1 (A. J. Moles 8*, G. J. Parsons 10*); Second day, Somerset 61-2 (R. J. Harden 11*, M. D. Crowe 9*).

Somerset

N. A. Felton c Milburn b Donald	21	– c Storie b Donald	25
J. J. E. Hardy c Storie b Smith	13	– c Humpage c Parsons	2
R. J. Harden lbw b Donald	1	– c Humpage b Gifford	32
M. D. Crowe not out	206	– run out	33
N. J. Pringle b Donald	79	– c Moles b Gifford	11
*V. J. Marks not out	60	– b Milburn	13
†N. D. Burns (did not bat)		– not out	50
G. D. Rose (did not bat)		– c sub b Gifford	6
G. V. Palmer (did not bat)		– not out	5
B 12, l-b 12, w 2, n-b 1	27	B 13, l-b 6, w 2, n-b 1	22

1/40 2/40 3/42 4/235   (4 wkts dec.) 407   1/14 2/48 3/95   (7 wkts dec.) 199
4/121 5/122
6/158 7/171

M. R. Davis and A. N. Jones did not bat.

Bonus points – Somerset 4, Warwickshire 1.

Bowling: *First Innings*—Donald 22-1-74-3; Smith 18-1-78-1; Parsons 21-4-90-0; Milburn 9-0-45-0; Moles 15-3-40-0; Gifford 15-4-56-0. *Second Innings*—Donald 16-2-40-1; Smith 1-0-5-0; Parsons 19-0-68-1; Gifford 13-3-41-3; Milburn 8-2-26-1.

Warwickshire

T. A. Lloyd b Jones	0	– lbw b Marks	35
A. J. Moles not out	145	– c Davis b Jones	7
G. J. Parsons c Rose b Marks	61	– (7) c Burns b Davis	2
A. C. Storie lbw b Palmer	17	– (3) lbw b Marks	32
P. A. Smith not out	62	– (8) not out	36
D. L. Amiss (did not bat)		– (4) c Burns b Davis	53
†G. W. Humpage (did not bat)		– (5) c sub b Marks	30
Asif Din (did not bat)		– (6) lbw b Davis	2
E. T. Milburn (did not bat)		– not out	1
B 1, l-b 9, w 4, n-b 2	16	L-b 7	7

1/0 2/114 3/144   (3 wkts dec.) 301   1/24 2/56 3/123 4/155   (7 wkts) 205
5/163 6/165 7/172

A. A. Donald and *N. Gifford did not bat.

Bonus points – Warwickshire 4, Somerset 1.

Bowling: *First Innings*—Jones 17-2-64-1; Rose 7-1-26-0; Palmer 19-6-52-1; Davis 18-1-75-0; Marks 21-6-52-1; Pringle 6-1-22-0. *Second Innings*—Jones 15-5-37-1; Palmer 12.4-2-42-0; Marks 22-8-76-3; Davis 15-2-43-3.

Umpires: J. H. Hampshire and D. O. Oslear.

At Worcester, July 4, 6, 7. WARWICKSHIRE drew with WORCESTERSHIRE.

WARWICKSHIRE v SUSSEX

At Nuneaton, July 15, 16, 17. Drawn. Warwickshire 5 pts, Sussex 8 pts. Toss: Warwickshire. Rain frustrated Sussex's attempt to force a win after attractive batting from the Wells brothers had given them a first-innings lead of 191. Colin Wells had an especially fine all-round match, taking five wickets and holding two catches on the first day, and on the second, after Alikhan had equalled his highest score, sharing a fifth-wicket partnership of 130 with his brother. Alan Wells went on to score 119 off 217 deliveries in a stay of 256 minutes, hitting thirteen fours.

Close of play: First day, Sussex 51-1 (R. I. Alikhan 19*, A. C. S. Pigott 9*); Second day, Sussex 302-6 (A. P. Wells 85*).

Warwickshire

A. J. Moles c Gould b Kimber	22	– (2) not out 41
T. A. Lloyd c C. M. Wells b le Roux	3	– (1) c A. P. Wells b le Roux 2
P. A. Smith c Gould b Pigott	10	– c Green b le Roux 14
D. L. Amiss c C. M. Wells b le Roux	35	– c Parker b le Roux 3
G. W. Humpage b C. M. Wells	22	– not out 17
Asif Din lbw b C. M. Wells	19	
†G. A. Tedstone c Gould b C. M. Wells	2	
G. J. Parsons b Pigott	26	
E. T. Milburn b C. M. Wells	10	
A. A. Donald not out	37	
*N. Gifford b C. M. Wells	8	
L-b 8, w 2, n-b 4	14	L-b 2, w 2 4

1/5 2/22 3/55 4/94 5/102   208   1/8 2/37 3/59   (3 wkts) 81
6/106 7/129 8/157 9/167

Bonus points – Warwickshire 2, Sussex 4.

Bowling: *First Innings*—le Roux 22-5-54-2; Pigott 17-4-46-2; Kimber 16-3-55-1; C. M. Wells 26.2-8-45-5. *Second Innings*—le Roux 11-1-31-3; Pigott 7-1-22-0; C. M. Wells 1-0-1-0; Kimber 1-0-8-0; Heseltine 6-5-1-0; Standing 1-0-11-0; Green 3-2-5-0.

Sussex

R. I. Alikhan b Smith	78	G. S. le Roux c Moles b Donald 34
A. M. Green c Asif Din b Donald	18	S. J. S. Kimber not out 19
A. C. S. Pigott b Donald	9	
P. W. G. Parker c Amiss b Parsons	1	B 4, l-b 8, w 1, n-b 12 25
A. P. Wells c Tedstone b Parsons	119	
C. M. Wells b Smith	71	1/34 2/57 3/62 (8 wkts dec.) 399
D. K. Standing retired hurt	2	4/134 5/264 6/302
*†I. J. Gould c Milburn b Donald	23	7/358 8/399

P. A. W. Heseltine did not bat.

Bonus points – Sussex 4, Warwickshire 3 (Score at 100 overs: 377-7).

Bowling: Donald 37-2-168-4; Smith 18-2-79-2; Parsons 30.1-5-90-2; Moles 10-2-22-0; Gifford 7-1-23-0; Milburn 1-0-5-0.

Umpires: B. Dudleston and R. A. White.

At Bournemouth, July 18, 19, 20. WARWICKSHIRE drew with HAMPSHIRE.

At Southport, July 22, 23. WARWICKSHIRE lost to LANCASHIRE by ten wickets.

WARWICKSHIRE v NORTHAMPTONSHIRE

At Birmingham, August 1, 3, 4. Drawn. Warwickshire 6 pts, Northamptonshire 7 pts. Toss: Warwickshire. A twenty-minute stoppage in the final hour thwarted a magnificent attempt by Northamptonshire to score 222 from a minimum of 31 overs. Larkins led the chase with 73 off 50 deliveries, hitting three sixes and eight fours, but Merrick's steadiness saved the home side. The two Warwickshire innings were notable for wicket-keeper Tedstone's first Championship fifty, and for Lloyd's running himself out on 99, having driven the ball too close to the substitute fielder, Harper.

Close of play: First day, Northamptonshire 75-1 (G. Cook 34*, R. J. Bailey 29*); Second day, Warwickshire 114-1 (T. A. Lloyd 56*, G. C. Small 4*).

Warwickshire

A. J. Moles c Bailey b N. G. B. Cook	33	– lbw b Davis ... 41
T. A. Lloyd c Walker b Capel	18	– run out ... 99
Asif Din lbw b Walker	27	– (4) c Ripley b Capel ... 10
D. L. Amiss b Capel	42	– (5) lbw b Capel ... 60
G. W. Humpage b N. G. B. Cook	16	– (6) not out ... 35
P. A. Smith c Davis b N. G. B. Cook	0	– (7) not out ... 4
†G. A. Tedstone c Ripley b Capel	51	
G. J. Parsons c Lamb b Capel	0	
G. C. Small c Williams b Capel	0	– (3) b Davis ... 8
T. A. Merrick lbw b Walker	9	
*N. Gifford not out	5	
L-b 12, n-b 22	34	L-b 16, w 2, n-b 5 ... 23

1/27 2/91 3/91 4/112 5/112   235   1/92 2/122 3/137   (5 wkts dec.) 280
6/188 7/188 8/191 9/221   4/218 5/266

Bonus points – Warwickshire 2, Northamptonshire 4.

Bowling: *First Innings*—Davis 18-4-55-0; Capel 16.4-3-45-5; Walker 14-5-25-2; Robinson 11-1-53-0; N. G. B. Cook 19-6-45-3. *Second Innings*—Davis 28-7-75-2; Capel 28-4-92-2; Walker 9-2-34-0; N. G. B. Cook 22-10-39-0; Robinson 4-1-13-0; Williams 9-4-11-0.

Northamptonshire

*G. Cook c Moles b Small	47	– lbw b Merrick ... 8
W. Larkins b Small	4	– b Merrick ... 73
R. J. Bailey b Merrick	29	– b Smith ... 28
A. J. Lamb lbw b Small	85	– c sub b Smith ... 28
D. J. Capel c Tedstone b Merrick	4	– b Smith ... 3
R. G. Williams lbw b Smith	7	– c Tedstone b Merrick ... 7
†D. Ripley lbw b Gifford	37	– not out ... 13
N. G. B. Cook c Humpage b Merrick	15	– (9) not out ... 1
W. W. Davis b Small	0	– (8) b Merrick ... 17
A. Walker not out	41	
M. A. Robinson c Tedstone b Merrick	0	
B 1, l-b 11, n-b 13	25	B 8, l-b 16, w 1, n-b 4 ... 29

1/13 2/79 3/107 4/114 5/132   294   1/9 2/128 3/128 4/137   (7 wkts) 207
6/228 7/228 8/228 9/259   5/172 6/175 7/206

Bonus points – Northamptonshire 3, Warwickshire 4.

Bowling: *First Innings*—Small 27-3-98-4; Merrick 30.5-1-102-4; Parsons 9-4-13-0; Gifford 20-9-41-1; Smith 7-1-28-1. *Second Innings*—Small 4-1-22-0; Merrick 12.5-0-58-4; Smith 10-1-103-3.

Umpires: B. Dudleston and P. B. Wight.

At Worksop, August 5, 6, 7. WARWICKSHIRE lost to NOTTINGHAMSHIRE by an innings and 34 runs.

At Hinckley, August 8, 10, 11. WARWICKSHIRE drew with LEICESTERSHIRE.

At Hove, August 15, 17, 18. WARWICKSHIRE drew with SUSSEX.

WARWICKSHIRE v GLOUCESTERSHIRE

At Birmingham, August 19, 20, 21. Gloucestershire won by four wickets. Gloucestershire 22 pts, Warwickshire 4 pts. Toss: Warwickshire. Two declarations in a high-scoring match left Gloucestershire with the task of scoring 329 at almost 5 an over. Athey, twice given sound support by Romaines, distinguished himself with a hundred in each innings, scoring his first off 190 deliveries (one six, sixteen fours) and his second off 67 fewer (two sixes, seven fours). To round off a personal triumph, he hit the last ball for six to win the match. Only 23 wickets were taken on a good batting pitch. For Warwickshire, Asif Din continued his improved form following his promotion to No. 3, hitting his first hundred of the season before the declaration at lunch on the third day. Merrick, in the first innings, scored a hurricane 74 off 50 deliveries, striking four sixes and six fours and sharing a last-wicket stand of 92 with Gifford.

Close of play: First day, Warwickshire 390; Second day, Warwickshire 66-2 (Asif Din 11*, D. L. Amiss 34*).

Warwickshire

A. J. Moles st Russell b Alleyne	50	– (2) c Russell b Sainsbury 7
T. A. Lloyd c Greene b Alleyne	45	– (1) c Russell b Greene 13
Asif Din c Russell b Greene	16	– not out 115
D. L. Amiss c Russell b Alleyne	7	– c Wright b Athey 64
G. W. Humpage c Russell b Alleyne	74	– not out 54
†G. A. Tedstone lbw b Greene	24	
A. C. Storie lbw b Sainsbury	5	
G. C. Small lbw b Greene	32	
T. A. Merrick not out	74	
T. A. Munton b Greene	0	
*N. Gifford b Athey	36	
B 8, l-b 11, w 1, n-b 7	27	B 1, l-b 5, w 1 7

1/101 2/104 3/116 4/126 5/179   390   1/20 2/20 3/146   (3 wkts dec.) 260
6/186 7/266 8/298 9/298

Bonus points – Warwickshire 3, Gloucestershire 2 (Score at 100 overs: 266-6).

Bowling: First Innings—Greene 35-6-108-4; Sainsbury 24-7-51-1; Lloyds 6-1-22-0; Graveney 12-3-27-0; Alleyne 31-6-128-4; Athey 13.4-1-35-1. *Second Innings*—Greene 13-0-65-1; Sainsbury 13-3-26-1; Alleyne 5-0-35-0; Athey 14-1-67-1; Graveney 11-1-61-0.

Gloucestershire

A. W. Stovold b Small	11	– b Munton	34
A. J. Wright b Merrick	9	– c Tedstone b Small	0
P. W. Romaines c and b Merrick	68	– c Small b Merrick	65
*C. W. J. Athey c Lloyd b Gifford	115	– not out	114
K. M. Curran not out	71	– b Merrick	33
M. W. Alleyne not out	24	– (8) not out	23
†R. C. Russell (did not bat)		– (6) run out	33
V. S. Greene (did not bat)		– (7) run out	8
L-b 21, n-b 3	24	B 1, l-b 21, n-b 1	23

1/20 2/20 3/195 4/236   (4 wkts dec.) 322   1/1 2/64 3/154   (6 wkts) 333
                                                      4/220 5/269 6/291

J. W. Lloyds, *D. A. Graveney and G. E. Sainsbury did not bat.

Bonus points – Gloucestershire 4, Warwickshire 1.

Bowling: *First Innings*—Small 20–3–48–1; Merrick 20–2–86–2; Munton 20–3–67–0; Moles 13–2–41–0; Gifford 19–6–51–1; Asif Din 1–0–8–0. *Second Innings*—Small 18–4–68–1; Merrick 20–2–99–2; Munton 15–1–60–1; Gifford 9–0–58–0; Moles 5–0–26–0.

Umpires: R. Julian and M. J. Kitchen.

WARWICKSHIRE v LANCASHIRE

At Birmingham, August 22, 24, 25. Lancashire won by 25 runs. Lancashire 21 pts, Warwickshire 5 pts. Toss: Warwickshire. Warwickshire's second successive home defeat came on a suspect pitch on which the scores declined in each innings. Although a career-best match return of thirteen for 115 by Merrick left Warwickshire needing 136 for victory, the home batsmen never looked likely to withstand the hostility of Patterson. Allott and Watkinson were the only batsmen to reach 50, Allott hitting a six and six fours to revive Lancashire after they had lost seven wickets in the 30 overs' play possible on the first day; Watkinson following his six wickets in Warwickshire's first innings with eight fours in his 56. Finally, both gave good support to Patterson as Lancashire pressed on to an important win.

Close of play: First day, Lancashire 91-7 (P. J. W. Allott 10*, J. Simmons 1*); Second day, Lancashire 76-6 (M. A. Atherton 12*, M. Watkinson 25*).

Lancashire

G. D. Mendis c Humpage b Small	0	– lbw b Merrick	12
G. Fowler b Merrick	34	– b Small	15
M. A. Atherton c Humpage b Merrick	18	– c Tedstone b Small	13
N. H. Fairbrother c Asif Din b Merrick	0	– c Moles b Merrick	0
M. Watkinson lbw b Munton	16	– (8) c Munton b Merrick	56
*D. P. Hughes b Merrick	6	– c Tedstone b Merrick	0
†W. K. Hegg b Munton	1	– c Moles b Merrick	0
P. J. W. Allott not out	62	– (9) c Storie b Merrick	1
J. Simmons b Merrick	2	– (10) c Tedstone b Small	1
I. Folley b Merrick	9	– (5) c Asif Din b Merrick	5
B. P. Patterson b Small	11	– not out	4
L-b 5, n-b 1	6	B 1, l-b 5, n-b 7	13

1/0 2/48 3/50 4/68 5/72   165   1/23 2/33 3/35 4/41 5/41   120
6/79 7/83 8/95 9/117   6/43 7/91 8/92 9/111

Bonus points – Lancashire 1, Warwickshire 4.

Bowling: *First Innings*—Small 18–3–69–2; Merrick 18–3–70–6; Munton 8–1–21–2. *Second Innings*—Small 19–1–69–3; Merrick 18.1–2–45–7.

Warwickshire

A. J. Moles c Hughes b Watkinson	33	– (2) c Simmons b Patterson	0
T. A. Lloyd c Fowler b Watkinson	44	– (1) b Patterson	18
Asif Din c and b Watkinson	10	– c Allott b Patterson	2
D. L. Amiss c Fowler b Allott	12	– c Hegg b Patterson	3
G. W. Humpage c Hegg b Watkinson	0	– b Allott	18
†G. A. Tedstone lbw b Allott	5	– lbw b Allott	1
A. C. Storie not out	16	– c Hegg b Watkinson	16
G. C. Small c Hegg b Allott	4	– lbw b Patterson	5
T. A. Merrick run out	9	– b Watkinson	9
T. A. Munton lbw b Watkinson	11	– not out	11
*N. Gifford c Hegg b Watkinson	0	– c Simmons b Patterson	0
L-b 5, w 1	6	B 9, l-b 9, w 9	27
	150		**110**

1/63 2/80 3/94 4/104 5/108
6/109 7/113 8/123 9/148

1/8 2/20 3/25 4/42 5/44
6/69 7/78 8/96 9/96

Bonus points – Warwickshire 1, Lancashire 4.

Bowling: *First Innings*—Patterson 22–3–58–0; Allott 17–10–22–3; Watkinson 29–10–65–6.
Second Innings—Patterson 17–4–40–6; Allott 16–8–24–2; Watkinson 12–4–28–2.

Umpires: R. Julian and M. J. Kitchen.

At Uxbridge, August 26, 27, 28. WARWICKSHIRE drew with MIDDLESEX.

WARWICKSHIRE v WORCESTERSHIRE

At Birmingham, August 29, 31, September 1. Drawn. Warwickshire 2 pts, Worcestershire 8 pts. Toss: Worcestershire. Put in to bat in conditions helpful for seam bowling, Warwickshire struggled against a keen Worcestershire attack, spearheaded by Radford, who began the match with 89 first-class wickets. Only Asif Din, with a patient 85, offered any resistance. Worcestershire strengthened their hold on the match through a solid batting performance. Hick's driving and square-cutting were imperious, and he hit a six and thirteen fours off 206 deliveries in a stay of three hours. Warwickshire began the final day 205 behind with nine wickets in hand, but Worcestershire's hopes of victory evaporated on a pitch which defied all their bowlers. Moles hit a superb 137, including 25 fours, and Amiss marked his penultimate first-class appearance at Edgbaston with a polished 97.

Close of play: First day, Worcestershire 122-1 (G. J. Lord 30*, G. A. Hick 65*); Second day, Warwickshire 57-1 (A. J. Moles 29*, Asif Din 13*).

Warwickshire

A. J. Moles c Rhodes b Radford	4	– (2) c Rhodes b Hick	137
T. A. Lloyd b Newport	14	– (1) b Newport	13
Asif Din c Hick b Radford	85	– c Rhodes b McEwan	41
D. L. Amiss lbw b Radford	4	– c Rhodes b Radford	97
†G. W. Humpage lbw b Newport	20	– b Newport	31
D. A. Thorne c Rhodes b Radford	6	– lbw b Radford	43
A. C. Storie c Rhodes b McEwan	8	– not out	7
G. C. Small c Lampitt b McEwan	20	– c Lord b Radford	2
T. A. Merrick not out	0	– not out	0
T. A. Munton c Rhodes b McEwan	0		
*N. Gifford not out	5		
L-b 11, w 1, n-b 9	21	L-b 10, w 1, n-b 9	20
	187	(7 wkts dec.)	**391**

1/14 2/22 3/31 4/58 5/75
6/121 7/151 8/153 9/160

1/24 2/140 3/286
4/309 5/356
6/385 7/391

Bonus points – Warwickshire 1, Worcestershire 4.

Bowling: *First Innings*—Radford 20.3–1–75–5; Newport 18–3–59–2; McEwan 14.4–4–29–3; Lampitt 5.2–0–13–0. *Second Innings*—Radford 36–6–141–3; Newport 31–11–84–2; McEwan 21–3–64–1; Hick 23–8–57–1; Lampitt 7–0–30–0; D'Oliveira 2–0–5–0.

Worcestershire

†S. J. Rhodes lbw b Merrick	4	P. J. Newport not out	28
G. J. Lord b Small	36	N. V. Radford b Merrick	6
G. A. Hick c and b Munton	126		
T. S. Curtis c Humpage b Small	94	B 15, l-b 25, w 8, n-b 12	60
D. B. D'Oliveira lbw b Merrick	43		
*P. A. Neale lbw b Gifford	50	1/6 2/131 3/261	(9 wkts dec.) 449
I. T. Botham c Small b Merrick	1	4/342 5/347 6/349	
S. R. Lampitt lbw b Merrick	1	7/355 8/442 9/449	

S. M. McEwan did not bat.

Bonus points – Worcestershire 4, Warwickshire 1 (Score at 100 overs: 322-3).

Bowling: Small 37–9–81–2; Merrick 34.4–4–160–5; Munton 38–9–110–1; Moles 12–2–32–0; Gifford 14–4–26–1.

Umpires: D. R. Shepherd and A. G. T. Whitehead.

WARWICKSHIRE v KENT

At Birmingham, September 2, 3, 4. Warwickshire won by 133 runs. Warwickshire 24 pts, Kent 6 pts. Toss: Warwickshire. Warwickshire played their most positive cricket of the summer to dominate the final day and take a rare maximum haul of 24 points. The win was set up by a magnificent first-innings 151 by Moles. On a difficult pitch, which afforded movement and inconsistent bounce to the quicker bowlers, he was never in trouble, and his second successive hundred was marked with square-cutting and pulling of splendid authority. His runs came out of 236 for six, and in the 280 minutes he batted, he faced 250 deliveries and hit 24 fours. Warwickshire's seam attack was more penetrative than Kent's, and although Benson, with his thirteenth Championship innings of 50 or more, and Baptiste, with 60 off 61 deliveries, gave their innings respectability, the visitors finished 59 behind. On the last morning, not even eight wickets by Baptiste in a career-best return could prevent the home side from setting a target of 280 in a minimum of 68 overs. After lunch, Munton, Merrick, Small and Smith were too much for Kent's frail batting.

Close of play: First day, Warwickshire 302-9 (G. C. Small 32*, N. Gifford 0*); Second day, Warwickshire 57-1 (T. A. Lloyd 34*, Asif Din 16*).

Warwickshire

A. J. Moles b Davis	151	– lbw b Penn	5
T. A. Lloyd b Cowdrey	16	– c Davis b Baptiste	41
Asif Din c Benson b Baptiste	12	– lbw b Baptiste	53
D. L. Amiss c sub b Penn	24	– c Aslett b Baptiste	2
†G. W. Humpage lbw b Igglesden	10	– b Baptiste	11
D. A. Thorne c Baptiste b Igglesden	13	– lbw b Baptiste	11
P. A. Smith c Marsh b Baptiste	12	– b Baptiste	36
G. C. Small not out	32	– c and b Baptiste	19
T. A. Merrick c Davis b Igglesden	18	– lbw b Baptiste	15
T. A. Munton c and b Igglesden	6	– not out	6
*N. Gifford not out	0	– not out	7
B 2, l-b 5, n-b 1	8	B 9, l-b 1, n-b 4	14

1/52 2/107 3/156 4/178 5/216	(9 wkts dec.) 302	1/10 2/64 3/66	(9 wkts dec.) 220
6/236 7/242 8/286 9/296		4/101 5/124 6/149	
		7/173 8/192 9/203	

Bonus points – Warwickshire 4, Kent 4.

Bowling: *First Innings*—Igglesden 20–3–60–4; Penn 23.2–4–84–1; Baptiste 25–6–70–2; Cowdrey 20–4–70–1; Davis 10–5–11–1. *Second Innings*—Igglesden 17–1–57–0; Penn 14–1–74–1; Baptiste 21–3–76–8; Cowdrey 2–0–3–0.

Kent

M. R. Benson c Asif Din b Smith	67	– b Munton	25
S. G. Hinks b Small	25	– b Small	5
S. C. Goldsmith c Humpage b Merrick	16	– c sub b Merrick	4
C. J. Tavaré c Humpage b Moles	14	– b Munton	6
D. G. Aslett lbw b Small	10	– lbw b Merrick	1
*C. S. Cowdrey lbw b Smith	9	– b Munton	17
E. A. E. Baptiste c Moles b Small	60	– b Merrick	0
†S. A. Marsh c Humpage b Merrick	0	– c Lloyd b Smith	28
C. Penn c Asif Din b Small	20	– c Thorne b Smith	8
A. P. Igglesden b Munton	0	– c Humpage b Munton	19
R. P. Davis not out	0	– not out	21
L-b 16, w 2, n-b 4	22	B 4, l-b 7, w 1	12

1/29 2/62 3/92 4/113 5/153　　243　　1/6 2/13 3/39 4/42 5/50　　146
6/162 7/164 8/242 9/243　　　　　　　6/50 7/66 8/93 9/115

Bonus points – Kent 2, Warwickshire 4.

Bowling: *First Innings*—Small 22.5–4–80–4; Merrick 18–8–52–2; Munton 16–5–50–1; Moles 6–3–9–1; Smith 8–1–36–2. *Second Innings*—Small 19–2–56–2; Merrick 12–4–21–3; Munton 13.2–4–33–4; Smith 7–0–25–1.

Umpires: D. R. Shepherd and P. B. Wight.

At Scarborough, September 9, 10, 11. WARWICKSHIRE drew with YORKSHIRE.

STATUS OF MATCHES IN THE UK

(*a*) **Automatic First-Class Matches**

The following matches of three or more days' duration should automatically be considered first-class:

　(i) County Championship matches.
　(ii) Official representative tourist matches from Full Member Countries, unless specifically excluded.
　(iii) MCC v any First-Class County.
　(iv) Oxford v Cambridge and either University against First-Class Counties.
　(v) Scotland v Ireland.

(*b*) **Excluded from First-Class Status**

The following matches of three or more days' duration should not normally be accorded first-class status:

　(i) County "friendly" matches.
　(ii) Matches played by Scotland or Ireland, other than their annual match against each other.
　(iii) Unofficial tourist matches, unless circumstances are exceptional.
　(iv) MCC v Oxford/Cambridge.
　(v) Matches involving privately raised teams, unless included officially in a touring team's itinerary.

(*c*) **Consideration of Doubtful Status**

Matches played by unofficial touring teams of exceptional ability can be considered in advance and decisions taken accordingly.
　Certain other matches comprising 22 recognised first-class cricketers might also be considered in advance.

WORCESTERSHIRE

Patron: The Duke of Westminster
President: D. Kenyon
Chairman: C. D. Fearnley
Chairman, Cricket Committee: M. G. Jones
Secretary: M. D. Vockins
   County Ground, New Road, Worcester
   WR2 4QQ (Telephone: 0905-422694)
Captain: P. A. Neale
Coach: B. L. D'Oliveira

A new era dawned at New Road in 1987 as Worcestershire, inspired almost inevitably by Ian Botham, captured their first trophy for thirteen years by becoming the first winners of the Refuge Assurance League. Much of their improvement on the previous season in the Sunday competition, when they finished sixteenth, could be credited to the England all-rounder. His arrival from Somerset, amid a blaze of publicity, had not met with the approval of all the members, nor with the unanimous backing of the committee. But come the final Sunday of the season, when for the first time since the days of Bradman the County Ground gates were locked behind a capacity crowd, there was no longer any doubting the wisdom of luring Botham to Worcester.

In that match, against Northamptonshire, Botham figured in a century opening stand with Tim Curtis for a record fourth successive game, providing the platform for Worcestershire's title-winning victory. He had promised the county's supporters a trophy on his arrival, and he had been true to his word. In eleven Sunday innings, he scored 578 runs, as well as taking nineteen economical wickets. Owing to injuries and Test calls, he appeared in only eleven Britannic Assurance Championship matches and made just one first-class century. That, almost predictably, came against his former county on his first return to Taunton.

Yet, over the season, not even Botham could match the supreme talents of Graeme Hick, who was only 30 runs short of scoring 3,000 in all matches for the county. But for the weather, he would surely have exceeded 2,000 runs in first-class cricket for the second year running. With 1,879 runs, all but 11 of them in the Championship, he was the leading run-scorer in the country. Eight hundreds, the last three in consecutive matches, took his tally to sixteen in 89 Championship innings for Worcestershire. Surprisingly, perhaps, he had still not managed his first hundred in the Sunday League. But in making his top score of 88 at Trent Bridge, he did, at the age of 21 years 29 days, become the youngest player to complete 1,000 runs in the competition.

In the first round of the NatWest Bank Trophy, Hick hammered the highest limited-overs score for Worcestershire in making 172 not out against Devon. The third-highest score in the history of the 60-overs competition, it included eight sixes, and exactly 100 of his runs came in boundaries. Worcestershire's total of 404 for three, of which Botham scored 101, was a record for limited-overs cricket in England, as was their winning margin of 299. However, they lost by 15 runs to Essex in the second round. In the Benson and Hedges Cup, they had been eliminated by Surrey in the quarter-finals.

In the Championship, Worcestershire lost the equivalent of more than twelve days to the weather and managed five wins compared with seven the previous year. That did not prevent Neal Radford from taking 100 wickets for the second time in his three years at New Road. His 109 wickets boosted his total for Worcestershire in that time to 288 and included the season's best return of eight for 55 against Nottinghamshire. He was also the joint leading wicket-taker on Sundays with 25. Winner of the Dick Lygon award for the best team man, both on and off the field, Radford was also the Worcestershire Supporters' Association Player of the Year.

Tim Curtis underlined his development as one of the most consistent openers in the country with a career-best aggregate of 1,601 runs. He compiled four Championship hundreds and in addition was the leading run-scorer in the Sunday competition with 617. Comfortably at ease against even the quickest bowlers, he has the technique and potential to graduate to Test level.

Graham Dilley's first season was restricted by Test calls and continued problems with a side injury. He appeared in only six Championship matches, but his 21 wickets, at 18.42 apiece, included a Championship-best six for 43 against Leicestershire the day he and Botham were awarded their county caps. It was also against Leicestershire, but at Grace Road, that Paul Pridgeon produced a career-best return of seven for 44. The highlight of the season for the left-arm spinner, Richard Illingworth, was with the bat rather than the ball. Going in as night-watchman against Warwickshire, he achieved a maiden century the next day with an unbeaten 120.

Phil Neale recovered from a traumatic start, in which after seventeen innings he was averaging only 12, to miss out by just 6 runs on his 1,000. Damian D'Oliveira, having dropped down the order from opening, achieved that target for the third successive year. Steven Rhodes was again a tidy performer behind the stumps, while Phil Newport was a reliable, perhaps somewhat underrated, all-rounder.

However, the departure of David Smith and Dipak Patel the previous winter left a hole in the batting line-up that remained unfilled. Martin Weston's top score all season was only 54, and neither Gordon Lord nor Lawrence Smith was able to command a regular place in the side. Stuart Lampitt deputised for Botham in thirteen Championship matches but managed only 111 runs. Efforts have to be made to fill the void if this otherwise well-balanced Worcestershire side is to figure prominently in the quest for the Championship. – Chris Moore.

WORCESTERSHIRE 1987

Back row: L. K. Smith, D. A. Leatherdale, S. R. Lampitt, J. P. Wright, I. T. Botham, G. R. Dilley, S. M. McEwan, P. Bent, G. J. Lord, C. M. Tolley.
Front row: B. L. D'Oliveira (*coach*), M. J. Weston, G. A. Hick, N. V. Radford, T. S. Curtis, P. A. Neale (*captain*), A. P. Pridgeon, D. B. D'Oliveira,
P. J. Newport, S. J. Rhodes, R. K. Illingworth.

[*Bill Smith*

WORCESTERSHIRE RESULTS

All first-class matches – Played 25: Won 5, Lost 4, Drawn 16.

County Championship matches – Played 24: Won 5, Lost 4, Drawn 15.

Bonus points – Batting 58, Bowling 68.

Competition placings – Britannic Assurance County Championship, 9th; NatWest Bank Trophy, 2nd round; Benson and Hedges Cup, q-f; Refuge Assurance League, winners.

BRITANNIC ASSURANCE CHAMPIONSHIP AVERAGES

BATTING

	Birthplace	M	I	NO	R	HI	Avge
‡R. K. Illingworth	Bradford	19	19	11	448	120*	56.00
§‡G. A. Hick	Salisbury, Rhodesia	24	37	2	1,868	173	53.37
‡T. S. Curtis	Chislehurst	24	39	6	1,566	138*	47.45
‡P. J. Newport	High Wycombe	24	25	12	534	64*	41.07
‡P. A. Neale	Scunthorpe	24	33	6	925	103*	34.25
‡D. B. D'Oliveira	Cape Town, SA	24	36	3	975	121*	29.54
I. T. Botham	Heswall	11	14	1	366	126*	28.15
‡S. J. Rhodes	Bradford	24	31	7	544	80	22.66
‡M. J. Weston	Worcester	14	21	2	426	54	22.42
G. J. Lord	Birmingham	11	18	2	347	66	21.68
‡G. R. Dilley	Dartford	6	4	1	40	29	13.33
‡N. V. Radford	Luanshya, N. Rhodesia	23	21	4	197	31	11.58
S. R. Lampitt	Wolverhampton	12	14	3	111	24	10.09
L. K. Smith	Mirfield	2	4	1	30	20*	10.00
‡A. P. Pridgeon	Wall Heath	17	10	2	57	19	7.12

Also batted: S. M. McEwan (*Worcester*) (5 matches) 1.

* Signifies not out.   ‡ Denotes county cap.   § Not qualified for England.

The following played a total of seventeen three-figure innings for Worcestershire in County Championship matches – G. A. Hick 8, T. S. Curtis 4, P. A. Neale 2, I. T. Botham 1, D. B. D'Oliveira 1, R. K. Illingworth 1.

BOWLING

	O	M	R	W	BB	Avge
G. R. Dilley	124	25	387	21	6-43	18.42
N. V. Radford	741.5	126	2,269	109	8-55	20.81
A. P. Pridgeon	334	77	891	28	7-44	31.82
I. T. Botham	125.3	17	450	14	3-51	32.14
G. A. Hick	301.2	59	980	25	4-31	39.20
R. K. Illingworth	466.2	115	1,331	33	4-28	40.33
P. J. Newport	496.3	79	1,803	42	4-28	42.92

Also bowled: T. S. Curtis 19-2-94-2; D. B. D'Oliveira 31.2-5-147-3; S. R. Lampitt 79.2-11-273-3; G. J. Lord 2-0-24-0; S. M. McEwan 88.4-12-298-9; P. A. Neale 3.1-0-12-0; L. K. Smith 7-2-20-1; M. J. Weston 96-18-326-7.

Wicket-keeper: S. J. Rhodes 51 ct, 6 st.

Leading Fielder: D. B. D'Oliveira 24.

WORCESTERSHIRE v KENT

At Worcester, April 25, 26, 27. Worcestershire won by two wickets. Worcestershire 20 pts, Kent 8 pts. Toss: Kent. A seventh-wicket stand of 87 between Rhodes, who hit a career-best 78 off 69 balls, and Newport swept Worcestershire towards an unexpected victory with thirteen balls to spare. Kent had controlled the match virtually throughout. Cowdrey's declaration at lunch had left Worcestershire needing 322 in 70 overs, which looked out of the question as they slipped to 164 for six. But Rhodes, with three sixes and six fours, helped reduce the target to 41 from seven overs. At the start of the match Dilley took two wickets in his second over against his former county. However, a third-wicket stand of 285 between Benson and Tavaré, whose 152 in more than four hours included 114 in boundaries, gave Kent an initiative which they did not relinquish until Worcestershire's tailenders wrenched it from their grasp on the final evening.

Close of play: First day, Worcestershire 1-0 (R. K. Illingworth 1*, T. S. Curtis 0*); Second day, Kent 80-0 (M. R. Benson 26*, N. R. Taylor 49*).

Kent

M. R. Benson c Newport b Illingworth	122	– c Rhodes b Weston	54
N. R. Taylor c Rhodes b Dilley	2	– lbw b Radford	66
S. G. Hinks b Dilley	0	– not out	44
C. J. Tavaré b Radford	152	– not out	14
D. G. Aslett c Rhodes b Botham	45		
*C. S. Cowdrey c D'Oliveira b Radford	10		
†S. A. Marsh c Curtis b Radford	7		
C. Penn c D'Oliveira b Botham	1		
A. P. Igglesden not out	0		
B 9, l-b 11, w 2, n-b 17	39	B 4, l-b 3, w 3, n-b 5	15

1/7 2/8 3/293 4/336 5/369 (8 wkts dec.) 378   1/115 2/162 (2 wkts dec.) 193
6/375 7/376 8/378

D. L. Underwood and K. B. S. Jarvis did not bat.

Bonus points – Kent 4, Worcestershire 1 (Score at 100 overs: 358-4).

Bowling: *First Innings*—Dilley 19-3-59-2; Radford 21.5-6-63-3; Newport 19-2-56-0; Botham 16-5-71-2; Weston 10-2-31-0; Illingworth 19-4-62-1; D'Oliveira 1-0-16-0. *Second Innings*—Dilley 10-2-36-0; Radford 15-4-23-1; Newport 12-2-58-0; Botham 13-0-54-0; Illingworth 1-0-1-0; Weston 5-1-14-1.

Worcestershire

R. K. Illingworth c Cowdrey b Igglesden	8	– (9) not out	25
T. S. Curtis lbw b Penn	41	– (1) b Penn	25
M. J. Weston c Hinks b Jarvis	0	– (2) b Jarvis	2
G. A. Hick c Cowdrey b Underwood	29	– (3) lbw b Jarvis	68
*P. A. Neale b Igglesden	41	– (4) c Igglesden b Cowdrey	7
D. B. D'Oliveira c and b Penn	0	– (5) c Tavaré b Underwood	18
I. T. Botham c Aslett b Underwood	46	– (6) c Penn b Igglesden	78
†S. J. Rhodes c Marsh b Penn	7	– (7) c Igglesden b Jarvis	78
P. J. Newport not out	28	– (8) run out	40
N. V. Radford c Tavaré b Penn	1	– not out	22
G. R. Dilley c Taylor b Penn	29		
B 1, l-b 2, w 3, n-b 14	20	L-b 6, w 3, n-b 6	15

1/37 2/38 3/89 4/89 5/89 250   1/3 2/85 3/95 4/116 (8 wkts) 325
6/167 7/182 8/190 9/195   5/150 6/164 7/251 8/297

Bonus points – Worcestershire 3, Kent 4.

Bowling: *First Innings*—Igglesden 19-1-88-2; Jarvis 20-5-45-1; Penn 21.4-5-71-5; Underwood 23-11-43-2. *Second Innings*—Jarvis 17-2-106-3; Igglesden 12-2-67-1; Penn 18.5-5-64-1; Underwood 11-3-33-1; Cowdrey 9-0-49-1.

Umpires: J. A. Jameson and A. G. T. Whitehead.

WORCESTERSHIRE v SUSSEX

At Worcester, May 6, 7, 8. Sussex won by three wickets. Sussex 22 pts, Worcestershire 8 pts. Toss: Worcestershire. A captain's innings by Gould saw Sussex home with three balls to spare after Neale's imaginative declaration had set them a target of 274 in 62 overs. Hick, whose tenth Championship hundred contained a six and sixteen fours, and Botham (54 off 58 balls) indulged in some explosive hitting on the opening day, but by way of contrast it was an obdurate 115 in 292 minutes from Green that left Sussex only 30 runs adrift on first innings. Radford took four wickets in one over and finished with seven for 82. Curtis batted throughout Worcestershire's second innings for his first century of the season, hitting a six and fourteen fours, and when Dilley broke through with two wickets in thirteen balls, Worcestershire held the advantage. However, Colin Wells's 61 off 52 balls, with a six and ten fours, redressed the balance and opened the way for Gould's match-winning contribution.

Close of play: First day, Sussex 32-0 (R. I. Alikhan 9*, A. M. Green 14*); Second day, Worcestershire 71-1 (T. S. Curtis 21*, G. A. Hick 15*).

Worcestershire

T. S. Curtis lbw b le Roux	11	– not out	106
M. J. Weston c Parker b C. M. Wells	52	– c Gould b le Roux	26
G. A. Hick lbw b le Roux	107	– b A. P. Wells	23
*P. A. Neale c Alikhan b C. M. Wells	0	– c C. M. Wells b A. P. Wells	9
D. B. D'Oliveira c Green b Waring	56	– c Alikhan b A. P. Wells	24
I. T. Botham lbw b Waring	54	– run out	12
†S. J. Rhodes not out	35	– c le Roux b Ricketts	7
P. J. Newport not out	21	– c Alikhan b Ricketts	13
N. V. Radford (did not bat)		– not out	9
B 6, l-b 10, w 3, n-b 11	30	B 1, l-b 8, w 2, n-b 3	14

1/16 2/170 3/170 4/217   (6 wkts dec.) 366   1/39 2/79 3/97   (7 wkts dec.) 243
5/297 6/311   4/142 5/182
                                              6/198 7/227

R. K. Illingworth and G. R. Dilley did not bat.

Bonus points – Worcestershire 4, Sussex 2.

Bowling: *First Innings*—le Roux 19–4–63–2; Pigott 7–1–25–0; C. M. Wells 24–2–105–2; Waring 26–7–76–2; Ricketts 20–3–81–0. *Second Innings*—le Roux 16–4–38–1; Waring 7–1–26–0; Ricketts 10.4–0–40–2; C. M. Wells 14–1–55–0; A. P. Wells 13–0–67–3; Standing 1–0–8–0.

Sussex

R. I. Alikhan c D'Oliveira b Dilley	13	– b Botham	26
A. M. Green c Rhodes b Botham	115	– c Weston b Dilley	7
P. W. G. Parker c Botham b Radford	51	– c Radford b Dilley	2
A. P. Wells b Illingworth	33	– c Botham b Illingworth	48
C. M. Wells lbw b Radford	39	– c Newport b Botham	61
D. K. Standing c D'Oliveira b Radford	1	– (8) c D'Oliveira b Dilley	4
*†I. J. Gould b Radford	25	– (6) not out	73
G. S. le Roux b Radford	0	– (7) c Illingworth b Dilley	25
I. C. Waring lbw b Radford	0		
C. I. O. Ricketts c D'Oliveira b Radford	29		
A. C. S. Pigott not out	5	– (9) not out	6
B 1, l-b 8, w 1, n-b 15	25	B 4, l-b 15, n-b 3	22

1/37 2/127 3/189 4/272 5/273   336   1/15 2/17 3/83 4/149   (7 wkts) 274
6/274 7/274 8/274 9/313   5/176 6/247 7/253

Bonus points – Sussex 4, Worcestershire 4.

Bowling: *First Innings*—Dilley 20–3–75–1; Radford 25.5–5–82–7; Botham 20–0–56–1; Newport 14–2–69–0; Illingworth 9–2–36–1; Weston 4–1–9–0. *Second Innings*—Dilley 18.3–1–67–4; Radford 13–2–50–0; Botham 12–0–57–2; Newport 4–0–21–0; Illingworth 13–3–48–1; Weston 1–0–12–0.

Umpires: J. H. Harris and B. Leadbeater.

WORCESTERSHIRE v DERBYSHIRE

At Worcester, May 20, 21, 22. Drawn. Worcestershire 7 pts, Derbyshire 6 pts. Toss: Worcestershire. Three stoppages for rain on the final afternoon during Derbyshire's last-wicket stand of 24 in seventeen overs left Worcestershire, who were without Dilley and Botham for the first time, to chase a near-impossible target of 225 from 28 overs. Hick, on the eve of his 21st birthday, raised their hopes, taking 19 runs off one over from Mortensen and 15 off one from Warner, but when he was brilliantly caught on the deep-square boundary by Wright, and D'Oliveira was bowled with the next delivery, the attempt was abandoned. Batting first on an untrustworthy pitch, Derbyshire profited from five dropped catches, but they paid a high price themselves as D'Oliveira, put down before he had scored and then twice more, rode his luck for an unbeaten 121 that included seventeen fours and two sixes.

Close of play: First day, Derbyshire 309; Second day, Derbyshire 63-0 (K. J. Barnett 38*, J. G. Wright 19*).

Derbyshire

*K. J. Barnett c Rhodes b Newport	16	– b Radford	59
J. G. Wright c Lampitt b Weston	50	– c Pridgeon b Radford	27
B. Roberts b Pridgeon	67	– run out	37
J. E. Morris c Neale b Newport	15	– c Rhodes b Newport	8
†B. J. M. Maher lbw b Pridgeon	58	– c and b Pridgeon	6
I. S. Anderson c Radford b Pridgeon	6	– lbw b Newport	4
R. J. Finney lbw b Radford	27	– lbw b Radford	6
P. G. Newman lbw b Radford	6	– not out	35
A. E. Warner c Rhodes b Pridgeon	13	– lbw b Radford	0
M. Jean-Jacques b Radford	13	– b Radford	2
O. H. Mortensen not out	2	– c and b D'Oliveira	11
B 6, l-b 15, w 3, n-b 12	36	B 1, l-b 8, w 1, n-b 10	20

1/40 2/112 3/152 4/188 5/206   309   1/84 2/103 3/120 4/142 5/149   215
6/255 7/275 8/288 9/299   6/158 7/169 8/169 9/191

Bonus points – Derbyshire 3, Worcestershire 3 (Score at 100 overs: 281-7).

Bowling: *First Innings*—Radford 37.5–7–107–3; Pridgeon 25–5–58–4; Newport 22–4–79–2; Weston 4–1–6–1; Illingworth 22–8–34–0; Lampitt 3–2–4–0. *Second Innings*—Radford 29–3–75–5; Pridgeon 19–4–71–1; Newport 23–9–44–2; Illingworth 14–10–9–0; D'Oliveira 1.1–0–7–1.

Worcestershire

T. S. Curtis lbw b Roberts	39	– b Newman	31
M. J. Weston c Maher b Newman	9	– b Newman	28
G. A. Hick c Finney b Warner	37	– c Wright b Warner	41
D. B. D'Oliveira not out	121	– b Warner	8
*P. A. Neale c Roberts b Mortensen	8	– (6) not out	8
†S. J. Rhodes b Warner	36	– (5) c Finney b Warner	1
S. R. Lampitt lbw b Jean-Jacques	5	– not out	7
P. J. Newport b Roberts	6		
N. V. Radford c Barnett b Roberts	0		
R. K. Illingworth not out	23		
B 2, l-b 10, n-b 4	16	B 3, l-b 10, n-b 4	17

1/23 2/73 3/103 4/113 5/198   (8 wkts dec.) 300   1/60 2/93 3/117   (5 wkts) 141
6/222 7/245 8/245   4/117 5/126

A. P. Pridgeon did not bat.

Bonus points – Worcestershire 4, Derbyshire 3.

Bowling: *First Innings*—Newman 15.2-4-62-1; Mortensen 20-6-51-1; Warner 19-4-44-2; Jean-Jacques 13-2-48-1; Finney 12-2-38-0; Roberts 7-1-45-3. *Second Innings*—Newman 12-0-56-2; Mortensen 7-0-41-0; Warner 6-0-28-3; Jean-Jacques 2-0-3-0.

Umpires: J. W. Holder and D. Lloyd.

At Manchester, May 23, 25, 26. WORCESTERSHIRE lost to LANCASHIRE by 117 runs.

WORCESTERSHIRE v ESSEX

At Worcester, May 30, June 1, 2. Drawn. Worcestershire 6 pts, Essex 4 pts. Toss: Worcestershire. Twenty-one wickets tumbled on the second day as the seam bowlers made full use of a wicket affected by the rain which had prevented any play after lunch on the opening day. Radford's seven for 51 included his 200th Championship wicket for Worcestershire in only 45 games – a strike-rate of 4.47 wickets per game – since he moved to New Road from Lancashire in April 1985. The rain prevented Worcestershire from pressing home their advantage by washing out the final day.

Close of play: First day, Worcestershire 106-2 (G. A. Hick 18*, D. B. D'Oliveira 17*); Second day, Worcestershire 127-3 (T. S. Curtis 45*, R. K. Illingworth 7*).

Worcestershire

T. S. Curtis c East b Foster	19	– not out	45
M. J. Weston lbw b Pringle	44	– c Lever b Topley	42
G. A. Hick c East b Foster	29	– c Gooch b Foster	1
D. B. D'Oliveira c Fletcher b Foster	17	– c East b Gooch	26
*P. A. Neale c East b Foster	11		
I. T. Botham c Gooch b Lever	22		
†S. J. Rhodes c Hardie b Topley	31		
P. J. Newport c Gooch b Foster	0		
N. V. Radford lbw b Pringle	17		
R. K. Illingworth not out	0	– (5) not out	7
A. P. Pridgeon c Pringle b Topley	0		
L-b 8, w 5	13	L-b 5, n-b 1	6
	203	(3 wkts)	127

1/56 2/77 3/115 4/122 5/147 6/151 7/153 8/203 9/203

1/66 2/67 3/120

Bonus points – Worcestershire 2, Essex 4.

Bowling: *First Innings*—Lever 20-6-64-1; Foster 26-8-74-5; Topley 9.2-2-20-2; Pringle 10-3-29-2; Childs 1-0-8-0. *Second Innings*—Foster 11-3-27-1; Lever 5-0-21-0; Topley 14-1-56-1; Pringle 4-1-15-0; Gooch 4-1-3-1.

Essex

*G. A. Gooch lbw b Botham	29	T. D. Topley lbw b Radford	4
I. Redpath c Hick b Botham	9	J. K. Lever c Rhodes b Radford	4
B. R. Hardie lbw b Radford	0	J. H. Childs not out	7
K. W. R. Fletcher lbw b Radford	8		
D. R. Pringle lbw b Botham	4	B 5, l-b 9, w 1	15
†D. E. East c Curtis b Radford	5		
N. A. Foster c Rhodes b Radford	17		121
C. Gladwin c Pridgeon b Radford	19		

1/20 2/21 3/44 4/54 5/60 6/73 7/89 8/96 9/108

Bonus points – Worcestershire 4.

Bowling: Radford 19.2-5-51-7; Pridgeon 3-1-5-0; Botham 16-3-51-3.

Umpires: J. W. Holder and D. R. Shepherd.

At Sheffield, June 3, 4, 5. WORCESTERSHIRE drew with YORKSHIRE.

At Leicester, June 6, 8, 9. WORCESTERSHIRE drew with LEICESTERSHIRE.

WORCESTERSHIRE v LEICESTERSHIRE

At Worcester, June 13, 15, 16. Drawn. Worcestershire 6 pts, Leicestershire 4 pts. Toss: Leicestershire. Dilley and Rhodes turned in Championship-best and career-best performances respectively in a rain-ruined match which was ultimately washed out by a thunderstorm five minutes after tea on the final afternoon. Dilley, looking to confirm his fitness in front of the England manager, did so emphatically with six wickets as only Willey and Gower put up any prolonged resistance.

Close of play: First day, Worcestershire 65-2 (I. T. Botham 42*, D. B. D'Oliveira 3*); Second day, Worcestershire 183-6 (S. J. Rhodes 44*, P. J. Newport 17*).

Leicestershire

L. Potter b Dilley	6	– c Rhodes b Dilley	0
R. A. Cobb c D'Oliveira b Dilley	3	– not out	36
*P. Willey c Rhodes b Radford	48	– c D'Oliveira b Botham	12
J. J. Whitaker b Botham	13	– not out	16
D. I. Gower c Rhodes b Pridgeon	33		
T. J. Boon b Dilley	6		
†P. Whitticase b Radford	16		
P. A. J. DeFreitas c Radford b Dilley	14		
W. K. M. Benjamin c Rhodes b Dilley	3		
J. P. Agnew b Dilley	3		
L. B. Taylor not out	0		
B 5, l-b 7, n-b 2	14	N-b 6	6

1/8 2/9 3/31 4/84 5/112   159   1/0 2/49   (2 wkts) 70
6/132 7/142 8/145 9/158

Bonus points – Leicestershire 1, Worcestershire 4.

Bowling: *First Innings*—Dilley 15.3–6–43–6; Radford 15–4–41–2; Botham 12–3–23–1; Newport 5–0–26–0; Pridgeon 7–2–14–1. *Second Innings*—Dilley 9–2–26–1; Radford 6–0–16–0; Botham 6–1–16–1; Pridgeon 4–0–12–0.

Worcestershire

T. S. Curtis c Potter b DeFreitas	10	N. V. Radford lbw b Agnew	2
I. T. Botham b Benjamin	49	G. R. Dilley not out	8
G. A. Hick lbw b Agnew	1		
D. B. D'Oliveira b DeFreitas	5	B 1, l-b 10, w 3, n-b 3	17
*P. A. Neale c DeFreitas b Willey	31		
M. J. Weston c Whitticase b Agnew	10	1/49 2/56 3/75 (9 wkts dec.) 234
†S. J. Rhodes c Potter b Agnew	80	4/77 5/91 6/151	
P. J. Newport c Gower b Agnew	21	7/192 8/194 9/234	

A. P. Pridgeon did not bat.

Bonus points – Worcestershire 2, Leicestershire 3 (Score at 100 overs: 208-8).

Bowling: Agnew 35.1–9–81–5; DeFreitas 36–13–62–2; Benjamin 30–8–74–1; Willey 3–1–6–1.

Umpires: B. Dudleston and N. T. Plews.

WORCESTERSHIRE v GLOUCESTERSHIRE

At Worcester, June 17, 18, 19. Drawn. Worcestershire 1 pt, Gloucestershire 4 pts. Toss: Gloucestershire. The weather restricted play to the second day only. Stovold (76 off 91 balls) and Wright rarely looked in trouble on an easy-paced pitch as they put on 136 for the first wicket, and Wright, hitting eleven boundaries, advanced sedately to 92 from 210 deliveries before becoming Radford's 39th Championship victim of the season.

Gloucestershire

A. W. Stovold lbw b Radford 76
A. J. Wright c Rhodes b Radford 92
P. W. Romaines c Neale b Newport ... 14
P. Bainbridge not out 56

J. W. Lloyds not out 29
    B 4, l-b 11, w 2, n-b 17 34

1/136 2/166 3/242   (3 wkts) 301

M. W. Alleyne, K. P. Tomlins, †R. C. Russell, *D. A. Graveney, C. A. Walsh and D. V.
Lawrence did not bat.

Bonus points – Gloucestershire 4, Worcestershire 1.

Bowling: Radford 24-2-87-2; Pridgeon 15-1-52-0; Newport 14.3-1-71-1; Illingworth
11-3-22-0; Weston 6-1-24-0; Hick 7-0-30-0.

Worcestershire

T. S. Curtis, M. J. Weston, G. A. Hick, D. B. D'Oliveira, S. R. Lampitt, *P. A. Neale,
†S. J. Rhodes, P. J. Newport, R. K. Illingworth, N. V. Radford and A. P. Pridgeon.

Umpires: B. Dudleston and J. H. Hampshire.

At Nottingham, June 20, 22, 23. WORCESTERSHIRE drew with NOTTINGHAMSHIRE.

At Gloucester, June 27, 29, 30. WORCESTERSHIRE beat GLOUCESTERSHIRE by
160 runs.

WORCESTERSHIRE v NOTTINGHAMSHIRE

At Kidderminster, July 1, 2, 3. Worcestershire won by ten wickets. Worcestershire 23 pts,
Nottinghamshire 4 pts. Toss: Worcestershire. Radford became the first bowler to 50
Championship wickets with the season's best return to date, his eight wickets including a
three-wicket maiden in a 27-ball spell of five for 13. Forced to follow on, Nottinghamshire
avoided the ignominy of an innings defeat, but Worcestershire needed just 62 for victory. On
the opening day of the first Championship game at Chester Road for fourteen years, Curtis
faced 286 balls in making 110 in five and a half hours, his third Championship hundred of the
summer. With Newport he put on 110 for the seventh wicket after Hadlee had taken three
wickets in seven balls, and as well as rescuing Worcestershire, their partnership broke the
county's 59-year-old record for that wicket against Nottinghamshire.
Close of play: First day, Worcestershire 328-9 (R. K. Illingworth 27*, A. P. Pridgeon 12*);
Second day, Nottinghamshire 177-6 (J. D. Birch 24*).

Worcestershire

T. S. Curtis c Randall b Afford ....110 – not out 42
L. K. Smith c Scott b Hadlee .... 2 – not out 20
G. A. Hick lbw b Pick 63
D. B. D'Oliveira c Hadlee b Afford 17
*P. A. Neale lbw b Hadlee 18
S. R. Lampitt lbw b Hadlee 0
†S. J. Rhodes lbw b Hadlee 0
P. J. Newport b Afford 60
R. K. Illingworth not out 43
N. V. Radford b Pick 8
A. P. Pridgeon c Johnson b Afford 17
    L-b 7, n-b 4 11

1/17 2/117 3/138 4/162 5/164   349   (no wkt) 62
6/164 7/274 8/289 9/308

Bonus points – Worcestershire 3, Nottinghamshire 3 (Score at 100 overs: 285-7).

Bowling: *First Innings*—Hadlee 22-6-58-4; Pick 27-5-111-2; Cooper 18-4-41-0;
Hemmings 8-1-30-0; Afford 39.4-11-102-4. *Second Innings*—Cooper 3-0-14-0; Pick
2-0-12-0; Afford 5-1-11-0; Birch 6.2-2-14-0; Johnson 2-0-11-0.

Nottinghamshire

D. W. Randall lbw b Radford	11	– c and b Pridgeon	34
M. Newell lbw b Radford	6	– c Rhodes b Newport	9
P. Johnson b Radford	0	– c D'Oliveira b Pridgeon	48
*C. E. B. Rice b Radford	0	– c Rhodes b Illingworth	21
J. D. Birch lbw b Radford	8	– lbw b Radford	34
R. J. Hadlee c Neale b Illingworth	84	– b Hick	21
†C. W. Scott b Radford	45	– c Rhodes b Illingworth	13
E. E. Hemmings c Rhodes b Radford	0	– c Rhodes b Radford	32
R. A. Pick c Rhodes b Illingworth	1	– b Hick	12
K. E. Cooper c Neale b Radford	1	– c Lampitt b Hick	0
J. A. Afford not out	0	– not out	5
B 5, l-b 2, w 1, n-b 3	11	L-b 6, w 4, n-b 4	14

1/13 2/13 3/13 4/25 5/40   167   1/35 2/66 3/104 4/121 5/146   243
6/160 7/164 8/165 9/167   6/177 7/194 8/227 9/227

Bonus points – Nottinghamshire 1, Worcestershire 4.

Bowling: *First Innings*—Radford 16.1-3-55-8; Pridgeon 12-3-34-0; Newport 6-0-44-0; Illingworth 14-4-27-2. *Second Innings*—Newport 11-0-43-1; Radford 20-3-63-2; Pridgeon 7-1-33-2; Illingworth 20-6-45-2; Hick 20-3-53-3.

Umpires: H. D. Bird and B. J. Meyer.

WORCESTERSHIRE v WARWICKSHIRE

At Worcester, July 4, 6, 7. Drawn. Worcestershire 7 pts, Warwickshire 7 pts. Toss: Warwickshire. A seventh-wicket stand of 82 between Rhodes and Newport spared Worcestershire's blushes after they were 70 for six in the final session with 27 overs remaining. In compiling his 101st hundred on the opening day, Amiss became the heaviest run-scorer against Worcestershire, overtaking the 3,391 runs totalled by Hampshire's C. P. Mead more than 50 years earlier. It was his ninth hundred against Worcestershire. Illingworth, sent in as nightwatchman, displayed unflagging concentration in batting for all but the first two balls of Worcestershire's first innings. His maiden century came in 320 minutes off 237 balls. Neither side held great hopes of forcing victory until Worcestershire, having been set a target of 281 in 47 overs, lost Curtis and Hick in the space of three balls from Donald and subsided alarmingly. However, Warwickshire's chance of pressing home their advantage disappeared soon after tea when Small retired from the attack because of an injury to his side.

Close of play: First day, Worcestershire 15-1 (L. K. Smith 0*, R. K. Illingworth 9*); Second day, Warwickshire 33-0 (T. A. Lloyd 11*, A. J. Moles 20*).

Warwickshire

T. A. Lloyd b Newport	23	– b Illingworth	67
A. J. Moles b Pridgeon	5	– st Rhodes b Curtis	67
A. C. Storie c Rhodes b Pridgeon	0	– c Curtis b Lampitt	0
D. L. Amiss run out	123	– c Rhodes b Curtis	45
†G. W. Humpage c Smith b Newport	52	– c Curtis b Smith	18
Asif Din c Rhodes b Newport	6	– not out	44
G. J. Parsons c Curtis b Hick	33	– not out	12
G. C. Small c D'Oliveira b Hick	17		
T. A. Munton c Illingworth b Hick	2		
A. A. Donald not out	12		
*N. Gifford not out	11		
L-b 12, w 2, n-b 3	17	B 2, l-b 5, w 1, n-b 3	11

1/16 2/18 3/42 4/153 5/165   (9 wkts dec.) 301   1/106 2/108 3/180   (5 wkts dec.) 264
6/254 7/263 8/267 9/278   4/191 5/225

Bonus points – Warwickshire 3, Worcestershire 4 (Score at 100 overs: 282-9).

Bowling: *First Innings*—Radford 11–3–17–0; Pridgeon 21–6–46–2; Lampitt 14–1–56–0; Newport 19–3–66–3; Illingworth 19–5–62–0; Hick 20–4–42–3. *Second Innings*—Pridgeon 12–5–28–0; Newport 15–3–52–0; Hick 7–1–35–0; Illingworth 10–4–36–1; Lampitt 4–2–6–1; Curtis 15–2–72–2; Smith 7–2–20–1; Neale 3–0–8–0.

Worcestershire

T. S. Curtis c Humpage b Donald	0	– c Parsons b Donald	4
L. K. Smith b Small	3	– b Munton	5
R. K. Illingworth not out	120	– (9) not out	4
G. A. Hick lbw b Munton	19	– (3) c Humpage b Donald	0
D. B. D'Oliveira c Lloyd b Parsons	19	– (4) c and b Parsons	34
*P. A. Neale c Humpage b Small	9	– (5) b Munton	2
S. R. Lampitt c Amiss b Donald	5	– (6) lbw b Small	10
†S. J. Rhodes c Humpage b Parsons	14	– (7) c Parsons b Asif Din	29
P. J. Newport b Donald	31	– (8) not out	64
N. V. Radford c Asif Din b Donald	8		
A. P. Pridgeon c Lloyd b Parsons	19		
B 15, l-b 17, w 4, n-b 2	38	B 5, l-b 11, w 1, n-b 1	18

1/0 2/45 3/70 4/115 5/142	**285**	1/6 2/6 3/29 4/57 (7 wkts) 170
6/167 7/192 8/240 9/250		5/68 6/70 7/152

Bonus points – Worcestershire 3, Warwickshire 4.

Bowling: *First Innings*—Donald 25–2–85–4; Small 23–7–43–2; Parsons 21.3–2–76–3; Munton 14–5–31–1; Gifford 7–2–15–0; Moles 5–3–3–0. *Second Innings*—Donald 12–4–15–2; Small 6.1–1–17–1; Munton 8.5–0–43–2; Parsons 8.4–3–55–1; Gifford 5–3–5–0; Asif Din 6–1–19–1.

Umpires: H. D. Bird and B. J. Meyer.

At Taunton, July 15, 16, 17. WORCESTERSHIRE drew with SOMERSET.

At Worcester, July 18, 19, 20. WORCESTERSHIRE drew with PAKISTANIS (See Pakistani tour section).

At The Oval, July 22, 23, 24. WORCESTERSHIRE drew with SURREY.

WORCESTERSHIRE v SOMERSET

At Worcester, July 25, 27, 28. Drawn. Worcestershire 6 pts, Somerset 5 pts. Toss: Somerset. The same parched pitch as used in the two previous games at New Road brought five more centuries, making nine in total in nine days' use. Hick's eleventh Championship hundred, including one six and eleven fours, off 128 balls, was almost to order for his parents' visit from Zimbabwe, and Worcestershire took a token lead of 12 to ensure Neale's first century of the season. He hit a six and twelve fours. In turn, Crowe (105 off 117 balls, including fifteen fours) and Roebuck put on 173 for the second wicket in the morning session after Harden had retired hurt from a blow to the face. Set a target of 285 in 60 overs, Worcestershire were floundering at 73 for five, but Neale and Rhodes salvaged the draw with an unbroken sixth-wicket stand of 94.

Close of play: First day, Somerset 308; Second day, Somerset 57-1 (P. M. Roebuck 30*, R. J. Harden 9*).

Somerset

N. A. Felton c Lord b Hick	110	– run out	16
*P. M. Roebuck c D'Oliveira b Radford	6	– not out	135
J. J. E. Hardy c Weston b Newport	24	– (6) b Illingworth	3
M. D. Crowe lbw b Radford	33	– c Radford b Hick	105
N. J. Pringle c Neale b Hick	74	– st Rhodes b Illingworth	4
R. J. Harden lbw b Radford	20	– (3) b Weston	11
†N. D. Burns b Radford	17	– st Rhodes b Hick	10
V. J. Marks b Radford	7	– not out	5
G. V. Palmer lbw b Radford	0		
M. D. Harman not out	4		
A. N. Jones b Radford	0		
L-b 4, w 1, n-b 8	13	B 2, l-b 4, n-b 1	7

1/11 2/58 3/113 4/256 5/275   308   1/38 2/235 3/236   (6 wkts dec.) 296
6/295 7/298 8/298 9/307   4/244 5/252 6/273

Bonus points – Somerset 3, Worcestershire 2 (Score at 100 overs: 281-5).

In the second innings R. J. Harden, when 11, retired hurt at 62 and resumed at 235.

Bowling: *First Innings*—Radford 29-5-86-7; Pridgeon 20-8-39-0; Hick 27-7-67-2; Newport 11-1-38-1; Illingworth 23-2-62-0; Weston 3-0-12-0. *Second Innings*—Radford 8-1-25-0; Pridgeon 4-0-13-0; Illingworth 22-4-80-2; Curtis 2-0-6-0; Newport 6-0-23-0; Weston 14-1-70-1; Hick 19-1-73-2.

Worcestershire

T. S. Curtis c Roebuck b Jones	17	– b Palmer	12
G. J. Lord lbw b Palmer	0	– lbw b Palmer	0
G. A. Hick c Felton b Marks	132	– c Felton b Jones	29
D. B. D'Oliveira c and b Harman	19	– lbw b Jones	4
*P. A. Neale not out	103	– not out	53
M. J. Weston lbw b Palmer	0	– c Roebuck b Palmer	13
†S. J. Rhodes b Palmer	0	– not out	51
P. J. Newport not out	31		
B 5, l-b 8, w 4, n-b 1	18	L-b 3, n-b 2	5

1/4 2/36 3/91 4/242   (6 wkts dec.) 320   1/4 2/41 3/45   (5 wkts) 167
5/242 6/242   4/45 5/73

R. K. Illingworth, N. V. Radford and A. P. Pridgeon did not bat.

Bonus points – Worcestershire 4, Somerset 2.

Bowling: *First Innings*—Jones 17-2-61-1; Palmer 24-5-67-3; Marks 20.3-4-69-1; Harman 19-3-77-1; Pringle 8-1-23-0; Roebuck 2-0-10-0. *Second Innings*—Jones 12-1-35-2; Palmer 13-0-57-3; Marks 16-1-60-0; Harman 8.3-6-8-0; Pringle 4-1-4-0.

Umpires: D. O. Oslear and N. T. Plews.

At Lord's, August 8, 10, 11. WORCESTERSHIRE drew with MIDDLESEX.

WORCESTERSHIRE v GLAMORGAN

At Worcester, August 15, 17, 18. Drawn. Worcestershire 7 pts, Glamorgan 7 pts. Toss: Glamorgan. Glamorgan incurred the wrath of the above-average home crowd by refusing to set Worcestershire even a token target in the final session, choosing instead to bat on until they were dismissed in the third of the last twenty overs. Their lead by then was 319. Todd's first Championship century for the Welsh county, compiled in 204 minutes from 175 deliveries, with three sixes and twenty fours, had staved off the threat of defeat after Glamorgan had been 40 for five on the third morning. Ontong helped Todd add 133 for the sixth wicket to present Morris with the opportunity of a declaration, but, remembering perhaps how Worcestershire had scored 225 off 32 overs to beat Glamorgan in Neath the previous year, Morris opted for caution ahead of entertainment. Shastri had provided some of the latter on the first day, benefiting from the absence of Dilley and Botham in the afternoon, both suffering from strains.

Close of play: First day, Worcestershire 42-1 (G. J. Lord 18*, G. A. Hick 21*); Second day, Glamorgan 6-0 (A. R. Butcher 6*, H. Morris 0*).

Glamorgan

A. R. Butcher b Radford	18	– b Radford	18
*H. Morris c Illingworth b Newport	35	– lbw b Radford	0
G. C. Holmes c D'Oliveira b Botham	6	– b Newport	9
M. P. Maynard c Neale b Newport	26	– c Hick b Newport	5
R. C. Ontong c Rhodes b Illingworth	33	– c Curtis b Illingworth	48
R. J. Shastri b Radford	99	– c and b Radford	0
P. A. Todd lbw b Newport	35	– c Neale b Illingworth	135
†C. P. Metson run out	15	– lbw b Illingworth	0
S. J. Base b Radford	1	– (10) st Rhodes b D'Oliveira	14
I. Smith not out	2	– (9) b Newport	19
S. R. Barwick c and b Radford	0	– not out	3
B 6, l-b 9, n-b 16	31	L-b 4, w 1, n-b 18	23
	301		**274**

1/55 2/65 3/65 4/106 5/169   301   1/7 2/31 3/35 4/37 5/40   274
6/216 7/286 8/293 9/301   6/173 7/173 8/215 9/269

Bonus points – Glamorgan 4, Worcestershire 4.

Bowling: *First Innings*—Dilley 6-3-8-0; Radford 26.2-3-73-4; Botham 8.3-1-38-1; Newport 16-3-66-3; Illingworth 25-7-82-1; Hick 9-3-19-0. *Second Innings*—Radford 34-5-110-3; Hick 11-3-34-0; Newport 23-2-86-3; Illingworth 17-8-40-3; D'Oliveira 1.1-1-0-1.

Worcestershire

T. S. Curtis c Metson b Base	3	– not out	0
G. J. Lord c Metson b Barwick	66	– not out	0
G. A. Hick c Metson b Smith	34		
D. B. D'Oliveira c Morris b Base	68		
*P. A. Neale lbw b Barwick	18		
I. T. Botham c Maynard b Shastri	5		
†S. J. Rhodes c Holmes b Barwick	12		
P. J. Newport retired hurt	19		
R. K. Illingworth not out	20		
N. V. Radford not out	3		
L-b 2, w 4, n-b 2	8		

1/11 2/75 3/124 4/164   (7 wkts dec.) 256   (no wkt) 0
5/173 6/210 7/219

G. R. Dilley did not bat.

Bonus points – Worcestershire 3, Glamorgan 3.

Bowling: *First Innings*—Barwick 31-7-93-3; Base 30-8-89-2; Ontong 3-1-12-0; Shastri 7-1-12-1; Smith 6-1-33-1; Holmes 5-1-15-0. *Second Innings*—Shastri 1-1-0-0.

Umpires: J. Birkenshaw and P. J. Eele.

At Northampton, August 19, 20, 21. WORCESTERSHIRE drew with NORTHAMPTON-SHIRE.

At Neath, August 22, 24, 25. WORCESTERSHIRE lost to GLAMORGAN by seven wickets.

WORCESTERSHIRE v HAMPSHIRE

At Worcester, August 26, 27, 28. Hampshire won by 31 runs. Hampshire 18 pts, Worcestershire 5 pts. Toss: Worcestershire. With four wickets in hand and needing 40 runs from the last seven overs, Worcestershire were within sight of their first Championship win in nine games until Marshall returned to take three for 3 in nine balls. Neale, the first to fall to him, had been Worcestershire's driving force, hitting 90 from 95 balls, including two sixes and fourteen fours, and adding 101 in twelve overs with Lampitt. Nicholas (fifteen fours) had held Hampshire's first innings together with an unbeaten 110 in 274 minutes after only two hours' play had been possible on the first day. Worcestershire declared at the start of the final day, still 86 runs behind, whereupon Smith's 118 not out off 120 balls allowed Nicholas to set them to score 273 in 59 overs.

Close of play: First day, Hampshire 89-3 (M. C. J. Nicholas 27*, R. A. Smith 39*); Second day, Worcestershire 152-2 (G. J. Lord 64*, D. B. D'Oliveira 20*).

Hampshire

V. P. Terry lbw b Newport	1	– c Curtis b Radford	9
C. L. Smith c Botham b Radford	14	– not out	118
*M. C. J. Nicholas not out	110	– retired hurt	0
D. R. Turner b Radford	0	– b McEwan	22
R. A. Smith c Rhodes b Newport	40	– b McEwan	4
K. D. James lbw b Newport	9	– not out	23
M. D. Marshall run out	24		
†R. J. Parks c D'Oliveira b McEwan	3		
T. M. Tremlett c Rhodes b McEwan	8		
R. J. Maru c Hick b Radford	9		
C. A. Connor c and b Newport	0		
B 1, l-b 9, w 3, n-b 7	20	L-b 4, n-b 6	10

1/11 2/22 3/22 4/93 5/116   238   1/21 2/70 3/78   (3 wkts dec.) 186
6/166 7/183 8/198 9/237

Bonus points – Hampshire 2, Worcestershire 4.

Bowling: *First Innings*—Radford 29-8-86-3; Newport 25-4-84-4; McEwan 10-1-32-2; Lampitt 10-3-26-0. *Second Innings*—Newport 9-2-38-0; Radford 7-0-25-1; McEwan 11-1-36-2; Hick 10-2-47-0; Lampitt 4-0-20-0; Curtis 2-0-16-0.

Worcestershire

T. S. Curtis b Connor	49	– c Maru b Tremlett	17
G. J. Lord not out	64	– c C. L. Smith b Marshall	12
G. A. Hick c R. A. Smith b Maru	5	– b Tremlett	16
D. B. D'Oliveira not out	20	– b Maru	31
*P. A. Neale (did not bat)		– b Marshall	90
I. T. Botham (did not bat)		– b Connor	12
S. R. Lampitt (did not bat)		– c Terry b James	24
†S. J. Rhodes (did not bat)		– c C. L. Smith b Maru	17
N. V. Radford (did not bat)		– lbw b Marshall	2
P. J. Newport (did not bat)		– not out	1
S. M. McEwan (did not bat)		– c Maru b Marshall	1
B 3, l-b 7, w 1, n-b 3	14	B 1, l-b 5, w 2, n-b 10	18

1/109 2/118   (2 wkts dec.) 152   1/33 2/42 3/73 4/89 5/104   241
6/205 7/233 8/239 9/239

Bonus points – Worcestershire 1.

Bowling: *First Innings*—Marshall 9-2-27-0; Connor 16-8-21-1; Tremlett 10-2-22-0; Maru 18-4-39-1; James 5-0-26-0; C. L. Smith 3-0-7-0. *Second Innings*—Marshall 9-1-23-4; Connor 9-1-36-1; Maru 21-3-77-2; Tremlett 9-0-29-2; James 7-0-70-1.

Umpires: J. W. Holder and A. A. Jones.

At Birmingham, August 29, 31, September 1. WORCESTERSHIRE drew with WARWICKSHIRE.

At Colchester, September 2, 3, 4. WORCESTERSHIRE beat ESSEX by 119 runs.

WORCESTERSHIRE v NORTHAMPTONSHIRE

At Worcester, September 12, 14, 15. Worcestershire won by four wickets. Worcestershire 20 pts, Northamptonshire 6 pts. Toss: Northamptonshire. Rain restricted Saturday's play to only seventeen overs, but the match took several remarkable turns on Monday and Tuesday to bring Worcestershire their fifth Championship win of the season, achieved with five balls to spare. Both sides made up for lost time with heavy scoring on the second day, 473 runs coming from 120 overs for the loss of seven wickets. Harper (seventeen fours) and Wild (one six, twelve fours) added 221 without being parted for the visitors' sixth wicket, but they were upstaged by Hick's unbeaten 140, his third consecutive Championship hundred and his eighth of the summer. From 145 deliveries, it included seventeen fours and took him past 1,000 first-class runs in a prolific seven-week period. When Neale declared at the start of the final day, Radford and Newport skittled out Northamptonshire for 101 in 37 overs and five balls, leaving Worcestershire a minimum of 64 overs in which to score 227.

Close of play: First day, Northamptonshire 82-4 (R. G. Williams 9*, R. A. Harper 2*); Second day, Worcestershire 215-6 (G. A. Hick 140*, P. J. Newport 10*).

Northamptonshire

*G. Cook c Rhodes b Newport	7	– c sub b Radford	0
W. Larkins c Lord b Radford	48	– b Newport	1
R. J. Bailey lbw b Radford	10	– b Weston	36
A. J. Lamb c Newport b Radford	2	– c sub b Newport	10
R. G. Williams b McEwan	25	– lbw b Radford	0
R. A. Harper not out	127	– retired hurt	8
D. J. Wild not out	102	– c Hick b Radford	10
†D. Ripley (did not bat)		– c Rhodes b Radford	16
N. G. B. Cook (did not bat)		– c Hick b Newport	4
G. Smith (did not bat)		– c Hick b Newport	6
M. A. Robinson (did not bat)		– not out	1
B 1, l-b 11, w 6, n-b 1	19	B 1, l-b 5, w 1, n-b 2	9

1/16 2/61 3/65 4/80 5/119   (5 wkts dec.) 340   1/0 2/4 3/34 4/41 5/67   101
6/89 7/94 8/100 9/101

Bonus points – Northamptonshire 4, Worcestershire 2.

Bowling: *First Innings*—Radford 17-3-47-3; Newport 14-1-65-1; McEwan 11-1-65-1; Hick 17-0-84-0; Weston 8-0-34-0; D'Oliveira 8-0-34-0. *Second Innings*—Radford 14-3-35-4; Newport 12.5-4-28-4; McEwan 6-0-20-0; Weston 5-1-12-1.

Worcestershire

T. S. Curtis lbw b Robinson	12	– c and b N. G. B. Cook	71
G. J. Lord lbw b Smith	10	– b Smith	6
G. A. Hick not out	140	– c sub b N. G. B. Cook	56
D. B. D'Oliveira c G. Cook b Smith	2	– b Williams	20
*P. A. Neale c and b N. G. B. Cook	14	– c Larkins b Williams	34
M. J. Weston c Wild b Robinson	2	– not out	28
†S. J. Rhodes c Smith b N. G. B. Cook	10	– (8) not out	0
P. J. Newport not out	10		
N. V. Radford (did not bat)		– (7) b Williams	0
L-b 8, n-b 7	15	B 6, l-b 6, n-b 1	13

1/21 2/40 3/46 4/99   (6 wkts dec.) 215   1/19 2/93 3/141   (6 wkts) 228
5/116 6/163   4/177 5/223 6/224

I. T. Botham and S. M. McEwan did not bat.

Bonus points – Worcestershire 2, Northamptonshire 2.

Bowling: *First Innings*—Robinson 18-3-53-2; Smith 9-2-32-2; Harper 4-1-9-0; Wild 7-0-27-0; N. G. B. Cook 21-3-62-2; Williams 5-1-24-0. *Second Innings*—Robinson 5-0-15-0; Smith 6-0-32-1; Wild 12-0-60-0; N. G. B. Cook 25.1-6-53-2; Williams 15-2-56-3.

Umpires: D. J. Constant and J. H. Harris.

YORKSHIRE

Patron: HRH The Duchess of Kent
President: The Viscount Mountgarret
Chairman: B. Walsh
Chairman, Cricket Committee: D. B. Close
Secretary: J. Lister
   Headingley Cricket Ground, Leeds LS6 3BU
   (Telephone: 0532-787394)
Captain: P. Carrick

Yorkshire, who began 1987 under a cloud of doubt, put most – if not all – their difficulties behind them and exceeded the expectations of even their most optimistic follower. The highlight of the season was the triumph in the Benson and Hedges Cup, in which they defeated Northamptonshire in an absorbing final from which both sides emerged with credit. It was a success which put Yorkshire in the company of Essex, Kent and Lancashire as the only other counties to capture all four major honours. In addition, they recorded seven victories in the Britannic Assurance Championship, the most since 1978. But there was a worrying decline in the second half of the summer as they faded – after heading the table for a long time – to finish eighth, only two places better than 1986.

Following the decision not to renew Geoffrey Boycott's contract, the most important move was the appointment of Phil Carrick as captain in place of David Bairstow. Bairstow quickly settled back into the role of senior professional, which suited his temperament. And, without the ultimate responsibility in the field, he refound much of his best form behind the stumps until injury, with which he wrestled bravely over a lengthy period, reduced his effectiveness. At the same time, the players appeared happier with Carrick's more relaxed style of leadership, which allowed them to make a number of decisions themselves. Confidence grew in the course of a splendid start which produced eight successive victories in the different competitions. To some extent Yorkshire had an advantage at Headingley, where the varying bounce unsettled a number of visiting sides, particularly in the Benson and Hedges Cup, but the team played positive cricket, with several of the younger members figuring prominently.

Paul Jarvis, although not consistent and sometimes vulnerable when adopting a defensive role, bowled above medium pace with genuine hostility, as did Arnie Sidebottom. Jarvis had easily the best striking-rate for Yorkshire in the Championship with a wicket every 47.7 balls, and his 75 wickets underlined both his potential and his importance to the county's attack. Among the batsmen, Richard Blakey made remarkable progress. The twenty-year-old Young England opener, who effectively stepped into Boycott's shoes, even though he batted at No. 3, became the youngest since Len Hutton to make 1,000 first-class runs in a season for Yorkshire and the youngest ever to complete a double-century. Displaying an impressive temperament, Blakey made his runs with a good deal of style – 51.8 per 100 balls – and fully earned his cap, which was awarded before the final fixture of the season, at Scarborough.

On July 12, Yorkshire beat Middlesex in the Refuge Assurance Sunday League while still basking in the glory of the previous day's Benson and Hedges Cup victory at Lord's. At that point they were very much in contention on all fronts, but it proved to be the high-water-mark in their fortunes. They fell away in disappointing fashion. In going through eight Sunday League fixtures without a win – five defeats with three abandoned – they endured their worst run at that level. Hopes of a serious challenge for the NatWest Bank Trophy disappeared when they collapsed dramatically under no more than steady pressure from Leicestershire.

They also lost momentum in the Championship in a sequence which spotlighted an unexpected weakness. The batting proved unreliable, despite the efforts of Martyn Moxon and Blakey. Ashley Metcalfe enjoyed considerable success in the limited-overs games, scoring 1,095 runs for an average of 49.77 in the three principal competitions, but was unable to develop that form in the three-day game. More importantly, Jim Love and Kevin Sharp lacked authority in the middle order. To compensate, Ian Swallow, although previously regarded as an off-spinner, did well with limited opportunities and Phil Robinson marked his belated call to the first team with a series of sturdy innings. It might be argued that these two should have been chosen more often.

Selection policy was often difficult to follow, and an insistence on using four seamers, supported by Carrick's slow left-arm, left Yorkshire with an unbalanced and limited attack in the Championship. Indeed, Carrick appeared to put too much faith in a satisfactory limited-overs formula, and in doing so he inadvertently helped create an air of complacency in the dressing-room. Certainly Yorkshire lost their keen edge once they had made sure of the Benson and Hedges Cup.

The bowling, from an attacking point of view, depended heavily on Jarvis and Sidebottom, who at 34 takes his benefit in 1988. Peter Hartley did enough to convince the cricket committee that he, too, deserved a cap. He had a fairly lean time in August and September, however, and proved more expensive than Stuart Fletcher, who might have been given more work. Chris Shaw could not force his way into the reckoning on anything like a regular basis. A failure to use an off-spinner meant that Swallow and the highly regarded Phil Berry were unable to advance their careers, leaving Carrick the only slow bowler with reasonable county experience. This is a matter which should receive attention in the near future.

Equally, Bairstow is the one specialist wicket-keeper equipped for senior duty. Blakey did a reasonable job when pressed into service, but here, too, the cricket committee will have to take positive action. On the credit side, Yorkshire proved that they can compete with the best, although they still have a lot to do before they can take real satisfaction from their team-building programme. The foundations have been laid. Much will depend on how Carrick handles the situation now that more is expected from his side; also on how much support he receives. – John Callaghan.

YORKSHIRE 1987

[Bill Smith]

Back row: W. Morton (physiotherapist) R. J. Blakey, S. D. Fletcher, M. D. Moxon, P. J. Hartley, S. N. Hartley, P. W. Jarvis, A. A. Metcalfe. Front row: J. D. Love, D. L. Bairstow, P. Carrick (captain), A. Sidebottom, K. Sharp. Insets: P. E. Robinson, C. Shaw, I. G. Swallow, S. J. Dennis.

YORKSHIRE RESULTS

All first-class matches – Played 24: Won 7, Lost 4, Drawn 13. Abandoned 1.

County Championship matches – Played 23: Won 7, Lost 3, Drawn 13. Abandoned 1.

Bonus points – Batting 52, Bowling 58.

Competition placings – Britannic Assurance County Championship, 8th; NatWest Bank Trophy, q-f; Benson and Hedges Cup, winners; Refuge Assurance League, 12th equal.

BRITANNIC ASSURANCE CHAMPIONSHIP AVERAGES

BATTING

	Birthplace	M	I	NO	R	HI	Avge
‡R. J. Blakey	Huddersfield	23	36	5	1,343	204*	43.32
‡M. D. Moxon	Barnsley	21	35	4	1,298	130	41.87
P. E. Robinson	Keighley	6	11	2	330	95	36.66
‡D. L. Bairstow	Bradford	19	22	1	695	128	33.09
‡A. A. Metcalfe	Horsforth	22	38	4	1,010	113	29.70
‡K. Sharp	Leeds	20	32	4	751	81*	26.82
‡J. D. Love	Leeds	20	28	6	590	79*	26.81
C. Shaw	Hemsworth	6	5	4	24	22*	24.00
I. G. Swallow	Barnsley	4	7	2	107	55	21.40
‡S. N. Hartley	Shipley	9	16	1	284	63	18.93
‡P. J. Hartley	Keighley	21	25	7	332	49	18.44
‡P. Carrick	Armley	23	28	2	450	61	17.30
‡P. W. Jarvis	Redcar	22	24	11	212	32	16.30
‡A. Sidebottom	Barnsley	17	21	5	260	33	16.25
S. D. Fletcher	Keighley	15	12	6	61	15	10.16

Also batted: ‡S. J. Dennis (*Scarborough*) (2 matches) 4, 1; P. J. Berry (*Saltburn*) (3 matches) did not bat.

* *Signifies not out.*   ‡ *Denotes county cap.*

The following played a total of nine three-figure innings for Yorkshire in County Championship matches – R. J. Blakey 4, D. L. Bairstow 2, M. D. Moxon 2, A. A. Metcalfe 1.

BOWLING

	O	M	R	W	BB	Avge
P. W. Jarvis	596.2	137	1,831	75	7-82	24.41
P. Carrick	534.4	189	1,199	48	5-42	24.97
I. G. Swallow	84	19	267	10	7-95	26.70
A. Sidebottom	425.1	80	1,182	42	4-46	28.14
S. D. Fletcher	276.3	54	903	32	4-22	28.21
P. J. Hartley	485	92	1,641	46	4-52	35.67

Also bowled: D. L. Bairstow 5-0-29-0; P. J. Berry 14-3-55-1; S. J. Dennis 47-8-168-2; S. N. Hartley 12-2-50-2; J. D. Love 99.2-13-345-4; A. A. Metcalfe 12.2-1-62-3; M. D. Moxon 29-7-78-1; K. Sharp 37.1-6-189-1; C. Shaw 95.2-21-268-9.

Wicket-keepers: D. L. Bairstow 31 ct, 4 st; R. J. Blakey 11 ct.

Leading Fielders: M. D. Moxon 23, R. J. Blakey 15.

At Lord's, April 25, 26, 27. YORKSHIRE beat MIDDLESEX by two wickets.

YORKSHIRE v HAMPSHIRE

At Leeds, May 6, 7, 8. Yorkshire won by 15 runs. Yorkshire 23 pts, Hampshire 3 pts. Toss: Yorkshire. On a pitch of uneven bounce, batting was a hazardous business and Moxon played a crucial innings which stretched over 338 minutes. His 98 came from 263 balls and included fourteen fours. Greenidge adopted a more aggressive approach, his 54 coming from only 70 balls (one six, nine fours) before he was brilliantly caught, wide down the leg side, by the stand-in wicket-keeper, Blakey. No-one else in the Hampshire line-up had a similar solution, and when Yorkshire collapsed in their second innings the second day realised just 239 runs for the loss of seventeen wickets. Hampshire's target on the last day was 263 in 97 overs and a tremendous tussle developed. Turner battled for two and a half hours, but could not quite turn the tide, and although Marshall hit out defiantly, Fletcher's spell of three for 18 proved more decisive. In dismissing Smith, Carrick took his 700th first-class wicket.

Close of play: First day, Hampshire 32-0 (C. G. Greenidge 29*, V. P. Terry 1*); Second day, Yorkshire 123-7 (A. Sidebottom 26*, P. J. Hartley 0*).

Yorkshire

M. D. Moxon c Parks b Tremlett	98	– c Parks b James	34
A. A. Metcalfe c Parks b Tremlett	30	– c Smith b Marshall	36
†R. J. Blakey b Marshall	17	– c Terry b Tremlett	1
K. Sharp c Maru b Marshall	16	– b Tremlett	2
J. D. Love c Parks b Tremlett	3	– c Greenidge b Connor	0
S. N. Hartley c Greenidge b Marshall	20	– lbw b Marshall	0
*P. Carrick c Terry b James	26	– lbw b Marshall	13
A. Sidebottom not out	22	– c Parks b Marshall	26
P. J. Hartley b James	8	– b Connor	0
P. W. Jarvis not out	18	– not out	0
S. D. Fletcher (did not bat)		– c Greenidge b Connor	0
B 4, l-b 11, w 2, n-b 11	28	B 4, l-b 6, w 1, n-b 1	12

1/39 2/71 3/119 4/125 5/198   (8 wkts dec.) 286   1/57 2/62 3/74 4/81 5/82   124
6/236 7/238 8/247   6/83 7/122 8/123 9/124

Bonus points – Yorkshire 3, Hampshire 3 (Score at 100 overs: 274-8).

Bowling: *First Innings*–Marshall 25-5-48-3; Connor 14-2-67-0; Maru 13-6-25-0; Tremlett 31-12-62-3; James 23-6-69-2. *Second Innings*–Marshall 16-5-37-4; Connor 12.4-2-32-3; Tremlett 13-7-21-2; James 8-3-18-1; Maru 3-1-6-0.

Hampshire

C. G. Greenidge c Blakey b P. J. Hartley	54	– c Blakey b Sidebottom	29
V. P. Terry b P. J. Hartley	23	– b Fletcher	35
*M. C. J. Nicholas c S. N. Hartley b Fletcher	0	– c Love b P. J. Hartley	8
C. L. Smith c S. N. Hartley b Sidebottom	11	– c Moxon b Carrick	8
D. R. Turner b Fletcher	0	– lbw b Fletcher	47
K. D. James run out	10	– c Blakey b Sidebottom	24
M. D. Marshall b Jarvis	22	– c Carrick b Sidebottom	44
T. M. Tremlett b Fletcher	0	– c Blakey b Fletcher	0
†R. J. Parks not out	14	– c Moxon b Fletcher	21
R. J. Maru lbw b Jarvis	1	– c Blakey b Sidebottom	12
C. A. Connor lbw b Jarvis	0	– not out	5
L-b 9, n-b 4	13	L-b 6, w 1, n-b 7	14

1/85 2/86 3/86 4/93 5/102   148   1/38 2/53 3/72 4/106 5/147   247
6/115 7/122 8/140 9/142   6/185 7/185 8/219 9/236

Bonus points – Yorkshire 4.

Bowling: *First Innings*—Jarvis 18.3–4–43–3; Sidebottom 19–3–56–1; Fletcher 12–5–26–3; P. J. Hartley 12–6–14–2. *Second Innings*—Sidebottom 23.4–6–46–4; Jarvis 7–0–25–0; P. J. Hartley 21–7–81–1; Fletcher 16–4–44–4; Carrick 23–7–38–1; Love 2–0–7–0.

Umpires: J. W. Holder and D. O. Oslear.

YORKSHIRE v SOMERSET

At Leeds, May 20, 21, 22. Drawn. Yorkshire 8 pts, Somerset 6 pts. Toss: Somerset. Roebuck took a battering on another pitch of uneven bounce, the index finger on his right hand being broken by a ball from Jarvis as he made 112 from 255 balls with thirteen boundaries. Blakey was also injured, having to retire after being hit on the elbow at 16, but he came back to record his highest score and see his side obtain a useful lead. Marks was resolute when Somerset batted again, staying 130 minutes for his unbeaten 63, and Roebuck went in last to use up an over, although he did not face a ball. Yorkshire, in pursuit of 160 from seventeen overs, launched a foolhardy charge and finished up having to defend anxiously after losing five wickets for 53 in nine overs.

Close of play: First day, Yorkshire 14-0 (M. D. Moxon 8*, A. A. Metcalfe 4*); Second day, Yorkshire 332-8 (P. J. Hartley 9*, P. W. Jarvis 12*).

Somerset

N. A. Felton c Bairstow b Jarvis	0	– c Blakey b Hartley	11
*P. M. Roebuck c Fletcher b Hartley	112	– (11) not out	0
J. J. E. Hardy c Carrick b Fletcher	8	– (2) c Metcalfe b Sidebottom	17
M. D. Crowe b Hartley	1	– (3) c Sharp b Fletcher	36
R. J. Harden c Jarvis b Sidebottom	17	– (4) c Bairstow b Moxon	28
V. J. Marks b Sidebottom	21	– (5) not out	63
†N. D. Burns b Sidebottom	0	– (6) b Jarvis	37
G. D. Rose b Hartley	43	– (7) c Sidebottom b Hartley	0
M. R. Davis c Moxon b Carrick	13	– (8) hit wkt b Sidebottom	3
N. A. Mallender not out	20	– (9) lbw b Hartley	0
A. N. Jones b Hartley	7	– (10) c Hartley b Jarvis	15
B 1, l-b 20, w 1, n-b 5	27	B 4, l-b 4, w 1, n-b 10	19
	269	(9 wkts dec.)	**229**

1/7 2/39 3/41 4/85 5/139 6/139 7/217 8/222 9/253

1/30 2/33 3/98 4/107 5/158 6/161 7/180 8/181 9/220

Bonus points – Somerset 3, Yorkshire 4 (Score at 100 overs: 257-9).

Bowling: *First Innings*—Sidebottom 24–7–51–3; Jarvis 20–4–54–1; Hartley 21.5–5–52–4; Fletcher 19–3–64–1; Carrick 14–3–23–1; Moxon 3–1–4–0. *Second Innings*—Sidebottom 14–3–28–2; Jarvis 19–4–68–2; Hartley 20–3–59–3; Fletcher 15–3–54–1; Carrick 2–0–6–0; Moxon 5–2–6–1.

Yorkshire

M. D. Moxon c Burns b Jones	24	– not out	29
A. A. Metcalfe lbw b Jones	66	– c Davis b Jones	0
R. J. Blakey lbw b Marks	99	– (7) c Burns b Rose	4
K. Sharp c Burns b Jones	32	– (3) c Rose b Jones	1
J. D. Love c Marks b Mallender	5	– b Rose	0
†D. L. Bairstow lbw b Rose	47	– (4) c Burns b Jones	23
*P. Carrick c sub b Rose	3	– (6) c Crowe b Jones	2
A. Sidebottom lbw b Mallender	12	– c Crowe b Jones	2
P. J. Hartley b Jones	9	– not out	9
P. W. Jarvis b Davis	19		
S. D. Fletcher not out	0		
L-b 8, w 1, n-b 14	23	L-b 3, w 1	4
	339	(7 wkts)	**74**

1/41 2/148 3/157 4/183 5/281 6/285 7/309 8/311 9/337

1/1 2/11 3/47 4/50 5/53 6/58 7/61

Bonus points – Yorkshire 4, Somerset 3 (Score at 100 overs: 311-7).

In the first innings R. J. Blakey, when 16, retired hurt at 70 and resumed at 148.

Bowling: *First Innings*—Jones 20–3–80–4; Mallender 20–2–67–2; Rose 19–6–76–2; Davis 21.5–6–43–1; Marks 24–5–56–1; Crowe 3–0–9–0. *Second Innings*—Jones 7–0–31–5; Mallender 3.4–1–23–0; Rose 5–1–17–2; Davis 1–1–0–0.

Umpires: H. D. Bird and J. Birkenshaw.

At Cardiff, May 23, 25, 26. YORKSHIRE lost to GLAMORGAN by 73 runs.

YORKSHIRE v NOTTINGHAMSHIRE

At Middlesbrough, May 30, June 1, 2. Drawn. Yorkshire 4 pts, Nottinghamshire 8 pts. Toss: Yorkshire. Yorkshire batted badly on a greenish pitch that allowed some extra bounce but lacked pace. Rice had a spell of three for 18 in twenty balls to break the back of the innings, and only a brave 52 in 107 minutes by Carrick brought a second batting point. Rice followed up with a fine 98 after Broad had retired hurt after five balls on the second morning, and it was later learnt that his left thumb had been broken by a ball from Agnew in the previous day's Refuge Assurance League match against Leicestershire. Rice batted for 166 minutes and, making the most of some wayward bowling, hit one six and fifteen fours. Yorkshire, batting again, collapsed badly and only rain, which washed out the last day, saved them from defeat.

Close of play: First day, Nottinghamshire 47-0 (B. C. Broad 27*, R. T. Robinson 17*); Second day, Yorkshire 42-4 (K. Sharp 20*, P. W. Jarvis 2*).

Yorkshire

M. D. Moxon c French b Rice	47	– c French b Rice	8
A. A. Metcalfe c Broad b Hadlee	13	– c Robinson b Saxelby	0
R. J. Blakey lbw b Rice	37	– lbw b Saxelby	9
K. Sharp c Johnson b Rice	9	– not out	20
J. D. Love c Randall b Hadlee	8	– c French b Rice	0
†D. L. Bairstow c French b Hadlee	20		
*P. Carrick c Broad b Hemmings	52		
A. Sidebottom c Johnson b Saxelby	5		
P. J. Hartley b Rice	12		
P. W. Jarvis c French b Hemmings	3	– (6) not out	2
S. D. Fletcher not out	0		
L-b 8, w 1, n-b 3	12	N-b 3	3

1/19 2/84 3/107 4/114 5/138   218   1/1 2/19 3/20 4/26   (4 wkts) 42
6/155 7/164 8/190 9/203

Bonus points – Yorkshire 2, Nottinghamshire 4.

Bowling: *First Innings*—Hadlee 19–8–35–3; Rice 27–8–68–4; Saxelby 27–12–58–1; Hemmings 7.4–0–29–2; Afford 2–0–13–0; Birch 2–0–7–0. *Second Innings*—Saxelby 8–1–22–2; Rice 8–5–8–2; Afford 1–0–12–0.

Nottinghamshire

B. C. Broad retired hurt	27	R. J. Hadlee not out	28
*R. T. Robinson c Bairstow b Jarvis	38	K. Saxelby c Sharp b Fletcher	4
D. W. Randall lbw b Hartley	58	J. A. Afford c Love b Fletcher	0
P. Johnson lbw b Jarvis	0		
C. E. B. Rice c Jarvis b Carrick	98	B 10, l-b 14, w 1, n-b 8	33
J. D. Birch c and b Carrick	45		
E. E. Hemmings lbw b Hartley	10		347
†B. N. French lbw b Jarvis	6	1/91 2/91 3/173 4/278 5/292	
		6/304 7/328 8/345 9/347	

Bonus points – Nottinghamshire 4, Yorkshire 2 (Score at 100 overs: 307-6).

B. C. Broad retired hurt at 48.

Bowling: Sidebottom 19–3–52–0; Jarvis 30–6–85–3; Hartley 17–1–79–2; Carrick 19–6–35–2; Fletcher 15.2–4–44–2; Moxon 2–0–14–0; Love 6–2–14–0.

Umpires: B. Leadbeater and N. T. Plews.

YORKSHIRE v WORCESTERSHIRE

At Sheffield, June 3, 4, 5. Drawn. Yorkshire 2 pts, Worcestershire 3 pts. Toss: Yorkshire. Bad weather ruined this game, with only eleven overs possible on the first day and none at all on the second. In order to make up for lost time, each side forfeited an innings and Worcestershire were set to make 231 in 48 overs. On a slow pitch that made timing difficult, they never really moved into an effective stride, being only 77 for one after twenty overs. Hick, who had a useful all-round match, taking wickets even when tactically offering Yorkshire runs, brought about an acceleration with 54 from 60 balls, hitting a six and nine fours, but the chance of a result was slim when bad light brought an early end.

Close of play: First day, Yorkshire 19-1 (M. D. Moxon 14*, R. J. Blakey 2*); Second day, No play.

Yorkshire

M. D. Moxon c Radford b Hick	82	*P. Carrick not out 40
A. A. Metcalfe c Weston b Pridgeon	3	A. Sidebottom not out 9
R. J. Blakey lbw b Radford	5	
K. Sharp st Rhodes b Hick	69	L-b 1, n-b 1 2
J. D. Love c Pridgeon b Hick	16	
†D. L. Bairstow c Illingworth b Hick	0	1/16 2/23 3/137 4/160 (7 wkts dec.) 230
S. N. Hartley c Rhodes b Illingworth	4	5/160 6/165 7/199

C. Shaw and S. D. Fletcher did not bat.

Bonus points – Yorkshire 2, Worcestershire 3.

Bowling: Radford 13-3-34-1; Pridgeon 14-5-24-1; Newport 8-1-25-0; Illingworth 16-2-63-1; Hick 11.2-0-83-4.

Yorkshire forfeited their second innings.

Worcestershire

Worcestershire forfeited their first innings.

T. S. Curtis not out	41	P. J. Newport not out 0
M. J. Weston c Bairstow b Sidebottom	1	
G. A. Hick c Love b Carrick	54	L-b 4, n-b 4 8
D. B. D'Oliveira b Sidebottom	14	
*P. A. Neale c Sharp b Carrick	9	1/10 2/84 3/105 (5 wkts) 128
†S. J. Rhodes lbw b Carrick	1	4/122 5/128

S. R. Lampitt, R. K. Illingworth, N. V. Radford and A. P. Pridgeon did not bat.

Bowling: Sidebottom 14-0-42-2; Fletcher 5-0-27-0; Carrick 14.4-4-30-3; Love 3-0-9-0; Shaw 3-1-16-0.

Umpires: B. Leadbeater and N. T. Plews.

YORKSHIRE v DERBYSHIRE

At Harrogate, June 6, 8, 9. Yorkshire won by an innings and 169 runs. Yorkshire 24 pts, Derbyshire 2 pts. Toss: Yorkshire. Only 47 overs were possible on the first day because of overnight rain, but on an easy-paced pitch Yorkshire batted solidly, and they continued well into the second day in the hope of enforcing the follow-on. Moxon's 130, the cornerstone of the innings, came from 255 balls and he struck one six and sixteen fours. Bairstow set about some dispirited bowling with 104 from only 149 deliveries, hitting four sixes and twelve fours as he and Moxon put on 196 in 48 overs. Derbyshire failed to take advantage of the conditions, which were still more than adequate for batting, although there was some slow turn from the pavilion end. Only Morris challenged the bowlers as seven wickets fell before the close, and on the final day Derbyshire fared even worse. Carrick claimed two wickets without conceding a run in 43 balls and finished with match figures of five for 10 in 26 overs. When, within fifteen minutes of the early finish, heavy rain began to fall, it seemed a natural indictment of the poor cricket played by the visiting side.

Close of play: First day, Yorkshire 121-3 (M. D. Moxon 53*, D. L. Bairstow 31*); Second day, Derbyshire 103-7 (P. G. Newman 24*, C. F. B. P. Rudd 2*).

Yorkshire

M. D. Moxon c Wright b Rudd 130	P. J. Hartley b Morris 24
A. A. Metcalfe c Wright b Newman ... 5	P. W. Jarvis not out 3
R. J. Blakey c Roberts b Jean-Jacques . 22	
K. Sharp c Maher b Jean-Jacques 0	B 5, l-b 7, w 3, n-b 12 27
†D. L. Bairstow run out 104	
J. D. Love not out 50	1/14 2/66 3/66 4/262 (7 wkts dec.) 393
*P. Carrick c Rudd b Finney 28	5/292 6/325 7/376

S. D. Fletcher and P. J. Berry did not bat.

Bonus points – Yorkshire 4, Derbyshire 2 (Score at 100 overs: 353-6).

Bowling: Newman 17–3–59–1; Warner 21–5–56–0; Rudd 19–4–89–1; Barnett 3–1–5–0; Jean-Jacques 23–4–86–2; Roberts 7–1–19–0; Finney 16–2–54–1; Morris 2.3–0–13–1.

Derbyshire

*K. J. Barnett b Jarvis	2	– c Carrick b Fletcher	11
J. G. Wright c Bairstow b Jarvis	6	– c Moxon b Jarvis	4
B. Roberts c Metcalfe b Hartley	9	– c Bairstow b Fletcher	5
J. E. Morris c Moxon b Fletcher	41	– c Blakey b Carrick	5
†B. J. M. Maher b Jarvis	10	– c Bairstow b Hartley	23
I. S. Anderson c Moxon b Carrick	1	– c Moxon b Carrick	2
R. J. Finney c Moxon b Fletcher	0	– c Love b Jarvis	0
P. G. Newman st Bairstow b Carrick	26	– c Carrick b Hartley	12
C. F. B. P. Rudd c Berry b Hartley	9	– not out	3
A. E. Warner lbw b Carrick	13	– c Berry b Fletcher	14
M. Jean-Jacques not out	0	– lbw b Fletcher	0
B 4, l-b 1, w 3, n-b 6	14	L-b 6, w 2, n-b 6	14

1/3 2/15 3/19 4/61 5/73		131	1/17 2/18 3/29 4/33 5/36	93
6/73 7/86 8/113 9/114			6/49 7/63 8/72 9/93	

Bonus points – Yorkshire 4.

Bowling: *First Innings*—Jarvis 13–2–40–3; Hartley 14–2–45–2; Berry 2–0–10–0; Fletcher 6–0–26–2; Carrick 13.1–9–5–3. *Second Innings*—Jarvis 6–0–26–2; Fletcher 7.1–1–23–4; Carrick 13–11–5–2; Hartley 7–0–33–2.

Umpires: M. J. Kitchen and R. A. White.

At Manchester, June 13, 14, 15. YORKSHIRE drew with LANCASHIRE.

At Basingstoke, June 17, 18, 19. YORKSHIRE drew with HAMPSHIRE.

YORKSHIRE v ESSEX

At Leeds, June 20, 22, 23. Yorkshire won by nine wickets. Yorkshire 24 pts, Essex 4 pts. Toss: Essex. Sidebottom, with wickets in each of his first two overs, destroyed Essex's confidence on a pitch of variable bounce. They needed eight overs for their first runs and only Gooch (87 balls), Lilley (101 balls) and Page (103 balls) checked Yorkshire's progress. The home batsmen, using experience of the conditions to get on the front foot, fared much better, with Moxon reaching a fine century from 180 balls (thirteen fours) out of 156. Topley bowled a long spell of tidy medium pace, but Yorkshire ground out a big lead and then struck early blows when Essex batted a second time. The match was prolonged by a workmanlike stand between East and Topley, who put on 67 in fifteen overs. Topley, who had come in as night-watchman, kept Yorkshire at bay for fractionally over four hours while he compiled his highest score in first-class cricket. Finally Sharp, an occasional off-spinner, forced an error and Yorkshire had time to win with ease.

Close of play: First day, Yorkshire 92-2 (M. D. Moxon 59*, K. Sharp 10*); Second day, Essex 25-3 (T. D. Topley 6*, D. E. East 0*).

Essex

*G. A. Gooch c Blakey b Jarvis	33	– b Sidebottom	5
I. Redpath lbw b Sidebottom	0	– lbw b Jarvis	0
B. R. Hardie lbw b Sidebottom	0	– (4) lbw b Jarvis	14
K. W. R. Fletcher c Bairstow b Hartley	19	– (6) c Fletcher b Hartley	6
G. Miller lbw b Jarvis	16	– (10) lbw b Jarvis	0
D. R. Pringle lbw b Jarvis	4	– (7) lbw b Sidebottom	7
A. W. Lilley b Carrick	22	– (8) b Hartley	15
H. A. Page c Hartley b Carrick	29	– (9) b Love	6
†D. E. East c Bairstow b Carrick	0	– (5) c Bairstow b Hartley	36
T. D. Topley c Hartley b Carrick	5	– (3) c Moxon b Sharp	66
J. H. Childs not out	15	– not out	4
B 4, l-b 4	8	B 9, l-b 14, w 4, n-b 2	29

1/0 2/0 3/34 4/71 5/72   151   1/5 2/5 3/25 4/92 5/110   188
6/83 7/119 8/119 9/133   6/127 7/154 8/174 9/174

Bonus points – Essex 1, Yorkshire 4.

Bowling: *First Innings*—Jarvis 20-8-34-3; Sidebottom 19-9-20-2; Fletcher 13-3-34-0; Hartley 11-0-45-1; Carrick 12.3-7-10-4. *Second Innings*—Jarvis 17-3-67-3; Sidebottom 12-1-30-2; Hartley 12-5-27-3; Fletcher 8-2-23-0; Carrick 16-11-8-0; Love 8-4-10-1; Sharp 1.1-1-0-1.

Yorkshire

M. D. Moxon run out	104		
A. A. Metcalfe c Miller b Topley	9	– lbw b Page	0
R. J. Blakey b Pringle	6		
K. Sharp b Topley	50	– (3) not out	1
J. D. Love not out	65	– (1) not out	10
†D. L. Bairstow lbw b Topley	0		
*P. Carrick c Hardie b Topley	5		
A. Sidebottom b Gooch	7		
P. J. Hartley b Page	49		
P. W. Jarvis not out	8		
L-b 17, n-b 11	28		

1/61 2/75 3/161 4/191 5/191 (8 wkts dec.) 331 1/6   (1 wkt) 11
6/203 7/226 8/313

S. D. Fletcher did not bat.

Bonus points – Yorkshire 4, Essex 3 (Score at 100 overs: 313-7).

Bowling: *First Innings*—Page 16-2-84-1; Pringle 28-4-87-1; Topley 38-12-75-4; Gooch 8-1-34-1; Childs 13-2-34-0. *Second Innings*—Topley 1-0-6-0; Page 1-0-5-1.

Umpires: J. A. Jameson and P. B. Wight.

At Northampton, June 27, 29, 30. YORKSHIRE lost to NORTHAMPTONSHIRE by seven wickets.

At Canterbury, July 1, 2, 3. YORKSHIRE beat KENT by two wickets.

At Nottingham, July 4, 6. YORKSHIRE lost to NOTTINGHAMSHIRE by eight wickets.

At The Oval, July 15, 16, 17. YORKSHIRE drew with SURREY.

At Hastings, July 18, 20, 21. SUSSEX v YORKSHIRE. Abandoned.

YORKSHIRE v GLAMORGAN

At Leeds, July 22, 23, 24. Drawn. Yorkshire 6 pts, Glamorgan 4 pts. Toss: Glamorgan. In the face of steady seam bowling, Yorkshire collapsed to 125 for seven after a delayed start because of overnight rain. They were troubled by bad light, but their problems had nothing to do with a good pitch that picked up pace as it dried out. Glamorgan, however, fared even worse, losing half their side for 31 as their batsmen played back instead of forward. Ontong showed what could be done, remaining unbeaten after 158 minutes. When Yorkshire batted a second time Glamorgan were missing their pace bowlers, van Zyl (stress fracture of the foot) and Smith (dislocated toe), but Yorkshire failed to score quickly enough to make the most of the situation. Another 30 overs were lost to rain on the last day and Glamorgan were set 246 in 61 overs. They again lost the top half of their order cheaply, but Ontong, dropped by Love at slip before he had scored, and Derrick hammered the spinners, who operated in poor light to keep things going until the weather closed in completely.

Close of play: First day, Yorkshire 181-9 (P. J. Hartley 28*, S. D. Fletcher 0*); Second day, Yorkshire 102-2 (M. D. Moxon 44*, J. D. Love 35*).

Yorkshire

M. D. Moxon lbw b van Zyl	1	– c Maynard b Derrick	56
A. A. Metcalfe c Holmes b Smith	32	– (5) not out	19
R. J. Blakey c Morris b van Zyl	13	– (2) lbw b Barwick	16
K. Sharp c James b Derrick	21	– (3) b Barwick	2
J. D. Love c Ontong b Barwick	31	– (4) run out	43
†D. L. Bairstow c Smith b Ontong	6	– b Derrick	4
*P. Carrick c James b Barwick	5		
A. Sidebottom lbw b van Zyl	25		
P. J. Hartley not out	43	– (7) not out	9
P. W. Jarvis b Ontong	6		
S. D. Fletcher c Holmes b Barwick	4		
L-b 9, w 1, n-b 3	13	W 1, n-b 4	5

1/6 2/24 3/70 4/72 5/97   200   1/25 2/27 3/122   (5 wkts dec.) 154
6/112 7/125 8/168 9/181   4/122 5/132

Bonus points – Yorkshire 2, Glamorgan 4.

Bowling: *First Innings*—van Zyl 13-2-35-3; Barwick 29-10-69-3; Smith 7-2-21-1; Derrick 5-1-20-1; Ontong 23-6-46-2. *Second Innings*—Barwick 17-1-54-2; Derrick 16-5-61-2; Ontong 7-0-20-0; Holmes 7-0-19-0.

Glamorgan

S. P. James c Bairstow b Jarvis	1	– c sub b Jarvis	27
*H. Morris b Sidebottom	9	– c Moxon b Hartley	29
G. C. Holmes lbw b Hartley	13	– c Blakey b Hartley	0
M. P. Maynard c Bairstow b Sidebottom	1	– b Hartley	19
R. C. Ontong not out	46	– not out	42
P. A. Todd lbw b Sidebottom	0	– c Bairstow b Jarvis	2
J. Derrick b Fletcher	10	– not out	47
†C. P. Metson c Moxon b Carrick	18		
I. Smith lbw b Jarvis	1		
C. J. P. G. van Zyl c Bairstow b Carrick	0		
S. R. Barwick lbw b Jarvis	4		
B 4, l-b 2	6	L-b 12, w 1, n-b 1	14

1/6 2/21 3/24 4/31 5/31   109   1/48 2/48 3/74   (5 wkts) 180
6/46 7/90 8/97 9/100   4/82 5/84

Bonus points – Yorkshire 4.

Bowling: *First Innings*—Jarvis 18–10–12–3; Sidebottom 14–4–34–3; Hartley 13–6–27–1; Fletcher 7–2–17–1; Carrick 9–4–13–2. *Second Innings*—Jarvis 12–2–42–2; Sidebottom 3–0–6–0; Hartley 12–3–34–3; Fletcher 6–1–9–0; Carrick 13–3–42–0; Love 10–0–35–0.

Umpires: B. Leadbeater and N. T. Plews.

At Leicester, July 25, 27, 28. YORKSHIRE beat LEICESTERSHIRE by an innings and 86 runs.

YORKSHIRE v LANCASHIRE

At Leeds, August 1, 3, 4. Drawn. Yorkshire 5 pts, Lancashire 4 pts. Toss: Yorkshire. Lancashire scored steadily on a pitch that offered no help to the bowlers after being subjected to fifteen tons of pressure in a rolling exercise undertaken to solve Headingley's problems of uneven bounce. Fowler set a hectic pace in the early stages, but Lancashire's innings lost momentum until Watkinson, hitting six fours and four sixes in 81 from 116 balls, ensured a fourth batting point. On the second day, Yorkshire also made comfortable progress, but when rain washed out play from late afternoon, Carrick had to give Lancashire a 106-run lead to keep the game alive. Mendis moved serenely to an unbeaten hundred, with fourteen fours, from 180 balls, whereupon Lancashire at last set a target of 287 in 65 minutes plus twenty overs. Yorkshire, however, showed no interest and the match drifted along to become the twelfth successive Roses draw. Remarkably, no wicket fell on the last day, which was uninterrupted, although six batsmen, Blakey, Sharp, Moxon and Metcalfe for Yorkshire, and Mendis and Atherton for Lancashire, were at the wicket at various times.

Close of play: First day, Lancashire 326-8 (J. Simmons 1*, I. Folley 1*); Second day, Yorkshire 168-2 (R. J. Blakey 52*, K. Sharp 27*).

Lancashire

G. D. Mendis b Shaw	22	– not out	100
G. Fowler c Bairstow b Hartley	83		
M. A. Atherton lbw b Jarvis	44	– (2) not out	76
N. H. Fairbrother c Metcalfe b Shaw	21		
M. Watkinson c sub b Shaw	81		
*D. P. Hughes c Hartley b Carrick	10		
†W. K. Hegg b Shaw	35		
P. J. W. Allott run out	9		
J. Simmons not out	14		
I. Folley b Shaw	6		
K. W. McLeod c Moxon b Shaw	9		
B 1, l-b 16, w 2, n-b 3	22	L-b 3, w 1	4

1/71 2/127 3/162 4/192 5/217   356   (no wkt dec.) 180
6/309 7/321 8/324 9/338

Bonus points – Lancashire 4, Yorkshire 2 (Score at 100 overs: 309-6).

Bowling: *First Innings*—Jarvis 16–3–54–1; Hartley 21–2–62–1; Shaw 28.5–7–64–6; Fletcher 21–3–56–0; Moxon 5–1–22–0; Carrick 22–3–81–1. *Second Innings*—Fletcher 6–0–24–0; Hartley 2–1–2–0; Love 17–3–51–0; Sharp 16–5–49–0; Bairstow 5–0–29–0; Metcalfe 4–0–16–0; Shaw 3.3–1–6–0.

Yorkshire

M. D. Moxon c sub b Folley	54	– not out	51
A. A. Metcalfe c Fairbrother b Watkinson	25	– not out	47
R. J. Blakey not out	79		
K. Sharp not out	81		
B 5, l-b 1, w 1, n-b 4	11	L-b 2, n-b 2	4

1/65 2/125   (2 wkts dec.) 250   (no wkt) 102

J. D. Love, †D. L. Bairstow, *P. Carrick, P. J. Hartley, P. W. Jarvis, C. Shaw and S. D. Fletcher did not bat.

Bonus points – Yorkshire 3.

Bowling: *First Innings*—Allott 17–1–67–0; McLeod 13–2–29–0; Watkinson 17–2–63–1; Simmons 12.4–5–23–0; Folley 23–4–62–1. *Second Innings*—McLeod 5–3–5–0; Allott 4–1–9–0; Folley 10–2–36–0; Watkinson 4–0–33–0; Atherton 6–1–17–0.

Umpires: K. J. Lyons and B. J. Meyer.

At Chesterfield, August 5, 6, 7. YORKSHIRE drew with DERBYSHIRE.

YORKSHIRE v SUSSEX

At Sheffield, August 8, 10, 11. Drawn. Yorkshire 4 pts, Sussex 6 pts. Toss: Yorkshire. Yorkshire collapsed badly on an easy-paced pitch which allowed a little extra bounce. Pigott used this admirably, and only a fighting half-century by Swallow – his first at this level – achieved a degree of respectability. Lenham broke a bone in his foot as Sussex, in turn, made heavy weather of batting, and it needed Pigott to strike some good blows for them to gain a useful lead. Metcalfe, with one six and fifteen fours, made his first century of the season, from 163 balls, but rain had already reduced the room for manoeuvre. And when Sussex were eventually given a target of 197 in 48 overs, another downpour finished things.

Close of play: First day, Yorkshire 116-7 (I. G. Swallow 25*, S. J. Dennis 0*); Second day, Yorkshire 15-0 (A. A. Metcalfe 5*, I. G. Swallow 8*).

Yorkshire

†R. J. Blakey run out	7	– (3) c Parker b Babington	0
A. A. Metcalfe c Lenham b Kimber	23	– (1) c Babington b Kimber	113
K. Sharp c and b Pigott	5	– (4) c C. M. Wells b Kimber	54
P. E. Robinson c Standing b C. M. Wells	21	– (5) not out	21
S. N. Hartley lbw b Kimber	8	– (6) c Parker b C. M. Wells	14
I. G. Swallow c Parker b Pigott	55	– (2) c Parker b Babington	27
*P. Carrick c Moores b Pigott	8		
P. W. Jarvis c A. P. Wells b Babington	11		
S. J. Dennis c Pigott b Babington	1		
S. D. Fletcher b Heseltine	15		
C. Shaw not out	0		
B 4, l-b 5, n-b 4	13	L-b 5, w 1, n-b 4	10

1/10 2/22 3/58 4/62 5/71   167   1/90 2/92   (5 wkts dec.) 239
6/93 7/115 8/118 9/163   3/195 4/203 5/239

Bonus points – Yorkshire 1, Sussex 4.

Bowling: *First Innings*—Pigott 29–13–49–3; Babington 16–3–49–2; C. M. Wells 18–3–39–1; Kimber 7–3–13–2; Heseltine 5–0–8–1. *Second Innings*—Pigott 10–1–26–0; Babington 11–4–32–2; Standing 7–1–36–0; Kimber 9–0–57–2; Heseltine 15–2–52–0; C. M. Wells 6–0–31–1.

Sussex

D. K. Standing c Hartley b Dennis	4	– not out		6
N. J. Lenham retired hurt	12			
P. W. G. Parker lbw b Shaw	18			
A. P. Wells c Jarvis b Fletcher	21			
C. M. Wells c Blakey b Fletcher	33			
*I. J. Gould c Robinson b Carrick	29			
†P. Moores c Carrick b Jarvis	5	– (2) not out		4
A. C. S. Pigott lbw b Fletcher	35			
S. J. S. Kimber b Fletcher	19			
P. A. W. Heseltine not out	24			
A. M. Babington not out	0			
L-b 8, n-b 2	10	L-b 6		6

1/9 2/35 3/91 4/94   (8 wkts dec.) 210   (no wkt) 16
5/103 6/166 7/166 8/205

Bonus points – Sussex 2, Yorkshire 3.

Bowling: *First Innings*—Jarvis 22–4–60–1; Dennis 14–3–40–1; Shaw 14–1–45–1; Fletcher 14–6–35–4; Carrick 12–5–22–1. *Second Innings*—Jarvis 4.5–3–1–0; Dennis 4–2–9–0.

Umpires: H. D. Bird and J. W. Holder.

At Taunton, August 15, 17, 18. YORKSHIRE drew with SOMERSET.

YORKSHIRE v LEICESTERSHIRE

At Scarborough, August 19, 20, 21. Drawn. Yorkshire 6 pts, Leicestershire 8 pts. Toss: Leicestershire. After a delayed start because of rain, Briers (210 balls, ten fours) and Whitaker (206 balls, one six, fifteen fours) put Leicestershire in a strong position. This became even stronger when, on the second day, Agnew hit a spectacular, career-best 90 from 68 balls, including six sixes and eight fours, and then took the first five Yorkshire wickets to fall. Bairstow saved his side with a typically gritty effort, scoring his 128 from 157 balls (three sixes, seventeen fours). Leicestershire, with Cobb, Whitaker, DeFreitas and Whitticase affected by illness or injury, were in trouble at 62 for five after Carrick had given them a lead of 100. But DeFreitas hit out strongly, and Yorkshire made no attempt to chase a target of 289 in 56 overs.

Close of play: First day, Leicestershire 253-3 (J. J. Whitaker 94*, J. P. Agnew 9*); Second day, Yorkshire 265-9 (A. Sidebottom 9*, P. W. Jarvis 0*).

Leicestershire

I. P. Butcher b Jarvis	11	– lbw b Sidebottom		9
N. E. Briers c Jarvis b Carrick	104	– c Blakey b Sidebottom		5
R. A. Cobb c Bairstow b P. J. Hartley	13	– (8) not out		26
J. J. Whitaker b Sidebottom	105	– (5) c Bairstow b Sidebottom		9
J. P. Agnew c Bairstow b Jarvis	90	– (9) c Robinson b Swallow		19
*P. Willey b Sidebottom	8	– (3) c Bairstow b P. J. Hartley		19
P. B. Clift c Metcalfe b Jarvis	5	– (4) c Bairstow b P. J. Hartley		14
P. A. J. DeFreitas not out	5	– (6) c Carrick b P. J. Hartley		58
†P. Whitticase c Bairstow b Sidebottom	0	– (7) b Swallow		8
G. J. F. Ferris (did not bat)		– not out		1
B 5, l-b 6, w 1, n-b 12	24	B 8, l-b 7, n-b 5		20

1/20 2/70 3/241 4/332 5/345   (8 wkts dec.) 365   1/14 2/27 3/39   (8 wkts dec.) 188
6/355 7/362 8/365   4/60 5/62 6/121
                                                7/149 8/182

P. M. Such did not bat.

Bonus points – Leicestershire 4, Yorkshire 3.

Bowling: *First Innings*—Jarvis 20–5–79–3; Sidebottom 20.4–1–71–3; P. J. Hartley 13–0–61–1; S. N. Hartley 4–1–15–0; Swallow 17–5–49–0; Carrick 21–6–79–1. *Second Innings*—Jarvis 8–1–30–0; Sidebottom 10–2–36–3; P. J. Hartley 14–1–77–3; Swallow 9–0–29–2; Carrick 2–1–1–0.

Yorkshire

M. D. Moxon lbw b Agnew	2	– c and b Such	80
A. A. Metcalfe b Agnew	34	– lbw b Agnew	8
R. J. Blakey b Agnew	30	– lbw b Agnew	3
P. E. Robinson b Agnew	2	– c Willey b Such	43
S. N. Hartley b Agnew	8	– c DeFreitas b Such	8
†D. L. Bairstow b Ferris	128	– not out	27
I. G. Swallow c DeFreitas b Clift	15	– not out	1
*P. Carrick b Such	5		
P. J. Hartley c DeFreitas b Such	0		
A. Sidebottom not out	9		
P. W. Jarvis not out	0		
B 4, l-b 4, n-b 24	32	B 4, l-b 7, n-b 3	14

1/14 2/60 3/69 4/86 5/88   (9 wkts. dec.) 265   1/9 2/53 3/131   (5 wkts) 184
6/206 7/229 8/255 9/261   4/144 5/167

Bonus points – Yorkshire 3, Leicestershire 4.

Bowling: *First Innings*—Ferris 19–3–60–1; Agnew 22.3–5–84–5; DeFreitas 5.3–1–13–0; Such 29–9–79–2; Clift 13–3–21–1. *Second Innings*—Agnew 13–2–46–2; Ferris 11–2–45–0; Clift 11–3–32–0; Such 10–1–50–3.

Umpires: J. H. Harris and R. A. White.

YORKSHIRE v GLOUCESTERSHIRE

At Leeds, August 26, 27, 28. Yorkshire won by 44 runs. Yorkshire 19 pts, Gloucestershire 1 pt. Toss: Gloucestershire. The first day having been washed out by heavy rain, and Moxon dismissed by the first ball of the game, Yorkshire struggled to maintain a reasonable tempo on a slow, low pitch which made timing difficult. Lloyds put in a long, accurate spell of off-spin, but eventually Blakey overcame his initial difficulties to become the youngest player to score a double-hundred for Yorkshire. His runs came from 375 balls and included 25 bound-aries. Love helped him add 190 from 50 overs. Each side forfeited an innings, so that Gloucestershire's target became 364 in what would have been 103 overs had they gone the distance. The run-chase was dominated by Athey, who completed his fourth successive century, hitting one six and twelve fours in 167 balls. Lloyds, missed before scoring, had two sixes and eleven fours in their stand of 154 from 38 overs, but Jarvis, keeping a full length and producing some extra pace, cut through the lower order. Athey made no noticeable attempt to protect the tail and also refused the offer to go off for poor light near the end of the innings.

Close of play: First day, No play; Second day, Yorkshire 363-4 dec.

Yorkshire

M. D. Moxon c Lloyds b Walsh	0	J. D. Love not out	79
A. A. Metcalfe c Russell b Sainsbury	23		
R. J. Blakey not out	204	L-b 18	18
P. E. Robinson b Walsh	24		
S. N. Hartley c Curran b Ibadulla	15	1/0 2/58 3/131 4/173 (4 wkts. dec.) 363

†D. L. Bairstow, *P. Carrick, P. J. Hartley, P. W. Jarvis and A. Sidebottom did not bat.

Bonus points – Yorkshire 3, Gloucestershire 1 (Score at 100 overs: 288-4).

Bowling: Walsh 23–2–64–2; Sainsbury 36–13–89–1; Alleyne 17–1–81–0; Lloyds 32–11–67–0; Athey 3–1–10–0; Ibadulla 10–1–33–1.

Yorkshire forfeited their second innings.

Gloucestershire

Gloucestershire forfeited their first innings.

A. W. Stovold c Love b Jarvis	15	K. B. K. Ibadulla b Carrick 5
A. J. Wright c Moxon b P. J. Hartley	52	C. A. Walsh c Robinson b Jarvis 12
P. W. Romaines lbw b Jarvis	29	G. E. Sainsbury b Jarvis 0
*C. W. J. Athey not out 101		
K. M. Curran c Robinson b Jarvis	1	B 5, l-b 13, n-b 4 22
J. W. Lloyds lbw b Jarvis	82	
M. W. Alleyne c Sidebottom b Jarvis ..	0	1/20 2/106 3/106 4/115 5/269 319
†R. C. Russell b Sidebottom	0	6/271 7/272 8/302 9/319

Bowling: Jarvis 29–8–82–7; Sidebottom 25–4–71–1; P. J. Hartley 16–4–56–1; Moxon 5–2–6–0; Carrick 16–6–53–1; Love 8–1–33–0.

Umpires: J. Birkenshaw and R. Julian.

At Scarborough, September 2, 3, 4. YORKSHIRE lost to MCC by six wickets (See Other Matches, 1987).

YORKSHIRE v WARWICKSHIRE

At Scarborough, September 9, 10, 11. Drawn. Yorkshire 8 pts, Warwickshire 7 pts. Toss: Warwickshire. Batsmen on both sides experienced problems on a pitch that was very slow and low. Amiss, in his last Championship match, fell first ball in the first innings and managed just three deliveries in the second. Warwickshire appeared on course for a substantial total when Moles (177 balls, sixteen fours) and Asif Din were adding 147 in 45 overs, but the rest of the batting rather fell away owing to careless strokeplay and some persistent bowling from Jarvis and Carrick. Yorkshire also had uncertain periods, but Love and Bairstow put on 96 from 23 overs to give their innings substance. Hopes of a home victory grew when Warwickshire lost four wickets on the second evening to Jarvis, who achieved a hostility unexpected in the conditions. However, he limped out of the attack on the last morning with a knee strain, the night-watchman, Munton, resisted for more than three and a half hours, and finally Smith hit a brisk 89 from 110 balls to take the game beyond Yorkshire's reach. A token declaration left an impossible target of 279 in 85 minutes plus twenty overs, and the sides had already settled for a draw before rain brought an early end to play.

Close of play: First day, Yorkshire 37-2 (A. A. Metcalfe 19*, I. G. Swallow 0*); Second day, Warwickshire 82-4 (G. W. Humpage 20*, T. A. Munton 1*).

Warwickshire

A. J. Moles c Swallow b Jarvis	101	– (2) b Jarvis	10
T. A. Lloyd b Jarvis	 12	– (1) b Jarvis	36
Asif Din c Robinson b Carrick	... 77	– lbw b Jarvis	0
D. L. Amiss c Bairstow b Sidebottom	 0	– c Blakey b Jarvis	4
†G. W. Humpage c Robinson b Carrick	... 12	– b Sidebottom	69
D. A. Thorne lbw b Jarvis	 0	– (7) lbw b Swallow	0
P. A. Smith c Bairstow b Carrick	... 21	– (8) c Sidebottom b Metcalfe	89
G. C. Small st Bairstow b Carrick	... 13	– (5) b Love	8
T. A. Merrick b Hartley	 5	– (10) not out	2
T. A. Munton b Jarvis	 13	– (6) b Metcalfe	38
*N. Gifford not out	 16		
B 1, l-b 12, w 2, n-b 7	 22	B 4, l-b 15, n-b 14	33

1/23 2/170 3/170 4/218 5/218	292	1/22 2/22 3/30	(9 wkts dec.) 289
6/222 7/243 8/248 9/268		4/75 5/143 6/144	
		7/254 8/285 9/289	

Bonus points – Warwickshire 3, Yorkshire 4.

Bowling: *First Innings*—Jarvis 20.1–2–76–4; Sidebottom 12–3–34–1; Hartley 18–4–53–1; Carrick 31–12–71–4; Swallow 15–5–45–0. *Second Innings*—Jarvis 14.1–2–39–4; Sidebottom 14–1–40–1; Carrick 26–12–53–0; Hartley 16.5–2–44–0; Swallow 19–7–26–1; Love 6.2–0–50–1; Metcalfe 4–1–18–2.

Yorkshire

M. D. Moxon lbw b Small	0	– b Merrick 6
A. A. Metcalfe lbw b Munton	60	– not out 58
R. J. Blakey c Thorne b Small	16	
I. G. Swallow c Moles b Small	0	
P. E. Robinson b Gifford	62	– (3) not out 5
J. D. Love not out	67	
†D. L. Bairstow c Lloyd b Munton	47	
*P. Carrick b Munton	5	
A. Sidebottom c Merrick b Gifford	3	
P. J. Hartley c Humpage b Gifford	9	
P. W. Jarvis not out	7	
B 9, l-b 12, n-b 6	27	L-b 1, n-b 1 2

1/0 2/35 3/37 4/132 5/158   (9 wkts dec.) 303   1/40   (1 wkt) 71
6/254 7/264 8/269 9/293

Bonus points – Yorkshire 4, Warwickshire 4.

Bowling: *First Innings*—Small 23–10–63–3; Merrick 11–2–44–0; Gifford 36.4–9–70–3; Moles 4–1–21–0; Munton 19–3–48–3; Asif Din 1–0–5–0; Smith 4–0–31–0. *Second Innings*—Small 8–0–33–0; Merrick 7–1–24–1; Gifford 2–1–12–0; Lloyd 1–0–1–0; Munton 0.2–0–0–0.

Umpires: J. Birkenshaw and N. T. Plews.

YOUNG CRICKETER OF THE YEAR

(Elected by the Cricket Writers Club)

1950	R. Tattersall	1970	C. M. Old
1951	P. B. H. May	1971	J. Whitehouse
1952	F. S. Trueman	1972	D. R. Owen-Thomas
1953	M. C. Cowdrey	1973	M. Hendrick
1954	P. J. Loader	1974	P. H. Edmonds
1955	K. F. Barrington	1975	A. Kennedy
1956	B. Taylor	1976	G. Miller
1957	M. J. Stewart	1977	I. T. Botham
1958	A. C. D. Ingleby-Mackenzie	1978	D. I. Gower
1959	G. Pullar	1979	P. W. G. Parker
1960	D. A. Allen	1980	G. R. Dilley
1961	P. H. Parfitt	1981	M. W. Gatting
1962	P. J. Sharpe	1982	N. G. Cowans
1963	G. Boycott	1983	N. A. Foster
1964	J. M. Brearley	1984	R. J. Bailey
1965	A. P. E. Knott	1985	D. V. Lawrence
1966	D. L. Underwood	1986	{ A. A. Metcalfe / J. J. Whitaker }
1967	A. W. Greig		
1968	R. M. H. Cottam	1987	R. J. Blakey
1969	A. Ward		

An additional award, in memory of Norman Preston, Editor of *Wisden* from 1952 to 1980, was made to C. W. J. Athey in 1980.

THE UNIVERSITIES IN 1987

OXFORD

President: M. J. K. Smith (St Edmund Hall)
Hon. Treasurer: Dr S. R. Porter (St Cross)

Captain: C. D. M. Tooley (St Dunstan's College and Magdalen)
Secretary: D. A. Hagan (Trinity School, Leamington Spa and St Edmund Hall)

Captain for 1988: M. J. Kilborn (Farrer Agric. HS, University of New South Wales and St John's)
Secretary: S. D. Weale (Westminster City and Keble)

Oxford University were victims of another depressingly wet season in The Parks and hardly a match in May and June was not affected by rain. The results show only one defeat in first-class matches, but rather than to Oxford's ability, this was due to the adverse weather and to a reluctance on the part of the opposition to enforce the follow-on.

The Dark Blues were looking for a general all-round improvement on the previous season and although overall their performances were marginally better, a wide gulf remained between the University and the first-class counties. The new captain, Chris Tooley, had a promising intake of freshmen in Mark Crawley, Rajdeep Sardesai, son of the former Indian Test batsman, D. N. Sardesai, Patrick Edwards and Andy Beech, and with the exception of Beech from Australia, who never adjusted to slow pitches, they enjoyed satisfactory first seasons.

Nevertheless, Oxford were weak in every aspect, not least in their opening batsmen, the area where they were strongest in 1986. The unavailability of David Hagan and Adrian Mee for the greater part of the season gave Beech and Russell Morris every opportunity to establish themselves, but both were disappointing and neither justified his inclusion at Lord's. Mike Kilborn and Tooley were always left with the task of building the innings, with never more than 20 on the board, and they were reasonably successful. Crawley, who is on the Lancashire staff, began with a pair against Kent, but a maiden half-century in the next match, against Hampshire, confirmed his potential. This was fully revealed in the University Match when he hit a career-best 140. Sardesai was the most consistent batsman, but his weakness at running between the wickets persisted all season.

The University's chief shortcoming, as in previous years, was the bowling. Tim Firth and Iain Henderson posed no threat with the new ball, and the performance of Henderson was most disappointing. He had little control or direction, added to which was a consistent problem with over-stepping. Even though Oxford had the benefit of Alan Carter, a National Cricket Association coach, throughout the term, the fast bowler was unable to correct these faults, which if anything became worse as the season wore on.

One of the few successes was Edwards, who developed into a useful slow left-arm bowler. He was not afraid to toss the ball up and he generally maintained a good length. His partner, Simon Weale, was not so successful in

OXFORD UNIVERSITY 1987

[*Bill Smith*]

Back row: R. E. Morris, T. Firth, S. D. Weale, I. M. Henderson, A. R. Beech, P. G. Edwards. *Front row*: M. R. Crawley, J. E. B. Cope, C. D. M. Tooley (*captain*), M. J. Kilborn, R. D. Sardesai.

terms of wickets taken, but he developed into a useful all-rounder, reserving his best batting for Lord's.

Not surprisingly, the county batsmen again enjoyed a feast of runs on good, if slow, pitches. The six first-class fixtures in The Parks produced nine centuries and some big stands. The biggest, 249 by James and Morris, was a Glamorgan second-wicket record. Others included 188 by Warwickshire's openers, Lloyd and Moles, 167 for the first wicket by Benson and Taylor of Kent, and 165 by Hampshire's James and Cowley for the fifth wicket.

Oxford's out-cricket was again of a low standard and provided no improvement on the previous year. Far too many catches were put down, and it is difficult to understand why the fielding has deteriorated so alarmingly in recent years. It used to be one aspect of the game in which University cricketers could match their opponents, and they pay heavily every time a catch is grounded. – Paton Fenton.

OXFORD UNIVERSITY RESULTS

First-class matches – Played 7: Lost 1, Drawn 6.

FIRST-CLASS AVERAGES

BATTING AND FIELDING

	Birthplace	M	I	NO	R	HI	Avge	Ct/St
R. D. Sardesai ...	*Ahmedabad, India*	6	8	1	220	63*	31.42	1
M. J. Kilborn	*Gunnedah, Australia*	7	11	2	266	59	29.55	8
M. A. Crawley ...	*Newton-le-Willows*	7	10	1	263	140	29.22	2
C. D. M. Tooley .	*Bromley*	7	9	1	178	61*	22.25	4
S. D. Weale	*Knightsbridge*	7	8	0	165	76	20.62	0
R. E. Morris	*St Asaph*	6	9	2	98	34	14.00	1
D. A. Hagan	*Wide Open*	3	4	0	52	37	13.00	3
P. G. Edwards ...	*Bradford-on-Avon*	7	7	4	23	8	7.66	3
A. R. Beech	*Perth, Australia*	4	7	0	49	33	7.00	1
I. M. Henderson .	*Glapthorn*	6	7	1	33	14	5.50	2
T. Firth	*Bristol*	6	6	0	32	10	5.33	1
J. E. B. Cope	*Leigh-on-Sea*	7	7	3	17	4	4.25	7/1

Played in one match: A. A. G. Mee (*Johannesburg, SA*) 6; J. D. Nuttall (*Fulford*) 3; R. A. Rydon (*Greatham*) 8 (1 ct); N. V. Salvi (*Gwalior, India*) 5 (1 ct).

* *Signifies not out.*

M. A. Crawley played the only three-figure innings for Oxford University.

BOWLING

	O	M	R	W	BB	Avge
P. G. Edwards	172.4	42	500	14	4-93	35.71
T. Firth	203.3	29	663	13	4-129	51.00
I. M. Henderson ...	111	13	437	7	3-48	62.42
M. A. Crawley	161.1	32	516	6	2-30	86.00
S. D. Weale	185	44	523	6	2-87	87.16

Also bowled: M. J. Kilborn 3-0-23-0; R. E. Morris 2-0-11-0; J. D. Nuttall 19-5-48-1; R. A. Rydon 13-3-47-1; C. D. M. Tooley 7.3-1-37-2.

OXFORD UNIVERSITY v KENT

At Oxford, April 22, 23, 24. Drawn. Toss: Kent. Benson and Taylor opened the first-class season at The Parks with a partnership of 167, and then Hinks took over. There were thirteen fours and a six in his unbeaten 104. The Dark Blues lost Hagan and Beech quickly, but Kilborn and Tooley prevented a collapse with a stand of 95. When they were all out for 155, 190 behind, Cowdrey chose not to enforce the follow-on and used the opportunity to become Kent's third century-maker. Oxford, left to score 368 in 265 minutes, lost four wickets for 85 before Tooley and Sardesai made a draw certain with an unbeaten partnership of 124 in two and a quarter hours.

Close of play: First day, Kent 345-3 (S. G. Hinks 104*, D. G. Aslett 31*); Second day, Kent 102-1 (C. S. Cowdrey 67*, D. G. Aslett 0*).

Kent

M. R. Benson run out	106		
N. R. Taylor c and b Edwards	58		
S. G. Hinks not out	104		
C. J. Tavaré c Kilborn b Crawley	35		
D. G. Aslett not out	31	– (3) c Cope b Firth	31
*C. S. Cowdrey (did not bat)		– (1) not out	100
†S. A. Marsh (did not bat)		– (2) c Firth b Nuttall	24
C. Penn (did not bat)		– (4) not out	9
B 4, l-b 3, w 2, n-b 2	11	B 5, l-b 1, w 1, n-b 6	13

1/167 2/185 3/263			(3 wkts dec.) 345		1/77 2/154		(2 wkts dec.) 177

A. P. Igglesden, D. L. Underwood and K. B. S. Jarvis did not bat.

Bowling: *First Innings*—Firth 26–2–76–0; Nuttall 14–4–30–0; Crawley 24–5–79–1; Weale 37–6–106–0; Edwards 19–8–47–1. *Second Innings*—Firth 15.2–1–37–1; Crawley 22–5–59–0; Weale 19–3–49–0; Nuttall 5–1–18–1; Edwards 2–0–8–0.

Oxford University

D. A. Hagan c Penn b Igglesden	0	– c Tavaré b Penn	37
A. R. Beech c Marsh b Jarvis	0	– c Cowdrey b Igglesden	0
M. J. Kilborn c Tavaré b Underwood	43	– c Penn b Underwood	38
*C. D. M. Tooley c Marsh b Igglesden	44	– (5) not out	61
M. A. Crawley c Hinks b Igglesden	0	– (4) c Tavaré b Underwood	0
R. D. Sardesai st Marsh b Underwood	17	– not out	63
S. D. Weale c Tavaré b Jarvis	19		
T. Firth b Underwood	0		
P. G. Edwards c Penn b Igglesden	4		
J. D. Nuttall c Tavaré b Penn	3		
†J. E. B. Cope not out	3		
L-b 5, w 1, n-b 16	22	B 1, l-b 5, w 1, n-b 3	10

1/1 2/5 3/100 4/102 5/106		155		1/6 2/68 3/71 4/85		(4 wkts) 209
6/142 7/142 8/142 9/147

Bowling: *First Innings*—Igglesden 15–2–49–4; Jarvis 14–6–23–2; Cowdrey 5–3–13–0; Penn 11–2–29–1; Underwood 19–7–28–3; Aslett 2–0–7–0; Tavaré 1–0–1–0. *Second Innings*—Igglesden 7–0–15–1; Jarvis 11–3–34–0; Underwood 17–7–32–2; Penn 13–2–53–1; Aslett 8–2–34–0; Hinks 8–2–22–0; Taylor 5–1–13–0.

Umpires: D. Lloyd and A. G. T. Whitehead.

OXFORD UNIVERSITY v HAMPSHIRE

At Oxford, April 29, 30, May 1. Drawn. Toss: Hampshire. Only 85 minutes' play was possible on the last day. Hampshire were given a sound start by Terry and Chris Smith, and after tea James and Cowley plundered 165 in under two hours off a tiring attack. Oxford batted for all but 35 minutes of the second day in scoring 176, with Crawley completing a maiden half-century, but Hampshire, who led by 167, preferred batting practice and did not enforce the follow-on. Rain prevented any play after lunch.

Close of play: First day, Hampshire 343-5 (K. D. James 103*, T. M. Tremlett 4*); Second day, Hampshire 10-0 (M. C. J. Nicholas 9*, C. L. Smith 1*).

Hampshire

V. P. Terry c Hagan b Edwards	71		
C. L. Smith c Cope b Henderson	29	– not out	28
*M. C. J. Nicholas c Morris b Henderson	7	– (1) not out	30
D. R. Turner c Kilborn b Crawley	17		
N. G. Cowley c Crawley b Tooley	96		
K. D. James not out	103		
T. M. Tremlett not out	4		
B 3, l-b 4, w 5, n-b 4	16	L-b 5, w 1, n-b 1	7

1/69 2/77 3/115 4/148 5/313   (5 wkts dec.) 343   (no wkt) 65

R. J. Maru, C. A. Connor, †R. J. Parks and S. J. W. Andrew did not bat.

Bowling: *First Innings*—Henderson 17–1–81–2; Firth 18–4–48–0; Weale 16–5–50–0; Crawley 16–2–78–1; Edwards 15–2–63–1; Tooley 2–0–16–1. *Second Innings*—Henderson 12–2–25–0; Firth 14.1–2–26–0; Weale 3–1–9–0.

Oxford University

D. A. Hagan c Smith b Connor	0	I. M. Henderson c Parks b Connor	3
R. E. Morris lbw b Cowley	31	P. G. Edwards c Smith b Andrew	0
M. J. Kilborn b Tremlett	22	†J. E. B. Cope not out	3
*C. D. M. Tooley lbw b Cowley	14		
M. A. Crawley c Smith b Maru	58	B 1, l-b 16, n-b 3	20
R. D. Sardesai c Smith b Cowley	15		
S. D. Weale c sub b Cowley	0	1/13 2/52 3/71 4/80 5/116	176
T. Firth b Andrew	10	6/116 7/141 8/150 9/151	

Bowling: Andrew 14–5–26–2; Connor 13–7–19–2; Tremlett 11–3–20–1; James 14–3–29–0; Maru 17–6–30–1; Cowley 18–6–35–4.

Umpires: A. A. Jones and M. J. Kitchen.

OXFORD UNIVERSITY v GLOUCESTERSHIRE

At Oxford, May 20, 21, 22. Drawn. Toss: Oxford University. Oxford's bowlers suffered another mauling after Gloucestershire were put in on an easy-paced wicket. After Romaines had scored 119 out of 226 for five, Tomlins and Greene added 109 in 75 minutes, Tomlins hitting three sixes and eleven fours. Greene followed up his unbeaten 38 with four for 41 as Oxford were bowled out next day for 161. Gloucestershire opted to bat again, and by declaring at the close left the University all of the last day to score 286, However, their sporting approach was ruined by the rain, which restricted play to 55 minutes before lunch and left another game abandoned as a draw.

Close of play: First day, Oxford University 37-2 (M. J. Kilborn 11*, M. A. Crawley 6*); Second day, Gloucestershire 103-5 dec.

Gloucestershire

A. W. Stovold b Firth	36	
P. W. Romaines c Hagan b Edwards	119	– (6) not out 12
A. J. Wright c Crawley b Firth	6	– (1) c Henderson b Edwards ... 41
P. Bainbridge c Tooley b Edwards	24	– (3) c and b Henderson 16
M. W. Alleyne c Cope b Edwards	9	– (2) b Henderson 0
K. P. Tomlins c Sardesai b Weale	100	
†R. C. Russell c Cope b Edwards	1	– (4) c Hagan b Henderson 7
V. S. Greene not out	38	
*D. A. Graveney (did not bat)		– (5) lbw b Firth 18
G. E. Sainsbury (did not bat)		– (7) not out 0
B 3, l-b 3, w 1, n-b 3	10	L-b 1, w 2, n-b 6 9

1/56 2/66 3/135 4/187 5/226   (7 wkts dec.) 343   1/1 2/22 3/35   (5 wkts dec.) 103
6/234 7/343   4/75 5/103

D. A. Burrows did not bat.

Bowling: *First Innings*—Henderson 10-2-48-0; Firth 13-1-52-2; Crawley 25-4-65-0;
Weale 23-6-79-1; Edwards 30-8-93-4. *Second Innings*—Firth 13-3-36-1; Henderson
8-1-48-3; Edwards 6-0-15-1; Weale 2-1-3-0.

Oxford University

D. A. Hagan b Greene	15	
R. E. Morris b Sainsbury	4	– (1) c Russell b Bainbridge 0
M. J. Kilborn st Russell b Bainbridge	41	– not out 15
M. A. Crawley lbw b Graveney	19	– (2) not out 20
*C. D. M. Tooley c Greene b Bainbridge	5	
R. D. Sardesai c Russell b Greene	48	
S. D. Weale b Greene	2	
T. Firth b Graveney	6	
I. M. Henderson c Russell b Greene	8	
†J. E. B. Cope not out	1	
P. G. Edwards c Romaines b Graveney	8	
B 1, l-b 2, n-b 1	4	

1/20 2/20 3/69 4/76 5/99   161   1/0   (1 wkt) 35
6/113 7/122 8/147 9/150

Bowling: *First Innings*—Greene 18-6-41-4; Sainsbury 13-3-26-1; Burrows 9-0-27-0;
Graveney 26.5-12-31-3; Bainbridge 13-3-33-2. *Second Innings*—Greene 7-3-13-0;
Bainbridge 4-0-9-1; Sainsbury 2-0-8-0; Graveney 5-3-5-0.

Umpires: J. H. Hampshire and D. S. Thompsett.

OXFORD UNIVERSITY v NOTTINGHAMSHIRE

At Oxford, May 23, 25, 26. Nottinghamshire won by an innings and 140 runs. Toss: Nottinghamshire. Oxford were outplayed by Nottinghamshire, who won by an innings with two hours to spare after rain had prevented any play on the first day. The Dark Blues were bowled out for 66 after being put in on a pitch which gave the slow bowlers some assistance. When Nottinghamshire replied with 258 for six, with French top scorer with a punishing 70, the University needed 192 to avoid an innings defeat. Their hopes of playing out for a draw were upset by Saxelby, who took three of the first four wickets. Afford and Hemmings did the mopping-up.

Close of play: First day, No play; Second day, Nottinghamshire 110-3 (M. Newell 42*, J. D. Birch 6*).

Oxford University

R. E. Morris c Randall b Saxelby	4	– b Hemmings	34
M. A. Crawley c Johnson b Hemmings	18	– b Pick	0
M. J. Kilborn c Robinson b Pick	4	– c Johnson b Saxelby	5
*C. D. M. Tooley b Afford	12	– b Saxelby	1
R. D. Sardesai st French b Hemmings	1	– c French b Saxelby	0
A. R. Beech c French b Pick	9	– b Afford	0
S. D. Weale c French b Hemmings	1	– b Afford	0
T. Firth b Saxelby	4	– (9) c Saxelby b Afford	6
I. M. Henderson c Newell b Somani	3	– (8) lbw b Hemmings	0
†J. E. B. Cope c Birch b Somani	3	– c Pick b Afford	4
P. G. Edwards not out	5	– not out	0
L-b 1, w 1	2	L-b 2	2

1/18 2/26 3/28 4/29 5/41   66   1/1 2/12 3/20 4/20 5/24   52
6/42 7/49 8/58 9/58   6/24 7/33 8/40 9/50

Bowling: *First Innings*—Pick 12–6–16–2; Saxelby 16–9–22–2; Hemmings 20–11–18–3; Afford 8–6–2–1; Somani 4.3–0–7–2. *Second Innings*—Pick 5–1–5–1; Saxelby 10–5–14–3; Hemmings 13–9–16–2; Afford 8–4–15–4.

Nottinghamshire

*R. T. Robinson b Firth	21	A. Somani not out	26
M. Newell c Kilborn b Firth	53	E. E. Hemmings not out	0
D. W. Randall c Kilborn b Edwards	21	B 1, l-b 4, w 7, n-b 7	19
P. Johnson st Cope b Edwards	5		
J. D. Birch c Kilborn b Firth	43	1/49 2/88 3/96	(6 wkts dec.) 258
†B. N. French c Beech b Firth	70	4/134 5/186 6/258	

R. A. Pick, K. Saxelby and J. A. Afford did not bat.

Bowling: Henderson 12–1–35–0; Firth 32–3–129–4; Weale 16–6–25–0; Edwards 21–3–64–2.

Umpires: J. H. Hampshire and K. Taylor.

OXFORD UNIVERSITY v WARWICKSHIRE

At Oxford, May 30, June 1, 2. Drawn. Toss: Warwickshire. Both Lloyd and Moles made the University pay heavily for dropped catches. Lloyd, whose score was the highest of the season in The Parks, was missed when 32 and Moles survived two chances before he had scored 20. In reply to the county's 279 for two, the Dark Blues lost their half their side for 89, but Gifford was saved from any decision about following on or taking batting practice by Sardesai and Weale, who added 41 in more than an hour. Weale batted on for a further two hours ten minutes for his highest first-class score before being last out. Rain prevented any play on the third day.

Close of play: First day, Warwickshire 279-2 (T. A. Lloyd 150*, D. L. Amiss 20*); Second day, Warwickshire 10-0 (D. L. Amiss 4*, G. W. Humpage 3*).

Warwickshire

T. A. Lloyd not out	150		
A. J. Moles c Cope b Weale	76		
A. C. Storie c Salvi b Firth	19		
D. L. Amiss not out	20	– (1) not out	4
†G. W. Humpage (did not bat)		– (2) not out	3
B 1, l-b 2, w 2, n-b 9	14	N-b 3	3

1/188 2/242   (2 wkts dec.) 279   (no wkt) 10

A. R. K. Pierson, Asif Din, G. J. Parsons, T. A. Munton, A. A. Donald and *N. Gifford did not bat.

Bowling: *First Innings*—Firth 23–3–88–1; Henderson 10–0–32–0; Crawley 15–2–51–0; Edwards 15–2–42–0; Weale 13–1–63–1. *Second Innings*—Firth 2–0–6–0; Henderson 1–0–1–0; Edwards 1–0–3–0.

Oxford University

R. E. Morris b Donald	8	T. Firth b Pierson	6
M. A. Crawley c Storie b Munton	8	†J. E. B. Cope c Humpage b Parsons	2
M. J. Kilborn c Pierson b Moles	22	P. G. Edwards not out	6
*C. D. M. Tooley lbw b Pierson	32		
R. D. Sardesai c Storie b Donald	36	B 8, l-b 4, w 2, n-b 9	23
N. V. Salvi st Humpage b Moles	5		
S. D. Weale c Asif Din b Moles	58	1/20 2/28 3/69 4/77 5/89	220
I. M. Henderson run out	14	6/130 7/165 8/180 9/187	

Bowling: Donald 20–1–44–2; Parsons 27–8–51–1; Munton 5–2–10–1; Pierson 24–4–59–2; Moles 8.5–0–21–3; Gifford 6–2–5–0; Asif Din 7–0–18–0.

Umpires: D. Lloyd and P. B. Wight.

†At Oxford, June 10, 11, 12. Drawn. MCC 306 for eight dec. (R. J. Lanchbury 36, Asif Din 115, S. C. Wundke 43, C. R. Trembath 35; S. D. Weale four for 86) and 139 for eight dec. (R. J. Robinson 60, S. C. Wundke 48; S. D. Weale three for 38); Oxford University 185 (C. D. M. Tooley 111, I. M. Henderson 32 not out; M. Frost five for 65, C. R. Trembath three for 50) and 189 for nine (S. D. Weale 89; D. Lloyd four for 16).

†At Oxford, June 13, 15, 16. Drawn. Combined Services 250 for eight dec. (C. Hobson 108; P. G. Edwards five for 51) and 72 for one; Oxford University 302 for five dec. (M. J. Kilborn 154 not out, S. D. Weale 87).

†At Oxford, June 27, 29, 30. Oxford University won by five wickets. Free Foresters 173 for nine dec. (C. Rowe 56; P. G. Edwards five for 38) and 224 (J. O. D. Orders 74; P. G. Edwards five for 42); Oxford University 252 (R. D. Sardesai 60) and 147 for five.

OXFORD UNIVERSITY v GLAMORGAN

At Oxford, June 20, 22, 23. Drawn. Toss: Oxford University. Heavy rain on the second day saved Oxford from the possibility of a heavy defeat in the last first-class match in The Parks. Glamorgan's response to being put in was a record county second-wicket partnership of 249 by James and Morris. It was dominated by Morris, who took 68 minutes less to complete his century than it took James to reach his maiden hundred in only his second first-class innings. Maynard hit an entertaining 52 off 44 balls before the declaration at lunch, and then helped himself to three wickets as Oxford, Beech excepted, made a feeble reply. Kilborn with 11 was the only other batsman to reach double figures.

Close of play: First day, Glamorgan 258-2 (S. P. James 98*, G. C. Holmes 0*); Second day, No play.

Glamorgan

S. P. James c Rydon b Weale	106	J. Derrick not out	18
J. A. Hopkins c Cope b Rydon	2		
*H. Morris c Edwards b Crawley	143	B 2, l-b 6, w 3, n-b 4	15
G. C. Holmes c Tooley b Weale	6		
M. P. Maynard c Edwards b Crawley	52	1/6 2/255 3/265	(6 wkts dec.) 373
P. A. Cottey c Tooley b Edwards	31	4/292 5/338 6/373	

†C. P. Metson, I. Smith, C. J. P. G. van Zyl and S. Monkhouse did not bat.

Bowling: Henderson 20–5–63–0; Rydon 13–3–47–1; Crawley 35–7–116–2; Weale 32–9–87–2; Edwards 19.4–3–52–1.

Oxford University

A. R. Beech c Metson b Maynard	33		R. A. Rydon b Monkhouse	8
A. A. G. Mee lbw b Smith	6		†J. E. B. Cope lbw b van Zyl	1
M. J. Kilborn c Hopkins b Maynard	11		P. G. Edwards not out	0
M. A. Crawley c Monkhouse b Morris	0		L-b 1, n-b 17	18
*C. D. M. Tooley b Maynard	4			
S. D. Weale b Monkhouse	9		1/20 2/58 3/60	(9 wkts dec.) 95
R. E. Morris not out	4		4/66 5/69 6/84	
I. M. Henderson c Metson b van Zyl	1		7/85 8/94 9/95	

Bowling: van Zyl 13.4–8–12–2; Monkhouse 12–3–21–2; Smith 6–2–19–1; Derrick 6–2–7–0; Holmes 4–2–8–0; Maynard 7–1–21–3; Morris 2–0–6–1.

Umpires: P. J. Eele and D. S. Thompsett.

At Lord's, July 1, 2, 3. OXFORD UNIVERSITY drew with CAMBRIDGE UNIVERSITY
(See Other Matches at Lord's, 1987).

CAMBRIDGE

President: Sir John Butterfield (Downing)

Captain: D. G. Price (Haberdashers' Aske's and Homerton)
Secretary: A. M. G. Scott (Seaford Head and Queens')

Captain for 1988: M. A. Atherton (Manchester GS and Downing)
Secretary: G. A. Pointer (St Dunstan's and St John's)

Another difficult season for Cambridge was brightened by the arrival of a talented Lancastrian cricketer in Michael Atherton. One of the country's most successful schoolboy cricketers, he arrived at Fenner's having led the England Young Cricketers' tour to Sri Lanka, where, despite his own indifferent form, he had impressed experienced observers with his captaincy. He lived up to his advance billing right from the start with a masterful unbeaten début innings of 73 out of 135 against Essex, following with 33* out of 71 in the second innings.

Against Derbyshire, Atherton scored the University's only century of the season, carrying his bat for 109. And although he failed, much to everyone's surprise, against Oxford at Lord's, where he managed only 7 runs in the first innings and 0 in the second, he finished with 411 runs at an average of 37.36. More important, he impressed his colleagues to such an extent that they took the unusual step of electing him as captain in his second year.

Nevertheless, there were disappointments. Paul Bail, who had been expected to build on his successful season as a freshman, discovered too many ways of being dismissed, particularly before he had settled in. He managed only 257 runs, of which 90 were scored in the second innings against Oxford. David Fell, another experienced batsman, who had scored a first-class hundred in each of his previous two seasons, averaged only 21 from thirteen innings, while the captain, David Price, was beset by injuries and loss of form. He needed an excellent University Match to improve his aggregate to 228 runs.

If there was a batting bonus, it came from the performances of Mike Tremellen who, having initially gained a place as an emergency seam bowler,

CAMBRIDGE UNIVERSITY 1987

[Bill Smith]

Back row: G. J. Saville (coach), A. M. Hooper, R. I. Clitheroe, M. R. Middleton, G. A. Pointer, J. N. Perry, J. M. Tremellen. Front row: M. A. Atherton, P. A. C. Bail, D. G. Price (captain), S. R. Gorman, D. J. Fell. Insets: A. M. G. Scott, J. E. Davidson.

averaged 32.75 with the bat. He was called upon when a disastrous run of injuries depleted a better-than-average Cambridge attack.

John Davidson, the match-winner at Lord's in 1986, took only six wickets against the counties and did not play against Oxford, while Alastair Scott showed signs of strain at the demands placed upon him. Jon Perry, a quickish right-armer, threatened to be the find of the season until injury curtailed his appearances. He was, however, the most economical of a predominantly seam attack. Atherton bowled his leg-spin energetically, but the other slow bowlers were disappointing.

Aware of the falling standards of cricket at Oxford and Cambridge, the latter have been making strenuous efforts to recruit better players. There are signs that their policy is being rewarded, and Atherton hopes to have several experienced players available in 1988. The evidence of the Benson and Hedges Cup matches, for which the Combined Universities side was open to students other than those at Oxford and Cambridge, was that there are many talented cricketers able to meet the increasingly exacting standards being demanded by admission tutors.

There were times during the season, however, when the quality of the players was overshadowed by worries about the quality of the pitches at Fenner's. Remedial work had been carried out during the winter, but the wickets were again slow and the bounce disappointingly low, leaving more work still to be done. – David Hallett.

CAMBRIDGE UNIVERSITY RESULTS

First-class matches – Played 8: Lost 3, Drawn 5.

FIRST-CLASS AVERAGES

BATTING AND FIELDING

	Birthplace	M	I	NO	R	HI	Avge	Ct/St
M. A. Atherton ..	Manchester	8	13	2	411	109*	37.36	6
J. M. Tremellen ..	Pendine	4	6	2	131	39	32.75	1
A. M. Hooper ...	Perivale	3	4	0	112	89	28.00	0
D. J. Fell	Stafford	8	13	1	252	67*	21.00	5
D. G. Price	Luton	7	11	0	228	57	20.72	0
P. A. C. Bail ...	Burnham-on-Sea	8	13	0	257	90	19.76	1
R. Bate	Finchley	3	4	0	65	36	16.25	1
R. I. Clitheroe ..	Radcliffe	3	4	0	63	36	15.75	5/2
G. A. Pointer	Lewisham	7	10	3	101	33	14.42	1
S. R. Gorman ...	Middlesbrough	7	11	1	117	39	11.70	4
S. D. Heath	Bristol	4	7	1	54	26	9.00	0
M. S. Ahluwalia .	Isleworth	4	7	0	53	17	7.57	1
R. J. Hart	Beckenham	6	9	1	46	12	5.75	1
A. M. G. Scott ...	Guildford	7	10	4	17	11*	2.83	3
J. E. Davidson ..	Aberystwyth	2	4	0	11	5	2.75	1

Also batted: M. R. Middleton (*Guildford*) (2 matches) 6; S. L. Palmer (*Brighton*) (1 match) 18; J. N. Perry (*Frimley*) (3 matches) 0, 10 (1 ct); T. M. Verghese (*Mulanthurthy, India*) (1 match) 2.

* *Signifies not out.*

M. A. Atherton played the only three-figure innings for Cambridge University.

BOWLING

	O	M	R	W	BB	Avge
J. N. Perry	66.5	12	193	8	3-56	24.12
A. M. G. Scott	250.3	50	744	18	5-97	41.33
J. E. Davidson	79	10	274	6	3-101	45.66
R. J. Hart	166.2	40	477	9	2-19	53.00
G. A. Pointer	171	25	543	10	3-52	54.30
M. A. Atherton ...	100.5	8	320	5	1-14	64.00

Also bowled: M. R. Middleton 36–5–119–1; S. L. Palmer 16–3–57–1; D. G. Price 5–1–24–1; J. M. Tremellen 35–4–179–1; T. M. Verghese 22.2–1–110–1.

†At Cambridge, April 17. Cambridge University won by one wicket. Loughborough University 165 for eight dec.; Cambridge University 166 for nine (M. S. Ahluwalia 56, S. R. Gorman 67; T. Barry four for 22).

CAMBRIDGE UNIVERSITY v ESSEX

At Cambridge, April 18, 20, 21. Essex won by 249 runs. Toss: Cambridge University. It was soon business as usual for Essex on a sunny and warm first day of the season. Gladwin overshadowed Gooch, but it was Hardie, again, who enjoyed the University bowling. He reached the season's first century in four and a half hours from 210 deliveries. The Cambridge reply was held together by the freshman, Atherton, who scored a patient 73 while most of his colleagues struggled against the South African, Page, Essex's new overseas fast bowler. Page took five wickets on his first appearance. Gooch did not enforce the follow-on, preferring to give his batsmen practice. Even so, the declaration before lunch on the third day left his bowlers plenty of time to bowl out Cambridge for a second time. Atherton batted 160 minutes for his 33.

Close of play: First day, Essex 335-5 (G. Miller 30*, D. E. East 7*); Second day, Essex 58-0 (P. J. Prichard 36*, K. W. R. Fletcher 19*).

Essex

*G. A. Gooch b Davidson	13		
C. Gladwin c Bail b Atherton	77		
B. R. Hardie c Gorman b Hart	143		
P. J. Prichard c Ahluwalia b Scott	28	– (1) not out	69
K. W. R. Fletcher lbw b Davidson	13	– (2) b Scott	30
G. Miller not out	30		
†D. E. East not out	7	– (4) c and b Scott	0
H. A. Page (did not bat)		– (3) c Davidson b Hart	0
N. A. Foster (did not bat)		– (5) c sub b Hart	15
B 11, l-b 6, w 2, n-b 5	24	L-b 1, w 4, n-b 1	6

1/39 2/142 3/214 4/248 5/318   (5 wkts dec.) 335   1/89 2/90 3/91   (4 wkts dec.) 120
                                                          4/120

J. K. Lever and J. H. Childs did not bat.

Bowling: *First Innings*—Davidson 32–5–109–2; Pointer 19–7–62–0; Scott 21–3–53–1; Hart 19–4–58–1; Atherton 8–1–30–1; Price 1–0–6–0. *Second Innings*—Davidson 1–0–3–0; Scott 15–1–68–2; Pointer 11–2–29–0; Hart 7.2–1–19–2.

Cambridge University

P. A. C. Bail lbw b Page	4	– c and b Lever	0
M. S. Ahluwalia c Childs b Lever	5	– c Fletcher b Foster	1
M. A. Atherton not out	73	– c East b Childs	33
†D. J. Fell c East b Page	0	– b Foster	6
*D. G. Price c Gooch b Lever	3	– c Miller b Foster	3
S. D. Heath b Page	4	– lbw b Lever	1
S. R. Gorman lbw b Page	0	– lbw b Page	0
R. J. Hart lbw b Page	2	– lbw b Miller	12
G. A. Pointer b Foster	30	– not out	6
J. E. Davidson b Foster	0	– b Childs	2
A. M. G. Scott c Hardie b Miller	2	– lbw b Childs	0
B 4, l-b 4, n-b 4	12	L-b 4, w 1, n-b 2	7

1/10 2/10 3/10 4/13 5/18	135	1/0 2/2 3/8 4/14 5/15	71
6/18 7/20 8/69 9/77		6/23 7/63 8/65 9/71	

Bowling: First Innings—Lever 18–7–34–2; Page 14–2–26–5; Childs 16–6–19–0; Foster 16–4–39–2; Miller 9.1–4–9–1. *Second Innings*—Lever 13–8–10–2; Foster 9–3–14–3; Page 7–2–13–1; Gooch 6–2–15–0; Miller 9–5–11–1; Childs 6.5–3–4–3.

Umpires: P. J. Eele and K. E. Palmer.

CAMBRIDGE UNIVERSITY v LANCASHIRE

At Cambridge, April 22, 23, 24. Drawn. Toss: Cambridge University. The day began auspiciously for Cambridge with Mendis caught off the first ball of the match, and until later in the day their seam bowlers made Lancashire work hard for their runs on a slow pitch providing some movement when the ball was kept up to the bat. This dictum was not always followed as Hughes, in his first match in England as county captain, and Simmons began to take toll of the tiring attack. Lancashire's elder statesmen struck twenty boundaries between them. Batting was even slower the next day. There were only 41 runs scored between lunch and tea as the young batsmen struggled against the contrasting spin of Simmons and Folley. Palmer made a valiant but unsuccessful attempt to pass the follow-on figure on the third morning, but Hughes was more concerned with practice and allowed Cambridge breathing time by giving his batsmen another chance in the middle.

Close of play: First day, Lancashire 278-8 (P. J. W. Allott 16*, I. Folley 10*); Second day, Cambridge University 137-9 (S. L. Palmer 5*).

Lancashire

G. D. Mendis c Atherton b Scott	0	– b Perry	6
G. Fowler lbw b Palmer	49	– run out	62
J. Abrahams c Atherton b Scott	10		
N. H. Fairbrother lbw b Scott	4	– (3) not out	47
S. J. O'Shaughnessy b Perry	27	– (4) not out	5
*D. P. Hughes c Fell b Hart	81		
A. N. Hayhurst lbw b Scott	8		
J. Simmons c Perry b Hart	64		
P. J. W. Allott b Perry	29		
I. Folley not out	14		
†J. Stanworth b Perry	6		
L-b 3, w 1, n-b 5	9	B 1, l-b 2, w 1	4

1/0 2/18 3/33 4/93 5/102	301	1/7 2/102	(2 wkts dec.) 124
6/113 7/238 8/263 9/295			

Bowling: First Innings—Scott 36–7–95–4; Perry 31.5–5–73–3; Palmer 12–2–41–1; Hart 27–9–53–2; Atherton 9–0–36–0. *Second Innings*—Scott 17–3–65–0; Perry 1–1–0–1; Palmer 4–1–16–0; Hart 12–2–40–0.

Cambridge University

P. A. C. Bail lbw b O'Shaughnessy	4	– lbw b O'Shaughnessy	17
M. S. Ahluwalia c O'Shaughnessy b Simmons	17	– lbw b Allott	8
M. A. Atherton c Stanworth b Hayhurst	12	– b Hughes	13
†D. J. Fell c Allott b Simmons	35	– b O'Shaughnessy	0
*D. G. Price run out	9	– c Allott b Simmons	37
S. D. Heath c Stanworth b Folley	2	– not out	11
S. R. Gorman st Stanworth b Folley	39	– not out	0
R. J. Hart lbw b Simmons	0		
S. L. Palmer b Allott	18		
J. N. Perry lbw b Allott	0		
A. M. G. Scott not out	0		
B 1, l-b 8, n-b 6	15	L-b 2, w 1, n-b 2	5

1/5 2/32 3/46 4/73 5/80   151   1/26 2/26 3/27   (5 wkts) 91
6/106 7/112 8/134 9/137   4/79 5/79

Bowling: *First Innings*—Allott 24.5–15–24–2; O'Shaughnessy 27–14–41–1; Hayhurst 10–1–17–1; Folley 21–12–33–2; Simmons 21–13–27–3. *Second Innings*—Allott 6–0–10–1; O'Shaughnessy 8–3–25–2; Folley 12–7–7–0; Simmons 6–5–1–1; Hughes 6–2–12–1; Hayhurst 9–1–34–0.

Umpires: P. J. Eele and K. E. Palmer.

CAMBRIDGE UNIVERSITY v LEICESTERSHIRE

At Cambridge, April 25, 27, 28. Leicestershire won by an innings and 220 runs. Toss: Cambridge University. Price, winning the toss for the third successive match, changed his tactics and opted to bat. His side were dismissed by tea, with Such, the county's newly acquired off-spinner, doing more or less as he used to do for Nottinghamshire against Oxford. Atherton again batted well for the University. Runs came more easily for Leicestershire's batsmen. Potter and Butcher put on 140 in a fraction over two hours, and Whitaker, producing the best batting of the match, reached his hundred in 167 minutes from 178 balls. Despite the efforts of Atherton, and two defiant sixes by Pointer, there was little prospect of Cambridge saving the game and they were all out soon after lunch on the final day. Price, who had injured a hand while fielding, did not bat in the second innings.

Close of play: First day, Leicestershire 129-0 (L. Potter 64*, I. P. Butcher 56*); Second day, Cambridge University 24-2 (M. S. Ahluwalia 3*).

Cambridge University

P. A. C. Bail b Taylor	3	– c Whitticase b Tennant	14
M. S. Ahluwalia c Potter b Agnew	11	– lbw b Willey	7
M. A. Atherton c Boon b Such	32	– (4) c Whitaker b Such	32
†D. J. Fell lbw b Taylor	6	– (5) b Willey	9
*D. G. Price c Tennant b Taylor	0	– absent injured	
S. D. Heath c Whitticase b Agnew	26	– c Boon b Potter	1
S. R. Gorman c Willey b Such	7	– b Willey	19
J. M. Tremellen not out	17	– (3) c and b Such	4
R. J. Hart b Tennant	4	– (8) c Butcher b Willey	1
G. A. Pointer b Such	1	– (9) st Whitticase b Such	28
A. M. G. Scott c Butcher b Such	0	– (10) not out	0
L-b 4, n-b 7	11	L-b 3, n-b 1	4

1/3 2/21 3/51 4/51 5/62   118   1/17 2/24 3/38 4/58 5/61   119
6/92 7/96 8/107 9/110   6/83 7/90 8/91 9/119

Bowling: *First Innings*—Agnew 17–4–36–2; Taylor 11–1–21–3; Tennant 14–3–41–1; Such 19.3–15–14–4; Willey 1–1–0–0; Potter 1–0–2–0. *Second Innings*—Agnew 10–8–6–0; Tennant 5–0–15–1; Such 18.1–7–42–3; Potter 12–3–21–1; Willey 21–9–32–4.

Leicestershire

L. Potter c sub b Scott	68	†P. Whitticase not out	12
I. P. Butcher run out	87		
D. I. Gower lbw b Scott	47	B 5, l-b 11, w 4	20
J. J. Whitaker c Atherton b Hart	126		
T. J. Boon lbw b Scott	70	1/140 2/213 3/217 (5 wkts dec.) 457	
*P. Willey not out	27	4/392 5/428	

L. Tennant, J. P. Agnew, L. B. Taylor and P. M. Such did not bat.

Bowling: Scott 35–7–111–3; Pointer 22–3–73–0; Tremellen 13–2–79–0; Hart 28–4–115–1; Atherton 20–1–63–0.

Umpires: B. Hassan and R. Julian.

CAMBRIDGE UNIVERSITY v NORTHAMPTONSHIRE

At Cambridge, April 29, 30, May 1. Drawn. Toss: Northamptonshire. The flirtation at Fenner's with summer passed; with May came rain to wash out all but 33 minutes of the final day. Northamptonshire batted soundly, if unspectacularly, the best innings coming from Boyd-Moss against his old university. He became the first victim of Clitheroe, the wicket-keeper, who was making his début and was later to prove himself a more-than-reliable lower-order batsman, top-scoring with 36 after batting for almost two hours. Northamptonshire's secretary/manager, S. P. Coverdale, who like Boyd-Moss won his Blue for Cambridge in four consecutive years, made his first first-class appearance for seven years.

Close of play: First day, Cambridge University 37-2 (M. A. Atherton 13*, P. A. C. Bail 6*); Second day, Northamptonshire 141-0 (R. J. Bailey 75*, D. J. Wild 50*).

Northamptonshire

*G. Cook run out	12		
R. J. Boyd-Moss c Clitheroe b Scott	77		
D. J. Wild c Hart b Pointer	5	– (2) not out	64
R. J. Bailey c Pointer b Verghese	21	– (1) not out	94
R. G. Williams not out	69		
D. J. Capel b Pointer	21		
†D. Ripley c Atherton b Hart	10		
N. G. B. Cook c Fell b Scott	9		
A. Walker st Clitheroe b Atherton	0		
B 1, l-b 3, w 3, n-b 5	12	B 6, l-b 5, w 1, n-b 9	21

1/39 2/51 3/95 4/145 5/175	(8 wkts dec.) 236	(no wkt) 179
6/205 7/235 8/236		

S. P. Coverdale and S. J. Brown did not bat.

Bowling: *First Innings*—Pointer 16–1–72–2; Scott 19–3–66–2; Verghese 6–0–36–1; Hart 14–3–36–1; Atherton 8.4–1–22–1. *Second Innings*—Pointer 1–0–1–0; Scott 8–2–25–0; Verghese 16.2–1–74–0; Hart 14–1–55–0; Atherton 5–1–13–0.

Cambridge University

M. A. Atherton lbw b Capel	14	R. J. Hart lbw b Walker	12
M. S. Ahluwalia lbw b Walker	4	G. A. Pointer b Walker	2
D. J. Fell b Wild	7	*A. M. G. Scott not out	0
P. A. C. Bail lbw b Brown	19		
R. Bate c and b N. G. B. Cook	15	B 6, l-b 18	24
S. R. Gorman c G. Cook b Brown	13		
T. M. Verghese b Wild	2	1/10 2/27 3/42 4/54 5/79	148
†R. I. Clitheroe lbw b Walker	36	6/82 7/105 8/142 9/147	

Bowling: Capel 12–6–13–1; Walker 16.3–7–22–4; Wild 15–9–11–2; Boyd-Moss 9–7–8–0; Bailey 4–2–8–0; N. G. B. Cook 22–7–37–1; Brown 13–5–25–2.

Umpires: B. Hassan and R. Julian.

CAMBRIDGE UNIVERSITY v DERBYSHIRE

At Cambridge, May 6, 7, 8. Derbyshire won by 164 runs. Toss: Cambridge University. With Barnett, Roberts and, to a lesser extent, Anderson among the runs, Derbyshire made sound and occasionally spectacular progress on a slow first-class pitch. The second day belonged to Atherton, who confirmed his initial promise with his maiden first-class hundred, reached in 257 minutes from 262 balls, thirteen of which he hit for four. Altogether, in carrying his bat for 109 out of Cambridge's total of 185, he batted for 284 minutes and faced 290 balls. Maher, with a half-century in the book by the close, replied with a hundred for Derbyshire in 241 minutes from 203 balls, hitting nine fours. The only resistance in Cambridge's second innings came from Bail as Barnett, prompted perhaps by the purveyances of Atherton, bowled his own under-used leg-breaks and picked up four wickets.

Close of play: First day, Cambridge University 24-1 (M. A. Atherton 15*, D. J. Fell 5*); Second day, Derbyshire 83-2 (B. J. M. Maher 50*, R. J. Finney 27*).

Derbyshire

*K. J. Barnett c Bate b Hart	59	
†B. J. M. Maher c Clitheroe b Pointer	18 – not out	100
B. Roberts c Clitheroe b Davidson	99	
J. E. Morris c Scott b Davidson	11	
I. S. Anderson b Davidson	44	
P. G. Newman c Atherton b Hart	8 – (1) b Davidson	1
A. E. Warner run out	0	
R. J. Finney not out	14 – (4) b Atherton	63
M. Jean-Jacques not out	3 – (6) not out	6
C. F. B. P. Rudd (did not bat)	– (3) c Clitheroe b Scott	1
M. Wakefield (did not bat)	– (5) st Clitheroe b Price	4
B 5, l-b 7, w 1, n-b 3	16	B 6, l-b 13, n-b 1	20

1/51 2/110 3/141 4/236   (7 wkts. dec.) 272   1/23 2/26 3/163   (4 wkts. dec.) 195
5/249 6/249 7/256   4/172

Bowling: *First Innings*—Pointer 16–2–54–1; Davidson 26–1–101–3; Scott 18–2–58–0; Hart 24–10–47–2. *Second Innings*—Pointer 11–1–27–0; Davidson 20–4–61–1; Scott 15–4–38–1; Hart 9–3–18–0; Price 4–1–18–1; Atherton 6–0–14–1.

Cambridge University

S. R. Gorman b Warner	1 – (6) b Rudd	7
M. A. Atherton not out	109 – c Barnett b Newman	1
D. J. Fell c Maher b Finney	13 – lbw b Barnett	22
P. A. C. Bail c Wakefield b Jean-Jacques	33 – b Rudd	49
*D. G. Price c Anderson b Jean-Jacques	0 – (1) lbw b Newman	1
R. Bate c Maher b Jean-Jacques	3 – (5) b Barnett	11
†R. I. Clitheroe c and b Newman	11 – lbw b Barnett	8
G. A. Pointer b Warner	1 – b Rudd	0
R. J. Hart b Warner	0 – not out	7
J. E. Davidson c Barnett b Rudd	4 – b Barnett	5
A. M. G. Scott lbw b Wakefield	0 – lbw b Anderson	3
L-b 8, w 2	10	B 1, l-b 2, n-b 1	4

1/7 2/35 3/122 4/122 5/128   185   1/2 2/5 3/57 4/87 5/89   118
6/160 7/165 8/173 9/184   6/97 7/97 8/103 9/115

Bowling: *First Innings*—Newman 18–7–31–1; Warner 19–6–32–3; Wakefield 12–5–30–1; Finney 16–0–48–1; Jean-Jacques 13–7–17–3; Anderson 7–1–13–0; Rudd 3–1–6–1. *Second Innings*—Warner 5–2–8–0; Newman 5–3–3–2; Roberts 7–0–23–0; Finney 5–2–12–0; Rudd 14–6–27–3; Barnett 20–8–31–4; Anderson 7.4–5–11–1.

Umpires: J. H. Hampshire and H. J. Rhodes.

CAMBRIDGE UNIVERSITY v MIDDLESEX

At Cambridge, May 20, 21, 22. Drawn. Toss: Cambridge University. Slack brightened a gloomy first day with a hundred off 127 balls in 149 minutes. The left-hander hit Atherton for two sixes, and there were another thirteen fours before he reached three figures; another six boundaries followed. With Atherton, Fell, Tremellen and Bate receiving considerable help from extras, Cambridge managed their best score of the season. Some of the county's work in the field was not exemplary. Rain washed out the final day completely.

Close of play: First day, Cambridge University 25-2 (M. A. Atherton 9*); Second day, Middlesex 9-0 (A. Needham 3*, A. J. T. Miller 6*).

Middlesex

W. N. Slack b Pointer	149	
A. J. T. Miller c Fell b Tremellen	27	– not out 6
C. T. Radley c Atherton b Pointer	61	
M. A. Roseberry not out	22	
R. O. Butcher lbw b Pointer	23	
*†P. R. Downton not out	4	
A. Needham (did not bat)		– (1) not out 3
B 2, l-b 14, w 2	18	

1/83 2/243 3/248 4/292   (4 wkts dec.) 304   (no wkt) 9

N. F. Williams, S. P. Hughes, W. W. Daniel and P. C. R. Tufnell did not bat.

Bowling: *First Innings*—Pointer 31–2–99–3; Scott 30–9–63–0; Tremellen 12–0–47–1; Hart 12–3–36–0; Atherton 9–1–43–0. *Second Innings*—Scott 3–2–5–0; Pointer 3–2–4–0.

Cambridge University

A. M. Hooper lbw b Williams	8	J. M. Tremellen c Roseberry b Daniel . 34
M. A. Atherton c Slack b Needham	41	R. J. Hart c Downton b Daniel 8
A. M. G. Scott c Roseberry b Tufnell	1	G. A. Pointer not out 0
†D. J. Fell c Downton b Daniel	39	
P. A. C. Bail c Radley b Needham	15	B 12, l-b 18, w 2, n-b 4 36
*D. G. Price c Roseberry b Needham	26	
R. Bate st Downton b Tufnell	36	1/18 2/25 3/88 4/112 5/135 253
S. D. Heath lbw b Hughes	9	6/168 7/193 8/203 9/250

Bowling: Hughes 19–2–73–1; Williams 16–2–39–1; Tufnell 19–9–45–2; Daniel 15.1–4–29–3; Needham 24–10–37–3.

Umpires: M. J. Kitchen and K. Taylor.

†At Cambridge, June 7. Cambridge University won by 26 runs. Cambridge University 229 for five (S. R. Gorman 92; T. A. Cotterell four for 80); Quidnuncs 203 (C. F. E. Goldie 70; A. M. G. Scott four for 36, M. R. Middleton four for 53).

†At Cambridge, June 10. Wales won by four wickets. Cambridge University 99 (B. Lloyd four for 20); Wales 103 for six.

†At Cambridge, June 13, 14, 15. Drawn. MCC 273 for six dec. (J. D. Robinson 102, N. R. C. MacLaurin 71, J. H. Hampshire 51; J. M. Tremellen three for 55) and 4 for one; Cambridge University 120 for one dec. (P. A. C. Bail 33, M. A. Atherton 50 not out, D. J. Fell 30 not out).

CAMBRIDGE UNIVERSITY v SURREY

At Cambridge, June 17, 18, 19. Drawn. Toss: Cambridge University. Surrey were 23 for four on the opening morning, but Greig, captain of Cambridge in 1979 and now captaining Surrey, prevented any embarrassment on his return to Fenner's by hitting a hundred in 147 minutes (134 balls, two sixes, thirteen fours). Cambridge made a spirited reply before rain interrupted their progress, and no play was possible on the final day.

Close of play: First day, Surrey 258-8 (I. A. Greig 104*, G. E. Brown 8*); Second day, Cambridge University 180-7 (J. M. Tremellen 9*, G. A. Pointer 0*).

Surrey

D. J. Bicknell c Clitheroe b Pointer	...	1
G. S. Clinton c Gorman b Pointer	....	11
A. J. Stewart b Perry	....	2
M. A. Lynch b Perry	....	63
T. E. Jesty c Gorman b Pointer	......	0
D. J. Thomas c Tremellen b Perry	....	23
*I. A. Greig not out	....	104
C. K. Bullen b Atherton	....	22

K. T. Medlycott c Gorman b Middleton 13
†G. E. Brown not out 8

B 1, l-b 7, n-b 3 11

1/1 2/12 3/18   (8 wkts dec.) 258
4/23 5/95 6/111
7/185 8/229

S. T. Clarke did not bat.

Bowling: Perry 12-3-56-3; Pointer 13-2-52-3; Tremellen 8-2-41-0; Middleton 21-4-72-1; Atherton 12.1-3-29-1.

Cambridge University

P. A. C. Bail c Clinton b Medlycott	...	4
M. A. Atherton c Brown b Lynch	.....	44
D. J. Fell c Brown b Clarke	....	48
A. M. Hooper c Greig b Bullen	....	0
*D. G. Price c Jesty b Medlycott	.....	46
S. R. Gorman lbw b Thomas	....	5
J. M. Tremellen not out	....	9

†R. I. Clitheroe lbw b Thomas 8
G. A. Pointer not out 0

B 9, l-b 4, n-b 3 16

1/21 2/58 3/61 4/131   (7 wkts) 180
5/158 6/159 7/172

J. N. Perry and M. R. Middleton did not bat.

Bowling: Clarke 16-3-37-1; Thomas 9-3-25-2; Medlycott 27-10-55-2; Bullen 20-9-29-1; Lynch 10-5-16-1; Greig 3-1-5-0.

Umpires: D. Lloyd and H. J. Rhodes.

---

†At Durham, June 20. Durham University won by 134 runs. Durham University 230 for five (50 overs) (A. Fordham 70, G. M. Charlesworth 57 not out); Cambridge University 96 (J. P. Stephenson four for 29).

---

†At Durham, June 21. No result. Durham University 245 for six (50 overs) (A. Fordham 85, G. M. Charlesworth 70); Cambridge University 132 for three (A. M. Hooper 57, P. A. C. Bail 50).

---

†At Portsmouth, June 27, 28, 29. Cambridge University won by 68 runs. Cambridge University 282 for five dec. (P. A. C. Bail 134, M. A. Atherton 74) and 163 (M. A. Atherton 53; A. W. Taylor seven for 73); Combined Services 250 for eight dec. (A. Ward 85) and 127 (M. V. Fleming 61; M. R. Middleton four for 21).

At Lord's, July 1, 2, 3. CAMBRIDGE UNIVERSITY drew with OXFORD UNIVERSITY (See Other Matches at Lord's, 1987).

OXFORD AND CAMBRIDGE BLUES

From 1946 to 1987, and some others

A full list of Blues from 1837 may be found in all Wisdens published between 1923 and 1939. Between 1948 and 1972 the list was confined to all those who had won Blues after 1880, plus some of "special interest for personal or family reasons". Between 1972 and 1982 the list was restricted to those who had won Blues since 1919. Such adjustments have been necessary owing to the exigencies of space.

OXFORD

Aamer Hameed (Central Model HS and Punjab U.) 1979
Abell, G. E. B. (Marlborough) 1924, 1926-27
Allan, J. M. (Edinburgh Academy) 1953-56
Allerton, J. W. O. (Stowe) 1969
Allison, D. F. (Greenmore Coll.) 1970
Altham, H. S. (Repton) 1911-12
Arenhold, J. A. (Diocesan Coll., SA) 1954

Baig, A. A. (Aliya and Osmania U., India) 1959-62
Baig, M. A. (Osmania U., India) 1962-64
Bailey, J. A. (Christ's Hospital) (Capt. in 1958) 1956-58
Barber, A. T. (Shrewsbury) (Capt. in 1929) 1927-29
Barker, A. H. (Charterhouse) 1964-65, 1967
Bartlett, J. H. (Chichester) 1946, 1951
Beech, A. R. (John XXIII Coll., Perth and Univ. of Western Australia) 1987
Bettington, R. H. B. (The King's School, Parramatta) (Capt. in 1923) 1920-23
Bird, W. S. (Malvern) (Capt. in 1906) 1904-06
Birrell, H. B. (St Andrews, SA) 1953-54
Blake, P. D. S. (Eton) (Capt. in 1952) 1950-52
Bloy, N. C. F. (Dover) 1946-47
Boobbyer, B. (Uppingham) 1949-52
Bosanquet, B. J. T. (Eton) 1898-1900
Botton, N. D. (King Edward's, Bath) 1974
Bowman, R. C. (Fettes) 1957
Brettell, D. N. (Cheltenham) 1977
Bristowe, W. R. (Charterhouse) 1984-85
Brooks, R. A. (Quintin and Bristol U.) 1967
Burchnall, R. L. (Winchester) 1970-71
Burki, J. (St Mary's, Rawalpindi and Punjab U.) 1958-60
Burton, M. St J. W. (Umtali HS, Rhodesia and Rhodes U.) (Capt. in 1970) 1969-71
Bury, T. E. O. (Charterhouse) 1980
Bush, J. E. (Magdalen Coll. Sch.) 1952

Campbell, A. N. (Berkhamsted) 1970
Campbell, I. P. (Canford) 1949-50
Campbell, I. P. F. (Repton) (Capt. in 1913) 1911-13
Cantlay, C. P. T. (Radley) 1975
Carr, D. B. (Repton) (Capt. in 1950) 1949-51

Carr, J. D. (Repton) 1983-85
Carroll, P. R. (Newington Coll. and Sydney U.) 1971
Chalk, F. G. H. (Uppingham) (Capt. in 1934) 1931-34
Chesterton, G. H. (Malvern) 1949
Claughton, J. A. (King Edward's, Birmingham) (Capt. in 1978) 1976-79
Clements, S. M. (Ipswich) (Capt. in 1979) 1976, 1979
Clube, S. V. M. (St John's, Leatherhead) 1956
Cope, J. E. B. (St John's, Leatherhead) 1986-87
Corlett, S. C. (Worksop) 1971-72
Corran, A. J. (Gresham's) 1958-60
Coutts, I. D. F. (Dulwich) 1952
Cowan, R. S. (Lewes Priory CS) 1980-82
Cowdrey, M. C. (Tonbridge) (Capt. in 1954) 1952-54
Coxon, A. J. (Harrow CS) 1952
Crawley, A. M. (Harrow) 1927-30
Crawley, M. A. (Manchester GS) 1987
Crutchley, G. E. V. (Harrow) 1912
Cullinan, M. R. (Hilton Coll., SA) 1983-84
Curtis, I. J. (Whitgift) 1980, 1982
Cushing, V. G. B. (KCS Wimbledon) 1973
Cuthbertson, J. L. (Rugby) 1962-63

Davidson, W. W. (Brighton) 1947-48
Davis, F. J. (Blundell's) 1963
Dawson, T. A. J. (Mill Hill) 1986
Delisle, G. P. S. (Stonyhurst) 1955-56
de Saram, F. C. (Royal Coll., Colombo) 1934-35
Divecha, R. V. (Podar HS and Bombay U.) 1950-51
Dixon, E. J. H. (St Edward's, Oxford) (Capt. in 1939) 1937-39
Donnelly, M. P. (New Plymouth BHS and Canterbury U., NZ) (Capt. in 1947) 1946-47
Dowding, A. L. (St Peter's, Adelaide) (Capt. in 1953) 1952-53
Drybrough, C. D. (Highgate) (Capt. in 1961-62) 1960-62
Duff, A. R. (Radley) 1960-61
Dyer, A. W. (Mill Hill) 1965-66
Dyson, E. M. (QEGS, Wakefield) 1958

Eagar, M. A. (Rugby) 1956-59
Easter, J. N. C. (St Edward's, Oxford) 1967-68
Edbrooke, R. M. (Queen Elizabeth's Hospital) 1984
Edwards, P. G. (Canford) 1987
Ellis, R. G. P. (Haileybury) (Capt. in 1982) 1981-83
Elviss, R. W. (Leeds GS) 1966-67
Ezekowitz, R. A. B. (Westville BHS, Durban and Cape Town U., SA) 1980-81

Faber, M. J. J. (Eton) 1972
Fane, F. L. (Charterhouse) 1897-98
Fasken, D. K. (Wellington) 1953-55
Fellows-Smith, J. P. (Durban HS, SA) 1953-55
Fillary, E. W. J. (St Lawrence) 1963-65
Findlay, W. (Eton) (Capt. in 1903) 1901-03
Firth, T. (Stockport GS) 1987
Fisher, P. B. (St Ignatius, Enfield) 1975-78
Foster, G. N. (Malvern) 1905-08
Foster, H. K. (Malvern) 1894-96
Foster, R. E. (Malvern) (Capt. in 1900) 1897-1900
Franks, J. G. (Stamford) 1984-85
Fry, C. A. (Repton) 1959-61
Fry, C. B. (Repton) (Capt. in 1894) 1892-95
Fursdon, E. D. (Sherborne) 1974-75

Gamble, N. W. (Stockport GS) 1967
Garofall, A. R. (Latymer Upper) 1967-68
Gibbs, P. J. K. (Hanley GS) 1964-66
Gibson, I. (Manchester GS) 1955-58
Gilliat, R. M. C. (Charterhouse) (Capt. in 1966) 1964-67
Gilligan, F. W. (Dulwich) (Capt. in 1920) 1919-20
Glover, T. R. (Lancaster RGS) (Capt. in 1975) 1973-75
Goldstein, F. S. (Falcon Coll., Bulawayo) (Capt. in 1968-69) 1966-69
Green, D. M. (Manchester GS) 1959-61
Grover, J. N. (Winchester) (Capt. in 1938) 1936-38
Groves, M. G. M. (Diocesan Coll., SA) 1964-66
Guest, M. R. J. (Rugby) 1964-66
Guise, J. L. (Winchester) (Capt. in 1925) 1924-25
Gurr, D. R. (Aylesbury GS) 1976-77

Hagan, D. A. (Trinity, Leamington Spa) 1986
Halliday, S. J. (Downside) 1980
Hamblin, C. B. (King's, Canterbury) 1971-73
Hamilton, A. C. (Charterhouse) 1975
Harris, C. R. (Buckingham RLS) 1964
Harris, Hon. G. R. C. (Lord Harris) (Eton) 1871-72, 1874

Hayes, K. A. (QEGS, Blackburn) (Capt. in 1984) 1981-84
Heal, M. G. (St Brendan's, Bristol) 1970, 1972
Heard, H. (QE Hosp. Sch.) 1969-70
Henderson, D. (St Edward's, Oxford) 1950
Henderson, I. M. (Laxton) 1987
Henley, D. F. (Harrow) 1947
Heseltine, P. J. (Holgate GS) 1983
Hiller, R. B. (Bec) 1966
Hobbs, J. A. D. (Liverpool Coll.) 1957
Hofmeyr, M. B. (Pretoria, SA) (Capt. in 1951) 1949-51
Holmes, E. R. T. (Malvern) (Capt. in 1927) 1925-27
Hone, B. W. (Adelaide U.) (Capt. in 1933) 1931-33
Howell, M. (Repton) (Capt. in 1919) 1914, 1919
Huxford, P. N. (Richard Hale) 1981

Imran Khan (Aitchison Coll., Lahore and Worcester RGS) (Capt. in 1974) 1973-75

Jakobson, T. R. (Charterhouse) 1961
Jardine, D. R. (Winchester) 1920-21, 1923
Jardine, M. R. (Fettes) (Capt. in 1891) 1889-92
Jarrett, D. W. (Wellington) 1975
Johns, R. L. (St Albans and Keele U.) 1970
Jones, A. K. C. (Solihull) (Capt. in 1973) 1971-73
Jones, P. C. H. (Milton HS, Rhodesia and Rhodes U.) (Capt. in 1972) 1971-72
Jose, A. D. (Adelaide U.) 1950-51
Jowett, D. C. P. R. (Sherborne) 1952-55
Jowett, R. L. (Bradford GS) 1957-59

Kamm, A. (Charterhouse) 1954
Kardar, A. H. (Islamia Coll. and Punjab U.) 1947-49
Kayum, D. A. (Selhurst GS and Chatham House GS) 1977-78
Keighley, W. G. (Eton) 1947-48
Kentish, E. S. M. (Cornwall Coll., Jamaica) 1956
Khan, A. J. (Aitchison Coll., Lahore and Punjab U.) 1968-69
Kilborn, M. J. (Farrer Agric. HS and Univ. of NSW) 1986-87
Kingsley, P. G. T. (Winchester) (Capt. in 1930) 1928-30
Kinkead-Weekes, R. C. (Eton) 1972
Knight, D. J. (Malvern) 1914, 1919
Knight, J. M. (Oundle) 1979
Knott, C. H. (Tonbridge) (Capt. in 1924) 1922-24
Knott, F. H. (Tonbridge) (Capt. in 1914) 1912-14
Knox, F. P. (Dulwich) (Capt. in 1901) 1899-1901

Lamb, Hon. T. M. (Shrewsbury) 1973-74

Lawrence, M. P. (Manchester GS) 1984-86

Lee, R. J. (Church of England GS and Sydney U.) 1972-74

Legge, G. B. (Malvern) (Capt. in 1926) 1925-26

L'Estrange, M. G. (St Aloysius Coll. and Sydney U.) 1977, 1979

Leveson Gower, H. D. G. (Winchester) (Capt. in 1896) 1893-96

Lewis, D. J. (Cape Town U.) 1951

Lloyd, M. F. D. (Magdalen Coll. Sch.) 1974

Luddington, R. S. (KCS, Wimbledon) 1982

McCanlis, M. A. (Cranleigh) (Capt. in 1928) 1926-28

Macindoe, D. H. (Eton) (Capt. in 1946) 1937-39, 1946

McKinna, G. H. (Manchester GS) 1953

MacLarnon, P. C. (Loughborough GS) 1985

Majendie, N. L. (Winchester) 1962-63

Mallett, A. W. H. (Dulwich) 1947-48

Mallett, N. V. H. (St Andrew's Coll. and Cape Town U.) 1981

Manasseh, M. (Epsom) 1964

Marie, G. V. (Western Australia U. and Reading U.) (Capt. in 1979, but injury prevented him playing v Cambridge) 1978

Marks, V. J. (Blundell's) (Capt. in 1976-77) 1975-78

Marsden, R. (Merchant Taylors', Northwood) 1982

Marshall, J. C. (Rugby) 1953

Marsham, C. D. B. (Private) (Capt. in 1857-58) 1854-58

Marsham, C. H. B. (Eton) (Capt. in 1902) 1900-02

Marsham, C. J. B. (Private) 1851

Marsham, R. H. B. (Private) 1856

Marsland, G. P. (Rossall) 1954

Martin, J. D. (Magdalen Coll. Sch.) (Capt. in 1965) 1962-63, 1965

Maudsley, R. H. (Malvern) 1946-47

May, P. (Prince Edward's, Salisbury and Cape Town U.) (Capt. in 1971) 1970-72

Mee, A. A. G. (Merchant Taylors', Northwood) 1986

Melville, A. (Michaelhouse, SA) (Capt. in 1931-32) 1930-33

Melville, C. D. M. (Michaelhouse, SA) 1957

Metcalfe, S. G. (Leeds GS) 1956

Millener, D. J. (Auckland GS and Auckland U.) 1969-70

Miller, A. J. T. (Haileybury) (Capt. in 1985) 1983-85

Minns, R. E. F. (King's, Canterbury) 1962-63

Mitchell, W. M. (Dulwich) 1951-52

Mitchell-Innes, N. S. (Sedbergh) (Capt. in 1936) 1934-37

Moore, D. N. (Shrewsbury) (Capt. in 1931, when he did not play v Cambridge owing to illness) 1930

Morgan, A. H. (Hastings GS) 1969

Morrill, N. D. (Sandown GS and Millfield) 1979

Morris, R. E. (Dyffryn Conwy, Llanrwst) 1987

Moulding, R. P. (Haberdashers' Aske's) (Capt. in 1981) 1978-83

Mountford, P. N. G. (Bromsgrove) 1963

Neate, F. W. (St Paul's) 1961-62

Newton-Thompson, J. O. (Diocesan Coll., SA) 1946

Niven, R. A. (Berkhamsted) 1968-69, 1973

O'Brien, T. C. (St Charles' College, Notting-Hill) 1884-85

Orders, J. O. D. (Winchester) 1978-81

Owen-Smith, H. G. (Diocesan College, SA) 1931-33

Palairet, L. C. H. (Repton) (Capt. in 1892-93) 1890-93

Pataudi, Nawab of (Chief's College, Lahore) 1929-31

Pataudi, Nawab of (Winchester) (Capt. in 1961, when he did not play v Cambridge owing to a car accident and 1963) 1960, 1963

Pathmanathan, G. (Royal Coll., Colombo and Sri Lanka U.) 1975-78

Paver, R. G. L. (Fort Victoria HS and Rhodes U.) 1973-74

Pawson, A. C. (Winchester) 1903

Pawson, A. G. (Winchester) (Capt. in 1910) 1908-11

Pawson, H. A. (Winchester) (Capt. in 1948) 1947-48

Pearce, J. P. (Ampleforth) 1979

Peebles, I. A. R. (Glasgow Academy) 1930

Petchey, M. D. (Latymer Upper) 1983

Phillips, J. B. M. (King's, Canterbury) 1955

Piachaud, J. D. (St Thomas's, Colombo) 1958-61

Pithey, D. B. (Plumtree HS and Cape Town U.) 1961-62

Porter, S. R. (Peers School) 1973

Potter, I. C. (King's, Canterbury) 1961-62

Potts, H. J. (Stand GS) 1950

Price, V. R. (Bishop's Stortford) (Capt. in 1921) 1919-22

Pycroft, J. (Bath) 1836

Quinlan, J. D. (Sherborne) 1985

Rawlinson, H. T. (Eton) 1983-84

Raybould, J. G. (Leeds GS) 1959

Ridge, S. P. (Dr Challenor's GS) 1982

Ridley, G. N. S. (Milton HS, Rhodesia) (Capt. in 1967) 1965-68

Ridley, R. M. (Clifton) 1968-70

Robertson-Glasgow, R. C. (Charterhouse) 1920-23

Robinson, G. A. (Preston Cath. Coll.) 1971

Robinson, H. B. O. (North Shore Coll., Vancouver) 1947-48

Rogers, J. J. (Sedbergh) 1979-81

Ross, C. J. (Wanganui CS and Wellington U., NZ) (Capt. in 1980) 1978-80

Rudd, C. R. D. (Eton) 1949

Rumbold, J. S. (St Andrew's Coll., NZ) 1946

Rutnagur, R. S. (Westminster) 1985-86

Rydon, R. A. (Sherborne) 1986

Sabine, P. N. B. (Marlborough) 1963

Sale, R. (Repton) 1910

Sale, R. (Repton) 1939, 1946

Salvi, N. V. (Rossall) 1986

Sanderson, J. F. W. (Westminster) 1980

Sardesai, R. D. (St Xavier's Coll., Bombay and Univ. of Bombay) 1987

Saunders, C. J. (Lancing) 1964

Savage, R. Le Q. (Marlborough) 1976-78

Sayer, D. M. (Maidstone GS) 1958-60

Scott, M. D. (Winchester) 1957

Singleton, A. P. (Shrewsbury) (Capt. in 1937) 1934-37

Siviter, K. (Liverpool) 1976

Smith, A. C. (King Edward's, Birmingham) (Capt. in 1959-60) 1958-60

Smith, G. O. (Charterhouse) 1895-96

Smith, M. J. K. (Stamford) (Capt. in 1956) 1954-56

Stallibrass, M. J. D. (Lancing) 1974

Stevens, G. T. S. (UCS) (Capt. in 1922) 1920-23

Sutcliffe, S. P. (King George V GS, Southport) 1980-81

Sutton, M. A. (Ampleforth) 1946

Tavaré, C. J. (Sevenoaks) 1975-77

Taylor, C. H. (Westminster) 1923-26

Taylor, T. J. (Stockport GS) 1981-82

Thackeray, P. R. (St Edward's, Oxford and Exeter U.) 1974

Thomas, R. J. A. (Radley) 1965

Thorne, D. A. (Bablake) (Capt. in 1986) 1984-86

Toft, D. P. (Tonbridge) 1966-67

Toogood, G. J. (N. Bromsgrove HS) (Capt. in 1983) 1982-85

Tooley, C. D. M. (St Dunstan's) (Capt. in 1987) 1985-87

Topham, R. D. N. (Shrewsbury and Australian National U., Canberra) 1976

Travers, B. H. (Sydney U.) 1946, 1948

Twining, R. H. (Eton) (Capt. in 1912) 1910-13

van der Bijl, P. G. (Diocesan Coll., SA) 1932

Van Ryneveld, C. B. (Diocesan Coll., SA) (Capt. in 1949) 1948-50

Varey, J. G. (Birkenhead) 1982-83

Wagstaffe, M. C. (Rossall and Exeter U.) 1972

Walford, M. M. (Rugby) 1936, 1938

Walker, D. F. (Uppingham) (Capt. in 1935) 1933-35

Waller, G. de W. (Hurstpierpoint) 1974

Walsh, D. R. (Marlborough) 1967-69

Walshe, A. P. (Milton HS, Rhodesia) 1953, 1955-56

Walton, A. C. (Radley) (Capt. in 1957) 1955-57

Ward, J. M. (Newcastle-under-Lyme HS) 1971-73

Warner, P. F. (Rugby) 1895-96

Watson, A. G. M. (St Lawrence) 1965-66, 1968

Weale, S. D. (Westminster City) 1987

Webb, H. E. (Winchester) 1948

Webbe, A. J. (Harrow) (Capt. in 1877-78) 1875-78

Wellings, E. M. (Cheltenham) 1929, 1931

Westley, S. A. (Lancaster RGS) 1968-69

Wheatley, G. A. (Uppingham) 1946

Whitcombe, P. A. (Winchester) 1947-49

Whitcombe, P. J. (Worcester RGS) 1951-52

Wiley, W. G. A. (Diocesan Coll., SA) 1952

Williams, C. C. P. (Westminster) (Capt. in 1955) 1953-55

Wilson, P. R. B. (Milton HS, Rhodesia and Cape Town U.) 1968, 1970

Wilson, R. W. (Warwick) 1957

Wingfield Digby, A. R. (Sherborne) 1971, 1975-77

Winn, C. E. (KCS, Wimbledon) 1948-51

Woodcock, R. G. (Worcester RGS) 1957-58

Wookey, S. M. (Malvern and Cambridge U.) 1978

Wordsworth, Chas. (Harrow) (Capt. both years, first Oxford Capt.) 1827, 1829

Worsley, D. R. (Bolton) (Capt. in 1964) 1961-64

Wrigley, M. H. (Harrow) 1949

CAMBRIDGE

Acfield, D. L. (Brentwood) 1967-68

Aers, D. R. (Tonbridge) 1967

Ahluwalia, M. S. (Latymer Upper) 1986

Aird, R. (Eton) 1923

Alexander, F. C. M. (Wolmer's Coll., Jamaica) 1952-53

Allbrook, M. E. (Tonbridge) 1975-78

Allen, G. O. (Eton) 1922-23

Allom, M. J. C. (Wellington) 1927-28

Andrew, C. R. (Barnard Castle) (Capt. in 1985) 1984-85

Ashton, C. T. (Winchester) (Capt. in 1923) 1921-23

Ashton, G. (Winchester) (Capt. in 1921) 1919-21

Ashton, H. (Winchester) (Capt. in 1922) 1920-22

Atherton, M. A. (Manchester GS) 1987

Atkins, G. (Dr Challenor's GS) 1960

Aworth, C. J. (Tiffin) (Capt. in 1975) 1973-75

Bail, P. A. C. (Millfield) 1986-87

Bailey, T. E. (Dulwich) 1947-48

Baker, R. K. (Brentwood) 1973-74

Bannister, C. S. (Caterham) 1976

Barber, R. W. (Ruthin) 1956-57

Barford, M. T. (Eastbourne) 1970-71

Barrington, W. E. J. (Lancing) 1982

Bartlett, H. T. (Dulwich) (Capt. in 1936) 1934-36

Beaumont, D. J. (West Bridgford GS and Bramshill Coll.) 1978

Benke, A. F. (Cheltenham) 1962

Bennett, B. W. P. (Welbeck and RMA Sandhurst) 1979

Bennett, C. T. (Harrow) (Capt. in 1925) 1923, 1925

Bernard, J. R. (Clifton) 1958-60

Bhatia, A. N. (Doon School, India) 1969

Bligh, Hon. Ivo F. W. (Lord Darnley) (Eton) (Capt. in 1881) 1878-81

Blofeld, H. C. (Eton) 1959

Bodkin, P. E. (Bradfield) (Capt. in 1946) 1946

Boyd-Moss, R. J. (Bedford) 1980-83

Brearley, J. M. (City of London) (Capt. in 1963-64) 1961-64

Breddy, M. N. (Cheltenham GS) 1984

Brodie, J. B. (Union HS, SA) 1960

Brodrick, P. D. (Royal GS, Newcastle) 1961

Bromley, R. C. (Christ's Coll. and Canterbury U., NZ) 1970

Brooker, M. E. W. (Lancaster RGS and Burnley GS) 1976

Brown, A. D. (Clacton HS) 1986

Brown, F. R. (The Leys) 1930-31

Browne, D. W. (Stamford) 1986

Burnett, A. C. (Lancing) 1949

Burnley, I. D. (Queen Elizabeth, Darlington) 1984

Bushby, M. H. (Dulwich) (Capt. in 1954) 1952-54

Calthorpe, Hon. F. S. G. (Repton) 1912-14, 1919

Cameron, J. H. (Taunton) 1935-37

Cangley, B. G. M. (Felsted) 1947

Carling, P. G. (Kingston GS) 1968, 1970

Chambers, R. E. J. (Forest) 1966

Chapman, A. P. F. (Oakham and Uppingham) 1920-22

Close, P. A. (Haileybury) 1965

Cobden, F. C. (Harrow) 1870-72

Cockett, J. A. (Aldenham) 1951

Coghlan, T. B. L. (Rugby) 1958

Conradi, E. R. (Oundle) 1946

Cook, G. W. (Dulwich) 1957-58

Cooper, N. H. C. (St Brendan's, Bristol and East Anglia U.) 1979

Cosh, N. J. (Dulwich) 1966-68

Cotterell, T. A. (Downside) 1983-85

Cottrell, G. A. (Kingston GS) (Capt. in 1968) 1966-68

Cottrell, P. R. (Chislehurst and Sidcup GS) 1979

Coverdale, S. P. (St Peter's, York) 1974-77

Craig, E. J. (Charterhouse) 1961-63

Crawford, N. C. (Shrewsbury) 1979-80

Crawley, E. (Harrow) 1887-89

Crawley, L. G. (Harrow) 1923-25

Croft, P. D. (Gresham's) 1955

Crookes, D. V. (Michaelhouse, SA) 1953

Curtis, T. S. (Worcester RGS) 1983

Daniell, J. (Clifton) 1899-1901

Daniels, D. M. (Rutlish) 1964-65

Datta, P. B. (Asutosh Coll., Calcutta) 1947

Davies, A. G. (Birkenhead) 1984-85

Davies, J. G. W. (Tonbridge) 1933-34

Davidson, J. E. (Penglais) 1985-86

Dawson, E. W. (Eton) (Capt. in 1927) 1924-27

Day, S. H. (Malvern) (Capt. in 1901) 1899-1902

Dewes, A. R. (Dulwich) 1978

Dewes, J. G. (Aldenham) 1948-50

Dexter, E. R. (Radley) (Capt. in 1958) 1956-58

Dickinson, D. C. (Clifton) 1953

Doggart, A. G. (Bishop's Stortford) 1921-22

Doggart, G. H. G. (Winchester) (Capt. in 1950) 1948-50

Doggart, S. J. G. (Winchester) 1980-83

Douglas-Pennant, S. (Eton) 1959

Duleepsinhji, K. S. (Cheltenham) 1925-26, 1928

Edmonds, P. H. (Gilbert Rennie HS, Lusaka, Skinner's and Cranbrook) (Capt. in 1973) 1971-73

Edwards, T. D. W. (Sherborne) 1981

Elgood, B. C. (Bradfield) 1948

Ellison, C. C. (Tonbridge) 1982-83, 1985-86

Enthoven, H. J. (Harrow) (Capt. in 1926) 1923-26

Estcourt, N. S. D. (Plumtree, Southern Rhodesia) 1954

Falcon, M. (Harrow) (Capt. in 1910) 1908-11

Farnes, K. (Royal Liberty School, Romford) 1931-33

Fell, D. J. (John Lyon) 1985-87

Field, M. N. (Bablake) 1974

Fitzgerald, J. F. (St Brendan's, Bristol) 1968

Ford, A. F. J. (Repton) 1878-81

Ford, F. G. J. (Repton) (Capt. in 1889) 1887-90

Ford, W. J. (Repton) 1873

Fosh, M. K. (Harrow) 1977-78

Gardiner, S. J. (St Andrew's, Bloemfontein) 1978

Garlick, P. L. (Sherborne) 1984

Gibb, P. A. (St Edward's, Oxford) 1935-38

Gibson, C. H. (Eton) 1920-21

Gilligan, A. E. R. (Dulwich) 1919-20

Goldie, C. F. E. (St Paul's) 1981-82

Golding, A. K. (Colchester GS) 1986

Goodfellow, A. (Marlborough) 1961-62

Goonesena, G. (Royal Coll., Colombo) (Capt. in 1957) 1954-57

Gorman, S. R. (St Peter's, York) 1985, 1987

Grace, W. G., jun. (Clifton) 1895-96

Grant, G. C. (Trinidad) 1929-30

Grant, R. S. (Trinidad) 1933

Green, D. J. (Burton GS) (Capt. in 1959) 1957-59

Greig, I. A. (Queen's Coll., SA) (Capt. in 1979) 1977-79

Grierson, H. (Bedford GS) 1911

Grimes, A. D. H. (Tonbridge) 1984

Griffith, M. G. (Marlborough) 1963-65

Griffith, S. C. (Dulwich) 1935

Griffiths, W. H. (Charterhouse) 1946-48

Hadley, R. J. (Sanfields CS) 1971-73

Hall, J. E. (Ardingly) 1969

Hall, P. J. (Geelong) 1949

Harvey, J. R. W. (Marlborough) 1965

Hawke, Hon. M. B. (Eton) (Capt. in 1885) 1882-83, 1885

Hayes, P. J. (Brighton) 1974-75, 1977

Hays, D. L. (Highgate) 1966, 1968

Hayward, W. I. D. (St Peter's Coll., Adelaide) 1950-51, 1953

Haywood, D. C. (Nottingham HS) 1968

Hazelrigg, A. G. (Eton) (Capt. in 1932) 1930-32

Henderson, S. P. (Downside and Durham U.) (Capt. in 1983) 1982-83

Hewitt, S. G. P. (Bradford GS) 1983

Hignell, A. J. (Denstone) (Capt. in 1977-78) 1975-78

Hobson, B. S. (Taunton) 1946

Hodgson, K. I. (Oundle) 1981-83

Hodson, R. P. (QEGS, Wakefield) 1972-73

Holliday, D. C. (Oundle) 1979-81

Hooper, A. M. (Latymer Upper) 1987

Howat, M. G. (Abingdon) 1977, 1980

Howland, C. B. (Dulwich) (Capt. in 1960) 1958-60

Hughes, G. (Cardiff HS) 1965

Human, J. H. (Repton) (Capt. in 1934) 1932-34

Hurd, A. (Chigwell) 1958-60

Hutton, R. A. (Repton) 1962-64

Huxter, R. J. A. (Magdalen Coll. Sch.) 1981

Insole, D. J. (Monoux, Walthamstow) (Capt. in 1949) 1947-49

Jackson, E. J. W. (Winchester) 1974-76

Jackson, F. S. (Harrow) (Capt. in 1892-93) 1890-93

Jahangir Khan (Lahore), 1933-36

James, R. M. (St John's, Leatherhead) 1956-58

Jameson, T. E. N. (Taunton and Durham U.) 1970

Jarrett, D. W. (Wellington and Oxford U.) 1976

Jefferson, R. I. (Winchester) 1961

Jenner, Herbert (Eton) (Capt. in 1827, First Cambridge Capt.) 1827

Jessop, G. L. (Cheltenham GS) (Capt. in 1899) 1896-99

Johnson, P. D. (Nottingham HS) 1970-72

Jones, A. O. (Bedford Modern) 1893

Jorden, A. M. (Monmouth) (Capt. in 1969-70) 1968-70

Kelland, P. A. (Repton) 1950

Kemp-Welch, G. D. (Charterhouse) (Capt. in 1931) 1929-31

Kendall, M. P. (Gillingham GS) 1972

Kenny, C. J. M. (Ampleforth) 1952

Kerslake, R. C. (Kingswood) 1963-64

Killick, E. T. (St Paul's) 1928-30

Kirby, D. (St Peter's, York) (Capt. in 1961) 1959-61

Kirkman, M. C. (Dulwich) 1963

Knight, R. D. V. (Dulwich) 1967-70

Knightley-Smith, W. (Highgate) 1953

Lacey, F. E. (Sherborne) 1882

Lacy-Scott, D. G. (Marlborough) 1946

Lea, A. E. (High Arcal GS) 1984-86

Lewis, A. R. (Neath GS) (Capt. in 1962) 1960-62

Lewis, L. K. (Taunton) 1953

Littlewood, D. J. (Enfield GS) 1978

Lowry, T. C. (Christ's College, NZ) (Capt. in 1924) 1923-24

Lumsden, V. R. (Munro College, Jamaica) 1953-55

Lyttelton, 4th Lord (Eton) 1838

Lyttelton, Hon. Alfred (Eton) (Capt. in 1879) 1876-79

Lyttelton, Hon. C. F. (Eton) 1908-09

Lyttelton, Hon. C. G. (Lord Cobham) (Eton) 1861-64

Lyttelton, Hon. Edward (Eton) (Capt. in 1878) 1875-78

Lyttelton, Hon. G. W. S. (Eton) 1866-67

McAdam, K. P. W. J. (Prince of Wales, Nairobi and Millfield) 1965-66

MacBryan, J. C. W. (Exeter) 1920

McCarthy, C. N. (Maritzburg Coll., SA) 1952

McDowall, J. I. (Rugby) 1969

MacGregor, G. (Uppingham) (Capt. in 1891) 1888-91

McLachlan, A. A. (St Peter's, Adelaide) 1964-65
McLachlan, I. M. (St Peter's, Adelaide) 1957-58
Majid Khan (Aitchison Coll., Lahore and Punjab U.) (Capt. in 1971-72) 1970-72
Malalasekera, V. P. (Royal Coll., Colombo) 1966-67
Mann, E. W. (Harrow) (Capt. in 1905) 1903-05
Mann, F. G. (Eton) 1938-39
Mann, F. T. (Malvern) 1909-11
Marlar, R. G. (Harrow) (Capt. in 1953) 1951-53
Marriott, C. S. (St Columba's) 1920-21
Mathews, K. P. A. (Felsted) 1951
May, P. B. H. (Charterhouse) 1950-52
Melluish, M. E. L. (Rossall) (Capt. in 1956) 1954-56
Meyer, R. J. O. (Haileybury) 1924-26
Middleton, M. R. (Harrow) 1987
Miller, M. E. (Prince Henry GS, Hohne, WG) 1963
Mills, J. M. (Oundle) (Capt. in 1948) 1946-48
Mills, J. P. C. (Oundle) (Capt. in 1982) 1979-82
Mischler, N. M. (St Paul's) 1946-47
Mitchell, F. (St Peter's, York) (Capt. in 1896) 1894-97
Morgan, J. T. (Charterhouse) (Capt. in 1930) 1928-30
Morgan, M. N. (Marlborough) 1954
Morris, R. J. (Blundell's) 1949
Morrison, J. S. F. (Charterhouse) (Capt. in 1919) 1912, 1914, 1919
Moses, G. H. (Ystalyfera GS) 1974
Moylan, A. C. D. (Clifton) 1977
Mubarak, A. M. (Royal Coll., Colombo and Sri Lanka U.) 1978-80
Murray, D. L. (Queen's RC, Trinidad) (Capt. in 1966) 1965-66
Murrills, T. J. (The Leys) (Capt. in 1976) 1973-74, 1976

Nevin, M. R. S. (Winchester) 1969
Norris, D. W. W. (Harrow) 1967-68

O'Brien, R. P. (Wellington) 1955-56
Odendaal, A. (Queen's Coll. and Stellenbosch U., SA) 1980
Owen-Thomas, D. R. (KCS, Wimbledon) 1969-72

Palfreman, A. B. (Nottingham HS) 1966
Palmer, R. W. M. (Bedford) 1982
Parker, G. W. (Crypt, Gloucester) (Capt. in 1935) 1934-35
Parker, P. W. G. (Collyer's GS) 1976-78
Parsons, A. B. D. (Brighton) 1954-55
Pathmanathan, G. (Royal Coll., Colombo, Sri Lanka U. and Oxford U.) 1983

Paull, R. K. (Millfield) 1967
Payne, M. W. (Wellington) (Capt. in 1907) 1904-07
Pearson, H. (King Alfred's and St Andrew's U.) 1969
Pearson, A. J. G. (Downside) 1961-63
Peck, I. G. (Bedford) (Capt. in 1980-81) 1980-81
Pepper, J. (The Leys) 1946-48
Perry, J. N. (Ampleforth) 1987
Pieris, P. I. (St Thomas's, Colombo) 1957-58
Pointer, G. A. (St Dunstan's) 1987
Pollock, A. J. (Shrewsbury) (Capt. in 1984) 1982-84
Ponniah, C. E. M. (St Thomas's, Colombo) 1967-69
Ponsonby, Hon. F. G. B. (Lord Bessborough) (Harrow) 1836
Popplewell, N. F. M. (Radley) 1977-79
Popplewell, O. B. (Charterhouse) 1949-51
Pretlove, J. F. (Alleyn's) 1954-56
Price, D. G. (Haberdashers' Aske's) (Capt. in 1986-87) 1984-87
Prideaux, R. M. (Tonbridge) 1958-60
Pringle, D. R. (Felsted) (Capt. in 1982, when he did not play v Oxford owing to Test selection) 1979-81
Pritchard, G. C. (King's, Canterbury) 1964
Pryer, B. J. K. (City of London) 1948
Pyemont, C. P. (Marlborough) 1967

Ranjitsinhji, K. S. (Rajkumar Coll., India) 1893
Ratcliffe, A. (Rydal) 1930-32
Reddy, N. S. K. (Doon School, India) 1959-61
Rimell, A. G. J. (Charterhouse) 1949-50
Robins, R. W. V. (Highgate) 1926-28
Roebuck, P. G. P. (Millfield) 1984-85
Roebuck, P. M. (Millfield) 1975-77
Roopnaraine, R. (Queen's RC, BG) 1965-66
Rose, M. H. (Pocklington) 1963-64
Ross, N. P. G. (Marlborough) 1969
Roundell, J. (Winchester) 1973
Russell, D. P. (West Park GS, St Helens) 1974-75
Russell, S. G. (Tiffin) (Capt. in 1967) 1965-67
Russom, N. (Huish's GS) 1980-81

Scott, A. M. G. (Seaford Head) 1985-87
Seabrook, F. J. (Haileybury) (Capt. in 1928) 1926-28
Seager, C. P. (Peterhouse, Rhodesia) 1971
Selvey, M. W. W. (Battersea GS and Manchester U.) 1971
Sheppard, D. S. (Sherborne) (Capt. in 1952) 1950-52
Short, R. L. (Denstone) 1969
Shuttleworth, G. M. (Blackburn GS) 1946-48

Silk, D. R. W. (Christ's Hospital) (Capt. in 1955) 1953-55
Singh, S. (Khalsa Coll. and Punjab U.) 1955-56
Sinker, N. D. (Winchester) 1966
Slack, J. K. E. (UCS) 1954
Smith, C. S. (William Hulme's GS) 1954-57
Smith, D. J. (Stockport GS) 1955-56
Smyth, R. I. (Sedbergh) 1973-75
Snowden, W. (Merchant Taylors', Crosby) (Capt. in 1974) 1972-75
Spencer, J. (Brighton and Hove GS) 1970-72
Steele, H. K. (King's Coll., NZ) 1971-72
Stevenson, M. H. (Rydal) 1949-52
Studd, C. T. (Eton) (Capt. in 1883) 1880-83
Studd, G. B. (Eton) (Capt. in 1882) 1879-82
Studd, J. E. K. (Eton) (Capt. in 1884) 1881-84
Studd, P. M. (Harrow) (Capt. in 1939) 1937-39
Studd, R. A. (Eton) 1895
Subba Row, R. (Whitgift) 1951-53
Surridge, D. (Richard Hale and Southampton U.) 1979
Swift, B. T. (St Peter's, Adelaide) 1957

Taylor, C. R. V. (Birkenhead) 1971-73
Thomson, R. H. (Bexhill) 1961-62
Thwaites, I. G. (Eastbourne) 1964
Tindall, M. (Harrow) (Capt. in 1937) 1935-37
Tordoff, G. G. (Normanton GS) 1952
Trapnell, B. M. W. (UCS) 1946
Tremellen, J. M. (Bradfield) 1987
Turnbull, M. J. (Downside) (Capt. in 1929) 1926, 1928-29

Urquhart, J. R. (King Edward VI School, Chelmsford) 1948

Valentine, B. H. (Repton) 1929
Varey, D. W. (Birkenhead) 1982-83

Wait, O. J. (Dulwich) 1949, 1951
Warr, J. J. (Ealing County GS) (Capt. in 1951) 1949-52
Watts, H. E. (Downside) 1947
Webster, W. H. (Highgate) 1932
Weedon, M. J. H. (Harrow) 1962
Wells, T. U. (King's Coll., NZ) 1950
Wheatley, O. S. (King Edward's, Birmingham) 1957-58
Wheelhouse, A. (Nottingham HS) 1959
White, R. C. (Hilton Coll., SA) (Capt. in 1965) 1962-65
Wilcox, D. R. (Dulwich) (Capt. in 1933) 1931-33
Wilenkin, B. C. G. (Harrow) 1956
Wilkin, C. L. A. (St Kitts GS) 1970
Willard, M. J. L. (Judd) 1959-61
Willatt, G. L. (Repton) (Capt. in 1947) 1946-47
Windows, A. R. (Clifton) 1962-64
Wood, G. E. C. (Cheltenham) (Capt. in 1920) 1914, 1919-20
Wookey, S. M. (Malvern) 1975-76
Wooller, W. (Rydal) 1935-36
Wright, S. (Mill Hill) 1973

Yardley, N. W. D. (St Peter's, York) (Capt. in 1938) 1935-38
Young, R. A. (Repton) (Capt. in 1908) 1905-08

NCA COMPETITION WINNERS, 1987

NCA County Championship: Nottinghamshire CA beat Essex CA by eight wickets.
NCA Six-a-Side Club Championship: St Lawrence and Highland Court (Canterbury) beat Pudsey St Lawrence by two wickets.
Dunlop 50-plus County Championship: Berkshire CA beat Lancashire CA by 15 runs.
Texaco Under-16 County Championship: Yorkshire CA won, having lost fewer wickets than Sussex CA in the final group matches, each county having won twice.
SunLife of Canada Under-15 Club Championship: Slazengers CC (Yorkshire) beat Crawley CC (Sussex) by eight wickets.
National Westminster Bank Under-13 Club Championship: Wycombe House CC (Middlesex).
President's Trophy: Durham County League beat Bassetlaw and District League by seven wickets.
Club Cricket Conference Inter-League: Thames Valley League beat Essex League by 49 runs.
Esso NAYC Under-19 Festivals: Cambridge Festival Final – Yorkshire beat Sussex by 33 runs. Oxford Festival Final – Hampshire beat Worcestershire by 12 runs. Final – Yorkshire beat Hampshire by 49 runs.

OTHER MATCHES, 1987

THE TILCON TROPHY

Rain ruined the Harrogate Festival, where all three Tilcon Trophy matches were decided by the system of each player bowling two balls at a single stump, the side scoring the most hits being declared the winners.

†June 10. Gloucestershire beat Derbyshire 3-2. Rain delayed the start until two o'clock and then permitted only 14.2 overs to be bowled. Derbyshire reached 43 without loss. In the ensuing bowling contest, R. C. Russell, K. P. Tomlins and J. W. Lloyds hit the stump once each for Gloucestershire, while C. F. B. P. Rudd and B. J. M. Maher were successful for Derbyshire.

†June 11. Glamorgan beat Worcestershire 3-2. With no orthodox play possible, C. P. Metson hit the stump once and S. J. Base twice for Glamorgan, while M. J. Weston and G. R. Dilley struck once each for Worcestershire.

†June 12. Gloucestershire beat Glamorgan 4-3. Rain prevented any play in the final, which was not decided until the fourth round of the bowling contest. In the first round, S. P. James of Glamorgan and K. P. Tomlins of Gloucestershire were successful; in the second round no-one managed a hit; in the third C. J. P. G. van Zyl and S. R. Barwick struck for Glamorgan, as did A. J. Wright and M. W. Alleyne for Gloucestershire; and in the fourth round J. W. Lloyds, the only player to hit the stump, won the Trophy for Gloucestershire.

†GLAMORGAN v GLOUCESTERSHIRE

At Cardiff, July 6. Gloucestershire won by seven wickets. Toss: Gloucestershire. This match, attended by the Prince and Princess of Wales, the patrons of the two counties, launched Glamorgan's centenary celebrations. That Gloucestershire would win the Severn Trophy, presented by British Gas (Wales), was never in doubt once Stovold and Wright had put on 126 in 25 overs. Wright, 99 not out, missed out on a century when Curran, with overs in hand, took to the bowling and scored the winning runs.

Glamorgan

J. A. Hopkins st Russell b Graveney	42	J. G. Thomas not out	16
S. P. James lbw b Sainsbury	9		
*H. Morris b Graveney	39	L-b 8, w 5, n-b 2	15
G. C. Holmes run out	29		
M. P. Maynard not out	68	1/28 2/67 3/106 (5 wkts, 40 overs) 218
P. A. Cottey lbw b Walsh	0	4/154 5/154

†C. P. Metson, S. R. Barwick, S. Monkhouse and C. J. P. G. van Zyl did not bat.

Bowling: Curran 5-0-27-0; Sainsbury 8-2-39-1; Lloyds 8-0-40-0; Graveney 8-1-31-2; Alleyne 3-0-22-0; Lawrence 4-0-31-0; Walsh 4-0-20-1.

Gloucestershire

A. W. Stovold b Maynard	52	K. M. Curran not out	45
A. J. Wright not out	99	L-b 9, w 4, n-b 6	19
P. W. Romaines c Metson b Maynard	0		
M. W. Alleyne b Maynard	5	1/126 2/126 3/134 (3 wkts, 37.5 overs) 220

G. E. Sainsbury, J. W. Lloyds, †R. C. Russell, *D. A. Graveney, C. A. Walsh and D. V. Lawrence did not bat.

Bowling: Thomas 7-0-37-0; van Zyl 6.5-0-30-0; Barwick 8-0-41-0; Maynard 8-0-54-3; Monkhouse 8-0-49-0.

Umpires: R. Julian and D. Lloyd.

IRELAND v SCOTLAND

At Coleraine, July 18, 19, 20. Drawn. Toss: Ireland. Rain and a wet outfield delayed the start until 4.45 p.m., and in the three hours' play that followed, Ireland reached 110 for seven. However, they were rescued by Corlett and McBrine, who on the second day took their eighth-wicket partnership to 150 in 156 minutes, passing by 44 the previous record for Ireland, set in 1928 by T. G. McVeagh and P. A. Thornton against the West Indians. McBrine, who faced 158 balls and hit twelve fours, became the first Irish player to score a century batting at No. 9. Scotland, who lost Philip for 0, were in trouble at 71 for five, but recovered through Smith, Snodgrass and Ker to enable Swan to declare at the overnight score. With the pitch taking spin, a Scottish victory looked a possibility when Ireland were 84 for six with 162 minutes remaining, but the later order ensured that defeat was avoided. When Scotland batted again, Russell suffered the ignominy of a pair, despite facing 32 balls in the first innings and 22 in the second.

Ireland

S. J. S. Warke lbw b Duthie	36	– c Govan b Snodgrass	18
M. F. Cohen c Russell b Ker	4	– c Snodgrass b Govan	12
M. P. Rea c Philip b Ker	13	– c Russell b Snodgrass	0
M. A. Masood c Brown b Ker	10	– c Stevenson b Govan	22
D. G. Dennison c Stevenson b Ker	3	– c Swan b Govan	12
G. D. Harrison c Smith b Duthie	17	– b Stevenson	14
J. D. Garth c Russell b Duthie	1	– c Duthie b Stevenson	11
S. C. Corlett c Brown b Stevenson	53	– not out	31
A. McBrine c Stevenson b Govan	102	– c Snodgrass b Stevenson	20
*†P. B. Jackson not out	1	– c Philip b Stevenson	4
H. Milling c Duthie b Govan	2	– not out	4
B 1, l-b 2, w 13, n-b 1	17	B 6, w 6, n-b 1	13

1/10 2/27 3/48 4/54 5/79   259   1/30 2/30 3/32   (9 wkts dec.) 161
6/82 7/102 8/252 9/256   4/65 5/67 6/84
                                          7/104 8/142 9/147

Bowling: First Innings—Duthie 29-7-99-3; Ker 23-4-54-4; Snodgrass 11-1-26-0; Govan 14.1-2-43-2; Russell 7-1-23-0; Stevenson 6-1-11-1. *Second Innings*—Duthie 11-5-26-0; Ker 6-3-7-0; Snodgrass 9-1-26-2; Govan 27-12-68-3; Stevenson 16-6-28-4.

Scotland

I. L. Philip c Warke b Corlett	0	– c McBrine b Milling	3
K. Scott c Corlett b Milling	33	– not out	14
*R. G. Swan c Corlett b Milling	26		
A. B. Russell lbw b McBrine	0	– (3) b Milling	0
†A. Brown c Cohen b Milling	2	– (4) lbw b McBrine	13
M. J. Smith c and b Milling	79	– (5) not out	0
D. L. Snodgrass b Harrison	49		
P. G. Duthie lbw b McBrine	3		
J. E. Ker not out	26		
J. W. Govan not out	5		
L-b 4, w 8, n-b 6	18	W 5, n-b 2	7

1/0 2/60 3/69 4/71 5/71   (8 wkts dec.) 241   1/5 2/12 3/32   (3 wkts) 37
6/155 7/164 8/228

A. W. J. Stevenson did not bat.

Bowling: First Innings—Corlett 12-0-28-1; Milling 24-4-81-4; Garth 13-3-34-0; McBrine 24-11-43-2; Harrison 18-3-51-1. *Second Innings*—Corlett 5-1-8-0; Milling 5-1-17-2; McBrine 2-1-4-1; Harrison 2-0-8-0.

Umpires: J. Doherty and P. Lunney.

CALLERS-PEGASUS FESTIVAL

†ENGLAND XI v REST OF THE WORLD XI

At Jesmond, July 30. England XI won by three wickets. Toss: Rest of the World XI.

Rest of the World XI

*C. G. Greenidge st Richards b Cowdrey	80
G. A. Hick c Richards b Dilley	12
D. B. Vengsarkar c Slack b Allott	0
D. M. Jones lbw b Cowdrey	64
S. R. Waugh not out	44
A. L. Logie b Emburey	22

R. J. Shastri not out	2
L-b 10, w 6	16
1/21 2/36 3/145 (5 wkts, 45 overs) 240	
4/180 5/233	

M. D. Marshall, Madan Lal, †T. E. Blain and A. H. Gray did not bat.

Bowling: Dilley 7–2–23–1; Cowans 5–1–13–0; Botham 8–0–54–0; Allott 7–0–35–1; Emburey 9–0–47–1; Cowdrey 9–0–58–2.

England XI

G. Fowler c Waugh b Madan Lal	27
W. N. Slack lbw b Madan Lal	85
M. C. J. Nicholas c Vengsarkar b Hick	27
N. H. Fairbrother st Blain b Hick	19
C. S. Cowdrey c Gray b Hick	9
I. T. Botham c Hick b Marshall	30
†C. J. Richards c Blain b Marshall	18

*J. E. Emburey not out	5
P. J. W. Allott not out	1
L-b 10, w 4, n-b 8	22
1/68 2/154 3/154 (7 wkts, 43 overs) 243	
4/177 5/186 6/212 7/237	

G. R. Dilley and N. G. Cowans did not bat.

Bowling: Gray 9–0–48–0; Marshall 7–0–40–2; Madan Lal 9–0–37–2; Shastri 4–0–28–0; Hick 6–2–15–3; Waugh 8–0–65–0.

Umpires: S. Levison and G. I. McLean.

†ENGLAND XI v REST OF THE WORLD XI

At Jesmond, July 31. Rest of the World XI won by three wickets. Toss: England XI.

England XI

G. Fowler c Shastri b Hick	57
W. N. Slack c Waugh b Hick	35
M. C. J. Nicholas st Blain b Shastri	4
N. H. Fairbrother run out	23
C. S. Cowdrey c Gray b Shastri	61
I. T. Botham c Waugh	21
†C. J. Richards b Marshall	4
*J. E. Emburey run out	4

P. J. W. Allott c Gray b Shastri	5
G. R. Dilley not out	3
N. G. Cowans b Gray	1
B 1, l-b 6, w 14, n-b 5	26
1/95 2/109 3/109 (53.4 overs) 244	
4/169 5/196 6/230	
7/232 8/240 9/240	

Bowling: Gray 8.4–0–32–1; Marshall 11–1–33–1; Shastri 11–0–68–3; Hick 11–0–47–2; Waugh 7–0–35–1; Border 5–0–22–0.

Rest of the World XI

*C. G. Greenidge b Allott	52
G. A. Hick c Nicholas b Emburey	58
D. B. Vengsarkar c Fairbrother b Cowdrey	35
A. L. Logie c Allott b Emburey	1
A. R. Border c Richards b Botham	15
D. M. Jones c Botham b Cowdrey	22

S. R. Waugh c Emburey b Allott	42
†T. E. Blain not out	7
R. J. Shastri not out	2
B 4, l-b 6, w 1	11
1/95 2/135 3/147 (7 wkts, 43.1 overs) 245	
4/151 5/175 6/222 7/241	

M. D. Marshall and A. H. Gray did not bat.

Bowling: Dilley 9–0–50–0; Cowans 4–0–33–0; Allott 8–0–47–2; Cowdrey 6–0–40–2; Fairbrother 2–0–25–0; Emburey 11–3–23–2; Botham 3.1–0–17–1.

Umpires: S. Levison and G. I. McLean.

†At Welshpool, August 9, 10, 11. Drawn. Ireland 321 (P. B. Jackson 89 not out, M. A. Masood 79, T. J. T. Patterson 43; J. Kitson five for 76); Wales 321 for eight dec. (N. Roberts 127, A. Puddle 110; M. Halliday four for 93, T. J. T. Patterson three for 44).

†At Aberdeen, August 12, 13, 14. Drawn. MCC 203 for eight dec. (R. D. V. Knight 36, B. T. Donelan 41; P. G. Duthie five for 55) and 125 for two (D. L. Hays 39, S. P. Henderson 41 not out); Scotland 188 for one dec. (K. Scott 72 not out, R. G. Swan 79 not out).

REST OF THE WORLD MATCHES

As preparation for the MCC Bicentenary match at Lord's, the Rest of the World squad, under the managership of C. H. Lloyd, undertook four warm-up matches.

†LAVINIA, DUCHESS OF NORFOLK'S XI v REST OF THE WORLD XI

At Arundel, August 9. Lavinia, Duchess of Norfolk's XI won by five wickets. Toss: Rest of the World XI. The target of Lavinia, Duchess of Norfolk's XI was reduced, because of rain, to 168 off 35 overs.

Rest of the World XI

S. M. Gavaskar c Neale b Pocock 26	†P. J. L. Dujon not out 22	
D. L. Haynes lbw b Merry 19	L-b 10, n-b 2 12	
D. M. Jones not out 143		
*A. R. Border b Pocock 29	1/46 2/52 3/149 (4 wkts, 55 overs) 262	
Kapil Dev lbw b Woolmer 11	4/176	

J. G. Bracewell, Maninder Singh, J. R. Ratnayeke, B. A. Reid and K. W. McLeod did not bat.

Bowling: Newport 8–1–37–0; van der Bijl 10–1–39–0; Merry 10–1–55–1; Pocock 13–1–51–2; Hick 6–0–37–0; Woolmer 8–0–33–1.

Lavinia, Duchess of Norfolk's XI

R. A. Woolmer lbw b Kapil Dev 1	*J. M. Brearley not out 21	
T. S. Curtis c Bracewell b Reid 22		
G. A. Hick not out 85	B 1, l-b 8, w 1, n-b 3 13	
D. B. D'Oliveira c Dujon b McLeod .. 7		
P. A. Neale b Kapil Dev 20	1/4 2/40 3/51 (5 wkts, 32.5 overs) 169	
P. J. Newport b Kapil Dev 0	4/118 5/118	

†C. F. E. Goldie, P. I. Pocock, V. A. P. van der Bijl and W. G. Merry did not bat.

Bowling: Kapil Dev 9-2-38-3; Reid 8.5-0-38-1; McLeod 10-0-47-1; Maninder 5-1-37-0.

Umpires: C. Cook and J. G. Langridge.

†LEAGUE CRICKET CONFERENCE v REST OF THE WORLD XI

At West Bromwich CC, August 11. No result.

Rest of the World XI

S. M. Gavaskar c Andrews b Estwick .. 1	*A. R. Border not out 26	
D. L. Haynes c Knowles b Estwick ... 14	L-b 8, w 3, n-b 2 13	
D. B. Vengsarkar not out 68		
Kapil Dev c Moseley b Andrews 18	1/1 2/28 3/82 (4 wkts, 39 overs) 149	
†P. J. L. Dujon c Foster b Andrews ... 9	4/102	

D. M. Jones, J. G. Bracewell, J. R. Ratnayeke, Maninder Singh and B. A. Reid did not bat.

Bowling: Moseley 6–3–10–0; Estwick 6–2–16–2; Frost 8–1–29–0; Greene 11–1–47–0; Andrews 7–0–27–2; Knowles 1–0–12–0.

League Cricket Conference

*P. Knowles, J. Foster, †J. McCauley, S. Dean, V. S. Greene, R. Steyn, W. S. Andrews, M. Frost, E. A. Moseley, S. C. Wundke and R. O. Estwick.

Umpires: G. Wenman and J. A. Potts.

†LANCASHIRE v REST OF THE WORLD XI

At Manchester, August 14. Rest of the World XI won by four wickets. Toss: Rest of the World XI. The game, originally scheduled as a first-class fixture for August 12, 13, 14, was reduced to a 50-over match when the first two days were lost to rain. Fairbrother, captaining Lancashire for the first time in a pointer to the future, gave their innings purpose with 62 in a fifth-wicket partnership of 96 with Abrahams. The Rest of the World were facing defeat until Dujon and Bracewell came together in an unbroken seventh-wicket partnership of 59 in ten overs.

Lancashire

M. R. Chadwick c Gavaskar b Bracewell	29	J. D. Fitton not out		0
N. J. Speak c Haynes b Bracewell	28			
M. A. Atherton st Dujon b Maninder	7	B 4, l-b 5, w 4, n-b 5		18
*N. H. Fairbrother b Maninder	62			
M. Watkinson c Gavaskar b Bracewell	1	1/58 2/69 3/71	(6 wkts, 50 overs)	180
J. Abrahams run out	35	4/80 5/176 6/180		

†W. K. Hegg, I. Folley, K. W. McLeod and B. P. Patterson did not bat.

Bowling: Kapil Dev 7–1–31–0; Reid 5–2–14–0; Ratnayeke 10–1–40–0; Bracewell 10–6–13–3; Maninder 10–2–44–2; Haynes 3–0–8–0; Jones 5–0–21–0.

Rest of the World XI

S. M. Gavaskar retired hurt	10	J. G. Bracewell not out		29
D. L. Haynes c Abrahams b Folley	27	†P. J. L. Dujon not out		18
J. R. Ratnayeke st Hegg b Fitton	17			
D. B. Vengsarkar lbw b Folley	0	B 4, l-b 9, w 8, n-b 6		27
*A. R. Border c Folley b Abrahams	28			
D. M. Jones c Chadwick b Fitton	15	1/54 2/54 3/70	(6 wkts, 47 overs)	181
Kapil Dev b Watkinson	10	4/110 5/116 6/122		

B. A. Reid and Maninder Singh did not bat.

Bowling: Patterson 8–0–40–0; McLeod 6–1–17–0; Folley 10–1–29–2; Fitton 10–1–35–2; Abrahams 6–1–16–1; Watkinson 7–0–31–1.

Umpires: J. A. Jameson and R. A. White.

GLOUCESTERSHIRE v REST OF THE WORLD XI

At Bristol, August 15, 16, 17. Drawn. Toss: Rest of the World XI. Practice, rather than a victory, was very much on Border's mind. He chose not to set the county side a realistic target on the third day, and when eventually Gloucestershire had only three wickets remaining, he did not claim the extra half-hour. Vengsarkar, coming in when Haynes was bowled by the first ball of the match, played a memorable innings, hitting 22 fours and all but carrying his bat for a sumptuous 173 not out in four and a half hours. He and Jones (one six, ten fours) put on 171 in 40 overs. Maninder, surprisingly not required for Lord's, then gave a beautiful demonstration of left-arm spin bowling, although Alleyne played him well. When Dujon was injured, Haynes and Jones took turns behind the stumps before J. S. Brooks, of the Clifton club, was pressed into service. A century in 215 minutes from Haynes (twenty fours) and fierce hitting from Border and Kapil Dev further increased the Rest's lead, but it took an over from Russell to provoke a declaration. This left Gloucestershire to score 386 in 280 minutes.

Close of play: First day, Gloucestershire 84-0 (A. W. Stovold 47*, K. B. K. Ibadulla 24*); Second day, Rest of the World XI 209-2 (D. L. Haynes 102*, Kapil Dev 25*).

Rest of the World XI

D. L. Haynes b Greene	0	– b Lloyds	130
J. R. Ratnayeke run out	11	– c Stovold b Greene	17
D. B. Vengsarkar not out	173		
Kapil Dev c Romaines b Greene	7	– b Greene	49
*A. R. Border b Greene	28	– (3) c Alleyne b Sainsbury	57
D. M. Jones b Alleyne	80	– (7) not out	21
†P. J. L. Dujon c Athey b Alleyne	0	– (5) not out	14
J. G. Bracewell st Russell b Athey	14	– (6) c and b Lloyds	6
Maninder Singh c Russell b Athey	1		
B. A. Reid c Ibadulla b Lloyds	9		
C. A. Walsh c Greene b Lloyds	2		
L-b 7, w 1, n-b 3	11	L-b 6, n-b 4	10

1/0 2/35 3/46 4/85 5/256   336   1/28 2/155 3/258   (5 wkts dec.) 304
6/256 7/315 8/319 9/332   4/263 5/272

Bowling: *First Innings*—Greene 20–0–76–3; Sainsbury 16–2–44–0; Alleyne 15–2–85–2; Lloyds 17.4–0–65–2; Athey 9–1–21–2; Ibadulla 8–0–38–0. *Second Innings*—Greene 22–5–64–2; Sainsbury 15–3–46–1; Alleyne 8–1–47–0; Lloyds 21–5–86–2; Athey 10–1–42–0; Ibadulla 3–0–6–0; Russell 1–0–7–0.

Gloucestershire

A. W. Stovold c Haynes b Reid	47	– c Haynes b Ratnayeke	8
K. B. K. Ibadulla c Haynes b Reid	28	– b Reid	4
M. W. Alleyne c Walsh b Maninder	78	– c Dujon b Bracewell	42
P. W. Romaines lbw b Kapil Dev	9		
O. C. K. Smith c Kapil Dev b Maninder	1	– (4) c Vengsarkar b Bracewell	14
*C. W. J. Athey b Maninder	14	– (5) c Border b Bracewell	26
K. M. Curran st Haynes b Maninder	22	– (6) c Kapil Dev b Bracewell	53
J. W. Lloyds c Kapil Dev b Maninder	17	– (7) c Bracewell b Haynes	37
†R. C. Russell not out	5	– (8) not out	6
V. S. Greene c Jones b Walsh	7	– (9) not out	0
G. E. Sainsbury b Walsh	1		
B 11, l-b 7, n-b 8	26	B 12, l-b 16, n-b 3	31

1/88 2/105 3/134 4/135 5/161   255   1/15 2/15 3/68 4/91   (7 wkts) 221
6/205 7/237 8/246 9/253   5/126 6/199 7/215

Bowling: *First Innings*—Kapil Dev 16–4–45–1; Reid 12–2–47–2; Walsh 13–4–20–2; Bracewell 23–8–54–0; Maninder 24–6–71–5. *Second Innings*—Reid 11–1–28–1; Ratnayeke 11–6–26–1; Maninder 21–10–42–0; Bracewell 27–12–57–4; Kapil Dev 6–0–30–0; Haynes 1–0–4–1; Jones 1–0–6–0.

Umpires: J. W. Holder and B. J. Meyer.

At Lord's, August 20, 21, 22, 24, 25. REST OF THE WORLD drew with MCC (See MCC section).

YORKSHIRE v MCC

At Scarborough, September 2, 3, 4. MCC won by six wickets. Toss: Yorkshire. Metcalfe took the opportunity of a very slow pitch to compile a career-best 152 from 284 balls, hitting sixteen fours and three sixes and passing 1,000 runs for the season in the process. He and Robinson (sixteen fours) took toll of some friendly bowling in a stand worth 170 from 42 overs. MCC struggled for a time, but Atherton and Radley put on 130 in 41 overs, the young Cambridge Blue reaching his highest score to date with a six and seventeen fours in an innings of 189 balls. Bairstow, nursing a damaged hand in the field, claimed career-best bowling figures when he joined the attack, and after Swallow had completed a maiden century in Yorkshire's second innings, MCC were set a target of 248 in 61 overs. They had slumped to 126 for four when Downton and Radley came together, and with Yorkshire keeping the game open by using the occasional off-spin of Love, their decisive partnership saw MCC to victory with eight balls to spare.

Close of play: First day, MCC 9-1 (M. A. Atherton 7*, P. R. Downton 0*); Second day, Yorkshire 44-3 (I. G. Swallow 27*, J. D. Love 8*).

Yorkshire

A. A. Metcalfe b Kippax	152	– c Downton b Cowans	0
I. G. Swallow b Cowans	28	– c Henderson b Kippax	114
†R. J. Blakey b Cowans	12	– lbw b Cowans	6
P. E. Robinson c Downton b Cowans	91	– lbw b Kippax	0
J. D. Love not out	17	– st Downton b Folley	32
S. N. Hartley not out	14	– b Folley	0
D. L. Bairstow (did not bat)		– c Kippax b Folley	41
P. J. Hartley (did not bat)		– st Downton b Kippax	15
*P. Carrick (did not bat)		– c Radley b Folley	21
A. Sidebottom (did not bat)		– not out	1
L-b 1, n-b 2	3	B 3	3

1/60 2/94 3/264 4/291   (4 wkts dec.) 317   1/0 2/14 3/23   (9 wkts dec.) 233
4/96 5/96 6/190
7/202 8/227 9/233

P. W. Jarvis did not bat.

Bowling: *First Innings*—Cowans 24–4–63–3; Fraser 25–12–65–0; Knight 3–2–4–0; Kippax 19–3–46–1; Carr 15–3–53–0; Folley 21–2–85–0. *Second Innings*—Cowans 9–4–18–2; Fraser 11–3–21–0; Kippax 23–2–71–3; Atherton 11–2–37–0; Carr 4–1–11–0; Folley 20.4–7–72–4.

MCC

J. D. Carr c Blakey b Sidebottom	0	– c S. N. Hartley b Carrick	57
M. A. Atherton b Swallow	110	– run out	27
†P. R. Downton c Swallow b Jarvis	4	– (6) not out	64
S. P. Henderson b Jarvis	9	– (3) c S. N. Hartley b Carrick	8
R. O. Butcher lbw b Carrick	25	– (4) c Bairstow b Love	25
C. T. Radley c Robinson b Bairstow	72	– (5) not out	58
*R. D. V. Knight not out	22		
I. Folley c Blakey b Bairstow	0		
P. J. Kippax c Swallow b Bairstow	3		
A. R. C. Fraser c Jarvis b P. J. Hartley	29		
N. G. Cowans not out	8		
B 1, l-b 11, w 4, n-b 5	21	B 8, l-b 3	11

1/3 2/19 3/39 4/84 5/214   (9 wkts dec.) 303   1/80 2/84 3/106 4/126   (4 wkts) 250
6/248 7/248 8/254 9/294

Bowling: *First Innings*—Jarvis 15.5–5–55–2; Sidebottom 15–2–48–1; Swallow 19–4–56–1; P. J. Hartley 10.2–43–1; Carrick 22–8–59–1; Bairstow 8–1–25–3; Love 5–1–5–0. *Second Innings*—Jarvis 9–2–31–0; Sidebottom 6.4–1–31–0; P. J. Hartley 6–1–42–0; Swallow 8–2–26–0; Carrick 19–1–65–2; Love 11–1–44–1.

Umpires: J. Birkenshaw and B. Leadbeater.

THE ASDA CHALLENGE

†DERBYSHIRE v LANCASHIRE

At Scarborough, September 6. Lancashire won on the toss of a coin after rain ended play.
Toss: Lancashire.
Man of the Match: K. J. Barnett.

Derbyshire

*K. J. Barnett run out	158	P. G. Newman b Watkinson		0
†B. J. M. Maher c Hughes b Hayhurst	11	F. A. Griffith not out		1
B. Roberts lbw b Abrahams	52			
J. E. Morris b Abrahams	4	L-b 13, w 4		17
M. A. Holding b Abrahams	0			
A. E. Warner b Hayhurst	2	1/47 2/173 3/205	(9 wkts, 50 overs)	256
C. J. Adams st Hegg b Abrahams	10	4/205 5/208 6/244		
R. J. Finney c Atherton b Abrahams	1	7/246 8/252 9/256		

O. H. Mortensen did not bat.

Bowling: Allott 5–1–20–0; Watkinson 10–0–44–1; O'Shaughnessy 8–0–43–0; Hayhurst 8–0–32–2; Simmons 10–0–61–0; Abrahams 9–0–43–5.

Lancashire

G. Fowler not out	25			
G. D. Mendis not out	15			
L-b 1, w 1	2			
		(no wkt, 7 overs)	42	

M. A. Atherton, J. Abrahams, M. Watkinson, *D. P. Hughes, S. J. O'Shaughnessy, A. N. Hayhurst, P. J. W. Allott, J. Simmons and †W. K. Hegg did not bat.

Bowling: Newman 4–1–22–0; Mortensen 3–0–19–0.

Umpires: J. Birkenshaw and B. Leadbeater.

†YORKSHIRE v HAMPSHIRE

At Scarborough, September 7. Yorkshire won by eight wickets. Toss: Yorkshire.
Man of the Match: A. A. Metcalfe.

Hampshire

V. P. Terry lbw b Jarvis	0	I. J. Chivers not out		15
C. L. Smith c Sidebottom b Carrick	35	C. A. Connor not out		4
R. A. Smith c Bairstow b P. J. Hartley	16			
*M. C. J. Nicholas run out	54	B 1, l-b 14, w 2, n-b 6		23
D. R. Turner c Carrick b Sidebottom	33			
N. G. Cowley b Fletcher	0	1/0 2/38 3/73	(8 wkts, 50 overs)	199
†R. J. Parks c Bairstow b P. J. Hartley	19	4/144 5/145 6/165		
T. M. Tremlett b P. J. Hartley	0	7/165 8/182		

P. J. Bakker did not bat.

Bowling: Jarvis 10–1–35–1; Sidebottom 10–0–32–1; Fletcher 10–0–29–1; P. J. Hartley 8–1–35–3; Carrick 7–0–28–1; Love 5–0–25–0.

Yorkshire

A. A. Metcalfe c and b Tremlett	80
K. Sharp not out	68
J. D. Love c Chivers b Bakker	29
P. E. Robinson not out	16
B 4, l-b 3	7

1/127 2/183   (2 wkts, 30.5 overs) 200

S. N. Hartley, †D. L. Bairstow, *P. Carrick, A. Sidebottom, P. J. Hartley, P. W. Jarvis and S. D. Fletcher did not bat.

Bowling: Bakker 7.5-0-49-1; Connor 5-0-42-0; Tremlett 6-0-35-1; Cowley 6-0-40-0; Chivers 6-0-27-0.

Umpires: J. Birkenshaw and B. Leadbeater.

FINAL

†YORKSHIRE v LANCASHIRE

At Scarborough, September 8. Yorkshire won by four wickets. Toss: Yorkshire. Watkinson hit six sixes and sixteen fours as he scored 149 out of 225.
Man of the Match: M. Watkinson.

Lancashire

G. D. Mendis lbw b Sidebottom	16	A. N. Hayhurst b Jarvis	13
G. Fowler c Carrick b Sidebottom	21	P. J. W. Allott not out	10
M. A. Atherton lbw b Love	2	†W. K. Hegg not out	0
J. Abrahams run out	6	B 4, l-b 12, w 4, n-b 1	21
M. Watkinson c Robinson b Sidebottom	149		
*D. P. Hughes c Metcalfe b Carrick	25	1/39 2/39 3/47 (8 wkts, 50 overs) 273	
S. J. O'Shaughnessy run out	10	4/49 5/140 6/177	
		7/238 8/272	

J. Simmons did not bat.

Bowling: Jarvis 10-1-41-1; Sidebottom 9-0-64-3; Carrick 10-1-33-1; Love 2-0-11-1; P. J. Hartley 10-1-59-0; Fletcher 9-0-49-0.

Yorkshire

K. Sharp b Abrahams	50	*P. Carrick b Allott	1
A. A. Metcalfe lbw b Watkinson	4	P. J. Hartley not out	8
J. D. Love c Watkinson b Hayhurst	22	L-b 7, w 5	12
P. E. Robinson c Hegg b Hayhurst	108		
†D. L. Bairstow not out	68	1/8 2/62 3/89 (6 wkts, 50 overs) 277	
S. N. Hartley c Hughes b Watkinson	4	4/249 5/257 6/260	

A. Sidebottom, P. W. Jarvis and S. D. Fletcher did not bat.

Bowling: Allott 10-0-36-1; Watkinson 10-1-61-2; O'Shaughnessy 9-0-58-0; Hayhurst 10-0-47-2; Simmons 7-0-42-0; Abrahams 4-0-26-1.

Umpires: J. Birkenshaw and B. Leadbeater.

NATWEST BANK TROPHY, 1987

Nottinghamshire, beaten by Essex in the 1985 NatWest Bank Trophy final, won their first limited-overs trophy when they defeated Northamptonshire by three wickets with three balls to spare. The match was played over two days, rain having delayed and then twice interrupted play on the Saturday; and because the start was not one and a half hours later than scheduled, each innings was limited to 50 overs. Nottinghamshire received £20,000, in addition to the NatWest Bank Trophy, while Northamptonshire, runners-up in their second Lord's final in 1987, received £10,000. The losing semi-finalists, Gloucestershire and Leicestershire, each received £4,750, and Derbyshire, Essex, Warwickshire and Yorkshire each received £2,375 as the losing quarter-finalists. For an innings of 70 that turned defeat into victory, Richard Hadlee was named Man of the Match by the England manager, M. J. Stewart, and received £550. The Man of the Match in the semi-finals received £275; in each quarter-final £200; in each second-round match £125; and in each first-round match £100. In addition, the Man of the Match also received a medal and a tie. Total prizemoney for the competition was £53,500, £2,500 more than in 1986.

FIRST ROUND

BUCKINGHAMSHIRE v SOMERSET

At High Wycombe, June 24. Buckinghamshire won by 7 runs. Toss: Somerset. Buckinghamshire became the fifth minor county to defeat a first-class county in the competition.
Man of the Match: S. J. Edwards.

Buckinghamshire

A. R. Harwood c Burns b Jones	47		A. W. Lyon b Rose		2
T. Butler c Hardy b Harman	16		†D. J. Goldsmith b Rose		4
D. E. Smith run out	12		C. D. Booden run out		3
S. Burrow lbw b Marks	5		L-b 11, w 10, n-b 3		24
*N. G. Hames lbw b Mallender	0				
G. R. Black st Burns b Mallender	1		1/31 2/57 3/83	(59.5 overs)	154
K. I. Hodgson c Felton b Jones	15		4/89 5/96 6/98		
S. J. Edwards not out	25		7/119 8/131 9/143		

Bowling: Jones 12–3–38–2; Mallender 12–1–27–2; Marks 12–7–10–1; Harman 12–1–38–1; Rose 11.5–4–30–2.

Somerset

*P. M. Roebuck c and b Booden	2		M. D. Harman run out		0
N. A. Felton c Burrow b Edwards	8		N. A. Mallender lbw b Burrow		6
J. J. E. Hardy c Edwards b Booden	4		A. N. Jones not out		1
M. D. Crowe c Hodgson b Edwards	2		B 4, l-b 4, w 3		11
R. J. Bartlett b Burrow	56				
V. J. Marks c and b Lyon	14		1/3 2/13 3/18	(59.3 overs)	147
G. D. Rose b Burrow	26		4/21 5/60 6/103		
†N. D. Burns c Smith b Black	17		7/134 8/137 9/145		

Bowling: Booden 12–5–12–2; Edwards 12–5–14–2; Lyon 12–4–28–1; Burrow 9–0–32–3; Black 11.3–1–37–1; Hodgson 3–0–16–0.

Umpires: C. Cook and B. J. Meyer.

CAMBRIDGESHIRE v DERBYSHIRE

At Wisbech, June 24. Derbyshire won by six wickets. Toss: Derbyshire.
Man of the Match: A. E. Warner.

Cambridgeshire

*N. T. Gadsby c Maher b Jean-Jacques	31	M. G. Stephenson b Newman	1
I. S. Lawrence lbw b Holding	0	D. C. Collard c Maher b Holding	4
†M. A. Garnham b Warner	31	A. P. Wykes not out	0
N. J. Adams c Barnett b Jean-Jacques	3	L-b 5, w 2, n-b 4	11
S. Turner c Maher b Warner	7		
A. D. Cuthill lbw b Warner	0	1/3 2/58 3/67	(40.3 overs) 91
C. Lethbridge lbw b Jean-Jacques	1	4/78 5/79 6/82	
R. A. Milne c Rudd b Newman	2	7/82 8/86 9/91	

Bowling: Holding 9.3–4–16–2; Mortensen 8–4–9–0; Newman 7–3–18–2; Warner 9–1–20–3; Jean-Jacques 7–2–23–3.

Derbyshire

*K. J. Barnett b Lethbridge	12	P. G. Newman not out	10
†B. J. M. Maher lbw b Lethbridge	2	B 1, l-b 3, n-b 3	7
B. Roberts c Adams b Wykes	33		
J. E. Morris c Milne b Wykes	16	1/13 2/25 3/65	(4 wkts, 38.4 overs) 92
I. S. Anderson not out	12	4/66	

M. A. Holding, A. E. Warner, M. Jean-Jacques, O. H. Mortensen and C. F. B. P. Rudd did not bat.

Bowling: Turner 10.4–3–23–0; Lethbridge 9–2–18–2; Stephenson 10–1–20–0; Collard 2–0–13–0; Wykes 7–1–14–2.

Umpires: R. A. Duckett and P. B. Wight.

DURHAM v MIDDLESEX

At Darlington, June 24. Middlesex won by seven wickets. Toss: Middlesex.
Man of the Match: P. J. Kippax.

Durham

J. W. Lister c and b Edmonds	21	P. J. Kippax not out	1
S. Greensword c Carr b Emburey	56	G. Johnson not out	1
Wasim Raja st Downton b Emburey	18		
*N. A. Riddell c Emburey b Fraser	2	L-b 15, w 1, n-b 3	19
A. S. Patel c Butcher b Needham	11		
P. Burn c Edmonds b Daniel	10	1/60 2/106 3/109	(8 wkts, 60 overs) 151
†A. R. Fothergill run out	12	4/118 5/126 6/141	
I. E. Conn b Daniel	0	7/142 8/149	

S. Ward did not bat.

Bowling: Daniel 8–3–16–2; Fraser 12–5–24–1; Emburey 12–7–14–2; Edmonds 12–2–31–1; Needham 12–2–29–1; Gatting 4–0–22–0.

Middlesex

W. N. Slack c Lister b Kippax	45	R. O. Butcher not out	16
J. D. Carr st Fothergill b Kippax	14	B 4, l-b 2, w 1	7
C. T. Radley c and b Conn	28		
*M. W. Gatting not out	45	1/44 2/75 3/106	(3 wkts, 50.2 overs) 155

†P. R. Downton, J. E. Emburey, P. H. Edmonds, A. R. C. Fraser, W. W. Daniel and A. Needham did not bat.

Bowling: Johnson 7–1–22–0; Ward 6–3–13–0; Kippax 12–4–24–2; Wasim Raja 12–5–22–0; Conn 8.2–0–49–1; Patel 5–0–19–0.

Umpires: J. H. Hampshire and T. G. Wilson.

GLAMORGAN v CHESHIRE

At Cardiff, June 24. Glamorgan won by 145 runs. Toss: Cheshire. Monkhouse's five wickets included a spell of four for 5 runs.
Man of the Match: G. C. Holmes.

Glamorgan

S. P. James run out	26	J. G. Thomas c Cockbain b Blackburn	34
J. A. Hopkins c N. T. O'Brien		†C. P. Metson not out	4
b J. F. M. O'Brien	33		
*H. Morris c Tansley b J. F. M. O'Brien	13	B 3, l-b 4, w 7	14
G. C. Holmes run out	57		
M. P. Maynard b Blackburn	10	1/66 2/66 3/103 (7 wkts, 60 overs)	230
R. J. Shastri c Hitchmough b Fox	37	4/125 5/165	
J. Derrick not out	2	6/210 7/225	

S. Monkhouse and S. R. Barwick did not bat.

Bowling: Fox 9–2–37–1; Crawley 6–0–17–0; J. F. M. O'Brien 12–1–38–2; N. T. O'Brien 12–0–47–0; De Prez 9–0–33–0; Blackburn 12–3–51–2.

Cheshire

I. J. Tansley c Holmes b Monkhouse	17	†S. Cummings b Monkhouse	0
J. J. Hitchmough c Metson b Thomas	0	P. H. De Prez c Hopkins b Shastri	11
I. Cockbain c Hopkins b Barwick	10	J. F. M. O'Brien not out	8
S. T. Crawley c Maynard b Barwick	7	B 2, l-b 6, w 4, n-b 6	18
*N. T. O'Brien b Barwick	0		
K. Teasdale lbw b Monkhouse	8	1/3 2/35 3/39 (38.1 overs)	85
G. J. Blackburn c Metson b Monkhouse	3	4/39 5/53 6/53	
A. Fox b Monkhouse	3	7/62 8/63 9/64	

Bowling: Thomas 4–0–8–1; Barwick 12–6–18–3; Monkhouse 12–3–32–5; Holmes 7–3–14–0; Shastri 3.1–1–5–1.

Umpires: D. J. Dennis and M. J. Kitchen.

HAMPSHIRE v DORSET

At Southampton, June 24. Hampshire won by 209 runs. Toss: Hampshire. Hampshire's victory was their largest margin of victory by runs in the 60-overs competition.
Man of the Match: C. L. Smith.

Hampshire

C. G. Greenidge lbw b Malone	0
C. L. Smith not out	140
*M. C. J. Nicholas b Stone	50
D. R. Turner not out	100
B 3, l-b 4, w 7	14

1/0 2/110 (2 wkts, 60 overs) 304

V. P. Terry, K. D. James, M. D. Marshall, †R. J. Parks, T. M. Tremlett, S. J. W. Andrew and R. J. Maru did not bat.

Bowling: Malone 12–0–82–1; Stuart 12–2–28–0; Stone 12–2–41–1; Wingfield Digby 12–0–62–0; Kennedy 7–0–45–0; Turrill 5–0–39–0.

Dorset

R. P. Merriman b Tremlett 17	A. R. Wingfield Digby b Maru 0
G. S. Calway c Greenidge b Marshall . 0	S. J. Malone b Maru 2
S. J. Halliday b Andrew 9	†A. R. Richardson lbw b James 0
*A. Kennedy c Smith b Tremlett 16	L-b 8, w 3, n-b 2 13
V. B. Lewis c Andrew b James 8	
C. Stone lbw b Tremlett 1	1/1 2/24 3/46 (29.4 overs) 95
S. J. Turrill c Greenidge b James 6	4/51 5/60 6/60
I. C. D. Stuart not out 23	7/80 8/81 9/93

Bowling: Marshall 5–1–9–1; Andrew 7–1–22–1; Tremlett 8–1–29–3; James 7.4–2–22–3; Maru 2–0–5–2.

Umpires: H. D. Bird and J. H. Harris.

LANCASHIRE v GLOUCESTERSHIRE

At Manchester, June 24. Gloucestershire won by 41 runs. Toss: Gloucestershire. This was Gloucestershire's first win over Lancashire in nine Gillette Cup/NatWest Bank Trophy matches. It was the first time since 1968 that Lancashire had not figured in the second round.
Man of the Match: D. A. Graveney.

Gloucestershire

A. W. Stovold st Stanworth b Simmons 41	M. W. Alleyne not out 0
A. J. Wright c Austin b Simmons 88	
C. W. J. Athey c Hayhurst b Watkinson 79	B 5, l-b 16, w 11, n-b 2 34
P. Bainbridge c Fowler b Simmons 4	
J. W. Lloyds b Hayhurst 3	1/87 2/195 3/212 (7 wkts, 60 overs) 277
K. M. Curran c Fairbrother b Watkinson 22	4/216 5/255
C. A. Walsh b Watkinson 6	6/277 7/277

†R. C. Russell, *D. A. Graveney and D. V. Lawrence did not bat.

Bowling: Patterson 12–1–51–0; Watkinson 12–0–64–3; Austin 12–1–50–0; Hayhurst 12–0–52–1; Simmons 12–0–39–3.

Lancashire

G. Fowler c Curran b Lawrence 9	J. Simmons b Walsh 12
G. D. Mendis c Lloyds b Walsh 11	†J. Stanworth b Lawrence 0
D. W. Varey c and b Graveney 38	B. P. Patterson not out 0
N. H. Fairbrother c Russell b Lawrence 87	B 1, l-b 13, w 12, n-b 4 30
*D. P. Hughes c Curran b Graveney ... 1	
M. Watkinson c Lloyds b Graveney ... 22	1/23 2/32 3/118 (55.2 overs) 236
A. N. Hayhurst b Walsh 16	4/122 5/156 6/188
I. D. Austin b Lawrence 10	7/210 8/234 9/234

Bowling: Walsh 10–1–25–3; Lawrence 10.2–1–49–4; Alleyne 4–0–16–0; Bainbridge 7–0–55–0; Lloyds 12–0–50–0; Graveney 12–1–27–3.

Umpires: J. Birkenshaw and B. Leadbeater.

LEICESTERSHIRE v OXFORDSHIRE

At Leicester, June 24. Leicestershire won by six wickets. Toss: Leicestershire.
Man of the Match: R. A. Cobb.

Oxfordshire

G. C. Ford b Agnew	26	D. A. Hale b Benjamin	2
M. D. Nurton c Whitticase b Agnew	0	R. N. Busby not out	9
P. A. Fowler c Willey b Lewis	15	B 4, l-b 7, w 14, n-b 8	33
*P. J. Garner lbw b Agnew	12		
C. J. Clements c Boon b Willey	3	(8 wkts, 60 overs)	181
†A. Crossley run out	37	1/2 2/32 3/60	
S. R. Porter run out	44	4/71 5/73 6/151	
		7/159 8/181	

K. A. Arnold and I. J. Curtis did not bat.

Bowling: Benjamin 12–3–23–1; Agnew 12–4–31–3; Clift 12–2–41–0; Lewis 12–2–30–1; Willey 12–0–45–1.

Leicestershire

R. A. Cobb not out	66	*P. Willey not out	3
N. E. Briers lbw b Arnold	9	L-b 2, w 8, n-b 1	11
D. I. Gower lbw b Curtis	52		
J. J. Whitaker b Hale	27	1/18 2/96 3/139	(4 wkts, 47.5 overs) 185
T. J. Boon c Nurton b Hale	17	4/177	

P. B. Clift, C. C. Lewis, W. K. M. Benjamin, †P. Whitticase and J. P. Agnew did not bat.

Bowling: Busby 6.5–2–29–0; Arnold 12–1–45–1; Curtis 12–2–34–1; Hale 10–1–35–2; Porter 5–0–26–0; Garner 2–0–14–0.

Umpires: B. Dudleston and D. R. Shepherd.

NORTHAMPTONSHIRE v IRELAND

At Northampton, June 24. Northamptonshire won by 88 runs. Toss: Ireland. Ireland bowled out a first-class county for the first time since entering the competition eight years earlier.
Man of the Match: A. Walker.

Northamptonshire

*G. Cook run out	50	N. G. B. Cook c Masood b Garth	4
W. Larkins c McBrine b Milling	16	W. W. Davis not out	14
R. J. Bailey c Masood b Milling	4	A. Walker run out	1
A. J. Lamb c Jackson b Masood	19	L-b 1, w 3, n-b 1	5
D. J. Capel c Milling b Halliday	48		
R. G. Williams lbw b Garth	30	1/23 2/29 3/65	(59.1 overs) 198
D. J. Wild c and b Garth	6	4/134 5/148 6/174	
†D. Ripley c Jackson b Milling	1	7/179 8/179 9/190	

Bowling: Milling 10–0–42–3; Jeffrey 3–0–16–0; Garth 11.1–1–28–3; Masood 12–0–42–1; McBrine 12–2–33–0; Halliday 11–1–36–1.

Ireland

S. J. S. Warke c Ripley b Walker	4	*†P. B. Jackson c Capel b N. G. B. Cook	1
M. F. Cohen lbw b Walker	9	H. Milling c Williams b N. G. B. Cook	9
M. A. Masood b Walker	0	A. S. Jeffrey absent injured	
D. G. Dennison lbw b Walker	1	B 1, l-b 6, w 9	16
G. D. Harrison b N. G. B. Cook	23		
J. D. Garth b Davis	17	1/8 2/8 3/14	(49.4 overs) 110
A. McBrine lbw b N. G. B. Cook	22	4/22 5/50 6/83	
M. Halliday not out	8	7/93 8/95 9/110	

Bowling: Davis 8–1–18–1; Walker 9–6–7–4; Capel 10–1–24–0; Wild 10–1–26–0; Williams 3–2–4–0; N. G. B. Cook 9.4–2–24–4.

Umpires: R. Palmer and R. A. White.

NORTHUMBERLAND v ESSEX

At Jesmond, June 24, 25, 26. Essex won by 176 runs. Toss: Northumberland. Close of play:
First day, Northumberland 40-3 (P. N. S. Dutton 13*, M. E. Younger 4*); Second day,
No play.

Man of the Match: N. A. Foster.

Essex

*G. A. Gooch c Corby b Purvis	76	N. A. Foster c Dutton b Graham		25
J. P. Stephenson c Corby b Graham	6	†D. E. East not out		0
B. R. Hardie b Younger	12			
K. W. R. Fletcher c Pearson b Younger	23	L-b 10, w 4, n-b 1		15
A. W. Lilley c Corby b Gillespie	13			
D. R. Pringle not out	63	1/55 2/84 3/127	(8 wkts, 60 overs)	247
G. Miller b Old	7	4/127 5/158 6/169		
H. A. Page run out	7	7/182 8/233		

T. D. Topley did not bat.

Bowling: Old 12–2–34–1; Scott 5–0–30–0; Graham 12–3–55–2; Gillespie 12–3–44–1; Purvis
10–0–42–1; Younger 9–0–32–2.

Northumberland

R. Dreyer c East b Page	5	†K. C. Corby b Foster		0
K. Pearson lbw b Topley	6	P. C. Graham b Foster		0
P. N. S. Dutton lbw b Topley	18	S. P. Scott not out		0
S. R. Gillespie lbw b Topley	3	B 4, l-b 1, w 6, n-b 1		12
*M. E. Younger c Miller b Page	14			
C. M. Old b Foster	1	1/16 2/21 3/29	(43.2 overs)	71
P. G. Cormack c East b Topley	12	4/57 5/57 6/71		
J. R. Purvis lbw b Foster	0	7/71 8/71 9/71		

Bowling: Foster 8–3–9–4; Page 12–4–10–2; Gooch 9–1–21–0; Topley 9.2–3–21–4; Pringle
5–2–5–0.

Umpires: D. B. Harrison and J. A. Jameson.

NOTTINGHAMSHIRE v SUFFOLK

At Nottingham, June 24. Nottinghamshire won by eight wickets. Toss: Suffolk.
Man of the Match: K. E. Cooper.

Suffolk

M. S. A. McEvoy c Rice b Cooper	27	H. J. W. Wright b Rice		16
J. W. Edrich lbw b Rice	17	R. C. Green b Rice		7
P. J. Hayes lbw b Cooper	0	M. D. Bailey not out		1
*S. M. Clements lbw b Cooper	0	L-b 3, w 2		5
G. Morgan c Cooper b Hemmings	1			
P. J. Caley b Hadlee	11	1/37 2/39 3/43	(49 overs)	94
K. G. Brooks c Hadlee b Rice	9	4/44 5/46 6/59		
†S. J. Halliday c Scott b Saxelby	0	7/69 8/69 9/88		

Bowling: Hadlee 10–3–12–1; Cooper 10–4–9–3; Rice 11–7–19–4; Saxelby 10–2–36–1;
Hemmings 8–1–15–1.

Nottinghamshire

B. C. Broad c and b Hayes		37
R. T. Robinson c Morgan b Hayes		34
D. W. Randall not out		18
P. Johnson not out		0
B 1, l-b 2, w 2, n-b 1		6

1/59 2/93   (2 wkts, 25.2 overs) 95

*C. E. B. Rice, J. D. Birch, R. J. Hadlee, †C. W. Scott, E. E. Hemmings, K. Saxelby and K. E. Cooper did not bat.

Bowling: Green 5-1-14-0; Wright 4-0-24-0; Bailey 5-1-28-0; Hayes 8-2-14-2; Caley 3-0-10-0; Edrich 0.2-0-2-0.

Umpires: R. Julian and K. E. Palmer.

SCOTLAND v KENT

At Edinburgh, June 24. Kent won by six wickets. Toss: Kent. Underwood's return of eight for 31 was the best by any bowler in the competition, while Scotland's total was their lowest in the competition.

Man of the Match: D. L. Underwood.

Scotland

I. L. Philip c C. S. Cowdrey b Pienaar		8
L. S. Rajput c Farbrace b Igglesden		2
*R. G. Swan c G. R. Cowdrey b Underwood		16
D. B. Pauline b Underwood		14
A. B. Russell c and b Underwood		2
D. L. Snodgrass c Pienaar b Underwood		1
†A. Brown lbw b Underwood		18
N. W. Burnett c Hinks b Underwood		2
P. G. Duthie c Kelleher b Underwood		4
E. J. McIntyre c Igglesden b Underwood		0
J. E. Ker not out		0
B 1, l-b 1, w 2, n-b 3		7

1/9 2/12 3/31 4/44   (35.1 overs) 74
5/46 6/51 7/59 8/71 9/73

Bowling: Igglesden 7-3-6-1; Kelleher 6-2-6-0; Pienaar 6-2-14-1; Underwood 11.1-2-31-8; G. R. Cowdrey 5-2-15-0.

Kent

M. R. Benson c Swan b Ker		2
S. G. Hinks c McIntyre b Duthie		0
D. G. Aslett c Philip b Pauline		19
C. J. Tavaré b Duthie		0
*C. S. Cowdrey not out		34
G. R. Cowdrey not out		18
B 1, w 1		2

1/1 2/14 3/19   (4 wkts, 23 overs) 75
4/29

R. F. Pienaar, †P. Farbrace, D. J. M. Kelleher, D. L. Underwood and A. P. Igglesden did not bat.

Bowling: Duthie 9-1-23-2; Ker 4-1-12-1; Pauline 4-1-16-1; Rajput 3-0-12-0; McIntyre 3-0-11-0.

Umpires: J. W. Holder and D. Lloyd.

STAFFORDSHIRE v WARWICKSHIRE

At Burton upon Trent, June 24. Warwickshire won by 77 runs. Toss: Staffordshire.

Man of the Match: G. W. Humpage.

Warwickshire

T. A. Lloyd b Patel	70	A. C. Storie not out	25
A. J. Moles c Griffiths b Benjamin	7	G. J. Parsons not out	2
P. A. Smith c Hawkins b Webster	16	L-b 4, w 1, n-b 5	10
D. L. Amiss c Banks b Hawkins	10		
†G. W. Humpage b Blank	76	1/12 2/43 3/71 (6 wkts, 60 overs) 226	
Asif Din lbw b Patel	10	4/167 5/185 6/218	

A. R. K. Pierson, A. A. Donald and *N. Gifford did not bat.

Bowling: Benjamin 12–2–65–1; Webster 12–2–44–1; Blank 11–1–38–1; Hawkins 11–1–38–1; Patel 12–0–26–2; Cartledge 2–0–11–0.

Staffordshire

S. J. Dean c Pierson b Gifford	72	D. C. Blank not out	3
J. P. Addison b Donald	3	J. E. Benjamin b Donald	5
D. N. Patel lbw b Smith	0	A. J. Webster b Donald	0
D. A. Banks b Parsons	18	B 6, w 1	7
D. Cartledge b Donald	19		
*N. J. Archer c Gifford b Parsons	10	1/11 2/16 3/64 (56.4 overs) 149	
†A. Griffiths c Parsons b Gifford	5	4/101 5/120 6/133	
A. Hawkins b Donald	7	7/134 8/142 9/149	

Bowling: Donald 10.4–3–24–5; Smith 8–1–18–1; Pierson 12–3–24–0; Parsons 11–2–39–2; Gifford 12–2–24–2; Moles 3–0–14–0.

Umpires: N. T. Plews and H. J. Rhodes.

SURREY v HERTFORDSHIRE

At The Oval, June 24. Surrey won by eight wickets. Toss: Surrey.
Man of the Match: A. J. Stewart.

Hertfordshire

R. Herbert b Clarke	37	W. G. Merry c Richards b Thomas	1
N. P. G. Wright c Jesty b Clarke	7	B. G. Collins not out	9
S. P. Henderson c Smith b Greig	16	B 1, l-b 6, w 6	13
S. A. Dean b Jesty	42		
M. C. G. Wright lbw b Greig	2	1/21 2/94 3/100 (8 wkts, 60 overs) 162	
*E. P. Neal lbw b Greig	10	4/103 5/123 6/124	
†M. W. C. Olley not out	19	7/138 8/142	
T. S. Smith c Clarke b Thomas	6		

R. J. Hailey did not bat.

Bowling: Clarke 12–2–20–2; Thomas 12–2–34–2; Bicknell 12–3–27–0; Greig 8–0–32–3; Bullen 12–4–36–0; Jesty 4–1–6–1.

Surrey

G. S. Clinton c Neal b Herbert	34		
D. M. Smith c Neal b Collins	1		
A. J. Stewart not out	66		
M. A. Lynch not out	53		
L-b 2, w 7, n-b 1	10		

1/9 2/82 (2 wkts, 45 overs) 164

T. E. Jesty, †C. J. Richards, *I. A. Greig, D. J. Thomas, C. K. Bullen, S. T. Clarke and M. P. Bicknell did not bat.

Bowling: Merry 6–1–20–0; Collins 9–2–22–1; Neal 4–0–11–0; Hailey 8–2–46–0; Herbert 11–3–36–1; Smith 7–1–27–0.

Umpires: A. Jepson and D. O. Oslear.

SUSSEX v CUMBERLAND

At Hove, June 24. Sussex won by eight wickets. Toss: Sussex.
  Man of the Match: A. M. Green.

Cumberland

M. D. Woods c Pigott b Babington	2		*J. R. Moyes lbw b le Roux	0
C. J. Stockdale c Moores b Pigott	10		†S. M. Dutton not out	2
G. D. Hodgson b Pigott	24		L-b 13, w 5	18
S. Sharp c Reeve b le Roux	38			
B. W. Reidy lbw b Pigott	0		1/5 2/27 3/47 (8 wkts, 60 overs)	182
G. J. Clarke run out	61		4/47 5/107 6/167	
G. Monkhouse b Reeve	27		7/170 8/182	

D. Halliwell and S. Wall did not bat.

  Bowling: le Roux 12–3–22–2; Babington 11–0–44–1; Pigott 12–2–25–3; C. M. Wells 9–2–29–0; Reeve 12–3–38–1; Ricketts 4–1–11–0.

Sussex

R. I. Alikhan lbw b Woods	37
A. M. Green b Woods	84
C. M. Wells not out	37
A. P. Wells not out	13
B 2, l-b 9, w 3, n-b 2	16

1/111 2/153   (2 wkts, 46.3 overs) 187

*I. J. Gould, D. A. Reeve, G. S. le Roux, †P. Moores, A. C. S. Pigott, C. I. O. Ricketts and A. M. Babington did not bat.

  Bowling: Halliwell 11.3–2–36–0; Wall 10–2–48–0; Monkhouse 9–0–34–0; Reidy 8–1–25–0; Woods 8–1–33–2.

Umpires: K. J. Lyons and C. T. Spencer.

WILTSHIRE v YORKSHIRE

At Trowbridge, June 24. Yorkshire won by 129 runs. Toss: Wiltshire.
  Man of the Match: A. A. Metcalfe.

Yorkshire

M. D. Moxon c Watts b Meehan	74		A. Sidebottom not out	1
A. A. Metcalfe b Cooper	85		P. J. Hartley not out	7
R. J. Blakey c Cullip b Inchmore	14		L-b 5, w 4, n-b 1	10
K. Sharp c Mercer b Cooper	13			
J. D. Love b Inchmore	62		1/161 2/165 3/183 (7 wkts, 60 overs)	304
†D. L. Bairstow c Mercer b Watts	28		4/207 5/278	
*P. Carrick run out	10		6/286 7/304	

P. W. Jarvis and S. D. Fletcher did not bat.

  Bowling: Simpkins 12–0–47–0; Meehan 12–0–61–1; Watts 10–2–57–1; Inchmore 12–0–62–2; Cooper 9–0–38–2; Trembath 5–0–34–0.

Wiltshire

B. H. White b Love	8	P. Meehan c Fletcher b Sharp	6
†J. J. Cullip c Sharp b Hartley	9	J. D. Inchmore c Sidebottom b Metcalfe	3
D. J. M. Mercer c Bairstow b Hartley	3	M. A. Watts not out	7
R. J. Lanchbury c Love b Sharp	40	L-b 3, w 5	8
C. R. Trembath c Blakey b Love	4		
J. J. Newman c Fletcher b Sharp	62	1/21 2/25 3/26	(58 overs) 175
*R. C. Cooper c Sidebottom b Metcalfe	15	4/33 5/118 6/139	
D. P. Simpkins c Love b Sharp	10	7/155 8/165 9/165	

Bowling: Jarvis 3–0–5–0; Sidebottom 4–1–3–0; Fletcher 5–0–8–0; Hartley 6–0–11–2; Love 12–3–39–2; Carrick 12–6–22–0; Sharp 9–0–40–4; Metcalfe 7–0–44–2.

Umpires: D. G. L. Evans and D. J. Halfyard.

WORCESTERSHIRE v DEVON

At Worcester, June 24. Worcestershire won by 299 runs. Toss: Devon. Worcestershire's total of 404 for three and their margin of victory were records for any county in limited-overs cricket in the United Kingdom. Hick's unbeaten 172 was the highest by a Worcestershire batsman in all one-day cricket; Botham scored his hundred before lunch, hitting three sixes and ten fours.

Man of the Match: G. A. Hick.

Worcestershire

T. S. Curtis c Ward b Tierney	79	*P. A. Neale not out	12
I. T. Botham lbw b Tierney	101	B 1, l-b 11, w 5, n-b 4	21
G. A. Hick not out	172		
D. B. D'Oliveira b Ward	19	1/152 2/279 3/321	(3 wkts, 60 overs) 404

†S. J. Rhodes, P. J. Newport, R. K. Illingworth, N. V. Radford, G. R. Dilley and A. P. Pridgeon did not bat.

Bowling: Yeabsley 12–1–50–0; Taylor 12–0–97–0; Allin 12–0–79–0; Tierney 12–0–82–2; Ward 12–0–84–1.

Devon

M. Olive b Pridgeon	9	M. A. Taylor c Dilley b Illingworth	5
K. G. Rice b Newport	11	A. W. Allin c Pridgeon b Curtis	5
N. A. Folland c Rhodes b Pridgeon	0	D. I. Yeabsley not out	5
N. R. Gaywood lbw b Pridgeon	0		
*J. H. Edwards c Hick b Illingworth	17	L-b 7, w 3, n-b 6	16
†R. C. Turpin c Radford b D'Oliveira	12		
J. K. Tierney c Dilley b Illingworth	12	1/26 2/26 3/27 4/34	(36 overs) 105
T. W. Ward st Rhodes b Illingworth	13	5/58 6/74 7/81 8/89 9/95	

Bowling: Dilley 5–0–13–0; Radford 3–0–11–0; Newport 5–2–5–1; Pridgeon 5–2–7–3; D'Oliveira 8–0–33–1; Illingworth 8–2–20–4; Curtis 2–0–9–1.

Umpires: B. Hassan and A. A. Jones.

SECOND ROUND

ESSEX v WORCESTERSHIRE

At Chelmsford, July 8. Essex won by 15 runs. Toss: Essex. Only Hick, with 55 off 63 balls, looked capable of mastering the Essex seam attack on a fast pitch full of assistance. When he was fourth out, the odds favoured Essex. Radford and Dilley added 48 adventurously but Lever, who had dismissed Botham first ball, had the last word.

Man of the Match: T. D. Topley.

Essex

*G. A. Gooch c Botham b Newport	34	†D. E. East b Radford	13
J. P. Stephenson c D'Oliveira b Dilley	0	T. D. Topley not out	15
B. R. Hardie lbw b Newport	21	J. K. Lever not out	3
K. W. R. Fletcher c Rhodes b Botham	7	L-b 15, w 5, n-b 5	25
D. R. Pringle c Botham b Dilley	10		
G. Miller c Rhodes b Radford	21	1/1 2/59 3/64 (9 wkts, 60 overs) 194	
A. W. Lilley c Rhodes b Pridgeon	19	4/70 5/102 6/118	
N. A. Foster b Radford	26	7/155 8/169 9/178	

Bowling: Dilley 12–3–38–2; Pridgeon 12–3–34–1; Radford 12–0–56–3; Newport 12–1–22–2; Botham 12–0–29–1.

Worcestershire

T. S. Curtis c Gooch b Topley	10	N. V. Radford b Lever	37
I. T. Botham c East b Lever	0	G. R. Dilley c Pringle b Lever	25
G. A. Hick c East b Topley	55	A. P. Pridgeon not out	0
D. B. D'Oliveira c East b Topley	9	L-b 4, w 8, n-b 1	13
*P. A. Neale b Pringle	27		
†S. J. Rhodes b Gooch	1	1/1 2/45 3/68 (56.3 overs) 179	
P. J. Newport c Gooch b Topley	1	4/81 5/88 6/98	
R. K. Illingworth c Gooch b Lever	1	7/99 8/125 9/173	

Bowling: Lever 10.3–3–39–4; Foster 10–1–31–0; Pringle 12–0–34–1; Topley 12–3–36–4; Gooch 12–0–35–1.

Umpires: R. Julian and R. A. White.

KENT v DERBYSHIRE

At Canterbury, July 8. Derbyshire won by one wicket. Toss: Derbyshire. Barnett and Roberts put on 101 in seventeen overs after Igglesden had removed Maher in the first over. Underwood checked Derbyshire's advance but they scored consistently until the final over when Mortensen, last man in, hit the second ball for the winning run. Kent were 136 after 40 overs but lost three wickets for 13 in six overs.

Man of the Match: M. A. Holding.

Kent

M. R. Benson c Roberts b Newman	20	†P. Farbrace run out	4
N. R. Taylor b Newman	85	D. J. M. Kelleher not out	0
D. G. Aslett lbw b Holding	32	B 1, l-b 14, w 3, n-b 2	20
C. J. Tavaré b Holding	0		
*C. S. Cowdrey run out	48	1/56 2/140 3/140 (8 wkts, 60 overs) 232	
G. R. Cowdrey c Morris b Jean-Jacques	9	4/153 5/170 6/199	
E. A. E. Baptiste lbw b Newman	14	7/218 8/232	

A. P. Igglesden and D. L. Underwood did not bat.

Bowling: Holding 12–3–30–2; Mortensen 12–2–34–0; Jean-Jacques 11–1–53–1; Newman 12–0–40–3; Warner 7–0–31–0; Sharma 6–0–29–0.

Derbyshire

*K. J. Barnett c and b Underwood	45	A. E. Warner lbw b C. S. Cowdrey	32
†B. J. M. Maher c Underwood b Igglesden	0	M. Jean-Jacques not out	10
B. Roberts c Underwood b Igglesden	60	O. H. Mortensen not out	1
J. E. Morris b Underwood	8		
I. S. Anderson c Farbrace b Kelleher	14	L-b 6, w 4	10
R. Sharma run out	21	1/8 2/109 3/109 (9 wkts, 59.2 overs) 233	
P. G. Newman lbw b Kelleher	11	4/117 5/145 6/161	
M. A. Holding c Farbrace b Igglesden	21	7/173 8/200 9/229	

Bowling: Igglesden 12–2–54–3; Kelleher 11.2–0–73–2; Baptiste 12–3–39–0; C. S. Cowdrey 12–3–40–1; Underwood 12–4–21–2.

Umpires: J. A. Jameson and B. Leadbeater.

LEICESTERSHIRE v HAMPSHIRE

At Leicester, July 8. Leicestershire won by 15 runs. Toss: Leicestershire. Hampshire scored the highest total by a side batting second in this competition and still lost, left to rue the 18 runs conceded in wides and no-balls. Andrew bowled five in his first over and four in his third, this spell costing 17 runs with only two scoring strokes. Willey (127 balls, fourteen fours) and Gower put on 158 in 30 overs; Willey and Whitaker 120 in sixteen.

Man of the Match: P. Willey.

Leicestershire

R. A. Cobb c Parks b Tremlett	8	W. K. M. Benjamin not out	2
N. E. Briers c C. L. Smith b James	9	P. A. J. DeFreitas not out	8
*P. Willey c R. A. Smith b Tremlett	154	L-b 11, w 15, n-b 3	29
D. I. Gower b Cowley	79		
J. J. Whitaker c Greenidge b Andrew	52	1/25 2/45 3/203 (6 wkts, 60 overs) 341	
P. B. Clift c Andrew b Marshall	0	4/323 5/325 6/330	

T. J. Boon, †P. Whitticase and J. P. Agnew did not bat.

Bowling: Marshall 12–2–32–1; Andrew 9–0–66–1; James 12–0–79–1; Tremlett 12–1–81–2; Cowley 12–1–48–1; Nicholas 3–0–24–0.

Hampshire

C. G. Greenidge b DeFreitas	22	T. M. Tremlett not out	43
C. L. Smith b Clift	40	†R. J. Parks c Cobb b Benjamin	3
*M. C. J. Nicholas c Clift b Benjamin	60	S. J. W. Andrew not out	0
D. R. Turner b Clift	18	B 1, l-b 5, w 6, n-b 2	14
R. A. Smith c Cobb b DeFreitas	49		
K. D. James c Agnew b Willey	10	1/34 2/108 3/140 (9 wkts, 60 overs) 326	
M. D. Marshall c Clift b Agnew	51	4/170 5/191 6/234	
N. G. Cowley c Cobb b Benjamin	16	7/277 8/287 9/302	

Bowling: Agnew 12–0–94–1; DeFreitas 12–2–55–2; Willey 12–0–54–1; Benjamin 12–1–57–3; Clift 12–1–60–2.

Umpires: A. G. T. Whitehead and P. B. Wight.

MIDDLESEX v NOTTINGHAMSHIRE

At Uxbridge, July 8. Nottinghamshire won by 60 runs. Toss: Middlesex. A fine catch by Carr on the mid-wicket boundary in the 28th over stopped a runaway start by Robinson (90 balls, twelve fours) and Broad. A post-lunch slump from 184 for two to 205 for five was resolved by Randall and Birch, who added 51 in nine overs. Gatting batted for 37 overs but lacked the support to threaten Nottinghamshire's hold.

Man of the Match: R. T. Robinson.

Nottinghamshire

B. C. Broad c Downton b Daniel	64	E. E. Hemmings c Slack b Emburey	4
R. T. Robinson c Carr b Needham	79	R. A. Pick b Daniel	0
P. Johnson b Edmonds	3	K. Saxelby not out	0
*C. E. B. Rice run out	39	B 1, l-b 14, w 9, n-b 10	34
R. J. Hadlee b Hughes	1		
D. W. Randall b Emburey	22	1/130 2/146 3/190 (59.3 overs) 279	
J. D. Birch c Gatting b Daniel	28	4/193 5/205 6/256	
†B. N. French lbw b Emburey	5	7/268 8/278 9/279	

Bowling: Hughes 12–1–41–1; Daniel 11.3–1–37–3; Edmonds 10–1–45–1; Emburey 12–0–58–3; Slack 3–0–27–0; Needham 9–0–45–1; Gatting 2–0–11–0.

Middlesex

W. N. Slack st French b Hemmings	26	A. Needham c Robinson b Saxelby	11
J. D. Carr b Pick	13	S. P. Hughes run out	1
*M. W. Gatting c Robinson b Saxelby	73	W. W. Daniel not out	3
C. T. Radley lbw b Hemmings	31	B 4, l-b 11, w 4, n-b 4	23
K. R. Brown lbw b Hadlee	24		
†P. R. Downton c and b Hemmings	3	1/34 2/40 3/130	(57.2 overs) 219
J. E. Emburey c Robinson b Pick	11	4/183 5/185 6/199	
P. H. Edmonds b Pick	0	7/204 8/205 9/205	

Bowling: Hemmings 12–0–51–3; Hadlee 12–3–32–1; Saxelby 10.2–0–43–2; Pick 12–0–39–3; Rice 11–3–39–0.

Umpires: A. A. Jones and D. O. Oslear.

NORTHAMPTONSHIRE v SURREY

At Northampton, July 8. Northamptonshire won by five wickets. Toss: Surrey. Northamptonshire played three spinners on a slow pitch taking turn, but when they batted they still found Clarke's pace a difficult proposition. Lamb took them to within 23 runs of victory, batting for 46 overs and hitting 88 off 130 balls with eight fours. He was missed behind the wicket when 63.

Man of the Match: A. J. Lamb.

Surrey

G. S. Clinton st Ripley b Harper	28	S. T. Clarke b Wild	5
D. M. Smith c Walker b Harper	35	C. K. Bullen not out	1
A. J. Stewart b N. G. B. Cook	44	M. P. Bicknell b Wild	0
M. A. Lynch c G. Cook b Harper	1	B 1, l-b 9, w 4	14
T. E. Jesty b N. G. B. Cook	35		
†C. J. Richards b Wild	27	1/67 2/72 3/75	(58.3 overs) 211
*I. A. Greig c G. Cook b Walker	13	4/151 5/159 6/195	
M. A. Feltham c and b Walker	8	7/199 8/209 9/211	

Bowling: Capel 5–2–19–0; Walker 7–2–27–2; Williams 12–1–33–0; Harper 12–3–40–3; N. G. B. Cook 12–1–39–2; Wild 10.3–0–43–3.

Northamptonshire

*G. Cook lbw b Clarke	7	R. A. Harper not out	4
W. Larkins lbw b Clarke	12		
R. J. Bailey c Feltham b Bullen	44	L-b 3	3
A. J. Lamb c Smith b Greig	88		
D. J. Capel not out	46	1/18 2/25 3/89	(5 wkts, 58.5 overs) 213
R. G. Williams b Lynch	9	4/189 5/208	

D. J. Wild, †D. Ripley, N. G. B. Cook and A. Walker did not bat.

Bowling: Clarke 12–2–41–2; Bicknell 12–1–44–0; Feltham 9–1–46–0; Bullen 12–1–38–1; Greig 9.5–0–30–1; Lynch 4–1–11–1.

Umpires: D. J. Constant and J. H. Harris.

SUSSEX v GLOUCESTERSHIRE

At Hove, July 8. Gloucestershire won by five wickets. Toss: Gloucestershire. Graveney's spell of four for 14 in four overs arrested Sussex after Green (131 balls) and Alan Wells (94 balls) had added 115. So well did Gloucestershire bowl and field that Sussex were limited to sixteen boundaries. Needing 4 an over, the winners were given a perfect start by Wright (120 balls) and Stovold (90 balls), who put on 145 in 31 overs.

Man of the Match: D. A. Graveney.

Sussex

R. I. Alikhan b Sainsbury	18	A. C. S. Pigott b Walsh		11
A. M. Green c Wright b Graveney	84	†P. Moores not out		3
P. W. G. Parker lbw b Sainsbury	0			
A. P. Wells st Russell b Graveney	55	L-b 14, w 2		16
C. M. Wells c Alleyne b Graveney	6			
*I. J. Gould b Graveney	15	1/43 2/43 3/158	(8 wkts, 60 overs)	242
G. S. le Roux lbw b Walsh	8	4/167 5/187 6/189		
D. A. Reeve not out	26	7/205 8/229		

A. M. Babington did not bat.

Bowling: Walsh 12–2–48–2; Curran 12–1–42–0; Sainsbury 12–2–30–2; Alleyne 4–0–17–0; Lawrence 8–0–43–0; Graveney 12–1–48–4.

Gloucestershire

A. W. Stovold b le Roux	69	†R. C. Russell not out		27
A. J. Wright c C. M. Wells b Pigott	76			
C. W. J. Athey not out	29	L-b 7, w 3, n-b 8		18
M. W. Alleyne b Pigott	9			
K. M. Curran c le Roux b Babington	0	1/145 2/172 3/187	(5 wkts, 58.3 overs)	243
J. W. Lloyds lbw b C. M. Wells	15	4/188 5/204		

G. E. Sainsbury, *D. A. Graveney, C. A. Walsh and D. V. Lawrence did not bat.

Bowling: le Roux 12–2–27–1; Babington 11–0–65–1; Reeve 11–0–51–0; Pigott 12–3–36–2; C. M. Wells 12–0–55–1; Green 0.3–0–2–0.

Umpires: J. Birkenshaw and K. J. Lyons.

WARWICKSHIRE v BUCKINGHAMSHIRE

At Birmingham, July 8. Warwickshire won by 201 runs. Toss: Buckinghamshire. Putting Warwickshire in first, Buckinghamshire saw their hopes of further glory evaporate as Moles (166 balls) hit his first hundred in limited-overs cricket. Warwickshire pressed home their advantage by adding 154 in the last twenty overs.

Man of the Match: A. J. Moles.

Warwickshire

A. J. Moles b Black	127	A. C. Storie not out		16
T. A. Lloyd b Lyon	61			
P. A. Smith run out	4	B 3, l-b 8, w 3, n-b 1		15
D. L. Amiss c Hodgson b Edwards	39			
†G. W. Humpage c Goldsmith b Black	42	1/120 2/154 3/208	(5 wkts, 60 overs)	329
Asif Din not out	25	4/276 5/299		

G. J. Parsons, T. A. Munton, A. A. Donald and *N. Gifford did not bat.

Bowling: Booden 8–2–55–0; Edwards 12–1–49–1; Black 10–1–54–2; Burrow 10–0–69–0; Lyon 12–2–43–1; Hodgson 8–0–48–0.

Buckinghamshire

A. R. Harwood c Moles b Gifford	57	†D. J. Goldsmith c Donald b Gifford		0
T. Butler b Smith	14	C. D. Booden b Donald		0
D. E. Smith c Amiss b Munton	9	A. W. Lyon b Donald		0
S. Burrow c Amiss b Munton	9	B 3, l-b 7, w 5, n-b 1		16
K. I. Hodgson c Storie b Gifford	24			
*N. G. Hames c Humpage b Donald	5	1/18 2/44 3/44	(41.4 overs)	128
G. R. Black not out	2	4/98 5/117 6/121		
S. J. Edwards b Gifford	1	7/124 8/127 9/128		

Bowling: Donald 9.4–0–27–3; Smith 7–1–20–1; Munton 6–0–22–2; Parsons 10–2–21–0; Moles 2–0–19–0; Gifford 7–4–9–4.

Umpires: J. H. Hampshire and D. Lloyd.

YORKSHIRE v GLAMORGAN

At Leeds, July 8. Yorkshire won by nine wickets. Toss: Yorkshire. Headingley, scene of England's demise in the preceding week, came under fire again after Glamorgan had been bowled out in 123 minutes. With the ball moving in the air and off the seam, Sidebottom had figures of five for 8 in his first seven overs. Morris survived, going on to carry his bat, while Thomas showed what could be done by playing forward, hitting six fours and a six in an innings of 26 balls. The match finished at 2.47 p.m.

Man of the Match: A. Sidebottom.

Glamorgan

S. P. James lbw b Sidebottom	6	I. Smith b Jarvis 5
*H. Morris not out	16	S. J. Base lbw b Jarvis 4
G. C. Holmes c Moxon b Sidebottom	0	S. R. Barwick c Sidebottom b Jarvis ... 5
M. P. Maynard c Moxon b Sidebottom	6	L-b 1, n-b 6 7
R. J. Shastri lbw b Sidebottom	0	
P. A. Todd c Bairstow b Sidebottom	1	1/10 2/10 3/18 (28.2 overs) 83
J. G. Thomas c Blakey b Hartley	33	4/18 5/22 6/56
†C. P. Metson c Blakey b Hartley	0	7/58 8/63 9/74

Bowling: Jarvis 10.2–1–31–3; Sidebottom 9–4–27–5; Fletcher 4–0–5–0; Hartley 5–0–19–2.

Yorkshire

M. D. Moxon not out	43
A. A. Metcalfe c Maynard b Smith	25
R. J. Blakey not out	4
L-b 2, w 4, n-b 6	12

1/68   (1 wkt, 24 overs) 84

K. Sharp, J. D. Love, †D. L. Bairstow, *P. Carrick, A. Sidebottom, P. J. Hartley, P. W. Jarvis and S. D. Fletcher did not bat.

Bowling: Thomas 8–0–24–0; Barwick 5–1–17–0; Base 3–0–12–0; Smith 4–0–18–1; Holmes 4–1–11–0.

Umpires: M. J. Kitchen and N. T. Plews.

QUARTER-FINALS

DERBYSHIRE v NOTTINGHAMSHIRE

At Derby, July 29, 30. Nottinghamshire won by 57 runs. Toss: Derbyshire. A crowd of 7,000, thought to be Derbyshire's biggest since the Gillette Cup semi-final at Chesterfield in 1969, saw Nottinghamshire in control throughout. In the absence of Newman and Warner, Derbyshire used seven bowlers, and in the final over Jean-Jacques, helped by two good catches, performed Derbyshire's first hat-trick in the competition. Although a delayed start and further interruptions had made a finish on the first day unlikely, Hemmings tilted the balance firmly towards Nottinghamshire by the close, dismissing Morris and Barnett in a seven-over spell which cost only 8 runs. Overnight, Derbyshire were 106 for four from 34 overs (I. S. Anderson 5*, R. J. Finney 9*), and when the game resumed on the second afternoon, the outcome was never in doubt.

Man of the Match: E. E. Hemmings.

Nottinghamshire

B. C. Broad c Maher b Malcolm	67	E. E. Hemmings not out 0
R. T. Robinson lbw b Holding	19	R. A. Pick not out 0
M. Newell c Barnett b Mortensen	60	
*C. E. B. Rice c Sharma b Mortensen	0	L-b 10, w 15, n-b 2 27
P. Johnson lbw b Holding	41	
R. J. Hadlee c Barnett b Jean-Jacques	34	1/35 2/153 3/153 (8 wkts, 60 overs) 268
J. D. Birch c Roberts b Jean-Jacques	20	4/186 5/237 6/268
†B. N. French c Maher b Jean-Jacques	0	7/268 8/268

K. Saxelby did not bat.

Bowling: Holding 12–1–33–2; Jean-Jacques 12–0–73–3; Mortensen 12–1–35–2; Malcolm 11–0–53–1; Sharma 7–1–32–0; Finney 2–0–17–0; Roberts 4–1–15–0.

Derbyshire

*K. J. Barnett lbw b Hemmings	53	M. Jean-Jacques run out	1
†B. J. M. Maher c Hadlee b Rice	11	O. H. Mortensen c French b Hadlee	1
B. Roberts c French b Hadlee	10	D. E. Malcolm b Hadlee	1
J. E. Morris c Robinson b Hemmings	15	L-b 8, w 2, n-b 1	11
I. S. Anderson not out	54		
R. J. Finney c Broad b Saxelby	40	1/38 2/59 3/83	(55.5 overs) 211
R. Sharma c Hemmings b Saxelby	5	4/92 5/161 6/168	
M. A. Holding c Saxelby b Hemmings	9	7/189 8/208 9/209	

Bowling: Saxelby 12–1–54–2; Pick 12–0–44–0; Rice 10–1–44–1; Hadlee 9.5–1–33–3; Hemmings 12–4–28–3.

Umpires: M. J. Kitchen and B. Leadbeater.

ESSEX v NORTHAMPTONSHIRE

At Chelmsford, July 29, 30. Northamptonshire won by six wickets. Toss: Essex. A commanding 121 not out from Larkins and a fine half-century by Lamb on a sluggish pitch prised the initiative from Essex after they had restricted Northamptonshire to 22 for two in the first thirteen overs. Larkins made his runs from 173 deliveries, with only 40 coming in boundaries (two sixes, seven fours). For Essex, Hardie and Fletcher put on 104 after the early departure of Gooch, and then Border, making his only county appearance of the season, battled it out for an undefeated 46. Rain had prevented any play on Wednesday.

Man of the Match: W. Larkins.

Essex

*G. A. Gooch c G. Cook b Davis	2	N. A. Foster not out	20
B. R. Hardie c G. Cook b Capel	56		
K. W. R. Fletcher lbw b Davis	49	B 2, l-b 13, w 3, n-b 1	19
A. R. Border not out	46		
D. R. Pringle c Larkins b Williams	8	1/4 2/108 3/127	(5 wkts, 60 overs) 204
A. W. Lilley b Williams	4	4/144 5/160	

G. Miller, †D. E. East, T. D. Topley and J. K. Lever did not bat.

Bowling: Davis 12–2–46–2; Capel 12–4–26–1; N. G. B. Cook 12–3–32–0; Wild 8–1–26–0; Walker 7–0–26–0; Williams 9–1–33–2.

Northamptonshire

*G. Cook c Gooch b Foster	8	R. G. Williams not out	1
W. Larkins not out	121	L-b 7, w 2	9
R. J. Bailey c East b Lever	2		
A. J. Lamb c Pringle b Gooch	50	1/11 2/22 3/142	(4 wkts, 56.4 overs) 205
D. J. Capel c Pringle b Border	14	4/204	

D. J. Wild, †D. Ripley, N. G. B. Cook, W. W. Davis and A. Walker did not bat.

Bowling: Lever 10–3–19–1; Foster 10–2–33–1; Topley 8–1–33–0; Pringle 9–0–46–0; Miller 12–1–46–0; Gooch 7–1–20–1; Border 0.4–0–1–1.

Umpires: J. H. Hampshire and R. Julian.

GLOUCESTERSHIRE v WARWICKSHIRE

At Bristol, July 29. Gloucestershire won by five wickets. Toss: Gloucestershire. Warwickshire, with Small not completely match fit, paid the price for dropping both Gloucestershire openers while they were in single figures. Stovold and Wright were not parted until they had put on 151, and Stovold (thirteen fours) had all but seen the match won when he was bowled.

He must have wondered what was happening as Gloucestershire got themselves into a minor tangle before meeting their target with more than thirteen overs in hand. Warwickshire would have had an even more modest total to defend had it not been for Amiss, who batted 37 overs for his 40 runs, and Tedstone, who played so well that 40 runs came from the last five overs.

Man of the Match: A. W. Stovold.

Warwickshire

T. A. Lloyd b Bainbridge	34	G. J. Parsons c Lawrence b Bainbridge		19
A. J. Moles c Russell b Lawrence	6	G. C. Small not out		5
Asif Din c Russell b Walsh	4	L-b 11, w 5, n-b 3		19
D. L. Amiss lbw b Walsh	40			—
†G. W. Humpage b Alleyne	2	1/29 2/34 3/56	(7 wkts, 60 overs)	203
P. A. Smith c Athey b Lloyds	19	4/59 5/102		
G. A. Tedstone not out	55	6/127 7/181		

A. A. Donald and *N. Gifford did not bat.

Bowling: Walsh 12–1–42–2; Lawrence 12–2–49–1; Bainbridge 12–1–42–2; Alleyne 6–1–12–1; Graveney 12–1–30–0; Lloyds 6–0–17–1.

Gloucestershire

A. W. Stovold b Parsons	94	M. W. Alleyne not out		0
A. J. Wright b Small	58			
C. W. J. Athey hit wkt b Donald	18	L-b 12, w 10, n-b 5		27
P. Bainbridge c Humpage b Donald	2			—
K. M. Curran c Asif Din b Parsons	0	1/151 2/191 3/198	(5 wkts, 46.2 overs)	207
J. W. Lloyds not out	8	4/198 5/203		

†R. C. Russell, *D. A. Graveney, C. A. Walsh and D. V. Lawrence did not bat.

Bowling: Donald 9–1–37–2; Small 12–1–53–1; Parsons 9.2–0–40–2; Gifford 9–1–27–0; Smith 3–0–17–0; Moles 4–0–21–0.

Umpires: D. J. Constant and K. E. Palmer.

YORKSHIRE v LEICESTERSHIRE

At Leeds, July 29, 30. Leicestershire won by 36 runs. Toss: Yorkshire. With Gower making the most of some wayward bowling by Fletcher and Shaw, Leicestershire recovered from a hesitant start after being put in on a pitch that allowed some movement off the seam. Yorkshire missed three straightforward catches (Whitaker when 3 and 21, Clift when 1), but they were regaining control as their early batsmen prospered. However, Willey took a fine catch to remove Metcalfe (88 balls, one six, nine fours), and when play ended in sunshine at 7.10 p.m. – to the derision of the 10,500 spectators who had stoically borne the earlier interruptions for rain – Yorkshire were 137 for three after 39 overs (K. Sharp 38*, J. D. Love 1*). DeFreitas, who had hit out to considerable effect in the later stages of the Leicestershire innings, produced a fine spell of bowling on the second day, claiming three for eight in 23 balls, and Clift disposed of Love and Bairstow in one over. Yorkshire's last seven wickets went down for 34 in ten overs as Leicestershire won with surprising ease.

Man of the Match: P. A. J. DeFreitas.

Leicestershire

R. A. Cobb c Bairstow b Jarvis	9	C. C. Lewis b Fletcher		18
N. E. Briers c Moxon b Jarvis	32	J. P. Agnew not out		8
*P. Willey c Moxon b Jarvis	2	G. J. F. Ferris not out		2
D. I. Gower c Metcalfe b Jarvis	49	B 2, l-b 6, w 12, n-b 1		21
J. J. Whitaker c Love b Shaw	39			—
P. B. Clift lbw b Carrick	20	1/17 2/21 3/103	(9 wkts, 60 overs)	236
P. A. J. DeFreitas c Jarvis b Hartley	33	4/109 5/149 6/187		
†P. Whitticase b Bairstow b Hartley	3	7/195 8/222 9/233		

Bowling: Jarvis 12–2–41–4; Hartley 12–0–43–2; Fletcher 12–2–55–1; Shaw 8–1–41–1; Carrick 12–3–33–1; Moxon 4–0–15–0.

Yorkshire

M. D. Moxon c DeFreitas	18	P. W. Jarvis b DeFreitas 0
A. A. Metcalfe c Willey b Ferris	73	C. Shaw not out 1
R. J. Blakey lbw b DeFreitas	0	S. D. Fletcher lbw b DeFreitas 0
K. Sharp b DeFreitas	50	L-b 4, w 6, n-b 4 14
J. D. Love c and b Clift	15	
†D. L. Bairstow b Clift	4	1/50 2/50 3/131 (56.5 overs) 200
*P. Carrick b Agnew	14	4/166 5/170 6/171
P. J. Hartley c Whitticase b Ferris	11	7/198 8/198 9/200

Bowling: Agnew 10-2-31-1; Ferris 11-1-47-2; DeFreitas 10.5-2-34-5; Clift 12-1-28-2; Lewis 4-0-26-0; Willey 9-0-30-0.

Umpires: B. Dudleston and R. Palmer.

SEMI-FINALS

GLOUCESTERSHIRE v NOTTINGHAMSHIRE

At Bristol, August 12. Nottinghamshire won by 143 runs. Toss: Nottinghamshire. Pick, bowling fast and straight with much hostility, overwhelmed Gloucestershire's early batting to shatter their hopes of reaching the final. It was a great disappointment for the many home supporters in the crowd of 8,000 who had seen Gloucestershire bowl steadily, even though Graveney, Walsh, Curran and Bainbridge were carrying injuries, and field marvellously to keep the Nottinghamshire total to 225. Russell was an inspiration to all the fieldsmen by the deftness of his work. All looked set for a tense struggle: but at 20 for four, Gloucestershire were as good as beaten. Bainbridge, bravely batting one-handed, delayed the inevitable, but there was no need for a tea interval. Pick polished off the tail to finish with five for 22 and consign Gloucestershire to their lowest total in the 60 overs competition.

Man of the Match: R. A. Pick.

Nottinghamshire

B. C. Broad c Wright b Graveney	65	E. E. Hemmings not out 19
R. T. Robinson b Sainsbury	24	R. A. Pick not out 6
M. Newell c Lloyds b Curran	2	
*C. E. B. Rice c Russell b Graveney	27	L-b 9, w 13, n-b 2 24
P. Johnson run out	28	
R. J. Hadlee run out	13	1/48 2/65 3/125 (8 wkts, 60 overs) 225
J. D. Birch c Russell b Walsh	15	4/141 5/170 6/180
†B. N. French c and b Bainbridge	2	7/184 8/198

K. Saxelby did not bat.

Bowling: Walsh 12-1-45-1; Sainsbury 12-2-29-1; Graveney 12-1-41-2; Curran 9-1-27-1; Bainbridge 11-1-55-1; Alleyne 4-0-19-0.

Gloucestershire

A. W. Stovold c Newell b Pick	14	C. A. Walsh b Pick 7
A. J. Wright b Pick	1	*D. A. Graveney not out 5
C. W. J. Athey c French b Hadlee	4	G. E. Sainsbury b Pick 2
M. W. Alleyne b Pick	0	L-b 3, w 1, n-b 2 6
K. M. Curran c Broad b Rice	2	
J. W. Lloyds c Johnson b Saxelby	9	1/10 2/20 3/20 (35.1 overs) 82
†R. C. Russell b Hemmings	14	4/20 5/33 6/33
P. Bainbridge c Broad b Hemmings	18	7/64 8/65 9/75

Bowling: Hadlee 6-1-15-1; Pick 9.1-2-22-5; Rice 5-2-5-1; Saxelby 8-1-24-1; Hemmings 7-1-13-2.

Umpires: J. H. Harris and J. W. Holder.

LEICESTERSHIRE v NORTHAMPTONSHIRE

At Leicester, August 12, 13. Northamptonshire won by 85 runs. Toss: Leicestershire. Northamptonshire became the third county, following Middlesex in 1975 and Essex in 1985, to reach both Lord's finals in the same year. A crowd of some 7,500, Grace Road's best for a number of years, saw Cook (108 balls) and Larkins (95 balls) put on 116 in 33 overs. With stoppages for bad light – there were three in all, amounting to three and a quarter hours – the middle innings developed unevenly, but thanks to Capel the last ten overs realised 68 runs. His 46, from 32 balls, included a six and six fours. Leicestershire were 37 for two off nine overs (P. Willey 9*, D. I. Gower 12*) when play stopped for the day, ironically in sunshine; but when it resumed next afternoon, they never got going. Larkins took a marvellous catch at cover to get rid of Gower, juggling the ball several times, and the run-out of Whitaker, stranded when Clift refused a run to Davis at third man, somehow summed up Leicestershire's lot.

Man of the Match: D. J. Capel.

Northamptonshire

*G. Cook c Briers b Willey	51	D. J. Wild c Lewis b Agnew	8
W. Larkins c Butcher b Lewis	58	†D. Ripley not out	2
R. J. Bailey b Clift	32	B 1, l-b 11, w 2, n-b 2	16
A. J. Lamb c Whitticase b Ferris	32		
D. J. Capel not out	46	1/116 2/120 3/181 (6 wkts, 60 overs) 249
R. G. Williams c Whitticase b DeFreitas	4	4/185 5/210 6/225	

N. G. B. Cook, W. W. Davis and A. Walker did not bat.

Bowling: Agnew 12–0–58–1; Ferris 8–1–43–1; Clift 12–1–42–1; DeFreitas 12–4–31–1; Lewis 11–0–47–1; Willey 5–0–16–1.

Leicestershire

N. E. Briers c Ripley b Capel	11	C. C. Lewis c Wild b Williams	15
I. P. Butcher c G. Cook b Capel	2	J. P. Agnew not out	5
*P. Willey b Capel	12	G. J. F. Ferris c Walker b N. G. B. Cook	0
D. I. Gower c Larkins b Wild	34	B 2, l-b 8, w 6, n-b 1	17
J. J. Whitaker run out	37		
P. B. Clift b Williams	14	1/14 2/23 3/51 (51.2 overs) 164
P. A. J. DeFreitas c Davis b Williams	13	4/81 5/119 6/124	
†P. Whitticase c Davis b Williams	4	7/142 8/142 9/164	

Bowling: Davis 7–0–20–0; Capel 10–2–43–3; Walker 7–0–20–0; Wild 8–2–24–1; N. G. B. Cook 11.2–3–37–1; Williams 8–2–10–4.

Umpires: K. J. Lyons and B. J. Meyer.

FINAL

NORTHAMPTONSHIRE v NOTTINGHAMSHIRE

At Lord's, September 5, 7. Nottinghamshire won by three wickets, their first victory in the final of a knockout competition. Yet when play resumed at 1.30 on Monday afternoon, overnight rain having prevented a prompt start, Northamptonshire were heavily backed to win. In 21 overs on Saturday evening, they had reduced Nottinghamshire to 57 for four, with Rice 20 not out and Birch 9 not out and only Hadlee of the recognised batsmen to come. Only Hadlee! When Birch was bowled in the 29th over and the New Zealand all-rounder walked bareheaded to the middle, neither his determination nor his self-belief could be denied. He and Rice added 62 in twelve overs. Northamptonshire were jubilant when Rice (96 balls, three fours) was caught at mid-on, but it was from then that they lost their grip on the game. Their cricket had been superb: fifteen overs had passed before the day's first boundary. But the 44th over, Williams's last, realised 15 runs and Hadlee might have been caught any one of three times – once when Lamb lost the ball as it was crossing the mid-wicket boundary for six.

When Davis was brought back to complete his spell, French set about him with full-blooded drives and confident flicks, and as the pressure mounted, Northamptonshire's fielders fumbled and conceded overthrows. A target of 51 off five overs was brought down to 8 off the last, to be bowled by Capel who was nursing a back strain. Off the first ball he ran out French when his on-drive was deflected off Hadlee's boot towards the bowler; but now Hadlee had the strike. Capel's next ball he drove high and straight for six, and then he pulled the third to the Tavern boundary. It was a magnificent finale to a calculated innings: 70 runs off 61 balls with two sixes and four fours. He and French (35 off 27 balls) had added 75 in eight overs to dash the cup of victory from Northamptonshire's lips.

Overnight rain, continuing into the morning, had made a 10.30 start impossible on Saturday. Play commenced at 11.45, with the match reduced to 50 overs each, as it had been in the 1983 final. When a thunderstorm in the 27th and further rain in the 41st over of Northamptonshire's innings resulted in the loss of 103 minutes, play had to be continued into a second day for the first time in a final. Twice before, in the Gillette Cup final of 1974 and the Benson and Hedges Cup final of 1980, there had been no play at all on the Saturday.

Put in, Northamptonshire batted steadily. The outfield was slow and conditions initially were overcast, but Larkins (124 balls, twelve fours) batted with much style and aggression and there was good running between the wickets. Not until Capel joined Bailey in the 43rd over, though, did the run-rate rise consistently above 4 an over. It was almost six o'clock when Nottinghamshire began their innings, and very soon Davis was bowling out of the shadow of the Pavilion, his arm whirling high into the sun behind it. He removed Robinson in his second over, the batsman nowhere in line with a ball rising sharply on off stump, and had Broad lbw in his third. When Randall, in his first first-team match since breaking a finger in July, played round a well-flighted ball from Nick Cook, and Johnson, in a terrible tangle, was unable to push his bat ahead of his front leg, Northamptonshire were in control. Knowing play had to stop at 7.10, and that Nottinghamshire could not afford to risk another wicket, Geoff Cook was able to bowl his spinners to decrease the overs available on Monday. Everything, it seemed, favoured Northamptonshire except Dame Fortune: she favoured Hadlee.

Man of the Match: R. J. Hadlee.

Attendance: 18,270 (excluding members).

Northamptonshire

*G. Cook c French b Saxelby		26
W. Larkins lbw b Pick		87
A. J. Lamb b Rice		41
R. J. Bailey not out		39
D. J. Capel not out		29
B 1, l-b 2, n-b 3		6

1/61 (1) 2/152 (2)   (3 wkts, 50 overs) 228
3/169 (3)

R. G. Williams, D. J. Wild, †D. Ripley, N. G. B. Cook, W. W. Davis and A. Walker did not bat.

Bowling: Hadlee 10-1-29-0; Pick 10-1-36-1; Rice 10-0-45-1; Saxelby 10-0-63-1; Hemmings 10-0-52-0.

Nottinghamshire

B. C. Broad lbw b Davis		3
R. T. Robinson c Ripley b Davis		2
D. W. Randall b N. G. B. Cook		10
*C. E. B. Rice c G. Cook b Williams		63
P. Johnson lbw b Walker		1
J. D. Birch b Walker		21
R. J. Hadlee not out		70
†B. N. French run out		35
E. E. Hemmings not out		0
L-b 18, w 8		26

1/11 (2) 2/12 (1)   (7 wkts, 49.3 overs) 231
3/31 (3) 4/38 (5)
5/84 (6) 6/146 (4)
7/221 (8)

R. A. Pick and K. Saxelby did not bat.

Bowling: Davis 10-1-45-2; Capel 6.3-1-31-0; Walker 10-0-38-2; N. G. B. Cook 10-2-30-1; Williams 10-0-48-1; Wild 3-0-21-0.

Umpires: D. R. Shepherd and A. G. T. Whitehead.

NATWEST BANK TROPHY RECORDS

(Including Gillette Cup, 1963-80)

Batting

Highest individual scores: 206, A. I. Kallicharran, Warwickshire v Oxfordshire, Birmingham, 1984; 177, C. G. Greenidge, Hampshire v Glamorgan, Southampton, 1975; 172 not out, G. A. Hick, Worcestershire v Devon, Worcester, 1987; 165 not out, V. P. Terry, Hampshire v Berkshire, Southampton, 1985; 158, G. D. Barlow, Middlesex v Lancashire, Lord's, 1984; 158, Zaheer Abbas, Gloucestershire v Leicestershire, Leicester, 1983; 156, D. I. Gower, Leicestershire v Derbyshire, Leicester, 1984; 155, J. J. Whitaker, Leicestershire v Wiltshire, Swindon, 1984; 154, P. Willey, Leicestershire v Hampshire, Leicester, 1987; 153, A. Hill, Derbyshire v Cornwall, Derby, 1986. (93 hundreds were scored in the Gillette Cup; 59 hundreds have been scored in the NatWest Bank Trophy.)

Fastest hundred: R. E. Marshall in 77 minutes, Hampshire v Bedfordshire at Goldington, 1968.

Highest innings totals (off 60 overs): 404 for three, Worcestershire v Devon, Worcester, 1987; 392 for five, Warwickshire v Oxfordshire, Birmingham, 1984; 371 for four, Hampshire v Glamorgan, Southampton, 1975; 365 for three, Derbyshire v Cornwall, Derby, 1986; 354 for seven, Leicestershire v Wiltshire, Swindon, 1984; 349 for six, Lancashire v Gloucestershire, Bristol, 1984; 341 for six, Leicestershire v Hampshire, Leicester, 1987; 339 for four, Hampshire v Berkshire, Southampton, 1985; 330 for four, Somerset v Glamorgan, Cardiff, 1978; 329 for five, Warwickshire v Buckinghamshire, Birmingham, 1987; 327 for seven, Gloucestershire v Berkshire, Reading, 1966; 327 for six, Essex v Scotland, Chelmsford, 1984; 326 for six, Leicestershire v Worcestershire, Leicester, 1979; 326 for nine, Hampshire v Leicestershire, Leicester, 1987; 321 for four, Hampshire v Bedfordshire, Goldington, 1968; 317 for four, Yorkshire v Surrey (*in the final*), Lord's, 1965; 317 for eight, Warwickshire v Durham, Birmingham, 1986; 312 for five, Worcestershire v Lancashire, Manchester, 1985; 306 for six (59.3 overs), Gloucestershire v Leicestershire, Leicester, 1983; 305 for five, Leicestershire v Ireland, Leicester, 1986; 304 for two, Hampshire v Dorset, Southampton, 1987; 304 for seven, Yorkshire v Wiltshire, Trowbridge, 1987.

Highest innings total by a minor county: 256 off 58 overs, Oxfordshire v Warwickshire, Birmingham, 1983.

Highest innings by a side batting first and losing: 302 for five (60 overs), Leicestershire v Gloucestershire, Leicester, 1983. *In the final:* 242 for eight (60 overs), Lancashire v Sussex, 1986.

Highest totals by a side batting second: 326 for nine (60 overs), Hampshire v Leicestershire, Leicester, 1987; 306 for six (59.3 overs), Gloucestershire v Leicestershire, Leicester, 1983; 298 (59 overs), Lancashire v Worcestershire, Manchester, 1985; 297 for four (57.1 overs), Somerset v Warwickshire, Taunton, 1978; 296 for four (58 overs), Kent v Surrey, Canterbury, 1985; 290 for seven (59.3 overs), Yorkshire v Worcestershire, Leeds, 1982; 287 for six (59 overs), Warwickshire v Glamorgan, Birmingham, 1976; 287 (60 overs), Essex v Somerset, Taunton, 1978; 282 for nine (60 overs), Leicestershire v Gloucestershire, Leicester, 1975. *In the final:* 279 for five (60 overs), Nottinghamshire v Essex, 1985.

Highest total by a side batting second and winning: 306 for six (59.3 overs), Gloucestershire v Leicestershire, Leicester, 1983. *In the final:* 243 for three (58.2 overs), Sussex v Lancashire, 1986.

Highest total by a side batting second and losing: 326 for nine (60 overs), Hampshire v Leicestershire, Leicester, 1987.

Lowest innings in the final at Lord's: 118 (60 overs), Lancashire v Kent, 1974.

Lowest completed innings totals: 39 (26.4 overs), Ireland v Sussex, Hove, 1985; 41 (20 overs), Cambridgeshire v Buckinghamshire, Cambridge, 1972; 41 (19.4 overs), Middlesex v Essex, Westcliff, 1972; 41 (36.1 overs), Shropshire v Essex, Wellington, 1974.

Lowest total by a side batting first and winning: 98 (56.2 overs), Worcestershire v Durham, Chester-le-Street, 1968.

Shortest innings: 10.1 overs (60 for one), Worcestershire v Lancashire, Worcester, 1963.

Matches re-arranged on a reduced number of overs are excluded from the above.

Record partnerships for each wicket

227 for 1st	R. E. Marshall and B. L. Reed, Hampshire v Bedfordshire at Goldington		1968
286 for 2nd	I. S. Anderson and A. Hill, Derbyshire v Cornwall at Derby		1986
209 for 3rd	P. Willey and D. I. Gower, Leicestershire v Ireland at Leicester		1986
234* for 4th	D. Lloyd and C. H. Lloyd, Lancashire v Gloucestershire at Manchester		1978
166 for 5th	M. A. Lynch and G. R. J. Roope, Surrey v Durham at The Oval		1982
105 for 6th	G. S. Sobers and R. A. White, Nottinghamshire v Worcestershire at Worcester		1974
160* for 7th	C. J. Richards and I. R. Payne, Surrey v Lincolnshire at Sleaford		1983
71* for 8th	R. C. Ontong and T. Davies, Glamorgan v Staffordshire at Stone		1986
87 for 9th	M. A. Nash and A. E. Cordle, Glamorgan v Lincolnshire at Swansea		1974
81 for 10th	S. Turner and R. E. East, Essex v Yorkshire at Leeds		1982

Bowling

Hat-tricks (6): J. D. F. Larter, Northamptonshire v Sussex, Northampton, 1963; D. A. D. Sydenham, Surrey v Cheshire, Hoylake, 1964; R. N. S. Hobbs, Essex v Middlesex, Lord's, 1968; N. M. McVicker, Warwickshire v Lincolnshire, Birmingham, 1971; G. S. le Roux, Sussex v Ireland, Hove, 1985; M. Jean-Jacques, Derbyshire v Nottinghamshire, Derby, 1987.

Four wickets in five balls: D. A. D. Sydenham, Surrey v Cheshire, Hoylake, 1964.

Best bowling: eight for 31, D. L. Underwood, Kent v Scotland, Edinburgh, 1987; seven for 15, A. L. Dixon, Kent v Surrey, The Oval, 1967; seven for 30, P. J. Sainsbury, Hampshire v Norfolk, Southampton, 1965; seven for 32, S. P. Davis, Durham v Lancashire, Chester-le-Street, 1983; seven for 33, R. D. Jackman, Surrey v Yorkshire, Harrogate, 1970; seven for 37, N. A. Mallender, Northamptonshire v Worcestershire, Northampton, 1984.

Results

Largest victories in runs: Worcestershire by 299 runs v Devon, Worcester, 1987; Sussex by 244 runs v Ireland, Hove, 1985; Warwickshire by 227 runs v Oxfordshire, Birmingham, 1984; Essex by 226 runs v Oxfordshire, Chelmsford, 1985; Leicestershire by 214 runs v Staffordshire, Longton, 1975; Hampshire by 209 runs v Dorset, Southampton, 1987; Derbyshire by 204 runs v Cornwall, Derby, 1986; Warwickshire by 201 runs v Buckinghamshire, Birmingham, 1987; Sussex by 200 runs v Durham, Hove, 1964. *In the final:* 175 runs, Yorkshire v Surrey, Lord's 1965.

Victories by ten wickets (6): Northamptonshire v Leicestershire, Leicester, 1964; Warwickshire v Cambridgeshire, Birmingham, 1965; Sussex v Derbyshire, Hove 1968; Hampshire v Nottinghamshire, Southampton, 1977; Middlesex v Worcestershire, Worcester, 1980; Yorkshire v Cheshire, Birkenhead, 1985.

Quickest finishes: both at 2.20 p.m. Worcestershire beat Lancashire by nine wickets at Worcester, 1963; Essex beat Middlesex by eight wickets at Westcliff, 1972.

Scores level: Nottinghamshire 215, Somerset 215 for nine at Taunton, 1964; Surrey 196, Sussex 196 for eight at The Oval, 1970; Somerset 287 for six, Essex 287 at Taunton, 1978; Surrey 195 for seven, Essex 195 at Chelmsford, 1980; Essex 149, Derbyshire 149 for eight at Derby, 1981; Northamptonshire 235 for nine, Derbyshire 235 for six in the final at Lord's, 1981; Middlesex 222 for nine, Somerset 222 for eight at Lord's, 1983; Hampshire 224 for eight, Essex 224 for seven at Southampton, 1985. Under the rules the side which lost fewer wickets won.

Wins by a Minor County (6): Durham v Yorkshire (by five wickets), Harrogate, 1973; Lincolnshire v Glamorgan (by six wickets), Swansea, 1974; Hertfordshire v Essex (by 33 runs), 2nd
round, Hitchin, 1976; Shropshire v Yorkshire (by 37 runs), Telford, 1984; Durham v Derbyshire (by seven wickets), Derby, 1985; Buckinghamshire v Somerset, High Wycombe, 1987.

WINNERS

Gillette Cup

1963 SUSSEX beat Worcestershire by 14 runs.
1964 SUSSEX beat Warwickshire by eight wickets.
1965 YORKSHIRE beat Surrey by 175 runs.
1966 WARWICKSHIRE beat Worcestershire by five wickets.
1967 KENT beat Somerset by 32 runs.
1968 WARWICKSHIRE beat Sussex by four wickets.
1969 YORKSHIRE beat Derbyshire by 69 runs.
1970 LANCASHIRE beat Sussex by six wickets.
1971 LANCASHIRE beat Kent by 24 runs.
1972 LANCASHIRE beat Warwickshire by four wickets.
1973 GLOUCESTERSHIRE beat Sussex by 40 runs.
1974 KENT beat Lancashire by four wickets.
1975 LANCASHIRE beat Middlesex by seven wickets.
1976 NORTHAMPTONSHIRE beat Lancashire by four wickets.
1977 MIDDLESEX beat Glamorgan by five wickets.
1978 SUSSEX beat Somerset by five wickets.
1979 SOMERSET beat Northamptonshire by 45 runs.
1980 MIDDLESEX beat Surrey by seven wickets.

NatWest Bank Trophy

1981 DERBYSHIRE beat Northamptonshire by losing fewer wickets with the scores level.
1982 SURREY beat Warwickshire by nine wickets.
1983 SOMERSET beat Kent by 24 runs.
1984 MIDDLESEX beat Kent by four wickets.
1985 ESSEX beat Nottinghamshire by 1 run.
1986 SUSSEX beat Lancashire by seven wickets.
1987 NOTTINGHAMSHIRE beat Northamptonshire by three wickets.

INTERNATIONAL YOUTH TOURNAMENT, 1987

The seventh International Youth Tournament, for cricketers aged under nineteen on January
1, 1987, was held at Belfast from July 28 to August 4. Six countries participated: Bermuda,
Canada, Denmark, England, Holland and Ireland. England were invited to send two teams,
as they had previously, and in the final, England South beat England North by 79 runs.

England South 152 (47.5 overs) (J. I. Longley 34; J. D. Batty three for 22); England North
73 (37.1 overs) (M. Cleal three for 10, N. Shahid four for 9).

The following players were selected for the two England teams: England North – K. M.
Krikken (Derbyshire) (*captain*), C. J. Adams (Derbyshire), J. D. Batty (Yorkshire), G. Coates
(Staffordshire), D. Colquhoun (Durham), A. Day (Durham), M. Doidge (Yorkshire), R. P.
Gofton (Yorkshire), P. Grayson (Yorkshire), I. J. Houseman (Yorkshire), P. J. Martin
(Yorkshire), D. B. Storer (Lincolnshire) and G. Wells (Lancashire). England South – H. R. J.
Trump (Somerset) (*captain*), M. Cleal (Somerset), S. J. Green (Warwickshire), R. Hanley
(Sussex), A. Hansford (Sussex), J. I. Longley (Kent), W. Noon (Lincolnshire), A. L. Penberthy
(Cornwall), A. R. Phillips (Somerset), M. Pooley (Cornwall), J. D. Ratcliffe (Warwickshire),
N. Shahid (Suffolk) and I. G. Steer (Warwickshire).

BENSON AND HEDGES CUP, 1987

Yorkshire, runners-up in the first Benson and Hedges Cup final, in 1972, won the sixteenth final at Lord's by displaying the tactics of a long-distance runner, being always in control and edging ahead in the final metres. They and Northamptonshire both scored 244 runs, but Yorkshire won on the rule giving victory to the side having taken the greater number of wickets. Had each side lost the same number of wickets, Yorkshire would still have won the trophy and a cheque for £20,000 by virtue of their superior score after 30 overs: 110 for three to 109 for four. Northamptonshire, winners in 1980, received £10,000 as losing finalists.

The beaten semi-finalists, Kent and Surrey, received £4,750 each, while Gloucestershire, Hampshire, Somerset and Worcestershire, the losing quarter-finalists, received £2,375. In addition, the winners of the group matches received £725.

Jim Love of Yorkshire, chosen by the England captain, Mike Gatting, as winner of the Gold Award in the final, received £550. The Gold Award winners in the semi-finals received £275 each, in the quarter-finals £200 each, and in the group matches £125 each.

Total prizemoney for the competition was £84,900, an increase of £2,500 over the previous year. Benson and Hedges increased their total sponsorship to the TCCB for 1987 to £436,770.

For the first time, cricketers from universities affiliated to the UAU, as well as those from Oxford and Cambridge, were considered for the Combined Universities team. The fourteen players selected are named at the beginning of the Group C matches.

FINAL GROUP TABLE

	Played	Won	Lost	No Result	Pts	Run-rate
Group A						
GLOUCESTERSHIRE	4	3	1	0	6	1.406
NORTHAMPTONSHIRE	4	2	2	0	4	1.259
Derbyshire	4	2	2	0	4	1.443
Nottinghamshire	4	2	2	0	4	1.720
Leicestershire	4	1	3	0	2	1.704
Group B						
YORKSHIRE	4	4	0	0	8	1.507
WORCESTERSHIRE	4	3	1	0	6	1.533
Warwickshire	4	1	2	1	3	1.675
Lancashire	4	1	2	1	3	1.744
Scotland	4	0	4	0	0	2.163
Group C						
SOMERSET	4	3	1	0	6	1.254
HAMPSHIRE	4	3	1	0	6	1.401
Essex	4	2	2	0	4	1.910
Middlesex	4	1	2	1	3	1.721
Combined Universities	4	0	3	1	1	1.666

	Played	Won	Lost	No Result	Pts	Run-rate
Group D						
SURREY	4	4	0	0	8	1.371
KENT	4	3	1	0	6	1.281
Glamorgan	4	1	3	0	2	1.449
Sussex	4	1	3	0	2	1.532
Minor Counties	4	1	3	0	2	1.682

The top two teams in each group qualified for the quarter-finals.

Where two or more teams finished with the same number of points, the position in the group was based on the faster run-rate in all group matches (calculated by balls bowled divided by runs scored) in which the side batting second was scheduled, at the start of their innings, to bat for 30 overs or more.

GROUP A

DERBYSHIRE v NORTHAMPTONSHIRE

At Derby, May 2, 4. Derbyshire won, having taken the greater number of wickets with the scores tied. Toss: Northamptonshire. Northamptonshire's total of 300 was the highest by a side batting second in the Benson and Hedges Cup, and the aggregate of 600 runs in the match was the second highest in the competition. In addition, each county's total was their highest in the competition. Close of play: Northamptonshire 78-0 (21 overs) (G. Cook 37*, W. Larkins 36*).

Gold Award: B. Roberts.

Derbyshire

*K. J. Barnett c Ripley b Capel	39	A. E. Warner not out	11
†B. J. M. Maher c N. G. B. Cook		M. A. Holding not out	16
b Wild	50		
B. Roberts c Boyd-Moss b Walker	100	B 1, l-b 17, w 2, n-b 3	23
J. E. Morris c Ripley b N. G. B. Cook	34		
I. S. Anderson lbw b Capel	0	1/76 2/108 3/184 (6 wkts, 55 overs)	300
P. G. Newman run out	27	4/191 5/267 6/275	

R. J. Finney, M. Jean-Jacques and O. H. Mortensen did not bat.

Bowling: Davis 11-0-79-0; Walker 11-1-60-1; Capel 11-0-41-2; N. G. B. Cook 11-0-52-1; Wild 11-0-50-1.

Northamptonshire

*G. Cook lbw b Mortensen	42	N. G. B. Cook c Maher b Jean-Jacques	12
W. Larkins c Maher b Mortensen	38	W. W. Davis not out	15
R. J. Boyd-Moss c Maher b Mortensen	4	A. Walker run out	0
A. J. Lamb lbw b Holding	83	B 2, l-b 13, w 8, n-b 5	28
R. J. Bailey run out	26		
D. J. Capel run out	13	1/82 2/88 3/99 (55 overs)	300
D. J. Wild c Warner b Newman	6	4/175 5/210 6/220	
†D. Ripley run out	33	7/240 8/260 9/292	

Bowling: Holding 11-0-46-1; Newman 11-0-43-1; Mortensen 11-1-50-3; Jean-Jacques 9-0-63-1; Warner 9-0-66-0; Finney 4-0-17-0.

Umpires: J. A. Jameson and D. Lloyd.

GLOUCESTERSHIRE v NOTTINGHAMSHIRE

At Bristol, May 2. Gloucestershire won by eight wickets. Toss: Gloucestershire.
Gold Award: A. W. Stovold.

Nottinghamshire

B. C. Broad run out	83	P. Johnson not out	4
R. T. Robinson c Lloyds b Walsh	89	B 8, w 1, n-b 1	10
D. W. Randall not out	40		
*C. E. B. Rice c Russell b Lawrence	2	1/155 2/195 3/210 (3 wkts, 55 overs)	228

C. D. Fraser-Darling, †B. N. French, R. A. Pick, E. E. Hemmings, J. A. Afford and
K. Saxelby did not bat.

Bowling: Walsh 10–0–37–1; Lawrence 11–0–52–1; Curran 8–0–27–0; Bainbridge
11–0–45–0; Graveney 10–0–30–0; Lloyds 5–0–29–0.

Gloucestershire

A. W. Stovold not out	101		
P. W. Romaines c French b Hemmings	11		
C. W. J. Athey c Randall b Saxelby	91		
P. Bainbridge not out	9		
L-b 10, w 7	17		

1/31 2/202   (2 wkts, 52.5 overs) 229

K. M. Curran, J. W. Lloyds, A. J. Wright, †R. C. Russell, *D. A. Graveney, C. A. Walsh
and D. V. Lawrence did not bat.

Bowling: Pick 10–0–52–0; Rice 9.5–1–39–0; Hemmings 11–3–25–1; Saxelby 11–2–36–1;
Afford 8–0–55–0; Fraser-Darling 3–0–12–0.

Umpires: B. Dudleston and A. G. T. Whitehead.

GLOUCESTERSHIRE v LEICESTERSHIRE

At Bristol, May 9. Gloucestershire won by 21 runs. Toss: Leicestershire.
Gold Award: J. P. Agnew.

Gloucestershire

A. W. Stovold lbw b Agnew	0	*D. A. Graveney not out	2
P. W. Romaines c and b Agnew	6	C. A. Walsh not out	7
C. W. J. Athey c Potter b DeFreitas	80		
P. Bainbridge c Whitticase b Agnew	59	B 6, l-b 15, w 6, n-b 3	30
K. M. Curran c Potter b Taylor	22		
A. J. Wright lbw b Agnew	13	1/0 2/26 3/152 (8 wkts, 55 overs)	234
M. W. Alleyne c Whitticase b Benjamin	8	4/181 5/202 6/203	
†R. C. Russell c Gower b Agnew	7	7/215 8/224	

D. V. Lawrence did not bat.

Bowling: Agnew 11–2–30–5; DeFreitas 11–0–46–1; Benjamin 11–0–44–1; Taylor
11–2–44–1; Willey 11–0–49–0.

Leicestershire

L. Potter c Wright b Curran	18	†P. Whitticase not out	9
I. P. Butcher c Graveney b Curran	80	J. P. Agnew run out	4
D. I. Gower c and b Curran	0	L. B. Taylor b Curran	1
*P. Willey b Alleyne	24		
J. J. Whitaker c Stovold b Bainbridge	45		
T. J. Boon lbw b Graveney	0	L-b 5, w 3, n-b 3	11
P. A. J. DeFreitas st Russell b Bainbridge	5	1/36 2/40 3/93 (53.2 overs)	213
W. K. M. Benjamin c Bainbridge b Walsh	16	4/157 5/157 6/162	
		7/197 8/202 9/210	

Bowling: Walsh 10-2-30-1; Lawrence 5-0-26-0; Bainbridge 11-0-54-2; Curran 10.2-1-43-4; Alleyne 6-0-24-1; Graveney 11-1-31-1.

Umpires: J. H. Harris and R. A. White.

NOTTINGHAMSHIRE v DERBYSHIRE

At Nottingham, May 9. Nottinghamshire won by 27 runs. Toss: Derbyshire.
Gold Award: E. E. Hemmings.

Nottinghamshire

M. Newell c Roberts b Warner	25	E. E. Hemmings c Roberts b Jean-Jacques	26
R. T. Robinson c Holding b Jean-Jacques	60	R. A. Pick b Jean-Jacques	1
D. W. Randall c Maher b Newman	30	L-b 15, w 9, n-b 1	25
*C. E. B. Rice b Warner	10		
P. Johnson c Maher b Warner	5	1/61 2/115 3/131 (8 wkts, 55 overs)	209
J. D. Birch not out	26	4/139 5/146 6/148	
†B. N. French b Warner	1	7/206 8/209	

K. Saxelby and K. E. Cooper did not bat.

Bowling: Newman 11-2-38-1; Holding 11-1-38-0; Mortensen 11-0-39-0; Jean-Jacques 6-0-22-3; Warner 11-0-36-4; Finney 5-0-21-0.

Derbyshire

*K. J. Barnett c Randall b Cooper	3	R. J. Finney c French b Saxelby	2
†B. J. M. Maher lbw b Pick	4	M. Jean-Jacques lbw b Pick	2
B. Roberts b Hemmings	61	O. H. Mortensen lbw b Pick	0
J. E. Morris run out	36	L-b 10, w 1, n-b 3	14
I. S. Anderson not out	28		
P. G. Newman c French b Cooper	10	1/8 2/8 3/95 4/121 (49.5 overs)	182
A. E. Warner lbw b Cooper	0	5/130 6/138 7/168	
M. A. Holding c Pick b Saxelby	22	8/173 9/182	

Bowling: Pick 10.5-3-23-3; Cooper 11-2-39-3; Saxelby 9-0-45-2; Rice 9-0-41-0; Hemmings 10-1-24-1.

Umpires: J. Birkenshaw and P. B. Wight.

LEICESTERSHIRE v NOTTINGHAMSHIRE

At Leicester, May 12, 13. Leicestershire won by eight wickets. Toss: Leicestershire. On the first day Benjamin took four wickets in six balls, the last three – those of Johnson, Hadlee and French – being a hat-trick. Nottinghamshire's total was their lowest in the competition. Close of play: Nottinghamshire 62-6 (25.3 overs) (M. Newell 26*, E. E. Hemmings 10*).
Gold Award: W. K. M. Benjamin.

Nottinghamshire

M. Newell lbw b Taylor	27	R. A. Pick b Taylor	4
R. T. Robinson b Willey	18	K. Saxelby b Benjamin	1
D. W. Randall lbw b Willey	0	K. E. Cooper not out	4
*C. E. B. Rice c Whitticase b Benjamin	0		
P. Johnson c Whitticase b Benjamin	0	L-b 2, w 7, n-b 1	10
R. J. Hadlee lbw b Benjamin	0		
†B. N. French lbw b Benjamin	0	1/43 2/43 3/46 4/46	(32.4 overs) 74
E. E. Hemmings lbw b Taylor	10	5/46 6/46 7/63 8/65 9/70	

Bowling: Agnew 6–1–17–0; DeFreitas 6–3–9–0; Willey 7–1–15–2; Benjamin 10–1–26–5; Taylor 3.4–1–5–3.

Leicestershire

L. Potter c Hemmings b Saxelby	21
I. P. Butcher b Pick	4
D. I. Gower not out	38
*P. Willey not out	12
W 1	1

1/9 2/50   (2 wkts, 18 overs) 76

J. J. Whitaker, T. J. Boon, P. A. J. DeFreitas, W. K. M. Benjamin, †P. Whitticase, J. P. Agnew and L. B. Taylor did not bat.

Bowling: Hadlee 5–2–6–0; Pick 6–0–36–1; Cooper 1–0–4–0; Hemmings 3–0–17–0; Saxelby 3–0–13–1.

Umpires: J. W. Holder and P. B. Wight.

NORTHAMPTONSHIRE v GLOUCESTERSHIRE

At Northampton, May 12, 13. Northamptonshire won by 58 runs. Toss: Gloucestershire. The second-wicket stand of 245 between Bailey and G. Cook, both of whom scored their first hundreds in the competition, was a county record for any wicket in the Benson and Hedges Cup. Bailey's 134 was also a Northamptonshire record for the competition. Close of play: Northamptonshire 148-1 (36.3 overs) (G. Cook 46*, R. J. Bailey 73*).

Gold Award: R. J. Bailey.

Northamptonshire

*G. Cook run out	108
W. Larkins c Russell b Lawrence	18
R. J. Bailey b Walsh	134
A. J. Lamb not out	1
L-b 14, w 6, n-b 2	22

1/29 2/274 3/283   (3 wkts, 55 overs) 283

D. J. Capel, R. G. Williams, D. J. Wild, †D. Ripley, N. G. B. Cook, W. W. Davis and A. Walker did not bat.

Bowling: Walsh 11–3–52–1; Lawrence 10–0–47–1; Curran 11–1–60–0; Bainbridge 11–1–55–0; Alleyne 2–0–6–0; Graveney 10–0–49–0.

Gloucestershire

A. W. Stovold c Lamb b Davis	11	*D. A. Graveney b Davis	11
P. W. Romaines lbw b Davis	7	C. A. Walsh b Williams	7
C. W. J. Athey c Larkins b Williams	95	D. V. Lawrence not out	1
P. Bainbridge run out	30	L-b 10, w 3, n-b 7	20
K. M. Curran b Walker	21		
A. J. Wright c Ripley b Capel	10	1/19 2/23 3/93	(52 overs) 225
M. W. Alleyne c and b Williams	4	4/170 5/189 6/195	
†R. C. Russell c Wild b Williams	8	7/197 8/214 9/220	

Bowling: Davis 9–0–34–3; Walker 9–2–26–1; Capel 10–1–38–1; N. G. B. Cook 11–0–49–0; Wild 4–0–27–0; Williams 9–0–41–4.

Umpires: J. H. Harris and D. O. Oslear.

LEICESTERSHIRE v DERBYSHIRE

At Leicester, May 14, 15. Derbyshire won on faster scoring-rate when a hailstorm ended play. Toss: Derbyshire. Close of play: Leicestershire 98-6 (41.1 overs) (P. Willey 39*, P. Whitticase 20*).

Gold Award: P. Willey.

Leicestershire

L. Potter run out	0	W. K. M. Benjamin run out	0
I. P. Butcher b Mortensen	7	J. P. Agnew run out	1
D. I. Gower lbw b Holding	10	L. B. Taylor not out	2
*P. Willey not out	80		
J. J. Whitaker c Anderson b Mortensen	0	L-b 8, w 7, n-b 1	16
T. J. Boon c Roberts b Mortensen	2		
P. A. J. DeFreitas c Jean-Jacques		1/0 2/18 3/19 (9 wkts, 55 overs) 168
b Finney	14	4/19 5/27 6/47
†P. Whitticase run out	36	7/155 8/156 9/161

Bowling: Mortensen 11–5–20–3; Holding 11–3–15–1; Newman 11–2–36–0; Warner 11–2–32–0; Finney 5–1–20–1; Jean-Jacques 6–0–37–0.

Derbyshire

*K. J. Barnett hit wkt b Taylor	29	P. G. Newman not out	0
†B. J. M. Maher run out	37	L-b 2, w 3, n-b 3	8
B. Roberts c Whitticase b Willey	6		
J. E. Morris not out	16	1/73 2/74 3/86 (4 wkts, 32 overs) 100
I. S. Anderson c Whitticase b DeFreitas	4	4/97

A. E. Warner, R. J. Finney, M. Jean-Jacques, O. H. Mortensen and M. A. Holding did not bat.

Bowling: Agnew 6–1–18–0; DeFreitas 8–1–13–1; Benjamin 6–1–30–0; Taylor 7–0–28–1; Willey 5–1–9–1.

Umpires: H. D. Bird and D. O. Oslear.

NOTTINGHAMSHIRE v NORTHAMPTONSHIRE

At Nottingham, May 14, 15. Nottinghamshire won by 15 runs. Toss: Nottinghamshire. Close of play: Nottinghamshire 130-3 (37 overs) (C. E. B. Rice 26*, P. Johnson 4*).

Gold Award: R. A. Pick.

Nottinghamshire

B. C. Broad c Ripley b Capel	6	†B. N. French not out	2
R. T. Robinson b Walker	37	R. A. Pick not out	2
D. W. Randall c G. Cook b Capel	45		
*C. E. B. Rice c Davis b N. G. B. Cook	64	B 3, l-b 5, w 7, n-b 2	17
P. Johnson c Bailey b Davis	49		
J. D. Birch c Walker b Capel	3	1/21 2/61 3/118 (8 wkts, 55 overs) 256
R. J. Hadlee b Walker	28	4/190 5/195 6/240
E. E. Hemmings c G. Cook b Walker	3	7/252 8/252

K. Saxelby did not bat.

Bowling: Davis 11–1–55–1; Capel 11–3–33–3; Wild 7–0–28–0; Walker 11–0–50–3; N. G. B. Cook 11–0–59–1; Williams 4–0–23–0.

Northamptonshire

*G. Cook b Pick	1
W. Larkins c Hadlee b Pick	4
R. J. Bailey b Pick	17
A. J. Lamb c Rice b Saxelby	116
D. J. Capel b Pick	0
R. G. Williams b Rice	23
D. J. Wild c French b Saxelby	8
†D. Ripley b Saxelby	18

N. G. B. Cook run out	21
W. W. Davis lbw b Hemmings	0
A. Walker not out	15
L-b 10, w 8	18

1/5 2/7 3/26   (53.2 overs) 241
4/36 5/84 6/100
7/122 8/191 9/195

Bowling: Hadlee 11–0–47–0; Pick 11–2–42–4; Rice 10–1–44–1; Saxelby 10.2–0–41–3; Hemmings 11–0–57–1.

Umpires: J. H. Hampshire and J. W. Holder.

DERBYSHIRE v GLOUCESTERSHIRE

At Derby, May 16, 18. Gloucestershire won by 4 runs. Toss: Derbyshire. Barnett's score was the highest by a Derbyshire player in the Benson and Hedges Cup. Close of play: Derbyshire 33-0 (8 overs) (K. J. Barnett 21*, B. J. M. Maher 5*).

Gold Award: K. J. Barnett.

Gloucestershire

A. W. Stovold c Newman b Holding	14
A. J. Wright c Maher b Mortensen	28
C. W. J. Athey lbw b Mortensen	0
P. Bainbridge b Newman	42
K. M. Curran c Jean-Jacques b Warner	57
J. W. Lloyds c Barnett b Jean-Jacques	27
M. W. Alleyne run out	36
†R. C. Russell not out	10

C. A. Walsh c Roberts b Newman	4
*D. A. Graveney not out	0
B 6, l-b 11, w 4, n-b 2	23

1/30 2/30 3/62   (8 wkts, 55 overs) 241
4/135 5/179 6/206
7/230 8/239

D. V. Lawrence did not bat.

Bowling: Holding 11–0–38–1; Mortensen 11–2–20–2; Finney 2–0–8–0; Jean-Jacques 9–0–42–1; Newman 11–1–55–2; Warner 11–0–61–1.

Derbyshire

*K. J. Barnett c Lloyds b Alleyne	115
†B. J. M. Maher c Lloyds b Graveney	42
B. Roberts b Lawrence	0
J. E. Morris b Walsh	29
I. S. Anderson c Russell b Walsh	11
M. A. Holding b Alleyne	8
R. J. Finney c sub b Alleyne	6
P. G. Newman c Alleyne b Bainbridge	1

A. E. Warner run out	1
M. Jean-Jacques not out	2
O. H. Mortensen not out	3
L-b 11, w 5, n-b 3	19

1/119 2/120 3/179   (9 wkts, 55 overs) 237
4/205 5/219 6/229
7/229 8/231 9/232

Bowling: Walsh 11–0–34–2; Lawrence 11–0–58–1; Bainbridge 11–1–37–1; Curran 7–0–37–0; Graveney 11–0–37–1; Lloyds 2–0–10–0; Alleyne 2–0–13–3.

Umpires: J. Birkenshaw and N. T. Plews.

NORTHAMPTONSHIRE v LEICESTERSHIRE

At Northampton, May 16. Northamptonshire won by 37 runs. Toss: Leicestershire.

Gold Award: D. Ripley.

Northamptonshire

*G. Cook c Whitticase b Agnew	9	N. G. B. Cook run out	0
W. Larkins lbw b Agnew	29	W. W. Davis not out	13
R. J. Bailey c Potter b Benjamin	18	A. Walker not out	12
A. J. Lamb lbw b Potter	44	B 5, l-b 6, w 6, n-b 2	19
D. J. Capel c Whitticase b Taylor	0		—
R. G. Williams b Willey	18	1/39 2/42 3/82 (9 wkts, 55 overs)	224
D. J. Wild c Whitticase b DeFreitas	36	4/83 5/126 6/132	
†D. Ripley c Whitticase b Benjamin	26	7/196 8/196 9/198	

Bowling: Agnew 8–2–40–2; DeFreitas 11–0–42–1; Taylor 8–1–22–1; Benjamin 10–1–44–2; Willey 11–1–31–1; Potter 7–0–34–1.

Leicestershire

L. Potter c Ripley b Capel	1	W. K. M. Benjamin c Davis b Walker	21
I. P. Butcher c Ripley b Davis	9	J. P. Agnew c G. Cook b Davis	20
D. I. Gower b Davis	1	L. B. Taylor not out	4
*P. Willey c Walker b Williams	35	B 1, l-b 8, w 2, n-b 1	12
J. J. Whitaker c Ripley b Capel	14		—
T. J. Boon not out	58	1/3 2/12 3/19 (9 wkts, 55 overs)	187
P. A. J. DeFreitas st Ripley b Williams	8	4/47 5/75 6/92	
†P. Whitticase c Davis b N. G. B. Cook	4	7/102 8/135 9/172	

Bowling: Davis 11–3–20–3; Capel 11–3–35–2; Walker 11–1–53–1; Williams 11–2–32–2; N. G. B. Cook 11–1–38–1.

Umpires: H. D. Bird and B. Leadbeater.

GROUP B

WARWICKSHIRE v YORKSHIRE

At Birmingham, May 2, 4. Yorkshire won by ten wickets. Toss: Warwickshire. The opening stand of 211 unbroken between Moxon and Metcalfe was the highest for any wicket for Yorkshire in one-day cricket. Close of play: Yorkshire 81-0 (24 overs) (M. D. Moxon 37*, A. A. Metcalfe 34*).

Gold Award: A. A. Metcalfe.

Warwickshire

T. A. Lloyd run out	67	T. A. Merrick not out	13
A. J. Moles lbw b Jarvis	0	T. A. Munton not out	6
A. C. Storie c Bairstow b Hartley	65		
D. L. Amiss b Hartley	3	L-b 11, w 2, n-b 1	14
†G. W. Humpage c and b Jarvis	25		—
Asif Din c Bairstow b Jarvis	2	1/0 2/138 3/140 (8 wkts, 55 overs)	208
D. A. Thorne b Hartley	7	4/145 5/154 6/181	
G. J. Parsons c Metcalfe b Sidebottom	6	7/181 8/193	

*N. Gifford did not bat.

Bowling: Sidebottom 11–1–48–1; Jarvis 11–4–30–3; Fletcher 7–0–32–0; Hartley 11–3–30–3; Carrick 11–1–33–0; Moxon 4–0–24–0.

Yorkshire

M. D. Moxon not out	93
A. A. Metcalfe not out	94
B 5, l-b 4, w 14, n-b 1	24

(no wkt, 50 overs) 211

R. J. Blakey, K. Sharp, J. D. Love, †D. L. Bairstow, *P. Carrick, A. Sidebottom, P. J. Hartley, P. W. Jarvis and S. D. Fletcher did not bat.

Bowling: Merrick 11–1–32–0; Parsons 9–1–36–0; Munton 11–1–41–0; Moles 6–0–31–0; Gifford 9–0–41–0; Thorne 4–0–21–0.

Umpires: K. E. Palmer and R. A. White.

WORCESTERSHIRE v LANCASHIRE

At Worcester, May 2. Worcestershire won by 87 runs. Toss: Lancashire.
Gold Award: G. A. Hick.

Worcestershire

T. S. Curtis c Stanworth b Hayhurst	62	†S. J. Rhodes c Hughes b Hayhurst	14
M. J. Weston c Stanworth b Hayhurst	18	P. J. Newport not out	3
G. A. Hick c Hughes b Simmons	88	L-b 7, w 2	9
I. T. Botham b Austin	3		
*P. A. Neale c Simmons b Hayhurst	22	1/39 2/162 3/169 (6 wkts, 55 overs)	257
D. B. D'Oliveira not out	38	4/193 5/213 6/244	

R. K. Illingworth, N. V. Radford and G. R. Dilley did not bat.

Bowling: McLeod 11–1–66–0; Hayhurst 11–1–50–4; O'Shaughnessy 11–2–45–0; Austin 11–3–41–1; Simmons 11–1–48–1.

Lancashire

G. D. Mendis c Rhodes b Radford	4	J. Simmons b Weston	1
G. Fowler c D'Oliveira b Dilley	16	K. W. McLeod c Botham b Radford	4
J. Abrahams c Rhodes b Newport	17	†J. Stanworth not out	7
N. H. Fairbrother b Newport	2	L-b 3, w 5, n-b 4	12
S. J. O'Shaughnessy run out	21		
*D. P. Hughes c Botham b Newport	5	1/21 2/21 3/30 (50.1 overs)	170
A. N. Hayhurst c D'Oliveira b Dilley	1	4/49 5/56 6/60	
I. D. Austin b Botham	80	7/95 8/101 9/119	

Bowling: Dilley 9–4–22–2; Radford 11–0–25–2; Botham 9.1–0–28–1; Newport 11–1–42–3; Weston 7–0–41–1; Illingworth 3–0–9–0.

Umpires: H. D. Bird and J. H. Hampshire.

SCOTLAND v WARWICKSHIRE

At Perth, May 9. Warwickshire won by 131 runs. Toss: Warwickshire.
Gold Award: A. J. Moles.

Warwickshire

T. A. Lloyd lbw b Donald	9	D. A. Thorne b Duthie	30
A. J. Moles b Burnett	72	G. J. Parsons not out	1
A. C. Storie lbw b Moir	66	L-b 9, w 3, n-b 4	16
D. L. Amiss not out	49		
†G. W. Humpage c Knight b Donald	4	1/32 2/138 3/177 (6 wkts, 55 overs)	260
P. A. Smith b Moir	13	4/190 5/207 6/255	

A. A. Donald, T. A. Munton and *N. Gifford did not bat.

Bowling: Burnett 7–0–31–1; Duthie 11–2–61–1; Donald 11–0–42–2; Henry 11–2–33–0; Stevenson 4–0–21–0; Moir 11–1–63–2.

Scotland

I. L. Philip lbw b Smith	1	P. G. Duthie not out		7
K. Scott c Humpage b Smith	12	A. W. J. Stevenson lbw b Munton		5
*R. G. Swan lbw b Donald	2	†J. D. Knight b Donald		4
W. A. Donald c Humpage b Moles	29	B 4, l-b 5, w 6, n-b 7		22
O. Henry c Munton b Gifford	5			
A. B. Russell b Donald	21	1/9 2/21 3/21	(46.2 overs)	129
N. W. Burnett c Gifford b Munton	17	4/44 5/63 6/90		
D. G. Moir b Donald	4	7/110 8/111 9/117		

Bowling: Donald 10.2–2–28–4; Smith 7–2–24–2; Parsons 8–3–12–0; Gifford 6–0–7–1; Moles 5–0–17–1; Munton 10–1–32–2.

Umpires: J. A. Jameson and R. Julian.

YORKSHIRE v LANCASHIRE

At Leeds, May 9. Yorkshire won by 75 runs. Toss: Yorkshire.
   Gold Award: A. A. Metcalfe.

Yorkshire

M. D. Moxon c Austin b O'Shaughnessy	11	*P. Carrick c and b Allott		1
A. A. Metcalfe c Stanworth b Simmons	84	P. J. Hartley not out		1
R. J. Blakey b Simmons	58	L-b 10, w 2		12
K. Sharp run out	19			
J. D. Love not out	47	1/41 2/138 3/173	(6 wkts, 55 overs)	269
†D. L. Bairstow c Abrahams b McLeod	36	4/183 5/258 6/261		

A. Sidebottom, P. W. Jarvis and S. D. Fletcher did not bat.

Bowling: Allott 11–1–44–1; McLeod 11–0–59–1; Austin 11–0–44–0; O'Shaughnessy 11–1–55–1; Simmons 11–0–57–2.

Lancashire

G. D. Mendis c Bairstow b Hartley	28	P. J. W. Allott b Fletcher		18
G. Fowler c Moxon b Sidebottom	2	†J. Stanworth lbw b Sidebottom		2
J. Abrahams c Bairstow b Fletcher	6	K. W. McLeod not out		5
N. H. Fairbrother c Sharp b Hartley	54	B 1, l-b 10, w 3, n-b 2		16
S. J. O'Shaughnessy c Carrick	9			
*D. P. Hughes c Bairstow b Jarvis	28	1/20 2/37 3/45	(51.2 overs)	194
I. D. Austin c and b Hartley	2	4/92 5/114 6/119		
J. Simmons c and b Sidebottom	24	7/148 8/174 9/179		

Bowling: Jarvis 11–1–33–1; Sidebottom 9.2–1–21–3; Hartley 11–0–40–3; Fletcher 9–1–37–2; Carrick 11–1–52–1.

Umpires: J. W. Holder and D. O. Oslear.

LANCASHIRE v SCOTLAND

At Southport, May 12, 13. Lancashire won by seven wickets. Toss: Scotland. There was no play on the first day.
   Gold Award: I. L. Philip.

Scotland

I. L. Philip lbw b Allott	71	P. G. Duthie b Allott		1
K. Scott c Allott b Watkinson	13	J. E. Ker b Allott		2
*R. G. Swan c and b Abrahams	40	†J. D. Knight not out		1
O. Henry run out	8	L-b 5, w 7, n-b 3		15
W. A. Donald b Abrahams	5			
A. B. Russell run out	0	1/53 2/138 3/140	(9 wkts, 55 overs)	168
N. W. Burnett c Hughes b Simmons	0	4/148 5/148 6/150		
D. L. Snodgrass not out	12	7/152 8/155 9/167		

Bowling: Allott 11–3–24–3; McLeod 6–0–14–0; Watkinson 9–2–25–1; O'Shaughnessy 4–0–19–0; Simmons 11–3–29–1; Hughes 6–0–20–0; Abrahams 8–2–32–2.

Lancashire

G. D. Mendis c Philip b Henry	29	J. Abrahams not out	31
G. Fowler c Knight b Ker	2	B 1, l-b 5, w 4, n-b 1	11
D. W. Varey c and b Duthie	27		
S. J. O'Shaughnessy not out	69	1/6 2/42 3/92 (3 wkts, 45 overs)	169

*D. P. Hughes, M. Watkinson, J. Simmons, K. W. McLeod, P. J. W. Allott and †J. Stanworth did not bat.

Bowling: Duthie 9–1–26–1; Ker 9–0–35–1; Donald 10–2–40–0; Henry 11–3–28–1; Burnett 5–0–29–0; Snodgrass 1–0–5–0.

Umpires: K. J. Lyons and R. A. White.

YORKSHIRE v WORCESTERSHIRE

At Leeds, May 12, 13. Yorkshire won by 12 runs. Toss: Yorkshire. Yorkshire's seventh successive victory of the season ensured them of a place in the quarter-finals. Close of play: Worcestershire 46-5 (17 overs) D. B. D'Oliveira 9*, S. J. Rhodes 8*).
Gold Award: A. Sidebottom.

Yorkshire

M. D. Moxon b Pridgeon	20	P. J. Hartley c Rhodes b Radford	1
A. A. Metcalfe c Botham b Dilley	9	P. W. Jarvis c Hick b Dilley	11
R. J. Blakey c Botham b Radford	5	S. D. Fletcher b Botham	1
K. Sharp not out	64	B 6, w 9	15
S. N. Hartley c Dilley b Pridgeon	7		
†D. L. Bairstow c Hick b Newport	0	1/11 2/20 3/47 (53.4 overs)	143
*P. Carrick c Rhodes b Radford	10	4/65 5/67 6/96	
A. Sidebottom c D'Oliveira b Newport	0	7/97 8/98 9/139	

Bowling: Dilley 10–3–17–2; Radford 11–2–35–3; Botham 10.4–1–31–1; Pridgeon 11–2–26–2; Newport 11–0–28–2.

Worcestershire

T. S. Curtis b Jarvis	14	N. V. Radford c Bairstow b Fletcher	9
M. J. Weston lbw b Sidebottom	0	G. R. Dilley c Moxon b S. N. Hartley	4
G. A. Hick b Blakey b Sidebottom	2	A. P. Pridgeon not out	4
*P. A. Neale c Bairstow b Sidebottom	4	L-b 12, w 1, n-b 6	19
D. B. D'Oliveira lbw b Fletcher	59		
I. T. Botham lbw b Sidebottom	0	1/9 2/19 3/23 (50.1 overs)	131
†S. J. Rhodes c Bairstow b P. J. Hartley	13	4/23 5/27 6/56	
P. J. Newport run out	1	7/57 8/86 9/95	

Bowling: Jarvis 11–4–25–1; Sidebottom 11–5–15–4; P. J. Hartley 11–2–28–1; Fletcher 9.1–2–21–2; Carrick 3–0–5–0; S. N. Hartley 5–0–25–1.

Umpires: R. Julian and D. Lloyd.

LANCASHIRE v WARWICKSHIRE

At Manchester, May 14, 15. No result. Toss: Warwickshire. Following heavy rain on the second afternoon, the match which began on the first day – when twelve overs were bowled – was abandoned: Warwickshire 203-8, Lancashire 34-1. A new match of 22 overs a side was begun, but this too was ended by rain.

Lancashire

G. D. Mendis c Lloyd b Donald	18	M. Watkinson not out	4
G. Fowler b Smith	1	J. Simmons not out	0
J. Abrahams b Smith	0	B 1, l-b 3, w 2	6
N. H. Fairbrother c Donald b Parsons	50		
S. J. O'Shaughnessy b Donald	0	1/4 2/12 3/33	(6 wkts, 17 overs) 93
*D. P. Hughes b Gifford	14	4/33 5/78 6/93	

K. W. McLeod, P. J. W. Allott and †J. Stanworth did not bat.

Bowling: Small 3–1–10–0; Smith 4–0–23–2; Donald 2–0–6–2; Gifford 4–0–23–1; Parsons 4–0–27–1.

Warwickshire

T. A. Lloyd, A. J. Moles, A. C. Storie, D. L. Amiss, †G. W. Humpage, P. A. Smith, D. A. Thorne, G. J. Parsons, G. C. Small, A. A. Donald and *N. Gifford.

Umpires: B. Leadbeater and R. Julian.

WORCESTERSHIRE v SCOTLAND

At Worcester, May 14, 15. Worcestershire won by eight wickets. Toss: Worcestershire. Hick retired hurt when 1 and returned at the fall of the second wicket. Close of play: Scotland 149.
Gold Award: T. S. Curtis.

Scotland

I. L. Philip c Botham b Newport	21	J. E. Ker c Rhodes b Dilley	3
K. Scott c Botham b Radford	1	A. W. J. Stevenson run out	1
*R. G. Swan c Rhodes b Radford	37	†J. D. Knight not out	0
W. A. Donald c Rhodes b Newport	20	L-b 12, w 5, n-b 6	23
O. Henry b Botham	8		
A. B. Russell c Rhodes b Botham	18	1/5 2/48 3/75	(54.5 overs) 149
D. L. Snodgrass lbw b Radford	0	4/94 5/110 6/110	
P. G. Duthie c Curtis b Botham	22	7/133 8/144 9/149	

Bowling: Dilley 11–2–24–1; Radford 11–1–25–3; Pridgeon 11–2–29–0; Botham 10.5–4–29–3; Newport 11–1–30–2.

Worcestershire

T. S. Curtis not out	64
M. J. Weston b Ker	3
G. A. Hick not out	73
*P. A. Neale c and b Donald	0
L-b 7, w 2, n-b 1	10

1/12 2/30   (2 wkts, 32 overs) 150

D. B. D'Oliveira, I. T. Botham, †S. J. Rhodes, P. J. Newport, N. V. Radford, G. R. Dilley and A. P. Pridgeon did not bat.

Bowling: Duthie 9–3–38–0; Ker 5–1–13–1; Henry 9–1–39–0; Donald 3–0–17–1; Snodgrass 2–0–12–0; Stevenson 4–0–24–0.

Umpires: D. Lloyd and K. J. Lyons.

SCOTLAND v YORKSHIRE

At Glasgow, May 16. Yorkshire won by seven wickets. Toss: Yorkshire.
Gold Award: A. A. Metcalfe.

Scotland

I. L. Philip run out	22	P. G. Duthie b Fletcher		0
K. Scott lbw b P. J. Hartley	29	A. W. J. Stevenson b P. J. Hartley		0
*R. G. Swan c Metcalfe b Fletcher	43			
W. A. Donald c Bairstow b P. J. Hartley	2	L-b 9, w 3, n-b 1		13
O. Henry lbw b Carrick	1			
A. B. Russell b Fletcher	35	1/45 2/56 3/65	(9 wkts, 55 overs)	164
N. W. Burnett not out	17	4/72 5/140 6/144		
D. G. Moir c Bairstow b Fletcher	2	7/152 8/153 9/164		

†J. D. Knight did not bat.

Bowling: Dennis 11–2–36–0; Fletcher 11–2–34–4; Pickles 11–3–28–0; Carrick 11–3–12–1; P. J. Hartley 11–1–45–3.

Yorkshire

M. D. Moxon b Burnett	2	C. S. Pickles not out		13
A. A. Metcalfe run out	91	B 1, l-b 11, w 9, n-b 1		14
R. J. Blakey not out	37			
K. Sharp c and b Stevenson	8	1/20 2/131 3/142	(3 wkts, 38 overs)	165

S. N. Hartley, †D. L. Bairstow, *P. Carrick, P. J. Hartley, S. J. Dennis and S. D. Fletcher did not bat.

Bowling: Duthie 11–2–28–0; Burnett 6–0–21–1; Donald 4–1–12–0; Moir 4–0–24–0; Henry 4–1–24–0; Stevenson 9–0–52–1.

Umpires: J. W. Holder and D. Lloyd.

WARWICKSHIRE v WORCESTERSHIRE

At Birmingham, May 16. Worcestershire won by 110 runs. Toss: Warwickshire.
Gold Award: S. J. Rhodes.

Worcestershire

T. S. Curtis lbw b Smith	3	†S. J. Rhodes not out		51
M. J. Weston c Storie b Small	8	N. V. Radford not out		9
G. A. Hick b Gifford	50	B 1, l-b 11, w 6, n-b 4		22
D. B. D'Oliveira st Humpage b Gifford	20			
*P. A. Neale c Storie b Small	52	1/9 2/15 3/84	(6 wkts, 55 overs)	233
I. T. Botham b Donald	18	4/91 5/137 6/189		

P. J. Newport, R. K. Illingworth and G. R. Dilley did not bat.

Bowling: Small 11–0–42–2; Smith 8–1–28–1; Donald 11–1–57–1; Parsons 11–3–35–0; Gifford 7–1–23–2; Moles 7–0–36–0.

Warwickshire

T. A. Lloyd b Dilley	12	G. C. Small lbw b Newport		0
A. J. Moles c Botham b Newport	8	A. A. Donald c Botham b Newport		0
A. C. Storie lbw b Newport	11	*N. Gifford b Newport		0
D. L. Amiss c Rhodes b Dilley	28	L-b 9, w 14, n-b 2		25
†G. W. Humpage b Illingworth	16			
P. A. Smith c Rhodes b Botham	5	1/18 2/31 3/58	(40 overs)	123
D. A. Thorne not out	10	4/82 5/97 6/106		
G. J. Parsons c D'Oliveira b Illingworth	8	7/123 8/123 9/123		

Bowling: Dilley 8–0–21–2; Radford 8–2–22–0; Botham 8–1–25–1; Newport 9–1–22–5; Illingworth 7–1–24–2.

Umpires: B. Dudleston and D. J. Constant.

GROUP C

The Combined Universities' squad of fourteen named for the competition was: J. P. Stephenson (Durham) (*captain*), M. A. Atherton (Cambridge), P. A. C. Bail (Cambridge), T. M. Barry (Loughborough), M. J. Cann (Swansea), M. A. Crawley (Oxford), J. E. Davidson (Cambridge), A. Fordham (Durham), N. Hussain (Durham), P. C. M. Perera (Exeter), D. G. Price (Cambridge), A. M. G. Scott (Cambridge), M. P. Speight (Durham) and C. D. M. Tooley (Oxford).

COMBINED UNIVERSITIES v HAMPSHIRE

At Oxford, May 2. Hampshire won by 93 runs. Toss: Combined Universities. Greenidge, who became the first Hampshire player to score 2,000 runs in the competition, scored a hundred before lunch off 107 balls and shared with Terry in a Hampshire record opening partnership.
Gold Award: C. G. Greenidge.

Hampshire

C. G. Greenidge b Cann	133	N. G. Cowley run out		7
V. P. Terry c Cann b Stephenson	54	T. M. Tremlett not out		6
*M. C. J. Nicholas run out	22	L-b 11, w 7, n-b 8		26
R. A. Smith c Fordham b Davidson	4			
D. R. Turner c Tooley b Perera	1	1/194 2/213 3/220	(8 wkts, 55 overs)	300
K. D. James c Speight b Scott	29	4/228 5/236 6/276		
M. D. Marshall b Perera	18	7/291 8/300		

†R. J. Parks and C. A. Connor did not bat.

Bowling: Davidson 11–0–53–1; Scott 11–2–47–1; Perera 11–1–52–2; Stephenson 9–0–48–1; Cann 11–0–67–1; Atherton 2–0–22–0.

Combined Universities

*J. P. Stephenson b Tremlett	24	M. J. Cann not out		13
M. A. Atherton b James	2			
A. Fordham c Parks b Tremlett	19	L-b 7, w 4, n-b 1		12
P. A. C. Bail run out	56			
N. Hussain not out	62	1/4 2/34 3/94	(5 wkts, 55 overs)	207
C. D. M. Tooley c Connor b Cowley	19	4/124 5/160		

†M. P. Speight, P. C. M. Perera, J. E. Davidson and A. M. G. Scott did not bat.

Bowling: Marshall 5–1–13–0; James 11–0–38–1; Connor 8–0–24–0; Tremlett 11–0–28–2; Cowley 11–0–41–1; Nicholas 8–0–54–0; Smith 1–0–2–0.

Umpires: A. A. Jones and M. J. Kitchen.

SOMERSET v ESSEX

At Taunton, May 2. Somerset won by 5 runs. Toss: Somerset.
Gold Award: M. D. Crowe.

Somerset

N. A. Felton run out	31	M. R. Davis run out		3
*P. M. Roebuck c and b Miller	52	A. N. Jones c Gooch b Pringle		0
J. J. E. Hardy c Gooch b Miller	8	N. A. Mallender run out		1
M. D. Crowe lbw b Page	70	L-b 5, w 3		8
R. J. Harden lbw b Miller	3			
V. J. Marks b Foster	12	1/66 2/82 3/107	(55 overs)	229
†N. D. Burns not out	41	4/133 5/163 6/209		
G. D. Rose run out	0	7/211 8/224 9/225		

Bowling: Lever 10–0–42–0; Foster 8–0–44–1; Page 8–2–22–1; Pringle 11–0–49–1; Miller 11–0–37–3; Gooch 7–0–30–0.

Essex

*G. A. Gooch c Crowe b Jones	0	N. A. Foster not out		37
C. Gladwin lbw b Davis	2	H. A. Page b Jones		23
B. R. Hardie run out	46	J. K. Lever not out		10
K. W. R. Fletcher lbw b Rose	18	L-b 4, w 2, n-b 1		7
D. R. Pringle lbw b Marks	37			—
A. W. Lilley b Mallender	24	1/0 2/10 3/44	(9 wkts, 55 overs)	224
G. Miller c Roebuck b Rose	19	4/101 5/108 6/142		
†D. E. East run out	1	7/146 8/157 9/205		

Bowling: Jones 10–2–41–2; Davis 7–1–23–1; Mallender 11–1–49–1; Rose 11–2–41–2; Marks 11–1–41–1; Crowe 5–0–25–0.

Umpires: D. G. L. Evans and R. Palmer.

HAMPSHIRE v MIDDLESEX

At Southampton, May 9. Hampshire won by nine wickets. Toss: Middlesex.
Gold Award: T. M. Tremlett.

Middlesex

A. J. T. Miller b Connor	1	N. F. Williams run out		5
W. N. Slack c Parks b Tremlett	16	S. P. Hughes not out		0
J. D. Carr c Nicholas b Tremlett	5			
C. T. Radley lbw b James	3	L-b 5, w 3, n-b 8		16
R. O. Butcher c Turner b James	50			—
†P. R. Downton not out	80	1/19 2/27 3/34	(8 wkts, 55 overs)	192
*J. E. Emburey b James	3	4/34 5/132 6/141		
P. H. Edmonds b Marshall	13	7/171 8/187		

W. W. Daniel did not bat.

Bowling: Marshall 11–2–30–1; Connor 11–1–51–1; Tremlett 11–3–25–2; James 11–0–31–3; Cowley 11–0–50–0.

Hampshire

C. G. Greenidge c Hughes b Edmonds	54
V. P. Terry not out	67
*M. C. J. Nicholas not out	59
L-b 4, w 2, n-b 7	13
	—
1/89	(1 wkt, 51.3 overs) 193

C. L. Smith, D. R. Turner, K. D. James, M. D. Marshall, N. G. Cowley, T. M. Tremlett, †R. J. Parks and C. A. Connor did not bat.

Bowling: Daniel 8–0–39–0; Williams 8–1–41–0; Hughes 11–0–49–0; Edmonds 11–1–27–1; Emburey 11–1–23–0; Carr 2–0–9–0; Radley 0.3–0–1–0.

Umpires: D. G. L. Evans and D. R. Shepherd.

SOMERSET v COMBINED UNIVERSITIES

At Taunton, May 9. Somerset won by 16 runs. Toss: Somerset. Mallender dismissed Cann, Speight and Crawley to become the eighth player, and the first for Somerset, to take a hat-trick in the competition.
Gold Award: V. J. Marks.

Somerset

N. A. Felton c Speight b Davidson	1	G. D. Rose b Barry	2
*P. M. Roebuck c Crawley b Davidson	120	A. N. Jones not out	4
J. J. E. Hardy c Atherton b Barry	20		
M. D. Crowe c Hussain b Barry	1	B 1, l-b 3, w 1, n-b 3	8
R. J. Harden run out	13		
V. J. Marks c Speight b Davidson	70	1/9 2/51 3/61 4/96 (7 wkts, 55 overs)	249
†N. D. Burns not out	10	5/231 6/231 7/236	

M. R. Davis and N. A. Mallender did not bat.

Bowling: Scott 11–1–37–0; Davidson 11–0–64–3; Barry 11–0–58–3; Cann 11–0–43–0; Crawley 11–0–43–0.

Combined Universities

*J. P. Stephenson c Marks b Crowe	75	T. M. Barry not out	3
M. A. Atherton c and b Davis	57	J. E. Davidson not out	3
M. J. Cann c Crowe b Mallender	46		
P. A. C. Bail c Roebuck b Rose	6	L-b 10, w 6, n-b 4	20
N. Hussain c Crowe	17		
C. D. M. Tooley run out	1	1/127 2/171 3/177 (8 wkts, 55 overs)	233
†M. P. Speight b Mallender	5	4/210 5/217 6/223	
M. A. Crawley b Mallender	0	7/223 8/228	

A. M. G. Scott did not bat.

Bowling: Jones 7–2–29–0; Mallender 11–1–44–3; Rose 9–1–53–1; Davis 7–0–30–1; Marks 11–2–25–0; Crowe 10–0–42–2.

Umpires: K. J. Lyons and A. G. T. Whitehead.

ESSEX v MIDDLESEX

At Chelmsford, May 12. Essex won by eight wickets. Toss: Essex.
Gold Award: G. A. Gooch (for a record thirteenth time).

Middlesex

M. A. Roseberry lbw b Foster	2	N. F. Williams lbw b Page	12
W. N. Slack lbw b Lever	0	S. P. Hughes not out	2
*M. W. Gatting lbw b Foster	0	W. W. Daniel b Page	17
C. T. Radley b Page	30	L-b 5, w 9	14
R. O. Butcher c Gooch b Lever	3		
†P. R. Downton c Miller b Gooch	19	1/2 2/2 3/3 4/10 (43.4 overs)	113
J. E. Emburey c East b Lever	0	5/53 6/54 7/74	
P. H. Edmonds c Foster b Gooch	14	8/91 9/94	

Bowling: Foster 9–0–13–2; Lever 11–3–31–3; Page 9.4–2–26–3; Pringle 6–0–19–0; Gooch 8–1–19–2.

Essex

*G. A. Gooch not out	53	
C. Gladwin b Hughes	24	
B. R. Hardie c Downton b Hughes	9	
K. W. R. Fletcher not out	13	
L-b 2, w 2, n-b 11	15	

1/79 2/96 (2 wkts, 25.1 overs) 114

D. R. Pringle, A. W. Lilley, G. Miller, †D. E. East, N. A. Foster, H. A. Page and J. K. Lever did not bat.

Bowling: Daniel 8–0–49–0; Williams 8–0–28–0; Gatting 5–1–17–0; Hughes 4.1–1–18–2.

Umpires: B. J. Meyer and K. E. Palmer.

HAMPSHIRE v SOMERSET

At Southampton, May 12. Somerset won by 71 runs and qualified for the quarter-finals. Toss: Hampshire. The third-wicket stand of 269 unbroken between Roebuck and Crowe was a record for that wicket in any domestic limited-overs competition. Somerset's total and Crowe's 155 not out, including five sixes and twelve fours, were records for the county in the Benson and Hedges Cup.

Gold Award: M. D. Crowe.

Somerset

N. A. Felton c James b Tremlett	......	11
*P. M. Roebuck not out	....	110
J. J. E. Hardy c Terry b Tremlett	.....	19
M. D. Crowe not out	....	155
L-b 11, w 10, n-b 3	....	24

1/27 2/50   (2 wkts, 55 overs) 319

R. J. Harden, V. J. Marks, †N. D. Burns, G. D. Rose, N. A. Mallender, A. N. Jones and G. V. Palmer did not bat.

Bowling: Marshall 11-1-42-0; Connor 11-2-72-0; Tremlett 11-1-60-2; James 10-0-61-0; Cowley 7-0-37-0; Nicholas 5-0-36-0.

Hampshire

C. G. Greenidge c Felton b Rose	.....	17	T. M. Tremlett c Hardy b Palmer	.....	10
V. P. Terry c Burns b Jones	....	63	†R. J. Parks c Roebuck b Marks	.....	3
*M. C. J. Nicholas c Burns b Crowe	..	26	C. A. Connor not out	....	0
D. R. Turner c Rose b Marks	.....	93	L-b 12, w 7	....	19
C. L. Smith c Burns b Jones	....	2			
K. D. James b Rose	.....	5	1/28 2/86 3/149	(49 overs)	248
M. D. Marshall b Rose	....	0	4/159 5/178 6/178		
N. G. Cowley b Mallender	....	10	7/199 8/240 9/248		

Bowling: Jones 8-0-34-2; Mallender 9-2-37-1; Rose 11-1-35-3; Palmer 7-0-36-1; Marks 7-0-48-2; Crowe 7-0-46-1.

Umpires: A. A. Jones and D. R. Shepherd.

ESSEX v HAMPSHIRE

At Chelmsford, May 14, 15. Hampshire won by 86 runs. Toss: Essex. Essex recorded their lowest total in the competition, while Gooch failed to score for the sixth time in ten innings. Close of play: Hampshire 186.

Gold Award: S. J. W. Andrew.

Hampshire

C. G. Greenidge c Lilley b Foster	.....	25	T. M. Tremlett lbw b Foster	....	1
V. P. Terry lbw b Topley	.....	23	†R. J. Parks lbw b Foster	....	0
*M. C. J. Nicholas c Gooch b Topley	.	3	S. J. W. Andrew not out	....	0
D. R. Turner c East b Gooch	....	28	L-b 10, w 21, n-b 4	....	35
C. L. Smith b Topley	....	2			
K. D. James c East b Gooch	....	8	1/54 2/61 3/65	(50.2 overs)	186
M. D. Marshall lbw b Foster	....	34	4/75 5/102 6/120		
N. G. Cowley c Foster b Gooch	......	27	7/184 8/184 9/185		

Bowling: Foster 10.2-1-32-4; Topley 11-3-29-3; Gooch 11-3-36-3; Page 9-0-52-0; Pringle 9-2-27-0.

Essex

*G. A. Gooch b Marshall	0	†D. E. East c Marshall b James	32
C. Gladwin lbw b Andrew	0	N. A. Foster c Parks b Marshall	29
B. R. Hardie c Greenidge b Marshall	0	T. D. Topley not out	3
K. W. R. Fletcher c Nicholas b Andrew	0	B 4, l-b 1, w 7, n-b 12	24
D. R. Pringle c Terry b Andrew	5		
A. W. Lilley c Parks b Andrew	1	1/5 2/6 3/7 4/12	(30.1 overs) 100
H. A. Page b Marshall	0	5/15 6/20 7/21	
G. Miller c Turner b Andrew	6	8/39 9/84	

Bowling: Marshall 10.1–0–33–4; Andrew 9–3–24–5; Tremlett 7–2–18–0; James 4–0–20–1.

Umpires: J. Birkenshaw and R. A. White.

MIDDLESEX v COMBINED UNIVERSITIES

At Lord's, May 14, 15. No result. Toss: Combined Universities. This fixture was unique in a knockout competition, for the teams began three matches yet could not finish. The first day was lost. A 54-over-a-side game achieved only fourteen overs in which Combined Universities scored 31 for two. In the afternoon a 25 overs-a-side game managed seventeen overs with Middlesex, put in, making 113 for one (Slack 57 not out). The last resort was the minimum ten-overs dash, but rain arrived again in the fifth over.

Middlesex

*M. W. Gatting b Cann	11
W. N. Slack not out	22
R. O. Butcher not out	2
B 3, l-b 5	8

1/40   (1 wkt, 4.2 overs) 43

M. A. Roseberry, C. T. Radley, †P. R. Downton, J. E. Emburey, A. Needham, N. F. Williams, S. P. Hughes and W. W. Daniel did not bat.

Bowling: Scott 2–0–18–0; Davidson 1–0–14–0; Cann 1–0–1–1; Crawley 0.2–0–2–0.

Combined Universities

*J. P. Stephenson, P. A. C. Bail, A. Fordham, C. D. M. Tooley, N. Hussain, T. M. Barry, M. J. Cann, †M. P. Speight, M. A. Crawley, J. E. Davidson and A. M. G. Scott.

Umpires: R. Palmer and P. B. Wight.

COMBINED UNIVERSITIES v ESSEX

At Cambridge, May 16. Essex won by three wickets. Toss: Essex. Gooch became the first player to score 3,000 runs in the Benson and Hedges Cup.
Gold Award: B. R. Hardie.

Combined Universities

*J. P. Stephenson lbw b Pringle	20	T. M. Barry b Pringle	13
M. A. Atherton c Foster b Topley	28	J. E. Davidson c Hardie b Lever	11
A. Fordham run out	14	A. M. G. Scott not out	2
P. A. C. Bail c and b Miller	6	B 8, l-b 7, w 4, n-b 1	20
N. Hussain lbw b Foster	8		
M. J. Cann c East b Miller	1	1/40 2/63 3/68	(54.5 overs) 154
†M. P. Speight c Gooch b Lever	18	4/68 5/83 6/92	
M. A. Crawley b Pringle	13	7/124 8/127 9/151	

Bowling: Foster 11–3–25–1; Lever 9–1–29–2; Topley 10–4–19–1; Pringle 10.5–1–32–3; Miller 11–4–24–2; Gooch 3–1–10–0.

Essex

*G. A. Gooch b Scott	16	†D. E. East c Crawley b Stephenson ... 3
C. Gladwin b Scott	1	N. A. Foster not out	10
B. R. Hardie not out	70	L-b 5, w 6, n-b 1	12
K. W. R. Fletcher b Barry	39		
D. R. Pringle c and b Barry	0	1/10 2/27 3/123 (7 wkts, 54.2 overs) 157
A. W. Lilley b Barry	3	4/123 5/129
G. Miller run out	3	6/137 7/140

T. D. Topley and J. K. Lever did not bat.

Bowling: Scott 11–3–32–2; Davidson 10.2–1–25–0; Cann 4–0–16–0; Barry 11–0–26–3; Crawley 11–3–26–0; Stephenson 7–0–27–1.

Umpires: J. H. Hampshire and K. J. Lyons.

MIDDLESEX v SOMERSET

At Lord's, May 16. Middlesex won by 15 runs. Toss: Somerset.
Gold Award: W. N. Slack.

Middlesex

W. N. Slack c Hardy b Rose	110	N. F. Williams c Burns b Jones	1
M. A. Roseberry b Mallender	6	S. P. Hughes not out	6
*M. W. Gatting st Burns b Marks	31	A. R. C. Fraser lbw b Mallender	4
C. T. Radley run out	0	B 1, l-b 9, w 8, n-b 2	20
R. O. Butcher b Crowe	22		
†P. R. Downton c Burns b Jones	51	1/12 2/99 3/101 (54.2 overs) 270
A. Needham run out	5	4/153 5/201 6/242
J. E. Emburey c Hardy b Mallender	14	7/242 8/244 9/264

Bowling: Jones 10–1–56–2; Mallender 10.2–1–47–3; Davis 7–0–32–0; Rose 11–0–55–1; Marks 9–3–40–1; Crowe 7–0–30–1.

Somerset

N. A. Felton c Downton b Hughes	8	A. N. Jones not out	2
*P. M. Roebuck hit wkt b Hughes	1	M. R. Davis lbw b Hughes	4
J. J. E. Hardy run out	19		
M. D. Crowe c and b Williams	13	B 2, l-b 6, w 14, n-b 5	27
R. J. Harden c Fraser b Gatting	35		
V. J. Marks b Gatting	53	1/13 2/15 3/52 (9 wkts, 55 overs) 255
†N. D. Burns b Hughes	51	4/52 5/130 6/170
G. D. Rose run out	42	7/248 8/251 9/255

N. A. Mallender did not bat.

Bowling: Williams 9–1–24–1; Hughes 7–0–34–4; Fraser 11–1–37–0; Needham 11–0–38–0; Emburey 9.5–0–76–0; Gatting 7.1–0–38–2.

Umpires: M. J. Kitchen and B. J. Meyer.

GROUP D

KENT v MINOR COUNTIES

At Canterbury, May 2. Kent won by 36 runs. Toss: Kent.
Gold Award: P. A. Todd.

Kent

M. R. Benson not out	107	†S. A. Marsh lbw b Green	1
S. G. Hinks b Greensword	63	L-b 7, w 7, n-b 4	18
C. J. Tavaré lbw b Merry	34		
*C. S. Cowdrey b Bunting	39	1/109 2/199 3/258 (5 wkts, 55 overs) 266	
G. R. Cowdrey c Roope b Green	4	4/263 5/266	

N. R. Taylor, C. Penn, A. P. Igglesden, D. L. Underwood and D. J. M. Kelleher did not bat.

Bowling: Green 8–1–54–2; Bunting 5–0–38–1; Greensword 11–2–28–1; Merry 11–0–51–1; Herbert 9–0–47–0; Plumb 11–0–41–0.

Minor Counties

S. R. Atkinson lbw b Igglesden	0	R. Herbert run out	7
*S. G. Plumb c Igglesden		R. C. Green not out	8
b C. S. Cowdrey	13	W. G. Merry not out	1
P. A. Todd c Kelleher b Hinks	87	L-b 22, w 2, n-b 9	33
G. R. J. Roope lbw b Kelleher	0		
S. P. Henderson c Penn b C. S. Cowdrey	18	1/2 2/35 3/56 (8 wkts, 55 overs) 230	
†M. A. Garnham c Tavaré b Underwood	17	4/89 5/130 6/176	
S. Greensword c Taylor b Penn	46	7/193 8/228	

R. A. Bunting did not bat.

Bowling: Igglesden 5–1–26–1; Penn 11–1–52–1; C. S. Cowdrey 11–0–40–2; Kelleher 11–1–30–1; Underwood 11–0–29–1; Hinks 4–0–26–1; Taylor 2–1–5–0.

Umpires: B. J. Meyer and P. B. Wight.

GLAMORGAN v SUSSEX

At Swansea, May 4. Glamorgan won by four wickets. Toss: Sussex. The match was rescheduled from May 2 because Swansea were appearing in the Welsh Rugby Union Cup final that day.

Gold Award: R. C. Ontong.

Sussex

A. M. Green c Metson b Barwick	7	*†I. J. Gould not out	17
R. I. Alikhan b Barwick	71	A. C. S. Pigott not out	0
P. W. G. Parker b Ontong	24	B 1, l-b 5, n-b 3	9
A. P. Wells b Barwick	72		
G. S. le Roux c Shastri b Holmes	19	1/20 2/67 3/183 (6 wkts, 55 overs) 224	
C. M. Wells c Ontong b Holmes	5	4/184 5/200 6/223	

D. K. Standing, C. I. O. Ricketts and I. C. Waring did not bat.

Bowling: Thomas 11–2–43–0; Barwick 11–3–36–3; Derrick 4–1–19–0; Ontong 11–0–49–1; Shastri 11–1–33–0; Holmes 7–0–38–2.

Glamorgan

J. A. Hopkins lbw b Pigott	1	M. P. Maynard not out	41
*H. Morris c Alikhan b Pigott	6	J. G. Thomas not out	2
A. R. Butcher b le Roux	5	B 5, l-b 4, w 3, n-b 2	14
R. J. Shastri c le Roux b Ricketts	28		
R. C. Ontong run out	72	1/6 2/9 3/15 (6 wkts, 54.4 overs) 225	
G. C. Holmes c Standing b Pigott	56	4/87 5/147 6/220	

†C. P. Metson, J. Derrick and S. R. Barwick did not bat.

Bowling: le Roux 10.4–2–44–1; Pigott 10–2–45–3; C. M. Wells 11–2–35–0; Waring 11–1–55–0; Ricketts 11–1–30–1; Standing 1–0–7–0.

Umpires: J. H. Harris and D. R. Shepherd.

SURREY v KENT

At The Oval, May 9. Surrey won by 6 runs. Toss: Surrey.
Gold Award: M. A. Lynch.

Surrey

G. S. Clinton c G. R. Cowdrey b Penn	16	D. J. Thomas not out	8
D. M. Smith c and b Baptiste	69		
M. A. Lynch not out	112	L-b 10, w 2, n-b 1	13
T. E. Jesty run out	6		
†C. J. Richards c Taylor b Penn	18	1/34 2/166 3/193 (5 wkts, 55 overs) 242
*I. A. Greig b Penn	0	4/232 5/233

D. M. Ward, C. K. Bullen, M. A. Feltham and S. T. Clarke did not bat.

Bowling: Igglesden 11–1–41–0; Baptiste 11–0–37–1; Penn 9–0–53–3; C. S. Cowdrey 11–0–52–0; Underwood 11–1–40–0; Hinks 2–0–9–0.

Kent

M. R. Benson b Greig	29	E. A. E. Baptiste not out	14
S. G. Hinks c Smith b Feltham	24	C. Penn not out	2
N. R. Taylor b Bullen	15	B 3, l-b 7, w 10, n-b 3	23
C. J. Tavaré c Richards b Feltham	33		
*C. S. Cowdrey b Clarke	52	1/61 2/66 3/96 (7 wkts, 55 overs) 236
G. R. Cowdrey c Feltham b Greig	40	4/119 5/210
†S. A. Marsh run out	4	6/215 7/221

A. P. Igglesden and D. L. Underwood did not bat.

Bowling: Clarke 11–2–43–1; Thomas 11–1–44–0; Feltham 11–0–41–2; Bullen 11–1–31–1; Greig 11–0–67–2.

Umpires: M. J. Kitchen and R. Palmer.

SUSSEX v MINOR COUNTIES

At Hove, May 9. Sussex won by 111 runs. Toss: Sussex.
Gold Award: C. M. Wells.

Sussex

R. I. Alikhan c Bunting b Greensword	54	D. A. Reeve not out	4
A. P. Wells c Herbert b Green	0		
P. W. G. Parker c Roope b Greensword	31	B 4, l-b 4, w 5, n-b 5	18
C. M. Wells not out	101		
*I. J. Gould c Bunting b Green	65	1/0 2/71 3/125 (5 wkts, 55 overs) 285
G. S. le Roux c Henderson b Green	12	4/237 5/268

†P. Moores, A. M. Babington, C. I. O. Ricketts and S. D. Myles did not bat.

Bowling: Bunting 8–2–46–0; Green 11–0–67–3; Greensword 11–3–34–2; Merry 8–1–39–0; Herbert 10–0–53–0; Plumb 7–0–38–0.

Minor Counties

S. R. Atkinson lbw b Babington	......	20
*S. G. Plumb c Moores b Babington	...	0
P. A. Todd run out	....	0
G. R. J. Roope b Ricketts	....	33
S. P. Henderson c Ricketts b Babington		51
†M. A. Garnham b Babington	....	7
S. Greensword c C. M. Wells		
b A. P. Wells	.	19
R. Herbert c Myles b Parker	....	9

R. C. Green c C. M. Wells b Gould	...	14
W. G. Merry lbw b Parker	....	0
R. A. Bunting not out	....	0
B 3, l-b 11, w 3, n-b 4	....	21
1/6 2/6 3/41	(54.2 overs)	174
4/99 5/123 6/133		
7/150 8/174 9/174		

Bowling: le Roux 6–0–14–0; Babington 11–3–30–4; Reeve 6–1–14–0; C. M. Wells 11–1–31–0; Ricketts 11–1–37–1; Myles 4–0–11–0; A. P. Wells 4–0–20–1; Parker 1–0–3–2; Gould 0.2–0–0–1.

Umpires: D. J. Constant and N. T. Plews.

KENT v SUSSEX

At Canterbury, May 12, 13. Kent won by 106 runs. Toss: Kent. Close of play: Kent 99-3 (32 overs) (S. G. Hinks 56*, C. S. Cowdrey 11*).

Gold Award: C. S. Cowdrey.

Kent

M. R. Benson c Gould b le Roux	.....	7
S. G. Hinks b C. M. Wells	....	85
D. G. Aslett b Pigott b Reeve	....	15
C. J. Tavaré b Reeve	....	1
*C. S. Cowdrey b Babington	....	21
G. R. Cowdrey st Gould b A. P. Wells .		69
E. A. E. Baptiste c Green b le Roux	..	21
†S. A. Marsh st Gould b Reeve	....	2

C. Penn lbw b Reeve	....	0
A. P. Igglesden not out	....	5
D. L. Underwood not out	....	3
B 3, l-b 3, w 3, n-b 5	......	14
		—
1/18 2/65 3/68	(9 wkts, 55 overs)	243
4/129 5/146 6/226		
7/230 8/230 9/234		

Bowling: Pigott 9–1–30–0; le Roux 11–1–45–2; C. M. Wells 11–1–42–1; Reeve 11–2–42–4; Babington 11–0–58–1; A. P. Wells 2–0–20–1.

Sussex

R. I. Alikhan c Marsh b C. S. Cowdrey		12
A. M. Green b C. S. Cowdrey	......	32
P. W. G. Parker b Igglesden	....	7
A. P. Wells b C. S. Cowdrey	....	12
C. M. Wells st Marsh b Underwood	..	10
N. J. Lenham b C. S. Cowdrey	......	0
*†I. J. Gould b Penn	....	3
G. S. le Roux c Igglesden b Underwood		2

D. A. Reeve not out	....	30
A. C. S. Pigott c Benson b Underwood .		12
A. M. Babington c Tavaré b Underwood		1
B 4, l-b 5, w 5, n-b 2	......	16
		—
1/25 2/35 3/65 4/74	(45.2 overs)	137
5/74 6/83 7/86 8/91 9/126		

Bowling: Baptiste 7–1–24–0; Igglesden 7–0–25–1; C. S. Cowdrey 11–4–14–4; Penn 9–1–21–1; Underwood 8.2–1–28–4; Hinks 3–0–16–0.

Umpires: B. Dudleston and J. A. Jameson.

SURREY v GLAMORGAN

At The Oval, May 12, 13. Surrey won by 48 runs. Toss: Glamorgan. Close of play: Glamorgan 59-2 (25 overs) (A. R. Butcher 33*, R. C. Ontong 10*).

Gold Award: S. T. Clarke.

Surrey

G. S. Clinton c Ontong b Holmes	71	*I. A. Greig c Metson b Thomas	10
N. J. Falkner c Derrick b Ontong	58		
M. A. Lynch c Morris b Holmes	28	L-b 13	13
D. M. Smith not out	29		
T. E. Jesty b van Zyl	4	1/123 2/154 3/171 (5 wkts, 55 overs) 241	
†C. J. Richards not out	28	4/179 5/200	

C. K. Bullen, D. J. Thomas, M. A. Feltham and S. T. Clarke did not bat.

Bowling: Thomas 11-0-50-1; van Zyl 11-2-45-1; Barwick 11-0-49-0; Derrick 6-1-20-0; Ontong 11-0-47-1; Holmes 5-1-17-2.

Glamorgan

J. A. Hopkins c Richards b Clarke	0	†C. P. Metson b Clarke	0
*H. Morris c Lynch b Thomas	12	C. J. P. G. van Zyl b Clarke	5
A. R. Butcher lbw b Clarke	65	S. R. Barwick c Bullen b Greig	1
R. C. Ontong run out	50	L-b 13, w 5, n-b 1	19
G. C. Holmes c sub b Greig	28		
M. P. Maynard run out	5	1/0 2/26 3/133 (51.1 overs) 193	
J. G. Thomas c Feltham b Greig	6	4/168 5/171 6/184	
J. Derrick not out	2	7/184 8/184 9/192	

Bowling: Clarke 9-3-25-4; Thomas 11-2-38-1; Feltham 9-1-33-0; Bullen 11-0-48-0; Jesty 8-0-23-0; Greig 3.1-0-13-3.

Umpires: J. H. Hampshire and R. Palmer.

MINOR COUNTIES v GLAMORGAN

At Christ Church College Ground, Oxford, May 14, 15. Minor Counties won by seven wickets. Toss: Minor Counties. Todd, whose innings was the highest in the competition by a Minor Counties player, reached his fifty and his hundred with a six, and in all hit seven sixes and six fours as Minor Counties achieved their fourth win ever in the competition. Close of play: Minor Counties 11-0 (4 overs) (S. R. Atkinson 6*, R. Herbert 5*).

Gold Award: P. A. Todd.

Glamorgan

J. A. Hopkins c Todd b Busby	0	G. C. Holmes run out	20
*H. Morris c Garnham b Bunting	20	M. P. Maynard not out	30
A. R. Butcher b Bunting	31	B 1, l-b 2, w 11, n-b 3	17
R. J. Shastri st Garnham b Greensword	8		
R. C. Ontong not out	77	1/1 2/50 3/68 (6 wkts, 55 overs) 220	
J. G. Thomas c Busby b Greensword	17	4/79 5/103 6/144	

†C. P. Metson, S. R. Barwick and I. Smith did not bat.

Bowling: Green 11-3-43-0; Busby 11-4-35-1; Bunting 11-0-43-2; Greensword 11-2-29-2; Plumb 6-0-37-0; Roope 5-0-30-0.

Minor Counties

S. R. Atkinson lbw b Barwick	18	S. P. Henderson not out	6
R. Herbert c Shastri b Holmes	24	B 3, l-b 4, w 3, n-b 5	15
P. A. Todd b Smith	107		
G. R. J. Roope not out	53	1/31 2/105 3/214 (3 wkts, 52.5 overs) 223	

*S. G. Plumb, †M. A. Garnham, S. Greensword, R. C. Green, R. N. Busby and R. A. Bunting did not bat.

Bowling: Thomas 7.5-1-42-0; Barwick 9-2-24-1; Shastri 11-0-29-0; Ontong 10-1-58-0; Holmes 11-1-42-1; Smith 4-0-21-1.

Umpires: D. G. L. Evans and A. G. T. Whitehead.

SUSSEX v SURREY

At Hove, May 14, 15. Surrey won by 20 runs in a match of twelve overs a side after a match of 23 overs a side had been abandoned (Surrey 58-5) following a shower. Toss: Sussex. There was no play on the first day.

Gold Award: M. A. Feltham.

Surrey

M. A. Lynch lbw b Babington	11	N. J. Falkner not out	1
D. M. Smith c le Roux b Heseltine	18		
†C. J. Richards c Green b Babington	9	L-b 4, w 2, n-b 4	10
*I. A. Greig b Heseltine	3		—
T. E. Jesty c A. P. Wells b le Roux	9	1/16 2/40 3/45 (7 wkts, 12 overs)	104
D. J. Thomas run out	22	4/45 5/63	
M. A. Feltham c Gould b Reeve	21	6/103 7/104	

G. S. Clinton, S. T. Clarke and M. P. Bicknell did not bat.

Bowling: Babington 3–0–30–2; C. M. Wells 2–0–12–0; Heseltine 2–0–12–2; le Roux 3–0–23–1; Reeve 2–0–23–1.

Sussex

A. M. Green b Thomas	7	N. J. Lenham not out	18
A. P. Wells c Thomas b Bicknell	2	D. A. Reeve not out	4
P. W. G. Parker lbw b Bicknell	1	L-b 6, w 8	14
C. M. Wells c Greig b Feltham	13		—
*I. J. Gould c Thomas b Feltham	9	1/9 2/12 3/15 (6 wkts, 12 overs)	84
G. S. le Roux c sub b Greig	16	4/39 5/39 6/73	

A. M. Babington, P. A. W. Heseltine and †P. Moores did not bat.

Bowling: Thomas 3–0–15–1; Bicknell 3–0–15–2; Feltham 2–0–15–2; Greig 2–0–16–1; Clarke 2–0–17–0.

Umpires: B. Dudleston and J. A. Jameson.

GLAMORGAN v KENT

At Cardiff, May 16. Kent won by 14 runs. Toss: Glamorgan. Glamorgan's total was their highest in the Benson and Hedges Cup, and Kent's was the highest by any team on a Welsh ground in the competition. Morris's innings was the highest by a Glamorgan player in the competition.

Gold Award: H. Morris.

Kent

M. R. Benson st Metson b Shastri	61	E. A. E. Baptiste not out	3
S. G. Hinks b Ontong	53		
D. G. Aslett b Base	41	L-b 9, w 5, n-b 1	15
C. J. Tavaré not out	61		—
*C. S. Cowdrey b Thomas	22	1/106 2/140 3/185 (5 wkts, 55 overs)	285
G. R. Cowdrey b Thomas	29	4/219 5/279	

C. Penn, †S. A. Marsh, K. B. S. Jarvis and D. L. Underwood did not bat.

Bowling: Ontong 11–1–33–1; Shastri 11–1–55–1; Thomas 11–0–67–2; Barwick 10–0–62–0; Base 9–0–43–1; Smith 3–0–16–0.

Glamorgan

J. A. Hopkins c Aslett b C. S. Cowdrey	25	†C. P. Metson b C. S. Cowdrey		7
*H. Morris b Baptiste	115	S. J. Base b C. S. Cowdrey		12
A. R. Butcher c Marsh b Penn	7	S. R. Barwick not out		8
R. J. Shastri c Aslett b Underwood	14	L-b 10, w 3, n-b 2		15
R. C. Ontong c Aslett b Underwood	11			
M. P. Maynard c Penn b Underwood	25	1/40 2/65 3/103	(54.4 overs)	271
J. G. Thomas b Hinks	32	4/127 5/184 6/228		
I. Smith c Underwood b C. S. Cowdrey	0	7/237 8/244 9/252		

Bowling: Penn 11–0–46–1; Underwood 11–1–50–3; C. S. Cowdrey 5.4–0–52–4; Jarvis 7–0–27–0; Hinks 9–0–49–1; Baptiste 11–1–37–1.

Umpires: R. Julian and K. E. Palmer.

MINOR COUNTIES v SURREY

At Christ Church College Ground, Oxford, May 16. Surrey won by seven wickets. Toss: Surrey.

Gold Award: T. E. Jesty.

Minor Counties

S. R. Atkinson c Richards b Thomas	10	S. Greensword lbw b Feltham		2
R. Herbert b Bullen	24	R. C. Green not out		9
P. A. Todd c Richards b Bicknell	5			
G. R. J. Roope c Smith b Bicknell	1	L-b 21, w 2		23
S. P. Henderson c Bullen b Feltham	24			
*S. G. Plumb run out	14	1/22 2/31 3/41 4/74	(7 wkts, 55 overs)	150
†M. A. Garnham not out	38	5/76 6/104 7/111		

W. G. Merry and R. A. Bunting did not bat.

Bowling: Clarke 11–2–26–0; Thomas 11–1–28–1; Bicknell 11–2–28–2; Feltham 11–3–18–2; Bullen 11–3–29–1.

Surrey

G. S. Clinton c Herbert b Bunting	65	†C. J. Richards not out		0
N. J. Falkner b Green	0	L-b 4, w 2, n-b 2		8
D. M. Smith c Roope b Herbert	23			
T. E. Jesty not out	57	1/1 2/53 3/149	(3 wkts, 35.2 overs)	153

*I. A. Greig, C. K. Bullen, D. J. Thomas, M. A. Feltham, S. T. Clarke and M. P. Bicknell did not bat.

Bowling: Green 4–0–17–1; Merry 4–2–11–0; Bunting 10–2–40–1; Greensword 5–2–13–0; Herbert 6.2–0–43–1; Plumb 6–1–25–0.

Umpires: J. H. Harris and A. A. Jones.

QUARTER-FINALS

GLOUCESTERSHIRE v KENT

At Bristol, May 27. Kent won by one wicket. Toss: Gloucestershire. Kent's tenth-wicket pair, Kelleher and Underwood, scampered a bye to the wicket-keeper off the last ball to decide a thrilling match. Kent had their task under control while the Cowdrey brothers were together for the fifth wicket, but they lost their way dramatically and 6 runs were needed from the last over with three wickets remaining. When the dismissals of Penn and Marsh left the last pair to make 5 from two balls, Underwood smote the penultimate ball from Lawrence for four. With limited bowling resources and Underwood hit out of the attack after five overs, Kent owed much to Chris Cowdrey's shrewd captaincy for having an attainable target.

Gold Award: C. S. Cowdrey.

Gloucestershire

A. W. Stovold c Kelleher	
b C. S. Cowdrey .	9
A. J. Wright b Hinks	58
C. W. J. Athey lbw b Baptiste	61
P. Bainbridge c Marsh b Penn	0
K. M. Curran not out	40
J. W. Lloyds b Penn	36
M. W. Alleyne run out	5

†R. C. Russell run out 11
C. A. Walsh not out 2

      B 1, l-b 14, w 12, n-b 1 28
                       —

1/28 2/136 3/138   (7 wkts, 55 overs) 250
4/158 5/210
6/222 7/247

*D. A. Graveney and D. V. Lawrence did not bat.

Bowling: Baptiste 11–2–34–1; Kelleher 11–0–36–0; C. S. Cowdrey 11–2–43–1; Penn 11–0–52–2; Underwood 5–0–45–0; Hinks 6–0–25–1.

Kent

M. R. Benson c Russell b Curran	34
S. G. Hinks run out	20
D. G. Aslett run out	56
C. J. Tavaré b Walsh	39
*C. S. Cowdrey c Russell b Lawrence	37
G. R. Cowdrey c Lawrence b Bainbridge	18
E. A. E. Baptiste c Lawrence	
b Bainbridge .	3
†S. A. Marsh run out	6

C. Penn c Athey b Lawrence 0
D. J. M. Kelleher not out 0
D. L. Underwood not out 4

      B 5, l-b 19, w 3, n-b 7 34
                       —

1/63 2/80 3/158   (9 wkts, 55 overs) 251
4/181 5/228 6/239
7/239 8/246 9/246

Bowling: Walsh 11–0–30–1; Lawrence 11–0–62–2; Bainbridge 11–1–44–2; Curran 11–0–35–1; Alleyne 7–0–32–0; Graveney 3–0–21–0; Lloyds 1–0–3–0.

Umpires: M. J. Kitchen and A. G. T. Whitehead.

SOMERSET v NORTHAMPTONSHIRE

At Taunton, May 27. Northamptonshire won by 29 runs. Toss: Northamptonshire. Following a brisk start, Northamptonshire lost four wickets in eighteen overs for 48 runs but were rescued by Williams, who hit two sixes and six fours in 93 balls. On a slightly grassy pitch in dull weather, Capel's three wickets in thirteen deliveries immediately undermined Somerset. Stoutly though Hardy, Harden, Marks and Burns batted, Northamptonshire's bowlers never let Somerset back into the match.

Gold Award: R. G. Williams.

Northamptonshire

*G. Cook c and b G. D. Rose	33
W. Larkins c Burns b Jones	5
R. J. Bailey c Harden b G. D. Rose	36
A. J. Lamb lbw b Crowe	0
D. J. Capel c Crowe b Marks	14
R. G. Williams c Marks b Mallender	72
D. J. Wild c Harden b Marks	23
†D. Ripley b Jones	4

N. G. B. Cook not out 2
W. W. Davis c Harden b Mallender 4
A. Walker c Crowe b Jones 0
      B 5, l-b 5, w 7, n-b 2 19

1/6 2/77 3/82   (54.2 overs) 212
4/86 5/125 6/172
7/204 8/206 9/211

Bowling: Jones 10.2–1–33–3; Mallender 11–1–43–2; Palmer 3–0–22–0; G. D. Rose 8–0–26–2; Crowe 11–0–43–1; Marks 11–2–35–2.

Somerset

N. A. Felton c G. Cook b Capel	10
B. C. Rose b Capel	0
J. J. E. Hardy c Capel b Wild	35
M. D. Crowe lbw b Capel	2
R. J. Harden b Walker	23
*V. J. Marks run out	37
†N. D. Burns not out	43
G. D. Rose c Wild b Capel	13

G. V. Palmer run out 4
N. A. Mallender lbw b Walker 0
A. N. Jones c Walker b Wild 8
      L-b 3, w 2, n-b 3 8

1/10 2/13 3/15   (50.5 overs) 183
4/51 5/99 6/149
7/149 8/160 9/161

Bowling: Davis 9–1–27–0; Capel 11–2–38–4; Walker 9–1–21–2; Williams 5–0–23–0; Wild 10.5–0–46–2; N. G. B. Cook 6–0–25–0.

Umpires: D. J. Constant and N. T. Plews.

SURREY v WORCESTERSHIRE

At The Oval, May 27. Surrey won by seven wickets. Toss: Worcestershire. Surrey's victory was a personal triumph for Smith, who had returned to The Oval after three seasons at Worcester. His fine century (one six, eight fours) was made in spite of a lingering back injury and, with Jesty, he removed Worcestershire from the competition with some ease. Worcestershire's 233 never looked sufficient on an excellent pitch, especially as Curtis and Hick had given evidence of its benefits in their stand of 106 for the second wicket in 28 overs. When they dismissed Bicknell, Stewart and Lynch, the last-mentioned two in the same over from Newport, Worcestershire were still in contention, but Smith was determined to make it his day. To add to Worcestershire's woes, they were fined for failing to achieve the required over-rate.

Gold Award: D. M. Smith.

Worcestershire

T. S. Curtis c Richards b Clarke	78	N. V. Radford b Clarke		0
M. J. Weston lbw b Clarke	7	P. J. Newport not out		2
G. A. Hick b Jesty	52	L-b 10, w 8, n-b 1		19
D. B. D'Oliveira c Greig b Jesty	11			
I. T. Botham c Bicknell b Bullen	5	1/11 2/117 3/135	(8 wkts, 55 overs)	233
*P. A. Neale c Bullen b Feltham	39	4/144 5/190 6/221		
†S. J. Rhodes c and b Clarke	20	7/229 8/233		

A. P. Pridgeon and G. R. Dilley did not bat.

Bowling: Clarke 11–1–47–4; Thomas 9–0–30–0; Feltham 9–0–52–1; Greig 4–1–16–0; Bullen 11–0–34–1; Jesty 11–0–44–2.

Surrey

D. J. Bicknell b Botham	17	T. E. Jesty not out		85
D. M. Smith not out	110	L-b 6, w 6, n-b 1		13
A. J. Stewart c Rhodes b Newport	9			
M. A. Lynch c Botham b Newport	0	1/58 2/75 3/75	(3 wkts, 53.4 overs)	234

†C. J. Richards, *I. A. Greig, D. J. Thomas, C. K. Bullen, M. A. Feltham and S. T. Clarke did not bat.

Bowling: Dilley 9–1–43–0; Radford 8.4–0–41–0; Botham 10–2–35–1; Newport 8–2–34–2; Pridgeon 10–0–45–0; Hick 8–0–30–0.

Umpires: D. G. L. Evans and B. Leadbeater.

YORKSHIRE v HAMPSHIRE

At Leeds, May 27. Yorkshire won by nine wickets. Toss: Yorkshire. Hampshire never really recovered from losing Greenidge for 13 – run out by quick work from Sharp in the gully. Against persistent seam bowling on an easy-paced pitch, they struggled to raise the rate above 3 an over, although Turner improvised skilfully. Metcalfe dominated Yorkshire's reply with a brilliant innings, his unbeaten 93, which included a six and ten fours, coming from 135 balls.

Gold Award: A. A. Metcalfe (his fourth in five matches in 1987).

Hampshire

C. G. Greenidge run out	13	†R. J. Parks not out	15
V. P. Terry c Moxon b Fletcher	21	T. M. Tremlett not out	5
D. R. Turner b Sidebottom	38		
*M. C. J. Nicholas c Bairstow b Fletcher	9	L-b 11, w 1, n-b 4	16
C. L. Smith b Fletcher	26		
K. D. James c Metcalfe b Carrick	4	1/23 2/50 3/68 (8 wkts, 55 overs) 174	
M. D. Marshall c Carrick b Hartley	24	4/107 5/120 6/134	
N. G. Cowley run out	3	7/145 8/154	

S. J. W. Andrew did not bat.

Bowling: Sidebottom 8–3–15–1; Jarvis 11–3–41–0; Hartley 11–1–37–1; Fletcher 11–0–41–3; Carrick 11–2–19–1; Moxon 3–0–10–0.

Yorkshire

M. D. Moxon b Marshall	21
A. A. Metcalfe not out	93
R. J. Blakey not out	52
L-b 10, w 2	12

1/78   (1 wkt, 45.5 overs) 178

K. Sharp, J. D. Love, †D. L. Bairstow, *P. Carrick, A. Sidebottom, P. J. Hartley, P. W. Jarvis and S. D. Fletcher did not bat.

Bowling: Marshall 9–1–18–1; Andrew 7–0–34–0; James 7.5–0–48–0; Tremlett 11–3–32–0; Cowley 11–1–36–0.

Umpires: B. J. Meyer and D. O. Oslear.

SEMI-FINALS

KENT v NORTHAMPTONSHIRE

At Canterbury, June 10. Northamptonshire won by five wickets. Toss: Northamptonshire. Kent recovered from an uncertain start as first Benson and Tavaré put on 57 off nineteen overs and then Tavaré and Chris Cowdrey added 115 off fifteen. Tavaré hit eight fours in his innings of 108 balls and Cowdrey, who faced 61 balls, hit four sixes and five fours. Northamptonshire were faltering until Lamb and Capel struck 111 from nineteen overs, and they still needed 97 off the last ten. However, Lamb now took control of the match and with superb limited-overs batting manufactured an exciting victory with two balls to spare. His unbeaten 126 came off 101 balls and included a six and ten fours. Kent were left reflecting on what might have been had Baptiste not been injured while fielding after bowling six overs for just 8 runs.

Gold Award: A. J. Lamb.

Kent

M. R. Benson b Davis	46	E. A. E. Baptiste not out	11
S. G. Hinks c Lamb b Capel	7	†S. A. Marsh c G. Cook b N. G. B. Cook	4
D. G. Aslett b Wild	11	B 1, l-b 9, w 10, n-b 2	22
C. J. Tavaré b Davis	78		
*C. S. Cowdrey c G. Cook b N. G. B. Cook	87	1/9 2/53 3/110 (7 wkts, 55 overs) 275	
		4/225 5/239	
G. R. Cowdrey c Ripley b Davis	9	6/268 7/275	

C. Penn, D. J. M. Kelleher and D. L. Underwood did not bat.

Bowling: Davis 11–1–37–3; Capel 11–0–51–1; Walker 10–0–58–0; Wild 11–1–23–1; N. G. B. Cook 10–0–64–2; Williams 2–0–32–0.

Northamptonshire

*G. Cook c G. R. Cowdrey	
b Underwood . 40	R. G. Williams b Underwood 6
W. Larkins c Marsh b Baptiste 3	D. J. Wild not out 10
R. J. Bailey c Marsh b Penn 29	B 1, l-b 7, w 10 18
A. J. Lamb not out 126	
D. J. Capel b Kelleher 47	1/12 2/76 3/89 (5 wkts, 54.4 overs) 279
	4/200 5/211

†D. Ripley, N. G. B. Cook, W. W. Davis and A. Walker did not bat.

Bowling: Baptiste 6–3–8–1; Kelleher 11–0–47–1; Penn 10.4–0–60–1; Underwood 11–0–64–2; C. S. Cowdrey 9–0–55–0; Hinks 3–0–19–0; G. R. Cowdrey 4–0–18–0.

Umpires: J. H. Hampshire and N. T. Plews.

YORKSHIRE v SURREY

At Leeds, June 10, 11, 12. Yorkshire won by 76 runs. Toss: Surrey. Yorkshire scored heavily after being put in on a good, firm pitch. Moxon led the way, his 97 coming from 160 balls, while Love was particularly severe on the left-arm medium pace of Thomas, hitting him for three sixes as he raced to 40 from nineteen balls. Surrey's innings was dogged by the weather, with play stretching into Friday when Thursday was washed out. Their cause was hopeless when, from 41 for three overnight after seventeen overs (G. S. Clinton 11*, C. K. Bullen 2*), half the side was out for 126 in the 36th over. Clinton was the last man out, but his 69 used up 132 balls and was too slow to be of real value. Bullen, promoted up the order, hit a good 33 from 54 deliveries.

Gold Award: M. D. Moxon.

Yorkshire

M. D. Moxon c Richards b Bicknell ... 97	A. Sidebottom lbw b Bicknell 0
A. A. Metcalfe c Thomas b Jesty 27	P. J. Hartley not out 7
R. J. Blakey c and b Bullen 2	B 2, l-b 5, w 1, n-b 2 10
K. Sharp c Lynch b Bullen 10	
†D. L. Bairstow lbw b Clarke 45	1/53 2/68 3/108 (7 wkts, 55 overs) 238
J. D. Love not out 40	4/186 5/190
*P. Carrick c Smith b Bicknell 0	6/190 7/190

P. W. Jarvis and S. D. Fletcher did not bat.

Bowling: Clarke 11–2–38–1; Thomas 8–1–70–0; Bicknell 11–2–29–3; Greig 3–0–21–0; Jesty 11–2–35–1; Bullen 11–1–38–2.

Surrey

G. S. Clinton b Sidebottom 69	D. J. Thomas b Fletcher 3
D. M. Smith c Fletcher b Sidebottom .. 5	S. T. Clarke lbw b Fletcher 1
A. J. Stewart lbw b Sidebottom 0	M. P. Bicknell not out 1
M. A. Lynch run out 6	B 3, l-b 8, w 12, n-b 2 25
C. K. Bullen b Jarvis 33	
T. E. Jesty c Bairstow b Jarvis 5	1/19 2/19 3/36 (48.2 overs) 162
†C. J. Richards b Hartley 8	4/114 5/126 6/137
*I. A. Greig c Jarvis b Fletcher 6	7/147 8/152 9/154

Bowling: Sidebottom 8.2–1–29–3; Jarvis 7–1–21–2; Hartley 11–1–28–1; Fletcher 10–0–33–3; Carrick 11–2–33–0; Love 1–0–7–0.

Umpires: J. Birkenshaw and D. J. Constant.

FINAL

NORTHAMPTONSHIRE v YORKSHIRE

At Lord's, July 11. Yorkshire won, having taken the greater number of wickets with the scores tied. Requiring an average of 4.45 runs per over, they had paced their reply almost to perfection, and when the scores were level with one ball remaining, Love, winner of the Gold Award, coolly blocked it.

Winning the toss gave Yorkshire the advantage of any moisture in the pitch on a morning of high summer. Jarvis, in his second over, forced it home when Cook played a sharply rising ball to forward short leg, and he then exposed Bailey's weakness against the ball seaming and lifting outside off stump. Nevertheless Bailey and Larkins were splendidly dismissive of everything within range of their strokeplay until, in the twelfth over, Larkins aimed to mid-wicket and instead sent the ball looping high to the long-waiting Carrick at cover. Three overs later, Moxon at slip took a tremendous two-handed catch, diving to his right, to cut short Bailey's promise. There were five boundaries in his 26, cracking shots, and Lamb was emulating him before he slashed at another rising delivery and Bairstow, tumbling to his right, held well a catch off the bottom edge. Now Carrick, from the Nursery End, applied further pressure, obtaining slight turn and benefiting from the irregular bounce. Five overs of tight control gave away just 6 runs; at lunch his figures were 8–2–18–0 and Northamptonshire after 36 overs were 128 for four. Thereafter, the pitch lost its sting and Capel and Williams put Northamptonshire on the way to the third-highest total in a Benson and Hedges final with some hard, straight hitting against the second-line seamers and quick running against keen Yorkshire fielding. It was good cricket. When Williams, driving, was caught in the 51st over, they had added 120 in 28 overs. Capel, whose 97 was his highest in the competition, was bowled, swinging, in the penultimate over; his innings of 139 minutes and 110 balls contained eleven fours, many from full, flowing drives.

Moxon and Metcalfe gave Yorkshire an assured start, and if Moxon was initially the more enterprising, Metcalfe was soon leaning into his strokes, the ball too fast over the outfield for fieldsmen. Nick Cook made the breakthrough in the 24th over, confusing Moxon with flight as he advanced and bowling him between bat and pad. Three overs later Metcalfe carelessly hoisted a full toss from Williams to deep mid-wicket; Blakey did the same to a long-hop in the off-spinner's next over. The two slow bowlers checked Yorkshire but, 119 for three at tea after 35 overs, they could afford to await the return of Capel, very wayward, and Walker to step up the rate. In seven overs from them, Love and the bustling Bairstow put on 54. A diving parry to Geoff Cook at cover by Walker in his follow-through led to Bairstow's run-out, but Carrick, bludgeoning Davis past point for four then short-arm hooking him to the square-leg fence, left his side needing 10 from the last two overs to level the scores. Yorkshire were 240 for six when Davis began the last over, and if Bailey's shy from mid-on had run out Sidebottom off the fifth ball, 1 run would still have been needed. Instead, Love, having hit five boundaries, was not required to score from the 93rd delivery he faced and Yorkshire's many and sporting supporters could come forward into the shadows in front of the pavilion to salute their native sons. The days of darkness were behind them.

Gold Award: J. D. Love.

Attendance: 18,513 (excluding members); *receipts:* £288,221.

Northamptonshire

*G. Cook c Blakey b Jarvis	1	†D. Ripley not out	6
W. Larkins c Carrick b Hartley	15		
R. J. Bailey c Moxon b Fletcher	26	B 2, l-b 3, w 2, n-b 4	11
A. J. Lamb c Bairstow b Jarvis	28		
D. J. Capel b Hartley	97	1/3 (1) 2/31 (2) (7 wkts, 55 overs) 244	
R. G. Williams c Bairstow b Jarvis	44	3/48 (3) 4/92 (4)	
D. J. Wild b Jarvis	6	5/212 (6) 6/226 (7)	
W. W. Davis not out	10	7/232 (5)	

N. G. B. Cook and A. Walker did not bat.

Bowling: Jarvis 11–2–43–4; Sidebottom 11–1–40–0; Fletcher 11–1–60–1; Hartley 11–0–66–2; Carrick 11–2–30–0.

Yorkshire

M. D. Moxon b N. G. B. Cook	45	A. Sidebottom not out	2
A. A. Metcalfe c Davis b Williams	47		
R. J. Blakey c Davis b Williams	1	B 1, l-b 4, w 4, n-b 7	16
K. Sharp b Williams	24		
J. D. Love not out	75	1/97 (1) 2/101 (2)	(6 wkts, 55 overs) 244
†D. L. Bairstow run out	24	3/103 (3) 4/160 (4)	
*P. Carrick run out	10	5/223 (6) 6/235 (7)	

P. J. Hartley, P. W. Jarvis and S. D. Fletcher did not bat.

Bowling: Davis 11-1-37-0; Walker 11-0-62-0; Capel 11-0-66-0; N. G. B. Cook 11-1-42-1; Williams 11-0-32-3.

Umpires: H. D. Bird and K. E. Palmer.

BENSON AND HEDGES CUP RECORDS

Highest individual scores: 198 not out, G. A. Gooch, Essex v Sussex, Hove, 1982; 173 not out, C. G. Greenidge, Hampshire v Minor Counties (South), Amersham, 1973; 158 not out, B. F. Davison, Leicestershire v Warwickshire, Coventry, 1972; 155 not out, M. D. Crowe, Somerset v Hampshire, Southampton, 1987; 154 not out, M. J. Procter, Gloucestershire v Somerset, Taunton, 1972. (148 hundreds have been scored in the competition.)

Highest totals in 55 overs: 350 for three, Essex v Oxford & Cambridge Univs, Chelmsford, 1979; 333 for four, Essex v Oxford & Cambridge Univs, Chelmsford, 1985; 327 for four, Leicestershire v Warwickshire, Coventry, 1972; 327 for two, Essex v Sussex, Hove, 1982; 321 for one, Hampshire v Minor Counties (South), Amersham, 1973. *In the final:* 290 for six, Essex v Surrey, 1979.

Highest total by a side batting second and winning: 291 for five (53.5 overs), Warwickshire v Lancashire, Manchester, 1981. *In the final:* 244 (55 overs), Yorkshire v Northamptonshire, 1987.

Highest total by a side batting second and losing: 300 (55 overs), Northamptonshire v Derbyshire, Derby, 1987. *In the final:* 255 (51.4 overs), Surrey v Essex, 1979.

Highest match aggregate: 601 for thirteen wickets, Somerset (307-6) v Gloucestershire (294-7), Taunton, 1982.

Lowest totals: 56 in 26.2 overs, Leicestershire v Minor Counties, Wellington, 1982; 59 in 34 overs, Oxford & Cambridge Univs v Glamorgan, Cambridge, 1983; 60 in 26 overs, Sussex v Middlesex, Hove, 1978; 62 in 26.5 overs, Gloucestershire v Hampshire, Bristol, 1975. *In the final:* 130 in 50.1 overs, Nottinghamshire v Somerset, 1982.

Best bowling: Seven for 12, W. W. Daniel, Middlesex v Minor Counties (East), Ipswich, 1978; seven for 22, J. R. Thomson, Middlesex v Hampshire, Lord's, 1981; seven for 32, R. G. D. Willis, Warwickshire v Yorkshire, Birmingham, 1981.

Hat-tricks (9): G. D. McKenzie, Leicestershire v Worcestershire, Worcester, 1972; K. Higgs, Leicestershire v Surrey in the final, Lord's, 1974; A. A. Jones, Middlesex v Essex, Lord's, 1977; M. J. Procter, Gloucestershire v Hampshire, Southampton, 1977; W. Larkins, Northamptonshire v Oxford & Cambridge Univs, Northampton, 1980; E. A. Moseley, Glamorgan v Kent, Cardiff, 1981; G. C. Small, Warwickshire v Leicestershire, Leicester, 1984; N. A. Mallender, Somerset v Combined Univs, Taunton, 1987; W. K. M. Benjamin, Leicestershire v Nottinghamshire, Leicester, 1987.

Record partnership for each wicket

241 for 1st	S. M. Gavaskar and B. C. Rose, Somerset v Kent at Canterbury ...	1980
285* for 2nd	C. G. Greenidge and D. R. Turner, Hampshire v Minor Counties (South) at Amersham	1973
269* for 3rd	P. M. Roebuck and M. D. Crowe, Somerset v Hampshire at Southampton	1987
184* for 4th	D. Lloyd and B. W. Reidy, Lancashire v Derby at Chesterfield	1980
160 for 5th	A. J. Lamb and D. J. Capel, Northamptonshire v Leicestershire at Northampton	1986
114 for 6th	Majid Khan and G. P. Ellis, Glamorgan v Gloucestershire at Bristol	1975
149* for 7th	J. D. Love and C. M. Old, Yorkshire v Scotland at Bradford	1981
109 for 8th	R. E. East and N. Smith, Essex v Northamptonshire at Chelmsford.	1977
83 for 9th	P. G. Newman and M. A. Holding, Derbyshire v Nottinghamshire at Nottingham	1985
80* for 10th	D. L. Bairstow and M. Johnson, Yorkshire v Derbyshire at Derby ..	1981

WINNERS 1972-87

1972 LEICESTERSHIRE beat Yorkshire by five wickets.
1973 KENT beat Worcestershire by 39 runs.
1974 SURREY beat Leicestershire by 27 runs.
1975 LEICESTERSHIRE beat Middlesex by five wickets.
1976 KENT beat Worcestershire by 43 runs.
1977 GLOUCESTERSHIRE beat Kent by 64 runs.
1978 KENT beat Derbyshire by six wickets.
1979 ESSEX beat Surrey by 35 runs.
1980 NORTHAMPTONSHIRE beat Essex by 6 runs.
1981 SOMERSET beat Surrey by seven wickets.
1982 SOMERSET beat Nottinghamshire by nine wickets.
1983 MIDDLESEX beat Essex by 4 runs.
1984 LANCASHIRE beat Warwickshire by six wickets.
1985 LEICESTERSHIRE beat Essex by five wickets.
1986 MIDDLESEX beat Kent by 2 runs.
1987 YORKSHIRE beat Northamptonshire, having taken more wickets with the scores tied.

WINS BY OXFORD AND CAMBRIDGE UNIVERSITIES

1973 OXFORD beat Northamptonshire at Northampton by two wickets.
1975 OXFORD & CAMBRIDGE beat Worcestershire at Cambridge by 66 runs.
1975 OXFORD & CAMBRIDGE beat Northamptonshire at Oxford by three wickets.
1976 OXFORD & CAMBRIDGE beat Yorkshire at Barnsley by seven wickets.
1984 OXFORD & CAMBRIDGE beat Gloucestershire at Bristol by 27 runs.

WINS BY MINOR COUNTIES AND SCOTLAND

1980 MINOR COUNTIES beat Gloucestershire at Chippenham by 3 runs.
1981 MINOR COUNTIES beat Hampshire at Southampton by 3 runs.
1982 MINOR COUNTIES beat Leicestershire at Wellington by 131 runs.
1986 SCOTLAND beat Lancashire at Perth by 3 runs.
1987 MINOR COUNTIES beat Glamorgan at Oxford (Christ Church) by seven wickets.

REFUGE ASSURANCE LEAGUE, 1987

Worcestershire, sixteenth in the 1986 John Player League and without a major trophy since winning the County Championship in 1974, won the inaugural Refuge Assurance League when, on the last Sunday of the season, they defeated Northamptonshire by nine wickets. Nottinghamshire, questing three trophies, had needed Worcestershire to lose – and to win themselves – and so had to settle for second place. Gloucestershire's win over Glamorgan and Somerset's over Derbyshire that same day lifted them to third and fourth respectively, leaving Derbyshire, who had been one of the leading three since the end of May, out of the prizemoney. Ironically, Somerset edged ahead of Derbyshire by beating them at Derby, which ensured them of one more away win. Gloucestershire's third place, a rise of fourteen over 1986, was their highest in the Sunday League.

In a season when a record 31 matches were without a result, Nottinghamshire's supporters could point to four "no results" against one by Worcestershire. However, the crux for Nottinghamshire, having gone eleven weeks without a loss, was defeat on the last two Sundays of August by Gloucestershire and Derbyshire. They had recalled Rice, Hadlee, Broad and French from the MCC Bicentenary match for the fixture at Moreton-in-Marsh, only to lose by 2 runs. Leicestershire were the hardest hit by the weather, seven of their sixteen matches being "no results". Twenty matches in all did not even

Continued over

REFUGE ASSURANCE LEAGUE

		P	W	L	T	NR	Pts	Sixes	4W	Away Wins
1	Worcestershire (16) ...	16	11	4	0	1	46	32	3	4
2	Nottinghamshire (3) ...	13	9	3	0	4	44	8	3	4
3	Gloucestershire (17) ...	16	9	4	1	2	42	17	4	3
4	Somerset (6)	15	8	4	0	4	40	27	3	4
5	Derbyshire (3)	14	8	4	1	3	40	29	2	3
6	Kent (6)	14	8	5	0	3	38	37	4	5
7	Hampshire (1)	14	6	6	2	2	32	32	1	3
7	Surrey (12)	14	6	6	0	4	32	33	1	2
9	Lancashire (12)	13	5	6	0	5	30	21	0	1
10	Middlesex (9)	13	5	7	0	4	28	13	2	1
10	Northamptonshire (5) .	12	4	6	0	6	28	31	2	1
12	Yorkshire (8)	14	5	8	0	3	26	45	3	1
12	Leicestershire (15)	12	3	6	0	7	26	13	0	2
14	Glamorgan (12)	14	5	9	0	2	24	18	4	4
14	Sussex (4)	13	4	8	0	4	24	37	3	2
14	Essex (2)	13	4	8	0	4	24	15	2	1
17	Warwickshire (9)	12	3	9	0	4	20	12	0	1

1986 positions in brackets.

No play was possible in the following twenty matches: May 7 – Northamptonshire v Hampshire. July 19 – Essex v Derbyshire, Glamorgan v Surrey, Kent v Northamptonshire, Nottinghamshire v Middlesex, Somerset v Leicestershire, Sussex v Lancashire. July 26 – Lancashire v Nottinghamshire. August 9 – Derbyshire v Surrey, Leicestershire v Warwickshire, Northamptonshire v Essex, Yorkshire v Sussex. August 23 – Northamptonshire v Middlesex, Warwickshire v Lancashire. September 6 – Leicestershire v Glamorgan, Nottinghamshire v Essex, Warwickshire v Middlesex, Yorkshire v Hampshire. September 13 – Kent v Warwickshire, Sussex v Leicestershire.

start, equalling the record 1983 total of matches abandoned without a ball bowled.

Although the title was not decided until the last round, Worcestershire, Nottinghamshire and Derbyshire had been the front-runners since July 5, when victory over Yorkshire took Nottinghamshire to the top of the League table and Worcestershire's win over Warwickshire settled them in behind Derbyshire. Hampshire, the defending Sunday League champions, had made the early running but by the middle of August had drifted. Kent, having trailed the leaders throughout July and August, could manage only four points from their last three games, twice losing out to the weather, and finished sixth.

Once Worcestershire went to the front on August 23, albeit having played one more match than Nottinghamshire, they were never headed. T. S. Curtis and I. T. Botham provided century opening partnerships in their last four games, a unique sequence in the Sunday League, although in 1975 G. Boycott and J. H. Hampshire had shared four century opening partnerships in May, June, July and August. In Curtis (617 runs, average 47.46), G. A. Hick (599 at 59.90) and Botham (578 at 57.80), Worcestershire had the three leading batsmen: the next, C. L. Smith (476) and C. S. Cowdrey (472), were more than 100 behind them. Furthermore, their opening bowler, N. V. Radford, with 25 at 21.36, was joint leading wicket-taker with Gloucestershire's C. A. Walsh (average 12.44), and S. J. Rhodes, with 24 dismissals, was the League's leading wicket-keeper. Botham proved his all-round value with nineteen wickets at 15.52 (4.25 runs an over) and six catches.

In their final seasons, D. L. Amiss took his record aggregate for the Sunday League past 7,000 runs, and C. E. B. Rice completed 6,000 runs. G. A. Gooch and T. E. Jesty both passed 5,000 runs, while Jesty also became the first to a "double" of 5,000 runs and 200 wickets. P. Bainbridge completed the "double" of 1,000 runs and 100 wickets in the League, and D. L. Bairstow, who at the end of the season was just four dismissals short of R. W. Taylor's career dismissals in the Sunday League, became the first wicket-keeper to take 200 catches.

DISTRIBUTION OF PRIZEMONEY

The total prizemoney was £75,625.

£20,000 and Refuge Assurance Trophy: WORCESTERSHIRE.
£10,000 to runners-up: NOTTINGHAMSHIRE.
£4,500 for third place: GLOUCESTERSHIRE.
£2,625 for fourth place: SOMERSET.
£275 each match to the winners – shared if tied or no result.

Batting award: £400 to C. S. Cowdrey (Kent) who hit eighteen sixes in the season.

Other leading six-hitters:

17 – C. G. Greenidge (Hampshire).
16 – G. S. le Roux (Sussex).
14 – I. T. Botham (Worcestershire).
11 – A. A. Metcalfe (Yorkshire).
10 – R. J. Bailey (Northamptonshire), M. A. Holding (Derbyshire), C. M. Wells (Sussex).
9 – R. J. Harden (Somerset).
8 – D. L. Bairstow (Yorkshire), J. D. Love (Yorkshire).
7 – J. J. E. Hardy (Somerset), S. N. Hartley (Yorkshire), A. J. Lamb (Northamptonshire), W. Larkins (Northamptonshire).
6 – N. H. Fairbrother (Lancashire), T. E. Jesty (Surrey), P. W. G. Parker (Sussex).

A total of 420 sixes were hit in the League in 1987.

Fastest televised fifty: £250 to M. P. Maynard (Glamorgan) – 34 balls v Somerset at Weston-super-Mare on August 2.

Bowling award: £400 to be shared between the following ten bowlers who took four wickets or more in an innings twice: P. Bainbridge (Gloucestershire), C. S. Cowdrey (Kent), G. R. Cowdrey (Kent), J. E. Emburey (Middlesex), G. C. Holmes (Glamorgan), P. W. Jarvis (Yorkshire), A. C. S. Pigott (Sussex), N. V. Radford (Worcestershire), K. Saxelby (Nottinghamshire) and C. A. Walsh (Gloucestershire).

S. R. Barwick (Glamorgan), I. T. Botham (Worcestershire), J. Derrick (Glamorgan), N. A. Foster (Essex), I. A. Greig (Surrey), M. A. Holding (Derbyshire), A. N. Jones (Somerset), G. S. le Roux (Sussex), J. K. Lever (Essex), M. D. Marshall (Hampshire), G. V. Palmer (Somerset), R. A. Pick (Nottinghamshire), G. D. Rose (Somerset), A. Sidebottom (Yorkshire), G. B. Stevenson (Northamptonshire), A. Walker (Northamptonshire) and A. E. Warner (Derbyshire) each took four wickets in an innings once.

DERBYSHIRE

DERBYSHIRE v NORTHAMPTONSHIRE

At Derby, May 3. Northamptonshire won by 22 runs. Toss: Derbyshire.

Northamptonshire

W. Larkins c and b Warner	44
R. J. Bailey not out	125
A. J. Lamb c Maher b Jean-Jacques	0
D. J. Capel not out	77
L-b 13, w 4, n-b 1	18

1/111 2/112   (2 wkts, 40 overs) 264

*G. Cook, S. J. Brown, R. A. Harper, D. J. Wild, N. G. B. Cook, A. Walker and †D. Ripley did not bat.

Bowling: Finney 7–0–32–0; Mortensen 8–0–48–0; Holding 8–0–45–0; Newman 7–0–57–0; Warner 5–1–30–1; Jean-Jacques 5–0–39–1.

Derbyshire

*K. J. Barnett b Harper	36	R. J. Finney not out	5
†B. J. M. Maher c Wild b Harper	36	M. Jean-Jacques b Walker	4
B. Roberts c Bailey b N. G. B. Cook	44	O. H. Mortensen run out	1
J. E. Morris b N. G. B. Cook	30	L-b 11, w 6	17
M. A. Holding c Lamb b Wild	3		
I. S. Anderson b Brown	3	1/68 2/94 3/143 (38 overs) 242
P. G. Newman run out	25	4/150 5/162 6/167	
A. E. Warner c Harper b Walker	38	7/228 8/231 9/235	

Bowling: Walker 6–0–29–2; Capel 6–0–43–0; Wild 8–0–42–1; Harper 7–0–39–2; N. G. B. Cook 8–0–49–2; Brown 3–0–29–1.

Umpires: D. Lloyd and J. A. Jameson.

At Hove, May 10. DERBYSHIRE beat SUSSEX by four wickets.

DERBYSHIRE v WORCESTERSHIRE

At Derby, May 24. Derbyshire won by three wickets. Toss: Worcestershire.

Worcestershire

T. S. Curtis lbw b Warner	55	P. J. Newport not out		4
M. J. Weston c Maher b Newman	0	R. K. Illingworth b Warner		2
G. A. Hick c Maher b Holding	16			
D. B. D'Oliveira b Holding	37	L-b 11, w 5, n-b 1		17
*P. A. Neale c Holding b Newman	22			
†S. J. Rhodes c Morris b Warner	15	1/1 2/38 3/109	(9 wkts, 40 overs)	175
S. R. Lampitt lbw b Holding	3	4/142 5/152 6/159		
N. V. Radford b Warner	4	7/164 8/171 9/175		

A. P. Pridgeon did not bat.

Bowling: Newman 8–0–39–2; Mortensen 8–3–20–0; Holding 8–2–17–3; Jean-Jacques 8–0–54–0; Warner 8–0–34–4.

Derbyshire

*K. J. Barnett b Radford	4	M. A. Holding b Radford		54
†B. J. M. Maher c Rhodes b Pridgeon	12	A. E. Warner not out		39
B. Roberts c Rhodes b Newport	9	B 1, l-b 4, w 4		9
J. E. Morris lbw b Newport	2			
I. S. Anderson not out	41	1/4 2/26 3/26	(7 wkts, 38.3 overs)	179
R. J. Finney c Neale b Newport	7	4/29 5/39		
P. G. Newman c Rhodes b Illingworth	2	6/45 7/121		

M. Jean-Jacques and O. H. Mortensen did not bat.

Bowling: Radford 8–0–49–2; Pridgeon 8–2–15–1; Newport 8–1–30–3; Weston 6.3–0–34–0; Illingworth 8–1–46–1.

Umpires: D. G. L. Evans and B. Leadbeater.

At Birmingham, May 31. DERBYSHIRE beat WARWICKSHIRE by two wickets.

At Sheffield, June 7. DERBYSHIRE beat YORKSHIRE by 19 runs.

At Southampton, June 14. DERBYSHIRE tied with HAMPSHIRE.

DERBYSHIRE v GLOUCESTERSHIRE

At Ilkeston, June 21. Derbyshire won by 18 runs. Toss: Gloucestershire.

Derbyshire

*K. J. Barnett c Romaines b Alleyne	28	I. S. Anderson not out		7
†B. J. M. Maher b Alleyne	30	C. F. B. P. Rudd not out		5
B. Roberts c Alleyne b Bainbridge	41			
J. E. Morris c Bainbridge b Lawrence	19	B 1, l-b 10, w 2, n-b 1		14
M. A. Holding c Graveney b Walsh	19			
P. G. Newman lbw b Walsh	2	1/49 2/70 3/106	(8 wkts, 40 overs)	165
A. E. Warner st Russell b Bainbridge	0	4/145 5/148 6/150		
M. Jean-Jacques b Bainbridge	0	7/150 8/150		

O. H. Mortensen did not bat.

Bowling: Lawrence 8–0–28–1; Walsh 8–0–34–2; Bainbridge 8–0–30–3; Alleyne 8–1–35–2; Lloyds 8–0–27–0.

Gloucestershire

A. W. Stovold c Jean-Jacques b Holding	21	*D. A. Graveney not out	....	9
A. J. Wright b Mortensen	12	C. A. Walsh c Rudd b Warner	....	33
P. W. Romaines c and b Jean-Jacques	9	D. V. Lawrence b Holding	....	3
P. Bainbridge c Holding b Newman ...	23	L-b 4, w 2	....	6
J. W. Lloyds lbw b Warner	9			
K. P. Tomlins c Roberts b Holding ...	10	1/26 2/37 3/60	(38.4 overs)	147
M. W. Alleyne c Barnett b Mortensen	7	4/76 5/78 6/91		
†R. C. Russell c Barnett b Holding	5	7/98 8/100 9/142		

Bowling: Newman 8-0-24-1; Mortensen 8-1-33-2; Jean-Jacques 4-0-7-1; Rudd 6-0-24-0; Holding 7.4-0-34-4; Warner 5-0-21-2.

Umpires: B. Dudleston and D. R. Shepherd.

At Manchester, June 28. LANCASHIRE v DERBYSHIRE. No result.

DERBYSHIRE v GLAMORGAN

At Cheadle, July 12. Derbyshire won by one wicket. Toss: Derbyshire.

Glamorgan

*H. Morris c Morris b Roberts	13	S. J. Base c Holding b Roberts	....	10
P. A. Cottey lbw b Mortensen	1	†C. P. Metson not out	....	8
G. C. Holmes c Maher b Holding	20	S. R. Barwick not out	....	2
M. P. Maynard c Finney b Jean-Jacques	2	B 1, l-b 7, w 2	....	10
R. J. Shastri c Maher b Holding	41			
P. A. Todd c Roberts b Jean-Jacques	31	1/3 2/33 3/36	(9 wkts, 40 overs)	173
J. Derrick c Maher b Jean-Jacques	1	4/51 5/110 6/114		
I. Smith c Anderson b Roberts	34	7/123 8/151 9/165		

Bowling: Newman 8-1-43-0; Mortensen 8-1-20-1; Jean-Jacques 8-0-38-3; Holding 8-2-20-2; Roberts 8-0-44-3.

Derbyshire

*K. J. Barnett c Cottey b Holmes	28	P. G. Newman run out	....	0
†B. J. M. Maher run out	8	M. Jean-Jacques c and b Barwick	....	8
B. Roberts b Holmes	6	O. H. Mortensen not out	....	4
J. E. Morris c Metson b Barwick	49	B 1, l-b 16, w 5	....	22
I. S. Anderson b Derrick	22			
M. A. Holding c Derrick b Smith	9	1/29 2/45 3/50	(9 wkts, 39.5 overs)	176
R. J. Finney c Morris b Barwick	1	4/107 5/132 6/136		
R. Sharma not out	19	7/137 8/139 9/165		

Bowling: Barwick 8-1-25-3; Base 4-0-26-0; Shastri 8-1-18-0; Holmes 7.5-0-32-2; Derrick 8-0-40-1; Smith 4-0-18-1.

Umpires: J. W. Holder and B. J. Meyer.

At Southend, July 19. ESSEX v DERBYSHIRE. No result.

At Lord's, July 26. DERBYSHIRE lost to MIDDLESEX by 71 runs.

At Canterbury, August 2. DERBYSHIRE lost to KENT by seven wickets.

DERBYSHIRE v SURREY

At Chesterfield, August 9. No result.

DERBYSHIRE v LEICESTERSHIRE

At Derby, August 16. Derbyshire won by three wickets. Toss: Leicestershire.

Leicestershire

I. P. Butcher run out	12	P. B. Clift not out	1
N. E. Briers c Roberts b Warner	50		
D. I. Gower st Maher b Sharma	47	L-b 6, w 3, n-b 4	13
*P. Willey run out	41		
J. J. Whitaker b Holding	45	1/28 2/104 3/141 (6 wkts, 40 overs) 222	
P. A. J. DeFreitas c Sharma b Holding	13	4/162 5/221 6/222	

†P. Whitticase, P. M. Such, G. J. F. Ferris and J. P. Agnew did not bat.

Bowling: Newman 8–2–52–0; Mortensen 8–2–15–0; Jean-Jacques 5–0–30–0; Holding 8–0–41–2; Warner 8–0–56–1; Sharma 3–0–22–1.

Derbyshire

*K. J. Barnett st Whitticase b Willey	82	R. Sharma not out	16
†B. J. M. Maher c Butcher b Agnew	2	P. G. Newman not out	11
B. Roberts c Ferris b Clift	31	L-b 9, w 2, n-b 3	14
J. E. Morris b Clift	11		
M. A. Holding b Clift	0	1/12 2/74 3/93 (7 wkts, 39.5 overs) 225	
I. S. Anderson c Gower b Willey	18	4/93 5/149	
A. E. Warner c Butcher b Willey	40	6/160 7/206	

M. Jean-Jacques and O. H. Mortensen did not bat.

Bowling: Ferris 6–0–23–0; Agnew 6–0–47–1; DeFreitas 7.5–0–55–0; Clift 8–1–23–3; Such 6–0–28–0; Willey 6–0–40–3.

Umpires: J. H. Harris and D. O. Oslear.

DERBYSHIRE v NOTTINGHAMSHIRE

At Derby, August 30. Derbyshire won by seven wickets. Toss: Derbyshire.

Nottinghamshire

B. C. Broad lbw b Mortensen	8	E. E. Hemmings not out	29
R. T. Robinson b Jean-Jacques	16	R. A. Pick run out	6
P. Johnson b Warner	15	K. Saxelby not out	4
*C. E. B. Rice c Sharma b Warner	2	L-b 7, w 3	10
J. D. Birch b Holding	2		
R. J. Hadlee b Holding	28	1/16 2/31 3/36 (8 wkts, 40 overs) 125	
†B. N. French c Newman b Jean-Jacques	5	4/43 5/53 6/63	
		7/98 8/114	

M. K. Bore did not bat.

Bowling: Newman 8–1–20–0; Mortensen 8–0–20–1; Warner 8–1–29–2; Jean-Jacques 8–1–29–2; Holding 8–1–20–2.

Derbyshire

*K. J. Barnett b Hadlee	63	M. A. Holding not out		4
†B. J. M. Maher c and b Hemmings	17	B 2, l-b 9, w 1		12
B. Roberts not out	32			
J. E. Morris b Hadlee	0	1/50 2/119 3/119	(3 wkts, 38 overs)	128

M. Jean-Jacques, R. J. Finney, R. Sharma, P. G. Newman, A. E. Warner and O. H. Mortensen did not bat.

Bowling: Saxelby 4–1–15–0; Bore 8–0–23–0; Hadlee 7–0–12–2; Rice 8–1–17–0; Hemmings 8–0–27–1; Pick 3–0–23–0.

Umpires: H. D. Bird and R. Palmer.

DERBYSHIRE v SOMERSET

At Derby, September 13. Somerset won by 14 runs. The third-wicket stand of 165 between Roebuck and Harden was a record for Somerset in the Sunday League. Toss: Derbyshire.

Somerset

*P. M. Roebuck b Warner	78	G. D. Rose run out		15
J. G. Wyatt c Maher b Mortensen	2	B 5, l-b 12, w 3		20
M. D. Crowe lbw b Newman	0			
R. J. Harden b Holding	73	1/3 2/5 3/170	(5 wkts, 40 overs)	204
J. J. E. Hardy not out	16	4/173 5/204		

V. J. Marks, †N. D. Burns, G. V. Palmer, N. A. Mallender and A. N. Jones did not bat.

Bowling: Newman 8–0–29–1; Mortensen 8–0–19–1; Jean-Jacques 4–0–19–0; Holding 8–0–36–1; Warner 8–0–59–1; Sharma 4–0–25–0.

Derbyshire

*K. J. Barnett c Burns b Jones	5	P. G. Newman not out		30
†B. J. M. Maher lbw b Mallender	10	M. Jean-Jacques c Burns b Rose		15
B. Roberts b Palmer	19	O. H. Mortensen not out		5
J. E. Morris c Burns b Palmer	41	L-b 18, w 1		19
M. A. Holding c Burns b Rose	7			
R. Sharma lbw b Marks	12	1/12 2/38 3/42	(9 wkts, 40 overs)	190
A. E. Warner b Rose	21	4/53 5/83 6/123		
R. J. Finney b Rose	6	7/123 8/138 9/180		

Bowling: Jones 8–0–57–1; Mallender 8–1–18–1; Palmer 8–0–38–2; Rose 8–0–28–4; Marks 8–0–31–1.

Umpires: J. Birkenshaw and J. A. Jameson.

ESSEX

At Taunton, May 3. ESSEX lost to SOMERSET by 36 runs.

ESSEX v LEICESTERSHIRE

At Chelmsford, May 17. No result. Toss: Essex.

Leicestershire

L. Potter c Pringle b Page	9	J. P. Agnew not out	0
*D. I. Gower b Topley	8	L-b 6, w 1	7
J. J. Whitaker c Lilley b Foster	95		
T. J. Boon c Pringle b Lever	61	1/17 2/21 3/172 (5 wkts, 40 overs) 191	
P. A. J. DeFreitas c Pringle b Foster	11	4/181 5/191	

N. E. Briers, P. B. Clift, †P. Whitticase, L. B. Taylor and P. M. Such did not bat.

Bowling: Foster 8–1–46–2; Lever 8–1–37–1; Topley 8–1–30–1; Pringle 8–0–36–0; Page 8–1–36–1.

Essex

*G. A. Gooch, J. P. Stephenson, B. R. Hardie, K. W. R. Fletcher, D. R. Pringle, A. W. Lilley, T. D. Topley, †D. E. East, N. A. Foster, H. A. Page and J. K. Lever.

Umpires: J. H. Hampshire and K. J. Lyons.

At The Oval, May 24. ESSEX lost to SURREY by five wickets.

At Worcester, May 31. ESSEX lost to WORCESTERSHIRE by nine wickets.

ESSEX v KENT

At Ilford, June 14. Kent won by 16 runs in a match restricted by rain to eighteen overs a side. Toss: Essex.

Kent

S. G. Hinks c Page b Topley	2	†S. A. Marsh run out	13
*C. S. Cowdrey c and b Pringle	60	N. R. Taylor not out	0
C. J. Tavaré b Foster	17	L-b 1, w 2	3
D. G. Aslett c Foster b Page	8		
R. F. Pienaar c Gooch b Page	13	1/3 2/41 3/54 (7 wkts, 18 overs) 127	
G. R. Cowdrey b Pringle	11	4/77 5/91 6/126 7/127	

C. Penn, D. J. M. Kelleher and A. P. Igglesden did not bat.

Bowling: Lever 4–0–32–0; Topley 3–0–12–1; Pringle 4–0–30–2; Foster 4–0–28–1; Page 2–0–15–2; Gooch 1–0–9–0.

Essex

*G. A. Gooch b G. R. Cowdrey	11	G. Miller not out	16
B. R. Hardie c Tavaré b Kelleher	1	†D. E. East run out	35
K. W. R. Fletcher c Igglesden b Kelleher	5	T. D. Topley not out	4
D. R. Pringle b Penn	8	B 3, l-b 8, w 6	17
A. W. Lilley b G. R. Cowdrey	10		
H. A. Page c Pienaar b G. R. Cowdrey	2	1/3 2/17 3/23 (8 wkts, 18 overs) 111	
N. A. Foster c Igglesden		4/40 5/49 6/49	
b G. R. Cowdrey	2	7/55 8/97	

J. K. Lever did not bat.

Bowling: Pienaar 3–0–16–0; Kelleher 4–0–25–2; Igglesden 3–0–13–0; G. R. Cowdrey 4–0–15–4; Hinks 1–0–11–0; Penn 3–0–20–1.

Umpires: M. J. Kitchen and D. R. Shepherd.

At Birmingham, June 21. ESSEX lost to WARWICKSHIRE on scoring-rate.

ESSEX v SUSSEX

At Chelmsford, July 5. Essex won by 1 run. Toss: Sussex.

Essex

*G. A. Gooch c Moores b le Roux	10	J. P. Stephenson not out	40
G. Miller c Gould b C. M. Wells	38	B 2, l-b 5, w 3	10
B. R. Hardie not out	102		
D. R. Pringle c Gould b Pigott	37	1/22 2/90 3/165 (3 wkts, 40 overs) 237	

N. Hussain, A. W. Lilley, †D. E. East, T. D. Topley, H. A. Page and J. K. Lever did not bat.

Bowling: Pigott 8–0–56–1; le Roux 8–1–36–1; C. M. Wells 8–0–31–1; Reeve 5–0–32–0; Babington 8–0–47–0; Kimber 3–0–28–0.

Sussex

A. M. Green c Hardie b Page	13	A. C. S. Pigott run out	2
*I. J. Gould c Stephenson b Page	74	†P. Moores not out	0
C. M. Wells b Pringle	65	L-b 11, w 4, n-b 1	16
A. P. Wells b Lever	27		
G. S. le Roux c Gooch b Page	7	1/18 2/136 3/171 (8 wkts, 40 overs) 236	
D. A. Reeve b Pringle	9	4/187 5/199 6/231	
R. I. Alikhan run out	23	7/235 8/236	

A. M. Babington and S. J. S. Kimber did not bat.

Bowling: Lever 8–0–44–1; Page 8–1–38–3; Topley 8–0–26–0; Miller 0.2–0–1–0; Gooch 7.4–0–48–0; Pringle 8–0–68–2.

Umpires: J. H. Hampshire and B. Leadbeater.

ESSEX v GLOUCESTERSHIRE

At Chelmsford, July 12. Gloucestershire won by 33 runs. Toss: Gloucestershire.

Gloucestershire

A. J. Wright b Foster	10	P. W. Romaines c Lever b Foster	33
†R. C. Russell c Gooch b Foster	7	M. W. Alleyne not out	4
*C. W. J. Athey c and b Lever	47	L-b 14, w 7	21
J. W. Lloyds c Fletcher b Foster	57		
K. M. Curran not out	36	1/17 2/20 3/136 (6 wkts, 40 overs) 228	
A. W. Stovold b Gooch	13	4/136 5/167 6/219	

G. E. Sainsbury, C. A. Walsh and D. V. Lawrence did not bat.

Bowling: Foster 8–0–39–4; Lever 8–0–56–1; Topley 7–1–30–0; Miller 8–0–30–0; Pringle 1–0–6–0; Gooch 8–0–53–1.

Essex

*G. A. Gooch c Russell b Lawrence	67	N. A. Foster not out	22
G. Miller lbw b Sainsbury	18	T. D. Topley b Walsh	7
B. R. Hardie b Lloyds b Curran	7	J. K. Lever b Walsh	0
J. P. Stephenson b Curran	2	B 3, l-b 4, w 7, n-b 4	18
K. W. R. Fletcher run out	1		
A. W. Lilley b Alleyne	24	1/35 2/48 3/69 (39 overs) 195	
D. R. Pringle c Athey b Walsh	23	4/73 5/112 6/148	
†D. E. East b Walsh	6	7/164 8/166 9/195	

Bowling: Walsh 8–0–28–4; Sainsbury 8–0–26–1; Curran 8–1–36–2; Lawrence 7–0–44–1; Lloyds 2–0–24–0; Alleyne 6–0–30–1.

Umpires: J. A. Jameson and P. B. Wight.

ESSEX v DERBYSHIRE

At Southend, July 19. No result.

At Portsmouth, July 26. ESSEX lost to HAMPSHIRE by four wickets.

At Northampton, August 9. NORTHAMPTONSHIRE v ESSEX. No result.

ESSEX v MIDDLESEX

At Chelmsford, August 16. Middlesex won by five wickets. Toss: Essex.

Essex

*G. A. Gooch c Roseberry b Cowans ..	10	†D. E. East c Fraser b Hughes	3
B. R. Hardie b Cowans	20	T. D. Topley not out	5
P. J. Prichard lbw b Emburey	0	I. L. Pont not out	12
D. R. Pringle b Emburey	3	B 1, l-b 6, w 6, n-b 3	16
J. P. Stephenson b Emburey	18		
A. W. Lilley run out	7	(9 wkts, 40 overs)	128
N. Hussain c Fraser b Emburey	22	1/27 2/32 3/32	
N. A. Foster b Fraser	12	4/47 5/61 6/70	
		7/92 8/104 9/107	

Bowling: Cowans 8–3–16–2; Fraser 8–1–28–1; Emburey 8–1–26–4; Hughes 8–1–25–1; Sykes 8–0–26–0.

Middlesex

M. A. Roseberry c Topley b Gooch ...	22	J. E. Emburey not out	26
J. D. Carr b Pringle	33		
M. R. Ramprakash lbw b Foster	0	L-b 11	11
K. R. Brown lbw b Gooch	10		
*M. W. Gatting b Topley	7	(5 wkts, 38.5 overs)	129
†P. R. Downton not out	20	1/58 2/62 3/62	
		4/83 5/83	

J. F. Sykes, S. P. Hughes, N. G. Cowans and A. R. C. Fraser did not bat.

Bowling: Foster 7.5–1–40–1; Pont 8–0–17–0; Topley 8–2–21–1; Pringle 7–2–18–1; Gooch 8–1–22–2.

Umpires: A. A. Jones and B. Leadbeater.

At Neath, August 23. ESSEX beat GLAMORGAN by 13 runs.

ESSEX v YORKSHIRE

At Colchester, August 30. Essex won by six wickets. Toss: Essex. Gooch, when 8, reached 5,000 runs in the Sunday League.

Yorkshire

M. D. Moxon c Prichard b Miller	16		P. J. Hartley c Hussain b Foster	7
A. A. Metcalfe c Hardie b Foster	0		P. W. Jarvis not out	0
J. D. Love st East b Miller	8			
†D. L. Bairstow run out	1		L-b 11, w 3, n-b 2	16
P. E. Robinson c Gooch b Pont	39			
S. N. Hartley b Hardie b Gooch	11		1/6 2/23 3/25	(8 wkts, 40 overs) 119
*P. Carrick b Topley	7		4/40 5/67 6/84	
A. Sidebottom not out	14		7/95 8/116	

S. J. Dennis did not bat.

Bowling: Foster 8–1–24–2; Pont 8–1–20–1; Miller 8–1–26–2; Topley 8–0–19–1; Gooch 8–1–19–1.

Essex

*G. A. Gooch not out	70		N. Hussain not out	26
B. R. Hardie c Bairstow b P. J. Hartley	4		B 4, l-b 4, n-b 1	9
P. J. Prichard b P. J. Hartley	4			
A. W. Lilley lbw b Carrick	4		1/25 2/39 3/44	(4 wkts, 36.3 overs) 120
J. P. Stephenson c Carrick b Sidebottom	3		4/53	

G. Miller, N. A. Foster, †D. E. East, T. D. Topley and I. L. Pont did not bat.

Bowling: Jarvis 7–1–25–0; Sidebottom 7–0–22–1; P. J. Hartley 7.3–6–10–2; Carrick 8–0–25–1; Love 4–0–14–0; Dennis 3–0–16–0.

Umpires: P. J. Eele and B. J. Meyer.

At Nottingham, September 6. NOTTINGHAMSHIRE v ESSEX. No result.

ESSEX v LANCASHIRE

At Chelmsford, September 13. Essex won by 32 runs in a match reduced by rain to 23 overs a side. Toss: Lancashire.

Essex

*G. A. Gooch c Hegg b Patterson	1		G. Miller b Patterson	11
B. R. Hardie c Hegg b Watkinson	9		I. L. Pont not out	1
A. W. Lilley b Simmons	15		J. K. Lever not out	1
D. R. Pringle b Hayhurst	7		B 1, l-b 3, w 1, n-b 4	9
N. Hussain c Hegg b Hayhurst	30			
J. P. Stephenson b Simmons	0		1/4 2/31 3/31	(9 wkts, 23 overs) 103
K. W. R. Fletcher c Simmons b Allott	5		4/59 5/60 6/74	
†D. E. East c Hughes b Patterson	14		7/76 8/98 9/101	

Bowling: Patterson 5–0–25–3; Allott 5–0–22–1; Simmons 5–0–21–2; Watkinson 4–0–22–1; Hayhurst 4–1–9–2.

Lancashire

G. D. Mendis b Miller	13		J. Simmons c Lever b Pont	2
G. Fowler lbw b Lever	6		†W. K. Hegg c and b Lever	4
M. A. Atherton b Pringle	22		B. P. Patterson not out	2
M. Watkinson b Pringle	1		L-b 7, w 1	8
J. Abrahams c East b Pringle	0			
*D. P. Hughes c Hussain b Miller	0		1/12 2/30 3/35	(20.4 overs) 71
A. N. Hayhurst c Lever b Miller	4		4/35 5/36 6/45	
P. J. W. Allott c Hardie b Pont	9		7/56 8/65 9/66	

Bowling: Pont 5–0–16–2; Lever 3.4–1–9–2; Miller 5–0–13–3; Pringle 4–1–12–3; Gooch 3–0–14–0.

Umpires: B. Dudleston and R. Palmer.

GLAMORGAN

GLAMORGAN v SUSSEX

At Cardiff, May 3. Sussex won by 70 runs. Toss: Glamorgan.

Sussex

A. M. Green b Ontong 36	*I. J. Gould not out 0
A. P. Wells run out 29	L-b 12, w 2, n-b 3 17
P. W. G. Parker not out 86	
C. M. Wells b Thomas 21	1/47 2/86 3/144 (4 wkts, 40 overs) 212
G. S. le Roux run out 23	4/206

S. D. Myles, A. C. S. Pigott, †P. Moores, D. K. Standing and I. C. Waring did not bat.

Bowling: Thomas 7–0–34–1; Barwick 8–0–60–0; Ontong 8–1–26–1; Shastri 8–0–31–0; Derrick 5–0–27–0; Holmes 4–0–22–0.

Glamorgan

J. A. Hopkins c Parker b Standing 35	J. Derrick c Pigott b le Roux 3
*H. Morris c Moores b C. M. Wells . . 7	†C. P. Metson b Pigott 3
A. R. Butcher b Waring 40	S. R. Barwick b A. P. Wells 2
R. J. Shastri b Pigott 7	L-b 13, w 1, n-b 1 15
R. C. Ontong b Waring 4	
J. G. Thomas b Pigott 3	1/13 2/81 3/93 (39.1 overs) 142
G. C. Holmes not out 23	4/102 5/107 6/107
M. P. Maynard b Waring 0	7/107 8/123 9/133

Bowling: C. M. Wells 8–1–27–1; le Roux 7–0–16–1; Standing 8–0–29–1; Waring 8–1–26–3; Pigott 8–0–31–3; A. P. Wells 0.1–0–0–1.

Umpires: J. H. Harris and D. R. Shepherd.

At Manchester, May 10. GLAMORGAN beat LANCASHIRE by three wickets.

GLAMORGAN v KENT

At Swansea, May 17. Kent won by 25 runs. The game was reduced to 35 overs a side after rain had delayed the start. Toss: Glamorgan.

Kent

M. R. Benson b Holmes 52	†S. A. Marsh lbw b Holmes 4
S. G. Hinks b Thomas 6	C. Penn not out 0
C. J. Tavaré c Shastri b Base 61	B 1, l-b 8, w 6 15
D. G. Aslett c and b Holmes 49	
*C. S. Cowdrey c Barwick b Thomas . . 3	1/24 2/108 3/161 (7 wkts, 35 overs) 200
G. R. Cowdrey c Ontong b Holmes . . . 10	4/166 5/194
E. A. E. Baptiste not out 0	6/194 7/198

R. P. Davis and K. B. S. Jarvis did not bat.

Bowling: Thomas 6–0–24–2; Barwick 8–1–30–0; Ontong 7–0–37–0; Holmes 6–0–30–4; Base 8–0–70–1.

Glamorgan

J. A. Hopkins lbw b Davis	16	†C. P. Metson lbw b Penn	8
*H. Morris c and b Jarvis	3	S. J. Base run out	19
A. R. Butcher c and b Baptiste	4	S. R. Barwick b Baptiste	14
R. J. Shastri st Marsh b Davis	2	L-b 7, w 4	11
R. C. Ontong not out	69		
G. C. Holmes c Benson b Penn	22	1/22 2/27 3/27	(35 overs) 175
M. P. Maynard c Tavaré b Penn	3	4/30 5/63 6/75	
J. G. Thomas b Davis	4	7/86 8/97 9/152	

Bowling: Baptiste 8-0-40-2; Jarvis 8-0-40-1; Davis 8-0-19-3; C. S. Cowdrey 4-0-20-0; Penn 7-1-49-3.

Umpires: R. Julian and K. E. Palmer.

GLAMORGAN v YORKSHIRE

At Cardiff, May 24. Glamorgan won by 23 runs. Toss: Glamorgan.

Glamorgan

J. A. Hopkins run out	58	J. Derrick b Jarvis	5
*H. Morris c Bairstow b Sidebottom	0	I. Smith not out	7
A. R. Butcher retired hurt	8		
R. J. Shastri c Bairstow b P. J. Hartley	13	B 4, l-b 13, w 4, n-b 2	23
R. C. Ontong c Bairstow b Fletcher	18		
G. C. Holmes b Sidebottom	37	1/2 2/53 3/102	(6 wkts, 40 overs) 195
M. P. Maynard not out	26	4/142 5/170 6/181	

†C. P. Metson and S. R. Barwick did not bat.

Bowling: Fletcher 8-0-34-1; Sidebottom 8-0-33-2; Jarvis 8-1-34-1; P. J. Hartley 8-0-51-1; Moxon 4-1-11-0; Carrick 4-0-15-0.

Yorkshire

M. D. Moxon b Smith	7	P. J. Hartley not out	17
A. A. Metcalfe c Ontong b Smith	14	P. W. Jarvis b Barwick	0
K. Sharp c Derrick b Ontong	25	S. D. Fletcher b Holmes	6
†D. L. Bairstow c Smith b Holmes	56	L-b 1, w 1, n-b 1	3
J. D. Love c Metson b Barwick	34		
S. N. Hartley b Barwick	5	1/15 2/31 3/58	(39.5 overs) 172
*P. Carrick c sub b Barwick	2	4/138 5/144 6/144	
A. Sidebottom run out	3	7/147 8/159 9/159	

Bowling: Smith 8-1-19-2; Barwick 8-1-23-4; Ontong 8-0-51-1; Shastri 8-0-17-0; Holmes 6.5-0-49-2; Derrick 1-0-12-0.

Umpires: A. G. T. Whitehead and P. B. Wight.

GLAMORGAN v NOTTINGHAMSHIRE

At Ebbw Vale, June 14. Nottinghamshire won by 70 runs. Toss: Glamorgan. Holmes dismissed Johnson, Fraser-Darling and French to become the first player since R. M. Ellison in 1983 to take a hat-trick in the Sunday League.

Nottinghamshire

R. T. Robinson c Metson b Smith	18	E. E. Hemmings run out	5
B. C. Broad b Holmes	32	K. Saxelby b Holmes	0
*C. E. B. Rice st Metson b Shastri	36	K. E. Cooper not out	0
R. J. Hadlee c Derrick b Shastri	5	B 1, l-b 3, w 11, n-b 1	16
P. Johnson b Holmes	51		
D. W. Randall c Maynard b Thomas	40	1/31 2/85 3/92	(39.3 overs) 203
C. D. Fraser-Darling lbw b Holmes	0	4/116 5/187 6/187	
†B. N. French st Metson b Holmes	0	7/187 8/197 9/201	

Bowling: Thomas 7.3–0–36–1; Smith 8–0–55–1; Base 4–0–27–0; Shastri 8–0–33–2; Holmes 8–0–27–5; Derrick 4–0–21–0.

Glamorgan

J. A. Hopkins b Cooper	12	I. Smith b Saxelby	3
*H. Morris c Robinson b Saxelby	7	†C. P. Metson not out	2
G. C. Holmes run out	14	S. J. Base run out	3
M. P. Maynard run out	47	B 1, l-b 12, w 4	17
R. J. Shastri lbw b Hemmings	11		
P. A. Cottey c French b Rice	10	1/23 2/25 3/47	(36 overs) 133
J. G. Thomas c Broad b Rice	7	4/71 5/102 6/116	
J. Derrick b Hadlee	0	7/118 8/126 9/128	

Bowling: Saxelby 6–2–17–2; Cooper 7–0–19–1; Hemmings 8–1–27–1; Hadlee 8–1–23–1; Rice 7–0–34–2.

Umpires: H. D. Bird and R. Palmer.

At Luton, June 21. GLAMORGAN beat NORTHAMPTONSHIRE by 6 runs.

At Lord's, June 28. GLAMORGAN lost to MIDDLESEX by four wickets.

At Cheadle, July 12. GLAMORGAN lost to DERBYSHIRE by one wicket.

GLAMORGAN v SURREY

At Cardiff, July 19. No result.

GLAMORGAN v WARWICKSHIRE

At Swansea, July 26. Warwickshire won by six wickets. Toss: Warwickshire.

Glamorgan

J. A. Hopkins c Gifford b Parsons	12	†C. P. Metson b Munton	11
*H. Morris c Tedstone b Parsons	17	I. Smith c Lloyd b Merrick	2
G. C. Holmes c Tedstone b P. A. Smith	20	S. R. Barwick not out	3
M. P. Maynard c Tedstone b Munton	13	L-b 7, w 7, n-b 3	17
R. J. Shastri c P. A. Smith b Munton	26		
R. C. Ontong c P. A. Smith b Gifford	9	1/18 2/50 3/58	(9 wkts, 40 overs) 144
P. A. Todd c and b Gifford	2	4/69 5/86 6/90	
J. Derrick not out	12	7/112 8/126 9/129	

Bowling: Merrick 8–2–29–1; Parsons 8–0–21–2; Gifford 8–0–13–2; P. A. Smith 5–0–26–1; Munton 8–0–32–3; Moles 3–0–16–0.

Warwickshire

A. J. Moles st Metson b Shastri	19	†G. A. Tedstone not out	31
T. A. Lloyd run out	38	L-b 5, w 7, n-b 2	14
Asif Din run out	16		
D. L. Amiss run out	10	1/40 2/61 3/91 (4 wkts, 38 overs) 145	
P. A. Smith not out	17	4/97	

N. M. K. Smith, T. A. Merrick, G. J. Parsons, T. A. Munton and *N. Gifford did not bat.

Bowling: Barwick 4–1–5–0; Smith 4–0–23–0; Shastri 8–0–27–1; Ontong 8–0–18–0; Derrick 7–0–29–0; Holmes 7–1–38–0.

Umpires: K. E. Palmer and P. B. Wight.

At Weston-super-Mare, August 2. GLAMORGAN beat SOMERSET by seven wickets.

At Bournemouth, August 9. GLAMORGAN beat HAMPSHIRE by five wickets.

GLAMORGAN v WORCESTERSHIRE

At Swansea, August 16. Worcestershire won by 30 runs in a match reduced to 39 overs a side. Toss: Glamorgan.

Worcestershire

T. S. Curtis c Ontong b Holmes	86	*P. A. Neale lbw b Barwick	0
I. T. Botham b Smith	57	S. R. Lampitt not out	12
G. A. Hick run out	21	B 4, l-b 12, w 11, n-b 2	29
D. B. D'Oliveira c Holmes b Ontong	28		
N. V. Radford not out	41	1/104 2/166 3/208 (6 wkts, 39 overs) 275	
†S. J. Rhodes b Barwick	1	4/235 5/236 6/236	

P. J. Newport, A. P. Pridgeon and R. K. Illingworth did not bat.

Bowling: Thomas 8–1–45–0; Barwick 8–0–68–2; Smith 6–0–44–1; Shastri 8–0–53–0; Ontong 8–0–46–1; Holmes 1–0–3–1.

Glamorgan

A. R. Butcher c Curtis b Pridgeon	6	I. Smith c Illingworth b Lampitt	14
P. A. Todd c Rhodes b Pridgeon	4	†C. P. Metson not out	16
M. P. Maynard b Illingworth	28	S. R. Barwick not out	1
R. J. Shastri c and b Lampitt	46	L-b 6, w 3	9
G. C. Holmes run out	51		
J. G. Thomas b Illingworth	8	1/7 2/15 3/68 (9 wkts, 39 overs) 245	
R. C. Ontong c Illingworth b Radford	46	4/120 5/141 6/160	
*H. Morris b Hick	16	7/191 8/210 9/243	

Bowling: Pridgeon 5–0–19–2; Newport 6–0–30–0; Radford 7–0–47–1; Illingworth 8–0–51–2; Lampitt 8–0–64–2; Hick 5–0–28–1.

Umpires: J. Birkenshaw and D. G. L. Evans.

GLAMORGAN v ESSEX

At Neath, August 23. Essex won by 13 runs. Toss: Essex.

Essex

B. R. Hardie c Metson b Base	23	N. A. Foster not out	35
J. P. Stephenson run out	39	†D. E. East not out	4
P. J. Prichard lbw b Holmes	2	B 2, l-b 3, w 2, n-b 1	8
D. R. Pringle run out	4		—
A. W. Lilley b North	12	1/47 2/50 3/58 (6 wkts, 40 overs) 179	
*K. W. R. Fletcher b Holmes	52	4/79 5/91 6/175	

G. Miller, J. K. Lever and T. D. Topley did not bat.

Bowling: Barwick 8-1-41-0; Base 8-0-26-1; Holmes 8-0-50-2; Ontong 8-1-27-0; North 8-1-30-1.

Glamorgan

A. R. Butcher st East b Miller	16	†C. P. Metson c Prichard b Lever	10
P. A. Todd b Lever	6	S. J. Base c Hardie b Lever	4
M. P. Maynard run out	16	B 3, l-b 5, w 4, n-b 2	14
R. C. Ontong b Foster	37		—
G. C. Holmes b Lever	34	1/15 2/40 3/41 (8 wkts, 40 overs) 166	
*H. Morris not out	27	4/117 5/121 6/131	
J. Derrick c Foster b Topley	2	7/161 8/166	

P. D. North and S. R. Barwick did not bat.

Bowling: Foster 8-1-35-1; Lever 8-1-28-4; Miller 8-0-23-1; Topley 8-0-34-1; Pringle 8-0-38-0.

Umpires: J. W. Holder and A. G. T. Whitehead.

At Leicester, September 6. LEICESTERSHIRE v GLAMORGAN. No result.

At Bristol, September 13. GLAMORGAN lost to GLOUCESTERSHIRE by six wickets.

GLOUCESTERSHIRE

GLOUCESTERSHIRE v WARWICKSHIRE

At Bristol, May 17. Gloucestershire won on faster scoring-rate when rain ended play after earlier showers had first reduced the match to 28 overs a side and then reduced Warwickshire's target to 144 off 26 overs. Toss: Warwickshire.

Gloucestershire

A. W. Stovold b Munton	45	*D. A. Graveney run out	0
A. J. Wright run out	21	G. E. Sainsbury not out	0
C. W. J. Athey c Thorne b Merrick	21	B 1, l-b 3, w 6	10
J. W. Lloyds b Gifford	7		—
*P. Bainbridge not out	38	1/46 2/76 3/88 (8 wkts, 28 overs) 154	
M. W. Alleyne c Munton b Merrick	4	4/105 5/127 6/146	
†R. C. Russell c Storie b Merrick	4	7/153 8/153	
C. A. Walsh c Humpage b Munton	4		

D. V. Lawrence did not bat.

Bowling: Merrick 8-2-29-3; Smith 5-0-18-0; Parsons 6-0-41-0; Munton 6-0-38-2; Gifford 3-0-24-1.

Warwickshire

A. J. Moles run out	1	†G. W. Humpage not out	3
T. A. Lloyd not out	57	L-b 7, w 4, n-b 1	12
D. A. Thorne st Russell b Bainbridge	14		
P. A. Smith c Russell b Walsh	18	1/2 2/44 3/101 (3 wkts, 20 overs)	105

A. C. Storie, Asif Din, G. J. Parsons, T. A. Merrick, T. A. Munton and *N. Gifford did not bat.

Bowling: Lawrence 4–0–19–0; Sainsbury 5–0–32–0; Bainbridge 6–1–32–1; Walsh 5–0–15–1.

Umpires: D. J. Constant and B. Dudleston.

At Taunton, May 24. GLOUCESTERSHIRE lost to SOMERSET by 29 runs.

At Southampton, May 31. GLOUCESTERSHIRE tied with HAMPSHIRE.

At Lord's, June 7. GLOUCESTERSHIRE beat MIDDLESEX by eight wickets.

GLOUCESTERSHIRE v SUSSEX

At Swindon, June 14. Gloucestershire won by four wickets. Toss: Gloucestershire.

Sussex

A. M. Green c Russell b Tomlins	31	S. D. Myles not out	1
*I. J. Gould c Athey b Lawrence	9		
C. M. Wells c Tomlins b Walsh	42	L-b 6, w 4, n-b 1	11
A. P. Wells b Alleyne	52		
G. S. le Roux not out	69	1/22 2/65 3/125 (5 wkts, 40 overs)	221
D. A. Reeve b Walsh	6	4/169 5/213	

†P. Moores, C. I. O. Ricketts, A. M. Babington and D. K. Standing did not bat.

Bowling: Walsh 8–0–26–2; Lawrence 8–0–33–1; Bainbridge 8–0–60–0; Alleyne 8–0–44–1; Tomlins 4–0–22–1; Graveney 4–0–30–0.

Gloucestershire

A. W. Stovold c Green b C. M. Wells	0	K. P. Tomlins c and b Standing	11
A. J. Wright lbw b le Roux	80	C. A. Walsh not out	3
C. W. J. Athey st Moores b Standing	70	B 5, l-b 13, w 4, n-b 3	25
P. Bainbridge b Standing	14		
J. W. Lloyds lbw b Reeve	3	1/0 2/138 3/174 (6 wkts, 40 overs)	224
M. W. Alleyne not out	18	4/185 5/190 6/208	

†R. C. Russell, *D. A. Graveney and D. V. Lawrence did not bat.

Bowling: C. M. Wells 8–1–19–1; le Roux 8–1–31–1; Reeve 8–0–36–1; Babington 6–0–40–0; Ricketts 4–0–32–0; Myles 2–0–20–0; Standing 4–0–28–3.

Umpires: A. A. Jones and B. J. Meyer.

At Ilkeston, June 21. GLOUCESTERSHIRE lost to DERBYSHIRE by 18 runs.

GLOUCESTERSHIRE v WORCESTERSHIRE

At Gloucester, June 28. No result, rain having ended play. Toss: Worcestershire.

Gloucestershire

A. J. Wright c Radford b Newport	1	*D. A. Graveney b Dilley	1
†R. C. Russell b Radford	70	D. V. Lawrence c Illingworth b Botham	1
C. W. J. Athey b Botham	17	G. E. Sainsbury b Botham	0
K. M. Curran c Pridgeon b Botham ..	6	L-b 8, w 4, n-b 2	14
P. Bainbridge c Pridgeon b Dilley	8		
J. W. Lloyds b Botham	7	1/10 2/54 3/69 (29.5 overs) 149	
C. A. Walsh run out	6	4/90 5/121 6/121	
M. W. Alleyne not out	18	7/139 8/144 9/147	

Bowling: Dilley 8–0–43–2; Newport 5–0–21–1; Botham 7.5–1–27–5; Radford 8–0–43–1; Pridgeon 1–0–7–0.

Worcestershire

T. S. Curtis not out	30
I. T. Botham c Alleyne b Sainsbury ...	11
G. A. Hick not out	18
L-b 3, w 4	7

1/33   (1 wkt, 14.5 overs) 66

D. B. D'Oliveira, *P. A. Neale, †S. J. Rhodes, P. J. Newport, N. V. Radford, R. K. Illingworth, G. R. Dilley and A. P. Pridgeon did not bat.

Bowling: Lawrence 5–0–22–0; Sainsbury 6–0–27–1; Walsh 2.5–0–13–0; Bainbridge 1–0–1–0.

Umpires: J. Birkenshaw and D. G. L. Evans.

At Chelmsford, July 12. GLOUCESTERSHIRE beat ESSEX by 33 runs.

GLOUCESTERSHIRE v YORKSHIRE

At Bristol, July 19. Gloucestershire won by four wickets. Toss: Gloucestershire. The match, already reduced to 29 overs, was interrupted by rain when Yorkshire had faced 26.3 overs, whereupon Gloucestershire were set a target of 140 off 26 overs.

Yorkshire

K. Sharp b Walsh	0	*P. Carrick not out	8
A. A. Metcalfe c Wright b Sainsbury ..	7		
J. D. Love b Lawrence	20	L-b 7, w 1, n-b 2	10
†D. L. Bairstow b Alleyne	14		
P. E. Robinson b Alleyne	41	1/2 2/15 3/43 (5 wkts, 26.3 overs) 142	
S. N. Hartley not out	42	4/47 5/116	

P. J. Hartley, A. Sidebottom, P. W. Jarvis and S. D. Fletcher did not bat.

Bowling: Walsh 5.3–2–12–1; Sainsbury 6–1–17–1; Lawrence 5–0–38–1; Alleyne 6–0–41–2; Graveney 4–0–27–0.

Gloucestershire

A. J. Wright c Bairstow b Jarvis	12	M. W. Alleyne not out	4
†R. C. Russell lbw b Sidebottom	1	C. A. Walsh not out	16
C. W. J. Athey b Fletcher	12	B 3, l-b 14, w 4	21
J. W. Lloyds c Sharp b Fletcher	47		
K. M. Curran c Bairstow b Jarvis	21	1/3 2/15 3/60 (6 wkts, 25.2 overs) 142
P. W. Romaines b Fletcher	8	4/110 5/120 6/120

*D. A. Graveney, D. V. Lawrence and G. E. Sainsbury did not bat.

Bowling: Sidebottom 7–2–20–1; Jarvis 6–1–27–2; P. J. Hartley 5.2–0–29–0; Fletcher 6–0–45–3; S. N. Hartley 1–0–4–0.

Umpires: H. D. Bird and A. A. Jones.

At Finedon, July 26. NORTHAMPTONSHIRE v GLOUCESTERSHIRE. No result.

GLOUCESTERSHIRE v LEICESTERSHIRE

At Cheltenham, August 2. Leicestershire won by seven wickets. Toss: Leicestershire.

Gloucestershire

A. W. Stovold b Lewis	37	C. A. Walsh b DeFreitas	0
C. W. J. Athey c Whitticase b Agnew	12	*D. A. Graveney b DeFreitas	4
K. M. Curran c Gower b Lewis	60	G. E. Sainsbury not out	1
J. W. Lloyds c Gower b Ferris	2	L-b 11, w 8, n-b 4	23
P. Bainbridge c Willey b Clift	11		
P. W. Romaines not out	29	1/18 2/130 3/130 (9 wkts, 40 overs) 198
M. W. Alleyne c Whitticase b Clift	0	4/132 5/154 6/155
†R. C. Russell run out	19	7/188 8/192 9/197

Bowling: Ferris 8–0–28–1; Agnew 8–1–40–1; DeFreitas 8–0–52–2; Lewis 8–1–40–2; Clift 8–1–27–2.

Leicestershire

I. P. Butcher lbw b Sainsbury	7	J. J. Whitaker not out	5
N. E. Briers c Athey b Lloyds	62	L-b 6, w 3	9
D. I. Gower c Russell b Bainbridge	24		
*P. Willey not out	95	1/29 2/56 3/167 (3 wkts, 37.3 overs) 202

P. B. Clift, †P. Whitticase, P. A. J. DeFreitas, C. C. Lewis, G. J. F. Ferris and J. P. Agnew did not bat.

Bowling: Sainsbury 6–0–31–1; Walsh 8–1–38–0; Bainbridge 7–1–27–1; Alleyne 3–0–24–0; Graveney 8–0–36–0; Lloyds 5.3–1–40–1.

Umpires: J. A. Jameson and D. R. Shepherd.

GLOUCESTERSHIRE v KENT

At Cheltenham, August 9. Gloucestershire won by five wickets. Toss: Gloucestershire.

Kent

M. R. Benson c Athey b Alleyne	50
S. G. Hinks c Tomlins b Sainsbury	23
C. J. Tavaré c Lloyds b Walsh	5
D. G. Aslett c Russell b Curran	6
*C. S. Cowdrey c Walsh b Curran	23
E. A. E. Baptiste c Lloyds b Walsh	20
N. R. Taylor c Curran b Walsh	10
†S. A. Marsh c Wright b Walsh	27

A. P. Igglesden not out 13
R. P. Davis c Sainsbury b Lawrence ... 4
K. B. S. Jarvis not out 0
B 2, l-b 5, w 5 12

1/38 2/45 3/70   (9 wkts, 40 overs) 193
4/106 5/123 6/135
7/174 8/185 9/185

Bowling: Lawrence 8-0-51-1; Sainsbury 8-0-36-1; Walsh 8-1-19-4; Curran 8-0-32-2; Alleyne 8-0-48-1.

Gloucestershire

A. J. Wright c Benson b Igglesden	14
*C. W. J. Athey lbw b Cowdrey	48
K. M. Curran c Benson b Jarvis	28
J. W. Lloyds b Igglesden	38
P. W. Romaines c Tavaré b Cowdrey	16
†R. C. Russell not out	11

M. W. Alleyne not out 23

B 4, l-b 6, w 6 16

1/22 2/74 3/122   (5 wkts, 36.4 overs) 194
4/159 5/160

K. P. Tomlins, C. A. Walsh, D. V. Lawrence and G. E. Sainsbury did not bat.

Bowling: Igglesden 7-0-33-2; Baptiste 6-0-26-0; Cowdrey 8-0-37-2; Davis 8-1-42-0; Jarvis 7.4-0-46-1.

Umpires: J. H. Harris and N. T. Plews.

GLOUCESTERSHIRE v NOTTINGHAMSHIRE

At Moreton-in-Marsh, August 23. Gloucestershire won by 2 runs in a match reduced by rain to 30 overs a side. Toss: Nottinghamshire. Saxelby took his 100th wicket in the Sunday League, when he dismissed Ibadulla.

Gloucestershire

†R. C. Russell b Pick	13
A. J. Wright c Hadlee b Bore	16
C. W. J. Athey c French b Pick	16
K. M. Curran c Rice b Pick	14
P. W. Romaines c French b Pick	13
M. W. Alleyne lbw b Hadlee	3
K. B. K. Ibadulla c French b Saxelby	12
J. N. Shepherd c and b Rice	1

C. A. Walsh run out 11
*P. Bainbridge not out 4
G. E. Sainsbury b Rice 2
L-b 4, w 1, n-b 1 6

1/22 2/38 3/56   (29.3 overs) 111
4/70 5/77 6/86
7/90 8/95 9/107

Bowling: Saxelby 6-1-21-1; Bore 6-0-23-1; Hadlee 6-1-13-1; Pick 6-1-32-4; Rice 5.3-0-18-2.

Nottinghamshire

B. C. Broad c Russell b Sainsbury	0
R. T. Robinson b Shepherd	19
P. Johnson run out	1
*C. E. B. Rice b Shepherd	17
J. D. Birch c and b Alleyne	18
R. J. Hadlee not out	36
E. E. Hemmings c Walsh b Alleyne	1

†B. N. French b Walsh 9
R. A. Pick not out 1

L-b 6, w 1 7

1/0 2/5 3/37   (7 wkts, 30 overs) 109
4/52 5/68 6/74 7/103

M. K. Bore and K. Saxelby did not bat.

Bowling: Sainsbury 6-1-11-1; Shepherd 6-1-20-2; Walsh 6-0-17-1; Alleyne 6-0-17-2; Bainbridge 6-0-38-0.

Umpires: K. J. Lyons and R. A. White.

At Manchester, August 30. GLOUCESTERSHIRE lost to LANCASHIRE by 13 runs.

At The Oval, September 6. GLOUCESTERSHIRE beat SURREY on faster scoring-rate.

GLOUCESTERSHIRE v GLAMORGAN

At Bristol, September 13. Gloucestershire won by six wickets. Toss: Gloucestershire.

Glamorgan

A. R. Butcher c Romaines b Curran ... 6	P. D. North c Russell b Walsh 0
J. A. Hopkins b Curran 23	†C. P. Metson not out 5
M. P. Maynard c Curran b Alleyne .. 66	
G. C. Holmes lbw b Sainsbury 14	L-b 7, w 5 12
P. A. Todd c Curran b Bainbridge .. 31	
*H. Morris b Walsh 2	1/10 2/52 3/83 (8 wkts, 40 overs) 191
I. Smith c Curran b Alleyne 11	4/148 5/150 6/155
J. Derrick not out 21	7/171 8/171

S. R. Barwick did not bat.

Bowling: Curran 8–1–24–2; Sainsbury 8–0–49–1; Walsh 8–0–27–2; Bainbridge 7–0–39–1; Alleyne 8–0–33–2; Graveney 1–0–12–0.

Gloucestershire

C. W. J. Athey c Metson b Smith 0	P. Bainbridge not out 5
†R. C. Russell not out 72	L-b 6, w 3 9
K. M. Curran st Metson b North 55	
J. W. Lloyds c Smith b Derrick 30	1/1 2/119 3/158 (4 wkts, 37.3 overs) 193
P. W. Romaines c Metson b Barwick .. 22	4/188

A. J. Wright, M. W. Alleyne, C. A. Walsh, *D. A. Graveney and G. E. Sainsbury did not bat.

Bowling: Barwick 7–1–26–1; Smith 8–1–29–1; North 8–0–51–1; Holmes 6.3–0–27–0; Derrick 8–0–54–1.

Umpires: J. W. Holder and R. A. White.

HAMPSHIRE

At Leicester, May 3. HAMPSHIRE beat LEICESTERSHIRE by 5 runs.

HAMPSHIRE v SURREY

At Southampton, May 10. Hampshire won by 75 runs. Toss: Surrey. The fourth-wicket stand of 219 between Greenidge and Smith was a record for the 40-overs competition. Greenidge's 172, which came off 142 balls, with ten sixes and thirteen fours, was the highest by a Hampshire player in the Sunday League.

Hampshire

C. G. Greenidge c Falkner b Greig ...172	M. D. Marshall not out 3
V. P. Terry lbw b Thomas 8	
*M. C. J. Nicholas b Thomas 0	L-b 12, w 2, n-b 10 24
D. R. Turner c Ward b Doughty 10	
C. L. Smith not out 60	1/23 2/23 3/54 (5 wkts, 40 overs) 281
K. D. James c Ward b Greig 4	4/273 5/278

N. G. Cowley, T. M. Tremlett, †R. J. Parks and C. A. Connor did not bat.

Bowling: Thomas 8–1–35–2; Gray 7–0–59–0; Feltham 8–0–53–0; Doughty 6–0–35–1; Greig 7–0–55–2; Bullen 4–0–32–0.

Surrey

N. J. Falkner c Nicholas b Marshall	52	R. J. Doughty b Marshall	18
G. S. Clinton c Greenidge b Tremlett	49	C. K. Bullen run out	25
T. E. Jesty c and b Connor	7	A. H. Gray not out	7
Zahid Sadiq lbw b Cowley	0	L-b 4, w 2	6
†D. M. Ward b Cowley	3		
D. J. Thomas c James b Tremlett	10	1/78 2/86 3/87	(36.4 overs) 206
*I. A. Greig c Terry b Cowley	16	4/111 5/117 6/130	
M. A. Feltham c Connor b Tremlett	13	7/150 8/162 9/189	

Bowling: James 7.4–0–41–0; Connor 6–1–35–1; Tremlett 8–0–56–3; Marshall 7–0–34–2; Cowley 8–0–36–3.

Umpires: D. G. L. Evans and D. R. Shepherd.

At Northampton, May 17. NORTHAMPTONSHIRE v HAMPSHIRE. No result.

At Manchester, May 24. HAMPSHIRE lost to LANCASHIRE by five wickets.

HAMPSHIRE v GLOUCESTERSHIRE

At Southampton, May 31. Tied. Toss: Gloucestershire.

Hampshire

V. P. Terry c Alleyne b Lloyds	32	T. M. Tremlett c Walsh b Bainbridge	2
R. J. Scott c Russell b Walsh	0	R. J. Maru not out	6
D. R. Turner c Russell b Bainbridge	9	C. A. Connor not out	0
K. D. James run out	37	L-b 4, w 5	9
*M. C. J. Nicholas c Athey b Bainbridge	60		
C. L. Smith lbw b Walsh	45	1/4 2/17 3/78	(9 wkts, 40 overs) 214
M. D. Marshall b Alleyne	4	4/84 5/189 6/195	
†R. J. Parks c Walsh b Bainbridge	10	7/199 8/206 9/208	

Bowling: Lawrence 8–0–29–0; Walsh 8–2–35–2; Bainbridge 8–0–50–4; Graveney 4–0–24–0; Alleyne 5–0–39–1; Lloyds 7–0–33–1.

Gloucestershire

A. W. Stovold b Marshall	33	M. W. Alleyne not out	5
C. W. J. Athey c Parks b Marshall	41		
K. M. Curran run out	69	B 1, l-b 7, w 6	14
J. W. Lloyds run out	11		
P. Bainbridge b Tremlett	36	1/53 2/110 3/127	(5 wkts, 40 overs) 214
P. W. Romaines not out	5	4/201 5/206	

†R. C. Russell, *D. A. Graveney, C. A. Walsh and D. V. Lawrence did not bat.

Bowling: James 8–0–37–0; Connor 8–1–36–0; Tremlett 8–0–47–1; Marshall 8–0–35–2; Nicholas 3–0–21–0; Maru 5–0–30–0.

Umpires: K. E. Palmer and A. G. T. Whitehead.

At Horsham, June 7. HAMPSHIRE lost to SUSSEX by one wicket.

HAMPSHIRE v DERBYSHIRE

At Southampton, June 14. Tied. Toss: Hampshire.

Derbyshire

*K. J. Barnett c Aymes b Marshall	37	C. F. B. P. Rudd run out	3
†B. J. M. Maher run out	5	M. Jean-Jacques lbw b Marshall	1
B. Roberts run out	2	O. H. Mortensen not out	1
J. E. Morris c Nicholas b Connor	81	B 4, l-b 8, w 3, n-b 1	16
I. S. Anderson st Aymes b Maru	32		
M. A. Holding b Marshall	26	1/19 2/24 3/64 (39.3 overs) 206	
P. G. Newman lbw b Marshall	0	4/133 5/191 6/191	
A. E. Warner c Aymes b Connor	2	7/194 8/201 9/204	

Bowling: Connor 7.3–0–33–2; James 8–0–44–0; Tremlett 7–0–25–0; Marshall 8–0–33–4; Maru 8–0–43–1; Nicholas 1–0–16–0.

Hampshire

V. P. Terry run out	69	M. D. Marshall c Holding	
D. R. Turner c Roberts b Mortensen	40	b Jean-Jacques	1
R. A. Smith run out	3	R. J. Maru not out	0
*M. C. J. Nicholas c Anderson		L-b 9, w 13, n-b 2	24
b Warner	49		
C. L. Smith c Anderson b Newman	11	1/81 2/87 3/166 (6 wkts, 40 overs) 206	
K. D. James not out	9	4/194 5/198 6/202	

†A. N. Aymes, C. A. Connor and T. M. Tremlett did not bat.

Bowling: Mortensen 8–0–30–1; Newman 8–0–35–1; Warner 8–0–44–1; Holding 8–0–41–0; Rudd 2–0–12–0; Jean-Jacques 6–0–35–1.

Umpires: K. J. Lyons and D. O. Oslear.

HAMPSHIRE v MIDDLESEX

At Basingstoke, June 21. Hampshire won by seven wickets. Toss: Middlesex.

Middlesex

W. N. Slack c James b Tremlett	18	N. F. Williams c Tremlett b Marshall	17
J. D. Carr c Parks b Connor	12	S. P. Hughes not out	8
C. T. Radley c and b James	17	A. R. C. Fraser c Parks b Connor	2
A. Needham b Marshall	9		
R. O. Butcher c and b Maru	11	L-b 5, w 2	7
M. R. Ramprakash c Tremlett			
b Marshall	1	1/24 2/47 3/48 (40 overs) 143	
*†P. R. Downton c James b Connor	30	4/63 5/70 6/74	
J. F. Sykes c and b Tremlett	11	7/105 8/132 9/135	

Bowling: James 8–0–26–1; Connor 8–0–39–3; Tremlett 8–0–23–2; Maru 8–1–23–1; Marshall 8–0–27–3.

Hampshire

D. R. Turner c Carr b Needham	12	V. P. Terry not out	7
C. L. Smith not out	71	L-b 4, w 1, n-b 1	6
R. A. Smith b Needham	12		
*M. C. J. Nicholas b Carr	38	1/31 2/51 3/134 (3 wkts, 38.2 overs) 146	

K. D. James, M. D. Marshall, †R. J. Parks, T. M. Tremlett, R. J. Maru and C. A. Connor did not bat.

Bowling: Williams 6–0–28–0; Fraser 8–0–28–0; Needham 8–1–13–2; Hughes 7–0–30–0; Sykes 7–0–33–0; Carr 2.2–0–10–1.

Umpires: H. D. Bird and J. H. Harris.

At Birmingham, June 28. HAMPSHIRE beat WARWICKSHIRE by 84 runs.

HAMPSHIRE v WORCESTERSHIRE

At Southampton, July 12. Worcestershire won by six wickets. Toss: Hampshire.

Hampshire

C. G. Greenidge c Botham b Dilley	0	†R. J. Parks b Botham		10
C. L. Smith b Botham	13	T. M. Tremlett not out		2
R. A. Smith c Botham b Illingworth	52	C. A. Connor not out		0
*M. C. J. Nicholas c Rhodes b Newport	24	B 1, l-b 7, w 4		12
D. R. Turner b Hick	11			
K. D. James c Curtis b Illingworth	10	1/0 2/37 3/94	(9 wkts, 40 overs)	183
M. D. Marshall c Botham b Dilley	35	4/95 5/116 6/122		
N. G. Cowley b Dilley	14	7/167 8/174 9/182		

Bowling: Dilley 8–1–38–3; Pridgeon 5–1–15–0; Botham 8–1–37–2; Radford 6–0–23–0; Newport 4–0–23–1; Illingworth 5–0–21–2; Hick 4–0–18–1.

Worcestershire

T. S. Curtis c Parks b Marshall	13	†S. J. Rhodes not out		19
I. T. Botham c Turner b Cowley	41	B 1, l-b 8, w 2, n-b 2		13
G. A. Hick lbw b Tremlett	53			
D. B. D'Oliveira c Parks b Marshall	22	1/24 2/82 3/134	(4 wkts, 38.1 overs)	188
*P. A. Neale not out	27	4/140		

P. J. Newport, N. V. Radford, R. K. Illingworth, G. R. Dilley and A. P. Pridgeon did not bat.

Bowling: Marshall 8–2–30–2; James 6.1–1–47–0; Connor 8–0–30–0; Cowley 8–1–37–1; Tremlett 8–0–35–1.

Umpires: K. E. Palmer and N. T. Plews.

HAMPSHIRE v ESSEX

At Portsmouth, July 26. Hampshire won by four wickets. Toss: Hampshire. The seventh-wicket stand of 75 unbroken between Marshall and Parks was a Hampshire record for the Sunday League.

Essex

*G. A. Gooch c Parks b Connor	4	†D. E. East not out		3
G. Miller c Parks b Marshall	2	T. D. Topley c C. L. Smith b Tremlett		4
B. R. Hardie lbw b Marshall	0	J. K. Lever c Parks b Marshall		0
D. R. Pringle st Parks b Tremlett	9	L-b 6, w 1		7
J. P. Stephenson run out	15			
A. W. Lilley c Terry b Cowley	55	1/5 2/5 3/11	(38.5 overs)	122
N. Hussain c Terry b Tremlett	13	4/34 5/34 6/93		
H. A. Page c Terry b Cowley	10	7/113 8/115 9/120		

Bowling: Connor 7–2–9–1; Marshall 7.5–0–21–3; Maru 8–2–19–0; Tremlett 8–1–27–3; Cowley 8–0–40–2.

Hampshire

C. G. Greenidge run out	10	N. G. Cowley c Topley b Lever		2
C. L. Smith c Stephenson b Topley	10	†R. J. Parks not out		38
R. A. Smith b East b Pringle	0	L-b 11, w 3, n-b 1		15
*M. C. J. Nicholas run out	0			
V. P. Terry c East b Gooch	9	1/12 2/14 3/17	(6 wkts, 39.2 overs)	125
M. D. Marshall not out	41	4/36 5/46 6/50		

T. M. Tremlett, R. J. Maru and C. A. Connor did not bat.

Bowling: Lever 8–2–17–1; Pringle 7.2–1–36–1; Topley 8–3–14–1; Page 8–1–21–0; Gooch 8–1–26–1.

Umpires: D. Lloyd and J. A. Jameson.

HAMPSHIRE v GLAMORGAN

At Bournemouth, August 9. Glamorgan won by five wickets by achieving a revised target of 113 in 22 overs. Toss: Glamorgan.

Hampshire

C. G. Greenidge c Shastri b Barwick ..	22	N. G. Cowley c Metson b Holmes	19
V. P. Terry c and b Smith	34	T. M. Tremlett not out	4
R. A. Smith c Metson b Holmes	3	L-b 8, w 13	21
*M. C. J. Nicholas not out	79		
C. L. Smith c Metson b Derrick	16	1/30 2/46 3/96 (6 wkts, 39 overs)	200
M. D. Marshall b Barwick	2	4/132 5/151 6/183	

†R. J. Parks, P. J. Bakker and C. A. Connor did not bat.

Bowling: Barwick 8–0–37–2; Monkhouse 4–0–23–0; Holmes 7–0–50–2; Derrick 8–0–26–1; Shastri 8–0–33–0; Smith 4–0–23–1.

Glamorgan

P. A. Todd b Connor	2	I. Smith not out	9
A. R. Butcher c Cowley b Tremlett ...	10		
M. P. Maynard c Terry b Connor	22	L-b 3, w 2	5
R. J. Shastri b Bakker	36		
G. C. Holmes not out	25	1/5 2/23 3/61 (5 wkts, 20.4 overs)	116
*H. Morris b Bakker	7	4/78 5/99	

S. Monkhouse, J. Derrick, †C. P. Metson and S. R. Barwick did not bat.

Bowling: Connor 6–1–33–2; Marshall 7–0–26–0; Tremlett 2–0–14–1; Bakker 5.4–0–40–2.

Umpires: R. Julian and D. O. Oslear.

At Nottingham, August 16. HAMPSHIRE lost to NOTTINGHAMSHIRE by seven wickets.

HAMPSHIRE v SOMERSET

At Bournemouth, August 23. Somerset won by 24 runs. Toss: Hampshire.

Somerset

*P. M. Roebuck c Tremlett b Connor ..	82	A. N. Jones b Bakker	5
J. G. Wyatt c James b Tremlett	52	N. A. Mallender not out	8
J. J. E. Hardy c C. L. Smith b James ..	14		
R. J. Harden c Cowley b James	2	B 1, l-b 7	8
G. D. Rose c Nicholas b Connor	15		
†N. D. Burns c Nicholas b Bakker	1	1/99 2/131 3/138 (8 wkts, 40 overs)	200
N. A. Felton c James b Bakker	3	4/165 5/171 6/175	
G. V. Palmer not out	10	7/177 8/190	

M. R. Davis did not bat.

Bowling: Connor 7–0–36–2; Bakker 8–0–27–3; Ayling 8–0–37–0; Tremlett 8–1–35–1; Cowley 4–0–28–0; James 5–0–29–2.

Hampshire

V. P. Terry c Rose b Palmer	29	†R. J. Parks not out	10
*M. C. J. Nicholas lbw b Davis	8	C. A. Connor not out	5
R. A. Smith c Harden b Jones	41		
K. D. James b Rose	21	B 4, l-b 8, w 4, n-b 1	17
C. L. Smith b Mallender	16		
J. R. Ayling c Wyatt b Rose	15	1/22 2/86 3/93 (8 wkts, 40 overs) 176	
N. G. Cowley c Burns b Jones	2	4/117 5/145 6/148	
T. M. Tremlett c Mallender b Jones	12	7/150 8/164	

P. J. Bakker did not bat.

Bowling: Jones 8–0–36–3; Mallender 8–1–22–1; Davis 8–0–32–1; Rose 8–0–29–2; Palmer 8–0–45–1.

Umpires: D. J. Constant and D. S. Thompsett.

At Maidstone, August 30. HAMPSHIRE beat KENT by 67 runs.

At Leeds, September 6. YORKSHIRE v HAMPSHIRE. No result.

KENT

At Nottingham, May 3. KENT lost to NOTTINGHAMSHIRE by nine wickets.

KENT v WORCESTERSHIRE

At Canterbury, May 10. Kent won by 49 runs. Toss: Kent.

Kent

S. G. Hinks c D'Oliveira b Dilley	6	E. A. E. Baptiste not out	3
N. R. Taylor c Rhodes b Botham	9		
C. J. Tavaré b Radford	12	L-b 15, n-b 2	17
D. G. Aslett not out	122		
*C. S. Cowdrey st Rhodes b Illingworth	58	1/11 2/31 3/33 (5 wkts, 40 overs) 270	
G. R. Cowdrey c Neale b Illingworth	43	4/168 5/259	

†S. A. Marsh, C. Penn, A. P. Igglesden and R. P. Davis did not bat.

Bowling: Dilley 8–1–57–1; Radford 8–0–34–1; Botham 7–0–36–1; Newport 6–0–31–0; Illingworth 8–0–66–2; Weston 3–0–31–0.

Worcestershire

T. S. Curtis lbw b C. S. Cowdrey	50	P. J. Newport c Penn b Baptiste	3
G. A. Hick c Hinks b C. S. Cowdrey	60	R. K. Illingworth not out	1
I. T. Botham c Baptiste b Penn	11	G. R. Dilley c Marsh b Baptiste	0
D. B. D'Oliveira b C. S. Cowdrey	17	L-b 10, w 1, n-b 3	14
*P. A. Neale c sub b Davis	18		
M. J. Weston c and b Davis	1	1/98 2/122 3/136 (37.5 overs) 221	
†S. J. Rhodes c sub b Baptiste	30	4/166 5/168 6/170	
N. V. Radford run out	16	7/195 8/220 9/220	

Bowling: Igglesden 7–0–34–0; Baptiste 6.5–0–31–3; Davis 8–0–56–2; Penn 8–0–47–1; C. S. Cowdrey 8–0–43–3.

Umpires: M. J. Kitchen and R. Palmer.

At Swansea, May 17. KENT beat GLAMORGAN by 25 runs.

KENT v MIDDLESEX

At Canterbury, May 24. Kent won by 103 runs. Toss: Kent. Middlesex failed to bowl their 40 overs in the allotted time. Williams took his three wickets in four balls.

Kent

M. R. Benson b Needham	87	C. Penn b Daniel 0
S. G. Hinks b Needham	64	D. J. Kelleher b Daniel 0
C. J. Tavaré run out	5	
D. G. Aslett c Carr b Daniel	19	L-b 10, w 1, n-b 1 12
*C. S. Cowdrey c Downton b Williams	18	
G. R. Cowdrey c Downton b Williams	0	1/123 2/137 3/168　(9 wkts, 38 overs) 212
E. A. E. Baptiste c Fraser b Williams	0	4/193 5/193 6/193
†S. A. Marsh not out	7	7/211 8/212 9/212

R. P. Davis did not bat.

Bowling: Williams 6-0-38-3; Hughes 6-0-40-0; Daniel 7-0-24-3; Fraser 8-0-34-0; Needham 8-0-38-2; Slack 3-0-28-0.

Middlesex

W. N. Slack c Marsh b Kelleher	2	S. P. Hughes not out 13
M. R. Ramprakash c Marsh b Kelleher	10	A. R. C. Fraser c Marsh b Penn .. 0
R. O. Butcher c and b Baptiste	4	W. W. Daniel b Baptiste 9
J. D. Carr c Kelleher b C. S. Cowdrey	17	
*†P. R. Downton c Baptiste b Davis	8	L-b 4, w 6, n-b 2 12
M. A. Roseberry c Marsh b Penn	26	
A. Needham c Marsh b C. S. Cowdrey	0	1/3 2/18 3/24 4/45　(32.2 overs) 109
N. F. Williams lbw b Penn	8	5/45 6/45 7/79 8/87 9/87

Bowling: Kelleher 8-0-25-2; Baptiste 4.2-1-9-2; Davis 8-2-17-1; C. S. Cowdrey 8-0-36-2; Penn 4-1-18-3.

Umpires: B. Dudleston and A. A. Jones.

At Middlesbrough, May 31. KENT lost to YORKSHIRE by nine wickets.

At Ilford, June 14. KENT beat ESSEX by 16 runs.

At Manchester, June 21. KENT beat LANCASHIRE by 52 runs.

KENT v SOMERSET

At Canterbury, June 28. Somerset won by 65 runs. Toss: Kent.

Somerset

*V. J. Marks c C. S. Cowdrey b Pienaar	26	G. V. Palmer c Wells b C. S. Cowdrey	2
N. A. Felton c Hinks b Igglesden	5	N. A. Mallender not out	9
J. J. E. Hardy c Wells b Pienaar	8	A. N. Jones not out	2
M. D. Crowe c Wells b C. S. Cowdrey	56		
R. J. Harden c Aslett b G. R. Cowdrey	20	L-b 9, w 2 11
J. C. M. Atkinson c Tavaré		
b C. S. Cowdrey	0	1/13 2/32 3/51　(9 wkts, 40 overs) 156
†N. D. Burns b C. S. Cowdrey	6	4/105 5/107 6/130
G. D. Rose b Igglesden	11	7/130 8/133 9/147

Bowling: Igglesden 8–2–15–2; Kelleher 8–0–14–0; Pienaar 8–0–33–2; G. R. Cowdrey 8–0–47–1; C. S. Cowdrey 8–0–38–4.

Kent

M. R. Benson run out 0	D. J. M. Kelleher c Burns b Palmer ... 0
S. G. Hinks b Jones 6	R. P. Davis not out 7
C. J. Tavaré c Hardy b Marks 25	A. P. Igglesden c Harden b Jones 7
D. G. Aslett c Jones b Palmer 12	
*C. S. Cowdrey c Harden b Palmer 7	L-b 7, n-b 1 8
G. R. Cowdrey c Burns b Palmer 2	
R. F. Pienaar c Jones b Palmer 15	1/1 2/19 3/45 4/50 (34.5 overs) 91
†V. Wells run out 2	5/54 6/57 7/61 8/62 9/75

Bowling: Jones 5.5–1–12–2; Rose 8–3–12–0; Mallender 5–0–14–0; Marks 8–1–22–1; Palmer 8–0–24–5.

Umpires: D. J. Constant and A. A. Jones.

KENT v NORTHAMPTONSHIRE

At Canterbury, July 19. No result.

KENT v DERBYSHIRE

At Canterbury, August 2. Kent won by seven wickets. Toss: Kent.

Derbyshire

*K. J. Barnett c Marsh b Cowdrey 20	M. Jean-Jacques run out 5
†B. J. M. Maher b Jarvis 5	M. Beardshall c Hinks b Baptiste 7
B. Roberts c Marsh b Jarvis 1	O. H. Mortensen not out 2
J. E. Morris b Penn 38	L-b 14, w 13 27
I. S. Anderson lbw b Penn 15	
M. A. Holding c Marsh b Penn 0	1/12 2/15 3/78 (38.4 overs) 147
R. J. Finney c Hinks b Cowdrey 14	4/88 5/88 6/110
R. Sharma c Taylor b Igglesden 13	7/116 8/123 9/142

Bowling: Jarvis 8–0–21–2; Baptiste 7–0–32–1; Igglesden 7.4–1–20–1; Cowdrey 8–0–29–2; Penn 8–0–31–3.

Kent

M. R. Benson c Maher b Jean-Jacques . 13	*C. S. Cowdrey not out 58
S. G. Hinks c Maher b Jean-Jacques .. 8	L-b 3, w 1 4
C. J. Tavaré c Morris b Holding 19	
D. G. Aslett not out 50	1/9 2/30 3/46 (3 wkts, 36.4 overs) 152

N. R. Taylor, E. A. E. Baptiste, †S. Marsh, A. P. Igglesden, C. Penn and K. B. S. Jarvis did not bat.

Bowling: Mortensen 8–0–34–0; Jean-Jacques 7–1–34–2; Holding 7–0–25–1; Beardshall 8–1–23–0; Finney 6.4–0–33–0.

Umpires: R. Julian and R. Palmer.

At Cheltenham, August 9. KENT lost to GLOUCESTERSHIRE by five wickets.

At The Oval, August 16. KENT beat SURREY by 9 runs.

At Leicester, August 23. KENT beat LEICESTERSHIRE by four wickets.

KENT v HAMPSHIRE

At Maidstone, August 30. Hampshire won by 67 runs. Toss: Hampshire.

Hampshire

*V. P. Terry lbw b Cowley	27	K. D. James not out		32
D. R. Turner b Underwood	45		B 4, l-b 10, w 5	19
R. A. Smith st Marsh b Underwood	35			
C. L. Smith not out	76	1/71 2/97 3/143	(3 wkts, 40 overs)	234

S. J. W. Andrew, J. R. Ayling, N. G. Cowley, †R. J. Parks, T. M. Tremlett and C. A. Connor did not bat.

Bowling: Jarvis 8-0-53-0; Baptiste 8-0-56-0; Penn 8-0-38-0; Cowdrey 8-0-40-1; Underwood 8-0-33-2.

Kent

M. R. Benson c Parks b Tremlett	21	C. Penn c Cowley b Andrew		30
S. G. Hinks b Ayling	25	D. L. Underwood b Connor		1
C. J. Tavaré lbw b Cowley	26	K. B. S. Jarvis b Connor		0
D. G. Aslett c Parks b Tremlett	2		L-b 6, n-b 1	7
*C. S. Cowdrey c James b Ayling	4			
E. A. E. Baptiste c Cowley b Ayling	8	1/48 2/48 3/54	(36.5 overs)	167
S. C. Goldsmith not out	43	4/63 5/85 6/99		
†S. A. Marsh b Cowley	0	7/101 8/162 9/167		

Bowling: Connor 6.5-0-25-2; Andrew 7-1-33-1; Ayling 8-0-30-3; Tremlett 7-1-28-2; Cowley 8-0-45-2.

Umpires: K. J. Lyons and N. T. Plews.

KENT v SUSSEX

At Canterbury, September 6. No result. Toss: Sussex.

Kent

M. R. Benson b C. M. Wells	17	D. G. Aslett not out		0
S. C. Goldsmith lbw b C. M. Wells	0		L-b 1, w 1	2
C. J. Tavaré c Gould b Reeve	9			
E. A. E. Baptiste c Babington b Reeve	5	1/1 2/23 3/33	(4 wkts, 13.3 overs)	35
*C. S. Cowdrey not out	2	4/35		

G. R. Cowdrey, †S. A. Marsh, C. Penn, R. P. Davis and K. B. S. Jarvis did not bat.

Bowling: C. M. Wells 7-0-17-2; Reeve 6.3-0-17-2.

Sussex

K. Greenfield, P. W. G. Parker, C. M. Wells, A. P. Wells, *†I. J. Gould, R. I. Alikhan, P. Moores, D. A. Reeve, A. C. S. Pigott, I. C. Waring and A. M. Babington.

Umpires: B. Dudleston and A. G. T. Whitehead.

KENT v WARWICKSHIRE

At Canterbury, September 13. No result.

LANCASHIRE

At Worcester, May 3. LANCASHIRE lost to WORCESTERSHIRE by six wickets.

LANCASHIRE v GLAMORGAN

At Manchester, May 10. Glamorgan won by three wickets. Toss: Lancashire.

Lancashire

G. D. Mendis run out	48	M. Watkinson run out	3
G. Fowler c and b Barwick	21	I. D. Austin not out	1
J. Abrahams c Butcher b Shastri	1	B 1, l-b 11	12
N. H. Fairbrother not out	102		
S. J. O'Shaughnessy c and b Holmes	32	1/32 2/48 3/95 (6 wkts, 40 overs) 236	
*D. P. Hughes c Morris b Holmes	16	4/170 5/210 6/228	

J. Simmons, P. J. W. Allott and †J. Stanworth did not bat.

Bowling: Thomas 8–1–45–0; Barwick 8–0–39–1; Ontong 8–0–32–0; Shastri 4–1–22–1; Holmes 8–0–58–2; Derrick 4–0–28–0.

Glamorgan

J. A. Hopkins c Allott b Hughes	52	J. G. Thomas b Watkinson	13
*H. Morris c Watkinson b Hughes	89	J. Derrick not out	6
A. R. Butcher b Abrahams	24	L-b 7, w 2	9
G. C. Holmes b Hughes	13		
R. C. Ontong not out	22	1/122 2/164 3/181 (7 wkts, 38.3 overs) 237	
R. J. Shastri c sub b Abrahams	6	4/185 5/197	
M. P. Maynard c Hughes b Watkinson	3	6/214 7/229	

†C. P. Metson and S. R. Barwick did not bat.

Bowling: Watkinson 7–0–40–2; Allott 6.3–1–38–0; Simmons 8–0–38–0; O'Shaughnessy 2–0–29–0; Austin 2–0–19–0; Hughes 8–0–47–3; Abrahams 5–0–19–2.

Umpires: J. H. Hampshire and P. B. Wight.

At The Oval, May 17. SURREY v LANCASHIRE. No result.

LANCASHIRE v HAMPSHIRE

At Manchester, May 24. Lancashire won by five wickets. Toss: Lancashire.

Hampshire

R. J. Scott c Austin b Simmons	48	N. G. Cowley b Watkinson	7
V. P. Terry c Stanworth b Austin	27	T. M. Tremlett not out	0
D. R. Turner c Stanworth b Simmons	10	L-b 6, w 5	11
*M. C. J. Nicholas run out	23		
C. L. Smith run out	18	1/66 2/91 3/94 (7 wkts, 40 overs) 175	
K. D. James c Fowler b Allott	4	4/133 5/135	
M. D. Marshall not out	27	6/146 7/166	

†R. J. Parks and S. J. W. Andrew did not bat.

Bowling: Allott 8–1–30–1; Watkinson 8–0–34–1; Austin 8–0–32–1; O'Shaughnessy 8–0–37–0; Simmons 8–1–36–2.

Lancashire

G. D. Mendis b Tremlett 43	M. Watkinson not out 6
G. Fowler c and b Cowley 58	
J. Abrahams c Nicholas b Marshall ... 3	L-b 7, w 1, n-b 1 9
N. H. Fairbrother st Parks b Cowley .. 9	
S. J. O'Shaughnessy not out 30	1/96 2/106 3/110 (5 wkts, 39.5 overs) 179
*D. P. Hughes b Nicholas 21	4/139 5/172

P. J. W. Allott, I. D. Austin, J. Simmons and †J. Stanworth did not bat.

Bowling: Tremlett 8–0–34–1; Cowley 8–0–34–2; Marshall 8–1–18–1; Andrew 6–0–35–0; James 7.5–0–40–0; Nicholas 2–0–11–1.

Umpires: J. A. Jameson and R. A. White.

LANCASHIRE v SOMERSET

At Manchester, May 31. Lancashire won by seven wickets. Toss: Lancashire.

Somerset

J. G. Wyatt lbw b Allott 13	†N. D. Burns not out 13
N. A. Felton c Fowler b Simmons 42	
J. J. E. Hardy lbw b Hughes 52	L-b 7, w 8 15
M. D. Crowe c Austin b Watkinson ... 27	
R. J. Harden b Hughes 35	1/30 2/105 3/122 (6 wkts, 40 overs) 227
*V. J. Marks c sub b Allott 30	4/166 5/191 6/227

G. D. Rose, G. V. Palmer, N. A. Mallender and A. N. Jones did not bat.

Bowling: Watkinson 8–0–54–1; Allott 8–0–30–2; Austin 8–0–30–0; Hayhurst 4–0–15–0; Simmons 8–0–59–1; Hughes 4–0–32–2.

Lancashire

G. D. Mendis lbw b Mallender 3	*D. P. Hughes not out 6
G. Fowler not out 100	
J. Abrahams c Marks b Palmer 12	L-b 6, n-b 1 7
N. H. Fairbrother c Crowe	
b Mallender .102	1/10 2/42 3/218 (3 wkts, 39.2 overs) 230

A. N. Hayhurst, I. D. Austin, M. Watkinson, J. Simmons, P. J. W. Allott and †J. Stanworth did not bat.

Bowling: Mallender 8–0–45–2; Jones 8–0–42–0; Rose 8–0–38–0; Palmer 4.2–0–32–1; Marks 8–0–48–0; Crowe 3–0–19–0.

Umpires: B. Dudleston and D. O. Oslear.

LANCASHIRE v KENT

At Manchester, June 21. Kent won by 52 runs. Toss: Lancashire. Kent's total was their highest and the highest by any county against Lancashire in the Sunday League, while the seventh-wicket stand of 130 between Hughes and Hayhurst of Lancashire was a record for the competition.

Kent

S. G. Hinks c O'Shaughnessy	D. G. Aslett not out 7
b Watkinson . 14	
M. R. Benson c O'Shaughnessy b Hughes 92	B 4, l-b 13, w 6 23
C. J. Tavaré c O'Shaughnessy b Hughes 90	
*C. S. Cowdrey not out 60	1/27 2/197 3/233 (4 wkts, 40 overs) 290
G. R. Cowdrey c Fairbrother b Hughes 4	4/252

R. F. Pienaar, †S. A. Marsh, D. J. M. Kelleher, R. P. Davis and A. P. Igglesden did not bat.

Bowling: Watkinson 8–1–48–1; Hayhurst 6–1–21–0; O'Shaughnessy 4–0–25–0; Austin 7–0–49–0; Folley 8–0–57–0; Hughes 7–0–73–3.

Lancashire

G. D. Mendis c Marsh b Igglesden	29	I. D. Austin run out	3
G. Fowler c Hinks b Kelleher	6	I. Folley c Marsh b Pienaar	3
D. W. Varey lbw b G. R. Cowdrey	15	†J. Stanworth not out	1
N. H. Fairbrother c Marsh b G. R. Cowdrey	5	B 1, l-b 11, w 10	22
S. J. O'Shaughnessy b G. R. Cowdrey	0		
*D. P. Hughes c Marsh b Igglesden	72	1/12 2/54 3/56 (38.1 overs) 238	
M. Watkinson b G. R. Cowdrey	21	4/56 5/61 6/99	
A. N. Hayhurst b Igglesden	61	7/229 8/230 9/235	

Bowling: Igglesden 7.1–0–40–3; Kelleher 8–0–53–1; Pienaar 7–0–41–1; G. R. Cowdrey 8–0–42–4; Davis 8–0–50–0.

Umpires: J. Birkenshaw and B. Leadbeater.

LANCASHIRE v DERBYSHIRE

At Manchester, June 28. No result, rain having ended play. Toss: Lancashire.

Derbyshire

*K. J. Barnett run out	18	I. S. Anderson not out	23
†B. J. M. Maher b Simmons	78	A. E. Warner not out	16
B. Roberts c Fowler b O'Shaughnessy	56	L-b 7	7
M. A. Holding b Simmons	5		
J. E. Morris run out	15	1/37 2/156 3/159 (6 wkts, 40 overs) 228	
P. G. Newman c Simmons b Allott	10	4/173 5/183 6/196	

M. Jean-Jacques, C. F. B. P. Rudd and O. H. Mortensen did not bat.

Bowling: Allott 8–1–37–1; Watkinson 7–0–35–0; Hayhurst 4–1–14–0; Austin 5–0–32–0; Simmons 8–0–43–2; O'Shaughnessy 8–0–60–1.

Lancashire

G. D. Mendis not out	8
G. Fowler not out	6

(no wkt, 1.5 overs) 14

S. J. O'Shaughnessy, N. H. Fairbrother, *D. P. Hughes, M. Watkinson, A. N. Hayhurst, I. D. Austin, J. Simmons, P. J. W. Allott and †J. Stanworth did not bat.

Bowling: Newman 1–0–7–0; Mortensen 0.5–0–7–0.

Umpires: N. T. Plews and A. G. T. Whitehead.

At Tring, July 5. LANCASHIRE lost to NORTHAMPTONSHIRE by 54 runs.

LANCASHIRE v LEICESTERSHIRE

At Manchester, July 12. Leicestershire won by 1 run. Toss: Lancashire. Leicestershire won their first Sunday match of the season in their seventh match.

Leicestershire

*P. Willey c Hegg b Watkinson	6	†P. Whitticase run out 1
N. E. Briers c Hegg b Watkinson	5	P. A. J. DeFreitas not out 20
D. I. Gower c Hughes b Simmons	67	L. B. Taylor not out 5
J. J. Whitaker c Simmons b Allott	46	L-b 6, w 4 10
T. J. Boon lbw b Simmons	10	
P. B. Clift c Hegg b O'Shaughnessy	23	1/10 2/29 3/121　　(8 wkts, 40 overs) 198
W. K. M. Benjamin c O'Shaughnessy		4/134 5/163 6/163
b Patterson	5	7/174 8/182

J. P. Agnew did not bat.

Bowling: Watkinson 8–1–30–2; Patterson 8–0–33–1; Allott 8–0–43–1; Hayhurst 4–0–36–0; Simmons 8–1–31–2; O'Shaughnessy 4–0–19–1.

Lancashire

G. D. Mendis c Whitticase b Clift	22	M. Watkinson run out 0
G. Fowler lbw b Agnew	87	B 1, l-b 6, w 4, n-b 1 12
N. H. Fairbrother b Taylor	29	
S. J. O'Shaughnessy not out	29	1/57 2/130 3/145　　(5 wkts, 40 overs) 197
*D. P. Hughes run out	18	4/185 5/197

A. N. Hayhurst, J. Simmons, P. J. W. Allott, B. P. Patterson and †W. K. Hegg did not bat.

Bowling: Agnew 8–0–40–1; DeFreitas 8–0–40–0; Clift 8–0–25–1; Willey 5–0–23–0; Benjamin 8–0–39–0; Taylor 3–0–23–1.

Umpires: R. Julian and D. O. Oslear.

At Hastings, July 19. SUSSEX v LANCASHIRE. No result.

LANCASHIRE v NOTTINGHAMSHIRE

At Manchester, July 26. No result.

At Scarborough, August 2. LANCASHIRE beat YORKSHIRE by four wickets.

At Lord's, August 9. LANCASHIRE beat MIDDLESEX by four wickets.

At Birmingham, August 23. WARWICKSHIRE v LANCASHIRE. No result.

LANCASHIRE v GLOUCESTERSHIRE

At Manchester, August 30. Lancashire won by 13 runs. Toss: Lancashire.

Lancashire

M. A. Atherton b Sainsbury	2	J. D. Fitton b Walsh 0
N. J. Speak c Athey b Sainsbury	13	†W. K. Hegg b Walsh 2
J. Abrahams c Walsh b Alleyne	24	I. Folley not out 1
M. Watkinson b Bainbridge	57	B 2, l-b 13, w 3 18
*D. P. Hughes run out	18	
S. J. O'Shaughnessy run out	0	1/7 2/40 3/46　　(9 wkts, 40 overs) 161
A. N. Hayhurst not out	26	4/90 5/94 6/147
I. D. Austin b Walsh	0	7/148 8/148 9/158

Bowling: Sainsbury 8–0–21–2; Walsh 8–2–19–3; Bainbridge 8–1–32–1; Alleyne 6–0–35–1; Lloyds 2–0–13–0; Graveney 8–0–26–0.

Gloucestershire

†R. C. Russell c and b Folley	43	*D. A. Graveney b O'Shaughnessy	6
A. J. Wright b Hayhurst	10	P. Bainbridge not out	0
C. W. J. Athey b Fitton	27		
K. M. Curran not out	35	B 1, l-b 6, w 3, n-b 1	11
J. W. Lloyds run out	4		
P. W. Romaines b Folley	0	1/27 2/81 3/91 (8 wkts, 40 overs)	148
M. W. Alleyne st Hegg b Folley	2	4/96 5/96 6/106	
C. A. Walsh b Watkinson	10	7/125 8/148	

G. E. Sainsbury did not bat.

Bowling: Watkinson 8–0–32–1; Austin 4–0–16–0; Hayhurst 5–0–17–1; O'Shaughnessy 7–0–28–1; Fitton 8–0–25–1; Folley 8–1–23–3.

Umpires: D. J. Constant and J. A. Jameson.

At Chelmsford, September 13. LANCASHIRE lost to ESSEX by 32 runs.

LEICESTERSHIRE

LEICESTERSHIRE v HAMPSHIRE

At Leicester, May 3. Hampshire won by 5 runs. Toss: Leicestershire.

Hampshire

C. G. Greenidge c Such b Willey	78	K. D. James not out	8
V. P. Terry c Such b Agnew	46	B 5, w 2, n-b 2	9
D. R. Turner b Such	1		
*M. C. J. Nicholas b DeFreitas	30	1/127 2/130 (4 wkts, 40 overs)	226
C. L. Smith not out	54	3/133 4/196	

M. D. Marshall, T. M. Tremlett, †R. J. Parks, N. G. Cowley and C. A. Connor did not bat.

Bowling: Agnew 8–0–28–1; DeFreitas 8–0–58–1; Willey 8–0–37–1; Such 8–1–43–1; Taylor 8–0–55–0.

Leicestershire

D. I. Gower c Tremlett b Cowley	94	P. A. J. DeFreitas b James	31
L. Potter c James b Connor	38		
J. J. Whitaker b Cowley	18	B 1, l-b 7, w 1, n-b 2	11
*P. Willey c Turner b Tremlett	10		
T. J. Boon run out	11	1/118 2/157 3/160 (6 wkts, 40 overs)	221
N. E. Briers not out	8	4/181 5/181 6/221	

†P. Whitticase, L. B. Taylor, J. P. Agnew and P. M. Such did not bat.

Bowling: Connor 8–1–40–1; James 8–0–52–1; Marshall 8–0–29–0; Tremlett 8–0–57–1; Cowley 8–0–35–2.

Umpires: J. W. Holder and N. T. Plews.

At Chelmsford, May 17. ESSEX v LEICESTERSHIRE. No result.

At Nottingham, May 31. LEICESTERSHIRE lost to NOTTINGHAMSHIRE by ten wickets.

LEICESTERSHIRE v WORCESTERSHIRE

At Leicester, June 7. Worcestershire won by 1 run. Toss: Leicestershire.

Worcestershire

T. S. Curtis c Gill b Taylor	0	P. J. Newport not out	26
M. J. Weston c and b Willey	44		
G. A. Hick c Taylor b Ferris	67	B 3, l-b 7, w 6, n-b 1	17
D. B. D'Oliveira c Boon b Ferris	26		
*P. A. Neale c Potter b Agnew	12	1/0 2/113 3/137 (5 wkts, 40 overs) 219
†S. J. Rhodes not out	27	4/160 5/163	

N. V. Radford, S. M. McEwan, R. K. Illingworth and A. P. Pridgeon did not bat.

Bowling: Taylor 8-1-45-1; Agnew 8-0-46-1; Lewis 8-0-47-0; Ferris 8-0-46-2; Willey 8-0-25-1.

Leicestershire

L. Potter c Rhodes b Newport	27	G. J. F. Ferris run out	0
N. E. Briers c and b Hick	79	L. B. Taylor b Pridgeon	0
J. J. Whitaker run out	49	†P. Gill not out	0
*P. Willey c Hick b Radford	16	B 2, l-b 8, w 7, n-b 2	19
T. J. Boon c Illingworth b Pridgeon	8		
P. D. Bowler run out	7	1/54 2/154 3/173 (9 wkts, 40 overs) 218
C. C. Lewis not out	12	4/192 5/201 6/205	
J. P. Agnew run out	1	7/208 8/208 9/209	

Bowling: Radford 8-0-45-1; Pridgeon 8-1-36-2; McEwan 4-0-26-0; Newport 4-0-20-1; Illingworth 8-0-38-0; Hick 8-0-43-1.

Umpires: D. Lloyd and K. E. Palmer.

LEICESTERSHIRE v SURREY

At Leicester, June 14. No result. Toss: Surrey.

Leicestershire

D. I. Gower c Stewart b Bicknell	26	C. C. Lewis not out	0
N. E. Briers c Stewart b Bicknell	2	P. B. Clift not out	0
J. J. Whitaker b Greig	29		
L. Potter b Greig	6	L-b 4	4
*P. Willey b Greig	8		
P. A. J. DeFreitas b Greig	1	1/8 2/38 3/66 (7 wkts, 16.1 overs) 77
W. K. M. Benjamin b Bullen	1	4/75 5/76 6/77 7/77	

†P. Whitticase and J. P. Agnew did not bat.

Bowling: Feltham 3-0-12-0; Bicknell 5-0-18-2; Gray 2-0-10-0; Bullen 3.1-0-20-1; Greig 3-0-13-4.

Surrey

G. S. Clinton, A. J. Stewart, M. A. Lynch, T. E. Jesty, †C. J. Richards, D. M. Ward, *I. A. Greig, M. A. Feltham, M. P. Bicknell, A. H. Gray and C. K. Bullen.

Umpires: J. A. Jameson and R. Julian.

At Lord's, July 5. LEICESTERSHIRE lost to MIDDLESEX by five wickets.

At Manchester, July 12. LEICESTERSHIRE beat LANCASHIRE by 1 run.

At Taunton, July 19. SOMERSET v LEICESTERSHIRE. No result.

LEICESTERSHIRE v YORKSHIRE

At Leicester, July 26. No result after rain ended play. Toss: Leicestershire.

Yorkshire

M. D. Moxon c Ferris b Willey	33	P. J. Hartley not out 2
A. A. Metcalfe c Lewis b Willey	59	
J. D. Love c Bowler b Willey	25	L-b 6, w 2 8
†D. L. Bairstow b Ferris	45	
P. E. Robinson c Whitaker b DeFreitas	9	1/94 2/94 3/126 (5 wkts, 40 overs) 211
S. N. Hartley not out	30	4/158 5/204

*P. Carrick, C. Shaw, P. W. Jarvis and S. D. Fletcher did not bat.

Bowling: Agnew 8–0–37–0; Ferris 7–0–37–1; DeFreitas 8–0–40–1; Lewis 3–0–21–0; Willey 7–1–40–3; Clift 7–0–30–0.

Leicestershire

N. E. Briers not out	11
L. Potter not out	15
L-b 5, w 1	6

(no wkt, 8 overs) 32

*P. Willey, J. J. Whitaker, P. D. Bowler, P. B. Clift, P. A. J. DeFreitas, †P. Whitticase, C. C. Lewis, G. J. F. Ferris and J. P. Agnew did not bat.

Bowling: Jarvis 4–0–17–0; Shaw 4–1–10–0.

Umpires: D. J. Constant and R. Palmer.

At Cheltenham, August 2. LEICESTERSHIRE beat GLOUCESTERSHIRE by seven wickets.

LEICESTERSHIRE v WARWICKSHIRE

At Leicester, August 9. No result.

At Derby, August 16. LEICESTERSHIRE lost to DERBYSHIRE by three wickets.

LEICESTERSHIRE v KENT

At Leicester, August 23. Kent won by four wickets after achieving a revised target of 187 off 38 overs. Toss: Kent.

Leicestershire

†I. P. Butcher run out	66	P. B. Clift c Marsh b Cowdrey	0
N. E. Briers c and b Cowdrey	30	C. C. Lewis not out	23
D. I. Gower c Taylor b Cowdrey	1	L-b 5, w 1, n-b 2	8
J. J. Whitaker b Penn	12		
*P. Willey c Davis b Cowdrey	0	1/68 2/70 3/88	(6 wkts, 40 overs) 196
L. Potter not out	56	4/89 5/148 6/149	

L. B. Taylor, J. P. Agnew and P. M. Such did not bat.

Bowling: Jarvis 8-2-42-0; Baptiste 8-0-63-0; Davis 8-0-35-0; Penn 8-0-34-1; Cowdrey 8-0-17-4.

Kent

M. R. Benson lbw b Agnew	17	N. R. Taylor not out	26
S. G. Hinks b Taylor	4	†S. A. Marsh not out	5
C. J. Tavaré b Clift	39	B 1, l-b 11, w 7, n-b 2	21
*C. S. Cowdrey lbw b Agnew	1		
D. G. Aslett c Butcher b Lewis	20	1/28 2/28 3/31	(6 wkts, 37.2 overs) 189
E. A. E. Baptiste b Taylor	56	4/75 5/117 6/181	

K. B. S. Jarvis, C. Penn and R. P. Davis did not bat.

Bowling: Taylor 7.2-0-27-2; Agnew 8-0-37-2; Lewis 8-0-32-1; Clift 8-0-47-1; Such 6-0-34-0.

Umpires: D. Lloyd and D. O. Oslear.

LEICESTERSHIRE v NORTHAMPTONSHIRE

At Leicester, August 30. Leicestershire won by 70 runs. Toss: Northamptonshire.

Leicestershire

L. Potter c sub b Bailey	76	W. K. M. Benjamin c Bailey b Harper	5
T. J. Boon run out	25	J. P. Agnew not out	1
D. I. Gower b Bailey	36	†P. Whitticase not out	1
J. J. Whitaker c G. Cook		B 4, l-b 7, w 2	13
b N. G. B. Cook	14		
P. A. J. DeFreitas c Larkins b Bailey	2	1/57 2/144 3/151	(8 wkts, 40 overs) 208
*P. Willey c Capel b Harper	27	4/158 5/166 6/194	
P. B. Clift c and b Harper	8	7/205 8/205	

L. B. Taylor did not bat.

Bowling: Robinson 8-1-33-0; Capel 8-0-30-0; Boyd-Moss 4-0-26-0; N. G. B. Cook 8-0-40-1; Harper 8-0-45-3; Bailey 4-0-23-3.

Northamptonshire

*G. Cook b Agnew	9	N. G. B. Cook c Potter b Clift	12
W. Larkins c Whitticase b Agnew	13	M. A. Robinson run out	1
A. J. Lamb c DeFreitas b Agnew	12	D. J. Wild absent injured	
R. J. Bailey lbw b DeFreitas	10	B 2, l-b 1, w 2, n-b 4	9
D. J. Capel c Potter b DeFreitas	0		
R. A. Harper lbw b DeFreitas	0	1/14 2/36 3/36	(34.4 overs) 138
R. J. Boyd-Moss c Benjamin b Clift	39	4/38 5/38 6/55	
†D. Ripley not out	33	7/111 8/135 9/138	

Bowling: Taylor 4-0-29-0; Agnew 6-0-16-3; DeFreitas 6-0-17-3; Willey 6-2-15-0; Clift 7.4-0-33-2; Benjamin 5-0-25-0.

Umpires: B. Leadbeater and R. A. White.

LEICESTERSHIRE v GLAMORGAN

At Leicester, September 6. No result.

At Hove, September 13. SUSSEX v LEICESTERSHIRE. No result.

MIDDLESEX

MIDDLESEX v SOMERSET

At Lord's, May 17. No result. Toss: Middlesex.

Somerset

N. A. Felton b Williams	20	R. J. Harden not out	5
*P. M. Roebuck c Daniel b Williams	6	W 4, n-b 2	6
J. J. E. Hardy c Roseberry b Williams	10		
M. D. Crowe not out	25	1/25 2/30 3/49 (3 wkts, 17.1 overs)	72

V. J. Marks, †N. D. Burns, G. D. Rose, M. R. Davis, A. N. Jones and N. A. Mallender did not bat.

Bowling: Hughes 4–0–7–0; Williams 7–1–46–3; Daniel 5–0–19–0; Needham 1.1–1–0–0.

Middlesex

W. N. Slack, M. R. Ramprakash, M. A. Roseberry, *M. W. Gatting, R. O. Butcher, †P. R. Downton, A. Needham, N. F. Williams, S. P. Hughes, A. R. C. Fraser and W. W. Daniel.

Umpires: M. J. Kitchen and B. J. Meyer.

At Canterbury, May 24. MIDDLESEX lost to KENT by 103 runs.

MIDDLESEX v GLOUCESTERSHIRE

At Lord's, June 7. Gloucestershire won by eight wickets. Toss: Gloucestershire. Bainbridge brought the Middlesex innings to a close with a spell of five for 7 in 21 balls.

Middlesex

W. N. Slack run out	25	S. P. Hughes st Russell b Bainbridge	3
J. D. Carr c Russell b Greene	8	A. R. C. Fraser c Curran b Bainbridge	6
M. R. Ramprakash c Greene b Alleyne	11	W. W. Daniel not out	3
R. O. Butcher c Russell b Tomlins	16	L-b 10, w 6, n-b 1	17
M. A. Roseberry c Russell b Bainbridge	27		
*†P. R. Downton c Stovold b Alleyne	10	1/16 2/46 3/53 (38.3 overs)	143
A. Needham c Lawrence b Bainbridge	12	4/77 5/109 6/126	
N. F. Williams c Lloyds b Bainbridge	5	7/127 8/131 9/138	

Bowling: Lawrence 8–0–27–0; Greene 4–0–22–1; Alleyne 8–1–25–2; Bainbridge 7.3–0–22–5; Tomlins 5–0–17–1; Graveney 6–0–20–0.

Gloucestershire

A. W. Stovold c Ramprakash b Hughes	24
A. J. Wright lbw b Daniel	12
K. M. Curran not out	69
P. Bainbridge not out	28
L-b 3, w 7, n-b 1	11

1/28 2/50   (2 wkts, 34.3 overs) 144

K. P. Tomlins, J. W. Lloyds, M. W. Alleyne, †R. C. Russell, V. S. Greene, *D. A. Graveney and D. V. Lawrence did not bat.

Bowling: Daniel 8-1-30-1; Williams 8-0-38-0; Hughes 5-0-16-1; Fraser 6-0-25-0; Needham 3.3-0-16-0; Slack 4-0-16-0.

Umpires: K. J. Lyons and D. O. Oslear.

At Worcester, June 14. MIDDLESEX lost to WORCESTERSHIRE by seven wickets.

At Basingstoke, June 21. MIDDLESEX lost to HAMPSHIRE by seven wickets.

MIDDLESEX v GLAMORGAN

At Lord's, June 28. Middlesex won by four wickets. Toss: Middlesex.

Glamorgan

J. A. Hopkins b Slack	68		†C. P. Metson not out	23
*H. Morris c Butcher b Slack	24		I. Smith not out	8
R. J. Shastri c Brown b Slack	14		B 1, l-b 10, w 2, n-b 2	15
M. P. Maynard lbw b Emburey	28			
P. A. Cottey c Downton b Fraser	1		1/72 2/106 3/141 (7 wkts, 40 overs) 188
J. G. Thomas b Emburey	3		4/146 5/152
J. Derrick c and b Emburey	4		6/153 7/172

S. Monkhouse and S. R. Barwick did not bat.

Bowling: Williams 8-0-30-0; Fraser 8-1-42-1; Gatting 8-0-40-0; Emburey 8-0-35-3; Slack 8-0-30-3.

Middlesex

J. D. Carr st Metson b Derrick	47		K. R. Brown not out	21
M. R. Ramprakash c Metson b Thomas	9		W. N. Slack not out	15
*M. W. Gatting b Derrick	48		L-b 7, w 8, n-b 2	17
R. O. Butcher c Monkhouse b Derrick	3			
†P. R. Downton c Morris b Derrick	19		1/28 2/116 3/121 (6 wkts, 39 overs) 189
J. E. Emburey c Monkhouse b Derrick	10		4/130 5/146 6/155

J. F. Sykes, N. F. Williams and A. R. C. Fraser did not bat.

Bowling: Smith 6-0-23-0; Thomas 7-0-25-1; Shastri 8-0-44-0; Barwick 6-0-34-0; Derrick 8-0-32-5; Monkhouse 4-1-24-0.

Umpires: J. H. Harris and J. A. Jameson.

MIDDLESEX v LEICESTERSHIRE

At Lord's, July 5. Middlesex won by five wickets. Toss: Middlesex.

Leicestershire

*P. Willey c Emburey b Williams	14	C. C. Lewis not out	0
N. E. Briers b Daniel	3	J. P. Agnew not out	2
J. J. Whitaker b Hughes	60		
L. Potter c Emburey b Needham	13	B 1, l-b 9, w 1, n-b 3	14
T. J. Boon b Hughes	17		
P. B. Clift c Radley b Emburey	31	1/16 2/29 3/59 (8 wkts, 40 overs)	170
P. A. J. DeFreitas c Needham b Hughes	2	4/100 5/135 6/137	
W. K. M. Benjamin run out	14	7/167 8/168	

†P. Gill did not bat.

Bowling: Williams 8-0-22-1; Daniel 8-0-35-1; Emburey 8-0-35-1; Needham 8-0-40-1; Hughes 8-0-28-3.

Middlesex

J. D. Carr b Agnew	10	K. R. Brown not out	40
W. N. Slack c Willey b Benjamin	27		
C. T. Radley c and b Clift	27	B 3, l-b 7, w 8, n-b 2	20
†P. R. Downton lbw b Benjamin	0		
A. Needham c Willey b Clift	15	1/28 2/55 3/55 (5 wkts, 38.3 overs)	172
R. O. Butcher not out	33	4/85 5/92	

*J. E. Emburey, N. F. Williams, S. P. Hughes and W. W. Daniel did not bat.

Bowling: DeFreitas 7.3-1-28-0; Agnew 8-0-18-1; Benjamin 8-0-39-2; Clift 8-0-35-2; Lewis 4-0-19-0; Willey 3-0-23-0.

Umpires: J. Birkenshaw and K. J. Lyons.

At Scarborough, July 12. MIDDLESEX lost to YORKSHIRE by 33 runs.

At Nottingham, July 19. NOTTINGHAMSHIRE v MIDDLESEX. No result.

MIDDLESEX v DERBYSHIRE

At Lord's, July 26. Middlesex won by 71 runs. Toss: Derbyshire.

Middlesex

W. N. Slack c Jean-Jacques b Sharma	49	N. F. Williams b Holding	0
J. D. Carr c Maher b Mortensen	17		
C. T. Radley run out	1	L-b 8, w 4	12
R. O. Butcher c Newman b Sharma	25		
K. R. Brown not out	26	1/51 2/53 3/85 (7 wkts, 40 overs)	161
*†P. R. Downton b Jean-Jacques	26	4/102 5/152	
J. F. Sykes lbw b Holding	5	6/159 7/161	

S. P. Hughes, N. G. Cowans and A. R. C. Fraser did not bat.

Bowling: Newman 8-0-38-0; Mortensen 8-3-18-1; Jean-Jacques 8-0-41-1; Sharma 8-3-25-2; Holding 8-0-31-2.

Derbyshire

*K. J. Barnett c Carr b Cowans	15	M. Jean-Jacques run out	10
†B. J. M. Maher run out	2	P. G. Newman c Carr b Hughes	4
B. Roberts b Fraser	13	O. H. Mortensen not out	0
J. E. Morris lbw b Cowans	1		
I. S. Anderson c Downton b Cowans	1	L-b 3, w 4, n-b 4	11
M. A. Holding run out	9		
R. J. Finney b Sykes	11	1/20 2/28 3/30 4/39	(32.4 overs) 90
R. Sharma b Sykes	13	5/41 6/50 7/70 8/81 9/90	

Bowling: Williams 8–0–30–0; Cowans 8–1–12–3; Hughes 6.4–0–19–1; Fraser 7–0–20–1; Sykes 3–0–6–2.

Umpires: H. D. Bird and R. A. White.

MIDDLESEX v SURREY

At Lord's, August 2. Surrey won by five wickets in a match reduced by rain to eighteen overs a side. Toss: Surrey.

Middlesex

J. D. Carr lbw b Thomas	6	†P. R. Downton not out	0
C. T. Radley st Richards b Thomas	13	L-b 4	4
*M. W. Gatting not out	96		
J. E. Emburey b Bullen	9	1/7 2/38 3/74	(4 wkts, 18 overs) 150
K. R. Brown run out	22	4/129	

R. O. Butcher, J. F. Sykes, N. G. Cowans, A. R. C. Fraser and S. P. Hughes did not bat.

Bowling: Feltham 4–0–25–0; Thomas 4–0–33–2; Greig 3–0–33–0; Bullen 4–0–30–1; Clarke 3–0–25–0.

Surrey

†C. J. Richards c Emburey b Cowans	1	A. J. Stewart not out	3
D. M. Smith run out	28		
T. E. Jesty c Gatting b Sykes	51	L-b 6, w 1	7
*I. A. Greig c Butcher b Hughes	19		
M. A. Lynch not out	44	1/2 2/75 3/84	(5 wkts, 18 overs) 153
D. M. Ward b Hughes	0	4/136 5/139	

D. J. Thomas, M. A. Feltham, C. K. Bullen and S. T. Clarke did not bat.

Bowling: Cowans 4–0–18–1; Fraser 4–0–29–0; Sykes 4–0–37–1; Emburey 3–0–44–0; Hughes 3–0–19–2.

Umpires: D. Lloyd and N. T. Plews.

MIDDLESEX v LANCASHIRE

At Lord's, August 9. Lancashire won by four wickets after rain had reduced their target to 152 off 33 overs. Toss: Lancashire.

Middlesex

W. N. Slack c O'Shaughnessy b Patterson	3	I. J. F. Hutchinson not out	22
R. O. Butcher b Watkinson	2	A. Needham run out	29
C. T. Radley c Hughes b O'Shaughnessy	56	L-b 7, n-b 8	15
K. R. Brown c Patterson b Simmons	41	1/7 2/7 3/96	(6 wkts, 40 overs) 184
*†P. R. Downton c Hegg b Hayhurst	16	4/116 5/131 6/184	

N. F. Williams, S. P. Hughes, N. G. Cowans and W. W. Daniel did not bat.

Bowling: Patterson 8–0–34–1; Watkinson 8–1–20–1; Allott 8–0–42–0; Simmons 8–0–41–1; O'Shaughnessy 6–0–33–1; Hayhurst 2–1–7–1.

Lancashire

G. D. Mendis run out	44	A. N. Hayhurst c Radley b Cowans	3
M. A. Atherton lbw b Cowans	1	P. J. W. Allott not out	5
N. H. Fairbrother c Downton b Daniel	60	B 5, l-b 6, w 2	13
M. Watkinson b Needham	6		
*D. P. Hughes c Butcher b Needham	3	1/9 2/98 3/112 (6 wkts, 31.3 overs) 154	
S. J. O'Shaughnessy not out	19	4/124 5/128 6/145	

J. Simmons, †W. K. Hegg and B. P. Patterson did not bat.

Bowling: Cowans 7–0–29–2; Williams 3–0–15–0; Daniel 7.3–0–40–1; Hughes 7–0–34–0; Needham 7–0–25–2.

Umpires: J. H. Hampshire and H. J. Rhodes.

At Chelmsford, August 16. MIDDLESEX beat ESSEX by five wickets.

At Wellingborough School, August 23. NORTHAMPTONSHIRE v MIDDLESEX. No result.

MIDDLESEX v SUSSEX

At Lord's, August 30. Middlesex won by 68 runs. Toss: Sussex.

Middlesex

J. D. Carr c Green b A. P. Wells	44	K. R. Brown not out	50
M. A. Roseberry b Babington	19	B 2, l-b 6, w 11	19
*M. W. Gatting b Pigott	0		
M. R. Ramprakash not out	82	1/48 2/50 3/97 (3 wkts, 40 overs) 214	

†P. R. Downton, J. E. Emburey, J. F. Sykes, S. P. Hughes, A. R. C. Fraser and N. G. Cowans did not bat.

Bowling: Reeve 8–1–56–0; C. M. Wells 8–0–24–0; Babington 8–0–39–1; Pigott 8–0–36–1; Waring 3–0–17–0; A. P. Wells 5–0–34–1.

Sussex

A. M. Green c Ramprakash b Cowans	6	A. C. S. Pigott c Emburey b Sykes	9
P. W. G. Parker c Downton b Cowans	19	K. Greenfield not out	8
C. M. Wells c Ramprakash b Hughes	17		
A. P. Wells c Carr b Sykes	14	L-b 7, w 4, n-b 1	12
*†I. J. Gould not out	56		
D. A. Reeve run out	1	1/24 2/46 3/47 (7 wkts, 40 overs) 146	
R. I. Alikhan b Sykes	4	4/85 5/88 6/99 7/122	

I. C. Waring and A. M. Babington did not bat.

Bowling: Cowans 8–2–23–2; Fraser 5–1–20–0; Hughes 6–1–19–1; Gatting 3–0–22–0; Emburey 8–0–24–0; Sykes 8–0–26–3; Ramprakash 1–0–4–0; Brown 1–0–1–0.

Umpires: B. Dudleston and A. A. Jones.

At Birmingham, September 6. WARWICKSHIRE v MIDDLESEX. No result.

NORTHAMPTONSHIRE

At Derby, May 3. NORTHAMPTONSHIRE beat DERBYSHIRE by 22 runs.

At Leeds, May 10. NORTHAMPTONSHIRE lost to YORKSHIRE by six wickets.

NORTHAMPTONSHIRE v HAMPSHIRE

At Northampton, May 17. No result.

NORTHAMPTONSHIRE v SUSSEX

At Northampton, May 31. Northamptonshire won by 43 runs. Toss: Sussex.

Northamptonshire

R. J. Bailey c Gould b C. M. Wells ...	5	*G. Cook run out	16
W. Larkins c le Roux b Heseltine	36	†D. Ripley not out	8
A. J. Lamb c Moores b C. M. Wells ..	2	L-b 5, w 1, n-b 1	7
D. J. Capel c Moores b Reeve	7		
R. A. Harper c A. P. Wells b Waring .	37	1/6 2/12 3/29 (7 wkts, 40 overs) 188	
R. G. Williams not out	63	4/71 5/108	
D. J. Wild c Moores b Waring	7	6/125 7/166	

N. G. B. Cook and A. Walker did not bat.

Bowling: C. M. Wells 8–1–17–2; le Roux 8–0–35–0; Reeve 8–0–46–1; Kimber 2–0–16–0; Heseltine 6–0–34–1; Waring 8–0–35–2.

Sussex

A. P. Wells run out	25	S. J. S. Kimber lbw b Capel	2
A. M. Green c and b Wild	14	P. A. W. Heseltine not out	6
C. M. Wells c Bailey b N. G. B. Cook .	36	A. M. Babington b Capel	1
*I. J. Gould c Lamb b N. G. B. Cook .	24	L-b 7, w 2	9
G. S. le Roux c and b N. G. B. Cook .	9		
D. A. Reeve c Ripley b Capel	13	1/29 2/47 3/90 (38.1 overs) 145	
†P. Moores b Harper	5	4/111 5/118 6/134	
I. C. Waring lbw b Walker	1	7/134 8/138 9/138	

Bowling: Walker 7–0–24–1; Capel 4.1–1–14–3; Harper 8–1–19–1; Wild 8–0–25–1; N. G. B. Cook 8–0–36–3; Williams 3–0–20–0.

Umpires: J. Birkenshaw and A. A. Jones.

NORTHAMPTONSHIRE v NOTTINGHAMSHIRE

At Northampton, June 7. Northamptonshire won by 26 runs. Toss: Nottinghamshire.

Northamptonshire

R. J. Bailey b Fraser-Darling	43	*G. Cook not out	1
W. Larkins c Johnson b Pick	91		
A. J. Lamb b Rice	43	L-b 15, w 3	18
R. G. Williams b Saxelby	9		
D. J. Capel c Scott b Saxelby	5	1/108 2/175 3/203 (5 wkts, 40 overs) 213	
R. A. Harper not out	3	4/205 5/210	

D. J. Wild, †D. Ripley, N. G. B. Cook and A. Walker did not bat.

Bowling: Pick 8–2–44–1; Saxelby 8–0–35–2; Hemmings 8–2–27–0; Hadlee 7–1–40–0; Rice 7–0–38–1; Fraser-Darling 2–0–14–1.

Nottinghamshire

D. J. R. Martindale b Walker	1	†C. W. Scott b Walker		14
D. W. Randall b Harper	25	R. A. Pick b Walker		12
*C. E. B. Rice run out	41	K. Saxelby not out		9
P. Johnson c Williams b N. G. B. Cook	32	L-b 18, w 2		20
R. J. Hadlee c Wild b N. G. B. Cook	20			
R. J. Evans lbw b Walker	2	1/4 2/59 3/106	(39.4 overs)	187
C. D. Fraser-Darling b Harper	11	4/117 5/125 6/145		
E. E. Hemmings run out	0	7/147 8/151 9/173		

Bowling: Walker 7.4–2–28–4; Capel 8–0–32–0; Wild 8–0–35–0; Harper 8–0–44–2; N. G. B. Cook 8–0–30–2.

Umpires: J. W. Holder and B. Leadbeater.

NORTHAMPTONSHIRE v GLAMORGAN

At Luton, June 21. Glamorgan won by 6 runs. Toss: Northamptonshire.

Glamorgan

J. A. Hopkins c Harper b Williams	36	I. Smith run out		18
*H. Morris c G. Cook b Harper	17	S. R. Barwick b Harper		0
G. C. Holmes not out	33	S. Monkhouse b Harper		0
P. A. Todd c Wild b N. G. B. Cook	0	B 5, l-b 10, w 2		17
M. P. Maynard c Bailey b Williams	7			
R. J. Shastri c Harper b Williams	4	1/36 2/65 3/68	(40 overs)	142
J. Derrick b Wild	0	4/79 5/104 6/104		
†C. P. Metson c G. Cook b Wild	10	7/120 8/142 9/142		

Bowling: Capel 7–2–21–0; Walker 4–0–19–0; Harper 8–3–19–3; N. G. B. Cook 8–5–11–1; Williams 8–1–24–3; Wild 5–0–33–2.

Northamptonshire

R. J. Bailey c Metson b Monkhouse	7	†D. Ripley not out		4
W. Larkins c Metson b Monkhouse	3	N. G. B. Cook not out		1
A. J. Lamb c Smith b Monkhouse	20			
D. J. Capel b Barwick	14	W 6		6
R. A. Harper hit wkt b Shastri	19			
R. G. Williams b Holmes	33	1/5 2/12 3/41	(8 wkts, 40 overs)	136
D. J. Wild c Monkhouse b Derrick	13	4/47 5/77 6/98		
*G. Cook lbw b Barwick	16	7/123 8/135		

A. Walker did not bat.

Bowling: Smith 6–1–13–0; Monkhouse 8–4–14–3; Barwick 8–0–46–2; Shastri 8–1–19–1; Derrick 5–0–20–1; Holmes 5–0–24–1.

Umpires: B. J. Meyer and R. Palmer.

At Guildford, June 28. NORTHAMPTONSHIRE lost to SURREY by 1 run.

NORTHAMPTONSHIRE v LANCASHIRE

At Tring, July 5. Northamptonshire won by 54 runs. Toss: Lancashire.

Northamptonshire

R. J. Bailey c Fowler b Folley	81	*G. Cook c Hegg b Allott		5
W. Larkins c Fowler b O'Shaughnessy	81	D. J. Wild not out		8
A. J. Lamb b O'Shaughnessy	5	L-b 15, w 2		17
R. A. Harper not out	65			
R. G. Williams c Allott b O'Shaughnessy	7	1/169 2/178 3/178	(6 wkts, 40 overs)	290
G. B. Stevenson b Austin	21	4/201 5/268 6/275		

†D. Ripley, N. G. B. Cook and M. A. Robinson did not bat.

Bowling: Allott 8–2–41–1; Watkinson 6–0–42–0; Austin 8–0–73–1; Folley 4–0–35–1; Simmons 8–0–62–0; O'Shaughnessy 6–0–22–3.

Lancashire

G. Fowler b Harper	42	J. Simmons c G. Cook b Williams		21
D. W. Varey c N. G. B. Cook b Wild	8	I. Folley c G. Cook b Williams		19
N. H. Fairbrother c Ripley b Wild	1	†W. K. Hegg not out		6
S. J. O'Shaughnessy b Stevenson	24	L-b 8, w 9, n-b 1		18
M. Watkinson lbw b Stevenson	21			
*D. P. Hughes b Stevenson	30	1/19 2/29 3/59	(38.4 overs)	236
P. J. W. Allott b Stevenson	34	4/98 5/103 6/163		
I. D. Austin b Williams	12	7/181 8/186 9/215		

Bowling: Robinson 8–0–50–0; Wild 5–0–16–2; Harper 5–0–28–1; N. G. B. Cook 8–1–37–0; Stevenson 8–0–55–4; Williams 3.4–0–32–3; Bailey 1–0–10–0.

Umpires: D. J. Constant and J. H. Harris.

At Canterbury, July 19. KENT v NORTHAMPTONSHIRE. No result.

NORTHAMPTONSHIRE v GLOUCESTERSHIRE

At Finedon, July 26. No result after rain ended play. Toss: Northamptonshire.

Northamptonshire

R. J. Bailey run out	24	†D. Ripley run out		3
W. Larkins st Russell b Lloyds	13	N. G. B. Cook not out		0
A. J. Lamb c and b Lloyds	36			
D. J. Capel c Alleyne b Bainbridge	3	B 1, l-b 13, w 3		17
R. A. Harper c Alleyne b Lawrence	28			
R. G. Williams b Lawrence	4	1/34 2/82 3/85	(8 wkts, 40 overs)	170
D. J. Wild not out	29	4/88 5/93 6/135		
*G. Cook c Wright b Greene	13	7/165 8/170		

A. Walker did not bat.

Bowling: Greene 8–1–25–1; Sainsbury 8–1–16–0; Lloyds 8–1–38–2; Bainbridge 4–0–15–1; Alleyne 4–0–13–0; Lawrence 8–0–49–2.

Gloucestershire

A. J. Wright b Williams	16
†R. C. Russell run out	17
K. M. Curran not out	1
J. W. Lloyds not out	1
L-b 3, w 1	4

1/32 2/38   (2 wkts, 14 overs) 39

A. W. Stovold, P. W. Romaines, M. W. Alleyne, *P. Bainbridge, V. S. Greene, D. V. Lawrence and G. E. Sainsbury did not bat.

Bowling: Capel 6–1–16–0; Walker 5–1–14–0; Williams 2–0–5–1; Harper 1–0–1–0.

Umpires: J. H. Hampshire and D. R. Shepherd.

At Birmingham, August 2. NORTHAMPTONSHIRE lost to WARWICKSHIRE by seven wickets.

NORTHAMPTONSHIRE v ESSEX

At Northampton, August 9. No result.

NORTHAMPTONSHIRE v MIDDLESEX

At Wellingborough School, August 23. No result.

At Leicester, August 30. NORTHAMPTONSHIRE lost to LEICESTERSHIRE by 70 runs.

At Taunton, September 6. SOMERSET v NORTHAMPTONSHIRE. No result.

At Worcester, September 13. NORTHAMPTONSHIRE lost to WORCESTERSHIRE by nine wickets.

NOTTINGHAMSHIRE

NOTTINGHAMSHIRE v KENT

At Nottingham, May 3. Nottinghamshire won by nine wickets. Toss: Nottinghamshire.

Kent

M. R. Benson c French b Saxelby	1	D. J. M. Kelleher c and b Saxelby	19
S. G. Hinks c French b Saxelby	15	A. P. Igglesden c Pick b Saxelby	5
C. J. Tavaré c Fraser-Darling b Saxelby	1	D. L. Underwood not out	1
N. R. Taylor run out	17		
*C. S. Cowdrey c Robinson b Fraser-Darling	59	L-b 6, w 3, n-b 1	10
G. R. Cowdrey c Pick b Evans	8	1/6 2/18 3/24 (39.2 overs)	174
†S. A. Marsh c Pick b Fraser-Darling	36	4/47 5/71 6/141	
C. Penn c and b Pick	2	7/144 8/148 9/166	

Bowling: Pick 8–0–36–1; Saxelby 7.2–0–21–5; Fraser-Darling 8–1–32–2; Evans 8–0–31–1; Hemmings 8–0–48–0.

Nottinghamshire

R. T. Robinson c Marsh b C. S. Cowdrey	45
D. W. Randall not out	73
P. Johnson not out	45
L-b 10, w 2	12

1/80   (1 wkt, 34 overs) 175

*C. E. B. Rice, J. D. Birch, †B. N. French, C. D. Fraser-Darling, K. P. Evans, E. E. Hemmings, R. A. Pick and K. Saxelby did not bat.

Bowling: Igglesden 6–2–16–0; Kelleher 8–0–28–0; C. S. Cowdrey 5–0–27–1; Penn 6–0–46–0; Underwood 7–0–34–0; Hinks 2–0–14–0.

Umpires: J. Birkenshaw and R. Julian.

NOTTINGHAMSHIRE v LEICESTERSHIRE

At Nottingham, May 31. Nottinghamshire won by ten wickets. Toss: Nottinghamshire.

Leicestershire

L. Potter c Hadlee b Saxelby	1	W. K. M. Benjamin run out		12
D. I. Gower b Pick	16	J. P. Agnew not out		23
J. J. Whitaker c and b Pick	7	L. B. Taylor not out		3
*P. Willey c Randall b Hemmings	3	L-b 2, w 3, n-b 1		6
T. J. Boon c Rice b Hadlee	5			
N. E. Briers c Hadlee b Rice	6	1/6 2/24 3/27	(9 wkts, 40 overs)	132
P. B. Clift c Hadlee b Saxelby	41	4/33 5/35 6/50		
†P. Whitticase c Scott b Pick	9	7/63 8/83 9/124		

Bowling: Pick 8–0–49–3; Saxelby 8–0–31–2; Hadlee 8–2–14–1; Hemmings 8–4–7–1; Rice 8–0–29–1.

Nottinghamshire

B. C. Broad not out	76
R. T. Robinson not out	50
L-b 1, w 4, n-b 2	7

(no wkt, 24.4 overs) 133

D. W. Randall, *C. E. B. Rice, P. Johnson, J. D. Birch, R. J. Hadlee, †C. W. Scott, R. A. Pick, E. E. Hemmings and K. Saxelby did not bat.

Bowling: Agnew 6.4–0–40–0; Benjamin 6–0–26–0; Clift 3–0–25–0; Taylor 6–0–25–0; Willey 3–1–16–0.

Umpires: J. H. Hampshire and M. J. Kitchen.

At Northampton, June 7. NOTTINGHAMSHIRE lost to NORTHAMPTONSHIRE by 26 runs.

At Ebbw Vale, June 14. NOTTINGHAMSHIRE beat GLAMORGAN by 70 runs.

NOTTINGHAMSHIRE v WORCESTERSHIRE

At Nottingham, June 21. Nottinghamshire won by four wickets. Toss: Nottinghamshire. Saxelby dismissed Rhodes, Neale and Radford to become the fourth bowler to take a hat-trick in limited-overs cricket in 1987, and the first ever to do so for Nottinghamshire in the Sunday League. When Hick reached 18, he became the youngest player to score 1,000 runs in the competition.

Worcestershire

T. S. Curtis b Pick	30	N. V. Radford c Hadlee b Saxelby	0
M. J. Weston c Scott b Cooper	1	R. K. Illingworth run out	0
G. A. Hick c and b Hadlee	88	B 2, l-b 2, w 2, n-b 1	8
D. B. D'Oliveira b Saxelby	56		
†S. J. Rhodes c Hemmings b Saxelby	39	1/5 2/83 3/164 (8 wkts, 40 overs)	229
*P. A. Neale b Saxelby	7	4/180 5/227 6/227	
P. J. Newport not out	0	7/227 8/229	

S. M. McEwan and A. P. Pridgeon did not bat.

Bowling: Cooper 8-1-28-1; Saxelby 8-1-54-4; Hadlee 8-0-33-1; Hemmings 8-0-53-0; Pick 4-0-32-1; Rice 4-0-24-0.

Nottinghamshire

D. W. Randall b Radford	82	E. E. Hemmings lbw b Radford	1
M. Newell c Rhodes b Newport	12	†C. W. Scott not out	1
*C. E. B. Rice b Radford	84	B 1, l-b 11, w 10, n-b 2	24
R. J. Hadlee b Pridgeon	18		
P. Johnson b Radford	4	1/28 2/196 3/213 (6 wkts, 39.3 overs)	231
J. D. Birch not out	5	4/222 5/223 6/225	

R. A. Pick, K. Saxelby and K. E. Cooper did not bat.

Bowling: Pridgeon 8-0-39-1; Radford 8-1-28-4; Newport 8-1-45-1; McEwan 3-0-22-0; Weston 4-0-27-0; Illingworth 5-0-38-0; Hick 3.3-0-30-0.

Umpires: R. Julian and K. E. Palmer.

At Hove, June 28. NOTTINGHAMSHIRE beat SUSSEX by six wickets.

NOTTINGHAMSHIRE v YORKSHIRE

At Nottingham, July 5. Nottinghamshire won by 85 runs. Toss: Yorkshire. Nottinghamshire's total was their highest and also the highest by any county against Yorkshire in the Sunday League, while Randall's innings of 123 was the best for Nottinghamshire in the competition.

Nottinghamshire

D. W. Randall c Robinson b P. J. Hartley	123	†C. W. Scott b Sidebottom	26
R. J. Hadlee lbw b Jarvis	23	E. E. Hemmings not out	2
P. Johnson b Fletcher	63	B 2, l-b 4, w 2, n-b 5	13
*C. E. B. Rice c Bairstow b Fletcher	7		
J. D. Birch run out	11	1/29 2/180 3/208 (6 wkts, 40 overs)	283
R. J. Evans not out	15	4/233 5/241 6/280	

R. A. Pick, K. Saxelby and K. E. Cooper did not bat.

Bowling: Jarvis 8-1-56-1; Sidebottom 8-1-56-1; Fletcher 8-0-43-2; P. J. Hartley 8-0-56-1; S. N. Hartley 2-0-22-0; Carrick 6-1-44-0.

Yorkshire

K. Sharp run out	7	A. Sidebottom c Hadlee b Saxelby	37
A. A. Metcalfe run out	96	P. W. Jarvis b Saxelby	11
J. D. Love c Scott b Hadlee	5	S. D. Fletcher not out	1
†D. L. Bairstow c Scott b Hadlee	3	L-b 11, w 4, n-b 1	16
P. E. Robinson b Pick	20		
S. N. Hartley b Pick	0	1/22 2/46 3/57	(38 overs) 198
*P. Carrick b Rice	2	4/138 5/139 6/146	
P. J. Hartley lbw b Pick	0	7/146 8/146 9/194	

Bowling: Cooper 4–1–12–0; Saxelby 7–1–32–2; Pick 8–2–28–3; Hadlee 8–0–37–2; Hemmings 5–0–37–0; Rice 6–0–41–1.

Umpires: B. Dudleston and A. G. T. Whitehead.

At Birmingham, July 12. NOTTINGHAMSHIRE beat WARWICKSHIRE by seven wickets.

NOTTINGHAMSHIRE v MIDDLESEX

At Nottingham, July 19. No result.

At Manchester, July 26. LANCASHIRE v NOTTINGHAMSHIRE. No result.

NOTTINGHAMSHIRE v SOMERSET

At Nottingham, August 9. No result.

NOTTINGHAMSHIRE v HAMPSHIRE

At Nottingham, August 16. Nottinghamshire won by seven wickets. Toss: Nottinghamshire.

Hampshire

C. G. Greenidge c Broad b Saxelby	17	T. M. Tremlett run out	0
V. P. Terry c Hemmings b Rice	80	C. A. Connor not out	0
R. A. Smith c Johnson b Pick	21		
*M. C. J. Nicholas c Birch b Hemmings	2	L-b 8, w 2, n-b 3	13
C. L. Smith c and b Hemmings	1		
M. D. Marshall c and b Hemmings	2	1/24 2/64 3/79	(8 wkts, 40 overs) 166
N. G. Cowley c Rice b Pick	0	4/86 5/92 6/94	
†R. J. Parks not out	30	7/164 8/164	

P. J. Bakker did not bat.

Bowling: Saxelby 7–3–33–1; Bore 6–0–22–0; Hadlee 8–1–30–0; Hemmings 8–0–26–3; Pick 8–0–28–2; Rice 3–0–19–1.

Nottinghamshire

B. C. Broad c Parks b Connor 7	J. D. Birch not out 20
R. T. Robinson c Terry b Cowley 33	L-b 6, w 1, n-b 1 8
P. Johnson c Parks b Marshall 55	
*C. E. B. Rice not out 47	1/16 2/79 3/128 (3 wkts, 38.1 overs) 170

R. J. Hadlee, †B. N. French, E. E. Hemmings, R. A. Pick, K. Saxelby and M. K. Bore did not bat.

Bowling: Marshall 8–0–20–1; Connor 7–1–16–1; Tremlett 7.1–0–48–0; Cowley 8–0–46–1; Bakker 8–0–34–0.

Umpires: N. T. Plews and R. A. White.

At Moreton-in-Marsh, August 23. NOTTINGHAMSHIRE lost to GLOUCESTERSHIRE by 2 runs.

At Derby, August 30. NOTTINGHAMSHIRE lost to DERBYSHIRE by seven wickets.

NOTTINGHAMSHIRE v ESSEX

At Nottingham, September 6. No result.

At The Oval, September 13. NOTTINGHAMSHIRE beat SURREY by three wickets.

SOMERSET

SOMERSET v ESSEX

At Taunton, May 3. Somerset won by 36 runs after Essex's target had been reduced by rain to 217 off 35 overs. Toss: Somerset.

Somerset

N. A. Felton b Miller 17	†N. D. Burns not out 4
*P. M. Roebuck c Stephenson b Miller . 35	
J. J. E. Hardy not out 94	B 1, l-b 9, w 7 17
M. D. Crowe run out 19	
R. J. Harden b Page 0	1/35 2/66 3/109 (5 wkts, 40 overs) 247
V. J. Marks b Lever 61	4/114 5/242

G. D. Rose, M. R. Davis, N. A. Mallender and A. N. Jones did not bat.

Bowling: Page 8–0–39–1; Lever 7–0–63–1; Miller 8–1–32–2; Gooch 4–0–12–0; Pringle 8–0–58–0; Childs 5–0–33–0.

Essex

*G. A. Gooch c Crowe b Mallender	27	G. Miller run out	4
J. P. Stephenson c Crowe b Jones	6	J. K. Lever not out	6
B. R. Hardie c Hardy b Marks	60	J. H. Childs c Crowe b Jones	10
D. R. Pringle c Mallender b Rose	10	L-b 6, w 1, n-b 1	8
A. W. Lilley c Feltham b Marks	1		
K. W. R. Fletcher c Jones b Rose	16	1/13 2/65 3/95	(34.3 overs) 181
H. A. Page run out	31	4/96 5/127 6/128	
†D. E. East c Marks b Jones	2	7/145 8/159 9/165	

Bowling: Jones 6.3–0–35–3; Davis 5–0–18–0; Mallender 8–0–42–1; Marks 8–0–49–2; Rose 6–0–26–2; Crowe 1–0–5–0.

Umpires: D. G. L. Evans and R. Palmer.

At Lord's, May 17. MIDDLESEX v SOMERSET. No result.

SOMERSET v GLOUCESTERSHIRE

At Taunton, May 24. Somerset won by 29 runs. Toss: Somerset.

Somerset

B. C. Rose c Russell b Sainsbury	3	G. V. Palmer c Stovold b Lawrence	5
N. A. Felton c Russell b Lawrence	4	N. A. Mallender not out	1
J. J. E. Hardy c Romaines b Alleyne	13		
M. D. Crowe c and b Bainbridge	22	L-b 12, w 4, n-b 1	17
R. J. Harden c Wright b Sainsbury	52		
*V. J. Marks run out	1	1/10 2/13 3/46	(9 wkts, 40 overs) 173
†N. D. Burns b Lloyds	5	4/60 5/62 6/77	
G. D. Rose b Sainsbury	50	7/131 8/158 9/173	

A. N. Jones did not bat.

Bowling: Lawrence 8–0–29–2; Sainsbury 8–0–57–3; Bainbridge 8–0–25–1; Alleyne 4–0–12–1; Lloyds 4–1–14–1; Graveney 8–2–24–0.

Gloucestershire

A. W. Stovold c Burns b Mallender	7	*D. A. Graveney not out	23
A. J. Wright c Hardy b Jones	12	D. V. Lawrence c Mallender b Jones	0
K. M. Curran c Felton b Palmer	15	G. E. Sainsbury c Burns b Jones	5
P. Bainbridge c Marks b Palmer	9	L-b 5, n-b 1	6
P. W. Romaines run out	33		
J. W. Lloyds c Marks b Palmer	7	1/9 2/30 3/38 4/47	(36.4 overs) 144
†R. C. Russell b Marks	10	5/65 6/96 7/97 8/125 9/125	
M. W. Alleyne c Burns b Jones	17		

Bowling: Jones 6.4–1–37–4; Mallender 7–0–29–1; G. D. Rose 7–0–36–0; Palmer 8–0–17–3; Marks 8–1–20–1.

Umpires: J. H. Harris and D. Lloyd.

At Manchester, May 31. SOMERSET lost to LANCASHIRE by seven wickets.

SOMERSET v WARWICKSHIRE

At Bath, June 14. Somerset won on faster scoring-rate when rain ended play. Toss: Warwickshire.

Somerset

J. J. E. Hardy c Humpage b Donald	..	0	G. V. Palmer b Donald	....	1
J. G. Wyatt run out	....	0	N. A. Mallender not out	....	8
M. D. Crowe c Asif Din b Donald	..	82			
R. J. Harden c Donald b Pierson	....	23	B 4, l-b 8, w 3, n-b 2	......	17
N. A. Felton c Lloyd b Gifford	....	29			
*V. J. Marks c Humpage b Smith	.....	6	1/0 2/8 3/55	(8 wkts, 40 overs)	195
†N. D. Burns c Pierson b Gifford	.....	3	4/127 5/139 6/155		
G. D. Rose not out	....	26	7/158 8/169		

A. N. Jones did not bat.

Bowling: Donald 8–2–22–3; Smith 8–1–47–1; Moles 1–0–2–0; Munton 8–0–36–0; Pierson 7–0–41–1; Gifford 8–0–35–2.

Warwickshire

A. J. Moles lbw b Rose	....	56	D. A. Thorne not out	....	1
T. A. Lloyd c and b Rose	....	36	L-b 3, w 1	....	4
P. A. Smith run out	....	6			
D. L. Amiss not out	....	9	1/95 2/100 3/111	(4 wkts, 24 overs)	113
†G. W. Humpage st Burns b Marks	...	1	4/112		

Asif Din, T. A. Munton, A. A. Donald, *N. Gifford and A. R. K. Pierson did not bat.

Bowling: Jones 3–0–19–0; Mallender 5–0–26–0; Palmer 6–0–27–0; Rose 5–0–16–2; Marks 5–0–22–1.

Umpires: J. W. Holder and R. A. White.

SOMERSET v SUSSEX

At Bath, June 21. Sussex won by seven wickets after achieving a revised target of 140 off 35 overs. Toss: Somerset.

Somerset

N. A. Felton c Reeve b C. M. Wells	..	5	G. V. Palmer not out	....	12
J. J. E. Hardy c le Roux b Pigott	.....	29	N. A. Mallender lbw b le Roux	....	0
M. D. Crowe c Myles b C. M. Wells	..	10	A. N. Jones not out	....	4
R. J. Harden c A. P. Wells b Babington		9	L-b 10, w 3	....	13
R. J. Bartlett c Moores b Babington	...	23			
*V. J. Marks c and b le Roux	....	19	1/14 2/42 3/51	(9 wkts, 36.2 overs)	145
†N. D. Burns b le Roux	....	4	4/72 5/101 6/106		
G. D. Rose c Reeve b le Roux	....	17	7/113 8/138 9/138		

Bowling: C. M. Wells 8–1–22–2; le Roux 8–0–33–4; Pigott 8–1–36–1; Reeve 6.2–0–19–0; Babington 6–0–25–2.

Sussex

*I. J. Gould b Mallender	....	3	G. S. le Roux not out	....	33
A. M. Green run out	....	36	B 1, l-b 5, w 6	....	12
C. M. Wells lbw b Marks	....	28			
A. P. Wells not out	....	29	1/12 2/75 3/79	(3 wkts, 34.2 overs)	141

R. I. Alikhan, D. A. Reeve, S. D. Myles, †P. Moores, A. C. S. Pigott and A. M. Babington did not bat.

Bowling: Jones 7.2–0–36–0; Mallender 8–1–21–1; Palmer 5–0–16–0; Rose 8–0–29–0; Marks 6–0–33–1.

Umpires: D. G. L. Evans and K. J. Lyons.

At Canterbury, June 28. SOMERSET beat KENT by 65 runs.

At The Oval, July 12. SOMERSET lost to SURREY by seven wickets.

SOMERSET v LEICESTERSHIRE

At Taunton, July 19. No result.

At Worcester, July 26. SOMERSET beat WORCESTERSHIRE on faster scoring-rate.

SOMERSET v GLAMORGAN

At Weston-super-Mare, August 2. Glamorgan won by seven wickets. Toss: Glamorgan.

Somerset

†N. D. Burns c Metson b Barwick	0	A. N. Jones not out 11
J. J. E. Hardy c Metson b Smith	1	M. D. Harman c Hopkins b Holmes ... 2
M. D. Crowe st Metson b Ontong	23	D. J. Foster not out 3
R. J. Harden b Barwick	61	L-b 8, w 3 11
*P. M. Roebuck c Metson b Shastri ...	38	
N. J. Pringle c Metson b Derrick	22	1/0 2/6 3/45 (9 wkts, 40 overs) 183
V. J. Marks run out	0	4/104 5/143 6/144
G. V. Palmer run out	11	7/167 8/170 9/174

Bowling: Barwick 8–1–23–2; Smith 5–0–17–1; Holmes 7–1–44–1; Ontong 8–1–40–1; Shastri 8–1–24–1; Derrick 4–0–27–1.

Glamorgan

P. A. Todd st Burns b Marks	33	R. C. Ontong not out 4
J. A. Hopkins b Marks	47	L-b 3, w 5, n-b 1 9
M. P. Maynard c Hardy b Jones	50	
R. J. Shastri not out	43	1/52 2/127 3/157 (3 wkts, 38.3 overs) 186

*H. Morris, G. C. Holmes, J. Derrick, †C. P. Metson, I. Smith and S. R. Barwick did not bat.

Bowling: Jones 8–0–28–1; Foster 8–1–31–0; Pringle 3–0–18–0; Marks 8–2–26–2; Palmer 8–0–55–0; Harman 3.3–0–25–0.

Umpires: J. Birkenshaw and J. H. Hampshire.

At Nottingham, August 9. NOTTINGHAMSHIRE v SOMERSET. No result.

SOMERSET v YORKSHIRE

At Taunton, August 16. Somerset won by five wickets. Toss: Yorkshire.

Yorkshire

K. Sharp st Burns b Marks	40	P. W. Jarvis not out		29
A. A. Metcalfe c Roebuck b Jones	9	S. D. Fletcher not out		0
J. D. Love b Rose	0			
†D. L. Bairstow c Pringle b Mallender	30	L-b 9, w 5, n-b 1		15
P. E. Robinson b Mallender	3			
S. N. Hartley run out	33	1/20 2/21 3/85	(8 wkts, 39 overs)	170
*P. Carrick c Burns b Mallender	5	4/91 5/91 6/105		
P. J. Hartley c Marks b Palmer	6	7/118 8/166		

C. Shaw did not bat.

Bowling: Jones 7–1–31–1; Rose 8–1–27–1; Palmer 8–0–46–1; Marks 8–0–32–1; Mallender 8–0–25–3.

Somerset

*P. M. Roebuck c Bairstow b Shaw	29	V. J. Marks not out		19
J. G. Wyatt lbw b P. J. Hartley	1			
J. J. E. Hardy c Metcalfe b Love	24	B 1, l-b 9, w 3, n-b 1		14
†N. D. Burns c Bairstow b P. J. Hartley	29			
R. J. Harden not out	48	1/8 2/50 3/89	(5 wkts, 38.5 overs)	171
N. J. Pringle c and b Love	7	4/93 5/110		

G. V. Palmer, G. D. Rose, N. A. Mallender and A. N. Jones did not bat.

Bowling: Jarvis 8–2–34–0; P. J. Hartley 8–0–32–2; Fletcher 4.5–0–24–0; Shaw 6–0–25–1; Carrick 6–1–29–0; Love 6–1–17–2.

Umpires: B. Dudleston and R. Julian.

At Bournemouth, August 23. SOMERSET beat HAMPSHIRE by 24 runs.

SOMERSET v NORTHAMPTONSHIRE

At Taunton, September 6. No result. Toss: Northamptonshire.

Somerset

J. G. Wyatt c Ripley b Robinson	1	R. J. Harden not out		1
*P. M. Roebuck c N. G. B. Cook				
b Harper	26	B 2, n-b 1		3
J. J. E. Hardy not out	33			
M. D. Crowe c Lamb b N. G. B. Cook	27	1/13 2/42 3/87	(3 wkts, 25 overs)	91

V. J. Marks, †N. D. Burns, G. D. Rose, G. V. Palmer, N. A. Mallender and A. N. Jones did not bat.

Bowling: Smith 4–0–17–0; Robinson 5–0–13–1; Harper 5–0–17–1; Wild 6–1–14–0; Larkins 4–0–25–0; N. G. B. Cook 1–0–3–1.

Northamptonshire

W. Larkins, R. J. Bailey, A. J. Lamb, R. J. Boyd-Moss, R. A. Harper, D. J. Wild, *G. Cook, †D. Ripley, N. G. B. Cook, G. Smith and M. A. Robinson.

Umpires: R. Julian and D. R. Shepherd.

At Derby, September 13. SOMERSET beat DERBYSHIRE by 14 runs.

SURREY

At Southampton, May 10. SURREY lost to HAMPSHIRE by 75 runs.

SURREY v LANCASHIRE

At The Oval, May 17. No result. Toss: Surrey.

Lancashire

G. D. Mendis not out	....	37
G. Fowler b Thomas	....	5
J. Abrahams c Bullen b Clarke	....	23
N. H. Fairbrother not out	....	2
L-b 9, n-b 1	....	10

1/21 2/72   (2 wkts, 22 overs) 77

S. J. O'Shaughnessy, *D. P. Hughes, M. Watkinson, I. D. Austin, J. Simmons, P. J. W. Allott and †J. Stanworth did not bat.

Bowling: Thomas 8–0–31–1; Bicknell 4–1–9–0; Feltham 4–0–15–0; Clarke 3–0–5–1; Greig 3–0–8–0.

Surrey

G. S. Clinton, N. J. Falkner, M. A. Lynch, T. E. Jesty, †C. J. Richards, *I. A. Greig, C. K. Bullen, D. J. Thomas, M. A. Feltham, M. P. Bicknell and S. T. Clarke.

Umpires: J. H. Harris and A. A. Jones.

SURREY v ESSEX

At The Oval, May 24. Surrey won by five wickets. Toss: Essex.

Essex

C. Gladwin c Bullen b Clarke	....	37	G. Miller c Stewart b Greig	....	19
†D. E. East c Ward b Greig	....	13	H. A. Page not out	....	4
B. R. Hardie not out	....	66	L-b 8, w 2	....	10
D. R. Pringle run out	....	1			
*K. W. R. Fletcher b Bicknell	....	14	1/27 2/83 3/85	(6 wkts, 40 overs) 167
A. W. Lilley c Jesty b Thomas	......	3	4/112 5/120 6/153	

I. Redpath, T. D. Topley and J. K. Lever did not bat.

Bowling: Thomas 8–1–24–1; Bicknell 8–0–26–1; Bullen 8–2–28–0; Greig 8–0–50–2; Clarke 8–0–31–1.

Surrey

G. S. Clinton c Miller b Pringle	......	52	D. M. Smith not out	....	8
†D. M. Ward lbw b Topley	....	7			
A. J. Stewart c East b Topley	....	4	L-b 5, w 6	....	11
M. A. Lynch c Miller b Lever	......	45			
T. E. Jesty b Topley	....	0	1/30 2/42 3/114	(5 wkts, 38.5 overs) 168
*I. A. Greig not out	....	41	4/115 5/136	

C. K. Bullen, D. J. Thomas, M. P. Bicknell and S. T. Clarke did not bat.

Bowling: Lever 7.5–1–32–1; Page 8–0–54–0; Topley 8–1–24–3; Miller 8–0–28–0; Pringle 7–0–25–1.

Umpires: R. Julian and K. J. Lyons.

SURREY v WARWICKSHIRE

At The Oval, June 7. Surrey won by three wickets. Toss: Surrey.

Warwickshire

T. A. Lloyd b Bullen	30	A. R. K. Pierson not out		8
A. J. Moles b Greig	21	A. A. Donald not out		2
D. A. Thorne b Bullen	9			
D. L. Amiss c Ward b Thomas	53	B 1, l-b 8, w 5, n-b 2		16
†G. W. Humpage c Richards b Bicknell	24			
Asif Din c and b Greig	25	1/53 2/53 3/81 4/128 (7 wkts, 40 overs)		209
G. J. Parsons b Gray	21	5/148 6/197 7/199		

T. A. Munton and *N. Gifford did not bat.

Bowling: Bicknell 8–0–33–1; Thomas 8–0–45–1; Greig 8–0–57–2; Bullen 8–1–29–2; Gray 8–0–36–1.

Surrey

G. S. Clinton c Donald b Pierson	45	D. J. Thomas not out		7
A. J. Stewart c Pierson b Donald	5	C. K. Bullen not out		7
M. A. Lynch c and b Pierson	32	L-b 9, w 8, n-b 1		18
†C. J. Richards run out	11			
D. M. Ward b Parsons	53	1/12 2/67 3/91 (7 wkts, 39.4 overs)		213
*I. A. Greig b Donald	34	4/114 5/191		
K. T. Medlycott b Parsons	1	6/192 7/199		

M. P. Bicknell and A. H. Gray did not bat.

Bowling: Donald 8–0–36–2; Parsons 8–0–40–2; Munton 8–0–46–0; Pierson 8–0–34–2; Gifford 7.4–0–48–0.

Umpires: J. H. Harris and A. G. T. Whitehead.

At Leicester, June 14. LEICESTERSHIRE v SURREY. No result.

At Leeds, June 21. SURREY lost to YORKSHIRE by 51 runs.

SURREY v NORTHAMPTONSHIRE

At Guildford, June 28. Surrey won by 1 run. Toss Northamptonshire.

Surrey

†C. J. Richards b Harper	41	T. E. Jesty not out		77
A. J. Stewart c Ripley b Wild	19	L-b 5, w 3		8
D. M. Smith not out	72			
M. A. Lynch b Wild	3	1/60 2/70 3/81 (3 wkts, 40 overs)		220

D. M. Ward, *I. A. Greig, M. A. Feltham, C. K. Bullen, A. H. Gray and M. P. Bicknell did not bat.

Bowling: Walker 7–0–52–0; Capel 6–0–30–0; Wild 8–0–28–2; Harper 8–0–34–1; N. G. B. Cook 7–0–50–0; Williams 4–0–21–0.

Northamptonshire

R. J. Bailey lbw b Bullen	36	D. J. Wild not out	1
W. Larkins c Richards b Feltham	49		
A. J. Lamb c Ward b Greig	47	B 4, l-b 2, w 3, n-b 4	13
D. J. Capel b Greig	52		
R. A. Harper c Richards b Lynch	16	1/93 2/97 3/190	(7 wkts, 40 overs) 219
R. G. Williams st Richards b Lynch	4	4/203 5/217	
*G. Cook run out	1	6/218 7/219	

†D. Ripley, N. G. B. Cook and A. Walker did not bat.

Bowling: Gray 8–0–39–0; Bicknell 8–0–60–0; Feltham 8–0–31–1; Bullen 8–1–37–1; Jesty 2–0–16–0; Greig 5–0–28–2; Lynch 1–0–2–2.

Umpires: R. A. White and P. B. Wight.

<h2 align="center">SURREY v SOMERSET</h2>

At The Oval, July 12. Surrey won by seven wickets. Toss: Somerset. Richards hit one six and thirteen fours, with his second fifty coming off 27 balls.

Somerset

*P. M. Roebuck c Bullen b Clarke	18	V. J. Marks run out	8
†N. D. Burns c Richards b Feltham	4		
J. J. E. Hardy b Feltham	40	L-b 17, w 7, n-b 1	25
M. D. Crowe c and b Feltham	56		
R. J. Harden c Lynch b Clarke	27	1/11 2/39 3/124	(6 wkts, 40 overs) 194
N. A. Felton not out	16	4/136 5/182 6/194	

D. J. Foster, G. V. Palmer, N. A. Mallender and A. N. Jones did not bat.

Bowling: Bicknell 8–0–35–0; Feltham 8–0–31–3; Clarke 8–0–21–2; Greig 8–0–51–0; Jesty 4–0–18–0; Bullen 4–0–21–0.

Surrey

G. S. Clinton c Burns b Jones	32	T. E. Jesty not out	0
†C. J. Richards b Palmer	113	L-b 8, w 5	13
D. M. Smith run out	28		
M. A. Lynch not out	9	1/100 2/183 3/185	(3 wkts, 35 overs) 195

D. M. Ward, *I. A. Greig, M. A. Feltham, C. K. Bullen, S. T. Clarke and M. P. Bicknell did not bat.

Bowling: Jones 8–0–26–1; Foster 8–0–38–0; Mallender 6–0–32–0; Marks 6–0–52–0; Palmer 7–0–39–1.

Umpires: J. Birkenshaw and M. J. Kitchen.

At Cardiff, July 19. GLAMORGAN v SURREY. No result.

At Lord's, August 2. SURREY beat MIDDLESEX by five wickets.

At Chesterfield, August 9. DERBYSHIRE v SURREY. No result.

SURREY v KENT

At The Oval, August 16. Kent won by 9 runs. Toss: Surrey.

Kent

M. R. Benson c Richards b Bicknell ...	40	†S. A. Marsh not out	1
N. R. Taylor lbw b Feltham	2		
C. J. Tavaré c Lynch b Feltham	79	L-b 13, w 5, n-b 1	19
*C. S. Cowdrey c Gray b Greig	77		—
E. A. E. Baptiste lbw b Gray	1	1/6 2/85 3/191 (5 wkts, 40 overs)	234
D. G. Aslett not out	15	4/194 5/230	

C. Penn, A. P. Igglesden, R. P. Davis and K. B. S. Jarvis did not bat.

Bowling: Bicknell 8–0–36–1; Feltham 8–1–31–2; Gray 8–1–37–1; Greig 8–0–48–1; Bullen 5–0–40–0; Jesty 3–0–29–0.

Surrey

G. S. Clinton c Marsh b Baptiste	23	C. K. Bullen c Marsh b Penn	1
†C. J. Richards c Tavaré b Jarvis	12	A. H. Gray b Igglesden	23
D. M. Smith c Aslett b Baptiste	16	M. P. Bicknell not out	12
T. E. Jesty c Benson b Baptiste	0	L-b 6, w 1, n-b 3	10
M. A. Lynch c Tavaré b Davis	53		—
D. M. Ward not out	73	1/16 2/54 3/54 (9 wkts, 40 overs)	225
*I. A. Greig b Davis	2	4/55 5/137 6/150	
M. A. Feltham b Davis	0	7/150 8/151 9/199	

Bowling: Jarvis 8–0–37–1; Igglesden 8–0–46–1; Baptiste 8–0–19–3; Davis 7–0–49–3; Penn 7–0–43–1; Cowdrey 2–0–25–0.

Umpires: J. H. Hampshire and D. Lloyd.

At Hove, August 23. SURREY beat SUSSEX by 60 runs.

At Hereford, August 30. SURREY lost to WORCESTERSHIRE by nine wickets.

SURREY v GLOUCESTERSHIRE

At The Oval, September 6. Gloucestershire won on faster scoring-rate. Toss: Surrey. Surrey's revised target of 107 from 21 overs was 0.69 of a run ahead of Gloucestershire's calculated total at 21 overs (106.31). Consequently, when Surrey fell 1 run short, the result was not a tie.

Gloucestershire

†R. C. Russell c Ward b Greig	18	*P. Bainbridge not out	4
C. W. J. Athey b Clarke	25	L-b 5	5
K. M. Curran c Richards b Greig	0		—
J. W. Lloyds c Bicknell b Bullen	37	1/33 2/34 3/73 (5 wkts, 21.2 overs)	108
P. W. Romaines c Medlycott b Bullen .	19	4/89 5/108	

A. J. Wright, M. W. Alleyne, C. A. Walsh, J. N. Shepherd and G. E. Sainsbury did not bat.

Bowling: Feltham 4–0–19–0; Bicknell 4–1–13–0; Greig 3–0–19–2; Clarke 5–1–27–1; Bullen 5.2–0–25–2.

Surrey

†C. J. Richards st Russell b Bainbridge	42
D. M. Smith c Wright b Bainbridge	37
T. E. Jesty c Russell b Walsh	5
M. A. Lynch run out	13
D. M. Ward b Walsh	2
K. T. Medlycott c Bainbridge b Walsh	0
*I. A. Greig not out	0

M. A. Feltham run out	1
L-b 5, w 1	6
1/74 2/85 3/89 (7 wkts, 21 overs)	106
4/103 5/103	
6/105 7/106	

C. K. Bullen, S. T. Clarke and M. P. Bicknell did not bat.

Bowling: Shepherd 6–0–40–0; Walsh 7–0–28–3; Bainbridge 4–0–24–2; Sainsbury 4–1–9–0.

Umpires: K. J. Lyons and D. S. Thompsett.

SURREY v NOTTINGHAMSHIRE

At The Oval, September 13. Nottinghamshire won by three wickets. Toss: Nottinghamshire.

Surrey

†C. J. Richards c Rice b Hemmings	27
D. M. Smith b Rice	36
A. J. Stewart run out	52
T. E. Jesty b Saxelby	19
M. A. Lynch c Rice b Saxelby	7
D. M. Ward run out	16
*I. A. Greig b Hadlee	19

M. A. Feltham not out	3
C. K. Bullen not out	1
B 11, w 4	15
1/47 2/114 3/127 (7 wkts, 40 overs)	195
4/147 5/155	
6/191 7/192	

S. T. Clarke and M. P. Bicknell did not bat.

Bowling: Saxelby 8–0–36–2; Pick 8–3–31–0; Hemmings 8–0–46–1; Hadlee 8–0–32–1; Rice 8–0–39–1.

Nottinghamshire

B. C. Broad b Bullen	48
R. T. Robinson c Richards b Bicknell	36
P. Johnson c Greig b Bullen	5
*C. E. B. Rice c and b Feltham	25
R. J. Hadlee c Ward b Feltham	16
D. W. Randall c Richards b Feltham	8
M. Newell not out	28

†B. N. French b Lynch	6
E. E. Hemmings not out	4
B 6, l-b 7, w 9	22
1/63 2/93 3/114 (7 wkts, 39.4 overs)	198
4/147 5/150	
6/166 7/194	

R. A. Pick and K. Saxelby did not bat.

Bowling: Clarke 8–1–30–0; Feltham 8–0–40–3; Bicknell 8–0–35–1; Greig 7–0–38–0; Bullen 8–0–38–2; Lynch 0.4–0–4–1.

Umpires: R. Julian and B. Leadbeater.

SUSSEX

At Cardiff, May 3. SUSSEX beat GLAMORGAN by 70 runs.

SUSSEX v DERBYSHIRE

At Hove, May 10. Derbyshire won by four wickets. Toss: Derbyshire.

Sussex

N. J. Lenham run out	22	†P. Moores not out	6
A. P. Wells run out	5	C. I. O. Ricketts b Newman	1
P. W. G. Parker c Krikken b Newman	1	A. M. Babington c Barnett b Newman	0
C. M. Wells b Mortensen	5	B 2, l-b 9, w 8, n-b 3	22
*I. J. Gould b Jean-Jacques	35		
G. S. le Roux b Jean-Jacques	66	1/12 2/19 3/37	(39.2 overs) 186
D. A. Reeve run out	21	4/40 5/148 6/149	
S. D. Myles b Jean-Jacques	2	7/161 8/184 9/186	

Bowling: Newman 7.2–0–31–3; Mortensen 8–1–26–1; Holding 8–0–27–0; Warner 8–0–43–0; Jean-Jacques 8–0–48–3.

Derbyshire

*K. J. Barnett c Moores b le Roux	1	P. G. Newman c Parker b A. P. Wells	10
I. S. Anderson c C. M. Wells b Babington	39	A. E. Warner b Ricketts	4
B. Roberts not out	101	R. J. Finney not out	10
J. E. Morris b Babington	0	B 1, l-b 3	4
M. A. Holding c C. M. Wells b Babington	18	1/5 2/101 3/101	(6 wkts, 40 overs) 187
		4/123 5/157 6/163	

†K. M. Krikken, M. Jean-Jacques and O. H. Mortensen did not bat.

Bowling: C. M. Wells 8–2–20–0; le Roux 8–0–46–1; Babington 8–0–33–3; Reeve 8–0–40–0; Ricketts 5–0–25–1; A. P. Wells 3–0–19–1.

Umpires: D. J. Constant and N. T. Plews.

At Northampton, May 31. SUSSEX lost to NORTHAMPTONSHIRE by 43 runs.

SUSSEX v HAMPSHIRE

At Horsham, June 7. Sussex won by one wicket. Toss: Sussex.

Hampshire

V. P. Terry c Green b C. M. Wells	75	†R. J. Parks not out	9
R. J. Scott run out	23	T. M. Tremlett not out	1
D. R. Turner c Moores b Reeve	1	L-b 5, w 5, n-b 4	14
*M. C. J. Nicholas lbw b Waring	1		
K. D. James run out	31	1/47 2/56 3/57	(7 wkts, 40 overs) 216
C. L. Smith c Moores b le Roux	54	4/104 5/167	
M. D. Marshall c Waring b le Roux	7	6/198 7/210	

R. J. Maru and C. A. Connor did not bat.

Bowling: C. M. Wells 8–0–39–1; le Roux 8–1–46–2; Waring 8–0–34–1; Reeve 8–0–33–1; Babington 6–0–42–0; Ricketts 2–0–17–0.

Sussex

A. P. Wells c Maru b James	10	C. I. O. Ricketts lbw b Connor	9
A. M. Green c Parks b Tremlett	17	I. C. Waring run out	8
C. M. Wells c Scott b Tremlett	70	A. M. Babington not out	0
*I. J. Gould b Tremlett	7	L-b 2, w 2	4
G. S. le Roux not out	83		
D. A. Reeve c Marshall b Maru	6	1/16 2/52 3/85	(9 wkts, 40 overs) 218
S. D. Myles b Maru	4	4/118 5/130 6/147	
†P. Moores run out	0	7/148 8/171 9/208	

Bowling: James 8–1–52–1; Connor 8–0–42–1; Marshall 8–0–29–0; Tremlett 8–0–36–3; Maru 8–1–57–2.

Umpires: R. Palmer and P. B. Wight.

At Swindon, June 14. SUSSEX lost to GLOUCESTERSHIRE by four wickets.

At Bath, June 21. SUSSEX beat SOMERSET by seven wickets.

SUSSEX v NOTTINGHAMSHIRE

At Hove, June 28. Nottinghamshire won by six wickets. Toss: Nottinghamshire.

Sussex

R. I. Alikhan run out	3	A. C. S. Pigott c Saxelby b Rice	3
*I. J. Gould b Cooper	38	†P. Moores not out	1
C. M. Wells c Pick b Rice	48	L-b 7, w 2	9
A. P. Wells c Cooper b Pick	27		
G. S. le Roux not out	56	1/6 2/89 3/95 (7 wkts, 40 overs) 194
D. A. Reeve lbw b Rice	6	4/147 5/177
S. D. Myles b Saxelby	3	6/186 7/193

D. K. Standing and I. C. Waring did not bat.

Bowling: Cooper 8–0–30–1; Saxelby 8–1–31–1; Pick 8–0–41–1; Hadlee 8–0–30–0; Rice 8–0–55–3.

Nottinghamshire

B. C. Broad c le Roux b Waring	45	D. W. Randall not out	9
R. T. Robinson c Moores b Pigott	78	B 1, l-b 9, w 2, n-b 1	13
P. Johnson c Moores b le Roux	14		
*C. E. B. Rice not out	30	1/100 2/134 (4 wkts, 39.4 overs) 195
R. J. Hadlee c A. P. Wells b C. M. Wells	6	3/168 4/181

K. E. Cooper, †C. W. Scott, J. D. Birch, R. A. Pick and K. Saxelby did not bat.

Bowling: C. M. Wells 4.4–0–23–1; le Roux 8–0–29–1; Reeve 8–0–42–0; Pigott 8–0–43–1; Standing 5–0–28–0; Waring 6–1–20–1.

Umpires: B. Leadbeater and D. Lloyd.

At Chelmsford, July 5. SUSSEX lost to ESSEX by 1 run.

SUSSEX v LANCASHIRE

At Hastings, July 19. No result.

SUSSEX v WORCESTERSHIRE

At Eastbourne, August 2. Worcestershire won by seven wickets after showers had caused their target to be reduced to 135 off 30 overs. Toss: Worcestershire.

Sussex

P. W. G. Parker c and b Newport	44	R. I. Alikhan run out	11
*†I. J. Gould b Radford	24		
C. M. Wells lbw b Botham	26	L-b 13, w 5, n-b 1	19
A. P. Wells c Newport b Botham	4		
G. S. le Roux run out	8	1/64 2/107 3/109 (6 wkts, 32 overs) 143
N. J. Lenham not out	7	4/120 5/126 6/143

S. J. S. Kimber, A. C. S. Pigott, A. M. Babington and I. C. Waring did not bat.

Bowling: Dilley 5–0–32–0; Pridgeon 8–0–24–0; Radford 7–0–28–1; Botham 8–0–31–2; Newport 4–0–15–1.

Worcestershire

T. S. Curtis c Gould b Waring	18	*P. A. Neale not out	23
I. T. Botham c Babington b C. M. Wells	27	L-b 7, w 7, n-b 1	15
G. A. Hick not out	52		
D. B. D'Oliveira b Babington	3	1/48 2/64 3/69 (3 wkts, 27.2 overs) 138

R. K. Illingworth, †S. J. Rhodes, P. J. Newport, N. V. Radford, A. P. Pridgeon and G. R. Dilley did not bat.

Bowling: C. M. Wells 8–1–21–1; Pigott 6–0–30–0; Waring 7–0–40–1; Babington 5–0–31–1; Alikhan 1–0–5–0; Parker 0.2–0–4–0.

Umpires: M. J. Kitchen and D. O. Oslear.

At Hull, August 9. YORKSHIRE v SUSSEX. No result.

SUSSEX v WARWICKSHIRE

At Hove, August 16. Sussex won by 7 runs. Toss: Sussex.

Sussex

A. M. Green b Small	24	R. I. Alikhan not out	18
P. W. G. Parker not out	106	B 2, l-b 7, w 4, n-b 1	14
C. M. Wells c Hodgson b Smith	59		
A. P. Wells c Pierson b Small	11	1/34 2/147 3/167 (3 wkts, 40 overs) 232

*†I. J. Gould, P. Moores, A. C. S. Pigott, D. A. Reeve, I. C. Waring and A. M. Babington did not bat.

Bowling: Merrick 8–2–33–0; Munton 7–0–35–0; Small 8–1–21–2; Moles 8–0–47–0; Pierson 2–0–28–0; Humpage 3–0–29–0; Smith 4–0–30–1.

Warwickshire

A. J. Moles c Gould b Pigott	83	N. M. K. Smith run out	22
*T. A. Lloyd c C. M. Wells b Reeve	16	G. C. Small not out	1
Asif Din b Babington	23	L-b 6, w 4, n-b 2	12
G. W. Humpage c Gould b Pigott	42		
T. A. Merrick b Pigott	0	1/39 2/101 3/162 (7 wkts, 40 overs) 225
G. D. Hodgson b Pigott	12	4/162 5/187	
†G. A. Tedstone not out	14	6/188 7/224	

A. R. K. Pierson and T. A. Munton did not bat.

Bowling: C. M. Wells 8–0–29–0; Babington 8–1–38–1; Reeve 8–0–36–1; Waring 8–0–56–0; Pigott 8–0–60–4.

Umpires: K. J. Lyons and A. G. T. Whitehead.

SUSSEX v SURREY

At Hove, August 23. Surrey won by 60 runs. Toss: Sussex.

Surrey

†C. J. Richards c Babington b Pigott . .	71	C. K. Bullen not out	8
D. M. Smith c Gould b Waring	47	S. T. Clarke not out	4
A. J. Stewart c Myles b Waring	25		
T. E. Jesty c Babington b Pigott	16	L-b 6, w 1	7
M. A. Lynch lbw b Pigott	1		
D. M. Ward c Parker b Pigott	4	1/98 2/136 3/155 (8 wkts, 40 overs) 223
*I. A. Greig b Wells	23	4/156 5/164 6/194
M. A. Feltham b Wells	17	7/198 8/211

M. P. Bicknell did not bat.

Bowling: Wells 8-0-47-2; Babington 8-1-31-0; Kimber 8-0-38-0; Waring 8-0-52-2; Pigott 8-0-49-4.

Sussex

A. M. Green b Lynch	62	S. J. S. Kimber run out	3
P. W. G. Parker lbw b Greig	24	I. C. Waring not out	2
C. M. Wells c Feltham b Bullen	13		
*†I. J. Gould b Bullen	17	B 2, l-b 7, w 3	12
R. I. Alikhan c and b Greig	3		
P. Moores st Richards b Bullen	2	1/53 2/70 3/98 (8 wkts, 40 overs) 163
S. D. Myles c Stewart b Lynch	15	4/105 5/112 6/137
A. C. S. Pigott not out	10	7/152 8/159

A. M. Babington did not bat.

Bowling: Bicknell 8-1-23-0; Feltham 8-0-31-0; Greig 8-1-29-2; Bullen 8-0-29-3; Clarke 4-0-13-0; Lynch 4-0-29-2.

Umpires: B. Leadbeater and B. J. Meyer.

At Lord's, August 30. SUSSEX lost to MIDDLESEX by 68 runs.

At Canterbury, September 6. KENT v SUSSEX. No result.

SUSSEX v LEICESTERSHIRE

At Hove, September 13. No result.

WARWICKSHIRE

WARWICKSHIRE v YORKSHIRE

At Birmingham, May 3. Yorkshire won by 51 runs after rain had reduced Warwickshire's target to 205 off 31 overs. Toss: Warwickshire.

Yorkshire

A. A. Metcalfe c Humpage b Thorne . .	67	A. Sidebottom run out	15
K. Sharp run out	17	P. J. Hartley not out	0
J. D. Love c Parsons b Thorne	43	B 6, l-b 9, w 1, n-b 1	17
†D. L. Bairstow not out	66		
P. E. Robinson b Moles	2	1/45 2/131 3/140 (7 wkts, 36 overs) 238
S. N. Hartley c and b Moles	7	4/159 5/187
*P. Carrick c Storie b Merrick	4	6/192 7/237

P. W. Jarvis and S. D. Fletcher did not bat.

Bowling: Merrick 8–1–38–1; Parsons 6–0–25–0; Munton 7–0–54–0; Gifford 7–0–54–0; Moles 5–0–27–2; Thorne 3–0–25–2.

Warwickshire

T. A. Lloyd c Bairstow b Sidebottom	.. 3	G. J. Parsons b P. J. Hartley	....	2
A. J. Moles c Sidebottom b Fletcher	... 11	T. A. Merrick not out	....	1
A. C. Storie b Jarvis	 55	L-b 8, w 2, n-b 2	....	12
D. L. Amiss c Fletcher b P. J. Hartley	. 15			
†G. W. Humpage b Jarvis	 47	1/8 2/18 3/63	(7 wkts, 31 overs)	154
Asif Din c and b Jarvis	 6	4/136 5/148		
D. A. Thorne not out	 2	6/148 7/151		

T. A. Munton and *N. Gifford did not bat.

Bowling: Fletcher 8–1–30–1; Sidebottom 8–1–20–1; Jarvis 8–0–54–3; P. J. Hartley 6–0–36–2; Carrick 1–0–6–0.

Umpires: K. E. Palmer and R. A. White.

At Bristol, May 17. WARWICKSHIRE lost to GLOUCESTERSHIRE on scoring-rate.

WARWICKSHIRE v DERBYSHIRE

At Birmingham, May 31. Derbyshire won by two wickets. Toss: Warwickshire.

Warwickshire

T. A. Lloyd c Roberts b Warner	 50	A. A. Donald b Holding	....	6
A. J. Moles lbw b Mortensen	 7	T. A. Munton not out	....	0
A. C. Storie lbw b Rudd	 15			
D. L. Amiss c Anderson b Warner	... 33	L-b 7, w 2	....	9
†G. W. Humpage b Holding	 32			
Asif Din lbw b Newman	 6	1/9 2/43 3/102	(8 wkts, 40 overs)	186
G. J. Parsons not out	 26	4/127 5/135 6/167		
A. R. K. Pierson b Holding	 2	7/169 8/183		

*N. Gifford did not bat.

Bowling: Newman 8–0–36–1; Mortensen 5–1–15–1; Holding 8–0–34–3; Rudd 5–0–20–1; Jean-Jacques 7–0–36–0; Warner 7–0–38–2.

Derbyshire

*K. J. Barnett c Humpage b Munton	.. 25	C. F. B. P. Rudd b Gifford	....	0
†B. J. M. Maher lbw b Donald	 3	M. Jean-Jacques not out	....	5
B. Roberts st Humpage b Pierson	... 13			
J. E. Morris c Moles b Munton	... 28	L-b 17, w 6	....	23
I. S. Anderson c Humpage b Parsons	.. 11			
P. G. Newman not out	 52	1/6 2/35 3/55	(8 wkts, 39.5 overs)	190
A. E. Warner lbw b Parsons	 10	4/92 5/107 6/133		
M. A. Holding c Moles b Donald	 20	7/163 8/172		

O. H. Mortensen did not bat.

Bowling: Donald 8–1–40–2; Parsons 8–0–49–2; Pierson 8–1–22–1; Munton 8–0–32–2; Gifford 7.5–0–30–1.

Umpires: D. Lloyd and P. B. Wight.

At The Oval, June 7. WARWICKSHIRE lost to SURREY by three wickets.

At Bath, June 14. WARWICKSHIRE lost to SOMERSET on scoring-rate.

WARWICKSHIRE v ESSEX

At Birmingham, June 21. Warwickshire won on faster scoring-rate when rain ended play.
Toss: Warwickshire.

Essex

*G. A. Gooch b Parsons	2	I. Redpath not out	11
G. Miller b Gifford	35	T. D. Topley b Donald	6
B. R. Hardie run out	13	J. K. Lever not out	1
D. R. Pringle b Smith	6	B 1, l-b 12, w 4, n-b 2	19
K. W. R. Fletcher lbw b Smith	3		
A. W. Lilley lbw b Smith	7	1/17 2/51 3/53 (9 wkts, 40 overs) 161	
H. A. Page c Parsons b Munton	39	4/66 5/73 6/79	
†D. E. East c Lloyd b Munton	19	7/135 8/137 9/154	

Bowling: Donald 8–1–31–1; Parsons 8–0–24–1; Gifford 6–1–11–1; Smith 8–0–35–3; Munton 8–1–31–2; Pierson 2–0–16–0.

Warwickshire

T. A. Lloyd b Pringle	19	A. A. Donald b Pringle	2
A. J. Moles lbw b Page	1	T. A. Munton not out	7
P. A. Smith b Page	19		
D. L. Amiss b Gooch	17	L-b 12, w 3	15
†G. W. Humpage b Topley	31		
Asif Din not out	42	1/8 2/44 3/46 (8 wkts, 38.5 overs) 160	
G. J. Parsons c Miller b Lever	7	4/87 5/101 6/138	
A. R. K. Pierson run out	0	7/140 8/142	

*N. Gifford did not bat.

Bowling: Lever 7.5–2–32–1; Page 8–2–22–2; Pringle 8–1–25–2; Topley 7–0–38–1; Gooch 8–0–31–1.

Umpires: J. H. Hampshire and D. Lloyd.

WARWICKSHIRE v HAMPSHIRE

At Birmingham, June 28. Hampshire won by 84 runs. Toss: Warwickshire.

Hampshire

D. R. Turner run out	60	N. G. Cowley not out	35
C. L. Smith c Smith b Pierson	31	†R. J. Parks not out	5
R. A. Smith c Humpage b Moles	7	B 1, l-b 7, w 8	16
*M. C. J. Nicholas c and b Moles	1		
V. P. Terry b Smith	24	1/54 2/79 3/92 (7 wkts, 40 overs) 210	
K. D. James b Donald	29	4/116 5/157	
M. D. Marshall b Donald	2	6/166 7/175	

T. M. Tremlett and C. A. Connor did not bat.

Bowling: Donald 8–1–34–2; Parsons 5–0–22–0; Pierson 8–0–34–1; Moles 8–0–39–2; Gifford 4–0–22–0; Smith 7–0–51–1.

Warwickshire

T. A. Lloyd b James	1	A. R. K. Pierson not out	21	
A. J. Moles b James	17	A. A. Donald not out	13	
P. A. Smith c Nicholas b Connor	8			
D. L. Amiss c Parks b James	2	B 4, w 5	9	
†G. W. Humpage b Tremlett	12		—	
Asif Din c Terry b Cowley	12	1/5 2/24 3/29	(8 wkts, 40 overs) 126	
A. C. Storie c Terry b Cowley	12	4/42 5/46 6/70		
G. J. Parsons run out	19	7/71 8/109		

*N. Gifford did not bat.

Bowling: James 8–1–26–3; Connor 8–0–29–1; Tremlett 8–0–22–1; Cowley 8–1–20–2; Marshall 4–0–7–0; Nicholas 4–0–18–0.

Umpires: J. H. Hampshire and D. O. Oslear.

At Worcester, July 5. WARWICKSHIRE lost to WORCESTERSHIRE by six wickets.

WARWICKSHIRE v NOTTINGHAMSHIRE

At Birmingham, July 12. Nottinghamshire won by seven wickets. Toss: Nottinghamshire.

Warwickshire

T. A. Lloyd b Bore	3	D. A. Thorne b Rice	3	
A. J. Moles b Pick	21	G. J. Parsons not out	1	
P. A. Smith lbw b Hadlee	56	L-b 5, w 1, n-b 1	7	
D. L. Amiss b Hadlee	11			
G. W. Humpage not out	42	1/9 2/55 3/89	(7 wkts, 40 overs) 175	
Asif Din b Pick	27	4/102 5/151		
†G. A. Tedstone c and b Rice	4	6/161 7/171		

T. A. Merrick and *N. Gifford did not bat.

Bowling: Saxelby 8–0–36–0; Bore 8–0–22–1; Hadlee 8–0–39–2; Pick 8–0–36–2; Rice 8–0–37–2.

Nottinghamshire

B. C. Broad not out	73	D. W. Randall not out	58	
R. T. Robinson lbw b Merrick	0	L-b 6, w 1, n-b 1	8	
P. Johnson b Merrick	0			
*C. E. B. Rice b Smith	40	1/1 2/1 3/70	(3 wkts, 38 overs) 179	

J. D. Birch, R. J. Hadlee, †B. N. French, M. K. Bore, R. A. Pick and K. Saxelby did not bat.

Bowling: Merrick 7–0–28–2; Parsons 8–0–31–0; Moles 8–0–29–0; Smith 7–0–44–1; Gifford 7–0–34–0; Thorne 1–0–7–0.

Umpires: B. Dudleston and A. A. Jones.

At Swansea, July 26. WARWICKSHIRE beat GLAMORGAN by six wickets.

WARWICKSHIRE v NORTHAMPTONSHIRE

At Birmingham, August 2. Warwickshire won by seven wickets. Toss: Warwickshire.

Northamptonshire

R. J. Bailey c Tedstone b Parsons	2	D. J. Wild lbw b P. A. Smith	3
*W. Larkins c Tedstone b Parsons	15	†D. Ripley not out	5
A. J. Lamb b Munton	68	L-b 5, w 11, n-b 4	20
D. J. Capel b Munton	50		
R. A. Harper c Tedstone b Merrick	12	1/4 2/22 3/133	(6 wkts, 40 overs) 205
R. G. Williams not out	30	4/157 5/164 6/187	

N. G. B. Cook, A. Walker and M. A. Robinson did not bat.

Bowling: Merrick 8–0–37–1; Parsons 8–0–22–2; Small 8–1–34–0; Moles 4–0–35–0; Munton 7–0–43–2; N. M. K. Smith 3–0–15–0; P. A. Smith 2–0–14–1.

Warwickshire

*T. A. Lloyd c and b Harper	42	G. W. Humpage not out	29
A. J. Moles run out	23	L-b 7, w 1	8
T. A. Merrick c Bailey b Wild	59		
Asif Din not out	46	1/70 2/73 3/155	(3 wkts, 38.3 overs) 207

P. A. Smith, †G. A. Tedstone, N. M. K. Smith, G. C. Small, G. J. Parsons and T. A. Munton did not bat.

Bowling: Capel 5–0–13–0; Walker 8–0–38–0; Harper 8–1–32–1; Wild 7–0–45–1; Cook 5–0–41–0; Robinson 5.3–0–31–0.

Umpires: B. Dudleston and P. B. Wight.

At Leicester, August 9. LEICESTERSHIRE v WARWICKSHIRE. No result.

At Hove, August 16. WARWICKSHIRE lost to SUSSEX by 7 runs.

WARWICKSHIRE v LANCASHIRE

At Birmingham, August 23. No result.

WARWICKSHIRE v MIDDLESEX

At Birmingham, September 6. No result.

At Canterbury, September 13. KENT v WARWICKSHIRE. No result.

WORCESTERSHIRE

WORCESTERSHIRE v LANCASHIRE

At Worcester, May 3. Worcestershire won by six wickets after rain had reduced their target to 117 off 25 overs. Toss: Worcestershire.

Lancashire

G. D. Mendis run out	13	J. Simmons lbw b Radford	3
G. Fowler c Illingworth b Newport	27	†J. Stanworth not out	4
J. Abrahams c Rhodes b Newport	4	K. W. McLeod run out	1
N. H. Fairbrother b Dilley	74	L-b 8, w 1, n-b 2	11
S. J. O'Shaughnessy b Botham	2		—
*D. P. Hughes lbw b Botham	0	1/35 2/41 3/64 (33.4 overs)	158
A. N. Hayhurst c Botham b Newport	5	4/68 5/68 6/93	
I. D. Austin lbw b Radford	14	7/149 8/151 9/156	

Bowling: Dilley 8–0–39–1; Radford 7.4–0–33–2; Botham 8–0–24–2; Newport 8–0–31–3; Weston 1–0–12–0; Illingworth 1–0–11–0.

Worcestershire

T. S. Curtis st Stanworth b Simmons	39	D. B. D'Oliveira not out	4
M. J. Weston c Fowler b McLeod	10	B 1, l-b 2, w 4, n-b 2	9
G. A. Hick b Austin	3		—
I. T. Botham b O'Shaughnessy	47	1/26 2/41 3/97 (4 wkts, 23.3 overs)	120
*P. A. Neale not out	8	4/107	

†S. J. Rhodes, P. J. Newport, R. K. Illingworth, N. V. Radford and G. R. Dilley did not bat.

Bowling: McLeod 6–1–19–1; Hayhurst 6.3–0–23–0; O'Shaughnessy 6–0–36–1; Austin 2–0–6–1; Simmons 3–0–33–1.

Umpires: H. D. Bird and J. H. Hampshire.

At Canterbury, May 10. WORCESTERSHIRE lost to KENT by 49 runs.

At Derby, May 24. WORCESTERSHIRE lost to DERBYSHIRE by three wickets.

WORCESTERSHIRE v ESSEX

At Worcester, May 31. Worcestershire won by nine wickets. Toss: Essex. Botham's first three-figure innings for Worcestershire included two sixes and sixteen fours.

Essex

*G. A. Gooch st Rhodes b McEwan	56	†D. E. East st Rhodes b Hick	0
C. Gladwin run out	6	N. A. Foster not out	28
B. R. Hardie c Neale b Hick	51		
D. R. Pringle not out	40	L-b 9, w 4	13
K. W. R. Fletcher c D'Oliveira b McEwan	2		—
H. A. Page c Newport b Botham	6	1/21 2/120 3/126 (6 wkts, 40 overs)	202
		4/131 5/140 6/141	

I. Redpath, T. D. Topley and J. K. Lever did not bat.

Bowling: Radford 7–1–24–0; Pridgeon 8–0–35–0; Botham 8–3–37–1; McEwan 8–0–37–2; Newport 2–0–13–0; Hick 7–0–47–2.

Worcestershire

T. S. Curtis c East b Page	20
I. T. Botham not out	125
G. A. Hick not out	41
B 1, l-b 10, w 4, n-b 2	17

1/58   (1 wkt, 31.3 overs) 203

M. J. Weston, D. B. D'Oliveira, *P. A. Neale, †S. J. Rhodes, N. V. Radford, P. J. Newport, S. M. McEwan and A. P. Pridgeon did not bat.

Bowling: Lever 7–0–33–0; Foster 5–0–42–0; Page 5–0–31–1; Pringle 5–0–20–0; Topley 5–0–32–0; Gooch 4.3–0–34–0.

Umpires: J. W. Holder and D. R. Shepherd.

At Leicester, June 7. WORCESTERSHIRE beat LEICESTERSHIRE by 1 run.

WORCESTERSHIRE v MIDDLESEX

At Worcester, June 14. Worcestershire won by seven wickets. Toss: Worcestershire.

Middlesex

W. N. Slack lbw b Pridgeon	9	J. E. Emburey not out	0
J. D. Carr c Botham b Dilley	84		
*M. W. Gatting run out	14	B 1, l-b 12, w 3	16
M. R. Ramprakash c Curtis b Hick	26		
R. O. Butcher not out	42	1/34 2/66 3/121 (5 wkts, 40 overs) 201
†P. R. Downton c Radford b Botham	10	4/169 5/197	

A. Needham, N. F. Williams, S. P. Hughes and A. R. C. Fraser did not bat.

Bowling: Dilley 7–0–24–1; Radford 8–1–31–0; Pridgeon 5–0–21–1; Newport 5–0–27–0; Botham 7–0–45–1; Hick 8–0–40–1.

Worcestershire

T. S. Curtis run out	11	*P. A. Neale not out	7
I. T. Botham b Emburey	62	L-b 6, w 2, n-b 1	9
G. A. Hick not out	83		
D. B. D'Oliveira c Downton b Williams	30	1/31 2/114 3/185 (3 wkts, 37.4 overs) 202

M. J. Weston, †S. J. Rhodes, P. J. Newport, N. V. Radford, G. R. Dilley and A. P. Pridgeon did not bat.

Bowling: Hughes 7–0–48–0; Williams 8–0–32–1; Fraser 8–1–26–0; Needham 7–0–44–0; Emburey 6–0–36–1; Gatting 1.4–0–10–0.

Umpires: B. Dudleston and N. T. Plews.

At Nottingham, June 21. WORCESTERSHIRE lost to NOTTINGHAMSHIRE by four wickets.

At Gloucester, June 28. GLOUCESTERSHIRE v WORCESTERSHIRE. No result.

WORCESTERSHIRE v WARWICKSHIRE

At Worcester, July 5. Worcestershire won by six wickets. Toss: Worcestershire. Amiss, when 10, became the first player to score 7,000 runs in the Sunday League.

Warwickshire

A. J. Moles c Rhodes b Newport	8	T. A. Merrick lbw b Radford	16
T. A. Lloyd c Rhodes b Newport	7	T. A. Munton b Radford	0
A. C. Storie c Radford b Newport	4	*N. Gifford not out	6
D. L. Amiss c Rhodes b Radford	29	B 1, l-b 3, w 4, n-b 5	13
†G. W. Humpage c Curtis b Lampitt	25		
Asif Din c Rhodes b Radford	6	1/16 2/21 3/24 (39.1 overs) 126	
G. J. Parsons st Rhodes b Illingworth	12	4/65 5/85 6/88	
G. C. Small b Radford	0	7/88 8/108 9/108	

Bowling: Pridgeon 8–0–20–0; Newport 8–0–25–3; Lampitt 8–0–36–1; Radford 8–0–32–5; Hick 7–1–9–0; Illingworth 0.1–0–0–1.

Worcestershire

T. S. Curtis c Humpage b Moles	34	†S. J. Rhodes not out	12
M. J. Weston lbw b Small	3	L-b 2, w 4	6
G. A. Hick b Merrick	11		
D. B. D'Oliveira not out	46	1/6 2/40 3/63 (4 wkts, 32.2 overs) 127	
*P. A. Neale c Amiss b Moles	15	4/81	

A. P. Pridgeon, P. J. Newport, S. R. Lampitt, N. V. Radford and R. K. Illingworth did not bat.

Bowling: Small 7–2–15–1; Merrick 6.2–0–32–1; Munton 6–0–33–0; Parsons 7–2–21–0; Moles 6–0–24–2.

Umpires: H. D. Bird and B. J. Meyer.

At Southampton, July 12. WORCESTERSHIRE beat HAMPSHIRE by six wickets.

WORCESTERSHIRE v SOMERSET

At Worcester, July 26. Somerset won on faster scoring-rate after rain ended play. Toss: Worcestershire.

Somerset

†N. D. Burns b Newport	6	N. J. Pringle not out	8
*P. M. Roebuck b Illingworth	51		
J. J. E. Hardy not out	84	L-b 7, w 6, n-b 4	17
M. D. Crowe c Hick b Illingworth	35		
R. J. Harden c Rhodes b Radford	26	1/12 2/89 3/131 (5 wkts, 40 overs) 230	
V. J. Marks run out	3	4/197 5/204	

G. V. Palmer, D. J. Foster, M. D. Harman and A. N. Jones did not bat.

Bowling: Pridgeon 8–0–46–0; Newport 8–0–37–1; Radford 8–0–40–1; Hick 8–0–34–0; Illingworth 6–0–49–2; Weston 2–0–17–0.

Worcestershire

T. S. Curtis lbw b Jones	47	M. J. Weston not out	3
G. J. Lord b Jones	6		
G. A. Hick c Burns b Palmer	25	L-b 3, w 2, n-b 2	7
D. B. D'Oliveira c Foster b Jones	9		
*P. A. Neale c Harman b Palmer	5	1/10 2/73 3/93 (5 wkts, 25.3 overs) 115	
†S. J. Rhodes not out	13	4/93 5/112	

P. J. Newport, R. K. Illingworth, N. V. Radford and A. P. Pridgeon did not bat.

Bowling: Jones 6–0–20–3; Foster 4–0–21–0; Harman 4.3–0–27–0; Marks 8–0–28–0; Palmer 3–0–16–2.

Umpires: D. O. Oslear and N. T. Plews.

At Eastbourne, August 2. WORCESTERSHIRE beat SUSSEX by seven wickets.

At Swansea, August 16. WORCESTERSHIRE beat GLAMORGAN by 30 runs.

WORCESTERSHIRE v YORKSHIRE

At Worcester, August 23. Worcestershire won by 72 runs in a match reduced to 23 overs a side, following heavy morning rain. Toss: Yorkshire.

Worcestershire

T. S. Curtis c Fletcher b Sidebottom	68	*P. A. Neale not out	6
I. T. Botham c Metcalfe b P. J. Hartley	56	P. J. Newport not out	5
G. A. Hick c Carrick b Sidebottom	6	B 1, l-b 12, w 2, n-b 2	17
D. B. D'Oliveira b Fletcher	3		
†S. J. Rhodes b Sidebottom	0	1/119 2/139 3/147 (6 wkts, 23 overs) 162	
N. V. Radford c Love b Sidebottom	1	4/147 5/148 6/149	

S. R. Lampitt, R. K. Illingworth and A. P. Pridgeon did not bat.

Bowling: Jarvis 5–0–24–0; Sidebottom 4–0–22–4; P. J. Hartley 5–0–33–1; Fletcher 5–0–37–1; Carrick 2–0–15–0; S. N. Hartley 2–0–18–0.

Yorkshire

M. D. Moxon c Rhodes b Radford	3	P. J. Hartley b Illingworth	1
A. A. Metcalfe c Rhodes b Radford	10	P. W. Jarvis b Hick	0
J. D. Love b Newport	4	S. D. Fletcher not out	0
†D. L. Bairstow run out	11		
P. E. Robinson b Lampitt	1	L-b 2, w 1, n-b 2	5
S. N. Hartley run out	22		
*P. Carrick c Newport b Illingworth	19	1/5 2/16 3/25 4/28 (19.4 overs) 90	
A. Sidebottom c and b Hick	14	5/35 6/65 7/82 8/90 9/90	

Bowling: Radford 3–0–13–2; Pridgeon 3–0–12–0; Newport 3–0–13–1; Lampitt 4–1–17–1; Illingworth 4–0–23–2; Hick 2.4–0–10–2.

Umpires: J. H. Harris and P. B. Wight.

WORCESTERSHIRE v SURREY

At Hereford, August 30. Worcestershire won by nine wickets. Toss: Surrey.

Surrey

†C. J. Richards c Neale b Botham	49
K. T. Medlycott c Rhodes b Weston ...	10
A. J. Stewart c Botham b Weston	9
T. E. Jesty b Pridgeon	2
M. A. Lynch lbw b Radford	5
D. M. Ward c Hick b Radford	8
*I. A. Greig c Weston b Hick	8
M. A. Feltham b Botham	1

C. K. Bullen b Botham	14
A. H. Gray b Radford	24
M. P. Bicknell not out	2
B 1, l-b 14, w 6, n-b 1	22
1/30 2/44 3/52 4/66 (40 overs) 154	
5/91 6/95 7/105 8/107 9/152	

Bowling: Pridgeon 8-0-27-1; Weston 8-0-24-2; Hick 8-0-33-1; Radford 8-0-31-3; Botham 8-1-24-3.

Worcestershire

T. S. Curtis not out	47
I. T. Botham c Bicknell b Medlycott ...	80
G. A. Hick not out	19
L-b 8, w 2, n-b 3	13

1/130   (1 wkt, 27.4 overs) 159

D. B. D'Oliveira, *P. A. Neale, †S. J. Rhodes, S. R. Lampitt, M. J. Weston, P. J. Newport, N. V. Radford and A. P. Pridgeon did not bat.

Bowling: Bicknell 2-0-16-0; Feltham 5-0-27-0; Gray 6-1-18-0; Bullen 8-0-37-0; Greig 2-0-7-0; Medlycott 4-0-39-1; Lynch 0.4-0-7-0.

Umpires: J. W. Holder and K. E. Palmer.

WORCESTERSHIRE v NORTHAMPTONSHIRE

At Worcester, September 13. Worcestershire won by nine wickets to become the Refuge Assurance League champions. Toss: Worcestershire. Curtis and Botham shared in their fourth consecutive century opening partnership in Sunday League matches.

Northamptonshire

R. J. Bailey c Rhodes b Newport	6
W. Larkins c Curtis b Pridgeon	3
A. J. Lamb b Pridgeon	17
D. J. Capel run out	0
R. A. Harper c Rhodes b Radford	55
R. G. Williams c D'Oliveira b Hick ...	53
D. J. Wild run out	1
*G. Cook b Botham	9

†D. Ripley run out	8
N. G. B. Cook c Rhodes b Botham ...	1
M. A. Robinson not out	0
L-b 6, w 9	15
1/7 2/11 3/24 4/28 (39.4 overs) 168	
5/113 6/130 7/154 8/164 9/168	

Bowling: Pridgeon 8-1-14-2; Newport 8-0-24-1; Weston 2-0-15-0; Radford 6-0-33-1; Hick 8-0-42-1; Botham 7.4-0-34-2

Worcestershire

T. S. Curtis not out	69
I. T. Botham b N. G. B. Cook	61
G. A. Hick not out	36
L-b 6	6

1/108   (1 wkt, 38 overs) 172

D. B. D'Oliveira, *P. A. Neale, M. J. Weston, †S. J. Rhodes, S. R. Lampitt, P. J. Newport, N. V. Radford and A. P. Pridgeon did not bat.

Bowling: Capel 7-1-17-0; Robinson 7-0-40-0; Wild 8-0-27-0; Harper 8-0-46-0; N. G. B. Cook 8-0-36-1.

Umpires: D. J. Constant and J. H. Harris.

YORKSHIRE

At Birmingham, May 3. YORKSHIRE beat WARWICKSHIRE by 51 runs.

YORKSHIRE v NORTHAMPTONSHIRE

At Leeds, May 10. Yorkshire won by six wickets. Toss: Yorkshire.

Northamptonshire

W. Larkins lbw b Fletcher	8	*G. Cook not out	11
R. J. Bailey c Sidebottom b S. N. Hartley	29		
A. J. Lamb c Moxon b Fletcher	61	L-b 12, w 2, n-b 4	18
D. J. Capel c Robinson b S. N. Hartley	27		
R. A. Harper c Bairstow b P. J. Hartley	17	1/23 2/55 3/89 (5 wkts, 40 overs) 192	
D. J. Wild not out	21	4/139 5/179	

†D. Ripley, N. G. B. Cook, A. Walker and S. J. Brown did not bat.

Bowling: Sidebottom 8-1-21-0; Fletcher 8-1-50-2; P. J. Hartley 7-0-27-1; Carrick 4-0-17-0; S. N. Hartley 8-0-43-2; Moxon 5-1-22-0.

Yorkshire

M. D. Moxon c and b Walker	64	S. N. Hartley not out	29
A. A. Metcalfe c G. Cook b Walker	2	B 4, l-b 9, w 2, n-b 1	16
K. Sharp b Brown	27		
†D. L. Bairstow c Larkins b Capel	19	1/12 2/77 3/117 (4 wkts, 37.2 overs) 194	
P. E. Robinson not out	37	4/152	

R. J. Blakey, *P. Carrick, A. Sidebottom, P. J. Hartley and S. D. Fletcher did not bat.

Bowling: Capel 8-0-28-1; Walker 6.2-1-13-2; Brown 8-1-35-1; Wild 7-0-48-0; Harper 5-0-38-0; N. G. B. Cook 3-0-19-0.

Umpires: J. W. Holder and D. O. Oslear.

At Cardiff, May 24. YORKSHIRE lost to GLAMORGAN by 23 runs.

YORKSHIRE v KENT

At Middlesbrough, May 31. Yorkshire won by nine wickets. Toss: Yorkshire.

Kent

M. R. Benson c Sharp b P. J. Hartley	9	C. Penn c Bairstow b P. J. Hartley	0
S. G. Hinks c and b Sidebottom	2	D. J. M. Kelleher lbw b Jarvis	0
C. J. Tavaré b Jarvis	1	R. P. Davis not out	3
D. G. Aslett b Jarvis	44	B 1, l-b 12, w 7, n-b 3	23
*C. S. Cowdrey c Bairstow b Fletcher	42		
G. R. Cowdrey run out	6	1/6 2/10 3/32 (39.3 overs) 175	
E. A. E. Baptiste lbw b Jarvis	20	4/116 5/125 6/135	
†S. A. Marsh b Fletcher	25	7/148 8/149 9/150	

Bowling: Sidebottom 8-0-32-1; Jarvis 8-1-19-4; Fletcher 7.3-0-33-2; P. J. Hartley 8-0-36-2; S. N. Hartley 6-0-28-0; Carrick 2-0-14-0.

Yorkshire

K. Sharp not out		70
A. A. Metcalfe c Benson b Hinks		74
J. D. Love not out		23
L-b 2, w 8		10

1/109   (1 wkt, 35 overs) 177

P. E. Robinson, S. N. Hartley, †D. L. Bairstow, *P. Carrick, A. Sidebottom, P. J. Hartley, P. W. Jarvis and S. D. Fletcher did not bat.

Bowling: Penn 6–0–17–0; Baptiste 7–0–32–0; Kelleher 8–1–31–0; C. S. Cowdrey 4–0–30–0; Davis 4–0–29–0; Hinks 4–0–27–1; G. R. Cowdrey 2–1–9–0.

Umpires: B. Leadbeater and N. T. Plews.

YORKSHIRE v DERBYSHIRE

At Sheffield, June 7. Derbyshire won by 19 runs in a match restricted by rain to nineteen overs a side. Toss: Yorkshire.

Derbyshire

*K. J. Barnett st Bairstow b Carrick	25	P. G. Newman not out		25
†B. J. M. Maher b S. N. Hartley	40			
B. Roberts not out	37	B 2, l-b 1, w 1		4
J. E. Morris run out	0			
M. A. Holding b Carrick	9	1/64 2/75 3/75	(5 wkts, 19 overs)	154
A. E. Warner c Sharp b Carrick	14	4/98 5/114		

I. S. Anderson, C. F. B. P. Rudd, M. Jean-Jacques and O. H. Mortensen did not bat.

Bowling: P. J. Hartley 4–0–26–0; Fletcher 4–0–35–0; Carrick 4–0–20–3; S. N. Hartley 1–0–9–1; Jarvis 4–0–40–0; Sidebottom 2–0–21–0.

Yorkshire

K. Sharp not out	57	S. N. Hartley not out		8
A. A. Metcalfe b Newman	17	L-b 3, w 1		4
J. D. Love c and b Mortensen	6			
†D. L. Bairstow c Roberts b Warner	25	1/24 2/39 3/82	(4 wkts, 19 overs)	135
P. E. Robinson c Roberts b Holding	18	4/115		

P. J. Hartley, *P. Carrick, S. D. Fletcher, A. Sidebottom and P. W. Jarvis did not bat.

Bowling: Rudd 3–0–15–0; Newman 4–0–30–1; Mortensen 4–0–29–1; Holding 4–0–26–1; Warner 4–0–32–1.

Umpires: M. J. Kitchen and R. A. White.

YORKSHIRE v SURREY

At Leeds, June 21. Yorkshire won by 51 runs. Toss: Surrey. Love, whose second fifty came off 21 balls, hit five fours and seven sixes – two on to the roof of the football stand.

Yorkshire

K. Sharp b Bullen	40	S. N. Hartley not out		3
A. A. Metcalfe c Greig b Bullen	10	L-b 22, w 7		29
J. D. Love not out	118			
†D. L. Bairstow c Clinton b Greig	24	1/39 2/81 3/134	(4 wkts, 40 overs)	245
P. E. Robinson c Stewart b Greig	21	4/212		

*P. Carrick, A. Sidebottom, P. J. Hartley, P. W. Jarvis and S. D. Fletcher did not bat.

Bowling: Thomas 8–0–64–0; Bicknell 8–0–35–0; Bullen 8–0–38–2; Greig 8–0–52–2; Clarke 8–0–34–0.

Surrey

G. S. Clinton lbw b Jarvis	7	C. K. Bullen b Fletcher	17
A. J. Stewart c Robinson b Jarvis	9	S. T. Clarke run out	15
†C. J. Richards b Fletcher	11	M. P. Bicknell not out	1
M. A. Lynch lbw b Sidebottom	2	L-b 11	11
T. E. Jesty b Carrick	48		
D. M. Ward b Jarvis	40	1/18 2/23 3/26	(39.5 overs) 194
*I. A. Greig lbw b Jarvis	9	4/42 5/118 6/132	
D. J. Thomas c P. J. Hartley b Fletcher	24	7/136 8/164 9/183	

Bowling: Sidebottom 8–1–25–1; Jarvis 8–0–19–4; Fletcher 8–1–29–3; Carrick 8–0–56–1; P. J. Hartley 7.5–0–54–0.

Umpires: J. A. Jameson and P. B. Wight.

At Nottingham, July 5. YORKSHIRE lost to NOTTINGHAMSHIRE by 85 runs.

YORKSHIRE v MIDDLESEX

At Scarborough, July 12. Yorkshire won by 33 runs. Toss: Middlesex.

Yorkshire

K. Sharp b Williams	16	P. J. Hartley not out	9
A. A. Metcalfe c Brown b Emburey	51	P. W. Jarvis not out	1
J. D. Love c Carr b Emburey	14		
†D. L. Bairstow c Gatting b Emburey	54	B 7, l-b 9, w 1, n-b 5	22
P. E. Robinson c Needham b Gatting	28		
S. N. Hartley c Emburey b Hughes	8	1/56 2/77 3/92	(8 wkts, 40 overs) 219
*P. Carrick c Brown b Emburey	15	4/156 5/192 6/194	
A. Sidebottom b Hughes	1	7/209 8/217	

S. D. Fletcher did not bat.

Bowling: Fraser 7–2–42–0; Williams 8–1–26–1; Hughes 8–1–41–2; Emburey 8–0–35–4; Gatting 7–0–36–1; Needham 2–0–23–0.

Middlesex

J. D. Carr run out	2	A. Needham b Carrick	19
W. N. Slack c Jarvis b Sidebottom	25	N. F. Williams b Jarvis	31
*M. W. Gatting c Fletcher b P. J. Hartley	73	S. P. Hughes c Jarvis b Carrick	0
K. R. Brown b Carrick	0	A. R. C. Fraser not out	6
†P. R. Downton c Bairstow b Fletcher	1	B 2, l-b 10, w 1, n-b 2	15
N. R. C. MacLaurin c Bairstow b Fletcher	2	1/3 2/56 3/64 4/65 5/71	(39 overs) 186
J. E. Emburey b P. J. Hartley	12	6/113 7/136 8/162 9/162	

Bowling: Jarvis 8–1–29–1; Sidebottom 8–1–31–1; P. J. Hartley 8–0–26–2; Fletcher 7–1–22–2; Carrick 8–0–66–3.

Umpires: B. Leadbeater and D. Lloyd.

At Bristol, July 19. YORKSHIRE lost to GLOUCESTERSHIRE by four wickets.

At Leicester, July 26. LEICESTERSHIRE v YORKSHIRE. No result.

YORKSHIRE v LANCASHIRE

At Scarborough, August 2. Lancashire won by four wickets. Toss: Lancashire. Lancashire's and Yorkshire's totals were their highest in the Sunday League "Roses" matches.

Yorkshire

M. D. Moxon st Hegg b Simmons	 36	*P. Carrick c Fowler b Watkinson	 4
A. A. Metcalfe c O'Shaughnessy b Simmons . 51		P. J. Hartley not out	6
J. D. Love b Simmons	7	L-b 8, w 3	11
†D. L. Bairstow c Hegg b O'Shaughnessy	5		
P. E. Robinson run out	41	1/73 2/93 3/102 (6 wkts, 40 overs) 244	
S. N. Hartley not out	83	4/112 5/193 6/207	

A. Sidebottom, P. W. Jarvis and S. D. Fletcher did not bat.

Bowling: McLeod 5-0-20-0; Watkinson 7-0-66-1; Simmons 8-0-26-3; Allott 8-0-43-0; O'Shaughnessy 8-0-51-1; Hayhurst 4-0-30-0.

Lancashire

G. D. Mendis c Bairstow b P. J. Hartley	26	A. N. Hayhurst not out	26
G. Fowler run out	33	P. J. W. Allott not out	16
N. H. Fairbrother b Jarvis	56	B 1, l-b 11	12
M. Watkinson c Sidebottom b Fletcher . 38			
*D. P. Hughes c Love b Carrick	8	1/63 2/64 3/139 (6 wkts, 39.4 overs) 248	
S. J. O'Shaughnessy c Carrick b Jarvis	33	4/155 5/185 6/224	

J. Simmons, K. W. McLeod and †W. K. Hegg did not bat.

Bowling: Jarvis 8-0-49-2; Sidebottom 8-0-51-0; Fletcher 7.4-1-34-1; P. J. Hartley 8-0-54-1; Carrick 6-0-37-1; S. N. Hartley 2-0-11-0.

Umpires: K. J. Lyons and B. J. Meyer.

YORKSHIRE v SUSSEX

At Hull, August 9. No result.

At Taunton, August 16. YORKSHIRE lost to SOMERSET by five wickets.

At Worcester, August 23. YORKSHIRE lost to WORCESTERSHIRE by 72 runs.

At Colchester, August 30. YORKSHIRE lost to ESSEX by six wickets.

YORKSHIRE v HAMPSHIRE

At Leeds, September 6. No result.

SUNDAY LEAGUE RECORDS

Batting

Highest score: 176 – G. A. Gooch, Essex v Glamorgan (Southend), 1983.

Most hundreds: 11 – C. G. Greenidge; 9 – K. S. McEwan and B. A. Richards. 295 hundreds have been scored in the League.

Most runs: D. L. Amiss 7,040; C. T. Radley 6,650; C. G. Greenidge 6,348; C. E. B. Rice 6,265; G. M. Turner 6,144; Younis Ahmed 5,897; D. R. Turner 5,856; P. Willey 5,807.

Most runs in a season: 814 – C. E. B. Rice (Nottinghamshire), 1977.

Most sixes in an innings: 13 – I. T. Botham, Somerset v Northamptonshire (Wellingborough School), 1986.

Most sixes by a team in an innings: 18 – Derbyshire v Worcestershire (Knypersley), 1985.

Most sixes in a season: 26 – I. V. A. Richards (Somerset), 1977.

Highest total: 310 for five – Essex v Glamorgan (Southend), 1983.

Highest total – batting second: 301 for six – Warwickshire v Essex (Colchester), 1982.

Highest match aggregate: 604 – Surrey (304) v Warwickshire (300 for nine) (The Oval), 1985.

Lowest total: 23 – Middlesex v Yorkshire (Leeds), 1974.

Shortest completed innings: 16 overs – Northamptonshire 59 v Middlesex (Tring), 1974.

Shortest match: 2 hr 13 min (40.3 overs) – Essex v Northamptonshire (Ilford), 1971.

Biggest victories: 190 runs, Kent beat Northamptonshire (Brackley), 1973.
    There have been nineteen instances of victory by ten wickets – by Derbyshire, Essex (twice), Hampshire, Leicestershire (twice), Middlesex (twice), Northamptonshire, Nottinghamshire, Somerset (twice), Surrey (twice), Warwickshire, Worcestershire and Yorkshire (three times). This does not include those matches in which the side batting second was set a reduced target.

Ties (25): Nottinghamshire v Kent (Nottingham), 1969, in a match reduced to twenty overs.
  Gloucestershire v Hampshire (Bristol), 1972; Gloucestershire v Northamptonshire (Bristol), 1972.
  Surrey v Worcestershire (Byfleet), 1973.
  Middlesex v Lancashire (Lord's), 1974; Sussex v Leicestershire (Hove), 1974.
  Lancashire v Worcestershire (Manchester), 1975; Somerset v Glamorgan (Taunton), 1975.
  Warwickshire v Kent (Birmingham), 1980.
  Kent v Lancashire (Maidstone), 1981.
  Yorkshire v Nottinghamshire (Hull), 1982; Hampshire v Lancashire (Southampton), 1982; Surrey v Hampshire (The Oval), 1982.
  Worcestershire v Nottinghamshire (Hereford), 1983; Lancashire v Worcestershire (Manchester), 1983, in a match reduced to nineteen overs; Warwickshire v Worcestershire (Birmingham), 1983, Warwickshire's innings having been reduced to ten overs.
  Middlesex v Essex (Lord's), 1984.
  Essex v Leicestershire (Chelmsford), 1985; Northamptonshire v Lancashire (Northampton), 1985; Lancashire v Glamorgan (Manchester), 1985.
  Kent v Surrey (Canterbury), 1986; Middlesex v Warwickshire (Lord's), 1986; Yorkshire v Warwickshire (Leeds), 1986.
  Hampshire v Gloucestershire (Southampton), 1987; Hampshire v Derbyshire (Southampton), 1987.

Record partnerships for each wicket

239 for 1st	G. A. Gooch and B. R. Hardie, Essex v Nottinghamshire at Nottingham	1985
273 for 2nd	G. A. Gooch and K. S. McEwan, Essex v Nottinghamshire at Nottingham	1983

215 for 3rd	W. Larkins and R. G. Williams, Northamptonshire v Worcestershire at Luton	1982
219 for 4th	C. G. Greenidge and C. L. Smith, Hampshire v Surrey at Southampton	1987
185 for 5th	B. M. McMillan and Asif Din, Warwickshire v Essex at Chelmsford .	1986
121 for 6th	C. P. Wilkins and A. J. Borrington, Derbyshire v Warwickshire at Chesterfield	1972
130 for 7th	D. P. Hughes and A. N. Hayhurst, Lancashire v Kent at Manchester	1987
95* for 8th	D. Breakwell and K. F. Jennings, Somerset v Nottinghamshire at Nottingham	1976
105 for 9th	D. G. Moir and R. W. Taylor, Derbyshire v Kent at Derby	1984
57 for 10th	D. A. Graveney and J. B. Mortimore, Gloucestershire v Lancashire at Tewkesbury	1973

Bowling

Best analyses: eight for 26, K. D. Boyce, Essex v Lancashire (Manchester), 1971; seven for 15, R. A. Hutton, Yorkshire v Worcestershire (Leeds), 1969; seven for 39, A. Hodgson, Northamptonshire v Somerset (Northampton), 1976; seven for 41, A. N. Jones, Sussex v Nottinghamshire (Nottingham), 1986; six for 6, R. W. Hooker, Middlesex v Surrey (Lord's), 1969; six for 7, M. Hendrick, Derbyshire v Nottinghamshire (Nottingham), 1972.

Four wickets in four balls: A. Ward, Derbyshire v Sussex (Derby), 1970.

Hat-tricks (18): A. Ward, Derbyshire v Sussex (Derby), 1970; R. Palmer, Somerset v Gloucestershire (Bristol), 1970; K. D. Boyce, Essex v Somerset (Westcliff), 1971; G. D. McKenzie, Leicestershire v Essex (Leicester), 1972; R. G. D. Willis, Warwickshire v Yorkshire (Birmingham), 1973; W. Blenkiron, Warwickshire v Derbyshire (Buxton), 1974; A. Buss, Sussex v Worcestershire (Hastings), 1974; J. M. Rice, Hampshire v Northamptonshire (Southampton), 1975; M. A. Nash, Glamorgan v Worcestershire (Worcester), 1975; A. Hodgson, Northamptonshire v Somerset (Northampton), 1976; A. E. Cordle, Glamorgan v Hampshire (Portsmouth), 1979; C. J. Tunnicliffe, Derbyshire v Worcestershire (Derby), 1979; M. D. Marshall, Hampshire v Surrey (Southampton), 1981; I. V. A. Richards, Somerset v Essex (Chelmsford), 1982; P. W. Jarvis, Yorkshire v Derbyshire (Derby), 1982; R. M. Ellison, Kent v Hampshire (Canterbury), 1983; G. C. Holmes, Glamorgan v Nottinghamshire (Ebbw Vale), 1987; K. Saxelby, Nottinghamshire v Worcestershire (Nottingham), 1987.

Most economical analysis: 8–8–0–0, B. A. Langford, Somerset v Essex (Yeovil), 1969.

Most expensive analyses: 8–0–88–1, E. E. Hemmings, Nottinghamshire v Somerset (Nottingham), 1983; 7.5–0–89–3, G. Miller, Derbyshire v Gloucestershire (Gloucester), 1984.

Most wickets in a season: 34 – R. J. Clapp (Somerset), 1974 and C. E. B. Rice (Nottinghamshire), 1986.

Most wickets: J. K. Lever 357; D. L. Underwood 346; S. Turner 303; N. Gifford 275; J. Simmons 275; J. N. Shepherd 267; T. E. Jesty 248; R. D. Jackman 234.

Wicket-keeping and Fielding

Most dismissals: R. W. Taylor 236 (187 ct, 49 st); D. L. Bairstow 232 (212 ct, 20 st); E. W. Jones 223 (184 ct, 39 st).

Most dismissals in a season: 28 (22 ct, 6 st) – J. T. Murray (Middlesex), 1975.

Most dismissals in an innings: 7 (6 ct, 1 st) – R. W. Taylor, Derbyshire v Lancashire (Manchester), 1975.

Most catches in an innings: 6 – K. Goodwin, Lancashire v Worcestershire (Worcester), 1969, and R. W. Taylor, Derbyshire v Lancashire (Manchester), 1975.

Most stumpings in an innings: 4 – S. J. Rhodes, Worcestershire v Warwickshire (Birmingham), 1986.

Most catches by a fielder: (not a wicket-keeper): J. F. Steele 101; C. T. Radley 90; G. Cook 87.

Most catches in a season: 16 – J. M. Rice (Hampshire), 1978.

Most catches in an innings: 5 – J. M. Rice, Hampshire v Warwickshire (Southampton), 1978.

CHAMPIONS: 1969-87

1969	Lancashire	1979	Somerset
1970	Lancashire	1980	Warwickshire
1971	Worcestershire	1981	Essex
1972	Kent	1982	Sussex
1973	Kent	1983	Yorkshire
1974	Leicestershire	1984	Essex
1975	Hampshire	1985	Essex
1976	Kent	1986	Hampshire
1977	Leicestershire	1987	Worcestershire
1978	Hampshire		

I ZINGARI RESULTS, 1987

Matches – 26: Won 7, Lost 3, Drawn 9, Abandoned 7.

May 2	Charterhouse	Lost by seven wickets
May 9	Eton College	Lost by 71 runs
May 9	Honourable Artillery Company	Won by four wickets
May 10	Sandhurst Wanderers	Won by 110 runs
May 17	Staff College	Won by six wickets
May 23	Eton Ramblers	Abandoned
June 6	Hurlingham CC	Won by three wickets
June 7	Lord Porchester's XI	Abandoned
June 16	Winchester College	Drawn
June 20	Guards CC	Drawn
June 27	Harrow School	Lost by 65 runs
June 28	Lavinia, Duchess of Norfolk's XI	Drawn
July 5	Hagley CC	Won by six wickets
July 11	Green Jackets Club	Drawn
July 12	Rickling Green CC	Drawn
July 18	Bradfield Waifs	Won by five wickets
July 18	Leicester Gentlemen	Drawn
July 19	Sir John Starkey's XI	Abandoned
July 25	Australian Crusaders CC	Drawn
July 26	Royal Armoured Corps	Won by 79 runs
August 1	Band of Brothers	Drawn
August 2	R. Leigh-Pemberton's XI	Abandoned
August 15, 16	South Wales Hunts XI	Drawn
August 26	Hampshire Hogs	Abandoned
September 5	J. H. Pawle's XI	Abandoned
September 6	Captain R. H. Hawkins' XI	Abandoned

MINOR COUNTIES CHAMPIONSHIP, 1987

By MICHAEL BERRY and ROBERT BROOKE

Minor Counties cricket glowed with health in 1987. A buoyant year saw a welcome win for the representative side over Glamorgan in the Benson and Hedges Cup in May, a famous victory in the NatWest Bank Trophy by Buckinghamshire over Somerset in June, and a thrilling conclusion to the Championship in September. Buckinghamshire emerged as the team of the season. For not only did they topple Somerset to become the fifth minor county to beat first-class opposition in the 60-overs competition, they also went on to win the Minor Counties Championship for the ninth time, so equalling Durham's record. However, a thought should be spared for Cambridgeshire, who went so close to glory themselves. Instead, they had to suffer the heartbreak of a fate that ran parallel with that of their first-class neighbours, Northamptonshire, reaching both of the season's finals but finishing runners-up each time.

Buckinghamshire's triumph was founded on a firm team fabric. There were no real stars, just a successful band of talented club cricketers blended together by their new captain, Neil Hames. In that respect, their title win was considerably more satisfying and more rewarding than had they been one of the counties employing former first-class professionals. The tonic of the NatWest Bank Trophy win was soon evident. They won four of their nine Championship games to finish above Berkshire at the head of the Western Division table. The runs of Malcolm Roberts, a Metropolitan Police officer, in his first season, and the 35 wickets of the veteran off-spinner, Andy Lyon, spearheaded their challenge. Roberts aggregated 475 runs in Western Division games, but his most vital innings came in the play-off with Cambridgeshire when he compiled a fine unbeaten 132.

Another Metropolitan policeman, Mark Stear, emerged as **Berkshire's** discovery of the season, taking 21 wickets at 21.09 apiece. His support of Jefferson Jones (31 wickets) and the arrival of another newcomer, Tim Dodd, provided a new cutting-edge to their attack, which Graham Roope backed up with 21 catches. Leading the way with the bat was Martin Lickley, whose aggregate of 594 runs was his best for the county.

Cheshire claimed their third trophy in five years when they lifted the knockout competition's Holt Cup in July. But their Championship hopes were set back by the weather, with six of their scheduled eight days of home Championship cricket being washed out without a ball bowled. Newcomers Geoff Blackburn, a slow left-armer, and Mark Boocock, a leg-spinner, joined forces with John O'Brien to give the county a strong spin triumvirate which shared 73 wickets, O'Brien taking 31 of them with his slow left-arm spin. Ian Tansley, their pocket-sized opener, returned from Derbyshire to make 519 runs, while Neil O'Brien, the new captain, and Ian Cockbain were again in good form.

John Inchmore, the former Worcestershire seam bowler, was recruited to bolster **Wiltshire**, and with twenty wickets and an ability to contribute runs in the lower order, he proved a useful acquisition. David Simpkins, an off-spinner, did much of the bowling and was rewarded with 34 wickets. Rob Savage, a former Hampshire Second XI player, scored the most runs, and Jeff Cullip, the wicket-keeper, also had a good year with the bat.

Devon were the only side to beat Buckinghamshire in the Championship, doing so in a last-over finish at Exmouth. Their failure to produce any young bowlers remains a problem, and again it was those veteran warriors, Doug Yeabsley, 45, and Paddy Considine, 47, who were the leading wicket-takers. The batting, however, continued to show some encouraging development, Nick Folland totalling 461 runs and Nick Gaywood not far behind with 449.

Leading run-scorer in the Championship was Richard Baigent of **Somerset II**, whose 713 at an average of 89.12 ensured that Somerset bowed out of the competition on an individual high note. In addition, Robert Woolston, a slow left-armer, claimed 32 wickets, the fifth-highest return in the Championship. In 1988, Somerset II are to be replaced by a Wales Minor Counties XI and so ends the competition's link with the first-class counties.

Shropshire were unable to improve on two wins from their first four matches, even though Steve Johnson made 643 runs and Mark Davies passed 500 runs for the first time. Joe Smith, acknowledged as one of their leading bowlers, enjoyed a memorable batting milestone against Cheshire at the start of August when he hit his maiden hundred for the county, nearly twenty years after making his Minor Counties début. Batting at No. 8, the 41-year-old Jamaican-born left-hander scored 101 off 113 balls as Shropshire, in disarray at 25 for six, recovered to 189 all out.

Oxfordshire struggled to live up to the mantle of being the 1986 Western Division winners, and with unavailability a key problem, they won only one Championship match. Mike Nurton's run-scoring showed no sign of waning – he made 597 at 59.70 – while Keith Arnold collected 29 wickets, forming with Roger Busby an opening partnership that was never an easy proposition for opposition batsmen.

Dorset and **Cornwall** joined Oxfordshire in failing to qualify for the 1988 NatWest Bank Trophy from the Western Division. Neither managed a win, although Cornwall will wonder for a long time how they failed to secure their first Championship victory in two decades. With nine balls left, they required just 3 runs to beat Buckinghamshire at Wadebridge and had four wickets in hand. Instead, a sequence of disasters ended with them losing all four wickets in seven balls to lose by 1 run. David Toseland's guile again produced most wickets, although he played in only five matches, but their crop of newcomers badly missed the experience of such men as Malcolm Dunstan and Trevor Angove. For Dorset, openers Graeme Calway (524 runs) and Richard Merriman (460 runs) scored freely, and Neil Taylor did well with the new ball in his first season. Chris Stone had an eventful season; against Wiltshire at Swindon he took an unusual first-ever "hat-trick" which spanned two days and two innings, having a couple of weeks earlier suffered the ignominy of seeing Shropshire's No. 11, Andy Barnard, hit his last ball for six to clinch a win at Wellington.

In the Eastern Division **Cambridgeshire's** campaign, their best for some two decades, owed much to Stuart Turner, the former Essex stalwart, who was recruited as their third professional alongside Michael Garnham and Chris Lethbridge. Turner had a marvellous summer, his 39 wickets including a historic day on June 7 when he became only the 22nd player in Minor Counties cricket to take ten wickets in an innings. On a wicket that was the source of much criticism – even from Turner himself – he returned the remarkable figures of 13.3–10–11–10, the best analysis recorded in the 93 years of the Minor Counties game, as Cumberland were bowled out for 47 in their second innings and Cambridgeshire won inside a day. It was one of five Championship wins which took them into the play-off, where they were beaten by Buckinghamshire, having experienced a similar disappointment at the hands of Cheshire in the Holt Trophy final at Oxford in July. Ian Lawrence was also a prime contributor to the Cambridgeshire season with 423 runs.

The sympathy felt for Cambridgeshire might also be extended to **Staffordshire**, who finished as Eastern Division runners-up for the fourth successive season. On this latest occasion, when they finished level at the top of the table with 59 points, their position was determined by the fact that their net batting average was inferior to that of Cambridgeshire. Phil Oliver, formerly of Warwickshire, added extra strength to their already powerful batting line-up and Joey Benjamin and Andy Webster bowled at times with real penetration. Once again, however, their leading wicket-taker was the 44-year-old slow left-armer, Russell Flower.

Durham unearthed a bright new talent in Paul Burn, a flame-haired batsman with great potential, but 46-year-old Peter Kippax kept the banner of experience aloft by capturing 24 wickets with his leg-breaks. John Lister made 572 runs, but Durham's late burst, reminiscent of the run that brought them the title in 1984, was frustrated by rain in their final fixture.

Cumberland played some enterprising and bold cricket, winning four and losing four of their nine matches. Three players, Bernard Reidy, Steven Sharp (546 runs) and Chris Stockdale all made notable centuries, Reidy's 144 not out off only 102 balls against Hertfordshire being a record score for the county. Sharp (119 not out) and Stockdale (103) shared a match-winning opening stand of 210 against Northumberland at Jesmond. David Halliwell picked up 28 wickets and enjoyed good support from Graham Monkhouse, who rejoined his native county after six years with Surrey.

Five defeats – the first four in their opening five matches – showed **Hertfordshire**, champions in 1983 and knockout winners in 1985, to be in a period of transition. Frank Collyer, who had been an inspirational captain, his right-hand man, Alan Garofall, David Ottley and Wayne Osman all retired, leaving the new captain, Peter Neal, with an unenviable job. He was not helped by the injury that prevented seam bowler David Surridge from appearing, and Bill Merry, although showing his worth with seventeen wickets, played only five times. On the credit side, Stephen Henderson and Reuben Herbert, two newcomers to the county, were members of the Minor Counties select XI, and there seemed to be no lack of talent, especially in the batting.

Lincolnshire engaged the former Northamptonshire opening bowler, Jim Griffiths, and his 36 wickets gave maximum value. With Mark Fell scoring 643 runs, the highest aggregate in the Eastern Division, and Neil Priestley 581, Lincolnshire made light of the loss of Paul Todd to Glamorgan, especially with Clive Wicks hitting his best-ever Minor Counties form after being recalled. **Suffolk**, a side of few individual stars, had Mike McEvoy in fine fettle with the bat, but their bowlers struggled to make the required impact. Russ Green, whom they would have looked to as the spearhead of the attack, was troubled by injury for part of the season. Tony Warrington, a 40-year-old called up for the first time since 1982, hit the county's only century.

Mike Morgan announced his decision to retire from the Minor Counties game after another season of under-achievement from **Bedfordshire**. The retirement of Keith Jones, save for one appearance late in the season, and the failure to tempt Les McFarlane to play again meant that their bowling was below par. Roger Knight, the former Surrey captain, did a good all-round job as their new professional and Northamptonshire's Alan Fordham again impressed. A solitary win over local rivals Hertfordshire was their one consolation.

At the foot of the Eastern Division, and without a win between them, were **Northumberland** and **Norfolk**. For Northumberland, Richard Dreyer showed plenty of spirit with the bat but their bowling was always weak. Chris Old had a disappointing time and was released during the winter. Norfolk, whose player problems could justifiably be described as chronic, suffered five defeats in their nine matches, a dismal record that equalled their unhappy performance in 1986. Steve Plumb, their new captain, and also captain of the representative side, finished with 508 runs but there were few other performances to enjoy.

MINOR COUNTIES CHAMPIONSHIP, 1987

Eastern Division

	Played	Won	Lost	Drawn Won 1st Inns	Lost 1st Inns	No Result	Points
Cambridgeshire^{NW}	9	5	0	2	1	1	59
Staffordshire^{NW}	9	5	0	2	1	1	59
Durham^{NW}	9	4	1*	3	0	1	54
Cumberland^{NW}	9	4	4	1	0	0	43
Hertfordshire^{NW}	9	2	5†	1	0	1	34
Lincolnshire^{NW}	9	2	3*	2	2	0	31
Suffolk^{NW}	9	2	3*	0	4	0	27
Bedfordshire	9	1	2	2	4	0	20
Northumberland	9	0	2*	1	4	2	14
Norfolk	9	0	5	2	0	2	10

Western Division

	Played	Won	Lost	Drawn Won 1st Inns	Lost 1st Inns	No Result	Points
Buckinghamshire^{NW}	9	4	1*	2	2	0	51
Berkshire^{NW}	9	3	0	4	2	0	44
Cheshire^{NW}	9	2	1*	2	1	3	36
Wiltshire^{NW}	9	2	1	2	3	1	31
Devon^{NW}	9	2	0	1	5	1	30
Somerset II	9	1	0	5	1	2	30
Shropshire^{NW}	9	2	3	1	3	0	26
Oxfordshire	9	1	3	2	3	0	19
Dorset	9	0	4*	4	1	0	16
Cornwall	9	0	4*	1	3	1	11

* Denotes first-innings points (3) in one match lost outright.
† Denotes first-innings points (3) in three matches lost outright.
^{NW} Denotes qualified for NatWest Bank Trophy in 1988.
Win = 10 pts, First-innings win = 3 pts, First-innings loss = 1 pt, No result = 2 pts.
In the Eastern Division, Cambridgeshire took precedence over Staffordshire on the basis of nett batting averages.

CHAMPIONSHIP PLAY-OFF

BUCKINGHAMSHIRE v CAMBRIDGESHIRE

At Worcester, September 10. Buckinghamshire won by virtue of losing fewer wickets with the scores level. Toss: Cambridgeshire. In a tense finish under darkening skies, Cambridgeshire's last pair could manage to score only 3 of the 4 runs needed off the last over, well bowled by Black. Such a finish had not looked remotely likely when Cambridgeshire were 43 for four with 193 runs needed off twenty overs, but a majestic 121 from Benson took them to the brink of victory. Buckinghamshire's innings was dominated by Roberts, who, dropped when 53 and 75, faced 166 balls for his unbeaten 132 and hit a six and thirteen fours.

Buckinghamshire

A. R. Harwood b Stephenson	20	G. R. Black c Turner b Lethbridge	4
M. J. Roberts not out	132	Extras	30
D. E. Smith c Garnham b Wing	12		
S. Burrow c Turner b Lethbridge	35	1/67 2/100 3/204 (5 wkts, 55 overs)	235
*N. G. Hames b Turner	2	4/220 5/235	

T. J. A. Scriven, S. J. Edwards, †C. J. Tungate, A. W. Lyon and C. D. Booden did not bat.

Bowling: Turner 11–3–34–1; Lethbridge 11–0–61–2; Collard 11–2–28–0; Wing 11–1–51–1; Stephenson 11–2–38–1.

Cambridgeshire

*N. T. Gadsby b Edwards	3	D. C. Collard not out	12
I. S. Lawrence c Tungate b Edwards	23	M. G. Stephenson b Burrow	0
†M. A. Garnham c Tungate b Edwards	9	D. C. Wing not out	5
J. D. R. Benson c Tungate b Burrow	121	Extras	22
S. Turner run out	2		
C. Lethbridge lbw b Lyon	11	1/7 2/30 3/41 (9 wkts, 55 overs)	235
A. D. Cuthill c and b Scriven	0	4/43 5/93 6/108	
C. W. A. Thornely c Smith b Burrow	27	7/178 8/216 9/216	

Bowling: Booden 11–1–35–0; Edwards 11–4–20–3; Lyon 11–1–44–1; Black 10–0–52–0; Scriven 6–0–26–1; Burrow 6–1–39–3.

Umpires: P. J. Eele and D. J. Halfyard.

HOLT CUP KNOCKOUT FINAL

CAMBRIDGESHIRE v CHESHIRE

At Christ Church College, Oxford, July 26. Cheshire won by eight wickets. Toss: Cheshire. Winning the toss gave Cheshire a match-winning advantage, enabling them to bowl first on a soft, moist wicket which particularly suited the seamers of their captain, O'Brien. Cambridgeshire were in serious straits at 86 for five after 29 overs, and Blackburn, prising out the tail, did not allow them to recover. Replying in improving conditions, Cheshire comfortably built on the solid foundation of 69 in 27 overs from Tansley and Crawley, despite the miserly bowling of Turner, who conceded only 10 runs in his eleven overs.

Cambridgeshire 131 (49.5 overs) (J. D. R. Benson 33; N. T. O'Brien four for 32, G. J. Blackburn four for 11); Cheshire 132 for two (47.4 overs) (I. J. Tansley 54, S. T. Crawley 30).

*In the averages that follow, * against a score signifies not out, * against a name signifies the captain and † signifies a wicket-keeper.*

BEDFORDSHIRE

Secretary – A. J. PEARCE, 15 Dene Way, Upper Caldecote,
Biggleswade SG18 9DL

Matches 9: Won – Hertfordshire. Lost – Cambridgeshire, Cumberland. Won on first innings –
Lincolnshire, Suffolk. Lost on first innings – Durham, Norfolk, Northumberland, Staffordshire.

Batting Averages

	M	I	NO	R	HI	100s	Avge
A. Fordham	4	7	1	343	126*	2	57.16
R. D. V. Knight	7	12	1	403	89	0	36.63
K. Gentle	8	14	1	349	108*	1	26.84
T. C. Thomas	8	13	2	242	71	0	22.00
N. A. Stanley	4	6	0	112	50	0	18.66
A. J. Moulding	5	8	0	140	33	0	17.50
P. D. B. Hoare	9	14	2	175	52	0	14.58
*M. Morgan	9	14	1	168	42	0	12.92
R. D. O. Earl	9	11	4	89	50*	0	12.71
†N. S. Randall	9	15	4	109	27*	0	9.90
K. Standring	7	7	5	12	3*	0	6.00

Played in four matches: P. A. Waterman 0, 2*, 3, 0. Played in three matches: M. R. Lester
21, 35, 0; J. R. Wake 0, 10*, 6, 33, 6. Played in two matches: S. D. L. Davis 23, 10, 9, 57;
S. J. Renshaw 0*, 0. Played in one match: A. Dean 1; D. J. Harris 16; K. V. Jones 41;
A. S. Pearson 3, 72; C. J. Proudman 1*, 3*; A. D. McCartney did not bat.

Bowling Averages

	O	M	R	W	BB	Avge
M. Morgan	80	16	298	14	6-55	21.28
P. A. Waterman	66.4	16	229	10	3-39	22.90
P. D. B. Hoare	96	19	293	10	4-40	29.30
R. D. O. Earl	150.1	49	397	13	3-13	30.53

Also bowled: S. D. L. Davis 2–0–17–1; A. Dean 5–3–12–0; K. V. Jones 13–7–14–2;
R. D. V. Knight 98–28–257–7; M. R. Lester 66–12–243–7; A. D. McCartney 11–3–32–1;
A. J. Moulding 28–7–86–3; C. J. Proudman 17.4–3–66–1; S. J. Renshaw 39.4–9–103–4;
K. Standring 122–31–340–8; N. A. Stanley 6–0–20–0; J. R. Wake 44–10–130–5.

BERKSHIRE

Secretary – C. F. V. MARTIN, Paradise Cottage, Paradise Road,
Henley-on-Thames, Oxon RG9 1UB

Matches 9: Won – Cornwall, Shropshire, Wiltshire. Won on first innings – Cheshire, Devon,
Oxfordshire, Somerset II. Lost on first innings – Buckinghamshire, Dorset.

Batting Averages

	M	I	NO	R	HI	100s	Avge
M. G. Lickley	9	17	3	594	100*	1	42.42
D. B. Gorman	8	13	5	255	53	0	31.87
K. S. Murray	4	6	0	149	95	0	24.83
T. P. J. Dodd	7	6	2	98	40*	0	24.50
*M. L. Simmons	9	15	4	261	115	1	23.72
M. G. Stear	7	8	2	139	57	0	23.16

	M	I	NO	R	HI	100s	Avge
G. R. J. Roope	9	14	1	295	62	0	22.69
G. E. Loveday	8	15	0	311	65	0	20.73
†M. E. Stevens	9	8	5	62	26*	0	20.66
S. Massey	6	9	1	150	52	0	18.75
J. H. Jones	8	6	2	58	21*	0	14.50

Played in eight matches: P. J. Lewington 0, 0, 6*. Played in three matches: P. M. New 9, 3, 3. Played in two matches: D. Hartley 9, 17, 26. Played in one match: J. F. Harvey 13, 0; J. A. Woollhead 24, 12.

Bowling Averages

	O	M	R	W	BB	Avge
J. H. Jones	211.5	57	497	31	5-22	16.03
M. G. Stear	180	54	443	21	4-37	21.09
P. J. Lewington	254.3	93	565	25	5-33	22.60
T. P. J. Dodd	170.3	32	491	20	5-15	24.55

Also bowled: D. Hartley 53.2–11–168–6; M. G. Lickley 12–6–18–1; G. E. Loveday 1–1–0–0; S. Massey 34–15–78–3; P. M. New 38–10–113–8; G. R. J. Roope 81–18–217–8.

BUCKINGHAMSHIRE

Secretary – S. J. TOMLIN, Orchardleigh Cottage, Bigfrith Lane, Cookham Dean SL6 9PH

Matches 9: Won – Cornwall, Dorset, Oxfordshire, Shropshire. Lost – Devon. Won on first innings – Berkshire, Wiltshire. Lost on first innings – Cheshire, Somerset II.

Batting Averages

	M	I	NO	R	HI	100s	Avge
M. J. Roberts	8	13	1	475	81	0	39.58
A. R. Harwood	9	16	1	431	59	0	28.73
S. Burrow	9	15	2	368	63	0	28.30
R. E. Hayward	8	14	1	347	54	0	26.69
*N. G. Hames	9	14	4	263	46	0	26.30
D. E. Smith	5	8	1	172	64	0	24.57
G. R. Black	7	8	2	130	80	0	21.66
A. W. Lyon	8	6	3	60	39	0	20.00
T. J. A. Scriven	5	7	1	105	46	0	17.50
S. J. Edwards	9	11	3	101	37	0	12.62

Played in seven matches: C. D. Booden 16*, 1, 1*. Played in five matches: †D. J. Goldsmith 6, 5*, 15. Played in four matches: †C. J. Tungate 3, 4*, 10, 20. Played in two matches: T. Butler 0, 4*, 23, 6. Played in one match: P. D. Atkins 40; K. I. Hodgson 14*, 8*; S. G. Lynch 4; R. W. M. Tredwell did not bat.

Bowling Averages

	O	M	R	W	BB	Avge
C. D. Booden	145.2	34	393	19	6-5	20.68
A. W. Lyon	280.3	76	735	35	6-12	21.00
S. J. Edwards	204.2	65	441	16	3-30	27.56
S. Burrow	166.4	40	473	16	6-66	29.56

Also bowled: P. D. Atkins 3–0–6–0; G. R. Black 63.1–17–166–5; N. G. Hames 3–2–4–1; A. R. Harwood 18–2–76–5; R. E. Hayward 2–1–1–0; K. I. Hodgson 16–4–57–0; S. G. Lynch 3–0–16–0; M. J. Roberts 2–2–0–0; T. J. A. Scriven 113.3–26–322–9; R. W. M. Tredwell 18–1–60–0.

CAMBRIDGESHIRE

Secretary – P. W. GOODEN, The Redlands, Oakington Road, Cottenham,
Cambridge CB4 4TW

*Matches 9: Won – Bedfordshire, Cumberland, Hertfordshire, Lincolnshire, Norfolk. Won on first
innings – Staffordshire, Suffolk. Lost on first innings – Durham. Abandoned – Northumberland.*

Batting Averages

	M	I	NO	R	HI	100s	Avge
I. S. Lawrence	7	12	4	423	100*	1	52.87
C. W. A. Thornely ...	5	7	3	195	65*	0	48.75
†M. A. Garnham	8	14	3	411	77*	0	37.36
A. D. Cuthill	6	7	1	176	66*	0	29.33
*N. T. Gadsby	8	13	1	335	66	0	27.91
R. A. Milne	7	7	1	113	44	0	18.83
C. Lethbridge	8	8	1	113	48*	0	16.14

Played in eight matches: D. C. Collard 9*, 2, 32, 0, 63; M. G. Stephenson 28*, 1, 23*, 26*, 4*, 3*. Played in six matches: C. R. F. Green 1, 0, 0; S. Turner 52, 39, 45, 2, 1. Played in three matches: N. J. Adams 43, 13, 5, 20, 10; S. Campin 23, 12. Played in two matches: A. P. A. Wykes 7*, 0*. Played in one match: J. D. R. Benson 8; S. Bishop 1*, 0; J. Stenner 5.

Bowling Averages

	O	M	R	W	BB	Avge
S. Turner	210.3	53	484	39	10-11	12.41
C. R. F. Green	88	31	216	12	5-78	18.00
D. C. Collard	149	37	445	23	5-35	19.34
M. G. Stephenson	172.1	48	395	17	4-37	23.23
C. Lethbridge	160	28	461	16	6-50	28.81

Also bowled: N. J. Adams 2.4-0-20-1; N. T. Gadsby 10-5-41-4; R. A. Milne 14.5-7-13-3; A. P. A. Wykes 29-9-72-2.

CHESHIRE

Secretary – J. B. Pickup, 2 Castle Street, Northwich CW8 1AB

*Matches 9: Won – Dorset, Shropshire. Lost – Wiltshire. Won on first innings – Buckinghamshire,
Oxfordshire. Lost on first innings – Berkshire. No result – Devon. Abandoned – Cornwall,
Somerset II.*

Batting Averages

	M	I	NO	R	HI	100s	Avge
I. J. Tansley	7	11	1	519	131*	2	51.90
I. Cockbain	6	9	1	330	100*	1	41.25
J. J. Hitchmough	7	12	5	274	59*	0	39.14
*N. T. O'Brien	7	11	2	337	103*	1	37.44
S. T. Crawley	7	11	0	282	87	0	25.63
K. Teasdale	7	9	0	125	37	0	13.88

Played in seven matches: G. J. Blackburn 36*, 10*, 51*, 4*, 9, 7*, 0, 7*, 19*, 18; M. G. Boocock 2*, 4*; J. F. M. O'Brien did not bat. Played in six matches: A. Fox 2*, 0, 10*, 21*. Played in four matches: †S. Cummings 4*, 6, 55, 5*, 11*. Played in three matches: N. Smith 1, 4. Played in one match: G. L. Bullock 4, 17; A. Cross did not bat.

Bowling Averages

	O	M	R	W	BB	Avge
J. F. M. O'Brien	203	54	540	31	5-60	17.41
G. J. Blackburn	172.3	51	474	25	5-45	18.96
M. G. Boocock	119.5	27	417	17	4-45	24.52
A. Fox	113	23	320	10	3-44	32.00

Also bowled: I. Cockbain 11–0–58–1; S. T. Crawley 62–18–195–5; A. Cross 4–1–24–0; J. J. Hitchmough 4–1–28–0; N. T. O'Brien 24–7–69–3; K. Teasdale 3–0–17–0.

CORNWALL

Secretary – T. D. MENEER, c/o L. P. Dawe, 22 Berkeley Vale, Falmouth

Matches 9: Lost – Berkshire, Buckinghamshire, Shropshire, Wiltshire. Won on first innings – Devon. Lost on first innings – Dorset, Oxfordshire, Somerset II. Abandoned – Cheshire.

Batting Averages

	M	I	NO	R	HI	100s	Avge
A. Penberthy	5	9	3	232	66	0	38.66
P. J. Stephens	6	10	0	288	86	0	28.80
S. Hooper	7	12	2	266	70*	0	26.60
C. C. Lovell	5	8	2	146	33	0	24.33
*E. G. Willcock	8	14	2	246	55*	0	20.50
M. W. Pooley	4	8	1	130	70	0	18.57
A. H. Watts	8	8	4	64	26*	0	16.00
D. A. Toseland	5	6	2	54	31	0	13.50
L. Bailey	4	7	0	79	21	0	11.28
C. J. Trudgeon	4	7	0	77	39	0	11.00
R. T. Walton	5	9	0	96	25	0	10.66
†D. J. Rowe	7	8	1	36	15	0	5.14

Played in five matches: R. J. Perry 1, 0, 4, 0, 0. Played in four matches: R. G. Furse 0, 50*, 28, 7, 9*. Played in three matches: A. J. Buzza 17, 19, 0, 12. Played in two matches: K. Blackburn 53, 8, 3, 11; T. M. Thomas 6*, 14, 1. Played in one match: M. S. T. Dunstan 15, 56*; S. P. Eva 23, 6; C. S. Kitt 10; K. Thomas 5.

Bowling Averages

	O	M	R	W	BB	Avge
D. A. Toseland	150.5	51	363	22	6-43	16.50
R. J. Perry	193.5	42	572	15	5-62	38.13
A. H. Watts	170	33	615	16	3-56	38.43

Also bowled: A. J. Buzza 34–5–142–2; R. G. Furse 40–6–141–3; C. S. Kitt 5–2–12–0; C. C. Lovell 116–8–534–9; A. Penberthy 64–10–236–7; M. W. Pooley 45–6–122–6.

CUMBERLAND

Secretary – M. BEATY, 9 Abbey Drive, Natland, Kendal, Cumbria LA9 7QN

Matches 9: Won – Bedfordshire, Hertfordshire, Norfolk, Northumberland. Lost – Cambridgeshire, Durham, Lincolnshire, Staffordshire. Won on first innings – Suffolk.

Batting Averages

	M	I	NO	R	HI	100s	Avge
B. W. Reidy	6	8	1	298	144*	1	42.57
S. Sharp	9	16	3	546	119*	2	42.00
*J. R. Moyes	9	13	3	350	62*	0	35.00
C. J. Stockdale	7	12	0	370	103	1	30.83
G. Monkhouse	6	8	1	134	56*	0	19.14
M. G. Scothern	9	8	3	88	39*	0	17.60
M. D. Woods	9	14	5	155	46*	0	17.22
C. R. Knight	4	7	1	66	35	0	11.00
†S. M. Dutton	9	11	4	66	36*	0	9.42
G. J. Clarke	5	7	0	60	43	0	8.57

Played in six matches: D. Halliwell 1, 20, 21. Played in four matches: R. Ellwood 7, 0. Played in three matches: R. I. Cooper 0, 0, 11; S. Wall 30*, 10, 22*, 0. Played in two matches: G. D. Hodgson 23, 24*, 55*, 7; P. Nixon 0, 6; S. D. Philbrook 1, 0, 3; S. M. Stuart 0, 14, 0. Played in one match; E. K. Sample 0, 0; P. Threlfall 0*, 1*.

Bowling Averages

	O	M	R	W	BB	Avge
D. Halliwell	168.4	38	462	28	5-45	16.50
G. Monkhouse	154.5	38	414	22	8-69	18.81
M. D. Woods	157.1	53	426	19	5-50	22.42
M. G. Scothern	149.1	29	454	19	4-40	23.89

Also bowled: S. M. Dutton 7-0-37-0; R. Ellwood 62.3-20-170-9; B. W. Reidy 85.1-19-226-9; E. K. Sample 3.5-0-18-4; P. Threlfall 10.5-1-78-3; S. Wall 33-2-120-0.

DEVON

Secretary – G. R. EVANS, Fountain Hill House, Fountain Hill, Budleigh Salterton EX9 6BX

Matches 9: Won – Buckinghamshire, Oxfordshire. Won on first innings – Wiltshire. Lost on first innings – Berkshire, Cornwall, Dorset, Shropshire, Somerset II. No result – Cheshire.

Batting Averages

	M	I	NO	R	HI	100s	Avge
N. A. Folland	6	11	2	461	98*	0	51.22
*J. H. Edwards	9	14	4	324	72	0	32.40
N. R. Gaywood	9	16	2	449	76	0	32.07
G. Randall-Johnson ..	4	7	2	139	42*	0	27.80
†R. C. Turpin	9	14	3	268	53	0	24.36
M. Olive	5	9	0	211	65	0	23.44
K. G. Rice	4	7	0	157	53	0	22.42
T. Farkins	5	9	0	200	54	0	22.22
N. White	8	14	2	264	57*	0	22.00
T. W. Ward	8	12	4	130	47*	0	16.25
P. G. Considine	8	6	3	37	15*	0	12.33
N. G. Folland	4	7	0	85	24	0	12.14

Played in five matches: D. I. Yeabsley 15*, 0*. Played in three matches: A. W. Allin 30*, 11*, 13*, 6*; M. A. Taylor 24, 4, 0, 6; M. C. Woodman 2*. Played in two matches: J. Jenkins 1. Played in one match: D. A. Tall 0; J. K. Tierney 3, 18*; G. Wallen 38, 24; M. Kingdon did not bat.

Bowling Averages

	O	M	R	W	BB	Avge
D. I. Yeabsley	173.2	43	476	20	6-68	23.80
P. G. Considine	144.2	24	531	22	4-25	24.13
A. W. Allin	100.1	19	317	13	4-49	24.38
M. C. Woodman	89	18	320	12	3-35	26.66
T. W. Ward	159	29	535	11	3-43	48.63

Also bowled: J. H. Edwards 11–2–45–2; N. A. Folland 32-4-143-7; J. Jenkins 73-15-182-9; M. Kingdon 23–12–39–1; K. G. Rice 1-0–4-0; D. A. Tall 4-0-30-0; M. A. Taylor 75-7-270-5; J. K. Tierney 6-1-16-1; N. White 1-0-16-0.

DORSET

Secretary – D. J. W. BRIDGE, Long Acre, Tinney's Lane,
Sherborne DT9 3DY

Matches 9: Lost – Buckinghamshire, Cheshire, Oxfordshire, Shropshire. Won on first innings – Berkshire, Cornwall, Devon, Wiltshire. Lost on first innings – Somerset II.

Batting Averages

	M	I	NO	R	HI	100s	Avge
I. C. D. Stuart	9	10	4	291	69*	0	48.50
*A. Kennedy	8	12	1	422	163*	1	38.36
G. S. Calway	9	14	0	524	155	1	37.42
R. P. Merriman	8	13	0	460	114	1	35.38
C. Stone	8	12	5	228	66*	0	32.57
R. V. Lewis	5	8	0	202	95	0	25.25
S. W. D. Rintoul	4	6	2	90	28	0	22.50
V. B. Lewis	7	10	1	153	82	0	17.00
†C. J. Wells	8	9	2	49	13	0	7.00

Played in eight matches: N. S. Taylor 4, 1, 0*, 9, 11. Played in five matches: P. L. Garlick 6*, 4*, 0, 2; S. Westlake 4, 5, 0, 4, 2*. Played in three matches: S. J. Halliday 9, 3, 11, 0; S. J. Turrill 0, 4*, 0, 30*. Played in two matches: R. V. J. Coombs 4*, 10; S. J. Malone 12*; A. R. Wingfield Digby 20*, 2. Played in one match: A. M. Marsh 0; A. B. O'Sullivan 7; S. Sawney 8.

Bowling Averages

	O	M	R	W	BB	Avge
N. S. Taylor	172.4	52	479	25	4-33	19.16
A. Kennedy	62	10	207	10	4-42	20.70
C. Stone	203	46	558	23	5-82	24.26
I. C. D. Stuart	122.1	20	468	13	4-46	36.00

Also bowled: G. S. Calway 18.2–3–88–3; R. V. J. Coombs 50–12–117–5; P. L. Garlick 81–13–298-9; S. J. Malone 32.2-5-116-2; A. M. Marsh 8-3-12-0; R. P. Merriman 3-0-10-0; A. B. O'Sullivan 10-0-58-1; S. Sawney 5-0-27-1; S. J. Turrill 8-0-43-0; C. J. Wells 0.3-0-7-0; A. R. Wingfield Digby 70-26-147-9.

DURHAM

Secretary – J. ILEY, Roselea, Springwell Avenue,
Durham DH1 4LY

Matches 9: Won – Cumberland, Hertfordshire, Lincolnshire, Suffolk. Lost – Staffordshire. Won on first innings – Bedfordshire, Cambridgeshire, Northumberland. No result – Norfolk.

Batting Averages

	M	I	NO	R	HI	100s	Avge
P. Burn	9	13	4	476	109*	2	52.88
J. W. Lister	9	15	2	572	97	0	44.00
*N. A. Riddell	9	14	3	479	97	0	43.54
A. S. Patel	9	16	5	402	61*	0	36.54
S. R. Atkinson	7	12	0	251	77	0	20.91
P. J. Kippax	7	8	2	125	67	0	20.83
S. Greensword	8	11	1	195	71	0	19.50
G. Hurst	5	7	1	113	38	0	18.83
†A. R. Fothergill	9	7	3	37	18	0	9.25

Played in seven matches: D. Beach 1, 1*, 1*; J. Johnston 0. Played in six matches: I. E. Conn 27*, 0. Played in four matches: S. Ward 7. Played in one match: P. B. Hill 24*; G. Johnson 4; W. Johnson 55, 2.

Bowling Averages

	O	M	R	W	BB	Avge
P. J. Kippax	164.4	50	376	24	5-62	15.66
J. Johnston	198	61	482	23	4-32	20.95
S. Greensword	113.3	31	287	13	5-69	22.07
D. Beach	136.3	25	507	20	6-45	25.35
I. E. Conn	102.2	13	363	12	5-64	30.25

Also bowled: P. Burn 5-2-8-1; G. Johnson 33-9-61-2; J. W. Lister 3-0-23-0; A. S. Patel 65-11-248-5; S. Ward 80.3-20-216-7.

HERTFORDSHIRE

Secretary – D. DREDGE, 38 Santers Lane, Potters Bar EN6 2BX

Matches 9: Won – Norfolk, Suffolk. Lost – Bedfordshire, Cambridgeshire, Cumberland, Durham, Lincolnshire. Won on first innings – Northumberland. No result – Staffordshire.

Batting Averages

	M	I	NO	R	HI	100s	Avge
S. P. Henderson	6	11	1	370	107	1	37.00
†M. W. C. Olley	9	11	4	219	67	0	31.28
B. G. Evans	8	16	1	447	93	0	29.80
N. P. G. Wright	7	13	0	383	83	0	29.46
M. C. G. Wright	6	9	2	206	71*	0	29.42
S. A. Dean	8	15	2	348	63	0	26.76
N. Gilbert	3	6	1	104	28	0	20.80
R. Herbert	9	17	1	320	89	0	20.00
*E. P. Neal	7	10	1	167	53	0	18.55
T. S. Smith	6	7	2	49	32*	0	9.80

Played in five matches: R. J. Hailey 2*, 0*, 0*; W. G. Merry 12, 12*, 0; A. P. Wright 0*, 22, 24, 24, 5. Played in four matches M. C. Ilott 0, 0*, 0. Played in two matches: F. E. Collyer 1, 5*, 0, 14; N. J. C. Gandon 37*, 3, 20; A. R. Garofall 16, 27, 9; A. M. W. Walters 5, 7*, 5. Played in one match: D. Perry 5, 2*; A. Devereux and T. C. E. Stancombe did not bat.

Bowling Averages

	O	M	R	W	BB	Avge
W. G. Merry	86.1	25	211	17	6-30	12.41
R. J. Hailey	143	33	447	22	5-40	20.31
T. S. Smith	174.5	53	399	16	3-36	24.93
A. P. Wright	90	21	310	11	5-44	28.18

Also bowled: S. A. Dean 5–0–45–0; A. Devereux 8–2–35–2; A. R. Garofall 43–17–115–3; R. Herbert 159.5–35–594–9; M. C. Ilott 32–7–120–1; E. P. Neal 95–21–321–9; D. Perry 10–3–31–0; T. C. E. Stancombe 14–1–68–3; A. M. W. Walters 23–3–89–2; N. P. G. Wright 0.3–0–7–0.

LINCOLNSHIRE

Secretary – D. H. WRIGHT, 18 Spencer Road, Ketton, Stamford

Matches 9: Won – Cumberland, Hertfordshire. Lost – Cambridgeshire, Durham, Staffordshire. Won on first innings – Northumberland, Suffolk. Lost on first innings – Bedfordshire, Norfolk.

Batting Averages

	M	I	NO	R	HI	100s	Avge
M. A. Fell	9	16	3	643	117	2	49.46
†N. Priestley	8	15	1	581	102*	1	41.50
C. Wicks	6	10	1	313	83	0	34.77
S. A. Bradford	5	7	2	155	59*	0	31.00
*H. Pougher	8	8	2	158	51	0	26.33
T. J. Hopper	9	14	7	162	34*	0	23.14
J. G. Franks	9	16	0	308	85	0	19.25
P. R. Butler	5	8	0	134	61	0	16.75
D. Marshall	8	7	0	72	36	0	10.28
R. L. Burton	7	8	2	39	18*	0	6.50

Played in eight matches: B. J. Griffiths 0*, 7, 0, 2, 2*. Played in two matches: D. J. Allen 2, 0, 0*; P. D. Johnson 31, 106, 12; D. B. Storer 1*, 3*; P. A. Todd 0, 14, 6, 13; S. D. Kelk did not bat. Played in one match: N. J. Illingworth 8, 4; T. F. Nicholls 16, 3; J. P. Quincey 3; H. S. Stroud 0, 17; L. A. Ward 8*, 0; S. N. Warman 2, 0; N. P. Dobbs did not bat.

Bowling Averages

	O	M	R	W	BB	Avge
B. J. Griffiths	258.5	67	701	36	7-48	19.47
D. Marshall	181.1	36	626	24	6-46	26.08
T. J. Hopper	186	33	604	22	3-52	27.45

Also bowled: D. J. Allen 15–4–49–1; S. A. Bradford 12.4–3–35–5; R. L. Burton 98.4–16–363–8; P. R. Butler 9–1–26–0; M. A. Fell 15–4–51–4; J. G. Franks 1–0–4–0; N. J. Illingworth 23–4–85–0; S. D. Kelk 52–10–188–2; T. F. Nicholls 21–6–56–0; N. Priestley 0.5–0–5–0; J. P. Quincey 19–2–50–1; D. B. Storer 3–1–11–1; L. A. Ward 5–0–16–0.

NORFOLK

Secretary – S. J. SKINNER, 27 Colkett Drive, Old Catton, Norwich NR6 7ND

Matches 9: Lost – Cambridgeshire, Cumberland, Hertfordshire, Staffordshire, Suffolk. Won on first innings – Bedfordshire, Lincolnshire. No result – Durham, Northumberland.

Batting Averages

	M	I	NO	R	HI	100s	Avge
*S. G. Plumb	9	15	3	508	131*	1	42.33
J. Whitehead	5	8	1	169	62	0	24.14
R. L. Bradford	5	7	0	168	43	0	24.00
R. D. Huggins	6	8	0	189	110	1	23.62
P. J. Ringwood	5	9	2	155	59	0	22.14
R. Kingshott	6	7	3	74	16	0	18.50
D. R. Thomas	5	6	1	91	48	0	18.20
D. J. Williams	4	7	1	107	37	0	17.83
†D. E. Mattocks	7	11	2	145	96	0	16.11
N. D. Cook	4	6	0	95	39	0	15.83
S. N. Waymouth	8	8	1	92	40*	0	13.14
R. A. Bunting	8	6	2	33	14	0	8.25

Played in four matches: F. L. Q. Handley 23, 4, 0, 2, 9; D. G. Savage 0, 31, 0, 19*; J. S. Tate 5, 0*, 0. Played in three matches: M. Ellis 0; G. M. Roff 4, 2, 6, 0. Played in two matches: J. C. M. Lewis 11*, 3, 19, 9; A. W. Payne did not bat. Played in one match: J. R. Carter 1, 1; K. P. Cooper 5*, 0; M. Rayner 13; D. W. Sands 15, 1; P. K. Whittaker 0, 8*.

Bowling Averages

	O	M	R	W	BB	Avge
R. Kingshott	143.5	37	410	18	4-9	22.77
R. A. Bunting . . . . , .	155.5	36	506	20	5-33	25.30
S. G. Plumb	112.5	26	396	15	3-17	26.40

Also bowled: K. P. Cooper 5.3–1–20–1; M. Ellis 24–6–61–3; J. C. M. Lewis 10–1–41–0; M. Rayner 18–3–55–3; G. M. Roff 31.1–8–98–6; D. G. Savage 4–0–22–0; J. S. Tate 94–24–242–7; D. R. Thomas 47.2–7–148–6; S. N. Waymouth 62–13–234–2; P. K. Whittaker 28–4–73–3.

NORTHUMBERLAND

Secretary – G. H. THOMPSON, Northumberland County Cricket Ground, Osborne Avenue, Jesmond, Newcastle upon Tyne NE2 1JS

Matches 9: Lost – Cumberland, Suffolk. Won on first innings – Bedfordshire. Lost on first innings – Durham, Hertfordshire, Lincolnshire, Staffordshire. No result – Norfolk. Abandoned – Cambridgeshire.

Batting Averages

	M	I	NO	R	HI	100s	Avge
J. R. Purvis	8	11	8	175	58*	0	58.33
R. Dreyer	6	11	2	398	94*	0	44.22
P. N. S. Dutton	8	15	4	380	51	0	34.54
K. Pearson	7	13	1	386	111	1	32.16
*M. E. Younger	7	9	2	211	39*	0	30.14
G. D. Halliday	6	10	2	220	65	0	27.50
G. R. Morris	6	10	2	192	53	0	24.00
C. M. Old	8	8	0	130	63	0	16.25

Played in eight matches: C. J. Harker 2, 1*, 0, 0. Played in six matches: †M. S. Tiffin 25, 31, 14, 31, 25. Played in five matches: P. C. Graham 0, 18*. Played in three matches: P. G. Cormack 1, 33*, 20*, 2; M. J. Green 11, 22, 2, 0; S. P. Scott 0*. Played in one match: M. B. Anderson 58*, 0; †K. C. Corby, C. Pleasants and B. Storey did not bat.

Bowling Averages

	O	M	R	W	BB	Avge
C. J. Harker	154.3	33	508	19	4-64	26.73
C. M. Old	201.4	45	619	19	6-98	32.57
P. C. Graham	128	27	416	12	3-37	34.66

Also bowled: R. Dreyer 12-3-39-1; P. N. S. Dutton 17.2-1-80-1; G. D. Halliday 62.4-15-186-5; C. Pleasants 6-1-20-0; J. R. Purvis 74.2-11-310-4; S. P. Scott 51-10-138-5; M. E. Younger 64-15-247-6.

OXFORDSHIRE

Secretary – J. E. O. SMITH, 2 The Green, Horton-cum-Studley, OX9 1AE

Matches 9: Won – Dorset. Lost – Buckinghamshire, Devon, Somerset II. Won on first innings – Cornwall, Shropshire. Lost on first innings – Berkshire, Cheshire, Wiltshire.

Batting Averages

	M	I	NO	R	HI	100s	Avge
M. D. Nurton	7	13	3	597	103*	1	59.70
T. A. Lester	6	11	4	202	61	0	28.85
*P. J. Garner	9	16	0	419	50	0	26.18
P. J. Densham	3	6	0	142	57	0	23.66
D. A. J. Wise	5	9	1	168	40	0	21.00
R. N. Busby	7	10	1	188	54	0	20.88
P. M. Jobson	6	12	1	229	57	0	20.81
†A. Crossley	7	10	2	139	45	0	17.37
K. A. Arnold	8	13	3	169	26	0	16.90
G. P. Savin	5	6	4	33	9	0	16.50
P. A. Fowler	6	11	0	172	51	0	15.63
S. R. Porter	5	8	3	71	24	0	14.20
R. A. Evans	8	10	1	61	24	0	6.77

Played in six matches: I. J. Curtis 0*, 0*, 4. Played in five matches: D. A. Hale 24, 2*, 2, 11, 21. Played in two matches: S. Partington 6, 1. Played in one match: P. L. Bradbury 17; C. J. Clements 2, 39; A. Sabin 45, 12; P. Hardiman did not bat.

Bowling Averages

	O	M	R	W	BB	Avge
K. A. Arnold	212.4	45	562	29	8-32	19.37
D. A. Hale	115.2	23	412	21	5-43	19.61
R. A. Evans	167.1	52	446	20	5-23	22.30
R. N. Busby	123	31	364	10	3-35	36.40
I. J. Curtis	113	30	447	10	3-72	44.70

Also bowled: P. L. Bradbury 16.3-2-59-1; P. J. Garner 28.2-9-82-3; P. Hardiman 15-3-67-1; P. M. Jobson 6-2-16-0; S. R. Porter 36-5-191-5; G. P. Savin 59.5-13-178-3.

SHROPSHIRE

Secretary – N. H. BIRCH, 8 Port Hill Close, Copthorne, Shrewsbury

Matches 9: Won – Cornwall, Dorset. Lost – Berkshire, Buckinghamshire, Cheshire. Won on first innings – Devon. Lost on first innings – Oxfordshire, Somerset II, Wiltshire.

Batting Averages

	M	I	NO	R	HI	100s	Avge
J. S. Johnson	9	18	3	643	98*	0	42.86
J. A. Smith	9	15	4	365	101	1	33.18
M. R. Davies	9	18	1	553	74	0	32.52
*J. Foster	9	18	2	453	79	0	28.31
S. C. Gale	7	13	1	240	78	0	20.00
K. Humphreys	9	17	1	271	47	0	16.93
P. B. Wormald	7	11	2	135	50	0	15.00
†D. J. Ashley	9	15	1	174	42	0	12.42
G. Edmunds	8	10	2	73	20*	0	9.12
J. S. Roberts	9	8	3	40	18	0	8.00

Played in four matches: A. S. Barnard 10*, 10*, 10, 12; J. P. Dawson 8, 0, 13, 4, 6. Played in two matches: A. N. Johnson 6, 4, 17, 8*. Played in one match: W. G. Bott 8*, 1; P. R. Lloyd 0; S. Ogrizovic 1*; D. Williamson 0.

Bowling Averages

	O	M	R	W	BB	Avge
J. P. Dawson	124.4	38	365	16	5-84	22.81
A. S. Barnard	101	28	282	12	5-68	23.50
G. Edmunds	226.3	65	660	25	5-19	26.40
J. A. Smith	195.5	37	624	19	4-81	32.84
J. S. Roberts	185.1	41	583	16	4-36	36.43

Also bowled: W. G. Bott 17-2-66-2; S. C. Gale 4-0-30-0; P. R. Lloyd 8-2-36-0; S. Ogrizovic 9-1-26-1; P. B. Wormald 110-21-354-9; D. Williamson 17-7-62-1.

SOMERSET SECOND ELEVEN

Secretary – A. S. BROWN, County Cricket Ground, Taunton TA1 1JT

Matches 9: Won – Oxfordshire. Won on first innings – Buckinghamshire, Cornwall, Devon, Dorset, Shropshire. Lost on first innings – Berkshire. No result – Wiltshire. Abandoned – Cheshire.

Batting Averages

	M	I	NO	R	HI	100s	Avge
R. Baigent	8	13	5	713	150*	1	89.12
J. G. Wyatt	6	9	1	444	129	2	55.50
R. J. Bartlett	6	7	1	223	84*	0	37.16
†T. Gard	7	6	3	103	84	0	34.33
J. C. M. Atkinson	8	11	1	281	109	1	28.10
P. A. C. Bail	6	10	1	208	102*	1	23.11

Played in seven matches: R. G. Woolston did not bat. Played in four matches: M. Cleal 13*, 0; C. H. Dredge 15; A. R. Phillips 0. Played in three matches: D. J. Foster 16; M. D. Harman 5*, 4*, 62; N. J. Pringle 10, 0, 32, 0, 22; H. R. J. Trump 10, 10, 7, 0, 1; R. Burt did not bat. Played in two matches: D. Beal 5*; P. J. Rendall 26, 27*, 12, 1*; R. D. Rose 10, 4; R. G. Twose 23, 38*, 42*. Played in one match: M. R. Davis 11*; J. M. Kerslake 8*, 2; N. A. Mallender 1, 8*; G. V. Palmer 0; B. C. Rose 27.

Bowling Averages

	O	M	R	W	BB	Avge
R. G. Woolston	192	48	576	32	7-47	18.00
A. R. Phillips	52	12	181	10	7-44	18.10

Also bowled: J. C. M. Atkinson 60–4–279–8; R. Baigent 1–0–8–0; P. A. C. Bail 3–0–19–0; R. J. Bartlett 1–0–4–0; D. Beal 49–7–184–5; R. Burt 59–15–176–5; M. Cleal 51–13–163–5; M. R. Davis 17–5–45–2; C. H. Dredge 63.4–15–131–7; D. J. Foster 62–10–180–9; M. D. Harman 63–22–122–3; N. A. Mallender 14–4–36–0; G. V. Palmer 22.2–4–68–6; N. J. Pringle 30–9–105–1; P. Rendall 32–6–105–5; H. R. J. Trump 37.1–6–139–3; R. G. Twose 18–0–62–0; J. G. Wyatt 1–0–6–0.

STAFFORDSHIRE

Secretary – W. S. BOURNE, 10 The Pavement, Brewood ST19 9BZ

Matches 9: Won – Cumberland, Durham, Lincolnshire, Norfolk, Suffolk. Won on first innings – Bedfordshire, Northumberland. Lost on first innings – Cambridgeshire. No result – Hertfordshire.

Batting Averages

	M	I	NO	R	HI	100s	Avge
P. R. Oliver	5	9	5	246	78*	0	61.50
*N. J. Archer	9	12	8	166	35	0	41.50
J. P. Addison	9	15	3	489	101	1	40.75
S. J. Dean	5	10	1	352	107	1	39.11
D. A. Banks	8	12	0	379	56	0	31.58
D. Cartledge	8	12	0	260	70	0	21.66
†A. Griffiths	9	8	3	102	30	0	20.40
J. E. Benjamin	9	6	1	68	33	0	13.60
D. C. Blank	9	7	4	14	9*	0	4.66

Played in nine matches: R. W. Flower 4*, 8*. Played in five matches: N. K. Davis 10, 0, 25, 0, 15; M. Frost 1*, 5. Played in four matches: A. J. Webster did not bat. Played in three matches: P. A. Marshall 48, 18*, 61, 1. Played in one match: S. Bailey 13, 7; G. S. Warner did not bat.

Bowling Averages

	O	M	R	W	BB	Avge
A. J. Webster	101.3	33	230	16	4–42	14.37
R. W. Flower	223.5	59	572	29	6–55	19.72
J. E. Benjamin	161.3	32	469	23	7–42	20.39
D. C. Blank	158	29	436	18	3–40	24.22
M. Frost	111	16	387	15	4–44	25.80

Also bowled: J. P. Addison 15–2–80–2; D. Cartledge 35–11–97–4; S. J. Dean 1.1–0–11–0.

SUFFOLK

Secretary – R. S. BARKER, 301 Henley Road, Ipswich IP1 6TB

Matches 9: Won – Norfolk, Northumberland. Lost – Durham, Hertfordshire, Staffordshire. Lost on first innings – Bedfordshire, Cambridgeshire, Cumberland, Lincolnshire.

Batting Averages

	M	I	NO	R	HI	100s	Avge
M. S. A. McEvoy	9	17	2	470	85	0	31.33
P. J. Caley	9	14	1	349	76	0	26.84
K. P. Offord	7	12	0	260	42	0	21.66
*C. M. Clements	8	13	1	246	44	0	20.50
†S. J. Halliday	9	16	0	277	58	0	17.31

	M	I	NO	R	HI	100s	Avge
K. G. Brooks	6	10	1	120	44	0	13.33
P. J. Hayes	9	14	2	147	35*	0	12.25
H. J. W. Wright	6	10	4	68	26*	0	11.33
M. D. Bailey	5	7	2	56	22*	0	11.20
R. J. Bond	8	13	2	116	37*	0	10.54

Played in five matches: R. A. Pybus 0, 4*, 0*, 2*, 0*, 21*. Played in four matches: R. C. Green 19*, 15, 0, 0*. Played in three matches: P. D. Barker 5, 5, 9, 12. Played in two matches: N. J. Crame 10, 11, 12*; C. C. Graham 0, 1*; A. J. King 3, 1, 11; R. J. Robinson 27, 9, 9; A. G. Warrington 112*, 14, 48, 2. Played in one match: K. J. Winder 1.

Bowling Averages

	O	M	R	W	BB	Avge
R. A. Pybus	122	29	360	19	4-34	18.94
R. C. Green	103	16	289	12	4-84	24.08
P. J. Hayes	176.2	55	426	17	4-10	25.05
P. J. Caley	161.1	36	502	19	5-66	26.42
K. G. Brooks	89.3	10	291	10	4-27	29.10
H. J. W. Wright	120	24	324	10	3-32	32.40

Also bowled: M. D. Bailey 57–13–153–5; P. D. Barker 14.4–1–87–1; S. M. Clements 7.1–1–39–0; C. C. Graham 50–9–141–4; K. P. Offord 7–0–52–0; R. J. Robinson 33–7–93–2; K. J. Winder 4–1–18–0.

WALES MINOR COUNTIES

Secretary – BILL EDWARDS, 59a King Edward Road, Swansea

WILTSHIRE

Secretary – C. R. SHEPPARD, 45 Ipswich Street, Swindon, Wiltshire SN2 1DB

Matches 9: Won – Cheshire, Cornwall. Lost – Berkshire. Won on first innings – Oxfordshire, Shropshire. Lost on first innings – Buckinghamshire, Devon, Dorset. No result – Somerset II.

Batting Averages

	M	I	NO	R	HI	100s	Avge
R. R. Savage	6	11	0	436	105	1	39.63
R. J. Lanchbury	5	9	1	282	77*	0	35.25
†J. J. Cullip	6	11	1	309	92	0	30.90
*R. C. Cooper	9	16	4	299	63	0	24.91
B. H. White	6	11	1	245	75	0	24.50
D. J. M. Mercer	9	17	1	368	101*	1	23.00
J. J. Newman	8	15	2	269	94	0	20.69
J. D. Inchmore	9	9	4	79	34	0	15.80
D. P. Simpkins	9	10	1	100	37*	0	11.11

Played in six matches: P. Meehan 21*, 0*, 8*, 13, 9, 30*. Played in four matches: K. St J. D. Emery 0, 18, 7*, 8. Played in three matches: R. J. Merryweather 2, 0, 3, 14; N. Newman 0, 15, 23, 1; C. J. Pike 64, 11, 0, 13; D. R. Pike 17, 9, 5, 1, 12*; C. R. Trembath 58, 30, 15, 7, 27. Played in two matches: R. Greatorix 0, 5, 0*, 0; A. J. Spencer 1*, 10, 1*; M. A. Watts 5*, 19*, 5, 4. Played in one match: M. C. Seaman 28, 0.

Bowling Averages

	O	M	R	W	BB	Avge
J. D. Inchmore	180.3	38	444	20	7-59	22.20
D. P. Simpkins	236.5	53	773	34	6-100	22.73
P. Meehan	122	29	363	14	8-61	25.92

Also bowled: R. C. Cooper 48.3–12–144–6; K. St J. D. Emery 72.1–11–260–4; R. J. Merryweather 23–4–66–1; N. Newman 11–2–37–2; A. J. Spencer 48–13–97–3; C. R. Trembath 39–9–94–4; M. A. Watts 29–3–118–3.

TOP TEN MINOR COUNTIES CHAMPIONSHIP AVERAGES, 1987

BATTING

(Qualification: 8 innings)

	M	I	NO	R	HI	100s	Avge
R. Baigent (*Somerset II*)	8	13	5	713	150*	1	89.12
P. R. Oliver (*Staffordshire*)	5	9	5	246	78*	0	61.50
M. D. Nurton (*Oxfordshire*) ...	7	13	3	597	103*	1	59.70
J. R. Purvis (*Northumberland*) .	8	11	8	175	58*	0	58.33
J. G. Wyatt (*Somerset II*)	6	9	1	444	129	2	55.50
P. Burn (*Durham*)	9	13	4	476	109*	2	52.88
I. S. Lawrence (*Cambridgeshire*)	7	12	4	423	100*	1	52.87
I. J. Tansley (*Cheshire*)	7	11	1	519	131*	1	51.90
N. A. Folland (*Devon*)	6	11	2	461	98*	0	51.22
M. A. Fell (*Lincolnshire*)	9	16	3	643	117	2	49.46

BOWLING

(Qualification: 20 wickets)

	O	M	R	W	BB	Avge
S. Turner (*Cambridgeshire*) ..	210.3	53	484	39	10-11	12.41
P. J. Kippax (*Durham*)	164.4	50	376	24	5-62	15.66
J. H. Jones (*Berkshire*)	211.5	57	497	31	5-22	16.03
D. Halliwell (*Cumberland*) ...	168.4	38	462	28	5-45	16.50
D. A. Toseland (*Cornwall*) ..	150.5	51	363	22	6-43	16.50
J. F. M. O'Brien (*Cheshire*) ..	203	54	540	31	5-60	17.41
R. G. Woolston (*Somerset II*) .	192	48	576	32	7-47	18.00
G. Monkhouse (*Cumberland*) .	154.5	38	414	22	8-69	18.81
G. J. Blackburn (*Cheshire*) ..	172.3	51	474	25	5-45	18.96
N. S. Taylor (*Dorset*)	172.4	52	479	25	4-33	19.16

THE MINOR COUNTIES CHAMPIONS

1885	Norfolk	1925	Buckinghamshire	1960	Lancashire II
	Durham	1926	Durham	1961	Somerset II
	Worcestershire	1927	Staffordshire	1962	Warwickshire II
1896	Worcestershire	1928	Berkshire	1963	Cambridgeshire
1897	Worcestershire	1929	Oxfordshire	1964	Lancashire II
1898	Worcestershire	1930	Durham	1965	Somerset II
1899	Northamptonshire	1931	Leicestershire II	1966	Lincolnshire
	Buckinghamshire	1932	Buckinghamshire	1967	Cheshire
1900	Glamorgan	1933	Undecided	1968	Yorkshire II
	Durham	1934	Lancashire II	1969	Buckinghamshire
	Northamptonshire	1935	Middlesex II	1970	Bedfordshire
1901	Durham	1936	Hertfordshire	1971	Yorkshire II
1902	Wiltshire	1937	Lancashire II	1972	Bedfordshire
1903	Northamptonshire	1938	Buckinghamshire	1973	Shropshire
1904	Northamptonshire	1939	Surrey II	1974	Oxfordshire
1905	Norfolk	1946	Suffolk	1975	Hertfordshire
1906	Staffordshire	1947	Yorkshire	1976	Durham
1907	Lancashire II	1948	Lancashire II	1977	Suffolk
1908	Staffordshire	1949	Lancashire II	1978	Devon
1909	Wiltshire	1950	Surrey II	1979	Suffolk
1910	Norfolk	1951	Kent II	1980	Durham
1911	Staffordshire	1952	Buckinghamshire	1981	Durham
1912	In abeyance	1953	Berkshire	1982	Oxfordshire
1913	Norfolk	1954	Surrey II	1983	Hertfordshire
1920	Staffordshire	1955	Surrey II	1984	Durham
1921	Staffordshire	1956	Kent II	1985	Cheshire
1922	Buckinghamshire	1957	Yorkshire II	1986	Cumberland
1923	Buckinghamshire	1958	Yorkshire II	1987	Buckinghamshire
1924	Berkshire	1959	Warwickshire II		

SECOND ELEVEN CHAMPIONSHIP, 1987

With first-team injuries frequently depriving them of regular members, **Derbyshire** called on a number of inexperienced players, and in the circumstances it was not unduly surprising that they dropped to the bottom of the table. Newcomers Mark Beardshall and Frank Griffith headed the bowling averages; the leading wicket-takers, Chris Rudd and Paul Taylor, were costly and were not retained. On the bright side, Andrew Brown scored more than 600 runs and Karl Krikken, with 23 dismissals, maintained his high promise as a wicket-keeper. "Reg" Sharma took six for 78 against Gloucestershire at Lydney.

Essex, rarely short of runs, were well served by Ian Redpath, whose aggregate was just 21 short of 1,000. Robert Pook hit two hundreds in his first full season, while Nasser Hussain, whose 157 not out against Northamptonshire was a particularly fine innings, earned his first-team call. Andrew Golding did well to take 43 wickets with his slow left-arm deliveries, and Ian Pont's 34 wickets cost only 17.79 apiece. Adrian Brown, the 1986 Cambridge Blue, kept wicket well in his first season with the club.

Improving from bottom place to seventh, **Glamorgan** were another strong batting side, with ten hundreds shared between six players. John Hopkins hit two in the match against Gloucestershire at Ammanford. Paul Roebuck was the outstanding batsman with 1,011 runs, including two hundreds, while Anthony Cottey's 697 runs included three hundreds. Nineteen-year-old Stephen James again headed the averages. Steven Monkhouse was the leading bowler, with 45 wickets, and Martin Roberts's 45 dismissals included six stumpings. Against Warwickshire at Olton, the slow left-arm spinner, Philip North, scored 82 and returned match figures of twelve for 142.

Gloucestershire, unable to improve on sixteenth position, relied for their runs on Kassim Ibadulla and Keith Tomlins, whose 616 runs included 135 not out against Warwickshire, 135 against Somerset – both at Bristol – and 103 against Hampshire at Bournemouth. "Vibert" Greene and John Shepherd were the most successful bowlers, although only Darren Chubbs took five wickets in an innings.

Rain and then successive defeats put paid to the hopes **Hampshire** had of winning the Championship. Once again they were weakened at vital times by first-team calls. Richard Scott, a left-hander, was their leading batsman, his three centuries including 136 against Middlesex at Southampton, when Cardigan Connor took six for 68. Jonathan Ayling emphasised his all-round promise with 621 runs and 23 wickets, and played for the first team, as did the leading wicket-taker, Dutchman Paul Jan Bakker.

Kent leapt twelve places to become joint winners with Yorkshire. In a season when extensive injuries to the club as a whole necessitated the involvement of many non-contracted players, this reflected an excellent team effort. Roy Pienaar, when he came into the side for the second half of the season, averaged just under 50; Trevor Ward topped 1,000 runs, including a magnificent innings of 212 not out against Hampshire; Vince Wells and Stephen Goldsmith both passed 900 runs; and there were promising innings from youngsters Mark Ealham, Mark Dobson and Jonathan Longley. The outstanding bowler was Richard Davis, slow left-arm, who took 49 wickets despite missing several games while deputising for Derek Underwood in the first team. Richard Hart, still at Cambridge University, also showed promise, while Paul Farbrace continued to make significant progress both as wicket-keeper and batsman.

Winners in 1986, **Lancashire** were pushed into third place by a narrow margin. In a season of memorable performances, with eleven hundreds coming from nine batsmen, the highlight was the performance of Dexter Fitton, who scored 616 runs, including the side's highest innings of 141 against Derbyshire at Derby, and took 68 wickets, more than any other bowler in the Championship. His returns included seven for 92 against Kent at Canterbury, six for 41 against Leicestershire at Middleton, six for 52 against Derby at Manchester, six for 70 against Leicestershire at Leicester and six for 74 against Warwickshire at Manchester. Other notable returns were Ian Austin's match figures of twelve for 74 against Warwickshire at Nuneaton and his six for 33 in the win over Somerset at Taunton.

For **Leicestershire**, who slipped down the table to tenth, Chris Lewis made an immediate impact, both with his fast bowling (46 wickets including twelve for 87 against Warwickshire at Moseley) and his batting (505 runs including 130 against Nottinghamshire at Hinckley).

Hundreds also came from the promising Justin Benson (156 against Warwickshire at Leicester) and Ian Butcher (100 against Northamptonshire at Market Harborough), while Lloyd Tennant, a Young England tourist to Sri Lanka, took six for 38 against Nottinghamshire at Hinckley and George Ferris returned eight for 33 against Surrey at Uppingham.

Despite being the only side to remain unbeaten, **Middlesex** won only twice and fell from fourth to fourteenth. Against Kent at Uxbridge, John Carr (193 not out) and Andy Miller (142) added 304 for the second wicket in 236 minutes, while Miller was involved in another big stand when he and Jamie Sykes took a heavy toll of Leicestershire's bowling at the Lensbury Club. Miller made 163, Sykes 125. Sykes took 26 wickets with his off-spinners and Philip Tufnell again bowled his left-arm spin to good effect, his 30 wickets including six for 30 against Surrey at Guildford.

With almost 40 per cent of their playing time lost to rain, **Northamptonshire's** young players struggled for consistent form. However, their cricket was positive, with encouraging batting form shown by Alan Fordham, when he returned from Durham University. The more experienced Robin Boyd-Moss and Stuart Waterton both passed 700 runs, while Waterton also claimed 33 victims behind the stumps. Neil Stanley batted well in his first full season, and Gareth Smith and Mark Robinson both maintained their promise as seam bowlers. With 34 wickets, as well as 481 runs, including an unbeaten century, Tim Scriven continued to develop as a slow left-arm bowler but, unable to challenge Nick Cook for a place, he was not retained.

Nottinghamshire, weakened by injury and calls to the first team, slid further down the table to fifteenth. None the less there were some good individual performances. Paul Pollard, the most prolific batsman, hit three hundreds; all-rounder Kevin Evans scored 604 runs and took 34 wickets; and David Millns, a right-arm fast-medium bowler, captured 44 wickets.

Failing to maintain their progress of 1986, **Somerset** dropped a place to equal eighth. Mark Greatbatch, a left-hand batsman on exchange from Central Districts in New Zealand, had a fine season, scoring more than twice as many runs as anyone else and averaging 59.28. Otherwise the batting was somewhat disappointing, with many of the younger players failing to progress as anticipated. Robert Woolston, a slow left-arm bowler from the Lord's groundstaff, had an excellent first season, earning himself a first-team place. He was well supported by off-spinner Mark Harman, whose 22 wickets included a return of seven for 41, Gary Palmer, who took six for 61 against Kent at Taunton, and Darren Foster, who returned six for 56 against Hampshire, also at Taunton.

Surrey's policy of attacking cricket occasionally resulted in their falling at the last when chasing a target; and at other times only the tail-end batsmen stood between their bowlers and victory. David Ward's aggregate of 1,161 runs, including 202 against Lancashire at Purley, was the highest in the Championship in 1987. Passing 1,000 runs for the second successive season, he averaged more than 60, as did Darren Bicknell, who, in his first season, quickly won promotion to the first team. His 806 runs included 142 and 111 against Hampshire at The Oval and 163 against Yorkshire at Scarborough, where he and Zahid Sadiq (180) put on 287 for the third wicket. The bowling honours were shared, with nine players taking more than ten wickets. Off-spinner Chris Mays, a medical student at Middlesex Hospital, took seven for 40 against Middlesex at Guildford, while Graham Boxall, who bowled in only one match, took seven for 25 against Leicestershire at Uppingham.

Sussex, positively captained by Ian Waring after Peter Moores became a regular first-team player, shot up from fifteenth place to fourth, thanks to some excellent batting when chasing runs. Four players scored centuries, Keith Greenfield's 123 against Middlesex helping the county decide to offer him a contract for 1988. Another to impress was the leg-spinner, Andy Clarke, who bowled consistently and produced the only five-wicket return. All-rounder Meyrick Pringle from South Africa, in his first year, showed considerable promise.

Seven **Warwickshire** batsmen hit hundreds. Geoff Tedstone, who scored 169 against Yorkshire at Solihull, could always be relied on with the bat and behind the stumps; Dean Hodgson worked hard on his batting to score the most runs, and Jason Ratcliffe and Gareth Williamson caught the eye. Allan Donald took eleven for 45 against Glamorgan at Swansea, while Dean Hoffman did all that was asked of him with the ball, his 34 wickets including six for 39 against Somerset at Taunton. Robert Weir showed promise as a medium-pace bowler, but was restricted by injuries, and there were valuable contributions from off-spinners Adrian Pierson and Neil Smith.

Worcestershire's season saw improvements in individual performances, although the collective results were less encouraging. No batsman passed 500 runs. Lawrence Smith was the leading run-getter without scoring the weight of runs anticipated. In the drawn game against Gloucestershire at Bristol, hundreds came from Martin Weston (170), Gordon Lord (121 not out) and David Leatherdale (109). Leatherdale had an encouraging first season on the staff, and Jonathon Wright continued to show potential as a batsman. The attack was more penetrative than of late, with Stuart Lampitt, Steve McEwan, Ricardo Ellcock and left-arm spinner Richard Stemp all taking their wickets economically. Stuart Bevins, who joined the staff early in the summer, impressed behind the stumps.

Yorkshire, who had occupied twelfth and fifth places since winning the Championship in 1984, returned to the top of the table as joint winners with Kent. Their batting was strong, with four players passing 500 runs. Neil Nicholson hit two hundreds and six fifties to total 1,051 runs at an average of 55.31 and David Byas again scored heavily. Ian Swallow, Simon Dennis and Paul Booth all took more than 30 wickets, while Stuart Fletcher, who headed the averages, took his twenty wickets in only three appearances.

SECOND ELEVEN CHAMPIONSHIP, 1987

		Played	Won	Lost	Drawn	Bonus Points Batting	Bonus Points Bowling	Total Points	Average
1	{ Kent (13)	15	5	1	9*	35	40	163	10.87
	{ Yorkshire (5)	15	5	2	8	35	48	163	10.87
3	– Lancashire (1)	17	5	1	11*	38	53	179	10.53
4	– Sussex (15)	10	3	4	3	24	29	101	10.10
5	– Hampshire (14)	12	3	2	7	27	43	118	9.83
6	– Warwickshire (2)	16	4	7	5	32	52	148	9.25
7	– Glamorgan (17)	17	4	4	9	42	49	155	9.12
8	{ Surrey (10)	15	3	5	7	42	45	135	9.00
	{ Somerset (7)	11	3	4	4	18	33	99	9.00
10	– Leicestershire (6)	15	4	1	10	29	40	133	8.87
11	– Essex (3)	13	3	3	7	23	36	107	8.23
12	– Worcestershire (8)	10	2	2	6	23	27	82	8.20
13	– Northamptonshire (12) . .	13	2	3	8	27	43	102	7.85
14	– Middlesex (4)	13	2	0	11	23	32	87	6.69
15	– Nottinghamshire (11) . .	16	2	5	9	21	44	93†	5.81
16	– Gloucestershire (16) . .	13	1	4	8	23	30	69	5.31
17	– Derbyshire (9)	13	0	3	10	23	37	60	4.62

Kent and Yorkshire became joint champions by virtue of gaining equal average points and an equal number of wins.

1986 positions in brackets.

* Includes one tied match (8 pts each).

† Includes 12 points for a win in a one-innings match.

Note: The averages to determine the positions in the Championship are shown to two corrected decimal places.

In the averages that follow, * against a score signifies not out, * against a name signifies the captain and † signifies a wicket-keeper.

DERBYSHIRE SECOND ELEVEN

Matches 14: Lost – Lancashire, Nottinghamshire, Worcestershire. Drawn – Gloucestershire (twice), Lancashire, Leicestershire (twice), Northamptonshire (twice), Yorkshire (twice). Abandoned – Worcestershire.

Batting Averages

	M	I	NO	R	HI	Avge
*A. Hill	13	18	12	340	45*	56.66
R. Sharma	8	13	1	412	87	34.33
C. F. B. P. Rudd	8	15	1	453	84	32.35
A. M. Brown	13	23	1	643	74	29.22
M. Beardshall	8	11	2	174	45	19.33
D. Hallack	12	21	1	376	53*	18.80
T. J. G. O'Gorman	7	12	0	221	77	18.41
M. Wakefield	12	18	3	262	57*	17.46
A. G. Pierrepont	8	13	1	188	41*	15.66
†K. M. Krikken	9	15	0	213	56	14.20
W. Harper	3	4	0	50	25	12.50
F. A. Griffith	6	10	2	81	23	10.12
J. P. Taylor	12	16	8	69	16*	8.62
C. Marples	4	6	0	47	17	7.83

Also batted: D. J. Adams 0, 33, 3; I. S. Anderson 2, 96*, 70, 31*; T. J. Barry 10, 31, 19; R. J. Blitz 0, 39, 5; G. J. Carr 2, 6; R. J. Finney 32, 65*; J. Hurst 4, 17; M. Jean-Jacques 2; T. Kirk 2, 0; D. E. Malcolm 2; P. G. Newman 4; C. J. Rogers 2; C. A. Smith 5, 22; J. P. Tebay 4, 94; J. Tindale 2, 34.

Bowling Averages

	O	M	R	W	Avge
F. A. Griffith	100.3	20	264	13	20.30
M. Beardshall	166	43	386	19	20.31
A. G. Pierrepont	64	15	169	7	24.14
R. Sharma	229.1	65	490	19	25.78
C. F. B. P. Rudd	282.4	66	721	24	30.04
J. P. Taylor	333.5	68	950	24	39.58
M. Wakefield	228.3	79	534	11	48.54

Also bowled: D. J. Adams 26–4–99–1; I. S. Anderson 21–3–83–0; T. J. Barry 17–0–43–1; A. M. Brown 2–1–2–0; R. J. Finney 19–5–57–2; D. Hallack 4–0–18–1; W. Harper 20–3–51–1; A. Hill 20.1–6–85–2; M. Jean-Jacques 26–4–82–2; D. E. Malcolm 36–5–130–1; C. Marples 8.1–1–51–3; P. G. Newman 35–9–100–1; T. J. G. O'Gorman 7–0–53–0; J. Tindale 5–1–24–1.

ESSEX SECOND ELEVEN

Matches 14: Won – Gloucestershire, Nottinghamshire, Sussex. Lost – Northamptonshire, Surrey, Sussex. Drawn – Kent (twice), Middlesex (twice), Northamptonshire, Nottinghamshire, Surrey. Abandoned – Hampshire.

Batting Averages

	M	I	NO	R	HI	100s	Avge
I. Redpath	12	22	6	979	115*	1	61.18
N. Hussain	7	12	2	505	157*	1	50.50
R. N. Pook	13	22	1	769	106	2	36.61
C. Gladwin	8	13	0	372	90	0	28.61
I. L. Pont	9	12	2	265	60*	0	26.50
M. G. Field-Buss	12	21	1	425	73	0	21.25
A. Seymour	5	10	0	189	68	0	18.90
†A. D. Brown	13	19	6	239	38	0	18.38
C. J. Grinyer	11	17	1	282	60	0	17.62
P. R. Bushnell	7	7	2	88	24*	0	17.60
T. D. Topley	3	4	0	60	42	0	15.00
A. K. Golding	13	19	3	203	26	0	12.68
F. Griffith	3	5	0	54	27	0	10.80
*D. L. Acfield	9	9	4	48	17*	0	9.60

Played in four matches: *R. E. East, 17*, 8*. Played in three matches: J. H. Childs, 16*, 29*. Played in two matches: G. Ecclestone 2, 11, 53*; J. A. C. Williams 92, 5, 2*, 8. Played in one match: I. Binns 6, 37; B. Debenham 23, 9; M. George 4; J. Gregersen 13; N. V. Knight 2, 16*; P. J. Prichard 0, 8; N. Shahid 23, 10*; B. Sharpe 1, 0*.

Bowling Averages

	O	M	R	W	BB	Avge
C. Gladwin	46.3	12	142	8	6-35	17.75
I. L. Pont	216.4	47	605	34	4-22	17.79
J. H. Childs	110.5	40	228	10	4-50	22.80
A. K. Golding	410	103	1,239	43	6-67	28.81
F. Griffith	61	13	222	7	3-64	31.71
M. G. Field-Buss	263.4	69	717	22	4-36	32.59
C. J. Grinyer	180	39	531	13	4-50	40.84
D. L. Acfield	79.4	18	189	4	1-7	47.25
P. R. Bushnell	102	15	379	8	2-35	47.37
T. D. Topley	74.5	12	222	4	4-98	55.50

Also bowled: G. Ecclestone 10–1–33–1; I. Redpath 7–2–45–2; A. Seymour 4–0–19–0; N. Shahid 55–11–168–3; J. A. C. Williams 10–1–44–0.

GLAMORGAN SECOND ELEVEN

Matches 17: Won – Leicestershire, Nottinghamshire, Warwickshire, Worcestershire. Lost – Kent, Somerset, Warwickshire, Yorkshire. Drawn – Gloucestershire (twice), Lancashire, Leicestershire, Nottinghamshire, Somerset, Surrey, Worcestershire, Yorkshire.

Batting Averages

	M	I	NO	R	HI	100s	Avge
S. P. James	6	10	1	470	113	1	52.22
P. G. P. Roebuck	16	27	3	1,011	132	2	42.12
*J. A. Hopkins	11	16	0	670	130	2	41.87
J. Derrick	4	8	2	204	80	0	34.00
P. A. Cottey	14	23	1	697	136*	3	31.68
S. L. Watkin	9	11	7	123	54*	0	30.75
S. Peterson	4	8	1	205	131*	1	29.28
*A. Jones	5	5	2	77	49	0	25.66
P. D. North	15	24	4	469	82	0	23.45
M. J. Cann	10	17	1	359	65	0	22.43
G. A. Headley	4	5	0	97	38	0	19.40
S. Monkhouse	14	12	9	53	13*	0	17.66
S. W. Maddock	7	9	0	157	51	0	17.44
†M. L. Roberts	14	19	6	206	42*	0	15.84
S. J. Base	9	11	2	123	25	0	13.66
R. B. Croft	8	9	1	108	53	0	13.50

Also batted: S. Ball 4, 18, 6, 0; A. R. Butcher 131, 27, 44, 72; †K. Corby 2, 39; A. Dale 78, 2, 11; P. Dutton 14, 1; †A. M. Fraine 0; †A. Hardman 9, 22*; R. James 43*, 12*; S. J. Moorcroft 0, 0, 0, 0*; M. J. Newbold 11, 0*, 3*, 0; R. C. Ontong 21, 34; M. Saxelby 0, 7; I. Smith 4, 10, 46, 22; P. J. Tebay 2, 18; J. G. Thomas 12; P. A. Todd 5, 63; C. J. P. G. van Zyl 25*, 6, 25; J. Williams 1, 6*; S. Williams 14, 0, 1.

Bowling Averages

	O	M	R	W	BB	Avge
S. J. Base	281.3	53	737	34	6-83	21.67
S. Monkhouse	375.4	92	1,016	45	5-62	22.57
J. Derrick	111	21	333	12	4-76	27.75
S. L. Watkin	221.2	53	654	22	4-42	29.72

	O	M	R	W	BB	Avg
P. D. North	403.1	99	1,086	34	7-91	31.9
M. J. Cann	200.3	47	623	16	5-59	38.9
M. Davies	66	22	166	4	3-70	41.5
R. B. Croft	114	36	313	7	2-62	44.7

Also bowled: S. Ball 30–10–80–1; A. R. Butcher 20–0–85–5; P. A. Cottey 4.3–1–26–0; G. A. Headley 21–2–97–1; J. A. Hopkins 2–0–3–0; S. J. Moorcroft 80.2–15–275–4; M. J. Newbold 21–4–80–1; R. C. Ontong 49–11–157–5; P. G. P. Roebuck 29–4–90–0; M. Saxelby 22–3–94–5; I. Smith 61–18–130–2; J. G. Thomas 20–2–60–2; C. J. P. G. van Zyl 51–11–151–3.

GLOUCESTERSHIRE SECOND ELEVEN

Matches 13: Won – Somerset. Lost – Essex, Hampshire, Warwickshire, Worcestershire. Drawn Derbyshire (twice), Glamorgan (twice), Hampshire, Somerset, Warwickshire, Worcestershire.

Batting Averages

	M	I	NO	R	HI	100s	Avg
K. P. Tomlins	7	13	2	616	135*	3	56.0
N. J. Heaton	3	5	1	189	101	1	47.2
K. B. K. Ibadulla	9	17	3	627	83	0	44.7
V. S. Greene	6	10	3	236	51*	0	33.7
W. Johnson	7	13	2	328	106	1	29.8
P. N. Weekes	2	4	0	116	57	0	29.0
W. M. Smith	6	12	1	312	89	0	28.3
A. D. A. Chidgey	3	6	0	153	100	1	25.5
D. J. Taylor	12	17	4	327	42	0	25.1
M. C. Seaman	3	6	0	141	84	0	23.5
O. C. K. Smith	4	7	1	140	50	0	23.3
W. Weekes	2	4	1	70	38	0	23.3
*J. N. Shepherd	12	11	2	202	76	0	22.4
M. W. Pooley	9	13	2	238	55*	0	21.6
G. E. Sainsbury	5	7	1	116	51	0	19.3
D. J. Chubbs	7	8	4	50	24	0	12.5
D. A. Burrows	7	6	1	61	28	0	12.2
N. J. Pitts	3	5	1	47	20*	0	11.7
†A. J. Brassington	13	12	2	103	30	0	10.3
B. J. Debenham	3	6	0	60	33	0	10.0
J. A. Smith	3	3	2	10	5*	0	10.0

Played in two matches: M. C. C. Cox 2, 0; I. McLaren 26, 8; K. Roscoe 4*, 1; A. M. Smith 10*, 0. Played in one match: M. W. Alleyne 77, 36*; I. P. C. Blakemore 18, 14; M. Challenger 32, 1; M. Collinson 1; D. A. Graveney 33*; P. I. King 3; B. A. Mayers 80, 0; N. M. Pritchard 5, 0; J. B. White 0; A. J. Wright 34, 2.

Bowling Averages

	O	M	R	W	BB	Avg
D. A. Graveney	55.2	24	103	8	4-51	12.8
K. P. Tomlins	13.4	2	33	2	2-11	16.50
V. S. Greene	163.5	37	344	19	4-42	18.10
G. E. Sainsbury	104	39	182	10	2-23	18.2
A. M. Smith	55	15	133	6	4-20	22.1
J. N. Shepherd	170	56	383	17	4-19	22.52
D. A. Burrows	60.2	18	171	7	2-7	24.42
D. J. Chubbs	131	35	325	9	5-65	36.11
W. M. Smith	69.3	17	183	5	3-30	36.60
K. Roscoe	96	34	221	6	4-71	36.8
M. W. Pooley	126.1	22	422	10	3-20	42.20
D. J. Taylor	294	60	929	19	3-44	48.89

Also bowled: M. W. Alleyne 3–0–11–0; I. P. C. Blakemore 10.1–2–37–0; M. Collinson 7–4–31–0; M. C. C. Cox 83–30–195–3; N. J. Heaton 9–1–24–0; K. B. K. Ibadulla 34.2–8–124–3; W. Johnson 6–3–14–1; P. I. King 21–2–63–1; I. McLaren 47–6–134–3; N. J. Pitts 54–12–172–2; J. A. Smith 25.3–7–73–0; O. C. K. Smith 39.3–7–125–1; P. N. Weekes 45.3–5–148–0; W. Weekes 38–5–142–2; J. B. White 2.2–1–1–0.

HAMPSHIRE SECOND ELEVEN

Matches 13: Won – Gloucestershire, Somerset, Surrey. Lost – Somerset, Sussex. Drawn – Gloucestershire, Kent (twice), Middlesex (twice), Surrey, Sussex. Abandoned – Essex.

Batting Averages

	M	I	NO	R	HI	100s	Avge
R. A. Smith	3	6	1	342	106	1	68.40
R. J. Scott	12	22	2	836	163*	3	41.80
J. R. Ayling	12	20	4	621	122	1	38.81
N. G. Cowley	4	7	1	220	91	0	36.66
K. D. James	2	4	0	131	55	0	32.75
*T. C. Middleton	12	22	2	585	84	0	29.25
R. R. Savage	2	4	1	82	51*	0	27.33
M. E. O'Connor	11	19	0	498	74	0	26.21
†A. N. Aymes	12	19	7	286	47*	0	23.83
I. J. Chivers	12	16	2	325	68	0	23.21
C. A. Connor	5	4	1	56	24	0	18.66
P. J. Bakker	11	11	5	97	40*	0	16.16
S. J. W. Andrew	3	4	2	30	22	0	15.00
R. M. F. Cox	6	9	0	129	39	0	14.33
M. R. Newton	7	6	1	68	26	0	13.60
S. D. Udal	3	3	1	26	11	0	13.00
K. J. Shine	12	9	3	14	7	0	2.33

Played in one match: R. J. Maru 14*, 9; V. P. Terry 72*; P. R. C. Came did not bat.

Bowling Averages

	O	M	R	W	BB	Avge
R. J. Maru	51.2	17	128	8	5-76	16.00
S. D. Udal	45.4	13	127	7	4-40	18.14
J. R. Ayling	153	46	428	23	5-61	18.60
P. J. Bakker	321.2	80	850	35	5-51	24.28
C. A. Connor	176.3	33	465	19	6-68	24.47
K. J. Shine	257.3	51	794	30	4-21	26.46
N. G. Cowley	138	38	358	13	5-94	27.53
S. J. W. Andrew	88.3	18	226	7	3-50	32.28
I. J. Chivers	365.1	105	1,070	29	4-99	36.89

Also bowled: K. D. James 14–8–26–1; T. C. Middleton 1–0–9–0; M. R. Newton 115–25–399–2; R. J. Scott 32–9–93–3; R. A. Smith 8.3–2–28–0.

KENT SECOND ELEVEN

Matches 16: Won – Glamorgan, Lancashire, Surrey, Sussex, Yorkshire. Lost – Surrey. Drawn – Essex (twice), Hampshire (twice), Middlesex (twice), Somerset, Yorkshire. Tied – Lancashire. Abandoned – Sussex.

Batting Averages

	I	NO	R	HI	100s	Avge
R. F. Pienaar	9	0	444	124	2	49.33
†V. J. Wells	26	4	926	153*	1	42.09
T. R. Ward	28	3	1,011	212*	1	40.44
S. C. Goldsmith	26	3	920	152*	3	40.00
*R. A. Woolmer	6	4	77	20	0	38.50
C. Penn	6	3	110	66*	0	36.66
M. A. Ealham	19	7	359	76	0	29.91
†P. Farbrace	18	5	346	87	0	28.83
D. J. Sabine	25	0	601	66	0	24.04
G. R. Cowdrey	8	0	181	46	0	22.62
M. C. Dobson	15	1	241	60	0	17.21
R. M. Ellison	8	1	112	30	0	16.00
D. J. M. Kelleher	13	3	130	29	0	13.00
P. Roshier	12	4	104	47	0	13.00
R. P. Davis	11	1	76	25	0	7.60
N. Llong	9	1	59	18	0	7.37

Also batted: E. A. E. Baptiste 0, 4; J. Creed 7, 8; J. Day 60, 0; M. V. Fleming 11, 41, 56*; R. Hart 15, 11; J. Hinks 3, 25; S. G. Hinks 0, 41*, 4, 29; A. P. Igglesden 3, 8, 23*, 5; K. B. S. Jarvis 15, 2*, 7; J. I. Longley 74, 31, 43; R. Thomas 15, 0, 2; T. Wren 31*; A. McAvan did not bat.

Bowling Averages

	O	M	R	W	Avge
E. A. E. Baptiste	25	8	53	4	13.25
M. V. Fleming	36.1	13	83	6	13.83
R. Hart	46	12	151	8	18.87
K. B. S. Jarvis	93.5	21	227	12	18.91
A. P. Igglesden	64	19	127	6	21.16
R. A. Woolmer	54	5	171	7	24.42
R. P. Davis	457.1	143	1,199	49	24.46
R. F. Pienaar	170.2	43	461	18	25.61
D. J. M. Kelleher	250.4	58	766	26	29.46
P. Roshier	255.4	60	787	18	43.72
N. Llong	105	26	359	8	44.87
M. C. Dobson	59	10	182	4	45.50
C. Penn	74	16	195	4	48.75
D. J. Sabine	169	23	655	9	72.77

Also bowled: G. R. Cowdrey 23–5–65–2; J. Day 11–3–24–2; M. A. Ealham 34–5–154–2; R. M. Ellison 10–2–34–1; S. C. Goldsmith 4–0–22–0; S. G. Hinks 7–1–17–1; A. McAvan 12–1–39–0; V. J. Wells 41–6–146–3; T. Wren 23–4–78–1.

LANCASHIRE SECOND ELEVEN

Matches 18: Won – Derbyshire, Northamptonshire, Somerset, Warwickshire (twice). Lost – Kent. Drawn – Derbyshire, Glamorgan, Leicestershire (twice), Northamptonshire, Nottinghamshire (twice), Surrey (twice), Yorkshire. Tied – Kent. Abandoned – Yorkshire.

Batting Averages

	M	I	NO	R	HI	100s	Avge
D. W. Varey	3	5	0	325	104	1	65.00
*J. Abrahams	11	14	3	697	112*	2	63.36
K. A. Hayes	9	11	2	452	115	1	50.22
M. A. Atherton	3	3	0	149	110	1	49.66
J. D. Fitton	16	19	6	616	141	1	47.38
M. Watkinson	3	5	1	185	85	0	46.25

	M	I	NO	R	HI	100s	Avge
*M. R. Chadwick	14	22	2	833	108	2	41.65
A. N. Hayhurst	12	16	2	548	91	0	39.14
N. J. Speak	15	22	1	736	101	1	35.04
S. Henriksen	5	6	2	118	53*	0	29.50
I. C. Davidson	15	19	9	290	104*	1	29.00
S. J. O'Shaughnessy	9	11	0	311	114	1	28.27
†C. Maynard	2	3	0	75	56	0	25.00
†W. K. Hegg	7	6	1	121	55*	0	24.20
I. D. Austin	11	13	1	282	84	0	23.50
†J. Macauley	8	6	3	59	29*	0	19.66
M. A. Crawley	3	4	1	59	50*	0	19.66
G. D. Lloyd	7	10	1	176	74	0	19.55
S. P. Titchard	5	8	2	91	45	0	15.16
K. W. McLeod	9	6	0	51	18	0	8.50
A. J. Murphy	10	5	2	9	7*	0	3.00

Played in two matches: G. J. Bolton 5*, 2; P. J. Martin 19*; B. P. Patterson did not bat.
Played in one match: P. Ferriday 2; I. Folley 30, 12; †J. Stanworth 18*, 9; I. Ali did not bat.

Bowling Averages

	O	M	R	W	BB	Avge
I. Folley	39	19	64	5	3-47	12.80
I. D. Austin	185.4	56	402	30	6-25	13.40
B. P. Patterson	51	14	139	10	7-51	13.90
I. Ali	34	8	84	5	3-37	16.80
J. Abrahams	124	27	313	18	4-60	17.38
J. D. Fitton	484.4	131	1,258	68	7-92	18.50
G. J. Bolton	39	9	109	4	3-39	27.25
S. Henriksen	78.2	18	225	8	3-33	28.12
A. N. Hayhurst	204.4	40	575	18	4-55	31.94
A. J. Murphy	194.2	41	584	18	3-73	32.44
K. W. McLeod	138.3	33	370	11	3-34	33.63
M. Watkinson	146.4	34	390	10	3-83	39.00
I. C. Davidson	218	46	705	18	3-66	39.16

Also bowled: M. A. Atherton 5-0-15-0; M. A. Crawley 22.5-3-95-2; P. Ferriday 1-0-3-0;
K. A. Hayes 4-2-8-2; P. J. Martin 22-4-80-0; C. Maynard 5-0-34-0; S. J. O'Shaughnessy
66-13-247-3; N. J. Speak 4-0-14-0.

LEICESTERSHIRE SECOND ELEVEN

Matches 17: Won – Nottinghamshire, Surrey, Warwickshire (twice). Lost – Glamorgan. Drawn – Derbyshire (twice), Glamorgan, Lancashire (twice), Middlesex, Northamptonshire, Nottinghamshire, Surrey, Worcestershire. Abandoned – Northamptonshire, Worcestershire.

Batting Averages

	I	NO	R	HI	100s	Avge
C. C. Lewis	13	4	505	130	1	56.11
P. B. Clift	4	0	192	99	0	48.00
L. Potter	11	2	357	85	0	39.66
P. Hepworth	17	5	413	83*	0	34.41
N. E. Briers	6	2	129	54	0	32.25
I. P. Butcher	9	0	255	100	1	28.33
J. D. R. Benson	19	0	486	156	0	25.57
R. A. Cobb	8	0	178	50	0	22.25
P. D. Bowler	24	4	444	63	0	22.20
W. K. M. Benjamin	7	1	131	49	0	21.83
†P. Gill	12	3	195	37*	0	21.66

	I	NO	R	HI	100s	Avge
D. J. Billington	13	3	216	61	0	21.60
L. Tennant	15	2	190	43*	0	14.61
M. Blackett	19	2	220	36	0	12.94
G. J. F. Ferris	5	1	35	14*	0	8.75
W. G. Lovell	8	6	9	6	0	4.50

Also batted: J. C. Balderstone 14, 41*, 20*, 26*; T. J. Boon 7, 4*; M. I. Gidley 24; J. E. S. Joseph 24, 11*; J. R. Lumley 3, 43; P. M. Such 6*; L. B. Taylor 4, 1, 14, 0.

Bowling Averages

	O	M	R	W	BB	Avge
P. B. Clift	102.5	40	147	14	4-18	10.50
G. J. F. Ferris	221.3	51	484	38	8-33	12.73
C. C. Lewis	338.4	84	816	46	6-35	17.73
W. K. M. Benjamin	130	26	262	13	3-25	20.15
L. B. Taylor	136	23	331	13	4-55	25.46
P. D. Bowler	184.4	44	446	16	4-54	27.87
L. Tennant	285.5	44	860	29	6-38	29.65
W. G. Lovell	178.1	42	479	14	5-65	34.21
L. Potter	131.4	51	283	7	3-22	40.42

Also bowled: J. D. R. Benson 29–7–85–2; M. Blackett 1–0–5–0; N. E. Briers 18–8–31–3; T. J. Boon 1–0–5–0; I. P. Butcher 6–2–15–1; M. I. Gidley 9.1–5–16–2; K. Higgs 2–0–6–0; J. E. S. Joseph 9–2–29–2; P. M. Such 84–7–193–3.

MIDDLESEX SECOND ELEVEN

Matches 15: Won – Surrey, Sussex. Drawn – Essex (twice), Hampshire (twice), Kent (twice), Leicestershire, Northamptonshire, Sussex, Warwickshire (twice). Abandoned – Northamptonshire, Surrey.

Batting Averages

	M	I	NO	R	HI	Avge
A. J. T. Miller	8	8	0	523	163	65.37
†K. R. Brown	7	10	2	405	100*	50.62
M. R. Ramprakash	3	5	0	224	84	44.80
J. F. Sykes	12	16	3	486	125	37.38
M. A. Roseberry	8	11	2	336	78	37.33
N. G. Cowans	7	4	3	32	15*	32.00
G. K. Brown	12	16	3	370	79	28.46
A. Needham	5	5	2	85	27*	28.33
C. T. Radley	2	3	0	80	75	26.66
N. R. C. MacLaurin	12	18	4	362	75	25.85
I. J. F. Hutchinson	12	18	4	243	42	17.35
N. F. Williams	4	3	1	32	27*	16.00
†C. H. H. Pegg	4	3	0	36	27	12.00
P. C. R. Tufnell	8	3	2	9	9*	9.00
A. G. J. Fraser	13	8	1	61	21	8.71
D. M. Kutner	2	3	0	16	13	5.33

Played in four matches: †R. J. Sims 12, 0. Played in three matches: A. R. C. Fraser 15*, 10; P. N. Weekes 9, 4*. Played in two matches: J. D. Carr 288 runs; R. A. Davidson 0; S. P. Hughes 21. Played in one match: A. A. Barnett 1; R. O. Butcher 59; M. Keech 8; C. Remy 2, 3; P. Malik, R. A. Nixon and J. C. Pooley did not bat.

Bowling Averages

	O	M	R	W	Avge
P. Malik	35.1	8	85	5	17.00
A. A. Barnett	49	23	75	4	18.75
N. G. Cowans	141	48	296	15	19.73
A. R. C. Fraser	109.3	33	234	11	21.27
P. C. R. Tufnell	275.3	96	647	30	21.56
J. F. Sykes	262	81	580	26	22.30
P. N. Weekes	69.5	19	256	11	23.27
A. Needham	65	18	193	7	27.57
D. M. Kutner	37	9	112	4	28.00
S. P. Hughes	70.1	25	165	5	33.00
A. G. J. Fraser	243.3	43	850	23	36.95
N. F. Williams	102	25	254	5	50.80

Also bowled: G. K. Brown 48–8–200–3; J. D. Carr 10–1–34–0; R. A. Davidson 28–6–86–3; N. R. C. MacLaurin 2–1–5–0; C. Remy 4–0–11–0.

NORTHAMPTONSHIRE SECOND ELEVEN

Matches 15: Won – Essex, Nottinghamshire. Lost – Lancashire, Yorkshire (twice). Drawn – Derbyshire (twice), Essex, Lancashire, Leicestershire, Middlesex, Nottinghamshire, Worcestershire. Abandoned – Leicestershire, Middlesex.

Batting Averages

	M	I	NO	R	HI	100s	Avge
A. Fordham	4	7	1	334	112*	1	55.66
R. J. Boyd-Moss	8	15	1	702	120	1	50.14
†S. N. V. Waterton	11	19	3	725	94	0	45.31
T. Scriven	12	19	6	481	101*	1	37.00
M. R. Gouldstone	4	8	0	226	92	0	28.25
G. B. Stevenson	13	22	3	493	95	0	25.94
N. A. Stanley	13	22	1	528	97	0	25.14
B. R. Hartland	12	22	2	502	71	0	25.10
*R. M. Carter	12	15	6	178	40*	0	19.77
S. J. Brown	5	5	3	38	23	0	19.00
G. Smith	11	14	2	143	40*	0	11.91
M. Baker	11	16	1	169	42*	0	11.26
M. A. Robinson	12	12	7	19	4*	0	3.80

Also batted: R. J. Bailey 4, 59; N. G. B. Cook 8, 6; A. Goldsmith 19, 12; J. Hughes 2; S. Inwood 23, 15; J. Lumley 1, 9, 2; †W. Noon 5*, 5; †M. Olley 4, 1; A. Penberthy 5, 54*; A. Proud 36, 10; A. Roberts 1; I. Salisbury 0, 20, 0, 4.

Bowling Averages

	O	M	R	W	BB	Avge
N. A. Stanley	27	1	105	4	2-38	26.25
T. Scriven	369.4	111	916	34	4-26	26.94
G. Smith	206.4	46	641	22	4-68	29.13
M. A. Robinson	277	54	853	29	5-72	29.41
R. J. Boyd-Moss	177	48	470	15	3-54	31.33
S. J. Brown	94	22	281	8	2-47	35.12
G. B. Stevenson	236.5	47	763	20	4-44	38.15
M. Baker	139	21	504	10	2-40	50.40

Also bowled: R. J. Bailey 5–0–24–1; R. M. Carter 13–0–77–1; N. G. B. Cook 47–12–124–3; M. R. Gouldstone 6–0–47–1; B. R. Hartland 3–0–19–0; J. Hughes 5–1–21–0; J. Lumley 5–0–30–1; A. Penberthy 4–1–15–0; A. Proud 10–1–22–2; A. Roberts 30.2–10–100–3.

NOTTINGHAMSHIRE SECOND ELEVEN

Matches 16: Won – Derbyshire, Warwickshire (one-innings match). Lost – Essex, Glamorgan, Leicestershire, Northamptonshire, Yorkshire. Drawn – Derbyshire, Essex, Glamorgan, Lancashire (twice), Leicestershire, Northamptonshire, Sussex, Yorkshire.

Batting Averages

	M	I	NO	R	HI	100s	Avge
J. D. Birch	2	4	0	150	89	0	37.50
R. J. Evans	9	15	0	559	109	1	37.26
P. Pollard	12	20	1	667	171	3	35.10
C. J. Stockdale	5	8	1	236	86	0	33.71
D. J. Millns	12	14	8	202	58*	0	33.66
N. Fenwick	2	4	2	67	31*	0	33.50
D. J. R. Martindale	10	17	3	437	67*	0	31.21
A. Somani	12	19	4	450	128	2	30.00
C. D. Fraser-Darling	15	20	4	429	111	1	26.81
K. P. Evans	16	26	3	604	100*	1	26.26
D. S. Morgan	2	3	0	75	36	0	25.00
†C. W. Scott	9	15	3	226	37	0	18.83
G. D. Harding	8	11	4	111	37	0	15.85
M. Newell	5	7	0	111	45	0	15.85
*M. K. Bore	7	8	1	107	30	0	15.28
K. Blackburn	2	4	0	58	29	0	14.50
G. W. Mike	13	15	1	179	64	0	12.78
N. R. Gaywood	2	3	0	33	19	0	11.00
F. J. Cooke	5	4	0	35	34	0	8.75
K. E. Cooper	7	8	1	52	13	0	7.42
J. A. Afford	7	6	2	27	13	0	6.75
S. M. Brogan	4	7	0	25	12	0	3.57

Played in one match: G. F. Archer 26; J. Bovill 4*, 0; N. D. J. Cartmell 40, 0; B. Cruse 0, 0; P. J. Delaney 13, 6; D. E. Ellcock 14, 0; D. W. Randall 50, 15; G. R. Sanders 25*; M. Saxelby 38; R. A. Pick did not bat.

Bowling Averages

	O	M	R	W	BB	Avge
M. K. Bore	223.2	92	406	26	5-30	15.61
K. E. Cooper	191.5	59	473	23	4-15	20.56
D. J. Millns	301.3	64	1,052	44	6-43	23.90
K. P. Evans	331.4	99	861	34	4-48	25.32
G. W. Mike	131.1	29	473	15	4-51	31.53
R. J. Evans	26	2	131	4	3-78	32.75
C. D. Fraser-Darling	277.1	63	914	26	5-54	35.15
J. A. Afford	152	38	417	7	3-27	59.57

Also bowled: J. Bovill 13–9–19–1; B. Cruse 4–1–23–0; D. E. Ellcock 39–7–129–1; N. Fenwick 8–0–34–1; G. D. Harding 57.2–8–214–2; D. J. R. Martindale 0.5–0–4–0; D. S. Morgan 6–1–23–0; M. Newell 2–1–4–1; P. Pollard 2–0–23–0; M. Saxelby 10–1–45–1; A. Somani 64–15–237–2; C. J. Stockdale 6.3–0–43–0.

SOMERSET SECOND ELEVEN

Matches 11: Won – Glamorgan, Hampshire, Worcestershire. Lost – Gloucestershire, Hampshire, Lancashire, Warwickshire. Drawn – Glamorgan, Gloucestershire, Kent, Worcestershire.

Batting Averages

	M	I	NO	R	HI	Avge
B. C. Rose	2	3	1	122	78*	61.00
M. J. Greatbatch	10	19	5	830	181	59.28
J. C. M. Atkinson	6	11	2	353	129	39.22
G. V. Palmer	3	4	2	78	33*	39.00
R. J. Bartlett	8	14	1	367	70	28.23
N. J. Pringle	6	11	1	256	104*	25.60
R. Baigent	5	10	0	247	99	24.70
R. J. Harden	4	7	0	157	66	22.42
J. G. Wyatt	10	19	2	374	113*	22.00
†T. Gard	10	14	2	244	66	20.33
M. D. Harman	5	8	3	74	18	14.80
P. A. C. Bail	3	6	0	75	23	12.50
M. Cleal	6	9	1	90	17	11.25
H. R. J. Trump	4	7	1	63	27*	10.50
R. G. Woolston	8	10	3	65	28*	9.28
A. R. Phillips	3	5	2	25	12*	8.33
D. J. Foster	9	10	2	54	14	6.75

Played in one match: D. Beal 27*, 3; R. Blackburn 8, 4; M. R. Davis 23, 22; N. A. Felton 14; R. G. Furse 2; S. Hooper 2, 1; C. C. Lovell 33, 31; P. J. Rendall 3, 2; P. J. Robinson 5*; P. M. Roebuck 53, 16; G. Townsend 115*, 81; R. G. Twose 1, 1; C. H. Dredge and A. Kite did not bat.

Bowling Averages

	O	M	R	W	BB	Avge
G. V. Palmer	102.3	31	212	18	6-61	11.77
M. D. Harman	206	62	463	22	7-41	21.04
R. G. Woolston	367.2	100	756	28	4-15	27.00
H. R. J. Trump	98.4	18	338	9	2-23	37.55
C. H. Dredge	33	7	113	3	2-22	37.66
D. J. Foster	206.3	21	722	19	6-56	38.00
N. J. Pringle	134.5	28	455	10	3-71	45.50
M. Cleal	83	12	292	6	4-74	48.66
J. C. M. Atkinson	73	10	242	4	2-67	60.50
A. R. Phillips	61.3	1	245	4	3-66	61.25

Also bowled: R. Baigent 7–1–35–1; R. J. Bartlett 20.5–3–90–1; D. Beal 13–0–54–1; M. R. Davis 29.4–4–84–3; R. G. Furse 10–4–14–1; M. J. Greatbatch 2–0–11–0; R. J. Harden 23–0–96–1; A. Kite 4–0–23–0; C. C. Lovell 6–0–28–0; P. J. Rendall 26–7–54–2; P. J. Robinson 7–3–27–1; P. M. Roebuck 1–0–11–0.

SURREY SECOND ELEVEN

Matches 17: Won – Essex, Kent, Sussex. Lost – Hampshire, Kent, Leicestershire, Middlesex, Yorkshire. Drawn – Essex, Glamorgan, Hampshire, Lancashire (twice), Leicestershire, Yorkshire. Abandoned – Middlesex, Sussex.

Batting Averages

	M	I	NO	R	HI	Avge
D. J. Bicknell	8	13	1	806	163	67.16
D. M. Ward	12	19	1	1,161	202	64.50
C. S. Mays	7	9	4	171	39*	34.20
P. D. Atkins	15	24	1	698	102*	30.34
N. J. Falkner	12	21	4	506	66*	29.76
Zahid Sadiq	14	22	1	612	180	29.14
M. P. Bicknell	5	7	3	109	50*	27.25

	M	I	NO	R	HI	Avge
R. J. Doughty	12	19	3	367	71	22.93
C. K. Bullen	7	12	0	268	77	22.33
J. D. Robinson	5	8	0	102	59	12.75
N. Peters	11	15	4	127	30*	11.54
N. M. Kendrick	12	13	3	96	17	9.60
*C. E. Waller	12	8	1	60	26	8.57
†G. E. Brown	10	11	1	54	12	5.40

Also batted: J. Boiling 4, 1; G. Boxall 80, 16*, 2, 0, 0; M. A. Feltham 9, 7, 20, 4; M. Frost 2, 4, 1*; A. H. Gray 2, 1, 2*; K. T. Medlycott 6, 14, 39, 0, 7; K. Piper 8, 5, 1, 25, 21; D. M. Smith 76; A. J. Stewart 20, 9; D. J. Thomas 45, 1, 9, 69.

Bowling Averages

	O	M	R	W	Avge
G. Boxall	16.5	5	43	7	6.14
A. H. Gray	46	9	119	9	13.22
M. P. Bicknell	128	32	299	20	14.95
K. T. Medlycott	79	21	228	13	17.53
D. J. Thomas	54	10	149	7	21.28
C. S. Mays	248.4	84	622	29	21.44
M. Frost	62	16	250	11	22.72
C. E. Waller	189	64	406	15	27.06
J. D. Robinson	57	15	143	5	28.60
R. J. Doughty	344.4	54	1,119	35	31.97
C. K. Bullen	212	70	470	14	33.57
N. Peters	183	50	559	16	34.93
N. M. Kendrick	310	60	794	19	41.78

Also bowled: P. D. Atkins 1–0–6–1; D. J. Bicknell 8–1–44–0; J. Boiling 19–5–47–0; M. A. Feltham 38–4–127–1; D. M. Ward 11–0–62–2.

SUSSEX SECOND ELEVEN

Matches 12: Won – Essex, Hampshire, Warwickshire. Lost – Essex, Kent, Middlesex, Surrey. Drawn – Hampshire, Middlesex, Nottinghamshire. Abandoned – Kent, Surrey.

Batting Averages

	M	I	NO	R	HI	100s	Avge
S. T. Jefferies	3	6	2	226	87*	0	56.50
R. I. Alikhan	2	4	0	187	115	1	46.75
S. J. S. Kimber	4	8	1	287	73	0	41.00
D. A. Reeve	3	6	0	245	162	1	40.83
M. W. Pringle	4	7	1	227	66	0	37.83
R. Hanley	3	5	1	150	64*	0	37.50
*†P. Moores	3	5	1	129	61	0	32.25
†S. D. Myles	9	17	1	461	101*	1	28.81
C. Wilkinson	3	5	1	106	52	0	26.50
K. Greenfield	7	13	0	336	123	1	25.84
J. R. Prentis	3	6	0	151	37	0	25.16
C. I. O. Ricketts	8	14	3	267	77	0	24.27
A. J. Pugh	7	13	2	235	72*	0	21.36
A. Hansford	2	4	1	58	23	0	19.33
A. R. Clarke	4	6	2	76	29	0	19.00
D. K. Standing	5	10	1	158	62	0	17.55
I. C. Waring	6	11	0	149	35	0	13.54
†M. P. Speight	5	9	0	98	44	0	10.88
P. V. Boarer	6	9	4	44	12*	0	8.80
P. A. W. Heseltine ...	5	5	2	26	15	0	8.66
A. M. Babington	3	3	2	7	4*	0	7.00

Played in two matches: R. A. Bunting 14, 9*; G. S. Garton 15, 2; C. Hartridge 40, 16. Played in one match: A. J. Goldsmith 24, 10; A. M. Green 36, 2; J. W. Hall 36, 17; N. J. Lenham 56, 0; D. J. Panto 14, 0*; J. Roycroft 11, 3; P. Smith 25, 1; A. P. Wells 48, 42. G. Spencer did not bat.

Bowling Averages

	O	M	R	W	BB	Avge
D. A. Reeve	80	21	187	12	4-35	15.58
A. M. Babington	86	16	225	11	4-44	20.45
M. W. Pringle	84.1	13	291	14	4-41	20.78
A. Hansford	36	8	118	5	3-51	23.60
A. R. Clarke	99.3	26	262	11	5-82	23.81
C. Wilkinson	47	14	110	4	4-45	27.50
S. T. Jefferies	85.1	11	280	10	4-52	28.00
D. K. Standing	47.4	11	144	5	2-31	28.80
S. J. S. Kimber	58.3	14	211	7	4-56	30.14
S. D. Myles	38.1	3	139	4	1-1	34.75
P. A. W. Heseltine	101.4	19	323	9	3-63	35.88
C. I. O. Ricketts	178.2	43	582	13	3-64	44.76
P. V. Boarer	103	19	372	8	3-57	46.50
I. C. Waring	101.5	18	321	5	2-46	64.20

Also bowled: R. I. Alikhan 2–0–9–0; R. A. Bunting 33–8–91–2; G. S. Garton 12–2–58–1; C. Hartridge 11.5–1–34–1; D. J. Panto 31–9–77–1; G. Spencer 7–1–37–1.

WARWICKSHIRE SECOND ELEVEN

Matches 17: Won – Glamorgan, Gloucestershire, Somerset, Yorkshire. Lost – Glamorgan, Lancashire (twice), Leicestershire (twice), Nottinghamshire (one innings match), Sussex. Drawn – Gloucestershire, Middlesex (twice), Worcestershire, Yorkshire. Abandoned – Worcestershire.

Batting Averages

	M	I	NO	R	HI	100s	Avge
A. J. Moles	2	3	1	163	122*	1	81.50
P. G. Clark	2	4	1	178	98	0	59.33
A. C. Storie	5	9	2	373	161*	1	53.28
D. A. Thorne	4	6	0	278	186	1	46.33
†G. A. Tedstone	11	17	3	576	169	1	41.14
G. D. Hodgson	9	17	1	625	110	1	39.06
Asif Din	3	6	0	172	84	0	28.66
D. C. Percival	8	15	1	377	101*	1	26.92
J. R. Lumley	2	4	0	102	39	0	25.50
A. A. Donald	6	11	4	175	40*	0	25.00
R. N. Abberley	11	11	1	242	94*	0	24.20
T. A. Merrick	4	5	0	121	67	0	24.20
J. D. Ratcliffe	9	15	0	344	76	0	22.93
L. A. Vorster	3	4	0	91	46	0	22.75
G. M. Charlesworth	4	8	1	152	66*	0	21.71
G. P. Williamson	7	11	1	210	125	1	21.00
A. R. K. Pierson	10	17	1	334	51	0	20.87
N. M. K. Smith	14	21	0	365	76	0	17.38
T. A. Munton	3	4	1	46	25*	0	15.33
S. J. Green	4	7	1	83	34	0	13.83
J. R. Riley	6	10	2	103	40	0	12.87
D. S. Hoffman	8	8	3	59	42	0	11.80
E. T. Milburn	11	16	0	172	40	0	10.75
R. S. Weir	6	7	3	38	11	0	9.50
†W. K. Badger	3	4	0	29	18	0	7.25
M. A. J. Bell	3	3	0	20	8	0	6.66
A. Smith-Butler	2	3	1	7	5*	0	3.50
I. G. Steer	4	5	0	14	6	0	2.80
O. Chagar	2	4	0	4	3	0	1.33

Played in two matches: K. A. Bridge 0, 4; C. Notton 0*, 7, 6*. Played in one match: M. Clewley 0*, 0*; S. D. Lerigo 0; M. Smith 5, 34; P. A. Smith 5; K. Thomas 8, 1; P. W. Threlfall 0*, 0.

Bowling Averages

	O	M	R	W	BB	Avge
T. A. Merrick	139.5	33	331	24	7-29	13.79
A. A. Donald	179	45	462	27	6-25	17.11
T. A. Munton	103.3	27	287	16	5-43	17.93
D. S. Hoffman	198.5	47	643	34	6-39	18.91
G. M. Charlesworth	59	15	160	6	2-51	26.66
A. R. K. Pierson	237.4	54	672	24	4-120	28.00
R. S. Weir	143	33	453	16	4-46	28.31
J. R. Riley	95.2	8	427	15	8-74	28.46
N. M. K. Smith	222.5	52	725	22	4-103	32.95
A. Smith-Butler	57	19	170	5	3-64	34.00
E. T. Milburn	154.2	28	478	14	4-45	34.14
M. A. J. Bell	60.2	8	231	6	3-57	38.50

Also bowled: Asif Din 12–3–28–2; O. Chagar 39–5–100–3; M. Clewley 12–0–89–0; S. J. Green 6–0–36–1; S. D. Lerigo 12–0–32–1; A. J. Moles 7–1–22–1; C. Notton 23–4–77–3; J. D. Ratcliffe 0.1–0–4–0; M. Smith 7–0–21–0; D. A. Thorne 3–1–3–0; P. W. Threlfall 10–1–42–1; G. P. Williamson 23–5–59–3.

WORCESTERSHIRE SECOND ELEVEN

Matches 13: Won – Derbyshire, Gloucestershire. Lost – Glamorgan, Somerset. Drawn – Glamorgan, Gloucestershire, Leicestershire, Northamptonshire, Somerset, Warwickshire. Abandoned – Derbyshire, Leicestershire, Warwickshire.

Batting Averages

	M	I	NO	R	HI	Avge
M. J. Weston	4	6	1	283	170	56.60
R. D. Stemp	5	3	2	48	38*	48.00
G. J. Lord	5	10	3	316	121*	45.14
M. S. Scott	10	10	7	113	30	37.66
P. Bent	9	13	3	338	166*	33.80
S. R. Lampitt	6	7	0	221	82	31.57
L. K. Smith	10	18	2	455	92	28.43
D. A. Leatherdale	9	13	1	326	109	27.16
J. P. Wright	10	16	1	407	85*	27.13
R. M. Ellcock	10	11	2	241	54*	26.77
C. M. Tolley	8	12	2	214	34*	21.40
S. M. McEwan	7	7	2	95	35	19.00
A. D. Breakwell	2	4	0	43	25	10.75
†S. R. Bevins	8	10	1	53	15*	5.88

Played in two matches: †S. Bramhall 16*. Played in one match: G. R. Haynes 51, 3*; R. K. Illingworth 5; R. F. Pienaar 112, 11*; A. P. Rees 23, 2; C. J. Stephens did not bat.

Bowling Averages

	O	M	R	W	Avge
R. K. Illingworth	61.5	34	65	9	7.22
P. Bent	79.2	29	155	9	17.22
S. R. Lampitt	114.3	31	292	15	19.46
R. D. Stemp	214.3	72	480	23	20.86
S. M. McEwan	250.4	57	672	29	23.17
R. F. Pienaar	41.5	9	130	5	26.00
R. M. Ellcock	281	52	821	31	26.48
D. A. Leatherdale	106	18	449	10	44.90
M. J. Weston	99	19	298	5	59.60

Also bowled: A. D. Breakwell 3–0–26–0; G. R. Haynes 24.1–4–100–3; G. J. Lord 10–2–15–0; M. S. Scott 12–4–27–0; C. J. Stephens 22–7–57–2; C. M. Tolley 9.2–0–44–1.

YORKSHIRE SECOND ELEVEN

Matches 16: Won – Glamorgan, Northamptonshire (twice), Nottinghamshire, Surrey. Lost – Kent, Warwickshire. Drawn – Derbyshire (twice), Glamorgan, Kent, Lancashire, Nottinghamshire, Surrey, Warwickshire. Abandoned – Lancashire.

Batting Averages

	M	I	NO	R	HI	100s	Avge
N. G. Nicholson	14	26	7	1,051	144	2	55.31
D. Byas	14	26	2	889	162*	2	37.04
P. E. Robinson	11	21	2	703	94	0	37.00
S. A. Kellett	12	22	0	612	147	1	27.81
C. S. Pickles	14	21	3	472	84	0	26.22
*S. Oldham	14	7	5	52	18*	0	26.00
I. G. Swallow	11	17	2	379	78	0	25.26
P. A. Booth	13	17	5	249	41	0	20.75
S. J. Dennis	13	13	5	116	43	0	14.50
P. J. Berry	12	14	4	139	65	0	13.90
†M. Redhead	5	7	1	82	24	0	13.66
C. Shaw	8	10	1	59	14	0	6.55

Played in three matches: S. D. Fletcher 48, 5, 0; †E. Greenwood 50*, 1, 23*; J. Robinson 100*, 10, 21, 63*, 34; †A. Court did not bat. Played in two matches: P. Anderson 1, 0, 15*; S. N. Hartley 38, 19, 55, 32; B. Parker 20, 6, 12; †D. N. Pike 6, 13, 0. Played in one match: A. J. Bethel 11, 8; †S. Holgate 7, 5; J. D. Love 68, 65*; K. Sharp 81*, 29.

Bowling Averages

	O	M	R	W	BB	Avge
S. D. Fletcher	95.2	19	265	20	5-20	13.25
S. Oldham	201.3	70	437	19	3-36	23.00
D. Byas	58.4	11	219	9	3-29	24.33
I. G. Swallow	290.5	84	830	34	4-58	24.41
C. Shaw	225.5	43	635	26	4-61	24.42
P. J. Berry	304.5	96	827	27	5-47	30.62
S. J. Dennis	337.3	65	1,021	33	6-77	30.93
C. S. Pickles	198.2	30	582	18	5-24	32.33
P. A. Booth	394.5	116	1,179	31	5-87	38.03

Also bowled: P. Anderson 50–7–172–4; S. N. Hartley 13–3–35–0; J. D. Love 15–8–16–3; J. Robinson 9–2–47–2; P. E. Robinson 5.4–0–48–0.

SECOND ELEVEN CHAMPIONS

1959	Gloucestershire	1969	Kent	1979	Warwickshire
1960	Northamptonshire	1970	Kent	1980	Glamorgan
1961	Kent	1971	Hampshire	1981	Hampshire
1962	Worcestershire	1972	Nottinghamshire	1982	Worcestershire
1963	Worcestershire	1973	Essex	1983	Leicestershire
1964	Lancashire	1974	Middlesex	1984	Yorkshire
1965	Glamorgan	1975	Surrey	1985	Nottinghamshire
1966	Surrey	1976	Kent	1986	Lancashire
1967	Hampshire	1977	Yorkshire	1987	{ Kent
1968	Surrey	1978	Sussex		{ Yorkshire

WARWICK UNDER-25 COMPETITION FINAL, 1987

WORCESTERSHIRE v YORKSHIRE

At Birmingham, August 30. Yorkshire won by eight wickets. Toss: Worcestershire.

Worcestershire

L. K. Smith b Fletcher	0	I. R. J. McLaren b Shaw	4
*J. P. Wright run out	30	†W. Noon b Fletcher	0
P. Bent c Byas b Pickles	13	P. Humphries b Shaw	1
D. A. Leatherdale c Swallow b Berry	36	R. J. Grant not out	0
M. A. G. Jones retired hurt	13	B 2, l-b 10, w 4, n-b 1	17
C. M. Tolley b Fletcher	9		
R. D. Stemp b Fletcher	1	(36.2 overs)	124

Bowling: Fletcher 6–2–13–4; Shaw 5.2–0–20–2; Booth 8–2–21–0; Pickles 4–1–15–1; Swallow 8–0–23–0; Berry 5–0–20–1.

Yorkshire

†R. J. Blakey c Noon b Humphries	17
D. Byas not out	70
S. A. Kellett lbw b Humphries	0
N. G. Nicholson not out	26
B 6, l-b 4, w 5	15

(2 wkts, 28 overs) 128

J. Robinson, *I. G. Swallow, C. S. Pickles, P. Booth, P. J. Berry, C. Shaw and S. D. Fletcher did not bat.

Bowling: Humphries 8–1–21–2; Grant 5–0–26–0; Stemp 8–0–38–0; Bent 6–1–22–0; Leatherdale 1–0–11–0.

BAIN DAWES TROPHY FINAL, 1987

HAMPSHIRE v DERBYSHIRE

At Southampton, September 17. Derbyshire won by seven wickets. Toss: Hampshire.

Hampshire

T. C. Middleton c Anderson b Taylor	12	M. R. Newton not out	11
R. J. Scott b Beardshall	1	S. J. W. Andrew b Beardshall	2
*K. D. James c Krikken b Taylor	7	K. J. Shine not out	1
M. E. O'Connor c Krikken b Taylor	0	L-b 18, w 14, n-b 4	36
J. R. Ayling c Krikken b Sharma	12		
R. R. Savage b Beardshall	61	1/6 2/25 3/25 (9 wkts, 55 overs) 166
†A. N. Aymes run out	0	4/33 5/68 6/69
R. J. Maru b Beardshall	23	7/124 8/157 9/165

Bowling: Beardshall 11–0–32–4; Malcolm 11–2–22–0; Jean-Jacques 11–1–40–0; Taylor 11–1–26–3; Sharma 11–3–28–1.

Derbyshire

I. S. Anderson c Savage b Shine	58	
A. M. Brown c Aymes b Andrew	65	
T. J. G. O'Gorman not out	3	
R. Sharma c Savage b Shine	12	

C. F. B. P. Rudd not out 6
B 1, l-b 8, w 11, n-b 3 23

1/140 2/146 3/159   (3 wkts, 46 overs) 167

†K. M. Krikken, M. Beardshall, *A. Hill, M. Jean-Jacques, J. P. Taylor and D. E. Malcolm
did not bat.

Bowling: Andrew 11–1–37–1; Shine 11–0–43–2; Maru 8–2–18–0; Ayling 10–2–31–0; James
5–0–26–0; Newton 1–0–3–0.

Umpires: D. J. Constant and K. E. Palmer.

CAREER FIGURES OF PLAYERS RETIRING OR NOT RETAINED

BATTING

	M	I	NO	R	HI	100s	Avge	1,000r in season
D. L. Acfield	420	417	212	1,677	42	0	8.18	0
D. L. Amiss	658	1,139	126	43,453	262*	102	42.89	23+1
I. S. Anderson	140	225	27	4,726	112	2	23.86	1
P. H. Edmonds	390	495	91	7,651	142	3	18.93	0
K. A. Hayes	44	71	4	1,595	152	2	23.80	0
S. Henriksen	3	4	3	17	10*	0	17.00	0
K. B. S. Jarvis	242	182	81	336	19	0	3.32	0
S. J. O'Shaughnessy	100	161	27	3,567	159*	5	26.61	0
C. T. Radley	558	878	133	26,311	200	46	35.31	16
B. C. Rose	270	448	50	13,236	205	25	33.25	8
G. E. Sainsbury	73	68	37	166	14*	0	5.35	0
G. B. Stevenson	188	229	34	3,965	115*	2	20.33	0
K. P. Tomlins	107	161	20	3,786	146	5	26.85	0
D. W. Varey	65	110	12	2,657	156*	2	27.11	0

* Signifies not out.

BOWLING AND FIELDING

	R	W	BB	Avge	5W/i	10W/m	Ct/St
D. L. Acfield	26,800	950	8-55	28.21	34	4	137
D. L. Amiss	718	18	3-21	39.88	0	0	418
I. S. Anderson	1,356	22	4-35	61.63	0	0	106
P. H. Edmonds	31,933	1,242	8-53	25.71	47	9	345
K. A. Hayes	537	17	6-58	31.58	1	0	15
S. Henriksen	105	2	1-26	52.50	0	0	2
K. B. S. Jarvis	18,763	634	8-97	29.59	19	3	56
S. J. O'Shaughnessy	3,947	110	4-66	35.88	0	0	52
C. T. Radley	160	8	2-38	20.00	0	0	516
B. C. Rose	289	8	3-9	36.12	0	0	124
G. E. Sainsbury	5,702	172	7-38	33.15	7	0	15
G. B. Stevenson	14,075	488	8-57	28.84	18	2	73
K. P. Tomlins	360	4	2-28	90.00	0	0	65
D. W. Varey	4	0	—	—	0	0	24/1

UAU CHAMPIONSHIP, 1987

April flattered to deceive, May was cold and grey, June was simply wet. The UAU Championship once more vied with both the elements and strange arrangements and yet, thanks to the patience and endurance of the students, the competition won through. Nevertheless, that patience was stretched to tolerance by the circumstances of the final between Durham and Exeter. It was to have been played in Southampton, at Hampshire's County Ground, but rain fell throughout the night, and at lunch it was decided to postpone the match until the next week.

This decision, however, meant that a new venue had to be found. That chosen, albeit in error, could not have been more ill suited. The Roweheath Recreation Ground in Birmingham was what its name implies. The wicket and surroundings proved unsuitable to both sides, and the fixture was hurriedly moved to the Birmingham University Second XI ground at Wast Hills, Redditch. It was an unsettling experience for the students, several of them with experience of first-class county cricket. By the time they began play on a green and unprepared wicket at 1.30 p.m., in a final reduced to 50 overs a side, much of the edge had gone.

The two teams are to be congratulated on their steadfastness and willingness to soldier on in such distracting circumstances. But the question has to be asked. Why is it, when Oxford and Cambridge are given three days each year at Lord's, two equally talented teams had to make do with such unequal provision? UAU cricket deserves a much better deal, and the proper recognition of student cricketers is long overdue.

Of the 41 universities who entered the competition in the zonal group matches, 26 moved through to the knockout stages: Aberystwyth, Birmingham, Bradford, Bristol, Brunel, Cardiff, Durham, Essex, Exeter, Keele, Kent, King's College London, Lancaster, Leeds, Loughborough, Manchester, Newcastle, Nottingham, Reading, Southampton, Sussex, Swansea, University College London, University College of North Wales (Bangor), UMIST and Warwick. While the last eight contained some old regulars, there were welcome new quarter-finalists in Bangor, Newcastle and Southampton. The appearance of Bangor, albeit fielding a side drawn primarily from the Home Counties, was of particular interest. They knocked out Birmingham in the second round, and in their quarter-final beat Manchester by the substantial margin of 67 runs in a match interrupted several times by rain (Bangor 157, Manchester 90).

Their semi-final opponents, Durham, had entertained Newcastle and won with ease. Batting first in threatening weather, Durham scored 266 for eight in 50 overs (Alan Fordham 78, Nassar Hussain 55). Although David Storer hit a dogged 59, Newcastle slipped farther and farther behind, and when rain stopped play after 46 overs, they were 127 for seven, well behind on run-rate. In the other half of the draw, Exeter had a surprisingly comfortable passage against their old rivals, Loughborough, who could muster only 130 in reply to Exeter's 220 for nine. Southampton, hosts to the final stages, met with disappointment against Reading. Batting first they could reach only 157, Adam Licudi taking four for 45; and although Andrew Hart's four for 51 kept up the pressure on Reading, an invaluable 57 not out by Dave Penny saw them through by four wickets in the 57th over.

The semi-finals, on June 16, brought together Exeter and Reading on Southampton University's First XI wicket, while Bangor and Durham were assigned the uncovered – and therefore rain-affected – Second XI wicket. Batting first, Reading struggled, especially against the left-arm seam bowling of Mike Smith (four for 44 off 21 overs). The first-ball dismissal of their Australian batsman, Tim Richings, a prolific run-maker, adjudged lbw playing well forward to Smith, was a setback from which Reading never recovered. David Orr batted resolutely for 58 not out, but a total of 158 for nine after 60 overs was insufficient. Exeter won in 35 overs for the loss of three wickets. Their opener, Ian Stuart, hit a sparkling, unbeaten 96, and in the closing stages there was some aggressive batting from Chan Perera.

In the other semi-final, Bangor batted first on a lively pitch and made 175 in 59 overs, Paul Hunter being the mainstay of their innings with 59. Durham, without their usual opening attack because of exams, eventually called on John Stephenson, an occasional bowler, whose 22 overs yielded 61 runs for four wickets. Durham suffered an early setback when Fordham was caught behind off his gloves in Matt Taylor's opening over. Clearly distrustful of the wicket, his colleagues chose to hit out, and with 31 from Stephenson, 48 from Hussain and 36 not out from Tim O'Gorman, Durham won by four wickets in the 36th over.

FINAL

DURHAM v EXETER

At Wast Hills, Redditch, June 23. Durham won by six wickets. Toss: Durham. Given the condition of the pitch, Harding had no hesitation in asking Exeter to bat and they were immediately in trouble. Stuart chopped the first delivery of Charlesworth's opening over on to his stumps; Cummins, with an ill-conceived cover drive, chipped the third ball to point, where O'Gorman took the catch with an athletic leap. By "lunch", taken at three o'clock, Exeter had struggled to 36 for four off 26 overs, and although they pressed on with a little more urgency after the interval, they continued to be pegged back by the accurate seam bowling of Fenton and Charlesworth. Exeter's total may have seemed modest, but on a green and unpredictable wicket it was a substantial target. Mike Smith, bowling left-arm over the wicket with an economic approach and waspish delivery, proved the point, removing Fordham, Hussain and Charlesworth. Stephenson, however, batted immaculately, making his last innings as a student a masterpiece of concentration, sound technique and good judgement. His undefeated 50 bore the hallmark of a player capable of reaching the highest level, and it steered Durham to their second successive UAU Championship title.

Exeter

I. C. D. Stuart b Charlesworth	0	R. J. Belmont not out		10
J. W. Smith b Fenton	15	M. A. Smith c Stephenson		
D. G. Cummins c O'Gorman			b Charlesworth	0
b Charlesworth	0	W. M. Tebbit not out		4
*W. J. Dean b Fenton	20	B 2, l-b 8		10
P. C. M. Perera c O'Gorman b Fenton	4			
J. G. A. Frost c Stephenson b Fenton	26	1/1 2/1 3/24	(9 wkts, 50 overs)	108
†H. J. Norman run out	9	4/24 5/43 6/62		
D. Umbers c Foster b Fenton	14	7/92 8/92 9/94		

Bowling: Fenton 25–11–39–5; Charlesworth 25–6–59–3.

Durham

A. Fordham lbw b Smith	10	T. J. G. O'Gorman not out		12
J. P. Stephenson not out	50	B 1, l-b 1, w 3, n-b 3		8
N. Hussain c Norman b Smith	5			
G. M. Charlesworth c Stuart b Smith	1	1/26 2/48	(4 wkts, 40.1 overs)	110
J. R. Prentis run out	14	3/50 4/81		

S. G. Foster, *G. D. Harding, †M. P. Speight, S. Easterbrook and N. C. W. Fenton did not bat.

Bowling: M. A. Smith 18–8–30–3; Belmont 2–0–13–0; Stuart 8–0–34–0; Tebbit 12–3–27–0; Perera 0.1–0–4–0.

THE LANCASHIRE LEAGUES, 1987

By CHRIS ASPIN

The idea of Viv Richards, captain of West Indies, playing for Rishton, a village club in the industrial North, caught the fancy of the cricket world. And although many thought Rishton had "bought" the Lancashire League championship by paying Richards a record fee – said to be in the region of £10,000 – things turned out differently. In 1986, with Winston Davis as their professional, Rishton finished third. With Richards, they finished fourth and went out of the Worsley Cup in the semi-finals. Batting on damp pitches – the season was the wettest ever – Richards made, for him, a modest 899 runs, including three centuries; but in spite of the dismal weather, the crowds paid £17,526 to see him. A record £1,805 for the semi-final at Ramsbottom helped to swell the "gates" at Rishton's home and away fixtures to almost half the takings for the entire programme.

Richards earned the League's respect by refusing to leave his club to play for the Rest of the World in the MCC Bicentenary match at Lord's, but three other professionals were each fined £500 for breaking their contracts. In mid-season, Andrew Zesers (Ramsbottom) and Bharat Arun (Accrington) returned home, the former to train for the World Cup and the latter at the request of his employer. Later, David Gilbert (East Lancashire) missed the last four games in order to take part in New South Wales' tour of Zimbabwe.

Haslingden, who won the championship for the third time in five years, and Rawtenstall, the runners-up, succeeded largely because of their amateurs. It is difficult to recall another season when the two leaders reached the top without consistent match-winning performances by their professionals. The leading amateurs were Ian Clarkson (Nelson) with 809 runs, average 38.52, Michael Ingham (Haslingden) with 724 (55.69), and Terry Little (Colne) 712 (33.90). The Haslingden opener, Bryan Knowles, who topped 500 for the twelfth successive season, hit the Rawtenstall bowlers for eight fours and a six off consecutive balls and completed the fastest fifty off 21. Keith Roscoe (Rawtenstall) took 49 wickets at 13.24. He was one of a growing number of spinners to top the averages, among them the former Lancashire and England batsman, David Lloyd, of Accrington. His seven for 28 against Ramsbottom were the season's best figures.

East Lancashire won the Worsley Cup for the fifteenth time. They held Ramsbottom to 155 for five in the final and passed the total with six wickets standing.

In the Central Lancashire League, the arrival of Joel Garner made Oldham firm favourites, but having established a fifteen-point lead, they began to falter and let in Norden, who took the title for the first time. Norden's professional, Gus Logie, scored 1,352 runs and took 52 wickets, and his 159 against Rochdale was the season's highest. The club's young fast bowler, Nigel Young, took 93 wickets at 14.86, the best return in the Central Lancashire League by an amateur. Carl Hooper, who set up a league batting record in 1986, blossomed as a bowler for runners-up Werneth. He took eight for 6 against Hyde and finished with 92 wickets at 10.88 each. Garner, who headed the averages with 90 wickets at 9.58, twice took nine for 37 – against Middleton and Castleton Moor – and destroyed Hyde and Stockport with returns of eight for 14 and eight for 15 respectively. The best all-round figures came from another West Indian, Ezra Moseley (Littleborough) with 119 wickets and 867 runs, while Dexter Fitton (Radcliffe), a member of the

Lancashire staff, scored 1,063 runs and took 82 wickets. Curtley Ambrose (Heywood), who is joining Northamptonshire, took 115 wickets, including nine for 42 against Littleborough.

The leading amateur batsmen were Gary Toshach (Walsden) with 851 runs (56.73), Mike Arnold (Milnrow) 815 (31.34), Steve Monty (Royton) 756 (29.07) and Gary Yates (Werneth) 729 (56.07). Dave Norris (Milnrow) took 93 wickets at 15.25 each and David Mellor (Ashton) 76 at 15.68.

Milnrow won the J. W. Lees Wood Cup. In the final they scored 193 for six and dismissed Royton for 137. It was the ninth time Royton had lost a final.

MATTHEW BROWN LANCASHIRE LEAGUE

	P	W	L	D	Pts	Professional	Runs	Avge	Wkts	Avge
Haslingden	26	15	3	7	76*	E. A. Brandes ..	267	16.69	52	17.71
Rawtenstall	26	14	4	8	71	P. King	581	30.58	34	26.47
Nelson	26	14	6	4	66	S. R. Waugh ...	851	56.73	69	19.35
Rishton	26	13	6	7	64	I. V. A. Richards	899	64.21	42	17.50
Enfield	26	12	5	9	63	B. W. Reidy	701	53.92	67	13.54
Ramsbotton ...	26	13	7	6	63	{ A. K. Zesers ...	67	11.17	22	20.36
						{ Ijaz Faqih	185	37.00	25	15.40
Todmorden	26	9	8	9	52	P. S. de Villiers .	242	16.13	60	15.93
Accrington	26	9	10	7	49	{ B. Arun	204	20.40	31	18.39
						{ I. D. Austin ...	428	61.14	13	28.08
Bacup	26	8	10	8	43	S. C. Wundke ..	740	41.11	64	20.03
Church	26	7	13	6	41	W. S. Andrews ..	771	38.55	67	15.15
Colne	26	7	15	4	41	W. T. Greenidge .	61	4.06	80	16.60
Lowerhouse ...	26	6	13	7	39	T. A. Hogan	360	21.18	61	15.07
East Lancashire	26	3	15	8	23	D. R. Gilbert ..	313	22.36	32	21.94
Burnley	26	3	16	6	22*	B. A. Matthews .	217	16.69	44	22.77

* *Includes 2 points for one tied match.*

Note: One point awarded for bowling out the opposition.

TSB CENTRAL LANCASHIRE LEAGUE

	P	W	L	D	Pts	Professional	Runs	Avge	Wkts	Avge
Norden	30	21	2	7	96	A. L. Logie	1,352	64.38	52	15.33
Werneth	30	19	3	8	92*	C. L. Hooper ...	819	51.18	92	10.88
Oldham	30	18	4	8	88	J. Garner	341	21.31	90	9.58
Middleton	30	17	7	6	79	K. C. Williams .	992	55.11	48	17.29
Milnrow	30	17	8	5	76	D. Tazelaar	220	13.75	111	14.00
Walsden	30	13	9	8	67	G. Codrington ..	508	29.88	58	16.67
Radcliffe	30	12	11	7	62*	J. D. Fitton	1,063	48.31	82	13.59
Littleborough ..	30	12	8	10	62*	E. A. Moseley ..	867	45.63	119	9.84
Rochdale	30	10	11	9	55	R. C. Haynes ...	944	39.33	81	16.24
Royton	30	9	13	8	44*	V. A. Holder ...	259	12.33	47	23.68
Heywood	30	7	16	7	40	E. L. C. Ambrose	220	11.57	115	12.96
Stockport	30	7	16	7	38	M. J. R. Rindel .	758	34.45	40	23.25
Castleton Moor	30	7	16	7	36	S. Dublin	775	31.00	81	19.75
Ashton	30	5	17	8	34*	R. Patel	534	41.07	49	22.32
Hyde	30	4	19	7	21	A. Malik	395	35.90	16	32.37
Crompton	30	2	20	8	16	Shahid Aziz	248	10.33	81	19.71

* *Includes 2 points for a tie.*

Note: Five points awarded for an outright win; three for a limited win.

IRISH CRICKET IN 1987

By DEREK SCOTT

Ireland had never before played ten matches in a season, the largest previous number being eight. The programme fell into two phases, with five limited-overs matches played first in May and June and the "real" cricket following in the second half of the season. Of the latter, the wet summer of 1987 prevented results in the annual three-day matches against Scotland and Wales.

Of the five limited-overs fixtures, the first two were fortuitous. If Yorkshire had been knocked out of the Benson and Hedges Cup, they, and not Ireland, would have played Pakistan. And those well-documented Irish traits of luck and gambling played their part in one of the two-day matches. The gamble was that Northamptonshire would not reach the Benson and Hedges final. When they did, Sussex at short notice became a very welcome substitute and a most exciting game eventuated.

For the first time in living memory, no new cap was awarded by Ireland. Only sixteen players were called on, and this could have been as few as twelve but for injuries. M. A. Masood scored 546 runs (avge 42), a record aggregate, with one century and four fifties in thirteen innings; M. F. Cohen was not far behind with 455 runs, while G. D. Harrison, A. McBrine, M. Rea and S. J. S. Warke all scored more than 200 runs. Eight players averaged 23 or more. However, the bowling, as usual in recent years, was another story. S. C. Corlett took fifteen wickets, but at a cost of over 39, and H. Milling's fourteen wickets cost just under 30. The overall bowling figure improved by 5 runs per wicket but was still an unacceptable 41.36.

At the end of the season Corlett retired, at the age of 37, and his fitness and dedication over fourteen seasons will be sadly missed. Since 1974 he had been the mainstay of the faster bowling and no mean bat. In 73 matches he took 233 wickets at an average of 23.12, which put him third behind J. D. Monteith's 326 wickets and J. C. Boucher's 307, and he finished with 1,045 runs (avge 17.41), having reached 1,000 runs at Lord's last year. His replacement as a seam bowler is not on the horizon.

The captaincy of the Irish team changed hands. After 25 matches at the helm (1981-87), M. Halliday resigned to make way for a younger man. His ill luck with the toss was a byword; he won only six of 25! The mantle fell on P. B. Jackson, a marvellous wicket-keeper and a pleasant and enthusiastic man.

Pakistan visited Dublin in May for two limited-overs matches. They won the first easily, with Cohen (53) the only Irish batsman to get above 25, and the second on run-rate when rain stopped Ireland's reply. The dashing Masood made 89 in 82 minutes, but Pakistan's run-rate, boosted by Manzoor Elahi's 109 in 79 minutes, was much superior. Two weeks later Gloucestershire, sponsored by Cawood Oil, paid a hurried visit to Downpatrick for two 55-overs matches in which Ireland put up a better show. In the first, Gloucestershire made 300 for five (P. W. Romaines 143), but Ireland managed 207 for five (Harrison 62). Next day, and for the first time in these four matches, Ireland batted first. Masood scored 110 in 144 minutes out of 218 for seven; Gloucestershire won by six wickets in 49 overs (A. J. Wright 84, K. P. Tomlins 62).

These matches were good preparation for the NatWest Bank Trophy match against Northamptonshire a week later. Ireland put the home team in, and for the first time in this competition they bowled a county out, despite losing an opening bowler after only three overs. The fielding and catching were of a high order and no bowler was collared. However, the pitch was damp from incessant rain and Walker (four for 7 in nine overs) was too much for part-time players. Ireland, chasing 199, staggered to 110 for nine.

Sussex were the next opponents, coming to Malahide, Dublin, in mid-July under the sponsorship of JMA. The wicket was a batsman's dream; 967 runs were scored and only fourteen wickets fell. There were nine scores of 50 or more, a record for a match involving Ireland, and century stands abounded. For Sussex, Standing (50 and 114) and Green (131 not out and 56) put on 176 and 124 for the first wicket. Ireland's opening pair, Warke and Cohen (118 and 45), managed 154 and 68. Masood's 84 in 80 minutes allowed Ireland to set Sussex 289 to win in 124 minutes plus twenty overs, and when they were 182 for one entering the last hour, all seemed lost to Irish eyes. However, a dazzling catch by Dennison dismissed Parker (81) off the third ball of the penultimate over, with 9 runs still required. Corlett prevented 7 being scored from the last over, despite 3 off the second ball, and Sussex were a run short at the end with six wickets down.

A week later, Scotland came to Coleraine. The match vacillated dramatically but the players could not make up for the four hours lost to rain before play could start. The report of the match may be found on page 662.

At the start of the biennial tour, at Lord's in early August, MCC batted evenly and well for 250 for seven. At close of play Ireland declared at 193 for nine, again being rescued by the tail, and MCC set up a generous declaration on the second day – 257 in 184 minutes plus twenty overs. Ireland won by four wickets with an over to spare thanks to a quick 91 by Masood, a sheet-anchor 91 by Cohen, and some faulty MCC catching.

Next day at Arundel, in a match sponsored by Allied Irish Banks, Ireland were put in by the Duchess of Norfolk's XI. They scored 216 for six, a fourth-wicket stand of 146 by Rea (60) and Harrison (84) being the essence of the innings. Robin Marlar gave the Irish captain, Jackson, the Man of the Match award for his generous declaration, which allowed 103 minutes and twenty overs. But Stuart Turner, the former Essex all-rounder, must have felt hard done by. He came in with the score 32 for three, saw it deteriorate to 65 for six, then made 109 not out in 114 minutes to draw the match at 159 for seven. He was 76 with two overs to go!

Welshpool was a well-named new venue for the match against Wales. Rain washed out the third day after each team had scored 321. Masood made 79 and Jackson, at No. 9, almost emulated McBrine's innings against Scotland with a century. He was 89 not out after 116 minutes when the last wicket fell. The bulk of the Welsh runs came from a fourth-wicket stand of 218 between N. Roberts (127) and A. Puddle (110).

In domestic competitions, the 22-year-old, six-team Interprovincial Tournament was won by Ulster Town for the fifth time. Jackson led his team from last place in 1986 to first in 1987. S. C. Corlett, who was in four of Ulster Town's Cup-winning teams, took his 200th wicket in this Tournament in his 60th and last match before retirement. The final of the Schweppes Cup, an All-Ireland club championship, was contested by two teams from the North-West whose grounds are only a few miles apart. St Johnston, from Co. Donegal, beat the Derry city-based Brigade in a disappointing final. It was the first win by a North-West team in the six-year history of this popular competition.

In the Northern Cricket Union (Belfast), Waringstown won their fourteenth John Player Cup in 23 years. In only three of those 23 years had they failed to win a trophy, having in the same period won thirteen league titles and a total of 27 out of a possible 46 trophies. Roy Harrison, the oldest of four brothers, all of whom played for Ireland, participated in all 27 trophy wins. Lurgan were the beaten finalists by 27 runs over two innings. North of Ireland Cricket Club won the Lombard and Ulster Bank League outright for the first time since 1965, having shared the title in 1986. In the North-West (Derry), Donemana notched up a hat-trick of league titles but were beaten in the Northern Bank Cup final by Strabane. Strabane were the only club in Ireland to win a trophy with the aid of a professional, J. Kitson; he made a major contribution in the final, taking twelve for 97.

The Leinster Union (Dublin) has two leagues. The Belvedere Bond league, in which time is the determining factor, was won by Phoenix, with a revitalised Dublin University in second place, while the Wiggins Teape (limited-overs) League was shared between Clontarf, the holders, and YMCA when the final was washed out. YMCA retained the Sportsgear knockout Cup. Masood averaged 107.75 for Phoenix and the young YMCA champion, J. D. Garth, scored 728 runs and took 62 wickets. In Munster, Cork County Cricket Club, founded in 1849, entered competitive cricket there for the first time. They won the Anglo-Irish Banks League and Waterford won the Cup.

The Under-19 International Tournament, inaugurated in 1975, was held in Ireland for the first time in 1987. Sponsored by the Ulster Bank, it centred around Belfast, and the organisers, Jim Boyce and Des McCall, along with the clubs of the Northern Cricket Union, did a magnificent job. England South beat England North in the final, with Ireland finishing a creditable third. However, the general standard did not appear to be as good as in other years. The Under-19 and Under-15 Interprovincial Tournaments were won by Ulster Country and North-West respectively, while Welsh Schools won the annual three-day match against Irish Schools, in Dublin, for the second successive year.

SCOTTISH CRICKET IN 1987

By WATSON BLAIR

Following their first success in the Benson and Hedges Cup, at the expense of Lancashire at Perth in 1986, Scotland's international squad entertained reasonably high expectations of further success in 1987. Unfortunately, blustery and damp conditions ruined the two one-day practices in mid-April at Stenhousemuir, and throughout the Benson and Hedges campaign, the playing conditions can best be described as inclement. It was mostly wet, with low temperatures, and this time round Scotland failed to win any of their matches. Only two Scottish batsmen scored more than 100 runs, Richard Swan, the captain, totalling 122 runs, with a highest score of 43, and Iain Philip 115 runs, with a highest score of 71 against Lancashire, for which he received the Gold Award.

In June, Pakistan, without Imran Khan, visited Titwood, Glasgow, for a one-day match that was reduced to 45 overs each because of early-morning drizzle. Rain restricted the tourists' innings to 42 overs (203 for six) and left Scotland to score 184 in 38 overs. At the close, they were 128 for eight. For this match Scotland introduced Lalchand Rajput of India as their overseas player in place of the South African, Omar Henry, who had had a poor Benson and Hedges series.

Myreside, in Edinburgh, was for the third successive year the venue for Scotland's NatWest Bank Trophy tie, Kent being the visitors. Another delayed start and another insertion brought disaster for Scotland, who were bundled out for 74 in 35.1 overs. It was their lowest total in a one-day competition. Derek Underwood did the damage with eight for 31 in 11.1 overs, a record for the competition, and the match was over in three and a half hours with Kent winning by six wickets.

Glamorgan travelled to Inverleith, Edinburgh, for a testimonial match for Gilbert Parkhouse who, confined to a wheelchair, had been forced to retire from schoolmastering at Stewart's-Melville College. Batting first, Glamorgan scored 204 for seven in their 55 overs, Steve James contributing an unbeaten 76 and Matthew Maynard 40. Scotland made a brave effort in mustering 181 for nine, with Philip (64) and Swan (45) again the principal providers. For Parkhouse, whose contribution to Glamorgan and Scottish cricket will long be remembered, July 13 was a memorable day.

The same week, Scotland crossed the Irish Sea for their annual first-class match against Ireland. Owing to holiday traffic, the Scottish party were forced to take the last ferry from Stranraer and arrived in Larne 30 minutes after midnight. By car, coach and van, the party then travelled to Coleraine, and it was early morning before everyone got to bed. When the first day's play was held up until late afternoon, it must have been one of the few times when rain was welcomed by cricketers. The report of this match may be found on page 662.

Before the final international of the season, against MCC at Aberdeen, a further trial was held at Stenhousemuir between an SCU Senior Select XI and SCU Under-19 on July 22. It was won by the Under-19s by one wicket (129; 130 for nine), and did not reveal anything not already known by the selectors. Sadly, the match against MCC was so badly affected by the weather that neither side completed an innings.

Scotland B embarked on a most ambitious programme when, at Penrith on June 17, they defeated Cumbria Second XI by 24 runs with 3.4 overs to spare. Mike Smith (52) and Ken Scott (50) were the main contributors to Scotland's 169, and Cumbria, unable to counter Henry's spin (six for 37), were bowled out for 145. The two-day match against Durham University, at the Race-course Ground on June 18, 19, produced an exciting draw, the University being nine wickets down and 11 runs short of victory when time ran out. Scotland B scored 130 (K. Scott 75) and 243 for eight declared (J. M. Taylor 49); Durham replied with 152 for nine declared and 211 for nine (A. Fordham 65, N. Hussain 61). Henry's match return was eleven wickets for 110 runs.

Mike Smith was Scotland's hero when the B team made their first visit to Old Trafford to play Lancashire Second XI on July 6, 7. His 76 in the first innings (194 for eight dec.) included four sixes and six fours off 131 balls, while his second-innings 54, in a total of 272 for eight declared, contained a similar number of sixes and fours. In his second visit to the wicket, the young

Aberdeenshire batsman swept Ian Davidson for four successive sixes, all at increasing elevation, into the Members' Stand. Lancashire replied with 202 for two declared (M. R. Chadwick 116 not out, M. A. Atherton 69) and 209 for eight (M. A. Atherton 80) and the match was drawn.

In late August, two two-day matches were scheduled against Leicestershire Second XI, at Grace Road, and Nottinghamshire Second XI, at the John Player ground. A delayed start at Leicester led to a 40-overs match being played on the first day; the home side won by nine wickets. The second day was washed out. Nottinghamshire reached 101 for three on the first day of their match before play was halted by rain, and after problems with the pitch on the second day, it was agreed to play a 40-overs match on the adjoining artificial strip. Unaccustomed to such a surface, the Scots were dismissed in 39.2 overs for 144, which the county overtook in 33 overs to win by five wickets.

In addition to Mike Smith, who was capped against Ireland, Scotland B players providing evidence of possible promotion to the senior side included Gordon McGurr (Uddingston), Bruce Patterson (Ayr), Jonathan Williams (West of Scotland) and David Johnston (Aberdeenshire). All, however, were batsmen. Bowlers of pace and penetration were still required for Scotland to come up to county standard. Another new cap was Jim Govan of Carlton, a slow bowler, while Aberdeen-born Duncan Pauline, formerly of Surrey and Glamorgan, made his Scottish début in the NatWest match against Kent. He could be a distinct asset to Scotland in 1988.

On the domestic front, some 30 league and cup competitions, involving around 300 clubs from the Shetlands to Stranraer, gave lie to any suggestion that cricket is dead in Scotland. Much credit must go to the Scottish Cricket Union for their enterprise and dedication to the game at all levels. Clydesdale, beaten finalists in 1986, won the Knight, Frank and Rutley Scottish Cup, defeating Perthshire by 31 runs at Hamilton Crescent, Glasgow. It was their fifth success, and in the 22 seasons of the Cup, clubs from the Western Union have won the trophy on thirteen occasions.

The Macallan North of Scotland League was won by Northern Counties, followed by Ross County and Huntly. The runners-up, although qualifying for the Scottish Cup in 1988, intimated that they would be unable to compete and consequently Huntly take their place. The North Knockout Cup final saw Ross County beat Huntly. Cults were champions of the Aberdeenshire Grade 1 League, while Dyce won the Knockout Cup. In the Strathmore Union, Aberdeen GSFP became champions for the first time since 1982, relegating Arbroath United, champions for the previous three years, to the runner-up spot. After an absence of ten years, the Three Counties Cup returned to Dundee HSFP. Rossie Priory won both the Perthshire League and Cup, with Strathern finishing second in the League.

The Stoddard Carpets Scottish County Championship was retained by Aberdeenshire; Perthshire, Ayrshire and Forfarshire took the minor placings. The Challenge Cup, also sponsored by Stoddard Carpets, went to Perthshire, who beat Aberdeenshire in the final. With Dumbartonshire forced to withdraw from the Championship early last season, the 1988 competition has been reduced to nine teams, but it is hoped to bring the total up to ten for 1989. Two Indian professionals, Rajput (Perthshire) and Sanju Mudkavi (Aberdeenshire), played major roles with the bat and ball respectively in their teams' success.

Cupar and Stirling County Second XI were the leading clubs in the Forth Cricket Union. In the Ryden & Partners East League, newly promoted Grange won the First Division title from Stenhousemuir, Carlton and Royal High FP. Fauldhouse were relegated to the Second Division, which was won by Dunnikier. The Masterton Trophy was retained by Stenhousemuir, who defeated Carlton in the final. A new name was inscribed on the Mann Investments SCU Small Clubs Cup following St Modon's HSFP's victory over Rossie Priory in the final. The Scottish New Towns Development Corporations Trophy, played on a league basis, ended in a three-way tie between East Kilbride, Livingston and Glenrothes, but East Kilbride were declared champions by virtue of their superior run-rate. Irvine, winners in 1986, were unplaced, while Cumbernauld withdrew at the start of the season to concentrate on their regional league programme.

In the Western Union, again sponsored by D. M. Hall and Son, Drumpellier won the title in a closely contested final month from Ayr, Greenock and Ferguslie. But with Clydesdale, who finished sixth, winning the Scottish Cup, and with only four clubs from the Western Union qualifying for the 1988 Cup, Ferguslie found there was no consolation in finishing fourth this time. Greenock won both the Rowan Charity and West League Cups, defeating Ayr and West of Scotland respectively in the finals. Although Drumpellier won the Scottish section of the Cockspur Cup with a win over Clydesdale in a rain-reduced final, they failed to negotiate their first hurdle south of the border.

Woodhall won the Strathclyde League, while the Abbey Life Glasgow and District League was retained by Irvine, with Motherwell runners-up. The League Knockout Cup was won by ERNKOA, the acronym for Express Removals–North Kelvinside FP–Old Aloysians. For the fourth season in succession, Kelso won the Edinburgh Woollen Mill Border League, with Gala second. The Border Knockout Cup and the Indoor Sixes Trophy also went to Kelso.

The 1987 "Famous Grouse" Team of the Year award went to Grange. Among the commended clubs were Kelso, Lawside, Northern Counties, Rossie Priory and St Modon's HSFP, while West District received a special award. For the fifth successive year, West District triumphed in the Clydesdale Bank Scottish Inter-District Championship, although they failed in the quarter-finals of the NCA County Championship. During the season, Arbroath United, Ferguslie and Woodhall each celebrated their centenary, and 125th anniversaries were celebrated by Greenock, Stirling County and West of Scotland.

The North District won both the Under-23 and Under-19 District Championships, while the West District triumphed at Under-16 level. The SCU Under-15 knockout competition was won by Stewart's-Melville College. At international level, the Under-19s and Under-16s lost to their English Schools counterparts; by an innings and 2 runs, and by nine wickets respectively. At Ynysygerwn, the seniors just failed to beat Welsh Schools – Graham Robertson scored an unbeaten 108 – while the Under-16s lost at Swansea by 21 runs to a South Wales League Select XI but rallied to beat Welsh Schools Under-15 by 30 runs at Briton Ferry.

SCHOOLS CRICKET IN 1987

In such a wet summer, the English Schools were fortunate to play as much of their representative programme as they did without greater interruption. None of the batsmen capped in 1986 was available, and it soon became evident that the high standard of batting seen then would not be repeated. M. R. Ramprakash, although still at school, was not considered because of his commitments to Middlesex. Of the bowlers, however, H. R. J. Trump, M. R. Newton, P. J. Martin and I. J. Houseman could all be called upon, but because the International Youth Tournament in Ireland clashed with the Schools international matches, only Newton, being too old for the Youth Tournament, was available for English Schools. Seventeen schoolboys were included in the two NCA teams for Ireland, and while depriving the selectors of their services, it had the advantage of enabling younger cricketers to participate at this level. Trump was the 1987 winner of the Gray-Nicolls Trophy for the year's most-improved schoolboy cricketer.

In the two representative matches, fourteen players appeared for English Schools. They were: G. P. Thorpe (*captain*), W. M. I. Bailey, I. Binns (The Plume School, Maldon), N. A. Derbyshire, D. N. Essien, M. I. Gidley, D. A. Graham, M. C. Ilott, M. J. Kellaway, N. V. Knight, J. L. P. Meadows, M. R. Newton, P. J. Rendall and R. W. Sladdin. Their schools may be found in the scorecards of matches played at the MCC Festival, Oxford.

Graham, Knight and Thorpe were the pick of the batsmen, and Binns and Rendall showed promise. But even without the experienced players, the bowling was the team's strength. The openers, Ilott, left-arm, and Derbyshire kept a good line and length at medium pace and were well supported by Rendall and Meadows, the two all-rounders. The two slow left-armers, Newton and Sladdin, both spun the ball, and when Newton was required by his county, Hampshire, Gidley's off-breaks provided a balanced attack against Scottish Young Cricketers. Bailey and Kellaway shared the wicket-keeping, and there was a good standard of ground fielding and catching, especially at slip by Thorpe, who captained the team quietly and efficiently.

Against Welsh Schools, at Morris Motors, Oxford, English Schools' inexperience was apparent in the first innings when, put in, they subsided from 158 for five to 170 all out off the last ball of their 60 overs. After the bowlers had restricted Welsh Schools to 150, however, Ilott taking four for 34 and Newton three for 64, the batsmen fared better in the second innings. Knight (88) and Thorpe (66 not out) added 111 for the third wicket, but the declaration, at 195 for four, did not leave enough time. Welsh Schools earned a comfortable draw, finishing with 145 for six (A. Dale 41).

The speed with which the team had developed its confidence was reflected in the victory, by an innings and 2 runs, over Scottish Young Cricketers at Grange CC, Edinburgh. Put in again, they lost an early wicket before Knight (22) and Graham took the score to 74. Graham went on to dominate the innings with an outstanding 111, scored out of 152 in 172 minutes and containing one six and eleven fours; and in their 60 overs English Schools scored 176 for nine. In reply, the Scots were dismissed for 65 in 39.3 overs; Derbyshire (20–11–27–2) had only thirteen scoring shots hit off his bowling, Ilott took three for 24 and Rendall's impressive figures were 10.3–6–5–5. Following on, the home side were undone by the spinners; 31 for four by the close, 103 for seven at lunch on the second day, and all out for 109 soon afterwards. Sladdin, backed up by good wicket-keeping from Kellaway and Thorpe's slip catching, had figures of 24.2–12–39–6; Gidley, with two for 25, was an admirable foil at the other end.

Welsh Schools, with five Glamorgan Colts at Under-19 level, beat Irish Schools by ten wickets and drew with Scotland Under-19 as well as English Schools. At the Carlisle club, Irish Schools were dismissed for 189 and 98, only S. Harrison (59) and F. O'Mahony (31) establishing themselves. C. Stephens impressed as a seam bowler, returning match figures of nine for 100, while D. Shufflebotham took three for 41 in the first innings and S. Moorcroft four for 21 in the second. The captain, S. Williams (56), and D. Hemp (50) took Welsh Schools to a first-innings total of 253, and when they batted again A. Dale and S. Evans comfortably collected the 35 needed for victory. It was a quite different story at Ynysygerwn, however. Outclassed by Scotland Under-19, the Welsh were saved only by a fighting knock from Shufflebotham, the tenth-wicket pair having to survive the last eight balls. The Scots, batting first, scored 241 for nine declared (G. Salmond 65, G. B. A. Dyer 45), to which the Welsh could reply with only 153 (G. Lucas 48). G. S. R. Robertson scored 108 not out in Scotland's second innings of 207, and at 141 for nine, 295 runs behind, Wales were relieved to secure a draw.

For the MCC Schools Festival at Oxford, selection was on merit and disregarded prior selection for the international tournament in Ireland, even though such players could not be considered for the coming Schools internationals. At a time when little first-class cricket was played elsewhere in England, the Festival did well to enjoy a full day's play on the first and third days, although the second and fourth days were affected.

HMC SOUTHERN SCHOOLS v THE REST

At Magdalen College School, Oxford, July 18, 19. Drawn. Although a full day's play was possible on Saturday, drizzle permitted only three and a half hours on Sunday. On a damp, slow wicket, the left-handed Forward, enjoying some luck against Daniels, and Shahid, an elegant batsman, gave Southern Schools a sound start, but the best batting of the first day came from Knight and Adams for The Rest. On the second day, Forward and Brown put on 147 for Southern Schools' first wicket, with Brown particularly punishing and Marcelline, a Sri Lankan batsman, dominated The Rest's innings before the rain returned. Of the bowlers, McCartney and Daniels looked the pick of the seamers, while Shahid overcame the conditions to bowl his leg-breaks well. Manasseh, slow left-arm, had some success on the first day. Bailey was the better of the two wicket-keepers, but no-one stood out in generally competent fielding sides.

HMC Southern Schools

C. H. Forward (*Canford*) c Marcelline b Manasseh	39	– c Manasseh b Derbyshire	53
N. Shahid (*Ipswich*) c Pegg b Manasseh	52		
*J. I. Longley (*Tonbridge*) st Pegg b Manasseh	0	– (5) not out	7
A. D. Brown (*Caterham*) b Derbyshire	27	– (2) c Pegg b Daniels	90
M. A. Slade (*St Dunstan's*) st Pegg b Gidley	12	– (6) not out	0
J. V. Zagni (*Ipswich*) not out	22	– (4) b Daniels	7
J. L. P. Meadows (*Clifton*) not out	5	– (3) c Knight b Daniels	16
Extras	20	Extras	7

1/91 2/95 3/128 4/137 5/167   (5 wkts dec.) 177   1/147 2/147   (4 wkts dec.) 180
3/165 4/177

†W. M. I. Bailey (*Clifton*), A. D. McCartney (*Bedford Modern*), S. J. Watkinson (*Cranleigh*) and D. W. R. Wiles (*Merchant Taylors', Northwood*) did not bat.

Bowling: *First Innings*—Daniels 10-3-33-0; Balderson 8-2-27-0; Derbyshire 16-7-39-1; Marcelline 5-1-8-0; Gidley 9-0-32-1; Manasseh 12-4-25-3. *Second Innings*—Daniels 13-2-45-3; Derbyshire 12-1-49-1; Balderson 7-0-39-0; Gidley 4-0-17-0; Manasseh 4-0-27-0.

The Rest

*R. S. M. Morris (*Stowe*) c Bailey b Meadows . .	22	– c Bailey b Wiles 0
C. J. Adams (*Repton*) b Longley b Watkinson . .	65	
N. V. Knight (*Felsted*) not out	44	
H. A. Marcelline (*Bishop's Stortford*) c Bailey b McCartney .	5	– (2) not out 72
A. J. Lee (*Chigwell*) not out	10	– (3) b McCartney 0
†C. H. H. Pegg (*Radley*) (did not bat)		– (5) not out 4
D. C. Manasseh (*Harrow*) (did not bat)		– (4) c and b Zagni 21
Extras	12	Extras 12

1/92 2/114 3/123　　　(3 wkts dec.) 158　　　1/0 2/7 3/97　　　(3 wkts) 109

H. J. A. Daniels (*Sedbergh*), T. P. B. Balderson (*Pocklington*), M. I. Gidley (*Loughborough GS*) and N. A. Derbyshire (*Ampleforth*) did not bat.

Bowling: *First Innings*—McCartney 10-2-36-1; Wiles 9-2-43-0; Shahid 10-1-41-0; Watkinson 5-0-15-1; Zagni 5-2-14-0; Meadows 6-5-4-1. *Second Innings*—Wiles 4-0-19-1; McCartney 3-1-4-1; Watkinson 7-2-21-0; Meadows 5-1-9-0; Zagni 9-3-22-1; Shahid 6-0-24-0; Brown 1-0-4-0.

ESCA NORTH v ESCA SOUTH

At Keble College, Oxford, July 18, 19. Drawn. ESCA North were restricted to 157 in their 60 overs by tight bowling from Essien and Ilott, the seamers, and spinners Trump and Newton. Thanks to a fine innings from Graham (eighteen fours), supported by Hanley and Essien, the South reached 246 for seven before declaring with four overs remaining. Batty, an off-spinner, was the pick of the bowlers with five wickets. Following a delayed start, the North batted with greater urgency on the second day, scoring 179 in 42 overs before rain stopped play.

ESCA North

J. D. Ratcliffe (*Solihull VI Form Coll.*) b Trump	49	– c Thorpe b Essien 29
R. P. Gofton (*Wolfreton, Hull*) c Kellaway b Trump .	55	– c Rendall b Trump 44
D. Adams (*Chesterfield Tech. Coll.*) c Trump b Newton .	1	– (4) not out 4
G. Haynes (*King Edward VI, Stourbridge*) c Hanley b Newton .	0	
G. Steer (*Sir Edmund Campion*) not out	21	– (3) c and b Ilott 67
†G. Wells (*Birkdale HS*) c Trump b Newton .	15	– not out 30
R. W. Sladdin (*Sowerby Bridge*) not out	4	
B 5, l-b 5, w 1, n-b 1	12	L-b 5 5

1/92 2/117 3/117 4/117 5/152　　　(5 wkts) 157　　　1/42 2/118 3/171　　　(3 wkts) 179

J. Batty (*Bingley GS*), *D. Evans (*Normanton Freeston*), P. J. Martin (*Danum, Doncaster*) and I. J. Houseman (*Harrogate GS*) did not bat.

Bowling: *First Innings*—Essien 8-4-9-0; Ilott 8-5-9-0; Rendall 6-1-22-0; Trump 16-4-53-2; Pritchard 9-2-31-0; Newton 13-8-23-3. *Second Innings*—Essien 5-1-20-1; Ilott 11-5-26-1; Rendall 2-0-26-0; Trump 13-2-39-1; Pritchard 9-5-23-0; Newton 2-0-19-0; Thorpe 3-0-21-0.

ESCA South

R. Hanley (*Eastbourne VI Form Coll.*)		H. R. J. Trump (*Millfield*)	
	b Batty . 39	c Houseman b Batty .	5
A. L. Penberthy (*Camborne*) b Houseman	1	M. R. Newton (*Peter Symonds,*	
D. A. Graham (*Chipping Camden*)		*Winchester*) c Adams b Batty .	1
c Wells b Houseman .	93	*M. J. Kellaway (*Eastleigh Coll.*)	
G. P. Thorpe (*Farnham Coll.*)		not out .	1
st Evans b Batty .	29	B 13, l-b 9, w 1, n-b 1	24
P. J. Rendall (*Broadoak,*			
Weston-super-Mare) b Batty .	16	1/6 2/105 3/157 (7 wkts dec.) 246	
D. N. Essien (*Queen's, Taunton*) not out	37	4/189 5/226 6/238 7/240	

J. S. Pritchard (*Reading*) and M. Ilott (*Francis Combe, Watford*) did not bat.

Bowling: Martin 4–2–12–0; Houseman 15.5–1–80–2; Batty 24–7–62–5; Sladdin 3–0–20–0; Adams 9–0–50–0; Haynes 0.1–0–0–0.

At Keble College, Oxford, July 20. J. I. Longley's XI won by three wickets. G. Wells's XI 163 (P. J. Rendall 93; P. J. Martin three for 31, N. Shahid three for 31); J. I. Longley's XI 164 for seven (R. Hanley 43, D. A. Graham 44; M. I. Gidley three for 46).

At St Edward's, Oxford, July 20. Drawn. R. S. M. Morris's XI 188 for seven dec. (A. L. Penberthy 59, G. P. Thorpe 53; M. Ilott three for 62); M. R. Newton's XI 95 for eight (H. R. J. Trump four for 23, D. C. Manasseh three for 22).

At Christ Church College, Oxford, July 21. Drawn. MCC Schools East 151 for nine dec. (G. P. Thorpe 53; J. L. P. Meadows four for 43); MCC Schools West 7 for no wkt.

The matches at Lord's between MCC and MCC Schools, and between MCC Schools and the National Association of Young Cricketers were abandoned owing to rain. The names of the players selected for those matches may be found in Other Matches at Lord's, 1987.

Reports from the Schools

The schools programme generally suffered less from the dismal weather than the first-class game, although the damp, slow wickets of May and June restricted strokeplay. None the less, six players from the schools reviewed here passed 1,000 runs; C. J. Adams of Repton (1,242), H. A. M. Marcelline of Bishop's Stortford (1,166), N. Martin of King Edward's, Birmingham (1,104), N. V. Knight of Felsted (1,027), R. M. Day of Eastbourne College (1,008) and J. I. Longley of Tonbridge (1,007). Marcelline averaged 145.75 as well as taking 32 wickets, Martin averaged 110.40, and Day in addition took 45 wickets. The bowlers prospered, four taking 60 wickets or more: P. J. Le Cornu of Victoria College, Jersey (70), M. P. Mernagh of King's, Rochester (63), S. J. White of King's, Macclesfield (62) and P. A. Mestecky of Ratcliffe College (61). Le Cornu was the leading all-rounder with 859 runs as well as his 70 wickets, and of the sixteen other bowlers who took 50 wickets, P. D. Lunn of Abingdon scored 721 runs, S. P. Howkins of Dover College 656, D. W. Headley of Royal GS, Worcester 627, S. J. Watkinson of Cranleigh 551 and S. W. Ellis of King William's College, Isle of Man 515. P. Rainey of Ballymena Academy GS averaged only 6.46 for his 52 wickets. Seven hat-tricks were reported: by N. E. Baig of Bloxham, D. L. Clift of Merchant Taylors', Crosby, H. J. A. Daniels of Sedbergh, T. Kemp of Royal GS, Colchester (twice), M. J. T. Jefferson of Stowe and J. S. Pritchard of Reading.

Abingdon, captained with enthusiasm and a sporting approach by G. D. Scott, played positive, exciting cricket. P. D. Lunn batted with classical elegance and sound technique to score 721 runs, including 119 v Magdalen College School, and also took 56 wickets with his leg-spin. S. J. Green and off-spinner R. J. Tilley backed him with the ball, although a lack of penetration – as well as their own weakness against spin bowling – prevented a more rewarding final record. The leading all-rounder for **Alleyn's** was B. T. L. Bennett, under whose captaincy they beat St John's Leatherhead, Wellingborough and MCC. As opening bowler, he was well supported by J. Papanastasiou (fast) and O. A. Lucking (slow). J. G. Davey, a fifteen-year-old, showed promise as an opening bat. **Allhallows**, defeated only twice by schools, owed much to their all-rounder, R. Enticott, who averaged 54 in his last eight innings. The most successful bowler was J. E. T. Clark. **Ampleforth's** strength lay in their bowling, with a well-balanced attack compensating for a weakness in the batting caused by term-long injuries to two key players and general inexperience. There were victories over Durham, Worksop, Oundle and Blundell's. N. A. Derbyshire, aged sixteen, bowled genuinely fast, took 34 wickets, including seven for 46 v Oundle, was selected for MCC Schools and went on to play for English Schools.

As expected, **Ardingly's** young side experienced a poor season, but with ten players expected to return in 1988, prospects are bright. **Arnold** defeated William Hulme's GS, Bolton School, Baines, Brighton College and King's, Macclesfield, with whom they later tied at the King's festival. Their captain, R. G. Halsall, led by example, heading the averages and going on to represent Lancashire Schools Under-19 and Lancashire Federation. Bowling right-arm slow, he and S. M. Aga (slow left-arm) took 75 wickets, including Halsall's return of six for 38 against Hutton GS. Wicket-keeper J. Muir claimed 33 dismissals, as well as scoring 443 runs. **Ashville College** beat Mount St Mary's, Batley GS, Bishop Vesey's, Old Ashvillians and the XL Club, while the scores were tied in the drawn match v Stamford.

Excellent team spirit helped **Ballymena Academy** enjoy one of their most successful seasons. Any weakness in the batting was offset by a strong attack, spearheaded by P. Rainey, whose 52 wickets cost only 6.46 apiece, and all-rounder J. Glass. These two took 90 wickets between them, the supporting bowlers adding another 76. R. Kennedy was an astute captain and his splendid wicket-keeping inspired a high standard of fielding. In a season of rebuilding, **Bancroft's** had the encouragement of five victories. Centuries were scored by A. E. Phillips and G. J. Norgate, and there were useful innings from A. C. H. Knight. The captain, R. W. Hubbard (fast-medium), headed the bowling with 43 wickets, although his batting suffered from his carrying the attack, while A. Azad (medium), maintaining a good line and length, took 27 wickets. Two young all-rounders, G. P. Brown (fast medium) and P. Brown (off-breaks), showed much promise. A young **Bangor GS** side won ten matches, their captain, C. C. Yeates, leading by example with 599 runs, including 105 not out against Campbell College. Fifteen-year-old M. W. McCord, a slow left-arm spinner, was the leading wicket-taker. **Barnard Castle**, an efficient all-round side, were defeated only once in schools matches and won their end-of-term festival for the fourth year running. N. J. Foster and the left-handed M. E. Jobling passed 500 runs, while R. J. Irving, left-arm fast-medium, took his tally of wickets for the XI to more than 150.

Bedford School's fast bowlers, J. E. Crooker and B. C. Banks, made life unpleasant for opposing batsmen, but only once, against Rugby, did they bowl a side out. Crooker again headed the batting, followed by A. B. Cartmell, the captain and wicket-keeper. **Bedford Modern** recorded wins over Kimbolton, Christ's College Cambridge, St Albans, RGS Colchester and Gentlemen of Bedfordshire. They were captained by A. J. Trott, whose 625 runs included 116 not out v Queens' College, Cambridge, and 104 v Oundle. P. A. Owen (slow left-arm) took seven for 26 v RGS Colchester, and all-rounder A. D. McCartney (fast) nine for 23 v Kimbolton: each finished with 45 wickets. Fifteen-year-old G. A. H. Awudu was a fine prospect with 324 runs and 21 wickets. Astutely led by M. J. Keen, **Beechen Cliff**, Bath, enjoyed a solid season, in which they were defeated only by Prior Park – having been 98 without loss after the first hour. Their bowling strength lay with the spinners, J. D. Colbourne (leg-spin) and S. M. Priscott (left-arm), backed up by all-rounder D. J. Adams (fast). Keen, the leading batsman, scored 101 v Cowney GS in his final game for the school.

Berkhamsted, defeated by Brentwood in their opening match, went on to beat Haberdashers' Aske's, Aldenham, St Albans, Framlingham, St Lawrence and Kimbolton. The averages were headed by the opening batsman and slow left-arm bowler, D. T. Hodges, a

Colt, while another Colt, E. Shek, was the next-highest run-scorer. M. R. Player (medium-fast) bowled well, if at times with little luck. Lacking quality batting, **Birkenhead** narrowly failed to clinch victory chasing runs in four of their drawn games. Notable contributions came from the captain, P. I. Rennie, who took the most wickets, and M. J. Wilkie, the wicket-keeper, who scored the most runs. Outstanding for a young **Bishop's Stortford College** side was a Sri Lankan, H. A. M. Marcelline, whose aggregate of 1,166 runs at 145.75 easily passed the school record of 799, made in eight more innings in 1897 by C. H. Titchmarsh, who toured Australia and New Zealand with MacLaren in 1922-23. A correct opening batsman, Marcelline scored five hundreds, his 176 v Kingswood being the second highest for the College, and shared with the captain, G. M. E. Hackwell, an unbeaten stand of 226 v Stamford – a College record for any wicket. Such strong batting was let down at times by poor fielding, especially in the slips, and weak bowling.

After a successful season, **Bloxham** undertook an enjoyable tour to Barbados. N. E. Baig, who played for Pakistan Under-19, was an outstanding all-rounder, and his six for 24 v Denstone included a hat-trick. S. M. Blayney developed as an opening bat of much promise. **Blundell's**, with talented players often failing to take advantage of their opportunities, suffered several heavy defeats and their only win was at the expense of Oundle. A highlight was I. C. Fudge's 108 in the drawn game against Sherborne. A mixed season was reported by **Bradfield College's** young side, who recorded two good wins but suffered some unnecessary losses. D. J. Wiggins, a powerful right-hand bat, in his second year at the school, was the pick of the batsmen, while the captain, W. A. Oscroft, an accurate fast-medium bowler, led the attack. A visit to Barbados was planned for 1988 to participate in the Sir Garfield Sobers International Cricket Festival.

For **Bradford GS** the season was one of learning and improvement. Handicapped by injuries to two key bowlers, the attack often failed to dominate, yet when it did – against Hymers, Woodhouse Grove and William Hulme's GS – victory resulted. The batting, headed by opener D. R. Chadwick, was more reliable, but the middle order at times lacked discipline and patience when chasing big totals. The opposite was the experience of **Brentwood School**, whose strong middle order featured left-hander M. D. Wilkins, P. A. Welton, the captain, and J. G. Northwood. After losing two of their first three matches, the side went undefeated, registering good wins over Berkhamsted, Framlingham and Young Essex. The attack did better than expected, despite a slow home pitch. Seam predominated, but there was success, too, for the leg-spinner, P. McGowan. With ten victories, **Brighton College** exceeded expectations, a highlight being the only defeat of Ipswich, against whom C. P. Sweet scored 189 off 121 balls at the King's, Macclesfield, festival. The batting was solid, with no one player dominating, while Sweet and the two spinners, C. M. Long and C. M. Oliphant-Callum, who took 107 wickets between them, carried the attack. **Bromsgrove**, unbeaten by schools, were a strong batting side but found it hard to bowl sides out. Four consecutive wins – over Dean Close, Kelvinside Academy, King's Worcester and King Edward's Birmingham – were achieved when batting second. **Bryanston's** leading batsman, with more than twice as many runs as anyone else, was S. C. Ecclestone, whose 745 included 119 not out v Free Foresters.

Canford enjoyed their best season for many years, numbering Downside, King's Bruton, Bryanston and MCC among the seven teams beaten. Their only loss, to Bradfield, was by 3 runs. Outstanding was the captain, C. H. Forward, whose aggregate of 854 included 218 not out in 183 minutes in a score of 294 for one declared v King's, Taunton, and 124 not out v Bryanston in a match-winning unbroken opening stand of 200 with wicket-keeper J. P. Blissard-Barnes. A. M. W. Groves (medium) bowled consistently well for his 40 wickets, while fifteen-year-old T. R. Murray-Walker (medium) showed promise in taking twenty. Prominent in a successful season for **Caterham** were the captain, J. A. Cox-Colyer, who was just one wicket short of the double of 500 runs and 50 wickets, and A. D. Brown, who in spite of the slow wickets scored 898 runs at 81.63, including an unbeaten double-century, as well as taking 37 wickets. Another batsman to average more than 80 was A. J. Lee, captain of **Chigwell**, who were unbeaten by schools and enjoyed convincing wins v City of London, Brentwood and Enfield GS. Highlights were Lee's unbeaten 112 v Bancroft's and a school record opening stand of 198 between the wicket-keeper, T. A. Coleman (101 not out), and D. J. Clark (87) v MCC. J. F. Carpenter, a left-handed all-rounder, played for Essex Schools Under-15, while Lee played for Young Essex and Essex Schools Under-19.

Christ College, Brecon never fulfilled their promise, failing to win when the opportunity was there and twice losing when a draw could have been gained. The captain, D. O. Lloyd-Jones, a useful all-rounder, set a fine example in the field. **Christ's Hospital's** promising start was followed by four defeats in five games before a recovery which saw Ardingly (by ten wickets), Epsom and Cranleigh beaten. A high standard of fielding and sportsmanship characterised the season, and there were notable performances by J. P. Williams, with two centuries, and opening bowlers M. G. Fooks and R. C. Phillips, who took 33 wickets apiece. The leading batsman for **Claysmore** was G. Owton, whose 626 runs included two hundreds. Two fifteen-year-old opening bowlers, J. Dike and J. Rumball, showed promise with 39 and 33 wickets respectively, and the school reached the regional final of the Barclays Bank Under-17 Cup, which they lost to Millfield. Although **Clifton College** were frustrated by the poor weather, they defeated Blundell's, Marlborough, Colston's, Eastbourne and Winchester, losing to Clifton CC, Malvern and Tonbridge. W. M. Lawry, an opening batsman, hit 103 before lunch v Downside, and J. L. P. Meadows an unbeaten 143 in 140 minutes v Eastbourne. W. M. I. Bailey was selected to keep wicket for MCC Schools and, with Meadows, played for English Schools. A strong commitment and all-round team effort brought **Colfe's** seven wins, including those v Alleyn's, Hampton, Emanuel and their first v MCC. D. Neil-Dwyer scored the side's only hundred, and his five consecutive fifties helped secure wins. The captain and opening bowler, J. Streeter, discomfited most opposing batsmen, especially those of Alleyn's, against whom he returned seven for 15, and Emanuel (eight for 47).

Colston's batsmen provided many fine displays, notably centuries from the captain, C. E. J. TenBroeke, and opening batsman R. L. Rees Jones, but the bowling could not offer the support necessary to obtain good results. **Coventry School – Bablake** retained the Warwickshire Knockout Cup, defeating King Edward's, Birmingham to win the final for the seventh time in nine seasons. This was particularly satisfying because the season had started badly with defeats by RGS Worcester, Loughborough, King Edward's Birmingham and King's, Worcester. **Cranbrook**, whose only defeat by a school was by 2 runs at the hands of Sevenoaks, achieved their four wins by bowling out the opposition. The drawn match v the Band of Brothers finished with the scores level. In a season of mixed fortunes, **Cranleigh** were frustrated by injuries and illness as well as the weather, yet remained capable of some impressive victories; St John's, Leatherhead were beaten by 202 runs. Two all-rounders made major contributions, R. G. Gutteridge scoring 110 v St John's and 115 v Merchant Taylors', Northwood, as well as taking 44 wickets, including six for 33 v Eastbourne. The captain, S. J. Watkinson, scored 551 runs and, with eight for 80 v Hurstpierpoint and six for 32 v St John's, took 50 or more wickets for the third successive season, increasing his tally for the XI to 159.

For **Dauntsey's**, strong batting but a limited attack was a formula resulting in too many inconclusive draws. J. W. S. Porter had a wonderful season, scoring five hundreds and more runs than any previous Dauntsey's batsman in recent memory, but his off-breaks and the slow left-arm spin of J. C. Frost were not enough to bowl the side to victory. **Dean Close's** season saw a positive result in all but two of their matches, both of which were rain affected. A young side depended heavily on T. A. Edginton (slow left-arm), who topped both averages, but there was a sound batting prospect in fourteen-year-old C. J. Townsend. Losing only to MCC, **Denstone** beat Wrekin, Trent, Nottingham HS, King's Macclesfield, Old Swinford Hospital School and Abbot Beyne, against whom A. J. Sloan (medium) returned nine for 16. Solid batting was complemented by an accurate attack headed by Sloan and P. R. Dennis-Jones (off-breaks). Dominant at **Dover College** was the captain, S. P. Howkins, whose all-round contribution of 52 wickets and 656 runs, including 103 not out in 87 balls v Dover GS, was a post-war best for the College. Steady bowling was supported by excellent out-cricket, K. G. Keats, D. J. Winwood and J. D. Rouse especially standing out.

Downside's young team were hampered by the absence through illness, for much of the term, of their captain and leading batsman, P. J. A. Baldwin. However, the improving G. C. J. Barrington looked a useful off-spinner and opening bat. Lacking a penetrative attack to complement a strong, quick-scoring batting line-up, **Dulwich College** failed to record as many victories as they would have liked. There was an exciting tied game v St Paul's, and fifteen-year-old N. K. M. Talonpoika, with 77 v Downside, became the youngest to score a half-century for the College since T. E. Bailey in 1939. In **Durham School's** young side, all-rounders A. Roseberry and N. Whitfield made a favourable impression and thirteen-year-old W. P. C. Weston looked an outstanding prospect. At their end-of-term festival the school entertained Manchester GS, Millfield and Western Australia Public Schools.

With a school-record eleven victories, including an eight-wicket win v Hurstpierpoint for the Langdale Trophy, **Eastbourne College** enjoyed their best season ever. The captain, R. M. Day, a left-hand bat and off-spinner, scored 1,008 runs and captured 45 wickets, including seven for 34 v King's, Canterbury. He was well supported by M. A. Chapple (right-hand bat and medium pace), who joined him in five century opening partnerships and returned seven for 10 v Worth. F. A. Ali took six for 16 v Christ's Hospital. **The Edinburgh Academy's** inexperienced side came together well under the captaincy of T. H. Duff to beat Watson's and St Bees, but Merchiston Castle, Pocklington and Nottingham HS proved too good for them. Duff's 101 not out v Stewart's (five sixes, twelve fours) and M. M. A. Simpson's opening spell v St Bees, in which he hit the stumps six times in twelve balls, finishing with six for 20 in ten overs, were the season's highlights. A well-balanced attack and sound batting ensured **Elizabeth College, Guernsey**, of ten wins, including those v King Edward VI Southampton, Guernsey Island CC and Victoria College, Jersey, against whom J. Walker took six for 30. In his fourth year in the XI, M. Bacon, an influential captain, took his aggregate to 1,233 runs.

C. M. Reed (medium-fast) was the foremost bowler for **Ellesmere College**, his 41 wickets being a school record. There were fine performances, too, from the captain, J. J. Birchall (fast-medium in-swing), and M. J. Marvell, who in his first season with the XI scored the most runs and bowled slow left-arm with accuracy and guile. Against Birkenhead, O. Braithwaite and T. A. R. Elston put on 117 runs for the first wicket. **Eltham College** maintained their commendable record of wins, despite injuries which prevented the captain, R. J. Churchill, from bowling. T. J. Prifti enjoyed an excellent all-round season, giving the innings a sound start and troubling opposing batsmen with his slow left-armers. **Enfield GS**, with an identical record to that of 1986, attributed their four defeats following declarations to the inconsistent bowling of their experienced players. However, encouragement came from the emergence of three talented fifteen-year-old batsmen, one of whom, D. Bowen, scored twice as many runs as anyone else.

A highlight for **Epsom College** was the nine-wicket victory over St George's, Weybridge (219 for four), in which J. Jessop (106 not out) shared in a school record second-wicket partnership of 193 unbroken with P. J. Williams, the captain and leading bowler. **Eton**, unbeaten for the first time since 1982 and excellently captained by R. D. O. MacLeay, defeated Winchester by six wickets, Tonbridge (in the first fixture between the schools) by seven wickets, Shrewsbury by four wickets, I Zingari, MCC and Eton Ramblers. The batting relied on the experienced MacLeay and J. B. A. Jenkins, while the attack was built on J. K. Erith's fast bowling and T. P. M. Fleming's slow left-arm spin. Positive results eluded **Exeter School**, their two wins, over Allhallows and Old Exonians, set against a solitary defeat by Queen's, Taunton. No one player was outstanding, although C. L. Bawden, a left-hand bat and leg-spin bowler, caught the eye as a future prospect.

A preponderance of drawn games also characterised the season for **Felsted**, most of whose young side are expected to return in 1988. The captain, N. V. Knight, was outstanding for English Schools, with 1,027 runs, the next-highest aggregate being S. E. Carson's 377. Although the off-spin of S. A. Pearce-Higgins was accurate and generally economical, and J. B. C. Gilsenan and T. F. C. Cooper, both fast-medium, were hostile on occasions – Cooper took six Winchester wickets for 60 runs – an inability to knock over the tailenders led frequently to stalemate. **Fettes** did not manage a single win but their inexperienced side exceeded expectations by having the better of drawn games v Strathallan and Kelvinside. The captain, M. A. M. Adam, was a technically correct batsman and also opened the bowling with J. L. MacLean, who enjoyed success with bat and ball. Athletic and enthusiastic fielding was a feature of the XI's season. **Forest**, while undefeated in schools matches, were not decisive enough to win more than twice – v Bancroft's and the KAP XI. Their leading player was the talented fourteen-year-old, A. C. Richards, who took the most wickets, scored more than twice as many runs as the next batsman, and with A. R. Heyes went forward for HMC Under-15 trials. With **Framlingham's** young side rarely scoring enough runs to press for victory, N. C. Gowing's 102 not out v St Joseph's, Ipswich, was a feature of the season.

Giggleswick had a disappointing season. Lacking support for M. P. Kaye, a left-handed batsman and left-arm spin bowler, they struggled to dismiss opposing batsmen, found it difficult to chase runs, and failed to register a win. Kaye, scoring 120 not out, featured with D. A. V. Caton in an unbroken opening partnership of 207 – a school record – against Hipperholme GS. **Glenalmond**, unbeaten by schools, enjoyed good victories over Fettes and

Loretto but lost their momentum towards the end of the season and were perhaps fortunate that rain fell in the matches v Strathallan and Sedbergh. Noteworthy performances came from the opening batsman, J. P. Brown, who scored a maiden hundred v Dollar Academy, P. N. Kay behind the stumps, and R. J. H. White, a wrist-spinner who took 27 wickets, mostly bowling accurate googlies. Also unbeaten by schools were **Gordonstoun**, who benefited from better weather in the north of Scotland, although their batsmen did struggle on the damp wickets of April and May. A number of good Colts were drafted into the side late in the season, giving rise to expectations for 1988. An excellent season for **Gresham's** was followed by a tour to Barbados in August. With everyone contributing at some time or other, S. Musselwhite showing potential as a batsman of real quality, and T. D. Berwick regularly picking up wickets with his well-flighted leg-spin, fine victories were achieved v Framlingham, The Leys, King's Ely and MCC.

Haileybury also enjoyed a successful season, their six wins including those v Uppingham, Oundle and Dulwich, as well as the only victory over Scots Collage, Sydney. Bowling away-swing, B. J. B. Hall took 52 wickets, including seven for 42 v Oundle, and with E. G. Erith (twin brother of the Eton opener) took 90 wickets, a record for a Haileybury opening attack. The introduction to the XI of two sixteen-year-olds, J. B. Jouning and D. C. L. Beynon, produced 668 and 403 runs respectively. A tour to Australia was planned for Christmas. The inexperience of **Hampton's** young side often found expression when they were chasing runs. Nevertheless, W. L. C. Taylor scored 552, with two hundreds, and A. J. B. Sales developed into a useful opening batsman, as well as keeping wicket reliably. With the seam attack restricted by injuries, S. Patel (slow left-arm) took 49 wickets, including eight for 34 v St Benedict's, and P. Laver's off-spin frequently confounded opposing batsmen. **Harrow**, well captained by D. Manasseh, were unbeaten by schools and defeated Bradfield, Winchester, Charterhouse and Haileybury. Although D. W. F. Berry-Green and A. C. W. Snow opened the attack effectively, and the medium-pace swing bowling of J. A. R. Hill was a welcome addition for the last four matches, it was the slow left-arm spin of Manasseh and R. D. Nelson's off-spin that provoked most dismissals. H. Boralessa batted with excellent concentration and technique, exemplified by his 127 in 380 minutes v Charterhouse and carrying his bat for 91 v I Zingari. Another schoolboy to carry his bat was D. Luka of **Highgate**, who did so for 82 v Abingdon.

Hipperholme GS's six wins came v Crossley Heath, Rishworth, Habergham, Fulneck, Read and Batley GS. The captain, W. Clarke, bowling fast-medium, took seven for 9 in 8.3 overs as Crossley Heath were despatched for 23, and P. Rawsden hit 102 v Rishworth in the Under-17 Barclays Bank English Schools Cup. **Hurstpierpoint**, helped by winning five successive matches in the last six days of the season, set a new record with eleven wins, while M. J. Hastwell's aggregate of 891 runs was the second highest ever for the school. **Ipswich**, unbeaten during the school term, had their most successful season of the 1980s. The captain, J. V. Zagni, compiled 136 v RGS Colchester and 103 not out v Woodbridge, as well as taking 37 wickets bowling slow left-arm. He took five wickets in an innings four times. N. Shahid scored the most runs, including 104 not out v Felsted, and took the most wickets bowling leg-spin and googlies. Both played in the MCC Schools Festival, with Shahid being selected for MCC Schools v MCC and for NAYC v MCC Schools, as well as playing for Essex Second XI. R. Heap was a consistent opening batsman, and wicket-keeper S. Burnell took thirteen catches and made ten stumpings.

A young **Kent College** side achieved a creditable record, losing only one schools match and beating Dover College, St Edmund's, Sir Roger Manwood's and Choughs CC, as well as tying with Chatham House. G. Jenkins, a left-handed bat and right-arm fast-medium bowler, was leading run-scorer and wicket-taker, while S. Warley, an off-break bowler, and J. Hooker revealed their potential as opening batsmen in their first season. All-round team effort brought its rewards for **King Edward VI College, Stourbridge**. The batting tended to be dominated by the captain, G. R. Haynes, whose 140 not out v the Gentlemen of Worcestershire was a school record, M. J. Smith (two hundreds) and M. Jones. Six drawn games reflected an inability to bowl sides out, and one of the two losses came in an unusual manner when the last man was out, handled the ball, off the last delivery of the game. **King Edward VI, Southampton**, varied from outstanding, on some occasions, to mediocre on others. They won the local Sixth Form trophy, and held the advantage in many of the eleven drawn games. J. D. Stanley, still with two more years in the XI, was a most consistent batsman, while P. D. Chrispin, a right-arm fast bowler and authoritative left-hand bat, played for Hampshire

Under-19. M. L. Tidby's figures were dented when he was hit for six sixes in an over by a club player from Guernsey. A feature of the season for **King Edward VII, Lytham**, was their excellent performance v University College School at the Barnard Castle festival.

Batting was the strong suit of **King Edward's, Birmingham**, for whom W. Martin hit 1,104 runs at 110.40 and P. N. J. Inglis 711 at 64.63. They put on an unbeaten 270 for the first wicket in the win v Gentlemen of Worcestershire; Martin 148 and Inglis 109. Their reputation, however, prompted opposing teams to make defensive declarations, and although J. P. Coates (off-spin) and M. J. Goodall (leg-spin) bowled well, their own attack had its limitations. **King William's College, Isle of Man**, reported one of their best seasons ever; they were unbeaten and their seven wins included defeats of Merchant Taylors' Crosby, Aldenham and Liverpool College. The captain, S. W. Ellis, set the tone with 515 runs and 50 wickets, bowling medium-fast with occasional off-spin. W. R. Ashbrook and J. C. Radford, both medium-fast, supported him well. Centuries came from the left-handed opener, P. W. Townsend (103 v Stockport GS), and Radford (115 v MCC), while the wicket-keeper, A. P. Woodward, put together 419 runs opening the batting. **King's College, Taunton**, batted consistently, passing 200 nine times. The captain, A. C. Berry, scored 673 runs, including 103 v Clifton, while the side's other three-figure innings came from D. J. Battishill, whose left-arm spin accounted for 33 batsmen, including six for 29 v Blundell's.

For their seven wins, **King's College School, Wimbledon**, owed much to their spinners, D. W. Talbot (slow left-arm), and the captain, R. M. Wight (off-breaks). Talbot took 58 wickets in his first season, capturing five or more in an innings six times including a return of eight for 46 v Kingston GS. Wight also headed the batting and was given solid support by his opening partner, I. B. M. Ratnayake. **King's, Bruton**, a young XI, played some good cricket but, lacking experience, were not consistent enough to win any matches. J. Petrie, the captain, bowling medium pace with control and variation, took 28 wickets, but he disappointed with the bat and the bulk of the runs came from the unorthodox R. Ashfield and the stylish M. Vaughan-Brown. Inexperience also handicapped **King's, Canterbury**, for whom J. R. Davies (fast-medium) took five or more wickets v Cranleigh, Sutton Valence and KCS Wimbledon. S. R. Turner was a consistent opening batsman, while the only three-figure innings came from A. E. Mitchell v the Old Boys. **King's, Chester**, drew eleven of their games, not helped by the inability of their captain and strike bowler, J. S. W. Hawkins, to prime the attack. None the less, in spite of a painful back injury, he led the side well. C. Goodier (off-spin) was outstanding, with a school record of 50 wickets in his first season, and A. R. H. Mais and G. W. Jones, a left-hander, batted consistently all season. **King's, Macclesfield**, beat Cheadle Hulme, Newcastle-under-Lyme HS, Merchant Taylors' Crosby and Abbot Beyne, as well as tying with Arnold, but their six defeats were all by schools. S. R. Swindells scored prolifically and effected 33 dismissals (19 ct, 14 st), while S. J. White's leg-spin brought him 62 wickets – one short of the school record – including eight and nine in consecutive matches.

King's, Rochester, enjoyed another successful season in which they were unbeaten by schools and defeated seven under the positive captaincy and example of M. P. Mernagh, whose 63 wickets, including nine for 26 v Wellingborough School, took his total to 210 in four seasons. The batting had depth and maturity. **King's, Worcester**, had an enjoyable season, but an occasional brittleness in the batting and a reluctance in the middle order to graft after the loss of early wickets revealed a weakness. Although J. R. Underwood (slow left-arm) took the most wickets in his first full season, the lack of an experienced seam attack was a handicap. Fielding perhaps the youngest side in the school's history, **Kingston GS** often struggled. For all that, there were two centuries – one off 58 balls – from the captain, R. J. Williams, and a return of six for 30 v Teddington CC by R. A. Chandler, a leg-spinner, to savour. **Kingswood's** strong all-round side celebrated the school's 125th year of cricket with an excellent season. In schools matches they beat Prior Park, King Edward's Bath, Bristol GS, The Perse and Bishop's Stortford, against whom R. W. Lewis took six for 84 before scoring 130 not out in a school record winning total of 243 for nine.

Lancing's attack, consisting of four spinners and three seamers, flourished on the wet wickets of May and June, but lacked the experience and penetration to extract wins from draws on the drier ones of July. With batting in depth and excellent ground fielding, they beat Sussex Martlets, Free Foresters, Brighton VIth Form College, Christ's Hospital, Seaford, Sussex Schools and Hurstpierpoint. **Leighton Park** struggled at times to dismiss the opposition, although the captain, J. P. Newell-Price (medium-fast) was unlucky not to take more than 24 wickets. M. Harris (medium-fast) swung the ball prodigiously – perhaps too much on occasions. Schools wins were at the expense of Lord Wandsworth College and Victoria College, Jersey. In a season of mixed fortunes, **The Leys** played some exciting games. The captain and opening batsman, C. W. Barker, scored 613 runs, while N. R. Lankester scored 423 runs and took 46 wickets with his leg-spinners, including six for 56 v Felsted. With only three victories against schools sides, **Liverpool College** reported an indifferent season. Apart from the excellent wicket-keeping of Clein, the fielding was lethargic, even careless, and provided little support to the bowlers. J. M. Bishop's off-spin accounted for 27 batsmen, and J. Q. Harrington, a Colt, took fifteen wickets in his three matches, bowling leg-spin. R. B. Downes and A. W. B. Smith, the seam attack, also opened the batting with some success, but they received little support down the order.

Lord Wandsworth College's inexperienced side also suffered a disappointing season, often either batting or bowling well, but never bringing both together in the same match. The batting of the captain, S. H. Blows, who hit the side's only hundred, and the leg-spin bowling of the young D. A. Berry were bright spots. Highlights for **Loretto** were an innings of 108 not out from the captain, T. R. McCreath, and a return of seven for 93 by M. C. Eglinton, both v Rossall. Finishing with ten wins, **Loughborough GS** built their success on all-round strength and hard, fast home wickets. S. Pickering (fast), M. I. Gidley (off-spin) and fourteen-year-old C. Hawkes (slow left-arm) all troubled opposing batsmen, while in the side's own strong batting line-up the captain, I. Bell, and the left-handed Gidley were particularly effective at Nos. 3 and 4. In the ten-wicket victory over the XL Club, openers S. Sawbridge (132 not out) and D. Jones (63 not out) put on 210 runs, while Gidley scored 132 not out v Abbott Beyne. He played for English Schools, as did Hawkes at Under-15 level.

Unbeaten by schools, and losing only to MCC, **Magdalen College School** recorded five wins, notably those v Lord Williams's College Thame, Dean Close and Latymer Upper. The batting, led by the captain, T. J. Stockwin, with 740 runs, was strong while the bowling, with T. E. J. Waters (medium-fast), S. N. Webb (slow left-arm) and R. J. Suckling (off-spin) prominent, was well supported in the field. Stockwin excelled behind the stumps. In August and September the team played in the Zimbabwe Schools Festival. **Malvern College** benefited from the fine team spirit engendered by the captaincy of G. N. Lunt, who batted responsibly and enjoyed success with his leg-breaks. The opener J. R. Wileman's 772 runs included 107 v Charterhouse, and the medium-pace all-rounder, E. G. Maughan, had figures of seven for 49 v Old Malvernians in his return of 38 wickets. H. C. Douglas-Pennant, B. C. Usher and S. Johnson-Marshall provided further seam bowling, while A. J. Hardwicke, a Colt, established himself as a wicket-keeper-batsman. **Manchester GS**, who beat Bury GS, Bradford GS and Lytham, boasted a powerful batting line-up, with J. P. Crawley, P. M. Crawley, I. R. Cross and A. B. Gaskarth all passing 200 runs. Although accurate, the attack generally lacked penetration, but D. J. Worsley's six for 70 v Shrewsbury was a fine performance. The XI's season was curtailed owing to the school's reaching the final of the Barclays Bank Under-17 Cup, which they lost by five wickets to Millfield.

Several close and exciting finishes characterised the later part of the season of **Merchant Taylors', Crosby**, who were captained by sixteen-year-old R. W. Glynne-Jones, their wicket-keeper. Against King's, Chester, D. L. Clift, in his first over for the XI, took four for 0, including a hat-trick, at medium pace. Another feature was the opening partnership of 149 in 102 minutes between Glynne-Jones and Clift v William Hulme's, and S. R. McGee (medium-fast) looked a fine prospect with six for 22 v St Mary's College, Crosby. **Merchant Taylors', Northwood**, reported a rather indifferent season, although they beat St Albans, Highgate, Watford GS, Enfield GS and St Peter's, York. K. J. Clifford opened the innings effectively but too often the middle order failed him. The most successful bowlers were A. P. Thompson, J. L. Hampel (slow left-arm), who took six for 39 v Watford GS, and the captain, D. W. R. Wiles, who returned six for 36 v Highgate. Success came for **Merchiston Castle** v The Edinburgh Academy, George Heriot's, St Bees and Stewart's-Melville. M. E. R. Paton, the captain N. R. Ballantyne, S. J. K. Laird and A. J. K. Wilson gave the batting authority, while S. D. L. Francis and D. M. Streek (both fast-medium) formed an effective new-ball partnership. Against Strathallan, F. W. Hunter, a slow left-armer, took nine for 58, thought to be the best return in the school's history.

Millfield were unbeaten for the second successive season, while their Under-17s won the Barclays Bank competition for the fourth year running. The high point for an XI of tremendous batting depth was an unbroken opening partnership of 252 between G. Lucas and P. Holloway. H. R. J. Trump played for MCC Schools and, as did A. R. Phillips, signed for Somerset. The season was also a notable one for **Mill Hill**, who undertook a tour to Barbados, established a cricket festival with Plymouth College, Norwich School and Warwick School, and won five of their schools matches, the most for ten years. Aldenham, Dulwich, Highgate, Haberdashers' Aske's and Norwich were the schools beaten. L. B. Braham, the captain, opened the batting with consistency to score 970 runs and was well supported by B. R. Hartman, who also took the most wickets, and C. R. Younger, the wicket-keeper. E. M. Latter, a Colt, took six for 25 v Hampstead CC bowling at medium pace. The batting of **Milton Abbey**, sound in schools matches, proved to be vulnerable against club sides. However, the success in this department of Colts S. J. E. Courage and C. P. Cook bodes well for the future. The attack lacked penetration, although there was some guile in the slow left-arm bowling of W. O. Quibell and the off-spin of H. G. H. Groves. After five early wins against schools, **Monkton Combe** lost momentum through exams and rain. Fast bowler J. A. Jenkins emerged as an all-rounder, and fifteen-year-old S. J. Kandavanam (also fast) showed promise for the future.

Playing positive cricket, **Newcastle-under-Lyme School** achieved five victories, including one by ten wickets over Abbot Beyne. Opening batsmen R. N. Clowes and R. W. Johnson complemented each other's style, while D. J. Brock proved an exceptional fast-medium bowler. In a transitional period, the batting of **Norwich School** was insecure, with only N. A. Colman showing any degree of aggression. Frequently the bowlers were required to defend totals of less than 100, and once did so v Wymondham. The only convincing win was v RHS Holbrook. The season began slowly for **Nottingham HS** with nine draws and just one win, but the second half brought some exciting games and five more victories, including that by 120 runs v Bedford Modern, against whom M. Saxelby made 131 in two hours. He was selected for NAYC at Lord's. Hundreds also came from P. R. D. Briggs and N. A. Hunt, who scored the most runs.

Enjoying a successful season with seven wins and just one defeat, **Oakham** had a solid batting line-up revolving round the captain, D. M. Robjohns, who, at No. 3, scored 918 runs and took his aggregate for the XI to 2,322, a school record. Opening bowler S. V. Aldis proved too quick for most schoolboy sides, and was instrumental in Kimbolton being dismissed for 30 and Christ's, Brecon, for 78. Although they were hard to beat, **The Oratory**'s lack of experience showed when chasing runs and they managed only two wins. However, with the entire XI expected to return in 1988, prospects are bright. Outstanding for **Oundle** was their captain, T. I. Macmillan, whose 924 runs included four centuries, his 161 not out v Bedford Modern and 125 v St Edward's, Oxford, coming on consecutive days. Another highlight was the first-wicket stand of 209 v MCC he shared with A. R. Turner. The lack of penetrative spin support for R. H. J. Jenkins (fast-medium), who took 46 wickets, restricted their wins to five – v Uppingham, St Edward's Oxford, Oundle Rovers, Northamptonshire Amateurs and Free Foresters.

In schools matches **The Perse** beat Newport FGS, Wellingborough, The Leys and RGS Newcastle. The batting, expected to be their strength, was disappointing later in the season when they failed to force wins from promising positions. N. M. Law, though failing to maintain his early form, again scored more than 500 runs, including 109 v King's, Ely, and another early century came from I. R. Styan with 100 not out v Newport FGS. The attack had depth and variety, with 30 wickets falling to Styan (left-arm medium), including six for 32 v RGS Newcastle and three for 7 in eleven overs v Ipswich. P. A. Bailey (slow left-arm) was the pick of the spinners. **Pocklington** suffered more than most from the weather, with six matches abandoned, yet still won eleven. Their captain, T. P. B. Balderson, scored 623 runs and took 40 wickets, helped with the bat by S. A. Clarke, who also passed 600 runs, and in the attack by J. R. L. Brown, who captured 44 wickets. **Prior Park College** enjoyed their best season for many years, beating six schools, among them Dauntsey's by nine wickets and King Edward's, Bath, by ten wickets (a first-wicket stand of 183). M. Woodhouse, J. Reid and A. Hadley all passed 400 runs, while G. Lee, a newcomer to the side, took 35 wickets with his off-spin and fast bowler J. Powell collected 28.

The captain of **Queen Elizabeth GS, Wakefield**, J. Wild, hit 106 not out v King William's College, Isle of Man, their only century. For their seven wins, countered by only one defeat, **Queen's College, Taunton**, owed much to their outstanding all-rounder, D. N. A. Essien, who scored the most runs and took the most wickets before going on to represent English Schools. J. J. A. Wilson, an excellent captain, played some fine innings in a strong batting line-up.

Radley were captained by C. H. H. Pegg, who continued to show promise as a wicket-keeper and, although his form with the bat was generally disappointing, compiled their only hundred – 117 v Bradfield. He played for Middlesex Second XI. R. E. Q. Gurney's aggregate included two innings of 97 not out, against Sherborne and Winchester. G. D. L. Powell (slow left-arm) had returns of seven for 61 v Sherborne, six for 38 v Cheltenham, five for 27 v Bradfield and six for 56 v Winchester, the last three schools all being beaten. A below-average season was reported by **Ratcliffe College**, whose batting was uncertain on the wet wickets. However, the bowling made amends and five wins were recorded. Bowling fast-medium, P. A. Mestecky was in exceptional form, taking 61 wickets at 9.31, including five in an innings seven times, and increasing his tally for the past two years to 119. He also played the side's only three-figure innings, 100 not out v Loughborough GS. **Reading School**, with eleven wins, enjoyed their most successful season for many years. The captain, J. S. Pritchard (fast-medium) took 52 wickets, his eight for 34 v Pangbourne College including a hat-trick, and O. D. Beckett hit 102 not out v Shiplake. T. J. C. Dance, a fifth former, looked a useful right-arm opening bowler but excelled mainly as a left-handed opening bat whose 709 runs included 123 not out v Leighton Park.

In a season of rebuilding, **Reed's** took comfort from winning more matches than they lost. **Reigate GS** fielded their best side for some years, only successive losses in the last three matches marring a healthy record. S. J. Virley led the side with assurance and topped the batting, while P. A. Radford, an opener, compiled a maiden century. In his third season, fast bowler M. T. Holman again spearheaded the attack, but really lacked support. It was an outstanding season for **Repton's** opening batsman, C. J. Adams. Combining power and a range of strokes, he scored four centuries on his way to 1,242 runs, passing 1,000 before the end of June and breaking R. A. Hutton's school record of 1,036. He was selected for MCC Schools. The captain, D. J. Anderson, led from the front, taking 56 wickets with his medium-paced seam bowling. Eight wins were recorded, v Shrewsbury, Cheltenham, Pocklington, Worksop, Oakham and Wrekin; defeat was inflicted by Rugby and Malvern. **Rossall's** strike bowlers proved too expensive, and their inability to bowl sides out led to ten draws and only one win – v King's, Macclesfield. However, there were many sound contributions from the batsmen, notably the captain and wicket-keeper, C. D. Foster, whose century v Loretto at the Merchant Taylors', Northwood festival was the first against a school for many years.

Royal GS, Guildford, attributed their success to a sound attack, for the batting was occasionally disappointing, with some players frustratingly failing to fulfil their potential. Their end-of-term festival was attended by RGS, High Wycombe, and **Royal GS Worcester**, who, although without their leading batsmen of 1986, were unbeaten by schools, recording thirteen victories. The side's outstanding player was D. W. Headley, son of R.G. and grandson of G.A., who took 57 wickets bowling at fast-medium and scored 627 runs. J. S. Waters, the leg-spinner, took more than 50 wickets for the third successive season. **Rugby**, beaten only by Bedford in schools matches, enjoyed a successful season in which the school's Colts won the Lord's Taverners *Cricketer* Trophy from Wellington College in the final. Twelve fifties and two hundreds shared by the XI's leading batsmen, with B. C. A. Ellison heading both sets of averages. Bowling fast-medium, he, A. L. C. Winchester and H. N. Bhatia (leg-spin) all took 40 or more wickets. Bhatia played in his fifth successive fixture v Marlborough. Excellent ground fielding characterised the performances of **Rydal**, with S. M. Williams, J. R. Hogg and P. S. Goldsmith outstanding. A. G. Moore and H. S. L. Bradley batted well, but in a season badly affected by the rain, the bowling tended to be weak.

St Albans were disappointed that their county Colts, A. Dalwood and G. Dill, did not find their form until after the exams. D. Barlow was the only batsman to score more than one fifty, and only J. Smart v Watford GS and G. Bandy v John Lyon took five wickets in an innings. Unbeaten and with eleven victories, **St Dunstan's** enjoyed their best season ever; with all but two members expected to return in 1988, they are optimistic for the college's centenary year, when a tour of Australia is planned for December. M. A. Slade, whose 687 runs included 108 not out v Trinity, Croydon, G. R. S. Scovell and M. J. Dowse (101 v Whitgift) all played for Kent Under-19. In a strong batting side at **St Edmund's Canterbury**, N. C. Kennett scored two unbeaten hundreds, putting on 156 with R. Hayes v the XL Club and sharing an unbroken opening stand of 141 with M. J. E. Horton v the Staff. The attack lacked penetration, although the bowlers worked hard. **St George's, Weybridge**, suffered their first defeats at the hands of schools since July 1982, four coming after declarations. Two fifth formers performed most encouragingly, I. Turner scoring 501 runs and taking 34 wickets, and C. M. Bennett scoring 568 runs, including 146 not out v Hampton. St George's won the South zone Barclays Bank Under-17 competition, only to lose to Millfield in the national semi-finals.

It was a disappointing season for **St John's, Leatherhead**, who beat only Seaford College but lost to Alleyn's, Whitgift and, heavily, Cranleigh. A redeeming feature was the batting of the captain, S. E. Penfold, whose 747 runs included 107 v XL Club, 113 v Epsom College and 143 not out v Christ's Hospital. **St Lawrence College**, with many young players, managed only three wins against five losses. A. O. Uzor, as well as being the leading wicket-taker, was their outstanding batsman, scoring fifty in eight of his thirteen innings and going on to 154 not out v the Band of Brothers. Memorable in an unbeaten season for **St Paul's** were an exciting tie v Dulwich off the last ball of the final twenty overs and a ten-wicket win v The Leys, against whom H. C. G. Boothroyd-Brooks (121 not out) and P. W. T. Neate (102 not out) put on a school record first-wicket partnership of 246. Fulfilling the promise shown in 1986, **St Peter's, York**, won eight matches and lost only to MCC and to their hosts at the Merchant Taylors', Northwood, end-of-term festival. They were ably captained by all-rounder N. D. Muirhead, who scored two centuries, and M. D. Donoghue bowled very well at fast-medium for his 55 wickets.

Never bowled out, **Sedbergh** were unbeaten and won four matches, including those v RGS Lancaster and Ampleforth. The absence of a good spinner prevented them from pressing for victory in games eventually drawn. H. J. A. Daniels and A. M. Skinner opened the bowling to good effect, dismissing Glenalmond for 28 and Ampleforth for 44, Daniels's six wickets against the latter including a hat-trick. Daniels, a fine left-handed bat, also hit a superb century v a Professionals XI at Glenalmond, and there were two other hundreds from J. R. C. Dakin. Along with the captain, C. D. H. Palmer, these three played for Cumbria Under-19. After narrowly losing their first match to St Dunstan's, **Sevenoaks** were not beaten and, as in beating Caterham and Cranbrook, showed considerable powers of recovery when defeat seemed likely. St George's, Weybridge, were beaten off the last ball. The captain and wicket-keeper, C. J. Crang, hit three unbeaten hundeds; A. Griffiths (right-hand opening bat and slow left-arm bowler) and J. D. Fry (right-hand bat and fast bowler) were useful all-rounders.

Sherborne, with a young side, did well to remain undefeated. Their four wins included those v Bradfield and Haileybury. Much depended on the captain, A. Kardooni, who batted and led the side with great authority; in a total of 188 for nine declared v Taunton, he hit an unbeaten 114. Some entertaining cricket was played by **Shiplake**, who beat Oratory, Leighton Park and Bearwood in schools matches. For the second successive season C. Haynes scored the most runs and, despite the lack of suitable wickets, A. Hyman bowled fast and well. M. Patel (slow left-arm) improved during the season. A good fielding side occasionally let itself down by dropping catches at vital times. **Shrewsbury's** experienced XI had a fair season, the most impressive of their seven victories being over MCC, Cheltenham and Uppingham. The batting depended largely on J. R. Prichard (left-hand), C. M. Bullock, the captain, and M. J. Lascelles, each of whom passed 500 runs, with a century and sixteen fifties between them. A balanced attack shared the wickets but struggled to work through opposing batting after making early inroads.

In an enjoyable season, the inexperienced side of **Sir Roger Manwood's** were well led by J. A. N. Goold. Although injured for nearly half the season, when available he bowled fast-medium to form an aggressive opening partnership with D. J. Hill (fast), but without consistent support for them the attack often looked unbalanced. Most runs came from M. D. Giles, who, while not always technically correct, hit the ball hard and with confidence. **Stamford School**, under the captaincy of R. P. C. Plant, who scored 618 runs and took 33 wickets, also enjoyed a good season. There were five good wins, and in two of the drawn games the scores were level with wickets in hand. **Stockport GS** won their first match, v Liverpool College, and their last, v RGS Newcastle, with four more victories in between. Batting highlights were 100 not out v Haslingden by the left-handed I. Millner and 111 by M. Baulkwill v Doncaster GS. The main strike bowler, M. Duckworth, returned six for 70 v Oakwood, R. Pailin (left-arm medium-fast) took six for 45 v Bangor GS, and there was good support from two leg-spinners, P. Duckworth and B. Anderson. The highlight of a festival held as part of the school's quincentenary celebrations was a first-ever fixture v MCC. Unbeaten, for the first time in some years, **Stonyhurst** attributed their success to the medium-pace bowling of all-rounders J. Barnes and G. O'Driscoll, although the victories v Ampleforth, Stonyhurst Wanderers and the XL Club resulted from all-round teamwork.

Stowe, a strong batting side, beat Dean Close, Free Foresters, Bedford Modern, Kelvinside Academy and Merchant Taylors', Northwood, losing only to Rugby. The captain, R. S. M. Morris, made an outstanding contribution, his 938 runs including centuries v Dean Close (138), Free Foresters (109 not out), Mill Hill (109), Repton (141 not out) and Kelvinside Academy, against whom he and W. J. P. Atkinson put on 156 in 21 overs. The attack was spearheaded by R. B. Pumphrey (fast-medium), who returned six for 47 v Rugby; balance was provided by the off-spin of Morris, who took seven for 38 v Radley, and the slow left-arm turn of fifteen-year-old M. J. T. Jefferson, whose six for 55 v Dean Close included a hat-trick. **Strathallan**, although unbeaten by schools in Scotland, reported a season of mixed fortunes. The bowling lacked support for K. D. Smith, an off-spinner, who took his wickets for the school to 120, and the batting was generally disappointing. Highlights were G. M. Adam's unbeaten century v MCC, and the young opening partnership of R. Moffat and J. A. Jacobsen, which showed its worth at the end of the season.

Taunton School, captained by J. C. Kerslake, son of R. C. Kerslake, were unbeaten for the first time, winning eight matches. A team which enjoyed their cricket, **Tiffin** beat MCC, Reigate GS, Monkton Combe, Emanuel, Latymer Upper, Reed's and St Benedict's, against whom A. J. M. Carnie (fast-medium) returned six for 47. They batted in depth with five batsmen passing 300 runs; but the only hundred was G. J. Affleck's 102 not out v Emanuel. The captain, N. P. Warren, who opened the bowling with Carnie, made a splendid all-round contribution and represented Surrey Schools Under-19. At **Tonbridge**, J. I. Longley passed 1,000 runs for the second successive season, carried the batting, not surprisingly, and played for Kent Second XI. J. S. Durling (slow left-arm) was by far the most accurate and penetrative bowler. Eton were the only school to beat them, and there were wins v Winchester, Clifton and Eastbourne at the end-of-term festival.

Playing positive cricket, the young side of **Trent College** achieved an encouraging record with six wins. They relied initially on the experience and all-round ability of the captain, R. D. Kerrell (fast-medium) and the batting of T. H. Smith, although the leg-spin bowling of I. R. Birch augured well for the future. **Trinity**, losing only one of their 30 fixtures to the rain, enjoyed fourteen wins, including those v Hampton, Reigate, Reed's, St Benedict's, Kingston GS, Emanuel and MCC – the latter by one wicket, having chased 204 to win. Some promising young batsmen benefited from the experience of K. P. Morley, while the bowling strength lay in the under-16 seam trio of J. D. Good, P. A. Gardner and D. M. P. Turner. **Truro** were led by S. Peters, who had a solid all-round season and was well supported by A. Johnston, a left-handed batsman.

A mixed season was reported by **Uppingham**. The middle-order batting was fragile, no batsman inspiring confidence, although E. R. Fowler, a Colt, looked an excellent prospect. The bowling, however, was always strong. P. J. E. Spencer (left-arm medium-fast) and D. B. J. Cooke (off-breaks) each took 48 wickets, Spencer's return including eight for 12 v Leicester Gentlemen, and G. M. Leather (fast-medium) looked useful in his first season. Prominent again for **Victoria College, Jersey**, was P. J. Le Cornu, who proved himself to be one of the school's best-ever all-rounders with 859 runs and 70 wickets.

Warwick School suffered three early defeats, but consistent progress as the XI gained experience brought three wins. The batting developed around C. G. Stanton, who was ably supported by J. D. Moffatt and A. J. Bolton. C. Oswald, who with P. M. A. Hulyer took up off-spin at the start of the season, returned six for 63 v Trent College, but the presence of three off-spinners at the top of the averages illustrated the weakness of the seam bowling. A record of eleven draws, against two wins – v MCC and Gentlemen of Hertfordshire – reflected in part **Watford GS's** inability to support with any variety the opening attack of P. G. Rimmer and J. G. E. Pepper. Despite depth in batting, no-one established the habit of playing big innings. **Wellingborough School**, winners against Wisbech GS, Trent College, Ratcliffe College, Lord Williams's Thame and Kingswood, had an experienced captain in M. I. Ingram, their wicket-keeper, and two interesting young bowlers in fourteen-year-old N. J. Haste (medium), who took seven for 14 v Kingswood, and the fifteen-year-old all-rounder, J. M. Attfield (off-breaks). R. J. Cousins (fast-medium) took the most wickets.

In an excellent season, **Wellington College** beat Cranleigh, Winchester, Bradfield, Radley, MCC, Free Foresters and the Royal Corps of Transport, all seven wins coming when batting second. Most players made a significant contribution, but noteworthy were J. R. H. Fenwick (fast-medium), whose 52 wickets included eight for 45 v Radley, and the captain, J. S. Hodgson. The latter's 542 runs included the first century by the school v Marlborough – 122 not out, featuring six sixes and eleven fours – and his off-breaks brought him six for 47 v Winchester. **Wellington School, Somerset**, enjoyed their best season for many years, with seven victories, the most notable being v Plymouth College and Royal Naval College, Dartmouth. Opener J. Clist, outstanding with 649 runs, provided a firm foundation, and M. Coleman competently captained a team committed to positive cricket. A succession of exciting finishes characterised **Westminster's** unbeaten season. A well-balanced side was ably captained by all-rounder J. D. R. Griffiths, whose century v Charterhouse was the high point. A tour of India was planned for December.

Whitgift reported fair results in schools matches, in which they beat Reigate GS, Kingston GS, Trinity and St John's, Leatherhead. Three batsmen dominated; N. S. Auer, who hit 100 not out v Dulwich, was the most prolific, followed by the captain and opening bat, I. L. H. Scarisbrick, and G. J. Thompson, who reached three figures v Reigate. Auer also headed the bowling averages, although J. A. M. Bullock (medium) took the most wickets. Enterprising cricket saw **William Hulme's GS** successfully chase large totals v Queen Elizabeth GS Wakefield, Stockport and Rydal, and bowl out St Mary's Crosby, Birkenhead and Bolton. Shrewsbury were also beaten, H. P. V. Scott-Gall (medium) reaping six for 19 on a green-top. Highlights were a school record 143 v QEGS by C. W. Timm, the captain and left-hand bat; three centuries from opening batsman D. M. J. Timm – 118 not out v Stockport, 125 not out v Rydal and 101 v King's, Macclesfield; and his six for 59 v Bolton.

As expected in a year of rebuilding, **Winchester's** young side experienced a poor season, yet they played better than a record of no wins and ten losses would suggest. Apart from some excellent innings by D. A. de Lanoy Meijer, a Colt, the batting was inconsistent, and the bowling, although supported by some occasionally brilliant fielding, lacked an incisive edge. The XI was captained by M. I. Riaz, a nephew of the Nawab of Pataudi, but while one link was renewed, another was broken with the retirement of V. Broderick, Winchester's professional for 28 years. **Woodhouse Grove**, another young team, were encouraged to beat William Hulme's GS, Bootham and Leeds GS. The attack lacked quality and variety, too much depending on the captain, L. Savill (fast-medium), who took 32 wickets, headed both averages, and was selected for Yorkshire Senior Schools. The opening batsman, L. Gomersall, developed well as the season progressed to score the most runs. **Worksop College**, after four decisive defeats in schools matches, finished on a high note with a six-wicket win over Bloxham. A thirteen-year-old left-hander, R. A. Kettleborough, was the most prolific batsman and with most of the side expected to return in 1988, prospects are good.

Wrekin College beat Shrewsbury, King's Worcester, MCC, Wellington CC and Old Wrekinians. The captain, C. A. Fenton, scored 657 runs, including two hundreds, but while runs often came quickly, the batting was occasionally exposed by accurate bowling. A hostile opening attack of J. R. Ford and I. Mirza received able support from Fenton (medium) and S. R. Jackson (left-arm medium), but the loss through injury of Ford for much of the season upset the balance, especially as the spin bowling was disappointing. The batting of **Wycliffe College** relied too heavily on the captain and opener, S. J. Reed, who with 643 runs broke his own school record of the previous season. A. Brown and S. G. Cady played some exciting free-scoring innings but overall the batting was too inconsistent. Although R. N. Giles (fast-medium) and Cady (left-arm fast) persevered on unhelpful wickets, the bowling generally struggled to bowl sides out. At **Wyggeston and Queen Elizabeth I College**, the batting was carried by the openers, S. C. Brammar, the captain, and the left-handed K. T. Roberts, who shared in partnerships of 119 v Wyggeston Masters and 138 unbroken in the victory v John Cleveland College in the Leicestershire Under-19 final. The only bowler to take ten wickets was J. L. Green (fast-medium), whose five for 18 were instrumental in the win v Ratcliffe College.

THE SCHOOLS

(Qualification: Batting 100 runs; Bowling: 10 wickets)

* On name indicates captain.   ** On figures indicates not out.*

Note: The line for batting reads Innings–Not Outs–Runs–Highest Innings–Average; that for bowling reads Overs–Maidens–Runs–Wickets–Average.

ABINGDON SCHOOL

Played 22: Won 6, Lost 5, Drawn 11

Master i/c: A. Mitra

Batting—P. D. Lunn 21–3–721–119–40.05; *G. D. Scott 22–2–595–87–29.75; R. J. Tilley 18–5–348–55*–26.76; N. D. Franklin 21–3–446–72–24.77; T. S. Greenland 15–2–256–39–19.69; S. J. Green 15–5–158–50*–15.80; N. J. Westwood 14–2–184–50*–15.33; G. R. Peddy 14–2–105–44*–8.75.

Bowling—M. Snow 73–29–205–13–15.76; P. D. Lunn 287–63–893–56–15.94; S. J. Green 183–28–563–34–16.55; P. J. Williams 123–29–291–14–20.78; R. J. Tilley 176–48–444–21–21.14; R. E. Clark 135–30–305–12–25.41.

ALDENHAM SCHOOL

Played 12: Won 2, Lost 3, Drawn 7. Abandoned 4

Master i/c: P. K. Smith

Batting—J. P. Patel 9–4–198–78*–39.60; K. Jahangir 11–1–338–87–33.80; *M. H. Moledina 12–1–310–69–28.18; G. E. Peel 11–0–251–70–22.81; N. J. Bayley 12–2–228–68–22.80; S. C. Munyard 11–0–245–43–22.27.

Bowling—M. A. Knopp 45–9–163–10–16.30; K. Jahangir 93–19–222–12–18.50; G. E. Peel 125–26–400–19–21.05.

ALLEYN'S SCHOOL

Played 18: Won 5, Lost 3, Drawn 10

Master i/c: S. E. Smith

Batting—*B. T. L. Bennett 15–3–628–85–52.33; J. G. Davey 15–1–469–76–33.50; O. A. Lucking 16–2–424–91–30.28; S. J. Clare 14–2–175–34–14.58; D. P. Pas 11–0–117–21–10.63; J. D. Athill 13–1–116–56*–9.66; E. H. R. de Mel 13–1–111–29–9.25.

Bowling—B. T. L. Bennett 125–41–264–27–9.77; O. A. Lucking 140.2–57–311–26–11.96; J. Papanastasiou 167.5–44–377–27–13.96; A. I. Ayoade 86–17–287–17–16.88; N. E. Humber 77–20–255–11–23.18.

ALLHALLOWS SCHOOL

Played 17: Won 4, Lost 5, Drawn 8

Master i/c: P. L. Petherbridge

Batting—R. Enticott 14–2–411–55–34.25; M. Sutton 14–2–293–73–24.41; J. M. Stamford 18–1–403–55*–23.70; *S. B. Claro 14–0–302–79–21.57; J. E. T. Clark 14–4–186–34–18.60; J. Chediak 13–0–190–54–14.61; C. D. Cuff 14–1–187–41*–14.38.

Bowling—S. B. Claro 121–26–377–23–16.39; J. E. T. Clark 163–31–585–33–17.72; R. Enticott 138–35–496–20–24.80; C. D. Cuff 92–9–359–12–29.91.

AMPLEFORTH COLLEGE

Played 15: Won 4, Lost 6, Drawn 5. Abandoned 1

Masters i/c: J. G. Willcox and Rev. J. F. Stephens OSB

Batting—B. T. Dow 16–0–367–90–22.93; J. R. Elliot 16–1–322–104*–21.46; *B. Beardmore-Grey 16–0–210–50–13.12; D. H. Churton 16–4–154–24–12.83; P. T. Lucas 12–1–134–32–12.18; N. A. Derbyshire 16–1–109–30–7.26.

Bowling—N. A. Derbyshire 179–54–385–34–11.32; W. J. Bianchi 106.1–26–322–28–11.50; B. R. Simonds-Gooding 84.4–26–217–17–12.76; D. H. Churton 145–40–452–19–23.78; B. T. Dow 87–21–242–10–24.20.

ARDINGLY COLLEGE

Played 15: Won 4, Lost 7, Drawn 4. Abandoned 2

Master i/c: T. J. Brooker

Batting—J. St G. L. Jessop 7–1–200–66–33.33; *T. W. Butterworth 15–2–302–57*–23.23; A. J. Butterworth 14–1–268–89*–20.61; G. Fagarazzi 15–2–207–33–15.92; G. Grove-Smith 14–2–168–49–14.00; N. P. Mather 13–2–153–64–13.90; A. J. Dear 12–0–160–43–13.33; C. D. J. Austin 13–2–146–37–13.27; P. R. Spencer 14–0–169–73–12.07.

Bowling—R. C. P. Maynard 99.2–7–435–19–22.89; T. W. Butterworth 89–8–349–14–24.92; P. R. Spencer 158.5–24–550–13–42.30; G. Fagarazzi 173.3–29–592–13–45.53.

ARNOLD SCHOOL

Played 19: Won 5, Lost 3, Drawn 10, Tied 1. Abandoned 2

Master i/c: S. Burnage

Batting—*R. G. Halsall 19–1–676–99–37.55; J. Muir 19–4–443–66–29.53; J. McFarlane 17–2–392–64–26.13; A. D. Jones 19–3–409–61*–25.56; P. Knapman 14–1–145–41*–11.15.

Bowling—R. G. Halsall 237.4–50–545–38–14.34; S. M. Aga 234–46–669–37–18.08; J. McFarlane 163.5–31–450–19–23.68; A. MacGregor 150.4–36–437–18–24.27.

ASHVILLE COLLEGE

Played 16: Won 5, Lost 5, Drawn 6

Master i/c: J. M. Bromley   Cricket professional: P. J. Kippax

Batting—S. C. Hitchen 16–4–524–94*–43.66; M. J. Smart 16–5–359–49*–32.63; S. J. Walmsley 13–0–316–76–26.33; *J. E. Hill 15–0–266–63–17.73; S. G. Peacock 16–1–238–57–15.86.

Bowling—M. W. Yates 105–20–310–22–14.09; J. A. Gunning 121–17–446–26–17.15; S. B. Henderson 64–9–227–13–17.46; S. C. Hitchen 79–18–283–14–20.21; M. J. Smart 198–42–659–29–22.72.

BALLYMENA ACADEMY GRAMMAR SCHOOL

Played 21: Won 14, Lost 5, Drawn 2

Master i/c: E. C. B. Jackson

Batting—J. Glass 18–6–318–44*–26.50; G. Crabbe 13–5–168–51*–21.00; J. Kennedy 18–5–240–39*–18.46; R. Kennedy 15–3–190–31*–15.83; M. Glass 14–0–176–86–12.57; S. McBurney 16–3–154–28–11.84.

Bowling—P. Rainey 152.3–47–336–52–6.46; J. Glass 143.2–31–383–38–10.07; D. Gillespie 36–2–119–10–11.90; M. Glass 140–30–335–26–12.88; S. McBurney 142.2–33–333–14–23.78.

BANCROFT'S SCHOOL

Played 16: Won 5, Lost 2, Drawn 8, Tied 1

Master i/c: J. G. Bromfield

Batting—A. E. Phillips 14–2–511–107*–42.58; G. J. Norgate 16–1–430–115*–28.66; A. C. H. Knight 17–1–360–76*–22.50; G. P. Brown 17–3–232–73*–16.57; P. Brown 16–0–262–69–16.37; G. A. Fisher 12–4–124–26–15.50; *R. W. Hubbard 17–1–231–67–14.43; G. J. Maynard 14–3–136–37–12.36.

Bowling—A. Azad 133.7–21–447–27–16.55; R. W. Hubbard 256–58–738–43–17.16; L. B. Smith 84.2–8–312–16–19.50; G. P. Brown 69.3–7–267–10–26.70.

BANGOR GRAMMAR SCHOOL

Played 22: Won 10, Lost 6, Drawn 6. Abandoned 3

Master i/c: C. C. J. Harte

Batting—*C. C. Yeates 19-3-599-105*-37.43; S. L. Mann 19-4-463-62*-30.86; N. S. Taylor 19-5-292-77*-20.85; A. P. Williamson 19-4-225-45-15.00; S. C. McKenna 20-2-219-61-12.16; D. J. J. Waugh 14-0-137-34-9.78.

Bowling—M. W. McCord 136.4-34-404-33-12.24; N. S. Taylor 178-61-374-30-12.46; S. L. Mann 83.2-20-227-17-13.35; S. J. Cummings 114-29-313-23-13.60; D. B. Curran 116.1-26-306-22-13.90; C. C. Yeates 48-5-187-13-14.38.

BARNARD CASTLE SCHOOL

Played 19: Won 10, Lost 3, Drawn 6. Abandoned 3

Master i/c: C. P. Johnson

Batting—*N. J. Foster 17-3-603-89-43.07; M. E. Jobling 19-2-587-84-34.52; T. Underwood 16-4-292-48-24.33; R. D. Whittaker 17-1-329-61-20.56; R. E. W. Shield 18-1-300-43*-17.64; G. D. Turnbull 15-3-163-51*-13.58; M. S. Plummer 16-6-123-38-12.30; A. J. Hetherington 15-2-154-19-11.84.

Bowling—R. J. Irving 221.2-71-467-46-10.15; C. M. Fairey 163.2-53-369-36-10.25; M. S. Plummer 99.3-15-349-18-19.38; N. J. Foster 195.1-38-627-29-21.62.

BEDFORD SCHOOL

Played 18: Won 3, Lost 4, Drawn 11. Abandoned 3

Master i/c: D. W. Jarrett   Cricket professional: R. G. Caple

Batting—J. E. Crooker 19-2-581-99-34.17; *A. B. Cartmell 20-1-524-87-27.57; B. C. Banks 17-6-282-38*-25.63; S. A. S. Cuthbert 20-0-471-60-23.55; R. W. H. Smith 9-0-210-50-23.33; J. C. White 19-5-304-56-21.71; S. G. Flude 20-0-408-74-20.40.

Bowling—B. C. Banks 241-60-669-33-20.27; J. E. Crooker 262-62-822-39-21.07; C. E. Parrish 147-17-570-22-25.90; R. A. Jones 125-33-375-11-34.09.

BEDFORD MODERN SCHOOL

Played 18: Won 5, Lost 2, Drawn 11. Abandoned 2

Master i/c: N. J. Chinneck

Batting—*A. J. Trott 17-4-625-116*-48.07; A. D. McCartney 16-3-472-82-36.30; G. A. H. Awudu 13-4-324-60-36.00; J. D. Cavanagh 18-3-453-97-30.20; G. C. Black 11-2-225-50*-25.00; J. C. Glanvill 12-1-217-74-19.72; D. J. Outtrim 13-3-154-36*-15.40.

Bowling—P. A. Owen 283.2-64-757-45-16.82; A. D. McCartney 267.2-45-759-45-16.86; G. A. H. Awudu 148.4-33-511-21-24.33.

BEECHEN CLIFF SCHOOL

Played 10: Won 5, Lost 1, Drawn 4. Abandoned 2

Master i/c: K. J. L. Mabe   Cricket professional: P. J. Colbourne

Batting—D. W. Benton 5-3-131-63*-65.50; *M. J. Keen 6-0-347-101-57.83; J. R. Dodd 6-0-219-66-36.50; D. J. Adams 7-1-192-56*-32.00; T. J. Sadgrove 7-3-105-50*-26.25; J. H. Crouch 7-2-124-44*-24.80.

Bowling—J. D. Colbourne 68-18-214-24-8.91; S. M. Priscott 95.2-24-260-24-10.83; D. J. Adams 94.2-27-282-15-18.80.

BERKHAMSTED SCHOOL

Played 12: Won 6, Lost 1, Drawn 5. Abandoned 3

Master i/c: F. J. Davis   Cricket professional: M. Herring

Batting—D. T. Hodges 12–2–422–80–42.20; E. Shek 10–2–289–92–36.12; S. T. Fox 10–1–250–71–27.77; C. Collett 10–2–188–55–23.50; *N. A. Allen 8–1–130–49*–18.57.

Bowling—D. T. Hodges 187–49–428–27–15.85; M. R. Player 195–47–442–24–18.41; S. T. Fox 83–21–224–10–22.40; C. M. Lovegrove 91–13–314–10–31.40.

BIRKENHEAD SCHOOL

Played 11: Won 3, Lost 2, Drawn 6. Abandoned 2

Master i/c: M. H. Bowyer

Batting—M. J. Wilkie 10–2–375–92–45.87; *P. I. Rennie 9–3–210–50*–35.00; A. G. Deakin 11–0–252–54–22.90; S. J. Cox 8–0–148–41–18.50.

Bowling—P. I. Rennie 123.4–33–288–23–12.52; G. McGowan 72.5–18–233–17–13.70; A. Allan 65–11–179–10–17.90; N. M. L. Jones 71–16–229–10–22.90.

BISHOP'S STORTFORD COLLEGE

Played 15: Won 3, Lost 5, Drawn 7. Abandoned 3

Master i/c: D. A. Hopper   Cricket professional: E. G. Witherden

Batting—H. A. M. Marcelline 15–7–1,166–176–145.75; *G. M. E. Hackwell 11–2–390–100*–43.33; J. C. Wright 13–2–275–61–25.00; J. R. Torrance 9–2–106–24–15.14; P. E. B. Armitage 14–4–146–41–14.60; C. C. Wright 13–1–130–33–10.83.

Bowling—H. A. M. Marcelline 185.2–43–491–32–15.34; P. E. B. Armitage 150–24–637–29–21.96; C. C. Wright 135.3–31–386–14–27.57; J. R. Torrance 123.4–24–429–11–39.00.

BLOXHAM SCHOOL

Played 20: Won 8, Lost 4, Drawn 8

Master i/c: I. K. George

Batting—N. E. Baig 20–2–657–85–36.50; S. M. Blayney 20–0–549–80–27.45; *N. A. Bertram 20–1–501–87–26.36; I. J. Turton 14–6–157–32*–19.62; D. A. Currall 15–3–226–63–18.83; T. M. Pears 14–0–234–52–16.71; M. J. Day 16–3–163–30–12.53; D. Hill 13–1–132–59*–11.00.

Bowling—M. J. Day 59.5–4–230–14–16.42; E. M. Hockey 161–34–490–25–19.60; N. E. Baig 206–39–614–31–19.80; S. M. Blayney 175–31–485–20–24.25; C. F. Wollerton 126–22–422–16–26.37.

BLUNDELL'S SCHOOL

Played 15: Won 1, Lost 4, Drawn 10. Abandoned 2

Masters i/c: T. I. Barwell and E. R. Crowe   Cricket professional: E. Steele

Batting—C. D. Bending 15–3–269–45–22.41; *R. K. Giles 15–1–283–61–20.21; J. P. Taylor 10–5–101–50*–20.20; I. C. Fudge 15–0–301–108–20.06; S. S. Patidar 15–0–286–59–19.06; N. E. Coleman 14–3–201–31–18.27; Y. A. Siddiqui 10–1–161–71*–17.88; P. G. Wilson 12–1–101–29–9.18.

Bowling—R. S. Castle 114.3–29–351–21–16.71; J. P. Taylor 137–33–460–20–23.00; S. S. Patidar 157.4–35–482–20–24.10; R. Norris 119.3–30–354–12–29.50.

BRADFIELD COLLEGE

Played 16: Won 2, Lost 5, Drawn 9. Abandoned 1

Master i/c: F. R. Dethridge   Cricket professional: J. F. Harvey

Batting—D. J. Wiggins 16–1–322–78–21.46; R. W. F. Perry 14–0–285–64–20.35; *W. A. Oscroft 15–1–218–55–15.57; W. Cairns 15–3–180–46–15.00; J. J. Bates 14–0–209–51–14.92; T. Findjan 16–0–229–45–14.31; B. Lauder 14–1–171–35–13.15; J. C. Adams 12–2–131–28*–13.10.

Bowling—W. A. Oscroft 171.3–32–463–33–14.03; J. D. Pearce 234–62–582–31–18.77; E. G. Browning 192–37–552–20–27.60.

BRADFORD GRAMMAR SCHOOL

Played 21: Won 5, Lost 4, Drawn 11, Tied 1. Abandoned 3

Master i/c: A. G. Smith

Batting—D. R. Chadwick 20–2–544–86–30.22; *P. R. Miles 19–4–339–71*–22.60; A. G. Webster 19–1–397–62–22.05; A. G. Stott 16–1–312–74*–20.80; S. Henry 9–0–183–57–20.33; J. P. Collen 19–2–320–73–18.82; P. A. Wallace 19–1–258–53–14.33; R. A. F. Kitchen 11–3–112–32–14.00; D. C. Whitfield 11–0–129–22–11.72.

Bowling—P. A. Wallace 180–36–529–28–18.89; C. M. Pawson 65.4–5–337–15–22.46; D. Priestley 117–18–477–21–22.71; R. A. F. Kitchen 125.1–26–420–17–24.70; P. R. Miles 130.4–18–673–21–32.04.

BRENTWOOD SCHOOL

Played 15: Won 4, Lost 2, Drawn 9

Master i/c: P. J. Whitcombe   Cricket professional: K. C. Preston

Batting—M. D. Wilkins 15–5–333–48*–33.30; *P. Welton 15–2–376–66–28.92; C. P. Davis 11–0–263–84–23.90; J. G. Northwood 14–0–237–77–16.92; M. A. Spackman 10–2–109–33–13.62; C. J. Wilkins 13–1–149–38–12.41; R. T. Goodey 13–0–142–31–10.92.

Bowling—P. Welton 197–59–429–29–14.79; A. A. Witney 170–44–482–29–16.62; P. McGowan 125–21–460–21–21.90; M. D. Wilkins 186–47–566–12–47.16.

BRIGHTON COLLEGE

Played 19: Won 10, Lost 3, Drawn 6. Abandoned 1

Master i/c: J. Spencer   Cricket professional: J. D. Morley

Batting—J. P. Gibson 19–4–508–93*–33.86; J. G. Forster 19–4–494–69*–32.93; C. P. Sweet 18–1–551–189–32.41; D. P. Cook 19–3–433–79–27.06; R. L. Chettleburgh 19–1–392–61–21.77; C. M. Gates 17–4–268–53–20.61; R. A. Iago 16–3–215–38–16.53; D. P. Andrews 11–3–129–31–16.12.

Bowling—C. M. Oliphant-Callum 333.1–82–931–59–15.77; C. M. Long 407.5–139–870–48–18.12; C. P. Sweet 172.4–27–531–26–20.42.

BROMSGROVE SCHOOL

Played 16: Won 6, Lost 1, Drawn 9. Abandoned 3

Master i/c: D. Langlands

Batting—R. J. Tattershaw 15–4–574–66–52.18; P. C. Duffy 15–3–574–79–47.83; *I. F. Barwick 16–3–412–106*–31.69; R. H. M. Beddall 6–1–146–42*–29.20; M. Fadlallah 9–4–117–43*–23.40; G. J. M. Cockburn 10–2–164–41–20.50; J. C. Reed-Daunter 7–0–139–41–19.85; D. Preston 15–1–191–51–13.64; A. Temple 9–1–106–39*–13.25.

Bowling—R. J. Tattershaw 147.1–39–467–32–14.59; J. C. Reed-Daunter 138.1–28–476–18–26.44; M. Fadlallah 132.4–25–424–14–30.28; P. C. Duffy 135–22–488–15–32.53.

BRYANSTON SCHOOL

Played 15: Won 6, Lost 4, Drawn 5

Master i/c: M. C. Wagstaffe

Batting—S. C. Ecclestone 15–3–745–119*–62.08; R. G. Lee 13–3–322–59–32.20; H. P. Cazalet 13–0–208–74–16.00; T. J. Millard 14–4–156–52*–15.60; D. J. Robinson 14–1–112–17–8.60.

Bowling—H. P. Cazalet 198–51–536–32–16.75; R. G. Lee 140–47–476–27–17.60; H. Astor 80–20–253–11–23.00; S. C. Ecclestone 198–42–616–23–26.90.

CANFORD SCHOOL

Played 15: Won 7, Lost 1, Drawn 7

Master i/c: H. A. Jarvis   Cricket professional: D. Shackleton

Batting—*C. H. Forward 14–3–854–218*–77.63; W. E. Johnson 13–2–344–88–31.27; J. P. Blissard-Barnes 13–4–258–51*–28.66; S. R. Knight 13–2–303–92–27.54; A. J. Ovendale 10–2–202–55*–25.25; A. J. Pope 11–2–165–39–18.33.

Bowling—A. M. W. Groves 201.2–62–439–40–10.97; T. R. Murray-Walker 118.4–39–346–20–17.30; T. C. Le Gallais 130–40–360–20–18.00; S. J. Hipwell 152.5–28–496–23–21.56; A. J. Ovendale 93–29–259–11–23.54.

CATERHAM SCHOOL

Played 16: Won 7, Lost 2, Drawn 7

Master i/c: A. Simon   Cricket professional: J. Wilson

Batting—A. D. Brown 16–5–898–204*–81.63; *J. A. Cox-Colyer 16–2–507–116*–36.21; K. J. Banks 15–3–318–56–26.50; N. B. Driscoll 4–0–100–34–25.00; M. G. Cole 11–2–213–60*–23.66; S. J. Dawes 10–1–201–101*–22.33; R. L. M. Mauger 10–1–112–28–12.44.

Bowling—J. A. Cox-Colyer 239.3–67–658–49–13.42; D. J. Paisey 123.5–32–277–18–15.38; A. D. Brown 225–50–651–37–17.59; S. A. Ghyas 78.2–8–271–12–22.58.

CHARTERHOUSE

Played 18: Won 4, Lost 4, Drawn 10

Master i/c: J. M. Knight   Cricket professional: R. V. Lewis

Batting—C. E. L. Simson 19–4–589–72*–39.26; A. E. Ivermee 20–0–507–101–25.35; A. T. Grundy 20–1–478–64–25.15; G. I. MacMillan 19–3–364–87–22.75; N. A. Stevens 10–2–174–65–21.75; *S. C. Mellstrom 18–2–341–83*–21.31; P. E. H. Morel 18–0–346–78–19.22.

Bowling—M. C. Gray 154–30–416–17–24.47; J. N. B. Borill 102–16–305–11–27.72; S. J. S. Townend 137.4–28–416–15–27.73; C. E. L. Simson 190–49–573–20–28.65; G. M. Bignell 115.4–20–384–12–32.00; A. E. Ivermee 207–18–621–18–34.50.

CHELTENHAM COLLEGE

Played 16: Won 5, Lost 5, Drawn 6. Abandoned 3

Master i/c: W. J. Wesson   Cricket professional: M. W. Stovold

Batting—G. F. Hill 19–4–655–96–43.66; D. J. Hampshire 17–1–500–91*–31.25; J. D. Hampshire 18–2–439–74–27.43; A. D. L. Thomas 9–3–163–51*–27.16; J. R. Boddington 14–4–257–51*–25.70; A. H. Turner 14–0–225–39–16.07.

Bowling—R. T. Davies 191–36–599–34–17.61; R. J. Jackson 98.4–11–367–18–20.38; D. J. Hampshire 164–35–513–25–20.52.

CHIGWELL SCHOOL

Played 11: Won 3, Lost 1, Drawn 7. Abandoned 4

Master i/c: D. N. Morrison

Batting—*A. J. Lee 9–2–581–112*–83.00; T. A. Coleman 11–3–259–101*–32.37; D. J. Clark 8–0–236–87–29.50; J. F. Carpenter 10–1–170–65–18.88.

Bowling—J. F. Carpenter 96.4–22–229–19–12.05; M. J. D. Haigh 62–8–179–12–14.91; M. G. Chalkley 132–35–336–21–16.00; A. C. M. Gallacher 86.1–26–181–10–18.10.

CHRIST COLLEGE, BRECON

Played 14: Won 2, Lost 3, Drawn 9. Abandoned 5

Master i/c: C. W. Kleiser

Batting—*D. O. Lloyd-Jones 11–2–472–102*–52.44; N. S. Johnson 11–1–323–84–32.30; M. Yendle 12–1–265–117*–24.09; K. L. Miller 11–3–172–51*–21.50; R. T. W. Horne 10–0–190–58–19.00; R. P. Sykes 12–2–186–49*–18.60.

Bowling—D. O. Lloyd-Jones 105.5–28–144–19–7.57; J. D. Shinton 139.4–23–445–22–20.22; K. L. Miller 125.1–44–262–12–21.83.

CHRIST'S HOSPITAL

Played 16: Won 4, Lost 7, Drawn 5

Master i/c: R. H. Sutcliffe   Cricket professional: A. Karim

Batting—J. P. Williams 14–2–421–116*–35.08; *R. T. Macro 14–0–287–68–20.50; C. F. Parsons 14–1–246–46–18.92; J. L. Tedder 13–2–191–32–17.36; J. R. Atkinson 13–3–156–33–15.60; J. D. English 10–3–108–27*–15.42; C. J. Thornham 12–3–120–34–13.33; R. C. Phillips 14–2–153–35–12.75.

Bowling—R. C. Phillips 167–36–493–33–14.93; M. G. Fooks 166–40–526–33–15.93; C. J. Thornham 82–11–283–13–21.76; J. R. Atkinson 97–17–351–16–21.93; A. H. G. Sharp 58–7–277–12–23.08.

CLAYESMORE SCHOOL

Played 18: Won 6, Lost 3, Drawn 9. Abandoned 1

Master i/c: R. P. Merriman

Batting—G. Owton 19–1–626–115–34.77; S. Thomatos 18–1–582–86–34.23; J. Gurdon 9–4–119–48*–23.80; C. Eitzen 17–3–324–62*–23.14; J. Rumball 16–2–297–68–21.21; J. Allen 11–4–107–24*–15.28; J. Dike 15–3–172–45*–14.33; D. Duffin 12–3–155–31–14.09.

Bowling—J. Dike 148.5–32–465–39–11.92; J. Rumball 177–52–495–33–15.00; S. Thomatos 115.5–25–354–16–22.12; J. Allen 99–5–429–11–39.00.

CLIFTON COLLEGE

Played 15: Won 5, Lost 3, Drawn 7. Abandoned 2

Master i/c: D. C. Henderson   Cricket professional: F. J. Andrew

Batting—J. L. P. Meadows 16–3–565–143*–43.46; W. M. Lawry 17–1–500–103–31.25; M. J. Munro 15–4–329–84–29.90; R. J. R. Clark 13–1–349–73–29.08; W. M. I. Bailey 15–2–296–81–22.76; *A. J. A. Cole 14–0–158–82–11.28.

Bowling—M. J. Munro 79.5–30–200–17–11.76; R. J. W. Holdsworth 215–48–653–42–15.54; I. K. R. Niven 158.1–37–466–25–18.64; M. D. Parish 76.3–26–221–10–22.10.

COLFE'S SCHOOL

Played 12: Won 7, Lost 1, Drawn 4. Abandoned 1

Master i/c: P. Hollingum

Batting—D. Neil-Dwyer 12–4–520–102–65.00; P. Whiteland 12–1–300–93–27.27; R. Harmer 12–0–307–71–25.58; G. Rameaux 12–1–251–59–22.81; G. Davies 8–2–112–45–18.66.

Bowling—*J. Streeter 218.3–48–530–47–11.27; S. Johnson 163.4–32–585–21–27.85.

COLSTON'S SCHOOL

Played 16: Won 3, Lost 7, Drawn 6. Abandoned 1

Master i/c: M. P. B. Tayler   Cricket professional: R. A. Sinfield

Batting—*C. E. J. TenBroeke 15–1–523–105–37.35; J. A. Franklin 9–2–255–51*–36.42; J. H. Fannon 16–2–361–68–25.78; D. J. Hobbs 15–2–314–67*–24.15; R. L. Rees Jones 14–2–282–113*–23.50; S. J. Harwood 10–2–159–37*–19.87; J. E. Vickery 10–0–134–36–13.40; M. N. Winrow 13–1–148–48–12.33.

Bowling—C. E. J. TenBroeke 54–10–229–10–22.90; M. Hitchings 165.2–21–671–26–25.80; M. R. R. Cruice 140.3–13–590–21–28.09.

COVENTRY SCHOOL – BABLAKE

Played 17: Won 5, Lost 5, Drawn 7

Master i/c: B. J. Sutton

Batting—D. Barr 15–3–501–75*–41.75; D. Hopkins 17–1–395–87–24.68; D. Ormerod 13–1–272–55–22.66; M. Enever 14–5–189–101*–21.00; S. Wain 9–0–178–50–19.77; R. Long 16–1–266–51–17.73; S. Jervis 11–4–115–37–16.42.

Bowling—A. Croston 48.5–10–129–14–9.21; B. Parham 88.1–24–241–22–10.95; D. Barr 89.1–13–296–14–21.14; D. Hopkins 171.1–31–584–24–24.33.

COVENTRY SCHOOL – KING HENRY VIII

Played 15: Won 3, Lost 3, Drawn 9. Abandoned 1

Master i/c: G. P. C. Courtois

Batting—P. M. D. Cunnington 12–6–371–78*–61.83; R. J. Harris 8–0–230–78–28.75; S. J. Payne 11–1–244–70–24.40; R. J. Field 14–4–232–38*–23.20; *A. G. Dow 15–2–269–57*–20.69.

Bowling—J. N. Plevin 73–20–168–10–16.80; I. J. Walters 94–23–272–16–17.00; A. G. Dow 86.2–12–284–16–17.75; K. P. Street 58–5–248–11–22.54; J. P. Pearson 130.1–18–474–18–26.33.

CRANBROOK SCHOOL

Played 12: Won 4, Lost 2, Drawn 6. Abandoned 1

Master i/c: J. A. Genton

Batting—S. C. Rayfield 10–2–276–68–34.50; H. R. J. Burrough 10–3–205–46–29.28; C. M. Taylor 11–2–233–50*–25.88; *S. P. Westerman 12–1–223–73–20.27; R. P. T. Lisle 11–1–199–75–19.90.

Bowling—J. M. R. Boughton 123.2–24–330–24–13.75; T. N. Hillier 122.2–30–311–20–15.55; M. D. Hall 146–36–395–22–17.95; S. France 78–18–247–10–24.70.

CRANLEIGH SCHOOL

Played 16: Won 6, Lost 6, Drawn 4. Abandoned 1

Master i/c: C. J. Lush

Batting—*S. J. Watkinson 16-2-551-104*-39.35; R. G. Gutteridge 16-2-475-115-33.92; W. J. Cardwell 16-0-443-90-27.68; J. Boatswain 10-1-215-65-23.88; R. A. J. Grove 16-0-192-45*-12.00.

Bowling—R. G. Gutteridge 213-53-528-44-12.00; S. J. Watkinson 285-60-834-52-16.03; T. Crouch 89-36-211-13-16.23; J. A. Letts 95-16-279-11-25.36.

DAUNTSEY'S SCHOOL

Played 12: Won 3, Lost 4, Drawn 5

Master i/c: M. K. F. Johnson   Cricket professional: A. Nuttall

Batting—J. W. S. Porter 12-5-874-180*-124.85; J. S. Brazier 11-0-237-45-21.54; C. R. B. Page 8-0-145-50-18.12; K. D. Tadhunter 11-0-166-47-15.09; R. P. M. Smith 11-0-120-26-10.90.

Bowling—J. C. Frost 114.5-18-444-36-12.33; J. W. S. Porter 140.2-22-563-27-20.85.

DEAN CLOSE SCHOOL

Played 16: Won 5, Lost 9, Drawn 2

Master i/c: C. M. Kenyon   Cricket professional: D. Walker

Batting—T. A. Edginton 16-1-469-93-31.26; J. T. Harcup 7-2-102-31-20.40; C. J. Townsend 15-2-239-65-18.38; *T. J. Harmer 12-0-201-63-16.75; S. K. Organ 14-1-213-36-16.38; A. J. Kerr 10-1-119-37-13.22; S. M. Cornish 16-0-210-31-13.12; S. K. S. Chua 12-1-144-73-13.09; E. C. M. B. Kikonyogo 14-1-158-51-12.15.

Bowling—T. A. Edginton 235.2-57-658-34-19.35; M. I. Cashmore 84-7-346-16-21.62; S. K. Organ 127.4-24-468-21-22.28; T. J. Harmer 87-14-335-12-27.91; C. N. C. Hodges 107.1-28-294-10-29.40.

DENSTONE COLLEGE

Played 12: Won 6, Lost 1, Drawn 5. Abandoned 2

Master i/c: A. N. James

Batting—J. H. A. Hughes 11-2-356-98-39.55; S. J. Martin 12-2-368-79-36.80; *D. J. Whittenbury 9-0-173-49-19.22; A. J. Sloan 9-2-134-74*-19.14; A. J. Gagie 12-1-157-70-14.27; E. W. H. Humphreys 10-1-113-41-12.55.

Bowling—A. J. Sloan 186-65-432-42-10.28; P. R. Dennis-Jones 128.2-48-247-24-10.29; C. H. C. Andrews 76-26-149-10-14.90; J. H. A. Hughes 101.1-17-271-17-15.94; R. J. Harris 75-19-202-10-20.20.

DOUAI SCHOOL

Played 9: Won 1, Lost 4, Drawn 4

Master i/c: J. Shaw

Batting—R. Lumb 8-2-198-46*-33.00; *C. Opia 8-1-216-69*-30.85; M. Allen 6-1-139-90*-27.80.

Bowling—R. Lumb 161-41-431-22-19.59; M. Allen 96-13-316-15-21.06; J. Joyce 75-18-317-14-22.64.

DOVER COLLEGE

Played 17: Won 4, Lost 8, Drawn 5

Master i/c: D. C. Butler

Batting—*S. P. Howkins 17–3–656–103*–46.85; J. D. Rouse 14–2–374–76*–31.16; K. G. Keats 16–5–190–43–17.27; D. J. Winwood 15–0–252–59–16.80; D. M. Rouse 15–0–243–73–16.20; S. M. Bradbrook 17–2–134–25–8.93.

Bowling—S. M. Bradbrook 152.5–22–580–30–19.33; S. P. Howkins 336.5–59–1,071–52–20.59; J. K. P. Boorman 192.1–33–606–20–30.30.

DOWNSIDE SCHOOL

Played 14: Won 3, Lost 7, Drawn 4. Abandoned 1

Master i/c: D. Baty

Batting—*P. J. A. Baldwin 9–1–252–71–31.50; J. M. R. Higgins 12–1–256–46–23.27; G. C. J. Barrington 14–1–289–61*–22.23; T. S. Pascal 12–1–209–45–19.00; C. E. Crossland 13–3–169–32*–16.90; D. O. Morris 10–1–106–41–11.77.

Bowling—R. M. Thesiger 59–10–187–12–15.58; C. E. Crossland 169.5–41–460–18–25.55; G. C. J. Barrington 173.5–35–579–22–26.31.

DULWICH COLLEGE

Played 17: Won 5, Lost 5, Drawn 6, Tied 1

Master i/c: N. D. Cousins   Cricket professionals: A. Ranson and W. A. Smith

Batting—G. N. Fisher 14–1–438–81–33.69; N. K. M. Talonpoika 6–2–119–77–29.75; R. F. Hollis 13–3–231–48*–23.10; A. P. Agar 14–3–246–50*–22.36; T. D. J. Ufton 17–4–268–53–20.61; *M. C. Lea 15–3–240–95*–20.00; M. E. Peffers 17–0–331–48–19.47; J. P. Howland 8–1–105–43–15.00; A. R. Lewis 9–0–112–29–12.44; D. V. Trivedi 13–0–137–39–10.53.

Bowling—A. J. Pearse 76–8–238–12–19.83; R. F. Hollis 186.2–32–620–26–23.84; T. D. J. Ufton 125–19–387–16–24.18; R. W. Penry-Jones 113–20–347–14–24.78; P. M. King 128.5–22–416–14–29.71.

DURHAM SCHOOL

Played 17: Won 2, Lost 2, Drawn 13. Abandoned 3

Master i/c: N. J. Willings   Cricket professional: M. Hirsch

Batting—A. Roseberry 17–2–605–120*–40.33; N. S. Whitfield 17–0–495–83–29.11; *A. G. Clayton 16–1–292–84–19.46; S. N. Monk 15–2–247–76–19.00; L. F. C. Ryan 12–6–100–33*–16.66; W. P. C. Weston 15–0–217–60–14.46; J. D. W. Gedye 13–3–108–33*–10.80.

Bowling—W. P. C. Weston 99–22–248–19–13.05; N. S. Whitfield 209–40–601–26–23.11; A. G. Clayton 191–45–558–23–24.26; A. Roseberry 179–35–524–20–26.20.

EASTBOURNE COLLEGE

Played 21: Won 11, Lost 2, Drawn 8

Master i/c: N. L. Wheeler   Cricket professional: A. E. James

Batting—*R. M. Day 21–2–1,008–127–53.05; T. C. Nicholson 19–5–470–71*–33.57; M. A. Chapple 21–1–654–111*–32.70; G. E. Thwaites 18–2–389–85–24.31; J. Toomer 16–6–208–61*–20.80; C. J. Stephenson 17–3–270–61–19.28; A. D. Ferrier 16–1–256–48–17.06.

Bowling—F. A. Ali 59–14–98–11–8.90; A. J. M. Crane 58–13–172–11–15.63; E. S. H. Giddins 159–34–458–28–16.35; M. A. Chapple 206.3–58–578–35–16.51; R. M. Day 268–57–819–45–18.20.

THE EDINBURGH ACADEMY

Played 14: Won 3, Lost 5, Drawn 6. Abandoned 2

Master i/c: A. R. Dyer

Batting—M. T. Innes 15–0–330–73–22.00; *T. H. Duff 15.2–285–101*–21.92; I. D. Lamond 11–5–128–26–21.33; S. Priyadarshi 12–0–191–38–15.91; M. K. Wilkinson 14–2–188–40–15.66; N. R. Dyer 13–1–136–64*–11.33; A. R. J. Monaghan 13–0–132–34–10.15; M. M. A. Simpson 15–2–113–19–8.69.

Bowling—I. D. Lamond 219.2–63–494–33–14.96; C. J. S. Cairns 123.1–34–364–23–15.82; J. D. Annan 95–17–307–17–18.05; N. R. Dyer 84.4–22–249–10–24.90; M. M. A. Simpson 140.2–23–440–15–29.33.

ELIZABETH COLLEGE, GUERNSEY

Played 17: Won 10, Lost 3, Drawn 4

Master i/c: M. E. Kinder

Batting—*M. Bacon 16–2–474–67–33.85; S. B. R. Mackay 15–3–328–56–27.33; P. J. Woods 15–0–377–68–25.13; D. Chadwick 10–4–126–30–21.00; D. J. Marshall 15–0–288–51–19.20; J. Walker 16–2–214–45–15.28; G. Robert 14–4–144–38–14.40; R. P. C. Cox 12–5–100–35–14.28.

Bowling—N. E. G. Garrett 119.3–29–311–25–12.44; J. Walker 140.2–35–455–34–13.38; R. P. C. Cox 182–56–477–35–13.62; R. C. Marshall 161.3–29–518–31–16.70.

ELLESMERE COLLEGE

Played 17: Won 3, Lost 2, Drawn 12. Abandoned 1

Master i/c: R. K. Sethi

Batting—M. J. Marvell 16–7–367–52–40.77; T. A. R. Elston 17–2–360–67–24.00; D. J. Marvell 15–2–291–75–22.38; C. M. Reed 16–2–294–57–21.00; *J. J. Birchall 15–1–283–93–20.21; J. S. Carver 10–4–119–43*–19.83; O. Braithwaite 14–0–217–63–15.50; W. J. Hart 12–3–102–35–11.33; D. R. Hopkins 13–2–124–35*–11.27.

Bowling—C. M. Reed 277.4–43–632–41–15.41; M. J. Marvell 217.3–56–518–28–18.50; J. J. Birchall 184.3–40–565–27–20.92; T. F. Bawtree 77–16–215–10–21.50.

ELTHAM COLLEGE

Played 21: Won 10, Lost 3, Drawn 8

Masters i/c: P. C. McCartney and B. M. Withecombe

Batting—T. J. Prifti 20–1–654–132–34.42; J. Peek 19–5–457–103–32.64; J. P. Chase 18–4–416–57*–29.71; R. J. Churchill 15–5–365–60–26.07; J. J. Guthrie 18–2–331–63*–20.68; N. A. O'Leary 16–4–248–84*–20.66; R. A. Morgan 17–1–220–36–13.75.

Bowling—S. J. Goodfellow 127.4–25–377–25–15.08; T. J. Prifti 200–42–671–40–16.77; J. P. Chase 193–40–540–32–16.87; S. P. Allen 52.5–3–204–11–18.54; S. H. Garnett 67–7–228–11–20.72; N. A. O'Leary 108–22–386–10–38.60.

EMANUEL SCHOOL

Played 16: Won 6, Lost 5, Drawn 5. Abandoned 1

Master i/c: R. Woodall   Cricket professional: M. G. D. Dimattina

Batting—S. Legg 16-3-357-75*-27.46; *C. Crouch 13-1-312-55-26.00; R. Ali Khan 15-2-249-63-19.15; D. Shore 10-0-179-61-17.90; Ahsan Din 11-3-142-71-17.75; I. Tournès 14-2-212-51-17.66; M. Coe 9-1-137-39-17.12.

ENFIELD GRAMMAR SCHOOL

Played 19: Won 4, Lost 8, Drawn 7. Abandoned 2

Master i/c: J. J. Conroy

Batting—D. Bowen 16-1-489-82*-32.60; R. Claypole 11-5-161-58*-26.83; N. Clydesdale 9-1-185-53*-23.12; J. King 13-1-216-62*-18.00; A. Griggs 13-0-212-62-16.30; S. Chandler 19-1-249-56*-13.83; N. Browne 17-1-190-64-11.87; M. King 14-1-116-21-8.92.

Bowling—M. Davies 202.5-43-570-32-17.81; R. Claypole 170.1-34-513-28-18.32; P. Nicholls 91-14-290-14-20.71.

EPSOM COLLEGE

Played 11: Won 3, Lost 3, Drawn 5. Abandoned 1

Master i/c: M. D. Hobbs

Batting—J. Jessop 11-1-424-106*-42.40; *P. J. Williams 10-3-278-95*-39.71; J. Saunders-Griffiths 10-0-205-75-20.50.

Bowling—P. J. Williams 123.1-26-367-19-19.31; P. Vickars 132.3-21-407-18-22.61.

ETON COLLEGE

Played 14: Won 6, Lost 0, Drawn 8. Abandoned 1

Master i/c: J. A. Claughton   Cricket professional: J. M. Rice

Batting—*R. D. O. MacLeay 14-3-548-84-49.81; J. B. A. Jenkins 15-2-486-59*-37.38; C. A. C. Winter 11-0-289-79-26.27; A. R. G. Lunt 15-4-253-83*-23.00; G. P. F. Selmon 12-1-149-38-13.54; J. B. Bowman-Shaw 14-0-167-52-11.92.

Bowling—T. P. M. Fleming 189.1-53-481-33-14.57; J. K. Erith 219.5-63-577-35-16.48; S. H. Shirazi 124.3-21-389-20-19.45; J. H. M. Fairbairn 155-39-471-24-19.62.

EXETER SCHOOL

Played 12: Won 2, Lost 1, Drawn 9. Abandoned 3

Master i/c: M. C. Wilcock   Cricket professional: D. Beckett

Batting—C. L. Bawden 11-2-318-85-35.33; *D. M. Richards 10-0-219-40-21.90; G. W. Evans 12-1-215-39*-19.54; R. P. Corney 11-0-189-33-17.18.

Bowling—N. J. J. Levitt 60.4-8-262-13-20.15; D. M. Richards 104-18-339-14-24.21; C. L. Bawden 87-11-358-11-32.54.

FELSTED SCHOOL

Played 19: Won 3, Lost 3, Drawn 13

Master i/c: A. N. Grierson Rickford   Cricket professional: G. Barker

Batting—*N. V. Knight 19–3–1,027–118*–64.18; S. E. Carson 18–2–377–58–23.56; J. D. Collard 16–0–367–81–22.93; T. F. C. Cooper 17–1–367–70–22.93; S. J. Keys 18–0–348–91–19.33; R. J. Bentley 16–3–176–37*–13.53; D. S. Grave 13–3–114–29–11.40.

Bowling—D. S. Grave 74–17–282–13–21.69; T. F. C. Cooper 166–67–589–25–23.56; I. F. Morgan 76–14–273–11–24.81; S. A. Pearce-Higgins 176–49–543–21–25.85; J. B. C. Gilsenan 198–28–699–26–26.88; B. R. G. Clover 106–25–330–12–27.50.

FETTES COLLEGE

Played 14: Won 0, Lost 6, Drawn 8. Abandoned 4

Master i/c: J. E. Tapp

Batting—*M. A. M. Adam 15–1–402–54*–28.71; J. L. MacLean 15–1–379–68–27.07; J. A. Cardwell-Moore 15–0–248–60–16.53; P. J. Hay 14–0–198–36–14.14; S. T. S. Cluin 10–0–115–33–11.50.

Bowling—J. L. MacLean 201.3–50–501–43–11.65; M. A. M. Adam 176–36–501–19–26.36.

FOREST SCHOOL

Played 14: Won 2, Lost 2, Drawn 10. Abandoned 5

Master i/c: K. A. Parsley   Cricket professional: S. Turner

Batting—A. C. Richards 14–2–631–99*–52.58; F. G. Cooke 11–1–218–63*–21.80; A. R. Heyes 14–0–296–72–21.14; B. J. Barnett 13–2–141–27*–12.81; L. Douris 12–2–128–37–12.80; P. I. O'Neill 10–1–110–66–12.22; *R. J. Davis 12–2–121–29*–12.10.

Bowling—R. J. Davis 182.4–46–516–24–21.50; A. C. Richards 235.3–37–842–28–30.07.

FRAMLINGHAM COLLEGE

Played 13: Won 2, Lost 6, Drawn 5. Abandoned 2

Master i/c: P. J. Hayes   Cricket professional: C. Rutterford

Batting—*N. C. Gowing 12–2–274–102*–27.40; R. W. Friend 10–0–199–51–19.90; M. A. C. Kimber 12–0–208–45–17.33; S. C. Giller 11–0–151–32–13.72; K. H. Ip 11–1–118–26*–11.80; S. E. Iliffe 12–2–114–25–11.40; P. C. E. Gubbins 11–0–108–38–9.81.

Bowling—M. A. C. Kimber 136.4–30–351–21–16.71; S. C. Giller 104–29–291–16–18.18; T. C. Woods 84.5–18–282–12–23.50; M. C. P. Davies 92–16–294–11–26.72.

GIGGLESWICK SCHOOL

Played 15: Won 0, Lost 3, Drawn 12. Abandoned 1

Master i/c: C. Green   Cricket professional: D. R. Gilbert

Batting—M. P. Kaye 15–3–536–120*–44.66; D. A. V. Caton 15–2–264–71*–20.30; G. B. Callan 9–2–129–34–18.42; *C. C. Haward 12–1–185–49–16.81; P. R. Boyle 12–1–148–36–13.45; W. P. D. Moss 12–2–113–20–11.30.

Bowling—M. P. Kaye 162–26–580–31–18.70; W. P. D. Moss 95–13–319–13–24.53; C. C. Haward 174–25–595–18–33.05; G. N. Topalian 162–31–467–14–33.35.

THE GLASGOW ACADEMY

Played 8: Won 2, Lost 4, Drawn 2

Master i/c: R. M. I. Williams Cricket professional: P. A. Cooper

Batting—G. T. McKay 8–1–287–91–41.00; *E. J. Miller 8–1–132–78–18.85; J. F. Mason 8–0–108–31–13.50.

Bowling—G. T. McKay 94.5–28–296–27–10.96; R. K. S. Fleming 78.3–19–188–15–12.53; D. J. Mowat 66.1–18–158–10–15.80; S. J. Miller 90–19–317–17–18.64.

GLENALMOND

Played 14: Won 3, Lost 2, Drawn 9. Abandoned 1

Master i/c: A. James Cricket professional: W. J. Dennis

Batting—J. P. Brown 13–1–375–102*–31.25; D. R. Oswald 12–2–211–56–21.10; J. R. Bassett 10–2–167–50*–20.87; I. M. S. Wilson 13–1–201–59–16.75; *J. A. Higgins 12–0–196–52–16.33; B. Hastie 11–3–125–27*–15.62; A. R. Linklater 11–0–144–33–13.09.

Bowling—R. J. H. White 126.4–40–372–27–13.77; I. M. S. Wilson 153.2–40–364–21–17.33; M. W. J. Crow 129–21–451–18–25.05.

GORDONSTOUN SCHOOL

Played 14: Won 6, Lost 4, Drawn 4

Master i/c: C. J. Barton

Batting—W. Hunnings 9–3–133–32*–22.16; B. McPherson 12–0–241–81–20.08; R. Thomas 11–4–103–32*–14.71; *H. Mason 14–1–191–77*–14.69; T. Scheel 11–0–153–28–13.90; A. Alireza 11–0–145–33–13.18.

Bowling—J. Reade 49–8–138–14–9.85; T. Ruane 30–4–168–12–14.00; T. Scheel 95–10–329–21–15.66; B. McPherson 103.2–12–413–21–19.66.

GRESHAM'S SCHOOL

Played 14: Won 7, Lost 2, Drawn 5. Abandoned 1

Master i/c: A. M. Ponder Cricket professional: K. Taylor

Batting—S. Mussellwhite 11–4–502–111*–71.71; A. C. Wheeler 13–4–394–61–43.77; H. E. M. Spence 11–1–329–71*–32.90; A. Clark 7–0–209–76–29.85; T. Allison 5–1–113–36*–28.25; *J. R. D. Allen 12–1–231–109–21.00.

Bowling—N. J. Roper 75.4–14–185–12–15.41; I. D. Barnett 64.4–11–181–11–16.45; C. Jackson 124–20–338–15–22.53; T. D. Berwick 212–27–883–38–23.23; R. M. Jackson 177–46–384–15–25.60.

HABERDASHERS' ASKE'S SCHOOL, ELSTREE

Played 19: Won 5, Lost 7, Drawn 7. Abandoned 3

Master i/c: D. I. Yeabsley

Batting—S. G. Lloyd 19–1–573–91–31.83; A. V. Spencer 19–1–547–80*–30.38; D. I. Chippeck 18–2–296–101*–18.50; D. B. Quinn 13–6–128–36*–18.28; S. T. Arumugam 12–3–138–65*–15.33; *M. R. Griffiths 15–1–189–34–13.50.

Bowling—R. P. Boseley 61–10–222–11–20.18; J. Atkins 87–16–306–15–20.40; J. D. Wellard 149–42–368–18–20.44; D. B. Quinn 146–26–596–29–20.55; M. R. Griffiths 203–33–749–27–27.74; S. T. Arumugam 197–45–510–18–28.33.

HAILEYBURY

Played 18: Won 6, Lost 2, Drawn 10. Abandoned 1

Master i/c: M. S. Seymour   Cricket professional: P. M. Ellis

Batting—J. B. Jouning 17–1–668–129*–41.75; A. M. Jouning 9–4–179–38–35.80; D. C. L. Beynon 17–4–403–69*–31.00; *J. M. Meacock 18–0–443–80–24.61; I. W. Pigott 16–5–221–59–20.09; B. J. B. Hall 10–4–114–48*–19.00; I. E. Simmons 6–0–114–25–19.00; A. G. van Hoffen 17–3–264–45–18.85; M. C. B. Butler 12–4–112–25–14.00.

Bowling—B. J. B. Hall 270–71–618–52–11.88; E. G. Erith 251.2–68–618–38–16.26; M. C. Herbert 127.4–25–351–15–23.40; A. M. Jouning 98.1–28–260–11–23.63.

HAMPTON SCHOOL

Played 16: Won 3, Lost 4, Drawn 9. Abandoned 1

Master i/c: G. R. Cocksworth

Batting—W. L. C. Taylor 14–3–552–131*–50.18; D. W. Rixon 16–4–415–71*–34.58; A. J. B. Sales 16–1–452–137*–30.13; J. P. Diprose 12–3–234–50–26.00; A. N. Westaway 15–1–285–62–20.35; V. Sheorey 16–0–292–58–18.25; J. J. Sanders 13–1–180–55*–15.00; P. Laver 13–3–121–26–12.10.

Bowling—S. Patel 278.5–88–752–49–15.34; J. C. Reeve 88–30–172–10–17.20; J. G. J. Alexander 125.2–35–308–12–25.66; J. J. Sanders 131–27–445–17–26.17; P. Laver 264.4–74–819–25–37.76.

HARROW SCHOOL

Played 15: Won 5, Lost 3, Drawn 7

Master i/c: S. J. Halliday   Cricket professional: P. Davis

Batting—H. Boralessa 15–1–575–127*–41.07; C. Keey 15–1–396–74–28.28; *D. C. Manasseh 15–0–410–85–27.33; R. C. Hamilton 15–1–336–64–24.00; M. B. T. de C. de Souza Girao 9–0–165–59–18.33; J. K. Bourne 15–5–156–35–15.60; R. D. Nelson 13–3–123–29–12.30; A. C. W. Snow 13–2–116–27–10.54; A. K. C. Green 12–0–119–42–9.91.

Bowling—J. A. R. Hill 69–19–155–11–14.09; D. W. F. Berry-Green 115–29–277–19–14.57; R. D. Nelson 151.5–28–434–28–15.50; A. C. W. Snow 124.4–18–332–21–15.80; D. C. Manasseh 190.3–47–540–29–18.62.

HEREFORD CATHEDRAL SCHOOL

Played 13: Won 7, Lost 1, Drawn 5

Master i/c: A. H. Connop

Batting—N. R. Denny 13–4–352–69*–39.11; *R. Binnersley 11–1–332–99–33.20; A. Mills 13–2–260–52–23.63; R. Wood 13–3–225–78*–22.50; G. Powell 13–0–281–70–21.61; A. Glinos 10–1–124–70–13.77.

Bowling—A. Herbert 131.3–41–229–30–7.63; C. Thomas 121.3–31–298–23–12.95; J. Price 47–10–162–11–14.72; G. Powell 110–19–401–18–22.27; A. Macdonald 98.1–20–348–12–29.00.

HIGHGATE SCHOOL

Played 14: Won 1, Lost 6, Drawn 7

Master i/c: C. J. Davies   Cricket professional: R. E. Jones

Batting—*D. N. Amato 15–1–483–91–34.50; D. Luka 14–3–357–82*–32.45; F. E. J. Wawn 15–0–284–52–18.93; N. Worthington 10–1–137–40–15.22.

Bowling—F. E. J. Wawn 97–18–270–18–15.00; D. N. Amato 276.4–82–718–42–17.09; J. A. Stoecker 170–34–455–19–23.94; R. A. Davenport 107–15–372–15–24.80.

HIPPERHOLME GRAMMAR SCHOOL
Played 13: Won 6, Lost 3, Drawn 4

Master i/c: I. Hugill

Batting—I. Crabtree 8-4-277-67*-69.25; P. Ramsden 11-1-330-102-33.00; J. Hemingway 5-1-111-44-27.75; L. Senior 8-2-119-42*-19.83; *W. Clarke 9-0-120-47-13.33; R. Sandford 11-0-145-46-13.18.

Bowling—W. Clarke 114.5-39-222-22-10.09; P. Ramsden 74.2-14-228-18-12.66; A. Kettle 69.2-11-240-17-14.11; C. Senior 62.3-12-160-10-16.00; J. F. Holt 83-11-299-17-17.58.

HURSTPIERPOINT COLLEGE
Played 21: Won 11, Lost 3, Drawn 7

Master i/c: M. E. Allbrook   Cricket professional: D. J. Semmence

Batting—M. J. Hastwell 21-2-891-97-46.89; W. J. Pike 15-5-298-67-29.80; S. A. Kerr 19-0-557-108-29.31; S. C. Twine 15-9-147-32*-24.50; A. J. Reid 20-1-447-116-23.52; *A. G. Dexter 19-1-415-61*-23.05; A. M. Ballamy 8-2-124-54*-20.66; M. J. K. Brown 13-2-205-46-18.63; M. D. Rose 18-0-310-70-17.22.

Bowling—C. D. J. Humphries 113-28-268-16-16.75; M. E. Barry 202.3-50-585-33-17.72; J. T. Beacham 57.4-9-298-14-21.28; A. G. Dexter 255.3-48-855-38-22.50; M. J. Hastwell 185-42-539-20-26.95; S. C. Twine 210.3-50-605-18-33.61.

IPSWICH SCHOOL
Played 14: Won 6, Lost 0, Drawn 8

Master i/c: P. M. Rees   Cricket professional: K. Winder

Batting—N. Shahid 14-2-523-104*-43.58; R. Heap 13-0-526-92-40.46; *J. V. Zagni 13-1-480-136-40.00; N. J. Gregory 14-4-287-62-28.70; C. Jermyn 10-1-174-63-19.33; D. Stone 10-4-112-28-18.66.

Bowling—J. V. Zagni 219-69-489-37-13.21; N. Shahid 281-101-590-43-13.72; C. Mallam 107-29-265-14-18.92.

KENT COLLEGE
Played 11: Won 4, Lost 3, Drawn 3, Tied 1

Master i/c: G. D. Opie

Batting—G. Jenkins 11-2-334-102*-37.11; S. Warley 11-0-253-71-23.00; R. Grove 10-3-156-45-22.28; *P. Glanfield 9-0-165-45-18.33; J. Barker 10-0-179-51-17.90; J. Hooker 9-0-148-37-16.44.

Bowling—K. Bullen 43-6-153-10-15.30; L. Sonaike 68-10-190-10-19.00; S. Warley 67.1-10-270-13-20.76; G. Jenkins 107.3-15-355-16-22.18.

KIMBOLTON SCHOOL
Played 14: Won 4, Lost 5, Drawn 5

Master i/c: T. J. Williams

Batting—A. W. T. Ramply 16-0-357-69-22.31; S. Skey 14-1-250-51*-19.23; R. J. T. Ramply 11-0-202-58-18.36; *R. L. Ward 15-5-162-31-16.20; S. D. Godden 10-3-113-28*-16.14; A. D. Moffat 14-0-197-52-14.07; R. Brittain 11-0-113-51-10.27; I. Goldberg 16-0-152-44-9.50.

Bowling—S. Adlam 66–16–182–13–14.00; R. L. Ward 192.4–46–521–30–17.36; R. J. T. Ramply 110–26–347–13–26.69; A. W. T. Ramply 141.1–30–496–15–33.06.

KING EDWARD VI COLLEGE, STOURBRIDGE

Played 14: Won 6, Lost 2, Drawn 6. Abandoned 4

Master i/c: M. Ryan

Batting—*G. R. Haynes 10–3–478–140*–68.28; M. Jones 13–1–451–78–37.58; A. W. Harris 7–0–220–92–31.42; M. J. Smith 10–2–221–103*–27.62; A. J. R. Hingley 9–4–137–54–27.40; G. O'Hanlon 10–2–153–61*–19.12.

Bowling—S. G. Potter 54–10–193–16–12.06; A. J. Bryan 122.2–22–341–20–17.05; J. M. Davies 86.5–18–240–14–17.14; G. R. Haynes 92.2–26–241–12–20.08; J. I. Hill 133.2–33–318–13–24.46.

KING EDWARD VI SCHOOL, SOUTHAMPTON

Played 24: Won 7, Lost 6, Drawn 11. Abandoned 1

Master i/c: R. J. Putt

Batting—J. D. Stanley 20–0–675–91–33.75; P. D. Chrispin 14–2–386–58–32.16; A. S. Wright 14–2–255–44–21.25; S. A. Fisher 23–3–401–70–20.05; C. L. W. Wotton 16–2–252–37–18.00; A. J. Donaldson 19–5–245–43*–17.50; J. A. Heywood 7–1–100–60*–16.66; A. J. Shepherd 15–0–202–34–13.46; *P. A. W. Holden 21–4–223–32–13.11.

Bowling—P. D. Chrispin 160–45–348–37–9.40; J. J. McGill 143–18–430–28–15.35; A. J. Donaldson 188–49–489–27–18.11; P. R. Cook 156–27–559–27–20.70; M. L. Tidby 88–19–323–15–21.53; P. A. W. Holden 103–17–372–17–21.88.

KING EDWARD VII SCHOOL, LYTHAM

Played 20: Won 7, Lost 4, Drawn 9

Master i/c: S. T. Godfrey

Batting—*M. C. Cope 17–1–532–74–33.25; G. A. Roberts 20–4–527–70–32.93; E. J. McKnight 18–2–466–61–29.12; J. A. Greenslade 20–2–405–48–22.50; S. J. Stammers 14–6–113–23*–14.12.

Bowling—S. J. Stammers 166.4–34–456–35–13.02; P. D. Shipston 118.3–24–382–26–14.69; P. C. Beverley 97–15–302–19–15.89; D. M. Robbins 107.5–7–405–23–17.60; J. G. Derbyshire 118.2–19–432–19–22.73.

KING EDWARD'S SCHOOL, BIRMINGHAM

Played 17: Won 4, Lost 2, Drawn 11. Abandoned 2

Master i/c: M. D. Stead   Cricket professional: P. J. Knowles

Batting—N. Martin 14–4–1,104–148*–110.40; P. N. J. Inglis 16–5–711–155–64.63; A. P. Hitchins 13–4–242–64–26.88; J. B. Pritchard 13–4–192–41–21.33; J. P. Coates 6–1–104–53–20.80; *M. J. Hills 12–2–187–84*–18.70; M. J. Goodall 8–2–103–35–17.16; P. J. N. Ashton 10–2–119–60–14.87.

Bowling—L. K. Rowley 96.5–20–284–16–17.75; N. Martin 71–16–229–10–22.90; J. P. Coates 166–22–622–20–31.10; J. B. Pritchard 100.5–10–437–13–33.61; M. J. Goodall 139–21–558–16–34.87.

KING WILLIAM'S COLLEGE, ISLE OF MAN

Played 15: Won 7, Lost 0, Drawn 8. Abandoned 1

Master i/c: T. M. Manning   Cricket professional: D. Mark

Batting—*S. W. Ellis 15-0-515-93-34.33; P. W. Townsend 15-2-439-103-33.76; P. A. Nicholson 11-7-132-39*-33.00; J. C. Radford 15-2-422-115-32.46; A. P. Woodward 15-0-419-68-27.93; M. F. Batey 15-3-334-67-27.83; C. J. McGowan 10-0-132-31-13.20.

Bowling—S. W. Ellis 231.3-58-582-50-11.64; J. C. Radford 119-31-378-25-15.12; W. R. Ashbrook 154.2-30-491-31-15.83.

KING'S COLLEGE, TAUNTON

Played 15: Won 7, Lost 3, Drawn 5

Master i/c: R. J. R. Yeates   Cricket professional: R. E. Marshall

Batting—*A. C. Berry 15-0-673-103-44.86; A. H. T. Jourdain 11-4-250-48-35.71; A. D. Bagshaw 4-0-129-67-32.25; N. K. L. Coulson 14-1-370-51-28.46; G. E. D. Davies 13-1-319-85-26.58; D. J. Battishill 11-1-247-100*-24.70; S. D. Painter 13-3-231-48*-23.10; G. P. Singh 13-1-275-59-22.91; A. J. Duncanson 8-2-123-49-20.50.

Bowling—D. J. Battishill 147.5-23-486-33-14.72; N. E. Keyte 172.4-45-506-27-18.74; M. J. E. W. Turner 85.3-19-306-16-19.12; S. D. Painter 74.3-12-295-13-22.69; A. J. Duncanson 105-19-305-12-25.41; A. C. Berry 104.4-22-360-12-30.00.

KING'S COLLEGE SCHOOL, WIMBLEDON

Played 15: Won 7, Lost 3, Drawn 5. Abandoned 2

Master i/c: A. G. P. Lang   Cricket professional: L. J. Moody

Batting—*R. M. Wight 15-1-566-99-40.42; I. B. M. Ratnayake 14-2-421-71-35.08; R. M. Hussey 13-0-341-87-26.23; J. Q. Cooper 13-2-260-51*-23.63; R. J. Nightingale 13-3-232-53-23.20; N. Ash 8-3-113-58*-22.60; E. J. Heaver 14-4-151-34-15.10.

Bowling—D. W. Talbot 281.2-107-650-58-11.20; R. M. Wight 243-78-635-29-21.89; W. Samad 63.3-16-233-10-23.30; J. Q. Cooper 144.1-24-553-18-30.72.

KING'S SCHOOL, BRUTON

Played 15: Won 0, Lost 5, Drawn 10

Master i/c: D. C. Elstone

Batting—T. Mornement 13-4-203-39*-22.55; R. Ashfield 14-0-315-72-22.50; M. Vaughan-Brown 14-0-262-48-18.71; E. Parham 14-3-140-50-12.72; R. Parker 13-3-125-39*-12.50; *J. Petrie 14-2-127-41-10.58; N. Allison 14-1-134-35-10.30.

Bowling—J. Petrie 136.3-29-404-28-14.42; R. Parker 137.1-20-477-20-23.85; E. Parham 127-24-452-18-25.11.

THE KING'S SCHOOL, CANTERBURY

Played 15: Won 2, Lost 3, Drawn 10

Master i/c: A. W. Dyer   Cricket professional: D. V. P. Wright

Batting—S. R. Turner 15-3-445-62-37.08; A. E. Mitchell 15-2-385-106-29.61; N. V. Daley 15-2-337-85*-25.92; *P. P. Lacamp 16-2-316-60-22.57; M. G. Le Huray 11-3-132-35*-16.50; A. J. H. Brown 10-3-100-27*-14.28; C. E. Butcher 12-3-101-27*-11.22.

Bowling—H. J. Andrée 138-36-349-23-15.17; J. R. Davies 180.4-45-472-31-15.22; N. V. Daley 109-20-312-20-15.60; R. R. Wallis 116-36-240-11-21.81; A. J. H. Brown 78-13-295-13-22.69.

THE KING'S SCHOOL, CHESTER

Played 16: Won 2, Lost 3, Drawn 11. Abandoned 4

Master i/c: K. H. Mellor

Batting—G. W. Jones 16–2–483–101*–34.50; A. R. H. Mais 14–0–442–58–31.57; C. Goodier 13–2–222–43–20.18; I. D. Kamaly-Asl 10–3–125–55*–17.85; G. Phillingham 10–3–113–40–16.14; J. A. Sowerby 16–3–207–42*–15.92; *J. S. W. Hawkins 13–0–171–61–13.15.

Bowling—C. Goodier 186.1–39–544–50–10.88; J. S. W. Hawkins 48.5–4–188–10–18.80; I. D. Kamaly-Asl 63–6–274–12–22.83.

THE KING'S SCHOOL, MACCLESFIELD

Played 23: Won 4, Lost 6, Drawn 12, Tied 1. Abandoned 1

Master i/c: D. M. Harbord

Batting—S. R. Swindells 22–4–763–92–42.38; A. J. Wilson 21–0–385–63–18.33; *C. W. Fitches 22–4–307–55*–17.05; P. R. Hammond 12–2–160–41–16.00; E. J. Fitzgerald 15–4–167–58–15.18; G. M. Simpson 17–4–182–47–14.00; R. J. Ward 22–0–282–64–12.81; S. J. White 15–3–108–32*–9.00.

Bowling—S. J. White 302–63–928–62–14.96; P. J. Riley 71–15–221–12–18.41; C. W. Fitches 265–60–683–31–22.03; P. R. Hammond 152–30–535–24–22.29; M. R. Palmer 100–16–335–13–25.76.

THE KING'S SCHOOL, ROCHESTER

Played 15: Won 9, Lost 2, Drawn 4. Abandoned 3

Master i/c: J. Irvine

Batting—*M. P. Mernagh 14–3–351–81–31.90; R. N. Eastburn 15–1–412–73–29.42; R. J. Bailey 14–0–410–67–29.28; N. D. Twiddy 13–2–306–84–27.81; M. R. Eastburn 14–2–325–70–27.08; C. J. Cowell 6–1–125–46*–25.00; P. E. Grainger 12–2–176–38*–17.60.

Bowling—M. P. Mernagh 285.5–56–780–63–12.38; R. J. Bailey 112.3–30–281–19–14.78; I. J. Nightingale 203.2–42–525–30–17.50.

THE KING'S SCHOOL, WORCESTER

Played 18: Won 5, Lost 6, Drawn 6, Tied 1

Master i/c: D. P. Iddon

Batting—J. R. I. Mills 15–4–441–113*–40.09; T. A. Preston 17–1–433–66–27.06; R. G. Tomlinson 14–6–293–70–24.41; J. A. Cooper 16–2–294–78*–21.00; C. M. Rogers 16–0–180–50–11.25.

Bowling—S. C. Thompson 38.4–4–177–10–17.70; M. J. Jelfs 72–14–220–11–20.00; J. R. Underwood 169.3–17–765–32–23.90; T. A. Preston 121.1–20–388–12–32.33; J. R. I. Mills 201.4–34–617–19–32.47.

KINGSTON GRAMMAR SCHOOL

Played 18: Won 2, Lost 11, Drawn 5. Abandoned 3

Master i/c: R. J. Sturgeon

Batting—*R. J. Williams 18–1–483–116–28.41; R. A. Iley 18–0–394–53–21.88; J. Snelling 16–2–258–45*–18.42; L. Chester 10–2–144–55*–18.00; M. Avoth 18–1–247–60*–14.52; R. J. Paler 18–0–225–36–12.50.

Bowling—L. Chester 55.5–4–243–12–20.25; R. J. Williams 157.2–28–533–20–26.65; S. J. Dowle 108.4–18–421–15–28.06; R. A. Chandler 149–18–659–22–29.95.

KINGSWOOD SCHOOL

Played 18: Won 6, Lost 5, Drawn 7

Master i/c: R. J. Lewis

Batting—R. W. Lewis 16–1–487–130*–32.46; J. K. Stinson 15–1–361–74–25.78; R. D. Udy 15–0–328–81–21.86; C. J. Riggs 15–3–226–71*–18.83; P. E. Mills 9–0–163–66–18.11; A. J. Sutherland 13–3–180–45–18.00; *T. Gleghorn 13–3–116–30*–11.60.

Bowling—M. D. Beresford-Smith 121.4–25–322–25–12.88; M. A. J. Earp 176.1–30–532–31–17.16; J. K. Stinson 106.5–21–313–16–19.56; R. W. Lewis 102.4–15–391–16–24.43; T. Gleghorn 72.5–11–316–11–28.72.

LANCING COLLEGE

Played 19: Won 7, Lost 4, Drawn 8. Abandoned 1

Master i/c: E. A. Evans-Jones   Cricket professional: R. G. Davies

Batting—A. A. Gosden 18–7–415–63*–37.72; J. A. Martin 19–3–465–76–29.06; P. M. Alcock 19–1–456–69–25.33; W. A. Gooda 19–1–396–60*–22.00; J. B. Higgo 19–0–393–83–20.68; A. S. Puddephatt 15–4–144–24–13.09; T. E. J. Selmon 15–0–188–64–12.53.

Bowling—*T. W. Poerscout-Edgerton 100.4–19–266–22–12.09; J. A. Martin 101.2–29–259–20–12.95; J. B. Higgo 49.2–24–234–15–15.60; A. S. Puddephatt 160.2–33–447–27–16.55; W. A. Gooda 94.2–24–271–14–19.35; A. A. Gosden 100–30–303–15–20.20; A. R. Hewitt 169–59–446–20–22.30.

LEIGHTON PARK SCHOOL

Played 16: Won 6, Lost 6, Drawn 4. Abandoned 3

Master i/c: R. C. Boyd

Batting—J. D. Thomas 14–4–409–75*–40.90; *J. P. Newell Price 12–6–206–45*–34.33; R. S. E. Sykes 14–2–265–53*–22.08; J. E. Shingles 9–2–135–31*–19.28; M. Harris 8–0–149–53–18.62; F. W. Brazell 13–1–211–43–17.58; J. J. Allen 8–0–119–36–14.87.

Bowling—F. W. Brazell 37–0–160–11–14.54; M. Harris 85–13–240–13–18.46; J. P. Newell Price 175–43–499–24–20.79; R. E. Cosstick 74–17–241–11–21.90.

THE LEYS SCHOOL

Played 19: Won 7, Lost 8, Drawn 4. Abandoned 2

Master i/c: P. R. Chamberlain   Cricket professional: D. Gibson

Batting—*C. W. Barker 19–0–613–105–32.26; P. R. Searle 16–3–368–91*–28.30; N. R. Lankester 19–1–423–87–23.50; D. O. Solomon 19–0–412–71–21.68; H. I. C. Finch 18–0–336–65–18.66; S. C. Hawtrey-Woore 11–5–101–42*–16.83; C. R. D. Bullen 19–2–190–38*–11.17; D. N. G. Farman 14–4–101–27–10.10.

Bowling—N. R. Lankester 225–26–860–46–18.69; C. R. D. Bullen 39–12–381–18–21.16; A. D. C. Spencer 86–7–333–15–22.20; R. C. S. Thompson 139.3–21–465–18–25.83; S. C. Hawtrey-Woore 130–23–487–18–27.05; P. R. Searle 129.1–38–352–12–29.33.

LIVERPOOL COLLEGE

Played 13: Won 4, Lost 4, Drawn 5. Abandoned 2

Master i/c: Rev. J. R. Macaulay   Cricket professional: W. Clutterbuck

Batting—R. B. Downes 12–2–397–86*–39.70; *A. W. B. Smith 11–2–338–86*–37.55; R. M. Bennett 8–3–102–39*–20.40; A. D. Payne 10–0–161–37–16.10.

Bowling—J. Q. Harrington 40–1–128–15–8.53; J. M. Bishop 113.1–20–374–27–13.85; R. B. Downes 125–34–313–18–17.38; A. W. B. Smith 112.1–19–381–20–19.05.

LLANDOVERY COLLEGE

Played 12: Won 3, Lost 3, Drawn 6. Abandoned 2

Master i/c: T. G. Marks

Batting—K. J. Whiskerd 15–2–350–64–26.92; *D. J. R. Evans 14–2–240–82–20.00;
G. T. Howells 10–2–157–30*–19.62; D. Simcock 15–3–206–37*–17.16; R. C. Jones
14–2–201–56*–16.75; N. G. Phillips 14–0–203–42–14.50.

Bowling—R. S. Williams 120–22–411–32–12.84; M. R. Patel 91–17–271–10–27.10; R. C. Jones
68–9–310–10–31.00; D. J. R. Evans 78–11–357–11–32.45.

LORD WANDSWORTH COLLEGE

Played 11: Won 0, Lost 5, Drawn 6

Master i/c: A. G. Whibley

Batting—*S. H. Blows 11–1–398–123*–39.80; M. J. Critchley 11–2–244–64–27.11; B. M.
Davies 10–0–176–70–17.60.

Bowling—D. A. Berry 76.4–6–278–18–15.44; B. M. Davies 99–24–234–11–21.27.

LORD WILLIAMS'S SCHOOL, THAME

Played 12: Won 3, Lost 3, Drawn 6. Abandoned 1

Master i/c: A. M. Brannan

Batting—M. Khan 4–3–122–45–122.00; S. Heyes 8–3–163–67*–32.60; M. Bateman
12–4–238–43*–29.75; T. Fairn 12–2–252–74–25.20; *S. Alexander 8–0–172–72*–21.50; T.
Jordan 12–0–188–64–15.66.

Bowling—M. Bateman 120–38–314–23–13.65; S. Alexander 79.2–15–218–13–16.76; R.
Stanley 110–22–312–15–20.80.

LORETTO SCHOOL

Played 13: Won 1, Lost 3, Drawn 9. Abandoned 5

Batting—*T. R. McCreath 13–3–391–108*–39.10; S. S. Hodgson 13–1–370–72*–30.83; A. G.
Shepherd-Cross 12–1–190–38–17.27; M. C. Eglinton 11–0–169–42–15.36.

Bowling—S. S. Hodgson 59–12–173–12–14.41; L. T. G. Craig 154–41–400–24–16.66; M. C.
Eglinton 288–61–814–47–17.31; C. Laird 123–28–338–12–28.16.

LOUGHBOROUGH GRAMMAR SCHOOL

Played 17: Won 10, Lost 1, Drawn 6. Abandoned 1

Master i/c: E. Thorpe

Batting—M. I. Gidley 10–4–341–112*–56.83; G. Leeson 7–3–218–51*–54.50; S. Sawbridge
12–2–446–132*–44.60; D. Jones 10–2–289–75–36.12; *I. Bell 16–1–511–93–34.06; C. Jones
9–3–195–68–32.50; W. Dessau 12–4–213–51*–26.62; S. Pickering 11–3–171–53*–21.37.

Bowling—A. Warnes 41.5–13–122–10–12.20; C. Hawkes 152.2–39–388–27–14.37; A.
Kaitiff 69.1–13–203–13–15.61; S. Pickering 145.3–36–371–23–16.13; M. I. Gidley
129–41–275–17–16.17; W. Dessau 101.4–21–268–13–20.61.

MAGDALEN COLLEGE SCHOOL

Played 15: Won 5, Lost 1, Drawn 9. Abandoned 3

Master i/c: N. A. Rollings

Batting—*T. J. Stockwin 14–3–740–108*–67.27; A. D. Redman 14–1–358–66–27.53; T. H. Boyles 14–2–281–62*–23.41; J. A. Turner 11–2–207–38*–23.00; J. M. Hutton 15–2–266–64–20.46.

Bowling—S. N. Webb 133.5–13–533–31–17.19; T. E. J. Waters 159.4–29–542–27–20.07; D. M. A. Andrews 63–10–204–10–20.40; R. J. Suckling 140.2–24–472–22–21.45; M. B. A. Reynolds 88.2–11–343–11–31.18.

MALVERN COLLEGE

Played 20: Won 5, Lost 2, Drawn 13

Master i/c: R. W. Tolchard   Cricket professional: G. D. Morton

Batting—J. R. Wileman 20–2–772–107–42.88; *G. N. Lunt 19–4–511–61–34.06; B. C. Usher 20–2–514–86–28.55; I. K. Timberlake 13–1–285–63*–23.75; S. Johnson-Marshall 15–3–274–50*–22.83; D. J. B. Read 11–5–129–41–21.50; E. G. Maughan 15–3–236–86*–19.66; A. J. Hardwicke 16–2–211–33–15.07.

Bowling—E. G. Maughan 205.4–52–545–38–14.34; B. C. Usher 80–14–295–16–18.43; G. N. Lunt 114.3–20–390–19–20.52; S. Johnson-Marshall 72.5–10–298–14–21.28; M. J. Barrett-Green 114.4–25–358–15–23.86; H. C. Douglas-Pennant 259.3–46–842–31–27.16.

MANCHESTER GRAMMAR SCHOOL

Played 14: Won 3, Lost 2, Drawn 9. Abandoned 2

Master i/c: D. Moss

Batting—J. P. Crawley 10–1–324–89–36.00; P. M. Crawley 13–1–365–52*–30.41; I. R. Cross 12–3–256–61–28.44; D. N. Dada 11–5–129–32*–21.50; P. D. Gibbon 11–4–141–41–20.14; A. B. Gaskarth 13–0–225–55–17.30; M. H. Taylor 12–0–193–65–16.08.

Bowling—R. B. Hennis 113.5–20–315–20–15.75; *R. J. A. Steele 160–38–413–18–22.94; D. J. Worsley 137.3–29–400–17–23.52; P. M. Crawley 190.3–57–440–18–24.44; A. M. Dodd 108.4–25–325–11–29.54.

MARLBOROUGH COLLEGE

Played 17: Won 5, Lost 1, Drawn 11. Abandoned 1

Master i/c: P. J. Lough   Cricket professional: R. R. Savage

Batting—G. W. Barker 17–3–535–108*–38.21; J. S. Kerr 17–2–498–122*–33.20; D. M. Bevan 13–5–219–47*–27.37; A. J. Robinson 17–0–404–90–23.76; N. J. Cook 11–4–151–27–21.57; M. A. Foulds 15–2–275–69*–21.15; S. C. G. Thomson 15–2–189–37*–14.53.

Bowling—D. M. Bevan 148–35–392–23–17.04; N. J. Cook 216.2–40–641–33–19.42; *A. B. Robb 239.3–68–547–26–21.03; S. C. Pole 213–52–639–26–24.57.

MERCHANT TAYLORS' SCHOOL, CROSBY

Played 19: Won 3, Lost 6, Drawn 10. Abandoned 1

Master i/c: Rev. D. A. Smith   Cricket professional: G. E. Trim

Batting—*R. W. Glynne-Jones 16–0–486–89–30.37; S. Bell 19–3–454–76–28.37; N. A. Hanley 12–1–227–59–20.63; M. Watkinson 14–2–242–70–20.16; M. W. Appleton 16–1–288–59–19.20; D. L. Clift 17–1–268–71–16.75; N. M. Dixon 12–1–172–48–15.63.

Bowling—S. R. McGee 127.5–34–375–24–15.62; A. J. Dawson 99–26–276–15–18.40; S. Bell 164.5–36–438–19–23.05; I. K. Wright 227.4–62–636–24–26.50.

MERCHANT TAYLORS' SCHOOL, NORTHWOOD

Played 20: Won 6, Lost 3, Drawn 11. Abandoned 4

Master i/c: W. M. B. Ritchie

Batting—J. R. Harrison 11–3–243–50–30.37; K. J. Clifford 20–3–513–92–30.17; *D. W. R. Wiles 15–5–249–42*–24.90; A. P. Solomons 16–1–316–50–21.06; S. Mediratta 12–6–104–39–17.33; J. L. Hampel 19–1–290–70*–16.11; A. J. Brand 20–1–301–42–15.84; G. J. Stamp 16–1–222–55*–14.80.

Bowling—J. L. Hampel 226.3–54–580–44–13.18; D. W. R. Wiles 243.3–46–725–35–20.71; A. P. Thompson 330.3–69–946–42–22.52; A. J. Brand 133–28–376–14–26.85.

MERCHISTON CASTLE SCHOOL

Played 15: Won 7, Lost 2, Drawn 6. Abandoned 2

Masters i/c: M. C. L. Gill and S. J. Dight

Batting—M. E. R. Paton 15–2–365–62*–28.07; *N. R. Ballantyne 15–3–305–60*–25.41; S. J. K. Laird 13–3–253–55*–25.30; A. J. K. Wilson 15–1–296–41*–21.14; P. Walton 11–1–176–42–17.60; D. M. Streek 13–2–170–35*–15.45; P. W. R. Martin 15–1–182–35*–13.00.

Bowling—S. D. L. Francis 147–57–318–33–9.63; D. M. Streek 150.5–40–304–29–10.48; F. W. Hunter 109–38–270–25–10.80; S. J. Elworthy 102–33–235–20–11.75; N. R. Ballantyne 45.3–9–145–10–14.50.

MILLFIELD SCHOOL

Played 14: Won 6, Lost 0, Drawn 8. Abandoned 1

Master i/c: A. D. Curtis   Cricket professional: G. C. Wilson

Batting—D. Luckes 13–4–579–132*–64.33; G. Lucas 10–3–386–101*–55.14; P. Holloway 10–3–284–103*–40.57; A. R. Phillips 12–2–374–85*–37.40; J. Humphrey 5–1–129–79*–32.25; H. R. J. Trump 12–0–386–107–32.16; J. Hallett 11–4–200–70–28.57; R. Dawson 6–0–123–69–20.50.

Bowling—H. R. J. Trump 173–54–390–24–16.25; J. Hallett 139.5–27–387–21–18.42; D. J. Knight 79.4–12–284–14–20.28; A. R. Phillips 177–29–564–25–22.56; M. Featherstone 110.1–19–383–14–27.35.

MILL HILL SCHOOL

Played 25: Won 8, Lost 9, Drawn 8. Abandoned 4

Master i/c: R. J. Denning   Cricket professional: G. A. R. Lock

Batting—*L. B. Braham 26–2–970–100–40.41; C. R. Younger 23–3–515–96–25.75; B. R. Hartman 22–2–504–76–25.20; I. M. Holmes 14–2–259–86–21.58; A. B. Dell 22–4–327–62–18.16; P. Achan 13–5–139–53*–17.37; M. R. Jacobson 11–3–113–37*–14.12; J. H. Bohn 19–2–209–48–12.29.

Bowling—P. Achan 160–25–451–29–15.55; E. M. Latter 135–19–435–21–20.71; B. R. Hartman 322–81–835–39–21.41; C. B. Forde 223–34–744–34–21.88; G. E. S. Brock 143–27–462–16–28.87.

MILTON ABBEY SCHOOL

Played 13: Won 4, Lost 5, Drawn 4

Master i/c: S. T. Smail

Batting—S. J. E. Courage 12–3–350–97–38.88; C. P. Cook 11–2–274–64–30.44; *J. M. A. Boscawen 12–1–304–74–27.63; R. F. Jessurun 11–4–132–30–18.85; W. O. Quibell 10–3–125–33–17.85; R. S. Padmore 10–0–111–29–11.10.

Bowling—H. G. H. Groves 56–11–169–13–13.00; W. O. Quibell 140.2–24–435–23–18.91; R. F. Jessurun 154.5–31–511–20–25.55; A. D. M. Cooke 86–19–306–10–30.60.

MONKTON COMBE SCHOOL

Played 13: Won 6, Lost 4, Drawn 3. Abandoned 2

Master i/c: P. C. Sibley   Cricket professional: N. D. Botton

Batting—*O. Q. Wyncoll 14–1–342–80–26.30; M. P. Davis 14–2–307–86*–25.58; J. F. Perry 10–0–240–51–24.00; J. A. Jenkins 11–3–168–44*–21.00; J. E. Harris 8–1–123–41*–17.57; J. M. Downey 8–1–107–43–15.28.

Bowling—J. A. Jenkins 138.4–38–309–25–12.36; J. M. Downey 74–5–270–19–14.21; R. S. Deacock 65–16–149–10–14.90; N. F. Robb 96–21–287–18–15.94; S. J. Kandavanam 100–20–294–14–21.00; O. Q. Wyncoll 82.2–11–306–14–21.85.

NEWCASTLE-UNDER-LYME SCHOOL

Played 12: Won 5, Lost 2, Drawn 5. Abandoned 1

Master i/c: R. K. Martindale

Batting—R. N. Clowes 11–4–247–45*–35.28; *J. J. Byrne 8–0–253–73–31.62; N. R. Hood 8–2–157–50*–26.16; R. W. Johnson 11–1–235–60*–23.50; D. J. Brock 6–0–119–39–19.83.

Bowling—D. J. Brock 128.2–42–319–26–12.26; J. M. Snape 87.4–18–264–21–12.57.

NORWICH SCHOOL

Played 14: Won 3, Lost 9, Drawn 2. Abandoned 3

Master i/c: P. J. Henderson

Batting—N. A. Colman 14–1–406–77–31.23; E. D. F. Cree 12–3–175–44–19.44; D. P. Heath 12–0–206–77–17.16; R. H. Onslow 8–0–133–43–16.62; J. S. Orr 12–0–133–40–11.08.

Bowling—P. B. Allen 44.2–11–135–10–13.50; *P. D. Lee 132–20–401–26–15.42; D. P. Heath 99.1–14–315–20–15.75; A. K. McCarter 107.2–22–366–12–30.50.

NOTTINGHAM HIGH SCHOOL

Played 19: Won 6, Lost 2, Drawn 11. Abandoned 1

Master i/c: P. G. Morris   Cricket professional: H. Latchman

Batting—M. Saxelby 6–1–254–131–50.80; N. A. Hunt 16–3–509–105*–39.15; P. R. D. Briggs 8–0–242–100–30.25; R. L. C. Jones 17–4–357–72*–27.46; R. I. Atkinson 6–1–130–52–26.00; S. A. O'Brien 9–4–115–67–23.00; N. P. Carr 12–3–192–61–21.33; *J. W. A. Morris 11–4–140–69–20.00; R. W. Dixon 10–1–153–37–17.00; T. R. Leman 10–0–124–28–12.40.

Bowling—S. A. O'Brien 85–32–190–15–12.66; T. J. Deas 299.2–74–677–49–13.81; A. J. Belfield 71–6–289–14–20.64; J. W. A. Morris 164.3–34–475–21–22.61.

OAKHAM SCHOOL

Played 21: Won 7, Lost 1, Drawn 13

Master i/c: J. Wills   Cricket professional: J. C. Balderstone

Batting—*D. M. Robjohns 20–4–918–123*–57.37; T. J. A. Graves 20–1–529–78*–27.84; C. W. Howard 8–4–109–44–27.25; C. W. Wood 20–3–411–74–24.17; P. J. R. Neild 18–5–303–85*–23.30; A. S. England 19–0–356–89–18.73; S. Millhouse 15–3–148–27–12.33.

Bowling—S. V. Aldis 254.2–60–782–45–17.37; C. W. Wood 140.3–24–479–22–21.77; D. M. Robjohns 48–4–219–10–21.90; D. J. Ross 138–26–406–18–22.55; P. J. R. Neild 206.2–30–660–19–34.73.

THE ORATORY SCHOOL

Played 13: Won 2, Lost 2, Drawn 9

Master i/c: P. L. Tomlinson

Batting—R. P. Unwin 12–2–246–62–24.60; J. N. Wallis 13–3–215–56–21.50; P. J. Coverdale 13–2–216–57–19.63; D. J. Sillence 13–1–225–43*–18.75; S. R. Wright 13–5–145–25*–18.12.

Bowling—R. P. Unwin 83–12–212–13–16.30; S. R. Wright 152–32–403–24–16.79; J. N. Wallis 102–18–307–17–18.05; M. D. Sillence 83–14–266–14–19.00.

OUNDLE SCHOOL

Played 18: Won 5, Lost 5, Drawn 8. Abandoned 2

Master i/c: V. G. B. Cushing   Cricket professional: T. Howorth

Batting—*T. I. Macmillan 18–1–924–161*–54.35; A. R. Turner 16–1–524–100*–34.93; T. Harrison 18–1–510–80–30.00; P. D. Eakins 14–3–300–47*–27.27; G. Spragg 15–4–278–60*–25.27; J. A. S. Shervington 14–1–243–40–18.69; R. H. J. Jenkins 16–3–223–45–17.15; T. Allerton 9–3–101–30–16.83; J. McAlpine 14–3–134–28*–12.18.

Bowling—A. Watson 82–19–290–18–16.11; R. H. J. Jenkins 272.5–79–876–46–19.04; T. Harrison 95–16–337–14–24.07; J. McAlpine 197–23–754–24–31.41; S. Means 105–20–362–11–32.90.

THE PERSE SCHOOL

Played 17: Won 6, Lost 3, Drawn 8. Abandoned 1

Master i/c: A. W. Billinghurst   Cricket professional: D. C. Collard

Batting—N. M. Law 15–1–512–109–36.57; *I. R. Styan 14–5–290–100*–32.22; R. J. Doel 14–0–376–62–26.85; P. J. Doel 12–3–231–48*–25.66; R. J. Sennitt 10–3–122–37*–17.42; P. J. Alexander 12–0–168–43–14.00; B. Melzer 10–0–103–42–10.30.

Bowling—I. R. Styan 181.4–65–406–30–13.53; P. A. Bailey 123–31–324–20–16.20; N. M. Law 79.2–18–235–14–16.78; T. F. P. Charlton 104–26–303–14–21.64; P. J. Alexander 74.1–15–237–10–23.70; M. A. Melford 137.4–35–419–15–27.93.

PLYMOUTH COLLEGE

Master i/c: T. J. Stevens

Batting—S. Stevenson 13–2–707–88–64.27; S. Summers 13–2–558–134–50.72; R. Colegate 12–4–337–98–42.12; G. Waldock 12–2–273–70–27.30; A. Kerr 10–2–168–66–21.00.

Bowling—B. Fox 151–24–571–33–17.30; C. Vinson 96–32–223–8–27.87; A. Lopes 116–23–420–14–30.00; S. Macartney 128–22–498–16–31.12.

POCKLINGTON SCHOOL

Played 20: Won 11, Lost 4, Drawn 4, Tied 1. Abandoned 6

Master i/c: D. Nuttall

Batting—*T. P. B. Balderson 18-3-623-100*-41.53; S. A. Clarke 18-3-608-102*-40.53; A. T. Pettinger 20-1-501-106-26.36; M. W. Wood 15-0-280-52-18.66; C. M. Haynes 15-4-178-43-16.18; J. R. L. Brown 14-0-206-50-14.71.

Bowling—J. A. Webster 72.2-18-205-18-11.38; J. R. L. Brown 225.1-64-593-44-13.47; M. W. Wood 123-26-383-28-13.67; R. J. Cox 118-39-279-17-16.41; T. P. B. Balderson 256.4-61-676-40-16.90; A. R. Dale 137-18-470-23-20.43.

PRIOR PARK COLLEGE

Played 17: Won 7, Lost 5, Drawn 5. Abandoned 1

Master i/c: W. E. Russell

Batting—A. Hadley 14-4-422-125*-42.20; J. Nwagbogu 7-2-179-44*-35.80; M. Woodhouse 16-2-464-107*-33.14; J. Reid 17-2-425-70-28.33; *B. Moorhouse 16-2-358-63-25.57; G. Lee 14-3-165-40-15.00; J. Powell 14-3-161-53-14.63.

Bowling—J. Reid 53.5-12-203-12-16.91; G. Adekoya 71-11-257-13-19.76; G. Lee 206.2-46-703-35-20.08; J. Powell 197.4-40-623-28-22.25; N. Corfield 143-35-493-19-25.94.

QUEEN ELIZABETH GRAMMAR SCHOOL, WAKEFIELD

Played 14: Won 5, Lost 4, Drawn 4, Tied 1

Master i/c: T. Barker

Batting—*J. Wild 12-4-430-106*-53.75; S. Barnsley 14-0-326-79-23.28; R. Littlewood 14-5-200-37*-22.22; P. Land 9-0-196-54-21.77; M. Philmore 11-1-174-59*-17.40.

Bowling—J. Wild 88.1-24-263-21-12.52; S. Bailey 145.1-31-454-21-21.61; G. Millman 110.4-18-446-16-27.87.

QUEEN'S COLLEGE, TAUNTON

Played 13: Won 7, Lost 1, Drawn 5. Abandoned 1

Master i/c: J. W. Davies

Batting—D. N. A. Essien 12-3-516-77-57.33; *J. J. A. Wilson 13-4-423-62*-47.00; M. Knight 10-4-202-34-33.66; J. R. Davey 13-1-343-60-28.58; B. Wixey 9-3-123-37*-20.50; S. Burt 10-1-128-31-14.22; P. Murphy 12-0-164-40-13.66.

Bowling—D. N. A. Essien 153.3-38-453-27-16.77; M. Irish 113.3-22-329-19-17.31; G. Harrison 97.3-20-308-16-19.25; C. Amor 116.1-25-344-14-24.57.

RADLEY COLLEGE

Played 15: Won 5, Lost 2, Drawn 8. Abandoned 1

Master i/c: A. C. Wallis   Cricket professionals: A. G. Robinson and A. R. Wagner

Batting—R. E. Q. Gurney 14-2-505-97*-42.08; M. J. Lowrey 14-1-317-71-24.38; *C. H. H. Pegg 14-1-315-117-24.23; R. B. Waller 11-5-123-34*-20.50; R. A. Jardine-Brown 8-2-118-28-19.66; A. C. I. Culley 8-0-157-91-19.62; M. Durden-Smith 9-1-146-68-18.25; C. J. Hayward 13-1-183-34-15.25; R. G. Fuller 13-1-170-37-14.16.

Bowling—G. D. L. Powell 189.2-73-491-37-13.27; S. J. Wilson-Stephens 77-16-228-16-14.25; M. J. Lowrey 125-57-423-22-19.22; R. B. Waller 108.1-23-367-14-26.21.

RATCLIFFE COLLEGE

Played 17: Won 5, Lost 7, Drawn 5. Abandoned 2

Master i/c: C. W. Swan

Batting—R. J. G. Adcock 15–4–324–70*–29.45; P. A. Mestecky 15–3–310–100*–25.83; N. J. Farnell 12–2–173–25*–17.30.

Bowling—P. A. Mestecky 244–71–568–61–9.31; R. J. G. Adcock 113–32–298–23–12.95; A. Copp 60–13–167–12–13.91.

READING SCHOOL

Played 17: Won 11, Lost 1, Drawn 5

Master i/c: R. G. Owen   Cricket professional: A. Dindar

Batting—T. J. C. Dance 16–3–709–123*–54.53; O. D. Beckett 15–3–604–102*–50.33; *J. S. Pritchard 14–5–353–70–39.22; G. J. Orpwood 13–2–342–73*–31.09; I. C. Orpwood 13–4–176–41–19.55; J. N. S. Hampton 11–1–175–55–17.50; R. M. Hawkins 10–2–102–25–12.75; P. R. Auty 12–3–102–39*–11.33.

Bowling—J. S. Pritchard 212.4–63–479–52–9.21; G. J. Orpwood 134.5–14–474–25–18.96; T. J. C. Dance 117.2–24–400–19–21.05; J. B. Hathaway 120–11–486–19–25.57.

REED'S SCHOOL

Played 19: Won 5, Lost 4, Drawn 10. Abandoned 1

Master i/c: G. R. Martin

Batting—J. R. Sharples 13–2–304–137–27.63; R. A. Blamey 15–5–264–52*–26.40; J. Dharmasena 18–6–295–76–24.58; D. J. D. Dominy 9–1–180–51–22.50; O. Pendered 18–1–361–96–21.23; N. Miller 15–3–208–74*–17.33; S. R. Shiells 20–1–309–48–16.26; S. C. W. Taylor 16–2–165–31–11.78; A. R. Balls 12–1–118–26–10.72; *T. T. Oliver 13–2–101–29*–9.18.

Bowling—J. R. Ovenden 81–16–216–13–16.61; T. T. Oliver 205.3–39–683–32–21.34; S. R. Shiells 47–5–215–10–21.50; J. Dharmasena 229.2–45–684–31–22.06; R. Pakenham 185.5–41–590–23–25.65; R. A. Blamey 104.4–12–423–16–26.43.

REIGATE GRAMMAR SCHOOL

Played 17: Won 6, Lost 5, Drawn 6. Abandoned 3

Master i/c: D. C. R. Jones   Cricket professional: H. Newton

Batting—*S. J. Virley 16–2–427–81–30.50; J. P. Jackson 14–2–357–61–29.75; P. A. Radford 15–0–390–114–26.00; D. M. Gregory 16–2–353–58–25.21; C. S. Bates 16–1–330–71–22.00; D. F. Rowlinson 8–2–109–32–18.16; J. S. Burrow 15–0–240–70–16.00; D. N. Abbott 14–5–137–20–15.22.

Bowling—M. T. Holman 227.1–48–662–41–16.14; D. F. Rowlinson 106–19–341–18–18.94; D. N. Abbott 129.5–28–418–22–19.00; M. P. Lander 120.3–31–360–17–21.17.

RENDCOMB COLLEGE

Played 13: Won 7, Lost 0, Drawn 6. Abandoned 1

Cricket professional: D. Essenhigh

Batting—W. Sherwood 10–5–262–79*–52.40; M. Astill 13–2–318–82–28.90; A. J. Brealy 7–3–108–37*–27.00; J. M. Fellows 13–1–285–61–23.75; *I. D. Whittaker 13–3–216–62–21.60; T. M. Burns 9–3–125–53–20.83.

Bowling—A. J. Brealy 179.5–54–473–45–10.51; B. M. Branston 48–9–171–16–10.68; N. L. Suffoll 93.2–12–277–17–16.29; C. G. Huck 96–23–276–14–19.71.

REPTON SCHOOL

Played 20: Won 8, Lost 3, Drawn 9. Abandoned 2

Master i/c: M. Stones   Cricket professional: M. K. Kettle

Batting—C. J. Adams 19–2–1,242–158–73.05; C. E. Wall 18–2–496–80–31.00; R. N. Wall 14–3–323–84–29.36; R. F. Williamson 12–0–351–63–29.25; S. C. Hall 14–3–317–100*–28.81; A. E. Jordan 12–0–249–77–20.75; A. P. Griffiths 13–4–152–29–16.88.

Bowling—*D. J. Anderson 246–65–632–56–11.28; C. E. Wall 241.2–54–648–34–19.05; C. J. Adams 99–16–354–17–20.82; A. J. Moxon 103–36–256–12–21.33; R. N. Wall 166–35–508–17–29.88.

ROSSALL SCHOOL

Played 16: Won 1, Lost 5, Drawn 10. Abandoned 3

Master i/c: R. J. Clapp

Batting—*C. D. Foster 16–0–453–106–28.31; S. S. Page 13–5–192–40*–24.00; D. M. Indo 17–0–358–87–21.05; A. D. Clark 9–1–167–49*–20.87; B. M. Evans 14–3–191–51*–17.36; P. L. Smith 16–1–249–61*–16.60; C. M. Cocker 10–0–134–43–13.40; J. G. Brown 9–1–103–36–12.87; W. E. Hayes 15–4–127–20*–11.54.

Bowling—B. M. Evans 103–22–370–21–17.61; S. D. Holmes 112–26–343–19–18.05; W. E. Hayes 218–32–676–30–22.53; A. G. Smith 223–33–723–19–38.05.

ROYAL GRAMMAR SCHOOL, GUILDFORD

Played 16: Won 6, Lost 3, Drawn 7

Master i/c: S. B. R. Shore

Batting—L. Jones 16–2–580–88*–41.42; P. Challinor 13–4–261–56*–29.00; N. Thomson 13–5–209–34–26.12; N. Canning 11–0–233–37–21.18; *T. Smith 15–2–237–41*–18.23.

Bowling—M. Pullen 49.1–8–142–12–11.83; P. Challinor 139–30–251–21–11.95; J. Hoyle 122–28–311–21–14.80; N. Canning 70–16–185–12–15.41; M. Gore 89–22–235–13–18.07; N. Thomson 154–44–372–20–18.60.

ROYAL GRAMMAR SCHOOL, NEWCASTLE

Played 15: Won 3, Lost 4, Drawn 8

Master i/c: D. W. Smith   Cricket professional: J. N. Graham

Batting—*A. Atkinson 10–5–252–63*–50.40; O. Youll 14–2–474–78–39.50; T. Meears-White 15–2–422–107*–32.46; S. Johnson 11–0–286–53–26.00; P. Venn 7–2–125–52*–25.00; C. Barnes 10–2–122–37–15.25; C. Graham 15–0–219–46–14.60.

Bowling—A. Atkinson 124.4–31–333–23–14.47; S. Ruddick 83.5–18–261–16–16.31; S. Johnson 167–24–430–25–17.20; O. Youll 89.5–9–260–13–20.00.

ROYAL GRAMMAR SCHOOL, WORCESTER

Played 22: Won 13, Lost 2, Drawn 7. Abandoned 3

Master i/c: B. M. Rees   Cricket professional: M. J. Horton

Batting—D. W. Headley 20–2–627–98–34.83; M. J. Ridlinton 21–5–447–70–27.93; J. S. Waters 17–9–218–56*–27.25; M. J. Walker 22–4–487–82–27.05; *G. T. G. Burrow 21–3–482–81–26.77; S. P. Chapman 6–1–114–71–22.80; B. P. C. Wilkes 6–0–124–60–20.66; S. D. Bradley 13–2–218–60*–19.81; P. C. Fearnley 13–2–173–36*–15.72.

Bowling—S. P. Chapman 43–10–99–11–9.00; D. W. Headley 280.1–67–551–57–9.66; J. S. Waters 359.1–82–650–52–12.50; M. J. Ridlinton 159.2–39–504–25–20.16; M. J. Walker 134.1–37–345–14–24.64; O. T. Pilgrim 227–36–389–11–35.36.

RUGBY SCHOOL

Played 18: Won 7, Lost 3, Drawn 8

Master i/c: K. Siviter   Cricket professional: W. J. Stewart

Batting—B. C. A. Ellison 17–2–437–72–29.13; Y. J. Khan 20–2–515–109–28.61; *T. H. A. Arulampalam 19–1–501–85*–27.83; R. R. Montgomerie 20–2–375–111*–20.83; G. W. Jepson 8–1–126–39–18.00; G. A. D. Whittaker 16–0–272–63–17.00; S. D. A. Drewett 9–0–142–59–15.77; M. Rowlands 18–1–184–37–10.82; H. N. Bhatia 14–3–117–18–10.63.

Bowling—B. C. A. Ellison 259.2–65–713–44–16.20; A. L. C. Winchester 231.3–37–772–42–18.38; H. N. Bhatia 280.5–71–835–40–20.87; M. Rowlands 178.5–41–517–24–21.54.

RYDAL SCHOOL

Played 11: Won 4, Lost 1, Drawn 6. Abandoned 4

Master i/c: M. H. Stevenson   Cricket professional: R. W. C. Pitman

Batting—A. G. Moore 11–1–331–98–33.10; H. S. L. Bradley 10–2–198–42–24.75; S. M. Williams 9–2–165–58–23.57; R. N. L. Harries 7–2–113–33*–22.60; J. R. Hogg 10–2–161–64*–20.12; *S. Dale-Jones 7–1–111–26–18.50.

Bowling—P. S. Goldsmith 94–19–260–22–11.81; P. A. Jeory 80–24–185–11–16.81; A. J. M. Higson 127–30–357–15–23.80.

ST ALBANS SCHOOL

Played 16: Won 3, Lost 4, Drawn 9

Master i/c: N. Woodsmith   Cricket professional: G. Cooper

Batting—D. Barlow 14–3–327–78–29.72; A. Dalwood 11–1–287–53–28.70; *T. Preest 14–1–298–70–22.92; M. Henculey 9–2–150–42–21.42; G. Dill 12–1–154–48–14.00; D. Rourke 13–0–177–34–13.61.

Bowling—J. Smart 161–26–498–24–20.75; E. Foster 75–15–209–10–20.90; G. Bandt 77–16–293–11–26.63.

ST DUNSTAN'S COLLEGE

Played 17: Won 11, Lost 0, Drawn 6

Master i/c: C. Matten

Batting—M. A. Slade 13–3–687–108*–68.70; G. R. S. Scovell 12–3–357–97*–39.66; D. A. Gale 4–1–114–57–38.00; M. J. Dowse 17–3–521–101–37.21; J. J. Platford 13–1–211–55*–17.58; L. Tyler 10–3–100–54*–14.28.

Bowling—G. R. S. Scovell 214–52–547–49–11.16; M. A. Slade 110–28–287–22–13.04; J. P. Andrews 141–32–355–25–14.20; J. D. M. Dall 81–15–266–18–14.77; H. R. Davies 78–10–267–13–20.53; T. R. E-Argent 121–26–319–14–22.78.

ST EDMUND'S SCHOOL, CANTERBURY

Played 12: Won 3, Lost 3, Drawn 6. Abandoned 1

Master i/c: H. W. Scott   Cricket professional: D. V. P. Wright

Batting—N. C. Kennett 10–3–438–115*–62.57; R. Hayes 9–1–261–97–32.62; P. J. Mitchell 9–1–212–53–26.50; M. J. E. Horton 10–1–157–63–17.44.

Bowling—D. Blench 110–23–317–18–17.61; P. J. Mitchell 88.4–9–334–16–20.87; *P. J. Bryant 123–10–517–20–25.85.

ST EDWARD'S SCHOOL, OXFORD

Played 13: Won 3, Lost 2, Drawn 8

Master i/c: P. G. Badger   Cricket professional: B. R. Edrich

Batting—O. A. C. Watson 11–1–334–102*–33.40; M. R. Jepp 13–1–255–55*–21.25; G. A. Wright 7–1–122–51–20.33; J. R. Kelly 13–4–171–33–19.00; N. K. T. Seddon 13–0–241–35–18.53; T. H. C. Hancock 9–0–165–40–18.33; J. M. Gray 9–0–144–44–16.00; J. P. Elvin 10–0–118–44–11.80.

Bowling—C. G. Sharp 219.3–41–579–33–17.54; R. J. Gaffney 142.5–19–513–20–25.65; J. R. Kelly 157.1–30–437–15–29.13.

ST GEORGE'S COLLEGE, WEYBRIDGE

Played 18: Won 4, Lost 6, Drawn 8

Master i/c: B. V. O'Gorman

Batting—C. M. Bennett 16–5–568–146*–51.63; J. H. C. Creber 16–5–540–85*–49.09; S. Henderson 12–3–291–51–32.33; I. Turner 18–2–501–73*–31.31; S. Cook 16–2–398–70–28.42.

Bowling—I. Turner 164–25–618–34–18.17; S. P. Cherriman 133.3–29–371–19–19.52; R. Aspinall 156.1–41–508–20–25.40; A. Regan 150.5–26–522–19–27.47.

ST JOHN'S SCHOOL, LEATHERHEAD

Played 16: Won 1, Lost 3, Drawn 12. Abandoned 1

Master i/c: A. B. Gale   Cricket professional: E. Shepperd

Batting—*S. E. Penfold 16–1–747–143*–49.80; M. E. Randall 7–0–215–71–30.71; I. B. George 16–1–321–56*–27.06; A. C. Hibbert 16–1–321–56*–21.40; D. Mahony 14–4–200–46–20.00; C. J. Bally 12–0–207–54–17.25; P. A. Prentice 11–1–111–21–11.10.

Bowling—A. C. Hibbert 145.1–29–475–24–19.79; O. D. M. Bell 210.1–41–653–31–21.06; T. P. Fairclough 191–22–707–29–24.37.

ST LAWRENCE COLLEGE

Played 14: Won 3, Lost 5, Drawn 6. Abandoned 3

Master i/c: N. O. S. Jones   Cricket professional: L. A. C. D'Arcy

Batting—*A. O. Uzor 13–2–722–154*–65.63; M. Carrington 10–4–225–65*–37.50; J. M. Winter 6–1–100–27–20.00; G. P. Carson 10–1–165–49*–18.33; P. N. Unachukwu 11–3–125–40*–15.62; R. S. Chhabra 14–0–215–43–15.35; L. M. Willsmer 12–0–148–43–12.33; A. Bird 10–1–100–28–11.11.

Bowling—C. P. Burr 72.1–16–268–16–16.75; A. O. Uzor 165–31–503–27–18.62; J. M. Winter 50–4–235–11–21.36; M. Carrington 100.5–20–330–14–23.57; L. M. Willsmer 125.2–16–365–13–28.07; A. Bird 137–26–438–11–39.81.

ST PAUL'S SCHOOL

Played 14: Won 5, Lost 0, Drawn 8, Tied 1. Abandoned 2

Master i/c: G. Hughes   Cricket professional: E. W. Whitfield

Batting—*H. C. G. Boothroyd-Brooks 16–3–537–121*–41.30; P. W. T. Neate 16–3–429–102*–33.00; S. W. Filmer 13–3–302–62–30.20; I. C. Colak-Antic 11–1–194–60–19.40; T. A. Kiggell 10–1–172–34–19.11; T. A. N. Bell 9–2–125–42–17.85; R. G. Burns 13–0–232–77–17.84; T. L. Morris 14–2–204–81*–17.00.

Bowling—T. A. Kiggell 178–44–404–24–16.83; H. C. G. Boothroyd-Brooks 132.4–31–322–19–16.94; D. J. Gordon-Smith 161.5–40–484–26–18.61; A. B. Turpin 163.1–33–470–21–22.38.

ST PETER'S SCHOOL, YORK

Played 18: Won 8, Lost 2, Drawn 8. Abandoned 3

Master i/c: D. Kirby   Cricket professional: K. F. Mohan

Batting—*N. D. Muirhead 14–4–503–102*–50.30; W. J. Robinson 13–3–458–101*–45.80; N. G. Wilkinson 18–6–391–54–32.58; R. Hutchinson 19–1–397–52*–22.05; M. Reid 18–1–332–75*–19.52; T. E. J. Cooper 14–1–218–72–16.76.

Bowling—M. D. Donoghue 231.1–62–655–55–11.90; P. F. Wand 215.3–80–459–37–12.40; N. G. Wilkinson 80.1–20–205–10–20.50; N. D. Muirhead 210.2–55–592–20–29.60.

SEDBERGH SCHOOL

Played 11: Won 4, Lost 0, Drawn 7. Abandoned 1

Master i/c: M. J. Morris

Batting—J. R. C. Dakin 12–3–592–112*–65.77; A. J. Meadows 9–6–183–62*–61.00; H. J. A. Daniels 11–1–386–114*–38.60; *C. D. H. Palmer 12–1–388–90–35.27; N. M. Poulsen 12–0–207–44–17.25; S. W. Gawthorpe 10–2–119–34–14.87.

Bowling—A. M. Skinner 137.4–40–360–29–12.41; H. J. A. Daniels 151–42–400–26–15.38; S. R. Farrow 55–11–211–12–17.58; A. J. Meadows 86–13–331–10–33.10.

SEVENOAKS SCHOOL

Played 16: Won 4, Lost 1, Drawn 11. Abandoned 2

Master i/c: I. J. B. Walker

Batting—*C. J. Crang 16–4–603–127*–50.25; J. D. Fry 15–3–355–72*–29.58; A. Griffiths 15–0–432–61–28.80; B. Shah 15–2–235–57*–18.07; S. A. Ford 12–2–160–47–16.00; S. M. Popham 10–1–102–26–11.33; G. M. Siddle 15–1–158–25–11.28.

Bowling—J. D. Fry 186.3–36–491–33–14.87; A. Griffiths 184.5–51–449–26–17.26; S. A. Ford 178.3–39–579–33–17.54.

SHERBORNE SCHOOL

Played 14: Won 4, Lost 0, Drawn 10. Abandoned 3

Master i/c: M. Cleaver   Cricket professional: C. Stone

Batting—*A. Kardooni 15–2–682–114*–52.46; B. Atwell 5–1–165–75*–41.25; A. James 15–3–344–62*–28.66; T. Ashworth 15–0–300–72–20.00; R. Youngman 14–2–228–43–19.00; S. Leeke 14–3–196–42–17.81; P. Hodges 14–2–195–40–16.25; T. Levy 11–3–121–26*–15.12.

Bowling—T. Levy 117.4–27–371–25–14.84; R. Bagnall 106–24–283–16–17.68; A. Macpherson 162.3–44–480–26–18.46; R. Springfield 112.2–27–327–15–21.80; P. Hodges 212–47–603–17–35.47.

SHIPLAKE COLLEGE

Played 12: Won 5, Lost 3, Drawn 4. Abandoned 2

Master i/c: P. M. Davey

Batting—C. Haynes 11–0–512–124–46.54; C. Keevil 11–5–248–82*–41.33; J. Adams 12–0–230–70–19.16; M. Patel 12–2–171–50*–17.10; *J. Bartlett 10–0–167–45–16.70.

Bowling—A. Hyman 121–25–301–26–11.57; T. Wilson 69–19–190–14–13.57; M. Patel 106–19–291–21–13.85; C. Haynes 53–8–232–11–21.09.

SHREWSBURY SCHOOL
Played 18: Won 7, Lost 4, Drawn 7

Master i/c: J. M. Williams   Cricket professional: P. H. Bromley

Batting—J. R. Prichard 18–2–595–84–37.18; M. J. Lascelles 17–2–543–89–36.20; *C. M. Bullock 18–1–594–104–34.94; P. J. Blanesley 10–3–108–24–15.42; C. W. Ransford 12–1–142–38–12.90; G. M. Hutchinson 19–4–191–21–12.73.

Bowling—D. J. Bowett 139–47–289–20–14.45; C. M. Bullock 52.1–16–155–10–15.50; P. J. Blanesley 192.1–42–511–29–17.62; D. M. W. Roberts 155–47–374–20–18.70; P. S. Bullock 168.4–31–533–28–19.03; M. J. Lascelles 189–31–669–29–23.06.

SIMON LANGTON GRAMMAR SCHOOL
Played 6: Won 3, Lost 1, Drawn 2. Abandoned 4

Master i/c: R. F. Harriott

Batting—P. C. Relf 6–1–184–116*–36.80; D. G. Newton 6–1–134–65*–26.80.

Bowling—T. Stevens 45.3–17–148–16–9.25; A. Judge 52.4–9–139–10–13.90.

SIR ROGER MANWOOD'S SCHOOL
Played 10: Won 3, Lost 4, Drawn 3

Master i/c: J. E. Newton

Batting—M. D. Giles 10–2–275–66*–34.37; *J. A. N. Goold 10–1–189–50*–21.00; M. J. May 9–0–147–53–16.33; D. T. Deadman 10–0–143–55–14.30; A. J. Crofts 10–1–103–32*–11.44.

Bowling—J. A. N. Goold 66.2–13–169–15–11.26; D. J. Hill 88.3–27–218–19–11.47; A. J. Crofts 66–13–217–12–18.08.

STAMFORD SCHOOL
Played 19: Won 5, Lost 2, Drawn 12

Master i/c: I. Poyser

Batting—*R. P. C. Plant 17–6–618–79–56.18; A. J. Smith 8–4–158–71*–39.50; J. R. Cobb 18–0–649–111–36.05; R. E. Moulton 6–1–164–59–32.80; D. Richardson 15–7–239–39*–29.87; D. M. Aldridge 18–2–401–105–25.06; C. P. Grindal 16–1–294–79–19.60; L. K. Tebb 14–2–148–37–12.33.

Bowling—S. A. Carruthers 47–5–176–14–12.57; R. P. C. Plant 204.4–41–625–33–18.93; D. Richardson 135.3–26–461–24–19.20; D. M. Aldridge 241.3–38–797–36–22.13.

STOCKPORT GRAMMAR SCHOOL
Played 20: Won 6, Lost 6, Drawn 8. Abandoned 1

Master i/c: C. Dunkerley

Batting—I. Millnur 19–2–515–100*–30.29; M. Seed 10–5–135–48–27.00; H. Grayson 17–1–412–78–25.75; M. Baulkwill 8–0–188–111–23.50; *N. Vernon 14–3–248–84*–22.54; J. Healey 14–2–232–72–19.33; M. Edmeston 14–2–197–45*–16.41; M. Duckworth 18–0–294–69–16.33.

Bowling—M. Duckworth 215–41–652–33–19.75; B. Anderson 129–32–513–23–22.30; R. Pailin 162–36–527–23–22.91; P. Duckworth 116–14–449–17–26.41; N. Ejje 160–24–568–16–35.50.

STONYHURST COLLEGE

Master i/c: J. M. Fairburn

Batting—G. O'Driscoll 10–0–246–69–24.60; J. Smith 7–0–125–44–17.85; P. Flood 10–2–116–33–14.50; P. Keown 8–0–110–61–13.75; J. Barnes 10–0–111–55–11.10.

Bowling—G. O'Driscoll 131–34–322–27–11.92; J. Barnes 170–45–428–31–13.80.

STOWE SCHOOL

Played 18: Won 5, Lost 1, Drawn 12. Abandoned 1

Master i/c: G. A. Cottrell   Cricket professional: M. J. Harris

Batting—*R. S. M. Morris 17–2–938–141*–62.53; W. J. P. Atkinson 11–3–322–60–40.25; J. C. Mahbubani 11–2–218–76–24.22; I. O. Bendell 15–0–292–59–19.46; D. T. H. Rotheroe 9–1–119–30–14.87; R. B. Pumfrey 12–2–130–38–13.00.

Bowling—R. B. Pumfrey 167.5–39–515–33–15.60; H. R. Thomas 111–27–298–18–16.55; R. S. M. Morris 231.4–72–525–30–17.50; A. R. Adam 103–14–354–19–18.63; M. J. T. Jefferson 176.2–48–592–26–22.76; R. B. K. Giles 111–16–377–11–34.27.

STRATHALLAN SCHOOL

Played 15: Won 4, Lost 4, Drawn 7. Abandoned 2

Master i/c: R. J. W. Proctor

Batting—J. A. Jacobsen 12–2–246–64–24.60; R. Moffat 11–1–230–78–23.00; *K. D. Smith 13–2–239–62*–21.72; G. M. Adam 10–1–191–100*–21.22; D. F. Lennox 13–1–183–38–15.25; A. G. A. Bullard 10–0–137–26–13.70; S. Neish 12–1–132–38–12.00; C. N. C. Henderson 11–1–105–37*–10.50.

Bowling—K. D. Smith 229–65–558–45–12.40; C. N. C. Henderson 164.3–38–438–27–16.22; G. N. Reid 67–15–228–10–22.80; A. H. Duff 98.5–26–254–11–23.09.

SUTTON VALENCE SCHOOL

Played 17: Won 7, Lost 2, Drawn 8. Abandoned 1

Master i/c: D. Pickard

Batting—N. Roberts 16–3–629–102*–48.38; *J. Crouch 15–0–584–100–38.93; A. Barr 13–2–236–66*–21.45; P. Heine 15–1–293–90–20.92; Y. Patel 14–3–203–47*–18.45; R. Harrison 16–0–256–59–16.00; C. Lakey 12–2–100–19–10.00.

Bowling—Y. Patel 40–19–70–10–7.00; C. Lakey 204–62–505–43–11.74; J. Crouch 136–36–372–25–14.88; N. Roberts 98–27–256–13–19.69; D. Patel 162–38–441–14–31.50.

TAUNTON SCHOOL

Played 19: Won 8, Lost 0, Drawn 11

Master i/c: R. P. Smith   Cricket professional: A. Kennedy

Batting—M. Van Der Walt 17–3–807–122–57.64; M. J. Amor 6–3–138–46–46.00; A. Habib 16–4–442–58–36.83; R. J. L. Craddock 17–1–511–68*–31.93; A. F. M. Dowdney 14–6–209–60*–26.12; V. J. Pike 9–3–139–28–23.16; N. A. Blake 10–2–134–40–16.75; M. Harris 12–1–176–61*–16.00.

Bowling—A. F. M. Dowdney 135.2–42–274–29–9.44; M. B. Goodman 148.4–39–318–23–13.82; V. J. Pike 230.2–53–632–42–15.04; M. Van Der Walt 99.5–22–289–18–16.05.

TIFFIN SCHOOL

Played 19: Won 7, Lost 3, Drawn 9. Abandoned 1

Master i/c: M. J. Williams

Batting—N. J. B. Howell 19–0–611–95–32.15; G. J. Affleck 19–2–508–102*–29.88; *N. P. Warren 19–3–474–83*–29.62; S. E. Fisher 11–6–139–33*–27.80; A. D. Young 17–5–300–72*–25.00; S. J. Crowter 19–1–414–73–23.00; A. W. Kennis 11–2–177–66–19.66; D. K. Jones 10–3–114–40–16.28; A. J. M. Carnie 14–1–160–61–12.30; J. Matthews 13–1–145–37–12.08.

Bowling—N. P. Warren 198.1–56–489–32–15.28; A. D. Young 147.5–25–487–26–18.73; A. N. Hones 218.3–45–664–33–20.12; A. J. M. Carnie 238.3–35–756–34–22.23.

TONBRIDGE SCHOOL

Played 17: Won 7, Lost 3, Drawn 7

Master i/c: S. J. G. Doggart   Cricket professional: H. Mutton

Batting—J. I. Longley 18–1–1,007–129–59.23; M. S. Nolan 13–6–180–50–25.71; D. R. Penfold 9–1–199–59–24.87; R. D. Gill 11–0–235–66–21.36; J. A. Richardson 16–3–262–78*–20.15; C. J. Althorp 11–3–141–40*–17.62; K. M. Seecharan 16–2–245–47–17.50; C. J. Hollins 14–2–208–48–17.33.

Bowling—A. G. Hunn 70.4–14–213–16–13.31; J. S. Durling 255.4–54–700–41–17.07; J. A. Richardson 106.1–30–303–17–17.82; C. J. Althorp 126.4–27–363–19–19.10.

TRENT COLLEGE

Played 17: Won 6, Lost 3, Drawn 8

Master i/c: T. P. Woods

Batting—T. H. Smith 17–2–461–94*–30.73; T. A. Ellis 7–1–161–35–26.83; S. H. Glover 14–0–344–54–24.57; J. D. Evans 14–1–244–60–18.76; I. R. Birch 12–1–200–35–18.18; N. A. Goulding 11–1–171–60–17.10; *R. D. Kerrell 17–2–252–51–16.80; T. C. White 17–0–272–48–16.00.

Bowling—I. R. Birch 114.3–22–315–22–14.31; R. D. Kerrell 190.3–36–624–30–20.80; I. W. McClean 84–12–364–15–24.26; J. S. Bocking 117–31–328–13–25.23; N. A. Goulding 98–23–319–10–31.90.

TRINITY SCHOOL

Played 29: Won 14, Lost 7, Drawn 8. Abandoned 1

Masters i/c: A. Gist and B. Widger

Batting—M. A. Butcher 5–2–134–77*–44.66; A. P. Hubbard 5–2–129–52*–43.00; K. P. Morley 21–4–578–70*–34.00; J. D. Good 14–9–153–42*–30.60; J. B. Orpin 19–1–482–77*–26.77; J. D. Morley 25–2–573–66*–24.91; P. A. Gardner 19–4–336–67–22.40; *P. J. Mander 29–2–584–61–21.62; C. Stokes 17–4–252–53–19.38; A. J. Budge 22–7–247–40*–16.46; D. M. P. Turner 22–3–268–42–14.10; J. W. Yarrow 23–3–203–31–10.15.

Bowling—D. M. P. Turner 311.4–73–808–56–14.42; J. A. Arthur 152.4–26–531–28–18.96; J. D. Good 268–66–771–40–19.27; P. A. Gardner 282.5–68–731–37–19.75; P. J. Mander 162.4–35–604–27–22.37.

TRURO SCHOOL

Played 10: Won 3, Lost 2, Drawn 5. Abandoned 2

Master i/c: A. J. D. Aldwinckle

Batting—A. Johnston 9–2–225–53*–32.14; *S. Peters 9–1–134–32–16.75.

Bowling—S. Peters 140.4–29–175–25–7.00; J. Berridge 60–7–182–13–14.00; A. Johnston 46.2–4–216–14–15.42; D. Johns 70–5–294–14–21.00.

UPPINGHAM SCHOOL

Played 18: Won 5, Lost 5, Drawn 8. Abandoned 1

Master i/c: P. L. Bodily   Cricket professional: M. R. Hallam

Batting—M. C. Renison 17–2–375–75–25.00; R. J. Howe 9–0–201–72–22.33; *D. B. J. Cooke 18–2–328–84–20.50; S. R. Green 11–3–158–56–19.75; E. R. Fowler 17–4–256–58–19.69; C. R. Saunders 18–1–307–78–18.05; T. J. Greer 13–3–161–72*–16.10; J. E. Greig 15–0–218–50–14.53.

Bowling—P. J. E. Spencer 275–70–660–48–13.75; D. B. J. Cooke 305.3–99–742–48–15.45; G. M. Leather 132.2–26–427–17–25.11; C. R. Saunders 158–26–526–20–26.30.

VICTORIA COLLEGE, JERSEY

Played 27: Won 11, Lost 9, Drawn 6, Tied 1. Abandoned 2

Master i/c: D. A. R. Ferguson   Cricket professional: R. A. Pearce

Batting—P. J. Le Cornu 28–5–859–106*–37.34; A. J. Clarke 28–4–692–80–28.83; I. R. Furness 25–3–541–79–24.59; D. J. Pearce 26–4–404–56–18.36; A. G. Sadarangani 22–2–334–38–16.70; G. C. Ferguson 12–4–128–60*–16.00; S. A. A. Gothard 19–5–222–45–15.85; N. F. Le Feuvre 10–1–127–42–14.11; M. E. Blumberg 13–1–152–31*–12.66; B. M. Vowden 19–4–143–30–9.53.

Bowling—I. R. Furness 84.5–21–266–28–9.50; P. J. Le Cornu 320.2–49–1,008–70–14.40; S. F. Thomas 51.1–7–222–15–14.80; S. A. A. Gothard 249–63–751–39–19.25; A. J. Clarke 163.4–33–501–26–19.26; B. Sarre 170.5–36–491–25–19.64.

WARWICK SCHOOL

Played 17: Won 3, Lost 5, Drawn 9. Abandoned 1

Master i/c: S. P. Sutcliffe   Cricket professional: N. Horner

Batting—C. G. Stanton 15–2–692–91–53.23; R. J. Cooke 5–0–154–86–30.80; J. D. Moffatt 15–0–279–69–18.60; A. J. Bolton 15–0–266–56–17.73; B. P. Dalby 13–3–146–41–14.60; C. J. French 14–3–151–25–13.72; J. R. Quinn 15–4–133–54–12.09; *J. J. C. Seccombe 16–2–167–46–11.92.

Bowling—P. M. A. Hulyer 42–9–175–11–15.90; C. Oswald 252–73–595–37–16.08; R. J. Cooke 91–20–359–16–22.43; J. N. Beachus 80–14–330–13–25.38; J. R. Quinn 93–23–427–14–30.50.

WATFORD GRAMMAR SCHOOL

Played 15: Won 2, Lost 2, Drawn 11. Abandoned 1

Master i/c: W. E. Miller

Batting—B. E. Watson 14–2–366–64–30.50; *G. D. Gregory 14–1–321–54–24.69; M. J. Roberts 15–0–339–82–22.60; D. W. Sharp 14–2–243–37–20.25; D. M. Armour 14–1–247–69*–19.00; N. R. Buirski 14–0–203–40–14.50; C. E. Mann 15–1–142–43–10.14; P. J. Windmill 13–1–121–29–10.08.

Bowling—P. G. Rimmer 182.2–44–471–28–16.82; G. D. Thomas 111–21–374–22–17.00; D. W. Sharp 105–11–405–18–22.50; J. G. E. Pepper 174.3–44–484–18–26.88.

WELLINGBOROUGH SCHOOL
Played 20: Won 5, Lost 4, Drawn 11

Master i/c: C. J. Ford   Cricket professional: J. C. J. Dye

Batting—*M. I. Ingram 20–3–658–101*–38.70; J. M. Attfield 20–7–486–63–37.38; N. J. Haste 15–7–181–35–22.62; M. I. Chacksfield 11–1–215–52–21.50; R. S. Morton 14–1–242–70–18.61; J. D. Dolman 10–2–110–33*–13.75; J. J. Attfield 17–2–198–46–13.20; A. D. Woodward 15–1–173–52–12.35.

Bowling—N. J. Haste 180–49–440–32–13.75; R. J. Cousins 249–57–611–39–15.66; J. M. Attfield 194.4–41–636–36–17.66; J. J. Attfield 131–15–455–14–32.50.

WELLINGTON COLLEGE
Played 17: Won 7, Lost 1, Drawn 9

Masters i/c: C. M. St G. Potter and K. M. Hopkins. Cricket professional: P. J. Lewington

Batting—*J. S. Hodgson 19–2–542–122*–31.88; N. H. Reynolds 18–7–330–69*–30.00; N. D. Jones 18–1–417–75–24.52; M. C. K. Hodgson 19–2–394–80*–23.17; W. R. D. Waghorn 17–1–366–68–22.87; J. S. White 18–3–260–64*–17.33; R. W. A. Sleigh 14–4–146–34*–14.60; J. R. H. Fenwick 14–2–114–31–9.50.

Bowling—J. R. H. Fenwick 274.5–57–688–52–13.23; R. J. H. Brett 124.4–27–328–20–16.40; J. S. Hodgson 206.5–60–528–29–18.20; B. P. Alexander 191.3–51–474–25–18.96; M. C. K. Hodgson 85–16–241–12–20.08.

WELLINGTON SCHOOL, SOMERSET
Played 16: Won 7, Lost 2, Drawn 7. Abandoned 1

Master i/c: P. M. Pearce

Batting—J. Clist 15–2–649–103*–49.92; R. Moysey 8–5–100–38*–33.33; S. Goodman 9–3–138–52*–23.00; *M. Colman 15–1–263–45–18.78; J. Govier 15–0–280–56–18.66; J. Smith 15–2–228–47–17.53; J. Austin 15–3–169–34–14.08; S. Kitto 11–1–133–41–13.30.

Bowling—S. Goodman 144–41–393–31–12.67; M. Coleman 140.1–29–455–29–15.68; S. Kitto 129–24–405–21–19.28; R. Moysey 85–16–334–17–19.64.

WESTMINSTER SCHOOL
Played 12: Won 4, Lost 0, Drawn 8. Abandoned 2

Master i/c: J. A. Cogan   Cricket professional: R. Gilson

Batting—J. R. D. Hyam 12–5–348–68*–49.71; *J. D. R. Griffiths 12–1–460–108–41.81; A. T. Coles 11–1–319–71*–31.90; J. Levine 9–2–166–38–23.71; T. Pinto 9–2–151–63–21.57; D. Cogan 7–1–118–58–19.66.

Bowling—M. Hashmi 54–16–137–10–13.70; A. Lancaster 75–13–248–17–14.58; G. Coren 124–23–418–22–19.00; D. Earle 58–11–195–10–19.50; J. D. R. Griffiths 112–14–389–16–24.31.

WHITGIFT SCHOOL
Played 15: Won 4, Lost 6, Drawn 5. Abandoned 2

Master i/c: P. C. Fladgate   Cricket professional: A. Long

Batting—N. S. Auer 16–3–614–100*–47.23; *I. L. H. Scarisbrick 16–0–462–74–28.87; G. J. Thompson 16–0–433–100–27.06; S. J. Clark 10–3–144–40–20.57; N. R. Carter 8–1–122–45–17.42; M. W. Wright 16–0–221–29–13.81; S. J. Hill 13–1–107–51*–8.91.

Bowling—N. S. Auer 77.4–19–240–21–11.42; J. A. M. Bulloch 201.5–48–505–29–17.41; H. Gallagher 150–24–484–22–22.00; S. J. Hill 234.2–46–694–24–28.91.

WILLIAM HULME'S GRAMMAR SCHOOL

Played 23: Won 10, Lost 5, Drawn 8

Master i/c: I. J. Shaw

Batting—D. M. J. Timm 22–2–705–125*–35.25; H. P. V. Scott-Gall 12–3–267–98*–29.66; N. J. Partington 15–9–158–44–26.33; *C. W. Timm 21–0–506–143–24.09; J. Hughes 11–0–255–62–23.18; M. J. Braddock 18–2–367–67–22.93; A. W. Kloss 18–4–248–63–17.71; I. D. Butler 18–4–193–44–13.78; D. Loveland 16–3–162–32*–12.46.

Bowling—H. P. V. Scott-Gall 113–20–336–21–16.00; S. V. Kapadia 209–39–730–38–19.21; I. R. Jordan 76–23–231–12–19.25; D. M. J. Timm 175–50–590–29–20.34; D. Loveland 106–18–284–13–21.84; A. P. Cleary 175–44–442–17–26.00.

WINCHESTER COLLEGE

Played 19: Won 0, Lost 10, Drawn 9

Master i/c: J. F. X. Miller   Cricket professional: V. Broderick

Batting—D. A. de Lanoy Meijer 19–2–471–72*–27.70; *M. I. Riaz 19–0–434–75–22.84; M. A. T. Hall 15–0–337–67–22.46; R. A. Sanders 12–0–232–63–19.33; D. A. Lewis 19–0–269–75–14.15; B. T. H. G. Pollard 19–3–223–38–13.93; M. W. Smith 13–5–111–24–13.87; A. P. S. Casstles 17–1–202–48–12.62; J. P. Maclay 16–5–133–28–12.09.

Bowling—J. R. Robinson 83.4–16–291–20–14.55; M. R. Dixon 261.3–47–869–34–25.55; M. W. Smith 280.4–51–932–32–29.12; B. T. H. G. Pollard 104.3–13–385–10–38.50; M. A. T. Hall 145.1–20–461–10–46.10.

WOODHOUSE GROVE SCHOOL

Played 12: Won 3, Lost 3, Drawn 6. Abandoned 2

Master i/c: E. R. Howard

Batting—*L. Savill 10–2–269–83*–33.62; L. Gomersall 12–1–317–68–28.81; M. Beever 8–2–155–40–25.83; D. Lawson 11–2–151–49–16.77; C. Miller 11–0–117–35–10.63.

Bowling—L. Savill 180–64–330–32–10.31.

WORKSOP COLLEGE

Played 15: Won 4, Lost 4, Drawn 7

Master i/c: N. S. Broadbent   Cricket professional: A. Kettleborough

Batting—*N. E. Green 15–2–387–76–29.76; R. A. Kettleborough 15–0–392–79–26.13; J. D. Goode 15–2–293–53*–22.53; M. D. Holden 9–4–101–28*–20.20; C. P. Green 15–2–239–38–18.38; C. R. G. Oldfield 13–3–130–51–13.00; D. Ellis 9–1–101–28–12.62; P. K. R. Patel 12–0–141–53–11.75.

Bowling—B. St J. B. Bowser 160–31–514–23–22.34; C. P. Green 188–23–593–26–22.80; P. K. R. Patel 83–9–297–11–27.00.

WREKIN COLLEGE

Played 17: Won 5, Lost 3, Drawn 8, Tied 1

Master i/c: T. J. Murphy   Cricket professional: T. Harrison

Batting—*C. A. Fenton 17–1–657–107–41.06; A. W. Ranaweera 12–5–210–80–30.00; S. R. Jackson 17–2–383–42–25.53; J. B. Rimmer 17–2–352–61*–23.46; R. W. Barker 17–0–242–83–14.23; I. Mirza 17–1–214–31–13.37; J. Mallinson 16–0–184–42–11.50.

Bowling—C. Fenton 90–21–223–20–11.15; S. R. Jackson 153–34–434–31–14.00; J. R. Ford 87–13–314–16–19.62; I. Mirza 104–12–310–14–22.14.

WYCLIFFE COLLEGE

Played 18: Won 2, Lost 6, Drawn 10

Master i/c: D. J. Trevis   Cricket professional: K. Biddulph

Batting—*S. J. Reed 14–1–643–101*–49.46; M. F. Brown 4–0–135–41–33.75; A. Brown 17–1–395–61–24.68; R. M. Giles 8–2–110–38–18.33; S. G. Cady 15–1–232–70*–16.57; G. Collins 15–1–202–51*–14.42; E. McDade 11–2–114–51*–12.66.

Bowling—A. Brown 39–6–180–12–15.00; R. N. Giles 170–31–486–21–23.14; M. Hair 70–12–254–11–23.09; S. G. Cady 133–28–392–15–26.13.

WYGGESTON & QUEEN ELIZABETH I SIXTH FORM COLLEGE

Played 9: Won 4, Lost 2, Drawn 3. Abandoned 3

Master i/c: G. G. Wells

Batting—*S. C. Brammar 8–2–244–71*–40.66; K. T. Roberts 8–1–213–54*–30.42; J. L. Green 6–0–100–35–16.66.

Bowling—J. L. Green 79.4–15–178–15–11.86.

THE DELOITTES RATINGS

Initiated by the former England captain, E. R. Dexter, and introduced prior to the Second Test between England and Pakistan in 1987, the Deloittes Ratings rank Test cricketers on a scale from 0 to 1,000 according to their form in Test matches since 1981. The ratings are calculated by computer and take into account playing conditions, the standard of the opposition and the nature and result of the match. Updated after every Test match, with a player's most recent performances carrying more weight than his earlier ones, the Deloittes Ratings therefore endeavour to provide a current assessment of a Test cricketer's form and his place among his peers. The leading twenty batsmen and bowlers in the Ratings after the 1987 England v Pakistan series were:

	Batsmen	Rating		Bowlers	Rating
1.	D. B. Vengsarkar (*India*)	893		R. J. Hadlee (*NZ*)	905
2.	C. G. Greenidge (*WI*)	875		Imran Khan (*Pak.*)	901
3.	D. M. Jones (*Aust.*)	844		J. Garner (*WI*)	835
4.	M. D. Crowe (*NZ*)	838		M. D. Marshall (*WI*)	813
5.	I. V. A. Richards (*WI*)	819		M. A. Holding (*WI*)	795
6.	D. L. Haynes (*WI*)	818		Tauseef Ahmed (*Pak.*)	684
7.	A. R. Border (*Aust.*)	792		Iqbal Qasim (*Pak.*)	678
8.	M. W. Gatting (*Eng.*)	788		R. A. Harper (*WI*)	675
9.	R. B. Richardson (*WI*)	784		A. H. Gray (*WI*)	674
10.	Javed Miandad (*Pak.*)	762		C. A. Walsh (*WI*)	654
11.	D. I. Gower (*Eng.*)	725		Wasim Akram (*Pak.*)	639
12.	A. Ranatunga (*SL*)	723		G. F. Lawson (*Aust.*)	635
13.	S. M. Gavaskar (*India*)	714		E. J. Chatfield (*NZ*)	609
14.	M. Azharuddin (*India*)	698		N. A. Foster (*Eng.*)	602
15.	J. V. Coney (*NZ*)	693		S. R. Waugh (*Aust.*)	591
16.	G. A. Gooch (*Eng.*)	683		G. C. Small (*Eng.*)	590
17.	Mudassar Nazar (*Pak.*)	680		B. A. Reid (*Aust.*)	578
18.	Imran Khan (*Pak.*)	678		B. P. Patterson (*WI*)	577
19.	Salim Malik (*Pak.*)	671		J. R. Ratnayeke (*SL*)	574
20.	B. C. Broad (*Eng.*)	666		Chetan Sharma (*India*)	572

OVERSEAS CRICKET, 1986-87

Note: Throughout this section, matches not first-class are denoted by the use of a dagger.

ENGLAND IN AUSTRALIA, 1986-87

By JOHN THICKNESSE

England's tour of Australia, under the captaincy of Mike Gatting, brought a timely and much-needed boost to English confidence after the tribulations of the previous months. Having flown from Heathrow in October carrying the prayers rather than the aspirations of their countrymen, following three lost series in succession – eight defeats in eleven Tests without a single win – they returned triumphantly in February not only with the Ashes safe till 1989 but also as winners of two one-day competitions in which West Indies were involved. It was an excellent performance, not least because at the outset England had given no sign of emerging from the pit. They lost to Queensland in the opening first-class fixture and were outplayed by Western Australia in the third on the eve of the First Test. Few, at that stage, would have given much for their retaining the Ashes against an Australian side which, during a hard-fought drawn series in India, had seemed capable of ending an equally depressing run of failure.

The recovery and subsequent success owed much to the efficient, friendly partnership of Peter Lush and Micky Stewart as managers, the confidence their encouragement gave Gatting, and the good team spirit that resulted. On and off the field it was a happy tour, in spite of an itinerary which could have been devised only by a group of men – the officials of both countries' Boards – who did not have to undergo it. Three trips to Perth raised the mileage flown internally to the equivalent of a trip around the Equator, while it was not until the thirteenth week that the team arrived in Sydney, favourite city of all touring teams and, with Melbourne, traditionally the focal point of cricket in Australia.

England's performance against Western Australia was woeful, and two of the state's new-ball bowlers, Bruce Reid and Chris Matthews, were in Australia's team across the continent at Brisbane three days later. When Allan Border won the toss and put England in to bat in helpful conditions for fast bowling, it required little imagination to see Australia going on to win and establishing an ascendancy that would take a lot of winning back. Instead, the opposite took place. Where on their form in Sheffield Shield cricket, Reid, Matthews and Merv Hughes, a bustling Victorian of lively pace, could have been expected to bowl England out for fewer than 250, the pressure of a Test exposed their inexperience. Lawson having surprisingly been named twelfth man, Australia's three fast bowlers at the 'Gabba had only nine Test caps between them; and when England scored 198 for two on a shortened opening day, the confidence they gained, as Australia's visibly declined, changed the outlook for the series.

Much of the credit belonged to Bill Athey who, having been forced on England as Chris Broad's opening partner through Wilf Slack's lack of form (and Gooch's decision not to tour), batted with judgement and composure to score 76 off 68 overs. Tactically, however, Gatting's switch to No. 3 in place of David Gower, who had bagged a "pair" at Perth, was of as much significance. After the early loss of Broad, Gatting helped Athey add 101 at a time when the quick capture of a second wicket might have been all the encouragement Australia's bowlers needed. Coming when it did, in the first session of the series, Gatting's unselfishness ensured him of his team's respect; its success was an obvious fillip to his self-assurance. With the exception of a silly incident on the first day of the Victoria match at Melbourne, when he overslept and was late arriving – a discourtesy for which the manager, over-reacting to the media for the only time in nineteen weeks, "severely reprimanded" him – Gatting's first taste of captaincy abroad was one he will recall with pride and pleasure.

Crucial as the first day had been for England in exposing the superficiality of Australia's presumed improvement, a missed catch early on the second morning may well, in retrospect, have decided the destination of the Ashes. For after Allan Lamb, then Athey, had fallen without addition to the overnight total, England would have slipped to 198 for five had Gower been caught in the slips before scoring. Instead, with Ian Botham, having gone 21 Tests without a hundred, hitting his fourteenth for England, a destructive 138 off 174 balls, England went on to reach 456. When Australia narrowly failed to save the follow-on, the tourists won by seven wickets, taking a lead that was never to be threatened.

One of the most pleasing aspects of the tour was the unity within the team and the way they dovetailed on the field. Broad, with the bat, and Graham Dilley, Gladstone Small and Phillip DeFreitas with the ball enjoyed outstanding personal success. But nearly everyone contributed and some, notably John Emburey and Phil Edmonds, the spinners, played a more important role than was suggested by their figures. Gower was fighting what looked to be a losing battle with his concentration early in the tour, a reaction possibly to being passed over as vice-captain. But his "life" at Brisbane proved his turning-point. Following 51 and 15 not out in the First Test, he made 136 and 48 at Perth, and scored 404 Test runs at 57.71 to be second in the averages. Gatting, who stayed at No. 3, scored 100 at Adelaide (Third Test) and a punishing 96 at Sydney (Fifth) which put England within reach of taking the series three-love until he was out in the second of the final twenty overs. He batted as he captained, without frills. His team knew where they stood with him.

It was in the Second Test that the left-handed Broad struck the prolific form that was to earn him the title of "International Player of the Season". His height, composure, concentration and sound technique were well suited to Australian pitches, and from the early matches he had batted impressively without taking full advantage of a series of good starts. All that changed at Perth, where his stylish 162 was the first of three hundreds in three successive Tests, an achievement equalled for England against Australia only by J. B. Hobbs, W. R. Hammond and R. A. Woolmer, the last-named in different series. Broad made 487 runs in the Tests at 69.57 and was a model of consistency in the one-day internationals; in fourteen innings he was out only five times for under 30, scoring another 559 for an aggregate of 1,046. Athey, though inevitably overshadowed, proved a determined foil, sharing two hundred opening stands in the Tests and in the field revealing as safe a pair of hands as any in the side, notably inside the "oblong" in the one-day games. Only a perfectly disguised yorker by Reid at Perth, bowling him for 96, denied him what would have been his first hundred in a Test.

Small was held back by a jarred knee in the first month, and with Dilley bowling some of the best spells of his career, and Botham and DeFreitas supporting him sufficiently, he was a bystander for three Tests. But when he was given his chance at Melbourne, in the Fourth Test, when Dilley was unfit, Small bowled his out-swingers with pace and excellent control to collect seven economical wickets and the Man of the Match award. Dilley and DeFreitas, who bowled with greater fire the longer the tour lasted, were England's fastest bowlers. But day in day out, in first-class games, Small was the most accurate and had the best control. It was clear he had the attributes of a valuable third seamer, and he was a force with the new ball because of his ability to swing it. DeFreitas, at twenty the youngest member of the party, looked a natural cricketer – a quick, aggressive bowler with an awkward skidding bounce and a great fielder in the deep. His batting did not live up to the promise of a clean-hit 40 in the Brisbane Test but the innings left no doubt of his potential. Emburey, the vice-captain, encountered problems with the leg-side winds in the Second and Third Tests but battled through with typical persistence, completing the series with a fine all-round performance which deserved to save the Sydney Test. He and Edmonds, who also played in every Test, enabled England to keep control when wickets were elusive, sharing almost 600 overs at 2.08 runs each, a huge contrast in economy to the Australian spinners.

Statistically, Botham had a modest series, scoring only 51 in five innings after Brisbane and finishing his Test career abroad with an untimely first-ball duck in Sydney. But in contrast to the West Indian tour of the previous winter, he was an asset to the side. He gave his all in every match and went out of his way to encourage younger players, especially DeFreitas. Reduced to bowling medium-pace after tearing a muscle in his ribs at Perth, he returned with five for 41 at Melbourne to help Small bowl Australia out for 141, and he made such a good adjustment to his loss of pace that he more than held his own as a defensive one-day bowler. In the Benson and Hedges Challenge at Perth and in the first final of the World Series Cup at Melbourne, where he slammed Australia for 68 off 39 balls and 71 off 52 respectively, he produced the two most memorable displays of controlled hitting of the tour.

Only Slack, who had the ill luck to encounter two difficult late out-swingers in the Queensland match and was unable to take his one subsequent chance to make up lost ground, appeared neither in a Test nor a one-day international. James Whitaker, the next least called upon, had the satisfaction of winning his first Test cap at Adelaide, where Botham was unfit, as well as scoring a hard-hit hundred against South Australia on his first appearance in a first-class game on tour; while Neil Foster, who did not play in a Test, did a good job in the later one-day internationals. Bruce French, number one wicket-keeper when the team was picked, enjoyed the ironic consolation of ousting Jack Richards from the last three World Series

Cup games after Richards had been preferred in the Tests because of his superior batting. Richards justified his elevation with 133 in the Second Test, and with a brilliant match behind the stumps at Melbourne, where by going two up England made certain of the Ashes. But when Richards lost his batting form, French seized the chance to show that, as a wicket-keeper, he was unmistakably the better of the two. His batting, similarly neat and tidy, looked to need only a tightening against fast bowling for French to be as valuable in England's tail as R. W. Taylor had made himself in Tests.

Australia ended the season on a note of hope by winning the Fifth Test, in which the 30-year-old Peter Taylor made a fairy-tale début, and by reaching the finals of the World Series Cup. But the absence in South Africa of five or six players who would have been pushing for inclusion in the Test team left a weakness in bowling that made them very vulnerable. Craig McDermott, their spearhead in England in 1985, was wrestling with conflicting advice concerning his best pace and method, and with Geoff Lawson out of favour with his captain and selectors, it left the 6ft 8in Reid, the fast-medium left-armer, as the only bowler of genuine Test class. Had England won the series 3-0, rather than 2-1, it would in fact have been a more accurate reflection of the disparity between the sides.

Batting was by far Australia's stronger wing. Geoff Marsh proved himself an adhesive opener of limitless endurance, and in Dean Jones and Stephen Waugh Australia had two youngsters of obvious class, both well equipped with strokes and always on the look-out to take the battle to the bowlers. After a poor First Test, Border was doggedly consistent and made two hundreds in the series; but as captain he lacked spark and the ability to inspire a young team much in need of it. Hard task as he had, he did not look the man to lead the Test team from its troubled run.

Overall, however, there could be little doubt that the responsibility for Australia's continued struggles rested squarely with their Board. Since the alliance with PBL Marketing was formed in 1979, the pursuit of money through a saturation of international one-day cricket, sapping players' stamina and leading to bad habits in technique, has too often seemed their main objective, if not the only one. A visitor's impression was that a wiser course might be the pursuit of excellence by giving greater encouragement to first-class cricket in the Sheffield Shield.

ENGLAND TOUR RESULTS

Test matches – Played 5: Won 2, Lost 1, Drawn 2.
First-class matches – Played 11: Won 5, Lost 3, Drawn 3.
Wins – Australia (2), South Australia, Tasmania, Victoria.
Losses – Australia, New South Wales, Queensland.
Draws – Australia (2), Western Australia.
Non first-class matches – Played 19: Won 14, Lost 4, Drawn 1. *Wins* – Australia (4), Pakistan (2), West Indies (4), Prime Minister's XI, South Australia Country XI, South-East Queensland Country XI, Western Australia Country XI. *Losses* – Australia (3), West Indies.
Draw – Queensland Country XI.

TEST MATCH AVERAGES

AUSTRALIA – BATTING

	T	I	NO	R	HI	100s	Avge
D. M. Jones	5	10	1	511	184*	1	56.77
G. R. J. Matthews ...	4	7	3	215	73*	0	53.75
A. R. Border	5	10	1	473	125	2	52.55
S. R. Waugh	5	8	1	310	79*	0	44.28
G. R. Marsh	5	10	0	429	110	1	42.90
G. M. Ritchie	4	8	2	244	46*	0	40.66
D. C. Boon	4	8	0	144	103	1	18.00
T. J. Zoehrer	4	7	1	102	38	0	17.00
C. D. Matthews	2	3	0	21	11	0	7.00
P. R. Sleep	3	4	0	25	10	0	6.25
M. G. Hughes	4	6	0	31	16	0	5.16
B. A. Reid	5	7	4	14	4	0	4.66

Played in one Test: G. F. Lawson 13; C. J. McDermott 0, 1; P. L. Taylor 11, 42; D. M. Wellham 17, 1; G. C. Dyer did not bat.

* Signifies not out.

BOWLING

	O	M	R	W	BB	Avge
P. L. Taylor	55	17	154	8	6-78	19.25
B. A. Reid	198.4	44	527	20	4-64	26.35
P. R. Sleep	136	43	316	10	5-72	31.60
S. R. Waugh	108.3	26	336	10	5-69	33.60
C. D. Matthews	70.1	14	233	6	3-95	38.83
M. G. Hughes	136.3	26	444	10	3-134	44.40

Also bowled: A. R. Border 16-6-32-1; G. F. Lawson 50-9-170-0; C. J. McDermott 26.5-4-83-4; G. R. J. Matthews 83-11-295-2.

ENGLAND – BATTING

	T	I	NO	R	HI	100s	Avge
B. C. Broad	5	9	2	487	162	3	69.57
D. I. Gower	5	8	1	404	136	1	57.71
M. W. Gatting	5	9	0	393	100	1	43.66
C. J. Richards	5	7	0	264	133	1	37.71
J. E. Emburey	5	7	2	179	69	0	35.80
C. W. J. Athey	5	9	0	303	96	0	33.66
I. T. Botham	4	6	0	189	138	1	31.50
P. A. J. DeFreitas ...	4	5	1	77	40	0	19.25
A. J. Lamb	5	9	1	144	43	0	18.00
G. C. Small	2	3	1	35	21*	0	17.50
P. H. Edmonds	5	5	1	44	19	0	11.00
G. R. Dilley	4	4	2	6	4*	0	3.00

Played in one Test: J. J. Whitaker 11.

* Signifies not out.

BOWLING

	O	M	R	W	BB	Avge
G. C. Small	78.4	23	180	12	5-48	15.00
G. R. Dilley	176.1	38	511	16	5-68	31.93
I. T. Botham	106.2	24	296	9	5-41	32.88
P. H. Edmonds	261.4	78	538	15	3-45	35.86
J. E. Emburey	315.5	86	663	18	7-78	36.83
P. A. J. DeFreitas	141.4	24	446	9	3-62	49.55

Also bowled: M. W. Gatting 23–7–39–0; A. J. Lamb 1–1–0–0.

ENGLAND AVERAGES – FIRST-CLASS MATCHES

BATTING

	M	I	NO	R	HI	100s	Avge
N. A. Foster	4	6	2	172	74*	0	43.00
B. C. Broad	10	18	2	679	162	3	42.43
I. T. Botham	8	14	2	481	138	1	40.08
B. N. French	3	5	2	113	58	0	37.66
D. I. Gower	9	16	2	508	136	1	36.28
A. J. Lamb	10	18	1	534	105	1	31.41
J. J. Whitaker	5	7	0	214	108	1	30.57
M. W. Gatting	10	18	0	520	100	1	28.88
C. W. J. Athey	9	16	1	422	96	0	28.13
C. J. Richards	9	14	1	335	133	1	25.76
J. E. Emburey	9	14	3	279	69	0	25.36
W. N. Slack	5	9	0	184	89	0	20.44
P. A. J. DeFreitas ...	7	10	2	130	40	0	16.25
G. R. Dilley	6	6	3	39	32	0	13.00
G. C. Small	8	11	3	100	26	0	12.50
P. H. Edmonds	9	10	2	95	27	0	11.87

* *Signifies not out.*

BOWLING

	O	M	R	W	BB	Avge
G. C. Small	258.4	72	626	33	5-48	18.96
M. W. Gatting	92	27	195	9	4-31	21.66
N. A. Foster	149	40	352	16	4-20	22.00
I. T. Botham	182.1	41	496	18	5-41	27.55
G. R. Dilley	231.1	44	685	21	5-68	32.61
J. E. Emburey	463.5	131	1,023	31	7-78	33.00
P. A. J. DeFreitas	239	43	754	22	4-44	34.27
P. H. Edmonds	428.4	122	929	25	3-37	37.16

Also bowled: C. W. J. Athey 4–0–25–0; A. J. Lamb 1–1–0–0.

FIELDING

28 – C. J. Richards (25 ct, 3 st); 11 – I. T. Botham, M. W. Gatting, A. J. Lamb; 10 – B. N. French (9 ct, 1 st); 7 – C. W. J. Athey, B. C. Broad, P. H. Edmonds; 6 – J. E. Emburey; 5 – W. N. Slack; 4 – N. A. Foster, D. I. Gower, G. C. Small; 2 – J. J. Whitaker, substitutes (P. A. J. DeFreitas, J. E. Emburey); 1 – P. A. J. DeFreitas, G. R. Dilley.

†QUEENSLAND COUNTRY XI v ENGLAND XI

At Bundaberg, October 18, 19, 20. Drawn. The loss of more than four hours on the last two days through heavy night-time rain, and Gatting's decision not to enforce the follow-on with 170 minutes left for play, hindered England's chance of starting the tour with a win. In perfect conditions, Broad and Slack won England the initiative with a partnership of 160 at a run a minute. Gower failed, but an inexperienced attack had no answer to Gatting, who struck 171 (two sixes, 28 fours) in two and a quarter hours in a fourth-wicket stand of 235 with Athey. Botham then hit 52 not out (two sixes, seven fours) off 26 balls in the final twenty minutes. Dilley, over-stepping, was no-balled sixteen times in eleven overs.

England XI 491 for four dec. (B. C. Broad 97, W. N. Slack 70, C. W. J. Athey 73 not out, M. W. Gatting 171, I. T. Botham 52 not out) and 129 for three (B. N. French 63 not out); Queensland Country XI 160 (L. Schulte 78 not out, J. Scuderi 30; P. A. J. DeFreitas four for 37).

†SOUTH-EAST QUEENSLAND COUNTRY XI v ENGLAND XI

At Queensland Agricultural College, Lawes, October 22. England XI won by 58 runs. Lamb's unbeaten hundred, his first innings since having an arthroscopic operation on his right knee at the end of the English season, carried England to an unassailable total on a stopping pitch. His last 61 came in 26 minutes as he completed the innings with 24 off the final over. A crowd of 4,500 watched the game.

England XI 245 for nine (50 overs) (W. N. Slack 31, A. J. Lamb 111 not out; S. Beattie four for 50); South-East Queensland Country XI 187 for six (50 overs) (M. Verenkamp 38, G. Stanley 34 not out).

QUEENSLAND v ENGLAND XI

At Brisbane, October 24, 25, 26, 27. Queensland won by five wickets. England never fully recovered from a calamitous first innings in which they were bowled out in 3 hours 50 minutes. Although Border had put them in in the hope that moisture beneath the surface would help his faster bowlers, it was lack of application that brought about England's downfall. Their inefficiency continued when Kerr and Courtice were given four "lives" during an opening stand of 154, the easiest chance being missed by French, standing back to Botham. Without wholly capitalising, Queensland were able to leave England twenty minutes batting on the second evening and benefited when Slack was brilliantly caught first ball by Henschell at first slip. Any hope of a recovery seemed gone at 99 for five but, helped by Lamb, Botham attacked judiciously to add 122 for the next wicket at 7 runs an over. Botham's 86, off 67 balls, contained eleven fours and four sixes, one of which shattered the secretary's window at long-off. England were still only 55 ahead when, at 231 for eight, he hooked Tazelaar, a sharp left-armer of 6ft 3in, to the finer of two long-legs; but Foster, who made his highest score in first-class cricket, ensured that the game would go into the fourth day with stands of 53 and 55 with DeFreitas and Small. Ritchie's polished 52 in 78 minutes took Queensland to a deserved win by lunch, their second victory in succession over an England touring team.

Close of play: First day, Queensland 52-0 (B. A. Courtice 19*, R. B. Kerr 29*); Second day, England XI 13-1 (B. C. Broad 9*, B. N. French 3*); Third day, Queensland 58-2 (B. A. Courtice 18*, A. B. Henschell 13*).

England XI

C. Broad c Henschell b McDermott	7	– b McDermott	18
N. Slack c Anderson b Frei	1	– c Henschell b Frei	0
I. Gower c Ritchie b McDermott	20	– (4) c Kerr b Frei	17
J. Lamb b Tazelaar	1	– (5) b McDermott	65
M. W. Gatting c Kerr b Frei	35	– (6) b Henschell	13
T. Botham c Border b Tazelaar	9	– (7) c McDermott b Tazelaar	86
E. Emburey lbw b Tazelaar	24	– (8) b McDermott	0
A. J. DeFreitas c Kerr b Tazelaar	5	– (9) b Hill	22
B. N. French not out	11	– (3) c Kerr b McDermott	6
A. Foster c Trimble b Henschell	2	– not out	74
C. Small c Tazelaar b Henschell	0	– c Courtice b Hill	16
B 1, l-b 6, n-b 13	20	L-b 5, w 1, n-b 16	22

1/4 2/37 3/40 4/44 5/57 **135** 1/4 2/27 3/47 4/50 5/99 **339**
110 7/118 8/129 9/135 6/221 7/221 8/231 9/284

Bowling: *First Innings*—McDermott 15–2–32–2; Frei 14–1–47–2; Tazelaar 14–4–34–4; Hill 5–9–0; Henschell 7.4–4–6–2. *Second Innings*—McDermott 19–1–93–4; Frei 11–0–69–2; Tazelaar 14–1–60–1; Henschell 8–0–80–1; Hill 10.2–1–31–2; Courtice 1–0–1–0.

Queensland

A. Courtice c Lamb b Foster	70	– (2) b DeFreitas	23
B. Kerr c Slack b Gatting	95	– (1) c Slack b Botham	8
S. Trimble c French b DeFreitas	24	– hit wkt b Botham	17
B. Henschell c Gatting b Botham	3	– not out	38
A. R. Border c Foster b Small	47	– (7) not out	10
P. W. Anderson c French b Small	20	– c Small b Emburey	9
J. McDermott c and b Small	18		
G. Hill not out	13		
Tazelaar not out	8		
M. Ritchie (did not bat)		– (5) run out	52
L-b 9, n-b 4	13	L-b 6, n-b 1	7

1/54 2/188 3/204 4/204 (7 wkts dec.) **311** 1/18 2/36 3/65 (5 wkts) **164**
5/251 6/284 7/291 4/139 5/150

Frei did not bat.

Bowling: *First Innings*—Botham 20–8–39–1; DeFreitas 26–5–61–1; Small 23–4–60–3; Foster 25–5–76–1; Emburey 20–4–63–0; Gatting 3–2–3–1. *Second Innings*—Botham 9–1–26–2; DeFreitas 13–3–40–1; Small 14.3–3–41–0; Foster 7–0–21–0; Emburey 7–2–30–1.

Umpires: M. W. Johnson and C. D. Timmins.

†SOUTH AUSTRALIA COUNTRY XI v ENGLAND XI

At Wudinna, October 29. England XI won by nine wickets after 33.4 overs (135 for one) and batted on. Of the home side, only Mitchell, seventh out in the 49th over, came to terms with accurate bowling and good catching on a slow, low-bouncing pitch. Broad and Slack shared their second three-figure opening stand against minor opposition, Broad's 59 coming off 81 balls.

South Australia Country XI 131 for nine (50 overs) (J. Mitchell 68; N. A. Foster three for 32); England XI 209 for three (47 overs) (B. C. Broad 59, W. N. Slack 55, C. J. Richards 40 not out).

SOUTH AUSTRALIA v ENGLAND XI

At Adelaide, October 31, November 1, 2, 3. England XI won by five wickets. When Botha
drove the winning runs ten minutes before tea on the last day, it marked the end of a fourtee
match sequence in first-class cricket in which England teams had gone without a victory,
last having been against Jamaica in the third match of their West Indian tour the previc
February. This was a well-earned success, stemming first from an attacking fourth-wick
partnership of 172 between Lamb and Whitaker on the second day, and then from Embure
patience and persistence as he took six for 102 in 38 overs of off-spin in South Australi
second innings. Though Parkinson, a stocky left-arm new-ball bowler, had a first spell of th
for 24, Emburey alone had the control and guile to dictate to batsmen on a pitch short of pa
and bounce following an unusually wet winter. Of the four hundreds, the fastest and mc
attractive was by Hookes (135 balls, two sixes, ten fours), who with his fellow left-hande
Phillips, threatened to take the game beyond England's reach as the England spinners brie
lost control. Lamb played well in both innings, but it was the inexperienced Whitaker
whom England owed most thanks. In his first innings in first-class cricket in Australia,
showed fine judgement of length and an urge to dominate the bowlers. He hit a six a
thirteen runs off 171 balls in three hours and a half.

Close of play: First day, South Australia 305-8 (P. R. Sleep 66*, S. D. H. Parkinson 11*
Second day, England XI 382-8 (P. H. Edmonds 15*, G. R. Dilley 20*); Third day, Sou
Australia 261-8 (T. B. A. May 2*, S. D. H. Parkinson 2*).

South Australia

A. M. J. Hilditch c Gatting b Small	11	– b Botham
A. S. Watson c Athey b Dilley	9	– lbw b Dilley
W. B. Phillips b Emburey	116	– c and b Emburey ... 7
G. A. Bishop b Edmonds	67	– c Edmonds b Emburey ... 3
*D. W. Hookes c Whitaker b Edmonds	0	– c Richards b Emburey ...10
P. R. Sleep not out	66	– b Emburey ... 2
†D. J. Kelly c and b Emburey	4	– c Gatting b Emburey
A. K. Zesers b Emburey	1	– c Edmonds b Emburey
T. B. A. May c Richards b Botham	15	– c Athey b Botham
S. D. H. Parkinson not out	11	– c Gatting b Dilley
P. W. Gladigau (did not bat)		– not out
L-b 3, n-b 2	5	B 4, l-b 3, n-b 7 ... 1-

1/16 2/42 3/186 4/186 5/216   (8 wkts dec.) 305   1/7 2/9 3/54 4/199 5/240   26-
6/224 7/234 8/283   6/256 7/257 8/257 9/265

Bowling: *First Innings*—Dilley 12-0-32-1; Botham 12-3-31-1; Emburey 33-8-76-3; Sma
9-4-43-1; Edmonds 29-5-97-2; Gatting 6-0-23-0. *Second Innings*—Dilley 13-2-61-2
Botham 7.1-1-17-2; Emburey 38-11-102-6; Edmonds 36-10-82-0; Gatting 1-1-0-0.

England XI

B. C. Broad lbw b Parkinson	0	– c Phillips b Hookes ... 6.
C. W. J. Athey c Phillips b Parkinson	18	– c Kelly b Gladigau ... (
*M. W. Gatting c Kelly b Parkinson	8	– c Kelly b Gladigau ... 4
A. J. Lamb st Kelly b Sleep	105	– c Sleep b Hookes ... 55
J. J. Whitaker c Watson b Parkinson	108	
I. T. Botham c Hookes b May	70	– not out ... 19
†C. J. Richards c Hookes b Sleep	24	– (5) b Hookes ... 9
J. E. Emburey st Kelly b May	4	– (7) not out ... 10
P. H. Edmonds c Hookes b Parkinson	27	
G. R. Dilley c Kelly b Sleep	32	
G. C. Small not out	0	
B 5, l-b 6	11	B 2, l-b 2, w 4, n-b 1 ... 9

1/1 2/15 3/38 4/210 5/294   407   1/15 2/23 3/129   (5 wkts) 169
6/325 7/347 8/347 9/407   4/130 5/143

Bowling: *First Innings*—Gladigau 14–2–56–0; Parkinson 22.4–2–87–5; Zesers 23–6–77–0; ay 23–0–111–2; Sleep 20–7–65–3. *Second Innings*—Gladigau 6–2–15–2; Parkinson 1–25–0; Zesers 4–0–15–0; Sleep 19–2–38–0; May 1–0–9–0; Hookes 15–5–58–3; Hilditch 0–1–0; Watson 0.2–0–4–0.

Umpires: A. R. Crafter and B. E. Martin.

†WESTERN AUSTRALIA COUNTRY XI v ENGLAND XI

 Kalgoorlie, November 5. England XI won by 117 runs. Athey, straight-driving three sixes d stroking sixteen fours all round the wicket, carried England to an easy win in the last of eir trio of Country XI matches.

England XI 293 for five (50 overs) (W. N. Slack 45, C. W. J. Athey 124, D. I. Gower 36, J. Whitaker 49); Western Australia Country XI 176 for nine (50 overs) (D. Wellington 39, Scott 36, C. Kerr 32; C. W. J. Athey three for 40).

WESTERN AUSTRALIA v ENGLAND XI

 t Perth, November 7, 8, 9, 10. Drawn. England lost what advantage there was in bowling rst by missing five catches, four of them in the slips. Marsh, however, did not require a prieve, holding an uneven innings together for 345 minutes in oppressive heat and hitting xteen fours, off-driving and square-cutting effectively before being ninth out. A discouraging ame for the touring side took a novel twist when, to protect Slack, Small was sent in as night- atchman for the final over. Rain, and a premature decision to abandon play for the day, mited Western Australia to 6.5 overs on the second day – time enough for Matthews to bowl mall – but on the third the two quick left-armers, Reid and Matthews, dismissed England in ree and a half hours. Reid enjoyed a spell of four for 5 in 27 balls as the Englishmen, batting osely, collapsed to 69 for six. Botham, at No. 8, drove and hooked 48 off 38 balls, but estern Australia had time to score 111 for two by stumps in spite of Marsh's slowness. When mall had him lbw on the final morning, he had batted 246 minutes for his 63, England aving mostly denied him room for his off-side strokes. Wood's punishing 53 enabled him to et England 331 in four hours, but with Slack out first ball, Gower completing a "pair", and atting also making nought, no attempt was made to get the runs. But for Botham being ropped at 4, at square leg off a well-hit hook, and fading light preventing Wood from using his fast bowlers in the final hour, Western Australia might have completed the win their ominance deserved.

Close of play: First day, England XI 1-0 (G. C. Small 0*, B. C. Broad 0*); Second day, England XI 19-1 (B. C. Broad 11*, W. N. Slack 3*); Third day, Western Australia 111-2 (G. R. Marsh 39*, G. M. Wood 16*).

Western Australia

G. R. Marsh b Botham	124	– lbw b Small	63
M. R. J. Veletta c Gatting b Botham	10	– c Broad b DeFreitas	2
T. M. Moody c Richards b DeFreitas	19	– st Richards b Edmonds	45
*G. M. Wood c Botham b DeFreitas	9	– c Gatting b Edmonds	53
W. S. Andrews b Dilley	31	– b Edmonds	9
K. H. MacLeay c Richards b DeFreitas	7	– run out	10
†M. J. Cox lbw b Dilley	1	– run out	8
T. G. Breman c Edmonds b DeFreitas	4	– c sub b Gatting	0
C. D. Matthews c Gower b Small	56	– not out	3
B. Mulder not out	1	– not out	2
B. A. Reid b Botham	0		
L-b 10, w 3	13	B 1, l-b 4, n-b 7	12

1/30 2/66 3/102 4/163 5/176	275	1/18 2/90 3/164 (8 wkts dec.) 207
6/185 7/190 8/274 9/275		4/178 5/186 6/196
		7/202 8/203

Bowling: *First Innings*—Dilley 16–4–43–2; DeFreitas 22–5–82–4; Small 18–4–67–1; Botham 14.4–1–42–3; Edmonds 9–1–31–0. *Second Innings*—Dilley 14–0–38–0; DeFreitas 14–2–51–1; Edmonds 13–1–37–3; Small 15.3–3–44–1; Botham 8–2–31–0; Gatting 1–0–1–1.

England XI

G. C. Small b Matthews	3	
B. C. Broad c Cox b MacLeay	33 – (1) c MacLeay b Reid	2
W. N. Slack b Reid	15 – (2) c Moody b MacLeay	
D. I. Gower b Reid	0 – (3) c Wood b MacLeay	
A. J. Lamb c Wood b Reid	0 – (4) c and b Mulder	6
*M. W. Gatting b Matthews	19 – (5) c Wood b Reid	
†C. J. Richards c Cox b Reid	3 – (6) c Cox b Mulder	1
I. T. Botham c Reid b Breman	48 – (7) not out	4
P. A. J. DeFreitas c Cox b Matthews	20 – (8) not out	
P. H. Edmonds b Matthews	1	
G. R. Dilley not out	1	
B 1, l-b 1, n-b 7	9	L-b 1, w 2, n-b 2

1/15 2/56 3/56 4/56 5/57   152   1/1 2/5 3/53 4/54   (6 wkts) 15
6/69 7/128 8/134 9/151   5/95 6/134

Bowling: First Innings—Reid 11-3-40-4; MacLeay 16-9-34-1; Matthews 14.5-3-30-
Breman 7-1-40-1; Mulder 2-1-6-0. *Second Innings*—Matthews 11-2-23-0; MacLe-
7-3-26-2; Reid 6-3-15-2; Breman 13-3-30-0; Mulder 16-5-46-2; Moody 3-2-2-0; Velet
1-0-1-0-0.

Umpires: C. Gannon and P. J. McConnell.

AUSTRALIA v ENGLAND

First Test Match

At Brisbane, November 14, 15, 16, 18, 19. England won by seven wickets. Followin
England's poor performance in their preceding match at Perth and the development of seven
of their own players on the recent tour of India, Australia were widely fancied to achiev
what would have been their seventh victory in eleven post-war Tests against Englan
at Woolloongabba. Lamb and Botham were the only England batsmen in good form, whi
Slack's failure against Western Australia left the tour selectors little alternative but to entru
Athey with the task of opening against the type of bowling – fast-medium left-arm – whic
had caused such problems in the state games. Another handicap for England was that on
ground on which, for several Tests, fast bowlers had been in their element, theirs had bee
inconsistent and the slip-catching unreliable. By contrast, Australia's batsmen with th
exception of Ritchie had been making runs, while Reid and Matthews, the left-arm new-ba
bowlers, had shared ten wickets for Western Australia the weekend before. It was understand
able therefore that, when Border won the toss and followed recent precedent by puttin
England in to bat, only their most phlegmatic supporters received the news with an outwar
show of confidence.

England's emphatic victory, which was completed 35 minutes after lunch on the fifth da
was a salutary reminder of the dangers of reading too much into omens and too little in
experience, especially in the first match of a series when nerves – and nerve – play such a par
Selection was another vital factor. Australia, uncertain of Lawson's stamina after his playin
only two Sheffield Shield games following a ten-month break with back trouble, omitted hi
before the start, thus committing themselves to three new-ball bowlers who had played on
nine Tests between them. England, despite the 'Gabba's reputation, chose both spinners ar
left out Small. Although Gatting, too, would have bowled first had he won the toss, the contr
exerted by Emburey and Edmonds in both Australian innings suggested that, had he done s
England's balance of three seamers and two spinners would still have proved his side's be
combination. C. D. Matthews (Australia) and Richards and DeFreitas (England) won the
first Test caps.

The opening session was to have a decisive bearing on how the match developed. Thoug
Reid moved one away to have Broad caught at the wicket after 35 minutes, Australia's attac
lacked the accuracy to put England under pressure, too many balls being bowled short or c
the stumps. Gatting, taking the onus of batting at No. 3 after Gower's failure at Perth, had a
edgy start, nearly playing on to Reid at 2; but Athey was composed, showing good judgeme
of the ball to leave alone. When England went in to lunch at 65 for one, much of th
advantage of the toss had disappeared.

Australia, ill served by their fast bowlers, at no stage promised to recover. Hughes ended
stand of 101 by bowling Gatting off his pads, but Lamb was soon into his stride. When ra

and bad light took 80 minutes off the final session, England at 198 for two were nicely placed. Athey had been a model of concentration and correct technique, his only blemishes two or three uppish strokes between the slips and gully from mistimed square-drives.

On the second morning, however, the game changed rapidly. Lamb was out first ball, Athey three overs later with the score unaltered, and still at 198 Gower was missed off Hughes by C. D. Matthews at third slip, a sharp chance off a slash two-handed to his right. The match turned in that instant. While Gower took half an hour to settle, Botham played with much authority; he dominated their stand of 118. Australia had an opening when C. D. Matthews had Gower caught at wide mid-on and bowled Richards in successive overs, but Border surrendered the initiative by pushing seven and sometimes eight fielders on to the boundary to deprive Botham of the strike. Emburey made only 8 before slicing Hughes to gully, but the lessening of pressure in the 40 minutes of his innings had much to do with DeFreitas's confident contribution as with Botham he added 92 in not much more than an hour. Botham's 138, which included an assault on Hughes which brought 22 in the over of his century, was comparable to his 118 at Old Trafford in 1981 for power and control. He batted 249 minutes (174 balls) and hit four sixes – straight drives – and thirteen fours before Hughes sprinted in to catch him at long-leg.

Australia lost Boon, pulling to mid-wicket, to close the second day at 33 for one. But on a pitch now free of moisture, there seemed little danger of their failing to score 257 to avoid the follow-on as Zoehrer, the night-watchman, was helping Marsh add 70. Dilley made the breakthrough with a highish lbw and Australia lost their grip as he maintained good line and pace to achieve his first five-wicket return in Tests. However, the critical dismissal was that of Border at 159. Tied down for an hour by Emburey, he made an ill-judged attempt to assert himself when Edmonds took over; the result was a skied catch to cover from a mis-hit drive. As they were to in the follow-on, the spinners played a crucial role by restricting Australia to 191 off 85 overs, when the new ball came due.

Marsh's disciplined 110 – he batted in great heat for 392 minutes (311 balls, twelve fours) – was the cornerstone of Australia's resistance in the follow-on. But three wickets, including Border's, fell for 92, and only while Ritchie shared a fourth-wicket stand of 113 in 175 minutes did Australia look to have a fair chance of survival. When DeFreitas ended that partnership with the new ball – a second debatable lbw decision – and G. R. J. Matthews was caught and bowled off a front edge by Dilley fifteen minutes from the close, Australia started the final day only 35 ahead at 243 for five, needing a lengthy stand between Marsh and Waugh to leave England a task against the clock.

They began with confidence, scoring 15 in two overs. Then, after 28 minutes, Marsh's gritty innings ended when he edged DeFreitas into his stumps, and in 31 minutes the last four wickets fell for 20. Emburey picked up three for 2 in 23 deliveries, belated reward for dismissing Border to a bat-pad catch in one of the best overs of the game. He finished with five for 80, claiming Waugh as his 100th Test victim in the process. England, needing 75, were certain winners from that point; but starting shakily they reminded their followers that the contest might have finished otherwise had Australia scored another 100 runs.

Man of the Match: I. T. Botham.   *Attendance:* 33,638.

Close of play: First day, England 198-2 (C. W. J. Athey 76*, A. J. Lamb 40*); Second day, Australia 33-1 (G. R. Marsh 17*, T. J. Zoehrer 0*); Third day, Australia 2-0 (D. C. Boon 1*, G. R. Marsh 1*); Fourth day, Australia 243-5 (G. R. Marsh 108*, S. R. Waugh 12*).

England

B. C. Broad c Zoehrer b Reid	8	– not out	35
C. W. J. Athey c Zoehrer b C. D. Matthews	76	– c Waugh b Hughes	1
*M. W. Gatting b Hughes	61	– c G. R. J. Matthews b Hughes	12
A. J. Lamb lbw b Hughes	40	– lbw b Reid	9
D. I. Gower c Ritchie b C. D. Matthews	51	– not out	15
I. T. Botham c Hughes b Waugh	138		
†C. J. Richards b C. D. Matthews	0		
J. E. Emburey c Waugh b Hughes	8		
P. A. J. DeFreitas c C. D. Matthews b Waugh	40		
P. H. Edmonds not out	9		
G. R. Dilley c Boon b Waugh	0		
B 3, l-b 19, n-b 3	25	B 2, n-b 3	5
	456		(3 wkts) 77

1/15 (1) 2/116 (3) 3/198 (4) 4/198 (2)   456   1/6 (2) 2/25 (3)   (3 wkts) 77
5/316 (5) 6/324 (7) 7/351 (8) 8/443 (6)   3/40 (4)
9/451 (9) 10/456 (11)

Bowling: *First Innings*—Reid 31–4–86–1; Hughes 36–7–134–3; C. D. Matthews 35–10–95–3; Waugh 21–3–76–3; G. R. J. Matthews 11–2–43–0. *Second Innings*—C. D. Matthews 4–0–11–0; Hughes 5.3–0–28–2; Reid 6–1–20–1; G. R. J. Matthews 7–1–16–0.

Australia

G. R. Marsh c Richards b Dilley	56	– (2) b DeFreitas	110
D. C. Boon c Broad b DeFreitas	10	– (1) lbw b Botham	14
†T. J. Zoehrer lbw b Dilley	38	– (8) not out	16
D. M. Jones lbw b DeFreitas	18	– (3) st Richards b Emburey	18
*A. R. Border c DeFreitas b Edmonds	7	– (4) c Lamb b Emburey	23
G. M. Ritchie c Edmonds b Dilley	41	– (5) lbw b DeFreitas	45
G. R. J. Matthews not out	56	– (6) c and b Dilley	13
S. R. Waugh c Richards b Dilley	0	– (7) b Emburey	28
C. D. Matthews c Gatting b Botham	11	– lbw b Emburey	0
M. G. Hughes b Botham	0	– b DeFreitas	0
B. A. Reid c Richards b Dilley	3	– c Broad b Emburey	2
B 2, l-b 8, w 2, n-b 6	18	B 5, l-b 6, n-b 2	13

1/27 (2) 2/97 (3) 3/114 (4) 4/126 (1)   248   1/24 (1) 2/44 (3) 3/92 (4)   282
5/159 (5) 6/198 (6) 7/204 (8) 8/239 (9)   4/205 (5) 5/224 (6) 6/262 (2)
9/239 (10) 10/248 (11)   7/266 (7) 8/266 (9) 9/275 (10)
                                                      10/282 (11)

Bowling: *First Innings*—DeFreitas 16–5–32–2; Dilley 25.4–7–68–5; Emburey 34–11–66–0; Edmonds 12–6–12–1; Botham 16–1–58–2; Gatting 1–0–2–0. *Second Innings*—Botham 12–0–34–1; Dilley 19–6–47–1; Emburey 42.5–14–80–5; DeFreitas 17–2–62–3; Edmonds 24–8–46–0; Gatting 2–0–2–0.

Umpires: A. R. Crafter and M. W. Johnson.

NEW SOUTH WALES v ENGLAND XI

At Newcastle, November 21, 22, 23. New South Wales won by eight wickets. High-class fast-medium seam bowling by Whitney and Gilbert swung a low-scoring game in favour of New South Wales on the second day after Holland, their 40-year-old night-watchman, and Waugh, who batted with greater freedom than anyone on either side, had closed England's lead to 16. The pitch, patchily damp as a result of the covers leaking in heavy rain the day before the match, crumbled as it dried in the wind and sun, and in their second innings England found no answer to the left-armer, Whitney, and Gilbert, whom Wellham was inspired to use ahead of Lawson, his senior new-ball bowler. Bowling straight and to a full attacking length, they extracted unpredictable movement at varied pace and height, sharing the attack until the score was 53 for seven. England, deprived of the services of Small by a foot injury received during a last-wicket stand of 25 with Edmonds, were unable to respond in kind and Wellham carried his team to victory with more than four sessions in hand. It was New South Wales' thirteenth victory over touring teams from England, but their first since E. R. Dexter's MCC side was defeated by an innings in 1962-63 on the Sydney Cricket Ground. England's second-innings 82 was the lowest by an England or MCC XI in Australia since New South Wales bowled out G. O. Allen's touring team for 73 in 1936-37.

Close of play: First day, New South Wales 15-2 (R. G. Holland 1*, D. M. Wellham 0*); Second day, England XI 66-9 (P. H. Edmonds 14*, G. C. Small 3*).

England XI

B. C. Broad lbw b Whitney	31	– lbw b Gilbert	0
C. W. J. Athey lbw b Lawson	3	– lbw b Whitney	0
W. N. Slack b Whitney	16	– b Gilbert	18
D. I. Gower c Wellham b Matthews	16	– (5) c Holland b Whitney	0
J. J. Whitaker c and b Matthews	4	– (4) c Waugh b Whitney	6
*J. E. Emburey c Waugh b Holland	10	– (8) c Dyer b Whitney	6
I. T. Botham c Taylor b Holland	14	– (6) b Gilbert	6
P. H. Edmonds b Matthews	6	– (9) not out	17
†B. N. French not out	38	– (7) lbw b Whitney	0
N. A. Foster c and b Lawson	25	– b Holland	0
G. C. Small b Holland	26	– lbw b Gilbert	14
B 3, l-b 2, n-b 3	8	L-b 10, n-b 5	15

1/16 2/51 3/61 4/74 5/75　　　　197　1/0 2/0 3/22 4/22 5/24　　　82
6/97 7/106 8/106 9/142　　　　　　　6/25 7/37 8/53 9/57

Bowling: *First Innings*—Lawson 16-3-42-2; Gilbert 5-1-16-0; Holland 27.3-11-58-3; Whitney 13-4-31-2; Matthews 19-6-33-3; Waugh 5-0-12-0. *Second Innings*—Gilbert 14.4-3-26-4; Whitney 17-4-39-5; Lawson 4-3-2-0; Holland 2-1-5-1.

New South Wales

S. M. Small c Edmonds b Emburey	8	– c Edmonds b Foster	9
M. A. Taylor st French b Emburey	4	– c Slack b Edmonds	31
R. G. Holland c French b Edmonds	36		
*D. M. Wellham lbw b Foster	18	– (3) not out	29
M. D. O'Neill b Foster	0	– (4) not out	13
G. R. J. Matthews b Emburey	25		
S. R. Waugh c French b Small	47		
†G. C. Dyer b Edmonds	4		
G. F. Lawson c French b Small	26		
D. R. Gilbert not out	10		
M. R. Whitney c French b Foster	1		
L-b 1, n-b 1	2	B 12, l-b 3, n-b 2	17

1/12 2/15 3/43 4/43 5/86　　　　181　1/23 2/57　　　(2 wkts) 99
6/110 7/118 8/165 9/170

Bowling: *First Innings*—Small 17-7-23-2; Foster 15.4-6-30-3; Emburey 29-9-65-3; Edmonds 31-13-55-2; Botham 2-0-7-0. *Second Innings*—Botham 3-1-7-0; Foster 13.1-7-24-1; Small 1-0-5-0; Emburey 15-7-16-0; Edmonds 16-4-32-1.

Umpires: R. A. French and A. G. Marshall.

AUSTRALIA v ENGLAND

Second Test Match

At Perth, November 28, 29, 30, December 2, 3. Drawn. After Border had lost the toss for the first time in nine Tests, Broad and Athey shared an opening stand of 223 which gave England control for much of the match, even if they were unable to turn their supremacy into victory. It was England's highest opening partnership for 39 Tests – Tavaré and Fowler scored the same number in 1983 against New Zealand at The Oval – and their fifth highest against Australia. England were denied victory first by a resolute and responsible 125 in 372 minutes by Border, who saved the follow-on in the company of the No. 11, Reid; secondly by an indecisive approach to their own second innings, which resulted in a delayed declaration; and finally by Australia's determined batting on the fifth day on a pitch which played truer than it had any right to on its appearance.

John Maley, who as travelling curator during the era of World Series Cricket had produced a number of true pitches under hot-house conditions, successfully transplanting them into non-cricket grounds, set out at Perth to prepare a surface which would be good for batting on the opening day; in contrast to recent Tests at the WACA ground, where not since 1977-78 had a captain chosen to bat first. This pitch started exceptionally dry by modern standards, with several cracks beginning to peep through, and finished resembling a giant jigsaw puzzle, split by a wavy crack (into which it was possible to slide a little finger) in line with the stumps at each end. Its appearance was alarming enough for Border to decline the use of a roller when Gatting's declaration left Australia to bat through the fifth day; but in the event the cracks proved an illusory advantage to England's bowlers, balls hitting them tending to deviate too much to create problems.

Australia made one change from the side beaten at Brisbane, Lawson coming in for Hughes while Sleep, South Australia's leg-spinning all-rounder, was omitted from their chosen twelve. England were unchanged. In the eighth over, Border at second slip missed Athey, two-handed to his left off C. D. Matthews, but that apart Australia's remodelled new-ball partnership never threatened to make inroads. Indeed, the new ball was wasted with more profligacy than at Brisbane. Broad played majestically throughout, never looking back after superbly struck fours to mid-wicket and extra-cover in Matthews's second over. When, by tea, England were 187 for no wicket, with Broad 2 runs away from his first Test hundred, a huge total was assured. Reid, the steadiest of Australia's bowlers, deprived Athey (286 minutes, eleven fours) of a well-deserved maiden Test hundred by yorking him for 96, and next over he had Lamb, cutting, caught at the wicket.

Australia lost their faint chance of recovering lost ground on the second morning when, shortly after Gatting had cut C. D. Matthews to gully, Broad was dropped Athey, two-handed to his left off C. D. Matthews, but that apart Australia's remodelled new-ball partnership at third slip in Lawson's best spell of the innings. Broad added only 15 more before Reid had him caught at the wicket, his innings having spanned 435 minutes and included 25 fours; but by then Gower, given the easiest of starts by C. D. Matthews with two loose balls on his legs, was in full stride with 35, pulling and off-driving with severity and perfect timing. After Botham, pushing on the off-side, had been caught off Reid at second slip, Richards in his second Test played with such assurance that Gower was content to let him dominate a sixth-wicket stand of 207, during which Richards became the first Surrey player since J. H. Edrich to make a hundred for England in a Test. They had been together 212 minutes when Gower (277 minutes, nineteen fours) was caught at cover after completing his sixth hundred against Australia and his second at Perth. Half an hour later, with a declaration imminent, Richards (sixteen fours) was caught at mid-off, 2 runs short of the highest score by an England wicket-keeper against Australia – A. P. E. Knott's 135 at Trent Bridge in 1977. Australia's attack, with the exception of Reid, was short of both accuracy and penetration, Richards relishing especially his off-spin of G. R. J. Matthews in a four-hour innings well attuned to England's aims.

Australia, left with half an hour's batting on the second day, needed 393 to save the follow-on and were at once in trouble when Boon played on to Dilley in the second over. Although Waugh, promoted four places, vindicated high opinions of his timing by making 71, which included the only six of the match, England, helped by a brilliant catch by Broad at backward short-leg off a well-hit hook by Marsh, worked steadily through the top half of the order. When, shortly before tea, Ritchie was caught at slip off a ball that hit a crack, turned and lifted, the prospects of a second win were good, but Border's technique, patience and relish for a fight were never better illustrated than in the next two sessions. Content to remain in occupation, yet missing next to nothing overpitched, he nursed four partners through successive stands of 81, 55, 26 and 25, so that when Reid came in at 385 for nine, only 8 runs were needed to make England bat again. Border himself made the decisive stroke three minutes before lunch on the third day, cutting Emburey for 4 and giving a little skip of joy as the ball crossed the line. When he was out ten minutes after the interval, having hit seventeen fours off 284 deliveries, England, 191 ahead, had 9 hours 40 minutes at their disposal to win the match.

Through good defensive bowling by Reid and Waugh, however, and concern that a start of 50 for three might lead to a collapse, England's second innings got going only while Gower was making 48 in 72 minutes. With Botham failing again, momentum was lost, and Gatting drew back from the declaration England had been aiming for before the close of play. Instead, he waited until the following morning.

Dilley at once made up lost time when, with the first ball of the last day, he had Boon caught by Botham at second slip, his 100th catch in Tests. But in Dilley's next over Botham missed a difficult low chance in the same position, and Marsh and Jones, both receiving the benefit on close lbw decisions, virtually made the game safe with a stand of 126. Soon after lunch, Botham tore a muscle in his left side delivering a bouncer, but when Edmonds had

Border caught at silly-point off bat and pad in the over after tea, England had another opening. However, the pitch remained true and slow with little turn, and despite many close calls against the spinners, with fielders clustered round the bat, Ritchie (135 minutes) and G. R. J. Matthews (95 minutes) held out until Gatting gave them best midway through the final twenty overs.

Man of the Match: B. C. Broad.   *Attendance:* 51,862.

Close of play: First day, England 272-2 (B. C. Broad 146*, M. W. Gatting 11*); Second day, Australia 19-1 (G. R. Marsh 6*, S. R. Waugh 8*); Third day, Australia 309-6 (A. R. Border 81*, T. J. Zoehrer 15*); Fourth day, England 199-8 (J. E. Emburey 4*).

England

B. C. Broad c Zoehrer b Reid	162	– lbw b Waugh 16
C. W. J. Athey b Reid	96	– c Border b Reid 6
A. J. Lamb c Zoehrer b Reid	0	– (4) lbw b Reid 2
*M. W. Gatting c Waugh b C. D. Matthews	14	– (3) b Waugh 70
D. I. Gower c Waugh b G. R. J. Matthews	136	– c Zoehrer b Waugh 48
I. T. Botham c Border b Reid	0	– c G. R. J. Matthews b Reid .. 6
†C. J. Richards c Waugh b C. D. Matthews	133	– c Lawson b Waugh 15
P. A. J. DeFreitas lbw b C. D. Matthews	11	– b Waugh 15
J. E. Emburey not out	5	– not out 4
B 4, l-b 15, w 3, n-b 13	35	B 4, l-b 9, n-b 4 17

1/223 (2) 2/227 (3) 3/275 (4)   (8 wkts dec.) 592   1/8 (2) 2/47 (1)   (8 wkts dec.) 199
4/333 (1) 5/339 (6) 6/546 (5)   3/50 (4) 4/123 (5)
7/585 (8) 8/592 (7)   5/140 (6) 6/172 (3)
                                                           7/190 (8) 8/199 (7)

P. H. Edmonds and G. R. Dilley did not bat.

Bowling: *First Innings*—Lawson 41–8–126–0; C. D. Matthews 29.1–4–112–3; Reid 40–8–115–4; Waugh 24–4–90–0; G. R. J. Matthews 34–3–124–1; Border 2–0–6–0. *Second Innings*—Reid 21–3–58–3; Lawson 9–1–44–0; Waugh 21.3–4–69–5; C. D. Matthews 2–0–15–0.

Australia

G. R. Marsh c Broad b Botham	15	– (2) lbw b Emburey 49
D. C. Boon b Dilley	2	– (1) c Botham b Dilley 0
S. R. Waugh c Botham b Emburey	71	
D. M. Jones c Athey b Edmonds	27	– (3) run out 69
*A. R. Border c Richards b Dilley	125	– (4) c Lamb b Edmonds 16
G. M. Ritchie c Botham b Edmonds	33	– (5) not out 24
G. R. J. Matthews c Botham b Dilley	45	– (6) not out 14
†T. J. Zoehrer lbw b Dilley	29	
G. F. Lawson b DeFreitas	13	
C. D. Matthews c Broad b Emburey	10	
B. A. Reid not out	2	
B 9, l-b 9, n-b 11	29	B 9, l-b 6, n-b 10 25

1/4 (2) 2/64 (1) 3/114 (3) 4/128 (4)   401   1/0 (1) 2/126 (3)   (4 wkts) 197
5/198 (6) 6/279 (7) 7/334 (8)   3/142 (2) 4/152 (4)
8/360 (9) 9/385 (10) 10/401 (5)

Bowling: *First Innings*—Botham 22–4–72–1; Dilley 24.4–4–79–4; Emburey 43–9–110–2; DeFreitas 24–4–67–1; Edmonds 21–4–55–2. *Second Innings*—Dilley 15–1–53–1; Botham 7.2–4–13–0; DeFreitas 13.4–2–47–0; Emburey 28–11–41–1; Edmonds 27–13–25–1; Gatting 5–3–3–0; Lamb 1–1–0–0.

Umpires: R. A. French and P. J. McConnell.

VICTORIA v ENGLAND XI

At Melbourne, December 6, 7, 8, 9. England XI won by five wickets. Victoria consigned themselves to a long struggle to avoid defeat by choosing to bat when the pitch was at its most unpredictable in pace and bounce. It was the season's first game on the Test ground. Gatting, having arrived late through over-sleeping, hastened the state side's collapse by having three men caught at long-leg, and then determined batting by Athey and French, plus attacking innings by Lamb and Foster, secured England a lead of 162. In much easier conditions, Victoria's stubborn second innings lasted 529 minutes. The left-handed Hibbert managed only six fours in nearly six hours over a holding outfield, while in contrast O'Donnell, badly missed at second slip at 8, drove and pulled vigorously, hitting a six and eight fours in 140 minutes. Persistent bowling by Small on the third day and three hard-earned wickets by Foster on the last left England 184 to win off a minimum of 46 overs. Whitaker made sure they had no problems by punching 48 off 64 balls, and Gower hit the winning boundary with 2.5 overs in hand, completing England's first win over Victoria since 1962-63.

Close of play: First day, England XI 128-6 (B. N. French 28*); Second day, Victoria 56-0 (D. F. Whatmore 39*, A. I. C. Dodemaide 11*); Third day, Victoria 296-6 (P. A. Hibbert 71*, M. G. D. Dimattina 17*).

Victoria

D. F. Whatmore c French b Small	4	– c and b Small	43
I. D. Frazer lbw b Foster	0	– (7) c Richards b Small	10
D. M. Jones c Lamb b Foster	4	– c Richards b Small	29
P. A. Hibbert c French b Foster	25	– c Gower b Edmonds	91
J. D. Siddons c Foster b Gatting	7	– c sub b Small	3
S. P. O'Donnell c Foster b Gatting	4	– st Richards b Edmonds	77
A. I. C. Dodemaide c Foster b Gatting	6	– (2) lbw b Small	24
†M. G. D. Dimattina not out	19	– c Lamb b Foster	20
M. G. Hughes c Gower b Gatting	17	– b Foster	20
*R. J. Bright c French b Small	0	– lbw b Foster	1
S. P. Davis b Small	2	– not out	0
B 1, l-b 3, w 1, n-b 8	13	B 9, l-b 8, n-b 10	27

1/7 2/7 3/16 4/33 5/37   101   1/60 2/106 3/107 4/112   345
6/55 7/63 8/91 9/92   5/239 6/263 7/308 8/342
                                      9/344

Bowling: *First Innings*—Small 15-3-30-3; Foster 15-6-29-3; Gatting 14-4-31-4; Edmonds 8-5-7-0. *Second Innings*—Small 40-9-81-5; Foster 42.1-9-115-3; Gatting 24-6-57-0; Edmonds 25-5-50-2; Athey 4-0-25-0.

England XI

W. N. Slack c sub b Hughes	10	– c Dimattina b O'Donnell	35
C. W. J. Athey c Hibbert b Hughes	58	– c Dimattina b Dodemaide	10
J. J. Whitaker c Frazer b Hughes	0	– c Whatmore b Bright	48
D. I. Gower c Dimattina b O'Donnell	23	– (5) not out	28
C. J. Richards c Dodemaide b O'Donnell	0	– (7) not out	0
*M. W. Gatting c Whatmore b Dodemaide	1	– (6) b Dodemaide	17
†B. N. French c Whatmore b Dodemaide	58		
A. J. Lamb c sub b Dodemaide	46	– (4) c Jones b Bright	36
P. H. Edmonds c Dimattina b Dodemaide	0		
N. A. Foster not out	46		
G. C. Small c Dodemaide b Bright	3		
B 10, l-b 6, w 1, n-b 1	18	L-b 1, w 8, n-b 1	10

1/28 2/30 3/58 4/78 5/83   263   1/14 2/88 3/112   (5 wkts) 184
6/128 7/193 8/199 9/238   4/140 5/180

Bowling: *First Innings*—Hughes 18-6-76-3; Davis 1-0-1-0; Dodemaide 23-6-76-4; O'Donnell 22-4-78-2; Bright 4.5-1-16-1. *Second Innings*—Hughes 8-0-24-0; Dodemaide 12-2-46-2; O'Donnell 12.1-3-36-1; Bright 10-1-54-2; Jones 3-0-23-0.

Umpires: R. C. Bailhache and D. W. Holt.

AUSTRALIA v ENGLAND

Third Test Match

At Adelaide, December 12, 13, 14, 15, 16. Drawn. A perfect batting pitch exposed the limitations of both sets of bowlers. Although late on the fourth evening there was an outside chance of a result when Australia lost two wickets for 8 runs at the start of their second innings, after leading by 59 on the first, in the conditions, and through the selection of the teams, a draw had looked the likely outcome from the time the captains tossed. In the event, only twenty wickets fell for 1,209 runs; four men made hundreds, Border and Broad their second in successive Tests, and there were nine scores between 41 and 93.

Sleep, the South Australian leg-spinner, and Hughes, who had been dropped after the First Test, replaced Lawson and C. D. Matthews from the team that drew in Perth; and when Zoehrer damaged a shoulder in practice, Dyer, his understudy on the tour of India, took his place. He had a tidy first Test match behind the stumps, although he experienced occasional difficulties taking Sleep and missed a stumping chance, given by Emburey, which might have earned Australia a three-figure lead. In England's second innings he suffered a broken nose when a ball from Sleep deflected off Broad's pads. Overall, however, he looked at least the equal of Australia's first choice.

The omission of Bright from the final XI was unsurprising in view of the slow left-armer's treatment by England in the state game earlier in the week. But it was a pawky move with Australia one down in the series; and in hindsight it was regretted by Border when, after winning a good toss, he was able to declare at 514 for five. Botham's rib muscle, which was proving slow to heal, obliged England to make their first change of the series, Whitaker winning his first cap on the ground where he had earlier scored 108. This left England a seam bowler short, a setback when Australia were in trouble early in their second innings, but as holders of the Ashes the tourists could be excused for consolidating their batting.

Whitaker, as it happened, spent an uncomfortable 51 minutes scoring 11 in his only innings. He went some way towards making up for his failure with the bat with the zeal with which he fielded during the eleven hours of Australia's first innings. With Gower, whose cutting-off was brilliant, and DeFreitas, whose speed over the ground and fine throwing arm saved many runs in the elongated outfield, Whitaker shared the distinction of being a member of the first trio of Leicestershire players to play in the same England team, though they had come from far and wide to do so.

Given the circumstances, a big Australian score was always on the cards, the more so when Dilley and DeFreitas, who was no-balled for over-stepping ten times in his first ten overs, made poor use of a new ball dampened by two showers. Marsh and Boon laid the foundations with Australia's first three-figure opening in a home Test against England since 1974-75 (I. R. Redpath and R. B. McCosker), but Edmonds and Emburey exercised their usual tight control and there was no worthwhile acceleration until just before the declaration when Matthews and Waugh added 49 in four overs. Jones did his best, repeatedly going down the pitch at Edmonds, only to be thwarted by the left-armer's subtleties of flight and the fielding of mid-off and mid-on set deep. Yet for all his aggression and swift running between the wickets, Jones batted 283 minutes for his 93 before being well caught, low on the leg-side, by Richards off a mis-hit hook. Boon, finding his confidence early on with a square cut and some good strokes off his legs, needed four hours for his first hundred against England, a strong, compact innings which contained fourteen fours and no chance. Border's range of strokes, and expert placing, enabled him to score 70 in 151 minutes before becoming the only batsman to fall to a defensive stroke, a looping leg-side bat-pad to Richards; but it was not until Waugh's improvisation and crisp driving wrung a response from Matthews that Australia scored with freedom.

England were never in danger of being asked to follow on. On the contrary, after Broad and Athey had put on 112 for the first wicket, and Broad and Gatting had added 161 for the second, they had prospects of taking a sizeable lead until Lamb and Gower were out within an over of each other in the last ten minutes of the third day. Without matching the majesty of his 162 in Perth, Broad played with smooth assurance, hitting a six and twelve fours in 308 minutes, while Gatting (180 minutes, fifteen fours) vigorously attacked the spin bowlers. Emburey, the night-watchman, held the innings together until after lunch on the fourth day, troubled only by Sleep, who turned and pitched his leg-breaks throughout.

Australia, left 2 hours 40 minutes batting before the close, were forced to consolidate when Boon and Jones fell to lively use of the new ball, but showers on the final morning made the last day academic. Border made a token declaration at tea after completing in 303 minutes his 21st Test hundred and his seventh against England; he survived a stumping chance off Embury at 85 and hit eleven fours. It was a disappointing match, played in mostly cool and cloudy weather, and crowds of 7,158 on the fourth day and 3,653 on the last reflected waning interest.

Man of the Match: A. R. Border.   *Attendance:* 46,720.

Close of play: First day, Australia 207-2 (D. M. Jones 27*, A. R. Border 19*); Second day, England 29-0 (B. C. Broad 18*, C. W. J. Athey 10*); Third day, England 349-5 (J. E. Emburey 5*, J. J. Whitaker 3*); Fourth day, Australia 82-3 (A. R. Border 31*, G. M. Ritchie 4*).

Australia

G. R. Marsh b Edmonds	43	– (2) c and b Edmonds	41
D. C. Boon c Whitaker b Emburey	103	– (1) lbw b DeFreitas	0
D. M. Jones c Richards b Dilley	93	– c Lamb b Dilley	2
*A. R. Border c Richards b Edmonds	70	– not out	100
G. M. Ritchie c Broad b DeFreitas	36	– not out	46
G. R. J. Matthews not out	73		
S. R. Waugh not out	79		
L-b 2, n-b 15	17	B 4, l-b 6, n-b 2	12

1/113 (1) 2/185 (2) 3/311 (4)   (5 wkts dec.) 514   1/1 (1) 2/8 (3)   (3 wkts dec.) 201
4/333 (3) 5/368 (5)   3/77 (2)

P. R. Sleep, †G. C. Dyer, M. G. Hughes and B. A. Reid did not bat.

Bowling: First Innings—Dilley 32-3-111-1; DeFreitas 32-4-128-1; Emburey 46-11-117-1; Edmonds 52-14-134-2; Gatting 9-1-22-0. *Second Innings*—Dilley 21-8-38-1; DeFreitas 16-5-36-1; Emburey 22-6-50-0; Edmonds 29-7-63-1; Gatting 2-1-4-0.

England

B. C. Broad c Marsh b Waugh	116	– not out	15
C. W. J. Athey b Sleep	55	– c Dyer b Hughes	12
*M. W. Gatting c Waugh b Sleep	100	– b Matthews	0
A. J. Lamb c Matthews b Hughes	14	– not out	9
D. I. Gower lbw b Reid	38		
J. E. Emburey c Dyer b Reid	49		
J. J. Whitaker c Matthews b Reid	11		
†C. J. Richards c Jones b Sleep	29		
P. A. J. DeFreitas not out	4		
P. H. Edmonds c Border b Sleep	13		
G. R. Dilley b Reid	0		
B 4, l-b 14, w 4, n-b 4	26	B 2, l-b 1	3

1/112 (2) 2/273 (1) 3/283 (3) 4/341 (4)   455   1/21 (2) 2/22 (3)   (2 wkts) 39
5/341 (5) 6/361 (7) 7/422 (8) 8/439 (6)
9/454 (10) 10/455 (11)

Bowling: First Innings—Hughes 30-8-82-1; Reid 28.4-8-64-4; Sleep 47-14-132-4; Matthews 23-1-102-0; Border 1-0-1-0; Waugh 19-4-56-1. *Second Innings*—Hughes 7-2-16-1; Waugh 3-1-10-0; Matthews 8-4-10-1; Sleep 5-5-0-0.

Umpires: A. R. Crafter and S. G. Randell.

TASMANIA v ENGLAND XI

At Hobart, December 18, 19, 20, 21. England XI won by an innings and 96 runs. No play was possible on the first day because rain had found a way through the covers. The pitch was still damp at one end on the second morning when, by winning the toss, England gained a big advantage. Harris and Bowler stayed in for 40 minutes, but once DeFreitas broke the stand, Tasmania lost their remaining nine wickets for 54 in an innings stretching over 200 minutes.

Small, battling into a strong headwind for thirteen successive overs, was the most impressive bowler. England, batting in easier conditions, were held together by Slack for four and a quarter hours; only Gatting and Emburey, whose 46 in 33 minutes came from boundaries (ten fours and a six), scored quickly. Emburey's innings surpassed the previous highest first-class score (44) made up entirely of boundaries. Of Tasmania's five missed catches, two were dropped off Ellison of Kent, whose loss of form in the English county season had deprived him of his chance of touring. Tasmania put up more resistance in their second innings, but with the bounce still inconsistent, England had the match won by tea.

Close of play: First day, no play; Second day, England XI 73-1 (W. N. Slack 37*, J. J. Whitaker 14*); Third day, Tasmania 43-3 (G. A. Hughes 18*, R. E. Soule 2*).

Tasmania

E. J. Harris c Athey b Small	14	– (2) b Gatting	12
P. D. Bowler lbw b DeFreitas	7	– (1) run out	1
K. Bradshaw c Lamb b Foster	7	– c Slack b Foster	4
G. A. Hughes lbw b Foster	0	– lbw b DeFreitas	24
*D. C. Boon c Broad b Foster	2	– (6) c Emburey b Gatting	29
D. J. Buckingham c Richards b Foster	0	– (7) not out	43
†R. E. Soule c Slack b Small	1	– (5) lbw b Gatting	21
R. M. Ellison c Richards b DeFreitas	13	– c Richards b Small	5
T. J. Cooley c Athey b DeFreitas	16	– (10) b DeFreitas	3
R. L. Brown c Richards b DeFreitas	9	– (9) c Lamb b Small	6
S. J. Milosz not out	0	– b Small	1
B 1, l-b 1, n-b 8	10	B 4, l-b 8, w 4, n-b 2	18

1/25 2/25 3/27 4/33 5/35	79	1/3 2/11 3/41 4/53 5/92	167
6/36 7/36 8/63 9/75		6/111 7/130 8/136 9/164	

Bowling: *First Innings*—DeFreitas 14.2-4-44-4; Small 14-9-8-2; Foster 16-5-20-4; Emburey 3-2-4-0; Gatting 3-2-1-0. *Second Innings*—Foster 15-2-37-1; Small 13.3-3-44-3; Gatting 17-5-40-3; DeFreitas 8-0-30-2; Emburey 3-2-4-0.

England XI

B. C. Broad c Milosz b Cooley	15	J. E. Emburey c Buckingham b Milosz	46
W. N. Slack c Ellison b Brown	89	N. A. Foster c and b Brown	25
J. J. Whitaker b Soule b Ellison	37	G. C. Small not out	3
A. J. Lamb c Buckingham b Ellison	19	B 3, l-b 5, w 1, n-b 18	27
†C. J. Richards lbw b Milosz	18		
P. A. J. DeFreitas c Bradshaw b Milosz	3	1/41 2/111 3/143	(9 wkts. dec.) 342
C. W. J. Athey not out	30	4/187 5/198 6/198	
*M. W. Gatting c Cooley	30	7/234 8/294 9/334	

Bowling: Cooley 21-0-85-2; Ellison 21.5-4-61-2; Brown 19-6-65-2; Milosz 31-8-104-3; Bowler 2-0-19-0.

Umpires: D. R. Gregg and S. G. Randell.

†PRIME MINISTER'S XI v ENGLAND XI

At Canberra, December 23. England XI won by four wickets. After two successful nets in Tasmania, Botham made his first appearance since his injury in Perth twenty days earlier. He bowled his ten overs barely at medium pace but experienced no discomfort and established his fitness for the Melbourne Test on Boxing Day. The Prime Minister's XI, led by Border, were on course for a big score when Bishop and Veletta put on 109 in 23 overs. However, England gained control through Botham and Edmonds, and on a good pitch the result was never in doubt. Gower scored 68 off 66 balls, and Botham, coming in with 67 needed, made good use of nearly an hour at the crease before being caught in the outfield within 2 runs of the target. The game was watched by 8,102 in beautiful weather.

Prime Minister's XI 240 for five (50 overs) (G. A. Bishop 49, M. R. J. Veletta 75, A. R. Border 41 not out); England XI 241 for six (47.4 overs) (B. C. Broad 47, D. I. Gower 68, M. W. Gatting 30, I. T. Botham 43).

AUSTRALIA v ENGLAND

Fourth Test Match

At Melbourne, December 26, 27, 28. England won by an innings and 14 runs. A combination of excellent out-swing bowling by Small, playing in his first Test of the series, and an inept appraisal by Australia of their best means of success, effectively decided the match, and the destination of the Ashes, by tea on the first day. Australia, put in on a pitch not fully dry, were bowled out for 141 in 235 minutes, Small maintaining a high degree of accuracy to take five for 48 in 22.4 overs. A last-minute replacement for Dilley, who failed a fitness test on a jarred knee on the morning of the match, Small amply justified his preference to Foster by dismissing five of the first seven batsmen in the order. With two more wickets in the second innings, including that of Border when with Marsh the captain was showing signs of keeping Australia in the match, a valuable 21 not out at No. 11, and a good catch in the deep to finish the game, Small was a deserving winner of the Man of the Match award in only his third Test.

Well as Small bowled, however, both he and more especially Botham, for whom Whitaker made way, were helped by Australia's ill-conceived approach. Botham, bowling off the shortened run he had used three days earlier in Canberra, took five for 41, a disproportionate reward for sixteen overs at medium pace with faster variations. The loss of Boon in Small's third over did nothing for Australia's confidence. But it was hard to disassociate the way they set about their innings from a well-publicised comment by Border, in a pre-match interview, that to revive their chance of winning back the Ashes, Australia needed to play boldly.

On quite a lively pitch, with a stronger growth of grass than for some years following a transplant of couch grass from a local golf course, Kingston Heath, Australia should have been content to let runs come. Jack Lyons's last Test pitch as head curator was never a straightforward one to bat on, yielding extra and variable bounce for the faster bowlers when they bent their backs, but the home side should have known from experience that at Melbourne, with its huge, slow outfield, a first-innings total of 250 would have given them at least an even chance. Marsh, for one, looked to lose his wicket through eagerness to follow the assumed instructions of his captain. Anything but a regular player of the hook – in some 30 hours' batting against England on the tour, he had produced no more than half a dozen – he attempted to hook a rising ball from Botham which pitched well outside off stump; Richards took the first of five catches in the innings with a gymnastic upward leap.

That wicket made the score 44 for two, and when, 40 minutes later, Richards took a second fine catch to dismiss Border, diving to his left, Australia were in trouble. Against the advice of Border and R. B. Simpson, Australia's cricket manager, the selectors had omitted Ritchie, a specialist batsman, in favour of an all-rounder, thought to be Matthews, to give the side an extra option in the field. In practice, with Matthews not called upon to bowl in an England innings lasting 120 overs, the decision served only to weaken their batting. McDermott, who in effect came in for Ritchie, and Zoehrer, who reclaimed his place from Dyer, were the changes from the team that drew at Adelaide.

Jones, who hit Emburey out of the attack with two lofted leg-side fours, was the one batsman to pass 20. He batted 154 minutes, hitting one glorious on-drive off DeFreitas, before being caught at mid-off off the leading edge, attempting to tuck Small to leg. A wonderful running catch by Richards, who sprinted 30 yards to square leg to take a mis-hit hook by McDermott, hastened Australia's downfall.

It was a lamentable piece of batting which was duly reflected in a second-day attendance more than 20,000 down on the 58,203 of Boxing Day. England had set themselves to bat for two days. But a mixture of over-attacking batting, and Australia's best bowling and fielding of the series – Matthews was outstanding in the field – saw them out for 349 at stumps, despite at one time being 163 for one through a second-wicket stand of 105 by Broad and Gatting. Broad was the one batsman who played the bowling strictly on its merits, while making due allowance for the foibles of the pitch. He demonstrated the right combination of patience and sound method to produce a lengthy innings, showing the bowlers the full face of the bat and waiting for the ball to drive. His 112 took 328 minutes, came off 255 balls, and included just nine fours. Reid was again the best Australian bowler, although Sleep played a part in fanning the impatience of the batsmen by bowling most of his overs round the wicket into the rough outside leg stump.

Australia, starting their second innings on the third morning with a deficit of 208, were never on course for the score of 450 that would have made a match of it. Border's dismissal at

113 after 85 minutes' resistance, superbly caught by Emburey at third slip after driving at a wideish ball from Small, wrecked their chances. Not until Marsh was run out by Edmonds in the covers, however, did England have prospects of an innings win. Unsettled by being given the benefit of the doubt by umpire French earlier that over, when a ball from Emburey bounced from his gloves to Athey at short leg, Marsh was sent back by Waugh after embarking on a risky single and never had a hope. He had batted determinedly for 213 minutes. On his departure Australia lost their will to battle on. The last six wickets fell for 41 in 80 minutes to the spin of Emburey and Edmonds; just 40 minutes after tea the game was over, leaving the Australian Board to rue attendance figures that were 125,000 down on those of 1982-83.

Man of the Match: G. C. Small.   *Attendance:* 107,817.

Close of play: First day, England 95-1 (B. C. Broad 56*, M. W. Gatting 8*); Second day, England 349.

Australia

G. R. Marsh c Richards b Botham	17	– (2) run out	60
D. C. Boon c Botham b Small	7	– (1) c Gatting b Small	8
D. M. Jones c Gower b Small	59	– c Gatting b DeFreitas	21
*A. R. Border c Richards b Botham	15	– c Emburey b Small	34
S. R. Waugh c Botham b Small	10	– b Edmonds	49
G. R. J. Matthews c Botham b Small	14	– b Emburey	0
P. R. Sleep c Richards b Small	0	– run out	6
†T. J. Zoehrer b Botham	5	– c Athey b Edmonds	1
C. J. McDermott c Richards b Botham	0	– b Emburey	1
M. G. Hughes c Richards b Botham	2	– c Small b Edmonds	8
B. A. Reid not out	2	– not out	0
B 1, l-b 1, w 1, n-b 7	10	L-b 3, w 1, n-b 2	6

1/16 (2) 2/44 (1) 3/80 (4) 4/108 (5)   141   1/13 (1) 2/48 (3) 3/113 (4)   194
5/118 (3) 6/118 (7) 7/129 (8)   4/153 (2) 5/153 (6) 6/175 (7)
8/133 (9) 9/137 (10) 10/141 (6)   7/180 (8) 8/185 (5)
                                                     9/189 (9) 10/194 (10)

Bowling: *First Innings*—Small 22.4-7-48-5; DeFreitas 11-1-30-0; Emburey 4-0-16-0; Botham 16-4-41-5; Gatting 1-0-4-0. *Second Innings*—DeFreitas 12-1-44-1; Small 15-3-40-2; Botham 7-1-19-0; Edmonds 19.4-5-45-3; Emburey 20-5-43-2.

England

B. C. Broad c Zoehrer b Hughes	112	J. E. Emburey c and b McDermott 22
C. W. J. Athey lbw b Reid	21	P. H. Edmonds lbw b McDermott 19
*M. W. Gatting c Hughes b Reid	40	G. C. Small not out 21
A. J. Lamb c Zoehrer b Reid	43	
D. I. Gower c Matthews b Sleep	7	B 6, l-b 7, w 1, n-b 11 25
I. T. Botham c Zoehrer b McDermott	29	
†C. J. Richards c Marsh b Reid	3	1/58 (2) 2/163 (3) 3/198 (1) 349
P. A. J. DeFreitas c Matthews		4/219 (5) 5/251 (4) 6/273 (6) 7/277 (7)
b McDermott	7	8/289 (8) 9/319 (9) 10/349 (10)

Bowling: McDermott 26.5-4-83-4; Hughes 30-3-94-1; Reid 28-5-78-4; Waugh 8-4-16-0; Sleep 28-4-65-1.

Umpires: A. R. Crafter and R. A. French.

BENSON AND HEDGES CHALLENGE

At Perth, December 30–January 7. England's four matches in this limited-overs tournament may be found in that section.

AUSTRALIA v ENGLAND

Fifth Test Match

At Sydney, January 10, 11, 12, 14, 15. Australia won by 55 runs. When, with one over left, Sleep bowled Emburey to complete Australia's first Test win in more than a year, it was an unexpected as well as welcome victory. Indeed, at the start of the final twenty overs England appeared to have the better chance. Recovering from the loss of four wickets in eight overs, among them Botham first ball to Taylor in his maiden Test, they had been carried to within 90 runs of their target (320) by the pugnacity of Gatting with determined help from Richards in a stand of 131, a record for England's sixth wicket on the ground. Only once before, in 633 Tests, had England scored more than 300 runs to win – at Melbourne in 1928-29 when Hobbs and Sutcliffe shared one of their most celebrated partnerships, 105 on a rain-affected pitch. However, at 230 for five, with Australia faltering, the odds had swung their way. Even when Gatting was caught and bowled by Waugh, 4 short of his hundred and with only another 3 on England's total, it was not until Sleep dismissed Richards and Edmonds with successive balls in the eleventh over of the final twenty that Australia scented victory.

Small defended resolutely through seven overs until, with only fourteen balls remaining, Border at first slip, one of eight men round the bat, claimed a sharp, low catch off Reid. Then, with 12,684 spectators in a state of high excitement, Sleep penetrated Emburey's defence with a "grubber" to give Australia their first win in fifteen Tests. Of Sleep's five for 72, his best figures in a Test, three were taken in his last five overs as England, through neither carelessness nor lack of fight, lost five for 31 in 70 tense minutes.

If their leg-spinner delivered Australia's *coup de grâce*, however, there was no question that their hero was the 30-year-old Taylor, a sandy-haired off-spinner from Sydney's Northern District club who had played only six first-class matches in his life, and only one that season, restricted to few appearances for New South Wales by their three Test spinners. So little was known about him that when Australia announced a twelve containing only one opening batsman, Marsh, there was speculation in some quarters that he owed selection to an error in transmission, confusing him with M. A. Taylor, a dour left-handed opener who had been making runs for New South Wales.

There was no substance to the allegations, and in a saga that developed along the lines of a story in *Boy's Own*, the unassuming Taylor gloriously vindicated the selectors' judgement, not to say courage, with a performance of such merit that he was named player of the match. Figures of six for 78 in England's first innings and two for 76 in the second revealed him as a thoughtful bowler with more than average powers of spin. But well as he did in his specialist department, it was his batting – angular, left-handed and blessed with common sense – that made possible Australia's win. Going in at No. 9, he batted for 244 minutes in both innings while 142 runs were scored, enabling Jones to add 111 with his last three partners in the first innings and sharing a stand of 98 with Waugh in the second when Australia's needs were even greater. Taylor, Ritchie and Wellham replaced Matthews (twelfth man), Boon and McDermott, while Dilley, fit again, returned for England at DeFreitas's expense.

Jones, whose 184 not out (540 minutes, 420 balls, one six, twelve fours) was his first Test hundred on home soil, was Australia's other match-winner in a game that produced more runs on every day than the bowlers should have allowed on a pitch which helped spin as well as seam. Faulty umpiring contributed to that, Jones, when 5, being the fortunate recipient of a benefit-of-doubt decision when Richards dived to take a leg-glance off Gower, when 62, surviving an lbw appeal when Taylor, over the wicket, got through a back-foot defensive stroke with a straight ball which kept low. Lack of confidence appeared to be at the root of the umpires' difficulties. It was to Jones's credit that he made the most of his luck while Gower failed to, driving a half-volley to extra-cover early on the following morning.

That England trailed by no more than 68 on first innings, bowled Australia out for 251 in their second, and came within a whisker of saving the match after Sleep's removal of Richards and Edmonds was due in large measure to Emburey, who with the ball and bat was in the thick of things for more than fourteen hours of the 30. Handicapped by a strained groin for most of his 210-minute 69, he went on to take seven for 78, his best figures in Test cricket, in Australia's second innings and finally logged another 68 minutes' batting in the last session. Like Gatting, Small and Richards, he deserved better than to finish on the losing side.

Man of the Match: P. L. Taylor.   *Attendance*: 93,429.
Man of the Series: B. C. Broad.

Close of play: First day, Australia 236-7 (D. M. Jones 119*, P. L. Taylor 0*); Second day, England 132-5 (D. I. Gower 62*, C. J. Richards 8*); Third day, Australia 74-2 (D. M. Jones 6*, A. R. Border 38*); Fourth day, England 39-1 (C. W. J. Athey 11*, D. I. Gower 7*).

Australia

G. R. Marsh c Gatting b Small	24	– (2) c Emburey b Dilley	14
G. M. Ritchie lbw b Dilley	6	– (1) c Botham b Edmonds	13
D. M. Jones not out	184	– c Richards b Emburey	30
*A. R. Border c Botham b Edmonds	34	– b Edmonds	49
D. M. Wellham c Richards b Small	17	– c Lamb b Emburey	1
S. R. Waugh c Richards b Small	0	– c Athey b Emburey	73
P. R. Sleep c Richards b Small	9	– c Lamb b Emburey	10
†T. J. Zoehrer c Gatting b Small	12	– lbw b Emburey	1
P. L. Taylor c Emburey b Edmonds	11	– c Lamb b Emburey	42
M. G. Hughes c Botham b Edmonds	16	– b Emburey	5
B. A. Reid b Dilley	4	– not out	1
B 12, l-b 4, w 2, n-b 8	26	B 5, l-b 7	12

1/8 (2) 2/58 (1) 3/149 (4) 4/184 (5) 343 1/29 (2) 2/31 (1) 3/106 (4) 251
5/184 (6) 6/200 (7) 7/232 (8) 4/110 (3) 5/115 (5) 6/141 (7)
8/271 (9) 9/338 (10) 10/343 (11) 7/145 (8) 8/243 (6) 9/248 (9)
 10/251 (10)

Bowling: *First Innings*—Dilley 23.5-5-67-2; Small 33-11-75-5; Botham 23-10-42-0; Emburey 30-4-62-0; Edmonds 34-5-79-3; Gatting 1-0-2-0. *Second Innings*—Dilley 15-4-48-1; Small 8-2-17-0; Edmonds 43-16-79-2; Emburey 46-15-78-7; Botham 3-0-17-0; Gatting 2-2-0-0.

England

B. C. Broad lbw b Hughes	6	– c and b Sleep	17
C. W. J. Athey c Zoehrer b Hughes	5	– b Sleep	31
*M. W. Gatting lbw b Reid	0	– (5) c and b Waugh	96
A. J. Lamb c Zoehrer b Taylor	24	– c Waugh b Taylor	3
D. I. Gower c Wellham b Taylor	72	– (3) c Marsh b Border	37
I. T. Botham c Marsh b Taylor	16	– c Wellham b Taylor	0
†C. J. Richards c Wellham b Reid	46	– b Sleep	38
J. E. Emburey b Taylor	69	– b Sleep	22
P. H. Edmonds c Marsh b Taylor	3	– lbw b Sleep	0
G. C. Small b Taylor	14	– c Border b Reid	0
G. R. Dilley not out	4	– not out	2
B 9, l-b 3, w 2, n-b 2	16	B 8, l-b 6, w 1, n-b 3	18

1/16 (2) 2/17 (3) 3/17 (1) 4/89 (4) 275 1/24 (1) 2/91 (3) 3/91 (2) 264
5/119 (6) 6/142 (5) 7/213 (7) 4/102 (4) 5/102 (6) 6/233 (5)
8/219 (9) 9/270 (10) 10/275 (8) 7/257 (7) 8/257 (9) 9/262 (10)
 10/264 (8)

Bowling: *First Innings*—Hughes 16-3-58-2; Reid 25-7-74-2; Waugh 6-4-6-0; Taylor 26-7-78-6; Sleep 21-6-47-0. *Second Innings*—Hughes 12-3-32-0; Reid 19-8-32-1; Sleep 35-14-72-5; Taylor 29-10-76-2; Border 13-6-25-1; Waugh 6-2-13-1.

Umpires: P. J. McConnell and S. G. Randell.

BENSON AND HEDGES WORLD SERIES CUP

January 17–February 11. England's ten matches in this limited-overs competition may be found in that section.

THE AUSTRALIANS IN INDIA, 1986-87

By R. MOHAN

The eleventh Test series between Australia and India earned its place in posterity when the first of the three matches, at the Chidambaram Stadium, Chepauk in Madras concluded excitingly in the second tie in Test cricket. It had taken almost 84 years and 498 Tests to produce the first tie, between Australia and West Indies at Brisbane in December 1960; the second came only 26 years later, but there have been so many Test matches of late that this was the 554th Test since that first historic finish at the 'Gabba.

The second tie was born of a quite different dramatic structure from the first, the prospect of a thrilling finish not being sprung on the crowd until the final day. At the 'Gabba, the teams had been evenly balanced and the scores suggest an intense drama which developed over the five days. At Chepauk, India were outplayed on the first three days and only just managed to avoid the follow-on before coming back strongly to level the scores. Allan Border's declaration at the overnight score had left India a target of 348 at exactly 4 runs an over on a wicket that remained hard. It was a practical rather than a sporting declaration, and the climax was shaped by India's bold bid to snatch victory in the limited-overs manner of a charge launched on the foundation provided by the first three men.

Apart from the fascination of such a rare result in five-day cricket, there was little of note in the series. A number of young Australian players seemed to benefit from the experience of playing in India, in particular Dean Jones, whose talents revealed a batsman of high class. That he possessed a temperament and the courage for Test cricket became apparent during his double-hundred in the First Test, in which David Boon and Border also scored hundreds. Boon and Geoff Marsh were efficient opening batsmen, while Greg Matthews thrived on the call to bowl long spells. An average of 29.07 is a reflection not so much of his ability as an off-spin bowler as of the slow easy-paced pitches which flattered the batsmen and deflated all the bowlers. These were the primary culprits in a series which produced little positive cricket in terms of attaining a victory, although the weather did not help by washing out the first three days of the Second Test. In the Third, all Australia sought was an honourable draw and this was achieved.

Kapil Dev went without a wicket in a series for the first time, and this certainly dented India's ambition of sustaining the winning vein struck several months earlier in England. Border, on the other hand, had cause to feel satisfied with the way the tour panned out for his young and inexperienced side, even though there was no escaping the conclusion that his side were still heavily reliant on him when they were under pressure. Neither captain, however, should have drawn any satisfaction from a series which saw relations on the field deteriorate from day to day. There were far too many incidents of gamesmanship, with the Indians reacting to the pattern of behaviour set by the visitors.

India won the limited-overs internationals 3-2, making sure of the series by winning successively at Delhi and Ahmedabad after the third match had been stopped by rain. Restricted to a low total in the Ahmedabad game, they struck back with a bowling and fielding performance reminiscent of that which had achieved many limited-overs triumphs. As many as eighteen umpires officiated in the three Tests and six one-day internationals, but the Australians' early misgivings over the standard of umpiring proved groundless. It was good to hear Border sing the Indian umpires' praises before embarking on the homeward journey and the Ashes series for which this tour was the preparation.

AUSTRALIAN TOUR RESULTS

Test matches – Played 3: Tied 1, Drawn 2.
First-class matches – Played 7: Tied 1, Drawn 6.
Tie – India.
Draws – India (2), Bombay, Delhi, Indian Board President's XI, Indian Under-25 XI.
Non first-class matches – Played 6: Won 2, Lost 3, No result 1. *Wins* – India (2). *Losses* – India (3). *No result* – India.

TEST MATCH AVERAGES

INDIA – BATTING

	T	I	NO	R	HI	100s	Avge
Kapil Dev	3	2	0	120	119	1	60.00
S. M. Gavaskar ...	3	4	0	205	103	1	51.25
C. S. Pandit	2	3	1	100	39	0	50.00
K. Srikkanth	3	4	0	142	53	0	35.50
M. Azharuddin	3	4	0	126	50	0	31.50
M. Amarnath	3	3	0	87	51	0	29.00
Chetan Sharma	2	2	0	53	30	0	26.50
N. S. Yadav	3	2	0	27	19	0	13.50
K. S. More	2	3	0	19	15	0	6.33

Played in three Tests: Maninder Singh 0*, 0; R. J. Shastri 62, 48*, 121*. Played in two Tests: D. B. Vengsarkar 22*, 164*. Played in one Test: R. R. Kulkarni did not bat.

* Signifies not out.

BOWLING

	O	M	R	W	BB	Avge
N. S. Yadav	136.3	25	359	8	4-84	44.87
R. J. Shastri	154.4	38	383	7	2-44	54.71
Maninder Singh	130	30	352	5	3-60	70.40

Also bowled: Chetan Sharma 30-2-123-2; Kapil Dev 45-12-124-0; R. R. Kulkarni 29-2-114-3; K. Srikkanth 6-0-19-0.

AUSTRALIA – BATTING

	T	I	NO	R	HI	100s	Avge
D. M. Jones	3	5	1	371	210	1	92.75
A. R. Border	3	4	1	245	106	1	81.66
D. C. Boon	3	5	0	325	122	1	65.00
G. R. J. Matthews	3	3	1	91	44	0	45.50
G. R. Marsh	3	5	0	165	101	1	33.00
G. M. Ritchie	3	3	0	72	31	0	24.00

Played in three Tests: R. J. Bright 30, 8; S. R. Waugh 12*, 2*, 39*, 6; T. J. Zoehrer 52*, 21.
Played in two Tests: D. R. Gilbert 1; B. A. Reid 2*; C. J. McDermott did not bat.

* Signifies not out.

BOWLING

	O	M	R	W	BB	Avge
G. R. J. Matthews	120.1	18	407	14	5-103	29.07
R. J. Bright	86	12	291	8	5-94	36.37

Also bowled: T. J. Boon 2-1-5-0; A. R. Border 13-3-41-0; D. R. Gilbert 35-4-119-1; D. M. Jones 1-1-0-0; C. J. McDermott 25-3-110-0; B. A. Reid 60-11-222-1; S. R. Waugh 35-5-130-2.

AUSTRALIAN AVERAGES – FIRST-CLASS MATCHES

BATTING

	M	I	NO	R	HI	100s	Avge
D. R. Gilbert	5	4	2	152	117	1	76.00
G. C. Dyer	3	3	0	208	106	1	69.33
D. C. Boon	6	8	1	476	122	1	68.00
A. R. Border	5	6	1	320	106	1	64.00
S. R. Waugh	6	7	3	227	82	0	56.75
D. M. Jones	7	9	1	438	210	1	54.75
G. R. J. Matthews	6	6	1	263	99	0	52.60
G. M. Ritchie	6	6	0	291	124	1	48.50
G. R. Marsh	6	8	0	328	139	2	41.00
T. J. Zoehrer	5	4	1	123	52*	0	41.00
M. R. J. Veletta	3	4	1	76	29	0	25.33
C. J. McDermott	5	3	0	62	23	0	20.66
R. J. Bright	7	6	1	66	30	0	13.20

Played in five matches: B. A. Reid 2*, 1*, 12*, 3. Played in two matches: S. P. Davis 3*, 0*.

* Signifies not out.

BOWLING

	O	M	R	W	BB	Avge
G. R. J. Matthews	179	29	601	20	5-103	30.05
D. R. Gilbert	107	23	367	11	4-92	33.36
S. P. Davis	48.4	12	175	5	3-52	35.00
S. R. Waugh	97	15	367	10	4-71	36.70
R. J. Bright	174.5	30	564	13	5-94	43.38
C. J. McDermott	99	13	355	7	3-85	50.71
B. A. Reid	116	18	394	7	2-34	56.28

Also bowled: A. R. Border 13-3-41-0; D. C. Boon 2-1-5-0; D. M. Jones 10-2-35-2; T. J. Zoehrer 1-0-8-0.

FIELDING

10 – T. J. Zoehrer (8 ct, 2 st); 7 – G. M. Ritchie; 4 – D. C. Boon, A. R. Border, G. R. Marsh, S. R. Waugh; 3 – R. J. Bright, G. C. Dyer, M. R. J. Veletta; 2 – D. M. Jones, C. J. McDermott, substitute (M. R. J. Veletta); 1 – S. P. Davis, G. R. J. Matthews.

INDIAN BOARD PRESIDENT'S XI v AUSTRALIANS

At Bangalore, August 30, 31, September 1. Drawn. Davis's use of the new ball from an altered run-up ensured that there would be some competitive interest in the match, and it needed Shastri and Viswanath, the former Test wicket-keeper, to rescue their side from 79 for five with a 130-run stand. Marsh and Boon resumed their partnership for Australia with a century opening stand, Marsh going on to his own hundred, and on the final day there was a prospect of an Australian victory until Viswanath masterminded another rearguard action. Rain at tea brought about an early finish. Shastri turned in a competent all-round performance, following his first-innings 63 with six wickets.

Close of play: First day, Australians 29-0; Second day, Australians 340-9.

Indian Board President's XI

L. S. Rajput c Zoehrer b Reid	15	– c Zoehrer b Davis	3
R. Lamba c Marsh b Davis	24	– c Marsh b Gilbert	44
M. Azharuddin lbw b Davis	4	– (4) c Zoehrer b Matthews	21
*M. D. Gunjal c and b Davis	3	– (5) c Boon b Jones	9
R. J. Shastri run out	63		
R. D. Kanwilkar c Border b Reid	12	– (3) b Gilbert	34
†S. Viswanath st Zoehrer b Matthews	70	– (6) not out	40
L. Sivaramakrishnan not out	11	– (7) not out	25
Gopal Sharma b Matthews	6		
P. Kasliwal b Matthews	4		
P. Sunderam st Zoehrer b Matthews	3		
B 10, l-b 7, w 3, n-b 4	24	B 9, l-b 3, n-b 2	14

1/37 2/42 3/51 4/60 5/79   239   1/16 2/85 3/94   (5 wkts) 190
6/209 7/211 8/221 9/233   4/115 5/129

Bowling: *First Innings*—Reid 14–1–56–2; Davis 17–3–52–3; Gilbert 12–4–45–0; Bright 18–3–55–0; Matthews 10.5–4–14–4. *Second Innings*—Reid 4–0–21–0; Davis 7–2–21–1; Bright 14–3–61–0; Gilbert 5–2–17–2; Matthews 10–3–40–1; Jones 5–0–18–1.

Australians

D. C. Boon c Kasliwal b Shastri	75	D. R. Gilbert not out	18
G. R. Marsh c and b Shastri	139	B. A. Reid b Shastri	3
D. M. Jones lbw b Shastri	20	S. P. Davis not out	0
*A. R. Border c Viswanath b Shastri	0	B 15, l-b 3, n-b 5	23
G. M. Ritchie c sub b Gopal	0		
G. R. J. Matthews c Shastri b Gopal	29	1/116 2/160 3/160	(9 wkts dec.) 340
†T. J. Zoehrer run out	16	4/161 5/251 6/275	
R. J. Bright st Viswanath b Shastri	17	7/300 8/317 9/339	

Bowling: Kasliwal 7–2–26–0; Sunderam 12–0–72–0; Gopal 38–7–96–2; Shastri 37–14–75–6; Sivaramakrishnan 15–1–53–0.

Umpires: P. D. Reporter and V. Vikramraju.

BOMBAY v AUSTRALIANS

At Gwalior, September 3, 4, 5. Drawn. This match, against the Irani Cup champions, Bombay, was added to the itinerary to fill several extra days on the tour, caused by the Australians' arriving in India earlier than originally anticipated. The teams agreed to limit their first innings to 110 overs so that the tourists could take the early afternoon flight to New Delhi on the third day. With Marsh resting, Ritchie used the opportunity of opening on a typical featherbed wicket to make a stroke-filled 124 from 125 balls and Border, Waugh and Matthews were also among the runs against a listless attack. Matthews hit 72 of his 99 runs in boundaries; two sixes and fifteen fours. Patil, who made 64, announced his retirement from first-class cricket immediately after his innings.

Close of play: First day, Australians 384-4; Second day, Bombay 181-5.

Australians

G. M. Ritchie c Kasliwal b Mokashi	124		
M. R. J. Veletta st Pandit b Mokashi	29	– not out	9
D. M. Jones lbw b Kasliwal	29		
*A. R. Border b Mokashi	75		
S. R. Waugh c Patil b Kasliwal	82		
G. R. J. Matthews c Kulkarni b Kasliwal	99		
†G. C. Dyer c and b Mokashi	41		
C. J. McDermott b Hattangadi b Mokashi	23		
R. J. Bright not out	2		
B. A. Reid not out	1		
D. C. Boon (did not bat)		– (1) not out	58
B 2, l-b 6, n-b 12	20	B 4, l-b 7, n-b 1	12

1/113 2/170 3/199 4/300　　　　　　　　(8 wkts) 525　　　　　　(no wkt) 79
5/424 6/477 7/521 8/523

Bowling: *First Innings*—Kulkarni 20-1-114-0; Kasliwal 30-1-143-3; Patil 5-0-24-0; Mokashi 32-4-156-5; Shastri 6-1-19-0; Rajput 17-3-61-0. *Second Innings*—Kasliwal 3-0-21-0; Sippy 5-0-12-0; Kulkarni 5-0-24-0; Mokashi 4-0-11-0.

Bombay

L. S. Rajput c Border b Waugh	25	R. R. Kulkarni c Veletta b Matthews	23
S. S. Hattangadi b McDermott	63	P. Kasliwal c Waugh b Bright	7
A. Sippy c Bright b McDermott	11	K. D. Mokashi not out	0
D. B. Vengsarkar lbw b McDermott	0	L-b 7, n-b 13	20
S. M. Gavaskar lbw b Bright	28		
†C. S. Pandit c Dyer b Reid	101	1/48 2/89 3/89	(9 wkts dec.) 353
S. M. Patil b Reid	64	4/131 5/153 6/290	
*R. J. Shastri retired hurt	11	7/341 8/353 9/353	

Bowling: McDermott 22-3-85-3; Reid 22-4-61-2; Waugh 10-0-70-1; Matthews 21-2-73-1; Bright 18.5-5-42-2; Jones 2-0-15-0.

Umpires: R. B. Gupta and P. G. Pandit.

†INDIA v AUSTRALIA

First One-day International

At Jaipur, September 7. India won by seven wickets with six overs to spare. A one-day international record first-wicket partnership of 212 between Boon and Marsh notwithstanding, the Australians managed only 250 and Srikkanth, with his maiden one-day international hundred, fired the Indian win. Marsh used up 140 balls for his hundred, compared with Boon's from

115 balls, and this left no time for the customary slog in the final stages. Moreover, India, after winning the toss, strategically slowed the over-rate so that they bowled only 47 overs, there being no penalty for bowling fewer than the stipulated 50 in the allotted time. Gavaskar, reinstated in the side after a public outcry over his omission, took a secondary role in the opening stand of 86, for there was no holding Srikkanth. He raced to 102 off 105 balls and his stand of 102 with Lamba came off 89 balls.

Man of the Match: K. Srikkanth.

Australia

G. R. Marsh run out	104	G. M. Ritchie not out		7
D. C. Boon c Shastri b Azharuddin	111	B 1, l-b 3, w 1, n-b 3		8
D. M. Jones not out	17			
*A. R. Border run out	3	1/212 2/225 3/228	(3 wkts, 47 overs)	250

S. R. Waugh, G. R. J. Matthews, †T. J. Zoehrer, C. J. McDermott, S. P. Davis and B. A. Reid did not bat.

Bowling: Kapil Dev 9-0-48-0; Binny 7-1-41-0; Shastri 10-1-31-0; Chetan 4-0-31-0; Maninder 10-0-42-0; Azharuddin 7-0-53-1.

India

K. Srikkanth c Jones b Reid	102	*Kapil Dev not out		26
S. M. Gavaskar run out	26	B 1, l-b 11, w 1, n-b 2		15
R. Lamba c Border b Matthews	64			
D. B. Vengsarkar not out	18	1/86 2/188 3/210	(3 wkts, 41 overs)	251

M. Azharuddin, R. M. H. Binny, †C. S. Pandit, R. J. Shastri, Chetan Sharma and Maninder Singh did not bat.

Bowling: McDermott 10-0-75-0; Davis 7-0-48-0; Reid 8-1-27-1; Waugh 7-0-42-0; Matthews 9-0-47-1.

Umpires: S. Banerjee and B. Nagaraja Rao.

†INDIA v AUSTRALIA

Second One-day International

At Srinagar, September 9. Australia won by three wickets. The Australians returned the compliment by inserting India and, by slowing the over-rate, bowling only 47 overs. India were coasting comfortably until Gavaskar was run out in the 25th over, and the attempts of Shastri and Pandit to make up for Azharuddin's slowness were not wholly successful. Vengsarkar had retired hurt because of back trouble. Kapil Dev and Binny made inroads on a wicket that held something for the seamers, but competent batting by Border swung the match Australia's way.

Man of the Match: A. R. Border.

India

K. Srikkanth c Zoehrer b Matthews	24	Chetan Sharma b Waugh		17
S. M. Gavaskar run out	52	R. M. H. Binny not out		11
R. Lamba c Zoehrer b Davis	1	Maninder Singh not out		2
D. B. Vengsarkar retired hurt	12	L-b 5, w 3, n-b 2		10
M. Azharuddin c Marsh b Waugh	16			
R. J. Shastri run out	37	1/50 2/51 3/108	(8 wkts, 47 overs)	222
†C. S. Pandit b Reid	24	4/123 5/161 6/192		
*Kapil Dev c Marsh b Davis	16	7/192 8/216		

Bowling: McDermott 9-1-37-0; Davis 10-1-51-2; Matthews 9-0-52-1; Reid 10-2-37-2; Waugh 9-0-40-2.

Australia

D. C. Boon c Lamba b Kapil Dev	 0	†T. J. Zoehrer c and b Kapil Dev	.....	1
G. R. Marsh c Pandit b Binny	 17	C. J. McDermott not out	......	7
D. M. Jones c Pandit b Binny	 12	B 1, l-b 12, w 1, n-b 6	....	20
*A. R. Border not out	 90			
G. M. Ritchie st Pandit b Shastri	 28	1/0 2/19 3/39	(7 wkts, 46 overs)	226
G. R. J. Matthews run out	 31	4/102 5/172		
S. R. Waugh st Pandit b Shastri	 20	6/213 7/216		

B. A. Reid and S. P. Davis did not bat.

Bowling: Kapil Dev 9-2-37-2; Binny 8-0-25-2; Chetan 9-0-41-0; Shastri 10-0-60-2; Maninder Singh 10-0-50-0.

Umpires: S. B. Kulkarni and R. S. Rathore.

INDIAN UNDER-25 XI v AUSTRALIANS

At Chandigarh, September 12, 13, 14. Drawn. An unremarkable match was played amidst tight security in the capital of Punjab and Haryana. Sidhu, a Test discard, and Kalyani, a young batsman from Maharashtra, were the only ones to make use of a good batting wicket after Viswanath had won the toss, while among the Australians, only Ritchie and Dyer, the reserve wicket-keeper, made half-centuries. The Under-25 XI second innings was even less noteworthy than the first.

Close of play: First day, Indian Under-25 XI 232; Second day, Australians 308-9.

Indian Under-25 XI

R. Poonawala c Dyer b McDermott	 14	– c Ritchie b Gilbert	....	21
N. S. Sidhu c Dyer b Gilbert	 63	– lbw b McDermott	....	36
C. Saldanha b Gilbert	 21	– c Veletta b Waugh	....	19
S. Kalyani not out	 62	– c Boon b Waugh	....	24
A. Sharma lbw b Waugh	 10	– c Boon b McDermott	....	18
S. Mudkavi lbw b Bright	 13	– lbw b Waugh	....	21
*†S. Viswanath c Ritchie b Waugh	 19	– lbw b Jones	....	44
L. Sivaramakrishnan b Waugh	 0	– c Ritchie b Waugh	....	0
Azim Khan b Bright	 6	– not out	....	60
B. Arun lbw b Gilbert	 2	– not out	....	0
R. P. Singh c Ritchie b Davis	 4			
B 2, l-b 5, w 1, n-b 10	 18	B 1, l-b 5, w 1, n-b 3	....	10

1/21 2/103 3/110 4/128 5/154   232   1/52 2/68 3/104   (8 wkts) 253
6/206 7/206 8/215 9/223   4/111 5/136 6/149
                                7/149 8/253

Bowling: *First Innings*—McDermott 6-1-13-1; Davis 18.4-6-57-1; Gilbert 17-5-51-3; Waugh 19-5-46-3; Bright 18-2-58-2. *Second Innings*—McDermott 22-4-59-2; Davis 6-1-45-0; Gilbert 14-3-43-1; Waugh 21-5-71-4; Bright 8-1-29-0; Jones 1-1-0-1.

Australians

G. R. Marsh lbw b Singh	 19	C. J. McDermott b Mudkavi	....	19
*D. C. Boon c and b Singh	 18	D. R. Gilbert not out	....	16
M. R. J. Veletta c Viswanath b Arun	.. 25	S. P. Davis not out	....	3
D. M. Jones b Azim	 13			
G. M. Ritchie b Sharma	 95	B 4, l-b 12, n-b 12	....	28
S. R. Waugh b Arun	 4			
†G. C. Dyer c Poonawala b Sharma	... 61	1/41 2/42 3/69	(9 wkts dec.)	308
R. J. Bright c Singh		4/107 5/114 6/215		
b Sivaramakrishnan .	7	7/225 8/260 9/294		

Bowling: Singh 14-1-50-2; Arun 13-1-64-2; Sivaramakrishnan 16-1-87-1; Azim 18-4-46-1; Sharma 9-3-21-2; Mudkavi 9-2-24-1.

Umpires: D. N. Dotiwala and V. K. Ramaswamy.

INDIA v AUSTRALIA

First Test Match

At Madras, September 18, 19, 20, 21, 22. Tied. On a hot and humid Monday, one of the most memorable Test match finishes was witnessed by some 30,000 spectators at Chepauk. For the second time in 1,052 Tests, the result was a tie, and coincidentally Australia had been involved each time. Yet there had been little hint of such a climax on the first four days; indeed, as India were being outplayed on the first three days, the thoughts of some Australians were possibly inclined to an innings victory. Only an inspired century against the odds by the Indian captain, Kapil Dev, precluded the possibility of India having to follow on after Australia had amassed their highest total in India – 574 in 742 minutes.

Border won the toss and Boon set the tone for positive Australian batting with his third Test hundred (331 minutes, 21 fours); all scored against India. On the second day, Jones cemented the solid start, first reaching his maiden Test hundred and then extending it to Australia's first double-hundred in a Test in India. Batting in all for 8 hours 23 minutes, facing 330 balls and hitting two sixes and 27 fours, Jones had to battle against the difficult weather conditions and overcome bouts of nausea and leg cramps. Yet he led the way in the partnership of 178 with Border, a record for Australia's fourth wicket against India. The Australian captain was dropped before scoring and twice more before reaching his nineteenth Test century in a little under four and a quarter hours.

Australia batted into the third day for 37 minutes; thereafter the Indians struggled against the workmanlike spin of Matthews and Bright. Srikkanth's aggressive 53 off 65 balls and a more chancy 50 off 59 balls by Azharuddin were entertaining but out of context, and by the close India still required 105 to make Australia bat again. Kapil Dev made sure they would with a free-flowing hundred off 109 balls. There were 21 fours in his 119, with 44 runs of his second fifty coming from boundaries. Matthews finished with five wickets in an innings for the first time.

Australia mustered 170 for five in the 49 overs available to them on the fourth day and Border declared first thing on the final morning, setting India 348 to win in a minimum of 87 overs. An opening stand of 55 announced what was assumed to be India's intention of a draw, but a century stand between Gavaskar, playing in his 100th consecutive Test match, and Amarnath pointed to different possibilities. When India went to tea at 190 for two, a last-session chase (158 off 30 overs) against an Australian side reduced to defence was on the cards, and when the final twenty overs began, India were suitably placed with 118 needed and seven wickets in hand. However, at 251 Gavaskar mistimed a cover drive after 259 minutes' batting, and Kapil Dev, having promoted himself in the order, went 2 runs later. Azharuddin unsuccessfully tried to charge Bright, but Shastri took control with a clever mixture of outright offence and the safe picking of runs.

With 18 needed off the last 30 balls, the match seemed to be India's, but when Chetan Sharma, caught on the boundary, and More were dismissed in one over by Bright, a third possible result – an Australian victory – was sighted for the first time that day. Yadav, who had struck Matthews for six to take India within 7 runs of victory, was next out, bowled off his pads by Bright, leaving India 344 for nine with eight balls remaining. Maninder Singh defended the last two balls from Bright, which gave Shastri the strike for the last over, from Matthews. He blocked the first ball and, scenting victory off the second, hit a shade too eagerly: the ball went in front of deep square leg off a thick inside edge and a misfield enabled 2 runs to be taken safely. The next ball he placed calmly towards mid-wicket for the single which eliminated the possibility of an Australian win. Maninder defended the fourth ball, with some difficulty, and at 5.18 p.m. was leg-before to Matthews's penultimate delivery. The Australians were jubilant, none more so than a tiring Matthews, who had been bowling since the ninth over and had taken his second five-wicket return, giving him ten in a match for the first time. With Bright also taking five wickets, all ten wickets in India's second innings had fallen to spin.

Close of play: First day, Australia 211-2 (D. M. Jones 56*, R. J. Bright 1*); Second day, Australia 556-6 (G. R. J. Matthews 34*, S. R. Waugh 5*); Third day, India 270-7 (Kapil Dev 33*, Chetan Sharma 14*); Fourth day, Australia 170-5 (G. R. J. Matthews 27*, S. R. Waugh 2*).

Australia

D. C. Boon c Kapil Dev b Chetan	122	– (2) lbw b Maninder	49
G. R. Marsh c Kapil Dev b Yadav	22	– (1) b Shastri	11
D. M. Jones b Yadav	210	– c Azharuddin b Maninder	24
R. J. Bright c Shastri b Yadav	30		
*A. R. Border c Gavaskar b Shastri	106	– (4) b Maninder	27
G. M. Ritchie run out	13	– (5) c Pandit b Shastri	28
G. R. J. Matthews c Pandit b Yadav	44	– (6) not out	27
S. R. Waugh not out	12	– (7) not out	2
B 1, l-b 7, w 1, n-b 6	15	L-b 1, n-b 1	2

1/48 2/206 3/282 4/460   (7 wkts dec.) 574   1/31 2/81 3/94   (5 wkts dec.) 170
5/481 6/544 7/574   4/125 5/165

†T. J. Zoehrer, C. J. McDermott and B. A. Reid did not bat.

Bowling: *First Innings*—Kapil Dev 18-5-52-0; Chetan 16-1-70-1; Maninder 39-8-135-0; Yadav 49.5-9-142-4; Shastri 47-8-161-1; Srikkanth 1-0-6-0. *Second Innings*—Chetan 6-0-19-0; Kapil Dev 1-0-5-0; Shastri 14-2-50-2; Maninder 19-2-60-3; Yadav 9-0-35-0.

India

S. M. Gavaskar c and b Matthews	8	– c Jones b Bright	90
K. Srikkanth c Ritchie b Matthews	53	– c Waugh b Matthews	39
M. Amarnath run out	1	– c Boon b Matthews	51
M. Azharuddin c and b Bright	50	– c Ritchie b Bright	42
R. J. Shastri c Zoehrer b Matthews	62	– (7) not out	48
C. S. Pandit c Waugh b Matthews	35	– (5) b Matthews	39
*Kapil Dev c Border b Matthews	119	– (6) c Bright b Matthews	1
†K. S. More c Zoehrer b Waugh	4	– (9) lbw b Bright	0
Chetan Sharma c Zoehrer b Reid	30	– (8) c McDermott b Bright	23
N. S. Yadav c Border b Bright	19	– b Bright	8
Maninder Singh not out	0	– lbw b Matthews	0
B 1, l-b 9, n-b 6	16	B 1, l-b 3, n-b 2	6

1/62 2/65 3/65 4/142 5/206   397   1/55 2/158 3/204 4/251 5/253   347
6/220 7/245 8/330 9/387   6/291 7/331 8/334 9/344

Bowling: *First Innings*—McDermott 14-2-59-0; Reid 18-4-93-1; Matthews 28.2-3-103-5; Bright 23-3-88-2; Waugh 11-2-44-1. *Second Innings*—McDermott 5-0-27-0; Reid 10-2-48-0; Matthews 39.5-7-146-5; Bright 25-3-94-5; Border 3-0-12-0; Waugh 4-1-16-0.

Umpires: D. N. Dotiwala and V. Vikramraju.

†INDIA v AUSTRALIA

Third One-day International

At Hyderabad, September 24. No result. Kapil Dev put Australia in so that he could apply the strategy of rationing the overs. India took the initiative after Boon, Marsh and Jones had played valuable innings, but Ritchie wrested it back in the later stages, blasting a fine 75 off 53 balls with seven fours and three sixes. He took 22 runs off one over from Madan Lal. In helpful conditions, the Australian seam bowlers had India in trouble before a thunderstorm washed out the match.

Man of the Match: No award.

Australia

D. C. Boon c Kapil Dev b Madan Lal	26	S. R. Waugh not out	25
G. R. Marsh run out	30		
D. M. Jones c Madan Lal b Shastri	48	B 2, l-b 5, w 3, n-b 1	11
*A. R. Border c Lamba b Shastri	7		
G. M. Ritchie st Pandit b Kapil Dev	75	1/55 2/78 3/111 (6 wkts, 47 overs) 242
G. R. J. Matthews c Maninder b Gopal	20	4/126 5/159 6/242

†G. C. Dyer, D. R. Gilbert, S. P. Davis and B. A. Reid did not bat.

Bowling: Kapil Dev 10–1–40–1; R. P. Singh 4–1–19–0; Madan Lal 9–0–60–1; Shastri 10–0–36–2; Maninder 7–0–42–0; Gopal 7–0–38–1.

India

K. Srikkanth b Reid		9
R. Lamba not out		20
M. Azharuddin not out		9
L-b 1, w 2		3
1/18	(1 wkt, 10.4 overs)	41

D. B. Vengsarkar, R. J. Shastri, *Kapil Dev, †C. S. Pandit, Madan Lal, R. P. Singh, Gopal Sharma and Maninder Singh did not bat.

Bowling: Davis 5.4–0–19–0; Reid 4–0–20–1; Gilbert 1–0–1–0.

Umpires: R. R. Kadam and R. V. Ramani.

INDIA v AUSTRALIA

Second Test Match

At New Delhi, September 26, 27, 28, 29, 30. Drawn. Heavy, unseasonal rain in the capital precluded the possibility of any play on the first two days, and poor covers had let the wicket get so damp that a start was finally possible only after tea on the fourth day. After Border had won the toss, Boon added to his run of big scores against India and the Australian wicket-keeper, Zoehrer, hit a maiden half-century before the token declaration. Vengsarkar, who had missed the First Test because of back trouble, made use of the time available to become the third Indian batsman to score 5,000 Test runs. The Australians had offered to play an alternative Test, provided this one was abandoned, but the Indian Board was a reluctant party to the negotiations.

Close of play: First, second, third days, No play; Fourth day, Australia 58-1 (D. C. Boon 37*, D. M. Jones 3*).

Australia

G. R. Marsh c Pandit b Chetan	11	†T. J. Zoehrer not out		52
D. C. Boon c Maninder b Shastri	67	L-b 2, w 4, n-b 3		9
D. M. Jones st Pandit b Shastri	29			
S. R. Waugh not out	39	1/34 2/110 3/118	(3 wkts dec.)	207

*A. R. Border, G. M. Ritchie, G. R. J. Matthews, R. J. Bright, C. J. McDermott and D. R. Gilbert did not bat.

Bowling: Kapil Dev 14–5–27–0; Chetan 8–1–34–1; Shastri 21.4–4–44–2; Maninder 19–4–54–0; Yadav 13–1–46–0.

India

S. M. Gavaskar b Gilbert	4	†C. S. Pandit not out		26
K. Srikkanth run out	26	L-b 5		5
M. Azharuddin c Zoehrer b Waugh	24			
D. B. Vengsarkar not out	22	1/9 2/57 3/59	(3 wkts)	107

M. Amarnath, R. J. Shastri, *Kapil Dev, Chetan Sharma, N. S. Yadav and Maninder Singh did not bat.

Bowling: McDermott 6–1–24–0; Gilbert 11–1–44–1; Waugh 6–0–29–1; Boon 2–1–5–0; Jones 1–1–0–0.

Umpires: V. K. Ramaswamy and P. D. Reporter.

†INDIA v AUSTRALIA

Fourth One-day International

At New Delhi, October 2. India won by three wickets, taking the lead in the one-day series thanks to a powerful innings by Lamba, whose 74 off 68 balls included eight fours and a six. The tactic of bowling first again favoured India, and the Australian innings did not get going until Waugh and Dyer added 102 for the seventh wicket in 12.4 overs. The century stand between Lamba and Vengsarkar gave the Indian innings momentum, and a burst of scoring from Kapil Dev and Shastri, who took 19 runs in a vital over off Matthews, hastened the finish. The Australians' criticism of the delaying tactics, which led to India's bowling only 45 overs in three and a half hours, was certainly warranted.

Man of the Match: R. Lamba.

Australia

D. C. Boon c Srikkanth b Binny	24	S. R. Waugh not out	57
G. R. Marsh lbw b Binny	5	†G. C. Dyer not out	45
D. M. Jones run out	43	B 3, l-b 4, w 1, n-b 1	9
*A. R. Border c Lamba b Maninder	5		
G. M. Ritchie lbw b Shastri	35	1/8 2/42 3/73　　(6 wkts, 45 overs) 238	
G. R. J. Matthews st Pandit b Maninder	15	4/85 5/118 6/136	

B. A. Reid, D. R. Gilbert and S. P. Davis did not bat.

Bowling: Kapil Dev 10-1-35-0; Binny 8-0-75-2; Madan Lal 8-0-45-0; Maninder 10-0-30-2; Shastri 9-2-46-1.

India

K. Srikkanth c Ritchie b Reid	9	M. Azharuddin c Ritchie b Reid	15
S. M. Gavaskar c Border b Davis	6	Madan Lal not out	9
R. Lamba c sub (M. R. J. Veletta) b Waugh	74	B 4, l-b 6, w 4	14
D. B. Vengsarkar c Matthews b Waugh	37		
*Kapil Dev c Dyer b Gilbert	36	1/7 2/24 3/126　　(7 wkts, 43.3 overs) 242	
†C. S. Pandit b Reid	13	4/141 5/168	
R. J. Shastri not out	29	6/193 7/232	

R. M. H. Binny and Maninder Singh did not bat.

Bowling: Davis 9.3-1-28-1; Reid 9-0-43-3; Gilbert 10-0-59-1; Waugh 10-0-48-2; Matthews 5-0-54-0.

Umpires: A. L. Narasimhan and J. D. Roy.

†INDIA v AUSTRALIA

Fifth One-day International

At Ahmedabad, October 5. India won by 52 runs, having come back into the match in fine style after batting unconvincingly. Only a partnership of 67 off 89 balls between Shastri and Madan Lal had given respectability to a mismanaged innings which had stood at 98 for six after Border had inserted India. Australia, having the full 50 overs available on account of their dismissing India, needed 108 off the last 25 overs with eight wickets in hand. But unnecessary risks in running sharp singles against a side fielding for its life in front of more than 60,000 fervent supporters swung the fortunes, and the series, India's way.

Man of the Match: R. J. Shastri.

India

S. M. Gavaskar b Davis 12	R. M. H. Binny c Boon b McDermott . 1
K. Srikkanth c Dyer b Gilbert 26	Gopal Sharma b Davis 7
R. Lamba run out 17	Maninder Singh not out 8
M. Azharuddin c and b Gilbert 10	L-b 3, w 11, n-b 1 15
*Kapil Dev c Boon b Waugh 6	
†C. S. Pandit c Border b Matthews 8	1/33 2/59 3/77 (47.4 overs) 193
R. J. Shastri c Jones b Davis 53	4/81 5/86 6/98
Madan Lal run out 30	7/165 8/166 9/181

Bowling: Davis 9.4-0-35-3; McDermott 8-1-24-1; Gilbert 10-0-52-2; Waugh 10-0-46-1; Matthews 10-1-33-1.

Australia

G. R. Marsh run out 43	C. J. McDermott st Pandit b Shastri . . 4
D. C. Boon c Madan Lal b Kapil Dev . 5	D. R. Gilbert not out 3
D. M. Jones c Lamba b Kapil Dev 2	S. P. Davis b Madan Lal 1
*A. R. Border run out 43	W 3 3
G. M. Ritchie run out 22	
G. R. J. Matthews c Srikkanth b Gopal 0	1/9 2/17 3/86 (43.3 overs) 141
S. R. Waugh c Pandit b Shastri 9	4/104 5/105 6/126
†G. C. Dyer run out 6	7/126 8/130 9/138

Bowling: Kapil Dev 8-1-17-2; Binny 6-0-27-0; Shastri 9-2-23-2; Gopal 10-0-42-1; Maninder 10-2-29-0; Madan Lal 0.3-0-3-1.

Umpires: B. R. Keshavamurthy and M. G. Mukherjee.

†INDIA v AUSTRALIA

Sixth One-day International

At Rajkot, October 7. Australia won by seven wickets after putting India in on a pitch that gave nothing to the bowlers. Lamba strengthened the good impression he had made in the series with his first hundred in a one-day international, off 118 balls with two sixes and eight fours, and Kapil Dev, who had extracted a concession from the selectors and was playing only as a batsman, struck what was possibly the quickest half-century in a one-day international. His first 50 runs came off 26 balls, including an onslaught on McDermott which yielded 24 in an over, and in all he hit two sixes and five fours. Jones set up the chase with a cultured 55 against some inexperienced bowling before Border saw his side home with an unbeaten 91 off 88 balls.

Man of the Match: A. R. Border.   *Man of the Series:* R. Lamba.

India

K. Srikkanth c McDermott b Matthews 23	†C. S. Pandit not out 14
R. Lamba b Reid 102	Madan Lal not out 1
M. Azharuddin run out 28	B 1, l-b 5, w 1 7
D. B. Vengsarkar c Marsh b Waugh . . . 25	
*Kapil Dev lbw b Waugh 58	1/59 2/143 3/179 (6 wkts, 48 overs) 260
R. J. Shastri run out 2	4/181 5/200 6/259

R. S. Ghai, R. P. Singh and Maninder Singh did not bat.

Bowling: Davis 9-0-34-0; McDermott 9-1-61-0; Waugh 10-1-50-2; Matthews 8-0-51-1; Reid 10-0-48-1; Border 2-0-10-0.

Australia

G. R. Marsh run out 39	G. M. Ritchie not out 35
D. C. Boon st Pandit b Shastri 39	L-b 4 4
D. M. Jones c Lamba b R. P. Singh . . . 55	
*A. R. Border not out 91	1/68 2/85 3/176 (3 wkts, 46.3 overs) 263

G. R. J. Matthews, S. R. Waugh, †G. C. Dyer, C. J. McDermott, B. A. Reid and S. P. Davis did not bat.

Bowling: Madan Lal 8–0–50–0; R. P. Singh 9.4–0–58–1; Ghai 6.2–0–37–0; Shastri 10–0–50–1; Maninder 10–0–49–0; Srikkanth 2–0–11–0; Azharuddin 0.3–0–4–0.

Umpires: K. R. Karimaniokam and R. Ravindram.

DELHI v AUSTRALIANS

At Baroda, October 10, 11, 12. Drawn. The touring team's three-day match against the Ranji Trophy champions produced maiden first-class hundreds for Dyer and Gilbert, who shared a 175-run partnership for the seventh wicket. Dyer, in 218 minutes, hit two sixes and ten fours and Gilbert had a six and seventeen fours in his 263-minute stay. When they came together, the Australians were well behind Delhi's first-innings 385, to which newcomers Nayyar and Ajay Sharma were prominent contributors. That only eighteen wickets fell in the three days reflected the type of pitches prevalent in India.

Close of play: First day, Delhi 275-5; Second day, Australians 79-4.

Delhi

†S. C. Khanna lbw b Gilbert	48	S. Sharma not out 4
M. Nayyar lbw b Bright	72	S. Srivastava not out 11
K. Bhaskar Pillai lbw b McDermott	41	
K. Azad c Marsh b Gilbert	60	B 2, l-b 14, n-b 12 28
M. Amarnath c Zoehrer b Gilbert	22	
R. Lamba c Waugh b Gilbert	9	1/93 2/169 3/186 (8 wkts dec.) 385
A. Sharma c McDermott b Reid	66	4/232 5/243 6/327
*Madan Lal b Veletta b Reid	24	7/361 8/373

A. Saini did not bat.

Bowling: Reid 16–2–34–2; McDermott 24–2–88–1; Gilbert 24–5–92–4; Waugh 12–0–50–0; Matthews 17–2–67–0; Bright 12–4–28–1; Jones 1–0–2–0; Zoehrer 1–0–8–0.

Australians

G. R. Marsh c Amarnath b S. Sharma	5	C. J. McDermott c Pillai b Azad 20
M. R. J. Veletta b Madan Lal	13	B. A. Reid not out 12
G. R. J. Matthews c Nayyar b Saini	44	*R. J. Bright c Srivastava b Azad ... 2
D. M. Jones run out	5	
S. R. Waugh c Nayyar b Azad	82	B 2, l-b 8, w 1, n-b 6 17
†T. J. Zoehrer b Srivastava	34	
G. C. Dyer c Lamba b A. Sharma	106	1/12 2/41 3/53 4/79 5/182 457
D. R. Gilbert c Saini b Azad	117	6/204 7/379 8/426 9/455

Bowling: S. Sharma 18–0–80–1; Madan Lal 14–1–63–1; Saini 12–1–68–1; A. Sharma 22–8–60–1; Azad 24.5–4–73–4; Srivastava 21–0–91–1; Lamba 3–0–12–0.

Umpires: J. D. Ghosh and R. B. Gupta.

INDIA v AUSTRALIA

Third Test Match

At Bombay, October 15, 16, 17, 18, 19. Drawn. Border having called correctly for the third time in the Test series to allow Australia the best of the batting conditions, Marsh established the innings with a slow first hundred against India before falling to Kulkarni, who had been drafted into the Indian side for his first Test as a replacement for the injured Chetan Sharma. But with the wicket seeming to help the spinners a shade on the second day, the safe total Australia were aiming for did not materialise. Gavaskar, batting just over five hours, compiled an immaculate century on his home ground, his 33rd in Tests, but India remained under some pressure as Matthews took all four wickets which fell on the third day. However, the fourth day belonged completely to the Bombay pair, Vengsarkar and Shastri, who put together a record, unfinished partnership of 298 for any wicket in India-Australia Tests; it was also the highest for India's sixth wicket against any country. While Vengsarkar made his twelfth Test century with classy elegance, a more stodgy Shastri burst into action every now and then to stroke six sixes – a record for an Indian in Tests. The Australians were in for the last nine overs of the fourth day but their real test came on the fifth, when Shastri disposed of Marsh and Boon. However, Jones and Border ensured the draw with an unbroken stand of 146, Border keeping the strike until lunch in order not to expose a nervy Jones to the turning ball. Afterwards Jones's confidence was in the ascendant and an interesting Test match meandered to a tame draw on a pitch which had lost its pace progressively. Not one wicket fell on the fourth day and only two on the final one.

Close of play: First day, Australia 217-2 (G. R. Marsh 89*, A. R. Border 34*); Second day, India 61-1 (S. M. Gavaskar 30*, K. S. More 0*); Third day, India 291-5 (D. B. Vengsarkar 41*, R. J. Shastri 37*); Fourth day, Australia 9-0 (D. C. Boon 5*, G. R. Marsh 2*).

Australia

G. R. Marsh c Gavaskar b Kulkarni	101	– (2) b Shastri 20
D. C. Boon c Gavaskar b Kulkarni	47	– (1) c More b Shastri 40
D. M. Jones c sub (L. Sivaramakrishnan) b Yadav	35	– not out 73
*A. R. Border st More b Maninder	46	– not out 66
G. M. Ritchie run out	31	
G. R. J. Matthews b Yadav	20	
S. R. Waugh b Yadav	6	
†T. J. Zoehrer c and b Maninder	21	
R. J. Bright lbw b Kulkarni	8	
D. R. Gilbert c sub (L. Sivaramakrishnan) b Yadav	1	
B. A. Reid not out	2	
B 5, l-b 12, n-b 10	27	B 5, l-b 5, n-b 7 17
	345	**(2 wkts) 216**

1/76 2/151 3/241 4/252 5/295 6/304 7/308 8/340 9/340   345   1/64 2/70   (2 wkts) 216

Bowling: *First Innings*—Kulkarni 23-2-85-3; Kapil Dev 6-1-16-0; Shastri 42-16-68-0; Yadav 41.4-8-84-4; Maninder 33-10-72-2; Srikkanth 2-0-3-0. *Second Innings*—Kapil Dev 6-1-24-0; Maninder 20-6-31-0; Shastri 30-8-60-2; Yadav 23-7-52-0; Kulkarni 6-0-29-0; Srikkanth 3-0-10-0.

India

S. M. Gavaskar c Ritchie b Matthews	103	M. Azharuddin c sub (M. R. J. Veletta) b Matthews 10
K. Srikkanth c Marsh b Bright	24	R. J. Shastri not out 121
†K. S. More c Jones b Matthews	15	B 9, l-b 15, n-b 21 45
M. Amarnath c sub (M. R. J. Veletta) b Matthews	35	
D. B. Vengsarkar not out	164	(5 wkts dec.) 517

1/53 2/119 3/194 4/205 5/219

*Kapil Dev, N. S. Yadav, R. R. Kulkarni and Maninder Singh did not bat.

Bowling: Reid 32-5-81-0; Gilbert 24-3-75-0; Matthews 52-8-158-4; Bright 38-6-109-1; Border 10-3-29-0; Waugh 14-2-41-0.

Umpires: J. D. Ghosh and R. B. Gupta.

THE WEST INDIANS IN PAKISTAN, 1986-87

By QAMAR AHMED

History was against Vivian Richards's West Indian team winning their Test series in Pakistan, even though under his captaincy West Indies had won their previous seven Test matches. Of their three predecessors to Pakistan, only Clive Lloyd's 1980-81 team had won a series; and that by only one victory in five matches. Of Lloyd's side then, Larry Gomes, Gordon Greenidge, Desmond Haynes and Malcolm Marshall, as well as the captain, had returned. It was much to the credit of Pakistan's young team that this series was drawn. They were shrewdly led by Imran Khan, who along with Abdul Qadir bowled admirably throughout. Each finished with eighteen wickets.

Only at Lahore, where they were furnished with a fast wicket, did the West Indian fast bowlers find conditions to their liking; elsewhere their powder was dampened. Unfortunately, the pitches too often produced uneven bounce which made strokeplay impossible, as is reflected by the failure, in a low-scoring series, of any batsman to score a hundred. Such was the paucity of run-making that there was only one partnership of more than 100, Javed Miandad and Ramiz Raja putting on 111 in the final, drawn Test at Karachi. Haynes's unbeaten 88 for West Indies in the second innings there was the highest score of either side in the Tests, while only Jeffrey Dujon, with an unbeaten 126 against the Punjab Governor's XI, reached three figures on the tour.

The series was evenly fought. Pakistan won the first Test by 186 runs, bowling out West Indies in their second innings for 53, their lowest total in Tests. But retribution was quickly forthcoming: an innings defeat in three days. The third Test was drawn after Imran and Tauseef Ahmed had defied the West Indians' attempt to end Pakistan's unbeaten record at Karachi. The limited-overs series, however, was one-sided, with West Indies winning 4-1.

Without a settled opening pair, Pakistan's batting struggled. Mohsin Khan and Mudassar Nazar began the series and ended it, while in between there were permutations, in the Test matches and one-day internationals, incorporating Shoaib Mohammad, Rizwan-uz-Zaman and Sajid Ali. No combination exceeded 25; and when Salim Malik's left arm was broken by a rising ball from Courtney Walsh in the first Test, the middle order also experienced difficulties. Ramiz Raja was below his best, as was Qasim Omar, but there were bonuses in the emergence of two young batsmen, Asif Mujtaba, who made his Test début after fine innings against the tourists at Rawalpindi and Sahiwal, and Ijaz Ahmed, who took 82 off them at Rawalpindi and was called up for three one-day internationals. Imran organised a defiant lower order, and in Saleem Jaffer Pakistan introduced a useful left-arm medium-pace bowler when Wasim Akram was unfit for the Third Test.

For West Indies, Richards failed repeatedly after struggling against illness during the First Test, twice being dismissed first ball in the limited-overs series. His best innings came at the end, when he laboured for 70 to under-pin his side's first innings at Karachi. Greenidge, Haynes and Ritchie Richardson each played useful innings. In the absence of Joel Garner and

Michael Holding, who chose not to tour, Tony Gray and Walsh bowled well to take 26 and 19 wickets respectively in all matches on the tour. Marshall, however, remained the greatest threat in the Test matches and always looked dangerous, even on slow wickets. He finished the series with sixteen wickets.

By way of experiment, neutral umpires stood in the Test series, V. K. Ramaswamy and P. D. Reporter of India officiating in the Second and Third matches. The Pakistan authorities were to be congratulated on this decision for, apart from an altercation between Marshall and umpire Reporter in Karachi, there was a welcome absence of bickering over decisions. Marshall was unhappy because he had twice been no-balled and twice refused appeals for lbw against Mohsin Khan early in the first innings.

WEST INDIAN TOUR RESULTS

Test matches – Played 3: Won 1, Lost 1, Drawn 1.
First-class matches – Played 6: Won 2, Lost 1, Drawn 3.
Wins – Pakistan, Baluchistan Governor's XI.
Loss – Pakistan.
Draws – Pakistan, President's XI, Punjab Governor's XI.
Non first-class matches – Played 5: Won 4, Lost 1. *Wins* – Pakistan (4). *Loss* – Pakistan.

TEST MATCH AVERAGES

PAKISTAN – BATTING

	T	I	NO	R	HI	100s	Avge
Javed Miandad ...	3	6	0	176	76	0	29.33
Imran Khan	3	6	2	115	61	0	28.75
Ramiz Raja	3	6	0	120	62	0	20.00
Salim Yousuf	3	6	0	114	61	0	19.00
Mudassar Nazar ...	2	4	0	69	26	0	17.25
Wasim Akram ...	2	4	0	67	66	0	16.75
Qasim Omar	3	6	1	71	48	0	14.20
Tauseef Ahmed ...	3	6	3	33	9*	0	11.00
Abdul Qadir	3	5	1	38	14	0	9.50
Mohsin Khan	3	6	0	48	40	0	8.00
Asif Mujtaba	2	4	0	32	12	0	8.00

Played in one Test: Rizwan-uz-Zaman 2, 1; Saleem Jaffer 9; Salim Malik 21*, 3*.

* *Signifies not out.*

BOWLING

	O	M	R	W	BB	Avge
Imran Khan	106.2	23	199	18	6-46	11.05
Wasim Akram	37	5	112	6	6-91	18.66
Abdul Qadir	132.2	19	361	18	6-16	20.05
Tauseef Ahmed	70	32	140	5	2-27	28.00

Also bowled: Asif Mujtaba 3-2-2-0; Mudassar Nazar 4-0-15-1; Saleem Jaffer 29-9-57-2.

WEST INDIES – BATTING

	T	I	NO	R	HI	100s	Avge
D. L. Haynes	3	5	1	149	88*	0	37.25
I. V. A. Richards	3	5	0	175	70	0	35.00
R. B. Richardson	3	5	0	148	54	0	29.60
C. G. Greenidge	3	5	0	132	75	0	26.40
H. A. Gomes	3	5	0	67	33	0	13.40
C. G. Butts	2	3	0	35	17	0	11.66
R. A. Harper	3	5	0	49	28	0	9.80
M. D. Marshall	3	5	1	32	13*	0	8.00
A. H. Gray	3	5	1	27	12*	0	6.75
P. J. L. Dujon	3	5	0	27	19	0	5.40
C. A. Walsh	3	5	1	12	8	0	3.00

Played in one Test: B. P. Patterson 0, 6*.

* Signifies not out.

BOWLING

	O	M	R	W	BB	Avge
C. G. Butts	60	24	95	6	4-73	15.83
A. H. Gray	99	27	227	14	4-39	16.21
M. D. Marshall	114	27	266	16	5-33	16.62
C. A. Walsh	97.3	27	195	11	4-21	17.72

Also bowled: R. A. Harper 36.5-9-69-2; B. P. Patterson 31-4-101-3; I. V. A. Richards 5-2-9-1.

WEST INDIAN AVERAGES – FIRST-CLASS MATCHES

BATTING

	M	I	NO	R	HI	100s	Avge
W. K. M. Benjamin	3	3	0	132	92	0	44.00
D. L. Haynes	5	8	2	259	88*	0	43.16
I. V. A. Richards	6	8	0	276	70	0	34.50
R. B. Richardson	6	10	1	264	67	0	29.33
P. J. L. Dujon	5	7	1	167	126*	1	27.83
C. G. Greenidge	6	10	1	225	75	0	25.00
A. L. Logie	2	3	0	58	29	0	19.33
H. A. Gomes	5	7	0	133	66	0	19.00
C. G. Butts	5	6	1	92	57*	0	18.40
R. A. Harper	6	8	0	146	77	0	18.25
M. D. Marshall	4	6	2	48	16*	0	12.00
T. R. O. Payne	2	2	0	14	14	0	7.00
B. P. Patterson	3	4	1	18	9	0	6.00
A. H. Gray	4	6	1	28	12	0	5.60
C. A. Walsh	4	6	1	12	8	0	2.40

* Signifies not out.

BOWLING

	O	M	R	W	BB	*Avge*
A. H. Gray	110	31	266	19	4-22	14.00
C. G. Butts	126.4	40	244	17	4-31	14.35
R. A. Harper	129.5	42	232	14	4-28	16.57
C. A. Walsh	117.3	29	265	14	4-21	18.92
M. D. Marshall	131	30	327	17	5-33	19.23
B. P. Patterson	54	11	173	8	3-34	21.62

Also bowled: W. K. M. Benjamin 34.2–3–120–3; I. V. A. Richards 14–3–35–1.

FIELDING

8 – R. B. Richardson; 7 – P. J. L. Dujon (6 ct, 1 st); 6 – C. G. Greenidge; 5 – R. A. Harper, D. L. Haynes; 4 – A. L. Logie, T. R. O. Payne, I. V. A. Richards, substitutes (A. H. Gray, A. L. Logie, T. R. O. Payne [1 ct, 1 st]); 2 – A. H. Gray, C. A. Walsh; 1 – C. G. Butts, B. P. Patterson.

BALUCHISTAN GOVERNOR'S XI v WEST INDIANS

At Quetta, October 12, 13, 14. West Indians won by an innings and 89 runs. Choosing to bat first on a spinners' wicket, the Governor's XI could find no-one to counter the off-spin of Harper and Butts, tall men whose height enabled them to obtain bounce. By the close, the West Indians were 9 runs ahead with five wickets in hand, Richards in an aggressive vein hitting all but 5 of his unbeaten 47 in boundaries. He was soon out next morning, but Harper and Butts took up with the bat what they had begun with the ball. Batting again, 198 runs in arrears, the home side were knocked back by a hostile burst from Gray. Harper took two wickets before the close to have them 89 for seven overnight, and it took the touring team only a quarter of an hour to complete their win on the final morning.

Baluchistan Governor's XI

Moin-ul-Atiq b Gray	24	– c Harper b Gray	5
Sajid Ali c Richardson b Harper	46	– c Richards b Gray	6
Ali Zia c Greenidge b Patterson	2	– lbw b Gray	0
Mansoor Rana lbw b Butts	6	– b Gray	3
*Ijaz Faqih lbw b Harper	8	– (6) b Harper	34
Zafar Ahmed c Haynes b Harper	6	– c sub b Patterson	12
†Anil Dalpat c Greenidge b Harper	8	– c Butts b Harper	17
Sajjad Akbar c Richards b Butts	3	– not out	0
Azeem Hafeez b Butts	2	– (10) b Butts	0
Asif Baloch not out	1	– (9) st sub b Butts	0
Habib Baloch b Butts	0	– b Harper	4
B 17, l-b 7, n-b 1	25	B 7, l-b 3, n-b 5	15

1/38 2/41 3/77 4/98 5/108   **131**   1/6 2/12 3/15 4/18 5/42   **109**
6/113 7/126 8/128 9/131   6/75 7/87 8/91 9/91

Bowling: *First Innings*—Patterson 5–1–19–1; Gray 5–1–17–1; Benjamin 3–0–12–0; Harper 19–6–28–4; Butts 16.4–4–31–4. *Second Innings*—Patterson 5–2–19–1; Gray 6–3–22–4; Benjamin 6–2–15–0; Harper 11–6–20–3; Butts 6–1–23–2.

West Indians

C. G. Greenidge c Sajjad b Ijaz	......	34
D. L. Haynes c Ali Zia b Ijaz	......	30
R. B. Richardson c Mansoor b Ijaz	....	7
H. A. Gomes st Anil b Sajjad	....	0
*I. V. A. Richards b Sajjad	....	47
†P. J. L. Dujon c Ali Zia b Ijaz	......	14
R. A. Harper b Sajjad	....	77
W. K. M. Benjamin c Ali Zia b Asif	..	38

A. H. Gray c Moin b Ijaz	....	1
C. G. Butts not out	....	57
B. P. Patterson st Anil b Ijaz	......	3
B 9, l-b 8, n-b 4	......	21
		329

1/65 2/72 3/73 4/87 5/140
6/140 7/215 8/216 9/310

Bowling: Azeem 4–0–26–0; Habib 5–0–31–0; Sajjad 34–5–92–3; Ijaz 37.1–8–103–6; Asif 12–1–43–1; Ali Zia 3–0–17–0.

Umpires: Shakeel Khan and Tariq Ata.

†PAKISTAN v WEST INDIES

First One-day International

At Peshawar, October 17. West Indies won by four wickets. Batting first on winning the toss, Pakistan never had enough runs to their credit once it became obvious that Greenidge was in form. But for a fourth-wicket stand of 57 between Ramiz Raja and Salim Malik, both of whom fell to Gray in successive overs, and 34 from Abdul Qadir (two sixes, four fours), West Indies' victory would have been even easier. Pitch invasions were twice met with teargas.
Man of the Match: C. G. Greenidge.

Pakistan

Mudassar Nazar lbw b Gray	....	15
Mohsin Khan lbw b Marshall	....	4
Ramiz Raja b Gray	....	31
Javed Miandad c Dujon b Benjamin	..	2
Salim Malik c Dujon b Gray	....	30
*Imran Khan not out	....	23
Wasim Akram run out	....	5

Abdul Qadir b Patterson	....	34
†Anil Dalpat not out	....	3
B 2, l-b 11, w 2, n-b 2	......	17
1/20 2/24 3/27 (7 wkts, 49 overs)		164
4/84 5/93		
6/141 7/158		

Tauseef Ahmed and Saleem Jaffer did not bat.

Bowling: Gray 10–1–20–3; Marshall 9–1–21–1; Benjamin 10–2–29–1; Harper 10–0–43–0; Patterson 10–0–38–1.

West Indies

C. G. Greenidge c Tauseef b Wasim	..	67
R. B. Richardson b Imran	....	10
H. A. Gomes b Tauseef	....	18
A. L. Logie run out	....	0
*I. V. A. Richards c Miandad b Jaffer	.	7
†P. J. L. Dujon c Miandad b Qadir	...	5

R. A. Harper not out	....	34
M. D. Marshall not out	....	0
B 8, l-b 11, w 3, n-b 2	......	24
1/24 2/89 3/96 (6 wkts, 45.3 overs)		165
4/117 5/118 6/150		

A. H. Gray, W. K. M. Benjamin and B. P. Patterson did not bat.

Bowling: Imran 7.3–2–22–1; Tauseef 10–2–29–1; Qadir 10–0–43–1; Wasim 10–2–28–1; Jaffer 8–0–24–1.

Umpires: Athar Zaidi and Shakoor Rana.

PRESIDENT'S XI v WEST INDIANS

At Rawalpindi, October 19, 20, 21. Drawn. Two four-wicket spells by the medium-fast bowler, Zakir Khan, brought him career-best figures and up-staged the touring team's rehearsal for the First Test. Put in after overnight rain had delayed the start by more than an hour, the West Indians were helped by fielding lapses as Richardson, with three lives, and

Gomes, surviving a stumping chance, put on 113. Richards and Harper checked the slide after Zakir's first strike, but next morning, again after a late start, Zakir took four wickets for just 15 runs. Positive batting, following early losses, saw Qasim Omar and Ijaz Ahmed add 121 in even time before the close, and when both were caught off Harper on the third morning, Asif Mujtaba brought his own magic to bear on the afternoon for President Zia-ul-Haq, who was visiting the ground.

Close of play: First day, West Indians 208-5 (I. V. A. Richards 40*, R. A. Harper 14*); Second day, President's XI 165-2 (Qasim Omar 72*, Ijaz Ahmed 60*).

West Indians

C. G. Greenidge lbw b Mohsin	4	– not out	25
R. B. Richardson c Salim b Zakir	67	– not out	16
H. A. Gomes c Salim b Zakir	66		
A. L. Logie lbw b Zakir	4		
*I. V. A. Richards b Zakir	54		
†T. R. O. Payne lbw b Zakir	0		
R. A. Harper c and b Nadeem	20		
M. D. Marshall not out	16		
W. K. M. Benjamin c Salim b Zakir	2		
C. G. Butts lbw b Zakir	0		
C. A. Walsh b Zakir	0		
B 5, l-b 3, n-b 6	14	L-b 5	5
	247		**(no wkt) 46**

1/10 2/123 3/137 4/158 5/158
6/227 7/239 8/241 9/247

Bowling: *First Innings*—Mohsin 11-4-29-1; Zakir 33.4-6-85-8; Nadeem 30-8-68-1; Riaz 7-1-32-0; Asif 4-2-14-0; Shoaib 3-1-11-0. *Second Innings*—Mohsin 4-1-19-0; Zakir 3-1-6-0; Nadeem 3-3-0-0; Asif 2-0-9-0; Shoaib 2-0-4-0; Ijaz 1-1-0-0; Omar 1-0-3-0.

President's XI

Masood Anwar c Payne b Walsh	11	Mohsin Kamal c Harper b Butts	0
Shoaib Mohammad c Payne b Marshall	5	Zakir Khan c Richardson b Benjamin	16
Qasim Omar c Greenidge b Harper	84	Nadeem Ghauri not out	0
Ijaz Ahmed c Logie b Harper	82		
*Javed Miandad lbw b Walsh	2	B 12, l-b 6, w 4, n-b 17	39
Asif Mujtaba c sub b Walsh	64		
Mohammad Riaz c Walsh b Harper	10	1/11 2/44 3/192 4/207 5/221	**317**
†Salim Yousuf c Richardson b Butts	4	6/239 7/245 8/251 9/313	

Bowling: Marshall 17-3-61-1; Walsh 20-2-70-3; Benjamin 13.3-0-56-1; Harper 32-7-73-3; Butts 16-3-39-2.

Umpires: Javed Akhtar and Mian Aslam.

PAKISTAN v WEST INDIES

First Test Match

At Faisalabad, October 24, 26, 27, 28, 29. Pakistan won by 186 runs. Devastating leg-spin and googly bowling by Qadir, well supported by Imran's fast-medium bowling and backed up by the brilliance of the close fielders, broke West Indies after tea on the fourth afternoon, taking Pakistan to the brink of victory with unexpected swiftness. West Indies' second-innings 53 was their lowest in Tests, their previous lowest having been 76, also against Pakistan, at Dacca in 1958-59, and was the lowest in a Test innings in Pakistan. The defeat was only their fourth in 57 Tests since 1979-80: they had in that time won 30.

West Indies' pace quartet dominated the opening day after Pakistan had chosen to bat first, only Imran resisting as he saw his side from 37 for five to 159. He lost Salim Malik at 90, his arm broken just above the wrist, but found an ally in Tauseef Ahmed and the last wicket put on 39. With Richards ill, West Indies' innings never developed against resourceful bowling by

Pakistan. Tauseef, dismissing Richardson and Dujon with successive balls, bowled a miserly spell in the afternoon, and then Wasim Akram swept away the tail to return his best figures in Test cricket. The loss of Mudassar and Ramiz before the close did not bode well for Pakistan with three days remaining, but they dug in on the third day, adding only 155 and, more important, losing only two more wickets. Salim Yousuf, having gone in as night-watchman, remained 46 overs for his 61, his maiden Test fifty, and both Mohsin and Miandad batted with great discipline, the latter eventually taking three hours over his 30.

It was Wasim Akram, with his first Test fifty, who swung the game away from West Indies. Pakistan's lead was 135 when he joined Imran. They added 34, and then with sixes off Marshall and Patterson he added 38 with the plucky Tauseef. Finally, Pakistan's courageous fightback was epitomised by Salim Malik, who came out to bat with his arm in plaster, faced fourteen balls, and helped Akram add a further 32. West Indies, with four sessions remaining, needed 240 to win; but after just one of them their innings was in a shambles – 43 for nine. Qadir had already taken five wickets (for 13) in a Test innings for the tenth time, and next morning he caught and bowled Marshall to finish with six for 16.

Man of the Match: Wasim Akram.

Close of play: First day, West Indies 54-1 (D. L. Haynes 18*, R. B. Richardson 20*); Second day, Pakistan 28-2 (Mohsin Khan 3*, Salim Yousuf 9*); Third day, Pakistan 183-4 (Qasim Omar 38*, Javed Miandad 15*); Fourth day, West Indies 43-9 (M. D. Marshall 6*).

Pakistan

Mohsin Khan lbw b Marshall	2	– (2) c Haynes b Walsh	40
Mudassar Nazar c Richardson b Marshall	26	– (1) c Haynes b Marshall	2
Ramiz Raja lbw b Marshall	0	– c Gray b Patterson	13
Javed Miandad c Dujon b Patterson	1	– (6) c sub (A. L. Logie) b Gray	30
Qasim Omar hit wkt b Gray	3	– lbw b Walsh	48
Salim Malik retired hurt	21	– (11) not out	3
*Imran Khan c and b Gray	61	– c Harper b Marshall	23
Abdul Qadir c and b Patterson	14	– lbw b Gray	2
†Salim Yousuf lbw b Gray	0	– (4) c Greenidge b Harper	61
Wasim Akram c Richardson b Gray	0	– (9) st Dujon b Harper	66
Tauseef Ahmed not out	9	– (10) b Walsh	8
B 1, l-b 11, n-b 10	22	B 7, l-b 8, w 2, n-b 15	32
	159		**328**

1/12 2/12 3/19 4/37 5/37   1/2 2/19 3/113 4/124 5/208
6/119 7/120 8/120 9/159   6/218 7/224 8/258 9/296

Bowling: *First Innings*—Marshall 10-2-48-3; Patterson 12-1-38-2; Gray 11.5-3-39-4; Walsh 5-0-22-0. *Second Innings*—Marshall 26-3-83-2; Patterson 19-3-63-1; Harper 27.5-9-36-2; Gray 22-4-82-2; Walsh 23-6-49-3.

West Indies

C. G. Greenidge lbw b Wasim	10	– lbw b Imran	12
D. L. Haynes lbw b Wasim	40	– lbw b Imran	0
R. B. Richardson b Tauseef	54	– c Ramiz b Qadir	14
H. A. Gomes c sub (Manzoor Elahi) b Qadir	33	– b Qadir	2
†P. J. L. Dujon c Ramiz b Tauseef	0	– (6) lbw b Imran	0
R. A. Harper c Yousuf b Wasim	28	– (7) c sub (Shoaib Mohammad) b Qadir	2
M. D. Marshall c Yousuf b Wasim	5	– (8) c and b Qadir	10
*I. V. A. Richards c Yousuf b Wasim	33	– (5) c Ramiz b Qadir	0
A. H. Gray not out	12	– b Qadir	5
C. A. Walsh lbw b Wasim	4	– b Imran	0
B. P. Patterson lbw b Wasim	0	– not out	6
B 9, l-b 8, n-b 12	29	L-b 2	2
	248		**53**

1/12 2/103 3/124 4/124 5/178   1/5 2/16 3/19 4/19 5/20
6/192 7/223 8/243 9/247   6/23 7/36 8/42 9/43

Bowling: *First Innings*—Wasim 25-3-91-6; Imran 21-8-32-1; Qadir 15-1-58-1; Tauseef 22-5-50-2. *Second Innings*—Imran 13-5-30-4; Wasim 3-0-5-0; Qadir 9.3-1-16-6.

Umpires: Khizar Hayat and Mian Mohammad Aslam.

PUNJAB GOVERNOR'S XI v WEST INDIANS

At Sahiwal, October 31, November 1, 2. Drawn. Put in, the West Indians again revealed their susceptibility to leg-spin as Nasir Javed, a youngster from Lahore, reduced them to 145 for seven. However, Dujon, who had made a "pair" in the Test match, was joined by Benjamin in a commanding partnership of 174 for the eighth wicket, his unbeaten 126 containing a six and sixteen fours while Benjamin hit two sixes and thirteen fours in his 92. The home side entered the final day needing 60 runs to avoid the follow-on, and with only three wickets in hand, but they were saved by the left-handed Asif Mujtaba, who followed his 64 at Rawalpindi with a defiant 70. West Indies used the afternoon session for batting practice and the match was called off half an hour after tea.

Close of play: First day, West Indians 238 for seven (P. J. L. Dujon 77*, W. K. M. Benjamin 52*); Second day, Punjab Governor's XI 128 for seven (Asif Mujtaba 31*, Ali Ahmed 5*).

West Indians

C. G. Greenidge c Masood Anwar b Mohsin	9	– lbw b Shahid Butt	21
D. L. Haynes c Mohsin b Ali Ahmed	30	– not out	50
R. B. Richardson c Mohsin b Ali Ahmed	22	– c Masood Anwar b Shahid Butt	4
P. J. L. Dujon not out	126		
A. L. Logie c Manzoor b Nasir	25	– (4) lbw b Mudassar	29
*I. V. A. Richards c and b Nasir	0		
†T. R. O. Payne c Shahid Anwar b Nasir	14		
R. A. Harper b Nasir	0		
W. K. M. Benjamin c Rizwan b Shahid Butt	92		
C. G. Butts b Rizwan	0		
B. P. Patterson c Ali Ahmed b Shahid Butt	9		
B 2, l-b 4, w 3, n-b 1	10	B 1, l-b 2, w 5, n-b 1	9

1/18 2/65 3/68 4/113 5/113   337   1/49 2/53 3/113   (3 wkts) 113
6/141 7/145 8/319 9/320

Bowling: First Innings—Mohsin 17-3-76-1; Ali Ahmed 10-1-50-2; Manzoor 9-1-38-0; Shahid Butt 30.4-6-73-2; Nasir 28-5-82-4; Asif 1-0-4-0; Rizwan 3-0-8-1. *Second Innings*—Mohsin 8-0-34-0; Ali Ahmed 5-0-20-0; Shahid Butt 6-1-31-2; Nasir 7-1-24-0; Asif 3-2-1-0; Mudassar 0.3-0-0-1.

Punjab Governor's XI

*Mudassar Nazar c Logie b Patterson	4	Ali Ahmed c Haynes b Patterson	28
Masood Anwar c Payne b Patterson	5	Mohsin Kamal lbw b Benjamin	10
Rizwan-uz-Zaman c Logie b Butts	28	Nasir Javed b Benjamin	3
Asif Mujtaba not out	70		
Shahid Anwar c Richards b Harper	6	B 9, l-b 10, w 2, n-b 8	29
Manzoor Elahi c Payne b Harper	26		
†Masood Iqbal c Logie b Butts	5	1/4 2/31 3/50 4/62 5/104	214
Shahid Butt b Butts	0	6/115 7/117 8/181 9/192	

Bowling: Patterson 13-4-34-3; Benjamin 11.5-1-37-2; Harper 31-14-42-2; Richards 9-1-26-0; Butts 28-8-56-3.

Umpires: Amanullah Khan and Mansoor Ali.

†PAKISTAN v WEST INDIES

Second One-day International

At Gujranwala, November 4. West Indies won on faster scoring-rate. Put in, West Indies collapsed to 67 for five but were again rescued by Dujon, who in 83 minutes with Marshall added 115, a record for the seventh wicket in one-day internationals. His unbeaten 57 contained two sixes and five fours; there were seven fours in Marshall's 66 of 66 balls. Saleem

Jaffer, opening the bowling in the absence of Imran Khan with a finger injury, started the collapse by taking three wickets in ten balls. Pakistan themselves slipped to 75 for six, but Miandad and Yousuf looked to be bringing victory into sight when the gathering gloom made the prospect of a finish impossible. West Indies had been bowling their overs at an average of five minutes each, and when it looked as if Pakistan were being denied the chance to win, the crowd began throwing bottles and firecrackers at the West Indian fielders. At this, Richards took his team off. Under the regulations of the series, the maiden overs were discarded in calculating the scoring-rate.

Man of the Match: M. D. Marshall.

West Indies

C. G. Greenidge c Yousuf b Jaffer	10	M. D. Marshall run out	66
D. L. Haynes c Yousuf b Jaffer	9	W. K. M. Benjamin not out	2
R. B. Richardson lbw b Manzoor	23		
A. L. Logie b Jaffer	0	B 1, l-b 4, w 2, n-b 4	11
*I. V. A. Richards c Tauseef b Qadir	17		
†P. J. L. Dujon not out	57	1/19 2/22 3/22 4/67 (7 wkts, 50 overs) 196
R. A. Harper lbw b Qadir	1	5/67 6/79 7/194

C. A. Walsh and B. P. Patterson did not bat.

Bowling: Wasim 10-2-41-0; Jaffer 10-0-49-3; Manzoor 10-2-25-1; Qadir 10-1-45-2; Tauseef 5-1-17-0; Asif 5-1-14-0.

Pakistan

Mohsin Khan b Marshall	4	Abdul Qadir c Dujon b Benjamin	0
Shoaib Mohammad run out	3	†Salim Yousuf not out	23
Ramiz Raja c Richards b Benjamin	30	B 1, l-b 9, w 7	17
Asif Mujtaba c Richardson b Marshall	0		
*Javed Miandad not out	74	1/5 2/22 3/23 (6 wkts, 43.5 overs) 155
Manzoor Elahi c Dujon b Benjamin	4	4/65 5/75 6/75

Wasim Akram, Tauseef Ahmed and Saleem Jaffer did not bat.

Bowling: Marshall 8-2-18-2; Patterson 7.5-2-33-0; Benjamin 10-1-21-3; Walsh 10-1-31-0; Harper 8-0-42-0.

Umpires: Khizar Hayat and Tariq Ata.

PAKISTAN v WEST INDIES

Second Test Match

At Lahore, November 7, 8, 9. West Indies won by an innings and 10 runs. Provided with a wicket that favoured their fast bowlers, West Indies levelled the series in three days. Ironically, they had omitted one of their pacemen, Patterson, in favour of the off-spinner, Butts, so going into a Test match with two specialist spin bowlers for the first time in 58 matches: such was the nature of the pitch, and the brittleness of Pakistan's batting against pace and unpredictable bounce, that they bowled one over between them. It was the briefest of respites.

For Pakistan, who won the toss and batted, Asif Mujtaba made his début in place of the injured Salim Malik. It was a fiery introduction, and he was to take 25 minutes getting his first run. Only Miandad, for three hours twelve minutes, had the class to survive long. West Indies also found batting difficult against the speed and spin combination of Imran and Qadir and owed much to Greenidge's skill and patience for a total in excess of 200. It was to prove enough, however; only 87 runs behind on first innings, Pakistan could not make West Indies bat a second time. Unlucky to lose Qasim Omar when he was struck on the face by a ball from Walsh, they were all out an hour after tea for 77, their second-lowest Test score and their lowest at home.

Man of the Match: M. D. Marshall.

Close of play: First day, West Indies 15-0 (C. G. Greenidge 9*, D. L. Haynes 6*); Second day, West Indies 185-7 (M. D. Marshall 3*, C. G. Butts 4*).

Pakistan

Mohsin Khan b Marshall	0 – (2) lbw b Gray	1
Rizwan-uz-Zaman c Richardson b Marshall	2 – (1) b Marshall	1
Qasim Omar lbw b Marshall	4 – retired hurt	10
Javed Miandad c Greenidge b Walsh	46 – b Walsh	19
Ramiz Raja b Gray	15 – lbw b Gray	1
Asif Mujtaba b Marshall	8 – lbw b Richards	6
†Salim Yousuf lbw b Walsh	8 – (8) lbw b Gray	13
Abdul Qadir run out	12 – (9) b Walsh	2
Wasim Akram lbw b Marshall	1 – (11) c Harper b Walsh	0
*Imran Khan not out	13 – (7) c Dujon b Walsh	2
Tauseef Ahmed c Dujon b Walsh	0 – (10) not out	6
B 9, l-b 4, n-b 9	22 B 4, l-b 9, w 1, n-b 2	16

1/0 2/6 3/9 4/46 5/75   **131**   1/3 2/3 3/33 4/44 5/54   **77**
6/95 7/98 8/99 9/129   6/64 7/69 8/71 9/77

Bowling: *First Innings*—Marshall 18–5–33–5; Gray 13–0–28–1; Walsh 21.4–3–56–3; Harper 1–0–1–0. *Second Innings*—Marshall 8–3–14–1; Gray 17–7–20–3; Walsh 14.5–5–21–4; Richards 5–2–9–1.

West Indies

C. G. Greenidge lbw b Qadir	75	C. G. Butts c Yousuf b Imran 6
D. L. Haynes b Tauseef	18	A. H. Gray b Imran 10
R. B. Richardson lbw b Qadir	4	C. A. Walsh b Imran 8
H. A. Gomes b Imran	9	
*I. V. A. Richards c Yousuf b Qadir	44	B 15, l-b 5, n-b 3 23
†P. J. L. Dujon b Imran	2	
R. A. Harper lbw b Qadir	6	1/49 2/71 3/107 4/153 5/160 **218**
M. D. Marshall not out	13	6/172 7/179 8/189 9/204

Bowling: Imran 30.5–4–59–5; Wasim 9–2–16–0; Qadir 32–5–96–4; Tauseef 19–8–27–1.

Umpires: V. K. Ramaswamy and P. D. Reporter.

†PAKISTAN v WEST INDIES

Third One-day International

At Sialkot, November 14. West Indies won by four wickets. Electing to bat first after heavy dew had delayed the start and reduced the format to 45 overs, Pakistan always struggled but appeared to be fighting back through some fine bowling by Qadir, Tauseef and Shoaib. West Indies were 87 for four when Richards played on to his first ball, but Logie and Dujon, with another useful innings (two sixes, four fours), rode the crisis. Prior to the start, a crowd of some 5,000 outside the ground, unable to join the 25,000 already inside, was shelled with teargas canisters and many were injured in the stampede that followed. In another incident, five people suffered broken limbs when the branch of a tree gave way under the weight of watchers.

Man of the Match: P. J. L. Dujon.

Pakistan

Rizwan-uz-Zaman c Greenidge b Walsh	4	Manzoor Elahi not out 24
Shoaib Mohammad c Dujon b Walsh	7	†Salim Yousuf not out 3
Ramiz Raja lbw b Benjamin	13	B 1, l-b 8, w 22, n-b 2 33
Javed Miandad b Marshall	34	
Abdul Qadir b Harper	2	1/25 2/29 3/70 (7 wkts, 45 overs) **148**
*Imran Khan c and b Walsh	9	4/77 5/101
Ijaz Ahmed b Marshall	19	6/104 7/140

Saleem Jaffer and Tauseef Ahmed did not bat.

Bowling: Marshall 9–2–29–2; Gray 9–1–28–0; Walsh 9–1–38–3; Benjamin 9–1–19–1; Harper 9–0–25–1.

West Indies

C. G. Greenidge lbw b Jaffer	1	R. A. Harper c Manzoor b Imran		1
D. L. Haynes run out	38	M. D. Marshall not out		1
R. B. Richardson run out	36	L-b 7, w 3, n-b 1		11
A. L. Logie not out	25			
*I. V. A. Richards b Shoaib	0	1/1 2/79 3/86	(6 wkts, 44.3 overs)	151
†P. J. L. Dujon b Jaffer	38	4/87 5/145 6/146		

W. K. M. Benjamin, A. H. Gray and C. A. Walsh did not bat.

Bowling: Imran 9-2-25-1; Jaffer 8-1-29-2; Tauseef 8.3-1-20-0; Qadir 9-0-30-0; Shoaib 7-0-31-1; Manzoor 3-0-9-0.

Umpires: Amanullah Khan and Shakeel Khan.

†PAKISTAN v WEST INDIES

Fourth One-day International

At Multan, November 17. West Indies won by 89 runs. Both teams agreed beforehand to limit the match to 45 overs each, but Pakistan, winning the toss and fielding, bowled only 44 overs. Batting consistently, with only Richards failing to reach double figures, West Indies were put in an impregnable position by Harper and Dujon, who put on 49 from the last six overs, Harper twice hitting Imran for six. Miandad and Imran led Pakistan's recovery from 30 for four with 64 in fourteen overs, but Gray's second spell of four for 16 in four overs was decisive.

Man of the Match: A. H. Gray.

West Indies

D. L. Haynes b Tauseef	21	R. A. Harper not out		34
R. B. Richardson c Tauseef b Jaffer	26			
A. L. Logie lbw b Imran	46	B 16, l-b 6, w 1		23
*I. V. A. Richards b Tauseef	4			
H. A. Gomes run out	38	1/50 2/51 3/61	(5 wkts, 44 overs)	202
†P. J. L. Dujon not out	10	4/153 5/153		

M. D. Marshall, A. H. Gray, W. K. M. Benjamin and C. A. Walsh did not bat.

Bowling: Imran 9-1-46-1; Jaffer 9-1-22-1; Tauseef 9-1-29-2; Qadir 9-1-32-0; Shoaib 4-0-25-0; Wasim 4-0-26-0.

Pakistan

Shoaib Mohammad c Richards b Benjamin	11	Wasim Akram c Richards b Gray		4
Sajid Ali lbw b Marshall	7	Tauseef Ahmed c Dujon b Gray		1
Ramiz Raja c Dujon b Walsh	7	Saleem Jaffer not out		2
Javed Miandad c Gomes b Gray	30			
Ijaz Ahmed c Dujon b Walsh	1	B 5, l-b 5, w 5, n-b 1		16
*Imran Khan c Logie b Gray	24	1/15 2/27 3/27	(38.2 overs)	113
Abdul Qadir run out	1	4/30 5/94 6/95		
†Salim Yousuf st Dujon b Gomes	9	7/96 8/100 9/108		

Bowling: Marshall 5-1-7-1; Gray 9-0-36-4; Walsh 5-4-7-2; Benjamin 9-3-27-1; Harper 9-1-22-0; Richards 1-0-3-0; Gomes 0.2-0-1-1.

Umpires: Mahboob Shah and Shakoor Rana.

†PAKISTAN v WEST INDIES

Fifth One-day International

At Hyderabad, November 18. Pakistan won by 11 runs. Winning the toss for the first time on the tour, Richards put Pakistan in and saw them recover from 24 for two through partnerships between Miandad and Ramiz, Manzoor and Ijaz (54 in seven overs) and finally Imran and Yousuf. Haynes and Richardson provided a platform for a later charge, but Pakistan's bowlers held a tight rein and ensured that West Indies would not enjoy a clean sweep of the one-day internationals. Qadir broke a finger on his left hand trying to catch Haynes off his own bowling but had the satisfaction of dismissing Richards first ball.

Man of the Match: Imran Khan.

Pakistan

Sajid Ali c Harper b Richards	10	*Imran Khan not out		27
Shoaib Mohammad c Richards b Patterson	3	†Salim Yousuf not out		23
Ramiz Raja st Dujon b Harper	32	B 3, l-b 15, w 7, n-b 3		28
Javed Miandad b Benjamin	30			
Manzoor Elahi c Patterson b Richardson	31	1/13 2/24 3/85	(6 wkts, 45 overs)	202
Ijaz Ahmed run out	18	4/85 5/139 6/150		

Abdul Qadir, Tauseef Ahmed and Saleem Jaffer did not bat.

Bowling: Patterson 9-3-46-1; Walsh 8-2-25-0; Richards 9-1-24-1; Benjamin 9-0-36-1; Harper 9-0-49-1; Richardson 1-0-4-1.

West Indies

C. G. Greenidge c Qadir b Manzoor	13	W. K. M. Benjamin c Shoaib b Jaffer		0
D. L. Haynes c Miandad b Shoaib	59	H. A. Gomes not out		8
R. B. Richardson c Shoaib b Imran	70	L-b 16, w 2, n-b 1		19
*I. V. A. Richards lbw b Qadir	0			
A. L. Logie c Manzoor b Jaffer	16	1/31 2/122 3/122	(7 wkts, 45 overs)	191
R. A. Harper b Imran	0	4/172 5/172		
†P. J. L. Dujon not out	6	6/175 7/175		

C. A. Walsh and B. P. Patterson did not bat.

Bowling: Imran 9-1-37-2; Jaffer 9-1-37-2; Manzoor 7-1-38-1; Tauseef 9-1-30-0; Qadir 9-0-21-1; Shoaib 2-0-12-1.

Umpires: Masroor Ali and Shakeel Khan.

PAKISTAN v WEST INDIES

Third Test Match

At Karachi, November 20, 21, 22, 24, 25. Drawn. Stubborn defence by Imran Khan and Tauseef Ahmed throughout the last session of the match was rewarded when bad light brought the match to an end with nine overs still to be bowled. For Pakistan, it had been a grim, day-long struggle to prevent West Indies from winning their eighth consecutive series.

Richards, having won the toss, played his most authoritative innings of the tour, batting without unnecessary flourish for two and threequarter hours to provide stability to the middle order. Next morning, however, West Indies' last three wickets fell in 40 minutes, and when Pakistan's openers also went quickly, Ramiz Raja settled in for a war of attrition, concentrating on tenure and not allowing himself to be rattled by Miandad's run-out after they had put on 111 for the third wicket. Ramiz's 50, in 317 minutes, was the third-slowest in Test matches after T. E. Bailey's in 357 minutes against Australia at Brisbane in 1958-59 and C. J.

Tavaré's in 352 minutes against Pakistan at Lord's in 1982; in all, he batted for 408 minutes. With Yousuf again providing valuable runs, Pakistan conceded only 1 run on the first innings, but they conceded the initiative to West Indies by giving lives to Greenidge (second ball), Haynes and Richardson before the end of the third day.

Imran, troubled by a stomach upset that afternoon, resumed fully fit after the rest day and in the late afternoon produced an outstanding display of fast bowling, twice taking two wickets with consecutive balls in a spell of five for 10 in six overs. Only Haynes held on, becoming the third West Indian to carry his bat through a Test innings. Pakistan, needing 213 to win, were left with five overs to negotiate before the close: time enough for West Indies to capture two wickets and put them on the defensive. Marshall then struck twice in the morning, dismissing Mohsin and Miandad, but once again Ramiz stood firm, batting another 236 minutes for 29. Mudassar, too, was obdurate, but a score of 97 for seven at tea favoured a West Indies win. Instead, Imran and Tauseef, last-wicket heroes in the first Test, took the match, and the series, to a draw. Imran, whose 34th birthday it was, received the Man of the Match award.

Close of play: First day, West Indies 212-7 (R. A. Harper 6*, C. G. Butts 1*); Second day, Pakistan 157-4 (Ramiz Raja 42*, Asif Mujtaba 6*); Third day, West Indies 84-1 (D. L. Haynes 46*, R. B. Richardson 21*); Fourth day, Pakistan 16-2 (Mohsin Khan 4*).

West Indies

C. G. Greenidge c Yousuf b Mudassar	27	– b Qadir	8
D. L. Haynes lbw b Imran	3	– not out	88
R. B. Richardson c Asif b Jaffer	44	– c Ramiz b Qadir	32
H. A. Gomes lbw b Qadir	18	– lbw b Qadir	5
*I. V. A. Richards c Ramiz b Tauseef	70	– c Yousuf b Imran	28
†P. J. L. Dujon c Yousuf b Qadir	19	– c Yousuf b Jaffer	6
R. A. Harper lbw b Imran	9	– b Imran	4
M. D. Marshall b Tauseef	4	– lbw b Imran	0
C. G. Butts lbw b Qadir	17	– c Mohsin b Imran	12
A. H. Gray c Imran b Qadir	0	– b Imran	0
C. A. Walsh not out	0	– b Imran	0
B 14, l-b 11, w 1, n-b 3	29	B 7, l-b 13, w 1, n-b 7	28
	240		**211**

1/14 2/55 3/94 4/110 5/172
6/204 7/210 8/227 9/234

1/36 2/107 3/128 4/159 5/171
6/185 7/185 8/209 9/211

Bowling: First Innings—Imran 19-4-32-2; Jaffer 15-5-34-1; Mudassar 4-0-15-1; Qadir 31.5-3-107-4; Tauseef 17-7-27-2. *Second Innings*—Imran 22.3-2-46-6; Jaffer 14-4-23-1; Tauseef 12-2-36-0; Qadir 44-9-84-3; Asif 3-2-2-0.

Pakistan

Mudassar Nazar b Gray	16	– (6) lbw b Butts	25
Mohsin Khan c Richards b Marshall	1	– (1) c Greenidge b Marshall	4
Ramiz Raja c Harper b Butts	62	– (4) b Butts	29
Javed Miandad run out	76	– (5) b Marshall	4
*Imran Khan lbw b Butts	1	– (8) not out	15
Asif Mujtaba c Dujon b Marshall	12	– (7) c Dujon b Walsh	6
Qasim Omar c Richardson b Butts	5	– (2) c Dujon b Gray	1
†Salim Yousuf c Walsh b Butts	22	– (3) c Haynes b Marshall	10
Tauseef Ahmed c Richardson b Gray	3	– not out	7
Saleem Jaffer b Gray	9		
Abdul Qadir not out	8		
B 9, l-b 12, w 1, n-b 2	24	B 17, l-b 6, w 1	24
	239	(7 wkts)	**125**

1/19 2/29 3/140 4/145 5/172
6/179 7/215 8/218 9/222

1/3 2/16 3/19 4/25
5/73 6/95 7/95

Bowling: First Innings—Marshall 33-9-57-2; Gray 21.1-6-40-3; Harper 7-0-31-0; Walsh 11-2-17-0; Butts 38-15-73-4. *Second Innings*—Marshall 19-5-31-3; Gray 14-7-18-1; Walsh 22-11-30-1; Butts 22-9-22-2; Harper 1-0-1-0.

Umpires: V. K. Ramaswamy and P. D. Reporter.

THE SRI LANKANS IN INDIA, 1986-87

By R. MOHAN

India's long-awaited success in a home series was made possible by the Sri Lankans' reluctance to come to terms with spin bowling on a sporting pitch in the Second Test and on a doubtful one in the Third. With their 2-0 victory in the Tests, India thus avenged their unexpected defeat in Sri Lanka the previous season.

There was little hint of the eventual collapse of Sri Lankan confidence as the visitors made runs in plenty in the run-in to the Test series; nor in the First Test, which was played on a placid green pitch at Kanpur. The change came about only when the Indian spinners gained purchase from the wickets in Nagpur and Cuttack, and it was Maninder Singh's astonishing improvement, plus the accompanying boost to his morale as he got among the wickets, which held the key to the series. Supported well by his spin colleagues against batsmen who were crease-tied and preoccupied with survival, Maninder proved a difficult prospect, and the Sri Lankans' cricket was on a down curve once they lost the second Test by an innings and more than 100 runs.

Although the tour had been hastily rearranged after the government of India came forward to clear the visit, the Sri Lankans had sufficient time in which to prepare for the test by spin which was bound to come once Kapil Dev had accepted that neither he nor his fellow seam bowlers could attain the strike-rate that had featured in India's Tests abroad in the immediately preceding seasons. But their senior batsmen, especially Duleep Mendis and Roy Dias, never aspired to take control of events. With three left-handers, including the makeshift opener, Ravi Ratnayeke, batting high in the order, it should have been possible for the visitors to counter the left-arm spin of Maninder; instead, they were let down by a lack of temperament, in the case of Asanka Gurusinha and Arjuna Ranatunga, or foxed by Shivlal Yadav's off-spin. On the other hand, Dilip Vengsarkar's masterly batting on these same spinners' pitches was a sparkling counterpoint to the domination by India's bowlers. It was no coincidence that, by the end of the series, Vengsarkar had scored centuries in each of India's last four Test wins – at Lord's and Leeds in 1986, and then in Nagpur and Cuttack. His contribution to those victories was direct and brilliant.

Apart from Ratnayeke, who bowled his medium pace steadily, and Asoka de Silva, whose leg-spin could have been a threat to batsmen less accustomed to spin, Sri Lanka had no bowling capable of controlling the flow of a Test match. Asantha de Mel was but a shadow of his former self, while it was a wasted effort for a young bowler like Graeme Labrooy to indulge in pseudo-intimidatory tactics.

There was a slight incident during the Nagpur Test when the Sri Lankans felt that the umpires were tardy in coming to the aid of the fielders with sawdust in wet conditions. Otherwise, it was a tour devoid of controversy. So affected was the visiting team by the loss of the Test series that the one-day series was handed over on a platter, despite the fact that Sri Lanka had won the first match convincingly. It may have been some consolation for Sri Lanka, however, that the emerging players made a greater impact overall than the experienced ones, for from the point of view of the country's cricket, this gave confidence for its future.

SRI LANKAN TOUR RESULTS

Test matches – Played 3: Lost 2, Drawn 1.
First-class matches – Played 5: Lost 2, Drawn 3.
Losses – India (2).
Draws – India, Indian Board President's XI, Indian Under-25 XI.
Non first-class matches – Played 5: Won 1, Lost 4. *Win* – India. *Losses* – India (4).

TEST MATCH AVERAGES

INDIA – BATTING

	T	I	NO	R	HI	100s	Avge
D. B. Vengsarkar ...	3	3	0	376	166	2	125.33
Kapil Dev	3	3	1	234	163	1	117.00
S. M. Gavaskar	3	3	0	255	176	1	85.00
R. Lamba	3	3	0	101	53	0	33.66
K. Srikkanth	3	3	0	62	40	0	20.66
R. J. Shastri	3	3	0	37	19	0	12.33

Played in three Tests: Maninder Singh 2; K. S. More 6*. Played in two Tests: M. Amarnath 131, 39; B. Arun 2*, 2; N. S. Yadav 3; Chetan Sharma did not bat. Played in one Test: M. Azharuddin 199.

* *Signifies not out.*

BOWLING

	O	M	R	W	BB	Avge
N. S. Yadav	61.1	19	150	11	5-76	13.63
Maninder Singh	103.5	33	279	18	7-51	15.50
R. J. Shastri	44	12	114	5	4-11	22.80
Kapil Dev	88	22	231	9	4-69	25.66
B. Arun	42	12	116	4	3-76	29.00

Also bowled: Chetan Sharma 41-4-162-3; K. Srikkanth 1-0-4-0.

SRI LANKA – BATTING

	T	I	NO	R	HI	100s	Avge
J. R. Ratnayeke	3	5	0	206	93	0	41.20
R. J. Ratnayake ...	2	4	2	60	32*	0	30.00
A. Ranatunga	3	5	0	148	59	0	29.60
R. L. Dias	3	5	0	116	50	0	23.20
A. P. Gurusinha ...	3	5	0	113	40	0	22.60
S. Wettimuny	3	5	0	109	79	0	21.80
P. A. de Silva	3	5	0	94	33	0	18.80
L. R. D. Mendis ...	3	5	0	76	38	0	15.20
E. A. R. de Silva ...	3	5	0	57	21	0	11.40
R. G. de Alwis ...	3	5	0	14	13	0	2.80

Played in one Test: S. D. Anurasiri 0*, 0*; A. L. F. de Mel 25; B. R. Jurangpathy 0, 0; G. F. Labrooy 5*.

* *Signifies not out.*

BOWLING

	O	M	R	W	BB	Avge
S. D. Anurasiri	26	3	71	4	4-71	17.75
J. R. Ratnayeke	92.4	9	306	9	5-85	34.00
R. J. Ratnayake	65	9	237	3	2-139	79.00

Also bowled: A. L. F. de Mel 31–4–119–1; E. A. R. de Silva 118–18–338–1; A. P. Gurusinha 8.5–0–67–2; B. R. Jurangpathy 21–3–69–1; G. F. Labrooy 35–4–164–1; A. Ranatunga 25–7–97–0; S. Wettimuny 2–0–16–0.

SRI LANKAN AVERAGES – FIRST-CLASS MATCHES

BATTING

	M	I	NO	R	HI	100s	Avge
S. Wettimuny	4	6	1	336	227*	1	67.20
P. A. de Silva	4	6	1	209	115*	1	41.80
J. R. Ratnayeke	4	6	0	244	93	0	40.66
A. Ranatunga	4	6	0	232	84	0	38.66
R. L. Dias	5	7	0	256	81	0	36.57
R. J. Ratnayake	3	4	2	60	32*	0	30.00
A. P. Gurusinha	4	6	0	172	59	0	28.66
A. L. F. de Mel	2	2	0	47	25	0	23.50
L. R. D. Mendis	5	7	0	156	65	0	22.28
B. R. Jurangpathy	3	3	1	27	27*	0	13.50
E. A. R. de Silva	4	5	0	57	21	0	11.40
R. G. de Alwis	5	6	0	27	13	0	4.50

Played in three matches: S. D. Anurasiri 0*, 0*. Played in two matches: G. F. Labrooy 5*, 0*; R. S. Madugalle 15*, 39. Played in one match: R. S. Mahanama 91.

* *Signifies not out.*

BOWLING

	O	M	R	W	BB	Avge
J. R. Ratnayeke	107.4	14	353	10	5-85	35.30
S. D. Anurasiri	64	8	207	5	4-71	41.40
G. F. Labrooy	68	8	301	5	4-137	60.20
R. J. Ratnayake	82	12	281	3	2-139	93.66

Also bowled: A. L. F. de Mel 60–7–213–2; E. A. R. de Silva 133–18–395–1; P. A. de Silva 7–0–35–0; R. L. Dias 6–0–39–0; A. P. Gurusinha 17.5–2–97–3; B. R. Jurangpathy 37–3–134–2; R. S. Madugalle 4–0–17–0; L. R. D. Mendis 6–0–20–0; A. Ranatunga 25–7–97–0; S. Wettimuny 2–0–16–0.

FIELDING

5 – R. G. de Alwis (4 ct, 1 st); 3 – B. R. Jurangpathy; 2 – E. A. R. de Silva, substitute (R. S. Mahanama); 1 – R. L. Dias, A. P. Gurusinha, A. Ranatunga, S. Wettimuny.

INDIAN BOARD PRESIDENT'S XI v SRI LANKANS

At Gwalior, December 7, 8, 9. Drawn. The Sri Lankans' introduction to Indian conditions was a happy one for the batsmen. On a placid wicket on which not even the first innings could be completed, Wettimuny batted through the first five sessions for his first-ever double-hundred (34 fours) and participated in three century partnerships as the other top-order batsmen attuned themselves well until the declaration. Of those in contention for a place in the Indian Test squad, Lamba remained in the limelight, his 113 containing two sixes and eleven fours.

Close of play: First day, Sri Lankans 259-2 (S. Wettimuny 113*, R. L. Dias 32*); Second day, Indian Board President's XI 80-1 (L. S. Rajput 29*, R. Lamba 19*).

Sri Lankans

S. Wettimuny not out 227	R. S. Madugalle not out 15		
J. R. Ratnayeke c Arun Lal b Gudge ... 38	B 5, l-b 9, n-b 5 19		
A. P. Gurusinha c Lamba b Gudge ... 59			
R. L. Dias c Lamba b Gudge ... 81	1/69 2/194 3/358 (4 wkts dec.) 504		
*L. R. D. Mendis c and b Gudge ... 65	4/465		

B. R. Jurangpathy, †R. G. de Alwis, R. J. Ratnayake, E. A. R. de Silva and S. D. Anurasiri did not bat.

Bowling: Ghai 19-2-95-0; Singh 16-4-46-0; Raman 51-15-108-0; Gudge 35-2-171-4; Srikkanth 13-3-27-0; Rajput 10-3-23-0; Arun Lal 6-1-20-0.

Indian Board President's XI

*K. Srikkanth c Dias b Ratnayeke 31	W. V. Raman not out 39		
L. S. Rajput b Anurasiri 82			
R. Lamba c Jurangpathy b Gurusinha .113	B 1, l-b 2, n-b 1 4		
Arun Lal b Jurangpathy 34			
M. Azharuddin not out 52	1/39 2/184 3/249 4/279 (4 wkts) 355		

K. Azad, †K. S. More, S. C. Gudge, R. P. Singh and R. S. Ghai did not bat.

Bowling: Ratnayeke 15-5-47-1; Ratnayake 17-3-44-0; de Silva 15-0-57-0; Anurasiri 23-3-78-1; Jurangpathy 16-0-65-1; Gurusinha 9-2-30-1; Dias 5-0-31-0.

Umpires: S. K. Ghosh and R. B. Gupta.

INDIAN UNDER-25 XI v SRI LANKANS

At Kolhapur, December 12, 13, 14. Drawn. The Sri Lankans amassed 500 for the second match in succession on another typically Indian wicket which offered nothing for bowlers of any variety. Aravinda de Silva batted aggressively for his hundred, hitting four sixes and ten fours in all; he and Mahanama had put on 191 when he was forced to retire hurt. Labrooy made an early breakthrough for the visitors, but Saldanha gave evidence of his promise with a polished 70 and then Pandit and Arun made centuries in the second unbroken partnership of more than 190 in three days.

Sri Lankans

R. S. Mahanama st Karim b Azim 91	B. R. Jurangpathy retired hurt 27		
†R. G. de Alwis c Sidhu b Arun 13	A. L. F. de Mel c Shome b Arun 22		
P. A. de Silva not out 115	G. F. Labrooy not out 0		
A. Ranatunga c Sidhu b Arun 84	B 4, l-b 10, w 6, n-b 17 37		
R. L. Dias b Shome 59			
*L. R. D. Mendis c Poonawalla b Shome 15	1/32 2/260 3/353 (7 wkts dec.) 502		
R. S. Madugalle c Karim b Sharma . . . 39	4/387 5/417 6/460 7/494		

S. D. Anurasiri did not bat.

Bowling: Arun 31-1-114-3; Shome 22-2-79-2; Poonawalla 3-1-10-0; Sidhu 3-1-15-0; Azim 25-3-116-1; Jadhav 21-2-95-0; Sharma 22-1-59-1.

Indian Under-25 XI

C. Saldanha b Labrooy	70	B. Arun not out	107
N. S. Sidhu c de Alwis b Labrooy	11		
R. Poonawalla b Labrooy	14	B 6, l-b 17, w 1, n-b 22	46
S. Kalyani lbw b Labrooy	41		
*C. S. Pandit not out	101	1/39 2/62 3/135 (5 wkts) 392	
A. Sharma c de Alwis b de Mel	2	4/193 5/199	

S. Jadhav, †S. S. Karim, G. Shome, jnr. and Azim Khan did not bat.

Bowling: de Mel 29-3-94-1; Labrooy 33-4-137-4; Dias 1-0-8-0; Anurasiri 15-2-58-0; de Silva 7-0-35-0; Madugalle 4-0-17-0; Mendis 6-0-20-0.

Umpires: R. Mehra and S. R. Ramachandra Rao.

INDIA v SRI LANKA

First Test Match

At Kanpur, December 17, 18, 20, 21, 22. Drawn. Sri Lanka, opting to bat on a grassy wicket, quickly found that it was ideal for strokeplay, and while Ratnayeke grafted his way to his highest Test score, Wettimuny took a more active role in Sri Lanka's first three-figure opening partnership in Tests. With no play on the second day, owing to rain and fog, it was three days later when Ratnayeke resumed, only to fall quickly to Kapil Dev, the Indian captain's first Test wicket in 106 fruitless overs since his dismissal of Athey at Birmingham in July. Dias, surviving a chance before he had scored, and Ranatunga hit stylish half-centuries to set Sri Lanka towards their highest score against India, and then, when the home team batted, Gavaskar compiled a typically sound and long innings until, in vexation over Labrooy's continued and unchecked use of the bouncer, he virtually gave his wicket away. He had, however, achieved his ambition of scoring a Test hundred (his 34th) in the city where his wife grew up. Azharuddin put behind him a lean patch with a marathon innings that had come almost to a standstill when he was leg-before on the threshold of a double-hundred. Both he and Kapil Dev (165 balls, one six, nineteen fours) made their highest scores in Tests, while their 272 for the sixth wicket, at more than 5 an over, was only 26 short of the record recently established in the series against Australia. However, India's 676 for seven was both their highest total in all Tests and the highest in a Test match in India.

Man of the Match: S. M. Gavaskar.

Close of play: First day, Sri Lanka 217-2 (J. R. Ratnayeke 93*, A. P. Gurusinha 0*); Second day, No play; Third day, India 74-1 (S. M. Gavaskar 39*, R. Lamba 13*); Fourth day, India 321-3 (S. M. Gavaskar 148*, M. Azharuddin 59*).

Sri Lanka

S. Wettimuny lbw b Chetan	79	A. L. F. de Mel c Arun b Shastri	25
J. R. Ratnayeke lbw b Kapil Dev	93	E. A. R. de Silva lbw b Arun	21
P. A. de Silva b Arun	26	G. F. Labrooy not out	5
A. P. Gurusinha b Kapil Dev	19		
R. L. Dias c Azharuddin b Arun	50	B 1, l-b 10, w 6, n-b 19	36
*L. R. D. Mendis lbw b Chetan	1		
A. Ranatunga lbw b Maninder	52	1/159 2/217 3/217 4/286 5/292	420
†R. G. de Alwis b Maninder	13	6/355 7/355 8/389 9/394	

Bowling: Kapil Dev 30-11-81-2; Arun 27-7-76-3; Chetan 31-4-122-2; Maninder 32-12-89-2; Shastri 17-6-37-1; Srikkanth 1-0-4-0.

India

S. M. Gavaskar c Wettimuny b Labrooy	176	*Kapil Dev lbw b Ratnayeke	163
K. Srikkanth c de Alwis b Ratnayeke	18	B. Arun not out	2
R. Lamba run out	24		
D. B. Vengsarkar c Gurusinha b de Mel	57	B 1, l-b 11, w 1, n-b 18	31
M. Azharuddin lbw b Ratnayeke	199	1/50 2/100 3/217 4/380 (7 wkts) 676	
R. J. Shastri lbw b Ratnayeke	6	5/399 6/671 7/676	

†K. S. More, Chetan Sharma and Maninder Singh did not bat.

Bowling: de Mel 31-4-119-1; Labrooy 35-4-164-1; Ratnayeke 37.1-2-132-4; E. A. R. de Silva 40-7-133-0; Ranatunga 15-4-58-0; Gurusinha 7-0-42-0; Wettimuny 2-0-16-0.

Umpires: R. B. Gupta and V. K. Ramaswamy.

†INDIA v SRI LANKA

First One-day International

At Kanpur, December 24. Sri Lanka won by 117 runs. The pitch which had played so well in the Test match was watered and used again for the one-day international, but it played so unreliably that only a ninth-wicket stand of 40 in the last four overs gave Sri Lanka a reasonable total after they had been put in. India collapsed against Ranatunga's accurate slow-medium pace and were dismissed for their lowest one-day score at home – a total only 16 runs higher than their record low.

Man of the Match: A. Ranatunga.

Sri Lanka

R. S. Mahanama c Vengsarkar b Kapil Dev .	13	†R. G. de Alwis b Maninder 15
J. R. Ratnayeke lbw b Kapil Dev	7	A. L. F. de Mel not out 23
A. P. Gurusinha c Madan Lal b Maninder .	35	R. J. Ratnayeke not out 19
P. A. de Silva c Maninder b Chetan ...	3	L-b 7, w 2, n-b 3 12
A. Ranatunga lbw b Arun	31	
R. L. Dias c and b Maninder	11	1/15 2/33 3/43　(8 wkts, 46 overs) 195
*L. R. D. Mendis b Chetan	26	4/95 5/101 6/117
		7/150 8/155

E. A. R. de Silva did not bat.

Bowling: Kapil Dev 7-3-10-2; Arun 8-0-43-1; Chetan 8-0-50-2; Madan Lal 8-1-36-0; Maninder 10-2-24-3; Shastri 5-0-25-0.

India

S. M. Gavaskar c de Alwis b Ratnayeke	2	Madan Lal c Mahanama b Ratnayeke . 1
K. Srikkanth c de Alwis b Ranatunga .	17	Chetan Sharma c Gurusinha b Ranatunga . 8
R. Lamba lbw b Ratnayeke	5	Maninder Singh not out 0
D. B. Vengsarkar run out	15	L-b 1, w 3, n-b 1 5
R. J. Shastri b Ranatunga	8	
*Kapil Dev c and b Ratnayeke	9	1/6 2/18 3/37 4/47 5/56　(24.1 overs) 78
†C. S. Pandit c and b Ranatunga	0	6/59 7/59 8/65 9/78
B. Arun c E. A. R. de Silva b Ratnayeke	8	

Bowling: de Mel 7-1-22-0; Ratnayeke 6-1-16-2; Ranatunga 6-1-14-4; E. A. R. de Silva 2-0-13-0; Ratnayeke 3.1-0-12-3.

Umpires: D. N. Dotiwala and S. R. Phookan.

INDIA v SRI LANKA

Second Test Match

At Nagpur, December 27, 28, 30, 31. India won by an innings and 106 runs to record their first victory in Tests against Sri Lanka. The Sri Lankans, having chosen to bat first, were disconcerted to see the ball turning so soon on a sporting pitch and were all out before tea on the first day. Ranatunga's brave, stroke-filled 59 from 77 deliveries provided their only relief as Yadav, with well-flighted off-spin, and Maninder Singh, slow left-arm, with good support from the close-in fieldsmen, exploited some nervous handling of spin bowling. Yadav's figures were his best in Tests. India's consolidation of their position was held up by bad light on the first day and rain and a damp outfield on the second, when the Sri Lankans were quirky about resuming in such conditions. Amarnath, returning after injury in place of the injured Azharuddin, and Vengsarkar drove home India's advantage after the former had shared a century stand with Lamba, who opened instead of Gavaskar. Amarnath batted for six minutes under six hours and became, at 61, the fourth to score 4,000 runs for India. His hundred was his eleventh in Tests, Vengsarkar's was his thirteenth. Gavaskar, recovered from the fever that had indisposed him, made possible a declaration at lunch on the fourth day with a versatile 74 off 79 balls, revealing his adaptability in a situation requiring quick runs. From one over from Ranatunga he took 18 runs, including two successive sixes. For three hours in the afternoon, Maninder mesmerised the opposition to return career-best figures of seven for 51 and finish with ten wickets in a Test for the first time. Only the left-handed Ratnayeke, batting for 2 hours 50 minutes, and Mendis, striking out boldly, provided any resistance.

Man of the Match: Maninder Singh and D. B. Vengsarkar (shared).

Close of play: First day, India 0-0 (K. Srikkanth 0*, R. Lamba 0*); Second day, India 54-1 (R. Lamba 19*, M. Amarnath 26*); Third day, India 324-3 (D. B. Vengsarkar 115*, S. M. Gavaskar 10*).

Sri Lanka

S. Wettimuny c Amarnath b Chetan	6	– c Srikkanth b Kapil Dev	6
J. R. Ratnayeke c Shastri b Kapil Dev	17	– c Gavaskar b Maninder	54
A. P. Gurusinha c Amarnath b Yadav	29	– c and b Yadav	15
R. L. Dias b Maninder	6	– b Maninder	2
P. A. de Silva lbw b Yadav	33	– c sub (Arun Lal) b Maninder	6
A. Ranatunga c Amarnath b Yadav	59	– (7) c Gavaskar b Maninder	5
*L. R. D. Mendis c Srikkanth b Maninder	1	– (6) b Maninder	38
B. R. Jurangpathy b Maninder	0	– c Vengsarkar b Yadav	0
†R. G. de Alwis c Vengsarkar b Yadav	1	– (11) c More b Maninder	0
R. J. Ratnayeke not out	32	– not out	4
E. A. R. de Silva c Shastri b Yadav	16	– (9) c Srikkanth b Maninder	0
B 2, l-b 1, n-b 1	4	B 4, l-b 5, n-b 2	11

1/7 2/38 3/52 4/66 5/105   204   1/15 2/42 3/47 4/57 5/122   141
6/110 7/110 8/129 9/160   6/132 7/137 8/137 9/141

Bowling: *First Innings*—Kapil Dev 10-3-29-1; Chetan 5-0-26-1; Maninder 20-6-56-3; Yadav 19.1-4-76-5; Shastri 5-2-14-0. *Second Innings*—Kapil Dev 6-1-16-1; Chetan 5-0-14-0; Yadav 14-6-21-2; Maninder 17.4-4-51-7; Shastri 6-0-30-0.

India

K. Srikkanth c de Alwis b Ratnayake	4	*Kapil Dev not out	11
R. Lamba c Jurangpathy b E. A. R. de Silva	53	R. J. Shastri c sub (R. S. Mahanama) b Gurusinha	12
M. Amarnath c sub (R. S. Mahanama) b Jurangpathy	131		
D. B. Vengsarkar c Jurangpathy b Ratnayeke	153	L-b 4, w 1, n-b 8	13
S. M. Gavaskar c E. A. R. de Silva b Gurusinha	74		

1/5 2/131 3/304   (6 wkts dec.) 451
4/420 5/428 6/451

†K. S. More, Chetan Sharma, N. S. Yadav and Maninder Singh did not bat.

Bowling: Ratnayake 35-4-139-2; Ratnayeke 28-4-89-0; Ranatunga 6-1-34-0; E. A. R. de Silva 38-5-91-1; Jurangpathy 21-3-69-1; Gurusinha 1.5-0-25-2.

Umpires: R. Mehra and P. D. Reporter.

INDIA v SRI LANKA

Third Test Match

At Cuttack, January 4, 5, 6, 7. India won by an innings and 67 runs. The Third Test began a day behind schedule as a mark of respect following the death on January 2 of Dr Harekrushna Mahtab, a former Chief Minister of the State of Orissa. Kapil Dev's reversal of fortune in winning the toss gave India an immediate and undeniable advantage as the wicket at the Barabati Stadium was virtually unprepared. It was an unpropitious stage for the city's first Test match, for the bounce and movement off the pitch were unpredictable from the start. In such conditions, Vengsarkar's highest Test innings of 166 (279 balls, fourteen fours) was especially praiseworthy. He was accompanied for much of the first day by the resolute Amarnath, who batted just over four hours for his 39, but there was a change of tempo on the second day when Kapil Dev joined Vengsarkar in a sixth-wicket stand of 111 in 25 overs.

That a total of 400 would be beyond Sri Lanka's reach became obvious as Maninder Singh and Kapil Dev, bowling at slow-medium pace and producing shooters almost at will, worked their way through the Sri Lankan batting. A seventh-wicket stand between Dias and Aravinda de Silva promised to save Sri Lanka from following-on, but when four wickets fell for 3 runs they were batting again before the close of the third day, 209 behind and soon losing wickets to the spinners. Next morning Kapil Dev scuttled Ratnayake with a low-bouncing delivery to claim his 300th wicket for India and, one day after his 28th birthday and soon into his 83rd Test, share with I. T. Botham the "double" of 3,000 runs and 300 wickets in Test cricket. Shastri, who had been under-bowled in the first innings, hastened the end with four for 11 in eleven overs, and within minutes after lunch India had registered their first series victory at home since K. W. R. Fletcher's England side were beaten in 1981-82.

Man of the Match: Kapil Dev. *Man of the Series:* D. B. Vengsarkar.

Close of play: First day, India 224-3 (D. B. Vengsarkar 98*, R. Lamba 24*); Second day, Sri Lanka 37-2 (A. P. Gurusinha 4*, E. A. R. de Silva 1*); Third day, Sri Lanka 51-3 (R. J. Ratnayake 0*).

India

S. M. Gavaskar lbw b Ratnayake	5	B. Arun c Ranatunga b Anurasiri	2
K. Srikkanth b Ratnayake	40	†K. S. More not out	6
M. Amarnath b Anurasiri	39	N. S. Yadav st de Alwis b Anurasiri	3
D. B. Vengsarkar lbw b Ratnayake	166	Maninder Singh lbw b Ratnayake	2
R. Lamba lbw b Ratnayake	24	B 8, l-b 19, n-b 7	34
R. J. Shastri c E. A. R. de Silva b Ratnayake	19		
*Kapil Dev b Anurasiri	60		400

1/18 2/70 3/164 4/225 5/272
6/383 7/385 8/387 9/397

Bowling: Ratnayake 30-5-98-1; Ratnayake 27.3-3-85-5; E. A. R. de Silva 40-6-114-0; Anurasiri 26-3-71-4; Ranatunga 4-2-5-0.

Sri Lanka

S. Wettimuny c Kapil Dev b Maninder	6	– b Shastri	12
J. R. Ratnayeke c Srikkanth b Yadav	20	– c Srikkanth b Yadav	22
A. P. Gurusinha c Lamba b Arun	40	– c Arun b Yadav	10
E. A. R. de Silva b Kapil Dev	1	– (9) st More b Yadav	19
*L. R. D. Mendis b Kapil Dev	9	– lbw b Shastri	27
A. Ranatunga lbw b Kapil Dev	30	– lbw b Maninder	2
R. L. Dias c Kapil Dev b Maninder	49	– b Shastri	9
P. A. de Silva lbw b Maninder	21	– c Shastri b Maninder	8
R. J. Ratnayake lbw b Maninder	0	– (4) b Kapil Dev	24
†R. G. de Alwis c Srikkanth b Kapil Dev	0	– lbw b Shastri	0
S. D. Anurasiri not out	0	– not out	0
B 1, l-b 11, n-b 3	15	B 2, l-b 5, n-b 2	9
	191		142

1/27 2/33 3/38 4/56 5/95 6/125
7/188 8/190 9/191

1/35 2/45 3/51 4/91 5/94
6/112 7/121 8/121 9/124

Bowling: *First Innings*—Kapil Dev 26-3-69-4; Arun 13-5-26-1; Maninder 17.1-6-41-4; Yadav 15-6-21-1; Shastri 5-0-22-0. *Second Innings*—Kapil Dev 16-4-36-1; Arun 2-0-14-0; Yadav 13-3-32-3; Maninder 17-5-42-2; Shastri 11-4-11-4.

Umpires: R. B. Gupta and V. K. Ramaswamy.

†INDIA v SRI LANKA

Second One-day International

At Gauhati, January 11. India won by eight wickets. The Sri Lankans' weakness against spin was anticipated by the preparation of a "turner" at the Nehru Stadium, nestling attractively in a valley. In a match restricted to 46 overs a side because of a damp pitch, caused by excessive watering the evening before, the Indian spinners held sway. Gavaskar dominated India's reply with an unbeaten 70, which brought him the Man of the Match award for the first time in limited-overs cricket.

Sri Lanka

J. R. Ratnayeke c Shastri b Yadav	11	R. J. Ratnayake run out	17
P. A. de Silva c Azharuddin b Madan Lal	3	A. L. F. de Mel c Azharuddin b Shastri	7
A. P. Gurusinha b Yadav	6	†R. G. de Alwis not out	6
R. L. Dias lbw b Shastri	26	B 4, l-b 8, w 3, n-b 1	16
A. Ranatunga c Srikkanth b Maninder	0		
*L. R. D. Mendis lbw b Kapil Dev	31	1/7 2/27 3/33 4/33 (8 wkts, 46 overs)	145
R. S. Madugalle not out	22	5/91 6/93 7/120 8/135	

E. A. R. de Silva did not bat.

Bowling: Kapil Dev 9-1-32-1; Madan Lal 9-1-25-1; Yadav 9-2-18-2; Maninder 10-1-30-1; Shastri 9-0-28-2.

India

K. Srikkanth lbw b Ratnayake 19
S. M. Gavaskar not out 70
R. Lamba lbw b Ratnayake 2
D. B. Vengsarkar not out 43
    L-b 1, w 9, n-b 2 12

1/44 2/50   (2 wkts, 27.3 overs) 146

M. Azharuddin, R. J. Shastri, *Kapil Dev, †C. S. Pandit, Madan Lal, Maninder Singh and N. S. Yadav did not bat.

Bowling: de Mel 7-0-43-0; Ratnayake 6-0-26-1; Ratnayeke 6.3-0-38-1; Ranatunga 5-0-24-0; E. A. R. de Silva 3-1-14-0.

Umpires: R. B. Gupta and P. G. Pandit.

†INDIA v SRI LANKA

Third One-day International

At New Delhi, January 13. India won by six wickets. By deliberately slowing down the over-rate after Gurusinha (two sixes, three fours) and Ranatunga (three sixes, two fours) had batted splendidly in ideal conditions, India, having put Sri Lanka in, were able to restrict them to 208. On a small ground like the Feroz Shah Kotla, this was a medium-sized target. Vengsarkar was in assertive form, and with Lamba he kept India ahead of the asking-rate.

Man of the Match: A. Ranatunga.

Sri Lanka

J. R. Ratnayeke c Pandit b Kulkarni . .	22	*L. R. D. Mendis not out	9
P. A. de Silva b Kulkarni	51	R. L. Dias not out	1
A. P. Gurusinha c Madan Lal			
b Azharuddin .	54	B 2, l-b 11, w 9, n-b 1	23
A. Ranatunga c Pandit b Kapil Dev . . .	41		
R. J. Ratnayake c Maninder b Kulkarni .	2	1/54 2/132 3/158 (6 wkts, 44 overs) 208	
A. L. F. de Mel b Kapil Dev	5	4/162 5/179 6/201	

R. S. Madugalle, †R. G. de Alwis and G. F. Labrooy did not bat.

Bowling: Kapil Dev 8-0-48-2; Madan Lal 7-1-21-0; Kulkarni 10-0-42-3; Maninder 10-2-30-0; Shastri 7-0-40-0; Azharuddin 2-0-14-1.

India

K. Srikkanth c Ranatunga b Ratnayeke	28	*Kapil Dev not out	16
S. M. Gavaskar c sub (R. S. Mahanama)			
b Ranatunga .	36	B 1, l-b 1, w 8	10
M. Azharuddin c Ranatunga b Labrooy	6		
D. B. Vengsarkar b Ranatunga	56	1/50 2/60 3/97 (4 wkts, 41.3 overs) 209	
R. Lamba not out	57	4/163	

R. J. Shastri, †C. S. Pandit, Madan Lal, Maninder Singh and R. R. Kulkarni did not bat.

Bowling: Ratnayake 8.3-0-48-1; Labrooy 10-0-48-1; de Mel 7-0-36-0; Ranatunga 10-0-42-2; Ratnayeke 6-0-33-0.

Umpires: S. K. Ghosh and R. R. Kadam.

†INDIA v SRI LANKA

Fourth One-day International

At Baroda, January 15. India won by 94 runs. India, although unable to maintain the frenetic rate provided by Srikkanth and Gavaskar, none the less put up a sizeable score after being put in on yet another pitch obviously prepared to suit the spinners. The Sri Lankan innings never developed as Yadav, Maninder and Shastri used the pitch to deny runs and also keep the batsmen on the hop.

Man of the Match: S. M. Gavaskar.

India

K. Srikkanth c Mahanama b Anurasiri .	63	M. Azharuddin lbw b Labrooy	5
S. M. Gavaskar c Mendis b Labrooy . .	69	R. R. Kulkarni not out	3
R. Lamba st de Alwis b Anurasiri	22	Maninder Singh not out	1
*Kapil Dev b Ratnayeke	5		
D. B. Vengsarkar c sub (A. L. F. de Mel)		B 2, l-b 7, w 2, n-b 2	13
b Labrooy .	22		
R. J. Shastri c Mendis b Labrooy	20	1/96 2/161 3/167 (8 wkts, 43 overs) 235	
†C. S. Pandit c sub (B. R. Jurangpathy)		4/169 5/199 6/224	
b Labrooy .	12	7/228 8/232	

N. S. Yadav did not bat.

Bowling: Ratnayake 10-0-34-0; Labrooy 10-0-57-5; Ratnayeke 8-0-52-1; Anurasiri 10-0-45-2; Ranatunga 4-0-30-0; Gurusinha 1-0-8-0.

Sri Lanka

R. S. Mahanama b Kulkarni	25	G. F. Labrooy lbw b Srikkanth	12
J. R. Ratnayeke st Pandit b Yadav	14	S. D. Anurasiri not out	0
A. P. Gurusinha st Pandit b Yadav	26	R. S. Madugalle absent ill	
R. L. Dias run out	0	L-b 7, w 2, n-b 2	11
A. Ranatunga b Maninder	20		
*L. R. D. Mendis c Azharuddin b Shastri	21	1/45 2/49 3/49 4/94	(36.3 overs) 141
R. J. Ratnayake c Lamba b Shastri	2	5/96 6/101 7/126	
†R. G. de Alwis c Srikkanth b Shastri	10	8/128 9/141	

Bowling: Kulkarni 8-1-31-1; Kapil Dev 6-1-15-0; Yadav 7-0-20-2; Maninder 10-1-38-1; Shastri 5-1-24-3; Srikkanth 0.3-0-6-1.

Umpires: P. G. Pandit and S. R. Ramachandra Rao.

†INDIA v SRI LANKA

Fifth One-day International

At Bombay, January 17. India won by 10 runs. A memorable match provided the highest runs-per-over quotient in international cricket as Sri Lanka bravely chased India's 299. Azharuddin hit his first hundred in one-day cricket and saw India to their highest score in a one-day international – compiled in just 40 overs after Mendis had asked them to bat. Mahanama (91 balls) laid the foundation for Sri Lanka's assault, which was at its peak when Gurusinha (34 balls, two sixes, five fours) was hitting Kapil Dev out of the ground. Such an extraordinary innings could not continue, however, and when Mahanama was run out soon after Gurusinha's dismissal, Sri Lanka's momentum was checked.

Man of the Match: R. S. Mahanama.

India

K. Srikkanth c Mahanama b Ranatunga	46	*Kapil Dev not out	4
S. M. Gavaskar c de Mel b Ranatunga	25		
M. Azharuddin not out	108	B 5, l-b 9, w 8, n-b 3	25
D. B. Vengsarkar c de Mel b Ratnayeke	52		
R. Lamba c sub (B. R. Jurangpathy) b Labrooy	39	1/67 2/88 3/203	(4 wkts, 40 overs) 299
		4/287	

Madan Lal, †C. S. Pandit, R. R. Kulkarni, Maninder Singh and N. S. Yadav did not bat.

Bowling: Ratnayake 10-1-63-0; Ratnayeke 6-0-50-1; de Mel 4-0-45-0; Ranatunga 10-0-59-2; Labrooy 10-0-68-1.

Sri Lanka

S. Wettimuny b Kulkarni	14	A. L. F. de Mel b Kapil Dev	7
†R. S. Mahanama run out	98	J. R. Ratnayeke not out	5
A. Ranatunga c Yadav b Madan Lal	29	L-b 7, w 4	11
*L. R. D. Mendis run out	30		
R. L. Dias st Pandit b Yadav	15	1/36 2/84 3/147	(7 wkts, 40 overs) 289
A. P. Gurusinha c Kapil Dev b Kulkarni	52	4/174 5/244	
R. J. Ratnayake not out	28	6/256 7/266	

S. D. Anurasiri and G. F. Labrooy did not bat.

Bowling: Kapil Dev 9-0-68-1; Kulkarni 9-0-57-2; Madan Lal 7-0-51-1; Maninder 10-0-69-0; Yadav 5-0-37-1.

Umpires: D. N. Dotiwala and R. R. Kadam.

THE WEST INDIANS IN AUSTRALIA, 1986-87

By TONY COZIER

West Indies suffered a sudden and dramatic reversal of their previous performances in one-day competitions in Australia when they returned there for the fifth time in seven seasons for the Benson and Hedges Challenge in Perth and the World Series Cup tournament. They had won the World Series Cup on each of the four occasions they had contested it; so convincingly in 1984-85 that they won twelve of their thirteen matches. Now they failed to qualify for the finals of either tournament as England won both, beating Pakistan in the Challenge and Australia in the World Series Cup.

There were advance signals of the eventual West Indian demise when they were beaten by Pakistan and England in their first two matches in Perth. By the time they had played their final match, their record was four wins against seven defeats in eleven one-day internationals. They had not lost as many in their four previous seasons, and they were also beaten in a one-day match at Townsville by a weakened Queensland state team.

West Indies failed because their batsmen failed, dismissed for fewer than 200 in each of their three World Series Cup defeats by England and the two by Australia. The loss of Gordon Greenidge for the last five matches with a strained hamstring and then of Desmond Haynes for the last two with a dislocated finger unsettled the batting order; the innings seldom got a start and recovery was rare as key batsmen lost form collectively. Vivian Richards himself was the leading West Indian batsman. But 240 of his 334 runs in the two competitions were made in four consecutive innings, and he was well short of the standards he had set in previous tournaments.

Apart from losing Greenidge and Haynes, West Indies were also hampered by other telling injuries. Michael Holding was twice forced out by strained muscles and Larry Gomes missed two matches with a stiff shoulder. While the fast bowling and fielding maintained their accustomed standards, it was obvious that the grind of international cricket had taken its toll of the principal members of the team, seven of whom were more than 30. Only two, the fast bowlers, Winston Benjamin and Tony Gray, were on their first tours to Australia. Joel Garner and Holding had returned to the team after opting out of the preceding tour of Pakistan, and Richards pleaded with the West Indies Board to reduce its international commitments even before a match was played. Greenidge reflected the general view when he spoke, in a newspaper interview, of being stale, homesick and tired. The fact that the team arrived in Perth early on Christmas morning did not improve morale.

This was Richards's first tour of Australia as captain and comparisons with his successful predecessor, Clive Lloyd, were inevitable. He could do little to prevent injuries or boost batting form, but he also appeared unable to motivate players deflated by the unaccustomed experience of failure.

WEST INDIAN TOUR RESULTS

First-class match – Played 1: Drawn 1.
Draw – Queensland.
Non first-class matches – Played 12: Won 4, Lost 8. *Wins* – Australia (3), England. *Losses* – Australia (2), England (4), Pakistan, Queensland.

West Indies' matches v Australia, England and Pakistan in the Benson and Hedges Challenge at Perth (December 30-January 4) may be found in that section.

†At Townsville, January 10. Queensland won by 25 runs. Queensland 214 for five (50 overs) (T. J. Barsby 61, A. B. Henschell 40*); West Indians 189 (47.3 overs) (M. D. Marshall 43).

QUEENSLAND v WEST INDIANS

At Townsville, January 11, 12, 13. Drawn. Toss: Queensland. The West Indians' decision to use the final day for batting practice condemned a match already dour to a dull draw. Yet it had begun spectacularly, with the state's bowlers having half the touring team's batsmen back in the pavilion for 90: four dismissed and Greenidge needing stitches after being struck on the cheekbone by a ball from McDermott. Harper, who hit three sixes and eleven fours, and Payne effected a recovery, as did Henschell the next day after an inspired spell by Holding had undermined the Queenslanders. Henschell hit two sixes and twelve fours, his 130 not out coming from 210 balls, while the game's third century-maker, Gomes, needed 236 balls for his unbeaten 164 (seventeen fours).

Close of play: First day, West Indians 277-8 (T. R. O. Payne 60*, C. A. Walsh 0*); Second day, West Indians 13-0 (D. L. Haynes 4*, R. B. Richardson 7*).

West Indians

C. G. Greenidge retired hurt	16				
D. L. Haynes lbw b McDermott	15	– (1) c and b Hill	67
R. B. Richardson c Henschell b McDermott	3	– (2) c Healy b McDermott	7
A. L. Logie b Polzin	25	– lbw b McDermott	36
H. A. Gomes c Kerr b Polzin	20	– (3) not out	164
†T. R. O. Payne not out	60		
R. A. Harper c Kerr b Polzin	118	– (5) b Inwood	20
W. K. M. Benjamin lbw b Polzin	1	– (6) not out	4
*M. A. Holding b Polzin	2		
J. Garner c Courtice b Tazelaar	1		
C. A. Walsh not out	0		
B 4, l-b 3, n-b 9	16	L-b 6, n-b 2	8

1/36 2/48 3/76 4/90 5/255   (8 wkts dec.) 277   1/14 2/131 3/214 4/291   (4 wkts) 306
6/257 7/271 8/277

Bowling: *First Innings*—McDermott 16-4-46-2; Tazelaar 20-1-76-1; Hill 17-2-49-0; Polzin 18-3-49-5; Henschell 16-1-50-0. *Second Innings*—McDermott 12-0-49-2; Tazelaar 15-2-50-0; Henschell 11-1-45-0; Polzin 11-0-27-0; Hill 24-4-93-1; Inwood 12-2-34-1; Barsby 2-0-2-0.

Queensland

B. A. Courtice c Haynes b Walsh	7	C. J. McDermott c Logie b Harper	0
*R. B. Kerr b Holding	14	D. Tazelaar not out	19
G. S. Trimble b Holding	10		
T. J. Barsby lbw b Holding	0	B 2, l-b 11, n-b 11	24
A. B. Henschell not out	130		
B. P. Inwood c Holding b Harper	15	1/17 2/24 3/24 4/43 (7 wkts dec.) 240
†I. A. Healy c sub b Gomes	21	5/109 6/179 7/179

M. A. Polzin and J. G. Hill did not bat.

Bowling: Garner 10-1-19-0; Walsh 17-1-57-1; Holding 11-3-18-3; Benjamin 12-1-30-0; Harper 19-5-65-2; Gomes 12-1-38-1.

Umpires: M. W. Johnson and C. D. Timmins.

West Indies' matches v Australia and England in the Benson and Hedges World Series Cup (January 17-February 6) may be found in that section.

THE WEST INDIANS IN NEW ZEALAND, 1986-87

By TONY COZIER

The unmistakable evidence after the West Indians' tour of New Zealand early in 1987 was that both teams were on the decline and faced a period of rebuilding. Each relied on the same players who had formed the nucleus of its sides for several years; most were over the age of 30 and several had passed their peak. The West Indians, particularly, lacked the all-round brilliance with which they had dominated international cricket for the better part of a decade, their enthusiasm diminished by a glut of cricket. They had come directly from a hectic one-day series in Australia.

The honours were even in the series of three Tests. New Zealand comfortably saved the first after a spirited recovery in their second innings, West Indies won the second, in spite of the loss of more than a day's play to the weather, and New Zealand levelled the rubber in convincing fashion in the last. In the one-day internationals that followed, the West Indians, largely through the batting of their captain, Vivian Richards, in the first and Gordon Greenidge in the last two, were irresistible.

The batting on both sides was inconsistent and depended heavily on the two outstanding individuals – Greenidge for West Indies and Martin Crowe for New Zealand. When they failed, the team failed. West Indies were dismissed for 100 and 264 in the Third Test when Greenidge was out twice for fewer than 20, and New Zealand were confined to 228 in the first innings of the First Test and 157 in the first innings of the Second when Crowe went similarly cheaply. Greenidge, after missing the last five matches in Australia through injury and nearly being replaced for the New Zealand tour, confirmed his standing as one of the most complete batsmen of modern times. His double-hundred in the Second Test and his centuries in the one-day internationals were masterpieces in their own ways. Crowe, the younger of two brothers in the New Zealand team and eleven years Greenidge's junior, enhanced his reputation as one of the finest young batsmen in the contemporary game with big scores in each of the Tests, all coming after the crisis of two early wickets.

The long-serving openers, Desmond Haynes of West Indies and John Wright of New Zealand, were the only others to score centuries. New Zealand could find no adequate successor to the reliable Bruce Edgar, who retired prior to the series, and West Indies' middle-order batting was repeatedly fragile, as it had been since the retirement of Clive Lloyd two years earlier.

Richard Hadlee again spearheaded New Zealand's attack magnificently, passing the landmark of 350 wickets in the final Test. He received admirable support from the 36-year-old Ewen Chatfield and, in the last Test, Martin Snedden. For West Indies, there was a noticeable changing of the guard in their attack. Michael Holding announced his retirement after the First Test, Joel Garner missed the Second through illness, and Malcolm Marshall found wickets hard to come by. With the additional responsibility placed on them, the younger fast bowlers, Courtney Walsh in particular and Tony Gray, showed their worth, especially in an explosive spell at the end of the Third Test. As Holding retired for West Indies, New Zealand also lost a tremendous servant of their game with the captain, Jeremy Coney, playing for the last time during the series. He had announced his intention earlier in the season.

It was the first visit to New Zealand by the West Indians since their ill-tempered tour of 1979-80, and the team manager, the former Test opening batsman and current Board secretary, Stephen Camacho, and captain Richards made a conscious effort to let bygones be bygones. Apart from exchanges during the Second Test between Richards and an umpire, Fred Goodall, which brought a protest from the New Zealand team management, the tour passed smoothly. Indeed, rather than any controversial incidents, it should best be remembered for the remarkable catching, mostly at short leg, and fielding of the little West Indian, Gus Logie, who captivated crowds and television viewers with his athleticism. He held eight catches in the three Tests and fourteen on the tour as a whole, many of them of breathtaking brilliance. Otherwise, the catching of both teams was unusually faulty, the West Indians falling well below their accepted standard by putting down fifteen catches in the Tests alone.

WEST INDIAN TOUR RESULTS

Test matches – Played 3: Won 1, Lost 1, Drawn 1.
First-class matches – Played 5: Won 1, Lost 1, Drawn 3.
Win – New Zealand.
Loss – New Zealand.
Draws – New Zealand, President's XI, Shell XI.
Non first-class matches – Played 4: Won 4. Abandoned 1. *Wins* – Auckland, New Zealand (3).
   Abandoned – New Zealand.

TEST MATCH AVERAGES

NEW ZEALAND – BATTING

	T	I	NO	R	HI	100s	Avge
M. D. Crowe	3	6	1	328	119	2	65.60
J. G. Bracewell	3	6	2	163	66	0	40.75
J. G. Wright	3	6	0	239	138	1	39.83
R. J. Hadlee	3	4	2	74	35*	0	37.00
J. J. Crowe	3	6	1	143	55	0	28.60
I. D. S. Smith	3	4	1	57	40*	0	19.00
J. V. Coney	3	6	0	77	36	0	12.83
D. N. Patel	3	6	0	73	21	0	12.16
K. R. Rutherford ...	2	4	0	29	12	0	7.25
E. J. Chatfield	3	4	2	5	4	0	2.50
S. L. Boock	2	3	0	7	4	0	2.33

Played in one Test: P. A. Horne 9, 0; M. C. Snedden 7.

* Signifies not out.

BOWLING

	O	M	R	W	BB	Avge
M. C. Snedden	24.3	3	82	5	5-68	16.40
R. J. Hadlee	113.1	20	354	17	6-50	20.82
S. L. Boock	67	24	180	7	3-76	25.71
E. J. Chatfield	114.3	39	282	10	4-30	28.20

Also bowled: J. G. Bracewell 45-9-147-1; J. V. Coney 14-2-30-0; M. D. Crowe 14-2-35-1; D. N. Patel 9-0-51-0.

WEST INDIES – BATTING

	T	I	NO	R	HI	100s	Avge
C. G. Greenidge ...	3	6	1	344	213	1	68.80
P. J. L. Dujon	3	4	0	144	77	0	36.00
R. B. Richardson	3	5	1	134	41	0	33.50
D. L. Haynes	3	6	1	160	121	1	32.00
C. A. Walsh	3	3	2	23	14	0	23.00
M. D. Marshall	3	4	0	83	45	0	20.75
I. V. A. Richards ..	3	4	0	77	38	0	19.25
H. A. Gomes	3	5	1	72	33	0	18.00
A. L. Logie	3	4	0	62	34	0	15.50
A. H. Gray	2	3	1	21	10*	0	10.50
J. Garner	3	3	0	11	11	0	3.66

Played in one Test: C. G. Butts 8*; M. A. Holding 0.

* Signifies not out.

BOWLING

	O	M	R	W	BB	Avge
J. Garner	77	16	205	12	5-51	17.08
A. H. Gray	49	10	150	8	3-45	18.75
C. A. Walsh	120.2	28	306	13	5-73	23.53
M. D. Marshall ...	119	21	289	9	4-43	32.11

Also bowled: C. G. Butts 38-10-82-2; H. A. Gomes 30-8-63-2; M. A. Holding 37-8-99-0; I. V. A. Richards 67-19-147-2; R. B. Richardson 4-1-4-0.

WEST INDIAN AVERAGES – FIRST-CLASS MATCHES

BATTING

	M	I	NO	R	HI	100s	Avge
C. G. Greenidge	4	7	1	383	213	1	63.83
D. L. Haynes	5	9	2	340	121	2	48.57
I. V. A. Richards ...	4	5	1	194	117*	1	48.50
R. B. Richardson ...	5	9	2	327	121	1	46.71
P. J. L. Dujon	4	6	1	223	77	0	44.60
C. L. Hooper	2	3	0	93	69	0	31.00
C. A. Walsh	4	3	2	23	14	0	23.00
H. A. Gomes	5	8	1	147	73	0	21.00
M. D. Marshall	3	4	0	83	45	0	20.75
A. L. Logie	5	6	0	71	34	0	11.83
A. H. Gray	4	3	1	21	10*	0	10.50
J. Garner	3	3	0	11	11	0	3.66

Played in three matches: C. G. Butts 3*, 8*. Played in two matches: M. A. Holding 34*, 0. Played in one match: T. R. O. Payne 0, 51; B. P. Patterson did not bat.

* Signifies not out.

BOWLING

	O	M	R	W	BB	Avge
J. Garner	96.5	18	265	17	5-51	15.58
H. A. Gomes	44.2	10	96	5	3-8	19.20
A. H. Gray	110	24	322	15	4-64	21.46
C. A. Walsh	156.2	37	397	15	5-73	26.46
M. D. Marshall	119	21	289	9	4-43	32.11
C. G. Butts	113	29	279	7	2-21	39.85
M. A. Holding	71	14	203	4	2-35	50.75

Also bowled: C. L. Hooper 7-0-50-0; B. P. Patterson 21-2-102-1; I. V. A. Richards 67-19-147-2; R. B. Richardson 4-1-4-0.

FIELDING

13 – P. J. L. Dujon (all ct); 11 – A. L. Logie; 6 – R. B. Richardson; 5 – I. V. A. Richards; 4 – A. H. Gray; 3 – J. Garner, C. G. Greenidge, M. A. Holding; substitutes (I. V. A. Richards 2, C. A. Walsh); 2 – C. G. Butts, D. L. Haynes, C. L. Hooper, B. P. Patterson; 1 – H. A. Gomes, T. R. O. Payne, C. A. Walsh.

†AUCKLAND v WEST INDIANS

At Auckland, February 14. West Indians won by five wickets, the result entirely of a dramatic innings by Richards. Victory appeared well beyond them when the captain came in at 146 for five with 76 runs required from 9.5 overs. However, he marked his first appearance in New Zealand with a succession of dazzling strokes, hitting 54 from 28 balls with three sixes and six fours. One six, over extra-cover, landed on the roof of a 70-foot high stand, one of the biggest hits seen at Eden Park. A crowd of 15,000 was well entertained by a match that yielded 446 runs from 89.5 overs.

Auckland 221 for four (45 overs) (P. A. Horne 30, R. B. Reid 97, J. J. Crowe 64; M. D. Marshall three for 41); West Indians 225 for five (44.5 overs) (R. B. Richardson 84, I. V. A. Richards 54 not out).

PRESIDENT'S XI v WEST INDIANS

At Hamilton, February 15, 16, 17. Drawn. The President's XI were twice rescued by late-order partnerships involving Stirling, their opening bowler. In the first innings, he recorded his highest first-class score in adding 139 in 93 minutes of positive strokeplay with the wicket-keeper, McSweeney, after the first seven wickets had fallen for 93. And on the last day, he found a stubborn partner in Morrison, with whom he added 43 for the last wicket to extend the innings and deny the West Indians a realistic chance of victory. Their target – 206 in 70 minutes plus twenty overs – was beyond them. The West Indians had themselves faltered in their first innings until Gomes, who batted solidly for four hours, and Dujon put on 108 in just under two hours. Next, Holding lashed four sixes in 34 before declaring with a lead of 18.

Close of play: First day, West Indians 49-1 (C. G. Greenidge 37*); Second day, President's XI 44-1 (R. H. Vance 28*, J. J. Crowe 0*).

President's XI

P. A. Horne c Holding b Gray	3	– c Dujon b Gray	10
R. H. Vance c Logie b Butts	12	– c Dujon b Walsh	34
*J. J. Crowe c Holding b Gray	2	– c Dujon b Gray	0
K. R. Rutherford b Holding	23	– c Logie b Butts	26
A. H. Jones c Walsh b Holding	7	– c Haynes b Gray	50
P. N. Webb c Greenidge b Butts	26	– c Butts b Holding	20
V. R. Brown c Hooper b Walsh	13	– c Hooper b Holding	0
†E. B. McSweeney c Greenidge b Gomes	76	– c sub b Butts	21
D. A. Stirling c Butts b Gomes	75	– not out	25
W. Watson c sub b Gomes	7	– c Dujon b Gray	0
D. K. Morrison not out	0	– not out	17
B 7, n-b 6	13	L-b 4, n-b 16	20

1/4 2/9 3/28 4/50 5/51   257   1/40 2/52 3/52   (9 wkts dec.) 223
6/81 7/93 8/232 9/253   4/104 5/146 6/146
                                  7/179 8/179 9/180

Bowling: *First Innings*—Walsh 14–6–22–1; Gray 17–6–39–2; Holding 24–5–69–2; Butts 26–7–78–2; Hooper 4–0–34–0; Gomes 4.2–0–8–3. *Second Innings*—Gray 22–3–64–4; Walsh 22–3–69–1; Butts 23–7–51–2; Holding 10–1–35–2; Gomes 1–1–0–0.

West Indians

C. G. Greenidge c Rutherford b Morrison	39		
D. L. Haynes c McSweeney b Stirling	11	– (1) not out	57
R. B. Richardson c McSweeney b Stirling	12	– (2) c Rutherford b Watson	10
H. A. Gomes c and b Brown	73	– (3) c McSweeney b Stirling	0
A. L. Logie c Crowe b Watson	9		
C. L. Hooper c McSweeney b Watson	19	– (4) c McSweeney b Watson	5
†P. J. L. Dujon c Brown b Stirling	62	– (5) not out	17
*M. A. Holding not out	34		
C. G. Butts not out	3		
B 4, l-b 1, n-b 8	13	W 2, n-b 2	4

1/49 2/63 3/63 4/85 5/119   (7 wkts dec.) 275   1/12 2/14 3/58   (3 wkts) 93
6/227 7/272

C. A. Walsh and A. H. Gray did not bat.

Bowling: *First Innings*—Stirling 18–1–99–3; Morrison 17–1–89–1; Watson 18–5–28–2; Brown 15–5–54–1; Jones 1–1–0–0. *Second Innings*—Stirling 5–1–30–1; Watson 8–3–20–2; Morrison 7–1–31–0; Brown 4–2–12–0.

Umpires: B. A. Aldridge and R. L. McHarg.

NEW ZEALAND v WEST INDIES

First Test Match

At Wellington, February 20, 21, 22, 23, 24. Drawn. When West Indies took the lead early on the third day with only two wickets down, they appeared to be building the foundation for victory. Yet New Zealand regained ground with characteristic determination. Their heroes were Wright, who batted for four hours five minutes for 75 during a difficult first innings and then for 9 hours 35 minutes in the second for 138, and Martin Crowe, with whom he added 241 for the third wicket in the second innings – New Zealand's highest for that wicket in Test matches. During their long partnership on the fourth day, West Indies had to contend with a strong, persistent and cool northerly wind and were handicapped by the absence of Marshall and Holding, both suffering from back strains. After the match Holding, who went without a wicket, announced his retirement after 60 Tests in which he took 249 wickets.

Richards's decision to bowl first on winning the toss produced quick returns. Wright found steady partners in Patel and Jeff Crowe, and Hadlee contributed a typically robust 35 not out, but New Zealand's total was disappointing on a generally good pitch. Patel, the Kenya-born former Worcestershire player, was making his début after his qualification had been cleared by ICC on the grounds that he was married to a New Zealander and had settled in the country. Jeff Crowe, one of Logie's three catches at short leg, was Garner's 250th Test wicket. In addition to his five wickets, Garner also held three sharp close catches, including that to remove Wright, cutting at Richards's off-spin.

Greenidge and Haynes, in their 58th Test together, gave West Indies another excellent start with their tenth century partnership, despite anxious moments early on. Haynes needed attention when hit on the jaw by Hadlee, and then survived an appeal for hit-wicket when the leg bail was dislodged as he set off for his 8th run. Greenidge played confidently until he was caught at short leg, and Haynes went past his ninth Test century before the close of the second day. However, when he was bowled by Bracewell next morning, offering no stroke to an off-break, the innings went into decline as New Zealand restricted the West Indians to 113 in three hours with steady, purposeful bowling. Haynes gave no chance in five hours eleven minutes' batting and struck twenty fours. When Smith caught Richards, he extended his New Zealand record of dismissals into three figures.

Rutherford and Coney again fell cheaply, both to Garner, but West Indies had to wait until after tea the following day for another wicket. In that time, Wright and Crowe became more and more entrenched as the weather, injuries and dropped catches wore the tourists' patience thin. Crowe survived a sharp, low chance to Logie at short leg off Walsh when 17; Wright should have been run out off the sixth ball of the fourth morning, and caught behind off Walsh when 44 and off Garner when 53. When bad light halted play 50 minutes early, New Zealand were 155 in front with seven wickets standing. Crowe, having reached his sixth Test century in mid-afternoon, had checked an on-drive off Richards and been caught at short mid-on after batting for 381 minutes, with fifteen fours.

Wright, resuming on the final morning, offered another chance at 115 off Garner and eventually was caught and bowled by Gomes from a tired stroke. He had fourteen fours from the 466 deliveries he faced for his sixth Test century. By then, New Zealand had made the match safe, and Richards, without two of his main bowlers, declined to change the ball, which had been in use for 177 overs when Coney declared at tea. No Test innings had seen so many overs bowled with the same ball. In the final session, Boock removed both openers as the ball turned sharply, provoking speculation that West Indies might have been further embarrassed had Coney declared sooner.

Man of the Match: J. G. Wright.

Close of play: First day, New Zealand 205-8 (R. J. Hadlee 16*, S. L. Boock 2*); Second day, West Indies 218-2 (D. L. Haynes 110*, R. B. Richardson 6*); Third day, New Zealand 91-2 (J. G. Wright 35*, M. D. Crowe 28*); Fourth day, New Zealand 272-3 (J. G. Wright 102*, D. N. Patel 4*).

New Zealand

J. G. Wright c Garner b Richards	75	– c and b Gomes	138
K. R. Rutherford c Logie b Garner	6	– lbw b Garner	6
*J. V. Coney c Logie b Marshall	3	– c Richards b Garner	4
M. D. Crowe lbw b Walsh	3	– c Holding b Richards	119
D. N. Patel c Garner b Walsh	18	– b Walsh	20
J. J. Crowe c Logie b Garner	37	– not out	27
J. G. Bracewell lbw b Garner	17	– not out	28
R. J. Hadlee not out	35		
†I. D. S. Smith lbw b Garner	0		
S. L. Boock c Garner b Marshall	3		
E. J. Chatfield lbw b Garner	0		
L-b 7, n-b 24	31	B 10, l-b 10, n-b 24	44

1/10 2/19 3/46 4/107 5/153   228   1/13 2/20 3/261   (5 wkts dec.) 386
6/181 7/192 8/192 9/226   4/301 5/331

Bowling: *First Innings*—Marshall 22-3-57-2; Garner 27-5-51-5; Walsh 12-1-46-2; Holding 16-4-34-0; Richards 11-3-32-1; Gomes 1-0-1-0. *Second Innings*—Marshall 20-6-43-0; Garner 30-9-72-2; Holding 21-4-65-0; Walsh 34-13-59-1; Richards 47-13-86-1; Gomes 21-6-37-1; Richardson 4-1-4-0.

West Indies

C. G. Greenidge c Rutherford b Chatfield	78	– c Rutherford b Boock	25
D. L. Haynes b Bracewell	121	– c Hadlee b Boock	13
H. A. Gomes c Smith b Hadlee	18	– not out	8
R. B. Richardson b Boock	37	– not out	1
*I. V. A. Richards c Smith b Chatfield	24		
A. L. Logie c Coney b Hadlee	3		
†P. J. L. Dujon c Smith b Chatfield	22		
M. D. Marshall c and b Boock	30		
M. A. Holding c sub (T. D. Ritchie) b Chatfield	0		
J. Garner c Hadlee b Boock	0		
C. A. Walsh not out	1		
B 1, l-b 8, w 1, n-b 1	11	B 3, l-b 1	4

1/150 2/208 3/232 4/278 5/287   345   1/33 2/46   (2 wkts) 50
6/289 7/339 8/343 9/344

Bowling: *First Innings*—Hadlee 31–9–77–2; Chatfield 39–14–102–4; Coney 3–0–8–0; Bracewell 14–5–47–1; Boock 35–14–76–3; M. D. Crowe 3–1–13–0; Patel 3–0–13–0. *Second Innings*—Hadlee 4–0–12–0; Chatfield 4–0–13–0; Boock 7–4–8–2; Bracewell 7–2–13–0.

Umpires: B. L. Aldridge and S. J. Woodward.

NEW ZEALAND v WEST INDIES

Second Test Match

At Auckland, February 27, 28, March 1, 2, 3. West Indies won by ten wickets with 4.3 overs to spare, their first victory in a Test in New Zealand since March 1969. Repeated interruptions for bad light and rain over the first four days caused the loss of almost eight and a quarter hours and led to a tense final day as New Zealand, through another dogged hundred by Martin Crowe, battled to avoid defeat. West Indies owed their substantial first-innings total to Greenidge's thirteenth century, and third double, in Tests, a triumph of technique and temperament on a pitch that encouraged the faster bowlers throughout.

Even though West Indies were without their two most experienced bowlers – Holding, by now back home, and Garner, who had developed a chest infection the day before the match – Richards's decision to bat first was surprising, considering the overcast conditions and the well-grassed pitch. Hadlee and Chatfield created problems throughout the first day, but with New Zealand playing both spinners they lacked seam-bowling support. It took all Greenidge's experience and skill to survive the difficult early period and he was 112 at the close of a shortened first day. West Indies quickly lost Logie next day to a smart gully catch by Martin Crowe, but Greenidge, surviving straightforward chances in the outfield at 131, 148 and 187, and the steady Dujon put on 165 to consolidate their position. Dujon's 77 was his highest score for fifteen Tests. The certainty of Greenidge's play was evidenced by his high number of boundaries: seven sixes, mostly off the spinners, and twenty fours. It was not until twenty minutes before the close of the second day that, driving at Hadlee, he lost his off stump. Hadlee dismissed Gray next day, Richards having needlessly extended the innings, and finished with five or more wickets in an innings for the 28th time in Tests.

New Zealand collapsed against the varied West Indies attack, and although Smith launched a stirring counter-attack to score 40 from 40 balls, the last wicket adding 39, it was not enough to prevent the follow-on. Only two and a quarter hours were possible between stoppages on the fourth day, when the Crowe brothers steadied the innings after the quick loss of the openers. Jeff took 35 balls to get off the mark, before which he was dropped at slip off Marshall, but he and Martin entered the last day at 64 for two.

With the weather mostly sunny, the cricket was tight and engrossing throughout. New Zealand were in trouble at 134 for five at lunch but Martin Crowe, dropped at slip off Walsh when 32, and the unflustered Bracewell put on 107 for the sixth wicket with positive play that brought an apparent concession from Richards when he introduced Gomes. The change proved decisive. Bracewell missed a pull and was lbw, whereupon Walsh and Gray set to work with the second new ball. Crowe eventually fell victim to Gray's bounce and Logie's remarkable reflexes and agility at short leg. His 382-minute innings was not without blemish, for he was missed again at 89, but his seventh Test century once more emphasised his class and temperament. He hit a six off Butts to raise his century and eight fours.

New Zealand started the final twenty overs needing 2 to make West Indies bat again and with three wickets standing. The loss of three overs to poor light heightened the tension, but Walsh, who had undeserving bad luck throughout, had Hadlee, Smith and Boock all caught off the outside edge for his first five-wicket haul in Tests. The West Indians were left with the formality of scoring 13 from six overs to record New Zealand's first defeat in a home Test for five seasons, and Greenidge and Haynes required only nine balls.

During the many breaks for rain and bad light, Richards engaged umpire Goodall in obviously animated discussion, and the New Zealand team manager, David Elder, afterwards alleged that the West Indies captain had "taunted and abused" the umpire and placed unwarranted pressure on him. The New Zealand Cricket Council made no comment.

Man of the Match: C. G. Greenidge.

Close of play: First day, West Indies 211-4 (C. G. Greenidge 112*, A. L. Logie 33*); Second day, West Indies 415-8 (C. G. Butts 7*, A. H. Gray 6*); Third day, New Zealand 1-0 (J. G. Wright 0*, K. R. Rutherford 0*); Fourth day, New Zealand 64-2 (J. J. Crowe 17*, M. D. Crowe 18*).

West Indies

C. G. Greenidge b Hadlee	213	– not out 10
D. L. Haynes c M. D. Crowe b Hadlee	1	– not out 6
H. A. Gomes c Smith b Chatfield	5	
R. B. Richardson c Smith b Hadlee	41	
*I. V. A. Richards b Hadlee	14	
A. L. Logie c M. D. Crowe b Hadlee	34	
†P. J. L. Dujon b Boock	77	
M. D. Marshall c J. J. Crowe b Boock	6	
C. G. Butts not out	8	
A. H. Gray lbw b Hadlee	8	
B 4, l-b 3, n-b 4	11	

1/7 2/14 3/109 4/131 5/219   (9 wkts dec.) 418   (no wkt) 16
6/384 7/400 8/402 9/418

C. A. Walsh did not bat.

Bowling: *First Innings*—Hadlee 41.4-7-105-6; Chatfield 37-14-88-1; Boock 25-6-96-2; Bracewell 17-2-53-0; Coney 11-2-22-0; M. D. Crowe 5-1-9-0; Patel 6-0-38-0. *Second Innings*—Hadlee 1-0-9-0; Chatfield 0.3-0-7-0.

New Zealand

J. G. Wright c Richardson b Marshall	11	– c Logie b Walsh 7
K. R. Rutherford b Marshall	12	– c Richardson b Walsh 5
J. J. Crowe c Dujon b Walsh	1	– c Gray b Walsh 21
M. D. Crowe c Dujon b Marshall	10	– c Logie b Gray 104
D. N. Patel c Greenidge b Butts	21	– lbw b Marshall 5
*J. V. Coney b Logie b Gray	15	– c Dujon b Gray 17
J. G. Bracewell c Richardson b Gray	7	– lbw b Gomes 43
R. J. Hadlee c Dujon b Butts	0	– c Richardson b Walsh 14
†I. D. S. Smith not out	40	– c Richards b Walsh 10
S. L. Boock c Dujon b Gray	0	– c Dujon b Walsh 4
E. J. Chatfield c Logie b Marshall	4	– not out 0
B 12, l-b 2, n-b 22	36	B 7, l-b 8, n-b 28 43

1/30 2/38 3/39 4/69 5/81   157   1/10 2/14 3/83 4/91 5/126   273
6/95 7/101 8/109 9/118   6/233 7/250 8/260 9/269

Bowling: *First Innings*—Marshall 17–3–43–4; Walsh 14–5–34–1; Butts 12–4–21–2; Gray 10–1–45–3. *Second Innings*—Marshall 33–7–71–2; Walsh 30.2–6–73–5; Butts 26–6–61–0; Gray 18–4–44–2; Gomes 4–1–9–1.

Umpires: F. R. Goodall and G. C. Morris.

SHELL XI v WEST INDIANS

At Napier, March 6, 7, 8. Drawn. A hard, true pitch allowed batsmen to exhibit their strokes and offered bowlers encouraging bounce. Haynes and Richardson put on 226 for the West Indians' third wicket and, after three wickets fell for 1 run late on the first day, Richards and Hooper added 187. Haynes hit ten fours in his second hundred of the tour while Richardson, after an unsteady start in which he was caught off a no-ball and hit on the back of the head ducking into a bouncer from Morrison, was in brilliant form, hitting a six and eighteen fours. Richards dominated the second day, his 35th birthday, with a succession of powerful strokes in his 93rd first-class century; his 117 came off 128 balls and included eighteen fours. The Shell XI were in trouble at 138 for six at the end of the second day, in spite of a dogged innings by the left-handed Horne, whose eventual 81 lasted four and threequarter hours. However, McSweeney and Snedden took hold of some loose bowling in a run-a-minute partnership of 161, with McSweeney also marking his birthday, his 30th, with a century. Cutting and pulling especially well, he hit fifteen fours. Garner, returning after the illness that kept him out of the Second Test, was by far the best West Indian bowler.

Close of play: First day, West Indians 290-5 (C. L. Hooper 23*, I. V. A. Richards 21*); Second day, Shell XI 138-6 (P. A. Horne 65*, E. B. McSweeney 2*).

West Indians

†T. R. O. Payne c Snedden b Wilson	0	– b Ritchie	51
D. L. Haynes b Wilson	112		
H. A. Gomes c Jones b Morrison	2		
R. B. Richardson c Ritchie b Wilson	121	– (2) not out	50
A. L. Logie lbw b Gray	0		
C. L. Hooper b Snedden	69		
*I. V. A. Richards not out	117		
L-b 4, n-b 8	12	L-b 2, n-b 2	4

1/2 2/19 3/245	(6 wkts dec.) 433	1/105 (1 wkt) 105
4/246 5/246 6/433		

J. Garner, C. G. Butts, A. H. Gray and B. P. Patterson did not bat.

Bowling: *First Innings*—Morrison 23–0–112–1; Wilson 22–2–109–3; Snedden 23.3–7–69–1; Gray 31–6–104–1; Jones 3–0–13–0; Blair 3–0–22–0. *Second Innings*—Morrison 5–0–30–0; Wilson 5–1–18–0; Snedden 4–0–14–0; Gray 4–0–21–0; Blair 4–1–4–0; Ritchie 3.3–0–16–1.

Shell XI

P. A. Horne c Patterson b Garner	81	†E. B. McSweeney not out	117
R. H. Vance c sub b Garner	12	*M. C. Snedden c Patterson b Garner	60
M. J. Greatbatch c Richardson b Garner	1	B 2, l-b 6, n-b 21	29
A. H. Jones c Payne b Butts	28		
B. R. Blair c Logie b Patterson	2	1/16 2/18 3/62 (8 wkts dec.) 348
T. D. Ritchie lbw b Gray	15	4/68 5/114 6/132
E. J. Gray lbw b Garner	3	7/187 8/348

D. K. Morrison and T. J. Wilson did not bat.

Bowling: Patterson 21–2–102–1; Gray 22–5–69–1; Garner 19.5–2–60–5; Butts 26–5–68–1; Gomes 9–1–25–0; Hooper 3–0–16–0.

Umpires: R. S. Dunne and T. A. McCall.

NEW ZEALAND v WEST INDIES

Third Test Match

At Christchurch, March 12, 13, 14, 15. New Zealand won by five wickets to square the series, inflicting on West Indies their first defeat in three days' play since 1965 when they were beaten by Australia at Port-of-Spain. Unfit conditions on certain parts of the outfield, caused by two days of heavy rain, had led to the abandonment of the first day and had also hindered the proper preparation of the pitch, which was slightly damp when play began promptly on the second morning. The toss provided New Zealand with an early advantage, and Hadlee and Chatfield capitalised on it against batting lacking application and discipline. The collapse started with the first ball of the third over, when Hadlee went through Haynes's defence to hit the off stump, and only the last-wicket partnership of Gray and Walsh lifted West Indies past 77, their previous lowest total against New Zealand. There were five slip catches as Hadlee, whose first four overs cost 25 runs, returned to maintain the pressure initiated by Chatfield, who bowled his eighteen overs unchanged, offering hardly a bad ball.

New Zealand lost both left-handed openers cheaply, Horne, on his début, and Wright falling to catches at first slip. But the Crowe brothers put them ahead by the end of the day. Both had been dropped by then, Jeff by the wicket-keeper off Marshall when 16, Martin at slip off Richards when 39, and Martin gave a chance to gully off Marshall next day when 75. Their stand was worth 156 when Martin, having struck thirteen hearty fours, got himself into a tangle over a pull shot against Marshall and was bowled 17 runs short of his third century of the series. Gray then claimed two quick wickets, only for Coney and Bracewell to consolidate New Zealand's advantage by adding 89. Bracewell took toll of his dispirited opponents with two sixes and four fours in his 66, the last 39 coming from 29 balls after tea.

West Indies had a deficit of 232 when Coney declared and Greenidge, who lifted Bracewell for six in the final over, and Haynes had reduced it by 35 at the close. When Haynes was out to the sixth ball and Greenidge to the seventh next morning, all fight seemed to leave the West Indians and they batted with carefree abandon as wickets fell at regular intervals. Richards epitomised his team's approach. Coming in at 80 for three after Hadlee had claimed his 350th Test wicket by having Richardson caught off a miscued hook, he took five cuts off the first seven balls he received from Hadlee and was then caught behind, cutting at a ball too close to him, the first of Snedden's five wickets. Dujon and Marshall delayed the end with a seventh-wicket partnership of 77, but New Zealand were left with the seeming formality of scoring 33. However, Walsh and Gray, bowling with real pace and hostility, made it anything but. Gray supplemented his bowling with two stunning catches, one at slip, the other at gully, but it was little more than a gesture. New Zealand completed their well-deserved victory with 25 minutes remaining of the day. Their fifth wicket in the second innings was that of Coney, their captain, who was given an emotional reception by the crowd in his last Test.

Man of the Match: E. J. Chatfield and R. J. Hadlee (shared).

Close of play: First day, No play; Second day, New Zealand 117-2 (J. J. Crowe 38*, M. D. Crowe 44*); Third day, West Indies 35-0 (C. G. Greenidge 16*, D. L. Haynes 17*).

West Indies

C. G. Greenidge b Chatfield	2 – c Smith b Hadlee	16
D. L. Haynes b Hadlee	0 – c Horne b Chatfield	19
R. B. Richardson c M. D. Crowe b Hadlee	37 – c M. D. Crowe b Hadlee	19
H. A. Gomes c J. J. Crowe b Chatfield	8 – c Coney b M. D. Crowe	33
*I. V. A. Richards c Smith b Hadlee	1 – c Smith b Snedden	38
A. L. Logie c Coney b Hadlee	6 – c J. J. Crowe b Snedden	19
†P. J. L. Dujon c Coney b Hadlee	6 – c M. D. Crowe b Snedden	39
M. D. Marshall c Snedden b Chatfield	2 – b Hadlee	45
J. Garner c Coney b Hadlee	0 – c Wright b Snedden	11
A. H. Gray not out	10 – c M. D. Crowe b Snedden	3
C. A. Walsh b Hadlee	14 – not out	8
L-b 6, n-b 8	14	B 2, l-b 4, n-b 8	14

1/2 2/6 3/44 4/56 5/56   100   1/37 2/37 3/80 4/129 5/133   264
6/64 7/67 8/70 9/75   6/160 7/237 8/241 9/255

Bowling: *First Innings*—Hadlee 12.3-2-50-6; Chatfield 18-8-30-4; Snedden 6-1-14-0. *Second Innings*—Hadlee 23-2-101-3; Chatfield 16-3-42-1; Bracewell 7-0-34-0; M. D. Crowe 6-0-13-1; Snedden 18.3-2-68-5.

New Zealand

J. G. Wright c Richards b Walsh	6	– c Richards b Gray	2
P. A. Horne c Richards b Garner	9	– c Gray b Walsh	0
J. J. Crowe c Dujon b Gray	55	– c Gray b Walsh	2
M. D. Crowe b Marshall	83	– not out	9
D. N. Patel c Dujon b Gray	0	– c Richardson b Walsh	9
*J. V. Coney run out	36	– c Gray b Garner	2
J. G. Bracewell c Haynes b Garner	66	– not out	2
R. J. Hadlee not out	25		
†I. D. S. Smith c Dujon b Garner	7		
M. C. Snedden c Logie b Garner	7		
E. J. Chatfield not out	1		
B 2, l-b 4, w 1, n-b 28	37	N-b 7	7

1/12 2/23 3/179 4/180 5/181   (9 wkts dec.) 332   1/1 2/3 3/13   (5 wkts) 33
6/270 7/294 8/307 9/330   4/27 5/30

Bowling: *First Innings*—Marshall 27-2-75-1; Garner 19-2-79-4; Walsh 24.5-3-78-1; Gray 17-4-47-2; Richards 9-3-29-0; Gomes 4-1-16-0. *Second Innings*—Walsh 5.1-0-16-3; Gray 4-1-14-1; Garner 1-0-3-1.

Umpires: G. C. Morris and S. J. Woodward.

†NEW ZEALAND v WEST INDIES

First One-day International

At Dunedin, March 18. West Indies won by 95 runs. A magnificent all-round performance by Richards, who became the first player to score a hundred and take five wickets in a one-day international, overshadowed all else. His 119, made from 113 balls with four sixes and ten fours, was his ninth at this level and his partnership of 120 with Hooper lifted West Indies from a shaky start after they had been put in. Hooper batted impressively on his international début. New Zealand never looked like getting close to their target as Richards captured his five wickets, mainly with slow-medium swing.

Man of the Match: I. V. A. Richards.

West Indies

C. G. Greenidge lbw b Snedden	15	A. H. Gray c Snedden b Hadlee	5
D. L. Haynes lbw b Hadlee	0	C. A. Walsh not out	7
R. B. Richardson run out	17	B. P. Patterson not out	0
C. L. Hooper c McSweeney b Snedden	48		
*I. V. A. Richards c Hadlee b M. D. Crowe	119	B 3, l-b 10	13
A. L. Logie st McSweeney b Coney	6	1/0 2/34 3/50 (9 wkts, 50 overs) 237	
†P. J. L. Dujon c J. J. Crowe b Coney	1	4/170 5/201 6/205	
J. Garner run out	6	7/215 8/227 9/233	

Bowling: Chatfield 10-2-35-0; Hadlee 10-1-46-2; Snedden 10-1-38-2; M. D. Crowe 7-0-26-1; Coney 9-1-34-2; Patel 2-0-19-0; Bracewell 2-0-26-0.

New Zealand

J. G. Wright st Dujon b Richards	34	R. J. Hadlee b Richards	11
†E. B. McSweeney run out	9	M. C. Snedden c Hooper b Walsh	7
M. D. Crowe c Richardson b Garner	7	E. J. Chatfield not out	2
P. A. Horne c Greenidge b Gray	17	B 4, l-b 10, w 1, n-b 2	17
J. J. Crowe c Dujon b Richards	7		
D. N. Patel c Dujon b Richards	15	1/15 2/44 3/72 (42.1 overs) 142	
*J. V. Coney c Patterson b Richards	7	4/78 5/100 6/105	
J. G. Bracewell b Gray	9	7/118 8/130 9/134	

Bowling: Garner 10-3-18-1; Patterson 6-0-15-0; Walsh 6.1-1-28-1; Gray 10-1-26-2; Richards 10-0-41-5.

Umpires: F. R. Goodall and G. C. Morris.

†NEW ZEALAND v WEST INDIES

Second One-day International

At Auckland, March 21. West Indies won by six wickets. After losing a wicket to the third ball, New Zealand, put in, were gathering momentum through a second-wicket partnership between Wright and Martin Crowe when Wright injured his knee badly enough to require a runner. His movement hindered, he virtually surrendered his wicket. Horne, first ball, and Crowe were out 1 run later. New Zealand's total became increasingly insignificant as Greenidge and Haynes shared an opening partnership of 134. Greenidge, badly dropped by the wicket-keeper off a skyer when 26, was in commanding form with four sixes and ten fours in making his eighth hundred in one-day internationals from 101 balls. After he was first out, the tempo changed so sharply that West Indies needed another twenty overs to score the remaining 80 to win.

Man of the Match: C. G. Greenidge.

New Zealand

†E. B. McSweeney c Richardson b Garner .	0	M. C. Snedden c Logie b Walsh	2
J. G. Wright c Logie b Richards	45	S. L. Boock not out	1
M. D. Crowe c Dujon b Gray	53	E. J. Chatfield run out	1
P. A. Horne lbw b Richards	0		
D. N. Patel c Hooper b Richards	15	L-b 6, w 2, n-b 4	12
*J. V. Coney c Richardson b Patterson .	52		
J. G. Bracewell c Logie b Patterson ..	14	(50 overs)	213
R. J. Hadlee c Dujon b Walsh	18		

1/0 2/105 3/106 4/106 5/134 6/172 7/204 8/211 9/211

Bowling: Garner 10-4-18-1; Patterson 9-2-52-2; Walsh 9-0-45-2; Gray 7-0-35-1; Richards 10-0-34-3; Hooper 5-0-23-0.

West Indies

C. G. Greenidge c Hadlee b Boock	104	*I. V. A. Richards not out	14
D. L. Haynes lbw b Bracewell	61	L-b 1	1
R. B. Richardson c Bracewell b Patel ..	12		
C. L. Hooper b Bracewell	10	(4 wkts, 49 overs)	217
A. L. Logie not out	15		

1/134 2/176 3/186 4/196

†P. J. L. Dujon, J. Garner, A. H. Gray, C. A. Walsh and B. P. Patterson did not bat.

Bowling: Chatfield 6-0-27-0; Hadlee 6-0-17-0; Snedden 4-0-27-0; Crowe 7-0-26-0; Coney 2-0-11-0; Boock 10-0-45-1; Bracewell 10-1-40-2; Patel 4-0-23-1.

Umpires: B. L. Aldridge and R. L. McHarg.

†NEW ZEALAND v WEST INDIES

Third One-day International

At Wellington, March 25, 26. Abandoned. Several days of heavy rain had left the Basin Reserve so wet that even the agreement of both teams to delay the match a day proved futile.

†NEW ZEALAND v WEST INDIES

Fourth One-day International

At Christchurch, March 28. West Indies won by ten wickets. After West Indies' bowlers had kept New Zealand to an inadequate total following Coney's decision to bat, Greenidge produced another outstanding innings as he, with Haynes an almost silent partner, swept them to victory with 10.4 overs remaining. His 133, from 140 balls, was his ninth and highest one-day hundred for West Indies and included four sixes, one a huge straight hit off Patel, and sixteen fours. New Zealand's scoring-rate never reached 4 an over, and when Patel and Coney seemed ready to accelerate, Hooper, at slow-medium, bowled them both and Bracewell as well while 7 runs were added.

Man of the Match: C. G. Greenidge.

New Zealand

P. A. Horne run out	15	†E. B. McSweeney not out	13
K. R. Rutherford b Garner	2	M. C. Snedden c Gray b Patterson	4
M. D. Crowe lbw b Walsh	42	E. J. Chatfield not out	3
J. J. Crowe c Richardson b Gray	2	B 3, l-b 9, w 12, n-b 5	29
D. N. Patel b Hooper	36		
*J. V. Coney b Hooper	21	1/3 2/63 3/74 (9 wkts, 50 overs) 191	
J. G. Bracewell b Hooper	0	4/77 5/138 6/138	
R. J. Hadlee c Payne b Walsh	24	7/145 8/174 9/180	

Bowling: Garner 10-1-33-1; Patterson 9-0-34-1; Walsh 7-0-18-2; Gray 10-2-30-1; Richards 8-0-37-0; Hooper 6-0-27-3.

West Indies

C. G. Greenidge not out	133
D. L. Haynes not out	53
L-b 3, w 2, n-b 1	6

(no wkt, 39.2 overs) 192

R. B. Richardson, C. L. Hooper, A. L. Logie, *I. V. A. Richards, †T. R. O. Payne, J. Garner, A. H. Gray, C. A. Walsh and B. P. Patterson did not bat.

Bowling: Chatfield 9-1-19-0; Hadlee 7-0-33-0; Snedden 7-0-37-0; Bracewell 5-0-26-0; M. D. Crowe 3-0-19-0; Coney 3-0-22-0; Patel 5-0-31-0; Rutherford 0.2-0-2-0.

Umpires: B. L. Aldridge and F. R. Goodall.

THE PAKISTANIS IN INDIA, 1986-87

By R. MOHAN

A run of eleven successive draws between India and Pakistan was dramatically arrested by the quality, or rather lack of quality, of a Test match pitch designed to produce a result. In contrast to the languorous pace at which the first four Tests had been played, the final Test in Bangalore, a centre notorious in the previous decade for flat wickets, was enthralling throughout. After pitches which had blunted the edge of Pakistan's pace attack and provided nothing for spin bowlers against Indian batsmen so accustomed to such bowling, it seemed at times that the batsmen were now treading through a minefield. It was a test of nerve which India, despite having dominated many phases of the first four Tests and having bundled out Pakistan for next to nothing in the first innings, failed. Imran Khan realised Pakistan's and his own ambition to beat India in India; but as much a victory for Pakistan's superior tactical approach to such conditions, it was also a victory born of the despair of the administrators, who sought to break the deadlock brought about by the teams' inability to bowl each other out on any surface other than an under-prepared one.

India, unable to develop the advantages won in the Second and Fourth Tests, relied heavily on their batsmen to run up huge totals which would put pressure on Pakistan batsmen lacking experience of slow, turning wickets. But this the Pakistanis, not having agreed to a minimum number of overs in a day's play, could counter tactically. Furthermore, the sharp decline of Kapil Dev as a strike bowler forced India to base their attack on the left-arm spin of Maninder Singh. He had improved enormously in the course of a long season, but he could not clinch the issue for India after opening up a golden avenue with seven for 27 on the first day of the Fifth Test. Considering the odds against which Pakistan's victory came – few sides have gone on to win a Test match after so inauspicious a first innings – theirs was a remarkable triumph.

In the limited-overs series, Pakistan's superiority was beyond dispute. They had a number of utility players in their ranks, any one of whom could fashion a match-winning effort with the bat, and they won the series 5-1. Even that solitary win for India came in somewhat contentious circumstances. Kapil Dev was unlucky with the toss, losing five of them, but these defeats went beyond the favour of the spin of the coin.

The touring team were subjected to a harrowing time by the crowds in Ahmedabad and Bangalore, where any convenient missile was thrown at the Pakistani players. However, Imran's sporting approach to the niggling problems which occur on a tour of India helped keep matters from getting out of proportion, including those instances when his own colleagues were guilty of over-dramatisation on the field. Their orchestrated appealing, and various other practices designed to put the umpires under severe pressure, gave an unhappy aspect to their cricket. Truth to tell, there were more than a fair share of errors of judgement by umpires in the series, but it could not be said that India benefited exceptionally from them. Indeed, Pakistan got away with a considerable amount and it was strange to hear the winning captain pursue his call for neutral umpires.

Sunil Gavaskar's feat of completing 10,000 runs, Imran's felicity with the bat, which belied the position at which he generally batted, the progress of Ramiz Raja as an opening batsman, the dashes of brilliance shown by Srikkanth, Vengsarkar and Azharuddin – easily the outstanding fielder in the two teams – and the wily performance of the spinners, Tauseef Ahmed, Iqbal Qasim and Maninder Singh: such were the high points of what would otherwise have been a not so memorable series.

PAKISTANI TOUR RESULTS

Test matches – Played 5: Won 1, Drawn 4.
First-class matches – Played 8: Won 1, Drawn 7.
Win – India.
Draws – India (4), Delhi, Indian Board President's XI, Indian Under-25 XI.
Non first-class matches – Played 9: Won 6, Lost 3. *Wins* – India (5), Indian XI. *Losses* – India, Cricket Club of India, Governor's XI.

TEST MATCH AVERAGES

INDIA – BATTING

	T	I	NO	R	HI	100s	Avge
D. B. Vengsarkar ..	5	8	2	404	109	1	67.33
M. Azharuddin	5	6	0	315	141	2	52.50
S. M. Gavaskar ...	4	6	0	295	96	0	49.16
K. Srikkanth	5	8	0	311	123	1	38.87
R. M. H. Binny ...	3	4	2	74	52*	0	37.00
Kapil Dev	5	6	1	182	66	0	36.40
R. J. Shastri	5	6	0	197	125	1	32.83
M. Amarnath	5	8	1	213	89	0	30.42
K. S. More	5	6	1	85	28	0	17.00
N. S. Yadav	4	5	2	18	8*	0	6.00
Maninder Singh ..	4	5	2	12	7*	0	4.00

Played in two Tests: Gopal Sharma 0; R. R. Kulkarni 2, 0. Played in one Test: Arun Lal 52, 70.

* *Signifies not out.*

BOWLING

	O	M	R	W	BB	Avge
R. M. H. Binny	49.1	12	126	8	6-56	15.75
Maninder Singh	260.2	96	478	20	7-27	23.90
Gopal Sharma	94.5	20	186	6	4-88	31.00
Kapil Dev	162	37	430	11	3-46	39.09
R. J. Shastri	200.5	54	422	9	4-69	46.88
N. S. Yadav	161.3	35	401	8	4-109	50.12

Also bowled: M. Amarnath 22-8-42-2; S. M. Gavaskar 5-1-19-0; R. R. Kulkarni 32-3-113-2; K. Srikkanth 7-0-17-0.

PAKISTAN – BATTING

	T	I	NO	R	HI	100s	Avge
Imran Khan	5	7	2	324	135*	1	64.80
Javed Miandad	4	7	1	302	94	0	50.33
Younis Ahmed	2	3	1	88	40	0	44.00
Ramiz Raja	5	9	0	381	114	1	42.33
Shoaib Mohammad ...	3	5	0	175	101	1	35.00
Rizwan-uz-Zaman ...	5	9	1	197	60	0	24.62
Tauseef Ahmed	4	5	3	48	15*	0	24.00
Salim Yousuf	5	7	1	134	43	0	22.33
Salim Malik	5	9	2	155	33	0	22.14
Manzoor Elahi	2	3	0	60	52	0	20.00
Wasim Akram	5	6	1	89	62	0	17.80
Iqbal Qasim	3	4	0	65	26	0	16.25
Abdul Qadir	3	3	0	48	25	0	16.00
Saleem Jaffer	2	3	1	8	8	0	4.00

Played in one Test: Ijaz Ahmed 3; Ijaz Faqih 105.

* Signifies not out.

BOWLING

	O	M	R	W	BB	Avge
Iqbal Qasim	154	46	367	12	5-48	30.58
Wasim Akram	159.2	31	413	13	5-96	31.76
Tauseef Ahmed	218.5	34	561	16	5-54	35.06
Imran Khan	123.1	21	392	8	2-28	49.00
Abdul Qadir	68	8	242	4	2-130	60.50

Also bowled: Ijaz Faqih 27-3-81-1; Saleem Jaffer 43-2-148-2; Manzoor Elahi 3-2-8-1; Rizwan-uz-Zaman 5-2-7-1; Shoaib Mohammad 9-1-32-1; Younis Ahmed 1-0-6-0.

PAKISTANI AVERAGES – FIRST-CLASS MATCHES

BATTING

	M	I	NO	R	HI	100s	Avge
Younis Ahmed	3	4	2	191	103*	1	95.50
Manzoor Elahi	4	6	3	215	65*	0	71.66
Javed Miandad	5	8	1	453	151	1	64.71
Imran Khan	6	8	2	343	135*	1	57.16
Ramiz Raja	7	11	0	594	167	2	54.00
Rizwan-uz-Zaman	7	12	2	491	193	2	49.10
Ijaz Ahmed	4	5	0	229	131	1	45.80
Shoaib Mohammad ...	5	9	1	362	116	1	45.25
Abdul Qadir	5	5	0	177	103	1	35.40
Salim Malik	8	14	2	304	53	0	25.33
Mudassar Nazar	3	4	1	76	31*	0	25.33
Tauseef Ahmed	5	5	3	48	15*	0	24.00
Salim Yousuf	6	8	1	151	43	0	21.57
Wasim Akram	6	7	2	90	62	0	18.00
Iqbal Qasim	4	4	0	65	26	0	16.25
Saleem Jaffer	4	5	3	13	8	0	6.50

Played in two matches: Zakir Khan 21; Zulqarnain did not bat. Played in one match: Asif Mujtaba 13; Ijaz Faqih 105.

* Signifies not out.

BOWLING

	O	M	R	W	BB	Avge
Manzoor Elahi	30.4	3	131	5	3-65	26.20
Iqbal Qasim	191	50	454	17	5-48	26.70
Tauseef Ahmed	244.5	41	620	21	5-54	29.52
Wasim Akram	184.2	35	487	14	5-96	34.78
Saleem Jaffer......	90	13	322	9	3-57	35.77
Imran Khan	143.1	26	437	12	3-38	36.41
Abdul Qadir	117	18	386	7	2-44	55.14

Also bowled: Asif Mujtaba 5-1-24-0; Ijaz Faqih 27-3-81-1; Mudassar Nazar 14-1-34-1; Rizwan-uz-Zaman 7-2-13-1; Salim Malik 1-0-1-0; Shoaib Mohammad 14-2-41-1; Younis Ahmed 1-0-6-0; Zakir Khan 44-11-126-2.

FIELDING

11 – Salim Yousuf (9 ct, 2 st); 7 – Iqbal Qasim; 6 – Manzoor Elahi; 4 – Salim Malik, substitutes (Asif Mujtaba 3, Ijaz Ahmed 1), Zulqarnain; 3 – Javed Miandad, Mudassar Nazar, Ramiz Raja, Tauseef Ahmed, Wasim Akram; 1 – Asif Mujtaba, Ijaz Ahmed, Rizwan-uz-Zaman.

†At Hyderabad, January 18. Governor's XI won by eight wickets. Pakistanis 176 for one (40 overs) (Shoaib Mohammad 30, Rizwan-uz-Zaman 97 not out); Governor's XI 177 for two. This was a charity match, organised by the National Institute of Social Action.

†At Brabourne Stadium, Bombay, January 20. Cricket Club of India won by six wickets. Pakistanis 189 (39.5 overs) (Mudassar Nazar 51, Ramiz Raja 34; R. J. Shastri three for 35); Cricket Club of India 190 for four (39 overs) (R. M. H. Binny 63, M. Azharuddin 80). This match was part of the Cricket Club of India's Golden Jubilee celebrations.

†At Jawaharlal Nehru Stadium, New Delhi, January 21 (day/night). Pakistanis won by 111 runs. Pakistanis 304 for four (40 overs) (Ijaz Ahmed 149, Rizwan-uz-Zaman 39, Salim Malik 65, Javed Miandad 34 not out); Indian XI 193 (Yashpal Sharma 34; Manzoor Elahi three for 45). Ijaz's 149 was off 92 balls and included six sixes and fourteen fours.

INDIAN BOARD PRESIDENT'S XI v PAKISTANIS

At Faridabad, January 23, 24, 25. Drawn. The Pakistani pace bowlers soon made their presence felt as they settled down to some hard work, with Imran Khan and Saleem Jaffer among the wickets. Only Viswanath and Azharuddin prevented the tourists from running through the innings. When the Pakistanis batted, Rizwan-uz-Zaman made a stolid 193, his highest score, in eight and a half hours, but Qadir's century, with eight sixes and six fours, put the bowling into truer perspective after the discarded Test off-spinner, Gopal Sharma, had undermined the innings with five wickets. Five of Qadir's sixes came off him.

Close of play: First day, Indian Board President's XI 215-6 (M. Azharuddin 55*, R. S. Ghai 0*); Second day, Pakistanis 195-6 (Rizwan-uz-Zaman 83*, Salim Yousuf 0*).

Indian Board President's XI

†S. Viswanath b Qadir	80	– c Yousuf b Jaffer	0
N. S. Sidhu lbw b Imran	15	– c Asif b Imran	4
Arun Lal c Mudassar b Zakir	10	– not out	18
K. P. Amarjit c Ijaz b Jaffer	9	– not out	6
M. Azharuddin not out	73		
*R. J. Shastri b Mudassar	38		
W. V. Raman c Mudassar b Qadir	3		
R. S. Ghai lbw b Imran	8		
Gopal Sharma b Jaffer	1		
K. K. Sharma b Jaffer	0		
N. Hirwani b Imran	4		
B 2, w 2, n-b 2	6	B 5, l-b 1, w 1	7

1/35 2/66 3/118 4/118 5/192   247   1/4 2/10   (2 wkts) 35
6/211 7/237 8/238 9/238

Bowling: *First Innings*—Imran 15–3–38–3; Jaffer 21–6–57–3; Mudassar 11–1–27–1; Zakir 19–5–53–1; Qadir 17–5–44–2; Rizwan 1–0–2–0; Asif 5–1–24–0. *Second Innings*—Imran 5–2–7–1; Jaffer 5–1–9–1; Zakir 3–2–6–0; Mudassar 3–0–7–0.

Pakistanis

Mudassar Nazar c and b Ghai	6	Zakir Khan lbw b K. K. Sharma	21
Rizwan-uz-Zaman c Arun Lal b Gopal	193	Abdul Qadir c Amarjit b Raman	103
Ramiz Raja c Arun Lal b Gopal	46	Saleem Jaffer not out	4
Salim Malik b Gopal	9		
Ijaz Ahmed b Raman	1	B 4, l-b 8, n-b 14	26
Asif Mujtaba b Gopal	13		
*Imran Khan c Arun Lal b Ghai	19	1/20 2/111 3/121 4/122 5/152	458
†Salim Yousuf st Viswanath b Hirwani	17	6/195 7/216 8/269 9/451	

Bowling: Ghai 21–1–92–1; K. K. Sharma 11–0–40–1; Gopal 47.1–6–165–5; Shastri 5–1–14–0; Raman 29–8–70–2; Hirwani 29–11–65–1.

Umpires: R. Mehra and S. R. Ramachandra Rao.

†INDIA v PAKISTAN

First One-day International

At Indore, January 27. Pakistan won by three wickets. India, put in to bat, were dealt early blows by Imran but recovered thanks to Shastri, captaining India for the first time as Kapil Dev had damaged a thigh muscle. Shastri's 50 off 67 balls began a counter-attack which saw India add 39 from the last three overs. Pakistan were in some difficulty against the Indian spinners, but Abdul Qadir, who was dropped at a crucial juncture, hit a brisk 39 off 46 balls. Imran and Manzoor saw them through with an over to spare. Run-making was always easier against the Indian seamers and the home side missed not having a third spinner.

Man of the Match: Abdul Qadir.

India

K. Srikkanth b Imran	2	Madan Lal c Imran b Mudassar	38
S. M. Gavaskar c Yousuf b Imran	10	Chetan Sharma not out	7
M. Azharuddin st Yousuf b Qadir	17	B 4, l-b 8, w 15, n-b 2	29
D. B. Vengsarkar c Ijaz b Jaffer	5		
*R. J. Shastri b Manzoor	50	1/10 2/19 3/29 (7 wkts, 45 overs) 196	
R. Lamba b Qadir	5	4/62 5/85	
†C. S. Pandit not out	33	6/123 7/188	

R. R. Kulkarni and Maninder Singh did not bat.

Bowling: Imran 10–1–41–2; Wasim 10–1–35–0; Jaffer 10–2–28–1; Mudassar 5–0–29–1; Qadir 8–1–42–2; Manzoor 2–0–9–1.

Pakistan

Mudassar Nazar c and b Shastri	43	Manzoor Elahi c Chetan b Srikkanth ... 27
Rizwan-uz-Zaman c Maninder b Chetan	2	†Salim Yousuf not out 0
Ijaz Ahmed c and b Shastri	17	B 4, l-b 5, w 1, n-b 4 14
Javed Miandad b Maninder	13	
Abdul Qadir c Lamba b Shastri	39	1/10 2/62 3/84 (7 wkts, 44 overs) 200
Salim Malik run out	23	4/86 5/137
*Imran Khan not out	22	6/156 7/196

Saleem Jaffer and Wasim Akram did not bat.

Bowling: Chetan 7-1-25-1; Madan Lal 10-1-37-0; Kulkarni 3-0-31-0; Maninder 10-1-31-1; Shastri 10-1-37-3; Azharuddin 3-0-20-0; Srikkanth 1-0-10-1.

Umpires: S. Banerjee and R. B. Gupta.

INDIAN UNDER-25 XI v PAKISTANIS

At Bombay, January 29, 30, 31. Drawn. It was the turn of Pakistan's two other openers to strike form as a hapless set of young bowlers tried to contain a powerful batting line-up on a perfect batting strip. After Ramiz Raja (193 balls, 25 fours) and Shoaib Mohammad (thirteen fours) had put on 287 in 240 minutes, Javed Miandad rattled up 151 off 126 balls, hitting three sixes and sixteen fours and quite overshadowing the aggressive knock of Ijaz Ahmed, who struck four sixes and thirteen fours in his 131 off 126 balls. A competent hundred by Sanjay Manjrekar, son of Vijay, was the Under-25's sole resistance against Tauseef Ahmed's off-spin. With little time left to make a follow-on meaningful, Miandad opted for batting practice.

Close of play: First day, Pakistanis 388-3 (Javed Miandad 50*, Ijaz Ahmed 5*); Second day, Indian Under-25 XI 112-4 (S. V. Manjrekar 14*, Deepak Sharma 12*).

Pakistanis

Ramiz Raja c and b S. Sharma	167			
Shoaib Mohammad b Manjrekar	116	– (3) not out		23
Salim Malik c Rajput b Azim	37	– (2) b S. Sharma		2
*Javed Miandad c Kalyani b Azim	151			
Ijaz Ahmed c Karim b Kalyani	131			
Manzoor Elahi not out	50			
Wasim Akram not out	1			
Mudassar Nazar (did not bat)		– (1) not out		31
B 3, l-b 12, n-b 6	21	B 1, n-b 1		2

1/287 2/313 3/363	(5 wkts dec.) 674	1/9 (1 wkt) 58
4/541 5/665		

Zakir Khan, Tauseef Ahmed and †Zulqarnain did not bat.

Bowling: *First Innings*—Arun 17-0-114-0; Patel 15-0-82-0; S. Sharma 25-1-105-1; Azim 30-2-175-2; Deepak 15-1-80-0; Rajput 7-1-15-0; Manjrekar 8-1-34-1; Kalyani 2-0-25-1; Saldanha 3-0-29-0. *Second Innings*—S. Sharma 7-2-32-1; Patel 4-0-13-0; Azim 3-0-8-0; Prakash 1-0-4-0.

Indian Under-25 XI

*L. S. Rajput lbw b Tauseef	34	†S. S. Karim lbw b Tauseef		0
C. Saldanha c Manzoor b Wasim	1	S. Sharma c Manzoor b Tauseef		0
P. C. Prakash b Zulqarnain b Manzoor	27	Rashid Patel not out		6
S. Kalyani c Zulqarnain b Manzoor	19			
S. V. Manjrekar lbw b Manzoor	128	B 4, l-b 2, n-b 6		12
Deepak Sharma c Zulqarnain b Zakir	21			
B. Arun c sub b Tauseef	14	1/4 2/62 3/82 4/96 5/130		281
Azim Khan c Wasim b Tauseef	19	6/175 7/232 8/234 9/234		

Bowling: Wasim 25-4-74-1; Zakir 22-4-67-1; Tauseef 26-7-59-5; Manzoor 16.4-1-65-3; Shoaib 5-1-9-0; Malik 1-0-1-0.

Umpires: S. B. Kulkarni and R. S. Rathore.

INDIA v PAKISTAN

First Test Match

At Madras, February 3, 4, 6, 7, 8. Drawn. An emotive and significant series got off to a fine start in a good atmosphere at a venue which was not on the original schedule. There was success for Kulkarni in his first over after Pakistan had chosen to bat, but Shoaib, with a painstaking maiden Test hundred, and Miandad, batting for 225 minutes, established the innings. Miandad was 6 short of his fifteenth Test century when he was smartly run out by Vengsarkar at silly point as he stepped out to Maninder. A middle-order collapse against the turning ball left Pakistan somewhat exposed before Imran Khan played a delightfully correct innings. Wasim Akram, with five sixes and six fours in his 62 off 102 balls, took the leading role in their stand of 112, a record for Pakistan's eighth wicket against India, with the result that Imran was still only 68 when the last man, Tauseef, joined him. However, they remained together for an hour and a half as first Imran reached his hundred, after six hours six minutes' batting, and then went on to his highest Test score, which contained five sixes and fourteen fours.

A marvellous 123 off 149 balls by Srikkanth, whose two sixes and eighteen fours included two fours and a six off successive balls by Imran, settled India well into their reply. His partnership of 200 with Gavaskar was the highest for the first wicket against Pakistan by any country. As well as Gavaskar, Vengsarkar and Amarnath were dismissed when in sight of their hundreds, and on a wicket that was still playing superbly the match meandered towards a draw. Of the bowlers, Maninder Singh performed well enough for the Pakistanis to draft the 39-year-old Younis Ahmed on to the tour as a left-handed counter to the potential threat of India's left-arm spinners.

Man of the Match: Imran Khan and K. Srikkanth (shared).

Close of play: First day, Pakistan 247-5 (Salim Malik 14*, Abdul Qadir 2*); Second day, India 15-0 (S. M. Gavaskar 10*, K. Srikkanth 5*); Third day, India 290-2 (M. Amarnath 33*, D. B. Vengsarkar 39*); Fourth day, India 527-9 (N. S. Yadav 6*, Maninder Singh 7*).

Pakistan

Rizwan-uz-Zaman c More b Kulkarni	1	– (3) not out	54
Shoaib Mohammad lbw b Maninder	101	– c Vengsarkar b Maninder	45
Ramiz Raja c Srikkanth b Maninder	24	– (1) c Azharuddin b Qadir	14
Javed Miandad run out	94	– st More b Maninder	54
Salim Malik b Maninder	19	– not out	6
Ijaz Ahmed c Vengsarkar b Maninder	3		
Abdul Qadir c Azharuddin b Shastri	21		
*Imran Khan not out	135		
Wasim Akram c Gavaskar b Yadav	62		
†Salim Yousuf c Kulkarni b Maninder	1		
Tauseef Ahmed not out	13		
L-b 11, w 1, n-b 1	13	L-b 3, n-b 6	9

1/2 2/60 3/215 4/237 5/244   (9 wkts dec.) 487   1/17 2/70 3/160   (3 wkts) 182
6/257 7/273 8/385 9/406

Bowling: *First Innings*—Kapil Dev 18-1-68-0; Kulkarni 7-0-41-1; Maninder 59-16-135-5; Yadav 41-3-127-1; Shastri 38-8-105-1. *Second Innings*—Kapil Dev 9-1-36-0; Kulkarni 5-0-15-1; Shastri 18-5-42-0; Maninder 26-10-47-2; Yadav 15-4-29-0; Srikkanth 3-0-6-0; Gavaskar 1-0-4-0.

India

S. M. Gavaskar c Tauseef b Qadir	91	R. R. Kulkarni c Yousuf b Imran	2
K. Srikkanth c Wasim b Tauseef	123	N. S. Yadav not out	6
M. Amarnath run out	89	Maninder Singh not out	7
D. B. Vengsarkar st Yousuf b Tauseef	96	B 9, l-b 5, n-b 5	19
M. Azharuddin st Yousuf b Tauseef	20		
R. J. Shastri c Yousuf b Imran	41	1/200 2/220 3/405	(9 wkts dec.) 527
*Kapil Dev c Ramiz b Qadir	5	4/424 5/429 6/453	
†K. S. More lbw b Wasim	28	7/494 8/498 9/515	

Bowling: Wasim 34–10–78–1; Imran 27–4–103–2; Qadir 39–4–130–2; Tauseef 67–6–189–3; Shoaib 3–0–13–0.

Umpires: R. Mehra and V. K. Ramaswamy.

INDIA v PAKISTAN
Second Test Match

At Calcutta, February 11, 12, 14, 15, 16. Drawn. Gavaskar's decision to opt out of this match for "personal reasons" – he was thought to be unhappy at his treatment by the Eden Gardens crowds – brought to a close his run of 106 consecutive Test matches. India, in trouble at 149 for five after being put in by Imran, fought their way to safety through a combative innings of 141 by Azharuddin, his fifth Test century. Kapil Dev, with 66 off 117 balls, joined him in a record 143 for India's sixth wicket partnership against Pakistan, and when he was out Binny, recalled to the Test team in place of Yadav, saw another hundred partnership posted. However, Binny's moment was still to come. On the third day, allying the new ball to the late evening breeze from the Hooghly, he sliced through the Pakistan middle order with a spell of four for 9 in 30 balls. Next morning he added the wickets of Qadir and Tauseef to finish with career-best figures in 28 Tests.

Thanks to Salim Yousuf, Pakistan had averted the follow-on, but there were almost two days remaining when India batted again. Arun Lal, who replaced Gavaskar, made his second fifty of the match, but India's batting was so slow that the declaration gave Binny little time to produce his late-evening formula again. He nevertheless accounted for Shoaib in the five overs before the close, a hint of what might have been. On the final day, the night-watchman, Salim Yousuf (216 minutes), Miandad (235 minutes) and Salim Malik (93 minutes) set about saving the match rather than considering the challenge of scoring 340 runs in just under even time. India were handicapped by an injury to Maninder, who had bruised his spinning finger in attempting to catch Ramiz Raja in the first innings, although the possibility of his bowling out the Pakistanis on the last day was remote. His economical first-innings figures were as much the product of the grim application of Rizwan-uz-Zaman and Ramiz, both of whom batted for approximately five hours, as of any spin on a pitch that became true and easy.

Man of the Match: R. M. H. Binny.

Close of play: First day, India 225-5 (M. Azharuddin 51*, Kapil Dev 39*); Second day, Pakistan 57-1 (Ramiz Raja 25*, Rizwan-uz-Zaman 0*); Third day, Pakistan 215-7 (Salim Yousuf 21*, Abdul Qadir 2*); Fourth day, Pakistan 16-1 (Ramiz Raja 7*, Salim Yousuf 4*).

India

K. Srikkanth c Malik b Wasim	22	– lbw b Imran	21
Arun Lal c Tauseef b Jaffer	52	– c Wasim b Imran	70
M. Amarnath run out	9	– b Tauseef	31
D. B. Vengsarkar c Yousuf b Wasim	38	– not out	41
M. Azharuddin b Wasim	141		
R. J. Shastri b Qadir	5		
*Kapil Dev c Miandad b Jaffer	66		
R. M. H. Binny not out	52		
†K. S. More run out	0		
R. R. Kulkarni lbw b Wasim	0		
Maninder Singh b Wasim	3		
B 1, l-b 8, w 1, n-b 5	15	B 4, l-b 12, n-b 2	18

1/30 2/73 3/104 4/144 5/149	403	1/37 2/100 3/181 (3 wkts dec.) 181
6/292 7/393 8/393 9/395		

Bowling: *First Innings*—Imran 27-2-93-0; Wasim 31-6-96-5; Jaffer 36-2-115-2; Tauseef 10-1-39-0; Qadir 14-3-51-1. *Second Innings*—Imran 7.1-0-28-2; Wasim 18-4-46-0; Tauseef 18-2-50-1; Qadir 2-0-8-0; Jaffer 7-0-33-0.

Pakistan

Shoaib Mohammad run out	24	– (2)	lbw b Binny	5
Ramiz Raja c sub (S. Viswanath) b Shastri	69	– (1)	c More b Binny	29
Rizwan-uz-Zaman b Kapil Dev	60	– (4)	b Shastri	8
Javed Miandad c More b Binny	17	– (5)	not out	63
Salim Malik lbw b Binny	0	– (6)	lbw b Kapil Dev	20
*Imran Khan c Kapil Dev b Binny	1	– (7)	not out	5
†Salim Yousuf lbw b Kapil Dev	33	– (3)	b Maninder	43
Wasim Akram b Binny	1			
Abdul Qadir b Binny	2			
Tauseef Ahmed c Vengsarkar b Binny	0			
Saleem Jaffer not out	0			
B 4, l-b 4, w 1, n-b 13	22		B 1, l-b 2, w 2, n-b 1	6

1/57 2/136 3/178 4/178 5/191   229   1/12 2/57 3/73   (5 wkts) 179
6/195 7/207 8/215 9/229   4/116 5/170

Bowling: *First Innings*—Kapil Dev 29-5-88-2; Binny 25.1-8-56-6; Maninder 20.1-11-21-0; Shastri 20.5-10-18-1; Kulkarni 13-1-38-0. *Second Innings*—Kapil Dev 19-7-41-1; Binny 21-4-45-2; Kulkarni 7-2-19-0; Shastri 24-6-41-1; Maninder 16-6-30-1.

Umpires: R. B. Gupta and P. D. Reporter.

†INDIA v PAKISTAN

Second One-day International

At Calcutta, February 18. Pakistan won by two wickets. A splendid 72 off 35 balls by Salim Malik brought Pakistan a remarkable victory before a crowd of 90,000-plus at the first one-day international at Eden Gardens. The match was seemingly in India's grasp after Srikkanth's 123 (one six, fourteen fours) and partnership of 145 for the fourth wicket with Azharuddin. Younis Ahmed, playing in his first one-day international in his 40th year, shared a century opening stand with Ramiz Raja, but in forcing the pace Pakistan slumped to 161 for five. Coming in when 78 runs were needed at more than 10 an over, Malik produced some amazing shots and hit a six and eleven fours as he turned the tables. Maninder, who played despite an injury, went for 70 runs in his ten overs.

Man of the Match: Salim Malik.

India

K. Srikkanth c Yousuf b Wasim	123	R. J. Shastri not out	21
L. S. Rajput b Imran	0	†C. S. Pandit not out	6
R. Lamba lbw b Imran	4	B 1, l-b 6, w 7, n-b 3	17
D. B. Vengsarkar c Yousuf b Jaffer	12		
M. Azharuddin c Younis b Wasim	49	1/3 2/13 3/58 (6 wkts, 40 overs) 238	
*Kapil Dev c and b Wasim	6	4/203 5/204 6/216	

Madan Lal, R. M. H. Binny and Maninder Singh did not bat.

Bowling: Imran 10-0-59-2; Wasim 10-0-49-3; Mudassar 4-0-30-0; Jaffer 10-0-49-1; Manzoor 6-0-44-0.

Pakistan

Ramiz Raja c Maninder b Shastri	....	58
Younis Ahmed c and b Shastri	......	58
Javed Miandad lbw b Maninder	.....	13
Abdul Qadir b Shastri	....	9
Manzoor Elahi lbw b Shastri	....	14
*Imran Khan b Kapil Dev	....	2
Salim Malik not out	....	72
Wasim Akram c Azharuddin		
b Kapil Dev	.	3

†Salim Yousuf run out	....	0
Mudassar Nazar not out	....	1
B 1, l-b 7, w 1, n-b 2	....	11
1/106 2/132 3/142	(8 wkts, 39.3 overs)	241
4/150 5/161 6/174		
7/224 8/232		

Saleem Jaffer did not bat.

Bowling: Kapil Dev 9.3–0–53–2; Binny 2–0–21–0; Madan Lal 5–0–33–0; Maninder 10–0–70–1; Shastri 10–0–38–4; Rajput 3–0–18–0.

Umpires: D. N. Dotiwala and R. V. Ramani.

INDIA v PAKISTAN

Third Test Match

At Jaipur, February 21, 22, 24, 25, 26. Drawn. Rajasthan's first Test match – the Sawai Mansingh Stadium became the 61st Test ground – was overtaken by events: first by the visit on the second day by General Zia, Pakistan's President, as part of his "Cricket for Peace" mission, and then by controversy over the repairs to the pitch following the thunderstorm and heavy winds which swept aside the covers and soaked the ground that evening.

Before these incidents, the talking points were the recall to Pakistan's Test team of Younis Ahmed after 17 years 111 days and the dismissal of Gavaskar, Imran's first ball taking the inside edge and ricocheting off Gavaskar's ultra-light pads, low to third slip. It was the third time in 123 Tests that the Indian opener had fallen to the first ball of a Test match. Thereafter, India's innings progressed laboriously. Azharuddin, revealing a penchant for successive centuries, took 183 balls for his sixth hundred in Tests, while Shastri appeared content on occupation, batting seven hours for his seventh.

Attention centred after the rest day centred on the pitch, which was sprinkled with sawdust. The Pakistanis claimed this had been used to dry the pitch, thus changing its nature; the Indian officials in defence claimed that it had been blown there from the outfield. The umpires dragged their feet over a resumption as Imran threatened to refuse to bat, and they eventually defused the situation by abandoning play for the day. This virtually condemned the match to yet another draw, which Pakistan ensured by batting until lunch on the final day. Ramiz, with 114 off 279 balls, was their bulwark after early Indian inroads and Imran, with eleven fours in his 140-minute 66, slipped his side past the follow-on figure next morning. India's attack, already without Maninder, was further depleted when Binny injured his ankle in the nets and was unable to bowl.

Man of the Match: R. J. Shastri.

Close of play: First day, India 228-4 (M. Azharuddin 72*, R. J. Shastri 22*); Second day, India 459-8 (R. M. H. Binny 3*, N. S. Yadav 5*); Third day, No play; Fourth day, Pakistan 228-6 (Imran Khan 21*).

India

S. M. Gavaskar c Miandad b Imran	....	0	– c Ramiz b Tauseef 24
K. Srikkanth lbw b Wasim	....	45	– c sub (Ijaz Ahmed) b Iqbal 51
M. Amarnath b Imran	....	49	– not out 15
D. B. Vengsarkar c Iqbal b Shoaib	....	30	– not out 21
M. Azharuddin c Yousuf b Tauseef	....	110	
R. J. Shastri c Ramiz b Iqbal	....	125	
*Kapil Dev c Yousuf b Rizwan	....	50	
†K. S. More c Miandad b Tauseef	....	22	
R. M. H. Binny not out	....	6	
N. S. Yadav not out	....	8	
B 2, l-b 10, w 1, n-b 7	....	20	L-b 2, n-b 1 3

1/0 2/74 3/114 4/156	(8 wkts dec.) 465	1/72 2/88	(2 wkts) 114
5/286 6/385 7/444 8/451			

Gopal Sharma did not bat.

Bowling: *First Innings*—Imran 35-7-93-2; Wasim 36.3-5-88-1; Iqbal 44-5-149-1; Tauseef 38-3-97-2; Shoaib 5-0-19-1; Rizwan 5-2-7-1. *Second Innings*—Wasim 5-1-17-0; Imran 5-2-8-0; Iqbal 13-4-34-1; Tauseef 13-3-47-1; Younis 1-0-6-0; Shoaib 1-1-0-0.

Pakistan

Ramiz Raja b Kapil Dev	114	†Salim Yousuf run out	14
Shoaib Mohammad c Gavaskar		Wasim Akram c Kapil Dev b Yadav	11
b Amarnath	0	Iqbal Qasim c Srikkanth b Gopal	20
Rizwan-uz-Zaman c More b Kapil Dev	10	Tauseef Ahmed not out	10
Javed Miandad lbw b Shastri	50	B 8, l-b 2, n-b 12	22
Younis Ahmed c sub (Arun Lal) b Gopal	14		
Salim Malik c Srikkanth b Gopal	10	1/0 2/28 3/122 4/162 5/174	341
*Imran Khan c Kapil Dev b Gopal	66	6/228 7/282 8/302 9/318	

Bowling: Kapil Dev 27-7-84-2; Amarnath 8-4-15-1; Shastri 36-12-79-1; Yadav 25-8-65-1; Gopal 32.5-3-88-4.

Umpires: V. K. Ramaswamy and P. D. Reporter.

DELHI v PAKISTANIS

At New Delhi, February 28, March 1, 2. Drawn. This fixture, against the Ranji Trophy champions, was approached in a relaxed mood by the touring team. Their principal players rested, and the only one with any motivation to impress was Younis, who hit a six and thirteen fours in his unbeaten hundred. Delhi's reply was built around Lamba's 131, which included fourteen fours, and enlivened by Madan Lal's three sixes and six fours in his 66. Dismissing Delhi on the third morning gave the Pakistanis further batting practice, which Rizwan-uz-Zaman used to score his second hundred of the tour and Ijaz Ahmed and Manzoor Elahi (seven sixes, two fours) enjoyed by smashing the bowling around. This offered some late entertainment in a match which was watched by fewer than 100 spectators.

Close of play: First day, Delhi 28-2 (R. Lamba 10*, S. Sharma 4*); Second day, Delhi 321-8 (A. Sharma 24*, Shashikant 20*).

Pakistanis

*Mudassar Nazar c Azad b Kumar	30	– b Madan Lal	9
Shoaib Mohammad c Lamba b Prabhakar	10	– c sub b Kumar	38
Rizwan-uz-Zaman b Prabhakar	0	– retired	101
Younis Ahmed retired	103		
Salim Malik c Nayyar b Azad	48	– c sub b Bhaskar Pillai	53
Ijaz Ahmed run out	14	– (4) lbw b Kumar	80
Manzoor Elahi not out	40	– (6) not out	65
Abdul Qadir c Kumar b A. Sharma	26		
Saleem Jaffer (did not bat)		– (7) not out	1
L-b 1, n-b 3	4	L-b 2, w 1	3

1/19 2/21 3/78 4/194   (6 wkts dec.) 275   1/9 2/82 3/252 4/328   (4 wkts) 350
5/238 6/275

Iqbal Qasim and †Zulqarnain did not bat.

Bowling: *First Innings*—Madan Lal 9-2-11-0; Prabhakar 10-2-26-2; S. Sharma 14-1-60-0; Kumar 13-1-51-1; Azad 16-0-84-1; A. Sharma 6.5-0-42-1. *Second Innings*—Prabhakar 8-2-25-0; Madan Lal 5-0-17-1; S. Sharma 15-0-67-0; Kumar 30-2-133-2; Azad 2-1-2-0; Nayyar 12-3-55-0; Bhaskar Pillai 8-0-49-1.

Delhi

M. Prabhakar c Manzoor b Jaffer	14	A. Sharma c Mudassar b Iqbal	40
R. Lamba c Zulqarnain b Manzoor	131	†Shashikant c and b Iqbal	34
M. Nayyar c Manzoor b Jaffer	0	R. Kumar not out	6
S. Sharma b Qadir	35		
K. Azad c sub b Iqbal	2		
S. C. Khanna b Iqbal	0	W 2, n-b 1	3
K. Bhaskar Pillai c sub b Iqbal	26		
*Madan Lal b Jaffer	66	1/22 2/22 3/101 4/104 5/104	357
		6/164 7/259 8/281 9/336	

Bowling: Jaffer 21–4–108–3; Manzoor 11–0–58–1; Iqbal 37–4–87–5; Qadir 32–5–100–1; Rizwan 1–0–4–0.

Umpires: R. R. Kadam and P. G. Pandit.

INDIA v PAKISTAN

Fourth Test Match

At Ahmedabad, March 4, 5, 7, 8, 9. Drawn. Gavaskar brought a sense of occasion to the eleventh consecutive draw between these two countries when, with a delectable late cut off Ijaz Faqih, he scored the 58th run needed for his 10,000 runs in Test cricket. The first to scale this summit, he achieved it in his 124th Test and 212th innings. Other Test landmarks were a maiden hundred by Ijaz – he also took a wicket with his first ball in the match – Yadav's 100th wicket, when he dismissed Iqbal Qasim, and Qadir's 150th wicket.

For the first time in ten years India played four spinners. Pakistan included Ijaz, who had arrived two days earlier to cover for Tauseef, who was ill; Manzoor Elahi and Qadir; Miandad was unfit with back problems. Electing to bat first on a pitch which looked under-prepared, Pakistan settled immediately for attrition, putting on a paltry 130 in 86 overs on the first day, although their tactics almost rebounded on them when they were 176 for six on the second. Ijaz and Imran revived the innings, putting on a record 154 for Pakistan's seventh wicket against India, and Ijaz went on to his hundred before the close, reaching both 50 and 100 with sixes off Maninder.

India batted from the second hour of the third day until almost the last of the fourth, when Wasim Akram brought their innings to an abrupt end by taking four for 10 in fourteen balls – three in one over. Gavaskar's feat put in the shade the competent hundred by Vengsarkar – his fifteenth in Tests – but Kapil Dev's 50 from 52 balls introduced a refreshing freedom to a match marked by slow batting. Indeed, the proceedings on the final day were unbearable. Only 33 runs were scored in the two hours to lunch, with Younis batting for 73 minutes for 2 runs; in all, 111 runs came in a day truncated by the decision to stop after ten of the final twenty overs. Rizwan took just over five hours for his 58, Younis four and a half hours for his unbeaten 34. The declining interest in the series could be understood.

The fourth day was marred by crowd disturbances in a city with a history of communal trouble. In the afternoon, the Pakistan outfielders were pelted with stones and, having with the umpires' consent taken his players off, Imran was reluctant to continue. Kapil Dev and Gavaskar appealed for calm over the public address system, and when play resumed after tea, some 50 minutes having been lost, the Pakistanis injected a dose of ironic humour as six of them took the field wearing helmets.

Man of the Match: Ijaz Faqih.

Close of play: First day, Pakistan 130-4 (Salim Malik 17*, Manzoor Elahi 19*); Second day, Pakistan 379-7 (Ijaz Faqih 104*, Abdul Qadir 20*); Third day, India 165-3 (D. B. Vengsarkar 62*, K. S. More 1*); Fourth day, Pakistan 25-0 (Ramiz Raja 14*, Rizwan-uz-Zaman 10*).

Pakistan

Ramiz Raja b Kapil Dev	41	– c Azharuddin b Maninder	21
†Salim Yousuf st More b Amarnath	2		
Rizwan-uz-Zaman c Kapil Dev b Maninder	5	– (2) c Azharuddin b Gopal	58
Younis Ahmed st More b Yadav	40	– (3) not out	34
Salim Malik c More b Yadav	20	– (4) not out	14
Manzoor Elahi c Kapil Dev b Yadav	52		
*Imran Khan b Gopal	72		
Ijaz Faqih lbw b Kapil Dev	105		
Abdul Qadir b Kapil Dev	25		
Wasim Akram not out	4		
Iqbal Qasim c More b Yadav	0		
B 6, l-b 20, n-b 3	29	N-b 8	8
	395	**(2 wkts)**	**135**

1/2 2/23 3/62 4/99 5/149 6/176 7/330 8/391 9/394   1/43 2/107

Bowling: *First Innings*—Kapil Dev 27–9–46–3; Amarnath 9–3–14–1; Maninder 54–21–106–1; Gopal 36–8–62–1; Yadav 48.3–13–109–4; Shastri 11–3–26–0; Srikkanth 2–0–6–0. *Second Innings*—Kapil Dev 10–3–19–0; Amarnath 2–0–6–0; Yadav 14–4–18–0; Gopal 26–9–36–1; Maninder 23–16–13–1; Shastri 18–6–23–0; Gavaskar 4–1–15–0; Srikkanth 2–0–5–0.

India

S. M. Gavaskar lbw b Imran	63	N. S. Yadav b Wasim	0	
K. Srikkanth b Ijaz	22	Gopal Sharma lbw b Wasim	0	
M. Amarnath c and b Iqbal	7	Maninder Singh b Wasim	0	
D. B. Vengsarkar c Malik b Wasim	109			
†K. S. More c Iqbal b Qadir	23	B 11, l-b 6, n-b 5	22	
M. Azharuddin b Imran	12			
R. J. Shastri c Iqbal b Manzoor	15	1/34 2/46 3/157 4/204 5/218	**323**	
*Kapil Dev not out	50	6/246 7/306 8/322 9/322		

Bowling: Imran 17–6–41–2; Wasim 21.5–2–60–4; Ijaz 27–3–81–1; Iqbal 30–11–63–1; Qadir 13–1–53–1; Manzoor 3–2–8–1.

Umpires: R. B. Gupta and S. R. Ramachandra Rao.

INDIA v PAKISTAN

Fifth Test Match

At Bangalore, March 13, 14, 15, 17. Pakistan won by 16 runs to record their first series win in India, their seventh Test win against India, and only their third victory in any series outside Pakistan. The behaviour of the pitch, so encouraging to spin bowling, provided a match of riveting theatre, although both captains had anticipated seaming conditions: India had included Binny for Gopal Sharma and Pakistan preferred Saleem Jaffer to Qadir. Miandad and Tauseef were again fit.

Batting first after winning the toss, Pakistan responded to panic induced by the turning ball with extravagant strokeplay that was not so much bold as foolish. Maninder, despite mixing the bad with the good, returned career-best figures of seven for 27, including a spell of four wickets in thirteen balls. Pakistan tumbled to their lowest score against India. The home side, in turn, were made to struggle, but Vengsarkar attained the right level of aggression, hitting a six and seven fours, to place India in a splendid position at 119 for four. His first misjudgement in lofting the ball opened the way for Pakistan's counter-attack. On a wicket getting worse by the hour, the Indian batsmen followed the example of their Pakistani counterparts and a lead of 29 was all that eventuated. Iqbal Qasim, who had joined the touring party in February, and Tauseef split the spoils.

The lead was erased by Imran's shrewd move in sending Miandad out to open with Ramiz, but Kapil was not so astute in keeping Maninder on when it became apparent that he was not bowling as effectively as in the first innings. Pakistan's middle order was allowed to prosper. Even so, only the ninth-wicket stand of 51, between Yousuf and Tauseef, put India in the disadvantageous position of having to score 221 in the fourth innings.

India's cause was not helped when they lost Srikkanth and Amarnath to successive balls and Vengsarkar was bowled on the eve of the rest day. But on the fourth day, on a pitch which allowed even an off-spinner to bowl bouncers, Gavaskar gave a masterly exhibition of technique and judgement. Only when he was out, having batted 5 hours 23 minutes and faced 266 balls for his 96, caught at slip off a ball which kicked off a good length, could Pakistan assume victory. A late, chancy charge by Binny cut the margin to 16, leaving India to consider what might have been had Kapil Dev and Shastri been able to resist the rush of blood that cost them their wickets.

Man of the Match: S. M. Gavaskar.   *Man of the Series:* Imran Khan.

Close of play: First day, India 68-2 (M. Amarnath 12*, D. B. Vengsarkar 9*); Second day, Pakistan 155-5 (Imran Khan 18*, Manzoor Elahi 1*); Third day, India 99-4 (S. M. Gavaskar 51*, M. Azharuddin 7*).

Pakistan

Ramiz Raja c Vengsarkar b Kapil Dev	22	– b Yadav 47
Rizwan-uz-Zaman b Kapil Dev	1	– (3) b Shastri 0
Salim Malik b Maninder	33	– (4) b Kapil Dev 33
Javed Miandad c Shastri b Maninder	7	– (2) c Srikkanth b Shastri 17
Manzoor Elahi c Azharuddin b Maninder	0	– (7) c More b Maninder 8
*Imran Khan c Amarnath b Maninder	6	– c Srikkanth b Shastri 39
Wasim Akram b Maninder	0	– (8) lbw b Maninder 11
†Salim Yousuf c and b Shastri	0	– (9) not out 41
Iqbal Qasim b Maninder	19	– (5) c Srikkanth b Yadav 26
Tauseef Ahmed not out	15	– c Malik b Shastri 10
Saleem Jaffer c Vengsarkar b Maninder	8	– c Gavaskar b Maninder 0
B 2, l-b 1, n-b 3	6	B 7, l-b 8, n-b 1 16

1/3 2/39 3/60 4/60 5/68   116   1/45 2/57 3/89 4/121 5/142   249
6/68 7/73 8/74 9/98   6/166 7/184 8/198 9/249

Bowling: *First Innings*—Kapil Dev 11-2-23-2; Binny 3-0-25-0; Amarnath 3-1-7-0; Maninder 18.2-8-27-7; Shastri 11-1-19-1; Yadav 3-0-12-0. *Second Innings*—Kapil Dev 12-2-25-1; Maninder 43.5-8-99-3; Shastri 24-3-69-4; Yadav 15-3-41-2.

India

S. M. Gavaskar b Tauseef	21	– c Rizwan b Iqbal 96
K. Srikkanth b Tauseef	21	– lbw b Wasim 6
M. Amarnath b Tauseef	13	– c Yousuf b Wasim 0
D. B. Vengsarkar c Manzoor b Tauseef	50	– b Tauseef 19
M. Azharuddin c Manzoor b Iqbal	6	– (6) c and b Iqbal 26
R. J. Shastri c Malik b Tauseef	7	– (7) c and b Iqbal 4
*Kapil Dev c Malik b Iqbal	9	– (8) b Iqbal 2
R. M. H. Binny c Tauseef b Iqbal	1	– (9) c Yousuf b Tauseef 15
†K. S. More not out	9	– (5) lbw b Tauseef 3
N. S. Yadav b Iqbal	0	– b Tauseef 4
Maninder Singh c Yousuf b Iqbal	0	– not out 2
B 4, l-b 4	8	B 22, l-b 5 27

1/39 2/56 3/71 4/102 5/126   145   1/15 2/15 3/64 4/80 5/123   204
6/130 7/135 8/137 9/143   6/155 7/161 8/180 9/185

Bowling: *First Innings*—Imran 5-0-26-0; Wasim 2-0-9-0; Iqbal 30-15-48-5; Tauseef 27-7-54-5. *Second Innings*—Wasim 11-3-19-2; Tauseef 45.5-12-85-4; Iqbal 37-11-73-4.

Umpires: R. B. Gupta and V. K. Ramaswamy.

†INDIA v PAKISTAN

Third One-day International

At Hyderabad, March 20. India won by virtue of having lost fewer wickets with the scores tied. In a sensational and controversial finish Abdul Qadir ran himself out off the last ball, attempting an impossible and unnecessary second run. Had he settled for the single which levelled the scores, Pakistan would have won on the tie-breaker, having scored more runs than India after 25 overs. To add to the confusion, the umpires had failed to notice an infringement of the field-placing restriction. Only three, instead of four, Indian fieldsmen were in the 30-yard circle as Kapil Dev bowled the last ball, and so it should have been a no-ball. Put in to bat, India had been struggling at 95 for four but were rescued by a stand of 112 between Shastri and Kapil – the best for India's fifth wicket in a one-day international.

Man of the Match: Not awarded.

India

S. M. Gavaskar c Manzoor b Wasim	1	Madan Lal run out	1
K. Srikkanth retired hurt	2	M. Prabhakar not out	0
R. Lamba c Miandad b Ijaz	41		
M. Azharuddin c Manzoor b Jaffer	18	L-b 5, w 11, n-b 4	20
†S. Viswanath c Wasim b Qadir	1		
R. J. Shastri not out	69	1/6 2/53 3/59 (6 wkts, 44 overs)	212
*Kapil Dev lbw b Imran	59	4/95 5/207 6/212	

Gopal Sharma and Maninder Singh did not bat.

Bowling: Imran Khan 9-2-27-1; Wasim 9-0-45-1; Jaffer 9-0-51-1; Qadir 9.2-0-44-1; Ijaz 6-0-31-1; Manzoor 1.4-0-9-0.

Pakistan

Ramiz Raja c Azharuddin b Kapil Dev	23	Abdul Qadir run out	1
Younis Ahmed st Viswanath b Gopal	26		
Salim Malik c Shastri b Gopal	84	B 2, l-b 2, w 7	11
Javed Miandad lbw b Shastri	25		
Manzoor Elahi not out	27	1/39 2/82 3/146 (7 wkts, 44 overs)	212
*Imran Khan c Maninder b Gopal	7	4/187 5/197	
Wasim Akram run out	8	6/209 7/212	

Ijaz Faqih, †Salim Yousuf and Saleem Jaffer did not bat.

Bowling: Kapil Dev 10-0-44-1; Prabhakar 8-1-32-0; Madal Lal 4-0-22-0; Maninder 10-0-41-0; Gopal 6-0-29-3; Shastri 6-0-40-1.

Umpires: S. K. Ghosh and V. Vikramraju.

†INDIA v PAKISTAN

Fourth One-day International

At Pune, March 22. Pakistan won by six wickets. Pakistan, with the advantage of the toss, cruised to an unbeatable 3-1 lead in the series of six internationals. All their bowlers benefited from a helpful pitch, none more so than Saleem Jaffer, the young left-arm fast bowler.

Man of the Match: Saleem Jaffer.

India

S. M. Gavaskar run out	7	R. R. Kulkarni c Tauseef b Qadir	15
R. Lamba c Qadir b Jaffer	27	Gopal Sharma run out	4
M. Azharuddin b Tauseef	0	Maninder Singh not out	2
D. B. Vengsarkar lbw b Jaffer	2	B 1, l-b 6, w 6, n-b 1	14
†S. Viswanath b Jaffer	5		
R. J. Shastri c Yousuf b Wasim	21	1/21 2/21 3/36 (9 wkts, 42 overs) 120	
*Kapil Dev lbw b Tauseef	6	4/44 5/49 6/63	
M. Prabhakar not out	17	7/88 8/109 9/114	

Bowling: Imran 7-2-20-0; Wasim 10-3-37-1; Tauseef 10-2-18-2; Jaffer 9-0-25-3; Qadir 6-0-13-1.

Pakistan

Ramiz Raja run out	33	Manzoor Elahi not out	7
†Salim Yousuf lbw b Kapil Dev	15		
Salim Malik c Vengsarkar b Maninder	17	B 4, l-b 3, w 1, n-b 2	10
Javed Miandad c sub (C. S. Pandit) b Kapil Dev	22	1/33 2/65 (4 wkts, 37.2 overs) 121	
*Imran Khan not out	17	3/77 4/114	

Wasim Akram, Ijaz Faqih, Saleem Jaffer, Tauseef Ahmed and Abdul Qadir did not bat.

Bowling: Kapil Dev 7-0-32-2; Kulkarni 2-0-10-0; Maninder 10-1-21-1; Gopal 10-0-28-0; Shastri 8.2-0-23-0.

Umpires: R. R. Kadam and S. R. Ramachandra Rao.

†INDIA v PAKISTAN

Fifth One-day International

At Nagpur, March 24. Pakistan won by 41 runs. Miandad and Imran (65 balls) put together a superlative stand of 142 to pull Pakistan from a crisis in the only match in which Kapil Dev won the toss and inserted Pakistan. Even so, India's target might still have been manageable but for an unbeaten 48 off 21 balls by Wasim Akram; he took 25 (266641) off one over by Chetan Sharma. Gavaskar (102 balls) and Shastri (39 balls) raised Indian hopes as they lashed out in a stand of 76 in defiance of an asking-rate which had climbed to 8 an over, but once past that threat Pakistan claimed the series 4-1 with one match remaining.

Man of the Match: Wasim Akram.

Pakistan

Ramiz Raja run out	8	Wasim Akram not out	48
Ijaz Ahmed b Maninder	34	†Salim Yousuf not out	3
Salim Malik c Azharuddin b Maninder	17	B 3, l-b 10, w 4, n-b 4	21
Javed Miandad c Shastri b Kapil Dev	78		
Manzoor Elahi lbw b Chetan	4	1/19 2/68 3/73 (6 wkts, 44 overs) 286	
*Imran Khan run out	73	4/83 5/225 6/245	

Tauseef Ahmed, Abdul Qadir and Saleem Jaffer did not bat.

Bowling: Kapil Dev 10-0-57-1; Prabhakar 4-0-24-0; Chetan 9-0-70-1; Maninder 10-1-43-2; Shastri 7-0-55-0; Rajput 4-0-24-0.

India

S. M. Gavaskar c Jaffer b Wasim	70	†S. Viswanath b Wasim	6
L. S. Rajput b Jaffer	8	M. Prabhakar not out	9
R. Lamba c Manzoor b Qadir	10	Maninder Singh not out	5
D. B. Vengsarkar b Qadir	34	L-b 8, w 18, n-b 2	28
*Kapil Dev b Qadir	6		
R. J. Shastri c Manzoor b Imran	52	1/25 2/40 3/105 (9 wkts, 44 overs) 245	
Chetan Sharma run out	5	4/115 5/191 6/202	
M. Azharuddin b Wasim	12	7/203 8/216 9/227	

Bowling: Imran 10–0–48–1; Wasim 10–1–26–3; Jaffer 6–0–31–1; Qadir 10–0–75–3; Tauseef 7–0–49–0; Manzoor 1–0–8–0.

Umpires: S. B. Kulkarni and R. S. Rathore.

†INDIA v PAKISTAN

Sixth One-day International

At Jamshedpur, March 26. Pakistan won by five wickets. Gavaskar and Prabhakar launched the Indian innings with 154 for the first wicket after Imran had put them in in ideal batting conditions. Prabhakar (thirteen fours), the replacement for Srikkanth, who was injured at Hyderabad, went on to his maiden hundred in a one-day international. Javed Miandad organised Pakistan's reply intelligently after Ijaz Ahmed had provided the thrust with 72 off 84 balls. The Indian bowlers wilted under the onslaught in the closing overs, and when 12 were needed off the final one, Miandad hit Gopal Sharma's first two balls for six.

Man of the Match: M. Prabhakar.   *Man of the Series:* R. J. Shastri.

India

S. M. Gavaskar c Manzoor b Qadir	...	69	R. J. Shastri not out	10
M. Prabhakar b Wasim	....	106	B 5, l-b 3, w 7, n-b 2	17
R. Lamba b Tauseef	....	9		
D. B. Vengsarkar, not out	....	54	1/154 2/171 3/247 (3 wkts, 44 overs)	265

M. Azharuddin, *Kapil Dev, R. R. Kulkarni, †S. Viswanath, Gopal Sharma and Maninder Singh did not bat.

Bowling: Imran 10–1–55–0; Jaffer 7–0–45–0; Qadir 10–0–52–1; Wasim 10–0–63–1; Tauseef 5–0–31–1; Manzoor 2–0–11–0.

Pakistan

Ramiz Raja c Viswanath b Kapil Dev	. 28	Wasim Akram not out	12
Ijaz Ahmed lbw b Maninder	 72		
Salim Malik lbw b Kulkarni	 13	B 3, l-b 10, w 3, n-b 6	22
Javed Miandad not out	 78		
*Imran Khan c Azharuddin b Gopal	.. 23	1/52 2/81 3/140 (5 wkts, 43.2 overs)	266
Manzoor Elahi b Kapil Dev	 18	4/195 5/247	

†Salim Yousuf, Abdul Qadir, Tauseef Ahmed and Saleem Jaffer did not bat.

Bowling: Kapil Dev 9.2–0–42–2; Prabhakar 6–0–36–0; Kulkarni 5–0–27–1; Maninder 10–0–45–1; Shastri 7–0–48–0; Gopal 6–0–55–1.

Umpires: S. Banerjee and V. Vikramraju.

THE NEW ZEALANDERS IN SRI LANKA, 1986-87

New Zealand's hastily arranged tour to Sri Lanka in mid-April was viewed by the New Zealand Cricket Council as a vital stage in rebuilding the national team. After five years of comparative stability, gaps had occurred and needed to be filled. Two stalwarts, Coney, the captain, and Edgar had retired during the season just finished, and with Wright, Edgar's opening partner for the previous eight years, being excused from the tour to allow him to arrange his benefit at Derbyshire, this meant that a new captain and vice-captain had to be selected. The Crowe brothers were the logical successors, with Jeff being appointed captain. It had been under his leadership that New Zealand won the Australasian Schoolboys' Championship in 1976-77, while Martin, leading by example, had won the Shell Trophy for Central Districts in the grand manner.

After the experience which many of the batsmen had undergone in the recent series against West Indies, it was essential that their confidence be restored. The programme of three Tests and four one-day internationals against Sri Lanka, preceded by a three-day match against an invitation side, was seen as an ideal preparation for the World Cup in India later in the year.

Four players were making their first tour for New Zealand: Phil Horne, a left-handed opening batsman who had represented New Zealand at badminton at the 1986 Commonwealth Games in Edinburgh and made his Test début against the West Indians; Andrew Jones, a right-handed middle-order batsman, aged 28, who made his first-class début in 1979-80; Dipak Patel, the former Worcestershire all-rounder; and Danny Morrison, a nuggety right-arm fast-medium bowler. A cricketer with a positive approach, Horne brought to the opener's role a sharp eye, an ever-improving technique and excellent judgement of a run. His fielding in the covers was first-class. Jones, whose tenacity and grit over the years had won him the respect of his Wellington team-mates, had forced his way into the side by scoring two hundreds and four fifties in eight Shell Trophy matches. He was preferred to Patel in the First Test match for the batting place resulting from Coney's retirement. Throughout the New Zealand season, the 21-year-old Morrison's bowling had developed appreciably. His greatest asset was his stamina; he was as determined and lively at the end of a hot day with the old ball as he was with the new at the start of the innings.

Unfortunately, and unhappily, the political troubles in Sri Lanka intensified while the team were there. While the first match was being played, at Galle, four passenger buses were sprayed with machine-gun fire by separatist rebels near Kandy, the venue of the Second Test. And on the evening that the First Test finished, a car bomb exploded near the team's hotel in Colombo, killing many people. Such an uneasy situation did not provide a satisfactory atmosphere for a young sports team – throughout their short stay they had been constantly under police surveillance – and in the interest of their safety the tour was cancelled three days later.

The Second and Third Test matches had been scheduled for Kandy (April 24–29) and Colombo (May 5–10), while the one-day internationals were to have been played at Moratuwa (May 2) and Colombo (May 3, 12, and 14). – Don Neely.

GALLE DISTRICT CRICKET ASSOCIATION
INVITATION XI v NEW ZEALANDERS

At Galle, April 11, 12, 13. Drawn. Crowe won the toss and gave his batsmen an opportunity to acclimatise on the first day. Career-best figures of eight for 81 by Bracewell, their off-spinner, on the second day, and a century and half-century by their opening batsmen, Rutherford and Horne, on the third, put the New Zealanders in good heart for the forthcoming international matches. However, Jones and Patel again missed out on a useful knock when Warnaweera, a quick off-spinner, struck a purple patch and prompted Crowe to declare a few minutes before tea. This allowed Mahanama, an exciting, cultured batsman, to display his range of strokes, with elegant drives and wristy cuts being interspersed with powerful hooks. He and Kuruppu gave the innings a lively start with five boundaries off the first eight balls.

New Zealanders

K. R. Rutherford c Wickremasinghe			
b Ramanayake	9	– c sub b Warnaweera	108
P. A. Horne c Gurusinha b Ramanayake	14	– c Silva b Warnaweera	56
A. H. Jones lbw b M. A. R. Samarasekera	4	– lbw b Warnaweera	0
D. N. Patel lbw b M. A. R. Samarasekera	6	– c de Silva b Warnaweera	9
*J. J. Crowe c Kuruppu b Gunasekera	58	– not out	1
E. J. Gray c Wickremasinghe b Warnaweera	42	– not out	0
E. B. McSweeney run out	28		
J. G. Bracewell lbw b Gunasekera	1		
†I. D. S. Smith c Wickremasinghe b Warnaweera	54		
M. C. Snedden c Silva b M. A. R. Samarasekera	2		
D. K. Morrison not out	3		
L-b 8, w 1, n-b 5	14	L-b 1, w 4, n-b 2	7

1/16 2/21 3/31 4/37 5/114   **235**   1/154 2/154   (4 wkts dec.) **181**
6/168 7/169 8/174 9/191   3/179 4/181

Bowling: *First Innings*—Ramanayake 11-1-32-2; M. A. R. Samarasekera 12-3-32-3; Gurusinha 4-1-7-0; Warnaweera 21.5-2-76-2; A. J. Samarasekera 19-6-44-0; Gunasekera 14-4-36-2. *Second Innings*—Ramanayake 9-0-37-0; M. A. R. Samarasekera 9-1-47-0; Warnaweera 13-3-51-4; A. J. Samarasekera 9-2-21-0; Gunasekera 7-0-24-0.

Galle District CA Invitation XI

R. S. Mahanama c Rutherford b Bracewell	20	– not out	41
D. S. B. P. Kuruppu c Crowe b Morrison	23	– c Jones b Morrison	9
A. P. Gurusinha c Morrison b Bracewell	14		
†S. A. R. Silva c McSweeney b Morrison	4	– (3) c Rutherford b Gray	16
M. A. R. Samarasekera c Jones b Bracewell	46		
*Y. Gunasekera c Rutherford b Bracewell	16		
D. C. Wickremasinghe lbw b Bracewell	1	– (4) not out	5
T. A. de Silva st Smith b Bracewell	38		
C. P. Ramanayake c Rutherford b Bracewell	4		
A. J. Samarasekera b Bracewell	0		
K. P. J. Warnaweera not out	24		
L-b 9, w 1, n-b 4	14	L-b 1, n-b 3	4

1/44 2/64 3/72 4/72 5/134   **204**   1/22 2/66   (2 wkts) **75**
6/135 7/140 8/150 9/150

Bowling: *First Innings*—Morrison 15-4-46-2; Snedden 11-2-42-0; Bracewell 32.2-10-81-8; Gray 15-6-26-0. *Second Innings*—Morrison 7-3-27-1; Snedden 6-3-20-0; Gray 4-1-15-1; Patel 5-0-12-0.

Umpires: M. D. D. N. Gunaratne and S. Ponnadurai.

SRI LANKA v NEW ZEALAND

First Test Match

At Colombo Cricket Club, Colombo, April 16, 18, 19, 20, 21. Drawn. Long, slow innings by Kuruppu, Sri Lanka's 25-year-old wicket-keeping opener, and Jeff Crowe, in his first Test as New Zealand's captain, sentenced this match to tedium and a draw. Broken records and personal achievements, however, meant it was not without historical significance. Kuruppu, who had previously played in 21 one-day internationals, became the first Sri Lankan to score a hundred on his Test début (361 minutes, 253 balls, fifteen fours); his unbeaten 201 was the highest for Sri Lanka in Tests and made him the third batsman to score a double-hundred in his first Test match. On the other side of the ledger, it was also the slowest Test double-hundred, taking 776 minutes during which he faced 517 balls and hit 25 fours. Only Hanif Mohammad (970 minutes) and L. Hutton (797 minutes) had batted longer in a Test match. Kuruppu then kept wicket throughout the New Zealand innings, the first time a player on his début had been on the field all five days. Like his counterpart, Smith, the New Zealand wicket-keeper, he did not let past one bye.

Jeff Crowe, who took his team to safety from a position of 99 for four, batted for 609 minutes, faced 397 balls and hit thirteen fours. His hundred, in 515 minutes off 331 balls, was the third slowest in Tests, while his unbeaten partnership of 246 with Hadlee was the highest for New Zealand's sixth wicket against any country. Hadlee's 151 not out, his second hundred and highest score in 70 Tests, came off 243 balls in 407 minutes and contained two sixes and fourteen fours. On the third morning, in dismissing Ratnayake, he drew level with D. K. Lillee (also 70 Tests) as the second-highest wicket-taker in Test cricket (355). Soon afterwards, Chatfield claimed his 100th Test wicket when Anurasiri was caught behind.

The docile nature of the pitch and the oppressive, humid atmosphere deprived New Zealand of any advantage they hoped to gain by inserting Sri Lanka. Only one wicket fell in each session on the first day. Dias sparkled briefly, but apart from Kuruppu, only Madugalle, who added 109 with him, batted with true authority. His 59 runs on the second afternoon came from 112 balls, and it needed a brilliant catch on the third morning by Hadlee, at gully, to dismiss him. In the field, New Zealand kept to their task well, but they paid heavily for dropping Kuruppu four times; at 31, 70, 165 and 181. Sri Lanka's declaration, 50 minutes before tea on the third day, came as a relief.

Bad light, which had cut short the first day by an hour and a half, took 39 minutes from the last session as New Zealand began their innings, and it cost another 80 minutes at the end of the fourth day. By then, Hadlee having struck 40 in 47 balls – in stark contrast to Jeff Crowe's 42 in 291 minutes – New Zealand had avoided the follow-on. Ratnayeke, taking two for 5 in six overs, had threatened to open up the game, but the New Zealand captain was immovable. Taking 80 balls to reach 10, he remained an hour on 15, added 61 with Gray in 175 minutes, and in the last session scored just 10 runs. Time had ceased to matter. The spectators lost interest, and not even free admission could attract them to watch as Crowe and Hadlee batted throughout the final day. The umpires drew stumps with sixteen overs remaining.

Close of play: First day, Sri Lanka, 141-3 (D. S. B. P. Kuruppu 66*, A. Ranatunga 3*); Second day, Sri Lanka 317-5 (D. S. B. P. Kuruppu 153*, R. S. Madugalle 59*); Third day, New Zealand 51-2 (A. H. Jones 19*, M. D. Crowe 0*); Fourth day, New Zealand 214-5 (J. J. Crowe 42*, R. J. Hadlee 40*).

Sri Lanka

R. S. Mahanama c Smith b Chatfield . .	16	R. J. Ratnayake c Bracewell b Hadlee .	17
†D. S. B. P. Kuruppu not not	201	S. D. Anurasiri c Smith b Chatfield . . .	1
A. P. Gurusinha lbw b Hadlee	22	A. K. Kuruppuarachchi not out	0
R. L. Dias c Bracewell b Hadlee	25		
A. Runatunga c Smith b Bracewell	15	L-b 4, w 1, n-b 11	16
*L. R. D. Mendis c Bracewell b Hadlee	12		
R. S. Madugalle c Hadlee b Gray	60	1/29 2/70 3/129 (9 wkts dec.) 397
J. R. Ratnayeke c M. D. Crowe		4/166 5/210 6/319	
b Bracewell .	12	7/342 8/382 9/383	

Bowling: Hadlee 38.5-10-102-4; Chatfield 38-11-104-2; M. D. Crowe 7-4-13-0; Snedden 16-4-41-0; Bracewell 47-14-98-2; Gray 27-12-35-1.

New Zealand

K. R. Rutherford c Madugalle		E. J. Gray c Ranatunga
b Ratnayake . 11		b Kuruppuarachchi . 31
P. A. Horne c Kuruppu b Anurasiri ... 16		R. J. Hadlee not out 151
A. H. Jones lbw b Ratnayeke 38		L-b 2, w 4, n-b 6 12
M. D. Crowe c Mendis b Ratnayeke .. 27		
*J. J. Crowe not out 120		1/20 2/51 3/90 4/99 5/160 (5 wkts) 406

J. G. Bracewell, †I. D. S. Smith, M. C. Snedden and E. J. Chatfield did not bat.

Bowling: Ratnayake 32–7–79–1; Kuruppuarachchi 20–3–64–1; Ranatunga 23–10–43–0; Ratnayeke 37–6–111–2; Anurasiri 36–13–67–1; Gurusinha 9–1–17–0; Madugalle 2–0–6–0; Dias 4–0–17–0.

Umpires: P. W. Vidanagamage and W. A. U. Wickremasinghe.

AUSTRALIA v NEW ZEALAND, 1987-88

Australia's last-wicket pair, C. J. McDermott and M. R. Whitney, held out for four overs in the Third Test to deny New Zealand the victory that would have squared the series. Following their success in the Reliance World Cup, Australia took the series 1-0, having won the First Test at Brisbane with a day to spare. The Second Test, a high-scoring match, was drawn. In the Third Test R. J. Hadlee took five wickets in a Test innings for the 31st and 32nd times and equalled I. T. Botham's record of 373 Test wickets. The New Zealander reached the landmark in 21 fewer Tests.

First Test: At Brisbane, December 4, 5, 6, 7. Australia won by nine wickets. New Zealand 186 (J. G. Wright 38, M. D. Crowe 67; C. J. McDermott four for 43, M. G. Hughes three for 40) and 212 (A. H. Jones 45, D. N. Patel 62; B. A. Reid four for 53, C. J. McDermott three for 79); Australia 305 (D. C. Boon 143, P. R. Sleep 39; R. J. Hadlee three for 95, D. K. Morrison four for 86) and 97 for one (G. R. Marsh 31 not out, D. M. Jones 38 not out).

Second Test: At Adelaide, December 11, 12, 13, 14, 15. Drawn. New Zealand 485 for nine dec. (J. G. Wright 45, A. H. Jones 150, M. D. Crowe 137, D. N. Patel 35, R. J. Hadlee 36, J. G. Bracewell 32; C. J. McDermott four for 135) and 182 for seven (A. H. Jones 64, D. N. Patel 40; P. R. Sleep three for 61, T. B. A. May three for 68); Australia 496 (G. R. Marsh 30, A. R. Border 205, S. R. Waugh 61, P. R. Sleep 62, G. C. Dyer 60; R. J. Hadlee five for 68).

Third Test: At Melbourne, December 26, 27, 28, 29, 30. Drawn. New Zealand 317 (J. G. Wright 99, A. H. Jones 40, M. D. Crowe 82, I. D. S. Smith 44; C. J. McDermott five for 97, M. R. Whitney four for 92) and 286 (J. G. Wright 43, M. D. Crowe 79, D. N. Patel 38; A. I. C. Dodemaide six for 58, P. R. Sleep three for 107); Australia 357 (A. R. Border 31, M. R. J. Veletta 31, S. R. Waugh 55, P. R. Sleep 90, A. I. C. Dodemaide 50, C. J. McDermott 33; R. J. Hadlee five for 109) and 230 for nine (D. C. Boon 54, A. R. Border 43, M. R. J. Veletta 39; R. J. Hadlee five for 67).

CHAMPIONS TROPHY, 1986-87

Immediately following their series in Pakistan, West Indies and Pakistan flew to Sharjah, where they joined India and Sri Lanka – themselves soon to embark on a Test series in India – in a six-match round-robin tournament for the Champions Trophy and £60,000 in prizemoney. West Indies won their three matches to add the trophy, and £22,000, to their successes in limited-overs internationals.

†INDIA v SRI LANKA

At Sharjah, November 27. India won by seven wickets. Toss: India. Srikkanth sparked India's reply, hitting two sixes and ten fours in his 92.
Man of the Match: K. Srikkanth.

Sri Lanka

R. S. Mahanama b Chetan	26	R. J. Ratnayake not out	8
P. A. de Silva c Azharuddin b Chetan	33	G. F. Labrooy run out	3
A. Ranatunga b Madan Lal	39	S. D. Anurasiri not out	0
*L. R. D. Mendis b Binny	35	L-b 19, n-b 1	20
A. P. Gurusinha b Binny	4		
H. P. Tillekeratne b Chetan	18	1/61 2/84 3/125 (9 wkts, 45 overs) 214
†R. G. de Alwis b Kapil Dev	17	4/138 5/159 6/185
A. L. F. de Mel c Maninder b Kapil Dev	11	7/199 8/204 9/213

Bowling: Kapil Dev 9-2-28-2; Binny 9-0-42-2; Chetan 8-0-40-3; Maninder 2-0-8-0; Madan Lal 9-0-37-1; Shastri 8-0-40-0.

India

K. Srikkanth b Gurusinha	92	*Kapil Dev not out	34
S. M. Gavaskar c de Alwis b Labrooy	27	B 1, l-b 3, w 8	12
R. Lamba b Labrooy	0		
M. Azharuddin not out	50	1/42 2/42 3/153 (3 wkts, 41.3 overs) 215

R. J. Shastri, R. M. H. Binny, Chetan Sharma, †C. S. Pandit, Madan Lal and Maninder Singh did not bat.

Bowling: de Mel 9-0-32-0; Ratnayake 7-1-44-0; Labrooy 8-1-32-2; Anurasiri 5-0-30-0; Ranatunga 4-0-28-0; Gurusinha 8.3-1-45-1.

Umpires: H. D. Bird and D. R. Shepherd.

†PAKISTAN v WEST INDIES

At Sharjah, November 28. West Indies won by nine wickets. Toss: Pakistan. A brilliant display of fielding by Logie supported West Indies' bowlers as Pakistan were dismissed for 143. In addition to his three catches, Logie effected both run-outs, the first accounting for Miandad just as he and Ramiz were threatening to establish Pakistan's innings. An error by England's two senior umpires allowed Walsh to commence a tenth over, in which he ended the Pakistan innings: the limit for each bowler was nine overs.
Man of the Match: A. L. Logie.

Pakistan

Mudassar Nazar c Logie b Benjamin ..	14
†Salim Yousuf c Logie b Gray	1
Ramiz Raja c and b Walsh	44
Javed Miandad run out	32
Manzoor Elahi b Gray	14
Ijaz Ahmed c Logie b Harper	4
*Imran Khan b Walsh	15
Asif Mujtaba run out	0

Wasim Akram c Benjamin b Walsh ...	2
Tauseef Ahmed not out	4
Saleem Jaffer b Walsh	0
L-b 7, w 6	13

1/5 2/31 3/87   (43.4 overs) 143
4/106 5/119 6/121
7/123 8/130 9/141

Bowling: Marshall 8-1-16-0; Gray 8-2-18-2; Benjamin 9-1-37-1; Walsh 9.4-1-31-4; Harper 9-1-34-1.

West Indies

D. L. Haynes not out	59
C. G. Greenidge c Yousuf b Manzoor .	74
R. B. Richardson not out	5
L-b 3, w 4	7

1/126   (1 wkt, 33.2 overs) 145

*I. V. A. Richards, A. L. Logie, †P. J. L. Dujon, R. A. Harper, M. D. Marshall, C. A. Walsh, A. H. Gray and W. K. M. Benjamin did not bat.

Bowling: Imran 6-0-33-0; Wasim 9-0-26-0; Jaffer 5-1-18-0; Tauseef 6-0-35-0; Mudassar 4-0-10-0; Manzoor 3.2-0-20-1.

Umpires: H. D. Bird and D. R. Shepherd.

†INDIA v WEST INDIES

At Sharjah, November 30. West Indies won by 33 runs. Toss: India.
Man of the Match: I. V. A. Richards.

West Indies

C. G. Greenidge lbw b Kapil Dev	0
D. L. Haynes c Srikkanth b Madan Lal	12
R. B. Richardson run out	18
*I. V. A. Richards c Binny b Maninder	62
A. L. Logie not out	58
†P. J. L. Dujon c Pandit b Azharuddin	9
R. A. Harper lbw b Azharuddin	1
M. D. Marshall run out	10

W. K. M. Benjamin run out	5
A. H. Gray not out	10
B 1, l-b 9, w 2, n-b 1	13

1/0 2/33 3/43   (8 wkts, 45 overs) 198
4/124 5/141 6/143
7/166 8/174

C. A. Walsh did not bat.

Bowling: Kapil Dev 9-2-33-1; Binny 9-0-41-0; Madan Lal 6-2-11-1; Shastri 4-0-32-0; Maninder 8-0-30-1; Azharuddin 9-1-41-2.

India

K. Srikkanth b Marshall	12
S. M. Gavaskar b Gray	63
R. Lamba c Dujon b Gray	0
D. B. Vengsarkar c Dujon b Benjamin .	2
M. Azharuddin b Gray	38
*Kapil Dev not out	23
R. J. Shastri b Benjamin	0
†C. S. Pandit c Greenidge b Walsh ...	3

Madan Lal b Marshall	8
R. M. H. Binny not out	1
B 4, l-b 9, w 2	15

1/17 2/22 3/31   (8 wkts, 45 overs) 165
4/123 5/130 6/131
7/136 8/161

Maninder Singh did not bat.

Bowling: Marshall 9-2-25-2; Gray 9-0-32-3; Benjamin 9-0-33-2; Harper 9-0-31-0; Walsh 9-0-31-1.

Umpires: H. D. Bird and D. R. Shepherd.

†PAKISTAN v SRI LANKA

At Sharjah, December 2. Pakistan won by four wickets. Toss: Pakistan.
Man of the Match: A. P. Gurusinha.

Sri Lanka

R. S. Mahanama lbw b Wasim	0	A. L. F. de Mel not out	21
P. A. de Silva c Miandad b Manzoor	3	J. R. Ratnayeke not out	17
A. P. Gurusinha run out	60	B 2, l-b 8, w 8	18
A. Ranatunga c Yousuf b Jaffer	14		
*L. R. D. Mendis b Mudassar	12	1/2 2/15 3/50 (7 wkts, 45 overs) 164	
H. P. Tillekeratne run out	19	4/71 5/119	
†R. G. de Alwis lbw b Imran	0	6/125 7/128	

R. J. Ratnayake and G. F. Labrooy did not bat.

Bowling: Imran 9-0-34-1; Wasim 9-0-25-1; Manzoor 7-0-21-1; Jaffer 9-0-40-1; Mudassar 6-0-16-1; Shoaib 5-1-18-0.

Pakistan

Mohsin Khan b Labrooy	7	Mudassar Nazar not out	6
Shoaib Mohammad c and b Gurusinha	19	Ijaz Ahmed not out	13
Ramiz Raja c Labrooy b de Mel	39	B 2, l-b 12, w 4, n-b 2	20
Javed Miandad c de Alwis b Ranatunga	32		
*Imran Khan c Mendis b Ratnayake	22	1/21 2/49 3/95 (6 wkts, 44 overs) 165	
Manzoor Elahi run out	7	4/124 5/137 6/142	

Wasim Akram, †Salim Yousuf and Saleem Jaffer did not bat.

Bowling: de Mel 9-1-29-1; Ratnayeke 9-0-27-1; Labrooy 8-1-29-1; Gurusinha 9-0-27-1; Ratnayeke 6-0-25-0; Ranatunga 3-0-14-1.

Umpires: H. D. Bird and D. R. Shepherd.

†SRI LANKA v WEST INDIES

At Sharjah, December 3. West Indies won by 193 runs. Richardson, dropped when 0, 6 and 35, hit his first one-day international hundred from 119 balls, with one six and eight fours. Toss: Sri Lanka.
Man of the Match: C. A. Walsh.

West Indies

C. G. Greenidge b de Mel	67	W. K. M. Benjamin b Ratnayeke	0
R. B. Richardson c Tillekeratne b Ratnayeke	109	M. D. Marshall not out	3
		B 1, l-b 5	6
*I. V. A. Richards b Ratnayeke	39		
R. A. Harper b Ratnayeke	15	1/132 2/220 3/221 (5 wkts, 45 overs) 248	
A. L. Logie not out	9	4/242 5/245	

H. A. Gomes, †P. J. L. Dujon, C. A. Walsh and A. H. Gray did not bat.

Bowling: de Mel 9-1-48-1; Ratnayeke 9-2-30-1; Labrooy 7-0-36-0; Ratnayeke 9-0-59-3; Gurusinha 9-0-51-0; Ranatunga 2-0-18-0.

Sri Lanka

R. S. Mahanama c Dujon b Marshall	13	J. R. Ratnayeke b Walsh	0
†D. S. B. P. Kuruppu run out	9	R. J. Ratnayake b Walsh	0
A. P. Gurusinha b Harper	15	G. F. Labrooy b Walsh	1
A. Ranatunga c Walsh b Harper	8	L-b 2	2
P. A. de Silva run out	3		
*L. R. D. Mendis c Dujon b Walsh	2	1/22 2/22 3/45 (28.3 overs) 55	
H. P. Tillekeratne not out	2	4/45 5/50 6/51	
A. L. F. de Mel b Walsh	0	7/51 8/51 9/51	

Bowling: Marshall 5–1–16–1; Gray 5–0–15–0; Benjamin 5–0–13–0; Harper 9–4–8–2; Walsh 4.3–3–1–5.

Umpires: H. D. Bird and D. R. Shepherd.

†INDIA v PAKISTAN

At Sharjah, December 5. Pakistan won by three wickets. Toss: Pakistan.
Man of the Match: Manzoor Elahi.

India

K. Srikkanth c Yousuf b Imran	3	Madan Lal run out		5
S. M. Gavaskar b Imran	0	R. M. H. Binny b Wasim		0
R. Lamba c Shoaib b Imran	6	Maninder Singh not out		1
D. B. Vengsarkar b Jaffer	6	B 1, l-b 8, w 9, n-b 1		19
M. Azharuddin c Miandad b Manzoor	49			
R. J. Shastri b Mudassar	1	1/2 2/8 3/16	(40.2 overs)	144
*Kapil Dev b Shoaib	36	4/39 5/42 6/110		
†C. S. Pandit b Wasim	18	7/128 8/136 9/136		

Bowling: Imran 8–0–27–3; Wasim 7.2–4–4–2; Jaffer 7–0–22–1; Mudassar 9–2–34–1; Manzoor 5–0–32–1; Shoaib 4–0–16–1.

Pakistan

Ramiz Raja c and b Shastri	21	Manzoor Elahi not out		50
Shoaib Mohammad c Gavaskar b Maninder	28	†Salim Yousuf not out		15
Asif Mujtaba c Gavaskar b Shastri	11	L-b 4, w 2, n-b 3		9
Javed Miandad c and b Maninder	0			
*Imran Khan c Vengsarkar b Maninder	0	1/51 2/53 3/53	(7 wkts, 43.3 overs)	145
Mudassar Nazar c Srikkanth b Maninder	1	4/53 5/65		
Ijaz Ahmed c Maninder b Madan Lal	10	6/65 7/108		

Wasim Akram and Saleem Jaffer did not bat.

Bowling: Kapil Dev 8–2–31–0; Binny 8.3–0–32–0; Maninder 9–2–22–4; Madan Lal 9–0–25–1; Shastri 9–1–31–2.

Umpires: H. D. Bird and D. R. Shepherd.

FINAL TABLE

	P	W	L	Pts
West Indies	3	3	0	6
Pakistan	3	2	1	4
India	3	1	2	2
Sri Lanka	3	0	3	0

BENSON AND HEDGES CHALLENGE, 1986-87

Cricket's contribution to the pot-pourri of events coinciding with the America's Cup yachting off Fremantle, the Benson and Hedges Challenge took the form of a limited-overs round-robin for four teams, with the two leading countries meeting in a final. All the matches were played at the Western Australian Cricket Association ground in Perth, where floodlights were used for the first time.

With New Zealand turning down an invitation to participate, though by no means without a presence around Perth, Pakistan joined Australia, England and West Indies (that season's World Series Cup contenders). They launched the tournament spectacularly by beating West Indies under the new lights and went on to reach the final. When West Indies lost to England four days later, it was the first time they had been beaten in consecutive one-day internationals since Australia and Pakistan beat them in the World Series Cup in 1981-82. Australia fared even worse, losing all their matches. But for England, fresh from retaining the Ashes in the Fourth Test at Melbourne, the tournament was a triumph, the second stage of a remarkable treble for Mike Gatting's team.

Yet again the popularity of the one-day game in Australia was evidenced by the attendances. More than 27,000, a record for the WACA and almost twice as many as attended any one day of the Second Test match a month earlier, saw England beat Australia; and some 22,000 watched Australia and West Indies decide the lesser placings. The fireworks which illuminated the sky after the final might have been lighting the future path of Australian cricket; the rockets, spent, falling to the ground, might as easily have symbolised the traditional game there.

†PAKISTAN v WEST INDIES

At Perth, December 30 (day/night). Pakistan won by 34 runs. Although West Indies were handicapped by the absence of Marshall and Garner with minor injuries, Pakistan, having been put in, were held to what seemed an insufficient total on a good pitch. Ramiz Raja and Javed Miandad put on in twenty overs for the third wicket, but when Miandad skied his 69th ball to mid-on, Pakistan lost six for 36 in the final seven overs. West Indies were well on course until Richardson failed to respond to Richards's call for a sharp single in the 29th over. When Mudassar won an lbw decision against Richards in the 30th, and Logie and Dujon followed by the 38th, they were struggling. With intelligent support Harper might still have rescued them, but Benjamin, Holding and Gray threw away their wickets.

Man of the Match: Mudassar Nazar. *Attendance:* 11,900.

Pakistan

Qasim Omar run out	30		Wasim Akram c Harper b Walsh	9	
Shoaib Mohammad c Richards b Benjamin	34		†Salim Yousuf not out	2	
Ramiz Raja c Richardson b Gray	42				
Javed Miandad c Richards b Walsh	53		L-b 3, w 3, n-b 1	7	
*Imran Khan c Benjamin b Gray	16				
Manzoor Elahi c Richardson b Gray	4		1/51 2/72 3/163 (8 wkts, 50 overs)	199	
Ijaz Ahmed c sub (H. A. Gomes) b Gray	2		4/166 5/177 6/188		
			7/188 8/199		

Mudassar Nazar and Saleem Jaffer did not bat.

Bowling: Gray 10-1-45-4; Walsh 10-0-48-2; Holding 10-0-30-0; Benjamin 10-2-35-1; Harper 10-0-38-0.

West Indies

C. G. Greenidge b Wasim	22	M. A. Holding b Shoaib		5
D. L. Haynes c Yousuf b Mudassar	25	A. H. Gray c Imran b Jaffer		3
R. B. Richardson run out	38	C. A. Walsh b Wasim		2
*I. V. A. Richards lbw b Mudassar	10	L-b 16, n-b 1		17
A. L. Logie c Yousuf b Mudassar	7			
†P. J. L. Dujon c Shoaib b Jaffer	13	1/40 2/71 3/105	(46.2 overs)	165
R. A. Harper not out	20	4/106 5/123 6/128		
W. K. M. Benjamin c Jaffer b Shoaib	3	7/139 8/150 9/155		

Bowling: Imran 7-2-18-0; Jaffer 10-2-29-2; Wasim 7.2-2-13-2; Manzoor 2-0-10-0; Mudassar 10-0-36-3; Shoaib 10-0-43-2.

Umpires: P. J. McConnell and S. G. Randell.

†AUSTRALIA v ENGLAND

At Perth, January 1 (day/night). England won by 37 runs. Broad, with a polished 76 in 37 overs, and Lamb and Botham, who added 106 in eleven, set up England's victory in front of a record crowd for the WACA on another beautiful evening. Botham hit Davis for 26 in an over (442466), the first of the sixes landing twenty rows back over long-on. He faced 39 balls and hit seven fours and three sixes, straight-driving with savage force. Australia were in the game until Border was yorked by Emburey after putting on 75 with Jones in thirteen overs. Jones, missed at slip at 16, used quick footwork to improvise some magnificent strokes on both sides of the wicket and as usual ran superbly. His 104 came off 129 balls (two sixes, nine fours), but he lacked support and England, who had won the toss, had the match in hand before he skied Dilley to mid-off in the 44th over.

Man of the Match: I. T. Botham.   *Attendance:* 27,125.

England

B. C. Broad run out	76	†C. J. Richards c Border b Reid		4
C. W. J. Athey c Zoehrer b O'Donnell	34	P. A. J. DeFreitas not out		0
D. I. Gower c Zoehrer b Whitney	6	B 2, l-b 6, w 4, n-b 1		13
A. J. Lamb c Zoehrer b Reid	66			
I. T. Botham c Zoehrer b Waugh	68	1/86 2/95 3/150	(6 wkts, 49 overs)	272
*M. W. Gatting not out	5	4/256 5/262 6/271		

J. E. Emburey, G. R. Dilley and G. C. Small did not bat.

Bowling: Davis 8-1-48-0; Whitney 10-0-56-1; MacLeay 9-0-51-0; Reid 10-1-46-2; O'Donnell 7-0-39-1; Waugh 5-0-24-1.

Australia

G. R. Marsh b Botham	28	M. R. Whitney run out		6
D. C. Boon c Emburey b DeFreitas	1	B. A. Reid b DeFreitas		10
D. M. Jones c Gower b Dilley	104	S. P. Davis not out		1
*A. R. Border b Emburey	26	L-b 7, w 10, n-b 4		21
S. R. Waugh c Richards b Small	16			
S. P. O'Donnell run out	0	1/7 2/50 3/125	(48.2 overs)	235
K. H. MacLeay c Emburey b Dilley	21	4/149 5/158 6/210		
†T. J. Zoehrer c Botham b DeFreitas	1	7/214 8/217 9/233		

Bowling: DeFreitas 9.2-0-42-3; Dilley 10-1-31-2; Botham 10-0-52-1; Small 9-0-62-1; Emburey 10-0-41-1.

Umpires: R. A. French and P. J. McConnell.

†AUSTRALIA v PAKISTAN

At Perth, January 2 (day/night). Pakistan won by one wicket. Toss: Australia. After being outplayed almost throughout the match, Pakistan snatched a seemingly impossible victory when Saleem Jaffer scooped Waugh for 2 over a close-set field off the last but one ball. Jones, making 121 (113 balls, two sixes, nine fours), his second hundred on successive days, and Waugh (82 off 102) added 173 for Australia's fourth wicket, a record in one-day internationals, and Australia looked unbeatable when Pakistan were 129 for six in the 30th over. But successive stands of 52, 43 and 43, in which Asif Mujtaba – a slightly built twenty-year-old left-arm spinner – was the common denominator, brought Pakistan to the final over needing only 7 to win, 39 runs having been plundered off the previous four. Wasim Akram was caught at deepish mid-off off the first ball, but Asif and Saleem Jaffer completed a humiliating half-hour for Australia, and a memorable one for Pakistan, by taking 1, 1, 3, 2 off the next four. Asif faced 56 balls, Manzoor Elahi 44 and Salim Yousuf 27.

Man of the Match: D. M. Jones.   *Attendance*: 17,144.

Australia

G. R. Marsh run out	28	S. P. O'Donnell not out	9
G. A. Bishop c Jaffer b Imran	6	K. H. MacLeay not out	1
D. M. Jones b Wasim	121	B 2, l-b 1, w 5, n-b 1	9
*A. R. Border b Mudassar	14		
S. R. Waugh b Imran	82	1/26 2/49 3/70 (6 wkts, 50 overs) 273	
G. R. J. Matthews b Wasim	3	4/243 5/254 6/271	

†T. J. Zoehrer, M. R. Whitney and B. A. Reid did not bat.

Bowling: Imran 10-0-43-2; Wasim 10-1-58-2; Jaffer 10-2-43-0; Mudassar 10-0-56-1; Asif 5-0-32-0; Shoaib 3-0-22-0; Manzoor 2-0-16-0.

Pakistan

Qasim Omar c Border b Waugh	67	†Salim Yousuf c O'Donnell b Whitney	31
Shoaib Mohammad lbw b MacLeay	9	Wasim Akram c Whitney b Waugh	5
Ramiz Raja c Bishop b MacLeay	0	Saleem Jaffer not out	3
Javed Miandad b Reid	7	L-b 15, w 1, n-b 1	17
Mudassar Nazar lbw b Waugh	7		
*Imran Khan c Zoehrer b Waugh	20	1/34 2/40 3/73 (9 wkts, 49.5 overs) 274	
Manzoor Elahi c and b Whitney	48	4/93 5/96 6/129	
Asif Mujtaba not out	60	7/181 8/224 9/267	

Bowling: MacLeay 10-0-36-2; Whitney 10-0-58-2; Reid 10-0-61-1; Waugh 9.5-0-48-4; O'Donnell 10-0-56-0.

Umpires: A. R. Crafter and S. G. Randell.

†ENGLAND v WEST INDIES

At Perth, January 3. England won by 19 runs. Cooler cricket at critical moments enabled England to make sure of reaching the final in the game that eliminated both West Indies and Australia. West Indies, putting England in, reduced them to 96 for five at the halfway point. But Lamb (108 balls) and Richards (63 balls) added 60 in eleven overs, and the recovery was continued through a solid effort by the bowlers. West Indies also began shakily, slipping to 104 for four when Richards mis-swept Emburey to deep square leg in the 28th over. Logie and Dujon added 74, but in the 42nd over, with only 51 runs wanted, Dujon took a needless risk in backing away to drive Dilley through the covers. Dilley took four for 7 in nineteen balls as West Indies collapsed, and an athletic diving stop by Athey at mid-on led to the running out of Harper.

Man of the Match: G. R. Dilley.   *Attendance*: 12,000.

England

B. C. Broad c Garner b Marshall	0
C. W. J. Athey c Richardson b Garner .	1
D. I. Gower c Dujon b Garner	11
A. J. Lamb c Harper b Marshall	71
*M. W. Gatting c Garner b Walsh	15
I. T. Botham c Greenidge b Harper ..	11
†C. J. Richards c Dujon b Garner	50
J. E. Emburey c Harper b Garner	18

P. H. Edmonds not out	16
G. R. Dilley c and b Garner	1
G. C. Small not out	8
L-b 10, w 8, n-b 8	26
1/3 2/10 3/35   (9 wkts, 50 overs) 228
4/67 5/96 6/156
7/194 8/209 9/211

Bowling: Marshall 10-1-30-2; Garner 10-0-47-5; Holding 10-0-33-0; Walsh 9-0-40-1; Harper 10-0-63-1; Richards 1-0-5-0.

West Indies

C. G. Greenidge b Small	20
D. L. Haynes lbw b Small	4
R. B. Richardson c Gatting b Botham .	12
*I. V. A. Richards c Broad b Emburey	45
A. L. Logie c Richards b Dilley	51
†P. J. L. Dujon b Dilley	36
R. A. Harper run out	4
M. D. Marshall b Dilley	7

M. A. Holding c Edmonds b Dilley ...	7
J. Garner not out	4
C. A. Walsh lbw b Emburey	0
B 4, l-b 9, w 4, n-b 2	19
1/9 2/39 3/51   (48.2 overs) 209
4/104 5/178 6/187
7/187 8/201 9/208

Bowling: Dilley 10-0-46-4; Small 10-1-37-2; Botham 10-1-29-1; Edmonds 9-1-53-0; Emburey 9.2-0-31-2.

Umpires: R. A. French and P. J. McConnell.

†AUSTRALIA v WEST INDIES

At Perth, January 4. West Indies won by 164 runs. Greenidge's first one-day international hundred against Australia, made without a chance off 120 balls, and an uncharacteristic miss by Waugh at long-off early in Holding's punishing 53 not out, set up West Indies' victory in a game in which only pride was at stake. West Indies had never lost three successive internationals and, having scored 255 for eight after being put in, they avoided that stigma without difficulty. A demoralised Australia were no match for Garner, Gray, Walsh and Holding on a bouncy pitch and were bowled out in 144 minutes. It was the first game in the tournament played in poor spirit, and Marsh was hit in the throat by one of several bouncers which West Indies appeared to bowl gratuitously and without regard to the possibility of being no-balled.

Man of the Match: C. G. Greenidge.   *Attendance*: 22,335.

West Indies

C. G. Greenidge b Waugh	100
D. L. Haynes c Zoehrer b MacLeay ...	18
H. A. Gomes b O'Donnell	18
*I. V. A. Richards lbw b O'Donnell ...	13
A. L. Logie b Reid	13
†P. J. L. Dujon c Zoehrer b O'Donnell .	9
R. A. Harper c Zoehrer b O'Donnell ..	2
M. A. Holding not out	53

J. Garner lbw b McDermott	1
A. H. Gray not out	10
L-b 13, w 3, n-b 2	18
1/46 2/95 3/127   (8 wkts, 50 overs) 255
4/176 5/176 6/180
7/203 8/210

C. A. Walsh did not bat.

Bowling: Reid 10-2-40-1; MacLeay 10-1-29-1; McDermott 10-0-67-1; Waugh 10-0-41-1; O'Donnell 10-0-65-4.

Australia

D. C. Boon b Garner	2		†T. J. Zoehrer lbw b Gray	4
G. R. Marsh c Richards b Gray	5		C. J. McDermott c Gomes b Gray	7
D. M. Jones c Harper b Garner	2		B. A. Reid not out	1
*A. R. Border c Greenidge b Holding	9		L-b 5, w 2, n-b 5	12
G. A. Bishop c Dujon b Holding	7			
S. R. Waugh b Harper	29		1/4 2/12 3/16 (35.4 overs) 91	
S. P. O'Donnell lbw b Harper	8		4/25 5/36 6/66	
K. H. MacLeay c Logie b Holding	5		7/78 8/78 9/89	

Bowling: Garner 6–2–10–2; Gray 7.4–0–9–3; Walsh 6–1–11–0; Holding 10–1–32–3; Harper 6–1–24–2.

Umpires: A. R. Crafter and S. G. Randell.

†ENGLAND v PAKISTAN

At Perth, January 5 (day/night). England won by three wickets. Toss: Pakistan. Broad's stylish innings – he faced 133 balls for his 97 – seemed to have put England on course for an uneventful victory in the dress rehearsal for the final until five wickets fell in ten overs. The last of them, Broad's, when he was adjudged caught at the wicket dabbing at Imran Khan in the 47th over, brought to light what had been a quiet game. Amid mounting excitement DeFreitas and Emburey added 15 off the next two overs and 5 more off the first three balls of the 50th; whereupon DeFreitas coolly won the match with a cover drive for four. In Pakistan's innings a blind spot in the umpires' knowledge of the Laws cost Ramiz Raja his wicket. Not hearing umpire Crafter's no-ball call, Ramiz began walking out when he clipped Gatting to Athey at wide mid-on, whence after hesitation Athey lobbed the ball to Richards. On appeal Ramiz was given out by umpire French at square leg in contravention of Law 38(2): "If a no-ball has been called, the striker shall not be given run out unless he attempts to run." Rarely as such an eventuality arises, two Test umpires should have known the Law.

Man of the Match: B. C. Broad.   *Attendance:* 9,304.

Pakistan

Qasim Omar b Botham	32		Manzoor Elahi not out	9
Shoaib Mohammad c DeFreitas			Wasim Akram not out	1
b Emburey	66		L-b 15, w 1, n-b 8	24
Ramiz Raja run out	15			
Javed Miandad c Athey b Emburey	59		1/61 2/98 3/156 (5 wkts, 50 overs) 229	
*Imran Khan c Gower b DeFreitas	23		4/198 5/225	

Mudassar Nazar, Asif Mujtaba, †Salim Yousuf and Saleem Jaffer did not bat.

Bowling: DeFreitas 9–1–24–1; Small 10–0–41–0; Foster 4–0–23–0; Botham 10–1–37–1; Gatting 7–0–24–0; Emburey 10–0–65–2.

England

B. C. Broad c Yousuf b Imran	97		P. A. J. DeFreitas not out	13
C. W. J. Athey b Manzoor	42		J. E. Emburey not out	11
D. I. Gower c Shoaib b Mudassar	2		B 1, l-b 13, w 3, n-b 1	18
A. J. Lamb c Miandad b Shoaib	32			
I. T. Botham c Ramiz b Wasim	10		1/104 2/108 3/156 (7 wkts, 49.4 overs) 232	
*M. W. Gatting run out	7		4/184 5/199	
†C. J. Richards run out	0		6/204 7/208	

N. A. Foster and G. C. Small did not bat.

Bowling: Wasim 9.4–1–28–1; Jaffer 10–2–43–0; Imran 9–0–41–1; Mudassar 10–0–39–1; Asif 3–0–19–0; Manzoor 5–0–24–1; Shoaib 5–0–24–1.

Umpires: A. R. Crafter and R. A. French.

QUALIFYING TABLE

	P	W	L	Pts
England	3	3	0	6
Pakistan	3	2	1	4
West Indies	3	1	2	2
Australia	3	0	3	0

FINAL

†ENGLAND v PAKISTAN

At Perth, January 7. England won by five wickets. Gatting won an important toss on the pitch on which the West Indian fast bowlers had routed Australia for 91 three days earlier, and except while Javed Miandad and Manzoor Elahi were adding 38 in seven overs for the sixth wicket, Pakistan were never in the game. Dilley bowled with pace and fire, swinging the ball dangerously away from the right-handers. He beat Shoaib Mohammad for speed in his first over, more than once hit batsmen on the gloves, and cracked Qasim Omar on the collar-bone as he was playing forward to a good-length ball. It was a disappointing pitch for a one-day match and turned the final into an anticlimax. None the less, Dilley deserved full credit for exploiting it and was a worthy candidate for the player of the match award, which R. W. Marsh, the former Australian wicket-keeper, gave to Miandad.

Pakistan, forced on to the defensive by Dilley and DeFreitas, were prevented from recovering lost ground by the accuracy of the supporting bowlers, losing wickets every time they tried to accelerate. The game would have been over even sooner had Gatting, at deep cover, been quicker to sight a ballooning drive by Miandad at 36 off Small. With Manzoor going for his strokes, Pakistan had half a chance at that stage. But then four wickets fell for 4 in fifteen balls, including two in two to Small, to make them 131 for nine. Miandad managed the strike adroitly to take all but five balls during his last-wicket stand with Saleem Jaffer, but 35 runs off the last nine overs were nothing like enough to make things difficult for England. In the event, they batted uncertainly, Athey, certainly, falling in the third over and umpire French adjudging Broad caught down the leg side off a ball that brushed his hip. Tactically it had to be right for Pakistan to attack, for if England batted 50 overs they were always going to win. But despite the encouragement of these two quick wickets, Imran stuck rigidly to conventional one-day patterns. Gower made a frisky 31, Lamb and Gatting added 89 in twenty overs, and Botham on-drove the winning hit with 9.5 overs in hand.

Man of the Match: Javed Miandad.   *Attendance:* 16,600.

Pakistan

Qasim Omar c Broad b Botham	21	
Shoaib Mohammad b Dilley	0	
Ramiz Raja c Athey b Botham	22	
Javed Miandad not out	77	
Asif Mujtaba c Gower b Botham	7	
*Imran Khan c Richards b Gatting ...	5	
Manzoor Elahi c Gower b Small	20	
†Salim Yousuf c Athey b Small	0	

Mudassar Nazar c Gower b Emburey ..	0
Wasim Akram c Gatting b Small	2
Saleem Jaffer not out	3
L-b 5, w 1, n-b 3	9

1/2 2/36 3/58   (9 wkts, 50 overs) 166
4/76 5/89 6/127
7/127 8/128 9/131

Bowling: DeFreitas 10-1-33-0; Dilley 10-0-23-1; Botham 10-2-29-3; Small 10-0-28-3; Emburey 8-0-34-1; Gatting 2-0-14-1.

England

B. C. Broad c Yousuf b Wasim	0
C. W. J. Athey c Yousuf b Imran	1
D. I. Gower c Shoaib b Imran	31
A. J. Lamb c Yousuf b Wasim	47
*M. W. Gatting b Wasim	49
I. T. Botham not out	23

†C. J. Richards not out	7
L-b 8, w 1	9

1/1 2/7 3/47   (5 wkts, 40.1 overs) 167
4/136 5/145

P. A. J. DeFreitas, J. E. Emburey, G. C. Small and G. R. Dilley did not bat.

Bowling: Imran 8-2-30-2; Wasim 10-2-27-3; Jaffer 10-1-43-0; Mudassar 5.1-0-22-0; Shoaib 2-0-11-0; Manzoor 5-0-26-0.

Umpires: A. R. Crafter and R. A. French.

BENSON AND HEDGES WORLD SERIES CUP, 1986-87

†ENGLAND v WEST INDIES

At Brisbane, January 17. England won by six wickets. Although Haynes and Logie added 86 in 22 overs, West Indies never recovered from losing Greenidge, Richardson and Richards in the first eleven. Moisture underneath the surface made the toss of more importance than it should have been, and Dilley, DeFreitas and Small took full advantage of Gatting's success, swinging and seaming the ball with immaculate control. Haynes and Logie were both caught on the boundary, Haynes brilliantly by DeFreitas ankle-high. With batting conditions steadily improving in 100-degree heat, there was no help for West Indies' fast bowlers and Richards, conceding defeat, withdrew them after England had reached 82 for one in 22 overs.

Man of the Match: G. R. Dilley.   *Attendance:* 13,630.

West Indies

C. G. Greenidge lbw b DeFreitas	0	M. A. Holding c Richards b Emburey	0
D. L. Haynes c DeFreitas b Emburey	48	J. Garner c Richards b Dilley	1
R. B. Richardson c Botham b Dilley	15	C. A. Walsh not out	3
*I. V. A. Richards b Dilley	0	L-b 4	4
A. L. Logie c Lamb b Emburey	46		
†P. J. L. Dujon b DeFreitas	22	1/1 2/26 3/26 (46.3 overs) 154
R. A. Harper lbw b Small	2	4/112 5/120 6/122
M. D. Marshall b Dilley	13	7/147 8/148 9/151

Bowling: Dilley 8.3–1–23–4; DeFreitas 9–2–17–2; Botham 10–1–46–0; Small 10–1–29–1; Emburey 9–0–35–3.

England

B. C. Broad b Richards	49	I. T. Botham not out	14
C. W. J. Athey c Dujon b Holding	14		
D. I. Gower c Garner b Harper	42	L-b 2, w 2, n-b 8	12
A. J. Lamb c sub (W. K. M. Benjamin) b Harper	22	1/30 2/91 3/134 (4 wkts, 43.1 overs) 156
*M. W. Gatting not out	3	4/140

†C. J. Richards, P. A. J. DeFreitas, J. E. Emburey, G. C. Small and G. R. Dilley did not bat.

Bowling: Marshall 5–1–11–0; Garner 4–0–17–0; Holding 6–0–33–1; Walsh 7.1–0–19–0; Harper 10–0–43–2; Richards 10–0–27–1; Richardson 1–0–4–0.

Umpires: M. W. Johnson and P. J. McConnell.

†AUSTRALIA v ENGLAND

At Brisbane, January 18. Australia won by 11 runs. A deceptively easy victory was set up by Jones, who shared a second-wicket stand of 178 in 30 overs with Marsh while making his third successive hundred against England. He faced 101 balls, hitting two sixes and six fours. For 40 overs England were never far behind the asking-rate. But when Gatting missed a swing at Taylor in the 43rd, Athey, drained by two days in the heat, was unable to take over the initiative. Up to that point he was an admirable anchor-man. His 111 lasted until the 48th over, used up more than half the strike (152 balls, ten fours) and put too much pressure on his partners.

Man of the Match: D. M. Jones.   *Attendance:* 21,060.

Australia

G. R. Marsh lbw b Dilley	93	S. P. O'Donnell not out		3
D. M. Wellham c Emburey b Small	26	L-b 9, w 3, n-b 1		13
D. M. Jones b Emburey	101			
*A. R. Border b Dilley	11	1/48 2/226 3/234	(4 wkts, 50 overs)	261
S. R. Waugh not out	14	4/246		

G. R. J. Matthews, K. H. MacLeay, †T. J. Zoehrer, P. L. Taylor and B. A. Reid did not bat.

Bowling: Dilley 10-2-40-2; DeFreitas 10-2-41-0; Small 10-0-57-1; Botham 10-0-54-0; Emburey 10-0-60-1.

England

B. C. Broad c Matthews b O'Donnell	15	J. E. Emburey not out		24
C. W. J. Athey c O'Donnell b Reid	111	G. C. Small run out		2
D. I. Gower b Waugh	15	G. R. Dilley not out		0
A. J. Lamb c Marsh b Matthews	6	B 1, l-b 10, n-b 1		12
I. T. Botham b O'Donnell	22			
*M. W. Gatting b Taylor	30	1/48 2/73 3/92	(9 wkts, 50 overs)	250
†C. J. Richards c O'Donnell b Reid	7	4/149 5/197 6/210		
P. A. J. DeFreitas c Border b Waugh	6	7/218 8/225 9/250		

Bowling: MacLeay 8-0-39-0; Reid 10-1-34-2; O'Donnell 10-0-59-2; Waugh 9-0-56-2; Matthews 10-0-34-1; Taylor 3-0-17-1.

Umpires: M. W. Johnson and P. J. McConnell.

†AUSTRALIA v WEST INDIES

At Melbourne, January 20 (day/night). West Indies won by seven wickets, recording their 100th win in 131 one-day internationals. Australia, sent in, were under pressure from the start, Marsh falling to Garner's second ball and Wellham taking nineteen balls to score his first run. They lost their fourth and fifth wickets at 74 in the 32nd over, but Border and O'Donnell added 91 in the next seventeen overs to set West Indies at least a modest challenge. O'Donnell's 52 from 64 balls included a straight six off Marshall, who then dismissed him to capture his 100th wicket in one-day internationals. Once Greenidge and Haynes had carefully put on 54 from 14.5 overs, West Indies were assured of victory. Haynes (67 from 121 balls) and Logie (44 from 71 balls) settled the issue by adding 79.

Man of the Match: D. L. Haynes. *Attendance:* 63,164.

Australia

G. R. Marsh c Dujon b Garner	1	S. P. O'Donnell c Holding b Marshall		52
D. M. Wellham run out	7	K. H. MacLeay not out		12
D. M. Jones lbw b Marshall	11	B 5, l-b 4, w 1, n-b 9		19
*A. R. Border not out	64			
S. R. Waugh hit wkt b Holding	15	1/2 2/23 3/30	(6 wkts, 50 overs)	181
G. R. J. Matthews run out	0	4/74 5/74 6/165		

†T. J. Zoehrer, P. L. Taylor and B. A. Reid did not bat.

Bowling: Marshall 9-0-40-2; Garner 9-1-47-1; Holding 10-1-15-1; Walsh 10-2-37-0; Harper 10-0-26-0; Richards 2-0-7-0.

West Indies

C. G. Greenidge c Border b Waugh	35	†P. J. L. Dujon not out		2
D. L. Haynes lbw b Matthews	67	B 7, l-b 3, w 1, n-b 3		14
R. B. Richardson b Taylor	20			
A. L. Logie not out	44	1/54 2/92 3/171	(3 wkts, 48.2 overs)	182

*I. V. A. Richards, R. A. Harper, M. D. Marshall, M. A. Holding, J. Garner and C. A. Walsh did not bat.

Bowling: MacLeay 6–0–20–0; Reid 8.2–2–33–0; O'Donnell 7–0–27–0; Waugh 7–0–30–1; Matthews 10–2–27–1; Taylor 10–1–35–1.

Umpires: A. R. Crafter and R. A. French.

†AUSTRALIA v ENGLAND

At Sydney, January 22 (day/night). England won by three wickets. Lamb struck Reid for 2, 4, 6, 2, 4 in the final over to blast England to a tremendous win with a ball to spare. Although the pitch lacked pace, Australia, who chose to bat first, should have scored more than 233 for eight after passing 150 in the 33rd over. Wellham played deftly (154 balls, five fours), but Australia lost momentum, adding only 43 in the last ten overs. England's innings followed a similar pattern, Broad's 45 coming off 58 balls and Gower and Lamb adding 86 off twelve overs. However, a clever spell by Matthews, supported by good fielding, left England needing 32 off three, 25 off two and 18 off the final over. Lamb, who until then had been at loggerheads with his timing and had not hit a boundary, was equal to the task, hauling Reid twice to square leg and once over deep mid-wicket.

Man of the Match: A. J. Lamb.   *Attendance:* 36,463.

Australia

G. R. Marsh c Richards b Edmonds	47	†T. J. Zoehrer not out	9
D. M. Wellham c Athey b Emburey	97	P. L. Taylor st Richards b Emburey	0
D. M. Jones c Athey b DeFreitas	34		
*A. R. Border c Dilley b Edmonds	13	B 2, l-b 5, n-b 2	9
S. R. Waugh c Athey b Dilley	10		
G. R. J. Matthews c DeFreitas		1/109 2/156 3/189 (8 wkts, 50 overs) 233	
b Emburey	2	4/205 5/208 6/208	
K. H. MacLeay b Dilley	12	7/230 8/233	

S. P. O'Donnell and B. A. Reid did not bat.

Bowling: Dilley 9–2–28–2; DeFreitas 10–0–46–1; Gatting 2–0–11–0; Botham 10–0–51–0; Emburey 9–0–42–3; Edmonds 10–0–48–2.

England

B. C. Broad c Matthews b Taylor	45	†C. J. Richards c Waugh b O'Donnell	3
C. W. J. Athey c Zoehrer b Reid	2	P. A. J. DeFreitas not out	6
D. I. Gower c Wellham b O'Donnell	50	L-b 16, w 2, n-b 1	19
A. J. Lamb not out	77		
*M. W. Gatting b O'Donnell	1	1/33 2/51 3/137 (7 wkts, 49.5 overs) 234	
I. T. Botham b Waugh	27	4/143 5/186	
J. E. Emburey run out	4	6/191 7/202	

P. H. Edmonds and G. R. Dilley did not bat.

Bowling: MacLeay 4–0–22–0; Reid 9.5–3–44–1; Taylor 10–0–42–1; Waugh 5–0–22–1; Matthews 10–1–36–0; Border 3–0–13–0; O'Donnell 8–0–39–3.

Umpires: A. R. Crafter and R. A. French.

†ENGLAND v WEST INDIES

At Adelaide, January 24. England won by 89 runs. Although England failed to make the most of an opening stand of 121 between Broad (96 balls) and Athey (110 balls) after West Indies had won the toss, two early wickets by DeFreitas set up a convincing win in good batting conditions. The decisive moment of West Indies' reply came in the 27th over when Broad sprinted twenty yards at wide long-on to snuff out a menacing innings by Richards (64 balls). Logie and Dujon added 44 in nine overs, but Emburey ended hopes of a recovery with four wickets in thirteen balls, three of them to catches in the deep.

Man of the Match: B. C. Broad.   *Attendance:* 11,178.

England

B. C. Broad st Dujon b Richards	55	†C. J. Richards b Marshall		18
C. W. J. Athey c Marshall b Harper	64	J. E. Emburey not out		16
D. I. Gower c Haynes b Gray	29	B 4, l-b 13, w 5, n-b 5		27
I. T. Botham c Logie b Walsh	7			
A. J. Lamb not out	33	1/121 2/148 3/161	(6 wkts, 50 overs)	252
*M. W. Gatting c Dujon b Walsh	3	4/177 5/182 6/220		

P. A. J. DeFreitas, G. R. Dilley and G. C. Small did not bat.

Bowling: Marshall 9-1-39-1; Gray 10-0-43-1; Garner 9-1-31-0; Walsh 10-0-55-2; Harper 9-0-46-1; Richards 3-0-21-1.

West Indies

C. G. Greenidge lbw b DeFreitas	3	J. Garner c DeFreitas b Emburey		0
D. L. Haynes b Small	22	A. H. Gray not out		7
R. B. Richardson c Lamb b DeFreitas	3	C. A. Walsh b DeFreitas		3
*I. V. A. Richards c Broad b Botham	43	W 2, n-b 5		7
A. L. Logie c Gower b Dilley	43			
†P. J. L. Dujon c Dilley b Emburey	25	1/3 2/15 3/60	(45.5 overs)	163
R. A. Harper c Dilley b Emburey	4	4/92 5/136 6/141		
M. D. Marshall c Athey b Emburey	3	7/150 8/150 9/157		

Bowling: Dilley 8-1-19-1; DeFreitas 7.5-1-15-3; Botham 10-0-46-1; Small 10-1-46-1; Emburey 10-0-37-4.

Umpires: B. E. Martin and S. G. Randell.

†AUSTRALIA v WEST INDIES

At Adelaide, January 25. West Indies won by 16 runs. Although without two of their most experienced players, Greenidge and Holding, both having strained hamstring muscles, West Indies won more comfortably than the final margin suggested. Gomes, in his first match of the competition, helped Richardson add 92 in an innings without a boundary, and when he was bowled in the 30th over, Richardson (134 balls, three fours) and Richards (64 balls, two sixes, seven fours) put on 74 in eleven overs. Marsh gave the Australian innings a solid base but lacked the power to dominate the closing overs; he was caught in the deep for 94 from 137 balls, having hit a six and three fours. The loss of Jones in the 27th over and Border in the 28th were setbacks from which Australia, who had decided to bat second, did not recover.

Man of the Match: G. R. Marsh.   *Attendance:* 23,908.

West Indies

D. L. Haynes c Zoehrer b Davis	3	R. A. Harper not out		13
R. B. Richardson b Waugh	72	B 3, l-b 15, w 7		25
H. A. Gomes b Matthews	43			
*I. V. A. Richards c Davis b Waugh	69	1/18 2/110 3/184	(5 wkts, 50 overs)	237
A. L. Logie run out	0	4/184 5/221		
†P. J. L. Dujon not out	12			

M. D. Marshall, J. Garner, A. H. Gray and C. A. Walsh did not bat.

Bowling: Davis 8-1-21-1; Reid 10-0-43-0; Waugh 7-0-41-2; Matthews 10-0-34-1; O'Donnell 7-0-31-0; Taylor 8-0-49-0.

Australia

G. R. Marsh c Harper b Walsh	94	†T. J. Zoehrer not out		22
D. M. Wellham c Dujon b Marshall	3	B. A. Reid b Walsh		1
D. M. Jones lbw b Garner	40	S. P. Davis not out		3
*A. R. Border b Harper	1	B 1, l-b 11, w 10, n-b 4		26
S. R. Waugh c Richards b Harper	24			
G. R. J. Matthews c and b Harper	3	1/4 2/85 3/86	(9 wkts, 50 overs)	221
S. P. O'Donnell c Dujon b Marshall	0	4/158 5/172 6/172		
P. L. Taylor b Walsh	4	7/183 8/199 9/217		

Bowling: Marshall 10-2-34-2; Gray 10-1-44-0; Garner 10-0-36-1; Walsh 10-0-46-3; Harper 10-0-49-3.

Umpires: R. C. Bailhache and A. R. Crafter.

†AUSTRALIA v ENGLAND

At Adelaide, January 26. Australia won by 33 runs. England paid the price for presumptuous strokes by Broad and Gatting when they could not stem the subsequent collapse and lost a game they should have won with ease – a "chuck" that was to imperil their chances of reaching the finals. Australia, who won the toss, had done well to recover from a hostile opening spell by DeFreitas, with Border and Waugh (120 balls) adding 164 for the fourth wicket, a World Series Cup record. Border (122 balls) had lives at 29, Dilley misjudging a skyer, and at 51, when Botham missed the stumps front-on from six yards. These lapses should have been inconsequential, because England were 125 for two after 31 overs. However, two careless strokes, followed by the running out of Lamb by Marsh with a direct hit from twenty yards, gave Australia control.

Man of the Match: S. R. Waugh.   *Attendance:* 24,664.

Australia

G. R. Marsh c Emburey b DeFreitas ..	8	G. R. J. Matthews c Lamb b Dilley ... 0
D. M. Wellham c Richards b DeFreitas	9	†T. J. Zoehrer not out 5
D. M. Jones c Richards b DeFreitas ...	8	B 1, l-b 8, w 4, n-b 2 15
*A. R. Border c Broad b DeFreitas	91	
S. R. Waugh not out	83	1/21 2/24 3/37 (6 wkts, 50 overs) 225
S. P. O'Donnell run out	6	4/201 5/211 6/219

K. H. MacLeay, P. L. Taylor and S. P. Davis did not bat.

Bowling: Dilley 10-1-41-1; DeFreitas 10-1-35-4; Botham 10-0-42-0; Small 10-0-42-0; Emburey 10-0-56-0.

England

B. C. Broad c Border b Waugh	46	P. A. J. DeFreitas c Jones b Taylor ... 8
C. W. J. Athey lbw b Davis	12	G. C. Small b MacLeay 2
D. I. Gower c Waugh b O'Donnell ...	21	G. R. Dilley not out 3
*M. W. Gatting b Taylor	46	L-b 8, w 1 9
A. J. Lamb run out	8	
I. T. Botham st Zoehrer b Taylor	18	1/23 2/55 3/125 (48.1 overs) 192
†C. J. Richards b Waugh	2	4/138 5/144 6/152
J. E. Emburey run out	17	7/168 8/184 9/188

Bowling: Davis 8-0-18-1; MacLeay 10-1-43-1; Matthews 4-0-21-0; O'Donnell 9-0-43-1; Waugh 10-1-30-2; Taylor 7.1-0-29-3.

Umpires: A. R. Crafter and S. G. Randell.

†AUSTRALIA v WEST INDIES

At Sydney, January 28 (day/night). Australia won by 36 runs. Australia could manage only a modest 194 after choosing to bat first on a pitch offering all bowlers assistance but, Richards apart, the West Indians lacked conviction and were dismissed for their lowest total in a one-day international on the ground. Border promoted himself to open, following Australia's sequence of poor starts, but although he and Marsh saw through the first fifteen overs, they put on only 33. Ritchie, returning to the team, hit 35 from 51 balls to boost the scoring-rate while Wellham provided middle-order stability. Dujon became the leading wicket-keeper in one-day international matches with 124 dismissals when he caught Taylor. Richards dominated West Indies' innings with 70 from 96 balls, including nine fours, but Harper's unbeaten 20 was their next highest score.

Man of the Match: S. P. O'Donnell.   *Attendance:* 36,439.

Australia

G. R. Marsh c Garner b Walsh	20	G. R. J. Matthews not out	13
*A. R. Border hit wkt b Walsh	19	P. L. Taylor c Dujon b Marshall	2
D. M. Jones c Richards b Benjamin	22	S. P. Davis run out	3
G. M. Ritchie c Haynes b Garner	35	B 3, l-b 10, w 3, n-b 2	18
D. M. Wellham c Dujon b Marshall	39		
S. R. Waugh run out	16	1/33 2/58 3/69	(50 overs) 194
S. P. O'Donnell run out	6	4/112 5/158 6/170	
†T. J. Zoehrer run out	1	7/173 8/179 9/187	

Bowling: Marshall 10-1-29-2; Garner 10-1-32-1; Walsh 10-1-41-2; Benjamin 10-0-45-1; Harper 10-0-34-0.

West Indies

D. L. Haynes b Matthews	17	W. K. M. Benjamin c Zoehrer	
R. B. Richardson c Zoehrer b O'Donnell	0	b O'Donnell	5
H. A. Gomes c and b O'Donnell	1	J. Garner c and b Taylor	18
*I. V. A. Richards c Zoehrer		C. A. Walsh c Border b Matthews	3
b Matthews	70	B 2, l-b 2, w 2	6
A. L. Logie c Wellham b Waugh	2		
†P. J. L. Dujon c Wellham b Waugh	14	1/12 2/14 3/40	(46.1 overs) 158
R. A. Harper not out	20	4/59 5/89 6/114	
M. D. Marshall c Waugh b O'Donnell	2	7/126 8/133 9/152	

Bowling: Davis 8-0-29-0; O'Donnell 10-2-19-4; Waugh 10-1-21-2; Matthews 8.1-2-32-3; Taylor 10-0-53-1.

Umpires: R. A. French and M. W. Johnson.

†ENGLAND v WEST INDIES

At Melbourne, January 30. West Indies won by six wickets. England, winning the toss, compounded the problems of an uneven pitch when Broad ran out Lamb and Gatting was bowled by Harper, making room to force his second ball square on the off side. Holding's swooping caught and bowled from Botham, taken at the expense of a damaged hamstring within a few feet of the batsman, wrecked England's prospects of recovery, and only Emburey's determination extended the innings until the 49th over. West Indies were lucky to lose only one early wicket against fine bowling by Small and DeFreitas. Richards, however, took command after nearly playing on in Emburey's first over, and when 21 became the first batsman to score 5,000 runs in one-day international cricket.

Man of the Match: I. V. A. Richards.   *Attendance*: 18,405.

England

B. C. Broad c Garner b Holding	33	P. A. J. DeFreitas c Haynes b Garner	13
C. W. J. Athey lbw b Garner	2	N. A. Foster b Marshall	5
D. I. Gower b Marshall	8	G. C. Small not out	1
A. J. Lamb run out	0	L-b 3, w 4, n-b 8	15
*M. W. Gatting b Harper	13		
I. T. Botham c and b Holding	15	1/11 2/27 3/37	(48.2 overs) 147
J. E. Emburey c Harper b Garner	34	4/61 5/77 6/84	
†C. J. Richards b Marshall	8	7/111 8/136 9/144	

Bowling: Marshall 9.2-2-30-3; Garner 9-1-37-3; Holding 8.3-2-19-2; Walsh 5-1-16-0; Harper 10-0-26-1; Richards 6.3-1-16-0.

West Indies

D. L. Haynes lbw b Foster	13	†P. J. L. Dujon not out	1
R. B. Richardson c Richards b DeFreitas	0	L-b 10, w 8, n-b 3	21
H. A. Gomes run out	36		
*I. V. A. Richards b Foster	58	1/7 2/49 3/98	(4 wkts, 48.3 overs) 148
A. L. Logie not out	19	4/146	

R. A. Harper, M. D. Marshall, M. A. Holding, J. Garner and C. A. Walsh did not bat.

Bowling: DeFreitas 10-2-15-1; Small 10-3-16-0; Botham 10-3-28-0; Foster 9-1-25-2; Embubery 9.3-1-54-0.

Umpires: R. C. Bailhache and S. G. Randell.

†AUSTRALIA v ENGLAND

At Melbourne, February 1. Australia won by 109 runs. A solid opening by Marsh and Border, followed by an aggressive 93 by Jones, gave Australia, who were put in, a score England never looked like challenging. Jones, facing 100 balls, won a critical tactical point with a successful assault on Emburey, who was taken out of the attack after his first three overs had gone for 25. Waugh, who helped Jones add 69 off ten overs for the fifth wicket, signed off in style with three successive fours off Gatting, scoring his 49 not out off 36 balls. Botham, promoted to open, made a disciplined 45 off 87 balls, but nobody supported him. Broad, Gower and Gatting fell to loose strokes, while Lamb, over-committing himself as non-striker, was run out for the third time in succession at the bowler's end, having been sent back.

Man of the Match: S. R. Waugh.　　　　*Attendance*: 58,580.

Australia

G. R. Marsh c Emburey b Foster	28	S. P. O'Donnell not out		4
*A. R. Border c Athey b Small	45			
D. M. Jones c Athey b Gatting	93	L-b 7, w 9, n-b 1		17
G. M. Ritchie st French b Gatting	9			
D. M. Wellham c Lamb b Gatting	3	1/61 2/127 3/144	(5 wkts, 50 overs)	248
S. R. Waugh not out	49	4/154 5/223		

G. R. J. Matthews, †T. J. Zoehrer, P. L. Taylor and S. P. Davis did not bat.

Bowling: DeFreitas 8-2-37-0; Small 10-0-49-1; Botham 10-0-35-0; Foster 7-1-20-1; Emburey 6-0-41-0; Gatting 9-0-59-3.

England

B. C. Broad b O'Donnell	2	N. A. Foster b Waugh		4
I. T. Botham c and b Matthews	45	†B. N. French not out		5
D. I. Gower c Taylor b Davis	11	G. C. Small c Matthews b Jones		4
A. J. Lamb run out	11	B 2, l-b 7, w 1		10
*M. W. Gatting c Davis b Waugh	6			
C. W. J. Athey lbw b O'Donnell	29	1/4 2/25 3/52	(47.3 overs)	139
J. E. Emburey b Waugh	1	4/65 5/87 6/90		
P. A. J. DeFreitas b Waugh	11	7/117 8/129 9/130		

Bowling: Davis 8-1-20-1; O'Donnell 9-2-33-2; Matthews 10-1-24-2; Waugh 10-0-26-3; Taylor 9-1-23-0; Jones 1.3-0-4-1.

Umpires: R. A. French and B. E. Martin.

†ENGLAND v WEST INDIES

At Devonport, February 3. England won by 29 runs. Richards's dismissal to his seventh ball, which he touched on to the stumps attempting to run Botham through the vacant slips, inspired a brilliant display of out-cricket which saw England home – and into the finals – with deceptive ease. Without Broad's measured 76 (142 balls) out of 158 for seven, England, put in, would not have had a target to defend, even though the seamers had a helpful pitch to bowl on and West Indies were without Haynes (dislocated finger) and Greenidge (damaged hamstring). Logie and Gomes added 46 for the third wicket to earn West Indies the advantage; but by dismissing Gomes – caught at leg slip – and Richards in successive overs, Botham swung the match. On five of the eight occasions on which Gatting changed the bowling, the man brought on took a wicket in the first over of his spell.

Man of the Match: B. C. Broad.　　　　*Attendance*: 9,848.

England

B. C. Broad c Dujon b Walsh	76	N. A. Foster run out	0
I. T. Botham c Richardson b Gray	8	†B. N. French b Marshall	0
D. I. Gower c Payne b Marshall	3	G. C. Small not out	6
A. J. Lamb c Logie b Harper	36	L-b 14, w 3, n-b 5	22
*M. W. Gatting c Richardson b Gray	6		
C. W. J. Athey lbw b Marshall	3	1/23 2/29 3/103 (9 wkts, 50 overs) 177	
J. E. Emburey c Garner b Walsh	2	4/129 5/133 6/143	
P. A. J. DeFreitas not out	15	7/158 8/159 9/160	

Bowling: Marshall 10–0–31–3; Gray 10–2–29–2; Garner 10–0–30–0; Walsh 10–1–31–2; Harper 10–0–42–1.

West Indies

R. B. Richardson c French b DeFreitas	2	J. Garner b Emburey	4
T. R. O. Payne c French b Botham	18	A. H. Gray c and b Emburey	0
A. L. Logie b Foster	31	C. A. Walsh not out	1
H. A. Gomes c Emburey b Botham	19	L-b 5, w 2	7
*I. V. A. Richards b Botham	1		
†P. J. L. Dujon c Gatting b Emburey	34	1/10 2/25 3/71 (48 overs) 148	
R. A. Harper c French b Small	4	4/73 5/90 6/95	
M. D. Marshall c Athey b DeFreitas	27	7/132 8/147 9/147	

Bowling: DeFreitas 9–1–20–2; Small 10–0–35–1; Foster 10–0–29–1; Botham 10–1–33–3; Emburey 9–0–26–3.

Umpires: A. R. Crafter and S. G. Randell.

†AUSTRALIA v WEST INDIES

At Sydney, February 6 (day/night). Australia won by two wickets. To reach the finals, West Indies had not only to win but to score 374 to surpass England's run-rate. They failed on both counts as their batting again let them down. It was the first time they had not qualified for the finals in five World Series Cup tournaments. After Richards had won the toss, Payne batted 42 overs for 60, many of his runs made with Logie as a runner after he strained a hamstring muscle sprinting for a quick single. Gray was recalled by Border after rightly being given out by umpire McConnell for obstructing the field – deliberately blocking the ball with his bat at the non-striker's end to baulk a run-out chance – but ironically he was run out soon afterwards. Zoehrer gave Australia an excellent start as makeshift opener with 50 from 59 balls, but the scoring slowed once he was out and the result was in doubt until O'Donnell thrashed 23 from fifteen balls at the end.

Man of the Match: T. J. Zoehrer.   *Attendance*: 32,537.

West Indies

R. B. Richardson c Ritchie b Davis	11	J. Garner run out	6
T. R. O. Payne c and b Taylor	60	A. H. Gray run out	1
A. L. Logie c Zoehrer b Waugh	14	C. A. Walsh not out	1
*I. V. A. Richards c and b Matthews	25	B 1, l-b 3, w 2	6
H. A. Gomes run out	38		
†P. J. L. Dujon lbw b Taylor	2	1/20 2/35 3/70 (49 overs) 192	
R. A. Harper c Wellham b Davis	20	4/148 5/152 6/174	
W. K. M. Benjamin c Wellham b Taylor	8	7/177 8/187 9/190	

Bowling: Davis 10–3–31–2; O'Donnell 10–1–33–0; Waugh 9–1–41–1; Matthews 10–0–47–1; Taylor 10–0–36–3.

Australia

G. R. Marsh c Richardson b Harper	33	G. R. J. Matthews b Richards	0
†T. J. Zoehrer c Richards b Walsh	50	P. L. Taylor not out	0
D. M. Jones c and b Harper	7		
G. M. Ritchie c and b Garner	25	B 8, l-b 3, w 2, n-b 1	14
D. M. Wellham c Garner b Gray	24		
S. R. Waugh st Dujon b Richards	11	1/74 2/87 3/106 (8 wkts, 49.1 overs) 195		
*A. R. Border b Richards	8	4/131 5/155 6/163	
S. P. O'Donnell not out	23	7/191 8/191	

S. P. Davis did not bat.

Bowling: Garner 10-1-37-1; Gray 8-0-48-1; Benjamin 3.1-1-15-0; Walsh 10-2-16-1; Harper 10-1-34-2; Richards 7-0-29-3; Gomes 1-0-5-0.

Umpires: R. A. French and P. J. McConnell.

QUALIFYING TABLE

	P	W	L	Pts
Australia	8	5	3	10
England	8	4	4	8
West Indies	8	3	5	6

†AUSTRALIA v ENGLAND

First Final Match

At Melbourne, February 8. England won by six wickets. Luck with the toss was the decisive factor: when Gatting won it on an overcast morning on which drizzle delayed the start by an hour, he earned England the equivalent of a 30- to 40-run advantage. In the event, victory should have come more easily than it did, for England failed with the ball to make the best use of the helpful conditions. They were additionally favoured in that by the time Broad and Botham opened England's innings, it was a perfect, sunny afternoon with not a cloud in sight. Botham set England up with an innings of powerful but mainly orthodox strokes which took heavy toll of the constraints placed on Border concerning the disposition of his field. As though to underline the point, Botham (52 balls) was caught just inside the long-off boundary as soon as Australia were permitted more than two men outside the 30-yard oblong. Only Athey's deliberation (12 off 57 balls) prolonged the innings into the 36th over. There was regular movement through the air and off the pitch when England bowled, both opening batsmen going to slip catches in the first two overs. But a surfeit of no-balls, from one of which Border (at 2) was also caught at slip, helped Australia gain a foothold. The third wicket added 103 in 27 overs, and until Ritchie was run out by Jones, Australia had a total of 200 in prospect. However, England's bowling tightened, and when five wickets fell for 30 in ten overs, the result was almost a formality.

Attendance: 51,589.

Australia

G. R. Marsh c Gatting b DeFreitas	2	P. L. Taylor not out	3
†T. J. Zoehrer c Gatting b Dilley	0	B. A. Reid not out	5
D. M. Jones b DeFreitas	67		
*A. R. Border c French b Foster	42	L-b 10, w 3, n-b 7	20
G. M. Ritchie run out	13		
S. R. Waugh c DeFreitas b Emburey	1	1/3 2/3 3/106 (8 wkts, 44 overs) 171		
S. P. O'Donnell b Dilley	10	4/134 5/137 6/146	
G. R. J. Matthews b Dilley	8	7/161 8/164	

S. P. Davis did not bat.

Bowling: Dilley 9-2-32-3; DeFreitas 9-0-32-2; Botham 9-0-26-0; Foster 9-0-42-1; Emburey 8-0-29-1.

England

B. C. Broad c Jones b Matthews	12	*M. W. Gatting not out	3
I. T. Botham c Marsh b Matthews	71	B 5, l-b 3, w 4, n-b 2	14
C. W. J. Athey c and b Matthews	12		
D. I. Gower c Taylor b Reid	45	1/91 2/93 3/147 (4 wkts, 36 overs)	172
A. J. Lamb not out	15	4/159	

J. E. Emburey, P. A. J. DeFreitas, N. A. Foster, †B. N. French and G. R. Dilley did not bat.

Bowling: Davis 4-0-17-0; O'Donnell 4-0-25-0; Reid 5-0-31-1; Waugh 8-1-36-0; Matthews 9-1-27-3; Taylor 5-0-24-0; Jones 1-0-4-0.

Umpires: P. J. McConnell and S. G. Randell.

†AUSTRALIA v ENGLAND

Second Final Match

At Sydney, February 11 (day/night), England won by 8 runs. O'Donnell, driving DeFreitas twice for six, made a valiant attempt to take the finals to a third match by scoring 40 off 27 balls; but England's 187 for nine proved out of range. Australia had seemed well placed when Marsh and Border opened with a stand of 55, but Border's dismissal by Botham in the nineteenth over, caught by French off an edged leg-glance, changed the game. On yet another pitch below standard for a one-day international, lacking pace and bounce and taking a considerable amount of turn, Botham and Emburey gained control by denying batsmen room to play square of the wicket. Botham had a spell of three for 7 in 27 balls and Emburey disposed of Jones with a diving caught and bowled, left-handed. From 80 for four in the 29th over, Wellham and Waugh added 44 in eleven, steadily picking up pace. Then Waugh, attempting a second run to deep third man, was unfortunate to be judged run out by Foster's pinpoint throw and Australia lost momentum. When Wellham and Zoehrer fell to successive balls in DeFreitas's second spell, Australia needed 53 at 8 an over, and only O'Donnell's power and determination kept the margin to single figures.

Botham's 25 off 31 balls had given England a rapid start after Gatting had won the toss and wisely chosen to bat. He straight drove Davis so devastatingly that Border placed a long-off, rather than long-leg, as one of the two men allowed outside the oblong. When Botham was out in the eighth over, well caught by Ritchie at square leg, Broad (87 balls) and Lamb (39) carried England to what proved a winning score.

Man of the Finals: I. T. Botham.   *Attendance:* 33,655.

England

B. C. Broad c O'Donnell b Matthews	53	N. A. Foster c Taylor b Davis	7
I. T. Botham c Ritchie b O'Donnell	25	†B. N. French not out	9
C. W. J. Athey b Matthews	16	G. R. Dilley not out	6
D. I. Gower c Wellham b Taylor	17	L-b 4, w 1	5
*M. W. Gatting run out	7		
A. J. Lamb c Zoehrer b O'Donnell	35	1/36 2/73 3/102 (9 wkts, 50 overs)	187
J. E. Emburey c Zoehrer b Waugh	6	4/120 5/121 6/143	
P. A. J. DeFreitas c Jones b Taylor	1	7/146 8/170 9/170	

Bowling: Davis 10-0-44-1; O'Donnell 10-1-37-2; Waugh 10-0-42-1; Matthews 10-1-31-2; Taylor 10-2-29-2.

Australia

G. R. Marsh lbw b Botham	28	†T. J. Zoehrer lbw b DeFreitas	0
*A. R. Border c French b Botham	27	G. R. J. Matthews run out	3
D. M. Jones c and b Emburey	13	P. L. Taylor not out	3
G. M. Ritchie c DeFreitas b Botham	4	B 1, l-b 6, w 2	9
D. M. Wellham c Gower b DeFreitas	30		
S. R. Waugh run out	22	1/55 2/70 3/72 4/80 (8 wkts, 50 overs)	179
S. P. O'Donnell not out	40	5/124 6/135 7/135 8/151	

S. P. Davis did not bat.

Bowling: Dilley 10-1-34-0; DeFreitas 10-1-34-2; Botham 10-1-26-3; Foster 10-0-51-0; Emburey 10-2-27-1.

Umpires: A. R. Crafter and R. A. French.

SHARJAH CUP, 1986-87

By GRAHAM OTWAY

England, the weakest of the four sides involved, won the fourth Sharjah Cup by virtue of their superior run-rate after Pakistan had chosen to put national pride before the £18,750 first prize in the final match of the round-robin tournament. Whereas India, their opponents, would have won the Cup had they maintained their unbeaten record in the competition, Pakistan's task was more complicated. To head the table, they had not only to win but also to beat England's run-rate of 4.46 per over. In the event, with India scoring 183 for eight in their 50 overs – a total insufficient to threaten England's run-rate if they lost – Pakistan had to score the 184 required in only 32.4 overs. Such is the rivalry between the neighbouring countries that Pakistan's early-order batsmen, fearing a possible collapse, refused to take the risks needed. And although an unbeaten partnership of 93 between Salim Malik and Javed Miandad won the match with eight wickets to spare, 41.4 overs were used in overtaking India's total. The match, billed as the final and sold out well in advance, was watched by a crowd of some 18,000 Indian and Pakistani expatriates living in the United Arab Emirates.

The performance of his batsmen was later criticised by Imran Khan, Pakistan's captain, but it was welcomed by an England side which, missing five of the top six batsmen from their tour to Australia, had begun the tournament 10-1 outsiders. They had lost their opening match to India by three wickets, but while Pakistan and India were recording victories over a disappointing Australian side which, apart from the injured Dean Jones, was virtually of Test strength, England's players found their touch by dint of hard work in the nets. A cultured 83 from Tim Robinson sent Pakistan crashing to a five-wicket defeat and Graham Gooch made 86 as Australia were beaten by 11 runs.

†ENGLAND v INDIA

At Sharjah, April 2. India won by three wickets. Toss: India. The combined effects of a slow pitch following a damp, early morning start and, for some of the batsmen, months out of action, were seen as England toiled to reach 211. Only Broad showed his true form. A typically flamboyant half-century by Srikkanth (one six, five fours) and an even harder-hit 64 off 54 balls by Kapil Dev steered India to a comfortable victory.

Man of the Match: Kapil Dev.

England

G. A. Gooch b Maninder	31	P. A. J. DeFreitas not out	18
B. C. Broad st Viswanath b Shastri	57	†C. J. Richards not out	14
R. T. Robinson c Srikkanth b Shastri	34		
N. H. Fairbrother c Azharuddin b Shastri	14	L-b 4, w 2	6
J. J. Whitaker b Gopal	4	1/60 2/106 3/134 (7 wkts, 50 overs) 211
D. J. Capel run out	8	4/143 5/145
*J. E. Emburey b Kapil Dev	25	6/167 7/184

P. H. Edmonds and N. A. Foster did not bat.

Bowling: Kapil Dev 8-1-30-1; Prabhakar 8-2-17-0; Arun 4-0-32-0; Gopal 10-0-38-1; Shastri 10-1-47-3; Maninder 10-0-43-1.

India

M. Prabhakar c Edmonds b Foster	....	4	†S. Viswanath b Emburey	 3
K. Srikkanth c Fairbrother b Capel	..	56	B. Arun not out	 7
R. Lamba c Whitaker b Edmonds	....	4	B 2, l-b 2, w 1	 5
D. B. Vengsarkar c Robinson b Edmonds		40		
R. J. Shastri c Edmonds b Emburey	...	7	1/22 2/33 3/86	(7 wkts, 48.5 overs) 214
*Kapil Dev c Capel b Emburey	......	64	4/97 5/146	
M. Azharuddin not out	....	24	6/194 7/200	

Gopal Sharma and Maninder Singh did not bat.

Bowling: DeFreitas 10–3–33–0; Foster 9–1–46–1; Capel 10–0–45–1; Edmonds 10–0–48–2; Emburey 9.5–0–38–3.

Umpires: D. P. Buultjens and P. W. Vidanagamage.

†AUSTRALIA v PAKISTAN

At Sharjah, April 3. Pakistan won by six wickets. Toss: Pakistan. Batting first on the livelier of Sharjah's two prepared pitches, Australia were immediately in trouble against hostile new-ball bowling from Wasim Akram and Manzoor Elahi. Boon and O'Donnell's century partnership lent the innings respectability, but with Miandad in the mood to take their attack apart, Australia never looked like winning.

Man of the Match: Mudassar Nazar.

Australia

G. R. Marsh c Yousuf b Manzoor	.....	1	P. L. Taylor run out	 0
M. R. J. Veletta b Wasim	....	0	B. A. Reid b Wasim	 0
D. C. Boon c Miandad b Mudassar	...	71	S. P. Davis not out	 2
*A. R. Border c Yousuf b Manzoor	...	5	L-b 11, w 3, n-b 1	 15
S. P. O'Donnell run out	....	54		
S. R. Waugh c Manzoor b Mudassar	..	8	1/1 2/1 3/8	(9 wkts, 50 overs) 176
G. R. J. Matthews not out	....	9	4/122 5/148 6/152	
†T. J. Zoehrer b Mudassar	....	11	7/171 8/171 9/172	

Bowling: Wasim 10–2–23–2; Manzoor 7–3–20–2; Qadir 10–1–26–0; Tauseef 8–2–19–0; Ijaz 5–0–33–0; Mudassar 10–1–44–3.

Pakistan

Ramiz Raja b Davis	....	3	Manzoor Elahi not out	 12
Mudassar Nazar run out	....	64	B 4, l-b 7, w 2, n-b 3	 16
Salim Malik c Waugh b Reid	....	9		
*Javed Miandad not out	....	74	1/13 2/28 3/144	(4 wkts, 46.4 overs) 180
Ijaz Ahmed c O'Donnell b Matthews	..	2	4/147	

Tauseef Ahmed, Abdul Qadir, Wasim Akram, †Salim Yousuf and Ijaz Faqih did not bat.

Bowling: Davis 10–2–26–1; Reid 8.4–3–26–1; O'Donnell 7–1–21–0; Waugh 6–0–34–0; Matthews 10–1–31–1; Taylor 5–0–31–0.

Umpires: D. P. Buultjens and P. W. Vidanagamage.

†AUSTRALIA v INDIA

At Sharjah, April 5. India won by seven wickets. Toss: India. Weakened by the absence of Border, their captain, with an injured finger, Australia suffered their second defeat of the tournament. India quickly recovered from the loss of Srikkanth in the first over, Gavaskar and Azharuddin putting on 165, a record for India's second wicket in one-day internationals.

Man of the Match: M. Azharuddin.

Australia

M. R. J. Veletta c Gavaskar b Prabhakar	5	D. M. Wellham not out 17
*G. R. Marsh c Vengsarkar b Gopal	39	G. R. J. Matthews not out 17
D. C. Boon c Vengsarkar b Kapil Dev	62	
S. R. Waugh c Gopal b Maninder	20	B 1, l-b 4, w 1, n-b 2 8
S. P. O'Donnell st Viswanath		
b Maninder	5	1/20 2/82 3/129　　(6 wkts, 50 overs) 176
G. M. Ritchie lbw b Kapil Dev	3	4/136 5/141 6/142

†T. J. Zoehrer, B. A. Reid and S. P. Davis did not bat.

Bowling: Kapil Dev 8-0-36-2; Prabhakar 10-2-18-1; Maninder 9-0-26-2; Arun 3-0-17-0; Gopal 10-0-46-1; Shastri 10-0-28-0.

India

K. Srikkanth c Matthews b Reid	0	R. J. Shastri not out 2
S. M. Gavaskar not out	78	B 3, l-b 5, w 1, n-b 2 11
M. Azharuddin c Marsh b O'Donnell	84	
*Kapil Dev b Waugh	2	1/0 2/165 3/169　　(3 wkts, 42 overs) 177

D. B. Vengsarkar, B. Arun, M. Prabhakar, Gopal Sharma, †S. Viswanath and Maninder Singh did not bat.

Bowling: Reid 10-1-35-1; Davis 7-2-22-0; O'Donnell 8-0-36-1; Matthews 9-0-43-0; Waugh 8-0-33-1.

Umpires: D. P. Buultjens and P. W. Vidanagamage.

†ENGLAND v PAKISTAN

At Sharjah, April 7. England won by five wickets. Toss: England. Out-fielding of the highest standard helped England beat Pakistan, the tournament favourites, by restricting them to 217 for nine. After the early loss of Gooch, the Nottinghamshire pair of Broad and Robinson set up England's victory with a second-wicket stand of 140.
Man of the Match: R. T. Robinson.

Pakistan

Mudassar Nazar c Richards b DeFreitas	3	†Salim Yousuf b Emburey 8
Ramiz Raja run out	44	Abdul Qadir not out 13
Ijaz Ahmed run out	1	Tauseef Ahmed not out 3
Javed Miandad run out	60	B 8, l-b 9, w 4, n-b 5 25
Salim Malik c Richards b Capel	1	
*Imran Khan c Richards b Foster	46	1/10 2/11 3/77　　(9 wkts, 50 overs) 217
Manzoor Elahi c and b Capel	3	4/83 5/175 6/175
Wasim Akram c Fairbrother b Capel	10	7/188 8/190 9/211

Bowling: DeFreitas 10-0-47-1; Small 10-2-25-0; Foster 10-0-47-1; Emburey 10-1-44-1; Capel 10-0-38-3.

England

G. A. Gooch c Malik b Imran	1	*J. E. Emburey not out 5
B. C. Broad c Ijaz b Mudassar	65	
R. T. Robinson c Manzoor b Qadir	83	B 2, l-b 9, w 3 14
J. J. Whitaker not out	44	
N. H. Fairbrother c Ramiz b Qadir	6	1/3 2/143 3/166　　(5 wkts, 47.2 overs) 220
D. J. Capel st Yousuf b Qadir	2	4/182 5/188

P. A. J. DeFreitas, †C. J. Richards, N. A. Foster and G. C. Small did not bat.

Bowling: Imran 9-2-24-1; Wasim 9.2-0-38-0; Qadir 10-0-47-3; Mudassar 10-0-41-1; Manzoor 6-0-39-0; Tauseef 3-0-20-0.

Umpires: D. P. Buultjens and P. W. Vidanagamage.

†AUSTRALIA v ENGLAND

At Sharjah, April 9. England won by 11 runs. Toss: Australia. England became the first side in the tournament to win after batting first, and with Gooch and Broad putting up 118 for the first wicket, they compiled the highest total as well. While Boon was making his third consecutive half-century and adding 159 with Border, the Australians had victory in their sights. But their later batsmen could not sustain the momentum.

Man of the Match: G. A. Gooch.

England

G. A. Gooch lbw b Waugh	86	*J. E. Emburey not out	18
B. C. Broad b Taylor	44	P. A. J. DeFreitas not out	1
R. T. Robinson lbw b O'Donnell	5	B 1, l-b 7, w 6, n-b 2	16
N. H. Fairbrother run out	32		
R. J. Bailey c O'Donnell b Reid	11	1/118 2/125 3/167 (6 wkts, 50 overs) 230	
D. J. Capel run out	17	4/188 5/193 6/229	

†C. J. Richards, N. A. Foster and G. C. Small did not bat.

Bowling: Reid 10-0-50-1; Davis 8-3-24-0; Matthews 7-0-31-0; Waugh 10-1-49-1; Taylor 7-0-41-1; O'Donnell 8-0-27-1.

Australia

G. R. Marsh lbw b DeFreitas	0	P. L. Taylor not out	14
D. C. Boon c Broad b Emburey	73	B. A. Reid run out	2
D. M. Wellham c Robinson b Small	2	S. P. Davis not out	3
*A. R. Border c Bailey b Emburey	84	L-b 6, n-b 1	7
S. P. O'Donnell run out	6		
S. R. Waugh b Foster	14	1/0 2/7 3/166 (9 wkts, 50 overs) 219	
G. R. J. Matthews c Gooch b DeFreitas	13	4/166 5/177 6/195	
†T. J. Zoehrer run out	1	7/200 8/200 9/204	

Bowling: DeFreitas 10-1-40-2; Small 9-1-23-1; Capel 5-0-28-0; Gooch 6-0-34-0; Emburey 10-1-38-2; Foster 10-0-50-1.

Umpires: D. P. Buultjens and P. W. Vidanagamage.

†INDIA v PAKISTAN

At Sharjah, April 10. Pakistan won by eight wickets. Toss: Pakistan.
Man of the Match: D. B. Vengsarkar.

India

K. Srikkanth c Yousuf b Wasim	5	B. Arun c Ramiz b Imran	6
S. M. Gavaskar b Imran	0	Maninder Singh not out	2
M. Azharuddin lbw b Imran	1		
D. B. Vengsarkar not out	95	B 1, l-b 6, w 3, n-b 2	12
M. Prabhakar run out	33		
R. J. Shastri c Miandad b Qadir	8	1/5 2/5 3/7 4/82 (8 wkts, 50 overs) 183	
*Kapil Dev c Yousuf b Imran	19	5/116 6/151	
†S. Viswanath run out	2	7/160 8/179	

Gopal Sharma did not bat.

Bowling: Imran 10-1-27-4; Wasim 10-2-21-1; Manzoor 5-0-29-0; Mudassar 10-0-39-0; Jaffer 5-0-21-0; Qadir 10-1-39-1.

Pakistan

Ramiz Raja c sub (C. S. Pandit) b Shastri . 53	Javed Miandad not out 52
Ijaz Ahmed b Maninder 9	B 3, l-b 6 9
Salim Malik not out 61	1/22 2/91 (2 wkts, 41.4 overs) 184

Mudassar Nazar, *Imran Khan, †Salim Yousuf, Manzoor Elahi, Abdul Qadir, Wasim Akram and Saleem Jaffer did not bat.

Bowling: Kapil Dev 8–1–27–0; Prabhakar 4–0–30–0; Maninder 10–2–28–1; Shastri 10–0–37–1; Gopal 7–0–36–0; Arun 2–0–11–0; Azharuddin 0.4–0–6–0.

Umpires: D. P. Buultjens and P. W. Vidanagamage.

FINAL TABLE

	P	W	L	Pts	*Run-rate*
England	3	2	1	4	4.46
Pakistan	3	2	1	4	4.17
India	3	2	1	4	4.07
Australia	3	0	3	0	3.80

Man of the Series: D. C. Boon.

FUTURE TOURS

1988	West Indians to England Sri Lankans to England
1988-89	Australians to Pakistan New Zealanders to India England to Sri Lanka and India West Indians and Pakistanis to Australia Pakistanis to New Zealand Indians to West Indies Pakistanis to Sri Lanka
1989	Australians to England
1989-90	Sri Lankans and Pakistanis to Australia Indians to Pakistan England to West Indies Indians to New Zealand and Sri Lanka Australians to New Zealand
1990	New Zealanders and Indians to England

1990-91	New Zealanders to Pakistan England to Australia West Indians to Sri Lanka and India Sri Lankans to Pakistan New Zealanders to Australia* Pakistanis to India* Sri Lankans to New Zealand* Australians to West Indies
1991	West Indians to England
1991-92	New Zealanders to Australia* Indians to Australia* West Indians to Australia Sri Lankans to India
1992-93	West Indians to Australia England to India* Indians to West Indies
1993	Australians to England*

* *Signifies unconfirmed.*

ENGLAND YOUNG CRICKETERS IN SRI LANKA, 1986-87

By BILL FRINDALL

England's Young Cricketers (under nineteen on September 1, 1986) undertook their first tour of Sri Lanka in January and February. Their visit, administered by the NCA and underwritten by the TCCB, lasted five weeks and included three four-day "Tests", three limited-overs internationals and three preliminary matches. This was Young England's fifth tour since these series were launched in 1970, when England were hosts to a West Indies side which included H. A. Gomes and D. A. Murray, and it reciprocated Young Sri Lanka's first visit to Britain the previous summer.

Although a solitary win, and that in a one-day match, would appear to signify a less than successful mission, the English players dominated all six of their longer matches and displayed a highly professional approach both on and off the field. Ably managed, coached and captained into a cheerful, competent and cohesive unit, they proved impressive ambassadors, and all should have gained valuable experience of touring and playing in front of attentive media. All six matches against Sri Lanka Young Cricketers were accorded ball-by-ball radio coverage and back-page leads in the national press, while the first match in the one-day series was televised in full. Celebrating the first anniversary of the Khettarama Stadium, a remarkable edifice housing an unsteady pitch constructed on reclaimed marsh, it was attended by 47,000 spectators, most of them children admitted free.

The tourists had little time to adapt to extremely slow pitches and a high degree of heat and humidity which swiftly drained even the fittest. However, their opponents, gathered from a 40-strong pool of youngsters, were often too ready to settle for a draw when victory was a strong possibility. The umpiring, by members of the Board's reserve Test match panel, was in the main fair and efficient. An exception, involving a crucial run-out, occurred in the penultimate over of the final one-day international and led to a diplomatic change of official for the final "Test".

Michael Atherton, a mature captain, sound opening bat and an exciting exponent of leg-spin and googly bowling, impressed in all departments. Trevor Ward, Nasser Hussain, Oliver Smith and Mark Ramprakash, the seventeen-year-old schoolboy who was named Player of the "Test" Series, all revealed sound temperaments and techniques. Mark Alleyne could not recapture his batting touch of the previous summer but always fielded outstandingly and bowled effectively in the limited-overs games. Martin Bicknell, the most consistent wicket-taker, employed a rhythmic approach and high right-arm action to extract lift from the most benign pitches. Harvey Trump, still in his penultimate year at Millfield, varied his off-spin and looked an all-rounder of promise, while Lloyd Tennant and Alastair Fraser earned scant reward for unsparing effort. All bowlers were well supported by the wicket-keeping of Warren Hegg and Martin Speight.

The tour party was: T. M. Lamb (*manager*), G. J. Saville (*assistant manager/coach*), M. A. Atherton (*captain*) (Lancashire), T. R. Ward (*vice-captain*) (Kent), M. W. Alleyne (Gloucestershire), M. P. Bicknell (Surrey),

S. J. Brown (Northamptonshire), M. A. Crawley (Lancashire), A. G. J. Fraser (Middlesex), W. K. Hegg (Lancashire), N. Hussain (Essex), M. R. Newton (Hampshire), M. R. Ramprakash (Middlesex), O. C. K. Smith (Gloucestershire), M. P. Speight (Sussex), L. Tennant (Leicestershire), H. R. J. Trump (Somerset).

RESULTS

Matches 9: Won 1, Lost 2, Drawn 6.

Note: None of the matches played was first-class.

v Sri Lanka Schools President's XI: at Nondescripts Cricket Club, Colombo, January 21, 22. Drawn. England Young Cricketers 175 for four dec. (M. A. Atherton 40, T. R. Ward 56) and 186 for six dec. (M. R. Ramprakash 84; L. Meegoda four for 50); Sri Lanka Schools President's XI 146 for four dec. (V. I. de Mel 63) and 162 for four (R. N. Z. Jaymon 52 not out).

v Sri Lanka Board President's XI: at P. Saravanamuttu Oval, Colombo, January 24, 25, 26. Drawn. Sri Lanka Board President's XI 217 for four dec. (U. C. Hathurusinghe 79, R. Rajapakse 41) and 153 (Chaminda Mendis 45; A. G. J. Fraser four for 38, L. Tennant four for 55); England Young Cricketers 194 for six dec. (M. A. Atherton 81) and 74 for no wkt (M. R. Ramprakash 40 not out).

v Kurunegala District Under-23 XI: at Welagedara Stadium, Kurunegala, January 28, 29, 30. Drawn. England Young Cricketers 271 for eight dec. (T. R. Ward 78, M. W. Alleyne 40; W. Kumara four for 60) and 228 for four dec. (T. R. Ward 94, M. A. Crawley 53, M. W. Alleyne 46); Kurunegala District Under-23 XI 251 for six dec. (S. Guneratne 65, P. Liyanage 61) and 94 for five.

v Sri Lanka Young Cricketers (First one-day international): at Khettarama Stadium, Colombo, February 1. Sri Lanka Young Cricketers won by two wickets. England Young Cricketers 131 for eight (45 overs); Sri Lanka Young Cricketers 132 for eight (43 overs). *Match award:* None.

SRI LANKA YOUNG CRICKETERS v ENGLAND YOUNG CRICKETERS

First "Test" Match

At Colombo Cricket Club Ground, Colombo, February 3, 4, 5, 6. Drawn. Toss: England. Deprived by injury of Atherton, Young England did well to dominate most of an interesting match. Both sides collapsed in the first innings after a sound opening on a pitch of uneven bounce, England losing six wickets for 32 runs and Sri Lanka losing all ten for 94. Ward's 60 off 77 balls included eight fours and a six as the tourists extended a lead of 41, but neither side was prepared to risk defeat in pursuit of victory on the final day, when England batted on for 40 minutes, extending a lead of 203 by 46 runs and allowing Bicknell to complete a maiden fifty. Missing Atherton's leg-spin, England claimed only four wickets as Hathurusinghe defended confidently for 265 minutes. The third day's play was interrupted by the stately progress of an iguana.

England Young Cricketers

M. R. Ramprakash c Kaluwitharna			
b Weerakkody	34	– c and b Jayasinghe	11
*T. R. Ward c Ranatunga b Jayasinghe	30	– c Kaluwitharna b Jayasinghe	60
M. W. Alleyne c Kaluwitharna b Mendis	37	– c Hathurusinghe b Thenuwara	0
N. Hussain b Mendis	42	– c Kaluwitharna b Jayasinghe	13
M. P. Speight b Madena	10	– c Allirajah b Thenuwara	6
O. C. K. Smith lbw b Madena	4	– c Jayasinghe b Thenuwara	21
A. G. J. Fraser c Kaluwitharna b Weerakkody	8	– st Kaluwitharna b Mendis	7
M. P. Bicknell b Madena	10	– not out	51
†W. K. Hegg lbw b Weerakkody	0	– (10) not out	29
H. R. J. Trump not out	17	– (9) c Jayasinghe b Mendis	0
L. Tennant b Madena	7		
B 4, l-b 3, w 8	15	B 3, l-b 4, w 2, n-b 1	10

1/72 2/72 3/146 4/153 5/168   214   1/60 2/73 3/73   (8 wkts dec.) 208
6/177 7/177 8/178 9/206   4/86 5/96 6/122
        7/134 8/137

Bowling: *First Innings*—Madena 27.4-8-58-4; Weerakkody 26-4-66-3; Jayasinghe 28-16-28-1; Hathurusinghe 10-1-28-0; Ranatunga 5-0-23-0; Mendis 6-5-4-2. *Second Innings*—Madena 7-1-22-0; Weerakkody 11-3-18-0; Thenuwara 34-13-70-3; Hathurusinghe 2-1-12-0; Mendis 11-2-19-2; Jayasinghe 22-8-60-3.

Sri Lanka Young Cricketers

R. Rajapakse lbw b Trump	31	– c and b Bicknell	6
A. Allirajah lbw b Bicknell	40	– b Tennant	19
U. C. Hathurusinghe lbw b Bicknell	1	– not out	62
V. I. de Mel c Alleyne b Tennant	6	– c and b Trump	4
S. Ranatunga lbw b Fraser	4	– c Trump b Hussain	28
Chaminda Mendis c Bicknell b Trump	17	– not out	26
†R. Kaluwitharna c sub (M. R. Newton) b Trump	11		
R. N. Weerakkody c Fraser b Bicknell	13		
C. R. Thenuwara st Hegg b Trump	23		
*D. R. Madena c Ramprakash b Bicknell	1		
S. K. Jayasinghe not out	10		
B 6, l-b 3, w 4, n-b 3	16	L-b 3, w 3, n-b 1	7

1/79 2/81 3/82 4/89 5/95 6/110   173   1/15 2/31 3/51 4/97   (4 wkts) 152
7/129 8/135 9/139

Bowling: *First Innings*—Fraser 21-12-19-1; Bicknell 27-10-46-4; Trump 25.5-9-51-4; Tennant 21-6-46-1; Alleyne 1-0-2-0. *Second Innings*—Fraser 12-1-31-0; Bicknell 13-4-22-1; Tennant 7-4-4-1; Trump 30-9-69-1; Smith 5-3-7-0; Hussain 7-2-16-1.

Umpires: L. Saverimuttu and W. A. U. Wickremasinghe.

SRI LANKA YOUNG CRICKETERS v ENGLAND YOUNG CRICKETERS

Second "Test" Match

At Asgiriya Stadium, Kandy, February 9, 10, 11, 12. Drawn. Toss: England. Sri Lanka made four changes in anticipation of a turning pitch, but their four spinners made little impression on a grassless surface which showed little sign of wear even after the final day. Atherton set his side to bat for five sessions, and Hussain (216 balls, 21 fours) and Smith (275 balls, eight fours) achieved this by adding 213 for the fifth wicket. Hussain, favouring the on-drive and pull, added 92 runs before lunch on the second day. The home side failed to avoid the follow-on but England's attack, with Bicknell absent from heat exhaustion, posed few threats in the final sessions. Unantenne reached his hundred in 148 minutes with his fifteenth boundary, a rocket-like flick to leg from an off-side ball.

England Young Cricketers

M. R. Ramprakash c Nadarajah b Perera	38	A. G. J. Fraser st Fernando b Perera	4
*M. A. Atherton c and b Perera	18	M. P. Bicknell not out	21
T. R. Ward c Nadarajah b Perera	67	B 5, l-b 9, n-b 1	15
M. W. Alleyne c Unantenne b Perera	13		
N. Hussain c Fernando b Perera	170	1/36 2/131 3/133 4/166 (7 wkts dec.)	451
O. C. K. Smith c and b Mendis	105	5/379 6/402 7/451	

†W. K. Hegg, H. R. J. Trump and L. Tennant did not bat.

Bowling: Madena 13-4-28-0; Weerakkody 13-4-35-0; Perera 53-8-162-6; Jayasinghe 28-13-55-0; Thenuwara 23-1-115-0; Mendis 10.5-1-42-1.

Sri Lanka Young Cricketers

R. Rajapakse b Atherton	39	c Alleyne b Tennant	16
A. Allirajah run out	0	b Atherton	53
D. Nadarajah b Trump	26	c Hussain b Trump	20
C. Unantenne c Atherton b Bicknell	15	not out	109
Chaminda Mendis c Hegg b Bicknell	96	lbw b Atherton	11
†N. V. Fernando c and b Bicknell	4	c Hegg b Fraser	0
R. N. Weerakkody c Hegg b Bicknell	11	st Hegg b Atherton	26
C. R. Thenuwara lbw b Tennant	22	not out	5
*D. R. Madena b Fraser	0		
D. C. M. Perera c Ward b Fraser	22		
S. K. Jayasinghe not out	8		
B 2, l-b 4, w 2, n-b 9	17	B 4, l-b 5, w 7, n-b 5	21

1/2 2/64 3/72 4/76 5/98 6/132	260	1/56 2/90 3/110 (6 wkts)	261
7/184 8/187 9/228		4/147 5/154 6/246	

Bowling: *First Innings*—Fraser 24-0-63-2; Tennant 22.5-65-1; Bicknell 27.2-11-37-4; Trump 28-14-49-1; Atherton 23-13-33-1; Alleyne 3-1-3-0; Ramprakash 1-0-4-0. *Second Innings*—Bicknell 4-2-4-0; Fraser 17-1-62-1; Tennant 10-3-40-1; Alleyne 3-1-5-0; Trump 31-5-73-1; Atherton 29-9-64-3; Hussain 1-0-4-0.

Umpires: B. C. Cooray and W. A. U. Wickremasinghe.

v Sri Lanka Young Cricketers (Second one-day international): at Singhalese Sports Club, Colombo, February 14. England Young Cricketers won by 88 runs. England Young Cricketers 229 for six (45 overs) (M. A. Atherton 48, T. R. Ward 41, N. Hussain 61 not out); Sri Lanka Young Cricketers 141 (39.1 overs) (M. W. Alleyne five for 31). *Match award*: N. Hussain.

v Sri Lanka Young Cricketers (Third one-day international): at Tyronne Fernando Stadium, Moratuwa, February 15. Sri Lanka Young Cricketers won by two wickets. England Young Cricketers 210 for seven (45 overs) (M. R. Ramprakash 61, M. A. Atherton 48); Sri Lanka Young Cricketers 212 for eight (44.2 overs) (U. C. Hathurusinghe 46, S. Ranatunga 52; M. A. Atherton four for 45). *Match award*: S. Ranatunga. *Player of the Series*: M. A. Atherton.

SRI LANKA YOUNG CRICKETERS v ENGLAND YOUNG CRICKETERS

Third "Test" Match

At Esplanade Ground, Galle, February 18, 19, 20, 21. Drawn. Toss: England. Moving south to a seaside ground in the shadow of a fort, England again amassed a substantial total but found it impossible to dismiss batsmen with sound front-foot techniques on a slow pitch of negligible bounce. Ward's absence through illness was scarcely noticed as Ramprakash (330 minutes, 273 balls, three sixes, nine fours) at last played the long innings that had eluded him;

and at the end of the England innings, Trump completed his half-century, scored in 34 minutes, by hitting 26 (446660) in one over from the Sri Lankan Test leg-spinner, Weerasinghe. Kaluwitharna, a diminutive seventeen-year-old wicket-keeper, dominated Sri Lanka's reply, reaching his hundred in 134 minutes and hitting two sixes and eighteen fours before the home side declared, 74 behind, on the final morning. Ramprakash hit seven sixes as he raced to his second hundred of the match and extended his tour aggregate to 587, average 58.70, in an unbroken stand of 208 in 220 minutes with his captain. Sri Lanka were set the token target of scoring 283 in two hours.

England Young Cricketers

M. R. Ramprakash b Chaminda Mendis	118	– not out	120
*M. A. Atherton c Unantenne b Weerasinghe	10	– not out	84
O. C. K. Smith c and b Chaminda Mendis	62		
M. W. Alleyne c Weerakkody b Perera	71		
N. Hussain c Kaluwitharna b Weerasinghe	37		
M. P. Speight c and b Weerasinghe	8		
M. P. Bicknell c Weerakkody b Perera	8		
A. G. J. Fraser st Kaluwitharna b Chaminda Mendis	23		
†W. K. Hegg b Chaminda Mendis	19		
H. R. J. Trump not out	50		
L. Tennant not out	8		
L-b 4, w 2	6	B 2, l-b 2	4

1/30 2/151 3/222 4/284 (9 wkts dec.) 420   (no wkt dec.) 208
5/312 6/312 7/325 8/359 9/366

Bowling: *First Innings*—Madena 9–2–33–0; Weerakkody 8–1–25–0; Weerasinghe 57–14–162–3; Hathurusinghe 2–0–9–0; Chaminda Mendis 30–8–68–4; Perera 45–13–98–2; Ranatunga 6–1–21–0. *Second Innings*—Madena 4–1–10–0; Weerakkody 4–0–11–0; Weerasinghe 22–6–73–0; Perera 20–6–38–0; Chaminda Mendis 9–0–38–0; Ranatunga 4–0–34–0.

Sri Lanka Young Cricketers

A. Allirajah c Hegg b Tennant	73		
U. C. Hathurusinghe c Trump b Bicknell	5	– (1) c Alleyne b Fraser	8
Chaminda Mendis c Hegg b Tennant	24		
C. Unantenne c Fraser b Atherton	11	– (3) not out	33
S. Ranatunga st Hegg b Atherton	37	– (4) not out	8
Chandima Mendis not out	53		
†R. Kaluwitharna c Atherton b Alleyne	119	– (2) c Speight b Fraser	10
R. N. Weerakkody not out	5		
B 7, l-b 3, w 7, n-b 2	19	L-b 2, w 2, n-b 1	5

1/17 2/47 3/71 4/140 (6 wkts dec.) 346   1/22 2/25 (2 wkts) 64
5/172 6/333

D. C. M. Perera, *D. R. Madena and C. D. U. S. Weerasinghe did not bat.

Bowling: *First Innings*—Bicknell 20–9–25–1; Fraser 20–2–62–0; Tennant 17–4–47–2; Trump 33–12–77–0; Atherton 24–5–61–2; Smith 8–1–28–0; Alleyne 12–3–36–1. *Second Innings*—Fraser 8–2–27–2; Tennant 7–3–20–0; Bicknell 6–3–7–0; Trump 5–2–8–0.

Umpires: B. C. Cooray and W. A. U. Wickremasinghe.

CRICKET IN AUSTRALIA, 1986-87

By JOHN MACKINNON

Western Australia regained the Sheffield Shield after three years in the most emphatic style. Their ability to win matches outright, which they did six times, gave them top place in the table by almost twenty points, and in the final they kept Victoria at bay almost nonchalantly.

For the 1986-87 season, yet another points system was devised "to introduce more positive, aggressive cricket"; and, predictably, it did no such thing. Six points were awarded for a win and two points for a first-innings lead, but the two points were forfeited in the event of the first-innings leader losing outright. However, captains were inevitably reluctant to risk losing their two points by making second-innings declarations. Ray Bright tried it in Sydney and Victoria lost. In addition, teams bowling fewer than 96 overs a day were penalised 0.1 of a point per over. New South Wales finished their match in Perth with a debit of minus 0.5, and it took them half the season to get out of the red. Nevertheless, the Australian Cricket Board did achieve something positive by enabling international players to be available for 21 of the 30 Shield matches, as well as for the final and the McDonald's Cup final.

Western Australia's superiority was most marked in their bowling, with the three left-arm fast-medium bowlers consistently effective. Bruce Reid established himself as the best bowler in the country, the burly Chris Matthews, although failing to keep his Test place, was one of the country's leading bowlers, and Peter Capes came through late in the season to play a decisive role in the final. Ken MacLeay was a model of steadiness and economy, and the recruitment of the Somerset off-spinner, Vic Marks, was a great success. His canny bowling gave the attack an ideal balance, and Brett Mulder, an emerging talent, should have benefited from Marks's presence. The batting was a blend of talented youth and experience, of right- and left-handed batsmen. Geoff Marsh scored more runs than anyone, while his opening partner, Mike Veletta, finished an excellent season sensationally, batting for more than two days in the final, indicating his ability both to concentrate and to eliminate error. Tom Moody, aged 21 and 6ft 8in tall, went in at No. 3, hit the ball tremendously hard, and, although benefiting from a successful opening partnership, looked an outstanding prospect. Graeme Wood and Wayne Andrews provided some left-handed dash in the middle order, and the batting gained further impetus from MacLeay, Marks and Tim Zoehrer. Zoehrer achieved some notoriety for his verbal antics, which ultimately brought him into conflict with the authorities, and his wicket-keeping, for all its periodic brilliance, was often undermined by lapses in concentration.

Victoria's improvement in recent years continued. They were worthy runners-up, without ever seriously threatening Western Australia's dominance; in the final, they were handicapped by the absence of Dean Jones and by injuries to three main bowlers, Simon O'Donnell, Simon Davis and Bright. Jones tasted success in international cricket, but his contribution to his Shield side was less significant. O'Donnell, who played many explosive innings, was quite their most consistent batsman. Jamie Siddons was a much improved player, and the veterans, Paul Hibbert and Dav Whatmore, provided invaluable experience. But the principal factor in Victoria's season was the fast bowling of Merv Hughes. He often presented a fearsome aspect and, even on placid pitches, was never less than wholehearted. The other bowlers were steady rather than penetrating, with Tony Dodemaide putting in some solid all-round performances. Bright, in his last season as captain, battled gamely against injury, and Paul Jackson looked to be his successor as Victoria's left-arm spinner.

South Australia finished the season strongly, as is their wont, but their two Shield wins were gained against sub-standard opposition and their success in the McDonald's Cup involved two victories against Tasmania and a fortuitous tie against Victoria. The most exciting development was in the medium-pace bowling of Andrew Zesers, who, just twenty at the end of the season, already showed remarkable control and maturity and had 100 first-class wickets to his name. Much was expected of Tim May, who at times looked a talented off-spinner; but there were times when his line was erratic. Peter Sleep bowled his leg-spinners steadily, but the faster bowling lacked a permanent presence. The batting was very much "as you were". Against Tasmania, David Hookes and Wayne Phillips, both left-handers, wrote their names in the record books with an unbroken partnership of 462, an Australian record for any wicket, which spectators and players alike will never forget. Phillips resumed as wicket-keeper, doing the job efficiently. Glenn Bishop played with his usual dash and earned fleeting selection for Australia's one-day squad, but the batting generally promised more than it achieved.

Queensland's fortunes slumped after a hat-trick of frustrating near misses. The most positive aspect of their season was the return to form of Craig McDermott, who regained his confidence and, by the end of the season, was bowling as fast and hostilely as ever. The umpires voted him "Sheffield Shield Player of the Year". Dirk Tazelaar's left-arm medium pace was a useful foil, and if the rest of the bowling was only spasmodically effective, Michael Polzin, an energetic fast bowler, made a dramatic début against South Australia. Allan Border's modest form meant that the batting depended a great deal on the success of the openers, Robbie Kerr and Andrew Courtice, the latter passing 50 seven times without going on to a hundred. Glenn Trimble had a reasonable season, but Greg Ritchie's form fell away after a promising start. Although Brett Henschell's batting developed more than his bowling, Queensland badly needed a good slow bowler and the improvement of his batting was something of a double-edged bonus.

New South Wales had some early encouragement with a decisive win over the touring England side, but it was to be virtually their only joy. Belated victories over Tasmania and Victoria, the latter rather hollow, served only to camouflage their deficiencies. Without the traditional help from the Sydney wicket – the pitches there were terribly slow – their spinners faded from the scene. Of the faster bowlers, Geoff Lawson missed much of the season through injury, but on his return showed signs of recovering some form; Mike Whitney was the pick, and Dave Gilbert bowled well below his best. The batting often failed in the first innings and usually compiled the bigger scores while saving games rather than winning them. Dirk Wellham, a thinking captain, was one who made most of his runs in the second innings; Stephen Small and Mark Taylor, the left-handed openers, each enjoyed one big innings; and Mark O'Neill was occasionally brilliant but never dependable. To add to their problems, the fielding was often poor, unforgettably so on the blameless surface of the Adelaide Oval.

The redeeming feature of Tasmania's season was their reaching the McDonald's Cup final, following a surprise win over Western Australia in Perth. However, they were easy pickings for South Australia in the final. In their Sheffield Shield matches, they struggled for much of the season, the loss of their English import, Richard Ellison, being a critical blow. Ellison's bowling gave the attack substance, as did the raw fast bowling of Troy Cooley, and serious injuries to this pair not only weakened the side but revealed a lack of reserve talent. For David Boon, the captain, it was a tough year – dropped from the Test team, suspended for one match from the Tasmanian team, and finally dispossessed of the captaincy, which passed to Brian Davison, now settled in Tasmania. Roger Woolley, Glenn Hughes and Danny Buckingham had their moments, and Richard Soule, a stocky little wicket-keeper, continued to impress.

By the season's end, the hard-pressed Australian Cricket Board had as much concern as ever for its ailing domestic competition. Nor was the departure of Kerry Packer, who sold his television (Channel 9) and marketing (PBL) interests in January to Alan Bond for $A1,100 million, likely to alter the format of the Australian season much. PBL's initial contract with the ACB expires in 1989, but the negotiation of a new, five-year contract means that the public and the players will continue to experience or endure a heavy emphasis on one-day cricket until 1994. As a major source of revenue, the "World Series" competition is vital for the funding of the Sheffield Shield, and under the revised agreement between the ACB and PBL, the state Associations should see a greater share of funds being channelled into cricket.

With Australian cricket at a low ebb in 1986-87, the availability for Shield cricket in 1987-88 of players from the unofficial tours of South Africa was seen in many quarters as a welcome infusion of lost talent. But with these same players also, in theory, being available to play for Australia in 1988-89, the ACB might have some interesting talks in store with those pragmatic souls from the Caribbean and the Asian sub-continent.

FIRST-CLASS AVERAGES, 1986-87

BATTING

(Qualification: 500 runs)

	I	NO	R	HI	100s	Avge
M. R. J. Veletta (*WA*)	19	6	971	262	2	74.69
W. S. Andrews (*WA*)	12	2	571	124*	2	57.10
W. B. Phillips (*SA*)	18	2	882	213*	3	55.12
D. W. Hookes (*SA*)	16	1	811	306*	2	54.06
A. R. Border (*Qld*)	22	2	1,002	125	2	50.10
S. P. O'Donnell (*Vic*)	21	3	892	108	1	49.55
G. R. Marsh (*WA*)	26	1	1,200	146	4	48.00
B. A. Courtice (*Qld*)	17	0	774	94	0	45.52
A. B. Henschell (*Qld*)	17	3	635	130*	3	45.35
D. M. Wellham (*NSW*)	19	3	715	166	2	44.68

	I	NO	R	HI	100s	Avge
T. M. Moody (*WA*)	18	1	746	111	2	43.88
D. M. Jones (*Vic*)	21	1	872	184*	2	43.60
G. M. Wood (*WA*)	17	4	560	107	2	43.07
R. D. Woolley (*Tas*)	18	4	587	108*	1	41.92
M. D. O'Neill (*NSW*)	19	4	627	110	2	41.80
P. A. Hibbert (*Vic*)	19	0	786	129	2	41.36
S. M. Small (*NSW*)	20	1	781	184	1	41.10
M. A. Taylor (*NSW*)	20	1	765	186	1	40.26
J. D. Siddons (*Vic*)	22	2	801	108	2	40.05
R. B. Kerr (*Qld*)	17	0	676	140	1	39.76
G. A. Bishop (*SA*)	17	0	675	135	1	39.70
A. M. J. Hilditch (*SA*)	14	1	510	131	1	39.23
S. R. Waugh (*NSW*)	21	2	741	89	0	39.00
G. M. Ritchie (*Qld*)	22	2	767	141	1	38.35
G. A. Hughes (*Tas*)	19	1	688	96	0	38.22
A. I. C. Dodemaide (*Vic*)	20	6	535	81*	0	38.21
G. S. Trimble (*Qld*)	15	0	562	115	1	37.46
G. R. J. Matthews (*NSW*)	20	4	578	104	1	36.12
D. J. Buckingham (*Tas*)	18	2	572	150	1	35.75
D. F. Whatmore (*Vic*)	23	0	741	137	2	32.21
D. C. Boon (*Tas*)	26	0	821	172	3	31.57

Signifies not out.

BOWLING

(Qualification: 20 wickets)

	O	M	R	W	Avge
M. A. Polzin (*Qld*)	160	31	458	23	19.91
P. A. Capes (*WA*)	181	50	458	22	20.81
C. J. McDermott (*Qld*)	404.3	55	1,296	58	22.34
A. K. Zesers (*SA*)	499	161	1,108	47	23.57
B. A. Reid (*WA*)	546.5	127	1,443	57	25.31
C. D. Matthews (*WA*)	526.4	110	1,502	57	26.35
R. M. Ellison (*Tas*)	266.5	53	646	23	28.08
M. G. Hughes (*Vic*)	571.1	113	1,623	57	28.47
K. H. MacLeay (*NSW*)	484	154	1,064	36	29.55
M. R. Whitney (*NSW*)	221.1	35	726	24	30.25
S. R. Waugh (*NSW*)	258.3	49	772	25	30.88
R. J. Bright (*Vic*)	409.1	123	911	29	31.41
V. J. Marks (*WA*)	456.4	153	955	30	31.83
P. R. Sleep (*SA*)	383.4	106	961	30	32.03
A. I. C. Dodemaide (*Vic*)	372.5	77	1,039	32	32.46
T. B. A. May (*SA*)	519.5	118	1,424	43	33.11
D. Tazelaar (*Qld*)	370.5	61	1,181	33	35.78
S. P. O'Donnell (*Vic*)	307.3	70	886	24	36.91
D. R. Gilbert (*NSW*)	285.5	53	910	23	39.56
S. J. Milosz (*Tas*)	362	66	1,216	27	45.03
A. B. Henschell (*Qld*)	401	96	1,121	23	48.73

WICKET-KEEPING

T. J. Zoehrer (*WA*) 38 (37 ct, 1 st), M. G. D. Dimattina (*Vic*) 31 (29 ct, 2 st), P. W. Anderson (*Qld*) 26 (22 ct, 4 st), R. E. Soule (*Tas*) 23 (21 ct, 2 st), M. J. Cox (*WA*) 18 (17 ct, 1 st), G. C. Dyer (*NSW*) 17 (16 ct, 1 st), W. B. Phillips (*SA*) 16 (all ct).

SHEFFIELD SHIELD, 1986-87

	Played	Won	Lost	Drawn	1st Inns Pts	Pts	Penalty Pts Deducted	Total
Western Australia ...	10	6	0	4	4	40	0.4	39.6
Victoria	10	3	3	4	2	20	0	20
South Australia	10	2	3	5	6	18	0	18
Queensland	10	2	1	7	6	18	0.3	17.7
New South Wales ...	10	2	3	5	4	16	0.6	15.4
Tasmania	10	0	5	5	4	4	0	4

Outright win = 6 pts ; lead on first innings in a drawn game = 2 pts.

WESTERN AUSTRALIA v SOUTH AUSTRALIA

At Perth, October 23, 24, 25, 26. Western Australia won by eight wickets. Western Australia 6 pts. Toss: Western Australia. Wood put the South Australians in and the supremacy of his bowlers was never seriously threatened, in spite of a maiden century in five hours ten minutes by the 31-year-old Watson. Hookes promised much but fell to Marks in both innings, aiming to hit him out of the ground. Wood and Veletta batted superbly for Western Australia, Wood's century, his fourth in six matches, containing fourteen fours. Gladigau, South Australia's best bowler, showed a fine turn of speed.

South Australia

A. M. J. Hilditch run out	0	– lbw b Matthews	11
A. S. Watson c and b Marks	117	– c Veletta b MacLeay	18
W. B. Phillips c Marks b MacLeay	28	– lbw b Matthews	0
G. A. Bishop c MacLeay b Breman	35	– c Veletta b MacLeay	6
*D. W. Hookes b Marks	33	– c Breman b Marks	77
P. R. Sleep c Reid b Marks	7	– lbw b Marks	17
†D. J. Kelly lbw b Matthews	2	– b Marks	14
J. K. Pyke c MacLeay b Matthews	1	– b Reid	32
A. K. Zesers c Zoehrer b MacLeay	19	– c Zoehrer b Reid	20
T. B. A. May not out	3	– not out	2
P. W. Gladigau b MacLeay	0	– c Zoehrer b Reid	0
L-b 5, w 1, n-b 7	13	B 2, l-b 2, w 1, n-b 4	9

1/0 2/37 3/116 4/179 5/221   **258**   1/31 2/31 3/31 4/56 5/117   **206**
6/232 7/234 8/235 9/258   6/140 7/153 8/197 9/206

Bowling: *First Innings*—Matthews 24-7-72-2; Reid 26-7-67-0; MacLeay 20.3-7-32-3; Marks 18-4-37-3; Breman 11-1-38-1; Andrews 2-0-7-0. *Second Innings*—Matthews 15-6-36-2; Reid 26.1-5-68-3; MacLeay 21-8-35-2; Marks 23-7-57-3; Breman 3-0-6-0.

Western Australia

G. R. Marsh c Hookes b Pyke	16	– b Gladigau	6
M. R. J. Veletta c Bishop b Zesers	58	– not out	72
T. M. Moody b Gladigau	29	– c Kelly b Gladigau	27
*G. M. Wood c Watson b Pyke	107	– not out	26
W. S. Andrews c Phillips b May	4		
†T. J. Zoehrer lbw b Zesers	6		
K. H. MacLeay b May	50		
T. G. Breman b Gladigau	13		
V. J. Marks b Gladigau	24		
C. D. Matthews not out	6		
B. A. Reid b Pyke	1		
B 6, l-b 7, w 1	14	B 1, l-b 7	8

1/26 2/84 3/139 4/144 5/157   **328**   1/24 2/82   (2 wkts) **139**
6/246 7/284 8/317 9/321

Bowling: *First Innings*—Gladigau 26–7–77–3; Pyke 19.3–5–66–3; Zesers 33–11–85–2; May 28–10–87–2. *Second Innings*—Gladigau 10–2–31–2; Pyke 5–1–18–0; Zesers 9–2–28–0; May 10–1–26–0; Sleep 7–1–24–0; Phillips 0.5–0–4–0.

Umpires: R. J. Evans and P. J. McConnell.

TASMANIA v VICTORIA

At Devonport, October 24, 25, 26, 27. Drawn. Victoria 2 pts. Toss: Victoria. With the first day lost to rain, Victoria made a spirited effort to gain outright points. Hughes, bowling fast, had all the Tasmanian batsmen in trouble and only Buckingham showed any enterprise. Jones was in fine form for Victoria, batting for four hours after Quinn had his hand broken by a rising ball from Brown. When Bright declared at lunch on the final day, Hughes again made early inroads, but a determined innings by Glenn Hughes, the former Australian captain's brother, making his Shield début, kept Victoria's bowlers at bay. Darren Close, at eighteen, became the youngest umpire to stand in an Australian first-class match.

Tasmania

E. J. Harris c Hibbert b Hughes	1	– (2) c Hibbert b Hughes	2
*D. C. Boon c Jones b Hughes	49	– (1) c Siddons b Hughes	0
K. Bradshaw c Dimattina b O'Donnell	40	– c Whatmore b Dodemaide	4
D. J. Buckingham c Dodemaide b Hughes	70	– (5) c Jones b Bright	11
R. D. Woolley c Whatmore b Hughes	7	– (6) not out	44
G. A. Hughes c Bright b Dodemaide	14	– (4) c Siddons b Dodemaide	52
†R. E. Soule c Hibbert b Hughes	14	– run out	6
R. M. Ellison not out	29	– not out	5
A. J. de Winter c Dimattina b Davis	2		
R. L. Brown c Hughes b O'Donnell	9		
S. J. Milosz b O'Donnell	1		
L-b 7	7	L-b 1, n-b 2	3
	243	(6 wkts)	127

1/4 2/70 3/115 4/133 5/179   1/0 2/6 3/36
6/188 7/209 8/216 9/239   4/94 5/112 6/118

Bowling: *First Innings*—Hughes 32–10–73–5; Davis 25–8–51–1; O'Donnell 22.1–9–37–3; Dodemaide 15–5–33–1; Bright 18–6–30–0; Jones 3–0–12–0. *Second Innings*—Hughes 15–4–20–2; Davis 6–3–11–0; O'Donnell 7–1–18–0; Dodemaide 11–2–23–2; Bright 19–4–48–1; Jones 2–0–6–0.

Victoria

M. B. Quinn retired hurt	1	S. P. O'Donnell not out	52
D. F. Whatmore b Milosz	33		
D. M. Jones c Soule b Ellison	111	L-b 5, n-b 6	11
P. A. Hibbert lbw b Ellison	43		
J. D. Siddons not out	76	1/100 2/179 3/201 (3 wkts dec.)	327

A. I. C. Dodemaide, †M. G. D. Dimattina, *R. J. Bright, M. G. Hughes and S. P. Davis did not bat.

M. B. Quinn retired hurt at 2.

Bowling: Ellison 32–6–80–2; Brown 27–3–96–0; Milosz 27–4–82–1; de Winter 14–2–49–0; Bradshaw 5–0–15–0.

Umpires: D. R. Close and S. G. Randell.

WESTERN AUSTRALIA v NEW SOUTH WALES

At Perth, October 29, 30, 31, November 1. Drawn. Western Australia 2 pts, New South Wales −0.5 pts. Toss: Western Australia. Western Australia's batting improved the longer their innings progressed, and by tea on the second day, MacLeay and Marks with an unbroken 168 had set a ninth-wicket record for the state in just two hours. MacLeay's hundred, his second in first-class cricket, took less than three hours and included two huge sixes off Matthews and ten fours. Zoehrer, having gone in at 122 for five, did much to set up the big Western Australian total, batting for 207 minutes and hitting a six and ten fours. The New South Wales batting foundered against the lively left-arm fast bowling of Matthews. Although Taylor held out for nearly seven hours, no-one else showed the same resolution until, following on, New South Wales batted comfortably through the last day.

Western Australia

G. R. Marsh c Waugh b Gilbert	5	C. D. Matthews c Wellham b Matthews	37	
M. R. J. Veletta c Dyer b Gilbert	1	K. H. MacLeay not out	114	
T. M. Moody c Waugh b Gilbert	57	V. J. Marks not out	66	
*G. M. Wood c Dyer b Lawson	13	B 1, l-b 30, n-b 10	41	
P. Gonnella c Taylor b Matthews	22			
W. S. Andrews b Bennett	67	1/5 2/15 3/65 4/109	(8 wkts dec.) 514	
†T. J. Zoehrer lbw b Whitney	91	5/122 6/245 7/314 8/346		

B. A. Reid did not bat.

Bowling: Gilbert 24–3–89–3; Lawson 29–6–70–1; Whitney 25–3–95–1; Bennett 17–5–43–1; Matthews 31–7–100–2; Waugh 18–3–51–0; O'Neill 5–0–35–0.

New South Wales

S. M. Small b Reid	16	– b Moody	76	
M. A. Taylor c Veletta b Reid	98	– lbw b MacLeay	0	
*D. M. Wellham b Matthews	12	– retired hurt	41	
G. R. J. Matthews c Zoehrer b Matthews	11	– c Moody b Matthews	29	
M. D. O'Neill lbw b Matthews	6	– not out	27	
S. R. Waugh c Zoehrer b Matthews	37	– c sub b Moody	0	
†G. C. Dyer c Zoehrer b MacLeay	6	– not out	7	
M. J. Bennett lbw b Reid	16			
D. R. Gilbert c Marsh b Matthews	22			
G. F. Lawson not out	36			
M. R. Whitney c Wood b Matthews	1			
L-b 5, n-b 10	15	B 6, l-b 10, w 4, n-b 3	23	

1/24 2/68 3/92 4/100 5/167	276	1/9 2/134 3/193 4/193 (4 wkts) 203
6/185 7/215 8/216 9/263		

Bowling: *First Innings*—Matthews 31.2–9–75–6; MacLeay 28–12–39–1; Reid 38–11–78–3; Marks 31–8–79–0. *Second Innings*—Matthews 17–4–36–1; MacLeay 20–6–50–1; Reid 14–6–18–0; Marks 26–10–61–0; Andrews 6–2–13–0; Moody 5–2–9–2.

Umpires: P. J. McConnell and T. A. Prue.

QUEENSLAND v TASMANIA

At Brisbane, October 31, November 1, 2, 3. Drawn. Tasmania 2 pts. Toss: Queensland. Put in, Tasmania made their highest score in the Sheffield Shield. Boon dominated an opening stand of 195, hitting nineteen fours in an innings lasting three hours, and while Harris could never match his partner's aggression, he batted solidly for five hours. Their bowlers having struggled on such a perfect wicket, Queensland's batsmen flourished, Trimble making 115 of his 163-run partnership with Kerr in two and threequarter hours and hitting one six and twenty fours. Ellison dismissed them both in six balls, and with the leg-spinner, Milosz, bowling steadily, Tasmania achieved first-innings points after lunch on the final day.

Tasmania

E. J. Harris c Trimble b Hill	108	– (2) c Kerr b Henschell	32	
*D. C. Boon b Henschell	117	– (1) c Ritchie b Tazelaar	19	
K. Bradshaw c Border b McDermott	45	– not out	21	
G. A. Hughes b McDermott	28	– c Anderson b Hill	1	
D. J. Buckingham c Anderson b Henschell	41	– c Anderson b Hill	0	

R. D. Woolley c Border b Hill	41	– (7) not out 35
†R. E. Soule lbw b Hill	14	
R. M. Ellison c Anderson b McDermott	54	
A. J. de Winter lbw b Henschell	1	– (6) c and b Hill 11
R. L. Brown b McDermott	30	
S. J. Milosz not out	0	
B 2, l-b 16, n-b 29	47	B 4, l-b 3, n-b 7 14

1/195 2/285 3/311 4/334 5/405	526	1/49 2/66 3/67 (5 wkts) 133
6/428 7/461 8/465 9/525		4/67 5/81

Bowling: *First Innings*—McDermott 31.1-2-125-4; Frei 20-3-75-0; Tazelaar 31-1-110-0; Henschell 46-6-112-3; Hill 31-11-80-3; Border 4-1-6-0. *Second Innings*—McDermott 5-1-18-0; Frei 8-0-20-0; Tazelaar 8-1-22-1; Henschell 22-11-24-1; Hill 15-11-16-3; Ritchie 5-1-26-0.

Queensland

R. B. Kerr c de Winter b Ellison	88	C. J. McDermott c Harris b Milosz ... 21
B. A. Courtice c Soule b Milosz	38	D. Tazelaar lbw b Milosz 19
G. S. Trimble c Woolley b Ellison	115	H. Frei not out 18
*A. R. Border c Soule b de Winter	47	
G. M. Ritchie c Boon b de Winter	30	B 7, l-b 9, w 2, n-b 14 32
A. B. Henschell c Soule b Milosz	10	
J. G. Hill c Hughes b Milosz	30	1/95 2/258 3/260 4/327 5/350 484
†P. W. Anderson c Bradshaw b Milosz	36	6/358 7/413 8/441 9/446

Bowling: Ellison 38-7-101-2; Brown 28-2-100-0; Milosz 49.5-9-153-6; de Winter 24-3-79-2; Hughes 6-1-13-0; Bradshaw 4-0-21-0; Boon 3-2-1-0.

Umpires: M. W. Johnson and P. D. Parker.

VICTORIA v NEW SOUTH WALES

At Melbourne, November 5, 6, 7, 8. Victoria won by four wickets. Victoria 6 pts. Toss: New South Wales. On an uneven pitch at St Kilda, Victoria's pace bowlers, Hughes and Dodemaide, reduced batting to a battle for survival. In their turn, the Victorians also struggled until O'Donnell, dropped by Bennett when 67, hit a sparkling hundred in three hours (two sixes, eight fours). A more determined effort in New South Wales' second innings left Victoria to score 126 for victory in 31 overs, and that they achieved their target with only three balls to spare was due to keen bowling and fielding from the defending holders.

New South Wales

S. M. Small c Dimattina b O'Donnell	17	– c Whatmore b Bright 54
M. A. Taylor c Dimattina b Davis	2	– run out 27
*D. M. Wellham c Dimattina b Dodemaide	19	– b Davis 14
G. R. J. Matthews c Whatmore b Hughes	37	– c Dodemaide b Bright 20
M. D. O'Neill c Bright b Hughes	1	– c Dimattina b Davis 36
S. R. Waugh b Hughes	6	– b Davis 59
†G. C. Dyer c Whatmore b Dodemaide	0	– c Frazer b Hughes 33
M. J. Bennett c O'Donnell b Dodemaide	18	– c Hughes b Bright 44
D. R. Gilbert c and b Bright	10	– b Jones 8
G. F. Lawson c Dodemaide b Bright	10	– b Hughes 1
R. G. Holland not out	0	– not out 3
L-b 5	5	B 4, l-b 5, w 1, n-b 6 16

1/14 2/22 3/62 4/69 5/81	125	1/67 2/95 3/111 4/130 5/184 315
6/86 7/86 8/113 9/125		6/250 7/267 8/300 9/301

Bowling: *First Innings*—Hughes 18-5-25-3; Davis 22-11-26-1; O'Donnell 7-4-9-1; Dodemaide 18-2-46-3; Bright 10.2-4-10-2; Jones 2-0-4-0. *Second Innings*—Hughes 38-5-89-2; Davis 44-11-66-3; Dodemaide 28-3-74-0; Bright 43.2-12-62-3; Jones 6-1-15-1.

Victoria

D. F. Whatmore b Gilbert	20	– (2) c Waugh b Gilbert	17
I. D. Frazer c Small b Matthews	45	– (1) run out	19
D. M. Jones b Gilbert	0	– c Holland b Waugh	30
†M. G. D. Dimattina c Small b Waugh	5	– (7) not out	1
P. A. Hibbert c Wellham b Matthews	35		
J. D. Siddons c Dyer b Gilbert	46	– (4) run out	9
S. P. O'Donnell lbw b Lawson	108	– (5) b Waugh	21
A. I. C. Dodemaide c O'Neill b Lawson	1	– (6) c Holland b Matthews	22
*R. J. Bright lbw b Gilbert	12	– (8) not out	1
M. G. Hughes b Lawson	20		
S. P. Davis not out	15		
L-b 3, n-b 5	8	B 2, l-b 4	6

1/27 2/27 3/41 4/108 5/111   315   1/26 2/59 3/77   (6 wkts) 126
6/223 7/234 8/279 9/279   4/78 5/122 6/122

Bowling: First Innings—Gilbert 33-4-103-4; Lawson 28-5-74-3; Waugh 19-5-42-1; Matthews 15-3-23-2; Bennett 14-2-38-0; Holland 13-4-32-0. *Second Innings*—Gilbert 7-1-27-1; Lawson 7-0-28-0; Waugh 8.3-0-39-2; Matthews 8-1-26-1.

Umpires: R. C. Bailhache and R. Guy.

SOUTH AUSTRALIA v QUEENSLAND

At Adelaide, November 7, 8, 9, 10. Drawn. South Australia 2 pts. Toss: Queensland. After controlling the match for the first three days, South Australia were hard pressed to avoid defeat. Queensland struggled in their first innings against the leg-spin of Sleep and the off-spin of May, only a partnership of 129 in two hours between Kerr and Border providing them with a respectable score. Bishop gave South Australia a flying start, but going for his hundred he drove rashly at Henschell after two and a half hours' batting. Phillips continued his good form and Sleep ensured a big first-innings lead with a patient century. Queensland began the final day with a deficit of 17 and only five wickets left, but Henschell took charge with a fine hundred in three and a quarter hours and South Australia faced a winning target of 200 in 41 overs. Hookes, opening, was promptly caught off his second ball, Phillips led a brief flurry, and when Sleep was out, South Australia were 88 for four. Survival became the priority.

Queensland

B. A. Courtice c Kelly b Parkinson	5	– (2) b May	64
R. B. Kerr c Hookes b Zesers	76	– (1) c Phillips b Zesers	1
G. S. Trimble c Kelly b Zesers	4	– lbw b Gladigau	49
*A. R. Border c Gladigau b May	77	– c Watson b Zesers	23
G. M. Ritchie c Kelly b Sleep	26	– c sub b Sleep	8
A. B. Henschell c May b Sleep	9	– (7) st Kelly b Sleep	111
†P. W. Anderson lbw b May	3	– (8) c Gladigau b May	24
C. J. McDermott c and b May	17	– (9) c Watson b May	29
J. G. Hill c Parkinson b Sleep	16	– (6) c Wundke b May	19
D. Tazelaar c Wundke b Sleep	6	– not out	6
H. Frei not out	0	– b Sleep	12
B 3, l-b 4, n-b 3	10	B 7, l-b 12, w 4, n-b 1	24

1/12 2/29 3/158 4/179 5/191   249   1/16 2/118 3/132 4/150 5/154   370
6/200 7/220 8/240 9/243   6/231 7/296 8/338 9/356

Bowling: First Innings—Gladigau 13-5-29-0; Parkinson 11-3-53-1; Zesers 19-4-55-2; May 25-5-57-3; Sleep 18.4-5-48-4. *Second Innings*—Gladigau 17-5-46-1; Parkinson 10-0-34-0; Zesers 30-15-41-2; May 42-5-146-4; Sleep 26-7-84-3.

South Australia

G. A. Bishop c Ritchie b Henschell	99	– c Anderson b Frei	12
A. S. Watson lbw b McDermott	9	– (7) c Border b Hill	8
W. B. Phillips c Henschell b Tazelaar	81	– b Tazelaar	38
*D. W. Hookes lbw b McDermott	20	– (2) c Kerr b Frei	0
P. R. Sleep lbw b McDermott	103	– (4) c Trimble b Tazelaar	26
S. C. Wundke lbw b Frei	36	– (5) c Courtice b Henschell	19
†D. J. Kelly c and b McDermott	43	– (6) st Anderson b Hill	6
S. D. H. Parkinson st Anderson b Border	1		
P. W. Gladigau not out	0		
T. B. A. May (did not bat)		– (8) not out	3
A. K. Zesers (did not bat)		– (9) not out	0
L-b 5, n-b 23	28	B 2, l-b 7, n-b 3	12

1/41 2/145 3/171 4/241 5/314 (8 wkts dec.) 420   1/2 2/22 3/81 4/88 (7 wkts) 124
6/419 7/420 8/420   5/108 6/116 7/124

Bowling: *First Innings*—McDermott 34-4-100-4; Frei 22-7-88-1; Tazelaar 30-5-84-1; Henschell 29-5-91-1; Hill 19-9-44-0; Courtice 2-0-8-0; Border 1.4-1-0-1. *Second Innings*—McDermott 9-0-43-0; Frei 5-0-33-2; Tazelaar 7-3-16-2; Henschell 8-3-14-1; Hill 12-7-9-2.

Umpires: B. E. Martin and R. B. Woods.

TASMANIA v WESTERN AUSTRALIA

At Devonport, November 21, 22, 23, 24. Western Australia won by ten wickets. Western Australia 6 pts. Toss: Tasmania. Victory was achieved before tea on the fourth day. Tasmania's batsmen were never able to cope with Western Australia's bowlers, Reid especially extracting bounce and movement from an excellent pitch. Only Woolley offered prolonged resistance, batting for almost three and a quarter hours. Western Australia's batsmen, however, revelled in the conditions, with Moody, batting brilliantly for three and a quarter hours, hitting twelve fours and dominating stands with Zoehrer and Andrews. For Tasmania, Brown bowled steadily but had little support from his colleagues.

Tasmania

E. J. Harris c and b Reid	15	– (2) c Zoehrer b Reid	16
*D. C. Boon c Andrews b Matthews	10	– (1) c Zoehrer b Matthews	2
K. Bradshaw c Marks b Reid	27	– c Zoehrer b Reid	9
G. A. Hughes c MacLeay b Reid	22	– c Marks b Reid	68
D. J. Buckingham c MacLeay b Matthews	11	– lbw b MacLeay	17
R. D. Woolley c Andrews b MacLeay	79	– b Marks	14
†R. E. Soule c Veletta b Mulder	8	– lbw b Mulder	30
R. M. Ellison st Zoehrer b Marks	42	– c Veletta b Mulder	10
A. J. de Winter c Marsh b Reid	35	– not out	25
R. L. Brown b MacLeay	0	– b Marks	2
S. J. Milosz not out	2	– c Veletta b MacLeay	1
L-b 5, n-b 8	13	L-b 8, n-b 11	19

1/12 2/44 3/80 4/84 5/101 264   1/14 2/31 3/60 4/125 5/125 213
6/132 7/216 8/238 9/238   6/153 7/180 8/187 9/200

Bowling: *First Innings*—Matthews 24-4-66-2; MacLeay 29-6-65-2; Reid 21.4-6-49-4; Marks 13-4-24-1; Mulder 14-5-39-1; Moody 5-1-16-0. *Second Innings*—Matthews 18-3-43-1; MacLeay 20.2-8-41-2; Reid 27-6-66-4; Marks 22-8-37-1; Mulder 4-0-18-2.

Western Australia

M. R. J. Veletta b Brown	21	– (2) not out	22
G. R. Marsh c Soule b Brown	48	– (1) not out	17
T. M. Moody st Soule b Milosz	111		
†T. J. Zoehrer c Soule b Brown	39		

W. S. Andrews c Ellison b Brown 64
K. H. MacLeay c Soule b Brown 27
*G. M. Wood c Soule b Ellison 5
V. J. Marks c Bradshaw b Ellison 45
C. D. Matthews b Boon 42
B. Mulder not out 12
B. A. Reid run out 5
    B 7, l-b 1, n-b 3 11   W 10, n-b 1 11

1/69 2/74 3/172 4/255 5/317   430   (no wkt) 50
6/326 7/326 8/407 9/415

Bowling: *First Innings*—Ellison 33–5–92–2; Brown 32–3–114–5; de Winter 14–2–62–0; Milosz 34–6–124–1; Hughes 4–0–12–0; Boon 6.2–1–18–1. *Second Innings*—Ellison 4–1–7–0; Brown 2–1–4–0; de Winter 5–1–34–0; Boon 0.5–0–5–0.

Umpires: B. Elliott and S. G. Randell.

VICTORIA v QUEENSLAND

At Wangaratta, November 21, 22, 23, 24. Drawn. Queensland 2 pts. Toss: Queensland. Border won the toss for the ninth consecutive time and his batsmen took heavy toll of a Victorian attack that was deprived of Bright's services when he fell heavily and injured his back. Ritchie dominated Queensland's innings, hitting fifteen fours and not giving a chance in a stay of four hours. The Victorian batsmen never came to terms with the pace of McDermott, only Siddons and Dodemaide threatening his domination. Dodemaide continued his good form when opening after Victoria followed on, and on a placid pitch the home side batted without difficulty through the final day. Whatmore was in for 219 minutes for his highest score. The MCG was unavailable owing to the ravages of the football season and the Wangaratta people turned out in good numbers to watch the match.

Queensland

R. B. Kerr c Hibbert b Hughes 4	J. G. Hill lbw b O'Donnell 10
B. A. Courtice b Jones 72	D. Tazelaar not out 18
G. M. Ritchie b Hughes 141	H. Frei c O'Donnell b Dodemaide 14
G. S. Trimble b O'Donnell 27	
*A. R. Border c Jones b Davis 67	B 1, l-b 13, w 5, n-b 5 24
A. B. Henschell b Dodemaide 93	
†P. W. Anderson c Dimattina b Davis . 42	1/4 2/188 3/243 4/259 5/346 523
C. J. McDermott run out 11	6/441 7/463 8/487 9/499

Bowling: Hughes 29–3–106–2; Davis 31–7–73–2; Dodemaide 26.3–4–91–2; O'Donnell 34–5–109–2; Bright 1.5–0–11–0; Jones 30.1–1–119–1.

Victoria

D. F. Whatmore b McDermott	13	– (2) c Anderson b Ritchie 137
I. D. Frazer c Border b McDermott	13	
D. M. Jones lbw b McDermott	20	– st Anderson b Hill 57
P. A. Hibbert run out	50	
†M. G. D. Dimattina c Border b Henschell	0	– not out 16
J. D. Siddons c Frei b McDermott	108	
S. P. O'Donnell c Border b Tazelaar	6	– (4) lbw b Courtice 50
A. I. C. Dodemaide not out	71	– (1) run out 47
*R. J. Bright lbw b McDermott	0	
M. G. Hughes b Tazelaar	25	– (6) not out 12
S. P. Davis c Henschell b McDermott	3	
B 1, l-b 5, n-b 19	25	B 8, l-b 12, w 1, n-b 6 27

1/38 2/62 3/63 4/146 5/164   334   1/110 2/240 3/274   (4 wkts) 346
6/188 7/250 8/254 9/312   4/334

In the first innings I. D. Frazer retired hurt at 14, and resumed at 146.

Bowling: *First Innings*—McDermott 36.1–4–89–6; Frei 17–5–55–0; Tazelaar 28–2–97–2; Henschell 28–5–73–1; Hill 4–0–14–0. *Second Innings*—McDermott 17–4–54–0; Frei 15–2–41–0; Tazelaar 15–3–43–0; Henschell 5–1–32–0; Hill 27–4–86–1; Courtice 16–4–42–1; Ritchie 6–2–10–1; Trimble 5–0–18–0.

Umpires: R. Guy and L. J. King.

QUEENSLAND v WESTERN AUSTRALIA

At Brisbane, November 28, 29, 30, December 1. Drawn. Toss: Western Australia. Rain restricted play on the first two days and prevented any on the last two. The medium-pacers, Capes and MacLeay, made good use of a helpful pitch, but Courtice batted stubbornly for four hours.

Queensland

B. A. Courtice c Wood b MacLeay	73	C. J. McDermott c Cox b Marks		0
*R. B. Kerr c Wood b MacLeay	17	J. G. Hill not out		0
T. J. Barsby c MacLeay b Capes	15			
G. S. Trimble b Capes	9	L-b 7, n-b 2		9
P. S. Clifford c Cox b Capes	24			
A. B. Henschell c Cox b MacLeay	9	1/37 2/60 3/82 4/121	(7 wkts)	162
†P. W. Anderson not out	6	5/154 6/159 7/160		

D. Tazelaar and H. Frei did not bat.

Bowling: Capes 26–9–38–3; MacLeay 29.1–12–55–3; Breman 22–3–55–0; Marks 4–0–7–1.

Western Australia

T. M. Moody, M. R. J. Veletta, M. W. McPhee, *G. M. Wood, W. S. Andrews, K. H. MacLeay, T. G. Breman, V. J. Marks, †M. J. Cox, P. A. Capes and B. Mulder.

Umpires: M. W. Johnson and P. D. Parker.

SOUTH AUSTRALIA v VICTORIA

At Adelaide, November 28, 29, 30, December 1. Victoria won by 117 runs. Victoria 6 pts. Toss: Victoria. Victoria's batsmen were well tested in the first innings by May's accurate off-spin, but Dodemaide established control in a last-wicket stand of 74 with Davis. Apart from Bishop, the South Australians were tied down by the Victorian bowling; but the opener was at his dashing best and was unfortunate to miss his century after two and a half hours' batting. In Victoria's second innings Hibbert hit a hundred in 192 minutes, and when Bright declared ahead of stumps on the third evening, he was rewarded with the valuable wicket of Bishop. On the last day, the pace of Hughes and the spin of Bright prevailed, but Hughes's success was tempered by a $A200 suspended fine for use of "crude language".

Victoria

D. F. Whatmore c and b May	82	(2) b Pyke	19
I. D. Frazer c Hookes b Schenscher	20	(1) b Zesers	57
P. A. Hibbert b May	48	c Wundke b May	101
G. L. Jordan c Phillips b May	7	b Zesers	25
J. D. Siddons c Bishop b Pyke	52	c Schenscher b Zesers	13
S. P. O'Donnell c Hookes b Schenscher	43	not out	0
A. I. C. Dodemaide c Schenscher b May	79		
†M. G. D. Dimattina c Pyke b May	4		
*R. J. Bright b Zesers	0		
M. G. Hughes c Kelly b Zesers	6		
S. P. Davis not out	6		
B 7, l-b 8, w 1, n-b 3	19	B 5, l-b 2, n-b 1	8

1/84 2/128 3/138 4/201 5/227   366   1/23 2/156 3/202   (5 wkts dec.) 223
6/275 7/282 8/282 9/292   4/222 5/223

Bowling: *First Innings*—Gladigau 18-2-68-0; Hookes 3-2-3-0; Zesers 24-5-68-2; Pyke 21-3-81-1; Wundke 5-0-16-0; May 45.5-16-88-5; Schenscher 9-0-27-2. *Second Innings*—Gladigau 8-3-19-0; Zesers 12.2-2-46-3; Pyke 8-2-19-1; May 26-4-101-1; Schenscher 9-0-31-0.

South Australia

G. A. Bishop b Hughes	93	– c Dimattina b O'Donnell	5
A. S. Watson c Hibbert b Hughes	1	– lbw b Dodemaide	48
W. B. Phillips c Jordan b Bright	35	– (4) c Hibbert b Bright	20
*D. W. Hookes b Bright	6	– (5) b Hughes	54
S. C. Wundke run out	10	– (6) c Dimattina b Bright	1
J. K. Pyke c Jordan b O'Donnell	32	– (7) c Dimattina b Hughes	27
†D. J. Kelly c O'Donnell b Davis	13	– (3) b Bright	17
A. K. Zesers c Jordan b Bright	13	– b Hughes	27
T. B. A. May c Jordan b Davis	9	– b Davis	3
P. M. Schenscher c Hibbert b Bright	8	– lbw b Hughes	15
P. W. Gladigau not out	10	– not out	7
L-b 1, n-b 2	3	B 4, l-b 9, n-b 2	15

1/4 2/83 3/133 4/139 5/161   233   1/9 2/60 3/88 4/94 5/103   239
6/187 7/206 8/214 9/215   6/172 7/185 8/190 9/214

Bowling: *First Innings*—Hughes 18-3-58-2; Davis 14-4-47-2; Dodemaide 10-5-21-0; O'Donnell 19-7-44-1; Bright 43.2-23-62-4; Whatmore 1-1-0-0. *Second Innings*—Hughes 24-3-69-4; Davis 10-2-27-1; Dodemaide 17-5-44-1; O'Donnell 13-3-34-1; Bright 30-13-50-3; Whatmore 1-0-2-0.

Umpires: A. R. Crafter and M. G. O'Connell.

QUEENSLAND v NEW SOUTH WALES

At Brisbane, December 5, 6, 7, 8. Queensland won by three wickets. Queensland 6 pts, New South Wales −0.1 pt. Toss: Queensland. Both captains deserved credit for an enterprising approach which led to a win for Queensland in the second-last over of the match. After a pedestrian first day (Queensland 251 for three), Border led an aggressive assault and declared on the second day at lunch. McDermott, producing his best form on a benign pitch, and Tazelaar forced New South Wales to follow on, whereupon they gave a more determined display. Wellham (nineteen fours) and O'Neill (fifteen fours) became so dominant that on the fourth morning New South Wales scored 191 in the two-hour session. When he reached his highest first-class score, Wellham declared, leaving Queensland 68 overs in which to score 289 for victory. Courtice and Kerr made a splendid start, and while Ritchie and Border were adding 111 in 86 minutes, a Queensland win seemed a formality. However, four wickets fell for 11 before Henschell and Anderson, with sensible batting, ensured victory.

Queensland

R. B. Kerr c Matthews b Waugh	82	– (2) c and b Matthews	22
B. A. Courtice c O'Neill b Matthews	94	– (1) c Dyer b Holland	63
T. J. Barsby c and b Gilbert	15	– (6) lbw b Waugh	2
P. S. Clifford c Gilbert b Whitney	60	– (5) c Bayliss b Whitney	7
G. M. Ritchie b Whitney	37	– (3) c Holland b Waugh	52
*A. R. Border b Waugh	49	– (4) run out	72
A. B. Henschell run out	21	– not out	26
†P. W. Anderson c O'Neill b Waugh	0	– c Waugh b Whitney	31
C. J. McDermott not out	20	– not out	5
B 3, l-b 8, w 1, n-b 22	34	B 5, l-b 4, n-b 1	10

1/177 2/199 3/224 4/308 5/322   (8 wkts dec.) 412   1/57 2/99 3/210 4/210   (7 wkts) 290
6/390 7/390 8/412   5/219 6/221 7/285

D. Tazelaar and H. Frei did not bat.

Bowling: *First Innings*—Gilbert 26-3-102-1; Whitney 29-3-117-2; Waugh 20.3-7-33-3; Holland 16-8-41-0; Matthews 31-7-108-1. *Second Innings*—Gilbert 13-3-38-0; Whitney 16.1-0-60-2; Waugh 13-0-60-2; Holland 13-0-76-1; Matthews 11-0-47-1.

New South Wales

S. M. Small c Clifford b McDermott	79	– c and b McDermott	50
M. A. Taylor lbw b Tazelaar	19	– lbw b Border	58
*D. M. Wellham c and b Tazelaar	24	– c Clifford b Border	166
M. D. O'Neill c Clifford b Border	2	– c Clifford b McDermott	110
G. R. J. Matthews c Tazelaar b McDermott	30	– c Clifford b Frei	9
†G. C. Dyer c Anderson b Tazelaar	3		
S. R. Waugh c Anderson b McDermott	1	– (6) not out	41
T. H. Bayliss not out	28	– (7) not out	11
D. R. Gilbert c Anderson b Tazelaar	9		
R. G. Holland lbw b McDermott	12		
M. R. Whitney b McDermott	0		
B 6, l-b 1, w 1, n-b 20	28	B 1, l-b 8, n-b 11	20

1/71 2/119 3/145 4/175 5/175   235   1/119 2/119 3/359   (5 wkts dec.) 465
6/181 7/183 8/197 9/229   4/387 5/444

Bowling: *First Innings*—McDermott 23.5-2-72-5; Frei 5-0-19-0; Courtice 5-1-12-0; Tazelaar 21-3-74-4; Henschell 22-9-46-0; Border 2-1-5-1. *Second Innings*—McDermott 23-1-96-2; Frei 21-2-92-1; Courtice 8-1-37-0; Tazelaar 15-0-62-0; Henschell 26-2-111-0; Border 20-7-58-2.

Umpires: M. W. Johnson and C. D. Timmins.

TASMANIA v SOUTH AUSTRALIA

At Launceston, December 5, 6, 7, 8. Drawn. Tasmania 2 pts. Toss: South Australia. The Tasmanians showed their best form for years and were unlucky when rain cut short the third day and washed out the fourth. Put in, they were soon in trouble as their batting collapsed on a lively pitch. But Boon, who had retired hurt from a blow on the chin, returned at the fall of the fifth wicket and began a recovery that ended abruptly when May took the last three wickets at no cost. South Australia's batsmen fared even worse and had no answer to the lively pace of the 20-year-old Cooley and the controlled swing of Ellison. Soule set a record for Tasmania in Shield cricket with six dismissals. When Tasmania batted again, Hughes played his second innings of high quality and made light of the allegedly sub-standard pitch.

Tasmania

E. J. Harris c Birchall b Gladigau	9	– (2) b Pyke	0
*D. C. Boon run out	46	– (1) c May b Gladigau	0
K. Bradshaw c May b Pyke	3	– not out	13
G. A. Hughes c Wundke b Gladigau	48	– not out	66
D. J. Buckingham c Hookes b Zesers	7		
R. D. Woolley c Wundke b Zesers	3		
†R. E. Soule c Hookes b Zesers	30		
R. M. Ellison not out	21		
R. L. Brown b May	49		
T. J. Cooley c Sleep b May	0		
S. J. Milosz c Phillips b May	0		
L-b 4, n-b 3	7	L-b 9	9

1/18 2/21 3/42 4/52 5/103   223   1/0 2/0   (2 wkts) 88
6/152 7/153 8/223 9/223

In the first innings D. C. Boon, when 7, retired hurt at 18, and resumed at 103.

Bowling: *First Innings*—Gladigau 17-5-36-2; Pyke 18-3-59-1; Wundke 7-2-14-0; Zesers 22-7-50-3; May 18.4-5-47-3; Sleep 1-0-6-0; Bishop 2-1-7-0. *Second Innings*—Gladigau 12.5-5-19-1; Pyke 13-5-33-1; Zesers 7-3-12-0; May 4-1-15-0.

South Australia

G. A. Bishop c Soule b Cooley	11	T. B. A. May c Boon b Milosz	42
A. S. Watson c Soule b Cooley	2	†J. T. W. Birchall c Soule b Cooley	6
W. B. Phillips lbw b Cooley	1	P. W. Gladigau not out	0
P. R. Sleep c Soule b Ellison	20		
*D. W. Hookes c Bradshaw b Ellison	4	L-b 10, n-b 6	16
S. C. Wundke c Cooley b Brown	30		
J. K. Pyke c Soule b Ellison	3	1/5 2/7 3/30 4/45 5/47	140
A. K. Zesers c Soule b Ellison	5	6/52 7/58 8/105 9/140	

Bowling: Cooley 21–9–41–4; Ellison 28–4–48–4; Brown 11–2–28–1; Milosz 13.2–8–13–1.

Umpires: D. R. Close and S. G. Randell.

NEW SOUTH WALES v WESTERN AUSTRALIA

At Sydney, December 12, 13, 14, 15. Drawn. New South Wales 2 pts. Toss: New South Wales. New South Wales took their first points of the season, but on a slow and lifeless pitch there was never any chance of a result. New South Wales' first innings took up eight hours as their batsmen toiled against the accurate spin of Marks and Mulder, and although Western Australia had similar problems against Holland and Bennett, Moody showed enterprise in 61 minutes of big hitting. Gilbert's back injury reduced New South Wales' bowling strength, and at one stage they were fielding three substitutes. One of them, R. J. Tucker, took four splendid catches off Holland.

New South Wales

S. M. Small c Breman b Mulder	59	– lbw b Matthews	0
M. A. Taylor c Matthews b Marks	70	– c McPhee b Matthews	9
*D. M. Wellham c Cox b Breman	35	– not out	66
M. D. O'Neill b Marks	66	– c Andrews b Matthews	50
T. H. Bayliss c Cox b Mulder	69	– c Moody b Marks	22
M. E. Waugh lbw b MacLeay	0	– c Veletta b Marks	26
M. J. Bennett c Moody b Marks	13	– not out	1
R. G. Holland run out	19		
M. R. Whitney lbw b MacLeay	0		
†D. J. A. Moore c Cox b MacLeay	4		
D. R. Gilbert not out	0		
B 1, l-b 4, w 2, n-b 3	10	B 5, l-b 6, w 1	12

1/131 2/144 3/188 4/269 5/274   345   1/5 2/16 3/96   (5 wkts dec.) 186
6/299 7/329 8/340 9/341   4/129 5/180

Bowling: *First Innings*—Matthews 27–4–106–0; MacLeay 31–12–60–3; Breman 10–4–21–1; Marks 49–15–105–3; Mulder 25–9–48–2. *Second Innings*—Matthews 21–2–51–3; MacLeay 15–4–38–0; Marks 30–8–42–2; Mulder 17–4–41–0; Andrews 1–0–3–0.

Western Australia

M. W. McPhee c sub b Holland	25	– b Waugh	28
M. R. J. Veletta c sub b Holland	91	– not out	26
T. M. Moody c and b Bennett	43	– not out	0
*G. M. Wood c sub b Holland	2		
W. S. Andrews lbw b Whitney	2		
K. H. MacLeay c Taylor b Holland	22		
V. J. Marks c Taylor b Holland	45		
†M. J. Cox c and b Bennett	28		
T. G. Breman c sub b Holland	5		
C. D. Matthews b Bennett	0		
B. Mulder not out	1		
B 10, l-b 3	13	B 3, l-b 1, n-b 1	5

1/55 2/115 3/126 4/143 5/170   277   1/58   (1 wkt) 59
6/243 7/244 8/259 9/260

Bowling: *First Innings*—Gilbert 4-2-6-0; Whitney 27-9-51-1; Waugh 7-1-30-0; Holland 42-9-86-6; Bennett 30.2-6-79-3; O'Neill 5-1-12-0. *Second Innings*—Whitney 5-1-8-0; Waugh 4-3-2-1; Holland 8-0-18-0; Bennett 12-5-16-0; O'Neill 6-1-10-0; Taylor 3-2-1-0.

Umpires: R. A. Emerson and A. G. Marshall.

NEW SOUTH WALES v SOUTH AUSTRALIA

At Sydney, December 18, 19, 20, 21. Drawn. South Australia 2 pts. Toss: South Australia. Bishop and Hilditch found few terrors in either the pitch or the bowling during a four-and-a-half-hour partnership. Bishop was especially impressive, hitting one six and fourteen fours, while Hilditch rewarded the state selectors' faith with a patient innings that included eleven fours. On the second day, however, South Australia's innings lost momentum as O'Connor battled away until the end, taking five and a half hours over his second century. When the New South Wales batting surrendered to the spinners, May, Sleep and Plummer, Hookes had no hesitation in enforcing the follow-on. With only a draw to play for, Taylor and Wellham concentrated superbly for five and a half hours, with Taylor's century being the third of his career, all of them against South Australia.

South Australia

G. A. Bishop c Wellham b Whitney	...	135
A. M. J. Hilditch c Dyer b Whitney	...	131
D. F. G. O'Connor lbw b Whitney	...	120
*D. W. Hookes b Whitney	...	0
W. B. Phillips c Taylor b Whitney	...	35
P. R. Sleep b Bennett	...	26
S. C. Wundke c Small b Bennett	...	8
N. R. Plummer b Bennett	...	0

T. B. A. May c Bennett b Matthews	...	4
A. K. Zesers run out	...	3
†J. T. W. Birchall not out	...	2
B 10, l-b 10, w 1, n-b 8	.....	29
		493

1/269 2/280 3/280 4/350 5/400 6/418 7/426 8/449 9/465

Bowling: Gilbert 24-2-70-0; Whitney 30-3-97-5; Holland 37-8-111-0; Waugh 9-1-28-0; Bennett 41-15-86-3; Matthews 20-6-56-1; O'Neill 5-0-25-0.

New South Wales

S. M. Small lbw b Sleep	...	52	– run out	5
M. A. Taylor c and b Sleep	...	26	– b Zesers	186
*D. M. Wellham c Bishop b May	...	48	– b Sleep	119
S. R. Waugh b Zesers	...	14	– c Birchall b Sleep	10
M. D. O'Neill lbw b Plummer	...	3	– (6) not out	5
G. R. J. Matthews b Plummer	...	0	– (7) not out	3
†G. C. Dyer c and b May	...	1	– (5) lbw b May	0
M. J. Bennett c Sleep b Zesers	...	39		
D. R. Gilbert c Plummer b Wundke	...	6		
R. G. Holland not out	...	11		
M. R. Whitney c Hilditch b Sleep	...	8		
L-b 3, n-b 7	...	10	B 6, l-b 5, n-b 3	14

1/81 2/84 3/121 4/126 5/126	**218**	1/9 2/270 3/306	(5 wkts) **342**
6/137 7/169 8/193 9/199		4/307 5/336	

Bowling: *First Innings*—Zesers 20-6-36-2; Hookes 6-1-18-0; Wundke 10-3-16-1; May 36-13-74-2; Sleep 31-6-48-3; Plummer 18-3-23-2. *Second Innings*—Zesers 14-3-36-1; Hookes 12-0-43-0; Wundke 7-0-30-0; May 35-12-59-1; Sleep 39-11-96-2; Plummer 26-7-67-0.

Umpires: R. A. Emerson and R. A. French.

WESTERN AUSTRALIA v VICTORIA

At Perth, December 18, 19, 20, 21. Western Australia won by six wickets. Western Australia 6 pts. Toss: Victoria. A splendid pitch provided an even contest between bat and ball. The Western Australian pace attack had Victoria struggling at 74 for four, but then Siddons, dropped by Veletta off MacLeay when 5, put on 158 in three hours with O'Donnell. O'Donnell smote four sixes in his splendid innings. Matthews cleaned up the Victorian tail, but Hughes responded by bowling very fast and Western Australia were soon in trouble. Andrews and Marks batted defiantly, but they finished 18 runs in arrears. However, when Victoria's second innings folded against Mulder's off-spin, Western Australia were left with a modest target. Matthews, sent in as night-watchman, launched a ferocious attack on Bright, hitting 18 off one over and going on to his highest first-class score.

Victoria

D. F. Whatmore c Andrews b MacLeay	11	– (2) c MacLeay b Capes	12
I. D. Frazer c Veletta b Matthews	25	– (1) lbw b MacLeay	6
D. M. Jones c MacLeay b Marks	26	– lbw b Capes	62
P. A. Hibbert c Andrews b Matthews	1	– c Marsh b Marks	25
J. D. Siddons lbw b Matthews	83	– c MacLeay b Matthews	23
S. P. O'Donnell c Cox b Capes	86	– lbw b Mulder	37
A. I. C. Dodemaide lbw b MacLeay	13	– c Cox b Matthews	9
†M. G. D. Dimattina b Matthews	8	– c Cox b Mulder	1
*R. J. Bright b Matthews	7	– c Cox b Mulder	2
M. G. Hughes lbw b Matthews	0	– not out	4
S. P. Davis not out	3	– c Veletta b Mulder	0
B 4, l-b 12, w 2, n-b 12	30	B 7, l-b 6, w 2, n-b 5	20

1/24 2/66 3/69 4/74 5/232   293   1/24 2/24 3/110 4/134 5/144   201
6/267 7/275 8/290 9/293   6/166 7/179 8/196 9/201

Bowling: *First Innings*—Matthews 24.4-2-84-6; MacLeay 32-7-78-2; Capes 21-8-36-1; Moody 6-2-19-0; Marks 14-4-35-1; Mulder 8-1-25-0. *Second Innings*—Matthews 22-6-58-2; MacLeay 12-3-37-1; Capes 14-3-35-2; Moody 7-4-6-0; Marks 15-6-35-1; Mulder 9-4-17-4.

Western Australia

G. R. Marsh b Hughes	4	– (2) lbw b Davis	20
M. R. J. Veletta hit wkt b Hughes	27	– (1) b Davis	59
T. M. Moody c Dimattina b Hughes	6	– (4) c Dimattina b Dodemaide	19
*G. M. Wood c Whatmore b Dodemaide	35	– (5) not out	34
W. S. Andrews c Jones b O'Donnell	69	– (6) not out	12
K. H. MacLeay c Dimattina b Bright	39		
V. J. Marks c Bright b Hughes	55		
†M. J. Cox b O'Donnell	13		
C. D. Matthews c Jones b O'Donnell	11	– (3) c Whatmore b Davis	65
P. A. Capes c Whatmore b Bright	2		
B. Mulder not out	0		
B 2, l-b 9, w 2, n-b 1	14	B 4, l-b 5, w 2, n-b 2	13

1/5 2/17 3/65 4/138 5/157   275   1/43 2/139 3/172   (4 wkts) 222
6/209 7/230 8/252 9/275   4/172

Bowling: *First Innings*—Hughes 20-5-59-4; Davis 15-2-46-0; O'Donnell 17-2-51-3; Bright 17.3-3-62-2; Dodemaide 12-3-46-1. *Second Innings*—Hughes 16-3-55-0; Davis 11-1-32-2; O'Donnell 16-5-38-0; Bright 6-0-39-0; Dodemaide 13-1-45-2; Frazer 0.4-0-4-0.

Umpires: R. J. Evans and W. M. Powell.

NEW SOUTH WALES v TASMANIA

At Newcastle, January 2, 3, 4, 5. Drawn. Toss: Tasmania. After the first day had been washed out, Jelich, in his first game for Tasmania since moving from Queensland, batted for seven hours, showing great concentration, although he could have been stumped twice by Dyer. Hughes, hitting one six and fourteen fours, scored his 96 in three and a half hours. Woolley's declaration left New South Wales all of the fourth day to try for first-innings points, but the rain returned to thwart both sides.

Tasmania

N. Jelich c M. A. Taylor		D. J. Buckingham not out	33
b P. L. Taylor	.126	*R. D. Woolley not out	2
P. D. Bowler c Bayliss b Gilbert	7	B 4, l-b 5, w 7, n-b 19	35
R. B. Gartrell c Holland b Bennett	20		
G. A. Hughes c Gilbert b Stepto	96	1/24 2/63 3/244 4/315 (4 wkts dec.) 319	

†R. E. Soule, R. M. Ellison, T. J. Cooley, R. L. Brown and S. J. Milosz did not bat.

Bowling: Gilbert 29–9–79–1; Stepto 21–3–59–1; Bennett 27–5–67–1; P. L. Taylor 26–3–58–1; Holland 15–2–47–0.

New South Wales

S. M. Small c Woolley b Milosz	86	T. H. Bayliss not out	9
M. A. Taylor c Soule b Brown	15	L-b 3, w 3, n-b 15	21
*D. M. Wellham run out	1		
M. D. O'Neill not out	44	1/68 2/69 3/161 (3 wkts) 176	

†G. C. Dyer, P. L. Taylor, M. J. Bennett, D. R. Gilbert, R. G. Holland and P. D. Stepto did not bat.

Bowling: Cooley 4–0–24–0; Ellison 14–4–33–0; Brown 22.4–3–55–1; Milosz 15–3–40–1; Bowler 3–0–21–0.

Umpires: R. A. Emerson and R. G. Harris.

QUEENSLAND v SOUTH AUSTRALIA

At Brisbane, January 2, 3, 4, 5. Drawn. Queensland 2 pts. Toss: South Australia. South Australia narrowly avoided defeat when their No. 11 batsman, Birchall, survived the last two balls from Tazelaar. Queensland had set a target of 286 at almost 4 runs an over and looked odds on to win when South Australia were 67 for four. Hookes and O'Connor added 87 in even time but their dismissals heralded another collapse. In Queensland's first innings, the South Australians dropped six catches, two of them off Inwood, who, on his début, hit ten fours in two and a half hours at the crease. When South Australia batted, the 22-year-old Polzin quickly made his mark, bowling superbly at medium pace to capture seven wickets for 59, the best figures by a Queensland bowler on his début. He finished the match with eleven for 103. In Queensland's second innings, Kerr batted brilliantly for four and a half hours to set up his declaration.

Queensland

B. A. Courtice c Birchall b Parkinson	9	– (2) run out		21
*R. B. Kerr c Birchall b Zesers	31	– (1) st Birchall b May		140
G. M. Ritchie c Pyke b May	43	– c Birchall b Zesers		0
G. S. Trimble c Hilditch b Zesers	24	– c Phillips b Zesers		10
P. S. Clifford lbw b Zesers	11	– lbw b May		18
A. B. Henschell c Birchall b Zesers	25	– c Birchall b Zesers		23
B. P. Inwood c Robertson b Parkinson	66	– not out		3
†P. W. Anderson lbw b Pyke	24	– not out		4
D. Tazelaar c Hookes b Pyke	19			
M. A. Polzin not out	18			
P. J. Carew b Zesers	5			
L-b 4, w 2, n-b 5	11	L-b 9, w 7		16

1/12 2/85 3/91 4/118 5/125   286   1/105 2/107 3/137   (6 wkts dec.) 235
6/150 7/208 8/255 9/268   4/166 5/227 6/227

Bowling: *First Innings*—Parkinson 25–7–63–2; Pyke 19–3–75–2; Zesers 39.5–12–74–5; Hookes 3–1–7–0; May 21–2–58–1; Sleep 2–1–5–0. *Second Innings*—Parkinson 8–1–19–0; Pyke 9–0–41–0; Zesers 31–4–78–3; Hookes 13–2–39–0; May 13–2–49–2.

South Australia

D. A. Robertson c Anderson b Carew	30	– (2) c Anderson b Polzin	25
A. M. J. Hilditch c Trimble b Polzin	14	– (1) lbw b Tazelaar	1
W. B. Phillips c Ritchie b Polzin	17	– lbw b Polzin	5
P. R. Sleep c Clifford b Carew	38	– c Ritchie b Carew	1
*D. W. Hookes c Inwood b Tazelaar	52	– c and b Polzin	78
D. F. G. O'Connor c Anderson b Polzin	18	– hit wkt b Henschell	55
J. K. Pyke c Courtice b Polzin	27	– c Kerr b Tazelaar	20
A. K. Zesers c Ritchie b Polzin	15	– c Kerr b Polzin	0
T. B. A. May c Ritchie b Polzin	5	– not out	3
S. D. H. Parkinson not out	4	– c Trimble b Tazelaar	0
†J. T. W. Birchall b Polzin	2	– not out	0
L-b 9, w 4, n-b 1	14	B 1, l-b 2, n-b 6	9

1/30 2/55 3/75 4/150 5/180	236	1/6 2/11 3/20	(9 wkts) 197
6/192 7/218 8/229 9/230		4/67 5/154 6/193	
		7/193 8/195 9/197	

Bowling: First Innings—Tazelaar 26–9–38–1; Polzin 28–7–59–7; Carew 21–5–66–2; Trimble 9–1–24–0; Henschell 16–4–40–0. *Second Innings*—Tazelaar 19–3–45–4; Polzin 19–7–44–4; Carew 15–3–45–0; Trimble 6–1–21–0; Henschell 15–5–39–1.

Umpires: M. W. Johnson and M. J. King.

SOUTH AUSTRALIA v NEW SOUTH WALES

At Adelaide, January 9, 10, 11, 12. South Australia won by 85 runs. South Australia 6 pts. Toss: South Australia. When Bishop was dropped by O'Neill off the fourth ball of the match, South Australia took control, running up 399 on the first day with brilliant innings from Bishop and Phillips, who batted for less than three hours for his 148. The New South Wales fielding was dreadful throughout the innings; O'Neill dropped four catches and six others went to ground. O'Neill made some amends with a century in three and a half hours, but New South Wales still fell short of the follow-on figure. However, Hookes agreed not to enforce the follow-on to give both sides a chance of outright points. More spectacular hitting by Bishop led to South Australia's setting New South Wales 347 to win in 380 minutes, but they never looked equal to the task. Six overs remained when Whitney succumbed to Zesers.

South Australia

G. A. Bishop c Taylor b Tucker	74	b Tucker	58
A. M. J. Hilditch c Taylor b Gilbert	66	– not out	52
D. A. Robertson b Holland	5		
*D. W. Hookes c Bower b Bennett	45		
†W. B. Phillips lbw b Whitney	148		
D. F. G. O'Connor c and b Whitney	46	– (3) not out	37
R. J. Zadow st Dyer b Holland	47		
J. K. Pyke run out	51		
T. B. A. May c O'Neill b Holland	9		
A. K. Zesers not out	3		
S. D. H. Parkinson c Gilbert b Holland	10		
B 4, l-b 7, n-b 19	30	L-b 4, n-b 2	6

1/131 2/164 3/164 4/312 5/386	534	1/83	(1 wkt dec.) 153
6/426 7/508 8/513 9/522			

Bowling: First Innings—Gilbert 25–1–95–1; Whitney 25–1–115–2; Tucker 23–1–81–1; Bennett 35–6–98–1; Holland 34.5–5–134–4. *Second Innings*—Gilbert 9–2–47–0; Whitney 4–0–40–0; Tucker 7–0–45–1; Bennett 2.2–0–17–0.

New South Wales

S. M. Small c Zesers b Parkinson	17	– c Robertson b May	38
M. A. Taylor c Phillips b Parkinson	59	– lbw b Pyke	28
R. J. Bower lbw b Parkinson	0	– lbw b May	22
M. D. O'Neill c Bishop b May	106	– b May	14
T. H. Bayliss c Phillips b Zesers	45	– b May	0
*†G. C. Dyer c Phillips b Parkinson	24	– c Phillips b Pyke	53
R. J. Tucker lbw b May	12	– c Phillips b Parkinson	25
M. J. Bennett not out	42	– lbw b Pyke	17
D. R. Gilbert c Bishop b Zesers	10	– not out	24
R. G. Holland c Zesers b May	2	– c Phillips b Zesers	2
M. R. Whitney not out	1	– c and b Zesers	19
B 6, l-b 15, w 1, n-b 1	23	B 9, l-b 6, w 2, n-b 2	19

1/20 2/20 3/169 4/247 5/247 (9 wkts dec.) 341
6/261 7/299 8/332 9/335

1/59 2/77 3/96 4/96 5/133 261
6/178 7/204 8/217 9/222

Bowling: *First Innings*—Parkinson 30-5-106-4; Zesers 39-14-82-2; Pyke 7-0-31-0; May 42-9-101-3. *Second Innings*—Parkinson 17-2-40-1; Zesers 31.4-10-68-2; Pyke 18-8-39-3; May 40-8-99-4.

Umpires: B. E. Martin and M. G. O'Connell.

VICTORIA v WESTERN AUSTRALIA

At Melbourne, January 9, 10, 11, 12. Drawn. Western Australia 2 pts. Toss: Victoria. Bright's decision to field first backfired as Western Australia spent nearly two days over their first innings. Victoria's batsmen seemed overawed by their task, but Whatmore kept his head and batted for five and threequarter hours in scoring his seventh century. He played another fine innings when Victoria followed on. Marks threatened to win the match for Western Australia with a fine spell of off-spin bowling, but the excellence of the pitch prevailed.

Western Australia

M. W. McPhee c Whatmore b Davis	99	C. D. Matthews c Dimattina b O'Donnell	2
M. R. J. Veletta c Quinn b O'Donnell	112	P. A. Capes not out	0
T. M. Moody b Dodemaide	100	L-b 18, w 1, n-b 2	21
*G. M. Wood c Quinn b McCarthy	3		
W. S. Andrews not out	124		
K. H. MacLeay b Bright	10	1/163 2/309 3/314 (8 wkts dec.) 529
V. J. Marks b Davis	47	4/345 5/374 6/478
†M. J. Cox lbw b O'Donnell	11	7/525 8/527

B. Mulder did not bat.

Bowling: McCarthy 31-8-81-1; Davis 38-8-115-2; Dodemaide 38-7-111-1; O'Donnell 33-6-82-3; Bright 34-5-116-1; Whatmore 2-0-6-0.

Victoria

M. B. Quinn c Cox b MacLeay	18	– (2) c Cox b Capes	28
D. F. Whatmore c Wood b Capes	113	– (1) hit wkt b Marks	64
P. A. Hibbert lbw b Matthews	4	– lbw b Marks	27
J. D. Siddons c Wood b Matthews	13	– c McPhee b Marks	10
G. L. Jordan c Mulder b Capes	2	– b Marks	8
S. P. O'Donnell c Cox b Capes	2	– st Cox b Marks	57
A. I. C. Dodemaide c Wood b MacLeay	30	– not out	12
†M. G. D. Dimattina b MacLeay	12	– not out	10
R. C. A. M. McCarthy b Capes	46		
*R. J. Bright not out	15		
S. P. Davis run out	7		
L-b 12, w 2, n-b 8	22	L-b 4, n-b 3	7

1/28 2/39 3/55 4/68 5/89 284
6/172 7/208 8/223 9/265

1/64 2/122 3/125 (6 wkts) 223
4/137 5/158 6/206

Bowling: *First Innings*—Matthews 32.4–5–78–2; MacLeay 29–8–65–3; Capes 28–8–77–4; Marks 14–5–28–0; Mulder 15–8–24–0. *Second Innings*—Matthews 18–3–61–0; MacLeay 11–2–24–0; Capes 10–0–39–1; Marks 34–14–55–5; Mulder 16–5–37–0; Moody 3–2–3–0; McPhee 2–2–0–0.

Umpires: R. C. Bailhache and L. J. King.

TASMANIA v QUEENSLAND

At Launceston, January 16, 17, 18, 19. Drawn. Queensland 2 pts. Toss: Tasmania. Put in, Queensland's batsmen were rarely troubled by Tasmania's bowlers, although Ellison's steadiness kept the run-scoring in check. When Tasmania batted, McDermott found conditions to his liking, and Tasmania never really recovered from his initial burst. By early on the rain-interrupted third day, they were following on. However, the wicket had eased and Boon, who had lost his Test place, found his best form, passing 50 for only the third time in the season. His 172 took five hours and his powerful strokes brought him 22 fours.

Queensland

*R. B. Kerr b Milosz	36	C. J. McDermott lbw b Ellison 10
B. A. Courtice b Ellison	73	D. Tazelaar c Boon b Milosz 3
G. S. Trimble c Soule b Ellison	63	M. A. Polzin not out 0
G. M. Ritchie c Hughes b Milosz	96	
T. J. Barsby run out	9	B 6, l-b 1, n-b 11 18
A. B. Henschell c Hughes b Ellison	1	
B. P. Inwood b Brown	57	1/61 2/179 3/216 4/232 5/235 406
†I. A. Healy c Brown b Milosz	40	6/325 7/385 8/396 9/406

Bowling: Cooley 20–1–75–0; Ellison 42–10–95–4; Brown 27–6–76–1; Milosz 38.5–10–127–4; Jelich 8–1–26–0.

Tasmania

N. Jelich c Henschell b McDermott	6	– (2) run out	40
*D. C. Boon c Trimble b McDermott	3	– (1) c Barsby b Henschell	172
R. B. Gartrell c Henschell b McDermott	8	– b Henschell	13
G. A. Hughes c Polzin b Tazelaar	44	– c Trimble b Tazelaar	55
D. J. Buckingham b Polzin	50	– c Kerr b Tazelaar	26
R. D. Woolley c Tazelaar b Henschell	31	– c Polzin b Barsby	22
†R. E. Soule b McDermott	8	– (8) not out	16
R. M. Ellison c Trimble b Polzin	15	– (7) b Tazelaar	0
T. J. Cooley not out	32	– c Tazelaar b Ritchie	7
R. L. Brown c Trimble b McDermott	11		
S. J. Milosz c Trimble b Tazelaar	4		
B 2, l-b 2, n-b 10	14	B 4, w 2, n-b 12	18

1/4 2/17 3/24 4/90 5/139	226	1/145 2/184 3/253 4/312 (8 wkts) 369
6/147 7/168 8/170 9/200		5/323 6/323 7/357 8/369

Bowling: *First Innings*—McDermott 21–4–54–5; Tazelaar 14.5–4–53–2; Polzin 14–2–42–2; Henschell 18–6–69–1; Courtice 5–3–4–0. *Second Innings*—McDermott 23–3–63–0; Tazelaar 26–10–80–3; Polzin 26–4–101–0; Henschell 25–5–71–2; Courtice 16–2–32–0; Inwood 8–3–8–0; Barsby 2–1–8–1; Ritchie 1–0–2–1.

Umpires: D. R. Close and J. T. Hinds.

VICTORIA v TASMANIA

At Melbourne, January 23, 24, 25, 26. Victoria won by six wickets. Victoria 6 pts. Toss: Tasmania. The speed and accuracy of Hughes and the batting of Hibbert were decisive elements in Victoria's impressive win, with Hughes taking ten wickets in a match for the first time. Victoria's batsmen also struggled, especially against the medium pace of Ellison, but Hibbert worked away for more than five hours over his second century of the season. It was a different story in the second innings as Victoria chased 195 to win in 59 overs, Hibbert and Siddons adding 143 in 94 minutes. In Tasmania's second innings, Gartrell was given out by umpire Holt for pushing the ball away after attempting to sweep a delivery from Jackson.

Tasmania

N. Jelich lbw b McCarthy	24	– (2) lbw b Hughes	3
*D. C. Boon c Dimattina b Hughes	69	– (1) c Dodemaide b Hughes	49
R. B. Gartrell c Siddons b Hughes	0	– handled the ball	43
G. A. Hughes c Jackson b Dodemaide	63	– b Bright	24
D. J. Buckingham lbw b Jackson	45	– (6) c McCarthy b Hughes	11
R. D. Woolley c Dimattina b Dodemaide	2	– (7) c Siddons b Hughes	1
†R. E. Soule lbw b Hughes	10	– (5) run out	28
R. M. Ellison c Whatmore b Hughes	28	– b Hughes	16
T. J. Cooley not out	20	– c Dimattina b Jackson	7
R. L. Brown b Dodemaide	6	– c Young b Jackson	8
S. J. Milosz b Hughes	0	– not out	1
L-b 13, w 2, n-b 2	17	B 1, l-b 5, w 4, n-b 4	14

1/93 2/93 3/102 4/189 5/195   284   1/31 2/64 3/130 4/132 5/169   205
6/209 7/237 8/274 9/283   6/171 7/175 8/190 9/196

Bowling: *First Innings*—Hughes 32.4–8–73–5; McCarthy 22–4–62–1; Dodemaide 23–7–59–3; Jackson 18–5–30–1; Bright 19–1–47–0. *Second Innings*—Hughes 26–3–61–5; McCarthy 7–1–32–0; Dodemaide 19–8–29–0; Jackson 13.1–2–56–2; Bright 12–5–21–1.

Victoria

M. B. Quinn c Soule b Ellison	49	– (2) b Cooley	19
D. F. Whatmore c Milosz b Brown	30	– (1) b Ellison	0
P. A. Hibbert c Brown b Ellison	129	– c sub b Hughes	88
P. W. Young c Gartrell b Ellison	31	– c Soule b Cooley	8
J. D. Siddons c Soule b Milosz	11	– not out	75
A. I. C. Dodemaide c Boon b Ellison	2	– not out	1
R. C. A. M. McCarthy c and b Ellison	11		
†M. G. D. Dimattina not out	7		
*R. J. Bright b Ellison	2		
P. W. Jackson not out	6		
L-b 7, n-b 10	17	B 1, l-b 2, w 1	4

1/64 2/117 3/221 4/257 5/266   (8 wkts dec.) 295   1/0 2/31 3/43 4/186   (4 wkts) 195
6/271 7/284 8/286

M. G. Hughes did not bat.

Bowling: *First Innings*—Ellison 42–11–77–6; Cooley 13–2–46–0; Milosz 35–5–89–1; Brown 24–4–55–1; Jelich 3–0–11–0; Boon 4–1–10–0. *Second Innings*—Ellison 12–1–52–1; Cooley 8–0–44–2; Milosz 7–0–38–0; Brown 3–0–13–0; Boon 8–0–38–0; Hughes 1–0–7–1.

Umpires: D. E. Holden and D. W. Holt.

QUEENSLAND v VICTORIA

At Brisbane, February 20, 21, 22. Queensland won by an innings and 43 runs. Queensland 6 pts. Toss: Queensland. Queensland needed only three days to defeat a Victorian side that found McDermott too much for them. Given the chance of bowling first on a lively pitch, the fast bowler was in his element, and only some big hitting by O'Donnell, including three sixes off Henschell, and more circumspect innings by Siddons and Dodemaide saved Victoria from embarrassment. Queensland began their innings cautiously, but as Victoria's fieldsmen dropped five catches, they increased their tempo. Henschell's hundred ensured a big first-innings lead and the stage was set for McDermott. Coming off his long run, he first struck Whatmore on the head and then, with carbon-copies of their first-innings dismissals, despatched both the opener and Hibbert for a "pair". Quinn won credit for his courageous defence, but when he was caught behind off Tazelaar, Victoria's resistance ended.

Victoria

M. B. Quinn c Kerr b Polzin	6	– (2) c Anderson b Tazelaar	42
D. F. Whatmore c Anderson b McDermott	0	– (1) c Anderson b McDermott	0
D. M. Jones c Kerr b Tazelaar	8	– lbw b McDermott	14
P. A. Hibbert b McDermott	0	– b McDermott	0
J. D. Siddons lbw b Henschell	40	– c Courtice b McDermott	4
S. P. O'Donnell c Carew b McDermott	86	– c Henschell b McDermott	0
A. I. C. Dodemaide b Tazelaar	45	– c Anderson b Carew	4
†M. G. D. Dimattina c Trimble b Henschell	4	– c Anderson b Tazelaar	7
*R. J. Bright b Carew	12	– c Border b Tazelaar	2
M. G. Hughes c Anderson b McDermott	1	– c Carew b Henschell	1
S. P. Davis not out	0	– not out	0
L-b 8, n-b 3	11	N-b 3	3
	213		**77**

1/7 2/7 3/8 4/29 5/110
6/156 7/166 8/201 9/213

1/0 2/28 3/28 4/52 5/52
6/59 7/73 8/76 9/77

Bowling: *First Innings*—McDermott 18.5-7-38-4; Polzin 14-2-52-1; Tazelaar 16-5-43-2; Carew 15-5-23-1; Henschell 20-5-48-2; Courtice 3-2-1-0. *Second Innings*—McDermott 13-0-48-5; Polzin 5-0-12-0; Tazelaar 4-0-6-3; Carew 7-4-7-1; Henschell 4.1-1-4-1.

Queensland

B. A. Courtice c O'Donnell b Hughes	31	C. J. McDermott c Jones b Dodemaide	10
R. B. Kerr c Dimattina b O'Donnell	20	D. Tazelaar b O'Donnell	13
G. M. Ritchie c Hughes b Davis	14	M. A. Polzin not out	3
*A. R. Border c and b Bright	34	P. J. Carew c O'Donnell b Jones	3
G. S. Trimble c Jones b Hughes	44	B 7, l-b 5, w 4, n-b 12	28
A. B. Henschell c Dimattina b Hughes	.125		
†P. W. Anderson c Dimattina b Dodemaide	8	1/38 2/62 3/96 4/137 5/189 6/222 7/244 8/301 9/325	**333**

Bowling: Hughes 32-4-110-3; O'Donnell 26-6-79-2; Davis 14-3-28-1; Dodemaide 19-3-41-2; Bright 24-6-61-1; Jones 1.4-0-2-1.

Umpires: M. W. Johnson and C. D. Timmins.

SOUTH AUSTRALIA v WESTERN AUSTRALIA

At Adelaide, February 20, 21, 22, 23. Western Australia won by eight wickets. Western Australia 6 pts. Toss: South Australia. On the first day, with their two fast left-arm bowlers, Reid and Matthews, bowling continuously from the Southern end, and helped by superb catching, Western Australia had South Australia out before stumps. In contrast, Western Australia's batsmen prospered on the perfect wicket against some erratic bowling. Marsh, dropped by Bishop when 98, batted soundly for five and a half hours, and there was an exciting innings from the giant Moody, who belted thirteen fours in a stay of 107 minutes. South Australia's second innings was as undistinguished as the first and Western Australia won with more than half a day to spare.

South Australia

G. A. Bishop c Marsh b Reid	10	– c Mulder b MacLeay	10
A. M. J. Hilditch c Marsh b Matthews	20	– b Marks	43
D. A. Robertson c Zoehrer b Reid	63	– lbw b Marks	48
P. R. Sleep c Marsh b Reid	31	– c Zoehrer b Reid	2
*†W. B. Phillips c Veletta b Matthews	5	– b Matthews	23
D. F. G. O'Connor run out	17	– not out	38
R. J. Zadow c MacLeay b Mulder	14	– c sub b Marks	4

J. K. Pyke c Wood b Reid	15	– c Marsh b Marks	5
T. B. A. May b Matthews	8	– c Moody b MacLeay	25
A. K. Zesers not out	2	– lbw b MacLeay	13
S. D. H. Parkinson c Mulder b Marks	0	– run out	2
L-b 5, w 1, n-b 4	10	B 3, l-b 8, n-b 5	16

1/18 2/37 3/90 4/98 5/126   195   1/12 2/84 3/95 4/133 5/133   229
6/158 7/167 8/183 9/195   6/141 7/157 8/198 9/224

Bowling: *First Innings*—Reid 22-5-59-4; MacLeay 12-2-24-0; Matthews 23-2-43-3; Marks 22.4-9-34-1; Mulder 10-1-30-1. *Second Innings*—Reid 26-6-55-1; MacLeay 17-5-32-3; Matthews 17-6-49-1; Marks 33-15-55-4; Mulder 10-1-27-0.

Western Australia

M. R. J. Veletta c Phillips b Pyke	9	– (2) not out	6
G. R. Marsh c Bishop b Parkinson	134	– (1) b Parkinson	0
T. M. Moody c Robertson b Sleep	85	– c Sleep b Zesers	10
*G. M. Wood c Phillips b Parkinson	42	– not out	0
W. S. Andrews lbw b Zesers	54		
K. H. MacLeay c Zadow b Zesers	39		
C. D. Matthews lbw b Parkinson	4		
†T. J. Zoehrer run out	11		
V. J. Marks b Zesers	8		
B. Mulder run out	4		
B. A. Reid not out	2		
B 5, l-b 6, w 6	17	L-b 1	1

1/46 2/170 3/245 4/329 5/339   409   1/0 2/13   (2 wkts) 17
6/344 7/365 8/385 9/404

Bowling: *First Innings*—Parkinson 20-2-89-3; Zesers 42.2-18-86-3; Pyke 26-7-72-1; May 24-3-87-0; Sleep 18-4-64-1. *Second Innings*—Parkinson 2.5-0-15-1; Zesers 2-1-1-1.

Umpires: A. R. Crafter and M. G. O'Connell.

TASMANIA v NEW SOUTH WALES

At Hobart, February 20, 21, 22, 23. New South Wales won by an innings and 6 runs. New South Wales 6 pts. Toss: Tasmania. Despite much of the game being spoilt by rain and bad light, New South Wales won their first match of the season. Tasmania's first-innings total owed everything to Woolley, who batted for three and a half hours, but with Ellison injured, and Cooley also breaking down, their bowling was very thin. Small batted for seven hours against his former state, hitting 23 fours in a career-best 184. The highlight of Tasmania's second innings was the return to form of Lawson, whose speed and accuracy forestalled any prospect of resistance.

Tasmania

*D. C. Boon c Lawson b Gilbert	28	– (2) c Waugh b Whitney	33
N. Jelich c Dyer b Lawson	12	– (1) run out	30
K. Bradshaw b Gilbert	8	– c Waugh b Whitney	5
G. A. Hughes c Waugh b Whitney	7	– c P. L. Taylor b Waugh	50
D. J. Buckingham c Dyer b Waugh	13	– b Gilbert	16
R. D. Woolley not out	108	– c P. L. Taylor b Lawson	46
†R. E. Soule c Matthews b Whitney	0	– b Lawson	10
T. J. Cooley c M. A. Taylor b Lawson	21	– lbw b Lawson	0
R. L. Brown b P. L. Taylor	13	– b Lawson	1
G. D. Campbell run out	8	– c Dyer b Lawson	0
S. J. Milosz c Dyer b Waugh	29	– not out	0
B 5, l-b 7, n-b 3	15	B 7, l-b 17, n-b 3	27

1/41 2/50 3/50 4/75 5/75   262   1/60 2/67 3/95 4/129 5/169   218
6/81 7/148 8/186 9/222   6/193 7/193 8/204 9/218

Bowling: *First Innings*—Gilbert 17–4–72–2; Lawson 17–4–40–2; Whitney 11–3–29–2; Waugh 12–1–48–2; P. L. Taylor 16–4–34–1; Matthews 9–1–27–0. *Second Innings*—Gilbert 13–3–35–1; Lawson 17.3–4–34–4; Whitney 11–2–23–2; Waugh 17–3–36–2; P. L. Taylor 15–0–49–0; Matthews 8–2–17–0.

New South Wales

S. M. Small c and b Milosz	184	†G. C. Dyer b Hughes		6
M. A. Taylor b Cooley	22	P. L. Taylor not out		0
*D. M. Wellham b Milosz	71	B 4, l-b 9, w 2, n-b 13		28
S. R. Waugh b Campbell	65			
M. D. O'Neill c Campbell b Milosz	59	1/57 2/188 3/307	(7 wkts dec.)	486
G. R. J. Matthews b Campbell	51	4/397 5/450 6/486 7/486		

G. F. Lawson, D. R. Gilbert and M. R. Whitney did not bat.

Bowling: Cooley 13–4–26–1; Brown 19–4–63–0; Campbell 24.3–2–115–2; Milosz 44–4–160–3; Jelich 25–2–78–0; Hughes 15–3–31–1.

Umpires: D. R. Close and P. Howard.

NEW SOUTH WALES v QUEENSLAND

At Sydney, February 27, 28, March 1, 2. Drawn. New South Wales 2 pts. Toss: New South Wales. Queensland needed points from this game if they were to qualify for the final and they were well on course when McDermott and Tazelaar fired out three New South Wales batsmen for 9. But the home side recovered through a fine innings by Waugh and determined batting from O'Neill and Dyer. Facing a modest target for first-innings points, Queensland succumbed to steady bowling, and by stumps on the second day New South Wales were in a position to push for victory. However, heavy rain washed out the last two days.

New South Wales

S. M. Small c Courtice b McDermott	0	– not out	29
M. A. Taylor b McDermott	5	– not out	34
*D. M. Wellham lbw b Tazelaar	0		
S. R. Waugh b Border b Hill	44		
M. D. O'Neill c Ritchie b Henschell	64		
G. R. J. Matthews st Anderson b Henschell	19		
†G. C. Dyer b Inwood b Henschell	70		
P. L. Taylor c Border b McDermott	1		
D. R. Gilbert not out	18		
G. F. Lawson c and b Henschell	2		
M. R. Whitney c Ritchie b McDermott	4		
L-b 2, n-b 3	5	B 1, n-b 4	5

1/0 2/5 3/9 4/73 5/99		232	(no wkt) 68
6/166 7/170 8/218 9/223			

Bowling: *First Innings*—McDermott 19.3–5–51–4; Tazelaar 17–2–65–1; Hill 21–5–66–1; Henschell 29–10–48–4. *Second Innings*—McDermott 5–1–20–0; Tazelaar 6–1–17–0; Hill 3–0–10–0; Henschell 7–1–20–0.

Queensland

R. B. Kerr c Waugh b Gilbert	16	C. J. McDermott lbw b Gilbert		30
B. A. Courtice c Waugh b Matthews	45	D. Tazelaar b Gilbert		3
G. M. Ritchie run out	3	J. G. Hill not out		0
*A. R. Border c Dyer b Lawson	11			
G. S. Trimble c Dyer b Waugh	57			
B. P. Inwood run out	21			
A. B. Henschell c Dyer b Waugh	0	B 7, l-b 4, n-b 7		18
†P. W. Anderson c M. A. Taylor				
b Waugh	16	1/31 2/37 3/58 4/137 5/145		220
		6/145 7/167 8/217 9/217		

Bowling: Gilbert 13.1–4–26–3; Lawson 10–4–16–1; Matthews 23–8–47–1; P. L. Taylor 18–2–50–0; Whitney 8–2–21–0; Waugh 12–1–49–3.

Umpires: R. A. Emerson and R. A. French.

VICTORIA v SOUTH AUSTRALIA

At Melbourne, February 27, 28, March 1, 2. Drawn. South Australia 2 pts. Toss: South Australia. When rain prevented play on the second day, the match became a contest for first-innings points, which Victoria appeared to be winning when they were 262 for six on the fourth morning. However, Young, having hit his highest first-class score, was caught down the leg side, and Zesers dismissed Dimattina and Hughes off successive balls to cap a superb display of medium-pace bowling. His seven for 67 were career-best figures. Victoria missed the batting of Jones, out with a knee injury. Phillips having been hit on the ankle while batting by a throw from O'Donnell, Hookes kept wicket for South Australia in both innings.

South Australia

G. A. Bishop lbw b O'Donnell	16	– c Dodemaide b Hughes	0
A. M. J. Hilditch c Dimattina b Hughes	15	– c Siddons b Jackson	51
D. A. Robertson c Jackson b Bright	24	– retired hurt	11
D. F. G. O'Connor c Young b Bright	51	– (8) not out	7
*D. W. Hookes c Quinn b Bright	32	– (4) st Dimattina b Jackson	0
P. R. Sleep c Siddons b Dodemaide	6	– c Young b Bright	13
†W. B. Phillips b Bright	33	– not out	14
J. K. Pyke c Whatmore b Jackson	27	– (5) c Jackson b Bright	59
T. B. A. May not out	31		
A. K. Zesers c Young b O'Donnell	23		
P. W. Gladigau b O'Donnell	15		
B 1, l-b 10	11	B 7, l-b 1, n-b 1	9

1/31 2/31 3/105 4/147 5/153   284   1/0 2/31 3/94   (5 wkts dec.) 164
6/155 7/213 8/213 9/263   4/134 5/152

In the second innings D. A. Robertson retired hurt at 29.

Bowling: *First Innings*—Hughes 27–6–78–1; O'Donnell 23.1–5–82–3; Bright 31–14–63–4; Dodemaide 10–1–36–1; Jackson 14–7–14–1. *Second Innings*—Hughes 5–2–8–1; Bright 8–1–18–2; Dodemaide 5–0–13–0; Jackson 14–0–83–2; Siddons 5–0–34–0.

Victoria

M. B. Quinn c Bishop b Zesers	25	– (5) not out	27
D. F. Whatmore c Gladigau b Zesers	19	– (1) c Hookes b Zesers	6
P. A. Hibbert b May	5		
J. D. Siddons c Hookes b Zesers	11	– (3) c Pyke b May	9
S. P. O'Donnell c Hookes b Zesers	73	– (4) c Gladigau b Sleep	22
P. W. Young c Hookes b Pyke	89	– (2) c Robertson b Zesers	9
A. I. C. Dodemaide lbw b Zesers	6	– (6) not out	11
P. W. Jackson c Robertson b May	14		
†M. G. D. Dimattina c Hookes b Zesers	8		
*R. J. Bright not out	3		
M. G. Hughes c Bishop b Zesers	0		
B 17, l-b 4, w 1, n-b 2	24	B 8	8

1/31 2/46 3/67 4/70 5/191   277   1/14 2/21 3/34 4/66   (4 wkts) 92
6/209 7/262 8/269 9/277

Bowling: *First Innings*—Gladigau 19–6–66–0; Pyke 13–6–21–1; Zesers 42.3–15–67–7; May 31–14–43–2; Sleep 25–8–59–0. *Second Innings*—Zesers 5–2–13–2; May 13–2–32–1; Sleep 9–2–27–1; O'Connor 1–0–5–0; Robertson 1–0–7–0.

Umpires: D. E. Holden and L. J. King.

WESTERN AUSTRALIA v TASMANIA

At Perth, February 27, 28, March 1, 2. Western Australia won by seven wickets. Western Australia 6 pts. Toss: Western Australia. A depleted Tasmanian side did well to extend this match into the final over. Boon and Hughes were suspended from the game following an alleged incident in a Hobart motel and Ellison could play only as a batsman. Western Australia, presented with some benign bowling, made their highest total against Tasmania, Wood needing 143 balls for his 103 and Andrews 201 balls for his 116. Tasmania's second innings was a triumph for Buckingham, who, although needing a runner, played superbly for four and a half hours, hitting 21 fours in his career-best 150. Western Australia, left just sixteen overs to score 94, did so easily enough. Their wicket-keeper, Zoehrer, was fined $A260 for using abusive language on the first day.

Tasmania

R. J. Bennett lbw b Matthews	78	– c Zoehrer b Reid	45
N. Jelich c Veletta b MacLeay	17	– lbw b MacLeay	6
D. J. Buckingham c MacLeay b Reid	28	– b Mulder	150
R. D. Woolley lbw b Matthews	13	– run out	52
*K. Bradshaw c Zoehrer b Matthews	16	– c Zoehrer b Reid	1
R. M. Ellison c Wood b Matthews	36	– c Zoehrer b Reid	5
†R. E. Soule lbw b Matthews	0	– (8) c Zoehrer b Reid	1
B. A. Cruse lbw b Reid	16	– (7) c Wood b Mulder	34
M. P. Tame c Zoehrer b MacLeay	14	– b Marks b MacLeay	5
R. L. Brown b Matthews	23	– b Matthews	29
S. J. Milosz not out	1	– not out	7
B 1, l-b 10, n-b 14	25	B 8, l-b 4, w 1, n-b 9	22
	267		**357**

1/46 2/96 3/122 4/172 5/177 6/177 7/209 8/235 9/266

1/17 2/124 3/214 4/227 5/267 6/274 7/288 8/301 9/327

Bowling: *First Innings*—Reid 27–3–85–2; MacLeay 33–8–56–2; Matthews 25–8–46–6; Marks 21–5–51–0; Mulder 5–1–6–0; Moody 7–1–12–0. *Second Innings*—Reid 31–6–90–4; MacLeay 25–6–76–2; Matthews 16.4–3–71–1; Marks 19–6–57–0; Mulder 25–11–51–2.

Western Australia

M. R. J. Veletta st Soule b Milosz	88	– (2) not out	40
G. R. Marsh lbw b Milosz	40	– (1) c and b Tame	18
T. M. Moody b Cruse	47	– c Ellison b Tame	4
*G. M. Wood c Ellison b Bradshaw	103	– (5) not out	21
W. S. Andrews c Jelich b Milosz	116		
K. H. MacLeay b Bradshaw	39		
†T. J. Zoehrer b Milosz	10		
V. J. Marks not out	20		
C. D. Matthews c Soule b Bradshaw	23	– (4) b Brown	5
B. Mulder lbw b Milosz	8		
B. A. Reid c sub b Brown	15		
L-b 9, w 1, n-b 12	22	B 1, l-b 8	9
	531		**(3 wkts) 97**

1/83 2/185 3/189 4/374 5/443 6/457 7/463 8/488 9/504

1/39 2/49 3/57

Bowling: *First Innings*—Brown 23.5-2-117-1; Tame 24-3-92-0; Milosz 33-3-140-5; Bradshaw 23-4-81-3; Cruse 17-2-64-1; Jelich 8-0-28-0. *Second Innings*—Brown 8-0-48-1; Tame 7.1-0-40-2.

Umpires: P. J. McConnell and T. A. Prue.

NEW SOUTH WALES v VICTORIA

At Sydney, March 6, 7, 8, 9. New South Wales won by one wicket. New South Wales 6 pts. Toss: Victoria. The excitement of the fourth evening, when Peter Taylor scored the winning run off the last ball, was in stark contrast to the first two days. Victoria's first innings was notable only for some rustic swings by Siddons and a meritorious maiden hundred by Young; the New South Wales senior batsmen pushed and prodded until Matthews came in and hit an entertaining 104 off 137 balls, his first hundred of the season. The Victorian captain then lived up to his name by declaring his second innings to leave New South Wales 69 overs in which to score 254 for victory. As Bright himself was unable to bowl, his move was especially generous. With Waugh making his highest score of the season, the target always seemed within reach, although New South Wales, having been outplayed for most of the match, were fortunate to win it.

Victoria

M. B. Quinn c Waugh b Gilbert	6	– (2) not out	78
D. F. Whatmore c Waugh b Matthews	39	– (1) c Waugh b Holland	44
P. A. Hibbert c Dyer b Lawson	32		
J. D. Siddons c P. L. Taylor b Lawson	102	– (3) c Wellham b Holland	39
S. P. O'Donnell c Waugh b Gilbert	2	– (4) not out	8
P. W. Young c Small b Matthews	111		
A. I. C. Dodemaide c Waugh b Matthews	58		
†M. G. D. Dimattina not out	7		
B 8, l-b 2, n-b 4	14	B 1, l-b 5	6

1/10 2/80 3/84 4/97 5/239   (7 wkts dec.) 371   1/96 2/161   (2 wkts dec.) 175
6/356 7/371

P. W. Jackson, *R. J. Bright and M. G. Hughes did not bat.

Bowling: *First Innings*—Gilbert 24-6-65-2; Lawson 28-11-34-2; Holland 27-0-89-0; Waugh 16-2-38-0; P. L. Taylor 22-5-69-0; Matthews 30.3-11-66-3. *Second Innings*—Gilbert 5-2-14-0; Lawson 10-3-26-0; Holland 16-0-69-2; P. L. Taylor 3-0-12-0; Matthews 15-1-48-0.

New South Wales

S. M. Small c Dimattina b Hughes	2	– b Jackson	0
M. A. Taylor c O'Donnell b Jackson	32	– c Siddons b Dodemaide	40
*D. M. Wellham c Jackson b Bright	20	– c and b Hughes	14
S. R. Waugh c Siddons b Dodemaide	18	– c Hughes b Jackson	89
M. D. O'Neill c Hibbert b Jackson	10	– (8) c Dimattina b Dodemaide	11
R. G. Holland b Bright	11	– (11) not out	1
G. R. J. Matthews c Dimattina b Hughes	104	– (5) c Siddons b Jackson	25
†G. C. Dyer c Whatmore b Jackson	14	– (6) c Dimattina b Dodemaide	46
P. L. Taylor not out	44	– (7) not out	16
D. R. Gilbert c Whatmore b Dodemaide	11	– (9) c Hughes b Jackson	4
G. F. Lawson c Young b Dodemaide	16	– (10) run out	0
B 3, l-b 6, w 1, n-b 1	11	B 4, l-b 3, n-b 1	8

1/2 2/53 3/65 4/86 5/96   293   1/2 2/26 3/81   (9 wkts) 254
6/126 7/176 8/235 9/257   4/122 5/207 6/229
                                      7/245 8/252 9/252

Bowling: *First Innings*—Hughes 20-4-41-2; O'Donnell 11-4-20-0; Bright 31-10-56-2; Jackson 51-18-120-3; Dodemaide 13.2-1-34-3; Whatmore 2-0-13-0. *Second Innings*—Hughes 14-3-41-1; O'Donnell 8-0-35-0; Jackson 29-3-111-4; Dodemaide 18-1-60-3.

Umpires: R. A. Emerson and R. A. French.

SOUTH AUSTRALIA v TASMANIA

At Adelaide, March 6, 7, 8, 9. South Australia won by an innings and 146 runs. South Australia 6 pts. Toss: Tasmania. The batting of Hookes and Phillips for the fourth wicket dwarfed all else. Coming together in mid-afternoon on the second day after Hookes had already put on 103 with Hilditch, they batted through until lunch on the third, when Hookes declared. Their unbroken partnership of 462 took 299 minutes, occupied 84.3 overs and broke every Australian partnership record; the previous highest partnership had been 456 by W. H. Ponsford and E. R. Mayne, for the first wicket, for Victoria against Queensland at Melbourne in 1923-24. Hookes, in 398 minutes, hit his first triple-hundred from 330 balls, 176 runs coming from two sixes and 41 fours; Phillips, whose third double-hundred this was, hit one six and 30 fours and played at each of the 253 balls bowled to him. Hookes did not give a chance, Phillips gave one. However, with Ellison and Cooley unavailable through injury, Tasmania's bowling was seriously undermanned. The South Australian bowler, Zesers, achieved a notable milestone by taking his 100th first-class wicket, two days before his twentieth birthday.

Tasmania

R. J. Bennett c Phillips b Gladigau	0	lbw b Pyke	15
*D. C. Boon b Gladigau	12	b Zesers	37
N. Jelich c Gladigau b Sleep	85	c Scott b Gladigau	57
G. A. Hughes c Hilditch b Zesers	8	c Pyke b May	18
R. D. Woolley c Gladigau b May	61	c Scott b May	26
B. A. Cruse b Zesers	7	c Phillips b Zesers	21
†R. E. Soule not out	30	retired hurt	53
W. S. Kirkman lbw b May	7	lbw b Zesers	0
R. L. Brown b May	15	c Scott b Sleep	9
M. P. Tame c Pyke b May	2	c Bishop b Sleep	15
S. J. Milosz c Scott b May	3	not out	0
L-b 9, n-b 1	10	B 2, l-b 4	6

1/5 2/18 3/29 4/147 5/179   **240**   1/52 2/58 3/128 4/132 5/158   **257**
6/179 7/195 8/223 9/233   6/204 7/204 8/217 9/250

Bowling: *First Innings*—Gladigau 12-3-44-2; Pyke 16-2-47-0; Zesers 25-11-40-2; Scott 2-1-1-0; May 20.2-4-60-5; Sleep 22-7-39-1. *Second Innings*—Gladigau 14-2-38-1; Pyke 7-2-31-1; Zesers 23.2-10-50-3; Scott 3-0-11-0; May 21-2-75-2; Sleep 10-2-42-2; Hookes 2-1-4-0.

South Australia

G. A. Bishop c Boon b Kirkman	13	†W. B. Phillips not out	213
A. M. Hilditch c Boon b Milosz	88	B 2, l-b 3, n-b 4	9
D. F. G. O'Connor c Boon b Brown	14		
*D. W. Hookes not out	306	1/21 2/78 3/181 (3 wkts dec.)	643

J. K. Pyke, P. R. Sleep, T. B. A. May, D. B. Scott, A. K. Zesers and P. W. Gladigau did not bat.

Bowling: Brown 13–1–81–1; Kirkman 29–0–164–1; Tame 21–2–98–0; Milosz 34–6–146–1; Jelich 13–3–61–0; Cruse 7–2–36–0; Boon 15–3–52–0.

Umpires: B. E. Martin and R. B. Woods.

WESTERN AUSTRALIA v QUEENSLAND

At Perth, March 6, 7, 8, 9. Western Australia won by six wickets. Western Australia 6 pts less 0.4 pt, Queensland –0.3 pt. Toss: Western Australia. Queensland had to win to qualify for the final for the fourth year in succession but, unable to cope with the Western Australian pace attack, they began badly and were bowled out on the first day. Western Australia in turn were unsettled by the speed and bounce gained by McDermott and owed their first-innings lead entirely to Marsh, who played superbly for his fourth hundred of the season. When Queensland's batting foundered a second time against pace, with Matthews again the spearhead, Western Australia had more than a day in which to score 194.

Queensland

B. A. Courtice c Veletta b Capes	54	– (2) c Zoehrer b Capes	32
R. B. Kerr c Moody b MacLeay	25	– (1) c Zoehrer b MacLeay	1
G. M. Ritchie b Matthews	2	– (5) c Zoehrer b Capes	19
*A. R. Border c Zoehrer b Matthews	39	– b Matthews	53
G. S. Trimble c Zoehrer b Reid	43	– (3) c Veletta b Matthews	66
A. B. Henschell c Wood b Reid	10	– c Capes b Matthews	1
†P. W. Anderson lbw b Capes	16	– c Capes b Matthews	10
C. J. McDermott c Moody b Matthews	12	– c Marks b Matthews	25
D. Tazelaar c Marsh b MacLeay	14	– c Marsh b Marks	2
M. A. Polzin c Veletta b Matthews	23	– c Zoehrer b Reid	15
P. J. Carew not out	0	– not out	0
B 1, l-b 8, n-b 6	15	B 1, l-b 4, n-b 9	14

1/36 2/39 3/118 4/132 5/174   253   1/7 2/90 3/126 4/161 5/163   238
6/184 7/202 8/212 9/249   6/191 7/206 8/220 9/221

Bowling: *First Innings*—Reid 24–3–77–2; MacLeay 27–9–66–2; Matthews 22.2–7–50–4; Capes 16–3–43–2; Marks 3–2–8–0. *Second Innings*—Reid 9.2–2–19–1; MacLeay 18–4–59–1; Matthews 20–5–60–4; Capes 18–5–57–3; Marks 10–1–38–1.

Western Australia

M. R. J. Veletta c Anderson b McDermott	5	– (2) not out	60
G. R. Marsh b McDermott	146	– (1) c McDermott b Henschell	44
T. M. Moody lbw b Tazelaar	11	– b Polzin	36
*G. M. Wood run out	11	– (5) c Anderson b Polzin	12
M. W. McPhee c Courtice b Henschell	26	– (6) not out	1
K. H. MacLeay lbw b McDermott	10		
†T. J. Zoehrer c Anderson b McDermott	0	– (4) b Polzin	23
V. J. Marks c Border b Polzin	44		
C. D. Matthews b Carew	22		
P. A. Capes lbw b McDermott	2		
B. A. Reid not out	2		
B 1, n-b 18	19	B 6, l-b 4, n-b 8	18

1/13 2/44 3/76 4/128 5/159   298   1/71 2/141 3/169   (4 wkts) 194
6/159 7/250 8/285 9/296   4/188

Bowling: *First Innings*—McDermott 20.1–6–55–5; Tazelaar 16–0–73–1; Polzin 13–2–45–1; Henschell 25–8–59–1; Carew 18–2–65–1. *Second Innings*—McDermott 16–0–67–0; Tazelaar 8–1–33–0; Polzin 12–4–27–3; Henschell 13.1–3–39–1; Carew 8–0–18–0.

Umpires: P. J. McConnell and T. A. Prue.

FINAL

WESTERN AUSTRALIA v VICTORIA

At Perth, March 20, 21, 22, 23, 24. Drawn. Toss: Victoria. By virtue of finishing top of the table, Western Australia had only to draw the final to win the Sheffield Shield, and this they did decisively. Victoria's only hope was to amass a big first-innings total and then bowl out their opponents twice, but on an excellent pitch this was a tall order. Having declared at 404 on the second afternoon, they did not dismiss Western Australia once until the fifth morning. For Victoria, O'Donnell's powerful hitting produced 80 in two and a half hours, Dodemaide compiled a more circumspect 81 not out, and Siddons promised great things until getting out when well set. Marsh took two sensational catches in the gully, and Capes was the best of Western Australia's left-arm pace triumvirate. Victoria needed early wickets, but Marsh and Veletta resisted every assault, and when after four and a half hours Marsh edged a drive to slip, Veletta batted on and on into the fourth day. Finally, after twelve and threequarter hours, he drove a catch to mid-off. His 262 was the highest score for Western Australia, beating Colin Milburn's 243 in 1968-69, an innings which, in contrast, occupied just two sessions; and Western Australia's 654 was their highest first-class total. In the field, Victoria never relented, and the enterprising Moody, just 3 runs short of his third hundred of the season, was run out by smart fielding from Dodemaide. Although Victoria's second innings was academic, O'Donnell again played well, hitting his tenth fifty of the summer.

Victoria

M. B. Quinn c Zoehrer b Capes	7	– (2) c Zoehrer b Capes	9
D. F. Whatmore b Capes	16	– (1) c Marsh b Capes	19
P. A. Hibbert run out	48	– b Marks	34
J. D. Siddons c Zoehrer b Capes	54	– c Marks b Matthews	13
S. P. O'Donnell c Marsh b Reid	80	– (6) c Capes b Reid	78
P. W. Young c Veletta b Reid	15	– (5) b Marks	1
A. I. C. Dodemaide not out	81	– not out	13
†M. G. D. Dimattina c Marsh b Capes	13	– not out	26
*R. J. Bright b Marks	29		
M. G. Hughes not out	33		
B 4, l-b 11, n-b 13	28	B 5, l-b 10, n-b 7	22

1/12 2/27 3/123 4/157 5/231   (8 wkts dec.) 404   1/27 2/38 3/61   (6 wkts) 215
6/232 7/268 8/339   4/62 5/106 6/170

S. P. Davis did not bat.

Bowling: *First Innings*—Capes 35-10-90-4; MacLeay 20-8-40-0; Reid 30-9-106-2; Matthews 18-2-84-0; Marks 24-4-67-1; Moody 1-0-2-0. *Second Innings*—Capes 13-4-43-2; MacLeay 11-5-32-0; Matthews 14-3-47-1; Marks 31-18-43-2; Reid 9-2-24-1; Andrews 1-1-0-0; Moody 5-0-11-0; Zoehrer 1-1-0-0.

Western Australia

M. R. J. Veletta c Dodemaide b Davis	262	C. D. Matthews c and b O'Donnell	6
G. R. Marsh c Whatmore b Dodemaide	86	P. A. Capes not out	6
T. M. Moody run out	97	B. A. Reid b Hughes	4
*G. M. Wood c sub b Hughes	84		
W. S. Andrews c sub b Davis	19	B 4, l-b 3, n-b 4	11
K. H. MacLeay c Dodemaide b Davis	10		
†T. J. Zoehrer st Dimattina b Siddons	53	1/152 2/316 3/508 4/545 5/554	654
V. J. Marks c sub b O'Donnell	16	6/592 7/631 8/642 9/643	

Bowling: Hughes 42-10-113-2; O'Donnell 37-6-134-2; Davis 34-5-127-3; Dodemaide 42-11-111-1; Bright 46-14-85-0; Siddons 14-1-44-1; Hibbert 3-0-9-0; Whatmore 13-7-24-0.

Umpires: P. J. McConnell and R. G. Bailhache.

SHEFFIELD SHIELD WINNERS

1892-93	Victoria	1939-40	New South Wales
1893-94	South Australia	1940-46	No competition
1894-95	Victoria	1946-47	Victoria
1895-96	New South Wales	1947-48	Western Australia
1896-97	New South Wales	1948-49	New South Wales
1897-98	Victoria	1949-50	New South Wales
1898-99	Victoria	1950-51	Victoria
1899-1900	New South Wales	1951-52	New South Wales
1900-01	Victoria	1952-53	South Australia
1901-02	New South Wales	1953-54	New South Wales
1902-03	New South Wales	1954-55	New South Wales
1903-04	New South Wales	1955-56	New South Wales
1904-05	New South Wales	1956-57	New South Wales
1905-06	New South Wales	1957-58	New South Wales
1906-07	New South Wales	1958-59	New South Wales
1907-08	Victoria	1959-60	New South Wales
1908-09	New South Wales	1960-61	New South Wales
1909-10	South Australia	1961-62	New South Wales
1910-11	New South Wales	1962-63	Victoria
1911-12	New South Wales	1963-64	South Australia
1912-13	South Australia	1964-65	New South Wales
1913-14	New South Wales	1965-66	New South Wales
1914-15	Victoria	1966-67	Victoria
1915-19	No competition	1967-68	Western Australia
1919-20	New South Wales	1968-69	South Australia
1920-21	New South Wales	1969-70	Victoria
1921-22	Victoria	1970-71	South Australia
1922-23	New South Wales	1971-72	Western Australia
1923-24	Victoria	1972-73	Western Australia
1924-25	Victoria	1973-74	Victoria
1925-26	New South Wales	1974-75	Western Australia
1926-27	South Australia	1975-76	South Australia
1927-28	Victoria	1976-77	Western Australia
1928-29	New South Wales	1977-78	Western Australia
1929-30	Victoria	1978-79	Victoria
1930-31	Victoria	1979-80	Victoria
1931-32	New South Wales	1980-81	Western Australia
1932-33	New South Wales	1981-82	South Australia
1933-34	Victoria	1982-83	New South Wales
1934-35	Victoria	1983-84	Western Australia
1935-36	South Australia	1984-85	New South Wales
1936-37	Victoria	1985-86	New South Wales
1937-38	New South Wales	1986-87	Western Australia
1938-39	South Australia		

New South Wales have won the Shield 39 times, Victoria 24, South Australia 12, Western Australia 10, Queensland 0, Tasmania 0.

†McDONALD'S CUP, 1986-87

At Perth, October 10. Western Australia won by 74 runs. Western Australia 248 for seven (50 overs) (T. M. Moody 70, P. Gonnella 58); Victoria 174 for eight (50 overs) (M. G. D. Dimattina 64).

At Hobart, October 11. Tasmania won on faster scoring-rate. Tasmania 231 for seven (44 overs) (E. J. Harris 54, D. J. Buckingham 48); Queensland 58 for four (21.2 overs).

At Adelaide, October 18. Queensland won by nine wickets after being set a revised target. South Australia 226 for five (47 overs) (G. A. Bishop 66, D. W. Hookes 46, P. R. Sleep 46 not out); Queensland 193 for one (35.1 overs) (T. J. Barsby 64, R. B. Kerr 95 not out).

At Adelaide, October 19. South Australia won on faster scoring-rate. South Australia 245 for five (50 overs) (A. M. J. Hilditch 109, S. C. Wundke 54 not out); Tasmania 175 for five (44 overs) (R. D. Woolley 43 not out, R. E. Soule 51 not out; T. B. A. May four for 9).

At Perth, November 2. Tied. New South Wales 243 for six (50 overs) (S. M. Small 85, T. H. Bayliss 43); Western Australia 243 for nine (50 overs) (G. M. Wood 71, W. S. Andrews 66 not out).

At Sydney, November 9. Victoria won by 1 run. Victoria 215 for seven (50 overs) (D. M. Jones 139 not out; M. R. Whitney four for 34); New South Wales 214 (50 overs) (G. R. J. Matthews 57, M. E. Waugh 46).

Semi-finals

At Adelaide, February 15. Tied. South Australia qualified for the final on their superior run-rate in the preliminary rounds. South Australia 222 for seven (50 overs) (D. F. G. O'Connor 46, J. K. Pyke 57, D. B. Scott 51 not out; M. G. Hughes four for 34); Victoria 222 for six (50 overs) (P. W. Young 51).

At Perth, February 15. Tasmania won by four wickets. Western Australia 266 for five (50 overs) (M. R. J. Veletta 69, T. M. Moody 42, G. M. Wood 96 not out); Tasmania 271 for six (49.3 overs) (D. C. Boon 80, R. D. Woolley 80 not out).

FINAL

†TASMANIA v SOUTH AUSTRALIA

At Hobart, March 15. South Australia won by 86 runs. Toss: Tasmania. Bishop's 116, off 128 balls, included three sixes and fourteen fours, while Phillips, with two sixes and nine fours, hit his 75 off 43 balls. South Australia's 325 was the highest total in a 50-overs innings in the final.
Man of the Match: G. A. Bishop.

South Australia

A. M. J. Hilditch c Soule b Tame	20	J. K. Pyke b de Winter	15
G. A. Bishop c and b de Winter	116	D. B. Scott not out	13
D. F. G. O'Connor c Bradshaw b de Winter	36	L-b 8, w 4, n-b 1	13
*D. W. Hookes b Bradshaw	37		
†W. B. Phillips run out	75		

1/45 2/131 3/188 (6 wkts, 50 overs) 325
4/241 5/288 6/325

S. C. Wundke, P. W. Gladigau, T. B. A. May and A. K. Zesers did not bat.

Bowling: Brown 10-0-53-0; Blizzard 10-1-38-0; Tame 6-0-64-1; de Winter 10-0-84-3; Hughes 10-0-47-0; Bradshaw 4-0-31-1.

Tasmania

N. Jelich c Hookes b Gladigau	10	R. L. Brown c sub b Bishop	22
*D. C. Boon c Pyke b Scott	38	P. A. Blizzard not out	1
D. J. Buckingham c Gladigau b May	56	M. P. Tame not out	0
R. D. Woolley c May b Scott	21	L-b 12, w 2, n-b 1	15
G. A. Hughes c Bishop b May	27		
A. J. de Winter b Zesers	4		
K. Bradshaw b May	8	1/54 2/62 3/122 (9 wkts, 50 overs) 239
†R. E. Soule b Wundke	37	4/137 5/141 6/155
		7/187 8/226 9/239

Bowling: Gladigau 10-2-38-1; Pyke 5-1-23-0; Scott 10-1-44-2; Zesers 10-0-45-1; May 10-0-50-3; Wundke 4-0-22-1; Bishop 1-0-5-1.

Umpires: D. R. Close and S. G. Randell.

CRICKET IN SOUTH AFRICA, 1986-87

By PETER SICHEL

For the second successive year, an Australian team toured South Africa, and again they provided the country's leading players with much needed international competition. It was noticeable that the Australians appeared more relaxed than on their first visit, and this was demonstrated in their approach to their matches. The development of Michael Haysman, John Maguire and Rod McCurdy was pleasing to see, and the experienced players, such as John Dyson, Steve Smith, Kim Hughes and Greg Shipperd, had good tours. However, Terry Alderman, Carl Rackemann and Mick Taylor disappointed.

The four five-day "Tests" were keenly contested, as the 1-0 scoreline, in South Africa's favour, illustrates. Dyson, Haysman and Smith produced innings of charm and character, but the bowlers, apart from McCurdy and Maguire, struggled to bowl out the South Africans, although Rodney Hogg, perhaps the quickest of all, did trouble them on more than one occasion. Similarly, the South Africans scored heavily through Peter Kirsten, Ken McEwan and Graeme Pollock, but it was left to Garth le Roux to provide the penetration necessary to bowl out sides on good pitches. At Newlands, Cape Town, and St George's Park, Port Elizabeth, the pitches were ideal for batting; and everywhere the matches were played in a fine spirit and attended by large crowds.

On the domestic scene, Transvaal regained the Currie Cup, but not quite as convincingly as hitherto. They were without Henry Fotheringham for part of the season, and consequently struggled to get the fine starts provided by Cook and him in recent years. Pollock, in his farewell season, also missed a few games but always looked dangerous at the crease. Clive Rice had a disappointing season, by his usual high standards, but Kevin McKenzie was in great form, hitting a career-best 188 against Eastern Province at the Wanderers. Brian McMillan, after his fine season with Warwickshire, was disappointing, as was Hugh Page, whose rhythm appeared to desert him. He was rather expensive. Transvaal's resilience was never better illustrated than against Western Province in the Currie Cup final, when Ray Jennings scored 99, having come in as night-watchman. Jennings also had a good season behind the stumps with 36 dismissals (32 ct, 4 st) in first-class matches, twice taking ten catches in a match – against Northern Transvaal at Verwoerdburg and Orange Free State at the Wanderers.

Western Province, by way of consolation, won the popular Benson and Hedges Trophy final against Transvaal a week later. Thanks to Kirsten, McEwan, Laurence Seeff, Darryl Cullinan and Terence Lazard, they made a great many runs throughout the season, yet inexplicably they were bowled out twice for moderate scores in Port Elizabeth to lose by an innings to Eastern Province. A certain looseness crept into their play from time to time, batsmen giving their wickets away when seemingly well set. Of the bowlers, le Roux, who had a fine season with bat and ball, Steve Jefferies, Brett Matthews, Adrian Kuiper and Eric Simons performed most creditably.

Eastern Province, strengthened by the arrival of Kepler Wessels as their new captain, again fell at the penultimate fence, being soundly beaten by

Western Province in their semi-final at Port Elizabeth. In Mark Rushmere they have as fine a young batsman as any in the country, but less reassuring was the reliance on Wessels, David Capel and, in the semi-final, Rod McCurdy, three imported players. Third in 1985-86, Northern Transvaal slipped to fourth after three heavy defeats early in the season. An unbeaten double-hundred by Vernon du Preez and an innings victory in the final match, against Border, showed what they were capable of. Mike Rindel, a left-hander, was their leading run-scorer in his first season of Currie Cup cricket, but Roy Pienaar, so prolific in limited-overs cricket (700 runs in sixteen innings), failed to reproduce this form in the first-class game. Cyril Mitchley and Rodney Ontong were the leading wicket-takers. Natal, although winning the Nissan Shield, also disappointed in the Currie Cup. However, potential there is evident. They had a comparatively young side, with a blend of maturity in Darryl Bestall, Rob Bentley, Brian Whitfield and Mark Logan, and with the emergence of such players as Chris Lister-James, David Norman and Andrew Hudson, they could hope for an improvement in the coming seasons.

Orange Free State were unfortunate to be without Corrie van Zyl for the greater part of the season, but in Allan Donald they had an exciting new prospect. He possessed a fast bowler's main attribute, speed, needing only to ally it to the ability to bowl a line and length. This should come with experience, and when it does, Donald and van Zyl could form the most dangerous opening partnership in South Africa. Joubert Strydom, the captain, is another who has youth on his side, with his best years undoubtedly ahead of him. Border found the standard of Currie Cup cricket extremely high, struggled, and returned to the Bowl section for 1987-88. Their batting was competent, but they lacked penetration in their attack. Emmerson Trotman and Lorrie Wilmot formed the backbone of their batting, with Wilmot, in his 43rd year, providing an object lesson to his younger team-mates with his courage and determination in adversity.

FIRST-CLASS AVERAGES, 1986-87

BATTING

(Qualification: 8 innings, average 35.00)

	M	I	NO	R	HI	100s	Avge
G. E. McMillan (*Transvaal/Transvaal B*)	7	10	4	628	156*	3	104.66
R. G. Pollock (*Transvaal*)	6	8	1	456	144	2	65.14
K. C. Wessels (*E. Province/Australian XI*) ...	12	20	2	1,160	137	5	64.44
A. J. Moles (*Griqualand W.*)	7	12	1	705	174	3	64.09
K. S. McEwan (*W. Province*)	10	17	4	830	138*	5	63.84
J. During (*W. Province B*)	6	9	5	255	66*	0	63.75
B. J. Whitfield (*Natal*)	10	18	3	845	129*	2	56.33
H. R. Fotheringham (*Transvaal/Transvaal B*)	5	8	1	358	134	1	51.14
V. F. du Preez (*N. Transvaal*)	5	9	1	399	200*	1	49.87
T. N. Lazard (*W. Province*)	6	11	1	495	166	2	49.50

	M	I	NO	R	HI	100s	Avge
P. N. Kirsten (*W. Province*)	12	21	2	921	204*	3	48.47
L. P. Vorster (*Transvaal/Transvaal B*)	9	14	3	516	74*	0	46.90
S. J. Cook (*Transvaal*)	10	18	2	748	110	3	46.75
M. D. Mellor (*Natal B*)	6	11	2	414	104*	1	46.00
K. A. McKenzie (*Transvaal*)	9	13	2	502	188	2	45.63
T. R. Madsen (*Natal*)	7	11	3	363	64	0	45.37
L. Seeff (*W. Province*)	8	15	3	534	141	3	44.50
D. Bestall (*Natal*)	7	12	5	301	113	1	43.00
A. I. Kallicharran (*OFS*)	7	13	0	555	110	1	42.69
W. M. van der Merwe (*W. Province B*)	4	8	3	204	79*	0	40.80
A. L. Wilmot (*Border*)	7	12	2	406	95*	0	40.60
K. J. Bridgens (*W. Province B*)	5	9	2	282	79	0	40.28
M. J. Mitchley (*Transvaal B*)	6	9	1	322	116*	1	40.25
T. B. Reid (*E. Province/E. Province B*)	6	10	2	320	79*	0	40.00
R. M. Bentley (*Natal/Natal B*)	7	12	2	389	79*	0	38.90
R. C. Ontong (*N. Transvaal*)	7	13	5	310	95	0	38.75
D. P. le Roux (*OFS*)	6	11	0	425	127	2	38.63
O. Henry (*Boland*)	6	9	1	307	114*	1	38.37
D. J. Ferrant (*E. Province B*)	6	9	4	191	66*	0	38.20
J. W. Furstenburg (*E. Province/E. Province B*)	5	9	1	303	73*	0	37.87

*Signifies not out.

BOWLING

(Qualification: 20 wickets)

	O	M	R	W	BB	Avge
J. During (*W. Province B*)	149.4	37	403	25	6-53	16.12
J. C. van Duyker (*N. Transvaal B*)	160.5	48	430	26	6-70	16.53
J. J. Hooper (*Transvaal/Transvaal B*)	193	50	456	24	7-29	19.00
G. S. le Roux (*W. Province*)	364.2	82	961	49	6-53	19.61
M. K. van Vuuren (*E. Province/E. Province B*)	167.1	36	469	23	4-44	20.39
C. D. Mitchley (*N. Transvaal*)	198.2	34	638	31	5-39	20.58
C. E. B. Rice (*Transvaal*)	216.1	63	495	24	4-19	20.62
K. J. Kerr (*Transvaal/Transvaal B*)	300.1	92	741	35	6-62	21.17
P. A. Rayment (*E. Province/E. Province B*)	164.3	34	446	21	5-51	21.23
A. J. Kourie (*Transvaal*)	280.5	87	641	30	6-67	21.36
D. J. Capel (*E. Province*)	148	33	473	21	5-43	22.52
A. A. Donald (*OFS*)	358.3	61	1,116	47	8-37	23.74
B. E. van der Vyver (*Griqualand W.*)	170.3	32	586	23	4-58	25.47
S. T. Jefferies (*W. Province*)	214.1	53	588	23	4-62	25.56
H. L. Alleyne (*Natal*)	177.5	29	582	22	4-30	26.45
N. V. Radford (*Transvaal*)	263	60	754	28	5-61	26.92
T. G. Shaw (*E. Province*)	391.2	132	793	27	6-49	29.37
R. L. S. Armitage (*E. Province*)	235	61	624	21	4-18	29.71
R. J. McCurdy (*E. Province/Australian XI*)	307.1	59	941	31	6-67	30.35
A. L. Hobson (*E. Province/E. Province B*)	236.5	49	734	24	7-42	30.58
B. T. Player (*OFS*)	194.4	41	620	20	5-31	31.00
M. B. Minnaar (*W. Province/W. Province B*)	320.4	93	721	23	4-73	31.34
O. Henry (*Boland*)	264.5	75	630	20	4-41	31.50
M. R. Hobson (*Natal/Natal B*)	223.5	33	734	22	5-72	33.36
H. A. Page (*Transvaal*)	386.3	71	1,077	32	4-68	33.65
R. C. Ontong (*N. Transvaal*)	248.2	55	682	20	5-96	34.10

CASTLE CURRIE CUP, 1986-87

	Played	Won	Lost	Drawn	Bonus Points Batting	Bowling	Total Pts
Transvaal	6	4	0	2	19	28	107
Eastern Province	6	4	2	0	14	24	98
Western Province	6	3	2	1	27	25	97
Northern Transvaal ...	6	1	4	1	15	23	53
Natal	6	1	0	5	14	22	51
Orange Free State	6	1	3	2	12	17	44
Border	6	0	3	3	8	17	25

Semi-final: Western Province beat Eastern Province by 47 runs.
Final: Transvaal drew with Western Province and won the trophy by virtue of finishing top of the qualifying table.

In the following scores, * by the name of a team indicates that they won the toss.

At Port Elizabeth, October 19, 20, 21. Eastern Province won by 212 runs. Eastern Province* 406 for five dec. (I. K. Daniell 59, K. C. Wessels 133, M. W. Rushmere 124, M. Michau 39; A. P. Beukes three for 90) and 229 for four dec. (I. K. Daniell 43, K. C. Wessels 78, R. L. S. Armitage 94 not out; A. A. Donald three for 48); Orange Free State 261 (A. M. Green 135; R. L. S. Armitage three for 39) and 162 (P. J. R. Steyn 44, A. I. Kallicharran 59; A. L. Hobson seven for 42). *Eastern Province 26 pts, Orange Free State 4 pts.*

At Bloemfontein, October 24, 25, 27. Drawn. Border* 350 for nine dec. (M. J. P. Ford 58, N. P. Minnaar 45, A. L. Wilmot 63, L. M. Phillips 30, I. L. Howell 39 not out; B. T. Player four for 81) and 207 for seven dec. (M. J. P. Ford 38, B. W. Lones 47, A. L. Wilmot 50 not out, L. M. Phillips 35; A. A. Donald three for 54, A. I. Kallicharran three for 63); Orange Free State 269 for five dec. (D. P. le Roux 127, J. J. Strydom 57, L. J. Wenzler 35 not out) and 266 for six (D. P. le Roux 109, A. I. Kallicharran 83). *Orange Free State 6 pts, Border 4 pts.*

At Cape Town, October 25, 26, 27. Drawn. Natal* 348 (D. Bestall 113, C. M. Lister-James 98, T. R. Madsen 60; M. B. Minnaar four for 92, B. A. Matthews three for 54) and 193 for five (B. J. Whitfield 77 not out, R. M. Bentley 57); Western Province 528 for seven dec. (A. G. Elgar 65, L. Seeff 141, P. N. Kirsten 204 not out, G. S. le Roux 39; H. L. Alleyne four for 105). *Western Province 8 pts, Natal 3 pts.*

At East London, November 21, 22, 23. Drawn. Border* 123 (H. L. Alleyne four for 30, R. K. McGlashan three for 44); Natal 129 for seven dec. (B. J. Whitfield 33, A. C. Hudson 51; G. M. Gower three for 21). *Border 3 pts, Natal 5 pts.*

At Johannesburg, November 21, 22, 23. Transvaal won by an innings and 17 runs. Transvaal* 397 for eight dec. (R. G. Pollock 107, K. A. McKenzie 188; W. K. Watson three for 96, D. J. Capel four for 71); Eastern Province 148 (R. L. S. Armitage 43, M. W. Rushmere 56; A. J. Kourie five for 5, N. V. Radford three for 39) and 232 (D. J. Richardson 64, D. J. Capel 46; N. V. Radford five for 61, B. M. McMillan four for 42). *Transvaal 28 pts, Eastern Province 3 pts.*

At Cape Town, November 22, 23, 24. Western Province won by 75 runs. Western Province* 260 (A. G. Elgar 33, K. S. McEwan 52, D. J. Cullinan 50, G. S. le Roux 59, S. T. Jefferies 37; C. D. Mitchley four for 56, R. C. Ontong three for 67) and 256 for four dec. (L. Seeff 46, K. S. McEwan 104 not out, A. P. Kuiper 42 not out; Northern Transvaal 218 (V. F. du Preez 41, L. J. Barnard 46, M. J. R. Rindel 43, R. C. Ontong 37 not out; S. T. Jefferies four for 62) and 223 (L. J. Barnard 77, A. M. Ferreira 31; G. S. le Roux four for 44, S. T. Jefferies three for 36, B. A. Matthews three for 49). *Western Province 23 pts, Northern Transvaal 5 pts.*

At Port Elizabeth, November 28, 29, 30. Eastern Province won by an innings and 35 runs. Western Province* 190 (L. Seeff 32, K. S. McEwan 102; T. G. Shaw four for 53, W. K. Watson three for 43) and 111 (E. O. Simons 57; R. L. S. Armitage four for 18, D. J. Capel three for 14); Eastern Province 336 (K. C. Wessels 40, M. Michau 47, D. J. Capel 134; G. S. le Roux four for 41). *Eastern Province 20 pts, Western Province 4 pts.*

At Durban, November 29, 30, December 1. Drawn. Transvaal 297 (S. J. Cook 43, H. R. Fotheringham 80, L. P. Vorster 48, C. E. B. Rice 77; H. L. Alleyne four for 98, D. Norman three for 61) and 233 for three dec. (S. J. Cook 109, H. R. Fotheringham 58, L. P. Vorster 35); Natal* 246 (M. B. Logan 44, A. C. Hudson 58, P. H. Rayner 31, N. P. Daniels 30; A. J. Kourie five for 75) and 143 for seven. *Natal 5 pts, Transvaal 7 pts.*

At Bloemfontein, December 6, 8, 9. Drawn. Natal* 277 (B. J. Whitfield 58, A. C. Hudson 46, R. M. Bentley 33, D. Bestall 47, C. M. Lister-James 44; F. J. C. Cronje three for 58) and 204 for three dec. (B. J. Whitfield 82, R. M. Bentley 79 not out; A. A. Donald three for 50); Orange Free State 200 (D. P. le Roux 36, A. I. Kallicharran 33, L. J. Wilkinson 36, F. J. C. Cronje 34 not out; R. K. McGlashan three for 100) and 256 for nine (P. J. R. Steyn 67, A. I. Kallicharran 69, J. J. Strydom 58 not out, R. J. East 33). *Orange Free State 4 pts, Natal 7 pts.*

At Verwoerdburg, December 12, 13, 15. Transvaal won by 120 runs. Transvaal 377 (B. M. McMillan 53, R. G. Pollock 61, C. E. B. Rice 37, K. A. McKenzie 121 not out, L. P. Vorster 46; C. D. Mitchley five for 88, M. D. Clare three for 88) and 220 for two dec. (S. J. Cook 105, M. Yachad 36, B. M. McMillan 51 not out); Northern Transvaal* 244 (M. J. R. Rindel 52, P. J. A. Visagie 71; C. E. B. Rice three for 45) and 233 (R. F. Pienaar 34, N. T. Day 34, P. J. A. Visagie 50; A. J. Kourie six for 67, H. A. Page three for 52). *Transvaal 25 pts, Northern Transvaal 5 pts.*

At Bloemfontein, December 12, 13, 15. Western Province won by ten wickets. Western Province* 406 for seven dec. (T. N. Lazard 166, K. S. McEwan 125, D. J. Cullinan 53) and 27 for no wkt; Orange Free State 115 (B. T. Player 51 not out; E. O. Simons three for 16, A. P. Kuiper four for 20) and 317 (D. P. le Roux 50, J. J. Strydom 107, L. J. Wilkinson 36, R. J. East 32; S. T. Jefferies three for 66, M. B. Minnaar four for 73). *Western Province 26 pts, Orange Free State 1 pt.*

At Verwoerdburg, December 19, 20, 21. Orange Free State won by 89 runs. Orange Free State* 272 (D. P. le Roux 54, A. I. Kallicharran 72, J. J. Strydom 38, C. J. P. G. van Zyl 30; C. D. Mitchley three for 40, A. M. Ferreira four for 49) and 154 (A. I. Kallicharran 50; C. D. Mitchley five for 39, M. D. Clare three for 63); Northern Transvaal 143 (B. T. Player five for 31, A. A. Donald three for 60) and 194 (R. F. Pienaar 57, M. J. R. Rindel 44; A. A. Donald four for 54). *Orange Free State 24 pts, Northern Transvaal 5 pts.*

At Johannesburg, December 19, 20, 21. Transvaal won by seven wickets. Western Province* 252 (P. N. Kirsten 69, E. O. Simons 47; N. V. Radford three for 89, H. A. Page four for 68) and 82 (N. V. Radford three for 21, H. A. Page three for 30); Transvaal 178 (M. Yachad 36, L. P. Vorster 34, A. J. Kourie 42 not out, R. V. Jennings 37; G. S. le Roux four for 42) and 159 for three (M. Yachad 33, L. P. Vorster 69 not out). *Transvaal 21 pts, Western Province 9 pts.*

At East London, December 19, 20, 21. Eastern Province won by eight wickets. Border* 165 (M. J. P. Ford 35, B. W. Lones 33; T. G. Shaw six for 49) and 122 (T. G. Shaw three for 33); Eastern Province 177 (D. J. Richardson 67; G. J. Thomas three for 8, H. Lindenberg three for 57) and 111 for two (K. C. Wessels 51 not out, M. W. Rushmere 32 not out). *Eastern Province 21 pts, Border 5 pts.*

At Port Elizabeth, December 26, 27, 28. Eastern Province won by two wickets. Northern Transvaal* 214 (V. F. du Preez 48, L. J. Barnard 48, M. J. R. Rindel 31, P. J. A. Visagie 32, A. M. Ferreira 35; D. J. Capel five for 43) and 179 (A. M. Ferreira 43; T. G. Shaw four for 52, R. L. S. Armitage three for 67); Eastern Province 244 (J. W. Furstenburg 47, M. W. Rushmere 36, T. B. Reid 63; R. C. Ontong five for 96, W. F. Morris three for 90) and 152 for eight (J. W. Furstenburg 49, D. J. Capel 36; W. F. Morris six for 69). *Eastern Province 21 pts, Northern Transvaal 7 pts.*

At Durban, January 1, 2, 3. Drawn. Northern Transvaal 352 for eight dec. (A. M. Ferreira 133, R. C. Ontong 95; R. M. Bentley three for 16) and 248 for seven dec. (R. F. Pienaar 58, M. J. R. Rindel 92; R. M. Bentley four for 69) Natal* 320 for seven dec. (M. B. Logan 113, A. C. Hudson 46, P. H. Rayner 52) and 60 for five. *Natal 9 pts, Northern Transvaal 5 pts.*

At East London, January 1, 2, 3. Drawn. Transvaal* 341 for nine dec. (M. Yachad 33, D. H. Howell 51, L. P. Vorster 40, R. V. Jennings 33, G. E. McMillan 60; I. Foulkes four for 115) and 171 for eight dec. (M. Yachad 31, W. Kirsh 36, K. J. Kerr 49 not out; H. Lindenberg four for 39, E. N. Trotman three for 48); Border 287 (E. N. Trotman 173; K. J. Kerr three for 125, G. N. MacNab three for 41) and 204 for eight (M. J. P. Ford 65, E. N. Trotman 56; K. J. Kerr three for 61, G. N. MacNab three for 51). *Border 7 pts, Transvaal 6 pts.*

At Cape Town, January 24, 25, 26. Western Province won by eight wickets. Border* 192 (A. L. Wilmot 52, G. M. Gower 30; G. S. le Roux three for 32) and 300 (B. W. Lones 68, E. N. Trotman 47, A. L. Wilmot 95 not out; G. S. le Roux three for 57, S. T. Jefferies three for 74, M. B. Minnaar three for 56); Western Province 439 for six dec. (T. N. Lazard 129, L. Seeff 114, P. N. Kirsten 50, A. P. Kuiper 57 not out, S. T. Jefferies 41 not out; E. N. Trotman four for 128) and 54 for two. *Western Province 27 pts, Border 4 pts.*

At Johannesburg, January 24, 25, 26. Transvaal won by nine wickets. Orange Free State* 137 (J. J. Strydom 47, R. J. East 39; B. M. McMillan four for 22) and 187 (C. J. van Heerden 75, A. I. Kallicharran 38; N. V. Radford five for 62); Transvaal 139 (L. P. Vorster 33; A. A. Donald eight for 37) and 186 for one (S. J. Cook 94 not out, M. Yachad 74 not out). *Transvaal 20 pts, Orange Free State 5 pts.*

At Durban, January 24, 25, 26. Natal won by five wickets. Eastern Province 231 (K. C. Wessels 48, M. W. Rushmere 57, M. Michau 64; C. M. Lister-James four for 42) and 209 (D. J. Richardson 44, M. Michau 83; N. P. Daniels four for 57); Natal* 213 for eight dec. (T. R. Madsen 64, C. L. King 30, N. P. Daniels 46; R. L. S. Armitage three for 43) and 231 for five (B. J. Whitfield 45, A. C. Hudson 63, P. H. Rayner 31). *Natal 22 pts, Eastern Province 7 pts.*

At Verwoerdburg, February 6, 7, 9. Northern Transvaal won by an innings and 122 runs. Northern Transvaal 427 for five dec. (V. F. du Preez 200 not out, M. J. R. Rindel 89, R. C. Ontong 49 not out; G. J. Thomas four for 142); Border* 76 (C. D. Mitchley four for 33, P. S. de Villiers four for 35) and 229 (B. W. Lones 55, G. L. Hayes 39, A. L. Wilmot 69; C. D. Mitchley three for 29, R. C. Ontong three for 45). *Northern Transvaal 26 pts, Border 2 pts.*

Semi-final

At Port Elizabeth, March 6, 7, 8, 9. Western Province won by 47 runs. Western Province* 288 for seven dec. (T. N. Lazard 62, K. S. McEwan 79, D. J. Cullinan 51 not out, G. S. le Roux 39; R. J. McCurdy five for 65) and 256 (T. N. Lazard 43, P. N. Kirsten 54, D. J. Cullinan 60, A. P. Kuiper 37; R. J. McCurdy four for 61, T. G. Shaw four for 110); Eastern Province 331 for seven dec. (P. G. Amm 30, K. C. Wessels 129, M. W. Rushmere 74) and 166 (P. G. Amm 40, K. C. Wessels 83; G. S. le Roux six for 53, M. B. Minnaar three for 26).

Final

At Johannesburg, March 13, 14, 15, 16. Drawn. Western Province* 280 for seven dec. (P. N. Kirsten 54, A. P. Kuiper 50, G. S. le Roux 71 not out) and 274 for three dec. (L. Seeff 122 not out, P. N. Kirsten 30, K. S. McEwan 37 not out, D. J. Cullinan 55); Transvaal 340 for seven dec. (S. J. Cook 110, R. V. Jennings 99, C. E. B. Rice 34, A. J. Kourie 31 not out) and 176 for two (H. R. Fotheringham 72 not out, R. G. Pollock 63 not out).

CURRIE CUP WINNERS

1889-90	Transvaal	1954-55	Natal
1890-91	Griqualand West	1955-56	Western Province
1892-93	Western Province	1958-59	Transvaal
1893-94	Western Province	1959-60	Natal
1894-95	Transvaal	1960-61	Natal
1896-97	Western Province	1962-63	Natal
1897-98	Western Province	1963-64	Natal
1902-03	Transvaal	1965-66	Natal/Transvaal (Tied)
1903-04	Transvaal	1966-67	Natal
1904-05	Transvaal	1967-68	Natal
1906-07	Transvaal	1968-69	Transvaal
1908-09	Western Province	1969-70	Transvaal/W. Province (Tied)
1910-11	Natal	1970-71	Transvaal
1912-13	Natal	1971-72	Transvaal
1920-21	Western Province	1972-73	Transvaal
1921-22	Transvaal/Natal/W. Prov. (Tied)	1973-74	Natal
1923-24	Transvaal	1974-75	Western Province
1925-26	Transvaal	1975-76	Natal
1926-27	Transvaal	1976-77	Natal
1929-30	Transvaal	1977-78	Western Province
1931-32	Western Province	1978-79	Transvaal
1933-34	Natal	1979-80	Transvaal
1934-35	Transvaal	1980-81	Natal
1936-37	Natal	1981-82	Western Province
1937-38	Natal/Transvaal (Tied)	1982-83	Transvaal
1946-47	Natal	1983-84	Transvaal
1947-48	Natal	1984-85	Transvaal
1950-51	Natal	1985-86	Western Province
1951-52	Natal	1986-87	Transvaal
1952-53	Western Province		

SAB BOWL, 1986-87

	Played	Won	Lost	Drawn	Bonus Points Batting	Bowling	Total Pts
Transvaal B	6	3	0	3	21	22	88
Natal B	6	3	0	3	18	21	84
Western Province B	6	3	3	0	14	20	79
Eastern Province B	6	2	2	2	9	21	60
Northern Transvaal B ...	6	2	4	0	2	27	59
Griqualand West	6	1	2	3	16	22	53
Boland	6	0	3	3	15	17	32

At Pietermaritzburg, October 25, 26, 27. Natal B won by eight wickets. Western Province B* 286 (F. B. Touzel 47, S. D. Bruce 41, W. M. van der Merwe 33, J. During 47 not out; M. R. Hobson five for 72) and 120 for seven dec. (W. M. van der Merwe 51 not out; E. J. Hodkinson three for 71, M. R. Hobson three for 36); Natal B 220 (M. D. Mellor 30, A. C. Hudson 37, K. D. Dawson 42; W. M. van der Merwe four for 48, J. During three for 46) and 187 for two (M. D. Mellor 63, L. M. Fuhri 81 not out). *Natal B 22 pts, Western Province B 8 pts.*

At Port Elizabeth, November 21, 22, 23. Drawn. Eastern Province B* 188 (T. B. Reid 69; K. J. Kerr six for 62) and 176 for four (T. B. Reid 79 not out, M. K. van Vuuren 47); Transvaal B 354 for six dec. (D. H. Howell 32, M. J. Mitchley 72, G. E. McMillan 110, B. McBride 47 not out, K. J. Kerr 62 not out). *Eastern Province B 3 pts, Transvaal B 7 pts.*

At Durban, November 21, 22, 23. Natal B won by 54 runs. Natal B 247 (M. B. Logan 64, P. H. Rayner 61; I. F. N. Weideman three for 56, C. R. Norris three for 53) and 191 for six dec. (M. B. Logan 75, L. M. Fuhri 35, P. H. Rayner 31 not out); Northern Transvaal B* 168 (M. W. Pfaff 48, P. J. A. Visagie 33; M. R. Hobson four for 74, C. A. Lowe four for 33) and 216 (P. J. A. Visagie 39, P. J. Symcox 53, J. Groenewald 66; M. R. Hobson three for 55, C. A. Lowe three for 33, P. J. Allan three for 20). *Natal B 22 pts, Northern Transvaal B 3 pts.*

At Kimberley, November 28, 29, 30. Drawn. Natal B* 364 for nine dec. (L. M. Fuhri 38, M. J. Pearse 33, K. D. Dawson 59, G. M. Walsh 95, C. A. Lowe 45; B. E. van der Vyver four for 58) and 267 for three (M. D. Mellor 104 not out, M. J. Pearse 30, M. A. W. Bowman 100 not out); Griqualand West 363 (J. M. Arthur 39, W. E. Schonegevel 64, A. D. Methven 78, A. P. Beukes 57; M. G. Holmes three for 73, M. D. Mellor three for 90). *Griqualand West 6 pts, Natal B 6 pts.*

At Stellenbosch, November 28, 29, December 1. Northern Transvaal B won by 24 runs. Northern Transvaal B* 145 (V. G. Cresswell 71; J. Hendricks four for 36, O. Henry four for 41) and 290 (C. R. Norris 71, P. J. A. Visagie 35, V. G. Cresswell 53, I. F. N. Weideman 30 not out, P. S. de Villiers 30; O. Henry four for 144); Boland 277 (J. D. du Toit 43, O. Henry 79, A. Watts 37 not out; I. F. N. Weideman three for 45, C. E. Eksteen three for 65) and 134 (H. W. H. Bergins 36; P. L. Symcox four for 61, C. E. Eksteen four for 40). *Northern Transvaal B 19 pts, Boland 8 pts.*

At Johannesburg, December 12, 13, 14. Transvaal B won by 4 runs. Transvaal B* 205 (D. H. Howell 49, G. E. McMillan 35, B. McBride 50; P. S. de Villiers three for 39, I. F. N. Weideman three for 56, J. C. van Duyker three for 47) and 172 (M. J. Mitchley 38, G. E. McMillan 57; P. S. de Villiers six for 57, J. C. van Duyker three for 37); Northern Transvaal B 191 (M. S. Venter 63, C. R. Norris 72; G. E. McMillan four for 36, B. Roberts three for 19) and 182 (P. L. Selsick 34, V. G. Cresswell 34, P. L. Symcox 35; K. J. Kerr four for 34, B. Roberts five for 68). *Transvaal B 22 pts, Northern Transvaal B 6 pts.*

At Cape Town, December 13, 14, 15. Western Province B won by 57 runs. Western Province B* 302 (K. J. Bridgens 79, R. P. Richardson 42, P. A. Koen 30, J. During 44 not out; G. J. Parsons four for 78, G. W. Symmonds three for 44) and 276 for nine dec. (F. B. Touzel 60, J. B. Commins 49, W. M. van der Merwe 79 not out, P. A. Koen 32); Griqualand West 351 (A. J. Moles 142, W. E. Schonegevel 40, B. E. van der Vyver 57, A. P. Beukes 42; J. During six for 53) and 170 (A. P. Beukes 61; W. M. van der Merwe four for 50). *Western Province B 21 pts, Griqualand West 9 pts.*

At Port Elizabeth, December 18, 19, 20. Eastern Province B won by 220 runs. Eastern Province B* 354 for six dec. (J. W. Furstenburg 50, P. G. Amm 31, D. G. Emslie 111, D. J. Callaghan 34, D. J. Ferrant 66 not out; B. E. van der Vyver three for 77) and 199 for four dec. (J. W. Furstenburg 73, P. G. Amm 90); Griqualand West 212 (W. E. Schonegevel 65, B. E. van der Vyver 58; M. K. van Vuuren four for 44, J. A. Carse three for 45) and 121 (J. A. Carse three for 15, K. G. Bauermeister three for 53). *Eastern Province B 23 pts, Griqualand West 4 pts.*

At Cape Town, December 19, 20, 21. Transvaal B won by an innings and 15 runs. Transvaal B* 404 for six dec. (W. Kirsh 90, M. J. Mitchley 116, R. W. Adair 59, G. E. McMillan 104 not out; W. M. van der Merwe three for 93); Western Province B 146 (K. J. Bridgens 78 not out; J. J. Hooper seven for 29) and 243 (A. G. Elgar 39, F. B. Touzel 64, K. J. Bridgens 34; K. J. Kerr five for 63). *Transvaal B 22 pts, Western Province B 2 pts.*

At Pietermaritzburg, January 1, 2, 3. Drawn. Boland* 322 for eight dec. (A. du Toit 31, S. Nackerdien 91, O. Henry 114 not out) and 197 for seven dec. (A. du Toit 31, S. Nackerdien 47; M. G. Holmes three for 26); Natal B 312 for nine dec. (M. J. Pearse 171, P. J. Allan 51; J. D. du Toit three for 52, O. Henry three for 17) and 144 for nine (K. D. Dawson 34, M. A. W. Bowman 41; P. Anker four for 51, O. Henry four for 73). *Natal B 6 pts, Boland 5 pts.*

At Verwoerdburg, January 16, 17, 18. Eastern Province B won by 50 runs. Eastern Province B* 165 (M. Michau 85; J. C. van Duyker four for 57, T. Bosch five for 58) and 127 (M. K. van Vuuren 39; J. C. van Duyker six for 70); Northern Transvaal B 75 (M. K. van Vuuren three for 14, A. J. Roberts five for 43) and 167 (C. P. L. de Lange 51; A. J. Roberts five for 43, J. A. Carse four for 38). *Eastern Province B 20 pts, Northern Transvaal B 5 pts.*

At Kimberley, January 16, 17, 18. Drawn. Griqualand West 343 (A. J. Moles 65, B. E. van der Vyver 120, F. W. Swarbrook 60; K. J. Kerr five for 86) and 312 for six (A. J. Moles 174, M. N. Kellow 37, F. W. Swarbrook 51; Transvaal B* 363 for four dec. (H. R. Fotheringham 134, B. Roberts 51, L. P. Vorster 58 not out, G. E. McMillan 82 not out; G. W. Symmonds three for 67). *Griqualand West 4 pts, Transvaal B 10 pts.*

At Uitenhage, January 23, 24, 25. Natal B won by five wickets. Eastern Province B 180 (D. G. Emslie 42, D. J. Ferrant 30, M. K. van Vuuren 33; C. A. Lowe four for 56) and 201 (P. G. Amm 30, I. K. Daniell 54, D. J. Ferrant 32 not out; S. R. Kimber four for 75; P. J. Allan four for 65); Natal B* 291 (M. D. Mellor 73, G. Walsh 112; P. A. Rayment five for 51) and 91 for five (M. D. Mellor 31 not out; P. A. Rayment three for 29). *Natal B 24 pts, Eastern Province B 4 pts.*

At Johannesburg, January 29, 30, 31. Transvaal B won by 81 runs. Transvaal B 388 for four dec. (K. J. Rule 36, B. Roberts 130, R. W. Adair 161 not out) and 183 for eight dec. (M. J. Mitchley 51, R. W. Adair 55); Boland* 311 (E. E. van Rooyen 36, S. A. Jones 87, J. D. du Toit 95; K. J. Kerr four for 60) and 179 (S. Nackerdien 50, N. M. Lambrechts 62; J. J. Hooper four for 46). *Transvaal B 24 pts, Boland 5 pts.*

At Verwoerdburg, January 30, 31, February 1. Northern Transvaal B won by three wickets. Western Province B* 257 (M. H. Austen 36, J. During 66 not out, A. J. McClement 72; M. D. Clare four for 53, J. C. van Duyker three for 55) and 196 for five dec. (M. H. Austen 54, J. B. Commins 42, A. M. Kirsten 45 not out); Northern Transvaal B 183 (C. P. L. de Lange 32, C. E. Eksteen 44; W. M. van der Merwe four for 49, A. J. McClement three for 21) and 271 for seven (M. S. Venter 61, K. D. Verdoorn 91, C. P. L. de Lange 42; C. R. Matthews four for 57). *Northern Transvaal B 21 pts, Western Province B 7 pts.*

At Stellenbosch, February 6, 7, 9. Drawn. Boland* 304 for seven dec. (A. du Toit 118, N. M. Lambrechts 38; M. K. van Vuuren three for 49, D. J. Ferrant three for 60) and 225 for nine dec. (A. du Toit 135; M. K. van Vuuren three for 34, D. J. Ferrant four for 70); Eastern Province B 250 for nine dec. (D. J. Callaghan 87, A. P. Nell 81; E. E. van Rooyen five for 56, J. Hendricks three for 54) and 36 for no wkt. *Boland 6 pts, Eastern Province B 4 pts.*

At Johannesburg, February 6, 7, 8. Drawn. Transvaal B* 364 for seven dec. (B. Roberts 47, G. E. McMillan 156 not out, B. McBride 49) and 114 for four (W. Kirsh 44, R. W. Adair 35 not out); Natal B 296 (M. D. Mellor 37, R. M. Bentley 55, C. M. Walsh 56, P. P. H. Trimborn 37 not out; J. J. Hooper three for 73). *Transvaal B 3 pts, Natal B 4 pts.*

At Cape Town, February 11, 12, 13. Western Province B won by six wickets. Eastern Province B* 314 for eight dec. (P. G. Amm 42, I. K. Daniell 94, D. G. Emslie 57, D. J. Callaghan 93; J. During six for 59) and 101 (P. A. Rayment 42; A. J. McClement six for 47); Western Province B 291 (J. B. Commins 89, K. J. Bridgens 50, J. During 32 not out; P. A. Rayment four for 65) and 128 for four (F. B. Touzel 42 not out). *Western Province B 20 pts, Eastern Province B 6 pts.*

At Kimberley, February 12, 13, 14. Drawn. Boland* 209 for nine dec. (N. M. Lambrechts 30, O. Henry 56); Griqualand West 211 for six (A. J. Moles 106 not out; G. Vermeulen four for 30). *Griqualand West 7 pts, Boland 5 pts.*

At Stellenbosch, March 6, 7, 9. Western Province B won by nine wickets. Western Province B* 281 for nine dec. (A. M. Kirsten 50, D. B. Rundle 87, J. During 37; R. Brown five for 64) and 27 for one; Boland 110 (C. Nolte four for 18) and 197 (S. A. Jones 52; I. Barnes four for 65). *Western Province B 21 pts, Boland 3 pts.*

At Verwoerdburg, March 6, 7, 8. Griqualand West won by eight wickets. Northern Transvaal B* 133 (G. J. Turner 36; G. J. Parsons three for 26, B. E. van der Vyver three for 32) and 181 (K. D. Verdoorn 56; G. J. Parsons four for 40); Griqualand West 245 (A. J. Moles 41, F. W. Swarbrook 50 not out, A. D. Methven 36, I. Human 30; T. Bosch five for 63) and 73 for two. *Griqualand West 23 pts, Northern Transvaal B 5 pts.*

OTHER FIRST-CLASS MATCH

At Kimberley, October 2, 3, 4. SA Defence Force won by ten wickets. Griqualand West* 242 (F. W. Swarbrook 50, A. J. Moles 72, A. D. Methven 51; A. A. Donald four for 80, B. T. Player three for 39) and 169 (A. J. Moles 46; A. A. Donald seven for 63); SA Defence Force 407 (P. G. Amm 37, P. H. Rayner 38, M. W. Pfaff 167, B. T. Player 36; P. McLaren three for 112, B. E. van der Vyver four for 113) and 5 for no wkt.

†NISSAN SHIELD, 1986-87

(50 overs per side)

At East London, November 1. Border won by 21 runs. Border 174 for six (J. G. Thomas 65 not out, I. L. Howell 33 not out); Northern Transvaal 153 (R. F. Pienaar 74).

At Cape Town, November 1. Western Province won by 2 runs. Western Province 236 for four (P. N. Kirsten 117 not out, D. J. Cullinan 44); Eastern Province 234 for eight (K. C. Wessels 46, M. W. Rushmere 99).

At Stellenbosch, November 1. Transvaal won by 26 runs. Transvaal 215 (S. J. Cook 62, R. G. Pollock 30, C. E. B. Rice 30; J. D. du Toit three for 53); Boland 189 (C. F. Spilhaus 38, N. M. Lambrechts 61; N. V. Radford three for 33, H. A. Page three for 34).

At Durban, November 1. Natal won by ten wickets. Orange Free State/Griqualand West 150 (J. J. Strydom 44, R. J. East 59 not out; D. Norman three for 14, H. L. Alleyne three for 36); Natal 151 for no wkt (B. J. Whitfield 68 not out, A. C. Hudson 62 not out).

At Stellenbosch, November 8. Natal won by eight wickets. Boland 106 (H. L. Alleyne three for 19); Natal 107 for two (B. J. Whitfield 38 not out, R. M. Bentley 33).

At Port Elizabeth, November 8. Eastern Province won on faster scoring-rate. Northern Transvaal 120 for six (L. J. Barnard 38 not out); Eastern Province 110 for four (K. C. Wessels 36, M. Michau 42 not out).

At Cape Town, November 8. Western Province won by 25 runs. Western Province 242 for nine (L. Seeff 66, A. P. Kuiper 104; B. M. Osborne five for 35); Border 217 (B. W. Lones 31, G. L. Hayes 49; G. S. le Roux four for 55).

At Kimberley, November 8. Transvaal won by nine wickets. Orange Free State/Griqualand West 104 for eight; Transvaal 109 for one (H. R. Fotheringham 63 not out).

At Johannesburg, November 15. Natal won by 23 runs. Natal 230 for seven (B. J. Whitfield 64, C. L. King 57; N. V. Radford five for 37); Transvaal 207 (H. R. Fotheringham 30, B. M. McMillan 43; H. L. Alleyne four for 31, C. M. Lister-James three for 34).

At Bloemfontein, November 15. Orange Free State/Griqualand West won by 4 runs. Orange Free State/Griqualand West 171 for five (J. J. Strydom 45 not out, B. T. Player 33 not out); Boland 167 (S. A. Jones 30; C. J. P. G. van Zyl five for 19).

At Verwoerdburg, November 15. Western Province won on faster scoring-rate. Northern Transvaal 202 for eight (A. M. Ferreira 57, M. J. R. Rindel 53; G. S. le Roux three for 33); Western Province 194 for five (L. Seeff 60, K. S. McEwan 68 not out).

At Port Elizabeth, November 15. Eastern Province won by four wickets. Border 207 for eight (E. N. Trotman 57, G. L. Hayes 33); Eastern Province 208 for six (K. C. Wessels 34, M. Michau 38, D. J. Richardson 57 not out, T. G. Shaw 34).

Semi-finals

First leg: At Johannesburg, February 18. Transvaal won by 20 runs. Transvaal 252 (S. J. Cook 59, R. G. Pollock 100; G. S. le Roux three for 49); Western Province 232 for seven (T. N. Lazard 50, P. N. Kirsten 44, E. O. Simons 30).

First leg: At Port Elizabeth, February 18. Natal won by 82 runs. Natal 260 for five (M. D. Logan 36, P. H. Rayner 76, T. R. Madsen 64 not out; C. L. King 33); Eastern Province 178 for eight (J. W. Furstenburg 31, K. C. Wessels 32, M. Michau 42; C. L. King three for 27).

Second leg: At Durban, February 21. Eastern Province won by four wickets. Natal 239 for eight (M. B. Logan 71, R. M. Bentley 47; D. J. Capel three for 48); Eastern Province 240 for six (K. C. Wessels 37, D. J. Richardson 53, D. J. Callaghan 37 not out, T. G. Shaw 44 not out).

Second leg: At Cape Town, February 21. Transvaal won by two wickets. Western Province 172 (P. N. Kirsten 38, G. S. le Roux 37; H. A. Page four for 25); Transvaal 176 for eight (R. G. Pollock 57).

Third leg: At Durban, February 22. Natal won by 27 runs. Natal 248 for eight (C. S. Stirk 55, A. C. Hudson 30, R. M. Bentley 52); Eastern Province 221 for eight (P. G. Amm 51, K. C. Wessels 55; H. L. Alleyne three for 41).

Final

At Johannesburg, February 28. Natal won on faster scoring-rate. Natal 236 for eight (50 overs) (R. M. Bentley 40, T. R. Madsen 70 not out, N. P. Daniels 43); Transvaal 201 for four (44.4 overs) (H. R. Fotheringham 42, M. Yachad 85 not out).

†BENSON AND HEDGES TROPHY, 1986-87

(*Day/night matches of 45 overs per side*)

At Johannesburg, October 15. Transvaal won on faster scoring-rate. Northern Transvaal 194 for seven (R. F. Pienaar 64, R. C. Ontong 35, K. D. Verdoorn 31; L. J. Barnard 30; C. E. B. Rice five for 43); Transvaal 106 for two (H. R. Fotheringham 47).

At Durban, October 17. Natal won by four wickets. Impalas 120 (D. Norman three for 13); Natal 122 for six (B. J. Whitfield 40, N. P. Daniels 31 not out).

At Port Elizabeth, October 22. Eastern Province won by 37 runs. Eastern Province 220 for nine (K. C. Wessels 78; P. N. Kirsten three for 26); Western Province 183 (P. N. Kirsten 54, G. S. le Roux 43; W. K. Watson three for 43).

At Johannesburg, October 24. Transvaal won by 94 runs. Transvaal 255 for four (M. Yachad 59, S. J. Cook 52, C. E. B. Rice 42 not out, H. R. Fotheringham 35, R. G. Pollock 33); Eastern Province 161 (M. W. Rushmere 34; C. E. B. Rice three for 32).

At Durban, October 29. Transvaal won on faster scoring-rate. Natal 117 for eight (T. R. Madsen 46 not out; H. A. Page three for 16); Transvaal 115 for five (C. E. B. Rice 32).

At Virginia, November 19. Western Province won by 134 runs. Western Province 239 for six (K. S. McEwan 63, L. Seeff 60); Impalas 105 (O. Henry 32; S. T. Jefferies four for 26).

At Pietermaritzburg, November 25. Eastern Province won by four wickets. Natal 196 for nine (A. C. Hudson 55, D. Bestall 34; W. K. Watson three for 35); Eastern Province 198 for six (P. G. Amm 70, I. K. Daniell 32, D. J. Richardson 31; H. L. Alleyne three for 37).

At Cape Town, December 3. Transvaal won by three wickets. Western Province 190 for seven (L. Seeff 57, K. S. McEwan 46; N. V. Radford three for 52); Transvaal 191 for seven (B. M. McMillan 43 not out).

At Verwoerdburg, December 4. Natal won by two wickets. Northern Transvaal 150 for eight (H. L. Alleyne three for 44); Natal 152 for eight (R. C. Ontong three for 14).

At Port Elizabeth, December 22. Impalas won by seven wickets. Eastern Province 167 (D. J. Capel 44; B. T. Player three for 24, O. Henry three for 9); Impalas 168 for three (E. N. Trotman 78 not out).

At Cape Town, January 9. Natal won by two wickets. Western Province 161 (L. Seeff 78; D. Norman three for 33, H. L. Alleyne three for 29); Natal 164 for eight (N. P. Daniels 51 not out, T. R. Madsen 35; A. P. Kuiper three for 25).

At Verwoerdburg, January 10. Northern Transvaal won by five wickets. Eastern Province 194 for six (K. C. Wessels 87, D. J. Capel 33; C. D. Mitchley three for 30); Northern Transvaal 195 for five (L. J. Barnard 70, R. F. Pienaar 68; D. J. Capel three for 36).

At Virginia, January 10. Transvaal won by 2 runs. Transvaal 161 for three (M. Yachad 87, W. Kirsh 55 not out); Impalas 159 for eight (O. Henry 37, D. P. le Roux 36, B. M. Osborne 34; H. A. Page three for 41).

At Cape Town, January 14. Western Province won by 16 runs. Western Province 208 for six (T. N. Lazard 67, G. S. le Roux 36 not out; A. M. Ferreira three for 34); Northern Transvaal 192 (V. F. du Preez 40, P. J. A. Visagie 36, N. T. Day 35, L. J. Barnard 31; E. O. Simons four for 21).

At Verwoerdburg, January 28. Northern Transvaal won on faster scoring-rate. Impalas 173 (J. J. Strydom 55 not out; W. F. Morris three for 31); Northern Transvaal 160 for seven (R. F. Pienaar 86).

Semi-finals

The first legs, Northern Transvaal v Transvaal at Verwoerdburg and Natal v Western Province at Durban, were both abandoned without a ball being bowled owing to rain.

Second leg: At Johannesburg, March 20. Transvaal won by 37 runs. Transvaal 241 for six (H. R. Fotheringham 108, R. G. Pollock 44, L. P. Vorster 36; P. S. de Villiers three for 47); Northern Transvaal 204 (M. J. R. Rindel 50; C. E. B. Rice four for 23, A. J. Kourie three for 44).

Second leg: At Cape Town, March 20. Western Province won by five wickets. Natal 208 for eight (R. M. Bentley 72 not out, N. P. Daniels 57; G. S. le Roux four for 44); Western Province 210 for five (T. N. Lazard 96 not out, P. N. Kirsten 49).

Final

At Cape Town, March 27. Western Province won by 41 runs. Western Province 205 for six (L. Seeff 84, D. J. Cullinan 49; N. V. Radford three for 39); Transvaal 164 (C. E. B. Rice 35; B. A. Matthews four for 22).

AUSTRALIAN TEAM IN SOUTH AFRICA, 1986-87

The following players toured South Africa: K. J. Hughes (*captain*), T. M. Alderman, J. Dyson, P. I. Faulkner, M. D. Haysman, T. G. Hogan, R. M. Hogg, T. V. Hohns, R. J. McCurdy, J. N. Maguire, C. G. Rackemann, S. J. Rixon, G. Shipperd, S. B. Smith, M. D. Taylor, K. C. Wessels, G. N. Yallop. The manager was B. C. Francis.

RESULTS

First-class matches – Played 12: Won 2, Lost 3, Drawn 7.
Non first-class matches – Played 8: Won 2, Lost 5, No result 1.

At Bloemfontein, November 21, 22, 24. Drawn. Australian XI 412 for nine dec. (S. B. Smith 47, J. Dyson 79, K. J. Hughes 100, M. D. Taylor 31, G. N. Yallop 31, T. V. Hohns 50 not out; C. J. P. G. van Zyl three for 79) and 100 for one (S. B. Smith 54 not out); Orange Free State* 367 (A. I. Kallicharran 110, J. Strydom 64, R. J. East 40, F. J. C. Cronje 43; C. G. Rackemann three for 77, J. N. Maguire three for 63).

At Virginia, November 27, 28, 29. President's XI won by three wickets. Australian XI* 347 for six dec. (M. D. Haysman 54, G. Shipperd 74, K. J. Hughes 79, M. D. Taylor 64, P. I. Faulkner 35; P. Anker three for 135) and 128 for five dec. (M. D. Haysman 39, T. G. Hogan 34 not out; C. M. Lister-James four for 38); President's XI 215 for five dec. (B. J. Whitfield 129 not out, B. M. McMillan 44) and 261 for seven (R. F. Pienaar 73, D. J. Cullinan 65, C. D. Mitchley 32 not out).

At East London, December 2, 3, 4. Drawn. Border* 358 (M. J. P. Ford 31, G. L. Hayes 74, A. L. Wilmot 44, B. M. Osborne 127, I. L. Howell 30; R. J. McCurdy four for 101, C. G. Rackemann three for 84); Australian XI 519 for eight (K. C. Wessels 137, G. N. Yallop 45, M. D. Haysman 180, P. I. Faulkner 48; E. N. Trotman four for 88).

†At Verwoerdburg, December 6 (day/night). South Africa won by six wickets. Australian XI 238 for five (44 overs) (S. B. Smith 59, K. C. Wessels 75 not out, P. I. Faulkner 37 not out); South Africa 239 for four (41.1 overs) (S. J. Cook 45, K. S. McEwan 68, R. G. Pollock 62, C. E. B. Rice 36 not out).

†At Johannesburg, December 8 (day/night). No result. Australian XI 149 (40 overs) (J. Dyson 45; B. M. McMillan four for 45); South Africa 3 for one (0.3 overs).

†At Cape Town, December 10 (day/night). South Africa won by eight wickets. Australian XI 85 (34 overs) (M. D. Taylor 36 not out; G. S. le Roux six for 21); South Africa 86 for two (15 overs) (S. J. Cook 47, P. N. Kirsten 30 not out).

At Port Elizabeth, December 12, 13, 14. Australian XI won by an innings and 84 runs. Eastern Province* 117 (M. W. Rushmere 60; R. M. Hogg four for 30, R. J. McCurdy three for 38, T. V. Hohns three for 34) and 125 (T. B. Reid 35 not out; J. N. Maguire seven for 46, T. G. Hogan three for 28); Australian XI 326 for seven dec. (K. C. Wessels 77, G. Shipperd 39, G. N. Yallop 96, M. D. Taylor 35, T. V. Hohns 37; A. J. Roberts three for 72).

†At Durban, December 17 (day/night). Australian XI won by six wickets (revised target 153 in 40 overs). South Africa 183 for nine (48 overs) (P. N. Kirsten 33, C. E. B. Rice 30; P. I. Faulkner three for 42); Australian XI 153 for four (39.1 overs) (G. Shipperd 33, K. J. Hughes 49, M. D. Taylor 39 not out).

At Durban, December 19, 20, 21. Natal won by six wickets. Australian XI* 227 for two dec. (G. Shipperd 78 not out, G. N. Yallop 34, M. D. Taylor 60, M. D. Haysman 32 not out) and 238 for six dec. (J. Dyson 63, T. V. Hohns 32, P. I. Faulkner 55; R. K. McGlashan four for 76); Natal 234 for three dec. (B. J. Whitfield 103 not out, T. R. Madsen 53 not out) and 232 for four (A. C. Hudson 55, R. M. Bentley 59, T. R. Madsen 60; T. V. Hohns three for 57).

SOUTH AFRICA v AUSTRALIAN XI

At Wanderers, Johannesburg, December 24, 26, 27, 28. South Africa won by 49 runs. Toss: Australian XI. Rixon, the Australians' wicket-keeper, took ten catches in the match, repeating his performance at this venue the previous season.

South Africa

B. J. Whitfield b Rackemann	17	– lbw b Maguire	23
S. J. Cook b McCurdy	28	– c Rixon b McCurdy	1
P. N. Kirsten c Wessels b McCurdy	14	– c Rixon b Maguire	19
B. M. McMillan c Rixon b McCurdy	1	– lbw b Maguire	30
*C. E. B. Rice c Rixon b Rackemann	61	– c Rixon b Maguire	18
K. A. McKenzie c Wessels b Rackemann	12	– lbw b Maguire	40
A. J. Kourie lbw b McCurdy	3	– c Haysman b Maguire	1
†D. J. Richardson c Rixon b McCurdy	29	– c Rixon b Rackemann	33
G. S. le Roux lbw b McCurdy	42	– c Rixon b Rackemann	0
H. A. Page c Rixon b Faulkner	5	– not out	7
S. T. Jefferies not out	27	– c Rixon b Rackemann	0
L-b 5, w 4, n-b 6	15	B 1, l-b 6, w 2, n-b 1	10

1/36 2/56 3/63 4/66 5/103   254   1/2 2/34 3/49 4/92 5/103   182
6/125 7/154 8/188 9/210   6/115 7/153 8/173 9/182

Bowling: *First Innings*—McCurdy 24.5-7-67-6; Rackemann 25-3-70-3; Maguire 18-4-54-0; Faulkner 21-2-58-1. *Second Innings*—McCurdy 19-4-58-1; Rackemann 19.19.4-3-54-3; Maguire 29-12-61-6; Faulkner 2-0-2-0.

Australian XI

S. B. Smith c Richardson b Rice	29	– c McKenzie b McMillan	36
J. Dyson b Jefferies	5	– b Kourie	16
K. C. Wessels c McMillan b le Roux	0	– c Richardson b McMillan	49
*K. J. Hughes lbw b le Roux	34	– not out	54
M. D. Taylor c Richardson b Rice	9	– c Richardson b Taylor	8
M. D. Haysman b Page	25	– c Kourie b Page	17
P. I. Faulkner b Page	9	– c McKenzie b McMillan	8
†S. J. Rixon lbw b Page	0	– b Page	16
J. N. Maguire c Richardson b Rice	3	– c Richardson b Rice	3
R. J. McCurdy not out	2	– b Jefferies	0
C. G. Rackemann b Rice	2	– c McKenzie b Rice	12
B 7, l-b 9, w 1, n-b 7	24	L-b 15, w 2, n-b 9	26

1/20 2/24 3/51 4/93 5/99   142   1/49 2/57 3/107 4/143 5/156   245
6/125 7/125 8/137 9/137   6/169 7/199 8/219 9/224

Bowling: *First Innings*—le Roux 11–4–25–2; Jefferies 8–0–29–1; Page 17–3–39–3; Rice 16–6–19–4; McMillan 9–3–14–0; Kourie 2–2–0–0. *Second Innings*—le Roux 14–3–39–0; Jefferies 17–5–42–1; Page 20–3–53–2; Rice 18.1–4–37–3; McMillan 15–2–44–3; Kourie 11–6–15–1.

Umpires: D. D. Schoof and F. E. Wood.

SOUTH AFRICA v AUSTRALIAN XI

At Newlands, Cape Town, January 1, 2, 3, 5, 6. Drawn. Toss: Australian XI.

South Africa

S. J. Cook c Rixon b McCurdy	6	– c and b Hohns	40
B. J. Whitfield st Rixon b Hohns	77	– c Hughes b Maguire	23
P. N. Kirsten c Hughes b Hohns	173	– not out	105
R. G. Pollock c sub (P. I. Faulkner) b Maguire	66		
*C. E. B. Rice lbw b Maguire	72		
K. A. McKenzie c Rixon b Maguire	24	– (4) lbw b Wessels	52
B. M. McMillan run out	30	– (5) not out	17
G. S. le Roux c Rixon b McCurdy	13		
†D. J. Richardson lbw b Maguire	1		
H. A. Page c Smith b McCurdy	7		
A. J. Kourie not out	2		
B 5, l-b 10, w 1, n-b 6	22	B 4, l-b 14, n-b 2	20

1/16 2/177 3/288 4/341 5/407   493   1/48 2/99 3/194   (3 wkts) 257
6/449 7/480 8/483 9/491

Bowling: *First Innings*—McCurdy 43–8–133–3; Rackemann 28–7–113–0; Maguire 46.4–8–116–4; Hohns 40–6–116–2. *Second Innings*—McCurdy 10–1–42–0; Rackemann 19–3–54–0; Maguire 16–3–53–1; Hohns 26–6–63–1; Wessels 12–6–18–1; Smith 2–0–9–0; Dyson 1–1–0–0.

Australian XI

S. B. Smith c McKenzie b le Roux	2	J. N. Maguire c Kirsten b McMillan	20
J. Dyson run out	198	C. G. Rackemann c Whitfield b Rice	8
K. C. Wessels lbw b le Roux	36	R. J. McCurdy not out	11
*K. J. Hughes c Richardson b le Roux	48		
M. D. Taylor c and b le Roux	0	L-b 19	19
M. D. Haysman c Kirsten b le Roux	153		
T. V. Hohns c Kirsten b McMillan	0	1/4 2/78 3/166 4/170 5/395	496
†S. J. Rixon c Richardson b McMillan	1	6/399 7/401 8/453 9/478	

Bowling: le Roux 42–13–85–5; Page 43–8–118–0; Kourie 39–10–87–0; McMillan 36–10–83–3; Rice 31–8–60–1; Kirsten 11–0–44–0.

Umpires: D. H. Bezuidenhout and O. R. Schoof.

At East London, January 9, 10, 11. Australian XI won by an innings and 46 runs. South African Invitation XI* 165 (J. J. Strydom 55, E. O. Simons 33 not out; P. I. Faulkner five for 49) and 121 (M. W. Rushmere 43 not out; R. M. Hogg four for 23, T. M. Alderman four for 24); Australian XI 332 (G. N. Yallop 182, M. D. Taylor 40; P. Anker four for 73, R. K. McGlashan three for 88).

At Pietermaritzburg, January 13, 14, 15. Drawn. South African Universities 240 for nine dec. (L. P. Vorster 47, B. McBride 88, D. J. Cullinan 41; T. V. Hohns five for 46) and 128 for two (L. P. Vorster 74 not out); Australian XI* 448 (S. B. Smith 119, J. Dyson 70, G. Shipperd 55, K. J. Hughes 95, T. G. Hogan 34 not out).

SOUTH AFRICA v AUSTRALIAN XI

At Kingsmead, Durban, January 17, 19, 20, 21, 22. Drawn. Toss: Australian XI.

Australian XI

S. B. Smith c Page b Henry	137	– b Page ... 5
J. Dyson c Richardson b le Roux	1	– c McMillan b Rice ... 101
K. C. Wessels c Richardson b le Roux	0	– c Richardson b Page ... 2
*K. J. Hughes c and b le Roux	25	– lbw b Page ... 9
G. N. Yallop c Page b Henry	36	– (7) c Henry b le Roux ... 26
M. D. Haysman c McKenzie b Kirsten	5	– (5) b Rice ... 115
T. V. Hohns c McKenzie b Kirsten	26	– (6) lbw b le Roux ... 10
†S. J. Rixon c Richardson b Page	13	– not out ... 42
J. N. Maguire c Richardson b le Roux	2	– run out ... 2
R. M. Hogg c Richardson b Page	6	– c McEwan b Kirsten ... 9
R. J. McCurdy not out	0	– c Whitfield b Kirsten ... 0
L-b 3, w 1, n-b 9	13	B 2, l-b 14, n-b 2 ... 18
	264	**339**

1/4 2/7 3/80 4/148 5/198   264   1/7 2/11 3/25 4/50 5/253   339
6/220 7/256 8/256 9/264   6/260 7/301 8/304 9/337

In the second innings J. Dyson, when 8, retired hurt at 23, and resumed at 50.

Bowling: *First Innings*—le Roux 13.3-1-33-4; Page 17-1-57-2; Rice 10-2-32-0; McMillan 10-0-57-0; Henry 23-4-58-2; Kirsten 15-4-24-2. *Second Innings*—le Roux 29-5-63-2; Page 35-6-87-3; Rice 19-4-38-2; McMillan 17-3-55-0; Henry 26-11-44-0; Kirsten 14.4-3-36-2.

South Africa

S. J. Cook b Hohns	44	– c Rixon b Hogg ... 23
B. J. Whitfield c Rixon b Hohns	59	– b Hogg ... 26
P. N. Kirsten c Yallop b Hohns	13	– lbw b Maguire ... 33
K. S. McEwan b McCurdy	101	– b Hohns ... 27
*C. E. B. Rice c Dyson b Hohns	22	– lbw b Hogg ... 0
K. A. McKenzie lbw b Hohns	14	– b Hohns ... 3
B. M. McMillan c Haysman b McCurdy	15	– not out ... 18
†D. J. Richardson not out	44	– c and b Hohns ... 0
G. S. le Roux c Rixon b McCurdy	6	
O. Henry c Yallop b Hogg	7	
H. A. Page c and b Hohns	2	
B 8, l-b 7, w 1, n-b 7	23	B 1, l-b 7, n-b 5 ... 13
	350	**(7 wkts) 143**

1/100 2/127 3/130 4/177 5/197   350   1/29 2/89 3/93 4/102   (7 wkts) 143
6/237 7/309 8/319 9/341   5/115 6/130 7/143

Bowling: *First Innings*—Hogg 28-5-87-1; McCurdy 22-2-76-3; Maguire 28-7-74-0; Hohns 47.4-13-98-6. *Second Innings*—Hogg 16-4-33-3; McCurdy 17-3-59-0; Maguire 7-3-16-1; Hohns 17.5-6-27-3.

Umpires: K. E. Liebenberg and L. J. Rautenbach.

At Verwoerdburg, January 24, 26, 27. Drawn. Northern Transvaal* 315 for eight dec. (V. F. du Preez 30, R. F. Pienaar 90, L. J. Barnard 33, A. M. Ferreira 69; J. N. Maguire four for 86, T. M. Alderman three for 89) and 217 for nine dec. (A. M. Ferreira 49, W. F. Morris 44; T. M. Alderman four for 49, C. G. Rackemann three for 67); Australian XI 281 for three dec. (S. B. Smith 73, G. Shipperd 110 not out, M. D. Taylor 47 not out) and 219 for seven (S. B. Smith 47, G. N. Yallop 69, S. J. Rixon 57).

SOUTH AFRICA v AUSTRALIAN XI

At St George's Park, Port Elizabeth, January 30, 31, February 1, 3, 4. Drawn. Toss: South Africa.

Australian XI

S. B. Smith lbw b le Roux	77	– b Rice	113
G. Shipperd c Whitfield b Donald	53	– b le Roux	0
J. Dyson lbw b le Roux	1	– c Kirsten b le Roux	8
*K. J. Hughes b Donald	42	– b Donald	44
K. C. Wessels b Henry	135	– not out	105
M. D. Haysman c Rice b Donald	19	– not out	53
T. V. Hohns hit wkt b Rice	37		
†S. J. Rixon c Page b Henry	61		
R. M. Hogg lbw b Henry	0		
R. J. McCurdy not out	6		
B 2, l-b 11, n-b 11	24	B 4, l-b 2, w 1, n-b 3	10

1/123 2/131 3/191 4/192 5/255   (9 wkts dec.) 455   1/26 2/26 3/142 4/198   (4 wkts) 333
6/308 7/442 8/442 9/455

T. M. Alderman did not bat.

Bowling: *First Innings*—le Roux 27-6-67-2; Donald 32-7-94-3; Page 27-4-95-0; Rice 19-5-43-1; Henry 36.5-10-96-3; Kirsten 22-6-47-0. *Second Innings*—le Roux 16-0-61-2; Donald 19-4-71-1; Page 19-1-40-0; Rice 10-1-25-1; Henry 35-14-63-0; Kirsten 15-4-42-0; Cook 2-1-1-0.

South Africa

S. J. Cook c Dyson b McCurdy	84	G. S. le Roux lbw b McCurdy	20
B. J. Whitfield c Rixon b Hogg	4	O. Henry c Hohns b Alderman	13
P. N. Kirsten lbw b Hogg	34	A. A. Donald c Haysman b Hohns	21
R. G. Pollock b Hogg	144		
K. S. McEwan not out	138	B 2, l-b 24, w 1, n-b 6	33
H. A. Page b Hohns	9		
*C. E. B. Rice lbw b Hogg	26	1/9 2/64 3/211 4/312 5/329	533
†D. J. Richardson lbw b Hogg	7	6/382 7/394 8/446 9/477	

Bowling: Hogg 39-7-97-5; Alderman 37-3-142-1; McCurdy 40-5-159-2; Hohns 51.2-12-109-2.

Umpires: K. E. Liebenberg and D. D. Schoof.

†At Port Elizabeth, February 7. South Africa won by 6 runs. South Africa 316 for six (50 overs) (S. J. Cook 70, R. F. Pienaar 74, P. N. Kirsten 87, R. G. Pollock 43); Australian XI 310 (49.5 overs) (J. Dyson 69, K. C. Wessels 122, K. J. Hughes 83; C. E. B. Rice five for 50).

†At Cape Town, February 10. South Africa won on faster scoring-rate. Australian XI 199 for seven (47.4 overs) (K. C. Wessels 35, M. D. Taylor 64 not out); South Africa 188 for two (40.3 overs) (S. J. Cook 65, P. N. Kirsten 82 not out, R. G. Pollock 30 not out).

†At Verwoerdburg, February 12. Australian XI won by five wickets. South Africa 237 for nine (50 overs) (R. G. Pollock 32, D. J. Richardson 54, G. S. le Roux 58, R. J. McCurdy four for 61); Australian XI 238 for five (48.5 overs) (S. B. Smith 37, J. Dyson 41, K. C. Wessels 43, K. J. Hughes 44).

†At Johannesburg, February 14. South Africa won by four wickets. Australian XI 175 for nine (50 overs) (J. Dyson 43, S. J. Rixon 33 not out; G. S. le Roux three for 31, H. A. Page three for 28); South Africa 176 for six (42.4 overs) (K. S. McEwan 59 not out).

CRICKET IN THE WEST INDIES, 1986-87

By TONY COZIER

Faced with financial difficulties exacerbated by the heavy losses from England's 1985-86 tour of the Caribbean, the West Indies Cricket Board of Control found it necessary to reduce the 1987 Shell Shield tournament by half. Instead of the usual format, in which each of the six teams played against the other, with the championship being determined on a league basis, the Board created two zones of three teams each, with the leaders in each zone contesting a final for the Shield. Coming at a time when the West Indies team was in a period of transition, and new players were needed to replace those approaching the end of their international careers, such a step was clearly negative, if necessary. The Shield, despite an annual subsidy of £100,000 from the sponsors, has consistently lost money and the Board said it could not afford to lose any at this time. It anticipated an improvement in its finances following several overseas tours and was confident it would revert to a full schedule in 1988.

Under the new arrangement, Guyana won the Shield by leading Leeward Islands on first innings in the final. Under the inspiring leadership of the all-rounder, Roger Harper, who enjoyed an outstanding season, the Guyanese made the most of the advantage of playing both their decisive zone match, against the 1986 champions, Barbados, and the final at home. The Bourda pitch at Georgetown was more suited to their strong spin-bowling attack than to the predominantly fast bowling of their opponents, and for these two matches they fielded four spinners and only one specialist new-ball bowler.

The Leewards qualified from the other zone through victories over Windward Islands and Jamaica which could hardly have been closer. They needed to go into the last over to beat the Windwards by three wickets, and then won a low-scoring match against Jamaica only through a last-wicket partnership of 23 which carried them from 86 for nine to the 109 they required. Jamaica, having beaten the Windwards in their other match, were thus denied a place in the final and a chance at the Shield, which they had won only once since its inception in 1965-66. Guyana's was their fourth tenure of the Championship.

The abbreviated season was boosted by two first-class matches prior to the Shield, Barbados playing at home against Guyana and at St Vincent against Windward Islands, and by pre-season tours by two English county teams. Yorkshire visited St Lucia and Barbados and Lancashire played in Jamaica, each including one first-class match on their schedule.

The short season provided encouraging returns, perhaps more so than might have been expected. After concern in recent years over the dearth of young batsmen, three young century-makers with less than half a dozen first-class matches behind them raised spirits. Sudesh Dhaniram, a slimly built, twenty-year-old Guyanese from the same area that produced R. B. Kanhai, B. F. Butcher and A. I. Kallicharran, was brought into the team for the last two matches and scored centuries against Barbados and the Leewards, showing himself to be a neat, composed player. Keith Arthurton, a stockily built 22-year-old left-hander from the tiny island of Nevis, fulfilled the potential he had shown at youth level with scores of 97 run out against the Windwards and 132 against Guyana in the final. Roland Holder, aged nineteen, a well-organised right-hander from Combermere School, alma mater of Sir Frank Worrell, J. E. D. Sealy and W. W. Hall, recorded his maiden hundred for Barbados in a second-wicket partnership of 306 with Gordon Greenidge against Trinidad & Tobago. Greenidge, in his only innings of the competition, made 202.

While these new names encouragingly emerged among the batsmen, the leading bowlers were familiar names. Clyde Butts (sixteen at 17.93), Winston Benjamin (fifteen at 19.60), Courtney Walsh (thirteen at 16.30) and Michael Holding (twelve at 14.08) had the most Shield wickets. All four had recently returned from West Indies' tours of Australia and New Zealand. Another bowler of experience who enjoyed a productive return to cricket in the West Indies, after missing the 1985-86 season while on contract in Tasmania, was Winston Davis; he took 21 wickets in the Windwards' four first-class matches.

There was, however, only one player of the season – Roger Harper. Dropped from the West Indian team as it moved from Australia to New Zealand, he returned home with a clear purpose. He started with a memorable all-round performance in the pre-Shield match against Barbados, scoring 120 and taking ten wickets in a losing cause, and followed that with crucial centuries against Trinidad & Tobago and against the Leewards in the final. In addition, he was at the wicket with an influential 40 when the lead was gained against Barbados. He picked up valuable wickets, fielded as always brilliantly, and confirmed the widely held impression that, at the age of 24, he is a future Test captain.

Harper's was an effort of inspiring commitment. Unfortunately, even though the Shield was delayed until the end of West Indies' tour of New Zealand – and the West Indies Board made participation mandatory for Test selection – only a few of the returning players found it possible to play in all matches. Desmond Haynes, ordered by a doctor to rest a finger dislocated in Australia, did not play at all. Nor did Larry Gomes, who remained in Australia, reportedly for dental treatment. Vivian Richards, Malcolm Marshall, Augustine Logie and Anthony Gray, in addition to Greenidge, each managed just one match. When Logie and Gray withdrew from Trinidad & Tobago's team for the opening match against Guyana the morning after their return from New Zealand, while Butts and Carl Hooper turned out for Guyana, the Trinidad & Tobago Cricket Board fined them $T500 each for failing to provide adequate cause.

Jamaica, denied a place in the Shell Shield final by what their captain, Holding, later claimed was "home-town umpiring", gained some consolation by retaining the Geddes Grant-Harrison Line Trophy limited-overs competition. Qualifying through victories by one wicket over the Windwards and by 1 run over the Leewards, Jamaica defeated Barbados by four wickets in a high-scoring final in which 501 runs were scored for the loss of only nine wickets in 95 overs.

Wary that the reduced Shell Shield schedule would be a disincentive to the island's young players, the Barbados Cricket Association used funds from its successful, long-running lottery to arrange two additional matches, against Guyana and the Windward Islands. Yorkshire, under their new captain, Phil Carrick, and with a full-strength team, drew a three-day, first-class match against the Windwards and lost only two of eight one-day matches on their tour – to the Windwards and to the Barbados Cricket League. In contrast, Lancashire struggled, being soundly beaten by Jamaica in both the three-day and the one-day matches. Another county team, Hampshire, toured Barbados in April for a series of one-day games as part of Marshall's benefit year, losing to Barbados off the last ball but winning the other four against club teams.

FIRST-CLASS AVERAGES, 1986-87

BATTING

(Qualification: 200 runs, average 25)

	M	I	NO	R	HI	100s	Avge
R. A. Harper (*Guyana*)	4	5	1	419	128	3	104.75
S. Dhaniram (*Guyana*)	3	3	0	236	131	2	78.66
K. L. T. Arthurton (*Leeward I*) ...	3	5	0	281	132	1	56.20
C. A. Davidson (*Jamaica*)	3	4	0	218	73	0	54.50
C. B. Lambert (*Guyana*)	5	7	0	328	94	0	46.85
J. C. Adams (*Jamaica*)	3	4	0	183	70	0	45.75
L. L. Lawrence (*Leeward I*)	3	6	1	225	67	0	45.00
R. I. C. Holder (*Barbados*)	4	6	0	256	115	1	42.66
C. A. Best (*Barbados*)	4	5	0	205	112	1	41.00
J. D. Charles (*Windward I*)	4	8	0	323	73	0	40.37
P. V. Simmons (*T & T*)	2	4	0	138	82	0	34.50
T. Mohamed (*Guyana*)	4	6	1	172	54*	0	34.40
R. Seeram (*Guyana*)	4	5	0	169	61	0	33.80
S. W. Julien (*Windward I*)	4	8	0	270	114	1	33.75
A. L. Kelly (*Leeward I*)	3	6	1	168	63	0	33.60
K. C. Williams (*T & T*)	2	4	0	127	58	0	31.75
T. Z. Kentish (*Windward I*)	4	7	3	118	28*	0	29.50
R. C. Haynes (*Jamaica*)	3	4	0	115	38	0	28.75
L. N. Reifer (*Barbados*)	4	6	1	143	48*	0	28.60
D. E. Ellcock (*Barbados*)	4	5	1	102	52	0	25.50

Signifies not out.

BOWLING

(Qualification: 8 wickets, 40 overs)

	O	M	R	W	BB	Avge
N. O. Perry (*Jamaica*)	46.5	16	92	9	5-39	10.22
V. S. Greene (*Barbados*)	68.5	18	186	15	4-15	12.40
W. E. Reid (*Barbados*)	62	20	125	9	4-46	13.88
M. A. Holding (*Jamaica*)	63	12	169	12	4-39	14.08
C. A. Walsh (*Jamaica*)	60.2	5	212	13	6-54	16.30
R. O. Estwick (*Barbados*)	52	15	132	8	4-59	16.50
C. G. Butts (*Guyana*)	162.5	49	287	16	5-67	17.93
C. L. Hooper (*Guyana*)	95	24	232	12	5-48	19.33
W. K. M. Benjamin (*Leeward I*) ...	111.1	25	294	15	6-50	19.60
R. A. Harper (*Guyana*)	162.4	38	355	18	6-63	19.72
R. C. Haynes (*Jamaica*)	119.4	47	244	11	3-13	22.18
T. Z. Kentish (*Windward I*)	141.3	22	341	15	4-72	22.73
W. W. Davis (*Windward I*)	166	22	510	21	4-60	24.28
G. L. Linton (*Barbados*)	84.2	22	202	8	5-67	25.25
D. E. Ellcock (*Barbados*)	71.3	13	246	8	3-49	30.75
S. Matthews (*Guyana*)	143	17	385	12	6-76	32.08
N. C. Guishard (*Leeward I*)	119	30	262	8	4-83	32.75

Note: Matches taken into account are Shell Shield, Guystac Trophy, Barbados v Guyana and Barbados v Windward Islands, and those against Yorkshire and Lancashire.

SHELL SHIELD, 1986-87

	Played	Won	Lost	Drawn	1st-inns lead in drawn match	Pts
Zone A						
Leeward Islands	2	2	0	0	0	32
Jamaica	2	1	1	0	0	16
Windward Islands	2	0	2	0	0	0
Zone B						
Guyana	2	1	0	1	1	24
Barbados	2	1	0	1	0	20
Trinidad & Tobago	2	0	2	0	0	0

Leeward Islands and Guyana qualified for the final.

Win = 16 pts; draw = 4 pts; 1st-innings lead in drawn match = 4 pts.

In the following scores, * by the name of the team indicates that they won the toss.

Zone A

At Kingston, April 3, 4, 5, 6. Jamaica won by nine wickets. Jamaica* 365 (C. A. Davidson 85, J. C. Adams 70, D. S. Morgan 48, F. A. Cunningham 47; T. Z. Kentish four for 72, W. W. Davis three for 97) and 65 for one; Windward Islands 163 (R. C. Haynes three for 13, M. A. Holding three for 40) and 266 (S. W. Julien 85, J. D. Charles 73; C. A. Walsh three for 47, M. A. Holding three for 53). *Jamaica 16 pts.*

At Castries, April 11, 12, 13, 14. Leeward Islands won by three wickets. Windward Islands* 370 (S. W. Julien 114, J. D. Charles 70, L. C. Sebastien 43, J. T. Etienne 32; G. J. F. Ferris four for 68, N. C. Guishard four for 83) and 198 (J. D. Charles 54, D. C. Collymore 35; W. K. M. Benjamin five for 68); Leeward Islands 388 (K. L. T. Arthurton 97, L. L. Lawrence 67, A. L. Kelly 63, N. C. Guishard 48, R. B. Richardson 44; W. W. Davis four for 94) and 181 for seven (R. M. Otto 45, A. L. Kelly 39, E. A. E. Baptiste 33 not out; W. W. Davis four for 60). *Leeward Islands 16 pts.*

At St John's, April 18, 19, 20, 21. Leeward Islands won by one wicket. Jamaica* 235 (C. A. Davidson 58, A. A. Daley 42, R. C. Haynes 38, J. C. Adams 36; W. K. M. Benjamin four for 39) and 112 (W. K. M. Benjamin six for 50); Leeward Islands 239 (L. L. Lawrence 57, I. V. A. Richards 42; M. A. Holding four for 39) and 109 for nine (K. L. T. Arthurton 32; C. A. Walsh six for 54). *Leeward Islands 16 pts.*

Zone B

At Port-of-Spain, April 3, 4, 5, 6. Guyana won by 91 runs. Guyana* 366 (R. A. Harper 109, A. F. D. Jackman 76, C. B. Lambert 58, G. E. Charles 37, R. Seeram 31; R. Nanan three for 80) and 239 for three dec. (C. B. Lambert 76, A. F. D. Jackman 75, T. Mohamed 54 not out); Trinidad & Tobago 260 (D. Deyal 63, K. C. Williams 58, P. V. Simmons 36; S. Matthews six for 76, C. G. Butts three for 71) and 254 (P. V. Simmons 82, A. Rajah 65; C. L. Hooper five for 48, C. G. Butts five for 67). *Guyana 16 pts.*

At Bridgetown, April 11, 12, 13, 14. Barbados won by an innings and 203 runs. Trinidad & Tobago 143 (K. C. Williams 36, D. I. Mohammed 35; V. S. Greene four for 48, M. D. Marshall three for 19) and 123 (M. D. Marshall four for 35, V. S. Greene three for 40); Barbados* 469 for three dec. (C. G. Greenidge 202, R. I. C. Holder 115, T. R. O. Payne 65 not out, L. N. Reifer 48 not out). *Barbados 16 pts.*

At Georgetown, April 18, 19, 20, 21. Drawn. Barbados 278 (A. L. Grant 89, C. A. Best 56; C. G. Butts five for 86); Guyana* 279 for seven (S. Dhaniram 102, R. A. Harper 40 not out, T. Mohamed 31; W. E. Reid three for 56, J. Garner three for 63). *Guyana 8 pts, Barbados 4 pts.*

Final

At Georgetown, April 24, 25, 26, 27. Drawn. Guyana won the trophy by virtue of their first-innings lead. Leeward Islands 317 (K. L. T. Arthurton 132, L. L. Lawrence 47, W. K. M. Benjamin 44; R. A. Harper four for 93, C. G. Butts three for 63) and 76 for no wkt (A. L. Kelly 35 not out, L. L. Lawrence 33 not out); Guyana* 485 (S. Dhaniram 131, R. A. Harper 128, C. B. Lambert 50, R. Seeram 50; N. C. Guishard three for 139).

SHELL SHIELD WINNERS

1965-66	Barbados	1976-77	Barbados
1966-67	Barbados	1977-78	Barbados
1968-69	Jamaica	1978-79	Barbados
1969-70	Trinidad	1979-80	Barbados
1970-71	Trinidad	1980-81	Combined Islands
1971-72	Barbados	1981-82	Barbados
1972-73	Guyana	1982-83	Guyana
1973-74	Barbados	1983-84	Barbados
1974-75	Guyana	1984-85	Trinidad & Tobago
1975-76 {	Trinidad	1985-86	Barbados
	Barbados	1986-87	Guyana

OTHER FIRST-CLASS MATCHES

At Bridgetown, March 13, 14, 15, 16. Barbados won by 68 runs. Barbados 318 (C. A. Best 112, D. E. Ellcock 47 not out, R. I. C. Holder 38; R. A. Harper four for 59) and 190 (N. A. Johnson 46, R. I. C. Holder 32; R. A. Harper six for 63). Guyana* 198 (R. Seeram 61, C. B. Lambert 30; W. E. Reid four for 46, R. O. Estwick three for 21) and 242 (R. A. Harper 120, T. Mohamed 38; R. O. Estwick four for 59, D. E. Ellcock three for 49).

At St Vincent, March 21, 22, 23. Drawn. Barbados* 252 (G. L. Linton 52 not out, D. E. Ellcock 52; T. Z. Kentish three for 60, W. W. Davis three for 69) and 143 (L. N. Reifer 30; W. W. Davis four for 63, T. Z. Kentish three for 21); Windward Islands 171 (D. Joseph 49, L. A. Lewis 36; G. L. Linton five for 57, V. S. Greene three for 30) and 143 for nine (L. D. John 50; V. S. Greene four for 15).

WINDWARD ISLANDS v YORKSHIRE

At Castries, March 24, 25, 26. Drawn. Toss: Yorkshire.

Yorkshire

M. D. Moxon b Kentish	75 –	c Collymore b Kentish ... 105
A. A. Metcalfe c Murray b Davis	5 –	lbw b Davis ... 6
R. J. Blakey lbw b Kentish	24 –	c and b Collymore ... 71
K. Sharp lbw b Davis	0 –	lbw b Collymore ... 0
J. D. Love b Kentish	23 –	lbw b Collymore ... 13
†D. L. Bairstow lbw b Murphy	18 –	not out ... 23
*P. Carrick c Collymore b Charles	22 –	not out ... 16
A. Sidebottom c Lewis b Charles	16	
P. J. Hartley lbw b Charles	12	
P. W. Jarvis c Collymore b Charles	1	
S. J. Dennis not out	6	
L-b 3, n-b 8	11	B 9, l-b 5, n-b 12 ... 26

1/37 2/106 3/107 4/127 5/148   213   1/20 2/159 3/159   (5 wkts dec.) 260
6/160 7/193 8/196 9/198   4/199 5/216

Bowling: *First Innings*—Davis 17–2–57–2; Murphy 14–2–47–1; Kentish 21–2–51–3; Collymore 11–2–35–0; Charles 7–1–20–4. *Second Innings*—Davis 16–2–62–1; Murphy 18–3–59–0; Kentish 14–0–50–1; Collymore 16–3–58–3; Charles 3–1–16–0; Mahon 1–0–1–0.

Windward Islands

D. Joseph b Sidebottom	34	– c Bairstow b Jarvis	6
L. A. Lewis lbw b Jarvis	32	– c Blakey b Dennis	18
†J. Murray c Dennis b Carrick	13		
S. W. Julien b Jarvis	37	– lbw b Jarvis	0
J. D. Charles c and b Hartley	21	– c Dennis b Carrick	35
L. C. Sebastien lbw b Jarvis	9	– not out	16
S. L. Mahon lbw b Sidebottom	8	– (3) lbw b Carrick	45
D. J. Collymore lbw b Dennis	12	– (7) not out	11
T. Z. Kentish not out	22		
W. W. Davis b Love	9		
S. A. E. Murphy hit wkt b Love	1		
B 3, l-b 12, n-b 13	28	B 6, l-b 1, w 1, n-b 1	9

1/67 2/79 3/99 4/147 5/162   226   1/15 2/30 3/103 4/128   (5 wkts) 140
6/175 7/186 8/199 9/224

Bowling: *First Innings*—Jarvis 14–3–47–3; Dennis 16–2–48–1; Sidebottom 13–2–34–2; Hartley 14–2–53–1; Carrick 18–2–29–1; Love 1.2–1–0–2. *Second Innings*—Jarvis 8–3–21–2; Dennis 4–0–27–1; Sidebottom 5–0–23–0; Hartley 4–0–17–0; Carrick 12–2–22–2; Love 8–1–23–0.

Umpires: S. Eudovic and C. Payne.

JAMAICA v LANCASHIRE

At Kingston, March 28, 29, 30. Jamaica won by nine wickets. Toss: Lancashire. In Lancashire's first innings, McLeod took the first three wickets in twelve balls at a cost of 4 runs.

Lancashire

G. D. Mendis lbw b McLeod	1	– c Morgan b Dennis	25
M. R. Chadwick c and b Haynes	12	– c Neita b McLeod	4
D. W. Varey c Adams b McLeod	0	– c and b Haynes	66
N. J. Speak c Cunningham b McLeod	4	– lbw b Dennis	0
A. N. Hayhurst c Davidson b Perry	19	– c sub b Perry	80
*D. P. Hughes c and b Haynes	4	– c McLeod b Perry	2
P. J. W. Allott c O'Connor b Haynes	18	– b Haynes	1
†W. K. Hegg c Neita b Perry	9	– lbw b Perry	6
I. Folley b Perry	19	– st Neita b Perry	4
I. C. Davidson b Perry	1	– b Perry	0
A. J. Murphy not out	4	– not out	1
B 1, l-b 1, w 3, n-b 1	6	B 6, l-b 1, n-b 5	12

1/6 2/10 3/36 4/46 5/46   97   1/19 2/29 3/34 4/168 5/177   201
6/73 7/73 8/82 9/97   6/178 7/187 8/200 9/201

Bowling: *First Innings*—McLeod 7–3–10–3; Dennis 9–4–8–0; Holding 4–1–7–0; Haynes 23–11–25–3; Perry 19.5–4–45–4. *Second Innings*—McLeod 14–3–36–1; Dennis 17–3–55–2; Holding 3–1–5–0; Haynes 34–15–59–2; Perry 27–10–39–5.

Jamaica

F. A. Cunningham lbw b Hayhurst	7	– not out 16
D. S. Morgan c Hegg b Murphy	14	– c Mendis b Hayhurst 15
C. St G. O'Connor c Allott b Folley	37	– not out 8
†M. C. Neita lbw b Hayhurst	0	
C. A. Davidson lbw b Hughes	73	
J. C. Adams c and b Folley	58	
R. C. Haynes st Hegg b Davidson	33	
K. W. McLeod lbw b Davidson	13	
N. O. Perry c Hughes b Folley	10	
K. Dennis not out	0	
B 6, l-b 7, w 4, n-b 2	19	

1/14 2/24 3/25 4/86 5/168   (9 wkts dec.) 264   1/18   (1 wkt) 39
6/223 7/241 8/259 9/264

*M. A. Holding did not bat.

Bowling: *First Innings*—Allott 11–4–15–0; Murphy 15.2–2–55–1; Hayhurst 9–1–37–2; Folley 19.3–4–44–3; Davidson 17–2–61–2; Hughes 19–4–39–1. *Second Innings*—Allott 4–1–23–0; Hayhurst 3–0–10–1; Varey 0.4–0–6–0.

GUYSTAC TROPHY, 1986-87

At Georgetown, November 21, 22, 23, 24. Drawn. Berbice 189 (C. B. Lambert 94; C. L. Hooper four for 21); Demerara* 165 for three (M. A. Harper 48 not out, S. Bamfield 36, A. A. Lyght 35).

†GEDDES GRANT-HARRISON LINE TROPHY

Zone A

At Kingston, April 1. Jamaica won by one wicket. Windward Islands 214 for six (50 overs) (L. D. John 84, L. A. Lewis 80); Jamaica 216 for nine (47.1 overs) (C. A. Davidson 86, J. C. Adams 40, R. C. Haynes 35 not out; W. W. Davis four for 26).

At Castries, April 9. Leeward Islands won by eight wickets. Windward Islands 212 for seven (50 overs) (L. D. John 74, S. W. Julien 49, I. Cadette 37); Leeward Islands 213 for two (43 overs) (L. L. Lawrence 88 not out, A. L. Kelly 60, R. B. Richardson 51).

At St John's, April 16. Jamaica won by 1 run. Jamaica 131 for nine (34 overs) (J. C. Adams 40, R. C. Haynes 40; R. M. Otto three for 29); Leeward Islands 130 for eight (34 overs) (R. B. Richardson 44, A. L. Kelly 37).

Zone B

At Port-of-Spain, April 1. Trinidad & Tobago won by four wickets. Guyana 236 for eight (50 overs) (A. F. D. Jackman 50, S. Dhaniram 40, R. A. Harper 38); Trinidad & Tobago 237 for six (49 overs) (D. I. Mohammed 80, A. Rajah 39, R. J. Bishop 30).

At Bridgetown, April 9. Barbados won by five wickets. Trinidad & Tobago 259 for four (50 overs) (A. L. Logie 107 not out, P. V. Simmons 58, R. J. Bishop 44); Barbados 263 for five (48.5 overs) (C. A. Best 137 not out, C. G. Greenidge 43).

At Georgetown, April 16. Barbados won by nine wickets. Guyana 126 (43.5 overs) (D. E. Ellcock four for 16, W. E. Reid three for 36); Barbados 129 for one (34.5 overs) (C. A. Best 77 not out, L. N. Reifer 48 not out).

Final

At Bridgetown, April 23. Jamaica won by four wickets. Barbados 249 for three (49 overs) (C. A. Best 74, C. G. Greenidge 65, T. R. O. Payne 55, A. L. Grant 36 not out); Jamaica* 252 for six (46 overs) (D. S. Morgan 59, P. J. L. Dujon 54, C. A. Davidson 44 not out, J. C. Adams 41). *Man of the Match:* P. J. L. Dujon.

CRICKET IN NEW ZEALAND, 1986-87

By C. R. BUTTERY

Against all predictions, and to the delight of their long-suffering supporters, Central Districts won the Shell Trophy for the first time, their last success in the three-day competition having been in 1970-71, when they won the Plunket Shield under the captaincy of B. E. Congdon. Their success in 1986-87 was almost solely due to the magnificent batting of Martin Crowe, their new captain, who scored six centuries in eight Shell Trophy games and followed these with two more in the three Test matches against the visiting West Indians later in the season. Not since Glenn Turner, in the 1970s, has one player so dominated the first-class batting averages. Crowe finished the season with 1,676 runs at an average of 93.11, so breaking Turner's record of 1,244 runs which had stood since 1975-76.

The Central Districts batting, uncertain in previous years, was built around Crowe, and it was significant that their only outright loss occurred when he failed in both innings. Nowhere was his influence more apparent than in the final game against Canterbury, a match Central Districts had to win to be sure of securing the Shell Trophy. Crowe scored 144 in the first innings and, when Central Districts were set a target of 374 to win, he played a fine captain's innings of 151 to take his side to a comfortable five-wicket victory. He was ably supported in that match, with innings of 48 and 126, by Mark Greatbatch, who with three centuries in all was the other outstanding batsman of the side. Derek Stirling and Gary Robertson were the most successful bowlers, but both suffered injuries during the season and neither played to his full potential. Fortunately, thanks to Crowe and Greatbatch, Central Districts' batting was strong enough to overcome any deficiencies in the bowling.

Otago, the previous year's winners, played the same positive cricket which had brought them the Trophy, and they shared the lead with Central Districts for most of the competition. Honours were about even. Otago lost to Central Districts the first time they met but defeated them by a wide margin in the return match, when Stephen Boock caught them on a wet wicket at Masterton and claimed six wickets in each innings. Only two points separated the two sides at the start of the final round, but an outright loss in Dunedin to Auckland cost Otago their chance of retaining the title. Ken Rutherford and Bruce Blair both had a satisfactory season with the bat, while Boock yet again was outstanding among the bowlers, particularly when the conditions favoured him. Otago were perhaps unfortunate in that several of their games were disrupted by rain, but the lack of consistent support for Rutherford, Blair and Boock was the main factor in the team's failure to win the competition for the second successive year.

Wellington finished in third place but should have done better. They had a well-balanced side which was particularly strong in batting, and once again they were the only team to go through the season without an outright defeat. Their problem was that the recognised batsmen seemed unable to force the pace when runs were required in a hurry. Against Auckland at the Basin Reserve they ran out of time when they were only 25 runs short of their target; in the return match, at Eden Park, stumps were drawn with Wellington needing 33 runs to win. Victory in these two matches would have put them in the lead by the fourth round, and might have provided the incentive necessary for them to maintain their position. Nevertheless, individual players did well. Bruce Edgar, who had announced his retirement from Test cricket, batted with unaccustomed freedom and made a significant score in nearly every match. Andrew Jones was the find of the season, scoring 710 runs in all first-class matches, with an average of 54.62, and gaining selection for the New Zealand touring team to Sri Lanka. Ewen Chatfield recorded some excellent bowling figures and finished the season with 48 wickets at a cost of 19.31 runs each.

Auckland were not the happiest of sides. The team was beset with internal bickering which eventually caused Peter Webb to step down as captain. Webb made his decision in the team's best interest; his tactics were being questioned and he felt he did not have the full support of some of his senior players. His replacement for the last two games was the experienced Worcestershire all-rounder, Dipak Patel. The unhappy atmosphere was undoubtedly a contributory factor to three losses in the first four matches, but although the team managed only two wins all season, the summer was not without its bright spots. Principal among these was the emergence of Phil Horne as a New Zealand opening batsman. The left-handed Horne, who had previously represented his country at badminton, scored 773 runs at an average of 51.53 and made his Test début against West Indies at Christchurch, where New Zealand squared the series. Patel scored three hundreds and was the other Auckland batsman to make his Test début in 1987. John Bracewell was the province's leading wicket-taker with 44 wickets, and Martin Snedden (32 wickets) and Danny Morrison (35) also bowled well. Morrison, a 21-year-old fast-medium opening bowler, showed distinct promise and went to Sri Lanka with the New Zealand side.

Canterbury had another mediocre season and had to rely heavily on John Wright and Richard Hadlee. In the Shell Trophy, Wright scored 780 runs for an average of 60.00 and Hadlee took 45 wickets at only 12.91 runs apiece, but not even these two fine players could prevent the team from finishing fifth. Paul McEwan, Rod Latham, Vaughan Brown and Anup Nathu, all experienced batsmen, did not score nearly as many runs as expected, while the bowlers were unable to give Hadlee the support he required. Unless the players are able to improve their game, Canterbury will continue to languish in the lower half of the competition.

Northern Districts lost five matches and struggled in nearly every game, their low scores evidence that they had still not recovered from the loss of experienced batsmen in recent years. Barry Cooper was the leading scorer with 532 runs, including a century in each innings against Canterbury, but his average was a modest 33.25. The bowling was also weak, with the leading wicket-taker, Murray Child, capturing his fifteen in just four matches. Hopes were higher for the future, however, with Graeme Hick, the Zimbabwean-born Worcestershire player, engaged to play for Northern Districts in 1988. The decision by Northern Districts to recruit a "name player" was no doubt influenced by the boost Martin Crowe had given to Central Districts.

The limited-overs Shell Cup competition was again closely contested, with the outcome not decided until the final match. Auckland and Canterbury each won four of their five games, and after a countback Auckland, with a higher runs-per-over rate, were declared the winners. The only century in the Shell Cup was made by Aucklander Derek Scott, whose quickly hit 140 out of a total of 246 against Northern Districts in the last game enabled Auckland to win the match and the series. Boock established a Shell Cup record for economical bowling when, for Otago against Northern Districts, he returned figures of 10–6–5–2 with his left-arm slow bowling.

History was made during the season when Pat Carrick of Christchurch became the first woman to umpire a men's first-class match in New Zealand. Mrs Carrick, a regular member of New Zealand women's teams between 1969 and 1978, joined the panel of first-class umpires and officiated in five Shell Cup and Trophy matches.

FIRST-CLASS AVERAGES, 1986-87

BATTING

(Qualification: 5 completed innings, average 25)

	M	I	NO	R	HI	100s	Avge
M. D. Crowe (*C. Districts*)	11	21	3	1,676	175*	8	93.11
E. B. McSweeney (*Wellington*) ...	10	12	4	495	117*	1	61.87
A. H. Jones (*Wellington*)	10	15	2	712	163*	2	54.76
B. A. Edgar (*Wellington*)	8	13	2	592	110	2	53.81
J. G. Wright (*Canterbury*)	11	21	2	1,019	192	3	53.63
P. A. Horne (*Auckland*)	9	17	2	773	150*	3	51.53
M. J. Greatbatch (*C. Districts*) ...	9	17	2	681	135	3	45.40
B. R. Blair (*Otago*)	9	15	1	623	120	3	44.50
D. N. Patel (*Auckland*)	11	21	2	796	170*	3	41.89
P. S. Briasco (*C. Districts*)	8	15	5	397	82*	0	39.70
P. N. Webb (*Auckland*)	9	16	4	475	82	0	39.58
T. D. Ritchie (*Wellington*)	9	13	1	469	95	0	39.08
T. E. Blain (*C. Districts*)	7	13	1	457	161	1	38.08
R. H. Vance (*Wellington*)	10	16	1	539	94	0	35.93
A. J. Hunt (*Auckland*)	5	7	1	200	87	0	33.33
B. G. Cooper (*N. Districts*)	8	16	0	532	105	2	33.25
K. R. Rutherford (*Otago*)	11	20	0	652	118	2	32.60
D. J. Boyle (*Canterbury*)	8	15	3	383	75*	0	31.91
D. J. Walker (*Otago*)	8	13	3	313	82*	0	31.30
J. J. Crowe (*Auckland*)	11	22	4	552	110	1	30.66
D. J. White (*N. Districts*)	8	16	1	455	109	1	30.33
R. T. Latham (*Canterbury*)	7	12	1	326	92	0	29.63
C. W. Flanagan (*Canterbury*)	5	6	1	148	69*	0	29.60
J. G. Bracewell (*Auckland*)	11	17	4	378	66	0	29.07
G. E. Bradburn (*N. Districts*)	5	10	1	249	104	1	27.66
B. A. Young (*N. Districts*)	8	16	3	358	89	0	27.53
V. R. Brown (*Canterbury*)	9	17	2	411	161*	1	27.40
L. M. Crocker (*N. Districts*)	5	10	0	267	91	0	26.70
R. N. Hoskin (*Otago*)	7	12	0	308	86	0	25.66
I. D. S. Smith (*C. Districts*)	11	17	6	280	50*	0	25.45
K. J. Burns (*Otago*)	8	14	0	352	60	0	25.14

*Signifies not out.

BOWLING

(Qualification: 15 wickets)

	O	M	R	W	BB	Avge
R. J. Hadlee (*Canterbury*)	407.2	106	935	62	7-49	15.08
S. L. Boock (*Otago*)	445	178	920	55	6-62	16.72
E. J. Chatfield (*Wellington*)	433.3	154	930	48	8-83	19.37
D. A. Stirling (*C. Districts*)	162	37	498	21	5-59	23.71
J. G. Bracewell (*Auckland*)	416	131	1,046	44	7-65	23.77
M. J. Child (*N. Districts*)	113	17	372	15	7-59	24.80
K. W. Martin (*C. Districts*)	203.1	41	676	27	6-25	25.03
G. K. Robertson (*C. Districts*) . .	198.5	39	628	25	6-47	25.12
T. J. Wilson (*Otago*)	246.5	49	821	30	6-73	27.36
M. C. Snedden (*Auckland*)	310.1	76	894	32	7-67	27.93
D. K. Morrison (*Auckland*)	313.1	70	1,053	35	7-82	30.08
S. W. Duff (*C. Districts*)	191.1	55	583	17	4-63	34.29
E. J. Gray (*Wellington*)	390.1	135	918	25	7-24	36.72
P. J. W. Allott (*Wellington*)	226.4	66	604	16	3-52	37.75
V. R. Brown (*Canterbury*)	307.1	81	942	20	4-106	47.10
D. J. Hartshorn (*Canterbury*) . . .	232.3	53	773	15	4-45	51.53

Note: Matches taken into account are Shell Trophy and those against the West Indian touring team.

SHELL TROPHY, 1986-87

	Played	Won	Lost	Drawn	1st Inns Pts	Pts
Central Districts	8	5	1	2	16	76
Otago	8	4	3	1	12	62*
Wellington	8	2	0	6	24	50*
Auckland	8	2	3	3	16	40
Canterbury	8	1	3	4	20	32
Northern Districts	8	1	5	2	4	16

Outright win = 12 pts; lead on first innings = 4 pts.

* First-innings points shared in one match.

In the following scores, * by the name of a team indicates that they won the toss.

At Trafalgar Park, Nelson, January 6, 7, 8. Central Districts won by 15 runs. Central Districts* 307 for four dec. (T. E. Blain 161, C. J. Smith 56, M. D. Crowe 56) and 208 for five dec. (T. E. Blain 46, C. J. Smith 34); Northern Districts 155 (B. A. Young 35; G. K. Robertson six for 47) and 345 (M. G. Harding 31, D. J. White 109, B. G. Cooper 67, C. W. Dickeson 55; G. K. Robertson five for 87, K. W. Martin three for 41). *Central Districts 16 pts.*

At Lancaster Park, Christchurch, January 6, 7, 8. Drawn. Canterbury 265 (J. G. Wright 51, A. Nathu 58, D. J. Boyle 40, P. E. McEwan 30; P. J. W. Allott three for 65) and 293 for nine (J. G. Wright 30, D. J. Boyle 42, P. E. McEwan 64, R. T. Latham 59, R. J. Hadlee 33; P. J. W. Allott three for 77); Wellington 383 for seven dec. (B. A. Edgar 94, T. D. Ritchie 50, J. V. Coney 47, E. J. Gray 54, E. B. McSweeney 79; V. R. Brown four for 106). *Wellington 4 pts.*

At Eden Park, Auckland, January 6, 7, 8. Otago won by 66 runs. Otago 218 (K. R. Rutherford 102, R. N. Hoskin 40; M. C. Snedden six for 57) and 213 (K. R. Rutherford 96, B. R. Blair 30, D. J. Boyle three for 59); Auckland* 157 (D. N. Patel 38, J. G. Bracewell 50 not out; T. J. Wilson six for 73) and 208 (P. A. Horne 62, P. N. Webb 53 not out; S. L. Boock five for 64, J. K. Lindsay four for 71). *Otago 16 pts.*

At Eden Park, Auckland, January 10, 11, 12. Canterbury won by 12 runs. Canterbury* 186 (J. G. Wright 72, P. E. McEwan 56; D. K. Morrison three for 24, J. G. Bracewell five for 31) and 197 (A. Nathu 45, D. J. Boyle 43, V. R. Brown 53; J. G. Bracewell five for 93); Auckland 154 (S. R. Gillespie 73; R. J. Hadlee five for 39, S. J. Roberts three for 47) and 217 (D. N. Patel 102; V. R. Brown three for 73, D. J. Hartsorn four for 45). *Canterbury 16 pts.*

At Levin Domain, Levin, January 10, 11, 12. Drawn. Central Districts* 308 for six dec. (M. J. Greatbatch 50, M. D. Crowe 160, P. S. Briasco 51) and 310 for four dec. (C. J. Smith 36, M. J. Greatbatch 117 not out, M. D. Crowe 73, I. D. S. Smith 34 not out); Wellington 318 for three dec. (B. A. Edgar 102, R. H. Vance 74, A. H. Jones 62 not out, T. D. Ritchie 63) and 244 for eight (T. D. Ritchie 95, E. B. McSweeney 40; D. A. Stirling five for 59). *Wellington 4 pts.*

At Seddon Park, Hamilton, January 10, 11, 12. Otago won by an innings and 37 runs. Otago 335 for six dec. (K. R. Rutherford 41, K. J. Burns 46, B. R. Blair 101, D. J. Walker 82 not out, T. J. Wilson 38); Northern Districts* 153 (C. W. Dickeson 46; N. A. Mallender four for 14, S. L. Boock three for 73) and 145 (B. G. Cooper 56, C. M. Kuggeleijn 30; S. L. Boock five for 61, J. K. Lindsay three for 30). *Otago 16 pts.*

At Basin Reserve, Wellington, January 14, 15, 16. Drawn. Auckland* 262 for five dec. (D. G. Scott 30, D. N. Patel 124, P. N. Webb 51) and 220 for eight dec. (D. G. Scott 38, D. N. Patel 33, P. N. Webb 63 not out, J. G. Bracewell 38); Wellington 263 for six dec. (B. A. Edgar 43, R. H. Vance 44, A. H. Jones 30, T. D. Ritchie 55, J. V. Coney 35; M. C. Snedden three for 76) and 195 for seven (B. A. Edgar 47, A. H. Jones 34, E. J. Gray 30, E. B. McSweeney 48; J. G. Bracewell four for 73). *Wellington 4 pts.*

At Harry Barker Reserve, Gisborne, January 14, 15, 16. Drawn. Northern Districts* 401 for eight dec. (G. W. McKenzie 115, B. G. Cooper 105, C. M. Kuggeleijn 49, B. A. Young 89; R. J. Hadlee five for 44) and 298 for six dec. (D. J. White 75, G. W. McKenzie 60, B. G. Cooper 100, C. M. Kuggeleijn 30); Canterbury 403 for four dec. (P. E. McEwan 59, V. R. Brown 161 not out, R. T. Latham 92, D. J. Hartshorn 35 not out, Extras 30) and 58 for three (J. G. Wright 32 not out). *Canterbury 4 pts.*

At Carisbrook, Dunedin, January 14, 15, 16. Central Districts won by 123 runs. Central Districts 216 (T. E. Blain 34, C. J. Smith 32, M. D. Crowe 73; J. A. Cushen three for 76, S. L. Boock four for 14) and 146 (M. D. Crowe 66; T. J. Wilson five for 90, J. A. Cushen three for 4); Otago* 166 (W. K. Lees 45; M. D. Crowe for 26, K. W. Martin three for 33) and 73 (G. K. Robertson four for 42, K. W. Martin six for 25). *Central Districts 16 pts.*

At Fitzherbert Park, Palmerston North, January 18, 19, 20. Central Districts won by 47 runs. Central Districts* 297 for four dec. (M. J. Greatbatch 48, M. D. Crowe 154 not out, I. D. S. Smith 50 not out) and 256 for nine dec. (T. E. Blain 33, M. J. Greatbatch 30, M. D. Crowe 45, P. Unwin 32, K. W. Martin 32 not out; J. G. Bracewell six for 116); Auckland 222 for two dec. (P. A. Horne 150 not out, D. G. Scott 44) and 284 (P. A. Horne 42, D. G. Scott 38, P. N. Webb 82, J. G. Bracewell 38; G. K. Robertson three for 45, S. W. Duff four for 90). *Central Districts 16 pts.*

At Molyneux Park, Alexandra, January 18, 19, 20. Otago won by four wickets. Canterbury* 207 (J. G. Wright 32, D. J. Boyle 75 not out; T. J. Wilson three for 55, S. L. Boock four for 68) and 217 for eight dec. (J. G. Wright 47, R. T. Latham 48 not out; S. L. Boock five for 53); Otago 174 (D. J. Walker 30; R. J. Hadlee five for 28, D. J. Hartshorn three for 55) and 253 for six (S. J. McCullum 71, K. J. Burns 38, B. R. Blair 100 not out; R. J. Hadlee four for 51). *Otago 12 pts, Canterbury 4 pts.*

At Basin Reserve, Wellington, January 18, 19, 20. Wellington won by ten wickets. Wellington 325 for eight dec. (B. A. Edgar 55, R. H. Vance 94, A. H. Jones 51, T. D. Ritchie 40; B. J. Barrett four for 68) and 26 for no wkt; Northern Districts* 153 (D. J. White 42; E. J. Chatfield three for 23, E. J. Gray three for 49) and 195 (L. M. Crocker 49, D. J. White 31, B. G. Cooper 47; P. J. W. Allott three for 52, E. J. Chatfield three for 42). *Wellington 16 pts.*

At Lancaster Park, Christchurch, January 24, 25, 26. Drawn. Central Districts* 335 for three dec. (T. E. Blain 34, M. D. Crowe 175 not out, P. S. Briasco 82 not out, Extras 31) and 321 for nine (T. E. Blain 49, M. J. Greatbatch 32, M. D. Crowe 50, P. S. Briasco 32, G. K. Robertson 50, K. W. Martin 47 not out; D. J. Hartshorn three for 74); Canterbury 337 for nine dec. (J. G. Wright 144, R. T. Latham 46, C. W. Flanagan 69 not out; P. J. Visser three for 71). *Canterbury 4 pts.*

At Eden Park, Auckland, January 24, 25, 26. Auckland won by 101 runs. Auckland* 302 for three dec. (P. A. Horne 52, R. B. Reid 40, D. N. Patel 170 not out) and 129 for eight dec. (M. J. Child three for 30, C. W. Dickeson four for 58); Northern Districts 183 (B. A. Young 43, M. J. Child 47; J. G. Bracewell seven for 65) and 147 (J. G. Bracewell four for 59, D. N. Patel three for 75). *Auckland 16 pts.*

At Carisbrook, Dunedin, January 24, 25, 26. Drawn. Otago* 311 (K. J. Burns 39, R. N. Hoskin 86, K. R. Rutherford 42, B. R. Blair 79; E. J. Chatfield eight for 83); Wellington 141 for four (A. H. Jones 54). *Otago 2 pts, Wellington 2 pts.*

At Eden Park, Auckland, January 28, 29, 30. Drawn. Auckland* 320 (P. A. Horne 30, A. J. Hunt 87, M. C. Snedden 56, G. B. Troup 60 not out, D. K. Morrison 36; E. J. Chatfield six for 64) and 183 for three dec. (P. A. Horne 79, J. J. Crowe 53 not out); Wellington 244 for eight dec. (B. A. Edgar 39, R. H. Vance 39, A. H. Jones 74, J. V. Coney 44) and 227 for eight (B. A. Edgar 48, R. H. Vance 47, A. H. Jones 30, J. V. Coney 43; D. K. Morrison three for 60, D. N. Patel three for 20). *Auckland 4 pts.*

At Queen Elizabeth Park, Masterton, January 28, 29, 30. Otago won by 245 runs. Otago* 275 (S. J. McCullum 60, R. N. Hoskin 64, K. R. Rutherford 33, W. K. Lees 31; G. K. Robertson three for 50, S. W. Duff four for 63) and 275 for nine dec. (K. J. Burns 56, K. R. Rutherford 118, D. J. Walker 40 not out; S. W. Duff three for 80); Central Districts 145 (P. S. Briasco 44; N. A. Mallender four for 44, S. L. Boock six for 62) and 160 (P. S. Briasco 31; S. L. Boock six for 64, J. K. Lindsay three for 45). *Otago 16 pts.*

At Lancaster Park, Christchurch, January 28, 29, 30. Northern Districts won by four wickets. Canterbury 178 (J. G. Wright 41; M. J. Child seven for 59) and 171 (A. Nathu 47; M. J. Child three for 57, C. M. Kuggeleijn four for 30); Northern Districts* 190 (Extras 30; R. J. Hadlee seven for 49) and 161 for six (D. J. White 78 not out, C. M. Kuggeleijn 33; R. J. Hadlee five for 32). *Northern Districts 16 pts.*

At Dudley Park, Rangiora, February 1, 2, 3. Drawn. Auckland 323 (R. B. Reid 71, P. A. Horne 68, J. J. Crowe 70, A. J. Hunt 51; R. J. Hadlee three for 32) and 257 for three dec. (P. A. Horne 119 not out, P. N. Webb 44, D. N. Patel 70); Canterbury* 252 (B. R. Hartland 52, J. G. Wright 54, R. J. Hadlee 50 not out; D. K. Morrison seven for 82) and 179 for six (P. E. McEwan 41, V. R. Brown 66; J. G. Bracewell four for 53). *Auckland 4 pts.*

At The Recreation Ground, Morrinsville, February 1, 2, 3. Central Districts won by eight wickets. Central Districts* 368 for three dec. (M. J. Greatbatch 135, M. D. Crowe 151, P. S. Briasco 30 not out) and 94 for two (P. S. Briasco 32 not out); Northern Districts 198 (G. E. Bradburn 37, K. B. Hancock 31; K. W. Martin five for 71) and 263 (G. E. Bradburn 104, L. M. Crocker 43, B. A. Young 39; G. R. Logan three for 75, M. D. Crowe three for 34). *Central Districts 16 pts.*

At Basin Reserve, Wellington, February 1, 2, 3. Wellington won by 94 runs. Wellington 297 for six dec. (B. A. Edgar 110, T. D. Ritchie 62, E. B. McSweeney 48 not out; J. A. Cushen three for 80) and 264 for nine dec. (R. H. Vance 77, A. H. Jones 163 not out); Otago* 267 (R. N. Hoskin 39, B. R. Blair 120, D. J. Walker 47; E. J. Chatfield seven for 65) and 200 (B. R. Blair 76; S. J. Maguiness three for 46, E. J. Gray three for 62). *Wellington 16 pts.*

At Carisbrook, Dunedin, February 5, 6, 7. Auckland won by nine wickets. Auckland 320 for nine dec. (J. J. Crowe 110, D. N. Patel 88, J. G. Bracewell 54; T. J. Wilson three for 99, S. L. Boock five for 61) and 109 for one (P. N. Webb 64, J. J. Crowe 33 not out); Otago* 165 (S. J. McCullum 54, B. R. Blair 37; D. K. Morrison three for 31, W. Watson five for 24) and 263 (K. J. Burns 60, K. R. Rutherford 72, B. R. Blair 32; M. C. Snedden seven for 67). *Auckland 16 pts.*

At Seddon Park, Hamilton, February 5, 6, 7. Drawn. Northern Districts* 89 (G. E. Bradburn 32; E. J. Gray seven for 24) and 263 for five (L. M. Crocker 91, B. G. Cooper 59, B. A. Young 44 not out); Wellington 296 for six dec. (R. H. Vance 31, A. H. Jones 105, T. D. Ritchie 31, J. V. Coney 50). *Wellington 4 pts.*

At Pukekura Park, New Plymouth, February 5, 6, 7. Central Districts won by five wickets. Canterbury* 435 for eight dec. (J. G. Wright 192, J. G. Boyle 39, D. J. Hartshorn 43, D. G. Farrant 33, V. R. Brown 42 not out; D. A. Stirling three for 70) and 235 for seven dec. (J. G. Wright 66, D. J. Boyle 56 not out, R. J. Hadlee 48 not out; G. R. Logan three for 28); Central Districts 297 for six dec. (M. J. Greatbatch 48, M. D. Crowe 144) and 375 for five (M. J. Greatbatch 126, M. D. Crowe 151). *Central Districts 12 pts, Canterbury 4 pts.*

CRICKET IN INDIA, 1986-87

By P. N. SUNDARESAN

Three Test-match tours, by Australia, Sri Lanka and Pakistan, including the usual quota of one-day internationals and other fixtures, made the 1986-87 Indian season a crowded one. An inevitable consequence was that the domestic competitions were pushed into the background, with the Indian Board of Control officials, including the selectors, too concerned with the international engagements to pay serious attention to events and trends in the domestic tournaments. Indeed, the international and domestic seasons seemed to run on separate, if parallel, lines instead of complementing each other.

One significant fact to emerge from the series with the three visiting countries was that the Indian bowling had lost much of its sting. The main cause was the decline in the striking power of Kapil Dev, who had provided the main thrust to the Indian attack for the past ten years. There was no emerging fast bowler, and the spinners were not of the calibre to offset this weakness, although the left-arm spinner, Maninder Singh, did show marked improvement. Nor could the selectors turn with confidence to the domestic tournaments to discover fresh bowling talent, for these were dominated extravagantly by batsmen.

The knockout stage of the Ranji Trophy championship reflected this fully, with 30 three-figure innings scored by as many as 23 batsmen; seven were double-hundreds. A total of 110 centuries marked the whole championship but, in sharp contrast, only seven bowlers took twenty or more wickets. So infrequently did bowlers dictate terms that the dearth of penetrative bowling, of any kind, was a distinctive and worrying feature of the Indian season. An interesting sidelight was that all the knockout matches were drawn, the winning teams being those with the first-innings lead.

Hyderabad, captained by M. V. Narasimha Rao, won the Ranji Trophy for the second time after a gap of 49 years. Their earlier triumph was notable because Hyderabad played only in the final against Nawanagar, the holders, after Madras and Southern Punjab had given them walkovers in the South Zone final and the semi-final respectively. Eddie Aibara, who played a great part in that victory with a gallant hundred in the final innings, had the satisfaction of seeing Hyderabad champions again. A national coach, he was one of two surviving members of the 1937-38 team.

With high scores so prevalent in the competition, a welcome feature of the final, played at the Feroz Shah Kotla in New Delhi, was the penetrative spell by Hyderabad's seamer, Rajesh Yadav, on the fourth morning. Delhi in response to Hyderabad's first-innings 457, were sitting pretty at 300 for three when Yadav, brother of the Test off-spinner, Shivlal Yadav, dismissed A. Sharma, Jaspal Singh, P. Jain and Shashikant to reduce them to 345 for seven. Delhi were all out for 433, 24 runs short, with Rajesh Yadav finishing with five for 114 and Shivlal three for 74.

The trend for big scores had been set earlier in the season in the Irani Cup and Duleep Trophy matches, with 300 passed in ten of the fifteen innings. Rest of India, who beat Delhi, the national champions, by an innings and 232 runs, amassed 637 runs, although it was fine bowling by the left-arm spinner, Azim Khan, with six for 29 in Delhi's second innings which clinched the Irani Cup for Rest of India. In the quarter-final of the Duleep Trophy, East

Zone scored 528 and 226 for two against Central Zone; in the semi-final they made 561, only for West Zone to reply with 567 for seven and gain a result on their first-innings lead. West Zone were on the receiving end in the final against South Zone, who, replying to 516, raised 740 runs. In their second innings West Zone were 472 for three.

In a season of such merry-making by batsmen, Arun Lal of Bengal was the outstanding peformer. Starting with 214 against Central Zone and 287 against West Zone in the Duleep Trophy, he went on to score 104 against Tripura, an unbeaten 200 against Assam and 45 against Bihar in the East Zone league of the Ranji Trophy before concluding with 287 against Rajasthan in the pre-quarter-final. At this stage he was recalled to the Test team for the matches against Pakistan, and what his absence meant to Bengal in their quarter-final against Delhi can be gauged from the scores: Bengal 464 for nine in reply to Delhi's 545 for seven declared. Arun Lal's 287 in the Duleep Trophy was the highest for the competition and his aggregate for the season was 1,388 runs, average 106.76.

The season's highest innings was Abdul Azeem's 303 not out for Hyderabad against Tamil Nadu. Carlton Saldanha of Karnataka scored the most runs in the Ranji Trophy, 785 for an average of 71.17, while S. Lahore of Madhya Pradesh led the bowlers with 32 wickets, all gathered from his four matches in the Central Zone league. Hat-tricks were performed by B. Burman of Bengal, against Tripura, and Bharat Arun of Tamil Nadu, against Goa. R. Pandit of Jammu and Kashmir returned the best all-round performance, his 158, five for 48 and eight for 33 against Services being chiefly responsible for his team's only victory of the season. K. Srikant (Services) and K. Chavan (Baroda) carried their bats through an innings while scoring 41 and 153 against Delhi and Gujarat respectively.

The Karnataka veteran and former Test batsman, B. P. Patel, was in excellent touch to record 611 runs, which took him past 6,000 runs in the Ranji Trophy; and with hundreds against Goa (115 not out) and Andhra (151), he increased his number of three-figure innings in the championship to 23. In achieving both landmarks he joined the company of V. S. Hazare (Baroda) and A. V. Mankad (Bombay).

FIRST-CLASS AVERAGES, 1986-87

BATTING

(Qualification: 600 runs)

	I	NO	R	HI	100s	Avge
Deepak Sharma (*Haryana*)	7	2	657	217	3	131.40
Arun Lal (*Bengal*)	15	2	1,388	287	5	106.76
M. Prabhakar (*Delhi*)	11	3	729	215	3	91.12
B. P. Patel (*Karnataka*)	10	3	611	151	2	87.28
S. Kalyani (*Maharashtra*)	11	3	686	200*	3	85.75
K. Bhaskar Pillai (*Delhi*)	12	2	855	222*	4	85.50
P. Roy (*Bengal*)	11	2	744	230*	4	82.66
D. B. Vengsarkar (*Bombay*)	16	4	987	166	6	82.25
A. Ayub (*Hyderabad*)	11	3	621	206*	2	77.62
M. Azharuddin (*Hyderabad*)	18	3	1,058	199	4	70.53
V. Mohanraj (*Hyderabad*)	13	2	751	211*	3	68.27

	I	NO	R	HI	100s	Avge
L. S. Rajput (*Bombay*)	15	2	881	136*	4	67.76
R. Lamba (*Delhi*)	14	1	873	131	5	67.15
R. J. Shastri (*Bombay*)	18	4	912	176*	4	65.14
C. Saldanha (*Karnataka*)	17	1	996	142	2	62.25
A. Azeem (*Hyderabad*)	14	1	753	303*	2	57.92
S. M. Gavaskar (*Bombay*)	17	0	897	176	2	52.76
M. R. Srinivasaprasad (*Karnataka*) ...	13	0	640	136	3	49.23
K. A. Qayyum (*Hyderabad*)	15	1	648	203	3	46.28
S. Viswanath (*Karnataka*)	17	1	715	91	0	44.68
K. Srikkanth (*Tamil Nadu*)	20	0	742	123	2	37.10
M. Amarnath (*Delhi*)	21	1	649	131	1	32.45

*Signifies not out.

BOWLING

(Qualification: 25 wickets)

	O	M	R	W	Avge
S. Lahore (*Madhya Pradesh*)	219.3	49	564	32	17.62
Deepak Sharma (*Haryana*)	253	54	656	26	25.23
Maninder Singh (*Delhi*)	670.4	200	1,522	60	25.36
M. V. Narasimha Rao (*Hyderabad*)	221.5	16	755	28	26.96
S. Talwar (*Haryana*)	273.5	50	731	27	27.07
P. Sunderam (*Rajasthan*)	231.4	30	866	31	27.93
A. R. Bhat (*Karnataka*)	312.3	75	870	26	33.46
W. V. Raman (*Tamil Nadu*)	332.5	83	935	27	34.62
N. S. Yadav (*Hyderabad*)	501.5	108	1,299	37	35.10
R. Yadav (*Hyderabad*)	230.5	25	963	26	37.03
R. J. Shastri (*Bombay*)	574.3	142	1,385	33	41.96

Note: Matches taken into account are Ranji Trophy, Duleep Trophy, Irani Trophy, and those against the Australian, Sri Lankan and Pakistani touring teams.

RANJI TROPHY, 1986-87

In the following scores, (M) indicates that the match was played on coir matting, (T) that it was played on turf, and * by the name of a team indicates that they won the toss.

Central Zone

At Indore (T), November 15, 16, 17. Rajasthan won by three wickets. Madhya Pradesh 177 (A. Vijayvargiya 39; P. Sunderam four for 65, Ratan Singh six for 56) and 278 for eight dec. (S. Ansari 115, A. Vijayvargiya 120 not out); Rajasthan* 160 (S. Mudkavi 36, D. Jain 45, Parminder Singh 43; J. Vaigad three for 38, S. Lahore three for 26) and 296 for seven (Padam Shastri 64, A. Asawa 101 not out; S. Lahore three for 90). *Rajasthan 13 pts, Madhya Pradesh 6 pts.*

At Nagpur (T), November 15, 16, 17. Drawn. Uttar Pradesh 183 (R. Sapru 30; S. Takle three for 31, S. Jugade three for 57) and 284 (S. S. Khandkar 35, S. Chaturvedi 36, S. P. Singh 116; B. Thakre five for 97, H. Wasu three for 87); Vidarbha* 309 (S. Phadkar 128; K. K. Sharma eight for 120) and 98 for three (U. Phate 42 not out). *Vidarbha 13 pts, Uttar Pradesh 8 pts.*

At Nagpur (T), November 21, 22, 23. Drawn. Vidarbha* 279 (U. Phate 41, P. Hingnikar 70, V. Gawate 68; P. Sunderam four for 63) and 251 (P. Shetty 44, U. Phate 43, P. Hingnikar 52, S. Hedaoo 45; Ratan Singh five for 68); Rajasthan 182 (J. Mathur 33, Padam Shastri 47, D. Jain 31, S. Vyas 35; H. Wasu five for 47) and 104 for three (A. Mudkavi 41 not out). *Vidarbha 15 pts, Rajasthan 11 pts.*

At Bhilai (T), November 21, 22, 23. Railways won by eight wickets. Madhya Pradesh* 191 (S. Ansari 34, C. P. Singh 55, A. Laghate 30; G. Tank three for 33) and 214 (A. Vijayvargiya 44, M. Sahni 32, C. P. Singh 57; Durga Prasad four for 45, H. Joshi four for 46); Railways 357 (P. Karkera 64, Yusuf Ali Khan 50, K. B. Kala 76, G. Tank 83; S. Lahore four for 113) and 50 for two. *Railways 16 pts, Madhya Pradesh 5 pts.*

At Agra (T), November 28, 29, 30. Uttar Pradesh won by 105 runs. Uttar Pradesh* 230 (S. S. Khandkar 30, S. Chaturvedi 33, R. Sapru 33, R. S. Hans 48; S. Lahore six for 58) and 195 for four dec. (S. S. Khandkar 38, S. P. Singh 51, S. Chaturvedi 68 not out; S. Lahore three for 101); Madhya Pradesh 114 (A. Laghate 34; M. A. Ansari five for 46, R. S. Hans four for 31) and 206 (S. Ansari 60, C. P. Singh 69; M. A. Ansari four for 70, R. S. Hans five for 75). *Uttar Pradesh 15 pts, Madhya Pradesh 5 pts.*

At Ajmer (M), November 28, 29, 30. Rajasthan won by three wickets. Railways 213 (D. Arora 36, Hyder Ali 48 not out; P. Sunderam five for 84) and 221 (P. Karkera 48, K. B. Kala 76; Ratan Singh five for 41); Rajasthan* 312 (S. Shastri 58, Padam Shastri 117, S. Mudkavi 32, D. Jain 34; Durga Prasad four for 62) and 123 for seven (S. Mudkavi 39 not out). *Rajasthan 19 pts, Railways 9 pts.*

At Orai (T), December 5, 6, 7. Drawn. Uttar Pradesh* 191 (R. Sapru 60, V. S. Yadav 35; Hyder Ali five for 19) and 288 for four dec. (S. S. Khandkar 118, S. P. Singh 32, R. Sapru 100 not out; H. Joshi three for 68); Railways 309 (P Karkera 61, Yusuf Ali Khan 72, D. Arora 34, Hyder Ali 39; M. A. Ansari six for 65) and 45 for no wkt. *Uttar Pradesh 6 pts, Railways 13 pts.*

At Rajpur (T), December 5, 6, 7. Drawn. Vidarbha 301 (U. Phate 118, P. Hingnikar 56, S. Hedaoo 31, V. Gawate 40; S. Lahore eight for 100) and 200 (Kawre 66; S. Lahore four for 57); Madhya Pradesh* 380 (S. Ansari 132, A. Vijayvargiya 60, C. P. Singh 43, R. Talwar 69) and 51 for four. *Madhya Pradesh 17 pts, Vidarbha 12 pts.*

At Karali (M), January 10, 11, 12. Drawn. Uttar Pradesh* 210 (R. Sapru 42, Gopal Sharma 47, M. A. Ansari 38 not out; P. Sunderam five for 57); Rajasthan 337 for five (A. Mudkavi 44, A. S. Negi 65, S. Mudkavi 102 not out, A. Asawa 78). *Rajasthan 11 pts, Uttar Pradesh 6 pts.*

At Nagpur (T), January 10, 11, 12. Drawn. Railways* 477 for four dec. (P. Karkera 47, Yusuf Ali Khan 227, R. D. Khanwilkar 41, K. B. Kala 59, D. Arora 36 not out, Durga Prasad 54 not out); Vidarbha 45 for no wkt. *Railways 4 pts, Vidarbha 1 pt.*

Rajasthan 54 pts, Railways 42 pts, Vidarbha 41 pts, Uttar Pradesh 35 pts, Madhya Pradesh 33 pts. Rajasthan and Railways qualified for the knockout stage.

East Zone

At Calcutta (T), December 5, 6, 7. Drawn. Orissa 430 for eight dec. (K. Dubey 139, D. Mahanty 128, A. Bharadwaj 39, S. Mitra 66; A. Saha three for 103); Tripura* 222 (S. Paul 31, U. Choudhry 30, S. Das Gupta 75; H. Praharaj five for 83, L. K. Mahapatra five for 60) and 54 for four. *Orissa 13 pts, Tripura 6 pts.*

At Gauhati (T), December 5, 6, 7. Drawn. Assam 287 (S. Dutta 35, S. Uzir 35, N. Konwar 78; Satish Singh three for 55, R. Arora three for 84, S. Sinha three for 40) and 100 for three (J. Choudhry 31 not out); Bihar* 362 for seven dec. (P. M. Khanna 80, Ujjal Das 104, S. Singh 112). *Bihar 14 pts, Assam 8 pts.*

At Gauhati (T), December 12, 13, 14. Drawn. Assam* 238 (J. Choudhry 42, Amal Das 77; H. Praharaj four for 83, S. Mitra three for 46) and 152 for three (J. Choudhry 72); Orissa 260 for seven dec. (D. Mahanty 47, S. Mitra 54; N. Konwar four for 51). *Orissa 12 pts, Assam 8 pts.*

At Calcutta (T), December 12, 13, 14. Bengal won by 351 runs. Bengal 309 for five dec. (P. Roy 121 not out, A. Verma 68, P. Nandy 41; A. Das three for 117) and 272 for six dec. (Arun Lal 104, A. Mitra 34, P. Nandy 37; T. Dam three for 74); Tripura* 102 (S. Bhattacharjee three for 21, S. Singh five for 33) and 128 (B. Burman seven for 56, including a hat-trick). *Bengal 24 pts, Tripura 5 pts.*

At Ranchi (T), December 17, 18, 19. No play, owing to rain. *Bihar 4 pts, Orissa 4 pts.*

At Gauhati (T), December 17, 18, 19. Drawn. Assam* 354 (R. Bora 46, S. Uzir 39, N. Konwar 128 not out, S. Chakravarthy 30; S. Singh three for 53, A. Bhattacharjee five for 79) and 176 for seven (Amal Das 32, P. Bora 39, R. Bora 50); Bengal 373 for four dec. (Arun Lal 200 not out, P. Nandy 41, A. Bhattacharjee 54 not out). *Bengal 16 pts, Assam 7 pts.*

At Calcutta (T), December 24, 25, 26. Drawn. Orissa 302 (S. Das 34, D. Mahanty 37, S. Mitra 114 not out; U. Chatterjee three for 54) and 218 for nine dec. (Sushil Kumar 53; P. Nandy five for 45); Bengal* 318 for seven dec. (P. Roy 146 not out, G. Shome, jun. 32; H. Praharaj three for 91, P. Agarwal three for 74) and 58 for four (A. Mitra 32; P. Agarwal three for 27). *Bengal 17 pts, Orissa 13 pts.*

At Jamshedpur (T), December 24, 25, 26. Bihar won by an innings and 160 runs. Bihar* 347 (A. Dayal 65, H. Gidwani 34, Ujjal Das 33, P. M. Khanna 63, Satish Singh 62, A. Kumar 33; A. Saha four for 114); Tripura 100 (A. Kumar five for 27, V. Venkatram four for 32) and 87 (D. Bhattacharjee 33; V. Venkatram five for 26). *Bihar 24 pts, Tripura 4 pts.*

At Silchar (T), January 8, 9, 10. Assam won by an innings and 53 runs. Tripura* 65 (N. Konwar six for 12) and 107 (N. Konwar seven for 26); Assam 225 for five dec. (Amal Das 37, R. Bora 88, S. Uzir 32 not out; T. Dam three for 93). *Assam 22 pts, Tripura 2 pts.*

At Calcutta (T), January 8, 9, 10. Drawn. Bihar 202 (B. D. Gossein 77, S. S. Karim 50; Satish Singh three for 26) and 274 (A. Dayal 35, B. D. Gossein 163 not out, S. S. Karim 45 not out); Bengal* 254 (R. Mitra 55, Arun Lal 45, S. Ganguly 57; S. Sinha four for 82, V. Venkatram four for 65). *Bengal 12 pts, Bihar 8 pts.*

Bengal 69 pts, Bihar 50 pts, Assam 45 pts, Orissa 42 pts, Tripura 17 pts. Bengal and Bihar qualified for the knockout stage.

North Zone

At Srinagar (T), September 16, 17, 18. Haryana won by an innings and 47 runs. Haryana 448 for nine dec. (Deepak Sharma 217, A. Malhotra 41, S. Talwar 42; I. Gandru three for 80); Jammu and Kashmir* 190 (S. Chowdhary 32, Nirmal Singh 55; R. Jolly five for 44) and 211 (R. Pandit 72, Vidya Bhaskar 59 not out; S. Talwar four for 77, Deepak Sharma four for 48). *Haryana 21 pts, Jammu and Kashmir 4 pts.*

At Srinagar (T), September 20, 21, 22. Punjab won by an innings and 60 runs. Jammu and Kashmir* 174 (Nayeem 56; R. S. Ghai three for 54) and 238 (R. Pandit 79; R. S. Ghai six for 117); Punjab 472 for six dec. (R. Kalsi 42, R. Puri 125, Yashpal Sharma 134, D. Chopra 50, R. S. Ghai 39). *Punjab 23 pts, Jammu and Kashmir 2 pts.*

At Srinagar (T), October 3, 4, 5. Drawn. Delhi 525 for eight dec. (S. C. Khanna 120, A. Mohindra 37, K. Bhaskar Pillai 160, M. Nayyar 100 not out; Ravi Kant four for 146); Jammu and Kashmir* 262 (S. Pervez 114; S. S. Saini five for 56) and 268 for nine (R. Pandit 75, Nirmal Singh 73 not out, Vidya Bhaskar 63; A. Sharma five for 34). *Delhi 14 pts, Jammu and Kashmir 8 pts.*

At Srinagar (T), October 7, 8, 9. Jammu and Kashmir won by nine wickets. Services 344 (S. Bhatnagar 44, B. Ghosh 45, C. Sharma 76, A. Jha 64, K. K. Gohil 30; R. Pandit five for 48) and 162 (K. Srikant 34, S. Bhatnagar 39; R. Pandit eight for 33); Jammu and Kashmir* 475 (R. Pandit 158, A. Gupta 152, Vidya Bhaskar 65, Nirmal Singh 39; K. K. Gohil seven for 144) and 32 for one. *Jammu and Kashmir 20 pts, Services 5 pts.*

At Mandi (T), November 15, 16, 17. Drawn. Jammu and Kashmir* 248 (Nirmal Singh 57, S. Chowdhary 69; P. Sen four for 56, Om Prakash three for 37) and 4 for one. Himachal Pradesh 250 for eight dec. (Darshan Singh 64, Inderjit Singh 33, V. Sen 53, Kamal Kant 40; Ravi Kant five for 64). *Himachal Pradesh 12 pts, Jammu and Kashmir 8 pts.*

At Mandi (T), November 20, 21, 22. Haryana won by an innings and 191 runs. Himachal Pradesh* 166 (Inderjit Singh 62; Deepak Sharma five for 56, Balkishan three for 23) and 65 (Deepak Sharma four for 35, Balkishan three for 13); Haryana 422 for four dec. (Deepak Sharma 169 not out, A. Sharma 97, A. Malhotra 65 not out, R. Chadda 37). *Haryana 24 pts, Himachal Pradesh 2 pts.*

At Una (T), November 25, 26, 27. Drawn. Delhi* 373 for eight dec. (K. Bhaskar Pillai 101, S. C. Khanna 110, A. Sharma 37, M. Prabhakar 42; P. Sen three for 100, J. Puri three for 67); Himachal Pradesh 146 (R. Nayyar 59 not out; K. Azad four for 33) and 34 for two. *Delhi 14 pts, Himachal Pradesh 6 pts.*

At Una (T), November 29, 30, December 1. Drawn. Himachal Pradesh 93 (R. S. Ghai three for 23, M. I. Singh six for 25) and 70 for six dec. (Inderjit Singh 32; R. S. Ghai three for 27); Punjab* 95 for five dec. (S. Agarwal 46) and 4 for no wkt. *Punjab 12 pts, Himachal Pradesh 5 pts.*

At Una (T), December 4, 5, 6. Services won by 266 runs. Services 319 (K. Srikant 45, S. Bhatnagar 90, B. Ghosh 49, C. Sharma 42) and 200 for six dec. (K. M. Roshan 52, B. Ghosh 55; Om Prakash three for 24); Himachal Pradesh* 189 (Darshan Singh 67, Jaswant Rai 47; S. Sadangi three for 48) and 64 (A. Jha three for 13, S. Sadangi five for 18). *Services 22 pts, Himachal Pradesh 8 pts.*

At Delhi (T), December 13, 14, 15. Delhi won by an innings and 78 runs. Delhi 310 for three dec. (M. Prabhakar 137, R. Lamba 115); Services* 145 (B. Ghosh 46; Maninder Singh six for 38) and 87 (K. Srikant 41 not out; Madan Lal three for 19, M. Prabhakar four for 31). *Delhi 24 pts, Services 1 pt.*

At Rohtak (T), December 18, 19, 20. Drawn. Delhi* 288 (A. Bharadwaj 45, K. Bhaskar Pillai 59, S. C. Khanna 56, S. Sharma 42 not out; S. Talwar four for 104, Deepak Sharma three for 44) and 191 for four (M. Prabhakar 108 not out, S. C. Khanna 37); Haryana 441 (K. P. Amarjeet 210 not out, A. Malhotra 73, Aman Kumar 51; P. Jain three for 88). *Haryana 14 pts, Delhi 8 pts.*

At Delhi (T), December 22, 23, 24. Drawn. Delhi* 329 for eight dec. (M. Prabhakar 80, K. Azad 86, S. C. Khanna 46, S. Sharma 40; D. Chopra three for 75, M. I. Singh four for 85) and 23 for no wkt; Punjab 175 (Gursharan Singh 39, D. Chopra 35; M. Prabhakar three for 31, S. Sharma four for 58) and 293 for six dec. (R. Kalsi 34, N. S. Sidhu 110, Gursharan Singh 103; A. Sharma three for 35). *Delhi 13 pts, Punjab 7 pts.*

At Delhi, December 26, 27, 28. Punjab won by an innings and 98 runs. Services* 165 (K. Srikant 63, K. M. Roshan 34; D. Chopra eight for 38) and 184 (B. Ghosh 58, B. Pathak 41; D. Chopra four for 71, M. I. Singh five for 70); Punjab 447 for seven dec. (N. S. Sidhu 131, Gursharan Singh 60, D. Chopra 42, R. S. Ghai 114 not out, M. I. Singh 54 not out). *Punjab 21 pts, Services 3 pts.*

At Delhi (T), January 8, 9, 10. Drawn. Services 212 (S. Bhatnagar 39, B. Ghosh 49, A. Jha 40; S. Talwar five for 64, Sharanjit Singh four for 46) and 310 (K. Srikant 47, S. Bhatnagar 31, B. Ghosh 68, V. Bakshi 55, S. Sadangi 32; S. Talwar four for 65); Haryana* 232 (A. Malhotra 80, R. Amarnath 32 not out; R. H. Khan seven for 49). *Haryana 11 pts, Services 8 pts.*

At Patiala (T), January 13, 14, 15. Drawn. Haryana* 501 for five dec. (Deepak Sharma 214 not out, R. Amarnath 62, K. P. Amarjeet 38, A. Malhotra 76; Harjinder Singh three for 95); Punjab 99 for four (A. Sharma 36; S. Talwar three for 48). *Haryana 5 pts, Punjab 2 pts.*

Haryana 75 pts, Delhi 73 pts, Punjab 65 pts, Jammu and Kashmir 42 pts, Services 39 pts, Himachal Pradesh 33 pts. Haryana and Delhi qualified for the knockout stage.

South Zone

At Panjim (T), November 15, 16, 17. Drawn. Goa 200 (N. Phadte 44, S. Kangralkar 78, S. Mahadevan 47; B. Arun four for 31, including a hat-trick) and 264 for eight (S. Tendulkar 38, N. Phadte 121; S. Vasudevan three for 53); Tamil Nadu* 426 (K. Srikkanth 57, P. C. Prakash 51, R. Madhavan 62, A. Jabbar 34, B. Arun 33, D. Girish 44, S. Vasudevan 59 not out; M. Desai three for 61). *Tamil Nadu 14 pts, Goa 8 pts.*

At Panjim (T), November 22, 23, 24. Drawn. Karnataka* 402 (M. R. Srinivasaprasad 32, C. Saldanha 89, S. M. H. Kirmani 107, B. P. Patel 115 not out; H. Angley six for 102) and 258 for three dec. (M. R. Srinivasaprasad 105, C. Saldanha 77, S. M. H. Kirmani 31 not out); Goa 295 (N. Phadte 49, S. Kangralkar 54, S. Mahadevan 44, H. Angley 56 not out; A. R. Bhat six for 56) and 48 for four (J. Abhiram four for 20). *Karnataka 18 pts, Goa 10 pts.*

At Bangalore (T), November 29, 30, December 1. Drawn. Karnataka* 452 (C. Saldanha 70, S. M. H. Kirmani 31, B. P. Patel 151, S. Viswanath 84, K. Jeswant 30; J. K. Ghiya three for 167, D. Sudhakar Reddy three for 76) and 228 for five dec. (C. Saldanha 74, S. Viswanath 76; M. N. Ravikumar four for 48); Andhra 435 (L. K. Adiseshu 35, S. Krishnamohan 74, M. F. Rehman 35, K. V. S. D. Kamaraju 120, K. B. Ramamurthy 80, J. K. Ghiya 31; K. Jeswant six for 114). *Karnataka 13 pts, Andhra 9 pts.*

At Trivandrum (T), November 29, 30, December 1. Drawn. Kerala 488 for six dec. (P. Ranganathan 64, S. Santosh 158, S. Rajesh 57, K. Jayaraman 125 not out, S. Ramesh 30 not out; S. Pednekar three for 102) and 28 for no wkt; Goa* 372 (S. Kangralkar 70, S. Mahadevan 109, D. Bangera 30, H. Angley 38, S. Pednekar 31; V. Hariharan three for 61, T. S. Mahadevan three for 89) and 20 for no wkt. *Kerala 12 pts, Goa 7 pts.*

At Panjim (T), December 5, 6, 7. Drawn. Goa* 402 (S. Shinde 49, N. Phadte 135, S. Mahadevan 113; J. K. Ghiya three for 99, D. Sudhakar Reddy four for 95) and 19 for no wkt; Andhra 416 for eight dec. (G. A. Pratapkumar 55, M. F. Rehman 37, K. B. Ramamurthy 117, D. Meher Baba 78, J. K. Ghiya 59 not out; G. Parikh three for 104). *Andhra 10 pts, Goa 8 pts.*

At Kothagudam (M), December 7, 8, 9. Drawn. Kerala 338 (T. Mathew 38, K. Jayaraman 133, S. Rajesh 51; M. V. Narasimha Rao four for 86) and 221 (T. Mathew 55, K. Jayaraman 58; N. S. Yadav three for 58, M. V. Narasimha Rao six for 75); Hyderabad* 349 for four dec. (A. Azeem 78, V. Mohanraj 180 not out) and 194 for eight (V. Jaisimha 66; V. Hariharan three for 68, S. Santosh three for 43). *Hyderabad 16 pts, Kerala 12 pts.*

At Srikakulam (M), December 12, 13, 14. Drawn. Andhra* 403 (L. K. Adiseshu 78, M. F. Rehman 31, M. N. Ravikumar 33, J. K. Ghiya 93, G. A. Pratapkumar 32, S. Krishnamohan 32; V. Hariharan three for 73, T. S. Mahadevan four for 68); Kerala 416 (T. Mathew 64, P. Ranganathan 38, T. P. Ajit Kumar 34, S. Santosh 74, K. Jayaraman 102, S. Rajesh 56). *Kerala 10 pts, Andhra 8 pts.*

At Hyderabad (T), December 13, 14, 15. Drawn. Hyderabad* 611 for four dec. (A. Azeem 303 not out, V. Mohanraj 115, K. A. Qayyum 104); Tamil Nadu 387 for six (V. B. Chandrasekhar 81, V. Sivaramakrishnan 94, R. Madhavan 57, R. Venkatesh 56, A. Jabbar 71 not out; Arshad Ayub three for 84). *Hyderabad 7 pts, Tamil Nadu 6 pts.*

At Trivandrum (T), December 19, 20, 21. Drawn. Kerala 284 (T. Mathew 59, K. Jayaraman 31, S. Rajesh 30, V. Hariharan 32, T. S. Mahadevan 35; L. Sivaramakrishnan four for 88) and 353 for eight dec. (K. Jayaraman 35, S. Rajesh 40, V. Hariharan 103, S. Ramesh 81 not out; S. Srinivasan three for 101); Tamil Nadu* 314 for six dec. (V. Sivaramakrishnan 57, P. C. Prakash 105, R. Madhavan 55) and 59 for four (V. Hariharan three for 12). *Tamil Nadu 16 pts, Kerala 10 pts.*

At Bangalore (T), December 20, 21, 22. Drawn. Karnataka* 368 (C. Saldanha 84, S. M. H. Kirmani 79, G. R. Viswanath 54, B. P. Patel 91; M. V. Narasimha Rao four for 96) and 239 for two dec. (M. R. Srinivasaprasad 123 not out, C. Saldanha 70); Hyderabad 272 (V. Mohanraj 30, D. Suresh 44, K. A. Qayyum 46, Ehtesham-ud-Din 70, R. Yadav 54; A. R. Bhat five for 107, H. Surendra four for 92) and 241 for five (A. Azeem 41, R. Yadav 68, Ehtesham-ud-Din 51 not out, Arshad Ayub 45 not out). *Karnataka 18 pts, Hyderabad 11 pts.*

At Anantapur (M), December 27, 28, 29. Drawn. Hyderabad 408 (A. Azeem 63, K. A. Qayyum 114, M. V. Narasimha Rao 61, Ehtesham-ud-Din 89, V. Jaisimha 38 not out; K. B. Ramamurthy three for 97, D. Meher Baba three for 71) and 108 for seven dec. (D. Suresh 42; S. Krishnamohan four for 44); Andhra* 477 (M. F. Rehman 108, K. V. S. D. Kamaraju 58, M. S. Kumar 93, K. B. Ramamurthy 128 not out; M. V. Ramanamurthy three for 63). *Andhra 14 pts, Hyderabad 9 pts.*

At Salem (T), December 27, 28, 29. Drawn. Karnataka* 550 (C. Saldanha 142, S. M. H. Kirmani 125, G. R. Viswanath 52, B. P. Patel 91, K. Jeswant 42; W. V. Raman six for 145); Tamil Nadu 296 (V. Sivaramakrishnan 38, P. C. Prakash 91, A. Jabbar 36, S. Vasudevan 52; H. Surendra four for 109, K. Jeswant four for 81). *Karnataka 13 pts, Tamil Nadu 7 pts.*

At Trivandrum (T), January 10, 11, 12. Drawn. Karnataka 475 (M. R. Srinivasaprasad 136, C. Saldanha 35, G. R. Viswanath 70, P. Ramesh Rao 60, K. Jeswant 97, H. Surendra 31 not out; V. Hariharan three for 98) and 139 for five (C. Saldanha 58 not out); Kerala* 350 (K. Jayaraman 105, S. Rajesh 45, T. C. Sudesh 84, Rammohan 32 not out; R. M. H. Binny four for 55, J. Abhiram three for 67). *Karnataka 13 pts, Kerala 12 pts.*

At Hyderabad (T), January 10, 11, 12. Hyderabad won by nine wickets. Goa* 134 (M. V. Narasimha Rao four for 25, Venkatapathy Raju three for 32) and 163 (M. V. Narasimha Rao five for 75, Arshad Ayub three for 39); Hyderabad 242 (V. Mohanraj 38, M. V. Narasimha Rao 31, Ehtesham-ud-Din 39 not out, Arshad Ayub 59; G. Parikh three for 43) and 57 for one. *Hyderabad 18 pts, Goa 4 pts.*

At Madras (T), January 10, 11, 12. Tamil Nadu won by four wickets. Andhra* 246 (M. F. Rehman 53, M. N. Ravikumar 31, K. B. Ramamurthy 79; Kanwaljit Singh three for 64, W. V. Raman four for 41) and 124 (K. V. S. D. Kamaraju 39; W. V. Raman six for 29); Tamil Nadu 163 (V. B. Chandrasekhar 38, A. Jabbar 30; M. N. Ravikumar four for 52, D. Meher Baba five for 38) and 208 for six (V. Sivaramakrishnan 41, P. C. Prakash 31, A. Jabbar 62). *Tamil Nadu 16 pts, Andhra 7 pts.*

Karnataka 75 pts, Hyderabad 61 pts, Tamil Nadu 59 pts, Kerala 56 pts, Andhra 48 pts, Goa 37 pts. Karnataka and Hyderabad qualified for the knockout stage.

West Zone

At Pune (T), November 15, 16, 17. Drawn. Gujarat* 398 (S. Talati 50, S. Pathak 85, A. Saheba 32, B. Mistry 64, J. Saigal 57, N. Patel 36; S. Jadhav six for 96) and 162 for one (S. Talati 100 not out, S. Pathak 60); Maharashtra 402 for eight dec. (R. Poonawala 128, M. D. Gunjal 57, B. Joglekar 31, Azim Khan 110 not out; R. Desai three for 87, J. Zinto three for 65). *Maharashtra 11 pts, Gujarat 10 pts.*

At Porbander (T), November 15, 16, 17. Bombay won by an innings and 11 runs. Saurashtra 181 (K. Chauhan 57; R. R. Kulkarni four for 27, D. Jadhav three for 49) and 153 (B. S. Sandhu three for 40, R. R. Kulkarni five for 49); Bombay* 345 (L. S. Rajput 112, J. Sanghani 66, A. Sippy 32, C. S. Pandit 44, R. J. Shastri 32; R. Jadeja three for 72). *Bombay 24 pts, Saurashtra 3 pts.*

At Navasam (M), November 22, 23, 24. Drawn. Saurashtra* 340 (K. Chauhan 53, R. Badiyani 66, A. Pandya 43, B. Jadeja 32, S. Keshwala 39; M. Kahar four for 75) and 95 for one (R. Badiyani 68 not out); Baroda 414 for six dec. (A. D. Gaekwad 30, K. Chavan 46, G. Tilakraj 46, M. Narula 105, T. Arothe 108; B. Radia three for 79). *Baroda 11 pts, Saurashtra 7 pts.*

At Thane (T), November 22, 23, 24. Drawn. Gujarat* 445 (S. Talati 51, S. Pathak 124, P. Desai 44, B. K. Patel 46, J. Zinto 85; B. S. Sandhu four for 95, K. D. Mokhasi three for 92); Bombay 293 (L. S. Rajput 57, S. S. Hattangadi 59, J. Sanghani 76, A. Sippy 34; D. Patel four for 41, J. Saigal three for 37) and 250 for seven (L. S. Rajput 31, S. S. Hattangadi 63, S. V. Manjrekar 32, B. S. Sandhu 51; J. Zinto four for 55). *Gujarat 14 pts, Bombay 12 pts.*

At Bombay (T), December 13, 14, 15. Bombay won by ten wickets. Baroda 234 (K. Chavan 31, K. S. More 74; R. R. Kulkarni three for 52, P. Kasliwal five for 73) and 208 (G. Tilakraj 59; B. S. Sandhu four for 24, P. Kasliwal four for 64); Bombay* 392 (D. B. Vengsarkar 109, S. L. Kulkarni 64, S. V. Manjrekar 100 not out; M. Kahar three for 71, R. Patel three for 142) and 53 for no wkt. *Bombay 19 pts, Baroda 6 pts.*

At Jamnagar (T), December 13, 14, 15. Drawn. Maharashtra 147 (A. Deshpande 36; S. Keshwala five for 69, C. Mankad three for 34) and 266 for seven dec. (M. D. Gunjal 67, P. R. Pradhan 98; C. Mankad four for 78); Saurashtra* 346 (K. Chauhan 52, R. Badiyani 65, A. Pandya 41, S. Keshwala 33, B. Jadeja 77; A. Walhekar four for 89, R. S. Hazare three for 85) and 8 for one. *Saurashtra 6 pts, Maharashtra 6 pts.*

At Surat (M), December 19, 20, 21. Drawn. Gujarat 324 (S. Pathak 38, B. Mistry 37, B. K. Patel 46, N. Patel 70, D. Patel 32; A. K. Patel three for 81, B. Radia four for 40) and 211 for seven dec. (S. Pathak 43, B. Mistry 72, B. K. Patel 42; B. Radia three for 70); Saurashtra* 310 (R. Badiyani 39, S. Keshwala 64, B. Pujara 91, S. Pillai 36; J. Saigal five for 63) and 119 for two (S. Pillai 37 not out). *Gujarat 14 pts, Saurashtra 12 pts.*

At Baroda (T), December 20, 21, 22. Maharashtra won by 61 runs. Maharashtra* 210 (R. Poonawala 65, N. Fadnis 78; R. Patel three for 47, D. V. Pardeshi five for 42) and 185 (S. Kalyani 64, M. D. Gunjal 37; D. V. Pardeshi three for 72, A. D. Gaekwad five for 29); Baroda 113 (T. Arothe 36 not out; R. S. Hazare three for 31, A. Walhekar three for 12) and 221 (R. Parikh 31, M. S. Patel 38, D. V. Pardeshi 49; V. V. Oak four for 55). *Maharashtra 17 pts, Baroda 5 pts.*

At Sholapur (T), December 26, 27, 28. Drawn. Maharashtra* 450 for eight dec. (S. Kalyani 200 not out, Azim Khan 68, M. D. Gunjal 50, S. C. Gudge 37; B. S. Sandhu three for 82); Bombay 255 for one (L. S. Rajput 136 not out, S. S. Hattangadi 111). *Bombay 7 pts, Maharashtra 6 pts.*

At Broach (T), December 26, 27, 28. Baroda won by nine wickets. Gujarat 251 (P. Bhatt 31, B. Mistry 83; R. Patel three for 62, T. Arothe three for 56) and 157 (R. Patel four for 27, A. Petiwale three for 52); Baroda* 326 (K. Chavan 153 not out, M. Narula 56, R. Patel 31) and 83 for one (G. Tilakraj 50 not out). *Baroda 19 pts, Gujarat 6 pts.*

Bombay 62 pts, Gujarat 44 pts, Baroda 41 pts, Maharashtra 40 pts, Saurashtra 28 pts. Bombay and Gujarat qualified for the knockout stage.

Pre-quarter-finals

At Calcutta (T), January 31, February 1, 2, 3. Drawn. Bengal declared winners by virtue of their first-innings lead. Bengal* 614 for seven dec. (P. Roy 134, Arun Lal 287, A. Mitra 40, P. Nandy 99) and 17 for two; Rajasthan 465 (A. Mudkavi 101, A. S. Negi 41, P. Shastri 69, D. Jain 50, S. Mudkavi 77, A. Asawa 87; P. Nandy four for 139).

At Patna (T), February 1, 2, 3, 4. Drawn. Bihar declared winners by virtue of their first-innings lead. Railways* 210 (Durga Prasad 76 not out; Randhir Singh five for 66, S. Sinha four for 64) and 394 for seven dec. (P. Karkera 70, K. B. Kala 122, D. Arora 38, G. Tank 42, Durga Prasad 50 not out); Bihar 422 (A. Dayal 69, H. Gidwani 109, Ujjal Das 35, V. Venkatram 84 not out; H. Joshi seven for 95) and 90 for one (P. M. Khanna 50, A. Dayal 31 not out).

Quarter-finals

At Bangalore (T), February 14, 15, 16, 17. Drawn. Karnataka declared winners by virtue of their first-innings lead. Karnataka* 465 (M. R. Srinivasaprasad 54, C. Saldanha 31, B. P. Patel 77, P. Ramesh Rao 75, J. Abhiram 102, T. Kothari 37, H. Surendra 37; R. Thakkar six for 170, K. D. Mokashi three for 141) and 166 for six (P. Ramesh Rao 70; Iqbal Karan three for 38); Bombay 404 (S. L. Kulkarni 175, S. V. Manjrekar 99; A. R. Bhat six for 148).

At Hyderabad (T), February 14, 15, 16, 17. Drawn. Hyderabad declared winners by virtue of their first-innings lead. Hyderabad* 605 for seven dec. (V. Mohanraj 32, V. Manohar 34, K. A. Qayyum 203, M. V. Narasimha Rao 114, V. Jaisimha 141 not out) and 224 for six dec. (V. Manohar 101 not out, Ehtesham-ud-Din 49; J. Zinto four for 42); Gujarat 314 (B. Mistry 32, P. Bhatt 69, J. Saigal 36, D. Patel 42 not out; R. Yadav three for 54, M. V. Ramanamurthy four for 88) and 129 for two (S. Talati 82, S. Pathak 33).

At Faridabad (T), February 14, 15, 16, 17. Drawn. Bihar declared winners by virtue of their first-innings lead. Bihar* 360 (H. Gidwani 137, Baldev Singh 63, Avinash Kumar 64, Randhir Singh 45 not out; Deepak Sharma three for 111, S. Talwar three for 142) and 283 for four (P. Khanna 91, Randhir Singh 39, S. S. Karim 72 not out, R. Deora 52 not out); Haryana 234 (K. P. Amarjeet 112; V. Venkatram four for 82, S. Ranjan three for 57).

At Calcutta (T), February 21, 22, 23, 24. Drawn. Delhi declared winners by virtue of their quotient of 77.85 compared with Bengal's quotient of 51.55. Delhi* 545 for seven dec. (R. Lamba 81, K. Azad 73, K. Bhaskar Pillai 60, Madan Lal 167, A. Sharma 101); Bengal 464 for nine (P. Roy 230 not out, A. Mitra 74, G. Shome, jun. 34; Madan Lal five for 127).

Semi-finals

At Hyderabad (T), March 7, 8, 9, 10. Hyderabad declared winners by virtue of their first-innings lead. Bihar* 468 (P. Khanna 145, H. Gidwani 179; R. Yadav five for 106, Arshad Ayub four for 109) and 87 for no wkt (P. Khanna 50 not out, H. Gidwani 33 not out); Hyderabad 783 for eight dec. (V. Mohanraj 93, K. A. Qayyum 55, M. V. Narasimha Rao 74, V. Jaisimha 120, Ehtesham-ud-Din 30, Arshad Ayub 206 not out, R. Yadav 37, M. V. Ramanamurthy 101 not out; S. Ranjan three for 145).

At Delhi (T), March 7, 8, 9, 10. Drawn. Delhi declared winners by virtue of their first-innings lead. Delhi 711 for three dec. (M. Nayyar 96, M. Prabhakar 215, K. Bhaskar Pillai 222 not out, R. Lamba 121 not out) and 247 for seven (M. Nayyar 103 not out, A. Sharma 105); Karnataka* 440 (M. R. Srinivasaprasad 88, S. M. H. Kirmani 48, P. Ramesh Rao 56, K. Jeswant 72, H. Surendra 40).

Final

At Delhi (T), March 21, 22, 23, 25, 26. Hyderabad declared winners by virtue of their first-innings lead. Hyderabad* 457 (A. Azeem 114, Arshad Ayub 174, N. S. Yadav 33; M. Amarnath three for 48) and 480 for seven (A. Azeem 43, V. Mohanraj 211 not out, M. V. Narasimha Rao 38, Arshad Ayub 80; Jaspal Singh four for 132); Delhi 433 (M. Nayyar 64, K. Bhaskar Pillai 160 not out, M. Amarnath 85; R. Yadav five for 114, N. S. Yadav three for 74).

RANJI TROPHY WINNERS

1934-35	Bombay	1961-62	Bombay
1935-36	Bombay	1962-63	Bombay
1936-37	Nawanagar	1963-64	Bombay
1937-38	Hyderabad	1964-65	Bombay
1938-39	Bengal	1965-66	Bombay
1939-40	Maharashtra	1966-67	Bombay
1940-41	Maharashtra	1967-68	Bombay
1941-42	Bombay	1968-69	Bombay
1942-43	Baroda	1969-70	Bombay
1943-44	Western India	1970-71	Bombay
1944-45	Bombay	1971-72	Bombay
1945-46	Holkar	1972-73	Bombay
1946-47	Baroda	1973-74	Karnataka
1947-48	Holkar	1974-75	Bombay
1948-49	Bombay	1975-76	Bombay
1949-50	Baroda	1976-77	Bombay
1950-51	Holkar	1977-78	Karnataka
1951-52	Bombay	1978-79	Delhi
1952-53	Holkar	1979-80	Delhi
1953-54	Bombay	1980-81	Bombay
1954-55	Madras	1981-82	Delhi
1955-56	Bombay	1982-83	Karnataka
1956-57	Bombay	1983-84	Bombay
1957-58	Baroda	1984-85	Bombay
1958-59	Bombay	1985-86	Delhi
1959-60	Bombay	1986-87	Hyderabad
1960-61	Bombay		

IRANI CUP, 1986-87

Ranji Trophy Champions (Delhi) v Rest of India

At Barkatulla Khan Stadium, Jodhpur (T), November 7, 8, 9, 11, 12. Rest of India won by an innings and 232 runs. Delhi* 266 (K. Azad 49, M. Prabhakar 75; R. S. Ghai three for 70, B. Arun four for 59) and 139 (Azim Khan six for 29); Rest of India 637 (L. S. Rajput 66, N. S. Sidhu 65, D. B. Vengsarkar 112, S. Kalyani 165, S. Viswanath 62, Azim Khan 41; S. Sharma three for 119, Maninder Singh five for 185).

DULEEP TROPHY, 1986-87

At Pune (T), October 20, 21, 22, 23. Drawn. East Zone declared winners by virtue of their first-innings lead. East Zone* 528 (Arun Lal 214, A. Mitra 120, D. Mohanty 35; H. Joshi three for 107) and 226 for two (P. Roy 76, S. Das 123 not out); Central Zone 330 (S. S. Khandkar 32, S. Mudkavi 41, Yusuf Ali Khan 111, R. Sapru 33; Randhir Singh six for 95, G. Shome, jun. three for 99).

Semi-finals

At Pune (T), October 25, 26, 27, 28. Drawn. West Zone declared winners by virtue of their first-innings lead. East Zone 561 (K. Dubey 76, Arun Lal 287, S. Das 33, V. Venkatram 43 not out; P. Kasliwal four for 87); West Zone* 567 for seven (L. S. Rajput 65, M. D. Gunjal 37, C. S. Pandit 78, S. M. Gavaskar 92, R. J. Shastri 176 not out, K. S. More 51; G. Shome, jun. three for 135).

At Wankhede Stadium, Bombay (T), October 25, 26, 27, 28. South Zone won by five wickets. North Zone* 283 (K. Azad 40, Madan Lal 55, Chetan Sharma 34, R. S. Ghai 49; B. Arun three for 89, R. Yadav three for 65) and 353 (R. Lamba 104, A. Malhotra 57, Yashpal Sharma 58; R. M. H. Binny four for 102, B. Arun four for 109); South Zone 364 (P. C. Prakash 81, M. Azharuddin 73, S. Viswanath 91, W. V. Raman 30; Maninder Singh three for 76) and 273 for five (M. Azharuddin 120 not out, S. Viswanath 56).

Final

At Wankhede Stadium, Bombay (T), October 31, November 1, 2, 4, 5. Drawn. South Zone declared winners by virtue of their first-innings lead. West Zone* 516 (A. D. Gaekwad 138, L. S. Rajput 105, R. J. Shastri 127, S. Keshwala 43, R. R. Kulkarni 38; N. S. Yadav three for 127, W. V. Raman six for 123) and 472 for three (A. D. Gaekwad 109, L. S. Rajput 101 not out, C. S. Pandit 88, R. J. Shastri 124 not out); South Zone 740 (K. Srikkanth 112, C. Saldanha 102, P. C. Prakash 34, M. Azharuddin 75, B. Arun 149, W. V. Raman 95, J. Abhiram 40; P. Kasliwal three for 179, R. J. Shastri three for 143).

CRICKET IN PAKISTAN, 1986-87

By ABID ALI KAZI

The 1986-87 season saw yet another record number of first-class matches played in Pakistan. As the result of a reshuffle of the formats of the existing competitions, and the introduction of a new tournament – the BCCP President's Cup – the total rose to 126, which was by far the most in a Pakistan season. The previous highest was 102 in 1985-86. The first-class season began with the tour by the West Indians, who came back to level the three-Test series after losing to Pakistan in the First Test at Faisalabad. In addition to the Test matches, the touring team played three first-class matches against invitation elevens, and there were the now-customary one-day internationals.

The BCCP Patron's Trophy, which had previously been restricted to divisional and zonal sides, was open to all first-class teams in 1986-87, with 36 teams, another record, participating. The preliminary league, comprising six groups which in turn were divided into two sub-groups each, was declared non first-class by the BCCP. The final knockout round, which was adjudged first-class, was played between the twelve teams who headed the twelve sub-groups. These same twelve teams also qualified for the Quaid-e-Azam Trophy. National Bank won the Patron's Trophy with an exciting victory over United Bank, beating them by 65 runs in the final.

Interestingly, National Bank had not played one first-class match the previous season as they had failed to qualify for the Quaid-e-Azam Trophy. The same fate befell such teams as PIA, Muslim Commercial Bank (MCB) and WAPDA, all of whom had played first-class cricket regularly till 1984-85, and a number of their players had consequently appeared for their divisional sides. However, for 1986-87 the Board introduced a new regulation which restricted a player to only one team throughout the season, and with a return to first-class cricket for many sides, the divisional teams had to make do with local talent. Because of this, Karachi, who won the Quaid-e-Azam Trophy in 1985-86 after a lapse of fifteen years, slumped to eleventh in the twelve-team tournament in 1986-87. National Bank took this trophy also, winning six of their eleven league matches and losing none. They were closely followed by United Bank, who also won six of their eleven matches but lost one.

The BCCP President's Cup was instituted for the 24 teams that did not qualify for the Quaid-e-Azam, and of these, seven decided not to enter the new competition. They were Pakistan Air Force, Pakistan Army, Pakistan Navy, Combined Universities, Hazara, Islamabad and Sukkur, the last two opting out at the last moment. Railways, beating Pakistan Customs by virtue of a first-innings lead in the final, became the first winners of the new competition – consolation for their exclusion from the Quaid-e-Azam. With one of the strongest sides on the national circuit, the Railmen had failed to make the top twelve because of a freak defeat at the hands of Peshawar. Overall the new competition was well contested and gave necessary experience to the lowly-rated first-class sides.

The format of the PACO Cup, which was previously contested by the five leading teams from the Quaid-e-Azam on a league basis, also changed, with the number of participants being raised to eight. They were divided into two groups, with two teams from each group qualifying for the semi-finals. With National Bank, winners of the other two first-class competitions, unable to call upon four of their leading players – one in India with the national team and another three touring Zimbabwe with Pakistan B – the PACO Cup went to PIA who, also without some of their players, did well to beat United Bank in the final by the narrow margin of 10 runs. Thus United Bank were the season's bridesmaid, finishing as runners-up in each of the three major first-class championships. Moreover, they were also the beaten finalists in the Wills Cup, the leading limited-overs tournament, losing by three wickets to Habib Bank. It was Habib Bank's second triumph in the six such competitions played since 1980-81.

Six batsmen scored more than 1,000 runs during the season, the highest aggregate coming from Mansoor Akhtar (United Bank), whose 1,503 runs earned him a place in the Pakistan team to tour England after four years out of the Test side. Ameer Akbar (National Bank) headed the batting averages with 1,349 runs at 67.45, including five hundreds. The others to pass 1,000 runs were Shafiq Ahmed (United Bank) 1,498, Zahid Ahmad (PIA) 1,167, Ashraf Ali (United Bank) 1,026, and Feroze Mehdi (PIA) 1,001. The highest individual score was Haider Jehangir's 171 for Lahore against National Bank in the PACO Cup. Among the bowlers, no fewer than seventeen took 50 or more wickets. The list was headed by the Rawalpindi captain, Raja Sarfraz, whose 91 wickets at 17.96 helped their revival. Other bowlers with 70 or more wickets were Nadeem Ghauri (Habib Bank) 83, Zulfiqar Butt (WAPDA) 81, Iqbal Sikandar (PIA) 78, Iqbal Qasim (National Bank) 75, Shahid Mahboob (PACO) 72 and Javed Hayat (WAPDA) 71. Kazim Mehdi (HBFC), Farrukh Zaman (MCB) and Pervez Shah (Lahore) were responsible for the season's three hat-tricks.

Two new records were set. United Bank's wicket-keeper, Ashraf Ali, edged past Anil Dalpat's previous record of 69 dismissals, set in 1983-84, by claiming 70 (62 ct, 8 st) in eighteen matches, and in the field Rawalpindi's all-rounder, Fahim Abbasi, in his début season, held 30 catches to pass the previous record, held by United Bank's Ali Zia with 25 catches. The other leading fielders were Sajid Ali (National Bank) 24, Faisal Rasheed (WAPDA) 21, and Rashid Khan (PIA) 20 catches.

FIRST-CLASS AVERAGES, 1986-87

BATTING

(Qualification: 500 runs, average 25)

	M	I	NO	R	HI	100s	Avge
Ameer Akbar (*National Bank*)	15	27	7	1,349	151*	5	67.45
Shafiq Ahmed (*United Bank*)	19	34	5	1,498	124	3	51.65
Ashraf Ali (*United Bank*)	18	29	9	1,026	113	2	51.30
Asif Mohammad (*PIA*)	9	13	2	535	89*	0	48.63
Mansoor Akhtar (*United Bank*)	19	34	3	1,503	167	3	48.48
Shaukat Mirza (*HBFC*)	12	21	3	835	125*	4	46.38
Arshad Pervez (*Habib Bank*)	12	20	1	835	144	2	43.94
Zahid Ahmad (*PIA*)	18	31	4	1,167	127	1	43.22
Raees Ahmed (*HBFC*)	14	25	3	912	147	1	41.45
Munir-ul-Haq (*HBFC*)	11	18	2	636	134*	1	39.75
Tahir Shah (*National Bank*)	15	26	1	993	150	4	39.72

	M	I	NO	R	HI	100s	Avge
Mazhar Hussain (*Lahore City/Lahore*)	12	23	3	767	139	1	38.35
Aamer Sohail (*Lahore City/Lahore*) ..	12	23	1	839	116	1	38.13
Feroze Mehdi (*PIA*)	16	29	2	1,001	135	3	37.07
Mujahid Hameed (*Rawalpindi*)	16	28	5	834	90*	0	36.26
Naved Anjum (*United Bank*)	13	20	1	683	111	2	35.94
Sajid Ali (*National Bank*)	16	29	2	958	150*	3	35.48
Asad Rauf (*National Bank*)	15	21	2	672	114	1	35.36
Sajid Khan (*Karachi*)	10	19	2	577	106*	1	33.94
Saeed Azad (*National Bank*)	15	26	2	804	121*	2	33.50
Amjad Siddiq (*WAPDA*)	13	22	3	630	100	1	33.15
Saeed Anwar (*Karachi*)	12	23	1	711	150	1	32.31
Wasim Ali (*Lahore City/Lahore*)	14	25	3	696	111*	1	31.63
Zaheer Abbas (*PIA*)	12	21	3	554	119*	1	30.77
Saadat Ali (*HBFC*)	15	27	2	766	100	1	30.64
Nasir Shah (*Karachi*)	12	23	1	673	124	3	30.59
Taslim Arif (*National Bank*)	15	24	6	550	126	1	30.55
Tanvir Razzaq (*WAPDA*)	15	26	2	724	131	1	30.16
Haseeb-ul-Hasan (*Karachi*)	11	21	1	582	104	1	29.10
Babar Basharat (*MCB*)	13	24	0	654	109	1	27.25
Anwar-ul-Haq (*MCB*)	12	23	2	569	132*	1	27.09
Umar Rasheed (*PACO*)	15	28	2	704	77	0	27.07
Shahid Javed (*Rawalpindi*)	16	29	1	746	103	1	26.64
Basit Ali (*Karachi*)	11	21	0	537	95	0	25.57
Tehsin Javed (*Habib Bank*)	12	22	1	532	112	1	25.33

Signifies not out.

BOWLING

(Qualification: 30 wickets)

	O	M	R	W	BB	Avge
Sajjad Akbar (*PNSC*)	197.2	40	473	35	5-28	13.51
Zia-ud-Din (*Pakistan Customs*)	161.4	34	425	30	5-69	14.16
Iqbal Qasim (*National Bank*)	566.3	128	1,145	75	7-77	15.26
Masood Anwar (*PACO*)	537.5	145	1,128	67	6-47	16.83
Naved Anjum (*United Bank*)	302.2	48	1,024	60	7-63	17.06
Iqbal Sikandar (*PIA*)	489.4	122	1,384	78	7-52	17.74
Raja Sarfraz (*Rawalpindi*)	630.4	127	1,635	91	8-58	17.96
Tanvir Ali (*PIA*)	492.4	145	1,167	64	8-28	18.23
Zulfiqar Butt (*WAPDA*)	643	168	1,484	81	7-16	18.32
Ijaz Faqih (*MCB*)	509	116	1,252	68	7-47	18.41
Nadeem Ghauri (*Habib Bank*)	685.3	197	1,566	83	6-25	18.86
Shakeel Ahmed (*Rawalpindi*)	235.2	31	691	35	6-86	19.74
Mohammad Asif (*Lahore*)	361	94	776	39	8-58	19.89
Sajid Bashir (*United Bank*)	213	43	667	33	5-52	20.21
Shahid Mahboob (*PACO*)	452.1	60	1,474	72	8-65	20.47
Kazim Mehdi (*HBFC*)	575.2	149	1,386	66	7-55	21.00
Barkatullah (*National Bank*)	383.1	44	1,386	66	7-49	21.00
Pervez Shah (*Lahore City/Lahore*) ..	327.4	75	930	44	7-68	21.13
Mian Fayyaz (*PACO*)	491.3	114	1,131	53	6-26	21.33
Raza Khan (*Karachi*)	336.4	58	944	44	7-66	21.45
Kamal Merchant (*United Bank*)	307.4	64	671	31	5-48	21.64
Shahid Aziz (*United Bank*)	257	62	758	35	7-56	21.65
Rashid Khan (*PIA*)	361.5	70	1,040	48	6-19	21.66
Zakaullah Khan (*Rawalpindi*)	365	63	957	44	6-48	21.75
Javed Hayat (*WAPDA*)	591.3	113	1,607	71	5-55	22.63
Farrukh Zaman (*MCB*)	382.5	81	1,043	46	7-42	22.67

	O	M	R	W	BB	Avge
Afzaal Butt (*National Bank*)	304.2	54	911	40	4-53	22.77
Zahid Ahmad (*PIA*)	475	141	1,061	45	6-58	23.57
Ali Ahmed (*HBFC*)	434.2	70	1,509	61	8-88	24.73
Sikander Bakht (*United Bank*)	378.5	70	1,246	50	6-37	24.92
Zulfiqar Ali (*PIA*)	408.3	75	1,386	55	6-38	25.20
Shahid Butt (*United Bank*)	505	118	1,286	49	5-59	26.24
Akram Raza (*Habib Bank*)	411.3	97	1,043	37	6-52	28.18
Aamer Sohail (*Lahore City/Lahore*) .	366.3	59	1,103	37	7-53	29.81
Hafeez-ur-Rehman (*National Bank*) .	590	104	1,586	46	5-122	34.47

WICKET-KEEPING

(Qualification: 25 dismissals)

Ashraf Ali (*United Bank*) 70 (62 ct, 8 st); Anil Dalpat (*PIA*) 55 (39 ct, 16 st); Taslim Arif (*National Bank*) 48 (40 ct, 8 st); Tahir Rasheed (*HBFC*) 42 (37 ct, 5 st); Sanaullah (*PACO*) 40 (34 ct, 6 st); Nadeem Abbasi (*Rawalpindi*) 27 (19 ct, 8 st); Sajid Abbasi (*MCB*) 26 (21 ct, 5 st).

   Nadeem Abbasi and Taslim Arif's dismissals include 3 and 2 catches respectively held while not keeping wicket.

Note: Matches taken into account are the BCCP Patron's Trophy, Quaid-e-Azam Trophy, BCCP President's Cup, PACO Cup and those against the West Indian touring team in Pakistan.

BCCP PATRON'S TROPHY, 1986-87

Note: First innings closed at 60 overs in pre-quarter finals and quarter-finals, and 85 overs in semi-finals and final.

Pre-Quarter-finals

At National Stadium, Karachi, November 28, 29, 30. MCB qualified for the quarter-finals by virtue of their first-innings lead. Drawn. PACO 127 (Junaid Alvi 30, Moin Mumtaz 36; Ijaz Faqih five for 43, Farrukh Zaman three for 42) and 392 for five dec. (Zahoor Elahi 107, Umar Rasheed 41, Moin Mumtaz 60, Nadeem Moosa 51, Shahid Mahboob 101 not out); MCB 196 for seven (Anwar-ul-Haq 33, Asad Mahmood 38, Mohiuddin Khan 34, Tahir Naqqash 31 not out; Mian Fayyaz three for 40) and 132 for seven (Anwar-ul-Haq 65; Mian Fayyaz five for 51).

At Iqbal Stadium, Faisalabad, November 28, 29, 30. National Bank won by two wickets. HBFC 258 for seven (Shaukat Mirza 125 not out, Raees Ahmed 60; Barkatullah three for 55) and 223 (Raees Ahmed 71, Rafat Alam 58, Ali Ahmed 44 not out; Barkatullah four for 74, Afzaal Butt four for 53); National Bank 169 (Sajid Ali 58, Ameer Akbar 43; Ali Ahmed five for 75, Sibtain Haider three for 74) and 314 for eight (Ameer Akbar 59, Hafeez-ur-Rehman 49, Barkatullah 41 not out, Iqbal Qasim 41 not out; Ali Ahmed three for 131, Sibtain Haider three for 89).

At Gaddafi Stadium, Lahore, November 28, 29, 30. PIA won by six wickets. Lahore City Blues 197 for six (Aamer Sohail 45, Wasim Ali 51) and 212 (Aamer Sohail 84, Wasim Ali 48, Haider Jehangir 35; Zulfiqar Ali four for 47, Iqbal Sikandar five for 80); PIA 195 (Zahid Ahmad 72 not out; Pervez Shah seven for 68) and 215 for four (R. I. Alikhan 47, Asif Mohammad 89 not out, Feroze Mehdi 31; Pervez Shah three for 71).

At Pindi Club Ground, Rawalpindi, November 29, 30, December 1. Rawalpindi won by six wickets. WAPDA 126 (Amjad Siddiq 49; Zakaullah Khan six for 48) and 218 (Saleem Rathore 36, Haafiz Shahid 64, Javed Hayat 31; Shakeel Ahmed four for 54); Rawalpindi 216 for nine (Nadeem Abbasi 33, Shahid Javed 86, Fahim Abbasi 46; Haafiz Shahid three for 23, Javed Hayat three for 58) and 129 for four (Shahid Javed 40, Mujahid Hameed 51 not out; Haafiz Shahid three for 29).

Quarter-finals

At Gymkhana Ground, Peshawar, December 3, 4. MCB won by ten wickets. Peshawar 119 (Aamer Mirza 34; Ijaz Faqih three for 42, Farrukh Zaman seven for 42) and 98 (Ijaz Faqih four for 28, Farrukh Zaman four for 41); MCB 176 (Babar Basharat 64, Ijaz Faqih 53; Iqbal Butt four for 56, Ishtiaq Ahmed five for 40) and 42 for no wkt.

At National Stadium, Karachi, December 3, 4, 5. Drawn. United Bank qualified for the semi-finals by virtue of their first-innings lead. United Bank 203 (Mansoor Akhtar 67, Moin-ul-Atiq 60; Nadeem Ghauri six for 75, Agha Zahid three for 32) and 348 (Mansoor Akhtar 32, Ali Zia 55, Nasir Valika 34, Naved Anjum 60, Ashraf Ali 43, Extras 43; Nadeem Ghauri three for 87, Anwar Miandad three for 31); Habib Bank 118 (Shahid Butt four for 28) and 54 for two (Tehsin Javed 33).

At Pindi Club Ground, Rawalpindi, December 3, 4, 5. Rawalpindi won by eight wickets. Karachi Blues 122 (Sajid Khan 41; Jamal Siddiqi four for 21, Shakeel Ahmed five for 18) and 261 (Nasir Shah 106 not out, Haseeb-ul-Hasan 63; Zakaullah Khan four for 65, Raja Sarfraz three for 31); Rawalpindi 205 for six (Nadeem Abbasi 38, Shahid Javed 37, Mujahid Hameed 50 not out) and 180 for two (Fahim Abbasi 86 not out, Noman Saeed 56).

At Gaddafi Stadium, Lahore, December 3, 4, 5. National Bank won by three wickets. PIA 250 for seven (Rizwan-uz-Zaman 114 not out, Asif Mohammad 60, Feroze Mehdi 42) and 187 (Rizwan-uz-Zaman 45, Asif Mohammad 81, Shahid Mohammad 30; Iqbal Qasim six for 29); National Bank 235 (Sajid Ali 51, Ameer Akbar 53, Shahid Tanvir 31; Zahid Ahmad three for 63, Tanvir Ali three for 28) and 203 for seven (Sajid Ali 44, Taslim Arif 63 not out; Tanvir Ali four for 63).

Semi-finals

At Gaddafi Stadium, Lahore, December 8, 9, 10. National Bank won by six wickets. MCB 193 (Babar Basharat 34, Mohiuddin Khan 32 not out; Barkatullah five for 74) and 95 (Salah-ud-Din 64 not out; Afzaal Butt three for 40, Barkatullah seven for 49); National Bank 168 (Tahir Naqqash four for 61, Mohiuddin Khan three for 64, Ijaz Faqih three for 39) and 123 for four (Ameer Akbar 43 not out).

At Iqbal Stadium, Faisalabad, December 8, 9, 10, 11. United Bank won by six wickets. Rawalpindi 130 (Shahid Javed 35, Mujahid Hameed 30; Naved Anjum six for 76) and 246 (Nadeem Abbasi 32, Shiraz Khan 51, Fahim Abbasi 48, Raja Sarfraz 52; Naved Anjum three for 37); United Bank 302 for six (Mansoor Akhtar 55, Shafiq Ahmed 68, Waheed Mirza 35, Nasir Valika 56 not out; Jamal Siddiqi three for 61) and 75 for four (Mansoor Akhtar 45 not out; Jamal Siddiqi three for 36).

Final

At Iqbal Stadium, Faisalabad, December 15, 16, 17, 18. National Bank won by 65 runs. National Bank 327 for seven (Saeed Azad 121 not out, Asad Rauf 85, Hafeez-ur-Rehman 49; Saleem Jaffer five for 117) and 187 (Tahir Shah 39, Taslim Arif 34; Saleem Jaffer four for 66, Sikander Bakht four for 59); United Bank 232 (Mansoor Akhtar 45, Shafiq Ahmed 84, Nasir Valika 37; Afzaal Butt four for 59, Iqbal Qasim three for 78) and 217 (Shafiq Ahmed 104 not out; Barkatullah three for 64, Hafeez-ur-Rehman three for 42).

QUAID-E-AZAM TROPHY, 1986-87

	Matches	Won	Lost	Drawn	Abandoned	Pts
National Bank	11	6	0	5	0	145
United Bank	11	6	1	4	0	144
WAPDA	11	5	3	3	0	126
HBFC	11	4	3	4	0	111
Rawalpindi	11	5	4	1	1	109
PIA	11	4	4	3	0	107
Lahore	11	3	2	6	0	103
PACO	11	3	3	5	0	99
Habib Bank	11	1	4	6	0	84
MCB	11	2	6	2	1	83
Karachi	11	1	5	5	0	76
Peshawar	11	2	7	2	0	65

Note: First innings closed at 85 overs.

At Sargodha Stadium, Sargodha, December 30, 31, January 1. HBFC won by 26 runs. HBFC 103 (Raees Ahmed 36; Ijaz Faqih four for 40, Ilyas Khan four for 12) and 213 (Saadat Ali 33, Shahid Saeed 33, Shaukat Mirza 60; Ijaz Faqih six for 76); MCB 220 (Pervez Akhtar 51, Salah-ud-Din 35; Kazim Mehdi four for 57) and 70 (Ijaz Faqih 34; Ali Ahmed five for 28, Kazim Mehdi five for 32). *HBFC 14 pts, MCB 6 pts.*

At Pindi Club Ground, Rawalpindi, December 30, 31, January 1. Rawalpindi won by an innings and 36 runs. Peshawar 91 (Rehmat Gul 30; Shakeel Ahmed three for 18, Raja Sarfraz four for 24) and 179 (Ibrar-ul-Haq 53, Pervez Chaughtai 33; Zakaullah Khan five for 66, Raja Sarfraz five for 76); Rawalpindi 306 for seven (Nadeem Abbasi 117, Farrukh Iqbal 31, Shahid Javed 33, Mujahid Hameed 56, Shiraz Khan 50; Pervez Chaughtai four for 62). *Rawalpindi 18 pts, Peshawar 4 pts.*

At National Stadium, Karachi, December 30, 31, January 1, 2. PIA won by 94 runs. PIA 287 for nine (Rizwan-uz-Zaman 53, Asif Mohammad 33, Zahid Ahmad 76 not out, Extras 38; Ali Akbar three for 76) and 213 (Asif Mohammad 32, Zahid Ahmad 38; Ali Akbar four for 63, Hasan Askari three for 50); Karachi 218 (Basit Ali 47, Zafar Ali 37; Zulfiqar Ali three for 43, Iqbal Sikandar three for 100, Tanvir Ali three for 32) and 188 (Zafar Ali 61, Haseeb-ul-Hasan 52; Iqbal Sikandar three for 41, Tanvir Ali four for 66). *PIA 18 pts, Karachi 6 pts.*

At Niaz Stadium, Hyderabad, December 30, 31, January 1, 2. Drawn. National Bank 241 (Sajid Ali 103, Ameer Akbar 45, Iqbal Qasim 44 not out; Yahya Toor five for 25) and 296 (Asad Rauf 76, Shahid Tanvir 63, Barkatullah 32 not out; Tahir Mahmood three for 52, Mian Fayyaz four for 96); PACO 215 (Nadeem Moosa 67; Afzaal Butt four for 57, Barkatullah four for 90) and 195 for five (Umar Rasheed 62, Tahir Mahmood 66 not out). *National Bank 9 pts, PACO 6 pts.*

At Zafar Ali Stadium, Sahiwal, December 30, 31, January 1, 2. WAPDA won by 33 runs. WAPDA 123 (Faisal Rasheed 37; Nadeem Ghauri six for 40, Akram Raza four for 35) and 252 (Faisal Rasheed 81, Haafiz Shahid 46, Zulfiqar Butt 39; Nadeem Ghauri three for 92, Akram Raza three for 61, Anwar Miandad three for 53); Habib Bank 137 (Tehsin Javed 30, Extras 31; Javed Hayat four for 27) and 205 (Arshad Pervez 61, Jamshed Hussain 32; Shakeel Khan three for 53, Javed Hayat three for 71, Zulfiqar Butt four for 60). *WAPDA 14 pts, Habib Bank 4 pts.*

At LCCA Ground, Lahore, December 30, 31, January 1, 2. Drawn. United Bank 327 for eight (Shafiq Ahmed 124, Nasir Valika 42, Waheed Mirza 40, Shahid Butt 50 not out; Mazhar Hussain four for 25) and 344 for five dec. (Mansoor Akhtar 65, Saifullah 71, Shafiq Ahmed 103 not out, Waheed Mirza 61); Lahore 293 for nine (Younis Ahmed 110, Pervez Shah 94; Shahid Butt five for 93) and 278 for eight (Aamer Sohail 52, Younis Ahmed 62, Wasim Ali 73 not out; Shahid Aziz three for 90, Waheed Mirza three for 68). *United Bank 10 pts, Lahore 8 pts.*

At POF Oval, Wah Cantt, January 5, 6, 7. HBFC won by ten wickets. HBFC 256 for six (Saadat Ali 34, Shaukat Mirza 64, Raees Ahmed 33, Tahir Rasheed 35 not out, Rafat Alam 43 not out; Raja Sarfraz three for 74) and 31 for no wkt; Rawalpindi 98 (Fahim Abbasi 38; Kazim Mehdi five for 30) and 188 (Fahim Abbasi 61, Raja Sarfraz 44; Ali Ahmed five for 72). *HBFC 18 pts, Rawalpindi 3 pts.*

At Services Ground, Peshawar, January 5, 6, 7. MCB won by 264 runs. MCB 259 for eight (Salah-ud-Din 37, Asif Ali 64, Nadeem Yousuf 59 not out) and 228 for one dec. (Anwar-ul-Haq 109 not out, Asif Ali 103); Peshawar 112 (Ijaz Faqih six for 41) and 111 (Rehmat Gul 32; Ijaz Faqih seven for 47, Farrukh Zaman three for 46). *MCB 18 pts, Peshawar 4 pts.*

At National Stadium, Karachi, January 5, 6, 7, 8. Drawn. PACO 132 (Umar Rasheed 54 not out; Rashid Khan five for 38) and 360 (Zahoor Elahi 33, Umar Rasheed 51, Tahir Mahmood 113, Masood Anwar 38 not out, Extras 39; Zulfiqar Ali six for 140); PIA 199 (Asif Mohammad 42, Zahid Ahmad 80; Shahid Mahboob four for 58, Yahya Toor three for 40) and 218 for six (Rizwan-uz-Zaman 39, Asif Mohammad 60, Zahid Ahmad 36 not out; Mian Fayyaz three for 45). *PIA 7 pts, PACO 4 pts.*

At Niaz Stadium, Hyderabad, January 5, 6, 7, 8. National Bank won by 129 runs. National Bank 335 for four (Sajid Ali 137 not out, Saeed Azad 38, Ameer Akbar 51, Asad Rauf 50 not out) and 271 for six dec. (Ameer Akbar 119 not out, Taslim Arif 58, Asad Rauf 38; Haseeb-ul-Hasan three for 23); Karachi 205 (Shoaib Habib 43, Haseeb-ul-Hasan 81; Afzaal Butt three for 42, Iqbal Qasim three for 33) and 272 (Saeed Anwar 150, Haseeb-ul-Hasan 55; Iqbal Qasim five for 62, Ameer Akbar three for 37). *National Bank 18 pts, Karachi 4 pts.*

At Gaddafi Stadium, Lahore, January 5, 6, 7, 8. United Bank won by five wickets. WAPDA 269 (Ali Bahadur 66, Amjad Siddiq 54, Zahid Umar 63, Shakeel Khan 31 not out; Sikander Bakht three for 76, Sajid Bashir three for 76) and 184 (Maqsood Raza 39, Tanvir Razzaq 51, Zulfiqar Saadat 33; Sikander Bakht four for 75, Sajid Bashir four for 65); United Bank 329 for eight (Waheed Mirza 58, Shafiq Ahmed 35, Ashraf Ali 112 not out, Sikander Bakht 48 not out; Shahid Pervez four for 82) and 125 for five (Moin-ul-Atiq 37, Nasir Valika 36 not out; Shakeel Khan three for 26). *United Bank 18 pts, WAPDA 8 pts.*

At LCCA Ground, Lahore, January 5, 6, 7, 8. Lahore won by one wicket. Habib Bank 268 for seven (Agha Zahid 39, Arshad Pervez 37, Tehsin Javed 76, Salim Malik 79; Aamer Sohail four for 118) and 138 (Agha Zahid 40, Tehsin Javed 34; Aamer Sohail seven for 53); Lahore 242 for six (Mohammad Ishaq 36, Aamer Sohail 45, Mazhar Hussain 79 not out, Pervez Shah 34 not out; Nadeem Ghauri four for 51) and 166 for nine (Aamer Sohail 77, Mazhar Hussain 34; Nadeem Ghauri five for 28). *Lahore 17 pts, Habib Bank 7 pts.*

At Services Ground, Peshawar, January 11, 12, 13. HBFC won by an innings and 118 runs. Peshawar 154 (Mohammad Shahid 53 not out, Mohammad Saleem 53; Ali Ahmed three for 39, Mohinder Kumar four for 35) and 84 (Ali Ahmed three for 36, Mohinder Kumar six for 45); HBFC 356 for six (Saadat Ali 57, Shaukat Mirza 117, Munir-ul-Haq 36, Tariq Alam 94). *HBFC 18 pts, Peshawar 4 pts.*

At National Stadium, Karachi, January 11, 12, 13, 14. Drawn. National Bank 327 for four (Sajid Ali 50, Taslim Arif 126, Saeed Azad 38, Ameer Akbar 88; Zahid Ahmad four for 106) and 251 for seven dec. (Saeed Azad 86, Saleem Pervez 59; Tanvir Ali four for 67); PIA 233 (Rizwan-uz-Zaman 51, Asif Mohammad 62, Zahid Ahmad 40; Iqbal Qasim five for 81, Hafeez-ur-Rehman five for 122) and 70 for one (Feroze Mehdi 32 not out). *National Bank 10 pts, PIA 5 pts.*

At Niaz Stadium, Hyderabad, January 11, 12, 13, 14. Drawn. Karachi 134 (Saeed Anwar 40; Shahid Mahboob seven for 69, Masood Anwar three for 32) and 299 (Basit Ali 30, Nasir Shah 124, Saeed Anwar 50, Haseeb-ul-Hasan 34; Shahid Mahboob four for 84, Masood Anwar four for 64); PACO 169 (Umar Rasheed 59; Raza Khan six for 78) and 60 for one (Zahoor Elahi 38 not out). *PACO 7 pts, Karachi 4 pts.*

At Gaddafi Stadium, Lahore, January 11, 12, 13, 14. Drawn. MCB 123 (Tahir Naqqash 40; Waheed Niazi four for 49, Atiq-ur-Rehman four for 41) and 186 for five (Anwar-ul-Haq 37, Babar Basharat 54, Ijaz Faqih 32); Habib Bank 256 (Arshad Pervez 33, Sultan Rana 36, Zaheer Ahmed 43, Akram Raza 75; Farrukh Zaman three for 69). *Habib Bank 10 pts, MCB 4 pts.*

At LCCA Ground, Lahore, January 11, 12, 13, 14. Drawn. Lahore 243 for four (Mohammad Ishaq 45, Aamer Sohail 85, Younis Ahmed 56 not out; Zulfiqar Butt three for 94) and 28 for two; WAPDA 238 (Ali Bahadur 43, Amjad Siddiq 100, Tanvir Razzaq 33; Younis Ahmed three for 43). *Lahore 9 pts, WAPDA 5 pts.*

At GHQ Ground, Rawalpindi, January 11, 12, 13, 14. United Bank won by six wickets. Rawalpindi 242 (Shiraz Khan 107, Nadeem Butt 46, Raja Sarfraz 37; Sikander Bakht six for 41) and 235 (Nadeem Abbasi 38, Mujahid Hameed 43, Shiraz Khan 75, Fahim Abbasi 30; Shahid Butt four for 48, Tariq Yousuf three for 50); United Bank 295 for six dec. (Mansoor Akhtar 88, Moin-ul-Atiq 43, Shafiq Ahmed 72, Nasir Valika 35; Fahim Abbasi four for 78) and 183 for four (Mansoor Akhtar 89, Moin-ul-Atiq 34, Shafiq Ahmed 41 not out). *United Bank 18 pts, Rawalpindi 6 pts.*

At Gaddafi Stadium, Lahore, January 17, 18, 19, 20. Drawn. Lahore 215 (Aamer Sohail 54, Younis Ahmed 40, Wasim Ali 49; Raza Khan five for 94) and 142 for four (Mazhar Hussain 51); Karachi 163 (Zafar Ali 35; Pervez Shah three for 50, Younis Ahmed three for 38). *Lahore 8 pts, Karachi 5 pts.*

At Municipal Stadium, Gujranwala, January 17, 18, 19, 20. National Bank won by eight wickets. MCB 208 (Babar Basharat 50, Ijaz Faqih 39; Iqbal Qasim six for 83, Hafeez-ur-Rehman three for 84) and 184 (Anwar-ul-Haq 30, Asif Ali 53; Barkatullah four for 82, Iqbal Qasim five for 54); National Bank 306 for six (Tahir Shah 46, Sajid Ali 34, Ameer Akbar 108, Shahid Tanvir 71 not out) and 89 for two (Sajid Ali 31). *National Bank 18 pts, MCB 5 pts.*

At Jinnah Stadium, Sialkot, January 17, 18, 19, 20. Drawn. PACO 165 (Nadeem Ghauri four for 51, Akram Raza four for 41) and 81 (Waheed Niazi three for 24, Nadeem Ghauri six for 25); Habib Bank 112 (Mian Fayyaz six for 26, Masood Anwar four for 37) and 115 for six (Agha Zahid 45; Mian Fayyaz three for 46, Masood Anwar three for 41). *PACO 7 pts, Habib Bank 4 pts.*

At Iqbal Stadium, Faisalabad, January 17, 18, 19, 20. Drawn. HBFC 228 (Shahid Saeed 31, Shaukat Mirza 102 not out; Haafiz Shahid six for 80) and 319 (Saadat Ali 37, Raees Ahmed 147; Zulfiqar Butt three for 76, Javed Hayat three for 48); WAPDA 262 for nine (Saleem Rathore 41, Tanvir Razzaq 96, Javed Hayat 50 not out; Mohinder Kumar five for 80) and 31 for one. *WAPDA 10 pts, HBFC 7 pts.*

At GHQ Ground, Rawalpindi, January 17, 18, 19, 20. Rawalpindi won by two wickets. PIA 143 (Raja Sarfraz four for 38, Fahim Abbasi three for 49) and 255 (Iqbal Sikandar 101, Zahid Ahmad 53; Zakaullah Khan three for 74, Raja Sarfraz six for 102); Rawalpindi 136 (Zulfiqar Ali five for 39, Rashid Khan three for 21) and 263 for eight (Noman Saeed 51, Shahid Javed 103; Zahid Ahmad three for 56). *Rawalpindi 14 pts, PIA 4 pts.*

At Services Ground, Peshawar, January 17, 18, 19, 20. Peshawar won by 18 runs. Peshawar 136 (Nadeem Yousuf 39; Sikander Bakht three for 23, Tariq Yousuf three for 25) and 177 (Aamer Mirza 53, Iqbal Butt 33; Shahid Aziz six for 92); United Bank 140 (Moin-ul-Atiq 70; Khurshid Akhtar seven for 51, Iqbal Butt three for 30) and 155 (Mansoor Akhtar 42, Ashraf Ali 69; Khurshid Akhtar five for 61, Shahid Hussain four for 23). *Peshawar 14 pts, United Bank 4 pts.*

At Gaddafi Stadium, Lahore, January 23, 24, 25, 26. Drawn. United Bank 270 for six (Mansoor Akhtar 30, Shafiq Ahmed 73, Mahmood Rasheed 34, Ashraf Ali 50 not out, Kamal Merchant 42 not out) and 398 for six dec. (Mansoor Akhtar 126, Moin-ul-Atiq 79, Saifullah 82, Naved Anjum 31, Ashraf Ali 37 not out); National Bank 265 (Ameer Akbar 120 not out, Asad Rauf 35, Shahid Tanvir 46; Sajid Bashir five for 52) and 93 for four. *United Bank 10 pts, National Bank 7 pts.*

At LCCA Ground, Lahore, January 23, 24, 25, 26. Drawn. PIA 244 (Feroze Mehdi 115, Anil Dalpat 58, Zahid Ahmad 35; Aamer Sohail three for 58) and 271 for five dec. (Zahid Ahmed 50, Zaheer Abbas 119 not out, Shahid Mohammad 52 not out); Lahore 152 (Mazhar Hussain 46; Tanvir Ali three for 49, Iqbal Sikandar six for 46) and 252 for eight (Mazhar Hussain 97, Wasim Ali 45, Irfan Gul 31; Zulfiqar Ali three for 39). *PIA 9 pts, Lahore 5 pts.*

At Jinnah Stadium, Sialkot, January 23, 24, 25, 26. WAPDA won by six wickets. MCB 159 (Ijaz Faqih 83; Haafiz Shahid three for 38, Shakeel Khan three for 30, Zulfiqar Butt four for 36) and 239 (Babar Basharat 94, Nadeem Yousuf 31 not out, Ijaz Faqih 33; Javed Hayat five for 74, Zulfiqar Butt three for 47); WAPDA 200 (Mohammad Ashraf 34, Dastgir Butt 38, Javed Hayat 30; Tahir Naqqash four for 78, Farrukh Zaman three for 33) and 199 for four (Saleem Rathore 34, Mohammad Ashraf 103, Maqsood Raza 40). *WAPDA 16 pts, MCB 5 pts.*

At Iqbal Stadium, Faisalabad, January 23, 24, 25, 26. Drawn. Habib Bank 272 for nine (Agha Zahid 62, Arshad Pervez 52, Zaheer Ahmed 45, Nadeem Ghauri 30 not out; Kazim Mehdi five for 88) and 295 for eight dec. (Arshad Pervez 44, Tehsin Javed 112, Azhar Khan 50; Kazim Mehdi three for 97, Raees Ahmed three for 110); HBFC 268 for nine (Shahid Saeed 36, Shaukat Mirza 67, Rafat Alam 46; Nadeem Ghauri six for 83) and 263 for six (Saadat Ali 35, Shaukat Mirza 102, Raees Ahmed 89 not out). *Habib Bank 10 pts, HBFC 8 pts.*

At GHQ Ground, Rawalpindi, January 23, 24, 25, 26. Rawalpindi won by 13 runs. Rawalpindi 153 (Noman Saeed 34; Masood Anwar six for 47) and 251 (Nadeem Abbasi 71, Shahid Javed 62; Shahid Mahboob three for 65, Masood Anwar five for 74); PACO 241 (Zahoor Elahi 54, Umar Rasheed 44, Shahid Mahboob 31; Raja Sarfraz five for 83, Zakaullah Khan five for 88) and 150 (Umar Rasheed 35; Raja Sarfraz three for 62, Zakaullah Khan five for 51). *Rawalpindi 15 pts, PACO 7 pts.*

At Services Ground, Peshawar, January 23, 24, 25, 26. Peshawar won by 124 runs. Peshawar 145 (Pervez Chaughtai 33; Haseeb-ul-Hasan three for 43) and 344 (Rehmat Gul 72, Irfan-ud-Din 48, Mohammad Shahid 32, Aamer Mirza 86, Ishtiaq Ahmed 31, Extras 30; Raza Khan three for 70, Shoaib Habib three for 88); Karachi 195 (Nasir Shah 50, Shoaib Habib 52 not out; Shahid Hussain four for 58, Faridoon Khan four for 49) and 170 (Nasir Shah 60, Zafar Ahmed 32; Shahid Hussain four for 55, Aamer Mirza three for 50). *Peshawar 14 pts, Karachi 5 pts.*

At National Stadium, Karachi, January 29, 30, 31, February 1. Habib Bank won by eight wickets. Karachi 160 for nine (Sajid Khan 51 not out; Nadeem Ghauri five for 49, Akram Raza three for 52) and 175 (Basit Ali 60, Saeed Anwar 58; Waheed Niazi five for 24, Akram Raza three for 42); Habib Bank 95 (Akram Raza 40; Raza Khan six for 42) and 241 for two (Agha Zahid 108, Tehsin Javed 84 not out). *Habib Bank 14 pts, Karachi 5 pts.*

At Gaddafi Stadium, Lahore, January 29, 30, 31, February 1. United Bank won by two wickets. PIA 145 (Zahid Ahmad 51; Naved Anjum five for 50, Kamal Merchant three for 15) and 374 (Feroze Mehdi 50, Zahid Ahmad 78, Zaheer Abbas 39, Anil Dalpat 45, Rashid Khan 65, Raja Akbar 35; Naved Anjum three for 67, Shahid Butt three for 92); United Bank 281 (Shafiq Ahmed 56, Naved Anjum 101; Rashid Khan three for 62, Zulfiqar Ali four for 114) and 242 for eight (Mansoor Akhtar 70, Saifullah 30, Shafiq Ahmed 57; Tanvir Ali four for 47). *United Bank 18 pts, PIA 4 pts.*

At LCCA Ground, Lahore, January 29, 30, 31, February 1. National Bank won by an innings and 38 runs. HBFC 142 (Raees Ahmed 30, Tahir Rasheed 45; Iqbal Qasim four for 57, Hafeez-ur-Rehman four for 58) and 139 (Saadat Ali 49, Rafat Alam 32; Iqbal Qasim five for 27); National Bank 319 for three (Tahir Shah 32, Ameer Akbar 151 not out, Saeed Azad 38, Saleem Anwar 87 not out). *National Bank 18 pts, HBFC 2 pts.*

At Municipal Stadium, Gujranwala, January 29, 30, 31, February 1. Lahore won by 134 runs. Lahore 314 for six (Aamer Sohail 116, Mazhar Hussain 42, Younis Ahmed 82, Pervez Shah 31 not out) and 160 (Wasim Ali 68; Zaigham Burki four for 58, Nadeem Yousuf four for 39); MCB 223 (Ijaz Faqih 96, Tahir Naqqash 51; Pervez Shah three for 58, Arshad Butt four for 46, Saleem Hussain three for 52) and 117 (Tahir Naqqash 46; Pervez Shah six for 35). *Lahore 18 pts, MCB 5 pts.*

At POF Oval, Wah Cantt, January 29, 30, 31, February 1. WAPDA won by 37 runs. WAPDA 231 (Amjad Siddiq 72; Raja Sarfraz four for 79) and 185 (Amjad Siddiq 59, Tanvir Razzaq 45 not out; Raja Sarfraz six for 65); Rawalpindi 219 (Mujahid Hameed 55, Raja Sarfraz 33 not out; Shahid Pervez four for 51) and 160 (Raja Sarfraz 33; Zulfiqar Butt five for 36). *WAPDA 17 pts, Rawalpindi 6 pts.*

At Services Ground, Peshawar, January 29, 30, 31, February 1. PACO won by 171 runs. PACO 205 (Zahoor Elahi 52, Yahya Toor 63; Aamer Mirza four for 33) and 220 (Zahoor Elahi 34, Umar Rasheed 31, Shahid Mahboob 34, Masood Anwar 44; Shahid Hussain four for 66, Khurshid Akhtar four for 78); Peshawar 104 (Pervez Chaughtai 40; Shahid Mahboob seven for 59, Umar Rasheed three for 30) and 150 (Aamer Mirza 53 not out; Shahid Mahboob four for 44, Masood Anwar four for 38). *PACO 16 pts, Peshawar 4 pts.*

At LCCA Ground, Lahore, February 4, 5. National Bank won by seven wickets. Lahore 184 (Younis Ahmed 81 not out; Iqbal Qasim seven for 77) and 69 (Mazhar Hussain 33; Barkatullah four for 37, Iqbal Qasim four for 14); National Bank 175 (Ameer Akbar 79; Mohammad Asif three for 62, Fayyaz Anwar four for 15) and 82 for three (Tahir Shah 30). *National Bank 15 pts, Lahore 5 pts.*

At Services Ground, Peshawar, February 4, 5, 6. WAPDA won by 333 runs. WAPDA 326 (Saleem Rathore 45, Mohammad Ashraf 66, Amjad Siddiq 81 not out, Javed Hayat 35; Shahid Hussain four for 72) and 302 (Tanvir Razzaq 131, Amjad Siddiq 42, Javed Hayat 36; Aamer Mirza three for 95); Peshawar 209 (Irfan-ud-Din 38, Pervez Chaughtai 56; Shahid Pervez four for 27, Zulfiqar Butt three for 64) and 86 (Haafiz Shahid three for 11, Javed Hayat four for 22). *WAPDA 18 pts, Peshawar 6 pts.*

At National Stadium, Karachi, February 4, 5, 6, 7. Karachi 256 for four (Sajid Khan 106 not out, Saeed Anwar 44, Zafar Ali 36) and 230 (Nasir Shad 103; Jamal Siddiqi six for 66); Rawalpindi 217 for nine (Mujahid Hameed 79 not out, Shiraz Khan 31; Syed Maqsood three for 55) and 163 (Akbar Siddiq 40; Raza Khan seven for 66). *Karachi 18 pts, Rawalpindi 4 pts.*

At Gaddafi Stadium, Lahore, February 4, 5, 6, 7. PIA won by three wickets. MCB 171 (Anwar-ul-Haq 39, Ilyas Khan 49 not out; Tanvir Ali four for 63, Iqbal Sikandar four for 42) and 230 (Babar Basharat 82; Zulfiqar Ali three for 50, Zahid Ahmad four for 48); PIA 216 (Zahid Ahmad 39, Zaheer Abbas 74, Iqbal Sikandar 51; Ijaz Faqih four for 48) and 188 for seven (Feroze Mehdi 58, Zaheer Abbas 70 not out; Farrukh Zaman four for 61 including a hat-trick). *PIA 16 pts, MCB 5 pts.*

At Jinnah Stadium, Sialkot, February 4, 5, 6, 7. Drawn. United Bank 305 (Saifullah 32, Mahmood Rasheed 42, Naved Anjum 111; Waheed Niazi four for 68, Nadeem Ghauri five for 116) and 359 for eight dec. (Mansoor Akhtar 45, Saifullah 44, Shafiq Ahmed 65, Naved Anjum 37, Ashraf Ali 85; Waheed Niazi three for 73); Habib Bank 345 for nine (Arshad Pervez 144, Azhar Khan 103 not out, Noman Shabir 30; Naved Anjum four for 46) and 173 for six (Arshad Pervez 53, Azhar Khan 47; Shahid Aziz three for 71). *Habib Bank 10 pts, United Bank 8 pts.*

At Iqbal Stadium, Faisalabad, February 4, 5, 6, 7. PACO won by five wickets. HBFC 199 (Raees Ahmed 46, Tahir Rasheed 62, Tariq Alam 44; Shahid Mahboob three for 45, Mian Fayyaz three for 68) and 92 (Shahid Mahboob eight for 65); PACO 179 (Moin Mumtaz 55, Mian Fayyaz 65; Ali Ahmed four for 70, Rafat Alam three for 30) and 116 for five (Zahoor Elahi 31, Mian Fayyaz 48; Sohail Khan four for 43). *PACO 15 pts, HBFC 5 pts.*

At Services Ground, Peshawar, February 10, 11. National Bank won by an innings and 110 runs. National Bank 383 for six (Tahir Shah 104, Ameer Akbar 135, Saleem Anwar 50); Peshawar 140 (Rehmat Gul 56; Iqbal Qasim six for 50, Hafeez-ur-Rehman three for 47) and 133 (Irfan-ud-Din 32, Khair Afzal 38; Tahir Shah three for 37, Iqbal Qasim four for 31). *National Bank 18 pts, Peshawar 3 pts.*

At GHQ Ground, Rawalpindi, February 10, 11, 12. Rawalpindi won by 179 runs. Rawalpindi 255 for five (Nadeem Abbasi 75, Mujahid Hameed 90 not out, Shiraz Khan 39) and 177 (Mujahid Hameed 68; Pervez Shah six for 40, including a hat-trick); Lahore 143 (Haider Jehangir 41, Aamer Sohail 30, Mazhar Hussain 38; Raja Sarfraz eight for 58) and 110 (Aamer Sohail 36; Shiraz Khan six for 42) *Rawalpindi 18 pts, Lahore 3 pts.*

At Gaddafi Stadium, Lahore, February 10, 11, 12, 13. PIA won by 170 runs. PIA 290 for six (Feroze Mehdi 100, Kamran Khan 39, Iqbal Sikandar 54 not out; Nadeem Ghauri three for 100) and 236 (Feroze Mehdi 48, Zahid Ahmad 55, Rashid Khan 39; Nadeem Ghauri three for 49, Agha Zahid three for 4); Habib Bank 247 (Arshad Pervez 93, Zaheer Ahmed 40; Raja Akbar three for 48, Iqbal Sikandar four for 7) and 109 (Arshad Pervez 36; Rashid Khan six for 19, Iqbal Sikandar three for 30). *PIA 18 pts, Habib Bank 6 pts.*

At LCCA Ground, Lahore, February 10, 11, 12, 13. PACO won by two wickets. WAPDA 255 (Zulfiqar-ul-Hasan 36, Mohammad Ashraf 51, Tanvir Razzaq 82; Mian Fayyaz four for 77, Masood Anwar four for 73) and 200 (Zulfiqar-ul-Hasan 62, Amjad Siddiq 30, Javed Hayat 34; Mian Fayyaz three for 64, Masood Anwar four for 47); PACO 235 (Farrukh Raza 49, Sanaullah 40, Umar Rasheed 42, Nadeem Moosa 42; Haafiz Shahid five for 43) and 221 for eight (Umar Rasheed 77, Moin Mumtaz 68; Shahid Pervez three for 43). *PACO 17 pts, WAPDA 8 pts.*

At Jinnah Stadium, Sialkot, February 10, 11, 12, 13. United Bank won by an innings and 99 runs. MCB 204 (Salah-ud-Din 44, Zaigham Burki 30, Extras 31; Naved Anjum three for 46, Sajid Bashir four for 60) and 63 (Naved Anjum four for 18, Sikander Bakht six for 37); United Bank 366 for nine (Mansoor Akhtar 45, Shafiq Ahmed 59, Naved Anjum 38, Ashraf Ali 113, Shahid Butt 52, Sajid Bashir 32 not out; Tahir Naqqash five for 108). *United Bank 18 pts, MCB 6 pts.*

At Aga Khan Gymkhana Ground, Karachi, February 10, 11, 12, 14. Drawn. HBFC 254 for eight (Saadat Ali 41, Raees Ahmed 73, Munir-ul-Haq 50, Tariq Alam 46 not out; Raza Khan three for 74, Syed Maqsood three for 90) and 351 for four dec. (Shahid Saeed 57, Shaukat Mirza 39, Munir-ul-Haq 134 not out, Tariq Alam 75 not out); Karachi 253 (Nasir Shah 43, Sajid Khan 40, Zafar Ali 32, Haseeb-ul-Hasan 45; Raees Ahmed six for 56) and 349 for eight (Sajid Khan 36, Saeed Anwar 33, Zafar Ali 60, Haseeb-ul-Hasan 104, Iqbal Saleem 35 not out; Ali Ahmed three for 114). *HBFC 10 pts, Karachi 8 pts.*

At Karachi Gymkhana Ground, Karachi, February 15, 16, 17, 18. HBFC won by 116 runs. HBFC 225 (Saadat Ali 100, Shaukat Mirza 42; Iqbal Sikandar three for 50, Tanvir Ali six for 62) and 162 (Munir-ul-Haq 59, Iqbal Sikandar seven for 52); PIA 139 (Faisal Qureshi 37; Kazim Mehdi four for 57, Sohail Khan four for 27) and 132 (Zaheer Abbas 42 not out; Kazim Mehdi seven for 55). *HBFC 17 pts, PIA 4 pts.*

At Aga Khan Gymkhana Ground, Karachi, February 16, 17, 18, 19. Drawn. WAPDA 236 (Mohammad Ashraf 31, Faisal Rasheed 34, Tanvir Razzaq 48, Ali Bahadur 50; Syed Maqsood three for 69) and 318 (Saleem Rathore 78, Zulfiqar-ul-Hasan 63, Tanvir Razzaq 94, Haafiz Shahid 47 not out; Syed Maqsood six for 104); Karachi 257 for nine (Sajid Khan 87, Zafar Ali 46, Saeed Anwar 56) and 211 for eight (Basit Ali 95; Zulfiqar Butt five for 53). *Karachi 10 pts, WAPDA 7 pts.*

At Montgomery Biscuit Factory Ground, Sahiwal, February 16, 17, 18, 19. Drawn. National Bank 345 for one (Tahir Shah 150, Sajid Ali 150 not out, Ameer Akbar 37 not out) and 323 for eight dec. (Tahir Shah 125, Asad Rauf 97; Nadeem Ghauri five for 110); Habib Bank 238 for seven (Azhar Khan 65, Akram Raza 50 not out) and 251 for seven (Arshad Pervez 65, Anwar Miandad 60, Akram Raza 63 not out; Barkatullah four for 81). *National Bank 10 pts, Habib Bank 4 pts.*

At Iqbal Stadium, Faisalabad, February 16, 17, 18, 19. United Bank won by six wickets. PACO 272 (Farrukh Raza 72, Umar Rasheed 36, Zahoor Elahi 50; Naved Anjum five for 97, Shahid Butt four for 91) and 225 (Farrukh Raza 62, Shahid Mahboob 49, Yahya Toor 31 not out, Imtiaz Ahmed 44; Sikander Bakht four for 60, Shahid Aziz three for 52); United Bank 276 (Mansoor Akhtar 41, Shafiq Ahmed 81, Ashraf Ali 76; Shahid Mahboob four for 77, Masood Anwar five for 60) and 222 for four (Ali Zia 41, Naved Anjum 81, Ashraf Ali 44 not out; Masood Anwar three for 55). *United Bank 18 pts, PACO 8 pts.*

At POF Oval, Wah Cantt, February 16, 17, 18, 19. Match abandoned without a ball bowled, owing to rain. *Rawalpindi 5 pts, MCB 5 pts.*

At Services Ground, Peshawar, February 16, 17, 18, 19. Drawn. Peshawar 158 (Aamer Mirza 38, Iqbal Butt 42 not out; Mohammad Asif eight for 58) and 98 for seven (Pervez Chaughtai 40 not out; Mohammad Asif four for 20); Lahore 254 for three dec. (Haider Jehangir 87, Wasim Ali 111 not out). *Lahore 10 pts, Peshawar 3 pts.*

At Karachi Gymkhana Ground, Karachi, February 21, 22, 23, 24. WAPDA won by 62 runs. WAPDA 182 (Faisal Rasheed 30, Javed Hayat 54; Iqbal Sikandar three for 38, Tanvir Ali five for 78) and 67 (Tanvir Ali eight for 28); PIA 89 (Zulfiqar Butt six for 28, Javed Hayat four for 49) and 98 (Zaheer Abbas 40; Zulfiqar Butt four for 36, Javed Hayat five for 55). *WAPDA 15 pts, PIA 4 pts.*

At Aga Khan Gymkhana Ground, Karachi, February 22, 23, 24, 25. Drawn. MCB 250 (Altaf Shaikh 37, Babar Basharat 109, Salah-ud-Din 38, Mohiuddin Khan 34; Raza Khan six for 84) and 314 for two dec. (Anwar-ul-Haq 132 not out, Altaf Shaikh 42, Babar Basharat 53, Salah-ud-Din 66 not out); Karachi 230 (Basit Ali 63, Zafar Ali 57; Zaigham Burki three for 43, Ijaz Faqih five for 80) and 236 for six (Sajid Khan 41, Nasir Shah 39, Saeed Anwar 66 not out, Haseeb-ul-Hasan 33; Ijaz Faqih three for 75). *MCB 10 pts, Karachi 7 pts.*

At Montgomery Biscuit Factory Ground, Sahiwal, February 22, 23, 24, 25. Drawn. Habib Bank 343 for six (Agha Zahid 62, Arshad Pervez 129, Sultan Rana 51, Akram Raza 33); Peshawar 200 (Rehmat Gul 57, Khurshid Akhtar 46, Qazi Shafiq 31; Nadeem Ghauri four for 76, Akram Raza six for 52). *Habib Bank 10 pts, Peshawar 5 pts.*

At LCCA Ground, Lahore, February 22, 23, 24, 25. Drawn. Lahore 100 (Munawwar Feroze 47; Shahid Mahboob seven for 70) and 51 for three (Aamer Sohail 31 not out); PACO 164 (Nadeem Moosa 48, Yahya Toor 46; Mohammad Asif four for 33). *PACO 7 pts, Lahore 4 pts.*

At Iqbal Stadium, Faisalabad, February 22, 23, 24, 25. Drawn. United Bank 237 (Mansoor Akhtar 33, Naved Anjum 40, Ashraf Ali 87 not out, Sajid Bashir 42; Ali Ahmed eight for 88); HBFC 43 for one. *United Bank 4 pts, HBFC 4 pts.*

At GHQ Ground, Rawalpindi, February 22, 23, 24, 25. Drawn. Rawalpindi 217 (Nadeem Abbasi 53, Shahid Javed 82; Shahid Tanvir five for 30); National Bank 98 for six (Saleem Anwar 43 not out; Shiraz Khan four for 40). *Rawalpindi 5 pts, National Bank 4 pts.*

At Karachi Gymkhana Ground, Karachi, February 28, March 1, 2, 3. United Bank won by an innings and 6 runs. Karachi 166 (Saeed Anwar 42; Kamal Merchant five for 48) and 144 (Sajid Khan 53; Shahid Aziz seven for 56); United Bank 316 for five (Moin-ul-Atiq 73, Mansoor Akhtar 167, Naved Anjum 48 not out; Nadeem Khan three for 117). *United Bank 18 pts, Karachi 4 pts.*

At Aga Khan Gymkhana Ground, Karachi, February 28, March 1, 2, 3. PIA won by an innings and 85 runs. Peshawar 102 (Khurshid Akhtar 36; Zulfiqar Ali six for 38) and 143 (Rehmat Gul 58; Zulfiqar Ali three for 47, Iqbal Sikandar three for 45); PIA 330 for seven dec. (R. I. Alikhan 33, Zahid Ahmad 127, Zaheer Abbas 33, Faisal Qureshi 55 not out; Ishtiaq Ahmed three for 68). *PIA 18 pts, Peshawar 4 pts.*

At Gaddafi Stadium, Lahore, February 28, March 1, 2, 3. MCB won by one wicket. PACO 151 (Nadeem Moosa 52 not out, Mian Fayyaz 35; Mohiuddin Khan six for 64, Tahir Naqqash three for 67) and 194 (Farrukh Raza 36, Shahid Mahboob 61; Mohiuddin Khan four for 33, Ilyas Khan three for 45); MCB 111 (Altaf Shaikh 37, Shahid Mahboob four for 69, Mian Fayyaz five for 5) and 238 for nine (Asad Mahmood 78, Mohiuddin Khan 34 not out; Masood Anwar three for 54, Mian Fayyaz three for 65). *MCB 14 pts, PACO 5 pts.*

At LCCA Ground, Lahore, February 28, March 1, 2, 3. Lahore won by 164 runs. Lahore 200 (Haider Jehangir 31, Aamer Sohail 41, Mazhar Hussain 53, Mohammad Asif 32; Kazim Mehdi three for 50, Raees Ahmed four for 66) and 404 (Aamer Sohail 59, Mazhar Hussain 139, Pervez Shah 90, Azhar Hussain 48; Raees Ahmed three for 99); HBFC 256 for eight (Raees Ahmed 86, Sagheer Abbas 35, Tahir Rasheed 39; Aamer Sohail four for 86) and 184 (Munir-ul-Haq 59, Saadat Ali 37; Azhar Hussain six for 22). *Lahore 16 pts, HBFC 8 pts.*

At GHQ Ground, Rawalpindi, February 28, March 1, 2, 3. Rawalpindi won by two wickets. Habib Bank 165 (Noman Shabbir 49; Raja Sarfraz five for 58, Shakeel Ahmed four for 39) and 113 (Shiraz Khan three for 31, Raja Sarfraz five for 47); Rawalpindi 174 for nine (Mujahid Hameed 65 not out, Raja Sarfraz 30; Akram Raza five for 65) and 105 for eight (Nadeem Ghauri four for 34). *Rawalpindi 15 pts, Habib Bank 5 pts.*

At Municipal Stadium, Gujranwala, February 28, March 1, 2, 3. National Bank won by six wickets. WAPDA 259 (Faisal Rasheed 118 not out, Javed Hayat 50; Afzaal Butt three for 43, Barkatullah three for 58) and 132 (Afzaal Butt three for 51, Barkatullah three for 26, Hafeez-ur-Rehman three for 32); National Bank 280 for nine dec. (Tahir Shah 43, Sajid Ali 63, Saeed Azad 79, Shahid Tanvir 50; Zulfiqar Butt three for 102, Javed Hayat five for 80) and 112 for four (Tahir Shah 35, Ameer Akbar 49; Shahid Pervez three for 48). *National Bank 18 pts, WAPDA 8 pts.*

QUAID-E-AZAM TROPHY WINNERS

1953-54	Bahawalpur	1973-74	Railways
1954-55	Karachi	1974-75	Punjab A
1956-57	Punjab	1975-76	National Bank
1957-58	Bahawalpur	1976-77	United Bank
1958-59	Karachi	1977-78	Habib Bank
1959-60	Karachi	1978-79	National Bank
1961-62	Karachi Blues	1979-80	PIA
1962-63	Karachi A	1980-81	United Bank
1963-64	Karachi Blues	1981-82	National Bank
1964-65	Karachi Blues	1982-83	United Bank
1966-67	Karachi	1983-84	National Bank
1968-69	Lahore	1984-85	United Bank
1969-70	PIA	1985-86	Karachi
1970-71	Karachi Blues	1986-87	National Bank
1972-73	Railways		

BCCP PRESIDENT'S CUP, 1986-87

Note: First innings closed at 60 overs in group matches, and 85 overs in semi-finals and final.

Group A

At Steel Mills Ground, Karachi, January 6, 7, 8. Drawn. Quetta 219 for five (Rashid Raza 45, Raj Hans 78, Imran Khan 47 not out) and 289 (Raj Hans 75, Imran Khan 48, Mansoor Khan 62, Aslam Shaikh 36; Jamal Zaidi four for 17); Pakistan Steel 267 for eight (Waqas Ukasha 55, Mohammad Sadiq 45, Jamal Zaidi 78; Raj Hans four for 91, Rashid Raza three for 7) and 24 for four. *Pakistan Steel 9 pts, Quetta 6 pts.*

At Aga Khan Gymkhana Ground, Karachi, January 6, 7, 8. Karachi Whites were awarded a walkover against Sukkur, who withdrew from the tournament. *Karachi Whites 14 pts.*

At Aga Khan Gymkhana Ground, Karachi, January 9, 10, 11. Quetta were awarded a walkover against Sukkur. *Quetta 14 pts.*

At Aga Khan Gymkhana Ground, Karachi, January 10, 11, 12. Karachi Whites won when Quetta conceded the match. Quetta 134 (Imran Khan 47; Shakeel Paul three for 24, Zafar Mehdi three for 27) and 34 for four; Karachi Whites 282 for six (Zafar Jamal 41, Mohammad Aslam 101, Asim Rizvi 39; Mohsin Raza four for 65). *Karachi Whites 18 pts, Quetta 3 pts.*

At Steel Mills Ground, Karachi, January 13, 14, 15. Pakistan Steel were awarded a walkover against Sukkur. *Pakistan Steel 14 pts.*

At Steel Mills Ground, Karachi, January 14, 15, 16. Drawn. Pakistan Steel 186 (Azhar Hussain 68; Shahab-ud-Din four for 38) and 122 for four (Waqas Ukasha 32, Imran Afzal 40); Karachi Whites 250 for eight (Azam Khan 37, Sajid Riaz 42, Asim Rizvi 81, Riaz Sheikh 43). *Karachi Whites 10 pts, Pakistan Steel 5 pts.*

Karachi Whites 42 pts, Pakistan Steel 28 pts, Quetta 23 pts, Sukkur 0 pt. Karachi Whites qualified for the group league.

Group B

At Government College Ground, Sargodha, January 5, 6, 7. Sargodha won by 64 runs. Sargodha 171 for four (Mohammad Nawaz 86, Zahid Malik 51 not out) and 133 (Zahid Malik 50; Imtiaz Ahmed four for 18); State Bank 186 (Ahsan Jawwad 31, Nasir Javed 64; R. Ghulam Abbas five for 48) and 54 (Naeem Khan eight for 25). *Sargodha 15 pts, State Bank 3 pts.*

At Iqbal Stadium, Faisalabad, January 5, 6, 7. Drawn. PNSC 202 for nine (Siddiq Patni 61, Sajjad Akbar 41 not out; Naved Nazir three for 35) and 185 for three (Shahid Anwar 36, Iqtidar Ali 53 not out, Azhar Sultan 63 not out); Faisalabad 240 for nine (Anwar Awais 32, Naseer Shaukat 89, Aamer Nazir 62 not out, Extras 31; Mohsin Kamal three for 66, Amin Lakhani three for 52). *Faisalabad 9 pts, PNSC 6 pts.*

At Sargodha Stadium, Sargodha, January 9, 10, 11. PNSC won by 175 runs. PNSC 210 for nine (Shahid Anwar 42, Iqtidar Ali 73 not out; Aziz-ur-Rehman five for 74) and 151 (Siddiq Patni 39 not out; Naeem Khan five for 53, R. Ghulam Abbas four for 35); Sargodha 72 (Azeem Hafeez four for 32, Sajjad Akbar three for 8) and 114 (Sajjad Akbar five for 48). *PNSC 16 pts, Sargodha 4 pts.*

At Iqbal Stadium, Faisalabad, January 9, 10, 11. Faisalabad won by seven wickets. State Bank 79 (Khwaja Iqtidar 38; Saadat Gul five for 34, Shahzad Ahmed five for 31) and 229 (Saleem Raza 77, Ahsan Jawwad 86, Imtiaz Ahmed 32 not out; Saadat Gul four for 35, Naseer Shaukat five for 50); Faisalabad 190 for nine (Gulzar Ali 53, Aamer Nazir 33, Saadat Gul 39 not out; Nasir Javed five for 64) and 121 for three (Gulzar Ali 30, Saadat Gul 45 not out). *Faisalabad 15 pts, State Bank 4 pts.*

At Sargodha Stadium, Sargodha, January 13, 14, 15. Drawn. Faisalabad 163 (Saadat Gul 73 not out; Irfan Akhtar three for 35, R. Ghulam Abbas six for 53) and 174 for five (Maqsood Ahmed 46, Naseer Shaukat 50; Aziz-ur-Rehman three for 43); Sargodha 201 for eight (Talat Imtiaz 39, Zahid Malik 50 not out; Shahzad Ahmed three for 28). *Sargodha 8 pts, Faisalabad 5 pts.*

At Iqbal Stadium, Faisalabad, January 13, 14, 15. PNSC won by an innings and 44 runs. State Bank 111 (Sajjad Akbar five for 28, Amin Lakhani four for 21) and 106 (Mohsin Kamal three for 55); PNSC 261 for six dec. (Shahid Anwar 101, Siddiq Patni 36, Azhar Sultan 45, Iqtidar Ali 32 not out). *PNSC 18 pts, State Bank 3 pts.*

PNSC 40 pts, Faisalabad 29 pts, Sargodha 27 pts, State Bank 10 pts. PNSC qualified for the group league.

Group C

At Montgomery Biscuit Factory Ground, Sahiwal, January 5, 6, 7. Multan won by an innings and 35 runs. Hyderabad 176 for nine (Zulfiqar Chaudhri 56, Anwar Iqbal 46; Bilal Rana three for 75) and 107 (Bilal Rana four for 42); Multan 318 for eight (Inzamam-ul-Haq 131, Mushtaq Ahmed 75; Sajid Asghar three for 74). *Multan 18 pts, Hyderabad 5 pts.*

At Zafar Ali Stadium, Sahiwal, January 5, 6, 7. Servis Industries won by an innings and 164 runs. Lahore Division 91 (Hamid Usman five for 22, Nasir J. Charlie four for 34) and 78 (Javed Iqbal 31; Nasir J. Charlie five for 21); Servis Industries 333 for seven (Rafaqat Ali 72, Rasheed Karimi 43, Farooq Bhatti 30, Haroon Abraham 49, Naeem Taj 41 not out, Anjum Bobby 41 not out; Mujahid Jamshed three for 68, Shahid Rasool three for 50). *Servis Industries 18 pts, Lahore Division 4 pts.*

At Montgomery Biscuit Factory Ground, Sahiwal, January 9, 10, 11. Multan won by ten wickets. Multan 325 for eight (Bilal Rana 121, Javed Mohammad 88, Sajid Waheed 36; Tahir Mahmood four for 55) and 65 for no wkt (Bilal Rana 41 not out); Lahore Division 147 (Mujahid Jamshed 76; Bilal Rana three for 48, Abubakar Siddiq four for 28) and 242 (Mujahid Jamshed 93, Tahir Mahmood 40; Bilal Rana six for 70). *Multan 18 pts, Lahore Division 4 pts.*

At Zafar Ali Stadium, Sahiwal, January 9, 10, 11. Servis Industries won by four wickets. Hyderabad 214 (Abdur Rauf 68, Extras 33; Nasir J. Charlie six for 56, Sikander Naqi three for 54) and 130 (Zulfiqar Chaudhri 33, Sajid Asghar 33; Nasir J. Charlie four for 52, Naeem Taj six for 55); Servis Industries 226 (Rasheed Karimi 36, Aamer Majeed 78, Naeem Taj 40; Munawwar Jafri six for 63) and 122 for six (Aamer Majeed 54 not out; Munawwar Jafri three for 39). *Servis Industries 17 pts, Hyderabad 6 pts.*

At Montgomery Biscuit Factory Ground, Sahiwal, January 12, 13, 14. Drawn. Servis Industries 202 (Akbar Khan 38, Aamer Majeed 44, Naeem Taj 46 not out; Bilal Rana four for 68); Multan 177 for four (Ayub Malik 42, Rizwan Sattar 59, Sajid Waheed 46 not out; Naeem Taj three for 85). *Multan 5 pts, Servis Industries 4 pts.*

At Zafar Ali Stadium, Sahiwal, January 12, 13, 14. Drawn. Lahore Division 204 (Tahir Mahmood 46 not out, Mujahid Jamshed 42, Javed Iqbal 53); Hyderabad 79 for three (Mehfooz Ali 33 not out). *Lahore Division 4 pts, Hyderabad 4 pts.*

Multan 41 pts, Servis Industries 39 pts, Hyderabad 15 pts, Lahore Division 12 pts. Multan qualified for the group league.

Groups D and E

At LCCA Ground, Lahore, January 18, 19, 20. Drawn. PWD 114 (Fareed Hasan 32; Zain-ul-Abideen three for 15, Haroon Rasheed five for 50); Lahore City Whites 120 for seven (Ghulam Ali three for 49, Fareed Hasan three for 34). *PWD 4 pts, Lahore City Whites 4 pts.*

At Zafar Ali Stadium, Sahiwal, January 18, 19, 20. Drawn. ADBP 227 (Aamer Malik 37, Mansoor Rana 81, Atif Rauf 35; Zia-ud-Din five for 69, Haaris A. Khan three for 71) and 187 for seven dec. (Atif Rauf 68 not out, Ghaffar Kazmi 41; Jalal-ud-Din three for 24); Pakistan Customs 164 (Haaris A. Khan 45, Zia-ud-Din 35; Qasim Shera four for 34; Khatib Rizwan three for 47) and 81 for six (Nadeem Jamal 41). *ADBP 9 pts, Pakistan Customs 5 pts.*

At Model Town Cricket Club Ground, Lahore, January 22, 23, 24. Pakistan Customs won by 132 runs. Pakistan Customs 226 (Nadeem Jamal 31, Tariq Mansoor 33, Farhat Javed 34, Nadeem Ahsan 60; Haroon Rasheed four for 95) and 246 for six dec. (Abid Javed 52, Tariq Mahmood 107, Tehsin Ahmed 34; Haroon Rasheed three for 78); Lahore City Whites 167 (Shahid Mahmood 39, Azhar Saeed 37 not out; Sohail Murtaza five for 62, Haaris A. Khan four for 33) and 173 (Ajmal Hussain 39, Shahid Mahmood 32, Haroon Rasheed 36; Jalal-ud-Din three for 45, Zia-ud-Din four for 31). *Pakistan Customs 17 pts, Lahore City Whites 5 pts.*

At Zafar Ali Stadium, Sahiwal, January 22, 23, 24. ADBP won by 169 runs. ADBP 245 for eight (Masood Anwar 53, Tanvir Ahmed 32, Aamer Malik 37, Mansoor Rana 38, Maqsood Kundi 35 not out; Sultan Kamdar four for 82, Hameed Rehmatullah three for 43) and 235 for five dec. (Masood Anwar 41, Mansoor Rana 37, Bilal Ahmed 42 not out, Atif Rauf 61 not out); PWD 163 (Sajjad Abbas 33; Raja Afaq four for 48, Khatib Rizwan four for 41) and 148 (Mohammad Asim 47; Raja Afaq six for 63, Khatib Rizwan four for 50). *ADBP 17 pts, PWD 5 pts.*

At Zafar Ali Stadium, Sahiwal, January 26, 27, 28. Pakistan Customs won by 151 runs. Pakistan Customs 251 (Muzaffer Abbasi 36, Mustanir Pervez 57, Zia-ud-Din 34; Hameed Rehmatullah three for 56, Sultan Kamdar three for 62) and 233 for eight dec. (Tariq Mahmood 101, Nadeem Ahsan 30, Farhat Javed 33; Sajjad Abbas three for 35); PWD 140 (Mohammad Asim 45; Zia-ud-Din four for 20) and 193 (Monis Qadri 42, Fareed Hasan 64; Zia-ud-Din four for 28). *Pakistan Customs 18 pts, PWD 4 pts.*

At Railways Stadium, Lahore, January 26, 27, 28. ADBP won by nine wickets. Lahore City Whites 158 for nine (Shahid Mahmood 39, Azhar Saeed 43; Raja Afaq four for 48) and 142 (Ajmal Hussain 35; Raja Afaq four for 48, Ghaffar Kazmi three for 34); ADBP 255 for nine (Atif Rauf 56, Ghaffar Kazmi 64; Sajid Bokhari for 71, Haroon Rasheed five for 115) and 49 for one. *ADBP 18 pts, Lahore City Whites 5 pts.*

ADBP 44 pts, Pakistan Customs 40 pts, Lahore City Whites 14 pts, PWD 13 pts. ADBP and Pakistan Customs qualified for the group league.

Group F

At Municipal Stadium, Gujranwala, January 5, 6, 7. Drawn. Railways 208 (Abid Sarwar 33, Hammad Butt 45, Musleh-ud-Din 45, Shahid Pervez 44; Sajjad Bashir six for 72); Gujranwala 63 (Musleh-ud-Din six for 32) and 61 for two. *Railways 8 pts, Gujranwala 4 pts.*

At Municipal Stadium, Gujranwala, January 9, 10, 11. Gujranwala were awarded a walkover against Islamabad, who withdrew from the tournament. *Gujranwala 14 pts.*

At Railways Stadium, Lahore, January 13, 14, 15. Railways were awarded a walkover against Islamabad. *Railways 14 pts.*

Railways 22 pts, Gujranwala 18 pts, Islamabad 0 pt. Railways qualified for the group league.

Group League, Round A

At Montgomery Biscuit Factory Ground, Sahiwal, January 18, 19, 20. PNSC won by eight wickets. ADBP 251 for five (Shahid Anwar 35, Siddiq Patni 50, Iqtidar Ali 63, Nasir Wasti 33) and 97 for two (Mutahir Shah 55 not out); Multan 97 (Sajjad Akbar four for 20, Amin Lakhani three for 22) and 250 (Ayub Malik 32, Rizwan Sattar 33, Inzamam-ul-Haq 94 not out; Amin Lakhani three for 77). *PNSC 18 pts, Multan 3 pts.*

At Montgomery Biscuit Factory Ground, Sahiwal, January 22, 23, 24. PNSC won by eight wickets. Karachi Whites 57 (Mohsin Kamal four for 16, Sajjad Akbar three for 4) and 292 (Zafar Mehdi 102, Riaz Sheikh 76; Amin Lakhani three for 56, Sajjad Akbar three for 119); PNSC 198 (Nasir Wasti 47; Riaz Sheikh seven for 71) and 154 for two (Shahid Anwar 89, Iqtidar Ali 44 not out). *PNSC 15 pts, Karachi Whites 4 pts.*

At Montgomery Biscuit Factory Ground, Sahiwal, January 26, 27, 28. Karachi Whites won by 73 runs. Karachi Whites 254 for nine (Zafar Mehdi 44, Riaz Sheikh 51, Shakeel Sajjad 55; Saleem Sajjad three for 40) and 199 (Asim Rizvi 51, Rashid Latif 54 not out; Saleem Sajjad three for 41); Multan 229 (Bilal Rana 72, Rizwan Sattar 75, Sajid Waheed 36; Riaz Sheikh three for 74, Zafar Mehdi three for 66, Shahab-ud-Din three for 41) and 151 (Tariq Chisti 43; Riaz Sheikh eight for 60). *Karachi Whites 18 pts, Multan 7 pts.*

PNSC 33 pts, Karachi Whites 22 pts, Multan 10 pts. PNSC and Karachi Whites qualified for the semi-finals.

Group League, Round B

At Model Town Cricket Club Ground, Lahore, February 4, 5, 6. Pakistan Customs won by six wickets. ADBP 229 (Mansoor Rana 30, Atif Rauf 55, Ghaffar Kazmi 41, Extras 30; Sohail Murtaza four for 63) and 212 for nine dec. (Najeeb Wahid 39, Ghaffar Kazmi 102; Athar Khan three for 55, Zia-ud-Din four for 57); Pakistan Customs 244 for seven (Tariq Mahmood 51, Mustanir Pervez 45 not out, Tariq Mansoor 35) and 201 for four (Nadeem Jamal 55, Tariq Mahmood 60, Zia-ud-Din 33). *Pakistan Customs 17 pts, ADBP 7 pts.*

At Municipal Stadium, Gujranwala, February 8, 9, 10. Drawn. Railways 131 (Aleem Dar 39, Babar Butt 37; Qasim Shera four for 57) and 295 for nine (Abid Sarwar 45, Musleh-ud-Din 69, Wasim Haider 31; Ghaffar Kazmi four for 82); ADBP 160 (Asif Faridi 44 not out; Musleh-ud-Din three for 45, Wasim Haider five for 73). *ADBP 7 pts, Railways 4 pts.*

At Model Town Cricket Club Ground, Lahore, February 12, 13, 14. Railways won by 2 runs. Railways 127 (Shahid Pervez 40; Jalal-ud-Din four for 36, Sohail Murtaza three for 51) and 197 (Hammad Butt 30, Shahid Pervez 60, Wasim Haider 31; Abid Pirzada five for 56); Pakistan Customs 206 for nine (Mustanir Pervez 30, Tariq Mansoor 70, Farhat Javed 41) and 116 (Haaris A. Khan 53; Mohammad Nazir four for 42, Asim Butt three for 11). *Railways 14 pts, Pakistan Customs 6 pts.*

Pakistan Customs 23 pts, Railways 18 pts, ADBP 14 pts. Pakistan Customs and Railways qualified for the semi-finals.

Semi-finals

At Model Town Cricket Club Ground, Lahore, February 17, 18, 19. Drawn. Railways were declared winners by virtue of their first-innings lead. PNSC 96 (Mohammad Nazir five for 31, Aamer Wasim four for 27) and 42 for two; Railways 130 (Abid Sarwar 51, Asim Butt 31; Sajjad Akbar four for 39, Afzal Saeed three for 19).

At LCCA Ground, Lahore, February 17, 18, 19. Drawn. Pakistan Customs were declared winners by virtue of their first-innings lead. Karachi Whites 171 for nine (Azam Khan 31, Sajid Riaz 52; Haaris A. Khan three for 52); Pakistan Customs 175 for eight (Muzaffar Abbasi 39, Tariq Mahmood 40, Zia-ud-Din 40 not out; Zafar Mehdi four for 60).

Final

At Gaddafi Stadium, Lahore, February 22, 23, 24, 25. Drawn. Railways were declared winners by virtue of their first-innings lead. Railways 259 (Babar Butt 81, Hammad Butt 30, Asim Butt 41; Sohail Murtaza three for 70, Haaris A. Khan three for 94, Zia-ud-Din four for 41); Pakistan Customs 102 (Wasim Haider five for 53, Mohammad Nazir four for 36) and 3 for no wkt.

PACO CUP, 1986-87

Note: First innings closed at 85 overs.

Group A

At Jinnah Stadium, Sialkot, March 9, 10, 11, 12. National Bank won by seven wickets. Lahore 312 (Haider Jehangir 171, Wasim Ali 80; Hafeez-ur-Rehman four for 111, Tahir Shah four for 109) and 255 (Irfan Gul 34, Saleem Hussain 91 not out, Azhar Hussain 34; Tahir Shah five for 129, Saleem Anwar three for 10); National Bank 209 (Tahir Shah 42, Taslim Arif 57; Azhar Hussain five for 46) and 359 for three (Saleem Pervez 145, Tahir Shah 108, Saeed Azad 61 not out). *National Bank 16 pts, Lahore 8 pts.*

At Model Town Cricket Club Ground, Lahore, March 9, 10, 11, 12. HBFC won by five wickets. WAPDA 219 (Maqsood Raza 91 not out; Kazim Mehdi four for 66) and 221 (Ali Bahadur 31, Maqsood Raza 66, Javed Hayat 34; Kazim Mehdi four for 74); HBFC 248 for seven (Shahid Saeed 68, Munir-ul-Haq 93; Zulfiqar Butt three for 93) and 193 for five (Shahid Saeed 54, Saadat Ali 64, Raees Ahmed 41; Javed Hayat five for 64). *HBFC 17 pts, WAPDA 6 pts.*

At LCCA Ground, Lahore, March 14, 15, 16. WAPDA won by an innings and 150 runs. Lahore 56 (Zulfiqar Butt seven for 16) and 78 (Wasim Ali 30; Javed Hayat four for 42, Zulfiqar Butt six for 30); WAPDA 284 for eight dec. (Ali Bahadur 130, Haafiz Shahid 67; Mohammad Asif seven for 108). *WAPDA 18 pts, Lahore 4 pts.*

At Zafar Ali Stadium, Sahiwal, March 14, 15, 16, 17. Drawn. National Bank 237 (Saeed Azad 65, Asad Rauf 114; Ali Ahmed three for 60, Shahid Saeed four for 26) and 291 for five (Tahir Shah 43, Saeed Azad 120, Asad Rauf 71; Kazim Mehdi four for 91); HBFC 276 for eight (Tahir Rasheed 32, Raees Ahmed 32, Munir-ul-Haq 91 not out, Ali Ahmed 33; Tahir Shah three for 120). *HBFC 10 pts, National Bank 7 pts.*

At Jinnah Stadium, Sialkot, March 19, 20, 21, 22. Abandoned without a ball bowled, owing to rain. *National Bank 5 pts, WAPDA 5 pts.*

At Railways Stadium, Lahore, March 19, 20, 21, 22. Abandoned without a ball bowled, owing to rain. *Lahore 5 pts, HBFC 5 pts.*

HBFC 32 pts, WAPDA 29 pts, National Bank 28 pts, Lahore 17 pts. HBFC and WAPDA qualified for the semi-finals.

Group B

At LCCA Ground, Lahore, March 9, 10, 11, 12. PIA won by 140 runs. PIA 314 for nine (Feroze Mehdi 135, Faisal Qureshi 56, Zahid Ahmad 71; Shakeel Ahmed five for 73) and 204 (R. I. Alikhan 55, Faisal Qureshi 34; Raja Sarfraz four for 44, Shakeel Ahmed six for 86); Rawalpindi 209 (Akbar Siddiq 40, Shiraz Khan 40, Raja Sarfraz 34; Iqbal Sikandar four for 66) and 169 (Mujahid Hameed 57; Iqbal Sikandar four for 52, Tanvir Ali five for 43). *PIA 18 pts, Rawalpindi 6 pts.*

At Iqbal Stadium, Faisalabad, March 9, 10, 11, 12. United Bank won by eight wickets. PACO 181 (Farrukh Raza 45, Yahya Toor 44; Sajid Bashir four for 62, Kamal Merchant four for 27) and 133 (Umar Rasheed 30, Masood Anwar 30; Naved Anjum seven for 63); United Bank 155 (Ali Zia 60 not out; Nadeem Moosa five for 30, Masood Anwar three for 26) and 163 for two (Mansoor Akhtar 75 not out, Shafiq Ahmed 50 not out). *United Bank 15 pts, PACO 5 pts.*

At Iqbal Stadium, Faisalabad, March 14, 15, 16, 17. Drawn. United Bank 157 (Kamal Merchant 30; Zulfiqar Ali three for 64, Rashid Khan six for 58) and 271 for eight (Mansoor Akhtar 36, Shafiq Ahmed 71, Kamal Merchant 53 not out; Rashid Khan five for 69); PIA 173 (R. I. Alikhan 50, Zahid Ahmad 36, Iqbal Sikandar 35; Sikander Bakht five for 82). *PIA 7 pts, United Bank 5 pts.*

At Municipal Stadium, Gujranwala, March 14, 15, 16, 17. PACO won by four wickets. Rawalpindi 211 (Akbar Siddiq 53, Mujahid Hameed 36; Shahid Mahboob five for 86) and 101 (Shahid Mahboob five for 50, Umar Rasheed three for 35); PACO 261 (Junaid Alvi 30, Farrukh Raza 32, Moin Mumtaz 75, Shahid Mahboob 38, Extras 30; Raja Sarfraz seven for 96) and 53 for six (Jamal Siddiqi four for 35). *PACO 18 pts, Rawalpindi 6 pts.*

At LCCA Ground, Lahore, March 19, 20, 21, 22. Drawn. PACO 101 for seven dec. (Moin Mumtaz 34; Rashid Khan three for 32); PIA 32 for no wkt. *PIA 4 pts.*

At Iqbal Stadium, Faisalabad, March 19, 20, 21, 22. Drawn. Rawalpindi 215 (Jamal Siddiqi 32, Shahid Javed 48, Mujahid Hameed 40, Shiraz Khan 33; Naved Anjum six for 56); United Bank 313 (Kamal Merchant 62, Mansoor Akhtar 101 not out, Ali Zia 68; Raja Sarfraz five for 70). *United Bank 10 pts, Rawalpindi 6 pts.*

United Bank 30 pts, PIA 29 pts, PACO 23 pts, Rawalpindi 18 pts. United Bank and PIA qualified for the semi-finals.

Semi-finals

At LCCA Ground, Lahore, March 24, 25, 26, 27. Drawn. PIA were declared winners by virtue of their first-innings lead. HBFC 221 (Saadat Ali 38, Raees Ahmed 33, Sagheer Abbas 85 not out; Iqbal Sikandar five for 59) and 259 for eight dec. (Shahid Saeed 53, Saadat Ali 32, Raees Ahmed 42, Tahir Rasheed 52 not out, Ijaz Ahmed 44); PIA 277 for eight (Feroze Mehdi 66, Zahid Ahmad 83, Asif Mohammad 50; Kazim Mehdi four for 107) and 146 for four (R. I. Alikhan 48, Zahid Ahmad 30).

At Iqbal Stadium, Faisalabad, March 24, 25, 26, 27. Drawn. United Bank were declared winners by virtue of their first-innings lead. United Bank 264 for nine (Saifullah 50, Moin-ul-Atiq 31, Shafiq Ahmed 85, Ali Zia 32; Zulfiqar Butt five for 77) and 346 (Mansoor Akhtar 57, Ali Zia 54, Naved Anjum 35, Ashraf Ali 44, Shafiq Ahmed 77, Kamal Merchant 39; Javed Hayat five for 122); WAPDA 205 (Maqsood Raza 67; Kamal Merchant three for 45, Shahid Butt three for 52) and 152 for one (Mohammad Ashraf 64 not out, Zulfiqar-ul-Hasan 34, Maqsood Raza 50).

Final

At LCCA Ground, Lahore, March 29, 30, 31, April 1. PIA won by 10 runs. PIA 146 (Naved Anjum three for 34, Shahid Butt five for 59) and 238 (Feroze Mehdi 94, Rizwan-uz-Zaman 39; Shahid Butt four for 82, Shahid Aziz five for 89); United Bank 232 (Manzoor Akhtar 32, Shafiq Ahmed 57, Ali Zia 32, Naved Anjum 34; Zahid Ahmed three for 49, Rizwan-uz-Zaman three for 43) and 142 (Ashraf Ali 32; Zahid Ahmed six for 58, Rizwan-uz-Zaman three for 55).

†WILLS CUP, 1986-87

Semi-finals

At Gaddafi Stadium, Lahore, October 6. Habib Bank won by 128 runs. Habib Bank 277 for two (50 overs) (Ijaz Ahmed 123 not out, Salim Malik 110 not out); ADBP 149 (43 overs) (Mansoor Rana 45; Anwar Miandad three for 17).

   At Shahi Bagh Stadium, Peshawar, October 6. United Bank won by 20 runs. United Bank 209 for eight (50 overs) (Moin-ul-Atiq 33, Mansoor Akhtar 51, Mudassar Nazar 64; Rashid Khan three for 34); PIA 189 (48.3 overs) (Zaheer Abbas 49, Zahid Ahmad 31, Anil Dalpat 40 not out; Saleem Jaffer three for 31).

Final

At Gaddafi Stadium, Lahore, October 10. Habib Bank won by three wickets. United Bank 154 (48.1 overs) (Moin-ul-Atiq 78; Akram Raza three for 38); Habib Bank 155 for seven (49.2 overs) (Mohsin Khan 54, Anwar Miandad 54; Saleem Jaffer three for 30).

PAKISTAN v ENGLAND, 1987-88

Pakistan beat England in four days in the First Test at Lahore, where Abdul Qadir took nine for 56 in the first innings and thirteen for 101 in the match. His first-innings return was the best by a Pakistan bowler, the fifth-best in all Tests, and the best by a bowler from any country against England. When the Second and Third Tests were both drawn, Pakistan had won their third successive series against England. In the Second Test at Faisalabad, the third day was lost as a result of a dispute between the England captain, M. W. Gatting, and the Pakistan umpire, Shakoor Rana.

First Test: At Lahore, November 25, 26, 27, 28. Pakistan won by an innings and 87 runs. England 175 (B. C. Broad 41, N. A. Foster 39, B. N. French 38 not out; Abdul Qadir nine for 56) and 130 (J. E. Emburey 38 not out; Abdul Qadir four for 45, Tauseef Ahmed three for 28, Iqbal Qasim three for 39); Pakistan 392 (Mudassar Nazar 120, Ramiz Raja 35, Javed Miandad 65, Ijaz Ahmed 44, Wasim Akram 40, Abdul Qadir 38, Extras 30; J. E. Emburey three for 109, N. G. B. Cook three for 87).

Second Test: At Faisalabad, December 7, 8, 9, 11, 12. Drawn. England 292 (B. C. Broad 116, M. W. Gatting 79; Abdul Qadir four for 105, Iqbal Qasim five for 83) and 137 for six dec. (G. A. Gooch 65; Abdul Qadir three for 45); Pakistan 191 (Salim Malik 60, Abdul Qadir 38; N. A. Foster four for 42, J. E. Emburey three for 49) and 51 for one.

Third Test: At Karachi, December 16, 17, 18, 20, 21. Drawn. England 294 (D. J. Capel 98, J. E. Emburey 70, B. N. French 31; Abdul Qadir five for 88) and 258 for nine (G. A. Gooch 93, J. E. Emburey 74 not out; Abdul Qadir five for 98); Pakistan 353 (Ramiz Raja 50, Salim Malik 55, Aamer Malik 98 not out, Wasim Akram 37, Abdul Qadir 61; P. A. J. DeFreitas five for 86).

   England won the one-day international series 3-0.

   Full details of England's tour of Pakistan will appear in the 1989 edition of Wisden.

CRICKET IN SRI LANKA, 1986-87

By GERRY VAIDYASEKERA

Civil unrest at home upset Sri Lanka's preparations for the forthcoming World Cup matches in Pakistan when New Zealand's hurriedly arranged tour of Sri Lanka was abandoned after only two matches. On the day that the First Test finished as a draw, a car bomb was detonated in Colombo, not far from where the New Zealanders were staying, and the authorities of the two countries agreed, in the interest of the players' safety, to call the tour off. The decision was a second setback for the Sri Lankan cricketers, because a planned tour of Pakistan by the Under-23 team in April had earlier been postponed until after the World Cup.

In the island's domestic cricket, nine districts contested the fourth National Cricket Tournament for the J. R. Jayawardena Trophy. Gampaha District, who won it the previous two seasons, and Colombo City were the finalists, and they shared the trophy when the match, played over four days, ended in a draw. The Robert Senanayaka Trophy was also shared when, for the second successive day, the weather ruined the three-day final at Maitland Place between Nationalised Services Cricket Association, the defending champions, and the Mercantile Cricket Association.

With Kurunegala and Negombo, the previous season's joint-champions of Division II, having been promoted, the full quota of twenty teams took part in the Lakspray Division I of the Inter-club Cricket Tournament. Singhalese Sports Club retained the Lakspray Trophy in a tense match against Colts CC, making their first appearance in the final in 23 years. In Division II, six more clubs entered to increase the number of participants to 29. Singhalese SC and Singha SC of Ambalangoda shared the Delmege Forsyth Trophy. Nondescripts CC, helped in the final by Kishan Dharmasena, a player with English league experience, regained the Division III Pure Beverages Trophy after four years; United Southern were runners-up.

In the Lakspray Division I, 40-year-old Owen Mottau of Colombo CC compiled the season's highest score, hitting 263 in 8 hours 25 minutes off 372 balls against the Tamils at Maitland Crescent. His innings included 25 fours, and his team totalled 677 from 170.5 overs in 12 hours 33 minutes. Somewhat quicker was Duleep Mendis's hundred in 99 minutes for Singhalese SC against Burgher Recreation Club at Maitland Place. T. H. Wijewardena of Saracens hit a hundred in 109 minutes against Panadura at Moratuwa. Prabath Senanayaka of Nomads took eight for 31 in an innings against Moratuwa, while Wasantha Kumara of Kurunegala Youth had match figures of thirteen for 83 against Negombo.

Scholarships, offered by the Sri Lanka Cricket Promoters' Association in England to play and coach there, were awarded to the Colts opening batsman, Dhammika Bulankulame, and to Colombo CC's wicket-keeper-batsman, Ashley de Silva. Dilhan Perera, the St Peter's College captain, won the Herman Claessen Memorial Trophy as the "Most Promising Under-17 Cricketer for 1986", following his outstanding batting achievements.

As part of the Asian Cricket Conference's promotion of the game in the Asian region, particularly in the non-Test playing countries, a Conference youth team of Sri Lankans, led by Roshan Mahanama, visited Hong Kong on a short tour. They played four matches, winning three and drawing one, with the first three games being played on astro-turf pitches and the final, two-day game on grass. Asanka Gurusinha, the left-handed Test batsman, scored three hundreds and had a batting average of 193.50, while he and three other bowlers – Graeme Labrooy, Sanjeewa Weerasinghe and C. P. Ramanayake – had bowling averages under 10.00.

In March, Gloucestershire, although without their international players, Walsh, Athey and Curran, made a three-week visit to Sri Lanka. They played ten matches, all but one of them being limited-overs games of 45 overs' duration. Of these, they won five and lost three, with one abandoned. The last fixture of the tour, a first-class match against a Board President's XI, was drawn. Andy Stovold struck form from the start and was a great success, although the only century was Tony Wright's 100 against Kandy District at Asgiriya. Phil Bainbridge returned the outstanding analysis of nine for 24 against Kurunegala District at Kurunegala, a record for a one-day game in Sri Lanka. Mark Alleyne, who earlier in the season had toured the island with the England Young Cricketers, also met with some success.

SRI LANKA BOARD PRESIDENT'S XI v GLOUCESTERSHIRE

At Singhalese Sports Club, Colombo, April 8, 9, 10. Drawn. Toss: Gloucestershire.

Gloucestershire

A. W. Stovold retired hurt	24		
A. J. Wright b Kuruppuarachchi	1	– b Kuruppuarachchi	6
P. W. Romaines b John	11	– b John	60
K. P. Tomlins c A. M. de Silva b Anurasiri	29	– c Kaluperuma b Anurasiri	65
M. W. Alleyne c A. M. de Silva b Kaluperuma	35	– b Anurasiri	22
P. Bainbridge b Wijegunaward	40	– c P. A. de Silva b Kaluperuma	15
†R. C. Russell c Kaluperuma b Wijegunaward	12	– not out	39
J. W. Lloyds c de Alwis b Kaluperuma	2	– run out	4
*D. A. Graveney not out	14	– not out	5
D. V. Lawrence c A. M. de Silva b Kaluperuma	0		
G. E. Sainsbury run out	12		
L-b 8, n-b 10	18	B 3, l-b 2	5

1/18 2/74 3/83 4/146 5/159   197   1/7 2/115 3/145   (6 wkts dec.) 221
6/166 7/166 8/166 9/197   4/166 5/191 6/196

Bowling: *First Innings*—John 15-4-45-1; Kuruppuarachchi 11-1-46-1; Wijegunaward 10-2-38-2; Anurasiri 11.4-3-33-1; Kaluperuma 14-3-28-3. *Second Innings*—John 13-1-30-1; Kuruppuarachchi 9-1-32-1; Wijegunaward 7-1-41-0; Anurasiri 19-3-64-2; Kaluperuma 15-4-49-1.

Sri Lanka Board President's XI

D. Ranatunga b Graveney	12	– lbw b Lawrence	0
A. M. de Silva st Russell b Graveney	70	– not out	58
S. K. Kaluperuma c Alleyne b Bainbridge	58	– c Russell b Lawrence	0
P. A. de Silva lbw b Bainbridge	1	– c Tomlins b Lawrence	71
*R. S. Madugalle not out	3	– b Lawrence	2
H. P. Tillekeratne c Wright b Graveney	10	– not out	13
†M. C. C. E. de Alwis c Lawrence b Bainbridge	4		
B 8, l-b 2, w 1	11	L-b 2, n-b 1	3

1/40 2/150 3/151 4/164 5/169   (6 wkts dec.) 169   1/0 2/2 3/123 4/128   (4 wkts) 147

S. D. Anurasiri, V. B. John, K. Wijegunaward and A. K. Kuruppuarachchi did not bat.

Bowling: *First Innings*—Lawrence 12-1-33-0; Sainsbury 5-2-15-0; Graveney 29-10-62-3; Bainbridge 16-4-33-3; Alleyne 3-0-15-0; Wright 1-0-1-0. *Second Innings*—Lawrence 11-1-46-4; Graveney 13-1-50-0; Bainbridge 8-0-23-0; Lloyds 4-0-26-0.

Umpires: A. C. Felsinger and W. A. U. Wickremasinghe.

CRICKET IN ZIMBABWE, 1986-87

By ALWYN PICHANICK

The 1986-87 season in Zimbabwe again saw two international teams visit the country. The first of the visitors were the third Young West Indies team to tour Zimbabwe since 1981, and on this occasion they were officially regarded as a "West Indies B" team. The tour schedule provided for four three-day matches against Zimbabwe, two three-day matches against President's XIs, five one-day matches against Zimbabwe, and one-day matches against a Zimbabwe President's XI and Zimbabwe Country Districts. However, owing to the period of mourning following the death of the President of Mozambique, the itinerary was hastily altered. One of the three-day matches against Zimbabwe was cancelled and another one was converted into a four-day fixture.

The visitors proved to be a most effective combination and won both series against Zimbabwe. In the first-class series, they won two of the three fixtures, with the third, played in Bulawayo, being drawn; in the one-day series, which was very exciting, they ultimately triumphed by three matches to two. The visitors also won the two other one-day fixtures, while the two first-class fixtures against President's XIs were drawn.

Although the results were somewhat disappointing from a Zimbabwean point of view, it was pleasing to observe the development of several of the younger Zimbabwean cricketers who played against the West Indians. The improvement shown by Christopher James was particularly noteworthy. The outstanding performers for Zimbabwe were the captain, David Houghton, and Andy Pycroft with the bat, while John Traicos, as ever, bowled immaculately and Peter Rawson turned in several good all-round performances.

The second visit of the season was undertaken by a Pakistan B team, which comprised several players with Test experience. The itinerary was a similar one to that undertaken by West Indies B and again the visitors won the five-match one-day series 3-2. It was a closely fought rubber, with Zimbabwe perhaps unfortunate in that the fourth fixture was interrupted by rain. The Pakistanis, batting second when it was apparent that their innings would not be completed, were able to adjust their manner of batting to achieve a match-winning run-rate.

The three first-class fixtures against Zimbabwe were all drawn, but interesting cricket was played. In the three-day fixture against Zimbabwe B, which was later ruled as first-class by the Pakistan Board of Control, Pakistan B won by three wickets after being 110 behind on the first innings and being set a target of 265 following an enterprising declaration by the Zimbabwe B captain, Ali Shah. The three one-day games against the President's XI were all won by the visitors.

From the Zimbabwean viewpoint, the highlight was the emergence of Kevin Arnott, who batted outstandingly in all the fixtures in which he played against the visitors. He was included in the Zimbabwean squad for the Reliance World Cup in India and Pakistan, which was announced at the conclusion of the Pakistan B tour. Otherwise, the squad was comprised almost entirely of players who had represented the country for some considerable time.

A pleasing feature of the season was the development and advancement through the various age groups in school teams of promising black players, and when Farayi Nhongerai was selected for one of the President's XI fixtures against Pakistan B, he became the first black cricketer to play in a major match. There is no doubt that he was the first of many who will soon be making their mark on the national scene for Zimbabwe.

WEST INDIES B IN ZIMBABWE, 1986-87

†At Harare South Country Club, Harare, September 30. West Indies B won by 172 runs. West Indies B 233 for seven (50 overs) (C. A. Best 40, L. L. Lawrence 59, R. M. Otto 46); Zimbabwe Country Districts 61 (25.5 overs) (V. S. Greene three for 15).

ZCU PRESIDENT'S XI v WEST INDIES B

At Harare Sports Club, Harare, October 2, 3, 4. Drawn. Toss: West Indies B. Butchart's seven catches were a record for a first-class match in Zimbabwe.

ZCU President's XI

R. D. Brown c Simmons b Merrick	13	– c Hooper b Merrick	9
G. A. Paterson run out	31	– c Best b Baptiste	31
A. Viljoen c Williams b Baptiste	10	– c Adams b Baptiste	2
G. C. Wallace c Best b Hooper	33	– c and b Simmons	27
*†D. L. Houghton c Simmons b Etienne	119	– b Baptiste	4
C. D. James c Merrick b Etienne	41	– c Williams b Baptiste	12
I. P. Butchart c Williams b Merrick	17	– c Williams b Baptiste	18
M. P. Jarvis c Otto b Merrick	5	– c Etienne b Simmons	4
D. H. Brain b Baptiste	6	– not out	6
C. J. Cox b Merrick	0	– c Hooper b Baptiste	2
K. G. Duers not out	1		
L-b 7, w 7, n-b 6	20	B 7, l-b 4, w 7, n-b 6	24

1/26 2/53 3/83 4/124 5/260   296   1/14 2/37 3/50   (9 wkts dec.) 139
6/267 7/281 8/294 9/296   4/68 5/93 6/111
                                                7/127 8/137 9/139

Bowling: *First Innings*—Merrick 18-7-33-4; Baptiste 20.3-2-84-2; Simmons 3-0-10-0; Adams 8-0-39-0; Etienne 22-4-50-2; Hooper 24-5-70-1; Best 1-0-3-0. *Second Innings*—Merrick 9-3-23-1; Baptiste 25-9-52-6; Simmons 16-3-53-2.

West Indies B

*C. A. Best lbw b Jarvis	7	– (3) c Butchart b Jarvis	0
P. V. Simmons c Butchart b Jarvis	7	– (1) c Brown b Jarvis	4
L. L. Lawrence c and b Duers	4	– (2) c Butchart b Cox	14
A. F. D. Jackman c Paterson b Duers	0	– (8) not out	45
R. M. Otto c Butchart b Cox	30	– (4) c Butchart b Cox	11
C. L. Hooper c Brain b Cox	21	– (5) c Paterson b Brain	88
E. A. E. Baptiste lbw b Jarvis	55	– (6) c Houghton b Jarvis	5
J. C. Adams c Butchart b Duers	2	– (7) b Brain	26
†D. Williams c Butchart b Jarvis	1	– st Houghton b Cox	25
T. A. Merrick c Brain b Cox	10	– not out	0
J. T. Etienne not out	19		
L-b 4	4	B 3, l-b 5, w 1	9

1/7 2/7 3/12 4/22 5/64   160   1/17 2/19 3/29 4/43   (8 wkts) 227
6/86 7/98 8/99 9/109   5/48 6/147 7/168 8/226

Bowling: *First Innings*—Duers 20-4-51-3; Jarvis 10.1-4-17-3; Butchart 7-1-17-0; Cox 14-0-71-4. *Second Innings*—Duers 7-2-20-0; Jarvis 19-6-49-3; Cox 29-7-94-3; Brain 14-3-44-2; Butchart 8-2-12-0.

Umpires: P. Latham and A. Stone.

†At Harare Sports Club, Harare, October 5. Zimbabwe won by 37 runs. Zimbabwe 213 for nine (50 overs) (A. C. Waller 35, D. L. Houghton 34, I. P. Butchart 52; V. S. Greene three for 41); West Indies B 176 (43.3 overs) (C. L. Hooper 84, E. A. E. Baptiste 38; A. J. Traicos three for 55).

†At Mutare, October 8. West Indies B won by six wickets. ZCU President's XI 189 for seven (50 overs) (G. A. Paterson 38, C. M. Robertson 31, C. D. James 42 not out; P. V. Simmons three for 33, C. L. Hooper three for 33); West Indies B 190 for four (42 overs) (L. L. Lawrence 63, A. F. D. Jackman 42, C. L. Hooper 34 not out).

ZIMBABWE v WEST INDIES B

At Harare Sports Club, Harare, October 10, 11, 13. West Indies B won by an innings and 58 runs. Toss: West Indies B.

Zimbabwe

R. D. Brown c Williams b Merrick	44	– c Jackman b Merrick 2
G. A. Paterson c Hooper b Merrick	20	– c Best b Baptiste 14
A. C. Waller c Williams b Merrick	6	– (4) lbw b Baptiste 28
*D. L. Houghton c Otto b Baptiste	10	– (5) c Williams b Ferris 0
G. C. Wallace c Williams b Baptiste	4	– (6) c Best b Baptiste 12
P. W. E. Rawson c Jackman b Hooper	18	– (7) lbw b Baptiste 0
I. P. Butchart c Jackman b Hooper	0	– (3) c Simmons b Merrick 6
E. A. Brandes lbw b Baptiste	22	– (3) c Greene b Baptiste 31
A. J. Traicos c Williams b Merrick	7	– c Simmons b Greene 10
M. P. Jarvis c Simmons b Ferris	7	– c Best b Greene 19
C. J. Cox not out	2	– not out 0
B 1, l-b 8, w 1, n-b 12	22	B 4, l-b 3, w 3, n-b 4 14
	162	**136**

1/45 2/54 3/71 4/79 5/120   1/12 2/56 3/63 4/67 5/96
6/120 7/121 8/129 9/154   6/96 7/101 8/114 9/135

Bowling: *First Innings*—Merrick 15-2-55-4; Ferris 15-3-32-1; Baptiste 15.2-5-32-3; Greene 10-3-22-0; Hooper 8-2-12-2. *Second Innings*—Merrick 19-6-41-2; Ferris 8-1-38-1; Baptiste 15-5-40-5; Hooper 2-0-9-0; Greene 1.3-0-1-2.

West Indies B

P. V. Simmons c Waller b Butchart	...107	E. A. E. Baptiste lbw b Rawson 11
L. L. Lawrence lbw b Rawson	3	V. S. Greene not out 14
*C. A. Best c Waller b Rawson	43	B 4, l-b 6 10
R. M. Otto c Brown b Traicos	16	
A. F. D. Jackman b Rawson	75	1/5 2/128 3/147 (6 wkts dec.) 356
C. L. Hooper not out	77	4/216 5/315 6/333

†D. Williams, T. A. Merrick and G. J. F. Ferris did not bat.

Bowling: Rawson 20-4-96-4; Brandes 15-0-77-0; Cox 13-1-51-0; Jarvis 14-6-32-0; Traicos 14-2-48-1; Butchart 8-0-42-1.

Umpires: K. Kanjee and P. Latham.

†At Harare Sports Club, Harare, October 12. West Indies B won by eight wickets. Zimbabwe 268 for six (50 overs) (G. A. Paterson 122, A. H. Shah 46, D. L. Houghton 48); West Indies B 272 for two (35.5 overs) (P. V. Simmons 166 not out, C. A. Best 30, A. F. D. Jackman 64 not out).

ZIMBABWE v WEST INDIES B

At Bulawayo, October 16, 17, 18. Drawn. Toss: Zimbabwe.

West Indies B

*C. A. Best c Jarvis b Butchart	47	– c Robertson b Rawson	6
P. V. Simmons lbw b Jarvis	11	– c Pycroft b Rawson	25
L. L. Lawrence c Brandes b Shah	42	– c Butchart b Traicos	6
A. F. D. Jackman lbw b Jarvis	2	– c Waller b Butchart	48
R. M. Otto c Traicos b Butchart	24	– not out	53
C. L. Hooper b Jarvis	32	– c Pycroft b Rawson	10
E. A. E. Baptiste c Robertson b Rawson	24	– lbw b Jarvis	10
V. S. Greene b Jarvis	10	– not out	2
†D. Williams b Traicos	1		
T. A. Merrick not out	16		
G. J. F. Ferris lbw b Jarvis	11		
L-b 12, w 2, n-b 1	15	L-b 4	4

1/20 2/28 3/81 4/110 5/167   235   1/16 2/35 3/41   (6 wkts dec.) 164
6/167 7/195 8/202 9/206   4/108 5/132 6/155

In the first innings L. L. Lawrence, when 4, retired hurt at 32 and resumed at 81.

Bowling: *First Innings*—Rawson 27-11-43-1; Jarvis 27.3-7-74-5; Butchart 21-10-40-2; Brandes 11-3-39-0; Shah 7-3-15-1; Traicos 4-1-12-1. *Second Innings*—Rawson 19-8-36-3; Jarvis 7-1-31-1; Traicos 13-0-56-1; Butchart 8-0-37-1.

Zimbabwe

G. A. Paterson b Ferris	4	– lbw b Ferris	10
A. H. Shah c Best b Merrick	1	– c Williams b Ferris	5
C. M. Robertson c Jackman b Ferris	17	– st Williams b Hooper	30
A. J. Pycroft c Hooper b Ferris	24	– b Hooper	42
*†D. L. Houghton b Ferris	0	– (6) c Simmons b Merrick	56
A. C. Waller c Williams b Baptiste	19	– (5) c Best b Merrick	31
P. W. E. Rawson b Merrick	22	– c Best b Ferris	51
I. P. Butchart not out	33	– c Best b Ferris	0
E. A. Brandes b Merrick	6	– not out	0
A. J. Traicos lbw b Merrick	0	– not out	0
M. P. Jarvis c Best b Greene	12		
L-b 5, n-b 1	6	B 3, l-b 11, w 2	16

1/5 2/5 3/42 4/42 5/63   144   1/13 2/18 3/86 4/121   (8 wkts) 241
6/83 7/99 8/111 9/111   5/133 6/239 7/239 8/241

Bowling: *First Innings*—Merrick 17-5-45-4; Ferris 15-3-57-4; Baptiste 12-4-36-1; Greene 0.3-0-1-1. *Second Innings*—Merrick 13-1-64-2; Ferris 12-3-40-4; Greene 14-5-28-0; Baptiste 6-1-25-0; Hooper 13-0-70-2.

Umpires: P. Latham and E. Gilmore.

†At Bulawayo, October 19. West Indies B won by 147 runs. West Indies B 280 for seven (50 overs) (P. V. Simmons 48, L. L. Lawrence 117 not out, C. A. Best 40, E. A. E. Baptiste 30; I. P. Butchart three for 52); Zimbabwe 133 (39.5 overs) (V. S. Greene three for 18, E. A. E. Baptiste four for 32).

ZCU PRESIDENT'S XI v WEST INDIES B

At Harare Sports Club, October 21, 22, 23. Drawn. Toss: ZCU President's XI.

West Indies B

P. V. Simmons c Houghton b Brandes . 21	†D. Williams c Shah b Brain 8
L. L. Lawrence c Walton b Cox 63	
J. D. Charles c and b Duers 185	B 1, l-b 5, w 4 10
*C. A. Best c Houghton b Brandes 52	
R. M. Otto not out 62	1/24 2/122 3/256 (6 wkts dec.) 414
J. C. Adams b Brain 13	4/369 5/400 6/414

C. L. Hooper, E. A. E. Baptiste, V. S. Greene and J. T. Etienne did not bat.

Bowling: Brandes 24–5–115–2; Duers 22–5–76–1; Brain 18–0–80–2; Cox 16–2–71–1; Shah 11–1–31–0; Meman 13–3–35–0.

ZCU President's XI

A. H. Shah c Williams b Baptiste 25	D. H. Brain c Greene b Baptiste 58
K. G. Walton lbw b Baptiste 6	C. J. Cox b Simmons 26
C. A. T. Hodgson c Etienne b Greene . . 52	K. G. Duers not out 12
E. A. Brandes c and b Baptiste 0	
C. D. James c Hooper b Baptiste 30	B 2, l-b 6, w 1, n-b 3 12
*D. L. Houghton lbw b Baptiste 5	
M. A. Meman c Williams b Baptiste . . . 0	1/11 2/59 3/63 4/98 5/114 239
†A. Flower c Hooper b Greene 13	6/114 7/123 8/199 9/200

Bowling: Baptiste 36–9–92–7; Greene 32–6–74–2; Adams 13–2–37–0; Etienne 12–9–4–0; Hooper 5–1–12–0; Best 3–1–6–0; Simmons 4–1–6–1.

Umpires: J. Bulling and K. Kanjee.

ZIMBABWE v WEST INDIES B

At Harare Sports Club, Harare, October 25, 27, 29. West Indies B won by ten wickets with a day to spare. There was no play on October 26 and 28, which were designated days of mourning for President Machel of Mozambique. Toss: Zimbabwe.

Zimbabwe

G. A. Paterson c Williams b Greene	15	– c Williams b Merrick	0
C. M. Robertson c Charles b Greene	13	– lbw b Ferris	0
A. J. Pycroft run out	1	– c Baptiste b Merrick	0
A. C. Waller c Williams b Baptiste	9	– b Ferris	18
*†D. L. Houghton c sub b Baptiste	39	– c Best b Greene	6
C. D. James lbw b Merrick	5	– c Best b Baptiste	9
P. W. E. Rawson not out	52	– c Williams b Greene	0
I. P. Butchart b Ferris	4	– not out	22
E. A. Brandes c Williams b Merrick	17	– c Best b Baptiste	7
A. J. Traicos lbw b Merrick	3	– c Hooper b Baptiste	0
M. P. Jarvis c Ferris b Merrick	0	– b Greene	2
L-b 6, w 1, n-b 5	12	L-b 8, n-b 4	12

1/25 2/26 3/32 4/49 5/59	170
6/98 7/112 8/154 9/169	
1/0 2/0 3/4 4/35 5/35	76
6/35 7/49 8/65 9/67	

Bowling: *First Innings*—Merrick 15.5–0–69–4; Ferris 16–4–38–1; Greene 15–4–20–2; Baptiste 17–3–29–2; Hooper 5–2–8–0. *Second Innings*—Merrick 13–2–29–2; Ferris 7–4–10–2; Greene 10.2–5–11–3; Baptiste 10–3–18–3.

West Indies B

*C. A. Best c Houghton b Jarvis	32	– not out	58
P. V. Simmons c Houghton b Brandes	0	– not out	15
J. D. Charles b Brandes	2		
A. F. D. Jackman c Houghton b Jarvis	19		
R. M. Otto c Pycroft b Rawson	29		
C. L. Hooper c Butchart b Brandes	34		
E. A. E. Baptiste c Houghton b Rawson	32		
V. S. Greene not out	10		
†D. Williams b Brandes	1		
T. A. Merrick lbw b Brandes	3		
G. J. F. Ferris lbw b Rawson	0		
B 2, l-b 4, w 2, n-b 4	12	L-b 2	2
	174	(no wkt)	75

1/1 2/17 3/48 4/76 5/94
6/155 7/160 8/163 9/171

Bowling: *First Innings*—Brandes 20–4–56–5; Jarvis 16–2–51–2; Rawson 18–4–44–3; Butchart 4–0–17–0; Traicos 1–1–0–0. *Second Innings*—Brandes 7.1–0–42–0; Jarvis 4–0–13–0; Rawson 3–1–18–0; Waller 1–1–0–0.

Umpires: K. Kanjee and D. C. Moore-Gordon.

†At Harare Sports Club, Harare, November 1. Zimbabwe won by 106 runs. Zimbabwe 261 for eight (50 overs) (D. L. Houghton 59, A. J. Pycroft 58, A. C. Waller 41; T. A. Merrick three for 57); West Indies B 155 (32 overs) (C. A. Best 57, R. M. Otto 31; I. P. Butchart three for 31).

†At Harare Sports Club, Harare, November 2. West Indies B won by eight wickets. After rain had interrupted play after 44 overs of Zimbabwe's innings, the match was reduced to 44 overs a side. Zimbabwe 128 for six (44 overs) (A. J. Pycroft 46 not out); West Indies B 132 for two (19 overs) (P. V. Simmons 75, L. L. Lawrence 32).

PAKISTAN B IN ZIMBABWE, 1986-87

†At Harare Sports Club, Harare, March 8. Zimbabwe won by six wickets. Pakistan B 173 for eight (50 overs) (Sajid Ali 32, Aamer Sohail 31, Asif Mujtaba 42 not out; P. W. E. Rawson three for 29); Zimbabwe 177 for four (38.3 overs) (A. J. Pycroft 47 not out, D. L. Houghton 86).

ZIMBABWE B v PAKISTAN B

At Harare South Country Club Ground, Harare, March 10, 11, 12. Pakistan B won by three wickets. Toss: Zimbabwe B.

Zimbabwe B

K. G. Walton c Zulqarnain b Zakir	0	– c Zulqarnain b Barkatullah	10
K. J. Arnott c Zulqarnain b Sajjad	70	– b Nadeem	54
D. G. Goodwin c Zakir b Nadeem	41	– c Zulqarnain b Barkatullah	10
*A. H. Shah c Sajjad b Asif	84	– c Sajid b Nadeem	42
C. D. James c Sajjad b Barkatullah	44	– b Nadeem	13
†W. R. James c Shaukat b Nadeem	19	– (9) not out	0
T. L. Penney not out	28		
K. J. Brunt c Sajid b Zakir	3	– (7) c Asif b Zakir	8
D. B. Lake not out	23	– (8) c Mazhar b Zakir	4
M. P. Jarvis (did not bat)		– (6) b Zakir	4
B 7, l-b 8, w 2, n-b 2	19	B 4, l-b 2, n-b 3	9

1/0 2/65 3/183 4/219 5/249   (7 wkts dec.) 331   1/39 2/57 3/87   (8 wkts dec.) 154
6/302 7/307   4/126 5/141 6/143
                                                    7/154 8/154

C. J. Cox did not bat.

Bowling: *First Innings*—Zakir 19-7-59-2; Mohsin 23-4-78-0; Barkatullah 18-3-74-1; Nadeem 22-8-35-2; Sajjad 15-2-48-1; Asif 11-2-22-1. *Second Innings*—Mohsin 10-4-27-0; Barkatullah 9-0-43-2; Ameer 2-1-7-0; Sajjad 2-1-1-0; Nadeem 9-2-23-3; Zakir 8.5-0-47-3.

Pakistan B

Sajid Ali c W. R. James b Jarvis	4	– c W. R. James b Brunt	89
Shaukat Mirza c W. R. James b Lake	30	– not out	105
Ameer Akbar c Cox b Lake	117	– b Jarvis	6
*Asif Mujtaba c W. R. James b Jarvis	9	– c Walton b Brunt	1
Mazhar Hussain c W. R. James b Cox	9	– run out	21
Sajjad Akbar c Walton b Jarvis	23	– run out	17
Zakir Khan c W. R. James b Lake	2	– (9) not out	3
†Zulqarnain b Cox	5	– (7) run out	3
Mohsin Kamal not out	13	– (8) run out	10
Barkatullah c Goodwin b Cox	0		
Nadeem Ghauri c Cox b Jarvis	2		
B 4, l-b 1, w 1, n-b 1	7	B 2, l-b 8	10

1/12 2/45 3/62 4/82 5/181   221   1/143 2/162 3/165   (7 wkts) 265
6/184 7/201 8/205 9/211   4/202 5/232
                                                   6/248 7/261

Bowling: *First Innings*—Jarvis 24.3-8-71-4; Lake 16-2-59-3; Cox 18-8-27-3; Brunt 11-1-51-0; Shah 6-1-8-0. *Second Innings*—Jarvis 11-0-84-1; Lake 15.2-2-67-0; Cox 12-1-61-0; Brunt 7-0-43-2.

Umpires: G. Batte and P. Latham.

†At Harare Sports Club, Harare, March 14. Pakistan B won by 98 runs. Pakistan B 284 for six (50 overs) (Sajid Ali 109, Zaheer Abbas 49, Asif Mujtaba 46 not out, Zulqarnain 30); Zimbabwe Cricket Union President's XI 186 (43.4 overs) (R. D. Brown 34, C. D. James 52; Nadeem Ghauri five for 40).

†At Harare Sports Club, Harare, March 15. Pakistan B won by four wickets. Zimbabwe 210 (50 overs) (A. H. Shah 35, A. J. Pycroft 30, I. P. Butchart 44); Pakistan B 211 for six (44.2 overs) (Aamer Sohail 72, Zaheer Abbas 35, Asif Mujtaba 37 not out).

ZIMBABWE v PAKISTAN B

At Bulawayo Athletic Club, Bulawayo, March 19, 20, 21. Drawn. Toss: Zimbabwe. Brown kept wicket in Pakistan B's second innings.

Zimbabwe

R. D. Brown b Zakir	5	– c Sohail b Zakir	20
G. A. Paterson lbw b Mohsin	19	– b Nadeem	26
K. J. Arnott c Sohail b Mohsin	55	– c Asif b Zakir	10
A. J. Pycroft c Nadeem b Nasir	0	– c Akbar b Nadeem	28
†D. L. Houghton b Mohsin	96	– c Akbar b Nadeem	21
A. H. Shah b Mohsin	22	– c Shaukat b Mohsin	0
P. W. E. Rawson lbw b Nadeem	10	– c and b Nadeem	48
M. A. Meman c Sohail b Mohsin	5	– (9) c Asif b Nasir	5
E. A. Brandes c Sohail b Mohsin	5	– (8) b Nasir	1
*A. J. Traicos b Mohsin	23	– not out	4
K. G. Duers not out	3	– not out	8
B 2, l-b 6, n-b 1	9	B 9, l-b 2, n-b 1	12

1/6 2/42 3/43 4/175 5/180   252   1/48 2/62 3/71   (9 wkts dec.) 183
6/213 7/213 8/222 9/225   4/100 5/100 6/163
                                    7/164 8/165 9/170

Bowling: *First Innings*—Zakir 21–6–48–1; Mohsin 30–7–87–7; Nasir 15–3–40–1; Nadeem 30–9–63–1; Mazhar 2–0–6–0. *Second Innings*—Zakir 13–3–32–2; Mohsin 17–6–42–1; Nadeem 26–5–80–4; Nasir 9–1–18–2.

Pakistan B

Sajid Ali b Duers	27	– c Pycroft b Rawson	2
†Aamer Sohail c Houghton b Rawson	3	– b Traicos	14
Ameer Akbar c Paterson b Duers	6	– c Brown b Duers	24
Shaukat Mirza b Brandes	17	– c Brown b Brandes	7
*Asif Mujtaba c and b Rawson	25	– not out	22
Anwar Miandad c Meman b Rawson	6	– c Brandes b Duers	8
Mazhar Hussain c and b Traicos	1	– c Brown b Duers	0
Mohsin Kamal lbw b Brandes	10		
Nasir Javed c Arnott b Duers	25	– (8) c Pycroft b Traicos	5
Nadeem Ghauri c Houghton b Rawson	18		
Zakir Khan not out	3	– (9) not out	0
L-b 3, n-b 1	4	L-b 3, n-b 4	7

1/13 2/28 3/37 4/66 5/86   145   1/2 2/24 3/35 4/66   (7 wkts) 89
6/87 7/89 8/97 9/124   5/81 6/81 7/87

Bowling: *First Innings*—Rawson 22–5–64–4; Duers 9.2–2–22–3; Traicos 16–7–24–1; Brandes 11–2–32–2. *Second Innings*—Rawson 8–3–15–1; Traicos 19–14–13–2; Brandes 7–1–22–1; Shah 6–4–3–0; Duers 13–7–20–3; Meman 3–0–13–0.

Umpires: E. Gilmour and R. Jackson.

†At Bulawayo, March 22. Zimbabwe won by six wickets. Pakistan B 125 (43 overs) (Asif Mujtaba 31; A. H. Shah three for 37, E. A. Brandes three for 4); Zimbabwe 126 for four (38 overs) (R. D. Brown 47, A. J. Pycroft 44 not out).

ZIMBABWE v PAKISTAN B

At Harare Sports Club, Harare, March 24, 25, 26. Drawn. Toss: Pakistan B.

Pakistan B

Sajid Ali c Houghton b Rawson	75	– c Pycroft b Rawson 0
Aamer Sohail c Shah b Rawson	21	– c Traicos b Brandes 24
Ameer Akbar b Brandes	6	– not out 30
Shaukat Mirza c Shah b Butchart	66	– c and b Brandes 26
*Asif Mujtaba c Butchart b Brandes	22	
Mazhar Hussain c Houghton b Brandes	0	– (5) c Houghton b Butchart 19
†Zulqarnain c Arnott b Butchart	13	
Zakir Khan c Arnott b Rawson	2	
Nasir Javed b Brandes	0	
Mohsin Kamal c Butchart b Traicos	5	
Barkatullah not out	0	
B 1, l-b 2, w 2, n-b 5	10	B 2, w 1, n-b 1 4

1/48 2/78 3/108 4/127 5/146   220   1/0 2/48 3/82 4/103   (4 wkts) 103
6/166 7/191 8/191 9/220

In the first innings Asif Mujtaba retired hurt at 116 and resumed at 166. In the second innings Ameer Akbar retired hurt at 36 and resumed at 82.

Bowling: *First Innings*—Rawson 25-7-88-3; Duers 9-3-30-0; Traicos 16.1-4-29-1; Brandes 25-9-57-4; Butchart 9-4-13-2. *Second Innings*—Rawson 7-0-25-1; Brandes 10.5-1-40-2; Duers 4-0-19-0; Butchart 7-2-10-1; Traicos 7-4-7-0.

Zimbabwe

R. D. Brown c Zulqarnain b Zakir	3	A. H. Shah not out 11
G. A. Paterson c Sohail b Zakir	7	
K. J. Arnott not out	45	L-b 3, w 5 8
A. J. Pycroft c Akbar b Zakir	3	
†D. L. Houghton b Mohsin	14	1/10 2/11 3/18 4/51 (4 wkts dec.) 91

P. W. E. Rawson, I. P. Butchart, E. A. Brandes, *A. J. Traicos and K. G. Duers did not bat.

Bowling: Zakir 16-2-46-3; Barkatullah 8-5-4-0; Mohsin 9-0-38-1.

Umpires: D. O. Oslear and I. Robinson.

†At Harare Sports Club, Harare, March 28. Pakistan B won by 64 runs. Pakistan B 268 for five (50 overs) (Ameer Akbar 125 not out, Asif Mujtaba 44, Sajjad Akbar 36 not out); Zimbabwe Cricket Union President's XI 204 (46 overs) (R. D. Brown 35, G. C. Wallace 36, D. L. Houghton 61; Nadeem Ghauri five for 51).

†At Harare Sports Club, Harare, March 29. Pakistan B won on faster scoring-rate. Zimbabwe 230 for seven (50 overs) (G. A. Paterson 88, R. D. Brown 45; Nadeem Ghauri three for 51); Pakistan B 117 for five (24 overs) (Ameer Akbar 35, Asif Mujtaba 37 not out; P. W. E. Rawson three for 47).

†At Triangle Country Club, Harare, April 1. Pakistan B won by 56 runs. Pakistan B 259 for four (50 overs) (Sajid Ali 87, Aamer Sohail 82, Shaukat Mirza 32); Zimbabwe Cricket Union President's XI 203 (46.5 overs) (K. J. Arnott 79, D. L. Houghton 56; Nadeem Ghauri three for 40, Sajjad Akbar three for 25).

ZIMBABWE v PAKISTAN B

At Harare Sports Club, Harare, April 3, 4, 6. Drawn. Toss: Zimbabwe.

Zimbabwe

R. D. Brown c Sohail b Nadeem	35	– c Sajid b Mohsin 8
G. A. Paterson c Zulqarnain b Mohsin	8	– c Nadeem b Mohsin 29
K. J. Arnott b Zakir	59	– retired hurt 0
A. J. Pycroft c Zulqarnain b Mohsin	34	– (5) b Zakir 57
†D. L. Houghton b Barkatullah	34	– (6) b Sajjad 65
A. H. Shah c Zulqarnain b Zakir	0	– (8) not out 19
P. W. E. Rawson lbw b Barkatullah	51	– (4) b Barkatullah 0
I. P. Butchart c Sohail b Barkatullah	23	– (7) c Sajjad b Zakir 0
M. A. Meman not out	2	
E. A. Brandes c Zulqarnain b Barkatullah	0	
*A. J. Traicos c Nadeem b Barkatullah	2	
L-b 10, w 1, n-b 9	20	B 1, l-b 14, n-b 1 16

1/18 2/62 3/143 4/147 5/154   268   1/22 2/31 3/74   (6 wkts dec.) 194
6/211 7/263 8/263 9/263   4/128 5/140 6/194

Bowling: *First Innings*—Mohsin 24-2-86-2; Zakir 22-8-46-2; Nadeem 20-6-38-1; Barkatullah 19.5-5-65-5; Sajjad 6-0-23-0. *Second Innings*—Mohsin 15-3-49-2; Barkatullah 8-2-31-1; Zakir 21-3-51-2; Nadeem 5-0-23-0; Asif 1-0-2-0; Sajjad 6.3-0-23-1.

Pakistan B

Sajid Ali b Brandes	66	– c Brandes b Rawson	12
Aamer Sohail c Houghton b Brandes	10	– lbw b Meman	11
Ameer Akbar c Paterson b Brandes	37	– lbw b Brandes	0
Shaukat Mirza b Brandes	9	– not out	27
*Asif Mujtaba c Meman b Brandes	1	– b Brandes	2
Sajjad Akbar c Pycroft b Meman	34	– not out	26
†Zulqarnain lbw b Butchart	3		
Zakir Khan c Pycroft b Meman	4		
Mohsin Kamal c Pycroft b Meman	13		
Barkatullah not out	5		
Nadeem Ghauri c Traicos b Brandes	0		
L-b 7, w 2, n-b 4	13	L-b 1, n-b 2	3

1/14 2/110 3/127 4/127 5/132   195   1/23 2/23 3/25 4/37   (4 wkts) 81
6/139 7/161 8/183 9/194

Bowling: *First Innings*—Rawson 20-6-59-0; Brandes 20.5-4-59-6; Butchart 11-2-31-1; Traicos 6-1-13-0; Shah 3-0-5-0; Meman 6-1-21-3. *Second Innings*—Rawson 17-6-27-1; Meman 9-3-23-1; Brandes 11-4-22-2; Traicos 8-5-6-0; Butchart 3-1-2-0.

Umpires: R. Jackson and K. Kanjee.

†At Harare Sports Club, Harare, April 5. Pakistan B won by four wickets. Zimbabwe 223 for eight (50 overs) (A. J. Pycroft 32, D. L. Houghton 50, I. P. Butchart 39 not out; Zakir Khan three for 16, Sajjad Akbar three for 32); Pakistan B 224 for six (48.5 overs) (Ameer Akbar 66, Asif Mujtaba 54 not out).

CRICKET IN DENMARK, 1987

Although the Danish national team ventured as far afield as Bermuda and hosted Holland for the first time in ten years in 1987, the greatest interest of the season finally centred on the local championship which, until ten days of its conclusion, might have been won by any of four teams. Esbjerg needed an outright victory over Herning to head the 1986 champions, Svanholm, and this they achieved, to take the title by a single point. At the foot of the table Aarhus and Ringsted, promoted after 1986, found the going too tough; they will give way in 1988 to the two Second Division winners, Skanderborg and Køge. A tendency towards inconsistency persisted throughout the season, but the player of the year was probably Esbjerg's Tim Jensen, whose performances included a good half-century against Holland.

At international level the Danish team was at its customary disadvantage, lacking the English county professionals, Mortensen and Henriksen, although the latter was nursing a back injury. A creditable draw in a two-day match was achieved in Bermuda, with Bredo, a young fast bowler, performing well. But both one-day games against Holland were lost, by margins which, local opinion considered, would hardly have been permitted had Mortensen been playing. If anything, the Danish fielding showed signs of a slight deterioration.

In the International Youth Tournament in Belfast, Denmark had one of its lean years, failing to achieve a win, but in Holland an Under-15 team won convincingly both its matches against the local side, which suggested better results ahead in two years' time. Winners of the national junior championship were Svanholm, against Esbjerg, while Nykøbing Mors triumphed over Nørrebro in the Boys (under 15). Nørrebro beat Herning in the Lilleput (under 13) – the former's teams consisting entirely of Pakistani players born in Denmark.

Denmark's women's teams proved too strong for a Holland junior women's team. The national women's title changed hands when Svanholm ended AB's reign of five seasons. In 1987, the Slagelse club became the fifth in Denmark to celebrate 100 years. In 1988 Dansk XL CC (Denmark's Forty Club) are 25 years old and host the Forty Clubs' tournament at Herning, in Jutland. – *Peter S. Hargreaves*.

CRICKET IN THE NETHERLANDS, 1987

Playing in the Reliance World Cup could have been Dutch cricket's finest hour, but the defeat by Zimbabwe in the 1986 ICC Trophy final, by 25 runs, meant that it was not to be. Inevitably, after such an eventful year, when in addition both India and New Zealand visited the Continent, 1987 was a comparatively quiet season. There was also a change of policy. Despite the success of the national team in 1986, in which "foreigners" Steve Atkinson (from England) and Rupert Gomes (Guyana), as well as the veteran wicket-keeper, Renee Schoonheim, played such a prominent part, the selectors decided to concentrate on Dutch nationals only – and in particular, young players.

In 1987, Holland entertained Surrey in May, playing and losing one limited-overs match. In July, a combined Oxford and Cambridge University team came to play two one-day games, one of which the Dutch won while the other was rained off, and then Holland travelled to Denmark, where they won both one-day matches comfortably. On a tour of Southern England that same month, Hampshire and Middlesex Second XIs, as well as Richmond CC, were beaten, but the Dutch lost to Surrey Second XI. Of other national teams in action, the Dutch

Ladies played their first three-day "Test" on home soil, losing to Ireland; the men's Under-21 team toured the West Midlands with great success, winning all five matches; and the Under-19 Colts performed creditably in the International Youth Tournament in Ireland.

VOC, of Rotterdam, won the First Division of the league championship for the fourth time in the 1980s, notably through the efforts of their captain and Dutch international, Roland Lefebvre, in the play-off matches. However, HBS The Hague jeopardised their chances of winning the league when they dismissed their Pakistani coach, Qasim Omar, before the end of the season. It was a brave decision. Meanwhile, in another part of The Hague, at HCC, for more than a century the bastion of Dutch cricket tradition, coloured clothing – pastel yellow – could be seen. – *David Hardy*.

PAKISTAN B IN KENYA, 1986-87

KENYA XI v PAKISTAN B

At Nairobi Gymkhana Club Ground, Nairobi, September 12, 13, 14. Pakistan B won by seven wickets. Toss: Kenya XI.

Kenya XI

B. Shah lbw b Mohsin	6	– b Nadeem		97
McDonald c Ijaz b Zakir	32	– c Ijaz b Sajjad		5
H. Mehta c Rizwan b Nadeem	33	– c Manzoor b Mohsin		23
Subtain b Manzoor	17	– c Zulqarnain b Mohsin		7
N. Verjee c Ijaz b Sajjad	22	– b Nadeem		16
T. Tikolo c Rizwan b Sajjad	79	– b Zakir		8
A. Boy c Zulqarnain b Sajjad	0	– c and b Sajjad		21
Muslim Kanji c Zulqarnain b Sajjad	2	– c and b Sajjad		2
Asif Karim lbw b Sajjad	0	– lbw b Rizwan		11
Zahoor Sheikh c Shahid b Sajjad	3	– not out		12
C. Udoyi not out	23	– b Sajjad		1
B 6, l-b 12, w 5, n-b 3	26	B 3, l-b 3, w 7, n-b 5		18
	243			**221**

1/10 2/73 3/107 4/121 5/180 6/184 7/202 8/204 9/209

1/27 2/70 3/86 4/114 5/125 6/188 7/193 8/196 9/218

Bowling: *First Innings*—Mohsin 12-0-63-1; Zakir 14-3-47-1; Nadeem 17-5-57-1; Sajjad 16.2-1-55-6; Manzoor 2-2-0-1; Rizwan 4-1-3-0. *Second Innings*—Mohsin 13-5-23-2; Zakir 13-4-18-1; Nadeem 27-6-64-2; Sajjad 32-8-78-4; Manzoor 6-0-28-0; Rizwan 3-0-4-1.

Pakistan B

Rizwan-uz-Zaman c Udoyi b Boy	66	– c Mehta b Asif		55
*Shoaib Mohammad c Muslim b Zahoor	6	– lbw b Asif		15
Shahid Anwar c Verjee b Mehta	80	– lbw b Asif		0
Sajjad Akbar lbw b Asif	0	– not out		23
Manzoor Elahi c Zahoor b Mehta	102			
Qasim Omar c Verjee b Mehta	0			
Ijaz Ahmed run out	34	– (5) not out		31
†Zulqarnain lbw b Asif	1			
Mohsin Kamal lbw b Asif	2			
Zakir Khan c Muslim b Zahoor	19			
Nadeem Ghauri not out	11			
L-b 7, w 1, n-b 1	9	B 1, l-b 9, w 1		11
	330	(3 wkts)		**135**

1/33 2/94 3/101 4/211 5/211 6/288 7/297 8/297 9/300

1/49 2/49 3/82

Bowling: *First Innings*—Zahoor 18-3-71-2; Udoyi 10-1-46-0; Boy 5-0-27-1; Asif 28-3-79-3; Verjee 3-0-26-0; Mehta 18-2-72-3; Tikolo 1-0-2-0. *Second Innings*—Zahoor 6-1-24-0; Udoyi 4-0-23-0; Boy 2-0-15-0; Asif 15-2-40-3; Mehta 9-1-23-0.

Umpires: M. Desai and S. Modi.

CRICKET IN CANADA, 1987

By KENNETH R. BULLOCK

Following the disappointment at Canada's seventh placing in the third ICC Trophy tournament in 1986, efforts in 1987 were concentrated on all aspects of rebuilding. This was particularly so at junior level. A most notable step was the establishment of a Development Programme Office in Regina, Saskatchewan, with a youth programme being developed in the city's schools. In addition, a junior tournament was held there for under-twelve and under-sixteen boys and girls.

Ontario's junior cricket continued its rapid expansion. In London, a programme involving 600 boys and girls from grades three to eight (ages eight to sixteen) culminated in a 48-team tournament. London also hosted an under-fifteen competition for teams from all Ontario leagues, while Toronto staged a similar six-a-side tournament for under-eighteens. In British Columbia, the Western Canada under-seventeen tournament attracted 37 boys from four provinces to Vancouver in July. In the national inter-provincial junior tournament, Ontario defeated Quebec.

On the international scene, Canada's under-nineteen team finished sixth of the seven entrants in the International Youth Tournament in Belfast, Northern Ireland, in July. Their only win was over Denmark, with their other five matches being lost. In October, a national senior side enjoyed a successful two-week tour of Barbados, where five matches were won, two lost and two rained off. The opposition was of a high calibre, with Gordon Greenidge playing in two of the matches and Joel Garner in one. Of the Canadians, Farouk Kirmani, Martin Johnson and Danny Singh were the leading batsmen while two spinners, Derek Etwaroo, an MCC Young Cricketer, and Kanti Patel, accounted for half the wickets taken.

At a national under-25 tournament held in Toronto in August, Alberta emerged as the winners. Cricket continues to grow in Alberta, with the game now very active in Red Deer, Lethbridge, Canmore and Medicine Hat, as well as the regular leagues in Calgary and Edmonton. Grace Church CC of the Toronto and District League won the Eastern final of the John Ross Robertson competition for clubs, but no winner was declared in the west. Highlights of activities in other provinces were visits made by New Brunswick and Quebec to Halifax, Nova Scotia, in July and by Nova Scotia to Saint John, New Brunswick, in August.

†CANADA v USA

At Winnipeg, Manitoba, September 5, 6, 7. Drawn. Toss: USA. Canada retained the K. Auty Trophy, which they have held since 1979, but the United States went closer than expected to pulling off a well-deserved upset. Although their decision to put Canada in produced an early success, Kirmani and Prashad then added 61 for the second wicket. Following Kirmani's departure at 69, Jayasekera held the innings together, hitting seven fours in his 76 before being ninth out. In reply, USA were 66 for two at the close and struggled on the second day to 160. Canada, having built on their lead, began the final day 135 ahead with seven wickets in hand, but from a promising position at 166 for four, they lost Jayasekera and Kirmani for the addition of 3 runs. When the last four wickets fell for just 25 more, the United States were left with four hours in which to score 220 to win. A shaky start to 76 for four was not promising, but Khan then hit a fine 74 not out which saw them finish only 29 runs short of their target.

Canada

O. Dipchand b Smythe	1	– b Lorrick 4
F. Kirmani b Shivnarine	33	– lbw b Khan 66
P. Prashad c and b Jackson	40	– c and b Stoute 42
†R. S. A. Jayasekera c Lashkari b Khan	76	– st Brearley b Stoute 8
S. Gounden c Lorrick b Jackson	2	– st Brearley b Renu 13
*M. Prashad b Smythe	18	– lbw b Khan 28
H. Grant run out	2	– c Jackson b Khan 19
D. Etwaroo c sub b Khan	2	– c Brearley b Stoute 2
R. Manosingh b Lorrick	0	– run out 0
K. Patel c Cohen b Lorrick	0	– not out 4
G. Porter not out	3	– st Brearley b Khan 0
L-b 3, n-b 5	8	B 4, w 3, n-b 1 8

1/8 2/69 3/90 4/96 5/141   185
6/160 7/169 8/171 9/177

1/7 2/62 3/96 4/117 5/166   194
6/169 7/182 8/189 9/189

Bowling: *First Innings*—Lorrick 15-2-40-2; Smythe 12-6-19-2; Khan 18.3-4-42-2; Renu 13-3-19-0; Stoute 10-2-18-0; Shivnarine 11-0-29-1; Jackson 10-0-15-2. *Second Innings*—Lorrick 10-2-36-1; Smythe 6-1-21-0; Khan 19.4-0-59-4; Stoute 22-5-35-3; Renu 6-1-8-1; Shivnarine 9-1-25-0; Jackson 5-1-6-0.

USA

N. Lashkari lbw b Grant	10	– lbw b Grant 0
W. Cohen c Jayasekera b Grant	25	– c Jayasekera b Dipchand 18
†M. Brearley c Jayasekera b Grant	24	– b Etwaroo 25
K. Khan run out	11	– (6) not out 74
L. Jackson c Jayasekera b Dipchand	4	– (9) not out 0
*S. Shivnarine c Grant b Patel	25	– (7) c M. Prashad b Grant 24
K. Lorrick c and b Patel	15	– (8) b Grant 2
S. Renu lbw b Patel	3	
P. Smythe c Gounden b Manosingh	11	– (4) b Patel 13
V. Stoute not out	5	– (5) c P. Prashad b Dipchand ... 10
R. Persaud c and b Manosingh	0	
B 4, l-b 6, w 10, n-b 7	27	B 2, l-b 9, w 5, n-b 9 ... 25

1/31 2/68 3/85 4/95 5/97   160
6/120 7/141 8/150 9/160

1/1 2/55 3/61 4/76   (7 wkts)   191
5/94 6/172 7/176

Bowling: *First Innings*—Grant 18-5-47-3; Porter 7-1-17-0; Gounden 1-0-2-0; Etwaroo 17-4-25-0; Patel 16-4-34-3; Manosingh 5-1-8-2; Dipchand 14-4-17-1. *Second Innings*—Grant 19-6-69-3; Porter 9-3-24-0; Dipchand 13-2-45-2; Etwaroo 4-1-18-1; Patel 6-1-24-1.

WOMEN'S CRICKET, 1987

THE GOLDEN JUBILEE OF TEST CRICKET IN ENGLAND

By NETTA RHEINBERG

In 1937, the first Australian women's touring team sailed for England for a three-Test series, the matches being of three days' duration. Twenty matches were played on a tour lasting four and a half months, including the sea voyage to and from Australia. These first Tests were played at Northampton, Blackpool and The Oval. The Australians paid their own fares, while at home the Women's Cricket Association raised over £1,000, which amply sufficed for hosting the tour. The series resulted in a win each and a draw.

Fifty years later, a younger Australian team flew to England for a tour lasting two months, including three four-day Test matches and three one-day internationals. Despite energetic efforts, the necessary major sponsorship failed to materialise. However, many free services and minor sponsorships were forthcoming, and these, together with one or two generous donations, permitted adequate hospitality to be shown to the Australian team. Furthermore, they removed the possibility of any cutting down of the tour.

For the second time this century, and after a gap of eleven years, MCC provided Lord's for a one-day international between England and Australia, a privilege gratefully accepted. Unfortunately, a period of fine weather broke the day before the match, and only after prolonged and dedicated work by the groundstaff, who sucked and mopped and extracted gallons of water, was play possible. The match began at two o'clock.

On this auspicious day, a bevy of WCA officers, as well as former players from both the inaugural tours – 1934-35 in Australia and 1937 in England – were entertained by the President of MCC, Colin Cowdrey, in his box and, after the match, in the Committee Room, making the occasion truly memorable. The President, always a great supporter of the women's game, acknowledged, in a short speech of welcome, the expertise of the leading women cricketers and the goodwill existing between men and women players. He expressed the hope that it would not be too long before ladies played again at Lord's.

Television coverage was provided by Channel 4 in an unprecedented ball-by-ball commentary, which resulted in good publicity and interest. The Billington Sugar Company generously donated £8,000 and a crystal bowl trophy which considerably brightened the whole tour.

THE ONE-DAY INTERNATIONALS

At Lord's, July 16. *First One-day International.* Australia won by 70 runs. England allowed Australia to stamp their authority completely on this match, which was reduced to 31 overs a side. Put in, Australia scored quickly against some erratic bowling. By the fifteenth over, 70 runs were on the board; 174 were scored in the overs allotted. Although England's fielders showed skill and agility, the field placing was poor. Against a tight attack, England's batsmen looked inexperienced and quite unable to attain the required run-rate of 5.6 an over. Only Jackie Court, the sole survivor of the first match played at Lord's in 1976, offered any lengthy resistance.

Australia 174 for three (31 overs) (L. Reeler 69, D. Annetts 36 not out); England 104 for five (31 overs) (J. Court 35; L. Fullston four for 12).

At Guildford, July 22. *Second One-day International*. Abandoned owing to rain.

At Canterbury, July 25. *Third One-day International*. England won by six wickets. A good crowd enjoyed a closely fought match played on an excellent artificial wicket. This had made play possible after heavy overnight rain had drenched the ground. England, winning the toss, again fielded first. Their opening bowling was more accurate and Australia began slowly at just over 2 runs an over. England's over-rate was also slow, with the result that only 53 overs were bowled within the three hours' limitation. Lindsay Reeler showed a fine range of strokes, while Denise Annetts, whose small stature did not hinder her quality batting, hit her half-century from 50 balls. England's fielding was of a high standard with Carole Hodges, the captain, holding three catches. Chasing a target of 3.3 runs an over, Janette Brittin went straight on to the attack and with Hodges kept the scoring-rate on schedule. Lyn Larsen's leg-breaks slowed England down, however, and they were faltering at 130 for four with ten overs remaining. But Jo Chamberlain launched an attack and, amid mounting excitement, the match was won in the 50th over with a scorching stroke over the long-off boundary. Her unbeaten 36 included seven boundaries.

With the games tied at one-all, the series was decided in Australia's favour because of their better run-rate.

Australia 177 for seven (53 overs) (L. Reeler 60, D. Annetts 50; S. Potter three for 41); England 178 for four (49.3 overs) (J. Brittin 38, C. Hodges 54, J. Court 42 not out, J. Chamberlain 36 not out).

ENGLAND v AUSTRALIA

First Test Match

At Worcester, August 1, 2, 3. Australia won by an innings and 21 runs with a day to spare. On a dull, damp morning, with the wicket taking some spin, England chose to bat and were soon in trouble against accurate bowling adhering to the principle of line and length. Indeed, Australia's attack was considerably superior to England's in this respect throughout the match. When Brittin was bowled in the first over, a defensive mood seemed to settle on the batsmen like a blanket. A sunny start to the afternoon and a score of 78 for two saw hopes rise among England's supporters, but after the dismissal of Hodges, Karen Brown's seam bowling removed three batsmen, including Wendy Watson, who had put together a good, fighting 50.

Australia also began slowly, scoring 44 for the loss of two wickets in the 73 minutes remaining. But it was well into the second day before England had another success. Belinda Haggett, her confidence given time to develop by much untidy bowling, thoroughly deserved her century, and although Gill McConway accounted for the middle order with steady seam bowling, the lower order dealt almost contemptuously with the bowling, putting on 89 runs to leave England 159 runs behind. Once again, their batting proved inadequate, only Hodges staying the course with a stubborn 55 before being the last wicket to fall. Jenny Owens took four wickets with her off-breaks, and England were all out a quarter of an hour before the close of the third day.

England

J. Brittin b Griffiths	0	b Griffiths 11
S. Potter c Matthews b Goss	18	run out 17
*C. Hodges c Griffiths b Fullston	27	b Owens 55
W. Watson c Fullston b Brown	50	b Larsen 7
J. Court c Reeler b Brown	15	b Brown 28
J. Chamberlain b Brown	0	b Goss 10
E. Wulcko c Annetts b Owens	12	c Matthews b Goss 2
K. Jobling b Goss	1	b Owens 5
G. McConway c Fullston b Owens	4	c Fullston b Owens 0
G. Smith c Annetts b Griffiths	4	c Larsen b Owens 0
†A. Stinson not out	1	not out 0
L-b 1, n-b 1	2	L-b 1, n-b 2 3

1/0 2/34 3/78 4/107 5/107   134   1/18 2/36 3/53 4/101 5/108   138
6/110 7/117 8/122 9/129   6/122 7/135 8/135 9/135

Bowling: *First Innings*—Griffiths 16.3–4–42–2; Goss 18–10–18–2; Brown 14–7–17–3; Owens 16–8–23–2; Fullston 14–5–33–1. *Second Innings*—Griffiths 16–6–23–1; Goss 21–10–38–2; Brown 13–4–31–1; Larsen 9–5–10–1; Fullston 15–8–17–0; Owens 16.5–7–18–4.

Australia

L. Reeler c Stinson b Chamberlain	3	S. Griffiths c Hodges b McConway	28
D. Emerson b Chamberlain	0	L. Fullston not out	41
B. Haggett hit wkt b McConway	126	J. Owens run out	14
D. Annetts c Jobling b McConway	34		
*L. Larsen c Stinson b McConway	25	B 8, l-b 4, w 1	13
Z. Goss c Hodges b McConway	1		
†C. Matthews c Court b Wulcko	4	1/3 2/4 3/100 4/194 5/195	293
K. Brown b McConway	4	6/196 7/200 8/204 9/264	

Bowling: Chamberlain 24–9–49–2; Smith 19–5–41–0; McConway 40–14–71–6; Jobling 11–4–36–0; Potter 10–5–15–0; Court 13–3–37–0; Wulcko 13.2–2–32–1.

Umpires: J. Burns and A. Garton.

ENGLAND v AUSTRALIA

Second Test Match

At Collingham & Linton CC, August 21, 22, 23, 24. Drawn. Only the perseverance of the groundsman rendered play possible, with overnight rain leaving the ground soaked on each morning. England chose to bat and at lunch were 79 for one. Even 160 for five at tea looked reasonable, but then off-spinner Owens settled into a good spell and the last five England wickets fell for just 29 runs. Watson's staunch unbeaten 69 contained some attractive drives.

The Australians resumed at 5 for one on a dull, drizzly second morning after a 30-minute delay and by tea had advanced to 169 for two, with the international record partnership of 309 between Reeler and Annetts well launched. It began at 2.16 p.m. and finished six and a quarter hours later, on the third day, when Annetts was run out for 193, having beaten by 2 runs the record set at Worcester in 1986 by S. Aggarwal of India. She batted beautifully, her innings full of memorable cuts, leg glides and pulls through mid-wicket on a pitch that was soft, very slow and turned appreciably throughout. Reeler remained unbeaten with 110 after a marathon 454 minutes, which included a record slowest century, in 440 minutes. First, they passed the third-wicket record partnership of 137, held by Edna Barker and Rachael Heyhoe Flint, and after 283 minutes together they eclipsed the previous highest partnership for any wicket, 235 set by Molly Hide and Betty Snowball.

Australia's declaration on the final day left England with 152 minutes and twenty overs in which to avoid an innings defeat. Although the day had dawned bright and sunny, the wet pitch prevented any play before two o'clock, which was to England's advantage. On the previous evening, more than an hour had been lost after the umpires decided that further play would be dangerous to the bowlers. Brittin batted throughout to ensure a draw, and early in her innings she passed 1,000 runs in Test cricket.

England

J. Brittin c Matthews b Brown	56	– not out	70
S. Potter c Reeler b Larsen	16	– b Fullston	8
*C. Hodges c Fullston b Owens	24	– c Annetts b Owens	0
W. Watson not out	69	– c Brown b Owens	13
J. Court b Griffiths	8	– c Reeler b Goss	16
†J. Powell c Reeler b Owens	0	– not out	9
J. Aspinall c Annetts b Goss	11		
K. Hicken c Matthews b Owens	2		
J. Chamberlain c Fullston b Owens	2		
E. Wulcko c Annetts b Brown	4		
G. McConway b Owens	1		
B 1, l-b 6, w 1	8		

1/34 2/94 3/100 4/131 5/138   201   1/44 2/44 3/70 4/87   (4 wkts) 116
6/172 7/191 8/193 9/200

Bowling: *First Innings*—Griffiths 12–2–32–1; Brown 17–7–30–2; Larsen 13–4–19–1; Goss 18–5–32–1; Fullston 9–3–26–0; Owens 20.2–3–55–5. *Second Innings*—Griffiths 18–7–38–0; Goss 11–10–1–1; Brown 9–4–14–0; Owens 14–4–36–2; Fullston 11–3–27–1.

Australia

L. Reeler not out	....	110
D. Emerson b Chamberlain	....	1
B. Haggett c Hicken b Chamberlain	...	21
D. Annetts run out	....	193
B 14, l-b 6, w 1	....	21

1/2 2/37 3/346 (3 wkts dec.) 346

*L. Larsen, Z. Goss, K. Brown, †C. Matthews, S. Griffiths, L. Fullston and J. Owens did not bat.

Bowling: Chamberlain 28–10–74–2; Aspinall 20–10–25–0; McConway 26.4–7–55–0; Potter 14–4–29–0; Hicken 25–6–48–0; Wulcko 15–1–62–0; Brittin 8–3–10–0; Hodges 5–0–23–0.

Umpires: S. Keen and J. West.

ENGLAND v AUSTRALIA

Third Test Match

At Hove, August 29, 30, 31, September 1. Drawn. England's improved performance in this match showed that they had gained in experience and were beginning to get the measure of their opponents. Their bowling was more controlled and backed up by excellent, nimble fielding which restricted the Australians after they were put in under cloudy skies. Reeler and Buckstein took two hours to reach their half-centuries, and although Annetts enlivened the batting with her 51, Larsen took four hours on the second day to compile an unbeaten 70. The declaration did not come until mid-afternoon, Australia having begun the day 230 for four.

England's innings began disastrously, and by the close they were 41 for four, three of their leading batsmen having succumbed to Brown's seamers. But on the third day, August Bank Holiday, the cricket and the weather sprang to life, providing much enjoyment for a good crowd. The two young Midlanders, Karen Hicken and Chamberlain, both new to Test cricket, came together at 108 for six and added 110 in a world record partnership for the seventh wicket to save the follow-on. With Hicken using her feet well and driving stylishly, while the more powerful Chamberlain scored strongly all round the wicket, the runs came in even time. England's challenging declaration at their overnight score of 265 for eight, 101 runs behind, was rejected by the Australians who, one-nil ahead in the series, chose to bat throughout the day for a draw.

Australia

L. Reeler run out	....	53	– lbw b Court	....	75
R. Buckstein run out	....	83	– run out	....	2
B. Haggett c Stinson b Chamberlain	.....	4	– c sub b McConway	.....	73
D. Annetts lbw b Hicken	....	51	– st Stinson b Hodges	.....	74
*L. Larsen not out	....	70			
K. Brown c and b Hicken	.....	24	– c Brittin b Chamberlain	.....	14
Z. Goss b Watson	.....	45	– st Stinson b McConway	.....	1
†C. Matthews b Hicken	.....	3	– c Court b Hodges	.....	4
S. Griffiths not out	.....	16	– b Court	.....	0
J. Owens (did not bat)	.....		– not out	.....	12
B 8, l-b 7, w 2	.....	17	B 5, w 2	.....	7

1/84 2/89 3/194 4/199 5/241 (7 wkts dec.) 366 1/25 2/122 3/203 (8 wkts dec.) 262
6/333 7/340 4/213 5/231 6/235
7/261 8/262

L. Fullston did not bat.

Bowling: *First Innings*—Chamberlain 35–11–64–1; Aspinall 10.3–4–14–0; Potter 14–4–37–0; McConway 49.3–19–100–0; Brittin 3–0–13–0; Hicken 39–16–63–3; Hodges 8–3–17–0; Court 4–0–17–0; Watson 8–1–26–1. *Second Innings*—Chamberlain 17–4–48–1; McConway 38–13–65–2; Hicken 18–5–37–0; Hodges 14–1–42–2; Potter 11–4–18–0; Court 11.5–3–31–2; Watson 5–1–16–0.

England

J. Brittin c Annetts b Brown	8	J. Aspinall not out 19
W. Watson b Brown	2	G. McConway not out 28
*C. Hodges c Matthews b Brown	46	
S. Potter c Reeler b Brown	4	B 4, l-b 3, w 1, n-b 1 9
J. Court c Reeler b Griffiths	7	
J. Powell c Larsen b Owens	19	1/12 2/13 3/24 (8 wkts dec.) 265
K. Hicken c Annetts b Brown	64	4/33 5/95 6/108
J. Chamberlain st Matthews b Larsen	59	7/218 8/218

†A. Stinson did not bat.

Bowling: Griffiths 34–15–57–1; Goss 22–9–36–0; Brown 32–19–32–5; Fullston 22–7–42–0; Owens 31–12–61–1; Larsen 13–3–30–1.

Umpires: J. Bragger and V. Williams.

CRICKET ASSOCIATIONS AND SOCIETIES

AUCKLAND CRICKET SOCIETY: *Secretary* J. H. Palmer, Eden Park, PO Box 2860, Auckland 1, New Zealand.

AUSTRALIAN CRICKET SOCIETY: Chris Harte, GPO Box 696, Adelaide, 5001, South Australia.

AUSTRALIAN CAPITAL TERRITORY BRANCH: Julian Oakley, GPO Box 50, Canberra, 2601, ACT.

NEW SOUTH WALES BRANCH: Ronald Cardwell, 92 Victoria Road, West Pennant Hills, 2120, NSW.

QUEENSLAND BRANCH: Robert Spence, GPO Box 1498, Brisbane 4001, Queensland.

SOUTH AUSTRALIAN BRANCH: Gerald Fishpool, 49 Johnstone Street, Glengowrie, 5044, South Australia.

VICTORIAN BRANCH: Leslie Hutchings, 7 Tree Top Drive, Kilsyth, 3137, Victoria.

WESTERN AUSTRALIAN BRANCH: Denis Tobin, 18 Lachlan Road, Crestwood, 6108, Western Australia.

BLACKLEY CRICKET SOCIETY: *Secretary* D. N. Butterfield, 7 Bayswater Terrace, Halifax, West Yorkshire, HX3 0NB.

CAMBRIDGE UNIVERSITY CRICKET SOCIETY: *Secretary* I. T. McDonald, Jesus College, Cambridge CB5 8BL.

CHELTENHAM CRICKET SOCIETY: *Secretary* N. Cooke, Wickets, 10 Welland Lodge Road, Cheltenham, Gloucestershire.

CHESTERFIELD CRICKET SOCIETY: *Secretary* J. S. Cook, 44 Morris Avenue, Newbold, Chesterfield, Derbyshire S41 7BA.

COUNCIL OF CRICKET SOCIETIES, THE: *Secretary* J. Featherstone, 205 Hyde Park Road, Leeds, Yorkshire LS6 1AH.

CRICKET MEMORABILIA SOCIETY: *Secretary* A. Sheldon, 29 Highclere Road, Crumpsall, Manchester M8 6WS.

CRICKET SOCIETY, THE: *Secretary* E. B. Budd, 180 Grove End Gardens, London NW8 9LS.

CRICKET SOCIETY, THE (Midland Branch): *Secretary* Dr A. A. Walker, "Sarnia", Hernes Nest, Bewdley, Worcestershire DY12 2ET.

CRICKET STATISTICIANS, ASSOCIATION OF: *Secretary* P. Wynne-Thomas, 23 Priory Road, West Bridgford, Nottingham.

CRICKET STATISTICIANS AND SCORERS OF INDIA, ASSOCIATION OF: *Secretary* Dr Vasant Naik, 102 B. Madhav Wadi, M.M.G. Road, Dadar, Bombay 400 014, India.

EAST RIDING CRICKET SOCIETY: *Secretary* R. P. Thompson, 151 Park Avenue, Hull HU5 3EX.

ESSEX CRICKET SOCIETY: *Secretary* P. Roberts, 5 Longacres, Hanover Square, Feering, Colchester, Essex CO5 9OP.

FYLDE CRICKET SOCIETY: *Secretary* W. J. Thompson, 26 Roseacre, Blackpool, Lancashire FY4 2PN.

HAMPSHIRE CRICKET SOCIETY: *Secretary* F. Bailey, 7 Lightfoot Grove, Basingstoke, Hampshire.

HEAVY WOOLLEN CRICKET SOCIETY: *Secretary* G. S. Cooper, 27 Milford Grove, Gomersal, Cleckheaton, West Yorkshire.

INDIA, THE CRICKET SOCIETY OF: *Secretary* Sandeep Singh Nakai, G-58, East of Kailash, New Delhi 110 065 India.

LANCASHIRE AND CHESHIRE CRICKET SOCIETY: *Secretary* H. W. Pardoe, "Crantock", 117a Barlow Moor Road, Didsbury, Manchester, M20 8TS.

LINCOLNSHIRE CRICKET LOVERS' SOCIETY: *Secretary* C. Kennedy, 26 Eastwood Avenue, Great Grimsby, South Humberside, DN34 5BE.

MERSEYSIDE CRICKET SOCIETY: *Secretary* W. T. Robins, 11 Yew Tree Road, Hunts Cross, Liverpool L25 9QN.

NATAL CRICKET SOCIETY: *Secretary* PO Box 3046, Durban 4000, South Africa.

NORTHERN CRICKET SOCIETY: *Secretary* K. Harvey, 1 Old Park Road, Roundhay, Leeds, Yorkshire LS8 1JT.

NOTTINGHAM CRICKET LOVERS' SOCIETY: *Secretary* G. Blagdurn, 2 Inham Circus, Chilwell, Beeston, Nottinghamshire, NG9 4FN.

PAKISTAN ASSOCIATION OF CRICKET STATISTICIANS: *Secretary* Abid Ali Kazi, 5-A, 11/1 Sunset Lane, Phase 11, Defence Housing Society, Karachi, Pakistan.

ROTHERHAM CRICKET SOCIETY: *Secretary* J. A. R. Atkin, 15 Gallow Tree Road, Rotherham, South Yorkshire S65 3FE.

SCOTLAND, CRICKET SOCIETY OF: *Secretary* A. J. Robertson, 5 Riverside Road, Eaglesham, Glasgow, G76 0DQ.

SOMERSET WYVERNS: *Secretary* M. J. W. Richards, The Wickets, 21 Vicarage Meadow, Southminster, Essex.

SOPHIANS, THE: *Secretary* A. K. Hignell, 79 Coed Glas Road, Llanishen, Cardiff.

SOUTH AFRICAN CRICKET SOCIETY: *Secretary* John Landau, PO Box 78040, Sandton, Transvaal, 2146, South Africa.

SRI LANKA CRICKET SOCIETY: M. Kamardeen, 25 Abdul Hamid Street, Colombo 12, Sri Lanka.

STOURBRIDGE AND DISTRICT CRICKET SOCIETY: *Secretary* R. Barber, 6 Carlton Avenue, Pedmore, Stourbridge, West Midlands DY9 9ED.

SUSSEX CRICKET SOCIETY: *Secretary* A. A. Dumbrell, 6 Southdown Avenue, Brighton, East Sussex, BN1 6EG.

UPPINGHAM SCHOOL CRICKET SOCIETY: *Secretary* Dr E. J. R. Boston, The Common Room, Uppingham School, Rutland.

WEST LANCASHIRE CRICKET SOCIETY: *Secretary* G. O. Shipton, 9 Breeze Road, Southport, Lancashire PR8 2HG.

WOMBWELL CRICKET LOVERS' SOCIETY: *Secretary* J. Sokell, 42 Woodstock Road, Barnsley, South Yorkshire, S75 1DX.

ZIMBABWE, CRICKET SOCIETY OF: *Secretary* L. G. Morgenrood, 10 Elsworth Avenue, Belgravia, Harare, Zimbabwe.

BIRTHS AND DEATHS OF CRICKETERS

The qualifications are as follows:

1. All players who have appeared in a Test match or a one-day international for a Test-match playing country.

2. Players who have appeared in 50 or more first-class matches during their careers and, if dead, were still living ten years ago.

3. Players who appeared in fifteen or more first-class matches in the 1987 English season.

4. English county captains, county caps and captains of Oxford and Cambridge Universities who, if dead, were still living ten years ago.

5. All players chosen as *Wisden* Cricketers of the Year, including the Public Schoolboys chosen for the 1918 and 1919 Almanacks. Cricketers of the Year are identified by the italic notation *CY* and year of appearance.

6. Players or personalities not otherwise qualified who are thought to be of sufficient interest to merit inclusion.

Key to abbreviations and symbols

CUCC – Cambridge University, OUCC – Oxford University.

Australian states: NSW – New South Wales, Qld – Queensland, S. Aust. – South Australia, Tas. – Tasmania, Vic. – Victoria, W. Aust. – Western Australia.

Indian teams: Guj. – Gujarat, H'bad – Hyderabad, Ind. Rlwys – Indian Railways, Ind. Serv. – Indian Services, J/K – Jammu and Kashmir, Karn. – Karnataka (Mysore to 1972-73), M. Pradesh – Madhya Pradesh (Central India [C. Ind.] to 1939-40, Holkar to 1954-55, Madhya Bharat to 1956-57), M'tra – Maharashtra, Naw. – Nawanagar, Raja. – Rajasthan, S'tra – Saurashtra (West India [W. Ind.] to 1945-46, Kathiawar to 1949-50), S. Punjab – Southern Punjab (Patiala to 1958-59, Punjab since 1968-69), TC – Travancore-Colchin (Kerala since 1956-57), TN – Tamil Nadu (Madras to 1959-60), U. Pradesh – Uttar Pradesh (United Provinces [U. Prov.] to 1948-49), Vidarbha (CP & Berar to 1949-50, Madhya Pradesh to 1956-57).

New Zealand provinces: Auck. – Auckland, Cant. – Canterbury, C. Dist. – Central Districts, N. Dist. – Northern Districts, Wgtn – Wellington.

Pakistani teams: B'pur – Bahawalpur, HBL – Habib Bank Ltd, HBFC – House Building Finance Corporation, IDBP – Industrial Development Bank of Pakistan, Kar. – Karachi, MCB – Muslim Commercial Bank, NBP – National Bank of Pakistan, NWFP – North-West Frontier Province, PIA – Pakistan International Airlines, Pak. Us – Pakistan Universities, Pak. Rlwys – Pakistan Railways, PWD – Public Works Department, R'pindi – Rawalpindi, UBL – United Bank Ltd.

South African provinces: E. Prov. – Eastern Province, Griq. W. – Griqualand West, N. Tvl – Northern Transvaal, NE Tvl – North-Eastern Transvaal, OFS – Orange Free State, Rhod. – Rhodesia, Tvl – Transvaal, W. Prov. – Western Province.

West Indies islands: B'dos – Barbados, BG – British Guiana (Guyana since 1966), Jam. – Jamaica, T/T – Trinidad and Tobago, Comb. Is. – Combined Islands.

* Denotes Test player. ** Denotes appeared for two countries. There is a list of Test players country by country from page 85.
† Denotes also played for team under its previous name.

Aamer Hameed (Pak. Us, Lahore, Punjab & OUCC) b Oct. 18, 1954

Abberley, R. N. (Warwicks.) b April 22, 1944

*A'Beckett, E. L. (Vic.) b Aug. 11, 1907

*Abdul Kadir (Kar. & NBP) b May 10, 1944

*Abdul Qadir (HBL, Lahore & Punjab) b Sept. 15, 1955

*Abel, R. (Surrey; *CY 1890*) b Nov. 30, 1857, d Dec. 10, 1936

Abell, Sir G. E. B. (OUCC, Worcs. & N. Ind.) b June 22, 1904

Aberdare, 3rd Lord (*see* Bruce, Hon. C. N.)

*Abid Ali, S. (H'bad) b Sept. 9, 1941

Abrahams, J. (Lancs.) b July 21, 1952

*Absolom, C. A. (CUCC & Kent) b June 7, 1846, d July 30, 1889

Acfield D. L. (CUCC & Essex) b July 24, 1947

*Achong, E. (T/T) b Feb. 16, 1904, d Aug. 29, 1986

Ackerman, H. M. (Border, NE Tvl, Northants, Natal & W. Prov.) b April 28, 1947

A'Court, D. G. (Glos.) b July 27, 1937

Adam, Sir Ronald, 2nd Bt (Pres. MCC 1946-47) b Oct. 30, 1885, d Dec. 26, 1982

Adams, P. W. (Cheltenham & Sussex; *CY 1919*) b 1900, d Feb. 28, 1962

*Adcock, N. A. T. (Tvl & Natal; *CY 1961*) b March 8, 1931

*Adhikari, H. R. (Guj., Baroda & Ind. Serv.) b July 31, 1919

*Afaq Hussain (Kar., Pak. Us, PIA & PWD) b Dec. 31, 1939

Afford, J. A. (Notts.) b May 12, 1964

*Aftab Baloch (PWD, Kar., Sind, NBP & PIA) b April 1, 1953

*Aftab Gul (Punjab U., Pak. Us & Lahore) b March 31, 1946

*Agha Saadat Ali (Pak. Us, Punjab, B'pur & Lahore) b June 21, 1929

*Agha Zahid (Pak. Us, Punjab, Lahore & HBL) b Jan. 7, 1953

*Agnew, J. P. (Leics; *CY 1988*) b April 4, 1960

*Ahangama, F. S. (SL) b Sept. 14, 1959

Ainsworth, Lt-Cdr M. L. Y. (Worcs.) b May 13, 1922, d Aug. 28, 1978

Aird, R. (CUCC & Hants; Sec. MCC 1953-62, Pres. MCC 1968-69) b May 4, 1902, d Aug. 16, 1986

Aitchison, Rev. J. K. (Scotland) b May 26, 1920

Alabaster, G. D. (Cant., N. Dist. & Otago) b Dec. 10, 1933

*Alabaster, J. C. (Otago) b July 11, 1930

Alcock, C. W. (Sec. Surrey CCC 1872-1907, Editor *Cricket* 1882-1907) b Dec. 2, 1842, d Feb. 26, 1907

Alderman, A. E. (Derbys.) b Oct. 30, 1907

*Alderman, T. M. (W. Aust. & Kent; *CY 1982*) b June 12, 1956

Aldridge, K. J. (Worcs & Tas.) b March 13, 1935

Alexander of Tunis, 1st Lord (Pres. MCC 1955-56) b Dec. 10, 1891, d June 16, 1969

*Alexander, F. C. M. (CUCC & Jam.) b Nov. 2, 1928

*Alexander, G. (Vic.) b April 22, 1851, d Nov. 6, 1930

*Alexander, H. H. (Vic.) b June 9, 1905

Alikhan, R. I. (Sussex & PIA) b Dec. 28, 1962

*Alim-ud-Din (Rajputna, Guj., Sind, B'pur, Kar. & PWD) b Dec. 15, 1930

*Allan, D. W. (B'dos) b Nov. 5, 1937

*Allan, F. E. (Vic.) b Dec. 2, 1849, d Feb. 9, 1917

Allan, J. M. (OUCC, Kent, Warwicks. & Scotland) b April 2, 1932

*Allan, P. J. (Qld) b Dec. 31, 1935

*Allcott, C. F. W. (Auck.) b Oct. 7, 1896, d Nov. 21, 1973

Allen, A. W. (CUCC & Northants) b Dec. 22, 1912

*Allen, B. O. (CUCC & Glos.) b Oct. 13, 1911, d May 1, 1981

*Allen, D. A. (Glos.) b Oct. 29, 1935

*Allen, Sir G. O. (CUCC & Middx; Pres. MCC 1963-64; *special portrait 1987*) b July 31, 1902

Allen, J. C. (Leewards) b Aug. 18, 1951

Allen, M. H. J. (Northants & Derbys.) b Jan. 7, 1933

*Allen, R. C. (NSW) b July 2, 1858, d May 2, 1952

Alletson, E. B. (Notts.) b March 6, 1884, d July 5, 1963

Alley, W. E. (NSW & Som.; *CY 1962*) b Feb. 3, 1919

*Alleyne, H. L. (B'dos, Worcs. & Natal) b Feb. 28, 1957

Alleyne, M. W. (Glos.) b May 23, 1968

*Allom, M. J. C. (CUCC & Surrey; Pres. MCC 1969-70) b March 23, 1906

Allott, P. J. W. (Lancs. & Wgtn) b Sept. 14, 1956

Altham, H. S. (OUCC, Surrey & Hants; Pres. MCC 1959-60) b Nov. 30, 1888, d March 11, 1965

Amalean, K. N. (SL) b April 7, 1965

*Amarnath, Lala (N. Ind., S. Punjab, Guj., Patiala, U. Pradesh & Ind. Rlwys) b Sept. 11, 1911

*Amarnath, M. (Punjab & Delhi; *CY 1984*) b Sept. 24, 1950

*Amarnath, S. (Punjab & Delhi) b Dec. 30, 1948

*Amar Singh, L. (Patiala, W. Ind. & Naw.) b Dec. 4, 1910, d May 20, 1940

*Amerasinghe, A. M. J. G. (SL) b Feb. 2, 1954

*Ames, L. E. G. (Kent; *CY 1929*) b Dec. 3, 1905

**Amir Elahi (Baroda, N. Ind., S. Punjab & B'pur) b Sept. 1, 1908, d Dec. 28, 1980

*Amiss, D. L. (Warwicks.; *CY 1975*) b April 7, 1943

Anderson, I. S. (Derbys. & Boland) b April 24, 1960

*Anderson, J. H. (W. Prov.) b April 26, 1874, d March 11, 1926

*Anderson, R. W. (Cant., N. Dist., Otago & C. Dist.) b Oct. 2, 1948

*Anderson, W. McD. (Otago, C. Dist. & Cant.) b Oct. 8, 1919, d Dec. 21, 1979

Andrew, C. R. (CUCC) b Feb. 18, 1963

*Andrew, K. V. (Northants) b Dec. 15, 1929

*Andrews, B. (Cant., C. Dist. & Otago) b April 4, 1945

*Andrews, T. J. E. (NSW) b Aug. 26, 1890, d Jan. 28, 1970

Andrews, W. H. R. (Som.) b April 14, 1908

Angell, F. L. (Som.) b June 29, 1922

*Anil Dalpat (Kar. & PIA) b Sept. 20, 1963

*Anurasiri, S. D. (SL) b Feb. 25, 1966

*Anwar Hussain (N. Ind., Bombay, Sind & Kar.) b July 16, 1920

*Anwar Khan (Kar., Sind & NBP) b Dec. 24, 1955

*Appleyard, R. (Yorks.; *CY 1952*) b June 27, 1924

*Apte, A. L. (Ind. Us, Bombay & Raja.) b Oct. 24, 1934

*Apte, M. L. (Bombay & Bengal) b Oct. 5, 1932

*Archer, A. G. (Worcs.) b Dec. 6, 1871, d July 15, 1935

*Archer, K. A. (Qld) b Jan. 17, 1928

*Archer, R. G. (Qld) b Oct. 25, 1933

*Arif Butt (Lahore & Pak. Rlwys) b May 17, 1944

Arlott, John, (Writer & Broadcaster) b Feb. 25, 1914

*Armitage, R. L. S. (E. Prov. & N. Tvl) b July 9, 1955

*Armitage, T. (Yorks.) b April 25, 1848, d Sept. 21, 1922

Armstrong, N. F. (Leics.) b Dec. 22, 1892

Armstrong, T. R. (Derbys.) b Oct. 13, 1909

*Armstrong, W. W. (Vic.; *CY 1903*) b May 22, 1879, d July 13, 1947

*Arnold, E. G. (Worcs.) b Nov. 7, 1876, d Oct. 25, 1942

*Arnold, G. G. (Surrey & Sussex; *CY 1972*) b Sept. 3, 1944

*Arnold, J. (Hants) b Nov. 30, 1907, d April 4, 1984

Arnold, P. (Cant. & Northants) b Oct. 16, 1926

Arshad Pervez (Sargodha, Lahore, Pak. Us, Servis Ind., HBL & Punjab) b Oct. 1, 1952

*Arun, B. (TN) b Dec. 14, 1962

*Arun Lal, J. (Delhi & Bengal) b Aug. 1, 1955

*Asgarali, N. (T/T) b Dec. 28, 1920

Ashdown, W. H. (Kent) b Dec. 27, 1898, d Sept. 15, 1979

*Ashley, W. H. (W. Prov.) b Feb. 10, 1862, d July 14, 1930

*Ashraf Ali (Lahore, Income Tax, Pak Us, Pak Rlwys & UBL) b April 22, 1958

*Ashton, C. T. (CUCC & Essex) b Feb. 19, 1901, d Oct. 31, 1942

*Ashton, G. (CUCC & Worcs.) b Sept. 27, 1896, d Feb. 6, 1981

Ashton, Sir H. (CUCC & Essex; *CY 1922*; Pres. MCC 1960-61) b Feb. 13, 1898, d June 17,1979

Asif Din, M. (Warwicks.) b Sept. 21, 1960

*Asif Iqbal (H'bad, Kar., Kent, PIA & NBP; *CY 1968*) b June 6, 1943

*Asif Masood (Lahore, Punjab U. & PIA) b Jan. 23, 1946

*Asif Mujtaba (Kar.) b Nov. 4, 1967

Aslett, D. G. (Kent) b Feb. 12, 1958

Aspinall, R. (Yorks.) b Nov. 27, 1918

*Astill, W. E. (Leics.; *CY 1933*) b March 1, 1888, d Feb. 10, 1948

Atherton, M. A. (CUCC & Lancs.) b March 23, 1968

*Athey, C. W. J. (Yorks. & Glos.) b Sept. 27, 1957

Atkinson, C. R. M. (Som.) b July 23, 1931

*Atkinson, D. St E. (B'dos & T/T) b Aug. 9, 1926

*Atkinson, E. St E. (B'dos) b Nov. 6, 1927

Atkinson, G. (Som. & Lancs.) b March 29, 1938

Atkinson, T. (Notts.) b Sept. 27, 1930

Attenborough, G. R. (S. Aust.) b Jan. 17, 1951

*Attewell, W. (Notts.; *CY 1892*) b June 12, 1861, d June 11, 1927

Austin, Sir H. B. G. (B'dos) b July 15, 1877, d July 27, 1943

*Austin, R. A. (Jam.) b Sept. 5, 1954

Avery, A. V. (Essex) b Dec. 19, 1914

Aworth, C. J. (CUCC & Surrey) b Feb. 19, 1953

Aylward, J. (Hants & All-England) b 1741, d Dec. 27, 1827

*Azad, K. (Delhi) b Jan. 2, 1959

*Azeem Hafeez (Kar., Allied Bank & PIA) b July 29, 1963

*Azhar Khan (Lahore, Punjab, Pak. Us., PIA & HBL) b Sept. 7, 1955

*Azharuddin, M. (H'bad) b Feb. 8, 1963

*Azmat Rana (B'pur, PIA, Punjab, Lahore & MCB) b Nov. 3, 1951

*Bacchus, S. F. A. F. (Guyana, W. Prov. & Border) b Jan. 31, 1954

*Bacher, Dr A. (Tvl) b May 24, 1942

*Badcock, C. L. (Tas. & S. Aust.) b April 10, 1914, d Dec. 13, 1982

*Badcock, F. T. (Wgtn & Otago) b Aug. 9, 1895, d Sept. 19, 1982

*Baichan, L. (Guyana) b May 12, 1946

*Baig, A. A. (H'bad, OUCC & Som.) b March 19, 1939

Bailey, Sir D. T. L. (Glos.) b Aug. 5, 1918

Bailey, J. (Hants) b April 6, 1908

Bailey, J. A. (Essex & OUCC; Sec. MCC 1974-87) b June 22, 1930

Bailey, R. J. (Northants) b Oct. 28, 1963

*Bailey, T. E. (Essex & CUCC; *CY 1950*) b Dec. 3, 1923

Baillie, A. W. (Sec. MCC 1858-63) b June 22, 1830, d May 10, 1867

Bainbridge, P. (Glos.; *CY 1986*) b April 16, 1958

*Bairstow, D. L. (Yorks. & Griq. W.) b Sept. 1, 1951

Baker, R. P. (Surrey) b April 9, 1954

*Bakewell, A. H. (Northants; *CY 1934*) b Nov. 2, 1908, d Jan. 23, 1983

*Balaskas, X. C. (Griq. W., Border, W. Prov., Tvl & NE Tvl) b Oct. 15, 1910

*Balderstone, J. C. (Yorks. & Leics.) b Nov. 16, 1940

Baldry, D. O. (Middx & Hants) b Dec. 26, 1931

Baldwin, H. G. (Surrey; Umpire) b March 16, 1893, d March 7, 1969

*Banerjee, S. A. (Bengal & Bihar) b Nov. 1, 1919

*Banerjee, S. N. (Bengal, Naw., Bihar & M. Pradesh) b Oct. 3, 1911, d Oct. 14, 1980

*Bannerman, A. C. (NSW) b March 21, 1854, d Sept. 19, 1924

*Bannerman, Charles (NSW) b July 23, 1851, d Aug. 20, 1930

Bannister, J. D. (Warwicks.) b Aug. 23, 1930

*Baptiste, E. A. E. (Kent & Leewards) b March 12, 1960

*Baqa Jilani, M. (N. Ind.) b July 20, 1911, d July 2, 1941

Barber, A. T. (OUCC & Yorks.) b June 17, 1905, d March 10, 1985

*Barber, R. T. (Wgtn & C. Dist.) b June 23, 1925

*Barber, R. W. (Lancs., CUCC & Warwicks.; *CY 1967*) b Sept. 26, 1935

*Barber, W. (Yorks.) b April 18, 1901, d Sept. 10, 1968

Barclay, J. R. T. (Sussex & OFS) b Jan. 22, 1954

*Bardsley, W. (NSW; *CY 1910*) b Dec. 7, 1882, d Jan. 20, 1954

Baring, A. E. G. (Hants) b Jan. 21, 1910, d Aug. 29, 1986

Barker, G. (Essex) b July 6, 1931

Barling, T. H. (Surrey) b Sept. 1, 1906

Barlow, A. (Lancs.) b Aug. 31, 1915, d May 9, 1983

Barlow, E. A. (OUCC & Lancs.) b Feb. 24, 1912, d June 27, 1980

*Barlow, E. J. (Tvl, E. Prov., W. Prov., Derbys. & Boland) b Aug. 12, 1940

*Barlow, G. D. (Middx) b March 26, 1950

*Barlow, R. G. (Lancs.) b May 28, 1851, d July 31, 1919

Barnard, H. M. (Hants) b July 18, 1933

Barnard, L. J. (Tvl & N. Tvl) b Jan. 5, 1956

Barnes, A. R. (Sec. Aust. Cricket Board 1960-81) b Sept. 12, 1916

*Barnes, S. F. (Warwicks. & Lancs.; *CY 1910*) b April 19, 1873, d Dec. 26, 1967

*Barnes, S. G. (NSW) b June 5, 1916, d Dec. 16, 1973

*Barnes, W. (Notts.; *CY 1890*) b May 27, 1852, d March 24, 1899

*Barnett, B. A. (Vic.) b March 23, 1908, d June 29, 1979

*Barnett, C. J. (Glos.; *CY 1937*) b July 3, 1910

Barnett, K. J. (Derbys. & Boland) b July 17, 1960

Barnwell, C. J. P. (Som.) b June 23, 1914

Baroda, Maharaja of (Manager, Ind. in Eng., 1959) b April 2, 1930

*Barratt, F. (Notts.) b April 12, 1894, d Jan. 29, 1947

Barratt, R. J. (Leics.) b May 3, 1942

*Barrett, A. G. (Jam.) b April 5, 1942

Barrett, B. J. (Auck., C. Dist., Worcs. & N. Dist.) b Nov. 16, 1966

*Barrett, J. E. (Vic.) b Oct. 15, 1866, d Feb. 9, 1916

Barrick, D. W. (Northants) b April 28, 1926

*Barrington, K. F. (Surrey; *CY 1960*) b Nov. 24, 1930, d March 14, 1981

Barron, W. (Lancs. & Northants) b Oct. 26, 1917

*Barrow, I. (Jam.) b Jan. 6, 1911, d April 2, 1979

Bartholomew, P. C. S. (T/T) b Oct. 9, 1939

*Bartlett, E. L. (B'dos) b March 18, 1906, d Dec. 21, 1976

*Bartlett, G. A. (C. Dist. & Cant.) b Feb. 3, 1941

Bartlett, H. T. (CUCC, Surrey & Sussex; *CY 1939*) b Oct. 7, 1914

Bartley, T. J. (Umpire) b March 19, 1908, d April 2, 1964

Barton, M. R. (OUCC & Surrey) b Oct. 14, 1914

*Barton, P. T. (Wgtn) b Oct. 9, 1935

*Barton, V. A. (Kent & Hants) b Oct. 6, 1867, d March 23, 1906

Barwick, S. R. (Glam.) b Sept. 6, 1960

Bates, D. L. (Sussex) b May 10, 1933

*Bates, W. (Yorks.) b Nov. 19, 1855, d Jan. 8, 1900

Bath, B. F. (Tvl) b Jan. 16, 1947

*Baumgartner, H. V. (OFS & Tvl) b Nov. 17, 1883, d April 8, 1938

Baxter, A. D. (Devon, Lancs., Middx & Scotland) b Jan. 20, 1910, d Jan. 28, 1986

*Bean, G. (Notts & Sussex) b March 7, 1864, d March 16, 1923

Bear, M. J. (Essex & Cant.) b Feb. 23, 1934

*Beard, D. D. (C. Dist. & N. Dist.) b Jan. 14, 1920, d July 15, 1982

*Beard, G. R. (NSW) b Aug. 19, 1950

Beauclerk, Lord Frederick (Middx, Surrey & MCC) b May 8, 1773, d April 22, 1850

Beaufort, 10th Duke of (Pres. MCC 1952-53) b April 4, 1900, d Feb. 5, 1984

*Beaumont, R. (Tvl) b Feb. 4, 1884, d May 25, 1958

*Beck, J. E. F. (Wgtn) b Aug. 1, 1934

Becker, G. C. (W. Aust.) b March 13, 1936

*Bedi, B. S. (N. Punjab, Delhi & Northants) b Sept. 25, 1946

*Bedser, A. V. (Surrey; *CY 1947*) b July 4, 1918

Bedser, E. A. (Surrey) b July 4, 1918

Beet, G. (Derbys.; Umpire) b April 24, 1886, d Dec. 13, 1946

*Begbie, D. W. (Tvl) b Dec. 12, 1914

Beldham, W. (Hambledon & Surrey) b Feb. 5, 1766, d Feb. 20, 1862

*Bell, A. J. (W. Prov. & Rhod.) b April 15, 1906, d Aug. 2, 1985

Bell, R. V. (Middx & Sussex) b Jan. 7, 1931

*Bell, W. (Cant.) b Sept. 5, 1931

Bellamy, B. W. (Northants) b April 22, 1891, d Dec. 20, 1985

*Benaud, J. (NSW) b May 11, 1944

*Benaud, R. (NSW; *CY 1962*) b Oct. 6, 1930

Benjamin, W. K. M. (Leewards & Leics.) b Dec. 31, 1964

Bennett, C. T. (CUCC, Surrey & Middx) b Aug. 10, 1902, d Feb. 3, 1978

Bennett, D. (Middx) b Dec. 18, 1933

Bennett, G. M. (Som.) b Dec. 17, 1909, d July 26, 1982

*Bennett, M. J. (NSW) b Oct. 16, 1956

Bennett, N. H. (Surrey) b Sept. 23, 1912

Bennett, R. (Lancs.) b June 16, 1940

*Benson, M. R. (Kent) b July 6, 1958

Bensted, E. C. (Qld) b Feb. 11, 1901, d Jan. 21, 1980

Bentley, R. M. (Rhod., Zimb. & Natal) b Nov. 3, 1958

Bernard, J. R. (CUCC & Glos.) b Dec. 7, 1938

Berry, L. G. (Leics.) b April 28, 1906, d Feb. 5, 1985

*Berry, R. (Lancs., Worcs. & Derbys.) b Jan. 29, 1926

Bessant, J. G. (Glos.) b Nov. 11, 1892, d Jan. 18, 1982

*Best, C. A. (B'dos) b May 14, 1959

Bestall, D. (N. Tvl, Natal & E. Prov.) b May 28, 1952

*Betancourt, N. (T/T) b June 4, 1887, d Oct. 12, 1947

Beukes, A. P. (Griq. W. & OFS) b May 24, 1953

Bezuidenhout, S. J. (E. Prov.) b July 11, 1946

Bhalekar, R. B. (M'tra) b Feb. 17, 1952

*Bhandari, P. (Delhi & Bengal) b Nov. 27, 1935

*Bhat, R. (Karn.) b April 16, 1958

Bick, D. A. (Middx) b Feb. 22, 1936

Bickmore, A. F. (OUCC & Kent) b May 19, 1899, d March 18, 1979

Biddulph, K. D. (Som.) b May 29, 1932

Biggs, A. L. (E. Prov.) b April 26, 1946

*Bilby, G. P. (Wgtn) b May 7, 1941

*Binks, J. G. (Yorks.; *CY 1969*) b Oct. 5, 1935

*Binny, R. M. H. (Karn.) b July 19, 1955

*Binns, A. P. (Jam.) b July 24, 1929

Birch, J. D. (Notts.) b June 18, 1955

Bird, H. D. (Yorks. & Leics.; Umpire) b April 19, 1933

*Bird, M. C. (Lancs. & Surrey) b March 25, 1888, d Dec. 9, 1933

Bird, R. E. (Worcs.) b April 15, 1915, d Feb. 20, 1985

*Birkenshaw, J. (Yorks., Leics. & Worcs.) b Nov. 13, 1940

*Birkett, L. S. (B'dos, BG & T/T) b April 14, 1904

Birrell, H. B. (E. Prov., Rhod. & OUCC) b Dec. 1, 1927

Bishop, G. A. (S. Aust.) b Feb. 25, 1960

*Bisset, Sir Murray (W. Prov.) b April 14, 1876, d Oct. 24, 1931

*Bissett, G. F. (Griq. W., W. Prov. & Tvl) b Nov. 5, 1905, d Nov. 14, 1965

Bissex, M. (Glos.) b Sept. 28, 1944

*Blackham, J. McC. (Vic.; *CY 1891*) b May 11, 1854, d Dec. 28, 1932

*Blackie, D. D. (Vic.) b April 5, 1882, d April 18, 1955

Blackledge, J. F. (Lancs.) b April 15, 1928

*Blain, T. E. (C. Dist.) b Feb. 17, 1962

Blair, B. R. (Otago) b Dec. 27, 1957

*Blair, R. W. (Wgtn & C. Dist.) b June 23, 1932

Blair, W. L. (Otago) b May 11, 1948

Blake, D. E. (Hants) b April 27, 1925

Blake, Rev. P. D. S. (OUCC & Sussex) b May 23, 1927

Blakey, R. J. (Yorks.) b Jan. 15, 1967

*Blanckenberg, J. M. (W. Prov. & Natal) b Dec. 31, 1893, 'presumed dead'

*Bland, K. C. (Rhod., E. Prov. & OFS; *CY 1966*) b April 5, 1938

Blenkiron, W. (Warwicks.) b July 21, 1942

Bligh, Hon. Ivo (*see* 8th Earl of Darnley)

Block, S. A. (CUCC & Surrey) b July 15, 1908, d Oct. 7, 1979

Blofeld, H. C. (CUCC) b Sept. 23, 1939

Blundell, Sir E. D. (CUCC & NZ) b May 29, 1907, d Sept. 24, 1984

*Blunt, R. C. (Cant. & Otago; *CY 1928*) b Nov. 3, 1900, d June 22, 1966

*Blythe, C. (Kent; *CY 1904*) b May 30, 1879, d Nov. 8, 1917

*Board, J. H. (Glos.) b Feb. 23, 1867, d April 16, 1924

*Bock, E. G. (Griq. W., Tvl & W. Prov.) b Sept. 17, 1908, d Sept. 5, 1961

Bodkin, P. E. (CUCC) b Sept. 15, 1924

*Bolton, B. A. (Cant. & Wgtn) b May 31, 1935

*Bolus, J. B. (Yorks., Notts. & Derbys.) b Jan. 31, 1934

*Bond, G. E. (W. Prov.) b April 5, 1909, d Aug. 27, 1965

Bond, J. D. (Lancs. & Notts.; *CY 1971*) b May 6, 1932

*Bonnor, G. J. (Vic. & NSW) b Feb. 25, 1855, d June 27, 1912

*Boock, S. L. (Otago & Cant.) b Sept. 20, 1951

Boon, D. C. (Tas.) b Dec. 29, 1960

Boon, T. J. (Leics.) b Nov. 1, 1961

*Booth, B. C. (NSW) b Oct. 19, 1933

Booth, B. J. (Lancs. & Leics.) b Dec. 3, 1935

Booth, F. S. (Lancs.) b Feb. 12, 1907, d Jan. 21, 1980

*Booth, M. W. (Yorks.; *CY 1914*) b Dec. 10, 1886, d July 1, 1916

Booth, P. (Leics.) b Nov. 2, 1952

Booth, R. (Yorks. & Worcs.) b Oct. 1, 1926

*Borde, C. G. (Baroda & M'tra) b July 21, 1934

*Border, A. R. (NSW, Glos, Qld & Essex; *CY 1982*) b July 27, 1955

Bore, M. K. (Yorks. & Notts.) b June 2, 1947

Borrington, A. J. (Derbys.) b Dec. 8, 1948

*Bosanquet, B. J. T. (OUCC & Middx; *CY 1905*) b Oct. 13, 1877, d Oct. 12, 1936

Bose, G. (Bengal) b May 20, 1947

Boshier, B. S. (Leics.) b March 6, 1932

*Botham, I. T. (Som. & Worcs.; *CY 1978*) b Nov. 24, 1955

*Botten, J. T. (NE Tvl & N. Tvl) b June 21, 1938

Boucher, J. C. (Ireland) b Dec. 22, 1910

Bourne, W. A. (B'dos & Warwicks.) b Nov. 15, 1952

*Bowden, M. P. (Surrey & Tvl) b Nov. 1, 1865, d Feb. 19, 1892

Bowditch, M. H. (W. Prov.) b Aug. 30, 1945

*Bowes, W. E. (Yorks.; *CY 1932*) b July 25, 1908, d Sept. 5, 1987

*Bowley, E. H. (Sussex & Auck.; *CY 1930*) b June 6, 1890, d July 9, 1974

Bowley, F. L. (Worcs.) b Nov. 9, 1873, d May 31, 1943

Bowman, R. (OUCC & Lancs.) b Jan. 26, 1934

Box, T. (Sussex) b Feb. 7, 1808, d July 12, 1876

*Boyce, K. D. (B'dos & Essex; *CY 1974*) b Oct. 11, 1943

*Boycott, G. (Yorks. & N. Tvl; *CY 1965*) b Oct. 21, 1940

Boyd-Moss, R. J. (CUCC & Northants) b Dec. 16, 1959

Boyes, G. S. (Hants) b March 31, 1899, d Feb. 11, 1973

*Boyle, H. F. (Vic.) b Dec. 10, 1847, d Nov. 21, 1907

*Bracewell, B. P. (C. Dist., Otago & N. Dist.) b Sept. 14, 1959

*Bracewell, J. G. (Otago & Auck.) b April 15, 1958

*Bradburn, W. P. (N. Dist.) b Nov. 24, 1938

*Bradley, W. M. (Kent) b Jan. 2, 1875, d June 19, 1944

*Bradman, Sir D. G. (NSW & S. Aust.; *CY 1931*) b Aug. 27, 1908

Bradshaw, J. C. (Leics.) b Jan. 25, 1902, d Nov. 8, 1984

Brain, B. M. (Worcs. & Glos.) b Sept. 13, 1940

*Brann, W. H. (E. Prov.) b April 4, 1899, d Sept. 22, 1953

Brassington, A. J. (Glos.) b Aug. 9, 1954

Bratchford, J. D. (Qld) b Feb. 2, 1929

*Braund, L. C. (Surrey & Som.; *CY 1902*) b Oct. 18, 1875, d Dec. 22, 1955

Bray, C. (Essex) b April 6, 1898

Brayshaw, I. J. (W. Aust.) b Jan. 14, 1942

Brazier, A. F. (Surrey & Kent) b Dec. 7, 1924

Breakwell, D. (Northants & Som.) b July 2, 1948

*Brearley, J. M. (CUCC & Middx; *CY 1977*) b April 28, 1942

*Brearley, W. (Lancs.; *CY 1909*) b March 11, 1876, d Jan. 30, 1937

*Brennan, D. V. (Yorks.) b Feb. 10, 1920, d Jan. 9, 1985

Brickett, D. J. (E. Prov.) b Dec. 9, 1950

Bridge, W. B. (Warwicks.) b May 29, 1938

Bridger, Rev. J. R. (Hants) b April 8, 1920, d July 14, 1986

Brierley, T. L. (Glam. & Lancs.) b June 15, 1910

Briers, N. E. (Leics.) b Jan. 15, 1955

*Briggs, John (Lancs.; *CY 1889*) b Oct. 3, 1862, d Jan. 11, 1902

*Bright, R. J. (Vic.) b July 13, 1954

*Briscoe, A. W. (Tvl) b Feb. 6, 1911, d April 22, 1941

*Broad, B. C. (Glos. & Notts.) b Sept. 29, 1957

Broadbent, R. G. (Worcs.) b June 21, 1924

Brocklehurst, B. G. (Som.) b Feb. 18, 1922

*Brockwell, W. (Kimberley & Surrey; *CY 1895*) b Jan. 21, 1865, d July 1, 1935

Broderick, V. (Northants) b Aug. 17, 1920

Brodhurst, A. H. (CUCC & Glos.) b July 21, 1916

*Bromfield, H. D. (W. Prov.) b June 26, 1932

*Bromley, E. H. (W. Aust. & Vic.) b Sept. 2, 1912, d Feb. 1, 1967

*Bromley-Davenport, H. R. (CUCC, Bombay Eur. & Middx) b Aug. 18, 1870, d May 23, 1914

*Brookes, D. (Northants; *CY 1957*) b Oct. 29, 1915

Brookes, W. H. (Editor of *Wisden* 1936-39) b Dec. 5, 1894, d May 28, 1955

Brooks, R. A. (OUCC & Som.) b June 14, 1943

*Brown, A. (Kent) b Oct. 17, 1935

Brown, A. S. (Glos.) b June 24, 1936
*Brown, D. J. (Warwicks.) b Jan. 30, 1942
Brown, D. W. J. (Glos.) b Feb. 26, 1942
Brown, E. (Warwicks.) b Nov. 27, 1911, 'dead'
*Brown, F. R. (CUCC, Surrey & Northants; *CY 1933*; Pres. MCC 1971-72) b Dec. 16, 1910
*Brown, G. (Hants) b Oct. 6, 1887, d Dec. 3, 1964
Brown, J. (Scotland) b Sept. 24, 1931
*Brown, J. T. (Yorks.; *CY 1895*) b Aug. 20, 1869, d Nov. 4, 1904
Brown, K. R. (Middx) b March 18, 1963
*Brown, L. S. (Tvl, NE Tvl & Rhod.) b Nov. 24, 1910, d Sept. 1, 1983
Brown, R. D. (Zimb.) b March 11, 1951
Brown, S. M. (Middx) b Dec. 8, 1917
*Brown, V. R. (Cant.) b Nov. 3, 1959
*Brown, W. A. (NSW & Qld; *CY 1939*) b July 31, 1912
Brown, W. C. (Northants) b Nov. 13, 1900, d Jan. 20, 1986
*Browne, C. R. (B'dos & BG) b Oct. 8, 1890, d Jan. 12, 1964
Bruce, Hon. C. N. (3rd Lord Aberdare) (OUCC & Middx) b Aug. 2, 1885, d Oct. 4, 1957
Bruce, S. D. (W. Prov. & OFS) b Jan. 11, 1954
*Bruce, W. (Vic.) b May 22, 1864, d Aug. 3, 1925
Bruyns, A. (W. Prov. & Natal) b Sept. 19, 1946
Bryan, G. J. (Kent) b Dec. 29, 1902
Bryan, J. L. (CUCC & Kent; *CY 1922*) b May 26, 1896, d April 23, 1985
Bryan, R. T. (Kent) b July 30, 1898, d July 27, 1970
*Buckenham, C. P. (Essex) b Jan. 16, 1876, d Feb. 23, 1937
Buckingham, J. (Warwicks.) b Jan. 21, 1903, d Jan. 25, 1987
Budd, E. H. (Middx & All-England) b Feb. 23, 1785, d March 29, 1875
Budd, W. L. (Hants) b Oct. 25, 1913, d Aug. 23, 1986
Buggins, B. L. (W. Aust.) b Jan. 29, 1935
Bull, C. L. (Cant.) b Aug. 19, 1946
Bull, D. F. E. (Qld) b Aug. 13, 1935
Bull, F. G. (Essex; *CY 1898*) b April 2, 1875, d Sept. 16, 1910
Buller, J. S. (Yorks. & Worcs.) b Aug. 23, 1909, d Aug. 7, 1970
Burden, M. D. (Hants) b Oct. 4, 1930, d Nov. 9, 1987
*Burge, P. J. (Qld; *CY 1965*) b May 17, 1932
*Burger, C. G. de V. (Natal) b July 12, 1935
Burgess, G. I. (Som.) b May 5, 1943
*Burgess, M. G. (Auck.) b July 17, 1944
Burke, C. (Auck.) b March 22, 1914
*Burke, J. W. (NSW; *CY 1957*) b June 12, 1930, d Feb. 2, 1979

*Burke, S. F. (NE Tvl & OFS) b March 11, 1934
*Burki, Javed (Pak. Us, OUCC, Punjab, Lahore, Kar., R'pindi & NWFP) b May 8, 1938
*Burn, E. J. K. (K. E.) (Tas.) b Sept. 17, 1862, d July 20, 1956
Burnet, J. R. (Yorks.) b Oct. 11, 1918
Burns, N. D. (Essex, W. Prov. & Som.) b Sept. 19, 1965
Burnup, C. J. (CUCC & Kent; *CY 1903*) b Nov. 21, 1875, d April 5, 1960
Burrough, H. D. (Som.) b Feb. 6, 1909
Burrow, B. W. (Griq. W.) b Feb. 8, 1940
Burton, D. C. F. (CUCC & Yorks.) b Sept. 13, 1887, d Sept. 24, 1971
*Burton, F. J. (Vic. & NSW) b 1866, d Aug. 25, 1929
Burtt, J. W. (C. Dist.) b June 11, 1944
*Burtt, T. B. (Cant.) b Jan. 22, 1915
Buse, H. T. F. (Som.) b Aug. 5, 1910
Bushby, M. H. (CUCC) b July 29, 1931
Buss, A. (Sussex) b Sept. 1, 1939
Buss, M. A. (Sussex & OFS) b Jan. 24, 1944
Buswell, J. E. (Northants) b July 3, 1909
*Butcher, A. R. (Surrey & Glam.) b Jan. 7, 1954
*Butcher, B. F. (Guyana; *CY 1970*) b Sept. 3, 1933
Butcher, I. P. (Leics.) b July 1, 1962
*Butcher, R. O. (Middx, B'dos & Tas.) b Oct. 14, 1953
*Butler, H. J. (Notts.) b March 12, 1913
Butler, L. C. (Wgtn) b Sept. 2, 1934
*Butler, L. S. (T/T) b Feb. 9, 1929
Butt, H. R. (Sussex) b Dec. 27, 1865, d Dec. 21, 1928
*Butts, C. G. (Guyana) b July 8, 1957
Butterfield, L. A. (Cant.) b Aug. 29, 1913
Buxton, I. R. (Derbys.) b April 17, 1938
*Buys, I. D. (W. Prov.) b Feb. 3, 1895, dead
*Bynoe, M. R. (B'dos) b Feb. 23, 1941

Caccia, Lord (Pres. MCC 1973-74) b Dec. 21, 1905
Caesar, Julius (Surrey & All-England) b March 25, 1830, d March 6, 1878
Caffyn, W. (Surrey & NSW) b Feb. 2, 1828, d Aug. 28, 1919
Caine, C. Stewart (Editor of *Wisden* 1926-33) b Oct. 28, 1861, d April 15, 1933
*Cairns, B. L. (C. Dist., Otago & N. Dist.) b Oct. 10, 1949
Calder, H. L. (Cranleigh; *CY 1918*) b 1900
*Callaway, S. T. (NSW & Cant.) b Feb. 6, 1868, d Nov. 25, 1923
*Callen, I. W. (Vic. & Boland) b May 2, 1955
*Calthorpe, Hon. F. S. Gough- (CUCC, Sussex & Warwicks.) b May 27, 1892, d Nov. 19, 1935
*Camacho, G. S. (Guyana) b Oct. 15, 1945
*Cameron, F. J. (Jam.) b June 22, 1923

*Cameron, F. J. (Otago) b June 1, 1932
*Cameron, H. B. (Tvl, E. Prov. & W. Prov.; CY 1936) b July 5, 1905, d Nov. 2, 1935
*Cameron, J. H. (CUCC, Jam. & Som.) b April 8, 1914
Campbell, K. O. (Otago) b March 20, 1943
*Campbell, T. (Tvl) b Feb. 9, 1882, d Oct. 5, 1924
Cannings, V. H. D. (Warwicks. & Hants) b April 3, 1919
Capel, D. J. (Northants & E. Prov.) b Feb. 6, 1963
Caple, R. G. (Middx & Hants) b Dec. 8, 1939
Cardus, Sir Neville (Cricket Writer) b April 3, 1888, d Feb. 27, 1975
*Carew, G. McD. (B'dos) b June 4, 1910, d Dec. 9, 1974
*Carew, M. C. (T/T) b Sept. 15, 1937
*Carkeek, W. (Vic.) b Oct. 17, 1878, d Feb. 20, 1937
Carlson, P. H. (Qld) b Aug. 8, 1951
*Carlstein, P. R. (OFS, Tvl, Natal & Rhod.) b Oct. 28, 1938
Carmody, D. K. (NSW & W. Aust.) b Feb. 16, 1919, d Oct. 21, 1977
Carpenter, D. (Glos.) b Sept. 12, 1935
Carpenter, R. (Cambs. & Utd England XI) b Nov. 18, 1830, d July 13, 1901
*Carr, A. W. (Notts.; CY 1923) b May 21, 1893, d Feb. 7, 1963
*Carr, D. B. (OUCC & Derbys.; CY 1960; Sec. TCCB 1974-86) b Dec. 28, 1926
*Carr, D. W. (Kent; CY 1910) b March 17, 1872, d March 23, 1950
Carr, J. D. (OUCC & Middx) b June 15, 1963
Carrick, P. (Yorks. & E. Prov.) b July 16, 1952
Carrigan, A. H. (Qld) b Aug. 26, 1917
Carrington, E. (Derbys.) b March 25, 1914
Carse, J. A. (Rhod., W. Prov., E. Prov. & Northants) b Dec. 13, 1958
*Carter, C. P. (Natal & Tvl) b April 23, 1881, d Nov. 8, 1952
*Carter, H. (NSW) b Halifax, Yorks. March 15, 1878, d June 8, 1948
Carter, R. G. (Warwicks.) b April 14, 1933
Carter, R. G. M. (Worcs.) b July 11, 1937
Carter, R. M. (Northants & Cant.) b May 25, 1960
Cartwright, H. (Derbys.) b May 12, 1951
*Cartwright, T. W. (Warwicks., Som. & Glam.) b July 22, 1935
Carty, R. A. (Hants) b July 28, 1922, d March 31, 1984
Cass, G. R. (Essex, Worcs. & Tas.) b April 23, 1940
Castell, A. T. (Hants) b Aug. 6, 1943
Castle, F. (Som.) b April 9, 1909
Catt, A. W. (Kent & W. Prov.) b Oct. 2, 1933

*Catterall, R. H. (Tvl, Rhod., Natal & OFS; CY 1925) b July 10, 1900, d Jan. 2, 1961
Causby, J. P. (S. Aust.) b Oct. 27, 1942
*Cave, H. B. (Wgtn & C. Dist.) b Oct. 10, 1922
Cederwall, B. W. (Wgtn) b Feb. 24, 1952
Chadwick, D. (W. Aust.) b March 29, 1941
Chalk, F. G. H. (OUCC & Kent) b Sept. 7, 1910, d Feb. 20, 1943
*Challenor, G. (B'dos) b June 28, 1888, d July 30, 1947
*Chandrasekhar, B. S. (†Karn.; CY 1972) b May 17, 1945
*Chang, H. S. (Jam.) b July 22, 1952
*Chapman, A. P. F. (Uppingham, OUCC & Kent; CY 1919) b Sept. 3, 1900, d Sept. 16, 1961
*Chapman, H. W. (Natal) b June 30, 1890, d Dec. 1, 1941
Chapman, T. A. (Leics. & Rhod.) b May 14, 1919, d Feb. 19, 1979
*Chappell, G. S. (S. Aust., Som. & Qld; CY 1973) b Aug. 7, 1948
*Chappell, I. M. (S. Aust. & Lancs.; CY 1976) b Sept. 26, 1943
*Chappell, T. M. (S. Aust., W. Aust. & NSW) b Oct. 21, 1952
*Chapple, M. E. (Cant. & C. Dist.) b July 25, 1930, d July 31, 1985
*Charlton, P. C. (NSW) b April 9, 1867, d Sept. 30, 1954
*Charlwood, H. R. J. (Sussex) b Dec. 19, 1846, d June 6, 1888
*Chatfield, E. J. (Wgtn) b July 3, 1950
*Chatterton, W. (Derbys.) b Dec. 27, 1861, d March 19, 1913
*Chauhan, C. P. S. (M'tra & Delhi) b July 21, 1947
Cheatle, R. G. L. (Sussex & Surrey) b July 31, 1953
*Cheetham, J. E. (W. Prov.) b May 26, 1920, d Aug. 21, 1980
Chester, F. (Worcs.; Umpire) b Jan. 20, 1895, d April 8, 1957
Chesterton, G. H. (OUCC & Worcs.) b July 15, 1922
*Chevalier, G. A. (W. Prov.) b March 9, 1937
Childs, J. H. (Glos. & Essex; CY 1987) b Aug. 15, 1951
Childs-Clarke, A. W. (Middx & Northants) b May 13, 1905, d Feb. 19, 1980
*Chipperfield, A. G. (NSW) b Nov. 17, 1905, d July 29, 1987
Chisholm, R. H. E. (Scotland) b May 22, 1927
*Chowdhury, N. R. (Bihar & Bengal) b May 23, 1923, d Dec. 14, 1979
*Christiani, C. M. (BG) b Oct. 28, 1913, d April 4, 1938
*Christiani, R. J. (BG) b July 19, 1920
*Christopherson, S. (Kent; Pres. MCC 1939-45) b Nov. 11, 1861, d April 6, 1949

*Christy, J. A. J. (Tvl & Qld) b Dec. 12, 1904, d Feb. 1, 1971

*Chubb, G. W. A. (Border & Tvl) b April 12, 1911, d Aug. 28, 1982

Clark, D. G. (Kent; Pres. MCC 1977-78) b Jan. 27, 1919

Clark, E. A. (Middx) b April 15, 1937

*Clark, E. W. (Northants) b Aug. 9, 1902, d April 28, 1982

Clark, L. S. (Essex) b March 6, 1914

Clark, T. H. (Surrey) b Oct. 4, 1924, d June 15, 1981

*Clark, W. M. (W. Aust.) b Sept. 19, 1953

*Clarke, Dr C. B. (B'dos, Northants & Essex) b April 7, 1918

Clarke, R. W. (Northants) b April 22, 1924, d Aug. 3, 1981

*Clarke, S. T. (B'dos, Surrey & Tvl) b Dec. 11, 1954

Clarke, William (Notts.; founded All-England XI & Trent Bridge ground) b Dec. 24, 1798, d Aug. 25, 1856

Clarkson, A. (Yorks. & Som.) b Sept. 5, 1939

Claughton, J. A. (OUCC & Warwicks.) b Sept. 17, 1956

*Clay, J. C. (Glam.) b March 18, 1898, d Aug. 12, 1973

Clay, J. D. (Notts.) b Oct. 15, 1924

Clayton, G. (Lancs & Som.) b Feb. 3, 1938

Clements, S. M. (OUCC) b April 19, 1956

*Cleverley, D. C. (Auck.) b Dec. 23, 1909

Clift, Patrick B. (Rhod., Leics. & Natal) b July 14, 1953

Clift, Philip B. (Glam.) b Sept. 3, 1918

Clinton, G. S. (Kent, Surrey & Zimb.-Rhod.) b May 5, 1953

*Close, D. B. (Yorks. & Som.; *CY 1964*) b Feb. 24, 1931

Cobb, R. A. (Leics.) b May 18, 1961

Cobham, 9th Visct (Worcs.) b Oct. 23, 1881, d July 31, 1949

Cobham, 10th Visct (Hon. C. J. Lyttelton) (Worcs.; Pres. MCC 1954) b Aug. 8, 1909, d March 20, 1977

*Cochrane, J. A. K. (Tvl & Griq. W.) b July 15, 1909, d June 15, 1987

*Coen, S. K. (OFS, W. Prov., Tvl & Border) b Oct. 14, 1902, d Jan. 28, 1967

*Colah, S. M. H. (Bombay, W. Ind. & Naw.) b Sept. 22, 1902, d Sept. 11, 1950

Colchin, Robert ("Long Robin") (Kent & All-England) b Nov. 1713, d April 1750

*Coldwell, L. J. (Worcs.) b Jan. 10, 1933

Coleman, C. A. R. (Leics.) b July 7, 1906, d June 14, 1978

*Colley, D. J. (NSW) b March 15, 1947

Collin, T. (Warwicks.) b April 7, 1911

*Collinge, R. O. (C. Dist., Wgtn & N. Dist.) b April 2, 1946

*Collins, H. L. (NSW) b Jan. 21, 1889, d May 28, 1959

Collins, R. (Lancs.) b March 10, 1934

*Colquhoun, I. A. (C. Dist.) b June 8, 1924

Coman, P. G. (Cant.) b April 13, 1943

*Commaille, J. M. M. (W. Prov., Natal, OFS & Griq. W.) b Feb. 21, 1883, d July 27, 1956

*Compton, D. C. S. (Middx & Holkar; *CY 1939*) b May 23, 1918

Compton, L. H. (Middx) b Sept. 12, 1912, d Dec. 27, 1984

*Coney, J. V. (Wgtn; *CY 1984*) b June 21, 1952

*Congdon, B. E. (C. Dist., Wgtn, Otago & Cant.; *CY 1974*) b Feb. 11, 1938

*Coningham, A. (NSW & Qld) b July 14, 1863, d June 13, 1939

*Connolly, A. N. (Vic. & Middx) b June 29, 1939

Connor, C. A. (Hants) b March 24, 1961

Constable, B. (Surrey) b Feb. 19, 1921

Constant, D. J. (Kent & Leics.; Umpire) b Nov. 9, 1941

*Constantine, Lord L. N. (T/T & B'dos; *CY 1940*) b Sept. 21, 1902, d July 1, 1971

Constantine, L. S. (T/T) b May 25, 1874, d Jan. 5, 1942

*Contractor, N. J. (Guj. & Ind. Rlwys) b March 7, 1934

*Conyngham, D. P. (Natal, Tvl & W. Prov.) b May 10, 1897

*Cook, C. (Glos.) b Aug. 23, 1921

*Cook, F. J. (E. Prov.) b 1870, dead

*Cook, G. (Northants & E. Prov.) b Oct. 9, 1951

Cook, G. G. (Qld) b June 29, 1910, d Sept. 12, 1982

*Cook, N. G. B. (Leics. & Northants) b June 17, 1956

Cook, S. J. (Tvl) b July 31, 1953

Cook, T. E. (Sussex) b Feb. 5, 1901, d Jan. 15, 1950

*Cooper, A. H. C. (Tvl) b Sept 2, 1893, d July 18, 1963

*Cooper, B. B. (Middx, Kent & Vic.) b March 15, 1844, d Aug. 7, 1914

Cooper, F. S. Ashley- (Cricket Historian) b March 17, 1877, d Jan. 31, 1932

Cooper, G. C. (Sussex) b Sept. 2, 1936

Cooper, H. P. (Yorks. & N. Tvl) b April 17, 1949

Cooper, K. E. (Notts.) b Dec. 27, 1957

Cooper, K. R. (Natal) b April 1, 1954

*Cooper, W. H. (Vic.) b Sept. 11, 1849, d April 5, 1939

Cope, G. A. (Yorks.) b Feb. 23, 1947

*Copson, W. H. (Derbys.; *CY 1937*) b April 27, 1908, d Sept. 14, 1971

Cordle, A. E. (Glam.) b Sept. 21, 1940

*Corling, G. E. (NSW) b July 13, 1941

Cornford, J. H. (Sussex) b Dec. 9, 1911, d June 17, 1985

*Cornford, W. L. (Sussex) b Dec. 25, 1900, d Feb. 6, 1964

Cornwallis, Capt. Hon. W. S. (2nd Lord Cornwallis) (Kent) b March 14, 1892, d Jan. 4, 1982

Corrall, P. (Leics.) b July 16, 1906

Corran, A. J. (OUCC & Notts.) b Nov. 25, 1939

*Cosier, G. J. (Vic., S. Aust. & Qld) b April 25, 1953

*Cottam, J. T. (NSW) b Sept. 5, 1867, d Jan. 30, 1897

*Cottam, R. M. H. (Hants & Northants) b Oct. 16, 1944

*Cotter, A. (NSW) b Dec. 3, 1884, d Oct. 31, 1917

Cotton, J. (Notts. & Leics.) b Nov. 7, 1940

Cottrell, G. A. (CUCC) b March 23, 1945

Coulson, S. S. (Leics.) b Oct. 17, 1898, d Oct. 3, 1981

*Coulthard, G. (Vic.) b Aug. 1, 1856, d Oct. 22, 1883

*Coventry, Hon. C. J. (Worcs.) b Feb. 26, 1867, d June 2, 1929

Coverdale, S. P. (CUCC, Yorks., & Northants) b Nov. 20, 1954

Cowan, M. J. (Yorks.) b June 10, 1933

Cowans, N. G. (Middx) b April 17, 1961

Cowdrey, C. S. (Kent) b Oct. 20, 1957

Cowdrey, G. R. (Kent) b June 27, 1964

*Cowdrey, M. C. (OUCC & Kent; *CY 1956*; Pres. MCC 1986-87) b Dec. 24, 1932

*Cowie, J. (Auck.) b March 30, 1912

Cowley, G. S. (E. Prov. & Natal) b March 1, 1953

Cowley, N. G. (Hants) b March 1, 1953

*Cowper, R. M. (Vic. & W. Aust.) b Oct. 5, 1940

Cox, A. L. (Northants) b July 22, 1907, d Nov. 1986

Cox, G., jun. (Sussex) b Aug. 23, 1911, d March 30, 1985

Cox, G. R. (Sussex) b Nov. 29, 1873, d March 24, 1949

*Cox, J. L. (Natal) b June 28, 1886, d July 4, 1971

*Coxon, A. (Yorks.) b Jan. 18, 1916

Crabtree, H. P. (Essex) b April 30, 1906, d May 28, 1982

Craig, E. J. (CUCC & Lancs.) b March 26, 1942

*Craig, I. D. (NSW) b June 12, 1935

Cranfield, L. M. (Glos.) b Aug. 29, 1909

Cranmer, P. (Warwicks.) b Sept. 10, 1914

*Cranston, J. (Glos.) b Jan. 9, 1859, d Dec. 10, 1904

Cranston, K. (Lancs.) b Oct. 20, 1917

*Crapp, J. F. (Glos.) b Oct. 14, 1912, d Feb. 15, 1981

*Crawford, J. N. (Surrey, S. Aust., Wgtn & Otago; *CY 1907*) b Dec. 1, 1886, d May 2, 1963

*Crawford, P. (NSW) b Aug. 3, 1933

Crawley, A. M. (OUCC & Kent; Pres. MCC 1972-73) b April 10, 1908

Crawley, L. G. (CUCC, Worcs. & Essex) b July 26, 1903, d July 9, 1981

Cray, S. J. (Essex) b May 29, 1921

*Cresswell, G. F. (Wgtn & C. Dist.) b March 22, 1915, d Jan. 10, 1966

*Cripps, G. (W. Prov.) b Oct. 19, 1865, d July 27, 1943

*Crisp, R. J. (Rhod., W. Prov. & Worcs.) b May 28, 1911

*Croft, C. E. H. (Guyana & Lancs.) b March 15, 1953

*Cromb, I. B. (Cant.) b June 25, 1905, d March 6, 1984

Crookes, N. S. (Natal) b Nov. 15, 1935

Cross, G. F. (Leics.) b Nov. 15, 1943

*Crowe, J. J. (S. Aust. & Auck.) b Sept. 14, 1958

*Crowe, M. D. (Auck., C. Dist. & Som.; *CY 1985*) b Sept. 22, 1962

Crump, B. S. (Northants) b April 25, 1938

Crush, E. (Kent) b April 25, 1917

Cuffy, T. (T/T) b Nov. 9, 1949

Cumbes, J. (Lancs., Surrey, Worcs. & Warwicks.) b May 4, 1944

*Cunis, R. S. (Auck. & N. Dist.) b Jan. 5, 1941

Cunningham, K. G. (S. Aust.) b July 26, 1939

*Curnow, S. H. (Tvl) b Dec. 16, 1907, d July 28, 1986

Curran, K. M. (Glos. & Zimb.) b Sept. 7, 1959

Curtis, T. S. (Worcs. & CUCC) b Jan. 15, 1960

Cuthbertson, G. B. (Middx, Sussex & Northants) b March 28, 1901

Cutmore, J. A. (Essex) b Dec. 28, 1898, d Nov. 30, 1985

*Cuttell, W. R. (Lancs.; *CY 1898*) b Sept. 13, 1864, d Dec. 9, 1929

*Da Costa, O. C. (Jam.) b Sept. 11, 1907, d Oct. 1, 1936

Dacre, C. C. (Auck. & Glos.) b May 15, 1899, d Nov. 2, 1975

Daer, A. G. (Essex) b Nov. 22, 1906, d July 16, 1980

Daft, Richard (Notts. & All-England) b Nov. 2, 1835, d July 18, 1900

Dakin, G. F. (E. Prov.) b Aug. 13, 1935

Dalmeny, Lord (6th Earl of Rosebery) (Middx & Surrey) b Jan. 8, 1882, d May 30, 1974

*Dalton, E. L. (Natal) b Dec. 2, 1906, d June 3, 1981

*Dani, H. T. (M'tra & Ind. Serv.) b May 24, 1933

*Daniel, W. W. (B'dos, Middx & W. Aust.) b Jan. 16, 1956

Daniels, N. P. (Natal & W. Prov.) b Jan. 28, 1956

Dansie, N. (S. Aust.) b July 2, 1928

*D'Arcy, J. W. (Cant., Wgtn & Otago) b April 23, 1936

Dare, R. (Hants) b Nov. 26, 1921

*Darling, J. (S. Aust.; *CY 1900*) b Nov. 21, 1870, d Jan. 2, 1946

*Darling, L. S. (Vic.) b Aug. 14, 1909

*Darling, W. M. (S. Aust.) b May 1, 1957

*Darnley, 8th Earl of (Hon. Ivo Bligh) (CUCC & Kent; Pres. MCC 1900) b March 13, 1859, d April 10, 1927

Davey, J. (Glos.) b Sept. 4, 1944

*Davidson, A. K. (NSW; *CY 1962*) b June 14, 1929

Davies, Dai (Glam.) b Aug. 26, 1896, d July 16, 1976

Davies, Emrys (Glam.) b June 27, 1904, d Nov. 10, 1975

*Davies, E. Q. (E. Prov., Tvl & NE Tvl) b Aug. 26, 1909, d Nov. 11, 1976

Davies, G. R. (NSW) b July 22, 1946

Davies, H. D. (Glam.) b July 23, 1932

Davies, H. G. (Glam.) b April 23, 1913

Davies, J. G. W. (CUCC & Kent; Pres. MCC 1985-86) b Sept. 10, 1911

Davies, T. (Glam.) b Oct. 25, 1960

Davis, B. A. (T/T & Glam.) b May 2, 1940

*Davis, C. A. (T/T) b Jan. 1, 1944

Davis, E. (Northants) b March 8, 1922

*Davis, I. C. (NSW & Qld) b June 25, 1953

Davis, M. R. (Som.) b Feb. 26, 1962

Davis, P. C. (Northants) b May 24, 1915

Davis, R. C. (Glam.) b Jan. 1, 1946

*Davis, S. P. (Vic.) b Nov. 8, 1959

*Davis, W. W. (Windwards, Glam., Tas. & Northants) b Sept. 18, 1958

Davison, B. F. (Rhod., Leics, Tas. & Glos.) b Dec. 21, 1946

Davison, I. (Notts.) b Oct. 4, 1937

Dawkes, G. O. (Leics. & Derbys.) b July 19, 1920

*Dawson, E. W. (CUCC & Leics.) b Feb. 13, 1904, d June 4, 1979

*Dawson, O. C. (Natal & Border) b Sept. 1, 1919

Day, A. P. (Kent; *CY 1910*) b April 10, 1885, d Jan. 22, 1969

Day, N. T. (Tvl & N. Tvl) b Dec. 31, 1953

*de Alwis, R. G. (SL) b Feb. 15, 1959

*Dean, H. (Lancs.) b Aug. 13, 1884, d March 12, 1957

*Deane, H. G. (Natal & Tvl) b July 21, 1895, d Oct. 21, 1939

*De Caires, F. I. (BG) b May 12, 1909, d Feb. 2, 1959

*De Courcy, J. H. (NSW) b April 18, 1927

Deed, J. A. (Kent) b Sept. 12, 1901, d Oct. 19, 1980

*DeFreitas, P. A. J. (Leics.) b Feb. 18, 1966

Delisle, G. P. S. (Middx & OUCC) b Dec. 25, 1934

*Dell, A. R. (Qld) b Aug. 6, 1947

*de Mel, A. L. F. (SL) b May 9, 1959

*Dempster, C. S. (Wgtn, Leics., Scotland & Warwicks.; *CY 1932*) b Nov. 15, 1903, d Feb. 14, 1974

*Dempster, E. W. (Wgtn) b Jan. 25, 1925

*Denness, M. H. (Scotland, Kent & Essex; *CY 1975*) b Dec. 1, 1940

Dennett, E. G. (Glos.) b April 27, 1880, d Sept. 14, 1937

Denning, P. W. (Som.) b Dec. 16, 1949

Dennis, F. (Yorks.) b June 11, 1907

Dennis, S. J. (Yorks. & OFS) b Oct. 18, 1960

*Denton, D. (Yorks.; *CY 1906*) b July 4, 1874, d Feb. 16, 1950

Denton, W. H. (Northants) b Nov. 2, 1890, d April 23, 1979

Deodhar, D. B. (M'tra; oldest living Ranji Trophy player) b Jan. 14, 1892

*Depeiza, C. C. (B'dos) b Oct. 10, 1927

Derrick, J. (Glam.) b Jan. 15, 1963

*Desai, R. B. (Bombay) b June 20, 1939

De Saram, F. C. (OUCC & Ceylon) b Sept. 5, 1912, d April 11, 1983

*de Silva, A. M. (SL) b Dec. 3, 1963

de Silva, D. L. S. (SL) b Nov. 17, 1956, d April 12, 1980

*de Silva, D. S. (SL) b June 11, 1942

*de Silva, E. A. R. (SL) b March 28, 1956

de Silva, G. N. (SL) b March 12, 1955

*de Silva, G. R. A. (SL) b Dec. 12, 1952

*de Silva, P. A. (SL) b Oct. 17, 1965

*de Smidt, R. W. (W. Prov.) b Nov. 24, 1883, d Aug. 3, 1986

De Vaal, P. D. (Tvl) b March 1, 1945

Devereux, L. N. (Middx, Worcs. & Glam.) b Oct. 20, 1931

Dewdney, C. T. (Jam.) b Oct. 23, 1933

*Dewes, J. G. (CUCC & Middx) b Oct. 11, 1926

Dews, G. (Worcs.) b June 5, 1921

*Dexter, E. R. (CUCC & Sussex; *CY 1961*) b May 15, 1935

*Dias, R. L. (SL) b Oct. 18, 1952

Dibbs, A. H. A. (Pres. MCC 1983-84) b Dec. 9, 1918, d Nov. 28, 1985

*Dick, A. E. (Otago & Wgtn) b Oct. 10, 1936

Dickeson, C. W. (N. Dist.) b March 26, 1955

*Dickinson, G. R. (Otago) b March 11, 1903, d March 17, 1978

*Dilley, G. R. (Kent, Natal & Worcs.) b May 18, 1959

Diment, R. A. (Glos. & Leics.) b Feb. 9, 1927

*Dipper, A. E. (Glos.) b Nov. 9, 1885, d Nov. 7, 1945

*Divecha, R. V. (Bombay, OUCC, Northants, Vidarbha & S'tra) b Oct. 18, 1927

Diver, A. J. D. (Cambs., Middx, Notts. & All-England) b June 6, 1824, d March 25, 1876

Dixon, A. L. (Kent) b Nov. 27, 1933

*Dixon, C. D. (Tvl) b Feb. 12, 1891, d Sept. 9, 1969

Dodds, T. C. (Essex) b May 29, 1919

Doggart, A. G. (CUCC, Durham & Middx) b June 2, 1897, d June 7, 1963

*Doggart, G. H. G. (CUCC & Sussex; Pres. MCC 1981-82) b July 18, 1925

Doherty, M. J. D. (Griq. W.) b March 14, 1947

*D'Oliveira, B. L. (Worcs.; *CY 1967*) b Oct. 4, 1931

D'Oliveira, D. B. (Worcs.) b Oct. 19, 1960

*Dollery, H. E. (Warwicks. & Wgtn; *CY 1952*) b Oct. 14, 1914, d Jan. 20, 1987

Dollery, K. R. (Qld, Auck., Tas. & Warwicks.) b Dec. 9, 1924

*Dolphin, A. (Yorks.) b Dec. 24, 1885, d Oct. 23, 1942

*Donnan, H. (NSW) b Nov. 12, 1864, d Aug. 13, 1956

*Donnelly, M. P. (Wgtn, Cant., Middx, Warwicks. & OUCC; *CY 1948*) b Oct. 17, 1917

*Dooland, B. (S. Aust. & Notts.; *CY 1955*) b Nov. 1, 1923, d Sept. 8, 1980

Dorrinton, W. (Kent & All-England) b April 29, 1809, d Nov. 8, 1848

Dorset, 3rd Duke of (Kent) b March 24, 1745, d July 19, 1799

*Doshi, D. R. (Bengal, Notts. & Warwicks.) b Dec. 22, 1947

*Douglas, J. W. H. T. (Essex; *CY 1915*) b Sept. 3, 1882, d Dec. 19, 1930

Dowding, A. L. (OUCC) b April 4, 1929

*Dowe, U. G. (Jam.) b March 29, 1949

*Dower, R. R. (E. Prov.) b June 4, 1876, d Sept. 15, 1964

Dowling, D. F. (Border, NE Tvl & Natal) b July 25, 1914

*Dowling, G. T. (Cant.) b March 4, 1937

*Downton, P. R. (Kent & Middx) b April 4, 1957

Draper, E. J. (E. Prov. & Griq. W.) b Sept. 27, 1934

*Draper, R. G. (E. Prov. & Griq. W.) b Dec. 24, 1926

Dredge, C. H. (Som.) b Aug. 4, 1954

*Druce, N. F. (CUCC & Surrey; *CY 1898*) b Jan. 1, 1875, d Oct. 27, 1954

Drybrough, C. D. (OUCC & Middx) b Aug. 31, 1938

*D'Souza, A. (Kar., Peshawar & PIA) b Jan. 17, 1939

*Ducat, A. (Surrey; *CY 1920*) b Feb. 16, 1886, d July 23, 1942

*Duckworth, C. A. R. (Natal & Rhod.) b March 22, 1933

*Duckworth, G. (Lancs.; *CY 1929*) b May 9, 1901, d Jan. 5, 1966

Dudleston, B. (Leics., Glos. & Rhod.) b July 16, 1945

*Duff, R. A. (NSW) b Aug. 17, 1878, d Dec. 13, 1911

*Dujon, P. J. L. (Jam.) b May 28, 1956

*Duleepsinhji, K. S. (CUCC & Sussex; *CY 1930*) b June 13, 1905, d Dec. 5, 1959

*Dumbrill, R. (Natal & Tvl) b Nov. 19, 1938

*Duminy, J. P. (OUCC, W. Prov. & Tvl) b Dec. 16, 1897, d Jan. 31, 1980

*Duncan, J. R. F. (Qld & Vic.) b March 25, 1944

*Dunell, O. R. (E. Prov.) b July 15, 1856, d Oct. 21, 1929

Dunning, B. (N. Dist.) b March 20, 1940

*Dunning, J. A. (Otago & OUCC) b Feb. 6, 1903, d June 24, 1971

*Du Preez, J. H. (Rhod. & Zimb.) b Nov. 14, 1942

Du Preez, V. F. (N. Tvl) b Sept. 6, 1958

*Durani, S. A. (S'tra, Guj. & Raja.) b Dec. 11, 1934

Durose, A. J. (Northants) b Oct. 10, 1944

*Durston, F. J. (Middx) b July 11, 1893, d April 8, 1965

*Du Toit, J. F. (SA) b April 5, 1868, d July 10, 1909

Dye, J. C. J. (Kent, Northants & E. Prov.) b July 24, 1942

Dyer, D. D. (Natal & Tvl) b Dec. 3, 1946

*Dyer, D. V. (Natal) b May 2, 1914

*Dyer, G. C. (NSW) b March 16, 1959

Dyer, R. I. H. B. (Warwicks.) b Dec. 22, 1958

*Dymock, G. (Qld) b July 21, 1945

Dyson, A. H. (Glam.) b July 10, 1905, d June 7, 1978

Dyson, J. (Lancs.) b July 8, 1934

*Dyson, John (NSW) b June 11, 1954

*Eady, C. J. (Tas.) b Oct. 29, 1870, d Dec. 20, 1945

Eagar, E. D. R. (OUCC, Glos. & Hants) b Dec. 8, 1917, d Sept. 13, 1977

Eagar, M. A. (OUCC & Glos.) b March 20, 1934

Eaglestone, J. T. (Middx & Glam.) b July 24, 1923

Ealham, A. G. E. (Kent) b Aug. 30, 1944

East, D. E. (Essex) b July 27, 1959

East, R. E. (Essex) b June 20, 1947

East, R. J. (OFS) b March 31, 1953

Eastman, G. F. (Essex) b April 7, 1903

Eastman, L. C. (Essex & Otago) b June 3, 1897, d April 17, 1941

*Eastwood, K. H. (Vic.) b Nov. 23, 1935

*Ebeling, H. I. (Vic.) b Jan. 1, 1905, d Jan. 12, 1980

Eckersley, P. T. (Lancs.) b July 2, 1904, d Aug. 13, 1940

Eddy, V. A. (Leewards) b Feb. 14, 1955

*Edgar, B. A. (Wgtn) b Nov. 23, 1956

Edinburgh, HRH Duke of (Pres. MCC 1948-49, 1974-75) b June 10, 1921

Edmeades, B. E. A. (Essex) b Sept. 17, 1941

*Edmonds, P. H. (CUCC, Middx & E. Prov.) b March 8, 1951

Edmonds, R. B. (Warwicks.) b March 2, 1941

Edrich, B. R. (Kent & Glam.) b Aug. 18, 1922

Edrich, E. H. (Lancs.) b March 27, 1914

Edrich, G. A. (Lancs.) b July 13, 1918

*Edrich, J. H. (Surrey; *CY 1966*) b June 21, 1937

*Edrich, W. J. (Middx; *CY 1940*) b March 26, 1916, d April 23, 1986

*Edwards, G. N. (C. Dist.) b May 27, 1955

*Edwards, J. D. (Vic.) b June 12, 1862, d July 31, 1911

Edwards, M. J. (CUCC & Surrey) b March 1, 1940

*Edwards, R. (W. Aust. & Vic.) b Dec. 1, 1942

*Edwards, R. M. (B'dos) b June 3, 1940

*Edwards, W. J. (W. Aust.) b Dec. 23, 1949

Eele, P. J. (Som.) b Jan. 27, 1935

Eggar, J. D. (OUCC, Hants & Derbys.) b Dec. 1, 1916, d May 3, 1983

Ehtesham-ud-Din (Lahore, Punjab, PIA, NBP & UBL) b Sept. 4, 1950

Elgie, M. K. (Natal) b March 6, 1933

*Elliott, C. S. (Derbys.) b April 24, 1912

*Elliott, H. (Derbys.) b Nov. 2, 1891, d Feb. 2, 1976

Elliott, Harold (Lancs.; Umpire) b June 15, 1904, d April 15, 1969

Ellis, G. P. (Glam.) b May 24, 1950

Ellis, J. L. (Vic.) b May 9, 1890, d July 26, 1974

Ellis, R. G. P. (OUCC & Middx) b Oct. 20 1960

*Ellison, R. M. (Kent & Tas.; *CY 1986*) b Sept. 21, 1959

Elms, R. B. (Kent & Hants) b April 5, 1949

*Emburey, J. E. (Middx & W. Prov.; *CY 1984*) b Aug. 20, 1952

*Emery, R. W. G. (Auck. & Cant.) b March 28, 1915, d Dec. 18, 1982

Emery, S. H. (NSW) b Oct. 16, 1885, d Jan. 7, 1967

*Emmett, G. M. (Glos.) b Dec. 2, 1912, d Dec. 18, 1976

*Emmett, T. (Yorks.) b Sept. 3, 1841, d June 30, 1904

*Endean, W. R. (Tvl) b May 31, 1924

*Engineer, F. M. (Bombay & Lancs.) b Feb. 25, 1938

Enthoven, H. J. (CUCC & Middx) b June 4, 1903, d June 29, 1975

*Evans, A. J. (OUCC, Hants & Kent) b May 1, 1889, d Sept. 18, 1960

Evans, D. G. L. (Glam.; Umpire) b July 27, 1933

*Evans, E. (NSW) b March 6, 1849, d July 2, 1921

Evans, G. (OUCC, Glam. & Leics.) b Aug. 13, 1915

Evans, J. B. (Glam.) b Nov. 9, 1936

*Evans, T. G. (Kent; *CY 1951*) b Aug. 18, 1920

Every, T. (Glam.) b Dec. 19, 1909

Eyre, T. J. P. (Derbys.) b Oct. 17, 1939

Faber, M. J. J. (OUCC & Sussex) b Aug. 15, 1950

*Fagg, A. E. (Kent) b June 18, 1915, d Sept. 13, 1977

Fairbairn, A. (Middx) b Jan. 25, 1923

*Fairbrother, N. H. (Lancs.) b Sept. 9, 1963

*Fairfax, A. G. (NSW) b June 16, 1906, d May 17, 1955

Fairservice, C. (Kent & Middx) b Aug. 21, 1909

Fairservice, W. J. (Kent) b May 16, 1881, d June 26, 1971

Falcon, M. (CUCC) b July 21, 1888, d Feb. 27, 1976

Fallows, J. A. (Lancs.) b July 25, 1907, d Jan. 20, 1974

*Fane, F. L. (OUCC & Essex) b April 27, 1875, d Nov. 27, 1960

Fantham, W. E. (Warwicks.) b May 14, 1918

*Farnes, K. (CUCC & Essex; *CY 1939*) b July 8, 1911, d Oct. 20, 1941

*Farooq Hamid (Lahore & PIA) b March 3, 1945

*Farrer, W. S. (Border) b Dec. 8, 1936

*Farrimond, W. (Lancs.) b May 23, 1903, d Nov. 14, 1979

*Farrukh Zaman (Peshawar, NWFP, Punjab & MCB) b April 2, 1956

*Faulkner, G. A. (Tvl) b Dec. 17, 1881, d Sept. 10, 1930

*Favell, L. E. (S. Aust.) b Oct. 6, 1929, d June 14, 1987

Fearnley, C. D. (Worcs.) b April 12, 1940

Featherstone, N. G. (Tvl, N. Tvl, Middx & Glam.) b Aug. 20, 1949

'Felix', N. (Wanostrocht) (Kent, Surrey & All-England) b Oct. 4, 1804, d Sept. 3, 1876

*Fellows-Smith, J. P. (OUCC, Tvl & Northants) b Feb. 3, 1932

Felton, N. A. (Som.) b Oct. 24, 1960

*Fender, P. G. H. (Sussex & Surrey; *CY 1915*) b Aug. 22, 1892, d June 15, 1985

Fenner, D. (Border) b March 27, 1929

Ferguson, W. (T/T) b Dec. 14, 1917, d Feb. 23, 1961

Fernandes, M. P. (BG) b Aug. 12, 1897, d May 8, 1981

Fernando, E. R. (SL) b Feb. 22, 1944

*Fernando, E. R. N. S. (SL) b Dec. 19, 1955

Ferrandi, J. H. (W. Prov.) b April 3, 1930

Ferreira, A. M. (N. Tvl & Warwicks.) b April 13, 1955

Ferris, G. J. F. (Leics. & Leewards) b Oct. 18, 1964

**Ferris, J. J. (NSW, Glos. & S. Aust.; *CY 1889*) b May 21, 1867, d Nov. 21, 1900
*Fichardt, C. G. (OFS) b March 20, 1870, d May 30, 1923
Fiddling, K. (Yorks. & Northants) b Oct. 13, 1917
*Fielder, A. (Kent; *CY 1907*) b July 19, 1877, d Aug. 30, 1949
Findlay, T. M. (Comb. Is. & Windwards) b Oct. 19, 1943
Findlay, W. (OUCC & Lancs.; Sec. Surrey CCC, Sec. MCC 1926-36) b June 22, 1880, d June 19, 1953
Fingleton, J. H. (NSW) b April 28, 1908, d Nov. 22, 1981
*Finlason, C. E. (Tvl & Griq. W.) b Feb. 19, 1860, d July 31, 1917
Finney, R. J. (Derbys.) b Aug. 2, 1960
Firth, J. (Yorks. & Leics.) b June 27, 1918, d Sept. 6, 1981
Firth, Rev. Canon J. D'E. E. (Winchester, OUCC & Notts.; *CY 1918*) b Jan. 21, 1900, d Sept. 21, 1957
Fisher, B. (Qld) b Jan. 20, 1934, d April 6, 1980
*Fisher, F. E. (Wgtn & C. Dist.) b July 28, 1924
Fisher, P. B. (OUCC, Middx & Worcs.) b Dec. 19, 1954
*Fishlock, L. B. (Surrey; *CY 1947*) b Jan. 2, 1907, d June 26, 1986
Fitzgerald, R. A. (CUCC & Middx; Sec. MCC 1863-76) b Oct. 1, 1834, d Oct. 28, 1881
Flanagan, J. P. D. (Tvl) b Sept. 20, 1947
*Flavell, J. A. (Worcs.; *CY 1965*) b May 15, 1929
Fleetwood-Smith, L. O'B. (Vic.) b March 30, 1910, d March 16, 1971
Fletcher, D. A. G. (Rhod. & Zimb.) b Sept. 27, 1948
Fletcher, D. G. W. (Surrey) b July 6, 1924
*Fletcher, K. W. R. (Essex; *CY 1974*) b May 20, 1944
Fletcher, S. D. (Yorks.) b June 8, 1964
*Floquet, C. E. (Tvl) b Nov. 3, 1884, d Nov. 22, 1963
*Flowers, W. (Notts.) b Dec. 7, 1856, d Nov. 1, 1926
Foat, J. C. (Glos.) b Nov. 21, 1952
*Foley, H. (Wgtn) b Jan. 28, 1906, d Oct. 16, 1948
Folley, I. (Lancs.) b Jan. 9, 1963
Foord, C. W. (Yorks.) b June 11, 1924
Forbes, C. (Notts.) b Aug. 9, 1936
Ford, D. A. (NSW) b Dec. 12, 1930
*Ford, F. G. J. (CUCC & Middx) b Dec. 14, 1866, d Feb. 7, 1940
Ford, N. M. (OUCC, Derbys. & Middx) b Nov. 18, 1906
Ford, R. G. (Glos.) b March 3, 1907, d Oct. 1981

Foreman, D. J. (W. Prov. & Sussex) b Feb. 1, 1933
Fosh, M. K. (CUCC & Essex) b Sept. 26, 1957
Foster, D. G. (Warwicks.) b March 19, 1907, d Oct. 13, 1980
*Foster, F. R. (Warwicks.; *CY 1912*) b Jan. 31, 1889, d May 3, 1958
Foster, G. N. (OUCC, Worcs. & Kent) b Oct. 16, 1884, d Aug. 11, 1971
Foster, H. K. (OUCC & Worcs.; *CY 1911*) b Oct. 30, 1873, d June 23, 1950
Foster, M. K. (Worcs.) b Jan. 1, 1889, d Dec. 3, 1940
*Foster, M. L. C. (Jam.) b May 9, 1943
Foster, N. A. (Essex; *CY 1988*) b May 6, 1962
Foster, P. G. (Kent) b Oct. 9, 1916
*Foster, R. E. (OUCC & Worcs.; *CY 1901*) b April 16, 1878, d May 13, 1914
*Fothergill, A. J. (Som.) b Aug. 26, 1854, d Aug. 1, 1932
Fotheringham, H. R. (Natal & Tvl) b April 4, 1953
Foulkes, I. (Border & OFS) b Feb. 22, 1955
*Fowler, G. (Lancs.) b April 20, 1957
Fowler, W. P. (Derbys., N. Dist. & Auck.) b March 13, 1959
*Francis, B. C. (NSW & Essex) b Feb. 18, 1948
Francis, D. A. (Glam.) b Nov. 29, 1953
*Francis, G. N. (B'dos) b Dec. 7, 1897, d Jan. 12, 1942
*Francis, H. H. (Glos. & W. Prov.) b May 26, 1868, d Jan. 7, 1936
Francke, F. M. (SL & Qld) b March 29, 1941
*Francois, C. M. (Griq. W.) b June 20, 1897, d May 26, 1944
*Frank, C. N. (Tvl) b Jan. 27, 1891, d Dec. 26, 1961
*Frank, W. H. B. (SA) b Nov. 23, 1872, d Feb. 16, 1945
Franklin, H. W. F. (OUCC, Surrey & Essex) b June 30, 1901, d May 25, 1985
Franklin, T. J. (Auck.) b March 18, 1962
Fraser, A. R. C. (Middx) b Aug. 8, 1965
*Frederick, M. C. (B'dos, Derbys. & Jam.) b May 6, 1927
*Fredericks, R. C. (†Guyana & Glam.; *CY 1974*) b Nov. 11, 1942
*Freeman, A. P. (Kent; *CY 1923*) b May 17, 1888, d Jan. 28, 1965
*Freeman, D. L. (Wgtn) b Sept. 8, 1914
*Freeman, E. W. (S. Aust.) b July 13, 1944
*Freer, F. W. (Vic.) b Dec. 4, 1915
*French, B. N. (Notts.) b Aug. 13, 1959
Frost, G. (Notts.) b Jan. 15, 1947
Fry, C. A. (OUCC, Hants & Northants) b Jan. 14, 1940
*Fry, C. B. (OUCC, Sussex & Hants; *CY 1895*) b April 25, 1872, d Sept. 7, 1956
*Fuller, E. R. H. (W. Prov.) b Aug. 2, 1931**

*Fuller, R. L. (Jam.) b Jan. 30, 1913, d May 3, 1987
*Fullerton, G. M. (Tvl) b Dec. 8, 1922
Fulton, R. W. (Cant.) b Aug. 5, 1951
Funston, G. K. (NE Tvl & Griq. W.) b Nov. 21, 1948
*Funston, K. J. (NE Tvl, OFS & Tvl) b Dec. 3, 1925
*Furlonge, H. A. (T/T) b June 19, 1934

Gabriel, R. S. (T/T) b June 5, 1952
*Gadkari, C. V. (M'tra & Ind. Serv.) b Feb. 3, 1928
*Gaekwad, A. D. (Baroda) b Sept. 23, 1952
*Gaekwad, D. K. (Baroda) b Oct. 27, 1928
*Gaekwad, H. G. (†M. Pradesh) b Aug. 29, 1923
Gale, R. A. (Middx) b Dec. 10, 1933
*Gallichan, N. (Wgtn) b June 3, 1906, d March 25, 1969
*Gamsy, D. (Natal) b Feb. 17, 1940
*Gandotra, A. (Delhi & Bengal) b Nov. 24, 1948
*Gannon, J. B. (W. Aust.) b Feb. 8, 1947
Gard, T. (Som.) b June 2, 1957
Gardiner, H. A. B. (Rhod.) b Jan. 3, 1944
Gardner, F. C. (Warwicks.) b June 4, 1922, d Jan. 13, 1979
Gardner, L. R. (Leics.) b Feb. 23, 1934
Garland-Wells, H. M. (OUCC & Surrey) b Nov. 14, 1907
Garlick, R. G. (Lancs. & Northants) b April 11, 1917
*Garner, J. (B'dos, Som. & S. Aust.; *CY 1980*) b Dec. 16, 1952
Garnham, M. A. (Glos. & Leics.) b Aug. 20, 1960
*Garrett, T. W. (NSW) b July 26, 1858, d Aug. 6, 1943
*Gaskin, B. M. (BG) b March 21, 1908, d May 2, 1979
*Gatting, M. W. (Middx; *CY 1984*) b June 6, 1957
Gaunt, R. A. (W. Aust. & Vic.) b Feb. 26, 1934
*Gavaskar, S. M. (Bombay & Som.; *CY 1980*) b July 10, 1949
*Gay, L. H. (CUCC, Hants & Som.) b March 24, 1871, d Nov. 1, 1949
Geary, A. C. T. (Surrey) b Sept. 11, 1900
*Geary, G. (Leics.; *CY 1927*) b July 9, 1893, d March 6, 1981
Gedye, S. G. (Auck.) b May 2, 1929
*Gehrs, D. R. A. (S. Aust.) b Nov. 29, 1880, d June 25, 1953
Ghai, R. S. (Punjab) b June 12, 1960
*Ghavri, K. D. (S'tra & Bombay) b Feb. 28, 1951
*Ghazali, M. E. Z. (M'tra & Pak. Serv.) b June 15, 1924
*Ghorpade, J. M. (Baroda) b Oct. 2, 1930, d March 29, 1978

*Ghulam Abbas (Kar., NBP & PIA) b May 1, 1947
*Ghulam Ahmed (H'bad) b July 4, 1922
*Gibb, P. A. (OUCC, Scotland, Yorks. & Essex) b July 11, 1913, d Dec. 7, 1977
Gibbons, H. H. (Worcs.) b Oct. 10, 1904, d Feb. 16, 1973
*Gibbs, G. L. (BG) b Dec. 27, 1925, d Feb. 21, 1979
*Gibbs, L. R. (†Guyana, S. Aust. & Warwicks.; *CY 1972*) b Sept. 29, 1934
Gibbs, P. J. K. (OUCC & Derbys.) b Aug. 17, 1944
Gibson, C. H. (Eton, CUCC & Sussex; *CY 1918*) b Aug. 23, 1900, d Dec. 31, 1976
Gibson, D. (Surrey) b May 1, 1936
Gibson, J. G. (N. Dist. & Auck.) b Nov. 12, 1948
*Giffen, G. (S. Aust.; *CY 1894*) b March 27, 1859, d Nov. 29, 1927
*Giffen, W. F. (S. Aust.) b Sept. 20, 1861, d June 29, 1949
*Gifford, N. (Worcs. & Warwicks.; *CY 1975*) b March 30, 1940
*Gilbert, D. R. (NSW) b Dec. 19, 1960
*Gilchrist, R. (Jam. & H'bad) b June 28, 1934
Giles, R. J. (Notts.) b Oct. 17, 1919
Gill, A. (Notts.) b Aug. 4, 1940
Gill, L. L. (Tas. & Qld) b Nov. 19, 1891, d Dec. 4, 1986
Gilhouley, K. (Yorks. & Notts.) b Aug. 8, 1934
Gillespie, S. R. (Auck.) b March 2, 1957
Gilliat, R. M. C. (OUCC & Hants) b May 20, 1944
*Gilligan, A. E. R. (CUCC, Surrey & Sussex; *CY 1924*; Pres. MCC 1967-68) b Dec. 23, 1894, d Sept. 5, 1976
*Gilligan, A. H. H. (Sussex) b June 29, 1896, d May 5, 1978
Gilligan, F. W. (OUCC & Essex) b Sept. 20, 1893, d May 4, 1960
Gilmour, G. J. (NSW) b June 26, 1951
*Gimblett, H. (Som.; *CY 1953*) b Oct. 19, 1914, d March 30, 1978
Gladstone, G. (*see* Marais, G. G.)
Gladwin, Chris (Essex) b May 10, 1962
*Gladwin, Cliff (Derbys.) b April 3, 1916
*Gleeson, J. W. (NSW & E. Prov.) b March 14, 1938
Gleeson, R. A. (E. Prov.) b Dec. 6, 1873, d Sept. 27, 1919
*Glover, G. K. (Kimberley & Griq. W.) b May 13, 1870, d Nov. 15, 1938
Glover, T. R. (OUCC) b Nov. 26, 1951
Goddard, G. F. (Scotland) b May 19, 1938
*Goddard, J. D. C. (B'dos) b April 21, 1919, d Aug. 26, 1987
*Goddard, T. L. (Natal & NE Tvl) b Aug. 1, 1931
*Goddard, T. W. (Glos.; *CY 1938*) b Oct. 1, 1900, d May 22, 1966

Goel, R. (Patiala & Haryana) b Sept. 29, 1942

Goldstein, F. S. (OUCC, Northants, Tvl & W. Prov.) b Oct. 14, 1944

*Gomes, H. A. (T/T & Middx; *CY 1985*) b July 13, 1953

Gomes, S. A. (T/T) b Oct. 18, 1950

*Gomez, G. E. (T/T) b Oct. 10, 1919

*Gooch, G. A. (Essex & W. Prov.; *CY 1980*) b July 23, 1953

Goodway, C. C. (Warwicks.) b July 10, 1909

Goodwin, K. (Lancs.) b June 25, 1938

Goodwin, T. J. (Leics.) b Jan. 22, 1929

Goonatillake, F. R. M. de S. (SL) b. Aug. 15, 1951

*Goonatillake, H. M. (SL) b Aug. 16, 1952

Goonesena, G. (Ceylon, Notts., CUCC & NSW) b Feb. 16, 1931

*Gopalan, M. J. (Madras) b June 6, 1909

*Gopinath, C. D. (Madras) b March 1, 1930

*Gordon, N. (Tvl) b Aug. 6, 1911

Gore, A. C. (Eton & Army; *CY 1919*) b May 14, 1900

Gothard, E. J. (Derbys.) b Oct. 1, 1904, d Jan. 17, 1979

Gould, I. J. (Middx, Auck. & Sussex) b Aug. 19, 1957

*Gover, A. R. (Surrey; *CY 1937*) b Feb. 29, 1908

*Gower, D. I. (Leics.; *CY 1979*) b April 1, 1957

Gower, G. M. (Border) b July 10, 1952

Gowrie, 1st Lord (Pres. MCC 1948-49) b July 6, 1872, d May 2, 1955

Grace, Dr Alfred b May 17, 1840, d May 24, 1916

Grace, Dr Alfred H. (Glos.) b March 10, 1866, d Sept. 16, 1929

Grace, C. B. (Clifton) b March 1882, d June 6, 1938

*Grace, Dr E. M. (Glos.) b Nov. 28, 1841, d May 20, 1911

Grace, Dr Edgar M. (MCC) (son of E. M. Grace) b Oct. 6, 1886, d Nov. 24, 1974

*Grace, G. F. (Glos.) b Dec. 13, 1850, d Sept. 22, 1880

Grace, Dr Henry (Glos.) b Jan. 31, 1833, d Nov. 15, 1895

Grace, Dr H. M. (father of W. G., E. M. and G. F.) b Feb. 21, 1808, d Dec. 23, 1871

Grace, Mrs H. M. (mother of W. G., E. M. and G. F.) b July 18, 1812, d July 25, 1884

*Grace, Dr W. G. (Glos.; *CY 1896*) b July 18, 1848, d Oct. 23, 1915

Grace, W. G., jun. (CUCC & Glos.) b July 6, 1874, d March 2, 1905

Graf, S. F. (W. Aust. & Hants) b May 19, 1957

*Graham, H. (Vic. & Otago) b Nov. 22, 1870, d Feb. 7, 1911

Graham, J. N. (Kent) b May 8, 1943

*Graham, R. (W. Prov.) b Sept. 16, 1877, d April 21, 1946

*Grant, G. C. (CUCC, T/T & Rhod.) b May 9, 1907, d Oct. 26, 1978

*Grant, R. S. (CUCC & T/T) b Dec. 15, 1909, d Oct. 18, 1977

Graveney, D. A. (Glos.) b Jan. 21, 1953

Graveney, J. K. (Glos.) b Dec. 16, 1924

*Graveney, T. W. (Glos., Worcs. & Qld; *CY 1953*) b June 16, 1927

Graves, P. J. (Sussex & OFS) b May 19, 1946

*Gray, A. H. (T/T & Surrey) b May 23, 1963

*Gray, E. J. (Wgtn) b Nov. 18, 1954

Gray, J. R. (Hants) b May 19, 1926

Gray, L. H. (Middx) b Dec. 16, 1915, d Jan. 3, 1983

Greasley, D. G. (Northants) b Jan. 20, 1926

Green, A. M. (Sussex & OFS) b May 28, 1960

Green, D. J. (Derbys. & CUCC) b Dec. 18, 1935

Green, D. M. (OUCC, Lancs. & Glos.; *CY 1969*) b Nov. 10, 1939

Green, Brig. M. A. (Glos. & Essex) b Oct. 3, 1891, d Dec. 28, 1971

*Greenhough, T. (Lancs.) b Nov. 9, 1931

*Greenidge, A. E. (B'dos) b Aug. 20, 1956

*Greenidge, C. G. (Hants & B'dos; *CY 1977*) b May 1, 1951

*Greenidge, G. A. (B'dos & Sussex) b May 26, 1948

Greensmith, W. T. (Essex) b Aug. 16, 1930

*Greenwood, A. (Yorks.) b Aug. 20, 1847, d Feb. 12, 1889

Greenwood, H. W. (Sussex & Northants) b Sept. 4, 1909, d March 24, 1979

Greenwood, P. (Lancs.) b Sept. 11, 1924

Greetham, C. (Som.) b. Aug. 28, 1936

*Gregory, David W. (NSW; first Australian captain) b April 15, 1845, d Aug. 4, 1919

*Gregory, E. J. (NSW) b May 29, 1839, d April 22, 1899

*Gregory, J. M. (NSW; *CY 1922*) b Aug. 14, 1895, d Aug. 7, 1973

*Gregory, R. G. (Vic.) b Feb. 26, 1916, d June 10, 1942

*Gregory, S. E. (NSW; *CY 1897*) b April 14, 1870, d August 1, 1929

*Greig, A. W. (Border, E. Prov. & Sussex; *CY 1975*) b Oct. 6, 1946

*Greig, I. A. (CUCC, Border, Sussex & Surrey) b Dec. 8, 1955

*Grell, M. G. (T/T) b Dec. 18, 1899, d Jan. 11, 1976

*Grieve, B. A. F. (Eng.) b May 28, 1864, d Nov. 19, 1917

Grieves, K. J. (NSW & Lancs.) b Aug. 27, 1925

*Grieveson, R. E. (Tvl) b Aug. 24, 1909

*Griffin, G. M. (Natal & Rhod.) b June 12, 1939

*Griffith, C. C. (B'dos; *CY 1964*) b Dec. 14, 1938

Griffith, G. ("Ben") (Surrey & Utd England XI) b Dec. 20, 1833, d May 3, 1879

*Griffith, H. C. (B'dos) b Dec. 1, 1893, d March 18, 1980

Griffith, K. (Worcs.) b Jan. 17, 1950

Griffith, M. G. (CUCC & Sussex) b Nov. 25, 1943

*Griffith, S. C. (CUCC, Surrey & Sussex; Sec. MCC 1962-74; Pres. MCC 1979-80) b June 16, 1914

Griffiths, B. J. (Northants) b June 13, 1949

Griffiths, Sir W. H. (CUCC & Glam.) b Sept. 26, 1923

Grimmett, C. V. (Wgtn, Vic. & S. Aust.; *CY 1931*) b Dec. 25, 1891, d May 2, 1980

Grimshaw, N. (Northants) b May 5, 1911

Gripper, R. A. (Rhod.) b July 7, 1938

*Groube, T. U. (Vic.) b Sept. 2, 1857, d Aug. 5, 1927

*Grout, A. T. W. (Qld) b March 30, 1927, d Nov. 9, 1968

Grove, C. W. (Warwicks. & Worcs.) b Dec. 16, 1912, d Feb. 15, 1982

Grover, J. N. (OUCC) b Oct. 15, 1915

Groves, B. S. (Border & Natal) b March 1, 1947

Groves, M. G. M. (OUCC, Som. & W. Prov.) b Jan. 14, 1943

Grundy, J. (Notts. & Utd England XI) b March 5, 1824, d Nov. 24, 1873

*Guard, G. M. (Bombay & Guj.) b Dec. 12, 1925, d March 13, 1978

*Guest, C. E. J. (Vic. & W. Aust.) b Oct. 7, 1937

Guha, S. (Bengal) b Jan. 31, 1946

**Guillen, S. C. (T/T & Cant.) b Sept. 24, 1924

Guise, J. L. (OUCC & Middx) b Nov. 25, 1903

*Gunasekera, Y. (SL) b Nov. 8, 1957

**Gul Mahomed (N. Ind., Baroda, H'bad, Punjab & Lahore) b Oct. 15, 1921

*Guneratne, R. P. W. (SL) b Jan. 26, 1962

*Gunn, G. (Notts.; *CY 1914*) b June 13, 1879, d June 28, 1958

Gunn, G. V. (Notts.) b June 21, 1905, d Oct. 14, 1957

*Gunn, J. (Notts.; *CY 1904*) b July 19, 1876, d Aug. 21, 1963

Gunn, T. (Sussex) b Sept. 27, 1935

*Gunn, William (Notts.; *CY 1890*) b Dec. 4, 1858, d Jan. 29, 1921

*Gupte, B. P. (Bombay, Bengal & Ind. Rlwys) b Aug. 30, 1934

*Gupte, S. P. (Bombay, Bengal, Raja. & T/T) b Dec. 11, 1929

*Gurusinha, A. P. (SL) b Sept. 16, 1966

Gurr, D. R. (OUCC & Som.) b March 27, 1956

*Guy, J. W. (C. Dist., Wgtn, Northants, Cant., Otago & N. Dist.) b Aug. 29, 1934

Hacker, P. J. (Notts., Derbys. & OFS) b July 16, 1952

*Hadlee, B. G. (Cant.) b Dec. 14, 1941

*Hadlee, D. R. (Cant.) b Jan. 6, 1948

*Hadlee, R. J. (Cant., Notts. & Tas.; *CY 1982*) b July 3, 1951

*Hadlee, W. A. (Cant. & Otago) b June 4, 1915

Hafeez, A. (*see* Kardar)

*Haig, N. E. (Middx) b Dec. 12, 1887, d Oct. 27, 1966

*Haigh, S. (Yorks.; *CY 1901*) b March 19, 1871, d Feb. 27, 1921

Halfyard, D. J. (Kent & Notts.) b April 3, 1931

*Hall, A. E. (Tvl & Lancs.) b Jan. 23, 1896, d Jan. 1, 1964

*Hall, G. G. (NE Tvl & E. Prov.) b May 24, 1938, d June 26, 1987

Hall, I. W. (Derbys.) b Dec. 27, 1939

Hall, Louis (Yorks.; *CY 1890*) b Nov. 1, 1852, d Nov. 19, 1915

Hall, T. A. (Derbys. & Som.) b Aug. 19, 1930, d April 21, 1984

*Hall, W. W. (B'dos, T/T & Qld) b Sept. 12, 1937

Hallam, A. W. (Lancs. & Notts.; *CY 1908*) b Nov. 12, 1869, d July 24, 1940

Hallam, M. R. (Leics.) b Sept. 10, 1931

*Halliwell, E. A. (Tvl & Middx; *CY 1905*) b Sept. 7, 1864, d Oct. 2, 1919

*Hallows, C. (Lancs.; *CY 1928*) b April 4, 1895, d Nov. 10, 1972

Hallows, J. (Lancs.; *CY 1905*) b Nov. 14, 1873, d May 20, 1910

*Halse, C. G. (Natal) b Feb. 28, 1935

Hamence, R. A. (S. Aust.) b Nov. 25, 1915

Hamer, A. (Yorks. & Derbys.) b Dec. 8, 1916

Hammond, H. E. (Sussex) b Nov. 7, 1907, d June 16, 1985

*Hammond, J. R. (S. Aust.) b April 19, 1950

*Hammond, W. R. (Glos.; *CY 1928*) b June 19, 1903, d July 1, 1965

*Hampshire, J. H. (Yorks., Derbys. & Tas.) b Feb. 10, 1941

*Hands, P. A. M. (W. Prov.) b March 18, 1890, d April 27, 1951

*Hands, R. H. M. (W. Prov.) b July 26, 1888, d April 20, 1918

*Hanif Mohammad (B'pur, Kar. & PIA; *CY 1968*) b Dec. 21, 1934

*Hanley, M. A. (Border & W. Prov.) b Nov. 10, 1918

Hanley, R. W. (E. Prov., OFS, Tvl & Northants) b Jan. 29, 1952

*Hanumant Singh (M. Pradesh & Raja.) b March 29, 1939

Harden, R. J. (Som.) b Aug. 16, 1965

Hardie, B. R. (Scotland & Essex) b Jan. 14, 1950

*Hardikar, M. S. (Bombay) b Feb. 8, 1936

*Hardinge, H. T. W. (Kent; *CY 1915*) b Feb. 25, 1886, d May 8, 1965

*Hardstaff, J. (Notts.) b Nov. 9, 1882, d April 2, 1947

*Hardstaff, J., jun. (Notts. & Auck.; *CY 1938*) b July 3, 1911

Hardy, J. J. E. (Hants & Som.) b Oct. 10, 1960

Harfield, L. (Hants) b Aug. 16, 1905, d Nov. 19, 1985

*Harford, N. S. (C. Dist. & Auck.) b Aug. 30, 1930, d March 30, 1981

*Harford, R. I. (Auck.) b May 30, 1936

Harman, R. (Surrey) b Dec. 28, 1941

*Haroon Rashid (Kar., Sind, NBP, PIA & UBL) b March 25, 1953

*Harper, R. A. (Guyana & Northants) b March 17, 1963

*Harris, 4th Lord (OUCC & Kent; Pres. MCC 1895) b Feb. 3, 1851, d March 24, 1932

Harris, David (Hants & All-England) b 1755, d May 19, 1803

Harris, M. J. (Middx, Notts., E. Prov. & Wgtn) b May 25, 1944

*Harris, P. G. Z. (Cant.) b July 18, 1927

*Harris, R. M. (Auck.) b July 27, 1933

*Harris, T. A. (Griq. W. & Tvl) b Aug. 27, 1916

Harrison, L. (Hants) b June 8, 1922

*Harry, J. (Vic.) b Aug. 1, 1857, d Oct. 27, 1919

Hart, G. E. (Middx) b Jan. 13, 1902, d April 11, 1987

Hart, R. T. (C. Dist.) b Nov. 7, 1961

*Hartigan, G. P. D. (Border) b Dec. 30, 1884, d Jan. 7, 1955

*Hartigan, R. J. (NSW & Qld) b Dec. 12, 1879, d June 7, 1958

*Hartkopf, A. E. V. (Vic.) b Dec. 28, 1889, d May 20, 1968

*Hartley, A. (Lancs.; *CY 1911*) b April 11, 1879, d Oct. 1918

*Hartley, J. C. (OUCC & Sussex) b Nov. 15, 1874, d March 8, 1963

Hartley, P. J. (Warwicks. & Yorks.) b April 18, 1960

Hartley, S. N. (Yorks. & OFS) b March 18, 1956

Harty, I. D. (Border) b May 7, 1941

Harvey, J. F. (Derbys.) b Sept. 27, 1939

*Harvey, M. R. (Vic.) b April 29, 1918

Harvey, P. F. (Notts.) b Jan. 15, 1923

*Harvey, R. L. (Natal) b Sept. 14, 1911

*Harvey, R. N. (Vic. & NSW; *CY 1954*) b Oct. 8, 1928

Harvey-Walker, A. J. (Derbys.) b July 21, 1944

Hasan Jamil (Kalat, Kar., Pak. Us & PIA) b July 25, 1952

*Haseeb Ahsan (Peshawar, Pak. Us, Kar. & PIA) b July 15, 1939

Hassan, B. (Notts.) b March 24, 1944

*Hassett, A. L. (Vic.; *CY 1949*) b Aug. 28, 1913

*Hastings, B. F. (Wgtn, C. Dist. & Cant.) b March 23, 1940

*Hathorn, C. M. H. (Tvl) b April 7, 1878, d May 17, 1920

*Hawke, 7th Lord (CUCC & Yorks.; *CY 1909*; Pres. MCC 1914-18) b Aug. 16, 1860, d Oct. 10, 1938

*Hawke, N. J. N. (W. Aust., S. Aust. & Tas.) b June 27, 1939

Hawker, Sir Cyril (Essex; Pres. MCC 1970-71) b July 21, 1900

Hawkins, D. G. (Glos.) b May 18, 1935

*Hayes, E. G. (Surrey & Leics.; *CY 1907*) b Nov. 6, 1876, d Dec. 2, 1953

*Hayes, F. C. (Lancs.) b Dec. 6, 1946

Hayes, G. L. (Border) b Nov. 6, 1955

*Hayes, J. A. (Auck. & Cant.) b Jan. 11, 1927

Hayes, K. A. (OUCC & Lancs.) b Sept. 26, 1962

Haygarth, A. (Sussex; Historian) b Aug. 4, 1825, d May 1, 1903

*Haynes, D. L. (B'dos) b Feb. 15, 1956

Haysman, M. D. (S. Aust. & Leics.) b April 22, 1961

Hayward, T. (Cambs. & All-England) b March 21, 1835, d July 21, 1876

*Hayward, T. W. (Surrey; *CY 1895*) b March 29, 1871, d July 19, 1939

Haywood, P. R. (Leics.) b March 30, 1947

*Hazare, V. S. (M'tra, C. Ind. & Baroda) b March 11, 1915

Hazell, H. L. (Som.) b Sept. 30, 1909

Hazlerigg, Lord, formerly Hon. A. G. (CUCC & Leics.) b Feb. 24, 1910

Hazlitt, G. R. (Vic. & NSW) b Sept. 4, 1888, d Oct. 30, 1915

*Headley, G. A. (Jam.; *CY 1934*) b May 30, 1909, d Nov. 30, 1983

*Headley, R. G. A. (Worcs. & Jam.) b June 29, 1939

Hearn, P. (Kent) b Nov. 18, 1925

*Hearne, Alec (Kent; *CY 1894*) b July 22, 1863, d May 16, 1952

**Hearne, Frank (Kent & W. Prov.) b Nov. 23, 1858, d July 14, 1949

*Hearne, G. A. L. (W. Prov.) b March 27, 1888, d Nov. 13, 1978

*Hearne, George G. (Kent) b July 7, 1856, d Feb. 13, 1932

*Hearne, J. T. (Middx; *CY 1892*) b May 3, 1867, d April 17, 1944

*Hearne, J. W. (Middx; *CY 1912*) b Feb. 11, 1891, d Sept. 13, 1965

Hearne, Thos. (Middx) b Sept. 4, 1826, d May 13, 1900

Hearne, Thos., jun. (Lord's Ground Superintendent) b Dec. 29, 1849, d Jan. 29, 1910

Heath, G. E. M. (Hants) b Feb. 20, 1913

Heath, M. (Hants) b March 9, 1934

Hedges, B. (Glam.) b Nov. 10, 1927

Hedges, L. P. (Tonbridge, OUCC, Kent & Glos.; *CY 1919*) b July 13, 1900, d Jan. 12, 1933

*Heine, P. S. (NE Tvl, OFS & Tvl) b June 28, 1928

*Hemmings, E. E. (Warwicks. & Notts.) b Feb. 20, 1949

Hemsley, E. J. O. (Worcs.) b Sept. 1, 1943

*Henderson, M. (Wgtn) b Aug. 2, 1895, d June 17, 1970

Henderson, R. (Surrey; *CY 1890*) b March 30, 1865, d Jan. 29, 1931

Henderson, S. P. (CUCC, Worcs. & Glam.) b Sept. 24, 1958

*Hendren, E. H. (Middx; *CY 1920*) b Feb. 5, 1889, d Oct. 4, 1962

*Hendrick, M. (Derbys. & Notts.; *CY 1978*) b Oct. 22, 1948

*Hendriks, J. L. (Jam.) b Dec. 21, 1933

*Hendry, H. L. (NSW & Vic.; oldest surviving Test & Sheffield Shield player) b May 24, 1895

Henry, O. (W. Prov., Boland & Scotland) b Jan. 23, 1952

Henschell, A. B. (Qld) b June 6, 1961

Henwood, P. P. (OFS & Natal) b May 22, 1946

Herman, O. W. (Hants) b Sept. 18, 1907, d June 24, 1987

Herman, R. S. (Middx, Border, Griq. W. & Hants) b Nov. 30, 1946

Heron, J. G. (Zimb.) b Nov. 8, 1948

*Heseltine, C. (Hants) b Nov. 26, 1869, d June 13, 1944

Hever, N. G. (Middx & Glam.) b Dec. 17, 1924

Hewetson, E. P. (OUCC & Warwicks.) b May 27, 1902, d Dec. 26, 1977

Hewett, H. T. (OUCC & Som.; *CY 1893*) b May 25, 1864, d March 4, 1921

Heyn, P. D. (SL) b June 26, 1945

*Hibbert, P. A. (Vic.) b July 23, 1952

Hick, G. A. (Worcs. & Zimb.; *CY 1987*) b May 23, 1966

Higgins, H. L. (Worcs.) b Feb. 24, 1894, d Sept. 15, 1979

*Higgs, J. D. (Vic.) b July 11, 1950

*Higgs, K. (Lancs. & Leics.; *CY 1968*) b Jan. 14, 1937

Hignell, A. J. (CUCC & Glos.) b Sept. 4, 1955

*Hilditch, A. M. J. (NSW) b May 20, 1956

Hill, Alan (Derbys. & OFS) b June 29, 1950

*Hill, Allen (Yorks.) b Nov. 14, 1843, d Aug. 29, 1910

*Hill, A. J. L. (CUCC & Hants) b July 26, 1871, d Sept. 6, 1950

*Hill, C. (S. Aust.; *CY 1900*) b March 18, 1877, d Sept. 5, 1945

Hill, E. (Som.) b July 9, 1923

Hill, G. (Hants) b April 15, 1913

*Hill, J. C. (Vic.) b June 25, 1923, d Aug. 11, 1974

Hill, L. W. (Glam.) b April 14, 1942

Hill, M. (Notts., Derbys & Som.) b Sept. 14, 1935

Hill, N. W. (Notts.) b Aug. 22, 1935

Hill, W. A. (Warwicks.) b April 27, 1910

Hills, J. J. (Glam.; Umpire) b Oct. 14, 1897, d Oct. 1969

Hills, R. W. (Kent) b Jan. 8, 1951

Hill-Wood, C. K. (OUCC & Derbys.) b June 5, 1907

Hill-Wood, Sir W. W. (CUCC & Derbys.) b Sept. 8, 1901, d Oct. 10, 1980

Hilton, C. (Lancs. & Essex) b Sept. 26, 1937

Hilton, J. (Lancs. & Som.) b Dec. 29, 1930

*Hilton, M. J. (Lancs.; *CY 1957*) b Aug. 2, 1928

*Hime, C. F. W. (Natal) b Oct. 24, 1869, d Dec. 6, 1940

Hinks, S. G. (Kent) b Oct. 12, 1960

*Hirst, G. H. (Yorks.; *CY 1901*) b Sept. 7, 1871, d May 10, 1954

*Hitch, J. W. (Surrey; *CY 1914*) b May 7, 1886, d July 7, 1965

Hitchcock, R. E. (Cant. & Warwicks.) b Nov. 28, 1929

*Hoad, E. L. G. (B'dos) b Jan. 29, 1896, d March 5, 1986

*Hoare, D. E. (W. Aust.) b Oct. 19, 1934

*Hobbs, Sir J. B. (Surrey; *CY 1909, special portrait 1926*) b Dec. 16, 1882, d Dec. 21, 1963

*Hobbs, R. N. S. (Essex & Glam.) b May 8, 1942

Hobson, D. L. (E. Prov. & W. Prov.) b Sept. 3, 1951

*Hodges, J. H. (Vic.) b July 31, 1856, d Jan. 17, 1933

Hodgkinson, G. F. (Derbys.) b Feb. 19, 1914, d Jan. 7, 1987

Hodgson, A. (Northants) b Oct. 27, 1951

Hoffman, D. S. (Warwicks.) b Jan. 13, 1966

Hofmeyr, M. B. (OUCC & NE Tvl) b Dec. 9, 1925

*Hogan, T. G. (Vic.) b Sept. 23, 1956

*Hogg, R. M. (S. Aust.) b March 5, 1951

Hogg, W. (Lancs. & Warwicks.) b July 12, 1955

Hohns, T. V. (Qld) b Jan. 23, 1954

Holder, V. A. (B'dos, Worcs. & OFS) b Oct. 8, 1945

*Holding, M. A. (Jam., Lancs., Derbys. & Tas.; *CY 1977*) b Feb. 16, 1954

*Hole, G. B. (NSW & S. Aust.) b Jan. 6, 1931

*Holford, D. A. J. (B'dos & T/T) b April 16, 1940

*Holland, R. G. (NSW) b Oct. 19, 1946

*Iddon, J. (Lancs.) b Jan. 8, 1902, d April 17, 1946

Igglesden, A. P. (Kent) b Oct. 8, 1964

*Ijaz Ahmed (Gujranwala & PACO) b Sept. 20, 1968

*Ijaz Butt (Pak. Us, Punjab, Lahore, R'pindi & Multan) b March 10, 1938

*Ijaz Faqih (Kar., Sind, PWD & MCB) b March 24, 1956

*Ikin, J. T. (Lancs.) b March 7, 1918, d Sept. 15, 1984

*Illingworth, R. (Yorks. & Leics.; *CY 1960*) b June 8, 1932

Illingworth, R. K. (Worcs.) b Aug. 23, 1963

*Imran Khan (Lahore, Dawood, Worcs., OUCC, PIA, Sussex & NSW; *CY 1983*) b Nov. 25, 1952

*Imtiaz Ahmed (N. Ind., Comb. Us, NWFP, Pak. Serv., Peshawar & PAF) b Jan. 5, 1928

*Imtiaz Ali (T/T) b July 28, 1954

Inchmore, J. D. (Worcs. & N. Tvl) b Feb. 22, 1949

*Indrajitsinhji, K. S. (S'tra & Delhi) b June 15, 1937

*Ingle, R. A. (Som.) b Nov. 5, 1903

Ingleby-Mackenzie, A. C. D. (Hants) b Sept. 15, 1933

Inman C. C. (Ceylon & Leics.) b Jan. 29, 1936

Innes, G. A. S. (W. Prov. & Tvl) b Nov. 16, 1931, d July 19, 1982

*Inshan Ali (T/T) b Sept. 25, 1949

*Insole, D. J. (CUCC & Essex; *CY 1956*) b April 18, 1926

*Intikhab Alam (Kar., PIA, Surrey, PWD, Sind & Punjab) b Dec. 28, 1941

*Inverarity, R. J. (W. Aust. & S. Aust.) b Jan. 31, 1944

*Iqbal Qasim (Kar., Sind & NBP) b Aug. 6, 1953

*Irani, J. K. (Sind) b Aug. 18, 1923, d Feb. 25, 1982

*Iredale, F. A. (NSW) b June 19, 1867, d April 15, 1926

*Iremonger, J. (Notts.; *CY 1903*) b March 5, 1876, d March 25, 1956

*Ironmonger, H. (Qld & Vic.) b April 7, 1882, d June 1, 1971

*Ironside, D. E. J. (Tvl) b May 2, 1925

*Irvine, B. L. (W. Prov., Natal, Essex & Tvl) b March 9, 1944

*Israr Ali (S. Punjab, B'pur & Multan) b May 1, 1927

*Iverson, J. B. (Vic.) b July 27, 1915, d Oct. 24, 1973

*Jackman, R. D. (Surrey, W. Prov. & Rhod.; *CY 1981*) b Aug. 13, 1945

*Jackson, A. A. (NSW) b Sept. 5, 1909, d Feb. 16, 1933

Jackson, A. B. (Derbys.) b Aug. 21, 1933

Jackson, Sir A. H. M. (Derbys.) b Nov. 9, 1899, d Oct. 11, 1983

*Jackson, Rt Hon. Sir F. S. (CUCC & Yorks.; *CY 1894*; Pres. MCC 1921) b Nov. 21, 1870, d March 9, 1947

Jackson, G. R. (Derbys.) b June 23, 1896, d Feb. 21, 1966

*Jackson, H. L. (Derbys.; *CY 1959*) b April 5, 1921

Jackson, John (Notts. & All-England) b May 21, 1833, d Nov. 4, 1901

Jackson, P. F. (Worcs.) b May 11, 1911

Jacques, T. A. (Yorks.) b Feb. 19, 1905

*Jahangir Khan (N. Ind. & CUCC) b Feb. 1, 1910

*Jai, L. P. (Bombay) b April 1, 1902, d Jan. 29, 1968

*Jaisimha, M. L. (H'bad) b March 3, 1939

Jakeman, F. (Yorks. & Northants) b Jan. 10, 1920, d May 18, 1986

*Jalal-ud-Din (PWD, Kar., IDBP & Allied Bank) b June 12, 1959

James, A. E. (Sussex) b Aug. 7, 1924

*James, K. C. (Wgtn & Northants) b March 12, 1904, d Aug. 21, 1976

James, K. D. (Middx, Hants & Wgtn) b March 18, 1961

James, R. M. (CUCC & Wgtn) b Oct. 2, 1934

*Jameson, J. A. (Warwicks.) b June 30, 1941

*Jamshedji, R. J. D. (Bombay) b Nov. 18, 1892, d April 5, 1976

*Jardine, D. R. (OUCC & Surrey; *CY 1928*) b Oct. 23, 1900, d June 18, 1958

Jardine, M. R. (OUCC & Middx) b June 8, 1869, d Jan. 16, 1947

*Jarman, B. N. (S. Aust.) b Feb. 17, 1936

Jarrett, D. W. (OUCC & CUCC) b April 19, 1952

*Jarvis, A. H. (S. Aust.) b Oct. 19, 1860, d Nov. 15, 1933

Jarvis, K. B. S. (Kent) b April 23, 1953

Jarvis, P. W. (Yorks.) b June 29, 1965

*Jarvis, T. W. (Auck. & Cant.) b July 29, 1944

*Javed Akhtar (R'pindi & Pak. Serv.) b Nov. 21, 1940

*Javed Miandad (Kar., Sind, Sussex, HBL & Glam.; *CY 1982*) b June 12, 1957

*Jayantilal, K. (H'bad) b Jan. 13, 1948

*Jayasekera, R. S. A. (SL) b Dec. 7, 1957

Jayasinghe, S. (Ceylon & Leics.) b Jan. 19, 1931

Jayasinghe, S. A. (SL) b July 15, 1955

Jean-Jacques, M. (Derbys.) b July 2, 1960

*Jefferies, S. T. (W. Prov., Derbys. & Lancs.) b Dec. 8, 1959

Jefferson, R. I. (CUCC & Surrey) b Aug. 15, 1941

*Jeganathan, S. (SL) b July 11, 1951

*Jenkins, R. O. (Worcs.; *CY 1950*) b Nov. 24, 1918

Jenkins, V. G. J. (OUCC & Glam.) b Nov. 2, 1911

*Jenner, T. J. (W. Aust. & S. Aust.) b Sept. 8, 1944

*Jennings, C. B. (S. Aust.) b June 5, 1884, d June 20, 1950

Jennings, K. F. (Som.) b Oct. 5, 1953

Jennings, R. V. (Tvl) b Aug. 9, 1954

Jepson, A. (Notts.) b July 12, 1915

*Jessop, G. L. (CUCC & Glos.; *CY 1898*) b May 19, 1874, d May 11, 1955

Jesty, T. E. (Hants., Border, Griq. W., Cant. & Surrey; *CY 1983*) b June 2, 1948

Jewell, Major M. F. S. (Sussex & Worcs.) b Sept. 15, 1885, d May 28, 1978

*John, V. B. (SL) b May 27, 1960

Johnson, C. (Yorks.) b Sept. 5, 1947

*Johnson, C. L. (Tvl) b 1871, d May 31, 1908

Johnson, G. W. (Kent & Tvl) b Nov. 8, 1946

*Johnson, H. H. H. (Jam.) b July 17, 1910, d June 24, 1987

Johnson, H. L. (Derbys.) b Nov. 8, 1927

*Johnson, I. W. (Vic.) b Dec. 8, 1918

Johnson, L. A. (Northants) b Aug. 12, 1936

*Johnson, L. J. (Qld) b March 18, 1919, d April 20, 1977

Johnson, P. (Notts.) b April 24, 1965

Johnson, P. D. (CUCC & Notts.) b Nov. 12, 1949

*Johnson, T. F. (T/T) b Jan. 10, 1917, d April 5, 1985

Johnston, B. A. (Broadcaster) b June 24, 1912

*Johnston, W. A. (Vic.; *CY 1949*) b Feb. 26, 1922

Jones, A. (Glam., W. Aust., N. Tvl & Natal; *CY 1978*) b Nov. 4, 1938

Jones, A. A. (Sussex, Som., Middx, Glam., N. Tvl & OFS) b Dec. 9, 1947

*Jones, A. H. (Wgtn) b May 9, 1959

Jones, A. L. (Glam.) b June 1, 1957

Jones, A. N. (Sussex, Border & Som.) b July 22, 1961

*Jones, A. O. (Notts. & CUCC; *CY 1900*) b Aug. 16, 1872, d Dec. 21, 1914

Jones, B. J. R. (Worcs.) b Nov. 2, 1955

*Jones, C. M. (C. E. L.) (BG) b Nov. 3, 1902, d Dec. 10, 1959

Jones, D. M. (Vic.) b March 24, 1961

Jones, Ernest (S. Aust. & W. Aust.) b Sept. 30, 1869, d Nov. 23, 1943

Jones, E. C. (Glam.) b Dec. 14, 1912

Jones, E. W. (Glam.) b June 25, 1942

Jones, I. J. (Glam.) b Dec. 10, 1941

Jones, K. V. (Middx) b March 28, 1942

*Jones, P. E. (T/T) b June 6, 1917

Jones, P. H. (Kent) b June 19, 1935

Jones, S. A. (W. Prov. & Boland) b April 14, 1955

*Jones, S. P. (NSW, Qld & Auck.) b Aug. 1, 1861, d July 14, 1951

Jones, W. E. (Glam.) b Oct. 31, 1916

Jordaan, A. H. (N. Tvl) b July 22, 1947

Jordan, A. B. (C. Dist.) b Sept. 5, 1949

Jordan, J. M. (Lancs.) b Feb. 7, 1932

Jorden, A. M. (CUCC & Essex) b Jan. 28, 1947

Jordon, R. C. (Vic.) b Feb. 17, 1937

*Joshi, P. G. (M'tra) b Oct. 27, 1926, d Jan. 8, 1987

Joshi, U. C. (S'tra, Ind. Rlwys, Guj. & Sussex) b Dec. 23, 1944

*Joslin, L. R. (Vic.) b Dec. 13, 1947

Judd, A. K. (CUCC & Hants) b Jan. 1, 1904

Judge, P. F. (Middx, Glam. & Bengal) b May 23, 1916

Julian, R. (Leics.) b Aug. 23, 1936

*Julien, B. D. (T/T & Kent) b March 13, 1950

*Jumadeen, R. R. (T/T) b April 12, 1948

Jupp, H. (Surrey) b Nov. 19, 1841, d April 8, 1889

*Jupp, V. W. C. (Sussex & Northants; *CY 1928*) b March 27, 1891, d July 9, 1960

Jurangpathy, B. R. (SL) b June 25, 1967

*Kallicharran, A. I. (Guyana, Warwicks., Qld, Tvl & OFS; *CY 1983*) b March 21, 1949

*Kaluperuma, L. W. (SL) b May 25, 1949

*Kaluperuma, S. M. S. (SL) b Oct. 22, 1961

*Kanhai, R. B. (†Guyana, Tvl, W. Aust., Warwicks. & Tas.; *CY 1964*) b Dec. 26, 1935

*Kanitkar, H. S. (M'tra) b Dec. 8, 1942

*Kapil Dev (Haryana, Northants & Worcs.; *CY 1983*) b Jan. 6, 1959

Kaplan, C. J. (OFS) b Jan. 26, 1909

**Kardar, A. H. (formerly Abdul Hafeez) (N. Ind., OUCC, Warwicks. & Pak. Serv.) b Jan. 17, 1925

Karnain, U. S. H. (SL) b Aug. 11, 1962

Katz, G. A. (Natal) b Feb. 9, 1947

*Keeton, W. W. (Notts.; *CY 1940*) b April 30, 1905, d Oct. 10, 1980

Keighley, W. G. (OUCC & Yorks.) b Jan. 10, 1925

*Keith, H. J. (Natal) b Oct. 25, 1927

Kelleher, H. R. A. (Surrey & Northants) b March 3, 1929

*Kelleway, C. (NSW) b April 25, 1886, d Nov. 16, 1944

Kelly, J. (Notts.) b Sept. 15, 1930

*Kelly, J. J. (NSW; *CY 1903*) b May 10, 1867, d Aug. 14, 1938

Kelly, J. M. (Lancs. & Derbys.) b March 19, 1922, d Nov. 13, 1979

*Kelly, T. J. D. (Vic.) b May 3, 1844, d July 20, 1893

*Kempis, G. A. (Natal) b Aug. 4, 1865, d May 19, 1890

*Kendall, T. (Vic. & Tas.) b Aug. 24, 1851, d Aug. 17, 1924

Kennedy, A. (Lancs.) b Nov. 4, 1949

*Kennedy, A. S. (Hants; *CY 1933*) b Jan. 24, 1891, d Nov. 15, 1959

*Kenny, R. B. (Bombay & Bengal) b Sept. 29, 1930, d Nov. 21, 1985

*Kent, M. F. (Qld) b Nov. 23, 1953

*Kentish, E. S. M. (Jam. & OUCC) b Nov. 21, 1916

*Kenyon, D. (Worcs.; *CY 1963*) b May 15, 1924

*Kerr, R. B. (Qld) b June 16, 1961

*Kerr, J. L. (Cant.) b Dec. 28, 1910

Kerr, K. J. (Tvl & Warwicks.) b Sept. 11, 1961

Kerslake, R. C. (CUCC & Som.) b Dec. 26, 1942

Kettle, M. K. (Northants) b March 18, 1944

*Khalid Hassan (Punjab & Lahore) b July 14, 1937

*Khalid Wazir (Pak.) b April 27, 1936

*Khan Mohammad (N. Ind., Pak. Us, Som., B'pur, Sind, Kar. & Lahore) b Jan. 1, 1928

Khanna, S. C. (Delhi) b June 3, 1956

Kidd, E. L. (CUCC & Middx) b Oct. 18, 1889, d July 2, 1984

Kilborn, M. J. (OUCC) b Sept. 20, 1962

*Killick, Rev. E. T. (CUCC & Middx) b May 9, 1907, d May 18, 1953

Kilner, Norman (Yorks. & Warwicks.) b July 21, 1895, d April 28, 1979

*Kilner, Roy (Yorks.; *CY 1924*) b Oct. 17, 1890, d April 5, 1928

Kimpton, R. C. M. (OUCC & Worcs.) b Sept. 21, 1916

*King, C. L. (B'dos, Glam., Worcs. & Natal) b June 11, 1951

*King, F. McD. (B'dos) b Dec. 14, 1926

King, I. M. (Warwicks. & Essex) b Nov. 10, 1931

King, J. B. (Philadelphia) b Oct. 19, 1873, d Oct. 17, 1965

*King, J. H. (Leics.) b April 16, 1871, d Nov. 18, 1946

*King, L. A. (Jam. & Bengal) b Feb. 27, 1939

Kingsley, Sir P. G. T. (OUCC) b May 26, 1908

*Kinneir, S. P. (Warwicks.; *CY 1912*) b May 13, 1871, d Oct. 16, 1928

*Kippax, A. F. (NSW) b May 25, 1897, d Sept. 4, 1972

Kirby, D. (CUCC & Leics.) b Jan. 18, 1939

*Kirmani, S. M. H. (†Karn.) b Dec. 29, 1949

Kirsten, P. N. (W. Prov., Sussex & Derbys.) b May 14, 1955

Kirton, K. N. (Border & E. Prov.) b Feb. 24, 1928

*Kischenchand, G. (W. Ind., Guj. & Baroda) b April 14, 1925

Kitchen, M. J. (Som.) b Aug. 1, 1940

*Kline, L. F. (Vic.) b Sept. 29, 1934

*Knight, A. E. (Leics.; *CY 1904*) b Oct. 8, 1872, d April 25, 1946

*Knight, B. R. (Essex & Leics.) b Feb. 18, 1938

*Knight, D. J. (OUCC & Surrey; *CY 1915*) b May 12, 1894, d Jan. 5, 1960

Knight, R. D. V. (CUCC, Surrey, Glos. & Sussex) b Sept. 6, 1946

Knight, W. H. (Editor of *Wisden* 1870-79) b Nov. 29, 1812, d Aug. 16, 1879

*Knott, A. P. E. (Kent & Tas.; *CY 1970*) b April 9, 1946

Knott, C. H. (OUCC & Kent; oldest living Blue) b March 20, 1901

Knott, C. J. (Hants) b Nov. 26, 1914

Knowles, J. (Notts.) b March 25, 1910

Knox, G. K. (Lancs.) b April 27, 1937

*Knox, N. A. (Surrey; *CY 1907*) b Oct. 10, 1884, d March 3, 1935

Kortright, C. J. (Essex) b Jan. 9, 1871, d Dec. 12, 1952

*Kotze, J. J. (Tvl & W. Prov.) b Aug. 7, 1879, d July 7, 1931

Kourie, A. J. (Tvl) b July 30, 1951

*Kripal Singh, A. G. (Madras & H'bad) b Aug. 6, 1933, d July 23, 1987

*Krishnamurthy, P. (H'bad) b July 12, 1947

Kuggeleijn, C. M. (N. Dist.) b May 10, 1956

Kuiper, A. P. (W. Prov.) b Aug. 24, 1959

*Kulkarni, R. R. (Bombay) b Sept. 25, 1962

*Kulkarni, U. N. (Bombay) b March 7, 1942

*Kumar, V. V. (†TN) b June 22, 1935

*Kunderan, B. K. (Ind. Rlwys & Mysore) b Oct. 2, 1939

*Kuruppu, D. S. B. P. (SL) b Jan. 5, 1962

*Kuruppuarachchi, A. K. (SL) b Nov. 1, 1964

*Kuys, F. (W. Prov.) b March 21, 1870, d Sept. 12, 1953

Kynaston, R. (Middx; Sec. MCC 1846-58) b Nov. 5, 1805, d June 21, 1874

*Labrooy, G. F. (SL) b June 7, 1964

Lacey, Sir F. E. (CUCC & Hants; Sec MCC 1898-1926) b Oct. 19, 1859, d May 26, 1946

*Laird, B. M. (W. Aust.) b Nov. 21, 1950

*Laker, J. C. (Surrey, Auck. & Essex; *CY 1952*) b Feb. 9, 1922, d April 23, 1986

*Lall Singh (S. Punjab) b Dec. 16, 1909, d Nov. 19, 1985

*Lamb, A. J. (W. Prov. & Northants; *CY 1981*) b June 20, 1954

Lamb, T. M. (OUCC, Middx & Northants) b March 24, 1953

*Lamba, R. (Delhi) b Jan. 2, 1958

Lambert, G. E. (Glos. & Som.) b May 11, 1919

Lambert, R. H. (Ireland) b July 18, 1874, d March 24, 1956

Lambert, Wm (Surrey) b 1779, d April 19, 1851

Lampard, A. W. (Vic. & AIF) b July 3, 1885, d Jan. 11, 1984

*Lance, H. R. (NE Tvl & Tvl) b June 6, 1940

Langdale, G. R. (Derbys. & Som.) b March 11, 1916

Langford, B. A. (Som.) b Dec. 17, 1935

*Langley, G. R. (S. Aust.; *CY 1957*) b Sept. 14, 1919

*Langridge, James (Sussex; *CY 1932*) b July 10, 1906, d Sept. 10, 1966

Langridge, J. G. (John) (Sussex; *CY 1950*) b Feb. 10, 1910

Langridge, R. J. (Sussex) b April 13, 1939

*Langton, A. B. C. (Tvl) b March 2, 1912, d Nov. 27, 1942

Larkins, W. (Northants & E. Prov.) b Nov. 22, 1953

*Larter, J. D. F. (Northants) b April 24, 1940

*Larwood, H. (Notts.; *CY 1927*) b Nov. 14, 1904

*Lashley, P. D. (B'dos) b Feb. 11, 1937

Latchman, A. H. (Middx & Notts.) b July 26, 1943

*Laughlin, T. J. (Vic.) b Jan. 30, 1951

*Laver, F. (Vic.) b Dec. 7, 1869, d Sept. 24, 1919

Lawrence, D. V. (Glos.) b Jan. 28, 1964

*Lawrence, G. B. (Rhod. & Natal) b March 31, 1932

Lawrence, J. (Som.) b March 29, 1914

*Lawry, W. M. (Vic.; *CY 1962*) b Feb. 11, 1937

Lawson, G. F. (NSW & Lancs.) b Dec. 7, 1957

Leadbeater, B. (Yorks.) b Aug. 14, 1943

*Leadbeater, E. (Yorks. & Warwicks.) b Aug. 15, 1927

Leary, S. E. (Kent) b April 30, 1933

Lee, C. (Yorks. & Derbys.) b March 17, 1924

Lee, F. S. (Middx & Som.) b July 24, 1905, d March 30, 1982

Lee, G. M. (Notts. & Derbys.) b June 7, 1887, d Feb. 29, 1976

*Lee, H. W. (Middx) b Oct. 26, 1890, d April 21, 1981

Lee, I. S. (Vic.) b March 24, 1914

Lee, J. W. (Middx & Som.) b Feb. 1, 1904, d June 20, 1944

Lee, P. G. (Northants & Lancs.; *CY 1976*) b Aug. 27, 1945

*Lee, P. K. (S. Aust.) b Sept. 14, 1904, d Aug. 9, 1980

*Lees, W. K. (Otago) b March 19, 1952

*Lees, W. S. (Surrey; *CY 1906*) b Dec. 25, 1875, d Sept. 10, 1924

Leese, Sir Oliver, Bt (Pres. MCC 1965-66) b Oct. 27, 1894, d Jan. 20, 1978

*Legall, R. A. (B'dos & T/T) b Dec. 1, 1925

Legard, E. (Warwicks.) b Aug. 23, 1935

*Leggat, I. B. (C. Dist.) b June 7, 1930

*Leggat, J. G. (Cant.) b May 27, 1926, d March 8, 1973

*Legge, G. B. (OUCC & Kent) b Jan. 26, 1903, d Nov. 21, 1940

Lenham, L. J. (Sussex) b May 24, 1936

Lenham, N. J. (Sussex) b Dec. 17, 1965

*le Roux, F. L. (Tvl & E. Prov.) b Feb. 5, 1882, d Sept. 22, 1963

le Roux, G. S. (W. Prov. & Sussex) b Sept. 4, 1955

le Roux, R. A. (OFS) b May 27, 1950

*Leslie, C. F. H. (OUCC & Middx) b Dec. 8, 1861, d Feb. 12, 1921

Lester, E. (Yorks.) b Feb. 18, 1923

Lester, G. (Leics.) b Dec. 27, 1915

Lester, Dr J. A. (Philadelphia) b Aug. 1, 1871, d Sept. 3, 1969

Lethbridge, C. (Warwicks.) b June 23, 1961

*Lever, J. K. (Essex & Natal; *CY 1979*) b Feb. 24, 1949

*Lever, P. (Lancs. & Tas.) b Sept. 17, 1940

*Leveson Gower, Sir H. D. G. (OUCC & Surrey) b May 8, 1873, d Feb. 1, 1954

*Levett, W. H. V. (Kent) b Jan. 25, 1908

Lewington, P. J. (Warwicks.) b Jan. 30, 1950

*Lewis, A. R. (CUCC & Glam.) b July 6, 1938

Lewis, C. (Kent) b July 27, 1908

Lewis, D. J. (OUCC & Rhod.) b July 27, 1927

*Lewis, D. M. (Jam.) b Feb. 21, 1946

Lewis, E. B. (Warwicks.) b Jan. 5, 1918, d Oct. 19, 1983

Lewis, E. J. (Glam. & Sussex) b Jan. 31, 1942

*Lewis, P. T. (W. Prov.) b Oct. 2, 1884, d Jan. 30, 1976

Lewis, R. V. (Hants) b Aug. 6, 1947

*Leyland, M. (Yorks.; *CY 1929*) b July 20, 1900, d Jan. 1, 1967

*Liaqat Ali (Kar., Sind, HBL & PIA) b May 21, 1955

Liddicutt, A. E. (Vic.) b Oct. 17, 1891, d April 8, 1983

Lightfoot, A. (Northants) b Jan. 8, 1936

Lill, J. C. (S. Aust.) b Dec. 7, 1933

*Lillee, D. K. (W. Aust.; *CY 1973*) b July 18, 1949

*Lilley, A. A. (Warwicks.; *CY 1897*) b Nov. 28, 1866, d Nov. 17, 1929

Lilley, A. W. (Essex) b May 8, 1959

Lilley, B. (Notts.) b Feb. 11, 1895, d Aug. 4, 1950

Lillywhite, Fred (Sussex; Editor of *Lillywhite's Guide to Cricketers*) b July 23, 1829, d Sept. 15, 1866

Lillywhite, F. W. ("William") (Sussex) b June 13, 1792, d Aug. 21, 1854

*Lillywhite, James, jun. (Sussex) b Feb. 23, 1842, d Oct. 25, 1929

*Lindsay, D. T. (NE Tvl, N. Tvl & Tvl) b Sept 4, 1939

*Lindsay, J. D. (Tvl & NE Tvl) b Sept. 8, 1909

*Lindsay, N. V. (Tvl & OFS) b July 30, 1886, d Feb. 2, 1976

*Lindwall, R. R. (NSW & Qld; *CY 1949*) b Oct. 3, 1921

*Ling, W. V. S. (Griq. W. & E. Prov.) b Oct. 3, 1891, d Sept. 26, 1960

*Lissette, A. F. (Auck. & N. Dist.) b Nov. 6, 1919, d Jan. 24, 1973

Lister, J. (Yorks. & Worcs.) b May 14, 1930

Lister, W. H. L. (Lancs.) b Oct. 7, 1911

Livingston, L. (NSW & Northants) b May 3, 1920

Livingstone, D. A. (Hants) b Sept. 21, 1933

Livsey, W. H. (Hants) b Sept. 23, 1893, d Sept. 12, 1978

*Llewellyn, C. B. (Natal & Hants; *CY 1911*) b Sept. 26, 1876, d June 7, 1964

Llewellyn, M. J. (Glam.) b Nov. 27, 1953

Lloyd, B. J. (Glam.) b Sept. 6, 1953

*Lloyd, C. H. (†Guyana & Lancs.; *CY 1971*) b Aug. 31, 1944

*Lloyd, D. (Lancs.) b March 18, 1947

*Lloyd, T. A. (Warwicks. & OFS) b Nov. 5, 1956

Lloyds, J. W. (Som., OFS & Glos.) b Nov. 17, 1954

*Loader, P. J. (Surrey and W. Aust.; *CY 1958*) b Oct. 25, 1929

Lobb, B. (Warwicks. & Som.) b Jan. 11, 1931

*Lock, G. A. R. (Surrey, Leics. & W. Aust.; *CY 1954*) b July 5, 1929

Lock, H. C. (Surrey) b May 8, 1903, d May 18, 1978

Lockwood, Ephraim (Yorks.) b April 4, 1845, d Dec. 19, 1921

*Lockwood, W. H. (Notts. & Surrey; *CY 1899*) b March 25, 1868, d April 26, 1932

Lockyer, T. (Surrey & All-England) b Nov. 1, 1826, d Dec. 22, 1869

*Logan, J. D. (SA) b June 24, 1880, d Jan. 3, 1960

*Logie, A. L. (T/T) b Sept. 28, 1960

*Lohmann, G. A. (Surrey, W. Prov. & Tvl; *CY 1889*) b June 2, 1865, d Dec. 1, 1901

Lomax, J. G. (Lancs. & Som.) b May 5, 1925

Long, A. (Surrey & Sussex) b Dec. 18, 1940

Longfield, T. C. (CUCC & Kent) b May 12, 1906, d Dec. 21, 1981

Lord, Thomas (Middx; founder of Lord's) b Nov. 23, 1755, d Jan. 13, 1832

*Love, H. S. B. (NSW & Vic.) b Aug. 10, 1895, d July 22, 1969

Love, J. D. (Yorks.) b April 22, 1955

Lowndes, W. G. L. F. (OUCC & Hants) b Jan. 24, 1898, d May 23, 1982

*Lowry, T. C. (Wgtn, CUCC & Som.) b Feb. 17, 1898, d July 20, 1976

*Lowson, F. A. (Yorks.) b July 1, 1925, d Sept. 8, 1984

*Loxton, S. J. E. (Vic.) b March 29, 1921

*Lucas, A. P. (CUCC, Surrey, Middx & Essex) b Feb. 20, 1857, d Oct. 12, 1923

Luckes, W. T. (Som.) b Jan. 1, 1901, d Oct. 27, 1982

*Luckhurst, B. W. (Kent; *CY 1971*) b Feb. 5, 1939

Lumb, R. G. (Yorks.) b Feb. 27, 1950

*Lundie, E. B. (E. Prov., W. Prov. & Tvl) b March 15, 1888, d Sept. 12, 1917

Lynch, M. A. (Surrey & Guyana) b May 21, 1958

*Lyon, B. H. (OUCC & Glos.; *CY 1931*) b Jan. 19, 1902, d June 22, 1970

Lyon, J. (Lancs.) b May 17, 1951

Lyon, M. D. (CUCC & Som.) b April 22, 1898, d Feb. 17, 1964

*Lyons, J. J. (S. Aust.) b May 21, 1863, d July 21, 1927

Lyons, K. J. (Glam.) b Dec. 18, 1946

*Lyttelton, Rt Hon. Alfred (CUCC & Middx; Pres. MCC 1898) b Feb. 7, 1857, d July 5, 1913

Lyttelton, Rt Rev. Hon. A. T. (MCC) b Jan. 7, 1852, d Feb. 19, 1903

Lyttelton, Rev. Hon. C. F. (CUCC & Worcs.) b Jan. 26, 1887, d Oct. 3, 1931

Lyttelton, Hon. C. G. (CUCC) b Oct. 27, 1842, d June 9, 1922

Lyttelton, Hon. C. J. (*see* 10th Visct Cobham)

Lyttelton, Rev. Hon. E. (CUCC & Middx) b July 23, 1855, d Jan. 26, 1942

Lyttelton, Hon. G. W. S. (CUCC) b June 12, 1847, d Dec. 5, 1913

Lyttelton, Hon. R. H. (MCC) b Jan. 18, 1854, d Nov. 7, 1939

*McAlister, P. A. (Vic.) b July 11, 1869, d May 10, 1938

*Macartney, C. G. (NSW & Otago; *CY 1922*) b June 27, 1886, d Sept. 9, 1958

*Macaulay, G. G. (Yorks.; *CY 1924*) b Dec. 7, 1897, d Dec. 14, 1940

*Macaulay, M. J. (Tvl, W. Prov., OFS, NE Tvl & E. Prov.) b April 19, 1939

*MacBryan, J. C. W. (CUCC & Som.; *CY 1925*) b July 22, 1892, d July 15, 1983

*McCabe, S. J. (NSW; *CY 1935*) b July 16, 1910, d Aug. 25, 1968

McCanlis, M. A. (OUCC, Surrey & Glos.) b June 17, 1906

*McCarthy, C. N. (Natal & CUCC) b March 24, 1929

*McConnon, J. E. (Glam.) b June 21, 1922

*McCool, C. L. (NSW, Qld & Som.) b Dec. 9, 1915, d April 5, 1986

McCorkell, N. T. (Hants) b March 23, 1912

*McCormick, E. L. (Vic.) b May 16, 1906

*McCosker, R. B. (NSW; *CY 1976*) b Dec. 11, 1946

McCullum, S. J. (Otago) b Dec. 6, 1956

McCurdy, R. J. (Vic., Derbys. & E. Prov.) b Dec. 30, 1959

*McDermott, C. J. (Qld; *CY 1986*) b April 14, 1965

*McDonald, C. C. (Vic.) b Nov. 17, 1928

*McDonald, E. A. (Tas., Vic. & Lancs.; *CY 1922*) b Jan. 6, 1891, d July 22, 1937

*McDonnell, P. S. (Vic., NSW & Qld) b Nov. 13, 1858, d Sept. 24, 1896

McEvoy, M. S. A. (Essex & Worcs.) b Jan. 25, 1956

McEwan, K. S. (E. Prov., W. Prov., Essex & W. Aust; *CY 1978*) b July 16, 1952

*McEwan, P. E. (Cant.) b Dec. 19, 1953

McFarlane, L. L. (Northants, Lancs. & Glam.) b Aug. 19, 1952

*McGahey, C. P. (Essex; *CY 1902*) b Feb. 12, 1871, d Jan. 10, 1935

*MacGibbon, A. R. (Cant.) b Aug. 28, 1924

*McGirr, H. M. (Wgtn) b Nov. 5, 1891, d April 14, 1964

*McGlew, D. J. (Natal; *CY 1956*) b March 11, 1929

*MacGregor, G. (CUCC & Middx; *CY 1891*) b Aug. 31, 1869, d Aug. 20, 1919

*McGregor, S. N. (Otago) b Dec. 18, 1931

McHugh, F. P. (Yorks. & Glos.) b Nov. 15, 1925

*McIlwraith, J. (Vic.) b Sept. 7, 1857, d July 5, 1938

Macindoe, D. H. (OUCC) b Sept. 1, 1917, d March 3, 1986

*McIntyre, A. J. (Surrey; *CY 1958*) b May 14, 1918

McIntyre, J. M. (Auck. & Cant.) b July 4, 1944

*Mackay, K. D. (Qld) b Oct. 24, 1925, d June 13, 1982

McKay-Coghill, D. (Tvl) b Nov. 4, 1941

McKechnie, B. J. (Otago) b Nov. 6, 1953

*McKenzie, G. D. (W. Aust. & Leics.; *CY 1965*) b June 24, 1941

McKenzie, K. A. (NE Tvl & Tvl) b July 16, 1948

*McKibbin, T. R. (NSW) b Dec. 10, 1870, d Dec. 15, 1939

*McKinnon, A. H. (E. Prov. & Tvl) b Aug. 20, 1932, d Dec. 2, 1983

*MacKinnon, F. A. (CUCC & Kent) b April 9, 1848, d Feb. 27, 1947

McLachlan, I. M. (CUCC & S. Aust.) b Oct. 2, 1936

*MacLaren, A. C. (Lancs.; *CY 1895*) b Dec. 1, 1871, d Nov. 17, 1944

*McLaren, J. W. (Qld) b Dec. 24, 1887, d Nov. 17, 1921

McLaughlin, J. J. (Qld) b Feb. 18, 1930

*Maclean, J. A. (Qld) b April 27, 1946

Maclean, J. F. (Worcs. & Glos.) b March 1, 1901, d March 9, 1986

*McLean, R. A. (Natal; *CY 1961*) b July 9, 1930

MacLeay, K. H. (W. Aust.) b April 2, 1959

*McLeod, C. E. (Vic.) b Oct. 24, 1869, d Nov. 26, 1918

*McLeod, E. G. (Auck. & Wgtn) b Oct. 14, 1900

*McLeod, R. W. (Vic.) b Jan. 19, 1868, d June 14, 1907

McMahon, J. W. (Surrey & Som.) b Dec. 28, 1919

*McMahon, T. G. (Wgtn) b Nov. 8, 1929

*McMaster, J. E. P. (Eng.) b March 16, 1861, d June 7, 1929

McMillan, G. E. (Tvl & N. Tvl) b Nov. 18, 1953

*McMillan, Q. (Tvl) b June 23, 1904, d July 3, 1948

*McMorris, E. D. A. (Jam.) b April 4, 1935

McNally, J. P. (Griq. W.) b Nov. 27, 1907

*McRae, D. A. N. (Cant.) b Dec. 25, 1912

*McShane, P. G. (Vic.) b 1857, d Dec. 11, 1903

McSweeney, E. B. (C. Dist. & Wgtn) b March 8, 1957

McVicker, N. M. (Warwicks. & Leics.) b Nov. 4, 1940

*McWatt, C. A. (BG) b Feb. 1, 1922

*Madan Lal (Punjab & Delhi) b March 20, 1951

*Maddocks, L. V. (Vic. & Tas.) b May 24, 1926

*Madray, I. S. (BG) b July 2, 1934

Madson, M. B. (Natal) b Sept. 29, 1949

*Madugalle, R. S. (SL) b April 22, 1959

*Maguire, J. N. (Qld) b Sept. 15, 1956

*Mahanama, R. S. (SL) b May 31, 1966

*Maher, B. J. M. (Derbys.) b Feb. 11, 1958

*Mahmood Hussain (Pak. Us, Punjab, Kar., E. Pak. & NTB) b April 2, 1932

*Mailey, A. A. (NSW) b Jan. 3, 1886, d Dec. 31, 1967

*Majid Khan (Lahore, Pak. Us, CUCC, Glam., PIA, Qld & Punjab; *CY 1970*) b Sept. 28, 1946

*Maka, E. S. (Bombay) b March 5, 1922

*Makepeace, H. (Lancs.) b Aug. 22, 1881, d Dec. 19, 1952

*Malhotra, A. (Haryana) b Jan. 26, 1957

Mallender, N. A. (Northants, Otago & Som.) b Aug. 13, 1961

*Mallett, A. A. (S. Aust.) b July 13, 1945

Mallett, A. W. H. (OUCC & Kent) b Aug. 29, 1924

*Malone, M. F. (W. Aust. & Lancs.) b Oct. 9, 1950

Malone, S. J. (Essex, Hants & Glam.) b Oct. 19, 1953

*Maninder Singh (Delhi) b June 13, 1963

*Manjrekar, V. L. (Bombay, Bengal, Andhra, U. Pradesh, Raja. & M'tra) b Sept. 26, 1931, d Oct. 18, 1983

*Mankad, A. V. (Bombay) b Oct. 12, 1946

*Mankad, V. (M. H.) (W. Ind., Naw., M'tra, Guj., Bengal, Bombay & Raja.; *CY 1947*) b April 12, 1917, d Aug. 21, 1978

*Mann, A. L. (W. Aust.) b Nov. 8, 1945

*Mann, F. G. (CUCC & Middx; Pres. MCC 1984-85) b Sept. 6, 1917

*Mann, F. T. (CUCC & Middx) b March 3, 1888, d Oct. 6, 1964

Mann, J. P. (Middx) b June 13, 1919

*Mann, N. B. F. (Natal & E. Prov.) b Dec. 28, 1920, d July 31, 1952

Manning, J. S. (S. Aust. & Northants) b June 11, 1924

Mansell, P. N. F. (Rhod.) b March 16, 1920

*Mansoor Akhtar (Kar., UBL & Sind) b Dec. 25, 1956

*Mantri, M. K. (Bombay & M'tra) b Sept. 1, 1921

*Manzoor Elahi (Multan, Pak. Rlwys & IDBP) b April 15, 1963

*Maqsood Ahmed (S. Punjab, R'pindi & Kar.) b March 26, 1925

*Marais, G. G. ("G. Gladstone") (Jam.) b Jan. 14, 1901, d May 19, 1978

Marie, G. V. (OUCC) b Feb. 17, 1945

*Markham, L. A. (Natal) b Sept. 12, 1924

*Marks, V. J. (OUCC, Som. & W. Aust.) b June 25, 1955

Marlar, R. G. (CUCC & Sussex) b Jan. 2, 1931

Marner, P. T. (Lancs. & Leics.) b March 31, 1936

*Marr, A. P. (NSW) b March 28, 1862, d March 15, 1940

*Marriott, C. S. (CUCC, Lancs. & Kent) b Sept. 14, 1895, d Oct. 13, 1966

Marsden, Tom (Eng.) b 1805, d Feb. 27, 1843

Marsh, F. E. (Derbys.) b July 7, 1920

*Marsh, G. R. (W. Aust.) b Dec. 31, 1958

*Marsh, R. W. (W. Aust.; *CY 1982*) b Nov. 11, 1947

*Marsh, S. A. (Kent) b Jan. 27, 1961

Marshal, Alan (Qld & Surrey; *CY 1909*) b June 12, 1883, d July 23, 1915

Marshall, J. M. A. (Warwicks.) b Oct. 26, 1916

*Marshall, M. D. (B'dos & Hants; *CY 1983*) b April 18, 1958

*Marshall, N. E. (B'dos & T/T) b Feb. 27, 1924

*Marshall, R. E. (B'dos & Hants; *CY 1959*) b April 25, 1930

Martin, E. J. (Notts.) b Aug. 17, 1925

*Martin, F. (Kent; *CY 1892*) b Oct. 12, 1861, d Dec. 13, 1921

*Martin, F. R. (Jam.) b Oct. 12, 1893, d Nov. 23, 1967

Martin, J. D. (OUCC & Som.) b Dec. 23, 1941

*Martin, J. W. (NSW & S. Aust.) b July 28, 1931

*Martin, J. W. (Kent) b Feb. 16, 1917, d Jan. 4, 1987

Martin, S. H. (Worcs., Natal & Rhod.) b Jan. 11, 1909

*Martindale, E. A. (B'dos) b Nov. 25, 1909, d March 17, 1972

Maru, R. J. (Middx & Hants) b Oct. 28, 1962

*Marx, W. F. E. (Tvl) b July 4, 1895, d June 2, 1974

*Mason, J. R. (Kent; *CY 1898*) b March 26, 1874, d Oct. 15, 1958

Masood Iqbal (Lahore, Punjab U., Pak. Us & HBL) b April 17, 1952

*Massie, H. H. (NSW) b April 11, 1854, d Oct. 12, 1938

*Massie, R. A. L. (W. Aust.; *CY 1973*) b April 14, 1947

*Matheson, A. M. (Auck.) b Feb. 27, 1906, d Dec. 31, 1985

*Mathias, Wallis (Sind, Kar. & NBP) b Feb. 4, 1935

*Matthews, A. D. G. (Northants & Glam.) b May 3, 1904, d July 29, 1977

*Matthews, C. D. (W. Aust.) b Sept. 22, 1962

Matthews, C. S. (Notts.) b Oct. 17, 1929

*Matthews, G. R. J. (NSW) b Dec. 15, 1959

*Matthews, T. J. (Vic.) b April 3, 1884, d Oct. 14, 1943

*Mattis, E. H. (Jam.) b April 11, 1957

Maudsley, R. H. (OUCC & Warwicks.) b April 8, 1918, d Sept. 29, 1981

*May, P. B. H. (CUCC & Surrey; *CY 1952*; Pres. MCC 1980-81) b Dec. 31, 1929

Mayer, J. H. (Warwicks.) b March 2, 1902, d Sept. 6, 1981

Mayes, R. (Kent) b Oct. 7, 1921

Maynard, C. (Warwicks. & Lancs.) b April 8, 1958

Maynard, M. P. (Glam.) b March 21, 1966

*Mayne, E. R. (S. Aust. & Vic.) b July 2, 1882, d Oct. 26, 1961

*Mayne, L. C. (W. Aust.) b Jan. 23, 1942

*Mead, C. P. (Hants; *CY 1912*) b March 9, 1887, d March 26, 1958

*Mead, W. (Essex; *CY 1904*) b March 25, 1868, d March 18, 1954

Meads, E. A. (Notts.) b Aug. 17, 1916

Meale, T. (Wgtn) b Nov. 11, 1928

*Meckiff, I. (Vic.) b Jan. 6, 1935

Medlycott, K. T. (Surrey) b May 12, 1965

*Meher-Homji, K. R. (W. Ind. & Bombay) b Aug. 9, 1911, d Feb. 10, 1982

*Mehra, V. L. (E. Punjab, Ind. Rlwys & Delhi) b March 12, 1938

*Meintjes, D. J. (Tvl) b June 9, 1890, d July 17, 1979

*Melle, M. G. (Tvl & W. Prov.) b June 3, 1930

Melluish, M. E. L. (CUCC & Middx) b June 13, 1932

*Melville, A. (OUCC, Sussex, Natal & Tvl; *CY 1948*) b May 19, 1910, d April 18, 1983

Mence, M. D. (Warwicks. & Glos.) b April 13, 1944

Mendis, G. D. (Sussex & Lancs.) b April 20, 1955

*Mendis, L. R. D. (SL) b Aug. 25, 1952

*Mendonca, I. L. (BG) b July 13, 1934

Mercer, J. (Sussex, Glam. & Northants; *CY 1927*) b April 22, 1895, d Aug. 31, 1987

*Merchant, V. M. (Bombay; *CY 1937*) b Oct. 12, 1911, d Oct. 27, 1987

*Merritt, W. E. (Cant. & Northants) b Aug. 18, 1908, d June 9, 1977

*Merry, C. A. (T/T) b Jan. 20, 1911, d April 19, 1964

Metcalfe, A. A. (Yorks.) b Dec. 25, 1963

Metson, C. P. (Middx & Glam.) b July 2, 1963

*Meuleman, K. D. (Vic. & W. Aust.) b Sept. 5, 1923

Meuli, E. M. (C. Dist.) b Feb. 20, 1926

Meyer, B. J. (Glos.) b Aug. 21, 1932

Meyer, R. J. O. (CUCC, Som. & W. Ind.) b March 15, 1905

Mian Mohammad Saaed (N. Ind. Patiala & S. Punjab; Pak.'s first captain) b Aug. 31, 1910, d Aug. 23, 1979

Middleton, J. (W. Prov.) b Sept. 30, 1865, d Dec. 23, 1913

**Midwinter, W. E. (Vic. & Glos.) b June 19, 1851, d Dec. 3, 1890

Milburn, B. D. (Otago) b Nov. 24, 1943

*Milburn, C. (Northants & W. Aust.; *CY 1967*) b Oct. 23, 1941

*Milkha Singh, A. G. (Madras) b Dec. 31, 1941

Miller, A. J. T. (OUCC & Middx) b May 30, 1963

*Miller, A. M. (Eng.) b Oct. 19, 1869, d June 26, 1959

Miller, G. (Derbys., Natal & Essex) b Sept. 8, 1952

*Miller, K. R. (Vic., NSW & Notts.; *CY 1954*) b Nov. 28, 1919

*Miller, L. S. M. (C. Dist. & Wgtn) b March 31, 1923

Miller, R. (Warwicks.) b Jan. 6, 1941

*Miller, R. C. (Jam.) b Dec. 24, 1924

*Milligan, F. W. (Yorks.) b March 19, 1870, d March 31, 1900

Millman, G. (Notts.) b Oct. 2, 1934

*Mills, C. H. (Surrey, Kimberley & W. Prov.) b Nov. 26, 1867, d July 26, 1948

Mills, G. H. (Otago) b Aug. 1, 1916

*Mills, J. E. (Auck.) b Sept. 3, 1905, d Dec. 11, 1972

Mills, J. M. (CUCC & Warwicks.) b July 27, 1921

Mills, J. P. C. (CUCC & Northants) b Dec. 6, 1958

Milner, J. (Essex) b Aug. 22, 1937

*Milton, C. A. (Glos.; *CY 1959*) b March 10, 1928

*Milton, W. H. (W. Prov.) b Dec. 3, 1854, d March 6, 1930

*Minnett, R. B. (NSW) b June 13, 1888, d Oct. 21, 1955

"Minshull", John (scorer of first recorded century) b *circa* 1741, d Oct. 1793

*Miran Bux, (Pak. Serv., Punjab & R'pindi) b April 20, 1907

*Misson, F. M. (NSW) b Nov. 19, 1938

*Mitchell, A. (Yorks.) b Sept. 13, 1902, d Dec. 25, 1976

*Mitchell, B. (Tvl; *CY 1936*) b Jan. 8, 1909

Mitchell, C. G. (Som.) b Jan. 27, 1929

**Mitchell, F. (CUCC, Yorks. & Tvl; *CY 1902*) b Aug. 13, 1872, d Oct. 11, 1935

*Mitchell, T. B. (Derbys.) b Sept. 4, 1902

*Mitchell-Innes, N. S. (OUCC & Som.) b Sept. 7, 1914

Mobey, G. S. (Surrey) b March 5, 1904

*Modi, R. S. (Bombay) b Nov. 11, 1924

*Mohammad Aslam (N. Ind. & Pak. Rlwys) b Jan. 5, 1920

*Mohammad Farooq (Kar.) b April 8, 1938

*Mohammad Ilyas (Lahore & PIA) b March 19, 1946

*Mohammad Munaf (Sind, E. Pak., Kar. & PIA) b Nov. 2, 1935

*Mohammad Nazir (Pak. Rlwys) b March 8, 1946

Mohsin Kamal (Lahore, Allied Bank & PNSC) b June 16, 1963

*Mohsin Khan (Pak. Rlwys, Kar., Sind., Pak. Us & HBL) b March 15, 1955

*Moir, A. McK. (Otago) b July 17, 1919

Moir, D. G. (Derbys & Scotland) b April 13, 1957

*Mold, A. W. (Lancs.; *CY 1892*) b May 27, 1863, d April 29, 1921

Moles, A. J. (Warwicks. & Griq. W.) b Feb. 12, 1961

*Moloney, D. A. R. (Wgtn, Otago & Cant.) b Aug. 11, 1910, d July 15, 1942

Monckton of Brenchley, 1st Lord (Pres. MCC 1956-57) b Jan. 17, 1891, d Jan. 9, 1965

Monkhouse, G. (Surrey) b April 26, 1954

*Moodie, G. H. (Jam.) b Nov. 25, 1915

*Moon, L. J. (CUCC & Middx) b Feb. 9, 1878, d Nov. 23, 1916

*Mooney, F. L. H. (Wgtn) b May 26, 1921

Moore, D. N. (OUCC & Glos.) b Sept. 26, 1910

Moore, H. I. (Notts.) b Feb. 28, 1941

Moore, R. H. (Hants) b Nov. 14, 1913

Moores, P. (Worcs. & Sussex) b Dec. 18, 1962

*More, K. S. (Baroda) b Sept. 4, 1962

Morgan, D. C. (Derbys.) b Feb. 26, 1929

Morgan, J. T. (CUCC & Glam.) b May 7, 1907, d Dec. 18, 1976

Morgan, M. (Notts.) b May 21, 1936

*Morgan, R. W. (Auck.) b Feb. 12, 1941

Morkel, D. P. B. (W. Prov.) b Jan. 25, 1906, d Oct. 6, 1980

*Morley, F. (Notts.) b Dec. 16, 1850, d Sept. 28, 1884

Morley, J. D. (Sussex) b Oct. 20, 1950

*Moroney, J. (NSW) b July 24, 1917

*Morris, A. R. (NSW; *CY 1949*) b Jan. 19, 1922

Morris, H. (Glam.) b Oct. 5, 1963

Morris, H. M. (CUCC & Essex) b April 16, 1898, d Nov. 18, 1984

Morris, J. E. (Derbys.) b April 1, 1964

Morris, R. E. T. (W. Prov.) b Jan. 28, 1947

*Morris, S. (Vic.) b June 22, 1855, d Sept. 20, 1931

Morrisby, R. O. G. (Tas.) b Jan. 12, 1915

*Morrison, B. D. (Wgtn) b Dec. 17, 1933

*Morrison, J. F. M. (C. Dist. & Wgtn) b Aug. 27, 1947

Mortensen, O. H. (Denmark & Derbys.) b Jan. 29, 1958

Mortimore, J. B. (Glos.) b May 14, 1933

Mortlock, W. (Surrey & Utd Eng. XI) b July 18, 1832, d Jan. 23, 1884

Moseley, E. A. (B'dos, Glam. & E. Prov.) b Jan. 5, 1958

Moseley, H. R. (B'dos & Som.) b May 28, 1948

Moses, H. (NSW) b Feb. 13, 1858, d Dec. 7, 1938

*Moss, A. E. (Middx) b Nov. 14, 1930

*Moss, J. K. (Vic.) b June 29, 1947

*Motz, R. C. (Cant.; *CY 1966*) b Jan. 12, 1940

Moulding, R. P. (OUCC & Middx) b Jan. 3, 1958

*Moule, W. H. (Vic.) b Jan. 31, 1858, d Aug. 24, 1939

**Moxon, M. D. (Yorks. & Griq. W.) b May 4, 1960

*Mudassar Nazar (Lahore, Punjab, Pak. Us, HBL, PIA & UBL) b April 6, 1956

*Muddiah, V. M. (Mysore & Ind. Serv.) b June 8, 1929

*Mufasir-ul-Haq (Kar., Dacca, PWD, E. Pak. & NBP) b Aug. 16, 1944, d July 27, 1983

Muncer, B. L. (Middx & Glam.) b Oct. 23, 1913, d Jan. 18, 1982

Munden, V. S. (Leics.) b Jan. 2, 1928

*Munir Malik (Punjab, R'pindi, Pak. Serv. & Kar.) b July 10, 1934

Munton, T. A. (Warwicks.) b July 30, 1965

**Murdoch, W. L. (NSW & Sussex) b Oct. 18, 1854, d Feb. 18, 1911

*Murray, A. R. A. (E. Prov.) b April 30, 1922

*Murray, B. A. G. (Wgtn) b Sept. 18, 1940

*Murray, D. A. (B'dos) b Sept. 29, 1950

*Murray, D. L. (T/T, CUCC, Notts. & Warwicks.) b May 20, 1943

*Murray, J. T. (Middx; *CY 1967*) b April 1, 1935

Murray-Willis, P. E. (Worcs. & Northants) b July 14, 1910

Murrell, H. R. (Kent & Middx) b Nov. 19, 1879, d Aug. 15, 1952

Murrills, T. J. (CUCC) b Dec. 22, 1953

*Musgrove, H. (Vic.) b Nov. 27, 1860, d Nov. 2, 1931

*Mushtaq Ali, S. (C. Ind., Guj., †M. Pradesh & U. Pradesh) b Dec. 17, 1914

*Mushtaq Mohammad (Kar., Northants & PIA; *CY 1963*) b Nov. 22, 1943

Muzzell, R. K. (W. Prov., Tvl and E. Prov.) b Dec. 23, 1945

Mynn, Alfred (Kent & All-Eng.) b Jan. 19, 1807, d Oct. 31, 1861

*Nadkarni, R. G. (M'tra & Bombay) b April 4, 1932

Naeem Ahmed (Kar., Pak. Us, NBP, UBL & PIA) b Sept. 20, 1952

*Nagel, L. E. (Vic.) b March 6, 1905, d Nov. 23, 1971

*Naik, S. S. (Bombay) b Feb. 21, 1945

*Nanan, R. (T/T) b May 29, 1953

*Naoomal Jaoomal, M. (N. Ind. & Sind) b April 17, 1904, d July 18, 1980

*Narasimha Rao, M. V. (H'bad) b Aug. 11, 1954

Naseer Malik (Khairpair & NBP) b Feb. 1, 1950

Nash, J. E. (S. Aust.) b April 16, 1950

*Nash, L. J. (Tas. & Vic.) b May 2, 1910, d July 24, 1986

Nash, M. A. (Glam.) b May 9, 1945

*Nasim-ul-Ghani (Kar., Pak. Us, Dacca, E. Pak., PWD & NBP) b May 14, 1941

*Naushad Ali (Kar., E. Pak., R'pindi, Peshawar, NWFP, Punjab & Pak. Serv.) b Oct. 1, 1943

Naved Anjum (Lahore & UBL) b July 27, 1963

Navle, J. G. (Rajputna, C. Ind., Holkar & Gwalior) b Dec. 7, 1902, d Sept. 7, 1979

*Nayak, S. V. (Bombay) b Oct. 20, 1954

*Nayudu, Col. C. K. (C. Ind., Andhra, U. Pradesh & Holkar; *CY 1933*) b Oct. 31, 1895, d Nov. 14, 1967

*Nayudu, C. S. (C. Ind., Holkar, Baroda, Bengal, Andhra & U. Pradesh) b April 18, 1914

*Nazar Mohammad (N. Ind. & Punjab) b March 5, 1921

*Nazir Ali, S. (S. Punjab & Sussex) b June 8, 1906, d Feb. 18, 1975

Neale, P. A. (Worcs.) b June 5, 1954

*Neblett, J. M. (B'dos & BG) b Nov. 13, 1901, d March 28, 1959

Needham, A. (Surrey & Middx) b March 23, 1957

Neilson, D. R. (Tvl) b Dec. 17, 1948

*Nel, J. D. (W. Prov.) b July 10, 1928

Nelson, G. W. (Border) b Nov. 14, 1941

Nevell, W. T. (Middx, Surrey & Northants) b June 13, 1916

*Newberry, C. (Tvl) b 1889, d Aug. 1, 1916

Newdick, G. A. (Wgtn) b Jan. 11, 1949

Newell, M. (Notts.) b Feb. 25, 1965

*Newham, W. (Sussex) b Dec 12, 1860, d June 26, 1944

Newland, Richard (Sussex) b *circa* 1718, d May 29, 1791

Newman, G. C. (OUCC & Middx) b April 26, 1904, d Oct. 13, 1982

*Newman, J. (Wgtn & Cant.) b July 3, 1902

Newman, J. A. (Hants & Cant.) b Nov. 12, 1884, d Dec. 21, 1973

Newman, P. G. (Derbys.) b Jan. 10, 1959

Newport, P. J. (Worcs.) b Oct. 11, 1962

*Newsom, E. S. (Tvl & Rhod.) b Dec. 2, 1910

Newstead, J. T. (Yorks.; *CY 1909*) b Sept. 8, 1877, d March 25, 1952

*Niaz Ahmed (Dacca, PWD, E. Pak. & Pak. Rlwys) b Nov. 11, 1945

Nicholas, M. C. J. (Hants) b Sept. 29, 1957

Nicholls, D. (Kent) b Dec. 8, 1943

Nicholls, R. B. (Glos.) b Dec. 4, 1933

*Nichols, M. S. (Essex; *CY 1934*) b Oct. 6, 1900, d Jan. 26, 1961

Nicholson, A. G. (Yorks.) b June 25, 1938, d Nov. 4, 1985

*Nicholson, F. (OFS) b Sept. 17, 1909, d July 30, 1982

*Nicolson, J. F. W. (Natal & OUCC) b July 19, 1899, d Dec. 13, 1935

*Nissar, Mahomed (Patiala, S. Punjab & U. Pradesh) b Aug. 1, 1910, d March 11, 1963

*Nitschke, H. C. (S. Aust.) b April 14, 1905, d Sept. 29, 1982

*Noble, M. A. (NSW; *CY 1900*) b Jan. 28, 1873, d June 22, 1940

Noblet, G. (S. Aust.) b Sept. 14, 1916

Noreiga, J. M. (T/T) b April 15, 1936

Norfolk, 16th Duke of (Pres. MCC 1957-58) b May 30, 1908, d Jan. 31, 1975

Norman, M. E. J. C. (Northants & Leics.) b Jan. 19, 1933

*Norton, N. O. (W. Prov. & Border) b May 11, 1881, d June 27, 1968

*Nothling, O. E. (NSW & Qld) b Aug. 1, 1900, d Sept. 26, 1965

*Nourse, A. D. ("Dudley") (Natal; *CY 1948*) b Nov. 12, 1910, d Aug. 14, 1981

*Nourse, A. W. ("Dave") (Natal, Tvl & W. Prov.) b Jan. 26, 1878, d July 8, 1948

Nugent, 1st Lord (Pres. MCC 1962-63) b Aug. 11, 1895, d April 27, 1973

*Nunes, R. K. (Jam.) b June 7, 1894, d July 22, 1958

*Nupen, E. P. (Tvl) b Jan. 1, 1902, d Jan. 29, 1977

*Nurse, S. M. (B'dos; *CY 1967*) b Nov. 10, 1933

Nutter, A. E. (Lancs. & Northants) b June 28, 1913

*Nyalchand, S. (W. Ind., Kathiawar, Guj. & S'tra) b Sept. 14, 1919

Nye, J. K. (Sussex) b May 23, 1914

Nyren, John (Hants) b Dec. 15, 1764, d June 28, 1837

Nyren, Richard (Hants & Sussex) b 1734, d April 25, 1797

Oakes, C. (Sussex) b Aug. 10, 1912

Oakes, J. (Sussex) b March 3, 1916

*Oakman, A. S. M. (Sussex) b April 20, 1930

Oates, T. W. (Notts.) b Aug. 9, 1875, d June 18, 1949

Oates, W. F. (Yorks. & Derbys.) b June 11, 1929

O'Brien, F. P. (Cant. & Northants) b Feb. 11, 1911

*O'Brien, L. P. (Vic.) b July 2, 1907

*O'Brien, Sir T. C. (OUCC & Middx) b Nov. 5, 1861, d Dec. 9, 1948

*Ochse, A. E. (Tvl) b March 11, 1870, d April 11, 1918

*Ochse, A. L. (E. Prov.) b Oct. 11, 1899, d May 6, 1949

*O'Connor, J. (Essex) b Nov. 6, 1897, d Feb. 22, 1977

*O'Connor, J. D. A. (NSW & S. Aust.) b Sept. 9, 1875, d Aug. 23, 1941

Odendaal, A. (CUCC & Boland) b May 4, 1954

*O'Donnell, S. P. (Vic.) b Jan. 26, 1963

Ogilvie, A. D. (Qld) b June 3, 1951

*O'Keeffe, K. J. (NSW & Som.) b Nov. 25, 1949

*Old, C. M. (Yorks., Warwicks. & N. Tvl; *CY 1979*) b Dec. 22, 1948

*Oldfield, N. (Lancs. & Northants) b May 5, 1911

*Oldfield, W. A. (NSW; *CY 1927*) b Sept. 9, 1894, d Aug. 10, 1976

Oldham, S. (Yorks. & Derbys.) b July 26, 1948

Oldroyd, E. (Yorks.) b Oct. 1, 1888, d Dec. 27, 1964

*O'Linn, S. (Kent, W. Prov. & Tvl) b May 5, 1927

Oliver, P. R. (Warwicks.) b May 9, 1956

*O'Neill, N. C. (NSW; *CY 1962*) b Feb. 19, 1937

Ontong, R. C. (Border, Tvl, N. Tvl & Glam.) b Sept. 9, 1955

Opatha, A. R. M. (SL) b Aug. 5, 1947

Ord, J. S. (Warwicks.) b July 12, 1912

*O'Reilly, W. J. (NSW; *CY 1935*) b Dec. 20, 1905

O'Riordan, A. J. (Ireland) b July 20, 1940

Ormiston, R. W. (C. Dist. & Wgtn) b Oct. 19, 1955

Ormrod, J. A. (Worcs. & Lancs.) b Dec. 22, 1942

O'Shaughnessy, S. J. (Lancs.) b Sept. 9, 1961

Oslear, D. O. (Umpire) b March 3, 1929

*O'Sullivan, D. R. (C. Dist. & Hants) b Nov. 16, 1944

Outschoorn, L. (Worcs.) b Sept. 26, 1918

*Overton, G. W. F. (Otago) b June 8, 1919

*Owen-Smith, H. G. O. (W. Prov., OUCC & Middx; *CY 1930*) b Feb. 18, 1909

Owen-Thomas, D. R. (CUCC & Surrey) b Sept. 20, 1948

*Oxenham, R. K. (Qld) b July 28, 1891, d Aug. 16, 1939

Packe, M. St J. (Leics.) b Aug. 21, 1916, d Dec. 20, 1978

*Padgett, D. E. V. (Yorks.) b July 20, 1934

*Padmore, A. L. (B'dos) b Dec. 17, 1946

Page, H. A. (Tvl & Essex) b July 3, 1962

Page, J. C. T. (Kent) b May 20, 1930

Page, M. H. (Derbys.) b June 17, 1941

*Page, M. L. (Cant.) b May 8, 1902, d Feb. 13, 1987

Pai, A. M. (Bombay) b April 28, 1945

*Paine, G. A. E. (Middx & Warwicks.; *CY 1935*) b June 11, 1908, d March 30, 1978

Pairaudeau, B. H. (BG & N. Dist.) b April 14, 1931

*Palairet, L. C. H. (OUCC & Som.; *CY 1893*) b May 27, 1870, d March 27, 1933

Palairet, R. C. N. (OUCC & Som.; Joint-Manager MCC in Australia 1932-33) b June 25, 1871, d Feb. 11, 1955

Palia, P. E. (Madras, U. Prov., Bombay, Mysore & Bengal) b Sept. 5, 1910, d Sept. 9, 1981

*Palm, A. W. (W. Prov.) b June 8, 1901, d Aug. 17, 1966

*Palmer, C. H. (Worcs. & Leics.; Pres. MCC 1978-79) b May 15, 1919

*Palmer, G. E. (Vic. & Tas.) b Feb. 22, 1860, d Aug. 22, 1910

Palmer, G. V. (Som.) b Nov. 1, 1965

*Palmer, K. E. (Som.) b April 22, 1937

Palmer, R. (Som.) b July 12, 1942

*Pandit, C. S. (Bombay) b Sept. 30, 1961

Pardon, Charles Frederick (Editor of *Wisden* 1887-90) b March 28, 1850, d April 18, 1890

Pardon, Sydney H. (Editor of *Wisden* 1891-1925) b Sept. 23, 1855, d Nov. 20, 1925

*Parfitt, P. H. (Middx; *CY 1963*) b Dec. 8, 1936

Paris, C. G. A. (Hants; Pres. MCC 1975-76) b Aug. 20, 1911

Parish, R. J. (Aust. Administrator) b May 7, 1916

*Park, R. L. (Vic.) b July 30, 1892, d Jan. 23, 1947

*Parkar, G. A. (Bombay) b Oct. 24, 1955

*Parkar, R. D. (Bombay) b Oct. 31, 1946

Parkar, Z. (Bombay) b Nov. 22, 1957

*Parker, C. W. L. (Glos.; *CY 1923*) b Oct. 14, 1882, d July 11, 1959

Parker, E. F. (Rhod. & Griq. W.) b April 26, 1939

*Parker, G. M. (SA) b May 27, 1899, d May 1, 1969

Parker, G. W. (CUCC & Glos.) b Feb. 11, 1912

*Parker, J. F. (Surrey) b April 23, 1913, d Jan. 27, 1983

*Parker, J. M. (N. Dist. & Worcs.) b Feb. 21, 1951

Parker, J. P. (Hants) b Nov. 29, 1902, d Aug. 9, 1984

*Parker, N. M. (Otago & Cant.) b Aug. 28, 1948

*Parker, P. W. G. (CUCC, Sussex & Natal) b Jan. 15, 1956

Parkhouse, W. G. A. (Glam.) b Oct. 12, 1925

*Parkin, C. H. (Yorks. & Lancs.; *CY 1924*) b Feb. 18, 1886, d June 15, 1943

*Parkin, D. C. (E. Prov., Tvl & Griq. W.) b Feb. 18, 1870, d March 20, 1936

Parks, H. W. (Sussex) b July 18, 1906, d May 7, 1984

*Parks, J. H. (Sussex & Cant.; *CY 1938*) b May 12, 1903, d Nov. 21, 1980

*Parks, J. M. (Sussex & Som.; *CY 1968*) b Oct. 21, 1931

Parks, R. J. (Hants) b June 15, 1959

Parr, F. D. (Lancs.) b June 1, 1928

Parr, George (Notts. & All-England) b May 22, 1826, d June 23, 1891

*Parry, D. R. (Comb. Is. & Leewards) b Dec. 22, 1954

*Parsana, D. D. (S'tra, Ind. Rlwys & Guj.) b Dec. 2, 1947

Parsons, A. B. D. (CUCC & Surrey) b Sept. 20, 1933

Parsons, A. E. W. (Auck. & Sussex) b Jan. 9, 1949

Parsons, G. J. (Leics., Warwicks., Boland & Griq. W.) b Oct. 17, 1959

Parsons, Canon J. H. (Warwicks.) b May 30, 1890, d Feb. 2, 1981

*Partridge, J. T. (Rhod.) b Dec. 9, 1932

Partridge, N. E. (Malvern, CUCC & Warwicks.; *CY 1919*) b Aug. 10, 1900, d March 10, 1982

Partridge, R. J. (Northants) b Feb. 11, 1912

*Pascoe, L. S. (NSW) b Feb. 13, 1950

Pasqual, S. P. (SL) b Oct. 15, 1961

*Passailaigue, C. C. (Jam.) b Aug. 1902, d Jan. 7, 1972

*Patankar, C. T. (Bombay) b Nov. 24, 1930

**Pataudi, Iftikhar Ali, Nawab of (OUCC, Worcs., Patiala, N. Ind. & S. Punjab; *CY 1932*) b March 16, 1910, d Jan. 5, 1952

*Pataudi, Mansur Ali, Nawab of (Sussex, OUCC, Delhi & H'bad; *CY 1968*) b Jan. 5, 1941

Patel, A. (S'tra) b March 6, 1957

*Patel, B. P. (Karn.) b Nov. 24, 1952

*Patel, D. N. (Worcs. & Auck.) b Oct. 25, 1958

Patel, J. M. (Guj.) b Nov. 26, 1924

Paterson, R. F. T. (Essex) b Sept. 8, 1916, d May 29, 1980

Pathmanathan, G. (OUCC, CUCC & SL) b Jan. 23, 1954

*Patiala, Maharaja of (N. Ind., Patiala & S. Punjab) b Jan. 17, 1913, d June 17, 1974

*Patil, S. M. (Bombay) b Aug. 18, 1956
*Patil, S. R. (M'tra) b Oct. 10, 1933
*Patterson, B. P. (Jam., Tas. & Lancs.) b Sept. 15, 1961
Pauline, D. B. (Surrey & Glam.) b Dec. 15, 1960
Paulsen, R. G. (Qld & W. Aust.) b Oct. 18, 1947
Pawson, A. G. (OUCC & Worcs.) b May 30, 1888, d Feb. 25, 1986
Pawson, H. A. (OUCC & Kent) b Aug. 22, 1921
Payn, L. W. (Natal) b May 6, 1915
*Payne, T. R. O. (B'dos) b Feb. 13, 1957
*Paynter, E. (Lancs.; *CY 1938*) b Nov. 5, 1901, d Feb. 5, 1979
Payton, D. H. (C. Dist.) b Feb. 19, 1945
Payton, W. R. D. (Notts.) b Feb. 13, 1882, d May 2, 1943
Pearce, G. (Sussex) b Oct. 27, 1908, d June 16, 1986
Pearce, T. A. (Kent) b Dec. 18, 1910, d Aug. 11, 1982
Pearce, T. N. (Essex) b Nov. 3, 1905
*Pearse, C. O. C. (Natal) b Oct. 10, 1884, d May 7, 1953
Pearse, D. K. (Natal) b May 1, 1958
Pearson, D. B. (Worcs.) b March 29, 1937
*Peate, E. (Yorks.) b March 2, 1856, d March 11, 1900
Peck, I. G. (CUCC & Northants) b Oct. 18, 1957
*Peebles, I. A. R. (OUCC, Middx & Scotland; *CY 1931*) b Jan. 20, 1908, d Feb. 28, 1980
*Peel, R. (Yorks.; *CY 1889*) b Feb. 12, 1857, d Aug. 12, 1941
*Pegler, S. J. (Tvl) b July 28, 1888, d Sept. 10, 1972
*Pellew, C. E. (S. Aust.) b Sept. 21, 1893, d May 9, 1981
Penn, C. (Kent) b June 19, 1963
*Penn, F. (Kent) b March 7, 1851, d Dec. 26, 1916
Pepper, C. G. (NSW and Aust. Serv.; Umpire) b Sept. 15, 1918
Perera, K. G. (SL) b May 22, 1964
Perkins, C. G. (Northants) b June 4, 1911
Perkins, H. (CUCC & Cambs.; Sec. MCC 1876-97) b Dec. 10, 1832, d May 6, 1916
*Perks, R. T. D. (Worcs.) b Oct. 4, 1911, d Nov. 22, 1977
Perrin, P. A. (Essex; *CY 1905*) b May 26, 1876, d Nov. 20, 1945
Perryman, S. P. (Warwicks. & Worcs.) b Oct. 22, 1955
*Pervez Sajjad (Lahore, PIA & Kar.) b Aug. 30, 1942
*Petherick, P. J. (Otago & Wgtn) b Sept. 25, 1942
Petrie, E. C. (Auck. & N. Dist.) b May 22, 1927
Pfuhl, G. P. (W. Prov.) b Aug. 27, 1947

*Phadkar, D. G. (M'tra, Bombay, Bengal & Ind. Rlwys) b Dec. 10, 1925, d March 17, 1985
Phebey, A. H. (Kent) b Oct. 1, 1924
Phelan, P. J. (Essex) b Feb. 9, 1938
*Philipson, H. (OUCC & Middx) b June 8, 1866, d Dec. 4, 1935
*Phillip, N. (Comb. Is., Windwards & Essex) b June 12, 1948
Phillipps, J. H. (NZ Manager) b Jan. 1, 1898, d June 8, 1977
Phillips, R. B. (NSW & Qld) b May 23, 1954
*Phillips, W. B. (S. Aust.) b March 1, 1958
Phillipson, C. P. (Sussex) b Feb. 10, 1952
Phillipson, W. E. (Lancs.) b Dec. 3, 1910
*Philpott, P. I. (NSW) b Nov. 21, 1934
Piachaud, J. D. (OUCC, Hants & Ceylon) b March 1, 1937
Pick, R. A. (Notts.) b Nov. 19, 1963
Pickles, L. (Som.) b Sept. 17, 1932
Pienaar, R. F. (Tvl, W. Prov., N. Tvl & Kent) b July 17, 1961
Pieris, H. S. M. (SL) b Feb. 16, 1946
*Pierre, L. R. (T/T) b June 5, 1921
*Pigott, A. C. S. (Sussex & Wgtn) b June 4, 1958
Pilch, Fuller (Norfolk & Kent) b March 17, 1804, d May 1, 1870
Pilling, H. (Lancs.) b Feb. 23, 1943
*Pilling, R. (Lancs.; *CY 1891*) b July 5, 1855, d March 28, 1891
Pinch, C. J. (NSW & S. Aust.) b June 23, 1921
Pithey, A. J. (Rhod. & W. Prov.) b July 17, 1933
Pithey, D. B. (Rhod., OUCC, Northants, W. Prov., Natal & Tvl) b Oct. 4, 1936
Pitman, R. W. C. (Hants) b Feb. 21, 1933
*Place, W. (Lancs.) b Dec 7, 1914
Platt, R. K. (Yorks. & Northants) b Dec. 21, 1932
*Playle, W. R. (Auck. & W. Aust.) b Dec. 1, 1938
Pleass, J. E. (Glam.) b May 21, 1923
*Plimsoll, J. B. (W. Prov. & Natal) b Oct. 27, 1917
Pocock, N. E. J. (Hants) b Dec. 15, 1951
*Pocock, P. I. (Surrey & N. Tvl) b Sept. 24, 1946
*Pollard, R. (Lancs.) b June 19, 1912, d Dec. 16, 1985
*Pollard, V. (C. Dist. & Cant.) b Burnley Sept. 7, 1945
Pollock, A. J. (CUCC) b April 19, 1962
*Pollock, P. M. (E. Prov.; *CY 1966*) b June 30, 1941
*Pollock, R. G. (E. Prov. & Tvl; *CY 1966*) b Feb. 27, 1944
*Ponsford, W. H. (Vic.; *CY 1935*) b Oct. 19, 1900
Pont, K. R. (Essex) b Jan. 16, 1953
*Poole, C. J. (Notts.) b March 13, 1921

Pooley, E. (Surrey & first England tour) b Feb. 13, 1838, d July 18, 1907

*Poore, M. B. (Cant.) b June 1, 1930

*Poore, Brig-Gen. R. M. (Hants & SA; *CY 1900*) b March 20, 1866, d July 14, 1938

Pope, A. V. (Derbys.) b Aug. 15, 1909

*Pope, G. H. (Derbys.) b Jan. 27, 1911

*Pope, R. J. (NSW) b Feb. 18, 1864, d July 27, 1952

Popplewell, N. F. M. (CUCC & Som.) b Aug. 8, 1957

Portal of Hungerford, 1st Lord (Pres. MCC 1958-59) b May 21, 1893, d April 22, 1971

Porter, A. (Glam.) b March 25, 1914

Porter, G. D. (W. Aust.) b March 18, 1955

Pothecary, E. A. (Hants) b March 1, 1906

*Pothecary, J. E. (W. Prov.) b Dec. 6, 1933

Potter, G. (Sussex) b Oct. 26, 1931

Potter, J. (Vic.) b April 13, 1938

Potter, L. (Kent, Griq. & Leics.) b Nov. 7, 1962

*Pougher, A. D. (Leics.) b April 19, 1865, d May 20, 1926

Pountain, F. R. (Sussex) b April 23, 1941

Powell, A. G. (CUCC & Essex) b Aug. 17, 1912, d June 7, 1982

*Powell, A. W. (Griq. W.) b July 18, 1873, d Sept. 11, 1948

*Prabhakar, M. (Delhi) b April 15, 1963

*Prasanna, E. A. S. (†Karn.) b May 22, 1940

Pratt, R. C. E. (Surrey) b May 5, 1928, d June 7, 1977

Pratt, R. L. (Leics.) b Nov. 15, 1938

Prentice, F. T. (Leics.) b April 22, 1912, d July 10, 1978

Pressdee, J. S. (Glam. & NE Tvl) b June 19, 1933

Preston, Hubert (Editor of *Wisden* 1944-51) b Dec. 16, 1868, d Aug. 6, 1960

Preston, K. C. (Essex) b Aug. 22, 1925

Preston, Norman (Editor of *Wisden* 1951-80) b March 18, 1903, d March 6, 1980

Pretlove, J. F. (CUCC & Kent) b Nov. 23, 1932

Price, D. G. (CUCC) b Feb. 7, 1965

Price, E. J. (Lancs. & Essex) b Oct. 27, 1918

*Price, J. S. E. (Middx) b July 22, 1937

*Price, W. F. (Middx) b April 25, 1902, d Jan. 13, 1969

Prichard, P. J. (Essex) b Jan. 7, 1965

*Prideaux, R. M. (CUCC, Kent, Northants, Sussex & OFS) b July 13, 1939

Pridgeon, A. P. (Worcs.) b Feb. 22, 1954

*Prince, C. F. H. (W. Prov., Border & E. Prov.) b Sept. 11, 1874, d March 5, 1948

*Pringle, D. R. (CUCC & Essex) b Sept. 18, 1958

Pritchard, T. L. (Wgtn, Warwicks. & Kent) b March 10, 1917

*Procter, M. J. (Glos., Natal, W. Prov. & Rhod.; *CY 1970*) b Sept. 15, 1946

Prodger, J. M. (Kent) b Sept. 1, 1935

*Promnitz, H. L. E. (Border, Griq. W. & OFS) b Feb. 23, 1904, d Sept. 7, 1983

Prouton, R. O. (Hants) b March 1, 1926

Puckett, C. W. (W. Aust.) b Feb. 21, 1911

Pugh, C. T. M. (Glos.) b March 13, 1937

Pullan, D. A. (Notts.) b May 1, 1944

*Pullar, G. (Lancs. & Glos.; *CY 1960*) b Aug. 1, 1935

Pullinger, G. R. (Essex) b March 14, 1920, d Aug. 4, 1982

*Puna, N. (N. Dist.) b Oct. 28, 1929

*Punjabi, P. H. (Sind & Guj.) b Sept. 20, 1921

Pycroft, A. J. (Zimb.) b June 6, 1956

Pydanna, M. (Guyana) b Jan. 27, 1950

*Qasim Omar (Kar. & MCB) b Feb. 9, 1957

Quaife, B. W. (Warwicks. & Worcs.) b Nov. 24, 1899, d Nov. 28, 1984

*Quaife, William (W. G.) (Warwicks. & Griq. W.; *CY 1902*) b March 17, 1872, d Oct. 13, 1951

Quick, I. W. (Vic.) b Nov. 5, 1933

*Quinn, N. A. (Griq. W. & Tvl) b Feb. 21, 1908, d Aug. 5, 1934

*Rabone, G. O. (Wgtn & Auck.) b Nov. 6, 1921

*Rackemann, C. G. (Qld) b June 3, 1960

*Radford, N. V. (Lancs., Tvl & Worcs.; *CY 1986*) b June 7, 1957

*Radley, C. T. (Middx; *CY 1979*) b May 13, 1944

*Rae, A. F. (Jam.) b Sept. 30, 1922

Raees Mohammad (Kar.) b Dec. 24, 1932

*Rai Singh, K. (S. Punjab & Ind. Serv.) b Feb. 24, 1922

Rait Kerr, Col. R. S. (Sec. MCC 1936-52) b April 13, 1891, d April 2, 1961

Rajah, A. (T/T) b July 30, 1955

*Rajindernath, V. (N. Ind., U. Prov., S. Punjab, Bihar & E. Punjab) b Jan. 7, 1928

*Rajinder Pal (Delhi, S. Punjab & Punjab) b Nov. 18, 1937

*Rajput, L. S. (Bombay) b Dec. 18, 1961

Ralph, L. H. R. (Essex) b May 22, 1920

*Ramadhin, S. (T/T & Lancs.; *CY 1951*) b May 1, 1929

*Ramaswami, C. (Madras) b June 18, 1896, 'presumed dead'

*Ramchand, G. S. (Sind, Bombay & Raja.) b July 26, 1927

*Ramiz Raja (Lahore, Allied Bank & PNSC) b July 14, 1962

*Ramji, L. (W. Ind.) b 1900, d Dec. 20, 1948

Ramsamooj, D. (T/T & Northants) b July 5, 1932

*Ranasinghe, A. N. (SL) b Oct. 13, 1956

*Ranatunga, A. (SL) b Dec. 1, 1963

*Randall, D. W. (Notts.; *CY 1980*) b Feb. 24, 1951

Randhir Singh (Orissa & Bihar) b Aug. 16, 1957
*Rangachari, C. R. (Madras) b April 14, 1916
*Rangnekar, K. M. (M'tra, Bombay & †M. Pradesh) b June 27, 1917, d Oct. 11, 1984
*Ranjane, V. B. (M'tra & Ind. Rlwys) b July 22, 1937
*Ranjitsinhji, K. S., afterwards H. H. the Jam Saheb of Nawanagar (CUCC & Sussex; *CY 1897*) b Sept. 10, 1872, d April 2, 1933
Ransford, V. S. (Vic.; *CY 1910*) b March 20, 1885, d March 19, 1958
Ransom, V. J. (Hants & Surrey) b March 17, 1918
*Rashid Khan (PWD, Kar. & PIA) b Dec. 15, 1959
Ratcliffe, R. M. (Lancs.) b Nov. 29, 1951
*Ratnayake, R. J. (SL) b Jan. 2, 1964
*Ratnayeke, J. R. (SL) b May 2, 1960
Rayment, A. W. H. (Hants) b May 29, 1928
Raymer, V. N. (Qld) b May 4, 1918
*Read, H. D. (Surrey & Essex) b Jan. 28, 1910
*Read, J. M. (Surrey; *CY 1890*) b Feb. 9, 1859, d Feb. 17, 1929
*Read, W. W. (Surrey; *CY 1893*) b Nov. 23, 1855, d Jan. 6, 1907
Reddick, T. B. (Middx, Notts. & W. Prov.) b Feb. 17, 1912, d June 1, 1982
*Reddy, B. (TN) b Nov. 12, 1954
Redman, J. (Som.) b March 1, 1926, d Sept. 19, 1981
*Redmond, R. E. (Wgtn & Auck.) b Dec. 29, 1944
*Redpath, I. R. (Vic.) b May 11, 1941
Reed, B. L. (Hants) b Sept. 9, 1937
*Reedman, J. C. (S. Aust.) b Oct. 9, 1865, d March 25, 1924
Rees, A. (Glam.) b Feb. 17, 1938
Reeve, D. A. (Sussex) b April 2, 1963
Reeves, W. (Essex; Umpire) b Jan. 22, 1875, d March 22, 1944
*Rege, M. R. (M'tra) b March 18, 1924
*Rehman, S. F. (Punjab, Pak. Us & Lahore) b June 11, 1935
*Reid, B. A. (W. Aust.) b March 14, 1963
*Reid, J. F. (Auck.) b March 3, 1956
*Reid, J. R. (Wgtn & Otago; *CY 1959*) b June 3, 1928
Reid, K. P. (E. Prov. & Northants) b July 24, 1951
*Reid, N. (W. Prov.) b Dec 26, 1890, d June 10, 1947
Reidy, B. W. (Lancs.) b Sept. 18, 1953
*Relf, A. E. (Sussex & Auck.; *CY 1914*) b June 26, 1874, d March 26, 1937
*Renneburg, D. A. (NSW) b Sept. 23, 1942
Revill, A. C. (Derbys & Leics.) b March 27, 1923
Reynolds, B. L. (Northants) b June 10, 1932

Reynolds, G. R. (Qld) b Aug. 24, 1936
Rhodes, A. E. G. (Derbys.) b Oct. 10, 1916, d Oct. 18, 1983
*Rhodes, H. J. (Derbys.) b July 22, 1936
Rhodes, S. D. (Notts.) b March 24, 1910
Rhodes, S. J. (Yorks. & Worcs.) b June 17, 1964
*Rhodes, W. (Yorks.; *CY 1899*) b Oct. 29, 1877, d July 8, 1973
Rice, C. E. B. (Tvl & Notts.; *CY 1981*) b July 23, 1949
Rice, J. M. (Hants) b Oct. 23, 1949
*Richards, A. R. (W. Prov.) b 1868, d Jan. 9, 1904
*Richards, B. A. (Natal, Glos., Hants & S. Aust.; *CY 1969*) b July 21, 1945
*Richards, C. J. (Surrey & OFS) b Aug. 10, 1958
Richards, G. (Glam.) b Nov. 29, 1951
*Richards, I. V. A. (Comb. Is., Leewards, Som. & Qld; *CY 1977*) b March 7, 1952
*Richards, W. H. M. (SA) b Aug. 1862, d Jan. 4, 1903
*Richardson, A. J. (S. Aust.) b July 24, 1888, d Dec. 23, 1973
Richardson, A. W. (Derbys.) b March 4, 1907, d July 29, 1983
Richardson, D. J. (E. Prov. & N. Tvl) b Sept. 16, 1959
*Richardson, D. W. (Worcs.) b Nov. 3, 1934
Richardson, G. W. (Derbys.) b April 26, 1938
*Richardson, P. E. (Worcs. & Kent; *CY 1957*) b July 4, 1931
*Richardson, R. B. (Leewards) b Jan. 12, 1962
*Richardson, T. (Surrey & Som.; *CY 1897*) b Aug. 11, 1870, d July 2, 1912
*Richardson, V. Y. (S. Aust.) b Sept. 7, 1894, d Oct. 29, 1969
*Richmond, T. L. (Notts.) b June 23, 1890, d Dec. 29, 1957
Rickards, K. R. (Jam. & Essex) b Aug. 23, 1923
Riddington, A. (Leics.) b Dec. 22, 1911
*Ridgway, F. (Kent) b Aug. 10, 1923
Ridings, P. L. (S. Aust.) b Oct. 2, 1917
*Rigg, K. E. (Vic.) b May 21, 1906
Riley, H. (Leics.) b Oct. 3, 1902
*Ring, D. T. (Vic.) b Oct. 14, 1918
Ripley, D. (Northants) b Sept. 13, 1966
Rist, F. H. (Essex) b March 30, 1914
Ritchie, G. G. (Tvl) b Sept. 16, 1933
*Ritchie, G. M. (Qld) b Jan. 23, 1960
*Rixon, S. J. (NSW) b Feb. 25, 1954
*Rizwan-uz-Zaman (Kar. & PIA) b Sept. 4, 1962
*Roach, C. A. (T/T) b March 13, 1904
*Roberts, A. D. G. (N. Dist.) b May 6, 1947
*Roberts, A. M. E. (Comb. Is., Leewards, Hants, NSW & Leics.; *CY 1975*) b Jan. 29, 1951
*Roberts, A. T. (Windwards) b Sept. 18, 1937

*Roberts, A. W. (Cant. & Otago) b Aug. 20, 1909, d May 13, 1978

Roberts, B. (Tvl & Derbys.) b May 30, 1962

Roberts, Pascal (T/T) b Dec 15, 1937

Roberts, W. B. (Lancs. & Victory Tests) b Sept. 27, 1914, d Aug. 24, 1951

*Robertson, G. K. (C. Dist.) b July 15, 1960

*Robertson, J. B. (W. Prov.) b June 5, 1906, d July 5, 1985

*Robertson, J. D. (Middx; *CY 1948*) b Feb. 22, 1917

Robertson, S. D. (Rhod.) b May 1, 1947

*Robertson, W. R. (Vic.) b Oct. 6, 1861, d June 24, 1938

Robertson-Glasgow, R. C. (OUCC & Som.) b July 15, 1901, d March 4, 1965

Robins, D. H. (Warwicks.) b June 26, 1914

Robins, R. V. C. (Middx) b March 13, 1935

*Robins, R. W. V. (CUCC & Middx; *CY 1930*) b June 3, 1906, d Dec. 12, 1968

Robinson, A. L. (Yorks.) b Aug. 17, 1946

Robinson, Emmott (Yorks.) b Nov. 16, 1883, d Nov. 17, 1969

Robinson, Ellis P. (Yorks. & Som.) b Aug. 10, 1911

Robinson, H. B. (OUCC & Canada) b March 3, 1919

Robinson, M. (Glam., Warwicks., H'bad & Madras) b July 16, 1921

Robinson, P. J. (Worcs. & Som.) b Feb. 9, 1943

Robinson, Ray (Writer) b July 8, 1908, d July 6, 1982

*Robinson, R. D. (Vic.) b June 8, 1946

*Robinson, R. H. (NSW, S. Aust. & Otago) b March 26, 1914, d Aug. 10, 1965

*Robinson, R. T. (Notts.; *CY 1986*) b Nov. 21, 1958

Robson, E. (Som.) b May 1, 1870, d May 23, 1924

Rochford, P. (Glos.) b Aug. 27, 1928

*Rodriguez, W. V. (T/T) b June 25, 1934

Roe, B. (Som.) b Jan. 27, 1939

Roebuck, P. M. (CUCC & Som.; *CY 1988*) b March 6, 1956

Rogers, N. H. (Hants) b March 9, 1918

Rogers, R. E. (Qld) b Aug. 24, 1916

Romaines, P. W. (Northants, Glos. & Griq. W.) b Dec. 25, 1955

*Roope, G. R. J. (Surrey & Griq. W.) b July 12, 1946

*Root, C. F. (Derbys. & Worcs.) b April 16, 1890, d Jan. 20, 1954

*Rorke, G. F. (NSW) b June 27, 1938

*Rose, B. C. (Som.; *CY 1980*) b June 4, 1950

Rose, G. D. (Middx & Som.) b April 12, 1964

Rosebery, 6th Earl of (see Dalmeny, Lord)

*Rose-Innes, A. (Kimberley & Tvl) b Feb. 16, 1868, d Nov. 22, 1946

Rosendorff, N. (OFS) b Jan. 22, 1945

Ross, C. J. (Wgtn & OUCC) b June 24, 1954

Rotherham, G. A. (Rugby, CUCC, Warwicks. & Wgtn; *CY 1918*) b May 28, 1899, d Jan. 31, 1985

Rouse, S. J. (Warwicks.) b Jan. 20, 1949

Routledge, R. (Middx) b July 7, 1920

*Routledge, T. W. (W. Prov. & Tvl) b April 18, 1867, d May 9, 1927

Rowan, A. M. B. (Tvl) b Feb. 7, 1921

*Rowan, E. A. B. (Tvl; *CY 1952*) b July 20, 1909

*Rowe, C. G. (Wgtn & C. Dist.) b June 30, 1915

Rowe, C. J. C. (Kent & Glam.) b May 5, 1953

Rowe, E. J. (Notts.) b July 21, 1920

*Rowe, G. A. (W. Prov.) b June 15, 1874, d Jan. 8, 1950

*Rowe, L. G. (Jam. & Derbys.) b Jan. 8, 1949

*Roy, A. (Bengal) b June 5, 1945

*Roy, Pankaj (Bengal) b May 31, 1928

*Roy, Pranab (Bengal) b Feb. 10, 1957

*Royle, Rev. V. P. F. A. (OUCC & Lancs.) b Jan. 29, 1854, d May 21, 1929

*Rumsey, F. E. (Worcs., Som. & Derbys.) b Dec. 4, 1935

*Russell, A. C. [C. A. G.] (Essex; *CY 1923*) b Oct. 7, 1887, d March 23, 1961

Russell, P. E. (Derbys.) b May 9, 1944

Russell, R. C. (Glos.) b Aug. 15, 1963

Russell, S. E. (Middx & Glos.) b Oct. 4, 1937

*Russell, W. E. (Middx) b July 3, 1936

Russom, N. (CUCC & Som.) b Dec. 3, 1958

Rutherford, I. A. (Worcs. & Otago) b June 30, 1957

*Rutherford, J. W. (W. Aust.) b Sept. 25, 1929

*Rutherford, K. R. (Otago) b Oct. 26, 1965

Ryall, R. J. P. (W. Prov.) b Nov. 26, 1959

Ryan, M. (Yorks.) b June 23, 1933

Ryan, M. L. (Cant.) b June 7, 1943

*Ryder, J. (Vic.) b Aug. 8, 1889, d April 3, 1977

Saadat Ali (Lahore, UBL & HBFC) b Feb. 6, 1955

*Sadiq Mohammad (Kar., PIA, Tas., Essex, Glos. & UBP) b May 3, 1945

Sadler, W. C. H. (Surrey) b Sept. 24, 1896, d Feb. 12, 1981

*Saeed Ahmed (Punjab, Pak. Us, Lahore, PIA, Kar., PWD & Sind) b Oct. 1, 1937

*Saggers, R. A. (NSW) b May 15, 1917, d March 1987

Sainsbury, G. E. (Essex & Glos.) b Jan. 17, 1958

Sainsbury, P. J. (Hants; *CY 1974*) b June 13, 1934

*St Hill, E. L. (T/T) b March 9, 1904, d May 21, 1957

*St Hill, W. H. (T/T) b July 6, 1893, d 1957

Sajid Ali (Kar. & NBP) b July 1, 1963

*Salah-ud-Din (Kar., PIA & Pak. Us) b Feb. 14, 1947

Sale, R., jun. (OUCC, Warwicks. & Derbys.) b Oct. 4, 1919, d Feb. 3, 1987

*Saleem Altaf (Lahore & PIA) b April 19, 1944

*Saleem Jaffer (Kar. & UBL) b Nov. 19, 1962

*Salim Malik (Lahore & HBL; *CY 1988*) b April 16, 1963

*Salim Yousuf (Sind, Kar., IDBP, Allied Bank & Customs) b Dec. 7, 1959

Samaranayake, A. D. A. (SL) b Feb. 25, 1962

Samarasekera, M. A. R. (SL) b Aug. 4, 1961

Sampson, H. (Yorks. & All-England) b March 13, 1813, d March 29, 1885

*Samuelson, S. V. (Natal) b Nov. 21, 1883, d Nov. 18, 1958

*Sandham, A. (Surrey; *CY 1923*) b July 6, 1890, d April 20, 1982

*Sandhu, B. S. (Bombay) b Aug. 3, 1956

*Sardesai, D. N. (Bombay) b Aug. 8, 1940

*Sarfraz Nawaz (Lahore, Punjab, Northants, Pak. Rlwys & UBL) b Dec. 1, 1948

*Sarwate, C. T. (CP & B, M'tra, Bombay & †M. Pradesh) b June 22, 1920

*Saunders, J. V. (Vic. & Wgtn) b Feb. 3, 1876, d Dec. 21, 1927

Saunders, S. L. (Tas.) b June 27, 1960

Savage, J. S. (Leics. & Lancs.) b March 3, 1929

Savage, R. Le Q. (OUCC & Warwicks.) b Dec. 10, 1955

Savill, L. A. (Essex) b June 30, 1935

Saville, G. J. (Essex) b Feb. 5, 1944

Saxelby, K. (Notts.) b Feb. 23, 1959

*Saxena, R. C. (Delhi & Bihar) b Sept. 20, 1944

Sayer, D. M. (OUCC & Kent) b Sept. 19, 1936

*Scarlett, R. O. (Jam.) b Aug. 15, 1934

Schmidt, E. (E. Prov. & OFS) b Sept. 21, 1950

Schofield, R. M. (C. Dist.) b Nov. 6, 1939

Scholes, W. J. (Vic.) b Feb. 5, 1950

Schonegevel, D. J. (OFS & Griq. W.) b Oct. 9, 1934

*Schultz, S. S. (CUCC & Lancs.) b Aug. 29, 1857, d Dec. 18, 1937

*Schwarz, R. O. (Middx & Natal; *CY 1908*) b May 4, 1875, d Nov. 18, 1918

*Scott, A. P. H. (Jam.) b July 29, 1934

Scott, Christopher J. (Lancs.) b Sept. 16, 1959

Scott, Colin J. (Glos.) b May 1, 1919

*Scott, H. J. H. (Vic.) b Dec. 26, 1858, d Sept. 23, 1910

Scott, M. E. (Northants) b May 8, 1936

*Scott, O. C. (Jam.) b Aug. 25, 1893, d June 16, 1961

*Scott, R. H. (Cant.) b March 6, 1917

Scott, S. W. (Middx; *CY 1893*) b March 24, 1854, d Dec. 8, 1933

*Scott, V. J. (Auck.) b July 31, 1916, d Aug. 2, 1980

*Scotton, W. H. (Notts.) b Jan. 15, 1856, d July 9, 1893

Seabrook, F. J. (CUCC & Glos.) b Jan. 9, 1899, d Aug. 7, 1979

*Sealey, B. J. (T/T) b Aug. 12, 1899, d Sept. 12, 1963

*Sealy, J. E. D. (B'dos & T/T) b Sept. 11, 1912, d Jan. 3, 1982

Seamer, J. W. (Som. & OUCC) b June 23, 1913

Sebastian, L. C. (Windwards) b Oct. 31, 1955

*Seccull, A. W. (Kimberley, W. Prov. & Tvl) b Sept. 14, 1868, d July 20, 1945

Seeff, L. J. (W. Prov.) b May 1, 1959

*Sekar, T. A. P. (TN) b March 28, 1955

*Selby, J. (Notts.) b July 1, 1849, d March 11, 1894

Sellers, A. B. (Yorks.; *CY 1940*) b March 5, 1907, d Feb. 20, 1981

*Sellers, R. H. D. (S. Aust.) b Aug. 20, 1940

*Selvey, M. W. W. (CUCC, Surrey, Middx, Glam. & OFS) b April 25, 1948

*Sen, P. (Bengal) b May 31, 1926, d Jan. 27, 1970

*Sen Gupta, A. K. (Ind. Serv.) b Aug. 3, 1939

*Serjeant, C. S. (W. Aust.) b Nov. 1, 1951

Seymour, James (Kent) b Oct. 25, 1879, d Sept. 30, 1930

*Seymour, M. A. (W. Prov.) b June 5, 1936

*Shackleton, D. (Hants.; *CY 1959*) b Aug. 12, 1924

*Shafiq Ahmed (Lahore, Punjab, NBP & UBL) b March 28, 1949

*Shafqat Rana (Lahore & PIA) b Aug. 10, 1943

*Shahid Israr (Kar. & Sind) b March 1, 1950

*Shahid Mahmood (Kar., Pak. Us & PWD) b March 17, 1939

*Shalders, W. A. (Griq. W. & Tvl) b Feb. 12, 1880, d March 18, 1917

*Sharma, Chetan (Haryana) b Jan. 3, 1966

*Sharma, Gopal (U. Pradesh) b Aug. 3, 1960

*Sharma, P. (Raja.) b Jan. 5, 1948

Sharma, R. (Derbys.) b June 27, 1962

Sharp, G. (Northants) b March 12, 1950

Sharp, H. P. (Middx) b Oct. 6, 1917

*Sharp, J. (Lancs.) b Feb. 15, 1878, d Jan. 28, 1938

Sharp, K. (Yorks. & Griq. W.) b April 6, 1959

*Sharpe, D. (Punjab, Pak. Rlwys, Lahore & S. Aust.) b Aug. 3, 1937

*Sharpe, J. W. (Surrey & Notts.; *CY 1892*) b
  Dec. 9, 1866, d June 19, 1936
*Sharpe, P. J. (Yorks. & Derbys.; *CY 1963*)
  b Dec. 27, 1936
*Shastri, R. J. (Bombay & Glam.) b May 27,
  1962
Shaw, Alfred (Notts. & Sussex) b Aug. 29,
  1842, d Jan. 16, 1907
Shaw, C. (Yorks.) b Feb. 17, 1964
Shaw, J. H. (Vic.) b Oct. 18, 1932
*Sheahan, A. P. (Vic.) b Sept. 30, 1946
Sheffield, J. R. (Essex & Wgtn) b Nov. 19,
  1906
*Shepherd, B. K. (W. Aust.) b April 23, 1937
Shepherd, D. J. (Glam.; *CY 1970*) b Aug.
  12, 1927
Shepherd, D. R. (Glos.) b Dec. 27, 1940
*Shepherd, J. N. (B'dos, Kent, Rhod. &
  Glos.; *CY 1979*) b Nov. 9, 1943
Shepherd, T. F. (Surrey) b Dec. 5, 1889, d
  Feb. 13, 1957
*Sheppard, Rt Rev. D. S. (Bishop of
  Liverpool) (CUCC & Sussex; *CY 1953*) b
  March 6, 1929
Shepstone, G. H. (Tvl) b April 8, 1876, d
  July 3, 1940
*Sherwell, P. W. (Tvl) b Aug. 17, 1880, d
  April 17, 1948
*Sherwin, M. (Notts.; *CY 1891*) b Feb. 26,
  1851, d July 3, 1910
*Shillingford, G. C. (Comb. Is. & Wind-
  wards) b Sept. 25, 1944
*Shillingford, I. T. (Comb. Is. &
  Windwards) b April 18, 1944
*Shinde, S. G. (Baroda, M'tra & Bombay) b
  Aug. 18, 1923, d June 22, 1955
Shipman, A. W. (Leics.) b March 7, 1901, d
  Dec. 12, 1979
Shipperd, G. (W. Aust.) b Nov. 11, 1956
Shirreff, A. C. (CUCC, Hants, Kent &
  Som.) b Feb. 12, 1919
*Shivnarine, S. (Guyana) b May 13, 1952
*Shoaib Mohammad (Kar. & PIA) b Jan. 8,
  1962
*Shodhan, R. H. (Guj. & Baroda) b Oct. 18,
  1928
Short, A. M. (Natal) b Sept. 27, 1947
*Shrewsbury, Arthur (Notts.; *CY 1890*) b
  April 11, 1856, d May 19, 1903
*Shrimpton, M. J. F. (C. Dist. & N. Dist.) b
  June 23, 1940
*Shuja-ud-Din, Col. (N. Ind., Pak. Us, Pak.
  Serv., B'pur & R'pindi) b April 10, 1930
*Shukla, R. C. (Bihar & Delhi) b Feb. 4,
  1948
*Shuter, J. (Kent & Surrey) b Feb. 9, 1855, d
  July 5, 1920
Shuttleworth, K. (Lancs. & Leics.) b Nov.
  13, 1944
*Sidebottom, A. (Yorks. & OFS) b April 1,
  1954
*Sidhu, N. S. (Punjab) b Oct. 20, 1963

*Siedle, I. J. (Natal) b Jan. 11, 1903, d Aug.
  24, 1982
*Sievers, M. W. (Vic.) b April 13, 1912, d
  May 10, 1968
*Sikander Bakht (PWD, PIA, Sind, Kar. &
  UBL) b Aug. 25, 1957
Silk, D. R. W. (CUCC & Som.) b Oct. 8,
  1931
*Silva, S. A. R. (SL) b Dec. 12, 1960
Sime, W. A. (Notts.) b Feb. 8, 1909, d May
  5, 1982
Simmons, J. (Lancs. & Tas.; *CY 1985*) b
  March 28, 1941
*Simpson, R. B. (NSW & W. Aust.; *CY
  1965*) b Feb. 3, 1936
*Simpson, R. T. (Notts. & Sind; *CY 1950*) b
  Feb. 27, 1920
*Simpson-Hayward, G. H. (Worcs.) b June
  7, 1875, d Oct. 2, 1936
Sims, Sir Arthur (Cant.) b July 22, 1877, d
  April 27, 1969
*Sims, J. M. (Middx) b May 13, 1903, d
  April 27, 1973
*Sinclair, B. W. (Wgtn) b Oct. 23, 1936
*Sinclair, I. McK. (Cant.) b June 1, 1933
*Sinclair, J. H. (Tvl) b Oct. 16, 1876, d Feb.
  23, 1913
*Sincock, D. J. (S. Aust.) b Feb. 1, 1942
*Sinfield, R. A. (Glos.) b Dec. 24, 1900
*Singh, Charan K. (T/T) b 1938
Singh, R. P. (U. Pradesh) b Jan. 6, 1963
Singh, Swaranjit (CUCC, Warwicks., E.
  Punjab & Bengal) b July 18, 1931
Singleton, A. P. (OUCC, Worcs. & Rhod.)
  b Aug. 5, 1914
*Sivaramakrishnan, L. (TN) b Dec. 31, 1965
*Skeet, C. H. L. (OUCC & Middx) b Aug.
  17, 1895, d April 20, 1978
*Skelding, Alec (Leics.) b Sept. 5, 1886, d
  April 17, 1960
*Skinner, A. F. (Derbys. & Northants) b
  April 22, 1913, d Feb. 28, 1982
Skinner, D. A. (Derbys.) b March 22, 1920
Skinner, L. E. (Surrey & Guyana) b Sept. 7,
  1950
*Slack, W. N. (Middx & Windwards) b Dec.
  12, 1954
Slade, D. N. F. (Worcs.) b Aug. 24, 1940
Slade, W. D. (Glam.) b Sept. 27, 1941
*Slater, K. N. (W. Aust.) b March 12, 1935
*Sleep, P. R. (S. Aust.) b May 4, 1957
*Slight, J. (Vic.) b Oct. 20, 1855, d Dec. 9,
  1930
Slocombe, P. A. (Som.) b Sept. 6, 1954
*Smailes, T. F. (Yorks.) b March 27, 1910, d
  Dec. 1, 1970
Smales, K. (Yorks. & Notts.) b Sept. 15,
  1927
*Small, G. C. (Warwicks. & S. Aust.) b Oct.
  18, 1961
Small, John, sen. (Hants & All-England) b
  April 19, 1737, d Dec. 31, 1826

*Small, J. A. (T/T) b Nov. 3, 1892, d April 26, 1958
*Small, M. A. (B'dos) b Feb. 12, 1964
Smart, J. A. (Warwicks.) b April 12, 1891, d Oct. 3, 1979
Smedley, M. J. (Notts.) b Oct. 28, 1941
*Smith, A. C. (OUCC & Warwicks.; Chief Exec. TCCB 1987-) b Oct. 25, 1936
Smith, A. J. S. (Natal) b Feb. 8, 1951
*Smith, Sir C. Aubrey (CUCC, Sussex & Tvl) b July 21, 1863, d Dec. 20, 1948
*Smith, C. I. J. (Middx; CY 1935) b Aug. 25, 1906, d Feb. 9, 1979
*Smith, C. J. E. (Tvl) b Dec. 25, 1872, d March 27, 1947
*Smith, C. L. (Natal, Glam. & Hants; CY 1984) b Oct. 15, 1958
Smith, C. S. (CUCC & Lancs.) b Oct. 1, 1932
*Smith, C. W. (B'dos) b July 29, 1933
*Smith, Denis (Derbys.; CY 1936) b Jan. 24, 1907, d Sept. 12, 1979
*Smith, D. B. M. (Vic.) b Sept. 14, 1884, d July 29, 1963
Smith, D. H. K. (Derbys. & OFS) b June 29, 1940
*Smith, D. M. (Surrey & Worcs.) b Jan. 9, 1956
*Smith, D. R. (Glos.) b Oct. 5, 1934
*Smith, D. V. (Sussex) b June 14, 1923
Smith, Edwin (Derbys.) b Jan. 2, 1934
*Smith, E. J. (Warwicks.) b Feb. 6, 1886, d Aug. 31, 1979
*Smith, F. B. (Cant.) b March 13, 1922
*Smith, F. W. (Tvl) No details of birth or death known
Smith, G. (Kent) b Nov. 30, 1925
Smith, G. J. (Essex) b April 2, 1935
*Smith, Harry (Glos.) b May 21, 1890, d Nov. 12, 1937
*Smith, H. D. (Otago & Cant.) b Jan. 8, 1913, d Jan. 25, 1986
Smith, I. (Glam.) b March 11, 1967
*Smith, I. D. S. (C. Dist.) b Feb. 28, 1957
Smith, K. D. (Warwicks.) b July 9, 1956
Smith, L. D. (Otago) b Dec. 23, 1914, d Nov. 1, 1978
Smith, M. J. (Middx) b Jan. 4, 1942
*Smith, M. J. K. (OUCC, Leics. & Warwicks.; CY 1960) b June 30, 1933
Smith, N. (Yorks. & Essex) b April 1, 1949
*Smith, O. G. (Jam.; CY 1958) b May 5, 1933, d Sept. 9, 1959
Smith, P. A. (Warwicks.) b April 5, 1964
Smith, Ray (Essex) b Aug. 10, 1914
Smith, Roy (Som.) b April 14, 1930
Smith, R. A. (Natal & Hants) b Sept. 13, 1963
Smith, R. C. (Leics.) b Aug. 3, 1935
*Smith, S. B. (NSW) b Oct. 18, 1961
*Smith, S. G. (T/T, Northants & Auck.; CY 1915) b Jan. 15, 1881, d Oct. 25, 1963

*Smith, T. P. B. (Essex; CY 1947) b Oct. 30, 1908, d Aug. 4, 1967
*Smith, V. I. (Natal) b Feb. 23, 1925
Smith, W. A. (Surrey) b Sept. 15, 1937
Smith, W. C. (Surrey; CY 1911) b Oct. 4, 1877, d July 16, 1946
*Smithson, G. A. (Yorks. & Leics.) b Nov. 1, 1926, d Sept. 6, 1970
*Snedden, C. A. (Auck.) b Jan. 7, 1918
*Snedden, M. C. (Auck.) b Nov. 23, 1958
Snellgrove, K. L. (Lancs.) b Nov. 12, 1941
*Snooke, S. D. (W. Prov. & Tvl) b Nov. 11, 1878, d April 4, 1959
*Snooke, S. J. (Border, W. Prov. & Tvl) b Feb. 1, 1881, d Aug. 14, 1966
*Snow, J. A. (Sussex; CY 1973) b Oct. 13, 1941
Snowden, A. W. (Northants) b Aug. 15, 1913, d May 7, 1981
Snowden, W. (CUCC) b Sept. 27, 1952
*Sobers, Sir G. S. (B'dos, S. Aust. & Notts.; CY 1964) b July 28, 1936
*Sohoni, S. W. (M'tra, Baroda & Bombay) b March 5, 1918
Solanky, J. W. (E. Africa & Glam.) b June 30, 1942
*Solkar, E. D. (Bombay & Sussex) b March 18, 1948
*Solomon, J. S. (BG) b Aug. 26, 1930
*Solomon, W. R. T. (Tvl & E. Prov.) b April 23, 1872, d July 12, 1964
*Sood, M. M. (Delhi) b July 6, 1939
Southern, J. W. (Hants) b Sept. 2, 1952
*Southerton, James (Surrey, Hants & Sussex) b Nov. 16, 1827, d June 16, 1880
Southerton, S. J. (Editor of Wisden 1934-35) b July 7, 1874, d March 12, 1935
*Sparling, J. T. (Auck.) b July 24, 1938
Spencer, C. T. (Leics.) b Aug. 18, 1931
Spencer, J. (CUCC & Sussex) b Oct. 6, 1949
Spencer, T. W. (Kent) b March 22, 1914
Sperry, J. (Leics.) b March 19, 1910
*Spofforth, F. R. (NSW & Vic.) b Sept. 9, 1853, d June 4, 1926
*Spooner, R. H. (Lancs.; CY 1905) b Oct. 21, 1880, d Oct. 2, 1961
*Spooner, R. T. (Warwicks.) b Dec. 30, 1919
Springall, J. D. (Notts.) b Sept. 19, 1932
*Srikkanth, K. (TN) b Dec. 21, 1959
Srinivasan, T. E. (TN) b Oct. 26, 1950
*Stackpole, K. R. (Vic.; CY 1973) b July 10, 1940
Standen, J. A. (Worcs.) b May 30, 1935
Standing, D. K. (Sussex) b Oct. 21, 1963
Stanyforth, Lt-Col. R. T. (Yorks.) b May 30, 1892, d Feb. 20, 1964
*Staples, S. J. (Notts.; CY 1929) b Sept. 18, 1892, d June 4, 1950
Starkie, S. (Northants) b April 4, 1926
*Statham, J. B. (Lancs.; CY 1955) b June 17, 1930

*Stayers, S. C. (†Guyana & Bombay) b June 9, 1937

Stead, B. (Yorks., Essex, Notts. & N. Tvl) b June 21, 1939, d April 15, 1980

Stead, D. W. (Cant.) b May 26, 1947

*Steel, A. G. (CUCC & Lancs.; Pres. MCC 1902) b Sept. 24, 1858, d June 15, 1914

*Steele, D. S. (Northants & Derbys.; *CY 1976*) b Sept. 29, 1941

Steele, J. F. (Leics., Natal & Glam.) b July 23, 1946

Stephens, E. J. (Glos.) b March 23, 1910

Stephenson, G. R. (Derbys. & Hants) b Nov. 19, 1942

Stephenson, H. H. (Surrey & All-England) b May 3, 1832, d Dec. 17, 1896

Stephenson, H. W. (Som.) b July 18, 1920

Stephenson, Lt-Col. J. R. (Sec. MCC 1987-) b Feb. 25, 1931

Stephenson, Lt-Col. J. W. A. (Essex & Worcs.) b Aug. 1, 1907, d May 20, 1982

Stevens, Edward ("Lumpy") (Hants) b circa 1735, d Sept. 7, 1819

*Stevens, G. B. (S. Aust.) b Feb. 29, 1932

*Stevens, G. T. S. (UCS, OUCC & Middx; *CY 1918*) b Jan. 7, 1901, d Sept. 19, 1970

*Stevenson, G. B. (Yorks. & Northants) b Dec. 16, 1955

Stevenson, K. (Derbys. & Hants) b Oct. 6, 1950

Stevenson, M. H. (CUCC & Derbys.) b June 13, 1927

Stewart, A. J. (Surrey) b April 8, 1963

*Stewart, M. J. (Surrey; *CY 1958*) b Sept. 16, 1932

*Stewart, R. B. (SA) b Sept. 3, 1856, d Sept. 12, 1913

Stewart, R. W. (Glos. & Middx) b Feb. 28, 1945

Stewart, W. J. (Warwicks. & Northants) b Aug. 31, 1934

*Stirling, D. A. (C. Dist.) b Oct. 5, 1961

Stocks, F. W. (Notts.) b Nov. 6, 1917

*Stoddart, A. E. (Middx; *CY 1893*) b March 11, 1863, d April 4, 1915

*Stollmeyer, J. B. (T/T) b April 11, 1921

*Stollmeyer, V. H. (T/T) b Jan. 24, 1916

*Storer, W. (Derbys.; *CY 1899*) b Jan. 25, 1867, d Feb. 28, 1912

Storey, S. J. (Surrey & Sussex) b Jan. 6, 1941

Storie, A. C. (Northants & Warwicks.) b July 25, 1965

Stott, L. W. (Auck.) b Dec. 8, 1946

Stott, W. B. (Yorks.) b July 18, 1934

Stovold, A. W. (Glos. & OFS) b March 19, 1953

*Street, G. B. (Sussex) b Dec. 6, 1889, d April 24, 1924

*Stricker, L. A. (Tvl) b May 26, 1884, d Feb. 5, 1960

Stringer, P. M. (Yorks. & Leics.) b Feb. 23, 1943

*Strudwick, H. (Surrey; *CY 1912*) b Jan. 28, 1880, d Feb. 14, 1970

Strydom, W. T. (OFS) b March 21, 1942

*Studd, C. T. (CUCC & Middx) b Dec. 2, 1860, d July 16, 1931

*Studd, G. B. (CUCC & Middx) b Oct. 20, 1859, d Feb. 13, 1945

Studd, Sir Peter M. (CUCC) b Sept. 15, 1916

Sturt, M. O. C. (Middx) b Sept. 12, 1940

*Subba Row, R. (CUCC, Surrey & Northants; *CY 1961*) b Jan. 29, 1932

*Subramanya, V. (Mysore) b July 16, 1936

Such, P. M. (Notts. & Leics.) b June 12, 1964

Sudhakar Rao, R. (Karn.) b Aug. 8, 1952

Sueter, T. (Hants & Surrey) b circa 1749, d Feb. 17, 1827

*Sugg, F. H. (Yorks., Derbys. & Lancs.; *CY 1890*) b Jan. 11, 1862, d May 29, 1933

Sullivan, J. (Lancs.) b Feb. 5, 1945

Sully, H. (Som. & Northants) b Nov. 1, 1939

*Sunderram, G. R. (Bombay & Raja.) b March 29, 1930

Sunnucks, P. R. (Kent) b June 22, 1916

*Surendranath, R. (Ind. Serv.) b Jan. 4, 1937

Surridge, W. S. (Surrey; *CY 1953*) b Sept. 3, 1917

*Surti, R. F. (Guj., Raja. & Qld) b May 25, 1936

*Susskind, M. J. (CUCC, Middx & Tvl) b June 8, 1891, d July 9, 1957

*Sutcliffe, B. (Auck., Otago & N. Dist.; *CY 1950*) b Nov. 17, 1923

*Sutcliffe, H. (Yorks.; *CY 1920*) b Nov. 24, 1894, d Jan. 22, 1978

Sutcliffe, S. P. (OUCC & Warwicks.) b May 22, 1960

Sutcliffe, W. H. H. (Yorks.) b Oct. 10, 1926

Suttle, K. G. (Sussex) b Aug. 25, 1928

Sutton, R. E. (Auck.) b May 30, 1940

*Swamy, V. N. (Ind. Serv.) b May 23, 1924, d May 1, 1983

Swanton, E. W. (Middx; Writer) b Feb. 11, 1907

Swarbrook, F. W. (Derbys., Griq. W. & OFS) b Dec. 17, 1950

Swart, P. D. (Rhod., W. Prov., Glam. & Boland) b April 27, 1946

*Swetman, R. (Surrey, Notts & Glos.) b Oct. 25, 1933

Sydenham, D. A. D. (Surrey) b April 6, 1934

Symington, S. J. (Leics.) b Sept. 16, 1926

*Taber, H. B. (NSW) b April 29, 1940

*Taberer, H. M. (OUCC & Natal) b Oct. 7, 1870, d June 5, 1932

*Tahir Naqqash (Servis Ind., MCB, Punjab & Lahore) b July 6, 1959

Tait, A. (Northants & Glos.) b Dec. 27, 1953

*Talat Ali (Lahore, PIA & UBL) b May 29, 1950
Talbot, R. O. (Cant. & Otago) b Nov. 26, 1903, d Jan. 5, 1983
*Tallon, D. (Qld; *CY 1949*) b Feb. 17, 1916, d Sept. 7, 1984
Tamhane, N. S. (Bombay) b Aug. 4, 1931
*Tancred, A. B. (Kimberley, Griq. W. & Tvl) b Aug. 20, 1865, d Nov. 23, 1911
*Tancred, L. J. (Tvl) b Oct. 7, 1876, d July 28, 1934
*Tancred, V. M. (Tvl) b 1875, d June 3, 1904
Tang Choon, R. P. (T/T) b 1914, d Sept. 5, 1985
*Tapscott, G. L. (Griq. W.) b Nov. 7, 1889, d Dec. 13, 1940
*Tapscott, L. E. (Griq. W.) b March 18, 1894, d July 7, 1934
*Tarapore, K. K. (Bombay) b Dec. 17, 1910, d June 15, 1986
Tarbox, C. V. (Worcs.) b July 2, 1891, d June 15, 1978
Tarrant, F. A. (Vic., Middx & Patiala; *CY 1908*) b Dec. 11, 1880, d Jan. 29, 1951
Tarrant, George F. (Cambs. & All-England) b Dec. 7, 1838, d July 2, 1870
*Taslim Arif (Kar., Sind & NBP) b May 1, 1954
*Tate, F. W. (Sussex) b July 24, 1867, d Feb. 24, 1943
*Tate, M. W. (Sussex; *CY 1924*) b May 30, 1895, d May 18, 1956
*Tattersall, R. (Lancs.) b Aug. 17, 1922
*Tauseef Ahmed (PWD, UBL & Kar.) b May 10, 1958
*Tavaré, C. J. (OUCC & Kent) b Oct. 27, 1954
Tayfield, A. (Natal, Tvl & NE Tvl) b June 21, 1931
*Tayfield, H. J. (Natal, Rhod. & Tvl; *CY 1956*) b Jan. 30, 1929
*Taylor, A. I. (Tvl) b July 25, 1925
Taylor, B. (Essex; *CY 1972*) b June 19, 1932
*Taylor, B. R. (Cant. & Wgtn) b July 12, 1943
*Taylor, Daniel (Natal) b Jan. 9, 1887, d Jan. 24, 1957
*Taylor, D. D. (Auck. & Warwicks.) b March 2, 1923, d Dec. 5, 1980
Taylor, D. J. S. (Surrey, Som. & Griq. W.) b Nov. 12, 1942
Taylor, G. R. (Hants) b Nov. 25, 1909, d Oct. 31, 1986
*Taylor, H. W. (Natal, Tvl & W. Prov.; *CY 1925*) b May 5, 1889, d Feb. 8, 1973
*Taylor, J. M. (NSW) b Oct. 10, 1895, d May 12, 1971
*Taylor, J. O. (T/T) b Jan. 3, 1932
*Taylor, K. (Yorks. & Auck.) b Aug. 21, 1935
Taylor, K. A. (Warwicks.) b Sept. 29, 1916
*Taylor, L. B. (Leics. & Natal) b Oct. 25, 1953

Taylor, M. D. (S. Aust.) b June 9, 1955
Taylor, M. L. (Lancs.) b July 16, 1904, d March 14, 1978
Taylor, M. N. S. (Notts. & Hants) b Nov. 12, 1942
Taylor, N. R. (Kent) b July 21, 1959
*Taylor, P. L. (NSW) b Aug. 22, 1956
Taylor, R. M. (Essex) b Nov. 30, 1909, d Jan. 1984
*Taylor, R. W. (Derbys.; *CY 1977*) b July 17, 1941
Taylor, T. L. (CUCC & Yorks.; *CY 1901*) b May 25, 1878, d March 16, 1960
Taylor, W. (Notts.) b Jan. 24, 1947
Tennekoon, A. P. B. (SL) b Oct. 29, 1946
*Tennyson, 3rd Lord (Hon. L. H.) (Hants; *CY 1914*) b Nov. 7, 1889, d June 6, 1951
*Terry, V. P. (Hants) b Jan. 14, 1959
*Theunissen, N. H. (W. Prov.) b May 4, 1867, d Nov. 9, 1929
Thomas, D. J. (Surrey & N. Tvl) b June 30, 1959
*Thomas, G. (NSW) b March 21, 1938
*Thomas, J. G. (Glam. & Border) b Aug. 12, 1960
Thompson, A. W. (Middx) b April 17, 1916
*Thompson, G. J. (Northants; *CY 1906*) b Oct. 27, 1877, d March 3, 1943
Thompson, J. R. (CUCC & Warwicks.) b May 10, 1918
*Thompson, Nathaniel (NSW) b April 21, 1838, d Sept. 2, 1896
Thompson, P. M. (OFS & W. Prov.) b April 25, 1948
Thompson, R. G. (Warwicks.) b Sept. 26, 1932
*Thoms, G. R. (Vic.) b March 22, 1927
*Thomson, A. L. (Vic.) b Dec. 2, 1945
*Thomson, J. R. (NSW, Qld & Middx) b Aug. 16, 1950
*Thomson, K. (Cant.) b Feb. 26, 1941
*Thomson, N. I. (Sussex) b Jan. 23, 1929
Thorne, D. A. (Warwicks & OUCC) b Dec. 12, 1964
Thornton, C. I. (CUCC, Kent & Middx) b March 20, 1850, d Dec. 10, 1929
*Thornton, P. G. (Yorks., Middx & SA) b Dec. 24, 1867, d Jan. 31, 1939
*Thurlow, H. M. (Qld) b Jan. 10, 1903, d Dec. 3, 1975
Tillekeratne, H. P. (SL) b July 14, 1967
Tilly, H. W. (Middx) b May 25, 1932
Timms, B. S. V. (Hants & Warwicks.) b Dec. 17, 1940
Timms, J. E. (Northants) b Nov. 3, 1906, d May 18, 1980
Timms, W. W. (Northants) b Sept. 28, 1902, d Sept. 30, 1986
Tindall, M. (CUCC & Middx) b March 31, 1914
Tindall, R. A. E. (Surrey) b Sept. 23, 1935
*Tindill, E. W. T. (Wgtn) b Dec. 18, 1910
Tissera, M. H. (SL) b March 23, 1939

*Titmus, F. J. (Middx, Surrey & OFS; *CY 1963*) b Nov. 24, 1932

Todd, L. J. (Kent) b June 19, 1907, d Aug. 20, 1967

Todd, P. A. (Notts. & Glam.) b March 12, 1953

Tolchard, J. G. (Leics.) b March 17, 1944

*Tolchard, R. W. (Leics.) b June 15, 1946

Tomlins, K. P. (Middx & Glos.) b Oct. 23, 1957

*Tomlinson, D. S. (Rhod. & Border) b Sept. 4, 1910

Tompkin, M. (Leics.) b Feb. 17, 1919, d Sept. 27, 1956

Toogood, G. J. (OUCC) b Nov. 19, 1961

Toohey, P. M. (NSW) b April 20, 1954

Tooley, C. D. M. (OUCC) b April 19, 1964

Tordoff, G. G. (CUCC & Som.) b Dec. 6, 1929

*Toshack, E. R. H. (NSW) b Dec. 15, 1914

Townsend, A. (Warwicks.) b Aug. 26, 1921

Townsend, A. F. (Derbys.) b March 29, 1912

*Townsend, C. L. (Glos.; *CY 1899*) b Nov. 7, 1876, d Oct. 17, 1958

*Townsend, D. C. H. (OUCC) b April 20, 1912

*Townsend, L. F. (Derbys. & Auck.; *CY 1934*) b June 8, 1903

Toynbee, M. H. (C. Dist.) b Nov. 29, 1956

*Traicos, A. J. (Rhod. & Zimb.) b May 17, 1947

*Travers, J. P. F. (S. Aust.) b Jan. 10, 1871, d Sept. 15, 1942

*Tremlett, M. F. (Som. & C. Dist.) b July 5, 1923, d July 30, 1984

Tremlett, T. M. (Hants) b July 26, 1956

*Tribe, G. E. (Vic. & Northants; *CY 1955*) b Oct. 4, 1920

*Trim, J. (BG) b Jan. 24, 1915, d Nov. 12, 1960

Trimble, S. C. (Qld) b Aug. 16, 1934

*Trimborn, P. H. J. (Natal) b May 18, 1940

**Trott, A. E. (Vic., Middx & Hawkes Bay; *CY 1899*) b Feb. 6, 1873, d July 30, 1914

*Trott, G. H. S. (Vic.; *CY 1894*) b Aug. 5, 1866, d Nov. 10, 1917

*Troup, G. B. (Auck.) b Oct. 3, 1952

*Trueman, F. S. (Yorks.; *CY 1953*) b Feb. 6, 1931

*Trumble, H. (Vic.; *CY 1897*) b May 12, 1867, d Aug. 14, 1938

*Trumble, J. W. (Vic.) b Sept. 16, 1863, d Aug. 17, 1944

*Trumper, V. T. (NSW; *CY 1903*) b Nov. 2, 1877, d June 28, 1915

Truscott, P. B. (Wgtn) b Aug. 14, 1941

*Tuckett, L. (OFS) b Feb. 6, 1919

*Tuckett, L. R. (Natal & OFS) b April 19, 1885, d April 8, 1963

Tufnell, N. C. (CUCC & Surrey) b June 13, 1887, d Aug. 3, 1951

Tuke, Sir Anthony (Pres. MCC 1982-83) b Aug. 22, 1920

Tunnicliffe, C. J. (Derbys.) b Aug. 11, 1951

Tunnicliffe, H. T. (Notts.) b March 4, 1950

Tunnicliffe, J. (Yorks.; *CY 1901*) b Aug. 26, 1866, d July 11, 1948

*Turnbull, M. J. (CUCC & Glam.; *CY 1931*) b March 16, 1906, d Aug. 5, 1944

*Turner, A. (NSW) b July 23, 1950

Turner, C. (Yorks.) b Jan. 11, 1902, d Nov. 19, 1968

*Turner, C. T. B. (NSW; *CY 1889*) b Nov. 16, 1862 d Jan. 1, 1944

Turner, D. R. (Hants & W. Prov.) b Feb. 5, 1949

Turner, F. M. (Leics.) b Aug. 8, 1934

*Turner, G. M. (Otago, N. Dist. & Worcs.; *CY 1971*) b May 26, 1947

Turner, S. (Essex & Natal) b July 18, 1943

*Twentyman-Jones, P. S. (W. Prov.) b Sept. 13, 1876, d March 8, 1954

Twining, R. H. (OUCC & Middx; Pres. MCC 1964-65) b Nov. 3, 1889, d Jan. 3, 1979

*Tyldesley, E. (Lancs.; *CY 1920*) b Feb. 5, 1889, d May 5, 1962

*Tyldesley, J. T. (Lancs.; *CY 1902*) b Nov. 22, 1873, d Nov. 27, 1930

*Tyldesley, R. K. (Lancs.; *CY 1925*) b March 11, 1897, d Sept. 17, 1943

*Tylecote, E. F. S. (OUCC & Kent) b June 23, 1849, d March 15, 1938

*Tyler, E. J. (Som.) b Oct. 13, 1864, d Jan. 21, 1917

*Tyson, F. H. (Northants; *CY 1956*) b June 6, 1930

Ufton, D. G. (Kent) b May 31, 1928

*Ulyett, G. (Yorks.) b Oct. 21, 1851, d June 18, 1898

*Umrigar, P. R. (Bombay & Guj.) b March 28, 1926

*Underwood, D. L. (Kent; *CY 1969*) b June 8, 1945

Unwin, F. St G. (Essex) b April 23, 1911

*Valentine, A. L. (Jam.; *CY 1951*) b April 29, 1930

*Valentine, B. H. (CUCC & Kent) b Jan. 17, 1908, d Feb. 2, 1983

*Valentine, V. A. (Jam.) b April 4, 1908, d July 6, 1972

Vance, R. H. (Wgtn) b March 31, 1955

*van der Bijl, P. G. (W. Prov. & OUCC) b Oct. 21, 1907, d Feb. 16, 1973

*van der Bijl, V. A. P. (Natal, Middx & Tvl; *CY 1981*) b March 19, 1948

Van der Gucht, P. I. (Glos. & Bengal) b Nov. 2, 1911

*Van der Merwe, E. A. (Tvl) b Nov. 9, 1904, d Feb. 28, 1971

*Van der Merwe, P. L. (W. Prov. & E. Prov.) b March 14, 1937

van Geloven, J. (Yorks. & Leics.) b Jan. 4, 1934

*Van Ryneveld, C. B. (W. Prov. & OUCC) b March 19, 1928

van Vuuren, M. K. (E. Prov.) b Aug. 20, 1958

Varachia, R. (First Pres. SA Cricket Union) b Oct. 12, 1915, d Dec. 11, 1981

Varey, D. W. (CUCC & Lancs.) b Oct. 15, 1961

*Varnals, G. D. (E. Prov., Tvl & Natal) b July 24, 1935

Vaulkhard, P. (Notts. & Derbys.) b Sept. 15, 1911

Vengsarkar, D. B. (Bombay; *CY 1987*) b April 6, 1956

*Veivers, T. R. (Qld) b April 6, 1937

Veletta, M. R. J. (W. Aust.) b Oct. 30, 1963

*Venkataraghavan, S. (†TN & Derbys.) b April 21, 1946

Venter, M. S. (Tvl & N. Tvl) b April 19, 1959

Verdoorn, K. D. (N. Tvl) b July 24, 1955

*Verity, H. (Yorks.; *CY 1932*) b May 18, 1905, d July 31, 1943

*Vernon, G. F. (Middx) b June 20, 1856, d Aug. 10, 1902

Vernon, M. T. (W. Aust.) b Feb. 9, 1937

Vigar, F. H. (Essex) b July 7, 1917

*Viljoen, K. G. (Griq. W., OFS & Tvl) b May 14, 1910, d Jan. 21, 1974

*Vincent, C. L. (Tvl) b Feb. 16, 1902, d Aug. 24, 1968

*Vine, J. (Sussex; *CY 1906*) b May 15, 1875, d April 25, 1946

*Vintcent, C. H. (Tvl & Griq. W.) b Sept. 2, 1866, d Sept. 28, 1943

Virgin, R. T. (Som., Northants & W. Prov.; *CY 1971*) b Aug. 26, 1939

*Viswanath, G. R. (†Karn.) b Feb. 12, 1949

*Viswanath, S. (Karn.) b Nov. 29, 1962

*Vivian, G. E. (Auck.) b Feb. 28, 1946

*Vivian, H. G. (Auck.) b Nov. 4, 1912, d Aug. 12, 1983

*Voce, W. (Notts.; *CY 1933*) b Aug. 8, 1909, d June 6, 1984

*Vogler, A. E. E. (Middx, Natal, Tvl & E. Prov.; *CY 1908*) b Nov. 28, 1876, d Aug. 9, 1946

*Vizianagram, Maharaj Kumar Sir Vijaya of (U. Prov.) b Dec. 28, 1905, d Dec. 2, 1965

Vonhagt, D. M. (SL) b March 31, 1965

*Waddington, A. (Yorks.) b Feb. 4, 1893, d Oct. 28, 1959

Waddington, J. E. (Griq. W.) b Dec. 30, 1918, d Nov. 24, 1985

*Wade, H. F. (Natal) b Sept. 14, 1905, d Nov. 22, 1980

Wade, T. H. (Essex) b Nov. 24, 1910, d July 25, 1987

*Wade, W. W. (Natal) b June 18, 1914

*Wadekar, A. L. (Bombay) b April 1, 1941

*Wadsworth, K. J. (C. Dist. & Cant.) b Nov. 30, 1946, d Aug. 19, 1976

*Wainwright, E. (Yorks.; *CY 1894*) b April 8, 1865, d Oct. 28, 1919

*Waite, J. H. B. (E. Prov. & Tvl) b Jan. 19, 1930

*Waite, M. G. (S. Aust.) b Jan. 7, 1911, d Dec. 16, 1985

*Walcott, C. L. (B'dos & BG; *CY 1958*) b Jan. 17, 1926

*Walcott, L. A. (B'dos) b Jan. 18, 1894, d Feb. 27, 1984

Walden, F. I. (Northants; Umpire) b March 1, 1888, d May 3, 1949

Walford, M. M. (OUCC & Som.) b Nov. 27, 1915

Walker, A. (Northants) b July 7, 1962

Walker, A. K. (NSW & Notts.) b Oct. 4, 1925

Walker, C. (Yorks. & Hants) b June 27, 1920

Walker, C. W. (S. Aust.) b Feb. 19, 1909, d Dec. 21, 1942

Walker, I. D. (Middx) b Jan. 8, 1844, d July 6, 1898

*Walker, M. H. N. (Vic.) b Sept. 12, 1948

*Walker, P. M. (Glam., Tvl & W. Prov.) b Feb. 17, 1936

Walker, W. (Notts.; oldest living County Champ. player) b Nov. 24, 1892

*Wall, T. W. (S. Aust.) b May 13, 1904, d March 25, 1981

*Wallace, W. M. (Auck.) b Dec. 19, 1916

Waller, C. E. (Surrey & Sussex) b Oct. 3, 1948

*Walsh, C. A. (Jam. & Glos.; *CY 1987*) b Oct. 30, 1962

Walsh, J. E. (NSW & Leics.) b Dec. 4, 1912, d May 20, 1980

*Walter, K. A. (Tvl) b Nov. 5, 1939

*Walters, C. F. (Glam. & Worcs.; *CY 1934*) b Aug. 28, 1905

*Walters, F. H. (Vic. & NSW) b Feb. 9, 1860, d June 1, 1922

Walters, J. (Derbys.) b Aug. 7, 1949

*Walters, K. D. (NSW) b Dec. 21, 1945

Walton, A. C. (OUCC & Middx) b Sept. 26, 1933

*Waqar Hassan (Pak. Us, Punjab, Pak. Serv. & Kar.) b Sept. 12, 1932

*Ward, Alan (Derbys., Leics. & Border) b Aug. 10, 1947

*Ward, Albert (Yorks. & Lancs.; *CY 1890*) b Nov. 21, 1865, d June 6, 1939

Ward, B. (Essex) b Feb. 28, 1944

Ward, D. (Glam.) b Aug. 30, 1934

*Ward, F. A. (S. Aust.) b Feb. 23, 1909, d March 25, 1974

*Ward, J. T. (Cant.) b March 11, 1937

*Ward, T. A. (Tvl) b Aug. 2, 1887, d Feb. 16, 1936

Ward, William (MCC & Hants) b July 24, 1787, d June 30, 1849

*Wardle, J. H. (Yorks.; *CY 1954*) b Jan. 8, 1923, d July 23, 1985

*Warnapura, B. (SL) b March 1, 1953
*Warnaweera, K. P. J. (SL) b Nov. 23, 1960
Warne, F. B. (Worcs., Vic. & Tvl) b Oct. 3, 1906
Warner, A. E. (Worcs. & Derbys.) b May 12, 1959
*Warner, Sir Pelham (OUCC & Middx; *CY 1904, special portrait 1921*; Pres. MCC 1950-51) b Oct. 2, 1873, d Jan. 30, 1963
*Warr, J. J. (CUCC & Middx; Pres. MCC 1987-88) b July 16, 1927
*Warren, A. R. (Derbys.) b April 2, 1875, d Sept. 3, 1951
*Washbrook, C. (Lancs.; *CY 1947*) b Dec. 6, 1914
*Wasim Akram (Lahore, PACO and PNSC) b June 3, 1966
*Wasim Bari (Kar., PIA & Sind) b March 23, 1948
*Wasim Raja (Lahore, Sargodha, Pak. Us, PIA, Punjab & NBP) b July 3, 1952
Wass, T. G. (Notts.; *CY 1908*) b Dec. 26, 1873, d Oct. 27, 1953
Wassell, A. (Hants) b April 15, 1940
*Watkins, A. J. (Glam.) b April 21, 1922
*Watkins, J. C. (Natal) b April 10, 1923
*Watkins, J. R. (NSW) b April 16, 1943
Watkinson, M. (Lancs.) b Aug. 1, 1961
*Watson, C. (Jam. & Delhi) b July 1, 1938
Watson, F. B. (Lancs.) b Sept. 17, 1898, d Feb. 1, 1976
*Watson, G. D. (Vic., W. Aust. & NSW) b March 8, 1945
Watson, G. G. (NSW, W. Aust. & Worcs.) b Jan. 29, 1955
*Watson, W. (Yorks. & Leics.; *CY 1954*) b March 7, 1920
*Watson, W. (Auck.) b Aug. 31, 1965
*Watson, W. J. (NSW) b Jan. 31, 1931
Watson, W. K. (Border, N. Tvl, E. Prov. & Notts.) b May 21, 1955
*Watt, L. (Otago) b Sept. 17, 1924
Watts, E. A. (Surrey) b Aug. 1, 1911, d May 2, 1982
Watts, H. E. (CUCC & Som.) b March 4, 1922
Watts, P. D. (Northants & Notts.) b March 31, 1938
Watts, P. J. (Northants) b June 16, 1940
*Waugh, S. R. (NSW & Som.) b June 2, 1965
*Wazir Ali, S. (C. Ind., S. Punjab & Patiala) b Sept. 15, 1903, d June 17, 1950
*Wazir Mohammad (B'pur & Kar.) b Dec. 22, 1929
*Webb, M. G. (Otago & Cant.) b June 22, 1947
*Webb, P. N. (Auck.) b July 14, 1957
Webb, R. J. (Otago) b Sept. 15, 1952
Webb, R. T. (Sussex) b July 11, 1922
Webb, S. G. (Manager Australians in England 1961) b Jan. 31, 1900, d Aug. 5, 1976

*Webbe, A. J. (OUCC & Middx) b Jan. 16, 1855, d Feb. 19, 1941
Webster, J. (CUCC & Northants) b Oct. 28, 1917
Webster, Dr R. V. (Warwicks. & Otago) b June 10, 1939
Webster, W. H. (CUCC & Middx; Pres. MCC 1976-77) b Feb. 22, 1910, d June 19, 1986
*Weekes, E. D. (B'dos; *CY 1951*) b Feb. 26, 1925
*Weekes, K. H. (Jam.) b Jan. 24, 1912
Weekes, R. T. (Warwicks.) b April 30, 1930
*Weerasinghe, C. D. U. S. (SL) b March 1, 1968
Weir, G. L. (Auck.) b June 2, 1908
*Wellard, A. W. (Som.; *CY 1936*) b April 8, 1902, d Dec. 31, 1980
Wellham, D. M. (NSW) b March 13, 1959
Wellings, E. M. (OUCC & Surrey) b April 6, 1909
Wells, A. P. (Sussex) b Oct. 2, 1961
Wells, B. D. (Glos. & Notts.) b July 27, 1930
Wells, C. M. (Sussex, Border & W. Prov.) b March 3, 1960
Wenman, E. G. (Kent & England) b Aug. 18, 1803, d Dec. 31, 1879
Wensley, A. F. (Sussex) b May 23, 1898, d June 17, 1970
Wesley, C. (Natal) b Sept. 5, 1937
*Wessels, K. C. (OFS, W. Prov., N. Tvl, Sussex, Qld & E. Prov.) b Sept. 14, 1957
West, G. H. (Editor of *Wisden* 1880-86) b 1851, d Oct. 6, 1896
Westcott, R. J. (W. Prov.) b Sept. 19, 1927
Weston, M. J. (Worcs.) b April 8, 1959
*Wettimuny, M. D. (SL) b June 11, 1951
*Wettimuny, S. (SL; *CY 1985*) b Aug. 12, 1956
Wettimuny, S. R. de S. (SL) b Aug. 12, 1956
*Wharton, A. (Lancs. & Leics.) b April 30, 1923
*Whatmore, D. F. (Vic.) b March 16, 1954
Wheatley, K. J. (Hants) b Jan. 20, 1946
Wheatley, O. S. (CUCC, Warwicks. & Glam.; *CY 1969*) b May 28, 1935
Whitaker, Haddon (Editor of *Wisden* 1940-43) b Aug. 30, 1908, d Jan. 5, 1982
*Whitaker, J. J. (Leics.; *CY 1987*) b May 5, 1962
Whitcombe, P. A. (OUCC & Middx) b April 23, 1923
White, A. F. T. (CUCC, Warwicks. & Worcs.) b Sept. 5, 1915
*White, D. W. (Hants & Glam.) b Dec. 14, 1935
White, E. C. S. (NSW) b July 14, 1913
*White, G. C. (Tvl) b Feb. 5, 1882, d Oct. 17, 1918
*White, J. C. (Som.; *CY 1929*) b Feb. 19, 1891, d May 2, 1961

White, Hon. L. R. (5th Lord Annaly) (Middx & Victory Test) b March 15, 1927

White, R. A. (Middx & Notts.) b Oct. 6, 1936

White, R. C. (CUCC, Glos. & Tvl) b Jan. 29, 1941

*White, W. A. (B'dos) b Nov. 20, 1938

Whitehead, J. P. (Yorks. & Worcs.) b Sept. 3, 1925

Whitehouse, J. (Warwicks.) b April 8, 1949

*Whitelaw, P. E. (Auck.) b Feb. 10, 1910

Whitfield, B. J. (Natal) b March 14, 1959

Whitfield, E. W. (Surrey & Northants) b May 31, 1911

Whiting, N. H. (Worcs.) b Oct. 2, 1920

Whitington, R. S. (S. Aust. & Victory Tests; Writer) b June 30, 1912, d March 13, 1984

*Whitney, M. R. (NSW & Glos.) b Feb. 24, 1959

Whittaker, G. J. (Surrey) b May 29, 1916

Whitticase, P. (Leics.) b March 15, 1965

Whittingham, N. B. (Notts.) b Oct. 22, 1940

*Whitty, W. J. (S. Aust.) b Aug. 15, 1886, d Jan. 30, 1974

*Whysall, W. W. (Notts.; *CY 1925*) b Oct. 31, 1887, d Nov. 11, 1930

*Wiener, J. M. (Vic.) b May 1, 1955

*Wight, C. V. (BG) b July 28, 1902, d Oct. 4, 1969

Wight, G. L. (BG) b May 28, 1929

Wight, P. B. (BG, Som., & Cant.) b June 25, 1930

*Wijesuriya, R. G. C. E. (SL) b Feb. 18, 1960

Wilcox, D. R. (CUCC & Essex) b June 4, 1910, d Feb. 6, 1953

Wild, D. J. (Northants) b Nov. 28, 1962

*Wiles, C. A. (B'dos & T/T) b Aug. 11, 1892, d Nov. 4, 1957

Wilkins, A. H. (Glam., Glos. & N. Tvl) b Aug. 22, 1953

Wilkins, C. P. (Derbys., Border, E. Prov. & Natal) b July 31, 1944

*Wilkinson, L. L. (Lancs.) b Nov. 5, 1916

Wilkinson, P. A. (Notts.) b Aug. 23, 1951

Wilkinson, Col. W. A. C. (OUCC) b Dec. 6, 1892, d Sept. 19, 1983

Willatt, G. L. (CUCC, Notts. & Derbys.) b May 7, 1918

*Willett, E. T. (Comb. Is. & Leewards) b May 1, 1953

Willett, M. D. (Surrey) b April 21, 1933

*Willey, P. (Northants, E. Prov. & Leics.) b Dec. 6, 1949

*Williams, A. B. (Jam.) b Nov. 21, 1949

*Williams, C. B. (B'dos) b March 8, 1926

Williams, Lord C. C. P. (OUCC & Essex) b Feb. 9, 1933

Williams, D. L. (Glam.) b Nov. 20, 1946

*Williams, E. A. V. (B'dos) b April 10, 1914

Williams, N. F. (Middx, Windwards & Tas.) b July 2, 1962

Williams, R. G. (Northants) b Aug. 10, 1957

*Williams, R. J. (Natal) b April 12, 1912, d May 14, 1984

Williamson, J. G. (Northants) b April 4, 1936

*Willis, R. G. D. (Surrey, Warwicks. & N. Tvl; *CY 1978*) b May 30, 1949

*Willoughby, J. T. (SA) b Nov. 7, 1874, d *circa* 1955

Willsher, E. (Kent & All-England) b Nov. 22, 1828, d Oct. 7, 1885

Wilmot, A. L. (E. Prov.) b June 1, 1943

Wilmot, K. (Warwicks.) b April 3, 1911

Wilson, A. (Lancs.) b April 24, 1921

Wilson, A. E. (Middx & Glos.) b May 18, 1910

*Wilson, Rev. C. E. M. (CUCC & Yorks.) b May 15, 1875, d Feb. 8, 1944

*Wilson, D. (Yorks. & MCC) b Aug. 7, 1937

Wilson, E. F. (Surrey) b June 24, 1907, d March 3, 1981

*Wilson, E. R. (CUCC & Yorks.) b March 25, 1879 d July 21, 1957

Wilson, J. V. (Yorks.; *CY 1961*) b Jan. 17, 1921

*Wilson, J. W. (Vic. & S. Aust.) b Aug. 20, 1921, d Oct. 13, 1985

Wilson, P. H. L. (Surrey, Som. & N. Tvl) b Aug. 17, 1958

Wilson, R. C. (Kent) b Feb. 18, 1928

Wiltshire, J. R. (Auck. & C. Dist.) b Jan. 20, 1952

*Wimble, C. S. (Tvl) b Jan. 9, 1864, d Jan. 28, 1930

Windows, A. R. (Glos. & CUCC) b Sept. 25, 1942

Winfield, H. M. (Notts.) b June 13, 1933

Wingfield Digby, Rev. A. R. (OUCC) b July 25, 1950

Winn, C. E. (OUCC & Sussex) b Nov. 13, 1926

*Winslow, P. L. (Sussex, Tvl & Rhod.) b May 21, 1929

Wisden, John (Sussex; founder John Wisden and Co. and *Wisden's Cricketers' Almanack*) b Sept. 5, 1826, d April 5, 1884

*Wishart, K. L. (BG) b Nov. 28, 1908, d Oct. 18, 1972

Wolton, A. V. G. (Warwicks.) b June 12, 1919

*Wood, A. (Yorks.; *CY 1939*) b Aug. 25, 1898, d April 1, 1973

*Wood, B. (Yorks., Lancs., Derbys. & E. Prov.) b Dec. 26, 1942

Wood, C. J. B. (Leics.) b Nov. 21, 1875, d June 5, 1960

Wood, D. J. (Sussex) b May 19, 1914

*Wood, G. E. C. (CUCC & Kent) b Aug. 22, 1893, d March 18, 1971
*Wood, G. M. (W. Aust.) b Nov. 6, 1956
*Wood, H. (Kent & Surrey; *CY 1891*) b Dec. 14, 1854, d April 30, 1919
*Wood, R. (Lancs. & Vic.) b March 7, 1860, d Jan. 6, 1915
*Woodcock, A. J. (S. Aust.) b Feb. 27, 1948
Woodcock, John C. (Editor of *Wisden* 1980-86) b Aug. 7, 1926
*Woodfull, W. M. (Vic.; *CY 1927*) b Aug. 22, 1897, d Aug. 11, 1965
Woodhead, F. G. (Notts.) b Oct. 30, 1912
Woodhouse, G. E. S. (Som.) b Feb. 15, 1924
**Woods, S. M. J. (CUCC & Som.; *CY 1889*) b April 14, 1867, d April 30, 1931
Wookey, S. M. (CUCC & OUCC) b Sept. 2, 1954
Wooler, C. R. D. (Leics. & Rhod.) b June 30, 1930
Wooller, W. (CUCC & Glam.) b Nov. 20, 1912
Woolley, C. N. (Glos. & Northants) b May 5, 1886, d Nov. 3, 1962
*Woolley, F. E. (Kent; *CY 1911*) b May 27, 1887, d Oct. 18, 1978
*Woolley, R. D. (Tas.) b Sept. 16, 1954
*Woolmer, R. A. (Kent, Natal & W. Prov.; *CY 1976*) b May 14, 1948
*Worrall, J. (Vic.) b May 12, 1863, d Nov. 17, 1937
*Worrell, Sir F. M. M. (B'dos & Jam.; *CY 1951*) b Aug. 1, 1924, d March 13, 1967
Worsley, D. R. (OUCC & Lancs.) b July 18, 1941
Worsley, Sir W. A. 4th Bt (Yorks.; Pres. MCC 1961-62) b April 5, 1890, d Dec. 4, 1973
*Worthington, T. S. (Derbys.; *CY 1937*) b Aug. 21, 1905, d Aug. 31, 1973
Wright, A. (Warwicks.) b Aug. 25, 1941
Wright, A. J. (Glos.) b July 27, 1962
*Wright, C. W. (CUCC & Notts.) b May 27, 1863, d Jan. 10, 1936
*Wright, D. V. P. (Kent; *CY 1940*) b Aug. 21, 1914
*Wright, J. G. (N. Dist. & Derbys.) b July 5, 1954
*Wright, K. J. (W. Aust. & S. Aust.) b Dec. 27, 1953

*Wright, L. G. (Derbys.; *CY 1906*) b June 15, 1862, d Jan. 11, 1953
Wright, M. J. E. (N. Dist.) b Jan. 17, 1950
Wyatt, J. G. (Som.) b June 19, 1963
*Wyatt, R. E. S. (Warwicks. & Worcs.; *CY 1930*) b May 2, 1901
*Wynne, O. E. (Tvl & W. Prov.) b June 1, 1919, d July 13, 1975
*Wynyard, E. G. (Hants) b April 1, 1861, d Oct. 30, 1936

Yachad, M. (N. Tvl & Tvl) b Nov. 17, 1960
*Yadav, N. S. (H'bad) b Jan. 26, 1957
*Yajurvindra Singh (M'tra & S'tra) b Aug. 1, 1952
*Yallop, G. N. (Vic.) b Oct. 7, 1952
*Yardley, B. (W. Aust.) b Sept. 5, 1947
*Yardley, N. W. D. (CUCC & Yorks.; *CY 1948*) b March 19, 1915
Yardley, T. J. (Worcs. & Northants) b Oct. 27, 1946
Yarnold, H. (Worcs.) b July 6, 1917, d Aug. 13, 1974
*Yashpal Sharma (Punjab) b Aug. 11, 1954
Yawar Saeed (Som. & Punjab) b Jan. 22, 1935
*Yograj Singh (Haryana & Punjab) b March 25, 1958
Young, D. M. (Worcs. & Glos.) b April 15, 1924
*Young, H. I. (Essex) b Feb. 5, 1876, d Dec. 12, 1964
*Young, J. A. (Middx) b Oct. 14, 1912
*Young, R. A. (CUCC & Sussex) b Sept. 16, 1885, d July 1, 1968
*Younis Ahmed (Lahore, Kar., Surrey, PIA, S. Aust., Worcs. & Glam.) b Oct. 20, 1947
*Yuile, B. W. (C. Dist.) b Oct. 29, 1941

*Zaheer Abbas (Kar., Glos., PWD, Dawood Indust., Sind & PIA; *CY 1972*) b July 24, 1947
*Zakir Khan (Sind, Peshawar & ADBP) b April 3, 1963
*Zoehrer, T. J. (W. Aust.) b Sept. 25, 1961
*Zulch, J. W. (Tvl) b Jan. 2, 1886, d May 19, 1924
*Zulfiqar Ahmed (B'pur & PIA) b Nov. 22, 1926
*Zulqarnain (Pak. Rlwys) b May 25, 1962

ADDRESSES OF REPRESENTATIVE BODIES

INTERNATIONAL CRICKET CONFERENCE: Lt-Col. J. R. Stephenson, OBE, Lord's Ground, London NW8 8QN.
ENGLAND: Cricket Council, A. C. Smith, Lord's Ground, London NW8 8QN.
AUSTRALIA: Australian Cricket Board, D. L. Richards, 70 Jolimont Street, Jolimont, Victoria 3002.

WEST INDIES: West Indies Cricket Board of Control, G. S. Camacho, 8B Caledonia Avenue, Kingston 5, Jamaica.

INDIA: Board of Control for Cricket in India, R. S. Mahendra, Vijay Nagar Colony, Bhiwani 125 021.

NEW ZEALAND: New Zealand Cricket Council, G. T. Dowling, OBE, PO Box 958, Christchurch.

PAKISTAN: Board of Control for Cricket in Pakistan, Ijaz Butt, Gaddafi Stadium, Lahore.

SRI LANKA: Board of Control for Cricket in Sri Lanka, Nuski Mohamed, 35 Maitland Place, Colombo 7.

SOUTH AFRICA: South African Cricket Union, Dr A. Bacher, PO Box 55009, Northlands 2116, Transvaal.

South African Cricket Board, A. I. Mangera, PO Box 54059, Vrededorp 2141, Transvaal.

ARGENTINA: Argentine Cricket Association, R. H. Gooding, c/o The English Club, 25 de Mayo 586, 1002 Buenos Aires.

BANGLADESH: Bangladesh Cricket Control Board, T. M. Islam, The Stadium, Dacca.

BERMUDA: Bermuda Cricket Board of Control, C. W. Butterfield, PO Box 992, Hamilton.

CANADA: Canadian Cricket Association, K. R. Bullock, PO Box 1364, Brockville, Ontario, K6V 5Y6.

DENMARK: Danish Cricket Association, Søren I. Nissen, Idraettens Hus, 2605 Brøndby.

EAST AFRICA: East and Central African Cricket Conference, S. Patel, PO Box 71712, Ndola, Zambia.

FIJI: Fiji Cricket Association, P. I. Knight, PO Box 300, Suva.

GIBRALTAR: Gibraltar Cricket Association, T. J. Finlayson, 21 Sandpits House, Withams Road.

HONG KONG: Hong Kong Cricket Association, S. K. Sipahimalani, Centre for Media Resources, University of Hong Kong, Knowles Bldg, Pokfulam Road.

ISRAEL: Israel Cricket Association, G. Kandeli, 35/7 Minz Street, Petach Tiqua.

KENYA: Kenya Cricket Association, P. S. Gill, PO Box 46480, Nairobi.

MALAYSIA: Malaysian Cricket Association, K. Sivanesan, c/o Perbadanan Kemajuan, Negeri Selangor, Persiaran Barat, P. Jaya, Selangor.

NETHERLANDS: Royal Netherlands Cricket Association, Hon. Secretary, Willem de Nevijgerlaan 96A, 2582 ET's – Gravenhage.

PAPUA NEW GUINEA: Papua New Guinea Board of Control, A. Lowther, c/o South Pacific Brewery Ltd, PO Box 6550, Boroko.

SINGAPORE: Singapore Cricket Association, R. Sivasubramaniam, 5000-D Marine Parade Road 22-16, Laguna Park, Singapore 1544.

USA: United States of America Cricket Association, Naseeruddin Khan, 2361 Hickory Road, Plymouth Meeting, Pennsylvania 19462.

WEST AFRICA: West Africa Cricket Conference, Chris Enahoro, National Sports Commission, National Stadium, PO Box 145 – Surulere, Lagos.

ZIMBABWE: Zimbabwe Cricket Union, A. L. A. Pichanick, PO Box 452, Harare.

BRITISH UNIVERSITIES SPORTS FEDERATION: 28 Woburn Square, London WC1.

CLUB CRICKET CONFERENCE: A. E. F. Stevens, 353 West Barnes Lane, New Malden, Surrey, KT3 6JF.

ENGLAND SCHOOLS' CRICKET ASSOCIATION: C. J. Cooper, 68 Hatherley Road, Winchester, Hampshire SO22 6RR.

IRISH CRICKET UNION: D. Scott, 45 Foxrock Park, Foxrock, Dublin 18, Ireland.

MINOR COUNTIES CRICKET ASSOCIATION: D. J. M. Armstrong, Thorpe Cottage, Mill Common, Ridlington, North Walsham, NR28 9TY.

NATIONAL CRICKET ASSOCIATION: B. J. Aspital, Lord's Ground, London NW8 8QN.

SCARBOROUGH CRICKET FESTIVAL: Colin T. Adamson, Cricket Ground, North Marine Road, Scarborough, North Yorkshire, YO12 7TJ.

SCOTTISH CRICKET UNION: R. W. Barclay, Admin. Office, 18 Ainslie Place, Edinburgh, EH3 6AU.

COMBINED SERVICES: Colonel R. M. Brennan, c/o ASCB, Clayton Barracks, Aldershot, Hampshire.

THE SPORTS COUNCIL: John Wheatley, Director-General, 16 Upper Woburn Place, London WC1 0QP.

ASSOCIATION OF CRICKET UMPIRES: L. J. Cheeseman, 16 Ruden Way, Epsom Downs, Surrey, KT17 3LN.

WOMEN'S CRICKET ASSOCIATION: 16 Upper Woburn Place, London WC1 0QP.

The addresses of MCC, the First-Class Counties, and Minor Counties are given at the head of each separate section.

OBITUARIES

ABRAHAM, NORMAN, died at Newport in South Wales in January, 1987, aged 98. In a few matches for Monmouthshire in 1925 and 1926, when they were very weak, he scored 473 runs with an average of 17.57.

ASHWELL, ARTHUR HARRY, who died at Birkenhead on August 19, 1985, aged 77, was on the Kent staff as a fast-medium opening bowler. In 1933 he headed the Second XI bowling averages with 40 wickets at 17.42, but in four matches for the county in 1933 and 1934 he failed to take a wicket and never quite looked what was wanted.

BAILEY, FREDERICK RAYMOND, who died at Wolstanton, Stoke-on-Trent, on May 8, 1985, aged 65, was a sound left-handed batsman who played for Staffordshire from 1939 to 1963 and also represented the Minor Counties. For Minor Counties against the Indians at Longton in 1959 he scored 79, putting on 284 for the second wicket with P. J. Sharpe, a stand which had much to do with his side making 334 in 290 minutes to win the match.

BANHAM, STANLEY TATTERSALL, died at Peterborough in December 1984, aged 71. A Bacup man, he was called upon by Lancashire to keep wicket against R. S. Grant's West Indians in 1939, took one catch, but in a match spoilt by rain, did not bat. It was his only first-class appearance, although he did play for the county's Second XI.

BOWES, WILLIAM ERIC (BILL), who died in hospital on September 5, 1987, aged 79, was one of the great bowlers of his day. He is often, for convenience, loosely classed as fast, but Robertson-Glasgow, writing in the early days of the war, described him, correctly, as the most difficult fast-medium bowler in England. It was, no doubt, partly because he never tried to acquire the extra yard or two of pace which would have put him indisputably in the ranks of the fast that he was such a fine bowler. And like most of the great, he came off the pitch faster than the batsman expected.

No man has ever worked harder at his art. He was constantly practising, constantly experimenting, but throughout he remained content with the ten yards to which that great coach, Walter Brearley, had cut his run when he first went to Lord's. He concentrated on control of length and direction and on moving the ball. He could always bowl a late in-swinger, but Brearley told him that he would never reach the top class unless he could make the ball run away as well. This it would occasionally do by a fluke, as at the Scarborough Festival in 1929, for example. George Hirst was persuaded to play and Bowes bowled him with one that pitched on the leg stump and took the off bail. Hirst, typically, said: "Well bowled. That would have been too good for me when I was good." Yet by the middle of 1931, after three years of trying, Bowes was no nearer to discovering how to produce this ball. Meanwhile he was already on the fringe of the England side. Most men in this position would have been satisfied, and concluded that away-swingers were not for them. Not so Bowes; he went on trying and finally found the required hint in an obscure coaching manual, which told him it was all in the position of the feet at the moment of delivery. Within a week or two he was bowling away-swingers as easily as in-swingers, with a barely perceptible change of action. Thenceforward the batsman who had successfully cut two or three in-swingers, and tried to repeat the stroke, was liable to find that he had picked the wrong ball and to chop it into his stumps. That season his wickets cost him 4 runs apiece fewer than in 1930.

Yorkshire had in those days no nursery; players were picked from the nets and graduated through the Second XI. Bowes, wanting a secure tenure, applied with typical enterprise, and with the approval of the county authorities, for a place on the groundstaff at Lord's. He was taken on for 1928, and in his first first-class match for MCC he took five for 69 against Wales; in his second, against Cambridge, he did the hat-trick. Naturally Yorkshire became interested, and after some complex negotiations it was agreed that, while his contract with MCC should stand, he should be released to play for Yorkshire unless MCC required him for a first-class match. As a result he played a few times for the county in 1929 and did enough to show his possibilities, his figures for all first-class matches being 65 wickets at 19 each. In 1930, after several successful matches for Yorkshire, culminating in eight for 69 against Middlesex at Sheffield, he received his county cap. From then on, though his contract with MCC did not end till 1937, they claimed his services only on special occasions and he was a regular member of the county side.

There can be no doubt that his engagement at Lord's had been an advantage to him. Not only had he received much admirable advice and coaching, but he had been carefully nursed and saved from the grind of bowling six days a week in county cricket before he was strong enough, something which has ruined so many promising bowlers. Now that he was a recognised member of the Yorkshire side, he was taken in hand by the senior professionals and taught his trade with a thoroughness which does much to explain why for so many years the county was by and large the most formidable in the Championship. Night after night he and Verity, who started at the same time, were taken up to a hotel bedroom and the day's cricket was discussed, the field set out on the bed with toothbrushes, shaving tackle and the like, and praise and blame administered impartially as required. At one of the first of these sessions Verity, who had accomplished his biggest performance to date, seven for 26 against Hampshire, was greeted with, "Seven for 26 and it ought to have been seven for 22! I never saw such bowling. Whatever wast thou doing to give A. K. Judd that four?" There is precedent for this attitude. In 1918 Eton dismissed Charterhouse for 13. That great man, C. M. Wells, for many years in charge of Eton cricket, entered the dressing-room with the words, "Should have been 9". But however outspoken the Yorkshire professionals were about anything of which they disapproved, there was no lack of praise either. Who could fail to learn in such an atmosphere? There can never have been a greater cricket school than the Yorkshire sides between the wars or two apter pupils than Bowes and Verity. And strong though Yorkshire were in every department, it was the bowling of these two more than anything else that won them their Championships in the 1930s.

There has probably never been a great cricketer who looked less like one than Bowes. Standing 6ft 4in, he was clumsily built and a poor mover. Wearing strong spectacles, he looked far more like a university professor, and indeed batted and fielded like one. However, no side has been so closely welded as Yorkshire in the 1920s and 1930s: every man knew just what he was expected to do and did it without being told. When Bowes suggested that it might be a good thing if he were taught the rudiments of batting, he was told firmly that his job was to take wickets; he was not to waste his valuable strength on making runs. If he ever showed signs of forgetting this, his partners were expected to run him out. Similarly in the field. He was stationed at mid-on and, if the ball came to him, he was to catch it or stop it as the case might be. But if it passed him, he was not to move; it was someone else's duty to chase it and throw it in. This was fully understood on the Yorkshire side. After all, Bowes was their great opener and they had no alternative to him.

But England had Larwood (and later Farnes), Voce and Allen, all faster than Bowes and all but Farnes far better bats and fields. Besides them there was always

[*Ken Kelly*

Bill Bowes, who served the game of cricket for six decades, first as a great fast-medium bowler in the Championship-winning Yorkshire teams of the 1930s and then as a journalist. A kind man, he was liked by all who met him.

Hammond, a much better bowler than was generally realised, to open if required. In those days three quick bowlers were usually regarded as ample; a place had to be kept for a slow left-arm bowler and a leg-spinner, if a good enough one could be found. So it is not surprising that selectors often passed Bowes over. Tests against Australia then stood on a footing of their own. Between 1932 and 1939, England played twenty Tests against Australia and Bowes was picked for six only; but as in these he took, in an era of mammoth scoring, 30 wickets at 24.70, it was clear that he was in no way out of his class. Yet even for the 1932-33 tour of Australia, his one tour abroad, he received his invitation only three days before the team sailed, having forced himself into the side by some superb bowling in the last weeks of the season.

One wicket on that tour in particular is remembered and deserves description. At Melbourne in the Second Test, Bradman, who had missed the First Test, came in to such tumultuous applause that Bowes had to stop in the middle of his run for it to subside, and "to fill in time" he moved mid-on to silly mid-on. Again he started, again he had to stop, and this time he moved his deep fine leg. He noticed that Bradman followed these moves with grave attention, and he felt sure that he expected a bouncer. So he ran up with his most threatening expression, but instead of digging the ball in he deliberately bowled one little more than stump high. Bradman, already halfway in position to hook, had suddenly to alter his stroke and in so doing pulled the ball into his wicket. In other words, a great piece of bowling. In fact, although with his height Bowes naturally had a steeper rise than most bowlers, and was always prepared to bowl a bouncer, he did not rely on it as a regular form of attack and, as he gained in experience, used it less and less. His use of the bouncer has probably been exaggerated by a famous incident at The Oval in 1932, a month or so before the start of this tour, when he bounced some at Hobbs. On that occasion, as far as the two protagonists were concerned there was no lasting ill feeling, though Hobbs never approved of the bodyline tactics.

Getting a commission in the war, Bowes was captured at Tobruk in 1942 and spent three years as a prisoner. By the time he returned home, he had lost four and a half stone and was not really fit to stand the rigours of first-class cricket. Moreover, at 38 he had reached an age at which a bowler of his type is sure to have lost some of his fire. His troubles were compounded by a severe strain to the muscles of his side and back. None the less, bowling at a reduced pace, he struggled bravely through two seasons, still taking wickets cheaply for the county and even playing against India at Lord's. In 1947 his benefit brought him £8,000, at that time a record, and he decided to retire, though Yorkshire were anxious to retain him even if he could bowl only off-spinners. Fortunately he had still 40 years of service to cricket in front of him. To the day of his death he wrote regularly on cricket for the papers, and with his profound knowledge of the game every word he wrote was worth reading. His autobiography, *Express Deliveries*, published in 1949, is probably the best book on cricket ever written by a professional; certainly the best since Albert Knight's *The Complete Cricketer* eighty years ago.

In his first-class career of 372 games, Bowes took 1,639 wickets at 16.76: as he made only 1,530 runs, his wickets outnumber his runs. In fifteen Tests, his figures were 68 wickets at 22.33.

BROOK, JAMES WILLIAM, who died at Halifax on July 12, 1985, aged 88, had a great local reputation as a batsman but, appearing in one match for Yorkshire in 1923, failed to score in his only innings.

BRUMFITT, JACK, died at Ilkley on March 16, 1987, aged 70. A well-known batsman in Yorkshire league cricket, he played once for the county as an amateur in 1938, when the side was weakened by the absence of Sutcliffe, Hutton and Turner, but met with no success.

BUCKINGHAM, JOHN, died in hospital in Birmingham on January 25, 1987, aged 84. Born in Yorkshire and going to the Midlands as a professional footballer, he kept wicket for Warwickshire II and first played for the county in 1933. In 1934 Jack Smart, their 'keeper, was injured in June and Buckingham took over, creating a good impression besides playing some useful innings. In 1935 and 1936, with Smart again available, he hardly played, but in 1937 he became the regular wicket-keeper and retained his place until the war. In 1937 he made the first of his three centuries, 109 at Gloucester, and in 1938 he came third in the averages, scoring 1,054 runs with an average of 31. Against Northamptonshire at Northampton, he made the highest score of his career, 137 not out, but more remarkable was his 124 at Derby. Warwickshire, set 311 to win, were 39 for five when he came in, but he and Dollery added 220 in two and a half hours, breaking the county's sixth-wicket record, and they won by four wickets. In all for Warwickshire he scored 2,840 runs with an average of 23.86, caught 133 batsmen and stumped 91. Never a sound or orthodox player, he had plenty of strokes and hit the ball astonishingly hard for so small a man. As a wicket-keeper, again he was brilliant rather than consistent and was apt to snatch. He is described as "a cheerful and plucky performer whose hilarious disregard of grammatical English was an unending source of amusement to the side". To the end of his life he was a constant visitor to the Edgbaston ground.

BURDEN, MERVYN DEREK, died at his home at Whitchurch, in Hampshire, on November 9, 1987, aged 57. Unlike so many Hampshire players, he was a genuine Hampshire man, born at Southampton and educated there at King Edward VI School. After a match or two for Hampshire in 1953, he became a regular member of the team in July 1954, when an analysis of seven for 48 against Leicestershire at Leicester showed how dangerous he could be when the wicket helped him. But like all save the really great slow off-spinners, he needed that help from the wicket to trouble the class batsmen; on a good wicket he lacked the spin and venom to be formidable to them. Still, without ever quite reaching the top flight, he did valuable service for the county for ten years and took 481 wickets at 26.11 runs each. His best season was 1955, when he took 70 at 21.75 and received his county cap. C. J. Knott, who played much for the county with him, writes: "He really did follow the mould of Lofty Herman, the jester of the dressing-room, and was a lovable and popular player." The value of such a man is not to be estimated in figures.

CARTY, RICHARD ARTHUR, who died at Bishops Waltham on March 31, 1984, aged 61, did useful work for Hampshire between 1949 and 1954 without quite getting an assured place in the side. He never lived up to the promise of his first appearance, against Oxford at Bournemouth, when, going in tenth, he contributed a hard-hit 53 and brought his side almost level on the first innings. This remained his highest score for the county and he followed it by taking five for 47. Fast-medium and at times, when fully fit, genuinely fast, he had to compete with several others of the same type and class, and tended to be the spare man of the side. Altogether he took 138 wickets at 30.17 and scored 798 runs with an average of 14.77. Against Oxford at Basingstoke in 1951, he took seven for 29.

CHANCE, GEOFFREY HENRY BARRINGTON, died on July 11, 1987, aged 93. At the end of June 1912, his last summer at Eton when he was seventeen and a half, he made his first appearance in the XI: it was against MCC and he took ten for 36, his victims including P. R. Johnson, F. A. Phillips, W. Findlay, E. M. Dowson and C. M. Wells, all experienced first-class batsmen and all, except perhaps Dowson, presumably in reasonable practice. The match was thirteen a side, so he did not take all ten wickets. MCC made 100 and bowled the boys out for 73, E. R. Wilson taking seven wickets. This was on Saturday. On the following Wednesday at Winchester, the ground was so wet that play could not start till 12.00, but by 1.30 Winchester, who had won the toss, were all out for 48, Chance having taken seven for 16. According to some accounts, in both these matches he was bowling slow leg-breaks. In fact there can be no doubt that he really bowled away-swingers. *The Times* on Eton and Winchester is precise – "Chance made good use of his wicket; he bowls fast to medium in pace over the wicket; he kept a length and made the ball get up quickly and go away just a little." Later, summing up the match, it said, "The Eton bowling was steady, but no one gave the impression he would be really difficult in fairly easy conditions". A writer in *The Wykehamist* said, "Chance did not seem to be making the ball break much or keeping a very steady length, tho' he varied his pace cleverly". This looks as if he had been expecting a leg-spinner. The accounts of Eton and Harrow, where he took three for 38 and three for 70, again lend no support to the leg-break theory, but they do say that the Eton batsmen shaped poorly at E. T. Buller's leg-breaks: ". . . it looked as if they had not had much experience of this style of bowling." Still, after what he had achieved, one would expect something fairly enthusiastic about his bowling, but one would look for it in vain. E. B. Noel, in his account of the season in *Wisden*, wrote: "Chance, medium-right, was also useful and he took thirty wickets for eight runs apiece." Yet his subsequent history suggests that this lukewarm language may well have been justified. In 1912 and 1913 he played a few matches for Berkshire, his native county. In 1913 he also appeared for Hampshire against MCC at Lord's and in 1922 for MCC against Scotland at Lord's. In none of these matches did he achieve anything. At the time of his death he was one of the few survivors of those who had played in first-class cricket before the Great War.

CHARI, S. V. T., who died at Madras on January 23, 1986, aged 71, had played for Madras in the inaugural match of the Ranji Trophy championship in 1934-35 and the next season represented India in an unofficial "Test" at Madras against Ryder's Australian team. A brilliant wicket-keeper with a somewhat unorthodox style, he gave up serious cricket to pursue his profession in medicine.

CHIPPERFIELD, ARTHUR GORDON, who died in Sydney on July 29, 1987, aged 81, played fourteen times for Australia in the 1930s and toured England twice and South Africa once. His selection for the 1934 team to England came as something of a surprise, following only three first-class innings. He was then 28, but 152 for Northern Districts at Newcastle against Jardine's 1932-33 MCC side had given notice of his ability, and with 84 against Queensland on his début for New South Wales he furthered the good impression already made. In England, he did not enjoy the best of health, but he finished the tour with 899 runs and an average of 40.86, having shown himself as a batsman who, while essentially a front-foot player, possessing a sound defensive technique, could when the occasion demanded hit hard and score at a good pace. He was an uncommonly good slip fielder and a useful bowler of leg-breaks.

A career-best 175 against Essex, in his first match in England, and 116 not out the following week against Hampshire, led to his inclusion for the First Test at Trent Bridge, where, having reached 99 by lunch on the second day, he was out without addition to the third ball afterwards, caught behind off Farnes. He was the first to be dismissed for 99 in his first Test, and had batted for three hours twenty minutes, his runs coming in the main from his square cutting. At Lord's, where Verity took fifteen wickets on a damp pitch, his unbeaten 37 was Australia's second-highest score of their first innings; his three for 91 in England's only innings were his best Test bowling figures. Chosen for the Manchester Test, despite suffering from an infection known colloquially as "Wimbledon Throat", he left hospital against medical advice to score 26, which helped Australia avoid the follow-on. He then returned to hospital, the instance being one of the few in Test cricket (weather-related instances apart) of a player batting but never fielding. He played in the next two Tests, but on his second trip to England, in 1938, played only at Lord's, where he split his finger stopping a shot from Hammond in his innings of 240. Later in the tour he had to undergo an operation because of appendicitis, and so Lord's was the last of his Tests, in which he scored 552 runs, with an average of 32.47, took five wickets at 87.40, and held fifteen catches. His only Test hundred was 109 against South Africa in Durban in 1935-36. Altogether, in 96 first-class games, he scored 4,295 runs, average 38.34, took 65 wickets at 39.72, and held 92 catches. His best bowling was eight for 66 for an Australian XI against MCC at Sydney in 1936-37, when he ended the touring team's first innings with a spell of four for 9. Two second-innings wickets gave him ten in the match.

COBBOLD, RALPH HAMILTON, who died in Ipswich Hospital on September 1, 1987, aged 81, was a player who never quite fulfilled his early promise. He was three years in the Eton XI and captain in the last, and in his first appearance at Lord's for them in 1923 he made 100. His average for his three matches against Harrow was 48. In 1924 he scored 149 against Winchester. At the same time he was one of the mainstays of three rather weak bowling teams, on the slow side of medium, often opening the bowling but sometimes slightly uncertain in length. Going up to Cambridge at a time when the University was extremely strong, he had a trial in his first year but did not get in. In his second year, 1927, he did nothing in the early trials, but late in May he made 104 for Perambulators against Etceteras and was given a place in the last two matches at Fenner's, against the Army and Free Foresters, when the University side was weakened by exams. An innings of 100 not out against the Foresters secured him a place on tour, when a series of useful scores got him his Blue. At Lord's, he failed. He was a good stylist and a particularly fine driver on both sides of the wicket.

COCHRAN, JOHN ALEXANDER KENNEDY, died in Johannesburg on June 15, 1987, aged 77. A tall, well-built fast bowler, able to move the ball both ways off the pitch, he opened the bowling against England at Durban in the final Test of the 1930-31 series. His 23 overs cost 47 runs without producing a wicket and he did not bowl in the second innings. It was his only match for South Africa. In a first-class career of three seasons, during which he represented Transvaal and Griqualand West, he took fifteen wickets at 24.06.

COLDHAM, JAMES DESMOND BOWDEN, who died on January 14, 1987, aged 63, was one to whom many other cricket writers owed a great debt. A tireless researcher, he was always delighted to place his knowledge at the disposal of anyone who wanted it, and the number of books and articles with which he helped must be legion. For years he had kept *Wisden* informed of deaths of which we would not otherwise have heard. If one wrote to him, one was certain of an answer and, if it did not come by return, it was because he was collecting the information required. He had moreover a passion for accuracy which is all too rare. He was himself responsible for a full and reliable history of Northamptonshire cricket and for a life of Lord Harris which won the praise even of those who had been brought up in the shadow of the great man. For years he edited the Cricket Society's *Journal* and himself wrote many learned articles for it.

COOPER, FREDERICK, died at Stourbridge in December 1986, aged 65. A younger brother of Edwin Cooper, who made many runs for Worcestershire, and like him born at Bacup, he played four times for Lancashire in 1946 and then moved to Worcestershire, for whom he had a good trial in 1947 and 1948, often opening the batting with his brother. His most notable performance was 113 not out in the second innings against Nottinghamshire at Trent Bridge in 1948, when he and Jenkins added 170 for the second wicket and secured an honourable draw. Although he did fairly well, he never quite secured a firm place in the side, and after a few matches in 1949 and 1950 he left the staff. It was a disappointing career, but his health had suffered in the war and it is pleasant to record that after retiring from serious cricket, he prospered in business and also served on the local council. Altogether, in 44 first-class matches he scored 1,369 runs with an average of 19.28.

COX, ARTHUR LEONARD, who died in November, 1986, aged 79, several times indicated that he might be of valuable service to Northamptonshire, but such expectations were never fulfilled. In a career stretching from 1926 to 1947, he played a number of useful innings but his lack of consistency was evidenced by his failing ever to get 1,000 runs. His only hundred, 104, was against Nottinghamshire at Trent Bridge in 1930. In 1932, bowling slow-to-medium leg-breaks, he took 54 wickets at 26.94, including seven for 91 against Derbyshire at Chesterfield, to complement his 967 runs, and this gave rise to hopes that he would establish himself as an all-rounder; but in the following season his batting and bowling both fell away as his confidence wavered. His father, Mark Cox, had been a stalwart of Northamptonshire at the turn of the century and his brother, also Mark, had a trial for the county in 1932.

DEACON, CHRISTOPHER FRANCIS, who died at his home in Cornwall on March 21, 1987, aged 64, played regularly for Dorset from 1951 to 1956. A compact left-handed batsman with a games-player's eye, he won a wartime Blue for Oxford in 1942 – he was there on a short course after three years in the St Edward's side – and scored heavily in club circles when the war was over. For Dorset his top score was 134 against Devon at Sherborne in 1951. From 1947 until 1982 he taught at Stowe School.

DE ZOETE, MILES HERMAN, who died on July 9, 1987, aged 79, was in the Eton XI in 1926, when he scored 73 and 30 at Lord's by some of the hardest hitting seen in the match for many years. Tall and strong, he drove with enormous power and never minded lifting the ball. In later life he was a menace in club cricket and a valuable addition to the Hertfordshire side whenever they could secure his services. His father had had a Blue at Cambridge.

DIVECHA, AJAY VITHALDAS, who died in Bombay on October 12, 1987, aged 47, was a younger brother of the Indian Test bowler, Remesh. For Maharashtra, Bombay and Delhi in the Ranji Trophy, he scored 226 runs, average 22.60, and, bowling medium pace, took 22 wickets at 32.45 between 1960-61 and 1964-65.

DODSWORTH, VICTOR EDWARD, who died at Healing, near Grimsby, on November 4, 1986, aged 75, played as a fast-medium right-arm bowler for Lincolnshire against Leicestershire II in 1949 and took four for 84. He was better known as a professional footballer.

DOLLERY, HORACE EDGAR (TOM), died in hospital in Birmingham on January 20, 1987, aged 72. Few players have done more for Warwickshire cricket. For twenty years he was one of the mainstays of their batting, usually top or second in the averages: he never had a bad season and seldom a bad patch. He was a tireless fieldsman and in the latter part of his career became the county's first official professional captain. When, under him, Warwickshire won the Championship for the first time in 40 years, *Wisden* described him as "the most skilful of all the county captains".

He was born at Reading next door to the Berkshire county ground, where the groundsman at the time was the father of Arthur Croom, of Warwickshire. Dollery was constantly on the ground, taking every opportunity to practise, and quite naturally, as he began to show promise, he conceived the ambition of playing for Warwickshire himself. He was five years in the XI at Reading School and captain in 1930 and 1931. In 1930 he made 101 out of 140 against MCC, but he put this completely in the shade next year when he carried his bat right through the innings for 104 not out in a total of 115, the next highest score being 3. Even admitting that the bowling was not strong, this is an almost incredible performance. To be able to keep the bowling over such a long period comes normally from years of experience, and many players never acquire the art. Moreover, the difficulty is multiplied when all the batsmen are schoolboys, who are as a race notoriously bad runners between the wickets.

That year he played a few matches for Berkshire as an amateur, and in 1932 and 1933 was a regular and valuable member of the side. In 1932, at the age of eighteen, he made a hundred in each innings against Monmouthshire at Newport, and in 1933 he had an average of 67 and represented the Minor Counties. Next year he became qualified for Warwickshire late in July and, without doing anything spectacular, showed clearly that he had not been overestimated. Innings of 34 and 46 against Middlesex created a particularly good impression. He did not waste time in proving his class. In 1935 he made his 1,000 runs, a feat he repeated every season until his retirement; in the opening match he saved the side from probable defeat by Gloucestershire with an innings of 100. Later in the season he hit Bowes off his back foot into the Edgbaston pavilion. He was indeed enormously strong and, though predominantly an off-side player, had strokes all round the wicket.

It seemed that he had only to strengthen his defence a little to become a great player. In this he never quite succeeded. He played in four Tests between 1947 and 1950, but did little, although against Australia at Lord's in 1948 he was top scorer in the second innings with 37. His runs on that occasion were scored almost entirely on the leg, the Australians typically knowing that he preferred the off. His innings ended ingloriously; he ducked to what he thought was a bumper from Lindwall and the ball skidded through to bowl him. He was only once picked for a tour abroad, to India in 1939, but it was cancelled because of the war. An innings of 70 that year on his first appearance for the Players at Lord's had doubtless helped.

Apart from this, the war also robbed him of six seasons' cricket between the ages of 25 and 32 and by that time the selectors preferred to experiment with younger players. So he will be remembered primarily as a great county player who, in an age when more and more batsmen were concentrating on defence, never lost his attacking instinct. In 1936 he scored 142 against Surrey at Edgbaston in 100 minutes, and as far on as 1949 his 200 against Gloucestershire at Gloucester took only 205 minutes. His highest score was 212 against Leicestershire at Edgbaston in 1952. In his early days, nothing escaped him at cover; later he developed into a reliable slip. In 1947, when for half the season the county lacked a trained wicket-keeper, he took over the position without any previous experience and performed adequately. After sharing the captaincy in 1948 with R. H. Maudsley, in 1949 he was appointed sole captain, a position he held until his retirement from first-class cricket at the end of 1955.

In his career he scored 24,413 runs (23,437 of them for Warwickshire) with an average of 37.50 and made 50 centuries. He caught 291 batsmen and stumped thirteen. His services to cricket did not end with his retirement. He became the county's coach and captain of the Second XI, which twice under him won the Minor Counties Championship, and from 1964 to 1972 he was a member of the Warwickshire committee. He was then made a life member of the club. In 1957 and 1958 he had been a Test selector.

DRAPER, ROBERT WILLIAM, who died at his home in Cowles Hill, Durban, on August 29, 1987, aged 84, made three appearances for Somerset as an amateur between 1925 and 1929. Left-handed both as a batsman and a bowler, he met with little success.

DUNBAR, JAMES GARRETT, who died after a long illness on February 24, 1987, aged 73, was one of the Assistant Secretaries at Lord's from 1949 to 1974. A chartered surveyor by profession, he had special responsibility for the maintenance of the grounds and buildings. This led him to become a leading authority on artificial pitches, and latterly he had been chairman of the London Playing Fields Association. He also took a great interest in youth cricket and had been chairman of the National Cricket Association. A man of boundless energy and enthusiasm, who threw himself wholeheartedly into everything that he undertook, he was an outstanding secretary of the Butterflies from 1949 to 1959 and managed five Butterfly tours to Germany, besides taking more than 400 wickets for the club. A fast-medium bowler with an easy action, which gave him some life off the pitch, he had been two years in the XI at Charterhouse. He was also a keen photographer and a number of his colour photographs appear in the first edition of E. W. Swanton's *The World of Cricket*.

EDGE, CYRIL ARTHUR, died on October 4, 1985, in Lancashire, aged 68. Tried for Lancashire as a fast-medium bowler between 1936 and 1938, he achieved little in his eight matches. In 1939 he played for the Minor Counties against the West Indians. His 29 wickets in first-class cricket cost 30.10 each.

EDWARDS, PHILIP GEORGE, who died in London on April 3, 1987, aged 80, had trials for Middlesex as a slow left-arm bowler in 1930 and 1933, but in four matches he took only one wicket and was not persevered with.

FAREBROTHER, MICHAEL HUMPHREY, died at Seaford on September 27, 1987, aged 67. Bowling left-arm fast-medium, with a good action, he was Eton's leading wicket-taker in 1938 and going up to Oxford played one first-class match for the University in 1939. Commissioned into the Grenadier Guards, he was erroneously reported in the 1945 *Wisden* as "killed in Italy". From 1956 till 1982, he was headmaster of St Peter's, Seaford.

FAVELL, LESLIE ERNEST, MBE, who died on June 14, 1987, aged 57, was one of South Australia's most popular players, having played more games (143), captained them more times (95) and scored more runs (9,656, average 38.17) than any other player. Twice, in 1963-64 and 1968-69, South Australia won the Sheffield Shield under his inspirational captaincy. But it was for his dashing style and fearless strokeplay as an opening batsman that the crowds loved him. From a crouching stance, with his grip low on the handle, he was especially strong on the square-cut and hook, while never averse to driving the fast bowlers straight back down the ground. When facing bowling he particularly fancied, he would allegedly sing "Happy Birthday" as a sign of his confidence. In the field, his throwing, as with so many Australians of his generation, was outstanding, even thrilling. Indeed, it had been his fielding that had taken him into first-grade cricket in his native Sydney as an eighteen year old. His chances of breaking into the strong New South Wales side were slim, however, and in 1951, when 22, he moved to

Adelaide. As fate would have it, his first match for South Australia, in 1951-52, was against his home state, and with 86 and 164 at Adelaide he embarked on a career which, until 1969-70, when he was in his 41st year, produced 8,269 runs in 121 Sheffield Shield matches, the most by any batsman for South Australia. In the twilight years of his career, with his stance becoming more upright, Favell had moved down the order.

Although he never toured England, he represented Australia in every other Test-playing country. The first of his nineteen Tests, nevertheless, was against England, at Brisbane in 1954-55 where he made 23; the last was at the Adelaide Oval in 1960-61, when he played in four of the five Tests against Worrell's West Indies, including the tied Test at Brisbane. In his 757 runs, average 27.03, there was only one hundred, an out-of-character 101 at Madras where, in January 1960, he batted throughout the opening day and was 100 not out at the close. Two years earlier, in South Africa, he had scored 190 against Griqualand West at more than a run a minute, including 114 before lunch. This was his highest score. In all first-class matches, he scored 12,379 runs, average 36.62, including 27 hundreds and twice scoring two hundreds in a match. His son, Alan, also played for South Australia.

The affection with which he was held was illustrated by 7,000 fans who attended, along with a host of Australia's legendary cricketers, a testimonial game for him several months before his death. Sir Donald Bradman went out with him to toss, a sincere tribute to a player who, Sir Donald had once said, set an example of sportsmanship which had never been bettered. In his later years he had become a journalist and broadcaster, and in these roles, as in his cricket, he demonstrated a generous and kindly spirit.

FULLER, RICHARD LIVINGSTON (DICKIE), died at his native Kingston, Jamaica, on May 3, 1987, aged 74. An aggressive right-hand bat and fast-medium bowler, he was selected in 1934-35 to play for West Indies against England in the Fourth Test at Kingston following performances of four for 69 and 113 not out in two and a half hours in the island's two matches against MCC. He scored 1, had match bowling figures of none for 12 from eight overs and it was his only Test. He later played in England in the Durham League and in Scotland.

FULLJAMES, GROUP CAPTAIN REGINALD EDGAR GILBERT, MC, who died on July 31, 1985, aged 88, played for the RAF from 1927 to 1932 as a slow left-arm bowler and in 1928 took seven for 25 against the Army at The Oval. He continued to play with success in good-class club cricket until a patriarchal age.

GILL, LYNWOOD LAWRENCE (LES), who died at Pullenvale, Queensland, on December 4, 1986, aged 95, was Australia's oldest surviving first-class cricketer, and indeed may have been the world's. A right-handed batsman and medium-pace bowler, he had already represented his native Tasmania against the 1911-12 MCC side and twice against Victoria the following season when he settled in Queensland after war service in the AIF. In 1926-27 and 1927-28 he played for the state in its first seasons in the Sheffield Shield, and in 1930-31, when many of the team were in dispute with the Queensland Cricket Association, he was recalled as captain for the final match against Victoria. Because of rain, the match was abandoned without a ball being bowled. In his ten first-class matches, he scored 447 runs, with an average of 29.80, and took eight wickets at 81.62. He was a Queensland selector from 1924 to 1944, with the exception of 1930-31. Although his birth registration shows his first name as Lynnwood, he always indicated it with only one "n".

GODDARD, JOHN DOUGLAS CLAUDE, OBE, died in hospital in London on August 26, 1987, aged 68. He had collapsed in his hotel while a guest of MCC at the Bicentenary match at Lord's. Goddard captained West Indies in 22 of his 27 Tests, most notably in England in 1950 when, after losing the first Test, they struck back to win the next three and their first series in England. In 1948-49, he had led West Indies to a 1-0 victory in India, where he won the toss in all five Tests, only the fourth captain so blessed by fortune. These two tours saw him popular with his players and in charge of happy sides, but this unhappily was not so in Australia in 1951-52. Riven by inter-island rivalries, a disillusioned team was conclusively beaten 4-1. Always a man who put the interests of his team ahead of his own, he stood down for the final Test, feeling that his form was a handicap; West Indies lost again and he returned to lead the side against New Zealand. Although when he went back to New Zealand in 1955-56, it was as player-manager with Atkinson as captain, Goddard was preferred as captain to take the West Indians to England in 1957. This time they lost the series 3-0; had it not been for his 40-minute 0 not out at Edgbaston and his 61 in 3 hours 40 minutes at Trent Bridge, this would surely have been 5-0.

Goddard was a fine all-round cricketer: left-hand bat, right-arm medium in-swing bowler or off-spinner, and an excellent fielder, especially close to the bat. He first played for Barbados in 1936-37 when he was seventeen, and in 1943-44 he scored a career-best 218 not out when he and Worrell shared an unbroken stand of 502 for the fourth wicket against Trinidad at Bridgetown. He played in all four Tests against England in 1947-48 and as captain at Georgetown and Kingston led West Indies to their two victories in the series. At Georgetown, where England in the first innings were dismissed for 111 on a drying pitch, he took five for 31 – his best Test figures – bowling medium-pace off-breaks to a leg-trap. In both these Tests he opened the batting, but really his place was further down the order. His highest score in Tests was 83 not out against New Zealand at Christchurch in 1955-56, and in all Tests he scored 859 runs with an average of 30.67; his 33 wickets cost 31.81 runs. He played his last first-class game in 1957-58, having scored 3,769 runs, average 33.35, hit five hundreds, and taken 146 wickets at 26.33.

GREEN, JOHN HERBERT, died on September 13, 1987, aged 79. He had a good record at Brighton College and in 1927, the year after he left, made one appearance for Warwickshire. But going up to Oxford that autumn, he did nothing in the Parks and was never tried for the University. He was a right-hand bat and a slow left-arm bowler. For years he was headmaster of a prep school in Broadstairs. He was also an ex-captain of the Royal St George's Golf Club.

HALL, GLEN GORDON, was found dead at his home in Ramsgate, Natal, on June 26, 1987, aged 49. A tall leg-spinner, quickish with both googly and top-spinner in his repertoire, he played just one Test for South Africa, against England at Cape Town in 1964-65 where for the first time in a Test match everyone bar the two wicket-keepers on either side bowled. His one wicket cost 94 runs; he failed to score in his only innings. He had, however, made a sensational entry into first-class cricket when he took four for 24 and nine for 122 for South African Universities against Western Province at Cape Town in 1960-61. In 32 first-class matches, during which he also appeared for North-Eastern Transvaal and Eastern Province, he took 110 wickets at 29.66; his batting average was 7.84.

HART, GEORGE EDMEAD, who died in hospital at Barnstaple, on April 11, 1987, aged 85, may well, in the course of a fourteen-year career for Middlesex, have been twelfth man more often than any other cricketer. For good measure, he had also acted as twelfth man for England in three Tests at Lord's, a position for which his faultless fielding admirably qualified him. Traditionally Middlesex had relied on a small staff of professionals supported by an apparently endless supply of talented amateurs, few of whom could play regularly. If in the 1920s and 1930s there was little sign of this supply drying up, the amount of time that the amateurs could give decreased rapidly. Hence the value of a professional such as Hart, who was always available to fill a vacancy, could field anywhere, and might make a few valuable runs at a crisis. Moreover, he was a good cutter and off-driver and was constantly raising hopes of developing into something better; hopes that were never fully realised. In 1928 he appeared in twenty matches and made 68 badly needed runs against Surrey at Lord's, but his aggregate was only 316 and his average 13.73. At last in 1934 he seemed to have made the grade. In consecutive matches at Lord's he scored 121 against Hampshire and 80 and 107 against Sussex, and though he had many failures later, he made 976 runs with an average of 24.40. He would doubtless have reached his thousand but for missing the last three matches through injury. By now he was regularly opening the batting, frequently with Price, the wicket-keeper, who a few years before had been No. 11. In 1936 he again topped 900 runs, but after that, with Edrich and Compton available, he reverted once more to being a regular twelfth man. In 1937 he made an admirable 118 against Kent at Lord's and in 1938 scored his fourth and last hundred, 105 against Nottinghamshire at Trent Bridge. In 1939 he and Hulme received a joint benefit and were not re-engaged, and from 1940 to 1964 he was the professional at Shrewsbury. Altogether, in 198 matches, 194 of them for Middlesex, he scored 5,786 runs with an average of 20.81.

HERMAN, OSWALD WILLIAM (LOFTY), who died in hospital in Southampton after a long illness on June 24, 1987, aged 79, was for years the mainstay of the Hampshire bowling. One of the many good cricketers whom Hampshire recruited from Oxfordshire (he was born at Horsepath), he played for them from 1929 to 1948, though that in fact meant for thirteen seasons: six he lost because of the war, and in 1939 he had succumbed to the lure of the Lancashire leagues and did not appear for the county. Luckily he returned in 1946 and was a great help when they were trying to rebuild the side. Very tall, with a high easy action which enabled him to bowl, as he often had to, for long periods, he was primarily a fast-medium in-swinger and, if sometimes he tended to bowl slightly short of a good length, it was because he could not, with so little support, afford to give runs away. In all he took 1,045 wickets at 27 runs each and scored 4,336 runs with an average of 11.08. Five times he took more than 100 wickets in a season, his best year being 1937 when he took 142 wickets at 22.07. In that year he also met with considerable success as a bat, scoring 801 runs with an average of 19.53, and might almost have been classed as an all-rounder. Against Leicestershire at Basingstoke he made 91 not out and against the New Zealanders 55 out of 77. In 1936 he had made 41 in eighteen minutes against Glamorgan at Bournemouth. Oddly enough, his highest score for the county he made only a few weeks before retirement, 92 against Leicestershire at Leicester: the score was 65 for six when he came in and he and Bailey put on 99. He batted after the old-fashioned tradition of fast bowlers, now alas abandoned. He put his foot out to the ball and hit it as hard as he could. In his last three seasons he took to bowling off-spinners when the shine was off or the wicket taking spin, often with considerable success. After leaving Hampshire he did valuable work for a season or two for Wiltshire, and from 1963 to 1971 he was on the list of first-class umpires. *C. J. Knott writes:* 'He was a grand fellow, whom I enjoyed playing with."

His son, R. S. Herman, also a fast-medium bowler, played for some years first for Middlesex then for Hampshire, and later, like his father, was a first-class umpire.

HERRING, LT-GEN. THE HON. SIR EDMUND FRANCIS, died in Melbourne on January 5, 1982, aged 89. Going to Oxford after graduating from Melbourne University, he played twice for the University as a right-hand bat but did not win a Blue. After the Second World War, he was appointed Lt-Governor of Victoria.

HIBBERT, HUGH WASHINGTON, died at Salisbury on March 12, 1985, aged 73. He had been in the XI at Downside, and in 1931 played one match for Northamptonshire as a bat without success.

HODGKINSON, GILBERT FRANK, who died in hospital at Mickleover, near Derby, on January 7, 1987, aged 73, played nineteen times for Derbyshire from 1935 to 1946. He had been in the XI at Derby School, primarily as a batsman, and in his first innings for the county, against the South Africans at Ilkeston, was top scorer with 44, which included nine fours, mainly from drives. This remained his highest score in first-class cricket. He played a few more matches before the war, during which in 1940 he was badly wounded in the head and taken prisoner: indeed the 1943 *Wisden* reported him killed in action. However, he was repatriated and had recovered sufficiently to captain the county in 1946, though he met with little personal success. In all matches for Derbyshire he scored 472 runs with an average of 14.75.

HORTON, ARNELL STANLEY, who died at Launceston, Tasmania, on September 15, 1987, six days before his 95th birthday, had been Australia's oldest surviving first-class cricketer following the death of L. L. Gill the previous December. A left-arm fast-medium bowler and right-hand bat, he failed to take a wicket or score in his sole first-class appearance, for Tasmania against the 1928-29 MCC side.

JACKBIR, SYDNEY, who died on October 16, 1986, played for Trinidad in the late 1940s and 1950s, chiefly as an orthodox left-arm spin bowler. He could, however, bowl to some effect with the new ball, and he appeared in this role in MCC's two games against the island in 1947-48.

JAMESON, CAPTAIN THOMAS GEORGE CAIRNES, RN, who died in hospital on January 18, 1987, aged 78, had represented the Navy as a batsman and in 1930 and 1931 appeared in three matches for Hampshire without much success.

JANES, DAVID ALLAN, who died in London on September 15, 1987, aged 43, was in the XI at Marlborough in 1960 and 1961 and, as a left-hand bat, strong on the front foot, played in the latter year for the Public Schools at Lord's. His county cricket was for Buckinghamshire, for whom from 1960 to 1976 he scored 3,802 runs, with an average of 26.59, in the Minor Counties Championship. In the Gillette Cup in 1972, he scored 95 when Buckinghamshire knocked out Cambridgeshire at Fenner's in the first round.

JEFFREY, CLINTON LINLEY, who died on February 11, 1987, aged 74, played fifteen times for Tasmania, making 530 runs with an average of 23.04 and taking nineteen wickets at 40.21 with medium pace. At Launceston, he took four for 70 against the 1934 Australian team before they left for England; his highest score was 80 not out against Victoria in 1938-39.

JOHNSON, HOPHNIE HOBAH HINES, who died in Miami, Florida, on June 24, 1987, aged 77, was a tall, slim fast bowler who took ten wickets (five for 41, five for 55) against England in 1947-48 when making his Test début in his native Jamaica. He was then 37 years old; with Goddard's side in England in 1950, he was 40 when he played in the second of his two Tests there. In the First Test, at Old Trafford, he pulled a muscle in his side early in his second spell and did not bowl again in the match, but in his first spell he had forced Hutton to retire hurt after being struck on the hand. This is not to suggest that Johnson was a dangerous bowler, for he disdained the bouncer, content to get his wickets through pace and accuracy. Altogether, in his three Tests he took thirteen wickets at 18.30, and in 28 first-class matches he took 68 wickets at 23.36. He represented Jamaica from 1934-35 until 1950-51.

JOSHI, PADMANABH GOVIND (NANA), died in Pune on January 8, 1987, aged 60. A sound wicket-keeper and useful, versatile right-hand batsman, he appeared in twelve Tests for India over nine seasons. He had already announced his possibilities as a batsman with a dour, unbeaten 100 for a combined team against "Jock" Livingstone's Commonwealth side at Nagpur in 1949-50 when he was called up by India in 1951-52 for the First Test against Nigel Howard's England side. He took two catches and made two stumpings in the first innings but was not required to bat, yet India dispensed with his services until the Fourth Test, then dropped him again for the Fifth, so establishing a pattern which prevailed until 1960-61, when he played in his final Test, against Pakistan at Bombay. He scored 52 not out and with R. B. Desai added 149 for the ninth wicket, which was still a record for India against all countries at the time of his death. His highest score in Tests, this took his aggregate to 207, with an average of 10.89; hardly, perhaps, what had been expected. In addition, he took eighteen catches and made nine stumpings. He had been on two tours, to the West Indies in 1952-53 and to England in 1959, when he played in three of the Tests. He played for Maharashtra from 1946-47 to 1964-65, captaining them from 1960-61 till 1962-63, and in 78 first-class matches scored 1,724 runs with an average of 17.06, caught 120 batsmen and stumped 61.

KRIPAL SINGH, AMRITSAR GOVINDSINGH, died in Madras on July 22, 1987, aged 53. Coming into the side for India's first Test match against New Zealand, at Hyderabad in 1955-56, he hit an unbeaten 100 on début and with Umrigar (223) added 171 for the fourth wicket. When India began uncertainly at Bombay in the next Test, he scored 63 and added 167 for the same wicket with Mankad, who emulated Umrigar's score of 223. With 36 in his only other innings, Kripal Singh finished the series with an average of 99.50. He did little in two Tests against Australia in 1956-57, but a half-century against West Indies at Madras in his one match of their 1958-59 series helped secure him a place in the 1959 team to England. There, however, he was a disappointment. He had taken to bowling off-breaks to improve his chances of Test selection, but a sore spinning finger limited his opportunities and his ten wickets in England cost 56.80 each. Of his 879 runs, average 33.80, 309 came after the Tests, including 178 against Lancashire in a high-scoring match. He had played only in the Lord's Test, scoring 41 in the second innings, and although he appeared another six times for India at home, he did nothing of note. In his fourteen Tests, he scored 422 runs, average 28.13, with just the one hundred, and took ten wickets at 58.40.

Recalled in 1961-62 for the series against England after taking a career-best six for 14 and six for 35 for Madras against Hyderabad, he appeared in the First Test alongside his brother, Milkha Singh. Their father, Ram Singh, had represented India in two unofficial "Tests" against Ryder's Australian team in 1935-36 and against Lord Tennyson's 1937-38 team, and two other brothers, Satwender and Harjinder, also played first-class cricket. In the Ranji Trophy, Kripal Singh first played for Madras in 1950-51; in 1954-55, when they won the Championship for the first time, he hit the highest of his ten hundreds: 208 against Travancore-

Cochin at Ernakulam. In 96 first-class matches, he scored 4,947 runs with an average of 40.88 and took 177 wickets at 28.41. He proved a sound tactical captain of Madras, later became a Test selector, and would have become the chairman of selectors in August 1987.

LASCELLES, REGINALD PETER, died at Nettleham, near Lincoln, on December 14, 1986, aged 62. An elegant right-hand batsman, he played for Lincolnshire from 1947 to 1959, scoring 1,842 runs with an average of 23.61. In 1952, when he headed the batting with an average of 61.66, he scored the only two centuries of his career, 163 not out against Yorkshire II at Barnsley and 104 not out against Cambridgeshire at Wisbech.

LING, ARTHUR JOHN PATRICK, died in hospital on January 12, 1987, aged 76. A left-handed batsman, he captained Stowe in 1928 and for the next few seasons was a pretty regular member of the Wiltshire side. From 1934 to 1936 he played for Glamorgan, doing sufficiently well to suggest that he could have become a useful member of the side, and in 1939 made five appearances for Somerset. In all first-class cricket he made 256 runs with an average of 16. His highest score was 41 not out for Glamorgan against Leicestershire at Swansea in 1934.

LUCK, ARTHUR, died on February 24, 1987, aged 72. He was tried for Northamptonshire as a medium-paced bowler in 1937 and 1938, but taking only two wickets was not considered for a further trial.

MACKESSACK, DOUGLAS, who died at Hopeman, Morayshire, on October 28, 1987, aged 84, achieved success as an all-rounder at Rugby in 1921, but on going up to Oxford he did nothing the following year in the Freshmen's match. In 1927, he played for Scotland against Ireland at Dublin, scoring 27 runs in his two innings and failing to take a wicket. It was his only first-class match.

MADDERN, JAMES GREGORY, who died on March 27, 1987, aged 73, played five times for Queensland between 1932-33 and 1936-37 as a right-hand bat but totalled only 51 runs. In 1936-37 he scored 62 for Queensland Country against MCC at Ipswich and again represented them against the Indian touring team in 1947-48.

MARTIN, JOHN WILLIAM, died in hospital after a short illness on January 4, 1987, aged 69. A tall, strongly built man, who bowled fast-medium to fast with a high action off a fairly short run, he showed distinct promise for Kent in three matches in 1939. Unfortunately he was never able to play more than a very few games a year, which he continued to do until 1953. However, in 1947, having taken four for 55 for MCC against the South Africans and followed it with three for 49 and six for 47 for Kent against Hampshire at Southampton, he was picked to open the England bowling with Bedser in the first Test at Nottingham. Nothing can show more clearly the weakness of English bowling in 1947, as in 1921, than that the selectors should have had to call upon one of so little experience and who had had so little chance of being in full practice. His one wicket (he bowled Alan Melville when he had made 189) cost 129 runs. None the less he was a good county bowler, and if Kent had been able to get his services regularly, they would have been several places higher in the table. In 1948 he again bowled Hampshire out at Southampton, taking six for 37, and in 1950 he had seven for 53 against Leicestershire at Folkestone. In all matches for Kent he took 129 wickets at 22.52 and in all first-class matches 162 at 24.00. He was of no great account as a batsman, but considered it his job to enliven the tail by hitting a few sixes if he could.

MERCER, JOHN (JACK), died on August 31, 1987, in London, aged 92. Born at Southwick, he joined the Sussex staff in 1913 but in 1914 was out of cricket and in Russia. In the war he was commissioned in the Royal Sussex and was wounded. Rejoining the county staff in 1919, he played twelve matches for Sussex between then and 1921, but eighteen wickets cost him more than 35 runs each, the side was rich in bowlers of his type, and he went away to Glamorgan, who, admitted to the Championship in 1921, were for lack of native players seeking far and wide for recruits. For a time it seemed that they might have made a bad bargain; in 1923 and 1924 he accomplished little, but in 1925 he took more than 100 wickets, a feat which he performed nine times in all, and from there he never looked back. Fast-medium, he had a beautiful and effortless action and could swing the ball either way late; he kept it well up and knew the value of a swinging yorker or half-volley. When the shine was off or the wicket was taking spin, he would turn to off-breaks.

Above all, he was a tireless trier, as the one reliable bowler on a weak side has to be. In his eighteen seasons with Glamorgan, the county was only twice higher than tenth and, until J. C. Clay developed into a great bowler, the only other bowler of any class was that wildly eccentric character, Frank Ryan, a slow left-hander, who had he not combined a passion for beer and women with the temperament of a spoilt *prima donna*, might have been one of the great bowlers of his own or indeed of any generation. In such circumstances many bowlers would have wilted, but Mercer's cheerfulness was proof against anything. Robertson-Glasgow called him the Mark Tapley of cricketers. To him, his tribulations and misfortunes were simply an endless cause of laughter and jesting. In 1936, at 41, he was still as good as ever; he took all ten wickets at Worcester for 51 and finished the season with 129 at 19.37. After this, however, the hard work began to tell. In the next three years, though the accuracy was there, the wickets became more expensive, and at the end of 1939 the county terminated his contract.

Even so, his career was not over. In 1947 he was appointed coach to Northamptonshire and indeed appeared once in the county side. Later he was their scorer. In addition to his bowling, he was in his early years a cheerful and successful hitter in the tail. In 1923 he made 48 in 35 minutes against Hampshire at Cardiff and next year created quite a sensation by hitting Rhodes for four sixes in an innings of 57 at Bradford. No-one can doubt that, had chances come his way in representative cricket, he would have shown himself worthy of them, but competition then was strong and his only MCC tour abroad was to India in 1926-27. In all first-class cricket he took 1,591 wickets at 23.38 and made 6,076 runs with an average of 11.77.

MERCHANT, VIJAYSINGH MADHAVJI, died in his native Bombay on October 27, 1987, aged 76. An opening batsman of orthodox technique and seemingly endless patience, on his two tours of England with Indian teams he was the leading batsman with 1,745 runs, average 51.32, in 1936 and 2,385, average 74.53, in 1946. In India, his runs were legion; his average in the Ranji Trophy championship was 98.75 from 3,639 runs. But often these runs were accumulated on surfaces almost too perfect, especially at the Brabourne Stadium in Bombay, and so it was his batting in English conditions which provided the measure of his greatness. On both tours he encountered a wet summer and rain-affected pitches, yet overcame them because of his excellent method, playing every ball on its merit, always in line and having time to play his strokes. His success against the moving ball, be it through the air or off the wicket, came from playing it with the swing or the spin; and he could play most strokes. He cut square and late quite brilliantly, his hooking and pulling were controlled, he turned the ball off his legs, through mid-wicket or fine, with a deft touch, and because his position when meeting the ball was secure, he drove with certainty along the ground. Not a tall man, only 5ft 7in, but strong, like Gavaskar in another generation he built his technique on classical footwork. And always there was his concentration and his determination.

All of Merchant's Test matches were against England, his first three coming at home against Jardine's 1933-34 side, when he batted in the middle order. In 1936, at Old Trafford, he scored the first of his three Test hundreds, 114 in the second innings when he and Mushtaq Ali put on 203 in 150 minutes for the first wicket. The second day's aggregate of 588 runs (England 398 for six, India 190 without loss) remains the highest for a day's play in Test cricket. In the first innings, a straightish drive by Merchant had led to the unfortunate run-out of Mushtaq Ali; as Mushtaq was backing up, the ball ricocheted from his bat to Fagg at mid-on, who threw down the bowler's wicket. In 1946, when he was vice-captain to Pataudi, he scored 245 in the three Tests with an average of 49; his 128 at The Oval, in addition to being the highest score for India against England at the time, was his sixth of seven hundreds on the tour. Two of these were double-hundreds, 242 not out against Lancashire and 205 against Sussex, and late in the tour he hit 181 against Essex, ninth out as the Indians successfully chased 367 and won in the last over. His third century for India was also his highest, scored when he was 40 in what was to be his final Test: 154 in Delhi in 1951-52 where he and Hazare added 211 for the third wicket. Throwing himself full length to stop the ball in England's second innings, he injured his shoulder and did not play again. Ill health had meant his missing India's post-war series in Australia and against West Indies.

In his ten Test matches, he scored 859 runs with an average of 47.72, and in his 146 first-class matches he totalled 13,248 runs for a career average of 71.22, which is second only to Sir Donald Bradman's of 95.14. He hit 44 hundreds, including ten double-hundreds and one triple: 359 not out in ten and threequarter hours for Bombay against Maharashtra at Bombay in 1943-44, adding 371 for the sixth wicket with R. S. Modi and 210 for the eighth with R. S. Cooper. As a bowler of off-breaks at around medium pace, he took 65 wickets at 31.87, including a hat-trick and hundred in a match at Bombay in 1946-47. Possessing a good, analytical cricket mind, he later became an administrator, selector, journalist and broadcaster.

MOBED, MINOCHER JAMSHEDJI (MANCHI) died in his native Karachi on December 29, 1986, aged 87. Much of his early career spanned an era when Indian cricket was developing, and by the time India became a Test-playing country he was past his peak. He first played for the Parsis in 1919 in the Sind Quadrangular Tournament, and he rendered yeoman service to various sides from Sind until 1943, scoring 1,456 runs for an average of 30. In his later years he became a useful all-rounder by bowling off-breaks with some degree of accuracy. He played against Gilligan's and Jardine's MCC teams to India, as well as Lord Tennyson's side of 1937-38, and in four seasons from 1938-39 he captained Sind in the Ranji Trophy. He later stood as an umpire in the two unofficial "Tests" played by MCC in Pakistan in 1951-52.

MORRISON, EWART GLADSTONE, died at Lewes on May 12, 1985, aged 87. Left-handed both as a batsman and a bowler, he appeared for Gloucestershire from 1926 to 1933, but only in his first season did he play at all frequently and it was then that he made his highest score, 59 in an hour against Worcestershire at Stonebridge. Altogether in his career he made 340 runs with an average of 10.30 and took three wickets for 209 runs.

MYBURGH, MAJOR CLAUDE JOHN, died suddenly at Hartley Wintney on October 10, 1987, aged 76. A fast-medium bowler, he headed the averages at St Lawrence, Ramsgate, and later played occasionally for the Army and for Devon. He also played soccer and hockey for the Army.

NEVINSON, JOHN HARCOURT, who died on August 22, 1987, aged 76, was in the Eton XI in 1928 and 1929. With a good action, he was distinctly fast for a schoolboy and in 1929 headed the averages with 44 wickets at 13.47. At Lord's he took six for 86 in the first innings. Going up to Oxford, he had a good trial for the University in 1930 and in his first match took four for 15 against Glamorgan; but after that he did nothing and later was never a serious contender for a Blue. In 1933 he played six matches for Middlesex, but, as his four wickets cost 92.25 runs each, he was not persevered with.

NEWNHAM, LESLIE, who died in Chelmsford on June 4, 1987, aged 67, had been for a number of years the official statistician for Essex, producing in that capacity a history of the county club in 1976, its centenary year.

NEWNHAM, STANLEY WILLIAM, died at Rhuddlan on December 2, 1985, aged 75. A slow left-arm bowler and useful batsman, he appeared once for Surrey in 1932 and later played for Denbighshire.

NUNN, DR JOHN AYSCOUGH, who died suddenly in Scotland on April 6, 1987, aged 81, had the curious experience of representing Oxford at both cricket and rugger for his first two years and failing to get a place in either side for the next two. The 1920s were a great era in University games, but in 1926 Oxford were for once short of talent at cricket. Their one player of distinction, E. R. T. Holmes, though dangerous, was not yet the consistent batsman he afterwards became. Similarly in rugger; after the great sides of 1923 and 1924, with their international threequarter lines, they were crushingly defeated at Twickenham in 1925 and 1926. It was in these circumstances that Nunn, coming up with a considerable reputation from Sherborne, gained his Blues. When higher standards returned, he could not retain them. At cricket he got the last place in 1926 on the morning of the match, as an opening bat, and justified it with admirable innings of 30 and 33 in a low-scoring match. Despite his humble record he was so highly regarded personally that he was elected secretary for 1927, clearly in the hopes that he would captain the side in 1928. No-one who knew him can doubt that he would have been an ideal captain. Unfortunately he had a poor season in 1927 and it was obvious that his place was no longer secure. He was dropped after the first match in 1928 and never appeared for the 'Varsity again. A beautiful upstanding stylist in minor cricket, with strokes on both sides of the wicket, he seemed at a higher level able to score solely by concentrating on dour defence, and it is significant that his only considerable scores for Oxford, 83 in 1926 and 98 in 1927, were made against the Army, whose bowling was distinctly below county standard. His greatest value to the side was his superb fielding at cover. In 1926 he was tried in three matches for Middlesex. Altogether in first-class cricket he scored 641 runs with an average of 18.85. Later he served for many years on the committee of the Free Foresters.

PAGE, MILFORD LAURENSON (CURLY), who died in Christchurch on February 13, 1987, aged 84, was the second of New Zealand's Test captains. A fine performer in whatever sport he chose, he was especially prominent in cricket and rugby; he was an All Black scrum-half in 1928. He was eighteen, still attending Christchurch Boys' High School, when selected to play for Canterbury against a strong Australian side in 1921 and he continued to represent the province until 1937. The Plunket Shield programme in those days provided for only three games, but none the less he scored 2,424 runs for Canterbury, with an average of 33.20. He made his highest score, 206, against Wellington in 1931-32. Altogether, he scored 5,857 runs in first-class cricket, averaging 29.88, and hit nine hundreds. He was a member of New Zealand's first team to England in 1927, when he passed 1,000 runs, returned in 1931 and was captain of the touring team in 1937. He played in fourteen Tests, scoring 492 with an average of 24.60. His one century, 104 at Lord's in 1931, was the first of New Zealand's dramatic comebacks. He was also a useful slow-medium bowler and an Astaire-like slip or gully. Self-effacing and modest, he was an unobtrusive captain, one of the game's quietly spoken, gentle figures.

PALMER, LT-COL. RODNEY HOWELL, MC, died suddenly on April 24, 1987, aged 79. Tall and strongly built, he bowled fast with a late swerve and was three years in the Harrow XI. He did not get a Blue at Cambridge but made three appearances for Hampshire between 1930 and 1933. His one notable performance was to take five for 93 against Yorkshire at Sheffield in 1933. He had also played for Berkshire.

PATEL, JAMSHED RUSTOM, died in Bombay on October 6, 1987. At Delhi in 1948-49, in the first Test between India and West Indies, he and D. K. Naik became the first Indian umpires to stand in a Test match. In all, between then and 1958-59, he officiated in nine Tests.

PICKERING, HARRY GORDON, who died at Seaford on March 4, 1984, aged 67, made three appearances for Essex in 1938 without much success, but in 1947, having a job in Leicester, he did enough in five matches for Leicestershire to suggest that he could have been valuable had he been able to play regularly. Against Derbyshire at Leicester, when 394 were needed to win, he joined Jackson at 236 for six and helped to add 140 in 90 minutes, his share being 62. Leicestershire won by three wickets with three balls to go. The finish, undeniably a fine one, was somewhat oddly described by Neville Cardus as "the most inspiring of our period". He followed this with 57 against Somerset, and finished the season, and indeed his first-class career, with 79, easily top score in a total of 208 at The Oval. For Leicestershire that year he scored 235 runs with an average of 23.50.

PILKINGTON, ALFRED FREDERICK, who died in October 1986, aged 85, was tried as a fast-medium opening bowler for Surrey against Cambridge University at The Oval in 1926; and though he took only one wicket, it was at least that of Duleepsinhji. He was better known as a footballer, playing for Dulwich Hamlet when they won the Amateur Cup in 1920 and later as a professional for Fulham.

PLANT, RICHARD HOWSON, who died on April 22, 1987, aged 75, did useful work as a batsman for Staffordshire for some twenty years. Later he was the club's president.

RUSSELL, DENIS LESLIE, died on December 29, 1986, aged 77. Captain of Beaumont College in 1927, he was four years at Oxford without getting a Blue, although in 1930 he scored 40 and 101 in the Seniors' match and, playing for H. D. G. Leveson Gower's XI at Eastbourne against the University in 1931 after the side had been made up, scored 92. Meanwhile he had made his mark for Middlesex, for whom he made 25 appearances between 1928 and 1932. In 1929 he scored 66 against Warwickshire at Birmingham and 52 against Kent at Dover, while in 1930 he enjoyed a triumph as a bowler, taking seven for 43 against Gloucestershire at Lord's. A right-handed bat, he had beautiful strokes, and with a slightly stronger defence, and perhaps a more stable temperament, he could have been a fine player. He was a slow-medium left-arm bowler who, if memory serves, relied more on length and a bit of pace off the wicket than on spin. He was also an excellent field. In all first-class matches he made 666 runs, with an average of 13.87, and took seventeen wickets at 31.00.

SAGGERS, RONALD ARTHUR, died in Australia in March 1987, aged 69. Although tall for a wicket-keeper, he was considered stylish by his contemporaries and was among the top flight of Australian 'keepers. Coming to England in 1948 as understudy to Tallon, he played in the Headingley Test, taking three catches, and then in 1949-50, with Tallon unavailable, he was the senior wicket-keeper in Hassett's team to South Africa. He played in all five Tests, effecting 21 dismissals with thirteen catches and eight stumpings. In 77 first-class matches – he represented New South Wales from 1939-40 to 1950-51 – he took 147 catches and made 74 stumpings, including ten dismissals (seven in one innings) for New South Wales against a Combined XI at Brisbane in 1940-41. A useful right-handed batsman, he scored 1,888 runs with an average of 23.89, his one century being his 104 not out against Essex in 1948 when the Australians put on 721 runs in one day.

SALE, RICHARD, died on February 3, 1987, aged 67. Going up to Oxford from Repton, he made his place in the side secure as a freshman in 1939 by consistent scoring. An aggressive right-hander, a particularly good off-driver and cutter, who also scored well off his legs, he opened the batting in the earlier matches with his captain, E. J. H. Dixon, and later with J. M. Lomas. Both were essentially solid players for whom Sale made an ideal partner. At Lord's in the first innings Oxford made a poor start and owed much to his 65, made out of 88, an innings regarded as quite outstanding by those who saw it. In the vacation he did well for Warwickshire, for whom he made 101 against Sussex at Edgbaston. Returning to Oxford in 1946, he was again a consistent opener and again held the side together at Lord's with an innings of 42 after they had lost two wickets cheaply. Later that summer he made the highest score of his career, 157 for Warwickshire against the Indians. He did not play for Warwickshire after 1947, but from 1949 to 1954 he appeared for Derbyshire, having gone as a master to Repton. For them his highest score was 146 against Lancashire in 1949. Altogether in first-class cricket he made 2,923 runs with an average of 27.31, including three centuries. Headmaster of Brentwood School from 1966 to 1981, he was responsible for changing them from direct grant status to full independence. His father, a housemaster at Shrewsbury, had been a member of H. S. Altham's famous Repton XI of 1908 and later gained Blues at Oxford for cricket and soccer, besides playing for Derbyshire.

SANTALL, JOHN FRANK EDEN, died at Bournemouth in May 1986, aged 78. He was given a good trial for Worcestershire as a batsman early in 1930, but in eight matches his highest score was 36 not out against Lancashire and the county did not persevere with him. Later he became a professional ice-skater. His father was long one of the mainstays of the Warwickshire attack and his elder brother was one of Warwickshire's leading batsmen between the wars.

TANNER, JOHN DENYS PARKIN, died at Ilkley on October 25, 1987, after a long illness, aged 66. A sound wicket-keeper of the modern school, who was happiest standing back, and a left-hander whose bat was sedulously straight, he was in the Charterhouse XI in 1938 and 1939 and, going up to Oxford after the war, narrowly missed a Blue in 1948. His only county cricket was a solitary appearance for Oxfordshire against Buckinghamshire in 1951, when he made 129, but he continued for many years to play with success in club cricket, largely in his native Yorkshire. He was a soccer player of great distinction, who captained Oxford and won several amateur international caps for England; on his first appearance, against Ireland, he scored three goals. He was a member of the Pegasus side which won the Amateur Cup in 1951 and had also played for Huddersfield Town.

TAYLOR, DERIEF DAVID SAMUEL, died in Kingston, Jamaica, on March 15, 1987, aged probably 78. Having formed a friendship with Tom Dollery while serving in North Africa in the war, he came to England and qualified for Warwickshire, for whom he played sixteen matches between 1948 and 1950. Tried primarily as a slow left-hander, he never looked like being a success in that role, and his fifteen wickets cost 40.46 runs each, but in 1949 he showed distinct promise as a left-handed bat, scoring 436 runs with an average of 43.60 and making 121 against Leicestershire at Edgbaston, when he and Dollery put on 178 for the fifth wicket. However, even this did not secure him a regular place, and in 1951 he became the county's coach, a post he retained until his return to his native Jamaica in 1982.

TAYLOR, REGINALD MINSHALL, died in Johannesburg in January 1984, aged 74. For Essex between 1931 and 1946 he scored 6,755 runs, with an average of 20.59 and took 92 wickets at 31.88. But most of those who remember him will feel that as a batsman he should have achieved more than he did. Only twice did he get his 1,000 runs, his average never reached 25, and he scored only five centuries. With a sound method and elegant strokes, which made him a pleasure to watch, he constantly got out, whether from over-confidence or from a lapse of concentration, just when he should have been setting himself to build one of the big innings of which he always looked capable. Arthur Shrewsbury used to say that when a batsman had made 30, he should play himself in again. Had Taylor adopted this policy he might have made twice as many runs. After a match or two in 1931, he got a regular place in 1932: his big performance was an innings of 106 against Yorkshire at Scarborough, and in those days a hundred against Yorkshire meant something. He and Nichols put on 153 for the sixth wicket in two hours. In 1933 he made his thousand runs and improved his average slightly, but in 1934 it dropped to 14 and in 1935 he did not appear for the county at all. Next year produced a partial recovery, and in 1937 he regained a regular place. In making 129 against Derbyshire at Colchester, he helped O'Connor to add 333 for the third wicket, a record for the county. In 1938 he made the highest score of his career, 193 against Sussex at Colchester. In 1939 his average dropped to 16, but he revealed unsuspected talents as a bowler of chinamen, capturing 56 wickets at 26.14. Against Kent he took five for 50 and against Somerset five for 23, and there were few innings in which he did not get one or two useful wickets. After serving in the war as an Air Force pilot with some distinction, he took a business appointment and played through 1946 as an amateur. In the first match he took seven for 99 against Somerset and in August made an admirable 143 against Warwickshire at Southend, but at the end of the season he emigrated to South Africa and his first-class career ended.

TEW, ANTHONY MARTIN, who died in hospital at Swindon on June 23, 1987, aged 78, was four years in the Winchester XI and, going up to Oxford, was immediately given a place in the University side in May 1928. However, he was dropped after two matches and did not receive another trial. Tall and strongly built, he was a fast-medium opener who could swing the ball and made some pace from the pitch, but against class batsmen he was steady and reliable rather than dangerous. He was later Superintendent of Constabulary for the Cleethorpes Division of Lincolnshire.

THOMPSON, EDDIE CLARKE, who died at Torquay on March 18, 1982, aged 75, played for Essex from 1926 to 1929. A sound left-hand batsman with a good style, he showed considerable promise, and it was thought that he needed only to increase the range of his scoring strokes and smarten up his fielding to become a valuable member of the side, especially as he could bowl a bit slow left-hand. Unfortunately the improvement never came, and in 44 matches his highest score was 45 not out.

TOWNSEND, LESLIE HYDE, who died at Brisbane on January 30, 1986, aged 71, stood as umpire in the Fifth Test of the 1958-59 series between Australia and England after McInnes, who had umpired in the previous four Tests, had been passed over. McInnes, one of Australia's senior umpires, subsequently retired. In Australia's first innings, while standing at square leg, Townsend was called on to adjudicate when the leg-side bail was seen to be on the ground after McDonald had glanced Trueman fine for four. He ruled in the batsman's favour and McDonald, 12 at the time, went on to score 133. In all, he stood in 37 first-class matches, but Melbourne in 1958-59 was his only Test match.

TRENTHAM, HERBERT, MBE, who died at Darlington on January 20, 1987, aged 79, had played for Durham. Secretary and treasurer for 48 years of the North Yorkshire and South Durham League, and a qualified football referee, he was decorated in 1984 for services to local sport.

TYLER, LT-COL. ARTHUR WELLESLEY, who died at Farnham on January 23, 1985, aged 77, kept wicket for the Army in 1931 and 1932 and had also played for Norfolk. He had been in the Cheltenham XI.

WADE, THOMAS HENRY, died in Colchester Hospital on July 25, 1987, aged 76. Batting left-handed and bowling right-arm, he was originally tried for Essex in 1929 as a slow off-spinner and met with considerable success. In one of his earliest matches he took four for 11 against Nottinghamshire, bowling two of their best batsmen, and followed it with four for 20 against Glamorgan. Later in the season he won a close match with Somerset at Chelmsford, taking five for 64 in the second innings. His final record that summer was 33 wickets at 25.57. However, he never fulfilled this promise and, after four seasons in and out of the side, took to practising wicket-keeping. He was so successful that in June 1934 he displaced in the side J. R. Sheffield, a far better batsman and the most reliable professional 'keeper they had had for many years. Indeed, when Sheffield regained a place it was as a bat and a slip fieldsman. For a few years Wade had to give way when that great wicket-keeper, A. G. Powell, was available, but after ill health ended Powell's county career in 1937, he held the position unchallenged till 1950. In 1936 an unexpected honour came to him. He was on a private visit to Australia when the two wicket-keepers on G. O. Allen's MCC side, Ames and Duckworth (and indeed a third possible 'keeper, Fagg) became casualties, and he was called in to keep against South Australia and Victoria. He acquitted himself so well and was so popular that he was awarded the rare distinction of an MCC touring cap. By 1950 fibrositis was beginning to trouble him and he retired at the end of the season, having received almost £4,000 for his benefit, at that time a record for Essex. Altogether he caught 414 batsmen and stumped 178, besides taking 48 wickets at 29.54. He never fulfilled the hopes that had once been entertained of his batting, but he played many useful innings of 40 or 50 and scored in all 5,024 runs with an average of 14.73. His highest score was 96.

WALKER, MALCOLM, who died in a motorcycle accident in August 1986, aged 52, went to Somerset in 1952 principally as an off-spinner, but for a time he looked to have possibilities as an opening batsman. In 1955, when he was 21, promoted to open the second innings against Essex at Romford, he hit 100 in three and a quarter hours, even though he was later discovered to be suffering from appendicitis. That same season he took five for 45 at Bristol as Gloucestershire sought a second-innings declaration, but these were to remain his best batting and bowling figures. Langford's success on his return from National Service blocked

Walker's bowling prospects and there was no place for him as a batsman. In 29 matches, from 1952 until 1958, he scored 574 runs, with an average of 11.71, and took 28 wickets at 34.85. He had played several times for Yorkshire II in 1950.

WALTER, IAN MALCOLM, who died in Wellington on July 17, 1987, aged 39, had been Television New Zealand's cricket producer since 1978. As such, he was instrumental in responding to and arousing the upsurge of interest in the game in New Zealand in the 1980s. His style of presentation sought a middle road between that of the BBC and the bolder delivery of Australian commercial television. As a left-handed batsman he represented New Zealand Under-20 and New Zealand Universities, and in 1973, when official scorer for the New Zealand touring team, he played for them against Scotland, scoring a quiet, undefeated 7.

WEST, ALBERT RICHARD, who died at his native place, Earl Shilton, on June 8, 1985, aged 64, was a slow left-arm bowler of considerable possibilities, but he did little on his three appearances for Leicestershire in 1939.

WILKINSON, FRANCIS WILLIAM, who died at Ely on October 26, 1987, aged 92, was a Cambridgeshire all-rounder who, in his only first-class match, for Minor Counties against Oxford University at Oxford in 1939, when he was 43, had to withdraw because of injury after bowling nine overs, in which he took one wicket. An Oxford undergraduate, D. J. F. Watson, took his place in the field and subsequently batted twice for him, an unusual occurrence which has not since been repeated in English first-class cricket. Watson himself played twice for the University that season and was killed in a flying accident while training in the United States in 1943.

YEATES, HERBERT NELSON McRAE, died at Kangaroo Point, Queensland, on March 28, 1987, aged 76. He was selected just the once for Queensland, against Victoria in Brisbane in 1930-31, but continuous rain led to the match being abandoned without a ball bowled. He was a right-hand bat and leg-spinner whose brother, S. F. M. Yeates, later played three times for the state.

THE LAWS OF CRICKET

(1980 CODE)

World copyright of MCC and reprinted by permission of MCC. Copies of the "Laws of Cricket" may be obtained from Lord's Cricket Ground.

INDEX TO THE LAWS

LAW 1. THE PLAYERS

1. Number of Players and Captain

A match is played between two sides each of eleven players, one of whom shall be captain. In the event of the captain not being available at any time, a deputy shall act for him.

2. Nomination of Players

Before the toss for innings, the captain shall nominate his players, who may not thereafter be changed without the consent of the opposing captain.

Note

(a) More or Less than Eleven Players a Side
A match may be played by agreement between sides of more or less than eleven players, but not more than eleven players may field.

LAW 2. SUBSTITUTES AND RUNNERS: BATSMAN OR FIELDSMAN LEAVING THE FIELD: BATSMAN RETIRING: BATSMAN COMMENCING INNINGS

1. Substitutes

In normal circumstances, a substitute shall be allowed to field only for a player who satisfies the umpire that he has become injured or become ill during the match. However, in very exceptional circumstances, the umpires may use their discretion to allow a substitute for a player who has to leave the field or does not take the field for other wholly acceptable reasons, subject to consent being given by the opposing captain. If a player wishes to change his shirt, boots, etc., he may leave the field to do so (no changing on the field), but no substitute will be allowed.

2. Objection to Substitutes

The opposing captain shall have no right of objection to any player acting as substitute in the field, nor as to where he shall field, although he may object to the substitute acting as wicket-keeper.

3. Substitute not to Bat or Bowl

A substitute shall not be allowed to bat or bowl.

4. A Player for whom a Substitute has Acted

A player may bat, bowl or field even though a substitute has acted for him.

5. Runner

A runner shall be allowed for a batsman who, during the match, is incapacitated by illness or injury. The person acting as runner shall be a member of the batting side and shall, if possible, have already batted in that innings.

6. Runner's Equipment

The player acting as runner for an injured batsman shall wear the same external protective equipment as the injured batsman.

7. Transgression of the Laws by an Injured Batsman or Runner

An injured batsman may be out should his runner break any one of Laws 33 (Handled the Ball), 37 (Obstructing the Field) or 38 (Run Out). As striker he remains himself subject to the Laws. Furthermore, should he be out of his ground for any purpose and the wicket at the wicket-keeper's end be put down he shall be out under Law 38 (Run Out) or Law 39 (Stumped), irrespective of the position of the other batsman or the runner, and no runs shall be scored.

When not the striker, the injured batsman is out of the game and shall stand where he does not interfere with the play. Should he bring himself into the game in any way, then he shall suffer the penalties that any transgression of the Laws demands.

8. Fieldsman Leaving the Field

No fieldsman shall leave the field or return during a session of play without the consent of the umpire at the bowler's end. The umpire's consent is also necessary if a substitute is required for a fieldsman, when his side returns to the field after an interval. If a member of the fielding side leaves the field or fails to return after an interval and is absent from the field for longer than fifteen minutes, he shall not be permitted to bowl after his return until he has been on the field for at least that length of playing time for which he was absent. This restriction shall not apply at the start of a new day's play.

9. Batsman Leaving the Field or Retiring

A batsman may leave the field or retire at any time owing to illness, injury or other unavoidable cause, having previously notified the umpire at the bowler's end. He may resume his innings at the fall of a wicket, which for the purposes of this Law shall include the retirement of another batsman.

If he leaves the field or retires for any other reason he may resume his innings only with the consent of the opposing captain.

When a batsman has left the field or retired and is unable to return owing to illness, injury or other unavoidable cause, his innings is to be recorded as "retired, not out". Otherwise it is to be recorded as "retired, out".

10. Commencement of a Batsman's Innings

A batsman shall be considered to have commenced his innings once he has stepped on to the field of play.

Note

(a) Substitutes and Runners
For the purpose of these Laws, allowable illnesses or injuries are those which occur at any time after the nomination by the captains of their teams.

LAW 3.   THE UMPIRES

1. Appointment

Before the toss for innings, two umpires shall be appointed, one for each end, to control the game with absolute impartiality as required by the Laws.

2. Change of Umpires

No umpire shall be changed during a match without the consent of both captains.

3. Special Conditions

Before the toss for innings, the umpires shall agree with both captains on any special conditions affecting the conduct of the match.

4. The Wickets

The umpires shall satisfy themselves before the start of the match that the wickets are properly pitched.

5. Clock or Watch

The umpires shall agree between themselves and inform both captains before the start of the match on the watch or clock to be followed during the match.

6. Conduct and Implements

Before and during a match the umpires shall ensure that the conduct of the game and the implements used are strictly in accordance with the Laws.

7. Fair and Unfair Play

The umpires shall be the sole judges of fair and unfair play.

8. Fitness of Ground, Weather and Light

(a) The umpires shall be the sole judges of the fitness of the ground, weather and light for play.

    (i) However, before deciding to suspend play, or not to start play, or not to resume play after an interval or stoppage, the umpires shall establish whether both captains (the batsmen at the wicket may deputise for their captain) wish to commence or to continue in the prevailing conditions; if so, their wishes shall be met.

    (ii) In addition, if during play the umpires decide that the light is unfit, only the batting side shall have the option of continuing play. After agreeing to continue to play in unfit light conditions, the captain of the batting side (or a batsman at the wicket) may appeal against the light to the umpires, who shall uphold the appeal only if, in their opinion, the light has deteriorated since the agreement to continue was made.

(b) After any suspension of play, the umpires, unaccompanied by any of the players or officials, shall, on their own initiative, carry out an inspection immediately the conditions improve and shall continue to inspect at intervals. Immediately the umpires decide that play is possible they shall call upon the players to resume the game.

9. Exceptional Circumstances

In exceptional circumstances, other than those of weather, ground or light, the umpires may decide to suspend or abandon play. Before making such a decision the umpires shall establish, if the circumstances allow, whether both captains (the batsmen at the wicket may deputise for their captain) wish to continue in the prevailing conditions; if so, their wishes shall be met.

10. Position of Umpires

The umpires shall stand where they can best see any act upon which their decision may be required.

Subject to this over-riding consideration, the umpire at the bowler's end shall stand where he does not interfere with either the bowler's run-up or the striker's view.

The umpire at the striker's end may elect to stand on the off instead of the leg side of the pitch, provided he informs the captain of the fielding side and the striker of his intention to do so.

11. Umpires Changing Ends

The umpires shall change ends after each side has had one innings.

12. Disputes

All disputes shall be determined by the umpires, and if they disagree the actual state of things shall continue.

13. Signals

The following code of signals shall be used by umpires who will wait until a signal has been answered by a scorer before allowing the game to proceed.

Boundary	– by waving the arm from side to side.
Boundary 6	– by raising both arms above the head.
Bye	– by raising an open hand above the head.
Dead Ball	– by crossing and re-crossing the wrists below the waist.
Leg-bye	– by touching a raised knee with the hand.
No-ball	– by extending one arm horizontally.
Out	– by raising the index finger above the head. If not out, the umpire shall call "not out".
Short run	– by bending the arm upwards and by touching the nearer shoulder with the tips of the fingers.
Wide	– by extending both arms horizontally.

14. Correctness of Scores

The umpires shall be responsible for satisfying themselves on the correctness of the scores throughout and at the conclusion of the match. See Law 21.6 (Correctness of Result).

Notes

(a) Attendance of Umpires
The umpires should be present on the ground and report to the ground executive or the equivalent at least thirty minutes before the start of a day's play.

(b) Consultation between Umpires and Scorers
Consultation between umpires and scorers over doubtful points is essential.

(c) Fitness of Ground
The umpires shall consider the ground as unfit for play when it is so wet or slippery as to deprive the bowlers of a reasonable foothold, the fieldsmen, other than the deep-fielders, of the power of free movement, or the batsmen of the ability to play their strokes or to run between the wickets. Play should not be suspended merely because the grass and the ball are wet and slippery.

(d) Fitness of Weather and Light
The umpires should suspend play only when they consider that the conditions are so bad that it is unreasonable or dangerous to continue.

LAW 4. THE SCORERS

1. Recording Runs

All runs scored shall be recorded by scorers appointed for the purpose. Where there are two scorers they shall frequently check to ensure that the score sheets agree.

2. Acknowledging Signals

The scorers shall accept and immediately acknowledge all instructions and signals given to them by the umpires.

LAW 5. THE BALL

1. Weight and Size

The ball, when new, shall weigh not less than 5½ ounces/155.9g, nor more than 5¾ ounces/163g; and shall measure not less than 8¹³⁄₁₆ inches/22.4cm, nor more than 9 inches/22.9cm in circumference.

2. Approval of Balls

All balls used in matches shall be approved by the umpires and captains before the start of the match.

3. New Ball

Subject to agreement to the contrary, having been made before the toss, either captain may demand a new ball at the start of each innings.

4. New Ball in Match of Three or More Days' Duration

In a match of three or more days' duration, the captain of the fielding side may demand a new ball after the prescribed number of overs has been bowled with the old one. The governing body for cricket in the country concerned shall decide the number of overs applicable in that country, which shall be not less than 75 six-ball overs (55 eight-ball overs).

5. Ball Lost or Becoming Unfit for Play

In the event of a ball during play being lost or, in the opinion of the umpires, becoming unfit for play, the umpires shall allow it to be replaced by one that in their opinion has had a similar amount of wear. If a ball is to be replaced, the umpires shall inform the batsman.

Note

> **(a) Specifications**
> The specifications, as described in 1 above, shall apply to top-grade balls only. The following degrees of tolerance will be acceptable for other grades of ball.
>
> (i) *Men's Grades 2–4*
> Weight: 5⁵⁄₁₆ ounces/150g to 5¹³⁄₁₆ ounces/165g.
> Size: 8¹⁄₁₆ inches/22.0cm to 9¹⁄₁₆ inches/23.0cm.
> (ii) *Women's*
> Weight: 4¹⁵⁄₁₆ ounces/140g to 5⁵⁄₁₆ ounces/150g.
> Size: 8¼ inches/21.0cm to 8⅞ inches/22.5cm.
> (iii) *Junior*
> Weight: 4⁵⁄₁₆ ounces/133g to 5¹⁄₁₆ ounces/143g.
> Size: 8¹¹⁄₁₆ inches/20.5cm to 8¹¹⁄₁₆ inches/22.0cm.

LAW 6. THE BAT

1. Width and Length

The bat overall shall not be more than 38 inches/96.5cm in length; the blade of the bat shall be made of wood and shall not exceed 4¼ inches/10.8cm at the widest part.

Note

> (a) The blade of the bat may be covered with material for protection, strengthening or repair. Such material shall not exceed ¹⁄₁₆ inch/1.56mm in thickness.

LAW 7. THE PITCH

1. Area of Pitch

The pitch is the area between the bowling creases – see Law 9 (The Bowling and Popping Creases). It shall measure 5ft/1.52m in width on either side of a line joining the centre of the middle stumps of the wickets – see Law 8 (The Wickets).

2. Selection and Preparation

Before the toss for innings, the executive of the ground shall be responsible for the selection and preparation of the pitch; thereafter the umpires shall control its use and maintenance.

3. Changing Pitch

The pitch shall not be changed during a match unless it becomes unfit for play, and then only with the consent of both captains.

4. Non-Turf Pitches

In the event of a non-turf pitch being used, the following shall apply:

    (a) Length: That of the playing surface to a minimum of 58ft/17.68m.

    (b) Width: That of the playing surface to a minimum of 6ft/1.83m.

See Law 10 (Rolling, Sweeping, Mowing, Watering the Pitch and Re-marking of Creases) Note (a).

LAW 8.   THE WICKETS

1. Width and Pitching

Two sets of wickets, each 9 inches/22.86cm wide, and consisting of three wooden stumps with two wooden bails upon the top, shall be pitched opposite and parallel to each other at a distance of 22 yards/20.12m between the centres of the two middle stumps.

2. Size of Stumps

The stumps shall be of equal and sufficient size to prevent the ball from passing between them. Their tops shall be 28 inches/71.1cm above the ground, and shall be dome-shaped except for the bail grooves.

3. Size of Bails

The bails shall be each 4⅜ inches/11.1cm in length and when in position on the top of the stumps shall not project more than ½ inch/1.3cm above them.

Notes

    (a) Dispensing with Bails
    In a high wind the umpires may decide to dispense with the use of bails.

    (b) Junior Cricket
    For junior cricket, as defined by the local governing body, the following measurements for the wickets shall apply:

        Width – 8 inches/20.32cm.
        Pitched – 21 yards/19.20m.
        Height – 27 inches/68.58cm.
        Bails – each 3⅞ inches/9.84cm in length and should not project more than ½ inch/1.3cm
            above the stumps.

LAW 9.   THE BOWLING, POPPING AND RETURN CREASES

1. The Bowling Crease

The bowling crease shall be marked in line with the stumps at each end and shall be 8 feet 8 inches/2.64m in length, with the stumps in the centre.

2. The Popping Crease

The popping crease, which is the back edge of the crease marking, shall be in front of and parallel with the bowling crease. It shall have the back edge of the crease marking 4 feet/1.22m from the centre of the stumps and shall extend to a minimum of 6 feet/1.83m on either side of the line of the wicket.

    The popping crease shall be considered to be unlimited in length.

3. The Return Crease

The return crease marking, of which the inside edge is the crease, shall be at each end of the bowling crease and at right angles to it. The return crease shall be marked to a minimum of 4 feet/1.22m behind the wicket and shall be considered to be unlimited in length. A forward extension shall be marked to the popping crease.

LAW 10. ROLLING, SWEEPING, MOWING, WATERING THE PITCH AND RE-MARKING OF CREASES

1. Rolling

During the match the pitch may be rolled at the request of the captain of the batting side, for a period of not more than seven minutes before the start of each innings, other than the first innings of the match, and before the start of each day's play. In addition, if, after the toss and before the first innings of the match, the start is delayed, the captain of the batting side shall have the right to have the pitch rolled for not more than seven minutes.

The pitch shall not otherwise be rolled during the match.

The seven minutes' rolling permitted before the start of a day's play shall take place not earlier than half an hour before the start of play and the captain of the batting side may delay such rolling until ten minutes before the start of play should he so desire.

If a captain declares an innings closed less than fifteen minutes before the resumption of play, and the other captain is thereby prevented from exercising his option of seven minutes' rolling or if he is so prevented for any other reason, the time for rolling shall be taken out of the normal playing time.

2. Sweeping

Such sweeping of the pitch as is necessary during the match shall be done so that the seven minutes allowed for rolling the pitch, provided for in 1 above, is not affected.

3. Mowing

(a) Responsibilities of Ground Authority and of Umpires
All mowings which are carried out before the toss for innings shall be the responsibility of the ground authority; thereafter they shall be carried out under the supervision of the umpires. See Law 7.2 (Selection and Preparation).

(b) Initial Mowing
The pitch shall be mown before play begins on the day the match is scheduled to start, or in the case of a delayed start on the day the match is expected to start. See 3(a) above (Responsibilities of Ground Authority and of Umpires).

(c) Subsequent Mowings in a Match of Two or More Days' Duration
In a match of two or more days' duration, the pitch shall be mown daily before play begins. Should this mowing not take place because of weather conditions, rest days or other reasons, the pitch shall be mown on the first day on which the match is resumed.

(d) Mowing of the Outfield in a Match of Two or More Days' Duration
In order to ensure that conditions are as similar as possible for both sides, the outfield shall normally be mown before the commencement of play on each day of the match, if ground and weather conditions allow. See Note (b) to this Law.

4. Watering

The pitch shall not be watered during a match.

5. Re-marking Creases

Whenever possible the creases shall be re-marked.

6. Maintenance of Foot-holes

In wet weather, the umpires shall ensure that the holes made by the bowlers and batsmen are cleaned out and dried whenever necessary to facilitate play. In matches of two or more days' duration, the umpires shall allow, if necessary, the re-turfing of foot-holes made by the bowler in his delivery stride, or the use of quick-setting fillings for the same purpose, before the start of each day's play.

7. Securing of Footholds and Maintenance of Pitch

During play, the umpires shall allow either batsman to beat the pitch with his bat and players to secure their footholds by the use of sawdust, provided that no damage to the pitch is so caused, and Law 42 (Unfair Play) is not contravened.

Notes

(a) Non-turf Pitches
The above Law 10 applies to turf pitches.

The game is played on non-turf pitches in many countries at various levels. Whilst the conduct of the game on these surfaces should always be in accordance with the Laws of Cricket, it is recognised that it may sometimes be necessary for governing bodies to lay down special playing conditions to suit the type of non-turf pitch used in their country.

In matches played against touring teams, any special playing conditions should be agreed in advance by both parties.

(b) Mowing of the Outfield in a Match of Two or More Days' Duration
If, for reasons other than ground and weather conditions, daily and complete mowing is not possible, the ground authority shall notify the captains and umpires, before the toss for innings, of the procedure to be adopted for such mowing during the match.

(c) Choice of Roller
If there is more than one roller available, the captain of the batting side shall have a choice.

LAW 11.   COVERING THE PITCH

1. Before the Start of a Match

Before the start of a match, complete covering of the pitch shall be allowed.

2. During a Match

The pitch shall not be completely covered during a match unless prior arrangement or regulations so provide.

3. Covering Bowlers' Run-up

Whenever possible, the bowlers' run-up shall be covered, but the covers so used shall not extend further than 4 feet/1.22m in front of the popping crease.

Note

(a) Removal of Covers
The covers should be removed as promptly as possible whenever the weather permits.

LAW 12.   INNINGS

1. Number of Innings

A match shall be of one or two innings of each side according to agreement reached before the start of play.

2. Alternate Innings

In a two-innings match each side shall take their innings alternately except in the case provided for in Law 13 (The Follow-on).

3. The Toss

The captains shall toss for the choice of innings on the field of play not later than fifteen minutes before the time scheduled for the match to start, or before the time agreed upon for play to start.

4. Choice of Innings

The winner of the toss shall notify his decision to bat or to field to the opposing captain not later than ten minutes before the time scheduled for the match to start, or before the time agreed upon for play to start. The decision shall not thereafter be altered.

5. Continuation after One Innings of Each Side

Despite the terms of 1 above, in a one-innings match, when a result has been reached on the first innings, the captains may agree to the continuation of play if, in their opinion, there is a prospect of carrying the game to a further issue in the time left. See Law 21 (Result).

Notes

> **(a) Limited Innings – One-innings Match**
> In a one-innings match, each innings may, by agreement, be limited by a number of overs or by a period of time.
>
> **(b) Limited Innings – Two-innings Match**
> In a two-innings match, the first innings of each side may, by agreement, be limited to a number of overs or by a period of time.

LAW 13.   THE FOLLOW-ON

1. Lead on First Innings

In a two-innings match the side which bats first and leads by 200 runs in a match of five days or more, by 150 runs in a three-day or four-day match, by 100 runs in a two-day match, or by 75 runs in a one-day match, shall have the option of requiring the other side to follow their innings.

2. Day's Play Lost

If no play takes place on the first day of a match of two or more days' duration, 1 above shall apply in accordance with the number of days' play remaining from the actual start of the match.

LAW 14.   DECLARATIONS

1. Time of Declaration

The captain of the batting side may declare an innings closed at any time during a match, irrespective of its duration.

2. Forfeiture of Second Innings

A captain may forfeit his second innings, provided his decision to do so is notified to the opposing captain and umpires in sufficient time to allow seven minutes' rolling of the pitch. See Law 10 (Rolling, Sweeping, Mowing, Watering the Pitch and Re-marking of Creases). The normal ten-minute interval between innings shall be applied.

LAW 15.   START OF PLAY

1. Call of Play

At the start of each innings and of each day's play, and on the resumption of play after any interval or interruption, the umpire at the bowler's end shall call "play".

2. Practice on the Field

At no time on any day of the match shall there be any bowling or batting practice on the pitch.

No practice may take place on the field if, in the opinion of the umpires, it could result in a waste of time.

3. Trial Run-up

No bowler shall have a trial run-up after "play" has been called in any session of play, except at the fall of a wicket when an umpire may allow such a trial run-up if he is satisfied that it will not cause any waste of time.

LAW 16. INTERVALS

1. Length

The umpire shall allow such intervals as have been agreed upon for meals, and ten minutes between each innings.

2. Luncheon Interval – Innings Ending or Stoppage within Ten Minutes of Interval

If an innings ends or there is a stoppage caused by weather or bad light within ten minutes of the agreed time for the luncheon interval, the interval shall be taken immediately.

The time remaining in the session of play shall be added to the agreed length of the interval but no extra allowance shall be made for the ten-minute interval between innings.

3. Tea Interval – Innings Ending or Stoppage within Thirty Minutes of Interval

If an innings ends or there is a stoppage caused by weather or bad light within thirty minutes of the agreed time for the tea interval, the interval shall be taken immediately.

The interval shall be of the agreed length and, if applicable, shall include the ten-minute interval between innings.

4. Tea Interval – Continuation of Play

If, at the agreed time for the tea interval, nine wickets are down, play shall continue for a period not exceeding thirty minutes or until the innings is concluded.

5. Tea Interval – Agreement to Forgo

At any time during the match, the captains may agree to forgo a tea interval.

6. Intervals for Drinks

If both captains agree before the start of a match that intervals for drinks may be taken, the option to take such intervals shall be available to either side. These intervals shall be restricted to one per session, shall be kept as short as possible, shall not be taken in the last hour of the match, and in any case shall not exceed five minutes.

The agreed times for these intervals shall be strictly adhered to, except that if a wicket falls within five minutes of the agreed time then drinks shall be taken out immediately.

If an innings ends or there is a stoppage caused by weather or bad light within thirty minutes of the agreed time for a drinks interval, there will be no interval for drinks in that session.

At any time during the match the captains may agree to forgo any such drinks interval.

Notes

(a) Tea Interval – One-day Match
In a one-day match, a specific time for the tea interval need not necessarily be arranged, and it may be agreed to take this interval between the innings of a one-innings match.

(b) Changing the Agreed Time of Intervals
In the event of the ground, weather or light conditions causing a suspension of play, the umpires, after consultation with the captains, may decide in the interests of time-saving to bring forward the time of the luncheon or tea interval.

LAW 17.   CESSATION OF PLAY

1. Call of Time

The umpire at the bowler's end shall call "time" on the cessation of play before any interval or interruption of play, at the end of each day's play, and at the conclusion of the match. See Law 27 (Appeals).

2. Removal of Bails

After the call of "time", the umpires shall remove the bails from both wickets.

3. Starting a Last Over

The last over before an interval or the close of play shall be started provided the umpire, after walking at his normal pace, has arrived at his position behind the stumps at the bowler's end before time has been reached.

4. Completion of the Last Over of a Session

The last over before an interval or the close of play shall be completed unless a batsman is out or retires during that over within two minutes of the interval or the close of play or unless the players have occasion to leave the field.

5. Completion of the Last Over of a Match

An over in progress at the close of play on the final day of a match shall be completed at the request of either captain, even if a wicket falls after time has been reached.

If, during the last over, the players have occasion to leave the field, the umpires shall call "time" and there shall be no resumption of play and the match shall be at an end.

6. Last Hour of Match – Number of Overs

The umpires shall indicate when one hour of playing time of the match remains according to the agreed hours of play. The next over after that moment shall be the first of a minimum of 20 six-ball overs (15 eight-ball overs), provided a result is not reached earlier or there is no interval or interruption of play.

7. Last Hour of Match – Intervals between Innings and Interruptions of Play

If, at the commencement of the last hour of the match, an interval or interruption of play is in progress or if, during the last hour, there is an interval between innings or an interruption of play, the minimum number of overs to be bowled on the resumption of play shall be reduced in proportion to the duration, within the last hour of the match, of any such interval or interruption.

The minimum number of overs to be bowled after the resumption of play shall be calculated as follows:

    (a) In the case of an interval or interruption of play being in progress at the commencement of the last hour of the match, or in the case of a first interval or interruption, a deduction shall be made from the minimum of 20 six-ball overs (or 15 eight-ball overs).

    (b) If there is a later interval or interruption, a further deduction shall be made from the minimum number of overs which should have been bowled following the last resumption of play.

    (c) These deductions shall be based on the following factors:

        (i) The number of overs already bowled in the last hour of the match or, in the case of a later interval or interruption, in the last session of play.

        (ii) The number of overs lost as a result of the interval or interruption allowing one six-ball over for every full three minutes (or one eight-ball over for every full four minutes) of interval or interruption.

        (iii) Any over left uncompleted at the end of an innings to be excluded from these calculations.

(iv) Any over left uncompleted at the start of an interruption of play to be completed when play is resumed and to count as one over bowled.

(v) An interval to start with the end of an innings and to end ten minutes later; an interruption to start on the call of "time" and to end on the call of "play".

(d) In the event of an innings being completed and a new innings commencing during the last hour of the match, the number of overs to be bowled in the new innings shall be calculated on the basis of one six-ball over for every three minutes or part thereof remaining for play (or one eight-ball over for every four minutes or part thereof remaining for play); or alternatively on the basis that sufficient overs be bowled to enable the full minimum quota of overs to be completed under circumstances governed by (a), (b) and (c) above. In all such cases the alternative which allows the greater number of overs shall be employed.

8. Bowler Unable to Complete an Over during Last Hour of the Match

If, for any reason, a bowler is unable to complete an over during the period of play referred to in 6 above, Law 22.7 (Bowler Incapacitated or Suspended during an Over) shall apply.

LAW 18. SCORING

1. A Run

The score shall be reckoned by runs. A run is scored:

(a) So often as the batsmen, after a hit or at any time while the ball is in play, shall have crossed and made good their ground from end to end.

(b) When a boundary is scored. See Law 19 (Boundaries).

(c) When penalty runs are awarded. See 6 below.

2. Short Runs

(a) If either batsman runs a short run, the umpire shall call and signal "one short" as soon as the ball becomes dead and that run shall not be scored. A run is short if a batsman fails to make good his ground on turning for a further run.

(b) Although a short run shortens the succeeding one, the latter, if completed, shall count.

(c) If either or both batsmen deliberately run short the umpire shall, as soon as he sees that the fielding side have no chance of dismissing either batsman, call and signal "dead ball" and disallow any runs attempted or previously scored. The batsmen shall return to their original ends.

(d) If both batsmen run short in one and the same run, only one run shall be deducted.

(e) Only if 3 or more runs are attempted can more than one be short and then, subject to (c) and (d) above, all runs so called shall be disallowed. If there has been more than one short run the umpires shall instruct the scorers as to the number of runs disallowed.

3. Striker Caught

If the striker is caught, no run shall be scored.

4. Batsman Run Out

If a batsman is run out, only that run which was being attempted shall not be scored. If, however, an injured striker himself is run out, no runs shall be scored. See Law 2.7 (Transgression of the Laws by an Injured Batsman or Runner).

5. Batsman Obstructing the Field

If a batsman is out Obstructing the Field, any runs completed before the obstruction occurs shall be scored unless such obstruction prevents a catch being made, in which case no runs shall be scored.

6. Runs Scored for Penalties

Runs shall be scored for penalties under Laws 20 (Lost Ball), 24 (No-ball), 25 (Wide-ball), 41.1 (Fielding the Ball) and for boundary allowances under Law 19 (Boundaries).

7. Batsman Returning to Wicket he has Left

If, while the ball is in play, the batsmen have crossed in running, neither shall return to the wicket he has left, even though a short run has been called or no run has been scored as in the case of a catch. Batsmen, however, shall return to the wickets they originally left in the cases of a boundary and of any disallowance of runs and of an injured batsman being, himself, run out. See Law 2.7 (Transgression by an Injured Batsman or Runner).

Note

(a) Short Run

A striker taking stance in front of his popping crease may run from that point without penalty.

LAW 19.   BOUNDARIES

1. The Boundary of the Playing Area

Before the toss for innings, the umpires shall agree with both captains on the boundary of the playing area. The boundary shall, if possible, be marked by a white line, a rope laid on the ground, or a fence. If flags or posts only are used to mark a boundary, the imaginary line joining such points shall be regarded as the boundary. An obstacle, or person, within the playing area shall not be regarded as a boundary unless so decided by the umpires before the toss for innings. Sightscreens within, or partially within, the playing area shall be regarded as the boundary and when the ball strikes or passes within or under or directly over any part of the screen, a boundary shall be scored.

2. Runs Scored for Boundaries

Before the toss for innings, the umpires shall agree with both captains the runs to be allowed for boundaries, and in deciding the allowance for them, the umpires and captains shall be guided by the prevailing custom of the ground. The allowance for a boundary shall normally be 4 runs, and 6 runs for all hits pitching over and clear of the boundary line or fence, even though the ball has been previously touched by a fieldsman. 6 runs shall also be scored if a fieldsman, after catching a ball, carries it over the boundary. See Law 32 (Caught) Note (a). 6 runs shall not be scored when a ball struck by the striker hits a sightscreen full pitch if the screen is within, or partially within, the playing area, but if the ball is struck directly over a sightscreen so situated, 6 runs shall be scored.

3. A Boundary

A boundary shall be scored and signalled by the umpire at the bowler's end whenever, in his opinion:

(a) A ball in play touches or crosses the boundary, however marked.

(b) A fieldsman with ball in hand touches or grounds any part of his person on or over a boundary line.

(c) A fieldsman with ball in hand grounds any part of his person over a boundary fence or board. This allows the fieldsman to touch or lean on or over a boundary fence or board in preventing a boundary.

4. Runs Exceeding Boundary Allowance

The runs completed at the instant the ball reaches the boundary shall count if they exceed the boundary allowance.

5. Overthrows or Wilful Act of a Fieldsman

If the boundary results from an overthrow or from the wilful act of a fieldsman, any runs already completed and the allowance shall be added to the score. The run in progress shall count provided that the batsmen have crossed at the instant of the throw or act.

Note

(a) Position of Sightscreens

Sightscreens should, if possible, be positioned wholly outside the playing area, as near as possible to the boundary line.

LAW 20. LOST BALL

1. Runs Scored

If a ball in play cannot be found or recovered, any fieldsman may call "lost ball" when 6 runs shall be added to the score; but if more than 6 have been run before "lost ball" is called, as many runs as have been completed shall be scored. The run in progress shall count provided that the batsmen have crossed at the instant of the call of "lost ball".

2. How Scored

The runs shall be added to the score of the striker if the ball has been struck, but otherwise to the score of byes, leg-byes, no-balls or wides as the case may be.

LAW 21. THE RESULT

1. A Win – Two-innings Matches

The side which has scored a total of runs in excess of that scored by the opposing side in its two completed innings shall be the winners.

2. A Win–One-innings Matches

(a) One-innings matches, unless played out as in 1 above, shall be decided on the first innings, but see Law 12.5 (Continuation after One Innings of Each Side).

(b) If the captains agree to continue play after the completion of one innings of each side in accordance with Law 12.5 (Continuation after One Innings of Each Side) and a result is not achieved on the second innings, the first innings result shall stand.

3. Umpires Awarding a Match

(a) A match shall be lost by a side which, during the match, (i) refuses to play, or (ii) concedes defeat, and the umpires shall award the match to the other side.

(b) Should both batsmen at the wickets or the fielding side leave the field at any time without the agreement of the umpires, this shall constitute a refusal to play and, on appeal, the umpires shall award the match to the other side in accordance with (a) above.

4. A Tie

The result of a match shall be a tie when the scores are equal at the conclusion of play, but only if the side batting last has completed its innings.

If the scores of the completed first innings of a one-day match are equal, it shall be a tie but only if the match has not been played out to a further conclusion.

5. A Draw

A match not determined in any of the ways as in 1, 2, 3 and 4 above shall count as a draw.

6. Correctness of Result

Any decision as to the correctness of the scores shall be the responsibility of the umpires. See Law 3.14 (Correctness of Scores).

If, after the umpires and players have left the field in the belief that the match has been concluded, the umpires decide that a mistake in scoring has occurred, which affects the result, and provided time has not been reached, they shall order play to resume and to continue until the agreed finishing time unless a result is reached earlier.

If the umpires decide that a mistake has occurred and time has been reached, the umpires shall immediately inform both captains of the necessary corrections to the scores and, if applicable, to the result.

7. Acceptance of Result

In accepting the scores as notified by the scorers and agreed by the umpires, the captains of both sides thereby accept the result.

Notes

(a) Statement of Results
The result of a finished match is stated as a win by runs, except in the case of a win by the side batting last when it is by the number of wickets still then to fall.

(b) Winning Hit or Extras
As soon as the side has won, see 1 and 2 above, the umpire shall call "time", the match is finished, and nothing that happens thereafter other than as a result of a mistake in scoring (see 6 above) shall be regarded as part of the match.

However, if a boundary constitutes the winning hit–or extras–and the boundary allowance exceeds the number of runs required to win the match, such runs scored shall be credited to the side's total and, in the case of a hit, to the striker's score.

LAW 22. THE OVER

1. Number of Balls

The ball shall be bowled from each wicket alternately in overs of either six or eight balls according to agreement before the match.

2. Call of "Over"

When the agreed number of balls has been bowled, and as the ball becomes dead or when it becomes clear to the umpire at the bowler's end that both the fielding side and the batsmen at the wicket have ceased to regard the ball as in play, the umpire shall call "over" before leaving the wicket.

3. No-ball or Wide-ball

Neither a no-ball nor a wide-ball shall be reckoned as one of the over.

4. Umpire Miscounting

If an umpire miscounts the number of balls, the over as counted by the umpire shall stand.

5. Bowler Changing Ends

A bowler shall be allowed to change ends as often as desired, provided only that he does not bowl two overs consecutively in an innings.

6. The Bowler Finishing an Over

A bowler shall finish an over in progress unless he be incapacitated or be suspended under Law 42.8 (The Bowling of Fast Short-pitched Balls), 9 (The Bowling of Fast High Full Pitches), 10 (Time Wasting) and 11 (Players Damaging the Pitch). If an over is left incomplete for any reason at the start of an interval or interruption of play, it shall be finished on the resumption of play.

7. Bowler Incapacitated or Suspended during an Over

If, for any reason, a bowler is incapacitated while running up to bowl the first ball of an over, or is incapacitated or suspended during an over, the umpire shall call and signal "dead ball" and another bowler shall be allowed to bowl or complete the over from the same end, provided only that he shall not bowl two overs, or part thereof, consecutively in one innings.

8. Position of Non-striker

The batsman at the bowler's end shall normally stand on the opposite side of the wicket to that from which the ball is being delivered, unless a request to do otherwise is granted by the umpire.

LAW 23. DEAD BALL

1. The Ball Becomes Dead

When:

    (a) It is finally settled in the hands of the wicket-keeper or the bowler.

    (b) It reaches or pitches over the boundary.

    (c) A batsman is out.

    (d) Whether played or not, it lodges in the clothing or equipment of a batsman or the clothing of an umpire.

    (e) A ball lodges in a protective helmet worn by a member of the fielding side.

    (f) A penalty is awarded under Law 20 (Lost Ball) or Law 41.1 (Fielding the Ball).

    (g) The umpire calls "over" or "time".

2. Either Umpire Shall Call and Signal "Dead Ball"

When:

    (a) He intervenes in a case of unfair play.

    (b) A serious injury to a player or umpire occurs.

    (c) He is satisfied that, for an adequate reason, the striker is not ready to receive the ball and makes no attempt to play it.

    (d) The bowler drops the ball accidentally before delivery, or the ball does not leave his hand for any reason.

    (e) One or both bails fall from the striker's wicket before he receives delivery.

    (f) He leaves his normal position for consultation.

    (g) He is required to do so under Law 26.3 (Disallowance of Leg-byes).

3. The Ball Ceases to be Dead

When:

    (a) The bowler starts his run-up or bowling action.

4. The Ball is Not Dead

When:

    (a) It strikes an umpire (unless it lodges in his dress).

    (b) The wicket is broken or struck down (unless a batsman is out thereby).

    (c) A unsuccessful appeal is made.

    (d) The wicket is broken accidentally either by the bowler during his delivery or by a batsman in running.

    (e) The umpire has called "no-ball" or "wide".

Notes

(a) Ball Finally Settled

Whether the ball is finally settled or not—see 1(a) above—must be a question for the umpires alone to decide.

(b) Action on Call of "Dead Ball"

    (i) If "dead ball" is called prior to the striker receiving a delivery, the bowler shall be allowed an additional ball.

    (ii) If "dead ball" is called after the striker receives a delivery, the bowler shall not be allowed an additional ball, unless a "no-ball" or "wide" has been called.

LAW 24. NO-BALL

1. Mode of Delivery

The umpire shall indicate to the striker whether the bowler intends to bowl over or round the wicket, overarm or underarm, right- or left-handed. Failure on the part of the bowler to indicate in advance a change in his mode of delivery is unfair and the umpire shall call and signal "no-ball".

2. Fair Delivery–The Arm

For a delivery to be fair the ball must be bowled, not thrown–see Note (a) below. If either umpire is not entirely satisfied with the absolute fairness of a delivery in this respect he shall call and signal "no-ball" instantly upon delivery.

3. Fair Delivery–The Feet

The umpire at the bowler's wicket shall call and signal "no-ball" if he is not satisfied that in the delivery stride:

(a) The bowler's back foot has landed within and not touching the return crease or its forward extension; or

(b) Some part of the front foot whether grounded or raised was behind the popping crease.

4. Bowler Throwing at Striker's Wicket before Delivery

If the bowler, before delivering the ball, throws it at the striker's wicket in an attempt to run him out, the umpire shall call and signal "no-ball". See Law 42.12 (Batsman Unfairly Stealing a Run) and Law 38 (Run Out).

5. Bowler Attempting to Run Out Non-striker before Delivery

If the bowler, before delivering the ball, attempts to run out the non-striker, any runs which result shall be allowed and shall be scored as no-balls. Such an attempt shall not count as a ball in the over. The umpire shall not call "no-ball". See Law 42.12 (Batsman Unfairly Stealing a Run).

6. Infringement of Laws by a Wicket-keeper or a Fieldsman

The umpire shall call and signal "no-ball" in the event of the wicket-keeper infringing Law 40.1 (Position of Wicket-keeper) or a fieldsman infringing Law 41.2 (Limitation of On-side Fieldsmen) or Law 41.3 (Position of Fieldsmen).

7. Revoking a Call

An umpire shall revoke the call "no-ball" if the ball does not leave the bowler's hand for any reason. See Law 23.2 (Either Umpire Shall Call and Signal "Dead Ball").

8. Penalty

A penalty of 1 run for a no-ball shall be scored if no runs are made otherwise.

9. Runs from a No-ball

The striker may hit a no-ball and whatever runs result shall be added to his score. Runs made otherwise from a no-ball shall be scored no-balls.

10. Out from a No-ball

The striker shall be out from a no-ball if he breaks Law 34 (Hit the Ball Twice) and either batsman may be run out or shall be given out if either breaks Law 33 (Handled the Ball) or Law 37 (Obstructing the Field).

11. Batsman Given Out off a No-ball

Should a batsman be given out off a no-ball the penalty for bowling it shall stand unless runs are otherwise scored.

Notes

(a) Definition of a Throw

A ball shall be deemed to have been thrown if, in the opinion of either umpire, the process of straightening the bowling arm, whether it be partial or complete, takes place during that part of the delivery swing which directly precedes the ball leaving the hand. This definition shall not debar a bowler from the use of the wrist in the delivery swing.

(b) No-ball Not Counting in Over

A no-ball shall not be reckoned as one of the over. See Law 22.3 (No-ball or Wide-ball).

LAW 25.   WIDE-BALL

1. Judging a Wide

If the bowler bowls the ball so high over or so wide of the wicket that, in the opinion of the umpire, it passes out of the reach of the striker, standing in a normal guard position, the umpire shall call and signal "wide-ball" as soon as it has passed the line of the striker's wicket.

The umpire shall not adjudge a ball as being wide if:

  (a) The striker, by moving from his guard position, causes the ball to pass out of his reach.

  (b) The striker moves and thus brings the ball within his reach.

2. Penalty

A penalty of 1 run for a wide shall be scored if no runs are made otherwise.

3. Ball Coming to Rest in Front of the Striker

If a ball which the umpire considers to have been delivered comes to rest in front of the line of the striker's wicket, "wide" shall not be called. The striker has a right, without interference from the fielding side, to make one attempt to hit the ball. If the fielding side interfere, the umpire shall replace the ball where it came to rest and shall order the fieldsmen to resume the places they occupied in the field before the ball was delivered.

The umpire shall call and signal "dead ball" as soon as it is clear that the striker does not intend to hit the ball, or after the striker has made an unsuccessful attempt to hit the ball.

4. Revoking a Call

The umpire shall revoke the call if the striker hits a ball which has been called "wide".

5. Ball Not Dead

The ball does not become dead on the call of "wide-ball"–see Law 23.4 (The Ball is Not Dead).

6. Runs Resulting from a Wide

All runs which are run or result from a wide-ball which is not a no-ball shall be scored wide-balls, or if no runs are made 1 shall be scored.

7. Out from a Wide

The striker shall be out from a wide-ball if he breaks Law 35 (Hit Wicket), or Law 39 (Stumped). Either batsman may be run out and shall be out if he breaks Law 33 (Handled the Ball), or Law 37 (Obstructing the Field).

8. Batsman Given Out off a Wide

Should a batsman be given out off a wide, the penalty for bowling it shall stand unless runs are otherwise made.

Note

(a) Wide-ball Not Counting in Over

A wide-ball shall not be reckoned as one of the over–see Law 22.3 (No-ball or Wide-ball).

LAW 26.   BYE AND LEG-BYE

1. Byes

If the ball, not having been called "wide" or "no-ball", passes the striker without touching his bat or person, and any runs are obtained, the umpire shall signal "bye" and the run or runs shall be credited as such to the batting side.

2. Leg-byes

If the ball, not having been called "wide" or "no-ball", is unintentionally deflected by the striker's dress or person, except a hand holding the bat, and any runs are obtained the umpire shall signal "leg-bye" and the run or runs so scored shall be credited as such to the batting side.

Such leg-byes shall be scored only if, in the opinion of the umpire, the striker has:

    (a) Attempted to play the ball with his bat; or

    (b) Tried to avoid being hit by the ball.

3. Disallowance of Leg-byes

In the case of a deflection by the striker's person, other than in 2(a) and (b) above, the umpire shall call and signal "dead ball" as soon as 1 run has been completed or when it is clear that a run is not being attempted, or the ball has reached the boundary.

On the call and signal of "dead ball" the batsmen shall return to their original ends and no runs shall be allowed.

LAW 27.   APPEALS

1. Time of Appeals

The umpires shall not give a batsman out unless appealed to by the other side which shall be done prior to the bowler beginning his run-up or bowling action to deliver the next ball. Under Law 23.1 (f) (The Ball Becomes Dead), the ball is dead on "over" being called; this does not, however, invalidate an appeal made prior to the first ball of the following over provided "time" has not been called-see Law 17.1 (Call of Time).

2. An Appeal "How's That?"

An appeal "How's That?" shall cover all ways of being out.

3. Answering Appeals

The umpire at the bowler's wicket shall answer appeals before the other umpire in all cases except those arising out of Law 35 (Hit Wicket) or Law 39 (Stumped) or Law 38 (Run Out) when this occurs at the striker's wicket.

When either umpire has given a batsman not out, the other umpire shall, within his jurisdiction, answer the appeal or a further appeal, provided it is made in time in accordance with 1 above (Time of Appeals).

4. Consultation by Umpires

An umpire may consult with the other umpire on a point of fact which the latter may have been in a better position to see and shall then give his decision. If, after consultation, there is still doubt remaining the decision shall be in favour of the batsman.

5. Batsman Leaving his Wicket under a Misapprehension

The umpires shall intervene if satisfied that a batsman, not having been given out, has left his wicket under a misapprehension that he has been dismissed.

6. Umpire's Decision

The umpire's decision is final. He may alter his decision, provided that such alteration is made promptly.

7. Withdrawal of an Appeal

In exceptional circumstances the captain of the fielding side may seek permission of the umpire to withdraw an appeal provided the outgoing batsman has not left the playing area. If this is allowed, the umpire shall cancel his decision.

LAW 28. THE WICKET IS DOWN

1. Wicket Down

The wicket is down if:

(a) Either the ball or the striker's bat or person completely removes either bail from the top of the stumps. A disturbance of a bail, whether temporary or not, shall not constitute a complete removal, but the wicket is down if a bail in falling lodges between two of the stumps.

(b) Any player completely removes with his hand or arm a bail from the top of the stumps, provided that the ball is held in that hand or in the hand of the arm so used.

(c) When both bails are off, a stump is struck out of the ground by the ball, or a player strikes or pulls a stump out of the ground, provided that the ball is held in the hand(s) or in the hand of the arm so used.

2. One Bail Off

If one bail is off, it shall be sufficient for the purpose of putting the wicket down to remove the remaining bail, or to strike or pull any of the three stumps out of the ground in any of the ways stated in 1 above.

3. All the Stumps Out of the Ground

If all the stumps are out of the ground, the fielding side shall be allowed to put back one or more stumps in order to have an opportunity of putting the wicket down.

4. Dispensing with Bails

If owing to the strength of the wind, it has been agreed to dispense with the bails in accordance with Law 8, Note (a) (Dispensing with Bails), the decision as to when the wicket is down is one for the umpires to decide on the facts before them. In such circumstances and if the umpires so decide, the wicket shall be held to be down even though a stump has not been struck out of the ground.

Note

(a) Remaking the Wicket
If the wicket is broken while the ball is in play, it is not the umpire's duty to remake the wicket until the ball has become dead–see Law 23 (Dead Ball). A member of the fielding side, however, may remake the wicket in such circumstances.

LAW 29. BATSMAN OUT OF HIS GROUND

1. When out of his Ground

A batsman shall be considered to be out of his ground unless some part of his bat in his hand or of his person is grounded behind the line of the popping crease.

LAW 30. BOWLED

1. Out Bowled

The striker shall be out *Bowled* if:

(a) His wicket is bowled down, even if the ball first touches his bat or person.

(b) He breaks his wicket by hitting or kicking the ball on to it before the completion of a stroke, or as a result of attempting to guard his wicket. See Law 34.1 (Out Hit the Ball Twice).

Note

(a) Out Bowled–Not lbw
The striker is out bowled if the ball is deflected on to his wicket even though a decision against him would be justified under Law 36 (lbw).

LAW 31. TIMED OUT

1. Out Timed Out

An incoming batsman shall be out *Timed Out* if he wilfully takes more than two minutes to come in–the two minutes being timed from the moment a wicket falls until the new batsman steps on to the field of play.

If this is not complied with and if the umpire is satisfied that the delay was wilful and if an appeal is made, the new batsman shall be given out by the umpire at the bowler's end.

2. Time to be Added

The time taken by the umpires to investigate the cause of the delay shall be added at the normal close of play.

Notes

    (a) Entry in Scorebook
    The correct entry in the scorebook when a batsman is given out under this Law is "timed out", and the bowler does not get credit for the wicket.

    (b) Batsmen Crossing on the Field of Play
    It is an essential duty of the captains to ensure that the in-going batsman passes the outgoing one before the latter leaves the field of play.

LAW 32. CAUGHT

1. Out Caught

The striker shall be out *Caught* if the ball touches his bat or if it touches below the wrist his hand or glove, holding the bat, and is subsequently held by a fieldsman before it touches the ground.

2. A Fair Catch

A catch shall be considered to have been fairly made if:

    (a) The fieldsman is within the field of play throughout the act of making the catch.

        (i) The act of making the catch shall start from the time when the fieldsman first handles the ball and shall end when he both retains complete control over the further disposal of the ball and remains within the field of play.

        (ii) In order to be within the field of play, the fieldsman may not touch or ground any part of his person on or over a boundary line. When the boundary is marked by a fence or board the fieldsman may not ground any part of his person over the boundary fence or board, but may touch or lean over the boundary fence or board in completing the catch.

    (b) The ball is hugged to the body of the catcher or accidentally lodges in his dress or, in the case of the wicket-keeper, in his pads. However, a striker may not be caught if a ball lodges in a protective helmet worn by a fieldsman, in which case the umpire shall call and signal "dead ball". See Law 23 (Dead Ball).

    (c) The ball does not touch the ground even though a hand holding it does so in effecting the catch.

    (d) A fieldsman catches the ball, after it has been lawfully played a second time by the striker, but only if the ball has not touched the ground since being first struck.

    (e) A fieldsman catches the ball after it has touched an umpire, another fieldsman or the other batsman. However, a striker may not be caught if a ball has touched a protective helmet worn by a fieldsman.

    (f) The ball is caught off an obstruction within the boundary provided it has not previously been agreed to regard the obstruction as a boundary.

3. Scoring of Runs

If a striker is caught, no run shall be scored.

Notes

(a) Scoring from an Attempted Catch

When a fieldsman carrying the ball touches or grounds any part of his person on or over a boundary marked by a line, 6 runs shall be scored.

(b) Ball Still in Play

If a fieldsman releases the ball before he crosses the boundary, the ball will be considered to be still in play and it may be caught by another fieldsman. However, if the original fieldsman returns to the field of play and handles the ball, a catch may not be made.

LAW 33. HANDLED THE BALL

1. Out Handled the Ball

Either batsman on appeal shall be out *Handled the Ball* if he wilfully touches the ball while in play with the hand not holding the bat unless he does so with the consent of the opposite side.

Note

(a) Entry in Scorebook

The correct entry in the scorebook when a batsman is given out under this Law is "handled the ball", and the bowler does not get credit for the wicket.

LAW 34. HIT THE BALL TWICE

1. Out Hit the Ball Twice

The striker, on appeal, shall be out *Hit the Ball Twice* if, after the ball is struck or is stopped by any part of his person, he wilfully strikes it again with his bat or person except for the sole purpose of guarding his wicket: this he may do with his bat or any part of his person other than his hands, but see Law 37.2 (Obstructing a Ball From Being Caught).

For the purpose of this Law, a hand holding the bat shall be regarded as part of the bat.

2. Returning the Ball to a Fieldsman

The striker, on appeal, shall be out under this Law if, without the consent of the opposite side, he uses his bat or person to return the ball to any of the fielding side.

3. Runs from Ball Lawfully Struck Twice

No runs except those which result from an overthrow or penalty – see Law 41 (The Fieldsman) – shall be scored from a ball lawfully struck twice.

Notes

(a) Entry in Scorebook

The correct entry in the scorebook when the striker is given out under this Law is "hit the ball twice", and the bowler does not get credit for the wicket.

(b) Runs Credited to the Batsman

Any runs awarded under 3 above as a result of an overthrow or penalty shall be credited to the striker, provided the ball in the first instance has touched the bat, or, if otherwise, as extras.

LAW 35. HIT WICKET

1. Out Hit Wicket

The striker shall be out *Hit Wicket* if, while the ball is in play:

(a) His wicket is broken with any part of his person, dress, or equipment as a result of any action taken by him in preparing to receive or in receiving a delivery, or in setting off for his first run, immediately after playing, or playing at, the ball.

(b) He hits down his wicket whilst lawfully making a second stroke for the purpose of guarding his wicket within the provisions of Law 34.1 (Out Hit the Ball Twice).

Notes

(a) Not Out Hit Wicket

A batsman is not out under this Law should his wicket be broken in any of the ways referred to in 1(a) above if:

    (i) It occurs while he is in the act of running, other than in setting off for his first run immediately after playing at the ball, or while he is avoiding being run out or stumped.

    (ii) The bowler after starting his run-up or bowling action does not deliver the ball; in which case the umpire shall immediately call and signal "dead ball".

    (iii) It occurs whilst he is avoiding a throw-in at any time.

LAW 36. LEG BEFORE WICKET

1. Out lbw

The striker shall be out *lbw* in the circumstances set out below:

(a) Striker Attempting to Play the Ball

The striker shall be out lbw if he first intercepts with any part of his person, dress or equipment a fair ball which would have hit the wicket and which has not previously touched his bat or a hand holding the bat, provided that:

    (i) The ball pitched in a straight line between wicket and wicket or on the off side of the striker's wicket, or in the case of a ball intercepted full pitch would have pitched in a straight line between wicket and wicket; and

    (ii) The point of impact is in a straight line between wicket and wicket, even if above the level of the bails.

(b) Striker Making No Attempt to Play the Ball

The striker shall be out lbw even if the ball is intercepted outside the line of the off stump if, in the opinion of the umpire, he has made no genuine attempt to play the ball with his bat, but has intercepted the ball with some part of his person and if the circumstances set out in (a) above apply.

LAW 37. OBSTRUCTING THE FIELD

1. Wilful Obstruction

Either batsman, on appeal, shall be out *Obstructing the Field* if he wilfully obstructs the opposite side by word or action.

2. Obstructing a Ball From Being Caught

The striker, on appeal, shall be out should wilful obstruction by either batsman prevent a catch being made.

This shall apply even though the striker causes the obstruction in lawfully guarding his wicket under the provisions of Law 34. See Law 34.1 (Out Hit the Ball Twice).

Notes

(a) Accidental Obstruction

The umpires must decide whether the obstruction was wilful or not. The accidental interception of a throw-in by a batsman while running does not break this Law.

(b) Entry in Scorebook

The correct entry in the scorebook when a batsman is given out under this Law is "obstructing the field", and the bowler does not get credit for the wicket.

LAW 38. RUN OUT

1. Out Run Out

Either batsman shall be out *Run Out* if in running or at any time while the ball is in play – except in the circumstances described in Law 39 (Stumped) – he is out of his ground and his wicket is put down by the opposite side. If, however, a batsman in running makes good his ground he shall not be out run out if he subsequently leaves his ground, in order to avoid injury, and the wicket is put down.

2. "No-ball" Called

If a no-ball has been called, the striker shall not be given run out unless he attempts to run.

3. Which Batsman Is Out

If the batsmen have crossed in running, he who runs for the wicket which is put down shall be out; if they have not crossed, he who has left the wicket which is put down shall be out. If a batsman remains in his ground or returns to his ground and the other batsman joins him there, the latter shall be out if his wicket is put down.

4. Scoring of Runs

If a batsman is run out, only that run which is being attempted shall not be scored. If, however, an injured striker himself is run out, no runs shall be scored. See Law 2.7 (Transgression of the Laws by an Injured Batsman or Runner).

Notes

(a) **Ball Played on to Opposite Wicket**
If the ball is played on to the opposite wicket, neither batsman is liable to be run out unless the ball has been touched by a fieldsman before the wicket is broken.

(b) **Entry in Scorebook**
The correct entry in the scorebook when a batsman is given out under this Law is "run out", and the bowler does not get credit for the wicket.

LAW 39. STUMPED

1. Out Stumped

The striker shall be out *Stumped* if, in receiving the ball, not being a no-ball, he is out of his ground otherwise than in attempting a run and the wicket is put down by the wicket-keeper without the intervention of another fieldsman.

2. Action by the Wicket-keeper

The wicket-keeper may take the ball in front of the wicket in an attempt to stump the striker only if the ball has touched the bat or person of the striker.

Note

(a) **Ball Rebounding from Wicket-keeper's Person**
The striker may be out stumped if, in the circumstances stated in 1 above, the wicket is broken by a ball rebounding from the wicket-keeper's person or equipment or is kicked or thrown by the wicket-keeper on to the wicket.

LAW 40. THE WICKET-KEEPER

1. Position of Wicket-keeper

The wicket-keeper shall remain wholly behind the wicket until a ball delivered by the bowler touches the bat or person of the striker, or passes the wicket, or until the striker attempts a run.

In the event of the wicket-keeper contravening this Law, the umpire at the striker's end shall call and signal "no ball" at the instant of delivery or as soon as possible thereafter.

2. Restriction on Actions of the Wicket-keeper

If the wicket-keeper interferes with the striker's right to play the ball and to guard his wicket, the striker shall not be out except under Laws 33 (Handled the Ball), 34 (Hit the Ball Twice), 37 (Obstructing the Field), 38 (Run Out).

3. Interference with the Wicket-keeper by the Striker

If in the legitimate defence of his wicket, the striker interferes with the wicket-keeper, he shall not be out, except as provided for in Law 37.2 (Obstructing a Ball From Being Caught).

LAW 41.   THE FIELDSMAN

1. Fielding the Ball

The fieldsman may stop the ball with any part of his person, but if he wilfully stops it otherwise, 5 runs shall be added to the run or runs already scored; if no run has been scored 5 penalty runs shall be awarded. The run in progress shall count provided that the batsmen have crossed at the instant of the act. If the ball has been struck, the penalty shall be added to the score of the striker, but otherwise to the scores of byes, leg-byes, no-balls or wides as the case may be.

2. Limitation of On-side Fieldsmen

The number of on-side fieldsmen behind the popping crease at the instant of the bowler's delivery shall not exceed two. In the event of infringement by the fielding side the umpire at the striker's end shall call and signal "no-ball" at the instant of delivery or as soon as possible thereafter.

3. Position of Fieldsmen

Whilst the ball is in play and until the ball has made contact with the bat or the striker's person or has passed his bat, no fieldsman, other than the bowler, may stand on or have any part of his person extended over the pitch (measuring 22 yards/20.12m × 10 feet/3.05m). In the event of a fieldsman contravening this Law, the umpire at the bowler's end shall call and signal "no-ball" at the instant of delivery or as soon as possible thereafter. See Law 40.1 (Position of Wicket-keeper).

4. Fieldsmen's Protective Helmets

Protective helmets, when not in use by members of the fielding side, shall be placed, if above the surface, only on the ground behind the wicket-keeper. In the event of the ball, when in play, striking a helmet whilst in this position, 5 penalty runs shall be awarded as laid down in Law 41.1 and Note (a).

Note

(a) **Batsmen Changing Ends**

The 5 runs referred to in 1 and 4 above are a penalty and the batsmen do not change ends solely by reason of this penalty.

LAW 42.   UNFAIR PLAY

1. Responsibility of Captains

The captains are responsible at all times for ensuring that play is conducted within the spirit of the game as well as within the Laws.

2. Responsibility of Umpires

The umpires are the sole judges of fair and unfair play.

3. Intervention by the Umpire

The umpires shall intervene without appeal by calling and signalling "dead ball" in the case of unfair play, but should not otherwise interfere with the progress of the game except as required to do so by the Laws.

4. Lifting the Seam

A player shall not lift the seam of the ball for any reason. Should this be done, the umpires shall change the ball for one of similar condition to that in use prior to the contravention. See Note (a).

5. Changing the Condition of the Ball

Any member of the fielding side may polish the ball provided that such polishing wastes no time and that no artificial substance is used. No-one shall rub the ball on the ground or use any artificial substance or take any other action to alter the condition of the ball.

In the event of a contravention of this Law, the umpires, after consultation, shall change the ball for one of similar condition to that in use prior to the contravention.

This Law does not prevent a member of the fielding side from drying a wet ball, or removing mud from the ball. See Note (b).

6. Incommoding the Striker

An umpire is justified in intervening under this Law and shall call and signal "dead ball" if, in his opinion, any player of the fielding side incommodes the striker by any noise or action while he is receiving the ball.

7. Obstruction of a Batsman in Running

It shall be considered unfair if any fieldsman wilfully obstructs a batsman in running. In these circumstances the umpire shall call and signal "dead ball" and allow any completed runs and the run in progress, or alternatively any boundary scored.

8. The Bowling of Fast Short-pitched Balls

The bowling of fast short-pitched balls is unfair if, in the opinion of the umpire at the bowler's end, it constitutes an attempt to intimidate the striker. See Note (d).

Umpires shall consider intimidation to be the deliberate bowling of fast short-pitched balls which by their length, height and direction are intended or likely to inflict physical injury on the striker. The relative skill of the striker shall also be taken into consideration.

In the event of such unfair bowling, the umpire at the bowler's end shall adopt the following procedure:

(a) In the first instance the umpire shall call and signal "no-ball", caution the bowler and inform the other umpire, the captain of the fielding side and the batsmen of what has occurred.

(b) If this caution is ineffective, he shall repeat the above procedure and indicate to the bowler that this is a final warning.

(c) Both the above caution and final warning shall continue to apply even though the bowler may later change ends.

(d) Should the above warnings prove ineffective the umpire at the bowler's end shall:

(i) At the first repetition call and signal "no-ball" and when the ball is dead direct the captain to take the bowler off forthwith and to complete the over with another bowler, provided that the bowler does not bowl two overs or part thereof consecutively. See Law 22.7 (Bowler Incapacitated or Suspended during an Over).

(ii) Not allow the bowler, thus taken off, to bowl again in the same innings.

(iii) Report the occurrence to the captain of the batting side as soon as the players leave the field for an interval.

(iv) Report the occurrence to the executive of the fielding side and to any governing body responsible for the match, who shall take any further action which is considered to be appropriate against the bowler concerned.

9. The Bowling of Fast High Full Pitches

The bowling of fast high full pitches is unfair. See Note (e).

In the event of such unfair bowling the umpire at the bowler's end shall adopt the procedures of caution, final warnings, action against the bowler and reporting as set out in 8 above.

10. Time Wasting

Any form of time wasting is unfair.

(a) In the event of the captain of the fielding side wasting time or allowing any member of his side to waste time, the umpire at the bowler's end shall adopt the following procedure:

(i) In the first instance he shall caution the captain of the fielding side and inform the other umpire of what has occurred.

(ii) If this caution is ineffective he shall repeat the above procedure and indicate to the captain that this is a final warning.

(iii) The umpire shall report the occurrence to the captain of the batting side as soon as the players leave the field for an interval.

(iv) Should the above procedure prove ineffective the umpire shall report the occurrence to the executive of the fielding side and to any governing body responsible for that match, who shall take appropriate action against the captain and the players concerned.

(b) In the event of a bowler taking unnecessarily long to bowl an over the umpire at the bowler's end shall adopt the procedures, other than the calling of "no-ball", of caution, final warning, action against the bowler and reporting.

(c) In the event of a batsman wasting time (See Note (f)) other than in the manner described in Law 31 (Timed Out), the umpire at the bowler's end shall adopt the following procedure:

(i) In the first instance he shall caution the batsman and inform the other umpire at once, and the captain of the batting side, as soon as the players leave the field for an interval, of what has occurred.

(ii) If this proves ineffective, he shall repeat the caution, indicate to the batsman that this is a final warning and inform the other umpire.

(iii) The umpire shall report the occurrence to both captains as soon as the players leave the field for an interval.

(iv) Should the above procedure prove ineffective, the umpire shall report the occurrence to the executive of the batting side and to any governing body responsible for that match, who shall take appropriate action against the player concerned.

11. Players Damaging the Pitch

The umpires shall intervene and prevent players from causing damage to the pitch which may assist the bowlers of either side. See Note (c).

(a) In the event of any member of the fielding side damaging the pitch, the umpire shall follow the procedure of caution, final warning, and reporting as set out in 10(a) above.

(b) In the event of a bowler contravening this Law by running down the pitch after delivering the ball, the umpire at the bowler's end shall first caution the bowler. If this caution is ineffective the umpire shall adopt the procedures, as set out in 8 above other than the calling and signalling of "no-ball".

(c) In the event of a batsman damaging the pitch the umpire at the bowler's end shall follow the procedures of caution, final warning and reporting as set out in 10(c) above.

12. Batsman Unfairly Stealing a Run

Any attempt by the batsman to steal a run during the bowler's run-up is unfair. Unless the bowler attempts to run out either batsman – see Law 24.4 (Bowler Throwing at Striker's Wicket before Delivery) and Law 24.5 (Bowler Attempting to Run Out Non-striker before Delivery) – the umpire shall call and signal "dead ball" as soon as the batsmen cross in any such attempt to run. The batsmen shall then return to their original wickets.

13. Player's Conduct

In the event of a player failing to comply with the instructions of an umpire, criticising his decisions by word or action, or showing dissent, or generally behaving in a manner which might bring the game into disrepute, the umpire concerned shall, in the first place, report the matter to the other umpire and to the player's captain requesting the latter to take action. If this proves ineffective, the umpire shall report the incident as soon as possible to the executive of the player's team and to any governing body responsible for the match, who shall take any further action which is considered appropriate against the player or players concerned.

Notes

(a) The Condition of the Ball
Umpires shall make frequent and irregular inspections of the condition of the ball.

(b) Drying of a Wet Ball
A wet ball may be dried on a towel or with sawdust.

(c) Danger Area
The danger area on the pitch, which must be protected from damage by a bowler, shall be regarded by the umpires as the area contained by an imaginary line 4 feet/1.22m from the popping crease, and parallel to it, and within two imaginary and parallel lines drawn down the pitch from points on that line 1 foot/30.48cm on either side of the middle stump.

(d) Fast Short-pitched Balls
As a guide, a fast short-pitched ball is one which pitches short and passes, or would have passed, above the shoulder height of the striker standing in a normal batting stance at the crease.

(e) The Bowling of Fast Full Pitches
The bowling of one fast, high full pitch shall be considered to be unfair if, in the opinion of the umpire, it is deliberate, bowled at the striker, and if it passes or would have passed above the shoulder height of the striker when standing in a normal batting stance at the crease.

(f) Time Wasting by Batsmen
Other than in exceptional circumstances, the batsman should always be ready to take strike when the bowler is ready to start his run-up.

INTERNATIONAL CRICKET CONFERENCE

On June 15, 1909, representatives of cricket in England, Australia and South Africa met at Lord's and founded the Imperial Cricket Conference. Membership was confined to the governing bodies of cricket in countries within the British Commonwealth where Test cricket was played. India, New Zealand and West Indies were elected as members on May 31, 1926, Pakistan on July 21, 1953, and Sri Lanka on July 21, 1981. South Africa ceased to be a member of the ICC on leaving the British Commonwealth in May, 1961.

On July 15, 1965, the Conference was renamed the International Cricket Conference and new rules were adopted to permit the election of countries from outside the British Commonwealth.

CONSTITUTION

Chairman: The President of MCC for the time being or his nominee.
Secretary: The Secretary of MCC.
Foundation members: United Kingdom and Australia.
Full members: India, New Zealand, West Indies, Pakistan and Sri Lanka.
Associate members*: Argentina (1974), Bangladesh (1977), Bermuda (1966), Canada (1968), Denmark (1966), East Africa (1966), Fiji (1965), Gibraltar (1969), Hong Kong (1969), Israel (1974), Kenya (1981), Malaysia (1967), Netherlands (1966), Papua New Guinea (1973), Singapore (1974), USA (1965), West Africa (1976) and Zimbabwe (1981).
Affiliate members*: Bahamas (1987), France (1987), Italy (1984), Switzerland (1985).

* Year of election shown in parentheses.

MEMBERSHIP

The following governing bodies for cricket shall be eligible for election.

Foundation Members: The governing bodies for cricket in the United Kingdom and Australia are known as Foundation Members, and while being Full Members of the Conference such governing bodies have certain additional rights as set out in the rules of the Conference.

Full Members: The governing body for cricket recognised by the Conference of a country, or countries associated for cricket purposes, of which the representative teams are accepted as qualified to play official Test matches.

Associate Members: The governing body for cricket recognised by the Conference of a country, or countries associated for cricket purposes, not qualifying as Full Members but where cricket is firmly established and organised.

Chairman: J. Buzaglo (*Gibraltar*). *Deputy Chairman:* K. R. Bullock (*Canada*). *Hon. Treasurer:* G. Davis (Israel).

TEST MATCHES

1. Duration of Test Matches

Within a maximum of 30 hours' playing time, the duration of Test matches shall be a matter for negotiation and agreement between the two countries in any particular series of Test matches.

When agreeing the Playing Conditions prior to the commencement of a Test series, the participating countries may:

(a) Extend the playing hours of the last Test beyond the limit of 30 hours, in a series in which, at the conclusion of the penultimate match, one side does not hold a lead of more than one match.

(b) Allow an extension of play by one hour on any of the first four days of a Test match, in the event of play being suspended for one hour or more on that day, owing to weather interference.

(c) Play on the rest day, conditions and circumstances permitting, should a full day's play be lost on either the second or third scheduled days of play.

(d) Make up time lost in excess of five minutes in each day's play owing to circumstances outside the game, other than acts of God.

Note. The umpires shall determine when such time shall be made up. This could, if conditions and circumstances permit, include the following day.

2. Qualification Rules

A cricketer is qualified to play in a Test match or one-day international either by birth or residence.

(a) Qualification by birth. A cricketer, unless debarred by the Conference, is always eligible to play for the country of his birth.

(b) Qualification by residence. A cricketer, unless debarred by the Conference, shall be eligible to play for any country in which he is residing and has been residing during the four immediately preceding years, provided that he has not played for the country of his birth during that period.

Note. Notwithstanding anything hereinbefore contained, any player who has once played in a Test match or one-day international for any country shall not afterwards be eligible to play in a Test match or one-day international against that country, without the consent of its governing body.

FIRST-CLASS MATCHES

1. Definitions

(a) A match of three or more days' duration between two sides of eleven players officially adjudged first-class shall be regarded as a first-class fixture.

(b) In the following Rules the term "governing body" is restricted to Foundation Members, Full Members and Associate Members of the conference.

2. Rules

(a) Foundation and Full Members of the ICC shall decide the status of matches of three or more days' duration played in their countries.

(b) In matches of three or more days' duration played in countries which are not Foundation Members or Full Members of the ICC:

    (i) If the visiting team comes from a country which is a Foundation or Full Member of the ICC, that country shall decide the status of matches.

    (ii) If the visiting team does not come from a country which is a Foundation or Full Member of the ICC, or is a Commonwealth team composed of players from different countries, the ICC shall decide the status of matches.

Notes

(a) Governing bodies agree that the interest of first-class cricket will be served by ensuring that first-class status is *not* accorded to any match in which one or other of the teams taking part cannot on a strict interpretation of the definition be adjudged first-class.

(b) In case of any disputes arising from these Rules, the Secretary of the ICC shall refer the matter for decision to the Conference, failing unanimous agreement by postal communication being reached.

3. First-class Status

The following matches shall be regarded as first-class, subject to the provisions of Definitions (a) being completely complied with:

(a) In the British Isles and Eire
The following matches of three or more days' duration shall automatically be considered first-class:

   (i) County Championship matches.

   (ii) Official representative tourist matches from Full Member countries unless specifically excluded.

   (iii) MCC v any first-class county.

   (iv) Oxford v Cambridge and either University against first-class counties.

   (v) Scotland v Ireland.

(b) In Australia

   (i) Sheffield Shield matches.

   (ii) Matches played by teams representing states of the Commonwealth of Australia between each other or against opponents adjudged first-class.

(c) In India

   (i) Ranji Trophy matches.

   (ii) Duleep Trophy matches.

   (iii) Irani Trophy matches.

   (iv) Matches played by teams representing state or regional associations affiliated to the Board of Control between each other or against opponents adjudged first-class.

   (v) All three-day matches played against representative visiting sides.

(d) In New Zealand

   (i) Shell Trophy matches.

   (ii) Matches played by teams representing major associations of the North and South Islands against opponents adjudged first-class.

(e) In Pakistan

   (i) Matches played by teams representing divisional associations affiliated to the Board of Control, between each other or against teams adjudged first-class.

   (ii) Matches between the divisional associations and the Universities past and present XI.

   (iii) Quaid-e-Azam Trophy matches.

   (iv) BCCP Patron's Trophy Tournament matches.

   (v) PACO Cup matches.

   (vi) BCCP President's Cup Championship matches.

(f) In Sri Lanka

   (i) Matches of three days or more against touring sides adjudged first-class.

(g) In West Indies

   (i) Matches played by teams representing Barbados, Guyana, Jamaica, Trinidad, the Windward Islands and the Leeward Islands, either for the Shell Shield or against other opponents adjudged first-class.

   (ii) The final of the inter-county tournament in Guyana between Berbice, Demerara and Essequibo.

(h) In all Foundation and Full Member countries represented on the Conference

   (i) Test matches and matches against teams adjudged first-class played by official touring teams.

   (ii) Official Test Trial matches.

   (iii) Special matches between teams adjudged first-class by the governing body or bodies concerned.

QUALIFICATION AND REGISTRATION

Regulations Governing the Qualification and Registration of Cricketers in
Test and Competitive County Cricket

1. QUALIFICATIONS FOR ENGLAND

Subject to the overriding discretion of the Test and County Cricket Board, acting with the
consent of the International Cricket Conference, the qualifications for playing for England shall
be:

(a) That the cricketer was born in the British Isles; or

(b) That the cricketer's father or mother was born in the British Isles and that he himself is
residing and has been resident therein during the preceding four consecutive years; or

(c) That the cricketer is residing and has been resident in the British Isles during the
preceding seven consecutive years; or

(d) That the cricketer is residing and has been resident in the British Isles during the
preceding four consecutive years and since the day before his fourteenth birthday.

All these qualifications apply only if the cricketer has not played for any other country in a
Test match or (if the Board so decides) any other international match during the specified period
of residence or in the case of (a) during the previous four years.

In the case of (b), if the cricketer has played first-class cricket in his country of origin before
commencing his period of residence in the British Isles, the four-year period shall be increased
to such number of years (not exceeding seven) as equals four years plus one year for each season
of first-class cricket he played in his country of origin. In the case of (b) and (c), if, following the
commencement of his period of residence in the British Isles, the cricketer plays first-class
cricket in his country of origin (other than as an overseas cricketer in circumstances approved
by the Board), then if previously qualified for England under (b) or (c) he shall cease to be so
qualified. If he was in the course of acquiring residential qualification, his period of residence in
the British Isles shall be treated as terminated, and a new period of residence will be required.

It is also required that the player shall have made a declaration in writing to the Board that it
is his desire and intention to play for England and in (b), (c) and (d) that he shall be a British or
Irish citizen.

2. QUALIFICATIONS FOR REGISTRATION FOR COMPETITIVE COUNTY CRICKET

(a) A cricketer qualified for England shall only be qualified for registration for:

(i) The county of his birth.
(ii) The county in which he is residing and has been resident for the previous twelve
consecutive months.
(iii) The county for which his father regularly played.

(b) In addition, a cricketer qualified for England shall be qualified for registration for a
county if:

(i) He has none of the above qualifications for any county and is not registered for
one; or

(ii) Although qualified for and/or registered by one or more counties, the county or
counties concerned have confirmed in writing that they do not wish to register him
or retain his registration.

This paragraph (b), however, will not permit registration of a player who has been under
contract to a county for the previous season and has failed to accept the offer of a new
contract for the new season. It does not prevent his application for a Special Registration.

3. REGISTRATION

Normally new registrations take place during the close season, but in exceptional circumstances
a county may apply to register a player in the course of a season.

No cricketer may be registered for more than one county at any one time or, subject to the overriding discretion of the Board, for more than one county during any one season. However, this shall not prevent a player qualified to play for England, and already registered for a minor county, from being registered for a first-class county with the consent of the minor county concerned, who will not lose his registration.

Except with the Board's approval no county may have registered for it more than 35 cricketers at any one time.

4. SPECIAL REGISTRATION

The qualification for county cricket may be wholly or partially waived by the Board and a cricketer qualified to play for England may be "specially registered" should the Board conclude that it would be in the best interest of competitive county cricket as a whole. For this purpose the Board shall have regard to the interests of the cricketer concerned and any other material considerations affecting the county concerned including, if applicable, the cricketer's age and the other Special Registrations of the county in previous years.

No application for Special Registration will be entertained in respect of a cricketer who has a contract of employment with another county in the absence of that county's consent, except during the period between January 1 and the start of the new season, if the cricketer's contract is due to expire in that period. However, in the instance of a player rejecting a new contract offered by his county, and insisting on moving, his registration will be regarded as "contested". A county may not make more than two contested registrations in any five years and not more than one in each twelve-month period.

5. CRICKETERS NOT QUALIFIED TO PLAY FOR ENGLAND

No county shall be entitled to play more than one unqualified cricketer in any competitive match, except where two unqualified cricketers were registered for the county on November 28, 1978 or if *bona fide* negotiations had been begun before that date and were completed before the 1979 season.

The player must have remained registered without a break and had a contract of employment with the county since the start of the 1979 season, except in any season during which he was a member of an official touring team to the British Isles.

Although there is no restriction on the number of unqualified cricketers who may be registered by a county, it is the Board's policy that in normal circumstances *not more than two unqualified cricketers should be registered by any one county.*

If a registered overseas player is invited to play for his country for the whole or part of a tour of the British Isles, his county must release him and, except with the prior consent of the Board, may not play him during that tour.

Note: A citizen of a country within the European Economic Community, although he is not qualified to play for England, is not regarded as an unqualified cricketer for the purposes of registration, provided he satisfies the requirements as set out in Regulation 1 (except that for "British Isles" read "EEC").

6. NEGOTIATIONS BETWEEN COUNTIES AND CRICKETERS

No county may approach or be involved in discussions with any unregistered cricketer who is not qualified for that county with a view to offering him a trial or registering him:

  (i) During the currency of a season without having given not less than fourteen days' previous notice in writing; or

  (ii) During the close season without having given notice in writing

to any county for which he is qualified for registration by virtue of birth or residence before making any such approach or engaging in any such discussions.

No county may approach or be involved in discussions with any cricketer under the age of sixteen on April 15 in the current year, unless the cricketer is qualified for registration by that county or is not qualified for registration by any other first-class county.

7. RESIDENCE

A player does not interrupt his qualifying period of residence by undertaking government service or occasional winter work for business reasons outside the county in which his residence is situated.

The qualifying period cannot run while the cricketer has a contract with or is registered by another county.

MAIN RULES AND PLAYING CONDITIONS
OF LIMITED-OVERS COMPETITIONS

The following rules, playing conditions and variations of the Laws of Cricket are common to all three county competitions – the Benson and Hedges Cup (55 overs a side), the NatWest Bank Trophy (60 overs) and the Refuge Assurance League (40 overs):

Status of Matches

Matches shall not be considered first-class.

Declarations

No declarations may be made at any time.

Restriction on Placement of Fieldsmen

At the instant of delivery a minimum of four fieldsmen (plus the bowler and wicket-keeper) must be within an area bounded by two semi-circles centred on each middle stump (each with a radius of 30 yards) and joined by a parallel line on each side of the pitch. In the event of an infringement, the square-leg umpire shall call "No-ball". The fielding circle should be marked by painted white "dots" at five-yard intervals.

Fieldsman Leaving the Field

In addition to Law 2.8, a player who suffers an injury caused by an external blow (e.g. not a pulled muscle) and has to leave the field for medical attention may bowl immediately on his return.

Mode of Delivery

No bowler may deliver the ball under-arm.

Limitation of Overs by Any One Bowler

No bowler may deliver more than one fifth of the allocated overs, except that where the total of overs is not divisible by five, an additional over shall be allowed to the minimum number of bowlers necessary to make up the balance.

Wide-ball – Judging a Wide

Umpires are instructed to apply a very strict and consistent interpretation in regard to the Law in order to prevent negative bowling wide of the wicket or over the batsman's head.

The following criteria should be adopted as a guide to umpires:

   1. If the ball passes either side of the wicket sufficiently wide to make it virtually impossible for the striker to play a "normal cricket stroke" both from where he is standing and from where he should normally be standing at the crease, the umpire shall call and signal "Wide".

   2. If the ball passes over head-height of the striker standing upright at the crease, the umpire shall call and signal "Wide".

Note: The above provisions do not apply if the striker makes contact with the ball.

The Bowling of Fast, Short-pitched Balls

A bowler shall be limited to one fast, short-pitched ball per over. If he bowls a second, the umpire shall call and signal "No ball". If the bowler is no-balled a second time in the innings for the same offence, the bowler shall be warned, and after a further offence he shall be taken off and not allowed to bowl again in the innings.

RULES COMMON TO THE BENSON AND HEDGES CUP AND THE NATWEST BANK TROPHY

The Result
1. *A Tie.*

In the event of a tie, the following shall apply:
  (i) The side taking the greater number of wickets shall be the winner.
  (ii) If both sides are all out, the side with the higher overall scoring-rate shall be the winner.
  (iii) If the result cannot be decided by either of the first two methods, the winner shall be the side with the higher rate after 30 overs or, if still equal, after twenty or, if still equal, after ten.

2. *Unfinished Match*

If a match remains unfinished after the allocated number of days, the winner shall be the side which has scored the faster in runs per over throughout the innings, provided that at least twenty overs have been bowled at the side batting second. If the scoring-rate is the same, the side losing fewer wickets in the first twenty overs of each innings shall be the winner.

If, however, at any time on the last day the umpires are satisfied that there is insufficient time remaining to achieve a definite result or, where applicable, for the side batting second to complete its maximum number of overs, they shall order a new match to be started, allowing an equal number of overs per side (minimum ten overs per side) bearing in mind the time remaining for play until scheduled close of play. In this event, team selection for the new match will be restricted to the eleven players and twelfth man originally chosen, unless authorised otherwise in advance by the Secretary of the Board. If, however, the team batting second has received twenty overs or more when the umpires decide that there is insufficient time remaining to achieve a definite result, the match shall not be resumed nor shall a new match be started.

In the event of no result being obtained within this rule, the captains should agree, if circumstances (outdoors or indoors) permit, to a bowling contest to achieve a result, five cricketers from each team to bowl overarm, two deliveries each, at three stumps at a distance of 22 yards. The team scoring the greater number of hits shall be the winner. If the scores are equal, the same cricketers will bowl one ball each alternately to achieve a result on a "sudden death" basis. If circumstances make this form of contest impossible, the match shall be decided by the toss of a coin, except in a Benson and Hedges zonal match which shall be declared to have "No Result".

3. *Over-rates*

All teams are expected to complete the bowling of their overs within an allotted playing time. In the event of their failing to do so, the full quota of overs will be completed but the fielding team will be fined £100 per over which it has failed to bowl in the allotted time. If the innings is limited in advance, the calculations will be revised accordingly.

RULES AND PLAYING CONDITIONS APPLYING ONLY TO THE BENSON AND HEDGES CUP

Duration of Play

The matches, of 55 overs per side, will be completed in one day, if possible, but two days will be allocated for zonal league matches and three days for knockout matches in case of weather interference. Matches started on Saturday but not completed may only be continued on Sunday with the approval of the Board.

Normal hours will be 11 a.m. to 7.00 p.m. (7.30 p.m. from 1988). The umpires may order extra time if they consider a finish can be obtained on any day.

Over-rates

The allotted playing-time for completing 55 overs is 3 hours, 25 minutes.

Qualification of Players

The University qualification will take precedence in respect of those players who are also qualified for county clubs and no cricketer may play for more than one team in the same year's competition.

Scoring System

In the zonal league matches the winning team scores two points. In a "no result" match each side scores one point.

   If two or more teams in any zone finish with an equal number of points, their position in the table shall be based on the faster run-rate in all zonal league matches. This is calculated by balls bowled, divided by runs scored.

RULES AND PLAYING CONDITIONS APPLYING ONLY TO THE NATWEST BANK TROPHY

Duration and hours of play

The matches, of 60 overs per side, will be completed in one day, if possible, but three days will be allocated in case of weather interference.

   Cup Final only: If the match starts not less than half an hour late, owing to weather or the state of the ground, and not more than one and a half hours late, each innings shall be limited to 50 overs. If, however, the start is delayed for more than one and a half hours, the 60-over limit shall apply.

   Normal hours will be 10.30 a.m. to 7.10 p.m. (7.30 p.m. from 1988). The umpires may order extra time if, in their opinion, a finish can be obtained on any day.

   The captains of the teams in the final shall be warned that heavy shadows may move across the pitch towards the end of the day and that no appeal against the light will be considered in such circumstances.

Over-rates

The allotted playing-time for completing 60 overs is 3 hours, 45 minutes.

RULES AND PLAYING CONDITIONS APPLYING ONLY TO THE REFUGE ASSURANCE LEAGUE

Hours of play

Normal hours of play shall be 2.00–7.00 p.m. (1.30–6.30 for televised matches) with a tea interval of twenty minutes at the end of the over in progress at 4.20 p.m. (3.50 for televised matches), or between innings, whichever is the earlier. The duration and time of the tea interval can be varied in the case of an interrupted match. Close of play shall normally be at 7.00 p.m. (6.30 for televised matches) but play may continue after that time if, in the opinion of the umpires, the overs remaining can be completed by 7.10 p.m. (6.40 p.m.)

Length of Innings

   (i) In an uninterrupted match:

      (a) Each side shall bat for 40 overs unless all out earlier.

      (b) If the side fielding first fails to bowl 40 overs by 4.20 p.m. (3.50 for televised matches), the over shall be completed and the side batting second shall receive the same number of overs as their opponents.

      (c) If the team batting first is all out within two minutes of the scheduled time for the tea interval, the innings of the side batting second shall be limited to the same number of overs as their opponents have received, the over in which the last wicket falls to count as a complete over.

(ii) In matches where the start is delayed or play is suspended:

(a) The object shall be to rearrange the number of overs so that both teams may receive the same number of overs (minimum ten each). The calculation of the overs to be bowled shall be based on an average rate of one over per $3\frac{1}{2}$ minutes or part thereof in the time remaining before 7.00 p.m. (6.30 p.m. for televised matches).

(b) If at the start is delayed by not more than an hour and the match is thereby reduced to no fewer than 31 overs a side, the time of the close of the first innings shall be fixed allowing $3\frac{1}{2}$ minutes for each over. If the team fielding first fails to bowl the revised number of overs by the agreed time, the principles set out in (i) b and c shall apply.

(c) Where play is suspended after the match has started on the basis of each team batting for more than twenty overs, the number of overs should be rearranged so that both teams may bat for the same number of overs (minimum of 20 each); the calculation as above.

(d) If, owing to a suspension of play during or immediately prior to the start of the innings of the team batting second, it is not possible for that team to have the opportunity of batting for the same number of overs (minimum 20 overs) as their opponents, they will bat for a number of overs to be calculated as above. The team batting second shall not bat for a greater number of overs than their opponents unless the latter have been all out in fewer than the agreed number of overs.

(e) If there is insufficient time to provide for a match as above (20 overs minimum), that match shall be void and, conditions permitting, a new match of ten overs each side shall be played provided play begins no later than 5.40 p.m. (5.10 for televised matches). If there is any suspension of play during the ten-overs match, it will be abandoned as a "No result".

(f) In the event of play being suspended in a match which began on the basis of each team batting for less than 20 overs (ten overs minimum), that match shall be void and, conditions permitting, a new match of ten overs per side shall be played as described in (e) above.

Over-rates

In uninterrupted matches or matches of not less than 31 overs per team, which are not subsequently interrupted, the team fielding first will be fined £100 for each over below the full quota bowled by the scheduled time for the tea interval and the team fielding second for each over below the full quota bowled by the scheduled time for the close of play. In matches of less than 31 overs, or in the event of interruptions after the start of play, teams will be expected to achieve a rate of eighteen overs per hour but no automatic fine will be imposed.

The Result

(i) Where both sides have had the opportunity to bat for the same number of overs and the scores are level, the result is a tie, no account being taken of the number of wickets which have fallen.

(ii) If, owing to suspension of play, the number of overs in the innings of the side batting second has to be revised, their target score, which they must exceed to win the match, shall be calculated by multiplying the revised number of overs by the average runs per over scored by the side batting first. If the target score involves a fraction, the final scores cannot be equal and the result cannot be a tie.

(iii) If a match is abandoned before the side batting second has received its allotted number of overs, the result shall be decided on the average run-rate throughout both innings, provided the team batting second has received not less than twenty overs.

(iv) If a result cannot be achieved as above, the match shall be declared "No result".

(v) If the team batting first has been all out without using its full quota of overs, the calculation of the run-rate shall be based on the full quota of overs to which it was entitled.

Scoring of points

(i) The team winning a match to score four points.

(ii) In a "tie" each team to score two points.

(iii) In a "No Result" match each team to score two points.

(iv) If two or more teams finish with an equal number of points for any of the first four places, their final positions will be decided by:

(a) The most wins or, if still equal

(b) The most away wins or, if still equal

(c) The higher run-rate throughout the season.

MEETINGS IN 1987

TCCB SPRING MEETING

At its Spring Meeting, held at Lord's on March 5, the TCCB appointed M. J. Stewart as England Team Manager for three years from April 1, 1987. Mr Stewart at the same time was appointed an England selector to join P. B. H. May (chairman), P. J. Sharpe and F. J. Titmus; A. C. Smith, the fourth selector in 1986, had since become Chief Executive of the TCCB. The appointment of an England Team Manager, which had the consent of all the counties, was seen as a way of building on the success achieved in Australia during the winter and of achieving continuity. During the season in England, the Chairman of Selectors would adopt the role filled on tour by the Tour Manager.

The meeting agreed, by a small majority, to pitches remaining uncovered in County Championship matches, but during the hours of play only and with the ends and run-ups being covered in the event of rain. It was hoped that this would encourage batsmen to develop better techniques and make the game more varied. A suggestion that only bowling bonus points be awarded in County Championship matches was rejected. The meeting did, however, approve a motion to the ICC to restrict short-pitched bowling, improve over-rates in Test cricket and, from 1990, limit bowlers' run-ups to 30 yards. The meeting stated that it was unhappy at any increase in the contested movement of players between counties. Recommendations would be made by the Registration Committee to the Summer Meeting to restrict moves that were not mutually agreeable to counties. With regard to qualification for England, a working party would consider this with a view to bringing England's period of qualification more into line with that permitted by the ICC.

INTERNATIONAL CRICKET CONFERENCE

A Special Meeting of the International Cricket Conference was held at Lord's on June 26 to discuss the position of cricketers who have sporting links with South Africa. West Indies proposed and India seconded a resolution that "Anyone who is now, or who may hereafter become qualified to participate in a match involving a member country of ICC, who on or after the date hereof makes or continues to have any sporting contact with South Africa shall be ineligible to participate in any match in a member country of ICC (save and except in the domestic cricket of a country if permitted by that country) or against any member country of ICC." Initially it had been expected that Zimbabwe would second the resolution, but alterations to the rules of ICC have to be proposed and seconded by Foundation and Full Member countries. The resolution was discussed at length, and it was the opinion of the meeting that the proposal contained a number of anomalies in the form expressed. Consequently an amended resolution was proposed by West Indies and seconded by Australia.

"Recognising the need to address the problem of cricketers having sporting contact with South Africa, it was resolved that the substance of the West Indies resolution be referred to a Select Committee of ICC, comprising one representative from each Foundation and Full Member, three representatives from the Associate Members [Gibraltar, Canada and Zimbabwe] and with the chairman of ICC as chairman of the committee, to produce a report by March 31, 1988 to enable the issue to be considered at the 1988 Annual Meeting of the International Cricket Conference. The committee will hold its first meeting in August 1987 with a second meeting in India during the World Cup and such subsequent meetings as are necessary." That amended resolution was carried unanimously and it was agreed that the original resolution by West Indies be left on the table. All Full Members were present at the meeting with the exception of New Zealand, who were represented. Of the Associate Members, Israel, Kenya and West Africa were not represented.

TCCB SUMMER MEETING

At its Summer Meeting, held at Lord's on July 31, the TCCB acted to stop the increase in the contested movement of cricketers between counties. In future, each first-class county shall, on or before September 20, send to the Board and to the other first-class counties a list of all cricketers who have a contract to play for it for the whole of the next season or, having had a contract in the season just ended, have been offered a contract for the next season (List I), and a list of all other cricketers who have had a contract with the county for the season just ended (List II). Should another county wish to register a cricketer who appears on List I, and that registration is contested by his current county, the application will be treated as one for Extraordinary Registration. Except in circumstances considered exceptional by the Board, no county shall be permitted more than one Extraordinary Registration in any twelve-month period or more than two in any five years. The meeting also overturned a decision made at the Board's 1986 Winter Meeting to do away with the quarter-finals in the league/knockout competition after 1987. It was decided to retain the present format.

INTERNATIONAL CRICKET CONFERENCE

At the Annual Meeting of the International Cricket Conference, held at Lord's on August 17, 18, it was agreed that from April 1, 1988 a minimum of fifteen overs an hour be bowled in Test cricket, the decision to be implemented first as an experimental rule for two or three years before being passed as a permanent one. The resolution, proposed by England and seconded by New Zealand, was passed by six votes to one (West Indies). However, the Conference took no action on the proposals by England to restrict short-pitched bowling in Test cricket to one such ball an over – save to urge umpires to enforce Law 42.8 – and to limit bowlers' run-ups to 30 yards from 1990. By nineteen votes to ten, the meeting did rule that five matches played in New Zealand in 1947-48 by the national Fiji team, captained by P. A. Snow, should be regarded as first-class, so overruling the original decision of the New Zealand Cricket Council. The five matches in question were the two against Auckland and those against Canterbury, Otago and Wellington. Member countries were asked to examine the machinery, role and method of the ICC's operations and have proposals ready for consideration at the 1988 Annual Meeting.

TCCB WINTER MEETING

At its Winter Meeting, held at Lord's on December 10, the TCCB reverted to the playing conditions which applied prior to 1987 with regard to the covering of pitches in the County Championship. In 1988, pitches will again be fully covered in the event of rain during the hours of play. Following the recommendations of its working party on the period of qualification for England, the Board reduced this from ten years to seven, the ruling being retrospective to the time when a player began his qualification period. The meeting, expressing concern at the increase in the use of substitute fielders, ruled that no substitute may take the field for five overs after a cricketer leaves it, no matter what the reason for his departure. The five-over period is not made null by any interval or close of play. A cricketer leaving the field may not bat for one to five overs, according to the length of his absence, or until five wickets have fallen, whichever is the sooner. To prevent time-wasting, protective equipment other than helmets, once on the field, must be worn until the fall of a wicket or until a natural break in play. In the two limited-overs knockout competitions, the time of the close of play when a result is not possible on that day will be 7.30 p.m. rather than 7.00/7.10 p.m. as previously. In the new Refuge Assurance Cup competition, it was agreed that an orange ball would be used.

UMPIRES FOR 1988

TEST MATCH UMPIRES

The panel for the Cornhill Test matches in 1988 between England and West Indies and England and Sri Lanka shows two changes from that of 1987. J. W. Holder, who played for Hampshire as a fast-medium bowler from 1968 to 1972 and has been on the first-class list since 1983, and N. T. Plews, on the first-class list since 1982, have replaced B. J. Meyer and A. G. T. Whitehead. However, Meyer joins the seven Test match umpires on the panel for the Texaco Trophy limited-overs internationals. The panel for the Test matches is: H. D. Bird, J. Birkenshaw, D. J. Constant, J. W. Holder, K. E. Palmer, N. T. Plews and D. R. Shepherd.

FIRST-CLASS UMPIRES

J. C. Balderstone, the former Yorkshire and Leicestershire batsman who played twice for England in 1976, and J. D. Bond, the former Lancashire captain and manager, come on to the first-class list for 1988 in place of J. A. Jameson, who has been appointed coach of Sussex, and D. Lloyd, who has joined the TCCB to promote Kwik Cricket. V. A. Holder, the former Worcestershire and West Indies fast bowler, K. Taylor, the former Yorkshire and England batsman, and R. C. Tolchard have gone on to the Reserve list. The full list is: J. C. Balderstone, H. D. Bird, J. Birkenshaw, J. D. Bond, D. J. Constant, B. Dudleston, D. G. L. Evans, J. H. Hampshire, J. H. Harris, J. W. Holder, A. Jones, R. Julian, M. J. Kitchen, B. Leadbeater, K. J. Lyons, B. J. Meyer, D. O. Oslear, K. E. Palmer, R. Palmer, N. T. Plews, D. R. Shepherd, R. A. White, A. G. T. Whitehead and P. B. Wight. *Reserves:* P. J. Eele, B. Hassan, V. A. Holder, H. J. Rhodes, K. Taylor, D. S. Thompsett and R. C. Tolchard.

MINOR COUNTIES UMPIRES

P. Adams, N. P. Atkins, K. Bray, C. J. Chapman, D. J. Dennis, R. H. Duckett, D. Fawkner-Corbett, W. H. Gillingham, D. J. Halfyard, D. B. Harrison, B. Knight, T. Lynan, G. I. McLean, T. G. A. Morley, D. Norton, M. K. Reed, K. S. Shenton, C. Smith, C. T. Spencer, G. A. Stickley, A. R. Tayler, R. C. Tolchard, R. Walker, T. V. Wilkins, R. T. Wilson and T. G. Wilson. *Reserves:* R. Bell, P. Brown, K. Coburn, R. K. Curtis, R. F. Elliott, R. G. Evans, J. B. Foulkes, P. Gray, M. A. Johnson, R. Pattinson, J. B. Seward, T. P. Stevens, J. Stobart, J. H. Symons and J. D. Thornton.

ERRATA

WISDEN, 1984

Page 450   In the Essex first innings, the 6th wicket fell at 118, not 112.
Page 780   The record partnership for the 9th wicket was:

88 S. N. Hartley and A. Ramage, Yorkshire v Middlesex at Lord's, 1982.

This amendment applies also to page 844 of Wisden 1983; a new record was set in 1984.

WISDEN, 1985

Page 915   In the First Test, R. M. H. Binny's bowling analysis was 18–2–42–0, not 18–3–72–0.

WISDEN, 1986

Page 284   I. T. Botham was 5th out at 160, not 6th as stated.
Page 296   When D. I. Gower reached his hundred, he had hit only nine boundaries, not fifteen.
Page 740   Middlesex beat Derbyshire by virtue of achieving a revised target of 121 (30 overs), not as stated. See also page 704.
Page 733   In Lancashire v Hampshire, J. Abrahams was c Connor b Tremlett.

WISDEN, 1987

Page 156   The recent instances of hat-tricks omit the following:
G. S. le Roux ⎱ South Africa v Australian XI at Johannesburg, 1985-86.
C. E. B. Rice ⎰
Page 273   M. W. Gatting's 183* was v India, not New Zealand.
Page 304   The match between India and Pakistan at Harrogate was not the first in England between the two countries.
Page 326   G. A. Gooch was at second slip when he caught B. A. Edgar, not first slip.
Page 327   M. W. Gatting reached his hundred in 239 minutes, not 288.
Page 328   K. R. Rutherford's 317 was the fourth-highest score by a New Zealander, not the third. The list omits B. Sutcliffe's 385 in 1952-53.
Page 404   G. R. Cowdrey, not C. S. Cowdrey, played for Kent v Glamorgan. C. J. Tavaré was Kent's captain.
Page 564   M. A. Feltham was c Smith, not Hick.
Page 580   The Middlesex captain was P. R. Downton. This applies also on page 629.
Page 589   D. L. Amiss in the first innings was c Radford b Patel.
Page 602   S. J. Rhodes was capped by Worcestershire in 1986.
Page 610   D. B. D'Oliveira in the first innings scored 5 and extras were 6 (L-b 1, n-b 5).
Page 614   A. L. Jones in the first innings was c Hick, not D'Oliveira.
Page 620   D. J. Makinson was c Sidebottom, not Bairstow.
Page 677   Lancashire's 4th wicket fell at 59, not 57, making the partnership between C. H. Lloyd and S. J. O'Shaughnessy 99, not 101.
Page 678   D. A. Reeve took four wickets for 12 runs in 45 balls, not 25.
Page 955   Sri Lanka's total of 479 was not their highest score in Test cricket (491-7 dec. v England, Lord's, 1984); it was, however, their highest v Pakistan.
Page 957   R. L. Dias resumed at 110, not 170.
Page 1140   In the match at Jodhpur on November 17, 18, 19, Vidarbha batted first and third, Rajasthan second and fourth. Because of the playing conditions in Indian domestic cricket, which provide for the addition of penalty points for slow over-rates, Rajasthan won by 9 runs, despite batting last.

CRICKET BOOKS, 1987

By JOHN ARLOTT

The review, of 91 cricket titles, contains the largest number of outstanding contributions to the literature of the game issued in a single year. That is not reckoned since the beginning of this feature in *Wisden*, but through the history of cricket writing, judged by the authoritative *Bibliography* of E. W. Padwick. These publications embrace a number of quite unique contributions to writings on cricket, and the quality is uniformly high. One criticism that may be made is of the number of books – not including the best – which carry no indices; that, of course, is not necessarily the fault of the authors but may often be explained by the parsimony of publishers.

The first title to call for examination is *Pageant of Cricket* (Macmillan; £30; de luxe edition of 200 copies, signed by the author and the writer of the foreword, £225), by David Frith, with a foreword by Sir Donald Bradman. This is a quite mighty and unique publication. It cannot be called simply a picture book, although it has an amazing range of 2,000 illustrations, for it has 120,000 words of completely relevant text within its 640 generous pages. It is difficult to resist the conclusion that this represents the peak of one man's – though not a narrowly personal – collection and study of the game. It is most impressively and unusually free from national bias; international in scope, and wide ranging in its type of illustration – in black and white and some fine colour – from reproduction of early paintings through to modern photographs. The text, a historical survey of cricket from the earliest days to the present, is the writing of a man deeply steeped in the literature of cricket. If the illustrations represent many years of collection, the accompanying history indicates long and patient study. The entire text is absorbing; the details interesting, valuable and often unusual. The true follower of cricket will find many hours of diversion and information in this book, which must stand alone on the shelves of the game.

Cricket Facts and Feats (Guinness; £11.95), by Bill Frindall, is both human and accurate, a sound work of reference which is almost compellingly easy to read. It is divided into early references; Test cricket; first-class cricket in Britain, Australia, South Africa, West Indies, New Zealand, India, Pakistan and Sri Lanka; first-class career records; women's cricket, limited-overs cricket, minor cricket, curiosities and a glossary. Legibly as well as attractively laid out, it is most intelligently indexed. Nothing else of its kind is quite so good.

The Formative Years of Australian Cricket 1803-93 (Angus & Robertson; £14.95), by Jack Pollard, is the work of a recognised historian of the game in that country. It is concerned with the way in which cricket grew, intimately and closely, with the social life of the growing country. Indeed, it is something of a social history in itself. Illuminatingly, and sometimes surprisingly, illustrated, carefully researched, conscientiously documented, and dealing with cricket on all levels through those formative years, it is an original contribution to the history as well as the literature of the game.

Wills Book of Excellence: Cricket (Orient Longman Ltd; Rs130.00), by Mudar Patherya, is the finest international study of cricket to come out of India. The author is described as "the youngest serious cricket writer today" and the authoritative editor is M. A. K. Pataudi – still generally remembered in England as the younger Nawab of Pataudi. It provides the phase of early history, up to Sir Donald Bradman and "Bodyline"; "Between the Wars"; and then branches out to the post-war great cricketers, West Indies, the emergence of India, "Modern Masters", and one-day play. The uniformly sound history is lifted by revealingly fresh information for the English reader in a section on Indian cricket. Production throughout is good; the statistics are clearly laid out, the index well made, and the reproduction at times is quite outstanding. If a couple of Hambledon surnames are misspelt, who is to worry? This is an extremely handsome 208-page book reflecting great credit on those who produced it.

The bicentenary of MCC was marked in many ways, but the study authorised by the club itself – *Double Century* (Hodder and Stoughton; £14.95), by Tony Lewis – is one of the most impressive tributes. The extent of the author's research is at once apparent. It is a substantial, 375-page work, immaculately and generously illustrated. There have, of course, been several histories of both Lord's and MCC, but this should remain the reference on the club for many years. The colour illustrations are impressive and tasteful; the writing style is ideal in its blend of ease and certainty.

Simultaneously comes another appreciable work of cricket chronicle in *The History of the Sheffield Shield* (Unwin Hyman; £19.95), by Chris Harte. It runs to 365 generous quarto pages, and covers the period from the inaugural match at Adelaide in 1892 until March 1986. The method is chronological, with seasonal surveys. It includes all 1,157 matches played in the competition to its date, together with statistics, major records, league tables, a list of individual records of batting and bowling, and a useful bibliography. The illustrations are neat and appropriate, and the personal studies perceptive. Although most of the scores are summarised, some of the more historic are valuably given in full.

New South Wales versus Queensland (from the author, GPO Box 1355, Perth, WA 6001, Australia; $A10.50; available in England from Appleby's Books, 5 St John's Street, Keswick, Cumbria; £5 plus postage), by John King, is a statistical history of the complete series of first-class matches between the two states from 1893 to 1986-87. A 58-page octavo, it is the sixth of the author's surveys of Australian state cricket; a seventh volume will be published in 1988. Mr King is very thorough, and the statistics will please the hungriest fact-hunter.

CCI & The Brabourne Stadium (The Cricket Club of India Ltd, Dinsha Wachha Road, Bombay 400 20; available in England from Martin Wood, 2 St John's Road, Sevenoaks, Kent; £5.75 plus postage), by Vasant Raiji and Anandji Dossa, celebrates the Golden Jubilees of the Cricket Club of India and its historic ground. It is a 114-page work, arranged in chronological terms, and illustrated with a colour plate of the ground and, otherwise and relevantly, in black and white. The authors are members of the club, and friends who watched Lord Tennyson's team play the inaugural match at the stadium in December 1937. The statistics at the end list the office-bearers of the club, CCI season captains, club colours awarded for meritorious performances since 1941, and the famous players who have played on the ground – an imposing list indeed.

Back Page Cricket: A Century of Newspaper Coverage (Macdonald/Queen Anne Press; £13.95), by E. W. Swanton, edited by George Plumptre, is a collection, some of it from Mr Swanton's own writings, of press reporting on cricket over the century since it became news. From Test matches to public schools, from Jack Hobbs beating W. G. Grace's record number of hundreds to the triumphs of Ian Botham – and sometimes moving by right to the front page from the back page – cricket's historic achievements are mustered as they were reported at the time. The press photo illustrations present the game as it seemed within its contemporary background. This is an absorbing and often surprising account, most knowledgeably edited.

Women's Test Cricket – The Golden Triangle 1934-1984 (The Book Guild Ltd, Lewes, Sussex; £15.00), by Joan L. Hawes, is the first major history of that branch of the game. Alec Bedser suggests, in his foreword, that "One could say, [it is] the last genuine amateur team sport left". In 1934-35 England Women played those of Australia and New Zealand in Australia. That was the beginning of a three-cornered competition which celebrated its 50th anniversary in 1984. Although South Africa, West Indies and India subsequently joined in, this date was perfect for a historian. The author was a player for Surrey Ladies and England, and a member of the touring side to New Zealand and Australia in 1957-58. She retired from active play in 1963 but has since become a qualified NCA coach. This carefully documented 422-page history, with its most adequate statistics and biographical sketches, serves women's cricket and its players handsomely.

Between the Wickets: The Who and Why of the Best in Cricket (Living Media [India], 316 Competent House, F-14, Connaught Place, New Delhi 110 001, India; Rs125.00), by Surjit S. Bhalla, is a quite unique book. It is an attempt to computerise and rank cricket performances. Surjit S. Bhalla holds a doctorate in economics from Princeton University and, until recently, was a senior economist at the World Bank, Washington DC; he is, at the moment, a senior fellow at the Policy Group, a research institute in New Delhi. He is also an immense cricket enthusiast, who determined to reduce the standards of cricketing performances to computerised figures. His 196-page quarto attempts to rank the Test-cricket batsmen, bowlers and all-rounders of history – and as an aside, those of the contemporary game – in a way that the normal averages have never allowed. As a single key, and example, batsmen are arranged by country, number of Tests and innings, average proportion of individual score to team score, percentage of innings in which the batsman scored 50 or more runs, percentage of innings in which the batsman's score was less than 10 runs, innings played to score first 2,000 runs, consistency of scoring runs defined as standard deviation divided by means, and, finally, standard deviation and percentage of team score. Of course, and as the author constantly points out, pitch conditions must always affect, indeed control, these figures. So far from this being ignored, however, one crucial heading is "Dead wickets, dying cricket". Ultimately it is the unassessable factor, but the author has done his best to meet all but that in a study which will intrigue those who evaluate the game by its numbers. It is a brave attempt to reduce to figures the values of players which cricket followers have based on personality, team loyalty, country loyalty and period loyalty.

Cricket's Silver Lining 1864-1914 (Collins Willow; £15) is a presentation by David Rayvern Allen of "The 50 Years from the birth of *Wisden* to the beginning of the Great War". It is a sensitively selected anthology; obviously not hurried, but the product of studious and appreciative reading. It comes, as the author points out, from "a time when the written word was the sole means of reporting matches and before broadcasting destroyed much of the mystique of the legendary characters of the game". C. W. Alcock ("Cricket under Queen Victoria"), Colonel Philip Trevor, A. C. MacLaren – there is an interview with him and one with W. G. Grace – Alec Waugh; a wittily selected and largely punning series of quotations from Shakespeare; Andrew Lang, Sir Neville Cardus, George Giffen and Edmund Blunden: the combination results in a collection of considerable character. This has all the making of a long, contemplative read.

The Faber Book of Cricket (Faber & Faber; £9.95) is an anthology edited by Michael Davie and Simon Davie. The introduction explains: "We wanted to make plain cricket's connection with the rest of life. So we settled on mainly abstract categories." There are some 170 items, including prose and poetry, with a range of admirable authors. Mary Russell Mitford, Francis Thompson, John Nyren, H. G. Wells, J. M. Barrie, C. L. R. James, John Masefield, Sir Neville Cardus, Sir Donald Bradman, George Orwell, Dylan Thomas, R. C. Robertson-Glasgow and James Joyce are a substantial proportion, but by no means all, of the names of a distinguished list.

Benny Green has also mustered a list of eminent contributors for his collection, *The Lord's Companion* (Pavilion/Michael Joseph; £16.95). It is a 460-page volume which covers its subject in time, atmosphere, history and personalities. Mr Green sets out to demonstrate that it is a story of almost continuous change, moderated only by "the inevitability of gradualness". Once again he has proved himself an excellent collector of considerable trifles.

Cricket is only one of the themes of *Sporting Literature* (Oxford University Press; £12.50), an anthology chosen by Vernon Scannell. The section "Bat and Pad" includes prose and verse by William Blake, Lord Byron, Sir Arthur Conan Doyle, Sir Neville Cardus and Andrew Lang. It is a collection of much literary sensibility.

The Guardian Book of Cricket (Pavilion/Michael Joseph; £14.95), edited by Matthew Engel, is within its divisions a chronologically ordered history, with a thoughtful introduction by the editor. It runs from September 7, 1880, with "Our special correspondent at The Oval", reporting "England v Australia, the Inaugural Home Test", to Frank Keating on the sacking of David Gower as England's captain at Lord's in June 1986. The list of contributors is generous: Cardus, of course, Denys Rowbotham, Paul Fitzpatrick, David Lacey, Eric Todd, Ian Peebles, John Woodcock, Terence Prittie, Henry Blofeld, Arlott, and a host of delightfully reminiscent names attached to first-class reports – Alistair Cooke, Geoffrey Moorhouse, James Cameron, Roy Hattersley, A. C. MacLaren, Stanley Reynolds, Norman Shrapnel and Don Davies. It is an utterly nostalgic collection, easy to read, most sensitively made, and by no means without humour; in its shaping, a genuine reminder of history and a demonstration of the *Guardian's* many yet mutually sympathetic styles.

The Observer on Cricket (Unwin Hyman; £11.95), edited by Scyld Berry, is an anthology of cricket writings from that paper. It is happily dedicated to "All the sub-editors unknown and unthanked", after which comes a poem by John Snow (Sussex and England) "On Being Dropped". The sections are of profiles, portraits, matches, occasional pieces and obituaries. Outstanding authors are H. S. Altham, R. C. Robertson-Glasgow, Michael Davie, Ted Dexter, Ian Peebles, Hugh McIlvanney, D. J. Knight, D. R. Jardine, Frank Worrell, an extremely impressive Tony Pawson, Alan Ross, Frank Tyson, Len Hutton and the editor. This is yet another quite charming collection in a year of unusual riches of this kind.

Much Ado about Cricket (Brewin Books; £5.95) is an extremely personal collection and survey, made by Derek Salberg, who was director of the Alexandra Theatre in Birmingham and whose four previous books were

about the theatre. He begins with a basic history of the game but soon launches out into a literary, romantic and often poetic survey of players, Test match grounds and general ideas about the game. This is the work of a well-read cricket enthusiast, who has crammed into his 140 pages much feeling for the game. His readers will share the pleasure Mr Salberg undoubtedly enjoyed in compiling this salute.

Michael Marshall has called his *Gentlemen and Players* (Grafton; £14.95) "Conversations with cricketers", but it is more than that. It is atmospheric, historical and, in the "playing foreword" by E. R. Dexter and Trueman, F. S., relishably personal. There are statistical appendices, scorecards, and records of Gentlemen v Players; but overwhelmingly, and somewhat picturesquely, this is a record of nostalgia. It has a fair weight of reminiscence and anecdote, with photographs that will jog the longest memories in a memorial to an ended, but still unforgotten, phase of English cricket.

Essex County Cricket Club: The Official History (The Kingswood Press; £15.95), by David Lemmon and Mike Marshall, is a substantial and workmanlike history of that county from its earliest days, through undistinguished times in the Championship, to the period of success which began with the winning of the Benson and Hedges Cup in 1979. The authors are clearly close to their subject in knowledge and feeling. They write with enthusiasm but not with bias, with humour but not too lightly, in what is a cut above the usual county history. The illustrations are apt; the index and the statistics (the latter compiled by Leslie Newnham, who died shortly before publication of this book) are both models of their kind.

The Cricket Grounds of Leicestershire (Association of Cricket Statisticians) is another in the Association's scholarly and workmanlike series. The ground records are compiled by Dennis Lambert. It deals with 22 First XI grounds within the county, including six in Leicester itself, five in Loughborough and three each in Colville and Hinckley, as well as listing 21 where Second XI matches have been played. The eventual complete set of these studies will be a most scholarly addition to the bookshelf of county cricket.

A Guide to First-Class and Other Important Cricket Matches in North and South America (The Association of Cricket Statisticians, West Bridgford, Nottingham; £2.50) is a further move by the Association towards the completion of the file of first-class and major play throughout the world.

Purple Patches (Collins; £12.95), by Ralph Barker, is the type of study the author does very well. Here he selects and describes eleven major individual performances by various English and Australian cricketers. Included among them are Arthur Booth, Bill Johnston, Frank Tyson, Jim Laker and Bob Massie. As usual, he makes the studies instinct with character, and once again, too, he has constructed a good "read" full of true cricketing atmosphere.

In *The Great All-Rounders* (Crowood Press; £12.95), David Lemmon is once more thorough and interesting in his examination of the subject – from "the Yardstick", W. G. Grace, to "Both", Ian Botham. He writes with a good background of research. It is a readable history which covers the subject thoroughly in its 180 quarto pages and has good illustrations.

In *Fifty Incredible Cricket Matches* (Stanley Paul; £10.95), Patrick Murphy has produced a series of reconstructions from Oxford v Cambridge 1870 to Pakistan v West Indies at Faisalabad, 1986. He is another who has read of the game as he writes – enthusiastically. Not only has he produced an

extremely readable collection, he has also included some delightful surprises. Older followers of the game, in particular, will find some familiar names and echoes of pleasurable feats.

Another offering in this presently popular field of research and reconstruction is *Cricket Mercenaries* (Pavilion/Michael Joseph; £10.95), by David Lemmon. It is concerned with overseas players in the English county game. It begins with William Midwinter, who was, in fact, born in Gloucestershire and joined their county team in 1878, having already played in the first of all Test matches for Australia in the previous season. In a way, probably, Midwinter does not strictly belong in the category, but it would have been strange indeed to have left him out. The last of the arrivals referred to here is Martin Crowe; but the story obviously, soon and healthily, will be continued. This is an aspect of cricket rarely previously examined, and even constant observers of the English scene will from time to time be surprised by names they had forgotten.

The scholarly pattern is continued in *The Men in White Coats* (Stanley Paul; £10.95), a study of umpires and umpiring by Teresa McLean. The author was the first woman to be given a cricket Blue from both Oxford and Cambridge, and she is a practising umpire for both men's and women's cricket in East Anglia. She has long had an interest in umpiring and has reinforced it by research and observation. She quotes, relevantly and often divertingly, and provides some pleasant illustrations – not simply technical, but often amusing, such as the reproductions of cartoons from *Punch*. Essentially, though, this is to be read as a serious, historical study of a crucial branch of the game.

Cricket Impressions (The Kingswood Press; £12.95), by Adrian Murrell, is the work of an established and expert cricket photographer whose work will be well known to readers of *The Cricketer* magazine. Its main value is as a well-made collection of the author's photographs. He also includes notes on technical photographic terms and information, and writes interestingly on his professional problems in cricket. The collection is a catholic one; pleasing, absorbing and, of its kind, outstanding. It will find a permanent place in many cricket libraries.

Cricket Characters (Stanley Paul; £14.95) is a collection of the cricket caricatures of John Ireland, with an informed accompanying text by Christopher Martin-Jenkins. Divided into sections on batsmen, all-rounders, wicket-keepers, bowlers, umpires and commentators, the selection is entirely modern. The drawings are made with a splendid blend of perception and humour. Reproduction is in generous quarto and full colour. Virtually every one of the subjects is instantly recognisable; and wittily perceptive enough to raise a grin even in the artist's victims.

Early Books on Cricket (Europa Publications; £12), by David Rayvern Allen, is a neatly informative survey of cricket books up to the publication of Alfred Gaston's *Bibliography* in 1895. The author is at pains to point out that it does not claim in any way to compete with the encyclopaedic *Bibliography* of E. W. Padwick. This is for the collector; thorough but, nevertheless, a guide. The research has obviously been considerable but is lightly borne.

Abridge Cricket Club, a Celebration of 150 Seasons (The Secretary, Abridge Cricket Club, 63 Hatch Road, Pilgrims Hatch, Brentwood, Essex CM15 9PU; £4.50), by Derrick Ferguson and Alan Lister, is a 110-page quarto most splendidly reproduced in the calligraphy of Denis Ferguson. It is illustrated largely in reproduction of black and white photographs, neatly drawn maps,

and a single, impressive, colour photograph. A sound club history, it is both readable and pleasant to handle.

Castle Cary Cricket Club 1837-1987 (The Secretary, Castle Cary Cricket Club, Donald Pither Memorial Sports Ground, Castle Cary, Somerset; no price given) is sub-titled "A Collection of Memorabilia from the Club Archives to Celebrate 150 Years of Cricket in Somerset". It is a 50-page quarto, in attractive covers, with many entertaining discoveries from old files and local papers.

Coromandel Cricket Club, 125 Years, 1862 to 1987 (The Secretary, Coromandel CC, 13 Young Street, Blackwood, Adelaide 5051, South Australia; no price given), by R. Mableson and C. Griffin, celebrates an anniversary of one of the oldest clubs in Australia. A 35-page octavo, it has sectionalised historical phases, statistics, and a foreword by J. W. Hewett, whose family has served the club, in a playing or official capacity, for more than 100 of its years.

Cricket on the Green; 200 Years of Cricket at Eversley, Hampshire (The Secretary, Eversley CC, Eversley Green, Eversley, Hampshire; no price given), by Andrew Renshaw, is a 50-page quarto. This is a workmanlike history, coming right up to the present day; generous, enthusiastic, and interestingly illustrated. Eversley was Charles Kingsley's parish, and that eminent author is quoted as saying "Cricket is better than beer".

The Erratics: 50 Not Out (from the Secretary, University of Exeter Staff Cricket Club, Exeter; no price given), edited by Stephen Fisher, is a history of the University of Exeter Staff Cricket Club 1934-1984. A 209-page octavo, it provides relevant statistics of all its players at the end; but before that it enjoys the club's progress, gives biographical and autobiographical notes on the players, retains a good sense of humour and, from time to time, breaks into verse. It is, too, brightly illustrated, partly with home-produced line drawings.

Ormskirk Cricket Club 1835-1985 (The Secretary, Ormskirk Cricket Club, Brook Lane, Ormskirk, Lancashire; no price given), by several hands, is another 50-page quarto. The contributors, while knowledgeable, also permit themselves plenty of pavilion-type humour. There are also accounts of triumphs, the outstanding one among them being Ormskirk's winning of the Lancashire knockout final of 1978.

Todmorden Cricket Club 1837-1987 (from C. J. W. Printers, Elland, Yorkshire; no price given), compiled and edited by Ron Wild, with special material by H. G. Stephenson, is a 96-page octavo with important scorecards, statistics, records and a running history. The foreword is by Peter Lever of Lancashire and England, himself a former Todmorden player.

Yorkshire Post 1987 Benefit Book (from Yorkshire CCC; £4.95), by various hands, has been compiled in aid of the county's indoor school appeal. It is based on drawings, character sketches and statistics of 25 great Yorkshire players; and it also carries several feature articles. It is a 96-page quarto, well produced, and with a most interesting quiz called "The Yorkshire Test".

Triumph in Australia (Macdonald/Queen Anne Press; £12.95) is the England captain, Mike Gatting's account of that successful tour of Australia in 1986-87. It is a companionable and personal account, written in the form of a diary, which does not shun such comments as "Another of those wasted days on tour" or "Disaster, absolute disaster. And I was the cause of it." It reads well as, indeed, a story of such success would be expected to. The illustrations are generous and the foreword, by Micky Stewart, gives it an official imprimatur.

Ashes to Ashes: England's Triumphant Test Series in Australia 1986-87 (The Kingswood Press; £9.95), by Peter Roebuck, is a thought-provoking book. The author writes perceptively about that successful tour, with excursions to the Davis Cup final and the America's Cup, both of which took place at the same period; and he also considers the Aborigine issue and the city of Darwin. He indulges in some humour, but his purpose is predominantly serious.

Grand Slam: England in Australia 1986-87 (Simon and Schuster; £7.95), by Christopher Martin-Jenkins, has photographs by Adrian Murrell and statistics by Richard Lockwood. It is "A *Cricketer* Special", capably and professionally written, with constantly valuable comment, not least on the World Series Cup. The listing of post-war England–Australia series is interesting, as are the limited-overs analyses for the season.

The Battle for The Ashes '87 (The Daily Telegraph; £5.95) is another account of that series which proved so attractive to British writers, if only by virtue of the English wins. It consists of reports by Peter West, Tony Lewis and Robert James; Australian viewpoint from Alan Shiell; expatriate viewpoint by Frank Tyson; preview and summary by Michael Melford; score charts, radial hundreds and Test averages by Wendy Wimbush. A generous centre section of action photographs rounds off a highly efficient tour account. Some may say it is in the old-fashioned mould, but it is completely satisfying to the committed follower.

Clean Sweep (W. H. Allen; £9.95), by Peter West, is his record of a new experience. In September 1986, Mr West retired from his post as television's senior cricket broadcaster, only to find himself, two months later, reporting England's matches in Australia for the *Daily Telegraph*. He had never covered an overseas tour before, and here he adds to his long experience the freshness and enthusiasm of one making a first trip. His style is, characteristically, friendly and engaging. "January 2: Last evening in addition to my match report, I filed another piece about Botham and Worcestershire, Graham Dilley and Kent, and the cancellation of Australia's tour to West Indies in early 1988. It was getting on for midnight when – these jobs completed – I hit the hay. It had been a long day. Telephone call from Sports Ed at 1.30 a.m. is not the best start to a new one." It was obviously a tough as well as an unexpected assignment; carried out as good naturedly as one would expect from Peter West.

Cricket XXXX Cricket (The Kingswood Press; £9.95), by Frances Edmonds, is essentially a personal book. The blurb announces categorically that "cricket bores her immeasurably". Nevertheless she enjoys Australia, and it is claimed that "Australia loves Frances". It is an amusingly irreverent, but at the same time, often perceptive, account of the cricketer, Philippe Edmonds's wife's three-and-a-half months' tour. Even those who do not approve of it will find it cheerfully easy to read.

The Independent World Cup Cricket '87 (Heinemann; £9.95), by Martin Johnson and Henry Blofeld, with photography by Michael Steele, is a 144-page account of that competition in which Australia so narrowly beat England in the final. There are previews of venues, teams and prospects, full scores of every match, and some evocative illustrations. A highly capable technical operation produced the book in less than a month of its final events.

One Good Season Deserved Another (from the author, The Coach House, Ponsonby, Seascale, Cumbria CA20 1BX; £3.25) is yet another of Nico Craven's cricket diaries. He is concerned with 1986 and 1987 and, of course, above all, with Gloucestershire. It is his usual enjoyable rumination.

It is not the practice in this review to deal with reprints; for that reason, the wholly admirable collection of The Pavilion Library reissues of classics is not dealt with at length. It seems, however, that two republications of 1987 demand mention. *The Cricketing Record of Major Warton's Tour 1888-9* (J. W. McKenzie; £30) was not widely published in the year (1889) of its first issue and it is now an extremely rare book. It is here reprinted in exact facsimile, plus a valuable four-page introduction by David Rayvern Allen. It runs to 219 pages; plus some intriguing advertisements. The style is period beyond question; there are some portrait illustrations and the whole is immensely readable. It is certainly a collectable piece for those who have not the rare good fortune to possess the original edition.

Another most interesting reprint is that of the first – 1888 – edition of the Badminton Library volume on *Cricket* (Ashford Press Publishing, Shedfield, Hampshire SO3 2HN; £16.95). "Edited by His Grace The Duke of Beaufort, KG, assisted by Alfred E. T. Watson", it was authoritatively written, largely by A. G. Steel and the Hon. R. H. Lyttelton, with contributions by Andrew Lang, W. G. Grace, R. A. H. Mitchell and Frederick Gale, and was in its day probably the most ambitious cricket publication ever produced. In a way a hinge publication, it is both readable and illuminating. The illustrations – engravings – are still not – as they were not originally – completely happy, but the rest of the production is good and the material, for those who do not already know it, is extremely valuable.

Run Chase (from the author, 20 Smallbrook Walk, Crewe, Cheshire CW2 6LX; £1.50, including postage), by Imogen Grosberg, is a 16-page octavo of poems. The author, who has established herself as a consistent sporting poet, remains largely faithful to her usual theme of cricket, but she also introduces horse-racing.

Cricket humour is a matter of taste, but *Marylebone versus The World* (Pavilion/Michael Joseph; £8.95), by William Rushton, will, by the author's reputation alone, commend itself to many readers. Mr Rushton knows his cricket history; he feels for the game with a genuine understanding. He draws a gloriously grotesque line – though he can be accurate when he wants to – and his text is of "in" humour. To quote a humorous book is to do it less than justice, but merely to skim this under the thumb is to be moved to laughter by many of the drawings. He protests that "historically his allegiance is to Surrey CCC, and he remains, in spirit, an Oval man".

Peter Tinniswood, author of *Tales from Witney Scrotum* (Pavilion/Michael Joseph; £7.95) has already created a collection of characters who are all too easily recognisable – Granny Swanton, Prodger the Poacher, Don "Sir Oswald" Mosey, Dame Peter West – and set them down in the setting of Witney Scrotum at Cowdrey's Bottom and Botham's Gut. It is an easy and literary laugh, maintaining the reputation created by *Tales from A Long Room* and echoed in the author's BBC television series, *I Didn't Know You Cared*. Once again there is a series of "in" jokes for cricket followers.

Passing from the irrelevant to the sublime, a new and newly illustrated edition of *The MCC Coaching Book* (The Kingswood Press; £10.95) is a valuable adjunct for all who seek to teach the methods of the game. It is approved and recommended by the National Cricket Association and,

despite the revisions, much of the original soundness has been retained. Some, though, will regret that a few of the old and classical photographs have been replaced, without necessarily being improved upon. That, though, is perhaps over-critical of a volume in the guidance of which Sir George Allen has long played a most important part.

Many will argue that *The MCC Coaching Book* has invalidated most other books of instruction. However, two of the year's other publications also make a genuine contribution to the technical study of the game. *The Test and County Cricket Board Guide to Better Cricket* (Octopus; £12.95), by Vic Marks, the Somerset and England all-rounder, presents a modern aspect; but respects past teachings. Assisted by sponsorship from National Westminster Bank, it is a handsome production, with photographs – many excellent ones in colour – and line-and-wash illustrations to complement the lively, discursive text. The views of leading cricketers, in addition to lending authority, are themselves of interest; recourse to *The Art of Cricket*, by Sir Donald Bradman, reinforces the importance of the basic principles. The whole is pleasingly presented, and as well as his scholarship, the author's wit is never far from the surface. "The sweep is usually played to a ball of good length pitching outside leg stump (unless you're Alan Knott)."

Masterstrokes: Cricket's Timeless Batting Lessons (The Kingswood Press; £14.95), is by Allen Synge and Derek Anns. Mr Synge, a great nephew of H. D. G. Leveson Gower, captained Millfield School; Mr Anns, a club cricketer in Essex, is also a student of cricket history. They have brought together the great classic action pictures of batting, from John Nyren to Geoffrey Boycott, David Gower, Barry Richards and Ian Botham. Along the way they have called in G. W. Beldam, C. B. Fry, Gilbert Jessop, Jack Hobbs, Victor Trumper, A. C. MacLaren, and Len Hutton. It is a splendid study of greatness in batsmanship; illustrating purity, classicism and creation; and to study the photographs is sheer delight. It is one of the few recent books to add anything to our knowledge – and appreciation – of the technique of batting.

Allan Border, An Autobiography (Methuen; £9.95) acknowledges help from Bob Spence and Ock, the author's manager. It shows Border as the "slow starter", the tentative New South Wales hopeful, who achieved some marked successes and was suddenly thrust into the captaincy of Australia. Though forthright and often humorous, he maintains his dignity through what has, at times, been an extremely difficult period for the game in his country and for the national team in particular.

The same author, in *A Peep at the Poms . . . the Australian Captain in England* (Arthur Barker; £9.95) writes both critically and with relish of his season with Essex in 1986. He played a significant part in their winning of the Championship that year, though the suddenly arranged Australian tour of India prevented him from joining in their end-of-season celebrations. He has much to say that is shrewd and salutary, and offers illuminating opinions on the leading players of the counties. If he is to return as captain of Australia, he has much useful material stored away in his mind. He analyses "the Essex Way"; and, in their turn, his team-mates there pass, invariably friendly, comments on him.

An unusual type of cricket autobiography is that of Ian Botham's wife, Kathy, which she has titled *Living with a Legend* (Grafton Books; £9.95). It was Brian Close who introduced the two when they were both eighteen, and he warned her of the perils of being married to a county or Test cricketer.

Now, a dozen years later, she has written an account of her married life; she did so in over-the-kitchen-table talk with her mother. The result is an honest story, not without its agonies but most certainly not without its giggles. Much of her life has been spent at home while her husband has been away – often abroad – playing cricket. She has then been at the mercy of the media. Her marriage has happily produced three children, and at the end of this account she says, "Life has been at times difficult, at times bloody impossible, but these times have been far outnumbered by the good, the funny, the tender and loving times. I look forward to the future, always conscious of the fact that to live with a legend can be wonderful but is seldom easy."

Boycott: The Autobiography (Macmillan; £14.95) is, as one might expect, not in the normal mould of cricketers' life stories. To begin with, it is weighty – a large octavo of some 300 pages. It is, of course, a record of immense statistical success; but it is also an argument of self-justification by a great player who felt himself frequently unjustly treated. This is not entirely a matter of protestation of injury. Boycott has many critics, but every one of them ought to read this book before condemning him. This man has been, technically, one of the greatest of all cricketers, and on that ground alone he is entitled to fair consideration. Whether one agrees or not with his point of view, his autobiography makes most absorbing reading.

Our Don Bradman (Collins Willow; £8.95), edited by Philip Derriman, is described as "the first anthology of writings about the world's greatest cricketer, Sir Donald Bradman". Much of it has not been collected before; some 40 per cent has been gathered from newspaper articles, about the same amount from books, and the remainder from poems, speeches and other miscellanea. Much of it was preserved in Sir Donald's scrapbooks. The editor is at pains to stress that Sir Donald is "in no way a patron of the book"; but he did answer queries about it and provide certain source materials. The material, which stretches over Bradman's entire career, runs to 222 pages and is an unusually complete collection of writings about one player. For Bradman idolators, it is a most satisfying array; historians of the future will find much in it to employ in their fashion.

Emburey: Autobiography (Partridge Press; £10.95) is the thoughtful life story of a thoughtful man, the Middlesex and England all-rounder. It can also be, as when he describes his dismissal from The Oval and the death of his father, extremely moving. He is acutely perceptive; so much so as to inspire hope that he will achieve his ambition of captaining a county. The chapter, "Captaincy – State of the Art", is a measure of his clarity of thought and understanding of his fellow cricketers. Cricketing events are described clear-sightedly and without bias. The philosopher in him produces the last line. "The moral is that there are always other chapters to be written."

Ray Illingworth: The Tempestuous Years 1979-83 (Sidgwick & Jackson; £10.95), which acknowledges assistance from Steve Whiting, was one of the books indicated, if not provoked, by the autobiographical writings of Geoffrey Boycott. Over the period under discussion, Ray Illingworth was the manager of Yorkshire. Before that, he had been a most capable cricket captain, whose scope in that capacity had been limited to leading Leicestershire and England with considerable success – but never his own county. There can be no doubt of his understanding and acumen so far as that field is concerned. This personal account was obviously something of a wrench to write; but after the three years he took deciding to do it, he pulled no punches: "I'm damned glad I no longer have anything at all to do with

Yorkshire County Cricket Club"; or again, "I reckon it was the skulduggery, the scheming and the downright dishonesty that sickened me most". Much of the undercurrent – in fact, the current – of the story concerns the clash between those two powerful and conflicting personalities, Illingworth and Boycott. It is yet another of the new style of highly revealing cricketing autobiographies of recent years.

Imran's Summer of Fulfilment (published by the author, c/o Beverston Printers, 111 Duke Street, St Helens, Merseyside; no price given), by Khadim Hussain Baloch, is announced as the author's first book. With a foreword by Imran Khan himself, it is the story of the Pakistani tour of 1987, rapidly and capably produced if the proof copy received is any criterion. Written from close to the action and to the players, it is an extremely readable account, with some perceptive and some quite charitable judgements, adequate statistics and pleasing illustrations. The author did well indeed to get his 160-page quarto within his deadline.

Archie Jackson: The Keats of Cricket (Pavilion/Michael Joseph; £10.95), by David Frith, is a revised and expanded edition of a study first published in a limited edition in 1974. Until now it has not, therefore, been easy to come by. The title indicates the quality of tragedy in this story of a gifted and attractive young Australian batsman who died all too early. Mr Frith is too wise to overplay the pathos of his story; he lets that come through naturally. This is one of the minor yet great stories of cricket, touching and haunting.

Kapil: The Autobiography of Kapil Dev (Sidgwick & Jackson; £9.95), which acknowledges the assistance of Mr R. Mohan of *The Hindu*, and Mr Bharat Reddy, is the story of the greatest modern Indian all-rounder. One must applaud, without by any means agreeing with it, his "So long as you are honest, sincere about your job and try 100 per cent, there is no reason why you cannot succeed at cricket". All too many desperate triers know it does not work quite like that. Kapil made his comment after India's Test win at Lord's; perhaps it is just a question of what you mean by success. There will be much greater support for the comment that leads one of his chapters: "Bowlers win Test matches." Many, too, will be pleased to read, "I hold Sunil Gavaskar in the highest esteem. He helped me at every stage of this successful campaign in England." There is much good thinking about cricket, and the reader will also be interested by the domestic side – Kapil's home life and marriage. The story is generous in manner and in presentation, and the statistical section emphasises the modesty of much of the text.

The autobiography of the West Indian and Hampshire fast bowler and all-rounder, Malcolm Marshall, is titled *Marshall Arts* (Macdonald/Queen Anne Press; £9.95). He takes a critical look at the English cricket scene, talks firmly about the personalities of the game in the Caribbean, and records the attempt, which he successfully resisted, to buy him into playing in South Africa. He is absorbing on such matters as his comparison of Lawrence Rowe with Viv Richards: "One of the reasons why Viv has already achieved what Lawrence should have done is, I suppose, the sheer strength of his personality. He expects to score runs and he usually does and, most importantly, he succeeds on all types of wickets and on all occasions. That is the hallmark of a truly great batsman and to that he owes not only his incredible talent but also his unshakable self-belief, strong ego and a fierce pride in his performance."

Percy (Clifford Frost Publications; £10.95), sub-titled "The Perspicacious Memoirs of a Cricketing Man", is the autobiography of Pat Pocock. It is

"written with Patrick Collins", and Mr Collins's achievement is to make it sound exactly like "Percy" Pocock himself talking. It is intelligent, perceptive, amusing and never more salutary than on the subject of over-limited cricket. "Until that time, the English professional had only one technique to learn. It was a method for playing three-day county cricket, and he acquired it, perfected it and carried it around with him like a badge of office. Now it was different; now there were bonus points, run-chases, slogging, unorthodox fields, manufactured shots and a heavy concentration upon results. People said it was a different game, and they were right. But this game demanded the kind of adaptability, discipline and physical fitness which would have crippled many of the old cricketers who were rushing to decry it." A book well worth reading and enjoying. It is necessary only to add that the production and reproduction are quite outstanding.

The next title, taken in due, alphabetical order, is almost diametrically different in feeling. It is called *The Harold Rhodes Affair* (Breedon Books; £7.95), and it relates the cricketing story of a Test bowler whose career never recovered from his being called for throwing. It has a most compassionate, but not lush, foreword by Fred Trueman, but the story is fundamentally sad; so near to high success only to be cast down. It is one of the truly tragic stories of cricket and should be read by everyone with a feeling for the literary truth of the game. If it should prove the selling success it deserves, it is no more than feeling would ask for its author. He shows compassion for others but he himself has so far had little luck.

Plum Warner (Unwin Hyman; £14.95), by Gerald Howat, is the work of a professional historian who has written four previous books on cricket. It is a most admirable piece of cricket research and reconstruction; scholarly, and by no means without humour. This is an honest attempt to set in perspective not only the playing performance but, more importantly, the administrative quality and achievements of one who held high standing at Lord's. "Plum" was not only, despite his physical frailty, a successful batsman and captain, a Test player and a fine competitor; he was also a writer, broadcaster, thinker, selector and, so many maintain, an *éminence grise* of the game. This is a soundly authoritative study which shows, too, an unexpectedly human side of a man who was, in his time, viewed perhaps with too great awe. Read, for instance, the rules of the Rat Hole Club.

Frank Worrell: A Biography (Lutterworth Press; £12.95), by Ivo Tennant, goes far towards filling too wide a gap which has existed for too long. Frank Worrell was the first black man regularly to captain a West Indian Test team. His achievement was not simply to win matches, but to unite the cricketers of those very mixed islands with such different histories and cultures. He was a likable man, cultured and courteous, but with a streak of steel in him; successful as a Test cricketer from the start. His death at 42 was an immense blow to West Indies cricket in almost every way; he was of a stature that made him virtually impossible to replace. There is a foreword by Clive Lloyd and a postscript by Richie Benaud, indicative, from two different angles, of his standing and the respect in which he was held. This, though slight physically, becomes a standard work.

The Demon and the Lobster (The Kingswood Press; £12.95), by Anthony Meredith, is a first book. The author teaches classics at Stowe, where he is a housemaster, and he has long and closely followed Essex cricket. This is a quite admirable study of Charles Kortright, of Essex, the legendary "fastest of them all", and Digby Jephson, the Surrey lob bowler; a pair labelled by

the author as "remarkable bowlers in the Golden Age". It is something of a period piece; both of these men were born in 1871 and this book is laced with quotations and illustrations from their days. There are, too, photographs which stir period memory and interest. This is a scholarly and valuable book, instinct with the age it records.

Hit for Six (The Basic Group of Companies; no price given) is a 14-page pamphlet recording the first year – 1986 – of the Basic Six 6-Hit Award. In the competition, Vivian Richards and Ian Botham finished equal with 34 sixes apiece, but Botham's nine in the match against Lancashire decided it in his favour. This is a pleasantly produced piece of cricket ephemera.

The ASDA Cricket Challenge 1987 (Dennis Fairey & Associates; £2), with its striking full-colour cover of David Bairstow taking a return from the field at full stretch, is a worthy successor to the earlier editions. Its colour illustration is generous; the text, from Peter Smith, Peter West, Ray Illingworth, Colin Cowdrey, Godfrey Evans, Christopher Martin-Jenkins and others, is most pleasingly readable.

Playfair Cricket Annual 1987 (Macdonald/Queen Anne Press; £1.75), edited by Bill Frindall, is, which some of the older generation may find difficult to believe, the 40th edition. This remains the ideal pocket reference of the game: 256 pages with biographical notes, wide-ranging statistics, Test career records for all nations, and first-class records for all English players. Neither does it neglect the one-day competitions nor the universities; even the umpires are covered.

Benson & Hedges West Indies Cricket Annual 1987 (Caribbean Communications, 116 Queens Road, Hersham, Walton-on-Thames, Surrey KT12 5LL; £3.40, including postage) is a most attractively produced 88-page quarto, edited once more by Tony Cozier. It covers Shell Shield and other domestic competitions; West Indies in Pakistan, New Zealand, Australia and Sharjah; West Indies B team to Zimbabwe; tours by Yorkshire, Lancashire and Hampshire to the islands; and a most valuable Who's Who in West Indies cricket. There is a full-length article by the editor on "The early trickle to the recent flood" of West Indian players in English cricket.

The Cricket Diary 1988 (from John Dixon, 18 Ashley Avenue, Lower Weston, Bath, BA1 3DS; £3.95) is once more edited and published by the former Gloucestershire slow left-arm bowler. It is thoroughly founded and soaked in cricket. The quotations are invariably relevant and often witty; the illustrations are pleasing and interesting. There is a scattering of statistics, county details include addresses, and there are locations of the governing bodies of the game. Made for enthusiasts by an enthusiast.

Wills Cricket Diary 1987-88 (Orient Longman; Rs75.00) runs from October 1, 1987 to December 31, 1988. It is a generous oblong quarto, three days to a page, most amply illustrated in black-and-white and colour, and with a sound statistical section. Many of the captions to the illustrations are lively and imaginative.

The Cricketer's Who's Who 1987 (Collins Willow; £8.95) continues, edited and compiled by Iain Sproat with Ralph Dellor as Associate Editor. Well illustrated with portraits of the players, and generous in its statistics and personal information about them, it is 503 pages long and should settle almost any argument that can be raised about contemporary English county players.

The following county cricket yearbooks, without exception, include the county's matches – first team and second team – in the preceding season, as well as indicated feature articles.

Essex County Cricket Club 1987 Handbook (Essex CCC, County Ground, Chelmsford; £3.50), edited by Peter Edwards, celebrates the county's 1986 successes in winning the County Championship and being runners-up in the John Player Special Sunday League. It has features by David Lemmon, Peter Edwards, Pat Murphy, Clem Driver, Graham Gooch, Doug Insole, Trevor Bailey (an obituary of Jim Laker), Mike Marshall, and numerous other writers in a quite unusually large, handsome and happy celebratory romp.

The Hampshire Handbook 1987 (Hampshire CCC, County Ground, Southampton; £3) runs to 200 pages and has features by Bob Parks, John Hughes, Mark Nicholas, Pat Symes, Vic Isaacs and Mike Neasom, and poems by Imogen Grosberg. Tony Mitchener, the editor, continues enthusiastically and ambitiously along his way.

Kent County Cricket Annual 1987 (Kent CCC, St Lawrence Ground, Canterbury; £2.50) has a rediscovery of Alec Skelding's verse, "The Umpire's lament", and features by Bernard Simmonds, Derek Carlaw, John Bray and Derek Ufton. Once again it is a pleasant addition to the county enthusiast's bookshelves.

Middlesex County Cricket Club Review 1986-87 (Middlesex CCC, Lord's Ground, London NW8 8QN; £4) has features by Mike Selvey, Mike Brearley, Simon Hughes, Derek Lodge, David Kendix, and Len Grimsey; and, sadly, tributes to Bill Edrich, "Tagge" Webster and Arthur Flower.

A new entrant to this field is *Northants '87* (The Northampton Mercury, PO Box 18, Upper Mounts, Northampton; £1.95), compiled by Peter Clifton. On unusually good paper for such a publication, it is an ambitious and generously illustrated 72-page quarto. The illustrations are far above the average county annual standard, and the features cover both the 1987 season – "How it fell apart" – and a passage of past history. It is a good money's-worth within its kind.

Irish Cricket Union Yearbook 1987 (Irish Cricket Union, Able Press, 22 St Catherine's Court, Newgrove Avenue, Sandymount, Dublin 4; £1) is the ninth edition. In addition to international matches, and Schweppes Cup and Bank and Youth competitions, it carries inter-provincial career records from 1966 to 1986. There are thoughtful articles by Sean Pender and John Elder.

The Wadham Stringer New Forest Club Cricket Association Handbook 1987 (from V. W. Loveless, "Pipers", Pear Tree Drive, Landford, Wiltshire SP5 2AY; no price given) continues in good health with addresses, fixtures, reports, averages and scores for that thriving competition.

The Journal of the Cricket Society (from Miss V. A. Hoggarth, 26 Thirlmere Rise, London Road, Bromley BR1 4HY; £3 to non-members) is edited by C. W. Porter and published seasonally. Spring 1987 has feature articles by G. H. G. Doggart, Stephen Green, Richard Cashman, Gerald Howat and many others; and Mike Brearley contributes to the Miscellany in this 76-page compilation.

The Cricketer International Quarterly (29 Cavendish Road, Redhill, Surrey RH1 4AH; £1.40), edited now by Richard Lockwood, maintains its statistical and scores bias. In this direction it is thorough, covering the world game and offering some pleasant illustrations.

The Cricketer International (29 Cavendish Road, Redhill, Surrey RH1 4AH; £1.10 monthly) continues under the editorship of Christopher Martin-Jenkins. It carries contributions from Peter Roebuck, Phil Edmonds, Wendy Wimbush, Cyril Berry, Alan Lee, Simon Hughes, E. W. Swanton, Alf Gover, Robert Brooke and the editor. Founded by Sir Pelham Warner in 1921, it has progressed with the times and is a most pleasantly produced periodical with some fine colour illustrations.

Wisden Cricket Monthly (6 Beech Lane, Guildown, Guildford, Surrey GU2 5ES; £1.10 monthly) continues under the editorship of David Frith, who misses no ideas. Regular contributors are Jack Bannister, David Foot, Neil Hallam, Doug Ibbotson, Jonathan Rice and the editor. It is generously and relevantly illustrated, partly in colour.

Cricketer (Newspress, 250 Spencer Street, Melbourne 3000, Australia; $A2.75 per issue) is the Australian magazine published monthly from October to April in each year. It runs to about 70 quarto pages an issue. Among its writers are Jack Pollard, Ashley Mallett, Greg Matthews and Chris Harte. It contains a poster-type colour spread and gives good news and feature coverage of the Australian scene.

New Zealand Cricket (RPL Sporting Publications, Third Floor, Communications House, 12 Heather Street, Parnell, Auckland, New Zealand; $NZ2.75 per issue) is published monthly from October to May. The editor is Don Cameron, while the leading contributors are Dick Brittenden, Andy Quick, John Harvey and Brent Edwards. Each issue consists of about 50 pages and covers the New Zealand scene conscientiously and competently.

Australian Cricket Journal (details of subscription from GPO Box 696, Adelaide 5001, South Australia), edited by Chris Harte, is a quarterly which, in 1987, went into its third annual volume. It is literate, thoughtful and invariably authoritative. Among the contributors are Richard Cashman, Keith Sandiford, Arthur Bryant and the editor.

THE ASHES

"In affectionate remembrance of English cricket which died at The Oval, 29th August, 1882. Deeply lamented by a large circle of sorrowing friends and acquaintances, R.I.P. N.B. The body will be cremated and the Ashes taken to Australia."

Australia's first victory on English soil over the full strength of England, on August 29, 1882, inspired a young London journalist, Reginald Shirley Brooks, to write this mock "obituary". It appeared in the *Sporting Times*.

Before England's defeat at The Oval, by 7 runs, arrangements had already been made for the Hon. Ivo Bligh, afterwards Lord Darnley, to lead a team to Australia. Three weeks later they set out, now with the popular objective of recovering the Ashes. In the event, Australia won the first Test by nine wickets, but with England winning the next two it became generally accepted that they brought back the Ashes.

It was long accepted that the real Ashes – a small urn believed to contain the ashes of a bail used in the third match – were presented to Bligh by a group of Melbourne women. At the time of the 1982 centenary of The Oval Test match, however, evidence was produced which suggested that these ashes were the remains of a ball and that they were given to the England captain by Sir William Clarke, the presentation taking place before the Test matches in Australia in 1883. The certain origin of the Ashes, therefore, is the subject of some dispute.

After Lord Darnley's death in 1927, the urn was given to MCC by Lord Darnley's Australian-born widow, Florence. It can be seen in the cricket museum at Lord's, together with a red and gold velvet bag, made specially for it, and the scorecard of the 1882 match.

FIXTURES, 1988

* Indicates Sunday play.   † Not first-class.

4d = Play over 4 days; where not indicated, first-class matches are of 3 days' duration.

Saturday, April 16

Cambridge	Cambridge U. v Derbys.
Oxford	Oxford U. v Leics.
Lord's*	MCC v Notts.

Wednesday, April 20

Cambridge	Cambridge U. v Warwicks.
Oxford	Oxford U. v Northants

Thursday, April 21

Derby (4d)	Derbys. v Leics.
Chelmsford (4d)	Essex v Kent
Bristol (4d)	Glos. v Glam.
Southampton (4d)	Hants v Surrey
Manchester (4d)	Lancs. v Worcs.
Lord's (4d)	Middx v Notts.
Hove (4d)	Sussex v Somerset

Tuesday, April 26

†Benson and Hedges Cup (1 day)

Bristol	Glos. v Combined Universities
Chelmsford	Essex v Surrey
Leicester	Leics. v Lancs.
Nottingham	Notts. v Minor Counties
Glasgow (Hamilton Crescent)	Scotland v Derbys.
Taunton	Somerset v Hants
Hove	Sussex v Kent
Leeds	Yorks. v Northants

Thursday, April 28

Cardiff (4d)	Glam. v Somerset
Bristol (4d)	Glos. v Sussex
Canterbury (4d)	Kent v Hants
Manchester (4d)	Lancs. v Warwicks.
Leicester (4d)	Leics. v Northants
Lord's (4d)	Middx v Essex
Worcester (4d)	Worcs. v Notts.
Leeds (4d)	Yorks. v Derbys.
Cambridge	Cambridge U. v Surrey

Tuesday, May 3

†Benson and Hedges Cup (1 day)

Oxford	Combined Universities v Somerset
Derby	Derbys. v Warwicks.
Southampton	Hants v Glam.
Lord's	Middx v Sussex
Swindon	Minor Counties v Worcs.
Nottingham	Notts. v Yorks.
Glasgow (Titwood)	Scotland v Leics.
The Oval	Surrey v Kent

Thursday, May 5

Chesterfield (4d)	Derbys. v Essex
Leicester (4d)	Leics. v Kent
Northampton (4d)	Northants v Glos.
Nottingham (4d)	Notts. v Lancs.
Taunton (4d)	Somerset v Worcs.
The Oval (4d)	Surrey v Middx
Birmingham (4d)	Warwicks. v Yorks.
Cambridge	Cambridge U. v Glam.
Oxford	Oxford U. v Hants

Saturday, May 7

Hove	Sussex v West Indians

Sunday, May 8

Arundel	†Lavinia, Duchess of Norfolk's XI v West Indians (1 day)

Tuesday, May 10

†Benson and Hedges Cup (1 day)

Southampton	Hants v Glos.
Canterbury	Kent v Essex
Liverpool	Lancs. v Derbys.
Darlington	Minor Counties v Northants
Taunton	Somerset v Glam.
The Oval	Surrey v Middx
Birmingham	Warwicks. v Scotland
Worcester	Worcs. v Notts.

Thursday, May 12

Southampton	†Hants v West Indians (1 day)

†Benson and Hedges Cup (1 day)

Chelmsford	Essex v Sussex
Cardiff	Glam. v Combined Universities
Bristol	Glos. v Somerset
Canterbury	Kent v Middx
Manchester	Lancs. v Scotland
Leicester	Leics. v Warwicks.
Northampton	Northants v Worcs.
Leeds	Yorks. v Minor Counties

Saturday, May 14

Taunton*	Somerset v West Indies

†Benson and Hedges Cup (1 day)

Cambridge	Combined Universities v Hants
Derby	Derbys. v Leics.
Swansea	Glam. v Glos.
Lord's	Middx v Essex
Northampton	Northants v Notts.
Hove	Sussex v Surrey
Birmingham	Warwicks. v Lancs.
Worcester	Worcs. v Yorks.

Tuesday, May 17

Northampton (4d)	Northants v Warwicks.

Wednesday, May 18

Bournemouth	Hants v Glam.
Leicester	Leics. v Middx
Nottingham	Notts. v Glos.
Worcester	Worcs. v Somerset
Cambridge	Cambridge U. v Essex
Oxford	Oxford U. v Kent

Thursday, May 19

Birmingham	ENGLAND v WEST INDIES (1st 1-day Texaco Trophy)

Saturday, May 21

Leeds	ENGLAND v WEST INDIES (2nd 1-day Texaco Trophy)
Swansea	Glam. v Derbys.
Canterbury	Kent v Yorks.
Leicester	Leics. v Worcs.
Nottingham	Notts. v Sussex
The Oval	Surrey v Northants
Birmingham	Warwicks. v Essex
Cambridge	Cambridge U. v Middx
Oxford	Oxford U. v Lancs.

Monday, May 23

Lord's	ENGLAND v WEST INDIES (3rd 1-day Texaco Trophy)

Wednesday, May 25

†Benson and Hedges Cup – Quarter-Finals (1 day)

Bristol	Glos. v West Indians (or another county if Glos. in B & H Cup quarter-finals)

Saturday, May 28

Worcester*	Worcs. v West Indians
Derby	Derbys. v Notts.
Chelmsford	Essex v Surrey
Swansea	Glam. v Glos.
Manchester	Lancs. v Somerset
Lord's	Middx v Sussex
Northampton	Northants v Leics.
Middlesbrough	Yorks. v Hants

Wednesday, June 1

Southampton	Hants v Somerset
Dartford	Kent v Notts.
Northampton	Northants v Yorks.
The Oval	Surrey v Sussex
Worcester	Worcs. v Lancs.
Oxford	Oxford U. v Glos.

Thursday, June 2

Nottingham	ENGLAND v WEST INDIES (1st Cornhill Test, 5 days)

Saturday, June 4

Cardiff	Glam. v Kent
Liverpool	Lancs. v Hants
Lord's	Middx v Worcs.
Taunton	Somerset v Northants
Horsham	Sussex v Derbys.
Birmingham	Warwicks. v Notts.
Harrogate	Yorks. v Surrey

Wednesday, June 8

†Benson and Hedges Cup – Semi-Finals (1 day)

Birmingham or Manchester	Warwicks. or Lancs. v West Indies
Harrogate	†Tilcon Trophy (3 days)

Saturday, June 11

Northampton*	Northants v West Indians
Derby	Derbys. v Glos.
Ilford	Essex v Sussex
Tunbridge Wells	Kent v Middx
Nottingham	Notts. v Glam.
Bath	Somerset v Warwicks.
The Oval	Surrey v Leics.
Worcester	Worcs. v Hants
Cambridge	Cambridge U. v Yorks.
Downpatrick*	†Ireland v MCC (3 days)

Wednesday, June 15

Ilford	Essex v Glos.
Basingstoke	Hants v Middx
Tunbridge Wells	Kent v Lancs.
Leicester	Leics. v Glam.
Bath	Somerset v Sussex
Leeds	Yorks. v Warwicks.
Oxford	Oxford U. v Notts.
The Oval	Surrey v Cambridge U.

Thursday, June 16

Lord's	ENGLAND v WEST INDIES (2nd Cornhill Test, 5 days)

Saturday, June 18

Derby	Derbys. v Worcs.
Southampton	Hants v Notts.
Manchester	Lancs. v Glos.
Leicester	Leics. v Sussex
Luton	Northants v Middx
Birmingham	Warwicks. v Kent
Sheffield	Yorks. v Essex

Wednesday, June 22

†NatWest Bank Trophy – First Round
(1 day)

Finchampstead	Berks. v Yorks.
Chester (Boughton Hall)	Cheshire v Northants
Torquay	Devon v Notts.
Darlington	Durham v Somerset
Chelmsford	Essex v Wilts.
Bristol	Glos. v Ireland
Canterbury	Kent v Bucks.
Manchester	Lancs. v Lincs.
Leicester	Leics. v Suffolk
Lord's	Middx v Herts.
Edinburgh (Myreside)	Scotland v Glam.
Telford (St George's)	Salop. v Hants

Burton upon Trent	Staffs. v Surrey
Hove	Sussex v Derbys.
Birmingham	Warwicks. v Cambs.
Worcester	Worcs. v Cumb.

Thursday, June 23

Cambridge	†Oxford & Camb. U. v West Indies (2 days)

Friday, June 24

Belfast (Ormeau)	†Ireland v Worcs. (1 day)

Saturday, June 25

Canterbury*	Kent v West Indians
Chelmsford	Essex v Middx
Swansea	Glam. v Lancs.
Gloucester	Glos. v Leics.
Nottingham	Notts. v Northants
The Oval	Surrey v Derbys.
Hove	Sussex v Yorks.
Derry (Beechgrove)	†Ireland v Worcs. (1 day)

Sunday, June 26

Dublin (Malahide)	†Ireland v Worcs. (1 day)

Wednesday, June 29

Gloucester	Glos. v Hants
Canterbury	Kent v Essex
Lord's	Middx v Yorks.
Taunton	Somerset v Glam.
Nuneaton (Griff & Coton)	Warwicks. v Lancs.

Thursday, June 30

Manchester	ENGLAND v WEST INDIES (3rd Cornhill Test, 5 days)

Saturday, July 2

Derby	Derbys. v Middx
Northampton	Northants v Lancs.
Taunton	Somerset v Essex
The Oval	Surrey v Warwicks.
Hastings	Sussex v Kent
Worcester	Worcs. v Glos.
Leeds	Yorks. v Leics.
Lord's*	Oxford U. v Cambridge U.

Wednesday, July 6

Derby	Derbys. v West Indians (if Derbys. not in NatWest Bank Trophy 2nd round)

†NatWest Bank Trophy – Second Round
(1 day)

Finchampstead or Leeds	Berks. or Yorks. v Middx or Herts.
Chester (Boughton Hall) or Northampton	Cheshire or Northants v Sussex or Derbys.
Torquay or Nottingham	Devon or Notts. v Worcs. or Cumb.
Chelmsford or Trowbridge	Essex or Wilts. v Staffs. or Surrey
Canterbury or to be arranged	Kent or Bucks. v Warwicks. or Cambs.
Leicester or Bury St Edmunds	Leics. or Suffolk v Glos. or Ireland
Glasgow (Titwood) or Cardiff	Scotland or Glam. v Lancs. or Lincs.
Telford (St George's) or Southampton	Salop. or Hants v Durham or Somerset

Saturday, July 9

Lord's	†BENSON AND HEDGES CUP FINAL (1 day)
Trowbridge*	†Minor Counties v West Indians (2 days)

Wednesday, July 13

Swansea	Glam. v West Indians
Southend	Essex v Derbys.
Bristol	Glos. v Northants
Manchester	Lancs. v Leics.
Nottingham	Notts. v Middx
Guildford	Surrey v Hants
Birmingham	Warwicks. v Worcs.

Saturday, July 16

Leicester*	Leics. v West Indians
Derby*	Derbys. v Northants
Southend	Essex v Lancs.
Bristol	Glos. v Somerset
Lord's	Middx v Glam.
Nottingham	Notts. v Worcs.
Guildford	Surrey v Kent
Birmingham	Warwicks. v Hants

Sunday, July 17

Dublin	†Ireland v Wales

Wednesday, July 20

Nantwich CC	†League Cricket Conference v Sri Lankans (2 days)
Cardiff	Glam. v Warwicks.
Portsmouth	Hants v Essex
Southport	Lancs. v Surrey
Leicester	Leics. v Derbys.
Northampton	Northants v Kent
Hove	Sussex v Glos.
Worcester	Worcs. v Yorks.
Lord's	†MCC v MCC Schools (1 day)

Thursday, July 21

Leeds	ENGLAND v WEST INDIES (4th Cornhill Test, 5 days)
Lord's	†MCC Schools v NAYC (1 day)

Friday, July 22

Lord's	NCA Young Cricketers v Combined Services (1 day)

Saturday, July 23

Manchesters* or Birmingham	Lancs. or Warwicks. v Sri Lankans
Cardiff	Glam. v Yorks.
Portsmouth	Hants v Derbys.
Folkestone	Kent v Worcs.
Leicester	Leics. v Essex
Lord's	Middx v Surrey
Northampton	Northants v Sussex
Taunton	Somerset v Notts.

Wednesday, July 27

To be arranged	First-class county v West Indians
Osterley	†Indian Gymkhana v Sri Lankans (1 day)

†NatWest Bank Trophy – Quarter-Finals
(1 day)

Thursday, July 28

Jesmond	†England XI v Rest of the World XI (1 day)

Friday, July 29

Arundel	†Lavinia, Duchess of Norfolk's XI v Sri Lankans (1 day)
Jesmond	†England XI v Rest of the World XI (1 day)

Saturday, July 30

Chelmsford*	Essex v West Indians
Lord's	Middx v Sri Lankans
Derby	Derbys. v Warwicks.
Cheltenham	Glos. v Surrey
Canterbury	Kent v Somerset
Worksop	Notts. v Leics.
Eastbourne	Sussex v Glam.
Worcester	Worcs. v Northants
Leeds	Yorks. v Lancs.

Wednesday, August 3

Cheltenham	Glos. v Warwicks.
Canterbury	Kent v Leics.
Northampton	Northants v Essex
Weston-super-Mare	Somerset v Surrey
Eastbourne	Sussex v Hants
Sheffield	Yorks. v Notts.
Swansea	†Glam. v Rest of the World XI (1 day)

Thursday, August 4

The Oval	ENGLAND v WEST INDIES (5th Cornhill Test, 5 days)
Sleaford	†Minor Counties v Sri Lankans (2 days)

Saturday, August 6

Nottingham*	Notts. v Sri Lankans
Swansea	Glam. v Surrey
Cheltenham	Glos. v Yorks.
Manchester	Lancs. v Middx
Leicester	Leics. v Hants
Weston-super-Mare	Somerset v Derbys.
Birmingham	Warwicks. v Northants
Kidderminster	Worcs. v Sussex

Wednesday, August 10

†NatWest Bank Trophy Semi-Finals (1 day)

Leeds	Yorks. v Sri Lankans (if Yorks. not in NatWest Bank Trophy semi-finals)

Saturday, August 13

The Oval*	Surrey v Sri Lankans
Chesterfield	Derbys. v Kent
Colchester	Essex v Notts.
Abergavenny	Glam. v Worcs.
Bournemouth	Hants v Northants
Lord's	Middx v Glos.
Hove	Sussex v Lancs.
Birmingham	Warwicks. v Leics.
Scarborough	Yorks. v Somerset

Sunday, August 14

†Warwick Under-25 Semi-Finals (1 day)
(or Sunday, August 21)

Wednesday, August 17

Bristol	Glos. v Sri Lankans
Chesterfield	Derbys. v Yorks.
Colchester	Essex v Glam.
Bournemouth	Hants v Kent
Lytham	Lancs. v Notts.
Uxbridge	Middx v Somerset
The Oval	Surrey v Worcs.
Hove	Sussex v Warwicks.

Friday, August 19

Lord's	†National Club Championship Final (1 day)

Saturday, August 20

Southampton*	Hants v Sri Lankans
Bristol	Glos. v Kent
Manchester	Lancs. v Derbys.
Leicester	Leics. v Somerset
Uxbridge	Middx v Warwicks.
Wellingborough School	Northants v Glam.
Nottingham	Notts. v Surrey
Worcester	Worcs. v Essex
Dumfries*	Scotland v Ireland
Lord's	†Norsk Hydro Village Championship Final (1 day)

Sunday, August 21

†Warwick Under-25 Semi-Finals (1 day)
(if not played on Sunday, August 14)

Thursday, August 25

Lord's	ENGLAND v SRI LANKA (Cornhill Test, 5 days)
Neath (4d)	Glam. v Leics.
Maidstone (4d)	Kent v Sussex
Northampton (4d)	Northants v Derbys.
Taunton (4d)	Somerset v Hants
The Oval (4d)	Surrey v Lancs.
Worcester (4d)	Worcs. v Warwicks.
Leeds (4d)	Yorks. v Middx

Tuesday, August 30

Southampton (4d)	Hants v Glos.
Manchester (4d)	Lancs. v Yorks.
Leicester (4d)	Leics. v Notts.
The Oval (4d)	Surrey v Essex
Hove (4d)	Sussex v Middx
Birmingham (4d)	Warwicks. v Glam.

Wednesday, August 31

Derby	Derbys. v Sri Lankans
Scarborough	Festival match (3 days)

Saturday, September 3

Lord's	†NATWEST BANK TROPHY FINAL (1 day)

Sunday, September 4

The Oval	†ENGLAND v SRI LANKA (Texaco Trophy, 1 day)
Birmingham	†Warwick Under-25 Final (1 day)
Scarborough	†Four Counties Knockout Competition (3 days)

Monday, September 5

†Bain Clarkson Trophy Final (1 day)

Wednesday, September 7

†Refuge Assurance Cup Semi-Finals (1 day)

Scarborough	†Yorks. v The Yorkshiremen (1 day)

Friday, September 9

Chelmsford* (4d)	Essex v Leics.
Cardiff* (4d)	Glam. v Hants
Bristol* (4d)	Glos. v Worcs.
Lord's* (4d)	Middx v Kent
Nottingham* (4d)	Notts. v Derbys.
Hove* (4d)	Sussex v Surrey
Birmingham* (4d)	Warwicks. v Somerset
Scarborough* (4d)	Yorks. v Northants

Wednesday, September 14

Derby (4d)	Derbys. v Lancs.
Chelmsford (4d)	Essex v Northants
Southampton (4d)	Hants v Sussex
Canterbury (4d)	Kent v Surrey
Nottingham (4d)	Notts. v Yorks.
Taunton (4d)	Somerset v Glos.
Worcester (4d)	Worcs. v Glam.

Sunday, September 18

Birmingham	†REFUGE ASSURANCE CUP FINAL

WEST INDIAN TOUR, 1988

MAY

7 Hove	v Sussex
8 Arundel	†v Lavinia, Duchess of Norfolk's XI (1 day)
12 Southampton	†v Hants (1 day)
14 Taunton*	v Somerset
19 Birmingham	†v ENGLAND (1st 1-day Texaco Trophy)
21 Leeds	†v ENGLAND (2nd 1-day Texaco Trophy)
23 Lord's	†v ENGLAND (3rd 1-day Texaco Trophy)
25 Bristol	v Glos. (or v another county if Glos. in B & H Cup quarter-finals)
28 Worcester*	v Worcs.

JUNE

2 Nottingham	v ENGLAND (1st Cornhill Test, 5 days)
8 Birmingham or Manchester	v Warwicks. or Lancs.
11 Northampton*	v Northants
16 Lord's	v ENGLAND (2nd Cornhill Test, 5 days)
23 Cambridge	†v Oxford & Camb. U. (2 days)
25 Canterbury*	v Kent
30 Manchester	v ENGLAND (3rd Cornhill Test, 5 days)

JULY

6 Derby	v Derbys. (if Derbys. not in NatWest Bank Trophy 2nd round)
9 Trowbridge*	†v Minor Counties (2 days)
13 Swansea	v Glam.
16 Leicester*	v Leics.
21 Leeds	v ENGLAND (4th Cornhill Test, 5 days)
27 To be arranged	v A first-class county
30 Chelmsford*	v Essex

AUGUST

4 The Oval	v ENGLAND (5th Cornhill Test, 5 days)

SRI LANKAN TOUR, 1988

JULY

20 Nantwich CC †v League Cricket
Conference (2 days)

23 Manchester* v Lancs. or Warwicks.
or
Birmingham

27 Osterley †v Indian Gymkhana
(1 day)

29 Arundel †v Lavinia, Duchess
of Norfolk's XI
(1 day)

30 Lord's v Middx

6 Nottingham* v Notts.

10 Leeds v Yorks. (if Yorks. not
in NatWest Bank
Trophy semi-finals)

13 The Oval* v Surrey

17 Bristol v Glos.

20 Southampton* v Hants

25 Lord's v ENGLAND (Cornhill
Test, 5 days)

31 Derby v Derbys.

AUGUST

4 Sleaford †v Minor Counties
(2 days)

SEPTEMBER

4 The Oval †v ENGLAND (1-day
Texaco Trophy)

†REFUGE ASSURANCE LEAGUE, 1988

APRIL

24–Derbys. v Leics. (Derby); Essex v Kent
(Chelmsford); Glos. v Glam. (Bristol);
Hants v Surrey (Southampton); Lancs. v
Worcs. (Manchester); Middx v Notts.
(Lord's); Sussex v Somerset (Hove).

MAY

1–Glam. v Somerset (Cardiff); Glos. v
Sussex (Bristol); Kent v Hants
(Canterbury); Lancs. v Warwicks.
(Manchester); Leics. v Northants
(Leicester); Middx v Essex (Lord's);
Worcs. v Notts. (Worcester); Yorks. v
Derbys. (Leeds).

8–Derbys. v Essex (Derby); Hants v
Glam. (Southampton); Leics. v
Kent (Leicester); Northants v Glos.
(Northampton); Notts. v Lancs.
(Nottingham); Somerset v Worcs.
(Taunton); Surrey v Middx (The Oval);
Warwicks. v Yorks. (Birmingham).

15–Essex v Northants (Chelmsford); Hants
v Middx (Southampton); Kent v
Lancs. (Canterbury); Notts. v Glos.
(Nottingham); Sussex v Surrey (Hove);
Warwicks. v Glam. (Birmingham);
Worcs. v Yorks. (Worcester).

22–Glam. v Derbys. (Newport); Kent
v Yorks. (Canterbury); Leics. v
Worcs. (Leicester); Notts. v Sussex
(Nottingham); Surrey v Northants (The
Oval); Warwicks. v Essex (Birmingham).

29–Derbys. v Notts. (Derby); Essex v Surrey
(Chelmsford); Glos. v Warwicks.
(Swindon); Lancs. v Leics. (Manchester);
Middx v Sussex (Lord's); Northants v
Kent (Northampton); Yorks. v Hants
(Middlesbrough).

JUNE

5–Glam. v Kent (Merthyr Tydfil); Lancs. v
Hants (Manchester); Middx v Worcs.
(Lord's); Somerset v Northants
(Taunton); Sussex v Derbys. (Horsham);
Warwicks. v Notts. (Birmingham);
Yorks. v Surrey (Leeds).

12–Derbys. v Glos. (Heanor); Essex v Sussex
(Ilford); Notts. v Glam. (Nottingham);
Somerset v Warwicks. (Bath); Surrey v
Leics. (The Oval); Worcs. v Hants
(Worcester).

19–Derbys. v Worcs. (Knypersley); Hants v
Notts. (Basingstoke); Lancs. v Glos.
(Manchester); Leics. v Sussex
(Leicester); Northants v Middx (Luton);
Somerset v Surrey (Bath); Warwicks. v
Kent (Birmingham); Yorks. v Essex
(Sheffield).

26–Glam. v Lancs. (Pontypridd); Glos. v
Leics. (Gloucester); Hants v Essex
(Bournemouth); Middx v Somerset
(Lord's); Notts. v Northants
(Nottingham); Surrey v Derbys. (The
Oval); Sussex v Yorks. (Hove).

JULY

3–Derbys. v Middx (Repton School); Kent v Notts. (Canterbury); Northants v Lancs. (Tring); Somerset v Essex (Taunton); Surrey v Warwicks. (The Oval); Sussex v Hants (Hastings); Worcs. v Glos. (Hereford); Yorks. v Leics. (Hull).

10–Essex v Glam. (Chelmsford); Hants v Glos. (Southampton); Kent v Middx (Canterbury); Lancs. v Somerset (Manchester); Northants v Yorks. (Northampton); Notts. v Leics. (Nottingham); Surrey v Worcs. (The Oval); Sussex v Warwicks. (Hove).

17–Essex v Lancs. (Southend); Glos. v Somerset (Bristol); Middx v Glam. (Lord's); Notts. v Yorks. (Nottingham); Surrey v Kent (The Oval); Warwicks. v Hants (Birmingham).

24–Glam. v Yorks. (Cardiff); Hants v Derbys. (Portsmouth); Kent v Worcs. (Folkestone); Leics. v Essex (Leicester); Middx v Warwicks. (Lord's); Northants v Sussex (Finedon); Somerset v Notts. (Taunton).

31–Derbys. v Warwicks. (Derby); Glos. v Surrey (Cheltenham); Kent v Somerset (Canterbury); Leics. v Middx (Leicester); Sussex v Glam. (Eastbourne); Worcs. v Northants (Worcester); Yorks. v Lancs. (Scarborough).

AUGUST

7–Glam. v Surrey (Ebbw Vale); Glos. v Yorks. (Cheltenham); Lancs. v Middx (Blackpool); Leics. v Hants (Leicester); Somerset v Derbys. (Weston-super-Mare); Warwicks. v Northants (Birmingham); Worcs. v Sussex (Worcester).

14–Derbys. v Kent (Chesterfield); Essex v Notts. (Colchester); Glam. v Worcs. (Swansea); Hants v Northants (Bournemouth); Middx v Glos. (Lord's); Sussex v Lancs. (Hove); Warwicks. v Leics. (Birmingham); Yorks. v Somerset (Scarborough).

21–Glos. v Kent (Moreton-in-Marsh); Lancs. v Derbys. (Manchester); Leics. v Somerset (Leicester); Northants v Glam. (Wellingborough School); Notts. v Surrey (Nottingham); Worcs. v Essex (Worcester).

28–Essex v Glos. (Chelmsford); Glam. v Leics. (Llanelli); Kent v Sussex (Maidstone); Northants v Derbys. (Northampton); Somerset v Hants (Taunton); Surrey v Lancs. (The Oval); Worcs. v Warwicks. (Worcester); Yorks. v Middx (Leeds).

†MINOR COUNTIES CHAMPIONSHIP, 1988

All matches are of two days' duration.

MAY

29–Berks. v Bucks. (Bracknell); Lincs. v Beds. (Sleaford); Northumb. v Herts. (Jesmond); Oxon. v Wales MC (Christ Church, Oxford).

30–Dorset v Salop. (Dorchester).

31–Cumb. v Herts. (Netherfield, Kendal); Durham v Beds. (Chester-le-Street); Northumb. v Suffolk (Jesmond).

JUNE

2–Cumb. v Suffolk (Workington); Staffs. v Herts. (Ind Coope, Burton upon Trent).

8–Cambs. v Herts. (March).

12–Beds. v Norfolk (Henlow); Lincs. v Northumb. (Bourne); Oxon. v Wilts. (Morris Motors, Oxford); Staffs. v Cumb. (Bignall End); Wales MC v Salop. (Colwyn Bay).

13–Cornwall v Cheshire (Wadebridge).

14–Cambs. v Northumb. (Wisbech).

15–Devon v Cheshire (Sidmouth).

26–Berks. v Oxon. (Falkland CC, Newbury); Bucks. v Dorset (High Wycombe); Cheshire v Salop. (Toft); Durham v Cumb. (Gateshead Fell); Staffs. v Beds. (Leek).

27–Herts. v Lincs. (Stevenage).

28–Berks. v Wales MC (Kidmore End).

JULY

4–Lincs. v Staffs. (Cleethorpes).

10–Cheshire v Bucks. (Bowdon); Cornwall v Wales MC (Falmouth); Cumb. v Lincs. (Barrow); Northumb. v Durham (Jesmond).

12–Devon v Wales MC (Exmouth); Salop. v Bucks. (Bridgnorth).

13–Cambs. v Staffs. (Cambridge).

17–Cumb. v Norfolk (Millom); Dorset v Wilts. (Dorchester); Salop. v Berks. (Shrewsbury).

18–Durham v Cambs. (Stockton on Tees); Herts. v Suffolk (St Albans); Oxon. v Cornwall (St Edward's School, Oxford).

19–Cheshire v Berks. (Warrington); Staffs. v Norfolk (Old Hill CC).

20–Wilts. v Cornwall (Trowbridge).

21–Dorset v Devon (Weymouth).

24–Suffolk v Lincs. (Ipswich School) (or on another date if either team is in the knockout final).

25–Bucks. v Wales MC (Manor Fields, Bletchley) (or on another date if either team is in the knockout final).

26–Cambs. v Suffolk (Cambridge); Herts. v Durham (Watford Town); Oxon. v Devon (Christ Church, Oxford); Wilts. v Berks. (Swindon).

28–Norfolk v Cambs. (Lakenham); Wilts v Devon (Chippenham).

31–Beds. v Northumb. (Southill Park); Berks. v Cornwall (Reading); Dorset v Cheshire (Sherborne School); Norfolk v Lincs. (Lakenham).

AUGUST

2–Beds. v Cambs. (Dunstable); Bucks. v Cornwall (Marlow); Norfolk v Northumb. (Lakenham); Suffolk v Durham (Mildenhall); Wales MC v Cheshire (Cardiff).

4–Dorset v Berks. (Dorchester); Norfolk v Durham (Lakenham).

7–Beds. v Cumb. (Bedford Town); Cheshire v Oxon. (Oxton); Lincs. v Cambs. (Lincoln Lindum).

8–Herts. v Norfolk (Letchworth); Northumb. v Staffs. (Jesmond).

9–Bucks. v Devon (Slough); Cambs. v Cumb. (Peterborough); Salop. v Oxon. (Wellington); Wales MC v Wilts. (Usk).

10–Durham v Staffs. (South Shields); Suffolk v Norfolk (Bury St Edmunds).

11–Berks. v Devon (Finchampstead).

14–Durham v Lincs. (Hartlepool); Oxon. v Dorset (Banbury XX); Wilts. v Bucks. (Devizes).

15–Beds. v Herts. (Luton Town); Cornwall v Salop. (St Austell).

16–Staffs. v Suffolk (Stone); Wales MC v Dorset (Ebbw Vale).

17–Devon v Salop. (Torquay).

21–Cornwall v Dorset (Truro); Cumb. v Northumb. (Carlisle); Salop. v Wilts. (Shifnal).

23–Cheshire v Wilts. (Chester).

24–Devon v Cornwall (Bovey Tracey).

28–Bucks. v Oxon. (Amersham); Suffolk v Beds. (Ransome's, Ipswich).

SEPTEMBER

11–Final (Worcester).

†MINOR COUNTIES KNOCKOUT COMPETITION, 1988

All matches are of one day's duration.

Qualifying Round

May 22 Cheshire v Staffs. (Nantwich); Cumb. v Lincs. (Penrith); Durham v Northumb. (Durham City); Wales MC v Salop (Welshpool).

First Round

June 5 Cambs. v Norfolk (Cambridge); Cornwall v Wilts. (Truro); Durham or Northumb. v Cumb. or Lincs. (Sunderland or Jesmond); Dorset v Devon (Sherborne School); Herts.

v Bucks. (Tring); Oxon. v Berks. (Christ Church, Oxford); Suffolk v Beds. (To be arranged); Wales MC or Salop. v Cheshire or Staffs. (Neath or Perkins, Shrewsbury).

Quarter-finals to be played on June 19.

Semi-finals to be played on July 3.

Final to be played on July 24.

†SECOND ELEVEN CHAMPIONSHIP, 1988

All matches are of three days' duration.

APRIL

20–Warwicks. v Leics. (Birmingham).

27–Somerset v Glam. (Bristol Imperial); Warwicks. v Lancs. (Birmingham).

MAY

4–Lancs. v Kent (Manchester); Leics. v Northants (Market Harborough); Sussex v Notts. (Hove); Worcs. v Derbys. (Worcester); Yorks. v Warwicks. (Elland).

11–Derbys. v Yorks. (Chesterfield); Glam. v Worcs. (Ammanford); Middx v Kent (Harrow CC); Surrey v Lancs. (Purley CC); Warwicks. v Somerset (Coventry & North Warwickshire CC).

18–Essex v Northants (Chelmsford); Glos. v Glam. (Bristol); Lancs. v Worcs. (Manchester); Notts. v Leics. (John Player, Nottingham); Surrey v Hants (The Oval); Yorks. v Somerset (York).

25–Derbys. v Lancs. (Ilkeston); Essex v Glos. (Leigh on Sea); Leics. v Middx (Leicester); Notts. v Warwicks. (Steetley); Surrey v Yorks. (Guildford); Sussex v Kent (Hastings); Worcs. v Northants (Worcester).

JUNE

1–Kent v Surrey (Canterbury); Lancs. v Notts. (Manchester); Leics. v Worcs. (Leicester); Middx v Warwicks. (Uxbridge); Somerset v Hants (Westland, Yeovil); Sussex v Essex (Eastbourne); Yorks. v Northants (Scarborough).

8–Derbys. v Northants (Chesterfield); Glam. v Notts. (Abergavenny); Hants v Essex (Bournemouth); Kent v Glos. (Folkestone); Leics. v Lancs. (Uppingham); Middx v Sussex (Harefield); Somerset v Surrey (Glastonbury CC); Warwicks. v Worcs. (Leamington Spa CC).

15–Glos. v Derbys. (Bristol); Glam. v Leics. (Gorseinon); Kent v Somerset (Canterbury); Lancs. v Northants (Manchester); Middx v Essex (Ealing CC); Sussex v Hants (Hove); Warwicks. v Yorks. (Studley CC).

22–Glam. v Glos. (Cardiff); Hants v Middx (Southampton); Kent v Sussex (Maidstone); Lancs. v Derbys. (Northern CC, Crosby); Leics. v Surrey (Hinckley); Northants v Essex (Northampton); Notts. v Yorks. (Worksop); Somerset v Warwicks. (Bath).

29–Essex v Kent (Ilford); Glam. v Somerset (Pontarddulais); Glos. v Worcs. (Bristol); Leics. v Notts. (Leicester); Northants v Middx (Northampton); Sussex v Warwicks. (Horsham); Yorks. v Lancs. (Todmorden).

JULY

6–Glos. v Warwicks. (Dowty Rotol, Cheltenham); Lancs. v Leics. (Manchester); Middx v Hants (Lensbury Club, Teddington); Northants v Derbys. (Bletchley Town CC); Surrey v Kent (The Oval); Worcs. v Glam. (Worcester); Yorks. v Notts. (Harrogate).

13–Derbys. v Leics. (Heanor); Kent v Essex (Gore Court, Sittingbourne); Northants v Yorks. (Wellingborough School); Notts. v Lancs. (Worthington Simpson, Newark); Surrey v Middx (The Oval); Worcs. v Warwicks. (Worcester); Hants v Glos. (Southampton).

20–Essex v Surrey (Chelmsford); Glos. v Hants (Lydney); Kent v Middx (Canterbury); Lancs. v Yorks. (Manchester); Leics. v Sussex (Hinckley); Northants v Notts. (Old Northamptonians CC); Somerset v Worcs. (Weston-super-Mare); Warwicks. v Glam. (Walmley CC).

24–Derbys. v Worcs. (Shipley).

27–Derbys. v Glos. (Ilkeston); Hants v Somerset (Bournemouth); Kent v Yorks. (Dover); Northants v Lancs. (Bedford School); Notts. v Essex (Worksop College); Surrey v Leics. (Guildford).

AUGUST

3–Derbys. v Notts. (Derby); Essex v Sussex (Romford); Hants v Kent (Southampton); Lancs. v Surrey (Manchester); Leics. v Warwicks. (Leicester); Middx v Northants (Harrow CC); Somerset v Glos. (Taunton).

v Hants (Southend); Lancs. v Somerset (Blackpool); Middx. v Surrey (Enfield CC); Northants v Sussex (Wolverton); Notts. v Glam. (Worthington Simpson, Newark); Warwicks. v Glos. (Moseley CC); Worcs. v Leics. (Worcester).

17-Essex v Notts. (Access, Southend); Glam. v Lancs. (Swansea); Kent v Hants (Canterbury); Northants v Leics. (Northampton); Surrey v Sussex (Banstead CC); Warwicks. v Middx (Griff and Coton, Nuneaton); Worcs. v Somerset (Old Hill CC); Yorks. v Derbys. (Park Avenue, Bradford).

24-Essex v Middx (Chelmsford); Glos. v Somerset (Bristol); Hants v Surrey (Southampton); Lancs. v Warwicks. (Manchester); Leics. v Glam. (Leicester);

Northants v Worcs. (Oundle School); Notts. v Derbys. (Steetley); Yorks. v Kent (Marske-by-Sea).

31-Glam. v Warwicks. (Cardiff); Kent v Lancs. (Canterbury); Leics. v Derbys. (Market Harborough); Notts. v Northants (Nottingham); Sussex v Middx (Hastings); Worcs. v Glos. (Worcester); Yorks. v Surrey (Leeds).

SEPTEMBER

7-Hants v Sussex (Southampton); Lancs. v Glam. (Manchester); Somerset v Yorks. (Taunton); Surrey v Essex (Banstead CC).

14-Sussex v Surrey (Hove).

†WARWICK UNDER-25 COMPETITION, 1988

All matches are of one day's duration.

MAY

3-Somerset v Glam. (Taunton).

9-Kent v Hants (Tonbridge School).

10-Glam. v Glos. (Pontarddulais).

17-Kent v Surrey (Canterbury).

23-Derbys. v Lancs. (Heanor); Glam. v Warwicks. (Croesyceilog); Northants v Leics. (Northampton).

30-Lancs. v Notts. (Heywood).

31-Somerset v Worcs. (Taunton); Warwicks. v Glos. (Birmingham).

JUNE

6-Yorks. v Derbys. (Bawtry Road, Sheffield); Essex v Northants (Wanstead CC); Glos. v Somerset (Bristol); Middx v Leics. (Ealing CC).

13-Hants v Sussex (Southampton); Warwicks. v Somerset (Birmingham).

14-Glos. v Worcs. (Bristol); Notts. v Yorks. (Thoresby Park); Sussex v Kent (Hove).

20-Essex v Leics. (Colchester); Surrey v Sussex (The Oval); Worcs. v Glam. (Worcester).

27-Derbys. v Notts. (Derby); Yorks. v Lancs. (Park Avenue, Bradford); Worcs. v Warwicks. (Worcester).

JULY

4-Middx v Essex (Ealing CC).

26-Hants v Surrey (Bournemouth).

AUGUST

14-Semi-Finals.

21-Semi-Finals (if not played on August 14).

SEPTEMBER

4-FINAL (Birmingham).

†BAIN CLARKSON TROPHY, 19

All matches are of one day's duration.

MAY

3–Leics. v Northants (Leicester).

9–Glam. v Worcs. (Swansea); Yorks. v Leics. (Leeds).

10–Northants v Derbys. (Northampton).

11–Sussex v Essex (Arundel Castle).

16–Derbys. v Yorks. (Chesterfield); Glos. v Warwicks. (Bristol); Hants v Surrey (Southampton).

17–Glos. v Worcs. (Bristol); Notts. v Leics. (Worthington Simpson, Newark); Sussex v Middx (Eastbourne).

23–Middx v Kent (South Hampstead CC); Somerset v Glos. (Taunton); Surrey v Hants (Guildford).

24–Derbys. v Lancs. (Ilkeston); Essex v Middx (Leigh on Sea); Glam. v Warwicks. (Abergavenny); Notts. v Northants (Collingham & District CC); Sussex v Surrey (Horsham).

30–Sussex v Hants (Arundel Castle).

31–Kent v Essex (Canterbury); Lancs. v Notts. (Middleton); Leics. v Derbys. (Leicester); Surrey v Sussex (The Oval); Yorks. v Northants (Scarborough).

JUNE

6–Surrey v Kent (The Oval); Worcs. v Warwicks. (Worcester).

7–Yorks. v Derbys. (Hull); Glam. v Somerset (Ynysygerwn); Hants v Essex (Bournemouth); Leics. v Lancs. (Uppingham); Middx v Sussex (Harefield); Worcs. v Glos. (Worcester).

13–Kent v Middx (Canterbury); Leics. v Yorks. (Leicester).

14–Lancs. v Northants (Manchester); Middx v Essex (Enfield CC); Warwicks. v Somerset (Birmingham).

21–Essex v Hants (Brentwood); Glam. v Glos. (Swansea); Lancs. v Derbys. (Preston); Notts. v Yorks. (Worksop College); Somerset v Warwicks. (Bath).

27–Hants v Middx (Sou....ton); Northants v Leics. (Northampto..).

28–Derbys. v Northants (Derby); Essex v Kent (Ilford); Glos. v Glam. (Bristol); Leics. v Notts. (Leicester); Yorks. v Lancs. (Elland).

JULY

4–Kent v Sussex (Canterbury).

5–Glos. v Somerset (Bristol); Lancs. v Leics. (Ramsbottom); Middx v Hants (Lensbury Club, Teddington); Yorks. v Notts. (Doncaster).

11–Derbys. v Notts. (Derby); Somerset v Glam. (Taunton); Surrey v Essex (The Oval); Warwicks. v Worcs. (Birmingham).

12–Derbys. v Leics. (Derby); Essex v Sussex (Wanstead); Northants v Yorks. (Northampton); Notts. v Lancs. (Worksop College); Surrey v Middx (The Oval); Warwicks. v Glos. (Moseley CC); Worcs. v Somerset (Worcester).

18–Kent v Surrey (Canterbury); Notts. v Derbys. (Farnsfield CC); Worcs. v Glam. (To be arranged); Northants v Middx (Woughton, Milton Keynes).

19–Lancs. v Yorks. (Manchester); Northants v Notts. (Peterborough); Somerset v Worcs. (Taunton); Surrey v Surrey (South Hampstead CC); Warwicks. v Glam. (Stratford upon Avon).

25–Essex v Surrey (Orsett); Hants v Sussex (Southampton).

26–Northants v Lancs. (Bedford Modern School); Sussex v Kent (Hastings).

AUGUST

2–Hants v Kent (Southampton).

16–Kent v Hants (Canterbury).

SEPTEMBER

5–FINAL.

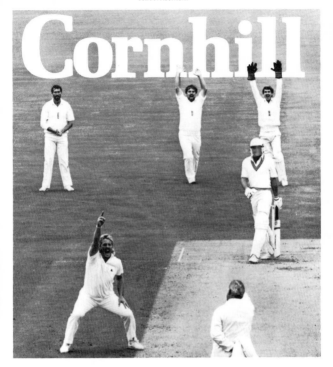

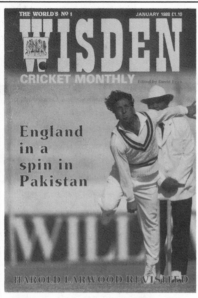